1,000,000 Books

are available to read at

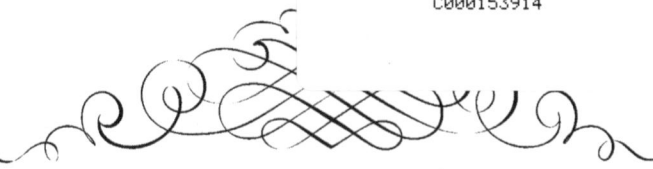

www.ForgottenBooks.com

Read online
Download PDF
Purchase in print

ISBN 978-1-5282-9208-5
PIBN 10989067

This book is a reproduction of an important historical work. Forgotten Books uses state-of-the-art technology to digitally reconstruct the work, preserving the original format whilst repairing imperfections present in the aged copy. In rare cases, an imperfection in the original, such as a blemish or missing page, may be replicated in our edition. We do, however, repair the vast majority of imperfections successfully; any imperfections that remain are intentionally left to preserve the state of such historical works.

Forgotten Books is a registered trademark of FB &c Ltd.
Copyright © 2018 FB &c Ltd.
FB &c Ltd, Dalton House, 60 Windsor Avenue, London, SW19 2RR.
Company number 08720141. Registered in England and Wales.

For support please visit www.forgottenbooks.com

1 MONTH OF FREE READING

at

www.ForgottenBooks.com

By purchasing this book you are eligible for one month membership to ForgottenBooks.com, giving you unlimited access to our entire collection of over 1,000,000 titles via our web site and mobile apps.

To claim your free month visit:

www.forgottenbooks.com/free989067

* Offer is valid for 45 days from date of purchase. Terms and conditions apply.

English
Français
Deutsche
Italiano
Español
Português

www.forgottenbooks.com

Mythology Photography **Fiction** Fishing Christianity **Art** Cooking Essays Buddhism Freemasonry Medicine **Biology** Music **Ancient Egypt** Evolution Carpentry Physics Dance Geology **Mathematics** Fitness Shakespeare **Folklore** Yoga Marketing **Confidence** Immortality Biographies Poetry **Psychology** Witchcraft Electronics Chemistry History **Law** Accounting **Philosophy** Anthropology Alchemy Drama Quantum Mechanics Atheism Sexual Health **Ancient History** **Entrepreneurship** Languages Sport Paleontology Needlework Islam **Metaphysics** Investment Archaeology Parenting Statistics Criminology **Motivational**

DEAN BROS. STEAM PUMP WORKS,

FIRST STREET (NEW TENTH STREET), NEAR NORTH SENATE AVENUE LONG DISTANCE TELEPHONE 9

BOILER FEEDERS, FIRE PUMPS, DUPLEX PUMPS, DISTILLERY PUMPS, AIR PUMPS and CONDENSERS, VACUUM PUMPS, BREWERY PUMPS, RAILROAD WATER STATION PUMPS, PUMPING MACHINERY FOR ALL PURPOSES. Send for ILLUSTRATED CATALOGUE.

INTERIOR VIEW, INDIANAPOLIS BUSINESS UNIVERSITY, WHEN BUILDING.

Showing skylight (30 x 142 feet), court, balconies, bridges, remodeled at an expense of tens of thousands of dollars, making for the University the finest quarters of any Business School in the land.

BUSINESS WORLD SUPPLIED WITH HELP

Our graduates in demand. Over 10,000 now in the best situations. Hundreds of the most prominent citizens graduated here. Our course of training opens the broadest avenue to immediate and permanent prosperity. Call for personal interview with

ELEVATOR FOR DAY AND NIGHT SCHOOL. **E. J. HEEB, President.**

ABEL & DOYLE

HENRY ABEL.
FRANK J. DOYLE.

AGENTS FOR

The Celebrated Peninsular Furnace

AND MANUFACTURERS OF

TIN, COPPER AND SHEET IRON WORK

Prompt attention Given to Job Work, Spouting and Guttering; Tin, Iron and Slate Roofing, Hotel and Restaurant Utensils, Copper Draining Boards, Etc.

31 INDIANA AVENUE, INDIANAPOLIS.

M. S. HUEY & SON

551 MASSACHUSETTS AVENUE,

MANUFACTURERS OF

WOOD MANTELS

FINE INTERIOR WOOD WORK

551 Massachusetts Avenue

MANTELS, TILING, GRATES, ETC., RETAILED AT FACTORY.

SEEDS

BULBS, GARDEN TOOLS, POULTRY SUPPLIES, LAWN GRASS SEED AND FERTILIZERS.

We Carry the Most Complete Stock in the City.

HUNTINGTON & PAGE, Seedsmen

Successors to THE HUNTINGTON SEED CO.

78 EAST MARKET STREET

WRITE FOR OUR ANNUAL CATALOGUE. TELEPHONE No. 129

ENGRAVER AND DIE SINKER.

GEO. J. MAYER

MANUFACTURER OF

Seals AND Stencils

Rubber Stamps, Steel Stamps, Badges, Checks, Burning Brands, Door Plates, Door Numbers, Check Protectors, Numbering Machines, Etc.

TELEPHONE 123. CATALOGUE FREE.

15 South Meridian Street, Ground Floor, Indianapolis, Indiana.

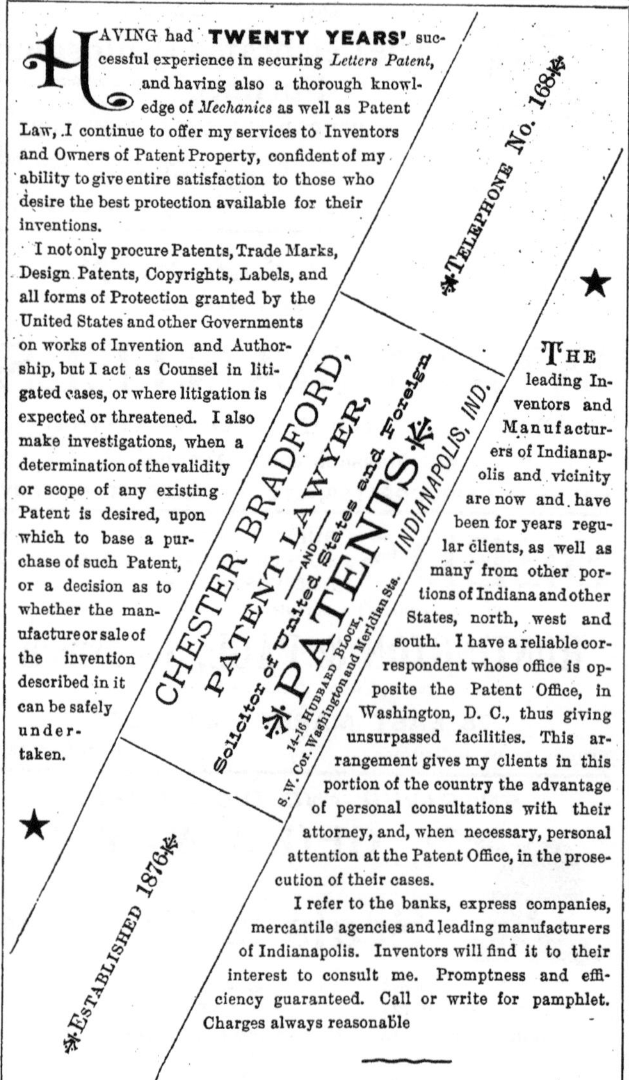
HAVING had TWENTY YEARS' successful experience in securing *Letters Patent*, and having also a thorough knowledge of *Mechanics* as well as Patent Law, I continue to offer my services to Inventors and Owners of Patent Property, confident of my ability to give entire satisfaction to those who desire the best protection available for their inventions.
I not only procure Patents, Trade Marks, Design Patents, Copyrights, Labels, and all forms of Protection granted by the United States and other Governments on works of Invention and Authorship, but I act as Counsel in litigated cases, or where litigation is expected or threatened. I also make investigations, when a determination of the validity or scope of any existing Patent is desired, upon which to base a purchase of such Patent, or a decision as to whether the manufacture or sale of the invention described in it can be safely undertaken.
TELEPHONE No. 168
CHESTER BRADFORD,
PATENT LAWYER,
Solicitor of United States — AND — Foreign
PATENTS
14-16 HUBBARD BLOCK,
S. W. Cor. Washington and Meridian Sts.
INDIANAPOLIS, IND.
ESTABLISHED 1876
THE leading Inventors and Manufacturers of Indianapolis and vicinity are now and have been for years regular clients, as well as many from other portions of Indiana and other States, north, west and south. I have a reliable correspondent whose office is opposite the Patent Office, in Washington, D. C., thus giving unsurpassed facilities. This arrangement gives my clients in this portion of the country the advantage of personal consultations with their attorney, and, when necessary, personal attention at the Patent Office, in the prosecution of their cases.
I refer to the banks, express companies, mercantile agencies and leading manufacturers of Indianapolis. Inventors will find it to their interest to consult me. Promptness and efficiency guaranteed. Call or write for pamphlet. Charges always reasonable

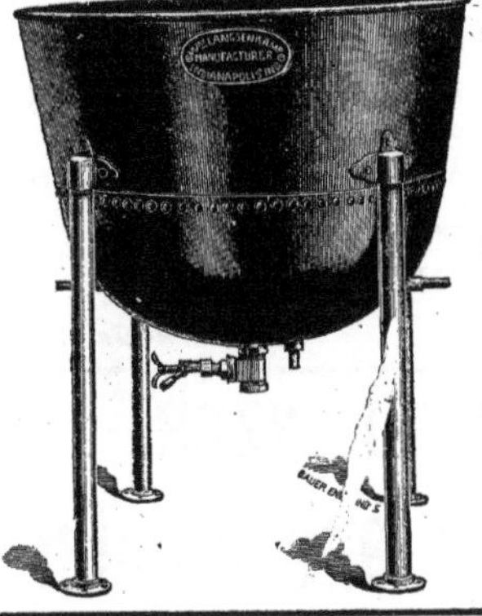

Wm. Langsenkamp

Coppersmith

MANUFACTURER OF

BREW, JACKET AND CANDY KETTLES, DYE CYLINDERS, COILS, SODA FOUNTAINS, ETC.

Also Dealer in Sheet Copper and Brass, and Copper and Brass Tubing and Rods

ALL ORDERS PROMPTLY ATTENDED TO.

Corner Georgia and Delaware Streets

Telephone 121

HENRY LANGSENKAMP. WILLIAM LANGSENKAMP, JR.

LANGSENKAMP BROS' BRASS WORKS

TEL. 121.

FOUNDERS AND FINISHERS

HEAVY AND LIGHT CASTINGS IN BRASS, ZINC, WHITE METAL, ALUMINUM, PHOSPHOR BRONZE, ETC.

SPECIAL ATTENTION GIVEN TO REPAIR WORK.

SHEET BRASS, BRASS TUBES AND RODS.

90-92 E. Georgia St., near Delaware, Indianapolis.

No. 1.

BABY SUPPLY MANUFACT'G CO.

No. 1 represents our Outing Canopy Hammock being carried on a Safety Bicycle. Just the thing for Bicyclists.

No. 2 represents our Outing Hammock with person taking a refreshing rest after hunting or fishing. These Hammocks can be tilt to any degree or arranged as desired, and are large enough for two persons to sleep in. When closed they are proof against flies and mosquitoes.

No. 2.

No. 3. Outing Hammock, being used as a Swinging Settee.

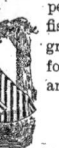

No. 3.

256 South East St., Indianapolis. THOMAS NESOM, Manager

JNO. M. LILLY,

HARDWOOD MANTELS,

LATEST DESIGNS.

Open Fireplaces, Andirons, Gas Logs, Tile Floors of Every Description. Bathroom Work a Specialty. Designs and Estimates Furnished.

SOLE AGENT TAYLOR GAS GRATES

78-80 MASSACHUSETTS AVE. TELEPHONE 207.

B. J. SCHLANZER,

Contractor and Builder

...PLANING MILL...

682 Charles Street, - Indianapolis, Ind.

WOOD TURNING DONE TO ORDER. TELEPHONE 864.

Columbian.....
Feather Cleaning & Dyeing Establishment,

147 Massachusetts Ave., Indianapolis, Ind.

Feathers and Tips Dyed and Curled EQUAL TO NEW.

FIRST-CLASS WORK. SATISFACTION GUARANTEED.

ALBERT MINTER,

MANUFACTURER OF AND DEALER IN

Tight Barrel Staves

South End California St.

Circled Heads, Square Heading and Cooperage. TELEPHONE 655.

MOFFAT & CO.,

402 LEMCKE BUILDING.

BROKERS IN

Glass House Supplies

Iron and Steel Manufacturers' Supplies,
Tin Plate Manufacturers' Supplies,

ARSENIC, SODA ASH, NITRATE OF SODA,
TIFFIN WOOD-BURNED LIME, GROUND AND BOLTED,
LAGOS PALM OIL,
MOUNT SAVAGE FIRE BRICK, SILICA BRICK.

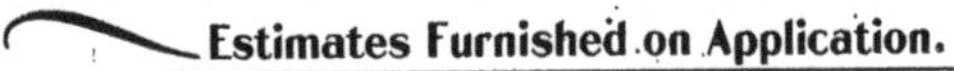
Estimates Furnished on Application.

LONG DISTANCE TELEPHONE 1218.

$100 CARRIED IN POCKET ONE YEAR EARNS 0.
DEPOSITED IN BANK ONE YEAR EARNS $4.
USED AS PER THE W. E. FOREST

"FLUCTUATION SYSTEM"

EARNS AN AVERAGE OF 5 PER CENT A WEEK

"SAFE AND SURE"; requires no time on your part. GET YOUR CASH EVERY SEVEN DAYS. "System" FREE. Call or send for it. We only ask your unprejudiced investigation to convince you that our claims are true. The W. E. FOREST CO.

THOS. S. S. KERR, Gen. Agent, 77½ E. Market St., Indianapolis, Ind.

McNAMARA, KOSTER & CO.

Foundry and Pattern Shop

ALL KINDS OF HEAVY AND LIGHT GRAY IRON CASTINGS.

Particular Attention Given to Job Pattern Work.

212 TO 218 SOUTH PENNSYLVANIA STREET,

TELEPHONE 1593. INDIANAPOLIS.

Wrought Iron Bridge Company

W. W. WINSLOW, General Agent.

Office, Room 1 Hubbard Block, S. W. Corner Washington and Meridian Sts.

TEL. 1190...... INDIANAPOLIS, INDIANA.

The Best Bridge in the State of Indiana

The new 500-foot Steel Bridge, with 36-foot Roadway and 2½ foot walk, across White River, Kentucky ave., cost $62,000.00. Washington street (Pogues Run) plate girders, with numerous other city and Marion County bridges, as well as throughout the State.

The Iron Work for the Union Railway Co.'s new Illinois Street Tunnel was furnished by us; also 375-foot Wrought Iron Bridge and a 400x30 Steel Bridge, (including masonry built by us) with many other Marion county and city bridges, across White River, and we refer to the workmanship and quality of material with pride.

Builders of Steel, Iron, Wood and Combination

RAILROAD AND HIGHWAY BRIDGES.

VIADUCTS, GIRDERS, ROOF TRUSSES, GENERAL STRUCTURAL WORK, TURNTABLES, IRON WHARFS, ETC. DYE FORGES, EYE BARS AND UPSET RODS A SPECIALTY.

The Fred Dietz Co.

370-406 MADISON AVENUE.

MANUFACTURERS OF

WOODEN PACKING BOXES,

Factory and Warehouse Trucks.

PAT. JULY 28, 1896.

Send for Catalogue. Tel. 654.

R. L. POLK & CO.'S

INDIANAPOLIS

CITY DIRECTORY

For 1897.

EMBRACING A COMPLETE ALPHABETICAL LIST OF BUSINESS FIRMS PRIVATE CITIZENS, A DIRECTORY OF THE CITY AND COUNTY OFFICERS, CHURCHES AND PUBLIC SCHOOLS, BENEVOLENT, LITERARY AND OTHER ASSOCIATIONS, BANKS, INCORPORATED INSTITUTIONS, INDIANA STATE GOVERNMENT, ETC.; ALSO A COMPLETE DIRECTORY OF MT. JACKSON, BRIGHTWOOD, HAUGHVILLE, IRVINGTON, WEST INDIANAPOLIS, AND MAPLETON

TO WHICH IS ADDED

A REVISED MAP OF THE CITY AND SUBURBS WITH STREET GUIDE

ALSO

A COMPLETE CLASSIFIED BUSINESS DIRECTORY

VOLUME XLIII.

INDIANAPOLIS:
COMPILED AND PUBLISHED BY R. L. POLK & CO.
CARLON & HOLLENBECK, PRINTERS AND BINDERS.
1897.

Entered according to Act of Congress, in the Year 1897, by R. L. Polk & Co., in the office of the Librarian of Congress at Washington, D. C.

FORTY-THIRD VOLUME.

1897.

1358771

INTRODUCTORY.

The publishers take pleasure in presenting to their patrons the forty-third annual volume of THE INDIANAPOLIS CITY DIRECTORY. They offer it with the assurance that it will equal former editions in completeness and accuracy.

The territory embraced this year is the same as in the past, including, in addition to the city proper, West Indianapolis, Irvington, Brightwood, Haughville, Mount Jackson, Mapleton, Woodside, Clifton-on-the-River, Marion Park and Emerichsville.

POPULATION.

This volume contains 65,320 names. By using a multiple of 2¾, a population of 179,630 is shown for the territory above mentioned. This multiple is used to include males under twenty years of age and females following no employment or living at home with their parents, many of whom have been included in former editions but excluded from this. In fixing the population of the city and suburbs at 179,630 it is believed that a just and fair estimate is given, and one which is borne out by the poll at the recent election, which gave the city over 41,000 voters. This would indicate a population of over 165,000 for that portion of the territory included within the city limits and about 15,000 for the above-named suburbs.

NEW STREET GUIDE.

The street guide given in the present work is entirely new and includes all the alterations in the names of streets contained in the ordinances recently passed by the city council. In this guide we have shown under the name of the old street its new name, and in the case of two or more streets of the same name, the ward in which each is contained. And under the new name has been included the names of the old street or streets which comprise that street under the new ordinance.

RENUMBERING OF HOUSES.

The city council has now under consideration the renumbering of houses on the decimal system, 100 to the block of the usual length, a system which is in vogue in nearly all large cities, and one that for simplicity and convenience can not be excelled. The number would indicate the exact number of blocks distant from the base or dividing line of the city.

CITY MAP.

In the revised edition of the city map, also presented by the publishers with this volume, all street changes have been made to accord with the city ordinance and our street guide above mentioned. At the foot of the map is also contained a street guide locating on the map by letter and figure the names of all streets. In this guide, also, the same rule has been followed in regard to the names of the old and new streets that we followed in our street guide referred to above.

Changes found in a city directory from year to year surely indicate the life and activity of its inhabitants, and the statistics which our columns from time to time present are bases on which to estimate the city's growth and prosperity. As the city increases in population demands for more commodious offices centrally located increase, and as real estate in the heart of the city becomes more valuable old buildings are torn down to make place for new ones more modern in style and more commodious in arrangement. Each of these buildings has its numerous tenants and the proportion who move yearly can only be appreciated by comparing one of our editions with its previous one. These changes make the Directory an absolute necessity in every store and business man's office.

In conclusion the publishers desire to thank their patrons for continued support, and the public generally for courtesy extended to their agents in collecting the required data. Neither effort nor expense have been spared to make the work accurate and reliable.

R. L. POLK & CO.

TABLE OF CONTENTS.

INDEX TO ADVERTISERS.

R. L. POLK & CO.'S

Indianapolis City Directory.

1897.

STREETS AND AVENUES.

For List of Abbreviations see page 139.

Abattoir—
(W I), from White river w to Dover, first s of Morris

Abbott—
From 320 S Missouri w to West

Abigail—
From Naomi s to Oscar, first e of Shelby
25 Beecher
50 Van Buren

Adair—
(B), from C C C & St L Ry n, first e of Bartholomew

Adams—
From Thirtieth n to Howland, second e of Ralston av
50 English

Adams—
(B), from Warren n, first e of Houston

Addison—
(4th Ward), see Twenty eighth

Addison—
(W I), from Washington s, first w of Laura
Jackson

Adelaide—
(Old Choptank al), from Walnut n to St Clair

Adler—
From Meridian e to Union, first n of Raymond

Agnes—
From 500 W New York n to Elizabeth
63 Vermont
112 Michigan
168 North

Alabama, N—
From 152 E Washington n to Thirtieth, third e of Meridian
25 Court
50 Market
75 Wabash
100 Ohio
125 Miami
150 New York
200 Vermont
256 Michigan
300 North
352 Walnut
392 St Clair
Ft Wayne av
470 Pratt
500 St Joseph
520 Tenth
574 Eleventh
650 Thirteenth
715 Fifteenth
800 Sixteenth
900 Seventeenth
960 Nineteenth
1000 Twenty first
1100 Twenty second
1160 Twenty third
1200 Twenty fourth
Twenty fifth
1300 Twenty eighth

Alabama, S—
From 149 E Washington s to Wyoming
25 Pearl
50 Maryland
Virginia av
100 Georgia
150 Louisiana
195 South
225 Bane
250 Garden
296 Merrill
360 Norwood
McCarty

Albemarle—
See Hamilton av

Albert—
From 675 W Vermont n to North Michigan

Aldrich—
From Cannon e to Freeland, third s of English av
Payne
Crawford
Canby
Dupont
Golay

Alexander av—
From Sherman Drive e to National av
Southeastern av

Allegheny, E—
From Meridian e to Delaware, bet Vermont and Michigan.
Pennsylvania

Allegheny, W—
From Meridian w to Senate av, bet Vermont and Michigan
50 Illinois
100 Capitol av

Allen—
From Laurel second n of English av, w to Leota

Allfree—
From W Twenty first n to Marlette Drive, second e of Northwestern av

Alvord—
From Malott av n to Twenty first, first e of Cornell av
50 Thirteenth
100 Fifteenth
200 Sixteenth
250 Seventeenth
300 Nineteenth
350 Twentieth
409 Twenty first

Amanda—
(B), from Morris e to Shade, first n of Twenty fifth
Ella

Anderson—
(1st Ward), see Twenty first

Anderson—
(3d Ward), from C C C & St L Ry w to Howard, first n of Fourteenth

Andrews—
From Twenty second n to Twenty fifth, first w of Illinois
Twenty third
Twenty fourth

Annette—
(N I), from Twenty fourth n to Thirty first, second w of Northwestern av
Chicago
Twenty fifth
Twenty sixth
Roache av
Twenty seventh
Twenty eighth
Udell
Twenty ninth
Eugene
Thirtieth

Apple Tree Lane—
From Hollis n to Stoughton av, first e of Sterling

Applegate—
From Iowa s to Raymond, third e of East
50 Beecher
100 Sanford

Aqueduct—
From Fall creek n. first w of the canal

Arbor av—
(W I), from Oliver av s to Woodburn av
Cottage av

Arch—
From Park av e to College av, first n of St Clair
40 Broadway

Archer—
See Highland av

Arden—
(B), from Shade e to Brightwood av, first n of Warren
Lawn
Depot
Poplar

Arizona, E—
From 679 S Meridian e to Chestnut
Union

Arizona, W—
From 678 S Meridian w to Dakota
50 Capitol av
100 Carlos
150 West

Arlington av—
(14th Ward), see Van Buren

Arlington av—
From Thirtieth n to Howland, third e of L E & W R R
50 Fleet
100 Heath

Armour—
From N Senate av w, second s of Twenty first
50 Highland pl

Armstrong—
(N I), see Thirtieth

Arrow av—
(Old Clarke), from Hillside av n e to Valley av, first n of Ludlow av
Nevada

Arsenal av, N—
From 752 E Washington n to Michigan
50 Market
100 Ohio
150 New York
200 Vermont
250 Sturm av

Arsenal av, S—
From 755 E Washington s to Southeastern av
50 Williams

Arthur—
From Cottage av s to Cypress, third e of Shelby

Asbury—
From Cottage av s to Cypress, first e of State av

Ash—
From 309 Mass av n to city limits
50 Pratt
72 Tenth
100 Eleventh
200 Thirteenth
236 Fourteenth
250 Fifteenth
300 Sixteenth
350 Seventeenth
400 Nineteenth
480 Twentieth
510 Twenty first
550 Twenty second
600 Twenty third
650 Twenty fourth
700 Twenty fifth
750 Twenty sixth
800 Twenty seventh

Ashland—
(W I), from Oliver av n, third w of Drover

Astor—
From Minkner e to Wilmot

Athon—
From Rhode Island n to Indiana av, first w of Blake

Atkinson—
From Washington n to Michigan, third e of Sherman Drive
Ohio

Atlantic—
(S I), from S Park av e to Aurora, first s of National av
Girard av
Penn av

Atlas—
(1st Ward), from Nowland av to C C C & St L Ry, see Steele

Atlas—
(1st Ward), from Nineteenth n to Belt R R, first e of Sheldon
50 Twentieth
74 Pike
100 Twenty first

Atlas—
(S I), from National av s to State av
Atlantic
Pacific

Atwood—
From Sanders n to Morris, first w of Shelby

Auburn—
From C, H & D R R s to city limits, fourth e of S State av
50 Graydon
100 Southeastern av
150 English av
200 Lester
250 Woodlawn av
300 Prospect
Stanton
Cypress

Aurora av—
(S I), from cor National av and Shelby s to State av
Atlantic
Pacific

Austin—
See Thirteenth

Austin—
(B), from C C C & St L Ry n, first e of Waverly
Glen Drive

Auvergne av—
(I), from Fletcher av s to Huron av, first e of Worcester

Avon—
(S), from McPherson n e to Stanton av

Avondale—
(Brooklyn H'ts), from Turner av w to Fremont av
LeGrand
Cooper av

Ayres—
(I), from Michigan and Star av e, first s of Long
Kingbridge
Temperance
Hawkins
Sugar

Bacon—
From Shelby w to Dexter

Bailey—
From Thirty fourth n to Thirty eighth, first w of Illinois
Thirty fifth
Thirty sixth
Thirty seventh

Baird—
(B), from C C C & St L Ry n, first e of Espy

Baker—
(C R), from Crescent w to Flora, first n of Grand av

Baltimore av—
From Twenty third n to Howland, fourth e of Ralston av
50 Twenty fourth
100 Twenty fifth
150 Twenty seventh
200 Twenty eighth
250 Twenty ninth
300 Thirtieth
400 English

Bane—
From Delaware e to New Jersey, first s of South
50 Alabama

Barnes av—
(Old Emma, N I), from Twenty seventh n to Thirty first, first w of Clifton
Twenty eighth
Udell
Twenty ninth
Eugene
Thirtieth

Barnhill—
From North n to Coe, seventh w of Blake
50 Elizabeth

Barrows—
See Columbia av

Barth av—
From Sanders s to city limits, first w of Shelby
Orange
Cottage av
Minnesota
Iowa
Naomi
Beecher
Sanford

Bartholomow—
(B), from C C C & St L Ry n, first e of Hare

Bates—
From S Liberty to State av, bet Georgia and Louisiana
Noble
25 Concordia
50 Benton
100 Pine
200 Shelby
288 Leota
320 Oriental
Quincy
Warren
Detroit
Summit

Bates alley—
See Bates

Baxter av—
(N I), from Twenty second s, second w of Fall creek

Bayard—
(Old Detroit), from Madison av e to Garfield Park, second s of Raymond

Beacon—
From Bloomington w to Miley av, third n of Washington
Decatur
Wilmot
Minkner
Richland

Beaty—
(Old Water), from 90 Stevens s to Buchanan, first w of Virginia av
50 McCarty

Bedford av—
See Sutherland av

Beech—
From Hillside av s e to Ingram, thence n e to Lawrence, first n of Eighth
Ingram
Valley Drive
Gertrude av
Langley av

Beech—
(B), from Brightwood av e, first n of C C C & St L Ry

Beecher—
From J M & I R R e to State av, first n of Belt R R
East
50 Singleton
100 Gray
150 Applegate
200 New
250 Napoleon
300 Ringgold av
350 Barth av
400 Shelby
450 Laurel
500 Spruce
550 Draper
600 St Elmo

Beechwood av—
(I), from Grand av s e, first s of Oak av

Bell—
From Michigan n to St Clair, bet

Highland av and Oriental
50 North

Belle—
See Twenty eighth

Bellefontaine—
From 370 Mass av n to city limits
50 Tenth
100 Eleventh
200 Thirteenth
250 Fourteenth
300 Fifteenth
350 Sixteenth
400 Seventeenth
500 Nineteenth
550 Twentieth
600 Twenty first
650 Twenty second
700 Twenty third
750 Twenty fourth
800 Twenty fifth
850 Twenty sixth
900 Twenty seventh

Bellis—
From Darwin n, first e of Hillside av

Belmont av, N—
From W Washington n to Michigan, at city limits west

Belmont av, S—
From W Washington s to Maryland

Belmont av—
(H), from White river s to city limits, first w of Sheffield

Belmont av—
(W I) from Maryland s to Johnson.

Belt—
(W I), from Nordyke av s e, first w of York
Lynn av

Benham av—
From Wagner av s to Ainsworth, first w of University av

Benton—
From 401 E Washington s to Harrison
56 Maryland
70 Meek
99 Georgia
125 Bates
150 Louisiana
175 Lord

Bentwood—
(B), from C C C & St L Ry n, first e of Morris

Berlin av—
From Fall creek n to Thirtieth, second w of Senate av
Twenty third
Twenty fourth
Twenty fifth
Twenty eighth
Twenty ninth

Berlin—
(H), from Crawfordsville Pike n, first w of Lafayette

Bertha—
(W I), from Harris av w to Lincoln av, first s of Jackson

Bethel av—
From Auburn av and Cypress s e
Calvin
Luther
Zwingley

Beville av, N—
From Washington n to Michigan, first e of Jefferson av

Beville av, S—
From Washington s, first e of Jefferson av

Bicking—
From 408 S Delaware e to East, second s of McCarty
38 Davis
74 High
100 New Jersey

Biddle—
From Pine e to C C C & St L Ry, first n of North

Birch av—
(W I), from Oliver av s w to Marion av, first w of Drover
50 Cottage av

Bird—
From Ohio n to Vermont, bet Illinois an Meridian
50 New York

Birkenmeyer—
See Downey

Bismarck—
From 439 Virginia av w to Wright

Bismarck av—
(H), crossing Michigan n and s, first w of Sheffield av

Bismarck—
(W I), crossing Morris n and s, first w of Sheffield av

Black—
(I), from Star av e to Temperance, third s of Engish av
Kingbridge

Blackford, N—
From 346 W Washington n to Indiana av
25 Court
50 Market
100 Ohio
150 New York
206 Vermont
260 Michigan
308 North

Blackford, S—
(Old Helen), from 349 W Washington s to Georgia
25 Pearl
50 Maryland
75 Chesapeake

Blackmore—
See Twenty third

Blake—
From 438 W Washington n to Pratt
50 Market
100 Ohio
152 New York
206 Vermont
252 Michigan
310 North
378 Elizabeth
408 Rhode Island
Indiana av

Bloomington—
From Washington n to White river, first w of Greely
Market
Beacon

Blount av—
(I), from Washington av n, first e of National av

Bloyd av—
From cor Hillside and Manlove avs to Rural, thence n e to Shade, first n of Lawrence
Greenbrier lane
Cooper
Paw Paw
Catharine
Line
Hazel
Bodley
Fountain
Cushing
Rural

Bloyd av—
(B), from School n e to Bartholomew, first s of Willow
James
Harriet
Morris
Waverly
Austin
Stuart

Bluff av—
From S Meridian s w to city limits, first s of Grand av

Bodley—
From Bloyd av n to Fountain, third w of Rural

Boland—
(N I), from Twenty fourth n to cor Northwestern av and Twenty eighth, first e of Annette
Chicago
Twenty fifth
Twenty sixth
Roache av
Twenty seventh

Bond—
(N I), from Collett av n, first w of Franklin
Hibberd

Boone—
From Shelby e to State av, bet Prospect and Woodlawn av

Boston—
From Penn e, first n of Twenty first
Talbott av
Delaware

Boswell—
From Twenty eighth n e to Bellefontaine

Bow—
From Larch e to Orchard av, first s of Coyner

Boyd av—
From Raymond s, second e of Shelby
Winchester
Bryan
Wade
Bradbury
Finley av

Bradbury—
From 744 Shelby e to State av
Boyd av

Bradley—
From E Washington n to Michigan, first e of Sherman Drive
100 Ohio

Bradshaw—
From 531 Virginia av w to Wright
74 Holmes

Brandt—
From Shelby e to Churchman av, first s of Cameron
Tindall
Dietz
Knox

Brett—
From cor Indiana av and Rembrandt e to Fall creek, see Fourteenth

Brett—
From N West w to Brooks, first n of Drake, see Thirteenth

Bridge—
(W I), from Morris s, first w of Drover
Nordyke av
Lynn av

Bright—
From Ohio n to Indiana av, third w of West
150 New York
208 Vermont
266 Michigan
North
Center
Elizabeth

Brighton Boulevard—
(Old Floral av), from Holton pl n to Fall creek, first w of canal

Brightwood av—
From Tenth n, first e of Ewing

Brightwood av—
(B), from Warren n, first e of Poplar
Arden
Brinkman
Willow
Schofield

Brinkman—
See Twenty fifth

Broadway—
From St Clair n to Thirtieth, second e of East
25 Arch
84 Pratt
110 Tenth
148 Eleventh
184 Twelfth
232 Thirteenth
282 Fifteenth
400 Sixteenth
450 Seventeenth
500 Nineteenth
550 Twentieth
690 Twenty first
750 Twenty second
800 Twenty third
850 Twenty fourth
900 Twenty fifth
Sutherland av
Brown
Twenty eighth
Twenty ninth

Brook—
(I), from Washington s to P C C & St L Ry, first e of National av
Church

Brooker—
(Old Brooker's al), from Thirteenth n to Sixteenth, bet Senate and Capitol avs
30 Fourteenth
80 Fifteenth

Brooker's alley—
See Brooker

Brookland av—
From Tenth n, first e of Rural
Progress av
Pope av

Brooks—
From cor Pratt and Tenth, n to McIntyre
Torbet
Eleventh
Darnell
Thirteenth

Brookside av—
From cor Highland av and Tenth n e to Parker av
56 Omer
126 Stoughton av
174 Lambeth
232 Newman
300 Commerce
Steele
Centennial
Samoa
Jupiter
Crown
Lilly
Valley av
Rural

Brookside av, S—
See Nowland av

Brookville Road—
From E Washington s e to National av
Thurman
Sherman Drive
Thomas
Worcester
Twenty second

Brouse av—
From Twenty fifth n to city limits, seventh e of Ralston av
Twenty seventh
Twenty eighth
Twenty ninth

Brown—
From Broadway e to L E & W R R, first n of Sutherland av
College av
Sheridan
Custer
Alger

Brown—
(I), from Star av e, first s of Pure
Kingbridge
Temperance

Brown av—
(15th Ward), see Bluff av

Brown av—
From W Twenty eighth n to Thirty second, first w of Indianapolis av
Twenty ninth
Thirtieth
Thirty first

Bruce—
See Twenty third

Brush—
(Old Noble, 5th Ward), from Washington n to White river
Market

Bryan—
From Shelby e to State av, sixth s of Belt R R
Boyd av
Mattie av

Buchanan—
From 508 S East e to Virginia av, first s of McCarty
36 Greer
87 Beaty
135 Wright
175 Holmes
213 McKernan

Buckeye—
(N I), from Thirtieth n to Thirty first, first e of canal

Budd—
From Ohio to Vermont, bet Alabama and New Jersey
30 Miami
50 New York

Burford—
From White river s to Ream
50 Romaine
100 Carleton

Burgess av—
(I), from National av e, first s of C H & D R R

Burton av—
(N I), from Twenty fifth n to Udell, first w of canal
Twenty sixth
Roache av
Twenty seventh
Twenty eighth

Butler—
See Twelfth

Butler av—
(I), from Burgess av n to P C C & St L Ry, first e of Butler University

Byram Place—
From Fifteenth to Sixteenth, bet Illinois and Capitol av

Cable—
From W New York s, third w of White river

Cairo—
(Old Fountain), from Floral av w, first s of Panzy

Caldwell—
From Michigan n to Elizabeth, first e of White river

Cale—
From Brightwood av e to Mineral, third n of Tenth

Calhoun—
(Old Oscar), from Shelby e, first s of Arlington (14th Ward)

California, N—
From 302 W Washington n to Indiana av, thence n w to First
25 Court
50 Market
75 Wabash
156 New York
196 Vermont
260 Michigan
300 North
340 Indiana av
418 St Clair
472 Pratt

California, S—
From 299 W Washington s to Georgia
25 Pearl
50 Maryland

Calvin—
From Bethel av s to Pleasant av, first e of Knox
Reformers av

Cameron—
From Shelby e, first s of McDougal

Camp—
From W St Clair n to Eleventh, first w of California
50 Pratt
100 Tenth
150 Torbet

Campbell—
(8th Ward), see E North

Campbell—
(I), from Walnut av n, first e of Pleasant

Canal The—
From cor St Clair and Missouri n w to city limits

Canal—
From Thirteenth n w to Fourteneth, first e of canal

Canby—
From English av s to Prospect, first e of Crawford
Lester
Woodlawn av
Aldrich

Cannon—
From English av s to Prospect, first e of Auburn av
Lester
Woodlawn av
Aldrich

Capitol—
See Kane

Capitol av, N—
From 100 W Washington n to Thirty eighth
50 Market
78 Wabash
100 Ohio
125 Miami
150 New York
200 Vermont
225 Allegheny
250 Michigan
300 North
350 Walnut
410 St Clair
454 Pratt
528 Tenth
579 Eleventh
651 Twelfth
696 Thirteenth
718 Fourteenth
776 Fifteenth
800 Sixteenth
834 Seventeenth
900 Eighteenth
960 Nineteenth
982 Twentieth
1100 Twenty first
1150 McLean pl
1175 Twenty second
1275 Twenty third
1325 Twenty fourth
1350 Twenty fifth
1450 Twenty seventh
Twenty eighth
Twenty ninth
Thirtieth
Thirty second
Thirty third
Thirty fourth
Thirty fifth
Thirty sixth
Thirty seventh

Capitol av, S—
(Utah), from 99 W Washington s to Minnesota

25 Pearl
48 Maryland
75 Chesapeake
100 Georgia
125 Mobile
150 Louisiana
200 South
250 Garden
300 Merrill
325 Norwood
400 McCarty
505 Ray
563 Wilkins
575 Morris
Kansas
Wisconsin
Arizona

Carleton—
From Daisy w to White river, third s of Raymond
Yassie
Burford
Oscar
Dett

Carlos—
From Ray s to city limits, second w of Capitol av
26 Wilkins
Morris
Wisconsin
Arizona
Shelby

Caroline av—
From Hillside av n to Thirtieth, first e of Baltimore av
Twenty fourth
Twenty fifth
Twenty seventh
Twenty eighth
Twenty ninth

Carson—
From Meridian e to Madison av, first s of Iowa

Carter—
(8th Ward), see Vermont

Carter—
From Thirty fourth n to Thirtieth, first w of Capitol av
Thirty fifth
Thirty sixth
Thirty seventh

Carter—
(I), from Lena n to Pan Handle R R, first w of Dale

Catalpa av—
See Thirty second

Catharine—
See Norwood

Caven—
(Old Nevada), from J M & I R R e to East, first s of Iowa (14th Ward)

Cedar—
From cor Harrison and Shelby s w to Virginia av
103 English av
155 Fletcher av
173 Huron
181 Elm
200 Hosbrook

Centennial—
From Bee Line Ry s to Nowland av, first e of Steele
Brookside av
Coyner

Centennial—
(H), crossing Michigan n and s, first w of Highland av

Center—
From Bright w to Douglass, first n of North

Central av—
From terminus of Ft Wayne av n to Twenty eighth
34 Eleventh
78 Twelfth
174 Thirteenth
237 Fifteenth
350 Sixteenth
400 Seventeenth
450 Nineteenth
500 Twentieth
550 Twenty first
600 Twenty second
650 Twenty third
700 Twenty fifth
750 Sutherland
800 Twenty eighth
850 Twenty ninth
900 Thirtieth
950 Thirty fourth
1000 Thirty eighth

Central av—
(I), crossing Washington av n and s, first e of Johnson av

Centre—
(I), from Line e, first s of Fourth

Chadwick—
From W McCarty s to Morris, first e of West
Ray
Wilkins

Chambers—
(I), from Ritter av e to Campbell, n of Elm av

Chapel—
From 26 E St Clair n to Tenth, first e of Meridian
50 Pratt
100 St Joseph

Charles—
From 23 E McCarty s to Palmer
Ray
Wilkins
Morris
Downey
Lockwood

Chase—
(W I), from Oliver av n, first e of Judge Harding
South

Cherry—
See Tenth

Cherry av—
(I), from Washington av s and e, first e of Downey av

Chesapeake, E—
From 75 S Meridian e to Delaware
50 Pennsylvania

Chesapeake, W—
From 76 S Meridian w to Helen
50 Illinois
100 Capitol av
Kentucky av
150 Senate av
175 Osage
200 Missouri
250 West
300 California

Chester—
From North to Elizabeth, first w of Capitol av

Chestnut—
From 232 Madison av s to Lockwood
264 Poplar
280 Ray
312 Wilkins
340 Morris
Downey

Chestnut—
(I), from Line e, first s of Washington av

Chicago—
(N I), from Michigan Road w to C C C & St L Ry, first n of Twenty fourth

Choptank alley—
See Adelaide

Christian—
From Washington s to R R tracks, second e of Rural

Christian av—
See Eleventh

Church—
From McCarty s to Morris, first w of Capitol av
McCauley
Ray
50 Wilkins

Church—
(I), from Brook e, first s of Washington
National av

Churchman av—
(Old Pleasant av), from Prospect s beyond city limits, first e of Harlan
50 Sycamore
100 Cypress
Knox

Cincinnati—
From Michigan n to Walnut, bet Liberty and Noble
50 North

Circle—
See Monument pl

Clara—
(N I), from Eighteenth n, first w of Schurmann av

Clark—
From Harvey n, third e of Shelby

Clark—
(H), from Belmont av w, first n of Mick

Clarke—
See Arrow av

Clay—
(1st Ward), see Progress av

Clay—
(15th Ward), see Schiller

Clayton—
See Fifteenth

Clermont—
(Brooklyn Hgts), from C C C & St L Ry w to Fremont av, sixth n of Tilden

Cleveland—
(H), from Frazee n, first w of Holmes

Clifford av—
See Tenth

Clifton—
(Old Lulu, N I), from Twenty sixth to Thirty third, third w of Northwestern av
Roache av
Twenty seventh
Twenty eighth
Udell
Twenty ninth
Eugene
Thirtieth
Thirty first
Congress av
Thirty second

Clinton—
From 226 E Ohio n to Michigan, bet New Jersey and East
25 Miami
50 New York
100 Vermont

Clinton—
(Brooklyn Hgts), from C C C & St L Ry w to Fremont av, first w of Tilden

Clyde—
(1st Ward), see Twenty second

Clyde—
From Spruce e to State av, first s of Willow
Draper
St Elmo

Clyde av—
(I), from Brookville Pike s to Huron av, first w of National av
English av
Fletcher av

Coble—
From Vermont s to New York, first e of Belt R R

Coburn—
See Prospect

Coe—
From Hiawatha w to Barnhill, first n of Elizabeth
Maxwell
Wilson

Coffey—
(W I), from Oliver av n, first w of Shover
South

Coleman av—
(I), from Washington s to P C C & St L Ry, first e of National av

Colfax—
(Old Osage av), from Tenth n, first e of Lancaster av
Progress av
Pope av

Colgrove—
See Raymond

College av—
From Mass av n to Thirtieth, first e of Broadway
20 Arch
50 Pratt
100 Tenth
150 Eleventh
200 Twelfth
250 Thirteenth
300 Fourteenth
350 Fifteenth
400 Sixteenth
450 Seventeenth
500 Nineteenth
550 Twentieth
600 Twenty first
650 Twenty second
700 Twenty third
750 Twenty fourth
800 Twenty fifth
850 Twenty sixth
900 Twenty seventh
950 Twenty eighth
1000 Twenty ninth

College av—
(N of city limits), from Thirtieth n to Western av, first w of L, N A & C Ry
Fleet

College av—
(I), n end of Central av

College Circle—
(I), Park enclosed by College av

Collett av—
(I), from Burgess av s, first e of National av

Collett av—
(N I), from the canal w to Schurmann av, second n of Twenty second
Franklin
Bond

Collins—
(Old Race), from Thirteenth n to Fourteenth, first w of West.

Colorado av—
From Washington n to Michigan, sixth e of Sherman Drive
Ohio

Columbia—
(5th Ward), see Market

Columbia alley—
See Toledo

Columbia av—
(8th Ward), see Tecumseh

Columbia av—
From e end Malott av n to Macy av, third e of L E & W R R
26 Thirteenth
120 Fifteenth
150 Sixteenth
200 Seventeenth
250 Nineteenth
300 Twentieth
550 Twenty first
Twenty second
Twenty third
Davidge
Twenty fifth
Twenty seventh
Twenty eighth
Twenty ninth
Thirtieth

Commerce av—
(Orange av and old Commercial av), from cor Hillside av and Ludlow lane s e to Brookside av, thence e to Rural
Pendleton Pike
300 Brookside av
Windsor av
Larch
Jefferson av
Ramsey av
Keystone av
Eureka av
Excelsior av

Commercial av—
(I), from Washington s to P C C & St L Ry, second e of National av
Irvington av

Concord—
See Oakland av

Concord—
(H), crossing Michigan n and s, first w of Haugh

Concordia—
From Maryland s to Harrison, first e of Noble
5 Meek
25 Georgia
50 Bates
75 Louisiana
100 Lord

Congress av—
(Old Walnut av, N I), from Northwestern av w to Clifton, first n of Rader

Cook—
From Maryland s to Louisiana, bet East and Liberty
50 Georgia

Cooper—
From Fernway n to Bloyd av, first e of Paw Paw

Cooper av—
(Brooklyn Hgts), from Lafayette Gravel Road n

Cora—
From Howard w to the canal, bet Thirteenth and Fourteenth

Coram—
From N Penn e to Talbott av, first n of Sixteenth

Cornell av—
From cor Mass av and Cherry n to Thirtieth, first e of Bellefontaine
50 Eleventh
150 Thirteenth
200 Fourteenth
240 Fifteenth
314 Sixteenth
374 Seventeenth
410 Nineteenth
500 Twentieth
550 Twenty first
600 Twenty second
650 Twenty third
700 Twenty fourth
750 Twenty fifth
850 Twenty seventh
900 Twenty eighth
950 Twenty ninth

Corral—
(N I), from Michigan Road w to Twenty fourth, first s of Chicago

Cottage av—
(Old Willow and Orphan), from East e to Graydon av
Wright
Shelby
50 Olive
100 Linden
150 Arthur
200 Laurel
250 Spruce
State av
Asbury

Cottage av—
(W I), from River av w, first n of Woodburn
Birch av
Marion av
Warren av
Division

Cottrell—
From Georgia s to Louisiana, first w of Missouri

Court, E—
From Penn e to Noble, bet Washington and Market
96 Delaware
127 Alabama
200 New Jersey
225 Clinton
250 East
275 Liberty

Court, W—
From Illinois w to Blackford, bet Washington and Market
100 Capitol av
150 Senate av
175 Osage
200 Missouri
250 West
280 California

Coyner—
From Centennial e to Orchard av, first s of Brookside av
Samoa
Jupiter

Crawford—
(5th Ward), see Elder av

Crawford—
From English av s to Prospect, first e of Payne
Lester
Woodlawn av
Aldrich

Crescent—
(C R), from Northwestern av n, opp Crown Hill Cemetery
Grand av
Baker

Cress—
See Thaddeus

Cross—
From Peru av e, first s of Mass av

Crown—
From Orchard av to Brookside av, first w of Rural

Crown Hill av—
(N I), from Meridian w to Crown Hill Cemetery, first n of Thirty fifth
Salem
Illinois
Bailey
Capitol av
Carter

Cruse, N—
From 600 E Washington n to Market

Cruse, S—
From 600 E Washington s to P C C & St L Ry
Southeastern av

Curtis—
From Orchard av n to Lily, first e of Rural

Cushing—
From Bloyd av n to Pruitt, first w of Rural

Custer—
From Twenty third to Brown, first e of Sheridan
Twenty fourth
Twenty fifth

Cypress—
From 275 Shelby e to city limits

25 Young
50 Olive
Lockwood
100 Laurel
125 Seibert
Arthur
Thaddeus
150 Spruce
175 Draper
St Elmo
200 State av
Harlan
300 Churchman av
350 Auburn

Daggy—
(I), from Star av e, first s of Keightley
Kingbridge
Temperance
Hawkins
Sugar

Daisy—
From Raymond s, second e of White river
Norman
Kelly
Romaine
Carleton
Ream

Dakota—
From Ray s to city limits, first w of West
25 Vinton
50 Wilkins
75 Jones
100 Morris
150 Wisconsin
350 Arizona

Daly—
(Old Wilson), from Benton e, first s of Washington (10th Ward)

Darnell—
From West w to Brooks, first n of Eleventh
50 Oregon

Darwin—
From Bloyd av n w to Hillside av, first n of Fernway

Date—
(I), from Lena n to Watkins, first w of National av

Davidge—
See Twenty fourth

Davidson—
From E Washington n to Peru av, third e of Noble
50 Market
98 Ohio
154 New York
184 Vermont
250 Michigan
299 North

Davis—
(4th Ward), see Tenth

Davis—
From Bicking s to Madison av, first e of Delaware (12th Ward)

Dawson—
(Old John), from Lexington av s to Orange, first e of State av (9th Ward)
Woodlawn av
Prospect

Dayton—
(I), from English av s to Huron av, first e of Earl av
Fletcher av

Dearborn—
From E Washington s, first e of Gray

Decatur—
From W Washington n to Beacon, first w of Richland
Market
90 Exeritt

Delaware, N—
From 100 E Washington n to Thirty eighth
25 Court
50 Market
80 Wabash
110 Ohio
125 Miami
147 New York
206 Vermont
250 Michigan
302 North
340 Walnut
351 Ft Wayne av
404 St Clair
434 Pratt
504 St Joseph
527 Tenth
570 Eleventh
675 Twelfth
711 Thirteenth
750 Fifteenth
800 Sixteenth
900 Seventeenth
980 Nineteenth
1000 Twentieth
1050 Twenty first
1100 Twenty second
1130 Twenty third
1150 Twenty fourth
1200 Twenty fifth
Twenty eighth
Thirtieth
Thirty second
Thirty third
Thirty fourth
Thirty sixth

Delaware, S—
From 99 E Washington s to Madison av
25 Pearl
45 Virginia av
50 Maryland
96 Georgia
150 Louisiana
200 South
225 Bane
250 Garden
300 Merrill
365 McCarty
389 Wyoming
409 Bicking

Deloss—
From Shelby e to State av, first n of English av
50 Olive
100 Leota
150 Laurel
200 Spruce

Denny—
From Washington n to Michigan, second e of Sherman Drive
New York

Denny—
(B), from James w to Rural, first n of Brinkman

Depot—
(B), from Warren n, first e of Lawn

Depot av—
(I), from Cherry av s w, first e of Central av

Detroit—
(14th Ward), see Bayard

Detroit—
(4th Ward), see Hobart

Detroit—
From Southeastern av s to Bates, first e of Warren (9th Ward)

Detroit av—
(I), from English av s to Huron, first e of Dayton av

Dett—
From Ream n, second e of White river

Dexter—
From Troy s to Martin
Knox
Bacon
Perry

Dexter—
(N I), from W Eighteenth n to Twenty second, first w of Sugar Grove av
Nineteenth
Twenty first

Dickson—
From E Market n to Ohio, first e of Cruse

Dietz—
From Glen Drive n w to Sutherland, first e of Fountain

Dietz—
(S of city limits), from Brandt n, fourth e of Shelby

Dillon—
See Shelby

Division—
(B), from Rural e to Bloyd av, first s of Glen Drive
James
Harriet
Wheeler
Morris
Waverly
Austin
Stuart

Division—
(W I), from Oliver s to Morris, first w of Warren
Cottage av
Woodburn
Standard av

Dora—
(I), from Line e, first s of Tenth
Leland
Ray
Euclid Drive

Dorcas—
From Henrietta w, first s of Washington

Dorman—
From E New York n to Tenth, first w of Highland av
50 Vermont
100 Michigan
173 North
256 St Clair
300 Pratt
350 Polk

Dougherty—
From 540 S East e to Virginia av, first s of Buchanan
133 Wright
197 McKernan
296 Hunter

Douglass—
From Market n to Indiana av, first e of Blake
100 Ohio
150 New York
202 Vermont
258 Michigan
320 North
350 Center
400 Elizabeth

Downey—
(Old Hanway, Downey and Birkenmeyer), from 633 S Meridian e to Edgewood
Charles
Union
Mulberry
Chestnut
Madison av
Kennington
New Jersey
East
Wright

Downey av—
(I), from Washington av e to Ritter av, first e of Ohmer av

Downing av—
(H), from Michigan s to Vermont, first e of Concord

Drake—
From N West w to Brooks, first n of Twelfth
50 Oregon

Draper—
(Old Draper and St Charles), from Clyde s to Van Buren, first e of Spruce
Cypress
Naomi

Drover—
(W I), from South s to Belt R R, first w of White river
Oliver av
Cottage av
Woodburn av
River av
Morris

Dugdale—
From Belt R R n, first e of Meridian

Duncan—
See Garden

Dunlop—
From 543 Madison av e to East, third s of Morris
40 Kennington
80 S New Jersey

Dupont—
From Southeastern av s to Prospect, first e of Canby
Lester
Woodlawn av
Aldrich

Dye—
From W Thirtieth n to Thirty second, first w of Brown
50 Thirty first

Earhart—
From Prospect to Wallace, third e of Belt R R

Earl—
From Cypress s to Laura av, first w of Fullenwider av

Earl av—
(I), from English av s to Huron, first w of Dayton av

East, N—
From 250 E Washington n to Tenth
25 Court
50 Market
82 Wabash
98 Ohio
125 Miami
150 New York
175 Lockerbie
198 Vermont
250 Michigan
250 Mass av
310 North
356 Walnut
402 St Clair
452 Pratt

East, S—
From 249 E Washington s to Garfield Park
25 Pearl
50 Maryland
100 Georgia
Bates
150 Louisiana
160 Lord
199 Virginia av
199 South
244 Stevens pl
265 Warsaw
299 Merrill
339 Stevens
Norwood
399 McCarty
475 Bicking
506 Buchanan
540 Dougherty
578 Prospect
600 Morris
624 Sanders
674 Downey
680 Dunlop
704 Nebraska
Cottage av
738 Weghorst
764 Lincoln
784 Minnesota
800 Iowa
824 Caven
860 Beecher
900 Sanford
Raymond

East av—
(I), from Grand av e, first s of P C C & St L Ry

Eastern av—
From Washington n to Michigan, first w of Temple av
New York

Eckert—
From 279 Kentucky av s to Merrill, first w of West

Economy—
From Biddle to St Clair, first e of Pine

Eddy—
From 75 W South s to Norwood
50 Garden
100 Merrill

Eden Place—
From 225 N Delaware e to Hudson, first n of Vermont

Edgewood—
From Sanders s, first e of Wright

Edward—
(B), from C C C & St L Ry n, first e of Lancaster

Edward—
(W I), from Oliver av n, fourth w of Drover

Eighteenth—
(Old Eighteenth), see Twenty sixth

Eighteenth, E—
(Old Ninth, from Meridian to Talbott av), from Meridian e to Talbott av, first n of Seventeenth
Pennsylvania

Eighteenth, W—
(Old Ninth, from Meridian to foot of Highland pl; old Tenth, from C C C & St L Ry to Northwestern av, and Vorster av, from Meridian w to city limits), first north of Seventeenth
Illinois
Hall pl
Capitol av
Senate av
C C C & St L Ry
Lenox
Mill
Northwestern av
Canal
Fall creek
Milburn
Montcalm
Rembrandt
Post av
Gent
Sugar Grove
Dexter
Schurmann av

Eighth—
See Seventeenth

Eitel av—
From Meridian e to Penn. first n of Thirty sixth

Elder av—
From Washington n to Vermont, second w of Belt R R

Eldridge—
(14th Ward), see Laurel

Eldridge—
From Fall creek n, third w of canal

Eleventh—
(Old Eleventh), see Twentieth

Eleventh, E—
(Old Second, Morrison and Christian av), from 571 N Meridian to L E & W R R
Penn
Delaware
Alabama
New Jersey
Central av
Fort Wayne av
Park av
Broadway
College av

Eleventh, W—
From 570 N Meridian w to Fall creek
50 Illinois
100 Capitol av
150 Senate av
C C C & St L Ry
218 Howard
Fayette
West
Brooks

Elgin—
From North n to Elizabeth, first w of Chester

Elizabeth—
From Bright w to city limits, first n of North
48 Douglass
82 Blake
149 Agnes
175 Locke
204 Patterson
224 Hiawatha
233 Maxwell
250 Wilson
300 Barnhill

Elk—
See Woodlawn av

Ella—
(B), from Brinkman n, first e of Waverly

Ellen—
See Bright

Elliott—
From Bloyd av n to Greenbrier lane

Ellis—
(14th Ward), see Swift

Ellis—
From Willard n to Tenth, first e of Watts

Ellsworth—
From New York n to Vermont, first w of Senate av

Elm—
From Noble s e to Shelby, first n of Virginia av
97 Pine
175 Cedar
225 Grove

Elm—
(B), from School e to Lancaster, first n of Willow

Elm av—
(I), from Washington av n, first e of Blount av

Elmira—
(N I), from C C C & St L Ry n to Thirty first, fifth w of Northwestern av
Twenty ninth
Eugene
Thirtieth

Elnora—
From Harvey n, first e of Shelby

Elwood—
From North n to Elizabeth, first w of Caldwell

Emma—
(N I), see Barnes av

Emma av—
From Colgrove s, first e of Mattie av
Winchester av
Bryan av
Wade
Bradbury av
Hunter
Walker av

Emmet—
From N Illinois w to Capitol av, bet Walnut and Pratt

Empire—
From S Capitol av w to S Senate av, first s of South

Emrich—
(H), from Belmont av w, first n of Clara

English—
From Harrison av e to Line av, first n of Thirtieth
Hamilton
Adams
Nicholas
Baltimore av
Hillside av
Brouse av

English av—
From 71 Harrison s e to Shelby, thence to city limits
11 Pine
100 Cedar
139 Shelby
200 Olive
242 Leota
276 Laurel
320 Spruce
450 State av
Auburn av
Southeastern av

English av—
(I), a continuation of English av
McPherson
Lake av
Thomas
Star av
Kingbridge
Temperance
Earl
Dayton av
Detroit av
Worcester av
Clyde av

Erie—
(8th Ward), see Gray

Erie—
From Pearl s, first e of Alabama (10th Ward)

Erwin—
(H), from Michigan n, first w of Merrit
Summit
Grandview av

Espy—
(B), from C C C & St L Ry n, first e of Edward

Ethel—
From Twenty fourth n, first e of Northwestern av

Ethel—
(W I), from Oliver av n, first w of Drover

Euclid av—
(4th Ward), see Moesch av

Euclid av—
From Washington n to Michigan, first e of Colorado av
Ohio

Euclid Drive—
(I), from Clifford av s, third e of Line
Dora
Frank

Eugene—
(N I), from Northwestern av w to C C C & St L Ry, second n of Udell
Annette
Rader
Clifton
Barnes av
Elmira

Eureka av—
From Michigan n to Orchard av, second w of Rural
Tilden
Pratt
Tenth
Progress av
Commerce av
Pope av
Nowland av

Eutaw—
From Paca n w to Tenth, first n of Indiana av

Everett—
From Bloomington w, second n of Washington
Decatur
Wilmot
Minkner
Richland

Evison—
From 251 Prospect s to Orange

Ewing—
From Willard n to Tenth, first e of Fay

Excelsior av—
See Temple av

Fairview—
From Fall creek n, second w of the canal

Fay—
From Willard n to Tenth, first e of Ellis

Fay—
(W I), from Judge Harding w to William, first s of Morris

Fayette—
From North n w to Tenth, thence n to Thirteenth, first e of West
56 Walnut
192 St Clair
198 Pratt
225 Tenth
252 Eleventh
300 Twelfth

Fenneman—
From Palmer s to Minnesota, first w of Madison av

Fernway—
From Lawrence n e to cor Bloyd av and Fountain
Cooper
Paw Paw
Katharine
Hazel

Fifteenth—
(Old Fifteenth), see Twenty third

Fifteenth, E—
(Old Sixth and Lincoln av), from 781 N Delaware e to Hillside av
Alabama
New Jersey
Central av
Park av
Broadway
College av
Ash
Bellefontaine
Garfield pl
Cornell av
L E & W R R
Alvord
Yandes
Columbia av
Martindale av
Newman
Sheldon

Fifteenth, W—
(Old Sixth and Clayton), from 778 N Illinois w to cor Indiana and Post avs
115 Capitol av
Brooker
170 Senate av
C C C & St L Ry
220 Howard
250 Mill
Canal
West
Fall creek
Milburn
Montcalm
Rembrandt

Fifth—
See Fourteenth

Finley av—
From Shelby e, first s of Bradbury
Boyd av

First—
See Tenth

Fitch—
(B), from Lancaster w to Pendleton Road

Flack—
(H), from Belmont av w, first n of Washington
Muir av

Fleet—
From Western av e to Ralston av, first n of Thirtieth
Park av
Broadway
College av
Macy av
Grand av
Royal av
Arlington av

Fletcher av—
From cor Noble and South s e to Shelby, thence e to city limits
49 Pine
98 Cedar
150 Shelby
200 Olive
250 Laurel
300 Spruce
400 State av
Harlan
St Paul

Fletcher av—
(I), from Temperance e, first s of English av
Earl
Dayton av
Detroit av
Worcester av
Auvergne av
Clyde av

Flora—
(C R), from Grand av n, second w of Crescent

Floral av—
(4th Ward), see Twenty first

Floral av—
(5th Ward), see Brighton boulevard

Florence—
(H), from Michigan n, first w of Erwin
Summit
Grandview av

Forest av, N—
From W Washington n to Michigan, first e of Keystone av
New York

Forest av, S—
(Old Range), from W Washington s to P C C & St L Ry, first e of Keystone av

Fort Wayne av—
From 300 N Penn n e to Central av
48 Walnut
88 St Clair
120 Pratt
150 St Joseph
194 Tenth

Foundry—
(B), from Beech n, first e of Brightwood av

Fountain—
(4th Ward), see Cairo

Fountain—
From Lawrence n to Hillside av, second w of Rural
Bloyd av
Bodley
Line av
Sutherland

Fourteenth—
(Old Fourteenth), see Twenty second

Fourteenth, E—
(Old Fifth and Irwin), from 710 N Meridian e to Delaware and from College av to L E & W R R
50 Penn
100 Delaware
College av
Ash
Bellefontaine
Cornell av

Fourteenth, W—
(Old Fifth, McIntyre and Brett), from 730 N Meridian w to Capitol av
Rembrandt
50 Illinois
100 Capitol av
125 Brooker
150 Senate av
173 C C C & St L Ry
198 Howard
265 Mill
Canal
West
Oregon
Collins
Fall creek
Trumbull
Milburn
Montcalm

Fourth—
See Thirtieth

Fourth—
(I), from Line e, first s of Third

Fowler—
(Old Oxford), from N Pine e to L E & W R R, first n of St Clair

Francis—
(4th Ward), see Twenty ninth

Francis—
(W of city limits), from North av n, second w of Schurmann av

Frank—
(9th Ward), see Nelson

Frank—
Between S Meridian and Union, s of Belt R R (15th Ward)

Frank—
(I), from Line e, second s of Tenth

Franklin—
(14th Ward), see S New Jersey

Franklin—
(N I), from Collett av n, second w of the canal
Hibberd av

Frazee—
(H), from Belt R R w, first n of Michigan

Freeland—
From Southeastern av s to Prospect, first e of Golay
Lester
Woodlawn av
Aldrich

Fremont—
(Brooklyn Hgts), from Monroe w to Avondale

Fremont—
(N I), from Schurmann av e, first n of Twenty second

French—
See Twentieth

Front—
(S), from Twin Lake av n w to Avon av, w of Sherman Drive

Front—
(W I), from Morris s to Lambert, first e of Belmont av

Fulton—
From 344 E Washington n e to St Clair, first e of L E & W R R
50 Market
100 Ohio
150 New York
200 Vermont
250 Michigan
300 North

Gale—
(B), from Glen Drive n, first e of Shade

Galena—
From Raymond n, second e of Shelby
Harvey

Garden, E—
(Old Duncan), from 250 S Meridian e to New Jersey
Madison av
Penn
Delaware
Alabama

Garden, W—
(Old Henry), from 250 S Meridian w to Kentucky av
50 Illinois
76 Eddy
100 Capitol av
125 Willard
Senate av
Missouri
West

Garfield av—
From Washington n to Tenth, fourth e of Sherman Drive
New York
Michigan
Byram

Garfield Place—
From Fifteenth n to Sixteenth, bet Bellefontaine and Cornell av

Garland—
(W I), from Oliver av n, second w of Drover

Gatling—
See Barth av

Geisendorff—
From 402 W Washington n to New York
50 Market
100 Ohio

Geneva—
From Auburn w, first s of English av

Geneva—
(H), from Lafayette w, first n of Plymouth

Gent—
(N I), from Eighteenth n, first w of Post av

Georgia, E—
From 99 S Meridian e to Shelby
50 Penn
100 Delaware
150 Alabama
200 New Jersey
250 East
Cook
300 Liberty
350 Noble
373 Concordia
399 Benton
439 Pine

Georgia, W—
From 100 S Meridian w to White river
50 Illinois
98 Capitol av
159 Kentucky av
150 Senate av
175 Osage
200 Missouri
225 Cottrell
250 West
300 California
350 S Blackford

Germania av—
(H), crossing Michigan n and s, first w of Tremont av

Gertrude av—
From cor Beach and Valley av to Lawrence, third e of Hillside av

Gilbert—
(W I), from Howard s to Miller, first e of Belmont av

Gillard av—
See Keystone av

Gimbel—
See Norwood

Girard av—
(I), from National av s to State av, second w of Aurora av

Gladstone av—
From E Washington n to Tenth, fifth e of Sherman Drive
New York
Michigan
Byram

Glen av—
From Crawfordsville Road n, second w of Fall creek
Twelfth

Glen Drive—
From cor Line av and Fountain e to Rural, n e to Morris, s e to C C C & St L Ry
James
Harriet
Wheeler
Morris
Waverly
Austin
Stuart
Shade
Gale
Station

Golay—
From Southeastern av s beyond C C C & St L Ry, first e of Dupont
Lester
Woodlawn av
Aldrich
Prospect

Good av—
(I), from P C C & St L Ry s to East av, first w of Line

Goodwin—
From E Michigan s to Washington, first w of Belt R R
Vermont
New York

Grace—
From Washington s to Moore av, first e of Rural

Graceland av—
From W Thirtieth n to Thirty fourth, first w of Capitol av
50 Thirty second
100 Thirty third

Graham—
From Hillside av e to Gertrude av, first n of Valley av
Thalman av
Holloway av

Graham—
(I), from Walnut av n, first e of Maxwell

Grand av—
From Thirtieth n to Heath, first e of L E & W R R
Fleet

Grand av—
(C R, n w of city limits), from Crescent w, first s of Baker

Grand av—
(I), from Ritter av n e to Irving av, thence s e to Line, first s of University av

Grand View—
From Sutherland av n to Thirtieth, second e of College av

Grand View av—
(H), from Lafayette Road w, fourth n of Michigan

Grant—
From 322 S West w to Rose

Gray, N—
(Old Erie), from E Washington n to New York and s to P C C & St L Ry, first e of Oxford

Gray, S—
From Gresham s to Raymond, second e of East
50 Beecher
100 Sanford

Graydon—
From Sycamore s, first e of Asbury

Graydon—
(W), from Auburn av e to Rural, first n of Southeastern av
Sharpe av

Greely—
(Old State), from Washington n to White river, first w of Wallace
Market

Green av—
From Auburn av s e to Prospect, first n of C C C & St L Ry
Aldrich

Green av—
(I), from Chambers s to Elm av, second e of Ritter av

Greenbrier lane—
From Lawrence n e to Hillside av
Bloyd av

Greencastle—
See Ninth.

Greenfield—
(I), from Ritter av e, first e of C H & D R R

Greenwood—
See Cornell av

Greer—
From 44 Stevens s to Buchanan
50 McCarty

Greer alley—
See River

Gregg—
See Ninth

Gresham—
See Minnesota

Grove—
From 540 Virginia av n e to cor of Shelby and Fletcher av
Hosbrook
Elm
Huron

Grove—
(N I), from North av n, fourth e of White river

Grove av—
(2d Ward), see MacPherson av

Grover—
(N I), from Ontario n to Roache av, second w of the canal
Wells

Guffin—
From Sixteenth n to Seventeenth, bet Bellefontaine and Cornell av

Hadley—
From Agnes w to Patterson, first n of North

Hadley av—
(W I), from Drover s w to Johnson, first s e of I & V Ry
Morris
York
Stack
Belt Ry
Miller

Hall—
(8th Ward), see Olney

Hall Place—
From 74 W Sixteenth n to Twenty first, first w of Illinois
50 Eighteenth
100 Nineteenth

Hamburg—
(Old Leonard), from Raymond n to Harvey, first e of Shelby

Hamilton—
From Thirtieth n to Howland, first e of Ralston av
English

Hamilton av—
(Old Johnson), from Washington n to Michigan, first e of Randolph
Ohio

Hamilton av—
(Old Albemarle), from Michigan n to Tenth, second e of Woodruff pl
Tilden

Hampton—
From Tenth s, first e of Rural

Hann—
From Greenbrier n e to Fountain, first e of Hillside av

Hanna—
See Oriental

Hanway—
See Downey

Hare—
(B), from Bee Line Ry n, first e of Wood

Harlan—
See Twenty fourth

Harlan—
(Old Hester and Sylvan), from English av s to Cypress, first e of State av
Spann av
Fletcher av
Hoyt av
Lexington av
Pleasant
Woodlawn av
Prospect
Orange
Sycamore

Harmon—
From 125 E South s to McCarty
24 Bane
47 Garden
89 Merrill

Harriet—
(B), from Bloyd av n, first e of James

Harris—
From North n to Elizabeth, first w of Blake

Harris av—
(W I), from Washington s, first w of Ruth
Jackson
Bertha
Ida
Victoria
Oliver av

Harrison—
From 176 S Noble e to Shelby
20 Concordia
46 Benton
67 English av
104 Pine
160 Ittenbach

Harrison av—
See Ralston av

Hart—
(Old Herman, 14th Ward), from Nelson e, first s of Prospect

Hartford—
From Sanders s, first w of Edgewood

Harvey—
(Old Le Grand av), from Shelby e to city limits, first n of Raymond
Leonard
Galena
Clark
Mabel

Haugh—
(H), from Vermont n to Summit, first w of Holmes av

Hawkins—
(I), from Huron av s to Ayres, first w of Sugar
Keightley
Daggy
Long

Hazel—
From Valley av n to Bloyd av, first w of Fountain
Lawrence

Heath—
From Grand av e to Ralston av, second n of Thirtieth
Royal av
Arlington av

Helen—
See Blackford

Helen—
(H), from Michigan n, first w of Florence
Summit
Grand View av

Hendricks—
From Nebraska s to Lincoln, second e of Madison av

Henrietta—
From Washington s to Maryland, first w of White river
Dorcas

Henry—
See Garden

Herbert—
See Twentieth

Herman—
See Hart

Hermann—
From 447 E Ohio s to Market

Herron Place—
See Twenty sixth

Hester—
See Harlan

Hiatt—
(W I), from Morris s to Miller, first e of Belmont av
Lambert
Howard

Hiawatha—
From W Vermont n to Davis, fourth w of Blake
Michigan
North
Elizabeth
Rhode Island
Margaret

Hibberd av—
(N I), from the canal w to Schurmann av, first n of Collett av
Franklin
Bond

High—
From 184 E McCarty s to Prospect
70 Bicking

Highland av—
(H), from Michigan n, first w of Concord

Highland av—
From Washington n to Marlowe av, fourth e of Noble
50 Market
100 Ohio

Highland av—
(4th Ward), see Thirty first

Highland Place—
From Nineteenth n, first w of Senate av
Armour
Twentieth
Twenty first
Marlette Drive
Fall creek

Highwater—
See Albert

Hill—
(14th Ward), see Lockwood

Hill—
From 691 S Meridian e to Chestnut, first s of Downey (15th Ward)
Locust
Union

Hill av—
(1st Ward), see Hillside av

Hillside av—
(Old Hill av), from Columbia and Thirteenth n e to city limits
Martindale av
Newman
Sheldon
Arrow av
Sixteenth
Ingram
Montana
Seventeenth
Beech
Nineteenth
Twentieth
Bloyd av
Twenty first
Twenty third
Baltimore av
Caroline av
Twenty fifth
Twenty seventh
Twenty eighth
Twenty ninth
Thirtieth

Hinton—
From Brightwood av e to Mineral, first n of Tenth

Hobart—
(Old Detroit), from Thirty eighth s, first w of Meridian

Hoefgen—
(Old Hoefgens's lane), from S Meridian e to Madison av, first s of Pleasant run

Hoefgen's lane—
See Hoefgen

Holborn—
From Hiawatha w, first s of Michigan

Hollis—
From Sterling e to Tecumseh, first n of Tenth

Holloway av—
From Beech n to Lawrence, first e of Thalman av

Holloway av—
(I), from Brookfield av n to C H & D R R, third e of National av

Holly av—
(W I), from Oliver av s'w, first w of Birch av

Holmes—
From Bradshaw s to Buchanan, first e of Wright

Holmes av—
(H), crossing Michigan n and s, first w of King av

Holton Place—
(Old Ninth), from first alley w of Senate av w to Northwestern av, first n of Seventeenth
Lenox
Mill

Home av—
See Thirteenth

Hooker—
See Twelfth

Hope—
(B), from Beech n, first e of Foundry

Hopkins av—
(I), from Brookville Road n e to Holloway av

Hosbrook—
From Cedar s e to Shelby, first n of Virginia av
81 Grove
Woodlawn av

Houston—
From Talbott av w, first s of Tenth

Houston—
(B), from Warren n to C C C & St L Ry, first e of Bentwood

Hovey—
(Old Jackson), from Belt R R n to Twenty fifth, first e of Sheldon
Twenty second
Twenty third
Twenty fourth

Howard—
From Tenth n to Sixteenth, first e of the canal
Eleventh
102 Twelfth
128 Smith
150 Thirteenth
184 Cora
218 Fourteenth
Fifteenth

Howard—
(W I), from Judge Harding w, second s of Morris
William
Reisner
McLain
Lee
Shepard
Gilbert
Belmont av

Howland—
From Macy av e to National av, third n of Thirteenth
Royal
Van Buren
Ralston av
Hamilton
Adams
Nicholas
Baltimore av
Line av
Brightwood av
School

Hoyt av—
From Shelby e to St Paul, first s of Fletcher av
50 Olive
100 Laurel
150 Spruce
200 State av

Hubbard—
From Tenth s, first e of Hampton

Hudson—
From E Vermont n to Ft Wayne av, bet Delaware and Alabama
126 Michigan
North
Walnut

Humboldt—
See Seventeenth

Humboldt av—
(B), from Howland s to Schofield, third e of University av

Hunter—
(Old Short), from 269 Dougherty s to Prospect, first w of Virginia av

Huntington—
See W Eleventh

Huron—
From 250 Virginia av e to Noble, thence s e to Shelby
10 Irving pl
48 Noble
89 Pine
175 Cedar
256 Grove

Huron av—
(I), from Temperance e, first s of Fletcher av
Hawkins
Sugar
Worcester av

Ida—
(W I), from Harris w, first s of Bertha

Illinois, N—
From 48 W Washington n to Thirty eighth
50 Market
75 Wabash
100 Ohio
150 New York
200 Vermont
250 Michigan
300 North
350 Walnut
400 St Clair
450 Pratt
500 St Joseph
526 Tenth
566 Eleventh
630 Twelfth
680 Thirteenth
730 Fourteenth
778 Fifteenth
827 Sixteenth
850 Seventeenth
902 Eighteenth
975 Nineteenth
1024 Twentieth
1100 Twenty first
1150 McLean Place
1162 Twenty second
1200 Twenty third
1250 Twenty fourth
1300 Twenty fifth
1350 Twenty sixth
Twenty seventh
Twenty eighth
Twenty ninth
Thirtieth
Thirty second
Thirty third
Thirty fourth
Thirty fifth
Thirty sixth
Thirty seventh

Illinois, S—
From 49 W Washington s to city limits
26 Pearl
50 Maryland
75 Chesapeake
100 Georgia
125 Mobile
150 Louisiana
175 McNabb
200 South
250 Garden
300 Merrill
340 Norwood
396 McCarty
474 Ray
527 Wilkins
576 Morris
600 Kansas
650 Wisconsin

Indiana av—
From cor Ohio and Illinois n w to Eighteenth
52 New York
100 Vermont
154 Michigan
200 North
252 California
300 Blackford
314 Bright
340 Paca
356 Douglass
400 Blake
428 Athon
Locke
Tenth
Milburn
Montcalm
Rembrandt
Post

Indianapolis av—
From Northeastern av and Fall creek n to Thirty second, first w of Paris av

Twenty third
Twenty fourth
Twenty fifth
Twenty sixth
Twenty eighth
Twenty ninth
Thirtieth
Thirty first

Ingram— From Hillside av n e to Beech, third n of C C C & St L Ry (1st Ward)
Nevada

Ingram— (14th Ward), see Vigo

Iowa— From S Meridian e to Shelby, first s of Minnesota
Union
Madison av
Singleton
Gray
Applegate
New
Napoleon
Ringgold av
Barth av

Iron av— (N I), from Twenty second s to Twenty first, third w of Fall creek

Irving av— (I), e end of University av

Irving Place— (Old School), from 329 E South s to Huron

Irvington av— (I), crossing Lake av e and w, first s of Washington av

Irwin— See Fourteenth

Isabella— (N I), from Twenty fourth n to North western av, first e of Annette

Ismond— (N I), from Eighteenth n, first w of Mansfield av

Ittenbach— From C C C & St L Ry s to Harrison, first e of Pine
Lord

Ivy— (Old Ivy lane), from Mass av s e to Taffe, first e of Rural

Jackson— (W I), from Harris w, first s of National Road

Jackson— (1st Ward), see Hovey

Jackson— (4th Ward), see Twenty second

Jackson Place— From McCrea pl w to Illinois, first s of Georgia

James— (B), from Bloyd av n, first e of Rural
Park
Division
Glen Drive

Jefferson— (9th Ward), see Woodlawn av

Jefferson av— From Washington n to Nowland av, third e of Woodruff pl
New York
Michigan
Tilden
Pratt
Tenth
Commerce av

Jennison— (1st Ward), see Twenty seventh

Jennison— (I), from Third n, first e of Line

John— (1st Ward), see Pratt

John— (9th Ward), see Dawson

Johnson— From Brightwood av e to Mineral, fourth n of Tenth

Johnson— (W I), from Judge Harding w to Belmont av, first s of Miller
Reisner
McLain
Lee

Johnson av— (8th Ward), see Hamilton av

Johnson av— (I), from Washington av s e, first e of Ritter av

Jones— (4th Ward), see Reno

Jones— From S West w to White river, first n of Morris
76 Dakota

Jones— (I), crossing Cherry n and s, first e of Line

Judge Harding— (W I), from W Washington s to Raymond, first w of Bloomington
Oliver av
Morris
Lambert
Howard
Miller
Johnson

Julia— (N I), from North av n, third w of Schurmann av

Julian av— (I), from Maple av e, first s of Washington av

Junction av— (I), from Ritter av s e to Central av, first w of C H & D R R

Jupiter— From C C C & St L Ry s to Coyner, first e of Samoa
Brookside av

Kane— (Old Capitol, 5th Ward), from North n to Elizabeth, first w of Parkman

Kankakee— From Michigan n to North, first e of Capitol av

Kansas— From 620 S Meridian w to Carlos
50 Illinois
100 Capitol av

Kappus— (W I), from Morris s to Miller, first w of Shepard

Katharine— From Fernway n to Bloyd av and s to Langley av, first e of Paw Paw

Keaton— (I), from Line e, first n of Walnut av

Keightley— (I), from Star av e, first s of Middle
Kingbridge
Temperance
Hawkins
Sugar

Keith— From Stoughton av n to Louise, first e of Newman

Kelly— (Old Spruce, 15th Ward), from Meridian w to Daisy, second s of Raymond
Race
Vine
Bluff av

Kennington— From 168 E Morris s to Lincoln
33 Sanders
43 Downey
66 Dunlop
100 Nebraska

Kentucky av— From cor Illinois and Washington s w to city limits
54 Maryland
100 Georgia
150 Louisiana
200 South
Garden
Eckert
Merrill
Sand

Kenwood av— From W Twenty eighth n to Thirty eighth, first w of Illinois
Twenty ninth
Thirtieth
Thirty second
Thirty third
Thirty fourth
Thirty fifth
Thirty sixth
Thirty seventh

Ketcham— From E Merrill s to Norwood, first e of S Alabama

Ketcham— (H), from Michigan s to Vermont, first w of Haugh

Keystone av— (Old Gillard and Keystone av), from E Washington n to Nowland av, first e of Beville av
New York
Michigan
Tilden
Pratt
Tenth
Progress
Commerce av
Pope av

Keystone av— (Old Gillard av), from E Washington s to P C C & St L Ry, first e of Beville av

King— From N Delaware w to Pennsylvania, first n of Thirteenth

King— (5th Ward), see Minkner

King— (8th Ward), see Sturm av

King av— (H), crossing Michigan n and s, first w of Germania av

Kingbridge— (I), from English av s to Ayres, first w of Temperance
Pure
Brown
Slack
Middle
Keightley
Daggy
Long

Knox—
From Shelby w to Dexter, second s of Brandt

Knox—
S e of city limits, a continuation of Auburn from Bethel av s
Reformers av
Churchman av
Raymond
Walker av

Koerner—
See Norwood

Koller—
See New York

Lafayette—
From Tenth n to Sixteenth, first e of Howard
Eleventh
Twelfth
Thirteenth
Fourteenth
Fifteenth

Lafayette av—
Continuation of Bloomington n to limits, first w of White river

Lafayette—
(Brooklyn Hgts), from Turner av w to Fremont av, second n of Monroe

Lafayette—
(H), from Crawfordsville Pike n, first w of White river

Lake—
See Twenty fourth

Lake av—
(I), from Washington av s, first e of National av

Lake av—
(S), from English av n e to Thomas, first e of McPherson
Sherman Drive

Lambert—
(W I), from Judge Harding w to Belmont av, first s of Morris
William
Reisner
McLain
Lee
Shepard
Kappus

Lancaster—
(B), from C C C & St L Ry n, first e of Adair

Lancaster av—
From Tenth n, first e of La Salle av
Progress av
Pope av

Langley av—
From Hillside av s e to Beech, thence n e to Hazel, first n of Valley av
Thalman av
Gertrude
Beech

Langsdale av—
From Northwestern av w, second s of Fall creek

Laporte av—
(B), from Howland s to Schofield, second e of University av

Larch—
From Commerce av n e, first w of Jefferson av

La Salle—
(4th Ward), see Montcalm.

La Salle—
(Old Watts and Lebanon), from Washington n, first e of Dearborn
New York
Michigan
Willard
Tenth
Nowland av

Laura—
(W I), from Washington s, first w of Belmont av
Jackson

Laurel—
(Old Linden and Eldridge), from Deloss to Van Buren, first e of Leota
English av
Spann av
Fletcher av
Hoyt av
Lexington av
Pleasant
Woodlawn av
Prospect
Orange
Smithson
Cottage av
Cypress
Vigo
Naomi

Lawn—
(B), from Warren n, first e of Shade

Lawrence—
From cor of Greenbrier lane and Hillside av s e to Rural
Gertrude av
Fernway
Beech
Hazel
Fountain

Lebanon av—
See La Salle

Lee—
(W I), from Johnson n to Morris, third e of Belmont av
Miller
Howard
Lambert

Leeds—
From Traub av w to Belmont av, first n of Washington

Le Grand—
(B H), from Monroe n to Avondale, second w of Turner av

Le Grand av—
(14th Ward), see Harvey

Leland—
(I), from Clifford av s, first e of Line

Lemcke—
From E Washington s, third w of Belt R R

Lena—
(I), from Worcester e to National av, first s of Watkinson

Lenox—
From Sixteenth n to Holton pl, first w of C C C & St L Ry
Seventeenth

Leon—
From Michigan n to North, bet East and Liberty

Leonard—
From Colgrove n to Harvey, first e of Shelby (14th Ward), see Hamburg

Leonard—
From Cottage av s to Minnesota, third w of Shelby (14th Ward)
Roll

Leota—
From 126 Southeastern av s to English av
50 Meek
100 Bates
C C C & St L Ry
Deloss

Lester—
From Auburn av e to Freeland, first s of English av
Cannon
Payne
Crawford
Canby
Dupont
Golay

Lexington av—
(4th Ward), see Sackville

Lexington av—
From Shelby e to city limits, first s of Hoyt av
50 Olive
100 Laurel
150 Spruce
200 State av
220 Dawson
270 Nelson
Villa av
Harlan

Liberty, N—
From 300 E Washington n to Mass av
25 Court
50 Market
78 Wabash
100 Ohio
125 Miami
150 New York
166 Lockerbie
213 Vermont
248 Michigan
296 North

Liberty, S—
From 299 E Washington s to South
50 Maryland
75 Meek
100 Georgia
150 Louisiana
Lord

Lily—
From cor Brookside av and Crown e to Parker av, first n of Orchard av
Rural
Urbana

Lincoln av—
See Fifteenth

Lincoln av—
(W I), from Jackson s to Victoria, first w of Harris

Lincoln lane—
See Lincoln

Lincoln—
(Old Lincoln lane), from Madison av e, fifth s of Morris
Kennington
Hendricks
East

Linden—
(1st Ward), see Twelfth

Linden—
From Harrison s to Prospect, see Laurel

Linden—
From Prospect s to Cypress, second e of Shelby
Orange
Cottage av
Swift

Line—
(I), crossing Washington av n and s, first e of Maple av

Line av—
From Bloyd av n to Thirty eighth, third e of Hillside av
Fountain
Sutherland
Twenty fifth
Twenty seventh
Twenty eighth
Twenty ninth
Thirtieth
Howland

Linwood av—
From Washington n to Michigan, seventh e of Sherman Drive
New York

Locke—
From 175 Elizabeth n to Indiana av
50 Rhode Island
111 Margaret
121 Maria

Lockerbie—
From East e to Noble, bet New York and Vermont
50 Liberty

Lockwood—
(Old Hill), from Cypress s, second e of Shelby (14th Ward)

Logan—
From Plymouth s to Raymond, first w of East

London av—
From Fall creek n to Thirtieth, first w of Senate av
Twenty third
Twenty fourth
Twenty fifth
Twenty eighth
Twenty ninth

Long—
(I), from Star av e, first s of Daggy
Kingbridge
Temperance
Hawkins
Sugar

Lord—
From 163 S East e to Shelby
Noble
Concordia
Benton
Pine
Ittenbach

Lorraine—
From Langley av n to Lawrence, first w of Hazel

Louise—
From Newman n e to Commerce av, first n of Stoughton av

Louise av—
(I), from Worcester av s e to English av

Louisiana, E—
From 149 S Meridian e to Noble
50 Pennsylvania
100 Delaware
150 Alabama
200 New Jersey
250 East
275 Cook
300 Liberty

Louisiana, W—
From 150 S Meridian w to Capitol av
McCrea
50 Illinois

Louthain—
From Cottage av s, first e of Spruce

Low—
(C R), from Grand av n, first w of Crescent

Lowell—
(W I), from Belmont av w, first n of Morris

Ludlow av—
From Hillside av n e to Valley av, first e of Sheldon
Nevada

Lulu—
See Clifton

Luther—
From Bethel av s, first e of Calvin
Reformer's av

Lynn—
(11th Ward), see Oriental

Lynn—
From I D & W Ry n to Michigan, first e of Belmont av (5th Ward)
50 New York
100 Vermont
130 Wilcox

Lynn av—
(W I), from Bridge s w to Belt R R, first e of Nordyke av

McCarty, E—
From 399 S Meridian e to Virginia av
31 Charles
51 Union
71 Mulberry
81 Madison av
C C C & St L Ry
114 Delaware
124 Harmon
150 Alabama
180 High
258 New Jersey
285 East
327 Greer
371 Beaty
412 Water
419 Sullivan

McCarty, W—
From 400 S Meridian w to White river
37 Illinois
76 Maple
99 Capitol av
123 Church
133 McGinnis
155 Senate av
165 Meikel
199 Missouri
233 Chadwick
247 West

McCarty—
(W I), from Belmont av w, first s of Oliver av

McCauley—
From 450 S Capitol av w to Missouri, first s of McCarty
19 Church
McGill
29 Meikel

McCord—
From Shelby e to Dietz, third s of Finley av
Tindall

McCormick—
From Miley av e, second n of Washington

McCrea—
From Georgia s to Louisiana, first w of Meridian

McDougal—
From Shelby e, first s of McCord

McGill—
From 188 W Louisiana s to South

McGinnis—
From W McCarty s to Ray, second w of Capitol av
McCauley

McIntire—
(4th Ward), see Fourteenth

McKenzie—
See Armour

McKernan—
From 213 Buchanan s to Sanders, second w of Virginia av
100 Dougherty
150 Prospect
200 Morris

McKim av—
From 729 E Washington s to Williams, between Oriental and Arsenal av

McLain, N—
(W I), from Morris n, first w of Reisner

McLain, S—
(W I), from Morris s, first w of Reisner
Lambert
Howard
Miller
Johnson

McLean Place—
(Old Thirteenth), from Meridian w to Senate av, first n of Twenty first
Illinois
Capitol av

McLene—
(4th Ward), see Roach av

McNabb—
From 184 S Meridian w to Illinois

McOuat—
From 176 Patterson w to Hiawatha

McPherson—
(E of city limits, S), from English av n, second w of Sherman Drive
Twin Lake av
Avon av
Stanton av

McRea—
(14th Ward), see Napoleon

Mabel—
From Harvey n, fourth e of Shelby

MacPherson—
(Old Grove av), from Twenty seventh n to Thirtieth, first e of Cornell av

Macy—
From Thirtieth n to Heath, first e of L E & W R R

Madeira—
S e of city limits, from Prospect s, first e of Miami

Madison—
See Polk

Madison av—
From cor Meridian and South s e to Morris, thence s to city limits
100 Merrill
125 Union
150 Norwood
187 McCarty
195 Ray
300 Delaware
350 Wilkins
400 Prospect
410 Davis
425 Morris
485 Sanders
500 Downey
550 Dunlop
582 Nebraska
Palmer
684 Lincoln av
692 Minnesota
Iowa
Sanford
Raymond

Malinda—
From Kelly w, first s of Smithson

Malott av—
From cor Eleventh and Cornell av n e to Columbia av
Alvord
64 Yandes

Manchester—
(1st Ward), see Thirtieth

Manhattan av—
(Brooklyn Hgts), from Smith av e, first n of Tilden

Mankedick—
From Spruce e to State av, first s of Orange

Manlove av—
From Hillside av n to Thirtieth, third e of Ralston av
Long Branch
Twenty third
Twenty fourth
Twenty fifth
Twenty seventh
Twenty eighth
Twenty ninth

Mansfield av—
(N I), from Eighteenth n, first w of Clara

Maple—
From 73 W McCarty s to Morris, second w of Meridian
94 Ray
142 Wilkins

Maple av—
(I), from Cherry av n, first e of Central av

Margaret—
From Rhode Island w to Hiawatha, fourth n of North
25 Locke

Maria—
From Rhode Island w to Locke

Marion av—
(W I), from Oliver av s to Woodburn av, first e of Warren av
Cottage av

Market, E—
From Monument pl e to State av, first n of Washington
50 Penn
100 Delaware
150 Alabama
190 New Jersey
250 East
300 Liberty
350 Noble
360 Spring
366 Fulton
396 Davidson
450 Pine
472 Hermann
592 Highland av
Oriental
721 Arsenal av

Market, W—
(Old Market, Columbia and Springfield), from Monument pl to Miley av, first n of Washington
50 Illinois
75 Muskingum
100 Capitol av
150 Senate av
175 Osage
208 Missouri
250 West
300 California
350 Blackford
400 Geisendorff
Blake
White river
Brush
Wallace
Greely
Bloomington
Decatur
Wilmot
Minkner
Richland

Markland—
(I), from Fourth s, first e of Jennison

Marlette Drive—
From N Senate av w to Northwestern av, first s of Fall creek
Highland Place
Shriver
Allfree
Wendell

Marlowe av—
A continuation of E Miami, from Preston e to Oriental, first n of Ohio

Martha—
(W I), from Belmont av w, between Howard and Miller

Martin—
From Shelby w to Dexter, fifth s of Brandt

Martindale av—
From Hillside av n to Thirtieth, first e of Columbia av
60 Fifteenth
132 Sixteenth
160 Seventeenth
210 Nineteenth
276 Twentieth
320 Twenty first
Twenty second
Twenty third
Twenty fourth
Twenty fifth
Twenty seventh
Twenty eighth
Twenty ninth
Thirtieth

Maryland, E—
From 49 S Meridian e to Alabama
50 Pennsylvania
100 Delaware

Maryland, W—
From 50 S Meridian w to city limits
50 Illinois
100 Capitol av
Kentucky av
148 Senate av
166 Osage
200 Missouri
249 West
300 California
339 Blackford
White river
Henrietta
Belmont av

Mason—
(9th Ward), see St Paul

Mason—
From Madison Road e, second s of Raymond

Massachusetts av—
From the cor of Ohio and Pennsylvania n e to L E & W R R
50 New York
100 Vermont
150 Michigan
200 North
250 Walnut
300 St Clair
304 College av
314 Oak
329 Fulton
330 Ash
370 Bellefontaine
450 Cornell av
500 Yandes
550 Columbia av
600 Martindale av
650 Newman
700 Sheldon
750 Orange
800 Atlas
850 Centennial
900 Samoa
950 Jupiter
1000 Nowland av

Mattie av—
(S e of city), from Warren av n to Colgrove av, first e of Bloyd av
Wade
Bryan av
Winchester av

Maxwell—
From North n to Tenth, fifth w of Blake
55 Elizabeth
100 Coe

Maxwell av—
(I), from Walnut av n, first e of Greene

Mayhew—
See Twelfth

Meadow—
From Fall creek and Hooker n, second e of Glen av

Mechanic—
From E South s to Garden, between Meridian and Pennsylvania

Meek—
From 64 S Liberty e to Leota
49 Noble
70 Concordia
102 Benton
152 Pine
208 Shelby

Meikel—
From McCarty s to Ray, first w of Senate av
50 McCauley

Meridian, N—
From 2 W Washington n to city limits, dividing the city e and w
22 Monument pl
94 Ohio
152 New York
210 Vermont
252 Michigan
304 North
350 Walnut
410 St Clair
450 Pratt
500 St Joseph
528 Tenth
566 Eleventh
680 Thirteenth
700 Fourteenth
800 Sixteenth
820 Seventeenth
836 Eighteenth
862 Nineteenth
1000 Twenty first
1028 McLean pl
1100 Twenty second
1130 Twenty third
1196 Twenty fourth
Twenty fifth
Twenty eighth
1700 Thirtieth
Thirty second
Thirty third
Thirty fourth
Thirty fifth
Thirty sixth
Thirty seventh
Thirty eighth

Meridian, S—
From 1 E Washington s to city limits, dividing the city e and w
25 Pearl
49 Maryland
57 Chesapeake
99 Georgia
135 Mobile
149 Louisiana
185 McNabb
199 South
225 Madison av
249 Garden
299 Merrill
349 Norwood
399 McCarty
493 Ray
543 Wilkins
587 Morris
620 Kansas
633 Downey
655 Wisconsin
Palmer
678 Arizona
Minnesota
Raymond

Merrill, E—
From 300 S Meridian e to Virginia av
50 Madison
Union
50 Pennsylvania
100 Delaware
125 Harmon
140 Ketcham
145 Alabama
200 New Jersey
250 East

Merrill, W—
From 300 S Meridian w to Kentucky av
50 Illinois
75 Eddy
100 Capitol av
125 Willard
150 Senate av
200 Missouri
250 West
292 Eckert
300 Rose

Merritt—
(H), from Michigan n, first w of Lafayette Road
Summit
Grand View av

Miami, E—
From N Meridian e to Noble and from Highland to Oriental, bet Ohio and New York
50 Pennsylvania
100 Delaware
150 Alabama
200 New York
225 Clinton
250 East
300 Liberty
Highland av
Oriental

Miami, W—
From Capitol av w

to West, bet Ohio and New York
Roanoke
50 Senate av
75 Osage
100 Missouri
130 Toledo

Miami—
S e of city limits, from Prospect s to Wallace, first w of Madeira

Michigan, E—
From 249 N Meridian e to city limits
50 Pennsylvania
75 Susquehanna
100 Delaware
150 Alabama
194 New Jersey
250 East
300 Liberty
310 Cincinnati
330 Noble
380 Spring
388 Fulton
402 Davidson
450 Pine
C C C &StL Ry
550 Dorman
600 Highland av
650 Bell
675 Oriental
700 Myla av
750 Arsenal av
850 State av
Walcott
Randolph
Woodruff Place
Columbia av
1034 Hamilton av
1050 Jefferson av
1070 Ramsey av
Keystone av
1106 Forest av
1112 Eureka av
1118 Tacoma av
1128 Excelsior av
1134 Temple av
Eastern av
Rural
La Salle
Belt R R
Sherman Drive
Bradley
Denny
Atkinson
Garfield av
Gladstone av
Colorado av
Euclid av

Michigan, W—
From 250 N Meridian w to city limits
50 Illinois
100 Capitol av
150 Senate av
200 Missouri
250 West
300 California
348 Blackford
366 Bright
400 Douglass
450 Blake
475 Minerva
571 Agnes
595 Patterson
604 Hiawatha
650 Albert
White river
Elwood
Caldwell

Michigan—
(I), from Wallace e, second n of Washington av

Michigan av—
(8th and 9th Wards), see Southeastern av

Michigan road—
See Northwestern av

Mick—
(H), from Belmont av w, first n of Grand View av

Middle—
From Senate av to Howard, between Tenth and Eleventh

Middle—
(I), from Star av e, first s of Slack
Kingbridge
Temperance

Middle Drive—
See Woodruff Place

Milburn—
From Indiana av n, first w of Trumbull

Miley av—
(Old Miley av and Taylor), from W Washington n to Vermont, first w of Belt R R
Market
McCormick
Decatur
Beacon
Astor
New York

Mill—
From Fourteenth n to Eighteenth, sixth w of Meridian
25 Fifteenth
Sumner
50 Sixteenth
Seventeenth

Miller—
(W I), from Judge Harding w to Eagle creek, between Howard and Johnson
William
Reisner
McLain
Lee
Shepard
Gilbert
Hyatt
Belmont av

Miller—
(4th Ward), see Nineteenth

Mineral—
From Tenth av n, first e of Brightwood av

Minerva—
From New York n to North, first w of Blake
70 Vermont
140 Michigan

Minkner—
(Old King, 5th Ward), from Washington n to New York, third w of Bloomington
Market
McCormick
Beacon
Astor

Minnesota, E—
(Minnesota and Gresham), from Meridian e to Shelby, first s of Palmer
Union
Chestnut
J M & I R R
Madison av
East
Gray
New
Leonard
Ringgold av

Minnesota, W—
From Meridian w to White river, first s of Palmer
Illinois
Capitol av
Carlos

Minter av—
(C R), from Northwestern av w, first s of Grand av

Mississippi, N and S—
See Senate av N and S

Missouri, N—
From 200 W Washington n to Tenth
25 Court
50 Market
75 Wabash
100 Ohio
125 Miami
150 New York
200 Vermont
250 Michigan
300 North
350 Walnut
500 St Clair
616 Pratt

Missouri, S—
From 199 W Washington s to Ray
25 Pearl
50 Maryland
75 Chesapeake
100 Georgia
150 Louisiana
200 South
262 Garden
280 Merrill
320 Abbott
347 Norwood
399 McCarty
494 Ray

Mobile—
From 124 S Meridian w to Capitol av
50 Illinois

Moesch—
(Old Euclid av, N I), from cor Michigan Road and Addison n e

Monroe—
(8th Ward), see Tilden

Monroe—
N e of city limits (Brooklyn Heights), from s end Turner av w to Fremont av

Montana—
From Sheldon e to Hillside av, first n of Sixteenth

Montcalm—
From Indiana av n to Shooting Park, first w of Milburn
Fourteenth
Fifteenth
Sixteenth
Seventeenth
Eighteenth

Monument place—
Formerly Circle

Moore av—
From Rural e to Grace, first s of Washington

Morgan—
(W I), from McLain w to Lee, first s of Miller

Morris, E—
From 582 S Meridian e to McKernan
22 Charles
50 Union
75 Mulberry
83 Chestnut
J M & I R R
150 Madison av
283 East
374 Wright
Atwood
McKernan

Morris, W—
From 588 S Meridian w to city limits
53 Illinois
61 Maple
100 Capitol av
172 Church
200 Carlos
253 West
333 Dakota
White river

Morris—
(B), from Bee Line Ry n, first e of Wheeler
Park
Division
Twenty fifth

Morris—
(W I), a continuation of W Morris, from White river w
Drover
Bridge
Nordyke av
Hadley av
River av
Division
Belt Ry
Judge Harding
Williams
Reisner
McLain
Lee
Belmont av

Morrison—
(2d Ward), see Eleventh

Morton—
See Iowa

Mozart—
From Madison av e to Chestnut, first n of Raymond

Muir—
(H), from Washington n, first w of Belmont av
Flack

Mulberry—
From 69 E McCarty s to Morris
Poplar
Ray
Wilkins

Mulberry Court—
Between Meridian and Delaware, first n of Thirty fifth

Muskingum—
From Washington n, between Illinois and Capitol av

Myla av—
From Ohio to Michigan, first e of Oriental
New York
Vermont

Myrtis—
From Northwestern av e, first n of Fifteenth

Naomi—
From Shelby e to State av, fourth s of Prospect
Laurel
Spruce
Draper

Napoleon—
(Old McRea), from Iowa s to Raymond, fifth e of East
50 Beecher
100 Sanford

National av—
(I), from Washington s to Ayres
Church
Lena
Nora
English av
Fletcher av
Huron av

National av—
(S I), from Shelby w to S Park av

National road—
See W Washington av

Nebraska—
From 581 Madison av e to East.
31 Kennington
Hendricks
90 S New Jersey

Neil—
From Washington s, second w of Belt R R

Nelson—
(Frank and Quince), from Lexington av s to Sycamore, second e of State av
Woodlawn av
Prospect
Orange

Nevada—
(14th Ward), see Caven

Nevada—
From Mass av n e to Sheldon (1st Ward)
Ludlow av
Arrow av
Vigo
Hillside av

New—
From Minnesota s to Raymond, fourth e of East
Iowa
Beecher
Sanford

New Jersey, N—
From 200 E Washington n to city limits
25 Court
48 Market
76 Wabash
96 Ohio
125 Miami
150 New York
191 Vermont
247 Michigan
300 North
352 Walnut
400 St Clair
449 Pratt
489 Ft Wayne av
491 St Joseph
500 Tenth
600 Eleventh
700 Thirteenth
770 Fifteenth
800 Sixteenth
870 Seventeenth
960 Nineteenth
1000 Twentieth
1050 Twenty first
Twenty second
Twenty third
Twenty fourth
Twenty fifth
Twenty eighth
Twenty ninth
Thirtieth
Thirty first
Thirty second

New Jersey, S—
(Old Franklin), from 199 E Washington s to Nebraska
24 Pearl
50 Maryland
100 Georgia
149 Louisiana
199 South
230 Bane
250 Garden
295 Merrill
348 Norwood
390 McCarty
478 Bicking
Prospect
Sanders
Downey
Dunlop

New York, E—
(Old Koller and old Ohio, from Randolph e to city limits), from 149 N Meridian e to city limits
50 Pennsylvania
98 Delaware
150 Alabama
175 Budd
200 New Jersey
225 Clinton
250 East
299 Liberty
350 Noble
372 Spring
384 Fulton
393 Davidson
406 Pine
C C C & St L Ry
550 Highland av
Oriental
Myla av
Arsenal av
N State av
Walcott
Randolph
Hamilton av
Jefferson av
N Beville av
Keystone av
Forest av
Tacoma av
Temple av
Eastern av
Rural
Oxford
Gray
LaSalle
Belt R R

New York, W—
From 150 N Meridian w to city limits
54 Illinois
102 Capitol av
150 Senate av
174 Ellsworth
212 Missouri
225 Toledo
254 West
296 California
352 Blackford
384 Bright
414 Douglass
432 Blake
472 Minerva
500 Agnes
White river
Minkner
Richland
Cable
Miley av
Elder av
Lynn

Newman—
From Tenth n to Stoughton, thence n w to Hillside av, thence n to Twenty fifth
Brookside av
Massachusetts av
Hillside av
Fifteenth
Sixteenth
Seventeenth
Nineteenth
Twenty first
Twenty second
Twenty third
Twenty fourth

Newport—
(Old Smith), from 39 Rhode Island n to Indiana av (4th Ward)
42 Maria
100 Rathbone

Nicholas—
From English n to Thirty eighth, third e of Ralston av
Howland

Nineteenth—
(Old Nineteenth), see Twenty seventh

Nineteenth, E—
(Old Tenth from Pennsylvania to Central av and old Ninth from Central av east), from Pennsylvania e to Hillside av, third n of Sixteenth
50 Talbott av
100 Delaware
150 Alabama
200 New Jersey
250 Central av
325 Ruckle
350 Park av
400 Broadway
450 College av
470 Ash
500 Bellefontaine
550 Cornell av
L E & W R R
600 Alvord
650 Yandes
700 Columbia av
788 Martindale av
Newman
Sheldon
Atlas

Nineteenth, W—
(Old Tenth), from 980 N Illinois w to Capitol av, third n of Sixteenth

Nineteenth—
(Old Miller av, N I), from Gent w, second n of Eighteenth

Ninth—
(From Central av n to Hillside av), see Nineteenth

Ninth—
(From gravel pit at foot of Highland Place to Talbott av), see Eighteenth

Ninth—
(From Northwestern av to first alley w of Senate av), see Holton Place

Noble—
(5th Ward), see Brush

Noble, N—
From 350 E Washington n to cor Massachusetts av and St Clair
50 Market
75 Wabash
100 Ohio
128 Miami
150 New York
178 Lockerbie
216 Vermont
250 Michigan
306 North
389 St Clair

Noble, S—
From 351 E Washington s to Virginia av
50 Maryland
64 Meek
100 Georgia
135 Bates
150 Louisiana
170 Lord
177 Harrison
200 South

200 Fletcher av
240 Huron
275 Woodlawn av

Nora—
(I), from Parker e to National av, first s of Lena

Nordyke av—
(W I), from Morris s w to I U Ry, bet Hadley and Lynn avs

Norman—
From Daisy w, first s of Raymond
Yassie

North, E—
From 297 N Meridian e to Oriental
50 Pennsylvania
50 Ft Wayne av
75 Susquehanna
100 Delaware
125 Hudson
150 Alabama
175 Tremont
200 New Jersey
250 Mass av
250 East
275 Leon
300 Liberty
318 Cincinnati
350 Noble
426 Spring
434 Fulton
Peru av
452 Davidson
Pine
Dorman
Highland av

North, W—
From 300 N Meridian w to White river
50 Illinois
100 Capitol av
150 Senate av
175 Wood
200 Missouri
225 Fayette
250 West
291 California
356 Blackford
400 Bright
428 Douglass
450 Blake
494 Minerva
540 Agnes
Patterson
566 Hiawatha
Maxwell
604 Albert
Wilson
Barnhill
Caldwell
Elwood
Porter
Parkman
Kane
Chester
Elgin
Sherman Drive

North av—
(N I), from Schurmann av w to White river, first n of Wells
Clara
Twenty ninth
Julia
White
Grove
Woodbine
Vale

North Brookside av—
See Brookside av

Northwestern av—
(Old Michigan Road), from cor West and Fifteenth n to Thirty eighth
Sixteenth
Seventeenth
Eighteenth
Nineteenth
Twenty first
Langsdale
Wilmington
Twenty third
Twenty fourth
Twenty seventh
Twenty eighth
Udell
Twenty ninth
Eugene
Thirtieth
Thirty first

Norwood, E—
(Old Phipps, Koerner, Sinker and Gimbel), from 349 S Meridian e to Virginia av
Union
Pennsylvania
Madison av
J M & I R R
Delaware
Harmon
Alabama
Ketcham
New Jersey
East
Greer
Beaty

Norwood, W—
(Old Norwood, Catharine and Roe), from 48 Russell av w to city limits, first s of Merrill
Illinois
Capitol av
Missouri
Chadwick
West
Rose
Dakota

Nowland av—
(Old S Brookside av), from cor Commerce av and Windsor n e to Parker av, thence e to Colfax
Larch
Jefferson av
Ramsey av
Keystone av
Eureka av
Temple av
Rural
Brookland av
Parker av
Oakland av
Waverly
LaSalle
Lancaster

Oak—
From Mass av n to Eleventh, first e of College av
65 Pratt
96 Tenth

Oak—
(B H), from Turner av w to Fremont av, first n of Monroe

Oak—
(I), from Walnut av n, first e of Line

Oakland av—
(Old Concord and Oakland av), from E Michigan n to Nowland av, first e of Hubbard
Topp Place
Tenth
Progress av
Pope av

Oakwood—
From Hillside av e to Line, first n of Fountain

Ohio, E—
From 99 N Meridian e to Randolph
50 Pennsylvania
100 Delaware
150 Alabama
200 New Jersey
224 Clinton
250 East
298 Liberty
350 Noble
360 Spring
386 Fulton
396 Davidson
400 Pine
450 Hermann
600 Highland av
645 Oriental
675 Myla av
700 Arsenal av
760 State av
Walcott

Ohio, W—
From 94 N Meridian w to city limits
50 Illinois
92 Capitol av
150 Senate av
196 Missouri
2.3 Toledo
248 West
Blackford
Geisendorff
Douglass
Blake

Ohio—
(From Randolph e to city limits), see New York

Ohio—
(I), from Wallace e, first n of Washington av

Ohmer av—
(I), from P C C & St L Ry s w to University av, thence s e to Downey, first e of Butler av

Old Mill Race—
From Maxwell w, n of West Washington av

Olin—
From Ohio s, first e of La Salle

Olive—
From Harrison s beyond Cypress, first e of Shelby
Deloss
English av
Spann av
Fletcher av
Hoyt av
Lexington av
50 Pleasant
75 Woodlawn av
100 Prospect
200 Orange
300 Cottage av

Oliver av—
(W I), from White river w, first s of South
Drover
Birch av
Ethel
Garland
Ashland
Marion av
Edward
Warren
Osgood
Division
Shover
Arbor
Chase
Judge Harding
Belmont av

Olney—
(Old Hall), from Washington s, first e of Tuxedo

Omer—
From Brookside av e to Lambeth, first n of Tenth

Ontario—
See Twenty fifth

Orange—
From Edgewood e to city limits, first s of Prospect
Ringgold av
Barth av
Shelby
Olive
Linden
Laurel
Spruce
Evison
State av
Harlan
Pleasant av

Orange av—
See Commerce av

Orchard—
(I), from Washington av s, first e of Line

Orchard av—
From Nowland av n e to Parker av, first s. of Brookside av
Crown
Eureka av
Temple av
Rural

Orchard av—
(N I), n e of city limits, from Schurmann av w to White river, first n of North av

Oregon—
From Darnell n to McIntyre, first w of West
85 Mayhew
100 Drake

Orient—
(N I), from Northwestern av w, first s of Lake

Oriental, N—
(Old Hanna), from Washington n to Tenth, first e of Highland av
50 Market
100 Ohio
Marlowe av
150 New York
200 Vermont
Sturm av
250 Michigan
300 North
350 St Clair
400 Pratt
450 Polk

Oriental, S—
(Oriental and Lynn), from 693 E Washington s to Bates
33 Williams
Southeastern av

Oriole—
From Nebraska to Lincoln, second w of East

Orphan—
See Cottage av

Osage—
N and s crossing Washington, first w of Senate av

Osage alley—
See Osage

Osage av—
See Colfax

Oscar—
(14th Ward), see Calhoun

Oscar—
From Ream n, third e of White river (15th Ward)

Osgood—
(W I), from Oliver av n, fourth e of Judge Harding

Oxford—
(2d Ward), see Fowler

Oxford—
From Washington n to New York, first e of Rural

Paca—
From cor Indiana av and St Clair n to Tenth
50 Pratt

Pacific—
(S I), from South Park av e to Aurora, second s of National av

Palmer—
From 835 S Meridian e to Madison av
25 Charles
50 Union
Chestnut
Fenneman
J M & I R R

Pansy—
From Brighton boulevard w to Fall creek, first s of Twenty first

Paris av—
From Fall creek n to Thirtieth, third w of Senate av
Twenty third
Twenty fourth
Twenty fifth
Twenty eighth
Twenty ninth

Park—
(B), from Rural e to Morris, first s of Division
James
Harriet
Wheeler

Park av—
From Massachusetts av n to Thirtieth, first e of East
52 St Clair
66 Arch
103 Pratt
120 Tenth
159 Eleventh
210 Twelfth
248 Thirteenth
336 Fifteenth
400 Sixteenth
450 Seventeenth
500 Nineteenth
550 Twentieth
600 Twenty first
650 Twenty second
700 Twenty third
Twenty fourth
Twenty fifth
Sutherland av
Twenty eighth
Twenty ninth

Park Front—
From Brookside av e to Lambeth, second n of Tenth

Parker—
(I), from Brookville av n, first w of National av

Parker av—
From Tenth and Massachusetts av n to C C C & St L Ry, first e of Brookland av
Progress av
Pope av
Nowland av
Orchard av
Lily
Urbana
Brookside av

Parkman—
From North n to Elizabeth, first w of Porter

Patterson—
From Vermont n to Elizabeth, third w of Blake
106 Michigan
162 North

Patton—
From Brightwood av e to Mineral, second n of Cale

Paw Paw—
From Fernway n to Bloyd av, first e of Cooper

Payne—
From English av s to Prospect, first e of Cannon
Lester
Woodburn av
Aldrich

Pearl, E—
From 24 S Meridian e to Pine
50 Pennsylvania
100 Delaware
150 Alabama
175 Erie
200 New Jersey
250 East
400 Benton

Pearl, W—
From 25 S Meridian w to White river
50 Illinois
100 Capitol av
150 Senate av
200 Missouri
250 West
300 California
350 Blackford

Peck—
From Nineteenth s, first w of Central av

Pendergast—
From Concord w, first n of Michigan

Pennsylvania, N—
From 50 E Washington n to Thirty eighth
24 Court
50 Market
75 Wabash
100 Ohio
149 New York
199 Vermont
258 Michigan
298 North
352 Walnut
402 St Clair
442 Pratt
498 St Joseph
570 Tenth
612 Eleventh
632 Thirteenth
700 Fourteenth
790 Sixteenth
830 Seventeenth
900 Nineteenth
1000 Twenty first
1100 Twenty second
1130 Twenty third
1164 Twenty fourth
1250 Twenty fifth
Twenty eighth
Thirtieth
Thirty second
Thirty third
Thirty fourth
Thirty sixth
Eitel av

Pennsylvania, S—
From 49 E Washington s to Madison av
25 Pearl
49 Maryland
75 Chesapeake
93 Georgia
146 Louisiana
200 South
287 Merrill

Pennsylvania av—
(S I), from National av s to State av, first w of Aurora

Perry—
From Shelby w to Dexter, fourth n of Brandt

Peru av—
From cor of Fulton and North n e to Mass av
25 St Clair
40 Pratt
100 Cross

Phipps—
See Norwood

Phipps—
(B), from Pendleton Road s, second w of Lancaster

Picken—
From Nineteenth n to Belt R R, second e of Sheldon
Twentieth
Twenty first

Pierce—
See Wilmot

Pike—
From Sheldon e to Hillside av, first n of Twentieth
Atlas
Picking
Tipton

Pine, N—
From 500 E Washington n to Peru av
50 Market
100 Ohio
150 New York
204 Vermont
254 Michigan
304 North
344 Biddle
400 St Clair
Fowler
Pratt

Pine, S—
From 501 E Washington s to Harrison, thence s w to 346 Virginia av
Daly
50 Maryland
55 Meek
100 Georgia
125 Bates
150 Louisiana
191 Lord
195 Harrison
200 English av
268 Fletcher av
300 Huron
340 Elm

Pleasant—
From Shelby e to St Paul, second n of Prospect
50 Olive
100 Laurel
150 Spruce
200 State av
Dawson
Nelson
Villa av
Harlan

Pleasant—
(I), from Washington n to Michigan, first e of Summit

Pleasant av—
(14th Ward), see Churchman av

Pleasant av—
(I), from Walnut av n w, first e of Graham

Plum—
From 539 W Washington s, second w of White river

Plum alley—
See Plum

Plymouth—
From Chestnut e to East, first n of Raymond
Webb
Randell
Logan

Plymouth av—
(H), from Lafayette w, first n Crawfordsville pike

Polk—
(Old Madison), from C C C & St L Ry e to Oriental, second n of St Clair
50 Dorman
100 Highland av

Pope av—
From Keystone av e to Colfax, third n of Tenth
Eureka av
Temple av
Rural
Brookland av
Parker av
Oakland av
Waverly av
La Salle
Lancaster

Poplar—
From Union e to Chestnut, first s of McCarty
Mulberry

Poplar—
(B), from Warren n, first e of Depot

Porter—
From North n to Elizabeth, first w of Elwood

Post av—
From Crawfordsville Pike n to Eighteenth, first e of Schurmann av
Indiana av
Fifteenth
Sixteenth
Seventeenth

Prairie—
See Tacoma

Pratt, E—
(Old Pratt, Gregg, Vine, John and Greencastle av), from 455 N Meridian e to city limits
Pennsylvania
Delaware
Alabama
Ft Wayne av
New Jersey
East
Park av
Broadway
College av
Oak
Ash
Bellefontaine
Massachusetts av
L E & W R R
Dorman
Highland Place
Oriental
U S Arsenal gr'nds
Woodruff Place
Tecumseh
Hamilton av
Jefferson av
Ramsey av
Keystone av
Eureka av
Temple av

Pratt, W—
From 456 N Meridian w to Paca, thence n w to Tenth
50 Illinois
100 Capitol av
125 Roanoke
150 Senate av
C C C & St L Ry
200 Missouri
225 Fayette
250 West
275 California
312 Camp
360 Paca
400 Blake

Preston—
From Ohio to Marlowe av, first w of Highland av

Progress av—
(Old Clay), from Keystone av e to Colfax, first n of Tenth
Eureka av
Temple av
Rural
Brookland av
Parker av
Oakland av
Waverly
La Salle
Lancaster av

Prospect—
(Old Coburn), from Madison av e beyond city limits, first n of Morris
High
New Jersey
East
Wright
McKernan
Hunter
Virginia av
Shelby
Olive
Linden
Laurel
Spruce
Evison
State av
Dawson
Nelson
Villa av
Harlan
Churchman av
St Paul
St Peter
Auburn av
Cannon
Payne
Crawford
Canby
Dupont
Golay
Freeland
Madeira
Earhart

Pure—
(I), from Star av e, first s of English av
Kingbridge
Temperance

Putnam—
(B)), from Shade e to Brightwood av, first s of Pendleton Road

Queen av—
(Old Spring, N I), from Fall creek e, first s of Lake

Quill—
From Naomi s, first w of State av

Quince—
See Nelson

Quincy—
From Southeastern av to Bates, first e of Oriental

Quincy—
(I), from Washington av n, first w of Summit

Race—
See Collins (4th Ward)

Race—
From Raymond s to Kelly, first w of S Meridian (15th Ward)
Tabor

Rachel—
From W Maryland s to I U Ry, first w of Blackford

Rader—
(N I), from cor C C C & St L Ry and Twenty fourth n, third w of Northwestern av
Chicago
Twenty fifth
Twenty sixth
Roache av
Twenty seventh
Twenty eighth
Udell
Twenty ninth
Eugene
Thirtieth
Thirty first
Ethel av
Congress
Thirty second

Railroad—
(I), from Line av e to East

Ralston av—
(Old Harrison av), from Twenty first n to L E & W R R, fifth e of Columbia av
Twenty second
Twenty third
Twenty fourth
Twenty fifth
Jennison
Twenty seventh
Twenty eighth
Twenty ninth
Thirtieth
Fleet
English
Heath
Howland

Ramsey av—
From Michigan n to Nowland av, fourth e of Woodruff pl
Tilden
Tenth
Commerce

Randolph—
(1st Ward), see Ninth

Randolph—
From 900 E Washington n to Michigan (8th Ward)
New York
Vermont
Sturm av

Range—
See Forest av

Ransdell—
From Raymond n to J M & I R R, second e of Madison av

Rathbone—
From Newport w, fourth n of Elizabeth

Rawles av—
(I), from Central av s e, first s of Beechwood av

Ray, E—
From 493 S Meridian e to Madison av
25 Charles
50 Union
77 Mulberry
100 Chestnut

Ray, W—
(Ray and Shearer), from 492 S Meridian w to White river
50 Illinois
75 Maple
100 Capitol av
125 Church
McGill
128 Meikel
138 Carlos
150 Missouri
175 Chadwick
West
Dakota

Ray—
(I), from Clifford av s, second e of Line

Raymond, E—
(Raymond and Colgrove), from S Meridian e to Knox, third s of Belt R R
Chestnut
Madison av
Webb
Ransdell

J M & I R R
Logan
East
Singleton
Gray
Applegate
New
Napoleon
Ringgold av
Barth av
Shelby
Hamburg
Galena
Boyd av
Mattie av

Raymond, W—
From S Meridian w, third s of Belt R R
Race
Vine
Bluff av
Daisy
Yassie
White river

Ream—
From Daisy w to White river, fourth s of Raymond
Yassie
Burford
Oscar
Dett

Ream—
(Brooklyn Hgts), from C C C & St L Ry w to Fremont av, fifth n of Monroe

Rebecca—
See Twenty ninth

Reformer's av—
From Knox e, first s of Bethel av

Reichwein—
From W Washington s, first w of Belt R R

Reisner, N—
(W I), from Morris n, first w of William

Reisner, S—
(W I), from Morris s, first w of William
Lambert
Howard
Miller
Johnson

Rembrandt—
From Indiana av n, first w of Montcalm

Reno—
(Old Jones, N I), from Sackville w to Schurmann av, first n of Jackson

Reuben—
From Reichwein w to Belmont av, first s of Washington
Neil
Lemcke
Thompson

Reynolds av—
(H), from Grand View av n, first w of Lafayette Road

Rhode Island—
From 408 Blake w to Hiawatha
25 Athon
63 Newport
75 Locke

Richard—
See Sixteenth

Richland—
(Old Wright), from Washington n, first w of King (5th Ward)
Market
Beacon

Ringgold av—
(Old Wallack,) from Sanders s to Raymond, second w of Shelby
Orange
Cottage av
Roll
Minnesota
Iowa
Beecher
Sanford

Ritter av—
(I), crossing Washington av n and s, first e of Elm av

River—
From Missouri w to White river, first n of Merrill

River—
(N I), from North av n, first e of White river

River av—
(W I), from intersection of Oliver av and White river s w to Morris
Cottage av
Woodburn av
Standard av
Division

Roache—
From Washington n, e of city limits, to New York, second w of Sherman Drive

Roache av—
(Old McLene, N I), from Northwestern av w to Schurmann av, fourth n of Chicago
Annette
Rader
Clifton
Burton av
Grover

Roanoke—
From Walnut n to Tenth, between Capitol av and Senate av
50 St Clair
100 Pratt

Rock—
From S Meridian e to Madison av, second s of Belt R R

Rockwood—
(13th Ward), see Lord

Roe—
See Norwood

Roll—
From Leonard e to Shelby, first s of Cottage av
Ringgold av
Barth av

Romaine—
From Daisy w to White river, second s of Raymond
Burford
Oscar

Root—
From 404 S West w to White river

Root—
(Brooklyn Hgts), from C C C & St L Ry n to Fremont av, fourth n of Monroe

Rose—
From Merrill s to Norwood, first w of West
Grant

Roseline—
From Brookside av to Orchard av, first e of Jupiter

Royal av—
From Thirtieth n, second e of L E & W R R

Rucker—
From Ream n, first e of White river

Ruckle—
From E Seventeenth n to Twenty first, first e of Central av
Nineteenth
Twentieth

Ruddell—
From N Illinois w to Capitol av, first n of Twenty seventh

Rural, N—
From Washington n to city limits, first e of Eastern av
New York
Michigan
Tenth
Progress av
Commerce av
Pope av
Nowland av
Orchard av
Lily
Urbana
Brookside av
Massachusetts av
C C C & St L Ry
Lawrence
Bloyd av
Park
Pruitt
Division
Glen Drive
Twenty fifth

Rural, S—
From Washington s to English av, first e of Eastern av
Moore

P C C & St L Ry
Southeastern av

Russ—
From Brightwood av e to Mineral, second n of Tenth

Russell av—
From 300 S Illinois (cor Merrill) s e to McCarty
61 Norwood

Ruth—
(W I), from W Washington s, first w of Addison
Jackson

Sackville—
(Old Lexington av, 4th Ward, N I), from W Twenty first n to Twenty third, first w of Fall creek

Sahm—
From Alabama e to Central av, first n of Pratt

St. Charles—
See Draper

St. Clair, E—
From 409 N Meridian e to Oriental
50 Pennsylvania
100 Delaware
150 Ft Wayne av
Alabama
200 New Jersey
250 East
Park av
300 Broadway
College av
Massachusetts av
Spring
424 Fulton
465 Peru av
553 Pine
C C C & StL Ry
600 Dorman
650 Highland av

St. Clair, W—
From 410 N Meridian w to Indiana av
25 Superior
50 Illinois
100 Capitol av
150 Senate av
200 Missouri
225 Fayette
250 West
270 California
300 Camp
350 Paca

St. Elmo—
From Naomi s to Van Buren, first w of State av

St. Joseph, E—
From 497 N Meridian e to Ft Wayne av
50 Pennsylvania
100 Delaware
140 Alabama

St. Joseph, W—
From N Meridian w to Illinois, fourth w of North

St. Marie av—
See Wade

St. Mary—
See Tenth

St. Paul—
(Old Mason and St Paul), from Southeastern av s to Bethel av, second w of Auburn av
English av
Spann av
Fletcher av
Geneva
Lexington av
Pleasant
Woodlawn av
Prospect
Stanton av

St. Peter—
From C C C & St L Ry s to Prospect, first w of Auburn av
Woodlawn av

Salem—
(Old Superior, 4th Ward), from W Thirty fourth n to Thirty sixth, first w of Meridian

Samoa—
From C C C & St L Ry s to Coyner, first e of Centennial

Sample—
(W I), from Judge Harding e to Belt R R, first n of Morris

Sand—
From Kentucky av s e to McCarty, first s of Merrill

Sanders—
From Madison av e to Shelby, first s of Morris
Kennington
New Jersey
East
Wright
Edgewood
Ringgold av
Barth av

Sanford—
From East e to Shelby, first n of Raymond
Singleton
Gray
Applegate
New
Napoleon
Ringgold av
Barth av

Sangster av—
From Twenty first n to Thirtieth, sec- e of Ralston av
Long Branch
Twenty third
Twenty fourth
Twenty fifth
Twenty seventh
Twenty eighth
Twenty ninth

Schofield—
(B), continuation of Thirtieth from Morris to National av
Shade
Gale
Station
Brightwood av
Foundry
Hope
School
Wood
Hare
Bartholomew
Adair
Lancaster
Edward
Espy
Baird

Schofield av—
From Twenty first n to Thirtieth, first e of Ralston av
Twenty third
Twenty fourth
Twenty fifth
Twenty seventh
Twenty eighth
Twenty ninth

School—
See Irving pl

School—
(B), from Warren s, first e of Brightwood av

Schurmann av—
(N I), from Indiana av n to junction C C C & St L Ry and Thirtieth
Eighteenth
Nineteenth
Twenty first
Twenty second
Fremont
Collett av
Hibbard av
North av
Roache av
Orchard av
Twenty eighth
Udell

Scioto—
N and s crossing Washington, first e of Meridian

Scott—
From Tenth to Eleventh, bet Illinois and Capitol av

Second—
(Old Second), from Delaware w to Fall creek, see Eleventh

Second—
(Old Second), from Delaware w to Central av, see Twelfth

Second—
(I), from Line e, first s of P C C & St L Ry

Senate av, N—
From 152 W Washington n to Thirty eighth
25 W Court
54 Market
75 Wabash
100 Ohio
128 Miami
152 New York
200 Vermont
225 Allegheny
252 Michigan
300 North
364 Walnut
400 St Clair
476 Pratt
526 Tenth
576 Eleventh
624 Twelfth
670 Thirteenth
724 Fourteenth
764 Fifteenth
822 Sixteenth
850 Seventeenth
900 Eighteenth
964 Nineteenth
Twentieth
Twenty first
Twenty third
Twenty fourth
Twenty fifth
Twenty sixth
Twenty seventh
Twenty eighth
Twenty ninth
Thirtieth
Thirty first
Thirty second
Thirty third
Thirty fourth
Thirty fifth
Thirty sixth
Thirty seventh

Senate av, S—
From 149 W Washington s to Merrill
25 Pearl
42 Maryland
100 Georgia
125 Mobile
150 Louisiana
200 South
242 Garden

Seventeenth—
(Old Seventeenth), see Twenty fifth

Seventeenth, E—
(Old Eighth), from N Meridian e to Hillside av, first n of Sixteenth
Pennsylvania
Talbott av
Delaware
Alabama
New Jersey
Central av
Ruckle
Park av
Broadway
College av
Ash
Bellefontaine
Guffin
L E & W R R
Alvord
Yandes
Columbia av
Martindale av
Newman
Sheldon

Seventeenth, W—
(Old Eighth and Humboldt), from N Meridian w to city limits, first n of Sixteenth
Illinois
Hall pl
Capitol av
Senate av
C C C & St L Ry
Lenox
Mill
Northwestern av
Canal
Fall creek
Milburn
Montcalm
Rembrandt
Post av
Sugar Grove av

Seventh—
See Sixteenth

Shade—
(B), from Warren av n, first e of Adams

Shank—
(I), from Line av e, first s of Walnut

Sharpe—
(12th Ward), see Garden

Sharpe av—
From P C C & St L Ry s, first e of Auburn av (9th Ward)
Southeastern av

Shearer—
See Ray

Sheffield—
(W I), crossing Morris n and s, first w of Belmont av

Sheffield av —
(H), from Vermont n, first w of Belmont av

Shelby—
(Old Dillon and Shelby), from Meek s to city limits, first e of Pine
Georgia
Bates
Lord
Harrison
Cedar
Deloss
English av
Spann av
Fletcher av
Grove
Hoyt av
Huron
Lexington av
Elm
Pleasant
Hosbrook
Woodlawn av
Boone
Prospect
Virginia av
Sanders
Orange
Cottage av
Pleasant Run
Twenty third
Cypress
Minnesota
Iowa
Naomi
Beecher
Belt R R
Van Buren
Sanford
Harvey
Raymond
Wincnester
Bryan
Wade
Bradbury
Finley av

Sheldon—
From Mass av n to city limits, first e of Newman
C C C & St L Ry
Hillside av
Sixteenth
Montana
Seventeenth
Nineteenth
Twentieth
Pike
Twenty first
Twenty second
Twenty fourth
Twenty fifth

Shepard—
(W I), from Lambert s to Miller, second e of Belmont av

Sheridan—
(4th Ward), see Wayne

Sherman Drive, E
From E Washington n to Tenth, fourth e of Belt R R

Sherman Drive, W
From E Washington s to Churchman av, fourth e of Belt R R

Shoemaker—
See Twenty seventh

Short—
(13th Ward), see Hunter

Short—
From Walker av e, first s of Bradbury (14th Ward)

Shover—
(W I), from Oliver av n, third e of Judge Harding

Shriver—
From W Twenty first n to Fall creek, third e of Northwestern av

Seibert—
From Cypress n, first e of Olive

Singleton—
From Iowa s to Raymond, first e of East
50 Beecher
100 Sanford

Sinker—
See Norwood

Sixteenth—
(Old Sixteenth), see Twenty fourth

Sixteenth, E—
(Old Seventh), from N Meridian e to Hillside av, first n of Fifteenth
50 Pennsylvania
Talbott av
100 Delaware
150 Alabama
200 New Jersey
250 Central av
300 Park av
350 Broadway
375 College av
400 Ash
500 Bellefontaine
550 Cornell av
L E & W R R
543 Alvord
560 Yandes
586 Columbia av
640 Martindale av
670 Newman
728 Sheldon

Sixteenth, W—
(Old Seventh and Richard), from N Meridian w to city limits, first n of Fifteenth
50 Illinois
Hall pl
100 Capitol av
150 Senate av
C C C & St L Ry
250 Lenox
252 Howard
260 Mill
Northwestern av
Canal
Fall creek
Milburn
Montcalm
Rembrandt
Post av
Indiana av

Sixth—
See Fifteenth

Slack—
(I), from Star av e, first s of Brown
Kingbridge
Temperance

Smith—
From N Illinois w to the canal, bet Twelfth and Thirteenth (3d Ward)
50 Capitol av
100 Senate av
C C C & St L Ry
Howard

Smith—
(13th Ward), see Alabama

Smith—
(5th Ward), see Newport

Smith av—
(Brooklyn Hgts), from Monroe n to Avondale, first w of Turner av

Smithson—
From Laurel e to Spruce, first s of Orange

South, E—
From 199 S Meridian e to Noble
49 Pennsylvania
99 Delaware
153 Alabama
199 New Jersey
249 East
309 Irving pl

South, W—
From 200 S Meridian w to Kentucky av
50 Illinois
75 Eddy
100 Capitol av
149 Senate av
183 McGill
195 Missouri
249 West

South—
(W I), from Drover w, first n of Oliver av
Ethel
Garland
Ashland
Edward
Osgood
Shover
Coffey
Chase
Judge Harding

South av—
(I), from Grand av s, first e of Central av

South Brookside av—
See Nowland av

South Park av—
(S I), from National av s to State av, fourth w of Shelby

Southeastern av—
From 503 E Washington s e to National av
Cruse
Shelby
128 Leota
167 Oriental
175 Quincy
219 Warren
McKim av
Arsenal av
Detroit
233 Summit
269 State av
St Paul
Auburn av
Woodside av
English av
Canby
Dupont
Golay
Freeland
Sherman Drive

Southern av—
From S Meridian e to Shelby, first s of Hoefgen
Madison av
J M & I R R
Bean creek

Spann av—
From Shelby, first s of English av, e to city limits
50 Olive
100 Laurel
150 Spruce
State av
Harlan
St Paul

Spencer av—
(B), from Brightwood av e to School, first n of Schofield

Spice lane—
From Glen Drive n to Sutherland, first w of Rural

Spratt av—
(I), from Ohmer n e, thence s e to Grand av, first s of P C C & St L Ry
Downey av
Ritter av

Spring—
(4th Ward), see Queen av

Spring—
From Market n to St Clair, first e of Noble
50 Ohio
100 New York
150 Vermont
200 Michigan
250 North
Walnut

Springdale Place—
From Oriental to Arsenal av, first n of Market

Springfield—
See Market

Spruce—
15th Ward), see Kelly

Spruce—
(Spruce and old Urbana, 14th Ward), from C C C & St L Ry e to Van Buren, third e of Shelby
Deloss
English av
Spann av
Fletcher av
Hoyt av
Lexington av
Pleasant
Woodlawn av
Boone
Prospect
Orange
Mankedick
Smithson
Cottage av
Clyde
Cypress
Naomi
Belt R R

Standard av—
(W I), from River av w to Division av, first s of Woodburn av

Stanton av—
(S), from McPherson e to Thomas, first s of C H & D R R
Avon av
Sherman Drive

Star av—
(I), from English av s to Ayres, first w of Kingbridge
Pure
Brown
Slack
Middle
Keightley
Daggy
Long

State—
(5th Ward), see Greely

State av, N—
From 826 E Washington n to Michigan
50 Market
100 Ohio
150 New York
200 Vermont
225 Sturm av

State av, S—
From 825 E Washington s to city limits
54 Williams
88 C H & D R R
100 Southeastern av
Bates
C C C & St L Ry
150 Deloss
175 English av
200 Spann av
225 Fletcher av
250 Hoyt av
275 Lexington av
410 Pleasant
550 Woodlawn av
Boone
600 Prospect
700 Orange
725 Mankedick
775 Sycamore
825 Cottage av
860 Clyde
900 Cypress
Naomi
Beecher
Van Buren
Harvey
Raymond
Winchester
Bryan
Wade
Bradbury
Finley av
Walker av

State av—
(S I), from South Park av e to Aurora

Station—
(B), from Glen Drive n, first e of Gale

Steele—
(Old Atlas), from Nowland av n w to Mass av, first w of Centennial
Brookside av

Sterling—
From Tenth n to Stoughton av, first e of Winsdor

Stevens—
From 328 S East e to Virginia av
91 Beaty

Stevens Place—
From 227 S New Jersey e to East

Stillwell—
From Tenth s to Polk, first e of Dorman

Stock—
(W I), from Hadley av s e to Nordyke av, bet York and I U Ry

Stoughton av—
From Brookside av e, second n of Tenth
Woodruff av
Newman
Windsor
Sterling

Stuart—
(B), from Bloyd av n, first e of Austin

Sturm av—
(Old King and Sturm av), from Highland av e to Randolph, first s of Michigan (8th Ward)
Oriental
Arsenal av
State av
Walcott

Sugar—
(I), from Huron av s to Ayres, first w of National av
Keightley
Daggy
Long

Sugar Grove av—
(N I); from Indiana av n to Twenty second, first w of Post av
Seventeenth
Eighteenth
Herbert
Nineteenth
Twenty first

Sullivan—
See Wright

Summit, N—
From E Ohio n to Vermont, bet Arsenal and State avs
New York

Summit, S—
From 817 E Washington s to Bates
Williams
C H & D R R
Southeastern av

Summit—
(H), from White river w, second n of Michigan
Merritt
Erwin
Florence
Helen

Summit—
(I), from Washington av n, first w of Pleasant

Sumner—
From Howard w to Mill, first n of Fifteenth

Superior—
(4th Ward), see Salem

Superior—
From North n to Eleventh, first w of Meridian
50 Walnut
110 St Clair
150 Pratt
200 St Joseph
228 Tenth

Susquehanna—
From New York n to North, bet Pennsylvania and Delaware
50 Vermont
100 Michigan

Sutherland—
From cor Fountain and Line n e to cor of Rural and Twenty fifth (1st Ward)

Sutherland av—
(Old Bedford av), from Central av n e to Thirtieth, first n of Twenty fifth
Park av
Broadway
College av
Twenty eighth
Twenty ninth

Swift—
(Old Ellis), from 381 Olive e to Linden, first s of Cottage av

Sycamore—
From State av e to Churchman av, first s of Orange
Graydon
Nelson
Villa av
Harlan

Sycamore—
(Brooklyn Hgts), from C C C & St L Ry w to Cooper av, third n of Monroe

Sylvan—
(14th Ward), see Harlan

Tabor—
From S Meridian w, first s of Raymond (15th Ward)
Vine
Race
Bluff av

Tacoma, N—
From E Washington n to Michigan, third w of Rural
New York

Tacoma, S—
(Old Prairie), from E Washington s to P C C & St L Ry, third w of Rural

Taffe—
From Parker av n to Lily
Orchard av

Talbott av—
From Sixteenth n to Twenty fifth, first e of Pennsylvania
156 Nineteenth
250 Twenty first
350 Twenty second
380 Twenty third
420 Twenty fourth

Taylor—
(8th Ward), see Miley av

Tecumseh—
(Old Columbia av and Tecumseh, 8th Ward), from E Michigan n to Commerce av, first e of Woodruff pl
Tilden
Pratt
Tenth
Hollis

Temperance—
(I), from English av s to Ayres, first w of Earl
Pure
Brown
Fletcher av
Slack
Middle
Huron av
Keightley
Daggy
Long

Temple av, N—
(Old Temple av and Excelsior av), from E Washington n to Orchard av, first e of Tacoma
New York
Michigan
Tilden
Pratt
Tenth
Progress av
Commerce av
Pope av
Nowland av

Temple av, S—
(Old Woodside), from Washington s to Southeastern av, first e of Tacoma
P C C & St L Ry
Graydon

Tennessee, N—
See N Capitol av

Tennessee, S—
See S Capitol av

Tenth—
(Old Tenth), from C C C & St L Ry w to Northwestern av, see Eighteenth

Tenth—
(Old Tenth), from Meridian e to Central av and from Meridian w to Highland pl, see Nineteenth

Tenth—
(Old Tenth), from Central av e to Martindale av, see Twentieth

Tenth, E—
(Old First, St Mary, Cherry and Clifford av), from N Meridian e to city limits, tenth n of Washington
Pennsylvania
Delaware
Alabama

New Jersey
East
Park av
Broadway
College av
Oak
Ash
Bellefontaine
Cornell av
Massachusetts av
Dorman
Stillwell
Brookside av
Highland av
Woodruff av
Newman
Windsor
Sterling
Tecumseh
Hamilton av
Jefferson av
Ramsey av
Keystone av
Eureka av
Temple av
Rural
Brookland av
Parker av
Oakland av
Waverly av
LaSalle
Lancaster av
Ellis
Colfax
Cleveland av

Tenth, W—
(Old First and Davis), from 528 N Meridian w to city limits, tenth n of Washington
Illinois
Capitol av
Senate av
C C C & St L Ry
Howard
Canal
Fayette
West
California
Camp
Paca
Pratt
Brooks
Indiana av
Locke
Maxwell
Fall creek
Sherman Drive
Lafayette Road
Grand View av

Thaddeus—
(Old Thaddeus and Cress), from Cypress s to Van Buren, first w of Spruce
Vigo
Naomi

Thalman av—
From Beech n e to Lawrence, first e of Hillside av
Langley

Thayer—
(W I), from National Road s, first e of Eagle creek

Third—
See Twelfth

Third—
(I), from Line av e, first s of Second

Thirteenth—
(Old Thirteenth, from Talbott av to Hillside av), see Twenty first

Thirteenth—
(Old Thirteenth, from first alley e of Highland pl to Meridian), see McLean pl

Thirteenth, E—
(Old Home av), from 632 N Pennsylvania e to Columbia av
100 Delaware
150 Alabama
200 New Jersey
250 Central av
322 Park av
333 Broadway
370 College av
Ash
Bellefontaine
500 Cornell av
L E & W R R
Alvord
Yandes

Thirteenth, W—
(Old Fourth, Brett, from West to Fall creek and Austin), from N Meridian w to Trumbull, first n of Twelfth
112 Capitol av
125 Brooker
150 Senate av
C C C & St L Ry
210 Howard
225 Fayette
West
Brooks
Fall creek

Thirtieth—
(Old Thirtieth), see Thirty eighth

Thirtieth, E—
(Old Twenty second and Manchester), from Meridian e to city limits, first n of Twenty ninth
Pennsylvania
Talbott av
Delaware
Alabama
New Jersey
Central av
Park av
Broadway
College av
Ash
Bellefontaine
Fleming av
Fall creek
Macy av
Columbia av
Martindale av
Grand av
Royal av
Arlington av
Ralston av
Schofield av
Sangster
Manlove av
Baltimore av
Caroline av
Hillside av
Brouse av
Line av

Thirtieth, W—
(Old Twenty second and Armstrong), from Meridian w to city limits
Illinois
Kenwood av
Capitol av
Graceland av
Senate av
London av
Berlin av
Paris av
Indianapolis av
Brown av
Dye
Northwestern av
Annette
Rader
Clifton
Barnes av
Elmira
Schurmann av

Thirty Eighth, E—
(Old Thirtieth), from N Meridian e, first n of Thirty seventh
Fall creek
Delaware
Central av

Thirty Eighth, W
(Old Thirtieth), from Meridian w to Northwestern av
25 Detroit
50 Illinois
75 Kenwood
100 Capitol av
125 Carter
150 Senate av

Thirty Fifth—
(Old Twenty seventh), from Illinois w to Senate av, first n of Thirty fourth
Kenwood av
Capitol av
Graceland av

Thirty First, E—
(Old Twenty third), from Meridian e to Central av, first n of Thirtieth
Pennsylvania
Delaware
New Jersey

Thirty First, W—
(Old Twenty third and Highland av), from Meridian w to city limits, first n of Thirtieth
Illinois
Kenwood av
Capitol av
Graceland av
Indianapolis av
Brown av
Dye
Northwestern av
Annette
Rader
Clifton
Barnes av
Elmira

Thirty Fourth, E—
(Old Twenty sixth), from Meridian e to Central av, first n of Thirty third
Pennsylvania
Delaware

Thirty Fourth, W
(Old Twenty sixth), from Meridian w to Senate av, first n of Thirty third
Salem
Illinois
Kenwood av
Capitol av
Graceland av

Thirty Second, E—
(Old Twenty fourth), from N Meridian e to Central av, first n of Thirty first
Pennsylvania
Delaware
New Jersey

Thirty Second, W
(Old Twenty fourth and Catalpa av), from N Meridian w to city limits, first n of Thirty first
50 Illinois
75 Kenwood av
100 Capitol av
125 Graceland av
150 Senate av
200 Indianapolis av
250 Brown av
275 Dye
Northwestern av
Rader
Clifton

Thirty Seventh—
(Old Twenty ninth), from N Meridian w to Crown Hill Cemetery, first n of Thirty sixth
Hobart
Illinois
Kenwood av
Capitol av
Carter
Senate av

Thirty Sixth, E—
(Old Twenty eighth), from N Meridian e to Central av, first n of Thirty fifth
Pennsylvania
Delaware

Thirty Sixth, W—
(Old Twenty eighth), from N Meridian w to Crown Hill Cemetery, first n of Thirty fifth
25 Salem
50 Illinois
75 Kenwood av
100 Capitol av
125 Carter
150 Senate av

Thirty Third, E—
(Old Twenty fifth), from N Meridian e to Delaware, first n of Thirty second
50 Pennsylvania

Thirty Third, W—
(Old Twenty fifth), from N Illinois w to Senate av, first n of Thirty second
Kenwood av

Capitol av
Graceland av

Thomas—
(15th W a r d), see Wilkins

Thomas—
(S), from Brookville Pike s to English av, first e of Sherman Drive
Stanton av
Twin Lake av
Lake av

Thompson—
From W Washington s, fourth w of Belt R R

Thurman—
From Brookville Road e, first s of Washington

Tilden—
(Old Monroe), from Woodruff pl to Keystone av, bet Michigan and Tenth
Hamilton av
Jefferson av
Ramsey av

Tilford av—
(I), from Elm n, first e of Ritter av

Tindall—
From Brandt n. second w of Knox

Tippecanoe alley—
See Tippecanoe

Tippecanoe—
E and w, crossing Meridian, first n of New York

Tipton—
From Hillside av n to Belt R R, third e of Sheldon

Toledo—
(Old Columbia al), from Wabash n to Michigan, first w of Missouri
12 Ohio
25 Miami
320 New York
900 Vermont

Tompkins—
See Beecher

Topp Place—
From Temple av e to Rural, first n of Michigan

Torbett—
From 512 N West w to city limits, bet Tenth and Eleventh
Camp
Brooks

Traub av—
From W Washington n, first e of Belmont av
Leeds

Tremont—
From Michigan n to Walnut, bet New Jersey and Alabama

Tremont av—
(H), from Vermont n, first w of Bismarck av

Tremont—
(W I), from Morris s, first w of Bismarck

Troy—
From Shelby w to Dexter, first south of Brandt

Trumbull—
From Austin s, first w of Fall creek
Hooker

Turner av—
(Brooklyn Hgts), from Monroe n to Avondale

Tutewiler—
From Morris s, first e of Madison av

Tuxedo—
From Washington s, first e of LaSalle

Twelfth—
(Old Twelfth), see Twenty first

Twelfth, E—
(Old Second and Butler), from Delaware e to College av, first n of Eleventh
Alabama
New Jersey
Central av
Park av
Broadway

Twelfth, W—
(Old Third, Mayhew and Hooker), from Illinois w to Indiana av, first n of Eleventh
Capitol av
Senate av
C C C & St L Ry
Howard
The canal
Fayette
West
Oregon
Brooks
Fall creek
Trumbull

Twentieth—
(Old Twentieth), see Twenty eighth

Twentieth, E—
(Old Eleventh, old Tenth from Central av to Martindale av and French), from Talbott av e to Hillside av, first n of Nineteenth
Delaware
Alabama
New Jersey
Central av
Ruckle
Park av
Broadway
College av
Ash
Bellefontaine
Cornell av
L E & W R R
Alvord
Yandes
Columbia av
Martindale av
Sheldon
Atlas
Picken
Tipton

Twentieth, W—
(Old Eleventh and Herbert), from N Meridian w to Highland pl
50 Illinois
100 Capitol av
150 Senate av

Twenty Eighth—
(Old Twenty eighth), see Thirty sixth

Twenty Eighth, E
(Old Twentieth and Belle), from N Meridian n to city limits, first n of Twenty seventh
Pennsylvania
Talbott av
Delaware
Alabama
New Jersey
Central av
Park av
Fleming av
Sutherland av
Ash
Boswell
Bellefontaine
Cornell av
MacPherson av
L E & W R R
Yandes
Columbia av
Martindale av
Ralston av
Schofield av
Sangster av
Manlove av
Baltimore av
Caroline av
Hillside av
Brouse av
Line av

Twenty Eighth, W
(Old Twentieth and Addison), from N Meridian w to city limits, first n of Twenty seventh
Illinois
Kenwood av
Capitol av
Senate av
London av
Berlin av
Paris av
Indianapolis av
Northwestern av
Isabelle av
Annette
Rader
Clifton
Barnes
The canal
Burton av
Sherman av

Twenty Fifth—
(Old Twenty fifth), see Thirty third

Twenty Fifth, E—
(Old Seventeenth), from N Meridian e to city limits, first n of Twenty fourth
Pennsylvania
Talbott av
Delaware
Alabama
New Jersey
Central av
Park av
Broadway
College av
Ash
Bellefontaine
Cornell av
L E & W R R
Yandes
Columbia av
Martindale av
Newman
Sheldon
Hovey
Ralston av
Schofield av
Sangster av
Manlove av
Baltimore av
Caroline av
Hillside av
Brouse av
Line av

Twenty Fifth, W—
(Old Seventeenth and Ontario), from N Illinois w to city limits, first n of Twenty fourth
Andrews
Capitol av
Senate av
London av
Berlin av
Paris av
Indianapolis av
Ethel av
Northwestern av
Isabella
Annette
Rader
Clifton
C C C & St L Ry
The canal
Belt R R
Burton av
Franklin
Grover

Twenty First, E—
(Old Twelfth, old Thirteenth e from Talbott av and Anderson), from Meridian e to Hillside av, first n of Twentieth
50 Pennsylvania
Talbott av
Delaware
Alabama
New Jersey
Central av
Ruckle
Park av
Broadway
College av
Ash
Bellefontaine
Cornell av
L E & W R R
Alvord
Yandes
Columbia av
Martindale av
Sheldon
Atlas
Ralston
Pickens
Tipton

Schofield av
Sangster

Twenty First, W— (Old Twelfth and Floral av, from canal w), from Meridian w to city limits, first n of Twentieth
50 Illinois
100 Capitol av
150 Senate av
200 Highland pl
250 Shriver
300 Allfree
350 Wendell
400 Northwestern av
Brighton boulevard
Sackville
Iron av
Post av
White av
Sugar Grove
Dexter
Schurmann av

Twenty Fourth— (Old Twenty fourth), see Thirty second

Twenty Fourth, E (Old Sixteenth, Davidge and Harlan), from N Meridian e to Baltimore av, first n of Twenty third
Pennsylvania
Talbott av
Delaware
Alabama
New Jersey
Central av
Park av
Broadway
College av
Sheridan
Ash
Bellefontaine
Cornell av
L E & W R R
Columbia av
Martindale av
Newman
Sheldon
Hovey
Ralston av
Schofield av
Sangster av
Manlove av

Twenty Fourth, W (Old Sixteenth and Lake), from N Meridian w to city limits, first n of Twenty third
Illinois
Andrews
Capitol av
Senate av
London
Berlin av
Paris av
Indianapolis av
Ethel av
Northwestern av
Isabelle
Annette
Rader
Canal
Fairview
Franklin

Twenty Ninth— (Old Twenty ninth), see Thirty seventh

Twenty Ninth, E— (Old Twenty first and Rebecca), e from Central av to city limits, first n of Twenty eighth
Park av
Broadway
College av
Fleming
Fall creek
Sutherland av
Bellefontaine
Cornell av
MacPherson
L E & W R R
Columbia av
Martindale av
Ralston av
Schofield av
Sangster av
Manlove av
Baltimore av
Caroline av
Hillside av
Brouse av

Twenty Ninth, W— (Old Twenty first and Francis), from Meridian w to city limits, first n of Twenty eighth
50 Illinois
100 Capitol av
150 Senate av
200 London av
250 Berlin av
300 Paris av
350 Indianapolis av
400 Brown
Northwestern av
Annette
Rader
Clifton
Barnes av
Elmira
The canal

Twenty Second— (Old Twenty second), see Thirtieth

Twenty Second, E (Old Fourteenth and Clyde), from Meridian e to Ralston av
Pennsylvania
Talbott av
Delaware
Alabama
New Jersey
Central av
Park av
Broadway
College av
Bellefontaine
Cornell av
L E & W R R
Yandes
Columbia av
Martindale av
Newman
Sheldon
Hovey

Twenty Second, W (Old Fourteeenth and Jackson), from N Meridian w to city limits, first n of Twenty first
50 Illinois
68 Andrews
100 Capitol av
Senate av
Fall creek
Iron av
Post av
White av
Sugar Grove av
Dexter
Schurmann av

Twenty Seventh— (Old Twenty seventh), see Thirty fifth

Twenty Seventh, E— (Old Nineteenth and Jennison), from Sutherland av e to Line av, first n of Twenty sixth
College av
Ash
Bellefontaine
Cornell av
L E & W R R
Yandes
Columbia av
Martindale av
Ralston av
Schofield
Sangster av
Manlove av
Baltimore av
Caroline av
Hillside av
Brouse av

Twenty Seventh, W— (Old Nineteenth), from N Meridian w to city limits, first n of Twenty sixth
50 Illinois
100 Capitol av
150 Senate av
200 London av
250 Berlin av
300 Paris av
350 Indianapolis av
Northwestern av
Isabelle
Annette
Rader
Clifton
Barnes av
The canal
Burton av

Twenty Sixth— (Old Twenty sixth), see Thirty fourth

Twenty Sixth, W— (Old Eighteenth and Wells), from Meridian w to city limits, first n of Twenty fifth
Illinois
Capitol av
Senate av
Northwestern av
Isabelle
Annette
Rader
Clifton
The canal
Burton av
Grover
Schurmann av

Twenty Third— (Old Twenty third), see Thirty first

Twenty Third, E— (Old Fifteenth, Bruce and Blackmore), from N Meridian e to Hillside av, first n of Twenty second
Pennsylvania
Talbott av
Delaware
Alabama
New Jersey
Central av
Park av
Broadway
College av
Ash
Bellefontaine
Cornell av
L E & W R R
Yandes
Columbia av
Martindale av
Newman
Sheldon
Hovey
Ralston av
Schofield av
Manlove av
Baltimore av

Twenty Third, W— (Old Fifteenth and Jones), from N Illinois w to Schurmann av, first n of Twenty second
Andrews
Capitol av
Senate av
London av
Berlin av
Paris av
Indianapolis av
Northwestern av
Fall creek
Aqueduct
Fair View

Twin Lake— (S), from McPherson n e to Sherman Drive, thence s e to Thomas

Udell— (N I), from Northwestern av w to Schurmann av, second n of Twenty seventh
Annette
Rader
Clifton
Barnes av
Elmira

Union— From cor of Madison av and Merrill s to city limits
44 Norwood
84 McCarty
201 Ray
229 Wilkins
272 Morris
325 Downey
400 Lockwood
450 Palmer
480 Harvey

University av— (I), from Butler av e, first s of P C C & St L Ry

Urbana— (14th Ward), see Spruce

Urbana— From Rural e to Parker av, first n of Lily

Utah—
See S Capitol av

Vale—
(N I), from North n to Orchard av, seventh w of Schurmann av

Valley—
(13th Ward), see Warsaw

Valley av—
(Old Valley Drive), from cor Beech and Gertrude av e to Brookside av, second s of Lawrence
Clark
Ludlow lane
Hazel
Brookside av

Van Buren—
(Old Arlington av), from Shelby e to city limits, first s of Naomi
50 Abigail
74 Laurel
100 Thaddeus
124 Spruce
150 Draper
174 St Elmo
200 State av

Vermont, E—
From 199 N Meridian e to Randolph
50 Pennsylvania
100 Delaware
146 Alabama
200 New Jersey
250 East
299 Liberty
330 Noble
422 Spring
432 Fulton
450 Davidson
462 Pine
L E & W R R
550 Dorman
600 Highland av
650 Oriental
Arsenal av
State av
Walcott

Vermont, W—
From 200 N Meridian w to city limits
50 Illinois
104 Capitol av
155 Senate av
175 Ellsworth
204 Missouri
226 Toledo
250 West
290 California
370 Blackford
374 Bright
400 Douglass
Blake
Minerva
600 Agnes
637 Patterson
680 Hiawatha
White river
Miley av
Elder av
Lyon
Belmont av

Victoria—
(W I), from Harris w, first s of Ida

Vigo—
(Old Ingram), from Abigail e, first n of Beecher (14th Ward)

Villa av—
(Old Villa av and William), from Lexington av s to Pleasant Run, third e of State av
Woodlawn av
Prospect
Orange

Vincennes—
(W I), from Morris n e, first w of Kentucky av

Vine—
(7th Ward), see Pratt

Vine—
From Raymond s to Kelly, second w of Meridian (15th Ward)
Tabor

Vinton—
From 528 S West to White river
Dakota

Violet—
From Wilmington n to Fall creek, first w of Northwestern av

Virginia av—
From cor of Pennsylvania and Washington s e to Prospect
50 Maryland
96 Georgia
150 Louisiana
199 South
230 Huron
250 Warsaw
293 Merrill
326 Pine
330 Stevens
Norwood
430 Cedar
450 McCarty
450 Bismarck
519 Bradshaw
528 Grove
577 Buchanan
600 Woodlawn av
619 Dougherty

Voight—
(B), from Pendleton Road s to Fitch, first w of Lancaster

Volney—
Running north and south, first e of Mineral

Vorster av—
See Eighteenth

Wabash, E—
From Pennsylvania e to Noble, between Market and Ohio
50 Pennsylvania
100 Delaware
150 Alabama
200 New Jersey
225 Clinton
250 East
300 Liberty

Wabash, W—
From 70 N Illinois w to Blackford
100 Capitol av
180 Senate av
200 Missouri
Toledo
250 West

Wacker—
(H), from Frazee n to Grand View av, first w of Summit

Wade—
(Old St Marie av), from Shelby e to State av, third s of Raymond
Walker av
Boyd av
Mattie av

Wagner av—
(I), from University av w, first w of Ainsworth av

Walcott—
From 842 E Washington n to Michigan, first e of State av
Ohio
New York
Vermont
Sturm av

Walker—
(B), from Pendleton Road s to Fitch, third w of Lancaster

Walker—
(H), from Frazee n to Summit, first w of Haugh

Walker av—
From Wade s e, thence e to Knox
Bradbury av
Short
Finley av

Wallace—
From Washington n to White river, first w of Brush (5th Ward)
Market

Wallace—
(I), from Washington av n, first w of Quincy

Wallack—
See Ringgold av

Walnut—
(15th Ward), see Tabor

Walnut, E—
From 350 N Meridian e to Noble (7th Ward)
50 Pennsylvania
100 Delaware
100 Ft Wayne av
150 Alabama
200 New Jersey
250 East
300 Park av

Walnut, W—
From 349 N Meridian w to West (6th Ward)
25 Superior
50 Illinois
98 Capitol av
150 Senate av
175 Wood
202 Missouri
210 Fayette

Walnut av—
(4th Ward), see Congress av

Walnut av—
(I), from College av n e and e, first n of Washington av

Warman av—
(H), from I D & W Ry s to Vermont, first w of Holmes av

Warren—
From Southeastern av s to Bates, first e of Quincy

Warren—
(B), from Pendleton Road e, first s of Bloyd av
Houston
Adams
Shade
Lawn
Depot
Poplar
Brightwood

Warren—
(I), from Washington av s, first e of Orchard

Warren av—
(W I), from Oliver av s to Woodburn av, first w of Marion av
Cottage av

Warsaw—
(Old Valley), from 279 S East e to Virginia av, bet South and Merrill

Washington, E—
From 1 N Meridian e to city limits, dividing the city n and s
50 Pennsylvania
100 Delaware
152 Alabama
200 New Jersey
224 Clinton
250 East
300 Liberty
348 Noble
406 Davidson
432 Benton
500 Pine
501 Southeastern av
600 Cruse
620 Highland av
650 Oriental
730 McKim av
762 Arsenal av
800 Summit
840 State av
858 Walcott
900 Randolph
1008 Hamilton av
1030 Jefferson av
1100 Beville av
1128 Keystone av
1132 Forest av
1150 Tacoma av

1164 Temple av
1200 Eastern av
1250 Rural
Grace
Oxford
Gray
Dearborn
LaSalle
Tuxedo

Washington, W—
From 2 S Meridian w to city limits, dividing the city n and s
48 Illinois
100 Capitol av
152 Senate av
200 Missouri
252 West
302 California
346 Blackford
402 Geisendorf
438 Blake
500 White river
Henrietta
Plum
736 Brush
792 Wallace
808 Greely
880 Bloomington
900 Decatur
Drake
Wilmot
Minkner
998 Richland
1003 Belt R R
1036 Miley av
1050 Elder av
1080 Traub av
1100 Belmont av

Washington av—
(I), from Wallace e, a continuation of E Washington

Washington Boulevard—
See Delaware

Water—
See Beaty

Water—
(I), from Parker av n w, second n of Brookside Road

Watkins av—
(I), from Worcester av e, first n of Lena

Watts—
See LaSalle

Waverly—
(B), from Bloyd av n to Twenty fifth, first e of Morris
Division
Glen Drive

Waverly av—
From Tenth n to Nowland av, fourth e of Rural

Wayne—
(Old Sheridan), from Brooks w to Fall creek, first n of Eleventh

Webb—
From Belt R R s to Raymond, first e of Madison av

Weghorst—
From East e, first n of Lincoln av

Wells—
See Twenty sixth

Wendell—
From W Twenty first n to Fall creek, first e of Northwestern av
Mariette Drive

West, N—
From 252 W Washington n to Indiana av, thence n w to Tenth and w to Fifteenth
25 Court
50 Market
75 Wabash
100 Ohio
154 New York
175 Miami
205 Vermont
250 Michigan
300 North
362 Walnut
400 St Clair
462 Pratt
500 Tenth
550 Eleventh
600 Twelfth
Thirteenth
Fourteenth

West, S—
From 249 W Washington s to city limits
25 Pearl
50 Maryland
75 Chesapeake
94 Georgia
150 Louisiana
200 South
Kentucky av
251 Garden
296 Merrill
316 Abbott
318 Grant
362 Norwood
388 McCarty
404 Root
498 Ray
510 Vinton
550 Wilkins
560 Jones
575 Morris
Wisconsin
Arizona
White river

West Drive—
See Woodruff pl

West Washington av—
(Old National Road, 5th Ward), from Blackford w to White river, first n of Washington

Western av—
Continuation of Sutherland av from Thirtieth n, thence e to L E & W R R
Fleet
Park av
Broadway
College av

Western av—
(I), from Washington av s, first w of National av

Westfield—
From Northwestern av e, first n of Thirtieth

Wheatley—
From McLain n to Murray, second e of Shelby

Wheeler—
(B), from Bloyd av n, first e of Harriet
Park
Division
Glen Drive

White—
(N I), from North av n, fourth w of Schurmann av

White av—
(N I), from Eighteenth n, first w of Ismond

Wilcox—
From Belmont av e, bet Vermont and Michigan
Lynn

Wilkins, E—
From 544 S Meridian e to Madison av
25 Charles
50 Union
75 Mulberry
100 Chestnut

Wilkins, W—
(Old Thomas), from 544 S Meridian w to Dakota
50 Illinois
75 Maple
100 Capitol av
Church
Carlos
Chadwick
West

Willard—
From Garden s to Merrill, first w of Capitol av (11th Ward)

Willard—
(E of city limits), from LaSalle e to Ewing, first s of Tenth
Ellis
Fay

William—
(9th Ward), see Villa av

William—
(W I), from Morris n and s, first w of Judge Harding

Williams—
From 33 Oriental e to State av, first s of Washington
50 Arsenal av
Summit

Willow—
(14th Ward), see Cottage av

Willow—
(B), from Shade e of Bartholomew, first n of Twenty fifth
Gale
Station
Brightwood
Foundry
Hope
School
Wood
Hare

Wilmington av—
From Northwestern av w, first s of Fall creek

Wilmot—
(Old Pierce), from W Washington n to Astor, first w of Decatur

Wilson—
(10th Ward), see Daly

Wilson—
From North n to Davis, fifth w of Blake (4th Ward)
Elizabeth
Coe

Winchester—
From Shelby e to State av, first s of Raymond
Boyd av
Mattie av

Windsor—
From Tenth n to Commerce, first e of Keith

Wisconsin—
From 655 S Meridian w to Dakota, second s of Morris
50 Illinois
100 Capitol av
Carlos
West

Wood—
(9th Ward), see Woodlawn av

Wood—
From Michigan n to North, first w of Senate av, (6th Ward)

Wood—
(B), from Bee Line Ry n, first e of School

Woodbine—
(N I), from North av n, third n of White river

Woodburn av—
(W I), from Drover w, first s of Cottage av
River av
Marion av
Warren
Division
Arbor av

Woodlawn av—
(Old Elk, Woodlawn av, Jefferson and Wood), from 360 Shelby e to city limits

50 Olive
100 Laurel
150 Spruce
State av
Dawson
Nelson
Villa av
Harlan
St Paul
St Peter
Auburn
Cannon

Woodruff av—
From Tenth n to Brookside av, first w of Newman

Woodruff Place—
Bounded by U S Arsenal Grounds, Tenth, Tecumseh and Michigan

Woodside—
See Temple av

Woodside av—
from P C C & St L Ry s to English av, second e of Auburn

Graydon
Southeastern av

Worcester av—
(I), from C H & D R R s to Huron av, first e of Detroit av
Watkins av
Lena
Young
Brookville pike
English av
Fletcher av

Wright—
(5th Ward), see Richmond

Wright—
(Old Sullivan and Wright), from E McCarty s to Cottage av, fourth e of East
Bismarck
Bradshaw
Buchanan
Dougherty
Prospect
Morris
Sanders
Downey
Carroll

Wyoming—
From 376 S Delaware e to East
Delaware
Alabama
High
New Jersey

Yale—
(N I), from North av n to Orchard av, second e of White river

Yandes—
From Malott av n to Thirtieth, second e of L E & W R R
Thirteenth
Fifteenth
Sixteenth
Seventeenth
Nineteenth
Twentieth
Twenty first
Twenty second
Twenty third
Twenty fourth
Twenty fifth
Twenty seventh
Twenty eighth
Twenty ninth

Yassie—
From Raymond s to Ream, first w of Daisy
Norman
Romaine
Carleton

Yeiser—
See Sanders

York—
(W I), from Hadley av s e, first n of Stock

Young—
(I), from Worcester av s e to Parker, first n of Brookville pike

Zwingley—
From Bethel av s, first e of Luther
Reformers av

1358771

WE RECEIVE many complaints from our patrons to the effect that they are bothered so much by **BORROWERS.** These parties are not the private citizen nor the stranger in the city, who steps in, looks at the Directory and goes out, but merchants, business and professional men, who need a Directory every day of the year, yet who are too close-fisted to buy one.

These same individuals are the ones that borrow your Directory "just for a minute," which, in the majority of cases, means a day or perhaps a week, unless you remember that they have it and send for it.

These same borrowers will tell the Directory canvasser that he has "no use for a Directory," that he "knows everybody," and, vice versa, "everybody knows him."

WARD BOUNDARIES.

FIRST WARD—

All of that part of said city bounded as follows shall be and constitute the First Ward: Commencing on the center line of Rural street at its intersection by the center line of Twenty-fifth street; thence south with the center line of Rural street to the center line of Tenth street; thence west with the center line of Tenth street to the center line of the Lake Erie & Western Railway tracks; thence north with the center line of the Lake Erie & Western Railway tracks to the center line of Eleventh street; thence west with the center line of Eleventh street to the center line of Cornell avenue; thence north with the center line of Cornell avenue to the center line of Twenty-third street; thence east with the center line of Twenty-third street to the center line of the Lake Erie & Western Railway tracks; thence north or northeasterly with the center line of the Lake Erie & Western Railway tracks to the city limits and city corporation line; thence east with the center line of Thirtieth street to the center line of Line avenue; thence south with the center line of Line avenue to the center line of Twenty-fifth street; thence east with the center line of Twenty-fifth street to the center line of Rural street, the place of beginning.

SECOND WARD—

All that part of said city bounded as follows shall be and constitute the Second Ward: Commencing at Thirtieth street and the center line of the Lake Erie & Western Railway tracks; thence running south with said center line of said railway tracks to the center line of Twenty-third street; thence west with the center line of Twenty-third street to the center line of Cornell avenue; thence south with the center line of Cornell avenue to the center line of Eleventh street; thence west with the center line of Eleventh street to the center line of Central avenue; thence south with the center line of Central avenue to the center line of Tenth street; thence west with the center line of Tenth street to the center line of Alabama street; thence north with the center line of Alabama street to the south bank of Fall creek; thence northeasterly with the south bank of Fall creek to Thirtieth street; thence east to the place of beginning.

THIRD WARD—

All that part of said city bounded as follows shall be and constitute the Third Ward: Commencing at the intersection of the south bank of Fall creek by the center line of Alabama street; thence running south with the center line of Alabama street to the center line of Eleventh street; thence west with the center line of Eleventh street to the center line of the canal; thence northerly with the center line of the canal to the center of Northwestern avenue; thence north with the center of Northwestern avenue to the south bank of Fall creek; thence easterly and northeasterly with the south bank of Fall creek, following the meanderings of said stream to the place of beginning.

FOURTH WARD—

All of that part of said city bounded as follows shall be and constitute the Fourth Ward: Commencing at the intersection of the center line of Tenth street with the center line of the canal; thence running northerly with the center line of the canal to the center of Northwestern avenue; thence north with the center of Northwestern avenue, to the south bank of Fall creek; thence easterly and northeasterly with the south bank of Fall creek, following the meanderings of said stream to a point in a line parallel with and three hundred and forty feet distant and east from the center line of Meridian street; thence north parallel with the center line of Meridian street, and three hundred and forty feet distant from said center line and north with the center line of Pennsylvania street to the center line of Thirty-second street; thence east with the center line of Thirty-second street to the center line of Delaware; thence north with the center line of Delaware street to the center line of Thirty-fourth street; thence west with the center line of Thirty-fourth street to the center line of Meridian street; thence north with the center line of Meridian street to the center line of Thirty-eighth street; thence west with the center line of Thirty-eighth street to the center line of Senate avenue; thence south with the center line of Senate avenue to a point on said city corporation line near the southeast corner of the Crown Hill cemetery; thence west with the city corporation line on the south of Crown Hill cemetery and following such corporation line to the center of Northwestern avenue; thence with the center of Northwestern avenue to the center of Thirty-second street, as shown by the plat of Keystone Park as recorded in Plat Book ten, page 123, in the office of the Recorder of Marion county, Indiana, thence west on the center of Thirty-second street to the center of Clifton street as shown by the above mentioned plat; thence south with the center of Clifton street to the center of Thirty-first street as shown by plat of Armstrong's first addition to North Indianapolis, as recorded in Plat Book seven, page 25, in the office of the Recoorder of Marion county, Indiana; thence west with the center of Thirty-first street to the center line of the canal; thence southeast with the center line of the canal to the center line of Schurmann avenue; thence south with the center line of Schumann avenue to the east bank of White river; thence south with the bank of White river to the center line of Tenth street; thence east with the center line of Tenth street to the place of beginning.

FIFTH WARD—

All that part of said city bounded as follows shall be and constitute the Fifth Ward: Commencing at the intersection of the center line of Tenth street by the center line of Paca street; thence running south with the center line of Paca street and the center line of Bright street to the center line of North street; thence east with the center line of North street to the center line of Blackford street; thence south with the center line of Blackford to the center line of Washington street; thence west with the center line of Washington street to the east bank of White river; thence south along the meanderings of said east bank of White river to Maryland street and the city corporation line; thence west in a direct line with the city corporation line to west line of Belmont avenue; thence north on Belmont avenue and the said township line to Michigan street; thence due east along the center line of Michigan street to the east bank of White river; thence north in a direct line from Michigan street to the south line of section thirty-four, township sixteen north, range three east; thence east along said section line extended to the east bank of Fall creek; thence northeasterly with the east bank of Fall creek to the center line of Indiana avenue; thence southeasterly with the center line of Indiana avenue to the center line of Tenth street; thence east with the center line of Tenth street to the place of beginning.

There shall be excepted from this ward so much of the incorporated town of Haughville as is embraced within the description of this ward.

SIXTH WARD—

All that part of said city bounded as follows shall be and constitute the Sixth Ward: Commencing at the intersection of the center line of Tenth street with the canal; thence running northerly with the canal to the center line of Eleventh street; thence east with the center line of Eleventh street to the center line of Alabama street; thence south with the center line of Alabama street to the center line of North street; thence west with the center line of North street to the canal; thence south with the canal to the center line of Vermont street; thence west with the center line of Vermont street to the center line of Blackford street; thence north with the center line of Blackford street to the center line of North street; thence west with the center line of North street to the center line of Bright street; thence north with the center line of Bright street and the center line of Paca street to the center line of Tenth street; thence east with the center line of Tenth street to the place of beginning.

SEVENTH WARD—

All that part of said city bounded as follows shall be and constitute the Seventh Ward: Commencing at the intersection of the center line of Alabama street by the center line of Tenth street; thence running east with the center line of Tenth street to the center line of Central avenue; thence north with the center line of Central avenue to the center line of Eleventh street; thence east with the center line of Eleventh street to the center line of Ash street; thence south with the center line of Ash street to the center line of Massachusetts avenue; thence southwest with the center line of Massachusetts avenue to the center line of St. Clair street; thence east with the center line of St. Clair street to the center line of Pine street; thence south with the center line of Pine street to the center line of Ohio street; thence west with the center line of Ohio street to the center line of Alabama street; thence north with the center line of Alabama street to the place of beginning.

EIGHTH WARD—

All that part of said city bounded as follows shall be and constitute the Eighth Ward: Commencing at the intersection of the center line of Eleventh street by the center line of Ash street; thence running east with the center line of Eleventh street to the center line of the Lake Erie & Western Railway tracks; thence south with the center line of the Lake Erie & Western Railway tracks to the center line of Tenth street; thence east with the center line of Tenth street to the center line of Rural street; thence south with the center line of Rural street to the center line of New York street; thence east with the center line of New York street to the west line of the Indianapolis Union Railway Company's right-of-way; thence south with said west line of the Indianapolis Union Railway Company's right-of-way to the north line of the right-of-way of the Pittsburg, Cincinnati, Chicago & St. Louis Railroad Company's railroad; thence west with the north line of said railway company's right-of-way to the center line of Pine street; thence north with the center line of Pine street to the center line of St. Clair street; thence west with the center line of St. Clair street to the center line of Massachusetts avenue; thence northeast with the center line of Massachusetts avenue to the center line of Ash street; thence north with the center line of Ash street to the place of beginning.

There shall be excepted from this ward the incorporated town of Woodruff place which lies within this description and is situated directly east of the Arsenal.

NINTH WARD—

All that part of said city bounded as follows shall be and constitute the Ninth Ward: Commencing at the intersection of the center line of the tracks of the Pennsylvania Railroad Company by the center line of Pine street; thence running east with the center line of the tracks of said railroad company to the center line of Rural street or said center line extended south across said track; thence south with the center line of Rural street and with the corporation line to English avenue; thence west on English avenue to Auburn avenue; thence south on Auburn avenue to the center line of Prospect street; thence west with the center line of Prospect street to the center line of Virginia avenue; thence northwest with the center line of Virginia avenue to the center line of Cedar street; thence northeast with the center line of Cedar street to the center line of Fletcher avenue; thence northwest with the center line of Fletcher avenue to the center line of Pine street; thence northeast and north with the center line of Pine street to the place of beginning.

TENTH WARD—

All of that part of said city bounded as follows shall be and constitute the Tenth Ward: Commencing at the intersection of the center line of Illinois street by the center line of Market street; thence running east with the center line of Market street and the center line of Monument place north of the monument, and the center line of Market street to the center line of Pennsylvania street; thence north with the center line of Pennsylvania street to the center line of Ohio street; thence east with the center line of Ohio street to the center line of Pine street; thence south and southwest with the center line of Pine street to the center line of Fletcher avenue; thence northwest with the center line of Fletcher avenue to the center line of South street; thence west with the center line of South street to the center line of Illinois street; thence north with the center line of Illinois street to the place of beginning.

ELEVENTH WARD—

All of that part of said city bounded as follows shall be and constitute the Eleventh Ward: Commencing at the intersection of the center line of the canal with the center line of North street; thence running east with the center line of North to the center line of Alabama street; thence south with the center line of Alabama street to the center line of Ohio street; thence west with the center line of Ohio street to the center line of Pennsylvania street; thence south with the center line of Pennsylvania street to the center line of Market street; thence west with the center line of Market street to the center of Monument place north of the monument, and the center line of Market street to the center line of Illinois street; thence south with the center line of Illinois street to the center line of Washington street; thence west with the center line of Washington street to the center line of Blackford street; thence north with the center line of Blackford street to the center line of Vermont street; thence east with the center line of Vermont street to the center line of the canal: thence north with the center line of the canal to the place of beginning.

TWELFTH WARD—

All of that part of the city bounded as follows shall be and constitute the Twelfth Ward: Commencing at the intersection of the east bank of White river by the center line of Washington street; thence running east with the center line of Washington street to the center line of Illinois street; thence south with the center line of Illinois street to the center line of South street; thence east with the center line of South street to the center line of the tracks of the Pennsylvania Railroad Company, Louisville division; thence south with the center line of the tracks of the Pennsylvania Railroad Company to the center line of McCarty street; thence west with the center line of McCarty street to the east bank of White river; thence north with the east bank of White river following the meanderings of said stream to the place of beginning.

THIRTEENTH WARD—

All of that part of said city bounded as follows shall be and constitute the Thirteenth Ward: Commencing at the intersection of the center line of the tracks of the Pennsylvania Railroad Company, Louisville division, by the center line of South street; thence running east with the center line of South street to the center line of Fletcher avenue; thence southeast with the center line of Fletcher avenue to the center line of Cedar street; thence southwest with the center line of Cedar street to the center line of Virginia avenue; thence southeast with the center line of Virginia avenue to the center line of Prospect street; thence west with the center line of Prospect street to the center line of Wright street; thence north with the center line of Wright street to the center line of Dougherty street; thence west with the center line of Dougherty street to the center line of East street; thence south with the center line of Prospect street to cener line of Prospect street; thence west with the center line of Prospect street to the center line of Madison avenue; thence northwest with the center line of Madison avenue to the center line of the tracks of the Pennsylvania Railroad Company, Louisville division; thence north with the center line of the tracks of said railroad company to the place of beginning.

FOURTEENTH WARD—

All of that part of said city bounded as follows shall be and constitute the Fourteenth Ward: Commencing at the intersection of the center line of Madison avenue by the center line of Prospect street; thence running east with the center line of Prospect street to the center line of East street; thence north with the center line of East street to the center line of Dougherty street; thence east with the center line of Dougherty street to the center line of Wright street; thence south with the center line of Wright street to the center line of Prospect street; thence east with the center line of Prospect street to Virginia avenue and on east with the center line of Prospect street to Auburn avenue; thence south on Auburn avenue and to the south line of the Belt railroad; thence west along the south line of the Belt railroad to the line running north and south from the center of section eighteen, township fifteen north, range four east; thence south from said line to the center of section nineteen, township fifteen north, range four east; thence west in a direct line to the center line of Madison avenue; thence north with the center line of Madison avenue to the place of beginning.

FIFTEENTH WARD—

All of that part of said city bounded as follows shall be and constitute the Fifteenth Ward: Commencing at the intersection of the east bank of White river by the center line of McCarty street; thence running east with the center line of McCarty street to the center line of the tracks of the Pennsylvania Railroad Company, Louisville division; thence south with the center line of said railroad tracks to the center line of Madison avenue; thence southeast and south with the center line of Madison avenue to the south corporation line of said city; thence west with said corporation line to the east bank of White river; thence north with the east bank of White river following the meanderings of said stream to the place of beginning.

R. L. POLK & CO.'S

Indianapolis City Directory.

1897.

MISCELLANEOUS INFORMATION.

INDIANA STATE GOVERNMENT, 1897.

Governor—James A. Mount. Term expires January, 1901.

Lieutenant-Governor — Wm. S. Haggard. Term expires January, 1901.

Secretary of State—Wm. D. Owen. Term expires January, 1899.

Treasurer—Frederick J. Scholz. Term ex- February, 1899.

Auditor—Americus C. Daily. Term expires January, 1899.

Attorney-General—Wm. A. Ketcham. Term expires November, 1898.

Superintendent Public Instruction—David M. Geeting. Term expires March, 1899.

Chief of Bureau of Statistics of Indiana—S. J. Thompson. Term expires November, 1898.

Clerk Supreme Court — Alexander Hess. Term expires November 22, 1898.

Reporter Supreme Court—Charles F. Remy. Term expires January 13, 1901.

Chief of Bureau of Geology—Willis S. Blatchley. Term expires November, 1898.

APPOINTED BY THE GOVERNOR.

Adjutant-General—James K. Gore.
Quartermaster-General—Benjamin A. Richardson.
Governor's Private Secretary—Charles E. Wilson.

APPOINTED BY THE LEGISLATURE.

State Librarian—Emma L. Davidson.

SUPREME COURT.

Judges—Timothy E. Howard, James McCabe, James H. Jordan, Leonard J. Hackney, Leander J. Monks.

APPOINTED BY THE SUPREME COURT.

Librarian—John C. McNutt.
Sheriff—David A. Roach.

APPELLATE COURT, STATE HOUSE.

Judges—Woodfin D. Robinson, Wm. J. Henley, James B. Black, Daniel W. Comstock, Ulric Z. Wiley.

STATE BOARD OF AGRICULTURE.

John L. Haines, Lake; Mason J. Niblack, Vincennes; W. W. Stevens, Salem; J. W. Lagrange, Franklin; V. K. Officer, Volga; W. W. Hamilton, Greensburg; H. B. Howland, Howland; Charles Downing, Greenfield; James M. Sankey, Terre Haute; John L. Davis, Crawfordsville; M. S. Claypool, Muncie; Wm. M. Blackstock, Lafayette; John L. Thompson, Gas City; Charles B. Harris, Goshen; Aaron Jones, South Bend; Jas. E. McDonald, Ligonier; Charles F. Kennedy, Secretary, 14 State House.

STATE BOARD OF HEALTH.

President, Douglas C. Ramsey, Mt. Vernon; Secretary, John N. Hurty, Indianapolis; L. L. Whitesides, Franklin; T. Henry Davis, Richmond; J. H. Forrest, Marion.

STATE BOARD OF CHARITIES.

The Governor, President ex officio; John R. Elder, Demarchus C. Brown, Timothy Nicholson, Thomas E. Ellison, Mary Spink, Margaret F. Peelle; Ernest Bicknell, Secretary, 52 State House.

STATE BOARD OF EDUCATION.

State Superintendent of Public Instruction, President; The Governor, Presidents of State University, Purdue University and State Normal School; Superintendents of Schools of Indianapolis, Evansville and Ft. Wayne.

BOARD OF REGENTS STATE SOLDIERS' AND SAILORS' MONUMENT.

President and Superintendent, Fred Knefler; G. V. Menzies, Jasper Packard; Edward P. Thompson, Secretary, 93 State House.

STATE BOARD OF TAX COMMISSIONERS.

The Governor, Chairman; Secretary of State, Auditor of State, I. N. Walker and D. F. Allen, Commissioners; Secretary, Wm. H. Hart, 35 State House.

STATE BUREAU OF PUBLIC PRINTING, BINDING AND STATIONERY.

The Governor, Secretary of State, Auditor of State; Thomas J. Carter, Clerk, 3 State House.

STATE DEPARTMENT OF GEOLOGY AND NATURAL RESOURCES, 89 STATE HOUSE.

State Geologist, Willis S. Blatchley; Inspector of Mines, Robert Fisher, Brazil; Supervisor of Natural Gas, J. C. Leach, 89 State House; Supervisor of Oil, Chester F. Hall, 92 State House.

STATE LIVE STOCK SANITARY COMMISSION.

George W. Hall, Raleigh; James M. Sankey, Terre Haute; M. S. Claypool, Muncie; Mortimer Levering, Secretary, Lafayette; F. A. Bolser, Veterinarian, New Castle.

CITY OFFICIALS.

Offices—Basement Court House.

Mayor—Thomas Taggart.
Clerk to Mayor—Charles H. Spencer.
City Clerk—Charles H. Stuckmeyer.
Deputy City Clerk—August Tamm jr.
Police Judge—Charles E. Cox.

Bailiff Police Court—John F. Kurtz.
City Comptroller—Eudorus M. Johnson.
Deputy City Comptroller—Martin J. Murphy.
Clerks—Charles H. Adam, Arthur H. Byfield.
City Attorney—James B. Curtis.
Deputy City Attorney—Joseph E. Bell.
City Civil Engineer—Bernard J. T. Jeup; Chief Clerk, Miles Grant Hornaday.
Assistant City Civil Engineers—J. H. Deane, J. H. Moore, George R. Boyce, Charles A. Brown.
City Building Inspector—George W. Bunting.
Foreman Street Repairs—George H. Herpick.
Assistant—Michael J. Burns.
Clerk—John T. Brennan.
Sweeping and Sprinkling Inspector—Charles A. Garrard.
City Weighmaster—Thomas F. Harrold.
City Veterinarian—Louis A. Greiner.
Custodian City Hall—Michael Gantner.

BOARD OF PUBLIC WORKS.

Members of the Board—Michael A. Downing, Chairman; Martin C. Anderson, W. Scott Moore; Secretary, Bart Parker; Assistant, John H. Reddington.

DEPARTMENT OF PUBLIC SAFETY.

Members of the Board—Charles Maguire, Chairman; Frederick J. Mack, Thomas J. Morse, Richard C. Herrick, Secretary; Thomas F. Colbert, Superintendent of Police; Thomas F. Barrett, Chief of Fire Department; George W. Bunting, Building Inspector.

BOARD OF PUBLIC HEALTH AND CHARITIES.

Frank A. Morrison, M. D., President.
Martin H. Field, M. D.
Lewis C. Cline, M. D.
Edmund D. Clark, M. D., City Sanitarian.
Wm. C. Ripley, Clerk.
Henry F. Kline, Thomas H. Neilan, Wm. M. Arnold, A. G. Sanborn, Bernard Frey, Jeremiah Collins, George Woessner, Sanitary Inspectors.
City Hospital, cor. Locke and Margaret, Charles E. Ferguson, M. D., Supt.
City Dispensary, 34 E. Ohio, Leonard Bell, M. D., Supt.

BUREAU OF ASSESSMENTS.

Wm. A. Hughes, Chief Clerk.
Assistants—Hubert L. Schonacker, Michael F. Lahey, Levi E. Christy, John W. Pfaff, Thomas W. Cecil.

COMMISSIONERS DEPARTMENT OF PUBLIC PARKS.

Edward F. Claypool, President; Wm. E. English, Oran Perry, Sterling R. Holt, Wm. H. Leedy; Wm. R. Holloway, Clerk; J. Clyde Power, Engineer and Superintendent.

COUNCILMEN AT LARGE.

George J. Dudley, Thomas J. Montgomery, Albert E. Rauch, Robert M. Madden, John O'Connor, Edward Sherer.

COMMON COUNCIL.

1st Ward—O. M. Murphy.
2d Ward—John R. Allen.
3d Ward—Gavin L. Payne.
4th Ward—Mahlon P. Woody.
5th Ward—Frank E. Wolcott.
6th Ward—John A. Puryear.
7th Ward—George W. Shaffer.
8th Ward—Duncan Dewar.
9th Ward—Frank S. Clark.
10th Ward—George R. Colter.
11th Ward—Wm. H. Cooper.
12th Ward—James H. Costello.
13th Ward—John H. Kirkhoff.
14th Ward—James T. Smith.
15th Ward—John G. Ohleyer.
James H. Costello, President.

STANDING COMMITTEES.

Accounts and Claims—O'Connor, Wolcott, Allen.
Contracts and Franchises—Montgomery, Smith, Rauch, Madden, Murphy, Shaffer, Colter.
Elections—Dudley, Colter, Payne.
Fees and Salaries — Madden, Ohleyer, Murphy.
Finance—Wolcott, Dewar, Kirchoff, Clark, Ohleyer, Cooper, Allen.
Judiciary—Rauch, Sherer, Cooper.
Ordinances—Clark, O'Connor, Allen.
Printing—Montgomery, O'Connor, Payne.
Public Health—Dewar, Wolcott, Woody.
Public Morals—Ohleyer, Rauch, Puryear.
Public Property and Improvements—Kirkhoff, Dudley, Cooper.
Public Safety and Comfort—Sherer, Clark, Woody.
Railroads—Smith, Colter, Shaffer.
Rules—Costello, Dudley, Peryear.
Sewers, Streets and Alleys—Montgomery, Dewar, Woody.

BOARD OF SCHOOL COMMISSIONERS.

1st—F. H. Blackledge, 634-635 Lemcke bldg. Term expires 1897.
2d—Wm. Scott, 48 S. Meridian. Term expires 1897.
3d—George W. Sloan, 22 W. Washington. Term expires 1899.
4th—Henry Russe, 23 N. Capitol av. Term expires 1898.
5th—Michael J. Burns, 14 Basement Court House. Term expires 1899.
6th—Herman E. Rinne, 182 W. Washington. Term expires 1899.
7th—Charles C. Roth, 62 Fletcher av. Term expires 1898.
8th—Charles H. Adam, City Comptroller's Office. Term expires 1898.
9th—Franklin Vonnegut, 184 E. Washington. Term expires 1899.
10th—H. C. Hendrickson, 68½ E. Market. Term expires 1897.
11th—John B. McNeely, Commercial Club bldg. Term expires 1897.
Attorney of the Board—Wm. T. Brown, 216-218 Indiana Trust bldg.

Regular meetings of the Board at its rooms in the Library Building on the first and third Friday evenings of each month at 8 o'clock.

Bill nights, the first and third Friday evenings of each month. Bills must be left at the office of the Board on the day previous (Thursday); if later they will lie over until the next bill night.

OFFICERS OF THE BOARD.

President—Wm. Scott.
Secretary—John B. McNeely.
Treasurer—George W. Sloan.
Superintendent of Schools—David K. Goss.
Assistant Superintendent—N. Cropsey.
Assistant Secretary—Emma B. Ridenour.
Superintendent of Buildings and Grounds and Supplies—P. J. O'Meara.
Office in Library Building, s. w. cor. Meridian and Ohio sts. Open from 7:30 a. m. to 6 p. m.

COMMITTEES.

Finance and Auditing—Blackledge, Rinne and Hendrickson. (Meets at office of Public Schools at 4:30 p. m., on first and third Fridays of each month.)
Buildings and Grounds—Sloan, Roth and Blackledge.
Furniture and Supplies—McNeely, Russe and Vonnegut.
Supervision, Examination and Manual Training—Roth, Burns and Adam.
Appointment of Teachers and Salaries—Adam, Vonnegut and Sloan.
High Schools—Vonnegut, McNeely, Russe, Roth and Hendrickson.
German, Music and Drawing—Rinne, Vonnegut and Burns.

Heating, Hygiene and Janitors—Russe, Hendrickson and McNeely.
Judiciary, Districts and Boundaries—Burns, Blackledge and Rinne.
Public Library—Russe, Adam, Hendrickson, Sloan and Blackledge.
Citizens' Advisory Library Committee—John B. Connor, Gavin L. Payne, Mrs. John Newman Carey, Miss Nebraska Cropsey. (Meets in the office of the Librarian on the Thursday preceding the first Friday of each month.)

FIRE DEPARTMENT.

Headquarters—Corner New York and Massachusetts av.
Chief Engineer—Thomas F. Barrett.
First Assistant Engineer—Charles E. Coots.
Second Assistant Engineer—Gustave Ernst.
Superintendent Fire Alarm Telegraph—George H. Holderman.
Veterinary Surgeon—Louis A. Greiner.
Engine Co. No. 1—147 Indiana av.; James O. George, Captain.
Engine Co. No. 2—Hillside av. and 7th; Ebenezer R. Leach, Captain.
Engine Co. No. 3—Prospect, near Virginia av.; John O'Brien, Captain.
Engine Co. No. 4—Cor. Madison av. and Morris; John Keating, Captain.
Engine Co. No. 5—North Side Sixth, near Capitol av.; John Fox, Captain.
Engine Co. No. 6—273 W. Washington; Walter Ripley, Captain.
Engine Co. No. 7—Headquarters; Wm. Gans, Engineer; Benedict Beck, Captain.
Engine Co. No. 8—Massachusetts av. near Noble st.; Jacob Petty, Captain.
Hose Reel Co. No. 9—North Indianapolis.
Hose Reel Co. No. 10—Cor. Illinois and Merrill; John Glazier, Captain.
Hose Co. No. 11—Virginia av. near Huron; Wm. Arnold, Captain.
Hose Co. No. 12—Beville av. south of Michigan; Simeon Hoyl, Captain.
Hose Co. No. 13—North side Maryland east of Meridian; Benedict Beck, Captain.
Hose Co. No. 14—Twenty-second and Kenwood av.; Charles Wesby, Captain.
Hose Co. No. 15—532 E Washington; John Loucks, Captain.
Hose Co. No. 16—Cor. Seventh and Ash; Thomas Howard, Captain.
Hose Co. No. 17—Cor. McCarty and West; Peter Delaney, Captain.
Hose Co. No. 18—W. Washington, opp. Traub av.; James Brannon, Captain.
Chemical Co. No. 1—Cor. New York and Massachusetts av.; Wm. Tobin, Captain.
Chemical Co. No. 2—125 E. South; John R. Robinson, Captain.
Chemical Co. No. 3—North side 6th near Capitol av; John Monaghan, Captain.
Hook and Ladder Co. No. 1—North side Maryland east of Meridian; James M. Campbell, Captain.
Hook and Ladder Co. No. 2—125 E South; Gustave Ernst, Captain.
Hook and Ladder Co. No. 3—North side 6th near Capitol av.; Thomas F. Quinn, Captain.
Hook and Ladder Co. No. 4—132 E. Washington; Albert Meurer, Captain.
Water Tower No. 1—Cor. New York and Massachusetts av.; George Diller, Driver.
Watchmen in Fire Tower—Frank Graham, John King, Samuel James.

FIRE-ALARM SIGNALS.

No. —Location of Boxes.—

4 Pennsylvania and Market.
5 English Opera House.
6 East and New York.
7 Noble and Michigan.
8 New Jersey and Massachusetts av.
9 Pine and North.
10 Market and Pine.
1—1 Vermont, bet. East and Liberty.
1—2 No. 13 Engine House.
1—3 Delaware and Walnut.
1—4 New Jersey and Ft. Wayne av.
1—5 Peru and Massachusetts av.
1—6 Christian av. and Ash.
1—7 Park av. and Butler.
1—8 Columbia and Malott avs.
1—9 Highland av. and John.
1—2—3 No. 9 Hose House, Ash and Seventh.
1—2—4 Alabama and Seventh.
1—2—5 Central and Lincoln avs.
1—2—6 Yandes and Lincoln av.
1—2—7 Brookside av. and Jupiter.
1—2—8 Central av. and Eighth.
1—2—9 Delaware and Tenth.
1—3—1 Alabama and Morrison.
1—3—2 Bellefontaine and Eighth.
1—3—4 College av. and Tenth.
1—3—5 Home av. and Delaware.
1—3—6 Alabama and North.
1—3—7 Atlas Works.
1—3—8 College av and Irwin.
1—3—9 Home and Cornell avs.
1—4—1 Yandes and Ninth.
1—4—2 Clifford and Highland avs
1—4—3 Clifford av. and Tecumseh.
1—4—5 Fourteenth and New Jersey.
1—4—6 Hillside av and Clark.
1—4—7 Eighth and Alvord.
1—4—8 College av. and Twelfth.
1—4—9 College av. and Eighteenth.
1—5—2 Park av. and Fourteenth.
1—5—3 L. E. & W. R. R. and Fifteenth.
1—5—4 Clifford and Ramsey avs.
1—5—6 Stoughton and Newman.
1—5—7 Hillside and Bloyd avs.
2—1 Illinois and St. Joseph.
2—3 Pennsylvania and Pratt.
2—4 Meridian and Second.
2—5 No. 5 Engine House.
2—6 Senate av. and St. Clair.
2—7 Illinois and Michigan.
2—8 Pennsylvania and Fifth.
2—9 Senate av. and Fourth.
2—1—2 Capitol av. and Eighth.
2—1—3 Pennsylvania and Michigan.
2—1—4 Illinois and Eleventh.
2—1—5 Colored Orphan Asylum.
2—1—6 Pennsylvania and Fourteenth.
2—1—7 Meridian and Seventh.
2—1—8 Capitol av. and Eighteenth.
2—1—9 Broadway and Cherry.
2—3—1 Illinois and Thirteenth.
2—3—4 No. 14 Hose Co.
2—3—5 Illinois and Twenty-fifth.
2—3—7 No. 9 Engine House.
3—1 No. 1 Engine House.
3—2 Meridian and Walnut.
3—4 California and Vermont.
3—5 Blake and New York.
3—6 Indiana av. and St. Clair.
3—7 City Hospital.
3—8 Blake and North.
3—9 Michigan and Agnes.
3—1—2 West and Walnut.
3—1—3 West and Third.
3—1—4 Seventh and Howard.
3—1—5 Torbet and Paca.
3—1—6 Capitol av. and First.
3—1—7 Northwestern av. and Twenty-first.
3—1—8 Vorster and Gent.
4—1 No. 6 Engine House.
4—2 Geisendorff and Washington.
4—3 Missouri and New York.
4—5 Meridian and Washington.
4—6 Illinois and Ohio.
4—7 Capitol av. and Washington.
4—8 Kingan's Pork House.
4—9 Indianola, three squares from river.
4—1—2 Missouri and Maryland.
4—1—3 Senate av. and Wabash.
4—1—5 Capitol av. and Georgia.
4—2—1 O. I. & W. Round House, west of river.
4—2—3 Insane Hospital.
4—2—4 Miley av. and Washington.
4—2—5 West Vermont and Belt R. R.
4—2—6 Capitol av. and Ohio.
5—1 No. 10 Hose House.
5—2 Illinois and Louisiana.
5—3 West and South.

5—4 West and McCarty.
5—6 Senate av. and Henry.
5—7 Meridian and Ray.
5—8 No. 4 Engine House.
5—9 Madison av. and Dunlop.
5—1—2 West and Ray.
5—1—3 Kentucky av. and Merrill.
5—1—4 Union and Morris.
5—1—6 Illinois and Kansas.
5—1—7 Morris and Dakota.
5—1—8 Morris and Church.
5—1—9 Capitol av. and McCarty.
5—2—1 Meridian and Palmer.
5—2—3 Pine and Lord.
5—2—4 Madison av. and Lincoln lane.
5—2—6 Meridian and Belt R. R.
5—2—7 Carlos and Ray.
5—2—8 No. 17 Engine House.
5—2—9 Meridian and Raymond.
6—1 No. 2 Hook and Ladder House.
6—2 Pennsylvania and Madison av.
6—3 Delaware and McCarty.
6—4 East and McCarty.
6—5 New Jersey and Merrill.
6—7 Virginia av. and Bradshaw.
6—8 East and Coburn.
6—9 Bicking and High.
6—1—2 McKernan and Dougherty.
6—1—3 East and Lincoln lane.
6—1—4 East and Beecher.
6—1—5 Wright and Sanders.
6—1—7 McCarty and Beaty.
7—1 No. 11 Engine House.
7—2 East and Georgia.
7—3 Cedar and Elm.
7—4 Benton and Georgia.
7—5 English av. and Pine.
7—6 Dillon and Bates.
7—8 No. 3 Engine House.
7—9 Fletcher av. and Dillon.
7—1—2 Spruce and Prospect.
7—1—3 English av. and Linden.
7—1—4 Olive and Willow.
7—1—5 Shelby and Beecher.
7—1—6 State av. and Orange.
7—1—8 Orange and Laurel.
7—1—9 Barth and Cottage avs.
7—2—1 Lexington av. and Linden.
7—2—3 Fletcher av. and Spruce.
7—2—4 State av. and Pleasant.
7—2—5 Prospect and Pleasant av.
7—2—6 Orange and Harlan.
7—2—8 Indiana Bicycle Works.
8—1 Market and New Jersey.
8—2 Washington and Delaware.
8—3 Washington and East.
8—4 New York and Davidson.
8—5 Deaf and Dumb Asylum.
8—6 U. S. Arsenal.
8—7 Oriental and Washington.
8—9 Female Prison.
8—1—2 No. 8 Hose House, East Washington.
8—1—3 Market and Noble.
8—1—4 Ohio and Highland av.
8—1—5 Michigan and Highland av.
8—1—6 Market and Arsenal av.
8—2—1 Panhandle Railway Shops.
8—2—3 Walcott and Carter.
8—2—4 State av. and Washington.
8—2—5 Madden's Lounge Factory.
8—2—6 Tucker & Dorsey.
8—2—7 Washington and Beville av.
8—2—9 No. 12 Hose House.
8—3—1 Michigan av. and Woodside.
8—3—2 Washington and Dearborn.
9—1 No. 7 Hose House.
9—2 Meridian and Georgia.
9—3 Meridian and South.
9—4 Pennsylvania and Louisiana.
9—5 Alabama and Virginia av.
9—6 Headquarters.
9—7 Grand Hotel.
9—8 Capitol av. and Ohio.

PRIVATE FIRE HYDRANTS.

Balke-Krauss Co....1
U. S. Arsenal Grounds....5
Parry Manufacturing Co....2
Deaf and Dumb Institute....1
Female Reformatory....1
Indianapolis Gas Works....2
Panhandle Shops....8
Sinker-Davis Co....1
Standard Wheel Co....3
Dugdale Can Co....1
Kingan & Co. (ltd)....1
Citizens' Street Car Co....1
Premier Steel Co....1

SPECIAL SIGNALS.

For the use of the Fire Department and Water Works Company.

First 2 strokes, Second Alarm.
Second 2 strokes, Third Alarm.
1—2—1 strokes, fire out and hose reeled up.
3 strokes calls off the Fire Pressure.
3—3 calls for Fire Pressure without pulling a box.
12 strokes at 12 m., struck at tower.

WEST INDIANAPOLIS BOXES.

(Telephone 543).
2 Car Works.
4 Judge Harding and Vandalia Line.
5 Indianapolis Stove Co.
6 Indianapolis Furniture Co.
8 Wheel Works.
15 York and Nordyke.
21 William and Howard.
22 Morris and Crawford.
23 Morris and Hadley.
24 Belt Railroad Office.
27 Marion and Cottage.
31 Howard and Lee.
33 Oliver av. and Birch.
35 Oliver and Osgood.
41 Belmont and Lambert.
42 Reisner and Miller.
45 River av. and Woodburn.
52 Morris and Reisner.
63 River av. and Morris.
72 Stock Yards.
89 Harding and Oliver av.

POLICE DEPARTMENT.

Headquarters—Southeast cor. Pearl and Alabama sts.
Police Surgeon—Thomas E. Courtney, M. D.
Superintendent—Thomas F. Colbert.
Clerk to Superintendent—John E. Engle.
Captains—James F. Quigley, Charles F. Dawson.
Sergeants — John Lowe, John Corrigan, Christian Kruger, Leonard Crane, Miller J. Laporte, Frank Schwab, Martin J. Hyland, Wm. F. Schweigert.
Doormen—G. A. Taffe, John Long.
Court Bailiff—John F. Kurtz.

DRIVERS OF PATROL WAGONS.

Charles Rogers, Albert Miller, John F. Loughlin, Joseph Steinruck.

IMPOUNDING OFFICER.

A. O. Robinson.

PATROLMEN.

Asch, Adolph.
Barlow, George F.
Bartleson, John A.
Beckman, Wm. F.
Bolen, Frank B.
Boylan, John P.
Bray, Edward S.
Butcher, Daniel A.
Byard, Jackson L.
Caplinger, Daniel B.
Carter, Daniel.
Clarke, Nelson E.
Conklin, Wm. H.
Coulson, Joseph E.
Cox, Wm. L.
Crabtree, James.
Crannon, Timothy.
Cronin, James J.
Curran, Patrick J.
Dilts, George W.
Dippel, Peter.
Dugan, Thomas F.
Fickle, Albert.
Gerber, Samuel S.
Giblin, Frank.
Grubb, Theodore.
Guntz, Simon J.
Hagerman, Green.
Haley, Daniel F.
Hanlon, Lawrence.
Harris, Edward.
Hart, Simpson T.
Hauser, Conrad.
Helm, John C.
Hite, Wm. D.
Hoffbauer, Nicholas J.
Hollahan, Jeremiah A.
Holtz, Wm. A.
Irish Samuel F.
Jackson, Newton.
Jones, Benjamin F.
Jordan, Robert H.
Kennaugh, Thos. C.
Kimpel, John N.

Kitzmiller, John C.
Knauss, Christian G.
Koons, George B.
Kurtz, Jacob D.
Lancaster, David R.
Leet, Ira L.
Leppert, Samuel.
Loughlin, John F.
Lund, Perry.
Lyons, Robert H.
McMullen, Valentine S.
Mackessey, Timothy.
Mahoney, Martin F.
Mathey, Alfred F.
Mefford, James O.
Milam, Wm. B.
Miller, Albert.
Monninger, Henry.
Moore, Terrance M.
Mulhall, Edward T.
O'Brien, Patrick W.
Panse, James B.
Pope, Henry T.
Pope, James P.
Rader, John D.
Raftery, Michael.
Recer, Joseph H.
Richardson, Josephus.
Rinker, A. Dayton.
Robinson, Albert O.
Rockafellow, C. W.
Rogers, Charles.
Rogers, Wm.
Ross, Robert.
Sangston, Wm.
Schrader, Henry C.
Scott, Lewis C.
Seamans, Joseph R.
Shaffer, Adolphus C.
Slate, Henry.
Smith, Allen F.
Spearing, Frederick.
Steinruck, Joseph.
Stephans, Andrew J.
Stevens, Bion R.
Streit, Jesse M.
Taffe, George A.
Temple, Carter.
Tieben, Garret H.
Tomlinson, George H.
Wallace, Harry R.
Ward, Nathan T.
Ware, Charles A.
Warren, Calvin M.
Weible, John.
Wheeler, Edward.
Wilson, James F.
Winn, James W.
Woodward, Wm.
Woolley, Oliver W.

DETECTIVE DEPARTMENT.

Chief—Timothy Splann.
Detectives—Benjamin T. Thornton, John Kaehn, Jeremiah E. Kinney, Martin McGuff, David S. Richards, Frank Wilson, Thomas L. Stout, John F. Manning.

POLICE COURT.

Court House.

Police Judge—Charles E. Cox.
Clerk—Charles H. Stuckmeyer.
Deputy Clerk—August Tamm.
Bailiff—John F. Kurtz.

MERCHANT POLICE.

Headquarters—10 Odd Fellows' Bldg.
Captain—Jasper N. Clary.
Lieutenant—John H. Whitman.
Secretary—Benjamin F. Wilson.
Treasurer—Benjamin F. Myers.
Patrolmen—Nelson Daubenspeck, Robert D. Bacon, George W. Fess, Christian Cook, Thomas M. Kingsbury, David F. Clary, George W. Cheatham, Michael Smiley, Wilford Bristow, Ira Hadley, Samuel Hice, James Breen, Wm. Hillman, John L. Elliott, Samuel Dever, Thomas C. Moore, Harry J. Thrush, Thomas Morton, John M. Shulse, John Minor, Milton H. Miller, Bennett Campbell, John C. Ballard, Joseph O'Donnell, Charles F. Reno, George W. Hancock, Frank S. Littlejohn, Bowen F. Julian, Thomas B. Archer, Samuel J. McClure, John T. Borgmann, John C. Whittinghill, Alonzo Gates, Wm. H. Harwood, Henry P. Thomas, Christian Hansing, Cyrenius E. Porteus, Mark A. Smith, Benjamin A. Bell, John M. Spears, Isaac N. Williams, Frank A. Arnold, John C. Johnson, Charles H. Dongers, Herman F. Ropkey, Foster Cunningham, Wm. Smith, Warren G. McCain, John Foltzenlogle, Abraham C. Fouty.

COUNTY OFFICERS.

Clerk (ex-officio of all courts)—James W. Fesler. Term expires December, 1898. Deputy, Clinton L. Hare.
Treasurer—Wm. H. Schmidt. Term expires September, 1899. Deputy, David Wallace.
Auditor—Harry B. Smith. Term expires November, 1899.
Recorder—Wm. E. Shilling. Term expires December, 1898. Deputy, Benjamin Franklin.
Sheriff—Thomas P. Shufelton. Term expires December, 1898.
Coroner—Alembert W. Brayton. Term expires November, 1898.
Commissioners—James E. Greer, term expires November, 1898; John McGregor, term expires November, 1899; Henry Harding, term expires November, 1901.
Assessor—Joseph E. Boswell. Term expires November, 1900.
Surveyor—John V. Coyner. Term expires November, 1898.
Superintendent of Schools—Wm. B. Flick. Term expires 1897.
Judge Marion Circuit Court—Henry Clay Allen. Term expires November, 1900.
Probate Commissioner—Gus O'Bryan, 51 Court House.
Judges Superior Court—Room 1—John L. McMaster. Term expires November, 1898. Room 2—Lawson M. Harvey. Term expires November, 1898. Room 3—Vinson Carter. Term expires November 15, 1898.
Judge Marion Criminal Court—Frank McCray. Term expires November, 1898.
Prosecuting Attorney—Charles S. Wiltsie. Term expires November, 1898.

TOWNSHIP OFFICERS.

Township Assessor—Eugene Saulcy. Term expires August 4, 1897.
Deputies—M. L. Jefferson, Edward A. Bretz, Benjamin F. Conner, Wm. U. Graham, James N. Shelton, John A. Porter.
Justices of the Peace—Charles A. Clark, Frank M. Hay, John H. Herig (W. I.); Wm. S. Lockman, Ezra G. Martin (H.); Carl Habich, Luke Walpole, John W. Sears (B.); Wm. H. Nickerson, Elmer B. Pentecost (I.)
Constables—A. A. Whitesell, C. J. Whitesell, Joseph B. Shores, Wm. H. Huston, Frank L. Glass, Philip Marer, David J. Smock, John F. Henninger.
Trustees—Center, Horace B. Makepeace, 10½ E. Washington street; Franklin, Wm. B. Pentecost; Perry, Benjamin M. Morgan; Pike, Sobiski Butler; Washington, Oliver J. Pursel; Wayne, Francis M. Clark; Warren, John Kitley; Lawrence, Michael M. Hindman; Decatur, Thornton A. Mills.
Time of Holding Elections—General, State and county elections are held on the first Tuesday after the first Monday in November. Township elections, first Monday in April. The general city election is held on the second Tuesday in October.

ASYLUMS, HOSPITALS, ETC.

Alpha Home for Aged Colored Women—Darwin, near Hillside av.
Asylum for Friendless Colored Children—Southwest cor. Twelfth and Senate av. Mrs. Alice R. Taylor, Pres.
Central Hospital for Insane—National road 3 miles west of city. George F. Edenharter, M. D., Supt.
City Dispensary—34 East Ohio street. Leonard Bell, M. D., Supt.
City Hospital—Northwest cor. Locke and Margaret streets. Charles E. Ferguson, M. D., Supt.
County Infirmary—Indiana av., four miles northwest of city. Flavious J. Meyers, Supt.
Friendly Inn—290 West Market street. Wm. R. Moore, Supt.
German Lutheran Orphans' Home—Northeast cor. Washington and Watts. Wm. C. Jaeger, Supt.
German General Protestant Orphan Asylum—South State av., opp. Sycamore street. Henry F. Roesener, Supt.
Guardians' Home—Southeast cor. Auburn av. and Prospect.
Home for Aged Poor—North side of Vermont, east of East street. In charge of the Little Sisters of the Poor.

Home of the Good Shepherd—57 West Raymond.

Indiana Institute for the Education of the Blind—North side of North, between Meridian and Pennsylvania streets. Wm. H. Glascock, Supt.

Indiana Institution for Educating the Deaf and Dumb—Southeast cor. Washington street and State av. R. O. Johnson, Supt.

Indiana Reform School for Girls and Woman's Prison—Southeast cor. Michigan and Randolph streets. Sarah F. Keely, Supt.

Indianapolis Home for Friendless Women—Corner Capitol av. and Eleventh street. Gertrude T. Marquess, Matron.

Indianapolis Orphan Asylum—Northeast cor. College and Home avs. Mrs. John A. Bradshaw, Pres.

Katharine Home—Southeast cor. Capitol av. and Eleventh street. Mary A. Hendricks, Supt.

Marion County Jail—Southwest cor. Delaware and Pearl streets. Thomas P. Shufelton, Sheriff.

Marion County Work House—South side Twelfth street, between Highland place and Northwestern av. Cornelius McGroarty, Supt.

Polyclinique in connection with Central College of Physicians and Surgeons—209 South Pennsylvania.

Protestant Deaconess Home—118 North Senate av. Bertha Schneider, Matron.

Rescue Home and Mission—49 East South. Wm. V. Wheeler, Supt.

St. Joseph's Home and Industrial School—397 South Alabama.

St. Vincent's Infirmary—Southeast cor. Delaware and South streets. In charge of the Sisters of Charity.

BANKS AND BANKERS.

Indianapolis Clearing House Association—8 Fletcher's Bank Bldg. Frederick Baggs, Mngr.

Capital National Bank—Commercial Club Bldg. Chartered 1889. Capital, $300,000; surplus, $45,000; undivided profits, $12,000. Medford B. Wilson, Pres.; W. F. Churchman, Cashr.

Indiana National Bank—Cor. Pennsylvania and Virginia av. Incorporated 1865. Capital, $300,000; surplus and undivided profits, $700,000. Volney T. Malott, Pres.; Edward L. McKee, Vice Pres.; Edward B. Porter, Cashr.; M. W. Malott, Asst Cashr.

Indianapolis National Bank—607 Indiana Trust Bldg. Edward Hawkins, Receiver.

Merchants' National Bank The—Southwest cor. Washington and Meridian streets. Incorporated 1865; charter extended 1885. Capital, $1,000,000; surplus, $90,000; John P. Frenzel, Pres.; Otto N. Frenzel, Vice Pres. and Cashr.; Frederick Fahnley, Second Vice Pres.; Oscar F. Frenzel, Asst. Cashr.

Fletcher's Bank (S. A. Fletcher & Co), 30, 32 and 34 E. Washington street. Capital, $1,000,000; surplus, $100,000.

State Bank of Indiana—Northwest cor. Washington and Illinois. Incorporated 1892. Capital, $200,000; surplus and undivided profits, $25,000. Hiram W. Miller, Pres.; David A. Coulter, Frankfort, Ind., Vice Pres.; James R. Henry, Cashr.

TRUST COMPANIES.

Indiana Trust Co.—Incorporated 1893. Capital, $1,000,000. Southeast cor. Virginia av. and Washington street. John P. Frenzel, Pres.; John A. Butler, Sec.

Lawyers' Loan and Trust Co.—Incorporated 1895. Capital, $300,000. 68½ E. Market. W. F. Churchman, Pres.; H. F. Stevenson, Sec.

Marion Trust Co.—Incorporated 1895. Capital, $300,000. Southeast cor. Market and Monument pl. Frank A. Maus, Pres.; Wm. T. Noble, Sec.

Union Trust Co.—Incorporated 1893. Capital, $600,000. 68 E. Market. J. H. Holliday, Pres.; Henry C. G. Bals, Sec.

BUILDERS' EXCHANGE.

—35 E. Ohio.—

Meeting of members 10 o'clock a. m. daily.
Meeting of Directors first Friday in each month.

Officers—George W. Stanley, Pres.; Stanton W. Hawkey, Vice Pres.; Theodore F. Smither, Treas.; Charles Balke, Sec.

MEMBERS.

Adamant Wall Plaster Co. of Indiana.
Adams Brick Co., brick mnfrs, box 151.
Adams Henry C., stone quarry.
Adams Joseph R., painter, box 5.
Andrews George W., press brick, box 23.
Archer Alexander M., wall plaster.
Aufderheide Henry, genl contr, box 102.
Bachman Frederick M., lumber.
Balke & Krauss Co., lumber, box 117.
Bender Conrad, genl contr, box 163.
Bernhardt Lorenz, stone contr, box 91.
Boring Ephraim, plastr, box 124.
Brown-Ketcham Iron Works, box 64.
Brown M. L., lumber.
Bruner Anderson, sewer contr, box 56.
Burnet & Lewis, box 121.
Capitol Lumber Co, box 4.
Clarke & Sons, plumbers, box 113.
Clements George, carp, box 126.
Clements Peter, carp, box 148.
Coburn Henry, lumber.
Cochrane S. W., carp, box 8.
Consolidated Coal and Lime Co, box 133.
Dalton & Merrifield, lumber.
Diamond Wall Plaster Co., box 63.
Dreier Ernest, brick contr, box 138.
Eldridge E. H. & Co., lumber, box 75.
Ernst Joseph, plastr, box 153.
Fertig & Kevers, painters, box 114.
Foster Lumber Co., box 3.
Francke & Schindler, hardware.
Fraser Bros. & Van Hoff, lumber, box 71.
Fritz Peter, stone contr, box 105.
Fulmer Leander A., excavator, box 46.
Gardner Joseph, tinner, box 131.
Greensburg Limestone Co., box 64.
Haugh-Noelke Iron Wks, box 22.
Hawkey Stanton W., brick contr, box 104.
Heintz Valentine, brick contr, box 13.
Hetherington & Berner, box 141.
Humphreys M. E. & Co., roof matrl, box 84.
Indianapolis Manufacturers' and Carpenters' Union, lumber, box 34.
Ittenbach G. & Co., cut stone contrs, box 83.
Jameson Thomas H., genl contr, box 95.
Johnson Wm. A., painter, box 74.
Kattau Wm. H., genl contr, box 15.
Keller Julius, cement walks, box 132.
Kirkhoff Bros., plumbers, box 31.
Koehring & Son, hardware, box 32.
Koss & Fritz, stone contrs, box 135.
Kraas Wm., contr, box 42.
Krauss Charles, pumps, box 25.
Kruse & Dewenter, heating furnaces.
Laakmann & Sherer, cement walks, box 35.
Lauck John, contr, box 164.
Laut H. W. & Co., tinners, box 38.
Lilly & Stalnaker, hardware, box 161.
Long Steel and Iron Roofing Co., box 37.
Luedeman Bros., brick mnfrs, box 21.
McGauly James, plumber, box 116.
McWorkman W., tinner and roofer, box 67.
Mack Frederick J., painter, box 145.
Marion Brick Works, brick mnfrs, box 62.
Martin John, brick contr, box 142.
Meyer A. B. & Co., lime and cement, box 24.
Michie Albert, bridge contr.
Michigan Lumber Co., box 54.
Morse Thomas J., genl contr, box 61.
Muecke Wm., painter, box 36.
Mueller J. A. D., stair builder, box 158.
Noe Nicholas, brick contr, box 98.
Nuerge & Reinking, genl contrs, box 66.
Otto Gas Engine Co., John Wallace, agt.

Pangborn George W., real est.
Pearce Charles, genl contr, box 72.
Petrie Wm., stone contr, box 96.
Pierson J. C. & Son, brick contrs, box 51.
Pierson Levi S., brick contr, box 14.
Pothast Christian, brick mnfr, box 27.
Preusch J. F., carp, box 33.
Pursell Peter M., heating furnaces, box 137.
Roberts Lemuel, stair builder, box 127.
Russell Isaac, lumber, box 6.
Salisbury & Stanley, genl contrs, box 65.
Schmid J. C. & Sons, stone contrs, box 94.
Schultz & Sommer, plasterers, box 147.
Shellhouse & Co., hardware, box 156.
Sheridan Brick Works, box 151.
Shover James E., genl contr, box 73.
Shover Oran D., excavator, box 12.
Schreiber Frederick, contr, box 82.
Schumacher John A. & Co., contrs, box 152.
Sims J. A., gravel roofer, box 146.
Smith George F., contr, box 155.
Smither Theodore F., roofer, box 85.
Smock Ferdinand C., carp, box 43.
Spielhoff Henry & Son, genl contrs, box 103.
Sullivan C. W., plasterer, box 101.
Tielking Henry W., stone contr, box 44.
Tall Wm R., plasterer, box 53.
Thurtle J. G., architect.
Twiname James E., brick mnfr, box 106.
Twiname John J., brick contr, box 45.
Van Camp Hardware and Iron Co.
Vater Thomas J., brick contr, box 112.
Vonnegut Clemens, hardware.
Wallace John, Otto gas engines.
Weaver George, brick contr, box 144.
Wehking Charles F., brick contr, box 162.

BUILDING, LOAN AND SAVINGS ASSOCIATIONS.

Acme Savings and Loan Association—W. H. Stringer, Sec., 428 N. Senate av.
Active Building Association—H. F. Shoemaker, Sec., 426½ Mass. av.
Advance Saving and Loan Association—Frank M. Hueber, Sec., 103½ E. Washington.
Aetna Savings and Loan Association—Howard Kimball, Sec., 89 E. Market.
Alabama Street Building, Loan and Savings Association—Wm. G. Holland, Sec., 915 N. Capitol av.
American Building and Loan Association—Jesse Summers, Sec., 42 Lombard bldg.
American Loan and Savings Society—S. L. Douglass, Sec., 529 Lemcke bldg.
American Union Savings Association—Jesse W. Brooks, Agt., 44½ N. Penn.
Arsenal Building and Loan Association—James R. Scott, Sec., 75 E. Seventh.
Atlas Savings Association—Robert Martindale, Sec., 84 E. Market.
Bee Hive Savings and Loan Association—Hugh Campbell, Sec., 641 Mass. av.
Big Four Building Association—Samuel E. Ellerman, Sec., 68½ E. Market.
Blake Street Savings and Loan Association No. 4—Joseph Hoy, Sec., 454 Blake.
Cabinet Makers' Building and Loan Association—Gustav G. Stark, Sec., 436 E. Market.
Capital City Building and Loan Association—Robert G. Brier, Sec., 78 N. Penn.
Celtic Savings and Loan Association—John R. Welch, Sec., 34 Monument pl.
Center Building and Loan Association—Samuel W. Wales, Sec., 387 Mass. av.
Central Savings and Loan Association No. 3—Theodore Stein, Sec., 229 Lemcke bldg.
Citizens' Mutual Building and Loan Association—Albert B. Carter, Sec., 29 Journal bldg.
Citizens' Savings and Loan Association No. 2—E. J. Hoffman, Sec., 161 Union.
City Savings and Loan Association—Joseph Buennagel, Sec., 174 Duncan.
College Avenue Savings and Loan Association—Fred C. Gardner, Sec., 292 Broadway.
Columbia Savings and Loan Association—James L. Kingsbury, Sec., 30½ N. Delaware.
Commercial Building and Loan Association—Levi Kennedy, Sec., 416 Indiana Trust bldg.
Commonwealth Loan and Savings Association of Indianapolis—Charles E. Dark, Sec., 18½ Waverly bldg.
Crescent Loan and Investment Company—James H. Lowes, Sec., 63 When bldg.
Dime Savings and Loan Association—W. A. Rhodes, Sec., 2 Plymouth bldg.
Downey Street Savings and Loan Association Nos. 1 and 2—Peter Ohleyer, Sec., 452 S. Meridian.
Dwelling Building Association—J. E. Pierce, Sec., 24 S. Penn.
East End Saving and Loan Association—L. D. Buenting, Sec., 27½ S. Delaware.
East Washington Street Building and Loan Association—Emil C. Rassmann, Sec., 31 Monument pl.
Eastern Savings and Loan Association—Conrad Mueller, Sec., Merchants' National Bank.
English Avenue No. 2 Building and Loan Association—J. F. Reinecke, Sec., 56 Fletcher av.
Economy Savings and Loan Association—M. Steinhauer, Sec., 201 Bates.
Equitable Savings and Loan Association—L. G. Dynes, Sec., 245 E. Washington.
Equitable State Building and Loan Association—H. D. Vories, Sec., 512 Indiana Trust Bldg.
Eureka Saving and Loan Asociation—T. C. Whitcomb, Sec., 60 E. Market.
Fidelity Building and Savings Union Nos. 1, 2, 3, 4 and 5—Edward J. Robinson, Sec., 81 W. Market.
Fidelity Savings and Loan Association—A. C. Simms, Sec., 184 Indiana av.
Fletcher Avenue Building and Loan Association—Nelson Yoke, Sec., 131 Fletcher av.
Fourteenth Street Saving and Loan Association—Sidney M. Dyer, Sec., 31 Monument pl.
Franklin Building and Loan Association—W. A. Rhodes, Sec., 72 E. Market.
Fraternal Building and Loan Association—George W. Powell, Sec., 51 Journal Bldg.
Fraternal Building and Loan Association No. 2—George W. Powell, Sec., 51 Journal Bldg.
Garfield Park Building and Loan Association—Joseph Ruff, Sec., 42 S. New Jersey.
German-American Building and Loan Association A and B—G. W. Brown, Sec., 100 N. Delaware.
German-American Perpetual Saving and Loan Association—H. W. Aldag, Sec., Merchants' National Bank.
German Home Building and Loan Association—H. W. Fechtman, Sec.
Globe Loan and Savings Association—Henry Thienes, Sec., 204 Clifford av.
Government Building and Loan Institution—H. E. Rose, Sec., 31 Journal Bldg.
Government Building and Loan Institution No. 2 and 3—H. E. Rose, Sec., 31 Journal Bldg.
Guardian Savings and Loan Association—Wm. H. Hobbs, Sec., 70 E. Market.
Guarantee Savings and Investment Association—S. D. La Fuze, Sec., 68 Lombard Bldg.
Hartford Saving and Investment Company—J. M. Spann, Sec., 84 E. Market.
Home Builders' Savings and Loan Association—Hugo Wuelfing, Sec., 35 S. Meridian.
Home Savings Association—Alice V. Mendenhall, Sec., 627 Lemcke Bldg.
Hoosier Savings and Loan Association The—W. H. Stringer, Sec., 428 N Senate av.
Ideal Society for Savings Association—G. L. Paetz, Sec., 36 Stevens.

Illinois and Seventh Street Savings and Loan Association No. 2—A. A. Young, Sec., 12 N. Meridian.
Imperial Savings and Loan Association—George W. Ryan, Sec., 719 Lemcke Bldg.
Independent Turners' Savings and Loan Association—August Doeppers, Sec., 700 E. Market.
Indiana Home and Savings Association—C. E. Galloway, Sec., 94 E. Market.
Indiana Mutual No. 1 Building and Loan Association—Charles Kahlo, Sec., 32 E. Market.
Indiana Mutual No. 2 Building and Loan Association—Charles Kahlo, Sec., 32 E. Market.
Indiana Mutual No. 3 Building and Loan Association—Charles Kahlo, Sec., 32 E. Market.
Indiana Mutual No. 4—Charles Kahlo, Sec., 32 E. Market.
Indiana Mutual No. 5—Charles Kahlo, Sec., 32 E. Market.
Indiana Savings and Investment Company—C. E. Holloway, Sec., 90 E. Market.
Indiana Savings and Loan Association No. 2—Jacob Buennagel, Sec., 387 S. East.
Indiana Society for Savings—C. A. Bookwalter, Sec., 214 Lemcke bldg.
Indianapolis Building and Loan Association—W. A. Rhodes, Sec., 72 E. Market.
Indianapolis Savings and Investment Company—George L. Raschig, Sec., 36 Monument pl.
Indianola Building and Loan Association—Frank B. Fowler, Sec., 601 Lemcke bldg.
Industrial Alliance Building and Loan Association—J. M. Heller, Sec., 35 Baldwin blk.
Industrial Savings and Loan Association No. 3—Peter Ohleyer, Sec., 452 S. Meridian.
International Building and Loan Association Nos. 1 and 2—Charles Schurmann, Sec., 83 E. Market.
Interstate Building and Savings Association—John H. Furnas, Sec., 112 N. Penn.
Knights of Labor Savings Association No. 2—Theodore C. Hoffmann, Sec., Merchants' National Bank.
Laborers' Savings and Loan Association No. 2—Frank H. Goheen, 348 Coburn.
Laborers' Savings and Loan Association No. 3—L. D. Buenting, 27½ S. Delaware.
Lombard Building and Loan Association—A. L. Cook, Sec., 97 Lombard bldg.
McCarty Street Savings and Loan Association—Rudolph P. Thiecke, 483 S. New Jersey.
Madison Avenue No. 4 Building and Loan Association—Jacob Buennagel, Sec., 387 S. East.
Madison Avenue No. 5 Building and Loan Association—Frank H. Goheen, Sec., 348 Coburn.
Madison Road Savings and Loan Association—John Brill, jr., Sec., 425 Madison av.
Madison Road Savings and Loan Association No. 2—John Brill, jr., Sec., 425 Madison av.
Marion County Savings and Loan Association—Joseph Buennagel, Sec., 174 Duncan.
Marion Trust and Loan Company—J. F. Fesler, Sec., 10 Clay.
Massachusetts Avenue and Michigan Street Building and Loan Association—E. M. Ogle, Sec., 400 N. Meridian.
Mechanics' Mutual Building and Loan Association—Albert Rabb, Assignee, 62 Lombard bldg.
Mechanics' Mutual Building and Loan Association No. 1—Albert Rabb, Assignee, 62 Lombard bldg.
Mechanics' Mutual Building and Loan Association No. 2—George L. Raschig, Receiver, 36 Monument pl.
Merrill Savings and Loan Association—Jacob Buennagel, Sec., 387 S. East.
Monument Savings and Loan Association—H. F. Stevenson, Sec., 68½ E. Market.
Morris Street Savings and Loan Association No. 2—Charles W. Drewes, Sec., 265 Union.
Mutual Home and Savings Association—W. A. Rhodes, Sec., 72 E. Market.
Mutual Savings Union and Loan Association—John Schley, Sec., 16 Masonic Temple.
National Savings and Loan Association—C. B. Feibleman, Sec., 90 E. Court.
New Massachusetts Avenue Savings and Loan—Wm. F. Wocher, Sec., 19½ N. Penn.
New Merrill Street Savings and Loan Association—H. A. Weber, Sec., 198 Virginia av.
New Shelby Street Building and Loan Association—Anton Schmidt, Sec., 362 Shelby.
New Year Savings and Loan Association—J. H. Smith, Sec., 36 W. Washington.
Noble Street Savings and Loan Association—Theodore Stein, Sec., 229 Lemcke bldg.
North East Savings and Loan Association—Newton Todd, Sec., 7 Ingalls blk.
North Side Savings and Loan Association—W. H. Stringer, Sec., 428 N. Senate av.
Occidental Savings and Loan Association—C. H. Rosebrock, Sec., 19 Thorpe blk.
Pan Handle Building, Savings and Loan Association—P. J. Landers, Sec., 774 E. Washington.
Parnell Building and Loan Association—Jeremiah Collins, Sec., 373 S. Illinois.
People's Building and Loan Association No. 5—J. F. Reinecke, Sec., 56 Fletcher av.
People's Mutual Savings and Loan—H. R. Martin, Sec., 25 Water.
Personal Property Saving and Loan Association—W. A. Zumpfe, Sec., 4 Lombard bldg.
Phoenix Savings and Loan Asociation—C. B. Feibleman, Sec., 90 E. Court.
Plymouth Savings and Loan Association—Edward Gilbert, Sec., 44½ N Penn.
Progress Savings and Loan Association—Peter Pfisterer, Sec., 103½ E. Washington.
Prospect Savings and Loan Association—John Schley, Sec., 16 Masonic Temple.
Provident Savings, Loan and Investment Association—Arthur B. Grover, Sec., 436 Lemcke Bldg.
Prudential Depository, Saving and Loan Association—C. R. Jones, Sec., 30 Monument pl.
Railroadmen's Building and Saving Association—W. T. Cannon, Sec., Union Station.
Reserve Fund Savings and Loan Association of Indiana—Charles H. Young, Sec., 55 When blk.
Royal Savings and Loan Association—Howard Kimbal, Sec., 89 E. Market.
Rural Savings and Loan Association—George H. McCaslin, Sec., 2½ W. Washington.
Security Savings and Loan Association—Kenneth G. Reid, Sec., 42 N. Delaware.
Southeastern Savings and Loan Association—C. H. Adam, Sec., 326 Orange.
South Meridian Street No. 3 Savings and Loan Association—J. G. Ohleyer, Sec., 29 W. Washington.
Standard Saving and Loan Association of Indianapolis—C. H. Rosebrock, Sec., 88½ E. Washington.
Standard Savings and Loan Association of Indiana—George R. Root, Sec., 27 Thorpe blk.
Star Savings and Loan Association—H. H. Fay, Sec., 40½ E. Washington.
State Building and Loan Association of Indiana Nos. 2 and 3—Frank H. Hovey, Sec., 31 S. Penn.
State Capitol Investment Company—John Furnas, Sec., 26-27 When Bldg.

State House Building Association—H. F. Hackedorn, Sec., 211-213 Indiana Trust bldg.
State House Dime Association—H. F. Hackedorn, Sec., 211-213 Indiana Trust bldg.
Sun Building, Loan and Investment Company—John Green, Sec., 12½ N. Delaware.
Sun Savings and Investment Company—L. G. Miller, Sec., 117 W. Georgia.
Teutonia No. 4 Savings and Loan Association—Conrad Mueller, Sec., Merchants' National Bank.
Thorpe Block Savings and Loan Association—J. K. Wright, Sec., 83 E. Market.
Triennial Savings and Loan Association—E. J. Hoffman, Sec., 161 Union.
Turner Building and Savings Association No. 2—Armin Bohn, Sec., 1060 N. Senate av.
Union Mutual Building and Loan Association—James E. Franklin, Sec., 87 W. Market.
Union National Savings and Loan Association The, Nos. 1 and 2—Nicholas Ensley, Sec., 65 E. Ohio.
United States Building and Loan Institution—Caleb N. Lodge, Sec., 721 Lemcke bldg.
United States Savings Fund and Investment Company—E. H. Hall, Sec., 42-44 Lorraine bldg.
Virginia Avenue Building and Loan Association—Oswald Thau, Sec., 430 Virginia av.
Washington Savings and Loan Association—John W. Hall, Sec., 18 Aetna bldg, 19½ N. Penn.
West Indianapolis Savings and Loan Association—B. W. Gillespie, Sec., Union Stock Yards (W. I.)
West Market Exchange Building and Loan Association—W. H. Stringer, Sec., 428 N. Senate av.
Western Savings and Loan Association—Theo. A. Pfafflin, Sec., 997 N. Senate av.
World Building, Loan and Investment Company—Everett Wagner, Sec., 36½ W. Washington.
Young Men's Saving and Loan Association—H. A. Weber, Sec., 198 Virginia av.

CEMETERIES.

Crown Hill Cemetery—Incorporated 1863. Situated on Northwestern av, three miles north of the city, and comprises about 400 acres of land. Allen M. Fletcher, Pres.; George P. Anderson, Sec.; office, 6 Ingalls blk. Frederick W. Chislett, Supt.; office at cemetery.
German Catholic Cemetery—Meridian street, south of city.
German Lutheran Cemetery—Meridian street, south of city.
Greenlawn Cemetery—West side Kentucky av., north of South street.
Holy Cross Cemetery (Roman Catholic)—Bluff road, south of city. Rev. F. H. Gavisk, Pres.; J. R. Welsh, Sec.; office, 34 Monument pl. Jeremiah Egan, Supt.
Jewish Cemetery—Spruce and South Meridian streets. Owned by the Indianapolis Hebrew Congregation.
Mount Jackson Cemetery—Mount Jackson. Wm. H. Speer, Mngr.

CHURCHES AND SUNDAY SCHOOLS.

ADVENTISTS.

Seventh Day Adventist Church—175 Central av. Rev. Wm. A. Young, pastor. Services Saturdays, 3:30 p. m., Sunday evening 7:30 p. m.; Sunday School (Saturday), 2:30 p. m.

BAPTIST.

Brightwood Baptist Church — Northwest cor. Bloyd av. and Stuart. Rev. Lee Fisher, pastor. Services 11 a. m., 7:30 p. m.; Sunday School, 9:30 a. m.
College Avenue Baptist Church—Northeast cor. College and Lincoln avs. Rev. Calvin A. Hare, D. D., pastor. Services 10:45 a. m., 7:30 p. m.; Sunday School, 9:30 a. m.
First Baptist Church—Northeast cor. Pennsylvania and New York streets. Rev. Daniel J. Ellison, pastor. Services 10:45 a. m., 7:30 p. m.; Sunday School, 9:30 a. m.
First Baptist Church (Haughville)—Rev. C. H. McDowell, pastor. Services 10:45 a. m.; Sunday School, 9:45 a. m.
Garden Baptist Church—168 Bright street. Rev. Charles L. Berry, pastor. Services 10:30 a. m., 7 p. m.; Sunday School, 2 p. m.
German Baptist Church—Northwest cor. North and Davidson streets. Rev. Andrew H. Freitag, pastor. Services 10 a. m., 7 p. m.; Sunday School, 2 p. m.
River Avenue Baptist Church (West Indianapolis)—Southwest cor. River and Standard avs. Services 10:30 a. m., 7:30 p. m.; Sunday School, 9:30 a. m.
Second Baptist Church (Irvington)—Services 11 a. m., 7:30 p. m.; Sunday School, 9:30 a. m.
South Street Baptist Church—Southwest cor. South and Noble streets. Rev. Charles E. W. Dobbs, pastor. Services 10:45 a. m., 7:30 p. m.; Sunday School, 9:30 a. m.
University Place Baptist Church—Southeast cor. Meridian and Twenty-fifth streets. Rev. C. H. McDowell, pastor. Services 7:30 p. m.; Sunday School, 10 a. m.
Woodruff Place Baptist Church—Southwest cor. Michigan and Walcott streets. Rev. Adrian D. Berry, pastor. Services 10:30 a. m., 7:30 p. m.; Sunday School, 2:30 p. m.

BAPTIST COLORED.

Antioch Baptist Church—Cor. Fourth and Howard streets. Rev. J. M. Morton, pastor. Services 11 a. m., 8 p. m.; Sunday School, 9 a. m.
Corinthian Baptist Church—Southwest cor. North and Fulton streets. Rev. John J. Blackshear, pastor. Services 10:30 a. m., 7:30 p. m.; Sunday School, 9 a. m.
Evergreen Baptist Church — 161 Shelby street. Rev. James Parker, pastor. Services 11 a. m., 7:30 p. m.; Sunday School, 9 a. m.
First Baptist Church (Irvington) — Rev. Ephraim Tyler, pastor. Services 11 a. m., 7:30 p. m.; Sunday School, 2:30 p. m.
First Baptist Church (North Indianapolis)—Rev. Anderson Simmons, pastor. Services 10:30 a. m., 7:30 p. m.; Sunday School, 9:30 a. m.
First Baptist Church (West Indianapolis)—Cor. Reisner and Johnson av. Rev. Marcellus Elzy, pastor. Services 10:30 a. m., 7:30 p. m.; Sunday School, 10 a. m.
Garfield Missionary Baptist Church—Perkins pike, near Bethel av., Rev. Robert H. Sample, pastor. Services 10:30 a. m., 7:30 p. m.; Sunday School, 9 a. m.
Mount Carmel Baptist Church—Southwest cor. James and Bedford av., Brightwood. Rev. John F. Broyles, pastor. Services 10:30 a. m., 7:30 p. m.; Sunday School, 9:30 a. m.
Mount Pilgrim Baptist Church—West side of Olive 1 n of Pleasant Run. Rev. James C. Harrison, pastor. Services 11 a. m., 7:30 p. m.; Sunday School, 9:30 a. m.
Mount Zion Baptist Church—Cor. Second street and Big Four R. R. Rev. Benjamin Farrell, pastor. Services 11 a. m., 3 and 8 p. m.; Sunday School 9 a. m.
New Bethel Baptist Church—83 Martindale av. Rev. Nathaniel Seymore, pastor. Services 11 a. m., 7 p. m.; Sunday School 9:30 a. m.
Olive Baptist Church—Cor. Coburn and McKernan. Rev. Thomas Byrd, pastor. Services 11 a. m., 7 p. m.; Sunday School 9 a. m.

St. James Baptist Church — Haughville, Tremont av., bet. Mick and Grandview avs. Services 11 a. m., 7:30 p. m.; Sunday School, 9 a. m. Rev. Nathan Payne, pastor.
Second Baptist Church—North side Michigan, east of West. Rev. James W. Carr, pastor. Services 11 a. m., 7:30 p. m.; Sunday School, 9 a. m.
South Calvary Church—Cor. Maple and Morris streets. Rev. C. F. Williams, pastor. Services 10:30 a. m., 7:30 p. m.; Sunday School, 9 a. m.
Third Baptist Tabernacle—130 Rhode Island street. Rev. Christopher C. Wilson, pastor. Services 10:30 a. m., 7:30 p. m.; Sunday School, 9 a. m.

FREEWILL BAPTIST.

Freewill Baptist Church—Cor. Rhode Island and Smith streets. Rev. Ollie S. J. Granderson, pastor. Services 11 a. m., 3:30 p. m.; Sunday School, 2 p. m.

CATHOLIC DIOCESE OF VINCENNES.

The southern half of the State of Indiana, including Marion county, is the Diocese of Vincennes, so called because the former Bishops lived at Vincennes.
Bishop—Rt. Rev. Francis Silas Chatard, D. D., Indianapolis, Ind.
Vicar General—Rt. Rev. Mgr. August Bessonies.
Vicar General—Very Rev. Anthony Scheideler.
Chancellor—Very Rev. D. O'Donaghue.
Offices—St. John's Clergy House, 76 W. Georgia.
Church of the Assumption—William street, West Indianapolis. Rev. Joseph F. Weber, rector. Mass, 7:30 and 9:30 a. m.; Vespers, 3 p. m.
Holy Cross Church—Southeast cor. Hanna and Ohio streets. Rev. Denis McCabe, rector. Mass, 8 and 10 a. m.; Vespers, 7:30 p. m.; Sunday School, 2:30 p. m.
Sacred Heart Church—Cor. Union and Palmer streets. Rev. Francis Haase, rector. Mass, 5:30 a. m., 7:30 a. m. and 10 a. m.; Vespers, 2:30 p. m.; Sunday School, 2:30 p. m.
St. Anthony's Church—Southeast cor. Warman avenue and New York, Haughville. Rev. Francis B. Dowd, rector. Mass, 8 and 10 a. m.; Sunday School, 2 p. m.; Vespers, 2:30 p. m.
St. Bridget's Catholic Church—Northeast cor. West and St. Clair streets. Rev. Daniel Curran, rector. Mass, 8 a. m. and 10 a. m.; Sunday School and Vespers, 2:30 p. m.
St. Francis De Sales—Brightwood. Rev. Simon Schwarz, rector. Mass, 10 a. m.; Vespers, 3 p. m.; Sunday School, 3 p. m.
St. John's Church—East side of Capitol av., between Georgia and Maryland. Clergy House, 76 W. Georgia street. Rev. Francis Henry Gavisk, rector; Revs. James A. O'Brien and Victor J. Brucker, assistants. Sunday services: Mass, 6, 7:30, 9 a. m.; High Mass, 10 a. m. Sermon at each mass. Sunday School, 2:30 p. m.; Society meetings, 4 p. m.; Vespers, 3 p. m. Mass daily, 6 and 8 a. m.
St. Joseph's Church—Southwest cor. Noble and North streets. Rev. H. Alerding, rector; Rev. George J. Lannert, assistant. Mass, 6 a. m., 8 a. m., 10 a. m. Vespers, 3 p. m.; Sunday School, 2:30 p. m.
St. Mary's Catholic Church—South side Maryland, west of Delaware street. Very Rev. Anthony Scheideler, rector; Rev. Adam Kohlmann, assistant rector. Mass, 6:30, 7:30 and 10 a. m.; Sunday School, 2:30 p. m.; Vespers, 3 p. m.
St. Patrick's Church—Southwest cor. Dougherty and Short streets. Very Rev. D. O'Donaghue, rector; Rev. Wm. A. Maher, assistant rector. Mass, 6 a. m., 8 a. m., 10 a. m.; Sunday School, 2:30 p. m., and Vespers, 3 p. m.
SS. Peter and Paul Cathedral—Cor. Meridian and Fifth. Right Rev. Francis S. Chatard, Right Rev. August Bessonies and Rev. Joseph Chartrand. Mass, 6, 8, 10 a. m.; Vespers, 3 p. m.

CHRISTIAN.

Central Christian Church—Northeast cor. Delaware and Fort Wayne av. Rev. John E. Pounds, pastor. Sunday services, 10:45 a. m. and 7:30 p. m.; Sunday School, 9:30 a. m.
Englewood Christian Church—40 N. Rural. Rev. Asa L. Orcutt, pastor. Services, 10:45 a. m. and 7:30 p. m.; Sunday School, 9:30 a. m.
Fourth Christian Church—449 N. West. Rev. G. H. Clarke, pastor. Services, 10:30 a. m., 7:30 p. m.; Sunday School, 2:30 p. m.
Haughville Christian Church—Haughville. Rev. Frank Findly, pastor. Services, 10:30 a. m.; Sunday School, 9:30 a. m.
Hillside Avenue Christian Church—East side Hillside av., between French and Ninth streets. Rev. W. C. Payne, pastor. Services, 10:30 a. m., 7:30 p. m.
Irvington Christian Church—Southeast cor. Downey and Houston avs., Irvington. Rev. E. P. Wise, pastor. Services, 10:45 a. m., 7:30 p. m.; Sunday School, 9:15 a. m.
Olive Branch Christian Church—556 S. Meridian. Rev. James C. Burkhardt, pastor. Services, 10:45 a. m., 7:45 p. m.; Sunday School, 3 p. m.
Second Christian Church (colored)—Northwest cor. Fourth and Howard. Rev. Mansfield F. Womack, pastor. Services, 10:30 a. m., 7 p. m.; Sunday School, 9:30 a. m.
Second Christian Church (W. I.)—Shepard street. Preaching every third Sunday of each month. Services every Sunday, 10:30 a. m.; Sunday School, 9:30 a. m.
Seventh Christian Church—Cor. Udell and Annette streets, North Indianapolis. Rev. Robert W. Clymer, pastor. Services, 11 a. m.; Sunday School, 9:30 a. m.
Sixth Christian Church—Southeast cor. Elm and Pine streets. Rev. D. R. Lucas, pastor. Services, 10:30 a. m., 7:30 p. m.; Sunday School, 9:15 a. m.
Third Christian Church—433 Home av. Rev. Burris A. Jenkins, pastor. Services, 10:30 a. m., 7:30 p. m.; Sunday School, 9 a. m.

CHRISTIAN SCIENTIST.

First Church of Christ—136 E. New York street. Mrs. A. Dorland, reader. Services, 10:30 a. m.

CHURCH OF CHRIST.

North Indianapolis Church of Christ—Rev. John W. Vandivier, pastor. Services, 10:30 a. m., 7:30 p. m.
West Indianapolis Church of Christ—Rev. Alvin M. Morris, pastor. Services, 10:30 a. m., 7:30 p. m.

CHURCH OF GOD.

Church of God—Cor. Le Grand av. and Leonard. Rev. John Vinson, pastor. Services, 10:30 a. m., 7:30 p. m.; Sunday School, 9:30 a. m.

CONGREGATIONAL.

Brightwood Congregational Church—Rev. Claude E. Grove, pastor. Services, 10:30 a. m., 7:30 p. m.; Sunday School, 9:30 a. m.
Fellowship Congregational Church—Southeast cor. Broadway and Eleventh. Rev. Frank M. Whitlock, pastor. Services, 10:45 a. m., 7:30 p. m.; Sunday School, 9:30 a. m.
Mayflower Congregational Church—Southwest cor. Delaware and Seventh streets. Rev. J. W. Wilson, pastor. Services, 10:45 a. m.; Sunday School, 9:30 a. m.

Northeast Congregational Church—Cor. Yandes and Eighth. Rev. George K. Miller, pastor. Services, 10:30 a. m.
People's Congregational Church—Southwest cor. Michigan and Blackford. Rev. Oren D. Fisher, pastor. Services, 10:45 a. m., 7:30 p. m.; Sunday School, 11:45 a. m.
Pilgrim Congregational Church—Cor. Woodburn and Warren av., West Indianapolis. Rev. Andrew F. Ayres, pastor. Services, 10:30 a. m., 7:30 p. m.; Sunday School, 9:30 a. m.
Plymouth Congregational Church—Southeast cor. New York and Meridian streets. Frederic E. Dewhurst, pastor. Services, 10:45 a. m., 7:45 p. m.; Sunday School, 9:30 a. m.
South Side Congregational Church—464 Virginia av. Rev. Franklin E. Jeffery, pastor. Services, 10:45 a. m., 7:45 p. m.; Sunday School, 9:30 a. m.
Union Congregational Church—Cor. La Salle and Richard streets, Marion Park. Rev. Oren D. Fisher, pastor. Services, 3 p. m.; Sunday School, 4 p. m.

EPISCOPAL DIOCESE OF INDIANA.

Bishop—Rt. Rev. John Hazen White, D. D., 242 N. Penn. street.
Secretary—Willis D. Engle, 432 Talbott av.
Treasurer—Charles E. Brooks.
Chancellor—Wm. Mack, Terre Haute, Ind.
Trustees—Aquilla Q. Jones, Lewis B. Martin, Edward Olcott, Nathan F. Dalton.
Christ Church—Northeast cor. Monument place and Meridian. Rev. Andrew J. Graham, pastor. Services 7:30 and 10:30 a. m. and 7:30 p. m.; Sunday School, 9:15 a. m.
Holy Innocents' Church—Northeast cor. Fletcher av. and Cedar. Rev. Edwin G. Hunter, rector. Services 7:30 and 10:30 a. m., 7:30 p. m.; Sunday School, 2:30 p. m.
Grace Cathedral—Southeast cor. Central av. and Seventh. Rev. Edgar F. Gee, rector. Holy communion every Sunday at 7:30 a. m.; service and celebration 10:30 a. m.; evening service 7:30; Sunday School, 3 p. m.
Grace Cathedral Mission—Cor. Illinois and Twenty-second streets. Services 4 p. m.; Sunday School 3 p. m.
St. George's Chapel—Northwest cor. Church and Morris streets. Rev. Andrew J. Graham, rector. Services every Thursday, 7:30 p. m.; Sunday School, 2:30 p. m.
St. Paul's Church—Southeast cor. New York and Illinois streets. Rev. Gustav A. Carstensen, rector. Services 10:45 a. m., 7:45 p. m.; Sunday School, 9:30 a. m.
Trinity Mission—Southeast cor. East and Lincoln lane. Rev. Andrew J. Graham, rector. Services second Sunday each month at 3:30 p. m.

EVANGELICAL CHURCH.

St. John's Evangelical Church—Northwest cor. East and Dunlop. Rev. Theodore Schorg, pastor. Services 10:30 a. m., 7:30 p. m.; Sunday School, 9 a. m.
St. Paul's German Evangelical—Southeast cor. of Columbia av. and Eighth. Rev. Henry F. Frigge, pastor. Services 10:30 a. m., 7:30 p. m.; Sunday School, 9:20 a. m.
Zion's German Evangelical Church—Cor. Ohio and Bird streets. Rev. J. C. Peters, pastor. Services 10:30 a. m., 7:30 p. m.; Sunday School, 9 a. m.

EVANGELICAL ASSOCIATION.

First Evangelical Church—Southeast cor. of New York and East streets. Rev. Frederick G. Schweitzer, pastor. Services 10:30 a. m., 7:30 p. m.; Sunday School, 9 a. m.

Second Evangelical Church—Northeast cor. Wilkins and Church streets. Rev. Joseph Fenkbeiner, pastor. Services 10 a. m., 7:30 p. m.; Sunday School, 2:15 p. m.

FRIENDS.

Friends' Church—Southeast cor. Alabama and Home av. Rev. Thomas C. Brown, pastor. Services 10:30 a. m., 7:45 p. m.; Sunday School, 9:15 a. m.; Wednesday 10:30 a. m.
Friends' Mission Church—Haughville, Frazee, near King av. Sunday, 10:30 a. m., 3 and 7:45 p. m.; Sunday School, 9:30 a. m.
Friends' River Side Church—West Indianapolis, southeast cor. Division and Standard av. Services 10:30 a. m.; Sunday School, 9:30 a. m.

REFORMED CHURCH IN THE U. S.

Church of Hope, German Reformed—Clifford av., bet. Waverly and Oakland avs. Rev. Julius Grauel, pastor. Services 10:30 a. m.; Sunday School, 9 a. m. Services at Brightwood, 2:30 p. m.
First German Reformed Church—Cor. Noble and Ohio. Rev. John G. Steinert, pastor. Services 10:30 a. m., 7:30 p. m.; Sunday School, 9 a. m.
Fourth German Reformed Church—75 N. Belmont av. (H). Rev. Frederick Kalbfleisch, pastor. Services 10:30 a. m.; Sunday School, 9 a. m.
St. John's Evangelical Reformed Church—Southeast cor. Merrill and Alabama streets. Rev. Max G. I. Stern, pastor. Services 10 a. m., 7:30 p. m.; Sunday School, 2 p. m.
Third (Immanuel) German Reformed Church—Northeast cor. Coburn and New Jersey streets. Rev. Alvin G. Gekeler, pastor. Services 10:30 a. m., 7:30 p. m.; Sunday School, 9 a. m.

HEBREW.

Congregation Indianapolis—South side of Market, west of East street. Rev. Meyer Messing, rabbi. Services 7:30 p. m. Friday, 10 a. m. Saturday.
Congregation Kennesses Israel—Northeast cor. Merrill and Eddy. Services Saturday 7:30 a. m., Friday 7:30 p. m.
Congregation Sharah Tefilla—552 South Meridian. Services 7:30 a. m. Saturday, sundown Friday.
Congregation Hungarian Ohew Zedeck—Southwest cor. Louisiana and Virginia av. Elias Klein, rabbi. Services Friday at sunset, Saturday 8 a. m.

LUTHERAN.

Danish Evangelical Lutheran Trinity Church—Southeast cor. of McCarty and Beaty streets. Rev. G. A. Christensen, pastor. Services Sunday 10:30 a. m., 7:30 p. m.; Sunday School, 12 m.
First (English) Lutheran Church—Northeast cor. Walnut and Penn. streets. Rev. David L. Mackenzie, pastor. Services 10:45 a. m., 7:30 p. m.; Sunday School, 9:30 a. m.
St. John's German Evangelical Lutheran Church—Haughville, Bismarck av., near Frazee. Rev. George Gotsch, pastor. Services 10 a. m.; Sunday School 11 a. m.
St. Paul's German Evangelical Lutheran Church—Northeast cor. New Jersey and McCarty streets. Rev. Frederick Wambsganns, pastor; Rev. J. G. Kunz and Rev. P. Eickstaedt, assistant pastors. Services 10 a. m., 7:30 p. m.
St. Peter's German Evangelical Lutheran Church—Southeast cor. Brookside av. and Jupiter streets. Rev. Charles W. Giese, pastor. Services 10 a. m., 8 p. m.; Sunday School, 2 p. m.
Second English Evangelical Lutheran Church—Hosbrook, near Elk. Rev. Isaac D. Worman, pastor. Services 10:30 a. m., 7:30 p. m.; Sunday School, 9:30 a. m.
Trinity German Evangelical Lutheran Church—Northeast cor. East and Ohio streets. Rev. Peter Seuel, pastor. Services 10 a. m., 7:30 p. m.; Sunday School, 2 p. m.

METHODIST EPISCOPAL.

Barth Place M. E. Church—Northwest cor. Shelby and Martin streets. Rev. Manuel Noble, pastor. Services 7:30 p. m.; Sunday School, 2 p. m.
Blackford Street M. E. Church—Southeast cor. Blackford and Market streets. Rev. Charles W. Crooke, pastor. Services 10:30 a. m., 7:30 p. m.; Sunday School, 2 p. m.; prayer meeting Thursday, 7:30 p. m.
Brightwood M. E. Church—Rev. Warren W. Reynolds, pastor. Services 10:30 a. m., 7:30 p. m.; Sunday School, 9 a. m.
Broadway M. E. Church—Cor. Broadway and Twelfth. Rev. L. F. Dimmitt, pastor. Services 10:30 a. m., 7:30 p. m.; Sunday School, 2:30 p. m.; prayer meeting Thursday, 7:30 p. m.
California Street M. E. Church—Southwest cor. North and California streets. Rev. Wm. S. Biddle, pastor. Services 10:30 a. m., 7:30 p. m.; Sunday School, 2 p. m.
Central Avenue M. E. Church—Northeast cor. Central av. and Butler street. Rev. Charles C. Lasby, D. D., pastor. Services 10:30 a. m., 7:30 p. m.; Sunday School, 2:30 p. m.
East Park M. E. Church—1090 E. Ohio street. Rev. Elbert L. Wimmer, pastor. Services 10:30 a. m. and 7:30 p. m.; Sunday School, 2:30 p. m.
Edwin Ray M. E. Church—Southwest cor. Woodlawn av. and Linden street. Rev. Edwin B. Rawls, pastor. Services 10:30 a. m., 7:30 p. m.; Sunday School, 2:30 p. m.
First German M. E. Church—Southwest cor. New York and New Jersey streets. Rev. Wm. F. Griewe, pastor. Services 10:30 a. m., 7:30 p. m.; Sunday School, 9 a. m. Prayer meeting Thursday evening, 7:30 p. m.
Fletcher Place M. E. Church—Cor. South street and Virginia av. Rev. Robert Roberts, D. D., pastor. Services 10:30 a. m., 7:30 p. m.; Sunday School, 2 p. m. Prayer meeting Thursday evenings.
Furnas Place M. E. Church—Southwest cor. Keystone and Clifford avs. Rev. James T. O'Neal, pastor. Services 10:30 a. m., 7:30 p. m.; Sunday School, 9 a. m.
Grace M. E. Church—Northeast cor. East and Market streets. Rev. Hickman N. King, pastor. Services 10:30 a. m., 7:30 p. m.; Sunday School, 2:15 p. m.
Hall Place M. E. Church—Northeast cor. Seventh street and Hall place. Rev. James A. Sargent, pastor. Services 10:30 a. m., 7:30 p. m.; Sunday School, 2 p. m. Prayer meeting Thursday evenings.
Hyde Park M. E. Church—Twenty-second, near Illinois. Rev. Robb E. Zaring, pastor. Services 10:30 a. m., 7:30 p. m.; Sunday School, 9 a. m.
Irvington M. E. Church—Rev. Thomas G. Cocks, pastor. Services 10:30 a. m., 7:30 p. m.; Sunday School 2:30 p. m.
Haughville M. E. Church—King av., Haughville. Rev. A. W. Wood, pastor. Services 10:30 a. m., 7:30 p. m.; Sunday School, 2:30 p. m.
Lincoln Avenue M. E. Church—Cor. Lincoln av. and Newman. Rev. Stephen W. Troyer, pastor. Services 10:30 a. m., 7:30 p. m.; Sunday School, 2:15 p. m.
Madison Avenue M. E. Church—Cor. Madison av. and Union street. Rev. W. M. Whitset, pastor. Services 10:30 a. m., 7:30 p. m.; Sunday School, 9:45 a. m.
Mapleton M. E. Church—Rev. Thomas W. Northcott, pastor. Services 10:30 a. m.; Sunday School, 3 p. m.
Meridian Street M. E. Church—Southwest cor. New York and Meridian streets. Rev. Charles N. Sims, D. D., pastor. Services 10:45 a. m., 7:30 p. m.; Sunday School, 9:30 a. m.
Nippert Memorial German M. E. Church—Northwest cor. Clifford and Keystone avs. Rev. Henry R. Bornemann, pastor. Services 10:30 a. m. and 7:30 p. m.; Sunday School, 2:30 p. m.
North Indianapolis M. E. Church—Rev. Madian H. Appleby, pastor. Services 7 p. m.; Sunday School, 2:30 p. m.
Oak Hill M. E. Church—Cor. Lawrence and Fountain. Rev. Benjamin F. Morgan, pastor. Services 10:30 a. m., 7:30 p. m.; Sunday School, 2:30 p. m.
Roberts Park M. E. Church—Northeast cor. Delaware and Vermont streets. Rev. T. I. Coultas, D. D., pastor. Services 11 a. m., 7:30 p. m.; Sunday School, 10 a. m.
Second German M. E. Church—Northeast cor. Prospect and Spruce. Rev. August F. Zarwell, pastor. Services 10:30 a. m., 7:30 p. m.; Sunday School, 9 a. m.
Simpson Chapel—Cor. Howard and Second streets. Rev. Louis M. Hagood, pastor. Services 10:30 a. m., 7:30 p. m.; Sunday School, 9 a. m.
Third German M. E. Church—Cor. Morris and Church streets. Rev. Matthias George, pastor. Services 10:30 a. m., 7:30 p. m.; Sunday School, 9 a. m.
Trinity M. E. Church—Division street, West Indianapolis. Rev. John W. J. Collins, pastor. Services 10:30 a. m., 7:30 p. m.; Sunday School, 2:30 p. m.
West Indianapolis M. E. Church—William street, West Indianapolis. Rev. J. Wesley Maxwell, pastor. Services 10:30 a. m., 7:30 p. m.; Sunday School, 3 p. m.
Woodside M. E. Church—Woodside. Rev. Merritt Machlan, pastor Services 10:30 a. m., 7:30 p. m.

AFRICAN METHODIST EPISCOPAL.

Allen Chapel A. M. E. Church—Broadway, near Cherry street. Rev. Abraham L. Murray, pastor. Services 10:45 a. m., 7:30 p. m.; Sunday School, 2 p. m.
Barnes Chapel A. M. E. Church—Ontario street, North Indianapolis. Rev. Thomas R. Prentiss, pastor. Services 11 a. m., 7:30 p. m.; Sunday School, 2 p. m.
Bethel A. M. E. Church—Northeast cor. Vermont and Columbia streets. Rev. David A. Graham, pastor. Services 10:45 a. m., 7:45 p. m.; Sunday School, 2 p. m.
St. Paul's A. M E. Church—Manlove av., near Brinkman street. Rev. George R. Collins, pastor. Services 10:30 a. m., 7:30 p. m.; Sunday School, 2:15 p. m.
South Mission A. M. E. Church—West McCarty street, near Pogues run. Rev. Wm. C. Irvin, pastor. Services 10:30 a. m., 7:30 p. m.; Sunday School, 2:30 p. m.
Trinity A. M. E. Church—568 Virginia av. Rev. Wm. Williams, pastor. Services 10:45 a. m., 7:30 p. m.; Sunday School, 2:30 p. m.

AFRICAN METHODIST EPISCOPAL ZION.

Jones Tabernacle A. M. E. Zion Church—Northwest cor. Blackford and North streets. Rev. Adam Wakefield, pastor. Services 10:30 a. m., 7:30 p. m.; Sunday School, 9:30 a. m.
Penick Chapel A. M. E. Zion Church—Earhart street, near Prospect street. Rev. Junius J. Kennedy, pastor. Services 10:30 a. m., 7:30 p. m.; Sunday School, 2 p. m.
Walters Chapel A. M. E. Zion Church—Cor. Barth av. and Sanders street. Rev. George B. Lynch. pastor. Services 11 a. m., 7:30 p. m.; Sunday School, 2 p. m.

METHODIST PROTESTANT.

First Methodist Protestant Church—Southeast cor. Dillon street and Hoyt av. Rev. Hugh Stackhouse, pastor. Services 10:30 a. m., 7:30 p. m.; Sunday School, 9:30 a. m.

MORAVIAN.

Moravian Church—Cor. Seventeenth and College av. Rev. Wm. H. Vogler, pastor. Services 10:45 a. m., 7:30 p. m.; Sunday School, 9:30 a. m.

PRESBYTERIAN.

East Washington Street Presbyterian Church—South side Washington, near State av. Rev. Frank C. Hood, pastor. Services 10:45 a. m., 7:30 p. m.; Sunday School, 9:15 a. m.

First Presbyterian Church—Southwest cor. Penn. and New York streets. Rev. Matthias L. Haines, D. D., pastor. Services 10:45 a. m., 7:30 p. m.; Sunday School, 9:30 a. m.; Bible class, 9:30 a. m.

Fourth Presbyterian Church — Northwest cor. Tenth and Alabama streets. Rev. G. L. Mackintosh, pastor. Services 10:30 a. m., 7:30 p. m.; Sunday School, 2:15 p. m.

Mayer Presbyterian Chapel—Northeast cor. Catharine and West streets. Rev. Edward Baech, pastor. Services 7:30 p. m.; Sunday School, 2:30 p. m.

Memorial Presbyterian Church—Northwest cor. Christian av. and Ash street. Rev. Frank O. Ballard, D. D., pastor. Services 10:30 a. m.; Sunday School, 9 a. m.; prayer meeting Thursdays, 7:30 p. m.

Ninth Presbyterian Church (Colored)—Northeast cor. Capitol av. and Michigan street. Rev. Oscar A. Williams, pastor. Services 10:30 a. m., 7:30 p. m.; Sunday School, 2:30 p. m.

Olive Street Presbyterian Church—East side Olive, north of Willow street. Rev. J. T. Orton, pastor. Services 10:30 a. m., 7:30 p. m.; Sunday School, 2:30 p. m.

Prospect Mission—East side Miami, first south of Prospect. Services 7:30 p. m.; Sunday School, 2:15 p. m.

Second Presbyterian Church — Northwest cor. Vermont and Penn. streets. Rev. Joseph A. Milburn, pastor; Rev. Edward Baech, associate pastor. Services 10:45 a. m., 7:30 p. m.; Sunday School, 9:45 a. m.

Seventh Presbyterian Church—East side Elm, north of Cedar street. Rev. Rice V. Hunter, pastor. Services 10:30 a. m., 7:30 p. m.; Sunday School, 2:30 p. m.

Sixth (Olivet) Presbyterian Church—Northeast cor. McCarty and Union. Rev. Eli A. Allen, pastor. Services 10:45 a. m., 7:30 p. m.; Sunday School, 9:30 a. m.

Tabernacle Presbyterian Church—Northeast cor. Second and Meridian streets. Rev. J. Cumming Smith, pastor; Rev. Warren B. Dunham, associate pastor. Services 10:30 a. m.; Sunday School, 9:30 a. m.

Tabernacle Chapel—Cor. Washington and Miley av. (W. I.) and Tabernacle Chapel, Mount Jackson. Services 10:30 a. m., 7:30 p. m.; Sunday School, 2:15 p. m. Rev. Warren B. Dunham, pastor.

Twelfth Presbyterian Church—269 W. Maryland. Rev. Wm. A. Hendrickson, pastor. Services 11 a. m., 7:30 p. m.; Sunday School, 9:30 a. m.

UNITED PRESBYTERIAN.

First United Presbyterian Church—Cor. East and Massachusetts av. Rev. Joseph Littell, pastor. Services 10:30 a. m., 7:30 p. m.; Sunday School, 2:30 p. m.

Woodruff Avenue United Presbyterian Church—Woodruff av., near Stoughton. Rev. J. P. Cowan, D. D., pastor. Services 10:30 a. m., 7:30 p. m.; Sunday School, 2:30 p. m.

SPIRITUALISTS.

First Spiritualist Church—Southwest cor. Alabama and New York streets. Services 10:45 a. m., 7:45 p. m.

SWEDENBORGIAN.

New Church Chapel—333 North Alabama street. Rev. Willis L. Gladish, pastor. Services Sunday 10:45 a. m.; Sunday School, 9:30 a. m.

UNITED BRETHREN.

First United Brethren Church—East side Oak, bet. Vine and Cherry streets. Rev. James E. Shannon, pastor. Services 10:30 a. m., 7:30 p. m.; Sunday School, 9:15 a. m.

Second U. B. Church—Rural street, bet. Clifford and Brookside avs. Services 10:30 a. m., 7:30 p. m.; Sunday School, 2 p. m. Prayer meeting Wednesday, 7 p. m.

UNIVERSALIST.

Central Universalist Church—Cor. Sixth and New Jersey. Rev. Thomas S. Guthrie, pastor. Services 10:45 a. m., 7:45 p. m.; Sunday School, 9:30 a. m.

CLUBS.

(See also Miscellaneous Societies.)

Albemarle Club—Cor. Ray and Church. John F. Barrett, Pres.; Wm. L. Rice, Sec.

Alhambra Club—20½ S. New Jersey. Henry Homer, Pres.; John Willmann, Sec.

American Whist Club—Thomas L. Sullivan, Pres.; Charles E. Coffin, Sec.; Charles E. Holloway, Treas. Meets every Tuesday night at The Denison.

Americus Club—Meets at Amuricus Club Hall, 116 N. Alamaba. C. B. Feibleman, Sec.

Augsburg Society Club—278 Cedar.

Boys' Club—64-66 E. Court. Mrs. Ed J. Foster, Pres.

Century Club—Meets Tuesday evenings at The Denison. Ernest P. Bicknell, Pres.; Herbert W. Foltz, Sec.

Cleveland Club—84½ W. Washington.

Clio Club—Meets every first and third Friday of each month at St. John's Hall, cor. Capitol av. and Georgia. John M. Sullivan, Pres.; M. P. Grady, Sec.

Columbia Club—73 Monument pl. M. G. McLain, Pres.; Horace F. Wood, Sec.; Charles H. Rouzer, Supt.

Commercial Club— Meets second Monday of each month in Commercial Club bldg. Daniel P. Erwin, Pres.; Wm. Fortune, First Vice-Pres.; Jacob P. Dunn, Second Vice-Pres.; A. B. Gates, Treas.; Evans Woollen, Sec.

Congregational Club—Rev. E. D. Curtis, D. D., Pres.; L. H. Wales, Sec. Meets second Tuesday in January, March, May and November.

Contemporary Club—Meets at Propylaeum fourth Wednesday of each month. J. E. Cleland, Pres.; George T. Porter, Sec.

Country Club—Joseph K. Lilly, Pres.; Charles M. Reynolds, Sec. Office at Capital National Bank

Deutscher Klub—Herman Lieber, Pres.; Theodore C. Stempfel, Sec. Meets at Deutscher Haus.

Dramatic Club—Meets at Propylaeum bldg. W. J. Brown, Pres.; Miss Louise Garrard, Sec.

Fairbanks C. W. Republican Club—337 Dillon. H. W. Denny, Sec.

Fortnightly Club—Meets every other Tuesday at St. Paul's Church parlor.

Franco-American Club—625 N. Meridian. Arthur D. F. Jaillet, Pres.

Hendricks Club—Organized December 29, 1885. 19½ N. Meridian.

Herculean Club—139 Indiana av. S. A. Furniss, Pres.; Charles Stapp, Sec.

Hoosier Kennel Club—Albert Lieber, Pres.; Harry F. Hildebrand, Sec.

Indiana Whist Club—Charles E. Coffin, Pres.; Dr. H. E. Green, Sec.; Edward B. Porter, Treas.

Indianapolis Baseball Club—13 When blk.

Indianapolis Caledonian Quoiting Club—Meets 36 W. Washington, second and fourth Tuesdays in each month. John A. McGaw, Pres.; John M. Clark, Sec.

Indianapolis Engineering Club—Charles C. Brown, Cor. Sec., 204 Lemcke bldg.

Indianapolis Flower Mission—Meets in Room 1, Plymouth bldg. weekly. Alma W. Wilson, Sec.
Indianapolis Literary Club—Plymouth bldg. Rev. M. L. Haines, Pres.; Louis Howland, Sec.; John N. Hurty, Treas.
Indianapolis Local Council of Women—Meets at Propylaeum first Tuesday in every month. Mrs. Emil Wulschner, Pres.; Mrs. S. E. Perkins, Sec.
Indianapolis Press Club—Meets at The Denison. Arthur C. White, Pres.; Miss Laura A. Smith, Sec.
Indianapolis Science Club—Meets at The Denison.
Indianapolis Shakspeare Club—Meets on call. Mrs. Charity Dye, Pres.; Mrs. W. H. Cook, Sec.
Indianapolis Single Tax Club—68 Lombard bldg. Meets monthly. John H. Bishop, Pres.; Conrad Rust, jr., Sec.
Indianapolis Whist Club—Meets at Commercial Club bldg. Frederick M. Herron, Pres.; Albert Daller, Sec. and Treas.
Indianapolis Women's Club—Meets first and third Fridays at Propylaeum. Mrs. Henry D. Pierce, Pres.; Mrs. Wm. L. Elder, Sec.
Indianola Athletic and Outing Club—906 W. Washington.
Limited Gun Club—27 Baldwin blk. Royal Robinson, Sec.
Lyra Casino Club—122 N. Meridian.
McCullough Club—Meets at Plymouth bldg. Charles S. Lewis, Pres.; Harry C. Hendrickson, Sec.
Magazine Club—Blind Asylum. Adelaide Carman, Pres.
Marion Club—25 E. Ohio. L. G. Rothschild, Pres.; S. P. Wellman, Sec.
Matinee Musicale—Mrs. A. M. Robertson, Pres.; Mrs. W. C. Lynn, Sec. Meets at Propylaeum fortnightly.
Montauk Club—572½ Virginia av. Charles Ruschaupt, Pres.; Edward Walsman, Sec.
Nauvoo Club—10 Blackford blk.
North Side Republican Club—424 College av. W. M. Gerard, Pres.; John R. Allen, Sec.
Over The Teacups—Meets every two weeks, 828 N. Penn. Mrs. D. W. Marmon, Pres.
Parlor Club—Meets semi-monthly. Elizabeth Nicholson, Pres.; Susan E. H. Perkins, Sec.
Portfolio Club—Meets at School of Music every other week. Herbert Foltz, Sec.
Progress Club—Meets at Mansur Hall every Sunday 3 p. m. Samuel D. La Fuze, Pres.; J. Howard Springer, Sec.
Pythagoras Athletic Club—F. G. Castor, Sec. Bellefontaine Hall.
Rosemary Club—Miss Anna L. Carter, Pres.; Miss Elizabeth K. Hough, Sec. Meets fortnightly, Saturday afternoon, at Propylaeum.
South Side Republican Club—323 E. Merrill. Wm. H. Leedy, Pres.; Frank Diller, Sec.
Tenanahaf Club—C. S. Carleton, Pres.; Guy A. Boyle, Sec.
Washington Club—Alexander Jackson, Pres.; John Woods, Sec.
White Cycle Club—332 E. Market. Joseph Pfleger, Pres.; Burt Gadd, Sec.
Willard Deaf Mute Club—10 Stewart pl. Harry C. Anderson, Pres.
Young Men's Gray Club—45½ N. Capitol av. Meets every Friday evening. John W. Kealing, Pres.
Zig-Zag Cycle Club—Meets at 84 N. Delaware. F. W. Erdelmeyer, Pres.; Oliver Light, Sec.

COURTS.

The United States is divided into nine Judicial Circuits, in each of which a Circuit Court is held for each district within each circuit. The act of Congress approved April 10, 1869, provides as follows: "The Circuit Court in each district shall be held by the Justice of the Supreme Court allotted to the circuit, or by the Circuit Judge of the circuit, or by the District Judge of the district, sitting alone, or by the Justice of the Supreme Court and Circuit Judge sitting together, in which case the Justice of the Supreme Court shall preside, or in the absence of either of them, by the other (who shall preside), and the District Judge." The State of Indiana comprises one Judicial District. The courts for the district are held in Indianapolis, New Albany, Evansville and Fort Wayne. The district is attached to the Seventh Judicial Circuit, which comprises the States of Wisconsin, Illinois and Indiana.
The United States Courts of the District of Indiana are organized as follows:

CIRCUIT COURT.

Associate Justice of the Supreme Court—Hon. Henry B. Brown.
Circuit Judges—Hon. Wm. A. Woods, Hon. James G. Jenkins, Hon. John W. Showalter.
Clerk—Noble C. Butler.
Master in Chancery—Wm. P. Fishback, Circuit and District Courts.
Deputy Clerk—Willard C. Nichols.
United States District Attorney—Frank B. Burke.
Assistant U. S. District Attorney—Edwin Corr.
United States Marshal—Wm. H. Hawkins.
Terms of Court—First Tuesdays in May and November, in the Circuit Court Room, Postoffice bldg.

UNITED STATES DISTRICT COURT.

District Judge—Hon. John H. Baker.
United States District Attorney—Frank B. Burke.
Assistant United States District Attorney—Edwin Corr.
United States Marshal—Wm. H. Hawkins.
Clerk—Noble C. Butler.
Terms of Court—Same as United States Circuit Court.

SUPREME COURT OF INDIANA.

Judges—Timothy E. Howard, Leonard J. Hackney, James McCabe, James H. Jordan, Leander J. Monks.
Clerk—Alexander Hess.
Terms of Supreme Court—Fourth Monday in May and fourth Monday in November.

APPELLATE COURT OF INDIANA.

Judges—Woodfin D. Robinson, Wm. J. Henley, James B. Black, Daniel W. Comstock, Ulric Z. Wiley.
Clerk—Alexander Hess.
Terms of Appellate Court—Fourth Monday in May and fourth Monday in November.

MARION CIRCUIT COURT.

Judge—Henry Clay Allen.
*Clerk—James W. Fesler.
Probate Commissioner—Gus O'Bryan.
Terms of Court—Second Monday in February, first Monday in May, fourth Monday in August and first Monday in December.
*The Clerk of the Circuit Court is ex officio Clerk of all the Courts.

MARION CRIMINAL COURT.

Judge—Frank McCray.
Prosecuting Attorney—Charles S. Wiltsie.

SUPERIOR COURT.

Judges—John L. McMaster, Room 1; Lawson M. Harvey, Room 2; Vinson Carter, Room 3.
Terms of Superior Court—This court is in session at all times, except during the months of July and August.

FEDERAL OFFICERS.

Circuit Justice of the Seventh Circuit and Associate Justice United States Supreme Court—Henry B. Brown, Postoffice bldg.
Judges United States Circuit Court—Hon. Wm. A. Woods, Hon. James G. Jenkins and Hon. John W. Showalter.
Judge United States District Court—Hon. John H. Baker, Postoffice bldg.
Official Reporter—Rowland Evans, Postoffice bldg.
Clerk United States Courts—Noble C. Butler, Postoffice bldg.
Deputies—Willard C. Nichols, Edward McDevitt.
United States District Attorney—Frank B. Burke, Postoffice bldg.
Assistant United States District Attorney—Edwin Corr, Postoffice bldg.
United States Marshal—Wm. H. Hawkins, 29½ N. Penn.
Chief Deputy—John E. Foley.
Deputies—Jerome C. Foley, Charles P. Taylor.
United States Pension Agent—M. V. B. Spencer, 67 W. Maryland.
Chief Clerk—Joseph Reiley.
Special Examiners Pension Bureau—H. L. McC. Taylor, W. L. Brooke, F. H. Austin.
United States Board of Pension Examiners—Wm. J. Browning, M. D., E. C. Reyer, M. D., R. French Stone, M. D.
Surveyor of Customs—Third floor Postoffice bldg. George G. Tanner.
Deputy—Austin H. Brown.
Inspector of Customs—Wm. K. Sproule.
Clerk—Alfred H. Johnson.
Warehouseman—Jeremiah Hollihan.
Collector of Internal Revenue—Wm. H. Bracken, Lawrenceburg, Ind.
Deputies—Postoffice bldg: P. J. Ryan, John P. Franz, John P. Schiltges.
Gauger—Jacob W. Hollenbeck.
Postmaster—Albert Sahm, Postoffice bldg.
Assistant Postmaster—W. O. Reveal, Postoffice bldg.
United States Commissioners—Henry Douglas Pierce, 18½ N. Meridian; Harold Taylor, 302 Indiana Trust bldg; Wm. A. Van Buren, 18½ N. Penn.; Charles W. Moores, 602 Lemcke bldg; Nathan Morris, 138 Commercial Club bldg; Alexander C. Ayres, 500 Indiana Trust bldg.
Bureau of Animal Industry—Joseph C. Roberts, inspector in charge, Kingan & Co.
Supervisor of Elections—Wm. A. Van Buren, chief, 18½ N. Penn.
United States Secret Service—Thomas B. Carter, chief, 29½ N. Penn.
Weather Bureau—Charles F. R. Wappenhans, Rooms 905-907 Majestic bldg.
United States Railway Mail Service—Charles D. Rogers, chief clk, Postoffice bldg.

INSURANCE.

Columbian Relief Fund Association—409-410 Lemcke bldg. Wm. H. Latta, Pres.; Everett Wagner, Vice-Pres. and Treas.; C. H. Brackett, Sec.
Commercial Travelers' Mutual Accident Association of Indiana—20-21 When bldg. Carey McPherson, Pres.; Benjamin H. Prather, Sec. and Treas.
German American Savings Life Association—718 Lemcke bldg. James W. Hess, Pres.; Austin T. Quick, Sec.; J. R. Henry, Treas.
German Fire Insurance Co. of Indiana—27-33 S. Delaware. Theodore Stein, Pres.; Lorenz Schmidt, Sec.; Theodore Reyer, Treas.
Globe Accident Insurance Co.—Aetna bldg, 19½ N. Penn. Albert Sahm, Pres.; Wm. A. Walker, Sec.; Union Trust Co., Treas.
Home Benefit Association of Indianapolis—67 Ingalls blk. Louis S. Smith, Pres.; Joseph B. Classick, Vice-Pres.; Samuel L. Morrow, Sec. and Treas.
Indiana Association of Underwriters—4 Hartford blk. John B. Cromer, Pres.; Isaac C. Hays, Sec. and Treas.
Indiana Insurance Co. of Indianapolis—83-85 E. Market. Chartered 1851. Reorganized 1875. Capital $150,000. M. V. McGilliard, Pres.; J. Kirk Wright, Sec.; E. G. Cornelius, Treas.
Indiana League of Fire Underwriters—Spencer House. D. A. Rudy, Pres.; John R. Engle, Sec. and Treas.
Indiana Millers' Mutual Fire Insurance Co.—32 Board of Trade bldg. Incorporated 1889. M. S. Blish, Pres.; E. E. Perry, Sec. and Treas.
Indianapolis German Mutual Fire Insurance Co.—156½ E. Washington. Incorporated 1884. Frank A. Maus, Pres.; Charlotte Dinkelaker, Sec.; Albert H. Krull, Treas.
Industrial Life Association of Indianapolis, Ind.—1 Hartford blk. Incorporated 1877. John O. Cooper, Pres.; J. W. Morris, Sec. and Treas.; John O. Copeland, Genl. Supt.
Masonic Mutual Benefit Society of Indiana—29½ E. Market. R. S. Robertson, Pres.; Harold C. Megrew, Sec.
Masons' Union Life Association—8-9 Masonic Temple. N. R. Ruckle, Pres.; James S. Anderson, Sec.
Mutual Life Insurance Co. of Indiana—30½ N. Delaware. Incorporated February, 1882. Wm. R. Myers, Pres.; Henry Malpas, Sec. and Treas.
Odd Fellows' Mutual Aid Association of Indiana—2 Odd Fellows' Hall. Organized Nov. 21, 1872. John F. Wallick, Pres.; David B. Schideler, Sec.; Charles P. Tulley, Treas.
Old Wayne Mutual Life Association—52-62 Commercial Club bldg. Reincorporated May, 1883. L. C. Stewart, Pres.; C. C. Gilmore, Sec.; John Furnas, Treas.
Railway Officials' and Employes' Accident Association—25-32 Ingalls blk. Chalmers Brown, Pres.; Wm. K. Bellis, Sec. and Genl. Mngr.; Samuel Bellis, Asst. Sec. and Treas.
State Life Insurance Co.—515-520 Lemcke bldg. Andrew M. Sweeney, Pres.; Wilbur S. Wynn, Sec.
Vernon Insurance and Trust Co. of Indianapolis—McGilliard Agency Co., 83-85 E. Market.

LABOR ORGANIZATIONS.

American Hod Carriers' Union No. 1—Meets at Colored Odd Fellows' Hall, Indiana avenue, first and third Mondays.
Architectural Iron Workers—Meets at 76½ S. Delaware, first and fourth Saturdays.
Auxiliary B. of L. E.—Meets every Thursday evening at Engineers' Hall.
Barbers' Union—Meets at 27 W. Pearl.
Blacksmiths' Union No. 27—Meets at 92½ E. Washington every Thursday night.
Bookbinders' Union No. 5—Meets first Thursday of each month in Pressmen's Hall.
Brewers' Union No. 77—Meets last Sunday of each month at Bernard's Hall.
Bricklayers' Union—78½ W. Washington.
Brotherhood of Locomotive Engineers, Indianapolis Division No. 11—Meets at Wallace blk every second and fourth Sundays. Auxiliary meets first and third Thursdays at Wallace Hall.
Brotherhood of Painters and Decorators, Local No. 47—Meets at 66½ N. Penn. Tuesday evenings.
Brotherhood of Railway Trainmen—Meets at Mansur Hall every Sunday at 2 p. m.
Carpenters' District Council—Meets every Thursday evening at 18½ S. Delaware.
Carpenters' Local Union No. 60—(German)—Meets at 27½ S. Delaware every Saturday night.

Carpenters' Local Union No. 446—Meets at 18½ S. Delaware Tuesdays.
Carpenters' Union No. 157—Meets at Haughville every Wednesday night.
Carpenters' Union No. 281—Meets Wednesdays at 18½ S. Delaware.
Central Labor Union—Meets second and fourth Monday evenings at 66½ N. Penn., Edgar A. Perkins, Sec.
Cigar Makers' Local Union No. 33—Meets in Bricklayers' Hall the first Wednesday of each month.
Cooper's International Union, Local No. 25—Meets at 66½ N. Penn. Friday evenings.
Furniture Workers' Local Union No. 36—Meets at Mozart Hall first and third Tuesday nights.
Garment Workers' Union—Meets in Mansur Hall.
Indiana Federation of Trade and Labor Unions—Edgar A. Perkins, Pres., Indianapolis; Robert E. Groff, Sec., Indianapolis.
Indianapolis Division 103, Order of Railway Conductors—Meets at 94 N. Meridian first and third Sundays of each month.
Indianapolis Musicians' Protective Association—Meets Mozart Hall every Sunday.
International Typographical Union—29½ E. Market. Wm. B. Prescott, Pres.; John W. Bramwood, Sec and Treas.; Hugo Miller, German Sec.
Iron Molders' No. 17 of N. A.—Meets Bricklayers' Hall Tuesdays.
Journeyman Bakers' and Confectioners' Local Union No. 18—Meets at Mozart Hall first and third Saturday nights.
Laundry Workers' Union No. 5254—Meets Griffith blk second and fourth Wednesday evenings.
Local Union No. 56 Iron Molders of North America—Meets in Carpenters' Hall, 18½ S. Delaware, Friday evenings.
Locomotive Engineers, L. A. Thomas Division No. 492—Meets Sundays at Odd Fellows' Hall, Virginia av.
Locomotive Firemen's Brotherhood—Meets Griffith blk. Tuesday evenings.
Metal Polishers' Union—Meets in Central Labor Union Hall.
National Alliance Theatrical Stage Employes, Local No. 30—Meets at 66½ N. Penn. second and fourth Sunday every month. Charles I. Burgan, Mngr.
National Brotherhood of Electrical Workers of America, Union No. 10 of Indianapolis—Meets in Cyclorama pl.
Operative Plasterers' International Association, Local No. 46—Meets Thursday evenings at 66½ N. Penn.
Order of Railway Telegraphers—Meets at When blk. second and fourth Thursdays.
Order of Railway Conductors—Meets in Wallace Hall first and third Sundays.
Paper Hangers' Union—Meets at 27 W. Pearl.
Patternmakers' National League of North America—Meets at corner of Penn. and Maryland every Friday.
Pressmen's Union—Meets the first Friday of each month at 27 W. Pearl.
Reed and Rattan Workers' Union—Meets first Tuesday in every month at Mozart Hall.
Retail Clerks' National Protective Association, Local No. 1—Meets at 66¼ N. Penn. first and third Wednesday evenings every month. C. Hoover, Sec.
Reform Club No. 1—Meets first and third Thursdays in DeSoto blk.
Sawmakers' Union No. 1—Meets at 33 S. Illinois the first and third Fridays.
Stationary Engineers' No. 25—37½ E. Washington.
Stonecutters' Association of North America, Indianapolis Branch—Meets at Griffith blk. first and third Friday nights.
Stone Masons' and Hard Stone Cutters' Union—Meets at 76½ S. Delaware second and fourth Monday nights.
Switchmen's Union—Meets second Sunday night and fourth Sunday afternoon at Machinists' Hall.
Teamsters' and Shovelers' Union No. 5486—Meets at Union Hall Wednesdays.
Tin, Sheet Iron and Cornice Workers' Local Union No. 44—Meets at Iron Hall Monday night of each week.
Typographical Union No. 1—Meets at Griffith blk. first Sunday in each month. C. E. McKee, Sec.
Typographical Union No. 14—Meets first Tuesday in every month and first Sunday in January and July at Mozart Hall.
United Association of Plumbers, Gas and Steam Fitters, Local Union No. 73—Meets at Griffith blk. Tuesday evening of each week.
Upholsterers' Union—Meets at 27 W. Pearl.

LIBRARIES.

Agricultural Library of the Indiana State Board of Agriculture—State House. Contains about 1,200 volumes.
Butler University Library—Irvington. Inclusive of societies, 5,075 volumes.
Carpenters' and Joiners' Library—16 Cyclorama pl.
Haughville Reading Room—East side Germania av., between Michigan and Frazee, Haughville.
Horticultural Library of the State Horticultural Society—Contains about 500 volumes. State House.
Indianapolis Bar Association Library—57 Court House. Established 1880. Contains 4,000 volumes.
Marion County Library—Court House. Established 1844. Contains 5,000 volumes. Open on Saturday from 9 to 12 a. m. and 2 to 5 p. m.
Public Library and Reading Room—Southwest cor. Meridian and Ohio. Established 1873 and maintained under the authority of the Board of School Commissioners, for which purpose it is authorized to levy a tax each year of not exceeding four cents on the hundred dollars of taxable property assessed for city taxes. Contains 65,000 volumes and 6,000 pamphlets. Open daily 9 a. m. to 10 p. m. Eliza G. Browning, Librarian. Branch Libraries: No. 1, cor. Udell and Clinton, North Indianapolis, Belle Abrams, Librarian in charge. No. 2, 48 Clifford av., Mary F. Algire, Librarian in charge. No. 3, 100 Woodlawn av., Alma W. Wilson. Librarian in charge. No. 4, 528 S. Meridian, Gustav C. Jose, Librarian in charge.
St. Aloysius Library—Northeast cor. Capitol av. and Georgia.
St. Cecilia's Library of the St. Cecilian Society—South side of Maryland, east of Capitol av. Contains 800 volumes.
State Law Library—Separated from State Library 1867. Contains 35,000 volumes. Rooms 64-65 State House. John C. McNutt, Librarian.
State Library—Established 1825. Contains 25,000 volumes. Emma L. Davidson, Librarian, 47 State House.
West Indianapolis Library—Opposite City Hall (W I). Gertrude Hilligos, Librarian.
Young Men's Christian Association Reading Room and Library—33 N. Illinois.

MEDICAL AND DENTAL COLLEGES AND SOCIETIES.

American Medical College—Southeast cor. Indiana av. and California. J. C. Hamilton, M. D., Pres.; Wm. H. Shackelton, Treas.; Russell C. Kelsey, M. D., Sec.
Central College of Physicians and Surgeons—Southeast cor. Penn. and South. Organized 1879. Joseph Eastman, M. D., Pres.; Samuel E. Earp, M. D., Sec.; John L. Masters, M. D., Treas.; Thomas B. Eastman, M. D., Asst. Sec.

Indiana Academy of Medicine—J. D. George, M. D., Pres.; R. C. Kelsey, M. D., Sec.
Indiana Dental College The—Incorporated 1879. 89 E. Ohio. George E. Hunt, Sec.
Indiana State Dental Association—Next meeting at Ft. Wayne, Ind. W. S. Rawls, Pres.; W. A. Mason, Ft. Wayne, Sec.
Indiana State Medical Society—Meets annually. Next meeting at Terre Haute, Ind., May, 1897. J. H. Ford, Pres., Wabash, Ind.; F. C. Heath, Sec.
Indiana State Physio-Medical Association—Meets at Physio-Medical College. Robert Smith, M. D., Pres.; Amos W. Fisher, M. D., Sec.
Indianapolis Odontological Society—Meets at Indiana Dental College. Merit Wells, Pres.; John Q. Byram, Sec. and Treas.
Indianapolis Physio-Medical Society—Meets first and third Thursday evenings of each month. J. J. Baker, M. D., Pres.; Amos W. Fisher, M. D., Sec.
Indianapolis Society of Hygiene—334 N. New Jersey. Rachel Swain, Pres.; Grace J. Clarke, Cor. Sec.
Marion County Medical Society—Meets every Tuesday evening in Criminal Court Room. H. M. Lash, Pres.; T. B. Noble, Sec.
Medical College of Indiana—Northwest cor. Senate av. and Market. Incorporated 1878. Annual session from October to March. Joseph W. Marsee, M. D., Dean.
Physio-Medical College of Indiana—Northwest cor. North and Alabama. Incorporated 1873. Collins S. T. Bedford, Sec.

MILITARY.

James K. Gore, Adjutant-General.
Benjamin A. Richardson, Quartermaster-General.
First Brigade Indiana National Guard—Brigadier-General W. J. McKee, Commanding, Indianapolis; Lieutenant Colonel F. W. Frank, A. Adjt.-Gen., Anderson; Lieutenant Colonel Wm. M. Wright, Med. Director, Indianapolis; Major W. W. Robbins, A. D. C., Indianapolis; Major Geo. W. Keyser, Chief Q. M., Indianapolis; Major H. O. Eagle, Chief Com. Sub., Indianapolis; Major Charles T. McIntire, Chief Sig. Officer, Indianapolis; Captain David I. McCormick, I. S. A. Prac., Indianapolis; First Lieutenant Henry W. Hageman, Aide-de-Camp, Fort Wayne; First Lieutenant Frank E. Strouse, Aide-de-Camp, Rockville.
First Regiment Infantry, Indiana National Guard—George H. Pennington, Col., New Albany; G. W. McCoy, Lt. Col., Vincennes; Lieutenant E. L. Dishman, Adjt., New Albany; T. F. Stunkard, Surgeon, Terre Haute; Edward Bierhaus, jr., Quartermaster, Vincennes; T. J. Louden, Batt. Major, Bloomington; D. McAuliff, Batt. Major, Brazil; J. F. Fee, Batt. Major, Greencastle.
Second Regiment Infantry, Indiana National Guard—James R. Ross, Col., Indianapolis; H. B. Smith, Lieut. Col., Indianapolis; George W. Powell, Adjt., Indianapolis; F. R. Charlton, Surgeon, Indianapolis; Oliver T. Logan, Asst. Surgeon, Indianapolis; John A. Conlen, Quartermaster, Indianapolis; Rev. G. A. Carstensen, Chaplain, Indianapolis; Edwin P. Thayer, Batt. Major, Greenfield; Charles B. Rockwood, Batt. Major, Indianapolis; W. S. Rich, Batt. Major, Indianapolis.
Company A, Indianapolis—Hall, 121 E. Pearl. H. C. Castor, Capt.; James Little, 1st Lieut.; Webb Irvin, 2d Lieut.
Company D, Indianapolis—Henry T. Conde, Capt.; Frank F. McCrea, 1st Lieut.; A. T. Isensee, 2d Lieut.
Company H, Indianapolis—C. S. Tarleton, Capt.; Harry Mahan, 1st Lieut.; C. B. Carr, 2d Lieut.

First Separate Company, Indianapolis—John J. Buckner, Capt.; John Edlin, 1st Lieut.; Jesse H. Ringgold, 2d Lieut.
Second Separate Company Infantry, Indiana National Guard—Sidney Moore, 1st Lieut.; Powell James, 2d Lieut.
First Regiment Light Artillery, Indiana National Guard—Captain J. B. Curtis, Com.; Lieutenant C. A. Garrard, Adjt.; Bert B. Adams, Quartermaster, Indianapolis.
Battery A, Indianapolis—Charles A. Garrard, Senior 1st Lieut. Com.; Edward Johnson, Junior 1st Lieut.; H. C. Cullen, 2d Lieut. Armory, corner 7th and Senate av.
United States Arsenal—Situated north end of Arsenal avenue, between Michigan street and Clifford avenue. Major A. L. Varney, Commandant.
Albert Lieber Zouaves—Jacob Fox, Capt.; Carl Mueller, Sec.
Hibernian Rifles—Wm. J. Welsh, Capt.; James Manley, 1st Lieut.; Wm. Carson, 2d Lieut.

MISCELLANEOUS SOCIETIES AND ORGANIZATIONS.

Badischer Benevolent Association—Meets third Sunday in each month at 2:30 p. m., at Columbia Hall.
Bakers' Mutual Benefit Association—Meets first Sunday in every month at 10 a. m., at Mozart Hall.
Baptist Ministers' Conference for Indianapolis and Vicinity—Meets second Monday of each month at First Baptist Church. Rev. Larkin W. Bicknell, Sec.
Bavarian Society—Meets every second Sunday in each month at 2 p. m., at 113 E. Washington.
Board of Children's Guardians of Marion County—1 Plymouth bldg. Julia H. Goodhart, Sec.
Boys' Home and Employment Association—64 E. Court. Thomas C. Day, Pres.; Miss Graydon, Supt.
Brewers' Benevolent Association—Meets first Sunday in every month at Columbia Hall.
Brothers of the Sacred Heart—In charge of St. Joseph's Institute, cor. Coburn and Short streets.
Bureau of Justice—68½ E. Market. Henry C. Long, Pres.; Samuel B. Ashby, Attorney.
Burford, Wm. B. Relief Association—21 W. Washington. A. W. Applegate, Pres.; James B. Thale, Sec.; Henry H. Thale, Treas.
Butchers' Association of Marion County—Meets first Thursday in each month at 8 p. m., at 113 E. Washington.
Catholic Ladies' Temperance Society—Northeast corner Georgia and Capitol av.
Charity Organization Society—C. S. Grout, Sec., 1 Plymouth bldg.
Christ Church Guild—Meets every Tuesday in Guild Rooms. Mrs. A. A. Cady, Pres.; Mrs. Mary F. Love, Sec.
Christian Church Union—George Fate, Sec.; meets at Central Christian Church first Friday of each month.
Christian Mothers' Society of the Sacred Heart Congregation—Meets second Sunday every month, at St. Cecelia Hall.
Christian Science—136 E. New York.
Christian Woman's Board of Missions of Christian Church—Mrs. O. A. Burgess, Pres.; Lois A. White, Sec., 160 N. Delaware.
Colored Benevolent Society of Indianapolis—Meets last Thursday of each month, at Plymouth Church. B. J. Morgan, Pres.; S. A. Fletcher, Sec.; Jacob Porter, Treas.
Commercial Travelers' Association of Indiana—Thomas P. Swain, Pres.; W. F. Henley, Sec.; S. Meridian.

Convent of the Sisters of St. Joseph—Cor. Palmer and Meridian.
Deutscher Frauen Unterstuetzung Verein—Meets the first and third Fridays of every month at 2 p. m., at Deutsche Haus.
Door of Hope Rescue Home—84 N. Alabama.
Eastern Indiana Fair Circuit—15 State House.
Epworth League Union of Indianapolis—Solomon M. Hoff, Pres.; Wm. L. Steeg, Sec. 19 Pembroke Arcade.
Flower Mission—1 Plymouth bldg. Alma W. Wilson, Sec.
Franciscan Convent — Cor. Union and Palmer. In charge of Franciscan Fathers.
Fresh Air Mission—1 Plymouth bldg. C. S. Grout, Sec.
Friends' Boarding Home for Young Ladies —155 N. Illinois. Rachel E. Clark, Matron.
Gardeners' Benefit Association—Meets the first Sunday of every month, at 2 p. m., at Mozart Hall.
General Contractors' Association of Indianapolis — Builders' Exchange, southwest cor. Ohio and Penn. J. A. Shoemaker, Pres.; Thomas H. Jameson, Sec.
German American Democratic Club—Meets third Thursday in every month, at Mozart Hall.
German House—Southeast cor. New Jersey and Michigan.
German Ladies' Benevolent Society of Indianapolis—Meets at Socialer Turnverein Hall every Tuesday at 2 p. m., cor. Michigan and New Jersey.
German Ladies' Mutual Benefit Society No. 1—Meets second and fourth Thursdays in every month, at 2 p. m., at Mozart Hall.
German Ladies' Mutual Benefit Society No. 25—Meets last Friday of every month, at Mozart Hall.
German Mutual Benefit Association—Meets every last Sunday in each month, at 2 p. m., in Mozart Hall.
German Pioneer Association— Meets the third Sunday in every month, at 2 p. m., at Mozart Hall.
German Veterean Association—Meets every Sunday of each month, at 2 p. m., at Deutsche Haus.
House of the Good Shepherd—South side Raymond, west of Meridian.
Independent Gymnastic Association—Northeast cor. Illinois and Ohio.
Independent Turnverein Hall Association of Indianapolis—Northeast cor. of Illinois and Ohio.
Indiana Association of Short Horn Breeders—State House. Organized May, 1872. E. C. Thompson, Sec. and Treas., Irvington.
Indiana Bee Keepers' Association—State House. Organized 1879. E. S. Pope, Sec., Indianapolis.
Indiana Car Service Association—D. T. Bacon, Mngr., Union Station.
Indiana Children's Home Society—Rev. Willis D. Engle, Sec., 46 Coffin blk.
Indiana Farmers' Reading Circle—State House. H. F. McMahan, Sec., Fairfield, Ind.
Indiana Horticultural Society—11 State House. Organized 1842. Prof. James Troop, Sec., Lafayette, Ind.
Indiana Humane Society—46 Lombard bldg. Incorporated 1882. D. W. Coffin, Sec.
Indiana Jersey Cattle Club—State House. Organized January, 1883. W. S. Budd, Sec., Indianapolis.
Indiana Master Plumbers' Association—84 N. Illinois. John S. Farrell, Pres.; W. W. Wilcox, Sec.
Indiana Retail Merchants' Association—46 Board of Trade bldg. W. Marshall Thomas, Sec.
Indiana State Dairy Association—H. C. Beckman, Sec., Brunswick, Ind.
Indiana State Florists' Association—State House. Organized 1887. Stuart Anderson, Pres.; Robert McKain, Sec.
Indiana State Liquor League—Meets at 39 Lorraine bldg.
Indiana State Poultry Association—Meets in State House. Wm. Tobin, Pres.; Thomas W. Pottage, Sec.
Indiana State Sunday School Association—C. D. Meigs, State Supt., 61 Central av.
Indiana Swine Breeders' Association—State House. Organized January, 1877. Harry Nowlin, Sec., Lawrenceburg, Ind.
Indiana Tract Society—John W. Moore, Sec., 175 Central av.
Indiana Wool Growers' Association—State House. Organized October, 1876. J. W. Robe, Sec., Greencastle.
Indianapolis Art Association—May Wright Sewall, Pres.; Mrs. Addison C. Harris, Sec. Pictures, property and meetings at Propylaeum.
Indianapolis Bar Association—Meets first Monday of each month at 55 Court House. Edward Daniels, Pres.; Jesse H. Blair, Treas.; Ernest R. Keith, Sec.
Indianapolis Benevolent Society—1 Plymouth bldg. Charles W. Moores, Sec.
Indianapolis Board of Trade—Board of Trade bldg. Justus C. Adams, Pres.; H. E. Kinney, Vice-Pres.; John Osterman, Treas.; Jacob W. Smith, Sec.
Indianapolis Christian Ministers' Association—W. E. Payne, Sec. and Treas. Meets third Monday of each month at 2 p. m.
Indianapolis Driving Club—T. S. Graves, Sec. Union Stock Yards (W. I.)
Indianapolis German Park Association—Northwest cor. Washington and Meridian. Otto Frenzel, Pres.; Paul H. Krauss, Sec.; Christ Off, Treas.
Indianapolis Industrial Union—135 N. Penn.
Indianapolis Joint Rate Association—J. B. Eckman, Sec. Board of Trade bldg.
Indianapolis Joint Weighing Association—J. B. Eckman, Supt. Board of Trade bldg.
Indianapolis Judische Bruder Verein—Meets first Sunday in every month at Hungarian Jewish Church. A. Rosenfeldt, Pres.; Joseph Winkler, Sec.
Indianapolis Master Plumbers' Association —84 N. Illinois. James McGauley, Pres.; W. W. Wilcox, Sec.
Indianapolis Ministerial Association—J. W. Cowan, Sec. Meets 10 a. m. first Monday of each month at Y. M. C. A. Hall.
Indianapolis News Mutual Relief Association—John Skidmore, Pres.; E. F. White, Sec.
Indianapolis Passenger Association—Southwest cor. Washington and Noble. John S. Lazarus, Chairman; Robison M. Case, Sec.
Indianapolis Propylaeum Association—25 E. North street. May Wright Sewall, Pres.; Margaret D. Chislett, First Vice-Pres.; Carrie F. Robertson, Second Vice-Pres.; Eliza G. Wiley, Sec.; Elizabeth V. Pierce, Treas.; Louise Garrard, Curator.
Indianapolis Young Men's Christian Association—29-37 N. Illinois. Wm. T. Brown, Pres.; O. H. Palmer, Sec.; G. V. Woolen, Treas.
Indianapolis Schweizerbund—Meets second Monday in each month at 113 E. Washington.
Indianapolis Target Shooting Association—Twelfth street west of Fall creek. Philip Zapf, Pres.; Ed Bretz, Sec.
Indianapolis Wholesale Confectioners' Association—Meets first and third Fridays in every month, 8 p. m., at Mozart Hall.
Institute of Psychology and Progressive Sciences—Office 113½ E. Washington. Irene W. Atkinson, Supreme Scribe.
Italian Mutual Benefit Society—Meets first Sunday in every month, 2 p. m., at 18½ S. Delaware. Domenico Montani, Pres.

League of American Wheelmen—29 S. Delaware.

Library Association of Indiana—Meets annually at State House last week in December. Elizabeth D. Swan, Pres., Lafayette, Ind.; J. N. Leach, Vice-Pres., Kokomo, Ind.; Mary E. Ahern, Sec. and Treas.

Liederkranz Gesang Verein—Meets second Sunday in every month at 2 p. m. at Mozart Hall.

Local Council of Women of Indianapolis, Branch National Council of Women—Meets 25 E. North monthly. Mrs. J. S. Jenckes, Sec.

Local Freight Agents' Association—Meets Board of Trade bldg. J. B. Eckman, Sec.

L'Union Fraternelle Francais—Meets first Monday in each month at 10½ E. Washington. Leon Boyer, Pres.; Alexander Chabloz, Sec.

Marion County Agricultural and Horticultural Society—14 State House. Ida F. Richardson, Sec.

Marion County Druggists' Association—Meets first Friday of each month at Board of Trade bldg. A. Timberlake, Pres.; M. Schwartz, Sec.

Masonic Burial Ground Association—86 W. Second. Rev. Willis D. Engle, Sec.

Masonic Relief Board—86 W. 2d, Willis D. Engle, Sec.

Master Steam and Hot Water Fitters' Association—84 N. Illinois. John S. Farrell, Vice-Pres.; James M. Haley, Sec.

Methodist Ministerial Association—Meets at Meridian Street M. E. Church at 10 a. m. every Monday, except first Monday of the month. Rev. W. M. Whitset, Sec.

Murphy Gospel Temperance League—Meets every Sunday at 3 p. m. and every Wednesday at 7:30 p. m., at G. A. R. Hall, 27½ N. Delaware.

Pentecost Bands—52 S. State av. Thomas H. Nelson, Supt.; Wm. S. Craig and Flora B. Nelson, Asst. Supts.; George E. Bula, Treas.

Pfaelzer Unterstuetzungs Verein—Meets the first Sunday of every Month at 2 p. m., Turn Halle, cor. Ohio and Illinois.

Plymouth Institute—Mary F. Allgire, Sec. Office Plymouth bldg.

Princely Knights of Character Castle—629 Lemcke bldg. Rev. J. R. Lucas, Pres.; Rev. Samuel M. Conner, Sec.; Rev. Cincinnatus H. McDowell, Treas.

Prussian Benefit Association—Meets last Sunday of every month at 2 p. m. at Columbia Hall. Wm. Kattau, Pres.; John Hoffmark, Sec.

Ramabai Circle—Mrs. May Wright Sewall, Pres. 345 N. Penn.

Rescue Mission Home—49 E. South. Mrs. Zerua J. P. Jaynes, Matron.

St. Aloysius Young Men's Society—Meets every Wednesday at St. Cecilia Hall.

St. Boniface Benevolent Society—Meets monthly at St. Mary's Hall.

St. Cecilia Men's Society—Meets Fourth Sunday of every month in St. Cecilia Hall.

St. Clare's Young Ladies' Society—Meets third Sunday of every month at St. Cecilia Hall.

St. Francis Mutual Aid Society—Meets first Sunday of every month in Sacred Heart Church.

St. Joseph's Benevolent Society—Meets monthly at St. Mary's Hall.

St. Vincent de Paul Men's Benevolent Society—Meets every fourth Sunday at St. Aloysius Library Hall, corner Capital av. and Georgia.

Salvation Army—84 W. Washington.

Schwaben Benefit Association—Meets every third Sunday at 2 p. m. in Mozart Hall.

Schweizer Bund—Meets first Sunday in every month, 2 p. m., at Mozart Hall.

Single Tax League—Meets at 68 Lombard bldg. J. M. Hislop, Pres.; Conrad Rust, jr., Sec.

Social Turnverein of Indianapolis—Southeast cor. Michigan and New Jersey.

South Side Turnverein—Henry Victor, Pres., s. s. Morris near Meridian.

Summer Mission for Sick Children—1 Plymouth bldg. C. S. Grout, Sec.

Sydenham Society of the Medical Society of Indiana—Meets every Saturday night at college. D. S. Wiggins, Pres.; A. W. Bloxsom, Treas.; W. F. Wittmer, Sec.

Theosophical Society—Meets at Propylaeum every Sunday at 7:30 p. m.

Training School Board—City Hospital.

Unabhaeniger Turnverein—Meets every second Wednesday in each month at Turn Halle, northeast cor. Ohio and Illinois streets.

Volunteers of America—33½ S. Illinois.

Woman's Exchange—125 N. Penn. Mrs. E. F. Hodges, Pres.

Woman's Sanitary Association—Meets first and third Tuesday mornings of each month at Plymouth Church. Mrs. Mary A. Gregory, Sec.

Women's Industrial Association for Practical Progress—Room 6, 156½ E. Washington. Mrs. L. L. Lawrence, Pres.; Miss Elsie Collins, Sec.; Mrs. Mary Wilson, Supt.

Young Men's Christian Association—33 N. Illinois street. Wm. T. Brown, Pres.; O. H. Palmer, Sec.; T. A. Hildreth, Genl. Sec.

Young Women's Christian Association—139 N. Meridian. Mrs. F. F. McCrea, Pres.; Miss Susan M. White, Genl. Sec.

Zweiundzwanziger Unterstuetzungs Verein—Meets first Sunday in each quarter at 10 a. m., at Mozart Hall.

MUSICAL SOCIETIES.

Apollo Zither Club—Meets every Thursday evening, at 262 S. Illinois. Miss Bertha Freiberg, Sec.

Crescendo Club—Meets monthly, at 134 N. Illinois. Miss Bessie Beck, Sec.

Concordia Society—Meets at Reichwein's Hall the first Sunday of each month. Eugene J. Hoffman, Sec.

Harugari Maennerchor—Meets every Sunday morning, 27 S. Delaware. Otto Isenthal, Sec.; Ernst F. Knodel, Musical Director.

Indianapolis Choral Union—Meets every Saturday evening at Second Presbyterian Church. F. A. McBride, Pres.; Andrew Smith, Sec.; F. X. Arens, Conductor.

Indianapolis Liederkranz—H. Zwicker, Sec.; Ernst F. Knodel, Musical Director. Meets in Mozart Hall every Wednesday night.

Indianapolis Mandolin Club—545 N. Illinois. Frank Z. Maffey, Pres.

Indianapolis Maennerchor — Rehearsals Tuesday and Friday evenings at Maennerchor Hall. Rudolph M. Mueller, Sec.; Alexander Ernestinoff, Director.

Ladies' Matinee Musicale—Mrs. Carrie F. Robertson, Pres. Meets first and third Wednesday afternoons in each month, from October to May, at 25 E. North.

Socialistischer Saengerchor—Meets at Columbia Hall.

BANDS OF MUSIC.

Hart's Orchestra—623 N. Capitol av. Henry V. Hart, Manager.

Houghton's Military Band and Orchestra—Alfred Houghton, Director; 383 E. New York.

Independent Veteran Drum Corps—91½ E. Court. George W. Glessner, Leader.

Indianapolis Military Band—72 E. Court.

Montani Bros.' Orchestra—168 N. Alabama.

Oak Hill Brass Band—Brightwood. John H. Fisse, Leader.

Panden Bros.' Orchestra—168 N. Alabama.

Union Band—435 E. McCarty. Robert A. W. Dehne, Leader.
When Band—70½ E. Court. George E. Mills, Leader.
Zumpfe's Orchestra—4 Lombard Bldg. Wm. A. Zumpfe, Leader.

NEWSPAPERS.

Agricultural Epitomist (monthly)—21½ W. Washington. Epitomist Publishing Co., pubs. 50 cents per annum.
American Nonconformist The (weekly)—70 E. Ohio. Est. 1879. Cuthbert Vincent, pub. $1 per annum.
American Tribune (weekly)—46 Journal bldg. American Tribune Co., proprs. $1 per year.
Awakener The (monthly)—61 Central av. Charles D. Meigs, pub. 50 cents per annum.
Butler Collegian The (monthly)—Educational. Est. 1886. Published by the faculty of Butler University, Irvington.
Catholic Record The—100 W. Georgia. Alexander Chomel, editor and propr. Issued every Thursday. $2 per annum.
Church Worker The (monthly)—279 Cedar. Episcopal. Rev. E. G. Hunter, pub. 50 cents per annum.
Clay-Worker (monthly)—5 Monument pl. T. A. Randall & Co., proprs. $2 per year.
Commercial Current (monthly)—82 When bldg. Indianapolis Business University, pub.
Courier The (weekly)—94 W. New York. Charles H. Stewart, pub.; $1.50 per annum.
Daily Reporter The (daily)—27½ S. Delaware. Reporter Pub. Co., pubs. $13 per year.
Drainage and Farm Journal (monthly)—Est. 1879. J. J. W. Billingsley, pub., 19 Talbott blk. $1 per year.
Eastern Star The (monthly)—Published by Ransford & Metcalf, 5 Windsor blk. $1 per annum.
Ensign The (weekly)—33 Talbott blk. A. E. Winters, editor. $1 per annum.
Fanciers' Gazette (monthly)—Est. 1896. Fanciers' Gazette Co., pubs., 49 Virginia av. 50 cents per annum.
Farm Record (monthly)—Cuthbert Vincent, pub., 70 E. Ohio. 50 cents per annum.
Freeman The—Published every Saturday by George L. Knox, 57½ Indiana av. $1.50 per year.
German Telegraph—Est. 1864. Published daily by the Gutenberg Co., 27 S. Delaware. $6 per annum.
Hotel and Sample Room The (monthly)—Devoted to the interests of the Indiana State Liquor League. F. J. Cailen, pub., 83 E. Court. $1 per annum.
Independent The (weekly)—Est. 1882. Published every Saturday by Sol. P. Hathaway, 19 Miller blk. $2 per year.
Indiana Baptist (weekly)—Indiana Baptist Pub. Co., pubs., 68 Baldwin blk. $1.50 per annum.
Indiana Boys' Brigades (monthly)—Frank R. Hale, pub., 32½ Clifford av.
Indiana Farmer—A weekly journal of the farm, home and garden. Indiana Farmer Co., proprs., 30½ N. Delaware. $1 per annum.
Indiana Journal of Commerce—Est. 1870. Wm. H. Drapier, pub., 12½ N. Delaware.
Indiana Labor Leader (weekly)—Hannegan & White, pubs, 25 S Delaware. $1 per year.
Indiana Medical Journal (monthly)—18 W. Ohio. Est. 1882. Indiana Medical Journal Pub. Co., proprs. $1 per year.
Indiana Newspaper Record The—Published at 32 W. Court. Indiana Newspaper Union, proprs.
Indiana Pharmacist (monthly)—Est. 1881. Indiana Pharmacist Pub. Co., 107 E. Ohio. $1 per year.
Indiana School Journal (monthly)—Est. 1856. W. A. Bell, editor, 66½ N. Pennsylvania. $1.50 per year.
Indiana State Journal (Republican)—Est. 1824. Published every Wednesday by the Indianapolis Journal Newspaper Co., n. e. cor. Monument pl. and Market. $1 per year.
Indiana State Sentinel (Democratic)—Est. 1822. Published every Wednesday by the Indianapolis Sentinel Co., 21 N. Illinois. $1 per year.
Indiana Tribune (daily and Sunday, German)—Philip Rappaport, pub., 18 S. Alabama. $7 per year.
Indiana Woman (weekly)—Published every Saturday by E. E. Stafford, 47-49 N. Illinois.
Indianapolis Bulletin (weekly)—84 E. Court. T. G. Harrison, propr. 50 cents per year.
Indianapolis Daily Live Stock Journal The (daily)—The Indianapolis Daily Live Stock Journal and Printing Co., proprs., Union Stock Yards (W. I).
Indianapolis Journal (Republican) — Est. 1824. Office, northeast cor. Monument pl. and Market. Indianapolis Journal Newspaper Co., pubs. Issued daily and Sunday. Daily, $8 per year; weekly, $1 per year; Sundays, $2 per year.
Indianapolis News The (Independent)—32 W. Washington. Est. 1869. Charles R. Williams, editor; Wm. J. Richards, manager. Published every afternoon except Sunday. $5.20 per annum by carrier or mail; 2 cents per copy.
Indianapolis Sentinel (Democratic) — Est. 1822. Published daily by the Indianapolis Sentinel Co., 21 N. Illinois. Daily, $6; including Sunday edition, $8 per year.
Indianapolis Trade Journal (weekly)—W. H. Robson, pub., 35 Commercial Club Bldg. $1 per year.
Indianapolis World (weekly)—38½ S. Illinois. Alexander E. Manning, pub. $1.50 per annum.
Inland Poultry (monthly)—O. L. Magill, pub., 10½ N. Delaware. 25 cents per year.
Inter-State and Indiana Official Railway Guide—126 W. Maryland. Journal Job Printing Co., pubs.
Ishmaelite The—Published by Mount Nebo Press, 35 Commercial Club Bldg. $1 per annum.
Jersey Bulletin (weekly)—76 S. Illinois. Est. 1883. D. H. Jenkins, pub. Issued every Wednesday. $2 per year.
Little Folks (monthly)—Little Folks Publishing Co., pubs, 5, 42 W. Market.
Marion County Gazette (weekly)—Est. 1890. S. J. MacDonald, pub., 22 Pembroke Arcade.
Masonic Advocate (monthly)—Martin H. Rice, editor and pub., 14 Masonic Temple. $1 per year.
Medical Epitomist (quarterly)—Russell C. Kelsey, pub., 109 E. Ohio.
Medical Free Press The—Russell C. Kelsey, editor, 105 E. Ohio. Terms, $1 per year.
Missionary Tidings—Published monthly by the Christian Woman's Board of Missions. 50 cents per year. 160 N. Delaware.
Municipal Engineering—Est. 1890. Municipal Engineering Co., pubs., 84 Commercial Club Bldg. Terms, $2 per year.
National Detective and Police Review (monthly) — Circulation, 20,000. 96½ E. Market. Review Publishing Co., pubs. $2 per annum.
Octographic Review (religious weekly)—454 W. Udell (N. I). Rev. Daniel Sommers, pub. $1.50 per annum.
Odd Fellows' Talisman (monthly)—3 Odd Fellows' Hall. John Reynolds, pub. $2 per year.
Organizer The (semi-monthly)—Organizer Pub. Co., pubs., 66½ N. Penn. Est. 1882. $1 per annum.

Patriot Phalanx (weekly)—Wm. F. and Wm. F. Clark, jr., pubs., 25 Cyclorama pl. $1 per year.
Pen The (monthly)—M. W. Carr, pub., 25½ W. Washington. $1.50 per year.
People The (weekly)—James B. Wilson, propr., 37½ Virginia av. Est. 1870.
Pentecost Herald (semi-monthly) — Est. April 1, 1894. Pentecost Bands, pubs., 52 S. State av.
Physio-Medical Journal (monthly)—George Hasty, editor and propr., 35 W. Ohio. $1.50 per annum.
Pythian Journal (monthly)—Est. 1874. A. M. Preston, pub., 398 S. Alabama. $1.50 per annum.
Reporter Daily The—Est. 1895. Reporter Publishing Co., pubs., 519 Indiana Trust bldg. $13 per year.
Rough Notes The (monthly)—Est. 1878. Published by the Rough Notes Co., 79 W. Market. $2 per year.
Silent Spectator (fortnightly)—Mansfield & Davis, pubs. 50 cents per annum.
South Side Sunday Mirror The (weekly)—Frank S. Blunk, pub., 37 Virginia av. $1 per annum.
Spottvogel (German)—Published every Sunday by the Gutenberg Co., 27 S. Delaware. $2 per year.
Sun The—79 E. Ohio. The Sun Publishing Co., proprs. Published every afternoon, except Sunday. $3 per annum by mail; by carrier, 6 cents per week.
Sunday Journal—Northeast cor. Monument pl. and market. Published every Sunday by the Indianapolis Journal Newspaper Co. $2 per year.
Sunday Sentinel—21 N. Illinois. Published every Sunday by the Indianapolis Sentinel Co. $2 per year.
Swine Breeders' Journal (semi-monthly)—467 S. Illinois. Morris Printing Co., pubs. $1 per year.
Typographical Journal The—John W. Bramwood, pub., 29½ E. Market. 25 cents per year.
Volksblatt (German weekly)—Published by the Gutenberg Co., 27 S. Delaware. $2 per year.
West Side Herald (weekly)—291 River av. (W. I). Brown & Smith, proprs. Terms, $1 per year.
Western Horseman—49 Monument pl. Published every Friday by Western Horseman Co. $2 per annum.
Wheelmen's Gazette (monthly)—Est. 1883. Ben. L. Darrow, pub., 31 W. Ohio. 50 cents per year.
Wood Worker—Est. 1882. Southeast cor. Meridian and Monument pl. S. H. Smith, propr. Published monthly. $1 per year.
World The (weekly)—Alexander E. Manning, pub., 40½ S. Illinois. $2 per year.
Young People's Journal—George F. Bass, editor, 132 Commercial Club bldg. Terms, $1 per year.
Zig Zag Cycler (weekly)—Cycler Printing Co., pubs., 30 Talbott blk. $1 per annum.

POST OFFICE.

Government Building — Southeast corner Penn. and Market streets.
Postmaster—Albert Sahm.
Assistant Postmaster—W. O. Reveal.
General Offices—East end of vestibule.
Office hours from 8 a. m. to 6 p. m. Sunday from 9 to 10 a. m.
Depot Branch—T. G. Hedian, Supt.

MONEY ORDER DEPARTMENT.

Superintendent—John L. F. Steeg.
Clerks—Charles W. Byfield, E. F. C. Bechert, O. A. Keely. John A. Hoffman, Lizzie Jeup.
Entrance to Money Order Office—East end of vestubule, cor. of Penn. and Market streets. Office hours from 9 a. m. to 5 p. m.

REGISTERED LETTER DEPARTMENT.

Superintendent—B. C. Shaw.
Registry Clerk—Lee S. Nicholson.
Depot Registry Clerks—Wm. J. Butler, Henry H. Harvey, James W. Mardick, Arthur M. Potts. Depot office open day and night.

MAILING DEPARTMENT.

Superintendent of Mails—Wm. O. Patterson.
Assistant Superintendent of Mails—Robert B. Mundelle.
Clerks—Charles H. Baughman, John E. Clinton, Wm. Curley, Charles E. Dynes, Walton L. Dynes, Walter P. Hanna, John T. Hedges, George McNutt, Virgil O. Moon, Allison B. Mundelle, Simpson P. Myers, Frank L. Rumford, Eugene M. Wilson, Wallace Buchanan.

CITY DELIVERY DEPARTMENT.

Superintendent—James H. Deery.
Assistant Superintendent—Edwin C. Weir.

GENERAL DELIVERY DEPARTMENT.

Clerks—Joseph H. Howes, John G. Edmunds. This department is open for business from 7 a. m. to 7 p. m., and on Sunday from 9 to 10 a. m.

SPECIAL DELIVERY DEPARTMENT.

Superintendent—Henry L. Canary.

STAMP DEPARTMENT.

Clerk—Wm. E. Miller.

CLERKS.

Distributing Department—George T. Cortleyon, Charles E. Cosler, John A. Lane, John H. McCloskey, Wm. R. Carson, Charles P. Sample, Joseph E. Tarkington, Raphael D. Van Wie.
Canceling Department—Charles G. Keiser, Harry B. Phillips, James M. Eades, Wm. H. Furniss, Julius R. Cox, Jesse A. Avery, Thomas C. Kelly, Charles E. Connor, Sampson R. Keeble.
Directory Department—B. L. Smith, Alva W. Gulley.
Dispatching Department—John F. Brasier, Louis J. Dochez, Wm. J. Jennings, James E. Lackey, Frank W. Williams, Bertrand L. Smith, Stephen R. Buck, Charles E. Finney.
Box Department—W. W. Jackson.
Cashier Second-class Mail—John F. Mullen.
Finance Clerk—David M. Elliott.
Night Superintendent—Clinton W. Parrish.
Messenger—Fred C. Vogt.
Timekeeper—Carlisle M. Smith.
Stenographer—Edna P. McGinnis.
Janitor—Conrad Beck.

LETTER CARRIERS.

District No. 1—John H. Garver.
District No. 2—Ellis W. Crane.
District No. 3—Robert H. McGinnis.
District No. 4—Sanford S. Tolin.
District No. 5—John P. Cochrane.
District No. 6—Walter N. Leonard.
District No. 7—James L. Moore.
District No. 8—Wm. Darby.
District No. 9—Frank H. Faris.
District No. 10—Jefferson D. Porter.
District No. 11—Omer Loyd.
District No. 12—Robert S. Cochrane.
District No. 13—Wm. R. Williams.
District No. 14—Alex. H. Arbuckle.
District No. 15—Jacob Mathias.
District No. 16—Frank A. Meredith.
District No. 17—Charles F. Doran.
District No. 18—Niels Jensen.
District No. 19—James K. Barnhill.
District No. 20—Wm. S. Warner.
District No. 21—Jacob C. Brown.
District No. 22—Frederick Ward.
District No. 23—Robert L. Maze.
District No. 24—Alexander McNutt.
District No. 25—Charles A. Boyl.
District No. 26—George W. Reid.

District No. 27—Joe A. Downey.
District No. 28—Walter W. Wilson.
District No. 29—John J. Turner.
District No. 30—Harry K. Milhouse.
District No. 31—James Leary.
District No. 32—Martin W. Healey.
District No. 33—Wm. W. Hall.
District No. 34—George W. Sulgrove.
District No. 35—Wm. C. Weber.
District No. 36—Benjamin J. Lantz.
District No. 37—Isaac N. Smock.
District No. 38—Edward L. Crawley.
District No. 39—John Wren.
District No. 40—John Amos.
District No. 41—Albert E. Smith.
District No. 42—James M. Stutsman.
District No. 43—Gustav Schmedel.
District No. 44—John N. Hobbs.
District No. 45—Fred A. Lorenz.
District No. 46—R. Douglas Wadsworth.
District No. 47—Wm. E. Jones.
District No. 48—Grant Smithson.
District No. 49—Wm. J. Hufford.
District No. 50—Frank L. Stilwell.
District No. 51—Isaac Doll.
District No. 52—Alfred A. Taylor.
District No. 53—Frank C. Rogers.
District No. 54—Albert E. Bragdon.
District No. 55—Wm. Kirschmeier.
District No. 56—Will S. Mitchell.
District No. 57—Aaron Stern.
District No. 58—Samuel M. Wallace.
District No. 59—Lewis W. Parrish.
District No. 60—George T. Nickerson.
District No. 61—Charles V. Hoover.
District No. 62—Charles Burris.
District No. 63—Albert M. Magley.
District No. 64—Henry M. Trimpe.
District No. 65—George Worthington.
District No. 66—James L. Tipton.
District No. 67—Charles W. Ensley.
District No. 68—C. Wm. Kuetemeier.
District No. 69—Andrew J. Wells.
District No. 70—Alonzo B. Clapp.
District No. 71—Richard O. Shimer.
District No. 72—Joseph M. Taylor.
District No. 73—James E. Cantlon.
District No. 74—Matthew A. Lockwood.
Substitute Carriers—John F. Quinn, Clarence E. Hibbs, Albert H. Tolin, Wm. F. Kiesle, George Deming, Joseph E. Carskadon, Michael E. Bradley, Robert S. Coxe, John C. Dehn, Wm. E. Pellett, James E. Nutt, Wm. H. Cobb, Wm. F. Hatfield, Jacob F. Poe, Oscar A. Soper, Leroy J. Silver.

PUBLIC BUILDINGS, HALLS, ETC.

Abbett's Building—31 Virginia av.
Adler Block—176-186 Virginia av.
Aaena Building—19 N. Penn.
Alpha Home—Darwin, near Hillside av.
Altman's Hall—618 S. Meridian.
Association Hall—Y. M. C. A. bldg, 33 N. Illinois.
Asylum for Friendless Colored Children—S. w. cor. Senate av. and Twelfth.
Athon Block—N. e. cor. Capitol av. and New York.
Bacon Block—122 Ft. Wayne av.
Baldwin Block—S. w. cor. Market and Delaware.
Bates House Block—N. w. cor. Washington and Illinois.
Beck Block—263 Mass. av.
Bellefontaine Hall—Cor. Mass. av. and Bellefontaine.
Blacherne The—N. w. cor. Meridian and Vermont.
Black's Block—51 Russell av.
Blackford Block—S. e. cor. Meridian and Washington.
Blake Block—S. w. cor. Washington and Kentucky av.
Blind Asylum—North side North, bet. Meridian and Penn.
Board of Trade—S. e. cor. Maryland and Capitol av.
Bonanza Block—Cor. Washington and West.
Boyd's Block—193 S. Illinois.
Braden Block—77 S. Illinois.
Bradshaw & Ayres Block—33 W. Washington.
Brandon Block—S. w. cor. Delaware and Washington.
Brennecke Building—N. w. cor. North and Illinois.
Bretz Block—S. w. cor. Illinois and Georgia.
Bricklayers' Hall—78½ W. Washington.
Brightwood Association Hall—Brightwood.
Bristor Block—559 Virginia av.
Brown's Building—N. w. cor. Pennsylvania and Washington.
Builders' Exchange—35 E. Ohio.
Burford Building—23-25 Pearl, bet. Meridian and Illinois.
Burns Hall—336 Indiana av.
Buschmann Block—Cor. Ft. Wayne av. and St. Mary.
Butler University—Irvington.
Caffee Block—Cor. Pendleton and Clifford avs.
Campbell Block—23 Indiana av.
Carlisle Block—N. w. cor. West and Washington.
Carpenters' Hall—18½ S. Delaware.
Catterson Block—22-30 Kentucky av.
Celtic Hall—286½ S. West.
Centennial Block—188 S. Meridian.
Central Black—60 E. Market.
Central Hospital for Insane—National road, 3 miles w. of city.
Central Station—S. e. cor. Alabama and Pearl.
Chalfant The—N. w. cor. Penn. and Michigan.
Chamber of Commerce—S. e. cor. Maryland and Capitol av.
Chatham Place Block—Cor. Mass. and Park avs.
Chislett Block—N. w. cor. Illinois and Seventh.
City Dispensary—34 E. Ohio.
City Hay Market—450 E. Washington.
City Hospital—N. w. cor. Locke and Margaret.
Claypool Block—N. e. cor. Illinois and Washington.
Cleaveland Block—S. w. cor. Capitol and Kentucky avs.
Coffin Block—90 E. Market.
Coffman Block—N. w. cor. Washington and Delaware.
Columbia Block—259 W. Washington.
Columbia Hall—401 S. Delaware.
Commercial Block—N. w. cor. Washington and Kentucky av.
Commercial Club Building—26 S. Meridian.
Condit Block—N. e. cor. Meridian and Pearl.
Conduitt Block—136 S. Meridian.
Cook's Hall—116 Hadley av (W. I.)
Cordova Block—25 W. Washington.
Corinthian Hall—N. w. cor. Central av. and St. Mary.
Council Chamber—Court House.
County Infirmary—Indiana av. 4 miles n. w. of city.
Court House—North side Washington bet. Delaware and Alabama.
Cyclorama Building—North side Market, bet. Illinois and Capitol av.
Danforth Block—South side Washington w. of Senate av.
Das Deutsche Haus—N. e. cor. Michigan and New Jersey.
Deaf and Dumb Institute—N. e. cor. Washington and State av.
De Soto Building—29 E. Market.
Door of Hope—84 N. Alabama.
Druid Hall—124 E. Maryland.
East End Block—N. w. cor. Washington and East.
East Market House—Northside Market, east of Delaware.
Elks' Hall—112 N. Meridian.

Elliott Block—20 W. Maryland.
Emerald Hall—284 S. West.
Empire Block—N. e. cor. Alabama and Mass. av.
Empire Theater—N. w. cor. Wabash and Delaware.
English Block—N. w. cor. Washington and Noble.
English's Opera House—West side Monument pl. between Market and Meridian.
Exchange Block—82 N. Penn.
Fair Block—Jackson pl.
Female Reformatory—S. e. cor. Michigan and Randolph.
Fletcher's Bank Building—30 E. Washington.
Franciscan Convert—Cor. Union and Palmer.
Frank Block—S. w. cor. California and Indiana av.
Franklin Fire Insurance Co.'s Building—S. e. cor. Monument place and Market.
Franklin Life Insurance Building—S. w. cor. Illinois and Kentucky av.
Friendly Inn—290 W. Market.
Gallup's Block—S. e. cor. Market and Capitol av.
Gaston Block—101 N. Delaware.
Gem Block—37 Indiana av.
Geological Museum—126 State House.
German General Protestant Orphan Asylum—S. State av. opp Sycamore.
German House—S. e. cor. Michigan and New Jersey.
German Lutheran Orphans' Home—N. e. cor. Washington and Watts.
German Mutual Insurance Block—29 S. Delaware.
Giezendanner Block—N. e. cor Vermont and Senate av.
Gramling Block—North side Washington, west of Penn.
Grand Opera House and Block—69 N. Penn.
Griffith Block—North side of Washington, east of Illinois.
Guardians' Home—S. e. cor. Prospect and Auburn.
Hahn's Building—17 E. Washington.
Halcyon Block—N. w. cor. Delaware and New York.
Hall Block—240 E. Washington.
Hammond Block—S. e. cor. Mass. av. and New York.
Hartford Block—84 E. Market.
Harugari Saenger Hall—29 S. Delaware.
Haueisen Block—27 W. Pearl.
Haughville Reading Room—Germania av., near Michigan (H).
Healey Hall—S. e. cor. McCarty and Maple.
Hendricks Block—S. w. cor. Market and Monument pl.
High School Building No. 1—N. e. cor. Michigan and Penn.
Home for Aged Poor—Vermont, e. of East.
Home for Friendless Women—Cor. Capitol av. and Eleventh.
Home of the Good Shepherd—57 W. Raymond.
Hord Block—18 Indiana av.
Howe Block—S. e. cor. Illinois and Georgia.
Hollywood Block—88 S. Illinois.
Holt Block—71 N. Illinois.
Hubbard Block—S. w. cor. Washington and Meridian.
Hutchings Block—N. w. cor Ohio and Penn.
Independent Turnverein Hall—101 N. Illinois.
Indiana Dental College Building—S. w. cor. Delaware and Ohio.
Indiana Institute for the Blind—North bet. Meridian and Penn.
Indiana Institution for the Deaf and Dumb —S. e. cor. Washington and State av.
Indiana Reform School for Girls and Woman's Prison—S. e. cor. Michigan and Randolph.
Indiana Trust Building—S. e. cor. Washington and Virginia av.
Indianapolis Home for Friendless Women—Cor. Capitol av. and 11th.
Indianapolis Light Artillery Armory—N. w. cor. Senate av. and 7th.
Indianapolis Orphan Asylum—N. e. cor. College and Home avs.
Industrial Training School Building—Madison av., Meridian and Merrill.
I. O. O. F. Building—N. e. cor. Washington and Penn.
I. O. O. F. Halls—462½ Virginia av. and s. w. cor. Central and Railroad (I).
Ingalls Block—S. w. cor. Washington and Penn.
Insane Asylum—Washington st., 2 miles west of city.
Iron Block—South side Washington st., west of Meridian.
Johnson Block—N. w. cor. Washington and East.
Journal Building—N. e. cor. Monument pl. and Market.
Judah Block—South side Washington st., east of Delaware.
Katherine Home—N. e. cor. Capitol av. and 11th.
Kealing Block—N. e. cor. Washington and Cruse.
Keeling's Building—Cor. Maryland and Virginia av.
Keller's Block—Cor. East and Coburn.
Kenmore Block—183 Mass. av.
Kerr's Block—Washington, bet. Senate av. and Missouri.
Kessler Block—N. w. cor. Mass. av. and St. Clair.
Knights of Labor Hall—115 E. Washington.
Knights of Pythias Hall—Talbott blk.
Knodel's Hall—113 E. Washington.
Koerner Block—N. w. cor. Delaware and Koerner.
Kregelo Block—52 Indiana av.
Lake Erie & Western Railroad Co.'s Building—S. w. cor. Washington and Noble.
Lemcke Building—N. w. cor. Penn. and Market.
Library Building—S. w. cor. Meridian and Ohio.
Lillian Hall—359½ Virginia av.
Lintner Block—184 Indiana av.
Littler's Hall—S. e. cor. Washington and Eastern av.
Lombard Building—24 E. Washington.
Lorraine Building—S. w. cor. Washington and Capitol av.
Ludwig Block—162 E. Washington.
Lyra Hall—86 W. Washington.
McDonald & Butler Block—18 N. Penn.
McDougall Block—62 S. Illinois.
McGinnis Block—280 E. Washington.
M. E. of N. A. Hall—92½ E. Washington.
Macy Block—South side Market, bet. Illinois and Monument pl.
Maennerchor Hall—181 E. Washington.
Majestic Building—N. e. cor. Penn. and Maryland.
Mansur Block—N. e. cor. Washington and Alabama.
Mansur Block—N. e. cor. Illinois and Market.
Marion Block—N. w. cor. Ohio and Meridian.
Marion County Jail—N. w. cor. Alabama and Maryland.
Marmont Hall—S. w. cor. Georgia and Illinois.
Marquette Block—26-34 Indiana av.
Masonic Hall—S. e. cor. Washington and Capitol av.
Masonic Temple—S. e. cor. Washington and Capitol av.
Massachusetts Avenue Depot—S. w. cor. Mass. and Clifford avs.
Maus Block—168 E. Washington.
Mayhew Block—27 Monument pl.
Meikel Block—12 W. Washington.
Meridian Building—114 N. Meridian.

Mick's Hall—N. w. cor. Illinois and Twenty-second.
Miller's Block—N. w. cor. Illinois and Market.
Milligan Block—289½ Mass. av.
Milton The—30 E. Pratt.
Mohs Block—S. e. cor. Shelby and Prospect.
Monument Place—Crossing Meridian and Market.
Moody Block—116 W. New York.
Moore Block—S. w. cor. Maryland and Penn.
Moore Block, No. 2—Cor. Mass av. and St. Clair.
Morgan Block—163 Mass. av.
Mozart Hall—37 S. Delaware.
Murphy Temperance League Hall—252 Columbia av.
National Hall—502 E. Washington.
Neerman Block—267 Mass. av.
New Block—84 N. Illinois.
New Denison House Block—S. e. cor. Penn. and Ohio.
Oakland Flats—239 N. Delaware.
Occidental Hall—488 Virginia av.
Old Library Building—S. w. cor. Penn. and Ohio.
Odd Fellows' Hall—N. e. cor. Washington and Penn.
Old Sentinel Building—S. w. cor. Monument pl. and Meridian.
O. I. H. Building—30 Monument pl.
Park Theater—N. e. cor. Washington and Capitol av.
Parnell Hall—73 W. McCarty.
Patriotic Sons of America Hall—92½ E. Washington.
Pembroke Arcade—Washington to Virginia av., w. of Delaware.
Pfaffiin Block—Cor. Senate and Indiana avs.
Phoenix Block—N. w. cor. Market and Delaware.
Phoenix Hall—590 S. Meridian.
Piel Block—29½ W. Ohio.
Pierce Block—See Stout Block.
Plaza The—18 Monument pl.
Plymouth Building—S. e. cor. New York and Meridian.
Poole's Hall—N. e. cor. Illinois and Twenty-second.
Post Hall (G. A. R.)—30½ N. Delaware.
Postoffice Building—S. e. cor. Market and Penn.
Press Building—S. e. cor. Monument pl. and Meridian.
Pressley Flats—175 N. Penn.
Protestant Deaconess Home—118 N. Senate av.
Propylaeum Building—25 E. North.
Ransdell Block—257 Mass. av.
Reaume Block—Maryland, between Capitol av. and Senate av.
Reichwein's Hall—S. w. cor. Market and Noble.
Rescue Home—49 E. South.
Rhodius Block—35 N. Capitol av.
Rialto Building—16-22 N. Penn.
Riley Block—N. e. cor. California and Washington.
Ripley Block—155 Indiana av.
Rowley Block—37 Kentucky av.
Royal Arcanum Hall—S. w. cor. Illinois and 7th.
Ryan Block—N. w. cor. Capitol and Indiana avs.
St. Aloysius Library Hall—N. e. cor. Capitol av. and Georgia.
St. Cecilia Hall—N. w. cor. Union and Palmer.
St. George's Hall—36½ E. Washington.
St. John's Hall—Cor. Capitol av. and Georgia.
St. Joseph's Hall—S. w. cor. North and Cincinnati.
St. Joseph's Home—397 S. Alabama.
St. Mary's Hall—82 S. Delaware.
St. Patrick's Hall—Dougherty, w. of Virginia av.
St. Vincent's Infirmary—S. e. cor. Delaware and South.
Sayles Block—18 E. Ohio.
Scholl Block—31 Indiana av.
Schrieber Block—N. w. cor. Coburn and Virginia av.
Scott Block—S. e. cor. Phipps and Meridian.
Scottish Rite Building—29-37 S. Penn.
Sentinel Building—21 N. Illinois.
Sentinel Printing Co. Building—77 W. Market.
Shea Hall—Cor. Belmont and Lambert (W. I).
Shiel Block—Cor. Indiana av. and Illinois.
Shiel The—120-122 N. Illinois and 25 Indiana av.
Sixth Street Station—North side Sixth, e. of Capitol av.
Smith Block—27 Virginia av.
Smith's Block—S. e. cor. Delaware and Ohio.
Snow Block—17 Virginia av.
Social Turnverein Building—Cor. Michigan and New Jersey.
South Meridian Hall—Cor. S. Meridian and Kansas.
South Side Turnverein Hall—S. s. Morris, near Meridian.
Spades Place—231 Mass. av.
Staley's Block—N. w. cor. Virginia av. and McCarty.
State Fair Grounds—Four miles n. e. of Monument pl.
State House—West side Capitol av., bet. Washington and Ohio.
State Museum—Dept. Geology and Natural History, 126 State House.
Stechhan Block—N. w. cor. Alabama and Pearl.
Sterling Block—Cor. Louisiana and Virginia av.
Stevenson Building—15-23 E. Washington.
Stewart Block—S. w. cor. Seventh and Illinois.
Stewart Place—S. e. cor. Illinois and Ohio.
Stock Yards—Hadley av. and Belt Railroad crossing (W. I.)
Stone Block—14-16 W. Ohio.
Stout Block—62-76 Mass av.
Sturm Place—E. Michigan, bet. Arsenal and State avs.
Surgical Institute Building—N. w. cor. Ohio and Capitol av.
Talbott Block—N. w. cor. Market and Penn.
Talbott & New's Block—East side Penn., s. of Market.
Telephone Building—S. w. cor. Illinois and Ohio.
Templeton Hall—36½ W. Washington.
Thompson's Block—S. w. cor. Ohio and Illinois.
Thorpe Block—83 E. Market.
Tomlinson Block—N. w. cor. Ohio and Indiana av.
Tomlinson Hall—N. e. cor. Market and Delaware.
Trade Block—15 McCrea.
Turne Hall—N. e. cor. Illinois and Ohio.
Union Building—67 W. Maryland.
Union Carpenters' Hall—25½ S. Meridian.
Union Hall—139 E. Washington.
Union Station—Cor. Illinois and Jackson pl.
U. S. Arsenal—North end of Arsenal av.
Vajen's Block—66 N. Penn.
Van Sickle's Hall—32½ Clifford av.
Van Vorhis Block—233 Mass. av.
Vinton Block—S. w. cor. Market and Penn.
Von Hake Block—30 N. Delaware.
Voss Block—Cor. 1st and Illinois.
Wachstetter's Hall—199 S. Capitol av.
Wallace Block—50 S. Delaware.
Wallace Block—S. e. cor. Mass. av. and New York.
Washington Hall—84 W. Washington.
Water Works Building—East bank White river, s. of Washington.

THE

CHICAGO, MILWAUKEE & ST. PAUL R'Y

With its 6,150 miles of thoroughly equipped road reaches all principal points in

Northern Illinois, Wisconsin, Iowa, Minnesota, South Dakota, North Dakota and Northern Michigan.

THE ONLY LINE

RUNNING ELECTRIC LIGHTED AND STEAM HEATED VESTIBULED TRAINS.

All Coupon Ticket Agents in the United States and Canada sell Tickets via the Chicago, Milwaukee & St. Paul R'y.

GEO. H. HEAFFORD,
Gen'l Pass. Agt., Chicago, Ill.

The Great Southwest System

Connecting the Commercial Centres and Rich Farms of

MISSOURI,

The Broad Corn and Wheat Fields and Thriving Towns of

KANSAS,

The Fertile River Valleys and Trade Centres of

NEBRASKA,

The Grand Picturesque and Enchanting Scenery, and the Famous Mining Districts of

COLORADO,

The Agricultural, Fruit, Mineral and Timber Lands, and Famous Hot Springs of

ARKANSAS,

The Beautiful Rolling Prairies and Woodlands of the

INDIAN TERRITORY,

The Sugar Plantations of

LOUISIANA,

The Cotton and Grain Fields, the Cattle Ranges and Winter Resorts of

TEXAS,

Historical and Scenic

OLD AND NEW MEXICO,

And forms, with its Connections, the Popular Winter Route to

ARIZONA AND CALIFORNIA.

For full descriptive and illustrated pamphlets of any of the above States, or Hot Springs, Ark., San Antonio, Tex., and Mexico, address Company's Agents, or the General Passenger Agent.

C. G. WARNER, Vice-President, **W. B. DODDRIDGE,** General Manager, **H. C. TOWNSEND,** Gen'l Passenger and Ticket Agent,

ST. LOUIS.

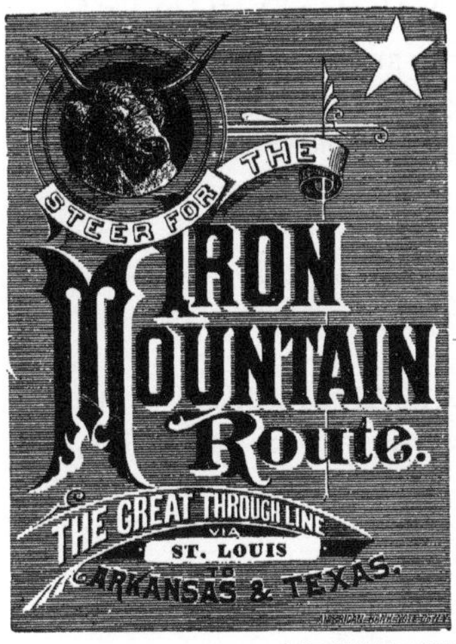

PULLMAN BUFFET SLEEPING CARS

—TO—

Memphis, Little Rock, Houston, Galveston, Dallas, El Paso, Austin, San Antonio and Los Angeles, without change.

FREE RECLINING CHAIR CARS

—TO—

Memphis, Little Rock, Fort Smith, Houston and Galveston.

4 DAILY TRAINS 4

St. Louis to Texas and the Southwest.

The Shortest and Quickest Line to the City of Mexico via Laredo, EAGLE PASS OR EL PASO.

Sleeping Cars through with only One Change.

NO CHANGE OF CARS, St. Louis to Los Angeles and Pacific Coast Points.

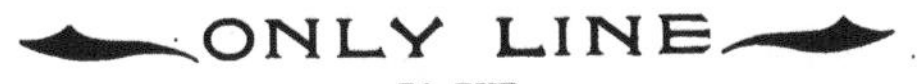

ONLY LINE

—TO THE—

GREAT HOT SPRINGS, OF ARKANSAS,

"The Carlsbad of America."

C. G. WARNER, Vice-President,

W. B. DODDRIDGE, General Manager,
H. C. TOWNSEND, Gen'l Pass. and Ticket Agent, } ST. LOUIS, MO.

10th YEAR OF PUBLICATION.

R. L. POLK & CO.'S
Medical and Surgical Register
OF THE UNITED STATES.

IT IS A FACT that the leading and progressive men in the medical profession regard the REGISTER as a standard book of reference which ought to be in every physician's library.

The Register is designed to so completely cover the medical directory field that further investment in that line will be unnecessary.

If you want to know the COLLEGE STANDING of the physicians you come in contact with, you will find it in the Register.

The Register will enable you to locate a LOST FRIEND if he is practicing anywhere in the United States.

The FOURTH EDITION will be revised to the latest possible date and will contain:

List of Physicians and Surgeons, arranged by States, giving Postoffice Address, with Population and Location of each place.

The School practiced.

College and Class of Graduation.

All the Existing and Extinct Medical Colleges in the United States and Canada, with Location, Faculty, etc.

The various Medical Societies, Medical Journals, Hospitals, Sanitariums, Asylums, and other Medical institutions

Boards of Health.

A Synopsis of the Laws for regulating the Practice of Medicine in each State.

Medical Departments of the U. S Army, Navy and Marine Hospital Servce.

Roster of Examining Surgeons of the U. S. Pension Department

A Descriptive Sketch of each State and Territory.

Climatological Statistics.

The Names and Location of Prominent Mineral Springs.

General Alphabetical list of Physicians, and reference to medical standing.

R. L. POLK & CO., PUBLISHERS.

Waverly Building—S. w. cor. Meridian and Monument pl.
Wesley Block—Indiana av., bet. Illinois and Capitol av.
Wheatley Block—N. e. cor. New Jersey and Ohio.
When Building—26-40 N. Penn.
White's Block—106 N. Meridian.
Wiley Block—N. w. cor. Penn. and Washington.
Wilson Block—S. e. cor. Illinois and Market.
Windsor The—S. w. cor. Illinois and Market.
Workhouse—South side Twelfth, bet. Highland pl. and Michigan rd.
Wright's Market Street Block—66 E. Market.
Wright's Pennsylvania Street Block—See Exchange Block.
Wyandot Block—N. e. cor. Ohio and Mass. av.
Yandes & Malott Block—East side Illinois, bet. Georgia and Louisiana.
Y. M. C. A. Building—33 N. Illinois.
Yohn Block—N. e. cor. Meridian and Washington.

PUBLIC PARKS.

Armstrong Park—North Indianapolis.
Fairview Park—Seven miles n. of city on the canal.
Garfield Park—South end of East.
Germania Park—Floral av. w. of canal.
Indianapolis Base Ball Park—E. Ohio, bet. Hanna and Arsenal av.
Irvington Park—Irvington.
Military Park—South side of New York, bet. Blackford and West.
Monument Place—Crossing Meridian and Market.
St. Clair Park—Meridian, Penn. and St. Clair.
University Square—West side Penn., bet. New York and Vermont.
West Indianapolis Park—Bet. Birch and Marion avs (W. I).
Wildwood—S. w. cor. Meridian and Seventeenth.
Woodruff Place—East of United States Arsenal, bet. Clifford av. and Michigan.

RAILROADS.

Belt Railroad and Stock Yards Company—W. P. Ijams, Pres.; Michael A. Downing, Vice-Pres.; John H. Holliday, Sec.; H. D. Lane, Auditor; Harry C. Graybill, Traffic Mngr. Office Union Stock Yards (W. I.)
Cincinnati, Hamilton & Dayton Railroad—From Indianapolis to Cincinnati, 123 miles; Cincinnati to Toledo, 202 miles. M. D. Woodford, Pres.; C. G. Waldo, Genl. Mngr. General offices, Cincinnati, O. Indianapolis offices, 2 W. Washington. H. G. Stiles, Genl. Agt, Freight Dept.; George W. Hayler, Dist. Pass. Agt.
Cleveland, Cincinnati, Chicago & St. Louis Railway (Big Four)—Total number of miles operated, 2,347. General offices, Cincinnati and Cleveland, O. M. E. Ingalls, Pres.; E. O. McCormick, Pass. Traffic Mngr.; D. B. Martin, Genl. Pass. Agt.; J. Q. Van Winkle, Genl. Supt.; Ford Woods, Genl. Freight Agt. P. & E. Ry.; George W. Bender, Supt. Chicago Division; J. A. Barnard, Genl. Mngr. P. & E. Division; J. W. Riley, Supt. P. & E. Division; Henry S. Frazer, Genl. Agt.; W. A. Sullivan, Freight Agt.; H. M. Bronson, Asst. Genl. Pass. Agt.; 1 E. Washington street, Indianapolis, Ind.
Cincinnati, Wabash & Michigan Railway—For general offices see Cleveland, Cincinnati, Chicago & St. Louis Railway.
Indiana, Decatur & Western Railway—From Indianapolis to Decatur, 153 miles. M. D. Woodford, Pres.; R. B. F. Pierce, Genl. Mngr.; George H. Graves, Supt.; J. S. Lazarus, Genl. Freight and Pass. Agt.; J. W. Connaty, Master Mechanic; George W. Lishawa, Auditor; F. H. Short, Treas.; George H. Graves, Supt.; George R. Balch, Purchasing Agt. General offices, Commercial Club bldg.
Indianapolis Union Railway Co. Lessees Belt Railroad—James McCrea, Pres.; W. N. Jackson, Sec.; W. T. Cannon, Treas. and Purchasing Agt.; C. A. Vinnedge, Auditor; A. A. Zion, Supt. Offices, Union Station.
Pennsylvania Lines—Indianapolis to Columbus, O., 188 miles. Louisville Division, Indianapolis to Louisville, Ky., 110 miles. Vincennes Division, Indianapolis to Vincennes, 116 miles. General offices, Pittsburg, Pa.; George B. Roberts, Pres., Philadelphia, Pa.; E. A. Ford, Genl. Pass. and Ticket Agt., Pittsburg, Pa.; John F. Miller, Genl. Supt., Columbus, O.; F. G. Darlington, Supt., Indianapolis. Indianapolis offices, Union Station. Oran Perry, Local Freight Agt.; S. F. Gray, Genl. Western Freight Agt.; George E. Rockwell, D. P. A.; George Rech, City Ticket Agt. Offices, n. e. cor. Illinois and Washington streets.
Lake Erie & Western Railway Co.—General offices, cor. Washington and Noble sts., Indianapolis, Ind. From Sandusky, O., to Peoria, Ill., 416 miles; from Indianapolis to Michigan City, Ind., 162 miles; from Fort Wayne to Connersville, Ind., 109 miles; from New Castle to Rushville, Ind., 24 miles; from St. Marys to Minster, 10 miles; total, 721 miles. C. S. Brice, Pres., New York; L. M. Schwan, Vice-Pres., New York; George L. Bradbury, Vice-Pres. and Genl. Mngr., Indianapolis, Ind.; Samuel B. Sweet, Genl. Freight Agt., Indianapolis, Ind.; Charles F. Daly, Genl. Passenger Agt., Indianapolis, Ind.; A. G. Young, Asst. Genl. Freight Agt., Indianapolis, Ind.; D. S. Hill, Genl. Supt., Indianapolis, Ind.; H. F. Bickell, Asst. Genl. Supt., Indianapolis, Ind.; T. H. Perry, Chief Engineer and Purchasing Agt., Indianapolis, Ind.; W. E. Hackedorn, Genl. Solicitor, Indianapolis, Ind.; John B. Cockrum, Genl. Attorney, Indianapolis, Ind.; A. D. Thomas, Asst. Treas., Indianapolis, Ind.; W. A. Wildhack, Auditor, Indianapolis, Ind.; E. N. Hicks, Trav. Pass, Agt., Indianapolis, Ind.; T. O. Baker, Trav. Freight Agt., Indianapolis, Ind. City ticket office, 26 S. Illinois. Local freight office, 51 S. Alabama street.
Louisville, New Albany & Chicago Railway (Monon Route)—From Indianapolis, Ind., to Chicago, Ill., 183 miles; from Indianapolis, Ind., to Michigan City, Ind., 154 miles; from Monon, Ind., to Louisville, Ky., 229 miles; branch from Orleans to French Lick Springs, 18 miles; from Bedford to Switz City, 41 miles. Samuel Thomas, Pres., New York City; W. H. McDoel, Vice-Pres. and Genl. Mngr., Chicago; J. L. Doherty, Asst. Auditor; Frank J. Reed, Genl. Passenger Agt., Chicago; E. C. Field, Genl. Solicitor, Chicago; A. J. O'Reilly, Genl. Agt., 1 Board of Trade bldg., Indianapolis, Ind.; George W. Hayler, District Passenger Agt., Indianapolis, Ind. Local ticket office, 2 W. Washington street. Local freight, corner New Jersey and Pearl.
Ohio, Indiana & Western Railway—For General Offices see Cleveland, Cincinnati, Chicago & St. Louis Railway.
Terre Haute & Indianapolis Railroad—Indianapolis to St. Louis, Mo., 240 miles. General Offices, Terre Haute, Ind. V. T. Malott, Receiver, Indianapolis, Ind.; J. J. Turner, Vice-Pres. and Genl. Mngr., St. Louis, Mo.; George E. Farrington, Genl. Agt. and Sec.; R. B. Thompson, Treas., Terre Haute, Ind.; E. A. Ford, Genl. Ticket and Passenger Agt.; W. F. Brunner, Asst. Genl. Passenger Agt., St. Louis,

Mo.; George E. Rockwell, District Passenger Agt.; A. D. Pendleton, Commercial Agt. Indianapolis Offices, northeast cor. Illinois and Washington streets.

RAILWAYS—STREET.

Citizens' Street Railroad Co.—Augustus L. Mason, Pres.; Wm. L. Elder, Vice-Pres.; Wm. F. Milholland, Sec. and Treas.; Miller Elliott, Supt., 750 W. Washington.

Indianapolis and Broad Ripple Rapid Transit Co.—Robert C. Light, Pres. and Genl. Mngr., 1-2 Lombard bldg.

Indianapolis, Greenwood & Franklin Electric Line—From Indianapolis to Greenwood, 30 miles. J. A. Polk, Greenwood, Pres.; Henry L. Smith, Genl. Mngr. General Offices, 731 Lemcke bldg.

SCHOOLS.

MISCELLANEOUS SCHOOLS.

Admire & McVeigh, 1½ E. Washington.

Assumption School—William, n of Morris (W. I.), in charge of Sisters of St. Benedict.

Boys' Classical School—783 N. Delaware. L. H. Baugher, Principal.

Butler College—Irvington, Ind. Scot Butler, President. A. M. Chamberlain, Sec. of Board.

Convent of the Good Shepherd—S. s. Raymond, w. of Meridian.

Convent of the Sisters of St. Joseph—Cor. Palmer and Meridian.

Duthie Lawson A.—11½ N. Meridian.

German Evangelical Lutheran Schools—387 S. New Jersey, cor. Pleasant and Spruce and Jupiter, near Brookside av.

German Lutheran Mission School—Cor. Jefferson and Orange avs.

German Lutheran School—481 E. Market. Adolphus C. F. Paar, Principal.

Girls' Classical School—426 N. Penn. May Wright Sewall, Principal.

Holy Cross School—S. e. cor. Hanna and Ohio. In charge of Sisters of Providence.

Independent Turn Verein School of Indianapolis—Adolph Mols, Instructor. Cor. Illinois and Ohio.

Indiana Boston School of Elocution and Expression of Indianapolis—Established 1879. Mrs. Hariet Augusta Prunk, Principal. 368 W. New York.

Indiana Law School—71 W. Market.

Indiana Kindergarten and Primary Normal Training School—Margaret, opp. City Hospital. Eliza A. Blaker, City Supt.

Indiana School of Art—N. w. cor. Monument Place and Market. Established 1889. Hilton U. Brown, Pres.; Carl H. Lieber, Sec.; Charles E. Hollenbeck, Treas.

Indiana School of Nursing (attached to City Hospital.)

Indianapolis Academy for Boys—498 N. Penn.

Indianapolis Business University—When bldg. Established 1850. Incorporated 1886. Emmett J. Heeb, Pres.

Indianapolis College of Music—Cor. Monument Place and Market. James M. Dungan, Mngr.

Industrial School for Colored Children—Jaillet Arthur, D. F., Ninth Presbyterian Church, 222 Keystone av.

Johnson John D.—156½ E. Washington.

Kindergarten No. 1—321 W. Pearl.

Kindengarten No. 2—68 Yandes.

Kindergarten No. 3—Margaret, opp. City Hospital.

Kindergarten No. 4—644 S. Illinois.

Kindergarten No. 5—10 N. Liberty.

Kindergarten No. 6—Cor. Catharine and Missouri.

Kindergarten No. 7—560 W. North.

Knickerbacker Hall The—Diocesan School for Girls, cor. 7th and Central av.

Metropolitan School of Music—134 N. Illinois. Franz X. Arens, Pres.; Oliver W. Pierce, Sec.

Nurses' Training School—735 N. Meridian.

St. Agnes Academy—702 N. Meridian. In charge of Sisters of Providence.

St. Ann's School (colored)—S. w. cor. Pratt and Fayette. In charge of the Sisters of St. Francis.

St. Anthony's School for Boys and Girls—East side of Warman av., 2 south of Vermont (H). In charge of Sisters of Providence.

St. Bridget's School—N. e. cor. West and St. Clair. In charge of the Sisters of St. Francis.

St. John's Academy and Boarding School for Girls—South side of Maryland e. of S. Capitol av. In charge of the Sisters of Providence.

St. John's German Evangelical Lutheran School—Bismarck av., near Frazee (H).

St. John's School for Boys—74 W. Georgia. In charge of the Brothers of the Sacred Heart.

St. Joseph's Academy—284 N. Noble. In charge of the Sisters of Providence.

St. Joseph's Home and Industrial School—397 S. Alabama. In charge of the Sisters of Providence.

St. Joseph's Institute—Cor. Coburn and Short. In charge of the Brothers of the Sacred Heart.

St. Joseph's School (for boys)—321 E. North. B. W. Bernhard Kingston, Principal.

St. Mary's School (for boys)—Rear 75 E. Maryland. Joseph P. Pfeiffer, Principal.

St. Mary's Academy and School (for girls)—South side Maryland w. of Delaware. In charge of the Sisters of St. Francis.

St. Patrick's School (for boys)—North side Dougherty w. of Virginia av. In charge of the Brothers of the Sacred Heart.

St. Patrick's Academy (for girls)—South side Dougherty w. of Short. In charge of the Sisters of Providence.

St. Peter and Paul School for Boys—In charge of Sisters of Providence. 672 N. Penn.

Sacred Heart School (for girls)—Cor. Meridian and Palmer. Mother Lidwina, Superior.

Sacred Heart School (for boys)—Cor. Union and Palmer.

Select Kindergarten—19 W. St. Joseph. Jennie M. Moore, Principal.

Select Kindergarten—571 N. Capitol av. Catherine O'Neill, Principal.

Select Kindergarten—435 Ash.

Shorthand Training School—49-55 Thorpe blk.

Sisters of the Good Shepherd—South side Raymond, near city limits.

University of Indianapolis—Meets at Assembly rooms, Commercial Club. Allen M. Fletcher, Pres.; George E. Hunt, Sec.; Herman Lieber, Treas.

University Extension, Indianapolis Center—Gustave A. Carstensen, Pres.; Harriet E. Jacobs, Sec.

Winona Assembly and Summer School—36 When bldg. Rev. S. C. Dickey.

PUBLIC SCHOOLS.

Superintendent of Schools—D. K. Goss, Library bldg.

Assistant Superintendent—Miss N. Cropsey—Office house, 4:30 to 5 p. m., Monday. Library bldg.

Clerk of Superintendent—Clara Stonebarger, Library bldg. Office hours of Superintendent, from 4:30 to 5:30 p. m. each week day, except Wednesday. Office hours of clerk, from 8:30 to 3 p. m.

Special Teachers—Wilhelmina Seegmiller, Supervisor of Drawing; Robert Nix, Supervisor of German; Perle Wilkison, Supervisor of Music; J. H. Woodruff, Supervisor of Penmanship; Curt Toll and Adolph Mols, Supervisors of Physical Culture. Office, Library bldg.

Normal School—In High School bldg. No. 1. Mary E. Nicholson, Principal.

HIGH SCHOOL NO. 1.

Corner Pennsylvania and Michigan. George W. Hufford, Principal.

INDUSTRIAL TRAINING SCHOOL.

Corner Meridian and Merrill and Madison av. Charles E. Emmerich, Principal.

PRIMARY GRAMMAR SCHOOLS.

No. 1—Cor. New Jersey and Vermont. Ida M. Andrus, Principal.
No. 2—Cor. Delaware and Walnut. Margaret Hamilton, Principal.
No. 3—Meridian, bet. Ohio and New York. M. Selma Ingersoll, Principal.
No. 4—Cor. Michigan and Blackford. Frances M. Brunton, Supervising Principal.
No. 5—Cor. Washington and California. Anna Courtney, Principal.
No. 6—Cor. Union and Phipps. Mary L. Colgan, Principal.
No. 7—Cor. Bates and Benton. Nelson Yoke, Supervising Principal.
No. 8—Oak Hill, northeast of Atlas Works. Georgia Alexander, Principal.
No. 9—Cor. Vermont and Davidson. Henrietta Schrake, Principal.
No. 10—Cor. Ash and Home av. Henrietta Colgan, Supervising Principal.
No. 11—Cor. 4th and Capitol av. Clara Washburn, Principal.
No. 12—Cor. West and McCarty. Mary H. Ingersoll, Principal.
No. 13—Cor. Buchanan and Beaty. Emma Donnan, Supervising Principal.
No. 14—South side Ohio, east of Highland av. Rauma W. Wales. Principal.
No. 15—Cor. Michigan and Keystone av. Sarah McFarland, Principal.
No. 16—Cor. Blomington and Springfield. Eliza M. Hopkins, Principal.
No. 17—Cor. West and 2d. Lavinia McFarland, Principal.
No. 18—Yandes, bet. Home and Lincoln avs. Victoria A. Willson, Principal.
No. 19—Shelby, south of Prospect. Marcellus Neal, Principal.
No. 20—Spruce, south of Prospect. Sadie L. Kirlin, Principal.
No. 21—Michigan av., s. e. of Institute for Deaf and Dumb. Florence Fay, Principal.
No. 22—Cor. Chestnut and Hill. Ada Duzan, Principal.
No. 23.—Cor. Fourth and Howard. Mary E. Willson, Principal.
No. 24—Cor. North and Minerva. John T. Smith, Principal.
No. 25—Cor. New Jersey and Merrill. Mary A. McKeever, Principal.
No. 26—Martindale av., bet. Lincoln av. and Seventh. Mary B. Knowlton, Principal.
No. 27—Cor. Park av. and Eighth. Margaret V. Marshall, Principal.
No. 28—Fletcher av., bet. Dillon and Cedar. Etta L. Miller, Principal.
No. 29—Cor. College av. and Eleventh. Jane W. Bass, Principal.
No. 30—Elder av. Martha Allgire, Teacher.
No. 31—Lincoln lane. Helen Hickey, Principal.
No. 32—Cor. Twelfth and Illinois. Cora M. Day, Principal.
No. 33—Cor. Sterling and Stoughton av. Kate Robson, Principal.
No. 34—Shelby, s. of Belt R. R. E. S. Skillen, Principal.
No. 35—Madison road, s. of Belt R. R. Flora Harvey, Principal.
No. 36—Cor. Capitol av. and Twentieth. Mary D. Stillwell, Principal.
No. 37—Seventeenth, e. of Baltimore av. James H. Young, Principal.
No. 38—Cor. Bloyd av. and Paw Paw. Mary A. Hancock, Principal.
No. 39—Cor. State and Lexington avs. Helen R. Lang, Principal.
No. 40—Cor. Penn. and North. Ella M. Christy, Principal.
No. 41—Cor. Armstrong and Rader (N. I.) Robert A. Smith, Principal.
No. 42—Cor. Wells and Rader (N. I.) Wm. M. Lewis, Principal.
No. 43—Mapleton. Alice O'Hair, Principal.
No. 44—Cerealine Works. Elizabeth Miller, Teacher.

SECRET AND BENEVOLENT ORGANIZATIONS.

MASONIC.

A. and A. Scotish Rite.
Indiana Sovereign Consistory—Jacob W. Smith, Commander-in-chief; Joseph W. Smith, Grand Sec.
Ancient Landmarks Lodge No. 319, F. and A. M.—Meets first Monday in each month in Masonic Temple. H. A. Sampsell, W. M.; Willis R. Miner, Sec.
Capital City Lodge No. 312—Meets first Tuesday of each month in Claypool blk. H. B. Fatout, W. M.; Thomas Oddy, Sec.
Center Lodge No. 23—Meets first Monday in each month in Claypool blk. C. C. Gilmore, W. M.; Albert Izor, Sec.
Grand Commandery K. T.—Meets third Wednesday of April.
Grand Lodge—Meets annually fourth Tuesday in May, hall southeast cor. Washington and Capitol av. Wm. H. Smythe, Grand Sec.
Indianapolis Chapter No. 5—Meets first Friday of each month in Claypool blk. Hugh J. Drummond, Sec.
Indianapolis Council No. 2—Meets in Masonic Temple. Henry Rebesberger, I. M.; Hugh J. Drummond, Recorder.
Keystone Chapter No. 6—Meets third Tuesday of each month in Masonic Temple. Hugh O. McVey, H. P.; J. W. Smith, Sec.
Logan Lodge No. 575—Meets first Monday of each month in Claypool blk. Hiram D. Harris, W. M.; John Schley, Sec.
Marion Lodge No. 35—Meets third Wednesday of each month in Masonic Temple. Jacob Watts, W. M.; H. J. Drummond, Sec.
Murat Temple, A. A. O. N. M. S.—Meets on Friday evenings. John T. Brush, Potentate; Joseph W. Smith, Recorder.
Mystic Tie Lodge No. 398—Meets second Monday of each month in Masonic Temple. Lewis E. Morrison, W. M.; Willis D. Engle, Sec.
Oriental Lodge No. 500—Meets cor. Central av. and St. Mary street. Albert T. Isensee, W. M.; Howard Kimball, Sec.
Pentalpha Lodge No. 564—Vestal W. Woodward, W. M.; Wm. H. Smythe, Sec. Meets first Thursday of each month in Masonic Temple.
Raper Commandery No. 1—Meets second Tuesday in each month in Masonic Temple. Wm. S. Rich, Eminent Commander; Wm. H. Smythe, Treas.; Jacob W. Smith, Recorder.

O. E. S.

Queen Esther Chapter No. 3—Mrs. Clara Holderman, W. M.; E. Nettie Ransford, Sec.; Masonic Temple.
Naomi Chapter No. 131—Mrs. Wilhelmina Brattain, W. M.; Aurelius Smith, Sec. Masonic Temple.

MASONIC (COLORED).

Central Lodge No. 1, F. and A. M.—Meets first Thursday of every month at northeast cor. Washington and Meridian. Jacob Porter, W. M.; Don Wells, Sec.
Waterford Lodge No. 13, F. and A. M.—Meets second Wednesday of every month at northeast cor. Washington and Meridian. Lawson Seaton, W. M.; Henry Terry, Sec.
Trinity Lodge No. 18, F. and A. M.—Meets first Wednesday of every month at northeast cor. Washington and Meridian. B. B. Biggins, W. M.; Thomas Bransford, Sec.

Cyrus Chapter No. 15, R. A. M.—Meets first Tuesday of every month at northeast cor. Washington and Meridian. A. J. Thompson, H. P.; Charles Chavis, Sec.

Zerubbabel Commandery No. 14, K. T.—Meets second Tuesday of every month at northeast cor. Washington and Meridian. Valuce Sanders, E. C.; Henry Moore, Recorder.

A. and A. Scotish Rite.

Constantine Consistory — Meets second Thursday in every month at northeast cor. Washington and Meridian. John J. Buckner, Commander-in-chief; Henry Moore, Sec.

Persian Temple, A. A. O. N. M. S.—Meets fourth Thursday in every month at northeast cor. Washington and Meridian. Henry Moore, Potentate; Wm. T. Floyd, Recorder.

O. E. S. (COLORED).

Union Chapter No. 1, O. E. S.—Meets first Monday of every month at northeast cor. Washington and Meridian. Roxabell Jones, R. M.; Etta Lewis, Sec.

Leah Chapter No. 2, O. E. S.—Meets second Monday in every month at northeast cor. Washington and Meridian. Fannie Lanier, R. M.; Jennie Lewis, Sec.

ODD FELLOWS.

Grand Lodge—Semi-annual Communication meets Wednesday following the third Tuesday in May. Annual Communication meets Wednesday following the third Tuesday in November. G. L. Reinhard, Grand Master; R. P. Davis, Deputy Grand Master; O. N. Cranor, Grand Warden; W. H. Leedy, Grand Sec.; James A. Wildman, Grand Treas. Odd Fellows' Hall.

Grand Encampment—Annual Communication meets the third Tuesday in November. J. E. Bodine, Grand Patriarch; J. I. McCoy, Grand High Priest; J. F. Mann, Grand Senior Warden; J. N. Nuzum, Junior Warden; W. H. Leedy, Grand Scribe; John Reynolds, Grand Treas.

Department Council Patriarchs Militant—Meets third Monday in November. J. E. Bodine, Pres.; Anderson McCrary, Clerk.

Samaritan Encampment No. 241 (West Indianapolis) — Meets second and fourth Monday. Edward H. Rose, Sec.

Metropolitan Encampment No. 5—Meets first and third Mondays in each month. George Rubush, Scribe.

Capitol Lodge No. 124—Meets every Friday evening in Grand Lodge bldg. Jacob W. Smith, Sec.

Mt. Jackson Encampment No. 231—Meets second and fourth Thursday. Samuel McBroom, Sec.

Center Lodge No. 18—Meets every Tuesday evening in Grand Lodge bldg. John H. Teckenbrock, Sec.

Germania Lodge No. 129—Meets every Thursday evening in Grand Lodge bldg. Henry Thoms, Sec.

Indianapolis Lodge No. 465—Meets every Friday evening at 467 Virginia av. H. J. Jacobson, Sec.

Meridian Lodge No. 480—Meets every Wednesday evening in Geizendanner Hall. H. C. Osborne, Sec.

Mozart Lodge No. 531—Meets every Friday evening at 27½ S. Delaware street. John Deitz, Sec.

Philoxenian Lodge No. 44—Meets every Wednesday evening in Grand Lodge bldg. Benjamin Franklin, Sec.

Puritan No. 678—Haughville. C. F. Childers, Sec. Meets every Friday.

Brightwood No. 655—Brightwood. W. Coldridge, Sec. Meets every Monday.

Samaritan No. 658—West Indianapolis. O. C. Chambers, Sec. Meets every Thursday.

Harris No. 644—Samuel McBroom, Sec. Meets every Monday at Mount Jackson.

Mapleton No. 690—Meets every Friday at Mapleton. Lewis G. Aiken, Sec.

Mapleton Encampment No. 209—Mapleton. L. G. Aiken, C. P.; Frank Jones, Sec. Meets second and fourth Monday.

Canton Indianapolis No. 2, P. M.—Meets every Thursday evening at Odd Fellows' Hall. Commander, J. E. Bodine; Lieutenant, Albert Lowes; Clerk, Edward Hoffer.

Canton Capital No. 42, P. M.—Meets every Tuesday evening, at 66½ E. Washington. Charles Westover, Clerk; E. L. Strong, Commandant.

REBEKAH DEGREE, I. O. O. F.

Olive Branch Lodge No. 10 D. of R.—Meets second and fourth Saturday evenings of each month at Grand Lodge Hall. S. O. Sharpe, Sec.

Indianapolis Lodge No. 520 D. of R.—Meets second and fourth Monday nights in Grand Lodge Hall. Jennie Condell, Sec., 27 Monument pl.

Fidelity Lodge No. 227 D. of R.—Meets every second and fourth Monday evening of each month at 467 Virginia av.

Myrtle Lodge No. 326 D. of R.—Mount Jackson.

Neolo Lodge No. 362 D. of R.—Brightwood.

Progress Lodge No. 395 D. of R.—Haughville.

Silvia Lodge No. 441 D. of R.—Mapleton, Ind.

West Indianapolis Lodge No. 418 D. of R.—Mrs. O. McGrew, Sec.

KNIGHTS OF PYTHIAS.

Grand Lodge of Indiana.

Headquarters, Rooms Talbott blk., northwest cor. Penn. and Market. Annual convocation first Tuesday in June. Frank Bowers, G. K. of R. S.

Marion Lodge No. 1—Meets Castle Hall, Talbott blk., every Wednesday evening. J. H. Moore, K. R. S.

Olive Branch No. 2—Meets Castle Hall, Talbott blk., every Saturday evening. A. H. Arbuckle, K. R. S.

Star Lodge No. 7—Meets Castle Hall, Talbott blk., every Tuesday evening. F. A. Blanchard, K. R. S.

Excelsior Lodge No. 25—Meets Castle Hall, Talbott blk., every Friday evening. W. W. Davy, K. R. S.

Indianapolis Lodge No. 56—Meets Castle Hall, Talbott blk., every Thursday evening. George T. Breunig, K. R. S.

Capitol City Lodge No. 97—Meets every Monday evening, 4½ E. Washington. W. S. Gordon, K. R. S.

Center Lodge No. 216—Meets I. O. O. F. bldg., Virginia av., every Tuesday evening. C. P. Balz, K. R. S.

Pythagoras Lodge No. 380—Meets every Monday evening in hall southwest cor. Mass. av. and Bellefontaine. Maurice Roche, K. R. S.

Damascus Lodge No. 384—Meets every Thursday evening in hall southwest cor. Illinois and 7th. W. D. Hoskins, K. R. S.

Arborvitae Lodge No. 318—Meets every Monday evening in Brightwood. George A. Sites, K. R. S.

Irvington Lodge No. 324—Meets every Friday evening. T. W. Wonnell, K. R. S.

West Indianapolis Lodge No. 244—Meets in Spencer Hall, West Indianapolis, every Wednesday evening. T. A. Schureman, K. R. S.

Arion Lodge No. 254—Meets in Haughville every Monday night. J. M. Brown, K. R. S.

General Relief Committee—Meets the first Thursday of each month in Castle Hall, Talbott blk.

UNIFORM RANK.

Headquarters Uniform Rank, K. of P.—James R. Carnahan, Major-General Commanding; Will J. McKee, A. G., Room 54 Journal bldg., northeast cor Market and Monument pl.

Indiana Brigade U. R. K. of P.—James R. Ross, Brig.-Gen. Commanding; Frank Bowers, A. A. G. Headquarters Journal bldg.

Indianapolis Division No. 2, U. R. K. of P.—Armory, Bricklayers' Hall. Meets every Friday evening. C. T. Bishop.

Excelsior Division No. 43.—Meets every Wednesday evening in armory, 121 E. Pearl.

Olive Branch Division No. 48—Meets every Thursday evening in armory, Court House.

Indiana Division No. 56—Meets every Friday in armory, Masonic Hall.

Pettibone Division No. 72—Meets every Friday evening in Spencer Hall, West Indianapolis.

RATHBONE SISTERS.

Grand Lodge Rathborne Sisters—Meets annually first Tuesday in June. Mabel Teague, G. M. of R. and C.

Myrtle Temple No. 7—Meets every Tuesday evening cor. Mass. av. and New York. Anna Kirkwood, M. E. C.; Hattie Ryder, Sec.

Brightwood Temple No. 79—Meets second and fourth Saturday evenings in Brightwood. Maggie Murray, Sec.

Banner Temple No. 37—Meets every Tuesday in Knights of Pythias Hall (W. I). Belle Salconbury, Sec.; Augusta Hagedon, M. of R. and C.

ANCIENT ORDER HIBERNIANS.

County Headquarters—S. w. cor. Georgia and Illinois sts. James McBride, C. P.; Jeremiah Kelly, C. S.; P. H. McNelis, C. T.

Division No. 1—Meets first and third Wednesday evenings of each month at Parnell Hall, 73 W. McCarty. Jeremiah Kelly, Sec.

Division No. 2—Meets S. w. cor. Illinois and Georgia first and third Monday evenings of each month. Thomas Brennan, Sec.

Division No. 3—Meets first and third Tuesdays of each month at 359½ Virginia av. Patrick J. Griffin, Sec.

Division No. 4—Meets first and third Thursday, Town Hall at Haughville. Jeremiah O'Connor, Sec.

Division No. 5—Meets cor. Rhode Island and Blake first and third Friday evenings of each month. Daniel O'Donnell, Sec.

ANCIENT ORDER OF UNITED WORKMEN.

Prospect Lodge No. 45—Meets Baldwin blk. Monday evenings.

BENEVOLENT PROTECTIVE ORDER OF ELKS.

Indianapolis Lodge No. 13—Meets in Elks' Hall, 112 N. Meridian, every Friday evening. H. S. Beissenherz, Sec.

GERMAN ORDER OF HARUGARI.

Hall, 27½ S. Delaware.

Harmonic Lodge No. 632—Meets every Tuesday evening. Carl Ziegler, Sec.

Hertha Lodge No. 43—Meets second and fourth Sundays of every month. Anna Pflueger, Sec.

Wodan Manie No. 42—Meets every Sunday. Carl Ziegler, Sec.

Schiller Lodge No. 381—Meets first and third Mondays of each month. Carl Waechter, Sec.

UNITED ANCIENT ORDER OF DRUIDS.

Hall, 124 E. Maryland.

Bos Chapter No. 5—Meets every first and third Sunday in each month, at 124 E. Maryland.

Capital City Grove No. 17—Meets at 41 N. Illinois every Thursday evening.

Germania Circle No. 1—Meets at 124 E. Maryland second and fourth Sundays of each month.

Humboldt Grove No. 8—Meets every Wednesday evening.

Mozart Grove No. 13—Meets every Tuesday evening.

Octavia Grove No. 3—Meets every Monday evening.

Washington S. A. Chapter No. 3—Meets every second and last Sunday in each month.

GRAND ARMY OF THE REPUBLIC.

Department Headquarters—Room 25 State House. Department Officers.

Department Commander—Henry M. Caylor, Post No. 133, Noblesville.

Sr. Vice Dept. Commander—Elmer Crockett, Post No. 8, South Bend.

Jr. Vice Dept. Commander—John E. Harrison, Post No. 59, Converse.

Medical Director—John H. Rerick, Post No. 104, Lagrange.

Chaplain—R. J. Parrett, Post 65, Frankfort.

Asst. Adjt.-General and Asst. Quartermaster General—R. M. Smock, Post No. 17, Indianapolis.

Department Inspector—C. J. McCole, Post No. 133, Noblesville.

Judge Advocate—C. M. Travis, Post No. 7, Crawfordsville.

Chief Mustering Officer—H. H. Woods, Post No. 77, Martinsville.

George H. Thomas Post No. 17—Meets first and third Tuesdays of each month at G. A. R. Hall, cor. Court and Delaware. C. S. Boynton, Commander; Wm. B. Downey, Adjutant; M. R. Smock, Quartermaster.

Martin R. Delaney Post No. 70—Meets first and third Thursdays of each month at Odd Fellows' Hall, Indiana av. Robert B. Bagby, Commander; Charles Brown, Adjutant; Henry Seaton, Quartermaster.

John F. Ruckle Post No. 165—Meets every Saturday evening, cor. Mass. av. and Bellefontaine. Thomas S. Lineger, Commander; John H. Kille, Adjutant; E. I. Saverage, Quartermaster.

George H. Chapman Post No. 209—Meets every Saturday evening in hall 66½ E. Washington. A. J. Buchanan, Commander; A. R. Seward, Adjutant; I. P. Tedrowe, Quartermaster.

Joseph R. Gordon Post No. 281—Meets every Wednesday evening at Odd Fellows' Hall, Virginia av., near McCarty. A. C. Staneart, Commander; John W. Scott, Adjutant; M. A. Daugherty, Quartermaster.

Major Robert Anderson Post No. 369—Meets Mansur Hall every Saturday night. Wm. H. Lester, Commander; Wm. H. Calvert, Adjutant; A. D. Miller, Quartermaster.

Phil H. Sheridan Post No. 539—Meets Mansur Hall second and fourth Friday every month. John C. Hamilton, Commander; James C. Slatery, Adjutant; C. S. Darnell, Quartermaster.

Alvin P. Hovey Post No. 559, West Indianapolis—Meets every Thursday evening at Spencer Hall, West Indianapolis. Abner D. Crull, Commander; Henry Hagerdorn, Quartermaster.

SONS OF THE AMERICAN REVOLUTION.

Headquarters—602 Lemcke bldg. S. B. Brown, M. D., Pres., Fort Wayne; Charles W. Moores, Sec.

DAUGHTERS OF THE AMERICAN REVOLUTION.

Chapter Regent—Mrs. Charles F. Sayles.
Caroline Scott Harrison Chapter—Mrs. E. S. Perkins, Sec.

WOMAN'S RELIEF CORPS.

National Headquarters—Room 41 When bldg. Mrs. Agnes Hitt, National Pres.; Mrs. Ida S. McBride, National Sec.
Major Robert Anderson Corps No. 44—Meets afternoon of first and third Mondays of each month at Mansur Hall. Mrs. Julia Tincher, Pres.
Phil H. Sheridan Corps No. 168—Meets Wednesday afternoons at Mansur Hall. Mrs. Louisa Byrkit, Pres.
George H. Chapman Corps No. 10—Meets Tuesdays at 60½ E. Washington. Mrs. Mollie Post, Pres.
Joseph R. Gordon Corps No. 43—Meets the first and third Wednesday afternoons of each month in Odd Fellows' Hall, Virginia av. Mrs. Dosia Dougherty, Pres.
John F. Ruckle Corps No. 40—Meets every Thursday afternoon at 2 o'clock in Bellefontaine Hall. Mrs. Laura Merritt, Pres.
George H. Thomas Corps No. 20—Meets afternoons first and third Tuesdays of each month at G. A. R. Hall, cor. Court and Delaware. Mrs. Margaret Sulgrove, Pres.
Martin R. Delaney Corps No. 118 (colored)—Meets at 184 Indiana av. Rosa Hamonds, Pres.
Alvin P. Hovey Corps No. 196—Meets second and fourth Wednesday afternoons of every month at G. A. R. Hall, West Indianapolis. Miss Augusta Hagedorn, Pres.

HEBREW SOCIETIES.

Independent Order B'nai Brith.

Abraham Lodge No. 58—Meets first and third Sunday evenings of each month in Hebrew Temple. I. N. Heims, Pres.; A. Weller, Treas.; Robert Stern, Sec.
Esther Lodge No. 323—Meets second and fourth Sunday evenings in each month at Americus Club Rooms. Isadore Feibleman, Pres.; Louis Efroymson, Sec.

Order Kesher Shal Barsel.

Indianapolis Lodge No. 149—Meets second and fourth Sunday afternoons at Hebrew Temple. Ed Ducas, Sec.

IMPROVED ORDER OF HEPTASOPHS.

Indianapolis Conclave No. 347—Meets first and third Wednesdays of each month in Iron Hall bldg. N. G. Smith, Archon; Bert A. Boyd, Sec.

IMPROVED ORDER OF RED MEN.

Hall in Griffith blk, 36½ W. Washington.
Great Council Improved Order of Red Men—Annual session third Tuesday in October. Charles R. McLeland, Madison, Ind., G. S.; Thomas G. Harrison, G. C. of R.
Comanche Tribe No. 128—Meets Tuesday nights in Red Men's Hall (W. I.) David Allen, C. of R.
Hiawatha Tribe No. 75—Meets every Tuesday evening in Red Men's Hall. R. E. Hopkins, C. of R.
Minnewa Tribe No. 38—Meets every Thursday evening in Red Men's Hall. Henry Wirtz, C. of R.; George Miller, S.
Newasa Tribe No. 190—Meets every Tuesday evening at Bellefontaine Hall. Frank G. Castor, C. of R.
Polmete Tribe No. 17 (German)—Meets every Monday evening at 124 E. Maryland. Herman Schlender, C. of R.
Red Cloud Tribe No. 18—Meets every Wednesday evening in Red Men's Hall. Edward Moriarty, Sachem, Wm. Buehrig, C. of R.
Tish-i-Mingo Tribe No. 210—Meets every Wednesday evening. S. A. Ogle, C. of R.
Wichita Tribe No. 139 (H.)—Meets every Wednesday evening in Red Men's Hall, Haughville. Charles F. White, C. of R.

D. OF P.

Great Council Degree of Pocahontas—60 Fletcher av. Hattie M. Hopkins, G. K. of R.
Alfarata Council No. 5—Meets first and third Friday night of each month at Red Men's Hall. Hattie M. Hopkins, K. of R.
Comanche Council No. 47—Meets every Friday night at K. P. Hall, West Indianapolis. Katie Tinsley, K. of R.
Kolola Council No. 70—Meets every Wednesday night, at I. O. O. F. Hall, West Indianapolis. Nellie Colvin, K. of R.
Mineola Council No. 31—Meets second and fourth Friday night of every month at Red Men's Hall. Mabel Teague, K. of R.
Winema Council No. 88—Meets every Saturday night at I. O. O. F. Hall, Brightwood. Daisy Partlow, K. of R.

UNITED ORDER GOLDEN CROSS.

Capital Commandery No. 466—Meets over 34 W. Washington second and fourth Monday evenings of each month. C. A. White, Noble Commander; Mrs. C. V. Bell, Keeper of Records.
Acme Commandery No. 537—Meets Wednesday nights at Flaskamp's Hall. E. A. Cole, N. C.; Mrs. Ellen M. Wimmer, K. of R. and S.
Star Commandery No. 586—Meets every Tuesday evening in Mansur Hall. George M. Duncan, Noble Commander; Jennie Matthews, Keeper of Records.
Independent Commandery No. 611—Meets every Thursday night at 361½ Virginia av. Ora Overhizer, K. of R. and S.

KNIGHTS AND LADIES OF HONOR.

Supreme Lodge Officers—Meets biennially second Tuesday in September. C. W. Harvey, Supreme Sec.; C. F. Dudley, Supreme Treas., 624 Lemcke bldg.
Grand Lodge of Indiana—Meets first Tuesday in October. George F. Lawrence, North Vernon, Ind., G. P.; A. S. Lane, G. S.
Compton Lodge No. 1137—Meets every Wednesday evening in Iron Hall bldg. Mary E. Weber, Sec.
Elizabeth Lodge No. 498 (German)—Meets every Friday evening at 124 E. Maryland. Charles G. Coulon, Sec.
Ethel Lodge No. 1936—Meets every Tuesday at Brightwood.
Garland Lodge No. 2010—Meets every Friday at cor. 8th and Hillside av. in Flaskamp's Hall. Jessie Prosser, Sec.
Hope Lodge No. 6—Meets Mansur Hall every Wednesday evening. Mrs. M. H. Greenwood, Sec.
Indianapolis Lodge No. 1900—Meets every Thursday at Moh's Hall. Wm. Trefz, Sec.
Martha Lodge No. 236 (German)—Meets every Tuesday evening in hall, 37½ S. Delaware. Adolph Wald, Sec.
Olive Branch No. 1868—Meets every Friday at New Hall. J. S. Thomas, Sec.
Phoenix Lodge No. 1337—Meets Van Sickle Hall every Tuesday evening. John E. Morris, Sec.
Washington Lodge No. 1352—Meets every Monday evening, cor. Senate av. and Vermont.
Pleasant Lodge No. 1338—Meets K. of H. Hall, Brightwood. A. L. Huff, Sec.
Gage Lodge No. 1163—Meets Mansur Hall second and fourth Mondays each month. Emma Boyd, Sec.

MILITARY ORDER LOYAL LEGION U. S.

Headquarters 41 When bldg. Commander Gen. Lew Wallace; Bvt. Col. Z. A. Smith, Recorder. Meets second Friday in February, May, October and December.

KNIGHTS OF THE ANCIENT ESSENIC ORDER.

Indianapolis Senate—Hugh S. Byrkit, Sec. Meets 66½ E. Washington Wednesday evenings.

KNIGHTS OF HONOR.

Supreme Lodge—Meets in May annually, next meeting in St. Louis, Mo. B. F. Nelson, Supreme Sec.
Grand Lodge—Meets the last Tuesday in February, biennially, Jeffersonville, Ind. J. W. Jacobs, Sec.
Eureka Lodge No. 24—Meets every Friday evening, 60 E. Market.
Germania Lodge No. 2634—Meets 27½ S. Delaware every Thursday. Albert Groenwoldt, Sec.
Schiller Lodge No. 40—Meets every Thursday evening, Druid Hall, E. Maryland. Gustav Thau, Pres.; Fred Weiffenbach, Sec.
Victoria Lodge No. 22—Meets every Monday evening, Red Men's Hall. H. T. Sinks, Dictator; J. W. Hosman, Reporter.

KNIGHTS OF THE MACCABEES.

Indianapolis Tent No. 35—Meets in Druid Hall, 39 N. Illinois, every Wednesday evening. C. W. Baird, Condr.; J. S. Dougherty, Record Keeper.

LADIES OF THE MACCABEES.

Indianapolis Hive No. 1—Meets every Tuesday afternoon in Iron Hall bldg. Frances Graham, L. C.; Norah Worden, L. R. K.

NATIONAL UNION.

Meridian Council No. 155—Meets first and third Friday of each month at Iron Hall bldg. C. J. Droege, Sec.; Charles E. Kershner, Treas.
Indianapolis R. R. Council No. 690—W. F. Goltra, Pres.; W. F. Fox, Rec. Sec.; H. L. Peck, Fin. Sec.; Ed. Graham, Treas. Meets second and fourth Friday nights in each month at Iron Hall bldg.
Hoosier Council No. 700—Ezra Eaton, Pres.; H. H. Hadley, Rec. Sec.; W. L. Hereth, Fin. Sec. Meets second and fourth Wednesday nights in each month at Iron Hall bldg.

CATHOLIC KNIGHTS OF AMERICA.

Branch No. 80—Meets at Sacred Heart Church first and third Monday every month.
Branch No. 563—Meets at St. Patrick's Hall second and fourth Sunday every month.

KNIGHTS OF FATHER MATHEW.

Bessonies Commandery No. 3—Meets every Sunday at 2 p. m. at n. e. cor. Georgia and Capitol av. J. V. Scanlan, C. S. K.

KNIGHTS OF ST. JOHN OF NORTH AMERICA.

Fourth District Commandery—Meets cor. Georgia and Capitol av. W. A. Kreber, Colonel; W. T. McHugh, Adjutant.
St. John's Commandery No. 175—Meets n. e. cor. Georgia and Capitol av. John F. Lavery, Sec.
St. Joseph's Commandery No. 191—Meets St. Joseph's Hall. John H. Reddington, Sec.
St. George's Commandery No. 192—Meets cor. Union and Palmer. Oscar Wuensch, Capt.
St. Francis De Sale's Commandery No. 273—Meets at Brightwood. P. S. Lavelle, Sec.

YOUNG MEN'S INSTITUTE.

Brownson Council No. 272—Meets at St. Joseph's Hall second and fourth Fridays of every month. J. H. Spellmire, Sec.
Weber Council No. 274—Meets at Wulf's Hall, West Indianapolis, John Britz, Sec.
Capitol Council No. 276—Meets at St. Patrick's Hall first and third Mondays of every month.
Wayne Council No. 288—Meets at Reading Room, Haughville; Anthony Gallagher, Sec.

INDEPENDENT ORDER OF FORESTERS.

Court Indianapolis 1820—Meets every fourth Friday night at northeast cor. Mass. av. and New York. Wm. M. Blythe, H. C. D.
Court Oak No. 1149—Meets at 36½ E. Washington.

ORDER OF CHOSEN FRIENDS.

Supreme Council—Meets third Monday in September, 1897. Office, 53 and 54 Commercial Club bldg.
Grand Council—Meets third Wednesday in March, 1897. E. A. Campbell, G. C.; W. S. Lockman, G. R. Office, 34 N. Delaware.
Alpha Council No. 1—Meets every Thursday evening in True Friends' Hall, southwest cor. New York and Alabama. R. L. Marrer, Councilor.
Crescent Council No. 8—Meets every Wednesday evening, southwest cor. New York and Alabama. W. A. Early, Sec., 1025 W. Washington.
Delta Council No. 2—Meets every Saturday evening in Equity Hall. John W. Byrkit, Sec., 11 Edwards (W I).
True Friend Council No. 23—Meets Tuesday evenings, southwest cor. New York and Alabama. A. Thompson, Councilor; Charles Jordan, Sec.
Union Council No. 15—Meets every Friday evening in K. of H. Hall, Brightwood. John Bradshaw, Sec., Brightwood.
Universal Council No. 28—Meets every Sunday afternoon at 3 o'clock, southwest cor. New York and Alabama. C. B. Feibleman, Councilor; M. Emden, Sec., 257 N. Liberty.
Venus Council No. 7—Meets every Tuesday evening at 62½ S. Illinois. F. H. Pillet, Sec., 55 Commercial Club bldg.

ORDER OF EQUITY.

Supreme Council.

Supreme Sec, Office, Suite 7, 156½ E. Washington street. Biennial session first Tuesday in October. Officers of the Supreme Council 1893-1897—Charles R. Jones, Supreme Councilor; Frank Bowers, Supreme V. C.; Wm. F. Lander, Supreme Sec.; Granville S. Wright, Supreme Treas.; James H. Taylor, M. D., Supreme Med. Dr.; J. H. Blair, Supreme Adjuster; Mrs. Emma J. Lander, Supreme Chaplain; J. H. Chamberlain, of Frankfort, Ind., Supreme Marshal; Mrs. A. B. Copeland, of Logansport, Supreme Guardian; E. A. Facer, of Chicago, Ill., Supreme Sentry.
Supreme Trustees — James C. Dickson, Chairman; Fred A. Lander, Sec., John Moore.
Committee on Laws and Supervision—Frank Bowers, George O. Lemming, Chicago, Ill.; Hon. J. B. Cheadle, Frankfort, Ind.
Committee on Finance and Accounts—Wm. A. Ball, Chicago, Ill.; J. H. Chamberlain, Frankfort, Ind.; J. A. Swartzel, M. D., Vincennes, Ind.

SUBORDINATE COUNCILS.

Officers elected annually in December.
Indianapolis Council No. 1—Meets second and fourth Monday evenings, 30 Monument pl. Fred A. Lander, Sec.
Equitas Council No. 2—Meets first and third Mondays. J. C. Ruckelhaus, Sec.

Taylor Council No. 3—Meets first and third Friday evenings at 30 Monument pl. J. H. Orndorff, Sec.
South Side Council No. 4—Meets first and third Mondays at 30 Monument pl. Earl Colden, Councilor; D. K. Partlow, Sec.; Charles R. Jones, Treas.
Hoosier Council No. 20.—Meets first and third Tuesdays in each month at 30 Monument pl. Mrs. Sarah M. Frank, Sec.

ORDER OF MIZPAH.

Supreme Lodge—11½ N. Meridian. Carlisle Gatewood, Supreme Sec.; T. B. Payton, Supreme Pres.; A. Alcorn, Supreme Treas. Meets every five years.
Oak Lodge No. 2—Meets every second and fourth Monday nights at Iron Hall bldg, Monument pl. J. W. Haughey, Sec.

ORDER OF GOLDEN CHAIN.

Hoosier Lodge No. 17—Meets second and fourth Wednesday evenings in each month at 110 English av. W. A. Rhodes, Commander; Milton H. Daniel, Sec. and Treas.

ORDER SONS OF ST. GEORGE.

Mayflower Lodge No. 324—Meets at 36½ E. Washington every Wednesday evening. Joseph Laycock, Pres.; Samuel Morgan, Sec.

PATRIOTIC ORDER SONS OF AMERICA.

Washington Camp No. 5—Meets every Friday evening, 92½ E. Washington.
Oriental League Supreme Council—Meets 88½ E. Washington.

ROYAL ARCANUM.

Grand Council—Meets first Thursday in April, 1897, at Indianapolis, Ind. J. F. Elder, Grand Regent, Richmond, Ind.; Edward E. Schroer, Grand Sec., 43 Thorpe blk., Indianapolis, Ind.; N. S. Byram, Grand Treas., Indianapolis, Ind.
Indiana Council No. 128—Meets every second and fourth Monday evenings each month in Griffith blk. E. H. Eldridge, Regent; J. A. Ehrensperger, Sec.
Indianapolis Council No. 328—Meets every second and fourth Tuesday evenings each month in Royal Arcanum Hall, cor. Illinois and 7th. Edward E. Schroer, Regent; A. B. Clark, Sec.
Hoosier Council No. 394—Meets every second and fourth Monday evenings each month in Royal Arcanum Hall, cor. Illinois and 7th. J. Burgess Brown, Regent; W. H. Webb, Sec.
Marion Council No. 399—Meets every second and fourth Friday evenings each month in Griffith blk. H. J. Craig, Regent; Frederick Poehler, Sec.

UNION VETERAN LEGION.

Encampment No. 80—Meets at G. A. R. Hall second Friday evening of each month. J. M. Paver, Colonel; W. B. Downey, Adjutant; A. D. Miller, Quartermaster.
Ladies Auxiliary—Meets at G. A. R. Hall second Friday afternoon of each month. Jennie Miller, Pres.; Lillie Gilbreath, Treas.; Emma Wilson, Sec.

Established 1879.

INDIANA

Boston School of Elocution AND Expression

OF INDIANAPOLIS.

MRS. HARRIET AUGUSTA PRUNK, Principal.

(Graduate of the Boston University School of Oratory, under the late Lewis B. Monroe.)

Elocution and Oratory Taught in all Branches of the Art, including the Delsarte System of Gesture and Dramatic Expression.
Instruction in Physical and Vocal Culture, Expressive Reading and Oratory. **Stammering and Defects of the Vocal Organs a specialty.** A Special Course intended for Teachers, Ministers and Law Students, in Bible, Oratorical and Shakesperean Studies. Essays revised. (Summer Term especially adapted to the wants of Teachers, Students and those unable to attend at other seasons of the year.)
Particular attention given in this school to the training of persons desirous of becoming **PUBLIC READERS** or **STUDENTS** of the **DRAMATIC ART.** Also **DIALECT** or **CHARACTER IMPERSONATIONS** and **THE ART of FENCING.** Pupils can enter at any time. BOSTON AND NEW YORK METHODS used and varied to suit individual needs. **DRAMATIC CLUBS** rehearsed and directed. For further information call on or address

368 W. New York St., Indianapolis, Ind.

Blake Street Cars Pass the School. Mrs. Harriet Augusta Prunk, Principal.

Additions, Removals, Etc.,

Received Too Late for Regular Insertion.

Aldrich Mary C, dancing academy, The Propylaeum, r 2 The Wyandot.
Allen David E, pres Ind Spoke Co and West Tenn Spoke and Lumber Co, 658 N Alabama, h same.
Allman Haman B, saloon, 67 Russell av, h 372 S Meridian.
AMERICAN BREWING CO, Joseph C Schaf Pres, Herman Habich Sec, Brewers and Bottlers, 175-197 W Ohio, Tel 935.
AMERICAN DETECTIVE AGENCY, Harry C Webster Genl Mngr, Rooms 12-15, 96½ E Market (Phoenix Blk). (See adv in classified Detective Agencies.)
Ansley Wm W, detective American Detective Agency, r 96½ E Market.
ARMSTRONG WM H & CO (Wm H Armstrong), Surgical Instrument Mnfrs, 77 S Illinois, Tel 928.
Aydelotte Wm M, lawyer, 504 Lemcke bldg, b 233 N Delaware.
Beebe Albert (Beebe & Brown), h 485 Central av.
Beebe & Brown (Albert Beebe. Gilbert H Brown), auctioneers, 132 Commercial Club bldg.
Biddle Wm S Rev, pastor California street M E Church, h 440 N California.
Blackshear John J Rev, pastor Corinthian Baptist Church, b 426 W Pratt.
Blair & Vazeille (Jesse H Blair, Etienne R Vazeille), lawyers, 112 Commercial Club bldg.
Booth John L, mngr Elite Cafe, 120-122 S Illinois, h same.
Bramwood John W, pub The Typographical Journal, 7 DeSoto blk, h 271 W Michigan.
Bridges Charles W, real est, 202 Lemcke bldg, h 442 Ash.
Brown Gilbert H (Beebe & Brown), h s e cor N New Jersey and 11th.
Bryan David C, investment banker, pres Union Construction Co and Indiana Land Co, 236 Lemcke bldg, h 18 W North.
Bullock Henry W, h 454 N California.
Bullock Jesse B, h 454 N California.
Callen Frank J, pub, 83 E Court, h 24 McKim av.
Carter Fletcher, architect, 427 Lemcke bldg, b 473 Central av.
Central Iron Works, Quincy, Ill, passenger and freight elevator mnfrs, James M Woods representative, 221-222 Lemcke bldg.
CENTRAL LOAN CO, Anson B Wiltse Mngr, Rooms 7-8 Talbott Blk.
Chapman Wm, jailer Marion County Jail, h 279 Douglass.
Clark Edmund D, phys, 22 E Ohio, and City Sanitarian, 10 Court House, h 401 N East.
Clarke Wm B, phys, 645 N Senate av, h same.
Coleman Henry, saloon, 723 N Senate av, h same.
Conlen Patrick, pawnbroker and jeweler, 14 Pembroke Arcade, h 246 Excelsior av.
Dedmon James E, phys, 327-329 The Shiel, h same.
Dreher Mathias, r 127 E Washington.
Edson Hanford A Rev, h 442 N Penn.
Elliott Larkin V, tel mnfr, 690 N Capitol av, h same.
Epworth League Headquarters, 19 Pembroke Arcade.
Falender Julius, saloon, 300 S Illinois, b 126 Maple.
Fitzgerald & Ruckelshaus (Frank N Fitzgerald, John C Ruckelshaus), lawyers, 37-40 Journal bldg.
Fox Oliver A, shoes, 68 E Washington, res Chicago, Ill.
Garver John J, phys, 14 W Ohio, h 888 N Penn.
Gee Harry F, trav agt Simmons Hardware Co, 83 Baldwin blk.
Habich Herman, sec American Brewing Co, h 269 N California.
Hannemann Albert, livery, rear 137 E Pratt, h 329 N Alabama.
Harger Frank D, sec Meridian Life and Trust Co, res Columbus, Ind.
Harrod Joel E, dressmkr, 9 Pembroke Arcade, h 14 Temple av.
Holtzman John W (Holtzman & Leathers), h 33 The Blacherne.
Imperial Savings and Loan Assn, 719 Lemcke bldg.
INDIANAPOLIS COLLECTING AND REPORTING AGENCY, John C Ruckelshaus Pres, Frank N Fitzgerald Sec and Treas, 39-40 Journal Building. (See adv opp p 485.)
Indiana Spoke Co, David E Allen pres, 658 N Alabama.
Jameson Walter (The Webb-Jameson Co), h 164 John.
Kelsey Preston, h 481 N Penn.
Lasby Charles C Rev, pastor Central Avenue M E Church, h 365 College av.
LITTLE FOLKS PUBLISHING CO, Charles A Suffrins Mngr, Publishers Little Folks, 5, 42 W Market.
McGroarty Cornelius, supt Marion County Workhouse.
McPherson Wm R, architect, 26 Warman av (H), b same.
Millner James W, restaurant, 35 E Market, h 95 W Vermont.
Pich Alfred, h 424 Union.
Prather Benjamin H, h 136 E North.
Suffrins Charles A, mngr Little Folks Publishing Co, h 36 Greer.
Swain George B, sign painter, 21 S Meridian, b Sherman House.
Sweetland Henry, transfer, 42 E Maryland, h 234 W 5th.
Taylor Charles P, dep U S Marshal, b 187 Broadway.
Tilton Harry W, salesman, h 139 N Meridian.
Stuart Romus F, lawyer, 202 Lemcke bldg, h 172 Huron.
Womack Mansfield F Rev, pastor Second Christian Church, b 220 W 4th.

R. L. POLK & CO.'S

Indianapolis City Directory.

1897.

ABBREVIATIONS

acct—accountant.
adv—advertisement.
agt—agent
al—alley.
asst—assistant.
assn—association.
av—avenue.
b—boards.
(B)—Brightwood.
blksmith—blacksmith.
bet—between.
bldg—building.
blk—block.
bkkpr—bookkeeper.
cabtmkr—cabinet maker.
carp—carpenter.
car rep—car repairer.
cashr—cashier.
civ engr—civil engineer.
clk—clerk.
collr—collector.
com mer—commission merchant.
confr—confectioner.
condr—conductor.
contr—contractor.
cor—corner.
(C R)—Clifton on the River.
dep—deputy.
dept—department.
e—east.
(E)—Emrichville.
engr—engineer.
e s—east side.
furngs—furnishings.
h—house.
(H)—Haughville.
(I)—Irvington.
Indpls—Indianapolis
ins—insurance.
insp—inspector.
lab—laborer.
la—lane.
lithog—lithographer.
mach—machinist.
mach hd—machine hand.
(M)—Mapleton.
(M J)—Mount Jackson.
(M P)—Marion Park.
mkr—maker.
mnfg—manufacturing.
mnfr—manufacturer.
mngr—manager.
Mass av—Massachusetts avenue.
(N I)—North Indianapolis.
n—north.
nr—near.
n e—northeast.
n s—north side.
n w—northwest.
opp—opposite.
opr—operator.
Penn—Pennsylvania
photog—photographer.
phys—physician.
pk—park.
pl—place.
plastr—plasterer.
P O—Postoffice.
pres—president.
prin—principal.
propr—proprietor.
pub—publisher.
r—rooms.
rd—road.
real est—real estate.
Rev—Reverend.
R M S—railway mail service.
(S)—Stratford.
(S I)—South Indianapolis.
solr—solicitor.
s—south.
s e—southeast.
s s—southside.
s w—southwest.
sec—secretary.
stenog—stenographer.
supt—superintendent.
tel—telegraph or telephone.
tmstr—teamster.
trav—traveling.
treas—treasurer.
uphlr—upholsterer.
vet surg—veterinary surgeon.
w—west.
(W)—Woodside.
(W I)—West Indianapolis.
(W P)—Woodruff Place.
whol—wholesale.
wid—widow.
w s—west side.

RAILROADS

C C C & St L Ry (Big Four)..................Cleveland, Cincinnati, Chicago & St. Louis
C H & D R R..................Cincinnati, Hamilton & Dayton
I C R R..................Illinois Central
I D & W Ry..................Indiana, Decatur & Western
I U Ry Co..................Indianapolis Union Railway Co
I & V Ry..................Indianapolis & Vincennes
J M & I R R (Penna Lines)..................Jeffersonville, Madison & Indianapolis
L E & W R R..................Lake Erie & Western
L N A & C Ry (Monon)..................Louisville, New Albany & Chicago
N P Ry Co..................Northern Pacific
Penna Lines..................Pennsylvania Lines
P & E Ry (Big Four)..................Peoria & Eastern
P C C & St L Ry (Pan Handle)..................Pittsburg, Cincinnati, Chicago & St. Louis
T H & I R R (Vandalia Line)..................Terre Haute & Indianapolis

For additions and removals, see opposite page.

Aaron Mark, trav agt, b Circle Park Hotel.
Abbett Archibald, h 282 S East.
Abbett Caroline (wid John B), h 553 Shelby.
Abbett Charles H, phys, 31½ Virginia av, h 82 W Vermont.
Abbett Ernest L, bill clk C C C & St L Ry, b 82 W Vermont.
Abbett Francis M, phys, 15½ Virginia av, r 227 The Shiel.
Abbett George W, clk, b 896 S Meridian.
Abbett John A, clk County Recorder, h 81 Woodburn av (W I).
Abbett John W, h 199 Bright.
Abbett Joseph S, tmstr, b 896 S Meridian.
Abbett Oliver H P Rev, h 277 S New Jersey.
Abbett Wm H, contr, 896 S Meridian, h same.
Abbitt Ora J, lab, b 368 W Maryland.
Abbitt Margaret M (wid Louis), h 368 W Maryland.
Abbitt Wm H, lab, b 368 W Maryland.
Abbott Adam, tmstr, b rear 117 Minerva.
Abbott Albert L, phys, 252 Bright, h same.
Abbott Alexis, lab, h 94 Bloomington.
Abbott Catherine E (wid Wm W), b 326 W 1st.
Abbott Delia (wid Wm F), h 298 W Maryland.

BUSINESS EDUCATION A NECESSITY.
TIME SHORT. DAY AND NIGHT SCHOOL.
SUCCESS CERTAIN AT THE PERMANENT, RELIABLE
Indianapolis BUSINESS UNIVERSITY

HENRY R. WORTHINGTON JET and SURFACE CONDENSERS 64 S. PENN. ST. Long Distance Telephone 284.

UNION CO-OPERATIVE LAUNDRY (COMPOSED OF UNION LAUNDRY GIRLS.) NOS. 38, 40 AND 42 VIRGINIA AVENUE. TELEPHONE 1269. INDIANAPOLIS, IND. T. E. SOMERVILLE, MANAGER

HORACE M. HADLEY
INSURANCE AND LOANS
66 E. Market Street, Basement
TELEPHONE 1540.

Abbott Diana (wid Isaac), b 50 Rhode Island.
Abbott Eli, carp, h e s Bradley 4 n of Ohio.
Abbott George, vault cleaner, h 171 S Alabama.
Abbott George L, b 702 Park.
Abbott Gertrude (wid Frank H), r 27½ Virginia.
Abbott James W, lab, h 575 W Michigan.
Abbott John, butcher, b 13 Sharpe.
Abbott John E, barber, h 473 Charles.
Abbott John W, foreman, h 33 Carson.
Abbott John W, lab, h 50 Rhode Island.
Abdon John, lab, b 57 Elm.
Abeck Catherina (wid Bernard), h 40 Arizona.
Abel, see also Apel and Ebel.
Abel Alexander, lab, h 344 W North.
Abel Alice (wid John), b 74 Dugdale.
Abel Edward W, molder, h 65 Smith.
Abel Frederick H, boilermkr, b 258 Lafayette av.
Abel Henry (Abel & Doyle), h 401 E New York.
Abel John T, barber, r 26 Grand Opera House blk.
Abel Mark M, clk, b 545 N Alabama.
Abel Wm, lab, h 142 Patterson.
ABEL & DOYLE (Henry Abel, Frank J Doyle), Tin, Copper and Sheet Iron Works; also Furnaces, 31 Indiana av. (See adv p 5.)
Aber Darius, lab, h 249 Alvord.
Aber Eva, dressmkr, b 249 Alvord.
Abercrombie Wm H, lab, b 11 Geneva.
Abernathey Almon, carp, h 81 W Walnut.
Abernathey Martha (wid Josiah), b 81 W Walnut.
Abernathey Richard, carp, h 141 N Alabama.
Abernathy Justus, plastr, 29 Palmer, h same.
Abernethy George, lab, h 200 W Ray.
Abner John V, painter, h 656 S Illinois.
Abney James W, stairbldr, h 29 Alvord.
Abraham Albert J, lab, b 181 English av.
Abraham August, lab, h 16 Arthur.
Abraham Henry, lab, h 16 Arthur.

COLLECTIONS
MERCHANTS' AND MANUFACTURERS' EXCHANGE
Will give you good service.
J. E. TAKKEN, Manager,
Union Building, over U. S. Pension Office.
73 West Maryland Street.

Abraham Herman L, h 181 English av.
Abraham John B (Abraham & Pein), h 887 N Senate av.
Abraham Wm, lab, h 12 Arizona.
ABRAHAM & PEIN, Propr North Side Laundry, 51-53 W 7th. (See adv in classified Laundries.)
Abrams Allen F, motorman, h 26 Byram pl.
Abrams Benjamin F, carp, h 464 W Eugene (N I).
Abrams Chester, porter, b 313 W North.
Abrams George, lab, b 27 Hosbrook.
Abrams John T, painter, b 437 N Senate av.
Abrams Lee, cook, r 18 S Senate av.
Abrams Lorenzo D, carp, h 437 N Senate av.
Abrams Max, tailor, h 15 Mulberry.
Abrams Milton, engr, h 91 Ash.
Abrams Nelson, lab, h 1476 Schurmann av (N I).
Abrams Perry A, blksmith, h 285 S Penn.
Abright Charles F, wagonmkr, 211 W Vermont, h 1100 N Meridian.
Abright Lena (wid August), h n s Grand View av, n end Germania av (H).
Abright Katherina, notions, 139 E Mkt House, h 1100 N Meridian.
Abromet Annie L, bkkpr State Life Ins Co, b 488 N Illinois.
Abromet Elizabeth (wid Adolphus) h 488 N Illinois.
Abromet John C, trav agt, b 488 N Illinois.
Abromet Lizzie C, bkkpr State Life Ins Co, b 488 N Illinois.
Abstine Israel, clothing, 239 E Washington, h same.
Abstome Wm, janitor, h 207 Alvord.
Achenbach Sadie C, dressmkr, 66 W New York, h same.
Achey Louis, lab, 327 W Market.
Achey Mary, h 327 W Market.
Achgill Andrew F, driver, h 165 Prospect.
Ackelow Herman, saloon, 269 Hadley av (W I), h same.
Acker, see also Aker.
Acker Joseph, brewer, h 72 High.
Acker Peter, painter, r 131½ E Washington.
Ackerman Frank, lab, b rear 512 S West.
Ackerman Frederick, salesman, h 726 N Capitol av.
Ackerman Howard U, trav agt, h 558 W 22d (N I).
Ackerman John J, printer, b rear 179 N California.
Ackerman Kate, h rear 512 S West.
Ackermann Andreas, h w s Belmont av 2 n of Morris (W I).
Acklin Samuel J, clk Stockton, Gillespie & Co, h 43 S McLain (W I).
Ackman Andrew, carp, b 125 E Washington.
Ackmann Charles W, clk Levey Bros, h 63 Wyoming.
Ackworth James H, fireman, h 27 N Station (B).
ACME CLOAK AND SUIT CO, H L Woelz Mngr, 6 Indiana av.
Acme Milling Co, Daniel C Robinson pres, Harvey Mullins sec and treas, 352 W Washington.
Acme Oil Co, Wm H Dye mngr, 401 Lemcke bldg.
ACME STEAM LAUNDRY, Mead & Adams Proprs, Office 13 N Illinois; Tel 696; Works s w cor 6th and C C C & St L Ry.

CLEMENS VONNEGUT 184, 186 and 192 E. Washington St. BUILDERS' HARDWARE, Building Paper. Duplex Joist Hangers

THE WM. H. BLOCK CO. DRY GOODS, DRAPERIES, RUGS, WINDOW SHADES.
7 AND 9 EAST WASHINGTON STREET.

Adail Elmer O, switchman, b 160 W Maryland.
Adair Charles A, condr, h 131 Yandes.
Adair Horace, barber, 216 W Washington, h same.
Adair Samuel S, carp, h 55 Columbia av.
Adair Wm, carp, h 75 Louise.
Adair Wm E, lab, h 333 Jackson.
Adair Wm S, condr, b w s Union 2 s of Washington (M J).
Adam Charles H, chief clk City Comptroller, h 326 Orange.
Adam Charlotte (wid Charles), b 85 Warren av (W I).
ADAM HERMAN F, Dealer in Fine Imported, Clear Havana and Domestic Cigars, Smokers' Articles, Etc, 15 N Illinois, h 345 Union.
ADAM LOUIS, Merchant Tailor, 17 Virginia av, h 260 S East.
Adam Louis G, trav agt, b 529 Ash.
Adam Philip, car rep, h 93 Decatur.
Adam Rachel H (wid Francis), b 681 N Capitol av.
Adam Wm A, clk, b 311 S East.
Adam Wm C, special police Merchants' Nat'l Bank, h 311 S East.
ADAMANT WALL PLASTER CO OF INDIANA, Alexander M Archer Pres, Martin T Ohr Vice-Pres, Harry M Ohr Sec and Treas, Charles G Root Genl Mngr, Office and Factory cor Phipps and J M & I R R; Tel 1512.
Adams Albert, driver, r 502½ E Washington.
Adams Alexander (Adams & Son), r 239 W Pearl.
Adams Alonzo G, actor, b 23 Ludlow av.
Adams Anna E (wid Wm D), h 52 Hosbrook.
Adams Benjamin, lab, r 154 N Belmont av (H).
Adams Bert B (Mead & Adams), gents furnishings, 13 N Illinois, h 765 N Alabama.
ADAMS BRICK CO THE (Capacity 50,000 per day), Justus C Adams Pres, Fred B Adams Sec, Robert Davis Supt, Office 2 Builders' Exchange, 35 E Ohio; Tel 535; Yards Le Grande av e of Shelby and Boyd and Finley av s e of Shelby pike; Tel 884.
Adams Charles, molder, h 182 S Judge Harding (W I).
Adams Charles O, lab, b 731 S East.
Adams Charles S, cooper, h 458½ W New York.
Adams Charles W, painter, b 7 Peru av.
Adams Clay F, saloon, 187 W 3d, h 160 Howard.
Adams Clifford C, lab, b 16 Haugh (H).
Adams Clyde A, hostler, b 222 E Court.
ADAMS C F CO, Edward E Wiley Mngr, Installment Goods, 93 N Illinois.
Adams David, lab, b 178½ Indiana av.
Adams Douglass, car rep, h 56 N Station (B).
Adams Edith, asst Public Library, b 211 Park av.
Adams Edward S, clk, b 40 Fletcher av.
Adams Eleanor E, teacher Public School No 25, b s s Bethel av 3 e of Zwingley.
Adams Eli S, molder, h 59 Sheffield (W I).
Adams Elizabeth B (wid Kneeland T), b 211 Park av.
Adams Estella A, teacher Public School No 6, b 98 Cypress.

Adams Ewing, lab, b s s Bethel av 3 e of Zwingley.
ADAMS EXPRESS CO, John J Henderson Agt, 25 S Meridian, Tel 101; and 147 S Meridian, Tel 332.
Adams Fay J, clk, b 16 Arch.
Adams Ferdinand L, broker, h 317 Ash.
Adams Foster T, butcher, b 26 N Station (B).
Adams Frank, clk The Adams Brick Co, h 58 Park av.
Adams Frank, printer, r 77½ S Illinois.
Adams Fred B, sec The Adams Brick Co, h 926 N New Jersey.
Adams George, fireman, h 23 Jefferson av.
Adams George, lab, b 20 Mill.
Adams George F (Adams & Williamson), h 148 E New York.
Adams George F, broommkr, b 16 Arch.
Adams George N, cupola tender, h 91 Minerva.
Adams George W, carp, h 731 S East.
Adams George W, cooper, h 458 W New York.
Adams George W, driver, h 21 Yandes.
Adams Hannah C (wid David M), b 1033 N New Jersey.
Adams Harry, lab, b 19 Oxford.
Adams Harry M, boilermkr, h 2 E Sutherland (B).
Adams Harvey A (J D Adams & Co), res Rockville, Ind.
ADAMS HENRY C, Propr St Paul Quarries and Agt Warren-Scharf Asphalt Paving Co, 6 Builders' Exchange; Tel 970, h 622 N Alabama.
Adams Henry C jr, clk, h 622 N Alabama.
Adams Henry C, b 160 Howard.
Adams Henry L, collr, h 16 Arch.
Adams Horace F, mngr, b 939 N Penn.
ADAMS H ALDEN, Physician (Eye, Ear and Nose), 21-23 W Ohio, h 211 Park av; Tel 731.
Adams Ira B, cabtmkr, h 633 W Eugene (N I).
Adams Isaac (Adams & Son), r 239 W Pearl.
Adams Isaac S, painter, h 101 N Noble.

GUIDO R. PRESSLER,
FRESCO PAINTER
Churches, Theaters, Public Buildings, Etc., A Specialty.
Residence, No. 325 North Liberty Street.
INDIANAPOLIS, IND.

INDIANAPOLIS STEEL ROOFING AND CORRUGATING WORKS, 23 and 25 East South Street. S. D. NOEL, Proprietor.

David S. McKernan, Rooms 2-5 Thorpe Block.
REAL ESTATE AND LOANS
Money to loan on real estate. Special inducements offered those having money to loan. It will pay you to investigate.

DIAMOND WALL PLASTER { Telephone 1410 BUILDERS' EXCHANGE.

Cor. E. Ohio St. and C., C., C. & St. L. R'y Tracks. BEST FACILITIES FOR STORING AND TRANSFERRING MACHINERY AND MERCHANDISE. UNION TRANSFER AND STORAGE CO.

W. McWORKMAN

FIRE SHUTTERS, FIRE DOORS, METAL CEILINGS.

930 W. Washington St. Tel. 1118.

Adams Isabelle N (wid Samuel), h 277 N Delaware.
Adams James, carp, b 35 E South.
Adams James B, mngr A M Eyster, h 602 N Senate av.
Adams James E, carp, h 68 W McCarty.
Adams James L, mach hd, h 520 W Addison (N I).
Adams James M, mach. h 56 Hazel.
Adams Jane, dressmkr, 267 N Noble, b same.
Adams Jasper H, woodcarver, h 631 W Eugene (N I).
Adams Jennie, h 126 N Missouri.
Adams Jesse N, b 277 N Delaware.
Adams John E, trav agt, b 7 Peru av.
Adams John H, lab, h 24 John.
Adams John J, lab, h 43 S Belmont av (W I).
Adams John M, gardener, h s s Bethel av 3 e of Zwingley.
Adams John Q (J Q Adams & Co), h 455 N Capitol av.
Adams John Q, lab, h 19 S Stuart (B).
Adams John T, engr, h 94 Oliver av (W I).
Adams Joseph, ins, 40½ Kentucky av, h 8 Wilcox.
Adams Joseph D (J D Adams & Co), h 1035 N Alabama.
ADAMS JOSEPH R, Painter, 177 Clinton, h 891 N Penn; Tel 909. (See adv in classified Painters.)
ADAMS JUSTUS C, Pres The Indpls Board of Trade and The Adams Brick Co, h 750 N Delaware; Tel 680.
ADAMS J D & CO (Joseph D and Harvey A Adams), Sewer Pipe, Stone Crushers, Road Graders and Iron Bridges, 30 Jackson Pl, opp north entrance to Union Station; Tel 487.
ADAMS J Q & CO (John Q Adams), House and Safe Movers, Office 26 Virginia av; Tel 1217; Yards 211 E Market. (See adv in classified House Movers.)
Adams J Will, lawyer, 76½ E Washington, b s s Bethel av 3 e of Zwingley.

GEO. J. MAYER, MANUFACTURER OF SEALS STENCILS, RUBBER STAMPS, CHECKS, BADGES, DOOR PLATES, ETC. 15 S. Meridian St., Ground Floor. TEL. 1386.

Adams Levi F (L F Adams & Co), b 317 Ash.
Adams Llewellyn, b 221 Hoyt av.
Adams Lou M, b 40 Fletcher av.
Adams L F & Co (Levi F Adams), com mer, 36 S Delaware.
Adams McClellan, boilermkr, h 2 Sutherland (B).
Adams Mack, hostler s w cor Washington and Ritter avs (I).
Adams Maggie E, dressmkr, 16 Haugh (H), h same.
Adams Margaret E (wid Byron F), h 98 Cypress.
Adams Marion, plastr, h 619 W 22d (N I).
Adams Martha J (wid Jesse J), h 31 Bismarck.
Adams Mary A, hairdresser, b 168 Agnes.
Adams Mary F, h 212 S William (W I).
Adams Mary F (wid Wesley M), h 40 Fletcher av.
Adams Mary M (wid Reuben), b 622 N Alabama.
Adams May, h 21 N East.
Adams Rachel J (wid Charles S), h 222 E Court.
Adams Robert B, embalmer D Kregelo & Son, h 361 N California.
Adams Robert H, solr N Y Life Ins Co, h 482 College av.
Adams Samuel, b 277 N Delaware.
Adams Sarah (wid Ira B), h 619 W 22d (N I).
Adams Sarah C (wid Stephen), h 7 Peru av.
Adams Thomas, agt, h 440 W Addison (N I).
Adams Thomas, lab, h 589 Virginia av.
Adams Thomas F, butcher, b 26 N Station (B).
Adams Thomas F, foreman John Scheid & Co, h 421 W 2d.
Adams Thomas J, clk Indpls Light and Power Co, h 146 N Illinois.
Adams Thomas J, engr, h 114 Dougherty.
Adams Viletta (wid Alexander), b 221 Bellefontaine.
Adams Walter A, lab, b 731 S East.
Adams Will H (Irvin & Adams), h 113 N Senate av.
Adams Willard, lab, h 391 Newman.
Adams Wm, lab, h 523 Mass av.
Adams Wm, lab, h 528 N Meridian.
Adams Wm, motorman, h 29 Tremont av (H).
Adams Wm B, driver, b 16 Arch.
Adams Wm C, cabtmkr, h 328 S State av.
Adams Wm E, cooper, h 19 Blake.
Adams Wm G, mach, h 19 Oxford.
Adams Wm L, r 300 E South.
Adams Wm L H, engr, h 322 Fletcher av.
Adams Wm T P, paparhanger, b 328 E Washington.
Adams Winnifred (wid Aaron), h 20 Mill.
Adams & Son (Alexander and Isaac), horsedealers, 239 W Pearl.
Adams & Williamson (George F Adams), veneer mnfrs, s e cor Clifford av and Bee Line Ry.
Adamson Dora, lab, b 359 S Illinois.
Adamson George, lab, b rear 233 Fayette.
Adamson John P, clk, b 500 N Alabama.
Addington John, brakeman, h 144 Cornell av.
Addington Warren B, lab, h 52 S California.
Addison James H, lab, h 17 Lafayette.
Addison Stanley L, dentist, 302½ N Senate av, r 28 Cincinnati.
Addison Wm A, trav agt Charles Mayer & Co, h 526 Park av.

A. METZGER AGENCY ESTABLISHED 1863. REAL ESTATE

LAMBERT GAS & GASOLINE ENGINE CO.
ANDERSON, IND. NATURAL GAS ENGINES.

Ade Wm F, lab, h 825 S East.
Adel John G, prin shorthand dept College of Commerce, h 559 Highland av (N I).
Adel Mildred C, dressmkr, 559 Highland av (N I), h same.
Adkins, see also Atkins.
Adkins Albert F, mach, b 45 Hoyt av.
Adkins Benjamin F, lab, h 437 W Addison (N I).
Adkins Clarence F, musician, h 437 W Addison (N I).
Adkins George M, switchman, b 548 Chestnut.
Adkins George W, carp, h 614 W Washington.
Adkins Ira, brakeman, r n e cor Jefferson and Frank.
Adkins James M, condr, h 45 Hoyt av.
Adkins Josiah, lab, b n s Pansy 1 w of Floral av.
Adkins Marcus G (Indiana Wall Paper Co), b 318 E McCarty.
Adkins Martin V, clk, h 84 Bright.
Adkins Riddle H, bkkpr Hollweg & Reese, h 437 Addison (N I).
Adkins Thomas A, jeweler Wm T Marcy, r 179 N Alabama.
Adkins Walter B, clk N Y Store, h 347 N Delaware.
Adkins Wm, carp, h 600 W Pearl.
Adkinson, see also Atkinson.
Adkinson Albert R, musician, b 472 N Alabama.
Adkinson Alonzo M, lab, b 81 Spann av.
Adkinson Eliza H (wid Wesley), h 616 Broadway.
Adkinson Herbert M (U S Artistic Co), b 616 Broadway.
Adkinson John M, carp, h 81 Spann av.
Adkinson Leonidas M, lineman, b 81 Spann av.
Adkinson Mary A, h 472 N Alabama.
Adkinson Omer E, barber, b 81 Spann av.
Adkinson Thomas, salesman, h 280 Indiana av.
Adkinson Wesley H, bkkpr, b 616 Broadway.
Adkinson Wm P, lawyer, 113½ E Washington, b 170 Maple.
Adkinson Winthrop R (U S Artistic Co), b 616 Broadway.
Adkisson Elizabeth W (wid John C), h 432 Cornell av.
Adler Catherine, h 760 Madison av.
Adler Julius, h 423 N New Jersey.
Adler Wolf (Gold & Adler), h 558 S Illinois.
Admire Allen, lab, h 162½ Indiana av.
Admire Ephraim E (Admire & McVeigh), r 85½ W Market.
Admire Henry, lab, b 162½ Indiana av.
Admire James, housemover, h 322 N Liberty.
Admire & McVeigh (Ephraim E Admire, Sherman McVeigh), business college, 1½ E Washington.
Adolay Edward A, ornamenter, b 475 S New Jersey.
Adolay Frank M, clk Indpls Brewing Co, b 475 S New Jersey.
Adolay Margaret J (wid Ernst E), h 475 S New Jersey.
Adolph Jacob S, plumber, 175 College av, h 213½ Christian av.
Adsit Jane M (wid Rev Samuel), h 861 N Meridian.
Advance Mnfg Co, furniture, n e cor Sheldon and Pike.
ADVANCE THRESHER CO, Michael H Snyder Genl Mngr, Office Room 3 Masonic Temple; Tel 1615.

THOS. C. DAY & CO.
INVESTING AGENTS,
TOWN AND FARM LOANS,
Rooms 325 to 330 Lemcke Bldg.

Aebker Charles, hostler, h 74 E Wilkins.
Aebker Christopher H, baker, 149 Prospect, h same.
Aebker Dietrich, mach hd, h 951 Madison av.
Aebker Henry C, lab, h 72 E Wilkins.
Aebker Herman W, cabtmkr, b 624 E Vermont.
Aebker Mary (wid Wm), h 624 E Vermont.
Aebker Richard W, sawyer, h 951 Madison av.
Aebker Wm, mach hd, b 72 E Wilkins.
Aebker Wm jr, lab, b 624 E Vermont.
Aetna Cabinet Co, Charles N Shockley pres, Victor H Rothley sec, furniture mnfrs, 168 W Georgia.
AETNA LIFE INSURANCE CO OF HARTFORD, CONN, R W Kempshall & Co Mngrs, James A Buchanan Special Agt, 214 Lemcke Bldg; Tel 1517.
AETNA LIFE INSURANCE CO OF HARTFORD, CONN (Accident Dept), Prather & Bangs Genl Agts for Indiana, Rooms 30-31 When Bldg.
AETNA SAVINGS AND LOAN ASSOCIATION, Howard Kimball Sec, 89 E Market; Tel 1494.
Aftung Anton, h 14 Deloss.
Agee Wm A, contr, n w cor Bismarck and Miller (W I), h same.
Ager George, mach, r 76 S Illinois.
Ager John, lab, b 73 Wheeler (B).
Aggart, see also Eckert and Eggert.
Aggart Ferdinand, lab, h 482 S Missouri.
Aggart Otto P, lab, b 482 S Missouri.
Agger Samuel, lab, b 275 N Noble.
Aggert Frederick W, checkman, h 67 Gresham.
Agnes Gideon, hostler, r 83 E Wabash.
Agnew Charles A, lab, b 358 Coburn.
Agnew Edward, lab, r 164 W Maryland.
Agnew John, lab, b 52½ S California.
AGNEW JOHN T, Saloon, 52 S Illinois, h 212 W South.
Agnew John W, lab, h 358 Coburn.
Agnew Will M, bkkpr The Capital Natl Bank, b 1157 N Illinois.

EAT
HITZ'S
CRACKERS
AND CAKES.
ASK YOUR GROCER FOR THEM.

BICYCLES $5 DOWN. MONTHLY. Best Wheels. Best Terms. WHEELMEN'S CO. 31 W. OHIO ST. LONG DISTANCE TEL. 1855.

J. H. TECKENBROCK General House Painter, 94 EAST SOUTH STREET.

Cutting

HAY & WILLITS MFG. CO.

76 N. Pennsylvania St. Phone 340.

C. ZIMMERMAN & SONS

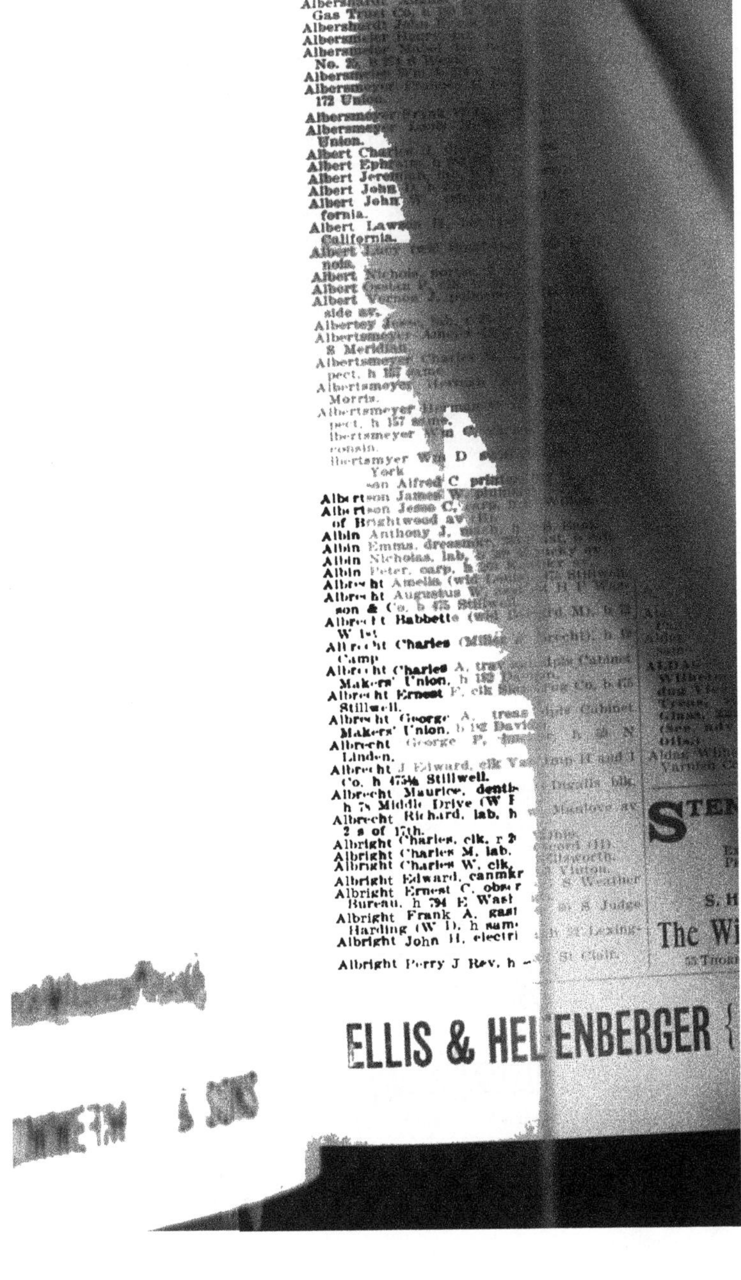

Albershardt
Gas Trust Co
Albershardt
Albersmeier
Albersmeier
No. 2
Albersmeyer
Albersmeyer
172 Union.
Albersmeyer
Albersmeyer
Union.
Albert Charles
Albert Ephraim
Albert Jeremiah
Albert John
Albert John
fornia.
Albert Lawson
California.
Albert Lucy
nois.
Albert Nichols
Albert Ossian
Albert Vernon J.
side av.
Albertey
Albertsmeyer
S Meridian.
Albertsmeyer Charles
pect, h 157 same.
Albertsmeyer
Morris.
Albertsmeyer Herman
pect, h 157 same.
lbertsmeyer Wm
consin.
lbertsmyer Wm D
York
son Alfred C
Albertson James W
Albertson Jesse C,
of Brightwood av
Albin Anthony J,
Albin Emma, dressmkr
Albin Nicholas, lab,
Albin Peter, carp, h
Albrecht Amelia (wid
Albrecht Augustus W
son & Co, h 475 Stillwell
Albrecht Babbette (wid
W 1st
Albrecht Charles (Miller & Albrecht), h
Camp
Albrecht Charles A, trav
Makers' Union, h 192 Dawson.
Albrecht Ernest F, clk
Stillwell.
Albrecht George A, treas
Makers' Union, b 192 Davidson
Albrecht George P,
Linden.
Albrecht J Edward, clk
Co, h 475½ Stillwell.
Albrecht Maurice, dentist
h 78 Middle Drive (W P
Albrecht Richard, lab, h
2 s of 17th.
Albright Charles, clk, r
Albright Charles M, lab,
Albright Charles W, clk,
Albright Edward, canmkr
Albright Ernest C, obser
Bureau, h 794 E Wash
Albright Frank A, gas
Harding (W I), h same
Albright John H, electri
Albright Perry J Rev, h

STE

S. H

The Wi

ELLIS & HELLENBERGER

FIDELITY MUTUAL LIFE—PHILADELPHIA, PA.
$75,000,000, Insurance In Force. $3,600,000, Death Losses Paid. $1,500,090, Surplus. A. H. COLLINS {General Agent, Baldwin Block.

Edwardsport Coal & Mining Co. ....BITUMINOUS COAL IN CAR LOADS TO DEALERS AND MANUFACTURERS. ROOMS 42 AND 43 WHEN BUILDING.

ESTABLISHED 1876. TELEPHONE 168.
CHESTER BRADFORD,
SOLICITOR OF PATENTS,
AND COUNSEL IN PATENT CAUSES.
(See adv. page 6.)
Office:—Rooms 14 and 16 Hubbard Block, S. W. Cor. Washington and Meridian Streets, INDIANAPOLIS, INDIANA.

Agricultural Epitomist, Epitomist Publishing Co pubs, 21½ W Washington.
Ahern Christina M (wid Christian), b 813 N Capitol av.
Ahern James, engr, h 45 Jefferson av.
Ahern John F, blksmith, h 60 Warren av (W I).
Ahern Michael, lab, h 532 S Illinois.
Ahern Wm, b 640 College av.
Ahern Wm D, millwright, h 407 W Udell (N I).
Ahlbrand Martin H, blksmith, h 12 Union.
Ahlders Ahlrich, notions, 539 S Meridian, h same.
Ahlders Albert A, clk, b 539 S Meridian.
Ahlders Bernard, bicycle rep, 539 S Meridian, b same.
Ahle Charles H, cashr The Bates, h 125 W North.
Ahlers Louis, carp, h 86 Chadwick.
Ahnefeld Edward W, uphlr, b 49 Jefferson.
Ahnefeld Wm, cabinetmkr, b 664 Chestnut.
Aholtz Everett, cook, r 230 N Senate av.
Ahrens, see also Arens.
Ahrens Charles N, mach hd, b 155 Eureka av.
Ahrens Christopher, tmstr, h 437 N Pine.
Ahrens Wm Rev, h 155 Eureka av.
Ahrens Wm M H, mach, h 61 Eureka av.
Aich, see also Eich.
Aich Wm, lab, h 456 E Washington.
Aichele, see also Eichel.
Aichele Charles A, painter, h 543 Madison av.
Aichele Charles G, clk U S Pension Agency, b 152 N Illinois.
Aichele Emil, baggageman, h 127 Palmer.
Aichele Eugene L, lab, b 448 Chestnut.
Aichele Henry D, packer, b 44 Dunlop.
Aichele Julius, brakeman, h 29 Haugh (H).
Aichele Otto, lab, h 44 Dunlop.
Aichele Wilhelmina (wid Emil E), h 448 Chestnut.
Aichhorn Christian H, mach, b 339 E Morris.
Aichhorn Frederick A, molder, b 339 E Morris.
Aichhorn Louis S, ironwkr, h 127 Cottage av.

Outing BICYCLES
..MADE BY..
HAY & WILLITS MFG CO.
76 N. Pennsylvania St. Phone 598.

Aichhorn Michael, patternmkr, b 339 E Morris.
Aichhorn Otto, mach, b 339 E Morris.
Aichhorn Sophia D (wid Wm), h 339 E Morris.
Aichhorn Wm, baker Insane Hospital, h 24 Haugh (H).
Aichinger Harley J, lab, h 19 Brett.
Aiken, see also Akin.
Aiken Daniel, boxmkr, h 958 Wilcox.
Aiken Lewis C, dep County Assessor, 35 Court House, h 1800 N Illinois.
Aiken Milton A, boxmkr, h 70 Germania (H).
Aikin George W, h 289 Davidson.
Aikin Homer L, collr, h 287 Davidson.
AIKINS BRONTE M, Attorney at Law, 425-426 Lemcke Bldg, h 12 The Blacherne; Tel 1847.
Aikman Samuel S Rev, evangelist, h 721 College av.
Aikman Wm H, trav agt Diamond Wall Plaster Co, h 71 Adams.
Ailiff Loury, tmstr, h 309 N West.
Ainsworth Charles L, trav agt, r 50 Hendricks blk.
Ainsworth Frank B, ins agt, 35 Talbott blk, r same.
Ainsworth Helen A, h 53 Hendricks blk.
Aippersbach John C, stonecutter, h 9 Margaret.
Aippersbach Wm, stonecutter, b 9 Margaret.
Aird John, tailor, h 68½ Mass av.
Aisenbrey Charles W, meats, 25 Virginia av, h n e cor Raymond and Ransdell.
Aitken David L, mach, h 70 Cornell av.
Aitken Elizabeth, h 456 W 1st.
Aitken James W, boilermkr, h 856 E Washington.
Akass Edward T A, clk L S Ayres & Co, h 1110 N Meridian.
Aker, see also Acker.
Aker Alice (wid J Theodore), h 609 W Pearl.
Aker Charlotte E (wid Ellis L), h 156 Elm.
Aker Lewis E, bookbndr, h 142 Elm.
Aker Lillie (wid Luther), b 176 Elm.
Aker Martin L, clk, b 156 Elm.
Akers Bettie C, stenog, b 325 N Illinois.
Akers David P, yardmaster, h 49 S Reisner (W I).
Akers Francis E, bricklyr, h 992 Cornell av.
Akers Peter C, clk R M S, h 372 Talbott av.
Akes James J, cooper, h 249 S West.
Akin, see also Aiken.
Akin Asbury R, collr, b 104 S Belmont av (W I).
Akin Frederick B, clk, b 1850 N Illinois.
Akin Lewis G, h 1850 N Illinois.
Akin Murry, lab, h 104 S Belmont av (W I).
Akin Wm B, b 28 Ft Wayne av.
Akins David, lab, h 35 Church.
Akins Oliver L, train desp I D & W Ry, h 136 E St Clair.
Akins Wm N, h 136 E St Clair.
Albee Wm, foreman Knight & Jillson, r 237 Mass av.
Alber Charles L, engr, h 415 W New York.
Alber Edward E, cigarmkr, h 87 S Liberty.
Alber Noah T, hackman, r 171 W Market.
Alber Thaddeus C, cigarmkr, b 87 S Liberty.
Albers Charles H, lab, h e s Rural 3 s of Sutherland (B).
Albers Sina L, tailoress, b 141 Woodlawn av.
Albershardt Anna L, b 326 E Vermont.

C. ZIMMERMAN & SONS | SLATE AND GRAVEL ROOFERS 19 South East Street.

DRIVEN WELLS And Second Water Wells and Pumps of all kinds at CHARLES KRAUSS', 42 S. PENN. ST., Telephone 465.

ERT ELSTEAM LAUNDRY 26 and 28 N. Senate Avenue. WE WILL CALL FOR AND DELIVER YOUR WORK. SATISFACTION GUARANTEED.

Albershardt August H, clk Consumers' Gas Trust Co, h 180 N Noble.
Albershardt John F, clk, h 271 N Liberty.
Albersmeier Henry, lab, h 274 S West.
Albersmeier Mabel, teacher Public School No. 25, b 274 S West.
Albersmeier Wm, b 274 S West.
Albersmeyer Frances M (wid Daniel J), h 172 Union.
Albersmeyer Frank W H, carp, b 172 Union.
Albersmeyer Louis H W, finisher, b 172 Union.
Albert Charles H, filer, h 255 Bates.
Albert Ephraim, h 382 Blake.
Albert Jeremiah, lab, h 209 W Merrill.
Albert John D, b 255 Bates.
Albert John W, trimmer, b 341 N California.
Albert Lawson H, baggageman, h 349 N California.
Albert Lucy (wid Singleton), h 169 N Illinois.
Albert Nichols, porter, h 58 John.
Albert Ossian P, clk, b 382 Blake.
Albert Vernon J, policeman, h 162 Brookside av.
Albertey Jesse, lab, r 23 N West.
Albertsmeyer Amelia (wid Charles), h 593 S Meridian.
Albertsmeyer Charles H, saloon, 155 Prospect, h 157 same.
Albertsmeyer Herman A, lab, b 341 E Morris.
Albertsmeyer Herman C, barber, 153 Prospect, h 157 same.
Albertsmeyer Wm C, varnisher, b 8 Wisconsin.
Albertsmyer Wm D, switchman, h 1072 W New York.
Albertson Alfred C, printer, h 552 E Ohio.
Albertson James W, plumber, b 552 E Ohio.
Albertson Jesse C, carp, h n s Willow 2 w of Brightwood av (B).
Albin Anthony J, mach, h 380 S East.
Albin Emma, dressmkr, 380 S East, b same.
Albin Nicholas, lab, b 269 Kentucky av.
Albin Peter, carp, h 269 Kentucky av.
Albrecht Amelia (wid Louis), h 475 Stillwell.
Albrecht Augustus W, asst supt H P Wasson & Co, b 475 Stillwell.
Albrecht Babbette (wid Bernhard M), b 72 W 1st.
Albrecht Charles (Miller & Albrecht), h 19 Camp.
Albrecht Charles A, trav agt Indpls Cabinet Makers' Union, h 182 Davidson.
Albrecht Ernest F, clk Sloan Drug Co, b 475 Stillwell.
Albrecht George A, treas Indpls Cabinet Makers' Union, b 182 Davidson.
Albrecht George P, huckster, h 59 N Linden.
Albrecht J Edward, clk Van Camp H and I Co, h 475½ Stillwell.
Albrecht Maurice, dentist, 61 Ingalls blk, h 78 Middle Drive (W P).
Albrecht Richard, lab, h w s Manlove av 2 s of 17th.
Albright Charles, clk, r 209 W Ohio.
Albright Charles M, lab, b Concord (H).
Albright Charles W, clk, h 15 Ellsworth.
Albright Edward, canmkr, h 23 Vinton.
Albright Ernest C, observer U S Weather Bureau, b 794 E Washington.
Albright Frank A, gasfitter, 60 S Judge Harding (W I), h same.
Albright John H, electrician, h 52 Lexington av.
Albright Perry J Rev, h 258 W St Clair.

EQUITABLE LIFE ASSURANCE SOCIETY OF THE UNITED STATES,
RICHARDSON & McCREA
Managers for Central Indiana,
79 East Market St. Telephone 182.

Albright Robert B, painter, h 262 W Michigan.
Albright Wm A, lab, h 10 Warman av (H).
Albritton Wm, lab, h 2 Peck.
Albro Frank T, candymkr, h 492 W New York.
Albro Henry O, b 492 W New York.
Albro Lorena S (wid Orville H), b 871 N Alabama.
ALCAZAR, Cigars and Tobaccos, Confectionery, Floral and Tonsorial Depts, Soda Dispensary, 30 W Washington; Tel 19.
Alcon Albert, agt, r 11½ N Meridian.
Alcon Caroline A, h 213 Ramsey av.
Alcon Charles, stenog Morris, Newberger & Curtis, b 213 Ramsey av.
Alcon Otto W, lab, b 213 Ramsey av.
Alcon Watson W, condr, b 213 Ramsey av.
Alcorn Charles, mach hd, b 541 Shelby.
Alcorn Charles C, cooper, b 175 Michigan av.
Alcorn Frank L, cooper, b 175 Michigan av.
Alcorn James, lab, b 56 High.
Alcorn Walter E, cooper, b 175 Michigan av.
Alcorn Wm, cooper, h 175 Michigan av.
Aldag August, h 583 E Washington.
Aldag Charles, h 644 E Washington.
Aldag Charles M, vice-pres The Aldag Paint and Varnish Co, b 583 E Washington.
Aldag Frank O, h 655 E Market.
Aldag Harry W, asst teller Merchants' Nat'l Bank, b 583 E Washington.
Aldag John E, sec and treas The Aldag Paint and Varnish Co, h 59 N Arsenal av.
Aldag Louis, shoes, 679 E Washington, h same.
ALDAG PAINT AND VARNISH CO THE, Wilhelm Aldag Pres, Charles M Aldag Vice-Pres, John E Aldag Sec and Treas, Paints, Oils, Varnish and Glass, 222 E Washington; Tel 334. (See adv in classified Paints and Oils.)
Aldag Wilhelm, pres The Aldag Paint and Varnish Co, h 456 E Market.

STENOGRAPHERS FURNISHED.
EXPERIENCED OR BEGINNERS, PERMANENT OR TEMPORARY.
S. H. EAST, State Agent,
The Williams Typewriter,
55 THORPE BLOCK, 87 EAST MARKET ST.

ELLIS & HELFENBERGER { ENTERPRISE FOUNDRY & FENCE CO. 162-170 S. Senate Ave. Tel. 958.

THE HOGAN TRANSFER AND STORAGE COMP'Y
Household Goods and Pianos Moved—Packed—Stored...... Baggage and Package Express Machinery and Safes a Specialty Cor. Washington and Illinois Sts. TELEPHONE No. 675.

Hose, Belting, Packing, Clothing, Druggists' Sundries, Bicycle Tires, Cotton Hose, Etc. New York Belting & Packing Co., L't'd.

THE CENTRAL RUBBER & SUP LY CO. PHONE 922. 79 S. ILLINOIS ST., INDIANAPOLIS, IND.

A death rate below all other American Companies, and dividends from this source correspondingly larger.
The Provident Life and Trust Company
Of Philadelphia.
D. W. EDWARDS, General Agent,
508 Indiana Trust Building.

Alden Herman L, clk, b 322 N New Jersey.
Alder John E, lab, b 231 Hadley av (W I).
Alderson Dora, clk, b 880 N Senate av.
Alderson George W, lab, h 546 W Washington.
Alderson James W, barber, 338 S West, h same.
Alderson Lafayette, lab, h 538 W Washington.
Alderson Moses S, lab, h 536 W Washington.
Alderson Phoebe, h n s 8th 2 n of canal.
Alderson Sarah J (wid Amos), h 880 N Senate av.
Alderson Thomas M, lab, b 546 W Washington.
Aldred Frederick H, saloon, 38 W Market, r 81½ same.
Aldred Reuben R, janitor Public School No 17, h n s 2d 1 w of West.
Aldrich Albert J, clk Penna Lines, h 1115 E Michigan.
Aldrich Charles O, painter, h 103 John.
Aldrich David E, trav agt, h 127 Talbott av.
Aldrich Frank, livery, 277 W Washington, h 426 Douglass.
Aldrich James F, city fireman, b 20 Orange av.
Aldrich John D, clk, h 189 College av.
Aldrich Joshua H, loans, 25 Thorpe blk, r 342 N Illinois.
Aldrich Mary C, clk, r 2 Wyandot blk.
Aldrich Royal, b 187 College av.
Aldridge, see also Eldridge.
Aldridge Benjamin, b 17 Cherry.
Aldridge Henry H, ins agt, b 17 Cherry.
Aldridge Hester A (wid Marcellus B), h 67 Clifford av.
Aldridge Jacob B, b 17 Cherry.
Aldridge John L, cigarmkr, b 17 Cherry.
Aldridge Joseph A, trav agt, b 17 Cherry.
Aldridge Melvina H (wid Worden A), b 81 N Capitol av.
Aldridge Oliver O, barber, b 274 W Washington.
Aldridge Sarah C, h 25½ Mass av.
Aldridge Susannah (wid Henry H), h 17 Cherry.

Julius C. Walk & Son,
Jewelers
Indianapolis.
12 EAST WASHINGTON ST.

Aldridge Winfield S, city agt, b 67 Clifford av.
Aleg Nicholas E, lab, h 29 Downey.
Alerding Bernard H, porter, h 75 High.
ALERDING HERMAN J REV, Rector St Joseph's Church, h 323 E North.
Alerding Leo, porter, b 75 High.
Alestock Walter, lab, h 297 E Court.
Alexander Albert M, cutter, b 291 S New Jersey.
Alexander Alexander, driver, h 91 Geisendorff.
Alexander Alexander, lab, h 445 W 1st.
Alexander Alice C, teacher Public School No 39, b 318 E Washington.
Alexander Carrie (wid Philip), dressmkr, 25½ W Washington, h 1096 N Penn.
Alexander Catherine, h 236 Clinton.
Alexander Charles, lab, h rear 138 E St Joseph.
Alexander Charles C, ironwkr, h 45 Bradshaw.
Alexander Coke, dist pass agt Mo Pac Ry, 7 Jackson pl, h 129 E St Joseph.
Alexander Cora M, stenog, b 399 N Penn.
Alexander David S W, lab, b 323 N California.
Alexander Earl, pressman, b 27 N New Jersey.
Alexander Elbridge G, tel opr C C C & St L Ry, h 733 N Illinois.
Alexander Emma B (wid James C), b 124 Butler.
Alexander Frank, lab, h 86 Yandes.
Alexander Fred W (Alexander & Co), sec Union Ins Co, b 785 N Illinois.
Alexander Frederick, porter, b 236 Clinton.
Alexander Frederick W, uphlr, h 286 Yandes.
Alexander George, porter, b 293 Indiana av.
Alexander George H, lab, h rear 626 Home av.
Alexander George M, clk, h 184 Hoyt av.
Alexander George W, trav agt, h 405 N Penn.
Alexander Georgia A, prin Public School No 8, b 405 N Penn.
Alexander Grace R, reporter, b 405 N Penn.
Alexander Harry, lab, r 19 Cincinnati.
Alexander Isadore, atttendant Insane Asylum.
Alexander James, farmer, b n s Wolf pike 1 e of School (B).
Alexander James, house cleaner, h 309 E Court.
Alexander James, janitor, b 26½ Chapel.
Alexander James, lab, h 28 Hadley.
Alexander James L, stair bldr, h 335 Cornell av.
Alexander James T, phys, 175½ Shelby, h 328 same.
Alexander Jefferson L, tmstr, h 10 Quince.
Alexander John, coachman 163 Central av.
Alexander John, lab, h 77 Nebraska.
Alexander John B, engr, b 159 N Pine.
Alexander John J, carp, h 429 W Eugene (N I).
Alexander John R, lab, h 166 Yandes.
Alexander John W, cabtmkr, b 291 S New Jersey.
Alexander Joseph, lab, h 576 S Meridian.
Alexander Joseph, lab, h 241 Orange.
Alexander Joseph A, mach hd, h 120 Ramsey av.
ALEXANDER JOSEPH C, Physician and Surgeon; Office Hours 9-10 A M, 1-3 and 7-8 P M, 123 S Noble; Tel 1071, h 146 Bates.

OTTO GAS ENGINES | BUILDERS' EXCHANGE S. W. Cor. Ohio and Penn. Telephone 535.

Becker & Son Charles Becker Jacob Becker Jr. Merchant Tailors. 21 N. Penn. St. Tel. 934

SALISBURY & STANLEY O HIDE, STORE AND BANK FIXTURES. Contractors and Builders. Repairing of all kinds done on short notice. 177 Clinton St., Indianapolis, Ind. Telephone 999.

Alexander Joseph G, driver, h 43 Barth av.
Alexander Joseph H, h 333 W Michigan (H).
Alexander Joseph L, lab, h rear 18 Bismarck.
Alexander Julia, h 28 Chapel.
Alexander Laura A, bkkpr, b 74 Lexington av.
Alexander Laura B, teacher Public School No. 8, h 184 Hoyt av.
Alexander Lawson, painter, h 180 Colburn.
Alexander Lillian M, h 313½ Mass av.
Alexander Martha (wid Stephen), b rear 234 W New York.
Alexander Mary A (wid Joseph), h 74 Lexington av.
Alexander Matthias, lab, b 183 Indiana av.
Alexander May J (wid James), r 116½ W New York.
Alexander Milton K, bkkpr, h 124 Butler.
Alexander Mitchel, cigarmkr, b 208 N Pine.
Alexander Norton E (Alexander & Co), h 785 N Illinois.
Alexander Oscar, mer police, b 180 Coburn.
Alexander Rhoda (wid Green), b 241 Orange.
Alexander Richard, lab, b 50 W 12th.
Alexander Robert, agt, h 61 Hosbrook.
Alexander Robert, dairy, n s Wolf pike 1 e of School (B), h same.
Alexander Robert, lab, h 166 Yandes.
Alexander Robert G, porter, h 320 W Court.
Alexander Robert P, clk C P Lesh Paper Co, r 86 N Senate av.
Alexander Rosanna E, b 164 Newman.
Alexander Safe A, lab, b 174 Bismarck av (H).
Alexander Samuel, lab, b 166 Yandes.
Alexander Samuel B, cabtmkr, h 40 Stevens.
Alexander Samuel M, tmstr, b 10 Quince.
Alexander Stephen, engr, r 323 N California.
Alexander Tubal, lab, b 1398 N Capitol av.
Alexander Wm, lab, r 197 N Missouri.
Alexander Wm F, tinner, h 212 River av (W I).
Alexander Wm H, grocer, 451 W 1st, h 453 W Pratt.
Alexander Wm P, painter, b 518 Udell (N I).
Alexander & Co (Norton E and Fred W Alexander), ins, 423 Lemcke bldg.
Alford Ambrose A, cigars, 21 S Meridian, h 491 Ash.
Alford Cora J (wid Sigel), h 29 Standard av (W I).
Alford Fremont (Alford & Partlow), h 424 Clifford av.
Alford Leland B, mach, h 51 Virginia av.
Alford Lurana E (wid Melvin Z), h 151 Virginia av.
Alford Tabitha (wid James R), b 1202 Morris (W I).
Alford Thomas A, clk A Kiefer Drug Co, b 162 N Illinois.
Alford Thomas G, salesman M O'Connor & Co, h 222 N Delaware.
Alford & Partlow (Fremont Alford, David K Partlow), lawyers, 37 Baldwin blk.
Alforth Henry P, cook, h 349 S East.
Alfreds Mortimer J, cementwkr, h 35 St Peter.
Algeo Amy B, teacher Public School No 33, b 130 Brookside av.
Algeo John, clk, h 306 Clifford av.
Algeo Robert P, clk C H & D R R, b 306 Clifford av.
Algeo Samuel, grocer, 49 Clifford av, h 130 Brookside av.
Alger Joseph, brakeman, h 7 Lynn.
Alhand John A, lab, h 125 River av (W I).
Alhand John L, b 345 S Olive.

Henry H. Fay, 40½ E. Washington St., REAL ESTATE, AND LOAN BROKER.

Alhand Mary (wid Lack), h 31 McCauley.
Alig George, pres The Home Stove Co, h 430 N New Jersey.
Alisch Emilie, teacher German Public School No 28, b 48 Barth av.
Alisch Herman O, car insp, h 35 Gatling.
Alisch John A, carp, 136 Spann av, b same.
Alisch Wilhelmina (wid Frederick L), h 48 Barth av.
Alisch Wm A, supt of circulation The Sun, h 48 Barth av.
Alkire Christina (wid John W), boarding 75 E Walnut.
Allard Albert R, optician, h 1126 N Penn.
Allardt Amanda J (wid Maximillian T), h 43 Lord.
Allardt Edwin W, bkkpr Postal Tel Cable Co, b 43 Lord.
Allbright George, lab, h 279 W Washington.
Allee Charles O, lab, h 214 Hoyt av.
Alleman Leon S, clk, b 294½ Mass av.
Alleman Martha N (wid Leonard), janitor, h 294½ Mass av.
Allen Addison B, barber, h 46 Stevens.
Allen Albert, waiter, h 180 Muskingum al.
Allen Alexander M, bartndr Hotel English, b same.
Allen Alonzo G, painter, h 436 W Udell (N I).
Allen Amanda M, b 273 River av (W I).
Allen Amsa, car rep, h 279 Springfield.
Allen Andrew, lab, h rear 430 Douglass.
Allen Andrew C, student, b 300 River av (W I).
Allen Andrew J, clk, b 19 N Arsenal av.
Allen Anna (wid John W), b 463 S Meridian.
Allen Arthur W, adv solr Indpls Journal, h 348 N New Jersey.
Allen Bros (Burgess F and Layton), draughtsmen, 61 Baldwin blk.
Allen Bryant D, carp, b 85 N Noble.
Allen Burgess (Allen Bros), h 1121 N Delaware.
Allen Burt, clk, b 299 Indiana av.
Allen Catherine, stenog Kennedy & Connaughton, b 184 Madison av.
Allen Charles, messenger, b 167 Spring.
Allen Charles, lab, h 154 Maple.
Allen Charles E, horseshoer, b 65 Columbia av.

MAYHEW 13 N. MERIDIAN STREET.

LIME, CEMENT, PLASTER FIRE BRICK AND CLAY SEWER PIPE, ETC. BALKE & KRAUSS CO., Cor. Market and Missouri Streets.

C. FRIEDGEN HAS THE FINEST STOCK OF LADIES' PARTY SLIPPERS and SHOES 19 NORTH PENNSYLVANIA ST.

SAMUEL LAING ▸ TIN, SLATE AND STEEL ROOFING 72 AND 74 EAST COURT STREET.

M. B. WILSON, Pres. W. F. CHURCHMAN, Cash.

THE CAPITAL NATIONAL BANK,
INDIANAPOLIS, IND.

Pays Interest on Time Certificates of Deposit.
Buys and Sells Foreign Exchange at Low Rates.

Capital, - - $300,000
Surplus and Earnings, 50,000

No. 28 S. Meridian St., Cor. Pearl.

Allen Charles G, barber, r 15 Monument pl.
Allen Charles H, cook, r 255 N West.
Allen Charles M, painter, h 361 English av.
Allen Charles S, trav agt, h 92 Harrison.
Allen Charles W, city fireman, h 465 Bellefontaine.
Allen Charles W, tmstr, h w s Gladstone av 1 n of Michigan.
Allen Cyrus, janitor, h 372 W 2d.
Allen David, roofer C Zimmerman & Sons, h n s Maryland 1 e of Oriental.
Allen David D, ins agt, h 185 Oliver av (W I).
Allen David E, h 658 N Alabama.
Allen David S, farmer, h e s College av 1 s of 31st.
Allen Edward, foreman, h 513 S Illinois.
Allen Edward, lab, h 121 Columbia al.
Allen Edward H, lab, h 107 Division (W I).
Allen Edwin G, stenog A B Meyer & Co, r 52½ W 7th.
Allen Edwin W, bkkpr Pearson's Music House, h 870 N Delaware.
Allen Eli A Rev, pastor Sixth Presbyterian Church, h 65 E McCarty.
Allen Elizabeth A (wid Rev Archibald C), b 61 Central av.
Allen Ella, dressmkr, 832 E 9th, b same.
Allen Ellen (wid George W), chief cook Insane Hospital.
Allen Elmer E, motorman, h 770 W Washington.
Allen Emma, h 1389 Annette (N I).
Allen Ethelbert, clk, b 299 Indiana av.
Allen Frank, engr, h 184 Madison av.
Allen Frank, molder, h 64½ N Illinois.
Allen Frank, phys, b 679 N Delaware.
Allen Fredonia, teacher Girls' Classical School, b 824 N Meridian.
Allen George, lab, h rear 108 Ash.
Allen George, lab, h 658 S Illinois.
Allen George, wood, h rear 310 E Washington.
Allen George B, huckster, b 389 S Delaware.
Allen George W, foreman, h 167 Spring.
Allen Granville G, vice-pres The A Burdsal Co, h 449 Broadway.

TUTTLE & SEGUIN,
28 E. Market Street.
Fire Insurance,
Real Estate, Loan
and Rental Agents.
TELEPHONE 1168.

Allen Harriet, h 679 N Delaware.
Allen Harry, lab, rear 119 Cornell av.
Allen Henry, lab, b 564 W North.
Allen Henry, switchman, h 3 Putnam (B).
Allen Henry Clay, judge Marion County Circuit Court, 45 Court House, h 782 N New Jersey.
Allen Horace R jr (The H R Allen National Surgical Institute), b 679 N Delaware.
ALLEN H R NATIONAL SURGICAL INSTITUTE THE, Horace R Allen jr, M D, Liberty C McLain, M D, and H Stewart Krug, M D, Proprietors, n w cor Ohio and Capitol av opp State House; Tel 22.
Allen Isaac, lab, h 65 Columbia av.
Allen Isaac, tmstr, h 198 W 2d.
Allen Jacob, r 89 N Delaware.
Allen Jacob H, lather, b 65 Columbia av.
Allen James, h 84 Columbia al.
Allen James, lab, b n s 8th 3 w of canal.
Allen Jaspar, lab, r 710 N Delaware.
Allen Jeremiah, porter, h rear 234 W New York.
Allen Jessie, attendant Public Library, b 249 S New Jersey.
Allen John, carp, b 300 River av (W I).
Allen John, city fireman, h 555 E 7th.
Allen John, driver, b rear 27 Cornell av.
Allen John, lab, b 27 Center.
Allen John, lab, b 242 W Maryland.
Allen John lab, b 48 N West.
Allen John, painter, r 190½ S Illinois.
Allen John D, barber, 322 Clifford av, h same.
Allen John H, porter, h 48 Elizabeth.
Allen John J, plastr, b 314 E Market.
Allen John J, plumber, b 184 Madison av.
Allen John R, pres Sensitive Governor Co, h 456 College av.
Allen John W, real est, h 71½ Lockerbie.
Allen Joseph, carp, b 123 Clarke.
Allen Joseph, silversmith, r 351 N Senate av.
Allen Joseph H, lab, h 225 S McLain (W I).
Allen Joseph M, steamfitter, h 472 Highland av.
Allen Kate (wid Stephen), h 19 N Arsenal av.
Allen Katherine M, stenog Ind Dental College, b 643 E Vermont.
Allen Laban B, clk, h n e cor Illinois and 29th.
Allen Laura, h 99 Malott av.
Allen Layton (Allen Bros), b 1121 N Delaware.
Allen Leroy, tel opr W U Tel Co, h 463 W Eugene (N I).
Allen Linton R (Shimer & Allen), h 285 N Noble.
Allen Lucy, grocer, 300 River av (W I), h same.
Allen Madge E, h 801 N Alabama.
Allen Margaret A (wid Stephen), h 436 W Udell (N I).
Allen Mary (wid Wm H), h 99 8th 1 w of canal.
Allen Mary A (wid James S), h 249 S New Jersey.
Allen Matthew B, gardener, h e s Central av 1 n of 15th.
Allen Maud, h 171 W Washington.
Allen Melvin S, opr W U Tel Co, h 350 Clifford av.
Allen Moses, lab, r 18 Lafayette.
Allen Nathan F, mach, h 299 Indiana av.
Allen Oliver M, sec Sensitive Governor Co, b 456 College av.

SULLIVAN & MAHAN Manufacturers of all kinds of PAPER BOXES 41 W. Pearl St.

DIAMOND WALL PLASTER { Telephone 1410 BUILDERS' EXCHANGE.

19 S. Illinois St. ☎ 1769. } THE HOME LAUNDRY { WORK CALLED FOR AND DELIVERED.

Allen Otto G, student, b 71½ Lockerbie.
Allen Powhattan, lab, h 1011 S Meridian.
Allen Priscilla (wid Henry), h 376 W 2d.
Allen Rachel, h 5 Wallace.
Allen Rachel (wid Robert), h 270 N Noble.
Allen Reuben C, lab, r 223 S Capitol av.
Allen Robert S, barber, r 84 W Ohio.
Allen Rose (wid George), b 16 Mill.
Allen Russell G (The A Burdsal Co), b 609 N Capitol av.
Allen Samuel, lab, h 44 Mill.
Allen Samuel J, express, h 10 Athon.
Allen Sidney F, trav agt, b Enterprise Hotel.
Allen Stephen T, live stock, Union Stock Yards (W I), h 67 Walcott.
Allen Theodore T, mach hd, h 492 S West.
Allen Thomas, h 1395 N Capitol av.
Allen Thomas C, ins agt, b 643 College av.
Allen Thomas W, clk R M S, b 378 N Alabama.
Allen Wm, clk, b 304 N Delaware.
Allen Wm, janitor, h 200 W 2d.
Allen Wm, lab, h 20 Everett.
Allen Wm A, engr, b 54 Yandes.
Allen Wm C (Mansfield & Allen), h 280 N New Jersey.
Allen Wm E, lab, h 529½ N Illinois.
Allen Wm E, lab, b 215 Spring.
Allen Wm H, student, b 236 E Vermont.
Allen Wm J, lab, h 85 N Noble.
Allen Wm P, phys, 297½ Mass av, h 57 Oak.
Allender Wm, engr, h 574 W Michigan.
Aller Benjamin, b 383 E New York.
Allerdice Esther M, teacher High School, b 226 Park av.
Allerdice Joseph (Joseph Allerdice & Co), pres Indpls Abattoir Co, h 226 Park av.
Allerdice Joseph jr, auditor Indpls Abattoir Co, b 226 Park av.
ALLERDICE JOSEPH & CO (Joseph Allerdice), Hides, 128 Kentucky av; Tel 644.
Allerman Henry, clk, b 200 Orange.
Alley Basil, lab, h 529 W Wells (N I).
Alley Frank B, engr, h n e cor 24th and Central av.
Alley James I, fireman, b 25 Fletcher av.
Alley Jesse L, electrician, b n e cor 24th and Central av.
Alley Rankin W, lab, b 31 Jefferson av.
Alley Walter R, helper, b 31 Jefferson av.
Allfree Ethel G, stenog J B Allfree Mnfg Co, b 137 Highland pl.
Allfree James B, vice-pres and genl mngr The J B Allfree Mnfg Co, h 137 Highland pl.
ALLFREE J B MANUFACTURING CO THE, Robert Shriver Pres, James B Allfree Vice-Pres and Genl Mngr, Joel W Hadley Sec and Treas, Mill Furnishers and Milling Engineers, 12th and Northwestern av; Tel 413.
Allgeier Simon, cabtmkr, h rear 92 English av.
Allgire Augusta W M, dressmkr, 205 E Ohio, h same.
Allgire Ethel O, teacher, b 66 Talbott av.
Allgire James R, mach, h 78 Woodruff av.
Allgire John R, veneerer, b 73 Woodruff av.
Allgire Joseph B, clk, h 479 Central av.
Allgire Martha C, teacher Public School No 30, b 66 Talbott av.
Allgire Mary A (wid Amon R), h 66 Talbott av.
Allgire Olive E, teacher Public School No 16, b 66 Talbott av.
Allgire Richard E, draughtsman J B Allfree Mnfg Co, b 73 Woodruff av.

FRANK NESSLER. WILL H. ROST.
FRANK NESSLER & CO.
Tailors
56 EAST MARKET ST. (Lemcke Building),
INDIANAPOLIS, IND.

Allgood George W, hackman, h 20 E Morris.
Alliga Erastus, cooper, h 125½ S Noble.
Allinder Adelia, clk Old Wayne Mut Life Ins Co, b 165 Hadley av (W I).
Allinder Charles E, mach, h 37 Standard av (W I).
Allinder Margaret J (wid Abram), h 247 Fletcher av.
Allinder Maria, dressmkr, h 247 Fletcher av.
Allinder Sarah B (wid Samuel), h 165 Hadley av (W I).
Allis Tabor S, clk, h 388 N West.
Allis Thomas, carp, h 243 Sheldon.
Allison Charles H, lawyer, 214 Lemcke bldg, h s e cor Houston and Cherry avs (I).
Allison Charles J, collr Jacob C Sipe, h 106 Greer.
Allison Charles M, photog, b 290 Christian av.
ALLISON COUPON COMPANY, John S Berryhill Pres, Wallace S Allison Sec, Manufacturers of Coupon Books, 69 W Georgia; Tel 1299.
Allison Deborah M, h 290 Christian av.
Allison Dellmore C, foreman, h 382 E 17th.
Allison Elmer, carp, h 11 Riley blk.
ALLISON-ENOS CO THE (John A Allison, T H K Enos), Sunday School Supplies, Books, Stationery, News and School Books, 92 N Meridian.
Allison George M, mason, b 24 S West.
Allison Granville E, h 313 N East.
Allison Harry, hackman, r 211 W Market.
Allison Harry S, foreman, h 1054 E Michigan.
Allison Henry B, clk, r 100 S Illinois.
Allison Herbert C, clk, b 768 Broadway.
Allison, Herschel V, lab, h 369 Jackson.
Allison James, lab, b 25 S West.
Allison James, lab, h 73 Meikel.
Allison James A, foreman, b 768 Broadway.
ALLISON JAMES A, Manufacturer of Allison's Perfection Fountain Pens, Fountain Inks and Combination Ink Bottle, Filler and Cleaner for Fountain Pens, 5 Stewart Pl, h 4 same.

Haueisen & Hartmann
163-169 E. Washington St.
FURNITURE,
Carpets,
Household Goods,
Tin, Granite and China Wares, Oil Cloth and Shades

THE WM. H. BLOCK CO. 7 AND 9 EAST WASHINGTON STREET. DRY GOODS, HOUSE FURNISHINGS AND CROCKERY.

London Guarantee and Accident Co. (Ltd.) Employers', Public and Teams' Liability, Workmen's Collective Insurance and Fidelity Bonds
GEORGE W. PANGBORN, General Agent, 704-706 Lemcke Bldg. Telephone 140.

FRANK K. SAWYER || Reliable Fire Insurance. Reasonable Rates.
74 E. MARKET STREET. Telephone 8.

JOSEPH GARDNER,
TIN, IRON, STEEL AND SLATE ROOFING,
GALVANIZED IRON CORNICES & SKYLIGHTS.
37, 39 & 41 KENTUCKY AVE. Telephone 322.

Allison James B, photog, 113 Mass av, h 290 Christian av.
Allison James M, mngr Tonica Temple, 86 N Penn, h 46 Tacoma av.
Allison James W, stonecutter, b 24 S West.
Allison John A (The Allison-Enos Co), b 95 N Meridian.
Allison John C, grocer, 1411 Annette, h 449 W Eugene (N I).
Allison John G, clk, b 24 S West.
Allison John W, b 148 Woodlawn av.
Allison Joseph E, contr, 148 Woodlawn av, h same.
Allison Lawrence E, city agt Columbus Butter and Cheese Co, h 533 N Alabama.
Allison Marie, bkkpr Allison-Enos Co, b 15 The Plaza.
Allison Myra J (wid Noah), h 768 Broadway.
Allison Olive, teacher Public School No 27, b 734 College av.
Allison Ora G, lab, h 55 Jones.
Allison Oscar P, mach hd, b 24 S West.
Allison Robert H, clk C C C & St L Ry, b 232 Central av.
Allison Wallace S, sec Allison Coupon Co, h 768 Broadway.
Allison Wm D (W D Allison Co), h 443 Park av.
Allison Wm J, fruits, 266½ W Washington, h 24 S West.
Allison Wm P, plumber, b 3 Riley blk.
ALLISON W D CO (Wm D Allison), Physicians' Chairs, Tables and Cabinets, Invalids' Rolling and Parlor Reclining Chairs, 85 E South; Tel 1176.
Allman Haman B, saloon, 67 Russell av, h same.
Allmeroth August, lab, h 412 Union.
Allmeroth John, sawyer, b 412 Union.
Alloways Anna L, clk Cathcart, Cleland & Co. b 109 E St Joseph.
Alloways Claude F, clk C H & I R R, b 109 E St Joseph.
Alloways Ella C, r 222½ E Washington.
Alloways James M (Alloways & Co), h 109 E St Joseph.
Alloways & Co (James M Alloways, Charles H Evans) shoemakers, 28 Mass av.

J. S. FARRELL & CO.
STEAM AND HOT WATER HEATING AND PLUMBING CONTRACTORS
84 North Illinois Street. Telephone 382.

Allred Edward, foreman Tanner & Sullivan, h 747 N Illinois.
Allred Wm, tinner, h w s Meridian 2 n of 29th.
Allstatt John W, lab, h 48 Osgood (W I).
Allstatt Wm D, lab, h 96 Bloomington.
Almack, Essie, h 210 N Meridian.
Almack Thomas S, b 97 Bright.
Almond Arvel E, fireman, b 106 Woodburn av (W I).
Almond Charles O, lab, b 332 W Vermont.
Almond Edward J, clk, b 51 Stevens.
Almond Enos A, trav agt, h 332 W Vermont.
Almond Etta J, stenog Milwaukee Harvester Co, h 75 W 1st.
Almond John, clk, b 500 N Alabama.
Alph Wallace, lab, h rear 273 Christian av.
Alred Jesse J, molder, b 24 Merrit (H).
Alred Lafayette C, molder, b 24 Merrit (H).
Alred Wm R, lab, h 24 Merrit (H).
Alsman Harvey G, clk When Clothing Store, h 554 N Alabama.
Alsmeyer Henry W, lab, h 183 S Linden.
Alsop Harry J, motorman, h 398½ College av.
Alsop Thomas V, painter, h 136 Lynn av (W I).
Altenbach Ferdinand, framemkr, b 80 Oak.
Altenbaugh Joseph H, fireman, h 27 N Gale (B).
Altenberger Frederick W, paste mnfr, 137 W Maryland, r same.
Altenburg Eugene, student, b 173 Bellefontaine.
Altenburg John D, clk, b 922 N New Jersey.
Altenburg Sarah C (wid Henry E), h 922 N New Jersey.
Althoff August, carp, b 630 S Meridian.
Althoff Felix H, engr, h 50 Chadwick.
Althouse Ellen W (wid Isaac), h 293 Virginia av.
Altland Hiram, h 43 Cornell av.
Altland Mary C, teacher Public School No 2, b 901 N Alabama.
Altland Samuel H, clk Dalton Hat Co, h 103 Highland pl.
Altland Sarah M, h 901 N Alabama.
Altland Titus, pressman, b 901 N Alabama.
Altland Wm H, lab, b 43 Cornell av.
Altland Wm L, ins agt, h 781 E Washington.
Altman Lloyd P, painter, h 385 S State av.
Altmann Charles, lab, h 84 Downey.
Altmann Frank, lab, h 927 Madison av.
Altmann Herman, saloon, 586 Morris (W I), h 23 Kansas.
Altman Katherina (wid Herman), h 927 Madison av.
Altmeyer Wm, lab, b 285 S Capitol av.
Alton Gustave, lab, b 297 W Merrill.
Altschul Adolph, clk Nathan Kahn, r 40 Nebraska.
Altum Reana, h 335 E Wabash.
Alums Frank, lab, h 327 S Delaware.
Alverson Harlan, jeweler, 547 W 22d (N I), h n e cor Eugene and Rader (N I).
Alvey James H, bkkpr Hendrickson, Lefler & Co, h 739 N Penn.
Alvis, see also Elvis.
Alvis James C, b 77 Middle Drive (W P).
Alvis Luther M, condr, h 17 Division (W I).
Alyea Ida B (W S Shellhouse & Co), b 168 E Vermont.
Alyea Jane M (wid John), h 168 E Vermont.
Amacher John M, canmkr, b 35 Hendricks.
Amacher Melchior, lab, h 35 Hendricks.

POLICIES IN UNITED STATES LIFE INSURANCE CO., offer indemnity against death, liberal cash surrender value or at option of policy-holder, fully paid-up life insurance or liberal life income.
E. B. SWIFT, M'g'r, 25 E. Market St.

WM. KOTTEMAN } WILL FURNISH YOUR HOUSE COMPLETE
89 & 91 E. Washington St. Telephone 1742

SHOW CASES | WILLIAM WIEGEL | 6 West Louisiana Street Opp. Union Station.

Amann Anna (wid Frederick G), b 377 S Capitol av.
Amann Gustave, porter Circle Park Hotel.
Amberg George, pub, b 134 W Ohio.
Ambrose Alvis D, fireman, b 176 S Senate av.
Ambrose Hannah (wid Maurice), h 251 Bates.
Ambrose Margeret (wid George W C), h 176 S Senate av.
Ambrose Sylvester, engr, h 504 S Capitol av.
Ambrose Wm, condr, b 176 S Senate av.
Ambuhl John F, blksmith, 125 W 18th, h 1345 N Senate av.
Amer Alfred E, carp, h 149½ English av.
America Loan and Savings Society, J M Cropsey pres, S L Douglass sec, 529 Lemcke bldg.

AMERICAN BONDING AND TRUST CO OF BALTIMORE CITY, W E Barton & Co Genl Agts, 504 Indiana Trust Bldg; Long Distance Tel 1918. (See right bottom cor cards.)

AMERICAN BUILDING AND LOAN ASSOCIATION OF INDIANA, David W Coffin Pres, Rollin H McCrea Vice-Pres, Jesse Summers Sec, George N Catterson Treas, Lewis C Walker Attorney, 42-43 Lombard Bldg; Tel 88.

American Buncher Mnfg Co, Arthur A McKain pres, Charles T Boyer vice-pres, Joseph K Sharpe jr sec, Abraham R Nicholas treas, 212 S Penn.

AMERICAN COLLECTING AND REPORTING ASSOCIATION, Wm H Groff Mngr, Room 41-42 Baldwin Blk.

AMERICAN DETECTIVE AGENCY, Harry C Webster Supt, Room 12-14, 96½ E Market.

AMERICAN EXPRESS CO, Joseph D Brown Agent, Offices 5 E Washington; Tel 376; and 145 S Meridian; Tel 1400; Stables 172, 174 and 176 W Georgia.

American Federation of Labor, Samuel Gompers pres, August McCraith sec, John B Lennon treas, 29½ E Market.
American Fruit Co, John Furnas pres, Wm H Cross sec, James H Smith treas, 36 W Washington.
American Hotel, Joseph C Drummond propr, 84 S Illinois.

AMERICAN MEDICAL COLLEGE, a University of Medicine, J C Hamilton Pres, Russell C Kelsey, M D, Sec, Wm H Shackleton Treas, s e cor Indiana av and California; Tel 1544.

AMERICAN NONCONFORMIST THE, Charles X Mathews Editor, 24 S Alabama.

American Paper Pulley Co (Rockwood Mnfg Co), 180 S Penn.

AMERICAN PLATE GLASS CO, Charles T Doxey Pres, Daniel M Ransdell Sec and Treas, 65-68 When Bldg; Tel 1822.

American Press Assn, Frank I Grubbs mngr, 67 W Georgia.

THOS. C. DAY & CO.
INVESTING AGENTS,
TOWN AND FARM LOANS,
Rooms 325 to 330 Lemcke Bldg.

AMERICAN STEEL CO THE, Daniel G Reid Pres, Clayton H Garvey Vice-Pres, Eugene J Buffington Sec, Wm B Leeds Treas, Clifford P Garvey Mngr, Mnfrs of Steel Ingots, Billets and Rails, Senate av and Merrill; Tel 303.

AMERICAN SURETY CO OF NEW YORK, Albert W Wishard 2d Res Vice-Pres, Ernest V Clark Res Asst Sec, Rooms 106-108 Commercial Club Bldg; Tel 1539.

AMERICAN TELEPHONE AND TELEGRAPH CO, Gouverneur Calhoun, Mngr, George G Martin Asst Mngr, 14 S Meridian and 131 W 22d.

AMERICAN TIN PLATE CO THE, W B Leeds Pres, John F Hazen Vice-Pres, D G Reid Treas, Rooms 805, 806 and 807 Majestic Bldg; Tel 73.

AMERICAN TOILET SUPPLY CO, Charles A Sellars Mngr, 26 S Illinois. (See adv in classified Toilet Supplies.)

AMERICAN TRIBUNE, American Tribune Co Publishers and Proprietors, 46 Journal Bldg.

AMERICAN TRIBUNE CO (Philander H Fitzgerald), Publishers and Proprietors American Tribune, 46 Journal Bldg.

American Tribune Soldier Colony Co, P H Fitzgerald pres and treas, B W Fitch sec, 46 Journal bldg.
American Truss Fence Co, Benjamin C Koch pres, Tremont, Ill, Thomas C Greene vice-pres, Tremont, Ill, Louis A Kinsey sec and treas, 11 W Pearl.
American Union Savings Assn, Sylvester Johnson pres, Jesse W Brooks agt, 44½ N Penn.

AMERICAN WRINGER CO, Frank E Fuller Mngr, 27 Indiana av.

Amick Charles P, contr, 1202 Morris (W I), b same.

EAT——
HITZ'S CRACKERS
AND CAKES.
ASK YOUR GROCER FOR THEM.

CARPETS AND RUGS RENOVATED.......... | **CAPITAL STEAM CARPET CLEANING WORKS M. D. PLUNKETT, TELEPHONE No. 818**

BENJ. BOOTH PRACTICAL EXPERT ACCOUNTANT. Accounts of any description investigated and audited, and statements rendered. Room 18, 82½ E. Washington St., Indianapolis, Ind.

The Best Place in the City to Get a Good Meal THE SHERMAN RESTAURANT 18 and 20 S. Meridian Street KERSHNER BROS., Proprs.

ESTABLISHED 1876. TELEPHONE 168.
CHESTER BRADFORD,
SOLICITOR OF PATENTS,
AND COUNSEL IN PATENT CAUSES.
(See adv. page 6.)
Office:—Rooms 14 and 16 Hubbard Block, S.W. Cor. Washington and Meridian Streets,
INDIANAPOLIS, INDIANA.

Amick Charles, condr, b 180 Christian av.
Amick David C, condr, h 502 E 9th.
Amick George L, fruits, 143 E Mkt House, h 488 N California.
Amick Howard H (Mahoney & Amick), h 180 Christian av.
Amick Louisa J, grocer, 1202 Morris (W I), h same.
Amiet Werner, mngr Circle Park Hotel.
Ammerman George L, lab, h 497 E 11th.
Ammerman Isaac N, lab, h 414 Newman.
Ammerman James W, lab, h 346 N Pine.
Ammerman Stephen A P, mach, h 114 Newman.
Ammerman Wm, hostler, b 346 N Pine.
Ammeroth August,, paperhngr, 412 Union, h same.
Ammeroth John, lab, b 412 Union.
Amos Arthur, blksmith, b 131 Union.
Amos Benjamin, lab, h 200 W 6th.
Amos Bertram, tel opr, h w s Harris av 5 s of C C C & St L Ry (M J).
Amos Henry C, tailor, r 27 Stewart pl.
Amos Henry J, feed, 21 Oriental, h 23 same.
Amos Isaac N, plumber, h 59 Traub av.
Amos Jacob H, clk, h 231 Christian av.
Amos James A, cook, r 193 W Washington.
Amos John, letter carrier P O, h 31 Wilcox.
Amos John C, mach, h 258 Lafeyette av.
Amos Lewis, lab, h 9 W Chesapeake.
Amos Lydia C (wid James), h 170 Beacon.
Amos Samuel, mach, h 247 Sheldon.
Amos Wm H, mason, h n s Pruitt 1 e of Fountain.
Amschler Frederick, lab, b 650 S Illinois.
Amsden Frederick E, watchman, h 203 N Noble.
Amschler Louisa, h 650 S Illinois.
Amsden Anna M (wid George W), h 203 N Noble.
Amsden George, engr, h 203 N Noble.
Amsler Frederick, lab, r 9½ Madison av.
Amt Benjamin, lab, h 100½ Downey.
Amt George (Surbey & Amt), h 24 Sullivan.
Amt Henry J, foreman, h 53 Hendricks.
Amthor Edwin J, clk, h 533 E Ohio.
Amthor Ida (wid Frederick), b 427 E Georgia.
Amthor Kate E, h 454 Virginia av.
Amthor Oscar W, clk, b 533 E Ohio.

O. B. Ensey
SLATE, STEEL, TIN AND IRON ROOFING.
Cor. 6th and Illinois Sts. Tel. 1562

AMTHOR WM L, Wall Paper, 454 Virginia av, h 533 E Ohio.

Anacker Christopher, carp, h 135 Lynn av (W I).
Anacker George, carp, h 139 Nordyke av (W I).
Anacker John, carp, h 195 Hadley av (W I).
Anderberg Martin, tailor, 29½ N Penn, h 212 N Noble.
Anderberg Nils, tailor, 43 Hubbard blk, h same.
Anderegg Christian, wheelmnfr, cor Osgood and Vandalia R R (W I), h 441 N Meridian.
Anderegg Edward C, bkkpr, b 441 N Meridian.
Anderegg John A, h 792 N Senate av.
Anders George R, tmstr, h 73 Oliver av (W I).
Anders Lank, lab, h 606 N West.
Andersen Anton C, lab, b 60 Gresham.
Andersen Lawrence A, clk, b 426 S East.
Andersen Martin, carp, h 60 Gresham.
Andersen Niels, coffee roaster, h 426 S East.
Anderson Addison L, grocer, 113 Ft Wayne av, h 111 same.
Anderson Albert, tinner, h 652 N West.
Anderson Albert C, engr, h 498 W Chicago (N I).
Anderson Alfred, lab, h n w cor Miller and Sheffield av (W I).
Anderson Allen S, dynamo opr, r 86 N Senate av.
Anderson Alma H (wid Edward), b 892 W Morris (W I).
Anderson Alvin C, molder, b 10 Minerva.
Anderson Aquilla, b 74 Fulton.
Anderson Arthur F, mach, h 645 Mass av.
Anderson Arvine P, clk C C C & St L Ry, b 24 Miley av.
Anderson August, bricklyr, b 39 N Alabama.
Anderson Benjamin F, finisher, b 10 Minerva.
Anderson Caroline (wid Henry S), h 71 Cornell av.
Anderson Catherine (wid Abner), h 788 E Market.
Anderson Charles, carp, 28 N New Jersey, h same.
Anderson Charles G, butcher, b 34½ Chadwick.
Anderson Clara, officer Indiana Reformatory, b same.
Anderson Clarence C, condr, h 98 Clifford av.
Anderson Clarence E, pressman, h 24 Newman.
Anderson C Wesley, student, h 42 Henry.
Anderson David E, vet surg, 266 E Washington, r 262½ same.
Anderson Don A, phys, 402 Virginia av, h same.
Anderson Edgar D, stenog C C C & St L Ry, b 286 Springfield.

ANDERSON ELI W, Dentist, 37½ E Washington (over Boyd, Besten & Langen Co), h 448 N Meridian; Tel 1315.

Anderson Emanuel, lab, r 31½ Columbia al.
Anderson Emma, stenog, b 217 Park av.
Anderson Fidelia, teacher High School, h 307 N Delaware.
Anderson Frank, lab, h 222 Yandes.
Anderson Frank, mach hd, h 43 Clifford av.
Anderson George, carp, 180 E Court, h 185 E Market.

TUTEWILER UNDERTAKER, No. 72 WEST MARKET STREET. TELEPHONE 216.

PROVIDENT LIFE AND TRUST CO. OF PHILADELPHIA. D. W. Edwards, G. A., 508 Indiana Trust Bldg. In form of policy; prompt settlement of death losses; equitable dealing with policy-holders; in strength of organization; and in everything which contributes to Security and Cheapness of life insurance, this company is unsurpassed.

Anderson George, lab, h rear 565 W Shoemaker (N I).
Anderson George, lab, b 73 Woodburn av (W I).
Anderson George, lab, b 100 Wright.
Anderson George E, farmer, h 113 W 10th.
Anderson George P, sec Crown Hill Cemetery, h 333 Michigan (H).
Anderson Grant U, brakeman, b 74 Fulton.
Anderson Hamilton, cook, b 270 Yandes.
Anderson Hans, lab, h 991 S Meridian.
Anderson Hans, molder, h 43 Haugh (H).
Anderson Harry, cabtmkr, b 74 Fulton.
Anderson Harvey, h 221 Pleasant.
Anderson Henry, collr, b 191 E Market.
Anderson Henry, lab, r 32 N Senate av.
Anderson Henry C, h 166 Pleasant.
Anderson Ida (wid Thomas), h rear 135 E Pratt.
Anderson Irvin E, barber, r 128 W Vermont.
Anderson James, dep constable, 20½ N Delaware, b 221 E Wabash.
Anderson James, egg packer, b 191 E Market.
Anderson James, lab, h 27 Meikel.
Anderson James, lab, r 182 W Market.
Anderson James B, lab, r 81 Muskingum al.
Anderson James E, phys, 2 Grand Opera House blk, h 871 N Meridian.
Anderson James G, plastr, b 66 Arbor av (W I).
Anderson James S, collr, h 251 Blake.
Anderson James S, sec Masons' Union Life Association, 8-9 Masonic Temple, h 980 N Illinois.
Anderson James T, agt, h 437 Ash.
Anderson James T jr, trav agt Van Camp H and I Co, h 794 N Capitol av.
Anderson James W, mach opr Indpls Journal, b 231 Hamilton av.
Anderson John, lab, b 41 Guffin.
Anderson John, lab, h 991 S Meridian.
Anderson John, trav agt, r 161½ Mass av.
Anderson John A, bartndr, h 269 N Noble.
Anderson John C, lab, h 54 Mayhew.
Anderson John C, lab, h 24 Miley av.
Anderson John F, barber, 108 Ft Wayne av, h same.
Anderson John H, h 181 Brookside av.
Anderson John H, teacher Public School No 40, h 186 Minerva.
Anderson John J, h 897 N Alabama.
Anderson John S, lab, h 184 N Dorman.
Anderson John W, cooper, h 10 Minerva.
Anderson John W, lab, b 788 E Market.
Anderson John W, switchman, h 311 N Pine.
Anderson Joseph, lab, b 149 Geisendorff.
Anderson Joseph, waiter, h 131 Douglass.
Anderson Joseph, fireman, h w s Cushing 1 s of 17th.
Anderson Julia (wid Winfield S), b 317 Davidson.
Anderson Leman C, notions, 177 W 12th, h same.
Anderson Lewis J, fireman, h 81 N Gillard av.
Anderson Lida M (wid James A), h 252½ Mass av.
Anderson Lou, waiter Ross House.
Anderson Lucien, trav agt, r 45 Indiana av.
Anderson L Emery, lab, h 511 Addison (N I).
ANDERSON MADS P, Furniture, Stoves, Coal, Coke, Wood, Kindling, Storage, Furniture Packer and Transfer, 381-385 Cedar, h 287 S East.
Anderson Margaret, stenog, b 217 Park av.
Anderson Margaret (wid John), b 48 S Gale (B).

THE WHEN IS A WORLD BEATER.

Anderson Martha, h 31½ Virginia av.
Anderson Martha E, teacher Public School No 42, b 49 Hosbrook.
Anderson Martin, lab, h 210 Miller (W I).
Anderson Martin C, contr, 41 Hoyt av, h same.
Anderson Mary J (wid Elijah J), h 49 Hosbrook.
Anderson Matthew H, mach, h 48 S Gale (B).
Anderson Morton, coachman 1012 N Penn.
Anderson Oliver P, plumber, h 304 S Penn.
Anderson Oliver R, woodwkr, b 24 Miley av.
Anderson Owen, carp, r 224 N New Jersey.
Anderson Park, clk, b 24 Miley av.
Anderson Peter, stairbldr, h 337 Bicking.
Anderson Reuben C, lab, b 312 E Court.
Anderson Robert, cook Hotel English.
Anderson Robert B, carp, h 177½ W 12th.
Anderson Robert B, porter, h 600 W North.
Anderson Robert G, h 5 Carlos.
Anderson Rolla D, clk, b 980 N Illinois.
Anderson Samuel, grocer, 97 Maple, h same.
Anderson Sarah A (wid Isaac J), h 607 W 22d (N I).
Anderson Sherman, mach hd, b 74 Fulton.
Anderson Stephen, foreman, h 191 Hoyt av.
Anderson Thomas, carp, h 635 N West.
Anderson Victoria (wid John J), b 159 Buchanan.
Anderson Walter, carp, h 441 W Addison (N I).
Anderson Willard C, cook, b 207 W 1st.
Anderson Wm, b 191 E Market.
Anderson Wm, coachman, h 5 Lafayette.
Anderson Wm, cook Sherman House, b 27 Meikel.
Anderson Wm, lab, h rear 237 Howard.
Anderson Wm, pipefitter, h 58 Walcott.
Anderson Wm, wagonmkr, h 265 English av.
Anderson Wm A, lab, b 991 S Meridian.
Anderson Wm E, carp, h 15 Hosbrook.
Anderson Wm H, b 500 N West.
Anderson Wm H, barber, r 175 W North.
Anderson Wm O, cashr The McGilliard Agency Co, h 217 Park av.
Anderson Willis, lab, h w s Caroline av 3 n of 17th.

The A. Burdsal Co. CELEBRATED HOMESTEAD READY MIXED PAINT. WHOLESALE AND RETAIL. 34 AND 36 SOUTH MERIDIAN STREET.

THEODORE F. SMITHER - GRAVEL ROOFING MATERIALS 2 and 3-Ply Building Paper, etc. Best of Materials. Telephone 861. Office, 151 West Maryland St.

ELECTRIC SUPPLIES We Carry a full Stock. Prices Right. C. W. MEIKEL, Tel. 466. 96-98 E. New York St.

DALTON & MERRIFIELD { LUMBER South Noble St., near E. Washington

INDIANA ELECTROTYPE CO. : BEST WORK. LOWEST PRICES. 23 WEST PEARL ST., INDIANAPOLIS, IND. JOB WORK. BOOK PLATES. All Orders Promptly Filled. BEST PATENT BASE ON THE MARKET.

KIRKHOFF BROS., Electrical Contractors, Wiring and Construction. 102-104 SOUTH PENNSYLVANIA ST. TELEPHONE 910.

Andes Nellie M, stenog Rockwood Mnfg Co, b 862 Grandview av.
Andies George, condr, b 678 W Washington.
Anding Charles, blksmith, b John H Anding.
Anding John H, bkkpr Home Brewing Co, h w s Auburn av 6 s of English av.
Andler Frederick, carriage trimmer, h 327½ E Washington.
Andler Rose A, h 316 E New York.
Andress John R, actor, h 192½ W Washington.
Andress Lan S, barber, s e cor 9th and Yandes, h same.
Andrew Grant L, lab, h 7 Hill.
Andrew Grant W, clk, b 7 Hill.
Andrew John B, real est, h 236 E Morris.
Andrew Margaret, b 198 Blake.
Andrew Mary R (wid Wm), b 46 Spann av.
Andrew Richard H, watchman, h 173 Yandes.
Andrews Abram, waiter, h 88 N New Jersey.
Andrews Albert A, cigarmkr, h 50 Wallack.
Andrews Almin W, lab, b 127 E 8th.
Andrews Charles, cook, b 141 W Washington.
Andrews Charles E, sawmkr, h 1674 N Penn.
Andrews Charles H, agt, b 80 W 5th.
Andrews Dora, motorman, h 321 S Delaware.
Andrews Dyke, porter, b 280 Fayette.
Andrews Earnest L, painter, 70½ E Court, h 629 Home av.
ANDREWS EDGAR C, Manufacturer of Laundry and Toilet Soaps, Factory Drover s of Morris Street Bridge (W I), h 261 Eureka av; Tel 404.
Andrews Edward, lab, b 631 W Michigan.
Andrews Edward G C, waiter, r 88 N New Jersey.
Andrews Emma M (wid Frank), r 171½ E Washington.
Andrews Frederick E, collr, b 261 Eureka av.
Andrews George, driver, h 73 Oliver av (W I).
Andrews George W, trav agt, h 10 Sterling.
Andrews Herbert E, clk, h 127 E 8th.

THE W. G. WASSON CO., 130 Indiana Ave. Tel. 989. STEAM COAL Car Lots a Specialty. Prompt Delivery. Brazil Block, Jackson and Anthracite.

Andrews John, lab, b w s Wheeler 1 n of Park (B).
Andrews John T, carp, h 129½ Newman.
Andrews John W, cooper, h rear 669 E Washington.
Andrews Josephine (wid Victor), h 127 E 8th.
Andrews Katherine, clk V T Malott, b 872 N Delaware.
Andrews Maria (wid Solomon), b 292 Clifford av.
Andrews Morgan, lab, h 319 W Morris.
Andrews Phoebe (wid Julius), h 17 Hill.
Andrews Richard H, watchman, h 173 Yandes.
Andrews Robert, lab, h 319 W Morris.
Andrews Sarah B (wid Edwin H), r 444 N Meridian.
Andrews Stella M, dressmkr, 45 Russell av, h same.
Andrews The Tailor, Manny E Cohen mngr, s e cor Illinois and Washington.
Andrews Thomas, driver, h 294 Highland av.
Andrews Wm, lab, h w s James 2 n of Bloyd av (B).
Andrews Wm, lab, b 23 N New Jersey.
Andrews Wm A, painter, b 241 N Delaware.
Andrews Wm H, mach, h 430 Martindale av.
Andrews Wm H, soapmkr, h 45 Russell av.
Andrews Wm W, clk Emil Wulschner & Son, h 162 Laurel.
Andri Wilhelmina (wid John), h 326 E New York.
Androvette Glass Co The, Edward Schurmann mngr, 6 Odd Fellows' blk, tel 1679.
Andrus Ida M, teacher Public School No 1, b 39 Christian av.
Andrus Matilda S (wid Reuben), r 39 Christian av.
Aneshaensel Adolph, mach, b 11 Carlos.
Aneshaensel Charles, h 55 Union.
Aneshaensel Charles jr (C Aneshaensel & Co), h 359 Park av.
ANESHAENSEL C & CO (Charles Aneshaensel Jr), Plumbers, Steam and Gas Fitters, Marion Blk, 102 N Meridian; Tel 850.
Aneshaensel Julius J, mach hd, h 11 Carlos.
Aneshaensel Otto (Aneshaensel & Prinzler), h 552 E Market.
Aneshaensel Walter, millinery trimmings, 143½ S Meridian, h 75 W Vermont.
Aneshaensel & Prinzel (Otto Aneshaensel, Louis V Prinzel) plumbers, 145 Virginia av.
Ange Mary F (wid Theodore), b 477 N New Jersey.
Anger Clara K, b 181 E South.
Anger Henry L, tinner, h 181 E South.
Angle Abel R, condr, h 23 W 1st.
Angove John A, r 88 W Ohio.
Angrick Andrew, butcher, b 326 Clifford av.
Angrick Anton, lab, h 247 W Morris.
Angrick August, lab, h 47 Vinton.
Angrick Carl, lab, b 23 Thomas.
Angrick Frank, lab, h 39 N Judge Harding (W I).
Angus Henry, lab, b 889 Morris (W I).
ANHEUSER-BUSCH BREWING ASSOCIATION, Jacob L Bieler Mngr Indianapolis Branch, 454-458 E Ohio; Tel 1687.
Anhier Anthony E, watchman, r 99 N New Jersey.
Ankenbrock C Wm, grocer, 326 Clifford av, h same.

W. H. Messenger FURNITURE, CARPETS, STOVES, 101 EAST WASHINGTON ST. TEL. 491.

McNamara, Koster & Co. | Foundry and Pattern Shop, 212-218 S. PENN. ST. . . . PHONE 1593.

THE FRED DIETZ CO. WOODEN PACKING BOXES MADE TO ORDER. FACTORY AND WAREHOUSE TRUCKS. 400 Madison Avenue. Telephone 69.

Ankenbrock Frank G, driver, h 83 High.
Ankenbrock Henry H, h 385 S Deleware.
Ankenbrock Henry W, bartndr, h 233 E Louisiana.
Ankenbrock Joseph F, trav agt, h 212 E Morris.
Ankenbrock Peter S, printer, h 385 S Delaware.
Ankeney Jacob, h 202 E Market.
Ankeney Sarah, b 202 E Market.
Annabil Anna M, h 79 N Alabama.
Annabil Ira M, h 79 N Alabama.
Annan Charles, lab 150 W Vermont.
Ansburg Joseph, lab, h 242 Tremont av (H).
Anschuetz Edward, cigarmkr, 548 Virginia av, b 7 Buchanan.
Anschuetz Gustav, patternmkr, h 7 Buchanan.
Anselm George G, molder, h 223 Bismarck av (H).
Anselm John J, printer, h 125 Laurel.
Anselm Mary A (wid Joseph F), h 6 Smithson.
Ansley Wm W, detective, r 17 Grand Opera House blk.
Ante Jacob J, lab, h 437 Union.
Ante Louis, painter, cor Meridian and Russell av, h 572 S Illinois.
Anterelli George L, paperhngr, h 306½ E Washington.
Anterelli James, paperhngr, b 308 E Washington.
Anterelli Louis, confr, 308 E Washington, h same.
Anthes Jacob, lab, h 500 S New Jersey.
ANTHONY EMANUEL, Physician, 90 Mass av, h 309 N New Jersey; Tel 1403.
ANTHONY E GROVE, Physician (Eye, Ear, Nose and Throat), 92 Mass av, h 309 N New Jersey; Tel 1403.
ANTHONY JAMES R, Physician, 405 College av, h same; Tels 1857 and 263.
Anthony Sarah M (wid Francis M), h 44 Catharine.
Anthony Virgil S T, clk, b 405 College av.
Anton Wm, engr, b 168½ W Washington.
Antrim Alfred W, bkkpr R W Furnas, h 28 Newman.
Antrim George D, buttermkr, h 99 N Beville av.
Antrim Joel B, engr, h 84 N Dorman.
Antrim Martin J, packer, b 167 E Vermont.
Antrobus Charles, lab, h 417 S Missouri.
Antrobus Elizabeth (wid John), b 417 S Missouri.
Antrobus Frank, lab, b 417 S Missouri.
Apel, see also Abel and Ebel.
Apel Harry, sander, b 182 N Senate av.
Apel Minnie, stenog H C Webster, b 210 Lexington av.
Apert Ellen (wid David), b 218 E Market.
Apert Joseph, enameler, b 218 E Market.
Appel Edward, bookbndr, r 382 N Senate av.
Appel John J (Gregory & Appel), h 387 Broadway.
Appel Joseph S, clk, h 180 Mass av.
Appel Lydia K, h 180 Mass av.
Apperson Mary, b 95 N Meridian.
Apple Anna L, confr, 750 N Senate av, h same.
Apple Rebecca A (wid James M), b 189 Columbia av.
Apple Elmer, condr, r 8 Poplar (B).
Apple Frank, switchtndr, b s s Pendleton av ¼ mile e (B).

Henry H. Fay, 40½ E. Washington St., REAL ESTATE, AND LOAN BROKER.

Apple Hervey, carp, h 128 Columbia av.
Apple Silas W, motorman, h 750 N Senate av.
Appleby Madian H Rev, pastor North Indianapolis M E Church, h 509 W Eugene (N I).
Appleby Sarah R (wid Robert), b 41 Highland pl.
Appleby Wm J, paperhngr, h 406 W Pratt.
Applegarth Susan W, b 172 E Ohio.
Applegate Augustus W, supt Wm B Burford, h 475 N Capitol av.
Applegate Cassius M, lab, b 162 Harrison.
Applegate David S, mail clk The Bates, r 24 Stewart pl.
Applegate Edgar T, clk Wm B Burford, h 484 N Senate av.
Applegate Edwin D, carp, h 245 N Liberty.
Applegate George, carp, b 127 N Alabama.
Applegate Harry R, student, r 124 N Meridian.
Applegate Hiram, huckster, h 150 Evison.
Applegate Ida M, bkkpr Elite Portrait and Frame Co, b 27 Hudson.
Applegate John H, switchman, h 53 Tacoma av.
Applegate Kate (wid Isaiah), teacher Public School No 5, b 39 Christian av.
Applegate Lauren F, com mer, 90 S Delaware, h 224 Muskingum al.
Applegate Stella, nurse, h 276 N Illinois.
Applegate Wm A (W A Applegate & Co), h 28 Central av.
Applegate Wm F, foreman, h 20 Woodside av.
Applegate W A & Co (Wm A Applegate), mdse brokers, 32 S Meridian.
Appleget Bert L, lab, h 65 Bismarck av (H).
Applegett George W, lab, h w s Waverly 4 n of Bloyd av (B).
Appleton Pearl E, stenog, r 137½ Mass av.
Appleton James A, buyer D P Erwin & Co 104 S Meridian, h 69 W 1st.
Arantz Wm F, filer, h 167 Coburn.
Arbaugh Archibald M, stenog Daniel Stewart Co, h w s National av 3 s of P C C & St L Ry (I).
Arbuckle Alexander H, letter carrier P O, h 1001 N Penn.

UNION CASUALTY & SURETY CO. OF ST. LOUIS, MO.
All lines of Personal Accident and Casualty Insurance, including Employers' and General Liability.
W. E. BARTON & CO., General Agents, 504 Indiana Trust Building.
LONG DISTANCE TELEPHONE 1918.

Indianapolis BUSINESS UNIVERSITY
Leading College of Business and Shorthand. Elevator day and night. Individual instruction. Large faculty. Terms easy. Enter now. See p. 4. When Block. E. J. HEEB, President.

NEW YORK FILTER MFG. CO.
Filters for Water-Works, Boiler Plants, Laundries, Hotels, Private Residences, Etc.
Henry R. Worthington, 64 S. Pennsylvania St. Long Distance Telephone 284.

UNION CO-OPERATIVE LAUNDRY (COMPOSED OF UNION LAUNDRY GIRLS.) NOS. 38, 40 AND 42 VIRGINIA AVENUE. T. E. SOMERVILLE, MANAGER — TELEPHONE 12. INDIANAPOLIS, IND.

HORACE M. HADLEY
REAL ESTATE AND INSURANCE
66 East Market Street, Basement
TELEPHONE 1540.

Arbuckle Alonzo A, clk Ward Bros, h 155 Elm.
Arbuckle Andrew L, blksmith, h 56 Holloway av.
Arbuckle Bennett M (M Arbuckle & Son), h 323 Bellefontaine.
Arbuckle Charles A, clk Ward Bros Drug Co, h 155 Elm.
Arbuckle Edward L, blksmith, b 175 Lawrence.
Arbuckle Edward O, condr, b 69 W 13th.
Arbuckle Frank, finisher, b 168 Bright.
Arbuckle George W, blksmith, h 235 Newman.
Arbuckle James F, blksmith, s e cor Pendleton av and Rural, h 175 Lawrence.
Arbuckle John W, painter, h 138 Lawrence.
Arbuckle Matthew (M Arbuckle & Son), h 181 College av.
ARBUCKLE M & SON (Matthew and Bennett M), Real Estate and Loans, 62 E Market; Tel 1680.
Arbuckle Oscar A, lab, h 175 Lawrence.
Arbuckle Samuel S, helper, h 168 Bright.
Arbuckle Susannah S (wid Samuel), h 57 Yandes.
Arbuckle Walter E, clk M Arbuckle & Son, b 181 College av.
Arbuckle Wm, brakeman, r 140 N East.
Arbuckle Wm E, helper, b 57 Yandes.
Archbold Charles E, music teacher, 25 N Spruce, h same.
Archbold Edgar P, mach, b 25 N Spruce.
Archbold John F, b 25 N Spruce.
Archdeacon Wm, pickles, 248 S Meridian, h 106 Ruckle.
Archdeacon Wm H, bkkpr, b 106 Ruckle.
Archer Alexander M, pres The Adamant Wall Plaster Co, h 34 Brookside av.
Archer Charles M, lab, h e s Baltimore av 2 n of 17th.
Archer Frank P, mngr Indianapolis Mortgage Loan Co, 10 Thorpe blk, h w s National av 1 s of C H & D R R (I).
Archer James C, condr, h 440 W Francis (N I).
Archer Thomas B, mer police, h 157 Harrison.

PERSONAL AND PROMPT ATTENTION GIVEN TO COLLECTIONS.
Merchants' and Manufacturers' Exchange
J. E. TAKKEN, Manager,
19 Union Building, 73 West Maryland Street.

Archer Tunis V, teacher Deaf and Dumb Inst, b 714 E Washington.
Archibald Garrett A (P B Ault & Co), h 30 The Blacherne.
Archibald Orson, teacher Deaf and Dumb Inst.
Archibald Wm, brakeman, b 29 Madison av.
Arens, see also Ahrens.
Arens Frank J, saloon, 249 E Morris, h 37 Coburn.
Arens Franz X, pres Metropolitan School of Music, h 678 N Capitol av.
Arens Hermon J, pressman, b 37 Coburn.
Arens Samuel, clk, h 240 E Vermont.
Arens Wm F, bottler, b 37 Coburn.
Argadine Elmer C, real est, h 543 Jefferson av.
Argue Mary J (wid John), b 928 N New Jersey.
Arheim Mary (wid Bernhard), b 419 S Capitol av.
Arington Samuel, lab, h 32 Becher.
Armack Frederick, mach, b 5 S Station (B).
Armacost Sarah (wid Aaron B), b 22 Ludlow av.
Armborst Frank, lab, b 620 S West.
Armbruster Eva M (Armbruster & Windhorst), h 79 S West.
Armbruster John J, h 79 S West.
Armburster John J jr, molder, b 79 S West.
Armbruster Julius, printer, b 74 Woodlawn av.
Armbruster & Windhorst (Eva M Armbruster, Anna M Windhorst), dressmkrs, 25½ W Washington.
Armel Albert, driver, h 76 S Spruce.
Armel Charles, driver, b 76 S Spruce.
Armel Clarence, shademkr, h 76 S Spruce.
Armentrout George S, lab, h 252 N California.
Armentrout James, b 33 W 22d.
Armer Albert W, packer, h 754 Chestnut.
Armer Austin, painter, b 754 Chestnut.
Armer David S, h 754 Chestnut.
Armer Flavius E, molder, b 754 Chestnut.
Armer Harry W, painter, h 591½ S Meridian.
Armer Lester, baker, b 754 Chestnut.
Armes Richard M, electrician, r 27 The Windsor.
Armistead George, lab, r 167 E South.
Armitage James E, bartndr, b 198½ Mass av.
Armitage James H, lab, h 198½ Mass av.
Armitage Wm, paperhngr, b 89 Indiana av.
Armitage Wm H, bartndr, b 198½ Mass av.
Armitstead Harry, carp, h 126 Clarke.
Armitstead James C, grocer, 36 Malott av, h 88 Ludlow av.
Armistead Mary E, dry goods, 36 Malott av, h 88 Ludlow av.
Armond David, carriagemkr, h 189 Highland av.
Armstead Wm A, carp, h 425 Lafayette.
Armstrong Albert A, lab, b 14 Concordia.
Armstrong Alonzo, lab, h 176½ Sheffield av (H).
Armstrong Calvin C, engr, h 29 Bloomington.
Armstrong Catherine E (wid Leander V), b 181 N California.
Armstrong Charles L, fireman, b 1100 W Washington (H).
Armstrong Charles W, clk John A Craig, r 84 W Vermont.
Armstrong Clarence M, drayman, h 84 Fletcher av.
Armstrong Dink, lab, b 32 Hiawatha.

CLEMENS VONNEGUT
184, 186 and 192 E. Washington St.
FOUNDRY AND MACHINISTS' SUPPLIES.
"NORTON" EMERY WHEELS
AND GRINDING MACHINERY.

THE WM. H. BLOCK CO. DRY GOODS, MILLINERY, CLOAKS AND FURS.
7 AND 9 EAST WASHINGTON STREET.

Armstrong Douglas K, teacher, h 916 Morris (W I).
Armstrong Douglass J, brakeman, b 245 W South.
Armstrong Edwin J (E J and J W Armstrong), h 550 W 22d (N I).
Armstrong Edwin J and James W, ice, 223 W Walnut.
Armstrong Fernando W, brakeman, h 216 Bates.
Armstrong Frank W, ins agt, h 396 Broadway.
Armstrong Franklin P, condr, h 61 S Summit.
Armstrong George, clk Indiana Paper Co, b 310 S Penn.
Armstrong George, lab, h e s Line 3 s of Washington av (I).
Armstrong George C, clk McCormick H M Co, b 500 Ash.
Armstrong George W (D H Baldwin & Co), r Cincinnati, O.
Armstrong Harvey J, mach hd, h 664 E St Clair.
Armstrong Hattie J (wid Thomas N), h 285 Sheffield av (H).
Armstrong Henry, collr, r 26 W New York.
Armstrong Ira, mach, b 383 Martindale av.
Armstrong James H, mach hd, h rear 664 E St Clair.
Armstrong James M, state mngr Covenant Mut Life Ass'n, 48 Journal bldg, h 194 N Delaware.
Armstrong James W (E J and J W Armstrong, h n s Highland av 1 w of Northwestern av (N I).
Armstrong John N, carp, b n s Willow 1 e of Brightwood av (B).
Armstrong John T, barber, h 122 W New York.
Armstrong John T, peddler, r 23 N West.
Armstrong John W, lab, h 34 Roanoke.

ARMSTRONG LAUNDRY, Armstrong & Reaume Proprietors, 126-130 W Maryland, Office 70 S Illinois; Tel 808.

Armstrong Lucius, lab, h 228½ Muskingum al.
Armstrong Morrow P, h 60 W 5th.
Armstrong Morton W, clk I D & W Ry, b 60 W 5th.
Armstrong Oscar G, engr, r 36 S Capitol av.
Armstrong Richard F, trav agt Wm H Armstrong, b 373 N Delaware.
Armstrong Robert B, helper, h 85 Cornell av.
Armstrong Robert M, clk The Progress Clothing Co, h 93 N Arsenal av.
Armstrong Royal O, clk Indiana Paper Co, b 310 S Penn.
Armstrong Russell B, barber, r 1 Ryan blk.
Armstrong Samuel C, lab, h 53 Tremont av (H).
Armstrong Sarah (wid Robert), nurse, 261 Mass av, h same.
Armstrong Sig M (Armstrong & Reaume and Mather & Armstrong), h 331 E Market.
Armstrong Thomas D, clk R M S, h 500 Ash.
Armstrong Thomas L (Armstrong & Carmony), b 143 N Alabama.
Armstrong Thomas P, carp, h 102 Bates.
Armstrong Washington, lab, h 349 Columbia av.
Armstrong Wm, supt of bldg Indiana Trust Co, h 133 W 6th.
Armstrong Wm H (Wm H Armstrong & Co), h 373 N Delaware.

ARMSTRONG WM H & CO (Wm H Armstrong, Emil Willbrandt), Surgical Instrument Mnfrs, 77 S Illinois; Tel 928.

Armstrong Wm J, engr, r 315 E Ohio.
Armstrong Wm M, lab, h 32 Hosbrook.
Armstrong & Carmony (Thomas L Armstrong, Fred Carmony), livery, 80 E Court.

ARMSTRONG & REAUME (Sig M Armstrong, Mrs John A Reaume), Proprs Armstrong Laundry, 126-130 W Maryland, Office 70 S Illinois; Tel 808.

Arn Kate M (wid Frederick J), h 623 E Market.
Arnald Thomas B, trav agt, h 351 Park av.
Arndt August F, shoemkr, 217 E Morris, h same.
Arndt Charles H, molder, b 889 Morris (W I).
Arndt Lillian M, teacher, b 894 Morris (W I).
Arnett Wm N, clk, b 2 Hill av.
Arnholter Edward F, harnessmkr, b 578 Virginia av.
Arnholter Henry, harness, 572 Virginia av, h 578 same.
Arnholter Henry jr, grocer, 564 Virginia av, b 578 same.
Arnholter Wm H, harnessmkr, b 578 Virginia av.
Arnold Abraham A, ironwkr, b 68 Yandes.
Arnold Alvin, attendant Insane Asylum.
Arnold Andrew, brakeman, h 175 Buchanan.
Arnold Anna M, housekpr 1094 N Meridian.
Arnold Arthur, engr, h 68 Miley av.
Arnold Barbara (wid Peter), h 84 Bright.
Arnold Benjamin F, student, r 367 N Alabama.
Arnold Charles, mach hd, r 156 W Washington.
Arnold Charles, plastr, h 191 Yandes.
Arnold Charles C, tmstr, h 188 Lexington av.
Arnold Charles H, watchman, h 402 Clifford av.
Arnold Charles P, lab, h 132 Winchester.

GUIDO R. PRESSLER,
FRESCO PAINTER
Churches, Theaters, Public Buildings, Etc., A Specialty.
Residence, No. 325 North Liberty Street.
INDIANAPOLIS, IND.

INDIANAPOLIS STEEL ROOFING AND CORRUGATING WORKS, 23 and 25 East South Street. S. D. NOEL, Proprietor.

David S. McKernan REAL ESTATE AND LOANS. Exchanging real estate a specialty. A number of choice pieces for encumbered property. Rooms 2-5 Thorpe Block.

DIAMOND WALL PLASTER { Telephone 1410 BUILDERS' EXCHANGE.

UNION TRANSFER AND STORAGE CO. Cor. E. Ohio St. and C., C., C. & St. L. R'y Tracks. Storage of Household Goods and Pianos a Specialty.

W. McWORKMAN,
Galvanized Iron Cornice Works
TIN AND SLATE ROOFING.
930 WEST WASHINGTON STREET.
TELEPHONE 1118.

Arnold Elizabeth (wid Eugene), h 10 Howard.
Arnold Eugene E, coachman, h 10 Howard.
Arnold Frances E, h 342 S New Jersey.
Arnold Frances G (wid Charles B), music teacher 513 W McLene (N I), b same.
Arnold Frank, lab, b 361 W Merrill.
Arnold Frank A, mer police, h 133 Forest av.
Arnold Franklin R, city fireman, b 227 Blake.
Arnold George, mach hd, b 271 N Noble.
Arnold George C, mach hd, b 225 Clinton.
Arnold George D, lab, b 116 Blackford.
Arnold George N, jeweler, b 227 Blake.
Arnold George S (Condit & Arnold), h 6 S Linden.
Arnold George S, driver Am Ex Co, h 68 W 6th.
Arnold George W, lab, h 148 Martindale av.
Arnold George W, lab, h 490 Sheldon.
Arnold Harriet A, (wid Theodore W), h rear 274 N Alabama.
Arnold Herman G, meats, 502 S Capitol av, h same.
Arnold Jacob (Clifford & Arnold), h 65½ Indiana av.
Arnold Jane (wid Willis), b 93 N Arsenal av.
Arnold John, bartndr, h 219 W Maryland.
Arnold John, lab, h 586 Jefferson av.
Arnold John, porter, b 25 S Delaware.
Arnold John, well driver, b 191 Yandes.
Arnold John B, expressman, b 233 Naomi.
Arnold John D, b 402 Clifford av.
Arnold John T, finisher, h 12 Ludlow av.
Arnold John W, h 372 N New Jersey.
Arnold Joseph, brakeman, h 1092 W New York.
Arnold Joseph, motorman, h w s Gladstone av 2 n of Washington.
Arnold Joseph C, ins agt, b 285 S Capitol av.
Arnold Justin A, trav agt Hide, Leather and Belting Co, h 484 Central av.
Arnold Louis, molder, h 306 S Meridian.
Arnold Martitia C, produce, 39 E Mkt House, b 139 Davidson.
Arnold Mary (wid Charles), b 26 Riley blk.

SEALS,
STENCILS,
STAMPS, Etc.
GEO. J. MAYER
15 S. Meridian St.
TELEPHONE 1386.

Arnold Mary E, h 116 Blackford.
Arnold Mary E (wid Taylor), h 212 E Vermont.
Arnold Michael F, city agt, h 227 Blake.
Arnold Philip H, driver, h rear 29 Palmer.
Arnold Richard C, janitor, h 102 Park av.
Arnold Richard C jr, trav agt, h 442 Talbott av.
Arnold Robert F, paperhngr, b 328 E Washington.
Arnold Thomas C, watchman, b 509 N Senate av.
Arnold Thomas J, huckster, b 139 Davidson.
Arnold Wm, bricklyr, b 131 Columbia av.
Arnold Wm A E, grocer, 534 Park av, h 722 Ash.
Arnold Wm E, capt Hose Co No 11, h 217 Fletcher av.
Arnold Wm H, coremkr, h 34 Gresham.
Arnold Wm M, city sanitary insp, h 217 Keystone av.
Arnouil Eugene, lab, b 247 W Morris.
Arnouil Louis, saloon, 253 W Morris, h 247 same.
Arnouil Louis C, clk, b 247 W Morris.
ARRICK CLIFFORD, Mngr Insurance Dept Union Trust Co and State Agt Washington Life Insurance Co of New York, 68 E Market, h 729 N Delaware; Tel 1576.
Arrold Martha (wid Wm), b 118 Woodlawn av.
Arschafsky David, shoemkr, b 283 E Washington.
Arschafsky Harris, shoemkr, 283 E Washington, h same.
Arszman Henry J, solr, h 95 Minerva.
Arterburn Anna C (wid Joseph), b 9 S Gale (B).
Arthur Charles H, condr, h 328 E 12th.
Arthur Eliza (wid Napoleon B), h rear 528 Virginia av.
Arthur Elizabeth, h rear 528 Virginia av.
Arthur Elizabeth (wid Wm), h 319 N California.
Arthur Frank W, clk, b 528 Virginia av.
Arthur Hamilton, student, r 4 Miller blk.
Arthur John, plumber, 238 Indiana av, h rear 319 N California.
Arthur Wm, clk, h 14 Cincinnati.
Artificial Ice and Cold Storage Co, Sterling R Holt pres, Mathias Garver vice-pres, Charles W Donson sec and treas, 197 W New York.
Artis Calvin, janitor, h 125 Darnell.
Artis Eli, barber, 145 W Merrill, h same.
Artist Everett D, grocer, n s Sutherland 1 e of Rural (B), b e s James 3 n of Division (B).
Artist Gray B, lab, h e s James 2 n of Division (B).
Artist Hannah (wid John), h e s James 1 n of Division (B).
Artist John, lab, b Margaret Artist.
Artist Margaret (wid Jonathan), h e s James 2 n of Division (B).
Artz Louis J C, mach hd, h 87 Wisconsin.
Asbury Benjamin S, lab, h 82 Bates.
Asbury John, lab, h 175 W 6th.
Asbury John G, trav agt, b 361 Ramsey av.
Asbury Joseph, lab, h 395 Columbia av.
Asbury Mary A, h 58 Thomas.
Asch Adolph, patrolman, h 124 S Olive.
Asch Louis, watchman, b 606½ Virginia av.
Ash Frank, h 12 Henry.
Ash Isaac, trav agt, h 544 Jefferson av.
Ash John, lab, h 298 S East.
Ash Richard, lab, h w s Miami 6 s of Prospect (N).

A. METZGER AGENCY ESTABLISHED 1863. L-O-A-N-S

LAMBERT GAS & GASOLINE ENGINE CO.
ANDERSON, IND. GAS ENGINES FOR ALL PURPOSES.

Ashbaugh Harry C, brakeman, h 7 Depot (B).
Ashbaugh John H, baggage master, h 161 Christian av.
Ashbaugh Walter E, bkkpr, b 161 Christian av.
Ashbey Jacob, hostler, b 195 Middle.
Ashbrook Nellie P, teacher Public School No. 3, b 1008 N Delaware.
Ashby Alice, nurse, r 147 N Penn.
Ashby Daniel W, lab, h 322 Blake.
Ashby John H, clk Dye, Valodin & Co, b 251 Howard (W I).
Ashby Samuel, lawyer, 68½ E Market, h 1673 N Capitol av.
Ashby Smith B, lab, b 322 Blake.
Ashcraft Henry B, lab, h 174 Trowbridge (W).
Ashcraft John M, lab, h 114 Trowbridge (W).
Asher Delaney, clk, h 107 Oliver av (W I).
Asher Lewis K, plumber, h 2½ Fletcher av.
Ashford Henry, lab, r 123 W Vermont.
Ashinger Wm H, switchman, h 647 Marlowe av.
Ashland J Harry, cook, b n e cor Brightwood av and C C C & St L Ry (B).
Ashley Anna C (wid Joseph L), b 136 W Michigan.
Ashley Charles J, tel opr P C C & St L Ry, h 136 W Michigan.
Ashley Julia E, teacher Public School No 10, h 196 Ash.
Ashley Marion, driver, h s w cor Waverly and Brookside avs.
Ashley Martha W (wid George T), h 196 Ash.
Ashley Thomas, trav agt, h 72 Ruckle.
Ashmead Seely W, engr, h 39 Brookside av.
Ashton Arthur F, photog, b 216 N Pine.
Ashton Harry B, photog, h 216 N Pine.
Askren Emma F, h 872 N Delaware.
Asmus Frederick, h 504 N West.
Asmus George C, huckster, h 131 Locke.
Asmus Louis, fruit, 2 E Louisiana, h 504 N West.
Asmus Louis, lab, h 174 Fayette.
Asmuessen Wm, lab, b 936 S East.
Asperger Frederick G, marblecutter, h 45 Ramsey av.
Aspinwall Annie, dressmkr, 28½ Indiana av, r same.
Aspinwall Frank P, clk Model Clothing Co, h 8 Water.
Aspinwall John, r 28½ Indiana av.
Astley Margaret, bkkpr, h 30 Hall pl.
Astley Sarah J (wid Samuel C), h n s Washington 1 e of Gladstone av.
Astley Wm, lab, r 290 W Market.
Atchison Harry O, clk, b 234 W New York.
Atchison James D, packer, h 234 W New York.
Atchison Mame C, bkkpr Polar Ice Co, b 324 N Delaware.
Atchison Maude, opr C U Tel Co, b 234 W New York.
Atchison Miranda V (wid John J), h 324 N Delaware.
Atchison Oliver N, clk, b 234 W New York.
Atchison Willis E, painter, b 234 W New York.
Aten Commodore P, trav agt, h 70 W 11th.
Atherton Alexander P, harnessmkr, h 136 Columbia av.
Atherton Charles H, cooper, h 141 Newman.
Atherton Clura G, opr W U Tel Co, b 262 S East.

THOS. C. DAY & CO.
Financial Agents and Loans.
We have the experience, and claim to be reliable.
Rooms 325 to 330 Lemcke Bldg.

Atherton Emery A, engr, b 136 Columbia av.
Atherton Ernest D, clk, h 131 W Ohio.
Atherton James P, b 131 W Ohio.
Atherton Jefferson, hostler, b 52 S Summit.
Atherton Jesse, lab, h e s Chester av 1 n of Washington.
Atherton Wm E, clk, b 131 W Ohio.
Atherton Wm F, printer, h 131 W Ohio.
Atherton Wm M, opr W U Tel Co, h 262 S East.
Athey George R, lab, h e s Lincoln av 3 s of Jackson (M J).
Athey Martha (wid James), h w s Harris av 2 s of W Washington (M J).
Athey Preston G, molder, h 181 Blake.
Athon James S, b 1030 N New Jersey.
Athon Lavinia D, h 96 W New York.
Atkins, see also Adkins.
Atkins Albert L, condr, h 172 Dougherty.
Atkins Elias C, pres E C Atkins & Co, h 666 N Meridian.
ATKINS E C & CO, Elias C Atkins Pres, Henry C Atkins Vice-Pres and Supt, Wm H Perkins Sec, Merritt A Potter Treas, Proprietors Sheffield Saw Works, 202-216 S Illinois; Tel 55.
Atkins George F, student, b 865 N Meridian.
Atkins Henry C, vice-pres and supt E C Atkins & Co, b 699 N Meridian.
Atkins Stephen, engr, h 234 Hamilton av.
Atkinson, see also Adkinson.
Atkinson Benjamin, engr, h 89 N Arsenal av.
Atkinson Charles E, clk, h 36 Thalman av.
Atkinson Charles E, printer, Indpls Sentinel, b 35 Highland pl.
Atkinson David C (Atkinson & Knipp), h 576 Central av.
Atkinson Edwin L, real est, h 25 Pleasant av.
Atkinson Elizabeth, laundress, r rear 77 W North.
Atkinson Frank P, rate clk C C C & St L Ry, b 132 N Capitol av.
Atkinson Harry N, driver, b 23 Keystone av.
Atkinson James, fireman, h 10 Depot (B).

EAT
QUAKER BREAD
ASK YOUR GROCER FOR IT.
THE HITZ BAKING CO.

BICYCLES $5 DOWN. MONTHLY. Best Wheels. Best Terms. WHEELMEN'S CO. 31 W. OHIO ST. LONG DISTANCE TEL. 1855.

J. H. TECKENBROCK | Grilles, Fretwork and Wood Carpets
94 EAST SOUTH STREET.

FIDELITY MUTUAL LIFE PHILADELPHIA, PA. A. H. COLLINS { General Agent, 52-53 Baldwin Block.

Edwardsport Coal & Mining Co. Rooms 42 and 43 When Building.

SUPERIOR BITUMINOUS COAL For Steam and Domestic . . Purposes . .

ESTABLISHED 1876. TELEPHONE 168.
CHESTER BRADFORD,
SOLICITOR OF PATENTS,
AND COUNSEL IN PATENT CAUSES.
(See adv. page 6.)
Office:—Rooms 14 and 16 Hubbard Block, S.W. Cor. Washington and Meridian Streets, INDIANAPOLIS, INDIANA.

Atkinson James H, sawmkr, b 89 N Arsenal av.
Atkinson John B, clk, h 153 S William (W I).
Atkinson Josephus, clk, b 120 Oliver av (W I).
Atkinson Mary (wid Henry),b 27 Hosbrook.
Atkinson Mary, nurse City Hospital.
Atkinson Newman, blksmith, 5 Hillside av, h 18 Holloway av.
Atkinson Oren, lab, b 117 N Illinois.
Atkinson Thomas E, h 117 N Illinois.
Atkinson Thomas J, painter, h 23 Keystone av.
Atkinson Wilbur, clk, b 153 S William (W I).
ATKINSON & KNIPP (David C Atkinson, Julius W Knipp), Lawyers, Rooms 521-523 Lemcke Bldg.
Atland Titus, pressman, h 901 N Alabama.
ATLAS ENGINE WORKS, Hugh H Hanna Pres, Robert M Coffin Sec, Julius F Pratt Treas, Matthew R Moore Supt, Manufacturers of Engines and Boilers, n e cor 9th and Martindale av; Tel 45.
Aton Charles W, switchman, h 50 S Gale (B).
Aton Thomas J, mach, b e s Miami 6 s of Wallace.
Attorney General's Office, Wm A Ketcham atty genl, 19 State House.
Atwood George C, lab, r 290 W Market.
Atwood James K, cutter, b 25 Birch av (W I).
Atwood Mary E (wid Robert), h 25 Birch av (W I).
Aubert Charles W, lab, b 440 S Delaware.
Aubrey Ella D, bkkpr, b 315 E St Clair.
Aubrey Henry C, painter, h 315 E St Clair.
Auch Andrew, finisher, h 78 N Dorman.
Auch Charles, mach A T Isensee, h 78 N Dorman.
Auch Henry, lab, b 78 N Dorman.
AUDITOR OF STATE'S OFFICE, Americus C Daily Auditor of State, Room 38 State House.

HAY & WILLITS MFG. CO.
76 N. PENNSYLVANIA ST.,
MAKERS
Outing BICYCLES
PHONE 598.

Auerbach Mark, cigar mnfr, 78 N Illinois, h 370 S Missouri.
Aufderheide Benjamin D, plater, b 272 Highland av.
Aufderheide Charles G, painter, b 58 Hillside av.
Aufderheide Charles J, carp, b 234 N Pine.
Aufderheide Gottfried, cigar mnfr, 52 Hillside av, h 58 same.
Aufderheide Henry, carp, 234 N Pine, h same.
Aufderheide Gottfried, cigarmkr, 52 Hillside av.
Aufderheide Henry C, bkkpr Michigan Lumber Co, h 407 S New Jersey.
Aufderheide Henry E, painter, h 96 Hill av.
Aufderheide John H (Aufderheide & Zumpfe), h 247 Central av.
Aufderheide Joseph, carp, h 272 Highland av.
Aufderheide Katherine (wid Ernst), b 318 N Delaware.
Aufderheide Walter H, blksmith, b 272 Highland av.
Aufderheide Wm, agt, b 58 Hillside av.
Aufderheide Wm, loans, 37½ E Washington, h 337 Central av.
AUFDERHEIDE & ZUMPFE (John H Aufderheide, Wm A Zumpfe), Real Estate and Investment Brokers, Room 4 Lombard Bldg.
Aug Jacob, lab, b 14 Athon.
Aughinbaugh Charles D, visitor Township Trustee's Office, h 1486 N Senate av.
Aughinbaugh Charles P, confr, 8 Malott av, h same.
Aughinbaugh Edward L, florist, 1572 N Meridian, h same.
Aughinbaugh Mary L, teacher, b 1572 N Meridian.
Aughinbaugh Sarah A (wid Henry P), b 1572 N Meridian.
Aughinbaugh Wm M, confr, 1149 N Alabama, h same.
Augstein Charles H, trav agt M O'Connor & Co, b 119 N Dorman.
Augstein Charles T, foreman, h 119 N Dorman.
Augstein Rudolph, clk, b 119 N Dorman.
Augusta Frederick, b 258 Alvord.
Ault Adam, engr, b e s Lincoln av 2 s of Jackson (M J).
Ault Percy B (P B Ault & Co), h 1104 N Penn.
AULT P B & CO (Percy B Ault, Garrett A Archibald), Gents' Furnishing Goods, 38 E Washington; Tel 830.
Aultman Co The, Edward T Kenney genl agt, agl implts, 3 Board of Trade bldg.
Aultman, Miller & Co, Henry J Prier genl agt, Buckeye Harvesting Machinery, 75-77 W Washington.
Aumann Charles F, sawmkr, h 19 Ketcham.
Aumann Henry H, tailor, h 103 N Senate av.
Auppely Conrad, lab, h 145 Sharpe av (W).
Aurine John, lab, h 533 W Francis (N I).
Austermiller Mary, bkkpr, b 142 N Senate av.
Austermiller Philip, engr, h 20 McGill.
Austermiller Wm, engr, h 157 W South.
Austermuehle Charles A, lab, h 207 E Morris.
Austermuhle Albert C (Linton & Co), h 1595 N Illinois.
Austin Albert A, mngr Austin & Tripp, b 23 S Summit.

ROOFING MATERIAL C. ZIMMERMAN & SONS, SLATE AND GRAVEL ROOFERS, 19 SOUTH EAST STREET.

DRIVEN WELLS And Second Water Wells and Pumps of all kinds at CHARLES KRAUSS', 42 S. PENN. ST., TEL. 465. REPAIRING NEATLY DONE.

Austin Algernon W, stenog, b 174 Bellefontaine.
Austin Benjamin, mach, b 88 Benton.
Austin Benjamin F, lab, h 61 S Noble.
Austin Cassius M, bricklyr, b 215 Spring.
Austin Catherine T (wid Algernon S), b 174 Bellefontaine.
Austin Charles D, carp, b 247 Huron.
Austin Charles H, lab, r 45½ Virginia av.
Austin Charles S, b 174 Bellefontaine.
Austin Charles S, contracting agt P C C & St L Ry, h 851 Ash.
Austin Edward A (Austin & Son and Austin & Tripp), h 23 S Summit.
Austin Elizabeth A, dressmkr, 128 Nordyke av (W I), h same.
Austin Ellen (wid John), h 276 Alvord.
Austin Frederick H, special examiner U S Pension Bureau, b 129 N Illinois.
Austin Gamaliel T, foreman, h 235 W Market.
Austin George, painter, h 234 S Missouri.
Austin Horace H, lab, b 171 W 5th.
Austin James J, saloon, 199 W Merrill, h same.
Austin Mary P, produce, 132 E Mkt House, h 215 Spring.
Austin Napoleon B, h 215 Spring.
Austin Richard J, mach hd, h 128 Nordyke av (W I).
Austin Wm W, engr, h 13 Paca.
Austin & Son (Edward A Austin), grocers, 852 E Washington.
Austin & Tripp (Edward A Austin, Albert E Tripp), driven wells, 31 W Maryland.
Avant Wm H (Wm Laurie & Co), h 380 N Delaware.
Avanthay Joseph, lab, b 164 W Maryland.
Avels Edward H, paperhngr, h 123 Kennington.
Avels George W, weighmstr, h 317 S Penn.
Avels Henry, paperhngr, 359 S Alabama, h same.
Avels Lulu, cashr George R Papp, b 317 S Penn.
Averdick Charles, bartndr, r 322 Clifford av.
Averett James R, barber, h 3 Carter.
AVERILL CHARLES E, Lawyer, 33-36 Thorpe Blk, h 121 Ruckle.
Averill Joseph A, yardmstr Vandalia Line, h 82 W 10th.
Averill Joseph T, clk, b 450 N East.
Averill Willis E, clk, b 82 W 10th.
Averitt T Alexander, carp, h 1379 N Senate av.
Avery Albert E, b 719 N Illinois.
Avery Catherine (wid Wm M), h 52 Johnson av.
Avery Edward E, printer, b 52 Johnson av.
Avery Edwin L, painter, 167½ W 1st, h 641 N Illinois.
Avery Elwood, real est, h 719 N Illinois.
Avery Eugene O E, brakeman, h 221 English av.
Avery Frank, painter, h 123 Clinton.
Avery Frank M, broommkr, b 56 Oak.
Avery Frank R, lab, h 215 E Wabash.
Avery George, lab, h 63 Camp.
Avery Guy C, grocer, 13 E Mkt House, h 164½ E Washington.
Avery Harry W, clk, b 719 N Illinois.
Avery Herschel, broommkr, b 56 Oak.
Avery Ida M, printer, b 52 Johnson av.
Avery Jesse A, canceling clk P O, h 193 Woodlawn av.
Avery John F, fitter, r 13 S Station (B).
Avery John L, b 449 N East.
Avery John P, phys, h 449 N East.

Richardson & McCrea,
REPRESENTING BEST KNOWN
FIRE INSURANCE COMPANIES.
Fidelity and Casualty Insurance Company of New York Represented.
Telephone 182. 79 East Market St.

Avery Leonard S, h 1197 N Capitol av.
Avery Matthias V, lab, h 56 Oak.
AVERY PLANTER CO, Frank Earnhart Mngr, Mnfrs of Engines, Threshers, Corn Planters and Cultivators, 45 Kentucky av; Tel 933.
Avery Ralph L, brakeman, h 33 Spann av.
Avery Sarah A (wid Enoch), r 12 Roanoke.
Avery Wm E, instructor Indianapolis Business University, When bldg, h 406 N Brookside av.
Avery Wm H, lab, h rear 301 N Pine.
Avey Harry, lab, b 117 N East.
Axelson Louis J, tailor, r 55 Dearborn.
Axman Louis H, jeweler, h 120 Mass av.
Axt Wm G, sec Indpls Abattoir Co, b Enterprise Hotel.
Axtell Adelbert, auctioneer, h 232½ S Meridian.
Axtell Cleo C, h 341 Central av.
Axtell Samuel P, cigars, 144 S Meridian, h 399 N East.
Axum Albert B, lab, h 88 Meikel.
Axum Wm, lab, h 88 Meikel.
Ayers Abraham, lab, b 412 S West.
Ayers Charles R, b 1190 N Illinois.
Ayers Cornelius, butler 530 N Delaware.
Ayers Edward, lab, h 219 Buchanan.
Ayers Elizabeth A (wid Pleasant), h 228 N East.
Ayers Fannie F, b 340 Cornell av.
Ayers Fay, nurse City Hospital.
Ayers Fenton E, molder, h 69 Haugh (H).
Ayers Frank S, clk, h 103 S William (W I).
Ayers George W, bartndr, b 412 S West.
Ayers James C, grocer, n e cor Washington and Denny, h same.
Ayers John C, lab, h 309 Yandes.
Ayers John O, boxmkr, b 412 S West.
Ayers John R, driver, b 1190 N Illinois.
Ayers Leonore, supt newspaper dept Organizer Pub Co, b 112 Park av.
Ayers Levi, carp, h 412 S West.
Ayers Morton G, carp, h w s Denny 2 n of Washington.
Ayers Nathan J, driver, h 208 Douglass.
Ayers Thomas E, watchman, h 61 Ludlow av.

The Williams Typewriter
Elegant Work, Visible Writing, Easy Operation, High Speed.
S. H. EAST, State Agent,
55 Thorpe Block, 87 E. Market St.

If You are not Satisfied with Your Laundry Work Give Us a Trial. ERTEL STEAM LAUNDRY 26 and 28 N. Senate Avenue. Telephone 1089.

ELLIS & HELFENBERGER Manufacturers of IRON and WIRE FENCES 162-170 S. SENATE AVE. TEL. 358.

THE HOGAN TRANSFER AND STORAGE COMP'Y
Household Goods and Pianos Moved—Packed—Stored...... Baggage and Package Express Machinery and Safes a Specialty Cor. Washington and Illinois Sts. TELEPHONE No. 675.

Hose, Belting, Packing, Clothing, Druggists' Sundries, Bicycle Tires, Cotton Hose, Etc. New York Belting & Packing Co., L't'd.
THE CENTRAL RUBBER & SUP LY CO. PHONE 922. 79 S. ILLINOIS ST., INDIANAPOLIS, IND.

HIGHEST SECURITY
LOWEST COST OF INSURANCE.
The Provident Life and Trust Co.
Of Philadelphia.
D. W. EDWARDS, Gen. Agent,
508 Indiana Trust Building.

Aylward Ellen (wid Thomas), b 30 Poplar (B).
Aylward James, lab, h 30 Poplar (B).
Ayres Albert F, lawyer, h 515 N New Jersey.
AYRES ALEXANDER C (Ayres & Jones), h 31 West Drive (W P).
Ayres Andrew F Rev, pastor Pilgrim Congregational Church, h s w cor Cottage av and Marion (W I).
Ayres A S (Brubaker & Ayres), h 179 N Alabama.
Ayres Charles A, bricklyr, b 258 S Olive.
Ayres David, woodturner, h 258 S Olive.
Ayres Ella J, stenog, b 258 S Olive.
Ayres Francis E, mach, h 217 Buchanan.
Ayres Frank L, mach, b 72 Bradshaw.
Ayres Frederick M, pres L S Ayres & Co, h 712 N Delaware.
Ayres Ida G, stenog Ayres & Jones, b 31 West Drive (W P).
Ayres Jesse O, lab, h w s Harris av 8 s of C C C & St L Ry (M J).
Ayres Julia E, stenog, b 258 S Olive.
Ayres Lucetta, boarding 86 E Ohio.
AYRES L S & CO, Frederick M Ayres Pres, Wm B Wheelock Vice-Pres, Maria H Ayres Sec and Treas, Dry Goods, Notions, Dressmaking, Millinery, Cloaks and Fur Goods, 33-37 W Washington; Tel 1007.
Ayres Maria H (wid Lyman S), sec and treas L S Ayres & Co, h 656 N Delaware.
Ayres Mary E (wid Thomas), b 189 E Market.
Ayres Sarah (wid Joseph), h 54 S Gale (B).
Ayres Wm D W, mach hd, h 72 Bradshaw.
Ayres Wm E, clk, b 79 Chadwick.
AYRES & JONES (Alexander C Ayres, Aquilla Q Jones), Lawyers, Rooms 500, 501, 502 Indiana Trust Bldg; Tel 148.

B

Baade Henry, blksmith, h 65 Germania av (H).

Julius C. Walk & Son,
Jewelers
Indianapolis.
12 EAST WASHINGTON ST.

Baar, see also Bahr, Barr, Bayer and Beyer.
Baar Bernhard J, tailor, h 187 N Liberty.
Baar George B, bartndr, b 187 N Liberty.
Baar Gerhard L, foreman, h 731 S Meridian.
Baar Joseph B, undertaker, r 276 E Market.
Baar Joseph C, cabtmkr, b 731 S Meridian.
Baar Leo A, tailor, b 187 N Liberty.
Baar Wm C, bkkpr, b 731 S Meridian.
Baas James W, huckster, h 138 Forest av.
Baase Charles G, clk Taylor & Smith, h 138 Dunlop.
Baase Christian L, express, h 14 Hendricks.
Baase Elizabeth M (wid Henry C), b 562 Chestnut.
Baase Henry C, foreman Outing Bicycle Co, h 244 Union.
Baase Henry L, express, h 562 Chestnut.
Baase Herman J, mach, b 14 Hendricks.
Baase John, express, h 347 Union.
Baase Wm, barber, h 26 Gresham.
Baaske Charles T, saloon, 20 N Delaware, h 35 N Beville av.
Babb Laurel V, teacher Public School No 22, b 524 N Capitol av.
Babb Robert A, collr, h 349 N Noble.
Babbitt Franklin, lab, h 48 Bismarck (W I).
Babbitt Isaac, mach, h 949 N Senate av.
Babbitt O'Bannon, carp, h 10 William.
Babbitt Wm A, lab, h 1183 Morris (W I).
Babbitt Wm A, painter The Blacherne, h 72 Fletcher av.
Babcock Adrian, cigar mnfr, 105½ Mass av, h 66 Clifford av.
Babcock Albert, clk, b 40 College av.
Babcock Charles E, clk The Indianapolis Journal, b 244 College av.
Babcock Edward E, trav agt, h 244 College av.
Babcock Frederick W, carp, h 62 Hoyt av.
Babcock Josephine (wid Wm M), h 40 College av.
Baber Adin (A Baber & Co), res Kansas, Ill.
Baber A & Co (Adin Baber, James B Sedwick, Edwin Nichols), live stock, Union Stock Yards (W I).
Baber Emma F, teacher Public School No 4, b 307 N Senate av.
BABY SUPPLY MANUFACTURING CO (Thomas Nesom), Mnfrs of Baby Supplies, Baby Hammocks, Folding Baby Cabs and Outing Tents, 256 S East. (See adv p 7; also classified Baby Buggies; also in Hammocks.)
Bache Henry, molder, h 180 N Belmont av (H).
Bacher Herman, saloon, 26 S Missouri, h same.
Bachman David, lab, b e s Northwestern av 1 n of 30th.
BACHMAN FREDERICK M, Lumber, s e cor Madison av and Lincoln la, h 670 N Meridian; Tel 920.
Bachman Louis, mach hd, h 436 E Vermont.
Bachman Narcissa, b 117 St Mary.
Bachman Thomas, tmstr, b 880 Milburn (M P).
Bachman Valentine, flour mill, n w cor Madison av and Ray, h 287 Union.
Backemeyer Charles H jr, driver, b 235 Union.
Backemeyer Frederick G, express, h 235 Union.
Backemier Charles H, grocer, 429 W Pratt, h same.

OTTO GAS ENGINES
BUILDERS' EXCHANGE S. W. Cor. Ohio and Penn. Telephone 535.

Becker & Son Charles Becker Jacob Becker Jr. Merchant Tailors. 21 N. Penn. St. Tel. 934

SALISBURY & STANLEY OF FC, SAND BANK FIXTURES.

Backer Frederick, molder, h 105 Tremont av (H).
Backer George, lab, h 1522 N Illinois.
Backer John A, blksmith, b 33 Clay.
Backley Leonard J, planer, h 139 Harrison.
Backley Susan (wid Isaac), h 425 Muskingum al.
Backmann Bernard, gardener, h 865 Madison av.
Backmann Frederick J, hostler, b 264 E Wabash.
Backmeyer Henry, produce, E Mkt House, h Madison rd 2 s of city limits.
Backus Catherine (wid Wm), b 215 Blake.
Backus Charles E, engr, r 18 Miley av.
Backus Frank, carp, b 140 Bellefontaine.
Backus Mary (wid Thomas), h 215 Dougherty.
Backus Thomas, waiter, b rear 121 N Senate av.
Backus Victor M, contr, h 773 N Meridian.
Bacon Bert, clk P L Chambers, b 243 Alvord.
Bacon Duncan T, mngr Indiana Car Service Assn, Union Station, h 200 N Illinois.
Bacon Edgar H, r 9½ Fletcher av.
Bacon Hattie C, phys, 9½ Fletcher av, h same.
Bacon Henry F, insp Cent U Tel Co, b 236 N Illinois.
Bacon Hiram, h 12 Ruckle.
Bacon Jasper N, trav agt, b 162 N Illinois.
Bacon Jennie, bkkpr Excelsior Laundry, b 236 N Illinois.
Bacon John L, dresser, h 243 Alvord.
Bacon Lambert L, clk, b 243 Alvord.
Bacon Mary E (wid Wm M), h 236 N Illinois.
Bacon Robert D, mer police, h 608 E Washington.
Bacon Wesley C, tilemkr, b 608 E Washington.
Bacon Wm T, trav agt George W Stout, h 471 Broadway.
Bade, se also Baade.
Bade Christina (wid Anthony F), h 209 S Alabama.
Bade Edward F, waiter, b 194 E Washington.
Bade Emma L (wid Charles H), b 266 E Ohio.
Bade George C, h 209 S Alabama.
Bade Henry C, clk Charles J Kuhn Co, r 69½ W Market.
Bade Henry F, checkman, h 136 E South.
Bade Lewis A, tmstr, h 30 N Olive.
Bade Wm F, supt Central Transfer Co, h 338 S New Jersey.
Bademan John, clk, r 75 Union.
Baden Charles N, collr, h 21 Dearborn.
Bader Albert, lab, b 42 Jones.
Bader Anna B, r 23 Hutchings blk.
Bader Edward W, mach hd, h 47 Iowa.
Bader Elizabeth (wid Jacob), barber, 320 E Washington, h 30 Dickson.
Bader Jacob, brewer, h 54 Morton.
Bader Wm, tuner Pearson's Music House, h 14 Tuxedo.
Bader Wm H, clk N Y Store, r 23 Hutchings blk.
Badger Albert, barber, b 278 Howard (W I).
Badger Charles H, pres and treas Badger Furniture Co, h 1160 N Alabama.
Badger David H, student, b 88 Hadley av (W I).
Badger Edward, sawmkr, h 278 Howard (W I).

Henry H. Fay, 40½ E. WASHINGTON ST., AGENT FOR Insurance Co. of North America, Pennsylvania Fire Ins. Co.

BADGER FURNITURE COMPANY, Charles H Badger Pres and Treas, M R Badger Sec, Furniture, Draperies, Upholstery, Etc, 75-77 E Washington and 20-24 Virginia av; Tel 291.
Badger John W, carver, b 88 Hadley av (W I).
Badger M R, sec Badger Furniture Co, h 1160 N Alabama.
Badger Sarah (wid Wm), h 436 W Udell (N I).
Badger Theodore, mach, h 88 Hadley av (W I).
Badger Wm E, mach, b 88 Hadley av (W I).
Badgley Richard, trav agt The H Lieber Co, b Spencer House.
Baech Edward Rev, associate pastor Second Presbyterian Church, h 296 S Meridian.
Baechler Jeremiah J, clk, b 83 N Noble.
Baehning Charles W, mach hd, b 467 E St Clair.
Baen Camille R, stenog Krag-Reynolds Co, b 23 Ft Wayne av.
Baer Isaac, foreman, h 183 N Pine.
Baer James H, messenger Am Ex Co, b 161 Meek.
Baerholdt Herman, hostler, b 43 Kansas.
Bagby Robert B, dep County Clerk, b 289 Blake.
Baggerly Charles W, cigar mnfr, 78 W Maryland, h 299 Cornell av.
Baggett Mary A (wid Wm), h 135 Agnes.
Baggott Frederick, lab, h rear 291 W Maryland.
Baggott John, peddler, h 82 Patterson.
Baggott John E, butcher, b 82 Patterson.
Baggott Thomas, grocer, 479 W Michigan, h 477 same.
Baggs Charles A, trav agt, h 413 N New Jersey.
Baggs Delbert K, clk, b 413 N New Jersey.
Baggs Frederick, mngr Indpls Clearing House Assn, h 548 N Capitol av.
Baggs Thomas B, bkkpr, h 167 E Walnut.
Bagley Alta J (wid Wm R), h 53½ Russell av.

MAYHEW'S SPECTACLES THE BEST IN USE SOLD ONLY AT 13 N. MERIDIAN ST.

Contractors and Builders. Repairing of all kinds done on short notice. 177 C... St. Indianapolis, Ind. Telephone 99

LUMBER Sash and Doors BALKE & KRAUSS CO., Corner Market and Missouri Sts.

Friedgen Has the BEST PATENT LEATHER SHOES AT LOWEST PRICES. 19 North Pennsylvania St.

SAMUEL LAING : HOT AIR FURNACES 72 AND 74 EAST COURT STREET.

M. B. Wilson, Pres. W. F. Churchman, Cash.
The Capital National Bank,
INDIANAPOLIS, IND.
Banking business in all its branches. Bonds and Foreign Exchange bought and sold.
Interest paid on time deposits.
Checks and drafts on all Indiana and Illinois points handled at lowest rates.
No. 28 South Meridian Street, Cor. Pearl.

Bagley Frank J, auditor, h 519 N Meridian.
Bagley Wm R, carp, 180 E Court, h 331 E New York.
Bagley Wm T, showman, h 53½ Russell av.
Bagnelle Alfaretta, h 388 N Alabama.
Bahle Herman H, carp, h 48 Sterling.
Bahr, see also Baar, Barr, Bayer and Beyer.
Bahr Elizabeth (wid Bernhard), h 431 Howard (W I).
Bahr Elizabeth (wid Bernhard), h 403 Madison av.
Bahr Josephine, clk The Wm H Block Co, b 403 Madison av.
Bahr Mary, clk Robert Keller, b 403 Madison av.
Bahr Max A, phys City Dispensary, 32 E Ohio, b 572 E Washington.
Bahr Michael, varnisher, b 403 Madison av.
Bahr Paul, music teacher, 572 E Washington, h same.
Bahr Wm J, varnisher, b 403 Madison av.
Baier George, lab, h 70 Kansas.
Bailey Allen H, actor, h 499 N West.
Bailey Andrew J, real est, 94½ E Washington, h 54 William (W I).
Bailey Charles, driver, h e s West 2 s of 1st.
Bailey Charles, lab, b n s 8th 3 w of canal.
Bailey Charles C, mach hd, h 227 Union.
Bailey Charles H (Bailey Mnfg Co), h 297 N Delaware.
Bailey Charles H, clk, b 54 William (W I).
Bailey Charles H, express, h 28 Oregon.
Bailey Charles M, tmstr, h 120½ Maple.
Bailey Charles P, tmstr, h 9 Taylor av.
Bailey Clara, b 58 Greer.
Bailey Curtis, lab, b 494 S West.
Bailey Doc, lab, h 10 Hiawatha.
Bailey Etta (wid Benjamin), h 29 W Michigan.
Bailey Francis M, clk, h 68 S McLain (W I).
Bailey Frank G, salesman, b 182 N Senate av.
Bailey Frank M, candymkr, b 188 W Vermont.
Bailey Frank P, vice pres L W Ott Mnfg Co, h 1030 N Capitol av.

Insure Against Accidents
WITH
TUTTLE & SEGUIN,
Agents for
Fidelity and Casualty Co., of New York.
$10,000 for $25. $5,000 for $12.50.
TEL. 1168. 28 E. MARKET ST.

Bailey Frederick T, tailor, b n w cor Michigan and State avs.
Bailey Frederick W, lab, h 57 Drake.
Bailey Grant, tmstr, b 273 S Capitol av.
Bailey Harry, lab, h e s Perkins pike 2 s of C C C & St L Ry.
Bailey Hassen E, packer, h 208 Lexington av.
Bailey Haven M, brakeman, h 443 W Michigan.
Bailey Henry, lab, b 66 S California.
Bailey Henry F, blksmith, h 414 Columbia av.
Bailey Iola, stenog Horace McKay, b 293 N Delaware.
Bailey Jacob, lab, h 79 Columbia al.
Bailey James, h 66 S California.
Bailey James, mach, r 101 N New Jersey.
Bailey James L, grocer, 326 S Olive, h 328 same.
Bailey James W, helper, h 350 S East.
Bailey John C, driver, h n w cor 4th and Lafayette.
Bailey John E, boarding n w cor Michigan and State avs.
BAILEY JOHN M, Lawyer, Rooms 1-2, 37½ E Washington, h 222 Walcott; Tel 276.
Bailey John T, switchman, h 260 Springfield.
Bailey John W, tmstr, h 275 Highland av.
Bailey Joseph M, b 1030 N Capitol av.
Bailey Leon O (Kern & Bailey), b Grand Hotel.
Bailey Lewis I, lab, h rear 468 Highland av.
Bailey L Foster, mngr furnaces 33 W Market, h 487½ W Addison (N I).
Bailey Manufacturing Co (Charles H Bailey, Finley B Pugh), clothing mnfrs, 196 S Meridian.
Bailey Mary (wid John), b 44 Leon.
Bailey Mary A (wid Joel), h 273 S Capitol av.
Bailey Mary A, b e s Capitol av 3 s of 30th.
Bailey Mary F, cook, h 306½ E Washington.
Bailey Mary H (wid Alvin L), h 344½ E St Clair.
Bailey Maud, h 123 Ft Wayne av.
Bailey Michael, b 1030 N Capitol av.
Bailey Oliver E, tinner, b 120½ Maple.
Bailey Otis, mach hd, b 120½ Maple.
Bailey Richard T, fireman, h 5 Traub av.
Bailey Robert, tmstr, h 113 Patterson.
Bailey Samuel C, tmstr, h w s Elwood 2 n of North.
Bailey Walter C, carpetlayer, b 499 N West.
Bailey Wiley, porter, h 210 Middle.
Bailey Wm, agt, r 31½ Virginia av.
Bailey Wm, tinner, h 33 Fletcher av.
Bailey Wm, trav agt, b 182 N Senate av.
Bailey Wm E, lab, b 480 W 22d (N I).
Bailey Wm E, lawyer, 20½ N Delaware, b 328 S Olive.
Bailey Wm S, trav agt, r 209 W Ohio.
Baillie Hamilton, coal, rear 148 S West, h 606 W Vermont.
Baillie Samuel F, grocer, 92 Agnes, h same.
Baily Jesse S, dentist, 18 E Ohio, h same.
Baily Samuel, saloon, 164 Indiana av, h same.
Baily Van Buren, lab, h 182 Lee (W I).
Baily Warren D, lab, h 184 Lee (W I).
Bain Catherine, stenog, b 434 Talbott av.
Bain David Z, blksmith, h w s Station 3 n of Schofield (B).
Bain John, fireman, b 32 Jefferson av.
Bain John, lab, b 328 E Washington.
Bain John R, saloon, 101 S Noble, h same.
Bain Karl J, stenog Francke & Schindler, b 434 Talbott av.

WEDDING CAKE BOXES · SULLIVAN & MAHAN 41 W. Pearl St.

DIAMOND WALL PLASTER { Telephone 1410 BUILDERS' EXCHANGE.

Best Work. Prompt Delivery. } THE HOME LAUNDRY 19 S. ILLINOIS ST. TEL. 1769. { Collars and Cuffs our Specialty.

Bain Margaret M (wid Wm C), b 101 S Noble.
Bain Patrick J, lab, b 271 W Market.
Bain Phoebe A (wid John I), h 434 Talbott av.
Bain Wm S, fireman, h 32 Jefferson av.
Bain Wm S, truckman, h 92 Spring.
Bainbridge Clinton, cigarmkr, b 82 Michigan av.
Bainbridge James, turner, b 82 Michigan av.
Bainbridge Lucien, helper, h 503 E Washington.
Bainbridge Margaret (wid Mahlon), h 82 Michigan av.
Baine Collins E, polisher, h 71 S Liberty.
Baine Jennie E (wid Thomas), h 134 Douglass.
Baine Ralph H, plumber, b 134 Douglass.
Baine Thomas W, fireman, h 227 English av.
Baine Wm W, agt, b 134 Douglass.
Baining Charles, b rear 555 E St Clair.
Bair Oliver P, mngr Warder, Bushnell & Glessner Co, 96 S Capitol av, h 94 Ruckle.
Bair Priscilla C (wid David), b 353 N Illinois.
Baird, see also Beard.
Baird Amos B, lab, b 175 W North.
Baird George W, cook, h s s Sturm av 1 e of N Arsenal av.
Baird Janet (wid Hugh), h 30 Elder av.
Baird Jeremiah W, waiter, r 175 W North.
Baird John C, bkkpr The Bowen-Merrill Co, h 1208 N Illinois.
Baird John W, lawyer, 19½ N Meridian, h 33 Christian av.
Baird Margaret A (wid Wm), b 721 N Illinois.
Baird Samuel F, lab, h 62 S Arsenal av.
BAIRD'S PHARMACY, Wm H Baird Propr, s e cor E Michigan and Highland av.
Baird Sarah A, h 108½ Mass av.
Baird Wm, brakeman, h 23 S Arsenal av.
Baird Wm E, porter, h 504 W Chicago (N I).
Baird Wm H, propr Baird's Pharmacy, h 222 Highland av.
Baist John R, saloon, 2 Warman av (H), h same.
Baity Carl, lab, b 146 S East.
Baity Estol, mach hd, b 146 S East.
Baity Henry R, brazier, h 146 S East.
Bake Jacob, painter, r 89½ N Delaware.
Bake John F, driver, h 44 Bismarck.
Bakemeier Charles H, collr Polar Ice Co, h 39 Sullivan.
Bakemeier Emma, dressmkr, 475 Virginia av, h same.
Bakemeier Mary (wid Henry), h rear 475 Virginia av.
Bakemeier Mary, b 475 Virginia av.
Bakemeyer Andrew H, tinner, 359 Indiana av, h 13 Hamilton av.
Bakemeyer Gertrude, bkkpr, h 41 Bradshaw.
Bakemeyer Harry, clk Frank K Sawyer, b 184 Broadway.
Bakemeyer Henry C, salesman Geo W Stout, h 184 Broadway.
Bakemeyer Henry F, foreman, h 41 Bradshaw.
Baker, see also Becker and Boecher.
Baker Aaron C, lab, h 56 Hazel.
Baker Albert (Baker & Daniels), h 760 N Penn.

FRANK NESSLER. WILL H. ROST.
FRANK NESSLER & CO.
Tailors
56 EAST MARKET ST. (Lemcke Building),
INDIANAPOLIS, IND.

Baker Albert J, barber, 508 E Washington, h 514 E Ohio.
Baker Alden H (Hinshaw & Baker), b 208 Ash.
Baker Alice, b 350 Park av.
Baker Alice I, b 367 N East.
Baker Alvia, watchman, b rear 339 S Delaware.
Baker Amanda, b 60 S Noble.
Baker Anna (wid Richard), b 119 N New Jersey.
Baker Anna M (wid Isaiah), b w s Grand av 4 s of University av (I).
Baker Arthur J, carp, b s w cor Moore av and Grace.
Baker Asa T, lab, b 507 S Capitol av.
Baker Austin, porter, r 19 W Pearl.
Baker Bertha (wid Jesse A), milliner, 214 E Washington, h same.
Baker Braxton, pres Standard S and L Assn, h 372 Park av.
Baker Bros (Omer G and Clarence I), furniture, 141 Mass av.
Baker Carleton, stenog, b 136 W 1st.
Baker Charles, brakeman, h 204 S Pine.
Baker Charles, lab, h 174 Indiana av.
BAKER CHARLES, Publisher Grand, English's and Park Theater Programmes, 39 Virginia av, h 24-25 Wyandot Blk; Tel 1220.
Baker Charles E D, janitor, b 5 Taylor av.
Baker Charles F, hostler, h 184 Bates.
Baker Charles W, cooper, b 125 N West.
Baker Charlotte F (wid Conrad), h 350 Park av.
Baker Christian H, lab, h 78 Arizona.
Baker Clarence I (Baker Bros), b 367 N East.
Baker Daniel, r 100 N Senate av.
Baker David F, mason, h 135 Martindale av.
Baker David M, barber Hotel English, b 367 Blake.
Baker Donnie, b 147 W South.
Baker Dora, h 89 N Delaware.
Baker Doras J, grocer, n w cor Washington and Crawfordsville rd (M J), h same.
Baker Edgar J (Baker & Flechart), h 245 Fletcher av.

Haueisen & Hartmann
163-169 E. Washington St.
FURNITURE,
Carpets,
Household Goods,
Tin, Granite and China Wares, Oil Cloth and Shades

THE WM. H. BLOCK CO. 7 AND 9 EAST WASHINGTON STREET. DRY GOODS, HOUSE FURNISHINGS AND CROCKERY.

London Guarantee and Accident Co. (Ltd.) All forms of Liability Insurance, Workmen's Collective Insurance, Fidelity Bonds and Individual Accident Insurance.
Geo. W. Pangborn, Gen. Agent, 704-706 Lemcke Bldg. Telephone 140.

FRANK K. SAWYER, AGENT 74 East Market Street. Telephone 863.

JOSEPH GARDNER,
TIN, COPPER AND SHEET-IRON WORK AND
HOT AIR FURNACES.
37, 39 & 41 KENTUCKY AVE. Telephone 322.

Baker Edward, lab, b Exchange Hotel (W I).
Baker Edward, waiter, r 103 W South.
Baker Edward R, condr, h 269½ E Washington.
Baker Edward S, printer, h 37½ W Washington.
Baker Elbert M, tel opr, b 25 Miley av.
Baker Elma M, nurse, r 149 N Penn.
Baker Elmer A, grocer, 303 Shelby, h same.
Baker Elmer C, stairbuilder, h 32 Marion av (W I).
Baker Elmer E, varnishmkr, h 33 Grant.
Baker E Brown, civ engr Central Engineering Co, 225 Lemcke bldg, b 29 Butler.
Baker Frank F, lab, b 530 S New Jersey.
Baker Frank P, carp, h n w cor Broadway and 22d.
Baker Frank P, student, h 411 Coburn.
Baker Frank W, phys, 31 W Market, h 812 N Meridian.
Baker Frederick, plastr, b 201 E Washington.
Baker Garrett, r 190½ S Illinois.
Baker George B H, plumber, b 520 College av.
Baker George E, clk, b 303 Shelby.
Baker George P, cooper, h rear 194 Dougherty.
Baker George W, h e s Addison 1 s of Washington (M J).
Baker George W, carp, h 50 Paw Paw.
Baker Georgia, dressmkr, 37½ W Washington, h same.
Baker Hattie (wid Henry), h 17 Center.
Baker Henry W, lab, h 11 Dawson.
Baker Hugh, b 190½ S Illinois.
Baker Jacob, cigar mnfr, 195 Virginia av, r 37½ W Market.
Baker Jacob E, bartndr, h 411 Coburn.
Baker Jacob P, lab, b 117 Lincoln la.
Baker James C, clk, r 127 W Maryland.
Baker James G, barber, h 239 S Senate av.
Baker James L, barber, b 105 N Alabama.
Baker James L, lab, b n w cor Glen Drive and Station (B).
Baker James M, lab, h 47 Michigan (H).
Baker James P, lawyer, 29-31 Thorpe blk, h 109 Central av.
Baker James T, barber, h 85 Park av.

J. S. FARRELL & CO.
STEAM AND HOT WATER
HEATING FOR STORES, OFFICES,
PUBLIC BUILDINGS,
PRIVATE RESIDENCES,
GREENHOUSES, ETC.
84 North Illinois St. Telephone 382.

Baker Jason E (Ritter & Baker), h w s Grand av 4 s of University av (I).
Baker Jennie (wid Henry), h rear 318 Indiana av.
Baker Jennie (wid Joseph), h w s Gale 3 n of Willow (B).
Baker Joel A, h 259 River av (W I).
Baker John, clk R M S, h 23 Ruckle.
Baker John, mach, r 23 N West.
Baker John A, lab, b 1541 N Capitol av.
Baker John H, carp, h 367 N East.
Baker John H, judge U S District Court, b The Denison.
Baker John J, phys, 37½ W Market, h 208 Ash.
Baker John M (Hussey & Baker), h 520 College av.
Baker John P, foreman, h 1094 E Ohio.
Baker John W, express, h rear 643 N Senate av.
Baker Joseph, lab, h rear 1867 E Washington.
Baker Joseph C, cooper, b n w cor Michigan and State avs.
Baker Joseph F, mngr, h 177 College av.
Baker Joseph L, cooper, b 67 S California.
Baker Joseph T, carp, 30 Tacoma av, h same.
Baker Julia B, h 120 W Maryland.
Baker J Corry, clk, r 82 W Ohio.
Baker Leo, barber, b 154 E Ohio.
Baker Louisa E, h 233 N Delaware.
Baker Lucy A (wid John), h 344 W North.
Baker Mamie, h 161½ W Washington.
Baker Mamie C (wid Alvia), stenog Tutewiler & Shideler, b 267 N New Jersey.
Baker Manville W, artist, 265 N New Jersey, h same.
Baker Margaret (wid Charles), h rear 612 N West.
Baker Margaret (Baker & Hartbeck), b 444 N New Jersey.
Baker Mary (wid Charles C), h 361 Cornell av.
Baker Milledge A (West Side Planing Mills), h 30 Coble.
Baker Nancy (wid George W), h 187 Brookside av.
Baker Noah P, lab, b 507 S Capitol av.
Baker Obadiah, lab, h 61 Catharine.
Baker Omer G (Baker Bros), h 367 N East.
Baker Oro E, packer, h 567½ Virginia av.
Baker Peter, foreman, h 5 Morgan (W I).
Baker Richard, lab, h 411 Coburn.
Baker Robert A, grocer, 71 Pendleton av (B), h same.
Baker Rosa (wid Santiago), h rear 472 W New York.
Baker Sarah, h 17 N East.
Baker Sarah E, h 85 Park av.
Baker Sarah E, h 239 S Senate av.
Baker Sarah E (wid Isaac), h 474 N California.
Baker Sarah M (wid Edward P), h 5 Taylor av.
Baker Sophia H (wid Stephen), h 520 College av.
Baker Thaddeus R, clk, b 350 Park av.
Baker Thomas E, carp, h rear 137 Martindale av.
Baker Thomas J, foreman, h 507 S Capitol av.
Baker Thomas M, clk The Gordon-Kurtz Co, h 233 N Delaware.
Baker Thomas O, trav agt, r 378 N Meridian.
Baker Thornton T, clk, b 303 Shelby.
Baker Victor W, pressman, h 431 S State av.

Prussian National Insurance Company OF STETTIN, GERMANY. ORGANIZED 1845.

United States Life Insurance Co., of New York.
E. B. SWIFT, M'g'r. 25 E. Market St.

WM. KOTTEMAN 89 & 91 E. Washington St. Telephone 1742 RUGS MATTINGS WINDOW SHADES

WILLIAM WIEGEL MANUFACTURER OF .... SHOW CASES 6 W. Louisiana St. Opposite Union Station.

Baker Wm, canmkr, b 869 S Meridian.
Baker Wm, lab, b 12 Eldridge (N I).
Baker Wm, mach, b 361 Cornell av.
Baker Wm E, carp, h s w cor Moore av and Grace.
Baker Wm H, lab, h 327½ E Washington.
Baker Wm H, propr Enterprise Hotel, h 191 N Delaware.
Baker Wm L (Baker & Thornton), h 440 Park av.
Baker Wm M, bottler, b 367 N East.
Baker Wm M, lab, h 84 Yandes.
Baker Wm W (Blair, Baker & Walter), h 1496 N Illinois.
Baker Winfield S, bartndr, h 587 Marlowe av.
BAKER & DANIELS (Albert Baker, Edward Daniels), Lawyers, 9, 10 and 11 Ingalls Blk; Tel 106.
Baker & Fleehart (Edgar J Baker, James E Fleehart), tinners, 141 Ash.
Baker & Hartbeck (Margaret Baker, Emma Hartbeck), milliners, 378 S East.
BAKER & THORNTON (Wm L Baker, Henry C Thornton), Stationers, Blank Book Mnfrs, Printers and School Goods, 38 S Meridian; Tel 1777.
Balay Etta (wid Benjamin C), h 15 E New York.
Balch John A, agt, h 56 Central av.
Balch Percy, barber, 287 Mass av, h 90 Ramsey av.
Balcom Otis J, trav agt, h 49 Beaty.
Balcom Stephen F, civ engr, h 449 N Senate av.
Baldock Elizabeth J (wid Wm), b 225 Eureka av.
Baldock Wm S, carp, h 225 Eureka av.
Baldon Lun, lab, b 46 Jones.
Baldon Stephen, lab, h 46 Jones.
Baldridge Jane (wid Charles), h 271 Lafayette.
Baldus Caroline (wid John), grocer, 42 Pendleton av (B), h same.
Baldus George F, lab, h 316 Excelsior av.
Baldus Henry P, helper, h n w cor Gale and Willow (B).
Baldus Ignatz F, engr, b 42 Pendleton av (B).
Baldus John J, clk, b 42 Pendleton av (B).
Baldus Joseph, saloon, 250 N Noble, h same.
Baldwin Amos J, fireman, b 287 Fletcher av.
Baldwin Benjamin, tmstr, h n w cor Berlin av and 20th.
Baldwin Benjamin jr, lab, b n w cor Berlin av and 20th.
Baldwin Celia, h 51 Rhode Island.
Baldwin Dwight H (D H Baldwin & Co), r Cincinnati, O.
BALDWIN D H & CO (Dwight H Baldwin, Lucien Wulsin, George W Armstrong, Albert A VanBuren, Clarence Wulsin), Pianos and Organs, 95-99 N Penn; Tel 47.
Baldwin Ebenezer, boarding 1 S Gale (B).
Baldwin Edward, tmstr, h 237 S Reisner (W I).
Baldwin Esther (wid Louis H), h 33 Tacoma av.
Baldwin Frank M, mnfrs agt, 83 Baldwin blk, h 1090 N Penn.
Baldwin George A, metalwkr Indpls Pattern Wks, b 184 E Vermont.
Baldwin Greene, lab, h 8 Hazel.
Baldwin Isaac D, r 23 Brandon blk.

THOS. C. DAY & CO.
Financial Agents and Loans.
We have the experience, and claim to be reliable.
Rooms 325 to 330 Lemcke Bldg.

Baldwin James H, office 83 Baldwin blk, h 385 N Penn.
Baldwin Jesse, brakeman, h 33 Tacoma av.
Baldwin John, lab, b 19 Woodburn av (W I).
Baldwin Lewis L, clk R M S, b Sherman House.
BALDWIN, MILLER & CO (Silas Baldwin, Enrique C Miller, Joseph E Reagan), Wholesale Watches, Clocks and Jewelry, 31-34 Commercial Club Bldg; Tel 932.
Baldwin Robert W, fireman, b 30 Oliver av (W I).
Baldwin Silas (Baldwin, Miller & Co), b 318 N Meridian.
Baldwin Stephen, lab, h 46 Jones.
Baldwin Thomas, lab, h 1373 N Capitol av.
Baldwin Thomas L, fireman, h 57 Pierce.
Baldwin Wm, lab, h 525 W Wells (N I).
Baldwin Wm R, brakeman, r 101 Bates.
Bales Arthur S, brakeman, h 49 S Gale (B).
Bales Berton B, clk Hord & Perkins, b 1105 N Senate av.
Bales Mack C, fireman, b 90 N Senate av.
Bales Otho D, clk When Clothing Store, b 1105 N Senate av.
Bales Solomon D, broker, Union Stock Yards (W I), b 94 S Reisner (W I).
Bales Walter, brakeman, b 23 Poplar (B).
Bales Wm P, clk Original Eagle, h 1105 N Senate av.
Balfe John, elev condr Murphy, Hibben & Co, b 350 E Morris.
Balfe Josephine C, bkkpr Acme Steam Laundry, b 350 E Morris.
Balfe Vitalis C (wid John), h 350 E Morris.
Balfour Alexander C (Balfour, Potts & Doolittle), h 124 Highland pl.
Balfour Charles O, clk Indiana Bicycle Co, b 290 Dillon.
Balfour James M (Balfour & Prasse), h 290 Dillon.
Balfour, Potts & Doolittle (Alexander C Balfour, Edward G Potts, Edwin F Doolittle), butter, 28 S Delaware.
Balfour & Prasse (James M Balfour, Christian Prasse), saloon, 559 Virginia av.

EAT
QUAKER BREAD
ASK YOUR GROCER FOR IT.
THE HITZ BAKING CO.

Capital Steam Carpet Cleaning Works
M. D. PLUNKETT Proprietor, Telephone 818

BENJ. BOOTH PRACTICAL EXPERT ACCOUNTANT. Complicated or disputed accounts investigated and adjusted. Room 18, 82½ E. Wash. St., Ind'p'l's, Ind.

18 and 20 South Meridian Street KERSHNER BROS., Proprs. THE SHERMAN RESTAURANT

ESTABLISHED 1876. TELEPHONE 168.
CHESTER BRADFORD,
SOLICITOR OF PATENTS,
AND COUNSEL IN PATENT CAUSES.
(See adv. page 6.)
Office:—Rooms 14 and 16 Hubbard Block, S.W. Cor. Washington and Meridian Streets, INDIANAPOLIS, INDIANA.

Balk Lizzie E, cigars, 80 E Market, b 223 W South.
Balk Wm A, h 308 Yandes.
Balke Charles R, pres Balke & Krauss Co, h 278 N Senate av.
Balke Louisa (wid Charles), b 278 N Senate av.
BALKE & KRAUSS CO, Charles R Balke Pres, Henry Griffiths Vice-Pres, Herman H Schulz Sec and Treas, Lumber, Lime and Coal and Planing Mill, cor Market and Missouri; Tel 1081. (See right bottom lines.)
Ball Addison W, phys, 132 Columbia av, h same.
Ball Albert J, clk R M S, b 327 N Illinois.
Ball Chauncey, lab, h w s James 1 n of Division (B).
Ball Courtland, r 37½ W Market.
Ball Cutler T (Ball & Maple), h 1609 N Illinois.
Ball Edward C, trav agt, h 39 Eastern av.
Ball Ellen, h 172 Blackford.
Ball Elmer M, architect, r 205 S Pine.
Ball Frank, lab, h 39 Brett.
Ball Frank W, printer, b 106 Oliver av (W I).
Ball George, r 212½ S Meridian.
Ball James T, flagman, h 240 W Market.
Ball Jeremiah C, hostler, r 120 E Wabash.
Ball Jessie M (wid Jerome C), boarding 68 S State av.
Ball John C, shoemkr, r 154 Madison av.
Ball John E, tel opr, b 74 W New York.
Ball John S, lab, h w s James 1 n of Division (B).
Ball Leila R, b 1609 N Illinois.
Ball Lily V, elocutionist, b w s Ritter av 6 n of Washington av (I).
Ball May, mngr Willcox & Gibbs Sewing Machine Co, 108 N Penn, r 124 E Ohio.
Ball Napoleon D, trav agt, h w s Ritter av 6 n of Washington av (I).
Ball Nathan, carp, h 98 Paca.
Ball Orlow B, city circulator The Indpls News, h 17 Hoyt av.
Ball Rinaldo L, polisher, b 495 E 9th.

Metal Ceilings and all kinds of Copper, Tin and Sheet Iron work.
O. B. ENSEY,
TELEPHONE 1562.
CORNER 6TH AND ILLINOIS STS.

Ball Susan A, h 63 Lexington av.
Ball Thomas, lab, r 355 S Capitol av.
Ball Wm, carp, b 240 W Market.
Ball Wm T, agt, h 55 Ellen.
Ball Wm T, tailor, h 39 Eastern av.
BALL & MAPLE (Cutler T Ball, Alfred L Maple), Proprs Electro Cure Institute, Rooms 1-2, 29½ W Ohio.
Ballance Robert J, mach, h 871 Cornell av.
Ballard Austin, engraver, h 52 Bellefontaine.
Ballard Celeste G, stenog Secretary of State, b 159 N Illinois.
Ballard Charles B (Russie & Ballard), h 44 Stevens.
Ballard David F, huckster, h 3 Hill.
Ballard Frank L F, gateman, h 1775 Graceland av.
Ballard Frank O Rev, pastor Memorial Presbyterian Church, h 401 Ash.
Ballard Granville M, real est, 19 Talbott blk, h 293 N Meridian.
Ballard Harrison W, h 287 N Meridian.
Ballard Harry C, clk Van Camp H and I Co, h 152 Dougherty.
Ballard Henry, lab, h w s Caroline av 3 n of Hillside av.
Ballard Henry C, plastr, h 44 Stevens.
Ballard H Wilfred, designer Indiana Illustrating Co, b 31 Dickson.
Ballard Isaac A, painter, b 168 E North.
Ballard James W, stonecutter, h 38 Henry.
Ballard James W, barber, 108 Michigan (H), h same.
Ballard Jane (wid Levering), b 158 Spring.
Ballard John C, mer police, h 333 W 2d.
Ballard John T, huckster, h 201 Union.
Ballard John W, cabtmkr, h 35 King av (H).
Ballard John W, cigarmkr, b 20 N West.
BALLARD JOSEPH H, Physician, Hours 8-10 A M, 2-4 and 7-8 P M, 108 Hill av; Tel 617; h 75 Woodruff av.
Ballard Judson, lab, h 410 N Brookside av.
Ballard Kate, h 142 Indiana av.
Ballard Levi C, clk, h 1059 N Senate av.
Ballard Luella, h 137 Downey.
Ballard Mabel, printer, b 165 N Capitol av.
Ballard Mary M (wid Jehu), r 296 Virginia av.
Ballard Myrtle, forewoman, r 187 E Ohio.
Ballard Nancy A (wid Wm), h 307½ N West.
Ballard Nellie (wid Wm O), r 296 Virginia av.
Ballard Nellie, teacher Public School No 1 (H), b 333 W 2d.
Ballard Orion C, h 416 Cornell av.
Ballard Ruth A (wid Cornelius W), b 158 Spann av.
Ballard Thomas, lab, h 142 Indiana av.
Ballard Walter M, bkkpr Indpls Abattoir Co, h 413 Ash.
BALLARD WM H, Ice Cream Mnfr, 102 N Delaware, h 364 College av; Tel 410.
Ballard Wm J, wirewkr, h 213 S Linden.
Ballard Wm P, agt, h 416 Cornell av.
Ballenger Carl C, cashr Nicoll The Tailor, b 204 Huron.
Ballenger Frank W, lawyer, b 273 Park av.
Ballenger Harvey, lab, h 204 Huron.
Ballenger Jennie L (wid Charles), h 530 College av.
Ballenger Luther H, carp, h 18 Wheeler.
Ballenger Walter S, mngr The Holt Ice and Cold Storage Co, b 530 College av.

TUTEWILER UNDERTAKER, No. 72 WEST MARKET STREET. TELEPHONE 216.

The Provident Life and Trust Co. Dividends are paid in cash and are not withheld for a long period of years, subject to forfeiture in the event of death or the termination of policy.
D. W. EDWARDS, GENERAL AGENT, 508 INDIANA TRUST BUILDING.

THEODORE F. SMITHER ROOFER
GRAVEL AND OTHER COMPOSITION
Yd 19 W. Maryland St. Telephone 861.
Of 15 W. Md. St.

Ballenger Wm T, barber, r 229 N New Jersey.
Ballinger Elijah M, carp, h 76 Yandes.
Ballinger John W, car rep, h 17 S Waverly (B).
Ballinger Marion F, carp, h 205 E Market.
Ballinger Nellie J (wid Jesse), h 426 Fulton.
Ballinger Linnie A, boarding 205 E Market.
Ballinger Wm S, broommkr, h 354 Ramsey av.
Ballinger Winston, motorman, h 99 Oliver av (W I).
Ballman Ernest, chairmkr, h 868 S Meridian.

BALLMANN J HENRY, House, Sign and Fresco Painter, 60 E Ohio, h 426 N New Jersey; Tel 757.

Ballnow Frank, mach, b Germania House.
Ballou Charles A, clk Board of State Charities, r 51 State House.
Ballou Frank, piano tuner Emil Wulschner & Son, b 136 N Penn.
Ballow Alice E (wid George S), b 232 S Capitol av.
Ballow George F, lab, h 232 S Capitol av.
Ballweg Alfred E, framemkr, h 1142 N Alabama.
Ballweg Amalie (wid Ambrose), h 171 Madison av.
Ballweg Charles F, picture framemkr 109½ E Washington, h rear 120 Wright.
Ballweg Clara, b 695 S Meridian.
Ballweg Frederick W (Ballweg & Co), h 695 S Meridian.
Ballweg Louis E, supt Ballweg & Co, b 695 S Meridian.

BALLWEG & CO (Frederick W Ballweg, Wm Blizard), Box Mnfrs, cor Wilkins and Pogue's run; Tel 903.

Balph Benjamin P, carp, h 449 W McLene (N I).
Bals Anthony H, h 892 N Senate av.
Bals Anthony H jr, clk, h 52 Sullivan.
Bals Christian F, h 950 N Capitol av.

BALS HENRY C G, Secretary Union Trust Co, 68 E Market, h 210 College av.

Bals Henry F, clk, h 892 N Senate av.
Baltimore & Ohio Express Co, 23 S Meridian; tel 378.
Baltutis Alfred A, cook, h 192 N Senate av.
Balz Charles P, clk Indpls Dist Tel Co, h 412 Cornell av.
Balz Christina (wid Peter), b 398 N West.
Balz Frederick, grocer, 400 N West, h 398 same.
Balz Frederick G, clk Indpls Dist Tel Co, h 509 N Senate av.
Balz Frederick G, clk Indpls Millinery Co, h 72 W 9th.
Balz John F, clk Lilly & Stalnaker, b 398 N West.
Balz John M, meats, 60 W 7th, h 72 W 9th.
Balz Lulu C, teacher Public School No 17, b 509 N Senate av.
Balz Peter, h 72 W 9th.
Balz Peter F, mngr Danbury Hat Co, h 334 Orange.
Balz Philip H, butcher, h 509 N Senate av.
Bamberger Edwin L, lawyer, 37 Journal bldg, b 321 N Alabama.
Bamberger Herman, trav agt Indpls Brewg Co, h 321 N Alabama.
Bamberger Isaac, b 5 Ft Wayne av.
Bamberger Michael, trav agt, b 204 N Illinois.

THE WHEN IS A WORLD BEATER.

Bamberger Ralph, lawyer 11 Aetna bldg, b 321 N Alabama.
Bandemer Albert O, lab, h 322 Columbia av.
Bandy Haskell R, polisher, h 321 Hillside av.
Bandy James E, motorman, h 69 W 6th.
Bandy Jonathan W, steamfitter, h 8 Cooper.
Bandy Wm E, bkkpr, h 8 Cooper.
Bandy Wm V, polisher, h 321 Hillside av.
Bane Jane, confr, 614½ S East, h same.
Bane John, lab, r 328 E Washington.
Bane Wm M, lab, h 614½ S East.
Banes Henry C, clk R M S, h 268 Brookside av.
Bangs Wendell O (Prather & Bangs), b 119 N Illinois.
Banier Anna M (wid Basil H), h 348 Union.
Baning Barbara (wid Jacob), b 55 Foundry (B).
Banke Elizabeth (wid John H), dressmkr, 218 S Olive, h same.
Banke Frederick H, mach, b 218 S Olive.
Bankert Ella, laundress, h 235 Muskingum al.
Bankert Jacob K, brakeman, b 1127 E Washington.
Bankett Theophilus, coachman 272 N Penn.
Banks Alfred, bartndr, h 445 N California.
Banks Andrew M, h 106 Columbia av.
Banks Bud, lab, h 124 N Missouri.
Banks Edward, lab, h 29 Maxwell.
Banks Eric Z, carp, h 131 Dougherty.
Banks Harry E, peddler, h 123 Newman.
Banks Irvin, blksmith, r s e cor Washington and National avs (I).
Banks Isaiah, lab, h 119 Newman.
Banks Isaiah jr, lab, b 119 Newman.
Banks James, lab, h 204 Middle.
Banks John, cook, h 329 W North.
Banks John, lab, b 119 Newman.
Banks John, lab, r 20 N West.
Banks Martha (wid John), h 518 W Maryland.
Banks Melvin, tinner, b 1655 Graceland av.
Banks Morris, porter Ross House.
Banks Reuben, farmer, h s s Washington 8 e of Sherman drive.

The A. Burdsal Co.
Manufacturers of
STEAMBOAT COLORS
BEST HOUSE PAINTS MADE.
Wholesale and Retail.
34 AND 36 SOUTH MERIDIAN STREET.

Electric Contractors
We are prepared to do any kind of Electric Contract Work.
C. W. MEIKEL. Telephone 466.
96-98 E. New York St.

DALTON & MERRIFIELD { LUMBER South Noble St., near E. Washington

LOWEST PRICES. BEST WORK. All Orders Promptly Filled. BEST PATENT BASE ON THE MARKET.

KIRKHOFF BROS.,
Sanitary Plumbers
STEAM AND HOT WATER HEATING.
102-104 SOUTH PENNSYLVANIA ST.
TELEPHONE 910.

Banks Silas, lab, b 119 Newman.
Banks Warren, hostler, b 131 Columbia al.
Banks Warren, lab, h 119 Newman.
Banks Wesley, lab, h 75 Torbet.
Banks Wesley S, restaurant, 31 Kentucky av, h same.
Banks Wm, janitor, h 294 Alvord.
Banks Wm H, lab, h n s Pendleton pike 1 mile e of (B).
Banks Wm M, cashr, b 112 Division (W I).
Banks Wm W, carp, b 85 Birch av (W I).
Banks Wyatt, porter N Y Store, h 285 Fayette.
Bannan Michael J, h 31 Vinton.
Bannan Richard, boarding 171 E Court.
Banner Hermann, lab, b 146 Michigan (H).
Banner John, lab, b e s Temperance 2 s of English av (I).
Banner Moses, lab, h e s Temperance 2 s of English av (I).
Banner Rudolph, porter, h 217½ W Maryland.
Banner Frank, gilder, h 59 Dunlop.
Banning James H, trav agt, h s s University av 1 e of Ritter av (I).
Bannon Andrew J, mach, h 21 Brett.
Bannon George (Bannon & Co), h 206 Dougherty.
Bannon John, car rep, h 74 N Gillard av.
Bannon Michael, lab, h 186½ Virginia av.
Bannon Thomas, barber, h 274 Lincoln la.
Bannon Wm R, student, b 206 Dougherty.
Bannon & Co (George Bannon, Michael K Stack), notions, 26 N Illinois.
Bannwarth Albert S, tel opr L W Louis, b 1455 E Ohio.
Bannwarth Benedict, h 175 Davidson.
Bannwarth Benjamin, clk, b 175 Davidson.
Bannwarth Carrie E, bkkpr, b 175 Davidson.
Bannwarth Charles E (O D Weaver & Co), h 158 N Pine.
Banse Theresa (wid Wm), h 195 S East.
Banta Dallas F, driver, h 58 S Judge Harding (W I).
Banta Florence, h 70 Buchanan.
Banta Horton F, clk, b 70 Buchanan.
Banta Isaac V, molder, h 38 Warman av (H).

Lime, Lath, Cement,
THE W. G. WASSON CO.
130 INDIANA AVE. TEL. 989.
Sewer Pipe, Flue Linings, Fire Brick, Fire Clay.

Banta Louisa J, dressmkr, 43 Bates, b same.
Banta Robert A, agt, h 216 Dougherty.
Banta Samuel, lab, h 43 Bates.
Bantz Jacob, stable boss, b 450 S Delaware.
Bany Adam, clk Indpls Drug Co, h 729 S Meridian.
Bany Bros (Henry A and Frank S), barbers, 97 E South.
Bany Edmund, barber, 105 Harrison, h 110 Cook.
Bany Frank A, driver, b 694 E Market.
Bany Frank S (Bany Bros), h 424 Union.
Bany Henry, driver, h 55 Yeiser.
Bany Henry A (Bany Bros), b 55 Yeiser.
Bany Peter, saloon, 257 E Washington, h 694 E Market.
Bany Philip, engr, h 17 Agnes.
Bany Simon, shoemkr, 832 E Market, h same.
Bany Simon jr, bartndr, h 87 Yeiser.
Banzhef Martin J, mach, h 74 Eastern av.
Banzing Charles, cigarmkr, b 630 S Meridian.
Baptist John H, contr, 61 Yandes, h same.
Baptist Outlook The, Indiana Baptist Publishing Co pubs, 68 Baldwin blk.
Barasch Leon, cigar mngfr, 233 E Washington, h same.
Barbee Harry C, mach, h 130 E Merrill.
Barbee Henry C, lab, h 168 W 2d.
Barbee James, lab, b rear 258 S Illinois.
Barbee Milton C, car rep, h 24 Hadley.
Barbee Robert B, wagonmkr, h 363 Orange.
Barber Angeline E (wid Luman), b n e cor Excelsior and Pope avs.
Barber Edward A, mach hd, h n e cor Excelsior and Pope avs.
Barber Elma E (wid Edwin), h 354 Talbott av.
Barber Emmons, lab, h 365 W North.
Barber Harry, mach, h 130 E Merrill.
Barber Harry R, insp Am Tel and Tel Co, h 381 N Delaware.
Barber Jackson, lab, r 338 Superior.
Barber James H, lab, h 178½ Indiana av.
Barber Johanna, b 346 Talbott av.
Barber Odie, lab, b 91 Locke.
Barber Lewis, lab, b 72 Oscar.
Barber Pell, lab, b 109 Kappus (W I).
Barber Simon, lab, h 91 Locke.
Barber Sarah (wid Milton C), h 24 Hadley.
Barber Sonny, lab, h 193 Patterson.
Barber Thomas, lab, b 109 Kappus (W I).
Barber Virgil, lab, h 109 Kappus (W I).
Barber Wm E, architect, h 293 N Senate av.
Barbour Ann (wid Edmund), b 119 W 6th.
Barbour Burr, lab, h 148 Lennox.
Barbour Charles, h 148 Lennox.
Barbour Edward E, student, h 150 E North.
Barbour Elizabeth (wid Thomas), h 64 W 1st.
Barbour Frederick J, lab, b 51 Brett.
Barbour George R, clk E C Atkins & Co, h 36 The Plaza.
Barbour Harriet (wid Samuel), b 597 N Capitol av.
Barbour Hough, lab, b 148 Lennox.
Barbour Isaac, driver, b 330 Douglass.
Barbour Jacob, lab, b 148 Lennox.
Barbour John M, mach hd, h 1410 Northwestern av.
Barbour Randolph E, barber, r 45 Brett.
Barbour Shadrach H, lab, h 90 W 8th.
Barbour Susan W, teacher Public School No 2, b 409 N Penn.
Barbour Thomas, lab, h 51 Brett.
Barbour Walker, lab, h 51 Howard.

INDIANA ELECTROTYPE CO. BOOK PLATES. JOB WORK. 23 WEST PEARL ST., INDIANAPOLIS, IND.

YOUR HOMES FURNISHED BY W. H. MESSENGER 101 East Washington St. Telephone 491.

McNamara, Koster & Co. { PATTERN MAKERS
Phone 1593. ◆ 212-218 S. PENN. ST.

Barckdall Daniel, confr, h 666 W Washington.
Barckdall George S, lab, b 67 Drake.
Barckdall Percival, city agt Gray & Gribben, h 67 Drake.
Barclay Isabella, housekpr, h n s Bedford av nr Park av.
Barcus James Q, mngr Northern Indiana N Y Life Ins Co, h 381 Broadway.
Barcus Joshua E, bkkpr, b 27 S McLain (W I).
Barcus Wm A, molder, b 27 S McLain (W I).
Bard Colbert A, clk R M S, h 247 N Capitol av.
Bareswilt Daniel, helper, b 21 Hope (B).
Barfield Isaac, lab, h 90 Newman.
Barge Gurley L, nailer, b 216½ S Meridian.
Barge Lewis S, clk, h 216½ S Meridian.
Barger George T, blksmith, 1352 N Senate av, h same.
Barger John G, student, h 420 S Illinois.
Barger Martin, lab, h e s Miami 4 s of Prospect (N).
Barger Milton E, bicyclemkr, b 1352 N Senate av.
Bargholt Frederick, news agt, r n w cor Union and Palmer.
Bario Lina, h 432 Talbott av.
Barkalow Albert V, furnishings, 20 Pembroke Arcade, b 203 N West.
Barkalow George, clk, b 203 N West.
Barkalow John W, bkkpr, h 523 Park av.
Barkau Wm, lab, b n s Howland av 2 w of Orchard.
Barkdall Wm A, turner, h 632 W Wells (N I).
Barker Averitte A, carp, b n w cor Floral av and Fountain.
Barker Bud, lab, h 86 S East.
Barker Charles S, clk E C Atkins & Co, h 145 Woodlawn av.
Barker Claude, boxmkr, b 75 Lockerbie.
Barker De Moss, weaver, b 105½ Broadway.
Barker Doctor, lab, h 568 W McLene (N I).
Barker Ellen M (wid Harry), b 211 Keystone av.
Barker Franklin H, carp, h 585 W Francis (N I).
Barker George, h 50 N William (W I).
Barker Harold, lab, b 105½ Broadway.
Barker Homer R, student, b 425 Talbott av.
Barker Jefferson B, waiter, r 75 Adams.
Barker John, waiter The Denison.
Barker John H, carp, h 555 W McLene (N I).
Barker John V, cashr, h 117 E Michigan.
Barker Joseph F, carp, h 538 W Shoemaker (N I).
Barker Lewis C, trav agt, h 1672 Kenwood av.
Barker Lydia J (wid Daniel), h 105½ Broadway.
Barker Nellie, seamstress Asylum for Friendless Colored Children.
Barker Oliver, brickmkr, h 103 Colgrove av.
Barker Peter F, fireman, b 568 McLene (N I).
Barker Robert P, carp, h 297 S Missouri.
Barker Sarah (wid Samuel), h 268 W Vermont.
Barker Sarah J, b 75 Lockerbie.
Barker Simeon, lab, b 65 Huron.
Barker Thomas J, plumber, h 289 N California.
Barker Wm, driver, h 71 Maxwell.
Barker Wm H, painter, h 69 Sheffield (W I).
Barkes Obadiah T, foreman, h 1006 W Washington.

Henry H. Fay,
40½ E. WASHINGTON ST.,
FIRE INSURANCE, REAL ESTATE,
LOANS AND RENTAL AGENT.

Barkes Sarah E (wid Wm), h 56 N Senate av.
Barkhau Agnes (wid Charles), h 432 S Meridian.
Barkhurst Drusilla (wid Wm), h n s Orchard av 3 w of Roseline.
Barkley John D, b 251 N Meridian.
Barkley Merrill B, b 251 N Meridian.
Barkley Minor, clk C C C & St L Ry, h 82 E North.
Barkley Wm S, h 251 N Meridian.
Barley John, carp, r 157 E Ohio.
Barley John, cooper, h 121 Haugh (H).
Barley Wm H, pressman, b 379 N California.
Barlow George F, patrolman, h 137 E South.
Barlow Harriet H (wid Frederick H), nurse, r 133 N Penn.
Barlow James M, ins agt, h 217 S New Jersey.
Barlow Jane J, milliner, b 137 E South.
Barlow John F, city fireman, h 18 Athon.
Barlow Raymond, brakeman, b 44 Lord.
Barlow Willard L, finisher, b 137 E South.
Barmeier Henrietta, music teacher, 867 N New Jersey, b same.
Barmfuhrer Charles, lab, h 325 S Olive.
Barmfuhrer Christian, lab, h 428 S State av.
Barmfuhrer Frederick, clk George's Hotel.
Barmfuhrer John J, cigarmkr, b 428 S State av.
Barmm Charles E, drugs, 452 Mass av, h same.
Barnaby George M, lab, h 2 Coe.
Barnaby Thomas J, lab, h 2 Coe.
Barnaby Wm O, foreman, h 241 Elizabeth.
Barnard, see also Barnhart and Bernhardt.
Barnard Frederick, shoes, 3 S Illinois, b 1733 N Illinois.
Barnard Henry, h 473 S Illinois.
Barnard Herman J, lumber inspr, h 71 Woodruff av.
Barnard Ida M, cashr C S Warburton, b 33 Newman.

BARNARD JOHN A, Genl Mngr Peoria & Eastern Division C C C & St L Ry, n e cor Delaware and South; Tel 484; b The Denison.

SURETY BONDS
American Bonding & Trust Co.
OF BALTIMORE, MD.
Authorized to act as Sole Surety on all Bonds.
Total Resources over $1,000,000.00.
W. E. BARTON & CO., General Agents,
504 INDIANA TRUST BUILDING.
Long Distance Telephone 1018.

THE FRED DIETZ CO.
WOODEN PACKING BOXES MADE TO ORDER.
FACTORY AND WAREHOUSE TRUCKS.
400 Madison Avenue. Telephone 654.

Business World Supplied with Help
GRADUATES ASSISTED TO POSITIONS
10,000 NOW IN GOOD SITUATIONS. TEL. 499. E. J. HEEB, PRES.
Indianapolis BUSINESS UNIVERSITY

Steam Pumping Machinery { HENRY R. WORTHINGTON, 64 S. PENNSYLVANIA ST. Long Distance Telephone 284.

UNION CO-OPERATIVE LAUNDRY (COMPOSED OF UNION LAUNDRY GIRLS.) NOS. 138, 140 AND 142 VIRGINIA AVENUE. T. E. SOMERVILLE, MANAGER — TELEPHONES. INDIANAPOLIS, IND.

HORACE M. HADLEY
Insurance, Real Estate, Loan and Rental Agent
66 EAST MARKET STREET,
Telephone 1540. Basement.

Barnard J Ott, barber, r 213 W Ohio.
Barnard Mary J (wid Wm D), h 33 Newman.
Barnard Nelson P, b 33 Newman.
Barnard Perry M, clk, b 146 Clifford av.
Barnard Warren G, clk, r 132 W Vermont.
Barnard & Leas Mnfg Co, T M Van Horn mngr, contrs, 49 Board of Trade bldg.
Barneclo Frank E, night foreman Frank Bird Transfer Co, h 149 S Noble.
Barneclo Henry D, molder, h 366½ Blake.
Barneclo Henry H, engr, h 84 Park av.
Barneclo Oliver M, grinder, h 22 Lord.
Barnell Oris P, city salesman Benjamin R Smith, h 109 Sanders.
Barner Caroline, laundress, h 173 E Court.
Barnes Albert A, woodenware mnfr, n w cor Addison and Emma (N I), h 850 N Meridian.
Barnes Albert H, lab, b 504 W Shoemaker (N I).
Barnes Alfred A, salesman Fahnley & McCrea, b 1063 N Illinois.
Barnes Andrew J, sec and treasurer College of Commerce, h 41 Huron.
Barnes Bert, bricklyr, h 884 Milburn (M P).
Barnes Catharine (wid James), h 17 Lockerbie.
Barnes Curtis E, carp, h 179 W 9th.
Barnes Dawson E, phys, 3 West Drive (W P), h same.
Barnes Douglass A, h 29 S California.
Barnes Edwin J, city fireman, h 1033 W Washington.
Barnes Frank, brakeman, r 39 N State av.
Barnes Frank, tailor, b 214 Middle.
Barnes Frank P, blksmith, h 88 S Shade (B).
Barnes George H, carp, h 95½ N Delaware.
Barnes George H, condr, h 178 Brookside av.
Barnes Granville, genl mngr The Newark Machine Co, 5 Board of Trade bldg, r 173 E Vermont.
Barnes Hamilton P, mach, h 57 Columbia av.
Barnes Henry F, phys, 1215 N Penn, h same.
Barnes Hugh, bartndr, h 89 Giesendorff.

Special Detailed Reports Promptly Furnished by Us.
MERCHANTS' AND MANUFACTURERS' EXCHANGE
J. E. TAKKEN, Manager,
19 Union Building, 73 West Maryland Street.

Barnes Jesse, tinner, h 228 W Ohio.
Barnes John, condr, h 502¼ College av.
Barnes John A, mngr, r 51 The Chalfant.
Barnes C F, carp, h 37 Samoa.
Barnes John E, electrician, h 17 Lockerbie.
Barnes John N, lab, b rear 518 Virginia av.
Barnes Jonas W, lab, h 115 Mulberry.
Barnes Laura A (wid Alfred R), h 1063 N Illinois.
Barnes Martin R, miller, b 19 Minerva.
Barnes Morris M, carp, b 37 Samoa.
Barnes Richard H, pres The Indpls Book and Stationery Co, h 454 Broadway.
Barnes Richard N, molder, h 154 Sheffield av (H).
Barnes Riley P, b 95½ N Delaware.
Barnes Sarah A (wid George D), h 416 W Addison (N I).
Barnes Solomon, waiter 400 N Illinois.
Barnes Turner, toolmkr, h 164 N Noble.
Barnes Walter, driver, b 574 N Penn.
Barnes Wm, lab, b 512 S Meridian.
Barnes Wm, lab, b 553 Virginia av.
Barnes Wm, lab, b 1 Willard.
Barnes Wm A, lab, r 166½ W Washington.
Barnes Wm H, undertaker, b 3 West Drive (W P).
Barnes Wm J, saloon, 353 W Washington, h same.
Barnes Wm T, elevator opr State House, b 416 W Addison (N I).
Barnes Wm T, sec and treas Vanguard Cycle Co, r 453 N Penn.
Barnett, see also Barnitt and Burnett.
Barnett Agnes, teacher Public School No 15, b 210 Randolph.
Barnett Benjamin B, lab, h 50 Thomas.
Barnett Bennett, h 288 N Liberty.
Barnett Charles L, trav agt, h 66 W Walnut.
Barnett Edward J, lab, h 260 W Pearl.
Barnett Emma, hairdresser, b 123 W Vermont.
Barnett Elizabeth (wid Daniel), h 131 N State av.
Barnett E Vawter (wid Wm H), b 43 Christain av.
Barnett Frank M, engr, h 41 Camp.
Barnett George W, blksmith, h 173 Columbia av.
Barnett Hattie (wid Wm), h 286 E Vermont.
Barnett James, coachman 808 N Meridian.
Barnett James H, condr, h 194 Spann av.
Barnett James T, salesman The Bowen-Merrill Co, b 210 Randolph.
Barnett Joel N, mach, h 185 Johnson av.
Barnett John F (Barnett & Weisenberger), h 1132 N New Jersey.
Barnett John M, clk R M S, b 276 N Penn.
Barnett Julia, costumer, 288 N Liberty, h same.
Barnett Lorena J (wid Nathaniel H), h 27 Johnson av.
Barnett Moses D, lab, b 142 Eddy.
Barnett Peter W, lab, h 356 Douglass.
Barnett Roscoe, painter, r 17 Franklin Life Ins bldg.
Barnett Salem C, yardmaster, b 130 S Judge Harding (W I).
Barnett Stewart W, car rep, h 75 Sheffield av (H).
Barnett Thomas, watchman Indiana Reformatory, h 210 Randolph.
Barnett Virginia, seamstress, h 294 N Liberty.
Barnett Wm, peddler, h 142 Eddy.
Barnett & Weisenberger (John F Barnett, Frank Weisenberger), livery, rear 478 N Penn.

CLEMENS VONNEGUT 184, 186 and 192 E. Washington St. | CABINET HARDWARE CARVERS' TOOLS. Glues of all kinds.

THE WM. H. BLOCK CO. DRY GOODS, MILLINERY, CLOAKS AND FURS.
7 AND 9 EAST WASHINGTON STREET.

Barney Amanda M (wid Chester), b 308 Home av.
Barney George L, mngr, h 28 West Drive (W P).
Barngrover George H, filer, b 130 N East.
Barngrover Hattie (wid Louis C), h 130 N East.
Barnhart, see also Barnard and Bernhardt.
Barnhart Alice, teacher Indiana Reformatory, b same.
Barnhart Charles E, finisher, h 27½ Athon.
Barnhart Emily (wid David), b 27½ Athon.
Barnhart Emma, music teacher, 220 E Louisiana, b same.
Barnhart Joel L, trav agt George W Stout, h 1359 N Illinois.
Barnhart John, electrician, b 220 E Louisiana.
Barnhart Joseph A, flagman, h 132 Newman.
Barnhart Philip A, elev opr, h 62 Traub av.
Barnhart Wm, baggageman, h 220 E Louisiana.
BARNHART WM H, Carriage and Wagonmaker, Repairs of All Kinds, 479 S Delaware, h 134 Church.
Barnhart Woodson G, lab, h 142 Church.
Barnhill Charles A, student, b w s Central av 2 s of Washington av (I).
Barnhill Jacob W, carp, 200 W Pearl, h 173 E Louisiana.
Barnhill James K, letter carrier P O, h s e cor Michigan and Auburn av.
Barnhill John C, h s s Washington av 2 e of Johnson av (I).
Barnhill John C jr, phys, h n s Central av 2 s of Washington av (I).
BARNHILL JOHN F, Physician, Limited to Nose, Throat and Ear, 516-518 Indiana Trust Bldg, r 81 W Vermont.
Barnhill Morton O, driver, h 560 W Francis (N I).
Barnhill Samuel, news agt, b 173 E Louisiana.
Barnhizer Martin N, clk, b 431 College av.
Barnitt, see also Barnett and Burnett.
Barnitt Anna J (wid Thomas), h 390 N Senate av.
BARNITT JAMES L, Insurance, Real Estate and Loans, 31 Lombard Bldg, b 513 N West.
Barnitt Thomas, bkkpr Kingan & Co ltd, h 513 N West.
Barnum George P, mach, b 143 N Alabama.
Barnum Pandora L, clk, h 190 E Market.
Barnum Wm W, grocer, 200 E Market, b 190 same.
BARON BROS (Charles F and Jacob J), Druggists, 703 E Washington; Tel 845.
Baron Charles F (Baron Bros), b 703 E Washington.
Baron George M, h 28 N Gillard av.
Baron Henry H, painter, h 57 Johnson av.
Baron Jacob, mach hd, h 34 Yeiser.
Baron Jacob J (Baron Bros), h 34 S Summit.
Baron John G, tailor, h 703 E Washington.
Baron John U, b 703 E Washington.
Baron Wm H, b 703 E Washington.
Barr, see also Baar, Bahr, Bayer and Beyer.
Barr Andre A, foreman, h 1161 N Capitol av.
Barr Anna (wid John H), h 217 Buchanan.

HEADQUARTERS PHOTOGRAPHIC OUTFITS AMATEUR OR PROFESSIONAL
THE H. LIEBER COMPANY, 33 S. MERIDIAN ST.

Barr Charles T, guard Marion County Work House, h 72 Chadwick.
Barr Emmet, lab, h 284 W 6th.
Barr Frank J, trav insp Joint Rate Assn, h 177 N Liberty.
Barr Jackson, lab, b 117 W 4th.
Barr Mary H (wid Jacob), b 577 Ash.
Barr Mary L (wid Rufus), h 1422 N Capitol av.
Barr Walter A, b 1422 N Capitol av.
Barr Wm D, train baggageman C C C & St L Ry, r 8, 10½ E Washington.
Barr Wm H, clk, h 1527 N Meridian.
Barr Wm H, switchman, b 176 S New Jersey.
Barr Wm H, shoes, 228 E Washington, h 68 Middle Drive (W P).
Barre John S, cashr, r 106½ N Meridian.
Barrett Andrew J, mach, h 174 Meek.
Barrett Ann V (wid Henry), h 6 Haugh (H).
Barrett Anthony, lab, h 408 Columbia av.
Barrett Bridget (wid John), h rear 577 S East.
Barrett Bridget (wid Richard), h 333 N Pine.
Barrett Catherine (wid Patrick), b 175 Duncan.
Barrett Charles, stenog, b 93 E South.
Barrett Charles E (Holstein, Barrett & Hubbard), h n w cor 18th and Ash.
Barrett Clinton T, harnessmkr, h 153 Buchanan.
Barrett Cyrus A, timekpr, b 228 Lexington av.
Barrett Edmund M, tel opr, b 6 Haugh (H).
Barrett Ernest C, bkkpr, h 867 N Delaware.
Barrett Haiman, second hd goods, 272 and 281 E Washington, h 272 E Washington.
Barrett Harry, clk, b 272 E Washington.
Barrett Harry, solr, b 103 W South.
Barrett James, lab, b rear 577 S East.
Barrett James, lab, b 346 N Pine.
Barrett James W, h 68 Cornell av.
Barrett James W, mach, b 174 Meek.
Barrett Jesse S, contr, 379 Ash, h same.
Barrett John, fireman, b n w cor Michigan and State avs.
Barrett John, lab, h rear 577 S East.

GUIDO R. PRESSLER, FRESCO PAINTER
Churches, Theaters, Public Buildings, Etc., A Specialty.
Residence, No. 325 North Liberty Street.
INDIANAPOLIS, IND.

INDIANAPOLIS STEEL ROOFING AND CORRUGATING WORKS, 23 and 25 East South Street. S. D. NOEL, Proprietor.

David S. McKernan REAL ESTATE AND LOANS
Houses, Lots, Farms and Western Lands for sale or trade.
ROOMS 2-5 THORPE BLOCK.

DIAMOND WALL PLASTER { Telephone 1410 BUILDERS' EXCHANGE.

Cor. E. Ohio St. and C., C., C. & St. L. R'y Tracks.

ISSUE NEGOTIABLE RECEIPTS ON MERCHANDISE AND HOUSEHOLD GOODS.

UNION TRANSFER AND STORAGE CO.

W. McWORKMAN,
ROOFING AND CORNICE WORKS,
930 W. Washington St. Tel. 1118.

Barrett John, lab, b 333 N Pine.
Barrett John A, car rep, h 34 Elder av.
Barrett John F, boilermkr, b 11 McGinnis.
Barrett John M, city fireman, h 228 Lexington av.
Barrett John T, clk, h 80 Chadwick.
Barrett Julia, cook The Denison.
Barrett Margaret (wid Edward), h 304 S Illinois.
Barrett Martin E, lab, b 11 McGinnis.
Barrett Mary A (wid Edward), h 11 McGinnis.
Barrett Mary E (wid James E), h 35 Broadway.
Barrett Michael J, baker Parrott & Taggart, b 11 McGinnis.
Barrett Oliver O, clk Frank Bird Transfer Co, h 184 Blackford.
Barrett Patrick, lab, h 174 Meek.
Barrett Patrick, peddler, b rear 577 S East.
Barrett Patrick J, opr W U Tel Co, b 174 Meek.
Barrett Philip, helper, b 333 N Pine.
Barrett Raymond, mach, b 1100 W Washington (H).
Barrett Richard, lab, b 56 McGinnis.
Barrett Richard J, carp, h 38 Michigan av.
Barrett Robert V, clk, r 209 W Ohio.
Barrett Roger, lab, b 56 McGinnis.
Barrett Rose (wid James), h 56 McGinnis.
Barrett Samuel, clk, b 272 E Washington.
Barrett Sarah E, dressmkr, 34 Elder av, h same.
Barrett Simpson K, h 499 E 7th.
Barrett Solomon, cigars, 93 E South, h same.
Barrett Thomas, paperhngr, h 72 Chadwick.

BARRETT THOMAS F, Chief Fire Department, Office s w cor Mass av and New York, h 281 E Merrill.

Barrett Thomas K, h 232 W Georgia.
Barrett Walter T, checkman Frank Bird Transfer Co, b 38 Michigan av.
Barrett Wm H, stenog, b 272 E Washington.
Barrick John R, bartndr, r 143 N Penn.
Barrick Kate, housekpr The Denison.

GEO. J. MAYER,
MANUFACTURER OF
SEALS
STENCILS, RUBBER STAMPS, CHECKS, BADGES, DOOR PLATES, ETC.
15 S. Meridian St., Ground Floor. TEL. 1386.

Barrick Valentine P, brakeman, b 28 S State av.
Barringer Samuel, mach, h n w cor Brown av and 22d.
Barrow George, plater, h 230 Dougherty.
Barrow James, lab, h 61 Beaty.
Barrow Maria O (wid Henry), h 667 Virginia av.
Barrows Charles L, spinner, h 41 Birch av (W I).
Barrows Edward H, driver, h 252 N Senate av.
Barrows Edward W, foreman, b 1700 N Illinois.
Barrows Frances J (wid Frederick A), h 2 Edgewood.
Barrows Wm F, pres Equitable Savings and Loan Assn, vice-pres Indiana Farmer Co, h 1700 N Illinois.
Barry Charles L, clk, h 20 Traub av.
Barry Edward, clk, b 209 W South.
Barry Ellen (wid Richard), b 209 W South.
Barry Ellen R (wid Charles L), h 281 N Liberty.
Barry Felix, coachman, b 225 W Vermont.
Barry George W, tinner, h 515 Armstrong (N I).
Barry John, tailor, 29 Indiana av, h 177 W Vermont.
Barry Josephine E, teacher, b 234 N Senate av.
Barry Mary (wid Edward), h 209 W South.
Barry Maurice J, mach, h 20 Traub av.
Barry Michael, engr, b 209 W South.
Barry Orla C, barber, b 289 Virginia av.
Barry Patrick, b 234 N Senate av.
Barry Paul, driver, b 1225 N Capitol av.
Barry Richard M, lab, b 209 W South.
Barry Samuel, sawmkr, r 256 S Delaware.
Barry Thomas, lab, h 12 Chadwick.
Barry Thomas G, asst mngr Daniel Stewart Co, h 553 N Meridian.
Barry Wm B (W B Barry Saw and Supply Co), h 224 College av.

BARRY W B SAW AND SUPPLY CO (Wm B Barry), 132-134 S Penn; Tel 628.

Barshier Wm H, helper, h 26 N Rural.
Bartel Celia, clk, b 206 E Morris.
Bartel John, paternmkr, h 97 Germania av. (H).
Bartel Samuel G, architect, 88 Germania av (H), h same.
Bartels Andrew, wheelmkr, h 352 S Olive.
Bartels Christian, lab, h 202 Highland av.
Bartenick Wm H, carp, h 40 S Stewart av, (B).
Barter Wm, lumberman, b 432 E Vermont.
Barth Charles H, collr, h 78 W 1st.
Barth Clayton A, bkkpr, h s w cor 24th and Central av.
Barth George W, trav agt, h 572 N Penn.
Barth Jacob S, bkkpr Scofield, Shurmer & Teagle, h s w cor Central av and 25th.
Barth John, mach, h 239 Blackford.
Barth John H Rev, h 161 Cottage av.
Barth John W, trav agt Clemens Vonnegut, h 385 N West.
Barth Mellville F, bkkpr, b 161 Cottage av.
Barth Ray M, clk P B Ault & Co, b 572 N Penn.
Barth Richard C, clk, h 30 S Senate av.
Barth Sebastian C Rev, h 387 N West.
Barth Wm, insp, r 18 Union.
Barthel Albert, meats, 754 E Washington, h same.

A. METZGER AGENCY ESTABLISHED 1863. REAL ESTATE

LAMBERT GAS & GASOLINE ENGINE CO.
ANDERSON, IND. GAS AND GASOLINE ENGINES, 2 TO 50 H. P.

BARTHEL BROS (Gustav, Oscar B and Frank), Grocers and Meat Market, 540 E Washington; Tel 1182.
Barthel Frank (Barthel Bros), b 540 E Washington.
Barthel Gustav (Barthel Bros), h 540 E Washington.
Barthel Johanna M (wid Bernhardt F W), h 540 E Washington.
Barthel Oscar B (Barthel Bros), b 540 E Washington.
Bartholomew Charles, h 277 E Washington.
Bartholomew Charles A, tagger Bureau Animal Industry, h 946 Ash.
Bartholomew Charles L, cushionmkr, b 58 Athon.
Bartholomew Clayton, engr, h 626 N West.
Bartholomew Deborah S (wid Harris), Employment Agency 30½ N Delaware, h 831 N Capitol av.
Bartholomew Edward W, waiter, b 58 Athon.
Bartholomew Ernest F, packer, b 58 Athon.
Bartholomew George H, cooper, h 7 Fay (W I).
Bartholomew Harry M, r 152 N Illinois.
Bartholomew John W, lab, b 277 E Washington.
Bartholomew Leila I, r 831 N Capitol av.
Bartholomew Lester C, barber, b 34 N New Jersey.
BARTHOLOMEW PLINY W, Lawyer, Ex-Judge Superior Court, 11-12 Baldwin Blk, h 526 College av.
Bartholomew Silas T, second hd store 255½ and 277 E Washington, h 255½ same.
Bartholomew Thomas S, cooper, h 58 Athon.
Bartholomew Thomas W, ins agt, b 262 S Missouri.
Bartholomew Walter T, agt, b 58 Athon.
Bartholomew Washington I, trav agt, h s s University av 1 w of Grand av (I).
Bartholomew Wm M, lab, b 255½ E Washington.
Bartle Frank H, mach, b 92 S Wheeler (B).
Bartleson John A, waiter, h 283 E Court.
Bartlett Arthur F, collr, h 205 E Morris.
Bartlett Cyrus, sawmkr, h 221 Sheldon.
Bartlett Edward H, lab, r 190 E Market.
Bartlett Franklin E, lab, h 130 Baltimore av.
Bartlett George, coachman 940 N Penn.
Bartlett George C, driver, h 53 Ellen.
Bartlett George E, lab, r 200 E Market.
Bartlett Harriet (wid Richard), h 39 Ellen.
Bartlett Harrison, janitor, b rear 123 Columbia al.
Bartlett Harry F, coachman 862 N Meridian.
Bartlett Jacob D, lab, h 18 Nordyke av (W I).
Bartlett James, lab, r 323 Clinton.
Bartlett James A, driver, h s e cor Manlove av and 17th.
Bartlett John, lab, h 100 Torbet.
Bartlett John C, peddler, h 521 W Maryland.
Bartlett John W, coremkr, h 14 Elliott.
Bartlett Joseph, lab, b rear 123 Columbia al.
Bartlett Joseph, lab, h 202 Elizabeth.
Bartlett Lydia (wid David), h rear 123 Columbia al.
Bartlett Nancy (wid Abraham), b 136 Columbia al.
Bartlett Phoebe (wid George), h 166 W 2d.
Bartlett Rena A (wid Matthew), h 332 S State av.
Bartlett Samuel E, lab, h 101 Maple.
Bartlett Stewart L, sawmkr, h 60 E Merrill.

We Buy Municipal ~ Bonds ~
THOS. C. DAY & CO,
Rooms 325 to 330 Lemcke Bldg.

Bartlett Susan (wid Charles), b 69 N Olive.
Bartlett Viola (wid Lee), h 395 Blackford.
Bartlett Wm H, driver, h 1391 N Capitol av.
Bartley Charles, lab, b 139 Fayette.
Bartley James M, carp, h 206 Hoyt av.
Bartley John B, fireman, h 100 Torbet.
Bartley Joseph, lab, b 389 Blackford.
Bartley Virgil B, lab, b 139 Fayette.
Bartling Wm F, driver, h 224 Cedar.
Bartlow John W, carp, h 8 N Dorman.
Bartmess Zora, teacher, r 155 N Illinois.
Bartol Harry B, route agt Am Ex Co, h 407 Talbott av.
Bartolles Mary A (wid Wm), b 1122 N Penn.
Barton Bridget, h 26 Chadwick.
Barton Charles A, trav agt, r 39½ Indiana av.
Barton Daniel, lab, b 26 Chadwick.
Barton David C, millwright, h 958 Sugar Grove av (M P).
Barton Frank, plumber, 15 Edward (W I), h same.
Barton George N, condr, b 123 N Illinois.
Barton Grace, h 33 N Noble.
Barton Ida M, b 45 Birch av (W I).
Barton James, lab, h 299 Blake.
Barton John R, stonecutter, h 217 River av (W I).
Barton Jones, lab, b 203 W 4th.
Barton Mary M (wid John), h 260 Roanoke.
Barton Patrick, lab, b 284 W Maryland.
Barton Sarah B, h 72 W Ohio.
Barton Wm B, carp, h 44 S Belmont (W I).
Barton Wm E (W E Barton & Co), b 404 N Delaware.
Barton Wm H, syrup refiner, 501 W Washington, h 273 River av (W I).
Barton Wm R, musician, r 87 E South.
Barton Wm T, blksmith, h 402 E Market.
BARTON W E & CO (Wm E Barton, Miles G O'Neall), Genl Agts American Bonding and Trust Co of Baltimore City and Union Casualty and Surety Co of St Louis, Mo, 504 Indiana Trust Bldg; Long Distance Tel 1918. (See right bottom cor cards.)
Bartsch Frank, blksmith, h 36 N Belmont av (H).

EAT HITZ'S CRACKERS AND CAKES.
ASK YOUR GROCER FOR THEM.

BICYCLES $5 DOWN, $1 MONTHLY. B & T Wheels. WHEELMEN'S CO. 31 W. OHIO ST. LONG DISTANCE TEL. 1855.

J. H. TECKENBROCK Painter and Decorator, 94 EAST SOUTH STREET.

FIDELITY MUTUAL LIFE—PHILADELPHIA, PA.
MATCHLESS SECURITY At LOW COST. } A. H. COLLINS { General Agent Baldwin Block.

Rooms 42 and 43 WHEN BUILDING.
Edwardsport and Mining Co. Miners and Shippers Steam and Domestic Coal.

ESTABLISHED 1876. TELEPHONE 168.
CHESTER BRADFORD,
SOLICITOR OF PATENTS,
AND COUNSEL IN PATENT CAUSES.
(See adv. page 6.)
Office:—Rooms 14 and 16 Hubbard Block, S. W. Cor. Washington and Meridian Streets,
INDIANAPOLIS, INDIANA.

Bartz Albert H, sawyer, b 314 Martindale av.
Bartz Charles F, mach, h 314 Martindale av.
Baruch Simon S, clk The Wm H Block Co, b 267 N New Jersey.
Barus Carl, music teacher, 243 N East, h same.
Barwise Richard M, clk Indiana Bicycle Co, b 433 N Illinois.
Base Ernest W, lab, h 63 Germania av (H).
Basey Andrew H, finisher, r 528 E Washington.
Basey Edward W H, mach, b 166 Harrison.
Basey Fannie (wid Andrew H), b 82 Michigan av.
Basey Frederick C, lab, h 324 E Vermont.
Basey Frederick H, mach, b 166 Harrison.
Basey Henry, carp, b 166 Harrison.
Basey Louis C, mach, b 324 E Vermont.
Basey Otto F, uphlr, h 287 Spring.
Basey Wm, lab, h 48 Michigan av.
Bash Hannah (wid Smith), h 1691 N Illinois.
Bash John F, mach hd, b 73 Yandes.
Bash Wm E, h 1691 N Illinois.
Bashford Harriet (wid Henry), h 13 Riley blk.
Baskerville Robert, mach, h 32 Standard av (W I).
Baskett John S, lab, h e s Muskingum al, 3 n of 1st.
Baskin Harry, produce, E Mkt House, h 117 Eddy.
Bason Alfred H, clk W U Tel Co, b 203 Douglass.
Bason Robert, mach, h 203 Douglass.
Bass Charles H, barber, r 128 W Vermont.
Bass Charles O, broom mnfr, 516 Ash, h same.
Bass Claude, lab, b 212 W St Clair.
Bass Edward, lab, b w s Graceland av, 2 s of 29th.
Bass Elias, condr, h 15 Shriver av.
Bass Ella, h 212 W St Clair.
Bass Eugene, waiter, b 26 W 1st.
Bass Florence, teacher Public School No 27, b 516 Ash.
Bass Frank, clk Cerealine Mnfg Co, r 220 N Capitol av.

Outing BICYCLES
$85.00.
MADE AND SOLD BY
HAY & WILLITS MFG. CO.

76 N. PENNSYLVANIA ST. PHONE 598.

Bass George F, editor Young People's Journa, h 674 Bellefontaine.
Bass George W, barber, h 187½ W 3d.
Bass Herbert L, draughtsman H C Hendrickson, b 674 Bellefontaine.
Bass Jane (wid Lovell), b 191 W 4th.
Bass Jane W, prin Public School No 28, b 555 College av.
Bass Kate W, teacher Public School No 3, b 144 Bellefontaine.
Bass Leonard, laundryman The Bates.
Bass Mary J (wid Thomas W), b 516 Ash.
Bass Walter G, insp, b 674 Bellefontaine.
Bass Wm H, teacher Industrial School, b 555 College av.
Bass Wm M, porter, h 208 W Ohio.
Bassett Edward E, b Enterprise Hotel.
Bassett Edward W (Bassett & Co), h 56 Bellefontaine.
Bassett George T, r 60 The Windsor.
Bassett Harry W, bookbinder, b 648 E Ohio.
Bassett Hiram H, agt, h 648 E Ohio.
Bassett Homer D, clk Navins' Pharmacy No 2, b 648 E Ohio.
Bassett John A, clk L S Ayres & Co, b 426 E 17th.
Bassett Ludlum G, trav agt, h 74 Tacoma av.
Bassett Samuel L, clk, h 4 Hollis.
Bassett Sarah M (wid Thomas M), h 599 N Penn.
Bassett Van G, clk, b Enterprise Hotel.
Bassett Walter B, mnfrs' agt, 18½ N Meridian, h 1016 N Capitol av.
Bassett Walter M, plumber, b 648 E Ohio.
Bassett Wm E, ins agt, h 50 Osgood.
Bassett & Co (Edward W Bassett), grain, 33 Board of Trade bldg.
Basso Philip G, reedworker, h 95 Yeiser.
Baster Wm E, electrotyper, h 102 Fayette.
Bastian Willits A, lawyer, 57 Journal bldg, h 1039 N Alabama.
Basye Otto, ins agt Coe & Roach, r 155 N New Jersey.
Batchelder Charles, carp, b 30 N West.
Batchelder Wm P, clk R M S, h 887 Bellefontaine.
Batcheler John J, clk H P Wasson & Co, b 83 N Noble.
Batchelor Dora (wid Frank), r 289½ E Washington.
Batchelor George H, lawyer, 5 Hubbard blk, b 191 Park av.
Batdorf Oliver C, uphlr, b 351 S New Jersey.
Bateman Harriet, stenog Union Nat S and L Assn, b 82 N East.
Bateman John W, clk Francke & Schindler, r 75 Union.
Bateman Louis E, clk, r 164 E New York.
Bates Albert, lab, h 1075 W New York.
Bates Carl A, student, b 326 Mass av.
Bates Catherine (wid Wm A), h 111 Yandes.
Bates Charles A, ins agt, 19 Monument pl, r 167 N Capitol av.
BATES CHARLES EDGAR, Architect, 323-324 Lemcke Bldg, h 583 Ash. (See adv in classified Architects.)
Bates Edna H, stenog, b 199 Woodlawn av.
Bates Eliza E, music teacher, 182 Brookside av, b same.
Bates Elizabeth C (wid Daniel T), h 199 Woodlawn av.
Bates Emery, r 60½ W Maryland.
Bates Frank P, pres Indpls Drop Forging Co, h 193 Prospect.
Bates Franklin P, baggageman, h 58 Michigan av.
Bates Frederick C, mach, b 193 Prospect.

C. ZIMMERMAN & SONS | SLATE AND GRAVEL ROOFERS 19 South East Street.

DRIVEN WELLS And Second Water Wells and Pumps of all kinds at CHARLES KRAUSS'. 42 S. PENN. ST. TELEPHONE 465.

Bates Hervey, pres Indpls Hominy Mills and Romona Oolitic Stone Co, h The Bates.
Bates Hervey jr, sec and treas Romona Oolitic Stone Co and Indpls Hominy Mills, h 623 N Penn.
BATES HOUSE PHARMACY, Deutsche Apotheke; Open all Night; 54 W Washington; Tel 964.
Bates Jacob L, painter, b 326 Mass av.
Bates James C, b 583 Ash.
Bates James E, engr, h 48 Cherry.
Bates John, h 95 Middle Drive (W P).
Bates John H, engr, h 48 Cherry.
Bates Marietta (wid Wm F), h 182 Brookside av.
Bates Maude B, stenog C C C & St L Ry, b 199 Woodlawn av.
Bates Ralph O, lecturer, h 154 N New Jersey.
Bates Raymond B, butcher, b 26 S Station (B).
Bates Rice T, salesman A B Meyer & Co, b 182 Brookside av.
Bates Samuel, lab, b 24 Sheffield av (H).
Bates The, Louis Reibold propr, n w cor Illinois and Washington.
Batley Celia D, confr, e s Lulu 4 n of Udell (N I), h 8 Madison.
Batley George C, condr, h 21 Russell av.
Batley Wm, h 16 Brookside av.
Batley Wm E, electrician, b 76 N Senate av.
Batliner John, patternmkr, h 53 Vine.
Batliner Josephine, dressmkr, 53 Vine, h same.
Batliner Otillia, clk, b 53 Vine.
Batly Grant, lab, b 750 N Senate av.
Batsel John, lab, h 489 S Capitol av.
Batt Horace M, ins agt, 31½ Virginia av, h same.
Battaw James V, tailor, r 284 E Michigan.
Battaw Mary (wid Isaac), h 30 Leonard.
Battey Robert C, lab, r 184 Indiana av.
Battie, see also Beattie.
Battie Willard, filer, h 75 Birch av (W I).
Battle Harriet, h 84 Maple.
Battle Isaac, lab, h 115 Kappus (W I).
Battley Robert S, lab, h 29 Miley av.
Batty Burn W (Batty & Co), b 1241 N Illinois.
Batty Edith (wid Robert P), h 1382 N Senate av.
Batty Edwin, carp, h 127 W 5th.
Batty Mary E (wid George W), h 1241 N Illinois.
Batty Robert, carp, r 184½ Indiana av.
Batty & Co (Burn W Batty, Homer M Smock), coal, 301 Indiana Trust bldg.
Bauchle Charles F, meats, 429 Madison av, h same.
BAUCUS WM I, Mngr The Wm H Block Co, h 1 Pressley Flats, 175 N Penn.
Bauer, see also Baur and Bower.
Bauer Albert, butcher, h 18 Dawson.
Bauer Albert, lab, b 175 W 9th.
Bauer Anna (wid Adolphus), r 5 Ryan blk.
Bauer Charles, produce, 130 High, h same.
Bauer Charles W, lab, h 243 Blake.
Bauer Charles W, lab, b 78 Wallack.
Bauer Conrad V, grocer, 148 N Capitol av, h same.
Bauer Elizabeth, clk John Wocher, b 435 Broadway.
Bauer Emil H, mach, b 243 Cornell av.
Bauer Ferdinand, mach, b 243 Cornell av.
Bauer Frank, bicycle rep, b 643 N Senate av.

RICHARDSON & McCREA, MANAGERS FOR CENTRAL INDIANA. EQUITABLE LIFE ASSURANCE SOCIETY Of the United States. 79 EAST MARKET STREET. TELEPHONE 182.

Bauer Frank, clk, b 84 W 10th.
Bauer Frank J, bartndr, b 207 Blake.
Bauer Frederick, lab, h n w cor Burton av and Shoemaker (N I).
Bauer Frederick, mach hd, b 100 Bernard av (N I).
Bauer Frederick M, filer, b 512 S Illinois.
Bauer Frederick W, engr, h 78 Wallack.
Bauer George (Kothe, Wells & Bauer), h 1532 N Illinois.
Bauer George, lab, h 74 Patterson.
Bauer George, lab, b 243 Blake.
Bauer George, uphlr, b 586 Morris (W I).
Bauer George H, filer, h 84 Benton.
Bauer George H, lab, h w s Burton av 3 s of McLene (N I).
Bauer George W, trav agt Indpls Cabtmkrs' Union, b 470 E Market.
BAUER HARRY C (The H C Bauer Engraving Co), 23 W Washington, h 549 E Market. (See adv opp classified Engravers.)
Bauer Henry, engr, h 219 N Beville av.
Bauer Henry, pres Indpls Cabinetmakers' Union, h 470 E Market.
BAUER H C ENGRAVING CO THE (Harry C Bauer), Designers and Wood Engravers, Half-Tone Engraving and Zinc Etching, 23 W Washington. (See adv opp classified Engravers.)
Bauer Jacob, h 22 Kansas.
Bauer Jacob, lab, h 95 N Dorman.
Bauer John, lab, b 310 Bismarck (H).
Bauer Joseph, coachman, r rear 643 N Senate av.
Bauer Joseph J, collr The Home Brewing Co, h 330 E South.
Bauer Josephine K, teacher Public School No. 10, b 243 Cornell av.
Bauer Katie, h 207 Blake.
Bauer Leona, h 669 Madison av.
Bauer Louis G, uphlr, h 27 Peru av.
Bauer Mary, clk Charles Mayer & Co, b 435 Broadway.
Bauer Mary S (wid George), h 435 Broadway.

Typewriter-Ribbons ALL COLORS FOR ALL MACHINES. THE BEST AND CHEAPEST. S. H. EAST, STATE AGENT. The Williams Typewriter.... 55 THORPE BLOCK, 87 E. MARKET ST.

ERTEL STEAM LAUNDRY LARGEST AND BEST IN THE STATE. PROMPT SERVICE. 26 and 28 N. Senate Ave. Telephone 1089.

ELLIS & HELFENBERGER Architectural Iron Work and Gray Iron Castings. 162-170 South Senate Ave. Tel. 958.

THE HOGAN TRANSFER AND STORAGE COMP'Y
Household Goods and Pianos Moved—Packed—Stored...... Baggage and Package Express Machinery and Safes a Specialty Cor. Washington and Illinois Sts. TELEPHONE No. 675.

Hose, Belting, Packing, Clothing, Druggists' Sundries, Bicycle Tires, Cotton Hose, Etc. New York Belting & Packing Co., L't'd.

THE CENTRAL RUBBER & SUP LY CO. PHONE 922. 79 S. ILLINOIS ST., INDIANAPOLIS, IND.

The Provident Life and Trust Company
Of Philadelphia.
Grants Certificates of Extension to Policyholders who are temporarily unable to pay their premiums
D. W. EDWARDS, Gen. Agt., 508 Indiana Trust Bldg.

Bauer Peter, lab, h 167 Sheffield av (H).
Bauer Peter, mach, h 243 Cornell av.
Bauer Peter, molder, r 29 Warman (H).
Bauer Philip, butcher, h 49 Bridge (W I).
Bauer Rosa, dressmkr, 22 Kansas, b same.
Bauer Rosetta (wid John G), h 292 S East.
Bauer Rudolph F, sawmkr, h 37 Holly av (W I).
Bauer Rudolph J, mach, b 243 Cornell av.
Bauer Theodore, saloon, 298 W Washington, b 207 Blake.
Bauer Valentine, blksmith, h 669 Madison av.
Bauer Wm A, agt, b 197 W Vermont.
Bauer Wm C, bkkpr N Y Store, h 84 W 10th.
Bauerle Joseph, lab, b 17 Oriole.
Baugh James C, packer, h 11 Garland (W I).
Baugh Thomas, lab, h 355 S Capitol av.
Baughan Charles J, switchman, h 371 N Noble.
Baugher Legh R, teacher, h 783 N Delaware.
Baughman, see also Bauman and Bowman.
Baughman Carrie P, drugs, 500 N Alabama, h same.
Baughman Catherine, teacher Public School No 24, b 50 Bradshaw.
Baughman Charles F, mach hd, b 310 Yandes.
Baughman Charles H, mailing clk P O, b 50 Bradshaw.
Baughman Herschel R A, b 292 Fletcher av.
Baughman Jacob A, carp, b 127 Winchester.
Baughman John, h 95 Geisendorff.
Baughman John, engr, h 127 Winchester av.
Baughman John U (John Baughman & Co), h 278 Douglass.
Baughman John & Co (John U Baughman, Wm C Holtsclaw), drugs, 248 Mass av.
Baughman Joseph S, porter, b 50 Bradshaw.
Baughman Leonard, carp, h 50 Bradshaw.
Baughman Wm H, h 118 W Vermont.
Baughn Anna, seamstress, b 209 Alvord.
Bauka Anton, driver, h 337 Fletcher av.
Baum Amon Z, molder, b 80 E New York.
Baum Lewis (Baum Pickle Co), h 233 E New York.
BAUM PICKLE CO (Lewis Baum), Mnfr Home-Made Dill Pickles, 201 Lemcke Bldg.

Julius C. Walk & Son,
Jewelers
Indianapolis.
12 EAST WASHINGTON ST.

Baum Samuel M, clk The Wm H Block Co, r 183 S Ohio.
Bauman, see also Baughman and Bowman.
Bauman Jacob M, mach hd, b w s James 3 n of Bloyd av (B).
Bauman Joseph H, lab, b 1378 N Capitol av.
Bauman Laura (wid Constantine), h 329 Columbia av.
Bauman Louis, lab, h 27 Warman av (H).
Bauman Wm M, carp, h 329 W Vermont.
Baumann Adam, lab, h 196 S Spruce.
Baumann Albert, carp, h 18 Singleton.
Baumann Charles H, mach, h 65 Wallack.
Baumann David, baker, 365 Indiana av, h same.
Baumann Eliza (wid Henry), h 76 Morton.
Baumann George H, leader of orchestra Empire Theater, b 135 W New York.
Baumann Henry, tmstr, h 935 S East.
Baumann John, car rep, h 74 N Gillard av.
Baumann Laura (wid Konstantine), grocer 449 Columbia av, h same.
Baumann Louisa (wid Henry), h 76 Morton.
Baumann Peter F, baker, rear 336 Indiana av, h same.
Baumann Sarah, clothing, 166 W Washington, h 280 N East.
Baumann Sebastian P, bottler, h 110 Dougherty.
Baumbach Christian, clk, b 80 McGinnis.
Baumbach Christian F, packer, h 80 McGinnis.
Baumbauer Albert, student, h 164 Davidson.
Baumgart Henry F, lab, h 182 Coburn.
Baumgart Gustave, baker, h 59 Leota.
Baumgart Wm, bartndr, b 59 Leota.
Baumgartner Wm H, vice pres Ind Paint and Color Co, h 1190 N Meridian.
Baumhoefer Matilda, dressmkr, 796½ N Alabama.
Baumhofer Bros (F Henry and Otto), grillewks, 163 Lambert (W I).
Baumhofer F Henry (Baumhofer Bros), h 42 S Reisner (W I).
Baumhofer Henry, carp, h 188 S William (W I).
Baumhofer Otto (Baumhofer Bros), h 163 Lambert (W I).
Baur, see also Bauer and Bower.
Baur Adolph J, painter, b 55 High.
Baur Adolph J G, printer, h 55 High.
Baus Adam J, condr, h 71 Lexington av.
Baus Mary (wid John), b 177 Hoyt av.
Baus Simon, engr, h 235 English av.
Baus Rosa (wid Oliver), h 1137 Northwestern av.
Bausch Frederick J V, butcher, b 764 S Meridian.
Baxley George, lab, b 159 W Merrill.
Baxter Armstead, lab, h 34 Howard.
Baxter Arthur R, collr, b 186 N Capitol av.
Baxter Charles N B, lab, h 157 W Merrill.
Baxter Edmund, driver, h 342 N Missouri.
Baxter Emory, b 186 N Capitol av.
Baxtel Ethel, bkkpr, b 332 W Washington.
Baxter Frank M, switchman, b 256 S Capitol av.
Baxter George W, foreman, h 365 S Olive.
Baxter G Harvey, bkkpr, b 108 Brookside av.
Baxter Jacob V, tmstr, h 2 Sylvan.
Baxter James B, tmstr, h 4 Sylvan.
Baxter James T, boilermkr, 332 W Washington.
Baxter Joseph W, driver, h 104 Shelby.
Baxter Mary L (wid John N), h 108 Brookside av.
Baxter May, teacher Public School No 8, b 365 S Olive.

OTTO GAS ENGINES | BUILDERS' EXCHANGE S. W. Cor. Ohio and Penn. Telephone 535.

Becker & Son Charles Becker Jacob Becker Jr. Merchant Tailors. 21 N. Penn. St. Tel. 934

Baxter Oliver R, carp, h 1 Bates al.
Baxter Samuel C, cashr C C C & St L Ry, b 293 N Delaware.
Baxter Sarah E (wid Wm A), h 123 St Marie.
Baxter Wm A, stock insp, b 123 St Marie.
Baxter Wm D, carp, h 1 Bates al.
Bay Alice M, teacher Public School No 7, b 314 E Ohio.
Bay Charles T, clk, b 314 E Ohio.
Bay Israel, trav agt, h 314 E Ohio.
Bayer, see also Baar, Bahr, Barr and Beyer.
Bayer Anton, packer, h n e cor Bluff rd and Raymond.
Bayer Frederick, h 925 S Meridian.
Bayer Harry, fruits, E Mkt House, b 365 E McCarty.
Bayer Ignatz, peddler, h 365 E McCarty.
Bayer Joseph, molder, h 35 Depot (B).
Bayless Minnie, dressmkr, h 19½ N Meridian.
Bayless Wm, carp, r 228 N Capitol av.
Bayliss Edwin L, carp, h 76 Springfield.
Baylor Rachel M (wid James J), h 29 Holmes av (H).
Baylor Wm J, toolmkr, h 163 Church.
Bazeille Etienne R, mngr, b 125 Fayette.
Bazel Cyrus, porter, h 145 Agnes.
Bazel Ford M, clk, r 175 W North.
Bea Charles, baggageman, h 406 S Delaware.
Beabar Wallace, b 131 N East.
Beach Arthur, driver, r 488½ E Washington.
Beach Charles, brakeman, b 656 S Illinois.
Beach Charles F Rev, h 1534 N Capitol av.
Beach Charles H, condr, r 199 W South.
Beach Joseph F, mach, b 471 S Illinois.
Beach Louis J, driver, h 471 S Illinois.
Beach Mark A, lab, b 471 S Illinois.
Beach Olive, h 301½ E Washington.
Beach Olive F, dressmkr, r 227 E Market.
Beach Oscar, hostler, r 488½ E Washington.
Beach Samuel, lab, h 241 S Capitol av.
Beach Wm G, r 10½ E Washington.
Beacham, see also Beecham.
Beacham Arthur B, h 83 Bismarck av (H).
Beacham Harry G, lineman, h 325 S East.
Beacham James H, trav agt, h 232 N Senate av.
Beacham Mack, clk H P Wasson & Co, b 232 N Senate av.
Beacham Margaret (wid Noah), b 83 Bismarck av (H).
Beachbard Thomas S, condr, h 501½ Bellefontaine.
Beachman Preston, waiter, r 104 S Illinois.
Beade Lee L, barber, h 424 College av.
Beadle Frank, printer, h 309 N Alabama.
Beal Arthur W, clk, h 74 W 10th.
Beal Joshua, paperhngr, h 517 Bellefontaine.
Beal Joshua jr, paperhngr, h 227 W 1st.
Beale Erastus H, carp, h 134 Fletcher av.
Beale James, porter, h 427 Muskingum al.
Beale James H, agt, h 120½ Oliver av (W I).
Bealer John A, b 150 Bates.
Beall Balcom, insp, h 269 River av (W I).
Beall David S, real est, h 25 Eureka av.
Beall Roscoe S, clk, b 220 E Walnut.
Beam George W, foreman Henry Coburn, h 274 N California.
Beam John, tuner Emil Wulschner & Son, h 77 E Walnut.
Beam Mary A (wid Wm), h 303½ E Washington.

Henry H. Fay,
40½ E. Washington St.,
REAL ESTATE,
AND LOAN BROKER.

Beam Robert, trimmer, b California House.
Beam Wm H, painter, h 259 Prospect.
Beaman Ora F, sander, b 621 Armstrong (N I).
Beamer Ezra, hostler, b 206 E Market.
Beamer Milo H, lab, b 326 W Vermont.
Beamouth Fanando A, phys, 123 W Vermont, b same.
Bean Arthur J, teacher Industrial School, h 1013 N Senate av.
Bean Robert, b California House.
Bean Wm F, doorkpr, r 19 Grand Opera House blk.
Beaning Henry, lab, h 72 Chadwick.
Beaning Wm, b 80 W 9th.
Beans Timothy S, carp, h 268 Bright.
Bear Ira, painter, h 188 River av (W I).
Beard, see also Baird.
Beard Alfred, porter The Bates.
Beard Alfred E, fruits, E Mkt House, b 70 S Pine.
Beard Alvin G, carp, 950 Ash, b same.
Beard Amos, lab, b 89 Camp.
Beard Anna (wid Harry), h 423 Clinton.
Beard Arthur L, teacher Indpls College of Music, b 1095 N Senate av.
Beard Charles A, paperhngr, b 123 N Illinois.
Beard Edgar C, agt, h 1095 N Senate av.
Beard Edward, porter, h 504 Chicago (N I).
Beard Edward O, b 123 N Illinois.
Beard Elisha, phys, 31½ Virginia av, h same.
Beard Elwood A, peddler, h 145 W North.
Beard Frank, trav agt, h 1133 N Delaware.
Beard George, lab, r 133 Allegheny.
Beard Hermann, brakeman, b 54 Belmont av (H).
Beard James, lab, h 411 Excelsior av.
Beard Jane, h w s Auburn av 2 s of English av.
Beard John A, h 467 S Missouri.
Beard John M, cashr local freight office L E & W R R, h 306 E South.
Beard Joseph E, tmstr, h 243 Eureka av.
Beard L Jennie, laundress, h 206 E Market.
Beard Rachel E (wid Wm M), h 257 W 5th.
Beard Samuel, lab, b 119 Ft Wayne av.
Beard Theodore G, b 113 Highland pl.

MAYHEW'S SPECTACLES
THE BEST IN USE
SOLD ONLY AT 13 N. MERIDIAN ST.

SALIS BEW & STANLEY • Office, Store and Bar Fixtures a Specialty. Repairing of all kinds done on short notice. 177 Clint or Street, Indianapolis, Ind. • Contractors and Builders TELEPHONE 999.

COAL AND LIME Cement, Hair, Sewer Pipe, etc. BALKE & KRAUSS CO. Cor. Missouri and Market Sts.

FRIEDGEN'S IS THE PLACE FOR THE NOBBIEST SHOES Ladies' and Gents' 19 North Pennsylvania St.

SAMUEL LAING || COPPER AND GALVANIZED IRON CORNICE MANUFACTURER
SKYLIGHTS AND VENTILATORS.
72 AND 74 E. COURT STREET.

M. B. WILSON, Pres. W. F. CHURCHMAN, Cash.

THE CAPITAL NATIONAL BANK,

INDIANAPOLIS, IND.

Our Specialty is handling all Country Checks and Drafts on Indiana and neighboring States at the very lowest rates. Call and see us.

Interest Paid on Time Deposits.

28 S. MERIDIAN ST., COR. PEARL.

Beard Urbana C (wid John O), dressmkr, 123 N Illinois, h same.
Beard Walter R (W R Beard & Co), h 114 Lincoln av.
Beard Wilbin E, h 336 S State av.
BEARD W R & CO (Walter R Beard) Agts' Specialties, 20 S Alabama; Tel 1122.
Beasley David K, car rep, h 1279 Morris (W I).
Beasley Ellen (wid James), h 23 Hadley.
Beasley Georgia A, b 23 Hadley.
Beasley Henry, restaurant, 155 Indiana av, h 306 Blackford.
Beasley James H, lab, h 226 E Pearl.
Beasley James J, salesman Clark, Wysong & Voris, h 78 S William (W I).
Beasley John, condr, h 538 W Udell (N I).
Beasley Lewis, lab, b 135 Lembert (W I).
Beasley Rosa (wid Wm S), b 31 Garden.
Beason, see Beeson.
Beattey James L, clk, h 329 W 1st.
Beattey James L, clk, h 132 W 1st.
Beattey Jesse H, lab, h 303 Shelby.
Beattey Joseph S, h 338 W 1st.
Beattey Wm, saloon, 541 Shelby, h same.
Beattie, see also Battie.
Beattie John M, carp, h 386 E Market.
Beatty Albert J, horseshoer, 675 N Senate av, h 38 Gatling.
Beatty Anna, cashr Great Atlantic and Pacific Tea Co, b 5 Broadway.
Beatty Charles E, foreman, h 543 W 22d (N I).
Beatty Charles M, horseshoer, r 128 W 5th.
Beatty Edward, lab, h 31 Blake.
Beatty Joseph, h 4 Jupiter.
Beatty Kate (wid Jonathan), h 5 Broadway.
Beatty Samuel L, porter 125 W Washington.
Beaty Catherine (wid John S), h 273 N California.
Beaty John, peddler, h rear 482 S West.
Beaty John R, confr, 207 Virginia av, h same.
Beauchamp Charles L, brakeman, h 81 Davidson.

TUTTLE & SEGUIN,

28 E. Market St. **Ground Floor.**

COLLECTING RENTS AND CARE OF PROPERTY A SPECIALTY.

Telephone 1168.

Beauchamp James M, clk Penna Lines, b 162 N Illinois.
Beaupre Charles, shoemkr, h 17 S Senate av.
Beaupre James, shoemkr, 291 Prospect, h same.
Beaupre Louis, vice-pres Pink Shoe Mnfg Co, h 188 E Morris.
Beaupre Macy A, restaurant, 141 W Washington, h 17 S Senate av.
Beaupre Sarah A (wid Frank X), h 253½ S Delaware.
Beaver, see also Beever and Bever.
Beaver Albert C, painter, b 110 Chadwick.
Beaver Charles H, lab, b 57 Peru av.
Beaver Daniel, painter, h 215 N Noble.
Beaver Horace, lab, b 215 N Noble.
Beaver John H, h 559 S New Jersey.
Beaver Joshua A, engr, h 57 Peru av.
Beaver Joseph A, lab, h 75 Montana.
Beaver Milton S, printer, h 462 W Francis (N I).
Beaver Thomas F, lab, b 57 Peru av.
Beazell Harry W, trav agt, b 47 Hall pl.
Beazell Harvey T, trav agt, h 47 Hall pl.
Bebinger, see also Biebinger.
Bebinger Charles, mach, b 140 Naomi.
Bebinger Oliver P, mach, h 392 Newman.
Becherer Constantine H, clk Charles Mayer & Co, b 33 King.
Becherer Julius, clk Charles Mayer & Co, b 33 King.
Becherer Maria (wid August), h 33 King.
Bechert Christian W, clk, b 296 S West.
Bechert Edward T C, M O clk P O, b 121 E New York.
Bechert Ferdinand W, grocer, 296 S West, h same.
Bechert Fred C, lab, b 210 W McCarty.
Bechert Frederick, junk, 210 W McCarty, h same.
Bechert Henry, clk, b 210 W McCarty.
Bechold Frederick, engr, h 508½ E 9th.
Bechtel Jacob, restaurant, 328 E Washington, h same.
Bechtel John, mill hd, b 187 S Capitol av.
Bechtel Laura, r 32 Hutchings blk.
Bechtel Wm, bartndr, b 448 S West.
Bechtell Charles F, mach hd, h 116½ W New York.
Bechtell Harry J, butcher, r 116½ W New York.
Bechtol Elmer G, mach hd, h 340 Bellefontaine.
Bechtold Elizabeth (wid George), h 272 W Merrill.
Bechtold George, plater, b 272 W Merrill.
Beck Alexander, bkkpr Indpls Paint and Color Co, r 101 N New Jersey.
Beck Benedict, capt Hose Co No 13, h 540 Chestnut.
Beck Benedict, engr, h 516 Union.
Beck Benedict C, engr, b 516 Union.
Beck Bessie, h rear 240 E Market.
Beck Clemens (F J Mack & Co), h 49 Dunlop.
Beck Conrad, baker, 671 E Washington, h same.
Beck Conrad, janitor P O, h 95 Dunlop.
Beck Edward, brakeman, r 233 Cedar.
Beck Edward, baker, b 222 W Washington.
Beck Eliza C (wid Henry), h 240 Oliver av (W I).
Beck Ella, b 131½ E Washington.
Beck Eman L, student, b 863 N Meridian.
Beck Frank, butcher, r 174 E Pearl.
Beck Frank A, propr Palace Stables, 25-27 W St Clair, r 77½ E Market.
Beck Frederick, h 756 S Meridian.

PAPER BOXES SULLIVAN & MAHAN 41 W. Pearl St.

DIAMOND WALL PLASTER { Telephone 1410 BUILDERS' EXCHANGE.

If your Laundry Work is not satisfactory, try

Beck Frederick, brewer, h 83 Lincoln la.
Beck Frederick D, baker, 34 E Mkt House and 311 Mass av, h 311 Mass av.
Beck George, lab, h 8 Gresham.
Beck George A, clk, b 635 N Meridian.
Beck George C, live stock purchasing agt, Union Stock Yards (W I), h 635 N Meridian.
Beck Harry, baker, b 671 E Washington.
Beck Henry, grocer, 280 S Olive, h same.
Beck Henry A, lawyer, 420 Lemcke bldg, b 863 N Meridian.
Beck James A, clk, h 28 S Reisner (W I).
Beck Jesse M, tiremkr, b rear 306 E Louisiana.
Beck John, watchman, h 28 Downey.
Beck John C, trav agt, h 132 Oliver av (W I).
Beck John M, motorman, h 108 Chadwick.
Beck Joseph L, painter, h 65 Dunlop.
Beck Joseph W, clk Van Camp H and I Co, b 548 N Capitol av.
Beck Julius, lab, h 72 Nebraska.
Beck Mary C (wid George W), h rear 306 E Louisiana.
Beck Otto C, grocer, 94 Indiana av, h 185½ N Senate av.
Beck Peter, shoemkr, h 34 N Sheffield (W I).
Beck Philomena (wid Charles), h 80 Greer.
Beck Ray M, storekpr, b 619 N Meridian.
Beck Roy, photog, h 378 Martindale av.
Beck Sabina (wid Frederick), b 461 Union.
Beck Samuel T, jeweler, r 91 S Illinois.
Beck Wm, carp, h 109 Fletcher av.
BECK WM, Meat Market, 187 E Washington and 78-80 E Mkt House; Tel 568, h 1350 E Washington.
Beck Wm M, waiter, r 10 Columbia blk.
Beck Wm O, undertaker Collier & Murphy, h 59 W Maryland.
Beck Wm S, phys, 42 W Market, h 863 N Meridian.
Becker, see also Baker and Boecher.
Becker Barbara, dressmkr, 305 S Penn, h same.
Becker Barbara (wid Frederick), b 621 S Meridian.
Becker Caroline (wid John), b 759 S East.
Becker Charles (Becker & Son), b 180 N New Jersey.
Becker Charles, produce, E Mkt House, h cor 32d and Meridian.
Becker Charles A, patternmkr, h 180 S Linden.
Becker Charles C, turner, h 68 N Liberty.
Becker Charles F, grinder, h 46 Dunlop.
Becker Charles T, barber, 548 S East, h same.
Becker Conrad, horseshoer, h 305 S Penn.
Becker David, peddler, h 422½ S Meridian.
Becker Edward, clk P O, r 160 S New Jersey.
Becker Edward J, barber, 760 S East, b 47 Iowa.
Becker Ernest R, clk, h 8 Stoughton av.
Becker Frank A, bicycle repr, h 448 Indiana av.
Becker Frank C, phys, 592 Morris (W I), h same.
Becker Frederick, clk, h 102 Keystone av.
Becker George P, cooper, h rear 194 Dougherty.
Becker Henry, janitor, h 118 Dunlop.
Becker Jacob, h 180 N New Jersey.
Becker Jacob jr (Becker & Son), h 286 E New York.
Becker Jacob, cigar mnfr, 47 Iowa, h same.
Becker Jacob, lab, h 5 Roseline.

FRANK NESSLER. WILL H. ROST.
FRANK NESSLER & CO.
Tailors
56 EAST MARKET ST. (Lemcke Building),
INDIANAPOLIS, IND.

Becker Jacob, lab, h 81 S Reisner (W I).
Becker John H, lab, h 887 S Meridian.
Becker Joseph, h 401 N Delaware.
Becker Julius D, grocer, 679 S East, b 20 Kansas.
Becker Louis, uphlr, h 589½ S Meridian.
Becker Robert, teacher German Public School No 27, h 271 N Alabama.
Becker Tobias, lab, h 27 Centennial (H).
Becker Wilhelmina (wid Henry J), h 20 Kansas.
Becker Wm, clk Ger Fire Ins Co of Indiana, b 621 S Meridian.
Becker Wm, lab, b 47 Iowa.
BECKER WM L, Druggist, Fine Cigars and Toilet Goods; Prescriptions Carefully Compounded; cor Hadley av and York (W I); h same; Tel 1323.
BECKER & SON (Charles and Jacob Jr), Merchant Tailors, 21 N Penn; Tel 934. (See right top lines.)
BECKERICH BROS (Wm P, Frank J and George), Grocers, 648 College av.
Beckerich Frank J (Beckerich Bros), b 601 Bellefontaine.
Beckerich George (Beckerich Bros), b 601 Bellefontaine.
Beckerich Wm P (Beckerich Bros), h 601 Bellefontaine.
Beckett Wymond J, lawyer, 68½ E Market, h 726 Ash.
Beckham Wesley, lab, b 16 Mill.
Beckley Fannie, h 75 Chapel.
Beckley Leonard J, lab, h 139 Harrison.
Beckley Martha A (wid George W), h 36½ W Washington.
Beckley Susan (wid Wm), h 425 Muskingum al.
Beckman Charles, lab, b 312 W Merrill.
Beckman Francis J, clk Am Ex Co, h 186 W Vermont.
Beckman Frank, driver, r 21 Catterson blk.
Beckman Frank H, clk Hide, Leather and Belting Co, h 180 Brookside av.
Beckman Fred, lab, b 312 W Merrill.
Beckman Henry, mach, b 119 Gillard av.
Beckman Hester (wid Wm), b 38 Ashland (W I).

THE HOME LAUNDRY
197 S. Illinois St. Telephone 1769.

ACORN STOVES AND RANGES
Haueisen & Hartmann
163-169 E. Washington St.
FURNITURE,
Carpets,
Household Goods,
Tin, Granite and China Wares, Oil Cloth and Shades

THE WM. H. BLOCK CO.
7 AND 9 EAST WASHINGTON STREET.
DRY GOODS,
MEN'S FURNISHINGS.

The Fidelity and Deposit Co. OF MARYLAND. Bonds signed for Administrators, Assignees, Executors, Guardians, Receivers, Trustees, and persons in every position of trust.
GEO. W. PANGBORN, General Agent, 704-706 Lemcke Building. Telephone 140.

INSURE YOUR PROPERTY WITH FRANK K. SAWYER

•JOSEPH GARDNER•
GALVANIZED IRON
CORNICES and SKYLIGHTS.
Metal Ceilings and Siding.
Tin, Iron, Steel and Slate Roofing.
37, 39 & 41 KENTUCKY AVE. Telephone 322.

Beckman Jason A, lab, b 368 Dillon.
Beckman Laura, r 155 N Illinois.
Beckman Louis, lab, h e s Woodside av 1 s of Washington.
Beckman Wm C, trav agt Holweg & Reese, h 876 N Penn.
Beckman Wm F, patrolman, h 497 Mulberry.
Beckmann Albert, lab, h 695 Chestnut.
Beckmann Emilia, b 106 Wisconsin.
Beckner Ethelbert, carp, h 11 S Senate av.
Beckner Henry W, farmer, h 1000 Grove av.
Beckner Iley H, clk, r Commercial blk.
Beckner John H, carp, b 1000 Grove av.
Beckner Van Amberg, plumber, b 206 W Walnut.
Becks John, lab, h 386 Clinton.
Becks John N, barber, h 233 W Ohio.
Becks John T, lab, b 386 Clinton.
Becks Osborn C, lab, b 386 Clinton.
Beckstedt George H, mach, h 860 E Washington.
Beckton Edward, clk, 156 N Illinois.
Beckwith Alexander, lab, h 240 Alvord.
Beckwith Alfred J, mach, b 46 Standard av (W I).
Beckwith Frank, plastr, h 94 Martindale av.
Beckwith J Frederick, mach, h 129 Fletcher av.
Beckwith Wm R, clk C C C & St L Ry, b 129 Fletcher av.
Bedell Andrew, h 90 W 1st.
Bedell George V, Gustav A Neerman assignee, planing mill, 399 E Market, h 468 Highland av.
Bedell Leonard J, clk, b 90 W 1st.
Bedell Marguerite A, stenog, b 90 W 1st.
Bedell Paul P, clk, h 38th cor Central av.
Bedford Archibald C, painter, b 319 N St Clair.
BEDFORD COLLINS T, Wholesale and Retail Druggist, 2 Indiana av; Tel 1258, Sec Physio-Medical College of Indiana, Physician, 185 Mass av; Tel 887, h 651 Broadway; Tel 1827.

J. S. FARRELL & CO.
Have Experienced Workmen and will Promptly Attend to your
PLUMBING
Repairs. 84 North Illinois Street. Telephone 382.

Bedford George T, mngr Collins T Bedford, 2 Indiana av, h 481 Broadway.
Bedford Indiana Stone Co, Allen W Conduitt pres, Harry G Coughlen sec and mngr, 26 Baldwin blk.
Bedford John H, h 319 W St Clair.
Bedford Thomas W E, h 2 S Waverly (B).
Bedford Wm L, painter, h 430 Indiana av.
Bedunnah John, driver, h 532 Chestnut.
Bee Hive Paper Box Co, Samuel H Richey pres, Charles F Moffitt sec and treas, 78½ W Washington.
Beeber John H, h 206 S East.
Beech, see Beach.
Beecham, see also Beacham.
Beecham Charles H, porter, h rear 117 St Mary.
Beecham Ella, laundress, h 321 E Court.
Beecham Fletcher L, waiter, h 272 Fulton.
Beecham Isabel (wid Wm), h 444 E 7th.
Beecham Maria A (wid Josiah), b 184 Minerva.
Beecham Wm, lab, b 415 Excelsior av.
Beechler James J, carp, b 70 Columbia av.
Beechler Laura, b 586 Broadway.
Beeks Cornelia C (wid Greenbury C), h 269 N Senate av.
Beeks Wm L, city agt, h 269 N Senate av.
Beelar Josephine (wid Benedict), b 68 W South.
Beeler, see also Bieler and Buehler.
Beeler Fielding, dep County Clerk, h Moorsville pike nr Maywood.
Beeler Frederick T, waiter Roosevelt House.
Beeler James, painter, b 8 Lawn (B).
Beeler Oscar B, clk, r 80 E Ohio.
Beeler Thomas, lab, b 26 Minerva.
Beeler Thomas J, carp, h 349 S Penn.
Beeler Willard D, plumber, h 74 Yandes.
Beem Cornelius L, mach, h 25 Bates.
Beem Jennie, stenog, b 102 N Capitol av.
Beem Phoebe (wid Henry), b 28 Warman av (H).
Beerbower Anna M (wid Edgar), h 105 N Linden.
Beerbower Charles, stonecutter, b 175 Mass av.
Beerbower Edgar P, b 5 Vine.
Beerbower Edgar S, clk, b 105 N Linden.
Beerbower Ella M (wid James), h 175 Mass av.
Beerbower Mary E, dressmkr, 11 Broadway, h same.
Beerbower Matilda L (wid E John), h 5 Vine.
Beerbower Robert W, clk C C C & St L Ry, b 105 N Linden.
Beerbower Stephen R, bicycle rep, h 11 Broadway.
Beerman August, carp 102 Dunlop, h same.
Beermann, August, bricklyr, b 38 Davis.
Beermann Henry B D, h 201 Minnesota.
Beermann Henry, car insp, h 441 E McCarty.
Beermann Henry L, clk, b 405 S New Jersey.
Beermann Louis, contr, 38 Davis, h same.
Beermann Louis jr, carp, b 38 Davis.
Beermann Wilhelmina (wid Henry), h 405 S New Jersey.
Beers John F, marble cutter, h 208 Clifford av.
Beesley Shadrach B, clk C C C & St L Ry, b 302 N Delaware.
Beeson, see also Beason.
Beeson Jehu W, b 1183 N Illinois.
Beeson Martha A, milliner, b 1183 N Illinois.

GUARANTEED INCOME POLICIES issued only by the United States Life Insurance Co.
E. B. SWIFT, Manager. 25 E. Market St.

Furniture Carpets } WM. KOTTEMAN { Stoves Ranges
89 and 91 East Washington Street. Telephone 1742.

Beeson Wm D, pres Indpls Tobacco Works, h 243 Fletcher av.
Beeson Wm M, boilermkr, h 48 Martin.
Beever, see also Beaver and Bever.
Beever Anna (wid Richard), h 380 N West.
Beff Bessie, stenog, b 166 N Alabama.
Begemann Adolph, sculptor, h 88 Benton.
Begemann Frederick, fireman, b 88 Benton.
Begemann Oswin, mach, b 88 Benton.
Beggs James M, engr, h 72 Hoyt av.
Beggs John J, lab, h 165 Beacon.
Beher Edward D, barber, r 85 N Alabama.
Behmer August E, stereotyper The Indpls Sentinel, h 118 High.
Behning August, baker, h 419 N New Jersey.
Behning August jr, trav agt, b 419 N New Jersey.
Behning Edwin F A, cigarmkr, b 419 N New Jersey.
Behnke Charles, propr Marion Park Hotel, cor Vorster and Post avs (M P).
Behnke Herman, lab, h 333 Columbia av.
Behnke Herman H, lab, h 324 Hillside av.
Behnke Marie P (wid Carl), b 338 Columbia av.
Behr Lena, grocer, 139 Cornell av, h same.
Behrendt Albert W, clk, h 59 High.
Behrendt Anna L, dressmkr, 59 High, b same.
Behrendt Rudolph, mach hd, b 59 High.
Behrens Louisa (wid Henry), h 25 Villa av.
Behrens Wm, car rep, h 23 Villa av.
Behrent Charles F, express, 199 Harrison, h same.
Behrent Frederick A, bkkpr Paul H Krauss, h 173 Fletcher av.
Behrent Henry, hackman, h 173 Harrison.
Behringer Emmett E, printer F H Smith, h 1122 N Penn.
Behringer Joseph (Groenwoldt & Behringer), h 150 Bates.
Behrmann Herman D, lab, h 38 Stevens.
Behrmann Wm F, express, h 132 Lexington av.
Behymer Belle, teacher Public School No 1 (H), h 108 Frazee (H).
Behymer Clement F, helper, h 183 Columbia av.
Behymer Frank, grocer, 302 Yandes, h 310 same.
Behymer, Lilian, teacher Public School No 1 (H), b 108 Frazee (H).
Behymer Omer T, clk L S Ayres & Co, b n s Eastern av 1 e of Good av.
Behymer Simeon, trav agt, h n s Eastern av 1 e of Good av (I).
Behymer Sylvester, lab, h 248 Martindale av.
Behymer Thomas, carp, h 108 Frazee (H).
Beiersdorf Clara, clk, b 194 N California.
Beiersdorf Helen (wid Leon), h 194 N California.
Beiersdorf Ida, stenog W D Allison Co, b 194 N California.
Beierstorfer Leonhardt, clk, b 389 N West.
Beigang Charles E, carp, h 253 Jefferson av.
Beinberg Edward B, plumber, b 990 N Senate av.
Beinberg Frederick, mach hd, b 990 N Senate av.
Beinberg Louis H, plumber, b 990 N Senate av.
Beinberg Wm H, plumber, h 174 W 9th.
Beindel John B, tailor, h 393 E Michigan.
Beine Frank A, gardener, h 1450 Schurman av (N I).
Beine Louisa (wid Charles), b 1450 Schurman av (N I).

We Buy Municipal ~ Bonds ~
THOS. C. DAY & CO,
Rooms 325 to 330 Lemcke Bldg.

Beinke Christian F, tmstr, h n s Lily 1 e of Rural.
Beirbusse Carl, clk, b 143 E Washington.
Beisel John J, lab, h 26 Lee (W I).
Beiser Edward, cabtmkr, b 70 High.
Beiser Henry, musician, h 745 Chestnut.
Beiser Katherine (wid August), b 70 High.
BEISSENHERZ HENRY D, Music Teacher, 529 N Alabama, h same.
Beissenherz Henry S, music teacher, b 529 N Alabama.
Beith James B, stenog P & E Ry, b 187 W New York.
Belcher Ralph E, clk, b 147 N Penn.
Belcher Thomas W S, music teacher, 147 N Penn, h same.
Belck Charles F, b rear 540 S East.
Belck Frederick C, h rear 540 S East.
Beldy Adam, lab, h 85 Lee (W I).
Beletzke Frank M, bartndr, b 342 E Morris.
Beletzke Joseph A, lab, h 342 E Morris.
Belk Sarah, nurse City Hospital.
Belke Wm C, carp, h 10 Eureka av.
Belknap James, millwright, h 158 S Linden.
Belknap James B, student, b 158 S Linden.
Bell Alma C, milliner, 172 Columbia av, h same.
Bell Anna L, h 427 Muskingum al.
Bell Benjamin A, mer police, h 162 Lexington av.
Bell Benjamin M, mach, h 73 Hudson.
Bell Bertha C, stenog, b 27 E 2d.
Bell Bessie, h 293 E Court.
Bell Catharine (wid James M), h 306 E South.
Bell Charles A, barber, r 127 W McCarty.
Bell Charles A, lab, h n e cor Brookside av and Jupiter.
Bell Charles C, brakeman, h 48 N Rural.
Bell Charles H, h 1½ Wood.
Bell Charles M, brakeman, h 464 Highland av.
Bell Charles W, mngr M S Huey & Son, b 322 N New Jersey.
Bell Cora, stenog, b 459 Broadway.
Bell Cora C, bkkpr, b 107 Oliver av (W I).
Bell Cornelia V (wid James H), h 73 Hudson.

EAT HITZ'S CRACKERS AND CAKES.
ASK YOUR GROCER FOR THEM.

WILLIAM WIEGEL { MANUFACTURER OF.... } SHOW CASES { 6 W. Louisiana St. Opposite Union Station.

CARPETS CLEANED LIKE NEW. TELEPHONE 818
CAPITAL STEAM CARPET CLEANING WORKS

BENJ. BOOTH PRACTICAL EXPERT ACCOUNTANT. Books Opened, Written Up, Posted and Balanced. Room 18, 82½ E. Washington St., Indianapolis, Ind.

IF YOU WANT A GOOD MEAL AND HAVE IT NICELY SERVED GO TO THE SHERMAN RESTAURANT 18 and 20 S. MERIDIAN STREET

ESTABLISHED 1876. TELEPHONE 168.
CHESTER BRADFORD,
SOLICITOR OF PATENTS,
AND COUNSEL IN PATENT CAUSES.
(See adv. page 6.)
Office:—Rooms 14 and 16 Hubbard Block, S. W. Cor. Washington and Meridian Streets, INDIANAPOLIS, INDIANA.

Bell David, porter, b 289 Indiana av.
Bell Edward, clk, h 51 Minnesota.
Bell Edward E, foreman Outing Bicycle Co, h 854 Rembrant (M P).
Bell Edward J, trav agt, r 28 Stewart pl.
Bell Eliza, cook, h rear 310 E Washington.
Bell Elizabeth, h 272 W Court.
Bell Emma, r 5½ Indiana av.
Bell Espy L, plastr, h 461 W Francis (N I).
Bell Esther R, sec Household Loan Assn, stenog George N Catterson, b 483 N Capitol av.
Bell Frank, lab, r 66 N Missouri.
Bell George, lab, b 167 Elm.
Bell George B, waiter, h 24 Seibert.
Bell George W, express, h 21 Mill.
BELL GUIDO, Physician, s w cor N East and E Ohio, h same; Tel 181.
Bell James, lab, h 436 W Chicago (N I).
Bell James A, lab, h 179 Minnesota.
Bell James M, surveyor, h 44 Tecumseh.
Bell James W, clk, r 1008 Majestic bldg.
Bell James W mach hd, h 461 W Francis (N I).
Bell Jessie L, bkkpr The Only Mnfg Co, r 52 Virginia av.
Bell John, coachman 660 N Meridian.
Bell John, lab, b 224 W 8th.
Bell John, lab, b 182 Muskingum al.
Bell John, lab, b rear 612 N West.
Bell John W, lab, h 105 Martindale av.
Bell John W, mach, h 20 Spann av.
Bell Joseph, lab, b 25 S Gale (B).
BELL JOSEPH E, Lawyer and Asst City Attorney, 77-78 Lombard Bldg, h 25 W Pratt.
Bell Joseph S, pipefitter Sanborn Electric Co, b 48 Buchanan.
Bell Leonard, supt City Dispensary, 32 E Ohio, b s w cor East and Ohio.
Bell Margaret G (wid Boaz), h 459 Broadway.
Bell Marshall, lab, h rear 42 Mill.
Bell Martha E (wid Henry W), h 27 E 2d.
Bell Mary H (wid James), h 837 N Capitol av.
Bell Mattie, h 210 W Court.
Bell Miletus, phys, h 172 Columbia av.

O. B. ENSEY
MANUFACTURER OF
GALVANIZED IRON CORNICE,
SKYLIGHTS AND WINDOW CAPS.
TELEPHONE 1562. Cor. 6th and Illinois Sts.

Bell Miletus F, grocer, 349 Yandes, h same.
Bell Morris B, mach hd, b 73 Hudson.
Bell Nancy A (wid Thomas), b 462 Indiana av.
Bell Orlando C, barber, b 72 S West.
Bell Oscar, lab, r 130 Allegheny.
Bell Prudence T (wid Wiley G), b 184 Broadway.
Bell Roxie (wid Wm A), b 289 Bright.
Bell Sarah (wid Peter), h 167 Elm.
Bell Sarah E (wid Wm J), h 38 College av.
Bell Squire, h 140 Hosbrook.
Bell Squire T, lab, b 140 Hosbrook.
Bell Stanley G, finisher, h rear 227 Virginia av.
BELL THOMPSON R, Patent Solicitor, 64 Ingalls Blk, h 52 Andrews. (See adv in classified Patent Attorneys.)
Bell Wm, lab, h 141 Elizabeth.
Bell Wm, mach, r 32 N Senate av.
Bell Wm A, pub Indiana School Journal, 66½ N Penn, h 223 Broadway.
Bell Wm E, cutter, b 118 Blackford.
Bell Wm P Q, janitor, h 497 N West.
Bell Wm O, insp Cent U Tel Co, b 27 Henry.
Bell Zachariah, barber, r 30 Columbia al.
Bellack Wm, violin teacher, r 39½ Indiana av.
Bellemore Charles L, cooper, h 374 S West.
Bellemore Scott A, baggageman, h 490½ S West.
Bellemore Wm H, cooper, h 517 S West.
Belles Alfred G, finisher, h 43 Buchanan.
Belles John J, trav agt, h 25 Fletcher av.
Bellew Frank, piano tuner, r 136 N Penn.
Bellis Cycle Co, Chalmers Brown pres, Wm H Schmidt vice-pres, Wm K Bellis sec, Benjamin L Webb treas, Elmer E Ruef supt, office 27 Ingalls blk, factory 124 S Penn.
Bellis John R, city fireman, h 71 Elm.
Bellis Samuel, asst sec and treas Railway Officials' and Employes' Accident Assn, b 564 N Meridian.
Bellis Wm, mach, h 557 N Illinois.
Bellis Wm K, sec Bellis Cycle Co, sec and genl mngr Railway Officials' and Employes' Accident Assn, h 564 N Meridian.
Bellis Wm W, mach, h 66 Andrews.
Bellman Joseph, lab, b 235 S Alabama.
Bellman Virginia M (wid James C), h 134 S Linden.
Belmont Blanche, h 159½ W Washington.
Belsier Joseph, brakeman, b e s Brightwood av 7 s of Willow (B).
Belt Joseph, lab, h rear 33 Columbia al.
BELT RAILROAD AND STOCK YARDS CO, Wm P Ijams Pres, Michael A Downing Vice-Pres, John H Holliday Sec, Harry D Lane Auditor, Harry C Graybill Traffic Mngr, Union Stock Yards (W I); Tel 196.
Belton Charles H, agt, h 5 Stoughton av.
Beltz Frank P (F P Beltz & Son), carriagemkr, 100 W Market, h 457 N California.
Beltz Frank R (F P Beltz & Son), h 185 W New York.
Beltz F P & Son (Frank P and Frank R), cigars, 29 S Illinois.
Beltz Jacob, plastr, 85 Stevens, h same.
Belzer Otto, custodian Military Park, h 241 N California.
Bemer Ezra, hostler, b 260 E Market.
Bemis Albert T, pres The Standard Dry Kiln Co, h 37 W Vermont.
Bemis Charles A, mach, b 357 S Illinois.

TUTEWILER, UNDERTAKER, No. 72 WEST MARKET STREET. TELEPHONE 216.

PARTNERSHIP INSURANCE At low cost. By which provision is made against the pecuniary loss and embarrassment resulting from the death of a member of a firm.
Provident Life and Trust Co. of Philadelphia, D. W. EDWARDS, Gen'l Agt., 508 Indiana Trust Bldg.

Bemis George W, patternmkr, h 357 S Illinois.
Bemis Stephen A, pres Indpls Bleaching Co, res St Louis, Mo.
Bemis Thomas, pres Specialty Mnfg Co, b 357 S Illinois cor Norwood. (See adv opp classified Photographers.)
Bemis Wm F, clk H P Wasson & Co, r 146 N Illinois.
Benbow Miles M, painter, h 163 Columbia av.
Bence Caroline (wid Robert F), b 80 Ash.
Bence Edwin C, clk The Wm H Block Co, h 799 N Illinois.
Bence Frank S, clk, h 1001 W Vermont.
Bender Charles W, basketmkr, h 40 Detroit.
Bender Conrad, contr, 180 W 5th, h 80 W 9th.
Bender Conrad S, carp, h 724 S East.
Bender Edward, cigarmkr, b 40 Detroit.
Bender George W, supt Chicago div C C C & St L Ry, n e cor Delaware and South, h 330 N Capitol av.
Bender Guy, tallyman, b 330 N Capitol av.
Bender Re, receiving clk C C C & St L Ry, b 330 N Capitol av.
Bender Robert, driver, h 26 Oriole.
Bender Samuel, engr, b 72 Elm.
Bene Philip, lab, h 17 Agnes.
Benedict Arthur C, insp Indpls Gas Co, h 97 Highland pl.
Benedict Charles A, carp, b 200 Columbia av.
Benedict Charles P (Benedict & Benedict), b 1091 N Meridian.
Benedict Dorothy A (wid Levi J), b 75 Sheffield av (H).
Benedict Jacob, lab, h 307 Columbia av.
Benedict James, lab, r 290 W Market.
Benedict John L (Benedict & Benedict), h 1091 N Meridian.
Benedict Olive (wid John A), b 1091 N Meridian.
Benedict Samuel A, h 200 Columbia av.
Benedict Samuel R, carp, b 77 Centennial.
Benedict Wm H, bkkpr, h 26 Tecumseh.

BENEDICT & BENEDICT (John L and Charles P), Lawyers, 33-34 Lombard Bldg; Tel 130.

Benefiel George F, lab, h 272 Union.
Benefiel Samuel M, b 325 S Meridian.

BENEPE JOHN L, Physician, Office Hours 9-11 A M and 2-4 P M, 209-210 Lemcke Bldg; Office Tel 453, r 10 The Blacherne; Tel 1616.

Benham Francelia N, h 134 Spring.
Benham John F, phys, 914 Morris (W I), h same.
Benham Mary A (wid James), housekpr 39 Broadway.
Beniger Ernest, lab, b e s Appelgate 1 n of Raymond.
Beninger John, carp, h 54 Yandes.
Benjamin Aaron, proofreader, b 11 Union.
Benjamin Eliza T, h 73 W 7th.
Benjamin George, b 136 W 1st.
Benjamin Samuel, tailor, b 23 Douglass.
Benner Arthur U, lab, h 327 W 23d.
Benner Henry, stonecutter, h 187 Elm.
Benner John M, supt, h n crossing of Belt Ry and Judge Harding (W I).
Benner Wm J, coal, 185 W 7th, b 327 W 23d.
Bennerscheidt August C, clk Consumers' Gas Trust Co, h 280 E North.
Bennerscheidt Carl, cabtmkr, b 39 N Alabama.

THE WHEN IS A WORLD BEATER.

Bennett Allan L, clk Indpls Fire Inspection Bureau, r 326 N Illinois.
Bennett Allen, carpetlyr, h 125 Allegheny.
Bennett Allen, carp, b 21 Grant.
Bennett Allen E, engr, h 48 Belmont av (H).
Bennett Alonzo L, brakeman, h 196 Fletcher av.
Bennett Carl H, clk, r 8, 161½ Mass av.
Bennett Catherine (wid Abraham), h 113 Blake.
Bennett Charles E, driver, b 344 Fletcher av.
Bennett Charles F, barber, b 36 S Station (B).
Bennett Daniel M, condr, h 474 E 9th.
Bennett David T, mngr South Bend Chilled Plow Co, h 231 S Olive.
Bennett Edward H, lab, h 21 Grant.
Bennett Elbert F, lab, h 22 Grace.
Bennett Ellen, stenog Kingan & Co (ltd), b 113 Blake.
Bennett Eliza L (wid George W), h 137 E Vermont.
Bennett Emery H, painter, h 41 Roe.
Bennett Ernest A, plumber, h 312 Cornell av.
Bennett Eunice, stenog Williams Bros, b 325 N Illinois.
Bennett Floyd E, millwright, h 21 Traub av.
Bennett Frederick, tel opr, b 294 Columbia av.
Bennett George, molder, r 58 Nordyke av (W I).
Bennett George H, electrician, h 16 Nordyke av (W I).
Bennett George W, contr, 509 Talbott av, h same.
Bennett Gilbert H, driver, h 250 W Market.
Bennett Harry, lab, h 51 Brett.
Bennett Hattie E (wid John K), b 264 W Michigan.
Bennett Henry W, pres The Indpls Stove Co, h 567 N Delaware.
Bennett Horace T, pres Capitol Lumber Co, h 123 E Pratt.
Bennett Ira H, carp, h 166 Laurel.
Bennett Isaac, lab, b 67 S Noble.

THE A. BURDSAL CO.
WINDOW AND PLATE
GLASS
Putty, Glazier Points, Diamonds.
Wholesale and Retail. 34 and 36 S. Meridian St.

THEODORE F. SMITHER, AGENT FOR WARREN'S ANCHOR BRAND ASPHALT ROOFING. OFFICE, 151 WEST MARYLAND ST. TEL. 861.

ELECTRIC CONSTRUCTION Isolated Plants Installed. Electric Wiring and Fittings of all kinds. C. W. Meikel. Tel. 466. 96-98 E. New York St

DALTON & MERRIFIELD { LUMBER South Noble St., near E. Washington

INDIANA ELECTROTYPE CO. :: BEST WORK LOWEST PRICES. 23 WEST PEARL ST., INDIANAPOLIS, IND. JOB WORK. BOOK PLATES. All Orders Promptly Filled. BEST PATENT BASE ON THE MARKET.

KIRKHOFF BROS.,
GAS AND ELECTRIC FIXTURES
THE LARGEST LINE IN THE CITY.
102-104 SOUTH PENNSYLVANIA ST.
TELEPHONE 910.

Bennett James B, carp, h 72 Fulton.
Bennett James E, foreman The J B Allfree Mnfg Co, h 601 N West.
Bennett John B, lab, h 863 S Meridian.
Bennett John J, lab, h 58 Gresham.
Bennett John W, mach hd, h 45 Nordyke av (W I).
Bennett J Wesley, photog, 38½ E Washington, h 762 N Senate av.
Bennett L da C, clk Kingan & Co (ltd), b 113 Blake.
Bennett Loren, engr, h 40 Lord.
Bennett Melissa J (wid Tarleton), h 15 Maple.
Bennett Montague G, grinder, h 488 W Eugene (N I).
Bennett Nannie J (wid Harvey), h 175 Bane.
Bennett Omer, lab, b 176 Patterson.
Bennett Philander L, car rep, h 144 Tacoma av.
Bennett Robert E, ice, h 197 Oliver av (W I).
Bennett Robert H, carp, h 234 S Penn.
Bennett Robert N, clk U S Pension Agency, h 536 Broadway.
BENNETT ROBERT R, Broker, 44 Lombard Bldg, h 429 N Meridian.
Bennett Sallie, h s s 8th 5 w of canal.
Bennett Solomon F, lab, b 136 W 1st.
Bennett Susannah (wid Joseph T), b 166 Laurel.
Bennett Theodore, condr, h 50 Cherry.
Bennett Warren G, undertaker, 20 Michigan (H), h 88 Tremont av (H).
Bennett Wm, h 5 Wallace.
Bennett Wm A, cutter Gem Garment Co, h 1689 Kenwood av.
Bennett Wm G, trav agt, h 452 N West.
Bennett Wm H, sec and treas The Indpls Stove Co, h 431 N Meridian.
Bennett Wm R, barber, b 863 S Meridian.
Bennett Wm S, driver, h 51 S Spruce.
Bennewitz George A, clk, b Hotel English.
Benney Wm C, bkkpr, h 468 W Addison (N I).
Benninger Frank, engraver, b 563 S East.
Benninger John, lab, b 42 McIntyre.
Benor Louis, clk, b 360 E New York.
Benor Morris, h 360 E New York.

COAL AND COKE
The W. G. Wasson Co.,
130 INDIANA AVE. TEL. 989
LIME AND LATH

Benor Paul, trav agt, b 360 E New York.
Benowitz George, clk, b Hotel English.
Benson Adelbert S (Middlesworth, Benson, Nave & Co), h 814 N Delaware.
Benson Annie (wid John A), h s s Washington 5 w of Harris av (M J).
Benson Edward J, lab, h 18 Wilcox.
Benson Hannah (wid Aaron), h 123 Eddy.
Benson Harry L, clk Order of Chosen Friends, h 115 Ash.
Benson Hiram P, coachman 79 E Pratt.
Benson Jane (wid Jeffrey), h rear 21 Center.
Benson John J, carp, h 184 Eureka av.
Benson Johnson, lab 400 Broadway.
Benson Joseph, tinner, h 213 S Reisner (W I).
Benson J Milton, teacher Public School No 24, b 109 Agnes.
Benson Luther, lecturer, h 873 N Delaware.
Benson Mabel, teacher Public School No 2, b 138 S William (W I).
Benson Margaret A (wid Julius L), b 75 Lockerbie.
Benson Mary L, h 477 N Meridian.
Benson Moses D, stenog L E & W R R, b 183 N Noble.
Benson Naphtali H, stenog L E & W R R, h 282½ S Illinois.
Benson Nathan H, clk, b 477 N Meridian.
Benson Sarah, stenog, b 183 N Noble.
Benson Susan M (wid James S), h 138 S William (W I).
Benson Theresa (wid David S), h 183 N Noble.
Benson Wm W, agt, b 229 N Penn.
Bentel Lewis D, fireman, h 56 Spann av.
Benthuysan George, lab, b 73 N Alabama.
Bentley Caroline (wid Albert), h 4 Willard.
Bentley George P, barber, 104 Mass av, h same.
Bentley James D, b 530 E Washington.
Bentley Robert, lab, b 28 Water.
Bentley Robert F, fireman, h 16 Depot (B).
Bentley Rose C (wid David E), h 58 S Gale (B).
Benton Allen R, LL D, prof Butler College, h w s Downey av 1 s of University av (I).
Benton Charlotte (wid Horatio), b 77 Adams.
Benton Delia H, cashr Mass Mut Life Ins Co, h 90 E Pratt.
Benton Eliza, teacher Girls' Classical School, h 90 E Pratt.
Benton George, lab, h 32 N Senate av.
Benton George, waiter, r 77 Adams.
Benton George W, clk Penna Lines, h 127 E 6th.
Benton George W, teacher High School, h 898 Broadway.
Benton Howard A, mnfrs' agt, 86 Lombard bldg, h 855 N Meridian.
Benton Justin W, bicycle rep, 86 E Georgia, h 86 Paca.
Benton Minnie E, stenog Parry Mnfg Co, b 221 Union.
Benton Rachel A (wid Joel C), h 221 Union.
Benton Walter P, ins, 7 Ingalls blk, h 362 College av.
Bentz August, mach, b 888 Madison av.
Bentz Barbara (wid Nicholas), h 888 Madison av.
Benz Wm, lab, h 109 Eureka av.
Benzel George, lab, h 149 N Dorman.
Benzel Henry, mach, b 149 N Dorman.
Benzing Charles W, cigar mnfr, 666½ S Meridian, b 630 same.
Benzinger August, mason, b 813 Chestnut.
Beplay Charles F, basketmkr, b 396 E Ohio.
Beplay Frederick W, engr, h 812 Cornell av.

W. H. MESSENGER COMPLETE HOUSE FURNISHER 101 East Washington Street, Telephone 491

Foundry and Pattern Shop } McNamara, Koster & Co. { PHONE 1593 212-218 S. Penn. St.

Beplay John McG, engr, h 396 E Ohio.
Berauer Joseph M, phys, 557½ Madison av, r same.
Berberich John L, driver, h 531 E Ohio.
Berch Wm E, packer, h 49 Garland (W I).
Berdel Barbara, h 45 Beaty.
Berdel Carl, paperhngr, 45 Beaty, b same.
Berdel John, shoemkr, 269 W McCarty, h same.
Berdel Louis J, clk When Clothing Store, h 560 S New Jersey.
Berdel Nellie, clk, b 45 Beaty.
Bereman Ernest, coremkr, b 88 Holmes (H).
Beretta Andrew, lab, h 242 S Alabama.
Berg Albert, teacher and librarian Deaf and Dumb Inst, h 65 Walcott.
Berg Augusta M S (wid Charles L), tailoress, b 332 E Wabash.
Berg Augustus, engr, h 342 S West.
Berg Charles L, lab, b 325 W Pearl.
Berg Flora, h 172 N Delaware.
Berg Frederick W, pressman, b 382 E New York.
Berg Fredericka (wid Charles), b 382 E New York.
Berg George F, pressman, h 382 E New York.
Berg George F jr, clk, b 382 E New York.
Berg Henrietta L (wid Henry L), h 456 N California.
Berg Jacob, filer, h 135 E New York.
Berg John F, mach, b 547 W Addison (N I).
Berg Michael, lab, b 160 W Maryland.
Berg Michael, shoemkr, 370½ S West, b 22 Lynn av (W I).
Berg Wm L, shoecutter, h 328 W Pearl.
Bergan, see also Burgan.
Bergan Frank, clk, b 528 E 9th.
Bergan Frederick J, lab, h 148 Carlos.
Bergan John F, mach, b 148 Carlos.
Bergan Wm F, asst bkkpr Charles Mayer & Co, b 148 Carlos.
Bergen Daniel, lab, b 62 Columbia av.
Bergen Edward W, lab, b 62 Columbia av.
Bergen Frank, lab, b 62 Columbia av.
Bergen Patrick, lab, b 62 Columbia av.
Bergen Wm P, stonecutter, h 62 Columbia av.
Bergener Emma (wid Herman), h 30 W Vermont.
Bergener Gustav J, house phys City Hospital, b 30 W Vermont.
Berger, see also Burger.
Berger Alfred, mach, h 9 Wendell.
Berger Ernest, clk, h 107 S Noble.
Berger Frank, mach hd, b 9 Wendell.
Berger Franz E, mach hd, b 9 Wendell.
Berger Fred T, with Charles Mayer & Co, h 324 N Capitol av.
Berger Henry G, mach, b 9 Wendell.
Berger Laura E (wid Michael R), h 17 The Blacherne.
Berger Peter, lab, h 103 Malott av.
Bergman, see also Borgman and Burgman.
Bergman John, architect, b 325 E Ohio.
Bergman John A, motorman, h 568 W Washington.
Bergmann Caroline (wid Francis), b 251 W Morris.
Bergmann Charles A, driver, b 484 S New Jersey.
Bergmann Elizabeth H, tailoress, h 100 Bradshaw.
Bergmann Francis J, soap mnfr, 251 W Morris, h 574 Bellefontaine.
Bergmann George A, bartndr, b 61 E South.
Bergmann Wm, driver, h 139 High.
Bergquist Edward, tailor, r 55 Dearborn.

Henry H. Fay,
40½ E. WASHINGTON ST.,
AGENT FOR
Insurance Co. of North America,
Pennsylvania Fire Ins. Co.

Bergquist John G, tailor, h 122½ Ft Wayne av.
Bergundthal David C, sec and treas Van Camp H and I Co, h 313 N Capitol av.
Berkholz Charles D, drayman, h 32 Smithson.
Berkle Charles, butcher, h 30 Oxford.
Berkley Albert, lab, b 210 Hamilton av.
Berkley James, lab, h 210 Hamilton av.
Berkley Jennie (wid James), h 216 S Meridian.
Berkowitz Armin, saloon, 484 E Washington, h same.
Berkowitz Bert, bartndr, b 484 E Washington.
Berkowitz Ignatz, saloon, 1102 E Washington, b 484 same.
Berkowitz Nathan, clk, b 290 Virginia av.
Berkshire Harry W, clk I D & W Ry, h 1059 E Michigan.
BERKSHIRE LIFE INSURANCE CO OF PITTSFIELD, MASS, John J Price Genl Agt, 207-208 Lemcke Bldg.
Berlet Christian, lab, h 8 Lynn av (W I).
Berlin Carl, lab, r 166½ W Washington.
Berlin James T, carp, h 120 Indiana av.
Berlt Charles A, clk, h 35 W Vermont.
Bernard Brother, teacher, b cor Coburn and Short.
Bernard Lydia A (wid Nelson), b 1259 N Penn.
Bernauer Charles, mach hd, r 2 Spann av.
Bernauer Charles A, bartndr, h 341 S Delaware.
Bernauer Edward E, saloon, 430 Virginia av, h 216 E Morris.
Bernauer Joseph, b 174 Laurel.
Bernauer Joseph, bartndr, h 410 Pleasant.
Bernauer Ursulla (wid Benedict), b 450 S Delaware.
Bernd Bros (Daniel and Peter), wagon mkrs, 71 W Morris.
Bernd Charles, painter, h 575 S Capitol av.
Bernd Daniel (Bernd Bros), h 63 W Morris.
Bernd George P, blksmith, h 618 S East.
Bernd George P M, wagonmkr, b 63 W Morris.
Bernd Peter (Bernd Bros), h 566 S Illinois.

Union Casualty & Surety Co.
of St. Louis, Mo.
Employers', Public, General, Teams and Elevator L a ; also Workmen's Collective, Steam Boiler, Plate Glass and Automatic Sprinkler Insurance.
W. E. BARTON & CO., General Agents,
504 Indiana Trust Building.
LONG DISTANCE TELEPHONE 1918.

THE FRED DIETZ CO.
WOODEN PACKING BOXES MADE TO ORDER
FACTORY AND WAREHOUSE TRUCKS.
400 Madison Avenue. Telephone 654.

Shorthand! BUSINESS UNIVERSITY. When Bl'k. Elevator day and night. Typewriting, Penmanship, Book-keeping, Office Training free. See page 4. Est. 1850. Tel. 499. E. J. HEEB, Proprietor.

Water Works Pumping Engines { HENRY R. WORTHINGTON, 64 SOUTH PENNSYLVANIA ST. Long Distance Telephone 284.

UNION CO-OPERATIVE LAUNDRY { (COMPOSED OF UNION LAUNDRY GIRLS.) NOS. 38, 40 AND 42 VIRGINIA AVENUE TELEPHONE 89 INDIANAPOLIS, IND. T. E. SOMERVILLE, MANAGER

HORACE M. HADLEY
REAL ESTATE AND LOANS....
66 East Market Street
Telephone 1540. BASEMENT.

Berndt August A, wood turner, b w s Oakland av 2 n of Clifford av.
Berndt August F, cabtmkr, h w s Oakland av 2 n of Clifford av.
Berndt Elnora S (wid John), h 180 Hillside av.
Berndt Harry O, mach, b 180 Hillisde av.
Berner Charles F, lab, h 254 Blake.
Berner Frederick, vice-pres Hetherington & Berner Co, h 40 Union.
Berner Frederick jr, treas Hetherington Berner Co, h 290 S Meridian.
Berner Gottlieb, h 21 Peru av.
Berner Louis E, clk, b 40 Union.
Berner Wm E, clk, b 254 Blake.
Bernhamer Louisa (wid Wm), b 997 N Senate av.
Bernhardt, see also Barnard and Barnhart.
Bernhardt Anna (wid Wm), h 220 Pleasant av.
Bernhardt Benjamin, butcher, h 149 Eddy.
Bernhardt Charles E, sawmkr, h n s Washington 3 e of Quincy.
Bernhardt Ernest, lab, h 120 W Morris.
Bernhardt Frank, clk, r 20½ N Delaware.
Bernhardt George, dairy, 60 W Raymond, h same.
Bernhardt John, driver, h e s Tremont av 1 n of Grandview av (H).
Bernhardt John C, clk, h 75 Shelby.
Bernhardt John C jr, clk, b 75 Shelby.
Bernhardt Lorenz, mason, 49 Wallack, h same.
Bernhardt Lorenz C, gilder, b 75 Shelby.
Bernhardt Olof L, painter, b 405 Coburn.
Bernhardt Wm, lab, b e s Tremont av 1 n of Grandview av (H).
Bernhart Frederick, saloon, 76 S Delaware, h same.
Bernhart John, saloon, 423 S Meridian, h 340 S New Jersey.
Bernhart John L, grocer, 38 Dunlop, h same.
Berninger Clarence O, student, r 367 N Alabama.
Bernloehr Charles, boxmkr, h 97 Chadwick.
Bernloehr Christopher, jeweler, 324 S Meridian. h same.

Merchants' and Manufacturers Exchange
Make Collections and Commercial Reports......
J. E. TAKKEN, MANAGER,
19 Union Building, 73 West Maryland Street

Bernloehr George, barber, 1 English av, h same.
Bernloehr John, baker, r 262½ E Washington.
Bernloehr John, janitor Court House, h 153 Meek.
Bernloehr John A, bkkpr, h 43 Russell av.
Bernloehr Lena (wid Jacob), b 39 Yeiser.
Bernloehr Margaret, midwife, 153 Meek, h same.
Berns Augustus F, music teacher, b 304 N New Jersey.
Berns George, carp, h 96 Oriole.
Bernstein, see also Borinstein.
Bernstein Jacob, clk, b 425 S Illinois.
Bernstein Joseph, furniture, 187 W Washington, stoves, 235 E Washington, junk, 189 Indiana av, h 425 S Illinois.
Bernstein Moses Z, clk, b 425 S Illinois.
Bernstein Nathan, clk, b 425 S Illinois.
Beronson Bernard, carver, b Illinois House.
Berringer John R, lab, h 42 McIntyre.
Berringer Wm H (Smock & Berringer), r 58 Hendricks blk.
Berringer Wm H, agt, h 36 N East.
Berry Abram S, mason, h 60 Johnson av.
Berry Adrian D Rev, pastor Woodruff Place Baptist Church, h 216 Randolph.
Berry Alice, h 4 Sheldon.
Berry Ann (wid Jeremiah), r 356 N Noble.
Berry Benjamin F, carp, h 9 Warren av (W I).
Berry Bros (John J and James E), plumbers, 374 Shelby.
Berry Bros (Madison N and Luther L), barbers, 205 Indiana av.
Berry Catherine (wid Michael), h 89 Buchanan.
Berry Charles, lab, b w s Sherman Drive 2 n of Michigan.
Berry Charles L, pastor Garden Baptist Church, b 228 W New York.
Berry Charles S, lab Spencer House.
Berry Clara J, b 27 Vine.
Berry Corinthia A (wid Frank), laundress, h 275 E Wabash.
Berry David L, carp, h 101 Geisendorff.
Berry Edward, carp, h 24 Mayhew.
Berry Edward C, mach, h 781 N Illinois.
Berry Eli, carp, h 529½ N Illinois.
Berry Eli F, blksmith, h 529½ N Illinois.
Berry Elizabeth M (George D Jones & Co), b 439 S Illinois.
Berry Ellen (wid George), h 298 S Capitol av.
Berry Frank D, clk, b 187 Buchanan.
Berry George, lab, h 298 S Capitol av.
Berry George H, cook, h 102 Hosbrook.
Berry George W, boarding, h 176 S New Jersey.
Berry Harry M, printer, b 529½ N Illinois.
Berry Henry M, molder, h 188 S Senate av.
Berry Isaac N, brakeman, b 176 S New Jersey.
Berry Isaiah, waiter, b 156 Michigan av.
Berry James, lab, h 65 Fayette.
Berry James, tmstr, b e s Baltimore av 2 n of 22d.
Berry James A, carp, 1 Hester, h same.
Berry James E (Berry Bros), b 89 Buchanan.
Berry James E, dry goods, 201 Hoyt av, h same.
Berry Jane (wid Benjamin), h s e cor Capitol av and 30th.
Berry John, r 251 S Meridian.
Berry John, lineman fire dept, b 364 S Illinois.
Berry John, gasfitter, h 140 Madison av.

CLEMENS VONNEGUT 184, 186 and 192 E. Washington St. | Wire Rope, Machinery, Lathes, Drills and Shapers

THE WM. H. BLOCK CO. DRY GOODS, DRAPERIES, RUGS, WINDOW SHADES.
7 AND 9 EAST WASHINGTON STREET.

Berry John J (Berry Bros), b 89 Buchanan.
Berry John M, brakeman, h 178 Hoyt av.
Berry Luther L (Berry Bros), h 386 N West.
Berry Lydia S, dressmkr, b s e cor Capitol av and 30th.
Berry Madison N (Berry Bros), b 386 N West.
Berry Marion, millwright, h 179 N Noble.
Berry Mary, h 3 Bates al.
Berry Michael, engr, h 299 E Merrill.
Berry Omer P, finisher, h 232 Douglass.
Berry Robert C, mach, h 361 Fletcher av.
Berry Vernon, printer, b 46 S Capitol av.
Berry Walter, lab, h 10 Vine.
Berry Walter J, carp, h 180 Douglass.
Berry Wm, h 310 E Georgia.
Berry Wm A, lab, h 226 Summit (H).
Berry Wm F, mach, h 301 Alvord.
Berry Wm H, carp, h 187 Buchanan.
Berry Wm H, porter, h 40 Guffin.
Berry Wm J, printer, b 140 Madison av.
Berry Wm M, painter, b 4 Sheldon.
Berryhill John S (Knefler & Berryhill), pres Allison Coupon Co, h 937 N Alabama.
Berryman Bert, collr The Indpls News, b 366 Cornell av.
Berryman Edward, lab, h 179 N Dorman.
Berryman Nellie E, bkkpr, b 366 Cornell av.
Berryman Presley, blksmith, h 129 Madison.
Berryman Wm, b 28 Eastern av.
Berryman Wm H, basketmkr, b 129 Madison.
Berryman Wm H, cooper, h 366 Cornell av.
Bersch George W, trav agt Schrader Bros, h 205 Bellefontaine.
Bert Mollie, r 307 The Shiel.
Bertel John, shoemkr, 269 W McCarty, h same.
Bertels Frank, baker, h 50 Paca.
Bertels Frank G, mason, b 107 Lexington av.
Bertels George, carp, 107 Lexington av, h same.
Bertelsman Charles, cigar mnfr, 264 Mass av, h 49 Windsor.
Bertelsman Henry W, storekpr, h 84 Stoughton av.
Bertelsman Lilly, agt, 262 Mass av, b 84 Stoughton av.
Bertelsman Wm, news, 264 Mass av, h same.
Bertermann Benedict, mech engr, b 244 N East.
BERTERMANN BROS (John and Wm G), Florists, 85 E Washington (30 Pembroke Arcade); Tel 840; Greenhouse, 1370 E Washington; Tel 198.
Bertermann Edward J, florist Bertermann Bros, h 80 Lockerbie.
Bertermann Irwin, student, b 1374 E Washington.
Bertermann John (Bertermann Bros), h 1374 E Washington.
Bertermann Walter, clk b 80 Lockerbie.
Bertermann Walter H, florist Bertermann Bros, b 1374 E Washington.
Bertermann Wm G (Bertermann Bros), h 244 N East.
Berth August, carp, h n s Michigan 2 e of Belt R R.
Berting Joseph F, train disp P C C & St L Ry, b 277 N Capitol av.
Bertram Sallie E (Union Co-Operative Laundry), r 5 Wyandot blk.
Bertram Wm, molder, b 52 Michigan (H).
Bertrand Charles, cook The Denison.
Bertsch Edward S, brakeman, b 779 E Washington.

Beschnack Franz, lab, h 353 S Capitol av.
Beskin Henry, grocer, 118 Indiana av, h same.
Bess Milton, waiter The Bates.
Bess Wm H, lab, r 283 Chapel.
Besse Henry, lab, r 130 Allegheny.
Bessel John B, baker, r 188 Virginia av.
Besser Eliza, r 178 S New Jersey.
Bessonies August Right Rev, vicar genl Diocese of Vincennes, h s e cor 5th and Meridian.
Best Isaiah, lab, h 34 Bates al.
Best John, car rep, h 351 Jefferson av.
Best Laura, h 167 W Maryland.
Best Mary (wid George), h 30 Bates al.
Best Wm J, lab, h 145 High.
Beston Michael, h s w cor Pine and Noble.
Beswick Ann T (wid Philip I), b 1007 N Capitol av.
Beswick Frank M, condr, h 22 Johnson av.
Beswick James H, carrier, b 270 S Delaware.
Beswick Margaret (wid James W), h 270 S Delaware.
Beswick Newton B, express, h 28 Wallace.
Betcone Donald S, trav agt, h 39 N Arsenal av.
Bethmann Louis F, lab, h 33 Holly av (W I).
Bethuram Alpha, mach hd, h Maywood, Ind.
Bettcher Elizabeth, teacher Public School No 1, b 204 N Illinois.
Bettcher Henry, tmstr, h 247 Lincoln la.
Bettcher John, car insp, h 249 Lincoln la.
Better Rudolph, harnessmkr, h 818 S East.
Bettes Mattie E, teacher Indiana Reformatory, b same.
Betts Howell T, tinner, rear 457 W Eugene, h 489 Francis (N I).
Betz Christian F, printer, h 28 Garland (W I).
Betz Lawrence, plumber, h 119 John.
Betz Wm B, foreman Allison Coupon Co, b 28 Garland (W I).
Betzler Charles W, carp, b 30 N West.
Betzner Charles A, condr, b 299 Columbia av.

GUIDO R. PRESSLER,
FRESCO PAINTER
Churches, Theaters, Public Buildings, Etc., A Specialty.
Residence, No. 325 North Liberty Street
INDIANAPOLIS, IND.

INDIANAPOLIS STEEL ROOFING AND CORRUGATING WORKS, 23 and 25 East South Street. S. D. NOEL, Proprietor.

David S. McKernan, REAL ESTATE AND LOANS
A number of choice pieces for subdivision, or for manufacturers' sites, with good switch facilities.
Rooms 2-5 Thorpe Block.

DIAMOND WALL PLASTER { Telephone 1410 BUILDERS' EXCHANGE.

UNION TRANSFER AND STORAGE CO., Cor. E. Ohio St. and C., C., C. & St. L. R'y Tracks. BRICK WAREHOUSE; CLEANEST AND SAFEST STORAGE IN CITY FOR HOUSEHOLD GOODS AND MERCHANDISE.

W. McWORKMAN,

METAL CEILINGS,
ROLLING SHUTTERS,
DOORS AND PARTITIONS.
930 W. Washington St. Tel. 1118.

Betzner Edward N, molder, h 299 Columbia av.
Beulah Logan, lab, b 166 Osage.
Beumer Henry, carp, h 136 Windsor.
Bevan John, trav agt, h 585 Ash.
Bevell Allen A, painter, h 1064 W Vermont.
Bevell Christian A, carp, h 490 W 1st.
Bever, see also Beaver and Beever.
Bever Charles M, clk Wm H Rolls' Sons, r 347 N Delaware.
Bever Ellsworth, clk, b 347 N Delaware.
Bever Fremont E, clk, b 340 N Meridian.
Bever Stallard J, clk, r 451 N Capitol av.
Beverly Battle, coachman, h 112 Roanoke.
BEVERIDGE ALBERT J, Lawyer, Rooms 1-4, 18½ N Penn, h 451 N Delaware; Tel 1184.
Beveridge Henry L, sec and treas Beveridge Paper Co, h 732 N New Jersey.
Beveridge Paper Co, Isaac V Stuphen pres, Henry L Beveridge sec and treas, cor Maryland and Geisendorff
Beverlin John, carp, h n s Oakwood 2 e of Hillside av.
Beville Burton L, clk, b s s E Washington 1 e of Belt R R.
Beville Henry H, real est, 2½ W Washington, h s s E Washington 1 e of Belt R R.
Beville Henry M, clk, b s s E Washington 1 e of Belt R R.
Bevington Samuel, fireman, r 104 English av.
Bevington Wm, engr, r 104 English av.
Bevis Andrew J, produce, E Mkt House, h n s Michigan 1 e of Belt R R.
Bevis Clemence V, painter, h w s Bradley 3 n of Ohio.
Bevis John A, painter, h w s Bradley 5 n of Ohio.
Bevis Stewart, painter, b e s Sherman Drive 1 n of Ohio.
Beyea Alfaretta J (wid Harrison G), b 424 Ash.
Beyer, see also Baar, Bahr, Barr and Bayer.
Beyer Anna, opr Cent U Tel Co, b 402 N California.
Beyer Caroline (wid Carl), b 48 Barth av.

SEALS,
STENCILS,
STAMPS, Etc.
GEO. J. MAYER
15 S. Meridian St.
TELEPHONE 1386.

Beyer Clara P (wid Christian), r 14 Stewart pl.
Beyer Edmund A, foreman Kahn Tailoring Co, r 12 Stewart pl.
Beyer Edward L, foreman, b 402 N California.
Beyer Elizabeth (wid Julius), h 610 S Meridian.
Beyer Francis A, coachman, h 175 N California.
Beyer Frank J, lab, h 16 Maple.
Beyer Gustav, cabtmkr, b 402 N California.
Beyer John, meats, 414 W North, h 416 same.
Beyer Katharina, b 669½ Madison av.
Beyer Max, produce, E Mkt House, h 213 Elm.
Beyer May (wid Frederick), h 331 E Georgia.
Beyer Otto E, lab, b 610 S Meridian.
Beyersdorfer John, bartndr, h 565 E 7th.
Bibbs Elizabeth, h e s Race 4 s of Raymond.
Bice Otis, tel opr, b 100 Camp.
Bichel Louis, brewer, b 476 E Washington.
BICKEL HARRISON C, Lawyer, Rooms 9-10, 82½ E Washington, h 228 Hoyt av.
Bickel John E, student, b 8 Detroit.
Bickel Michael T, mach, h 8 Detroit.
Bickel Milton O, switchman, h 287 Fletcher av.
Bickell Harvey F, asst genl supt L E & W R R, s w cor Washington and Noble, h 357 N New Jersey.
Bicker Frank A, mach, h 448 Indiana av.
Bickers John, millwright, h rear 67 Minerva.
Bickett Augusta, bkkpr Samuel Kealing, b 30 N West.
Bickett John, lab, b 83 Geisendorff.
Bickett Martha A (wid John E), r 30 N West.
Bicknell Andrew J, painter, b California House.
Bicknell Ernest, sec Board of State Charities, 52 State House, h 64 Ruckle.
Bicknell Larkin W Rev, h 218 E South.
Bicknell Myron D, lab, r 232 S Capitol av.
Biddinger James H, engr, h 28 School.
Biddinger James H jr, clk Kingan & Co (ltd), b 28 School.
Biddle Charles C, molder, b 224 Blake.
Biddle Frederick S, photog, 16½ E Washington, h same.
Biddle Henry P, millwright, h 224 Blake.
Biddle Horace P, clk, b 519 N Alabama.
Biddle Stephen V, music teacher, h 519 N Alabama.
Biddle Wm P, packer, b 224 Blake.
Biddle Wm S Rev, pastor California Street M E Church, h 221 Douglass.
Biddy James M, janitor High School, h 298 N Capitol av.
Biddy Lemuel F, clk, r 298 N Capitol av.
Bidwell Charles W, carp, h 24 Pleasant av.
Bidwell Elizabeth, dressmkr, 24 Pleasant av, h same.
Bidwell Harry M, clk C H & E H Schrader, b 24 Pleasant av.
Biebinger, see also Bebinger.
Biebinger Jacob, grocer, n s 30th 2 e of Illinois, h s w cor Capitol av and 30th (M).
Biebinger Mary A, dressmkr, 94 N East, r same.
Biedenmeister Charles A, h 265 E New York.
Biedenmeister Charles A jr, clk Daggett & Co, h 271 S Senate av.

A. METZGER AGENCY ESTABLISHED 1863. INSURANCE

LAMBERT GAS & GASOLINE ENGINE CO.
ANDERSON, IND. PORTABLE GASOLINE ENGINES, 2 TO 25 H. P.

Biedenmeister Daisy, teacher Public School No 15, h 265 E New York.
Biedenmeister Mary J, teacher Public School No 14, b 265 E New York.
Biegler George Q, register clk C C C & St L Ry, b 175 Hoyt av.
Biegler Portia E (wid John C), h 175 Hoyt av.
Biehl Nicholas, lab, h 673 Union.
Bieler, see also Beeler and Buehler.
Bieler Charles L, cashr D P Erwin & Co, h 41 West Drive (W P).
BIELER JACOB L, Mngr Indianapolis Branch Anheuser-Busch Brewing Association, 454-458 E Ohio; Tel 1687; h 1052 N Alabama.
Biemer Martin, blksmith, h 52 Division (W I).
Bier Charles E, tinner, h 32 Temple av.
Bier John W, tinner, h 34 Temple av.
Bierhaus Henry, teacher Deaf and Dumb Inst, h 610 E Washington.
Bierman, see Beermann.
Biffel Isom, lab, h rear 29 Cornell av.
BIG FOUR BUILDING ASSOCIATION, John H Furnas Pres, Samuel E Ellerman Sec, Rooms 11-12, 68½ E Market.
BIG FOUR ROUTE (C C C & St L Ry), Henry M Bronson Asst Genl Pass Agt, Henry S Fraser Genl Agt Freight Dept, W A Sullivan Commercial Agt, Benjamin C Kelsey City Ticket Agt, Wright S Jordan Trav Pass Agt, 1 E Washington; Tel 374; Samuel M Hice Ticket Agt, 36 Jackson Pl; Tel 388.
Bigelow David, mach hd, b 739 E Michigan.
Bigelow Eliza J (wid James F), b 69 N East.
Bigelow George W, mach hd, h 318 Martindale av.
Bigelow Ira G, tinner, h 157 Yandes.
Bigelow Isaac, cigarmkr, b 90 Sheldon.
Bigelow Isaac K, plastr, h 157 Yandes.
Bigelow Isaac M, tinner Van Camp H and I Co, b 157 Yandes.
Bigelow John, mach hd, b 739 E Michigan.
Bigelow John S, plastr, h 90 Sheldon.
Bigelow Wm H, mach hd, h 739 E Michigan.
Bigger Richard F (R H & R F Bigger), phys, 102 N Alabama, h same; tel 1023.
Bigger Robert H (R H & R F Bigger), phys, 429 Virginia av, h 102 N Alabama; tel 1023.
BIGGER R H & R F (Robert H and Richard F), Physicians and Surgeons, 429 Virginia av; Tels Office 1090, Res 1023.
Bigger Wm H, insp City Engineer, r 127 N Alabama.
Biggins Benjamin B, lab, h 4 Arthur.
Biggins Hugh, porter, h 605 W Vermont.
Biggins James M, phys, 117½ W Washington, h same.
Biggs Wm F, cooper, b 18 Caldwell.
Bigham Alice K (wid Hayden S), h 171 Park av.
Bihlmaier Frank, driver, h 381 W Washington.
Bilby Elmer W, lab, h 219 Hoyt av.
Bilger Grace (wid Joseph), h 240 Spring.
Bilger Nellie (wid John), b 316 Spring.
Billeter Francis E, driver, h 567 E Washington.
Billeter Zora, engr, b 75 River av (W I).
Billger Wm, carp, h 20 Merrit (H).
Billhauser Sophia (wid John), h 2 Hanway.

Farm and City Loans
25 Years' Successful Business.
THOS. C. DAY & CO,
Rooms 325 to 330 Lemcke Building.

Billigheimer Lee W, clk Elite Portrait and Frame Co, r 28½ Indiana av.
Billing Augusta (wid Andrew), h 30 Yeiser.
Billing Gustav, clk, b 30 Yeiser.
Billing Oscar J, clk C C C & St L Ry, b 30 Yeiser.
Billings Albert H, clk McCormick H M Co, b 179 E St Clair.
Billings Frederick H, clk Parry Mfg Co, b s s Oak av 2 e of Central av (I).
Billings George M, trav agt, h s s Oak av 2 e of Central av (I).
Billings Henry M, painter, h 128 Walcott.
Billingsley Alexander D, b w s Orchard 1 n of Howland av.
Billingsley Denton F (T A Randall & Co), h 622 E Washington.
Billingsley James H (D A Williams & Co), clk Penna Lines, h 910 Broadway.
Billingsley John J W, pub The Drainage Journal, 19 Talbott blk, h w s Orchard 1 n of Howland av.
Billingsley Joseph, blksmith, b 150 Cypress.
Billingsley, Judson J W, dairy, w s Orchard 1 n of Howland av, b same.
Billingsworth, John W, peddler, h 1696 N Senate av.
Billman Gustus S, phys, 643 Virginia av, h same.
Billman Joseph, lab, b 235 S Alabama.
Billman Nicholas, motorman, r 22 Columbia blk.
Billmire Claude L, lab, b 693 W Udell (N I).
Billmire Dalzell, cabtmkr, b 693 W Udell (N I).
Billmire Elizabeth (wid Charles W), h 693 W Udell (N I).
Billo Julius, cabtmkr, r 428½ Virginia av.
Bills Ella, music teacher, b s e cor 24th and Central av.
Bills Harry G, bkkpr Nelson Morris & Co, b 309 Fletcher av.
Bills James T, bicycle rep, h rear 175 S East.
Bills Nelson M, car insp, h 2 E Willow (B).
Bills Ora E, salesman Emil Wulschner & Son, h 243 Shelby.
Bills Sylvester, lab, h 155 Locke.

EAT
QUAKER BREAD
ASK YOUR GROCER FOR IT.
THE HITZ BAKING CO.

BICYCLES $5 DOWN. $5 MONTHLY. Big Wheels. Big Terms. WHEELMEN'S CO. 31 W. OHIO ST. LONG DISTANCE TEL. 1858.

J. H. TECKENBROCK House, Sign and Fresco Painter, 94 EAST SOUTH STREET.

FIDELITY MUTUAL LIFE PHILADELPHIA, PA. A. H. COLLINS, Gen. Agt. Baldwin Blk. } RATES REASONABLE. SOUND BEYOND QUESTION. BUSINESS-LIKE IN PRACTICE.

BITUMINOUS COAL ▸▸ Edwardsport Coal and Mining Company ROOMS 42 AND 43 WHEN BUILDING.

ESTABLISHED 1876. TELEPHONE 168.
CHESTER BRADFORD,
SOLICITOR OF PATENTS,
AND COUNSEL IN PATENT CAUSES.
(See adv. page 6.)
Office:—Rooms 14 and 16 Hubbard Block, S. W. Cor. Washington and Meridian Streets, INDIANAPOLIS, INDIANA.

Bills Thomas, lab, h 42 Athon.
Bills Thomas, lab, h rear 175 S East.
Biltimier Carrie R (wid Henry A), clk, b 434 Cornell av.
Binager Bruce J, billposter, h 36 Garfield pl.
Binager George T, agt, h 22 Sterling.
Binager Vintzson B (Binager & Reinert), h 324 N Alabama.
Binager & Reinert (Vintzson B Binager, John G Reinert), broom mnfrs, n e cor St Clair and Bee Line Ry.
Binan James, lab, h 42 S Liberty.
Binger Henry, butcher, h 141 S Summit.
Binger Otto, butcher, b 141 S Summit.
Bingham Edmund H, railroad editor The Indianapolis Sentinel, r 546 N Meridian.
Bingham Francis L, clk, h 32 W St Joseph.
Bingham George U, clk, h 146 East Drive (W P).
Bingham Harriett A (wid Wm P), b 110 Middle Drive (W P).
Bingham Joseph J, h 546 N Meridian.
Bingham Pearl W, barber, h 166 W Michigan.
Bingham Wheelock, fireman, b 17 McKim av.
Binkley Benjamin R, mach, h 148 Elm.
Binkley Carra A, clk Am Detective Agency, b 45 Warren.
Binkley Edward H, finisher, b 148 Elm.
Binkley Emma (wid John), h 45 Warren.
Binkley Joshua, b 148 Elm.
Binkley Ruth A, stenog, b 45 Warren.
Binkley Wm H, sawyer, b 148 Elm.
Binninger Christian, lab, h e s Applegate 2 n of Raymond.
Binninger Ernst, lab, h e s Applegate 2 n of Raymond.
Binninger Frank, lithog, b 563 S East.
Binninger Freda (wid John), h 563 S East.
Binninger Wm, lab, h e s Applegate 2 n of Raymond.
Binsac Anna (wid Wm), h 68 N Noble.
Binsac Emma C, clk, b 68 N Noble.
Binzer Henry E, coachman 803 College av.
Binzer Michael, trav agt, h 387½ N Noble.
Binzer Solomon, dry goods, 286 S Illinois, h 300 S Meridian.

BUY THE BEST.
Outing BICYCLES $85
MADE BY

76 N. PENN. ST. Phone 598.

Birch Mary (wid James), h 82 Torbet.
Birch Rebecca (wid Wm), h 466 W 2d.
Birch Richard E, h 178 Broadway.
Birchard Sarah C (wid Plaudin), b 704 Ash.
Birchfield James W, mngr, h 16 Stoughton av.
Birchman Wm, confr, 36 Hill av, b 24 Columbia av.
Birck John C, grinder, h 192 Nebraska.
Birck Nicholas, lab, h 25 Carson.
Birck Peter A, driver, h 366 N West.
Bird, see also Byrd.
Bird Ann M (wid Abraham), h 32 The Windsor.
Bird Asa, blksmith, h 164 W Maryland.
Bird Edward F, lab, h 95 Bradshaw.
Bird Elmer E, plumber, h 114 Fayette.
Bird Eugene E, mach, h 323 Columbia av.
Bird Frank, pres Frank Bird Transfer Co, h 683 N Illinois; Tel 258.
BIRD FRANK TRANSFER CO, Frank Bird Pres, George B Gaston Sec and Treas, General Office 24 Pembroke Arcade; Tel 534; Branch Offices, 115 N Delaware; Tel 444; Bates House and Union Station. (See adv in classified Omnibus Lines; also Transfer Companies.)

FRANK BIRD TRANSFER CO.
General Office, 24 Pembroke Arcade.
Offices { Union Station. 115 North Delaware and Bates House.
Stable, 115 North Delaware.
Order by Telephone Day or Night. | Baggage Checked at Residence | Carriages for Parties, Weddings, Depot, etc.
Telephone 534.

Bird Gustav A, huckster, h 230 S Olive.
Bird Henry, lab, h 624 Home av.
Bird James, lab, h rear 606 N West.
Bird James A, lab, b 235 Mass av.
Bird James D, foreman, h 561½ Virginia av.
Bird John, tmstr, b 297 W Merrill.
Bird Mary C (wid Wm A), h 155 Cornell av.
Bird Oliver, lab, h 398 Yandes.
Bird Richard, h 297 W Merrill.
Bird Stanton, lab, b 297 W Merrill.
Bird Thomas V, lab, b 230 S Olive.
Bird Wm C, blksmith, r 235 Mass av.
Bird Wm M jr (W M Bird jr & Co), r 81 W Vermont.
BIRD W M JR & CO (Wm M Bird Jr, John C Test), Rambler Bicycles, Densmore Typewriters, 29 E Market; Tel 1549.
Bireley Harvey F, condr, h 66 Tacoma av.
Birge James A, flagman, h 174 Davidson.
Birge Otis A, clk, b 174 Davidson.
Birge Warren A, lab, h 408 Dillon.
Birk, see also Burk.
Birk Andrew W, car rep, b n w cor Brightwood av and Wolf pike (B).
Birk Christian, engr, h 313 W Morris.
Birk Harry A, student, b 294 N West.
Birk Martin, h 294 N West.
Birk Martin J, meats, 298 N West, b 294 same.
Birk Otto E (Frenk & Birk), b 294 N West.
Birk Wm M, pharmacist Sloan Drug Co, b 294 N West.
Birket Charles T, phys, 187 Columbia av, b same.

ROOFING MATERIAL C. ZIMMERMAN & SONS, SLATE AND GRAVEL ROOFERS, 19 SOUTH EAST STREET.

PUMPS Chain Pumps, Driven Wells and Deep Water Wells. Repairing Neatly Done. Cisterns Built. CHARLES KRAUSS', 42 S. PENN. ST. TELEPHONE 465.

Birket Margaret J (wid Charles W), h 187 Columbia av.
Birkner George H, lab, h 307 Columbia av.
Birkner Peter, lab, h 277 Yandes.
Birmingham Thomas, lab, h 44 Geisendorff.
Birr Herman, blksmith, h 101 Gray.
Birrell James, hostler 215 Dougherty.
Birt, see also Burt.
Birt Henry W, waiter, r 25 S West.
Birt John J, finisher, h 379 S East.
Birtch Stephen, lab, h 40 Summit (H).
Bischel Louis, brewer, b 476 E Washington.
Bischoff George (Bischoff & Fisse), h e s Rural 3 n of Belt R R (B).
Bischoff George, butcher, b 112 Chadwick.
Bischoff & Fisse (George Bischoff, John H Fisse), feed, s e cor Rural and Belt R R (B).
Bisese Michael, peddler, h 222 S East.
Bish Philippa (wid Victor), h 807 N Meridian.
Bishoff Jacob (Wulf & Bishoff), res Augusta, Ind.
Bishop Aaron, mach, b 289 W Merrill.
Bishop Benjamin F, lab, h 231 Huron.
Bishop Charles T (Koehler & Bishop), h 564 E Vermont.
Bishop Edward, carp, h 612 W Washington.
Bishop Edward F, carp, h 239 Kentucky av.
Bishop Elias C, attendant, h n s W Washington 3 w of Insane Hospital gate (M J).
Bishop Ellsworth D, bkkpr Reeves & Co, h 152 E New York.
Bishop George W, cooper, r 45 Helen.
Bishop Harry E, musician, b 38 E 24th.
Bishop Henry H, jeweler, 580 Virginia av, h 151 Cottage av.
Bishop James, lab, b 234 Muskingum al.
Bishop James D, driver, r 580 N Senate av.
BISHOP JAMES L, Mngr Indianapolis Calcium Light Co, rear 126 W Maryland and 127 W Pearl, h 38 E 24th.
Bishop Joel C, carp, h 147 River av (W I).
Bishop John E, motorman, h 180 N Missouri.
Bishop Lewis P, well driver, 391 N New Jersey, h same.
Bishop Mary, h 70 S Senate av.
Bishop Nona M, h 151 N Alabama.
Bishop Samuel, lab, h 145 Miller (W I).
Bishop Sarah, dressmkr, 373 W Vermont, h same.
Bishop Wm F, polisher, b 110 Bates.
Bishop Wm J, lab, b 402½ College av.
Bishop Wm M, porter, h 149 Geisendorff.
Bisig Andrew J (Bisig & Lange), h e s Sherman Drive 1 s of Brookville rd (S).
Bisig Andrew J, mach hd, h 74 Laurel.
Bisig & Lange (Andrew J Bisig, Edward F Lange), dairy, e s Sherman Drive 1 s of Brookville rd (S).
Bismarck John, lab, r 144 N Capitol av.
Bisplinghoff Susannah (wid Herman), h 10 Beecher.
Bisselberg, see Buesselberg.
Bissell Charles J, gasfitter, h 284 W St Clair.
Bissell Daniel P, h 73 Lockerbie.
Bissell Frank P, salesman Central Cycle Mnfg Co, h 279 E Vermont.
Bissell Frederick L, bicycle rep, h 404 W Pratt.
Bistline Arvilla M, phys, 394 N New Jersey, b same.
Bistline Henry E, grocer, 187 S Illinois, h 1164½ E Washington.
Bittinger Jesse W, collr Albert Gall, h 850 N New Jersey.
Bittner Wm A, lab, h 220 W Merrill.

Richardson & McCrea, 79 East Market Street, FIRE INSURANCE, REAL ESTATE, LOANS, AND RENTAL AGENTS. Telephone 182.

Bittrich Wm S, meats, 56 E Mkt House, res Maywood, Ind.
Bitzer Conrad S, trav agt, h 770 N Senate av.
Bius Reece, condr, b 678 W Washington.
Biven Anthony, lab, h rear 738 N West.
Biven George, lab, r 187 Indiana av.
Bivens Ellen S (wid John), h w s Miami 9 s of Prospect.
Bivens Melissa (wid Wm), h 30 Drake.
Bivens Reuben A, finisher, h s s Prospect 1 e of Madeira.
Bivins Hampton S, lab, h n w cor Mill and 9th.
Bixby Allan S, supt Metallic Mnfg Co, h 301 Cornell av.
Bixby Burton L, b 92 Bellefontaine.
Bixby Charles W, trav agt Moline Plow Co, h 92 Bellefontaine.
Bixby Jennie M, teacher, b 92 Bellefontaine.
Bixler Edward J, watchman, h 24 Hope (B).
Bixler Henry W, lab, h 26 Hope (B).
BLACHERNE THE, Henry L Wallace Agt, Joseph W Nethery Supt, n w cor Meridian and Vermont; Tel 1183.
Black August, b 483 E Georgia.
Black Austin, fireman, h 32 Hoyt av.
Black Burton, lab, b 205 W 2d.
Black Carl S, motorman, b 563 W Francis (N I).
Black Charles C, lab, h 337 N Noble.
Black Charles H, carriage mnfr, 44 E Maryland, h 274 E Ohio.
Black Charles S, barber, 206 S Meridian, h same.
Black David M, janitor, h 296 Fayette.
Black Drew, student, b 403 Cornell av.
Black Elizabeth (wid Bernard), b 37 Eastern av.
Black Frank B, messenger, b 255 S Penn.
Black Frank J, mach, h 11 Temple av.
Black Frank M, clk H P Wasson & Co, b 325 Home av.
Black George, engr, b 942 Gent (M P).
Black George W (Warman, Black, Chamberlain & Co), res Greencastle, Ind.

SHORTHAND REPORTING...... CONVENTIONS, SPEECHES, SERMONS. COPYING ON TYPEWRITER. S. H. EAST, State Agent, THE WILLIAMS TYPEWRITER 55 Thorpe Block, 87 East Market Street.

Collars and Cuffs Laundered in Best of Style. Do it or High Gloss Finish.

ERTEL STEAM LAUNDRY 26 and 28 N. Senate Ave. Telephone 1089.

ELLIS & HELFENBERGER Manufacturers of Iron Vases, Setees and Hitch Posts. 162-170 South Senate Ave. Tel. 958.

THE HOGAN TRANSFER AND STORAGE COMP'Y
Household Goods and Pianos Moved—Packed—Stored...... Baggage and Package Express Machinery and Safes a Specialty Cor. Washington and Illinois Sts. TELEPHONE No. 675.

Hose, Belting, Packing, Clothing, Druggists' Sundries, Bicycle Tires, Cotton Hose, Etc. New York Belting & Packing Co., L't'd.
THE CENTRAL RUBBER & SUPPLY CO. PHONE 922. 79 S. ILLINOIS ST., INDIANAPOLIS, IND.

The Provident Life and Trust Co.
OF PHILADELPHIA.
Small Death Rate. Small Expense Rate. Safe Investments.
Insurance in force $115,000,000
D. W. EDWARDS, General Agent, 508 Indiana Trust Building.

Black George W, filer, h 1400 Northwestern av (N I).
Black George W, trav agt, h 325 Home av.
Black Grace, teacher Public School No 38, b 403 Cornell av.
Black Hannah M (wid Samuel), milliner, 23½ W Washington, h same.
Black Helen (wid Charles), h 571 Mass av.
Black James B (Black & Pugh), Judge Appellate Court of Indiana, 98 State House, h 397 N Penn.
Black James O, lab, b 23 S Arsenal av.
BLACK JAMES S, Vocalist, Voice Builder, Musical Director, Teacher of Vocal Technique, English and Italian Singing; Pupils Qualified for Teachers, Church and Concert Singers, 10 E 7th, h same.
Black Jennie M (wid Robert), h 403 Cornell av.
Black Jeremiah, carp, h 410 Blake.
Black John, art stained glass, 159 Mass av, h 1112 N Meridian; tel 1074.
Black John, lab, h 346 W North.
Black John A (The Grocers' Mnfg Co), h 23 Gregg.
Black Kimball, waiter, b 219 N West.
Black Lydia A (wid George H), h 86 N Liberty.
Black Marcus, uphlr, h 14 Germania av (H).
Black Napoleon R, carp, h 563 W Francis (N I).
Black Oscar E, filer, h 188 S Senate av.
Black Robert, lab, h 1476 Schumann av (N I).
Black Robert H, polisher, h 178 Harrison.
Black Ruth A (wid Washington), b 32 Hoyt av.
Black Thomas F, carp, h 255 S Penn.
Black Warren P, fireman, h 42 Harrison.
Black Wm, mach, h 510½ E 9th.
Black Wm A, mach, h 22 Lawn.
Black Wm H, tinner, h 1016 E Washington.
BLACK & PUGH (James B Black, Edwin B Pugh), Lawyers, 57-58 Lombard Bldg; Tel 1773.
Blackburn Albert, lab, b 342 N Missouri.

Julius C. Walk & Son, Jewelers Indianapolis.
12 EAST WASHINGTON ST.

Blackburn Cassius, lab, r 424 Muskingum al.
Blackburn Eugene, clk R M S, h 117 S Illinois.
Blackburn Frederick H, porter, b 55 Torbet.
Blackburn George, lab, h 55 Torbet.
Blackburn George jr, nurse, b 55 Torbet.
Blackburn Grace V, teacher Knickerbocker Hall, b e s Central av nr 7th.
Blackburn John C, porter, b 55 Torbet.
Blackburn Roderick, lab, h 382 N California.
Blackburn Wm, porter, b 354 W 2d.
Blacker Marshall D, carp, h 820 E 9th.
Blacketter George E, clk, r 42 Hendricks blk.
Blackford Clarence, waiter, h 18 S Senate av.
Blackford George, lab, r 480 W Lake (N I).
Blackford Wm, lab, r 354 W 2d.
Blackledge Albert S, vice-pres and treas The Mullen-Blackledge Co, b 975 N Meridian.
Blackledge Frank H (Blackledge & Thornton), h 205 N East.
Blackledge Irene L, teacher Girls' Classical School, b 975 N Meridian.
Blackledge John W, trav agt Mullen-Blackledge Co, b 975 N Meridian.
Blackledge Mame S, stenog Williams Bros, b 131 W St Clair.
Blackledge Susan K (wid Thomas G), h 975 N Meridian.
BLACKLEDGE & THORNTON (Frank H Blackledge, Wm W Thornton), Lawyers, 634-635 Lemcke Bldg; Tel 1580.
Blackman Eliza (wid John L), h 65 Buchanan.
Blackman Joseph B, meats, 19 E Mkt House, h 133 Dougherty.
Blackman Joseph E, clk, b 133 Dougherty.
Blackman Lloyd J, meats, 95 E Mkt House, b 133 Dougherty.
Blackman Wm W, carp, h 42 Woodlawn av.
Blackmeier Henry C, collr, r 100 N Alabama.
Blackmore Charles, lab, b 466 Indiana av.
Blackwell Albert, lab, b 319 Alvord.
Blackwell Bernard F, mach, b 25 Carlos.
Blackwell Charles, molder, h 2 Draper.
Blackwell Elmer W, clk, b 987 N Delaware.
Blackwell Frederick, saloon, 528 E 9th, h same.
Blackwell George W, tmstr, h w s Thaddeus 1 s of Cypress.
Bleckwell Henry, lab, h s s English av 3 e of Belt R R.
Blackwell Henry, lab, h n s Finley av 6 e of Shelby.
Blackwell James, mach, b 25 Carlos.
Blackwell, Jesse, tmstr, h 29 Athon.
Blackwell John tmstr, h w s Earhart 6 s of Prospect.
Blackwell John I, huckster, h 479 N California.
Blackwell John J (Renihan, Long & Blackwell), h 216 N West.
Blackwell John W, agt, b 912 S Meridian.
Blackwell John W, lab, h e s Waverly av 3 n of Clifford av.
Blackwell Julius, porter, h 483 W Ontario (N I).
Blackwell Nathan, lab, h s e cor Elizabeth and Barnhill.
Blackwell Nathaniel, lab, b 111 Shepard (W I).
Blackwell Nelson J, porter, h 157 Alvord.

OTTO GAS ENGINES
BUILDERS' EXCHANGE S. W. Cor. Ohio and Penn. Telephone 535.

Becker & Son Charles Becker Jacob Becker Jr. Merchant Tailors. 21 N. Penn. St. Tel. 934

Blackwell Otis L, bookbndr, b 1109 E Washington.
Blackwell Peter, lab, b 29 Athon.
Blackwell Roten M (Blackwell & Gates), h 987 N Delaware.
Blackwell Thomas, h 25 Carlos.
Blackwell Thomas F, mach, b 25 Carlos.
Blackwell Wm H, lab, h 319 Alvord.
Blackwell & Gates (Roten M Blackwell, Peter M Gates), grocers, n e cor Delaware and 10th.
Blades Bert J, pressfeeder, r 27 Ft Wayne av.
Blaes John G, mach, h 96 Eureka av.
Blaich Catharine (wid Wm F), b 127 W St Clair.
Blaich Lydia R, critic Public School No 28, b 232 Fulton.
Blaich Martha K, teacher, b 232 Fulton.
Blaich Mary (wid Gottlieb F), h 232 Fulton.
Blaich Mary S, stenog, b 232 Fulton.
Blaine Charles H, plumber, h 214 N Pine.
Blaine Mary (wid John), h 227 Bright.
Blaine Samuel N, dentist, r 29½ S Illinois.
Blair Aaron H (Blair & Failey), h 581 N Delaware.
Blair Amelia (wid John R), h 28 Cornell av.
Blair Andrew J, porter, h 179 Muskingum al.
Blair, Baker & Walter (Willet B Blair, Wm W Baker, James P Walter), live stock com, Union Stock Yards (W I).
Blair Benjamin L (B L Blair & Co), r 23 W Maryland.
BLAIR B L & CO (Benjamin L Blair), County and Township Supplies, State Agts Austin Road Goods, 23 W Maryland; Long Distance Tel 1501.
Blair Cornelius A, tmstr, h 2 Reynolds av (H).
Blair Esther M (wid Solomon), h 868 N Delaware.
Blair Flora A, dressmkr, 197 N Illinois, h same.
Blair Frank W, elev opr, b 120 S Olive.
Blair George W, paperhngr, h 302 Yandes.
Blair Harry H, lab, b 120 S Olive.
Blair Jesse H, lawyer, 112 Commercial Club bldg, h 1023 N New Jersey.
Blair Joseph, lab, h 21 Center.
Blair Joseph L, trav agt, b 276 N New Jersey.
Blair Willet B (Blair, Baker & Walter), h 226 Randolph.
Blair Wm, boilermkr, b 285 S Capitol av.
Blair Wm H, collr A Metzger Agency, h 120 S Olive.
Blair Wm M, mach, b 28 Cornell av.
Blair & Failey (Aaron H Blair, James F Failey), heading mnfrs, 2 Ingalls blk.
Blaisdell Charles C, claywkr, b 13 Coble.
Blaisdell Elijah, watchman, h 13 Coble.
Blaisdell Guy C, lab, b 13 Coble.
Blaisdell Leonard C, lawyer, h 1695 N Illinois.
Blaisdell Walter E, tmstr, b 13 Coble.
Blaisdell Wm F, lab, b 13 Coble.
Blaize Rose, governess Indpls Orphan Asylum, n e cor College and Home avs.
Blake Albert E, checkman, b 67 Madison av.
Blake Augustus, fitter, h 130 Church.
Blake Edward L, cigarmkr, b n e cor Centennial and Coyner.
Blake Frederick, lab, h 269 Coburn.
Blake Frederick jr, lab, b 269 Coburn.
Blake Henry, lab, h 115 Wisconsin.
Blake James, mach hd, h 737 N Senate av.
Blake John, stonecutter, h 175 S New Jersey.

Henry H. Fay,
40½ E. WASHINGTON ST.,
FIRE INSURANCE, REAL ESTATE,
LOANS AND RENTAL AGENT.

Blake John S, tilesetter, b 741 N Senate av.
Blake John W, h 513 W McLene (N I).
Blake Josephine, h 151½ W McCarty.
Blake Laura, h 20 N West.
Blake Laura F (wid John A), h 421 N Pine.
Blake Lulu, photog, b 88 Hillside av.
Blake Marshall H, salesman, h 200 S William (W I).
Blake Myra (wid Francis), h 20 N West.
Blake Solomon E, hatter, b 200 N Capitol av.
Blake Zachariah T, driver, h 270 E Miami.
Blakeman Andrew W, carp, h 232 Northwestern av.
Blakeman Colby C, fireman, h 61 Tacoma av.
Blakeman Grant, lab, b rear 218 Charles.
Blakeman Grant, molder, h 20 Oriole.
Blakeman John, lab, h w s James 2 n of Sutherland (B).
BLAKEMAN ROBERT I, Dentist, 3-6 Marion Blk, h 305 Broadway.
Blakemore Edward G, mason, b 171 W 5th.
Blakemore Harvey, barber, 169 Virginia av, h 126 Hudson.
Blaker Eliza A, city supt Indpls Free Kindergarten, office Margaret opp City Hospital, h 1196 N Meridian.
Blaker Louis J, agt White Line Fast Freight, 1 E Washington, h 1196 N Meridian.
Blakey Chapman J, porter, h 382 Clinton.
Blakey Wm, barber, b 122 Osage al.
Blakie Joseph, barber, h 134 Columbia al.
Blalock-Jones Matilda J (wid Stephen), dressmkr, 217½ Mass av, h same.
BLANCHARD FRANK A, Undertaker and Embalmer, 99 N Delaware; Tel 411; h 294 N Meridian; Tel 659.
Blanchard Ida M, flour mill, e s Highland av 1 s of Clifford av, b 51 Clifford av.
Blanchard James R, painter, b 419½ Indiana av.
Blanchard June L, mach, b 273 N Noble.
Blanchard Louisa, h 419½ Indiana av.
Blanchard Mary A (wid Edward), h 51 Clifford av.

JAS. N. MAYHEW,
MANUFACTURING
OPTICIAN
LENSES AND FRAMES A SPECIALTY.
No. 13 North Meridian St., Indianapolis.

SALISBURY & STANLEY. Office, Store and Bank Fixtures a Specialty. Repairing of all kinds done on short notice. 177 Clinton Street, Indianapolis, Ind. Contractors and Builders TELEPHONE 999.

LUMBER | Sash, Door and Planing Mill Work. | Balke & Krauss Co. Cor. Market and Missouri Streets.

FRIEDGEN'S TAN SHOES are the Newest Shades Prices the Lowest. 19 North Pennsylvania St.

SAMUEL LAING General Job Work in Sheet Metal of all Kinds 72 AND 74 E. COURT STREET.

M. B. WILSON, Pres. W. F. CHURCHMAN, Cash.
THE CAPITAL NATIONAL BANK,
INDIANAPOLIS, IND.
Make collections on all points in the States of Indiana and Illinois on the most favorable rates.
Capital, - - $300,000
Surplus and Earnings, 50,000
No. 28 S. Meridian St., Cor. Pearl.

Blanchard Thomas G, mattressmkr, b 419½ Indiana av.
Blanchard Wm H, clk, b 419½ Indiana av.
Blancher Isaac, lab, b 381 W 1st.
Blanchfield Joseph P, molder, r 71½ N Illinois.
Blanck Richard, butcher, h 58 Wisconsin.
Bland Wm I, ins agt, 42 W Market, r 226½ W Washington.
Blandford Bertha, printer, 40½ S Illinois, b w s Sherman Drive 3 s of Brookville rd (S).
Blandford Henry S, printer, h w s Sherman Drive 3 s of Brookville rd (S).
Blandford Henry S jr, lab, r 86 N Senate av.
Blandford Raymond, lab, b 289 Indiana av.
Blank Adolph G, painter, h 38 Langley av.
Blank Caspar, farmer, b 966 N Delaware.
Blank Ida M (wid Maximillian), h 431 Home av.
Blank Richard, butcher, h 58 Wisconsin.
Blankenship Charles, lab, b 252 E Washington.
Blankenship Elmina (wid George), b 18 Seibert.
Blankenship Walter, lab, h 113 Harrison.
Blankinship Elulia (wid James O), b 134 N Liberty.
Blankinship Mary (wid Frank), h 263 Lafayette.
Blanker Charles J, finisher, b 274 E Court.
Blanton Emma M (wid Alexander), b 596 N Penn.
Blanton Llewellyn H, pres Blanton Milling Co, h 596 N Penn.
BLANTON MILLING CO, Llewellyn H Blanton Pres, Henry D Yoder Sec and Treas, 200 W Maryland; Tel 321.
Blaschke Joseph, lab, h 59 Sheffield (W I).
Blase Frederick, mach, b 169 Union.
Blase Henry, porter, h 169 Union.
Blase Henry F, salesman Indpls Fancy Grocery Co, b 169 Union.
Blasengym Walter, mngr Gerrone W Burns, r 24 N Delaware.
Blasengyn Wm, welldriver, h 82 S West.

MONEY
Loaned on Short Notice at Lowest Rates.
TUTTLE & SEGUIN,
Tel. 1168. 28 E. Market St.

Blasingham Edward, watchman, r 80 W Market.
Blatchley Willis S, State Geologist, 89 State House, h 492 Broadway.
Blatz Helena (wid John), b 232 N California.
Blatz Leo A, clk, h 440½ S Illinois.
Blauvelt George W, lab, h 52 Carlos.
Blauvelt James A, car rep, h 59 S Arsenal av.
Blauvelt Jane E (wid Alexander), h 375 E Ohio.
Blauvelt Jane J (wid Charles S), h 23 Williams.
Blaydes Robert B, carp, b 31 Ashland (W I).
Blaylock Samuel J, cook, h 383 W 1st.
Bleck August, b 483 E Georgia.
Bleck August C, drayman, h 385 Union.
Bleck Frederick W, drayman, h 215 E Morris.
Bledsoe Elizabeth F, h 203 Alvord.
Bledsoe James P, collr, h 395 Cornell av.
Bledsoe Louis, switchman, b 203 Alvord.
Bledsoe Thomas T, condr, b 203 Alvord.
Bleistein Adam, cigar mnfr, 128 N Noble, h 541 E Ohio.
Bleistein Regina (wid Peter), h 541 E Ohio.
Bleistein Wm H, cigarmkr, b 541 E Ohio.
Blemer Frederick W, mach, b 11 Torbet.
Blemer Henry, molder, b 175 Meek.
Blenker Charles J, finisher, h 274 E Court.
Bless Frank, tmstr, h 454 Martindale av.
Blessing Walter, student, r 320 N Delaware.
Blettner George T, h 284 E Louisiana.
Blettner John, printer, h 270 S East.
Blettner Kate, b 329 E Louisiana.
Blettner Mary (wid John), h 329 E Louisiana.
Blevins Oscar, lab, b 54½ S California.
Blevins Sarah M, h 54½ S California.
Blew Wm C, trav agt, h 88 Stoughton av.
Blickenstaff Harry, driver, b 27 Lynn av (W I).
Bliss George W (Bliss, Swain & Co), h 284 N Meridian.
Bliss Henry R, sec and treas The Sinker-Davis Co, 112-150 S Missouri, h 16 West Drive (W P).
BLISS, SWAIN & CO (George W Bliss, Thomas A Swain), Proprs The Progress Clothing Co, 6-8 W Washington; Tel 1630.
Blizard Wm (Ballweg & Co), b 920 N Illinois.
Blizzard Charles T, clk, b 219 Huron.
Blizzard James L, salesman Krag-Reynolds Co, h 219 Huron.
Blizzard Omer C, clk, b 219 Huron.
Blizzard Silas W, flagman, h 41 Elm.
Block Clara A, teacher German Public School No 9, b 189 N East.
Block Edward, r 59½ N Illinois.
Block Henry W, foreman, h 341 N Pine.
Block Samuel H, trav agt, b 414 S Illinois.
BLOCK WM H (The Wm H Block Co), h 957 N Penn.
BLOCK WM H CO THE (Wm H Block), Dry Goods, Millinery, Cloaks and House Furnishings, 7-9 E Washington; Tel 1921. (See right top and bottom lines.)
BLODAU ROBERT P, Druggist and Mnfr of Blodau's Specialties, Cocoa Almond Cream, Corn Remedy, Headache Powders, Etc, 102 Indiana av; Tel 1692, h 235 N Senate av.

PAPER BOXES, MANUFACTURED BY SULLIVAN & MAHAN 41 W. PEARL STREET.

DIAMOND WALL PLASTER { Telephone 1410 BUILDERS' EXCHANGE.

Blodel Ann (wid Albert), b 90 Indiana av.
Blodgett Frederick, supt Elevator "A", h 1022 N Senate av.
Blodgett Wm G, carp, b 1725 N Illinois.
Blodgett Wm H, reporter The Indpls News, h 17 Hall pl.
Bloemker Ernst W, grocer, 602 E New York, h same.
Bloemker Frederick W, clk, b 602 E New York.
Bloess Theodore H, bkkpr Jung Brewing Co, h 78 Lexington av.
Blohm John W F, b 101 Lincoln la.
Blomberg Ernst F W, lab, h 347 English av.
Blomeyer Henry, fireman, h 957 Morris (W I).
Blonda Harrison C, cigarmkr, b 324 N Alabama.
Blood Lillian, bkkpr, b 173 Bellefontaine.
Bloom, see also Blume.
Bloom Edward, clk, b n w cor School and Spencer (B).
Bloom Elizabeth (wid Conrad), h n w cor School and Spencer (B).
Bloom Ernest, lab, b n w cor School and Spencer (B).
Bloom Harry H, tailor, h 249 S Pine.
Bloom Henry, engr, h 48 Foundry (B).
Bloom John, blksmith, h n s Spencer 1 w of School (B).
Bloom Joseph, barber, h 517 S Capitol av.
Bloom Samuel, grocer, 28 S Station (B), h 26 same.
Bloom Samuel, trav agt, r 2 Cleaveland blk.
Bloomer Abram, lab, h 90 Cypress.
Bloomer Isaac L, lawyer, 33-34 Baldwin blk, h 457 N Penn.
Bloomer John J, watchman, b 296 Blackford.
Bloomer Lewis H, grocer, 68 N Delaware, h 1401 E Washington.
Bloomer Mary E, dressmkr, 296 Blackford, h same.
Bloomer Susan (wid James), h 499 Virginia av.
Blosier Harry, brakeman, r e s Brightwood av 8 s of Willow (B).
Blossom Dallas E, tinner, b 345 Yandes.
Blossom Jeremiah A, clk, h 345 Yandes.
Blough Albert R, polisher, b 254 E Georgia.
Blough Simon D, carp, h 254 E Georgia.
Blount Barzillai M Rev, h n s Washington av 1 w of Maple av (I).
Blount David D, trav agt, h 11 S Senate av.
Blount Eli J, h 325 S Alabama.
Blount Grace D, teacher, b n s Washington av 1 w of Maple av (I).
Blount Homer S, clk, b n s Washington av 1 w of Maple av (I).
Blount Marvin E, clk, b n s Washington av 1 w of Maple av (I).
Blount May L, dressmkr, 11 S Senate av, h same.
Blount Rollin A, clk, h 72 W 6th.
Blount Sarah W (wid Robert S), h n w cor Ritter and University avs (I).
Blu Uriah L, phys, 65 Indiana av, h 117 N Senate av.
Blue Albert (Blue Bros), h cor Illinois and 38th.
Blue Alice M, cashr, h 33 Hadley av (W I).
Blue Augustus M, lab, b 185 N Liberty.
Blue Blanche B, teacher Public School No 41, b Elizabeth F Blue.

FRANK NESSLER. WILL H. ROST.
FRANK NESSLER & CO.
Tailors
56 EAST MARKET ST. (Lemcke Building),
INDIANAPOLIS, IND.

Blue Bros (Albert, Cortez D and George T), fruit growers, cor Illinois and 38th.
Blue Charles A, mach, h 64 Birch av (W I).
Blue Charles B, mach, b 894 W Washington.
Blue Charles G, gasfitter, b 185 N Liberty.
Blue Cortez D (Blue Bros), h cor Illinois and 38th.
Blue Edward, lab, b e s Sangster av 2 s of 17th.
Blue Edward, lab, r 1065 W Washington.
Blue Edward F, stenog The Indiana Mnfg Co, r 1065 W Washington.
Blue Elizabeth (wid Cyrus B), h 185 N Liberty.
Bule Elizabeth F (wid Peter), h cor Illinois and 38th.
Blue Flame Oil Burner Co, David Fitz Gibbon pres, Harry C Hornish vice-pres and mngr, George W Weir sec, 87 N Delaware.
Blue George, condr, b 75 W 13th.
Blue George T (Blue Bros), h cor Illinois and 38th.
Blue George W, fruit grower, h n w cor Illinois and 35th.
Blue Gerard, h 498 N Illinois.
Blue Hiram, coachman, h 195 W 4th.
Blue Irving P, student, b n w cor Illinois and 35th.
Blue James C, tmstr, b 69 Quince.
Blue John, city agt C F Adams & Co, h 108 Woodburn av (W I).
BLUE LINE, Chauncey R Watson Agt, 1 Board of Trade Bldg; Tel 255.
Blue Peter F, bkkpr, b 128 W Ohio.
Blue Rose (wid John), h e s Sangster av 2 s of 17th.
Blue Susan (wid Charles C), h 69 Quince.
Blue Thomas, lab, h 759 Brooker's al.
Blue Thomas, lab, h 190 W 3d.
Blue Wm G, farmer, h e s Nicholas 3 n of English av.
Blue Wm S, hostler, b 20 Bismarck av (H).
Bluemel Ernst, lab, h 128 S Summit.
Bluemel Gustav C, lab, b 128 S Summit.
Blum, see also Bloom and Blume.
Blum John, lab, h 595 Madison av.

Haueisen & Hartmann
163-169 E. Washington St.
FURNITURE,
Carpets,
Household Goods,
Tin, Granite and China Wares, Oil Cloth and Shades

Fine Laundry Work our Specialty. Collars and Cuffs our Hobby. THE HOME LAUNDRY 197 S. Illinois St. Telephone 1769.

THE WM. H. BLOCK CO. 7 AND 9 EAST WASHINGTON STREET. DRY GOODS, MEN'S FURNISHINGS.

Fidelity and Deposit Co. of Maryland. BONDS SIGNED.—LOCAL BOARD John B. Elam, Albert Sahm, Smiley N. Chambers, John M. Spann.
GEORGE W. PANGBORN, General Agent, 704-706 Lemcke Building. Telephone 140.

Insure Your Property With FRANK K. SAWYER || 74 EAST MARKET STREET Telephone 863.

JOSEPH GARDNER,
Hot Air Furnaces
With Combination Gas Burners for Burning Gas and Other Fuel at the Same Time.
37, 39 & 41 KENTUCKY AVE. Telephone 322.

Blum Samuel, gardener, h rear 1023 S Meridian.
Blumberg Charles H, watchman, h 203 Naomi.
Blumberg Ernest, tmstr, h 42 Barth av.
Blumberg John, com mer, 133 E Maryland, h 86 Prospect.
Blumberg Samuel, finisher, b 203 Naomi.
Blumberg Theodore, driver, b 203 Naomi.
Blumberg Wm F, milk, b 203 Naomi.
Blume, see also Bloom and Blum.
Blume Edward D, clk, b 494 N West.
Blume Guy E, barber, 64 Michigan (H), h same.
Blume Guy E, ins agt, h 114 Michigan (H).
Blume Herman A, carpet cutter, h 65 Sheldon.
Blume John L, clk, b 130 W Vermont.
Blume Rufus B, clk, b 494 N West.
Blume Rufus N, h 494 N West.
Blume Samuel, trav agt, h 202 S Meridian.
Blume Sophia C (wid Hans), h 142 Buchanan.
Blume Wm, pressman, b 58 Sinker.
Blume Wm C, car rep, h 286 E Merrill.
Blume & Co (Edward M Wood), com mers, 52 Virginia av.
Blumlein Adolph, baker, h 126 N Dorman.
Blumlein Louis P (Blumlein & Roach), h 615 Marlowe av.
Blumlein Otto H, b 295 S Missouri.
Blumlein & Roach (Louis P Blumlein, Michael R Roach), barbers, s e cor Washington and Illinois.
Blunk Frank S, printer, h 164 Coburn.
Blunk Margaret S, cashier R M Foster, r 143 N Penn.
Blurock Carl, b s e cor Rural and Pope av.
Blurock Charles P, cabtmkr, b 32 Leon.
Bly David, tmstr, h 155 English av.
Bly Ellsworth M, bartndr, h 137 Davidson.
Bly John, condr, h 49 Harlan.
Bly John S, lab, h n s Highland av 1 e of canal (N I).
Bly Mary (wid Oliver H P), b 191 E Market.
Bly Mathilda C (wid John), b 49 Harlan.
Blythe Daniel, lab, b 468 N Capitol av.
Blythe Harry F, meats, 58 E Mkt House, b 131 S East.

J. S. FARRELL & CO.
Plumbing
Natural and Artificial Gas Fitting.
84 N. ILLINOIS STREET.
TELEPHONE 382.

Blythe Wm M, h 287 N Pine.
Boals, see also Boles and Bowles.
Boales Thomas, condr, b 75 W 13th.
Board Ambrose, lab, h 121 Clinton.
Board Clarence, lab, b 121 Clinton.
Board James, mach, h 39 Harris.
Board John E Rev, b n w cor Nicholas and English.
BOARD OF CHILDREN'S GUARDIANS, Rev Nathaniel A Hyde Pres, Julia H Goodhart Sec and Treas, 400 Prospect; Tel 1398.
BOARD OF COUNTY COMMISSIONERS, 43 Court House.
BOARD OF PUBLIC HEALTH AND CHARITIES, Wm C Ripley Clk, 10 Basement Court House; Tel 538.
BOARD OF PUBLIC SAFETY, Richard C Herrick Sec, 2 Basement Court House; Tel 1390.
BOARD OF PUBLIC WORKS, Bart Parker Sec, 5 Basement Court House; Tel 1789.
Board of Regents State Soldiers' and Sailors' Monument, 93 State House.
BOARD OF SCHOOL COMMISSIONERS, Emma B Ridenour Asst Sec, City Library Bldg; Tel 202.
BOARD OF TRADE, Jacob W Smith Sec, s e cor Capitol av and Maryland; Tel 340.
Boardman Elbert S, real est, h 178 E Walnut.
Boardman Lillie, r 155 N Illinois.
Boardman Rebecca (wid David), b 989 N Alabama.
Boarman Sarah, h 86 Maple.
Boatman Frank J, clk, b 299 N New Jersey.
Boatman Frank P, supt, h 299 N New Jersey.
Boatright Wm, attendant Insane Asylum.
Boatright Wm W (Carter & Boatright), b 90 N Dorman.
Boaz Aurelius, peddler, h 40 S Belmont (W I).
Boaz Burling, clk R M S, h 323 S Penn.
Boaz Charles G, clk R M S, h 360 E McCarty.
Boaz Charles W, teacher Industrial School, b 360 E McCarty.
Boaz Edwin, polisher, b 40 S Belmont (W I).
Boaz Mary J (wid Wm), h 321 S Penn.
Boaz Robert L, piano tuner, b 40 S Belmont (W I).
Boaz Wm M, clk L E & W R R, h 910 N New Jersey.
Bobbs' Free Dispensary, n w cor Senate av and Market.
Bobbs John A, b 810 N Delaware.
Bobbs Wm C, sec The Bowen-Merrill Co, h 810 N Delaware.
Bobolz Herman, cook, b 251 E Washington.
Bobson Charles H, waiter, h 25 Roanoke.
Bobson Ernest, waiter Kershner Bros, r 23 Chapel.
Bock Anton C, lab, h 207 Newman.
Bock Christian, carp, h 476 N East.
Bock Frank, soldier, h 116 Clarke.
Bock George W, carp, b 476 N East.
Bock John E, mason, b 476 N East.
Bock Louisa (wid Henry), h 283 Davidson.
Bockhelt Wm P, framemkr, h 135 N Noble.
BOCKHOFF BROS (Wm F and Louis F), Sales Agts The National Cash Register Co, Grand Hotel Blk, 65 S Illinois; Tel 418.

IF CONTINUED to the end of its dividend period, policies of the UNITED STATES LIFE INSURANCE CO., will equal or excel any investment policy ever offered to the public. | E. B. SWIFT, Manager, 25 E. Market St.

Wm. Kotteman 89 & 91 E. Washington St. TELEPHONE 1742 Furniture

SHOW CASES WILLIAM WIEGEL 6 West Louisiana Street Opp. Union Station.

Bockhoff Ella, bkkpr Bockhoff Bros, b 15 West Drive (W P).
Bockhoff Louis F (Bockhoff Bros), h 364 Clifford av.
Bockhoff Wm F (Bockhoff Bros), h 15 West Drive (W P).
Bockstahler Alma R, music teacher, 410 S Illinois, h same.
Bockstahler Charles F, carp, h 49 Weghorst.
Bockstahler Sophia (wid Martin), h 410 S Illinois.
Bockstahler Wm H, clk Belt R R and Stock Yards Co, h 939 Ash.
Bockus Charles L, supt, h 515 W Eugene (N I).
Bockus Merton E, toolmkr, b 515 W Eugene (N I).
Boclair Oscar, lab, b 430 Blake.
Boda Orvill S, ins agt, h 126 E 14th.
Bode Charles H, cigarmkr, r 58 Roanoke.
Bodenmiller Frederick L, clk C C C & St L Ry, b 303 E St Clair.
Bodenmiller Louisa (wid Leonard), b 303 E St Clair.
Bodine Alva A, painter, h w s Bradley 1 n of Washington.
Bodine Elizabeth E (wid John), b 922 N New Jersey.
Bodine James E (J E Bodine & Co), h 943 N New Jersey.
Bodine J E & Co (James E Bodine), dental depot, 27 Monument pl.
Bodkin Elizabeth H (wid Wm A), b 343 Cornell av.
Bodtke Albert, harnessmkr, h 256 Roanoke.
Body Wm, driver, b 250 W 3d.
Boecher Henry, meats, 549 N West, h same.
Boecher Oscar H, musician, b 495 N West.
Boeckling Amos J, clk Albert Gall, h n s Ohio 4 e of Rural.
Boeckling Anton, h 52 Highland pl.
Boeckling Anton R (A R Boeckling & Co), b 52 Highland pl.
Boeckling Arthus A, bicycle rep, 65 W 7th, b 52 Highland pl.
Boeckling A R & Co (Anton R Boeckling), real est, 60 When bldg.
Boeckling George A, real est, 59 When bldg, b 52 Highland pl.
Boehm August, clk Power & Drake, r 239 W Market.
Boehm Caroline (wid John), h 42 Lord.
Boehm Charles, cabtmkr, b 42 Lord.
Boehm Frank, h s s Ohio 4 e of Rural.
Boehm Henry G, sawmkr, b s s Ohio 4 e of Rural.
Boehm John, baker, h 1019 E Washington.
Boehm Joseph F, lab, b 1019 E Washington.
Boehm Joseph F, boilermkr, h n w cor Rural and Pope av.
Boehm Raymond F, sawmkr, b s s Ohio 4 e of Rural.
Boehm Raymond M, carp, b 42 Lord.
Boehrnloehr George, baker, b 421 S Meridian.
Boekenkroeger Charles H, cabtmkr, h 51 Arbor av (W I).
Boeldt August C, car rep, h 205 Orange.
Boeldt Charles W, carp, h 68 Dunlop.
Boeldt Elizabeth M (wid Henry), b 111 Orange.
Boeldt Frederick, car rep, h 857 Cornell av.
Boeldt Henry F, lab, h 111 Orange.
Boeldt Joachim, drayman, h 67 Downey.
Boeldt Wm G, driver, h 71 Downey.
Boeling Ferdinand P, h 484 W 1st.
Boeling Peter, b 442 W 1st.

Farm and City Loans
25 Years' Successful Business.
THOS. C. DAY & CO,
Rooms 325 to 330 Lemcke Building.

Boerstler Frank, carp, h 22 Lynn av (W I).
Boerswill Daniel, lab, b 32 Hope (B).
Boerswill Jacob, lab, h 32 Hope (B).
Boerum Mary (wid Joseph S),) h 414 N Delaware.
Boesche Christian, watchman, h 246 River av (W I).
Boese, see also Boose and Bose.
Boese Edward W H, mach, b 166 Harrison.
Boese Frederick, lab, b 166 Harrison.
Boese George W, lab, h 124 Douglass.
Boese Henry, car rep, h 166 Harrison.
Boese Henry C, driver, h 267 N Liberty.
Boeseke Edgar A, mech engr, b 106 Nordyke av (W I).
Boetcher Augustus W, mach hd, h 524 W Francis (N I).
Boethel Wm P, gilder, h 132 Spring.
Boettcher Frederick, meats, 77 E Mkt House, h 150 Randolph.
Boettcher John, mach hd, h 48 Kennington.
Boettcher Rudolph, butcher, h 163 Davidson.
Bogan Addie, h 53 Brett.
Bogan Charles E, lab, h 21 Sumner.
Bogan Wm, porter, h 33 Howard.
Bogardus Arthur B, finisher, b 241 Buchanan.
Bogardus Charles H, butcher, h 19 Lynn av (W I).
Bogardus Edward D, foreman, h 373 Talbott av.
Bogardus Walter, bookbndr, h 241 Buchanan.
Bogardus Wm A, solr Frank K Sawyer, b 373 Talbott av.
Bogardus Wm B, h 241 Buchanan.
Bogert Charles C, grocer, 26 Minerva, h same.
Bogert Jacob A (James Bogert & Sons), h 364 N Senate av.
Bogert James & Sons (Jacob A and W James Bogert), trunks, 40 W Washington.
Bogert Ralph E, salesman Indpls Abattoir Co, h 513 Ash.
Bogert Stephen T, trav agt, h 1179 E Washington.
Bogert W James (James Bogert & Sons), h 1125 E Washington.

EAT
QUAKER BREAD
ASK YOUR GROCER FOR IT.
THE HITZ BAKING CO.

TURKISH RUGS AND CARPETS RESTORED TO ORIGINAL COLORS LIKE NEW | Capital Steam Carpet Cleaning Works M. D. PLUNKETT, Telephone 818

BENJ. BOOTH PRACTICAL EXPERT ACCOUNTANT.
Thirty years' experience. First-class credentials.
Room 18, 82½ E. Washington St. Indianapolis, Ind.

18 and 20 S. Meridian St. Established 8.
The Old Reliable Sherman European Restaurant

ESTABLISHED 1876. TELEPHONE 168.
CHESTER BRADFORD,
SOLICITOR OF PATENTS,
AND COUNSEL IN PATENT CAUSES.
(See adv. page 6.)
Office:—Rooms 14 and 16 Hubbard Block, S.W. Cor. Washington and Meridian Streets,
INDIANAPOLIS, INDIANA.

Boggiano Antonia, confr, 190 S Illinois, h same.
Boggiano Louis, b 190 S Illinois.
Boggs Anna M (wid Wm A), b 735 N Penn.
Boggs Charles E, tmstr, b 26 S Summit.
Boggs Charles H, lab, b 5 Minerva.
Boggs Curtis, engr, b 28 Eastern av.
Boggs Henry, painter, h 287 W Pearl.
Boggs Henry C, lab, h 5 Minerva.
Boggs Henry C, painter, 177 Clinton, h 316 W Pearl.
Boggs John A L, fireman, h 26 S Summit.
Boggs Mahlon, clk, h 28 Eastern av.
Boggs Martha (wid Peter M), h 383 S Delaware.
Boggs Newton E, engr Indpls Light and Power Co, h 467 S Capitol av.
Boggs Orlando, lab, b 160 W Maryland.
Boggs Peter E, fireman, h 27 S Summit.
Boggs Thomas J, lab, h 383 S Delaware.
Boggs Wm A, clk Ellen Donlon, b 952 N Senate av.
Bogle Frank L, clk, h 184 Dearborn.
Bogle Wm, condr, b 419 W Eugene (N I).
Bogren John C, lab, h 182 Cleveland.
Bohannon Ambrose G, livery, 855 E Michigan, h 23 Woodlawn av.
Bohannon Edmund, lab, h 57 Bismarck (W I).
Bohdenberg Wm, drayman, h 316 Bates.
Bohl Adam, painter, h w s Madeira 4 s of Prospect.
Bohlen Andrew J, mach hd, h 1 Geneva.
BOHLEN D A & SON (Oscar D Bohlen, Hugo A Zigrosser), Architects, 16-17 Brandon Blk, 95 E Washington; Tel 262.
Bohlen Oscar D (D A Bohlen & Son), h 350 Broadway.
Bohlen Ursula F (wid Diedrich A), h 412 Broadway.
Bohlinger Joseph, lab, h 234 S West.
Bohm, see Boehm.
BOHMIE JOHN M, Carriage and Wagon Mnfr, 180 E Pearl, h 99 Highland Pl.
Bohn Armin, salesman, h 1060 N Senate av.
Bohn Arthur (Vonnegut & Bohn), h 294 E New York.

CORRUGATED IRON CEILINGS AND SIDING.
ALL KINDS OF REPAIRING.
O. B. ENSEY,
TELEPHONE 1562.
COR. 6TH AND ILLINOIS STREETS.

Bohn George, trav agt, b 258 W Michigan.
Bohn Joseph, saloon, n s Grandview av n end Germania av (H), h 169 Grandview av (H).
Bohn Julia (wid Gustav), h 295 S Alabama.
Bohne Charles W A, gardener, h 750 Shelby.
Bohne Louisa (wid Henry), h 750 Shelby.
Bohnstadt Charles, porter, h 29 Carlos.
Bohnstadt Charles J, clk R M S, h 310 Fletcher av.
Bohon Daniel V, clk The Wm H Block Co, r 169 N Illinois.
Bohren Frank C, printer, b 136 Oliver av (W I).
Bohrmann Frederick, lab, b 122 S Noble.
Bohrmann Louisa (wid Henry), h 122 S Noble.
Boice, see also Boyce.
BOICE AUGUSTIN, Lawyer, 18½ N Meridian, Tel 562; b 275 N Delaware.
Boice Mary (wid Wm), h 433 N Illinois.
Boice & Dark (Augustine Boice, Charles E Dark), real est, 18½ N Meridian.
Boicourt Beverly S, plastr, h 1202 Morris (W I).
Boicourt Charles, city mngr The McGilliard Agency Co, h 299 Bellefontaine.
BOICOURT, TYNER & CO (Zachariah T Boicourt, Frank Tyner), Monuments, 121 N Delaware.
Boicourt Zachariah T (Boicourt, Tyner & Co), h 182 E North.
Bokeloh Ada (wid John F), h 112 Spann av.
Bokeloh Henry, engr, h 4 Hoyt av.
Bolan John, lab, b 39 N Alabama.
Bolan Thomas, lab, b 359 S Illinois.
Bolander Alma E, barber, 628 E 9th, b 75 Hill av.
Bolander Charles, lab, h 29 Quince.
Bolander Charles N, tailor, r 55 Dearborn.
Bolander George W, carp, h 75 Hill av.
Bolander Samuel P, grocer, 398 College av, h 460 Ash.
Bold Fannie (wid James), h 52½ S California.
Bolden Lincoln, lab, h rear 102 Howard.
Bolden Thomas, lab, h 66 Mankedick.
Bolder Henry, lab, h rear 610 N Penn.
Boldt George J, lab, h 438 S State av.
Boldt Henry, lab, h 1029 N Senate av.
Bolen Belle (wid Wm), h 194 N Delaware.
Bolen Daniel W, real est, 38 When bldg, h e s Kenwood av 1 n of 22d.
Bolen Frank B, patrolman, h 276 Douglass.
Bolen George W, lab, h 227 S Capitol av.
Bolen Leroy, electrician, b e s Kenwood av 1 n of 22d.
Bolen Wm, cook, h 169 W Wabash.
Bolen Wm N, printer, b 194 N Delaware.
Boler Henry, hostler, h rear 610 N Penn.
Boles, see also Boals and Bowles.
Boles Alexander, polisher, h 321 E Merrill.
Boles James, tmstr, h 10 St Paul.
Boles Sidney, tmstr, b 10 St Paul.
Bolg John M, dyer, h 212 E Vermont.
Bolger Wm T, h 59 W 14th.
Bolin George, grocer, 101 Shephard (W I), h 105 same.
Bolin Margaret E (wid John), grocer, 1173 E Washington, h 1169 same.
Bolin Roger M, grocer, 552 S West, h same.
Bolin Sidney J, shoes, 509½ S West, h same.
Boling Peter, b 442 W 1st.
Bolinger John C, watchman, h 48 Gresham.
Boll Andrew, clk C Maus Branch Indpls Brewing Co, b 128 Blake.

TUTEWILER UNDERTAKER,
NO. 72 WEST MARKET STREET.
TELEPHONE 216.

THE PROVIDENT LIFE AND TRUST CO. OF PHILADELPHIA. Endowment Insurance presents the double attraction of relieving manhood and middle age from anxiety and old age from want.
For particulars apply to D. W. EDWARDS, General Agent, 508 Indiana Trust Building.

THEODORE F. SMITHER

Boll George, lab, b 333 W Morris.
Boll John P, shoemkr, h 57 Kansas.
Bollen Wm T, lab, h n s Lake 5 e of C C C & St L Ry (N I).
Boller George, lab, b 61 Paw Paw.
Boller George, painter, b 282 N Pine.
Boller Mary, h 5 Leota.
Boller Peter, painter, 282 N Pine, h same.
Boller Thomas, lab, h 66 Mankedick.
Bollier Adolph G, uphlr, h 841 S East.
Bolling Richard, porter, r 14 Michigan (H).
Bollinger George A, molder, b 413 E McCarty.
Bollinger Harry P, driver, b 413 E McCarty.
Bollinger Henry M, insp, h 413 E McCarty.
Bollinger John, watchman, h 48 Gresham.
Bollinger Mamie J, milliner, 89 Mass av, b 413 E McCarty.
Bollinger Sadie M, milliner, b 413 E McCarty.
Bollnow Christopher, mach, r 27 Coburn.
Bolman Albert F, cigarmkr, h 760 S Meridian.
Bolser Charles, clk, r 31, 113 S Illinois.
Bolser Francis A, painter, h 274 S Noble.
Bolser Frank, painter, b 274 S Noble.
Bolser George, agt, r 31, 113 S Illinois.
Bolser George A, b 413 E Pearl.
Bolser Gilbert, saloon, 251 Columbia av, h same.
Bolser Horace A, condr, h 413 E Pearl.
Bolser Jane (wid Samuel L), h 113 S Illinois.
Bolser John W, grocer, 113 River av (W I), h same.
Bolt Mary D (wid Michael), h 73 Gimbel.
Bolte Henry, lab, h 277 N Noble.
Bolte Henry F, sawmkr, h 331 E Michigan.
Bolte Wm C, mach hd, b 277 N Noble.
Bolton Ella (wid Leon), b 167 River av (W I).
Bolton Frank T, real est, 36 N Delaware, h 17 Eureka av.
Bolton Isaac P, r 23 Brandon blk.
Bolton James P, yard master, h 43 N Judge Harding (W I).
Bombarger David E, h 82 Camp.
Bombarger Jacob E, mngr The Indpls Dist Tel Co, h 46 Camp.
Bombei John, driver, h 24 Thomas.
Bome Abraham L, cook, r 108 Eddy.
Bomer Robert, lab, h 629 W Michigan.
Bomgardner Emsley E, lab, h 560 W Shoemaker (N I).
Bomgardner Isaac, farmer, h 560 W Shoemaker (N I).
Bomstrup Wm, painter, h 279 Bates.
Bonar Sarah I (wid Matthew L), h 130 S Judge Harding (W I).
Bond Charles, plumber, b 71 S Summit.
Bond Frederick T, car rep, h 71 S Summit.
Bond George T, lab, h 78 S Missouri.
Bond Henry F, tailor, b 71 S Summit.
Bond Jesse, lab, h 278 Fulton.
Bond John, lab, r 24 Willard.
Bond Leo A, dist land agt I C R R Union Station, b Spencer House.
Bond Mary E, stenog, b 105 Huron.
Bond Pleasant, ins, 412 Indiana Trust bldg, h 446 Park av.
Bond Sarah L (wid Riley), h 203 Newman.
Bond Stephen D, clk U S Pension Agency, r 400 N Illinois.
Bond Thomas J, barber, 1560 N Illinois, h 31 Howard.
Bond Wm E, tmstr, h 211 E Washington.
Bone Anna, ensign, b 380 S Delaware.

THE WHEN IS A WORLD BEATER.

Bone Charles, clk Buddenbaum Bros, b 117 Lexington av.
Bone Charles A, stage carp, b 264 Indiana av.
Bone Edward E, stage hd, b 264 Indiana av.
Bone Frederick W, clk, b 78 W 19th.
Bone George W (W H Roberts & Co), h 84 W 14th.
Bone George W, clk, h 117 Lexington av.
Bone Henry W, porter, h 27 Center.
Bone James M, trav agt, h 407 Indiana av.
Bone James S, painter, b 264 Indiana av.
Bone Lena (wid Wm), h 264 Indiana av.
Bone Wm M, trav agt, h 78 W 19th.
Bonesteel Wm C, barber, 606 S Meridian, h same.
Bonham Alfred N, phys, 201 The Majestic, h 96 Ash.
Bonham Charles O, laundryman, h 4 Roseline.
BONHAM EVAN A, State Mngr Preferred Accident Insurance Co of New York, Rooms 15-16 Hartford Blk, 84 E Market, h 69 Fletcher av.
Bonham Nettie M, dressmkr, 236½ S Meridian, h same.
Boniface John, lab, h w s Baltimore av 1 n of 17th.
Bonifield Frank, motorman, b 1063 N Capitol av.
Bonke Charles F, lab, h 92 W Morris.
Bonke Robert R, grocer, 152 Church, h same.
Bonn Barbara (wid Philip), h 132 Ruckle.
Bonn Emma, seamstress, b 132 Ruckle.
Bonn George, lab, b 114 Buchanan.
Bonn Peter J, clk When Clothing Store, h 604 Central av.
Bonn Philip, mach, b 132 Ruckle.
Bonnell Margaret, h 199 E Washington.
Bonnemeyer Henry, driver, b 125 Kennington.
Bonner Frederick E, lab, b 108 S McLain (W I).
Bonner Paul, saloon, 201 W South, h 220 S Missouri.
Bonner Wiley D, foreman, h 64 Smith.
Bonner Wm S, mach, h 108 S McLain (W I).

THE A. BURDSAL CO.
Manufacturers of
Paints and Colors
VARNISHES,
Brushes, Painters' and Paper Hangers' Supplies.
34 and 36 South Meridian Street.

COMPOSITION ROOFING MATERIALS. BEST IN THE MARKET. TELEPHONE 861. OFFICE, 151 WEST MARYLAND ST.

ELECTRICIANS | DON'T FORGET US. ALL WORK GUARANTEED. C. W. MEIKEL, Tel. 466. 96-98 E. New York St.

DALTON & MERRIFIELD { LUMBER South Noble St., near E. Washington

INDIANA ELECTROTYPE CO. : BEST WORK. LOWEST PRICES.
23 WEST PEARL ST., INDIANAPOLIS, IND. JOB WORK. BOOK PLATES. All Orders Promptly Filled. BEST PATENT BASE ON THE MARKET.

KIRKHOFF BROS.
Steam and Hot Water Heating Apparatus,
Plumbing and Gas Fitting.
102-104 SOUTH PENNSYLVANIA ST.
TELEPHONE 910.

Bonnett Jacob L, driver, h 154 Cornell av.
Bonneville S Earl, clk The Denison, b same.
Bonniwell Wm A, dentist, 66½ N Penn, r same.
Bonowski Felix, lab, h 141 High.
Bonsall Nathaniel, b 170 Fayette.
Bonseck John R, carp, h 96 Cornell av.
Bonta Nettie, h 76 W South.
Booan Jennie, h 232 W North.
Booker Isaac, porter, b 216 W Chesapeake.
Booker John, lab, h 42 Lincoln la.
Booker Nellie F (wid Wm), r 1½ Wood.
Bookwald Henry, watchman, h 459 W Francis (N I).
Bookwalter Charles A (Hanaway, Bookwalter & Co), sec and treas Indiana Society for Savings, h 1656 N Illinois.
Bookwalter Sarah A (wid John), b 180 E North.
Boone Charles, lab, b 267 Spring.
Boone Frank M, furniture, 141 E Washington, b 79 Torbet.
Boone Frank P, carp, b 77 N Alabama.
Boone Gabriel, lab, h 265 Shelby.
Boone James A, carp, h 838 E Market.
Boone Mollie A, dressmkr, 210 Madison av, h same.
Boone Peter, carp, h e s Garfield av 3 n of Washington.
Boone Ralsemore M, h 48 N Haugh (H).
Boone Susan H (wid Francis M), b 79 Torbet.
Boone Willis N, engr, h 85 Bradshaw.
Boos David C, engr, b 38 S State av.
Boos Maurice, cooper, b 38 S State av.
Boose, see also Boese and Bose.
Boose Charles E, condr, h 409 Lexington av.
Boose Daniel M, lab, h s w cor Brookside av and Roseline.
Boote Daniel, reporter R G Dun & Co, h 340 E 10th.
Boote Fannie M, stenog Indiana Bicycle Co, b 340 E 10th.
Bootes Jesse B, dentist, b 117 N Senate av.
Bootes Ralstone D, mach hd, b 117 N Senate av.
Bootes Wm E, furnacewkr, b 117 N Senate av.

LIME
BUILDING SUPPLIES,
Hair, Plaster, Flue Linings,
The W. G. Wasson Co.
130 INDIANA AVE. Tel. 989.

BOOTH BENJAMIN, Public Accountant, Room 18, 82½ E Washington, h same. (See left top lines.)
Booth Benjamin, trav agt, h 78 W 5th.
Booth Edwin, foreman, h 96 Decatur.
Booth Elbert L, window decorator N Y Store, r 38 The Windsor.
Booth Erastus L, phys, b 453 N Senate av.
Booth George W, decorator, h 49 Arch.
Booth Jennie M, h 38 The Windsor.
Booth John jr, supt Herman Lauter, h 616 Bellefontaine.
Booth John L, restaurant, 122 N Illinois, h 453 N Senate av.
Booth John S (Booth & Johnson), lawyer, 77½ E Market, h 31 Park av.
Booth Joseph P, carp, h 33 Samoa.
Booth Mary F (wid Elijah), bkkpr, b 317 E St Clair.
Booth Minnie, dressmkr, 122 Indiana av, h same.
Booth Robert, woodturner, h 59 Pierce.
Booth Robert H, wood turner, b 59 Pierce.
Booth & Johnson (John S Booth, Wm M Johnson), real est, 77½ E Market.
Boothby Arthur, draughtsman Dean Bros' Steam Pump Works, h 1713 N Penn.
Boots Benjamin F, bartndr, r 67 N Alabama.
Boots Michael, trav agt, b 411 E Pearl.
Boots Wm, lodging 27 N New Jersey.
Boots Wm H, grinder, r 133 King av (H).
Booz Edward G, bkkpr Frank G Kamps, h 128 W New York.
Booz J Jordan, phys, 128 W New York, h same.
Bopp Emma, teacher German Public School No 2, b 120 E 6th.
Bopp Lena (wid Christian), teacher German Public School No 11, h 120 E 6th.
Borchardt Albert, propr Mueller's Hotel, 213 S Alabama.
Borchardt Louis, lab, b 213 S Alabama.
Borcherding Henry, carp, h 55 S Arsenal av.
Borchers Edward E, clk, b 346 N Senate av.
Borchers Herman, carp, h 346 N Senate av.
Borchert August, saloon, 425 S Delaware, h same.
Borchert Augusta (wid Frederick), h 63 Dunlop.
Borchert Charles, porter, b 324 S Delaware.
Borchert Clara W, h 605 N Senate av.
Borck Valentine, lab, h 14 Wilcox.
Borde Philip, peddler, h 434½ S Capitol av.
Bordenkecher Andrew, finisher, res Malott Park, Ind.
Bordenkecher Charles T, insp Indiana Bicycle Co, h 186 Spann av.
Bordenkecher George J, driver, h 334 Spring.
Borell Louis C, lab, h 254 W Pearl.
Boren Edwin D, bkkpr D P Erwin & Co, h 47 Chadwick.
Boren Wm A, clk Parry Mnfg Co, b 47 Chadwick.
Borger Conrad W, clk, b 191 Orange.
Borger John H, carver, b 191 Orange.
Borger John W, tmstr, h 191 Orange.
Borger John W jr, uphlr, b 191 Orange.
Borgerding Frank H, shoemkr, 356 S New Jersey, h same.
Borgerding Henry F, clk, b 356 S New Jersey.
Borgert Anna (wid Anthony), h 744 S Meridian.
Borgert Edward J, uphlr, b 744 S Meridian.
Borgert Henry A, clk The H Lieber Co, b 744 S Meridian.

Parlor, Bed Room, Dining Room, Kitchen, Furniture W. H. MESSENGER, 101 E. Wash. St., Tel. 491.

ALL KINDS OF HEAVY AND LIGHT GRAY IRON CASTINGS } McNamara, Koster & Co. Phone 1593. 212-218 S. Penn. St. { Foundry and Pattern Shop

Borgert Wm, tailor, h 744 S Meridian.
Borgmann, see also Bergman and Burgman.
Borgmann Frederick F, lab, h 724 Shelby.
Borgmann Frederick J H, carp, h 150 Pleasant av.
Borgmann Henry, lab, h s s Bethel av 1 e of Zwingley.
Borgmann Herman, driver, h 724 Shelby.
Borgmann John T, mer police, h 125 Chadwick.
Borgmann Wm, mason, h 237 English av.
Borgmann Wm, saloon, 359 Virginia av, b same.
Boring Edward E, plastr, 400 W 1st, h same.
Boring Ephraim, plastr, 345 N West, h same.
Boring Jennie, grocer, 400 W 1st, h same.
Borinstein, see also Bernstein.
Borinstein Abraham, clothing, 233 E Washington, h same.

BORINSTEIN A, Dealer in Rags, Paper Stock, Old Metal, Rubber, Scrap Iron, Etc, 109-115 S East; Tel 586; h 314 S Illinois.

Borinstein Joseph, junk, h 314 S Illinois.
Borinstein Moses, clk A Borinstein, h 377 S Illinois.
Borinstein Samuel, peddler, h 132 Maple.
Borinstein Wm, carver, h 536 S Capitol av.
Borkin Wm, painter, h 29 Shover (W I).
Borman Charles E, trav agt, h 577 Charles.
Borman Engel S (wid Ernest), h 252 Union.
Borman Wm E C, sawmkr, b 252 Union.
Borman Wm F, checkman, h 110 W Ray.
Born Charlotte (wid Nicholas), h 122 Yandes.
Born Frank S, bkkpr, b 121 W 7th.
Born Frederick, grocer, 3 Shelby, h 21 same.
Born Frederick W, cooper, h 261 S West.
Born George, polisher, b 114 Buchanan.
Born Harry L, clk, h 28 S LaSalle.
Born Henry, lab, r 158 Madison av.
Born Jacob, switchman, h 23 Bloomington.
Born John, h 251 S West.
Born Joseph, foreman Rockwood Mnfg Co, h 146 Lexington av.
Born Valentine, furniture, 62 E Washington, h 121 W 7th.
Bornemann Charles H, lab, h 380 Martindale av.
Bornemann Frederick, b 43 Wright.
Bornemann Henry R Rev, pastor Nippert Memorial German M E Church, h 394 Clifford av.
Bornemann Rudolph, h 394 Clifford.
Bornemeier Herman, grocer, 157 High, h same.
Bornemeier Herman B, clk, h 242 Minnesota.
Bornemeier Herman B, cabtmkr, h 799 S East.
Bornkamp Caroline (wid Wm), b 69 Chadwick.
Bornkamp Christopher F, sawmkr, h 69 Chadwick.
Bornkamp Wm F, clk E C Atkins & Co, h 20 Division (W I).
Bornman Henry L, foreman E C Atkins & Co, h 739 S Meridian.
Borsheim Alfred F, jeweler George G Dyer, b 570 Park av.
Borst Albert W, mach, b 76 Kansas.
Borst Emil H, h 71 Wisconsin.
Borst Frederick J, butcher, h 76 Kansas.

Henry H. Fay, 40½ E. WASHINGTON ST., FIRE INSURANCE, REAL ESTATE, LOANS AND RENTAL AGENT.

BORST GEORGE F, Drugs, Paints, Oils, Stationery, Etc, cor Meridian and Russell av; Tel 640; h same.

Borst Harry J, clk George F Borst, b 76 Kansas.
Borst Joseph B, lab, b 125 W Washington.
Borst Matilda M, stenog Indpls Mnfg Co, b 76 Kansas.
Bortlein John, lab, h 68 Hadley av (W I).
Bortlein John B, lab, b 68 Hadley av (W I).
Borton Emmor, turner, h 458 N New Jersey.

BOS JACOB, Wholesale Wines and Liquors, 35-37 S Delaware; Tel 1669; h 896 N Capitol av.

Bosan Shelby, lab, h 252 W 6th.
Bosard Edgar M, photog, 164 Virginia av, h 256 W St Clair.
Bosart Timothy L, sec, h n s Washington 1 e of Linwood av.
Bosdorfer Emilie (wid George), b 198 Shelby.
Bosdorfer Wm, cigarmkr, r 27½ Virginia av.
Bose, see also Boese and Boose.
Bose Henry A, driver, h 461 S Illinois.
Bose Henry A, solr, h 516 S Capitol av.
Bose Mary C (wid Wm H), b 280 E Market.
Bosler Emily (wid Joseph), b 587 Park av.
Bosler Frank A, mngr, h 587 Park av.
Bosler Frederick J, h 968 N Delaware.
Bosley Thomas J, clk R M S, h 196 Hoyt av.
Boss Adolph, barber, 356 Dillon, h 61 Buchanan.
Boss Albert J, tinner, h 444 Charles.
Boss John A, barber, h 87 Buchanan.
Bosserman Charles H, condr, h 42 Eastern av.
Bossert Conrad, bartndr, h 54 Dougherty.
Bossert Wm, contr, 7 Pembroke Arcade, h 128 W 2d.
Bosson Thomas M, lumber, h 675 College av.
Bosson Wm, lawyer, 83 Lombard bldg, h w s Illinois 1 s of 35th (M).
Bost John, car rep, h 351 Jefferson av.
Bostic Elmer, painter, r 423 W 2d.
Bostic Franklin J, painter, b 49 Wyoming.
Bostic John S, cooper, b 806 W Washington.

WILL GO ON YOUR BOND
American Bonding & Trust Co.
Of Baltimore, Md. Approved as sole surety by the United States Government and the different States as Sole Surety on all Forms of Bonds.
W. E. BARTON & CO., General Agents,
504 Indiana Trust Building.
LONG DISTANCE TELEPHONE 1918.

THE FRED DIETZ CO. WOODEN PACKING BOXES MADE TO ORDER FACTORY AND WAREHOUSE TRUCKS. 40 Madison Avenue. Telephone 69.

BUSINESS EDUCATION A NECESSITY. TIME SHORT. DAY AND NIGHT SCHOOL. SUCCESS CERTAIN AT THE PERMANENT, RELIABLE Indianapolis BUSINESS UNIVERSITY

Water and Oil Meters { HENRY R. WORTHINGTON, 64 S. PENNSYLVANIA ST. Long Distance Telephone 284.

UNION CO-OPERATIVE LAUNDRY { (COMPOSED OF UNION LAUNDRY GIRLS.) NOS. 138, 140 AND 142 VIRGINIA AVENUE. TELEPHONE 1269. INDIANAPOLIS, IND. T. E. SOMERVILLE, MANAGER

HORACE M. HADLEY
INSURANCE AND LOANS
66 E. Market Street, Basement
TELEPHONE 1540.

Bostic Rose, r 423 W 2d.
Boswell Charles E, die cutter, h 440 Cornell av.
Boswell David A, medicines, b e s Sutherland av 1 n of 20th.
Boswell Frank W, porter, h 147 Huron.
Boswell George G F, inventor, h n w cor 16th and Bellefontaine.
Boswell James F, phys, e s Sutherland av 1 n of 20th, b same.
BOSWELL JOSEPH E, Assessor Marion County, 35 Court House; Tel 912; h e s Sutherland av 1 n of 20th.
Boswell Samuel, farmer, h 652 W Washington.
Boteler Edward M, condr, h 124 Spann av.
Botkin Seymour H, lab, h 87 Chadwick.
Botkin John, lab, h 106 S Linden.
Botscheller Valetine, baker, h 318 E Miami.
Bott Conrad, uphlr N Y Store, h s w cor Orange av and Larch.
Bott Edward D, produce, 35 E Mkt House, b 439 S Delaware.
Bott Henry, carp, h 216 Hamilton av.
Bottin Herman, lab, h 43 Detroit.
Bottler Julius, saloon, 233 S Delaware, h 559 Madison av.
Bottler Rudolph, b 559 Madison av.
Bottom Bluford, lab, r 191½ Indiana av.
Bottom George, lab, r 191½ Indiana av.
Bottom Henry, lab 413 N Capitol av.
Bottom Henry, janitor, r 29½ E Market.
Bottom Thomas, lab, r 191½ Indiana av.
Bottome Turner D, pres The Faradizer Co, b 371 E 19th.
Bottorff James H, carp, h 670 Chestnut.
Bottorff John L, clk Indpls Gas Co, h 2 Andrews.
Botts Charles, lab, b 59 Superior.
Boucher Michael, lab, b 196 W Merrill.
Bouchie Lida C, h 301½ E Washington.
Boughner Sarah (wid John H), b 49 Arch.
Boughton John, cabtmkr, b 313 W Washington.
Boughton Wm C, paperhngr, h n w cor 8th and Lennox.
Bouldin Frederick, sawmkr, h 113 Huron.

COLLECTIONS
MERCHANTS' AND MANUFACTURERS' EXCHANGE
Will give you good service.
J. E. TAKKEN, Manager,
Union Building, over U. S. Pension Office,
73 West Maryland Street.

Bouncer Hattie A (wid Wm C), h 127 N Alabama.
Bounsell George W, mach, h 434 Martindale av.
Bourdalme August, lab, h 254 W Ray.
Bourgonne Charles L, clk Otto Schopp, b 441 Charles.
Bourgonne Otto S, drugs, 399 S Capitol av, b 441 Charles.
Bourgonne Stephen B, cigar mfr, 140 Union, b 441 Charles.
Bourne Samuel S, condr, b 792 W Washington.
Bourne Wm A, lab, h 118 Deloss.
Bouslog Charles, trav agt, b 475 E Market.
Bousum Abraham L, brakeman, h 121 Bismarck av (H).
Boury John L, coppersmith, b 319 Coburn.
Boury Julius H, tinner, 533 Virginia av, h 328 Coburn.
Bowe James C, painter, 32 S Meridian, h 1729 N Meridian.
Bowen Albert A, grainer, h 152 Michigan av.
Bowen Albert D, cutter, h 684 Broadway.
Bowen Ann (wid John), h 514 N West.
Bowen Anthony W, r 70 W New York.
Bowen Ara H, carp, h 93 Fayette.
Bowen Benjamin, porter, h 187 W 3d.
Bowen Benjamin F, painter, h 1385 N Senate av.
Bowen Charles, waiter, r 16 Commercial blk.
Bowen Cora B (wid John), h 186½ W Washington.
Bowen Curtis J, hostler, h 33 N Olive.
Bowen George E (Bowen & Secrest), res Carmel, Ind.
Bowen Harry, tmstr, b 1350 N Senate av.
Bowen Harry B, trimmer, h 41 Stevens.
Bowen James, b 270 Bates.
Bowen James A, mach, b 20 Traub av.
Bowen John, call boy, b 20 Traub av.
Bowen Josephine (wid George), b n s Washington 1 w of Maple av (I).
Bowen Katherine, usher Insane Hospital.
Bowen Laura E (wid Silas T), h 44 W North.
BOWEN-MERRILL CO THE, Wm H Elvin Pres, Wm C Bobbs Sec, Charles W Merrill Treas, John J Curtis Supt, Publishers, Booksellers, Stationers and Paper Dealers, 9-11 W Washington and 10-12 W Pearl; Tel 1779.
Bowen Thomas, lab, b 130 Allegheny.
Bowen Wm, painter, b 229 W Washington.
Bowen Wm E, restaurant 1085 E Washington, h same.
Bowen Wm W, mach, b 33 N Olive.
Bowen & Secrest (George E Bowen, Charles R Secrest, real est, 17 Fair blk.
Bowens Adrian, drugs, 316 S West, h same.
Bowens George W, lab, h 420 Superior.
Bowens Lee, porter, r 113 Indiana av.
Bower, see also Bauer and Baur.
Bower Catherine B, h 444 N New Jersey.
Brower Louis, peddler, h 450 S Capitol av.
Bower Louise, h e s Baltimore av 3 n of 22d.
Bower Mahala C, h e s Baltimore av 3 n of 22d.
Bower Rose, teacher Public School No 1 (H), b 63 Germania av (H).
Bowers Albert, lab, b n e cor 7th and Lenox.
Bowers Albert A, h 233 S Spruce.
Bowers Bena (wid John), housekpr 434 S Illinois.

CLEMENS VONNEGUT
184, 186 and 192 E. Washington St.
BUILDERS' HARDWARE,
Building Paper. Duplex Joist Hangers

THE WM. H. BLOCK CO. DRY GOODS, DRAPERIES, RUGS, WINDOW SHADES.
7 AND 9 EAST WASHINGTON STREET.

Bowers Benjamin, brakeman, r 839 E Washington.
Bowers David, lab, b 79 Lee (W I).
Bowers Emma A P (wid Isaac S), b 683 N Delaware.
Bowers Ethelinda J (wid John F), h 803 E Washington.
Bowers Frank, Grand K of R and S Knights of Pythias and treas Fraternal B-L Assn, 49 Journal bldg, h 309 College av.
Bowers Frank, mach, h 5½ Brookside av.
Bowers Frank J, condr, h 61 N Gale (B).
Bowers Freeman, carp, h 79 Lee (W I).
Bowers George B, lawyer, h 93 Yandes.
Bowers Henry, barber, 205 E Washington, b 124 N Liberty.
Bowers Hugh T, grinder, h 180 E South.
Bowers Isaac H, phys, 803 E Washington, b same.
Bowers James C, japanner, r 217½ E Washington.
Bowers James M, h 491 Highland av (N I).
Bowers Jesse H, tel opr, h 16 Tacoma av.
Bowers Jonas H, weighmaster, b 803 E Washington.
Bowers Joseph, waiter 599 N Penn.
Bowers Levi B, brakeman, h 217½ E Washington.
Bowers Mary (wid John), h 69 Yandes.
Bowers Thomas L, ccremkr, b 153 Newman.
Bowersmith Charles E, painter, h 127 N State av.
Bowersmith Wm C, clk Dalton Hat Co, b 127 N State av.
Bowes Henry J, lab, h 358 W 1st.
Bowie Alexander, carp, b 43 S West.
Bowie Walter, millwright, b 43 S West.
Bowlby Edward, engr, b 55 English av.
Bowlby Elmer T, treas Grand Opera House, b 67 Union.
Bowlby John H, solr, h 67 Union.
Bowlby John W, electrician English Opera House, b 37 Hudson.
Bowlby Sarah T (wid Abner P), b 527 E 8th.
Bowlby Walter G, asst treas English Opera House, b 67 Union.
Bowlby Wm W, painter, h 37 Hudson.
Bowlen Charles R, carp, r 23 N West.
Bowlen Leonidas, carp, n s Ohio 9 e of Rural, h same.
Bowler George, lab, h 61 Paw Paw.
Bowler John C, printer, b 72 Morton.
Bowler Thomas E, lab, h 66 Smithson.
Bowler Wm H, flagman, h 16 N State av.
Bowles, see also Boals and Boles.
Bowles Burkley C, cook, h 274 W North.

BOWLES DUANE H, Lawyer, 625-626 Lemcke Bldg; Tel 1886; b 493 N Meridian.

Bowles Elvira (wid Frank), h 44 Warman av (H).
Bowles Jesse R, lab, h 129 Walcott.
Bowles John A, engr monument, h 182 Yandes.
Bowles John H, waiter, h 226 W Vermont.
Bowles Kate M (wid Thomas H), h 493 N Meridian.
Bowles Osbourne, clk Indiana Mutual B and L Assn, b 493 N Meridian.
Bowles Thomas, driver, r 340 Superior.

BOWLEY GEORGE J, Designer and Wood Engraver, Room 14 Yohn Blk, n e cor Meridian and Washington, h 319 N Noble. (See adv in classified Wood Engravers.)

Bowling Casinda (wid Ormstead), h 228 Howard.
Bowling John H, carp, 176 Spann av, h same.
Bowlus Elmer, condr, b 75 W 13th.
Bowlus George W, foreman, h 174 Pleasant.
Bowlus John W, lawyer, 26 N Delaware, h 1508 N Meridian.
Bowlus Walter J, clk C C C & St L Ry, b 174 Pleasant.
Bowman, see also Baughman and Bauman.
Bowman Abraham, stenog Schnull & Co, b 451 S Capitol av.
Bowman Albert, lab, h 226 W Market.
Bowman Almon L, clk Van Camp H and I Co, h 568 E Washington.
Bowman Alonzo A, painter, h 26 Dearborn.
Bowman Anna L, stenog, b 132 Christian av.
Bowman Archibald, express, r 165 Indiana av.
Bowman Archibald P, driver, b 63 John.
Bowman Benjamin A, packer, b 63 John.
Bowman Byron L, candymkr, b 10 Lord.
Bowman Charles J, salesman, b e s Downey av 3 s of Houston av (I).
Bowman Charles P, painter, h 636 W Udell (N I).
Bowman Charles P, trav agt, h 50 W St Joseph.
Bowman Clinton D, winder, h w s Downey av 2 s of Washington av (I).
Bowman Clyde E, barber, b 921 Bellefontaine.
Bowman Ella, milliner, 28 S Illinois, h 18½ N Penn.
Bowman Franklin A, lab, b 177 Blake.
Bowman Frederick, cutter, b 122 S Noble.
Bowman Frederick, waiter, r 32 Grand Opera House blk.
Bowman Frederick L, cook, b w s Downey av 2 s of Washington av (I).
Bowman George, lab, h 28 Holborn.
Bowman George W, mach, h 30 Clark.
Bowman George W, solr N Y Life Ins Co, h 96 Lexington av.
Bowman Harry, insp City Engineer, b 236 Virginia av.

GUIDO R. PRESSLER,
FRESCO PAINTER
Churches, Theaters, Public Buildings, Etc., A Specialty.
Residence, No. 325 North Liberty Street.
INDIANAPOLIS, IND.

INDIANAPOLIS STEEL ROOFING AND CORRUGATING WORKS, 23 and 25 East South Street. S. D. NOEL, Proprietor.

David S. McKernan, REAL ESTATE AND LOANS
Money to loan on real estate. Special inducements offered those having money to loan. It will pay you to investigate.
Rooms 2-5 Thorpe Block.

DIAMOND WALL PLASTER { Telephone 1410 Builders' Exchange.

UNION TRANSFER AND STORAGE CO. Cor. E. Ohio St. and C., C., C. & St. L. R'y Tracks. BEST FACILITIES FOR STORING AND TRANSFERRING MACHINERY AND MERCHANDISE.

W. McWORKMAN

FIRE SHUTTERS,
FIRE DOORS,
METAL CEILINGS.

930 W. Washington St. Tel. 1118.

Bowman Harry C, fireman, h w s Walker 2 s of Pendleton av (B).
Bowman Henry, baker, b 320 S Missouri.
Bowman Ida M (wid Frederick E), b 24 Broadway.
Bowman Isaac M, huckster, h 381 W North.
Bowman Jacob, trav agt, h 236 Virginia av.
Bowman James, clk, b 290 E Washington.
Bowman James H, collr, b 542 W Addison (N I).
Bowman Jeremiah, lab, h 486 W Francis (N I).
Bowman John, carp, h 359 S West.
Bowman John, whitewasher, h 10 Mulberry.
Bowman John A, carp, h 40½ Grant.
Bowman John B, agt, h 58 Roanoke.
Bowman John C, brakeman, h 129 Hoyt av.
Bowman Levi, sawyer, h 328 Yandes.
Bowman Louis, bkkpr Indiana Car Service Assn, b 451 S Capitol av.
Bowman Louisa (wid Henry), h 122 S Noble.
Bowman Lucius S, bkkpr, h e s Downey av 3 s of Houston av (I).
Bowman Martin G, clk, b 451 S Capitol av.
Bowman Mary F (wid Andrew J), h 320 S Missouri.
Bowman Mary F (wid Wm), b 198 W 1st.
Bowman Moses, stenog, b 451 S Capitol av.
Bowman Nathan, peddler, h 451 S Capitol av.
Bowman Nellie M, teacher Public School No. 28, b 132 Christian av.
Bowman Oliver, fireman, b 124 English av.
Bowman Oliver F, collr H T Conde Implement Co., h 28 Hall pl.
Bowman Owen M, h 39 Wyoming.
Bowman Richard, lab, b 451 S Illinois.
Bowman Robert, tmstr, h 516 W Shoemaker (N I).
Bowman Rolla F, tmstr, h 516 W Shoemaker (N I).
Bowman Sarah N, h 20 N West.
Bowman Simeon C, cabtmkr, h 507 Sheldon.
Bowman Thomas, lab, h 20 Brett.
Bowman Wm, janitor, b 11 S Gillard av.
Bowman Wm, lab, h e s Bismarck 2 s of Grandview av (H).
Bowman Wm, lab, b 326 W Maryland.
Bowman Wm F, butcher, h 41 Rockwood.

GEO. J. MAYER,
MANUFACTURER OF
SEALS
STENCILS, RUBBER STAMPS, CHECKS, BADGES, DOOR PLATES, ETC.
5 S. Meridian St., Ground Floor. TEL. 1386.

Bowman Wm F, clk, b 367 S East.
Bowman Wm H, carp, 132 Christian av, h same.
Bowman Wm H, lab, h 380 N California.
Bowman Wm H, painter, h e s Burton av 1 s of McLene (N I).
BOWMAN WM H, Architect, 13-14 Ingalls Blk; Tel 747; b e s Downey av 3 s of Houston av (I).
Bowman Wm S, clk N A Moore & Co, h 577 W 22d (N I).
Bowman Willis M, cabtmkr, h 63 John.
Bowne Albert P, lab, h 51 Arch.
Bowne Nathan E, lab, h 779 E Market.
Bowser Adeline (wid Andrew), h s s Walnut 1 w of Sherman Drive.
Bowser Allen A (Prather & Co), state agt Daugherty Typewriter, 225-226 Lemcke bldg, b 121 E New York.
Bowser Harry, lawyer, 46 Lombard bldg, h 996 N Delaware.
Bowser Jacob, engr, h 629 S East.
Bowser Jerome, lab, b s s Walnut 1 w of Sherman Drive.
Bowser Levi C, watchman, h 59 Woodlawn av.
Bowser Thomas A, supt Outing Bicycle Co, h 624 Miller av (M P).
Bowsher George W, lineman, h 508 N West.
Bowsher Samuel, foreman Cent U Tel Co, h 282 W Michigan.
Bowsher Wm A, lab, h 258 Douglass.
Bowyer Wm T, huckster, h 5 Wendell av.
Boxley George, lab, h 33 Hosbrook.
Boxley George W, lab, b 33 Hosbrook.
Boyce, see also Boice.
Boyce Ellis W, janitor State House.
Boyce George C, tinner, b 265 Lincoln la.
Boyce George R, asst City Engr, h 71 Talbott av.
Boyce James E, lab, b 265 Lincoln la.
Boyce John E, grocer, 265 Lincoln la, h same.
Boyd Adam R, farmer, h 424 W Udell (N I).
Boyd Addison, cook, r 79 W Wabash.
Boyd Addison E, shoemkr, 144 Howard (W I), h 445 same.
BOYD ALONZO, Plumber, 816 N Illinois; Tel 1618; h 767 N Capitol av. (See adv in classified Plumbers.)
Boyd Amanda J, h 493 N New Jersey.
Boyd Anna B (wid Augustus), h 330 Lafayette.
Boyd Augustus, genl agt J I Case Threshing Machine Co, h 250 N Senate av.
Boyd Aura, second asst State Librarian, b 280 N Penn.
Boyd Bert, lab, b 175 Woodlawn av.
Boyd Bert A, bkkpr F P Rush & Co, h 1526 N Capitol av.
BOYD, BESTEN & LANGEN CO, Henry Besten Pres, E O Langen Sec and Treas, Walter H Boyd Mngr, Cloak Dealers and Furriers, 39 E Washington; Long Distance Tel, 1912.
Boyd Catherine, b 367 English av.
Boyd Clyde R, lab, b 549 E Michigan.
Boyd Edward H, bartndr, r 3 Cleaveland blk.
Boyd Edwin S, clk, r 68 W New York.
Boyd Elizabeth, r 223 N Alabama.
Boyd Elmer H, carp, h 697 W Udell (N I).
Boyd Emma F, clk K and L of H, b 238 N West.
Boyd Evelyn H (wid Augustus), h 619 N Meridian.

A. METZGER AGENCY ESTABLISHED 1863. REAL ESTATE

LAMBERT GAS & GASOLINE ENGINE CO.
ANDERSON, IND. NATURAL GAS ENGINES.

Boyd Felix, lab, h rear 422 N East.
Boyd Frances (wid Wm), h 34 Guffin.
Boyd Francis, clk Kingan & Co (ltd), h 238 N West.
Boyd Frank, clk, r 92 N Illinois.
Boyd Frank A, clk, h 74 Ft Wayne av.
Boyd James, mach, h rear 344 Blake.
Boyd James G, coppersmith, b 198 Bates.
Boyd James M, engr, h 198 Bates.
Boyd James T, phys, 76 E Ohio, h 957 N Alabama.
Boyd James T, waiter, h 168 Muskingum al.
Boyd Jasper N, clk Am Ex Co, h 73 W 12th.
Boyd John, lab, b 210 W Ohio.
Boyd John M, blksmith, 3 N Judge Harding, h 445 Howard (W I).
Boyd Joseph W, helper, h 126 Trowbridge (W).
Boyd Lewis O, baggageman, h 355 English av.
Boyd Margaret A, teacher Public School No 2, b 424 E Udell (N I).
Boyd Martha, h 175 Woodlawn av.
Boyd Martindale, pumps, 45 Mass av, h 324 E 17th.
Boyd Mary L, music teacher, 238 N West, b same.
Boyd Olin S, bkkpr D H Baldwin & Co, r 282 N Senate av.
Boyd Richard M, lab, h 325 W Morris.
Boyd Robert E, barber, 814 E Washington, h same.
Boyd Robert G, lab, h 463 Sheldon.
Boyd Robert H, b 957 N Alabama.
Boyd Thomas M (Gage & Boyd), res Hamilton, O.
Boyd Walter H, mngr Boyd, Besten & Langen Co, b 376 Park av.
Boyd Wm E (Boyd & Miller), h 323 Park av.
Boyd Wm H, agt Lake Shore-Lehigh Valley Route, n e cor Delaware and South, h 18 E Vermont.
Boyd Wm H, loans, 63 Baldwin blk, h 717 N Capitol av.
Boyd Wm H, plumber, h 442 Chestnut.
Boyd Wm K, condr, h 24 S Judge Harding (W I).
Boyd Wm R, ins agt, h 195 Prospect.
Boyd Wm R, lab, h w s Burgess av 4 s of C H & D Ry (I).
Boyd Zoreldah M (wid James W), h 376 Park av.
Boyd & Miller (Wm E Boyd, J Martin Miller), loans, 63 Baldwin blk.
Boyden David E, flagman, h 48 Sycamore.
Boyer Adam E, carp, h e s Guffin 1 n of 8th.
Boyer Byron J, carp, h 318 Yandes.
Boyer Carroll C, clk I & V R R, b 906 Broadway.
Boyer Charles E, lab, h 109 Wright.
Boyer Charles T, genl mngr Am Buncher Mnfg Co, h 303 E McCarty.
Boyer Emma (wid Thomas B), h 110 S Noble.
Boyer Isaac S, baggage agt, h 906 Broadway.
Boyer James, lab, h 228 Muskingum al.
Boyer James A, clk, h e s Rural 3 n of Clifford av.
Boyer John S, carp, h 169 N East.
Boyer Leon, lab, h 54 Hosbrook.
Boyer Martha J (wid Jacob), h 104 Park av.
Boyer Otis W, mailing clk Indpls Daily Live Stock Journal, b 82 S Reisner (W I).
Boyer Richard A, printer, h 303 S East.
Boyer Samuel A, cook, h 485 Lafayette.
Boyer Thomas B, pressman F H Smith, h 53 Stevens.

THOS. C. DAY & CO.
INVESTING AGENTS,
TOWN AND FARM LOANS,
Rooms 325 to 330 Lemcke Bldg.

Boyer Walter L, lab, b 228 Muskingum al.
Boyers Martha J (wid Jacob), h 104 Park av.
Boykin Wm, finisher, h 29 Shover (W I).
Boyl Baird J, mach, b 6 Lord.
Boyl Charles A, letter carrier P O, b 6 Lord.
Boyl James H, h 6 Lord.
Boyl Louis, b 6 Lord.
Boylan John P, patrolman, b 392 S Capitol av.
Boylan Michael T, saloon, 300 S Capitol av, b 392 same.
Boylan Patrick, h 392 S Capitol av.
Boylan Thomas, grocer, 53 Church, h same.
Boylan Thomas F, mach, r 29 Holmes av (H).
Boyle Bernard, lab Insane Hospital.
Boyle Charles E, mach opr The Indpls Sentinel, h 125 Pleasant.
Boyle Elisha E, clk, b 133 Michigan av.
Boyle Guy A, clk, b 422 Talbott av.
Boyle John J, head porter The Bates.
Boyle John M, molder, h 27 Catharine.
Boyle John T, carp, h 133 Ft Wayne av.
Boyle Joseph P, bookbndr, h 5½ Wilcox.
Boyle Patrick, lab, b 252 E Washington.
Boyle Wm H, gas insp, h 422 Talbott av.
Boyles Ellen, teacher Public School No 14, b e s Grand av 3 s of University av (I).
Boyles Francis K, h e s Grand av 3 s of University av (I).
Boyles Michael W, real est, 98 E Market, r 36 Ash.
Boynton Charles S, phys, 164 E New York, h same.
Boys Gilbert J, h 571 E Market.
Bozell Arthur L, lab, b 1125 E Michigan.
Bozell Jennie (wid Joseph), b 1125 E Michigan.
Bozell Walter V, clk Geo W Stout, h 204 Wright.
Bozzart Conrad, bartender, b 252 S Pine.
Brace Minta (wid Oscar B), milliner, 39 W Washington, r 16 Halcyon blk.
Bracken Albert N, ins agt, r 229 E Market.
Bracken Allen, lab, h 19 Springfield.
Bracken Elmer N, lab, h 476 Union.
Bracken John C, ins agt, r 229 E Market.

EAT
HITZ'S
CRACKERS
AND CAKES.
ASK YOUR GROCER FOR THEM.

BICYCLES $5 DOWN. MONTHLY. Best Wheels. Best Terms. WHEELMEN'S CO. 31 W. OHIO ST. LONG DISTANCE TEL. 1858.

J. H. TECKENBROCK General House Painter, 94 EAST SOUTH STREET.

FIDELITY MUTUAL LIFE—PHILADELPHIA, PA.
$75,000,000, Insurance In Force. $3,500,000, Death Losses Paid. $1,500,090, Surplus. A. H. COLLINS {General Agent, Baldwin Block.

BITUMINOUS COAL IN CAR LOADS TO DEALERS AND MANUFACTURERS. ROOMS 42 AND 43 WHEN BUILDING. Edwardsport Coal & Mining Co.

ESTABLISHED 1876. TELEPHONE 168.
CHESTER BRADFORD,
SOLICITOR OF PATENTS,
AND COUNSEL IN PATENT CAUSES.
(See adv. page 6.)
Office:—Rooms 14 and 16 Hubbard Block, S. W. Cor. Washington and Meridian Streets, INDIANAPOLIS, INDIANA.

Bracken John S, lab, h 154½ Martindale av.
Bracken Wm H, collr Internal Revenue, P O bldg, res Lawrenceburg, Ind.
Brackensiek Caspar H, cigarmkr, b 201 E Washington.
Brackett Charles H, sec Columbian Relief Fund Assn, h 199 Cornell av.
Brackett Mary, h 40 Chadwick.
Brackin Thomas R, lab, h 156 Elm.
Bracking Frank, trav agt, h 30 E Pratt.
Brackmeier Adolph H, driver, b 180 Virginia av.
Brackmeier George O, baker, 180 Virginia av, h same.
BRACKNEY GEORGE H, Genl Solicitor The Central Law Union, 425-426 Lemcke Bldg, h 223 E North.
Bradburn Charles E, motorman, h 263 S East.
Bradburn Homer, blksmith, b 54 Belmont av (H).
Bradburn Sarah A (wid Isaac), b 263 S East.
Bradburn Wm A, carp, h w s Sheffield av 1 n of Clark (H).
Bradbury Daniel M, lawyer, 403 Lemcke bldg, h 273 Park av.
Bradbury Edward A, opr W U Tel Co, h 439 E St Clair.
BRADBURY GEORGE L, Vice-Pres and Genl Mngr L E & W R R, s w cor Washington and Noble, b The Denison.
Bradbury Henry, lab, b 130 Allegheny.
Bradbury Henry R, sec Warren-Scharf Asphalt Paving Co, res New York City.
Bradbury James, barber, b 323 N Liberty.
Bradbury Walter H, engraver, r 11½ N Meridian.
Bradbury Wm, painter, b 799 N Illinois.
Braddock Newton A, sawmkr, h 219 Bright.
Brade Otto, furniture, 486 Virginia av, h 108 Spann av.
Bradehaft Annie, news, h 260 Shelby.
Bradehaft Louis, driver, h 260 Shelby.
Brademeyer Ann C (wid John F), h 59 N Dorman.

Outing BICYCLES
..MADE BY..
HAY & WILLITS MFG CO.
76 N. Pennsylvania St. Phone 598.

Brademeyer Christopher C, condr, h 172 N Dorman.
Braden David, trav agt, h 978 N Capitol av.
Braden Eben D, salesman Wm B Burford, h 1106 N Senate av.
Braden Hervey B, clk, b 978 N Capitol av.
Braden James, h n e cor Houston and Downey avs (I).
Braden Mary C (wid Whitson), h 174 Mass av.
Braden Robert B, real est, 77 E Market, h 1144 N Alabama.
Braden Ruth (wid Hugh), h 27 Hall pl.
Bradford Algernon, dairy, 72 Michigan (H), b same.
Bradford Clarence U, mach hd, b 635 Madison av.
BRADFORD CHESTER, Patent Lawyer and Solicitor, Established 1876, Rooms 14-16 Hubbard Blk, s w cor Washington and Meridian, Tel 168; b 1088 N Illinois, Tel 217. (See left top cor cards, p 6 and opp classified Patent Solicitors.)
Bradford Clifford C, lab, b 635 Madison av.
Bradford David E, lab, h 428 Lafayette.
Bradford Edward T, cashr, b 80 Fletcher av.
Bradford Eliza A, h 635 Madison av.
Bradford George F, musician, b 82 W North.
Bradford Hunter, printer, 92 E Court, h 473 E Market.
Bradford Hunter jr, printer, b 473 E Market.
Bradford James M, cigars, Commercial Club bldg, h 80 Fletcher av.
Bradford Jesse G, painter, h 426 W 2d.
Bradford John, lab, h 246 Lafayette av.
Bradford Joseph L, lab, b s s Washington 1 e of Sherman Drive.
Bradford Joseph S, printer, b 1095 W Michigan.
Bradford Louis A, lab, r 540 Superior.
Bradford Margaret (wid Sidney), h 13 Mill.
Bradford Margaret T (wid John), h 1095 W Michigan.
Bradford Oliver R, salesman Wheeler Dressed Beef Co, h 58 River av (W I).
Bradford Ira G, molder, b 635 Madison av.
Bradford Otto M, lab, h 72 W Michigan (H).
Bradford Sarah E (wid Oscar), h 91 Hadley av (W I).
Bradford Sidney, lab, r 169 W Wabash.
Bradford Theodore A, b 982 N Delaware.
Bradford Ward, lab, b 428 Lafayette.
Bradford Wm, dairyman, h e s Denny 3 n of Washington.
Bradley Andrew J, lab, b 175 River av (W I).
Bradley Anthony T, janitor, h 71 Martindale av.
Bradley Charles, lab 808 Park av.
Bradley Charles P, lab, h 563 E St Clair.
Bradley Edward G, lab, b 10 W Morris.
Bradley George F, lab, b 53 Buchanan.
Bradley Giles S (Bradley & Denny), h 612 College av.
Bradley Homer, farmer, h 1740 N Capitol av.
Bradley James K, lab, h 472 Clifford av.
Bradley James L, h 494 N Capitol av.
Bradley James N, b 175 River av (W I).
Bradley Jasper, lab, h 458 Charles.
Bradley John R, molder, h 85 Tremont (H).
Bradley Leland J, carp, h 485 Bellefontaine.
Bradley Logan L, attendant Insane Asylum.

C. ZIMMERMAN & SONS | SLATE AND GRAVEL ROOFERS 19 South East Street.

DRIVEN WELLS And Second Water Wells and Pumps of all kinds at CHARLES KRAUSS', 42 S. PENN. ST., Telephone 465.

ERTEL STEAM LAUNDRY 26 and 28 N. Senate Avenue. Telephone 18 ◄ WE WILL CALL FOR AND DEIVER YOUR WORK. SATISFACTION GUARANTEED.

Bradley Michael E, sub letter carrier P O, b 53 Buchanan.
Bradley Richard A P, engraver, b 53 Buchanan.
Bradley Thomas J, blksmith, h 175 River av (W I).
Bradley Wm, bartndr, r 153 N West.
Bradley Wm, fireman, b 124 English av.
Bradley Wm, plumber, h 71 Martindale av.
Bradley Wm F, pressman, h 929 N Senate av.
Bradley Wm J, lab, b 53 Buchanan.
Bradley Wm M, condr, h 22 Randolph.
Bradshaw Adeline, pres Board of Mngrs Indpls Orphan Asylum, h 26 E Vermont.
Bradshaw Alice (wid John W), h 174-176 N Illinois.
Bradshaw Charles, lab, b 35 Athon.
Bradshaw Frank, lab 416 N Illinois.
Bradshaw George, driver, h 574 E St Clair.
Bradshaw Harmon, bkkpr, b 18 W New York.
Bradshaw James, cook Roosevelt House.
Bradshaw Jeremiah, lab, h 35 Athon.
Bradshaw John A, clk, b 2 N Brightwood av (B).
Bradshaw John A, live stock, h 26 E Vermont.
Bradshaw John W, restaurant 56 S Illinois, h 18 W New York.
Bradshaw Julia, seamstress, b 64 Talbott av.
Bradshaw Melville H, b 571 Bellefontaine.
Bradshaw Oran, molder, h 73 Sheffield av (H).
Bradshaw Oran, molder, h 3 Frazee (H).
Bradshaw Owen, music teacher, h 171 W 5th.
Bradshaw Samuel, clk, b 2 N Brightwood av (B).
Bradshaw Wm A, clk, h 571 Bellefontaine.
Bradshaw Wm A, grocer, 2 N Brightwood av (B), h same.
Bradshaw Wm A jr, clk, b 2 N Brightwood av (B).
BRADSTREET COMPANY THE, Improved Mercantile Agency, H N Castle Supt, n w cor Meridian and Washington; Tel 305.
Bradway Angeline (wid Wm L), b 100 Eureka av.
Bradway Archibald L, lab, h 274 S William (W I).
Bradway Charles O, insp, h 141 Forest av.
Bradway Olna H, trav agt, h 100 Eureka av.
Bradwell Isaac N, lawyer, 32 Thorpe blk, h 386 N New Jersey.
Brady Bert, clk Indpls B and S Co, b 1133 E Michigan.
Brady Catherine (wid James), b 131 Michigan av.
Brady Charles H, meats, 104 E Mkt House, h 263 N Noble.
Brady Charles J, mach hd, b 470 Stillwell.
Brady Edward, lab, b 594 Morris (W I).
Brady Edward, tmstr, h 15 Chadwick.
Brady Florence M (wid Calvin C), h 460 N New Jersey.
Brady Frank, gasfitter, r 60 S Delaware.
Brady George, coremkr, h 114½ Hill av.
Brady George W, welldriver, 473 Lincoln av, h same.
Brady James, boilermkr, b 47 Empire.
Brady James A, molder, h 266 W Vermont.
Brady James J, dry goods, 911 S Meridian, h same.
Brady James T, lab, b 71 Peru av.
Brady Jane (wid John), h 47 Empire.

EQUITABLE LIFE ASSURANCE SOCIETY OF THE UNITED STATES, RICHARDSON & McCREA Managers for Central Indiana, 79 East Market St. Telephone 182.

Brady Jeremiah, lab, b 13 Chadwick.
Brady John, trav agt, b 53 Central av.
Brady John J, mach, b 157 Sheldon.
Brady John M, lab, b 51 Koller.
Brady John P, bricklayer, h 172 Fayette.
Brady John R, mach, h 651½ E Michigan.
Brady Joseph, distributer, b 60½ S Delaware.
Brady J Wm, trav agt M O'Connor & Co, r 30 W Vermont.
Brady Margaret (wid Patrick H), h 60½ S Delaware.
Brady Martin, soldier, h 51 N Summit.
Brady Matthew J, bricklyr, b 717 N Senate av.
Brady Mary A (wid Henry), b 601 N Delaware.
Brady Michael A, lab, h 333 W Morris.
Brady Peter D, tinner, b 242 English av.
Brady Richard, blksmith, h 87 Newman.
Brady Stephen, lab, h 193 W 9th.
Brady Thomas J, barber, 304 Blake, h same.
Brady Wm, cook, h 119 W Vermont.
Brady Wm F, painter, b 600 Ash.
Brady Wm R, painter, h 1133 E Michigan.
Braendlein Charles J, carver, b 376 Coburn.
Braendlein Henry J, carpet weaver, 376 Coburn, h same.
Braendlein Henry M, designer, h 426 S State av.
Braendlein Louis F, cashr Francke & Schindler, b 376 Coburn.
Braendlein Martin, florist, e s Senate av 2 s of 26th, h same.
Braendlein Paul, meats, 38 Gresham and 91 E Mkt House, h 38 Gresham.
Braffett Volney M, ins, h 430 College av.
Bragdon Albert E, letter carrier P O, h 86 Clark.
Bragg Stokely S, clk, h 81 Pleasant.
Bragg Thomas F, lawyer, 10½ N Delaware, h same.
Braham James A, lab h 180 W 2d.
Brake John B C, driver, b 180 Bates.
Brake Thomas, lab, h 33 Vinson.
Braley Charles H, chiropodist, 77 W Ohio, b same.
Bramblett Charles C, peddler, b s e cor LaSalle and Richard (M P).

STENOGRAPHERS FURNISHED. EXPERIENCED OR BEGINNERS, PERMANENT OR TEMPORARY. S. H. EAST, State Agent, The Williams Typewriter, 55 THORPE BLOCK, 87 EAST MARKET ST.

ELLIS & HELFENBERGER { ENTERPRISE FOUNDRY & FENCE CO. 162-170 S. Senate Ave. Tel. 958.

THE HOGAN TRANSFER AND STORAGE COMP'Y
Household Goods and Pianos Moved—Packed—Stored...... Baggage and Package Express Machinery and Safes a Specialty Cor. Washington and Illinois Sts. TELEPHONE No. 675.

Hose, Belting, Packing, Clothing, Druggists' Sundries, Bicycle Tires, Cotton Hose, Etc. New York Belting & Packing Co., L't'd.

A death rate below all other American Companies, and dividends from this source correspondingly larger.
The Provident Life and Trust Company
Of Philadelphia.
D. W. EDWARDS, General Agent,
508 Indiana Trust Building.

Bramblett Elmer A, peddler, b s e cor La-Salle and Richard (M P).
Bramblett Nancy (wid John), h s e cor La-Salle and Richard (M. P).
Bramblett Perry E, peddler, h 167 Elizabeth.
Bramblett Wm A, lab, h rear 333 S Alabama.
Bramkamp Wm H, barber, 146 Fletcher av, h 16 Dawson.
Bramwell Albert A, engr, h 48 Randolph.
Bramwell Wm A, carp, h 1655 Graceland av.
Branch John, lab, h 619 W Pearl.
Brand, see also Brandt and Brant.
Brand George P, blksmith, h 618 S East.
Brand Hattie W (wid John), b 309 Ash.
Brand Michael, blksmith, h 307 W Morris.
Brand Rebecca M, printer, r 87 The Windsor.
Brandenburg Charles, harnessmkr, h 235 S Alabama.
Brandenburg Sadie, watchwoman Deaf and Dumb Inst.
Brandenburg Thomas E, condr, h 305 Blake.
Brandenburger Adolph (Brandenburger Bros), b 65 S Linden.
Brandenburger Bros (Charles and Adolph), photogs, 65 S Linden.
Brandenburger Charles (Brandenburger Bros), b 65 S Linden.
Brandenburger Elizabeth (wid Ludwig), h 65 S Linden.
Brandenburger John, photog, b 65 S Linden.
Brandenburger Martin, tinner, b 65 S Linden.
Brandes Benjamin H, mach hd, h 257 S Penn.
Brandes Bernhard J, mach, b 257 S Penn.
Brandes George J, tailor, b 257 S Penn.
Brandes Henry N, lab, b 257 S Penn.
Brandes Herman F, grocer, s e cor Madeira and Prospect, h same.
Brandes John E, city fireman, h 502 Madison av.
Brandon Alonzo D, brakeman, h 56 S Summit.
Brandon Calvin F, salesman C A Heath, b 177 Christian av.
Brandon Eugene E, painter, h 331 Bates.

Julius C. Walk & Son,
Jewelers
Indianapolis.
12 EAST WASHINGTON ST.

THE CENTRAL RUBBER & SUPPLY CO. PHONE 922. 79 S. ILLINOIS ST., INDIANAPOLIS, IND.

Brandon James A, clk, h 124 Blackford.
Brandon Joseph H, bartndr, h 185 Coburn.
Brandon Lavinia (wid Marshall), b 56 S Summit.
Brandon Thomas L, mach, h 225 W South.
Brandon Victor J, student, b 330 Broadway.
Brandon Wm, lab, h 482 Chapel.
Brandstetter Anthony, carp, h 119 Palmer.
Brandt, see also Brand and Brant.
Brandt Adolph G (A G Brandt & Co), b 182 E McCarty.
Brandt Albert H (A G Brandt & Co), b 182 E McCarty.
Brandt A G & Co (Adolph and Albert H Brandt), bookbndrs, 64 S Penn.
Brandt Bertha (wid Herman T), h 182 E McCarty.
Brandt Charles, lab, h e s Auburn av 3 s of Bethel av.
Brandt Christian F W, grocer, 543 E Washington; h 52 Michigan av.
Brandt Dederich H, carp, h 349½ S Meridian.
Brandt Edward, florist, b 421 Bellefontaine.
Brandt Frank F, cutter Kahn Tailoring Co, b 424 N Illinois.
Brandt Fred, saloon, 44 W Washington, h 424 N Illinois.
Brandt Frederick, car insp, h 205 Fletcher av.
Brandt Frederick W, boxmnfr and cooper, 85 California, h 80 Vine.
Brandt Henry, uphlr, b 421 Bellefontaine.
Brandt Henry A, clk, b 52 Michigan av.
Brandt Henry F, carp, b 303 English av.
Brandt Henry G, lab, h 37 Parker.
Brandt Julius, uphlr, h 421 Bellefontaine.
Brandt Louis C, carp, h 186 Pleasant.
Brandt Oscar F, agt John Wocher, b 182 E McCarty.
Brandt Wm, lab, h 114 S Summit.
Brandt Wm F, clk, h 7 Allfree av.
Brandt Wm F, lab, h 24 Dawson.
Brandt Wm F C, clk, h 173 Madison av.
Branham Adeline N (wid George F), h 399 N Penn.
Branham Bush, lab, h 134 Lee (W I).
Branham Cynthia A (wid David C), b 22 Lockerbie.
Branham Edward, r 334 N Illinois.
Branham Edward T, trav agt McKee Shoe Co, h n e cor Arlington and Walnut avs (I).
Branham Elizabeth N (wid Charles E), clk, b 548 Chestnut.
Branham Ernest J, salesman, b 45 S Arsenal av.
Branham George B, car rep, h 134 Lee (W I).
Branham George E, contr, h 399 N Penn.
Branham George T (Branham & Lowther), r 215½ E Washington.
Branham Jennings W, baggageman, h 45 S Arsenal av.
Branham Kate V, cataloguer Public Library, r 334 N Illinois.
Branham Lynn C, fireman, h 35 N Station (B).
Branham Nannie E, teacher Indpls College of Music, b 139 E 12th.
Branham Priscilla A (wid Joseph W), h 110 Shelby.
Branham Wm, engr, h 138 Lee (W I).
Branham & Lowther (George T Branham, Nimrod R Lowther), tinners, 294 E Washington.
Branneman Wm C, carp, h n s Brookside av 3 e of Jupiter.

OTTO GAS ENGINES | BUILDERS' EXCHANGE S. W. Cor. Ohio and Penn. Telephone 535.

Becker & Son Charles Becker Jacob Becker Jr. Merchant Tailors. 21 N. Penn. St. Tel. 934

SALISBURY & STANLEY OFFICE, STORE AND BANK FIXTURES. Contractors and Builders. Repairing of all kinds done on short notice. 177 Clinton St., Indianapolis, Ind. Telephone 999.

Brannen Elizabeth (wid Thomas), r 70 W 11th.
Brannen Wm, lab, b 207 W 4th.
Brannen Wyatt, lab, h 207 W 4th.
Brannigan Frank, butcher, b 125 N West.
Brannon, see also Brennan.
Brannon James, capt Engine Co No 3, h 30 Prospect.
Brannon Thomas L, policeman Union Station, h n e cor 17th and N Senate av.
Bransford Hazy, waiter, b 176 Patterson.
Bransford Thomas, lab, h 27 Howard.
Bransford Thomas H, coachman 366 N Capitol av.
Bransford Wm, lab, b 289 Yandes.
Branson Joseph W, motorman, h w s Harris av 4 s of W Washington (M J).
Branson Walter E, driver, h 126 N Dorman.
Branson Walter E, driver, b 127 N East.
Branson Wm, mach, h 17 Bridge (W I).
Brant, see also Brand and Brandt.
Brant Henry, lab, b 23 Helen.
Brant John F, lab, b 23 Helen.
Brant Margaret (wid Robert), h 23 Helen.
Branthoover Bertha M, tel opr, b 78 Park av.
BRANTHOOVER FRANK M, Attorney at Law, 87 Baldwin Blk; Tel 1922, r same.
Brantlinger Theodore E, foreman, h 84 S Shade (B).
Brantlinger Wm H, cigarmkr, b 181 S New Jersey.
Bramwood John W, sec-treas International Typographical Union, pub Typographical Journal, 29½ E Market, h 271 W Michigan.
Branyan James A, city fireman, h 35 Carlos.
Brash Samuel J, condr, h 576 College av.
Brasher Florence, b 222 Lexington av.
Brasher Mary (wid John), b 222 Lexington av.
Brasier John F, dispatching clk P O, h 335 N Liberty.
Brathuer Wm, lab, b 141 Wisconsin.
Brattain Amanda E (wid Henry), h rear 195 Buchanan.
Brattain Edgar H, bkbinder, b rear 195 Buchanan.
Brattain Earl J, clk, b 66 Huron.
Brattain Frank D, clk, b 172 N Senate av.
Brattain George A, bookbndr, b rear 195 Buchanan.
Brattain John W, grocer, 414 W New York, h same.
Brattain John R, clk, h 172 N Senate av.
Brattain Mary E (wid Wm J), b 263 N California.
Brattain Omer, painter, b rear 195 Buchanan.
Brattain Russell H, clk, b 414 W New York.
Brattain Silas H, city fireman, h 66 Huron.
Brande Benjamin, clk, b 398 S Illinois.
Braughton Frederick L, tinner, b n w cor Clifford and Brookland avs.
Braughton Guy A, condr, b n w cor Clifford and Brookland avs.
Braughton Harry D, condr, h n e cor Parker and Clifford av.
Braughton McCullough A, tinner, b n w cor Clifford and Brookland avs.
Braughton McCullough C, tinner, 250 Mass av, h n w cor Clifford and Brookland avs.
Braun, see also Brown.
Braun Albert E, cabtmkr, h 762 Chestnut.
Braun Bertha, clk Robert Keller, b 105 Buchanan.
Braun Charles S, lithog, b 105 Buchanan.

Henry H. Fay,
40½ E. Washington St.,
REAL ESTATE,
AND LOAN BROKER.

Braun Ernest J, filer, b 22 Wyoming.
Braun Frank C, cabtmkr, b 1655 Graceland av.
Braun, Franz, cabtmkr, h 76 Weghorst.
Braun Frederica (wid John), h 774 Charles
Braun, George A, lab, h 5 S Beville av.
Braun Henry W, plumber, b 22 Wyoming.
Braun Joseph, lab, b 1640 N Illinois.
Braun, Joseph, tailor, b 300 S Meridian.
Braun Julius, printer, 149 Virginia av, b 105 Buchanan.
Braun, Louis B, lab, h 1129 E Washington.
Braun Mary (wid Paul), b 427 Union.
Braun Peter, lab, h 38 Fenneman.
Braun Reinhard, gasfitter, h 857 S East.
Braun Sophia, h 141 E South.
Braun Wilhelmina (wid Albert), h 22 Wyoming.
Braun Wm, mach, b 173 E Market.
Braun Wm B, lab, h 105 Buchanan.
Braun Wm D jr, mach, b 105 Buchanan.
Braune Paul, clk, b 163 Central av.
Braune Paul G, packer, h 165 Central av.
Brauntz Elizabeth (wid Louis), h 125 Blake.
Braudigam Charles, lab, h 97 Weghorst.
Braudigam Charles C, pictureframer, b 97 Weghorst.
Brautigam Edward F, canmkr, b 11 St Charles.
Brautigam Elias C, miller, h 11 St Charles.
Brautigam John M, tailor, 149 Mass av, h 386 E Michigan.
Brautigam Martin C, gunsmith, h 319 E Merrill.
Braxton Harvey L, attendant Insane Asylum.
Bray Alfred J, filer, h 320 S Illinois.
Bray Anna, h 382 Union.
Bray Augustus, carp, r 277 W Washington.
Bray David B, mach, b 501 Ash.
Bray Delbert S, mach, b 501 Ash.
Bray Edward S, patrolman, h 501 Ash.
Bray Edward W, r 96 N Alabama.
Bray James C, lab, h 248 Alvord.
Bray John, lab, b 372 S Capitol av.
Bray Mary E (wid Peter L), h 250 N East.
Bray Oliver P, condr, h 326 E 12th.

LIME, CEMENT, PLASTER FIRE BRICK AND CLAY SEWER PIPE, ETC. BALKE & KRAUSS CO., Cor. Market and Missouri Streets.

C. FRIEDGEN HAS THE FINEST STOCK OF LADIES' PARTY SLIPPERS and SHOES 19 NORTH PENNSYLVANIA ST.

SAMUEL LAING ▸ TIN, SLATE AND STEEL ROOFING, 72 AND 74 EAST COURT STREET.

M. B. WILSON, Pres. W. F. CHURCHMAN, Cash.
THE CAPITAL NATIONAL BANK,
INDIANAPOLIS, IND.
Pays Interest on Time Certificates of Deposit.
Buys and Sells Foreign Exchange at Low Rates.
Capital, - - $300,000
Surplus and Earnings, 50,000
No. 28 S. Meridian St., Cor. Pearl.

Bray Redding, bridgebldr, h w s Grand av 1 s of University av (I).
Bray Thomas A, steelwkr, h 372 S Capitol av.
Bray Wm L, tel opr, h 18 Temple av.
BRAYTON ALEMBERT W, Physician, 26½ E Ohio, Tel 1231; and Coroner Marion County, Coroner's Office, 59 Court House, h 615 Broadway, Tel 1279.
Brayton May, teacher Public School No 29, b 615 Broadway.
Brayton Nelson D, student, b 615 Broadway.
Brazington Wm C, artist, 53 Ingalls blk, b 186 N Delaware.
Breach Charles K, plastr, h 47 Dunlop.
Breadheft Henry D, dry goods, 319 Clifford av, h same.
Brearley Charles W, student, r 39½ Indiana av.
Breckenridge Charlotte, h 237 E Michigan.
Breckenridge Gabriel, lab, b 296 Blake.
Brecount Edward, stenog, b 23 Poplar (B).
Brecount Eveline (wid Nimrod D), boarding 23 Poplar (B).
Bredell George W, clk, h 52 Bismarck.
Bredell Jesse B, driver, b 52 Bismarck.
Bredewater George H, bartndr, h 599 W Michigan.
Breeden Edwin W, polisher, h 19 N Sheffield (W I).
Breeding Harry E, ins agt, b 433 Dillon.
Breeding James A, barber, 64 N Illinois, h s e cor Chester av and Ohio.
Breeding John H, lab, h 217 W 3d.
Breeding Martha J (wid Alexander), b 412 N New Jersey.
Breeding Sherman, lab, b 451 S Illinois.
Breedlove Berryman E, car rep, h 110 S William (W I).
Breedlove Earl L, stockkpr, b 130 Bates.
Breedlove Maybel E, teacher, b 131 S Reisner (W I).
Breedlove Samuel M, brazier, b 130 Bates.
Breedlove Stephen H, filer, h 130 Bates.
Breedlove Thomas J, agt, h 131 S Reisner (W I).

TUTTLE & SEGUIN,
28 E. Market Street.
Fire Insurance, Real Estate, Loan and Rental Agents.
TELEPHONE 1168.

Breedlove Wm B, waiter, b 226 W Vermont.
Breedlove Wm J, car rep, h 71 S McLain (W I).
Breedon Wm, brakeman, h 44 Martin.
Breen Bridget (wid Dennis), b 45 Michigan (H).
Breen Edward F, tinner, h 45 Michigan (H).
Breen Ellen (wid Martin), b 49 N Dorman.
Breen James, mer police, h 318 S Illinois.
Breen James A, switchman, h 52 N Gale (B).
Breen James E, packer, h 19 Agnes.
Breen Johanna (wid James), h 339 N Pine.
Breen Michael E, lab, b 339 N Pine.
Breen Patrick, lab, b 55 Gatling.
Breen Patrick J, lab, b 339 N Pine.
Breen Timothy F, foreman, b 339 N Pine.
Brees Isaac, carp, b 506 E Georgia.
Brees James, insp City Engineer, r 506½ E Washington.
Breese Winfield S, salesman, h 35 N Beville av.
Brehm Bernhard, drugs, 400 Mass av, b 34 Bellefontaine.
Brehm Otto, barber, h w s Burton av 2 s of McLene (N I).
Brehmer John J, carp, h 211 Hadley av (W I).
Brehob Christian N, driver, h 181 Wright.
Breil John, lab, h 93 Fremont av (H).
Breithaupt John, lab, h 211 Hamilton av.
Breithaupt Wm, finisher, h 45 Davis.
Brelsford Charles L, lab, h 85 Lord.
Bremer Frederick, brick mnfr, e s Sherman Drive 2 s of Prospect, h same.
Bremer Harmon J, lab, h e s Zwingley 1 s of Bethel av.
Bremer John D, bartndr, h 100 Laurel.
Bremer Wm, tmstr, b e s Sherman Drive 2 s of Prospect.
Bremer Wm M, express, h 785 Mass av.
Bremerman Charles E, packer, h 525 W 22d (N I).
Bremerman Frank B, guitarmkr, h 560 W Eugene (N I).
Bremerman Frederick, mining, h 293 N Alabama.
Bremerman Wm, packer, r 15 The Chalfant.
Brendel Charles R, lab, h 544 W Shoemaker (N I).
Breneman Sarah A (wid Henry), b 29 Newman.
Breneman Walter, lab, h 29 Newman.
Breneman Wm T, mach, b 29 Newman.
Brenham John, foreman, b 294 Christian av.
Brenizer George W, mail driver, h 57 Laurel.
Brenn Eliza (wid Frederick E), h 49 Bradshaw.
Brennan, see also Brannon.
Brennan Catherine (wid Richard), h 30 S Dorman.
Brennan Edward E, student, b 240 N Capitol av.
Brennan Edward J, phys, 240 N Capitol av, h same.
Brennan James, engr, b 173 E Market.
Brennan James, lab, b 320 W Maryland.
Brennan James M, plumber, h 5 Shriver av.
Brennan James P, lab, r 405 Madison av.
Brennan James P, weighmaster, b 320 W Maryland.
Brennan Johanna (wid Donald), h 27 Thomas.
Brennan John, city fireman, h 1361 N Capitol av.
Brennan John, lab, b 117 Kappus (W I).
Brennan John D, lab, h 321 S Missouri.
Brennan John T, clk Board of Public Wks, b 188 Woodlawn av.

SULLIVAN & MAHAN Manufacturers of all kinds of PAPER BOXES 41 W. Pearl St.

DIAMOND WALL PLASTER { Telephone 1410 BUILDERS' EXCHANGE.

Telephone 1769. 197 S. Illinois St. } THE HOME LAUNDRY } WORK CALLED FOR AND DELIVERED.

Brennan John V, plumber, h 44 Fayette.
Brennan Joseph, mach, b 188 S Senate av.
Brennan Joseph, contr, h 883 N Senate av.
Brennan Julia (wid Patrick), h 304 W 7th.
Brennan Lawrence A, janitor Court House, h 218 Elm.
Brennan Lawrence M, plumber, h 463 S Delaware.
Brennan Louis, foreman, r 168½ E Washington.
Brennan Mary (wid Thomas), h 320 W Maryland.
Brennan Michael, mason, h 252 W 7th.
Brennan Michael, lab, h 173 Johnson (W I).
Brennan Michael, janitor Public School No 28, h 115 Fletcher av.
Brennan Michael A, cashr Indpls Gas Co, h 56 Woodruff av.
Brennan Patrick, grocer, 326 S State av, h same.
Brennan Patrick, h 188 Woodlawn av.
Brennan Richard A, clk, b 30 S Dorman.
Brennan Thomas, butcher, b 320 W Maryland.
Brennan Thomas E, cabtmkr, b 23 Grant.
Brennan Thomas J, lab, h 33 Carlos.
Brennan Vincent G, phys, 240 N Capitol av, b same.
Brennan Wm, foreman, b 132 Michigan (H).
Brennan Wm, lab, b 86 N East.
Brennan Wm, winder, b 188 Woodlawn av.
Brennan Wm H, sawmkr, h 278 S Senate av.
Brenneke David B, dancing academy, n w cor Illinois and North, r 199 N Penn.
Brennen John, lab, b 294 Christian av.
Brennen Robert J, student Finch & Finch, b 583 College av.
Brenner Harry D, tel opr, b 120 Yeiser.
Brenner Minerva (wid George W), h 120 Yeiser.
Brentlinger Wm H, b 181 S New Jersey.
Brenton George, lab, b 827 S East.
Brenton John E, lab, b 827 S East.
Brenton Robert C, laborer, h 827 S East.
Bresett Marshall H, trav agt, h 174 Brookside av.
Bresinger Frank, lab, h 107 Sheffield av (H).
Bresnahan Edward J, cooper, h 206 W McCarty.
Bresnahan John P, lab, h 273 W Merrill.
Bresnahan Michael F, uphlr, b 273 W Merrill.
Bresnan, see also Brosnan.
Bresnan Ellen (wid Mark), h 25½ Chadwick.
Bresson Apollinaire J, carp, h 504 E 9th.
Brester John, gardener, h e s Ransdell 2 s of Southern av.
Brester John H, wiper, b 91 Weghorst.
Brester Wm, carp, h 91 Weghorst.
Brester Wm F, molder, b 91 Weghorst.
Bretney Eugene, vice-pres Crystal Ice Co, h 242 W New York.
Bretney Harry R, lab, b 242 W New York.
Bretz Adam, grocer, 106 S Illinois, h 825 N Capitol av.
Bretz Adolph J, clk, r 106½ S Illinois.
Bretz Arthur G, b 825 N Capitol av.
Bretz Edward A, clk Township Assessor, h 31 W St Joseph.
Bretz Otto, clk, r 102 S Illinois.
Bretzloff Adolph H, driver, h 129 W 2d.
Bretzloff Theodore R, gardener, b s s E Washington 2 e of Belt R R.
Breuer Kleues, carp, b 286 W Washington.
Breunig Charles, coachman 575 N Penn.

FRANK NESSLER. WILL H. ROST.
FRANK NESSLER & CO.
Tailors
56 EAST MARKET ST. (Lemcke Building),
INDIANAPOLIS, IND.

Breunig George T, bkkpr S A Fletcher & Co, h 241 Park av.
Breunig LeRoy C, clk S A Fletcher & Co, b 241 Park av.
Breuninger August H, agt, h 81 Elizabeth.
Breuninger Carl G, clk Clemens Vonnegut, b 81 Elizabeth.
Breuninger Gustav, baker, b 81 Elizabeth.
Brewer Albert C, trav agt Jacob Metzger & Co, b 213 Buchanan.
Brewer Albert H, barber, 75 N Alabama, h 38 Sullivan.
Brewer Alfred (A Brewer & Son), h 114 Hoyt av.
Brewer Alvin E, filer, h 307 N Delaware.
Brewer A & Son (Alfred and Calvin L), carps, 114 Hoyt av.
Brewer Calvin L (A Brewer & Son), b 114 Hoyt av.
Brewer Charles L, carp, h 126 Yandes.
Brewer Edward, barber, h 439 Lincoln av.
Brewer Edward jr, barber, b 439 Lincoln av.
Brewer Edward, carp, h 219 Alvord.
Brewer Edward, clk, r 36 Hendricks blk.
Brewer Edward A, lithog, h 364 N California.
Brewer Fielding, bricklyr, h 135 Elm.
Brewer Gurley, teacher, b 439 Lincoln av.
Brewer Harry, plumber, b 32 S Linden.
Brewer Hubbard Rev, b 439 Lincoln av.
Brewer James A, bkkpr, h 36 Warren av (W I).
Brewer Jesse M (wid John H), b 32 S Linden.
Brewer John A, engr, h 567½ Virginia av.
Brewer John C, clk, h 23 Traub av.
Brewer Marie S (wid Ambrose), dressmkr, 364 N California, h same.
Brewer Thomas F, clk, h 137½ Mass av.
Brewer Walter R, chief clk R G Dun & Co, b 135 Elm.
Brewin Anna E (wid Dillard A), b 165 S Alabama.
Brewster Charles J, engr, b 40 English av.
Breyer Avon, actor, h 44 Barth av.
Breyer Margaret (wid John F), h 44 Barth av.
Brian, see also Bryan and O'Brien.

Haueisen & Hartmann
163-169 E. Washington St.
FURNITURE,
Carpets,
Household Goods,
Tin, Granite and China Wares, Oil Cloth and Shades

THE WM. H. BLOCK CO. 7 AND 9 EAST WASHINGTON STREET. DRY GOODS, HOUSE FURNISHINGS AND CROCKERY.

London Guarantee and Accident Co. (Ltd.) Employers', Public and Teams' Liability, Workmen's Collective Insurance and Fidelity Bonds
GEORGE W. PANGBORN, General Agent, 704-706 Lemcke Bldg. Telephone 140.

FRANK K. SAWYER Reliable Fire Insurance. Reasonable Rates. 74 E. MARKET STREET. Telephone 8.

JOSEPH GARDNER,
TIN, IRON, STEEL AND SLATE ROOFING,
GALVANIZED IRON CORNICES & SKYLIGHTS.
37, 39 & 41 KENTUCKY AVE. Telephone 322.

Brian Eveline (wid James M), milliner, 58 N Illinois, r 212 The Shiel.
Brice Sarah E, h 25 Helen.
Briceland Howard M, tel editor The Indpls Sentinel, h 359 N Illinois.
Briceland Joseph N, clk John G Williams, b 225 N Delaware.
Brick Margaret (wid Patrick), h 293 S Alabama.
Brickert Senah E (wid David P), b 71 Maple.
Brickert Wm H, trav agt, h 1103 N Alabama.
Brickley Frank B, clk A Kiefer Drug Co, b 530 N Illinois.
Brickley Margaret (wid David E), h 640 Charles.
Brickley Patrick, lab, h 416 S Capitol av.
Brickley Wm, lab, h 416 S Capitol av.
Bricmont Frank, tile setter, b 46 S Capitol av.
Briddell Sidney L, lab, h 4 Pleasant.
Bridenbaugh Anna E (wid David), h Valley Drive nr Ludlow la.
Bridenbucher George (C H Johnson & Co), h Cambridge City, Ind.
Bridenstein Daniel, cook, r 67 N Alabama.
Bridge Catherine, h 182 E Court.
Bridge Henry, porter, b 182 E Court.
Bridge Thomas W, condr, h 28 Randolph.
Bridges Alvin D, tmstr, h s s Clifford av 1 e of Watts.
Bridges Benjamin S, lab, h 121 Newman.
Bridges Charles, produce, h 999 W Vermont.
Bridges Charles M, waiter, r 26 Roanoke.
Bridges Charles W, real est, h 442 Ash.
Bridges D Alexander, cook 771 N Alabama.
Bridges Emiline (wid Richard), b 121 Newman.
Bridges Emily (wid David), b rear 102 Howard.
Bridges Frank, coachman 251 Broadway.
Bridges George C, solr, b 74 W New York.
Bridges George W, carp, h 632 Bellefontaine.
Bridges Henry E, lab, h 43 Hosbrook.
Bridges James K, condr, r 175 S Illinois.
Bridges John W, paperhanger, h rear 304 College av.

J. S. FARRELL & CO.
STEAM AND HOT WATER HEATING AND PLUMBING CONTRACTORS
84 North Illinois Street. Telephone 382.

Bridges Marvin, lab, b rear 102 Howard.
Bridges Mary E (wid Isham V), h 10 Huron.
Bridges Philip, lab, b 173 Harmon.
Bridges Rebecca (wid Wm), h 328 Lincoln av.
Bridges Robert, lab, b 6 Emerson pl.
Bridges Thomas, lab The Bates.
Bridges Thomas J, tel opr, r 137 W New York.
Bridges Walter, mach, b 328 Lincoln av.
Bridgewater Samuel I, agt, h 15 Central av.
Bridgewater Thomas, lab, h rear 324 W 2d.
Bridgewater Wm H, lab, h 112 Shepard (W I).
Bridgins James H, driver, h 130 W 5th.
Bridwell George W, painter, h 344 English av.
Bridwell Sarah J (wid Wm S), h 299 Spann av.
Bridwell Wm, painter, b 299 Spann av.
Briean Ella, dresmkr L S Ayres & Co, b 95 N Meridian.
Brier Edwin C, student, b 419 N East.
Brier Robert G, bkkpr Emil Wulschner & Son, h 112 Talbott av.
Briese Herman, clk A Kiefer Drug Co, b 39½ Indiana av.
Briggs Carrie M (wid Andrew J), h 116 Indiana av.
Briggs Erastus M, contr, r 130 W Vermont.
Briggs Frank J, lab, b 17 Paca.
Briggs Harriet (wid Wm), h 180½ Indiana av.
Briggs Harry, clk, h 232 S Capitol av.
Briggs Harry, mill hd, r 76 W South.
Briggs James B, lab, h 18 Wilcox.
Briggs John R, beamer, h 266 River av (W I).
Briggs John W, lab, h 17 Paca.
Briggs Mary H (wid John G), b 918 N New Jersey.
Briggs Robert, lab, b 272 W Maryland.
Briggs Wm G, contr, h 126 W 9th.
Briggs Wm L, tmstr, h 473 Martindale av.
Brigham Charles E, clk Wm B Burford, h 945 N Senate av.
Brigham Charles F, clk, b 945 N Senate av.
Brigham Edwin B, phys, 153 Columbia av, h 385 Martindale av.
Brigham Lou, b 945 N Senate av.
Bright Charles, lineman, b 127 N East.
Bright Chester W, lineman, h 49 S Gale (B).
Bright David L, b 48 Edward (W I).
Bright Edward, clk, h 48 Edward (W I).
Bright Henry J, lab, h 27 Biddle.
Bright Louis G, sign writer, r 174 W Washington.
Bright Marshall E, clk, h 48 Edward (W I).
Bright Martha, r 149 N Penn.
Bright Wilson, lab, h 34 St Paul.
Brighton Walter, mach, h 122 S Pine.
Brill Albert, shoes and furngs, 314 E Washington, h same.
BRILL JAMES H, Physician, 310 N New Jersey, h same; Tel 1135.
Brill Jennie, h 18 Columbia al.
Brill John C, dyer, 95 N Illinois and 38 Mass av, h 86 Greer.
Brill John C, tmstr, h w s Sherman Drive 2 n of Michigan.
BRILLHART CLAUD I, Contractor for All Kinds of Sewers, 130 Michigan av, b same.
Brillhart George A, foreman Claud I Brillhart, h 130 Michigan av.

POLICIES IN UNITED STATES LIFE INSURANCE CO., offer indemnity against death, liberal cash surrender value or at option of policy-holder, fully paid-up life insurance or liberal life income. E. B. SWIFT, M'g'r, 25 E. Market St.

WM. KOTTEMAN } WILL FURNISH YOUR HOUSE COMPLETE
89 & 91 E. Washington St. Telephone 1742

SHOW CASES || WILLIAM WIEGEL || 6 West Louisiana Street Opp. Union Station.

Brimm Sallie H (wid George M), dressmkr, 170 Madison av, h same.
Brindley Henry G, foreman, h 339 S Alabama.
Briner Ellen, b 474 Bellefontaine.
Bringham Margaret (wid John), h 170 Dougherty.
Brinicombe Harry, mach, h 438 Cornell av.
Brininstool Carrie, milliner, 1556 N Illinois, h same.
Brininstool Joseph L, solr N Y Life Ins Co, h 1556 N Illinois.
Brink August W, tailor, h 733 E 7th.
Brink Caroline (wid Wm), h 504 S East.
BRINK CHRISTIAN, Trust Officer The Indiana Trust Co, h 333 N Capitol av.
Brink Frederick W, h 451 Madison av.
Brink Frederick W jr, mach hd, b 451 Madison av.
Brink Henry F, mach, h 347 E Morris.
Brink Henry W, mach, h n w cor Wallack and Raymond.
Brink Lina, dressmkr, 504 S East, b same.
Brink Louis H, cutter Wm Schoppenhorst, h 14 Barth av.
Brink Wm F, uphlr, h w s Wallack 2 n of Raymond.
Brink Wm H, cabtmkr, b 563 Madison av.
Brinker August, h 174 W New York.
Brinker Frederick W, clk, b 1098 N Meridian.
Brinker Frederick W, mach hd, b 174 W New York.
Brinker Henry C (Brinker & Habeney), h 1098 N Meridian.
BRINKER & HABENEY (Henry C Brinker, Henry F Habeney), Mnfrs of Cigar Boxes and Dealers in Cigar Mnfrs' Supplies, Labels, Ribbons, Flavors, Etc, 174-180 W Court; Tel 1685. (See adv in classified Box Manufacturers—Cigar.)
Brinkley Jonas P, clk, h 31 Garfield pl.
Brinkman Anton C, grocer, 765 S East, h same.
Brinkman Catherine, seamstress, b s e cor Mass av and Atlas.
Brinkman Catherine (wid Frederick J), h 277 Keystone av.
Brinkman Catharine M (wid Joseph H), h 48 S Stuart (B).
Brinkman Charles F, car rep, h 178 Jefferson av.
Brinkman Charles F jr, pressfeeder, b 178 Jefferson av.
Brinkman Charles H, watchmkr, b 526 E Ohio.
Brinkman Charles O, mach, b 48 S Stuart (B).
Brinkman Christian, lab, b 128 Blake.
Brinkman Christian F, clk, b 765 S East.
Brinkman Frank F, gasfitter, b 526 E Ohio.
Brinkman Frank H, carp, h 526 E Ohio.
Brinkman Frederick, carp, 229 Keystone av, h same.
Brinkman Herman H, foreman E C Atkins & Co, h 273 Jefferson av.
Brinkman John, lab, h 829 E 9th.
Brinkman John C, boilermkr, h 42 S Stuart (B).
Brinkman John H, bricklyr, h 264 S Alabama.
Brinkman Joseph, lab, h 6 Roseline.
Brinkman Joseph H, saloon, 195 Shelby, h 33 Willow.
Brinkman Louis P, presser, h 44 S Shade.
Brinkman Samuel, lab, h 128 Blake.

THOS. C. DAY & CO.
INVESTING AGENTS,
TOWN AND FARM LOANS,
Rooms 325 to 330 Lemcke Bldg.

Brinkman Wm F, cigarmkr, h 161 Laurel.
Brinkmann Arnold H, cigarmkr, h 573 E St Clair.
Brinkmann Christian F, carp, h n e cor Jefferson and St Peter.
Brinkmann Mary S L (wid Christian), h 191 Lincoln la.
Brinkmeyer Edward G F, bkkpr Woodford & Pohlman, h 636 E Ohio.
Brinkmeyer Frederick J, trav agt J C Perry & Co, b 240 Davidson.
Brinkmeyer George C (J C Perry & Co), h 640 N Penn.
Brinkmeyer Gustave H, bkkpr J C Perry & Co, b 240 Davidson.
Brinkmeyer John F, clk Woodford & Pohlman, h 234 Davidson.
Brinkmeyer John H, pres Pioneer Brass Works, h 630 E Ohio.
Brinkmeyer Louis G, janitor, b 48 Randolph.
Brinkmeyer Mary C (wid George H), h 240 Davidson.
Brinnick Wm E, switchman, h 168½ N Pine.
Brisbin George, molder, b 337 Elizabeth.
Brisbin Jefferson M, lab, h 28 Morton.
Brisbin Robert S, tmstr, h 337 Elizabeth.
Brisbin Timothy, mach hd, h 339 Elizabeth.
Briscoe John, lab, b 330 Douglass.
Briscoe John W, lab, h 37 Eastern av.
Briscoe Jordan, express, r 318 E Court.
Briscoe Thomas J, driver, h 330 Douglass.
Briscoe Wm, lab, r 374 Muskingum al.
Brisentine Edmond, mach hd, b e s Rural 2 s of Park (B).
Brisky Moses L, shoemkr, 29 W Ohio, r 187 S Illinois.
Brison Martin, clk Original Eagle, h 28 Bismarck av (H).
Bristol Charles, fireman, b 55 English av.
Bristol Charles W, foreman, h 293 N Liberty.
Bristor Wm A, h 95 Highland pl.
Bristor Wm A, h 536 N Capitol av.
Bristow David H, carp, h 154 Shelby.
Bristow Frank W, tmstr, b 244 Coburn.
Bristow George V, clk, h 422 Central av.
Bristow Joseph, h 422 Central av.
Bristow Joseph A, painter, h 58 Mayhew.
Bristow Lew C, waiter, b 194 E Washington.

EAT——
HITZ'S
CRACKERS
AND CAKES.
ASK YOUR GROCER FOR THEM.

Capital Steam Carpet Cleaning Works
M. D. PLUNKETT Proprietor, Telephone 818

BENJ. BOOTH PRACTICAL EXPERT ACCOUNTANT. Accounts of any description investigated and audited, and statements rendered. Room 18, 82½ E. Washington St., Indianapolis, Ind.

The Best Place in the City to Get a Good Meal THE SHERMAN RESTAURANT ; 18 and 20 S. Meridian Street KERSHNER BROS., Proprs.

ESTABLISHED 1876. TELEPHONE 168.
CHESTER BRADFORD,
SOLICITOR OF PATENTS,
AND COUNSEL IN PATENT CAUSES.
(See adv. page 6.)
Office:—Rooms 14 and 16 Hubbard Block, S.W. Cor. Washington and Meridian Streets, INDIANAPOLIS, INDIANA.

Bristow Thomas J, filer, b 303 S Meridian.
Bristow Wilford, mer police, h 244 Coburn.
Bristow Wm, motorman, h 216 Ash.
Bristow Wm, lab, h 550 N Missouri.
Bristow Wm M, painter, h 170 W Market.
Britan Willis W, printer, h 138 S Summit.
Britt Jerome J, sawyer, h 133 Fulton.
Britt Peter H, clk, h 308 Shelby.
Brittain James F, lab, b 623 W Vermont.
Brittenback J Wm, carp, h cor Russell av and S Illinois.
Britton Arthur A, carp, h 582 W Pearl.
Britton Artie A, lab, h 260 W Washington.
BRITTON CHARLES O, Funeral Director and Embalmer, 51 Indiana av, cor Capitol av, Tel 1579; h 114 Chadwick.
Britton Charles O, loans, 12 Fletcher Bank bldg, b 115 E Michigan.
Britton George, lab, h 191 W 9th.
Britton George, lab, h 24 Tacoma av.
Britton George P, carp, h 156½ Martindale av.
Britton George P, carp, h 484 W Ontario (N I).
Britton John F, mach hd, h 103 Birch av (W I).
Britton Martin L, trav agt Ry Officials' and Employes' Accident Assn, h 243 N Delaware.
Britton Mary, h 243 N Delaware.
Britton Oscar F, dentist, 28½ E Ohio, h 115 E Michigan.
Britton Theodore, mach, b 103 Birch av (W I).
Britton Wm M, lab, h 242 W 22d.
Britz John, clk Nordyke & Marmon Co, h 194 Nebraska.
Broader Lew, brakeman, b 13 Belmont av.
Broadhurst Joseph H, painter, b 101 Shelby.
Broadie George, cook, h 224 W Wabash.
Broadnax Wm H, porter, r 350 Superior.
Broadstreet George F, lab, h s s 6th 1 e of Capitol av.
Broadus Philip, porter Kahn Tailoring Co, h 163 Alvord.
Broady George A, supt South Side Dispensary, h 588 Virginia av.

O. B. Ensey
SLATE, STEEL, TIN AND IRON ROOFING.
Cor. 6th and Illinois Sts. Tel. 1562

Brochhausen Anna M, critic Public School No 4, b 174 Madison av.
Brochhausen Peter J, h 174 Madison av.
Brochhausen Swebert J, saloon, 2 Buchanan, b 174 Madison av.
Brochhausen Wm R, stereotyper, b 174 Madison av.
Brock Charles A, clk, b 1094 W Vermont.
Brock Claude, lab, b 120 Duncan.
Brock Benjamin, foreman, b 86 E Ohio.
Brock Edward, lab, b 90 W McCarty.
Brock Elizabeth (wid James), h 395 S Capitol av.
Brock Elizabeth S (wid Gaines R), music teacher, 23 Hosbrook, h same.
Brock George H, carp, h w s Arlington av 1 n of Walnut av (I).
Brock Henry L, lab, h 137 King av (H).
Brockt John W, motorman, h 1094 W Vermon.
Brock Joseph, foreman, b 86 E Ohio.
Brock Thomas, livery, 407 Virginia av, h 264 Huron.
Brocking August E, cabtmkr, h 234 Hoyt av.
Brocking Carl L, clk, b 43 Wyoming.
Brocking Ernest D, drayman, h 43 Wyoming.
Brocking Henry, pressfeeder, b 43 Wyoming.
Brockmeier Charles, gardener, b s w cor Raymond and Ransdell.
Brockway Asahel, carp, b 477 Charles.
Brockway Charles A, helper, b 420 N Pine.
Brockway Henry R, lab, h 420 N Pine.
Brockway Osmer C, h 1055 N Capitol av.
Brockway Wm H, clk, h 76 W Walnut.
Brodbeck Harry C (H C Brodbeck & Co), h 923 N Alabama.
Brodbeck H C & Co (Harry C and Townsend C Brodbeck), mnfrs' agts, 146 S Meridian.
Brodbeck Percy R, clk, b 923 N Alabama.
Brodbeck Townsend C (H C Brodbeck & Co), b 923 N Alabama.
Broden Fannie K, clk, b 379 Beville av.
Broden Frank J, pressman, b 379 Ramsey av.
Broden James, mach, h 50 Sinker.
Broden James, molder, h 271 E New York.
Broden James jr (M O'Connor & Co), h n w cor 10th and Alabama.
Broden James F, tel opr Indpls Brewg Co, b 122 High.
Broden Michael J, printer, h 379 Ramsey av.
Broden Thomas J, molder, h 122 High.
Brodon James, lab, h 633 W Vermont.
Broderick Daniel J, lab, h 41 Davis.
Broderick Daniel, lab, b 179 W South.
Broderick James, bartndr, b 220 S Missouri.
Broderick John, coremkr, b 25 Holmes av (H).
Broderick John, driver, b Enterprise Hotel.
Broderick Martin, lab, b 25 Holmes av (H).
Broderick Mary A (wid Michael), h 13 Garland (W I).
Broderick Michael, lab, b 58 Church.
Broderick Michael, lab, h 25 Holmes av (H).
Broderick Michael jr, molder, b 25 Holmes av (H).
Broderick Michael H, lab, b 13 Garland (W I).
Broderick Patrick, lab, b 179 W South.
Broderick Patrick H, bartndr, b 25 Holmes av (H).
Broderick Thomas, lab, b 179 W South.
Broe Andrew, sawmkr, b 298 S Capitol av.
Broecker Paul, butcher, b 326 W Vermont.

TUTEWILER UNDERTAKER, NO. 72 WEST MARKET STREET. TELEPHONE 216.

PROVIDENT LIFE AND TRUST CO. OF PHILADELPHIA. D. W. Edwards, G. A., 508 Indiana Trust Bldg. In form of policy; prompt settlement of death losses; equitable dealing with policy-holders; in strength of organization; and in everything which contributes to Security and Cheapness of life insurance, this company is unsurpassed.

THEODORE F. SMITHER Competent and Responsible ROOFER Office, 151 W Maryland St. ☎ 86

Brocking Augusta (wid Christian), b 144 Union.
Broeking Charles D, clk Francke & Schindler, h 246 Bellefontaine.
Broeking Edward D, finisher, b 168 Huron.
Broeking Frank A, clk Francke & Schindler, h 143 Union.
Broeking Frederick H, lab, h 168 Huron.
Broeking Louis F, mach, b 168 Huron.
Brogan Anna (wid Patrick), b 24 Jones.
Brogan Ellen (wid Dennis), b 28 Abbott.
Brogan James M, collarmkr, h 157 Woodlawn av.
Brogan Richard, lab, b 28 Abbott.
BROICH CHARLES H, Druggist, 588 S Meridian, h 326 Union, Tel 280.
Broich Max, driver, b 514 E Washington.
Brokaw Isaac E, bkkpr, h 576 Bellefontaine.
Brokaw Samuel H, condr, r 59½ N Illinois.
Bromberger Maurice, agt, b 505 S Capitol av.
Bromley, see also Brumley.
Bromley Charles D, clk, h 954 W Vermont.
Bromley Wm J, ins, b 123 E Michigan.
Bromm Christian, baker, 17 Shelby, confr, 20 E Mkt House, h 17 Shelby.
Brommer Frederick, painter, rear 524 E Washington, h same.
Brommer Frederick jr, city fireman, h 524 E Washington.
Brommer Wm F, bartndr, b rear 524 E Washington.
Bromstrup Henry, lab, h 279 Bates.
Bromstrup Wm C, painter, b 279 Bates.
Bromwell Harry P, lab, b 275 E Ohio.
Bronaugh John W, clk, b 247 N West.
Bronk Eugene, clk, r 171 W Ohio.
Bronner Lawson, lab, h 186 Miami.
Bronson, see also Brunson.
Bronson Bessie, stenog, b 1696 N Illinois.
Bronson Charles S, supt E C Atkins & Co, h 63 Middle Drive (W P).
Bronson Eveline A (wid Reese H), b 102 Park av.
Bronson Frank, sawyer, h 440 Chestnut.
Bronson Frank F, teacher Industrial School, b 225 N Capitol av.
Bronson Harry B, bridge carp C C C & St L Ry, h 261 English av.
BRONSON HENRY M, Asst Genl Pass Agt C C C & St L Ry (Big Four Route), 1 E Washington, Tel 374; h 225 N Capitol av.
Bronson Mary, r 26 Ryan blk.
Bronson Mary (wid Ely M), h 517 N New Jersey.
Bronstein Jacob, h 96 Eddy.
Brooke Thomas H C, h 308 W Michigan.
Brooke Wm L, special examiner U S Pension Bureau, h 61 Ash.
Brookman Wm, motorman, b 770 W Washington.
Brooks Albert S, lab, b 229 W Washington.
Brooks Alice D (wid Bennett), h 30 S Gale (B).
Brooks Anna (wid Peter), b 94 N Judge Harding (W I).
Brooks Archibald C, coachman 374 College av.
Brooks Arthur J, lumber, r 75 E Ohio.
Brooks Bartholomew D, planing mill, N Judge Harding nr Morris, h 94 N Judge Harding (W I).
Brooks Burrell, lab, b 229½ E Washington.
Brooks Calvin F, barber, h 30 Chapel.
Brooks Charles E, asst treas Natl Malleable Castings Co, r 294 N Meridian.

THE WHEN IS A WORLD BEATER.

Brooks Clementine, h s e cor Schofield av and Belle.
Brooks Daisy, teacher Public School No 9, b 131 N New Jersey.
Brooks David J, temperer, h 400 S East.
Brooks Edmund P, clk L E & W R R, h 154 Randolph.
Brooks Edward, bricklyr, b 477 S Meridian.
Brooks Edward, lab, b 132 W Ohio.
Brooks Edward, carp, b George Brooks.
Brooks George, carp, h w s Judge Harding 1 s of Washington (W I).
Brooks Harriet (wid Samuel), h 99 Division (W I).
Brooks Harry, motorman, b 1063 N Capitol av.
Brooks Horatio M, policeman Insane Hospital, h e s Laura 2 s of Washington (M J).
Brooks Jacob R, engr, h 437 E Washington.
Brooks James W H, driver, h 30 N Judge Harding (W I).
Brooks Jeremiah, lab, h w s Burgess av 1 s of C H & D Ry (I).
Brooks Jesse, painter, 325 N Noble, b same.
Brooks Jesse W, agt, r 564 N Meridian.
Brooks John, h 325 N Noble.
Brooks John, agt, h w s Schurman av 3 s of Wells (N I).
Brooks John W, bricklyr, h 291 Broadway.
Brooks John W, lab, b 48 Vincennes (W I).
Brooks Joseph E, bricklyr, r 268 S Illinois.
Brooks Laura (wid Samuel), h e s Miami 9 s of Prospect.
Brooks Leroy D, fireman, h 55 Foundry (B).
Brooks Louis C, cook, b 139 E Washington.
Brooks Margaret M (wid Frank), h 800 E Market.
Brooks Noah, brick mnfr, w s Sherman Drive 1 s of Clifford av, h e s Ellis 1 s of Clifford av.
BROOKS OIL CO, J Francis Burt Pres, Walter C Davisson Sec and Treas, 488 E Michigan, Tel 460.
Brooks Orion W, fireman, h 855 Cornell av.
Brooks Porter D, fireman, h 283 Fletcher av.
Brooks Sabie J (wid Nathan), h 87 Springfield.

The A. Burdsal Co. CELEBRATED HOMESTEAD READY MIXED PAINT. WHOLESALE AND RETAIL. 34 AND 36 SOUTH MERIDIAN STREET.

ELECTRIC SUPPLIES We Carry a full Stock. Prices Right. C. W. MEIKEL, Tel. 466. 96-98 E. New York St.

DALTON & MERRIFIELD { LUMBER South Noble St., near E. Washington

INDIANA ELECTROTYPE CO. : BEST WORK LOWEST PRICES.
23 WEST PEARL ST., INDIANAPOLIS, IND. JOB WORK. BOOK PLATES. All Orders Promptly Filled. BEST PATENT BASE ON THE MARKET.

KIRKHOFF BROS.,
Electrical Contractors, Wiring and Construction.
102-104 SOUTH PENNSYLVANIA ST.
TELEPHONE 910.

Brooks Salena (wid John), h 477 S Meridian.
Brooks Thomas, bookbndr Wm B Burford, h 112 Shelby.
Brooks Thomas E, brakeman, h 14 Detroit.
Brooks Violet (wid Henry), h rear 422 N East.
Brooks Warren, lab, b 55 Foundry (B).
Brooks Willard M, lab, h 631 S West.
Brooks Wm E, finisher, h 110 River av (W I).
Brooks Wm S, lab, b e s Perkins pike 2 s of C C C & St L Ry.
Brookshire Frederick, druggist Henry J Huder, r 150 N Illinois.
Brooksmith George, clk N Y Store, r 131 W Ohio.
Brooksmith Louis, b 168 Fletcher av.
Broom John E, h 223 W South.
Brophy Peter, watchman, b Senate Hotel.
Broshear Ephraim, lab, h 29 Poplar.
Brosius George W, lab, h 299 N Pine.
Brosnan, see also Bresnan.
Brosnan Bros (John D and Daniel D), dry goods, 39 S Illinois.
Brosnan Daniel D (Brosnan Bros), h 745 N Delaware.
Brosnan Dennis, polisher, b 272 W Merrill.
Brosnan Frederick, h 310 N Noble.
Brosnan James Y, cloaks, 52 N Illinois, h 495 N West.
Brosnan John D (Brosnan Bros), h 749 N Delaware.
Brossel Hubert, shoemkr, 78 N Illinois, h same.
Brothers Charles H, waiter, r 222 W Maryland.
Brothers of the Sacred Heart, s w cor Coburn and Short.
Brough Andrew, sawmkr, b 298 S Capitol av.
Brough Benjamin F, trav agt, h 284 E Ohio.
Brough John G, agt, b 284 E Ohio.
Brough John W, r 27 Brandon blk.
Broughton Moses T, huckster, h 102 Chadwick.
Broughton Perry, lab, h 95 S William (W I).
Brouhard John A, lab, h 543½ W Udell (N I).

THE W. G. WASSON CO.,
130 Indiana Ave. Tel. 989.
STEAM
COAL
Car Lots a Specialty. Prompt Delivery.
Brazil Block, Jackson and Anthracite.

Brouhard Lote, lab, r 163 W Washington.
Brounley Florence A (wid Bassett B), r 29 W Vermont.
Brouse Charles W (Charles W Brouse & Co), h e s Ritter av 2 s of University av (I).
Brouse Charles W & Co (Charles W Brouse, Wm H H Graham), real est, 96½ E Market.
Brouse David W, asst undertaker F A Blanchard, h 391 N East.
Brouse Elmer M, driver, h 1536 N Meridian.
Brouse, Hattie E, cashr, b 391 N East.
Brouse Louise, teacher, b e s Ritter av 2 s of University av (I).
Brouse Mary T, teacher Public School No 6, b e s Ritter av 2 s of University av (I).
Brouse Thomas W, h 72 Broadway.
Brouse Wm. A, bkkpr, b 391 N East.
Browder Cornelius D (Browder & Shover), h 390 Ash.
Browder Daniel, lab, h 1659 N Senate av.
Browder Wilbur F (Clifford, Browder & Moffett), h 358 Talbott av.
Browder & Shover (Corneluis D Browder, Amos F Shover), contractors, 54 Ingalls blk.
Brower Abraham G (Brower & Love Bros), res Utica, N Y.
Brower Daniel W, agt, h 443 E Ohio.
Brower Ellen M, dressmkrs, 443 E Ohio, h same.
Brower Henry, r 268 W Merrill.
BROWER & LOVE BROS (Abram G Brower, John R and Hugh M Love), Proprs Indiana Warp Mills, e bank of White River n of National road. Tel 622.
Brown, see also Braun.
Brown Aaron, lab, b 119 Martindale av.
Brown Aaron, carriagemkr, h 223 E Vermont.
Brown Ada B, asst bkkpr Globe Accident Ins Co, b 383 N Alabama.
Brown Adelene C (wid Erbin H), b 516 Park av.
Brown Adam, cook, b 214 Middle.
Brown Agnes C (wid James W), h cor Broadway and Bedford av.
Brown Albert, butcher, r 117 Lincoln la.
Brown Albert, carp, h 503 E 11th.
Brown Albert, carp, h 21 Sharpe.
Brown Albert, lab, r 166½ W Washington.
Brown Albert, photog, 72½ E Washington, h same.
Brown Albert, waiter, r 293 E Miami.
Brown Albert, weaver, b 14 Stoughton av.
Brown Albert C, painter, b 163 W South.
Brown Albert F, lab, h 15 McCauley.
Brown Albert G, butter, h 184 Bellefontaine.
Brown Albert H, sander, b 226 Lexington av.
Brown Albert J, teacher, h s s University av 4 w of Central av (I).
Brown Albert L, barber, r 105 E Washington.
Brown Alexander, bellboy The Denison.
Brown Alexander, hostler, h 40 Paca.
Brown Alexander G, mach hd, h 524 E Ohio.
Brown Alexander M, trav agt McKee Shoe Co, r 102 S Meridian.
Brown Alfred B, salesman Indpls Abattoir Co, h 38 Hoyt av.
Brown Alfred M, cabtmkr, h 226 Fayette.
Brown Alonzo C, clk, h 226 N Illinois.
Brown Alonzo F, lab, b 330 N California.

W. H. Messenger FURNITURE, CARPETS, STOVES, 101 EAST WASHINGTON ST. TEL. 491.

McNamara, Koster & Co. | Foundry and Pattern Shop, 212-218 S. PENN. ST. . . . PHONE 1593.

Brown Alonzo F, mach, h s s Pendleton av 2 w Brightwood av (B).
Brown Alonzo F C, lab, b 226 N Illinois.
Brown Alvin, carp, h 134 Lynn av.
Brown Alvin W, clk, b 31 Fletcher av.
Brown Amanda, h 178 E Washington.
Brown Amanda M, janitress, h 1171 Northwestern av.
Brown Andrew, lab, b 91 Woodruff av.
Brown Andrew, lab, b 466 W 2d.
Brown Andrew O, driver, h 68½ Mass av.
Brown Anna (wid Antonio), h 297 Alvord.
Brown Anna M (wid Charles), h 402 Talbott av.
Brown Artie W (wid Henry J), h 28 W New York.
Brown Arthur G, clk, b 411 Park av.
BROWN ARTHUR V, Lawyer, 12-13 Fletcher's Bank Bldg, h 299 N Meridian, Tel 1470.
Brown Asbury C, carp, h 430 Cornell av.
Brown August, bartndr, b 64 Shelby.
Brown August J, student, b 227 E Vermont.
Brown Agusta, stenog, b 304 N Delaware.
Brown Austin, lab, h 100 E Campbell.
Brown Austin H, dep Surveyor of Customs P O bldg, b 316 N Meridian.
Brown A Swan, pres Pettis Dry Goods Co, res New York City.
Brown Bedford, lab, h 347 S Brookside av.
Brown Benjamin, lab The Bates.
Brown Benjamin A, phys, 59 E Sutherland (B), h 15 same.
Brown Benjamin F, lab, h 384 S Capitol av.
Brown Benjamin W, clk Bellis Cycle Co, r 2 Stewart pl.
Brown Bert, gardener, b 1052 W Vermont.
Brown Bessie, clk, h 19½ N Meridian.
Brown Brazelton T, supt, h 39 E South.
Brown Brice P, trav agt Indpls Fancy Grocery Co, h 120 Spann av.
Brown Calvin S, lab, h 567 W Shoemaker (N I).
Brown Carl M, photog, h 29 Harlan.
Brown Caroline (wid Henry), h 157 Agnes.
Brown Carrie (wid George), h rear 23 W Ohio.
Brown Carrie P, b 300 W Addison (N I).
Brown Cary H, clk, h 491 Broadway.
Brown Cassander (wid Alexander), b 525 N Alabama.
Brown Chalmers, pres Railway Officials' and Employes' Accident Assn and pres Bellis Cycle Co, h 72 The Blacherne.
Brown Charles, barber, 342 E Washington, h same.
Brown Charles, buyer, h 32 N Reisner (W I).
Brown Charles, photog, 121 W Washington, r 413 N Illinois.
Brown Charles, plastr, b 93 Division (W I).
Brown Charles, porter, h 38½ S Illinois.
Brown Charles, tel opr, b n s Prospect 1 e of Belt R R.
Brown Charles A, asst City Engineer, h 163 Hoyt av.
Brown Charles B, waiter, r 190 E Market.
Brown Charles C, collr O J Conrad, h 158 E St Joseph.
Brown Charles C, consulting engr Central Engineering Co, 225 Lemcke bldg, h 525 N Delaware.
Brown Charles E, lab, b 26 McCauley.
Brown Charles F, cabtmkr, h 374 Orange.
Brown Charles H, clk, h 292 N California.
Brown Charles H, cutter Grafftey, Ault & Co, b 413 N Illinois.
Brown Charles H, mach, h 1105 E Ohio.

Henry H. Fay,
40½ E. Washington St..
REAL ESTATE,
AND LOAN BROKER.

Brown Charles J, switchman, h 305 N Senate av.
Brown Charles W, barber, h 289 Blake.
Brown Charlotte (wid Oliver J), b 536 College av.
Brown Christopher C, barber, 441 W Michigan, h 146 Minerva.
Brown Clara, h 123 Yandes.
Brown Clark Rev (Brown & Smith), h 92 Division (W I).
Brown Danforth, ins agt, h 1124 N Meridian.
Brown Daniel H, student, b 458 N California.
BROWN DANIEL L, State Mngr Massachusetts Benefit Life Association, Rooms 9-10 Baldwin Blk, h 249 N Delaware.
Brown Daniel L jr, student, b 249 N Delaware.
Brown Darwin, collr C F Adams Co, b 205 Dougherty.
Brown David, lab, h 307 Fayette.
Brown David M, carp, r 351 N Senate av.
Brown Della, teacher, h 33 Rockwood.
Brown Demarchus C, librarian and prof Butler College, h s w cor Washington and National avs (I).
Brown Dennis, cooper, h 228 Hamilton av.
Brown Dora W, b 141 Locke.
Brown Drucy, h e s Auburn av 6 s of Bethel av.
BROWN EDGAR A, Lawyer, 88-90 Lombard Bldg, Tel 1527; h 200 Broadway.
Brown Edgar B, molder, h 10 Belmont av (H).
Brown Edgar M, trav agt, b 1020 N Capitol av.
Brown Edward, lab, b 142 Lynn av (W I).
Brown Edward A, student, r 106½ E New York.
Brown Edward F, b 24 S Summit.
Brown Edward G, mach hd, b 202 W Walnut.
Brown Edward J, tmstr, b Jacob Brown.
Brown Edward L, barber, r 128 Indiana av.
Brown Edward L, fireman, h 256 Huron.

UNION CASUALTY & SURETY CO.
OF ST. LOUIS, MO.
All lines of Personal Accident and Casualty Insurance, including Employers' and General Liability.
W. E. BARTON & CO., General Agents,
504 Indiana Trust Building.
LONG DISTANCE TELEPHONE 1918.

THE FRED DIETZ CO.
WOODEN PACKING BOXES MADE TO ORDER. FACTORY AND WAREHOUSE TRUCKS.
400 Madison Avenue. Telephone 654.

Indianapolis BUSINESS UNIVERSITY
Leading College of Business and Shorthand. Elevator day and night. Individual instruction. Large faculty. Terms easy. Enter now. See p. 4. When Block. E. J. HEEB, President.

HENRY R. WORTHINGTON JET and SURFACE CONDENSERS 64 S. PENN. ST. Long Distance Telephone 284.

UNION CO-O ERATIPE LAUNDRY (COMPOSED MENU LAUNDRY GIRLS.) NOS. 138, 140 & 142 VIRGINIA AVENUE
T. E. SOMERVILLE, MANAGER TELEPHONE 1269. INDIANAPOLIS, IND.

HORACE M. HADLEY
REAL ESTATE AND INSURANCE
66 East Market Street, Basement
TELEPHONE 1540.

Brown Edwin R, porter, r 139 W Washington.
Brown Eleanore (wid Wm L), attendant Insane Hospital.
Brown Eli F, phys, 296 E Michigan, h same.
Brown Eli P (Eli P Brown & Co), h 1187 N Illinois.
Brown Eli P & Co (Eli P Brown), brokers, 25 Board of Trade bldg.
Brown Elijah P, editor, h 220 Ash.
Brown Elisha M, mach hd, b 115 River av (W I).
Brown Eliza, h 227½ Muskingum al.
Brown Eliza (wid Abram), h 18 N Rural.
Brown Eliza J (wid Thomas D), r 61½ N Penn.
Brown Elizabeth (wid George P C), h 383 N Alabama.
Brown Elizabeth (wid Levi), b 38 Arbor av (W I).
Brown Elizabeth (wid Louis), h 125 Blake.
Brown Ellis, cooper, h 5 Bates al.
Brown Elmer, coachman, h rear 811 N Meridian.
Brown Elmer E, sewing machines, 194 Virginia av, r 38½ Kentucky av.
Brown Elmer W, chemist, b 360 S New Jersey.
Brown Emma V (wid Wm H), teacher Public School No 23, h 215 Northwestern av.
Brown Emory F, brakeman, h 1608 N Illinois.
Brown Ernest, filer, b 22 Wyoming.
Brown Ernest F, clk Brown-Ketcham Iron Wks, b 280 N Meridian.
Brown Ernest M, dairy, n w cor 22d and Baltimore av, h same.
Brown Ethan A, storekpr, h 132 Bellefontaine.
Brown Everett, molder, h 105 Germania av (H).
Brown E Walker, b 24 S Summit.
Brown Fanny (wid Wm), b 1125 N Meridian.
Brown Fanny (wid John), b 30 Hiatt (W I).
Brown Flora (wid Henry), b 750 N Illinois.
Brown Francis M, engr, h 170 Columbia av.
Brown Frank, coachman 960 N Penn.
Brown Frank, confr, h 297 Bright.

PERSONAL AND PROMPT ATTENTION GIVEN TO COLLECTIONS.
Merchants' and Manufacturers' Exchange
J. E. TAKKEN, Manager,
19 Union Building, 73 West Maryland Street.

Brown Frank, driver, h 190 E Ohio.
Brown Frank, lab, r 175½ E Washington.
Brown Frank D, brakeman, h 238 Brookside av.
Brown Frank E, shoes, 156 E Washington, b 82 N East.
Brown Frank F, h 200 E St Joseph.
Brown Frank L, driver, h 190 E Market.
Brown Frankland T, lab, h 37 N McLain (W I).
Brown Frederick, clk, h 414 W Udell (N I).
Brown Frederick L, clk, h 14 S Gillard av.
Brown Garrett, lab, h e s Rural 7 s of Sutherland (B).
Brown Garrett A, salesman Indpls Abattoir Co, b 437 Central av.
Brown George, baker, b 77 Columbia av.
Brown George, bellboy The Denison.
Brown George, lab, h 26 Leon.
Brown George, lab, b 227½ Muskingum al.
Brown George, lab, b 382½ E 9th.
Brown George, lab, b 114 Roanoke.
Brown George, lab, b 21 Sharpe.
Brown George, lab, b 381 N Senate av.
Brown George, marshal, h 226 Lexington av.
Brown George H, engr, h 185 Brookside av.
Brown George O, h 127 W Michigan.
Brown George P, h s s Railroad 1 w of Central av (I).
Brown George R, stenog Ferdinand Winter and notary public, b 200 Broadway.
Brown George T, dairy, n s Bethel av 1 e of Auburn av, h same.
Brown George T, painter, h 370 Orange.
Brown George W, h s w cor University and Downey avs (I).
Brown George W, boarding 76 E New York.
Brown George W, in charge of salesmen Nordyke & Marmon Co, h 120 Middle Drive (W P).
Brown George W, lab, h 341 W Market.
Brown George W, lab, h 1180 Northwestern av (N I).
Brown George W jr, lab, h 1176 Northwestern av (N I).
Brown George W, painter, h w s Addison 2 s of Washington (M J).
Brown George W, painter, 29 Keith, h same.
Brown George W, salesman Indpls Abattoir Co, h 437 Central av.
Brown George W, sec Ger Am Bldg Assn, h 375 N Alabama.
Brown Georgiana, b rear 226 E Washington.
Brown G Charles, saloon, 66 Shelby, h 64 same.
Brown Grace C (wid Nicholas H), bkkpr, h e s Butler av 1 s of P C C & St L Ry (I).
Brown Grant, lab, b 137 Broadway.
Brown Gussie F, attendant Public Library, b 132 Bellefontaine.
Brown Guy C, collr, b 1308 N Capitol av.
Brown Harmon, lab, b 71 Minerva.
Brown Harold C, printer, b 1308 N Capitol av.
Brown Harriet (wid Ellison), h 414 W Udell (N I).
Brown Harrison, lab, h 30 St Peter.
Brown Harry, lab, h 881 Mass av.
Brown Harry, mach hd, b 58 Temple av.
Brown Harry E, rep, b 308 N Pine.
Brown Harry G, reporter The Indpls Sentinel, h 42 The Blacherne.
Brown Harry S (Reagan & Brown), r 76 W North.
Brown Harry T, lab, b 37 N McLain (W I).
Brown Harry W, lab, b 344 W North.
Brown Henry W, plumber, b 22 Wyoming.
Brown Helena C (wid Adrian D), drugs, 1310 N Capitol av, h 1308 same.

CLEMENS VONNEGUT 184, 186 and 192 E. Washington St. FOUNDRY AND MACHINISTS' SUPPLIES. "NORTON" EMERY WHEELS AND GRINDING MACHINERY.

THE WM. H. BLOCK CO. DRY GOODS, MILLINERY, CLOAKS AND FURS.
7 AND 9 EAST WASHINGTON STREET.

Brown Henry, carp, h 25 Palmer.
Brown Henry, lab, b 114 Roanoke.
Brown Henry E, molder, h 36 Bismarck av (H).
Brown Henry H, polisher, h 80 Weghorst.
Brown Henry L, cashr Daniel Stewart Co, h 286 Lincoln av.
Brown Henry L, grocer, 356 Indiana av, h same.
Brown Henry O, stenog, b 227 E Vermont.
Brown Herbert P, lawyer, 720 Lemcke bldg, r 421 Broadway.
Brown Herman, lab, h 71 Minerva.
Brown Hilton U, city editor The Indpls News, h s w cor National and Washington avs (I).
Brown Hiram, chief clk Thomas C Day & Co, h 520 Central av.
Brown Horace G, r 137½ Mass av.
Brown Hubert, clk, b 203 N West.
Brown Hugo R, clk, b 276 Spring.
Brown Ignatius (I & L M Brown), r 23 Baldwin blk.
Brown Irving S, asst supt N Y Store, h 805 N Meridian.
Brown Isaac B, lab, h 152 Lee (W I).
Brown Isaac I, plastr, h 359 S East.
Brown Isaac L, carp, h e s Brightwood av 7 s of Willow (B).

BROWN I & L M (Ignatius and Lyndsay M), Abstracts of Titles, 66 E Market.

Brown Jacob, farmer, h e s Lincoln av 2 s of C C C & St L Ry (M J).
Brown Jacob C, letter carrier P O, h 120 Weghorst.
Brown Jacob M, clk, h 159 Michigan (H).
Brown Jacob P, electrician, r 8 Grand Opera House blk.
Brown James, carp, h s e cor Davidge and Sheldon.
Brown James, lab, b 82 Yandes.
Brown James, lab The Bates.
Brown James, lab, b n s Bethel av 1 e of Auburn av.
Brown James, plastr, b 86 Martindale av.
Brown James A, barber, 174 Virginia av, h same.
Brown James A, driver, h 33 Rockwood.
Brown James A, lab, b 384 S Capitol av.
Brown James B, plastr, h 1354 N Capitol av.
Brown James D, paperhngr, b 132 E Walnut.
Brown James E, coachman, h 200 Middle.
Brown James E (Brown & Jones), h 448 Park av.
Brown James H, foreman, h 11 S Gale (B).
Brown James M, assembler, h 202 W Walnut.
Brown James O, lab, b 26 Eastern av.
Brown James W, brakeman, h 3 Taylor av.
Brown James W, lab, h 13 Frazee (H).
Brown James W, lab, h 71 Hazel.
Brown Jeanette, stenog McKee Shoe Co, b 312 College av.
Brown Jennie M, nurse Asylum for Friendless Colored Children.
Brown Jeremiah, h 450 N West.
Brown Jesse C, janitor Public School No 25, h 272 S New Jersey.
Brown Jesse H, h 421 Broadway.
Brown John, h 347 S State av.
Brown John, clk H P Wasson & Co, r 291 E New York.
Brown John, lab, b 199 W 3d.
Brown John, lab, b 326 W Maryland.
Brown John, lab, r 190 E Market.

Brown John, plastr, h 229 Mass av.
Brown John, sawmkr, h 430 S Illinois.
Brown John, waiter, b 307 Fayette.
Brown John A, blksmith, h 150 Lee (W I).
Brown John D, carp, 824 College av, h same.
Brown John E, horseshoer, b 174 Talbott av.
Brown John G, h 304 N New Jersey.
Brown John H, car rep, b 35 Spann av.
Brown John H F, tinner, h 205 Dougherty.
Brown John J, lab, h 26 McCauley.
Brown John L, clk, b 125 Lynn av (W I).
Brown John O, fireman, b 3 N Gale (B).
Brown John R, phys, 8 Sterling, h same.
Brown John S, clk, h 33 Rockwood.
Brown John T, bartndr, h 45½ Virginia av.
Brown John W, appraiser Ger Am Bldg Assn, h 82 N East.
Brown John W, fireman, h 1 Taylor av.
Brown John W, harnessmkr, h 180 Elm.
Brown John W, ironwkr, r 94 N New Jersey.
Brown John W, janitor Wilson blk, h same.
Brown John W, shoemkr, h 11½ W Washington.
Brown John W jr, collr People's Outfitting Co, b 11½ W Washington.
Brown Joseph, clk Exchange Hotel (W I).
Brown Joseph, lab, h 82 Adams.
Brown Joseph, tmstr, b 222 W 8th.
Brown Joseph A, checkman, h 1125 E Michigan.
Brown Joseph B, carp, b 29 Nebraska.
Brown Joseph B, lab, h 7 Hillside av.

BROWN JOSEPH D, Agt American Express Co, 5 E Washington, h 1125 N Meridian; Tel 376.

Brown Joseph F, dep County Clerk, h 92 N State av.
Brown Joseph H, cementer, r 190½ S Illinois.
Brown Joseph H, clk, h 420 W Michigan.
Brown Joseph H, tinner, 18 Prospect, h 43 Woodlawn av.
Brown Joseph P, h 1058 N New Jersey.
Brown Josephus, hostler, h 226 W Vermont.
Brown Julia, h 177 N West.
Brown J Burgess, h 1501 N Illinois.
Brown J Burgess jr, b 1501 N Illinois.

GUIDO R. PRESSLER,
FRESCO PAINTER
Churches, Theaters, Public Buildings, Etc., A Specialty.
Residence, No. 325 North Liberty Street.
INDIANAPOLIS, IND.

INDIANAPOLIS STEEL ROOFING AND CORRUGATING WORKS, 23 and 25 East South Street. S. D. NOEL, Proprietor.

David S. McKernan REAL ESTATE AND LOANS. Exchanging real estate a specialty. A number of choice pieces for encumbered property. Rooms 2-5 Thorpe Block.

DIAMOND WALL PLASTER { Telephone 1410 BUILDERS' EXCHANGE.

UNION TRANSFER AND STORAGE CO. Cor. E. Go St. and C., C., C. & St. L. R'y Tracks. Storage of Household Goods and Pianos a Specialty.

W. McWORKMAN,
Galvanized Iron Cornice Works
TIN AND SLATE ROOFING.
930 WEST WASHINGTON STREET.
TELEPHONE 1118.

Brown J Wyley, plastr, h 192 Hillside av.
Brown Kate (wid Anderson T), b 378 Lafayette.
Brown Katherine W (wid George), h 12 The Blacherne.
BROWN-KETCHAM IRON WORKS THE, Wm H Brown Pres, John L Ketcham Sec and Treas, Wm R Brown Supt, Michigan, Haughville; Tel 5.
Brown Laura S, h 20½ N Delaware.
Brown Leathey (wid Wm D), h 229 E Market.
Brown Leonard H, county rd supervisor, h e s Baltimore av 2 n of 22d.
Brown Leroy, clk P C C & St L Ry, h 14 S Gillard av.
Brown Lewis, barber, h 173 W North.
Brown Lewis J, collr Indpls Abattoir Co, b 437 Central av.
Brown Lot H, clk H P Wasson & Co, h 1112 N Penn.
Brown Louis, overall mnfr, 82 N Liberty, h same.
Brown Louis jr, clk, b 82 N Liberty.
Brown Louisa K (wid Henry T), h 227 E Vermont.
Brown Louise S (wid Frank), h 499 E 9th.
Brown Lourie O, clk, h 33 Rockwood.
Brown Lucia L, teacher Public School No 39, b 347 S State av.
Brown Lucille (wid Benjamin M), h 116 Spann av.
Brown Lulu, stenog Kingan & Co ltd, b 257 N Illinois.
Brown Lundy J, lab, b 168 Martindale av.
Brown Lydia F, teacher Public School No 3, b 437 Central av.
Brown Lyndsay M (I & L M Brown), r 276 N Alabama.
Brown L Elmer, clk Ry Officials' and Employers' Accident Assn, r 2 Stewart pl.
Brown Mahlon S, salesman Daggett & Co, h 234 Brookside av.
Brown Malcom C, clk, b 296 E Michigan.
Brown Malitha A (wid Elisha W), fitter, b 29½ Mulberry.
Brown Mamie I, teacher Public School No 23, b 349 Columbia av.

SEALS, STENCILS, STAMPS, Etc.
GEO. J. MAYER
15 S. Meridian St.
TELEPHONE 1386.

Brown-Manly Plow Co, Isaac B Pickett agt, 170 S Penn.
Brown Marcus L, mnfrs' agt, 6 Builders' Exchange, h 1020 N Capitol av.
Brown Margaret (wid Robert L), laundress, h 312 E Court.
Brown Margaret E, dressmkr, 263½ N New Jersey, h same.
Brown Maria J (wid John), b 289 N California.
Brown Marion L, stenog, b 304 N Delaware.
Brown Martha E (wid Emanuel), h 181 East Drive (W P).
Brown Martha L (wid Wm), h 3 N Gale (P).
Brown Mary (wid Alvin M), h 341 W Maryland.
Brown Mary (wid Henry), b 158 Sheldon.
Brown Mary (wid Kinzey), h 370 N Senate av.
Brown Mary (wid Matthew), h 341 W Maryland.
Brown Mary (wid Nicholas), h 215 Douglass.
Brown Mary (wid Richard), b 118 N East.
Brown Mary A, stenog Griffiths & Potts, b 438 Central av.
Brown Mary A, b 470 Stillwell.
Brown Mary A (wid Samuel), b 139 Woodlawn av.
Brown Mary C, stenog H T Conde Implement Co, b 210 Broadway.
Brown Mary E, b 565 S Meridian.
Brown Mary H (wid Wm), h 1680 Kenwood av.
Brown Mary I, teacher Public School No 13, b 203 E South.
Brown Mary J, h 115 Darnell.
Brown Mary W (wid Benjamin F), b w s Grand av 3 s of University av (I).
Brown Mason P, plumber, b 308 N Pine.
Brown Maurice H, clk Erie Despatch, h 204 Fayette.
Brown May, b 229 E Market.
Brown May (wid Joseph), h rear 384 Indiana av.
Brown Merritt, lab, b 312 E Court.
Brown Michael, waiter, h 50 Mayhew.
Brown Minnie (wid Albert), h 22 Wyoming.
Brown Mittie (wid Elisha), h 158 Chestnut.
Brown Nancy A, dressmkr, 484 W North, h same.
Brown Nancy L (wid Walter S), h 346 N Delaware.
Brown Nancy T (wid Ryland T), h 13 Central av.
Brown Nathaniel J, engr, h 208 Fayette.
Brown Nellie A, opr C U Tel Co, b 1354 N Capitol av.
Brown Nicholas, lab, b 498 Chestnut.
Brown Oliver W, chemist, b 35 Morrison.
Brown Oscar A J, cigarmkr, h 176 Spring.
Brown Oscar H, filer, b 87 N Noble.
Brown Owen A, baggageman, h 470 Stillwell.
Brown Patrick, janitor, h 498 Chestnut.
Brown Patrick jr, lithog Empire Theater, b 498 Chestnut.
Brown Percy G, b 1680 Kenwood av.
Brown Peter G, candy, b 332 E Washington.
Brown Pius E, carp, h 332 Spann av.
Brown Rebecca (wid Edward), b 27 S Station (B).
Brown Reuben T, lab, h 150 Bloyd av.
Brown Richard, driver, h 4 Yandes.
Brown Richard, foreman Mads P Anderson, h 70 Quince.

A. METZGER AGENCY ESTABLISHED 1863. L-O-A-N-S

LAMBERT GAS & GASOLINE ENGINE CO.
ANDERSON, IND. GAS ENGINES FOR ALL PURPOSES.

Brown Richard H, city fireman, h 255 S New Jersey.
Brown Richard H, trav agt, b 118 N East.
Brown Robert, lab, b 26 Church.
Brown Robert, lab h 86 Martindale av.
Brown Robert, waiter, r 4 Sterling blk.
Brown Robert A, dep Sec of State, 2 State House, h 911 N Capital av.
Brown Robert A, horseshoer, 29 Bird, h 174 Talbott av.
Brown Robert D, motorman, h 139 Tacoma av.
Brown, Robert J, clk, r 143½ Virginia av.
Brown Robert P, cigars, 137 River av (W I), h 115 same.
Brown Robert W, baggagemstr, h 53 Omer.
Brown Roy D, mach hd, b 115 Dunlop.
Brown Rudolph A, car rep, h 276 Spring.
Brown Samuel, lab, b Jacob Brown.
Brown Samuel, porter, h 458 N California.
Brown Samuel E, trav agt, h 1080 N Capitol av.
Brown Samuel H, fireman, h 140 Cypress.
Brown Samuel L, brakeman, h 315 Fletcher av.
Brown Samuel T, mngr pork dept Indpls Abattoir Co, h 735 N New Jersey.
Brown Sarah, hairdresser, h 289 Blake.
Brown Sarah (wid James), h 230 W 3d.
Brown Sarah A (wid John W), b 71 Louise.
Brown Sarah A W (wid George), b 1015 N Penn.
Brown Sarah E, housekpr 134 Spann av.
Brown Scott, driver, h 277 Fayette.
Brown Scott, lab, h rear e s Woodside av 1 s of Washington.
Brown Sidney V, cashr, r 115 N New Jersey.
Brown Solomon, lab, b 127 E Ohio.
Brown Spencer, lab, b 65 S East.
Brown Straw Binder Co, Albert Izor pres, Eli L Segar sec, George H Bryce treas, 39-41 E South.
Brown Taylor, carp, b 5 S Station (B).
Brown Theodore E, livery, 163 W Washington, h 38 N West.
Brown Thomas, lab, b 82 Yandes.
Brown Thomas B, boarding 127 E Ohio.
Brown Thomas C Rev, pastor Friends Church, h 35 Morrison.
Brown Thomas F, lab, b 498 Chestnut.
Brown Thomas F, painter, h rear 226 Park av.
Brown Thomas L, lab, b 520 N California.
Brown Thomas W, cashr Indpls Brewing Co, h 45 Ruckle.
Brown Tunstall O, music teacher, 169 W 5th, h same.
Brown Turner, driver, h 150 Bloyd av (B).
Brown Vallorus J, painter, h 172 N Missouri.
Brown Walker, coachman, h 19 Maria.
Brown Walter, mach, h 111 Walcott.
Brown Walter S, barber, h 91 Howard.
Brown Walter W, engr, h 33 Rockwood.
Brown Warren, lab, h 119 Allegheny.
Brown Wheeler, lab, b 348 W 2d.
Brown Wm, barber, b 237 W Michigan.
Brown Wm, buyer The Wm H Block Co, h 321 N Illinois.
Brown Wm, hostler, r 52½ Indiana av.
Brown Wm, lab, b 33 Howard.
Brown Wm, lab, h 119 Martindale av.
Brown Wm jr, lab, b 119 Martindale av.
Brown Wm, lab, b 182 Muskingum al.
Brown Wm, lab, b 1180 Northwestern av (N I).
Brown Wm, lab, b 21 Sharpe.
Brown Wm, lab, b 776 E 10th.

THOS. C. DAY & CO.
Financial Agents and Loans.
We have the experience, and claim to be reliable.
Rooms 325 to 330 Lemcke Bldg.

Brown Wm A, draughtsman, r 217 N Capitol av.
Brown Wm C, waiter, h 574 N Senate av.
Brown Wm E, clk, h 218 Spann av.
Brown Wm E, lab, b 175 W McCarty.
Brown Wm E, lab, r 139 W Washington.
Brown Wm G, phonographs, 26 Pembroke Arcade, b 92 N State av.
Brown Wm H, architect, b 422 N Illinois.
Brown Wm H, bkkpr, h 18 Stuart (B).
Brown Wm H, collr, h 139 Woodlawn av.
Brown Wm H, insp, h 26 King av (H).
Brown Wm H, painter, b 5 Bates al.
Brown Wm H, pres Brown-Ketcham Iron Works, h 280 N Meridian.
Brown Wm H, trav agt, h 41 The Blacherne.
Brown Wm J, agt, h 257 N Illinois.
Brown Wm J, barber, h 176 W 2d.
Brown Wm J, fireman, b Jacob Brown (M J).
Brown Wm J, vice-pres The Indpls Stove Co, h 499 N Delaware.
Brown Wm L, grocer, 125 Lynn av (W I), h same.
Brown Wm M, carp, h 114 Pleasant.
Brown Wm P, h 685 N Capitol av.
Brown Wm R, supt Brown-Ketcham Iron Works, h 859 N Penn.
Brown Wm S, b 702 E 9th.
Brown Wm T, car rep, b 5 S Station (B).
Brown Wm T, clk, b Stubbins Hotel.
BROWN WM T, Lawyer, 216-218 Indiana Trust Bldg, Tel 1208; h 291 Park av.
Brown Winfield S, carp, h 51 Oriental.
Brown Winfield S, cigarmkr, b 330 N California.
Brown W Dayton, clk R M S, h 225 N Linden.
Brown Zachariah, lab, h 12 Barrows.
Brown Zachariah A, carp, r 139½ E Washington.
Brown & Jones (James E Brown, W Franklin Jones), livery, 278 E Washington.
Brown & Smith (Rev Clark Brown, Wm J Smith), pubs West Side Herald, 291 River av (W I).

EAT
QUAKER BREAD
ASK YOUR GROCER FOR IT.
THE HITZ BAKING CO.

BICYCLES $5 DOWN, $5 MO. Best Wheels. Best Terms. WHEELMEN'S CO. 31 W. OHIO ST. LONG DISTANCE TEL. 1865.

J. H. TECKENBROCK | Grilles, Fretwork and Wood Carpets
94 EAST SOUTH STREET.

FIDELITY MUTUAL LIFE PHILADELPHIA, PA. A. H. COLLINS { General Agent, 52-53 Baldwin Block.

Edwardsport Coal & Mining Co. Rooms 42 and 43 When Building.

ESTABLISHED 1876. TELEPHONE 168.
CHESTER BRADFORD,
SOLICITOR OF PATENTS,
AND COUNSEL IN PATENT CAUSES.
(See adv. page 6.)
Office:—Rooms 14 and 16 Hubbard Block, S.W. Cor. Washington and Meridian Streets, INDIANAPOLIS, INDIANA.

Browne Joseph J, bkkpr Evans Linseed Oil Works, h 43 West Drive (W P).
Brownell Charles C, feed, 148 Blake, h 451 W New York.
Brownell Walter H, bkkpr, h 121 St Mary.
Brownfield James S, clk, b 312 E North.
Brownfield John, ironwkr, b 285 S Capitol av.
Browning Belle, h 121 Agnes.
Browning Blanche, h 27 N East.
Browning Cyrene T (wid Robert), r 448 N Meridian.
Browning Edgar N, lab, h 25 Maria.
Browning Eli W, trav agt, h 294 Union.
BROWNING ELIZA G, Librarian and Sec Indianapolis Public Library, Tel 202; b 605 N Capitol av.
Browning Elizabeth A (wid John A), b 216 W McCarty.
Browning Frank, trav agt A Kiefer Drug Co, h 299 N Alabama.
Browning Harry S, fireman, h s s Bloyd av 2 e of Morris (B).
Browning Henry L, sec C B Cones & Son Mnfg Co, h 605 N Capitol av.
Browning John W, condr, h 80 W St Clair.
Browning Mary A (wid Woodvill), b 605 N Capitol av.
Browning Mary S, housekpr Wyandot blk, r 38 same.
Browning Nannie, housekpr 327 Jefferson av.
Browning Reson, lab, h 136 Church.
Browning Robert C (Browning & Son), h n e cor Washington and Central avs (I).
Browning Thomas, b 135 Tacoma av.
Browning Thomas C, bkkpr Govt B and L Inst, h 82 E Vermont.
Browning Wm J, phys, 19 W Ohio, b 605 N Capitol av.
BROWNING & SON (Robert C Browning), Druggists, 15 W Washington, Tel 823.
Brownlee Ray (Daglish & Brownlee), b 137 Woodlawn av.
Brownlee Rolla A, driver, h 36 Union.
Brownlee Thomas, carp, h 137 Woodlawn av.

Hay & Willits Mfg Co.
76 N. PENNSYLVANIA ST.,
MAKERS
Outing BICYCLES
PHONE 598.

Broyles Frances E (wid Moses), h 258 Alvord.
Broyles George, lab, b 199 S Capitol av.
Broyles George W, lab, b 9 Henry.
Broyles Joseph H, clk County Recorder, h 412 Blake.
Broz Frank, gilder, b 431 Madison av.
Broz Joseph, framemkr, b 431 Madison av.
Broz Mary (wid Frank), h 431 Madison av.
Brubaker Arthur, student, b 368 N New Jersey.
Brubaker A Grant S, phys, b 527 College av.
Brubaker A S (Brubaker & Ayres), h 527 College av.
BRUBAKER SAMUEL H, Architect, 37½ E Washington, h 672 Park av. (See adv in classified Architects.)
BRUBAKER & AYRES (A S Brubaker, A M, M D, A S Ayres, M D), Physicians and Surgeons, 1-5 Fair Blk, opp Union Station.
Bruce Alexander, b 598 Virginia av.
Bruce Andrew J, h 224 Michigan (H).
Bruce Augusta G (wid James A), b 564 Broadway.
Bruce Bella, teacher Blind Institute.
Bruce Charles L, student, b 700 College av.
Bruce Charles M, lab, h 411 S State av.
Bruce David K, h 411 S State av.
Bruce Ella F, matron Indiana Reformatory.
Bruce Frank A, shadecutter, h 414 N California.
Bruce George Q, student, b 700 College av.
Bruce George W, claim agt, h 73 Woodlawn av.
Bruce Green, lab, h 63 Maxwell.
Bruce Ida B, dressmkr, 173 Hadley av (W I), h same.
BRUCE JAMES P, Baker and Confectioner, 598-600 Virginia av, h same. (See adv in classified Bakers.)
Bruce James W, mach, h 924 Gent (M P).
Bruce John W, h 701 Ash.
Bruce Joseph G, driver Adams Ex Co, h 122 Woodlawn av.
Bruce Louis G, lab, h 63 Maxwell.
Bruce Margaret (wid James A), h 700 College av.
Bruce Melissa H (wid Isaac N), h 15 Centennial (H).
Bruce Robert, clk, b 73 Woodlawn av.
Bruce Robert, mach, h s s Bloyd av 1 e of Morris (B).
Bruce Thomas, lab, h rear 68 S State av.
Bruce Thomas, mach, b s s Bloyd av 1 e of Morris (B).
Bruce Wallace, baker, h 19 Iowa.
Bruce Wilbert A, plastr, b 25 Elm.
Bruce Wm A, civil engr Indpls Water Co, h 701 Ash.
Bruce Wm F, porter, h 132 Spann av.
Bruce Wm J, baker, h 173 Hadley av (W I).
Bruck John, brewer, h 26 Deloss.
Brucker Victor J Rev, asst rector St John's Catholic Church, h 76 W Georgia.
Bruckman Wm, motorman, b 770 W Washington.
Bruckmann George W, lab, h w s Line 1 s of Grand av (I).
Bruder Charles A, painter, h 198 W Merrill.
Bruder Ignatius, huckster, b 44 Athon.
Bruder Jacob, huckster, h 127 Elizabeth.
Brueckner Frederick C, brewer, h 488 S New Jersey.
Brueckner Mary (wid Robert), h 25 Davis.

SUPERIOR BITUMINOUS COAL For Steam and Domestic . . Purposes . .

ROOFING MATERIAL C. ZIMMERMAN & SONS, SLATE AND GRAVEL ROOFERS, 19 SOUTH EAST STREET.

DRIVEN WELLS And Second Water Wells and Pumps of all kinds at CHARLES KRAUSS', 42 S. PENN. ST., TEL. 465. REPAIRING NEATLY DONE.

Bruenhoefer Christopher, bricklayer, b 199 Lincoln la.
Bruenhoefer Sophia (wid Christopher), h 199 Lincoln la.
Bruening Henry, carp, b 415 S Delaware.
Bruening John F, h 415 S Delaware.
Bruer John, lab, h e s Colorado av 1 n of Ohio.
Bruggner Blasius, finisher, b 1018 S Meridian.
Bruggner John, lab, b 1018 S Meridian.
Bruggner Joseph, varnisher, h 1018 S Meridian.
Bruhm August D, porter, b 96 Hendricks.
Bruhm Mary A (wid August), h 96 Hendricks.
Bruhn Wm C, lab, h 6 Iowa.
Brumbaugh David E, barber, r 69 E Washington.
Brume David L, switchman, h 50 N Belmont av (H).
Brumfield Carl, lab Deaf and Dumb Inst.
Brumfield Elizabeth J, b 12 Hiawatha.
Brumfield Martha (wid Samuel H), dressmkr, 266 Indiana av, h same.
Brumfield Perry W, carp, h 497 N California.
Brumit Robert, carp, h 24 S Rural.
Brumit Wm, carp, h 79 Cornell av.
Brumley, see also Bromley.
Brumley Nancy C (wid John A), h 140 Elm.
Brumley Wm F, lab, b 140 Elm.
Brummell Anna L, dressmkr, 53 Fayette, h same.
Brummell Edward, barber, b 238 S Reisner (W I).
Brummell Robert D, barber Union Stock Yards (W I), h 238 S Reisner (W I).
Brummer Robert, finisher, b 356 S New Jersey.
Brundage Edgar, clk, h 225 English av.
Brundage John E, opr W U Tel Co, h 23 McKim av.
Brundage Samuel M, clk When Clothing Store, h 1226 N Penn.
Brundy Mattie E, r 565 S Meridian.
Brune August, molder, h 66 Fayette.
Brunehler Charles, filer, h 174 Church.
Brunell August, driver, h 128 N Pine.
Bruner Abraham, driver, b 46 Torbet.
Bruner Alphonse, stonecutter, h 1323 N Alabama.
Bruner Anderson, sec The Diamond Steam Laundry and Toilet Supply Co, b 399 N New Jersey.
Bruner Augustus, pres The Diamond Steam Laundry and Toilet Supply Co, h 399 N New Jersey.
Bruner Blanche E, clk, b 64 Ludlow av.
Bruner Charles A, contr, h 43 Park av.
Bruner Elias D, carp, h 64 Ludlow av.
Bruner Harry H, brakeman, r 19, 113 S Illinois.
Bruner Henry E, baker, 94 W 7th, h same.
Bruner Henry L, prof Butler College, b same.
Bruner Jacob M, foreman C C C & St L Ry, h 111 Oak.
Bruner Orlando, clk, b 399 N New Jersey.
Bruner Thomas R, lab, h 313 N East.
Bruning Carl, harnessmkr, h 558 Muskingum al.
Bruning Mary H (wid J Frederick), h 439 S Meridian.
Brunnemer George C, city fireman, h 59 Rockwood.
Brunner Albert S, baker, b 14 Ketcham.
Brunner Bertha, h 173 W Court.
Brunner Frederick, foreman, h 38 Smithson.

Richardson & McCrea, REPRESENTING BEST KNOWN FIRE INSURANCE COMPANIES. Fidelity and Casualty Insurance Company of New York Represented. Telephone 182. 79 East Market St.

Brunner John J, clk, b 14 Ketcham.
Brunner Samuel G, mach, h 85 Yeiser.
Brunner Wm (Reinhardt & Brunner), h 188 W Court.
Brunning Charles E, phys, 101 Coburn, h same.
Brunning Charles J, pump cleaner, b 101 Coburn.
Brunning George, b 101 Coburn.
Bruns Charles, driver, r 224 S Delaware.
Bruns Charles H, bricklayer, h 25 Yeiser.
Bruns Frederick D, lab, h 118 Downey.
Brunsma John H, foreman, h 24 Auburn av.
Brunson, see also Bronson.
Brunson Benjamin R, boxmkr, b 1528 N Meridian.
Brunson Charles M, b 1528 N Meridian.
Brunson George R, live stock dealer, Union Stock Yards, h 472 Broadway.
Brunson Henry C (H C Brunson & Co), h 1528 N Meridian.
Brunson H C & Co (Henry C Brunson), box mnfrs, s e cor St Clair and canal.
BRUNSWICK-BALKE-COLLENDER CO THE, Emile Lang and Frank S Buttweiler Agts, 138-140 S Illinois.
Brunswick Maurice (Brunswick & Kahn), b 128 N East.
Brunswick & Kahn (Maurice Brunswick, Eli Kahn), clothing, 3 E Washington.
Brunton Frances M (wid Parker S), prin Public School No 4, b 489 Broadway.
Brush George E, clk When Clothing Store, h 1500 N Senate av.
Brush John T (Owen Bros & Co), h s s E Washington 2 e of Belt R R.
Bruton Edward, molder, h 221 Hadley av (W I).
Bryan, see also Brian and O'Brien.
Bryan Albert, student, b 748 N Illinois.
BRYAN ALMA L MRS, Teacher of Stenography and Typewriting; Individual Instruction; 135 E Pratt, h same.
Bryan Annie E, h 94 W 1st.
Bryan Bertha M, teacher Public School No 28, b 616 Virginia av.
Bryan Charles O, clk Dean Bros Steam Pump Works, b 1369 N Capitol av.

The Williams Typewriter Elegant Work, Visible Writing, Easy Operation, High Speed. S. H. EAST, State Agent, 55 Thorpe Block, 87 E. Market St.

If You are not Satisfied with Your Laundry Work Give Us a Trial. ERTEL STEAM LAUNDRY 26 and 28 N. Senate Avenue. Telephone 19.

ELLIS & HELFENBERGER Manufacturers of IRON and WIRE FENCES 162-170 S. SENATE AVE. TEL. 358.

THE HOGAN TRANSFER AND STORAGE COMP'Y
Household Goods and Pianos Moved—Packed—Stored...... Baggage and Package Express Machinery and Safes a Specialty Cor. Washington and Illinois Sts. TELEPHONE No. 675.

Hose, Belting, Packing, Clothing, Druggists' Sundries, Bicycle Tires, Cotton Hose, Etc. New York Belting & Packing Co., L't'd.

HIGHEST SECURITY
LOWEST COST OF INSURANCE.
The Provident Life and Trust Co.
Of Philadelphia.
D. W. EDWARDS, Gen. Agent,
508 Indiana Trust Building.

Bryan David C, real est, h 18 W North.
Bryan Dennis (D Bryan & Sons), h 990 S Meridian.
Bryan Dennis F (D Bryan & Sons), b 990 S Meridian.
Bryan D & Sons (Dennis, Dennis F, Edward and Patrick H), whol meats, Indpls Abattoir.
Bryan Edward (D Bryan & Sons), b 990 S Meridian.
Bryan Edward, b 432 N East.
Bryan Elmer B, prof Butler College, h 779 N New Jersey.
Bryan Felix A, h 185 N Alabama.
Bryan Franklin A, supt Kingan & Co (ltd), h 1104 N Senate av.
Bryan Harry, clk Union Line, b 166 E Michigan.
Bryan Harvey A, lab, h 14 Minerva.
BRYAN JAMES W, Druggist, n e cor Illinois and Jackson Pl, h 748 N Illinois.
Bryan John, molder, h 26 Nordyke av (W I).
Bryan John A, clk R M S, b Circle Park Hotel.
Bryan John M, druggist, h 630 N Capitol av.
Bryan John S, barber, h 251 N West.
Bryan John T, watchman, h 1369 N Capitol av.
Bryan Lewis, helper, h 119 River av (W I).
Bryan Louis, lab, h 13 Sharpe.
Bryan Louisa (wid Wiley), b 390 N California.
Bryan Martha (wid Joseph T), h 18 Villa av.
Bryan Maud L, teacher, b 18 W North.
Bryan Patrick H (D Bryan & Sons), b 990 S Meridian.
Bryan Philip L, butcher, h 134 Bright.
Bryan Rachel, h 101 Douglass.
Bryan Rebecca J (wid Joseph), h 75 Wilson.
Bryan Samuel, butcher, b 43 S West.
Bryan Solon L, lab, h 616 Virginia av.
Bryan Thomas J, lab, b 134 Bright.
Bryan Thomas N, phys, 346 E South, h same.

Julius C. Walk & Son,
Jewelers
Indianapolis.
12 EAST WASHINGTON ST.

Bryan Will E, clk C C C & St L Ry, h 18 Villa av.
Bryant Amanda (wid David), h 58 Minerva.
Bryant Benjamin, lab, h 123 E McCarty.
BRYANT'S BUSINESS COLLEGE, Consolidated Indianapolis Business University, When Bldg, N Penn, Tel 499; E J Heeb Propr. (See front cover, right bottom lines and p 4.)
Bryant Charles R, hostler, h 447 E Ohio.
Bryant David C, photog, h 1306 N Penn.
Bryant Edwin D, clk City Comptroller, h 126 W Michigan.
Bryant Emanuel, lab, h 1224 Northwestern av (N I).
Bryant Frank L, jeweler, 89 Mass av, h 176½ N Alabama.
Bryant Frank U, lab, h 415 N East.
Bryant Frances V, clk, b w s Euclid av 1 n of Washington.
Bryant Harry, switchman, h 995 W Vermont.
Bryant John W, reporter The Bradstreet Co, b 405 N Illinois.
Bryant Joseph, lab, b 58 Minerva.
Bryant Kate, photog, 88 S Illinois, h 1306 N Penn.
Bryant Laura (wid Lewis), h 160 Howard.
Bryant Mary A (wid Aaron), h 128 Anderson.
Bryant Milus J, propr Roosevelt House, 80 E Ohio, h same.
Bryant Nellie, h 289 E Court.
Bryant Rachel, h 101 Douglass.
Bryant Richard, engr, h 415 S Delaware.
Bryant Rose, opr Cent U Tel Co, b 58 Minerva.
Bryant Thomas M, lab, h rear 165 Minerva.
Bryant Wm, lab, b 128 Anderson.
Bryant Wm E, carp, h w s Euclid av 1 n of Washington.
Bryant Wm H, lab, b 23 Athon.
Bryant Wm H, plastr, h 224½ W Washington.
Bryant Wm L, woodwkr, b 186 W Merrill.
Bryant Willis, clk The Webb-Jameson Co, h 18 Bismarck.
BRYANT & STRATTON BUSINESS COLLEGE, Consolidated Indianapolis Business University, When Bldg, N Penn, Tel 499; E J Heeb Propr. (See front cover, right bottom lines and p 4.)
Bryce George H, propr Commercial Club Restaurant, treas Brown Straw Binder Co and mngr Peter F Bryce, h 285 E South.
Bryce John K, driver, h 110 Yeiser.
Bryce Patrick, lab, b 107 W South.
BRYCE PETER F, Baker, 14-16 E South, Tel 270; Res Chicago, Ill.
Bryce Robert J, driver, h 31 N Olive.
Brydon Reuben S, lab, b 103 Geisendorff.
Bryles George, lab, b 9 Henry.
Bryson Rachel A, phys, 431 Mass av, h same.
Bryson Robert H, mngr Fleischmann & Co, h 1279 N Meridian.
Buch Henry, trav agt, h 717 E Ohio.
Buch Nelson C, foreman, h 906 S Meridian.
BUCHANAN ALBERT E, Dentist, 32-33 When Bldg, b 922 N Delaware.
Buchanan Andrew J, mach hd, h 64 Hoyt av.
Buchanan Anna C W (wid James), h 502 Ash.

THE CENTRAL RUBBER & SUPPLY CO. PHONE 922. 79 S. ILLINOIS ST., INDIANAPOLIS, IND.

OTTO GAS ENGINES | BUILDERS' EXCHANGE S. W. Cor. Ohio and Penn. Telephone 585.

Becker & Son Charles Becker Jacob Becker Jr. Merchant Tailors. 21 N. Penn. St. Tel. 934

SALISBURY & STANLEY OFFICE, BANK FIXTURES, ... AND
... and Builders. Repair ... al kinds done on short notice. 177 Clinton St. Indianapolis, Ind. Telephone 99

Buchanan Annie, police matron, h 344 S Olive.
Buchanan Benjamin, hostler, r 475 Superior.
Buchanan Benjamin F, lab, h 310 Fayette.
Buchanan Charles E, b 64 Hoyt av.
Buchanan Charles E, brakeman, h e s Gale 6 n of Glen Drive (B).
Buchanan Charles E, cook, h 552 E Market.
Buchanan Charles J (Flanner & Buchanan), h 922 N Delaware.
Buchanan Edward A, dentist, b 952 N Delaware.
Buchanan Eli, policeman (W I), h 53 Sheffield av (W I).
Buchanan Elizabeth S (wid Royal D), h 349 N New Jersey.
Buchanan Fletcher W, clk, b 349 N New Jersey.
Buchanan Fred H, mach, r 174 S Capitol av.
Buchanan Frederick N, flagman, b 22 S State av.
Buchanan George H, lab, h 27 Wilcox.
Buchanan George W, condr, r 4 S Station (B).
Buchanan Gertrude J, stenog, b 64 Hoyt av.
Buchanan Harry S, paperhgr, h 169 W Ohio.
Buchanan Howard W, weigher, h 29 Wilcox.
Buchanan James, cook, r 52½ Indiana av.
BUCHANAN JAMES A, Special Agt Aetna Life Insurance Co of Hartford, Conn, 214 Lemcke Bldg, Tel 1517; h 95 Middle Drive (W P).
Buchanan James M, engr Indiana Reformatory, h 210 Walcott.
Buchanan John C, millwright, h 530 Broadway.
Buchanan Joseph F, insp, h 631 E Vermont.
Buchanan Joseph W, wagonmkr, 302 E Washington, h 128 Fletcher av.
Buchanan Mary (wid John), b 530 Broadway.
Buchanan Melvin R, clk, b 64 Hoyt av.
Buchanan Nancy (wid Andrew A), h 190 Woodlawn av.
Buchanan Nancy A (wid Ezra), h 42 Tecumseh.
Buchanan Orrie E, clk F M Hay, b 64 Hoyt av.
Buchanan Richard T, reporter The Sun, r 355 N Illinois.
Buchanan Sarah J (wid Oliver H), h 169 W Ohio.
Buchanan Warren, lab, b 552 E Market.
Buchanan Wallace W, mailing clerk P O, b 42 Tecumseh.
Buchanan Wm T, barber, 1 Michigan (H), h 29 Wilcox.
Buchanan Wm W, clk, h 876 N Delaware.
Buchel Otto G, bkkpr, b 14 Bedford av.
Bucher August, brewer, b 40 Nebraska.
Buchhorn Albert W, b 114 S Noble.
Buchhorn Christian, b 47 Buchanan.
Buchhorn Edward H, carver, b 114 S Noble.
Buchhorn Frederick W, driver, h 199 N Pine.
Buchhorn Frederick W jr, driver, h 843 E Michigan.
Buchhorn John C, mach, b 114 S Noble.
Buchhorn Sophie L (wid Christian), h 114 S Noble.
Buchhorn Walter, clk, b 199 N Pine.
Buchmeier Michael, tailor, h 109 N State av.
Buchner Augustus J, plumber, 62 Virginia av, h 267 Prospect.

Henry H. Fay,
40½ E. WASHINGTON ST.,
AGENT FOR
Insurance Co. of North America,
Pennsylvania Fire Ins. Co.

Buchner Mamie, bkkpr, b 267 Prospect.
Butchtel S Ellsworth, clk The Indpls Millinery Co, b Enterprise Hotel.
Buchter Mary (wid Theodore), h 506 W Addison (N I).
Buck Almira F (wid Thomas H), h 131½ E Washington.
Buck Cassius C, carp, h e s Bond 3 n of Chicago (N I).
Buck Cora A (wid Adolphus), b 86 Park av.
Buck George, bartndr, b 129 S Noble.
Buck Grant, driver, h 391 N West.
Buck Hiram F, painter, b 63 Yandes.
Buck Jesse D, axle setter, h 56 Sinker.
Buck Jesse T, painter, h 170 E Michigan.
Buck John P, h 550 W Francis (N I).
Buck John W, lumber, h 494 College av.
Buck Louie, teacher Public School No 41, b 550 W Francis (N I).
Buck Minnie C, stenog John S Spann & Co, b 33 College av.
Buck M Elizabeth (wid John A), h 227 E Court.
Buck Rebecca E (wid Philip), h 33 College av.
Buck Robert A, carp, h 542 W McLene (N I).
Buck Sander J H, h 133 E St Joseph.
Buck Stephen R, mailing clerk P O, h 340 Cornell av.
Buck Sylvester T, confr, 60 Indiana av, h same.
Buck Wm F, clk, b 133 E St Joseph.
Buckdall Wm, lab, h 632 Wells (N I).
Bucker Henry, horseshoer, 18 Cherry, h 486 N East.
Buckingham Edward D, ins agt, h 57 Catharine.
Buckingham Sarah (wid Thomas), b 219 W Ohio.
Buckler Elizabeth A (wid Greene B), h 284 River av (W I).
Buckler Frank P, lab, b 284 River av (W I).
Buckles James S, lab, h 20 Roanoke.
Buckley Anne, nurse, r 84 E New York.
Buckley Edward E, motorman, h 362 Fulton.
Buckley Hannah (wid John), h 32 Lord.
Buckley James J, clk, b 32 Lord.

MAYHEW'S
SPECTACLES
THE BEST IN USE
SOLD ONLY AT 13 N. MERIDIAN ST.

LUMBER Sash and Doors
BALKE & KRAUSS CO.,
Corner Market and Missouri Sts.

Friedgen Has the BEST PATENT LEATHER SHOES AT LOWEST PRICES. 19 North Pennsylvania St.

SAMUEL LAING: HOT AIR FURNACES 72 AND 74 EAST COURT STREET.

M. B. WILSON, Pres. W. F. CHURCHMAN, Cash.
The Capital National Bank,
INDIANAPOLIS, IND.
Banking business in all its branches. Bonds and Foreign Exchange bought and sold. Interest paid on time deposits. Checks and drafts on all Indiana and Illinois points handled at lowest rates.
No. 28 South Meridian Street, Cor. Pearl.

Buckley Jay J, mach, b 90 S Wheeler (B).
Buckley Jeremiah, b 259 River av (W I).
Buckley John M, foreman, h 90 S Wheeler (B).
Buckley Mary E, teacher Public School No 20, b 32 Lord.
Buckley Nellie J, laundress, b 165 Meek.
Buckley Patrick, lab, h 96 Sharpe av (W).
Buckley Patrick J, lab, h 237 Huron.
Buckner Alexander, barber, 206 W Washington, h same.
Buckner Aylett, lab, h 51 Sheffield (W I).
Buckner Daniel, porter, r 37½ Virginia av.
Buckner Edwin, polisher, b 51 Sheffield (W I).
Buckner Frank, waiter, r 38½ S Illinois.
Buckner George, coachman 410 Park av.
Buckner George, lab, r 323 N California.
Buckner George H, lab, h 301 N California.
Buckner Horace, polisher, h 46 Sheffield (W I).
Buckner Isaac B, lab, h 149 Patterson.
Buckner James, A, carp, h 84 Dougherty.
Buckner John, lab, h 217½ Indiana av.
Buckner John J, porter, r 35½ Kentucky av.
Buckner Mary, cook, h rear 25 Center.
Buckner Nathaniel, waiter, r 37½ Virginia av.
Buckner Robert, cupolatndr, h 16 Mill.
Buckner Simeon, lab, r 422 Superior.
Bucksot Charles A, truckman, h 140 Laurel.
Bucksot George F, molder, h 125 Shelby.
Bucksot Henry F, carp, h 23 Columbia av.
Bucksot Sina (wid Frederick), h 17 Hamilton av.
Bucksot Walter, sawmkr, b 23 Columbia av.
Bucksot Wm, molder, b 125 Shelby.
Bucy Carl E, ironwkr, b 144 Columbia av.
Bucy Lydia P (wid Hartwell), h 144 Columbia av.
Budd David S (J R Budd & Co), b 364 Park av.
Budd Frank, locksmith, 321 Clifford av, h same.
Budd George W, clk, h 541 Central av.
Budd Jacob E, trav agt, b 449 S Capitol av.
Budd John R (J R Budd & Co), h 364 Park av.
Budd Joseph E, b 45 S Capitol av.

Insure Against Accidents
WITH
TUTTLE & SEGUIN,
Agents for
Fidelity and Casualty Co., of New York.
$10,000 for $25. $5,000 for $12.50.
TEL. 1168. 28 E. MARKET ST.

Budd J R & Co (John R and David S Budd), poultry, 283 W Washington.
Budd Mary (wid Casper), h 449 S Capitol av.
Budd Wm S, ice, n w cor 6th and canal, h 274 Central av.
Budde Frederick H, car rep, h 122 Spring.
BUDDENBAUM BROS (John A and Frederick), Grocers, 2 Fletcher av.
Buddenbaum Charles H (Buddenbaum & Heller), h 97 Prospect.
Buddenbaum Frederick (Buddenbaum Bros), h 4 Fletcher av.
Buddenbaum Harry E (F J Meyer & Co), b 390 S East.
Buddenbaum John A (Buddenbaum Bros), h 83 S Noble.
Buddenbaum Louis G (Buddenbaum Lumber Co), b 96 N Arsenal av.
BUDDENBAUM LUMBER CO (Wm C and Louis G Buddenbaum), Building Material, Rough and Dressed Lumber, Doors, Sash and Blinds, s e cor New York and Pine, Tel 353.
Buddenbaum Mary C (wid Henry), b 96 N Arsenal av.
Buddenbaum Wm C (Buddenbaum Lumber Co), h 96 N Arsenal av.
BUDDENBAUM & HELLER (Charles H Buddenbaum, Ellsworth H Heller), Grocery and Meat Market; Free Delivery; 327 Prospect.
Budenz Henry J, paying teller The Capital Natl Bank, h 581 Shelby.
Budenz Julia A (wid Henry), b 581 Shelby.
Budenz Louis, tailor, h 229 Union.
Budenz Louis A, clk The Capital Natl Bank, h 51 Highland pl.
Budweitsky Joseph, clothing, 293 E Washington, h same.
Budwig Edwin J, trav agt, h 240 Cornell av.
Buechsenmann Martin, saloon, 288 W 6th, h same.
Buechert Frederick, junk, 212 W McCarty, h same.
Buechert Frederick C, agt, b 212 W McCarty.
Buecker Adolph, lab, b 159 Hoyt av.
Buecker Dora (wid Wm), b 159 Hoyt av.
Buecker John, brass finisher, b 185 W Washington.
Buehler Anna M (wid George), h 20 Downey.
Buehler Eugene, student, b 856 N New Jersey.
Buehler George C, painter, b 26 Buchanan.
Buehler Jacob, supt Indiana Lying-In Hospital, phys, 120 E McCarty, h same.
Buehler John, mach, b 20 Downey.
Buehler John, painter, h 329 Clifford av.
Buehler John, supt The H Lieber Co, h 633 S Meridian.
Buehler John H, mach, b 329 Clifford av.
Buehler Josephine (wid John), h 32 Wyoming.
Buehler Maximilian, trav agt The H Lieber Co, h 856 N New Jersey.
Buehler Rudolph, carp, h 12 Allfree av.
Buehrig Rebecca (wid Henry E), b n e cor 8th and Lennox.
Buehrig Wm T, h 768 N Capitol av.
Buell Caroline Y (wid Chester H), h 17 Omer.
Buell Jared R, b 392 S Delaware.
Buell Wm H, b 17 Omer.
Buenamann Herman W, tailor, h 468 S Missouri.
Buennagel Charles W, sawyer, b 70 Sanders.

WEDDING CAKE BOXES · SULLIVAN & MAHAN 41 W. Pearl St.

DIAMOND WALL PLASTER { Telephone 1410 BUILDERS' EXCHANGE.

Best Work. Prompt Delivery. } THE HOME LAUNDRY 197 S. ILLINOIS ST. TEL 1769. { Collars and Cuffs our Specialty.

Buennagel Charles W, mason, h 364 S East.
Buennagel Elizabeth (wid Frederick), h 70 Sanders.
Buennagel Frank J, packer, b 174 Duncan.
Buennagel George J, printer, 95½ E South, b 70 Sanders.
Buennagel Jacob (Paetz & Buennagel), h 387 S East.
Buennagel John J, mach hd, b 70 Sanders.
Buennagel Joseph, foreman, h 174 Duncan.
Buenting Gerhard C, tinner Christian Off & Co, h 485½ Stillwell.
Buenting Lueppo D, lawyer, 27½ S Delaware, h 216 Ramsey av.
Buergelin Fred T, blksmith, b 1349 Isabella (N I).
Buergelin Willis E, blksmith, 1364 Northwestern av, h 1349 Isabella (N I).
Buesking, see also Busking.
Buesking Frederick, lab, b 78 N Gillard av.
Buesselberg Christian F, sweeper, h 123 Williams.
Buffington Eugene J, sec American Steel Co, res Anderson, Ind.
Bufkin Samuel, b 408 N Delaware.
BUGBEE IRA B, Dealer in Lumber, Shingles, Doors, Sash, Blinds, Mouldings, Etc, s e cor Lincoln av and L E & W R R, Tel 1186; b 579 College av.
Bugbee Sarah H (wid John), h 434 College av.
Bugbee S Carrol, chief asst Theodore Stein, b 434 College av.
Bugby Parker E, engr, h 103 Cornell av.
Bugg Susan (wid Samuel), h 276 E Court.
Bugg Wm H (Bugg & Mays), h 276 E Court.
Bugg & Mays (Wm H Bugg, Wm C Mays), coal, 294 E Washington.
Bugh Harry, brakeman, r 21 S Station (B).
Buhneing Ernest, vault cleaner, 32 N Delaware, h 87 Meikel.
Buhr Herman F, bartender, h 18 Shelby.
Buhr John H, painter, h 425 Highland av.
Buhrlage Albert J, clk, h e s Western av 4 n of 22d.
BUILDERS' EXCHANGE OF INDIANAPOLIS, George W Stanley Pres, Stanton W Hawkey Vice-Pres, Charles R Balke Sec, Theodore F Smither Treas, Charles A Richart Supt, 35 E Ohio, Tel 535.
Buis Walter, condr, b 1063 N Capitol av.
Bula George E, mngr The Pentecost Herald, b 52 S State av.
Bula Rolla W, phys, 33 W Ohio, h 284 N Senate av.
Buley Nathan, lab, b 21 Alvord.
Bull Fannie N (wid George W), h 234 W New York.
Bull George W, clk T C Potter, r 300 N Penn.
Bull Wm C, trav agt, b 333 Michigan (H).
Bullard Charles, overseer George Merritt & Co, h 93 Blake.
Bullard Emily (wid Charles G), b 117 John.
Bullard John D, carder, b 93 Blake.
Bullen Wm H, lithog, 23 Keith.
Bullett Wm, lab, b 36 Rhode Island.
Bullington Frank L, drugs, n s Washington 1 e of Sherman Drive, b same.
Bullington Harvey H, h n s Washington 1 e of Sherman Drive.
Bullitt Mary R (wid Willitt), b 364 N New Jersey.

FRANK NESSLER. WILL H. ROST.
FRANK NESSLER & CO.
Tailors
56 EAST MARKET ST. (Lemcke Building),
INDIANAPOLIS, IND.

Bullock Burford, r 18 W Michigan.
Bullock Harriet N, teacher Public School No 5, r 18 W Michigan.
Bullock Henry J, millwright, h 18 Dougherty.
Bullock Henry W, lawyer, 95 E Washington, h 53 Keystone av.
Bullock Jesse R, b 448 Blake.
Bullock Onslow L, carp, h 82 Sheldon.
Bulmahn Charles (Hartman & Bulmahn), h 149 Harrison.
Bulmahn Edward C F, blksmith, b 149 Harrison.
Bumb Charles H, produce, E Mkt House, h 92 Nordyke av (W I).
Bumgardner John, herbalist, 108 E Mkt House, h 714 S Chestnut.
Bumgardner John J, wheelwright, b 714 Chestnut.
Bunce Charles D, mach hd, h 66 Warren av (W I).
Bunce James R, mach, h e s Bond 2 n of Chicago (N I).
Bunce John S, lab, h 65 King.
Bunce Thomas b 20 Roe.
Bunce Wm R, mach, h 65½ King.
Bunch Albert N, carp, h 264 Alvord.
Bunch Perry J Rev, h 381 S Olive.
Bundchu, see also Pundchu.
Bundy Albert W, fireman, h 50 Cornell av.
Bundy Benjamin F, carp, h 38 N Olive.
Bundy Charles E, barber, 197 W Washington, h 27 Ingram.
Bundy Charles H (C P Lesh Paper Co), b 22 Sterling.
Bundy Charles V, jeweler, b 38 N Olive.
Bundy Edward, engr, r 209 W South.
Bundy John P, carp, h 121 Ash.
Bundy John R, carp, h 54 Hoyt av.
Bundy Luther, lab, h 195 Bismarck av (H).
Bundy Morris E, engr, h 111 Ash.
Bundy Samuel E, barber, h 37 Harris.
Bundy Simon, bartndr, r 25 Kentucky av.
Bundy Wm, lab, h 1203 Indianapolis av.
Bunger John W, trav agt Clemens Vonnegut, h 416 College av.
Bunger Joseph F, clk Indpls Coffin Co, b 416 College av.

Haueisen & Hartmann
163-169 E. Washington St.
FURNITURE,
Carpets,
Household Goods,
Tin, Granite and China Wares, Oil Cloth and Shades

THE WM. H. BLOCK CO. 7 AND 9 EAST WASHINGTON STREET. DRY GOODS, HOUSE FURNISHINGS AND CROCKERY.

National Insurance Company

FRANK K. SAWYER, Agent

London Guarantee and Accident Co.

JOSEPH GARDNER
TIN, COPPER AND SHEET-IRON WORK
HOT AIR FURNACES

BUNTING GEORGE W,

BUREAU OF ASSESSMENTS,

BURFORD WM B, Lithographer,

...RRELL & CO.

...es Life Insurance Co., of New York

Wm. B. Burford
Manufacturer of
Blank Books,
Printer,
Lithographer,
Correspondence Solicited.
Estimates Furnished.
Over 1000 Varieties of Legal Blanks Kept in Stock.
Office & Salesroom, 21 & 23 West Washington St.
Factory: 17, 19, 21 & 23 West Pearl St.
Stationer.
Photo-Gravures for Catalogues, Portraits, Buildings, Commercial and Artistic Work of Every Description.
Indianapolis, Ind.

London Guarantee and Accident Co. (Ltd.) All forms of Liability Insurance, Workmen's Collective Insurance, Fidelity Bonds and Individual Accident Insurance.
Geo. W. Pangborn, Gen. Agent, 704-706 Lemcke Bldg. Telephone 140.

Prussian National Insurance Company OF STETTIN, GERMANY. ORGANIZED 1845. FRANK K. SAWYER, AGENT 74 East Market Street. Telephone 863.

JOSEPH GARDNER,
TIN, COPPER AND SHEET-IRON WORK AND
HOT AIR FURNACES.
37, 39 & 41 KENTUCKY AVE. Telephone 322.

Bunker Mary E (wid Robert A), b 338 W New York.
Bunnell Anna (wid Wm), h 651 E Market.
Bunnell Catherine A (wid Charles H), b 79 E Vermont.
Bunnell Charles D, lab, h 153 Hillside av.
Bunnell Frederick, clk, b 651 E Market.
Bunnell Julius C, dairy, s e cor Wolf pike and Baltimore av, h same.
Bunte Anna E, h 579 N Senate av.
Buntel Charles, trav agt Charles Mayer & Co, r 473 N Senate av.
Bunten Oscar H, tinner, b 31 Ashland (W I).
Buntin Davis C (Buntin, Shryer & McGannon), b The Denison.
Buntin, Shryer & McGannon (Davis C Buntin, Mark H Shryer, John R McGannon), curbing, 421 Lemcke bldg.
Bunting Charles, engr, b n w cor Michigan and State avs.
BUNTING GEORGE W, Building Inspector, 2 Basement Court House, h 180 N West, Tel 1390.
Bunting George W jr, architect, b 180 N West.
Bunting Wm P, lab, h 7 Grove.
Bunty Simon, lab, b 25½ Kentucky av.
Burbank Henry H, engr, h 148 N Illinois.
Burbank Lizzie L, boarding 148 N Illinois.
Burbridge Benjamin, lab, h 40 Lincoln la.
Burbridge James S, lab, h 426 Clinton.
Burbridge John W, lineman, h 88 Shelby.
Burbridge Wm A, lab, b 9 Center.
Burch Albert L, switchman, h 1083 W New York.
Burch Emmerson, lab, h 342 Yandes.
Burch Hampton J, mach, r 256 S Delaware.
Burch John A, plastr, 200 St Marie, h same.
Burch Oscar, painter, h 400 S West.
Burch Theodore, lab, h 616 W Eugene (N I).
Burch Wm, contr, h 342 Yandes.
Burcham Charles E, coffee roaster, h 183 Hoyt av.
Burcham Frank E, shoemkr, b 95 Hoyt av.
Burcham James H, oils, h 14 Marion (W I).
Burcham Joseph E, shoemkr, 163 Virginia av, h 95 Hoyt av.

J. S. FARRELL & CO.
STEAM AND HOT WATER HEATING FOR STORES, OFFICES, PUBLIC BUILDINGS, PRIVATE RESIDENCES, GREENHOUSES, ETC.
84 North Illinois St. Telephone 382.

Burchett Douglas, fireman, r 219 Fletcher av.
Burchett Lindsey L, engr, h 106 Spann av.
Burck Jacob, lab, h 135 Weghorst.
Burckhardt Louis, phys, 18 E Ohio, h 400 S Alabama.
Burckle George, coffinmkr, h 654 N West.
Burd, see also Bird and Byrd.
Burd Andrew C, fireman, h 126 River av (W I).
Burden Clark, bartndr, r 236 W Wabash.
Burden Wm, waiter, r 20 W Michigan.
Burdett Mary A (wid Ulysses), h 24 S Beville av.
Burdette Wm C, trav agt, h 230 N Liberty.
Burdge Margaret (wid Jonathan), b 112 Blackford.
Burdlow August, lab, h rear 498 S West.
Burdsal Alfred, pres The A Burdsal Co, h 454 N Capitol av.
BURDSAL A CO THE, Alfred Burdsal Pres, Granville C Allen Vice-Pres, Wm H Meier Sec and Treas, Mnfrs Paints and Varnishes, Wholesale Dealers Painters' Supplies, Glass, Etc; Office 34-36 S Meridian, Factory 241-253 S Penn; Tel 709. (See right bottom cor cards.)
Burdsal Huldah H (wid Thomas C), h 545 N Meririan.
Burdsal Olive S, h 545 N Meridian.
BUREAU OF ASSESSMENTS, Wm A Hughes, Chief Clk, Room 12 Basement Court House.
Bureau of Public Printing, Binding and Stationery, 3 State House.
Bureau of Statistics, 33 State House.
Burford Ernest H, collr, b 700 N Meridian.
Burford John T, phys, h 498 N Capitol av.
Burford Miles W, with Wm B Burford, b 700 N Meridian.
Burford Wesley B, b 498 N Capitol av.
BURFORD WM B, Lithographer, Engraver, Printer, Bookbinder, Etc, 21 W Washington, Tel 310; h 700 N Meridian. (See adv opp.)
Burgan, see also Bergan.
Burgan Charles I (J C Burgan & Co), h 312 Spann av.
Burgan Harvey H, lab, h 86 Lexington av.
Burgan James H, tel opr, b 29 N State av.
Burgan John C (J C Burgan & Co), h 1726 N Capitol av.
Burgan J C & Co (John C and Charles I Burgan), wagonmkrs, 114 E Ohio.
Burgan Tranum A, blksmith, h 177½ Indiana av.
Burgat Magdelena (wid Peter), h 22 Dougherty.
Burge Elizabeth (wid Thomas), b rear 111 Minerva.
Burger, see also Berger.
Burger Charles B, clk, h 564 Broadway.
Burges Edward, painter, 325 Davidson, h same.
Burges Elliott E, uphlr, h 215 N Pine.
Burges George S, peddler, b 169 N Noble.
Burges Mary A (wid Cornelius N), boarding 169 N Noble.
Burgess Alvin B, grocer, 252 N Noble, h same.
Burgess Anne J (wid Caleb C), h 1029 N Capitol av.
Burgess Benjamin F, grocer, 143 Newman, h same.
Burgess Clyde, lab, h 289 Kentucky av.
Burgess Everett E, cigarmkr, h 49 Wright.

United States Life Insurance Co., of New York.
E. B. SWIFT, M'g'r. 25 E. Market St.

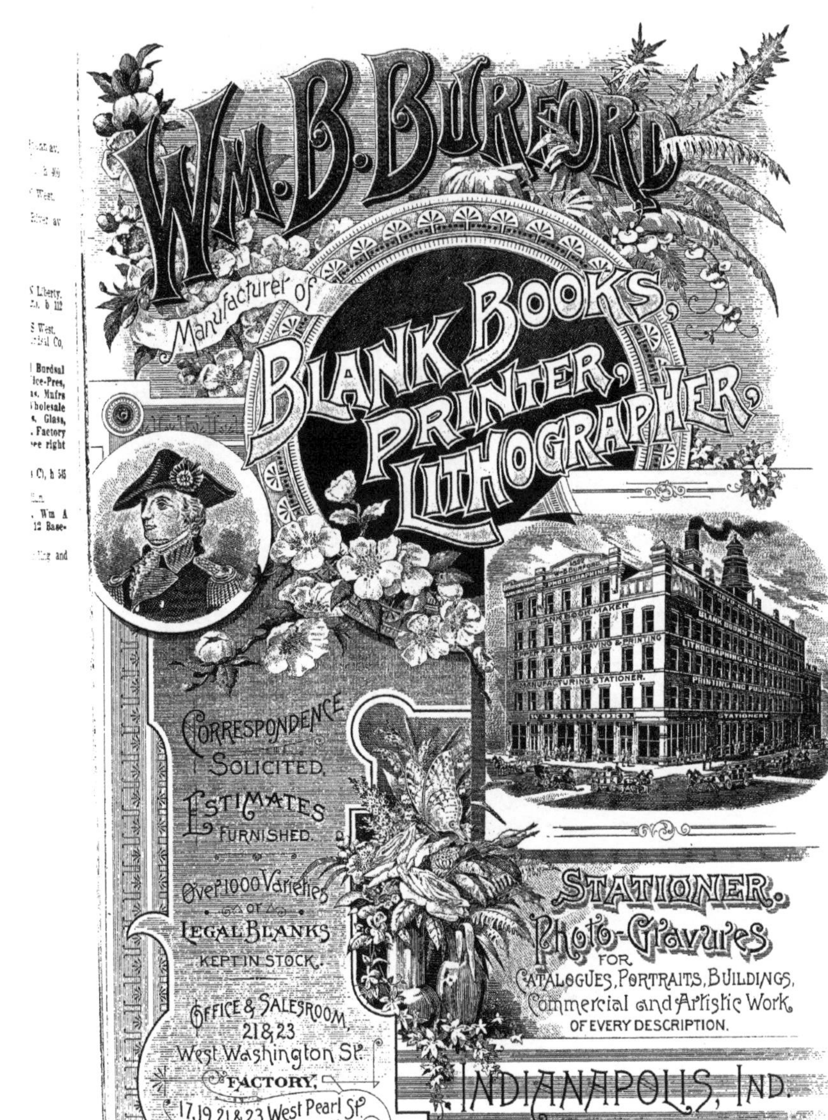

Wm. B. Burford
Manufacturer of
Blank Books,
Printer,
Lithographer,
Correspondence Solicited.
Estimates Furnished.
Over 1000 Varieties of Legal Blanks Kept in Stock.
Office & Salesroom, 21 & 23 West Washington St.
Factory, 17, 19, 21 & 23 West Pearl St.
Stationer.
Photo-Gravures for Catalogues, Portraits, Buildings, Commercial and Artistic Work, of Every Description.
Indianapolis, Ind.
Manufacturing Stationer.

WM. KOTTEMAN } 89 & 91 E. Washington St. Telephone 1742 { RUGS MATTINGS WINDOW SHADES

WILLIAM WIEGEL { MANUFACTURER OF..... } SHOW CASES { 6 W. Louisiana St. Opposite Union Station.

Burgess James C, h 86 Bradshaw.
Burgess Nancy J (wid Otis A), h 366 Bellefontaine.
Burgess Samuel, lab, h 125 Spring.
Burgett Aaron J, carp, h 215 Bismarck av (H).
Burgett Enoch D, boarding 36 S Capitol av.
Burgett Wm O, lab, h 210 Sheffield av (H).
Burgett Louisa H (wid Washington), b 86 Hoyt av.
Burgheim Charles, jeweler, r 353 N Illinois.
Burgheim Henry D, jeweler, 41 W Washington, h 452 S West.
Burgheim Louis, jeweler, h 625 N Meridian.
Burgin Isam S, hostler, r 290 W Pratt.
Burgman, see also Bergmann and Borgmann.
Burgman Frederick, h rear 64 Shelby.
Burgman Frederick H, carp, h 198 Shelby.
Burgman Louis, driver, h 266 Olive.
Burgner John, mason, h 303 E St. Clair.
Burgoyne Frank, notions, 5 Madison av, h same.
Burgoyne Mary L, h e s Butler av 1 s of P C C & St L Ry (I).
Burgoyne Wm, engr, h 171 Spann av.
Burk Anna (wid John), h 429½ S Meridian.
Burk Annis, reporter The Indpls Sentinel, h 159 E Ohio.
Burk Bridget (wid Martin), b 613 W Vermont.
Burk Caroline (wid Louis), h 16 Sharpe.
Burk Charles, cigars, h 145 E Merrill.
Burk Edgar H, paperhanger, h 21 Highland av (H).
Burk Frances (wid John), b 63 Middle Drive (W P).
Burk George, b 23 Russell av.
Burk George, butcher, h 44 Clark.
Burk Henry, condr, h 35 Hudson.
Burk Jacob E, driver, h 33 Coburn.
Burk James M, lab, h 19 Vinton.
Burk Jesse A, lab, r 336½ E Washington.
Burk John, sawmkr, b 429½ S Meridian.
Burk John E, shoes, 102 S Reisner (W I), h 100 same.
Burk John L, lab, h 40 Russell av.
Burk Joseph, lab, b 14 Wilcox.
Burk Joseph F, shoemkr, h 116 N Pine.
Burk Katharine (wid George W), h 159 E Ohio.
Burk Lemuel, live stock, h n s Amanda 1 w of Shade (B).
Burk Lewis C, lab, h 472 Stillwell.
Burk Lizzie, b 176 Douglass.
Burk Luke, driver, r 286 Douglass.
Burk Oliver, porter Insane Hospital.
Burk Patrick, lab, h 36 W Vermont.
Burk Philip, lab, h 51 Maple.
Burk Raymond E, clk Am Press Assn, b 35 Hudson.
Burk Stephen, lab, b 59 Peru av.
Burk Wm, h 59 Peru av.
Burk Wm, watchman, h 138 Fayette.
Burk Wm A, lab, h 21 Vinton.
Burk Wm H, lab, r 336½ E Washington.
Burkam Joseph K, condr, h 1093 W Michigan.
Burke Amanda (wid Ulich G), h 79 E 15th.
Burke Anna, cook The Denison.
Burke Bridget (wid Martin), b 218 Bates.
Burke Christopher, stoker, h 211 Union.
Burke Clemens, bkkpr, 24 W Maryland.
Burke Clement P, lab, b 79 E 15th.
Burke Corinne (wid John), dressmkr, h 61 Cornell av.
Burke Eliza (wid James), h 40 English av.
Burke Frank B, U S district attorney P O bldg, h 356 N Alabama.

THOS. C. DAY & CO.
Financial Agents and Loans.
We have the experience, and claim to be reliable.
Rooms 325 to 330 Lemcke Bldg.

Burke Franklin, lab, b 272 W Maryland.
Burke Frederick M, clk, h 55 Woodruff av.
Burke Henry, h 388 S Delaware.
Burke James, boilermkr, b 267 W Maryland.
Burke James, lab, r 82 Cleaveland blk.
Burke James A, porter R M S, h 186 Fayette.
Burke John, lab, h 206 Bates.
Burke John, lab, h 218 Bates.
Burke John A, fireman, b 207 Meek.
Burke Joseph, brakeman, b 40 English av.
Burke Marcus, lab, b 272 W Maryland.
Burke Mary, dressmkr, 5½ Blackford, h same.
Burke Mary E (wid John J), b 290 E St Clair.
Burke Mary J, teacher Shorthand Training School, b 48 W St Joseph.
Burke Michael J, lab, h 79 Leota.
Burke Nellie L, clk, b 138 Fayette.
Burke Orin T, lab, b 79 E 15th.
Burke Owen, motorman, h 169 Johnson av.
Burke Patrick, lab, h 205 Meek.
Burke Thomas, fireman, b 21 Miley av.
Burke Thomas P, lab, h 366 W Maryland.
Burke Wm, bricklyr, h 786 S East.
Burke Wm H, salesman Louis G Deschler, h 34 Hall pl.
Burke Wm T, caster Am Press Assn, b 211 Union.
Burkett Henry, lab, b 1052 S Meridian.
Burkett Wm, tmstr, h 924 Madison av.
Burkhalter Abraham, brakeman, b 99 Lexington av.
Burkhalter John J, mach, h 33 Smithson.
Burkhard Henry, dynamo tndr, r 86 N Senate av.
Burkhard Jacob, mach, r 118 Blackford.
Burkhard Adam, turner, h 127 E South.
Burkhardt Alexander, mach, h 100 Downey.
Burkhardt Edward E, lab, h 6 Ingram.
Burkhardt Ellsworth, trav agt, h 122 Pleasant.
Burkhardt George W, lab, h 459 Charles.
Burkhardt James C Rev, pastor Olive Branch Christian Church, h e s Ritter av 2 n of University av (I).

EAT
QUAKER BREAD
ASK YOUR GROCER FOR IT.
THE HITZ BAKING CO.

CARPETS CLEANED LIKE NEW. TELEPHONE 818
CAPITAL STEAM CARPET CLEANING WORKS

BENJ. BOOTH PRACTICAL EXPERT ACCOUNTANT. Complicated or disputed accounts investigated and adjusted. Room 18, 82½ E. Wash. St., Ind'p'l's, Ind.

18 and 20 South Meridian Street KERSHNER BROS., Proprs. THE SHERMAN RESTAURANT

ESTABLISHED 1876. TELEPHONE 168.
CHESTER BRADFORD,
SOLICITOR OF PATENTS,
AND COUNSEL IN PATENT CAUSES.
(See adv. page 6.)
Office:—Rooms 14 and 16 Hubbard Block, S.W. Cor. Washington and Meridian Streets, INDIANAPOLIS, INDIANA.

Burkhardt John J, shoemkr, 104 N Noble, h 333 Jefferson av.
Burkhardt Samuel, lab, b 333 Jefferson av.
Burkhardt Thomas, baker, r 323 W Washington.
Burkhart James F, clk, b 248 N Senate av.
Burkhart James H, polisher, b 320 E Louisiana.
Burkhart John, bartndr, b 1 Madison av.
Burkhart Joseph, polisher, h 74 Dugdale.
Burkhart Joseph S, h 567 Union.
Burkhart Julius C, trav agt, h 24 S Pine.
Burkhart Louis, saloon, 1 Madison av, h same.
Burkhart Susan E (wid Andrew J), h 248 N Senate av.
Burkher Louis, attendant Insane Hospital.
Burking Harry, lab, h 245 Orange.
Burkle Charles H, butcher, r 187 E Washington.
Burkley James, porter, r 35½ Kentucky av.
Burkline John, helper, b 12 S Gale (B).
Burkline John C, postmaster Brightwood, h 12 S Gale (B).
Burks Cora, dressmkr, n w cor Michigan and Bismarck av (H), h same.
Burks David C, mach hd, h 282 Howard.
Burks James, trav agt McKee Shoe Co, h 1044 N Alabama.
Burks John R, janitor, b 399 W North.
Burks Silas, lab, h rear 77 W North.
Burks Thomas L, watchman, h 913 N Senate av.
Burleson Dempsy D, plastr, h n s Schofield 1 w of School (B).
Burleson Elmer E, plastr, h w s Morris 4 s of Division (B).
Burleson George S, patternmkr, h 170 King av (H).
Burley Andrew L, porter, h 235 W Michigan.
Burley John, lab, b 235 W Michigan.
Burley Sarah A (wid Conrad), h 83 Howard.
Burlington John W, lab, h 368 Newman.
Burlington Naomi (wid Wm), b 398 Columbia av.
Burnell John H, brakeman, b 4 Walcott.
Burnell Wm E, lab, h 493 W Francis (N I).
Burnet George, lab, b 47 Agnes.

Metal Ceilings and all kinds of Copper, Tin and Sheet Iron work.
O. B. ENSEY,
TELEPHONE 1562.
CORNER 6TH AND ILLINOIS STS.

Burnet Harry B (Burnet & Lewis), h 463 Park av.
BURNET & LEWIS (Harry B Burnet, Thomas R Lewis), Lumber and Mill Work; Office and Yard 553 Dillon, Tel 530.
Burnett Arthur, wireman Sanborn Electric Co, b 71 Kansas.
Burnett Bros (James A and Wm M), grocers, 138 W Michigan (H), h 104 King av (H).
Burnett Caroline (wid Peter), b 169 Minerva.
Burnett Charles, caller, h 40 Warman av (H).
Burnett Charles, lab, b 1075 W Washington.
Burnett Charles E, clk, b 266 S Penn.
Burnett Daniel L, contr, h 288 E Market.
Burnett Dora M, dressmkr, 266 S Penn, h same.
Burnett Edward, lab, h 22 McCauley.
Burnett Frank, driver, h 281 Chapel.
Burnett Frank R, cashr, b 82 E Vermont.
Burnett Frederick, clk, b 266 S Penn.
Burnett George C, plastr, 266 S Penn, h same.
Burnett Henry N, driver, h 538 S Illinois.
Burnett Homer, porter, b 147 Minerva.
Burnett James A (Burnett Bros), b 104 King av (H).
Burnett John A, shoemkr, rear 271 Minerva, h 104 King av (H).
Burnett John W, lab, h 1075 W Washington.
Burnett John W, mach, b 65 Oak.
BURNETT LEE, Propr Park Theater Restaurant, Lunch Room and Bakery; Open all Night, 100 W Washington, r Senate Hotel, Tel 1361.
Burnett Levi M, grocer, 71 Minerva, h same.
Burnett Maria (wid John), h 40 Lincoln la.
Burnett Mary (wid James), b 20 Pleasant av.
Burnett Mary L (wid Levi L), h 77 W Michigan.
Burnett Omer, porter, b 147 Minerva.
Burnett Oren E, shoemkr, h 71 Kansas.
Burnett Ozro H, polisher, b 320 E Louisiana.
Burnett Peter M, cigarmkr, b 20 Pleasant av.
Burnett Samuel C, trav agt Parrott-Taggart Bakery, r 215 N Illinois.
Burnett Seth, plastr, h 105 N Gillard av.
Burnett Thomas, lab, b 22 McCauley.
Burnett Wm M (Burnett Bros), b 104 King av (H).
Burney Michael, lab, b 293 Blake.
Burnham George M, driver, h 76 S Missouri.
Burnham Gilbert L, baggageman, h 90 Clifford av.
Burns Alexander, mach hd, h 140 N Pine.
Burns Anna (wid Dorris), h 83 W Walnut.
Burns Augustine J, uphlr, b 110 Church.
Burns Charles, tmstr, h w s Daisy 1 n of Ream.
Burns Charles E, miller, b 110 Church.
Burns Charles E, watchmkr, b 447 N Senate av.
Burns Charles T, bkkpr, b 204 Douglass.
Burns Chemical Co The (Harvey D Burns, Levi Sutherland), polish mnfrs, 24 S New Jersey.
Burns Christine, dressmkr, 577 W Michigan, h same.
Burns Christopher, lab, h 250 N Liberty.
Burns Cornelius, lab, h 250 Springfield.

TUTEWILER UNDERTAKER, No. 72 WEST MARKET STREET. TELEPHONE 216.

Burns Daniel M, jeweler, b 252 Blake.
Burns Edward R, lab, h 110 Church.
Burns Edwin A, tailor, b 43 S Summit.
Burns Elizabeth (wid Thomas J), dressmkr, 187 Hoyt av, h same.
Burns Emma, h 260 W Washington.
Burns Emma R, housekpr, r 17 N East.
Burns Frank, lab, b 204 Douglass.
Burns Frank, roofer, h 12 Elizabeth.
Burns George, lab, h 232 W Wabash.
Burns George W, cigarmkr, r 8 Indiana av.
Burns Gerrone W, cigarmnfr., 252 Blake.

THE WHEN IS A WORLD BEATER.

THEOD

Harvey A. Burkhart & Sons

492 SOUTH MERIDIAN STREET,

Residence, Three Miles South of City.

DEALERS AND GROWERS OF

TREES AND PLANTS

Also Agents for the HOME NURSERIES

We will keep this spring, a Full Line of Fruit and Ornamental Trees

COR. OF WASHINGTON AND ALABAMA STREETS

IN REAR OF THE MANSUR BLOCK.

Expert Trimmers of Trees and Vines. Large Trees a Specialty. Keep in stock Hydrangea Honeysuckle, Clematis, Etc. Call and See Stock. Sixteen years' experience

Indianapolis, Ind.

BENJ. BOOTH PRACTICAL EXPERT ACCOUNTANT. Complicated or disputed accounts investigated and adjusted. Room 18, 82½ E. Wash. St., Ind'p'l's, Ind.

uth Meridian Street
ER BROS., Proprs.

ESTABLISHED 1876. TELEPHONE 168.
CHESTER BRADFORD,
SOLICITOR OF PATENTS,
AND COUNSEL IN PATENT CAUSES.
(See adv. page 6.)
Office:—Rooms 14 and 16 Hubbard Block, S.W. Cor. Washington and Meridian Streets, INDIANAPOLIS, INDIANA

Burnet Harry B (Burnet & Lewis), h 463 Park av.

BURNET & LEWIS (Harry B Burnet, Thomas R Lewis), Lumber and Mill Work; Office and Yard 553 Dillon, Tel 530.

Burnett Arthur, wireman Sanborn Electric Co, b 71 Kansas.

Burnett Bros (James A and Wm M), grocers, 138 W Michigan (H), h 104 King av (H).

THE SH

Tin and Sheet Iron work.
O. B. ENSEY,
TELEPHONE 1562.
CORNER 6TH AND ILLINOIS STS.

Burns Charles E, miller, b 110 Church.

Burns Charles E, watchmkr, b 447 N Senate av.

Burns Charles T, bkkpr, b 204 Douglass.

Burns Chemical Co The (Harvey D Burns, Levi Sutherland), polish mnfrs, 24 S New Jersey.

Burns Christine, dressmkr, 577 W Michigan, h same.

Burns Christopher, lab, h 250 N Liberty.

Burns Cornelius, lab, h 250 Springfield.

TUTEWILER UNDERTAKER, No. 72 WEST MARKET STREET. TELEPHONE 216.

The Provident Life and Trust Co. Dividends are paid in cash and are not withheld for a long period of years, subject to forfeiture in the event of death or the termination of policy.
D. W. EDWARDS, GENERAL AGENT, 508 INDIANA TRUST BUILDING.

THEODORE F. SMITHER,

Burns Daniel M, jeweler, b 252 Blake.
Burns Edward R, lab, h 110 Church.
Burns Edwin A, tailor, b 43 S Summit.
Burns Elizabeth (wid Thomas J), dressmkr, 187 Hoyt av, h same.
Burns Emma, h 260 W Washington.
Burns Emma R, housekpr, r 17 N East.
Burns Frank, lab, b 204 Douglass.
Burns Frank, roofer, h 12 Elizabeth.
Burns George, lab, h 232 W Wabash.
Burns George W, cigarmkr, r 8 Indiana av.
Burns Gerrone W, cigarmnfr, 252 Blake, saloon, 24 N Delaware, h 252 Blake.
Burns Harrison, lawyer, 42 W Market, r 19 Wyandot blk.
Burns Harry, h 191 W Market.
Burns Harvey, tmstr, h s e cor Yassie and Carlton.
Burns Harvey D (The Burns Chemical Co), h 230 Yandes.
Burns Herman, jeweler, r 8 Indiana av.
Burns Homer, lab, b 385½ E 7th.
Burns Hugh, bartndr, h 89 Geisendorff.
Burns James, molder, h 44 Sheffield (W I).
Burns James (McNelis & Burns), saloon, 263 Hadley av (W I), h same.
Burns James A, polisher, b 110 Church.
Burns James D, brakeman, h 9 Warren av (W I).
Burns Jedidiah W (Indpls Suspender Co), bkkpr The Capital Nat'l Bank, r 74 W Vermont.
Burns John, lab, b 300 W Maryland.
Burns John, lab, r 152 W Washington.
Burns John, shoemkr, b 58 Beaty.
Burns John B, engr, h 1050 W Washington.
Burns John F, blksmith, h 627 Mass av.
Burns Joseph, lab, h 15 Bismarck (H).
Burns Kate, grocer, 184 Fayette, h same.
Burns Louis G, candymkr, b 187 Hoyt av.
Burns Louisa (wid Henry), h 25 Villa av.
Burns Margaret (wid Le Roy), h 54 Dougherty.
Burns Margaret L, milliner, b 180 E North.
Burns Margery (wid Michael), b 1101 N Meridian.
Burns Mary A (wid John V), h 43 S Summit.
Burns Michael, lab, b 250 N Liberty.
Burns Michael J, agt, r 23 Stewart pl.
Burns Michael J, asst foreman street repairs, h 798 W Washington.
Burns Oscar, lab, b 140 N Pine.
Burns Patrick, lab, h 204 Douglass.
Burns Peter, clk, h 184 Fayette.
Burns Peter, lab, h 255 W McCarty.
Burns Robert E, waiter, r 191 W Market.
Burns Robert T, candymkr, b 187 Hoyt av.
Burns Sarah W (wid Wm V), h 46 Henry.
Burns Theodore, driver, b 140 N Pine.
Burns Theresa (wid Edward), h 241 W Maryland.
Burns Wm, brakeman, h 1081 W New York.
Burns Wm, lab, b 337 W Maryland.
Burns Wm, tmstr, b 860 E Washington.
Burns Wm C, lab, b 668 Park av.
Burns Wm F, jeweler and cigar mnfr, 8 Indiana av, h 447 N Senate av.
Burns Wm G, engr, b 182 N State.
Burns Wm L, trav agt The Bowen-Merrill Co, r 16 Wyandot blk.
Burns Wm R, porter, r 18 Yohn blk.
Burns Wm W, messenger Am Ex Co, h 52 Traub av.
Burnside Andrew D, clk Francke & Schindler, h 308 Clifford av.
Burnside Lily L, laundress, h rear 66 E Michigan.
Burr Jesse T, h 7 Wendell av.

THE WHEN IS A WORLD BEATER.

Burr Nathaniel B, h 169 N Senate av.
Burrage Charles R, drugs, 131 Mass av, h same.
Burrell Alcid C, teacher High School, r 156 E Michigan.
Burrell Wm E, lab, h 493 W Francis (N I).
Burris Abram L, lab, h 134 Patterson.
Burris Albert H, mach, h 48 Buchanan.
Burris Albert J, h rear 63 N East.
Burris Alice M (wid Luke), b 961 N New Jersey.
Burris Anna, h 23 Detroit.
Burris Charles, lab, r 374 Muskingum al.
Burris Charles, letter carrier P O, h 141 Agnes.
Burris Charles T, ins agt, b 31 Fletcher av.
Burris Erie A (wid Jacob), b 7 Stoughton av.
Burris Harry C, mach, h 48 Buchanan.
Burris Henry J (Thomas Burris & Son), h 125 E Washington.
Burris John S, painter, h 521 W Addison (N I).
Burris Thomas (Thomas Burris & Son), h 127 Meek.
Burris Thomas & Son (Thomas and Henry J), restaurant, 125 E Washington.
Burris Thompson, lab, h 141 Agnes.
Burris Walter M, driver, h 91 Decatur.
Burris Wm R, lab, b 33 Bloomington.
Burris Wm W, lineman, h 91 Decatur.
Burroughs Catherine (wid James), b 537 Virginia av.
Burroughs Elkanah, b 523 Central av.
Burroughs George F, mngr furnishing dept When Clothing Store, h 1662 N Illinois.
Burroughs John A (Peebles & Burroughs), r 48 The Chalfant.
Burrows Erie A (wid Jacob), b 7 Stoughton av.
Burrows Walter, sawmkr, h 961 N Senate av.
Burrows Wm H, painter, 176½ N Missouri, h same.
Bursott John W, feed, 263 Indiana av, h 362 N California.
Burt Albert, trav agt, h 317 S Alabama.
Burt Alphonso S, h 48 English av.
Burt Gustav, electrician Indpls Dist Tel Co, b 17 S Senate av.

The A. Burdsal Co.
Manufacturers of
STEAMBOAT COLORS
BEST HOUSE PAINTS MADE.
Wholesale and Retail.
34 AND 36 SOUTH MERIDIAN STREET.

AGENT FOR WARREN'S ANCHOR BRAND —ASPHALT ROOFING— OFFICE, 151 WEST MARYLAND ST TEL. 861.

Electric Contractors | We are prepared to do any kind of Electric Contract Work. C. W. MEIKEL. Telephone 466. 96-98 E. New York St.

DALTON & MERRIFIELD { LUMBER South Noble St., near E. Washington

INDIANA ELECTROTYPE CO. : BEST WORK. LOWEST PRICES.
23 WEST PEARL ST., INDIANAPOLIS, IND. JOB WORK. BOOK PLATES. All Orders Promptly Filled. BEST PATENT BASE ON THE MARKET.

KIRKHOFF BROS.,
Sanitary Plumbers
STEAM AND HOT WATER HEATING.
102-104 SOUTH PENNSYLVANIA ST.
TELEPHONE 910.

Burt Harry L, tel opr P C C & St L Ry, h 85 English av.
Burt James C Rev, h 56 Lexington av.
Burt J Francis, pres Brooks Oil Co, h 47 West Drive (W P).
Burtin Louis F, carp, h rear 18 Prospect.
Burting Joseph, tel opr, b 187 N Alabama.
Burton Anna L, teacher Public School No 13, b 285 E South.
Burton Charles F, buyer N Y Store, h 215 Hamilton av.
Burton Charles F, engr, h 18 Hoyt av.
Burton Clark, porter, r 236 W Wabash.
Burton Daniel, cooper, h 129 W New York.
Burton Doc, lab, b rear 608 N West.
Burton Edgar, collr The Bowen-Merrill Co, b 74 W 5th.
Burton Edward C, route agt Am Ex Co, h n s 11th 4 e of College av.
Burton Eliza (wid Thornton), b 955 N New Jersey.
Burton Ellen M (wid Wm W), r 253 Mass av.
Burton Elmer, trav agt, h 494 Bellefontaine.
Burton Frank C, cooper, b 129 W New York.
Burton Frederick, mach, h 45 Arizona.
Burton Frederick C, sawmkr, b 45 Arizona.
Burton George, tmstr, h 16 Sylvan.
Burton George jr, engr, b 16 Sylvan.
Burton George, motorman, b 490 Bellefontaine.
Burton George W, driver, b 111 Sanders.
Burton Isaac, carp, h 490 Bellefontaine.
Burton James M, mnfrs' agt, 1½ E Washington, h 74 W 5th.
Burton James W, clk, h 300 Fletcher av.
Burton John C, oils, h 524 W 22d (N I).
Burton John J, condr, b 1063 N Capitol av.
Burton Joseph E, plastr, h 612 W Eugene (N I).
Burton J Wesley, tmstr, h e s Caroline av 2 n of 17th.
Burton Martin, h 1096 N Capitol av.
Burton Nellie M, dressmkr, b 253 Mass av.
Burton Phoebe, dressmkr, b 253 Mass av.
Burton Sadie, h 208 N Illinois.
Burton Samuel C, baker, h rear 63 Wyoming.

Lime, Lath, Cement,
THE W. G. WASSON CO.
130 INDIANA AVE. TEL. 989.
Sewer Pipe, Flue Linings, Fire Brick, Fire Clay.

Burton Thornton, lab, b e s Caroline av 2 n of 17th.
Burton Wesley, lab, h 503 Jones (N I).
Burton Wm, clk, r 323 W North.
Burton Wm H, cooper, 487 W New York, h 462 same.
Burton Wm I, meats, 158 E 7th, h 494 Bellefontaine.
Burton Zania, lab, h 278 Alvord.
Busald George F, carp, h 211 Minnesota.
Busas August, mach, h 332 Hillside av.
Busby Charles E (Patterson & Busby), h 340 Central av.
Busch, see also Bush.
Busch Benjamin F, gasfitter, h 222 E Merrill.
Busch Charles A, shoemkr, 495 College av, h e s Addison 3 s of Washington (M J).
Busch Christian, shoemkr, s s Washington 17 w of Harris av (M J), h same.
Busch Emma S (wid Charles), h 13½ S Alabama.
Busch George, clk, b 174 W Ohio.
Busch George C, painter, h 1 N Dorman.
Busch Herman, lab, h 29 Weghorst.
Busch Johanna D (wid Jacob), b 233 N Noble.
Busch John A, carp, h 22 Iowa.
Busch Joseph C, foreman Natl Malleable Castings Co, b s s Washington 17 w of Harris av (M J).
Busch Wm C, molder, h 93 Weghorst.
Buscher Edward F, policeman, h 749 N Illinois.
Buscher Henry H, clk, b 282 Virginia av.
Buscher Sophie (wid Henry), r 282 Virginia av.
Buscher Wm, clk, h 177 St Mary.
Busching G Otto, clk Merchants' Natl Bank, b 250 N East.
Buschman Charles L (Lewis Meier & Co), h 1152 N Penn.
Buschman Edward, ins agt, r 289½ Mass av.
Buschman Louis F (Lewis Meier & Co), h 776 N New Jersey.
BUSCHMANN AUGUST, Groceries and Meats, 148-150 College av, Tel 973; h 193 Broadway.
Buschmann August W (Wm Buschman & Co), b 150 Central av.
Buschmann Emma W, h 150 Central av.
Buschmann Ernest F, bartender, b Circle Park Hotel.
Buschmann Ernest H, car rep, h 178 S Linden.
Buschmann George H, clk, b 150 Central av.
Buschmann Harry C, clk, b 150 Central av.
Buschmann Henry H, gilder, b 178 S Linden.
Buschmann Wm F (Wm Buschmann & Co), h 150 Central av.
BUSCHMANN WM & CO (Wm F and August W Buschmann), Dry Goods, Notions, Boots, Shoes, Groceries, Meats, Hardware, Queensware and Bicycles, 192-200 Ft Wayne av, Tel 261.
Buschor Julius, mach, h 1143 E Washington.
Buselmyer John, blksmith, h 115 Meek.
Buser Charles O, grocer, 250 Yandes, h 223 same.
Buser Daniel T, meats, 392 College av, h 394 same.
Buser Jacob, lab, r 19 Russell av.

YOUR HOMES FURNISHED BY W. H. MESSENGER 101 East Washington St. Telephone 491.

BUTLER COLLEGE

DEPARTMENT OF ARTS

UNIVERSITY OF INDIANAPOLIS

Irvington, the site of the College, is an attractive suburb of Indianapolis, four miles east of the center of the city, and connected with it by electric street cars, making quick trips every fifteen minutes. The population of the village consists mainly of those who have been drawn thither by its educational inducements. This gives it a special character of cultivation and good order, while, as a home for students, it is singularly free from the temptations and dangers often surrounding college life.

The College, in its literary and scientific departments, maintains a full corps of instructors, and offers every facility for thorough college work. Instruction in elocution, and regular and systematic training in physical exercises are furnished without extra charge. An excellent preparatory school fits students for college classes. Residence for young ladies is offered in a carefully conducted boarding hall on the college campus, where young ladies only are received. All the buildings are supplied with steam heat and electric lights. Tuition and living expenses low. For catalogue and information, address

SCOT BUTLER, President
IRVINGTON, IND.

McNamara, Koster & Co. Phone 1593. ♦ 212-218 S. PENN. ST. } PATTERN MAKERS

Buser John P, cigarmkr, 142 River av (W I), h same.
Buser Olive, milliner, r 9 Stewart pl.
Buser Wm S, molder, h 123 River av (W I).
Bush, see also Busch.
Bush Ada E, stenog The Gordon-Kurtz Co, b 8 Eden pl.
Bush Annie (wid Jeremiah), h 408 N Pine.
Bush Calvin W, foreman, h 10 S Station (B).
Bush Charles, janitor, b 548 N Missouri.
Bush Dennis B, boilermkr, b 408 N Pine.
Bush Edward T, trav agt, r 334 N Illinois.
Bush Ellen (wid Michael), h 17 S Pine.
Bush Fannie, h 15 Anderson.
Bush Hannah, h 296 N Liberty.
Bush Irvin, lab, h 639 E 8th.
Bush John, lab, h rear 636 Home av.
Bush John, saloon, 172 W Washington, h same.
Bush John H, switchman, h 147 W Morris.
Bush John W, teacher, h e s Commercial av 8 s of Washington av (I).
Bush Lyman F, engr, h 34 S State av.
Bush Michael, engr, b 296 N Liberty.
Bush Morton, hostler, h 15 N New Jersey.
Bush Nelson, h 906 S Meridian.
Bush Rebecca (wid Calvin), h 15 Mill.
Bush Thomas N, trav agt, b 328 W New York.
Bush Wm C, waiter, b 126 Duncan.
Bushnell Paul F, trav agt, h 199 E Morris.
Bushong Charles D, bkkpr, b 47 Fayette.
Bushong Deniza, grocer, 225 W Walnut, h 47 Fayette.
Bushong Frank B, gardener, h s s Shearer pike 1 e of Belt R R (B).
Bushong George L, clk, h 47 Fayette.
Bushong John A Rev, h e s Watts 1 n of Michigan.
Bushong Wm L, draughtsman, h 50 Fayette.
Bushrod Thomas W, barber, h 115 W 6th.
Buskel James H, carp, h 450 Newman.
Buskel Robert G, carp, b w s Bailey 3 s of 30th.
Buskel Wm, h w s Bailey 3 s of 30th.
Buskin Thomas, clk Supervisor C C C & St L Ry, b 6 Henry.
Busking, see also Buesking.
Busking Charles G, lab, b 154 Huron.
Busking Edward, patternmkr, b 144 Huron.
Busking Ellen (wid Wm F), h 144 Huron.
Busking Frank, mach, b 144 Huron.
Busking Henry C, h 154 Huron.
Busking Henry F, foreman Sinker-Davis Co, h 469 Park av.
Busking Wm, carp, h rear 526 S Meridian.
Busking Wm F, lather, b 154 Huron.
Buskirk Edward C, lawyer, h 116 Ruckle.
Buskirk Elizabeth (wid Peter Y), h 38 S Judge Harding (W I).
Buskirk Florence W (wid John), clk U S Pension Agency, b 325 N Noble.
Buskirk Frank, clk, h 37½ W Market.
Buskirk George A, clk Union Trust Co, h 1002 N Capitol av.
Buskirk Horace O, tel opr, r 35 Hendricks blk.
Buskirk Joseph L, condr, h 249 Blake.
Buskirk Roscoe W, tel opr, h 38 S Judge Harding (W I).
Bussell Louisa (wid Erastus T), h 780 N Illinois.
Bussell Wm J, mach opr Indpls Journal, r 11 E New York.
Busselle Elmer T, electrician, b 487 N Illinois.
Busselle Kate (wid Rue), h 487 N Illinois.

Henry H. Fay,
40½ E. WASHINGTON ST.,
FIRE INSURANCE, REAL ESTATE,
LOANS AND RENTAL AGENT.

Busselle Mary A (wid Wm), h 157 Fayette.
Busselle Ruby, trimmer New York Store, b 487 N Illinois.
Busselle Viola F, teacher Public School No 4, b 157 Fayette.
Busselle Wm L, bookbinder, b 157 Fayette.
Bussey Beulah (wid John), b 467 Virginia av.
Bussey Emma (wid Jesse G), h 29 Highland pl.
Bussey Frank, lab, b 67 Malott av.
Bussey John W (Bussey & Deitz), b 29 Highland pl.
Bussey Moses, lab, h 149 Hillside av.
Bussey & Dietz (John W Bussey, Oscar Dietz), meats, 903 N Senate av.
Buswell Agnes (wid John), b 116 Lexington av.
Butcher Daniel A, patrolman, h 219 Blake.
Butcher Edward, lab, b w s Elm av 1 n of Washington av (I).
Butcher Ellen, florist, 84 E Mkt House, h n end Maxwell av (I).
Butcher George L, gardener, h s s Walnut av 2 w of Maple av (I).
Buthe Augustus L, saloon, 171 W Washington, h w s Graceland av 2 n of 26th.
Butler Alexander L, janitor Public Library, h 389 S Delaware.
Butler Andrew, driver, h 191 W 2d.
Butler Andrew jr, lab, b 191 W 2d.
Butler Annie, cook Hotel English.
Butler A Ellsworth, foreman Western Horseman, h 33 Highland pl.
Butler Benjamin F, molder, h 129 Shepard (W I).
Butler Catherine M (wid Daniel K), h 25 School.
Butler Charles A, clk, b 495 E 9th.

BUTLER COLLEGE, A F Armstrong Pres Board of Directors, Albert M Chamberlain Sec Board of Directors, Scot Butler, A M, Pres Faculty and Treas Board of Directors, West End University av (Irvington). See adv opp.)

Butler Cora I (wid Lawrence), b 469 N New Jersey.

SURETY BONDS
American Bonding & Trust Co.
OF BALTIMORE, MD.
Authorized to act as Sole Surety on all Bonds.
Total Resources over $1,000,000.00.
W. E. BARTON & CO., General Agents,
504 Indiana Trust Building.
Long Distance Telephone 1918.

THE FRED DIETZ CO. WOODEN PACKING BOXES MADE TO OR. FACTORY AND WAREHOUSE TRUCKS. 400 Madison Avenue. Telephone 654.

Business World Supplied with Help
GRADUATES ASSISTED TO POSITIONS
10,000 NOW IN GOOD SITUATIONS. TEL. 499. E. J. HEEB, PRES.
Indianapolis BUSINESS UNIVERSITY

NEW YORK FILTER MFG. CO. Filters for Water-Works, Boiler Plants, Laundries, Hotels, Private Residences, Etc. | Henry R. Worthington, 64 S. Pennsylvania St. Long Distance Telephone 284.

UNION CO-OPERATIVE LAUNDRY (COMPOSED OF UNION LAUNDRY GIRLS.) NOS. 3, 40 AND 42 VIRGINIA AVENUE. TELEPHONES INDIANAPOLIS, IND. T. E. SOMERVILLE, MANAGER

HORACE M. HADLEY

Insurance, Real Estate, Loan and Rental Agent

66 EAST MARKET STREET,

Telephone 1540. Basement.

Butler Darwin W, live stock agt C H & D R R Union Stock Yards (W I), h 115 Park av.
Butler Edwin, painter, b 193 Elm.
Butler Ellen (wid Michael), b 534 S Illinois.
Butler Ernest J, distributer, b 41 Vine.
Butler Evelyn M, asst preparatory school Butler College, b w s Downey av 3 s of Washington av (I).
Butler Frank D, huckster, b 33 W Morris.
Butler George W, carp, h 343 Alvord.
Butler Hampton, lab, h 30 N Cruse.
Butler Harry C, plumber, h 77 E Walnut.
Butler Henry M, trav agt, b Grand Hotel.
Butler Houston, lab, b 232 W 5th.
Butler Ida C (wid James), h 210½ S Meridian.
Butler James, lab, b 410 S Capitol av.
Butler James H, lab, h 280 Howard (W I).
Butler Jennie, h 135 Allegheny.
Butler Job, well driver, 171 S Reisner (W I), h same.
Butler John A, mach, h 36 Standard av (W I).
BUTLER JOHN A, Sec The Indiana Trust Co, h 700 N New Jersey.
Butler John H, b 210 Park av.
Butler John H, fireman, h w s McPherson 1 n of English (S).
Butler John H, hostler, h 41 Vine.
Butler John S, student, b w s Downey av 3 s of Washington av (I).
Butler Lulu, clk, b 79 W Morris.
Butler Mahlon D, mngr W U Tel Co, 19 S Meridian, b 159 Christian av.
Butler Mary, h 654 N Alabama.
Butler Mary, b 359 Blake.
Butler Mary (wid Michael), h 410 S Capitol av.
Butler Mary J (wid Joseph), b 120 Ruckle.
Butler Michael F, sawmkr, b 410 S Capitol av.
Butler Nancy L, b 448 College av.
Butler Noble C, clk U S Courts P O bldg, h 210 Park av.
Butler Noble C jr, clk, b 210 Park av.
Butler Oscar, painter, b 193 Elm.
Butler Ovid D (Elliott & Butler), h 67 The Blacherne.

Special Detailed Reports Promptly Furnished by Us.

MERCHANTS' AND MANUFACTURERS' EXCHANGE

J. E. TAKKEN, Manager,

19 Union Building, 73 West Maryland Street.

Butler Randall, driver, h 23 Mill.
Butler Reuben J, h 193 Elm.
Butler Robert, farmer, h w s Earhart 3 s of Prospect.
Butler Robert, lab, h 227 W 3d.
Butler Samuel, tmstr, h 76 S Belmont av (W I).
BUTLER SCOT, A M, Pres Faculty and Treas Board of Directors Butler College, h w s Downey av 3 s of Washington av (I).
Butler Stephen H, clk, b 45 Bradshaw.
Butler Susan W (wid John M), h 166 N Meridian.
Butler Thomas, lab, b 337 W Maryland.
Butler Thomas H, trav agt, h 404 N Delaware.
Butler Thomas L, h 654 N Alabama.
Butler Timothy W, barber, b 40 Howard.
Butler Wm, broommkr, h 268 N Noble.
Butler Wm, lab, h s s Pansy 4 w of Floral av.
Butler Wm F, phys, 599 N Senate av, h same.
Butler Wm J, registry clk P O Depot Branch, h 25 School.
Butler Wm T, draughtsman Brown-Ketcham Iron Wks, r 378 N Meridian.
Butler Willis, bricklayer, h 210 W 10th.
Butler Winifred E, stenog J D Adams & Co, b 410 S Capitol av.
Butner Alonzo M, condr, h 218 Blake.
Butsch Frank G, nailer, b 507 S West.
Butsch Frank J, salesman Jacob Metzger & Co, b 118 Greer.
Butsch George W, mach, h 537 S Capitol av.
Butsch John, salesman, h 538 S East.
Butsch Joseph, h 789 N Delaware.
Butsch Mary (wid Peter), h 118 Greer.
Butsch Philip L, mach, h 436 S State av.
Buttel Morris, lab, b 224 W Maryland.
Butterfield Albert F, mach, h 76 Arbor av (W I).
Butterfield Caroline (wid Abram), b s w cor University and Downey avs (I).
Butterfield Cyrus S, printer, h 790 N Illinois.
Butterfield Edward T, printer, r 146 W Vermont.
Butterfield Manly, carp, h 538 W Wells (N I).
Butterfield Thomas M, carp, h 462 Shoemaker (N I).
Butterfield Tyranis P, carp, h 538 W Wells (N I).
Butterfield Velorus, clk Knight & Jillson, h 1119 E Michigan.
Butterfield Wm A, baker, b 287 S Penn.
Butterworth Charles W L, tailor, h 116 Lexington av.
Butterworth Elizabeth (wid Charles), h 78 Hoyt av.
Butterworth G Clarence, tailor, h s s Wolf pike 2 e of Baltimore av.
Butterworth James H, trav agt, h 483 Stillwell.
Butterworth John E, tailor, h 289 Huron.
Butterworth Lyda, h 37½ W Market.
Buttler Joseph (Ruemmele & Buttler), h 171 S Reisner (W I).
Button Lewis B, lab, h 47 Depot (B).
Butts Charles S, roadmaster, h 446 W Francis (N I).
Butts Frank C, well builder, 133 Indiana av, h 35 Ellsworth.
Buttweiler Frank S, agt The Brunswick-Balke-Collender Co, 138 S Illinois, b 28 Ft Wayne av.
Buttz Henry, plumber, h 141 S Olive.
Buttz John W, h 357 N East.

CLEMENS VONNEGUT 184, 186 and 192 E. Washington St. | CABINET HARDWARE CARVERS' TOOLS. Glues of all kinds.

THE WM. H. BLOCK CO. DRY GOODS, MILLINERY, CLOAKS AND FURS.
7 AND 9 EAST WASHINGTON STREET.

Buttz John W, gasfitter, h 396 W Pratt.
Buttz Pearl D, milliner, 54 Mass av, b 357 N East.
Butzke Paul E, packer, h 830 Rembrandt.
Buzan Mollie A, manicure, 25½ W Washington, r same.
Buzan Rex, printer, b 25½ Mass av.
Buzatt Carey, mngr Bicycle Academy Cyclorama bldg, r 104 S Noble.
Buzatt Joseph, clk, r 104 S Noble.
Buzatt Walter, lab, b 191 N New Jersey.
Buzzard Wm D, condr, h 533 College av.
Byard Jackson L, patrolman, h 164 Coburn.
Bybee Addison, pres Mnfrs' Bldg and Power Co, r 60 The Blacherne.
Bybee Cornelius, lab, b 184 Howard.
Bybee Frank, house mover, h 318 E Court.
Bybee Rhyul H, lab, h 211 W 3d.
Bye Benjamin F, phys, 170 N Illinois, h 130 W 2d.
Bye Charles E, phys, 170 N Illinois, h 410 E McCarty.
Bye David M, phys, 170 N Illinois, h 492 N Capitol av.
Bye George, ins agt, h 485 Highland av.
Bye Wm O, phys, 170 N Illinois, b 492 N Capitol av.
Byer August, cabtmkr, b 402 N California.
Byer Edward, clk, b 402 N California.
Byer Margaret (wid Lawrence), h 402 N California.
Byers, see also Baar, Bahr, Barr, Bayer and Beyer.
Byers Augusta, seamstress, r 5½ Indiana av.
Byers Clarence H, motorman, b 533 College av.
Byers Daniel H, switchtndr, h 345 English av.
Byers David A, engr, h 179 N California.
Byers Frank C, photog, h 260 W Washington.
Byers Herbert, coachman 493 N Capitol av.
Byers Joseph H, trav agt, h 518 N Illinois.
Byers Noah L, barber, b 371 English av.
Byers Wm J, baggageman, h 24 S Dorman.
Byers Wm J, blksmith, h 50 Fletcher av.
Byers Wm L, painter, h 324 W Pearl.
Byers Wm O, supt Inquiry Dept Indpls Bureau of Inquiry and Investigation, h 181 N Alabama.
Byfield Arthur H, bkkpr City Comptroller's Office, b 909 N Illinois.
Byfield Charles H, stair builder, h 458 Highland av.
Byfield Charles W, M O clk P O, b 909 N Illinois.
Byfield Delilah E, clk 198 Virginia av, h 271 English av.
Byfield Harry W, printer, b 86 Union.
Byfield Henry N, clk Knight & Jillson, b 909 N Illinois.
Byfield Jessie M (wid Cass), h 909 N Illinois.
Byfield Louise G, bkkpr G W Pangborn, b 86 Union.
Byfield Vincent D, molder, h 271 English av.
Byfield, Whitcomb, janitor Public School No 6, h 86 Union.
Bynum James, lab, b rear 119 Meek.
Bynum Thomas, lab, h 286 Alvord.
Bynum Wm D, lawyer, 534-535 Lemcke bldg, h 527 Ash.
Byram, Cornelius & Co (Norman S Byram, Edward G Cornelius), loans, 15 Thorpe blk.
Bynum Henry G, pres Cleaveland Fence Co, h 21 W 12th.
Byram John, engr, h 558 Union.

Byram John Q, dentist, n w cor Central av and P C C & St L Ry (I), h w s Ritter av 2 s of Washington av (I).
Byram Norman S (Byram, Cornelius & Co), sec and treas Cleaveland Fence Co, h 956 N Illinois.
Byram Norman S jr, trav agt, b 956 N Illinois.
Byram Oliver T, b 956 N Illinois.
Byram Perry M, prin High School (I), b w s Ritter av 2 s of Washington av (I).
Byrd, see also Bird and Burd.
BYRD JOSEPH W, Lumber, Shingles, Sash, Doors and Blinds, 323 Lemcke Bldg, Tel 1740; h Lake av nr Washington (I). (See adv opp Lumber Mnfrs and Dealers.)
Byrd Lewis, clk, h 130 St Mary.
Byrd Thomas Rev, pastor Olive Baptist Church, h 412 S State av.
Byrket Walter, fireman, r 12 N State av.
Byrkit Albert, engr, h 24 Garland (W I).
Byrkit Anna M (wid Davis Y), h 169 Ash.
Byrkit Davis Y, draughtsman C C C & St L Ry, b 169 Ash.
Byrkit Edwin A, opr W U Tel Co, b 1182 N Illinois.
Byrkit Elizabeth P (wid Martin), h 42 Marion av (W I).
Byrkit Frank, molder, h 39 W Morris.
Byrkit Henry, candymkr, h 4 Spann av.
Byrkit Hiram R, supt, h 75 W 2d.
Byrkit Hugh S, asst sec The Indpls Board of Trade, b 169 Ash.
Byrkit John W, clk Henry Coburn, h 11 Edward (W I).
Byrn James C, motorman, h 76 Holmes av (H).
Byrn Wm O, copycutter The Indpls News, h 87 W 20th.
Byrne Christopher, h 250 N Liberty.
Byrne Cornelius, boilermkr, b 250 N Liberty.
Byrne Ella, b 474 College av.
Byrne Frank, mach, b 213 S Alabama.
Byrne Joseph J, contr agt Nickel Plate Line, b 138 Mass av.
Byrne Michael, finisher, b 250 N Liberty.

GUIDO R. PRESSLER,
FRESCO PAINTER
Churches, Theaters, Public Buildings, Etc., A Specialty.
Residence, No. 325 North Liberty Street.
INDIANAPOLIS, IND.

INDIANAPOLIS STEEL ROOFING AND CORRUGATING WORKS, 23 and 25 East South Street. S. D. NOEL, Proprietor.

David S. McKernan REAL ESTATE AND LOANS
Houses, Lots, Farms and Western Lands for sale or trade.
ROOMS 2-5 THORPE BLOCK.

DIAMOND WALL PLASTER { Telephone 1410 BUILDERS' EXCHANGE.

Cor. E. Ohio St. and C., C., C. & St. L. R'y Tracks. ISSUE NEGOTIABLE RECEIPTS ON MERCHANDISE AND HOUSEHOLD GOODS. UNION TRANSFER AND STORAGE CO.

W. McWORKMAN,
ROOFING AND CORNICE WORKS,
930 W. Washington St. Tel. 1118.

Byrne Patrick, lab, h 4 Hadley av (W I).
Byrne Stephen T, furnacefitter, b 215 S Alabama.
Byrum Mary R (wid Thomas M), b 184 Hoyt av.

C

Cabalzer Joseph C, driver, h 114 Bright.
Cabbell George, lab, h 8 Wallack.
Cabbell Henry, hostler s w cor Washington and National avs.
Cable George W, clk R M S, h 246 N California.
Cable Mary E, teacher Public School No 19, 246 N California.
Cabman Ernest, peddler, r 266 W Court.
Cade John D, civil engr, h 5 Birch av (W I).
Cade Thomas B, boilermkr, h 872 Cornell av.
Cadres Edmund A, painter, b 30 McGill.
Cadwallader Adoniram E, tiremkr, b 170 Harrison.
Cadwallader Duke, packer, b 86 Downey.
Cadwallader Smith, baker, h 170 Harrison.
Cadwallader Wm, carp, b 23 Helen.
Cadwell Charles R, molder, h 158 Nordyke av (W I).
Cady Abigail A (wid Charles W), b 627 N Illinois.
Cady David, clk George J Marott, h 1024½ N Meridian.
Cady Elmer, b 1024½ N Meridian.
Cady Frederick W, lawyer, 8½ N Penn, h 903 Broadway.
Caesar August, baker, h 50 Morton.
Caesber Frank A, mach, b 2½ Shriver av.
Caesber Jesse H, mach, b 2½ Shriver av.
Caesber John S, millwright, h 2½ Shriver av.
Caffee, see also Coffay.
Caffee Amos H, student, h 186 N Senate av.
Caffery Mary, laundress, h 309 E Court.
Caffrey John A, trav agt, b Grand Hotel.
Caffrey John J, electrician, h w s Addison 3 s of Washington (M J).
Caffyn Ellsworth, h 289 Union.
Caffyn Frank E, b 271 Union.

GEO. J. MAYER,
MANUFACTURER OF
SEALS
STENCILS, RUBBER STAMPS, CHECKS, BADGES, DOOR PLATES, ETC.
15 S. Meridian St., Ground Floor. TEL. 1386.

Caffyn John, circulator, r 220½ S Meridian.
Caffyn Sarah J (wid James W), h 271 Union.
Cage John, lab, h 330 W 2d.
Cahalane Cornelius C, insp, b 252 Bates.
Cahalane Hanora (wid Patrick J), h 252 Bates.
Cahalane John F, mach, b 252 Bates.
Cahalane Michael S, fireman, b 252 Bates.
Cahalane Patrick J, engr, b 252 Bates.
Cahalane Thomas B, insp, b 252 Bates.
Cahill Alfred, blksmith, h 462½ N West.
Cahill Bartholomew, lab, b 11 Meikel.
Cahill Daniel, mach, h 416½ S Meridian.
Cahill George W, plumber, b 603 N West.
Cahill Henry F, b 323 Fletcher av.
Cahill Hiram J, carp, h 603 N West.
Cahill James B, foreman Sentinel Printing Co, h 430 S Meridian.
Cahill James R, glazier, b 323 Fletcher av.
Cahill John, lab, h 16 Meikel.
Cahill John, h 323 Fletcher av.
Cahill John S, uphlr, b 323 Fletcher av.
Cahill Joseph, spinner, h 347 W Washington.
Cahill Kate (wid John), h 3 Riley blk.
Cahill Lillie, cashr, b 462½ N West.
Cahill Martin, lab, b 271 W Market.
Cahill Mary, dressmkr, 414 S Meridian, r same.
Cahill Mary (wid John T), h 106 Agnes.
Cahill Mary A (wid John), dressmkr, 217 W Michigan, b same.
Cahill Patrick, b 160 Fletcher av.
Cahill Sadie (wid Dudley F), h 440½ S Meridian.
Cahill Thomas, lab, h 17 Meikel.
Cahill Thomas B, artist, 619 Virginia av, h same.
Cahn, see also Kahn.
Cahn Felix R, solr R L Polk & Co, 23-24 Journal bldg.
Cain, see also Kahn, Kane and O'Cain.
Cain Absalom F, lab, b e s Cornelius 1 n of Carlton (M).
Cain Edward M, cooper, h 47 Edward (W I).
Cain Frank T, motorman, r 193½ S Illinois.
Cain Hulda M (wid Marion), b 55 S California.
Cain James, b 47 Edward (W I).
Cain James, peddler, r 23 N West.
Cain John A, lab, h 170 S Judge Harding (W I).
Cain John C, waiter, b 130 Columbia al.
Cain John C, phys, 57 King av (H), h same.
Cain Joseph D, student, h 464 N West.
Cain Luke T, lab, b 262 S Missouri.
Cain Martin, lab, b 399 S Missouri.
Cain Mary A, b 464 N West.
Cain Michael, h 399 S Missouri.
Cain Michael D, agt, h 143 W Morris.
Cain Michael H, chief engr State House, h 905 N Capitol av.
Cain Nathan, lab, h e s Cornelius 1 n of Carlton (M).
Cain Samuel, b 46 Stevens.
Cain Sarah E, nurse, 28 Evison, h same.
Cain Taylor R, druggist, h 39 Hudson.
Cain Thomas, lab, b 29 Blackford.
Cain Thomas C, asst engr State House, h 25 Paca.
Cain Winifred (wid Michael), b 356 S Illinois.
Caine James H, clk Wm Laurie & Co, r 357 S Alabama.
Caird Robert N (Caird, Vial & Co), b 145 Highland pl.

A. METZGER AGENCY REAL ESTATE ESTABLISHED 1863.

LAMBERT GAS & GASOLINE ENGINE CO.
ANDERSON, IND. GAS AND GASOLINE ENGINES, 2 TO 50 H. P.

BICYCLES $5 DOWN. $5 MONTHLY. Bs Wheels. Bs Terms. WHEELMEN'S CO. 31 W. OHIO ST. LONG DISTANCE TEL. 1855.

Caird, Vial & Co (Robert N Caird, James M Vial), bicycles, 16 Monument pl.
Cairns James, lab, h 79 E McCarty.
Caito Michael, peddle fruits, h 218 S East.
Calbert, see also Colbert.
Calbert Felix M, oil, h 22 Excelsior av.
Calbert General F, oil, h 88 Keystone av.
Calbert James N, brakeman, b 124 English av.
Calderhead James, baker, 343 W Vermont.
Calderhead Margaret S, asst cashr, b 343 W Vermont.
Caldo Maria (wid Perry), h 220 W Wabash.
Caldwell, see also Cadwell, Cauldwell, Coldwell and Colwell.
Caldwell Albert, clk Parry Mnfg Co, b 156 N Illinois.
Caldwell Andrew J, bartndr, h 23 Bryan pl.
Caldwell Anna (wid Wm), h 86 W 8th.
Caldwell Arthur B, cashier Van Camp H and I Co, b 785 N Penn.
Caldwell Arthur C, clk, b 537 E Ohio.
Caldwell Austin, engr, b 211½ E Washington.
Caldwell Benjamin F, grocer, 188 W 7th, h 880½ N Senate av.
Caldwell Charles, bartndr, r 252 S Capitol av.
Caldwell Charles C, clk Hollweg & Reese, h 785 N Penn.
Caldwell Edmund J, clk When Clohing Store, b 1110 N New Jersey.
Caldwell Edward E, clk W U Tel Co, h 1182 N Illinois.
Caldwell Elizabeth (wid Thomas G), h 169 W New York.
Caldwell Emma, h 211½ E Washington.
Caldwell Frank W, mngr, h 530 W Francis (N I).
Caldwell Harry, porter, h 202 Agnes.
Caldwell James, h rear 175 N West.
Caldwell James, grocer, 65 E 14th, h 1110 N New Jersey.
Caldwell Jane (wid Henry), h 46 Vincennes (W I).
Caldwell Jefferson, real est, h 1059 N Delaware.
Caldwell Jesse, custodian, r 36 Bird.
Caldwell John, bartndr, b 771 N Senate av.
Caldwell John B, lab, b 269 W Market.
Caldwell John P, carp, h 791 E Market.
Caldwell Joseph W, painter, h 738 E 8th.
Caldwell Marion (Caldwell & Deacon), r 171 N Capitol av.
Caldwell Nelson, lab, h 94 Fayette.
Caldwell Oscar, tailor, 50½ S Illinois, b 771 N Senate av.
Caldwell Sarah (wid John), b 1007 N Capitol av.
Caldwell Sarah (wid Nelson), b 94 Fayette.
Caldwell Wm L, trav agt, h 976 N Capitol av.
Caldwell Wm P, claim clk C C C & St L Ry, h 154 Lexington av.
Caldwell Wilson, trav agt, h 537 E Ohio.
Caldwell W Hampton, phys, 143 N Penn, h same.
Caldwell & Deacon (Marion T Caldwell, Alfred L Deacon), real est, 52 Journal bldg.
Cale David H, student, b 111 Ruckle.
Cale Franklin N, carp, h 144 Martindale av.
CALE HOWARD, Lawyer, Room 24, 68½ E Market, h 111 Ruckle, Tel 824.
Cale Robert F, h 142 Martindale av.
Cale Wm D, lab, h 150 Martindale av.
Calef Lizzie R (wid Arthur), b 23 Division (W I).
Calhoun Frank, switchman, b 182 Meek.

We Buy Municipal ~ Bonds ~
THOS. C. DAY & CO,
Rooms 325 to 330 Lemcke Bldg.

Calhoun Franklin J, condr, h 4 S Station (B).
Calhoun Gouverneur, mngr Am Tel and Tel Co, h Cincinnati, O.
Calhoun Pamelia (wid Wm), b 4 S Station (B).
Calhoun Robert, lab, h 331 W Maryland.
Calhoun Wm A, fireman, h 353 English av.
California House, 184-186 S Illinois.
Calkins, see also Caulkins.
Calkins Mary I, h n e cor Downey and University avs (I).
Calkins Philip L, carp, h 26 Sheldon.
Call Clarence A, clk, h 18 Osgood (W I).
Call Dominick F, clk, b 116 Oak.
Call John J, mach, b 116 Oak.
Call Mary H (wid Hugh), h 116 Oak.
Callaghan Daniel, lab, h 229 W Merrill.
Callaghan Jeremiah M, lab, b 229 W Merrill.
Callahan Albert L, condr, h 66 N Beville av.
Callahan Charles F, blksmith, h 335 W 2d.
Callahan Daniel, lab, h 77 Meek.
Callahan Daniel W, horseshoer, b 31 Oliver av (W I).
Callahan Dennis, fireman, r 83 English av.
Callahan Elmer E, lab, h 89 Paca.
Callahan Frank B, clk, h 113 Lexington av.
Callahan George F, lab, b 106 Church.
Callahan James, lab, h 482 S West.
Callahan James, clk, b 70 Fayette.
Callahan James E, mach hd, h 233 English av.
Callahan James H, carp, h 70 Fayette.
Callahan James M, sawyer, h 376 N Missouri.
Callahan Jeremiah, lab, h 16 Minerva.
Callahan Jeremiah F, mach, h 305 Cornell av.
Callahan John, grocer, 152 Johnson (W I), h same.
Callahan John, lab, b 70 Fayette.
Callahan John, lab, h 31 Oliver av (W I).
Callahan John P, grocer, 109 Lexington av, h same.
Callahan John R, grocer, 101 S Reisner (W I), h same.
Callahan Judson E, clk, b 563 Broadway.
Callahan Louis A, printer, h 59 Willow.
Callahan Mary A (wid Wm), b 283 E Georgia.

EAT HITZ'S CRACKERS AND CAKES.
ASK YOUR GROCER FOR THEM.

J. H. TECKENBROCK Painter and Decorator, 94 EAST SOUTH STREET.

FIDELITY MUTUAL LIFE—PHILADELPHIA, PA.
MATCHLESS SECURITY At LOW COST. A. H. COLLINS General Agent Baldwin Block.

Rooms 42 and 43 WHEN BUILDING.

ESTABLISHED 1876. TELEPHONE 168.
CHESTER BRADFORD,
SOLICITOR OF PATENTS,
AND COUNSEL IN PATENT CAUSES.
(See adv. page 6.)
Office:—Rooms 14 and 16 Hubbard Block, S. W. Cor. Washington and Meridian Streets,
INDIANAPOLIS, INDIANA.

Callahan Michael, h 202 W Walnut.
Callahan Michael, clk, h 36 Lord.
Callahan Michael, fireman, b 106 Church.
Callahan Michael H, molder, h 325 W 2d.
Callahan Morris, lab, b 77 Meek.
Callahan Patrick, lab, b 532 S Capitol av.
Callahan Shafer, mach, b 36 Lord.
Callahan Thomas, clk, h 174 Bird.
Callahan Thomas M, mach, b 305 Cornell av.
Callahan Timothy E, condr, h 92 Bates.
Callahan Timothy E, molder, h 71 Paca.
Callahan Wm H, finisher, b 163 S Linden.
Callahan Wm J, ins agt, b 152 Johnson (W I).
Callaway Frank B, r 115 N New Jersey.
Callaway Thomas, lab, h 63½ Superior.
Callaway Wm J, clk Belt R R and Stock Yards Co, h 215 N Illinois.
Callen Frank J, pub, h 24 McKim av.
Callender Amanda (wid Isaac), b rear 626 Home av.
Calley Alexander, foreman, h 607 Bellefontaine.
Callis Hampton, carp, h 73 Minerva.
Callis Joseph, grocer, 183 Elizabeth, h same.
Callis Theodore O, mngr Enterprise Hotel, b same.
Callon Frank T, plumber, b 197 N Noble.
Callon Harry A, plumber, b 197 N Noble.
Callon James F, plumber, h 197 N Noble.
Calloway Ida, h rear 309 E Washington.
Calloway Thomas, lab, r 10 Roanoke.
Caltrider Kate, seamstress, h 193½ E Washington.
Calvelage August H, foreman Natl Malleable Castings Co, h 112 King (H).
Calvelage George B, molder, b 112 King (H).
Calvelage Louis B, asst foreman Natl Malleable Castings Co, b 112 King (H).
Calvelage Robert H, lab, b 112 King (H).
Calvert Belle C (wid David H), h 11 The Blacherne.
Calvert Frederick, chef The Bates.
Calvert George C, lawyer, 18½ N Penn, r 11 The Blacherne.
Calvert Mary E, dressmkr, 195 Bellefontaine, h same.
Calvert Wm H, clk Mut Life Ins Co of Ind, h 195 Bellefontaine.

Calvin, see also Colvin.
Calvin Charles H, molder, h 237 Columbia av.
Calvin Elizabeth (wid Joseph A), b 237 Columbia av.
Calvin Otha F, grocer, 203 W Washington, h 239 W Market.
Calvin Peter, lab, b 178 S Illinois.
Calvin Wm J, molder, b 69 Yandes.
Cambridge Charles M, farmer, h e s Daisy 1 n of Ream.
Cambridge James, lab, h 16 N McLain (W I).
Camden James O, lab, h 533 W 22d (N I).
Camden Wm T, lab, b 533 W 22d (N I).
Cameron Carl W, musician, b 26 School.
Cameron Clare G, clk The Progress Clothing Co, b 26 School.
Cameron Elizabeth F, r 106½ N Meridian.
Cameron James D, well driver, h 200 E St Joseph.
Cameron John B, clk engr m of w C C C & St L Ry, b 173 E Vermont.
Cameron John D, blksmith, h 1821 N Senate av.
Cameron Joseph B, salesman Emil Wulschner & Son, h 26 School.
Cameron Margaret (wid John), h 200 E St Joseph.
Cameron Sarah E, dressmkr, 200 E St Joseph, b same.
Cameron Wm H H, trav agt, b 422 N Illinois.
Camp, see also Kemp.
Camp Clayton E, car rep, h 31 S Stuart (B).
Camp David, lab, h e s Waverly 1 n of Division (B).
Camp David E, condr, h 58 Russell av.
Camp Edward, clk Commercial Hotel, r 285 S Capitol av.
Camp George T, lather, b 24 Brett.
Camp Joseph D, lab, h 24 Brett.
Campau Henry L, trav agt, r Grand Hotel.
Campbell Ada (wid John), b 74 W New York.
Campbell Adam, lab, h 118 N Belmont av (H).
Campbell Addie (wid John D), h 130 W New York.
Campbell Albert, condr, b 105 Minerva.
Campbell Albert, fireman, b 377 English av.
Campbell Albert E, lab, h 180 Douglass.
Campbell Albert E, lab, b 264 W Michigan.
Campbell Alexander, lab, h 92 N Dorman.
Campbell Amanda (wid Wellon), h 72 Martindale av.
Campbell Amaziah, carp, h 105 Newman.
Campbell Andrew, lab, h e s Hampton 1 s of Clifford av.
Campbell Andrew jr, lab, h w s Hampton 3 s of Clifford av.
Campbell Arthur B, cigars, 2 Malott av, b 579 E St Clair.
Campbell Belle, housekpr Blind Inst.
Campbell Benjamin J, clk Postal Tel Cable Co, b 794 E Washington.
Campbell Bennett, mer police, h 615 W Pearl.
Campbell Catherine, actress, b 243 Alvord.
Campbell Catherine (wid Dennis), h 106 Cherry.
Campbell Catherine (wid Edward), h 1065 W Michigan.
Campbell Charles, engr, h 229 English av.
Campbell Charles A, lab, h 44 N Rural.
Campbell Charles E, carp, h 210 W 6th.
Campbell Charles W, condr, h 83 Pleasant.
Campbell Chester E, grocer, 59 Howard, h same.

Edwardsport Coal and Mining Co. Miners and Shippers Steam and Domestic Coal.

C. ZIMMERMAN & SONS | SLATE AND GRAVEL ROOFERS 19 South East Street.

DRIVEN WELLS And Second Water Wells and Pumps of all kinds at CHARLES KRAUSS', 42 S. PENN. ST. TELEPHONE 465.

ERTEL STEAM LAUNDRY LARGEST AND BEST IN THE STATE. PROMPT SERVICE. 26 and 28 N. Senate Ave. Telephone 1089.

Campbell Clayton C, clk, b 66 Yeiser.
Campbell Clyde C, foreman, h 617 W Michigan.
Campbell Cornelius, molder, b 8 Yandes.
Campbell Daniel, saloon, 471 E St Clair, h 469 same.
Campbell Daniel A, fireman, b 8 Yandes.
Campbell Daniel B, plumber, h 244 W McCarty.
Campbell David, lab, b rear 232 S Missouri.
Campbell Eddy Morris (Campbell, Wild & Co), h 107 Middle Drive (W P).
Campbell Edward, paperhngr, b 1065 W Michigan.
Campbell Edward H, engr, h 374 Fulton.
Campbell Edward R, lab, h 654½ Virginia av.
Campbell Elizabeth A (wid James S), h 227 E New York.
Campbell Elizabeth J (wid Wm), h 84 W Ohio.
Campbell Emma, h 282 W Market.
Campbell Ezra N, foreman, h 58 Randolph.
Campbell Flora, h w s Auburn av 2 s of Bethel av.
Campbell Frank, lab, h 330 Indiana av.
Campbell Frank, painter, b 55 Dougherty.
Campbell Frank E, lab, b 615 W Pearl.
Campbell Frank O, engr, h 361 S Delaware.
Campbell Frederick G, clk G W Stout, b 471 Broadway.
Campbell Frederick M, brickmason, b 641 Mass av.
Campbell George, brakeman, h 800 E Market.
Campbell George D, mngr The Geo D Campbell Co, h 89 N State av.

CAMPBELL GEO D CO THE, George D Campbell Mngr, Mnfrs of Pickles, Preserves, Fruit Butter, Chow Chow, Mustard, Vinegar, Sauces, Etc, 593-599 E Washington.

Campbell George H, mach hd, h e s Sherman Drive 1 n of Washington.
Campbell Godfrey J, barber, r 141 W Washington.
Campbell Guy, lab, b 452 Chicago (N I).
Campbell Harrison, lab, h e s Baltimore av 2 n of Hillside av.
Campbell Henry, houseman, h 170 Bird.
Campbell Henry C, real est, 435 Lemcke bldg, h 1065 N Illinois.
Campbell Herbert J, clk, b 227 E New York.
Campbell Hester (wid Jacob), b 315 Fletcher av.
Campbell Hezekiah, carp, h 54 Carlos.
Campbell Hugh, carp, h 641 Mass av.
Campbell Irene (wid James D), b 73 Columbia av.
Campbell James, carp, b 55 Dougherty.
Campbell James, lab, h 124 W Miami.
Campbell James E, molder, b 1065 W Michigan.
Campbell James K, mach hd, h 10 Lynn av (W I).
Campbell James M, city fireman, b 54 Carlos.
Campbell Jennie (wid Laury), h 10½ Clifford av.
Campbell Jeremiah R, carp, h 55 Dougherty.
Campbell John F, fireman, b 115 Meek.
Campbell John H, carp, h 503 Martindale av.
Campbell John J, bookbinder, b 106 Cherry.
Campbell John W, trav pass agt Penna Lines, h s e cor Cherry and Houston avs (I).
Campbell Joseph, lab, h 41 Church.

RICHARDSON & McCREA, MANAGERS FOR CENTRAL INDIANA. EQUITABLE LIFE ASSURANCE SOCIETY Of the United States. 79 EAST MARKET STREET, TELEPHONE 182.

Campbell Joseph, tmstr, h 243 Eureka av.
Campbell Joshua T, h 155 Hoyt av.
Campbell Kate (wid Henry C), h 25½ Mass av.
Campbell Kate L (wid Thomas S), h 327 N Illinois.
Campbell Kate M (wid Allen), h 270 Fletcher av.
Campbell Len, barber, 115½ Mass av, r 24 Empire blk.
Campbell Leonard L, student, b 107 Middle Drive (W P).
Campbell Lester E, trav agt, b 808 Park av.
Campbell Levi S, phys, 65 Indiana av, r 73 same.
Campbell Louis, clk, h 431 Ash.
Campbell Lucinda (wid James E), h 594 E 10th.
Campbell Luther T, engr, h 424 E Georgia.
Campbell Marcia (wid Joseph), h 105 Minerva.
Campbell Mary (wid Morris), h 8 Yandes.
Campbell Mary A (wid Reuben), boarding 29 Madison av.
Campbell May, bkkkpr Frank M Dell, b 309 E Ohio.
Campbell Milton T, jeweler, 134 Mass av, h 754 Nevada.
Campbell Morris, lab, b 8 Yandes.
Campbell Newton M, engr, h 127 Fletcher av.
Campbell Ora A (wid Patrick), b 278 Michigan (H).
Campbell Orlando G, b n s Brookside av 1 e of Rural.
Campbell Patrick, clk, b Roosevelt House.
Campbell Prudence (wid James), b 212 N West.
Campbell Richard H, waiter, h 81 Muskingum al.
Campbell Richard W, carp, b 610 S Meridian.
Campbell Robert, policeman, h 84 Harrison.
Campbell Robert W, molder, h 18 Highland av (H).
Campbell Rose (wid Andrew), b 471 Broadway.
Campbell Ruth A (wid Joseph), h 794 E Washington.

Typewriter-Ribbons ALL COLORS FOR ALL MACHINES. THE BEST AND CHEAPEST. S. H. EAST, STATE AGENT, The Williams Typewriter.... 55 THORPE BLOCK, 87 E. MARKET ST.

ELLIS & HELFENBERGER Architectural Iron Work and Gray Iron Castings. 162-170 South Senate Ave. Tel. 958.

THE HOGAN TRANSFER AND STORAGE COMP'Y
Household Goods and Pianos Moved—Packed—Stored..... Baggage and Package Express Machinery and Safes a Specialty Cor. Washington and Illinois Sts. TELEPHONE No. 675.

Hose, Belting, Packing, Clothing, Druggists' Sundries, Bicycle Tires, Cotton Hose, Etc. New York Belting & Packing Co., L't'd.

The Provident Life and Trust Company
Of Philadelphia.
Grants Certificates of Extension to Policyholders who are temporarily unable to pay their premiums
D. W. EDWARDS, Gen. Agt., 508 Indiana Trust Bldg.

Campbell Samuel L, bookbndr, b 327 N Illinois.
Campbell Sarah, seamstress, b 8 Indiana av.
Campbell Simeon, lab, h 27 Springfield.
Campbell Susan G (wid James M), b 61 Highland pl.
Campbell Thomas, ballplyr, b 105 Newman.
Campbell Thomas C, broommkr, h 651½ E Michigan.
Campbell Thomas D, cabtmkr, h n s Brookside av 1 e of Rural.
Campbell Thomas H, lab, h 238 Keystone av.
Campbell Thomas R, fireman, b 794 E Washington.
Campbell Thomas W, driver, h 225 W Walnut.
Campbell Walter, lab, h 20 Ludlow av.
Campbell Walter, waiter, r 275 Chapel.
CAMPBELL, WILD & CO (Eddy Morris Campbell, John F Wild), Bankers, Municipal and Corporation Bonds Bought and Sold, Room 205 Indiana Trust Bldg, Tel 1880.
Campbell Wm, fireman Insane Hospital, r 61 Nordyke av (W I).
Campbell Wm, molder, b 1065 W Michigan.
Campbell Wm, tmstr, h 569 Mass av.
Campbell Wm jr, mach hd, h 61 Nordyke av (W I).
Campbell Wm B, clk H E Kinney, h 18 Grace.
Campbell Wm B, feed, 2 Malott av, h 11 Ludlow av.
Campbell Wm E, b n s Brookside av 1 e of Rural.
Campbell Wm P, condr, h 77 Lexington av.
Campbell Wm S, clk, h 66 Yeiser.
Campfield George W, carp, h 49 Leota.
Camphausen Gottlieb, mach, h 81 W Morris.
Camphausen Louisa (wid Emil), grocer, 53 River av (W I), h same.
Camplin Charles, brakeman, h 25 Belmont av.
Camplin Richard S, shoes, 71 E Washington, h s s Washington nr Belmont av.
Canaan Frank, b 71 Hoyt av.

THE CENTRAL RUBBER & SUPPLY CO. PHONE 922. 79 S. ILLINOIS ST., INDIANAPOLIS, IND.

Julius C. Walk & Son,
Jewelers
Indianapolis.
12 EAST WASHINGTON ST.

Canaan George B, engr, b 71 Hoyt av.
Canaan John J, engr, h 71 Hoyt av.
Canaan Wm H, fireman, b 71 Hoyt av.
Canada James F, mach, b 390 W 1st.
Canada James L, b e s Northwestern av 1 n of 24th.
Canada Mattie (wid Wm), h 390 W 1st.
Canady Daniel, lab, h 180 Bismarck av (H).
Canady Harvey, barber, r 175 N West.
Canady Perry W, mach hd, h 164 Davidson.
Canan Alice L (wid John T), h 519 N Alabama.
Canan Wm S, boxmkr, h 136 Madison av.
Canary Abraham L, foreman, h 72 Lexington av.
Canary Arthur B, printer, b 108 Hosbrook.
Canary Byron E, clk, b 1139 E Michigan.
Canary Henry L, supt special delivery P O, b 1139 E Michigan.
Canary Peter A, trav agt, h 1139 E Michigan.
Canary Wm S, bricklyr, h s w cor Michigan and Auburn avs.
Canatsey Allen S, checkman, h 612 S Meridian.
Canatsey, Andrew J, carp, h 111 Sanders.
Canauer Otto, lab, b 66 Geisendorff.
Canavan Martin, gasfitter, b 157 E Ohio.
Canfield Benton V, phys, 325 Virginia av, r same.
Canfield Byron W, bkkpr L S Ayres & Co, h 955 N Senate av.
Canfield Charles, painter, b s s Sturm av 1 e Arsenal av.
Canfield Hamilton A, lab, b 522 E Ohio.
Canfield Harry B, printer, b s s Sturm av 1 e Arsenal av.
Canfield John M Rev, h 61 Ft Wayne av.
Canfield Warren, painter, h s s Sturm av 1 e Arsenal av.
Canfield Wm S, printer, 31 Virginia av, b 61 Ft Wayne av.
Canfield Woods P, ins agt, 155 Michigan (H), h same.
Cangany Patrick, carp, h 19 Meikel.
Canine Blanche, teacher Public School No 11, b 113 Highland pl.
Canine Elizabeth (wid James F), b 861 N Illinois.
Canine Fred L, lawyer and mngr collection dept 11-12 Baldwin blk, b 160 Hoyt av.
Canine Hal B, trav agt Woodford & Pohlman, b 861 N Illinois.
Canning Mary (wid John), h rear 296 S West.
Canning Patrick H, lab, b rear 296 S West.
Cannmann Edward H, draughtsman, h 1016 N Senate av.
Cannon Conrad, lab, b 26 Clay.
Cannon Cornelius, lab, h 52 W Raymond.
Cannon George, mach hd, r 319 E Washington.
Cannon Harriet, b 826 College av.
Cannon Harry M, cigarmkr, h Mapleton, Ind.
Cannon John, painter, h 83 Bradshaw.
Cannon Martha (wid George), b 826 College av.
Cannon Patrick, lab, h 26 Clay.
Cannon Thomas L, carp, h 28 S Linden.
Cannon Wm T, sec Railroadmen's Building and Savings Assn, Union Station, h 826 College av.
Cantay Edward, lab, h 342 E New York.
Cantlon James E, letter carrier P O, h 1012 E Washington.
Cantlon John, lab, b 228 S West.
Cantlon Patrick, lab, b 98 Fayette.

OTTO GAS ENGINES | BUILDERS' EXCHANGE S. W. Cor. Ohio and Penn. Telephone 535.

CAPITOL LIFE

INSURANCE COMPANY

OF INDIANA

29 NORTH
PENNSYLVANIA
STREET.

Prompt Pay Wins the Day.

GREAT COMBINATION POLICY.

Settlements are made within and claims paid at sight by **24 Hours**

Sickness is indemnified for in sums of $1 to $12 a week regardless of occupation. Benefits take effect immediately on prepaid premium policies; on ordinary policy, ninety days after date of policy. No arbitrary restrictions; a fair, clear and concise contract.

Accidents covered by any other accident company are indemnified for by our policy in sums of $1 to $12. All adjustments promptly and fairly made. No quibbling or delays.

Death. Insurance against death in sums from $20 to $5,000. Cost, five cents and upward.

POLICIES PLAIN.
CONDITIONS FAIR.
PLANS MODERN.
COST REASONABLE.

Company also issues ordinary life, ten, fifteen and twenty year term and option policies at natural premium rates.

Under supervision of Insurance Department of the State of Indiana.

Becker & Son Charles Becker Jacob Becker Jr. Merchant Tailors. 21 N. Penn. St. Tel. 934

Cantlon Thomas, h 98 Fayette.
Cantlon Thomas E, trav agt, b 424 W New York.
Cantlon Wm E, plumber, b 98 Fayette.
Cantrell Augustin, lab, b 34 Torbet.
Cantrell Daniel M, printer, r 75½ Mass av.
Cantrell Nelson, hostler, r 36 W Ohio.
Cantrell Reuben, lab, b 34 Torbet.
Cantrell Sallie (wid Nelson), h 34 Torbet.
Cantrell Sarah (wid Reuben), h 173 W 5th.
Cantwell Edward J, opr W U Tel Co, h 132 N Pine.
Cantwell Thomas E, opr W U Tel Co, h 21 Eureka av.
Canty Ellen, cook, r 13 Fair blk.
Capen Philip M B C, painter, b 110 Ludlow av.
Capen Phoebe A (wid Nathan B), b 116 Bright.
CAPITAL CITY STEAM BOILER AND SHEET IRON WORKS, Kennedy & Connaughton Proprs, 207-209 S Illinois, Tel 1748. (See adv in classified Boilermakers.)
Capital House, Carlin Hamlin propr, 193 W Washington.
Capital Live Stock Commission Co The, John W Fort pres, Robert F Helm treas, Harrison E Lewis sec, Union Stock Yards (W I).
CAPITAL NATIONAL BANK THE, Medford B Wilson Pres, Wm F Churchman Cashier, Commercial Club Bldg, Tel 228. (See backbone and left top cor cards.)
CAPITAL RUBBER STAMP WORKS, George J Mayer Propr, 15 S Meridian, Tel 1386. (See left bottom cor cards and p 5.)
CAPITAL STEAM CARPET CLEANING WORKS THE, M D Plunkett Propr, cor 9th and Lennox (Big Four R R). (See right bottom lines and classified Carpet Cleaners.)
Capito Anna B, clk, b 50 S West.
Capito Harry A, propertyman, r 116½ W New York.
CAPITOL LIFE INSURANCE CO OF INDIANA, Henry Seyfried Pres, John Wagner Vice-Pres and Treas, John W Krick Sec, Dudley M Culver Medical Director, 29 N Penn. (See adv opp.)
CAPITOL LUMBER CO, Horace T Bennett Pres, Milton S Huey Vice-Pres, John R Hussey Sec and Treas, 331-335 Mass av, Tel 721.
CAPITOL PAVING AND CONSTRUCTION CO, W W Winslow Pres, Charles L James Vice-Pres and Supt, R A Lloyd Sec and Treas, Room 1 Hubbard Blk, s w cor Washington and Meridian, Tel 1190.
Caplinger Daniel D, patrolman, h 102 Shelby.
Caplinger Jacob, tmstr, b Paul Caplinger.
Caplinger James B, tmstr, h w s Laura 2 s of Washington (M J).
Caplinger Paul, h e s Laura 3 s of Washington (M J).
Caplinger Robert, b 24 William.
Caplinger Robert F, carp, h 825½ N Illinois.

Henry H. Fay, 40½ E. Washington St., REAL ESTATE, AND LOAN BROKER.

Caplinger Thomas A, lab, h w s Addison 4 s of Washington (M J).
Capner Jeremiah, lab, h s s Pansy 3 w of Floral av.
Caraway Samuel H, phys, r cor LaSalle and Humboldt av.
Carbary Edward, sergt U S Arsenal.
Carbaugh Wm L, lab, b 529 W Eugene (N I).
Carbee Wm H, messenger Am Ex Co, h 122 College av.
Carbox George, lineman, h 218 Yandes.
Card Arthur R, lab, b 229 N Penn.
Card John, agt, h 274 W New York.
Carder Harry, clk Van Camp H and I Co, h 351 N Senate av.
Cardon Joseph E, h 19 Russell av.
Cardon Wm, lab, h 41 Grant.
Carehoof Lafayette F, filer, b 325 E Ohio.
Carey, see also Cary.
Carey Ada M (wid Jason S), h 675 N Delaware.
Carey Adam, lab, r 12½ Indiana av.
Carey Angeline P, teacher High School, b 34 W St Joseph.
Carey Benjamin F, sewing mach, 211 W Washington, h 53 Brookside av.
Carey Bertha, clk, r 155 N Illinois.
Carey Beverly, lab, r 277 Bright.
Carey Charles C, engr, r 37 Bloomington.
Carey Elizabeth A (wid Samuel W), h 5½ Brookside av.
Carey George A E, phys, 413 College av, h same.
Carey Harriett, h 201 Belmont av (H).
Carey Hubbard, lab, b 183 Tremont av (H).
Carey John, lab, h 136 W 6th.
Carey John, pensioner, h 199½ Bates.
Carey John N (Daniel Stewart Co), h 660 N Meridian.
Carey Lowe, ice, h 34 W St Joseph.
Carey Mary A (wid James), h 33 Buchanan.
Carey Mary N (wid Harvey G), h 48 W North.
Carey Michael, lab, h 171 English av.
Carey Nellie (wid Michael), h 171 English av.
Carey Patrick, b 38 N William (W I).

MAYHEW'S
SPECTACLES
THE BEST IN USE
SOLD ONLY AT 13 N. MERIDIAN ST.

SALISBURY & STANLEY. 177 & 179 Indianapolis, Ind. • Contractors and Builders
Office, Store and Bar Fixtures a Specialty. Repairing of all kinds done on short notice. TELEPHONE 999.

COAL AND LIME Cement, Hair, Sewer Pipe, etc. BALKE & KRAUSS CO. Cor. Missouri and Market Sts.

FRIEDGEN'S IS THE PLACE FOR THE NOBBIEST SHOES
Ladies' and Gents' 19 North Pennsylvania St.

SAMUEL LAING || COPPER AND GALVANIZED IRON CORNICE MANUFACTURER
72 AND 74 E. COURT STREET. SKYLIGHTS AND VENTILATORS.

M. B. WILSON, Pres. W. F. CHURCHMAN, Cash.
THE CAPITAL NATIONAL BANK,
INDIANAPOLIS, IND.
Our Specialty is handling all Country Checks and Drafts on Indiana and neighboring States at the very lowest rates. Call and see us.
Interest Paid on Time Deposits.
28 S. MERIDIAN ST., COR. PEARL.

Carey Rachel (wid Benjamin W), b 10 Woodruff av.
Carey Samuel, lab, r 182½ E Washington.
Carey Samuel C (Layman & Carey Co), h 600 N Delaware.
Carey Simeon B (Layman & Carey Co), h 325 N Penn.
Carey Thomas, clk The Denison.
Carey Wm, shoemkr, 52 W Georgia, h 166 Douglass.
Carey Wm G, trav agt G W Stout, h 447 Park av.
Carey Wm J (Holmes & Carey), b 33 Buchanan.
Carey Wm M, lab, b 166 Douglass.
Carey Wm R, collr, h 280 Bright.
Carfield John R, horseshoer, 210 S Meridian, h same.
Cargett Johanna (wid Jacob), h 362 Coburn.
Carico Nancy E (wid John M), h 53 Dougherty.
Cariekro Wm, lab, h rear 643 N Senate av.
Carini Louis, mosaicwkr, b 214 E Washington.
Carle, see also Karle.
Carle Lowden H, bkkpr, b 271 Virginia av.
Carle Lucy T, teacher Public School No 7, b 271 Virginia av.
Carle Mary, stenog, b 271 Virginia av.
Carle Pearl, lab, b 23 Woodlawn av.
Carle Wm H, h 271 Virginia av.
Carlee Wm, brakeman, b 131 S East.
Carleson Nicolie, lab, b 1016 N Penn.
Carleton Charles W, r 63 N East.
Carleton Claude M, gasfitter, b 1501 N Capitol av.
Carleton George T, bkkpr Wm B Burford, h 735 N Penn.
CARLETON THOMAS L, Sanitary Plumbing, 6 Central av, Tel 261; h 1501 N Capitol av. (See adv in classified Plumbers.)
Carleton Wellington J, vulcanizer, h 136 Park av.
Carlin, see also Carlon.
Carlin Charles, barber, b n w cor Floral av and Fountain.

TUTTLE & SEGUIN,
28 E. Market St. Ground Floor.
COLLECTING RENTS AND CARE OF PROPERTY A SPECIALTY.
Telephone 1168.

Carlin Frank J (Carlin & Lennox), h 776 N Penn.
Carlin Harry M, lab, h 1122 N Rural.
Carlin James, sawmkr, h 371 S East.
Carlin Job D, student, b n w cor Floral av and Fountain.
Carlin Martha E (wid John D F), h 1122 N Rural.
Carlin Robert L, trav agt Emil Wulschner & Son, h 499 Ash.
Carlin Wm M (Carlin & Lennox), b 130 Christian av.
Carlin Wm R, tmstr, h n w cor Floral av and Fountain.
CARLIN & LENNOX (Frank J and Wm M Carlin, Edwin L Lennox), Pianos and Musical Merchandise, 31 E Market.
Carlisle Burford, enamler, b 509 Talbott av.
Carlisle Daniel, bkkpr John Rauch, r 404 N Illinois.
Carlisle Harry, lab, r 93 Cleaveland blk.
Carlisle James R, painter, h 93 Geisendorff.
Carlisle Margaret, teacher Public School No 36, r 404 N Illinois.
Carlisle Mary J (wid Wm), produce, 103 E Mkt House, h 66½ N Delaware.
Carlisle Mason B, lab, b 509 Talbott av.
Carlisle Robert E, carp, h rear 470 E Washington.
Carll Charles P, printer, b 168 E North.
Carll Clarence A, bkkpr Standard Oil Co, h 188 Elm.
Carll Samuel P, carp, h 412 E McCarty.
Carll Wm, clk, h 412 E McCarty.
Carlon, see also Carlin.
Carlon George T, bkkpr Carlon & Hollenbeck, b 79 W North.
Carlon John (Carlon & Hollenbeck and Welch & Carlon), h 79 W North.
Carlon Joseph M, clk, b 79 W North.
Carlon Patrick J (Harrington & Carlon), h 79 W North.
CARLON & HOLLENBECK (John Carlon, Charles E Hollenbeck), Book and Job Printers, Bookbinders and Publishers, s e cor Monument Pl and Meridian, Tel 267. (See adv opp.)
Carlsen Carl, bricklayer, h 197 Michigan (H).
Carlson Gustav, tailor, 27 Commercial blk, r same.
Carlstedt Alvin, gardener, h w s Schurman 1 n of Fremont (N I).
Carlstedt Everett A, clk, b 416 Indiana av.
Carlton, see Carleton.
Carlue Wm H, butcher, h 32 Carlos.
Carmack Harry W, brakeman, h 285 Huron.
Carman Adelaide, teacher Blind Institute.
Carman Eliza A (wid Abraham), h 35 Division (W I).
Carman Frank, clk, r 222 S Meridian.
Carman Oscar M, lineman, b 35 Division (W I).
Carman Rosa A (wid Henry), b 162 Howard.
Carman Victor H, electrician, h 35 Division (W I).
Carman Wm E, molder, h Haugh (H).
Carmichael Fernando W, harness cutter, h 9 Fletcher av.
Carmichael James L, hostler, b 19 Maria.
Carmichael John, lab, h 521 Mass av.
Carmody Michael A, lab, h 416 S Delaware.
Carmony Daniel, lab, b 127 W Maryland.
Carmony Fred (Armstrong & Carmony), b 75 Highland av.
Carmony Montgomery Z, bartndr Exchange Hotel (W I).

PAPER BOXES: SULLIVAN & MAHAN 41 W. Pearl St.

CARLON & HOLLENBECK
PRINTERS, BINDERS
AND BLANK BOOK
MANUFACTURERS
INDIANAPOLIS, INDIANA

MONUMENT PLACE
CORNER MERIDIAN AND CIRCLE
STREETS

DIAMOND WALL PLASTER { Telephone 1410 BUILDERS' EXCHANGE.

If your Laundry Work is not satisfactory, try

Carnagey John W, clk, b 145 Dougherty.
Carnagey Wm H, finisher, h 145 Dougherty.
Carnagua James W, sawyer, h 470 W Chicago (N I).
Carnagua John W, painter, h 470 W Chicago (N I).
Carnahan James R, lawyer, 54 Journal bldg, h 8 West Drive (W P).
Carnes Lewis C, clk, r The Plaza.
Carney, see also Kearney.
Carney Amos M, carp, h 14 Cooper.
Carney Bros (Wm M and George S), meats, 773 N Illinois.
Carney George S (Carney Bros), h 773 N Illinois.
Carney James R, tinner, b 77 Columbia.
Carney John A, lab, h 50 Foundry (B).
Carney Joseph E, tmstr, h e s Madeira 2 s of Prospect.
Carney Patrick, watchman, h 488 S Missouri.
Carney Patrick, ins agt, h 294½ Mass av.
Carney Thomas S, blksmith, h 371 E McCarty.
Carney Wm H, lab, h cor Kentucky av and White river.
Carney Wm M (Carney Bros), h 773 N Illinois.
Carnine Louisa (wid Nelson), h 79 Norwood.
Carnine Obie A, clk C H & D R R, b 79 Norwood.
Carnine Wm, lab, h 75 Norwood.
Carny Mary E, h rear 1 Rathbone.
Carothers L May, clk Knight & Jillson, h 860 N New Jersey.
Carothers Milton, lab, h 243 Orange.
Carothers Wm M (Wm M Carothers & Co), h 860 N New Jersey.
Carothers Wm M & Co (Wm M Carothers, Flora Nelson), plumbers, 62 W 7th.
Carpenter Addison H, clk Natl Malleable Castings Co, b Laura H Carpenter.
Carpenter Arthur, wheeltruer, b 430 E McCarty.
Carpenter Clarence, student, r 308 N Illinois.
Carpenter Clark, saloon, 86 W Market, h 150 W New York.
Carpenter Claude, mach, h 97 Bright.
Carpenter Conrad F, painter, h 171 Hoyt av.
Carpenter Edwin T, condr, h 118 Wright.
Carpenter James A, lab, b 351 S New Jersey.
Carpenter Jessie A, stenog The Hay & Willits Mnfg Co, b 171 Hoyt av.
Carpenter Jessie L, stenog Richardson & McCrea, b 30 Garfield pl.
Carpenter John I, flagman, h 229 Virginia av.
Carpenter Laura H (wid Henry W), h s e cor Harris av and W Washington (M J).
Carpenter Louis, tinner, r 113 Indiana av.
Carpenter Morell, lab, h 50 McGinnis.
Carpenter Olive A, h 229 Fayette.
Carpenter Ophelia (wid Anthony), h 90 Torbet.
Carpenter Perry, barber, 299 W Washington, h same.
Carpenter Peter, lab, b 90 Torbet.
Carpenter Ransom A, lab, h 53 Athon.
Carpenter Thomas J, carp, 891 Bellefontaine, h same.
Carpenter Walter N (Garber & Carpenter), h 51 West Drive (W P).
Carpenter Wm, engr, h 97 Bright.
Carpenter Wm A, painter, h 1098 W Vermont.
Carpenter Wm H, lab, h 13 Fayette.
Carr, see also Kerr.

FRANK NESSLER. WILL H. ROST.
FRANK NESSLER & CO.
Tailors
56 EAST MARKET ST. (Lemcke Building),
INDIANAPOLIS, IND.

Carr Ada, nurse 583 E St Clair, h same.
Carr Albert D, hostler, h 19 S Alabama.
Carr Albert W, driver, b 583 E St Clair.
Carr Amanda (wid Robert), h 130 Allegheny.
Carr Arthur E, condr, r 212 E Ohio.
Carr Attie G, teacher Public School No 12, b 530 Ash.
Carr Carroll B, bkkpr Mas Mut Ben Soc, h 370 N Meridian.
Carr Charles, lab Insane Hospital.
Carr Charles W, bricklyr, h 274 E Louisiana.
Carr Christian F, tmstr, h Michigan av (W).
Carr Cornelius, lab, h 436 E 7th.
Carr Edward, clk, b 274 E Louisiana.
Carr Edward M, jeweler, h e s Rural 6 n of Clifford av.
Carr Erskine, mach, h 56 Randolph.
Carr Essex, lab, h rear 115 W 6th.
Carr Frank, bkkpr, h 24 Church.
Carr Frank, tmstr, h 415 Excelsior av.
Carr Hannah (wid Thomas), grocer, 296 S Missouri, h same.
Carr Harry C, dentist Lida Pursell Page, b 281 N Liberty.
Carr James, b 111 N Dorman.
Carr James, lab, b 107 W South.
Carr James A, bookbndr, r 158 E Michigan.
Carr James P, plastr, h 48 Stevens.
Carr James W Rev, pastor Second Baptist Church, h 259 N West.
Carr John, plastr, r 82½ E Washington.
Carr John A, draughtsman, h 250 N Pine.
Carr John E, asst supt Prud Ins Co, h 113 Dougherty.
Carr John J, steelwkr, h 36 Henry.
Carr John T, lab, h 224 W Merrill.
Carr Joseph, b 44 Grant.
Carr Martin, clk, b 40 S West.
Carr Martin C, foreman Kingan & Co, h 607 W Vermont.
Carr Mary (wid Alexander C), h n w cor Brookside and Waverly avs.
Carr Mary A (wid Richard), h 530 Ash.
Carr Mary J (wid Thomas), b 221 Christian av.
Carr Michael W, editor and pub The Pen, 25½ W Washington, h 420 N Penn.

THE HOME LAUNDRY

ACORN STOVES AND RANGES
Haueisen & Hartmann
163-169 E. Washington St.
FURNITURE,
Carpets,
Household Goods,
Tin, Granite and China Wares. Oil Cloth and Shades

197 S. Ill St.
Telephone 1769.

THE WM. H. BLOCK CO. DRY GOODS,
7 AND 9 EAST WASHINGTON STREET. MEN'S FURNISHINGS.

The Fidelity and Deposit Co. OF MARYLAND. Bonds signed for Administrators, Assignees, Executors, Guardians, Receivers, Trustees, and persons in every position of trust.
GEO. W. PANGBORN, General Agent, 704-706 Lemcke Building. Telephone 140.

INSURE YOUR PROPERTY WITH FRANK K. SAWYER

• JOSEPH GARDNER •
GALVANIZED IRON
CORNICES and SKYLIGHTS.
Metal Ceilings and Siding.
Tin, Iron, Steel and Slate Roofing.
37, 39 & 41 KENTUCKY AVE. Telephone 322.

Carr Moses, lab, h 256 W 7th.
Carr Nathan, watchman, h n s 23d 2 e of Northwestern av.
Carr Patrick, lab, b 111 N Dorman.
Carr Roland S, agt John Wocher, r 34 The Windsor.
Carr Roland T, clk Louis S Stockman, h 8 Eden pl.
Carr Samuel J, clk, r 31 N New Jersey.
Carr Sylvanus, lab, h 21 Hill.
Carr Thomas, fireman, r 22 S State av.
Carr Thomas, lab, h 181 Elm.
Carr Thomas M, driver, h 138 Prospect.
Carr Wm A, lab, h 172 Buchanan.
Carr Wm M, chemist, b 1226 N Illinois.
Carr Wm S, wheelmkr, h 15 Woodburn av (W I).
Carrick Malachi, lab, h 277 W Maryland.
Carrico Frank D, millwright, b 50 Elizabeth.
Carrico George, lab, b 138 W 9th.
Carrico Sarah H (wid John), h 50 Elizabeth.
Carrigan Ellen (wid James), b 32 S McLain (W I).
Carrigan Thomas C, clk, r 30 W Vermont.
Carriger John J, real est, h 67 Central av.
Carriger Theodore M, real est, h 608 Central av.
Carroll Artemisia E, b 38 S State av.
Carroll Arthur L, tmstr, b 197 Bates.
Carroll Bell, teacher Board of Children's Guardians, b 467 Broadway.
Carroll Charles C, foreman, h 356 Union.
Carroll Charles P, lawyer, 12 Fletcher's Bank bldg, h 276 S Meridian.
Carroll Charles W, plastr, h 14 Torbet.
Carroll Edward, lab, b 79 Fayette.
Carroll Edward M, switchman, h 333 Fletcher av.
Carroll Elmer, lab, h 553 E 12th.
Carroll George J, brakeman, b 685 E Washington.
Carroll George W, clk Schrader Bros, b Stubbins Hotel.
Carroll James, plastr, h 232 S Olive.
Carroll James E, plastr, b 210 Douglass.
Carroll James H (Carroll & Copeley), h 299 S Missouri.
Carroll James P, tinner, h 212 Buchanan.
Carroll James W, huckster, h 176 Laurel.

J. S. FARRELL & CO.
Have Experienced Workmen and will Promptly Attend to your
PLUMBING
Repairs. 84 North Illinois Street. Telephone 382.

Carroll Jennie D (wid Patrick F), h 178 East Drive (W P).
Carroll Jeremiah, lab, h 223 Dillon.
Carroll John, checkman, h 457 Park av.
Carroll John, city fireman, b 188 W Merrill.
Carroll John, lab, h 305 S West.
Carroll John S, lab, b 340 Superior.
Carroll Laura, teacher, r 57 The Windsor.
Carroll Margaret, b 1360 Indianapolis av.
Carroll Margaret (wid Maurice), h 224 W Maryland.
Carroll Margaret A, teacher Public School No 4, b 224 W North.
Carroll Michael, watchman, h 409 S Missouri.
Carroll Michael F, lab, h 224 W Maryland.
Carroll Patrick, lab, h 188 W Merrill.
Carroll Patrick, repairman Insane Hospital.
Carroll Richard, lab, h 340 Superior.
Carroll Robert J, phys, 276 S Meridian, h same.
Carroll Roger, ship clk, b 73 W Georgia.
Carroll Thomas, steelwkr, b 46 S Capitol av.
Carroll Thomas P, clk, b 188 W Merrill.
Carroll Wm, foreman, h 202 W McCarty.
Carroll Wm J, stenog Fitzgerald & Delp, b 409 S Missouri.
Carroll & Copeley (James H Carroll, Henry Copeley), real est, 299 S Missouri.
Carrothers Thomas, plastr, b 863 S Meridian.
Carruthers Minnie, h 230 W Ohio.
Carskadon James, U S mail contr, h 866 S Meridian.
Carskadon Joseph E, sub letter carrier P O, b 866 S Meridian.
Carson Calvin, saloon, 176 Elizabeth, h same.
Carson Carl, foreman, b 167 N Capitol av.
Carson Charles C, painter, r 314 N East.
Carson Edgar M, clk, b 156 Hoyt av.
Carson Edward, lab, h 122½ Ft Wayne av.
Carson Elhanan L, lab, h 9 Grove.
Carson Francis P, clk, b 144 Gillard av.
Carson Frank, lab, b 176 Elizabeth.
Carson Frank T, clk, b 121 Dougherty.
Carson George A, mach, b 609 Bellefontaine.
Carson Harry, hostler, r 239 W Washington.
Carson Helen P (wid John B), h 1106 N Capitol av.
Carson James I, collarmkr, h 76 Laurel.
Carson Jessie, bkkpr U S Encaustic Tile Wks, b 1106 N Capitol av.
Carson John F (Carson & Thompson), h 831 N Penn, Tel 492.
CARSON JOHN H, Physician and Druggist, cor Illinois and 30th, Tel 1265, h 1777 N Illinois.
Carson John W, watchman, h 61 Laurel.
Carson Joseph O, bicycle rep, b 609 Bellefontaine.
Carson Lafayette S, brazier, h 121 Dougherty.
Carson Laura (wid John), b 259 Lincoln la.
Carson Margaret D, asst supt Door of Hope, 84 N Alabama.
Carson Mary (wid Peter), h 534 S Capitol av.
Carson Melvina (wid Alfred), b 18 Brett.
Carson Oliver H, lawyer, 88 Lombard bldg, h 1122 N Delaware.
Carson Parker S, h 156 Hoyt av.
Carson Robert J, driver, h s s Jackson 4 w of Lincoln av (M J).

GUARANTEED INCOME POLICIES issued only by the United States Life Insurance Co.
E. B. SWIFT, Manager. 25 E. Market St.

Furniture Carpets } WM. KOTTEMAN { Stoves Ranges
89 and 91 East Washington Street. Telephone 1742.

WILLIAM WIEGEL } MANUFACTURER OF..... } SHOW CASES } 6 W. Louisiana St. Opposite Union Station.

Carson Samuel J, millwright, h 126 Duncan.
Carson Wm, lab, h 436 S Missouri.
Carson Wm A, patternmkr, h n s Jackson 2 w of Lincoln av (M J).
Carson Wm L, ins agt, b 61 Laurel.
Carson Wm R, city dis clk P O, b 156 Hoyt av.
CARSON & THOMPSON (John F Carson, Charles N Thompson), Lawyers, 525-528 Lemcke Bldg, Tel 810.
Carstan Mads, patternmkr, h 26 Miley av.
Carstan Torval, mach hd, b 26 Miley av.
Carstensen Christian, carp, h 29 S Gale (B).
Carstensen Gustav A Rev, rector St. Paul's Episcopal Church, b 77 W North.
Carter Alice L (wid Henry C), h 42 Ruckle.
Carter Ann (wid John A), h 107 Highland pl.
Carter Anson B, b 765 N New Jersey.
Carter Arlando B, mason, h 823 E Market.
Carter Beatrice, b 215 W Maryland.
Carter Beedy, cook, r 215 W Maryland.
Carter Benjamin F, ins agt, h 88 Cornell av.
Carter Benjamin T, tmstr, h 18 Hill.
Carter Chapin, porter, h 41 Roanoke.
Carter Charles A, phys, 122 W Maryland, h same.
Carter Charles C, tinner, h 90½ Bright.
Carter Charles E, confr, 59 N Illinois, h same.
Carter Charles H, lab, h 738 N West.
Carter Charles P, lab, h 146 Miami.
Carter Charles W, ironwkr, h 88 Cornell av.
Carter Daniel, hatter, h 17 Woodburn av (W I).
Carter Daniel, patrolman, h 85 N Dorman.
Carter Delphia C, paperhngr, h 222 W 4th.
Carter Douglas, lab, h 115 Shepard (W I).
Carter Edward, lab, h w s Northwestern av 5 s of 30th (N I).
Carter Edward P, clk, b 68 N East.
Carter Esther N, bkkpr, b 765 N New Jersey.
Carter Fannie, h 559 E Walnut.
Carter Fanny D, teacher Public School No 37, b 107 Highland av.
Carter Fletcher, architect, b 473 Central av.
Carter Frank H, drugs, 298 Mass av, h 391 Broadway.
Carter Frank L, clk, b 765 N New Jersey.
Carter Frederick L (Carter, Lee & Co), b 1574 N Illinois.
CARTER GEORGE, Lawyer, 94½ E Washington, h 72 W 2d.
Carter George A, lab, h 174 John.
Carter George H (Carter, Lee & Co), h 1574 N Illinois.
Carter George W, carp, h 446 W 1st.
Carter Grace S (wid Alpha L), clk State Board of Health, h 430 The Shiel.
Carter Gray W, carp, h 485 W Walnut av (N I).
Carter Harlen W, drugs, n e cor Hillside av and Clarke, h same.
Carter Harriet D (wid Edward), h 742 N Senate av.
Carter Harry, clk, r 381 N Senate av.
Carter Harry, lab, h 117 Mulberry.
Carter Hattie, dressmkr, 25 Elm, b same.
Carter Henry, lab, b 230 Clinton.
Carter Henry, lab, b 129½ W McCarty.
Carter Henry, lab, h 83 Rhode Island.
Carter Henry J, lab, b 106 Agnes.
Carter Herbert R, clk, b 122 Christian av.

We Buy Municipal ~ Bonds ~
THOS. C. DAY & CO,
Rooms 325 to 330 Lemcke Bldg.

Carter Indiana H (wid James W), h e s Grand av 1 s of University av (I).
Carter Isaac, waiter, h 29 Roanoke.
Carter Jacob, lab, h 427 W Chicago (N I).
Carter James, lab, b 391 W 2d.
Carter James, phys, 210 Prospect, h 19 Dawson.
Carter James D, express, h 42 Heury.
Carter James E, hatter, b 479 S Capitol av.
Carter James F, confr, h e s Watts 1 n of Ohio.
Carter James W, h 442 N Illinois.
Carter Jesse, bartndr, r 300 S Illinois.
Carter John, h 1018 E Washington.
Carter John, lab, b 75 Chapel.
Carter John, lab, h rear n s Ohio 8 e of Rural.
Carter John A, produce, b 107 Highland pl.
Carter John H, clk, h 179 Patterson.
Carter John V, h 325 N Illinois.
Carter John W, hardware, 296 Mass av, h 122 Christian av.
Carter John W, janitor, h 28 Rhodes av.
Carter Joseph B, lab, b 75 Chapel.
Carter Joshua, lab, r 261½ Mass av.
Carter, Lee & Co (George H and Frederick L Carter, Frank J Lee), lumber, 995 W Washington.
Carter Levi, lab, h rear 330 Broadway.
Carter Linden, lab, b 159 W Merrill.
Carter Louis, lab, h 75 Chapel.
Carter Louis, lab, h 230 Clinton.
Carter Louis, lab, b rear 127 E St Joseph.
Carter L Jay (Carter & Boatright), b 189 N Noble.
Carter Margaret (wid Stephen), h 25 Elm.
Carter Margery A (wid John E), h 103 Geisendorff.
Carter Mary (wid John), h 765 N New Jersey.
Carter Mary, h 188 Agnes.
Carter Mary B, h 415 Bellefontaine.
Carter Mary G, teacher Public School No 24, b 107 Highland pl.
Carter Mattie (wid Daniel), dressmkr, 306½ E Washington, h same.

EAT
HITZ'S CRACKERS
AND CAKES.
ASK YOUR GROCER FOR THEM.

TURKISH RUGS AND CARPETS RESTORED TO ORIGINAL COLORS LIKE NEW | Capital Steam Carpet Cleaning Works
M. D. PLUNKETT, Telephone 818

The Fidelity and Deposit Co. OF MARYLAND. Bonds signed for Administrators, Assignees, Executors, Guardians, Receivers, Trustees, and persons in every position of trust. GEO. W. PANGBORN, General Agent, 704-706 Lemcke Building. Telephone 140.

INSURE YOUR PROPERTY WITH FRANK K. SAWYER

• JOSEPH GARDNER •
GALVANIZED IRON
CORNICES and SKYLIGHTS.
Metal Ceilings and Siding.
Tin, Iron, Steel and Slate Roofing.
37, 39 & 41 KENTUCKY AVE. Telephone 322.

Carr Moses, lab, h 256 W 7th.
Carr Nathan, watchman, h n s 23d 2 e of Northwestern av.
Carr Patrick, lab, b 111 N Dorman.
Carr Roland S, agt John Wocher, r 34 The Windsor.
Carr Roland T, clk Louis S Stockman, h 8 Eden pl.
Carr Samuel J, clk, r 31 N New Jersey.
Carr Sylvanus, lab, h 21 Hill.
Carr Thomas, fireman, r 22 S State av.
Carr Thomas, lab, h 181 Elm.
Carr Thomas M, driver, h 138 Prospect.
Carr Wm A, lab, h 172 Buchanan.
Carr Wm M, chemist, b 1226 N Illinois.
Carr Wm S, wheelmkr, h 15 Woodburn av (W I).
Carrick Malachi, lab, h 277 W Maryland.
Carrico Frank D, millwright, b 50 Elizabeth.
Carrico George, lab, b 138 W 9th.
Carrico Sarah H (wid John), h 50 Elizabeth.
Carrigan Ellen (wid James), b 32 S McLain (W I).
Carrigan Thomas C, clk, r 30 W Vermont.
Carriger John J, real est, h 67 Central av.
Carriger Theodore M, real est, h 608 Central av.
Carroll Artemisia E, b 38 S State av.
Carroll Arthur L, tmstr, b 197 Bates.
Carroll Bell, teacher Board of Children's Guardians, b 467 Broadway.
Carroll Charles C, foreman, h 356 Union.
Carroll Charles P, lawyer, 12 Fletcher's Bank bldg, h 276 S Meridian.
Carroll Charles W, plastr, h 14 Torbet.
Carroll Edward, lab, b 79 Fayette.
Carroll Edward M, switchman, h 333 Fletcher av.
Carroll Elmer, lab, h 558 E 12th.
Carroll George J, brakeman, b 685 E Washington.
Carroll George W, clk Schrader Bros, b Stubbins Hotel.
Carroll James, plastr, h 232 S Olive.
Carroll James E, plastr, b 210 Douglass.
Carroll James H (Carroll & Copeley), h 299 S Missouri.
Carroll James P, tinner, h 212 Buchanan.
Carroll James W, huckster, h 176 Laurel.

J. S. FARRELL & CO.
Have Experienced Workmen and will Promptly Attend to your
PLUMBING
Repairs. 84 North Illinois Street. Telephone 382.

Carroll Jennie D (wid Patrick F), h 178 East Drive (W P).
Carroll Jeremiah, lab, h 223 Dillon.
Carroll John, checkman, h 457 Park av.
Carroll John, city fireman, b 188 W Merrill.
Carroll John, lab, h 305 S West.
Carroll John S, lab, b 340 Superior.
Carroll Laura, teacher, r 57 The Windsor.
Carroll Margaret, b 1360 Indianapolis av.
Carroll Margaret (wid Maurice), h 224 W Maryland.
Carroll Margaret A, teacher Public School No 4, b 224 W North.
Carroll Michael, watchman, h 409 S Missou
Carr
Carr
Carr
tal.
Carroll Richard, lab, h 340 Superior.
Carroll Robert J, phys, 276 S Meridian, h same.
Carroll Roger, ship clk, b 73 W Georgia.
Carroll Thomas, steelwkr, b 46 S Capitol av.
Carroll Thomas P, clk, b 188 W Merrill.
Carroll Wm, foreman, h 202 W McCarty.
Carroll Wm J, stenog Fitzgerald & Delp, b 409 S Missouri.
Carroll & Copeley (James H Carroll, Henry Copeley), real est, 299 S Missouri.
Carrothers Thomas, plastr, b 863 S Meridian.
Carruthers Minnie, h 230 W Ohio.
Carskadon James, U S mail contr, h 866 S Meridian.
Carskadon Joseph E, sub letter carrier P O, b 866 S Meridian.
Carson Calvin, saloon, 176 Elizabeth, h same.
Carson Carl, foreman, b 167 N Capitol av.
Carson Charles C, painter, r 314 N East.
Carson Edgar M, clk, b 156 Hoyt av.
Carson Edward, lab, h 122½ Ft Wayne av.
Carson Elhanan L, lab, h 9 Grove.
Carson Francis P, clk, b 144 Gillard av.
Carson Frank, lab, b 176 Elizabeth.
Carson Frank T, clk, b 121 Dougherty.
Carson George A, mach, b 609 Bellefontaine.
Carson Harry, hostler, r 239 W Washington.
Carson Helen P (wid John B), h 1106 N Capitol av.
Carson James I, collarmkr, h 76 Laurel.
Carson Jessie, bkkpr U S Encaustic Tile Wks, b 1106 N Capitol av.
Carson John F (Carson & Thompson), h 831 N Penn, Tel 492.
CARSON JOHN H, Physician and Druggist, cor Illinois and 30th, Tel 1265, h 1777 N Illinois.
Carson John W, watchman, h 61 Laurel.
Carson Joseph O, bicycle rep, b 609 Bellefontaine.
Carson Lafayette S, brazier, h 121 Dougherty.
Carson Laura (wid John), b 259 Lincoln la.
Carson Margaret D, asst supt Door of Hope, 84 N Alabama.
Carson Mary (wid Peter), h 534 S Capitol av.
Carson Melvina (wid Alfred), b 18 Brett.
Carson Oliver H, lawyer, 88 Lombard bldg, h 1122 N Delaware.
Carson Parker S, h 156 Hoyt av.
Carson Robert J, driver, h s s Jackson 4 w of Lincoln av (M J).

GUARANTEED INCOME POLICIES issued only by the United States Life Insurance Co.
E. B. SWIFT, Manager. 25 E. Market St.

Furniture Carpets } WM. KOTTEMAN { Stoves Ranges
89 and 91 East Washington Street. Telephone 1742.

Carson Samuel J, millwright, h 126 Duncan.
Carson Wm, lab, h 436 S Missouri.
Carson Wm A, patternmkr, h n s Jackson 2 w of Lincoln av (M J).
Carson Wm L, ins agt, b 61 Laurel.
Carson Wm R, city dis clk P O, b 156 Hoyt av.
CARSON & THOMPSON (John F Carson, Charles N Thompson), Lawyers, 525-528 Lemcke Bldg, Tel 810.
Carstan Mads, patternmkr, h 26 Miley av.
Carstan Torval, mach hd, b 26 Miley av.
Carstensen Christian, carp, h 29 S Gale (B).
Carter Albert B (Ralph & Carter), sec Citizens' Mutual B and L Assn, h 68 N East.
Carter Albert H, clk, b 122 Christian av.
Carter Alice E, h s w cor Illinois and 29th.
Carter Alice L (wid Henry C), h 42 Ruckle.
Carter Ann (wid John A), h 107 Highland pl.
Carter Anson B, b 765 N New Jersey.
Carter Arlando B, mason, h 823 E Market.
Carter Beatrice, b 215 W Maryland.
Carter Beedy, cook, r 215 W Maryland.
Carter Benjamin F, ins agt, h 88 Cornell av.
Carter Benjamin T, tmstr, h 18 Hill.
Carter Chapin, porter, h 41 Roanoke.
Carter Charles A, phys, 122 W Maryland, h same.
Carter Charles C, tinner, h 90½ Bright.
Carter Charles E, confr, 59 N Illinois, h same.
Carter Charles H, lab, h 738 N West.
Carter Charles P, lab, h 146 Miami.
Carter Charles W, ironwkr, h 88 Cornell av.
Carter Daniel, hatter, h 17 Woodburn av (W I).
Carter Daniel, patrolman, h 85 N Dorman.
Carter Delphia C, paperhngr, h 222 W 4th.
Carter Douglas, lab, h 115 Shepard (W I).
Carter Edward, lab, h w s Northwestern av 5 s of 30th (N I).
Carter Edward P, clk, b 68 N East.
Carter Esther N, bkkpr, b 765 N New Jersey.
Carter Fannie, h 559 E Walnut.
Carter Fanny D, teacher Public School No 37, b 107 Highland av.
Carter Fletcher, architect, b 473 Central av.
Carter Frank H, drugs, 298 Mass av, h 391 Broadway.
Carter Frank L, clk, b 765 N New Jersey.
Carter Frederick L (Carter, Lee & Co), b 1574 N Illinois.
CARTER GEORGE, Lawyer, 94½ E Washington, h 72 W 2d.
Carter George A, lab, h 174 John.
Carter George H (Carter, Lee & Co), h 1574 N Illinois.
Carter George W, carp, h 446 W 1st.
Carter Grace S (wid Alpha L), clk State Board of Health, h 430 The Shiel.
Carter Gray W, carp, h 485 W Walnut av (N I).
Carter Harlen W, drugs, n e cor Hillside av and Clarke, h same.
Carter Harriet D (wid Edward), h 742 N Senate av.
Carter Harry, clk, r 381 N Senate av.
Carter Harry, lab, h 117 Mulberry.
Carter Hattie, dressmkr, 25 Elm, b same.
Carter Henry, lab, b 230 Clinton.
Carter Henry, lab, b 129½ W McCarty.
Carter Henry, lab, h 83 Rhode Island.
Carter Henry J, lab, b 106 Agnes.
Carter Herbert R, clk, b 122 Christian av.

We Buy Municipal ~ Bonds ~
THOS. C. DAY & CO,
Rooms 325 to 330 Lemcke Bldg.

Carter Indiana H (wid James W), h e s Grand av 1 s of University av (I).
Carter Isaac, waiter, h 29 Roanoke.
Carter Jacob, lab, h 427 W Chicago (N I).
Carter James, lab, b 391 W 2d.
Carter James, phys, 210 Prospect, h 19 Dawson.
Carter James D, express, h 42 Henry.
Carter James E, hatter, b 479 S Capitol av.
Carter James F, confr, h e s Watts 1 n of Ohio.
Carter James W, h 442 N Illinois.
Carter Jesse, bartndr, r 300 S Illinois.
Carter John, h 1018 E Washington.
Carter John, lab, b 75 Chapel.
Carter John, lab, h rear n s Ohio 8 e of Rural.
Carter John A, produce, b 107 Highland pl.
Carter John H, clk, h 179 Patterson.
Carter John V, h 325 N Illinois.
Carter John W, hardware, 296 Mass av, h 122 Christian av.
Carter John W, janitor, h 28 Rhodes av.
Carter Joseph B, lab, b 75 Chapel.
Carter Joshua, lab, r 261½ Mass av.
Carter, Lee & Co (George H and Frederick L Carter, Frank J Lee), lumber, 995 W Washington.
Carter Levi, lab, h rear 330 Broadway.
Carter Linden, lab, b 159 W Merrill.
Carter Louis, lab, h 75 Chapel.
Carter Louis, lab, h 230 Clinton.
Carter Louis, lab, b rear 127 E St Joseph.
Carter L Jay (Carter & Boatright), b 189 N Noble.
Carter Margaret (wid Stephen), h 25 Elm.
Carter Margery A (wid John E), h 103 Geisendorff.
Carter Mary (wid John), h 765 N New Jersey.
Carter Mary, h 188 Agnes.
Carter Mary B, h 415 Bellefontaine.
Carter Mary G, teacher Public School No 24, b 107 Highland pl.
Carter Mattie (wid Daniel), dressmkr, 306½ E Washington, h same.

EAT HITZ'S CRACKERS AND CAKES.
ASK YOUR GROCER FOR THEM.

WILLIAM WIEGEL } MANUFACTURER OF . . . . . } SHOW CASES { 6 W. Louisiana St. Opposite Union Station.

TURKISH RUGS AND CARPETS RESTORED TO ORIGINAL COLORS LIKE NEW | Capital Steam Carpet Cleaning Works M. D. PLUNKETT, Telephone 818

BENJ. BOOTH PRACTICAL EXPERT ACCOUNTANT. Books Opened, Written Up, Posted and Balanced. Room 18, 82½ E. Washington St., Indianapolis, Ind.

18 and 20 S. MERIDIAN STREET THE SHERMAN RESTAURANT IF YOU WANT A GOOD MEAL AND HAVE IT NICELY SERVED GO TO

ESTABLISHED 1876. TELEPHONE 168.
CHESTER BRADFORD,
SOLICITOR OF PATENTS,
AND COUNSEL IN PATENT CAUSES.
(See adv. page 6.)
Office:—Rooms 14 and 16 Hubbard Block, S. W. Cor. Washington and Meridian Streets, INDIANAPOLIS, INDIANA.

Carter Oliver L, clk The Indpls Journal, b 765 N New Jersey.
Carter Orlando M, carp, h 10 Elliott.
Carter Otto E, carp, h 763 N Senate av.
Carter Patrick, h 479 S Capitol av.
Carter Philip, lab, b 33 Athon.
Carter Rachel, h 84 S East.
Carter Robert, student, r 83 E Michigan.
Carter Thomas B, U S Treasury Agt, 29½ N Penn, h 134 E North.
Carter Thomas J, clk State Board of Public Printing, 3 State House, h 69 W 2d.
CARTER VINSON, Judge Superior Court Room 3, Court House, h 582 N Penn.
Carter Walker J, carp, h 290 Union.
Carter Walter, lab, h 6 Lafayette.
Carter Wm, fireman, b 291 Miller (W I).
Carter Wm, lab, b 390 N California.
Carter Wm, lab, h 235 Clinton.
Carter Wm, lab, r 381 N Senate av.
Carter Wm E, livery, 233 W Maryland, r same.
Carter Wm F, painter, h 9 Oxford.
Carter Wm H, painter, h 452 E Georgia.
Carter Wm M, barber, h 751 Brookers al.
Carter Wm P (Carter & Vetter), h 124 W Maryland.
Carter Wm W, clk The Progress Clothing Co, b 247 N Meridian.
Carter & Boatright (L Jay Carter, Wm W Boatright), real est, 13 Baldwin blk.
Carter & Vetter (Wm P Carter, John J Vetter), auctioneers, 252 E Washington.
Cartheuser Christian, driver, h 54 Morton.
Cartheuser Louis P, brewer, h 109 Gray.
Cartman Joseph, lab, b 211½ E Washington.
Cartmill Emma, h 402 Blackford.
Carton Anna, clk, b 520 S Capitol av.
Carton John H, lab, b 520 S Capitol av.
Carton Wm T, boilermkr, h 520 S Capitol av.
Cartwright Frederick, boarding 132 W Ohio.
Cartwright Jesse D, clk P C C & St L Ry, h 158 Pleasant.
Carty Wm, lab, h 121 Rhode Island.
Caruso Angelo, fruits, h 268 S East.

O. B. ENSEY
MANUFACTURER OF
GALVANIZED IRON CORNICE, SKYLIGHTS AND WINDOW CAPS,
TELEPHONE 1562. Cor. 6th and Illinois Sts.

Caruso Antonio, fruits, h 268 S East.
Carver Alfred, carp, h 17 Dawson.
Carver Charles G, ironwkr, b 17 Dawson.
Carver Charles W, real est, h 490 W Shoemaker (N I).
Carver David K, real est, h w s Downey av 2 s of Washington av (I).
Carver Edwin A, agt, h 31 Maxwell.
Carver John A, cooper, h 172 Lexington av.
Carver Wm, cupola tndr, b 107 W South.
Carvin Ella, h 412 N New Jersey.
Carvin Frank A, uphlr, b 473 Stillwell.
Carvin Frank F, salesman Wm L Elder, h 553 Central av.
Carvin Hannah E (wid Armel A), dressmkr 473 Stillwell, h same.
Carvin James M, phys, 113 S Illinois, h 397½ Bellefontaine.
Carvin Orville O, trav agt The Indpls Millinery Co, h s s Washington 2 w of Ritter av (I).
Carvon Wm, watchman, r 120 E Wabash.
Cary, see also Carey.
Cary Charles M, lab, h 367 Fletcher av.
Cary Elmer E, phys, 151 N Illinois, h same.
Cary Kittie I, artist, 151 N Illinois, h same.
Cary Wm I, ins agt, r 28 W Vermont.
Casad Walter S, carp, b 620 Bellefontaine.
Casady, see also Cassady and Cassidy.
Casady Elmer O, plater, b Robert Casady.
Casady Herbert, finisher, b Robert Casady.
Casady Horace G, lab, b Robert Casady.
Casady Robert, dairy, n w cor Clifford and Waverly avs, h same.
Casanova John, repairer, b 675 Union.
Case Alice T, dressmkr, 32 S Spruce, h same.
Case Creacy, laundress, h 331 Superior.
Case David H, r 13 Catterson blk.
Case Eugene, clk H P Wasson & Co, r 93 N Alabama.
Case Florence E, b 235 E South.
Case Frank M, tinner, h 7 Cottage av (W I).
Case George A, lab, h 611 W Pearl.
Case Hiram M, driver, h 58 Andrews.
Case Horace A, clk, h 235 E South.
Case John, lab, b 394 Blackford.
Case J I Threshing Machine Co, R B Coleman agt, 42 Kentucky av.
Case J Wylie, printer, h 32 Spruce.
Case Lester W, clk W H Block Co, b 235 E South.
Case Martha A (wid Berrien L), h 56 N State av.
Case Mary A (wid John L), h 32 S Spruce.
CASE ROBISON M, Chief Clerk Genl Pass Dept L E & W W R R, s w cor Washington and Noble, and Sec Indianapolis Pass Assn, h 322 Ash, Tel 1472.
Case Sarah A (wid John B), h 50 Concordia.
Case Wm, helper, b 221 W Pearl.
Casebeer Jacob B, phys, 173 Bellefontaine, h same.
Casey Bridget (wid Patrick), b 37 King av (H).
Casey Catherine (wid Michael), h 174 N Dorman.
Casey Charles A, lab, b 43 S West.
Casey Cornelius, lab, h 416 Highland av.
Casey Daniel, lab, b 126 Blackford.
Casey Daniel, lab, b 174 N Dorman.
Casey Dennis, lab, h rear 501 E Georgia.
Casey Dennis, lab, h 15 Sharpe.
Casey Dennis, lab, b 17 Spann av.
Casey Ellen (wid John), h 274 W McCarty.
Casey Ellen (wid Patrick), h 278 W McCarty.

TUTEWILER UNDERTAKER, NO. 72 WEST MARKET STREET. TELEPHONE 216.

PARTNERSHIP INSURANCE At low cost. By which provision is made against the pecuniary loss and embarrassment resulting from the death of a member of a firm.
Provident Life and Trust Co. of Philadelphia, D. W. EDWARDS, Gen'l Agt., 508 Indiana Trust Bldg.

THEODORE F. SMITHER ROOFER
GRAVEL AND OTHER COMPOSITION
Office, 15 W. Maryland St. Telephone 861.

Casey George, lab, h 611 W Pearl.
Casey Herman, lab, h 20 Hill.
Casey James, lab, b 274 W McCarty.
Casey Jeremiah, lab, b 174 N Dorman.
Casey Jeremiah, lab, b 416 Highland av.
Casey John, lab, b 185 Meek.
Casey John A, plumber, b 237 W Maryland.
Casey John E, route agt Am Ex Co, h 676 Broadway.
Casey John P, lab, b 278 W McCarty.
Casey Kate, governess Blind Institute.
Casey Mary, (wid Michael), b 83 N Gillard av.
Casey Mary (wid Patrick), h 185 Meek.
Casey Michael A, helper, b 416 Highland av.
Casey Michael M, condr, h 650 E 8th.
Casey Patrick J, lab, h 193 S Pine.
Casey Robert, lab, h 8 Douglass.
Casey Robert A, plastr, h e s Rural 4 s of Clifford av.
Casey Thomas, fireman, b 115 Meek.
Casey Thomas M, clk R M S, h 101 N New Jersey.
Casey Wm, lab, r 249 W 3d.
Casey Wm, station agt Consumers' Gas Co, b 197 W Maryland.
Casey Wm H, towerman, b 237 W Maryland.
Casey Wm M, printer, b 221 W Pearl.
Cash Allison O, carp, 108 Jefferson av, h same.
Cash Dudley O, trav agt, b 255 N Alabama.
Cash George T, driver, h 46 Oliver av (W I).
Cash Glenn A, student, b 180 Jefferson av.
Cash Hugh M (L E and H M Cash), r 853 E Michigan.
Cash John, lab, h 369 Lafayette.
Cash Lawrence E (L E and H M Cash), h 853 E Michigan.
Cash L E & H M (Lawrence E and Hugh M), medicine mnfrs, 853 E Michigan.
Cash Milton, clk Rich & McVey, b 283 W Michigan.
Cash Mina, teacher Public School No 4, b 283 W Michigan.
Cash Richard M, carp, h 351 N California.
Cash Willard, lab, h 412 E Pearl.
Cash Wm P, carp, h 102 Warren av (W I).
Cashman Daniel W, gas inspr, b 90 Belmont av (H).
Cashman George, lab, b 90 Belmont av (H).
Cashman Jacob, lab, h 312 W Merrill.
Cashman John, lab, b 90 Belmont av (H).
Cashman Timothy, shoemkr, h 90 Belmont av (H).
Caskey Alice E (wid James), b 54 N Station (B).
Caskey Effie M, clk J B Caskey & Son, b 9 N Station (B).
Caskey Jacob B (J B Caskey & Son), b 9 N Station (B).
Caskey James B, engr, h 9 N Station (B).
CASKEY J B & SON (Jacob B and Walter L), Druggists, 1 N Station (B).
Caskey Walter L (J B Caskey & Son), b 9 N Station (B).
Caskey Wm G, lab, b 36 Henry.
Casman George, fireman, r 34 N East.
Casner Edward, tiremkr, b 235 S Noble.
Cass Alice (wid Keirn G), h 150 Union.
Cass John F, wheelmkr, b 150 Union.
Cass Ray D, barber, 29 N Illinois, h 344 N Alabama.
Cass Sara A, teacher Public School No 22, b 150 Union.
Cass Wm H, wheelmkr, b 150 Union.
Cassady, see also Casady and Cassidy.
Cassady George D, porter, h 337 Coburn.

THE WHEN IS A WORLD BEATER.

Cassady James J, b 371 E McCarty.
Cassady James S, city fireman, h 312 E North.
Cassady Ulysses G, designer, h 773 E Washington.
Cassatt Frank, butcher, h 74 Bradshaw.
Cassatt Mary (wid Higgins), b 74 Bradshaw.
Cassel Charles, carp, b 216 Ash.
Cassel Chester R, driver, b 14 Park av.
Cassel Earl R, brakeman, b 14 Park av.
Cassel Jefferson M, bkkpr, h 14 Park av.
Cassell Harry L (Cassell & Karnatz), b 83 Greer.
Cassell Henry, h 15 Morrison.
Cassell Roy O, driver, b 14 Park av.
Cassell Winfield S, tel opr, h 83 Greer.
Cassell & Karnatz (Harry L Cassell, Jesse F Karnatz), adv agts, 52½ S Illinois.
Casserly John, motorman, h rear 256 Blake.
Casserly Michael, lab, b 279 W Pearl.
Casserly Patrick, lab, h 671 W Vermont.
Casserly Thomas, b 279 W Pearl.
Cassidy, see also Casady and Cassady.
Cassidy Anna (wid Wm), b 11 McGinnis.
Cassidy Clinton W, engr, b 99 Lexington av.
Cassidy Edward A, blksmith, b 225 E Market.
Cassidy Joseph, ironwkr, b 285 S Capitol av.
Cassidy Katherine (wid James), chief cook Insane Hospital.
Cassidy Louis B, carp, h 325 E Merrill.
Cassidy Patrick, lab, b 246 W Washington.
Cassidy Peter L, brakeman, h 287 N Noble.
Cassidy Richard T, fireman, h 294 Springfield.
Cassidy Wm, sawyer, h 272 S West.
Cassiero Frank A, fruits, h 118 N Capitol av.
Cassin Michael, lab, b 107 High.
Cassius Brother, teacher, b n w cor Coburn and Short.
Castello Maria (wid Charles), h 161 Buchanan.
Castenholz Richard C, h 335 E Morris.
Caster, see also Castor and Costor.
Caster Wm M, lab, h 191 Huron.
Castetter Hiram D, lab, h 65 Ruth (M J).
Castle Charles B, lab, h 10 Michigan (H).

THE A. BURDSAL CO.
WINDOW AND PLATE
GLASS
Putty, Glazier Points, Diamonds.
Wholesale and Retail. 34 and 36 S. Meridian St.

ELECTRIC CONSTRUCTION Isolated Plants Installed. Electric Wiring and Fittings of all kinds. C. W. Meikel. Tel. 466. 96-98 E. New York St

DALTON & MERRIFIELD { LUMBER South Noble St., near E. Washington

INDIANA ELECTROTYPE CO. :: BEST WORK. LOWEST PRICES. 23 WEST PEARL ST., INDIANAPOLIS, IND. JOB WORK. BOOK PLATES. All Orders Promptly Filled. BEST PATENT BASE ON THE MARKET.

KIRKHOFF BROS.,
GAS AND ELECTRIC FIXTURES
THE LARGEST LINE IN THE CITY.
102-104 SOUTH PENNSYLVANIA ST.
TELEPHONE 910.

Castle Charles L, engr, h 29 Decatur.
Castle Ernest V, electrician, b 206 S East.
Castle Frank B, confr, b 6 Cornell av.
Castle George, lab, b 10 Michigan (H).
Castle Harry T, painter, b 66 Cornell av.
Castle Henry N, supt The Bradstreet Co, h 15 Morrison.
Castle James F, clk, b 66 Cornell av.
Castle Mary J (wid James), h 66 Cornell av.
Castle Oliver H, ice machinery, 19 W South, b 311 N Alabama.
Castle Otto W, paperhanger, b 206 S East.
Castle Richard C, carp, h 10 Michigan (H).
Castle Robert E, b 66 Cornell av.
Castle Wm M, lab, h 206 S East.
Castleman David M, lab, h 320 Michigan (H).
Castleton George, lab, r 66 N Missouri.
Castor Lewis, b 583 N Rural.
CASTOR BROS (Frank G Castor), Book and Job Printers, 77 Mass av, Tel 124.
Castor Frank G (Castor Bros), b 72 Cornell av.
Castor Gertrude, h 139 N Gillard av.
Castor Harry G, cabtmkr, h 480 Brookside av.
CASTOR HIRAM C, Physician and Surgeon, 288 Mass av, Tel 235; h 91 Brookside av, Tel 608.
Castor Jesse W, printer, b 72 Cornell av.
Castor John W, fireman, b 504 Virginia av.
Castor Mary, r 175 E Louisiana.
Castor Samantha W (wid Edwin A), h 72 Cornell av.
Caswell Omer H, decorator N Y Store, b 31 N Liberty.
Caswell Wm H, plumber, 305 E Washington, h 31 N Liberty.
Catalani Frank, barber, 48 W Washington, h 115 W New York.
Catalano John, musician, h 494½ Virginia av.
Catalano Mary (wid Nicholas), h 494½ Virginia av.
Catellier Didier, shoecutter, h 1 Putnam (B).

COAL AND COKE
The W. G. Wasson Co.,
130 INDIANA AVE. TEL. 989
LIME AND LATH

Catellier Leda, milliner, 1 Putnam (B), h same.
Cates John M, carp, h 195½ E Washington.
Cates John W, real est, h 47 Frank.
Cates Wm, brakeman, b 23 Poplar (B).
Cathcart Albert E, collr, b 21 Cherry.
CATHCART, CLELAND & CO (Robert W Cathcart, John E Cleland, Wm F Coughlen), Books, Stationery and Wall Paper, 6 E Washington, Tel 330.
Cathcart John W Rev, h 21 Cherry.
Cathcart Kate, teacher Industrial School, b 439 N Penn.
Cathcart Robert W (Cathcart, Cleland & Co), h 439 N Penn.
Cathcart Wm, clk, b 21 Cherry.
Cather Dana G, hostler, r Union Stock Yards.
Cather Wallace E, condr, b 351 Mass av.
Catherwood Ellen (wid Joseph), b 128 E St Joseph.
Catherwood Frederick B, clk, h 258 Talbott av.
Catherwood Lilly (wid Albert S), r 71 The Windsor.
Cathiser James K, mach hd, b 58 Thomas.
Cathiser Louis A, lab, b 58 Thomas.
Catholic Record The, Alexander Chamel pub, 100 W Georgia.
Cathro David R, clk, h 579 N West.
Cathro Elizabeth, dry goods, 579 N West, h same.
Catlin Mary J (wid Harry), h 386 N New Jersey.
Catlin Mary J (wid Wm W), h 1099 N Penn.
Cato Mack, lab, h 90 Bradshaw.
Caton Andrew P, lab, h 360 S Delaware.
Caton John, lab, h 176 Harrison.
Caton Edward G, meats, 102 E Mkt House, h 40 Kappus (W I).
Caton Peter A, sawmkr, b 360 S Delaware.
Catt Joseph L, clk, h 466 S Illinois.
Catt L A (L A Catt & Co), h 150 N Senate av.
CATT L A & CO (L A and Wilson Catt), Dealers in Flour and Feed; also Boarding Stable, 192-194 W Maryland and 193-195 W Pearl, Tel 770.
Catt Omer L, clk, b 466 S Illinois.
Catt Sarah, dressmkr, 466 S Illinois, h same.
Catt Wm F, clk, b 466 S Illinois.
Catt Wilson (L A Catt & Co), h 150 N Senate av.
Catterson Charles C, painter, b 40 Bismarck.
Catterson Elizabeth A (wid Robert W), h 266 Union.
Catterson Frank, waiter, h 73 N Alabama.
Catterson George E, clk, b 40 Bismarck.
Catterson George N (R F Catterson & Son), h 808 N Meridian.
Catterson Missouri (wid Abel), h 40 Bismarck.
Catterson Robert F (R F Catterson & Son), r 1 Catterson blk.
CATTERSON R F & SON (Robert F and George N), Real Estate, Loans and Rents, 24 Kentucky av, Tel 359.
Caudell Eli N, lab, h 943 Mass av.
Caudell Elijah W, lab, b 99 N Rural (B).
Caudell Henry J, lab, h 99 N Rural (B).
Caudell Jacob W, helper, h 30 Cushing.
Caudell John F, lab, h 103 N Rural (B).
Caudell Marion O, lab, b 103 N Rural (B).
Caudell Otto E, lab, b 103 N Rural (B).
Caughlin, see also Coughlin.

W. H. MESSENGER COMPLETE HOUSE FURNISHER 101 East Washington Street, Telephone 491

Foundry and Pattern Shop } McNamara, Koster & Co. { PHONE 1593 212-218 S. Penn. St.

Caughlin Ella D, dressmkr, r 63 W Ohio.
Caughthran David B, trav agt, h 520 N Senate av.
Cauldwell, see also Caldwell.
Cauldwell David J, h 61 Camp.
CAULDWELL E H & CO (Edward H Cauldwell), Contractors and Builders, Screen Doors, 147 Ash. (See adv in classified Carpenters, Contractors and Builders.)
Cauldwell Susan A (wid Jasper), b 213½ Christian av.
Cauley Edward, lab, h 53 Maple.
Cauley Michael, lab, h 39 Williams.
Cauley Wm, lab, b 53 Maple.
Caulkins, see also Calkins.
Caulkins Aloc M, druggist, 109 E Washington, r 103½ same.
Cavaliero Nicholas, fruits, h 411 E Pearl.
Cavanaugh Joseph R, supt car service dept C C C & St L Ry, h 734 N New Jersey.
Cavanaugh Bartholomew, lab, b 271 W Market.
Cavanaugh Catherine (wid Edward), h 241 W Maryland.
Cavanaugh Ella (wid Wm), r 120 S Noble.
Cavanaugh Irvin, wheelmkr, b 108 S Judge Harding (W I).
Cavanaugh James, cook, h 23 Shelby.
Cavanaugh James, lab, b 342 W 1st.
Cavanaugh James J (McCaslin & Cavanaugh), h 428 N California.
Cavanaugh John, b 342 W 1st.
Cavanaugh John, lab, h 405 W New York.
Cavanaugh John, wheelmkr, b 108 S Judge Harding (W I).
Cavanaugh Lawrence, lab, b 107 Eddy.
Cavanaugh Margaret (wid Joseph), b 29 Oxford.
Cavanaugh Margaret (wid Matthias), h 107 Eddy.
Cavanaugh Patrick, lab, b 271 W Market.
Cave Clarissa (wid Jonas), b 36 N Gale (B).
Cave George W, foreman, h 40 N Gale (B).
Cave John D, foreman, h 36 N Gale (B).
Cave Omer, barber, 123 Ft Wayne av, h same.
CAVEN JOHN, Vice-Pres Indianapolis Light and Power Co, Suite 2-4, 81½ W Market, b Circle Park Hotel.
Cavender Frank P, tel opr, b 287 Lincoln av.
Cavender Harry H, clk When Clothing Store, b 287 Lincoln av.
Cavender Harvey J, carp, h 287 Lincoln av.
Cavett Alven, clk Exchange Hotel (W I).
CAVETT HENRY, Propr Exchange Hotel, Union Stock Yards (W I).
Cavin Michael, lab, h 502 E Georgia.
Cavin Wm J, mach, b 502 E Georgia.
Cavolt George E, lab, h 553 S Illinois.
Cawby James W, tinner, h s e cor Elizabeth and Caldwell.
Cawby Martin, b 297 N California.
Caylor, see also Kaler, Kaylor, Koehler and Kuler.
Caylor Allen, h 460 N West.
Caylor Edward A, dairy, s w cor Brookside and Lebanon avs, h same.
Caylor Elizabeth S, mach opr The Indpls News, b 315 Mass av.
Caylor Henry, lab, h 318 W Pearl.
Caylor Jefferson, trav agt Hendricks & Cooper, h 276 Bellefontaine.
Caylor Oliver P, clk, h 156 John.
Caylor Rachel W (wid George), h 315½ Mass av.

Henry H. Fay, 40½ E. WASHINGTON ST., AGENT FOR Insurance Co. of North America, Pennsylvania Fire Ins. Co.

Caylor Susan E, printer, b 315½ Mass av.
Cazat Warren, r 42½ Mass av.
Cebulla Sebastian P Rev, asst Sacred Heart Church, h n w cor Union and Palmer.
Cecil Thomas W, clk Assessment Bureau, h 176 E St Clair.
Cedan Annie, h 139 Eddy.
Cedan Frank, bartndr, b 139 Eddy.
Cedan Thomas, lab, b 139 Eddy.
Cederholm Charles A, mach, h 236 N Pine.
Cella John A (Cella & Geis), b 74 N Illinois.
Cella & Geis (John A Cella, Jacob J Geis), mantels, 23 W Ohio.
CENTER TOWNSHIP ASSESSOR'S OFFICE, Eugene Saulcy Assessor, 35 Court House, Tel 912.
CENTRAL ADVERTISING CO (Mayne C P Parker, George B Swain), Advertisers' Agts, Advertising Specialties and Novelties; Display and Scenic Signs a Specialty, 83 W Georgia.
Central Chair Co, Thomas L Thompson pres, Charles F Woerner vice-pres, B Frank Schmid sec and treas, s w cor Georgia and Missouri.
CENTRAL CHRISTIAN CHURCH, Rev John E Pounds Pastor, n e cor Walnut and Ft Wayne av.
Central College of Physicians and Surgeons, Joseph Eastman pres, John L Masters treas, Samuel E Earp dean and sec, Thomas B Eastman asst sec, s e cor Penn and South.
CENTRAL CYCLE MANUFACTURING CO, Lucius M Wainwright Pres, Albert D Johnson Sec and Treas, Bicycle Mnfrs and Retail Dealers; General Office and Factory 238-240 S Meridian, Tel 1636; Retail Store 52 N Penn, Tel 1846.
CENTRAL ENGINEERING CO, Charles C Brown Consulting Engineer, E Brown Baker Civil Engineer, 225-226 Lemcke Bldg.

Union Casualty & Surety Co. of St. Louis, Mo.
Employers', Public, General, Teams and Elevator Liability; also Workmen's Collective, Steam Boiler, Plate Glass and Automatic Sprinkler Insurance.
W. E. BARTON & CO., General Agents, 504 Indiana Trust Building.
LONG DISTANCE TELEPHONE 1918.

THE FRED DIETZ CO
WOODEN PACKING BOXES MADE TO ORDER FACTORY AND WAREHOUSE TRUCKS. 400 Madison Avenue. Telephone 65.

Shorthand! BUSINESS UNIVERSITY. When Bl'k. Elevator day and night. Typewriting, Penmanship, Book-keeping, Office Training free. See page 4. Est. 1850. Tel. 499. E. J. HEEB, Proprietor.

Steam Pumping Machinery { HENRY R. WORTHINGTON, 64 S. PENNSYLVANIA ST. Long Distance Telephone 284.

UNION CO-OPERATIVE LAUNDRY { LAUNDRY GIRLS.) NOS. 8, 40 AND 42 VIRGINIA AVENUE
T. E. SOMERVILLE, MANAGER — TELEPHONES NOS. 8, 40 AND 42 INDIANAPOLIS, IND.

HORACE M. HADLEY
REAL ESTATE AND LOANS....
66 East Market Street
Telephone 1540. BASEMENT.

CENTRAL INDIANA HOSPITAL FOR THE INSANE, George F Edenharter, M D, Supt, National road 3 miles west of city, Tel 389.
CENTRAL LAW UNION THE (Bronte M Aikins, Salem P Welman, George H Brackney), Law and Collections, 425-426 Lemcke Bldg, Tel 1847. (See adv under classified Collection Agents.)
CENTRAL LOAN CO, Anson B Wiltse Mngr, Room 5 Yohn Blk, 11½ N Meridian.
CENTRAL PRINTING CO, Sauer & Conner Proprs, Book and Job Printers, 83 E Court.
CENTRAL RUBBER AND SUPPLY CO THE, Edward C Deardorff Pres, Theodore H Deardorff Sec and Treas, Wholesale and Retail Dealers in Rubber Goods, Belting, Packing, Mill and Railroad Supplies, 79 S Illinois, Tel 922. (See left side lines.)
CENTRAL STATES DISPATCH FAST FREIGHT LINE, Thomas H Noonan Genl Mngr, Lynn E Stone Agt, Rooms 1-10 Lorraine Bldg, Tel 1396.
CENTRAL UNION TELEPHONE CO, Wm W Rider State Supt, Tel 43; Nathaniel G Warth Asst State Supt, Tel 43; Walter L Hill Exchange Mngr, Tel 1 (or 319), s w cor Illinois and Ohio.
CEREALINE MANUFACTURING CO THE, Thomas T Gaff Pres, Joseph F Gent Vice-Pres, Richard Thomas Sec and Treas, 950 Gent (M P); Tel Office 1460.
Chabloz Alexander, lab, h 58 Jones.
Chadwell Harry, coachman 854 N Penn.
Chadwick James F, stonecutter, h 380 S West.
Chadwick Levi, carp, h 314 E Georgia.
Chadwick Wm, carp, b 158 S William (W I).

Merchants' and Manufacturers' Exchange
Make Collections and Commercial Reports......
J. E. TAKKEN, MANAGER,
19 Union Building, 73 West Maryland Street

Chafee Wm T, trav agt Fahnley & McCrea, h 179 N State av.
Chaille Emerson W, student, b 241 Cornell av.
Chaille Uriah M, treas Ind Bap Pub Co, h 241 Cornell av.
Chalfant The, n w cor Penn and Michigan.
Chalk John R, bkkpr, h 228 Prospect.
Challenger Frank C, clk, b 288 E Market.
Chalmers Allen, lab, h 31 Bismarck av (H).
Chalmers James H, solr, h 21 Laurel.
Chalmers Mary (wid Andrew), h 242 Indiana av.
CHAMBERLAIN ALBERT M, Sec Board of Directors and Genl Representative Butler College, h w s Downey av 1 s of Washington av (I).
Chamberlain Jenner H (Warman, Black, Chamberlain & Co), b 99 Highland av.
Chamberlin Andrew B, tile setter, h 239 Blake.
Chamberlin Clarence O, lab, h 48 Coffey (W I).
Chamberlin Hannah J, grocer, 242 Oliver av, h 22 N Judge Harding (W I).
Chamberlin James F, saloon, 1321 Northwestern av, h same.
Chamberlin John F, clk, b 323 W Michigan.
Chamberlin John L, carp, h 327 E Wabash.
Chamberlin Wm H, h 323 W Michigan.
Chamberlin Wm H jr, scale rep, b 323 W Michigan.
Chambers Avery St C (Chambers Bros), b 915 Morris (W I).
CHAMBERS BROS (Oscar C and Avery St C), Druggists, 199 Howard (W I), Tel 1387.
Chambers Ferdinand, lawyer, 18½ N Penn, b 399 N Alabama.
Chambers James, novelties, 159 E Washington, h 427 Bellefontaine.
Chambers James H, lab, h 50 Springfield.
Chambers John W, lab, b 427 Bellefontaine.
Chambers Joseph M, express, h 40 Oliver av (W I).
Chambers Martha (wid John), h 404 N West.
Chambers Nancy J (wid George), h w s Euclid av 2 n of Ohio.
Chambers Nellie (wid John), h 604 N New Jersey.
Chambers Oscar C (Chambers Bros), b 915 Morris (W I).
CHAMBERS PERLEE L, Wholesale and Retail Dealer in Cigars, Tobacco and Smokers' Supplies, 56 W Washington and 59 N Penn, Tel 83; h 399 N Alabama.
CHAMBERS, PICKENS & MOORES (Smiley N Chambers, Samuel O Pickens, Charles W Moores), Lawyers, 602-610 Lemcke Bldg, Tel 787.
Chambers Smiley N (Chambers, Pickens & Moores), h 294 College av.
Chambers Thomas J, driver, r 138 E New York.
Chambers Wm, foreman, b 646 Herbert (M P).
Chambers Vance Z, porter, r 90 S Illinois.
Chamness Dayton C, lab, h 92 Woodburn av (W I).
Chamness James A, molder, h 26 Germania av (H).
Chamness Luke B, lab, h 193 Belmont av (H).
Chamness Mary, r 21 Bismarck av (H).

CLEMENS VONNEGUT || Wire Rope, Machinery, Lathes, Drills and Shapers
184, 186 and 192 E. Washington St.

THE WM. H. BLOCK CO. DRY GOODS, DRAPERIES, RUGS, WINDOW SHADES.
7 AND 9 EAST WASHINGTON STREET.

Chamness Rufus E, student, r 140 N Alabama.
Champe Charles G, painter, b 293 Virginia av.
Champe Eliza P (wid John L), h 293 Virginia av.
Champe Wm E, checkman, h 329 Virginia av.
Champion Coffee and Spice Mills, 31-33 E Maryland, see Krag-Reynolds Co.
Champion Edwin M, pressman, b 221 E Georgia.
Champion Elizabeth A, h 83 W Michigan.
Champion George, pressman, b 474 N Alabama.
Champion Isaac N, carp, h 101 Hoyt av.
Champion John A, printer, b 221 E Georgia.
Champion Joseph B, stenog, h 105 N New Jersey.
Champion Thomas, lab, b 287 E Georgia.
Champion Wm, foreman, h 221 E Georgia.
Champion Wm H, b 221 E Georgia.
Chance Frank S, sec Chance Matthews Printing Co, h 41 Colorado av.
Chance George, lab, h 7 Church.
Chance John W, lab, h 496 S Capitol av.
Chance Matthews Printing Co, E Edwin Matthews pres, Frank S Chance sec, Henry W Paine treas, 2 News bldg.
Chandler, see also Chantler.
Chandler Albert G, printer, b 51 Greer.
Chandler Arthur B, clk, b 30 Park av.
Chandler Charles, clk, r 90 N New Jersey.
Chandler Charles, cook, b 93 Columbia al.
Chandler Edward M, millwright, b 571 Broadway.
Chandler Elias, lab, r 66 N Missouri.
Chandler Eliza (wid Sylvester), h 54 Rockwood.
Chandler Emma K (wid Hadley), b 160 Broadway.
Chandler Frank, bartndr, h 567 N West.
Chandler George M, sec and purchasing agt Chandler & Taylor Co, b 350 College av.
Chandler George R, printer, h 51 Greer.
Chandler Harry A, engraver, h 429 N Senate av.

CHANDLER HENRY C, Wood Engraver, Rooms 13-14, 47½ N Illinois, s e cor Market, Tel 1077; h 278 W Vermont. (See adv in classified Engravers.)

Chandler Isaac, lab, h 37 Elizabeth.
Chandler Isabella (wid Wm), h 755 Bookers al.
Chandler Jacob, lab, h 18 Cora.
Chandler James H, cook, r 251 E Washington.
Chandler James L D, treas The Indpls Millinery Co, b 603 Broadway.
Chandler John H, mach, b 571 Broadway.
Chandler Lillian, stenog, b 160 Broadway.
Chandler Lora B (wid Wm), h 30 Park av.
Chandler Louis, clk, h 133 Highland av.
Chandler Mark, clk Roosevelt House.
Chandler Martha A (wid James W), h 161 Osage.
Chandler Mary, h 93 Columbia al.
Chandler Olive K, stenog, b 429 N Senate av.
Chandler Pearl, b 143 N West.
Chandler Theodore R, diesinker, h 443 Union.
Chandler Thomas, inspr, r 23 N West.
Chandler Thomas E, pres Chandler & Taylor Co, h 284 W Vermont.

Chandler Thomas E, student, b 571 Broadway.
Chandler Walter, clk, b 30 Park av.
Chandler Wm E, millwright, h 571 Broadway.
Chandler Wm G, millwright, b 571 Broadway.
Chandler Wm G, supt N Y Store, r 400 N Illinois.

CHANDLER & TAYLOR COMPANY, Thomas E Chandler Pres, Wm M Taylor Vice-Pres and Treas, George M Chandler Sec and Purchasing Agt, Engines and Saw Mill Machinery, 370 W Washington, Tel 320.

Chaney, see also Cheney.
Chaney George F, clk, b 58 Highland pl.
Chaney Mary (wid Wm), b 650 Madison av.
Chaney Phoebe E (wid Fernando C), h 58 Highland pl.
Chaney Stewart H, carp, h 555 W Addison (N I).
Chaney Wm A, train disp, h 58 Highland pl.
Chaney Wm H, carp, b 555 W Addison (N I).
Chantler, see also Chandler.
Chantler Mary A (wid Thomas), b 66 Oak.
Chantler Stephen, ins agt, b 177 Columbia av.
Chapel Anna, dressmkr, 158 N Senate av, b same.
Chapin Edward J, tool mnfr, 500 W Washington, h 204 Blackford.
Chapin Elijah, lab, h rear 163 St Mary.
Chapin Frances M, retoucher, b 204 Blackford.
Chapin George W, condr, h 949 Wilcox.
Chapin James W, h 405 Central av.
Chapin Wm G, cashr freight office C C C & St L Ry, h 275 W Michigan.
Chaplin Edward, meats, 78 E Mkt House, h 101 Pleasant.
Chaplin Vincent H, butcher, b 101 Pleasant.
Chapman Alfred P, engr, h 57 Jones.
Chapman Alonzo B, engraver Julius C Walk & Son, h 483 N Capitol av.
Chapman Anna L (wid John S), h 46 Lexington av.

GUIDO R. PRESSLER,
FRESCO PAINTER
Churches, Theaters, Public Buildings, Etc., A Specialty.
Residence, No. 325 North Liberty Street
INDIANAPOLIS, IND.

INDIANAPOLIS STEEL ROOFING AND CORRUGATING WORKS, 23 and 25 East South Street. S. D. NOEL, Proprietor.

David S. McKernan, REAL ESTATE AND LOANS
Rooms 2-5 Thorpe Block.
A number of choice pieces for subdivision, or for manufacturers' sites, with good switch facilities.

DIAMOND WALL PLASTER { Telephone 1410
BUILDERS' EXCHANGE.

UNION TRANSFER AND STORAGE CO. Cor. E. Ohio St. and C., C., C. & St. L. R'y Tracks.
BRICK WAREHOUSE; CLEANEST AND SAFEST STORAGE IN CITY FOR HOUSEHOLD GOODS AND MERCHANDISE.

W. McWORKMAN,

METAL CEILINGS,
ROLLING SHUTTERS,
DOORS AND PARTITIONS.

930 W. Washington St. Tel. 1118.

Chapman Blanche, stenog Old Wayne Mut Life Assn, b 208 Spann av.
Chapman Carey, fireman, b 308 S Illinois.
Chapman Carey E, clk, b 217 Huron.
Chapman Charles E, decorator, h n s Ohio av 1 w of Elm av (I).
Chapman Elizabeth (wid Nathan), r 213 S Pine.
Chapman Erastus P, insp, h 49 Thomas.
Chapman Harry, barber, 325 E Washington, b 208 Spann av.
Chapman Harry C, engr, h 69 Agnes.
Chapman James, porter R M S, b 46 Lexington av.
Chapman John, hostler, b 32 Byram pl.
Chapman John F, switchman, h 463 Stillwell.
Chapman John W, guard Marion County Workhouse, h 10 Allfree av.
Chapman Maria, b 95 N Meridian.
Chapman Mary E (wid Samuel), h 208 Spann av.
Chapman Page, clk S A Fletcher & Co, b n e cor Senate av and 30th (M).
Chapman Samuel B, decorator, h n s Ohio av 1 w of Elm av (I).
Chapman Thomas S, carp, 38 Camp, h same.
Chapman Tracy J, millwright, h 217 Huron.
Chapman Wm D, bkkpr Indpls Dist Tel Co, b w s Linwood av 4 n of Washington.
Chapman Wilson, lab, h 105 Locke.
Chappell Dorothy, b 51 Sullivan.
Chappell Holly F, carp, b 144 N Senate av.
Chapple Walter A, hostler, h 17 Douglass.
Chapple Wm, carp, h 407 Coburn.
Chapple Wm T, propertyman, h 120 Hosbrook.
CHARITY ORGANIZATION SOCIETY, Charles S Grout Genl Sec, 1 Plymouth Bldg, s e cor New York and Meridian, Tel 613.
Charles Aaron B, paperhngr, h 188 Fayette.
Charles Abraham B, carp, h 311 N West.
Charles Abraham L, painter, h 187 Douglass.
Charles Benjamin, h 41 Brett.
Charles Charles J, h 836 S Meridian.
Charles Fannie, b 57 Drake.

SEALS,
STENCILS,
STAMPS, Etc.
GEO. J. MAYER
15 S. Meridian St.
TELEPHONE 1386.

Charles George, waiter, r 163 Bird.
Charles Henry, waiter, r 66 N Missouri.
Charles Horace H, paperhngr, b 311 N West.
Charles Joseph, b 41 Brett.
Charles Louis J, foreman, h 137 N State av.
Charles Marion E, b 311 N West.
Charles Mary (wid Thomas), h 109 S Noble.
Charles Peter, lab, h 179 W 7th.
Charleston Thomas, lab, h 289 Yandes.
Charlton Arthur, carp, b 244 Huron.
Charlton Frederick R, phys, 16 E Ohio, r same.
Charpie Avery B Rev, h 17 Keystone av.
Charpie Leonard S, stenog Indpls Foundry Co, b 17 Keystone av.
Charron Claude, agt, h 15 W North.
Chartrand Joseph Rev, asst S S Peter and Paul Cathedral, h s e cor 5th and Meridian.
Chase Clarence J, ins agt, h 612 E Washington.
Chase Elmer, lab, b 17 Deloss.
Chase Hiram H, stonecutter, h 220 Fulton.
Chase Nina H, bkkpr, b 612 E Washington.
Chase Wm H, engr, h 225 N Noble.
Chase Wm P, mach, h 56 Thalman av.
Chastain Charles, lab, b 60 Hazel.
Chastain Edward, lab, h 52 Hazel.
Chastain John A T, poultry, E Mkt House, h 60 Hazel.
Chasteen Samuel W, cooper, h 35 Beacon.
Chasteen Wm, cooper, h Ida (M J).
Chastine Charles, driver, b 211 W Market.
Chastine Clyde P, lab, b 1360 Indianapolis av.
CHATARD FRANCIS SILAS RIGHT REV, Bishop of Vincennes, h s e cor 5th and Meridian.
Chatfield George L, mach, b Illinois House.
Chatman George H, lab, b 613 Miller av (M P).
Chatman George W, peddler, h 354 N Pine.
Chatman John, lab, b 72 Harlan.
Chatman Wm, lab, b 154 Hosbrook.
Chatten Charles M, finisher, h 38 Camp.
Chavis Charles, clk, r 300 E North.
Chavis Wm M, phys, 187½ Mass av, h same.
Chawner Chalmers, driver, r 27 Grand Opera House blk.
Cheatham Charles, cook, r 285 Chapel.
Cheatham Charles, porter, h 57 Mayhew.
Cheatham George W, mer policeman, h 525 N Senate av.
Cheatham Nancy J (wid John E), b 850 N Penn.
Cheatham Richard M, barber, r 35½ Kentucky av.
Cheatham Thomas W, lab, h 140 Harlan.
Cheatham Wm, plastr, h w s Madeira 8 s of Prospect.
Cheek Bond, lab, h n e cor Hazel and Lawrence.
Cheek John, student, r 71 Madison av.
Cheek John W, engr, h 251 Fletcher av.
Cheek Wm, lab, h w s Rural 2 n of Brookside av.
Cheely Edward W, patternmkr, b 41 Belmont av.
Cheely George W (Cheely & Son), tobacco mnfrs, 41 Belmont av, h same.
Cheely Harry (Cheely & Son), b 41 Belmont av.
Cheely & Son (George W and Harry), grocers, s e cor Washington and Addison (M J).
Cheeseman Henry, lab, b 27 Woodlawn av.

A. METZGER AGENCY ESTABLISHED 1863. INSURANCE

LAMBERT GAS & GASOLINE ENGINE CO.
ANDERSON, IND. PORTABLE GASOLINE ENGINES. 2 TO 25 H. P.

BICYCLES $5 { DOWN. MONTHLY. } Best Terms. { Best Wheels. } WHEELMEN'S CO. 31 W. OHIO ST. LONG DISTANCE TEL. 1855.

Cheeseman Sarah A (wid John), h 27 Woodlawn av.
Cheeseman Thomas, lab, b 27 Woodlawn av.
Cheezum Wm W, printer, h 256 S West.
Cheney, see also Chaney.
Cheney George M, civil engr, h 241 Ramsey av.
Cheney Marvell C, blksmith, b 201 N California.
Chenkey Andrew, polisher, h 947 Madison av.
Chenoweth Daniel A, office 66 E Market, h 441 N Delaware.
Chenoweth James C, motorman, h 142 Columbia av.
Chenoweth Jennie, boardinig 181 N Delaware.
Cherdron Charles, sawyer, b 217 N Pine.
Cherdron Frank, tel opr, b 217 N Pine.
Cherdron Henry, lab, b 217 N Pine.
Cherdron Martha E (wid Charles), h 217 N Pine.
Cherdron Oscar L, clk C Friedgen, b 217 N Pine.
Cherry David, lab, b 166 Osage.
Cherry Horace O, clk, b 235 Broadway.
Cherry James P, printer, h 497 N Senate av.
Cherry Mary M (wid Andrew O), h 235 Broadway.
Cherry Wm C, insp Indpls Fire Insp Bureau, b 235 Broadway.
Cherry Wm M, lab, h 380 N Brookside av.
Cheseldine Anna (wid Andrew), h 36 Stevens.
Cheslyn John W, finisher, h 37 Brett.
Chester Albert A, carp, h 38 Eureka av.
Chester Charles N, mach hd, h 19 Keith.
Chester Dick H, mngr Henry R Worthington, 64 S Penn, b 185 N Delaware.
Chester James, tel opr, r 211 N Illinois.
Chester Oil Co, George C Webster pres, Ernest W Dawson sec, 51 Lombard bldg.
Chester Ola (wid Thomas E), b 22 Oriental.
Chester Oriel E, carp, h 107 Malott av.
CHESTER PIPE AND TUBE CO THE (John H Dilks), 203 Majestic Bldg.
Chesterfield Oscar, attendant Insane Hospital.
Chestnutt John, sec Moore & Co, auditor Kingan & Co, h 814 N Alabama.
Chestnutt John W, clk Kingan & Co, b 370 N Meridian.
Chetester Barbara (wid George), h 101 Nebraska.
CHEVALIER PERCY R, Propr Lion Mantel and Grate House, 114 N Delaware, Tel 1437; h 57 Ruckle.
Cheyne Frederick H, electrician, h 219 Cornell av.
Chicago Belting Co, Harry L Whaley agt, 38 Kentucky av.
CHICAGO BRIDGE AND IRON CO, Albert Michie Agt, Engineers and Contractors, Office Room 6 Builders' Exchange, 35 E Ohio, Tel 970. (See adv in classified Contractors—Bridge.)
Chidester Daniel, lab, b 129 S Reisner (W I).
Chidester Wm J, trav agt, h 196 N Delaware.
Child Harry H, mngr Fairbanks, Morse & Co, b 265 N Illinois.
Childers Alonzo, b 127 Hoyt av.
Childers Calvin F, foreman Natl Malleable Castings Co, h 68 Germania (H).
Childers Edward H, agt, b 66 Wallack.

Farm and City Loans
25 Years' Successful Business.
THOS. C. DAY & CO,
Rooms 325 to 330 Lemcke Building.

Childers Frank R, collr, b 66 Wallack.
Childers Harry R, mach, h 9 Frazee (H).
Childers James, switchman, b 183 Yandes.
Childers James P, city salesman Nelson Morris & Co, h 127 Hoyt av.
Childers John R, solr, h 66 Wallack.
Childers Joshua F, lab, h 255½ E Washington.
Childers Perry P, lab, 65 N New Jersey.
Childers Robert S, drayman, h 1 Gatling.
Childers Stephen L, city fireman, h 278 N Liberty.
Childers Wm, welldriver, h e s Nicholas 2 n of English av.
Childers Wm H, carp, h 66 Wallack.
Childress Andrew, lab, h 12 Sheridan.
Childress Charles, lab, h 179 W 5th.
Childress Mary G (wid Albert), b 128 W North.
Childs George, painter, b 65 Ludlow av.
Childs Joseph, lab, b 324 W 2d.
Childs Leroy, lab, h 1387 N Capitol av.
Childs Peter, lab, h 324 W 2d.
Childs Roy, h 197½ Christian av.
Childs Wm, lab, b 33 Willard.
Childs Wm, lab, b 324 W 2d.
Chill Albert L, student, b 169 Yandes.
Chill Anna M (wid Charles W), b 169 Yandes.
Chill Annie E, teacher, b 169 Yandes.
Chill Ida E, nurse, b 48 Cornell av.
Chill Julia, h 62 Jefferson.
Chill Thomas M, h 169 Yandes.
Chillson Marshall D, h 43 Morrison.
Chilton Margaret (wid Thomas L), h 121 Frazee (H).
Chinn Maria (wid John H), h 140 Agnes.
Chipman John W, sec Wanamaker Car Scale Co, h 23 Home av.
Chipwood Wm, barber, r 193½ E Washington.
Chrisholm Robert C, lab, h 352½ W North.
Chislett Frederick V, vice-pres and treas Indpls Warehouse Co, h Crown Hill Cemetery.
CHISLETT FREDERICK W, Supt Crown Hill Cemetery, h same, Tel 555.

EAT
QUAKER BREAD
ASK YOUR GROCER FOR IT.
THE HITZ BAKING CO.

J. H. TECKENBROCK House, Sign and Fresco Painter, 94 EAST SOUTH STREET.

FIDELITY MUTUAL LIFE PHILADELPHIA, PA. A. H. COLLINS, Gen. Agt. Baldwin Blk. RATES REASONABLE. SOUND BEYOND QUESTION. BUSINESS-LIKE IN PRACTICE.

BITUMINOUS COAL ▸▸ Edwardsport Coal and Mining Company ROOMS 42 AND 43 WHEN BUILDING.

ESTABLISHED 1876. TELEPHONE 168.
CHESTER BRADFORD,
SOLICITOR OF PATENTS,
AND COUNSEL IN PATENT CAUSES.
(See adv. page 6.)
Office:—Rooms 14 and 16 Hubbard Block, S. W. Cor. Washington and Meridian Streets, INDIANAPOLIS, INDIANA.

Chislett John, asst supt Crown Hill Cemetery, h same.
Chism Clinton, cook, h 83 Fayette.
Chisman James M, fireman, h 59 S Belmont av (W I).
Chittick Barnard F, mach opr Indpls Journal, b 132 W Ohio.
Chitwood George R, phys, 31 N East, h same.
Chitwood Joseph D, painter, h 52 Poplar (B).
Chitwood Maria J, dry goods, 241 English av, h same.
Chitwood Martha (wid Elisha), b 53 N Brightwood av (B).
Chives Enos B, shoemkr, 19 Clifford av, h 318 N Liberty.
Chives James A, shoemkr, 247 Indiana av, h 318½ same.
Chomel Alexander, pub The Catholic Record, 100 W Georgia, h same.
Chomel Alexander jr, foreman The Catholic Record, b 100 W Georgia.
Chomel Anselm J, student, b 100 W Georgia.
Chomel Wm J, printer, b 100 W Georgia.
Chowning Emmett, porter, r 135 Allegheny.
Chowning Frank, tmstr, h 216 W Chesapeake.
Chowning Louis, lab, b 216 W Chesapeake.
Chrisman James W, bartndr, h 177½ Indiana av.
Christ, see also Crist.
Christ Anna, r 649½ Virginia av.
Christ Charles, lab, r 129 Virginia av.
Christ Ernest, student, r 585 N Senate av.
Christ Harry, peddler, r 166½ W Washington.
Christ Henry, butcher, h 152 Harlan.
Christena George E, cabtmkr, h 424 E Ohio.
Christena John, cabtmkr, h 324 Spring.
Christena Wesley C, carp, h 32 King.
Christena Wm H, cabtmkr, h 34 King.
Christensen Christian, tailor, 99½ Mass av, h same.
Christensen Frederick P, lab, h 425 W McLene (N I).
Christensen Gustavus A Rev, pastor Danish Evan Lutheran Church, h 43 Beaty.

BUY THE BEST.

76 N. PENN. ST. Phone 598.

Christensen Hans, grocer, 80 Tremont av (H), h 82 same.
Christensen Hans, hostler, 111 Dunlop.
Christensen Louis G, clk, 1202 Fairview (N I).
Christensen Mathew, driver, h 1202 Fairview (N I).
Christenson Gunder K, shoemkr, h 354 Clinton.
Christenson Thomas W, brickmason, h n e cor Mill and 9th.
Christian Elizabeth (wid Wilson), h 424 Lafayette.
Christian Eugene, foreman, b 237 W Maryland.
Christian Frederick E, civil engr, 364 Ramsey av, h same.
Christian Harry A, lab, h 59 Kansas.
Christian Harry E, insp, b 206 N Alabama.
Christian John E (J E Christian & Co), h 137 E Pratt.
Christian Joseph C, barber, 78 E Ohio, h 320 N Delaware.
Christian J E & Co (John E Christian), lumber, 475 E Michigan.
Christian Mary, b 113 Dunlop.
Christian Theodore R, architect, 364 Ramsey av, h same.
Christian Thomas J, lumber, 71 Alvord, h 78 W North.
Christian Wilmer F, farmer, h 206 N Alabama.
Christian Wilmer F jr, phys City Hospital, b 206 N Alabama.
Christie, see also Christy.
Christie Charles B, mach, b 104 Spring.
Christie Frank D, b 29 Hall pl.
Christie George W, clk, h 29 Hall pl.
Christie John L, switchman, b 124 Trowbridge (W).
Christie John W, carp, h 1103 N New Jersey.
Christie Joseph, brakeman, b 22 S State av.
Christie Thomas E, h 124 Trowbridge (W).
Christie Thomas E jr, clk, b 124 Trowbridge (W).
Christison Hadley, lab, b 150 Elm.
Christison Linda (wid David), h 150 Elm.
Christison Orlando H, nailer, b 150 Elm.
Christison Wm F, lab, b 150 Elm.
Christman Wm C, porter, h 278 Chapel.
Christofferson Christian A, supt, h 466 W New York.
Christoph Wm F, cigar mnfr, 85 Kansas, h same.
Christy, see also Christie.
Christy Cora L, teacher Public School No 24, b 367 Blake.
Christy Ella M, prin Public School No 40, r 99 Yandes.
Christy Frank W, plater, b 136 S East.
Christy Israel, lab, h 195 Agnes.
Christy Jacob H, 106 Shepard (W I).
Christy James F, h 391 S Missouri.
Christy Jennie, tailoress, h 27½ Monument pl.
Christy John, lab, b 34 S West.
Christy Levi, clk Assessment Bureau, h 99 Yandes.
Christy Rachel C (wid John), h 136 S East.
Christy Samuel A, news dealer, 259 Mass av, h same.
Christy Walter W, porter, h 356 Clinton.
Christy Wm W, laundry, 367 Blake, h same.
Chryst John W, stereotyper, h 29 Traub av.
Church Andrew S, architect, 352 Ramsey av, h same.
Church Barbara E (wid Joseph H), h 166 Blake.

ROOFING MATERIAL C. ZIMMERMAN & SONS, SLATE AND GRAVEL ROOFERS, 19 SOUTH EAST STREET.

PUMPS Chain Pumps, Driven Wells and Deep Water Wells. Repairing Neatly Done. Cisterns Built. CHARLES KRAUSS', 42 S. PENN. ST. TELEPHONE 465.

Collars and Cuffs Laundered in Best of Style. Dull or High Gloss Finish. ERTEL STEAM LAUNDRY 26 and 28 N. Senate Ave. Telephone 1089.

Church Edward W, hostler, r 33 N Alabama.
Church Frank L, toolmkr, h 856 La Salle (M P).
Church George, lab, r 659½ Virginia av.
Church Henry S, lab, h 11 Minerva.
Church Ida (wid Zenus K), h 22 Jefferson av.
Church John D, bkkpr, h 872 N Delaware.
Church Joseph A, h 274 N Alabama.
Church Luretta M, music teacher, 137 N Arsenal av, b same.
Church Richard H, painter, h 137 N Arsenal av.
Church Sherman T, miller, b 274 N Alabama.
Church Wm A, mattressmkr, b 378 Blake.
Churchill Albert A, dentist, r 18 Grand Opera House blk.
Churchill Alexander, lab, b 287 W North.
Churchill Alfred, lab, b 287 W North.
Churchill Cadd, lab, b 287 W North.
Churchill Charles D, foreman, r 76 N East.
Churchill Charles E, basketmkr, h 86 N East.
Churchill Charles J, blksmith, b 71 Minerva.
Churchill Daniel J, clk Morrow & McKee, b 314 N Alabama.
Churchill Henry, paperhngr, b 71 Dearborn.
Churchill John W, lab, h e s Race 4 s of Raymond.
Churchill Joshua, lab, h 71 Dearborn.
Churchill Morton C, lab, h 31 Traub av.
Churchill Richard, lab, h 287 W North.
Churchill Richard jr, lab, b 287 W North.
Churchman Edward M, sec The Mullen-Blackledge Co, 62 S Alabama, h 618 N Penn.
Churchman Frank F (Jeffery, Fuller & Co), h Churchman pike 6 miles s e of city limits.
CHURCHMAN WM F, Cashier The Capital National Bank, h Churchman pike 6 miles s e of City.
Ciato Michael, fruits, h 218 S East.
Ciener Isaac, liquors, 167 W Washington, h 215 W New York.
CINCINNATI, HAMILTON & DAYTON R R, George W Hayler District Pass Agt, Edward R Ingersoll City Ticket Agt, Henry G Stiles Genl Agt Freight Dept, 2 W Washington, Tel 737.
Ciphers, see also Cyphers.
Ciphers Wm L, waiter, r 128 W Ohio.
CIRCLE PARK BARBER SHOP, George Fate Mngr, 15 Monument Pl.
Circle Park Hotel, Mrs Mary Rhodius propr, 13 Monument pl.
CIRCLE TRANSFER CO (Isom C Hall, Thomas H Tanner, Albert Smith), 90 W Market, Tel 1569.
Ciriakolias John, candymkr, r 17 Kentucky av.
Cissell Felix W, wagonmkr, h 65 W McCarty.
Citizens' Mutual Building and Loan Assn, Wm Downey pres, Albert B Carter sec, Wm H Latta treas, 29 Journal bldg.
CITIZENS' STREET RAILROAD CO THE, Augustus L Mason Pres, Wm L Elder Vice-Pres, Wm F Milholland Sec and Treas, Miller Elliott Supt, 750 W Washington, Tel 85.

Richardson & McCrea, 79 East Market Street, FIRE INSURANCE, REAL ESTATE, LOANS, AND RENTAL AGENTS. Telephone 182.

CITY BOARD OF PUBLIC HEALTH AND CHARITIES, Wm C Ripley Clerk, Room 10 Basement Court House, Tel 538.
CITY BOARD OF PUBLIC SAFETY, Richard C Herrick Sec, Room 2 Basement Court House, Tel 1390.
CITY BOARD OF PUBLIC WORKS, Bart Parker Sec, Room 5 Basement Court House.
CITY BUILDING INSPECTOR'S OFFICE, George W Bunting Inspector, Room 2 Basement Court House, Tel 1390.
CITY CIVIL ENGINEER'S OFFICE, Bernard J T Jeup City Civil Engineer, Rooms 13-15 Basement Court House, Tel 512.
CITY CLERK'S OFFICE, Charles H Stuckmeyer Clerk, Room 6 Basement Court House, Tel 542.
CITY COMPTROLLER'S OFFICE, Eudorus M Johnson City Comptroller, Room 1 Basement Court House, Tel 1890.
CITY DIRECTORY OFFICE, R L Polk & Co Publishers, 23-24 Journal Bldg; Directories of All the Principal Cities on File for Reference.
CITY DISPENSARY, L Bell Supt, 32-34 E Ohio, Tel 470.
CITY HOSPITAL, Charles E Ferguson, M D, Supt, n w cor Locke and Margaret, Tel 828.
CITY MAYOR'S OFFICE, Thomas Taggart Mayor, Room 7 Basement Court House, Tel 874.
City Police Court, 21 basement Court House.
City Police Station, s e cor Alabama and Pearl.
CITY TREASURER'S OFFICE, Wm H Schmidt City Treas, 23 Court House.

SHORTHAND REPORTING...... CONVENTIONS, SPEECHES, SERMONS. COPYING ON TYPEWRITER. S. H. EAST, State Agent, THE WILLIAMS TYPEWRITER 55 Thorpe Block, 87 East Market Street.

ELLIS & HELFENBERGER Manufacturers of Iron Vases, Setees and Hitch Posts. 162-170 South Senate Ave. Tel. 958

THE HOGAN TRANSFER AND STORAGE COMP'Y
Household Goods and Pianos Moved—Packed—Stored...... Baggage and Package Express Machinery and Safes a Specialty Cor. Washington and Illinois Sts. TELEPHONE No. 675.

Hose, Belting, Packing, Clothing, Druggists' Sundries, Bicycle Tires, Cotton Hose, Etc. New York Belting & Packing Co., L't'd.
THE CENTRAL RUBBER & SUPPLY CO. PHONE 922. 79 S. ILLINOIS ST., INDIANAPOLIS, IND.

The Provident Life and Trust Co.
Small Death Rate. Small Expense Rate. Safe Investments. OF PHILADELPHIA. Insurance in force
D. W. EDWARDS, $115,000,000
General Agent, 508 Indiana Trust Building.

Claffey Charles C W, blksmith, h 870 E Vermont.
Claffey Christian C, city fireman, h 152 Pleasant.
Claffey Conrad, h 91 English av.
Claffey Edward L, mach, h 128 N Gillard av.
Claffey Edward W, lab, b 91 English av.
Claffey Frederick, carp, h e s Hope 2 s of Willow (B).
Claffey Frederick, mach, b 91 English av.
Claffey George C, glasscutter, h 1102 E Michigan.
Claffey John W, clk Model Clothing Co, b 79 S Linden.
Claffey Lewis F, driver, h 443 S State av.
Claffey Wm, blksmith, h 79 S Linden.
Claffey Wm C, blksmith, b 79 S Linden.
Claffey Wm F, packer, b 91 English av.
Claiborne, see also Claybourne.
Claiborne Leonard A, trav agt, h 201 N State av.
Clair James, lab, h 74 Benton.
Claman Eugene B, mach hd, b 136 W Vermont.
Claman Isaac, h 136 W Vermont.
Claman Wm R, clk, b 136 W Vermont.
Clampitt Charles F, clk, h 114 Willow (B).
Clancy Benjamin M, uphlr, b 11 Tecumseh.
Clancy Charles L, livery, rear 224 N Meridian, h 32 Johnson av.
Clancy Ella F (wid Wm W), h 53 Lexington av.
Clancy James, buyer N Y Store, r 279 N Capitol av.
Clancy James, lab, h 102 S Linden.
Clancy John D, lab, h 11 Tecumseh.
Clancy John J, bookbinder, b 11 Tecumseh av.
Clancy John J, brakeman, b 102 S Linden.
Clancy Leslie D, clk, b 53 Lexington av.
Clancy Thomas, car rep, h 48 N State av.
Clapp Alonzo B, letter carrier P O, h 501 N Alabama.
Clapp Charlotte (wid George W), b 20 Leonard.
Clapp Herbert E, watchman, h 28 Yandes.
Clapp Jennie B (wid Thomas H), h 531 N Delaware.

Julius C. Walk & Son, Jewelers Indianapolis.
12 EAST WASHINGTON ST.

Clapp Roger O, clk Union Trust Co, b 531 N Delaware.
Clapp Thomas C, collr, h 144 Ft Wayne av.
Clapp Wm H, bkkpr Richardson & McCrea, b 531 N Delaware.
Clare John, lab, h 131 Bates.
Clare Wm, poultry, E Mkt House, b 414 Newman.
Clark, see also Clarke.
Clark Alexander N, real est, h 239 N Capitol av.
Clark Alfred, h 266 N West.
Clark Alfred, trav agt, h 247 N Delaware.
Clark Alfred jr, stenog Parry Mufg Co, b 247 N Delaware.
Clark Alice J, dressmkr, 244½ E Washington, h same.
Clark Alice M, dressmkr, 47 Peru av, h same.
Clark Alonzo B, trav agt, h 1483 N Illinois.
Clark Alonzo E, fireman, h 186 S Judge Harding (W I).
Clark Alvin T, trav agt, h 1211 N Capitol av.
Clark Andrew J, mach, b 312 S West.
Clark Andrew J, phys, 338 N New Jersey, h same.
Clark Anna, matron Asylum for Friendless Colored Children, s w cor Senate av and 12th.
Clark Ansel C, b 71 Birch av (W I).
Clark Benjamin A, engr, h 8 N Station (B).
Clark Benjamin F, real est, h 487 W Udell (N I).
Clark Benjamin T, lab, h 5 Jefferson.
Clark Bradley, bricklayer, b 29 Madison av.
Clark Carey E, lab, b 97 N Beville av.
Clark Catherine M (wid James B), h 181 W Vermont.
Clark Charles, lab, h 21 Downey.
Clark Charles, packer, b 297 N California.
CLARK CHARLES A, Justice of the Peace, 88½ E Washington, h 183 Bellefontaine.
Clark Charles E, feedmaster, h 210 W South.
Clark Charles F, brakeman, h 71 Lord.
Clark Charles J, clk, h 23 Church.
Clark Charles L, grocer, 4 N Station (B), b 8 same.
Clark Charles L, trav agt, h 906 N New Jersey.
Clark Charles W, mach, b 66 S West.
Clark Charlotta (wid John T), b 12 Minnesota.
Clark Chauncey H (Stockton, Gillespie & Co), h 239 N Capitol av.
Clark Clarence E, electrician, h 223 W New York.
Clark Cyrus J (Clark, Wysong & Voris), h 461 Walnut av (N I).
Clark Daniel W, electrician, r 351 N Senate av.
Clark David H, carp, b 291 Miller (W I).
Clark Edgar H, page Superior Court No 3, b 600 Ash.
Clark Edmund D, phys, 14 W Ohio, and City Sanitarian, 10 Court House, h 401 N East.
Clark Edward, cook, h 325 E Court.
Clark Edward, lab, h 209 Minnesota.
Clark Edward, packer, b Marion Park Hotel (M P).
Clark Edward A, cigars, 150 Mass av, h 164 N Alabama.
Clark Edward J, lab, h 59 Germania av (H).
Clark Edward J, mach, b 524 Jefferson av.
Clark Edward S, photog, r 66 E Washington.

OTTO GAS ENGINES | BUILDERS' EXCHANGE S. W. Cor. Ohio and Penn. Telephone 535.

Becker & Son Charles Becker Jacob Becker Jr. Merchant Tailors. 21 N. Penn. St. Tel. 934

SALISBURY & STANLEY • Office, Store and Bar Fixtures a Specialty. Repairing of all kinds done on short notice. 177 Clinton St, Indianapolis, Ind. • Contractors and Builders TELEPHONE 999.

Clark Edward W, circulator Patriot Phalanx, b 95 N Meridian.
Clark Elisha A, lab, r 439 E Washington.
Clark Eliza J (wid Samuel), h s e cor Fernway and Catharine.
Clark Elizabeth, h 2 W Miami.
Clark Elizabeth (wid Timothy J), h 105 Bates.
Clark Elizabeth E (wid George M D), h 1374 N Senate av.
Clark Elliott D, saloon, 274 W Washington, h same.
Clark Ellsworth E, clk, h 938 N Alabama.
Clark Elmer H, ironwkr, h 71 Birch av (W I).
Clark Elmer J, lab, b 675 Mass av.
Clark Emma (wid Harry), notions, 17 Hillside av, h same.
Clark Ephraim, farmer, h 291 Miller (W I).
CLARK ERNEST V, Res Asst Sec American Surety Co of New York, 106-108 Commercial Club Bldg, Tel 1539, h 678 Broadway.
Clark Ewing P, supt agts Commercial B and L Assn, h 277 E Miami.
Clark Fannie, h 327 E New York.
Clark Frances G, propr White Ribbon House, 95 N Meridian.
Clark Frank U, trav agt, h 447 N East.
Clark Frank S, engr, h 211 Huron.
Clark Frank W, lab, h 483 Union.
Clark Franklin, lab, h 108 Bright.
Clark Frederick, fireman, h 27 N Gillard av.
Clark Frederick A (Clark & Roberts), b 856 N Meridian.
Clark George, b 956 Grove av.
Clark George, cook, b 191 N New Jersey.
Clark George, lab, h 37 Gatling.
Clark George H, city fieman, h 131 Huron.
Clark George L, engr, h n s Sutherland 1 w of Station (B).
Clark George M, clk, r 252 Mass av.
Clark George W, engr, h 12 N Station (B).
Clark Grace, b 1374 N Senate av.
Clark Harry F, clk R B Grover & Co, b 229 Coburn.
Clark Harry R, painter, h 610 W Eugene (N I).
Clark, Hattie (wid Charles), dressmkr, 252 E Washington, b same.
Clark Henry H, welldriver, 136 Martindale av, h same.
Clark Henry T, clk, h 8 Shriver av.
Clark Henry W, lab, h 66 S West.
Clark Herschel G, student, b 401 N East.
Clark Hiram, painter, b 402 E Market.
Clark Horace A, barber, 357 Virginia av, h same.
Clark Hugh, carriagemkr, h 233 W Michigan.
Clark Isaac, janitor Public School No 40, h 297 N Penn.
Clark James, brakeman, b 162 Harrison.
Clark James, painter, b 402 E Market.
Clark James, trav agt, h 202 Lincoln la.
Clark James F, mach hd, b 312 S West.
Clark James H, lab, h 963 S Meridian.
Clark James H, photog, 66 E Washington, h 1014 N Senate av.
Clark James H, umbrellas, 11 Indiana av, h 80 Mayhew.
Clark James M, waiter, h 9 Fayette.
Clark James, miller, h 327 E New York.
Clark John, b 579 N Penn.
Clark John, agt, r 77½ S Illinois.
Clark John, carp, h 421 W Addison (N I).
Clark John, mach, h 32 Cincinnati.

Henry H. Fay, 40½ E. WASHINGTON ST., FIRE INSURANCE, REAL ESTATE, LOANS AND RENTAL AGENT.

Clark John, molder, h 271 W Market.
Clark John C, cabtmkr, h 675 Mass av.
Clark John C, clk S F Muhl, r 523 N Illinois.
Clark John E, harnessmkr, b Germania House.
Clark John E, painter, b 437 N Senate av.
Clark John F, clk, b 105 Bates.
Clark John J, trav agt, h 175 Pleasant.
Clark John S, bricklayer, h 484 Chestnut.
Clark John T, horseshoer, 98 Kentucky av, h 2 Short.
Clark John W, driver, h 223 E Wabash.
Clark John W, lumber, 79 Alvord, h 866 N Penn.
Clark Jonathan M, bkkpr Krag-Reynolds Co, h 279 N Capitol av.
Clark Joseph, lab, h 42 Chadwick.
Clark Joseph H, grain agt, h 288 N Liberty.
Clark Joseph H, real est, h 856 N Meridian.
Clark Joseph W, tmstr, h 24 Hamilton av.
Clark Josephine E, teacher, b n e cor N Meridian and 24th.
Clark Joshua J, clk, h 164 N Alabama.
Clark Jossius M, agt, h 40 Drake.
Clark Katherine C, librarian Indpls Bar Library Assn, b 105 Bates.
Clark Laura (wid Richard), h 444 W Washington.
Clark Laura R, h 240 S Capitol av.
Clark Leander C, lab, h 190 Virginia av.
Clark Levi, clk, b 184 E Vermont.
Clark Levi, grain, h 229 Coburn.
Clark Levi, janitor, h 88 S Reisner (W I).
Clark Lewis A, carp, h 100 Kappus (W I).
Clark Lucy J, h 193 W Ray.
Clark Luther R, fruits, 73 E Mkt House, h 442 W Michigan.
Clark Margaret A, stenog, b 105 Bates.
Clark Margaret B (wid Charles), h 299 Bates.
Clark Margaret T (wid Reuben O), b 479 N Illinois.
Clark Mary M (wid Orrin B), matron Girls' Classical School, h 345 N Penn.
Clark Michael, h 312 S West.
Clark Michael F, lab, b 312 S West.

JAS. N. MAYHEW, MANUFACTURING OPTICIAN LENSES AND FRAMES A SPECIALTY. No. 13 North Meridian St., Indianapolis.

LUMBER | Sash, Door and Planing Mill Work. | Balke & Krauss Co. Cor. Market and Missouri Streets.

FRIEDGEN'S TAN SHOES are the Newest Shades
Prices the Lowest. 19 North Pennsylvania St.

SAMUEL LAING General Job Work in Sheet Metal of all Kinds
72 AND 74 E. COURT STREET.

M. B. WILSON, Pres. W. F. CHURCHMAN, Cash.
THE CAPITAL NATIONAL BANK,
INDIANAPOLIS, IND.
Make collections on all points in the States of Indiana and Illinois on the most favorable rates.
Capital, - - $300,000
Surplus and Earnings, 50,000
No. 28 S. Meridian St., Cor. Pearl.

Clark Miles E, mach, h s w cor Elizabeth and Caldwell.
Clark Millie, housekpr 224 S West.
Clark Milton, lab, b 154 N Belmont av (H).
Clark Milton C, driver, b 136 Martindale av.
Clark Nannie A, dressmkr, 306 N Delaware. h same.
Clark Nelson E, policeman, h 39 Mayhew.
Clark Noah A, engr, r 315 Mass av.
Clark Oliver, lab, b 183 Blake.
Clark Oliver, porter 206 N Alabama.
Clark Orian W, driver, h 787 N Senate av.
Clark Otis G, del clk Insane Hospital.
Clark Perry, mach, h 68 S Spruce.
Clark Purdue R, trav agt Pearson & Wetzel, b 275 N New Jersey.
Clark Rachel E, matron Friends' Boarding Home for Young Ladies, h 155 N Illinois.
Clark Richard, lab, b 169 W 5th.
Clark Richard, plastr, r 53 S California.
Clark Rilla, waiter, r 108½ Mass av.
Clark Robert, mach hd, h 324 Mass av.
Clark Robert, solr N Y Life Ins Co, h 115 Ruckle.
Clark Robert L, ins agt, 20½ N Delaware, h 84 N New Jersey.
Clark Samuel D, motorman, h 516 Bellefontaine.
Clark Samuel J, carp, h 243 Huron.
Clark Sarah, h 108½ Mass av.
Clark Sarah A, boarding 184 E Vermont.
Clark Sarah H (wid Benjamin F), h 600 Ash.
Clark Stephen A, trimmer, h 215 N New Jersey.
Clark Thomas F, flagman, h 224 S West.
Clark Thomas J, sawmkr, h 105 Fayette.
Clark Thomas W, plastr, b 135 N Illinois.
Clark Wallace H, foreman, h 646 E Market.
Clark Walter E, blksmith, h 643 E 7th.
Clark Willard, harnessmkr, r 172½ E Washington.
Clark Wm, b 233 W Michigan.
Clark Wm, carp, b 201 E Washington.
Clark Wm, lab, h 245 S Spruce.
Clark Wm A, painter, h 64 Camp.
Clark Wm F, uphlr, h 286 Fletcher av.
Clark Wm F (Wm F and Wm F Clark jr), b 95 N Meridian.

MONEY
Loaned on Short Notice at Lowest Rates.
TUTTLE & SEGUIN,
Tel. 1168. 28 E. Market St.

Clark Wm F jr (Wm F and Wm F Clark jr), b 95 N Meridian.
Clark Wm F and Wm F jr, pubs Patriot Phalanx, 25 Cyclorama pl.
Clark Wm H, phys, 27½ Monument pl, h same.
Clark Wm J, carp, h 244½ E Washington.
Clark Wm J, mach, b 105 Bates.
Clark Wm L, engr, h 142 Lexington av.
Clark Wm M, poultry, 178 E Wabash, h 384 Blake.
Clark Wm P, carp, h 505 E 11th.
Clark Wm R, lab, h 182 Columbia av.
Clark Wm T, painter, h 225 Naomi.
Clark Wilson, agt, h 184 E Vermont.
Clark, Wysong & Voris (Cyrus J Clark, Benjamin F Wysong, Wm C Voris), live stock, Union Stock Yards (W I).
Clark & Roberts (Frederick H Clark, Richard B Roberts), phys' chairs, 114 N Delaware.
Clarke Catherine (wid Michael F), h 160 Fletcher av.
Clarke Charles A, lab, b e s Sherman Drive 1 s of Washington.
Clarke Charles B (Means & Clark), h e s Central av 2 s of Washington av (I).
Clarke Frank J, janitor, h rear 52 Prospect.
Clarke George H Rev, pastor Fourth Christian Church, h 337 W 2d.
CLARKE GOOD H, Restaurant, 98 N Illinois, h 80 N Illinois.
CLARKE HENRY P, Physician and Surgeon, 2 Mansur Blk, cor Washington and Alabama, h 28 Ft Wayne av.
Clarke James E, engr, h 462 S Illinois.
Clarke Jennie E, midwife, 462 S Illinois, h same.
Clarke John C, lab, b 540 W Washington.
Clarke John E, plumber, b 160 Fletcher av.
Clarke John G, engr, b rear 29 Cornell av.
Clarke Joseph D, clk C C C & St L Ry, h 119 Broadway.
Clarke Joseph H, fireman, h 206 English av.
Clarke Katie L, bkkpr, b 160 Fletcher av.
Clarke Mary A (wid Alfred D), h 801 N New Jersey.
Clarke Sarah M, microscopist, b 801 N New Jersey.
Clarke Thomas J (Clarke & Sons), h 160 Fletcher av.
Clarke Wm H, lab, h 70 S William (W I).
CLARKE & SONS (Thomas J Clarke), Plumbers, Steam and Gas Fitters, 98 N Delaware, Tel 1401.
Clarkson Clyde, carp, b 408 S Meridian.
Clary, see also Cleary.
Clary Alonzo E, druggist, 102 Hoyt av, h same.
Clary Ara G, clk, h 172 Hoyt av.
Clary David F, mer police, h 291 S Alabama.
Clary Grafton A, farmer, h 20 Shelby.
Clary Jasper N, capt mer police, h 291 S Alabama.
Clary Kate, seamstress, b 7 Detroit.
Clary Oliver E, clk, b 171 Fletcher av.
Clary Worthington J P, h 171 Fletcher av.
Class, see also Klass.
Class Christopher, furnacewkr, h 17 Keith.
Class Michael, furnacewkr, h 46 Newman.
Classick James, lab, h 16 Chadwick.
Classick James A, wheelmkr, b 16 Chadwick.

PAPER BOXES, MANUFACTURED BY SULLIVAN & MAHAN 41 W. PEARL STREET.

DIAMOND WALL PLASTER { Telephone 1410 BUILDERS' EXCHANGE.

Fine Laundry Work our Specialty. Collars and Cuffs our Hobby. ‖ THE HOME LAUNDRY ‖ 197 S. Illinois St. Telephone 1769.

Classick Joseph B, vice-pres The Home Benefit Assn, b 16 Chadwick.
Claudius Brother, teacher, b cor Coburn and Short.
Clavelin Victor, lab, h 1049 S Meridian.
Clawson Edwin M, buyer W H Messenger, h 140 E St Joseph.
Clawson Frederick, lab, b 889 Morris (W I).
Clawson James G, carp, b 136 W 1st.
Clawson John, lab, b 397 Yandes.
Clawson John B, mailer The Indpls Sentinel, h 1299 N Penn.
Clawson John W, tmstr, h 308 Lambert (W I).
Clawson Thomas A, condr, h 5 Coble.
Clay Aaron, lab, r 236 E Wabash.
Clay Andrew J, grocer, 549 Shelby, h same.
Clay Charlotte (wid John H), h 647 E 7th.
Clay Edward, foreman, b 549 Shelby.
Clay Eliza (wid Coleman C), h 233 W 3d.
Clay Ella, teacher Public School No 24, b 434 Blake.
Clay Frederick, cooper, h 25 Grant.
Clay Grant H, dentist, h 433 Blake.
Clay Henry, lab, h 19 Torbet.
Clay Henry, lab, h 742 N West.
Clay Henry W, janitor, h 329 W North.
Clay Herbert J, lab, b 321 Blake.
Clay Hilliary, ins agt, r 84 W Ohio.
Clay Ira, shoemkr, h 16 Elizabeth.
Clay James, cooper, h 93 Lord.
Clay Jordan, lab, h 189 W 9th.
Clay Joseph, lab, b 25 Grant.
Clay Joseph F (Stockton, Gillespie & Co), h 426 Ash.
Clay Maria B (wid Henry), h 46 Brett.
Clay Mary J (wid Henry), h 201 W 4th.
Clay Mathew, lab, h 186 Meek.
Clay Oliver S, lab, b 647 E 7th.
Clay Richard, hostler, h 28 Columbia al.
Clay Shingle Co, John R Elder pres, Edward C Elder sec, 1 Ingalls blk.
Clay Solomon, watchman, h 166 Ft Wayne av.
Clay Thomas, lab, h 106 Howard.
Clay Wm O, carp, h 16 Leonard.
Clay Worker The, T A Randall & Co proprs, 5 Monument pl.
Clay Zina (wid Benjamin), h 321 Blake.
Clayborn Albert G, barber, r 299 Bright.
Claybourne, see also Claiborne.
Claybourne Colin W, h 948 N New Jersey.
Claybourne Wm F, b 948 N New Jersey.
Claybrook Moses, janitor, h 141 S Linden.
Claycomb Samuel, driver, h 111 Malott av.
Claycraft Los, watchman Kingan & Co, r same.
Claypool Edward F, h 182 N Meridian.
Claypool Jefferson H, lawyer, 14 Talbott blk, h 663 N Meridian.
Claypool John W (Claypool & Claypool), b 1088 N Illinois, tel 217.
Claypool Solomon (Claypool & Claypool), h 1088 N Illinois, tel 217.

CLAYPOOL & CLAYPOOL (Solomon and John W), Lawyers, Rooms 1-2 Blackford Blk, s e cor Washington and Meridian, Tel 780.

Clayton Amos, lab, h rear 125 E Pratt.
Clayton Anna E (wid John W), h 127 N East.
Clayton Charles J, carp, h 105 Bradshaw.
Clayton Henry, coachman 268 Park av.
Clayton Hiram, cook 268 Park av.
Clayton John F, baggageman, h 31 Sullivan.
Clayton Joseph S, paperhngr, h 291 Cornell av.

FRANK NESSLER. WILL H. ROST.
FRANK NESSLER & CO.
Tailors
56 EAST MARKET ST. (Lemcke Building),
INDIANAPOLIS, IND.

Clayton Leonidas W, trav agt The Indpls Stove Co, h 275 Broadway.
Clayton Thomas H, engr, b 340 S Meridian.
Clayton Wm W, trav agt The Indpls Stove Co, h 424 Central av.
Clear John, lab, h 151 Bates.
Clearwater Harry S, h 1106 N Delaware.
Clearwater Hiram R, h 173 Pleasant.
Cleary, see also Clary.
Cleary Andrew F, lab, h 254 Douglass.
Cleary Benedict, lab, b 390 Coburn.
Cleary Elmer S, clk, b 232 Huron.
Cleary John W, electrical engr, h 232 Huron.
Cleary May C, nurse, r 133 N Penn.
Cleary Michael D, contr, b Grand Hotel.
Cleary Patrick, watchman, h 523 N West.
Cleary, Wm F, clk, b 232 Huron.
Cleary Wm L, clk, h 108½ Mass av.
Cleaveland, see also Cleveland.
Cleaveland Calvin C, painter, 15 S Meridian, h 445 S Delaware.
Cleaveland Charles F, phys, 425 N Capitol av, h same.

CLEAVELAND FENCE CO, Henry G Byram Pres, Norman S Byram Vice-Pres, Sec and Treas; Office 21 Biddle, Factory 18-22 Biddle; Tel 328.

Cleaveland John B, mngr The Wire Fence Supply Co, h 351 Clifford av.
Cleaveland Wm V, painter, b 445 S Delaware.
Cleaver Charles E, bricklyr, b 109 Highland pl.
Cleaver Jefferson, bricklyr, h 371 E Ohio.
Cleaver John D, tile setter, b 371 E Ohio.
Cleaver Mary E (wid John W), b 109 Highland pl.
Cleaver Wm T, trav agt, h 109 Highland pl.
Cleckner Eliza T (wid Simon S), h 260 S Capitol av.
Clee Frank W, barber, h 405 Indiana av.
Cleet James, lab, h 510 S West.
Cleet Joseph F, helper, h n e cor English av and Belt R R.
Cleet Soloman, lab, h n s English av 2 w of Auburn av (W).
Clegg Clarence W, motorman, h 27 Beacon.

ACORN STOVES AND RANGES
Haueisen & Hartmann
163-169 E. Washington St.
FURNITURE,
Carpets,
Household Goods,
Tin, Granite and China Wares, Oil Cloth and Shades

THE WM. H. BLOCK CO. 7 AND 9 EAST WASHINGTON STREET. DRY GOODS, MEN'S FURNISHINGS.

Fidelity and Deposit Co. of Maryland. BONDS SIGNED.—LOCAL BOARD John B. Elam, Albert Sahm, Smiley N. Chambers, John M. Spann.
GEORGE W. PANGBORN, General Agent, 704-706 Lemcke Building. Telephone 140.

74 EAST MARKET STREET Telephone 863. Insure Your Property With FRANK K. SAWYER

JOSEPH GARDNER,
Hot Air Furnaces
With Combination Gas Burners for Burning Gas and Other Fuel at the Same Time.
37, 39 & 41 KENTUCKY AVE. Telephone 322.

Clegg John, lab, h 640 N Senate av.
Clegg John M, contr, h 1745 N Penn.
Clegg Owen E, carp, h 1680 Kenwood av.
Clegg Wm H, carp, h n s 30th 2 e of Illinois.
Cleland John E (Cathcart, Cleland & Co), h 32 W St Clair.
Clem Aaron, grocer, 86 Christian av, h 256 same.
Clem Edwin A, clk, b 256 Christian av.
Clemens Henry D, mach, h 127 John.
Clemens Wm E, clk, b 939 N Alabama.
Clemens W Frank, bicycles, 36 Mass av, h 107 Ft Wayne av.
Clement John, carp, h 10 Harrison.
Clements Charles I, lab, h 601 W Shoemaker (N I).
Clements Charles J, motorman, b 120 W Maryland.
Clements Christian, b 679 Madison av.
Clements Cyrus, lab, r 23 N West.
Clements Eliza E (wid Wm A), h 126 Bright.
Clements Flora J (wid Thomas L), h 108½ Mass av.
Clements Frank, barber, b 323 Clifford av.
Clements George, carp, 494 Madison av, h same.
Clements Harry B, painter, 194 Davidson, h same.
Clements Horace, waiter, r 287 N California.
Clements John B, dairy, 30 W 20th, h same.
Clements John J, agt, h 1660 Graceland av.
Clements John R, flagman, h 348 N Pine.
Clements John S, fireman, h 206 Spann av.
Clements Michael, carp, h 131 High.
Clements Michael E, lab, h 37 S California.
Clements Milton H, packer, r 23 N West.
Clements Nicholas J, lab, h 1261 Morris (W I).
Clements Oren R, clk Parry Mnfg Co, h 251 S Alabama.
Clements Peter, carp, 679 Madison av, h same.
Clements Robert E, lab, b 126 Bright.
Clements Silas, lab, h e s Orchard 3 n of Howland av.

J. S. FARRELL & CO.
Plumbing
Natural and Artificial Gas Fitting.
84 N. ILLINOIS STREET.
TELEPHONE 382.

Clements Theodore, woodwkr, b 121 W Maryland.
Clemmer Eugene P, music teacher, 130 N Illinois, h same.
Clemmer Ferd O, phys, 130 N Illinois, h same.
Clendening Albert S, carpetlayer W H Messenger, h 297 E Georgia.
Clendening Annie, h 403 W 2d.
Clendening Franklin H, lab, h 297 E Georgia.
Clendening Thomas J, carp, h 159½ E Washington.
Clette James J, lab, h 456 S West.
Cleveland, see also Cleaveland.
Cleveland Charles, molder, h w s Sherman Drive 1 s of C C C & St L Ry.
CLEVELAND, CINCINNATI, CHICAGO & ST LOUIS RY (Big Four Route), Henry M Bronson Asst Gen Pass Agt, Henry S Fraser Gen Agt Freight Dept, W A Sullivan Commercial Agt, Benjamin C Kelsey City Ticket Agt, Wright S Jordan Trav Pass Agt, 1 E Washington, Tel 374; Samuel M Hice Ticket Agt, 36 Jackson Pl, Tel 388.
Clevenger Harriet H, reader, r 78 E North.
Clevenger Oscar F, agt, r 42 S Capitol av.
Clevenger Viola (wid Oscar), h 231 W Vermont.
CLEVENGER WM F, Physician (Practice Limited to Throat, Nose and Ear), 19 E Ohio, h same, Tel 44.
Click Jesse D, lab, h 229 Buchanan.
Click John, saloon, 349 English av, h same.
Click Nettie (wid Nathan), b 105 English av.
Clickard George, lab, h 77 Drake.
Clidence John, lab, b e s Brown 2 n of 23d.
Clifford Alfred S, porter, b 200 Virginia av.
Clifford Amos, h 374 N West.
Clifford Bernard, lab, b 268½ W Washington.
CLIFFORD, BROWDER & MOFFETT (Vincent G Clifford, Wilbur F Browder, Winfield S Moffett), Lawyers, 72½ E Washington, Tel 1314.
Clifford Edward H, reporter, b 270 N West.
Clifford Harry C, lab, h 340 Coburn.
Clifford John C, lab, h 349½ S Meridian.
Clifford John F, brakeman, b 18 N Gale (B).
Clifford Mary (wid Bernard), b 230 W Maryland.
Clifford Michael L, bartndr, b 251 E Washington.
Clifford Patrick, carp, h 144 N Dorman.
Clifford Vincent G (Clifford, Browder & Moffett), h 174 Bellefontaine.
Clifford Wm, carp, h 493 N Senate av.
Clifford Wm L (Clifford & Arnold), h 487 N Senate av.
Clifford & Arnold (Wm L Clifford, Jacob Arnold), plumbers, 67 Indiana av.
Clift Frances (wid John M), b 270½ W Washington.
Clift Mahala J (wid Wm), b rear 265 Mass av.
Clifton Arthur J, lab, h 13 Sample (W I).
Clifton Benjamin, grocer, 355 Indiana av, h same.
Clifton Charles S, carp, h 317 Fletcher av.
Clifton Charles W (John G Clifton & Son and C W Clifton & Co), b 80 Ft Wayne av.
Clifton C W & Co (Charles W and John G Clifton), grocers, 80 Ft Wayne av.

IF CONTINUED to the end of its dividend period, policies of the UNITED STATES LIFE INSURANCE CO., will equal or excel any investment policy ever offered to the public. | E. B. SWIFT, Manager, 25 E. Market St.

Wm. Kotteman 89 & 91 E. Washington St. TELEPHONE 1742 Furniture

SHOW CASES

Clifton John G (John G Clifton & Son and C W Clifton & Co), h 80 Ft Wayne av.
Clifton John G & Son (John G and Charles W), produce, 94 E Mkt House.
Clifton Nelson, lab, h 15 Sample (W I).
Clifton Oliver, lab, b 15 Sample (W I).
Clifton Stephen A, agt, h 7 Ludlow av.
Climax Baking Powder Co, Alfred B Gates pres, Harry B Gates sec, Wm N Gates treas, 124 E Maryland.
Cline, see also Klein and Kline.
Cline Abraham, collr, b 395 E McCarty.
Cline Albert, real est, b 852 Cornell av.
Cline Benjamin F, carp, 573 Broadway, h same.
Cline David C (Smith, Curtis & Co), h 1003 E Washington.
Cline Edward H, lab, h 57 Hosbrook.
Cline Edward S, lab, h 110 Yandes.
Cline Frederick, real est, b 852 Cornell av.
Cline Henry, lab, h 140 Martindale av.
Cline Henry, peddler, h 433 S Capitol av.
Cline Jacob W, engr, h 10 N Dorman.
Cline James H, painter, b 619 N Capitol av.
Cline James W, condr, h 17 Henry.
Cline John, driver, r 114 N Meridian.
Cline John C, mngr A J Conroy & Co, 23 Indiana av, h 58 Warren av (W I).
Cline Joseph M, b 146 W Vermont.
Cline Julia, h 202 W Maryland.
CLINE LEWIS C, Physician (Limited to Throat, Nose and Ear), 42 E Ohio, h 862 N Meridian.
Cline Margaret (wid David), h 72 Buchanan.
Cline Martha, h s w cor Baltimore av and 17th.
Cline Martin L, real est, h 576 W 22d (N I).
Cline Mary A (wid Isaac H), h 619 N Capitol av.
Cline Noah A, driver, b 1055 W Michigan.
Cline Samuel, lab, h 572 W Washington.
Cline Walter, lab, b 140 Martindale av.
Cline Wm, h 64 S Summit.
Cline Wm, real est, 12½ N Delaware, h 852 Cornell av.
Cline Wm jr, real est, h 51 Bellefontaine.
Clinebick, Louis, cook, r 19 Russell av.
Clingerman Charles H, lab, h 63 Ft Wayne av.
Clingler Albert G, bicycle rep, 63 Indiana av, h 180 Elizabeth.
Clingler Henry S, finisher, h 180 Elizabeth.
Clingman Alexander, lab, b 381 W 1st.
Clingman August, lab, b 87 Rhode Island.
Clingman John A, lab, h 542 Chestnut.
Clingman Junius, driver, h 396 S Delaware.
Clingman Rufus A, lab, h 87 Rhode Island.
Clingman Wm, lab, h 79 W North.
Clinkert Wm C, plumber, h 39 Oliver av (W I).
Clinton Emma L, clk Probate Commissioner, b 736 N New Jersey.
Clinton George B, trav agt, h 307 N Senate av.
Clinton John E, mailing clk P O, b 548 E Ohio.
Clinton John R, dep clk Marion County, h 548 E Ohio.
Clinton Moses M, boys' supervisor Deaf and Dumb Inst, h 27 Walcott.
Clinton Nellie (wid James), h 393 W 2d.
Clinton Otis, packer, b 124 E North.
Clinton Wharton R, bkkpr, b 736 N New Jersey.
Clippinger Wm H, clk The H Lieber Co, h 75 Fletcher av.
Clites Willard K, trav agt, h 74 Highland pl.

Farm and City Loans
25 Years' Successful Business.
THOS. C. DAY & CO,
Rooms 325 to 330 Lemcke Building.

Cloak Albert, baggageman, h 1 Jefferson.
Clodfelter Noah J, h 140 East Drive (W P).
Cloe Freeman M, driver, h 75 Rockwood.
Clore Albert, lab, b 29 College av.
Clore James A, lab, b 382 E Michigan.
Close George A, printer, h 187 N Pine.
Closser Louise M (wid Joseph A), h 409 N Delaware.
Closson Charles P, h 329 N Illinois.
Cloud Albert D, carp, h 40 Standard av (W I).
Cloud Bruce R, engr, b 67 Minerva.
Cloud Charles E, clk Henry F Cloud, r 115 Bryan.
Cloud Charles F, switchman, b 421 Broadway.
Cloud Charles O, lab, b 9 Cleveland (H).
Cloud Dudley T (Cloud & Co), h 158 Prospect.
Cloud Edward, lab, h 32 N McLain (W I).
Cloud Emmett, molder, r 85 Holmes av (H).
CLOUD HENRY F, Dealer in Coal, Wood, Coke, Flour and Feed, 587 W McLene (N I), h 115 Bryan.
Cloud John W, barber, b 32 N McLain (W I).
Cloud Jonathan, carp, 40 Standard av (W I), b same.
Cloud Luther L, carp, h 159 Osage.
Cloud Margaret L, nurse, 18 Cornell av, b same.
Cloud Owen, hostler, r 181 Virginia av.
Cloud Peter, b 59 Bridge (W I).
Cloud Robert T S, b 158 Prospect.
Cloud Wm E, tmstr, b 115 Bryan.
Cloud Wm H, painter, h 76 Thalman av.
Cloud & Co (Dudley T Cloud, George P Gaddis), contrs, 246 Virginia av.
Clouds George C, gateman Union Station, h 124 Brookside av.
Clough John L, bkkpr, h 236 Clifford av.
Clough Susan N (wid Wm), h 236 Clifford av.
Clouse Wm, lab, b 324 E Michigan.
Clover Samuel, engr, b n w cor Michigan and State avs.
Clow Anna (wid Charles L), h 32 Chadwick.

EAT
QUAKER BREAD
ASK YOUR GROCER FOR IT.
THE HITZ BAKING CO.

WILLIAM WIEGEL 6 West Louisiana Street Opp. Union Station.

CARPETS CLEANED LIKE NEW. TELEPHONE 818
CAPITAL STEAM CARPET CLEANING WORKS

BENJ. BOOTH PRACTICAL EXPERT ACCOUNTANT.
Thirty years' experience. First-class credentials.
Room 18, 82½ E. Washington St. Indianapolis, Ind.

The Old Reliable Sherman European Restaurant || 18 and 20 S. Meridian St. Established 1880.

ESTABLISHED 1876. TELEPHONE 168.
CHESTER BRADFORD,
SOLICITOR OF PATENTS,
AND COUNSEL IN PATENT CAUSES.
(See adv. page 6.)
Office:—Rooms 14 and 16 Hubbard Block, S.W. Cor. Washington and Meridian Streets, INDIANAPOLIS, INDIANA.

Cluckner Martha (wid John), h 13 N California.
Clune James M, 2d hd goods, 209 E Washington, h 186 College av.
CLUNE JOHN, Propr World's Fair, 101-113 W Washington and Ladies' Home, 11-13 E Washington, Tel 1296; h 1054 N Alabama.
Clune Joseph, clk, b 186 College av.
Clune Michael, furniture mnfr, 700 S Meridian, h 619 N Penn.
Clune Patrick, b 186 College av.
Clune Wm J, bkkpr, b 619 N Penn.
Clune Wm P, clk, b 186 College av.
Clymer Anna, h 10 S Gillard av.
Clymer Henry F, agt, h 194 N Beville av.
Clymer Robert W Rev, pastor Seventh Christian Church, h 442 W Shoemaker (N I).
Coan, see Coen and Cohen.
Coates Clinton T, blksmith, h 94 S Shade (B).
Coates Leander D, brakeman, r 57 English av.
Coatney Benjamin H, photog, h 161½ Jefferson av.
Coats Francis E, teacher Girls' Classical School, b 345 N Penn.
Coats Jesse, condr, h 71 Hill av.
Cobb Amos B, porter, b 80 Elizabeth.
Cobb Arthur W, paymaster Udell Woodenware Works, h 612 Miller av (M P).
Cobb Campbell H, bkkpr, b 324 Park av.
Cobb Carroll C, cashr Central Union Tel Co, h 443 Talbott av.
Cobb David, hostler, r 23 Monument pl.
Cobb Edgar M, mach hd, h 131 Oliver av (W I).
Cobb Harriet M, b 324 Park av.
Cobb Henry, mach hd, h 131 Oliver av (W I).
Cobb Jane E (wid John W), h 584 W Addison (N I).
Cobb John M, salesman Bockhoff Bros, h 139 E 12th.
Cobb Julia B (wid Edward A), b 324 Park av.
Cobb Reuben R, b 12 W North.

CORRUGATED IRON CEILINGS AND SIDING.
ALL KINDS OF REPAIRING.
O. B. ENSEY,
TELEPHONE 1562.
COR. 6TH AND ILLINOIS STREETS.

Cobb Samuel H, h 22 Lockerbie.
Cobb Thomas A, lab, h 54 Sheffield av (H).
Cobb Thomas R, b 1699 N Illinois.
Cobb Wm A, mach hd, b 131 Oliver av (W I).
Cobb Wm F, chief carp Insane Hospital.
Cobb Wm H, sub letter carrier P O.
Cobbs Stephen, lab, b 85 Howard.
Coble George jr, saloon, 52 Pendleton av (B), h 5 Poplar (B).
Coble Harry, lab, b 103 Blake.
Coble John, b s s Walnut 2 w of Sherman Drive.
Coble Laura A, clk, b 383 W New York.
Coble Margaret (wid David), h 198 Bright.
Coble Mary (wid Daniel), h 115 Hosbrook.
Coble Mary A (wid George), h 383 W New York.
Coble Preston T, watchman, h 900 Morris (W I).
Coble Wm H, carp, b s s Walnut 2 w of Sherman Drive.
Coble Wm O, clk, h w s Sherman Drive 1 n of Michigan.
Cobler James L, driver, h 158½ W Washington.
Cobler Jesse, stable foreman Frank Bird Transfer Co, h 226½ E Washington.
Cobler Lawrence, mach hd, b 888 S Noble.
Cobler Marshal F, h 355 E Market.
Cobler Milton, lab, h 88 S Noble.
Cobler Ora, clk George J Marott, h 87 W McCarty.
Cobler Sherman C, b 88 S Noble.
Cobler Wm, car rep, h 106 Deloss.
COBURN AUGUSTUS, Mngr Michigan Lumber Co, 436 E North, h 887 N Penn.
Coburn Frederick E, fireman, h 244 Huron.
Coburn George E (Holmes & Co), b 264 Talbott av.
COBURN HENRY, Vice-Pres Consumers' Gas Trust Co, Lumber Yard and Planing Mill, cor Kentucky av and Georgia, Tel 612; h 751 N Penn.
Coburn Henry, wireman Sanborn Electric Co, b 935 Morris (W I).
Coburn Henry P, clk Henry Coburn, b 751 N Penn.
Coburn Henry R, electrician, b 30 S McLain (W I).
Coburn John, mach hd, h 1 Clinton.
Coburn John, lawyer, 531 Lemcke bldg, h 40 Hendricks, tel 1163.
Coburn Joseph A, lab, h 28 Thomas.
Coburn Minerva (wid Willard H), b 818 N Delaware.
Coburn Lydia C (wid James F), h 30 S McLain (W I).
Coburn Walter F, lab, b 30 S McLain (W I).
Coburn Willard H (Coburn & Weelburg), h 818 N Delaware.
Coburn Wm H, mngr Henry Coburn, b 779 N Penn.
Coburn & Weelburg (Willard H Coburn, George F Weelburg), live stock, Union Stock Yards (W I).
Coby Joseph, watchman, r 31 Garden.
Cocanaugher Joseph, janitor, h 60 Dawson.
Cocherl Dora J (wid Wm S), h 268 W 6th.
Cochran Alexander, clk, b 31 Fletcher av.
Cochran Andrew J, supt industrial dept Blind Institute, h 43 Highland pl.
Cochran Andrew J jr, clk C C C & St L Ry, h 170 E Merrill.
Cochran Cerilda (wid Thomas), h 224½ W Washington.

TUTEWILER UNDERTAKER, NO. 72 WEST MARKET STREET. TELEPHONE 216.

THE PROVIDENT LIFE AND TRUST CO. OF PHILADELPHIA. Endowment Insurance presents the double attraction of relieving manhood and middle age from anxiety and old age from want.
For particulars apply to D. W. EDWARDS, General Agent, 508 Indiana Trust Building.

THEODORE F. SMITHER

Cochran Charles, lab, h 165 Sheffield av (H).
Cochran Eck, drug clk, b 31 Fletcher av.
Cochran Effie N, boarding 1139 N Illinois.
Cochran Eli, carp, r 156 W Washington.
Cochran Ellen (wid Thomas), b 33 Bloomington.
Cochran Ford, lab, h 564½ W Washington.
Cochran Joseph, motorman, h 1139 N Illinois.
Cochran Robert, pottery, 564 W Washington, h same.
Cochran Wm A, cashr The Grand Hotel, r 151 N Alabama.
Cochran Wm A, contr, 322 Union, h same.
Cochran Wm C, huckster, h 217 E Washington.
Cochran Wm E, trav agt Elmer E Nichols Co, 74 S Meridian.
Cochran Wm M, h 304 College av.
Cochrane Arthur, motorman, r 23 N West.
Cochrane George W, carp, b 424 N Senate av.
Cochrane Jean M, cashr, b 415 N Illinois.
Cochrane John, carp, h 415 N Illinois.
Cochrane John P, letter carrier P O, h 190 Lexington av.
Cochrane Katrina, teacher Public School No 32, b 415 N Illinois.
Cochrane Robert S, letter carrier P O, b 415 N Illinois.
Cochrane Samuel W, contr, h 424 N Senate av.
Cochrane Wm T, city fireman, h 481 Stillwell.
Cockburn Henry D, trav agt Emil Wulschner & Son, h 117 E Vermont.
Cocke John S, lab, h 960 N New Jersey.
Cockerell Marshall H, carp, h 469 W Eugene (N I).
Cockley Jacob, r 146 S Noble.
Cocks Thomas G Rev, pastor Irvington M E Church, h n s Maple av 2 e of Central av (I).

COCKRUM JOHN B, General Attorney L E & W R R, s w cor Washington and Noble, Tel 1472; h 311 College av.

Codori Charles, mach, b 292 E South.
Cody Albert E, bkkpr, h 532 W Addison (N I).
Cody Edward, waiter, r 225 W Washington.
Cody James, h 499 E Georgia.
Cody James P, lab, h 20 Poplar (B).
Cody John J, mach hd, b 499 E Georgia.
Cody Minnie B, milliner, 46 N Illinois, h 532 W Addison (N I).
Coe Edwin H, bkkpr Schnull & Co, h Ritter av (I).
Coe Adellah W (wid Charles B), h 110 Talbott av.
Coe Henry (Coe & Roache), r 277 N Delaware.
Coe James M, mach hd, b 18 Allfree.
Coe Joseph E, crater, h 438 Charles.
Coe Katharine, h 80 E New York.
Coe Marion, lab, h 217 Minnesota.
Coe Matilda F (wid Orris K), b 182 S New Jersey.

COE & ROACHE (Henry Coe, Addison L Roache Jr), Loans and Insurance, 300 Indiana Trust Bldg, Tel 501.

Coen Frank, carp, b 143 E Washington.
Coen John J, grocer, 50 S Capitol av, h 50½ S Illinois.
Coen Robert J, lab, b 187 S Capitol av.

THE WHEN IS A WORLD BEATER.

Coen Samuel B, trav agt, h 888 Bellefontaine.
Coerper Henry J, trav agt, h 1064 N Delaware.
Cofer Albert C, lab, r 141 W Washington.
Coffay, see also Caffee.
Coffay Eleanor W (wid John), b 1101 N Penn.
Coffay Emily, teacher Public School No 17, b 1101 N Penn.
Coffelt Carl F, pressman, b Enterprise Hotel.
Coffelt Carl L, checkman, b 137 Martindale av.
Coffelt Wm A, mach, h rear 137 Martindale av.
Coffey, see also Coffy.
Coffey David, lab, h 283 E Court.
Coffey James W, drayman, 177 E Washington, h 319 E Wabash.
Coffey Michael, lab, h 114 Meek.
Coffie Cornelia, h rear 18 W Michigan.
Coffie Lafayette, lab, h e s Auburn av 4 s of Bethel av.
Coffield Thaddeus, painter, h 198 Walcott.
Coffin Abraham P, tmstr, h 195 S Pine.
Coffin Albert W (Coffin, Fletcher & Co), h 393 Park av.
Coffin Arthur, clk, h 355 Bellefontaine.
Coffin Bessie C, clk, b 76 W Walnut.
Coffin Carrie E (wid Erastus K), h 431 Home av.
Coffin Charles E (C E Coffin & Co), pres Indiana Savings and Investment Co, b The Denison.

COFFIN CHARLES F, Lawyer, Rooms 15-19 Aetna Bldg, 19½ N Penn, Tel 1161, h 382 Broadway.

Coffin Charles P, polisher, b 195 S Pine.
Coffin Charles Z, teller Indiana Natl Bank, h 93 Prospect.

COFFIN C E & CO (Charles E Coffin, Charles E Holloway), Investment Bankers, Brokers and Dealers in Real Estate, Mortgage Loans, Fire Insurance, 90 E Market, Tel 518.

Coffin David W, pres Am Bldg and Loan Assn, h 643 N Illinois.

THE A. BURDSAL CO.
Manufacturers of
Paints and Colors
VARNISHES,
Brushes, Painters' and Paper Hangers' Supplies.
34 AND 36 SOUTH MERIDIAN STREET.

COMPOSITION ROOFING MATERIALS. BEST IN THE MARKET. TELEPHONE 861. OFFICE, 151 WEST MARYLAND ST.

ELECTRICIANS | DON'T FORGET US. ALL WORK GUARANTEED. C. W. MEIKEL, Tel. 466. 96-98 E. New York St.

DALTON & MERRIFIELD { LUMBER South Noble St., near E. Washington

INDIANA ELECTROTYPE CO. :: BEST WORK. LOWEST PRICES.
23 WEST PEARL ST., INDIANAPOLIS, IND. JOB WORK. BOOK PLATES. BEST PATENT BASE ON THE MARKET.
All Orders Promptly Filled.

KIRKHOFF BROS.
Steam and Hot Water Heating Apparatus,
Plumbing and Gas Fitting.
102-104 SOUTH PENNSYLVANIA ST,
TELEPHONE 910.

Coffin, Fletcher & Co (Albert W Coffin, Lafayette W and Samuel H Fletcher), pork packers, n s Ray w of West.
Coffin Frank M, gas insp, h 556 N Alabama.
Coffin George, trav agt, r 146 N Illinois.
Coffin George W, butcher, h 135 Fletcher av.
Coffin Jennie (wid Junius M), b 510 S West.
Coffin Lydia B (wid Robert), b 356 Bellefontaine.
Coffin Maggie, governess Asylum for Friendless Colored Children.
Coffin Mary E, nurse 124 N Alabama.
Coffin Olga, student, b 1306 N Delaware.
Coffin Robert K, mach, b 355 Bellefontaine.
Coffin Robert M, sec Atlas Engine Works, h 356 Bellefontaine.
Coffin Thomas W, h 75 Cornell av.
Coffin Wm J, cigar mnfr, 72 Frank, h same.
Coffin Wm N, engr, h 556 Broadway.
Coffin Zeno W, h 93 Prospect.
Coffland Harry E, lineman, h 43 W Morris.
Coffman, see also Kauffman.
Coffman Catherine (wid George A), b 281 W 16th.
Coffman Charles, hostler, b State Fair Grounds.
Coffman Ella, buyer N Y Store, b 348 N Illinois.
Coffman Harry E, pressman, b 267 S New Jersey.
Coffman Henry C, salesman George Hitz & Co, h 123 Prospect.
Coffman Jackson D, carp, h 323 N Liberty.
Coffman Jacob, drugs, 540 S East, h 542½ same.
Coffman Jerome B, driver, h 235 Hoyt av.
Coffman John S, carp, h 119 Buchanan.
Coffman Joshua S, salesman Indpls Drug Co, h 267 S New Jersey.
Coffman Ralph B, mach, h 281 W 16th.
Coffman Walter M, mach, h 1700 Graceland av.
Coffman Wm F, wirewkr, b 103 N Senate av.
Coffy, see also Coffey.
Coffy Adelbert B, coffees, 130 Mass av, h 29 Garfield pl.
Cogan James, flagman, r 771 N Senate av.
Coghill Thomas S, carp, r 528 N Meridian.

LIME
BUILDING SUPPLIES,
Hair, Plaster, Flue Linings,
The W. G. Wasson Co.
130 INDIANA AVE. Tel. 989.

Cogle John H, foreman, h 240 English av.
Cogswell Anna P, elocutionist, 283 Douglass, b same.
Cogswell Malcolm W, clk, b 283 Douglass.
Cogswell Stacy H, carp, h 283 Douglass.
Cohee Morris M, clk, r 51 Indiana av.
Cohee Wm H, trav agt, h 1436 Rader (N I).
Cohen Abraham, h 157 N East.
Cohen Abraham, peddler, h 274 S Illinois.
Cohen Abraham B, solr New England Mut Life Ins Co, b 156 N East.
Cohen Alexander, junk, 359 W Washington, h 307 S Meridian.
Cohen Benjamin B, bartndr, b 284 E New York.
Cohen Bros (Isaac and Herman), dry goods, 228 W Washington.
Cohen David, peddler, h 441 S Illinois.
Cohen Harris, junk, 291 W Washington, h 132 Eddy.
Cohen Harry, bkkpr, b 307 S Meridian.
Cohen Henry E, clk, b 156 N East.
Cohen Herman (Cohen Bros), h 73 Madison av.
Cohen Hyman, pawnbroker, 31 S Illinois, h 156 N East.
Cohen Isaac (Cohen Bros), h 223 E Ohio.
Cohen John, lab, r 30 Roanoke.
Cohen Joseph, barber, 306 S Illinois, h 517 S Capitol av.
Cohen Joseph, bkkpr, b 307 S Meridian.
Cohen Louis, clk, h 418 S Delaware.
Cohen Louisa (wid Wm), b 401 N New Jersey.
Cohen Manny E, mngr Andrews The Tailor, b Circle Park Hotel.
Cohen Marcus, grocer, 127 Eddy, h same.
Cohen Simon, clothing, 592 Virginia av, h same.
Cohen Thomas, cutter, h 293 E Washington.
Cohn, see also Kahn.
Cohn Abraham, clk, h 497 N Capitol av.
Cohn Albert W, clk, b 221 Hadley av (W I).
Cohn Fabian, agt, h 20 Cornell av.
Cohn Isaac, tailor, h 470 N New Jersey.
Cohn Michael, h 87 N East.
Cohn Morris F, trimmer Kahn Tailoring Co, b 497 N Capitol av.
Cohn Myer, mngr Santa Clara Wine Co, 33 W Ohio, h 410 N Delaware.
Coine Michael, lab, h 54 Minerva.
Coit George F, tel opr, h Grand av (I).
Cokayne Edwin S, clk, h 81 College av.
Cokefair Edgar O, carp, b 115 High.
Cokefair Sophia O, h 115 High.
Colbert, see also Calbert.
Colbert Dennis J, clk R M S, h 29 Coburn.
Colbert John H, roll hd, r 78 W Georgia.
Colbert John J, steelwkr, h 29 Church.
Colbert Joseph, porter, h rear 632 N Penn.
Colbert Patrick, lab, h 438 S Illinois.
Colbert Thomas F, supt of police Police Station, s e cor Alabama and Pearl, h 449 N California.
Colbert Wm A, clk, b 438 S Illinois.
Colburn Wm, ironwkr, r 164 W Maryland.
Colby Elmira (wid Jonas), h 140 St Mary.
Colclazier George W, painter, h 134 N Liberty.
Colclazier Mary, dressmkr, 134 N Liberty, h same.
Colclazier Thomas J, lab, h 1155 Michigan av.
Colclazier Wm L, painter, h 96 Cornell av.
Colden Earl, clk, b 824 College av.
Coldo James, lab, h 19 Roanoke.
Coldo Maria (wid Perry), b 442 Superior.
Coldwell, see also Caldwell, Cauldwell and Colwell.

Parlor, Bed Room, Dining Room, Kitchen. Furniture W. H. MESSENGER, 101 E. Wash. St., Tel. 491.

ALL KINDS OF HEAVY AND LIGHT GRAY IRON CASTINGS } McNamara, Koster & Co. { Foundry and Pattern Shop
Phone 1593. 212-218 S. Penn. St.

Coldwell Horace G (H G Coldwell & Co), h 147 East Drive (W P).
Coldwell H G & Co (Horace G Coldwell, Frank Woodbridge), contrs, 74 E Market.
Cole, see also Kahl and Kohl.
Cole Abraham, lab, h 4 Wisconsin.
Cole Albert B, clk, b 528 Broadway.
Cole Albert B, lawyer, 17 Thorpe blk, r 516 N New Jersey.
Cole Albert M, phys, 173 N Penn, h same.
Cole Allen, lab, h 80 Arizona.
Cole Ambrose E, fireman, h 228 Newman.
Cole Anna (wid Henry), h rear 249 W South.
Cole Barton W (Cole & Pease), h 221 Christian av.
Cole Charles, huckster, b 358 S Delaware.
Cole Charles B, insp, h 402 N East.
Cole Charles M, wagonmkr, h 358 S Delaware.
Cole Clarence I, carp, h 588 W Eugene (N I).
Cole Dock, lab, h 352½ W North.
Cole Elizabeth (wid Thomas K), h 33 Hudson.
Cole Ernest B, clk R M S, h 528 Broadway.
Cole Frank L, carp, h 119 Ramsey av.
Cole F M, sec to genl frt agt L E & W R R, h 402 N East.
Cole George, trav agt, h 609 N West.
Cole Isaac C, carp, h 588 W Eugene (N I).
Cole Isabel, dressmkr, 507 E Market, h same.
Cole James A, carp, 148 Harlan, h same.
Cole James E, barber, b 1373 N Senate av.
Cole James H, medicines, 71 Indiana av, h 271 W Vermont.
Cole James J, phys, 507 E Market, b same.
Cole Jennie (wid James), h 63 Rhode Island.
Cole Joseph, lab, h 6 Drake.
Cole Joseph E, lab, h 438 Charles.
Cole Lee, coachman 98 W Vermont.
Cole Mary (wid Emery), h 111 Locke.
Cole Mary C (wid Albert M), b 440 Park av.
Cole Pasquale, huckster, b 336½ E Washington.
Cole Ross E, painter, h Union (M J).
Cole Samuel C, ydmaster, h 1085 W New York.
Cole Seth M, clk P B Ault & Co, b 82 E Vermont.
Cole Thomas, lab, b 14 Willard.
Cole Thomas A, trav agt, h 507 E Market.
Cole Wm H, printer, 80½ E Market.
Cole Wm S, bartndr, r n e cor Rural and Bloyd av (B).
Cole & Pease (Barton W Cole, Theodore W Pease), real est, 18 Baldwin blk.
Colebrook Edward W, janitor Crown Hill Cemetery, h 251 W 23d.
Colebrook Frederick J, lab, h 371 Cornell av.
Coleman, see also Cullmann and Kuhlman.
Coleman Abigail B (wid Harvey B), b 1021 N Alabama.
Coleman Abraham L, lab, h 53 Wallack.
Coleman Albert, finisher, b 267 N Pine.
Coleman Albert S, b 629 N Senate av.
Coleman Alphonsus L, mach hd, b 267 N Pine.
Coleman Alvey, lab, b 53 Wallack.
Coleman Anson D, clk, b 1164 E Washington.
Coleman Arthus R, b 18 Columbia al.
Coleman Benjamin F, painter, h 304 Virginia av.
Coleman Benjamin F, switchman, h 203 Belmont av (H).

Henry H. Fay,
40½ E. WASHINGTON ST.,
FIRE INSURANCE, REAL ESTATE,
LOANS AND RENTAL AGENT.

Coleman Cassius M, printer, h 709 N Senate av.
Coleman Celia, h 259 E New York.
Coleman Charles, lab, h rear 738 N West.
Coleman Charles, lab, b 16 Columbia al.
Coleman Charles F, soldier U S Arsenal.
Coleman Clark, lab, h 420 W 2d.
Coleman Columbus, lab, h 420 W 2d.
Coleman Eli, lab 512 N Illinois.
Coleman Eli, tmstr, h 210 St Mary.
Coleman Elias, lab, b 230 Roanoke.
Coleman Frances, tailoress, h 133½ Martindale av.
Coleman Frank G, painter, h 304 Virginia av.
Coleman George, waiter, r 356 Douglass.
Coleman George W, lab, h 297 N Senate av.
Coleman Georgia, b 90 Stevens.
Coleman Helen M (wid James P), h 170 Deloss.
Coleman Henry, h 883 Morris (W I).
Coleman Henry, lab, h 420 S Olive.
Coleman Henry, lab, r 483½ E Washington.
Coleman Henry, meats, 402 S West, h 308 same.
Coleman Henry, soldier U S Arsenal.
Coleman Herbert B, mnfrs' agt, 503 Lemcke bldg, h 1021 N Alabama.
Coleman Isabella (wid Thomas J), h rear 21 Cornell av.
Coleman James, clk, b 1164½ E Washington.
Coleman James, lab, h w s Caroline av 2 n of Hillside av.
Coleman James, tmstr, h e s Milburn 1 n of Indiana av (M P).
Coleman James M, phys, 187 Shelby, h 277 Virginia av.
Coleman James T, b 189 S Illinois.
Coleman John, bartndr, r 224 E Market.
Coleman John, lab, h 391 Clinton.
Coleman John A, monuments, h 366 N Alabama.
Coleman John C, lab, r 66 N Missouri.
Coleman John G, h 378 Blake.
Coleman John L, lab, b 203 Belmont av (H).
Coleman John T, lab, h 408 W North.
Coleman John W, lab, h 1014 N Senate av.
Coleman Joseph, lab, b rear 21 Cornell av.

WILL GO ON YOUR BOND
American Bonding & Trust Co.
Of Baltimore, Md. Approved as sole surety by the United States Government and the different States as Sole Surety on all Forms of Bonds.
W. E. BARTON & CO., General Agents,
504 Indiana Trust Building.
LONG DISTANCE TELEPHONE 1918.

THE FRED DIETZ CO.
WOODEN PACKING BOXES MADE TO OR. FACTORY AND WAREHOUSE TRUCKS. 40 Madison Avenue. Telephone 69

BUSINESS EDUCATION A NECESSITY.
TIME SHORT. DAY AND NIGHT SCHOOL.
SUCCESS CERTAIN AT THE PERMANENT, RELIABLE
Indianapolis BUSINESS UNIVERSITY

Water Works Pumping Engines { HENRY R. WORTHINGTON, 64 SOUTH PENNSYLVANIA ST. Long Distance Telephone 284.

UNION CO-OPERATIVE LAUNDRY (COMPOSED OF UNION LAUNDRY GIRLS.) NOS. 138, 140 AND 142 VIRGINIA AVENUE. —T. E. SOMERVILLE, MANAGER— TELEPHONE 1269. INDIANAPOLIS, IND.

HORACE M. HADLEY
INSURANCE AND LOANS
66 E. Market Street, Basement
TELEPHONE 1540.

Coleman Julia (wid Elias), r 136 N Penn.
COLEMAN LEWIS AUSTIN, Lawyer, 81 Baldwin Blk, r 294 N Capitol av.
Coleman Lewis H, porter, h 181 W 2d.
Coleman Louisa (wid Charles), b 403 W North.
Coleman Martin, boilermkr, b 267 N Pine.
Coleman Mary (wid Martin), h 267 N Pine.
Coleman Mary E (wid Wm F), h 90 Stevens.
Coleman Matthew P, boilermkr, h 141 Yandes.
Coleman Milton H, agt, h 76 Michigan (H).
Coleman Myrtle, teacher Liberty Street Free Kindergarten, b 277 Virginia av.
Coleman Naldo R, barber, 96 Russell av, h same.
Coleman Nancy (wid John), h rear 135 E Pratt.
Coleman Nicholas, mach, b 267 N Pine.
Coleman Patrick A, saloon, 59 Beacon, h same.
Coleman Richard M (Haughey & Coleman), b 118 W Vermont.
Coleman Rome B, agt J I Case Mach Co, 42 Kentucky av, r same.
Coleman Samuel J, lab, b rear 21 Cornell av.
Coleman Thaddeus, h 26 Hill.
Coleman Thomas, lab, h 9 McIntyre.
Coleman Thomas A, painter, b 26 Hill.
Coleman Walter, polisher, b e s Milburn 1 n of Indiana av (M P).
Coleman Wm, lab, b 615 N Senate av.
Coleman Wm, h 82 Ft Wayne av.
Coleman Wm H, h 34 W 2d.
Coleman Wm S, lab, h 150 Maple.
Coleman Willis, lab, h 176 Agnes.
Coleman Willis R, lab, h 37 W McCarty.
Coleman Woodson J, h 629 N Senate av.
Colerick E Fenwick, journalist, b Hotel English.
Coles George A, blksmith, h 1147 E Washington.
Coles Josie, b 867 S Meridian.
Coles Peter R, tmstr, b 22 Woodside av (W).
Colestock Frank E, lab, h 161½ Mass av.

COLLECTIONS
MERCHANTS' AND MANUFACTURERS' EXCHANGE
Will give you good service.
J. E. TAKKEN, Manager,
Union Building, over U. S. Pension Office.
73 West Maryland Street.

Colestock George, bookbndr, r 71½ N Illinois.
Colestock Wesley S, carp, r 95½ N Delaware.
Coley Grant G, h 10 Howard.
Coley Richard, carp, h 202 W 1st.
Coley Wm E, restaurant, 191 W Washington, h 232½ same.
Colgan Henrietta, prin Public School No 10, h 298 Park av.
Colgan Mary E, teacher Girls' Classical School, b 298 Park av.
Colgan Mary L, prin Public School No 6, b 298 Park av.
Colgrove Charles H, tel opr, b 36 Dickson.
Colgrove Oscar, collr J S Farrell & Co, h 36 Dickson.
Colin August, bartender, r 220½ S Meridian.
Colip Erastus H, fireman, h 362 Cedar.
Coll Dennis C, horseshoer, b 432 S Illinois.
Coll Dominick, clk, h 116 Oak.
Coll John J, mach, b 116 Oak.
Coll Mary A (wid Dominick), h 432 S Illinois.
Coll Mary H (wid Hugh), b 116 Oak.
Coll Wm J, lithog, h 143 Ft Wayne av.
Collamore Edward W, trav agt, b 64 Cherry.
Collamore Wm A, watchman, h 64 Cherry.
COLLEGE AVENUE PHARMACY, Smith H Mapes Propr, 501 College av.
Collester Clara A, bkkpr Thomas H Nelson, b 63 Tremont av (H).
Collester Franklin, lab, h 60 Tremont av (H).
Collett John, geologist, h 60½ N Illinois.
Collett Wm A, foreman, h 449 Ash.
Collette Harry S, tel opr, r 348 N Illinois.
Colley Charles A, coachman 25 Monument pl.
Colleys Henry E, cooper, h 29 N Dorman.
Colleys Nicholas, cooper, b 29 N Dorman.
Collier Bertha E, h 171 W Ohio.
Collier Charles R, mach, h 420 S East.
Collier Edward, brakeman, b 648 Marlowe av.
Collier James (Collier & Murphy), h 501 S Capitol av.
Collier James, switchman, b 201 E Washington.
Collier James L, lab, h 24 Crawford.
Collier Joseph, lawyer, 215 Indiana Trust bldg, h 648 Marlowe av.
Collier Louisa, teacher Public School No 30, b 18 Temple av.
Collier Mary E (wid Thomas), h 56 S Summit.
Collier Mary L, asst prin Public School No 6, b 1227 N Illinois.
Collier Nancy E, teacher Public School No 31, b 1227 N Illinois.
COLLIER PETER F, Book Publisher, 93 N Delaware, Res New York City.
Collier Wm H, painter, r 16 Ryan blk.
Collier Wm S, real est, h 1227 N Illinois.
COLLIER & MURPHY (James Collier, Martin J Murphy), Undertakers and Embalmers, 59 W Maryland, Tel 439.
Collinge Robert, boarding 88 W Ohio.
Collings Franklin C, money clk U S Exp Co, h 59 Hoyt av.
Collings George J, h s s Moore av 1 w of Dearborn.
Collins Absalom, lab, h e s Calvin 1 s of Bethel av.

CLEMENS VONNEGUT
184, 186 and 192 E. Washington St.
BUILDERS' HARDWARE,
Building Paper. Duplex Joist Hangers

THE WM. H. BLOCK CO. DRY GOODS, DRAPERIES, RUGS, WINDOW SHADES.
7 AND 9 EAST WASHINGTON STREET.

COLLINS ALBERT H, State Mngr Fidelity Mutual Life Insurance Co of Philadelphia, 52 Baldwin Blk, b 776 N Penn. (See left top lines.)
Collins Albert N, phys City Dispensary, 32 E Ohio.
Collins Anna B, teacher, b e s Denny 2 n of Washington.
Collins Anna M, boarding 28 S State av.
Collins Augustus F, watchman Marion County Workhouse, h 13 Shriver av.
Collins Charles S, b 60 Oak.
Collins Charles S, driver, h 138 Lexington av.
Collins Cornelius, lab, h 145 Geisendorff.
Collins Daniel, h 229½ E Washington.
Collins David, trav agt McCormick H M Co, h 92 W 7th.
Collins Edgar W, agt, h 271 W Michigan.
Collins Edward H, uphlr, b 123 Davidson.
Collins Elisha J, carp, h 8 Emerson pl.
Collins Eliza, h 315 W Maryland.
Collins Elizabeth A, teacher Public School No 8, b 316 N New Jersey.
Collins Elizabeth E, h 88 S Senate av.
Collins Elsie, sec Women's Industrial Assn for Practical Progress, b 73 Division (W I).
Collins Emanuel, cigars, 179 Indiana av, h 229½ E Washington.
Collins Frederick L, clk, b 477 N Alabama.
Collins George R Rev, pastor St Paul's A M E Church, h e s Manlove av 2 s of 17th.
Collins Gilbert, lab, h 230 W Chesapeake.
Collins Harry, engr, h 79 Hoyt av.
Collins James A, clk, h 103 N Gillard av.
Collins James L, baggageman, h 3 Empire.
Collins James M, painter, h 92 Columbia av.
Collins Jeremiah, city sanitary inspr, r 185 Meek.
Collins Jeremiah, clk, b 373 S Illinois.
Collins Jesse, lab, h 571 Shelby.
Collins Jesse, lab, h 130 Winchester av.
Collins John, carp, h 373 S Illinois.
Collins John, lab, b 150 Belmont av (W I).
Collins John, lab, b 124 S Pine.
Collins John F, insp, h 43 Vinton.
Collins John W (Weser & Collins), h 92 Ramsey av.
Collins John W, butcher, h 491 N California.
Collins John W J, pastor Trinity M E Church, h 15 Division (W I).
Collins Joseph, waiter 400 N Illinois.
Collins Joseph C, fireman, b 803 E Washington.
Collins Joshua, porter, h rear 166 E Michigan.
Collins Laura A (wid John W), h 123 Davidson.
Collins Levi, tmstr, b 247 Bates.
Collins Librain H, mach, h 535 College av.
Collins Lida E, h 334 E Ohio.
Collins Luman J, photog, b 3 Empire.
Collins Mahlon V, cabtmkr, h 351 S Brookside av.
Collins Major, pres Indiana Car and Foundry Co, res Brazil, Ind.
Collins Malachi, condr, b 1139 N Illinois.
Collins Malachi P, bartndr, h 281 W Pearl.
Collins Margaret (wid Thomas E), h 235 E Michigan.
Collins Marion, lab, b 40 Athon.
Collins Martha (wid Henry), h 114 Roanoke.
Collins Martin, lab, b 51 Blake.
Collins Martin F, printer, h 138 Lynn av (W I).
Collins Mary (wid Wm F), nurse Orphans' Home.

Collins Mary F (wid Edward), b 1542 N Senate av.
Collins Mayberry L, pressman, b 12 N State av.
Collins Michael J, b 469 W Shoemaker (N I).
Collins Oran P, fireman, h 28 S State av.
Collins Orrie M (wid Hiram), b 283 Hillside av.
Collins Patrick, b 412 Indiana av.
Collins Patrick, lab, b 520 W Maryland.
Collins Patrick H, tailor, 149½ E Washington, h 113 N Dorman.
Collins Robert, butcher, b 520 W Maryland.
Collins Robert, lab, h 60 Oak.
Collins Robert, lab, b 434 W 2d.
Collins Robert K, h 12 N State av.
Collins Sallie E (wid Wm A), h 477 N Alabama.
Collins Samuel E, photog, h 73 Division (W I).
Collins Sarah (wid Wm H), h 316 W Court.
Collins S Herbert, pres U S Lounge Mnfg Co and propr Natl Saw Guard Co, h 128 N Meridian.
Collins Thomas, porter Blind Inst.
Collins Thomas E, drugs, 52 Indiana av, r 7 Halcyon blk.
Collins Wm, carver, b Illinois House.
Collins Wm D, mach hd, h 665 W Eugene (N I).
Collins Wm G, trav agt, r 19 Stewart pl.
Collins Wm H, painter, h 455 S Missouri.
Collins Wm R, bartndr, b 12 N State av.
Collins Willis, waiter 400 N Illinois.
Collmann George, lab, h 423 S State av.
Collmann Wm, lab, b 423 S State av.
Colly Charles, driver, r 23 Monument pl.
Colman Samuel A, artist, 302½ N Senate av, h same.
Colon August P, bartndr, r 222 S Meridian.
Colon Nicholas, bartndr, r 5½ Madison av.
Colson Charles A, lineman, h 331 W Michigan.
Colson Charles H, lab, h 548 Chestnut.
Colson Elnora, dressmkr, 548 Chestnut, h same.
Colter, see also Coulter.
Colter Andrew, wheelmkr, b 140 Madison av.
Colter Andrew J, mach, b 361 E McCarty.

GUIDO R. PRESSLER,
FRESCO PAINTER
Churches, Theaters, Public Buildings, Etc., A Specialty.
Residence, No. 325 North Liberty Street.
INDIANAPOLIS, IND.

INDIANAPOLIS STEEL ROOFING AND CORRUGATING WORKS, 23 and 25 East South Street. S. D. NOEL, Proprietor.

David S. McKernan, Rooms 2-5 Thorpe Block.
REAL ESTATE AND LOANS
Money to loan on real estate. Special inducements offered those having money to loan. It will pay you to investigate.

DIAMOND WALL PLASTER { Telephone 1410 BUILDERS' EXCHANGE.

UNION TRANSFER AND STORAGE CO. Cor. E. Ohio St. and C., C., C. & St. L. R'y Tracks. BEST FACILITIES FOR STORING AND TRANSFERRING MACHINERY AND MERCHANDISE.

W. McWORKMAN

FIRE SHUTTERS,
FIRE DOORS,
METAL CEILINGS.

930 W. Washington St. Tel. 1118.

Colter George R, cigar mnfr, 139 Virginia av, h 172 E South.
Colter John A, city fireman, h 256 S Delaware.
Colter Mamie, cashr, b 361 E McCarty.
Colter Margaret (wid Archibald), h 256 S Delaware.
Colter Nellie, cashr, b 361 E McCarty.
Colter Richard S, h 361 E McCarty.
Colter Richard S, lineman, b 140 Madison av.
Colter Charles E, painter, b 120 Hosbrook.
Colter Edward, clk, r 169 N Illinois.
Colton Elizabeth (wid Elijah), b 120 Hosbrook.
Colton Elizabeth, teacher Public School No 6, b 76 Vine.
Colton John, lab, b 407 Coburn.
Coltrain Bay, blksmith, b 162 Madison av.
Coltrain Jarrett N, confr, 15 Madison av, h 162 same.
COLUMBIA CLUB, Charles H Rouzer Supt, 73 Monument Pl, Tel 56.
COLUMBIAN FEATHER CLEANING AND DYEING ESTABLISHMENT, Samuel Heath Mngr, 147 Mass av. (See adv p 8.)
COLUMBIAN RELIEF FUND ASSOCIATION, Wm H Latta Pres, Everett Wagner Vice-Pres and Treas, C H Brackett Sec, 409-410 Lemcke Bldg.
COLUMBUS BUGGY CO, Albert H Snider State Agt, 12-14 Monument Pl.
Colver Mary L (wid Hiram W), b 359 N Penn.
Colvin, see also Calvin.
Colvin Alexander, h 59 Dougherty.
Colvin George T, car rep, h 134 S Judge Harding (W I).
Colvin Henry, porter, b 154 W North.
Colvin Horace G, carp, h 6 Standard av (W I).
Colvin Jeremiah, engr, h 322 Union.
Colvin Rachel (wid Scott), h 154 W North.
Colvin Thomas S, lab, b 75 Centennial.
Colvin Wm H, lab, h 180 Anderson.
Colwell, see also Caldwell, Cauldwell and Coldwell.

GEO. J. MAYER,
MANUFACTURER OF
SEALS
STENCILS, RUBBER STAMPS, CHECKS, BADGES, DOOR PLATES, ETC.
.. S. Meridian St., Ground Floor. TEL. 1386.

Colwell Albert, clk, r 156 N Illinois.
Colwell Andrew J, clk, h 23 Byram pl.
Colwell David H, lab, b 413 Howard (W I).
Colwell Faires, horseshoer, 424 Mass av, h 27 Orange av.
Colwell Mary (wid Lucas), h 225 Elm.
Colwell Wm F, carp, h 413 Howard (W I).
Coman Charles, lab, h rear 740 N West.
Combs, see also Coombs.
Combs Ambrose (Combs & Triggs), h 619 S Meridian.
Combs Charles, lab, b 997 W Vermont.
Combs Edward, brakeman, b 54 Belmont av (H).
Combs Elias A, clk, h 27 Sheffield av (H).
Combs Francis C, h 253 Huron.
COMBS GEORGE W, Physician, 30 E Ohio, b The Denison, Office Tel 968, Res Tel 1484.
Combs John H, carp, h 629 Madison av.
Combs Julia (wid Jerome F), h 200 W New York.
Combs Newton, coachman, h 16 Leon.
Combs Olin, mach, h 997 W Vermont.
Combs Rolley, lab, b 27 Sheffield av (H).
Combs & Triggs (Ambrose Combs, James M Triggs), hardware, 496 Madison av.
Comer Georgie L, stenog C C C & St L Ry, b 192 Bellefontaine.
Comer Jeannette (wid George), h 192 Bellefontaine.
Comer John C, h 180 Ash.
Comer Martha H, bkkpr J A Lemcke, b 180 Ash.
Comer Martin J, butcher, h 29 Yandes.
Comer Mary E (wid Jonathan), dressmkr, 224 Ramsey av, b same.
Comer Robert J, bkkpr, b 180 Ash.
Comfort James W Rev, prof Butler College, h 253 Bellefontaine.
Comfort Joseph C, clk The Bowen-Merrill Co, b 253 Bellefontaine.
Comfort Wm E, bkkpr, b 253 Bellefontaine.
Comingor John A, phys, 34 When bldg, h 520 N Illinois.
Comingore Alice P (wid Wm H), h 124 E Vermont.
Comingore George R, b 853 N New Jersey.
Comingore Wm P, electrotyper, r 23 W Georgia.
Comley Edward B, clk, h 160 N Liberty.
Comley Sarah (wid Clifton), b 22 Home av.
Comley Wm G, bkkpr S A Fletcher & Co, b 22 Home av.
COMMERCE DESPATCH LINE, Eugene H Darrach Mngr, 1011-1012 Majestic Bldg, Tel 833.
COMMERCIAL BUILDING AND LOAN ASSOCIATION, John W Fort Pres, Levi Kennedy Sec, Henry L Brown Treas, 416-418 Indiana Trust Bldg, Tel 1241.
COMMERCIAL CLUB RESTAURANT, George H Bryce Propr, Commercial Club Bldg.
COMMERCIAL CLUB THE, Daniel P Erwin Pres, Wm Fortune 1st Vice-Pres, Jacob P Dunn 2d Vice-Pres, Evans Woollen Sec, Austin B Gates Treas, 128-129 Commercial Club Bldg, Tel 785.
COMMERCIAL CURRENT, Published by Indianapolis Business University, 82 When Bldg.

A. METZGER AGENCY ESTABLISHED 1863. REAL ESTATE

LAMBERT GAS & GASOLINE ENGINE CO.
ANDERSON, IND. NATURAL GAS ENGINES.

COMMERCIAL ELECTRIC CO, Joseph R Evans Pres, S Lee Hadley Sec, Willard A Evans Treas, Motors and Dynamos, cor Merrill and Willard, Tel 615.

COMMERCIAL TRAVELERS' MUTUAL ACCIDENT ASSOCIATION OF INDIANA, Carey McPherson Pres, Benjamin H Prather Sec, Home Office 20-21 When Bldg.

Commins George W, clk, h 322 E New York.
Commiskey Charles A, engr, h 547 S Capitol av.
Commiskey Henry, engr, h 39 Warren av (W I).
Commiskey Jane K, b 39 Warren av (W I).
Commiskey Susan, supervisor Insane Hospital.
Commons Josephine, stenog Wm H Smythe, b 363 N Alabama.
Commons Rosa A (wid Henry), b 162 Howard.
Commons Wm B, train disp, h 363 N Alabama.

COMMONWEALTH LOAN AND SAVINGS ASSOCIATION OF INDIANA, Addison H Nordyke Pres, Charles E Dark Sec, Wm H Hubbard Treas, Waverly Bldg, 18½ N Meridian, Tel 562.

Compton Arunah B, soldermkr, h 227 N California.
Compton, Ault & Co, Robert Hawkins mngr, willowware, 82 S Penn.
Compton Charles E, lawyer, 111 Commercial Club bldg, b 276 W North.
Compton Charles W, trav agt, h 464 E Washington.
Compton Frank, motorman, h 22 Crawford.
Compton George, lab, h 166 S Judge Harding (W I).
Compton George E, trav agt The McElwaine-Richards Co, r 230 N West.
Compton Hugh, condr, b 770 W Washington.
Compton Jacob D, h 453 N Illinois.

COMPTON JOSHUA A, Homeopathic Physician and Surgeon, Office Hours 1-4 and 7-9 P M, 75 E Ohio, h same, Tel 125.

Compton Lewis F, lab, h 46 S Belmont av (W I).
Compton Preston, lab, h w s Central av 2 s of C H & D R R (I).
Compton Ralph, b 453 N Illinois.
Compton Samuel W (Compton & Rice), h 172 N Delaware.
Compton Wesley, lab, h 133 Douglass.
Compton & Rice (Samuel M Compton, George L H Rice), grocers, 49 Mass av.

COMPUTING SCALE CO OF DAYTON, O, Spear & Co Genl Agts, 50, 51 and 52 When Bldg.

Comrie Margaret (wid Alexander), b 68 Downey.
Comstock Albert S, pres Comstock & Coonse Co, h 790 N Meridian.
Comstock Anna J, b 632 N Penn.
Comstock Charles H, vice-pres and mngr The Interior Hardwood Co, h 429 N Delaware.
Comstock Daniel W, judge Appellate Court of Indiana, 113 State House.
Comstock Frederick B, foreman Major Taylor, h 1217 N Penn.
Comstock Henry, carp, h 3 Walcott.

THOS. C. DAY & CO.
Financial Agents and Loans.
We have the experience, and claim to be reliable.
Rooms 325 to 330 Lemcke Bldg.

Comstock Horace A, jeweler, 16 E Washington, b 470 Ash.
Comstock James M, jeweler, h 279 N East.
Comstock John C, trav agt, b 279 N East.
Comstock Lyman W, adv agt The American Nonconformist, 24 S Alabama.
Comstock Margaret J (wid Thomas C), h 279 N East.

COMSTOCK & COONSE CO, Albert S Comstock Pres, George W Coonse Vice-Pres and Treas, Henry M Stackhouse Sec, Pump Mnfrs and Dealers in Carriages and Sleighs, 193-199 S Meridian, Tel 631.

Conant Charles O, mach hd, b E P Conant.
Conant Elisha P, mach, h w s Meridian 2 s of 30th.
Conant Harry W, mach, b E P Conant.
Conard Charles P, constable Carl Habich, h cor 22d and Morris.
Conarroe Martin M, h s s Clifford av 1 e of Ritter av (I).
Conaty, see also Connaty.
Conaty James B, h 297 N Liberty.
Conaway Charles, lab, b 41 S Reisner (W I).
Conaway Edward, lab, h 41 S Reisner (W I).
Conber Charles A, helper, b 162 John.
Conber Sarah E (wid John), h 162 John.
Conde Henri T, pres H T Conde Implement Co, h 210 Broadway.

CONDE H T IMPLEMENT CO, Henri T Conde Pres, Wm A Moore Vice-Pres, Will Cumback Jr Sec, Sanford C Conde Treas, Wholesale Agricultural Implements, Binder Twine, Carriages, Bicycles and Seeds, 27-33 N Capitol av, Tel 162.

Conde Sanford C, treas H T Conde Implement Co, h 10 Lincoln av.
Condell Harry A, fireman, b 201 Davidson.
Condell James S, lab, b 201 Davidson.
Condell Jennie R, bkkpr, b 201 Davidson.
Condell Mary J (wid James S), h 201 Davidson.
Condit, see also Conduitt.

EAT HITZ'S CRACKERS AND CAKES.
ASK YOUR GROCER FOR THEM.

BICYCLES $5 DOWN. MONTHLY. Best Wheels. Best Terms. WHEELMEN'S CO. 31 W. OHIO ST. LONG DISTANCE TEL. 1855.

J. H. TECKENBROCK General House Painter, 94 EAST SOUTH STREET.

FIDELITY MUTUAL LIFE—PHILADELPHIA PA.
$75,000,000, Insurance in Force. $3,600,000, Death Losses Paid. $1,500,000, Surplus.
A. H. COLLINS {General Agent, Baldwin [illegible]

BITUMINOUS COAL IN CAR LOADS TO DEALERS AND MANUFACTURERS. ROOMS 42 AND 43 WHEN BUILDING.

ESTABLISHED 1876. TELEPHONE 168.
CHESTER BRADFORD,
SOLICITOR OF PATENTS,
AND COUNSEL IN PATENT CAUSES.
(See adv. page 6.)
Office:—Rooms 14 and 16 Hubbard Block, S. W. Cor. Washington and Meridian Streets, INDIANAPOLIS, INDIANA.

Condit Harry H (Condit & Arnold) h 184 N Capitol av.
Condit & Arnold (Harry H Condit, George S Arnold), mnfrs' agents, 35 W Pearl.
Condo Charles B, foreman Penna Lines h 198 Woodlawn av.
Condon Ann (wid Thomas) h 87 Church.
Condon Charles P, cigarmkr, h 87 Church.
Condon Edward, butcher, h 77 Thomas.
Condon James T, uphlr, h 116½ W Ray.
Condon John, clk Hollweg & Reese, h 87 Church.
Condon John, lab, h 77 Thomas.
Condon Thomas jr, lab, h 77 Thomas.
Condon Joseph, uphlr, h 87 Church.
Condon Thomas, janitor, r 102 State House.
Condon Wm, molder, h 425 S West.
Condrey Edward M, clk, h 428 Douglass.
Condrey Emma F (wid James B) h 1125 N Penn.
Condrey John W, car rep, h 20 Miley av.
Condrey Rose, dressmkr, 428 Douglass, h same.
Condrey Samuel H, foreman, h 20 Miley av.
Condrey Wm J, condr, h 451 W 22d (N I).
Condron John J, molder, h 126 Belmont av (H).
Condron Michael, grocer, 124 Belmont av (H), h 126 same.
Conduitt, see also Condit.
Conduitt Alexander B, h 186 N Delaware.
Conduitt Allen W, pres Bedford Indiana Stone Co, sec and treas Indiana Bermudez Asphalt Co, h 380 Park av.
Conduitt Harold, student, h 380 Park av.
Conduitt Henry C, farmer, h 186 N Delaware.
Cone Frank, lab, h 530½ S Meridian.
Cones Constantine B, pres C B Cones & Son Mnfg Co, h 225 N Penn.
Cones C B & Son Manufacturing Co, Constantine B Cones pres, John W Murphy treas, Henry L Browning sec, clothing mnfrs, 12 N Senate av.
Cones Harry, plate printer F H Smith, h 402 N Senate av.
Conger Caroline, h 23 N California.
Conger Charles W, student, h 32 Hillside av.

Outing BICYCLES
..MADE BY..
HAY & WILLITS MFG. CO.
76 N. Pennsylvania St. Phone 598.

Edwardsport Coal & Mining Co.

Conger David, lab, h 74 S McLain.
Conger Frank J, driver, h 71 W [illegible]
Conger Herbert M, clk, h 130 E [illegible]
Conger Manuel H, fireman, h 267 [illegible]
Conger Oliver H, clk, h 433 Dill[on]
Conger Orner T Rev, h 32 Hillside [av]
Conger Rose, h 74 S McLain (W I)
Conger Samuel L, painter, h 128 [Dela]ware.
Conger Thomas A, clk, h 267 S E [illegible]
Con[illegible] Anna H (The Grocery) [illegible] 304 College av.
Conkle Wm W, clk, h 95 E Ot[illegible]
Conklin [illegible]
Conklin [illegible]
Conklin [illegible]
Conklin [illegible]
Conklin [illegible], lab, h Hanna Hotel.
Conklin Eugene H, stenog Cont[inental] Mnfg Co, r 94 W Vermont.
Conklin Fred H, lab, h 114 N S[illegible]
Conklin Harry, sawmkr, h 222 C[illegible]
Conklin Jennie M, stenog, h 1282 [illegible]
Conklin K[illegible], messenger 119 W M[illegible]
Conklin [illegible], h 22 Oregon.
Conklin Lester J, lab, h 62 M[illegible]
Conklin Margaret (wid Israel) [illegible] 39 W [illegible]
Conklin Thomas, carp, h 1282 N I[illegible]
Conklin [illegible], reporter The I[ndianapolis] Journal, r [illegible] blk.
Conklin [illegible] H, brakeman, h [illegible]
Conklin Warren A, condr, h [illegible]
Conklin Wm H, patrolman, h [illegible]
Con[illegible] Thomas A, agt Deere & [illegible] 77 W Wash[in]gton, h 171 W 12th.
Con[illegible] Edward F, sawyer, h 20 M[illegible] av.
Con[illegible] Edward F jr, lab, h 20 M[illegible]
Con[illegible] John A, pawnbroker [illegible] [Wash]ington, h 435 College av.
Con[illegible] M[illegible], clk, h 305 Kentucky av.
Con[illegible] Patrick, h 306 Excelsior.
Con[illegible], see also Conney.
Conley Bros (Daniel J and De[illegible]) [illegible] 17 W Pearl.
Con[illegible] Charles, clk, r 360 N Senate.
Con[illegible] Daniel J (Conley Bros) [illegible]
Conley Dennis (Conley Bros) h [illegible] [illegible]
Conley Frank, boiler insp, h 4 Gr[illegible]
Conley George R, bather, h 20 Ingr[aham]
Conley George W, lab, h 20 Ingraham.
Conley John, lab, h 122 Blackford.
Conley Ora R, h 26 Martindale av.
Conley Stanley, carp, h 40 Tecumseh.
Conley Wm, student, r 222 W Mary[land] [illegible]
Conley Wm H, lab, h 9 Willard.
Conlin Annie (wid Patrick) h 122 [Blackfo]rd.
Conlin John, bricklyr, h 126 Dunlap.
Conlin Peter, lab, h 122 Blackford.
Conn, see also Kahn.
Conn Clay, driver, r 173 W North.
Conn Frank, lab, h 40 Beacon.
Conn Henry C, lab, h 699 W North.
Conn John, cabtmkr, 135 Indiana [av, h] same.
Connally Austin, soldier U S Arsenal.
Connell John, [illegible] Kingan & Co (ltd), [h] Blackford.
Connell Patrick, h 1 Kauffmann [illegible]
Connelly, see also Conaty.
Connelly James W, master mechanic [illegible] & W Ry, h 17 S Belmont av (W I).
Connaughton John, lab, h 483 S W[illegible]
Connaughton John P (Kennedy & [Connaughton]) h 74 S Summit.

C. ZIMMERMAN & SONS SLATE AND GRAVEL ROOFERS 19 South East Street

DRIVEN WELLS And Second Water Wells and Pumps of all kinds at CHARLES KRAUSS', 42 S. PENN. ST., Telephone 465.

ERTEL STEAM LAUNDRY 26 and 28 N. Senate Avenue. Telephone 1089.
WE WILL CALL FOR AND DELIVER YOUR WORK. SATISFACTION GUARANTEED.

CONNECTICUT MUTUAL LIFE INSURANCE CO, Charles P Greene Genl Agt, F Wayland Douglas Asst Genl Agt, 78 Commercial Club Bldg.

Conn[illegible] O'Connell
Con[illegible] [illegible] Edward) h 93 Agnes.
Conn[illegible] A [illegible] John), h w s Miami 9 s of [illegible] (N).
Con[illegible] [illegible] h 213 S Alabama
Con[illegible] J [illegible] h [illegible] Maple
Connell M [illegible] packer h [illegible] Henry.
Conne[illegible] M [illegible] lab h [illegible] McGinnis
Con[illegible] [illegible] lab, h w s Hope [illegible] n of
Conne[illegible] packer h [illegible] Henry
Connel[illegible] plumber h [illegible] Columbia av.
Connel[illegible] [illegible] h 13 Benton
Conne[illegible] lab h [illegible] McGinnis
Connel[illegible] [illegible] Conley.
Conne[illegible] J trainmaster C C C & St L R [illegible] Bellefontaine
Connel[illegible] J [illegible] h 14 Hoyt
Co[illegible] [illegible] N Alabama
[illegible] Andrew J), h [illegible] N
[illegible] E M S h [illegible] S Mc-
[illegible]
[illegible] candymkr h 16 Arbor av
[illegible] lab h [illegible] Jackson and
[illegible] h [illegible] E Washington.
[illegible] trav agt M Kee [illegible] Co,
[illegible] h [illegible] N Illinois

EQUITABLE LIFE ASSURANCE SOCIETY OF THE UNITED STATES.

RICHARDSON & McCREA

Managers for Central Indiana.

79 East Market St. Telephone 182.

Conner James W Rev, h w s Hunter av 1 n of Washington av (I).
Conner John B, pres Indiana Farmer Co, h 30 Park av.
Conner John F, saloon, 296 S West, b 225 S Capitol av.
Conner Lee, clk, h 26½ N California.
Conner Maude, bkkpr Singer Mnfg Co, b 57 Eureka av.
Conner May B, stenog, h w s Omer 1 n of University av (I).
Conner Otto E, clk, h 1 Spann av.
Conner Richard A, trav agt, h 57 Eureka av.
Conner Sabra teacher Public School No 2, b w s Omer 1 n of University av (I).
Conner Samuel M, butcher, h w s Omer 1 n of University av (I).
Conner Sarah (wid Wm H), h s s Orange av 2 e of Hamilton av.
Conner Thomas, lab, h 32 W Francis (N I).
Conner Thomas H, h 112 Oliver av (W I).
Conner Timothy J, fireman, h 25 N Gillard av
Conner Wm, lab, h 252 Kentucky av.
Conner Wm A, trav agt Eli Lilly & Co, h 40 Hamilton av
Conner Wm E, lab, h 22 W Udell (N I).
Conner Wm R, mdse broker 25 W Georgia, b 21 Bellefontaine.
Conner Wm S, supt h 1044 N New Jersey.
Conner Wm W, student, h 240½ E Washington.
Connett James lab h rear 608 N West.
Connett Joseph lab, h rear 614 N West.
Connett Millard F, supt h 252 Bright.
Connett Walter R, stenog, b 252 Bright.
Connette John B, filer, h 634 Chestnut.
Connolly, see also Conley and Connelly.
Connolly Joseph W, bkkpr Wm H Armstrong & Co h 705 N Illinois.
Connor see also Conner and O'Connor.
Connor Bridget, h 440 S West.
Connor Catherine (wid John), h 225 S Capitol av.
Connor Charles, baggageman, h 130 N East.
Connor Charles E (Sauer & Connor), b n w cor 9th and Illinois.

STENOGRAPHERS FURNISHED.
EXPERIENCED OR BEGINNERS, PERMANENT OR TEMPORARY.
S. H. EAST, State Agent,
The Williams Typewriter,
55 Thorpe Block, 87 East Market St.

ELLIS & HELFENBERGER { ENTERPRISE FOUNDRY & FENCE CO. 162-170 S. Senate Ave. Tel. 958.

FIDELITY MUTUAL LIFE—PHILADELPHIA, PA.
$75,000,000, Insurance In Force. $3,500,000, Death Losses Paid. $1,500,090, Surplus. A. H. COLLINS {General Agent, Baldwin Block.

BITUMINOUS COAL IN CAR LOADS TO DEALERS AND MANUFACTURERS. ROOMS 42 AND 43 WHEN BUILDING. ••••• Edwardsport Coal & Mining Co.

ESTABLISHED 1876. TELEPHONE 168.
CHESTER BRADFORD,
SOLICITOR OF PATENTS,
AND COUNSEL IN PATENT CAUSES.
(See adv. page 6.)
Office:—Rooms 14 and 16 Hubbard Block, S. W. Cor. Washington and Meridian Streets, INDIANAPOLIS, INDIANA.

Condit Harry H (Condit & Arnold), b 1096 N Capitol av.
Condit & Arnold (Harry H Condit, George S Arnold), mnfrs' agents, 35 W Pearl.
Condo Charles B, foreman Penna Lines, h 198 Woodlawn av.
Condon Ann (wid Thomas), h 87 Church.
Condon Charles P, cigarmkr, b 87 Church.
Condon Edward, butcher, b 77 Thomas.
Condon James T, uphlr, h 116½ W Ray.
Condon John, clk Hollweg & Reese, b 87 Church.
Condon John, lab, h 77 Thomas.
Condon Thomas jr, lab, b 77 Thomas.
Condon Joseph, uphlr, b 87 Church.
Condon Thomas, janitor, r 102 State House.
Condon Wm, molder, h 425 S West.
Condrey Edward M, clk, h 428 Douglass.
Condrey Emma F (wid James B), b 1129 N Penn.
Condrey John W, car rep, b 20 Miley av.
Condrey Rose, dressmkr, 428 Douglass, h same.
Condrey Samuel H, foreman, h 20 Miley av.
Condrey Wm J, condr, h 451 W 22d (N I).
Condron John J, molder, b 126 Belmont av (H).
Condron Michael, grocer, 124 Belmont av (H), h 126 same.
Conduitt, see also Condit.
Conduitt Alexander B, h 186 N Delaware.
Conduitt Allen W, pres Bedford Indiana Stone Co, sec and treas Indiana Bermudez Asphalt Co, h 380 Park av.
Conduitt Harold, student, b 380 Park av.
Conduitt Henry C, farmer, b 186 N Delaware.
Cone Frank, lab, h 530½ S Meridian.
Cones Constantine B, pres C B Cones & Son Mnfg Co, h 225 N Penn.
Cones C B & Son Manufacturing Co, Constantine B Cones pres, John W Murphy treas, Henry L Browning sec, clothing mufrs, 12 N Senate av.
Cones Harry, plate printer F H Smith, b 402 N Senate av.
Conger Caroline, h 23 N California.
Conger Charles W, student, b 32 Hillside av.

Outing BICYCLES
..MADE BY..
HAY & WILLITS MFG CO.
76 N. Pennsylvania St. Phone 598.

Conger David, lab, b 74 S McLain (W I).
Conger Frank J, driver, h 71 W 5th.
Conger Herbert M, clk, b 198 E South.
Conger Manuel H, fireman, h 247 S East.
Conger Oliver H, clk, h 418 Dillon.
Conger Omer T Rev, h 32 Hillside av.
Conger Rose, h 74 S McLain (W I).
Conger Samuel L, painter, h 122 N Delaware.
Conger Thomas A, clk, b 247 S East.
Conkle Anson B (The Grocers' Mnfg Co), h 304 College av.
Conkle Wm W, clk, b 86 E Ohio.
Conklin, see also Coughlen.
Conklin Albert, lab, r 336½ E Washington.
Conklin Charles, clk, h 22 Gregg.
Conklin David, r 336½ E Washington.
Conklin Elijah, b Hanna Hotel.
Conklin Eugene H, stenog Central Cycle Mnfg Co, r 84 W Vermont.
Conklin Fred B, lab, b 114 N Summit.
Conklin Harry, sawmkr, h 333 Coburn.
Conklin Jessie M, stenog, b 1352 N Illinois.
Conklin Kate, housekpr 119 W Maryland.
Conklin Len D, clk, h 22 Gregg.
Conklin Luther J, lab, h 42 Miley av.
Conklin Margaret (wid Israel), h 119 W Maryland.
Conklin Pierson, carp, h 1352 N Illinois.
Conklin Roscoe, reporter The Indpls Journal, r 11 Hutchings blk.
Conklin Seth R, brakeman, b 541 Shelby.
Conklin Warren A, condr, b 541 Shelby.
Conklin Wm H, patrolman, h 114 N Summit.
Conlee Thomas A, agt Deere & Co, 75-77 W Washington, h 131 W 12th.
Conlen Edward F, sawyer, h 39 Malott av.
Conlen Edward F jr, lab, b 39 Malott av.
Conlen John A, pawnbroker, 57 W Washington, h 825 College av.
Conlen Michael, clk, h 245 Kentucky av.
Conlen Patrick, h 246 Excelsior av.
Conley, see also Connelly.
Conley Bros (Daniel J and Dennis), platers, 17 W Pearl.
Conley Charles, clk, r 100 N Senate av.
Conley Daniel J (Conley Bros), h 1778 Graceland av.
Conley Dennis (Conley Bros), h 113 S Illinois.
Conley Frank, boiler insp, h 4 Orange av.
Conley George R, lather, b 20 Ingram.
Conley George W, lab, h 20 Ingram.
Conley John, lab, b 132 Blackford.
Conley Ora B, b 56 Martindale av.
Conley Stanley, carp, h 49 Tecumseh.
Conley Wm, student, r 222 W Maryland.
Conley Wm H, lab, h 9 Willard.
Conlin Annie (wid Patrick), h 132 Blackford.
Conlin John, bricklyr, h 124 Duncan.
Conlin Peter, lab, b 132 Blackford.
Conn, see also Kahn.
Conn Clay, driver, r 175 W North.
Conn Frank, lab, h 40 Beacon.
Conn Henry C, lab, h 490 W North.
Conn John, cabtmkr, 185 Indiana av, h same.
Connally Austin, soldier U S Arsenal.
Connan John, clk Kingan & Co (ltd), h 293 Blackford.
Connan Patrick, h 1 Kauffmann pl.
Connaty, see also Conaty.
Connaty James W, master mechanic I D & W Ry, h 17 S Belmont av (W I).
Connaughton John, lab, b 483 S West.
Connaughton John P (Kennedy & Connaughton), h 74 S Summit.

C. ZIMMERMAN & SONS | SLATE AND GRAVEL ROOFERS 19 South East Street.

DRIVEN WELLS And Second Water Wells and Pumps of all kinds at CHARLES KRAUSS', 42 S. PENN. ST., Telephone 465.

ERTEL STEAM LAUNDRY 26 and 28 N. Senate Avenue. Telephone 18 WE WILL CALL FOR AND DELIVER YOUR WORK. SATISFACTION GUARANTEED.

CONNECTICUT MUTUAL LIFE INSURANCE CO, Charles P Greene Genl Agt, F Wayland Douglas Asst Genl Agt, 76 Commercial Club Bldg.

Connell, see also O'Connell.
Connell Anna (wid Edward), h 93 Agnes.
Connell Anna (wid John), h w s Miami 9 s of Prospect (N).
Connell Daniel, mason, b 213 S Alabama.
Connell John, lab, h 34 Maple.
Connell Maurice, packer, b 18 Henry.
Connell Michael, lab, h 25 McGinnis.
Connell Pizarro D, lab, h w s Hope 3 n of Willow (B).
Connell Thomas, packer, b 18 Henry.
Connell Thomas, plumber, b 200 Columbia av.
Connell Thomas A, mach, h 13 Benton.
Connell Timothy, lab, h 32 McGinnis.
Connelly, see also Conley.
Connelly Andrew J, trainmaster C C C & St L Ry, h 847 Bellefontaine.
Connelly Cornelius J, finisher, h 14 Hoyt av.
Connelly Ella, nurse 124 N Alabama.
Connelly Emily J (wid Andrew J), h 909 N New Jersey.
Connelly James, porter R M S, h 306 S Meridian.
Connelly John, boilermkr, b 79 Leota.
Connelly Nathalie, teacher Public School No 2, b 909 N New Jersey.
Connelly Patrick B, molder, h 6 Highland av (H).
Connelly Patrick T, horseshoer, h 433 S Missouri.
Connelly Thomas, lab, h 19 Patterson.
Connelly Thomas, stoker, h 378 S Missouri.
Conner, see also Connor and O'Connor.
Conner Abner, barber, r 31½ Indiana av.
Conner Adah, teacher Public School No 29, b 360 Park av.
Conner Albert, tmstr, b 252 E Washington.
Conner Alice C (wid Wm M), h 1116 N Delaware.
Conner Archibald, carp, h 622 W Udell (N I).
Conner Benjamin F, clk Township Assessor's Office, h 472 N East.
Conner Charles E (Central Printing Co), b 934 N Illinois.
Conner Charles H, molder, h 30 Holmes av (H).
Conner Charles W, watchmkr J P Wimmer, h 435 Talbott av.
Conner Clarence H, switchman, h 75 Lexington av.
Conner Eliza L (wid Robert), b 1007 N Capitol av.
Conner Ellsworth, horseshoer, b 252 E Washington.
Conner Ernest L, candymkr, h 16 Arbor av (W I).
Conner Flavius, lab, h s e cor Jackson and 17th.
Conner Frances A, h 175½ E Washington.
Conner Frank H, trav agt McKee Shoe Co, b 472 N East.
Conner Franklin M, tel opr, h 1078 W Vermont.
Conner George C, draughtsman, b w s Omer 1 n of University av (I).
Conner Hannah (wid James), b 25 N Gillard av.
Conner Helen, b 874 N Penn.
Conner James, hostler, b 1699 N Illinois.
Conner James C, carp, b 578 W Udell (N I).

EQUITABLE LIFE ASSURANCE SOCIETY OF THE UNITED STATES,
RICHARDSON & McCREA
Managers for Central Indiana,
79 East Market St. Telephone 182.

Conner James W Rev, h w s Hunter av 1 n of Washington av (I).
Conner John B, pres Indiana Farmer Co, h 360 Park av.
Conner John F, saloon, 286 S West, b 225 S Capitol av.
Conner Lee, clk, h 248½ N California.
Conner Maude, bkkpr Singer Mnfg Co, b 57 Eureka av.
Conner May B, stenog, b w s Omer 1 n of University av (I).
Conner Otto E, clk, h 1 Spann av.
Conner Richard A, trav agt, h 57 Eureka av.
Conner Sabra, teacher Public School No 2, b w s Omer 1 n of University av (I).
Conner Samuel M, butcher, h w s Omer 1 n of University av (I).
Conner Sarah (wid Wm H), h s s Orange av 2 e of Hamilton av.
Conner Thomas, lab, h 582 W Francis (N I).
Conner Thomas H, b 132 Oliver av (W I).
Conner Timothy J, fireman, h 25 N Gillard av.
Conner Wm, lab, h 252 Kentucky av.
Conner Wm A, trav agt Eli Lilly & Co, h 249 Hamilton av.
Conner Wm E, lab, b 622 W Udell (N I).
Conner Wm R, mdse broker, 25 W Georgia, b 221 Bellefontaine.
Conner Wm S, supt, h 1044 N New Jersey.
Conner Wm W, student, h 244½ E Washington.
Connett James, lab, h rear 608 N West.
Connett Joseph, lab, h rear 614 N West.
Connett Millard F, supt, h 252 Bright.
Connett Walter R, stenog, b 252 Bright.
Connette John B, filer, h 634 Chestnut.
Connolly, see also Conley and Connelly.
Connolly Joseph W, bkkpr Wm H Armstrong & Co, b 705 N Illinois.
Connor, see also Conner and O'Connor.
Connor Bridget, h 440 S West.
Connor Catherine (wid John), h 225 S Capitol av.
Connor Charles, baggageman, b 130 N East.
Connor Charles E (Sauer & Connor), b n w cor 9th and Illinois.

STENOGRAPHERS FURNISHED.
EXPERIENCED OR BEGINNERS, PERMANENT OR TEMPORARY.
S. H. EAST, State Agent,
The Williams Typewriter,
55 THORPE BLOCK, 87 EAST MARKET ST.

ELLIS & HELFENBERGER { ENTERPRISE FOUNDRY & FENCE CO. 162-170 S. Senate Ave. Tel. 958.

THE HOGAN TRANSFER AND STORAGE COMP'Y
Household Goods and Pianos Moved—Packed—Stored...... Baggage and Package Express Machinery and Safes a Specialty Cor. Washington and Illinois Sts. TELEPHONE No. 675.

A death rate below all other American Companies, and dividends from this source correspondingly larger.
The Provident Life and Trust Company
Of Philadelphia.
D. W. EDWARDS, General Agent,
508 Indiana Trust Building.

Connor David J, opr W U Tel Co, b 362 S West.
Connor Dennis J, janitor, h 143½ Virginia av.
Connor Edward J, propertyman, h 230½ E Washington.
Connor George A, clk, b 225 S Capitol av.
Connor Hannah (wid Mark), h 1 Elizabeth.
Connor Harry, clk, b 58 S West.
Connor James, horseshoer, b 202 W South.
Connor James, lab, n 9 Spann av.
Connor James M, collr, b 225 S Capitol av.
Connor John, condr, h 279 Christian av.
Connor John, foreman Levey Bros, h 21 Buchanan.
Connor John, grocer, 362 S West, h same.
Connor John, horseshoer, Union Stock Yards (W I), h 29 Holly av (W I).
Connor John, lab, b 48 N West.
Connor, molder, h 29 Highland (H).
Connor John E, clk, b 217½ Mass av.
Connor John E, tmstr, h rear 430 E McCarty.
Connor John F, mason, h 234 S Olive.
Connor John F jr, mason, b 234 S Olive.
Connor John H, agt, h 56 S William (W I).
Connor Mark, clk W U Tel Co, b 176 Huron.
Connor Martha (wid Nicholas), h 217½ Mass av.
Connor Mary (wid Michael), h 34 Dougherty.
Connor Mary, critic Public School No 13, b 234 S Olive.
Connor Mary B (wid Charles H), h 82 Ft Wayne av.
Connor Michael, lab, b 298 S Capitol av.
Connor Michael, lab, h 21 Roe.
Connor Michael, molder, r 24 N West.
Connor Michael, tel opr E P Brown & Co, b 362 S West.
Connor Michael O, horseshoer, 56 W Wabash, h 202 W South.
Connor Oliver I, trav agt, h 100 Pleasant.
Connor Patrick, boilermkr, h 36 Chadwick.
Connor Patrick, lab, b 126 Blackford.
Connor Thomas, lab, b 222 S Missouri.
Connor Thomas C, bricklayer, h 638 N Senate av.

Julius C. Walk & Son,
Jewelers
Indianapolis.
12 EAST WASHINGTON ST.

Connor Thomas J, blksmith, b 202 W South.
Connor Wm, horseshoer, b 202 W South.
Connor Wm W, molder, b 225 S Capitol av.
Connors Hannah (wid Max), h 276 Bright.
Connors Thomas M, train desp C H & D R R, h 108 Walcott.
Connors Margaret, h 260 W Washington.
Conover Axey, h 17 Holly av (W I).
Conover George R, dentist, 852½ E Washington, b 75 N State av.
Conover Wm A, housemover, 297 W Washington, h 17 Holly av (W I).
Conover Wm C, carp, h 1389 N Senate av.
Conover Wm F, dyer, 336 E Market, h same.
Conrad Armilda, h 571 W Michigan.
Conrad Coston W, carp, h 588 W McLene (N I).
Conrad Edward, plumber, b 109 N New Jersey.
Conrad Emerson L, musician, h 481 W 22d (N I).
Conrad George E, plumber, b 109 N New Jersey.
Conrad George J, lather, h 606 W Francis (N I).
Conrad Josephine B (wid Leonidas P), cook, b 164½ E Washington.
Conrad Lycurgus, carp, h 440 W McLene (N I).
Conrad Moses, agt, r 42½ Mass av.
CONRAD OWEN J, Dealer in Clothing, Musical Instruments, Etc, Cash or Installments, 70-72 Mass av, Tel 1329; h 426 E 12th.
Conrad Winburn F, lab, h 526 W Shoemaker (N I).
Conrath Joseph, musical instruments, 195 Virginia av, h Hubbard rd 1 mile s e of city limits.
CONROY A J & CO, John C Cline Mngr, Household Specialties, 23 Indiana av.
Conroy Bernard, lab, h 44 N California.
Conroy Bridget (wid Martin), h 228 S West.
Conroy John, dairy, n w cor Brookside and Waverly avs, h same.
Conroy Martin, h 249 S West.
Conroy Patrick, lab, b 228 S West.
Conroy Patrick, helper St Vincent's Hospital.
Conselman Jacob, r 74 Indiana av.
Considine Michael, lab, h 88 McGinnis.
CONSOLIDATED COAL AND LIME CO, August M Kuhn Pres, Albert H Goepper Sec and Treas, Office 13 Virginia av, Tel 273; Yards Madison av, Ray and J M & I R R.
Consolus Wm H, watchman Insane Hospital.
Constantine John L, messenger Am Ex Co, h 34 Newman.
Constantine Rutherford C, trav agt, b 34 Newman.
CONSUMERS' GAS TRUST CO, Robert N Lamb Pres, Henry Coburn Vice-Pres, Bement Lyman Sec and Genl Mngr, Julius F Pratt Treas, Wm H Shackleton Supt, 43-49 N Capitol av, Tel 26.
Convent of the Good Shepherd, 57 W Raymond.
Convent of the Sacred Heart, cor Meridian and Palmer.
Conver Charles A, mach, b 162 John.
Conver Sarah E (wid John), h 162 John.
Converse Eleanor M (wid Joel), h 123 Hosbrook.

The Central Rubber & Supply Co. PHONE 8. 79 S. ILLINOIS ST., INDIANAPOLIS, IND. Hose, Belting, Packing, Clothing, Druggists' Sundries, Bicycle Tires, Cotton Hose, Etc. New York Belting & Packing Co., L't'd.

OTTO GAS ENGINES | BUILDERS' EXCHANGE S. W. Cor. Ohio and Penn. Telephone 535.

Becker & Son Charles Becker Jacob Becker Jr. Merchant Tailors. 21 N. Penn. St. Tel. 934

SALISBURY & STANLEY OFFICE, STORE AND BANK FIXTURES. Contractors and Repairing of all kinds done on short notice. 177 Clinton St., Indianapolis, Ind. Telephone 99.

Converse John S, train disp P C C & St L Ry, b 33 Hudson.
Convery Jerome B, clk L E & W R R, h 489 E Market.
Conway Cecilia (wid Michael), h 36 Dougherty.
Conway Charles W, clk R M S, h 457 E McCarty.
Conway Delia A (wid Edward J), h 1015 N Senate av.
Conway Edward J, reporter, b 1015 N Senate av.
Conway Elihu W, painter, h 207½ Indiana av.
Conway Emily (wid Wm), b e s Elm av 1 n of Washington av (I).
Conway Irvin, foreman, h 255 Lincoln la.
Conway James J, molder, h 7 Cleveland (H).
Conway James M, lab, h 255 Lincoln la.
Conway James M, lab, h 160 S Linden.
Conway Jessie A, bkkpr, r 31 E McCarty.
Conway John, lab, h 8 Church.
Conway Margaret (wid Michael), h 378 S Delaware.
Conway Mattie L (wid Edward), b 63 Howard.
Conway Michael J, clk H P Wasson & Co, b 36 Dougherty.
Conway Philip, florist, b 22 Gatling.
Conway Walter T, clk, b 1015 N Senate av.
Conway Wm J, woodwkr, b 11 Russell av.
Conwell Cornelius, agt, h 140 W Vermont.
Conwell James, lab, b 140 W Vermont.
Conyers Ora A, switchman, h 320 Spann av.
Conzelmann Michael, h 220 Eureka av.
Conzelmann Wm F J, bkkpr, b 220 Eureka av.
Cooby Joseph, watchman, b 31 Garden.
Cook, see also Cooke and Koch.
Cook Ambrose, butcher, h 233 Buchanan.
Cook Abe L, sec Lombard B and L Assn, h 63 Ruckle.
Cook Abraham J, lab, b 72 Oliver av (W I).
Cook Abram B, carp, h 37 Woodside av (W).
Cook Albert F, wheel truer, b 84 John.
Cook Alfred E, clk Penna Lines, b 1137 N Meridian.
Cook Alva S, blksmith, h 394 Blake.
Cook Ambrose W, lab, h 233 Buchanan.
Cook Amelia (wid Ambrose), h 127 W North.
Cook Andrew, molder, h 23 Bismarck (H).
Cook Andrew L, fireman, h 84 John.
Cook Annie (wid Wm H), h 14 Athon.
Cook Anthony F, car rep, h 101 Harlan.
Cook Benjamin, cloth coverer, h 14 Athon.
Cook Benjamin C, printer, h 150 Lincoln av.
Cook Bessie J, cashr The Progress Clothing Co, b 150 Lincoln av.
Cook Caleb, lab, h 177 Mass av.
Cook Charles, lab, h 26 Holborn.
Cook Charles, mach, r 166½ W Washington.
Cook Charles, mailer, r 32 W Court.

COOK CHARLES A, Competent Chemist and Druggist, Prescriptions a Specialty, 361 Shelby at Belt R R, h same.

Cook Charles C, lab, h 330 E Market.
Cook Charles E, bricklyr, h 162 Patterson.
Cook Charles E, printer, h 53 Elm.
Cook Charles F (Cook & Nackenhorst), h 119 Elm.
Cook Charles F, ins agt, h 960½ N Alabama.
Cook Charles H, butcher, b 604 E Market.
Cook Charles G, janitor, h 87 S West.

Henry H. Fay, 40½ E. Washington St., REAL ESTATE, AND LOAN BROKER.

Cook Charles W, clk, b 22 E North.
Cook Charles W, pressman, b 86 Downey.
Cook Christian, mer police, h 24 Bicking.
Cook, Christian F W, bkkpr, h 417 S New Jersey.
Cook Carkson T, h 543 W Francis (N I).
Cook Corydon Y, h 56 Oscar.
Cook David L, plumber, r 289 E New York.
Cook David P, h 1382 N Senate av.
Cook Edward, driver, h 137 Eddy.
Cook Edward N, butcher, h 604 E Market.
Cook Ella H (wid Jesse), h 53 N State av.
Cook Emanuel, plumber, b 289 E New York.
Cook Francis, b 1061 W Washington.
Cook Francis T, h 543 W Francis (N I).
Cook Frank C, agt, h 133 Huron.
Cook Frederick, h 249 S Alabama.
Cook Frederick, driver, h 1007 W Vermont.
Cook Frederick C, drayman, h 650 E Ohio.
Cook Frederick H, bricklyr, b 38 Park av.
Cook Frederick J, mach, h 127 Nordyke av (W I).
Cook Frederick W, clk, h 593 Madison av.
Cook Frederick W jr, grocer, 593 Madison av, h same.

COOK GEORGE (Mabrey & Cook), Livery, Boarding, Hack and Sale Stable, 30 E Maryland, h 78½ E Maryland.

Cook George, printer, b 604 E Market.
Cook George, tel opr, b w s Gale (B).
Cook George J, phys, 18 W Ohio, r 24 The Windsor.
Cook George R, molder, h 32 Centennial (H).
Cook George W, b 38 Park av.
Cook Harry, driver, b 194 E Washington.
Cook Harry, lab, b 394 Blake.
Cook Harry L, mach hd, b 71 Peru av.
Cook Henry, bricklyr, h 38 Park av.
Cook Henry, head waiter Hotel English.
Cook Henry G, fireman, h 272 N Noble.
Cook Henry L, mach hd, h 13 Bridge (W I).
Cook Homer, cooper, h 280 E Louisiana.
Cook Homer, prin Public School (M J), res Bridgeport, Ind.
Cook Ira C, lab, h 217½ E Washington.
Cook James E, lab, h 86 Downey.

MAYHEW 13 N. MERIDIAN STREET.

LIME, CEMENT, PLASTER FIRE BRICK AND CLAY SEWER PIPE, ETC. BALKE & KRAUSS CO., Cor. Market and Missouri Streets.

C. FRIEDGEN HAS THE FINEST STOCK OF LADIES' PARTY SLIPPERS and SHOES 19 NORTH PENNSYLVANIA ST.

SAMUEL LAING ▸ TIN, SLATE AND STEEL ROOFING 72 AND 74 EAST COURT STREET.

M. B. WILSON, Pres. W. F. CHURCHMAN, Cash.
THE CAPITAL NATIONAL BANK,
INDIANAPOLIS, IND.
Pays Interest on Time Certificates of Deposit.
Buys and Sells Foreign Exchange at Low Rates.
Capital, - - $300,000
Surplus and Earnings, 50,000
No. 28 S. Meridian St., Cor. Pearl.

Cook Jane, laundress, h 158 Michigan av.
Cook Jay D, brakeman, h 53 Walcott.
Cook Jerome P, butcher, b 604 E Market.
Cook Jesse E, plastr, h 97 Greencastle av.
Cook John, engr, h 5 Lynn.
Cook John, grocer, 899 Morris (W I), h same.
Cook John, lab, h 41 Harris.
Cook John, mach, h 348 Spring.
Cook John A, clk, h 118 E Pratt.
Cook John B, cooper, h 229 Michigan (H).
Cook John F, clk L E & W R R, b 249 S Alabama.
Cook John J, plastr, h 66 Arch.
Cook John R, draughtsman, h 461 Ontario (N I).
Cook John W, h 446 W Pratt.
Cook Joseph, h 4 N Gale (B).
Cook Joseph, meats, 55 E Mkt House, b 604 E Market.
Cook Joseph, patternmkr, h 76 Belmont av (H).
Cook Joseph P, stonecutter, b 255 Coburn.
Cook Julia, b 714 Morris (W I).
Cook Levi, h 289 E New York.
Cook Lewis C, waiter, h 30 Bird.
Cook Louis, sawmkr, h 481 Union.
Cook Mary (wid George W), h 27 Blackford.
Cook Mary (wid Harry), b 431 Ash.
Cook Matthew D, phys, 20 Thalman av, h same.
Cook Matthew J, helper, b 4 N Gale (B).
Cook Minnie (wid James F), b 22 Lawn (B).
Cook Minnie, h rear 139 St Mary.
Cook Nicholas J, carp, 34½ S Penn, h 221 S McLain (W I).
Cook Norton W, lab, b 446 W Pratt.
Cook Patrick, lab, b 41 Madison av.
Cook Prudence, teacher Public School No 26, b 150 Lincoln av.
Cook Richard, bkkpr H J Heinz & Co, h 49 Park av.
Cook Robert B, live stock, Union Stock Yards (W I), h 544 Ash.
Cook Samuel, lab, b 176 Agnes.
Cook Samuel R, printer, h 161½ Jefferson av.

TUTTLE & SEGUIN,
28 E. Market Street.
Fire Insurance,
Real Estate, Loan
and Rental Agents.
TELEPHONE 1168.

Cook Sarah A (wid John), evangelist, b 52 S State av.
Cook Susan (wid Pleasant), b 169 Minerva.
Cook Susie V, clk, b 604 E Market.
Cook Thomas J, lab, h 543 W Francis (N I).
Cook Thomas J, trav agt Daniel Stewart & Co, h 425 Park av.
Cook Thomas V, painter, 36 Monument pl, h 551 S State av.
Cook Thomas V jr, painter, b 551 S State av.
Cook Ulysses G, brakeman, b 37 Woodside av (W).
Coo Walter, lab, h 565 W Shoemaker (N I).k
Cook Wilder, clk Schauroth & Co, b 441 College av.
Cook Wm, clk Clemens Vonnegut, b 107 Broadway.
Cook Wm, lab, b 650 E Ohio.
Cook Wm, lab, b 166 Osage.
Cook Wm, lab, b 380 S West.
Cook Wm, mach, h 15 S Station (B).
Cook Wm, molder, b 101 Harlan.
Cook Wm E, h 429 S New Jersey.
Cook Wm F, bkkpr Germania Life Ins Co, h 27 E St Joseph.
Cook Wm G, insp City Civil Engineer's Office, r 85½ W Market.
Cook Wm G, lab, h 47 Camp.
Cook Wm H, lab, h 42 Kansas.
Cook Wm H, driver, b 14 Athon.
Cook Wm H, porter, r 351 Superior.
Cook Wm H, salesman Fahnley & McCrea, h 705 N Alabama.
Cook Wm L, attendant Insane Asylum.
Cook Wm O, paperhngr, h 15 Stevens.
Cook Zay, molder, h 58 Nordyke av (W I).
Cook & Nackenhorst (Charles F Cook, Wm Nackenhorst), grocers, 622 Virginia av.

COOKE BENJAMIN J, Ph D, Physician and Surgeon, Office Hours 8-10 A M, 2-4 and 7-8 P M, 228 W Michigan, h same, Tel 1346.

Cooke George P, trav agt, h 355 N Alabama.
Cooke George T, printer, b 77 Johnson av.
Cooke Harlan E, lab, b 255 N Alabama.
Cooke James H, mailer Indpls Journal, h 61 Oak.
Cooke James M, meats, 47 E Mkt House, h 219 Davidson.
Cooke John M, h 300 E St Clair.
Cookerly John M, trav agt, b 406 N Brookside av.
Cookingham Philippena (wid Jacob), h 862 N Alabama.
Cookman Margaret (wid Wm), h 165 E Washington.
Cooksey Wm H, h 249½ W Maryland.
Cookson Thomas T, insp Indpls Gas Co, h 555 N West.
Cookus John T, agt, h 351 Bellefontaine.
Cooley Henry E, cooper, h 29 N Dorman.
Cooley Samuel M, musician, b 81 N Illinois.
Coolman Benjamin F, engr, h 798 LaSalle (M P).
Coolman Charles (Forrest & Coolman), b 798 LaSalle (M P).
Coolman Wm, drayman, b 798 LaSalle (M P).
Coombs, see also Combs.
Coombs Curtis C, meats, 440 Mass av, h 223 N Illinois.
Coombs Eli, butcher, h 305 Blake.

SULLIVAN & MAHAN Manufacturers of all kinds of PAPER BOXES 41 W. Pearl St.

DIAMOND WALL PLASTER { Telephone 1410 BUILDERS' EXCHANGE.

Telephone 1769. 197 S. Illinois St. } THE HOME LAUNDRY { WORK CALLED FOR AND DELIVERED.

Coombs James V Rev, h e s Lake av 6 s of Washington av (I).
Coombs James W, driver, h 148 Clark.
Coombs Thomas B, trav agt, h 223 N Illinois.
Coombs Wm H, cigars, 15 Virginia av, h 211 Douglass.
Coomes Charles E, lab, h 182 Lexington av.
Coon, see also Kuehn and Kuhn.
Coon Roy, b 326 E Louisiana.
Coon Wm, mach, h 59 N Judge Harding (W I).
Coon Wm P, baggageman, h 326 E Louisiana.
Cooney Edward J, insp Indpls Gas Co, b 104 S McLain (W I).
Cooney Elizabeth R, teacher, b 15 Vine.
Cooney Fenton G, painter, h 14 Lynn.
Cooney Frank L, clk, b 15 Vine.
Cooney Henry, lab, h 87 Patterson.
Cooney James W, molder, h 104 S McLain (W I).
Cooney John, lab, b n s Washington 2 e of Quincy.
Cooney John D, condr, h 183 Hadley av (W I).
Cooney Michael, lab, h 41 Iowa.
Cooney Patrick E, ydmastr, h 154 Spann av.
Cooney Rebecca E (wid George T), h 15 Vine.
Cooney, Seiner & Co (Thomas E Cooney, Charles F Seiner, Henry C Geiger), tinware, 17 E South.
Cooney Thomas E (Cooney, Seiner & Co), b 204 N Noble.
Coonfield Emanuel, lab, h Ivy la (B).
Cooning James, bartndr, h 476 S Capitol av.
Coons, see also Koons.
Coons Arlie B, paperhanger, b 563 E Washington.
Coons Charles, lab, b 44 Edward (W I).
Coons Frank M, carp, b 563 E Washington.
Coons Frederick A, clk Theodore Stein, h 309 E Market.
Coons Henry G, pressman The Indpls News, b 98 W Ohio.
Coons John W (Coons & Witty), h 1216 N Penn.
Coons Sanford F, ins, b 1216 N Penn.
Coons Wm I, druggist, n w cor Central av and P C C & St L Ry (I), r same.
Coons & Witty (John W Coons, John B Witty), ins agts, 15 When bldg.
Coonse George W, vice-pres and treas Comstock & Coonse Co, h 1100 N Penn.
Coonse Harvey W, dairy, n s Washington 2 e of Quincy, h same.
Cooper Alonzo F, finisher, h 176 Brookside av.
Cooper Andrew J, lab, h 245 W 5th.
Cooper Armstead, lab, b w s Hillside av 1 s of 17th.
Cooper Benjamin W, coachman, r 215½ Indiana av.
Cooper Caroline L, h 124 W 4th.
Cooper Charles, mnfrs' agt, 66½ N Penn, r same.
Cooper Charles A, h 173 Lexington av.
Cooper Charles B, student, b 350 College av.
Cooper Charles M, barber, h 305½ E Washington.
Cooper Charles M, lawyer, 51 Lombard bldg, b 400 N Meridian.
Cooper Charles S, trav agt, h rear 277 S New Jersey.
Cooper Daniel, barber, r 117 Indiana av.
Cooper Daniel, lab, b 181 W 4th.

FRANK NESSLER. WILL H. ROST.
FRANK NESSLER & CO.
Tailors
56 EAST MARKET ST. (Lemcke Building),
INDIANAPOLIS, IND.

Cooper Daniel L F, lab, h 368 S Delaware.
Cooper David T, ins agt, h 571 S Illinois.
Cooper Edward C, lawyer, b 173 Lexington av.
Cooper Elijah, h 142 S Judge Harding (W I).
Cooper Elizabeth A, stenog W U Tel Co, b 260 W St Clair.
Cooper Ella (wid Alvin), h 2 Douglass.
Cooper Ellsworth, car rep, b 142 S Judge Harding (W I).
Cooper Ernest, student, b 171 N Senate av.
Cooper Ethel A, teacher, b e s Grand av 1 s of Oak av (I).
Cooper Eugene A (Cooper & Wood), h 32 The Chalfant.
Cooper Everett, student, b 90 E Market.
Cooper Francis M, miller, h e s Grand av 1 s of Oak av (I).
Cooper Frank, lab Exchange Hotel (W I).
Cooper Frank, watchman, h 41 Helen.
Cooper Frederick D, baggageman, b 602 E Washington.
Cooper George, bartndr, r 305½ E Washington.
Cooper Hamilton, tailor, h 260 W St Clair.
Cooper Harry M, lab, b 362 W Vermont.
Cooper Homer O, jeweler Jacob C Sipe, b 248 Talbott av.
Cooper India (wid Wm), h 171 N Senate av.
Cooper James, lab, b 368 S Delaware.
Cooper Jennie, h 157 W Maryland.
Cooper Jeremiah, lab, h 223 Columbia av.
Cooper John, boilermkr, b 249½ W Washington.
Cooper John, b 221 W Michigan.
Cooper John, engr, h 94 Hadley av (W I).
Cooper John, supt Public Schools (B), h Brightwood av (B).
Cooper John J, pres U S Encaustic Tile Wks, h 400 N Meridian.
Cooper John O (J O Cooper & Co), pres Industrial L Assn of Ind, h 116 College av.
Cooper J O & Co (John O and Thomas Cooper), rug mnfrs, 223 Mass av.
Cooper John W (Cooper & Singleton), r s e cor Michigan and Columbia (N I).
Cooper John W, pres Indiana Bermudez Asphalt Co, h 390 College av.

Haueisen & Hartmann
163-169 E. Washington St.
FURNITURE,
Carpets,
Household Goods,
Tin, Granite and China Wares, Oil Cloth and Shades

THE WM. H. BLOCK CO. 7 AND 9 EAST WASHINGTON STREET. DRY GOODS, HOUSE FURNISHINGS AND CROCKERY.

London Guarantee and Accident Co. (Ltd.) Employers', Public and Teams' Liability, Workmen's Collective Insurance and Fidelity Bonds
GEORGE W. PANGBORN, General Agent, 704-706 Lemcke Bldg. Telephone 140.

FRANK K. SAWYER || Reliable Fire Insurance. Reasonable Rates. 74 E. MARKET STREET. Telephone 5.

JOSEPH GARDNER,
TIN, IRON, STEEL AND SLATE ROOFING,
GALVANIZED IRON CORNICES & SKYLIGHTS.
37, 39 & 41 KENTUCKY AVE. Telephone 322.

Cooper Joseph A, clk C P Lesh Paper Co, h 602 E Washington.
Cooper Joseph K, contr, 341 Talbott av, h same.
Cooper Joseph W, engr, h 130 W Vermont.
Cooper Lafayette M, clk U S Encaustic Tile Wks, h 1066 N Capitol av.
Cooper Leon J, clk, b 341 Talbott av.
Cooper Louis W, salesman Hendricks & Cooper, h 342 Broadway.
Cooper Lucretia, b 1148 N Delaware.
Cooper Luther, painter, h 323 W Morris.
Cooper Malinda (wid Richard), b 258 W 5th.
Cooper Martha G (wid Cornelius), h 45 Smith.
Cooper Mary Jane (wid Jacob L), b 1196 N Meridian.
Cooper Milton J, foreman, h 721 E Ohio.
Cooper Nathan E, carp, h 595 W Udell (N I).
Cooper Otto L, photog, h 176 Brookside av.
Cooper Pius J, cook, h 251 N West.
Cooper Rebecca J (wid John), b 305 E McCarty.
Cooper Richard D, barber, r 117 Indiana av.
Cooper Ronoldo M, student, b 75 E Walnut.
Cooper Rose M, student, r 62½ N Delaware.
Cooper Samuel, bartndr, r 285 E Washington.
Cooper Thomas (J O Cooper & Co), b 116 College av.
Cooper Thomas, lab, h 274 Martindale av.
Cooper Thomas A, condr, h 1067 W Vermont.
Cooper Wm D (Hendricks & Cooper), h 350 College av.
Cooper Wm H (Osterman & Cooper), h 181 N Capitol av.
Cooper Wm H, prin Dist School No 2, h 227 Ramsey av.
Cooper Wm R, clk Indpls Gas Co, b 181 N Capitol av.
Cooper Wilmington K, foreman, b 341 Talbott av.
Cooper Zachariah, lab, h 447 W 2d.
Cooper & Singleton (John W Cooper, Richard Singleton), billiards, 499 W Shoemaker (N I).

J. S. FARRELL & CO.
STEAM AND HOT WATER HEATING AND PLUMBING CONTRACTORS
84 North Illinois Street. Telephone 382.

COOPER & WOOD (Eugene A Cooper, Charles H Wood), Proprs Meridian Stables, 114-116 N Meridian, Tel 1502. (See adv in classified Livery.)
Co-Operative Carriage and Wagon Co (John Frank, Charles M Halstead, Joseph Koehler, Frank A Stiening), 115 N Alabama.
Coots, see also Coutts.
Coots Charles E, asst chief fire dept, h 331 Ash.
Cope Belle, bkkpr People's Outfitting Co, b 71 W Michigan.
Cope Julia A (wid Wm), h 312 N Pine.
Copeland Albert E, clk, b 271 S Illinois.
Copeland Andrew J, lab, b n w cor Brown av and 22d.
Copeland Anna B (wid John), b 78 W Maryland.
Copeland Charles F, agt Hood, Foulkrod & Co, h 579 Broadway.
Copeland Charles O, clk, b 372 N Meridian.
Copeland Edgar A, h 118 Ruckle.
Copeland Elihu, hostler, r cor Court and Missouri.
Copeland Frank E, bartndr, b n w cor Station and Glen Drive (B).
Copeland George H, porter, h 50 Drake.
Copeland George W, lab, h rear 606 S Meridian.
Copeland Isaac B, cigarmkr, h 9 Waverly (B).
Copeland James M, mach, b 63 Davidson.
Copeland John, lab, h 479 W Addison (N I).
Copeland John O, genl supt Ind Life Assn of Indpls, h 1170 N Illinois.
Copeland Joshua W, h 372 N Meridian.
Copeland Martha F, boarding 125 W Maryland.
Copeland Robert, cigarmkr, h 269½ Mass av.
Copeland Wm S, bricklyr, h 477 W Addison (N I).
Copeley Henry (Carroll & Copeley), h 196½ W McCarty.
Copelin Samuel, blksmith, h 109 W Ray.
Copelin Wm J, blksmith, h 54 Carlos.
Copenhaver Agnes, teacher School No 4 (W I), b 898 Morris (W I).
Copenhaver Charles E, clk, b 79 Tacoma av.
Copenhaver Emily (wid Andrew S), h 898 Morris (W I).
Copenhaver Henry, lab, h 137 Patterson.
Copenhaver Jasper, carp, h 79 Tacoma av.
Copenhaver John W, lab, h 79 Tacoma av.
Copenhaver Newton, carbldr, h 129 Walcott.
Copenhaver Wm A, finisher, h 681 Wells (N I).
Coppin Luther, lab, r 113 Indiana av.
Copple Harvey, car repr, h 263½ N New Jersey.
Coppock Andrew J (Coppock Bros), h 70 Spruce.
COPPOCK BROS (Andrew J and McClellan), Wall Paper, 187 Virginia av and 15 Pembroke Arcade.
Coppock Charles M, fireman, h 14 Elder av.
Coppock Henry C, painter, h 64 Arbor av (W I).
Coppock James L, clk Knight & Jillson, h 11 Quince.
Coppock McClellan (Coppock Bros), h 229 E Louisiana.
Coppock Thomas A, paperhngr, b 169 English av.
Coppock Wesley, engr, h 112 N Dorman.
Coppock Wm A, paperhngr, b 169 English av.

POLICIES IN UNITED STATES LIFE INSURANCE CO., offer indemnity against death, liberal cash surrender value or at option of policy-holder, fully paid-up life insurance or liberal life income. E. B. SWIFT, M'g'r, 25 E. Market St.

WM. KOTTEMAN 89 & 91 E. Washington St. Telephone 1742 **WILL FURNISH YOUR HOUSE COMPLETE**

SHOW CASES WILLIAM WIEGEL 6 West Louisiana Street Opp. Union Station.

Coppock Zillah (wid Nathan), h 169 English av.
Copsey George W, motorman, h 261 Alvord.
Copsey John E, sawfiler, h 302 Howard (W I).
Corbaley Cynthia J, h 509 N Alabama.
Corbaley George M, bkkpr, C H & D R R, h 416 W New York.
Corbaley Samuel B, clk, h 418 W New York.
Corbett Benjamin, peddler, h 125 Douglass.
Corbett Catherine (wid Edward), h 329 Coburn.
Corbett Charles A, clk, h 121 John.
Corbett Edward C, painter, h w s Miami 7 s of Prospect.
Corbett Jacob, lab, b 125 Douglass.
Corbin Wm H, barber, 142 S Illinois, h 318 N California.
Corby John, bricklyr, h 1 Sumner.
Corcan John T, pressman, h 343 S Olive.
Corci Peter, fruits, 49 S Illinois, h s w cor Georgia and Illinois.
Corcoran Catharine (wid John), h 48 S State av.
Corcoran Christopher H, oil mnfr, 192 W Chesapeake, h 191 W Maryland.
Corcoran James, clk, b 191 W Maryland.
Corcoran John E, clk, r 130 N Senate av.
Corcoran Nellie E, bkkpr, b 48 S State av.
Corcoran Patrick, pressman, b 191 W Maryland.
Corcoran Thomas, boilermkr, h 23 Ludlow av.
Cord Jesse, lab, r 66 N Missouri.
Cord John, watchman St Vincent's Hospital.
Cordary George, lab, b 390 N Brookside av.
Cordell Edward A, clk George J Marott, h 54 Birch av (W I).
Cordell Harry, brakeman, b 31 Jefferson av.
Cordell John E, agt, h 171 Bane.
Cordell Richard, confr, h 82 Erie.
Corder Charles, lab, h 738 N West.
Cordes Henry, trimmer, b California House.
Cordier Peter H, drayman, h 12 Dawson.
Cording Ferdinand, watchman, h 194 Minnesota.
Cordon Nelson, lab, h 19 Center.
Cordon Thomas, checkman, h 580 S West.
Cordon Wm, lab, b 272 W Maryland.
Cordry Henry E, clk, b 182 Minerva.
Cordry Thomas J, lab, h 182 Minerva.
Cordry Willard, clk, 182 Minerva.
Core George E, hostler, b 552 Virginia av.
Core John M, h 421 S New Jersey.
Core Wm F, asst mngr, b 421 S New Jersey.
Corey, see also Cory.
Corey Harry S, mach, h 26 La Salle (M P).
Corey Orrin J, janitor Public School No 11, h 122 W 4th.
Corey Virginia B (wid Leander H), b 26 La Salle (M P).
Corhan Elmer L, boxmkr, h 25 Douglass.
Corhan George N, cooper, h 216 Bright.
Corhan John D, carp, h w s Denny 4 n of Washington.
Corhan Wm C, driver, h 258½ W Washington.
Coridan Thomas J, clk R M S, h 910 N Senate av.
Coridan Wm, lab, h 41 Grant.
Cork Charles, mach, h 46 Clarke.
Corkin Elmer, brakeman, b 54 Belmont av (H).
Corkin Patrick, lab, h 500 Columbia av.

THOS. C. DAY & CO.
INVESTING AGENTS,
TOWN AND FARM LOANS,
Rooms 325 to 330 Lemcke Bldg.

Corley Guy, coachman 325 N Penn.
Corley John R, nurse, h 131 N Meridian.
Corliss Sally E, b 1057 N Illinois.
Cormack James, agt, r 72 E Vermont.
Corn Mary J (wid Gabriel), b 605 E Washington.
Corneal Hardin, tmstr, h 217 Le Grand av.
Cornehl Christian, lab, b Hanna Hotel.
Cornelius Albert B, cashr Thomas C Day & Co, h 571 Central av.
Cornelius Archibald C, clk, b 254 S Alabama.
Cornelius Augustus D, clk U S Pension Agency, h 334 E Ohio.
Cornelius Edward Y (Byram, Cornelius & Co), pres Indpls Chair Mnfg Co, h 521 N Meridian.
Cornelius Frederick W, clk, 334 E Ohio.
Cornelius George G, mach, b 334 E Ohio.
Cornelius Henry D, bkkpr, r 334 E Ohio.
Cornelius Pembroke S, mngr safety vault dept Indiana Trust Co, h 223 N Delaware.
Cornelius Ruth A (wid Cassius), h 254 S Alabama.
Cornelius Wilbur F, plater, h 254 S Alabama.
Cornelius Wm, collr, b 334 E Ohio.
Cornet Bros (John G and Louis P), grocers, 498 College av.
Cornet James, lab, h rear 608 N West.
Cornet James J, bookbndr, b 390 S New Jersey.
Cornet John G (Cornet Bros), b 570 Ash.
Cornet Leon P, bkkpr Indpls Gas Co, b 390 S New Jersey.
Cornet Louis, clk, r 174 N Illinois.
Cornet Louis P (Cornet Bros), h 570 Ash.
Cornet Matthew P, bookbndr, b 390 S New Jersey.
Cornet Nicholas S, clk, h 535 Bellefontaine.
Cornet Peter P, bkkpr, h 390 S New Jersey.
Corns Harrison, lab, h 74 Lee (W I).
Cornwall Alfred E, r 69½ W Market.
Cornwell Caroline (wid George W), h 51 Depot (B).
Cornwell Harry, hatter, h 117½ W Washington.

EAT—
HITZ'S CRACKERS
AND CAKES.
ASK YOUR GROCER FOR THEM.

Capital Steam Carpet Cleaning Works
M. D. PLUNKETT Proprietor, Telephone 818

BENJ. BOOTH PRACTICAL EXPERT ACCOUNTANT. Accounts of any description investigated and audited, and statements rendered. Room 18, 82½ E. Washington St., Indianapolis, Ind.

The Best Place in the City to Get a Good Meal THE SHERMAN RESTAURANT ♦♦♦♦ 18 and 20 S. Meridian Street KERSHNER BROS., Props.

ESTABLISHED 1876. TELEPHONE 168.
CHESTER BRADFORD,
SOLICITOR OF PATENTS,
AND COUNSEL IN PATENT CAUSES.
(See adv. page 6.)
Office:—Rooms 14 and 16 Hubbard Block, S.W. Cor. Washington and Meridian Streets,
INDIANAPOLIS, INDIANA.

Corr Edwin, asst U S Atty P O bldg, b 150 N Illinois.
Correll Elizabeth (wid Andrew J), h 477 Stillwell.
Correll Mark, carp, b 132 W Ohio.
Correll Otto W, clk, b 477 Stillwell.
Correll Way J, barber, b 477 Stillwell.
Correthers Wm G, stereotyper, h 18 Buchanan.
Corriden John W, b 354 S West.
Corriden Lawrence, h 354 S West.
Corrigan John, lab, b 105 N Noble.
Corrigan John, lab, h 133 N State av.
Corrigan John J, sergt of police, h 49 N Dorman.
Corrigan Patrick, lab, h 47 Henry.
Corrigan Thomas F, plumber, b 105 N Noble.
Corse Clarence S, trav agt, h 612 Central av.
Corse Peter, fruits, r 102 S Illinois.
Cortleyon George T, city dis clk P O, b 45 Arch.
Corwin Mary, teacher Deaf and Dumb Inst, b 32 W St Clair.
Corwin Sadie J, teacher Deaf and Dumb Inst, h 42 S Arsenal av.
Cory, see also Corey.
Cory Edward, wheelmkr, b 415 E McCarty.
Cory Robert F, condr, h 415 E McCarty.
Cory Scott, mach hd, h 711 Mass av.
Cory Thomas, clk, b 415 E McCarty.
Cory Walter, clk, b 899 Morris (W I).
Corya Louis W, restaurant, 135 Hadley av (W I), h same.
Corydon Thomas, lab, h 580 S West.
Coryell Alma (wid Frank), h 201 S Illinois.
Cosand Charles, lab, h 179 S Reisner (W I).
Cosby Ella (wid Donald), h 344 Yandes.
Cosby Harvey, driver, h 363 Fulton.
Cosby Hiram H, h 1923 N Illinois.
Cosby Richard M, h 192 Cornell av.
Cosgrove Bridget (wid Patrick), h 29 Henry.
Cosgrove Kate, h 483 N Meridian.
Cosgrove Maggie, cook, h 170 E Washington.
Cosgrove Peter M, student, b 153 W New York.

O. B. Ensey
SLATE, STEEL, TIN AND IRON ROOFING.
Cor. 6th and Illinois Sts. Tel. 1562

Cosgrove Wm P, tel opr, b 29 Henry.
Cosler Alpha B, student, b 504 Central av.
Cosler Charles E, city dis clk P O, h 24 Broadway.
Cosler Curtis, lab, h 473 S West.
Cosler Elizabeth T (wid Wm H), h 436 W Eugene (N I).
Cosler Isaac, h 504 Central av.
Cosler Orval D, h 1402 Rader (N I).
Coslin Richard, driver, h 5 Carter.
Coslow Jacob, ironwkr, b 201 E Washington.
Cosner Alfred C, cabtmkr, h 4 Madison.
Coss Henry T, hostler, h 526 Mulberry.
Cost George P, clk, r 75 W Vermont.
Costamagna Charles, painter, h 78 Cincinnati.
Costamagna James H, painter, h 268 Fulton.
Costello Alice, h 266 S Capitol av.
Costello Anna (wid James), b 117 Maple.
Costello David J, helper, b 30 Stevens.
Costello James H, b 276 W Maryland.
Costello Jeremiah, grocer, 401 S Capitol av, h same.
Costello John, city fireman, h 117 Maple.
Costello John, lab, h 76 Meikel.
Costello John J, h 276 W Maryland.
Costello John M, insp City Civil Engineer's Office, b 401 S Capitol av.
Costello Martin, flagman, h 30 Stevens.
Costello Martin F, clk, b 30 Stevens.
Costello Michael, saloon, 490 S Meridian, h 423 S Illinois.
Costello Michael R, switchman, h 344 Fletcher av.
Costello Nancy (wid James), b 117 Maple.
Costello Patrick, molder, h 135 Church.
Costello Patrick F, salesman George W Stout, b 401 S Capitol av.
Costello Patrick J (Costello & Riordan), h 195 Meek.
Costello Thomas W, clk, b 401 S Capitol av.
Costello & Riordan (Patrick J Costello, Daniel Riordan), horseshoers, 108 E Wabash.
Coster, see also Caster and Castor.
Coster Robert H, mach, b s s Bloyd av 1 w of Rural.
Coster Wm, engr, b Robert H Coster.
Costigan Frank, clk Occidental Hotel.
Costin Earl M, train disp C C C & St L Ry, h 168 Ash.
Coston George E, painter, h rear 524 N Senate av.
Coston George W, lab, h n s Lake 5 e of C C C & St L Ry (N I).
Coston Wm, lab, h n s Lake 5 e of C C C & St L Ry (N I).
Cotten Manson B, clk, h 290 E St Clair.
Cotter Elizabeth, notions, 130 Belmont av (H), h same.
Cotter Hannah (wid Terrence), h 144 East Drive (W P).
Cotter James, tailor, r 8½ E Washington, h 220 Douglass.
COTTER JAMES A C, Lawyer, 74 S Meridian, h 144 East Drive (W P).
Cotter James B, tailor, b 220 Douglass.
Cotter Thomas F, tailor, b 220 Douglass.
Cottingham Joshua J, h 96 W 1st.
Cottingham Lucy D, h 356½ Clifford av.
Cottle Alonzo J, painter, b 111 Sanders.
Cottle Grand O, butcher, b 111 Sanders.
Cottle James C, attendant Insane Hospital.
Cottman George S, printer, b John A Cottman.
Cottman John A, h s s University 3 w of Grand av (I).

TUTEWILER ▲ UNDERTAKER, ▲ No. 72 WEST MARKET STREET. TELEPHONE 216.

PROVIDENT LIFE AND TRUST CO. OF PHILADELPHIA. D. W. Edwards, G. A., 508 Indiana Trust Bldg. In form of policy; prompt settlement of death losses; equitable dealing with policy-holders; in strength of organization; and in everything which contributes to Security and Cheapness of life insurance, this company is unsurpassed.

THEODORE F. SMITHER ROOFER Competent and Responsible Office, 151 West Maryland St. Telephone 861.

Cottom George M, barber, 168 E Washington, h 426 E New York.
Cotton, see also Cotten.
Cotton Albert E, carp, h 43 Jefferson av.
Cotton Allen C, mach, h 3 Water.
Cotton Allen W (Neidlinger & Cotton), h 1510 Northwestern av (N I).
Cotton Alphonso C, trav agt, h 331 E South.
Cotton Charles C, bartndr, b 105 Mass av.
Cotton Edward N, lab, h 129 Newman.
Cotton Elizabth J, teacher Public School No 6, b 76 Vine.
Cotton Ella M (wid Charles W), h 76 Vine.
Cotton Fassett A, dep State Supt of Public Instruction, h 912 N Alabama.
Cotton Isaac M, grocer, 1158 E Washington, h same.
Cotton Jennie, dressmkr, 331 E South, b same.
Cotton John W, policeman, h 330 N California.
COTTON MADISON M, Propr Fulton Fish Market, Oysters, Fish and Game, 61 N Illinois, Tel 599; h same.
Cotton Mary E, teacher Public School No 16, b 76 Vine.
Cotton Oliver E, lab, h 586 W 22d (N I).
Cotton Ostorius W, lab, h 5 Minkner.
Cotton Sarah (wid Perry), h 290 E St Clair.
Cotton Sarah E, teacher Public School No 36, b 912 N Alabama.
Cottrel John, carp, b 5 S Station (B).
Cottrell John, clk, b 131 N New Jersey.
Cottrell Thomas, poultry, 355 W Washington, h 131 N New Jersey.
Cotty Horace L, barber, h 263½ Indiana av.
Couchman James B, dentist, 23 Cherry, h same.
Couger John, car rep, h 39 Wright.
Coughlen, see also Conklin.
Coughlen Edward, b 400 N Capitol av.
Coughlen Frank W, b 400 N Capitol av.
Coughlen Harriet (wid Wm), h 400 N Capitol av.
Coughlen Harry G, sec and mngr Bedford Indiana Stone Co, h 773 N Capitol av.
Coughlen Wm F (Cathcart, Cleland & Co), h 400 N Capitol av.
Coughlin Cornelius, lab, h 128 Newman.
Coughlin Geroge E (Coughlin & Wilson), h 494 N Penn.
Coughlin Mamie, housekpr Deaf and Dumb Inst.
Coughlin & Wilson (George E Coughlin, James F Wilson), dentists, 44½ N Penn.
Couk Clifton E, ins agt, h 820 E Market.
Coull Joseph, painter, h 954 Grove av.
Coulon Charles G, clk, h 48 Oriole.
Coulon Douglas H, printer, h 124 Fulton.
Coulon Josephine (wid Charles), b 200 College av.
Coulon Louis, barber, b 175 N East.
Coulon Oscar F, pressman, h 175 N East.
Coulson Joseph E, lab, h 338 S East.
Coultas Thomas I Rev, pastor Roberts Park M E Church, 73 Butler.
Coulter, see also Colter.
Coulter Bertha A, teacher of music, 189 Fayette, b same.
Coulter David A, real est, 94 E Market, b 189 Fayette.
Coulter David A, vice-pres The State Bank of Indiana, res Frankfort, Ind.
Coulter James, plumber, h 189 Fayette.
Coulter James A, student, b 189 Fayette.
Coulter Wm J, printer, b 189 Fayette.
Coultis America, dressmkr, 50 Ruckle, b same.

THE WHEN IS A WORLD BEATER.

Coultis George F, bkkpr, b 50 Ruckle.
Coultis Margaret (wid John) h 50 Ruckle.
Coulton John, lab, b 407 Coburn.
Counsilman Jacob, porter, b 78 Indiana av.
Counsilman John H, turner, h 427 W New York.
COUNTY ASSESSOR'S OFFICE, Joseph E Boswell Assessor, 35 Court House, Tel 912.
COUNTY AUDITOR'S OFFICE, Harry B Smith Auditor, 41 Court House, Tel 912.
COUNTY CLERK'S OFFICE, James W Fesler Clerk, 24-29 Court House, Tel 230.
COUNTY COMMISSIONERS' OFFICE, 43 Court House, Tel 912.
COUNTY CORONER'S OFFICE, Alembert W Brayton Coroner, 59 Court House.
COUNTY RECORDER'S OFFICE, Wm E Shilling Recorder, 44 Court House, Tel 912.
COUNTY SHERIFF'S OFFICE, Thomas P Shufelton Sheriff, 34 Court House.
County Supt of Public Schools, Wm B Flick supt, 57 Court House.
County Surveyor's Office, John V Coyner surveyor, 31 Court House.
COUNTY TREASURER'S OFFICE, Wm H Schmidt Treas, 23 Court House.
Courier The, Charles H Stewart pub, 94 W New York.
Courtney Albert, carp, h 111 Sharpe av (W).
Courtney Ann (wid Wm), h 860 N Penn.
Courtney Anna, prin Public School No 5, b 860 N Penn.
Courtney Catherine F, teacher Public School No 3, b 860 N Penn.
Courtney Charles, cook, r 52½ S Illinois.
Courtney Dennis, lab, h 7 Spann av.
Courtney Honora A, teacher, b 860 N Penn.
Courtney James F, lab, b 11 S Gillard av.
Courtney James H, porter, b 24 Chapel.
Courtney John, lab, b 51 Blake.

The A. Burdsal Co. CELEBRATED HOMESTEAD READY MIXED PAINT. WHOLESALE AND RETAIL. 34 AND 36 SOUTH MERIDIAN STREET.

ELECTRIC SUPPLIES We Carry a full Stock. Prices Right. C. W. MEIKEL, Tel. 466. 96-98 E. New York St.

DALTON & MERRIFIELD { LUMBER South Noble St., near E. Washington

INDIANA ELECTROTYPE CO. :: BEST WORK LOWEST PRICES.
23 WEST PEARL ST., INDIANAPOLIS, IND. JOB WORK. BOOK PLATES. All Orders Promptly Filled. BEST PATENT BASE ON THE MARKET.

KIRKHOFF BROS.,
Electrical Contractors, Wiring and Construction.
102-104 SOUTH PENNSYLVANIA ST.
TELEPHONE 910.

Courtney John, stoker, h 147 Lexington av.
Courtney John G, clk C C C & St L Ry, h 364 N Noble.
Courtney John W, carp, h 54 Columbia av.
Courtney Joseph C, plumber, b 347½ N California.
Courtney Maria, housekpr 134 Lynn av (W I).
Courtney Mary E, teacher Public School No 36, b 860 N Penn.
Courtney Samuel, b 364 N Noble.
Courtney Thomas E, phys, 501 Virginia av, b 860 N Penn.
Courtney Timothy, lab, h 347½ N California.
Courtney Zachary T, teas, 122 Mass av, h same.
Courtright Julia A, r 5½ Indiana av.
Cousin Edward, lab, b 190 Agnes.
Cousin Faithy (wid Wm), h 190 Agnes.
Cousin Ida B, h 325 Blake.
Cousin James, lab, b 190 Agnes.
Cousin Mary, h 23 Willard.
Cousin Oliver I, porter, h rear 310 E Washington.
Cousin Silas, lab, b 174 Bismarck av (H).
Cousins George E, printer, b 121 E Ohio.
Cousins Sarah (wid Oliver), h 44½ Malott av.
Coutts, see also Coots.
Coutts John M, buyer N Y Store, b 102 Meek.
Coval Bros (Lewis O and Edward C), grocers, 61 S West.
Coval Charles H, insp, h 108 King.
Coval Edward C (Coval Bros), h 217 W Maryland.
Coval Eliza J (wid Willis), b 812½ E Washington.
Coval Harry, lab, b 103 Blake.
Coval Lena (wid Alexander), b 61 S West.
Coval Lewis O (Coval Bros), h 61 S West.
Coval Mary (wid Peter), h 103 Blake.
Coval Nathaniel, confr, 810 E Washington, h 812½ same.
Coval Russell, lab, h 87 Belmont av.
Coval Wm M (Coval & Lemon), h 543 Central av.
Coval & Lemon (Wm M Coval, Albert E Lemon), abstracts, 96½ E Market.

THE W. G. WASSON CO.,
130 Indiana Ave. Tel. 989.
STEAM
COAL
Car Lots a Specialty. Prompt Delivery.
Brazil Block, Jackson and Anthracite.

Covall Maude W, stenog I & V Ry, b 175 N Delaware.
Covalt Sarah A (wid George W), b 227 Hoyt av.
Coveles Charles G, peddler, b 332 E Washington.
COVENANT MUTUAL LIFE ASSOCIATION OF GALESBURG, ILL, J M Armstrong State Mngr, 48 Journal Bldg.
Cover Catherine (wid Daniel), h 1542 N Capitol av.
Cover Isaac, lab, h 613 Miller av (M P).
Coverdill Charles, molder, b 40 Beacon.
Coverdill Charles V, uphlr, h 298½ Mass av.
Coverdill Frank, lab, b 40 Beacon.
Coverdill Harvey, hostler, h 14 Wallace.
Coverdill Henry F, tmstr, b 59 N Dorman.
Coverdill Wm, molder, b 40 Beacon.
Coverdill Wm, molder, h Lincoln av (M J).
Covert Amanda F (wid John B), h 431 Home av.
Covert Arthur L, janitor Public School No 36, h 86 W 20th.
Covert Charles E, ironwkr, h 32 S Linden.
Covert Elmer E, carp, h 31 Willow.
Covert John P, clk, b 512 Park av.
Covers Joseph E, foreman, h n s Bethel av 2 w of Perkins pike.
Covert Libbie (wid Charles L), b 72 W New York.
Covert Wm E, trav agt, b 105 Agnes.
Covert Wm T Rev, h 512 Park av.
Covert Wm T, baker, 105 Agnes, h same.
Covey Frank C, mach hd, h 373 W North.
Covington Cyrus, porter, r 79 W Wabash.
Covington Ephraim B, janitor, r 44½ N Penn.
Covington James E, lab, b 331 Bates.
Covington James M, engr, b 862 Cornell av.
Covy Frank S, lab, h 379 W North.
Cowan Charles L, lab, h 256 W 5th.
Cowan David L, ins, h 50 Windsor.
Cowan George, lab, h 76 Cleaveland blk.
Cowan James P E, special Pension Examiner, h 197 N Alabama.
Cowan James P Rev, pastor Woodruff av United Presbyterian Church, h 44 Windsor.
Cowan Joshua, lab, r 117 Indiana av.
Cowan Mary J (wid Wm), h 76 Cleaveland blk.
Cowan Robert P, lab, h 185 Yandes.
Cowan Samuel, driver, h 77 S Liberty.
Cowan Samuel, waiter, r 23 Roanoke.
Cowan Wm A, vice-pres Indpls Live Stock Journal and Printing Co, h 233 S Olive.
Coward Eliza, b rear 163 St Mary.
Coward Joseph, lab, h 37 Church.
Coward Joshua, lab, r 78 Columbia al.
Coward Matilda (wid Joseph), h 169 W Wabash.
Cowen Jennie W, teacher Public School No 32, b 246 Talbott av.
Cowen Robert B, bkkpr, h 246 Talbott av.
Cowden Wm, lab, h 274 W Maryland.
Cowger Albion E, canmkr, b 112 N Gillard av.
Cowger Arville J, agt, 37 N Gillard av.
Cowger James M, polisher, b 311 S Missouri.
Cowger John, car rep, h 39 Wright.
Cowger Moses T, lab, h 12 N Gillard av.
Cowger Noah N, carp, h 311 S Missouri.
Cowger Remus A, grinder, b 311 S Missouri.
Cowgill Ernest C, mach, h 83 Johnson av.
Cowgill Jay E, actuary, 537 Lemcke bldg, r Wyandot blk.
Cowgill Loy L, tinner, b 501 N California.

W. H. Messenger FURNITURE, CARPETS, STOVES, 101 EAST WASHINGTON ST. TEL. 491.

McNamara, Koster & Co. | Foundry and Pattern Shop, 212-218 S. PENN. ST. . . . PHONE 1593.

THE FRED DIETZ CO. WOODEN PACKING BOXES MADE TO ORDER. FACTORY AND WAREHOUSE TRUCKS. 40 Madison Avenue. Telephone 654.

Cowherd Charles M, lab, b 269 N West.
Cowherd James R, porter, b 269 N West.
Cowherd John, lab, b 269 N West.
Cowherd Martha J (wid Aaron), h 269 N West.
Cowherd Richard, lab, b rear 738 N West.
Cowherd Wimlock A, b 269 N West.
Cowie Rosanna (wid John R), b 287 Douglass.
Cowles Roswell B, engr, b 45 Bloomington.
Cox Aaron, b 1107 N Delaware.
Cox Albert, lab, r 205½ W Ohio.
Cox Albert G, pres Globe Machine Works and treas The Wanamaker Car Scale Co, h 564 N Penn.
Cox Alden J, electrician, h 519 College av.
Cox Alice B, stenog Kahn Tailoring Co, b 714 E Washington.
Cox Allen S, lab, h 77 Martindale av.
Cox Alonzo H, engr, h 160 Blake.
Cox Andrew J, lab, h 39 Oliver av (W I).
Cox Ann M, h 254 W Market.
Cox Ansel, lab, b 39 Oliver av (W I).
Cox Arthur T, trav agt, b 575 N Penn.
Cox Benjamin, clk N Y Store, h 443 W Eugene (N I).
Cox Bert, trav agt Daggett & Co, 20 W Georgia.
Cox Bettie E (wid Andrew J), b 575 N Penn.

COX CHARLES E, Judge Police Court, Room 20 Basement Court House, h 820 Park av.

Cox Charles E, lab, h 94 Woodburn av (W I).
Cox Charles H, driver, h 79 Wilson.
Cox Edmond M, mach, b 273 Christian av.
Cox Edward, engr, h 11 Astor.
Cox Edward C, lab, b 39 Oliver av (W I).
Cox, Emma (wid Gillum H), b 19 School.
Cox Ernest G, bkkpr Commercial Electric Co, h 361 Talbott av.
Cox Eugene T, subscription books, 17 Talbott blk, r same.
Cox Eunice M, clk, b 195 N Alabama.
Cox Francis M, shoes, 310 Indiana av, h same.
Cox Frank, waiter, r 409 W North.
Cox Frank H (wid Wm C), h 1197 N Illinois.
Cox Frederick, lab, r 24 N West.
Cox George, clk Consumers' Gas Trust Co, h 87 Park av.
Cox George A, engr, h 77 Meikel.
Cox George E, tentmkr, b 193 S New Jersey.
Cox George H, carp, 155 English av, h same.
Cox George M, horseshoer, 108 S Belmont av (W I), h same.
Cox Greeley, lab, b 564 N Senate av.
Cox Green, lab, b w s Caldwell 2 n of North.
Cox Harriet (wid John B), b 580 N Alabama.
Cox Harry, uphlr, b 351 S New Jersey.
Cox Harry E, clk L E & W R R, h Shearer pike beyond limits.
Cox Harry G, teacher Industrial School, b 564 N Penn.
Cox Henry C, b 37 English av.
Cox Henry C, lawyer, 47 Thorpe blk, h Railroad (I).
Cox Ira E, phys, 469 W Addison (N I), h same.
Cox Irvin, clk, h 443 W Eugene (N I).
Cox Irvin S, lab, b 275 E Ohio.
Cox Isaac S, confr, 88 Mass av, h 113 Talbott av.

Henry H. Fay, 40½ E. Washington St., REAL ESTATE, AND LOAN BROKER.

Cox Jacob A, trav agt, b 858 Bellefontaine.
Cox James P, blksmith, b 32 N Liberty.
Cox Jane (wid David), b 155 N Capitol av.
Cox Jane (wid Henry), h 167 W 3d.
Cox Jesse, lab, h rear 704 N Illinois.
Cox Jesse C, clk, h 193 S New Jersey.
Cox John, clk, b 87 Park av.
Cox John A M, ironwkr, h 193 S New Jersey.
Cox John B, h 273 Christian av.
Cox John C, lodgekpr Indiana Reformatory.
Cox John H, molder, h 2 Vermont (H).
Cox Joseph, carp, b 273 Christian av.
Cox Joseph D, trav agt, h 123 E Ohio.
Cox Joseph E, lab, h 310 E Louisana.
Cox Joseph S, carp, b 37 Highland pl.
Cox Julius R, dty dis clk P O, h 7 Quince.
Cox Leslie A, reporter The Sun, b 1107 N Delaware.
Cox Linton A (Pickens & Cox), h 1576 N Meridian.
Cox Lydia E (wid Jeremiah), h 1097 W Washington.
Cox Margaret A (wid Emery), h 928 N New Jersey.
Cox Martha G (wid James M), h 275 E Ohio.
Cox Millard F, lawyer, 7-8 When bldg, h 665 Broadway.
Cox Milton, lab, b 44 Edward (W I).
Cox Nora J (wid Walter W), h 343 Mass av.
Cox Oliver F, policeman Insane Hospital.
Cox Oliver T, bkkpr Domestic Laundry, h 431 Indiana av.
Cox Perry, mach, h 18 Orange av.
Cox Porter H, clk, b 275 E Ohio.
Cox Richard, tinner, 516 E 7th, h same.
Cox Richard M J, civ engr, h 858 Bellefontaine.
Cox Samuel, lab, h rear 42 Mill.
Cox Sarah J (wid Wm), b 361 Talbott av.
Cox Thomas, carp, b 516 E 7th.
Cox Thomas, lab, b 564 N Senate av.
Cox Thomas F, lab, h 270 Springfield.
Cox Walter G, miller, h 77 S West.
Cox Walter H, lab, h 29 Gatling.

UNION CASUALTY & SURETY CO. OF ST. LOUIS, MO. All lines of Personal Accident and Casualty Insurance, including Employers' and General Liability. W. E. BARTON & CO., General Agents, 504 Indiana Trust Building. LONG DISTANCE TELEPHONE 1918.

Indianapolis BUSINESS UNIVERSITY Leading College of Business and Shorthand. Elevator day and night. Individual instruction. Large faculty. Terms easy. Enter now. See p. 4. When Block. E. J. HEEB, President.

Water and Oil Meters { HENRY R. WORTHINGTON, 64 S. PENNSYLVANIA ST. Long Distance Telephone 284.

UNION CO-OPERATIVE LAUNDRY { NOS. 8, 40 AND 142 VIRGINIA AVENUE (COMPOSED OF UNION LAUNDRY GIRLS.) T. E. SOMERVILLE, MANAGER — TELEPHONE 199 . INDIANAPOLIS, IND.

HORACE M. HADLEY
REAL ESTATE AND INSURANCE
66 East Market Street, Basement
TELEPHONE 1540.

Cox Walter T, pres Monument Savings and Loan Assn, res Cincinnati, O.
Cox Warner M L, mach, h 40 Smith.
COX WM A, Propr Domestic Laundry, 73 N Illinois, h 329 N West, Tel 1585.
Cox Wm A, trav agt, b 1197 N Illinois.
Cox Wm B, hostler, h 90 Hoyt av.
Cox Wm E, trav agt, b 858 Bellefontaine.
Cox Wm H, lab, h 242 Spring.
Cox Wm H, painter, h 35 Eastern av.
Cox Wm H jr, bartndr, b 242 Spring.
Cox Wm J, lab, b 40 Smith.
Cox Wm L, patrolman, h 743 E Ohio.
Cox Wm T, painter, h 32 N Liberty.
Cox Wm W, printer Wm B Burford, h 253 S Olive.
Cox Woodson H, coachman 818 N Delaware.
Cox Zachariah M, h 93 W 14th.
Coxe John, cigar mnfr, 262 W Washington, h 380 W 2d.
Coxe Robert S, sub letter carrier P O, h 59 Mayhew.
Coxley Joseph, harnessmkr, 585 Morris (W I), r same.
Coy Arthur St C, lab, h 287 E Washington.
Coy Jesse T, mach, h 471 Martindale av.
Coy John, lab, r 268 S Illinois.
Coy Martha A, h 183 Columbia av.
Coy Wm M, clk, r 107 Malott av.
Coyle Anna (wid Michael), r 175 W Ohio.
Coyle Bernard, saloon, 849 S Meridian, h same.
Coyle Derby, saloon, 240 W Maryland, b 230 same.
Coyle Frank, lab, b 78 N Gillard av.
Coyle James B, carp, h 187 W South.
Coyle John, mach, b 2 McGill.
Coyle Margaret (wid Michael), h 2 McGill.
Coyle Margaret E, clk U S Pension Agency, b n e cor New York and West.
Coyle Robert, mach, h 250 S Alabama.
Coyle Sabina (wid James), h 153 W New York.
Coyle Susan (wid Wm B), h 224 Hamilton av.
Coyle Thomas J, student, b 153 W New York.
Coyne Michael, lab, h 32 S West.

PERSONAL AND PROMPT ATTENTION GIVEN TO COLLECTIONS.
Merchants' and Manufacturers' Exchange
J. E. TAKKEN, Manager,
19 Union Building, 73 West Maryland Street.

Coyner John V, Surveyor Marion County, 31 Court House, h n w cor Orchard av and Coyner.
Coyner Mary A, teacher Public School No 2, b 149 N Penn.
Coyner Susan M (wid Martin L), h 85 E Pratt.
Cozatt Charles E, bricklyr, h 158 Newman.
Cozier Benton, lab, h 41 Beacon.
Crabb James N, clk, h 264 Lincoln av.
Crabb John H, lab, h 1343 Isabella (N I).
Crabb John S, meats, 493 W Addison (N I), h 450 same.
Crabb John W, bartndr, h 26 Blackford.
Crabb Keller E, cigars, 64 Virginia av, h same.
Crabill Benjamin F, carp, h 20 S Pine.
Crabill Bros (John M and George W), grocers, 400 Talbott av.
Crabill George W (Crabill Bros), b 400 Talbott av.
Crabill John M (Crabill Bros), b 400 Talbott av.
Crabill Michael R, clk, h 400 Talbott av.
Crabill Zelma L, stenog, b 111 Meek.
Crabtree Abraham, bellboy, b rear 624 Home av.
Crabtree Amanda (wid Abram), h rear 624 Home av.
Crabtree Chalmers L, polisher, h 1211 Morris (W I).
Crabtree James, patrolman, h w s Cushing 2 s of Sutherland.
Crabtree Lovell B, grocer, 352 Mass av, h 354 same.
Crabtree Thomas H, painter, h 57 Sheffield (W I).
Craddick Laura (wid John), h 1389 Annette (N I).
Craft, see Kraft.
Craft Alvin C, student, b 720 N Illinois.
Craft Augustus P (Craft & Koehler), h 468 Broadway.
Craft Caleb, lab, b 326 W Maryland.
Craft Charles O, florist, 1541 N Capitol av, h same.
Craft Edward R, cupolatndr, h 68 Bates.
Craft Elizabeth (wid George), b 68 Bates.
Craft Ernest H, bkkpr, h 720 N Illinois.
Craft Frank (Craft & Payne), h 425 W Udell (N I).
Craft Harlan W, trav agt Peoria Rubber and Mnfg Co, b 471 N East.
Craft Lucinda B (wid Homer), h 613 Mass av.
Craft Moreland, plumber, b 286 Indiana av.
Craft Philip, lab, b 326 W Maryland.
Craft Richard P, chief deputy County Sheriff, h 897 N Delaware.
Craft Russell J, electrotyper, b 126 Yandes.
Craft Smith, blksmith, h 286 Indiana av.
Craft Wm B, ins agt, h 613 Mass av.
Craft Wm H (W H Craft & Co), h 720 N Illinois.
Craft Wm H, clk R M S, h 620 Park av.
Craft W H & Co (Wm H Craft), real est, 47½ N Illinois.
Craft & Koehler (Augustus P Craft, Emil W Koehler), jewelers, 27½ S Meridian.
Craft & Payne (Frank Craft and Charles Payne), grocers, 426 W Udell (N I).
Crafton Nelson J, lab, b 128 Columbia al.
Craghan James, lab, h 275 W Maryland.
Crago Eugene, painter, b 413 N Pine.
Crago George L, buttermkr, b 413 N Pine.
Crago John, harnessmkr, h 413 N Pine.
Cragun Lorenzo D, clk, h 123 W 5th.
Crahan John, lab, b 99 Geisendorff.

CLEMENS VONNEGUT 184, 186 and 192 E. Washington St. | FOUNDRY AND MACHINISTS' SUPPLIES. "NORTON" EMERY WHEELS AND GRINDING MACHINERY.

THE WM. H. BLOCK CO. DRY GOODS, MILLINERY, CLOAKS AND FURS.
7 AND 9 EAST WASHINGTON STREET.

Crahan Margaret (wid Patrick), h 99 Geisendorff.
Crahan Thomas W, lab, b 99 Geisendorff.
Crahen James M, mach, b 64 S California.
Crahen Martin, h 64 S California.
Craig Alexander, trav agt, h 951 N Alabama.
Craig Alexander, b 951 N Alabama.
Craig Andrew J, plumber, 197 W Maryland, h same.
Craig Arthur, lab, b 440 E 7th.
Craig Benjamin F, molder, h 28 N Haugh (H).
Craig Catherine L (wid Isaac), b 383 Mass av.
Craig Charles F, engr, b 452 E Market.
Craig Charles M, mach, h 135 William (W I).
Craig Charles W, clk, b 482 N Illinois.
Craig Columbus C, lab, h 119 S Reisner (W I).
Craig Edward, trav agt, h 356 N Noble.
Craig Edward J, foreman Salisbury & Stanley, h 36 Hoyt av.
Craig Eliza (wid John), b 60 Omer.
Craig Emanuel S, lab, b 195 W Maryland.
Craig Eva (wid David), notions, 136 Minerva, h same.
Craig Frank R, clk C C C & St L Ry, h 486 Stillwell.
Craig Frederick W, bartndr, h 79 W 8th.
Craig Frederick W, clk Penna Lines, h 138 Tacoma av.
Craig George W, lab, b 119 S Reisner (W I).
Craig Harry J, supt Lilly Varnish Co, h 1022 N Capitol av.
Craig Helen (wid James), b 309 S Brookside av.
Craig Helen P, officer Indiana Reformatory.
Craig Henry, wheelwright, h 48 Lafayette av.
CRAIG HENRY J, Wholesale Cigar Dealer, 15 Indiana av, r 122 The Shiel.
Craig Herimon T, contr, 452 E Market, b same.
Craig Hiram L, lab, h 78 Germania av (H).
Craig James, dry goods, 190 Indiana av, h 515 N West.
Craig James, lab, r 338 Superior.
Craig James F, mach, h 98 Bismarck av (H).
Craig James R, dairy, 309 S Brookside av, h same.
Craig Jesse, cashr Wm Beck, b 98 Bismarck av (H).
Craig John, tmstr, h 16 Root.
CRAIG JOHN A, Mnfr of Candies, 20 E Washington, h 482 N Illinois.
Craig John E, engr, h 34 Poplar (B).
Craig John F, carp, h 200 W 8th.
Craig John F, real est, 104 Michigan (H), h 143 King av (H).
Craig John F, baggageman, h 35 Clifford av.
Craig John T (Craig & Co), h 23 Ashland (W I).
Craig John W, h 86 S William (W I).
Craig Joshua W, butcher, b 597 W Michigan.
Craig Louisa (wid Isaac), h 383 Mass av.
Craig Modesta, h 380 Muskingum al.
Craig Porter J, soldier, h 60 Omer.
Craig Richard C, tmstr, h 27 Geneva.
Craig Robert, butcher, b 43 S West.
Craig Robert, lab, h 307 Shelby.
Craig Robert A, condr, h 143 Bellefontaine.

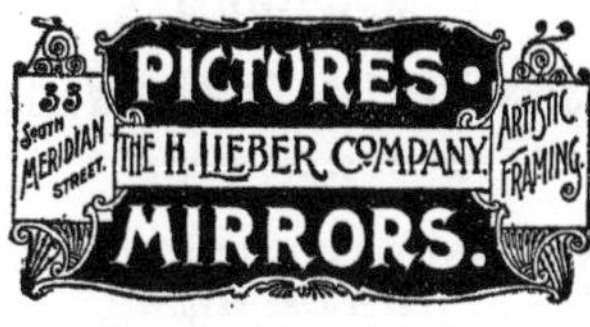

Craig Robert C, agt Janesville Machine Co, h 442 Broadway.
Craig Samuel I, h 205 Yandes.
Craig Stuart A, clk, b 515 N West.
Craig Wm, agt, h 439 W Udell (N I).
Craig Wm, lab, b 70 S Belmont av (W I).
Craig Wm, lab, h 56 Bismarck (W I).
Craig Wm B, vet surg, 23 Monument pl, b 80 W Market.
Craig Wm E, mach hd, b rear 119 Meek.
Craig Wm H, lab, b 70 S Belmont (W I).
Craig Wm R, clk, b 143 Bellefontaine.
Craig Wm S, asst supt The Pentecost Bands, b 52 S State av.
Craig Wm S, clk, b 452 E Market.
Craig Wm W, trav agt McCormick H M Co, b Spencer House.
Craig & Co (John T Craig, Harvey Lee), grocers, 75 Oliver av (W I).
Craighead Alexander A, waiter, h 66 Columbia av.
Craighead Gibson, cook, b 146 Michigan (H).
Craigie Wm, lab, h 58 Sanders.
Craigle Barbara (wid Christopher), b 167 Columbia av.
Craigle Charles T, foreman, h 248 S Missouri.
Craigle John E, switchman, h 279 S Missouri.
Crail Albert, mach, h 273 Alvord.
Crail Catherine (wid Aaron), b 311 Alvord.
Crail George, lab, h 541 Yandes.
Crail John V T, watchman, h 311 Alvord.
Crail Thomas M, lab, h 94 Oriole.
Crain Armena (wid Benjamin F), b 271 W Vermont.
Crain Lydia (wid Jehiel), b 49 Central av.
Crall John H, foreman George Hitz & Co, h 380 Talbott av.
Cramer, see also Creemer, Cromer and Kramer.
Cramer Charles, lather, r 93 N New Jersey.
Cramer Charles G, mngr Peter Merkle & Son, r The Windsor.
Cramer Charles H, trav agt Famous Stove Co, h 395 Ash.

GUIDO R. PRESSLER,
FRESCO PAINTER
Churches, Theaters, Public Buildings, Etc., A Specialty.
Residence, No. 325 North Liberty Street.
INDIANAPOLIS, IND.

INDIANAPOLIS STEEL ROOFING AND CORRUGATING WORKS, 23 and 25 East South Street. S. D. NOEL, Proprietor.

David S. McKernan REAL ESTATE AND LOANS. Exchanging real estate a specialty. A number of choice pieces for encumbered property. Rooms 2-5 Thorpe Block.

DIAMOND WALL PLASTER { Telephone 1410 BUILDERS' EXCHANGE.

Cor. E. Ohio St. and C., C., C. & St. L. R'y Tracks. UNION TRANSFER AND STORAGE CO. Storage of Hbuseho d Goods and Pianos a Specialty.

W. McWORKMAN,
Galvanized Iron Cornice Works
TIN AND SLATE ROOFING.
930 WEST WASHINGTON STREET.
TELEPHONE 1118.

Cramer Edgar L, color mixer, h 174 Dougherty.
Cramer Ella V, stenog, b 60 Cherry.
Cramer Harry C, ironwkr, r 174 E Washington.
Cramer Harry W, barber, b 206 Fletcher av.
Cramer Henry W, plastr, h 593 W Francis (N I).
Cramer Horace H, plastr, h 17 Ludlow av.
Cramer Joseph W, colormkr, h 537 S New Jersey.
Cramer Samuel B, carp, b 206 Fletcher av.
Cramer Wm, lab, b Exchange Hotel (W I).
Cramer Wm E, grocer, 59 E Mkt House, h 1211 Northwestern av.
Cramer Winfield S, plastr, 206 Fletcher av, h same.
Crampton Mary E (wid Wm), r 39 The Windsor.
Crandall Andrew M, engr, h 5 Walcott.
Crandall Charles A, mach, b 52 N State av.
Crandall George T, agt, h 247½ S Capitol av.
Crandall Joseph L, engr, h 52 N State av.
Crandall Joseph M, agt, h 894 N Illinois.
Crandall Laura L (wid Madison), h 380 N Senate av.
Crandall Tryphena (wid James M), h 164½ E Washington.
Crane, see also Crahan and Crain.
Crane Benjamin F, agt, h 1028 N Penn.
Crane Benjamin J, h 886 N Senate av.
Crane Charles J, ticket receiver Penna Lines, Union Station, h 56 Highland pl.
Crane Dennis, motorman, h 24 Osgood (W I).
Crane Elevator Co, Albert Nelson agt, 41 Lombard bldg.
Crane Ellis W, letter carrier P O, h 70 Harrison.
Crane Ernest C, clk, r 75 W Vermont.
Crane Frank, cigarmkr, b 435 E Washington.
Crane George W, bkkpr, h 135 E North.
Crane Irka M, clk, h 167½ E Washington.
Crane Isaac, lab, h 16 Center.
CRANE ISAIAH C, Watches, Clocks and Jewelry, 135 Virginia av, h 134 Dougherty.

SEALS,
STENCILS,
STAMPS, Etc.
GEO. J. MAYER
15 S. Meridian St.
TELEPHONE 1386.

Crane James P, h 106 Fayette.
Crane Johanna (wid Dennis), h 29½ Roe.
Crane John, driver, b 508 W Maryland.
Crane John, lab, h 60 Grant.
Crane John F, painter, h 556 W Washington.
Crane Julia F (wid Henry A), h 456 W 1st.
Crane Leonard, sergt of police, h 638 W Vermont.
Crane Maria E (wid Amos C), h 125 Yandes.
Crane Peter, b s w cor Washington and Downey avs (I).
Crane Richard J, molder, b 106 Fayette.
Crane Sarah (wid George S), b 433 Virginia av.
Crane Stephen D, shoes, 162 Virginia av, h same.
Crane Thomas W, brickmason, b w s Brookland av 2 n of Progress av.
Crane Wm A, cabtmkr, h 44 Ingram.
Crane Wm H, blksmith, h 72 Prospect.
Cranfill David, lab, h 94 Warren av (W I).
Crank Otto G, carp, h 73 Woodburn av (W I).
Crannon Timothy, patrolman, h 357 S Delaware.
Cranor Andrew P, grocer, n s Vorster av 1 w of Belt R R (M P), h same.
Cranor John H, loans, 723 Lemcke bldg, h 183 E St Clair.
Crans James T, phys, 243 Jefferson av, h same.
Cranshaw, see also Crenshaw.
Cranshaw Fleming, lab, h 61 Superior.
Crary Mary (wid Samuel), b 23 Brett.
Crather Thomas H, meats, 11 E Mkt House, h 4½ Malott av.
Craven Charles G, barber, 103 Indiana av, h 197 W Vermont.
Craven John, lab, h 126 Darnell.
Craven John, produce, 33 E Mkt House, h 298 E North.
Craven Patrick, lab, b 41 Minerva.
Craven Primus, lab, h 59 Smith.
Craven Riley, harnessmkr, 64 W 7th, h same.
Craven Schuble C, lab, h 34 Sheffield (W I).
Craven Theodore D, trav agt Murphy, Hibben & Co, b 600 Park av.
Craven Wm, lab, r 15 Rhode Island.
Cravens Charles, mach hd, h 22 King.
Cravens Jessie, b 13 Dougherty.
Cravens Joshua, lab, h rear 474 N California.
CRAVENS JUNIUS E, Dentist, 23-24 Marion Blk, h 370 N Meridian.
Cravens Randolph, lab Insane Hospital.
Cravens Thomas S, lawyer, 18½ N Penn, b 219 N Alabama.
Cravens Wm S, lab, h 72 Kennington.
Crawford Anna, nurse, r 84 E New York.
Crawford Benjamin, bkkpr, b 218 E Market.
Crawford Charles, tmstr, h rear 33 Woodlawn av.
Crawford Charles C, clk, b 23 N State av.
Crawford Constant G, patternmkr, b 511 Bellefontaine.
Crawford Curtis L, harnessmkr, h 50 Hoyt av.
Crawford David N, printer The Sun, b 600 Cornell av.
Crawford David T, lab, h 86 Holmes av (H).
Crawford Davis A, carp, b 265 N Senate av.
Crawford Edward M, clk, r 82½ E Washington.
Crawford Edward, gilder, b 26 N State av.

A. METZGER AGENCY ESTABLISHED 1863. L-O-A-N-S

LAMBERT GAS & GASOLINE ENGINE CO.
ANDERSON, IND. GAS ENGINES FOR ALL PURPOSES.

Crawford Elizabeth (wid Darius), h 200 W South.
Crawford Emory C, clk Great Atlantic and Pacific Tea Co, b 593 N Senate av.
Crawford Francis N, clk, h 213 W Maryland.
Grawford Green, lab, h 73 Torbet.
Crawford Harry, farmer, h 91 Woodburn av (W I).
Crawford Harry J, driver, b 26 N State av.
Crawford Henry J, lab, r 199½ Mass av.
Crawford James B, pres Meridian L and T Company, res Atlanta, Ga.
Crawford James W, clk, r 60½ S Delaware.
Crawford James W, foreman, h 174½ Brookside av.
Crawford John C, brakeman, h 1094 W New York.
Crawford John H, driver, b 23 N State av.
Crawford John W, sawyer, b 511 Bellefontaine.
Crawford Joseph A, lab, h 418 Columbia av.
Crawford Josephine (wid Abel), h 760 N Illinois.
Crawford Josephine E, h 511 Bellefontaine.
Crawford Julia (wid Thomas), h rear 81 Cornell av.
Crawford Lucetta (wid Wm), h 1556 Graceland av.
Crawford Luther W, roofer, b 553 S Meridian.
Crawford Michael B, bkkpr Lombard B and L Assn, b 218 E Market.
Crawford Morris A, barber, r 39 Hosbrook.
Crawford Nancy (wid David), b 20 Mill.
Crawford Nancy D (wid Thomas E), h 23 N State av.
Crawford Phyllis (wid Cator), h 75 Torbet.
Crawford Samuel, mach, b 252 N California.
Crawford Samuel M, collarmkr, b 23 N State av.
Crawford Smith, janitor, h 225 W Vermont.
Crawford Stephen M, whol meats, Indpls Abattoir (W I), h 377 N Senate av.
Crawford Thomas C, lab, h 513 English av.
Crawford Wm, mach, b 203 N West.
Crawford Wm F, real est, 72½ E Washington, h Greenwood, Ind.
Crawford Wm R, clk, b 213 W Maryland.
Crawford Wm T, lab, b 513 English av.
Crawford Zachariah T, salesman S M Crawford, h 593 N Senate av.
Crawley, see also Crowley.
Crawley Edward L, letter carrier P O, h 278 Douglass.
Crawley Hiram C, shoemkr, 183 S Meridian, h 166 Maple.
Crawley Lillie M, milliner, 428 S Meridian, b 166 Maple.
Crayton Wm D, mach hd, h 90 Kappus (W I).
Creager Homer, lab, b 235 W South.
Creagh Lizzie (wid John), h 109 Harrison.
Creasey Charles E, stockkpr, h 13 Smithson av.
Creasey Wm L, filer, h 82 N Olive.
Creasy Charles J, bicyclemkr, h 292 E South.
Creasy Maud, music teacher, 292 E South, h same.
Creeden Hannah R, stenog U S Pension Agency, b 437 S Delaware.
Creeden Jeremiah, foreman, h 437 S Delaware.
Creeden Joseph A, vet surg, 550 Virginia av, h same.
Creegan Bridget, h 116 Laurel.
Creelman George P, clk C C C & St L Ry, b 224 Clifford av.

THOS. C. DAY & CO.
INVESTING AGENTS,
TOWN AND FARM LOANS,
Rooms 325 to 330 Lemcke Bldg.

Creevy E Forest, salesman Smith Premier Typewriter Co, r 143 N Penn.
Cregg John C, real est, 94½ E Washington, h 178 S Judge Harding (W I).
Crenshaw John, lab, h 456 W Lake (N I).
CRESCENT LOAN AND INVESTMENT CO, John T Brush Pres, James H Lowes Sec, James R Henry Treas, 63-64 When Bldg.
Crescent Oil Co, Harry B Smith pres, Benjamin F Howard sec and treas, 34 E South.
Cress, see also Kress.
Cress Charles F, bookbndr, b s e cor Brookside av and Atlas.
Cress Henry, barber, 247 Mass av, h 56 Martindale av.
Cress Henry, farmer, h Ritter av (I).
Cress John V, produce, E Mkt House, h 56 Martindale av.
Cress Laura B, stenog Jenney Electric Motor Co, b 121 E New York.
Cress Lucien E, mach, b 56 Martindale av.
Cress Wm H, music teacher, s e cor Brookside av and Atlas, h same.
Cress Wm R, bartndr, b 80 Columbia av.
Cresshull Charles S, mngr Cresshull Novelty Mnfg Co, h 596 Chestnut.
CRESSHULL NOVELTY MANUFACTURING CO, Charles S Cresshull Mngr, Toys, Games, Etc, 596 Chestnut.
Cressler Clara (wid David W), h 886 W Washington.
Cressler Lillian, stenog, b 886 W Washington.
Cressler Nellie, teacher Public School No 5, b 886 W Washington.
Crewett George W, waiter, r rear 173 E St Joseph.
Crews Henry C, lather, b 1148 E Ohio.
Crews Isaac, clk, r 200½ W Washington.
CREWS JOHN W, Real Estate, Insurance and Rentals, Office n w cor Walnut and Northwestern av (N I), h 446½ W Udell (N I).
Crews Sewell W, clk, r 113 S Illinois.
Cribbs Harry A, stenog C C C & St L Ry, h 74 W 18th.

EAT
QUAKER BREAD
ASK YOUR GROCER FOR IT.
THE HITZ BAKING CO.

BICYCLES $5 DOWN. MONTHLY. Best Wheels. Best Terms. WHEELMEN'S CO. 31 W. OHIO ST. LONG DISTANCE TEL. 1855.

J. H. TECKENBROCK Grilles, Fretwork and Wood Carpets
94 EAST SOUTH STREET.

FIDELITY MUTUAL LIFE PHILADELPHIA, PA. A. H. COLLINS { General Agent, 52-53 Baldwin Block.

Edwardsport Coal & Mining Co. Rooms 42 and 43 When Building.

ESTABLISHED 1876. TELEPHONE 168.
CHESTER BRADFORD,
SOLICITOR OF PATENTS,
AND COUNSEL IN PATENT CAUSES.
(See adv. page 6.)
Office:—Rooms 14 and 16 Hubbard Block, S.W. Cor. Washington and Meridian Streets,
INDIANAPOLIS, INDIANA.

Cribbs Wm O B, clk Badger Furniture Co, h 118 N Summit.
Crichlow Wm A, painter, h 118 Maple.
Crickmore Jesse A, fireman, h 535 E Washington.
Crider Louis, carp, h 146 Miami.
Crider Robert S, carp, b 146 Miami.
Crider Thomas H, lab, b 146 Miami.
Crillman Harry R, collr, b 697 Park av.
Crim Albert R, broommkr, b 124 S Summit.
Crim John F, h 124 S Summit.
Crimans Alexander S, condr, h 40 Johnson av.
Crimans Wm, b 40 Johnson av.
Crimins John C, trimmer, b 76 E New York.
Cripe, Harris & Co (Sarah Cripe, Emma P Harris, John C Hall), novelty mnfrs, 82 Baldwin blk.
Cripe Sarah (Cripe, Harris & Co), r 92½ N Delaware.
Cripe Sarah E (wid Daniel E), r 24 Hutchings blk.
Crippen Charles W, lab, h 29 McCormick.
Crippen Ira L, photog, 278 English av, h same.
Crippin Clarence E, printer, h 165 Walcott.
Cripple Frederick, carp, r 149½ E Washington.
Criqui Mary (wid Mitchell), h 512 Shelby.
Crisman Isaac, carp, h 45 Frank.
Criss Harry J, lab, b 11 Astor.
Crist, see also Christ.
Crist Daniel O, phys, 22 W Ohio, h n w cor English av and Sherman Drive (S).
Crist George R, molder, h 455 W Francis (N I).
Crist George W, express, h 447 W Shoemaker (N I).
Crist John M, foreman, h 87 Holmes av (H).
Crist Marvin B, h 416 Ash.
Crist Melvin A, finisher, h 474 W Udell (N I).
Crist Robert E, agt, h 641 Eugene (N I).
Critchard Christian, coachman 712 N Meridian.
Critchlow Wilmer W, clk, r 276 N Delaware.
Critser Burtis A, lab, b 307 E Court.
Critser Fleming M, lab, h 376 Martindale av.

HAY & WILLITS MFG. CO.
76 N. PENNSYLVANIA ST.,
MAKERS
Outing BICYCLES
PHONE 598.

Crittenden Thomas, plastr, h rear 79 W North.
Crivel George F, trav agt, r 25 The Blacherne.
Crockett Daniel W, reporter, h 77 E St Joseph.
Crockett Frank L, lab, h 63 Maxwell.
Crockett George F, painter, h 1173 E Washington.
Crockett Harvey S, engr, b 161 Woodlawn av.
Crockett John D, watchman, h 161 Woodlawn av.
Crockett Laura, b 1373 Graceland av.
Crockett Oscar L, engr, h 55 Walcott.
Crockett Wm C, lab, b 63 Maxwell.
Crockett Wyatt C, lab, h 778 E 10th.
Croft Arthur A, trav agt Nordyke & Marmon Co, h 427 E 12th.
Croft Fannie M, milliner, 83 Mass av, h same.
Croghan James, switchman, h 48 Oriental.
Croif Abraham, shoemkr, 45 Mass av, r same.
Crombatch Marcus, notions, 13 E Mkt House, h 441 N Alabama.
Cromer, see also Cramer and Kramer.
Cromer Jennie E, cashr, b 585 E Washington.
Cromer John B, ins agt, h 450 N Alabama.
Cromlich Omar G, plumber, b 127 Michigan av.
Cromlich Sarah E (wid George W), h 127 Michigan av.
Crompton, see also Crampton and Crumpton.
Crompton Ebenezer R, tinner, 86 Mass av, h 169 E St Joseph.
Cromwell Tunie, stenog Frick Co, b 1091 W Washington.
Cron Adam, grocer, 449 Newman, h same.
Cron Frederick, grinder, b 449 Newman.
Cron Frederick A, mach, h 63 Oriole.
Cronbach Jennie (wid Samuel), h 517 W Maryland.
Crone Herman, clk, b 321 E Ohio.
Crone Jacob, saloon, 74 N Delaware, h 261 Bellefontaine.
Crone John H, bartndr, b 261 Bellefontaine.
Crone Louis D, engr Court House, h 129 King av (H).
Cronenberger Charles, waiter, r 90½ Mass av.
Croner Edgar B, clk, b 56 Omer.
Croner John H, blksmith, h 56 Omer.
Cronin Cornelius, clk, h 126 High.
Cronin Dennis, lab, h 80 Spann av.
Cronin Frank G, tel opr, b 627 E New York.
Cronin James A, saloon, 73 W McCarty, b 87 same.
Cronin James J, patrolman, h 28 McGill.
Cronin John, lab, h 289 Bates.
Cronin John, lab, h 87 W McCarty.
Cronin John E, stonecutter, b 87 W McCarty.
Cronin John P, bartndr, b 28 McGill.
Cronin Mary (wid John), h 28 McGill.
Cronin Michael J, condr, h 627 E New York.
Cronkhite Apollos B, boarding 272 N Meridian.
Cronkhite Levi A, carp, h 536 W Wells (N I).
Cronnon Elizabeth (wid John), nurse, 275 S Delaware, b same.
Cronnon Owen, molder, h 44 Bismarck av (H).
Cronstein Herman B, h 14 Mulberry.

SUPERIOR BITUMINOUS COAL For Steam and Domestic . . Purposes . .

ROOFING MATERIAL C. ZIMMERMAN & SONS, SLATE AND GRAVEL ROOFERS, 19 SOUTH EAST STREET.

DRIVEN WELLS And Second Water Wells and Pumps of all kinds at CHARLES KRAUSS', 42 S. PENN. ST., TEL. 465. REPAIRING NEATLY DONE.

Cronyn Wm M, treas The Indpls Book and Stationery Co, h 331 N Alabama.
Crook Hubert B, millwright, b 301 River av (W I).
Crooks John W, meats, 578 E St Clair, h same.
Crook Raymond R, lab, h 390 Highland av.
Crooke Asa E, foreman, h 24 Thalman av.
Crooke Charles W Rev, pastor Blackford St M E Church, cor Blackford and Market.
Crooker Edward C, baggageman, h 287 S Penn.
Croom Wm, lab, h w s Wallack 1 n of Pleasant run.
Croom Wm L, carp, h 173 Laurel.
Croones John H, hostler J H Spahr, r 75 E Wabash.
Croons Elizabeth (wid Felix), h 2 Susquehanna.
Cropper Charles G, bricklayer, h 575 W Francis (N I).
Cropper Eva A, mngr The Viavi Co, b 859 Bellefontaine.
Cropper James W, engr, h 23 N Gale (B).
Cropper Marion F, blksmith, h 514 W Udell (N I).
Cropper Roland T, brickmason, h 597 W 22d (N I).
Cropper Walter, driver, h 59 Muskingum al.
Cropper Wm B, mach, h 699 W Udell (N I).
Cropsey James M (Cropsey & Marshall), h 235 College av.
Cropsey Nebraska C, asst supt Public Schools, h 235 College av.
CROPSEY & MARSHALL (James M Cropsey, Elmer E Marshall), Lawyers, 529-530 Lemcke Bldg, Tel 1587.
Crosbie Wm J, cooper, h 221 S West.
Crosby Albert H, tel opr, b 177 Michigan av.
Crosby Charles E, helper, h 126 S Pine.
Crosby George, ball player, b 177 Michigan av.
Crosby Johanna (wid John), h 177 Michigan av.
Crosby John, engr, b 223 W New York.
Crosby John S, butcher, h 998 W Washington.
Crosby John W, butcher, r 77 N Alabama.
Crosby Mary, h 73 W Georgia.
Crosby Mary (wid David), h 79 Dougherty.
Crosby Mary E (wid Tolliver), h 755 Brookers al.
CROSBY MICHAEL, Genl Furniture Repair Shop, Mattresses and Upholstering, Second-Hand Furniture and Stoves Bought and Sold, 465-467 S Meridian, h same.
Crosby Wm, hostler, h Downey av (I).
Crosby Wm, lab, b 23 Mill.
Crosby Wm M, finisher, h 83 Dougherty.
Crose Benjamin D, reporter The Sun, b 408 N Illinois.
Crose Elizabeth K (wid Andrew J), b 56 Mass av.
Crose Mary E (wid John A), b 408 N Illinois.
Crose Samuel E, phys, 117½ W Washington, h 408 N Illinois.
Crose Willard J, clk, h 9 Emerson pl.
Crosley Charles, mason, h 606 W 22d (N I).
Crosley Clayton H, carp, h Brightwood av (B).
Crosley Charles, carp, h 628 W Francis (N I).

Richardson & McCrea, REPRESENTING BEST KNOWN FIRE INSURANCE COMPANIES. Fidelity and Casualty Insurance Company of New York Represented. Telephone 182. 79 East Market St.

Crosley Charles S, storekpr, h 624 N Penn.
Crosley Frank, painter, h 133 Martindale av.
Crosley Harry E, clk H H Lee, h 274 N Alabama.
Crosley Robert J, lab, h 197 Hillside av.
Crosley Sarah (wid James), h 12 Cooper.
Crosley Wm T H, lab, h 112 N Pine.
Cross Addie, h 79 W Wabash.
Cross Amelia M (wid Frank M), grocer, 140 Spring, h 365 E New York.
Cross Anna E (wid Joseph), h 440 S Illinois.
Cross Charles M (Charles M Cross & Co), h s e cor Washington and Ritter av (I).
CROSS CHARLES M & CO (Charles M Cross), Real Estate, Loans and Insurance, Room 1, 19½ N Meridian.
Cross Charles W, draughtsman Brown-Ketcham Iron Wks, b 413 N Capitol av.
Cross Emma (wid James), h 21 Chapel.
Cross Frank P, butter, 105 E Mkt House, h 103 Ft Wayne av.
Cross George, lab, b 172 W Wabash.
Cross George W, lab, h 82 Muskingum al.
Cross George W H, sec Red Clay Orchard Co, h 174 Fletcher av.
Cross Horace G, clk, r 45 Huron.
Cross James, lab, h 105 Maple.
Cross John G, condr, h 523 Talbott av.
Cross John H, lab, h 110 Rhode Island.
Cross John H, tmstr, h 1201 Morris (W I).
Cross John M, dynamo opr, r Hendricks blk.
Cross John T, baker, h 138 Buchanan.
Cross Mary A (wid Daniel), h 480 W Udell (N I).
Cross Newton, lab, r 130 Allegheny.
Cross Oliver, lab, b 889 Morris (W I).
Cross Rachel, boarding 889 Morris (W I).
Cross Richard C, huckster, h 168 N Pine.
Cross Shadrach, mach hd, h 364 Newman.
Cross Wm, mach, h 309 Alvord.
Crossen Charles E, driver, h 217½ Alvord.
Crossen James, lab, h 319 E Miami.
Crossen Thomas F, lab, h 35 Ellen.
Crossen Thomas F jr, lab, b 35 Ellen.
Crossland Drusilla W (wid Jacob A), b 80 W St Clair.

The Williams Typewriter Elegant Work, Visible Writing, Easy Operation, High Speed. S. H. EAST, State Agent, 55 Thorpe Block, 87 E. Market St.

If You are not Satisfied with Your Laundry Work Give Us a Trial . . ERTEL STEAM LAUNDRY 26 and 28 N. Senate Avenue. Telephone 1089.

ELLIS & HELFENBERGER Manufacturers of IRON and WIRE FENCES 162-170 S. SENATE AVE. TEL. 758.

THE HOGAN TRANSFER AND STORAGE COMP'Y
Household Goods and Pianos Moved—Packed—Stored...... Baggage and Package Express Machinery and Safes a Specialty Cor. Washington and Illinois Sts. TELEPHONE No. 675.

Hose, Belting, Packing, Clothing, Druggists' Sundries, Bicycle Tires, Cotton Hose, Etc. New York Belting & Packing Co., L't'd.

HIGHEST SECURITY
LOWEST COST OF INSURANCE.
The Provident Life and Trust Co.
Of Philadelphia.
D. W. EDWARDS, Gen. Agent,
508 Indiana Trust Building.

Crossland Harry A, sec Indpls Warehouse Co, h 768 N Alabama.
Crossley Erastus M, lab, b 46 Standard av (W I).
Crossman Elizabeth A (wid James K), artist, 1285 N Meridian, h same.
Crothers Mary F (wid John P), h 801 N Delaware.
Crouch Addison M, grocer, 31 Clifford av, b 480 Stillwell.
Crouch Cornelius M, mach hd, h 123 Division (W I).
Crouch Curtis, lab, h 47 Sheffield (W I).
Crouch Daniel P, lab, h 56 Bates.
Crouch David, lab, h 324 Mass av.
Crouch George S, cutter, r 144 Cypress.
Crouch George W, plastr, h 113 Woodlawn av.
Crouch Ira M, woodwkr, h 1774 Graceland av.
Crouch John A, millwright, b 25 Sycamore.
Crouch John B, millwright, h 25 Sycamore.
Crouch John L, carp, b 23 Cincinnati.
Crouch John W, clk R M S, h 873 Grandview av.
Crouch Mary (wid James), b 1774 Graceland av.
Crouch Sophia E (wid John L), h 180 Dearborn.
Crouch Warren M, driver, h 176 N Pine.
Crouch Wesley A, musician, b 151 Lambert (W I).
Crouch Wm C, carp, r rear 176 E Washington.
Crouch Wm H, lab, b 180 Dearborn.
Crouch Wm J, lab, h 125 S Reisner (W I).
Crouch Wm T, lab, h 77 High.
Crouse, see also Cruse, Kraus and Kruse.
Crouse Francis M, books, 38 N Delaware, h 37 Park av.
Crouse Jeannette, piano teacher, b 37 Park av.
Crouse Kate (wid Wm), b 797 N New Jersey.
Crouse Wm S, mngr Indpls Desk, File and Paper Box Manufactory, 143½ S Meridian, h 220 Randolph.
Crout Elmer C, real est, h 312 Park av.

Julius C. Walk & Son,
Jewelers
Indianapolis.
12 EAST WASHINGTON ST.

CROW CHARLES R, Physician, Office Hours 7-9 A M, 1-4 and 7-9 P M, 32 Monument Pl, h same, Tel 158.
Crow Forest M, clk, b 118 E Pratt.
Crow Harry, bartndr, r 60½ Mass av.
Crow James W, paperhngr, h 133 Shepard (W I).
Crow Rebecca (wid James V), baker, E Mkt House, b 133 Shepard (W I).
Crowder Burrel, carp, r 546½ W Udell (N I).
Crowder Charles J, elevator opr, b 129 Ash.
Crowder James T, painter, h 129 Ash.
Crowdis Hans, lab, h s w cor English av and Temperance (I).
Crowdus Edward, waiter, b 120 Columbia al.
Crowdus Wm, lab, h w s Perkins pike 3 n of Bethel av.
Crowe Charles W, baggageman, h 433 S Delaware.
Crowe Edward, brakeman, b 1100 W Washington (H).
Crowe Frederick V, paperhngr, h 40 Lee (W I).
Crowe George W, blksmith, h 118 E Pratt.
Crowe John F, tel opr W B Overman & Co, h ½ mile north of State Fair Grounds.
Crowe Samuel, engr, b 839 E Washington.
Crowe Walter B, opr W U Tel Co, h 65 Ft Wayne av.
Crowe Wm M, horseshoer, 87 Hadley av, h 52 Birch av (W I).
Crowell Melvin E, school supplies, 24 E Market, h 339 N Penn.
Crowl Wm T, mach, h 888 S Meridian.
Crowley, see also Crawley.
Crowley Anna, stenog, b St John's Academy.
Crowley Bridget (wid Daniel), h 271 E Merrill.
Crowley Bridget (wid Patrick), h 429 S Missouri.
Crowley Ella, stenog McCormick H M Co, b 229 N Penn.
Crowley James, lab, b 429 S Missouri.
Crowley John C, tel opr, b 78 Park av.
Crowley Timothy E, b 271 E Merrill.
Crowley Wm, lab, h 264 W 7th.
CROWN HILL CEMETERY, Allen M Fletcher Pres, George P Anderson Sec, Frederick W Chislett Supt; Entrance N Senate av and 26th, also Northwestern av (N I); Office at Cemetery, Tel 555.
Croy Harry E, condr, h 18 Poplar (B).
Crozier Amanda A (wid Amos W), h 1089 E Michigan.
Crozier Benton, lab, h 41 Beacon.
Crozier Margaret J (wid George), b 745 N New Jersey.
Crozier Warren, condr, b 1089 E Michigan.
Crudup David, lab, h 183 Tremont av (H).
Cruger Frank, clk Van Camp H and I Co, h 98 Ramsey av.
Cruikshank Orris G, student, b 154 Union.
Crull Abner D, brakeman, h 116 Nordyke av (W I).
Crull Albert, h 478 Park av.
Crull Alfred W, molder, h 950 Morris (W I).
Crull Charles A, carp, b s s 11th 1 e of Bellefontaine.
Crull David, carp, h 249 E 11th.
Crull Elizabeth (wid Jacob R), h 357 N Pine.
Crull Frank D, molder, b 950 Morris (W I).
Crull Frank F, trav agt Murphy, Hibben & Co, h 145 Hoyt av.
Crull Jerome, lab, b 116 Nordyke av (W I).
Crull John H, carp, h 82 Nordyke av (W I).

The Central Rubber & Supply Co. PHONE 8. 79 S. ILLINOIS ST., INDIANAPOLIS, IND.

OTTO GAS ENGINES | BUILDERS' EXCHANGE S. W. Cor. Ohio and Penn. Telephone 535.

Becker & Son Charles Becker Jacob Becker Jr. Merchant Tailors. 21 N. Penn. St. Tel. 934

SALISBURY & STANLEY OFFICE, STORE AND BANK FIXTURES. Contractors and Builders. Repairing of all kinds done on short notice. 177 Clinton St., Indianapolis, Ind. Telephone 999.

Crump Wiley, lab, b 237 Elizabeth.
Cruse, see also Crouse and Kruse.
Cruse Bros (Michael and John), boilermkrs, 284 S Capitol av.
Cruse Henry W, mach, h 293 English av.
Cruse Isaac, clk, r 200½ W Washington.

CRUSE JAMES S, Real Estate and Rentals, 92 E Market, h 66 Fletcher av, Tel 1088.

Cruse John (Cruse Bros), h 508 S Illinois.
Cruse Michael (Cruse Bros), h 492 S Illinois.
Cruse Warren, lab, h rear 432 E St Clair.
Crutcher Charles B, lab, b 220 Yandes.
Crutcher Christian, coachman, h 6 Peck.
Crutcher Henry, barber, 186 W 7th, h 483 Lafayette.
Crutchfield Ernest W, lab, b 529 W Washington.
Crutchfield Robert, lab, h 235 W 7th.
Crutchfield Stapleton, lab, h 235 W 7th.
Crutchfield Wm H, lab, h 313 S Missouri.
Crutchley Wm, driver, h 514 S West.
Crute Austin M, macu hd, b 125 N West.
Cruzan John T, engr, h 421 Chestnut.

CRYAN JOHN, Elevator Expert, 96 S Delaware, cor Georgia, Tel 121; h 52 S Alabama. (See adv in classified Elevators.)

Cryer Harry, trav agt, b 277 Virginia av.
Crystal Ice Co, Frank A Maus pres, Eugene Bretney vice-pres, Joseph C Schaf sec and treas, 181 W Ohio.
Crystal Laundry, Samuel J Ritchey propr, 10 Clifford av.
Cubberley Susan B, retoucher, r 35 The Windsor.
Cubel Adolph, lab, h 483 Union.
Cubel Edward J, lithog, b 483 Union.
Cubel Mary, restaurant, 315 E Washington, h 297 E Market.
Cubert George W, lab, b 149 Locke.
Cubert John W, driver, h 149 Locke.
Cuckow George, lab, h 597 W Michigan.
Cudworth Wm D, lab, h 218 Douglass.
Cuer Edward J, clk, b 234 N East.
Cuer Fannie R, teacher Public School No 31, b 234 N East.
Cuer Robert F, clk Model Clothing Co, h 234 N East.
Culbertson Squire, lab, h 26 Bates al.
Culbertson Walter L, carver, h 68 Cypress.
Culbertson Wm D, trav agt, h 996 N Senate av.
Cullen Alice, teacher Public School No 6, r 34 The Wyandot.
Cullen Charles T, bkkpr, b 422 N Meridian.
Cullen Edward M, b 33 Henry.
Cullen John B, lab, b 33 Henry.
Cullen John J, lab, h 33 Henry.
Cullen Joseph A, grocer, 120 Oliver av (W I), h same.
Cullen Mary A (wid Edward F), h 33 Henry.
Cullen Michael, h 107 W South.
Cullen Terry J, treas and mngr Erwin Hotel Co, h 422 N Meridian.
Cullen Thomas, tailor, r 127½ E Washington.
Cullen Wm, lab The Bates.
Culley Charles P, architect, h 278 Keystone av.
Culley David L, lab, b 33 Bradshaw.
Culley Elizabeth (wid James), h 33 Bradshaw.
Culley Susan, stenog Mass Mut Ben Soc, b 414 N Delaware.
Culley Thomas J, driver, h 16 Detroit.
Culley Wm I, blksmith, b 33 Bradshaw.

Henry H. Fay,
40½ E. WASHINGTON ST.,
AGENT FOR
Insurance Co. of North America,
Pennsylvania Fire Ins. Co.

Cullings, see also Collings.
Cullings Alice R, h 70 Torbet.
Cullings Andrew J, molder, h 304 Jackson.
Cullings James J, city fireman, h 835 N Capitol av.
Cullins Jane (wid Larkin), b 499 Mulberry.
Cullity Angeline, stenog Singer Mnfg Co, b 49 Eureka av.
Cullity Dennis, h 49 Eureka av.
Cullity Dennis E, clk, b 49 Eureka av.
Culloden Grace, b 1033 N Alabama.
Culloden Wm G, student, b 301 N Delaware.
Cullum Eberle, pressman, h 270 Blackford.
Cullum John M, printer Wm B Burford, b 270 Blackford.
Cullum Silas E, pressman Wm B Burford h 282 Blackford.
Cullumber Mary M (wid George H), b 123 Spann av.
Cully Stoughton, lab, r 32 N Senate av.
Culmann, see also Coleman and Kuhlman.
Culmann Daniel, finisher, h 240 Lincoln la.
Culmann Frederick R O, mach, b 187 Harrison.
Culmann George, carp, h 108 Gray.
Culmann John, baker, 614 N Senate av, h same.
Culmann Louis, blksmith, b 240 Lincoln la.
Culmann Louis J, baker, b 614 N Senate av.
Culmann Wilhelmina (wid Conrad), h 187 Harrison.
Culmer Laura (wid Harry H), h 250 S East.
Culmer Pearl W, teacher Public School No 2, b 250 S East.
Culp Albert W, waiter, b 176 W 7th.
Culp Arthur D, lab, h 114 N Gillard av.
Culp David S, grinder, h 26 Garland (W I).
Culver, see also Colver.
Culver Benjamin S, clk, h 177 W 9th.
Culver Dudley M, phys, 410 Virginia av, h 49 Fletcher av.
Culver Ellen M (wid Leven F), h 741 N Senate av.
Culver John M, teacher Industrial Training School, h 264 E 9th.
Culver Nancy W (wid Elihu), b 83 Birch av (W I).

MAYHEW'S SPECTACLES
THE BEST IN USE
SOLD ONLY AT 13 N. MERIDIAN ST.

LUMBER Sash and Doors BALKE & KRAUSS CO., Corner Market and Missouri Sts.

Friedgen Has the BEST PATENT LEATHER SHOES AT LOWEST PRICES. 19 North Pennsylvania St.

SAMUEL LAING ! HOT AIR FURNACES 72 AND 74 EAST COURT STREET.

M. B. WILSON, Pres. W. F. CHURCHMAN, Cash.
The Capital National Bank,
INDIANAPOLIS, IND.
Banking business in all its branches. Bonds and Foreign Exchange bought and sold. Interest paid on time deposits. Checks and drafts on all Indiana and Illinois points handled at lowest rates.
No. 28 South Meridian Street, Cor. Pearl.

Culver Raymond E, dentist, 262 E South, b 244 Central av.
Culver Thomas M, phys, 379 S Meridian, b St Charles Hotel.
Culver Wm F, lab, b 741 N Senate av.
Cumback James M, printer, h 357 Jefferson av.
Cumback Oliver T, engraver H C Chandler, h 458 Highland av.
Cumback Will jr, sec H T Conde Implement Co, h 446 N Alabama.
Cumberworth Wilbur W, clk L E & W R R, b 280 E New York.
Cummings Albert L, cashr, h 341 Bellefontaine.
Cummings Anna (wid James), h 800 N New Jersey.
Cummings Charles, lab, h 46 Rockwood.
Cummings Charles A, foreman, h 1035 E Michigan.
Cummings Charles A, painter, h 230 Coburn.
Cummings Charles F, baker, h 328 E Michigan.
Cummings Cornelius, foreman, b 39 N Alabama.
Cummings Dora T, laundress, b 312 Coburn.
Cummings Edwin B, h 10 N Gillard av.
Cummings George, driver, h 204 E McCarty.
Cummings Harry F, finisher, b 201 E Washington.
Cummings Harvey, carp, r 103 S New Jersey.
Cummings Henry, molder, h rear 221 S West.
Cummings Hugh, teacher, b 133 Clinton.
Cummings James, h 12½ Indiana av.
Cummings James M, carp, h 1152 E Washington.
Cummings James R, paperhanger, b 800 N New Jersey.
Cummings Jean, clk Deaf and Dumb Inst.
Cummings John, carp, h 115 W 10th.
Cummings John, fireman, b 22 S State av.
Cummings John F, plumber, h 201 E Washington.
Cummings Pierce, printer, r 19 Miller blk.
Cummings Lincoln A, lab, b 174 Martindale av.

Insure Against Accidents
WITH
TUTTLE & SEGUIN,
Agents for
Fidelity and Casualty Co., of New York.
$10,000 for $25. $5,000 for $12.50.
TEL. 1168. 28 E. MARKET ST.

Cummings Losey C, painter, h 341 Bellefontaine.
Cummings Margaret (wid Thomas), h 39 Walcott.
Cummings Marshall F, turner, 87 E South, h 12 Carlos (W I).
CUMMINGS MATTHEW M, Flour, Feed and Groceries, 62 N Delaware, Tel 703; h 320 Park av.
Cummings Nancy J (wid Joseph M), h 174 Martindale av.
Cummings Patrick, boilermkr, h 109 Martindale av.
Cummings Richard, furniture, 25 Madison av, h 800 N New Jersey.
Cummings Sarah C, h 115 N Illinois.
Cummings Sarah J, stenog, b 39 Walcott.
Cummings Thomas A, brakeman, b 1152 E Washington.
Cummings Wm, foreman, r 31 E McCarty.
Cummins Claude J, lab, b 439 N Pine.
Cummins George W, clk, h 322 E New York.
Cummins Milton, carp, h 25 Jefferson av.
Cummins Patrick, lab, b 635 W Vermont.
Cunliffe Joseph T, foreman, r 433 W New York.
Cunning James, genl supt Kingan & Co (ltd), b 228 E North.
Cunningham Adam A, lab, h 571 W Shoemaker (N I).
Cunningham Adelaide E (wid James S), b 146 N Dorman.
Cunningham Charles E, mach, b 341 Ash.
Cunningham Charles M, teacher, h 505 Ash.
Cunningham Christopher, b 75 Centennial.
Cunningham Cornelius W, insp, h 623 N Meridian.
Cunnigham Foster, mer police, h cor New Jersey and 22d.
Cunningham Francis M, lab, h 168 Martindale av.
Cunningham George W, condr, h 57 W 14th.
Cunningham George W, mach hd, h 74 Thalman av.
Cunningham Harry S, paperhngr, h 23 Harvey.
Cunningham Helen (wid Wm), b 71 W 2d.
CUNNINGHAM HENRY S, Physician, Office Hours 10-11 A M, 2-3 and 7-8 P M, 85½ W Market, Tel 960; Res 392 Bellefontaine, Tel 1319.
Cunningham Jacob C, driver, h 5 Fay (W I).
Cunningham James F, clk W U Tel Co, b 105 N Dorman.
Cunningham James H, bricklyr, b 69 Malott av.
Cunningham John, h 44 Jefferson av.
Cunningham John, hostler, b 40 Elizabeth.
Cunningham John D, lab, h 105 N Dorman.
Cunningham John J, bartndr, b 105 N Dorman.
Cunningham Jonathan, lab, b 5 Bates al.
Cunningham Joseph J, paperhngr, h 624 W Eugene (N I).
Cunningham Joseph W, lab, h 69 Malott av.
Cunningham Louisa, h 25 Virginia av.
Cunningham Margaret A (wid Francis M), h 68½ Indiana av.
Cunningham Mary J (wid John), h 206 S William (W I).
Cunningham Michael, lab, b 29 Blake.
Cunningham Oliver H, molder, h 217 S McLain (W I).
Cunningham Robert, watchman, r 735 N Senate av.

WEDDING CAKE BOXES • SULLIVAN & MAHAN 41 W. Pearl St.

DIAMOND WALL PLASTER { Telephone 1410 BUILDERS' EXCHANGE.

Best Work. Prompt Delivery. } THE HOME LAUNDRY 197 S. ILLINOIS ST. TEL. 1769. } Collars and Cuffs a Specialty.

Cunningham Robert L, printer, h 448 N West.
Cunningham Sarah (wid Thomas), h 29 Cincinnati.
Cunningham Scobey, salesman Pearson's Music House, h 517 Broadway.
Cunningham Tevis O, lab, b 168 Martindale av.
Cunningham Thomas, finisher, h 265½ Mass av.
Cunningham Thomas, lab, h 253 N Noble.
Cunningham Thomas H, brakeman, h 321 W Market.
Cunningham Wallace E, lab, b 69 Malott av.
Cunningham Wm, driver, b 304 S Meridian.
Cunningham Wm F, condr, h 341 Ash.
Cunningham Wm G, molder, h 219 S McLain (W I).
Cunningham Wm H, lab, h 486 W Ontario (N I).
Cunningham Wm H, mach hd, h 620 W Francis (N I).
Cunningham Wm I, mngr Huldah A Stout, r 236 E Market.
Cunningham Wm M, boilermkr, b 105 N Dorman.
Cupp Walter J, clk, b 446 W Francis (N I).
Curch Ernest, lab, b 149 Wisconsin.
Curd James E, brakeman, h 88 Lee (W I).
Curfiss Mabel I, bkkpr Charles Willig, b 195 N Alabama.
Curley Edward, lab, h 10 McGinnis.
Curley Hugh S, b 231 E New York.
Curley James J, engraver, h 128 Cornell av.
Curley Martin, flagman, h 231 E New York.
Curley Mary (wid John R), h 57 Stevens.
Curley Richard, printer, b 102 S Linden.
Curley Wm, mailing clk P O, b 57 Stevens.
Curnell Charles, engr, h 14 W Sutherland (B).
Curran, see also Kern and Kerns.
Curran Barbara (wid Richard), h 163 English av.
Curran Bridget (wid Michael), h 278 Bates.
Curran Bridget, housekpr 251 Broadway.
Curran Daniel Rev, rector St Bridget's Catholic Church, h n e cor West and St Clair.
Curran Daniel F, driver, h rear 431 N Pine.
Curran David J, chief clk local freight office C H & D R R, b 62 Huron.
Curran Dennis, driver, h rear 431 N Pine.
Curran Dennis, shoemkr, h 215 Dillon.
Curran Elizabeth, bkkpr, b 163 English av.
Curran Elizabeth, teacher Public School No 25, b 62 Huron.
Curran Eugene D, agt, h 87 Bradshaw.
Curran Henry P, driver, h n w cor Ohio and Linwood av.
Curran Johanna (wid John), h 166 English av.
Curran Johanna F (wid John), h 19 Oxford.
Curran John, lab, h 15 Deloss.
Curran John, lab, b 215 Dillon.
Curran John, plumber, b 278 Bates.
Curran John D, driver, h s w cor Euclid av and Ohio.
Curran Matthew F, lab, h w s Colorado av 1 n of Ohio.
Curran Michael, flagman, h 194 Bates.
Curran Michael, hostler, r 18 S East.
Curran Michael J, boilermkr, b 166 English av.
Curran Michael T, lab, h 153 N Dorman.
Curran Michael T, mach hd, b 19 Oxford.
Curran Patrick, lab, h 259 English av.
Curran Patrick, lab, b 359 S Illinois.
Curran Patrick J, lab, h 154 N Dorman.

FRANK NESSLER. WILL H. ROST.
FRANK NESSLER & CO.
Tailors
56 EAST MARKET ST. (Lemcke Building),
INDIANAPOLIS, IND.

Curran Patrick J, patrolman, h 19 Oxford.
Curran Thomas, lab, b 327 Bates.
Curran Thomas, lab, r 275 W Market.
Curran Thomas, lab, b 300 W Maryland.
Curran Timothy, b 166 English av.
Curran Timothy, carp, b 281 W Pearl.
Curran Wm J, clk, b 163 English av.
Currens George E, driver, h 345 S New Jersey.
Currens Hamilton K, clk H P Wasson & Co, b 58 Barth av.
Currens Harry C, salesman Pearson's Music House, h 1281 N Meridian.
Currens James, b 558 Union.
Currens Wm N, custodian Majestic bldg, office 216 same, h 328 S East.
Currens Wm P, tailor, b 328 S East.
Currie May D, nurse, 285 Virginia av, b same.
Currie Robert I, mach, h 23 Lawn (B).
Currier Frank, fireman, b 882 W Washington.
Curry Dora (wid David), h 72 E Ohio.
Curry Dorcas (wid Hamilton), b 83 Howard.
Curry Emma (wid John), h 406 Clinton.
Curry George W, restaurant, 234 Indiana av, h same.
Curry James P, engr, h 298 Blake.
Curry James W, cooper, h 220 Bright.
Curry Jane (wid Peter), h 478 Lincoln av.
Curry Jesse B, plumber, b 173 N Pine.
Curry John, lab, h 7 Mill.
Curry John S, engr, b 189 W Maryland.
Curry John S, patternmkr, h 28 St Peter.
Curry Mary E (wid Joseph P), b 56 Highland pl.
Curry Patrick J, lab, h 38 Springfield.
Curry Peter, polisher, b 283 E Georgia.
Curry Rachel, r 37½ W Market.
Curry Robert, lab, h rear 39 Center.
Curry Sarah A, stenog A Kiefer Drug Co, b 56 Highland pl.
Curry Solomon L, gasfitter, 173 N Pine, h same.
Curry Wm, weaver, b 406 Clinton.
Curry Wm, clk, h 78 W McCarty.
Curry Wm G, engr, h 210 Douglass.
Curry Wm H, polisher, b 210 Douglass.
Curry Wm M, lab, h 104 Hadley av (W I).

Haueisen & Hartmann
163-169 E. Washington St.
FURNITURE,
Carpets,
Household Goods,
Tin, Granite and China Wares, Oil Cloth and Shades

THE WM. H. BLOCK CO. 7 AND 9 EAST WASHINGTON STREET. DRY GOODS, HOUSE FURNISHINGS AND CROCKERY.

London Guarantee and Accident Co. (Ltd.) All forms of Liability Insurance, Workmen's Collective Insurance, Fidelity Bonds and Individual Accident Insurance.
Geo. W. Pangborn, Gen. Agent, 704-706 Lemcke Bldg. Telephone 140.

Prussian National Insurance Company OF STETTIN, GERMANY. ORGANIZED 1845. FRANK K. SAWYER, AGENT 74 East Market Street. Telephone 863.

JOSEPH GARDNER,
TIN, COPPER AND SHEET-IRON WORK AND HOT AIR FURNACES.
37, 39 & 41 KENTUCKY AVE. Telephone 322.

Curry Wm N, porter, r 212 W St Clair.
Curryer Wm F, phys, 40 E Ohio, h 286 College av.
Curryer Louis H, loans, b 286 College av.
Cursey Simon, barber, h 40 Mill.
Curshon James, helper, b 102 Harrison.
Curson Edward, lab, h 122½ Ft Wayne av.
Curson George W, candymkr, h 442 S Delaware.
Curson Harry, lab, h 124½ Ft Wayne av.
Curson John F, gas insp, h 43 N Brightwood av (B).
C son Letitia (wid Josiah), b 43 N Brightwood av (B).
Curson Wm A, painter, h 336 Spring.
Curson Wm J, painter, b 43 N Brightwood (B).
Curtin Christopher, b 217 S Illinois.
Curtin David, sec Monarch Supply Co, h 271 N New Jersey.
Curtis Alfred, wagonmkr, h 58 Clifford av.
Curtis Cassius P, painter, h 229 Alvord.
Curtis Caswell B, mnfrs' agt, 114 Commercial Club bldg, b 92 W Ohio.
Curtis Charles W, carp, 191 N New Jersey, h same.
Curtis Edward D Rev, supt Home Missions, Congregational Church of Indiana, h 452 N Delaware.
Curtis Frank M, bkkpr, h 376 Ash.
Curtis Hamilton C (Smith, Curtis & Co), h 135 Ludlow av.
Curtis Harry, mach hd, r 191 W Market.
Curtis Harry S E, barber, 290 Mass av, h 479 Stillwell.
Curtis Harry W, clk, r cor Illinois and 30th.
Curtis Henry, foreman, h 448 E Georgia.
Curtis Hiram K, h 53 Ash.
Curtis Ira A, mach, b 596 N West.
Curtis James B (Morris, Newberger & Curtis), city attorney, h 616 N Penn.
Curtis John E, phys, 1056 W Washington, h same.
Curtis John J, supt The Bowen-Merrill Co, b 53 Ash.
Curtis John W, painter, h 665 Madison av.
Curtis Joseph, porter, h 12 Howard.
Curtis Joseph, clk, b 426 S Illinois.
Curtis Mary (wid Andrew), b 144 St Mary.
Curtis Nellie, dressmkr, 36 Fayette, b same.

J. S. FARRELL & CO.
STEAM AND HOT WATER HEATING FOR STORES, OFFICES, PUBLIC BUILDINGS, PRIVATE RESIDENCES, GREENHOUSES, ETC.
84 North Illinois St. Telephone 382.

Curtis Ruth B (wid Thomas), h 665 Madison av.
Curtis Wm, coachman, r 263½ N New Jersey.
Curtiss John M, b Ross House.
Cusack John T, crockery, 103 S Illinois, h Washington av (I).
Cushing Edward L, collr, b 85 Hoyt av.
Cushing Emma (wid Charles), r 469 Virginia av.
Cushing Isabelle, dressmkr, 85 Hoyt av, h same.
Cushing James, lab, h 102 Harrison.
Cushing John R, agt, h 85 Hoyt av.
Cushing Oliver E, paperhngr, b 85 Hoyt av.
Cushingberry James, driver, h 229 Columbia av.
Cushion Car Wheel Co The, office 143½ S Meridian.
Cushionberry Tobias, lab, h 77 Clarke.
Cushman George C, waiter, h 10 Gatling.
Custer, see also Koester and Kuster.
Custer Carl C, timekpr, b 308 N Illinois.
Custer George D, trav agt McCormick H M Co, h Ritter av (I).
Custer George S, molder, h 251 S Senate av.
Custer Grace, stenog Indpls Water Co, b 33 W Vermont.
Custer John W, h Jackson (M J).
Cuthrell Albert, lab, b 87 Rhode Island.
Cuthrell John, tmstr, h 48 Locke.
Cuthrell Malinda (wid Thomas), h 87 Rhode Island.
Cuthrell Thomas, lab, b 87 Rhode Island.
Cutshall Peter, h 14 Lynn.
Cutshall Robert, carp, h 11 Lynn.
Cutshall Wm A, printer Indpls Journal, h 99 Keystone av.
Cutshaw Almira (wid Joseph F), b 74 W 10th.
Cutsinger Wm E, b 443 N New Jersey.
Cutter Florence E, h 640 N Illinois.
Cutter Frank C, lawyer, 1 Fletcher's Bank bldg, h 640 N Illinois.
Cutter Frederick P, h 640 N Illinois.
Cutting John A J, b 894 N Illinois.
Cutts John H, restaurant, 1412 Lulu (N I), h 552 W Addison (N I).
Cutts Silas M, lab, h 440 W Udell (N I).
Cutts Walter L, clk, b 552 W Addison (N I).
Cutworth Wm, lab, h 218 Douglass.
Cuykendall Frank F, lab, b 53 Bates.
Cuykendall Harry L, b 53 Bates.
Cuykendall John, hostler, b 53 Bates.
Cuykendall Warren A, engr, b 304 E Georgia.
Cuyler Frederick M, clk Thomas C Day & Co, h 399 N Capitol av.
CYCLER PRINTING CO, A E Winters Mngr, Publishers The Zig-Zag Cycler 33 Talbott Blk. (See adv opp classified Newspapers.)
Cyphers James F, carp, h 6 Morgan (W I).
Cyphers Wm, lab, h 8 Drake.
Czinczoll Charles, lab, h 19 Singleton.

D

Daa Wm, lab, b 200 S Meridian.
Daab George W, carp, h 148 Sheffield av (H).
Dacon Henry C, packer, b 3 Hiawatha.
Dacy James, lab, b 31 Maple.
Dacy John P, lab, b 31 Maple.
Dacy Patrick, h 31 Maple.
Dade John L, barber, h 3 Susquehanna.
Dade Millie (wid Townsend), h 472 W Chicago (N I).
Dagey Herman, mach hd, h 51 Mayhew.

United States Life Insurance Co., of New York.
E. B. SWIFT, M'g'r. 25 E. Market St.

WM. KOTTEMAN } 89 & 91 E. Washington St. Telephone 1742 { RUGS MATTINGS WINDOW SHADES

WILLIAM WIEGEL } MANUFA OF.... } SHOW CASES } 6 W. Louisiana St. Opposite Union Station.

Daggett Robert F, architect, b 293 W Vermont.
Daggett Robert P (R P Daggett & Co), h 293 W Vermont.
DAGGETT R P & CO (Robert P Daggett, James B Lizius), Architects, 28-32 Marion Blk, Tel 619. (See adv in classified Architects.)
Daggett Wm, pres Daggett & Co, h 280 N New Jersey.
Daggett Wm H, clk Daggett & Co, h 136 W Merrill.
DAGGETT & CO, Wm Daggett Pres, John F Messick Vice-Pres, James H Wilson Sec and Treas, Wholesale Confectioners, 18-20 W Maryland, Tel 367.
Daggy Edward W, clk, r 28 W Vermont.
Daggy George H, clk I D & W Ry, r 455 N Capitol av.
Daggy James A, clk, h 83 Birch av (W I).
Daggy Wm, nurse, b Enterprise Hotel.
Dagley Carrie, h 468 N New Jersey.
Daglish Annie (Daglish & Brownlee), b 179 Ash.
Daglish Frank J, clk, h 278 Mass av.
Daglish John, buyer, h 179 Ash.
Daglish John, lab, h 63 Minerva.
Daglish & Brownlee (Annie Daglish, Ray Brownlee), milliners, 240 Indiana av.
Dagner, see Degner.
Dague Cyrus A, driver, h 224½ W Washington.
Dahinten George, lab, h 453 S Missouri.
Dahl, see also Dale.
Dahl Catherine (wid Andrew P), h 131 E McCarty.
Dahl Charles F, baggageman, h 384 S Delaware.
Dahl Peter M, mach, h 28 Cooper.
Dahlmann Charles C, clk Clemens Vonnegut, h 637 Marlowe av.
Dahrenstaedt Ernest, watchman The Bates.
Dailey, see also Daley and Daly.
Dailey Cora, h 159½ W Washington.
Dailey Benjamin F Rev, h e s Ritter av 3 n of Washington av (I).
Dailey Harry C, grocer, 56 Kentucky av, h 36 S Capitol av.
Dailey Hezekiah, lawyer, 95 E Washington, h 36 Central av.
Dailey James T, plumber, b 382 Indiana av.
Dailey Matilda A (wid James J), h s s University av 3 w of Grand av (I).
Dailey May E, h 79 E Michigan.
Dailey Wm C, bartndr, b 359 Virginia av.
DAILY AMERICUS C, Auditor State of Indiana, 38 State House, h 830 N Meridian.
Daily Earl C, student, b 830 N Meridian.
Daily Edward A (Daily & Pfeffer), h 33 Clark.
Daily Harry M, clk Holliday & Wyon, b 1024 N Meridian.
Daily Irvin J, trav agt, h 513 Broadway.
Daily James M, lab, b 6 Coe.
Daily John H, helper, h 77 Harmon.
Daily Mary J (wid Joseph H), h 6 Coe.
Daily Reporter The, Reporter Publishing Co pubs, 519 Indiana Trust bldg.
Daily Thomas A, student, r 88 Lombard bldg.
Daily & Pfeffer (Edward A Daily, Edward C Pfeffer), painters, 66 W Market.
Dain Edward T, gasfitter, b Thomas N Dain.

THOS. C. DAY & CO.
Financial Agents and Loans.
We have the experience, and claim to be reliable.
Rooms 325 to 330 Lemcke Bldg.

Dain Thomas N, gasfitter, h s e cor Post av and Richard (M P).
Dair Frank, lab, h 189 Hillisde av.
Dalato Philip, huckster, h 278 S Delaware.
Dalbey Edward R, cigarmkr, h 24 Grace.
Dalbey Russell J, cigarmkr, h rear 425 Madison av.
Dale, see also Dahl.
Dale Annie, h 67 Fayette.
Dale Burnham C, phys, b 524 Broadway.
Dale Charles A, real est, 18½ N Penn, h 865 N Meridian.
Dale George, barber, b 41 N Capitol av.
Dale Elizabeth M (wid David D), h 140 Bellefontaine.
Dale Oliver S, h 524 Broadway.
Dale Salathiel B, barber, 554 W Udell and 216 E Washington, b 595 W Eugene (N I).
Dale Zerelda E (wid James I N), b 1111 N Senate av.
Daley, see also Dailey and Daly.
Daley Daniel T, lab, h 44 Grant.
Daley James E, condr, h 49 Warman av (H).
Daley Jane, h s s 8th 4 w of canal.
Daley John, paperhngr, b 406½ W Washington.
Daley Kate (wid Ernest), h 406½ W Washington.
Dallas Belle, clk, r 146 N Illinois.
Dallas James A, mach opr The Indpls News, h 71 Pleasant.
Daller Albert, chief clk Indiana Car Service Assn, h 138 N Senate av.
Dalrymple John M (Indpls Harness Co), h 183 Park av.
Dalrymple Joseph A, foreman Indpls Harness Co, h w s Commercial av 5 s of Washington av (I).
Dalrymple Virgil S, student, b w s Commercial av 5 s of Washington av (I).
Dalton Christopher, stonecutter, h 774 N Senate av.
Dalton Edward J, clk, b 774 N Senate av.
Dalton Edward J, engr, h 29 Eastern av.
Dalton Hannah V, cashr Dalton Hat Co, b 218 Buchanan.
DALTON HAT CO, John C Dalton Mngr, Bates House, 64 W Washington.

EAT
QUAKER BREAD
ASK YOUR GROCER FOR IT.
THE HITZ BAKING CO.

CARPETS AND RUGS RENOVATED........ | CAPITAL STEAM CARPET CLEANING WORKS M. D. PLUNKETT, TELEPHONE No. 818

BENJ. BOOTH PRACTICAL EXPERT ACCOUNTANT. Complicated or disputed accounts investigated and adjusted. Room 18, 82½ E. Wash. St., Ind'p'l's, Ind.

18 and 20 South Meridian Street KERSHNER BROS., Proprs. THE SHERMAN RESTAURANT

ESTABLISHED 1876. TELEPHONE 168.
CHESTER BRADFORD,
SOLICITOR OF PATENTS,
AND COUNSEL IN PATENT CAUSES.
(See adv. page 6.)
Office:—Rooms 14 and 16 Hubbard Block, S.W. Cor. Washington and Meridian Streets,
INDIANAPOLIS, INDIANA.

Dalton James F, lab, b 373 S Missouri.
Dalton James P, lab, b 413 S Missouri.
Dalton Jesse H, turner, h 169 Fayette.
Dalton John, lab, b 187 S Capitol av.
Dalton John C, mngr Dalton Hat Co, h 913 N Capitol av.
Dalton John F, lab, h 373 S Missouri.
Dalton Knowlton, lab, h rear 15 Cornell av.
Dalton Mary C (wid Michael), h 413 S Missouri.
Dalton Maurice, brakeman, b 218 Buchanan.
Dalton Maurice, engr, h 135 N Arsenal av.
Dalton Nathan F (Dalton & Merrifield), h 40 The Blacherne.
Dalton Noah, lab, b 170 Yandes.
Dalton Thomas, h 218 Buchanan.
Dalton Thomas, baggageman, r 362 S Illinois.
Dalton Thomas J, cigar mnfr, 659 N Senate av, b 774 same.
Dalton Thomas S, lab, b 413 S Missouri.
Dalton Wm D, clk, b 218 Buchanan.
Dalton Wm J, lab, b 373 S Missouri.
DALTON & MERRIFIELD (Nathan F Dalton, Charles E Merrifield), Lumber, Sash, Doors and Blinds, 30-50 S Noble, near E Washington, Tel 952. (See left top lines.)
Daly, see also Dailey and Daley.
DALY CHARLES F, Genl Pass and Ticket Agt L E & W R R, s w cor Washington and Noble, Tel 1472; h 857 N Illinois, Tel 1821.
Daly C is op e C, watchman, h 163 W South.hr t h r
Dal Daniel A, butcher, h 64 River av (W I).
Daly Frank, molder, r 19 S West.
Daly George W, molder, b 19 S West.
Daly Peter, janitor, r 5½ Indiana av.
Daly Wm C (Daly & Raub), h 124 E 14th.
DALY & RAUB (Wm C Daly, Edward B Raub), Attorneys at Law, Rooms 11, 12 and 13 Aetna Bldg, 19½ N Penn, Tel 1911.
Dalzell Armilda (wid Abraham W), h 20 Warman av (H).

Matal Ceilings and all kinds of Copper, Tin and Sheet Iron work.
O. B. ENSEY,
TELEPHONE 1562.
CORNER 6TH AND ILLINOIS STS.

Dalzell Fred C, molder, b 20 Warman av (H).
Dalzell Samuel, b Grand Hotel.
Dambacher Anton, car rep, b 745 E Ohio.
Dambacher Barbara (wid John), h 745 E Ohio.
Dambacher John T, car rep, b 745 E Ohio.
Dame Daisy, music teacher, 374 E 7th, b same.
Dame Eliza, baker, 374 E 7th, h same.
Dame Frank A, broommkr, h 263 Howard.
Dame Frederick B, bartndr, r 175 S Illinois.
Dame Jason, solr, h 374 E 7th.
Dame Mary A, bkkpr, b 307 N Alabama.
Damewood Wm, mach, b 118 W Vermont.
Damme Hermine (wid Frank E), h 67 Beaty.
Dammel Mary, stenog, b 75 Downey.
Dammel Michael W, contr, 75 Downey, h same.
Dammeyer Bros (Charles G, Henry G and Theodore H), grocers, 247 E Washington.
Dammeyer Charles, h 124 N East.
Dammeyer Charles G (Dammeyer Bros), h 464 E Market.
Dammeyer Edward H, clk, b 667 E Washington.
Dammeyer Henry G (Dammeyer Bros), h 527 E Ohio.
Dammeyer Louisa M (wid Anton G), h 667 E Washington.
Dammeyer Theodore H (Dammeyer Bros), b 124 N East.
Dammeyer Wm E, clk George R Popp, b 124 N East.
Damon Anna C (wid Charles L), r 316½ Virginia av.
Dampier Wm, lab, b e s Auburn av 1 s of Prospect.
Danacker Charles A, engr, h 260 Charles.
Danahey Florance, bartndr, h 23 Johnson av.
Donahue John A, steward, r 26, 113 S Illinois.
Danbury Hat Co, Peter F Balz mngr, 8 E Washington.
Dande Frederick, lab, h 25 Thomas.
Danely Nancy E (wid Leander), b 1614 N Illinois.
Danewood Albert, brakeman, r 39 N State av.
Danforth Ozias J, h 89 Indiana av.
Dangdahl Charles, mach, h 504 S West.
Dangler Christopher F, clk Indiana Rubber Co, h 468 E Market.
Daniel Adam, lab, h 50 Kappus (W I).
Daniel Charles A, carp, b 50 Kappus (W I).
Daniel Frank E, driver, h 25 Sinker.
Daniel Frank N, bkkpr, b 230 E McCarty.
Daniel Wm, lab, h 230 E McCarty.
Daniels Anna E, phys, 55 N State av, h same.
Daniels Cornelius, driver, b 16 Darnell.
Daniels Edward (Baker & Daniels), h 883 N Penn.
Daniels Elijah, cook, h 484 N East.
Daniels George, student, b 395 N West.
Daniels George B, bartndr, r 395 N Senate av.
Daniels George T, mach, h 55 N State av.
Daniels Henry, lab, h 520 N West.
Daniels Henry L, carp, h 46 Eureka av.
Daniels Isabella N, cashr, b 452 N New Jersey.
Daniels James, bartndr, r 161½ Mass av.
Daniels James, lab, h rear 329 E Michigan.
Daniels James T, ins, b 245 N Delaware.
Daniels John, b 395 N Senate av.
Daniels John, lab, h 16 Darnell.

TUTEWILER UNDERTAKER, No. 72 WEST MARKET STREET. TELEPHONE 216.

The Provident Life and Trust Co. Dividends are paid in cash and are not withheld for a long period of years, subject to forfeiture in the event of death or the termination of policy.
D. W. EDWARDS, GENERAL AGENT, 508 INDIANA TRUST BUILDING.

THEODORE F. SMITHER ~

Daniels Leopold, r 29½ N Penn.
Daniels Mary M (wid Samuel P), h 181 Fletcher av.
Daniels Matilda, h 415 S West.
Daniels Mattie, clk Order of Chosen Friends, r 309 The Shiel.
Daniels Milton H, lawyer, 110 English av, h same.
Daniels Oscar, car rep, h 152 Trowbridge (W).
Daniels Phoebe J, dressmkr, 152 E 7th, b 890 N Alabama.
Daniels Rolla E, clk, h 472½ Virginia av.
Daniels Thomas, lab, h 70½ W Maryland.
Daniels Walton H, clk Wm B Burford, h 24 The Chalfant.
Daniels Wm E, insp City Engineer, h 395 N Senate av.
Danielson August, helper, b 152 Trowbridge (W).
Danihy Peter, lab, h 63 Spann av.
Danihy Peter J, tel opr, b 63 Spann av.
Danke Albert, saloon, 250 S Meridian, h same.
Danke August, bartndr, h 26 Weghorst.
Dannan Thomas F, clk R M S, r 119 S Illinois.
Dannar Frederick, lab, h 313 S Reisner (W I).
Dannar Thomas P, butcher, h 213 S Reisner (W I).
Dannecker Wm L, cabtmkr, h 524 S Capitol av.
Danner Andrew F, clk, b 129 N Dorman.
Danner Charles F, horseshoer, 860 S Meridian, h S Meridian 1½ miles s of Belt R R.
Danner Edward, h 1206 N Illinois.
Danner James H (Danner & Lund), h 54 Tremont av (H).
Danner James M, trav agt, b 14 Wisconsin.
Danner John D, horseshoer, h 33 Clay.
Danner & Lund (James H Danner, Asher W Lund), horseshoers, 68 W 7th.
Dannie Catherine A (wid Joseph M), grocer, 207 Davidson, h same.
Dannie Joseph, baker, h 207 Davidson.
Danninburg James W, lab, h 76 E Morris.
Dansky John, lab, b 213 S Alabama.
Dansky John, r 19 Franklin Life Ins bldg.
Dantzer Albert G, bartndr, b California House.
Dantzer Charles V, h 112 Highland pl.
Dantzer Henry, uphlr, b 112 Highland pl.
Dantzer Louis J, mach, b 288 S East.
Dantzer Mary P, dressmkr, 270 Douglass, b same.
Danz Catherine E (wid Casper), h 17 Edward (W I).
Danz Frederick W, millwright, b 109 Cherry.
Danz John M, bookbndr, b 17 Edward (W I).
Danz George W F, plumber, 17 Edward (W I), b same.
Danziger George E, tailor, h 270 E Court.
Darby Andrew B, tmstr, h 72 N Beville av.
Darby Laura C, stenog Penna Lines, b 156 N Illinois.
Darby Wm, letter carrier P O, h 161 Spann av.
Darby Wm H, lab, h 1045 E Michigan.
Darby Wm T, clk The Wm H Block Co, r 181 N Delaware.
Darcy John, lab, h 30 Dougherty.
Darcy Peter J, lab, h 41 Buchanan.
Dare Zoa, h 497 S Illinois.
Dargar Michael, lab, b 99 Lexington av.
Dargitz Charles S, clk R M S, h 1450 N Illinois.

THE WHEN IS A WORLD BEATER.

Dargitz Dorretta, b 1450 N Illinois.
Daringer Nancy J (wid David), h 569 Union.
Dark Charles E (Boice & Dark), sec Commonwealth L and S Assn of Indiana, h 567 N Illinois.
Dark Edward H, student, b 567 N Illinois.
Dark Ira, carp, b 58 Michigan (H).
Dark Jesse, lab, b 31 Garden.
Dark Rosa E, teacher Public School No 9, b 299 Bellefontaine.
DARK STEPHEN C, Architect, 31-32 Cordova Bldg, 25½ W Washington, h 429 N Capitol av, Tel 753. (See adv in classified Architects.)
Dark Wilbur W, clk, b 567 N Illinois.
Dark Wm, carp, b 29 Nebraska.
Dark Wm C, carp, h 58 Michigan (H).
Dark Wm R, mach hd, h 31 Garden.
Darling Arthur H, checkman, h 163 Johnson av.
Darling Charles, barber, 13 Mass av, b 312 N New Jersey.
Darling Henry H, pressfeeder, r 326 E South.
Darling Ilas, lab, h 430 W Udell (N I).
Darling James, tilemkr, h 270 W 7th.
Darling Lorinda, b 625 N West.
DARLINGTON FRANK G, Supt Indianapolis Division P C C & St L Ry, Union Station, Tel 99; h 676 N Delaware, Tel 72.
Darmer Lydia L, h 34 N McLain (W I).
Darmody John, lab, b 107 W South.
Darmody John F, sec The Darmody-Morrison Co, b 31 Sinker.
Darmody Joseph M, tailor, b 31 Sinker.
Darmody-Morrison Co The, Frank Morrison pres, John F Darmody sec and treas, confrs, 84 S Penn.
Darmody Richard J, tailor, h 141 Lynn av (W I).
Darmody Thomas, h 31 Sinker.
Darmody Thomas F, trav agt, h 230 Ramsey av.
Darmody Wm, helper, b 860 E Washington.
Darmody Wm P, clk, r 565 Jefferson av.
Darnaby Robert E, printer, h 80 N Noble.

The A. Burdsal Co.
Manufacturers of
STEAMBOAT COLORS
BEST HOUSE PAINTS MADE.
Wholesale and Retail.
34 AND 36 SOUTH MERIDIAN STREET.

C. ROOFING CO.
2 and 3-Ply Ready Roofing, Paper, etc. Best of Materials.
Telephone 86. Office, 15 W Maryland St.

Electric Contractors
We are prepared to do any kind of Electric Contract Work.
C. W. MEIKEL. Telephone 466.
96-98 E. New York St.

DALTON & MERRIFIELD { LUMBER South Noble St., near E. Washington

INDIANA ELECTROTYPE CO. : BEST WORK. LOWEST PRICES.
23 WEST PEARL ST., INDIANAPOLIS, IND. JOB WORK. BOOK PLATES. All Orders Promptly Filled. BEST PATENT BASE ON THE MARKET.

KIRKHOFF BROS.,
Sanitary Plumbers
STEAM AND HOT WATER HEATING.
102-104 SOUTH PENNSYLVANIA ST.
TELEPHONE 910.

Darnall James P, condr, h 14 Belmont (H).
Darnall Jesse L, clk, b 159½ E Washington.
Darneal Robert, janitor, h 198 W 1st.
Darnell Alphine, clk, b 56 Ramsey av.
Darnell Calvin F, supt, h 738 N Illinois.
Darnell Charles, engr, h 14 W Sutherland (B).
Darnell Charles S, clk, h 56 Ramsey av.
Darnell Charles W, driver, h 51 S Belmont av (W I).
Darnell Frank A, student, b 14 W Sutherland (B).
Darnell Isom, lab, b 399 Lafayette.
Darnell Levi M, clk, h 84 S Judge Harding (W I).
Darnell Louis L, switchman, h 463 S East.
Darnell Sarah A, stenog, b 14 W Sutherland (B).
Darnell Walter S, mach, b 463 S East.
Darnell Zarelda (wid Wm W), h 463 S East.
Darrach Charles S, clk, r 101 N New Jersey.
Darrach Eugene H, mngr Commerce Despatch Line, h 1028 N New Jersey.
Darrach, Frank M, clk, r 101 N New Jersey.
Darragh Catherine (wid John), h 272 E Court.
Darragh Katherine, matron Indpls Orphan Asylum, n e cor College and Home avs.
Darrah Samuel F, dairy w s Colorado av 3 n of Ohio, h same.
Darrah Thomas, dairy w s Garfield av 2 n of Ohio, h same.
Darrah Walter H, drugs, 1099 E Washington, h same.
Darrell George, well driver, b 169 N East.
DARROW BEN L, Editor and Publisher Wheelmen's Gazette and Propr Wheelmen's Co, 31 W Ohio, h 80 Randolph, Tel 1855. (See right side lines.)
Darrow Edward R, sec for Receiver of Terre Haute and Indpls R R Co, b The Denison.
Darrow George G, gasfitter, b 193 N East.
Darrow Lillie, h 164½ W Washington.
Darrow Nelson E, baker, h 193 N East.
Darrow Travilla C (wid Benjamin C), b 80 Randolph.
Darter Charles E, lab, b 24½ S New Jersey.

Lime, Lath, Cement,
THE W. G. WASSON CO.
130 INDIANA AVE. TEL. 989.
Sewer Pipe, Flue Linings, Fire Brick, Fire Clay.

Darter James K P, postmaster and grocer, n w cor Illinois and 30th (M), h same.
Darter Robert L, clk, b James K P Darter.
Darter Sarah E (wid Amos R), h 24½ S New Jersey.
Daschler Veronica, nurse, 851½ S Meridian, h same.
Dasher Elwood M, h 245 N Illinois.
Dasher Grace L, h 245 N Illinois.
Dashiell Charles F, clk R M S, h 941 N Senate av.
Dashiell Masten, b 194 Bright.
Dashiell Myers T, bkkpr Indiana National Bank, b 82 E Vermont.
Dashiell Newton H, clk N Y Life Ins Co, b 82 E Vermont.
Datesman Frederick, clk Frank E Wolcott, r 372 W New York.
Daub Emma (wid Louis), r 177 Shelby.
Daubenspeck Nelson, mer police, h 25 W 1st.
Dauby Helen (wid David), milliner, h 5 Ft Wayne av.
Dauch David J, baker, 187 Elizabeth, h same.
Dauer Nellie L, b 156 Chestnut.
Dauffalder Louis, musician, h 97 Dearborn.
Daugherty, see also Doherty and Dougherty.
Daugherty Austin, mach, h 80 Barth av.
Daugherty Belle L, b 77 W 10th.
Daugherty Charles, engr, b 582 Virginia av.
Daugherty Christopher C, lab, b 167 John.
Daugherty Clifton L, news agt, h 222 Fletcher av.
Daugherty Elsie E, teacher, b 234 Fletcher av.
Daugherty James A, asst bkkpr Nordyke & Marmon Co, b 397 E 9th.
Daugherty James M, chairmkr, h 11 Quince.
Daugherty John H, phys and postmaster, w s Central av 3 s of Railroad (I), h n s University av 4 w of Central av (I).
Daugherty John H S, stairbldr, h 70 W 4th.
Daugherty Joseph F, h 77 W 10th.
Daugherty Joseph F jr, b 77 W 10th.
Daugherty Louis M, lab, h 1325 Isabella (N I).
Daugherty Louis W, trav agt Fahnley & McCrea, b 157 N State av.
Daugherty Lucy S (wid Wm W), h 58 Vine.
Daugherty Morton A, mngr Indiana Oil Tank Line, h 221 River av (W I).
Daugherty Samuel A, agt, b 234 Fletcher av.
Daugherty Solomon C, jeweler, h 1368 N Illinois.
Daugherty Sylvester, h 164 Pleasant.
Daugherty Theodosia (wid George), r 70 W 11th.
Daugherty Ulysses S, collr, b 234 Fletcher av.
Daugherty Wm, lab, h 82 Newman.
Daugherty Wm T, mach, h 397 E 9th.
Daum August, finisher, b 172 Blake.
Daupert Belle S, stenog The Hay & Willits Mnfg Co, b 1071 W Vermont.
Daupert George H, carp, h 62 Tremont av (H).
Dausch Wm F, butcher, h 208 Oliver av (W I).
Davar, see also Dever.
Davar David, janitor, b 27 King av (H).
Davee George W, bartndr, b 178 S Illinois.
Davenport Anna (wid Thomas), notions, 184 Virginia av, h same.
Davenport Catherine (wid Andrew), h 71 Foundry (B).

YOUR HOMES FURNISHED BY W. H. MESSENGER 101 East Washington St. Telephone 491.

McNamara, Koster & Co. Phone 1593. 212-218 S. PENN. ST. PATTERN MAKERS

Davenport Charles C, brakeman, h 18 Marion av (W I).
Davenport Clara (wid Henry), h 284 Fulton.
DAVENPORT FRANK B, Genl Mngr Mutual Life Insurance Co of Indiana, 727-728 Lemcke Bldg, h w s Ritter av 9 n of Washington av (I).
Davenport Frank J, uphlr, b 63 Dougherty.
Davenport Jerome B (Goodin & Davenport), h 22 Newman.
Davenport John, b w s Ritter av 9 n of Washington av (I).
Davenport John, cooper, h 28 N West.
Davenport John, plastr, b 63 Dougherty.
Davenport John F, lab, h w s Burgess av 3 s of C H & D R R (I).
Davenport Louisa E, housekpr 524 E Washington.
Davenport Martin, plastr, b 63 Dougherty.
Davenport Thomas, h 63 Dougherty.
Davenport Wm, farmer, b 74 S William (W I).
Davenport Wm, lab, b 284 Fulton.
Davey, see also Davy.
Davey Frank M, cutter Nicoll The Tailor, h 1439 N Illinois.
Davey Sidney, lab, h 644 W Washington.
David Alice K, teacher Public School No 6, b 816 N Alabama.
David Charles, lab, r 23 N West.
David Dorothy, teacher Public School No 7, b 816 N Alabama.
David George F, trainmaster, h 258 Christian av.
David Grace, clk, b 316 Ash.
David Guinetta E (wid Thomas S), h 816 N Alabama.
David Jacob, barber, h 132 N Capitol av.
David Joseph F, lab, h 63 Hosbrook.
David Lillian R, clk H T Conde Implement Co, b 816 N Alabama.
David Max A, bricklayer, h 12 Hendricks.
David Thomas H, b 816 N Alabama.
David Wm C, clk, h 126 E New York.
David Wm T, miller, h 15 Minerva.
Davids Herman, bricklayer, b 623 Madison av.
Davids Wm, bricklayer, h 623 Madison av.
Davidson, see also Davidson.
Davidson Alexander D (Howard & Davidson), b 441 E St Clair.
Davidson Allen, lab, b 228 W Wabash.
Davidson Cassandra (wid Jethro), h 421 N California.
Davidson Charles, peddler, h 89 S Belmont av (W I).
Davidson Charles E, clk L E & W R R, b 170 Hoyt av.
Davidson Charles L, lab, b 40 McIntyre.
Davidson Charles M, clk, b 441 E St Clair.
Davidson Daniel, painter, h 40 McIntyre.
Davidson Daniel M, lab, b e s Waverly av 2 s of Brookside av.
Davidson David, coachman 252 N Meridian.
Davidson Dorman N, real est, 15 Baldwin blk, h 424 Broadway.
Davidson Emeline (wid John), h 228 W Wabash.
DAVIDSON EMMA L (wid Albert J), State Librarian, Room 47 State House, h 417 N Capitol av.
Davidson Frank, lab, b e s Belmont 1 s of Johnson (W I).
Davidson Gaylon, farmer, h s s Johnson opp Reisner (W I).
Davidson George P, clk U S Lounge Mnfg Co, h 74 Hanna.

Henry H. Fay,
40½ E. WASHINGTON ST.,
FIRE INSURANCE, REAL ESTATE,
LOANS AND RENTAL AGENT.

Davidson Harry St J, clk N Y Store, b 1899 N Illinois.
Davidson Harvey C (Davidson & Nelson), b 875 Mass av.
Davidson Hazzard W, porter, b 421 N California.
Davidson Howard, janitor State Library, b 417 N Capitol av.
Davidson Isidor, bartndr, b 215 W New York.
Davidson Isom, peddler, r 228 W Wabash.
Davidson James, finisher, h 103 Nebraska.
Davidson James, plastr, h rear 16 Brett.
Davidson James H, mach hd, h rear 512 W Maryland.
Davidson James R, carp, h e s Waverly av 2 s of Brookside av.
Davidson James S, h 875 Mass av.
Davidson James S jr, lab, b 875 Mass av.
Davidson Jane (wid George H), b 186 Dougherty.
Davidson Jefferson T, lab, r 37½ Kentucky av.
Davidson Jefferson W, driver, b 490 W New York.
Davidson Jennie L, teacher Public School No 10, h 424 Broadway.
Davidson John, h 170 Davidson.
Davidson John, lab, r 228 W Wabash.
Davidson John W, h 316 Park av.
Davidson Lawson W, gas insp, h e s Illinois 1 s of 29th.
Davidson Leon T, barber, b 421 N California.
Davidson Lida J, h 176 Douglass.
Davidson Marion D, lab, h 1219 N Penn.
Davidson Mary, b 75 Drake.
Davidson Mary A (wid John T), h 441 E St Clair.
Davidson Minnie A (wid Daniel H), h 8 Lord.
Davidson Morris J, tailor, b 300 S Meridian.
Davidson Morton G W, carp, b 875 Mass av.
Davidson Noah N, h Highland av nr New York.
Davidson Oscar L, sign writer, h 130 W Pratt.
Davidson Richard, clk, h 177 Johnson (W I).

SURETY BONDS
American Bonding & Trust Co.
OF BALTIMORE, MD.
Authorized to act as Sole Surety on all Bonds.
Total Resources over $1,000,000.00.
W. E. BARTON & CO., General Agents,
504 INDIANA TRUST BUILDING.
Long Distance Telephone 1918.

THE FRED DIETZ CO.
WOODEN PACKING BOXES MADE TO ORDER.
FACTORY AND WAREHOUSE TRUCKS.
400 Madison Avenue. Telephone 654.

Business World Supplied with Help
GRADUATES ASSISTED TO POSITIONS
10,000 NOW IN GOOD SITUATIONS. TEL. 499. E. J. HEEB, PRES.
Indianapolis BUSINESS UNIVERSITY

HENRY R. WORTHINGTON JET and SURFACE CONDENSERS 64 S. PENN. ST. Long Distance Telephone 284.

UNION CO-OPERATIVE LAUNDRY (COMPOSED OF UNION LAUNDRY GIRLS.) NOS. 38, 40 AND 42 VIRGINIA AVENUE. INDIANAPOLIS, IND. TELEPHONES. T. E. SOMERVILLE, MANAGER

HORACE M. HADLEY
Insurance, Real Estate, Loan and Rental Agent
66 EAST MARKET STREET,
Telephone 1540. Basement.

Davidson Robert F, lawyer, 609 Lemcke bldg, b 316 Park av.
Davidson Robert H, h 61 Paca.
Davidson Thomas, condr, b 583 W Washington.
Davidson Thomas C, ins, h 137 Tacoma av.
DAVIDSON THOMAS H, Dentist, 9-10 Marion Blk, h 131 Highland Pl.
Davidson Wayne, barber, b 421 N California.
Davidson Wesley, farmer, h e s Belmont 1 s of Johnson (W I).
Davidson Wm, brickmkr, b 40 McIntyre.
Davidson Wm, lab, h 325 W Maryland.
Davidson Wm A, cabtmkr, h 170 Hoyt av.
Davidson Wm A, clk, h 61 Paca.
Davidson Wm E, mach hd, b 8 Lord.
Davidson Wm J, contr, 186 Dougherty, h same.
Davidson & Nelson (Harvey C Davidson, Bird Nelson), novelty works, s s Bloyd av 1 e of Belt R R (B).
Davie Frank, boxmkr, h 31 Thomas.
Davie George, lab, h 213 W Merrill.
Davies Arthur E, clk The Wm H Block Co, b 4 Cornell av.
Davies Jacob, shoemkr, 119 Mass av, b 283 E Washington.
Davies Mary L, teacher Industrial School, b 4 Cornell av.
Davis Aaron, lab, h 604 Virginia av.
Davis Abbie (wid James E), b 217 S Olive.
Davis Abel E, h 346 N West.
Davis Abijah A, musician, b 122 W Maryland.
Davis Abner, lab, h 212 Middle.
Davis Abraham, tailor, b 249 S Pine.
Davis Agnes, h 311 W Pratt.
Davis Alexander, lab, h 20 Holborn.
Davis Alexander H, h 81 W 11th.
Davis Allen, lab, h 98 Martindale av.
Davis Allen, trav agt, b 27 Prospect.
Davis Allen, lab, b 228 W Wabash.
Davis Anderson, waiter The Bates.
Davis Andrew P, lab, b 411 S Olive.
Davis Anna B, cook, b 328 E Washington.
Davis Arthur G, lawyer, 38 Thorpe blk, h 359 N California.

Special Detailed Reports Promptly Furnished by Us.
MERCHANTS' AND MANUFACTURERS' EXCHANGE
J. E. TAKKEN, Manager,
19 Union Building, 73 West Maryland Street.

Davis Bartholomew, painter, h 42 Smith.
Davis Belle, teacher Public School No 2 (H), b 155 Sheffield av (H).
Davis Benjamin, h w s Harriet 3 s of Sutherland (B).
Davis Benjamin, r 62½ S Illinois.
Davis Benjamin, lab, h 125 Eddy.
Davis Benjamin M, lab, h 22 S West.
Davis Benjamin M, prof Butler College, h w s Central av 2 s of Grand av (I).
Davis Benjamin N, grocer, 526 N Senate av, h 528 same.
Davis Benjamin S, acrobat, b 56 Columbia av.
Davis Calvin M, sawyer, h 84 Temple av.
Davis Caroline, h 31 E Wilkins.
Davis Catherine M, h 17 Lockerbie.
Davis Charles, b 206 Christian av.
Davis Charles, clk, b 148 N East.
Davis Charles, driver, h 125 W 6th.
Davis Charles, hostler, b 249 E Louisiana.
Davis Charles, lab, h 477 Lafayette.
Davis Charles A, yardmaster C C C & St L Ry, h 50 Wallack.
Davis Charles C, city fireman, h 1356 N Illinois.
Davis Charles C, painter, b 121 Williams.
Davis Charles E, lab, h 1286 Morris (W I).
Davis Charles L, bartndr, h 132 Gillard av.
Davis Charles R, lab, r 181 Virginia av.
Davis Charles W, clk, b 43 Bellefontaine.
Davis Charles W, lab, h 477 Lafayette.
Davis Charlotte (wid George), h 411 S Olive.
Davis Clara, queensware, 136 Minerva, h same.
Davis Clarence C, lab, b 125 Lambert (W I).
Davis Clarence K, treas Davis Mnfg Co, h n s Washington av 1 w of Central av (I).
Davis Clinton E, h 177 S New Jersey.
Davis Daniel B, carp, b 125 Lambert (W I).
Davis Daniel E, heater, h 581 S Illinois.
Davis David, clothing, 231 E Washington, h same.
Davis David, mach, b 24 Brookside av.
Davis David S, painter, h 188 Patterson.
Davis Dexter D, car rep, h 1286 W Morris.
Davis Donald, coachman 82 W Vermont.
Davis Edgar W, engr, h 231 English av.
Davis Edward, cook, h 581 E 8th.
Davis Edward, reporter, b 223 E New York.
Davis Edward, student, b 466 N Senate av.
Davis Edward H, tmstr, h 36 Arizona.
Davis Edward W, painter, h 34 Wyoming.
Davis Elisha, porter Spencer House.
Davis Eliza (wid John W), h 161 Jefferson av.
Davis Elizabeth, dressmkr, h s s Oak av 1 e of Central av (I).
Davis Elizabeth (wid Robert T), h 28 College av.
Davis Elizabeth C, h 329 N Illinois.
Davis Elliott W, clk Kingan & Co (ltd), b 170 Talbott av.
Davis Emeline (wid John M), h 69 W 13th.
Davis Emerson, pres Davis Mnfg Co, h 135 E North.
Davis Emery E, lab, h 221 S West.
Davis Emily J, phys, 125 Lambert (W I), h same.
Davis Emma M (wid Isaac), h 170 Talbott av.
Davis Enos, bricklyr, h 1512 Kenwood av.
Davis Ernest G, trimmer, h 658 Park av.
Davis Eugene J, phys, 399 College av, h same.
Davis Felix, contr, 154 Bird, h same.
Davis Fleming E, lab, h 205 Le Grand av.

CLEMENS VONNEGUT 184, 186 and 192 E. Washington St. | CABINET HARDWARE CARVERS' TOOLS. Glues of all kinds.

THE WM. H. BLOCK CO. 7 AND 9 EAST WASHINGTON STREET. DRY GOODS, MILLINERY, CLOAKS AND FURS.

Davis Francis M, painter, h 486 W Shoemaker (N I).
Davis Frank, boxmkr, b 504 S West.
Davis Frank, checkman, h 277 E Georgia.
Davis Frank, lineman, b 415 E Washington.
Davis Frank, switchman, r 539 E Washington.
Davis Frank N, barber, h 605 N West.
Davis Frank P, mach hd, h 262 W 7th.
Davis Frank V, clk, h 107 Bright.
Davis Frank W, spec agt State House Bldg Assn, h 123 Cottage av (W I).
Davis Frederick A W, vice-pres and treas The Indpls Water Co and treas Mnfrs' Natural Gas Co, h 677 N Alabama.
Davis George, carp, h 4½ Malott av.
Davis George, lab, h 176 Bismarck av (H).
Davis George, lab, b 1373 N Capitol av.
Davis George B, foreman, h 150 Cornell av.
Davis George L, lab, h 175 Alvord.
Davis George L, vice-pres Indpls Electrotype Foundry, h 360 Bellefontaine.
Davis George P, electrotyper, b 289 W Vermont.
Davis George U, foreman, h 252 W 22d.
Davis George W, lab, b 42 Smith.
Davis Harriette A (wid Henry), h 155 Sheffield av (H).
Davis Harris, carp, b 170 Cornell av.
Davis Harry G, lab, b 607 Mass av.
Davis Harry L, steamfitter, h 280 E Miami.
Davis Harry M, city fireman, h 552 Mulberry.
Davis Harvey L, carp, 73 W 19th, h same.
Davis Henderson, porter, h 746 Brooker's al.
Davis Henry, driver, h 12 Mill.
Davis Henry, lab, h 120 Dougherty.
Davis Henry A, mngr Huber Mnfg Co, h 277 E New York.
Davis Henry C, bkkpr Cerealine Mnfg Co, b Stubbins Hotel.
Davis Henry E, ins, r 35 W Vermont.
Davis Herbert L, lab, h 36 Samoa.
Davis Horace D, mach hd, h 421 Highland av.
Davis Inez, bkkpr, b 161 Jefferson av.
Davis Ira J, carp, b 123 Clarke.
Davis Isaac B, waiter, h 29 Center.
Davis Isaac D, switchman, h 1011 E Washington.
Davis Isaac E, musician, b 634 N Capitol av.
Davis Isabel R (wid Milton), b 180 N Illinois.
Davis Jacob D, carp, h 327 Yandes.
Davis James, lab, b rear 258 S Meridian.
Davis James, lab, h 36 St Paul.
Davis James, waiter, h 113 Indiana av.
Davis James B, fireman, h 486½ Virginia av.
Davis James B, lab, b rear 151 Spann av.
Davis James C (Warman, Black, Chamberlain & Co), res Lebanon, Ind.
Davis James C, produce, E Mkt House, h rear 149 Bellefontaine.
Davis James E, h 303 S Meridian.
Davis James E, clk, h 80 Division (W I).
Davis James H (Davis & Nealis), h 33 Camp.
Davis James H, insp Indpls Gas Co, h 148 N East.
Davis James P, trav agt, h 118 Forest av.
Davis James W, lab, h rear 80 Yandes.
Davis Jeannette (wid Charles C), h 478 N Penn.
Davis Jennie (wid Charles), b 227 Bright.
Davis Jennie (wid Robert F), h 124 Christian av.
Davis Joel R, phys, 125 Lambert (W I), h same.

HEADQUARTERS PHOTOGRAPHIC OUTFITS AMATEUR OR PROFESSIONAL THE H. LIEBER COMPANY 33 S. MERIDIAN ST.

Davis John, barber, r 42½ Mass av.
Davis John, lab, h 46 Locke.
Davis John, lab, h 39 Rhode Island.
Davis John, lab, b 228 W Wabash.
Davis John A, bartndr, b 289 W Vermont.
Davis John A, lab, b 407 S Olive.
Davis John D, porter, r 305 E Court.
Davis John D, lab, h 501 E 9th.
Davis John E, bartndr, b 81 W 11th.
Davis John F, brakeman, h 42 Gresham.
Davis John F, electrician, b 567 W 22d (N I).
Davis John L, tmstr, h 20 Woodside av (W).
Davis John M, lab, b 104 Hadley av (W I).
Davis John P, trav agt Hendrickson, Lefler & Co, h 1157 N Alabama.
Davis John R, messenger, b 217 S Olive.
Davis John R, fireman, h rear 151 Spann av.
Davis John W, brakeman, b 62 Spann av.
Davis John W, bricklyr, h 81 Leota.
Davis John W, clk Boyd, Besten & Langen Co, b 43 Bellefontaine.
Davis John W, student, b 220 N Capitol av.
Davis Joseph, h 79 W Ohio.
Davis Joseph, car rep, h 81 Wright.
Davis Joseph, tmstr, h 253 S Capitol av.
Davis Joseph M, lab, b 407 S Olive.
Davis Joseph F, mach hd, h 99 John.
Davis Joseph T (Joseph T Davis & Co), b 289 W Vermont.
Davis Joseph T & Co (Joseph T Davis), well drivers, 289 W Vermont.
Davis Joseph W, brakeman, b 62 Spann av.
Davis Lambert D, furniture, 300 W Washington, h 59 Hadley av (W I).
Davis Lawrence B, student, b 340 N Meridian.
Davis Lee, lab, b 444 E 7th.
Davis Lewis B, furniture, 405 Virginia av, r same.
Davis Lillie M (wid John P), h 496 W 22d (N I).
DAVIS LOUIS J, Bicycle Repairer, Bicycles Built to Order, 18 N West, h 3 Guffin.
Davis Louisa, b 180 N Illinois.
Davis Laura L, opr C U Tel Co, b 11 Greenwood.
Davis Lulu M (wid Rutledge), b 110 Shelby.

GUIDO R. PRESSLER, FRESCO PAINTER Churches, Theaters, Public Buildings, Etc., A Specialty. Residence, No. 325 North Liberty Street. INDIANAPOLIS, IND.

INDIANAPOLIS STEEL ROOFING AND CORRUGATING WORKS, 23 and 25 East South Street. S. D. NOEL, Proprietor.

David S. McKernan REAL ESTATE AND LOANS Houses, Lots, Farms and Western Lands for sale or trade. ROOMS 2-5 THORPE BLOCK.

DIAMOND WALL PLASTER { Telephone 1410 BUILDERS' EXCHANGE.

UNION TRANSFER AND STORAGE CO. Cor. E. Ohio St. and C., C., C. & St. L. R'y Tracks. ISSUE NEGOTIABLE RECEIPTS ON MERCHANDISE AND HOUSEHOLD GOODS.

W. McWORKMAN,
ROOFING AND CORNICE WORKS,
930 W. Washington St. Tel. 1118.

Davis Luther M, student, r 367 N Alabama.
Davis L Adele, bkkpr State House Bldg Assn, b 84 Temple av.
Davis Madison H, clk R M S, h 393 W 22d.
Davis Mnfg Co, Emerson Davis pres, Clarence K Davis treas and mngr, 68½ E Market.
Davis Marcus J, carp, b 436 Martindale av.
Davis Margaret A (wid Calvert), dressmkr, 463 S Meridian, h same.
Davis Maria (wid Franklin J), b 15 Ketcham.
Davis Maria M (wid Jesse W), b 21 S East.
Davis Marietta A (wid Jefferson C), h 1030 N New Jersey.
Davis Marks C, real est, 47½ N Illinois, b 340 N Meridian.
Davis Marshall W J, barber, b 348 W 2d.
Davis Martha E, dressmkr, 420 E Pearl, b same.
Davis Mary (wid John), h 289 W Vermont.
Davis Mary A (wid Wm H), h 108½ Mass av.
Davis Mary E (wid Charles A), janitress Stout blk.
Davis Mary H (wid Charles), dressmkr, 26 Wilcox, h same.
Davis Mary J, b 292 Broadway.
Davis Maude, clk Met Life Ins Co, b 177 S New Jersey.
Davis Minerva J (wid Wm M), h 172 Cornell av.
Davis Moses, h 607 Mass av.
Davis Nathan D, musician, b 634 N Capitol av.
Davis Nathaniel, lab, h 158 Martindale av.
Davis Nelson, lab, h 303 Alvord.
Davis Norwood B, carp, b 225 N Senate av.
Davis Oliver O, b 84 Temple av.
Davis Ora O (wid Deskin E), h 185 N Capito av.
Davis Patrick, saloon, 101 Patterson, h 103 same.
Davis Peter, lab, b 411 S Olive.
Davis Ransom, lab, b 42 Smith.
Davis Riley, lab, h 422 Muskingum al.
Davis Robert, lab, b 310 E Court.
Davis Robert, peddler, h rear 738 N West.

GEO. J. MAYER,
MANUFACTURER OF
SEALS
STENCILS, RUBBER STAMPS, CHECKS, BADGES, DOOR PLATES, ETC.
15 S. Meridian St., Ground Floor. TEL. 1386.

Davis Robert, supt The Adams Brick Co, h 203 Le Grand av.
Davis Robert G, lab, h 101 Hill av.
Davis Robert G, painter, h 63 Bismarck (W I).
Davis Robert H, lab, h 363 S West.
Davis Robert T, clk, b 124 Christian av.
Davis Rollo W, condr, r 102 S State av.
Davis Rose M, b 69 W 13th.
Davis Ruby (wid John), h 23 N East.
Davis Samantha G (wid John W), h n s University av 3 w of Central av (I).
Davis Samuel, driver, r 32 W Court.
Davis Samuel, lab, h 187 Middle.
Davis Samuel, meats, 43 E Mkt House, h 90 S Noble.
Davis Samuel, shoemkr, 275 E Washington, h same.
Davis Samuel, tinner, h 466 N Senate av.
Davis Samuel H, b 501 E 9th.
Davis Sarah (wid George), b 15 Stevens.
Davis Sarah (wid Henry K), h 97 Division (W I).
Davis Sarah (wid Holden), h 726 N Senate av.
Davis Sarah E (wid Samuel A), b 299 Kentucky av.
Davis Scott, lab, h rear 671 N Senate av.
Davis Scott W, lab, h 16 Sumner.
Davis Sherman T, lab, b 44 Paca.
Davis Stephen, lab, r 205 W North.
Davis Susan (wid Stephen), h 275 Chapel.
Davis Susan F (wid Quincy), b 399 College av.
Davis Susannah (wid Mason T), h 154½ Martindale av.
Davis Theodore P (Gavin & Davis), res Noblesville, Ind.
Davis Tevis A, finisher, b 168 Martindale av.
Davis Thomas, lab, h 28 Bates al.
Davis Thomas C, lab, b 849 S East.
Davis Thomas E, lab, b 103 Patterson.
Davis Thomas G, blksmith, h 312 E North.
Davis Thomas P, cook, h rear 13 Cornell av.
Davis Thomas W, carp, h 529 W Udell (N I).
Davis Ulysses G, lab, h 4 Standard av (W I).
Davis Virginia E, dressmkr, s s Oak av 1 e of Central av (I), h same.
Davis Waldo T, real est, h 43 Bellefontaine.
Davis Wallace S, huckster, h 30 Seibert.
Davis Walter J, lab, b 99 John.
Davis Walter L, carp, h w s Kenwood av 2 s of 30th.
Davis Walter W, helper, b 188 Patterson.
Davis Wilburn, carp, b 294 Christian av.
Davis Wiley, porter, r 28 Bates al.
Davis Willard, ins agt, h 178 Pleasant.
Davis Wm, lab, h 203 Belmont av (H).
Davis Wm, lab, h 240 Blake.
Davis Wm, lab, h 17 Center.
Davis Wm, lab, b 334 N Illinois.
Davis Wm, lab, h 10 Sharpe.
Davis Wm, lab, b 229 S West.
Davis Wm, lineman, r 46 Hendricks blk.
Davis Wm, presser, h 20 N Gale (B).
Davis Wm, waiter, r 250 S Senate av.
Davis Wm A, carp, h 574 Morris (W I).
Davis Wm B, farmer, h 634 N Capitol av.
Davis Wm B, steelwkr, h 56 Columbia av.
Davis Wm C, engr, h 184 N Beville av.
Davis Wm C, lab, h 149 W South.
Davis Wm E, clk Indpls Gas Co, b 271 Bright.
Davis Wm E, condr, h 304 E Market.
Davis Wm E, lab, b 407 S Olive.

A. METZGER AGENCY ESTABLISHED 1863. REAL ESTATE

LAMBERT GAS & GASOLINE ENGINE CO.
ANDERSON, IND. GAS AND GASOLINE ENGINES, 2 TO 50 H. P.

Davis Wm H, painter, h 406 W Addison (N I).
Davis Wm H, painter, b 97 Division (W I).
Davis Wm H, b 433 Dillon.
Davis Wm I, engr, h 194 English av.
Davis Wm J, lab, h 346 W North.
Davis Wm K, carp, h 436 Martindale av.
Davis Wm M, polisher, b 289 W Vermont.
Davis Wm M, temperer, b 172 Cornell av.
Davis Wm S, lab, h 217 W 6th.
Davis Wm W, b 268 W Merrill.
Davis & Nealis (James H Davis, Mary Nealis), platers, 92 S Delaware.
Davison, see also Davidson.
Davison Edward M, clk Great Atlantic and Pacific Tea Co, b 351 Talbott av.
Davison Owen, carp, h 351 Talbott av.
Davisson Walter C, sec and treas Brooks Oil Co, h 308 Park av.
Davy, see also Davey.
Davy Elizabeth, teacher Public School No 4, b 510 N California.
Davy Frank P, boxmkr, h 505 S West.
Davy Isaac R, clk, b 81 W St Clair.
Davy James, boxmkr, b 884 S Meridian.
Davy James, lab, h 170 Ramsey av.
Davy John, saloon, 169 Michigan (H), h same.
Davy John C, gasfitter, b 366 N Brookside av.
Davy John D, bkkpr Williams Bros, b 702 N Illinois.
Davy John E, clk Kingan & Co (ltd), b 510 N California.
Davy Joshua, lab, h 81 W St Clair.
Davy Josiah C, h 366 N Brookside av.
Davy Louis, lab, h 408 W Wilkins.
Davy Mabel S, teacher Public School No 3, b 510 N California.
Davy Nora, opr C U Tel Co, b 81 W St Clair.
Davy Walter W, printer, h 510 N California.
Dawkins Alfred, lab, h 2 Lyman (W I).
Daws Henry J, mach, r 168 Union.
Dawsey Edward, lab, h 2 Lafayette.
Dawson Abraham H, h 105 Wright.
Dawson Alfred, lab, h 563 E 8th.
Dawson Arthur W, clk Syerup & Co, h 326 W 1st.
Dawson Charles, lab, h 140 W 6th.
Dawson Charles F, capt of police, h 286 Dillon.
Dawson Charles J, bookbndr, b 144 Greer.
Dawson Charles L, lab, b 94 S West.
Dawson Charles W, motorman, h 177 Fletcher av.
Dawson David, peddler, r 77 Kentucky av.
Dawson Edward F, mach, b e s Hubbard 1 s of Clifford av.
Dawson Edward F, fireman, r 24 Ryan blk.
Dawson Edward W, sec Chester Oil Co, h 474 Bellefontaine.
Dawson Francis M, molder, b 94 S West.
Dawson Frank, waiter, h 163 Bird.
Dawson George H, insp Indpls Gas Co, b 163 Cornell av.
Dawson George J, barber, 515 E 8th, b 458 N California.
Dawson George L, painter, b 284 E Louisiana.
Dawson Henry C, huckster, h 144 Greer.
Dawson Herbert O, engr, b n w cor 7th and Alvord.
Dawson Iram D, welldriver, h 747 N Capitol av.
Dawson James, lab, b 184 Bismarck av (H).
Dawson James M, tmstr, b 233 Prospect.
Dawson James R, printer, b 103 Hoyt av.

Farm and City Loans
25 Years' Successful Business.
THOS. C. DAY & CO,
Rooms 325 to 330 Lemcke Building.

Dawson James W, truckman, h 154 Pleasant.
Dawson John B, condr, h 33 Wilcox.
Dawson John L, lab, h 173 E Walnut.
Dawson John W, h 233 Prospect.
Dawson Joseph, driver, h 94 S West.
Dawson Josie, h 175 W Ohio.
Dawson Louise (wid Scott R), r 27 Hutchings blk.
Dawson Luther, waiter, r 32 Bird.
Dawson Maria A, r 143½ Virginia av.
Dawson Mary A (wid Timothy), h 103 Hoyt av.
Dawson Matthew, tmstr, b 177 Fletcher av.
Dawson Richard, lab, h 167 Tremont av (H).
Dawson Thomas B, dairy, e s Hubbard 1 s of Clifford av, h same.
Dawson Thomas M, blksmith, h 223 Douglass.
Dawson Wm, mach, r 174 S Capitol av.
Dawson Wm P, carp, b 254 S Olive.
Day, see also O'Day.
Day Allie M, b 144 Madison av.
Day Benjamin D, lab, h w s Foundry 2 s of Schofield (B).
Day Budd, janitor, h 24 W 1st.
Day Carl E, motorman, b 489 College av.
Day Carl R, lab, h 158 Buchanan.
Day Charles, lab, h 393 Yandes.
Day Charles E, cook, h 37½ Kentucky av.
Day Charles H, motorman, h 44 Leon.
Day Charles W, lab, h 57 Bloomington.
Day Clifford I, clk, b 294 Christian av.
Day Cora M, prin Public School No 32, h 125 W 2d.
Day Daniel W, vise hd, b 120 Blackford.
Day Daniel, lab, h 269½ Mass av.
Day David N, carp, h 624 Ontario (N I).
Day Edgar, porter, h rear 115 W 6th.
Day Florence, b 213 W Ohio.
Day Frank T, clk, b 10 E 7th.
Day Frank W, buyer D P Erwin & Co, b 10 E 7th.
Day Frederick W, trav agt Smith, Day & Co, h 243 S Olive.
Day Harry A, lab, h e s Fairview 1 s of Lake (N I).

EAT
HITZ'S
CRACKERS
AND CAKES.
ASK YOUR GROCER FOR THEM.

BICYCLES $5 ... Best Wheels. Best Terms. WHEELMEN'S CO. 31 W. OHIO ST. LONG DISTANCE TEL. 1855.

J. H. TECKENBROCK Painter and Decorator, 94 EAST SOUTH STREET.

FIDELITY MUTUAL LIFE—PHILADELPHIA, PA.
MATCHLESS SECURITY At LOW COST. A. H. COLLINS General Agent Baldwin Block.

Rooms 42 and 43 WHEN BUILDING.

Edwardsport Al and Mining Co. Miners and Shippers Steam and Domestic Coal.

ESTABLISHED 1876. TELEPHONE 168.
CHESTER BRADFORD,
SOLICITOR OF PATENTS,
AND COUNSEL IN PATENT CAUSES.
(See adv. page 6.)
Office:—Rooms 14 and 16 Hubbard Block, S. W. Cor. Washington and Meridian Streets, INDIANAPOLIS, INDIANA.

Day Harry A, news dealer, 100 Meek, h same.
Day Harry McC, b 122 N Penn.
Day Harvey A, lab, b 539 Madison av.
Day Henry Rev, b 122 N Penn.
Day Henry B, car rep, h 17 W Sutherland (B).
Day Henry C, driver, h 343 N Pine.
Day James, lab, b 31 Madison av.
Day James M, foreman, h 41 Mayhew.
Day Jeremiah L, tmstr, h 406 Bates.
Day Joel, agt, r 117 N Illinois.
Day Joel, phys, h rear 16 Sullivan.
Day John A, clk R M S, h 23 Clifford av.
Day John H, printer, h 100 Geisendorf.
Day Kate, h 35 Garden.
Day Laura H, artist, 176 N California, h same.
Day Louis L, huckster, h rear 190 E Market.
Day Lucinda (wid Wm N), b 213 W Ohio.
Day Margaret (wid Elihu), b 343 N Pine.
Day Martha M (wid Richard L), b 125 W 2d.
Day Mary A (wid John W), h 176 Patterson.
Day Mary E (wid Lafayette), h 871 N New Jersey.
Day Mary E (wid Wm), b n e cor Maple and Walnut avs (I).
Day Oscar P, lab, h 1360 Indianapolis av.
Day Reginald H, trav agt, b 125 W 2d.
Day Thomas Rev, h 510 Central av.
Day Thomas C (Thos C Day & Co), h 820 N Meridian.
DAY THOS C & CO (Thomas C Day, George W Wishard), Mortgage Loans, Bonds and Financial Agts, Rooms 325-330 Lemcke Bldg, Tel 1325. (See right top cor cards.)
Day Walter L, mngr Smith, Day & Co, b 243 S Olive.
Day Walter S, grocer, 158 W Washington, h 176 N California.
Day Wm E, driver, h 150½ College av.
Day Worthington W, poultry, E Mkt House, h 294 Christian av.
Deacon Alfred L (Caldwell & Deacon), h 171 N Capitol av.

Outing BICYCLES
$85.00.
MADE AND SOLD BY
HAY & WILLITS MFG CO.
76 N. PENNSYLVANIA ST. PHONE 598.

Deacon Wm A, adv mngr The Indpls Sentinel, h 132 W Pratt.
Deady Margaret (wid Michael), restaurant, 66 N Delaware, h same.
Deakin Wm, h 43 Carlos.
Deakins Albert T, tinner, h 53 N Linden.
Deal Frank E, helper, b 77 N Gillard av.
Deal John, carp, h 77 N Gillard av.
Dean, see also Dehn.
Dean Allen, lab, r 66 N Missouri.
Dean Arvillo F, carp, h 42 Oliver av (W I).
DEAN BROS STEAM PUMP WORKS, Edward H Dean Pres, Wilfred R Dean Vice-Pres, John C Dean Sec and Treas, Ward H Dean Supt, 1st near cor Senate av, Tel 9. (See adv p 3.)
Dean Benjamin F, engr, h 44 Harrison.
Dean Charles, hostler, h 172½ W New York.
Dean Charles G, mach Dean Bros Steam Pump Works, b 549 N Capitol av.
Dean Charles H, lab, r rear 428 N Alabama.
Dean Claude, janitor, b 331 Clinton.
Dean Dunlap G, clk, h 16 Division (W I).
Dean Edward H, pres Dean Bros Steam Pump Works, h 673 N Meridian.
DEAN E S CO THE, M E Massey Agt, Stock and Grain Brokers, Room 51 Commercial Club Bldg. (See adv in classified Brokers.)
Dean Frank B, fireman, b 44 Harrison.
Dean George, steelwkr, b 52 McGinnis.
Dean George C, printer, h 14 S Senate av.
Dean Harriet (wid King D), h 331 Clinton.
Dean Irving M, trav agt, h 183 Fayette.
Dean James H, carp, h 377 W Shoemaker (N I).
Dean Jasper J, carp, h 452 W Eugene (N I).
Dean Joel D, agt, h 38 Arbor av (W I).
Dean John C, carp, h 36 Ketcham (H).
Dean John C, sec and treas Dean Bros Steam Pump Works, h 571 N Penn.
Dean John K, mach Dean Bros Steam Pump Works, b 549 N Capitol av.
Dean Joseph H, engr, b 233 Elizabeth.
Dean Lillian (wid Ward H), h 71 E St Clair.
Dean Mathew E, engr, b 160 S Noble.
Dean Melvin F, coachman 1108 N Meridian.
Dean Noble, lab, b 317 Clinton.
Dean Sarah, laundress, h 325 E Wabash.
Dean Stuart, molder Dean Bros Steam Pump Works, b 620 N Meridian.
Dean Terrence, h 331 E New York.
Dean Thomas, bookbndr, h 181 Buchanan.
Dean Thomas, trav agt Dean Bros Steam Pump Wks, h 559 N Capitol av.
Dean Thomas E, proof reader Indpls Journal, b 872 N Delaware.
Dean Thomas W, mach opr Indpls Journal, b 872 N Delaware.
Dean Walter, packer, h rear 95 John.
Dean Ward H, supt Dean Bros Steam Pump Works, h 600 N Penn.
Dean Wilfred R, vice-pres Dean Bros Steam Pump Works, h 620 N Meridian.
Dean Wm, coremkr, h 233 Elizabeth.
Dean Wm J, lab, h 384 N California.
Deane Charles H, h 282 Indiana av.
Deane Daisy D, stenog Thurman & Silvius, b 33 W Vermont.
Deane John H, asst City Engineer, 2 basement Court House, b 282 Indiana av.
Deane Thomas J, trav agt, b 282 Indiana av.
Dear Milton H, molder, h 804 S East.
Dearborn Anna B (wid Orin J), b 1012 N Alabama.

C. ZIMMERMAN & SONS | SLATE AND GRAVEL ROOFERS 19 South East Street.

DRIVEN WELLS And Second Water Wells and Pumps of all kinds at CHARLES KRAUSS'. 42 S. PENN. ST. TELEPHONE 465.

ERTEL STEAM LAUNDRY || LARGEST AND BEST IN THE STATE. PROMPT SERVICE. 26 and 28 N. Senate Ave. Tel 1089.

Dearborn Claire S, sec Ward Bros Drug Co, h 1012 N Alabama.
Deardorff Edward C, pres The Central Rubber and Supply Co, r 53 The Chalfant.
Deardorff Theodore H, sec and treas The Central Rubber and Supply Co, b Grand Hotel.

DEARINGER EDWARD A, Paper Hanger and Decorator; Orders Receive Prompt Attention and Satisfaction Guaranteed; 118 Ft Wayne av, h same. (See adv in classified Paper Hangers.)

Dearinger Frank B (Dearinger & Rogers), tool mnfr, rear 313 E Georgia, h 336 E South.
Dearinger James, carp, b 1210 Northwestern av (N I).
Dearinger Mary E (wid George W), h 1210 Northwestern av (N I).
Dearinger Simeon, plastr, h 599 W Pearl.
Dearinger Wm R, carp, h 187 Dougherty.
Dearinger & Rogers (Frank B Dearinger, Benjamin F Rogers), cement contrs, rear 313 E Georgia.
Dearman Anna (wid John B), h 38 Leon.
Dearmin Robert G, trav agt Indpls B and S Co, h 20 Pleasant av.
DeArmond John O, mach opr, b 351 S New Jersey.
DeArmond Luella, stenog, b 249 W New York.
DeArmond Thomas J, carriagemkr, h 281 Highland av.
Dearn Lydia (wid Eli), b 148 Eddy.
Dearth John P, cigars, 303 Virginia av, h 207½ same.
Dearth Wm L, livery, rear 162 E North, h 873 N New Jersey.
Deathe James C, trav agt, h 372 E Georgia.
Deatley Wm H, carp, h 63 Ingraham.
Deaty Margaret (wid Michael), h 86 E Ohio.
Deavers James, lab, h 94 Cleaveland blk.
DeBaun Samuel, r 283 N East.
Deboes Henry, lab, h 294 Indiana av.
DeBolt Clinton H, h 1174 N Illinois.
DeBolt Wm, clk Charles Mayer & Co, b 1174 N Illinois.
Debow Perry A, lab, h 23½ S West.
DeBowes Henry, lab, b 75 Elizabeth.
DeBruler David W, lab, h 2 e of 463 Ontario (N I).
DeBruler Margaretta (wid Oscar), teacher Indiana Industrial School, b 399 N Penn.
DeBruyn Charles H, lithog, r 27 Ryan blk.
Deburger Charles P, molder, h 19 Warman av (H).
DeBurger Edward, brakeman, b 38 Elder av.
DeBurger Mary (wid George), h 38 Elder av.
DeBusk John W, overall mnfr, 292 Mass av, h 177 College av.
DeCamp Cassius M, carp, h 43 S Austin (B).
DeCamp Oliver M, carp, b 43 S Austin (B).
Decher Augustus, lab, h 64 Downey.
Deciem Charles, brakeman, b e s Brightwood av 7 s of Willow (B).
Deck James M, trav agt, h 104 Walcott.
Decker Charles M, driver, b 104 Martindale av.
Decker Edward H, blksmith, h 130 Clifford av.
Decker Elizabeth (wid Conrad), b 130 Clifford av.
Decker Frank, tinner, b 287 S Penn.

RICHARDSON & McCREA, MANAGERS FOR CENTRAL INDIANA. EQUITABLE LIFE ASSURANCE SOCIETY Of the United States. 79 EAST MARKET STREET, TELEPHONE 182.

Decker George E, surrey hanger, h 233 Madison av.
Decker Harry C, carp, h 1737 Graceland av.
Decker Henry, cashr Indpls Gas Co, b 146 Union.
Decker John B, baggageman, h 25 Sullivan.
Decker John D, clk C C C & St L Ry, b 329 N New Jersey.
Decker Joseph F, driver, h 270 E Merrill.
Decker Mary (wid Ernst), h 11 Hendricks.
Deckert Christopher, lab, h 43 Grant.
Deckert Frank A, tinner, b 287 S Penn.
Deckert Harrison S, mach, h rear 152 Spann av.
Dedert Charles, packer, h 201 Orange.
Dedert Edward C, clk Buddenbaum Bros, h 134 N Summit.
Dedert Herman C, clk, b 519 E Ohio.
Dedert Louis F H, clk Murphy, Hibben & Co, b 56 N Arsenal av.
Dedert Wm F, checkman, h 56 N Arsenal av.
Dee Mollie, attendant Blind Institute.
Dee Wm D, lab, b Germania House.
Deeder Harry, mach, b 399 Yandes.
Deeds Harry W, state insp C U Tel Co, tel 43, h 176 N Senate av, tel 727.
Deeds Oreno O, lab, b 296 E Market.
Deeds Otto J, patternmkr, h 15 N Spruce.
Deeds Walston R, mach, b 296 E Market.
Deem, see also Dehm.
Deem Charles M, mach, h 42 Temple av.
Deem Frederick W, trav agt, h 23 Riley blk.
Deer, see also Doerr.
Deer Charles M, fireman, h 559 E St Clair.
Deer Harry, varnisher, h 9 Harvey.
Deer Henry, lab, h s w cor Judge Harding and Johnson (W I).
Deer John, tailor, h 107 Benton.
Deer John W, dry goods, 131 William (W I), h same.
Deer Joseph E, engr, h 14 Arbor av (W I).
Deer Louis N, cigarmkr, h 26 Bismarck av (H).
Deer Wm E, clk, h 163 Nordyke av (W I).
Deerberg Charles W, tailor, h 52 Beaty.
Deerberg Christian, lab, b 305 English av.
Deerberg Henry, lab, h 305 English av.

Typewriter-Ribbons ALL COLORS FOR ALL MACHINES. THE BEST AND CHEAPEST. S. H. EAST, STATE AGENT, The Williams Typewriter.... 55 THORPE BLOCK, 87 E. MARKET ST.

ELLIS & HELFENBERGER || Architectural Iron Work and Gray Iron Castings. 162-170 South Senate Ave. Tel. 958.

THE HOGAN TRANSFER AND STORAGE COMP'Y
Household Goods and Pianos Moved—Packed—Stored...... Baggage and Package Express Machinery and Safes a Specialty Cor. Washington and Illinois Sts. TELEPHONE No. 675.

The Central Rubber & Supply Co. ◆◆◆ Hose, Belting, Packing, Clothing, Druggists' Sundries, Bicycle Tires, Cotton Hose, Etc. New York Belting & Packing Co., L't'd. PHONE 92 . 79 S. ILLINOIS ST., INDIANAPOLIS, IND.

The Provident Life and Trust Company
Of Philadelphia.
Grants Certificates of Extension to Policyholders who are temporarily unable to pay their premiums
D. W. EDWARDS, Gen. Agt., 508 Indiana Trust Bldg.

Deere, Mansur & Co, Samuel W Smith agt, farm impLts, 75 W Washington.
DEERE & CO, Thomas A Conlee Agt, Plows and Cultivators, 75-77 W Washington, Tel 1198.
Deerhake Ernest H, carp, h 312 Fletcher av.
Deerham James, lab, h 18 Sumner.
Deering Harvester Co, James W Keogh agt, 192 W Market.
Deery Alice (wid Henry), h 385 N New Jersey.
Deery James H, supt city delivery P O, h 339 N Pine.
Deery John A, paperhngr, h 434 E North.
Deery Patrick E, paperhngr, h 86 Fayette.
Deeter Franklin S, fireman, b w s Station 4 s of Sutherland (B).
Deeter Royal L, brakeman, h 32 N Gillard av.
Deeter Wm W, condr, h 200 Clifford av.
Deetring George W, lab, b 325 E Ohio.
DeFalco Thomas A, barber, b 83½ Mass av.
Defendserfer Charles, lab, r 268 S Illinois.
Deffaulx Elizabeth (wid Louis F), b 127 Madison.
Deffaulx Louis F, carp, h 127 Madison.
Defibaugh Charles C, foreman The Sun, h 1780 Graceland av.
Defibaugh Wm J, driver, h 1780 Graceland av.
DeFord John A, carp, h 93 N Beville av.
Defrance John, cook, r 128 Allegheny.
Defrayne George A, mach The Sun, h 34 Leon.
Defrees Fred D, student, b 74 W Michigan.
Defrees Morris M, civ engr, 62 Ingalls blk, h 74 W Michigan.
Defrees Rollin E, draughtsman Atlas Engine Wks, h 524 E 8th.
Defrees Thomas M, lieut U S A, r 74 W Michigan.
Degan Nellie, b 157 Bates.
Degering Christian, farmer, h s s Washington 6 e of Sherman Drive.
Degnan Patrick, blksmith, h 95 Quincy.
Degnan Thomas F, engr, b 95 Quincy.
Degner Charles, driver, h 53 Carlos.
Degner Eva E, cashr John A Craig, b 1032 E Michigan.

Julius C. Walk & Son,
Jewelers
Indianapolis.
12 EAST WASHINGTON ST.

Degner Lydia E, bkkpr, b 1032 E Michigan.
Degner Wm E, carp, h 1032 E Michigan.
Degner Wm T, cigarmkr, b 53 Carlos.
DeGolyer Lauren F, mngr J A Everitt, h 70 W 4th.
Degorham Delano, polisher, h 223½ W Maryland.
DeHaas Charles L, lawyer, 729 Lemcke bldg, b 1108 N Alabama.
DeHaas Thomas W, phys, 36 W 13th, h 1108 N Alabama.
DeHart Edward J, lab, h 21 Ludlow av.
DeHart Juriah L (wid Austin), h 374 Fulton.
DeHart Pauline (wid Oliver M), meats, 401 W Udell (N I), h same.
DeHart Sylvanus, lab, h e s Bond 1 n of Chicago (N I).
DeHaven Anna E (wid Andrew J), b 114 College av.
DeHaven Edward C, trav agt, h 211 Ash.
DeHaven Edward E, painter, h 32 Leon.
DeHaven George W, paperhngr, h 923 N Senate av.
DeHaven George W, sawmkr, b 319 S Meridian.
DeHaven Hattie L, boarding 319 S Meridian.
DeHaven Jennie (wid John C), h 301 Yandes.
Dehm, see also Deem.
Dehm Wm F, clk, b 143 N Alabama.
Dehmel Louis C, fireman, b 1 S Gale (B).
Dehmer Charles, florist Insane Hospital.
Dehn, see also Dean.
Dehn John C, sub letter carrier P O, h 36 S Gale (B).
Dehne Charles (Charles Dehne & Bro), h 248 S Penn.
Dehne Charles & Bro (Charles and Wm), feed, 26 N Liberty.
Dehne Edward, driver, r 262½ E Washington.
Dehne Louis C, clk, b 419½ Indiana av.
Dehne Robert A W, music teacher, 435 E McCarty, h same.
Dehne Wm (Charles Dehne & Bro), h 215 Davidson.
Dehne Wm G F, lab, h 19 N Dorman.
Dehne Wm G F jr, cabtmkr, h 19 N Dorman.
Dehne Wm H, clk, b 248 S Penn.
Dehner, see also Diener.
Dehner Charles, lab, b 183 S William (W I).
Dehner Edward, foreman, h 230 Lincoln la.
Dehner Elizabeth (wid Joseph F), h 72 S Spruce.
Dehner Harry, painter, b 19 Buchanan.
Dehner Henry, boxmkr, h 521 S Capitol av.
Dehner Henry, huckster, h 19 Buchanan.
Dehner John, lab, h 183 S William (W I).
Dehner John jr, lab, b 183 S William (W I).
Dehner Peter, lab, b 183 S William (W I).
Dehner Urban J, lab, h 80 S Brightwood av (B).
Dehoff Emory S, carp, h 506 N West.
Dehoney Clark, lab, h 235 S Reisner (W I).
Dehoney Isaac, lab, h 184 Minerva.
Dehoney James R, barber, 596 N West, b 235 S Reisner (W I).
Dehoney John, lab, b 583 W Washington.
Dehoney Reason, lab, b 235 S Reisner (W I).
Dehorney Elzie, lab, r 29 Ellsworth.
Dehorney Peter, lab, h 326 W 2d.
Dehorney Washington, lab, h 183 Muskingum al.
Dehune John, plastr, b 553 W Washington.
Deibold John, steelwkr, b 14 Church.
Deichler Anna (wid George P), h 319 Virginia av.

OTTO GAS ENGINES | BUILDERS' EXCHANGE S. W. Cor. Ohio and Penn. Telephone 535.

Becker & Son Charles Becker Jacob Becker Jr. Merchant Tailors. 21 N. Penn. St. Tel. 934

SALISBURY & STANLEY · Office, Store and Bank Fixtures a Specialty. All kinds of Repairing done on short notice. 177 Clinton St., Indianapolis, Ind. · Contractors and Builders TELEPHONE 999.

Deichler Anna P, h 71 Peru av.
Deischer Lucy, nurse, 7 Miller blk, h same.
Deissler Henry F, baker, h 226 Coburn.
Deitch Clarence C, clk, r 24 Mansur blk.
Deitch Guilford A, lawyer, 26 Thorpe blk, h 237 Virginia av.
Deitch Henry, clk, h 237 E Vermont.
Deitch Joseph G, clk Model Clothing Co, h 1144 N Penn.
Deitch Oscar S, phys, 2 Bloomington, h 24 same.
Deitch Othello L, phys, 158 River av (W I), h same.
Deitch Otto A, druggist, 880 W Washington, h same.
Deitch Rachel A (wid Joseph L), b 400 W New York.
Deitch Robert P, lawyer, h 175 N Penn.
Deitchman Charles, lab, b 89 Lord.
Deitchman Nancy J, h 89 Lord.
Deitchman Wm, engr, b 14½ Bates.
Delaloye Eugene, lab, b 164 W Maryland.
Delaney Catherine (wid Michael), h 57 S California.
Delaney Cornelius, stoker, h 37 Henry.
Delaney Edward J, clk, b 301 S West.
Delaney Frances B, dressmkr, 388 S Capitol av, h same.
Delaney Hannah M, grocer, 301 S West, h same.
Delaney Joseph A, lab, h 292 Indiana av.
Delaney Kate (wid Michael), h 57 S California.
Delaney Margaret, clk, b 107 High.
Delaney Margaret (wid Michael), h 388 S Capitol av.
Delaney Patrick, lab, b 324 W Maryland.
Delaney Peter J, b 173 E Morris.
Delaney Peter W, city fireman, b 173 E Morris.
Delaney Philip, bookbndr, b 37 Henry.
Delaney Theresa M, nurse, 465½ S Meridian, h same.
Delaney Thomas F, finisher, b 173 E Morris.
Delaney Wm, lab, h 107 High.
Delaney Wm C, lab, b 37 Henry.
De Lano Charles J, trav agt, r 81½ W Market.
De Lapp Ida M, janitress, h 31½ Virginia av.
Delapp Joseph H, janitor, r 20 Hutchings blk.
De La Tour Marie (wid Herbez), music teacher, 191 N New Jersey, b same.
Delbrugge Catherine, forewoman, h 187 Church.
Delbrugge Walter, clk, b 187 Church.
Delbrugge Wm F, city fireman, h 187 Church.
Delehanty Patrick, switchman, h 232 Michigan (H).
Delker Christian, butcher, h rear e s Arlington av 3 n of Walnut av (I).
Delks, see also Dilks.
Delks Francis M, lab, h 54 Jones.
Delks Frank, mach, b 54 Jones.
Delks Harry, uphlr, b 54 Jones.
Dell Frank M, coal and wood, 378 E Washington, h 655 same.
Dell Margaret (wid Edward J), h 52 S Alabama.
Dell Wm A, horseshoer, 595 Morris (W I), h 30 N Judge Harding (W I).
Dell Wm H A, bkkpr, r 12 Hubbard blk.
DELLETT JACOB, Physician, Office Hours 9-11 A M, 1-3 and 7-8 P M, Sundays 10-12 A M, Office 77½ S Illinois, h 458 S Delaware.

Henry H. Fay,
40½ E. Washington St.,
REAL ESTATE,
AND LOAN BROKER.

Dellinger Andrew J, carp, h w s Union 2 s of Washington (M J).
De Long Catherine (wid Joseph), b 350 E Morris.
Delong Frank O, clk, b 142 Bates.
Delong John M, cooper, h 142 Bates.
De Long John W, mach, b 29 Madison av.
Delorenzo Dominick, fruits, 90 E Mkt House, h 21 S Liberty.
Delp Bertram, clk Fitzgerald & Delp, b 914 N Senate av.
Delp Otto (Fitzgerald & Delp), h 914 N Senate av.
Delury Francis M, lab, h 50 Nordyke av (W I).
Deluse George, saloon, 20 Kentucky av, h 214 Union.
Deluse John P, saloon, 99 E South, h same.
Deluse Otto P, bkkpr Indpls Brewing Co, b 214 Union.
Delveaux Clarence W, condr, b 547 College av.
Delveaux Eugene, stonecutter, b 547 College av.
Delveaux John B, mach, h 547 College av.
Delzell Samuel A, mach, h 661 Mass av.
Demar Lucas, lab, b 430 Blake.
Demaree Alice J, boarding 98 N Alabama.
Demaree Charles A (Demaree & Fisse), b 98 N Alabama.
Demaree Claude R, tailor, 12 Commercial blk, h 124 W New York.
Demaree Daniel L, carp, h 219 W 1st.
Demaree Fannie (wid John), h 81 Garden.
Demaree Frank, fruits, h 79 Harmon.
Demaree Frank S, ins, h 160 Newman.
Demaree John W, engr, h 270 Martindale av.
Demaree Robert P, lab, h 312 Columbia av.
Demaree Samuel F, mach, b 160 Newman.
Demaree Samuel J, paperhngr, b 283 Bates.
Demaree Samuel W, millwright, h 98 N Alabama.
Demaree Violet A, teacher Industrial School, r The Wyandot.
Demaree & Fisse (Charles A Demaree, John H Fisse), tailors, 41 Virginia av.
Demarest Thomas W, asst master mechanic P C C & St L Ry, b 714 E Washington.

COAL AND LIME Cement, Hair, Sewer Pipe, etc. BALKE & KRAUSS CO. Cor. Missouri and Market Sts.

THE HOGAN TRANSFER AND STO
Household Goods and Pianos Moved—Packed—Stored...... Baggage and Package Express Machinery and Safes a Specialty Cor. TELE

The Provident Lif and Trust Company
Of Philadelphia
Grants Certificates of Extension to I[illegible] who are temporarily unable to pay th[illegible]
D. W. EDWARDS, Gen. Agt., 508 Indiana Tr[illegible]

Deere, Mansur & Co. Samuel [illegible] farm impl[illegible], 75 W Wash[illegible]
DEERE & CO, Thomas A [illegible] Agt. Plows and Cultivators, 7[illegible] W Washington, Tel 1108.
Deerhake Ernest H, carp, h [illegible]
Deerham James, lab, h [illegible]
Deering Harvester Co. J [illegible] agt, 192 W Market.
Deery Alice (wid Henry) [illegible] New Jersey.
Deery James H, supt city [illegible] h 339 N Pine.
Deery John A, paperhngr, h [illegible]
Deery Patrick E, paperhngr [illegible]
Deeter Franklin S, fireman [illegible] 4 s of Sutherland (B)
Deeter Royal L, brakeman [illegible] av.
Deeter Wm W, condr, h [illegible]
Deetring George W, lab, h [illegible]
DeFalco Thomas A, barber [illegible]
Defendserfer Charles, lab [illegible]
Deffaulx Elizabeth (wid [illegible]) Madison.
Deffaulx Louis F, carp, h [illegible]
Defibaugh Charles C, forem [illegible] 1780 Graceland av.
Defibaugh Wm J, driver, h [illegible] av.
DeFord John A, carp, h [illegible]
Defrance John, cook, r [illegible]
Defrayne George A, mach [illegible] Leon.
Defrees Fred D, student [illegible]
Defrees Morris M, civ [illegible] h 74 W Michigan.
Defrees Rollin E, draughtsm [illegible] gine Wks, h 524 E [illegible]
Defrees Thomas M, lieut [illegible] Michigan.
Degan Nellie, h 157 Bates.
Degering Christian, farmer [illegible] ton 6 e of Sherman Drive.
Degnan Patrick, blksmith [illegible]
Degnan Thomas F, engr [illegible]
Degner Charles, driver, h [illegible]
Degner Eva E, cashr John [illegible] E Michigan.

Degner Lydia E[illegible]
Degner Wm F [illegible]
Degner Wm T [illegible]
DeGroyer Laure[illegible] 76 W 4th.
DeHaas Charles [illegible] bldg, h 1[illegible] N
DeHaas [illegible] 1[illegible] N Alabama
DeHart Edward
DeHart Josiah [illegible]
DeHart [illegible] W [illegible]
DeHart Sylvan[illegible] Chicago [illegible]
DeHaven Anna [illegible] College av.
DeHaven Edwar[illegible]
DeHaven Edwar[illegible]
DeHaven George [illegible] Senate av.
DeHaven George [illegible] ridian.
DeHaven Hattie [illegible]
DeHaven Jenn[illegible]
Dehm, see also [illegible]
Dehm Wm F [illegible]
Dehmel Louis C [illegible]
Dehmer Charles [illegible]
Dehn, see also [illegible]
Dehn John [illegible]
Dehne Charles [illegible] 30 S Penn.
Dehne Charles [illegible] food, 3[illegible] N Liberty
Dehne Edward.
Dehne Louis C [illegible]
Dehne Robert A [illegible] McCarty, h [illegible]
Dehne Wm [illegible] Davidson.
Dehne Wm G F [illegible]
Dehne Wm G F [illegible] man.
Dehne Wm H [illegible]
Dehner, see also [illegible]
Dehner Charles.
Dehner Edward.
Dehner Elizabeth [illegible] Spruce.
Dehner Harry [illegible]
Dehner Henry [illegible]
Dehner Henry [illegible]
Dehner John, lab [illegible]
Dehner John jr [illegible]
Dehner Peter, h[illegible]
Dehner Urban [illegible] av (B).
Dehoff Emory S [illegible]
Dehoney Clark [illegible]
Dehoney Isaac [illegible]
Dehoney James [illegible] 35 S Reisner
Dehoney John, [illegible]
Dehoney Rosco[illegible] (W I).
Dehorney Elzie [illegible]
Dehorney Peter [illegible]
Dehorney Wa[illegible] kingum al.
Dehune John, pl[illegible]
Deibold John, s[illegible]
Deichler Anna [illegible] ginia av.

Julius C. Walk & Son, Jewelers Indianapolis. 12 EAST WASHINGTON ST.

OTTO GAS ENGINES | S. W

The Central Rubber & Supply Co. PHONE 922. 79 S. ILLINOIS ST., INDIANAPOLIS, IND. Hose, Belting, Packing, Clothing, Druggists' Sundries, Bicycle Tires, Cotton Hose, Etc. New York Belting & Packing Co., L't'd.

Becker & Son Charles Becker Jacob Bucking Merchant Tailors. 21 N. Penn St. Tel. 934

SALISBURY & STANLEY. Office, Store and Bank Fixtures a Specialty. 177 Clinton St., Indianapolis, Ind. Contractors and Builders TELEPHONE 999.

Deichler Anna P, h 71 Peru av.
Deischer Lucy, nurse, 7 Miller blk, h same.
Deissler Henry F, baker, h 226 Coburn.
Deitch Clarence C, clk, r 24 Mansur blk.
Deitch Guilford A, lawyer, 26 Thorpe blk, h 237 Virginia av.
Deitch Henry, clk, h 237 E Vermont.
Deitch Joseph G, clk Model Clothing Co, h 1144 N Penn.
Deitch Oscar S, phys, 2 Bloomington, h 24 same.
Deitch Othello L, phys, 158 River av (W I) h same.
Deitch Otto A, druggist, 880 W Washington, h same.
Deitch Rachel A (wid Joseph L), b 400 W New York.
Deitch Robert P, lawyer, h 175 N Penn.
Deitchman Charles, lab, b 89 Lord.
Deitchman Nancy J, h 89 Lord.
Deitchman Wm, engr, b 14½ Bates.
Delaloye Eugene, lab, b 164 W Maryland.
Delaney Catherine (wid Michael), h 57 S California.
Delaney Cornelius, stoker, h 37 Henry.
Delaney Edward J, clk, b 301 S West.
Delaney Frances B, dressmkr, 388 S Capitol av, h same.
Delaney Hannah M, grocer, 301 S West, h same.
Delaney Joseph A, lab, h 292 Indiana av.
Delaney Kate (wid Michael), h 57 S California.
Delaney Margaret, clk, b 107 High.
Delaney Margaret (wid Michael), h 388 S Capitol av.
Delaney Patrick, lab, b 324 W Maryland.
Delaney Peter J, b 173 E Morris.
Delaney Peter W, city fireman, [illegible] Morris.
Delaney Philip, bookbndr, b 37 [illegible]
Delaney Theresa M, nurse, [illegible] ian, h same.
Delaney Thomas F, finish[illegible] ris.
Delaney Wm, lab, h [illegible]
Delaney Wm C, lab, b [illegible]
De Lano Charles J, tra[illegible] ket.
De Lapp Ida M, janit[illegible] av.
Delapp Joseph H, jan[illegible] blk.
De La Tour Marie [illegible] teacher, [illegible] N New J[illegible]
Delbrugge [illegible]rine, Church.
Delbrug[illegible] clk[illegible]
Delbru[illegible] Church[illegible]
Delehan[illegible] igan [illegible]
Delker [illegible] lingt[illegible]
Delks, [illegible]
Delks [illegible]
Delks [illegible]
Delks [illegible]
Dell [illegible] ingt[illegible]
Dell M[illegible] bama.
Dell W[illegible] h 3[illegible]
Dell W[illegible]
DELL[illegible] Hour[illegible] Sunday[illegible] nois.

Henry H. Fay,
40½ E. Washington St.,
REAL ESTATE,
AND LOAN BROKER.

Dellinger Andrew J, carp, h w s Union 2 s of Washington (M J).
De Long Catherine (wid Joseph), b 350 E Morris.
Delong Frank O, clk, b 142 Bates.
Delong John M, cooper, h 142 Bates.
De Long John W, mach, b 29 Madison av.
Delorenzo Dominick, fruits, 90 E Mkt House, h 21 S Liberty.
Delp Bertram, clk Fitzgerald & Delp, b 914 N Senate av.
Delp Otto (Fitzgerald & Delp), h 914 N Senate av.
Delury Francis M, lab, h 50 Nordyke av (W I).
Deluse George, saloon, 20 Kentucky av, h 214 Union.
Deluse John P, saloon, 99 E South, h same.
Deluse Otto P, bkkpr Indpls Brewing Co, h 214 Union.
Delveaux Clarence W, condr, b 547 College av.
Delveaux Eugene, stonecutter, b 547 College [illegible]
Delveaux John B, mach, h 547 College av.
Delzell Samuel A, mach, h 661 Mass av.
Demar Lucas, lab, b 430 Blake.
Demaree Alice J, boarding 98 N Alabama.
Demaree Charles A (Demaree & Fisse), b [illegible] Alabama.
[illegible] Claude R, tailor, 12 Commercial [illegible] 4 W New York.
[illegible] Daniel L, carp, h 219 W 1st.
[illegible] Fannie (wid John), h 81 Garden.
[illegible] Frank, fruits, h 79 Harmon.
[illegible] Frank S, ins, h 160 Newman.
[illegible] n W, engr, h 270 Martindale [illegible]
[illegible]ert P, lab, h 312 Columbia av.
[illegible]uel F, mach, b 160 Newman.
[illegible]el J, paperhngr, b 283 Bates.
[illegible]el W, millwright, h 98 N Al[illegible]
[illegible]t A, teacher Industrial [illegible] Wyandot.
[illegible]se (Charles A Demaree, [illegible] tailors, 41 Virginia av.
[illegible]s W, asst master mechan[illegible] Ry, b 714 E Washington.

[illegible]W'S SPECTACLES [illegible]ST IN USE [illegible]3 N. MERIDIAN ST.

CO[illegible] BALKE & KRAUSS CO. Cor. Missouri and Market Sts.

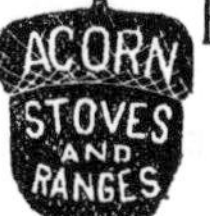

FRIEDGEN'S IS THE PLACE FOR THE NOBBIEST SHOES Ladies' and Gents' 19 North Pennsylvania St.

SAMUEL LAING | COPPER AND GALVANIZED IRON CORNICE MANUFACTURER
72 AND 32 COURT STREET. SKYLIGHTS AND VENTILATORS.

M. B. WILSON, Pres. W. F. CHURCHMAN, Cash.
THE CAPITAL NATIONAL BANK,
INDIANAPOLIS, IND.
Our Specialty is handling all Country Checks and Drafts on Indiana and neighboring States at the very lowest rates. Call and see us.
Interest Paid on Time Deposits.
28 S. MERIDIAN ST., COR. PEARL.

Demarr John, lab, h 15 Northwestern av.
DeMarr Stephen, lab, h 446 E 7th.
DeMarr Walter, coachman 247 Park av.
Demars Edward, waiter The Denison.
DeMartine Antonio A, fruits, 124 S Illinois, b same.
DeMartine Henry C, clk, b 124 S Illinois.
DeMartine Kate (wid Louis), h 124 S Illinois.
Demby Thomas, lab, r 433 Blake.
DeMiller Wm C, reporter, r 221 N Capitol av.
Deming Eli R, trav agt, h 71 W 2d.
Deming George, sub letter carrier P O, h 56 Dougherty.
Demmer Peter, carp, h 21 Coburn.
Demmerer Edna, h rear 227 Blake.
Demmerly Thomas W, embalmer F A Blanchard, h 316 N Alabama.
Demmy Jacob W, finisher, b 526½ S Meridian.
Demmy John R, lab, h 526½ S Meridian.
Demmy Wm H, b 98 Bates.
Demmy Wm J, agt, b 27 N New Jersey.
Demont Edward, clk, b 431 Ash.
DeMoss Calvin, peddler, h 5 Brown av (H).
DeMoss Charles E, butcher, h 460 W New York.
DeMott Elmer E, engr, h 98 Nordyke av (W I).
DeMott Wm S, b 98 Nordyke av (W I).
Demott Wm S, motorman, h 67 W 13th.
DeMotte David S, driver, h 84 Cypress.
DeMotte Garrett F, driver, b 70 Cypress.
Demotte Margaret, stenog, b 147 Huron.
DeMotte Mary (wid Garrett), n 70 Cypress.
DeMotte Orville, clk R M S, h 216 Clifford av.
DeMotte Wm H, teacher Deaf and Dumb Inst, h 121 Walcott.
Dempsey Clayton E, painter, r 152 N Senate av.
Dempsey Daniel O, stairbldr, h 577 E Market.
Dempsey Elmer, lab, b 18 Cora.
Dempsey Frank, lab, h 25 Roanoke.
Dempsey Frank E, insp City Engineer, b 577 E Market.
Dempsey Harry, mach, h 265 Davidson.

TUTTLE & SEGUIN,
28 E. Market St. Ground Floor.
COLLECTING RENTS AND CARE OF PROPERTY
A SPECIALTY.
Telephone 1168.

Dempsey Harvey, coachman 285 N Illinois.
Dempsey James W, bkkpr, h 132½ Ruckle.
Dempsey Wm E, lab, h 1375 Graceland av.
Denane Alman, lab, h 12 Holborn.
Denison Agnes H, music teacher, 103 Andrews, b same.
Denison Casino Co The, saloon, 81 N Penn.
Denison Frederick H, timekpr E C Atkins & Co, h 103 Andrews.
DENISON THE, Erwin Hotel Co Proprs, s e cor Penn and Ohio, Tel 471.
Deniston Charles E, clk L E & W R R, h 124 S Noble.
Deniston James J, harnessmkr, b 306 S Meridian.
Denker Charles, tailor, 594 Virginia av, h 93 Sanders.
Denker Christian W, car rep, h 22 Dawson.
Denker Henry C, car insp, h 962 Grove av.
Denker Wm, tailor, b 93 Sanders.
Denmead Anna, clk, r 405 N Penn.
Denmire Emma (wid Wm), r 11 Columbia blk.
Dennenberg Christine (wid Wm), h 660 Fremont (N I).
Denner Pauline (wid Frederick), h 68 S West.
Denner Wm F, mach hd, b 68 S West.
Dennett John, h 282 E St Clair.
Denney Anna (Pugh & Denney), b 177 Fletcher av.
Dennie Levi H, lab, h 52 S Austin (B).
Dennin Thomas, clk R M S, r 77½ S Illinois.
Denning Charles B, saloon, 1008 E Washington, b 18 Johnson av.
Denning Joseph, lab, b Exchange Hotel (W I).
Denning Joseph N, clk L S Ayres & Co, b 74 W New York.
Dennis Archibald R, clk A W Thompson, r 292 N Illinois.
Dennis Charles, editorial writer The Indpls News, h 813 N Alabama.
Dennis David, bell boy The Bates.
Dennis Elvira R (wid John), h 71 Davidson.
Dennis Henry L, engr, b 1027 E Washington.
Dennis James E, driver, h 21 Warren av (W I).
Dennis Jerome D, tel opr, h 15 Woodlawn av.
Dennis John, h 16 Warren av (W I).
Dennis John, bricklyr, b 36 Buchanan.
Dennis Louise E, b 71 Davidson.
Dennis Joseph M, engr, h 66 Ludlow av.
Dennis Martin L, baker, h 465 E St Clair.
Dennis Peter, contr, 36 Buchanan, h same.
Dennis Wilber, draughtsman Chandler & Taylor Co, b 216 W New York.
DENNY ALBERT W, Real Estate, Rentals and Insurance, 30 N Delaware, r same.
Denny Augustus, lab, h 114½ Hill av.
Denny Austin, crater, r 19 Russell av.
Denny Austin Flint (Stanton & Denny), h 847 N Delaware.
Denny Caleb S (McBride & Denny), h 673 N Penn.
Denny Charles, lab, b California House.
Denny Edward L, dep County Auditor, 41 Court House, h 252½ Mass av.
Denny Elmer E, brakeman, b 345 Prospect.
Denny George M, carp, b 288 Jefferson av.
Denny Harry W, bkkpr W J Holliday & Co, h 197 Woodlawn av.
Denny John, painter, h w s Denny 2 n of Ohio (B).

PAPER BOXES: SULLIVAN & MAHAN 41 W. Pearl St.

DIAMOND WALL PLASTER { Telephone 1410 BUILDERS' EXCHANGE.

If your Laundry Work is not satisfactory, try THE HOME LAUNDRY

Denny John E, carp, h 288 Jefferson av.
Denny Mary (wid Wm H), h 117½ W Washington.
Denny Owen L, painter e s Nicholas 1 s of Howland, h same.
Denny Robert, lab, h 67 Maple.
Denny Samuel, vice-pres Indpls Fancy Grocery Co, h 230 N West.
Denny Samuel H, trav agt, h 31 Ashland (W I).
Denny Scott L, clk, r 298 E South.
Denny Wm C, h 345 Prospect.
Densmore, see also Dinsmore.
Densmore Calvin E, engr, b 145 Bellefontaine.
Densmore Samuel, engr, h 145 Bellefontaine.
Denson Charles W, cigars, 149½ Mass av, r 269 N Alabama.
Denson Henry A, phys, 16 E Ohio, h 269 N Alabama.
Denson John A, fireman, h 27 Decatur.
Dent Edward J, clk Kingan & Co (ltd), b 533 College av.
Dent Ella, h 227 Fayette.
Dent Wm, coachman, 377 College av.
Dent Wm W, condr, h 15 Paca.
Denton Claude C, photog, r 9 Stewart pl.
Denton Frank J, cooper, r 72 S West.
Denton James, harnessmkr, b 306 S Meridian.
Denton Mary R, dressmkr, 145½ W Washington, h same.
Denton Robert G, mach hd, b 125 N West.
Denton Thomas B, cooper, h 125 N West.
Denwood Elmer E, lab, h n w cor English and Auburn avs (W).
Denwood George, mach hd, h s s Michigan av 2 w Auburn av (W).
Denwood John L, lab, b s s Michigan av 3 w of Auburn av (W).
Denwood Wm, lab, h s s Michigan av 3 w of Auburn av (W).
Denzer Louis J, mach, h 288 S East.
Denzer Mary A (wid John), h 147 S Noble.
Denzer Peter, cigarmkr, b 147 S Noble.
Denzler Gustav A, fireman, b 860 E Washington.
Denzler Herman, foreman, h 114 S State av.
DEPARTMENT PUBLIC PARKS, Wm R Holloway Sec, 619-625 Indiana Trust Bldg, Tel 1859.
Depew Joseph, lab 166 N Meridian.
DePew Richard J, h 50 Park av.
Depp George, h 228 E Pearl.
Deppe Wm A, molder, h 1 Walker (H).
Deppert Wm, driver, h 108 Geisendorff.
Depue Clayton M, carp, h 264 Highland av.
DePue Charles F, printer, b 71 E St Clair.
DePue Louisa J (wid James M), b 71 E St Clair.
Deputy Addison C, dentist, 91 Lombard bldg, h 1568 N Illinois.
Deputy Bros (Ivan D and Solomon D), creamery, 231 Mass av.
Deputy Charles, driver, r 152 W Washington.
Deputy Edward H, tinner, b 553 Virginia av.
Deputy Ivan D (Deputy Bros), h 231 Mass av.
Deputy John, switchman, b 1169 E Washington.
Deputy Joseph J, forger, b 336 N Liberty.
Deputy Luther, filer, h 4 Edward (W I).
Deputy Solomon D (Deputy Bros), b 231 Mass av.
Deputy Thomas M, r 116½ W New York.
DePuy Wm M, hatter, 47 Mass av, h 130 W Ohio.

FRANK NESSLER. WILL H. ROST.
FRANK NESSLER & CO.
Tailors
56 EAST MARKET ST. (Lemcke Building),
INDIANAPOLIS, IND.

DeQuesada Carlos V, musician, h 286 W 6th.
Derbyshire Elizabeth (wid Benjamin C), b 234 W Michigan.
Derleth George, meats, 234 W McCarty, h same.
Derleth Michael, painter, 31 Downey, h same.
Derleth Peter, carp, h 31 Gatling.
Derleth Wm, meats, 50 E Mkt House and 189 W Washington, h 497 Madison av.
Derndinger Oscar, trav agt Baldwin, Miller & Co, h 316 N Meridian.
Derrick Jesse T, ball player, h 124 Broadway.
Derrick Walker, lab, b rear 738 N West.
Derrick Ramsey, lab, b 189 W 3d.
Derricks Sarah (wid John), h 189 W 3d.
Derring Wm, lab, h 17 Athon.
Derritt Cain, lab, b 126 Hudson.
Derry Edward H, grocer, 1381 W Washington (M J), h 1379 same.
Dersch Ida, b 1289 N New Jersey.
Dersch John, h 1289 N New Jersey.
DeRuiter Derk, pres Indiana Construction Co, h 1026 N Meridian.
DeSanno James, tilesetter, h 747 E Michigan.
DeSanno Walter, mach, b 640 E Ohio.
Deschler Charles F, clk, b 159 Park av.
Deschler Frederick J, real est, h 159 Park av.
Deschler George, h 371 N Senate av.
Deschler John, meats, 31 E Mkt House, h 235 N California.
Deschler John H, butcher, b 235 N California.
DESCHLER LOUIS G, Wholesale and Retail Cigars and Tobacco, 51 N Penn (Lemcke Bldg), and Retail Cigars, Tobacco and News Dealer, The Bates House, Tel 1718; h 775 N Meridian.
Deschler Nettie (wid Charles J), h 275 Prospect.
Desebrock Bernard, mach, b 315 E New York.

Haueisen & Hartmann
163-169 E. Washington St.
FURNITURE,
Carpets,
Household Goods,
Tin, Granite and China Wares, Oil Cloth and Shades
197 S. Illinois St. Telephone 1769.

THE WM. H. BLOCK CO. 7 AND 9 EAST WASHINGTON STREET. DRY GOODS, MEN'S FURNISHINGS.

The Fidelity and Deposit Co. OF MARYLAND. Bonds signed for Administrators, Assignees, Executors, Guardians, Receivers, Trustees, and persons in every position of trust. GEO. W. PANGBORN, General Agent, 704-706 Lemcke Building. Telephone 140.

INSURE YOUR PROPERTY WITH FRANK K. SAWYER

• JOSEPH GARDNER •
GALVANIZED IRON
CORNICES and SKYLIGHTS.
Metal Ceilings and Siding.
Tin, Iron, Steel and Slate Roofing.
37, 39 & 41 KENTUCKY AVE. Telephone 322

Desebrock Henry, custodian German House, h same.
Deshong Harry, b 459 E Georgia.
Deshong Jemima (wid Hiram), h 459 E Georgia.
Deslan James, lab, b 21 Cleveland (H).
Deslan Michael, lab, b 21 Cleveland (H).
Desmond James L, blksmith, r 5 Columbia blk.
DeSouchet Augustus M, real est, 231 Lemcke bldg, h 32 The Blacherne.
Despo Alfred O, carp, 200 Fletcher av, h same.
Despo James I, clk, b 200 Fletcher av.
Dessauer Max, clk, h 108 Fletcher av.
DeTamble Edward S, pres Union Embossing Machine Co; h 695 N Alabama.
Detrick John C, clk, h 224 Buchanan.
Deugan Wm P, lab, h n s Pansy 1 w of Floral av.
Deupree Daniel E, draughtsman, h 117 Colgrove.
Devany Owen, lab, b 40 S West.
DeVar Elmer, clk, r 228 N Capitol av.
DeVay Pierre W, trav agt The Indiana Paper Co, b The Denison.
Devenish Edward C, mach, h 269 Alvord.
Devenish John J, molder, h 78 Cornell av.
Deveny Martin, lab, b 335 W Maryland.
Deveny Michael, lab, h 335 W Maryland.
Dever, see also Davar.
Dever Edward S, lab, b 27 Palmer.
Dever Helen (wid Charles), h 27 Palmer.
Dever John C, finisher, b 27 Palmer.
Dever Lydia (wid Eli), b 148 Eddy.
Dever Samuel, mer police, h 24 Athon.
Dever Thomas H, varnisher, b 27 Palmer.
Dever Wm G, finisher, b 27 Palmer.
DeVersey Elizabeth (wid Joseph), grocer, 697 S Meridian, h same.
DeVinay Effie (wid Willis), b 57 Camp.
Devine, see also Divine.
Devine Agnes (wid Patrick), h 155 W McCarty.
Devine Edward P, mach, b 156 S Noble.
Devine Frank J, mach, b 1143 E Washington.
Devine Isaac P, waiter, h 209 W North.
Devine John, b 215 Northwestern av.

J. S. FARRELL & CO.
Have Experienced Workmen and will Promptly Attend to your
PLUMBING
Repairs. 84 North Illinois Street. Telephone 382.

DeVine John A, mach, h 456 E Michigan.
Devine Thomas, baker Parrott & Taggart, b 155 W McCarty.
Devine Wm, lab, b 890 W Washington.
Devine Wm A, printer, h 601 Marlowe av.
Deviney Frank L, condr, h 931 Martindale av.
Deviney Thomas, lab, b 79 W McCarty.
Devir John, trav agt, h 270 N Liberty.
Devit Richard, coremkr, b 482 E Georgia.
Devlin John, clk Knight & Jillson, h 86 N New Jersey.
Devney Delia M, stenog Carson & Thompson, b 261 S East.
Devney Malachi, flagman, h 261 S East.
De Vore Charles S, chemist, b 83 Huron.
De Vore Clara B (wid Calvin E), r 183 Dearborn.
De Vore Eliza (wid James), h 79 W 7th.
Devore James C, civil engr, h 500 N Alabama.
De Vore James E, clk, h 228 N Capitol av.
De Voss Daniel, carp, h 125 Woodlawn av.
De Voss James D, millwright, b 125 Woodlawn av.
De Voss Samuel H, cigars, 308 Virginia av, b 125 Woodlawn av.
Devries Benjamin D, carver, h 114 Kennington.
Devries Byron, carver, h 43 Nebraska.
Dew Peter, lab, h 427 W 2d.
De Wald Frank, clk N Y Store, r 28 Hubbard blk.
Dewald Frank M, cigarmkr, h 2 Hermann.
Dewald Joseph, clk, h 233 N Noble.
Dewald Matthias, porter, h 238 Fulton.
Dewar Andrew J, mach, h 19 N Beville av.
Dewar Duncan, electrician, h 41 N Arsenal av.
Deweese Charles G, opr W U Tel Co, h 137 W New York.
Dewenter Herman C (Kruse & Dewenter), h 698 N Alabama.
Dewerson Alander, lab, b e s Sangster av 4 n of Belle.
Dewhurst Frederic E Rev, pastor Plymouth Church, h 28 Christian av.
Dewire Charles A, painter, h 88 Newman.
Dewire Nancy A (wid Charles), b 38 Newman.
DE WITT CARROLL L, Special Agt Glens Falls Insurance Co, 311-312 Lemcke Bldg, h 988 N Penn, Tel 1740.
DeWitt Charles A, brakeman, r 852½ E Washington.
DeWitt Martha M, cook, r 180 E Washington.
DeWitt Milton, foreman, b 295 E Court.
DE WITT WM L, Grocer, 877 Cornell av, h same.
DeWolf Harry E, clk, h 252 W Michigan.
Deyson Francis M, lab, h 161 Meek.
Dial Amelia S (wid Frank A), h 330 College av.
Diamond Joseph, mill hd, b 187 S Capitol av.
DIAMOND SAMPLE ROOM, Henry Kleine Propr, Headquarters for the Celebrated Blue Grass Club Whisky, 265 Mass av.
Diamond Steam Laundry and Toilet Supply Co The, Augustus Bruner pres, Anderson Bruner sec, 146 Ft Wayne av.
DIAMOND WALL PLASTER CO, Office Room 3 Builders' Exchange, Factory cor E North and Bee Line Ry, Tel 1410. (See top lines and opp classified Business Directory.)

GUARANTEED INCOME POLICIES issued only by the **United States Life Insurance Co.** E. B. SWIFT, Manager. 25 E. Market St.

Furniture Carpets } WM. KOTTEMAN { Stoves Ranges
89 and 91 East Washington Street. Telephone 1742.

WILLIAM WIEGEL } MANUFACTURER OF . . . . } SHOW CASES } 6 W. Louisiana St. Opposite Union Station.

Dichmann, see also Dickman.
Dichmann Anthony G, finisher Wm Wiegel, b 450 S East.
Dichmann George W, cabtmkr, h 48 Dougherty.
Dichmann John P, cabtmkr Wm Weigel, h 438 E McCarty.
Dichmann Philip, cabtmkr, h 450 S East.
Dichmann Wm J, cabtmkr Wm Weigel, h 46 Woodlawn av.
Dick, see also Dicks and Dix.
Dick Charles A, condr, h 351 S State av.
Dick George B, switchman, h 180 Hoyt av.
Dick George W, plater, 33 Virginia av, r 236 E Market.
Dick Sanford M, steamfitter, r 163 N Capitol av.
Dickens Fannie (wid Henry), h rear 490 W North.
Dicker Harriet (wid James), h 1559 N Illinois.
Dickerson, see also Dickinson, Dickson and Dixon.
Dickerson Albert R, asst Henry W Tutewiler, b 205 Blake.
Dickerson Alice, h 109 Locke.
Dickerson Belle K, dressmkr, 1129 N Delaware, b same.
Dickerson Charles S, engr, h 1680 Graceland av.
Dickerson Edward, lab, h 534 W Ontario (N I).
Dickerson George L, phys, 80 Dawson, h same.
Dickerson Harry, lab, b 182 Newman.
Dickerson Harry W, sawyer, b 445 Talbott av.
Dickerson Henry L Rev, h 108 Lexington av.
Dickerson Howard K, trav agt, b 445 Talbott av.
Dickerson James, lab, h 390 S State av.
Dickerson James A, mach, b 109 Locke.
Dickerson James A, porter, h 133 Columbia al.
Dickerson Jefferson, lab, b 97 Darnell.
Dickerson Jesse, lab, r rear 33 S Alabama.
Dickerson John L, h 1129 N Delaware.
Dickerson John A, horsedealer, h 861 N Delaware.
Dickerson Louise, b 597 W Pearl.
Dickerson Martha (wid Nelson), b 390 S State av.
Dickerson Mary (wid Frank), h 14 Holborn.
Dickerson Rolla E, plumber, b 109 Locke.
Dickerson Walker T, bkkpr Indiana Rubber Co, r 12 Wyandot blk.
Dickerson Wm, lab, b 34 Howard.
Dickerson Wm M, supt Indiana Lumber and Veneer Co, h 445 Talbott av.
Dickert Frank A, clk Wm Kotteman, h 290 Highland av.
Dickert Jacob, h 220 N West.
Dickert Jane E, dessmkr, 271 Union, h same.
Dickert Norbert A, grocer, 271 Union, h same.
Dickey Addison J, clk, h 550 N Illinois.
Dickey Alexander, city mngr Singer Mnfg Co, h 347 N Capitol av.
Dickey Alfred E, lawyer, 9 Ingalls blk, b 75 E Walnut.
Dickey Almon H, lawyer, 91½ E Court, r same.
Dickey Blanche, bkkpr, b 661 S Meridian.
Dickey Burton L, clk, h 186 Dougherty.
Dickey Charlotte J, stenog, b 564 College av.

We Buy Municipal ~ Bonds ~
THOS. C. DAY & CO,
Rooms 325 to 330 Lemcke Bldg.

Dickey Cyrus C, clk, h 661 S Meridian.
Dickey Edward T, lawyer, 4 Lombard bldg, h 744 N Alabama.
Dickey Frank, bottler, b 135 Madison.
Dickey George C, trav agt, h 28 N Senate av.
Dickey George R, gasfitter, b 224 E Court.
Dickey Harry E, agt, b 347 N Capitol av.
Dickey Jeremiah W, porter, h 135 Madison.
Dickey Marshall, clk, b 135 Madison.
Dickey Mary A (wid James B), h 55 Dougherty.
Dickey Samuel, b 347 N Capitol av.
Dickey Sarah I (wid Hezekiah), b 186 Dougherty.
DICKEY SOLOMON C REV, Sec and Mngr Winona Assembly and Summer School, h 564 College av.
Dickey Sophronia E, (wid James M), h 82 Greer.
Dickhut Frederick W, clk R M S, h 81 Hoyt av.
Dickhut Harry J, trav agt Kingan & Co (ltd), b 81 Hoyt av.
Dickie Frank E, bkkpr Central Cycle Mnfg Co, h 151 Woodlawn av.
Dickinson, see also Dickerson, Dickson and Dixon.
Dickinson Edward (G W Miller & Co), h w s Graceland av 3 n of 26th.
Dickinson Edwin P, butcher, b 516 S East.
Dickinson Elizabeth R (wid John C), h 331 N Penn.
Dickinson George, ins, h 516 S East.
Dickinson Theodore, lab, h rear 85 Cornell av.
Dickison Cassius R, polisher, h 79 Sanders.
Dickison Frank, motorman, h 62 Sheffield av (H).
Dickman, see also Dichmann.
Dickman Edward C, actor, b 91 N East.
Dickman Frank C, actor, b 91 N East.
Dickman Frederick B, h 91 N East.
Dickman Maria L (wid Charles W), h n s Washington av 2 w of Elm av (I).
Dickmann Wm A, watchmkr Wm T Marcy, h 24 W Walnut.
Dicks, see also Dick and Dix.

EAT HITZ'S CRACKERS AND CAKES.
ASK YOUR GROCER FOR THEM.

TURKISH RUGS AND CARPETS RESTORED TO ORIGINAL COLORS LIKE NEW | Capital Steam Carpet Cleaning Works M. D. PLUNKETT, Telephone 818

BENJ. BOOTH PRACTICAL EXPERT ACCOUNTANT. Books Opened, Written Up, Posted and Balanced. Room 18, 82½ E. Washington St., Indianapolis, Ind.

IF YOU WANT A GOOD MEAL AND HAVE IT NICELY SERVED GO TO THE SHERMAN RESTAURANT 18 and 20 S. MERIDIAN STREET

ESTABLISHED 1876. TELEPHONE 168.
CHESTER BRADFORD,
SOLICITOR OF PATENTS,
AND COUNSEL IN PATENT CAUSES.
(See adv. page 6.)
Office:—Rooms 14 and 16 Hubbard Block, S. W. Cor. Washington and Meridian Streets, INDIANAPOLIS, INDIANA.

Dicks Clarence W, student, b 310 N East.
Dicks Emory G, driver, h 18 Sharpe.
Dicks Francis M, butcher, h 310 N East.
Dicks George E, driver, r 355 S Capitol av.
Dicks Harry, tel opr, h 83 S Reisner (W I).
Dicks Harry E, meats, 32 Indiana av, r 69 N Illinois.
Dicks Ilva A, meats, 27 E Mkt House and 197 Mass av, h 310 N East.
Dickson, see also Dickerson, Dickinson and Dixon.
Dickson Arthur, b 474 N Penn.
Dickson Andrew, solr A Metzger Agency, b 506 N Senate av.
Dickson Annie, h 323 N California.
Dickson Arvenia (wid Barrett L), h 265 N East.
Dickson Beulah A (wid Wm), h w s Ritter av 2 s of C H & D R R (I).
Dickson Charles M, chief train disp Belt R R, h 135 Nordyke av (W I).
Dickson Effie (wid George), b 18 Cora.
Dickson Eliza (wid Charles), b 184 N Noble.
Dickson George A (Dickson & Talbott), h 644 N Penn.
Dickson George M, trav agt Hay & Willits Mnfg Co, b 55 Ruckle.
Dickson Hugh E, bartndr, h 250 S Capitol av.
Dickson James, lab, r 131 Allegheny.
DICKSON JAMES C (Agt), Lumber, 480 E Michigan, h 240 N East.
Dickson Jasper N, motorman, h 13 Sumner.
Dickson John, lab, h rear 33 S Alabama.
Dickson John, lab, h s e cor Jefferson and William.
Dickson John, lab, b 272 W Maryland.
Dickson John A, motorman, h 206 W St Clair.
Dickson John M, carpetlyr, h e s Ritter av 4 n of Washington av (I).
Dickson John T, pres Indpls Cabinet Wks, h 644 N Penn.
Dickson Joseph L, prin High School (W I), b 84 S Reisner (W I).
Dickson Josephine M A (wid Andrew), h 55 Ruckle.
Dickson Letitia (wid Hugh B), b 621 E Market.

O. B. ENSEY
MANUFACTURER OF
GALVANIZED IRON CORNICE,
SKYLIGHTS AND WINDOW CAPS.
TELEPHONE 1562. Cor. 6th and Illinois Sts.

Dickson Lewis M, lab, b 206 W St Clair.
Dickson Mahlon C, lab, b 206 W St Clair.
Dickson Margaret A (wid John B), h 310 N East.
Dickson Margaret I, sec Woman's Foreign Missionary Society of M E Church, b 310 N East.
Dickson Mary, h 132 N Liberty.
Dickson Mary A (wid James), b 578 N Penn.
Dickson Mary W, stenog Bellis Cycle Co, b 55 Ruckle.
Dickson Nathan, b 250 S Capitol av.
Dickson Nelson, lab, h 214 Middle.
Dickson Robert, h 474 N Penn.
Dickson Santford S, agt, h 387 Bellefontaine.
Dickson Simon, driver, h 422 E Walnut.
Dickson Simon G, lab, h 422 E Walnut.
Dickson Thomas M, lumber, h 500 E Market.
Dickson Wm, lab, h 207 W Walnut.
Dickson Wm, plumber, r 23 N West.
Dickson Wm C, h 474 N Penn.
Dickson Wm L, lab, b 206 W St Clair.
Dickson Wm R, baker, h e s Ritter av 4 n of Washington av (I).
DICKSON & TALBOTT (George A Dickson, Henry M Talbott), Proprs Grand, Park and English Opera Houses, 61½ N Penn, Ticket Office 8 Pembroke Arcade.
Dickten Wm, polisher, h rear 90 S Noble.
Diddel Andrew J, ins, h 469 College av.
Diddel Lelia E, stenog, b 469 College av.
Didlein Herman A, brewer, h 122 Kennington.
Didway Harriet D (wid John W), b 1273 N Delaware.
Didway Melville D, clk, h 1273 N Delaware.
Dieckmeyer Catherine (wid Wm), h 120 N Dorman.
Dieckmeyer Wm F, butcher, b 120 N Dorman.
Diederich John, cabtmkr, r 177 S Alabama.
Diefenbach Jacob, grocer, 210 W 1st, h same.
Diehl Kate (wid August), r 5½ Indiana av.
Diehm Christopher, lab, h 83 Davidson.
Diener, see also Dehner.
DIENER AUGUST, Marble and Granite Monuments and Statuary, Marble and Filing, 243 E Washington; Branch Works opp East Entrance Crown Hill Cemetery; h 1438 N Illinois. (See adv front edge and opp classified Monuments.)
Diener George, marblewkr August Diener, b 1438 N Illinois.
Diener Minnie, organist, b 1438 N Illinois.
Dierdorf John, tuner, h 514 Park av.
Dieringer Mary (wid Maker), h 21 Minnesota.
Dierking Charles A F, paperhngr, h 101 Naomi.
Dieter Ernest, shoemkr, 57 College av, h 74 Vine.
Dietrich, see also Dittrich.
Dietrich Albert, lab, h 81 Arizona.
Dietrich Edward, mach, b 391 Bellefontaine.
Dietrich Frank, miller, b 70 Fletcher av.
Dietrich Herman, mach, b 90 Union.
Dietrich John, driver, h 100 S Linden.
Dietrich Otto, lab, b 81 Arizona.
Dietrich Robert A, lab, b 81 Arizona.
Dietrich Wm D, tel opr, h 70 Fletcher av.

TUTEWILER UNDERTAKER, No. 72 WEST MARKET STREET. TELEPHONE 216.

PARTNERSHIP INSURANCE At low cost. By which provision is made against the pecuniary loss and embarrassment resulting from the death of a member of a firm.
Provident Life and Trust Co. of Philadelphia, D. W. EDWARDS, Gen'l Agt., 508 Indiana Trust Bldg.

THEODORE F. SMITHER, AGENT FOR WARREN'S ANCHOR BRAND ASPHALT ROOFING. OFFICE, 151 WEST MARYLAND ST. TEL. 861.

Dietrichs August E (M Dietrichs & Co), buyer Fahnley & McCrea, h 335 N Penn.
Dietrichs Dorothea (wid John), b 81 Kansas.
Dietrichs Margaret (wid Wm M; M Dietrichs & Co), b 335 N Penn.
Dietrichs M & Co (Margaret and August E Dietrichs), milliners, 10 E Washington.
Dietrick Joseph, lab, b 438 Mulberry.
Dietz August, baker, 44 Pendleton av (B), h same.
Dietz Charles E, clk George Hitz & Co, b 68 Pleasant.
Dietz Charles L, broker, 52 Virginia av, h n e cor Charles and 30th.
Dietz, Charles T, condr, h 60 N Noble.
Dietz Christian, farmer, h rear s e cor Line and P C C & St L Ry (I).
Dietz Edward A, finisher, b 50 Singleton.
Dietz Edward L, framemkr, b 194 E Morris.
Dietz Emil, pres and treas The Fred Dietz Co, h 224 S Alabama.
Dietz Ernst, butcher, b 579 Madison av.
Dietz Frank F, foreman The Fred Dietz Co, h 1376 E Washington.
Dietz Fred, coachman 619 N Penn.
DIETZ FRED CO THE, Emil Dietz Pres and Treas, George W Dietz Vice-Pres, Albert H Thoms Sec, Mnfrs of Packing Boxes and Warehouse Trucks, 370-406 Madison av, Tel 654. (See right side lines and p 10.)
Dietz Frederick A, mach, h 133 Newman.
Dietz Frederick G, clk Edward C Reick, b 293 Union.
Dietz Frederick P, lab, b 50 Singleton.
Dietz Frederika (wid Ferdinand), b 310 N Capitol av.
Dietz George W, vice-pres The Fred Dietz Co, h 293 Union.
Dietz, Harry A, clk, b 122 Yandes.
Dietz Helen F (wid Charles L), h 987 N Penn.
Dietz Henry, tinner, h 661 Charles.
Dietz Jacob J, clk George Hitz & Co, h 68 Pleasant.
Dietz James, tmstr, h 466 Chestnut.
Dietz John, h rear s e cor Line and P C C & St L Ry (I).
Dietz John C, farmer, h s e cor Line and P C C & St L Ry (I).
Dietz John C F, engr The H Lieber Co, h 136 Agnes.
Dietz John G, clk, h 203 E Morris.
Dietz Louis, lab, b s e cor Line and P C C & St L Ry (I).
Dietz Mary (wid Frederick), h 141 E South.
Dietz Oscar (Bussey & Dietz), b 400 Central av.
Dietz Otto, clk, b 203 E Morris.
Dietz Resenzia (wid Peter), h 50 Wallack.
Dietz Theodore, meats, 453½ Central av, h 400 same.
Dietz Theodore A, saloon, 299 S Delaware, h 269 S Alabama.
Dietz Webster, clk A Metzger Agency, b 987 N Penn.
Difel John, mach hd, b 212 Madison av.
Diffley Mary A, nurse Deaf and Dumb Inst.
Diggins Maurice, lab, h 520 N California.
Diggins Michael, lab, h 8 Meikel.
Diggins Thomas, lab, h 77 Camp.
Diggs Arthur E, attendant Public Library, b 263 N California.
Diggs George W, lab, h 456 E Washington.
Diggs Harry E, clk, b 263 N California.
Diggs Sarah A (wid John H), h 344 Cornell av.

THE WHEN IS A WORLD BEATER.

Diggs Thomas, tilesetter, b 181 S New Jersey.
Diggs Wm T, bricklyr, h 263 N California.
Dildine Alfred E, lab, b 260 Martindale av.
DILDINE BERT B, Merchant Tailor, The Lemcke Bldg, 64 E Market, h 36 Hall Pl.
Dildine Elizabeth (wid Henry), h 260 Martindale av.
Dildine Emery, electrotyper, b 260 Martindale av.
Dildine Erwin E, foreman, h 29 Temple av.
Dildine Frances E (wid Henry J), h 260 Martindale av.
Dildine George, ironwkr, b 260 Martindale av.
Dildine James A, clk P C C & St L Ry, h 75 N Arsenal av.
Dilg Louisa, seamstress, h 80 Meek.
Dilger Ignatz, lab, h s w cor West and Wisconsin.
Dilges Jacob, blksmith, n e cor Rural and Clifford av, h same.
Dilks, see also Delks.
Dilks John H (The Chester Pipe and Tube Co and Charles L Wayne & Co), h 20 The Blacherne.
Dill Chester E, mach, b 70 E Vermont.
Dill Edward J, tmstr, r 294½ Mass av.
Dill Elmer E, clk, r 340 E Market.
Dill Emanuel, lab, h 255½ E Washington.
Dill Emily (wid Wm G), dressmkr, 239 Shelby, h same.
Dill Ezekiel B, b 199 Sheffield av (H).
Dill Jane M (wid John C), b 858 Cornell av.
Dill J B, sec and treas Specialty Mnfg Co, h 70 E Vermont. (See adv opp classified Photographers.)
Dill Peter M, spec agt Mut Life Ins Co, h 872 N Penn.
Dillard Wm M, tmstr, h 34 Athon.
Dillehey Samuel C, polisher, h 268 S Illinois.
Dillen Nathan Y, carp, b 40 S Capitol av.
Dillen Susan, h 40 S Capitol av.
Dillenbeck Caroline M (wid Charles A), dressmkr, 217 Dougherty, h same.
Diller Elizabeth (wid Adam), b 27 School.
Diller Frank H, clk County Treasurer's Office, h 27 School.

THE A. BURDSAL CO.
WINDOW AND PLATE
GLASS
Putty, Glazier Points, Diamonds.
Wholesale and Retail. 34 and 36 S. Meridian St.

ELECTRIC CONSTRUCTION Isolated Plants Installed. Electric Wiring and Fittings of all kinds. C. W. Meikel. Tel. 466. 96-98 E. New York St

DALTON & MERRIFIELD { LUMBER South Noble St., near E. Washington

INDIANA ELECTROTYPE CO. BEST WORK. LOWEST PRICES. 23 WEST PEARL ST., INDIANAPOLIS, IND. JOB WORK. BOOK PLATES. All Orders Promptly Filled. BEST PATENT BASE ON THE MARKET.

KIRKHOFF BROS.,
GAS AND ELECTRIC FIXTURES
THE LARGEST LINE IN THE CITY.
102-104 SOUTH PENNSYLVANIA ST.
TELEPHONE 910.

Diller George W, city fireman, h 282 W St Clair.
Dillinger Earl V, mach, h 125 Lawrence.
Dillinger Everett B, carp, b 23 Elliott.
Dillinger James H, carp, h w s Harriet 2 n of Bloyd av (B).
Dillinger John W, grocer, 31 Cooper, h same.
Dillinger Matthew, lab, h 23 Elliott.
Dillingham Albert, foreman, r Mt Jackson.
Dillingham Vannie, school teacher, b 155 N Illinois.
Dillman Edward P, clk Atlas Engine Wks, b 191 Pleasant.
Dillman Ella J, dressmkr, 28 Evison, h same.
Dillman James A, carp, h 483 W Udell (N I).
Dillman Melissa R (wid Milton), h 28 Evison.
Dillman Oscar M, salesman C F Meyer & Bro, h 256 Talbott av.
Dillman Samuel, tmstr, h 553 Virginia av.
Dillman Uris A, lab, h 483 W Udell (N I).
Dillon Daniel, flagman, h 61 Maple.
Dillon David B, mach, b 564 S East.
Dillon George A, bicyclemkr, h 313 E Georgia.
Dillon Horace H, elev opr, b 40 S Capitol av.
Dillon James F, coremkr, b 30 Highland av (H).
Dillon Jane (wid John), h 564 S East.
Dillon John, molder, h 30 Highland av (H).
Dillon John B, foreman, h 21 Mayhew.
Dillon Katherine, asst postmaster Haughville, b 314 Michigan (H).
Dillon Lee, polisher, h 404 Columbia av.
Dillon Martin, boilermkr, b 419 S Missouri.
Dillon Mary, h 330 W Court.
Dillon Mary (wid Thomas), b 21 Mayhew.
Dillon Michael, cigarmkr, b 419 S Missouri.
Dillon Missouri (wid Levi), b 175 W Ohio.
Dillon Patrick, postmaster Haughville, 155 Michigan (H), h 314 same.
Dillon Thomas, lab, h 25 Helen.
Dillon Thomas, lab, h 419 S Missouri.
Dillon Thomas jr, boilermkr, b 419 S Missouri.

COAL AND COKE
The W. G. Wasson Co.,
130 INDIANA AVE. TEL. 989
LIME AND LATH

Dillon Thomas J, city fireman, h 364 S Illinois.
Dillon Wm J, mach, b 321 Jefferson av.
Dillow Samuel S, farmer, h w s Bluff rd 2 s of Raymond.
Dilts Charles O, lab, b 44 Yandes.
Dilts Edward, foreman, h w s Sugar Grove av 2 n of Vorster av (M P).
Dilts George W, patrolman, h 44 Yandes.
Dilts Harry E, condr, b 770 W Washington.
Dilts Oliver, mill hd, h 679 Wells (N I).
Dilts Sarah (wid Hoffman W), h 252½ Mass av.
Dimatteo Giovanni, peddler, b 121 Bright.
Dime Savings and Loan Assn, Wm A Rhodes sec, 2 Plymouth bldg.
Dimmitt Lewis F Rev, pastor Broadway M E Church, h 533 Bellefontaine.
Dimock Daniel J, restaurant, 74 N Illinois and 25 S Penn, h 25 Hall pl.
Dimock Daniel J jr, clk, r 74½ N Illinois.
Diner Thomas, lab, h Reisner (W I).
Dinges Henry W, plumber H A Goth, b 38 Hosbrook.
Dinges Margaret (wid Henry), h 38 Hosbrook.
Dingle Henry R, lab, h 124 Lee (W I).
Dingley Homer R, clk C C C & St L Ry, h 132 Cornell av.
Dingman Frederick D, barber, 452 W New York, h 53 Minerva.
Dinius Mary (wid John G), h 140 N East.
Dink Johanna C (wid John M), b 17 Shelby.
Dink John A, lab, h 64 Warren av (W I).
Dink Katharine (wid John), b 400 Central av.
Dinkelaker Charles A, clk, h 168 N Noble.
Dinkelaker Charlotte, sec Indpls German Mut Fire Ins Co, b 166 N Noble.
Dinkins James A, carp, h 77 Oliver av (W I).
Dinn Wm, lab, b 209 Douglass.
Dinnage Arthur W, mach, h 443 S Missouri.
Dinnage Mary A (wid Samuel), h 108 Wisconsin.
Dinnage Samuel, millwright, b 108 Wisconsin.
Dinnin Porter D, r 100 E Washington.
DINNIN SAMUEL E, Propr The Fan Saloon, 100 E Washington, cor Delaware, h 240 E Market, Tel 1259.
Dinsmore Thomas H, fireman, h 567½ Virginia av.
Dinwiddie Charles R, clk, h 766 N Senate av.
Dinwiddie Lottie E, stenog, b 766 N Senate av.
Dinwiddie Sophia (wid Hugh), h 366 W 2d.
Dinwiddie Wyatt E, hostler, h 766 N Senate av.
Dippel Catherine (wid Henry), h 60 Downey.
Dippel Charles L, tailor, 420 S Meridian, h same.
Dippel Dora (wid Henry), b 401 E New York.
Dippel Edward J, collr Hay & Willits Mnfg Co, b 244 N Pine.
Dippel Ferdinand F, carver, h 25 Frank.
Dippel Frederica (wid Frederick), nurse, 191 Coburn, b same.
Dippel Gottlieb L, framer, b 60 Downey.
Dippel Harry L, mach Dickson & Beaning, b 191 Coburn.
DIPPEL HENRY C, Cafe, 60 N Delaware, Tel 1430; h 48 Broadway.
Dippel John, h 244 N Pine.
Dippel John C, painter, b 98 N Dorman.

W. H. MESSENGER COMPLETE HOUSE FURNISHER 101 East Washington Street, Telephone 491

Foundry and Pattern Shop } McNamara, Koster & Co. { PHONE 1593 212-218 S. Penn. St.

Dippel Otto A, driver, h 21 Frank.
Dippel Peter, patrolman, h 195 N Noble.
Dirk George, baker, b 529 S New Jersey.
Dirk John V, lab, b 529 S New Jersey.
Dirk Kate A (wid Joseph), h 529 S New Jersey.
Dirk Magdalena (wid George), b 364 S East.
Dirks Margaret (wid Bernhard), b 621 S East.
Dirks Sarah J (wid John W), h 189 W 3d.
Disch Gabriel, gardener, h 955 S Meridian.
Disch John A, cabtmkr, h 1014 S Meridian.
Disch Louis, h 1012 S Meridian.
Disher Herman W, engr, b 222 Alvord.
Disher Joseph B, trav agt Ry Officials' and Employes' Accident Assn, h 731 N Illinois.
Disher Mary C, dressmkr, 731 N Illinois, h same.
Disher Mary E (wid John), h 125 E 6th.
Disher Peter L, lab, h 222 Alvord.
Disher Susan H, stenog, b 125 E 6th.
Disher Thomas G, horseshoer, 378 E 7th, h 874 Bellefontaine.
Dishman Jackson E, driver, h 178 Muskingum al.
Dishon Elizabeth (wid John), b 239 S Alabama.
Dismuke John, lab, h 99 Nebraska.
Disney Lydia A, h 862 N Alabama.
Dissette Charles K, bkkpr Indpls Foundry Co, b 309 E South.
Dissette Edward, h n e cor University and Omer avs (I).
Dissette James I, sec and treas Indpls Foundry Co, h 309 E South.
Dissler Edward G, switchman, h 2 Detroit.
Dissler Ella, h 92 W Ohio.
Dissler Harry J, fireman, h 92 W Ohio.
Disson John, lab, b Ross House.
Dithmer Agnes I, teacher Public School No 9, b 231 N Liberty.
Dithmer Henry L, sec Polar Ice Co, h 231 N Liberty.
Ditmer Calvin B, painter, h 648 Virginia av.
Ditmer Charles E, lab, b 648 Virginia av.
DiTrani Dominico, jeweler, b 191 N East.
DiTrani Francesco, confr, 227 E Washington, h same.
DiTrani Nicola, saloon, 125 E Maryland, h same.
Dittelhausen Michael F, baker, h rear 514 E Ohio.
Dittemore John V, trav agt, h 598 N Illinois.
Dittemore John W, h 18 Central av.
Dittman Frederick G (F G Dittman & Co), h 902 N Senate av.
Dittman F G & Co (Frederick G Dittman, Wm Quinot), grocers, 750 N Capitol av.
Dittman John H, h 904 N Senate av.
Dittman John H jr, clk, b 177 W 9th.
Dittmer Frederick H, driver, h 77 Pleasant.
Dittrich, see also Dietrich.
Dittrich Edward A, jeweler, 182 Virginia av, h same.
Dittrich Herman J, patternmkr, b 194 E Washington.
Dittrich Mary E (wid Christian G), h 467 E Market.
Diveley George, condr, b 788 E Market.
Diver Frank, engr, h 236 Fletcher av.
Divine, see also Devine.
Divine Calvin L, adv solr The Indpls Journal, r 17 The Chalfant.
Divine Charles C, trav freight agt I D & W Ry, h 337 Talbott av.
Dix, see also Dick and Dicks.

Henry H. Fay,
40½ E. WASHINGTON ST.,
AGENT FOR
Insurance Co. of North America,
Pennsylvania Fire Ins. Co.

Dix John, carpetlayer, b 229½ E Washington.
Dix Levi, lab, r 147 Eddy.
Dixlhan Ignatz, lab, h 21 Cleveland (H).
Dixon, see also Dickerson, Dickinson and Dickson.
Dixon Albert, poultry, 172 W Maryland, h same.
Dixon Cyrus A, real est, h 26 Gillard av.
Dixon Edgar, condr, b 489 College av.
Dixon Elmer, filer, b 382 Indiana av.
Dixon Frank C, clk, b 1148 N Alabama.
Dixon Franklin H, clk, b 646 W Vermont.
Dixon Green, lab, h 24 Smithson.
Dixon Henry S, lineman, b 95 N Meridian.
Dixon James A, mach, h 856 Cornell av.
Dixon James H, waiter, b 131 Allegheny.
Dixon John A, trav agt, h 993 N Penn.
Dixon John H, clk, h 1148 N Alabama.
Dixon John T, carp, b 646 W Vermont.
Dixon Minnie, clk Insane Asylum.
Dixon Norval H, mach hd, h 57 John.
Dixon Otto, lab, b 438 W Pratt.
Dixon Prophet, express, h rear 242 W New York.
Dixon Rollo B, clk, b 132 Hosbrook.
Dixon Samuel, lab, h 241 Orange.
Dixon Sheppard, lab, h 422 S Olive.
Dixon Sterling P, lawyer, 30½ N Delaware, h 451 N New Jersey.
Dixon Theodore P, b 26 Gillard av.
Dixon Wm, b 119 Ft Wayne av.
Dixon Wm, barber, h 366 W Vermont.
Dixon Wm jr, barber, b 207 W Walnut.
Dixon Wm, plumber, b 23 N West.
Dixon Williamson, engr, h 173 English av.
Dixon Willis C Rev, b 422 S Olive.
Dixson George F, carriagemkr, h e s Becker 3 s of Washington (M J).
Doan Elias C, tmstr, h 29 Clarke.
Doan John A, bricklyr, h 891 Morris (W I).
Doan Martha J, teacher Industrial School, b 592 Ash.
Doan Sarah E (wid John), h 92 Indiana av.
Doan Virgil, bricklyr, b 891 Morris (W I).
Doan Wilson S, lawyer, h e s Elm av 4 n of Washington av (I).
Doane Bland W, bricklyr, h 144 Lee (W I).
Doane Oscar E, bricklyr, h 142 Lee (W I).

Union Casualty & Surety Co.
of St. Louis, Mo.
Employers', Public, General, Teams and Elevator Liability; also Workmen's Collective, Steam Boiler, Plate Glass and Automatic Sprinkler Insurance.
W. E. BARTON & CO., General Agents,
504 Indiana Trust Building.
LONG DISTANCE TELEPHONE 1918.

THE FRED DIETZ CO. WOODEN PACKING BOXES MADE TO ORDER. FACTORY AND WAREHOUSE 400 Madison Avenue. Telephone 654.

Shorthand! BUSINESS UNIVERSITY. When Bl'k. Elevator day and night. Typewriting, Penmanship, Book-keeping. Office Training free. See page 4. Est. 1850. Tel. 499. E. J. HEEB, Proprietor.

NEW YORK FILTER MFG. CO. Filters for Water-Works, Boiler Plants, Laundries, Hotels, Private Residences, Etc. | Henry R. Worthington, 64 S. Pennsylvania St. Long Distance Telephone 284.

UNION CO-OPERATIVE LAUNDRY (COMPOSED OF LAUNDRY GIRLS.) NOS. 38, 40 AND 42 VIRGINIA AVENUE T. E. SOMERVILLE, MANAGER TELEPHONE 1 INDIANAPOLIS, IND.

HORACE M. HADLEY
REAL ESTATE AND LOANS....
66 East Market Street
Telephone 1540. BASEMENT.

Dobbelhoff Charles, collr, h 233 Fayette.
Dobbins Calvin, barber, h 303½ E Washington.
Dobbins Frances, r 175 E Louisiana.
Dobbins Joseph, carp, b 233 Virginia av.
Dobbins Wm A, condr, h 606 Central av.
Dobbins Wilson T, motorman, h 279 Blake.
Dobbs Charles E W Rev, pastor South St Baptist Church, h 59 Fletcher av.
Dobbs Leslie E, oil, h 49 Spann av.
Dobbs Scipio, lab, h 80 Maxwell.
DoBell Wm L, clk Daniel Stewart Co, h 1319 N Alabama.
DoBell Wm L jr, clk, b 1319 N Alabama.
Doblein Henry, cook, h 119 E Market.
Dobrowitz Henry, meats, 51 Russell av, h same.
Dobson Alfred P, clk The Wm H Block Co, b 349 N New Jersey.
Dobson America J (wid Scipio), b 183 Indiana av.
Dobson James, coal, 265 Michigan av, h same.
Dobson John W, opr Postal Tel Cable Co, b 265 Michigan av.
Dobson Laura E, teacher Public School No 1 (H), b 99 Greenwood.
Dobson Lena L, seamstress, b 304 College av.
Dobson Martin J, clk, b 265 Michigan av.
Dobson Thomas J, lab, h 35 Woodside av (W).
Dobters Anton, molder, b 106 W Michigan.
Dobyns Wm J, clk, b w s Central av 3 s of Washington av (I).
Dochez Alfred E (Guarantee Roofing Co and A E Dochez & Co), b 475½ N Illinois.
DOCHEZ A E & CO (Alfred E Dochez), Druggists, 82 Mass av, Tel 1345.
Dochez Charles A, b 475½ N Illinois.
Dochez Louis A, h 475½ N Illinois.
Dochez Louis J, mailing clk P O, b 475½ N Illinois.
Dochez Raymond A, b 475½ N Illinois.
Docktor John F, finisher, h 683 Charles.
Dockweiler Charles, engr, h 184 Clifford av.
Dockweiler Henry G (Dockweiler & Kingsbury), h 501 E Market.

Merchants' and Manufacturers Exchange
Make Collections and Commercial Reports......
J. E. TAKKEN, MANAGER,
19 Union Building, 73 West Maryland Street

Dockweiler & Kingsbury (Henry G Dockweiler, Edward D Kingsbury), fertilizers, 67 S Meridian.
Dodd Charles F, bricklyr, h 1541 N Illinois.
Dodd David, lab, h 40½ Malott av.
Dodd Harry P, condr, b 1156 N Capitol av.
Dodd James A, grocer, 184 Hill av, h same.
Dodd James H, lab, b 25 S Arsenal av.
Dodd John W, h 476 N Illinois.
Dodd Martha, h 82 The Windsor.
Dodd Philip H, engr, b 73 Johnson av.
Dodd Richard, lab, r 90 Locke.
Dodd Thomas, mach, h n s Orchard av 2 w of Roseline.
Dodd Wm, waiter, b 362 W Vermont.
Dodd Wm A, lab, h 25 S Arsenal av.
Dodd Wm J, lab, b 25 S Arsenal av.
Dodd Wm L, clk, b 184 Hill av.
Dodd Wm S, clk, b 476 N Illinois.
Dodd Wm T, cutter, b n s Orchard av 2 w of Roseline.
Dodds Elihu, draughtsman, h 305 Clifford av.
Dodds Wm T S, student Dr W N Wishard, r 345 N Senate av.
Dodge Daniel, engr, h 494 Stillwell.
Dodge Edward, engr, r 225 Michigan av.
Dodge Martha (wid John H), h 23 Blake.
Dodson, see also Dotson and Dutson.
Dodson Edgar, barber, b 76 Benton.
Dodson Ella, tailoress, r 11 Columbia blk.
Dodson Elmer E, barber, 103 S Noble, h 76 Benton.
Dodson Frank, lab, b 95 S West.
Dodson George, agt, h 15 W North.
Dodson Harry S, brakeman, h 29½ Holmes av (H).
Dodson Oliver M, condr, h 1147½ N Illinois.
Doebber Gustav, mach, h 19 Temple av.
Doehleman John, lab, h 735 E 7th.
Doenges August, carp, h 521 S Meridian.
Doenges Casper, grocer, 436 S Meridian, h same.
Doenges Wm H, clk, b 436 S Meridian.
Doeppers August B, special agt German Fire Insurance Co of Indiana, h 700 E Market.
Doeppers James W, mach, h 147 N West.
Doering Rudolph, coachman 194 E Michigan.
Doerr, see also Deer.
Doerr Elizabeth (wid John), h 41 Yandes.
Doerr George W, h 256 N Pine.
Doerr John H, engr, h 110 Clifford av.
Doerr John N, clk Ward Bros Drug Co, h 535 S Meridian.
Doerr Sebastian, lab, h 708 Charles.
Doerr Wm, carver, b 181 N Pine.
Doerschel Louis B, bottler, h 224 Fulton.
Doffee Mary A (wid Thomas), seamstress, h 17½ S Alabama.
Doheny James, clk R M S, r 90 N Senate av.
Doherty, see also Daugherty and Dougherty.
Doherty Bernard M, lab, b 76 Arizona.
Doherty Charles A, lab, b 76 Arizona.
Doherty James, cigars, 60 S Illinois, h same.
Doherty John, bartndr, h 820 W Washington.
Doherty Mary F (wid Andrew), b 20 Traub av.
Doherty Michael, h 76 Arizona.
Doherty Patrick J, collr Indpls Brewing Co, b 76 Arizona.
Doherty Timothy, switchman, h 188 Pleasant.
Doherty Wm J, lab, h 82 Newman.

CLEMENS VONNEGUT 184, 186 and 192 E. Washington St. | Wire Rope, Machinery, Lathes, Drills and Shapers

THE WM. H. BLOCK CO. DRY GOODS, DRAPERIES, RUGS, WINDOW SHADES.
7 AND 9 EAST WASHINGTON STREET.

Dohn Edward, sawyer, b 63 High.
Dohn Henry L, foreman, b 83 Morton.
Dohn Peter, engr, h 63 High.
Dohn Wm, mach, h 53 Cleaveland blk.
Dohrer Charles, hostler, h 148 Hadley av (W I).
Doing Nancy E (wid James R), h 104 W Vermont.
Doke Henry W., lab, h 377 Lincoln av.
Dolan Annie, b 217 N Capitol av.
Dolan John A, clk, h 12 N Liberty.
Dolan Margaret, b 30 W Walnut.
Dolan Mary, h 217 N Capitol av.
Dolan Mary (wid Timothy), b 72 W Vermont.
Dolan Wm, fireman, b 99 Lexington av.
Dolan Wm, hostler, r 175 E Michigan.
Dolas Catherine (wid John), h 260 S East.
Dolby Edward, mach hd, h 26 S Stuart (B).
Dolby James H, well driver, 81 W 7th, h 1282 Northwestern av.
DOLD ARNOLD F (Nick The Tailor), Dyeing, Cleaning and Repairing, 78 N Illinois, r 46½ Indiana av. (See adv opp classified Tailors.)
Dold Conrad L, printer, b 169 Laurel.
Dold Frank J, loungemkr, b 169 Laurel.
Dold Frederick, blksmith, h 169 Laurel.
Dolen James E, lab, b 50 Ellsworth.
Dolen Susie O (wid Creighton W), h 160 King.
Dolen Thomas, lab, h 616 N Meridian.
Dolen Timothy M, cooper, h 50 Ellsworth.
Dolen True K, press feeder, b 50 Ellsworth.
Doles Axie P, seamstress, b 54 S Arsenal av.
Doles Isaac, musical instmts, h 1567 N Illinois.
Dolfinger John O, ins agt, b 737 N Penn.
Dolfinger Otto F, h 737 N Penn.
Dolin Arthur, driver Wm B Burford, r 21 W Washington.
Doll Chester W, draughtsman H W Foltz, b 40 Garfield pl.
Doll Clarence A, soldier U S A, h 60 Omer.
Doll Clarence W, pressman, h 677 E Market.
Doll Frank G, condr, h 120 N Gillard av.
Doll Frederick M, clk, b 439 E McCarty.
Doll George G, clk, b 439 College av.
Doll Isaac, letter carrier P O, h 639 Marlowe av.
Doll Jacob L, druggist, h 439 College av.
Doll Louis, h 439 E McCarty.
Doll Wm H, clk, h 40 Garfield pl.
Dollarheid Charles A, lab, b 16 Warman av (H).
Dollarheid James H, clk, b 16 Warman av (H).
Dollarheid Jeannette M (wid Joel J), h 16 Warman av (H).
Dollarhide Columbus T (Laz Noble & Co), h 239 Cornell av.
Dollarhide Margaret A, h 509 Ash.
Dollens Harry C, clk Traders' Despatch, b 407 N Delaware.
Dollens Robert W, clk Rich & McVey, h 407 N Delaware.
Dolleris Sebastian, mason, h e s Applegate 1 n of Raymond.
Dolley John A, h 90 Fulton.
Dollihan Joseph, driver, b 46 Torbet.
Dollin Edward G, molder, b 349 S Alabama.
Dollman Henry L, carp, 25 William and 66 E Market, h 53 William.
Dollman Wilhelmina (wid Gottlieb), h 53 William.
Dollman Wm, carp, b 53 William.

Dolmetsch Eugene C, clk Charles Mayer & Co, h 473 N Senate av.
Dolph George A, engr, h 24 Carlos.
Dom August, finisher, h 172 Blake.
Dom Josiah, plastr, h 262 W Court.
Dombroski John J, foreman Natl Malleable Castings Co, h 62 King av (H).
DOMESTIC LAUNDRY, Wm A Cox Propr, 73 N Illinois, Tel 1585.
Domm Clifford B, clk Standard Oil Co, b 368 N New Jersey.
Domm Walter, asst bkkpr Standard Oil Co, b 368 N New Jersey.
Domroese Charles R, mach hd, h 44 Arizona.
Domroese Frederick C, asst mail clk The Sun, b 44 Arizona.
Domroese Paul E, asst stereotyper The Sun, b 44 Arizona.
Donaghue Patrick, lab, h 507 E Georgia.
Donaghue Thomas J, lab, h 21 Henry.
Donahoe, see also Donohue and O'Donaghue.
Donahoe Darby J, lab, h 171 S New Jersey.
Donahoe Honora (wid Martin), h 171 S New Jersey.
Donahoe John, brakeman, r 175 S New Jersey.
Donahue Daniel E, electrician, h 48 Geisendorff.
Donahue Daniel J, boilermkr, b 53 N Dorman.
Donahue Edward, boilermkr, b 53 N Dorman.
Donahue George, lab, b 48 Geisendorff.
Donahue Hannah (wid James), h rear 398 Mass av.
Donahue James F, foreman, b 53 N Dorman.
Donahue Jeremiah (Holland & Donahue), grocer, 249 W McCarty, h same.
Donahue Jeremiah F, coremkr, b 249 W McCarty.
Donahue John, lab, h 119 W South.
Donahue John T, butcher, b 249 W McCarty.

GUIDO R. PRESSLER,
FRESCO PAINTER
Churches, Theaters, Public Buildings, Etc., A Specialty.
Residence, No. 325 North Liberty Street
INDIANAPOLIS, IND.

INDIANAPOLIS STEEL ROOFING AND CORRUGATING WORKS, 23 and 25 East South Street. S. D. NOEL, Proprietor.

David S. McKernan, Rooms 2-5 Thorpe Block.
REAL ESTATE AND LOANS
A number of choice pieces for subdivision, or for manufacturers' sites, with good switch facilities.

DIAMOND WALL PLASTER { Telephone 1410 BUILDERS' EXCHANGE.

UNION TRANSFER AND STORAGE CO. Cor. E. Ohio St. and C., C., C. & St. L. R'y Tracks. BRICK WAREHOUSE; CLEANEST AND SAFEST STORAGE IN CITY FOR HOUSEHOLD GOODS AND MERCHANDISE.

W. McWORKMAN,

METAL CEILINGS,
ROLLING SHUTTERS,
DOORS AND PARTITIONS.

930 W. Washington St. Tel. 1118.

Donahue Katherine (wid James T), h 53 N Dorman.
Donahue Martin, h 28 S Dorman.
Donahue Martin jr, lab, b 28 S Dorman.
Donahue Michael, bartndr, r 113 S Illinois.
Donahue Michael, tmstr, h rear 51 Ash.
Donahue Patrick, car rep, h 44 Hope (B).
Donahue Patrick, paver, h 23 S East.
Donahue Robert, lab, h 94 Deloss.
Donahue Robert F, switchman, b 94 Deloss.
Donahue Thomas, foreman, h e s Senate av 2 s of 30th.
Donahue Wm T, lab, b e s N Senate av 2 s of 30th.
Donald Elmer, butler, h 425 W 2d.
Donaldson Elmer O, engr, h 13 Lexington av.
Donaldson Orville J, clk, b 17 Lexington av.
Donaldson Wm H, trav loan agt State B and L Assn, h 716 Broadway.
Donaldson Wm L, stage mngr Empire Theater, b 72 E Ohio.
Donavan, see also Donovan.
Donavan Caroline (wid Wm), h 6 S Poplar (B).
Donavan Daniel F, pressman, b 108 Dougherty.
Donavan John, engr, h 863 Cornell av.
Donavan John L, plumber, b 108 Dougherty.
Donavan Mary L (wid Lawrence), h 108 Dougherty.
Donavan Michael T, fireman, b 6 Poplar (B).
Donavan Wm, city fireman, h 129 W 5th.
Donavon Dennis J, molder, h 41 Madison av.
Donavon Grace A, boarding 41 Madison av.
Donelson Alfred L, condr, h 868 Cornell av.
Donelson Wm G, assembler, b rear 88 S Noble.
Donelson Wm J, huckster, h rear 83 Morton.
Doney Charles P, trav agt, h 225 Park av.
Donges Charles H, mer police, h 199 Elizabeth.
Donges Frederick E, molder, h 547 S State av.
Donges John P, trimmer, b 444 S Illinois.

SEALS,
STENCILS,
STAMPS, Etc.
GEO. J. MAYER
15 S. Meridian St.
TELEPHONE 1386.

Dongus Gustav A, baker Kershner Bros, h 54 Nebraska.
Dongus John M, lab, h 100 Dunlop.
Donlan Anna, h 79 W McCarty.
Donlan Michael, boilermkr, h 37 Bismarck av (H).
Donlan Michael E, lab, b 37 Bismarck av (H).
Donley Edward, b 122 W 2d.
Donley James, butcher, b 224 W Maryland.
Donley Wm H, music teacher, 42 W Market, h 122 W 2d.
Donlon Ellen (wid Timothy), grocer, 901 N Senate av, h 782 N Illinois.
Donlon John J, b 782 N Illinois.
Donnan Barbara (wid David), h 126 N Capitol av.
Donnan Emma, supervising prin Public School No 13, b 126 N Capitol av.
Donnan Laura, teacher High School, b 126 N Capitol av.
Donnan Theodore, packer, b 126 N Capitol av.
Donnan Wallace, tinner, 74 Mass av, h 902 N Delaware.
Donnell, see also O'Donnell.
Donnell Dollie, hair goods, 19½ N Meridian, h same.
Donnell James K, blksmith, h 466 Indiana av.
Donnell Maude, hairdresser, b 19½ N Meridian.
Donnelley Michael, foreman, r 56 N Senate av.
Donnelley Michael E, stereotyper The Indpls Journal, b 332 W Washington.
Donnelley Wm, insp, b 332 W Washington.
Donnelly Alexander F, watchman, h 24 St Peter.
Donnelly Anna H, milliner, h 26 Henry.
Donnelly Elizabeth (wid John), h 86 Tremont av (H).
Donnelly Ellen (wid Cornelius), h 21 Shriver av.
Donnelly James, butcher, h 329 W Maryland.
Donnelly James, lab, b 40 S West.
Donnelly Mary (wid Joseph), b 24 Osgood (W I).
Donnelly Maurice (Landers & Donnelly), mngr Terre Haute Brewing Co, h 194 Pleasant.
Donnelly Mollie, b 35 Garden.
Donnelly Robert F, carp, h w s Hester 1 s of English av.
Donnelly Thomas S, lab, h rear 22 Prospect.
Donnelly Walter, lab, b 31 Helen.
Donner Joseph C, condr, b 610 S Meridian.
Donnery Patrick, condr, h 89 Bright.
Donnery Thomas J, cutter, b 89 Bright.
Donnin Thomas, lab, h 238 W Wabash.
Donohue, see also Donahoe and O'Donaghue.
Donohue John, collr, h 113 Chadwick.
Donohue John, tmstr, h 203 W McCarty.
Donohue John L, lab, b 203 W McCarty.
Donohue Mary (wid Michael), b 70 English av.
Donohue Matthew, lab, b 203 W McCarty.
Donohue Michael, lab, b rear 240 S Missouri.
Donohue Michael, lab, b 12 Sharpe.
Donohue Patrick, lab, b 12 Sharpe.
Donohue Patrick, lab, b rear 240 S Missouri.
Donohue Patrick, mach, h 1106 E Washington.

A. METZGER AGENCY ESTABLISHED 1863. INSURANCE

LAMBERT GAS & GASOLINE ENGINE CO.
ANDERSON, IND. PORTABLE GASOLINE ENGINES. 2 TO 25 H. P.

Donohue Wm, lab, h rear 240 S Missouri.
Donohue Wm, lab, h 12 Sharpe.
Donough Abraham M, switchman, h 423 N Pine.
Donough Daniel R, genl ticket agt I U Ry Co, h 266 S Meridian.
Donough Louis, b 266 S Meridian.
Donovan, see also Donavan.
Donovan Alfred E, painter, h 131 Maxwell.
DONOVAN BENJAMIN C, Undertaker, 40 Division (W I), h same, Tel 1469.
Donovan Carl, blksmith, b 40 Division (W I).
Donovan Elizabeth A (wid James), b 125 Walcott.
Donovan George W, caner, h 39 Helen.
Donovan James B, lab, h 131 Maxwell.
Donovan James E, ballplayer, b 741 E Michigan.
Donovan James R, watchman, h 741 E Michigan.
Donovan Jesse F, plumber, b 741 E Michigan.
Donovan John H, lab, r 46 Leon.
Donovan John N, mason, h w s Bradley 2 n of Ohio.
Donovan John W, baggageman, h 563 E Washington.
Donovan Mary (wid Harvey), r 271 Mass av.
Donovan Thomas, hostler, h Noblesville rd e of city limits.
Donovan Wm M, ballplayer, b 741 E Michigan.
Donson Charles W, sec and treas Artificial Ice and Cold Storage Co, h 1523 N Meridian.
Donson Cyrus S, lab, r 158 N New Jersey.
Doody Wm, lab, b 486 S Capitol av.
Doolan Wesley, lab, h 951 N New Jersey.
Dooley Clayton C, blksmith, b 154 N Pine.
Dooley Elwood, lab, b 575 Highland av (N I).
Dooley Moses B, h w s Central av 1 n of 21st.
Dooley Moses E, wagonmkr, h 154 N Pine.
Dooley Ora, peddler, h 224 W Pearl.
Dooley Scott S, painter, h 410 Hanna.
Dooley Wm H, clk Kingan & Co (ltd), h 295 Blackford.
Dooley Willis P, student, h 47 N East.
Doolittle Amanda M (wid Wm), h 825 E Market.
Doolittle Charles A, mach hd, h 109 Fayette.
Doolittle Charles B, lab, b 244 Alvord.
Doolittle Edwin F (Balfour, Potts & Doolittle), h 723 College av.
Doolittle George H, driver, h 718 E Ohio.
Doolittle Harry, coachman 772 N Alabama.
Doolittle Harry R, motorman, h 426 E 10th.
Doolittle John F, lab, b 44 N Belmont av (H).
Doolittle Joseph B, confr, E Mkt House, b 4 Mass av.
Doolittle Lucinda (wid Franklin J), h 44 N Belmont av (H).
Doolittle Rachel A (wid Wm M), h 244 Alvord.
Doolittle Samuel O, messenger Am Ex Co, b 86 Ramsey av.
Doolittle Wm H, molder, b 44 N Belmont av (H).
Door of Hope Rescue Home, Celia Smock supt, 84 N Alabama.
Dopfer Oscar, butcher, h rear 247 S West.
Doppis Andrew, molder, b 160 Michigan (H).
Doran Charles F, letter carrier P O, h 60 N Beville av.

Farm and City Loans
25 Years' Successful Business.
THOS. C. DAY & CO,
Rooms 325 to 330 Lemcke Building.

Doran Charles J, paperhngr, b 164½ E Washington.
Doran Henry S, tinner, h 254 Cornell av.
Doran Josephine, dressmkr, 18½ N Meridian, r same.
Doran Mary J (wid Michael W E), h 150½ College av.
Doran Wm J, condr, h 51 Rockwood.
Dorband Henry, bricklyr, b 114 S Summit.
Dorbecker Henry, clk, b 77 N New Jersey.
Dorbecker Jacob H, mach, h 79 N New Jersey.
Dorbecker Louisa (wid John), h 77 N New Jersey.
Dorbin Joseph, lab, r 66 N Missouri.
Doremus Charles E, blksmith, h 111 Shelby.
Doremus Frank H, lab, h 24 Leonard.
Doremus George E, wagonmkr, h 641 S Meridian.
Doremus Harry C, uphlr, h 10 W Morris.
Dorey, see also Dory.
DOREY EDWARD R, Druggist, 144 College av, h 150½ same.
Dorey Louise J, h 531 E 7th.
Dorey Wm, clk, h 24 Garfield pl.
Dorgan Patrick, foreman, h 87 Leota.
Dorland Annie, christian scientist, h 129 N Penn.
Dorman Zachary, lab, h rear 61 Maxwell.
Dormire Jonathan C, shoemkr, h 355 S State av.
Dormire Wm O, switchman, b 355 S State av.
Dorn Adam, lab, h rear 296 S Missouri.
Dorn Charles, shoemkr, b 510 Chestnut.
Dorn Frank, baker, b 510 Chestnut.
Dorn Louis, cabtmkr W H Messenger, h 510 Chestnut.
Dorn Louis C, packer, b 510 Chestnut.
Dorner Charles T, clk, r 284 S West.
Dorrah David S (Moore & Dorrah), h 27 Centennial.
Dorrah Robert L, lab, h s e cor Washington av and Orchard (I).
Dorrah Wm, b 27 Centennial.
Dorscher Ernest H, mach, h 222 Hamilton av.
Dorsey Alvin E, h 1394 N Senate av.

EAT
QUAKER BREAD
ASK YOUR GROCER FOR IT.
THE HITZ BAKING CO.

BICYCLES $5 DOWN. MONTHLY. Best Wheels. Best Terms. WHEELMEN'S CO. 31 W. OHIO ST. LONG DISTANCE TEL. 1655.

J. H. TECKENBROCK House, Sign and Fresco Painter, 94 EAST SOUTH STREET.

FIDELITY MUTUAL LIFE PHILADELPHIA, PA. A. H. COLLINS, Gen. Agt. Baldwin Blk. } RATES REASONABLE. SOUND BEYOND QUESTION. BUSINESS-LIKE IN PRACTICE.

Edwardsport Coal and Mining Company ROOMS 42 AND 43 WHEN BUILDING. BITUMINOUS COAL

ESTABLISHED 1876. TELEPHONE 168.
CHESTER BRADFORD,
SOLICITOR OF PATENTS,
AND COUNSEL IN PATENT CAUSES.
(See adv. page 6.)
Office:—Rooms 14 and 16 Hubbard Block, S. W. Cor. Washington and Meridian Streets,
INDIANAPOLIS, INDIANA.

Dorsey Anna (wid Thomas), h 300 S Missouri.
Dorsey Charles B, mach, h e s Rural 1 s of Division (B).
Dorsey Daniel L, bkkpr, b 233 Central av.
Dorsey Edward, lab, h 333 W Chesapeake.
Dorsey Effie (wid Michael), b 1394 N Senate av.
Dorsey Elizabeth (wid Michael), b 20 Ketcham.
Dorsey Ezra, shoemkr, 86 Lincoln la, h same.
Dorsey Francis O, phys, b 233 Central av.
Dorsey James W, driver Charles Mayer & Co, h e s Auburn av 5 s of Bethel av.
Dorsey Katherine (wid Robert S), b 233 Central av.
Dorsey Mary, laundress, h 333 Superior.
Dorsey Peter J, lab, h 41 Buchanan.
Dorsey Robert L, sec Tucker & Dorsey Mnfg Co, h 233 Central av.
Dorsey Samuel, city fireman, h 271 Cornell av.
Dorsey Wm B, engr, h 19 N State av.
Dory, see also Dorey.
Dory Harry E, cigarmkr, b 361 W Michigan.
Dory James, filer, b 361 W Michigan.
Dory Joseph, engr, h 361 W Michigan.
Dosch Charles O, clk P C C & St L Ry, h 116 S Noble.
Dosch Wm D, driver, h 106½ Fayette.
Dosenbeck Anna (wid Oswald), weaver, h 197½ E Washington.
Dotey A Isaac, teacher High School, r 220 Bellefontaine.
Dotson, see also Dodson and Dutson.
Dotson James P, painter, h 460 W Francis (N I).
Dotson Jeremiah, painter, h 94½ E South.
Dotson Malinda A (wid Jacob), b 92 S West.
Dotson Wm, clk, h 25 Riley blk.
Dotson Wm E, clk, b 300 W Washington.
Dotson Wm T, clk, h 300 W Washington.
Dottolo Frederick, fruits, 41 E Mkt House, h 278 S Delaware.
Doty Arthur W, forgeman, h 72 S Noble.
Doty Charles H, boilermkr, h 13 Lawn (B).
Doty Check L, pressman The Indpls News, b 154 Madison av.

BUY THE BEST.
Outing BICYCLES $85
MADE BY
HAY & WILLITS MFG. CO.
76 N. PENN. ST. Phone 598.

Doty Clara, artist, b 19 Greer.
Doty Harriet J (wid Cary C), b 111 Shelby.
Doty John, tmstr, h 236 S Spruce.
Doty Morris E, brakeman, h e s Foundry 2 s of Willow (B).
Doty Taylor E, confr, 267 Mass av, h same.
Doublin Henry, cook, r 190 E Market.
Doudle John, lab, h 17 Chadwick.
Doudy Frederick, lab, h 25 Thomas.
Douge Charles S, carp, h 578 S West.
Dougherty, see also Daugherty and Doherty.
Dougherty Albert U, grocer, 28 Meikel, h same.
Dougherty, Bernard S, lab, b 254 Douglass.
Dougherty Charles E, janitor The Indpls Sentinel, h 465 S Illinois.
Dougherty Dennis, clk, r 117 W Maryland.
Dougherty Edward J, ironwkr, b 88 W Market.
Dougherty Edward J, trav agt, h 15 The Blacherne.
Dougherty Frank L, sec K of P Castle Hall Assn, h w s N Illinois 2 n of 28th.
Dougherty George E, clk, b 468 N East.
Dougherty George W, subscription agt The Bradstreet Co, b 861 N Penn.
Dougherty Horace W, bkkpr, b 468 N East.
Dougherty John, mach, h 217 Hamilton av.
Dougherty Katherine (wid John), b 216 W New York.
Dougherty Mary (wid James), b 233 Hamilton av.
Dougherty Mary (wid Wm), h 22 Wisconsin.
Dougherty Thomas, clk, b 399 N West.
Dougherty Wm D, gas insp, 468 N East, h same.
Doughty Ernest M, meats, 304 N Illinois, h 35 W St Clair.
Doughty Richard L, lab, h 116 Blackford.
Douglas Claude N, reporter, b 154 E Ohio.
Douglas Frederick, lab, h 33½ W South.
Douglas F Wayland, asst genl agt Connecticut Mutual Life Ins Co, h 959 N Capitol av.
Douglas Howard, lab, h 612 N West.
Douglas Ida M (wid Horace G), r 31 Camp.
Douglas Laura B (wid Stephen M), stenog The Hay & Willits Mnfg Co, b 59 Woodlawn av.
Douglas Levi S, lab, h 393 Lafayette.
Douglas Louis, lab, h 15 Anderson.
Douglass Andrew F, lab, h 280 Howard (W I).
Douglass Booker, lab, b n w cor Berlin av and 20th.
Douglass Clyde M, steelwkr, b 232 S Missouri.
Douglass Eugene W, teacher, h 189 Fletcher av.
Douglass Frank J, tel opr, h 455 N California.
Douglass Fred, driver, r 68½ N Delaware.
Douglass George, lab, h e s Rural 6 s of Sutherland (B).
Douglass Jason, lab, h 276 S Capitol av.
Douglass Jefferson B, baggagemaster, h 1113 N Delaware.
Douglass John W, lab, h 90 Lincoln la.
Douglass Mattie, h 147 W Maryland.
Douglass Nelson, lab, b 90 Lincoln la.
Douglass Richard, bricklyr, r 195 W South.
Douglass Robert, meats, 193 Howard (W I), h 59 S McLain (W I).
Douglass Robert, books, 11½ N Meridian, res, Princeton, Ind.
Douglass Rusha, carp, h 294½ Mass av.
Douglass Samuel, porter, h 5 Susquehanna.

ROOFING MATERIAL C. ZIMMERMAN & SONS, SLATE AND GRAVEL ROOFERS, 19 SOUTH EAST STREET.

PUMPS Chain Pumps, Driven Wells and Deep Water Wells. Repairing Neatly Done. Cisterns Built. CHARLES KRAUSS', 42 S. PENN. ST. TELEPHONE 465.

Douglass Samuel L (Faught & Co), sec America Savings and Loan Soc, h 638 Broadway.
Douglass Wm E, brakeman, h 114 College av.
Douglass Wm M, lab, h 676½ N Senate av.
Douglass Wm W, pub, 11½ N Meridian, h 409 N New Jersey.
Doup Delia, h 168 W Michigan.
Doutherd Levi, driver, h 443 W 1st.
Douthit Austin, trimmer, h 154 Union.
Douthitt Elisha M, carp, h 539 W 22d (N I).
Douthitt Frank W, clk, b 539 W 22d (N I).
Dove David M, carp, h n e cor Chambers and Ritter av (I).
Dove Elisha, farmer, h w s Morris 2 s of Division (B).
Dove Harry E, lab, b n e cor Chambers and Ritter av (I).
Dowd Francis B Rev, rector St Anthony's Church, h 55 Warman av (H).
Dowd Mary A (wid Morris), h 275 S Penn.
Dowd Morris M, clk Wm B Burford, b 275 S Penn.
Dowdel Michael J, brakeman, h 30 Carlos.
Dowdell Earl, driver, b 95 Pleasant.
Dowden Albert, lab, r 15 Rhode Island.
Dowden Charles, lab, h rear 28 Sinker.
Dowden James, mill hd, b 187 S Capitol av.
Dowden Lourie, plastr, b 125 W Maryland.
Dowdle John, lab, h 90 Chadwick.
Dowdy Wm, coachman 224 N Meridian.
Dowe Bernard, lab, h 421 S State av.
Dowell Elmer E, weigher, h 426 Cornell av.
Dowell Frederick, rollman, b 646 Herbert (M P).
Dowell George W, phys, 613 W 22d (N I), h same.
Dowell James W, paperhngr, b 37 Bates.
Dowell Wm H H, bricklyr, h 37 Bates.
Dowins George R, engr Consumers' Gas Trust Co, h 709 Mass av.
Dowlin Edward, molder, b 349 S Alabama.
Dowling Henry M, lawyer, 506 Indiana Trust bldg, h 382 Broadway.
Dowling James T, sawmkr, h 52 Church.
Dowling Kate, h rear 348 Douglass.
Dowling Mary A, dressmkr, 311 N California, b same.
Downes Elmer N, clk Indpls Rubber Co, r 116 S East.
Downey Bertrand B, teacher High School, b 4 Cornell av.
Downey Brandt C, reporter The Bradstreet Co, b 4 Cornell av.
Downey Charles E, whol confr, 255 E Washington, h 382 S East.
Downey Charles M, mach, h 505 Virginia av.
Downey Frank B, electrician, b 4 Cornell av.
Downey George N, lab, h 1364 N Senate av.
Downey James R, mach hd, h 669½ Madison av.
Downey James W, mach, b 505 Virginia av.
Downey John, lab, h 109 English av.
Downey John B, tel opr, b 109 English av.
Downey Joseph A, letter carrier P O, h 13 Water.
Downey Joseph E, lineman, h 131 W 22d.
Downey Maud (wid John T), b 21 Ft Wayne av.
Downey Prudence (wid Paul), b 382 S East.
Downey Rufus K, blksmith, h s e cor Washington av and Line (I).
Downey Sarah, h 123 W Michigan.
Downey Thomas, sawmkr, h 239 E Morris.

Richardson & McCrea, 79 East Market Street, FIRE INSURANCE, REAL ESTATE, LOANS, AND RENTAL AGENTS. Telephone 182.

Downey Thomas F, boilermkr, b 109 English av.
Downey Wm, pres Citizens' Mutual B and L Assn, res Martinsville, Ind.
Downey Wm, waiter The Denison.
Downey Wm B, clk, h 4 Cornell av.
Downey Wm E, clk Oliver Chilled Plow Wks, h 26 Ft Wayne av.
Downie Alexander, papermkr, h 617 W Pearl.
Downie George, lab, b 287 Douglass.
Downie George, lab, b 432 National rd.
Downie James, papermkr, b 617 W Pearl.
Downie Samuel C, grocer, 289 Prospect, h same.
Downie Wm M, lab, h 287 Douglass.
Downin Wm M, broommkr, h 95 John.
Downing Clarissa A (wid Wm), b Hanna Hotel.
Downing Frank A, tinner, h 150 N Rural.
Downing Frank J, condr, h 395 N New Jersey.
Downing Horace G, clk, h 79 E 7th.
Downing Indiana (wid James), b 71 N Arsenal av.
Downing Louisa, h 394 Blackford.
Downing Michael A, vice-pres Belt R R and Stock Yards Co and the Holt Ice and Cold Storage Co, h 224 N Meridian.
Downing Minerva, h 21 Columbia al.
Downing Sarah E, sec Indiana Reformatory, b same.
Downing Walter, lab, b 19 Columbia al.
Downing Wellington, carp, h w s Layman av 5 n of Washington av (I).
Downs Annie (wid Thomas), h 147 High.
Downs Cyrus F, foreman Sinker-Davis Co, h 148 W Maryland.
Downs Elizabeth (wid Charles), h 180 Blackford.
Downs E, engr Consumers' Gas Trust Co, h 709 Mass av.
Downs George W, carp, b 556 W Eugene (N I).
Downs Ida, dressmkr, 148 W Maryland, b same.
Downs Montgomery, com mer, b 307 E Court.

SHORTHAND REPORTING...... CONVENTIONS, SPEECHES, SERMONS. COPYING ON TYPEWRITER. S. H. EAST, State Agent, THE WILLIAMS TYPEWRITER 55 Thorne Block, 87 East Market Street.

Collars and Cuffs Laundered in Best of Style. Domestic or High Gloss Finish.

ERTEL STEAM LAUNDRY 26 and 28 N. Senate Ave. Telephone 1089.

ELLIS & HELFENBERGER Manufacturers of Iron Vases, Setees and Hitch Posts. 162-170 South Senate Ave. Tel. 958

THE HOGAN TRANSFER AND STORAGE COMP'Y
Household Goods and Pianos Moved—Packed—Stored...... Baggage and Package Express Machinery and Safes a Specialty Cor. Washington and Illinois Sts. TELEPHONE No. 675.

The Central Rubber & Supply Co. PHONE 2. 79 S. ILLINOIS ST., INDIANAPOLIS, IND. Hose, Belting, Packing, Clothing, Druggists' Sundries, Bicycle Tires, Cotton Hose, Etc. New York Belting & Packing Co., L't'd.

The Provident Life and Trust Co.
Small Death Rate. Small Expense Rate. Safe Investments. OF PHILADELPHIA. Insurance in force $115,000,000
D. W. EDWARDS, General Agent, 508 Indiana Trust Building.

Downs Richard, presser, b 90 S Wheeler (B).
Doxey Charles T, pres American Plate Glass Co, res Anderson, Ind.
Doyel Elisha G L, clk, h 144 Cypress.
Doyle Andrew, lab, h 94 Agnes.
Doyle Ann (wid Lawrence), h rear 9 Rose.
Doyle Charles W, trav agt, b 455 N Meridian.
Doyle Christopher, plastr, h e s Lincoln av 8 s of C C C & St L Ry (M J).
Doyle Daniel, car insp, h 56 Jefferson.
Doyle Edward T, bartndr, b 94 Agnes.
Doyle Edward X (E X Doyle & Co), h 50 Newman.
Doyle Ellen (wid John), h 313 N Pine.
Doyle E X & Co (Edward X Doyle), grocers, 401 Mass av.
Doyle Frances D, stenog Frank K Sawyer, b 257 Talbott av.
Doyle Francis C L, bookbndr, b 313 N Pine.
Doyle Frank J (Abel & Doyle), r 133 N Senate av.
Doyle Harry, clk Kingan & Co (ltd), b 271 W Maryland.
Doyle James, lab, b 31 Dougherty.
Doyle John F, lab, b 31 Dougherty.
Doyle John J, bartndr, b 94 Agnes.
Doyle Mary, printer, b 31 Dougherty.
Doyle Michael, lab, h 231 Minnesota.
Doyle Parker H, fireman, h 314 Cedar.
Doyle Patrick, foreman, b 29 Blake.
Doyle Patrick T, stoker, h 31 Dougherty.
Doyle Sarah (wid Philip), h 271 W Maryland.
Doyle Stephen A, lab, h 325 Lafayette.
Doyle Thomas J, pressman, b 31 Dougherty.
Doyle Thomas N, gasfitter, h 23 N Spruce.
Doyle Wm A, mach, b 94 Agnes.
Doyle Wm D, carp, h 22 Woodside av (W).
Dozier James V, stenog, h 433 W Eugene (N I).
Dozzle Kate, h 72 Hill av.
Dozzle May I, dressmkr, b 74 Hill av.
Draa John W, brakeman, b 99 Lexington av.
Draeger Charles W, packer, b 215 Coburn.
Draeger Frederick, sawyer, h 215 Coburn.

Julius C. Walk & Son, Jewelers Indianapolis.
12 EAST WASHINGTON ST.

Drager Christian P, carp, h 25 St Peter.
Drain Guy, lab, b 57 Warren av (W I).
Drainage Journal The, John J W Billingsley pub, 19 Talbott blk.
Draisin Maurice, peddler, h 155 Maple.
Drake Albert A, lab, b 398 S East.
Drake Alonzo D, carp, h 186 Spann av.
Drake Ambrose F, foreman, b 398 S East.
Drake Catherine (wid Henry), h 640 Charles.
Drake Emma G, milliner, 472 Virginia av, h same.
Drake Frank B, stonecutter, h 46 Torbet.
Drake Hiram J, driver, b 47 Harris.
Drake General L, lab, h 127 Locke.
Drake Harry E, baggagemstr, b 84 Pleasant.
Drake Helen, b 501 W Washington.
Drake Herman S, driver, h 627 Marlowe av.
Drake Hiram J, tmstr, b 323 Blake.
Drake Isaac, cook, b 93 Columbia al.
Drake James F, lab, h 534 W Washington.
Drake Lee, porter, h 127 Locke.
Drake Lola M, stenog, b 203 Orange.
Drake Nancy, h 292 Indiana av.
Drake Orrin L, blksmith, h 203 Orange.
Drake Rebecca L (wid Edward), b 84 Pleasant.
Drake Robert (Power & Drake), h 1031 N Alabama.
Drake Robert B, contr, 526 N Brookside av, h same.
Drake Wm E, photog, h 472 Virginia av.
Drake Wm G, paperhngr, h 400½ S Meridian.
Drake Wm J, h 398 S East.
Drake Wm W, barber, b 398 S East.
Drake Wm W, trimmer, b 400½ S Meridian.
Dransfield John, lab, h 331 W Market.
Dransfield Reuben, lab, h 98 Bloomington.
Dransfield Sarah E (wid Ezra), h 66 Geisendorff.
Dransfield Thomas D, lab, h 26 Douglass.
Draper Elizabeth (wid George), cook Insane Asylum.
Draper Martin F, bartndr, h 224 N Missouri.
Draper Thomas E, lab, h 456 Charles.
Drapier Wm H, pub Indiana Journal of Commerce, 78½ S Delaware, h 513 N New Jersey.
Drapier Wm H jr, notary public, clk Mas Mut Ben Soc, r 26 The Chalfant.
Draut Conrad (West Side Planing Mill Co), h 35 Crawford.
Drechsel George H, vice-pres The Emrich Furniture Co, h 24 Carlos.
Drehr Mathias, r 348 N Illinois.
Dreier Ernest, contr, 112 English av, h same.
Dreiss Otto, clk Charles Mayer & Co, h 473 N Senate av.
Dreithaler Gustav W, dyer, h 625 W Michigan.
Drescher Henry, carp, h 105 Hill av.
Dressendorfer Charles A, clk, h 510 N Alabama.
Dressendorfer Jacob G, clk, b Enterprise Hotel.
Dressendorfer Wm A, clk, b 117 N Senate av.
Dresser Alice W, teacher, b 531 N Delaware.
Dresser Mary E, teacher, b 531 N Delaware.
Dresser Nathaniel A, painter, h 47 Newman.
Dresser Otto W, mach, b 47 Newman.

OTTO GAS ENGINES | BUILDERS' EXCHANGE S. W. Cor. Ohio and Penn. Telephone 535.

Becker & Son Charles Becker Jacob Becker Jr. Merchant Tailors. 21 N. Penn. St. Tel. 934

Dresser Wm L, fireman, b 47 Newman.
Dreuhann Frank, cigar mnfr, 762 S Meridian, h same.
Drew Harry E, pres Wanamaker Car Scale Co, h 705 N Penn.
Drew John A, bkkpr, b 72 W New York.
Drew Lucius W, b Grand Hotel.
Drewes Charles W, foreman, h 265 Union.
Drewes Frederick, lab, b 265 Union.
Drews Anton, lab, h 56 Jones.
Drews Paul, lab, h 618 S West.
Drexler Catherine (wid David W), h 15 Oriole.
Dreyer August, gardener, h 903 S Meridian.
Dreyer John H, carp, h 147 Newman.
Dreyer Lewis S, motorman, h 1063 N Capitol av.
Dreyfoos Leo (Dreyfoos & Co), h 1099 N Meridian.
Dreyfoos & Co (Leo Dreyfoos, Samuel Fox, George A Solomons), proprs The Globe Clothing Co, 97-99 E Washington.
Driesbach Amandus G, carp, h 96 Yeiser.
Driesbaugh Catherine M (wid Simon L), b 133 S East.
Driftmeyer George C, butcher, b 52 Sanders.
Driftmeyer Henry, h 52 Sanders.
Driftmeyer Henry E, mach hd, b 52 Sanders.
Driftmeyer Wm H, trav agt, b 52 Sanders.
Driggs Nathaniel S, drugs, 850 E Washington, h 983 N Illinois.
Drinkard Clarence L, sawmkr, b 420 Bellefontaine.
Drinkard Wm R, trav agt, h 420 Bellefontaine.
Drinkout Charles, fireman, h 270 E Louisiana.
Drinkut Charles W, car insp, h 28 Gatling.
Drinkut Christina (wid Wm), b 258 S East.
Drinkut Frederick W, coachman 582 E Washington.
Drinkut Wm F, engr, h 259 S New Jersey.
Drischel Andrew E, carp, h 38 Thalman av.
Driscoll Cornelius, hostler, h 41 Nordyke av (W I).
Driscoll Richard, lab, b 224 W Maryland.
Driskell Bert, lab, b 80 Clifford av.
Driskell Eliza (wid Jacob), h 139 E Maryland.
Driskell Ella (wid Wm H), h 14 Cleaveland blk.
Driskell Florence, h 53½ Russell av.
Driskell Jasper N, lab, h 80 Clifford av.
Driskell Wm A, lab, b 139 E Maryland.
Droege Charles J, clk Cathcart, Cleland & Co, h 422 N East.
Droege Edward T, mach, h e s Hillside av 2 n of Belt R R.
Droege Lucy (wid Edward H), h 302 Coburn.
Drohan Daniel G, stoker, b 339 S Alabama.
Drohan John J, stoker, h 137 Wright.
Drohan Michael M, lab, b 130 Wright.
Drohan Patrick, h 130 Wright.
Drohan Thomas J, stoker, b 130 Wright.
Drole August, clk, b 630 S Meridian.
Drotz Emil, h 19 Laurel.
Drotz Harry, gasfitter, b 19 Laurel.
Drotz Wm, lab, h 47 Wallack.
Drought John, lab, h 145 Elm.
Drozdowitz Michael, pawnbroker, 149 E Washington, h same.
Drucker Samuel, bkkpr, b 268 E St Clair.
Drudy Mary (wid James), h 131 N Noble.
Drudy Winifred V, milliner, 173 E Washington and 131 N Noble, b same.

Henry H. Fay,
40½ E. WASHINGTON ST.,
FIRE INSURANCE, REAL ESTATE,
LOANS AND RENTAL AGENT.

Druley Wm S, trav agt Nat Coll Agency, h 85 Ft Wayne av.
Drum Charles, horseshoer, 25 S William (W I), h 55 Martha (W I).
Drum George T, painter, h 14 Martha (W I).
Drum Robert, lab, h 77 Dougherty.
Drumm Luther, lab, h 32 Brett.
Drumm Melvina A, h 220½ S Meridian.
Drummond Hugh J, with Consolidated Coal and Lime Co, h 266 S Senate av.
Drummond Joseph C, propr American Hotel, h 84 S Illinois.
Drummond Wm M, bkkpr Indpls Gas Co, h 221 W New York.
Drury George H, clk Van Camp H and I Co, h 79 E St Joseph.
Drury Harry, adv agt Empire Theater, b 137 E North.
Drury Mason, lab, h rear 275 Christian av.
Dry John M, lab, h 133 Allegheny.
Dry Nancy, h 133 Allegheny.
Dry Wm, lab, h 24 Willard.
Drybread Seneca, attendant Insane Asylum.
Dryden Bernard, h 255½ E Washington.
Dryden Edward L, tinner, h 124 S Pine.
Dryer Charles A, lawyer, 408 Indiana Trust bldg, h 368 Central av.
Dryer George H, car sealer, h rear 172 Bird.
Dryer George J, millwright, b 326 W Vermont.
Dryer George W, photog, 96½ S Illinois, h 1011 N Penn.
Dryer Hans I, clk, h 326 W Vermont.
Dryer James W, druggist, h 1008 N Delaware.
Drysdale Knowlton P, clk, r 52 The Chalfant.
Dubbs Eugene C, porter, h 283 S Missouri.
Dubiel Julius, chemist, r 39½ Indiana av.
DuBois Benjamin F, feather renovator, 116 Mass av, h same.
DuBois Calista (wid Peter), b 267 N East.
DuBois Edward, teacher, r 381 N Delaware.
Dubois Robert, clk, h 502½ N West.
DuBois Robert A, mach, b 179 Oliver av (W I).

JAS. N. MAYHEW,
MANUFACTURING
OPTICIAN
LENSES AND FRAMES A SPECIALTY.
No. 13 North Meridian St., Indianapolis.

SALISBURY & STANLEY. Contractors and Builders
177 Clint or Street, Indianapolis, Ind. TELEPHONE 999.
Of all kinds done on short

LUMBER | Sash, Door and Planing Mill Work. | Balke & Krauss Co. Cor. Market and Missouri Streets.

FRIEDGEN'S TAN SHOES are the Newest Shades Prices the Lowest. 19 North Pennsylvania St.

SAMUEL LAING General Job Work in Sheet Metal of all Kinds 72 AND 74 E. COURT STREET.

M. B. WILSON, Pres. W. F. CHURCHMAN, Cash.
THE CAPITAL NATIONAL BANK,
INDIANAPOLIS, IND.
Make collections on all points in the States of Indiana and Illinois on the most favorable rates.
Capital, - - $300,000
Surplus and Earnings, 50,000
No. 28 S. Meridian St., Cor. Pearl.

DuBois Samuel, engr, h 179 Oliver av (W I).
DuBois Wm, b 175 W South.
Dubowich Louis, pdlr, h 441½ S Illinois.
Dubs Lewis, lab, b n w cor Morris and Tremont av (W I).
Ducas Edward, mngr, h 157 N East.
Ducas Fannie, jeweler, 115 W Washington, h 157 N East.
Duchemin Elias P, contr, 325 S Meridian, b same.
Duchemin John W D, lab, r 290 W Market.
Duchene Alford J, harnessmkr, b 411 E Washington.
Duchene Charles, stage mngr Park Theater, b 411 E Washington.
Duchene Charles J, restaurant, 411 E Washington, h same.
Ducker Charles M, condr, h w s Brightwood av 2 n of Willow (B).
Duckett Wm, lab, b 27 Bates.
Duckum Thomas, carp, h rear e s Line 3 n of Washington av (I).
Duckwall Herbert R, broker, h 1108 N Senate av.
Duckwall John S, com mer, h 974 N Capitol av.
Duckwall Thomas, h 1108 N Senate av.
Duckworth Adonis N, brakeman, h 21 Poplar (B).
Duckworth James A, clk, h 181 N Liberty.
Duckworth John W, engr, h 295 Cornell av.
Duckworth Minnie G, bkkpr The Rough Notes Co, b 102 Broadway.
Duckworth Wm T, milk, b 18 Wheeler.
Dudanske Frank, mach, b 48 Dunlop.
Dudanske Wm, brewer, h 48 Dunlop.
Dudbridge Lewis B, clk, h 201 N Penn.
Dudbridge Sarah B (wid Wm), b 201 N Penn.
Duddy Edward C, porter R M S, h 551 W Eugene (N I).
Duddy Richard, blksmith, h 424 W McLene (N I).
Duddy Virgil W, painter, b 424 W McLene (N I).
Duden August (August Duden & Co), h 51 Huron.
Duden August & Co (August and Hans Duden), chemists, 51 Huron.

MONEY
Loaned on Short Notice at Lowest Rates.
TUTTLE & SEGUIN,
Tel. 1168. 28 E. Market St.

Duden Hans (August Duden & Co), b 51 Huron.
Duderstadt Henry, florist, h 27 Byram pl.
Dudgeon James W, clk Kingan & Co (ltd), h 551 Union.
Dudium Harry, tel opr, h 416 N New Jersey.
Dudley Aaron, lab, b 112 Howard.
Dudley Allen, lab, r 10 Mulberry.
Dudley Charles F, supreme treas Knights and Ladies of Honor, b 212 N West.
Dudley Darius, lab, b 450 Lincoln av.
Dudley Edward, tmstr, h 367 English av.
Dudley Edward M, painter, r 300 W New York.
Dudley Frank, driver, b 208 E Morris.
Dudley F & Co (Maud and Sarah F Dudley), drugs, 600 Central av.
Dudley George J (G J Dudley & Co), h 184 Coburn.
Dudley G J & Co (George J Dudley), clothing, 669 Virginia av.
Dudley Hubert W, phys, h 600 Central av.
Dudley Marshall R, painter, r 300 W New York.
Dudley Maud (F Dudley & Co), h 600 Central av.
Dudley Sarah (wid Allen), b 118 Martindale av.
Dudley Sarah F (F Dudley & Co), b 600 Central av.
Dudley Thomas, janitor Wyandot blk, h same.
Dudley Wm, driver, r 84 S Illinois.
Dudley Wm J, clk, b 184 Coburn.
Due Peter, lab, h 427 W 2d.
Duecker Bernard, mach hd, h 96 Marion av (W I).
Duerson Orlando, waiter, r 163 Bird.
Duff Christopher, h 173 E Morris.
Duff Richard T, driver, b 173 E Morris.
Duffecy Frank F, engr, b 172 Walcott.
Duffecy Michael M, bartndr, b 172 Walcott.
Duffecy Patrick H, engr, b 172 Walcott.
Duffecy Thomas, flagman, h 172 Walcott.
Duffecy Thomas O, fireman, b 172 Walcott.
Duffey Bernard A, tel opr, b 256 S Missouri.
Duffey Catherine (wid John), h 359 W Pearl.
Duffey Ellen (wid James), h 402½ S West.
Duffey James, saloon, 157 W McCarty, h same.
Duffey John B, lab, h 256 S Missouri.
Duffey John C, tel opr, b 256 S Missouri.
Duffey John P, lab, h 43 Blake.
Duffey John T, clk, b 402½ S West.
Duffey Joseph, bartndr, b 157 W McCarty.
Duffey Thomas, lab, h 97 William (W I).
Duffie Frank, painter, r 22 N Delaware.
Duffield Minnie (wid Dr James T), r 250½ S Meridian.
Duffy Agnes M, stenog Lamb & Hill, b 202 W St Clair.
Duffy Bridget (wid Patrick), h 359 W Pearl.
Duffy Charles, mach hd, b 71 E McCarty.
Duffy Edward, baggageman, h 60½ S Illinois.
Duffy Ernest J, lab, b 202 W St Clair.
Duffy James, mach hd, b 71 E McCarty.
Duffy John, lab, b 29 Blake.
Duffy John, lab, h 62 Pierce.
Duffy John F, lab, b 202 W St Clair.
Duffy John H, tilesetter, h 21 S East.
Duffy Joseph, fireman, b 71 E McCarty.
Duffy Joseph A, lab, b 109 Wright.
Duffy Kate (wid James), h 71 E McCarty.
Duffy Lawrence, b 71 E McCarty.
Duffy Lewis, lab, b 202 W St Clair.
Duffy Louisa (wid Thomas), b 204 Dougherty.

PAPER BOXES, MANUFACTURED BY SULLIVAN & MAHAN 41 W. PEARL STREET.

DIAMOND WALL PLASTER { Telephone 1410 BUILDERS' EXCHANGE

Fine Laundry Work our Specialty. Collars and Cuffs our Hobby. THE HOME LAUNDRY 197 S. Illinois St. Telephone 1769.

Duffy Mary (wid James), h 202 W St Clair.
Duffy Philip W, motorman, h 915 N Senate av.
Duffy Sabina (wid Luke), b 22 Quincy.
Duffy Thomas, lab, h 18 Lynn.
Duffy Wm P, clk U S Pension Agency, h 204 Dougherty.
Dufner Frederick, baker, b 187 Elizabeth.
Dufresne Leon, huckster, h 197 S Spruce.
Dugan Bernard W, barber, rear 370 S West, b 39 Roe.
Dugan Bridget (wid George), h 183 W South.
Dugan Charles E, painter, b 304 S Meridian.
Dugan Cornelius, flagman, h 98 Spann av.
Dugan Cornelius, lab, b 179 W South.
Dugan Daniel, saloon, 200 W Washington, h same.
Dugan Daniel, tmstr, r 2 McGill.
Dugan Daniel S, driver, b 263 Hadley av (W I).
Dugan Elizabeth C, stenog, b 1025 N Penn.
Dugan Ellen (wid John), attendant Insane Hospital.
Dugan Henry, h 31 Roe.
Dugan Hubert, bartndr, b 25 Ketcham (H).
Dugan James, lab, h 27 S California.
Dugan James F, shaper, b 74 Laurel.
Dugan James P, lab, b 183 W South.
Dugan James W, lab, b 84 N Belmont av (H).
Dugan John, lab, h 41 King av (H).
Dugan John, lab, b 220 S Missouri.
Dugan John, lab, b 31 Roe.
Dugan John, lab, b 107 W South.
Dugan John, lab, b 39 S West.
Dugan John, saloon, 38 Michigan (H), h same.
Dugan John A, butcher, b 39 Roe.
Dugan John A, treas G F Wittmer Lumber Co, trav agt Hollweg & Reese, h 1225 N Capitol av.
Dugan John F, lab, b 98 Spann av.
Dugan John M, clk John L Moore, b 183 W South.
Dugan Joseph A, trav agt, b 1025 N Penn.
Dugan Joseph M, clk, b 183 W South.
Dugan Kate (wid Henry), h 84 N Belmont av (H).
Dugan Lawrence E, bartndr, b 39 Roe.
Dugan Martin, lab, b 84 N Belmont av (H).
Dugan Martin, lab, b 267 W Maryland.
Dugan Martin, lab, h 364 W Maryland.
Dugan Martin, lab, b 113 Minerva.
Dugan Martin, lab, b 39 S West.
Dugan Martin M, grocer, 571 W Michigan, h rear 114 Agnes.
Dugan Martin S, lab, b 39 S West.
Dugan Mary (wid John), h 39 Roe.
Dugan Michael, lab, b 84 N Belmont av (H).
Dugan Michael, lab, h 80 Holmes av (H).
Dugan Michael, lab, b 230 W Maryland.
Dugan Michael, tmstr, b 31 Roe.
Dugan Michael J, tailor, b 140 King av (H).
Dugan Milton G, driver, h 367 S Capitol av.
Dugan Nicholas, bricklyr, h 1025 N Penn.
Dugan Neil, cigars, h 220 Blake.
Dugan Patrick, lab, h 10 Douglass.
Dugan Patrick, lab, b 140 King av (H).
Dugan Patrick, lab, b 950 W Vermont.
Dugan Peter, lab, h 140 King av (H).
Dugan Thomas, bartndr, b 246 W Washington.
Dugan Thomas, lab, h 25 Ketcham (H).
Dugan Thomas, lab, h 361 W Pearl.
Dugan Thomas, lab, b 31 Roe.
Dugan Thomas F, patrolman, b 88 Greer.
Dugan Valentine, butcher, h 39 Roe.
Dugan Valentine, lab, b 140 King av (H).

FRANK NESSLER. WILL H. ROST.
FRANK NESSLER & CO.
Tailors
56 East Market St. (Lemcke Building),
Indianapolis, Ind.

Dugan Wm, lab, h 309 S West.
Dugdale Benjamin H (Wadde & Dugdale), h 401 Broadway.
DUGDALE CAN CO THE, Wm Dugdale Pres, Tin Can Mnfrs, cor S Meridian and Belt R R, Tel 795.
Dugdale Wm, pres The Dugdale Can Co, h 617 N Meridian.
Duggan Leslie J, collr, b 63 Oak.
Duggan Walter C, horseshoer, h 63 Oak.
Dugged Mattie, b 18½ Indiana av.
DuGranrut Charles J, clk, h 450 N California.
DuGranrut George F, driver, h 282 N Senate av.
DuGranrut John L, butcher, b 282 Douglass.
DuGranrut Joshua W, tmstr, h 1849 N Illinois.
DuHadway Mary A (wid Porter), b 120 S Noble.
Duhadway Wm, ins agt, h 158 Wright.
Duhm Henry, driver, h 548 S Capitol av.
Duke Calvin F, mach, h 63 Jefferson.
Duke Daniel W, tmstr, h 170 Laurel.
Duke Wm A, lab, b 170 Laurel.
Duke Wm A, molder, h 325 Columbia av.
Dukes Davis, confr, h 410 N West.
Dukes Mary A, confr, 410 N West, h same.
Dukes Robert P, lab, h 444½ W Washington.
Dumas Arthur B, transfer, h 405½ S Delaware.
Dumas James T, transfer, b 27 Bicking.
Dummich Charles E, tinner, h 1356 N Senate av.
Dumont Elwood, clk, h 531 Ash.
Dumont Mary A (wid Ebenezer), b 705 N Penn.
Dumray Fannie, h 88 Garden.
Dumser John, brickmkr, h s w cor Colgrove and Mattie av.
DUN R G & CO THE, Mercantile Agency, Joseph A Kebler Mngr, 1 Waverly Bldg, 18½ N Meridian, Tel 708.
Dunaway John W, tailor, b 60 Chapel.

Haueisen & Hartmann
163-169 E. Washington St.
FURNITURE,
Carpets,
Household Goods,
Tin, Granite and China Wares, Oil Cloth and Shades

THE WM. H. BLOCK CO. 7 AND 9 EAST WASHINGTON STREET. DRY GOODS, MEN'S FURNISHINGS.

Fidelity and Deposit Co. of Maryland. BONDS SIGNED.—LOCAL BOARD John B. Elam, Albert Sahm, Smiley N. Chambers, John M. Spann.
GEORGE W. PANGBORN, General Agent, 704-706 Lemcke Building. Telephone 140.

74 EAST MARKET STREET Telephone 863. Insure Your Property With FRANK K. SAWYER

JOSEPH GARDNER,
Hot Air Furnaces
With Combination Gas Burners for Burning Gas and Other Fuel at the Same Time.
37, 39 & 41 KENTUCKY AVE. Telephone 322

Dunbar Alonzo G, barber, r 9 Grand Opera House blk.
Dunbar Clarence E, helper, h e s Rural 4 n of Bloyd av (B).
Dunbar Colin, b 1361 N Capitol av.
Dunbar Elmer L, boilermkr, h 45 Peru av.
Dunbar Esther (wid Frank), h 439 Blake.
Dunbar Frank E, welldriver, b 365 E Market.
Dunbar Nancy, dresmkr, 25½ W Washington, h 734 N Capitol av.
Dunbar Sarah (wid Melzar), h 734 N Capitol av.
Duncan Alexander, lab, h 421 S West.
Duncan Arthur L, student, b 275 W Vermont.
Duncan Carrie, boarding 118 S Judge Harding (W I).
Duncan Charles A, foreman Frank G Kamps, b 103 Agnes.
Duncan Clara J (wid James R), h rear 490 W North.
Duncan Cruz, lab, h 118 Columbia al.
Duncan Curtis, mach, b 118 S Judge Harding (W I).
Duncan David W, painter, b 639 E Wabash.
Duncan Edward, lab, h 111 Locke.
Duncan Eldridge, lab, r 48½ S Capitol av.
Duncan Finley P, driver, h 11 Holly av (W I).
Duncan Finus, lab, b 185 Minerva.
Duncan Frank E, fireman, h 57 Tacoma av.
Duncan Frank H, painter, b 103 Brookside av.
Duncan Frank J, lab, h 19 S Senate av.
Duncan Frank M, lab, b 260 Indiana av.
Duncan George M, clk, h 178 E South.
Duncan Gilbert A, cigarmkr, b 444 Indiana av.
Duncan Harry S, bkkpr A B Wiltse, 5, 11½ N Meridian, h 54-55 The Chalfant.
Duncan Henry W, tailor, b 88 Hoyt av.
Duncan Horace T, butcher, h 246 S Missouri.
Duncan Ira L, motorman, h 56 Arbor av (W I).
Duncan James B, patternmkr, b 91 River av (W I).
Duncan James N, paymaster, h 88 Hoyt av.

J. S. FARRELL & CO.
Plumbing
Natural and Artificial Gas Fitting.
84 N. ILLINOIS STREET.
TELEPHONE 382.

Duncan James S, trav agt Comstock & Coonse Co, h 147 Bellefontaine.
Duncan James W, clk Hotel English.
Duncan John, packer, h 15 Brett.
Duncan John, lab, r 291 Christian av.
Duncan John A, engr, h 27 Henry.
Duncan John C, clk U S Pension Agency, h 275 W Vermont.
Duncan John O, tinner, b 111 Locke.
Duncan John R (J R Duncan & Co), h 71 River av (W I).
Duncan John S (Duncan, Smith & Hornbrook), h 680 N Alabama.
Duncan John W, b 680 N Alabama.
Duncan Joseph G, trav agt, h 999 N New Jersey.
Duncan J R & Co (John R Duncan), patternmkrs, 168 W Georgia.
Duncan Kate (wid David W), h 444 Indiana av.
Duncan Leonard, lab, b 118 S Judge Harding (W I).
Duncan Mary A R, h rear 67 Minerva.
Duncan Minnie O, dressmkr, 444 Indiana av, b same.
Duncan Nancy B (wid John), b 45 Peru av.
Duncan Orville C, brakeman, b 103 Brookside av.
Duncan Rebecca H (wid David), h 291 E New York.
Duncan Robert, fruits, 119 E Mkt House, h 91 Camp.
Duncan Robert, liquors, 340 Blake, h same.
Duncan Robert B, b 174 Central av.
Duncan Robert P, mngr The Normandie European Hotel, 101-109 S Illinois.
Duncan Samuel, fireman, h 221 Elm.
Duncan Samuel E, sewer pipe, 157 Mass av, h 103 Brookside av.
Duncan Sherman F, mach, b 275 W Vermont.

DUNCAN, SMITH & HORNBROOK (John S Duncan, Charles W Smith, Henry H Hornbrook), Lawyers, Rooms 1-4, 76½ E Washington, Tel 342.

Duncan Thomas J, h 429 W Highland av (N I).
Duncan Wm, patternmkr, h 91 River av (W I).
Dundon Bridget (wid Patrick), b 199 Meek.
Dundon Wm, bartndr, b 123 Meek.
Dunfee Charles W, clk, b Enterprise Hotel.
Dungan Clara L, h rear 276 S Meridian.

DUNGAN JAMES M, Mngr Indianapolis College of Music and Director Dept of Music Franklin College, h 188 Ash.

Dungan Robert B, opr W U Tel Co, h 336 S New Jersey.

DUNGAN SAMUEL O, Mngr Polk's Milk Depot, 325 E 7th, h 399 Park av.

Dungan Stephen, painter, h 57 Elm.
Dunger Frank, lab, h 454 W 2d.
Dungey Augusta (wid James), r 271 Mass av.
Dungey James R, barber, 37½ Virginia av, r 125 Ft Wayne av.
Dunham Charles H, clk, b 268 S Noble.
Dunham Lizzie (wid George), h 268 S Noble.
Dunham Martha, stenog, h 160 N Delaware.
Dunham Mary E, h 268 S Noble.
Dunham Samuel L, well driver, h 330 Martindale av.
Dunham Wallace E, engr, h 186 N State av.

IF CONTINUED to the end of its dividend period, policies of the UNITED STATES LIFE INSURANCE CO., will equal or excel any investment policy ever offered to the public. | E. B. SWIFT, Manager, 25 E. Market St.

Wm. Kotteman 89 & 91 E. Washington St. TELEPHONE 1742 Furniture

SHOW CASES | WILLIAM WIEGEL | 6 West Louisiana Street Opp. Union Station.

Dunham Warren B Rev, pastor West Washington St Chapel, h 32 Elder av.
Dunham Wm P, mach, h 93 Brookside av.
Dunica James H, lab, h 6 Thalman av.
Dunica James T, horseshoer, h 64 Yandes.
Dunigan Stephen, painter, h 57 Elm.
DUNKINSON JOHN W, Sculptor, 17 Bell, h same.
Dunkle Alfred W, real est, 22 Thorpe blk, h 108 Ruckle.
Dunkle Will R, clk The McGilliard Agency Co, b 108 Ruckle.
Dunklebarger John E, freight receiver, h 176 Davidson.
Dunkman Rudolph, cabtmkr, b 450 S East.
Dunkmann Wm R, carver, h rear 164 S Noble.
Dunlap Charles H, plastr, b 197 N Noble.
Dunlap Clarence E, barber, r 18½ Indiana av.
Dunlap Dane S, student, r 410 N Penn.
Dunlap Elizabeth B, h 600 N Alabama.
Dunlap Henry L, bellman, h 26 Roanoke.
Dunlap James S, r 250 N Senate av.
Dunlap John, waiter, r 111 Indiana av.
Dunlap John M, phys, 19 W Ohio, r same.
Dunlap Joseph A, plastr, 200 Elm, h same.
Dunlap Livingston, h 600 N Alabama.
Dunlap Sarah B (wid Charles), b 482 Bellefontaine.
Dunlap Simon L, plastr, h e s Park av 1 n of 22d.
Dunlap Wm, waiter, r 148 W Maryland.
Dunlap Wm M, bkkpr H S Paramore, h 18 Topp pl.
DUNLAVY IRA E, Physician, 493 College av, b 533 same, Tel 648.
Dunlea Arthur, fruits, E Mkt House, b 518 W Addison (N I).
Dunlea John F, brakeman, h 85 Leota.
Dunlop Frank A, collr J S Cruse, b n s Bethel av 1 e of Auburn av.
Dunlop Robert M, foreman, h 198 Lexington av.
Dunlop Wm W, finisher, b 198 Lexington av.
Dunmeyer Charles H, gasfitter, b 266 E Ohio.
Dunmeyer Edward C, bkkpr Consumers' Gas Trust Co, h 636 E Market.
Dunmeyer Frederick W (F Dunmeyer & Co), h 266 E Ohio.
Dunmeyer F & Co (Frederick W Dunmeyer, Charles F W Resener), grocers, 15 E Mkt House.
Dunmeyer George H, clk Indpls Drug Co, b 266 E Ohio.
Dunmeyer Mary A (wid Harry), b 34 Oliver av (W I).
Dunn Albert A, carp, h 90 Tremont av (H).
Dunn Albert E, car insp, h 231 Michigan av.
Dunn Alfred C, condr, h 145½ Oliver av (W I).
Dunn Alonzo, foreman, b 46 Fletcher av.
Dunn Benjamin A, condr, h 138 Spann av.
Dunn Catherine, teacher Public School No 11, b 401 N Senate av.
Dunn Charles, waiter, r 77 N Alabama.
Dunn Charles C, attendant Insane Asylum.
Dunn Charles O, clk H P Wasson & Co, h w s Garfield av 3 n of Washington.
Dunn Charles W, clk, b 563 Park av.
Dunn Clement T, grocer, 148 Brookside av, h same.
Dunn Daniel, h 52 Fayette.
Dunn David, lab, h cor Belmont av and Vincennes bridge.

We Buy Municipal ~ Bonds ~
THOS. C. DAY & CO,
Rooms 325 to 330 Lemcke Bldg.

Dunn Edward, grain insp Indpls Board of Trade, b 1031 N Alabama.
Dunn Edward F, opr Postal Tel Cable Co, b 148 Huron.
Dunn Ernest E, driver, b 368 Cornell av.
Dunn Francis M, contr, 563 Park av, h same.
Dunn Frank J, clk, b 289 N Pine.
Dunn George, lab, h 33 Athon.
Dunn George E, contr, 128 King av (H), h same.
Dunn Grant R, lab, h 132 S Summit.
Dunn Harriet L (wid Jacob), b 401 N Senate av.
Dunn Harry C, plumber, h 58 W 8th.
Dunn Henry, lab, b 218 E Wabash.
Dunn Hubert, gilder, b 262 Lincoln la.
Dunn Jacob P, editorial writer The Indpls Sentinel, b 467 N Penn.
Dunn James, agt, h 289 N Pine.
Dunn James H, opr W U Tel Co, b 148 Huron.
Dunn James O, contr, 91 Germania av (H), h same.
Dunn Jane, h rear 21 Center.
Dunn Jeremiah, lab, h 44 King av (H).
Dunn Jesse E, trav agt, h 116 Yandes.
Dunn Jesse L, supt public schools (H), h 116 Germania av (H).
Dunn John, lab, h 162½ Indiana av.
DUNN JOHN C, Plumber, Gasfitter and Nickel-Plater, 63 N Illinois, Tel 632; h 878 N Senate av.
Dunn John E, clk L S Ayres & Co, h 368 Cornell av.
Dunn John G, bkkpr John C Dunn, h 1420 N Capitol av.
Dunn John H, carp, h 35 Bismarck av (H).
Dunn John M, foreman I U Ry Co, b 91 N State av.
Dunn Joseph, grocer, 297 S Illinois, h same.
Dunn Joseph, lab, h 106 Shepard (W I).
Dunn Joseph D, lab, b 257 Michigan av.
Dunn Joseph E, trav agt, h 148 Huron.
Dunn Lena, stenog, b 26 Elm.
Dunn Louis, lab, h 51 Davis.
Dunn Louis jr, oiler, b 51 Davis.
Dunn Marion A, chemist, b 257 Michigan av.

EAT
QUAKER BREAD
ASK YOUR GROCER FOR IT.
THE HITZ BAKING CO.

CARPETS CLEANED LIKE NEW. TELEPHONE 818
CAPITAL STEAM CARPET CLEANING WORKS

BENJ. BOOTH PRACTICAL EXPERT ACCOUNTANT. Thirty years' experience. First-class credentials. Room 18, 82½ E. Washington St. Indianapolis, Ind.

The Old Red Lion German European Restaurant || 18 and 20 S. Meridian St. Established 8.

ESTABLISHED 1876. TELEPHONE 168.
CHESTER BRADFORD,
SOLICITOR OF PATENTS,
AND COUNSEL IN PATENT CAUSES.
(See adv. page 6.)
Office:—Rooms 14 and 16 Hubbard Block, S.W. Cor. Washington and Meridian Streets,
INDIANAPOLIS, INDIANA.

Dunn Mary J (wid Felix C), b 10 Union.
Dunn Medora E (wid Armstrong I), h 257 Michigan av.
Dunn Michael, h 91 N State av.
Dunn Michael, lab, b 32 Lynn.
Dunn Morton E, clk, h 1096 N Senate av.
Dunn Patrick H, lab, h 32 Lynn.
Dunn Philip R, ornamenter, b 262 Lincoln la.
Dunn Rachel, h 81 Torbet.
Dunn Sallie (wid Wm), h 32 Drake.
Dunn Spencer, lab, b rear 204 Elizabeth.
Dunn Stephen, driver, h 14 Hadley.
Dunn Thomas, lab, r 172 Bismarck av (H).
Dunn Thomas F, mach hd, b 91 N State av.
Dunn Warren, lab, h 29 Hadley.
Dunn Wm, lab, h 42 Elder av.
Dunn Wm, porter The Denison.
Dunn Wm J, lab, b 257 Michigan av.
Dunn Wm L, insp, h 53 Birch av (W I).
Dunn Willis S, plumber, h 916 N Senate av.
Dunnavant Wm T, engr, h 234 S Missouri,
DUNNING LEHMAN H, Pres Indiana Medical Journal Publishing Co; Physician and Surgeon; Diseases of Women and Abdominal Surgery, 249 N Alabama, h same, Tel 1253.
Dunning Robert P, contr, 426 N California, h same.
Dunning Samuel M, printer, h 72 W 18th.
Dunnington Adeline J, music teacher, 92 Eureka av, h same.
Dunnington Gertrude L, stenog John J Price, b 228 E North.
Dunnington Guy W, clk E C Atkins & Co, b 228 E North.
Dunnington Harry, lab, b 207 W North.
Dunnington Mary H (wid Andrew), h 228 E North.
Dunnington Sarah, h 207 W North.
Dunnington Wm, whitewasher, r 215½ Indiana av.
Dunnington Wm J, ins agt, h 92 Eureka av.
Dunnington Wm N, clk Wm B Buford, h 160 N West.
Dupee Edward, lab, h 224 Howard.
Dupee Edward V, mattressmkr, r 183½ W Washington.

CORRUGATED IRON CEILINGS AND SIDING.
ALL KINDS OF REPAIRING.
O. B. ENSEY,
TELEPHONE 1562.
COR. 6TH AND ILLINOIS STREETS.

Dupee Frank, lab, h 314 W Court.
Dupee Joel, butler, h 43 Rhode Island.
Dupont Henry H, draughtsman, b 24 W Pratt.
Dupont Mary M (wid Aristides R), b 24 W Pratt.
Dupree Elizabeth (wid Edward), b rear 1 Rathbone.
Dupuis Delphine (wid John), b 110 Huron.
Dura Stanley, lab, b 63 Lynn av (W I).
Durand Charles H, lab, h 3 W Chesapeake.
Durand Ella (wid John T), h 56 Yandes.
Durant Wm E, mason, h 132 Newman.
Durbin Clinton T, fireman, h 160 Johnson av.
Durbin Lloyd W, clk, b 78 Dougherty.
Durbon Charles R, driven wells, 103 Yeiser, h same.
Durbon Nellie, b 103 Yeiser.
Durbon Walter S, pumpmkr, h 352 S Meridian.
Durborow Harry C, tinner, h 1057 N Senate av.
Durdel Frederick H, varnisher, h 271 Coburn.
Durfee Harvey F, trav agt Murphy, Hibbon & Co, h 447 College av.
Durfeld Angelica A, dressmkr, 308 Blake, h same.
Durfeld Katherine (wid John F), h 308 Blake.
Durflinger Harry A, carp, b 632 E New York.
Durflinger Oliver L, carp, h 632 E New York.
Durflinger Wm D, clk, b 632 E New York.
Durga Celia F (wid Harrison S), h 159½ E Washington.
Durham Charles, r 190½ S Illinois.
Durham Charles O, phys, 302 S Illinois, h 153 Union.
Durham Ewing, tiremkr, b 283 E Georgia.
Durham Frank C (Durham & Erganbright), r 302 S Illinois.
Durham James, lab, h 445 Blake.
Durham James B, driver, h 293 Douglass.
Durham James L, driver, h rear 628 Home av.
Durham James W, lab, h 50 Depot (B).
Durham Joseph, lab, b 427 W 2d.
Durham Joseph P, bkkpr Kahn Tailoring Co, h 102 Cherry.
Durham Nancy M (wid Leonard), b 24 Poplar (B).
Durham Raymond W, clk, b 102 Cherry.
Durham Robert L, lab, h 24 Poplar (B).
Durham Thomas A, driver, h 214 Newman.
DURHAM & ERGANBRIGHT (Frank C Durham, Luther L Erganbright), Lawyers, 629-630 Lemcke Bldg, Tel 1886.
Durie John E, lab, h 8 Standard av (W I).
Durin Ferdinand A, engraver, h 37 Cherry.
Durk Ramsey, coachman 785 N Meridian.
Durkee Ernest J, hostler, b 426 Columbia av.
Durkin James, lab, b 8 Church.
Durler Edward, pressman, r 601 E New York.
Durler George, cooper, h e s Garfield av 2 n of Ohio.
Durler George H, clk, h e s Garfield av 1 n of Ohio.
Durler John W, bookbndr Wm B Burford, h 437 E Vermont.
Durler May, stenog, b e s Garfield av 2 n of Ohio.
Durman Loda L, clk Original Eagle, h 217 E St Clair.

TUTEWILER UNDERTAKER, No. 72 WEST MARKET STREET. TELEPHONE 216.

THE PROVIDENT LIFE AND TRUST CO. OF PHILADELPHIA. Endowment Insurance presents the double attraction of relieving manhood and middle age from anxiety and old age from want. For particulars apply to D. W. EDWARDS, General Agent, 508 Indiana Trust Building.

THEODORE F. SMITHER ROOFER
GRAVEL AND OTHER COMPOSITION
Yard, 19 W. Maryland St. Telephone 861.
Office 15 W. Maryland St.

Durning Bernard, tailor, h 204 N Pine.
Durning Hugh, cutter, b 204 N Pine.
Durrett John T, lab, h rear 626 Home av.
Durrett Matilda (wid John), h 10 Sheridan.
Durrett Richard, lab, h 55 Drake.
Durrett Robert, lab, h rear 636 Home av.
Durson Frank, waiter, r 163 Bird.
Durst Ernest A, engraver, b 616 W Michigan.
Durst Ora L, springmkr, b 616 W Michigan.
Dury Margaret F (wid John), h 184 Mass av.
Dushmann Minnie (wid David), confr, 298 S Illinois, h same.
Duterstadt Henry L, florist, h 27 Byram pl.
Duthie Alice S, teacher Public School No 13, b 120 Hoyt av.
Duthie Archibald, turner, h 120 Hoyt av.
Duthie James, mach, h 240 Fletcher av.
Duthie Lawson A, college, 11½ N Meridian, b 240 Fletcher av.
Duthie Wm E, supt Indiana Chain Co, h 240 Fletcher av.
Dutot George F, clk County Recorder, h 86 Patterson.
Dutson, see also Dodson and Dotson.
Dutson James E, painter, h 21 Stevens.
Dutton Albert H, clk, r 154 N New Jersey.
Dutton Elizabeth F, b 571 E 9th.
Dutton Ellen (wid George), h 624 Madison av.
Dutton Harry L, engr, h 939 Madison av.
Dutton John L, engr, h 82 Dugdale.
Dutton Walter E, varnisher, h 26 Downey.
Dutton Wm, molder, b 143 N Alabama.
Duty Frank, lab, r 290 W Market.
Duty Harry M, brakeman, b 44 Lord.
Duvall Alfred B, janitor, h 65 Harlan.
Duvall Charles E, draperies, 44 N Illinois, h 537 same.
Duvall Charles G, baggageman, h 179 Hoyt av.
Duvall Charles H, solr A C Jones, b 171 W 3d.
Duvall Edwin D, trav agt, h 113 Hoyt av.
Duvall Ely A, lab, h 120½ Woodlawn av.
Duvall Gertrude, h 159 N Illinois.
Duvall Grace, h 159 N Illinois.
Duvall Howard, lab, h 69 Harlan.
Duvall Joseph P, city fireman, h 28 Jefferson av.
Duvall Theresa (wid Charles), h 245½ E Washington.
Duwe Wm, h 460 S Missouri.
Dux Edward F, stonecutter, b 158 Harrison.
Dux Emil A, cabtmkr, h 44 Lord.
Dux Jacob, clk, h 158 Harrison.
Duzan Ada, prin Public School No 22, b 858 N Penn.
Duzan Ada A (wid Wm N), h 858 N Penn.
Duzan George, condr, b 121 E New York.
Duzan Grace E, teacher Public School No 22, b 858 N Penn.
Duzan Jefferson C, foreman, h 595 W Eugene (N I).
Duzan Jessie F, teacher Public School No 11, b 858 N Penn.
Duzan Nellie R (wid George N), r 139 N Penn.
Duzan Samuel, barber, 94 S Belmont av W I), h same.
Duzan Wm F, lab, h 489 W Udell (N I).

DWELLING BUILDING ASSOCIATION, John Q Van Winkle Pres, David S Hill Vice-Pres, James E Pierce Sec, Wm T Cannon Treas, 24 S Penn.

Dwenger Wm, driver, h 467 S Delaware.
Dwenger Wm jr, clk, b 467 S Delaware.

THE WHEN IS A WORLD BEATER.

Dwight Huldah (wid Salmon H), b 489 N Illinois.
Dwinnell Charles L (Dwinnell & Jontz), r 12 Halcyon blk.
Dwinnell & Jontz (Charles L Dwinnell, John A Jontz), restaurant, 75 N Delaware.
Dwire Lewis S, fireman, h 135 Walcott.
Dwyer Anna M, teacher Public School No 12, b 138 S Olive.
Dwyer Arthur N, supt Nordyke & Marmon Co, h 869 N Penn.
Dwyer Dennis, brakeman, h 3 Wallace.
Dwyer Dennis, lab, h 3 Minkner.
Dwyer Edward, r 201 S Illinois.
Dwyer James A, boilermkr, b 138 S Olive.
Dwyer James J, boilermkr, h 138 S Olive.
Dwyer James J, saloon, 820 W Washington, h 3 Minkner.
Dwyer John A, engr, h 514 E 9th.
Dwyer John M, lab, h 229 W Chesapeake.
Dwyer John T, engr, h 269 Springfield.
Dwyer Joseph J (Toomey & Dwyer), r 649½ Virginia av.

DWYER JOSEPH M, Pharmacist and Druggist, Fancy and Toilet Goods, School Books, Paints, Oils and Glass; Night Bell, 425 Madison av, Tel 282; b 36 Coburn.

Dwyer Julia A, teacher Public School No 31, b 138 S Olive.
Dwyer Mary E, music teacher, 36 Coburn, b same.
Dwyer Michael A, engr, h 1008 W Washington.
Dwyer Patrick, lab, h 64 S Brightwood av (B).
Dwyer Thomas, b 229 W Chesapeake.
Dwyer Thomas, h 36 Coburn.
Dwyer Thomas, boilermkr, h 89 Decatur.
Dwyer Thomas, foreman, h 44½ Edward (W I).
Dwyer Thomas, lab, h 416 S West.
Dye Alexander, baggageman, r 5 Bretz blk.
Dye Alfred, lab, h 860 Milburn (M P).
Dye Alonzo M, helper, h 193 Trowbridge (W).

THE A. BURDSAL CO. Manufacturers of Paints and Colors VARNISHES, Brushes, Painters' and Paper Hangers' Supplies. 34 AND 36 SOUTH MERIDIAN STREET.

ELECTRICIANS DON'T FORGET US. ALL WORK GUARANTEED. C. W. MEIKEL, Tel. 466. 96-98 E. New York St.

DALTON & MERRIFIELD { LUMBER South Noble St., near E. Washington

INDIANA ELECTROTYPE CO. : BEST WORK. LOWEST PRICES.
23 WEST PEARL ST., INDIANAPOLIS, IND. JOB WORK. BOOK PLATES. BEST PATENT BASE ON THE MARKET.
All Orders Promptly Filled.

KIRKHOFF BROS.
Steam and Hot Water Heating Apparatus,
Plumbing and Gas Fitting.
102-104 SOUTH PENNSYLVANIA ST.
TELEPHONE 910.

Dye Charity, teacher High School, h 188 Broadway.
Dye George W, tmstr, h n w cor Northwestern av and 13th.
DYE JOHN T, Genl Counsel C C C & St L Ry, 101-102 Commercial Club Bldg, Tel 1347; h 599 N Delaware.
Dye Mary A, attendant Public Library, b 188 Broadway.
Dye, Valodin & Co (Washington W Dye, Charles M Valodin), live stock com, Union Stock Yards (W I).
Dye Washington W (Dye, Valodin & Co), h Washington twp.
DYE WM H, Attorney and Counselor at Law, 507 Indiana Trust Bldg, Tel 174; h 29 Morrison.
Dye Wm H, mngr Acme Oil Co, h 952 N Penn.
Dyer Andrew J, lab, b 316 W Maryland.
Dyer Effie, stenog, b 155 N Illinois.
Dyer Frederick, bricklyr, h 28 Villa av.
DYER GEORGE G, Mnfg Jeweler and Diamond Setter, 16 Waverly Bldg, 18½ N Meridian, h 570 Park av.
Dyer John A, student, b 570 Park av.
Dyer Parlee S, patternmkr, h 491 Dillon.
Dyer Sidney (Dyer & Rassmann), h 48 W 12th.
Dyer Wm B (Leonard & Dyer), h 436 N East.
DYER & RASSMANN (Sidney M Dyer, Emil C Rassmann), Real Estate, Rents and Insurance, 31 Monument Pl, Tel 1159.
Dynes Charles E, mailing clk P O, h 581 S State av.
Dynes Eldon L (Dynes & Greig), bkkpr Equitable Savings and Loan Assn, b 45 S Linden.
Dynes Joel A, execution dep sheriff, h 250 S Olive.
Dynes John F, lab, h 55 Barth.
Dynes Leonidas G, sec Equitable Savings and Loan Assn, 245 E Washington, h 45 S Linden.

LIME
BUILDING SUPPLIES,
Hair, Plaster, Flue Linings,
The W. G. Wasson Co.
130 INDIANA AVE. Tel. 989.

Dynes Walton L, mailing clk P O, b 45 S Linden.
Dynes & Greig (Eldon L Dynes, Alexander Greig), bicycle rep, 96 N Delaware.
Dysart Alexander C, carp, h 258 S New Jersey.
Dyson Edward, lab, b 116 Rhode Island.

E

Eacock George J, sec Natl Coll Agency, res Lafayette, Ind.
Eacock John M, pres Natl Coll Agency, h 176 Christian av.
Eacock J Smiley, vice-pres Natl Coll Agency, b 176 Christian av.
Eacret John D, meats, 24 Michigan (H), h same.
Eades James M, canceling clk P O, h 10 Hoyt av.
Eador Charles V T, cooper, b 456½ W New York.
Eador Russell, cooper, b 456½ W New York.
Eador Sarah A (wid Stephen), h 456½ W New York.
Eador Wm J, cooper, b 456½ W New York.
Eads Edgar T, asst bkkpr W H Messenger, b 77 Clifford av.
Eads John E, lab, b 202 Elizabeth.
Eads John M, lab, b 19 N Sheffield (W I).
EADS ROBERT I, Pharmacist, 100 E New York, Tel 888; h 247 N Meridian.
Eagan, see also Egan.
Eagan George, bartndr, b 175 S Capitol av.
Eagan James, lab, h 1020 S Meridian.
Eagan John, engr, b 125½ Hadley av (W I).
Eager Thomas, lab, h 75 S Wheeler (B).
Eagle Bessie M, stenog, b 120 Christian av.
Eagle Charles D, clk, b 56 Andrews.
Eagle Harry O, carpet cutter, h 188 Ramsey av.
Eagle John H, grocer, 348 N Delaware, h 338 same.
Eagle Mary E (wid John D), h 56 Andrews.
Eagle Wm O, mngr, b 338 N Delaware.
Eaglehoff Christian, woodwkr, r 177 E Washington.
Eaglen Joseph W, hostler, h s s Grandview av 1 n of Home.
Eaglen Mary (wid Silas), h 69 E McCarty.
Eaglesfield Caleb S, foreman Wm Eaglesfield Co, h 559 College av.
Eaglesfield James T (Wm Eaglesfield Co), h 808 Park av.
EAGLESFIELD WM CO (James T Eaglesfield, Alonzo E Robbins), Coal, Lumber and Planing Mill, s w cor Alvord and 9th, Tel 176.
Eagleson Wm B, lab, b 21 Agnes.
Eaglin George R, car insp, h 22 Miley av.
Eaker George, carp, h 402 W 1st.
Eaker Joseph, driver, b 402 W 1st.
Eaker Wm H, lab, h 8 Coe.
Eakins Otwell W, mach hd, b 234 E Washington.
Ealand Charles E, lab, b n s E Washington 5 e of Belt R R.
Ealand John, flagman, h n s E Washington 5 e of Belt R R.
Earhart David, livery, 671 Madison av, h 630 same.
Earhart George, driver, b 630 Madison av.
Earhart George W, grocer, 188 S William (W I), h same.
Earhart Perry W, dentist, 16½ E Washington, h 297½ Virginia av.
Earhart Sylvester F, dentist, 16½ E Washington, b 297½ Virginia av.

Parlor, Bed Room, Dining Room, Kitchen. Furniture W. H. MESSENGER, 101 E. Wash. St., Tel. 491.

ALL KINDS OF HEAVY AND LIGHT GRAY IRON CASTINGS | McNamara, Koster & Co. Phone 1593. 212-218 S. Penn. St. | Foundry and Pattern Shop

THE FRED DIETZ CO.

Earhart Wm I, grocer, 412 W North, h same.
Earl, see also Erle.
Earl Charles I, carp, b 489 College av.
Earl Edward H, carp, b 489 College av.
Earl Edwin C, stenog, b s s University av 1 w of Central av (I).
Earl Ernest E, bill poster, b 1228 N Illinois.
Earl Ernest F, clk, b s s University av 1 w of Central av (I).
Earl Henry S Rev, h s s University av 1 w of Central av (I).
Earl Howard, brakeman, h 6 Walcott.
Earl John, engr, h 150 Beacon.
Earl Martin T, carp, h 96 Jefferson.
Earl Robert A, car insp Kingan & Co, h 45 Miley av.
Earl Simeon D, clk, h 1228 N Illinois.
Earles Silas J, cigar mnfr, 46 Kappus (W I), h same.
Earley George, condr, b 28 S State av.
Earls Andrew, stock dealer, h 107 Colgrove.
Earls Charles B, fireman, h 28 Belmont av (H).
Early Anna, teacher Public School No 13, b 30 Union.
Early Catherine (wid John), h 30 Union.
Early Dennis, flagman, h 311 Cornell av.
Early Ella F, teacher Public School No 1 (H), b 30 Union.
Early Henry P, bkkpr, h 93 Union.
Early Hermann, lab, h s s Vorster 2 w of LaSalle (M P).
Early Jennie E, dressmkr, 414 Clifford av, h same.
Early John, lab, h 209 Northwestern av.
Early Margaret G, prin Public School No 4 (W I), b 30 Union.
Early Richard J, mach, 311 Cornell av.
Early Wm A, trav agt, h 190 N Capitol av.
Earnhart Jessie, stenog Holstein, Barrett & Hubbard, b 38 Walcott.
Earnheart Frank, mngr Avery Planter Co, h 141 St Mary.
Earnheart Lesley R, clk Avery Planter Co, 141 St Mary.
Earnshaw Joseph, h 38 Huron.
Earnest Sarah, nurse, 285 Virginia av, b same.
Earp Henry, carp, 214 Fletcher, h same.
Earp Ralph B, student, r 24½ Kentucky av.
EARP SAMUEL E, Physician and Sec Central College of Physicians and Surgeons, 24½ Kentucky av, Tel 1196; h 124 N Capitol av, Tel 1441.
Earsman Wm, ins agt, b 72 Harrison.
Earsom Alice E, dressmkr, 156 E St Joseph, b same.
Earsom Charles N, condr, b 141 Highland pl.
Earsom Nellie, dressmkr, r 19½ N Meridian.
Earsom Wm, stenog, r 72 Harrison.
Earsom Wm M, bkkpr, h 156 E St Joseph.
Ease Ernest G W, finisher, b 63 Germania av (H).
Easley Amanda, h 296 Highland av.
Easley Carrie, h 158 Chestnut.
Easley Carrie B, h 29½ Mulberry.
Easley Doc, janitor, b 237 W Michigan.
Easley Kate, h 158 Chestnut.
Easley Richmond, coachman 503 N Penn.
Easley Roland T, janitor, r 60 Hubbard blk.
Easley Scott, lab, h 560 N Senate av.
Easley Wesley, porter, r 26 Roanoke.
East Catherine (wid Isaac), h rear 9 Lexington av.

Henry H. Fay, 40½ E. WASHINGTON ST., FIRE INSURANCE, REAL ESTATE, LOANS AND RENTAL AGENT.

East Isaac W, lab, b rear 9 Lexington av.
East James R, farmer, h 292 N Illinois.
EAST STEPHEN H, Propr Shorthand Training School, State Agt Williams' Typewriter, 55 Thorpe Blk, b 302 N Delaware.
East Thomas J, real est, h 98 Highland pl.
Eastabrook, see also Estabrook.
Eastabrook Charles N, carp, h 634 Marlowe av.
Eastabrook Frederick, paperhanger, b 634 Marlowe av.
Eastabrook, George S, printer, b 634 Marlowe av.
Easter Edwin, foreman, h 16 Frazee (H).
Easterday Joseph W, gardener, h n s Wolf pike 3 e of Orchard.
Easterday Victor R, lab, h 107 Minerva.
Easterday Walter R, clk, h 241 River av (W I).
Easterday Wm O, foreman, h 188 Columbia av.
Eastern Star The (Ransford & Metcalf), pubs, 5 The Windsor.
Eastes Abraham, h 250 N Pine.
Eastes Dora R, teacher, b 258 W St Clair.
Eastes Ellsworth, clk R M S, h 57 Cornell av.
Eastham Robert S, barber, r 147 W Washington.
Eastman David C, carp, b 346 N West.
Eastman Henry C Rev, r 432 The Shiel.
Eastman Joseph, phys, 197 N Delaware, h 195 same.
Eastman Joseph R, phys, 197 N Delaware, b same.
Eastman Thomas B, phys, 197 N Delaware, h same.
Eastman Walter H, h 750 N Meridian.
Eastman Wm, lab, h 314 W St Clair.
Eastmann Charles, mach, h 61 Sanders.
Easton Charles W, lab, h 267 Spring.
Easton John, fireman, h 89 Darnell.
Eaton Art E, clk, b 1466 N Capitol av.
Eaton Claude W, carp, h 1377 London av.
Eaton Edward, hostler, h 23½ S Alabama.
Eaton Ezra F (Henley, Eaton & Co), h 1027 N Meridian.

WILL GO ON YOUR BOND
American Bonding & Trust Co.
Of Baltimore, Md. Approved as sole surety by the United States Government and the different States as Sole Surety on all Forms of Bonds.
W. E. BARTON & CO., General Agents, 504 Indiana Trust Building.
LONG DISTANCE TELEPHONE 1918.

WOODEN PACKING BOXES MADE TO ORDER FACTORY AND WAREHOUSE TRUCKS. 40 Madison Avenue. Telephone 69.

BUSINESS EDUCATION A NECESSITY. TIME SHORT. DAY AND NIGHT SCHOOL. SUCCESS CERTAIN AT THE PERMANENT, RELIABLE Indianapolis BUSINESS UNIVERSITY

Steam Pumping Machinery { HENRY R. WORTHINGTON, 64 S. PENNSYLVANIA ST. Long Distance Telephone 284.

UNION CO-OPERATIVE LAUNDRY (COMPOSED OF UNION LAUNDRY GIRLS.) NOS. 8, 40 AND 42 VIRGINIA AVENUE. T. E. SOMERVILLE, MANAGER —— TELEPHONE 8. INDIANAPOLIS, IND.

HORACE M. HADLEY
INSURANCE AND LOANS
66 E. Market Street, Basement
TELEPHONE 1540.

Eaton Frank H, brakeman, h 34 S Rural.
Eaton Helen A (wid George), b 90 W Walnut.
Eaton James E, lab, h 311 N Alabama.
Eaton James W, engr, h n e cor Senate av and 9th.
EATON MARION, Livery, Boarding and Sale Stable; Prompt Attention and Satisfaction Guaranteed Patrons; 25-27 W 7th, Tel 996; h 1466 N Capitol av.
Eaton Mary A (wid Elijah), b 65 W Michigan.
Eaton Mary J (wid James), b 311 N Alabama.
Eaton May, b 1466 N Capitol av.
Eaton Millard F, brickmason, h 33 S Reisner (W I).
Eaton Obadiah, fruits, 96 E Mkt House, h 199½ E Washington.
Eaton Pearl F, retoucher, b 46 Garfield pl.
Eaton Sylvester, lab, h 318 E Georgia.
Eaton Thomas, lab, h e s Miami 7 s of Prospect.
Eaton Eudolpho, roofer, h 172 Spann av.
Eaton Walter R, trimmer, h 1381 Berlin av.
Eaton Wm, cigarmkr, r 27½ Virginia av.
Eaton Wm J, roofer, h 190 Spann av.
Eaton Wm S, h w s Good av 4 s of Railroad (I).
Eaves George W, mach hd, b 293 W Morris.
Eaves James H, lab, h 296 W Morris.
Eaves Samuel, h 293 W Morris.
Eaves Samuel jr, mach hd, h 26 Maple.
Eaves Thomas, boxmkr, b 293 W Morris.
Ebaugh Philip K, watchman, h 155 Spring.
Ebel, see also Abel and Apel.
Ebel Bertha (wid Charles), b 706 E Washington.
Eberding Ernest, driver, b 531 S Meridian.
Eberhardt Clark E, elev opr, b 283 Douglass.
Eberhardt Alphonse C, finisher, b 5 Dawson.
Eberhardt Ernest S, clk Guarantee Sav and Inv Assn, b 173 E Merrill.
Eberhardt Ernst G, chemist, h 74 N Arsenal av.

COLLECTIONS
MERCHANTS' AND MANUFACTURERS' EXCHANGE
Will give you good service.
J. E. TAKKEN, Manager,
Union Building, over U. S. Pension Office.
73 West Maryland Street.

Eberhardt Ferdinand, tentmkr, h 187 River av (W I).
Eberhardt Frank G, clk, b 368 S East.
Eberhardt Frederick, collr Indpls Brewg Co, b 173 E Merrill.
Eberhardt Frederick F, collr, h 173 E Merrill.
Eberhardt George, cabtmkr, h 5 Dawson.
Eberhardt George C, lab, h 289 W Morris.
Eberhardt George J, mngr Eberhardt & Co, h 368 S East.
Eberhardt George J, foreman Natl Electric Headlight Co, h 524 S New Jersey.
Eberhardt George J jr, mach, b 524 S New Jersey.
Eberhardt George W, lab, r 193 W Washington.
Eberhardt John, h w s McPherson 1 n of English av (S).
Eberhardt John, h 257 W Morris.
Eberhardt John, fireman, h 37 Wisconsin.
Eberhardt John, mach, b 423 S New Jersey.
Eberhardt John C, student, h 189 N East.
Eberhardt Katharine, teacher Public School No 8, b 524 S New Jersey.
Eberhardt Moses F, lab, b 257 W Morris.
EBERHARDT & CO, George Eberhardt Mngr, Tent and Awning Mnfrs, 80 S Capitol av, Tel 1226.
Eberhart John C, dentist, h 189 N East.
Eberle Charles F, engraver, b 669 Mass av.
Eberle Carl, packer, h 72 Cincinnati.
Eberle Frank, veneerer, h 669 Mass av.
Eberle Frederick, baker, b 72 Cincinnati.
Ebersole Frank A, clk C H & D R R, h 289 N New Jersey.
Ebersole Georgia A (wid Charles F), b 289 N New Jersey.
Ebert Burd P, mach, h 218 W New York.
Ebert Charles C, mach opr The Sun, h 332 W 1st.
Ebert Charles D, clk, b 570 N Penn.
Ebert George W, mach, b 218 W New York.
Ebert John, lumber, h 570 N Penn.
Ebert Ulysses S G, patternmkr, r 218 W New York.
Ebert Wm H, trav agt, h 77 Highland pl.
Eberts John, lab, h 474 W 22d (N I).
Eberts John jr, mach, b 474 W 22d (N I).
Eblein John, shoemkr, 143 S New Jersey, r same.
Eblen Mary J (wid Wm B), b 131 Windsor.
Eblin Charles, brasswkr, b 12 Warman av (H).
Eblin Emily I (wid Jasper), h 12 Warman av (H).
Ebmeier Mathilda, teacher Public School No 6, b 326 Union.
Ebner Adolph, dry goods, 136 Michigan (H), h same.
Ebner Bertha E, sec Indpls Varnish Co, b 316 S East.
Ebner Edward J, b 316 S East.
Ebuer Emil, vice-pres Indpls Varnish Co, h 150 Buchanan.
Ebner Fannie M (wid Matthew), b 266 E Wabash.
Ebner Frank, bkkpr Indpls Varnish Co, b 316 S East.
Ebner John, pres Indpls Varnish Co, h 316 S East.
Ebner John, saloon, 154 W Washington, h 44 N Senate av.
Ebner Wm F, varnishmkr, b 316 S East.
Eburg Louis H, mach hd, h 58 Gresham.
Eccles Wm H, collr, r 174 N Illinois.
Echolds Joseph W, lab, h 64 Wisconsin.
Echols Alice (wid Wm S), h 42 S Capitol av.

CLEMENS VONNEGUT 184, 186 and 192 E. Washington St. | BUILDERS' HARDWARE, Building Paper. Duplex Joist Hangers.

THE WM. H. BLOCK CO. DRY GOODS, DRAPERIES, RUGS, WINDOW SHADES.
7 AND 9 EAST WASHINGTON STREET.

Echols Christopher C, condr, h 14 Minnesota.
Echols Henry H, carp, h 202 Bellefontaine.
Echols James A, cigarmkr, h s w cor Brookland and Progress avs.
Echols John T, condr, r 581 Morris (W I).
Echols Wm A, cigar mnfr, 289 Mass av, h 480 Highland av.
Echols Wm C, canmkr, b 14 Minnesota.
Eck George, lab, h 37 King av (H).
Eck George D, molder, b 100 N Belmont av (H).
Eck Harry E, clk, b 100 Belmont av (H).
Eck Mary J (wid Ferdinand), b 221 Virginia av.
Eck Teterick, grocer, 62 Michigan, h 100 Belmont av (H).
Eckel Edward, gunsmith Van Camp H and I Co, h 113 Benton.
Eckel George F, cutter, h 157 Huron.
Eckel Ingram, repr Van Camp H and I Co, b 113 Benton.
Eckel Thomas J, cutter, b 113 Benton.
Eckels Jonathan H, trav agt, h 112 Bright.
Eckenrode Wm D, die cutter, h 54 Greer.
Ecker Anna M (wid John), b 639 W Vermont.
Ecker Louis, peddler, b 265 S Capitol av.
Eckert, see also Aggart and Eggert.
Eckert Alton W, collarmkr, b 413 S State av.
Eckert Carl, baker, b 365 Indiana av.
Eckert Charles, h 29 Nebraska.
Eckert Charles E, painter, b 79 E Ray.
Eckert Charles W, collarmkr, h 413 S State av.
Eckert Fanny W, h 39 W Pratt.
Eckert Francis S, uphlr, b 79 E Ray.
Eckert Frank, foreman Indpls Daily Journal, h 87 N State av.
Eckert George R, music teacher, 87 N State av, h same.
Eckert Jacob, baker, 614 S East, h same.
Eckert Jacob, lab, h n w cor Burton av and Shoemaker (N I).
Eckert James, agt, r 80 N New Jersey.
Eckert Joseph, butcher, b 424 S Illinois.
Eckert Susan (wid Michael), h 79 E Ray.
Eckert Theodore M, agt, b 90 N Delaware.
Eckert Valentine, engr, b 927 N Meridian.
Eckert Wm, cigarmkr, h 111 Blake.
Eckert Wm, shoemkr, 119 Mass av, r 354 S Meridian.
Eckert Wm J, bricklyr, b 40 Samoa.
Eckfeldt Edward R, carp, h 15 Chadwick.
Eckhart Louis, baker, b 59½ N Illinois.
Eckhouse Bros (Joseph and Moses), whol liquors, 56 S Meridian.
Eckhouse Horace H, clk, b 994 N Meridian.
Eckhouse Joseph (Eckhouse Bros), h 994 N Meridian.
Eckhouse Moses (Eckhouse Bros), h 821 N Meridian.
Ecklin Charles A, trav agt Indpls Varnish Co, b 341 S New Jersey.
Ecklin Elizabeth (wid Andrew), h 341 S New Jersey.
Eckman John B, sec Joint Rate Assn and supt Weighing and Inspection Bureau, h 155 Bellefontaine.
Eckman John M, clk Joint Rate Assn, b 155 Bellefontaine.
Eckman Murray H, clk, b 155 Bellefontaine.
ECKMAN RUSSELL, Loans, 49 Board of Trade Bldg, h 458 N West.
Eckman Wm C, weighmaster, b 155 Bellefontaine.

Economist Plow Co, D P McKee agt, 10 Masonic Temple.
Eddie John A, bkkpr, h 259 N Delaware.
Eddings Milton W, molder, h 592 W North.
Eddleman Fred, motorman, h 533 College av.
Eddy Charles A, constable, 34 N Delaware, b 704 Ash.
Eddy Charles L, ins agt, h 217½ E Washington.
Eddy Elijah F N, collr, h 704 Ash.
Eddy Frank, mach opr The Indpls Sentinel, b 704 Ash.
Eddy Harry F, bkkpr, b 704 Ash.
Eddy Horace J, supt's office P C C & St L Ry, Union Station, h 56 West Drive (W P).
Eddy Hugh, lab, b 272 W Maryland.
Eddy Joseph A, acct, r 257 N Delaware.
Eddy Mary (wid Thomas E), h 530 W Washington.
Eddy Sarah J (wid John R), r 257 N Delaware.
Edelman Frederick, motorman, b 533 College av.
Eden Asa, contr, h 371 N Capitol av.
Eden August, lab, r Union Stock Yards (W I).
Eden Charles M, condr, b 371 N Capitol av.
Eden Harry G, contr, r 23 W 1st.
Eden Henry, car rep, h 41 Lexington av.
Eden James H, actor, b 371 N Capitol av.
Eden Samuel C, mach hd, h 175 Yandes.
Eden Wm H, cigarmkr, b 371 N Capitol av.
Edenharter Frank T (Edenharter & Mull), h 152 E New York.
EDENHARTER GEORGE F, M D, Supt Central Indiana Hospital for the Insane, National road 3 miles w of City, h same, Tel 389.
Edenharter, John, b 42 Tacoma av.
Edenharter Marion E, matron Insane Hospital.
EDENHARTER & MULL (Frank T Edenharter, George F Mull), Lawyers, 204-206 Indiana Trust Bldg, Tel 1464.

GUIDO R. PRESSLER,
FRESCO PAINTER
Churches, Theaters, Public Buildings, Etc., A Specialty.
Residence, No. 325 North Liberty Street.
INDIANAPOLIS, IND.

INDIANAPOLIS STEEL ROOFING AND CORRUGATING WORKS, 23 and 25 East South Street. S. D. NOEL, Proprietor.

David S. McKernan, Rooms 2-5 Thorpe Block.
REAL ESTATE AND LOANS
Money to loan on real estate. Special inducements offered those having money to loan. It will pay you to investigate.

DIAMOND WALL PLASTER { Telephone 1410 BUILDERS' EXCHANGE.

UNION TRANSFER AND STORAGE CO. Cor. E. Ohio St. and C., C., C. & St. L. R'y Tracks. BEST FACILITIES FOR STORING AND TRANSFERRING MACHINERY AND MERCHANDISE.

W. McWORKMAN

FIRE SHUTTERS, FIRE DOORS, METAL CEILINGS.

930 W. Washington St. Tel. 1118.

Edgar May, h 79 Kentucky av.
Edgar Mortimer S, bkkpr, h 54 Park av.
Edgar Richard, lab, b 331 W 1st.
Edgerton Dixon, mnfrs' agt, 77 E Market, h 110 Highland pl.
Edgerton Frank A, condr, h 52 Fletcher av.
Edgerton Harry H jr, trav agt, b 110 Highland pl.
Edgeworth Jennie, teacher Public School No 15, b Mary Edgeworth.
Edgeworth Mary (wid Preston), h e s National av 3 s of Washington av (I).
Edgeworth Mary H, stenog Indiana Soc for Savings, b 236 Broadway.
Edgey George, lab, b 233 S West.
Edgey John, packer, h 233 S West.
Edgey John D, marker, b 233 S West.
Edgey Wm J, packer, b 233 S West.
Edgington John F, trav agt, h n s University av 2 w of Ritter av (I).
Edgington Orla, lab, h 81 W Georgia.
Edighoffer George, mach, h 23 Hendricks.
Edington James T, harnessmkr, h w s Senate av 1 n of Lynn (M).
Edison James, r 186 N Senate av.
Edlen Daniel, lab, h e s Miami 4 s of Prospect.
Edlen John, porter, r 35½ Kentucky av.
Edlen Louisa (wid Scott), h 38 Pleasant av.
Edmiston Kate, b 308 E Ohio.
Edmonds James, lab, h 747 Brooker's al.
Edmonds James H, baggagemaster, h 6 Holmes.
Edmonds John C, carp, h 71 Madison av.
Edmonds John P, blksmith, r 19 Russell av.
Edmonds Reuben, lab, h 14 Howard.
Edmondson George F, bricklyr, h 35 Hoyt av.
Edmondson Major, hostler, h 569 S West.
Edmondson Milton J, barber, 116 Agnes, h 285 Chapel.
Edmonston Charles T, engr, h 287 E Georgia.
Edmunds Arthur R, clk R M S, b 1700 N Illinois.
Edmunds John G, gen delivery clk P O, h 1626 N Illinois.
Edmunds Manuel, lab, b 14 Howard.

GEO. J. MAYER, MANUFACTURER OF SEALS STENCILS, RUBBER STAMPS, CHECKS, BADGES, DOOR PLATES, ETC.
; S. Meridian St., Ground Floor. TEL. 1386.

Edmunds Rodger, lab, h rear 671 N Senate av.
Edmunds Wm, h 1626 N Illinois.
Edmunds Wm, lab, h rear 1383 N Senate av.
Edmundson Henry C, switchman, b 249 S Delaware.
Edson Carl C, mach hd, h 110 Shelby.
Edson Daniel M, contr, h 880 Milburn (M P).
Edson Edgar, bartndr, h 86 N New Jersey.
Edson James, lab, b n s 8th 1 w of canal.
Edson Lewis, lab, h 540 W North.
Edson Robert, barber, r 35 Kentucky av.
Edson Wm H, lab, h 431 W Chicago (N I).
Edson Wilson, porter, h 1009 S Meridian.
Edung Otto, driver, h 372 S Capitol av.
Edwards Albert J, switchman, h 116 N Pine.
Edwards Alexander, baker, h 307 Coburn.
Edwards Amanda (wid John W), b 138 N New Jersey.
Edwards Anna E (wid Wm T), h 75 Martindale av.
Edwards Burt, lab, b 174 S Missouri.
Edwards Cass, coremkr, h 21 S Belmont av (W I).
Edwards Catherine (wid John J), h 212 E Market.
Edwards Charles, r 167 N Capitol av.
Edwards Charles, b 272 E Court.
Edwards Charles, coal, 50 Sheffield (W I), h same.
Edwards Charles, lab, h 62 Chapel.
Edwards Charles D, mach, b 212 E Market.
Edwards Charles F, packer, b 23 Meikel.
Edwards Christopher C, watchman, h 34 Bird.
Edwards David J, rollturner, b 25 Gregg.
EDWARDS D W, Genl Agt The Provident Life and Trust Co of Philadelphia, Rooms 508-510 Indiana Trust Bldg, Tel 350; h 1042 N New Jersey. (See right top lines and left top cor cards and adv opp.)
Edwards Edward, fireman, b 28 S State av.
Edwards Edward, harnessmkr, b 312 N California.
Edwards Eliza D, teacher Public School No 40, b 679 N Senate av.
Edwards Emma (wid David M), h 133 Union.
Edwards Emma, dressmkr, 163 S East, h same.
Edwards Emory J, clk, h 29 Vine.
Edwards Frank, lab, h 774 E 10th.
Edwards Franklin, clk, r 76 N New Jersey.
Edwards George W, farmer, h w s N Illinois 3 s of 29th.
Edwards Grant, hostler, r Union Stock Yards.
Edwards Henry C, carp, r 25½ Kentucky av.
Edwards Henry, driver Sanborn Electric Co, b 774 E 10th.
Edwards Henry, lab, h n s Haughey av 2 w of Senate av.
Edwards Henry L, mach hd, h 152 Brookside av.
Edwards Homer J, sawyer, b 246 Yandes.
Edwards Hussey C, cook, h 90 Columbia al.
Edwards Isaac, lab, h 390 Clinton.
Edwards James, lab, h 322 W Court.
Edwards James, lab, b 1032 S Meridian.
Edwards James, lab, b 172 S Missouri.
Edwards Jet D (Sowders & Edwards), h 272 E Court.

A. METZGER AGENCY ESTABLISHED 1863. REAL ESTATE

THE PROVIDENT LIFE & TRUST CO.

ORGANIZED IN 1865.

Insurance in Force, $115,000,000
Assets, - - - - - - $32,000,000

The **Provident** has been conducted in accordance with the idea that Life Insurance is a sacred trust, and that the best management is that which secures permanence,

Unquestioned Safety,
Low Cost for Insurance,
Fair and Liberal Treatment,

and which best adapts plans of insurance to the needs of insurers. That the Company has not been excelled in accomplishing these results is a matter of record.

For particulars as to rates, plans of insurance, etc., apply to

D. W. EDWARDS, General Agent,

TELEPHONE 350. 508 Indiana Trust Bldg., INDIANAPOLIS, IND.

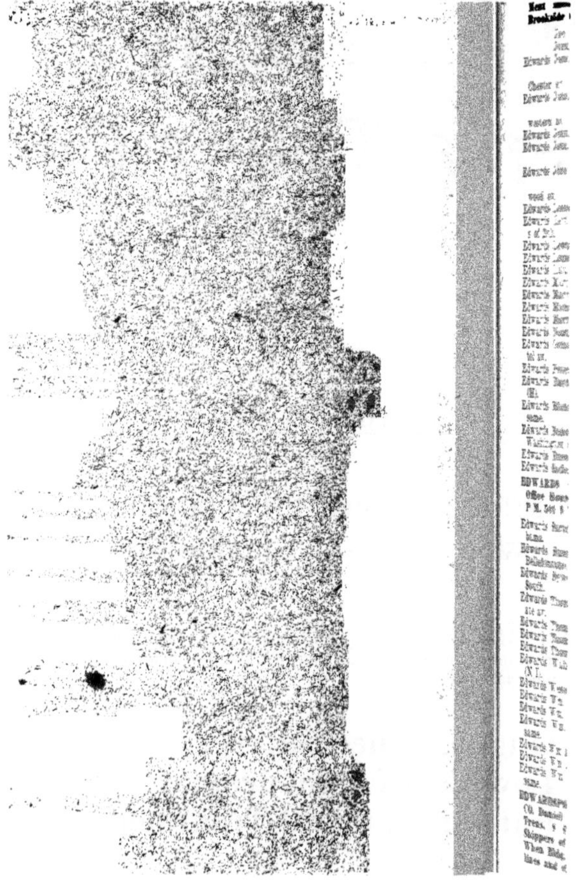

Next
Brookside

Edwards Jno.

Chester
Edwards Jno.

western
Edwards Jno.
Edwards Jno.

Edwards Jno.

wood
Edwards
Edwards
Edwards
Edwards
Edwards
Edwards
Edwards
Edwards
Edwards
Edwards
Edwards
tel av.
Edwards
Edwards
(H)
Edwards
same.
Edwards
Washington
Edwards
Edwards
EDWARDS
Office Hours
P M.
Edwards
bama.
Edwards
Bellefontaine
Edwards
South.
Edwards Thos.
ate av.
Edwards Thos.
Edwards Thos.
Edwards Thos.
Edwards
(N I.
Edwards W
Edwards Wm.
Edwards Wm.
Edwards Wm.
same.
Edwards Wm
Edwards Wm
Edwards Wm
same.
EDWARDS
(O. Daniel)
Treas.
Shippers of
When Bldg.
lines and

LAMBERT GAS & GASOLINE ENGINE CO.
ANDERSON, IND. NATURAL GAS ENGINES.

BICYCLES $5 DOWN. MONTHLY. Best Wheels. Best Terms. WHEELMEN'S CO. 31 W. OHIO ST. LONG DISTANCE TEL. 1855.

Edwards James A, lab, h 259 Lincoln la.
Edwards James F, collr, b 76 N New Jersey.
Edwards James M, gardener, h rear 1031 W Washington.
Edwards James W, clk Ward Bros Drug Co, h 28 Vine.
EDWARDS JEROME B, Grocery and Meat Market, 444 Mass av, h 61 Brookside av.
Edwards Joel B, h 207 Ash.
Edwards John, lab, b 64 Chapel.
Edwards John, lab, b 322 W Court.
Edwards John, lab, h n s Michigan 2 w of Chester av.
Edwards John, lab, r 338 Superior.
Edwards John, millwright, h 1149 Northwestern av.
Edwards John, plastr, h 199 Agnes.
Edwards John, tel opr, b 334 N Illinois.
Edwards John M, mach, h 369 Fletcher av.
Edwards John P, sup, h 25 Gregg.
Edwards Leonidas J, brakeman, b 1518 Kenwood av.
Edwards Leutelas S, mach, h 347 S East.
Edwards Levi W, lab, b w s N Illinois 3 s of 29th.
Edwards Lewis, bkkpr, h 459 E North.
Edwards Louisa (wid Charles), h 164 Bird.
Edwards Lulu (wid John W), h 280 Fulton.
Edwards Mary, h 269 Madison av.
Edwards Mary L (wid Wm), h 26 Meikel.
Edwards Michael, lab, h 679 N Senate av.
Edwards Morris F, clk, h 751 N Capitol av.
Edwards Noah, lab, b 680 W Vermont.
Edwards Octavius S, printer, r 171 N Capitol av.
Edwards Peter, lab, h 440 E 7th.
Edwards Raymond, lab, b 27 Reynolds av (H).
Edwards Richard H, carp, 15 S Alabama, r same.
Edwards Robert T, claim agt, h n e cor W Washington and Crawfordsville rd (M J).
Edwards Russell, horseshoer, b 134 S East.
Edwards Sadie, clk, b 459 E North.
EDWARDS SAMUEL G, Physician, Office Hours 8-10 A M, 1-3 and 6-8 P M, 501 N West, h same.
Edwards Sarah E (wid John), h 239 S Alabama.
Edwards Susan E (wid Robert D), b 82 Bellefontaine.
Edwards Sylvester, nurseryman, h 151 W South.
Edwards Thomas, barber, h rear 671 N Senate av.
Edwards Thomas, drayman, r 122 E Ohio.
Edwards Thomas, lab, h 114 Cook.
Edwards Thomas, lab, h 218 Miller (W I).
Edwards Walter H, carp, h 431 W Udell (N I).
Edwards Wesley, wagonmkr, h 220 Huron.
Edwards Wm, clk, b 75 Martindale av.
Edwards Wm, coachman 754 N Delaware.
Edwards Wm, vet surg, 134 W Pearl, h same.
Edwards Wm A, carp, h 246 Yandes.
Edwards Wm A, student, r 367 N Alabama.
Edwards Wm H, junk, 81 Norwood, h 73 same.
EDWARDSPORT COAL AND MINING CO, Daniel Lesley Pres, R E Moore Treas, S Frazier Sec, Miners and Shippers of Bituminous Coal, 42-43 When Bldg, Tel 1916. (See left side lines and classified Coal Miners.)

THOS. C. DAY & CO.
Financial Agents and Loans.
We have the experience, and claim to be reliable.
Rooms 325 to 330 Lemcke Bldg.

Effey August, lab, b 123 N Belmont av (H).
Efroymson Dinah (wid Meyer), h 475 S Meridian.
Efroymson Gustav A (Efroymson & Wolf), h 361 N East.
Efroymson Harry, stoves, 157 E Washington, h 41 Maple.
Efroymson Isaac, clk, b 475 S Meridian.
Efroymson Jacob, clk, b 475 S Meridian.
Efroymson Jacob, dry goods, 462 S Meridian, h 464 same.
Efroymson Louis M, clk, b 464 S Meridian.
Efroymson Meyer, clk, b 464 S Meridian.
Efroymson Philip B, clk, b 464 S Meridian.
Efroymson & Wolf (Gustave A Efroymson, Louis Wolf), props Star Store, 194-198 W Washington, tel 1744.
Egan, see also Eagan.
Egan Anna (wid John), h 339 S East.
Egan Benjamin F, driver, r 273 S West.
Egan David T, mach, b 805 E Market.
Egan Dennis, horseshoer, 112 N Delaware, h 1011 N Senate av.
Egan Dennis F, lab, h 353 S West.
Egan Dominick J (Egan & Son), h 53 Holmes av (H).
Egan Edward, mach, b 53 Holmes av (H).
Egan Edward P, mach, b 805 E Market.
Egan Henry F (Egan & Son), b 53 Holmes av (H).
Egan Irwin D, clk R G Dun & Co, b 805 E Market.
Egan James (Maloy & Egan), h 1 Lynn.
Egan James engr, h 492 W Eugene (N I).
Egan Jeremiah A, supt, h 805 E Market.
Egan Jeremiah A jr, insp Indpls Gas Co, b 805 E Market.
Egan John, engr, b 107 W South.
Egan Joseph, b 124 E Ohio.
Egan Kate, h 124 E Ohio.
Egan Kate B, h 226 N East.
Egan Mary A, microscopist, b 805 E Market.
Egan Mary (wid Michael), b 272 W Maryland.
Egan Michael, engr, h 18 Lee (W I).
Egan Michael, engr, h 492 W Eugene (N I).
Egan Michael, storekpr, b 38 Johnson av.

EAT
HITZ'S CRACKERS AND CAKES.
ASK YOUR GROCER FOR THEM.

J. H. TECKENBROCK General House Painter, 94 EAST SOUTH STREET.

FIDELITY MUTUAL LIFE—PHILADELPHIA, PA.
$75,000,000, Insurance In Force. $3,500,000, Death Losses Paid. $1,500,090, Surplus. A. H. COLLINS General Agent, Baldwin Block.

Edwardsport Coal & Mining Co. BITUMINOUS COAL IN CAR LOADS TO DEALERS AND MANUFACTURERS. ROOMS 42 AND 43 WHEN BU UD NG.

ESTABLISHED 1876. TELEPHONE 168.
CHESTER BRADFORD,
SOLICITOR OF PATENTS,
AND COUNSEL IN PATENT CAUSES.
(See adv. page 6.)
Office:—Rooms 14 and 16 Hubbard Block, S. W. Cor. Washington and Meridian Streets, INDIANAPOLIS, INDIANA.

Egan Michael W, trav agt, b 53 Holmes av (H).
Egan Patrick, trav agt, b 53 Holmes av (H).
Egan Peter, driver, h 46 S William (W I).
Egan Thomas (Egan & Sawders), b 215 S East.
Egan Thomas F, tailor, b 53 Holmes av (H).
Egan Thomas J, lab, b 339 S East.
Egan Thomas P, mngr Egan & Co, h 217 N Illinois.
Egan Wm, h 11 Warren av (W I).
Egan & Co, Thomas P Egan mngr, tailors, 22 Pembroke Arcade.
Egan & Son (Dominick J and Henry F Egan), grocers, 53 Holmes av (H).
Egan & Sowders (Thomas Egan, Wm M Sowders) oysters, 286 E Washington.
Egbert Harry C, lab, b rear 192 W Merrill.
Egbert Wm P, brakeman, h 24 Oriental.
Ege Charles, mach hd, b 86 N East.
Ege Charles F, sawyer, h 436 W Ontario (N I).
Ege Wm S, lab, h rear 342 Highland av.
Egelhoff Christian, wagonmkr, h s s Prospect 2 w of Madeira.
Egelhoff Henry, horseshoer, 901 Madeira av, h 906 same.
Egelhoff John J, bartndr, h 366 Prospect.
Egelhoff Margaret (wid John), grocer, s s Prospect 3 e of Madeira, h same.
Egelus Frederick, cabtmkr, h 130 N Noble.
Egelus Frederick W, grocer, 49 N Brightwood av (B), h same.
Egelus Pauline H (wid Daniel A), h 165 Fulton.
Egenolf Jacob, clk Charles Mayer & Co, h 73 Yeiser.
Eger Michael, mach, b 34 N Brightwood av (B).
Egerton Albert, bartndr, b 280 S Illinois.
Egerton Charles, saloon, 280 S Illinois, h same.
Egerton Charles H, b 280 S Illinois.
Egger Charles J, clk County Auditor, h 180 Dougherty.
Eggert, see also Aggert and Eckert.
Eggert Dorothea (wid Henry), b 65 Barth av.
Eggert Joseph, lab, h 68 Morton.

Outing BICYCLES
..MADE BY..
HAY & WILLITS MFG CO.
76 N. Pennsylvania St. Phone 598.

Eggert Paul W, pressman, b 22 Gresham.
Eggert Wm, drayman, h 22 Gresham.
Eggleson James, b 327 S Alabama.
Eggleston Wm W, farmer, b 120 Cornell av.
Egmont Sander, b 506 Madison av.
Ehart Albert, varnisher, b 920 Madison av.
Ehhart Charles S, r 131 W Ohio.
Ehlen Zachary P Rev, asst rector Sacred Heart Church, h cor Union and Palmer.
Ehler Henry, motorman, b 454 W Eugene (N I).
Ehlers Albert C, uphlr, b 647 S Meridian.
Ehlers Christian, lab, h 647 S Meridian.
Ehlers Edward J, baker, b cor Senate av and 27th.
Ehlers Frederick M, condr, h 454 W Eugene (N I).
Ehlert Albert, clk Chas H Schwomeyer & Co, b 315 S Meridian.
Ehlert Carl F, bkkpr, h 315 S Meridian.
Ehlert Ferdinand, lab, b 557 S New Jersey.
Ehlert Ferdinand B, lab, b 65 Buchanan.
Ehmann Gustav, butcher, b 28½ King av (H).
Ehrensperger Charles L, cashr L N A & C Ry, h 479 N New Jersey.
Ehrensperger Edward H, clk L N A & C Ry, h 215 Highland av.
Ehrensperger Elizabeth C (wid Frank X), h 170 N New Jersey.
Ehrensperger John A (J A Ehrensperger & Co), h 170 N New Jersey.
Ehrensperger Joseph F, clk L N A & C Ry, b 170 N New Jersey.
EHRENSPERGER J A & CO (John A Ehrensperger, Adolph Emmerich), Proprs Big Four Shoe Store, Fine Boots and Shoes a Specialty, 188 W Washington.
Ehrgott Emil, mach opr Indpls Journal, b 908 Broadway.
Ehrgott Gustav, clk, h 32 Bismarck.
Ehrgott Julius, engraver, b 908 Broadway.
Ehrgott Mary D (wid Martin), h 908 Broadway.
Ehrgott Otto, engraver, b 908 Broadway.
Ehrich Edward E, tinner, b 175 Elm.
Ehrich Wm G, tinner, 63 W Washington, h 175 Elm.
Ehricke Charles, musician, 298 Lincoln av, h same.
Ehrisman Jacob, mngr, b 51 Clifford av.
Ehrisman May (wid Samuel), h 71 Peru av.
Ehrmann Louis, r 319 Coburn.
Eich, see also Aich.
Eich Edward E, painter, h 43 N State av.
Eichel, see also Aichele.
Eichel August J, sawmkr, h 260 W 22d.
Eichel Herman, agt, b 175 Bane.
Eichel Jacob, collr, r 195 W Vermont.
Eicher John N, meats, 34 E Mkt House, h 589 Marlowe av.
Eichholtz George W, lumber, 95 E Market, h 445 N East.
Eichholtz Ida A, stenog, b 445 N East.
Eichhorn, see Aichhorn.
Eichler Julius, porter, b 202 Walcott.
EICHRODT CHARLES W, Pharmacist, s e cor West and 1st, Tel 634; h 736 N New Jersey.
Eichrodt Helen M, clk Probate Commissioner, b 778 N New Jersey.
Eichrodt Louis, clk Indpls Gas Co, b 778 N New Jersey.
Eicke Louis, lab, h 288 Columbia av.
Eicke Louis jr, gasfitter, h 288 Columbia av.
Eickenberg Alonzo, lab, b rear 277 S West.

C. ZIMMERMAN & SONS | SLATE AND GRAVEL ROOFERS 19 South East Street.

DRIVEN WELLS And Second Water Wells and Pumps of all kinds at CHARLES KRAUSS', 42 S. PENN. ST., Telephone 465.

ERTEL STEAM LAUNDRY 26 and 28 N. Senate Avenue. Tel 921. WE WILL CALL FOR & DELIVER. SATISFACTION GUARANTEED.

Eickenberg Julius K, shoemkr, b 9 Shelby.
Eickman Harry, lab, b 81 Stevens.
Eickman Henry C, carp, 40 N Gillard av, h same.
Eickmann Christian H, carp, b 151 N Gillard av.
Eickstaedt Paul W Rev, pastor St Paul's German Evangelical Lutheran Church, h 160 Pleasant.
Eidson Wm H, cabtmkr, h 202 N West.
Eidson Wm M, porter, h 1009 S Meridian.
Eifert Edward C, caller, b 71 Clifford av.
Eifert Harry W, bartndr, h 376 Highland av.
Eifert Justin, ruler, b 71 Clifford av.
Eifert Katherine (wid Henry), h 71 Clifford av.
Eifert Wm J, tel opr Police Headquarters, h 88 Clifford av.
Eigelberg Charles A, molder, h 27 King (H).
Eikenberry Jonas, carp, b 325 S Meridian.
Eilering Benjamin, porter, h 49 Evison.
Eilering Herman, lab, b s s Bethel av 2 e of Zwingley.
Eilering Levi, h n e cor Pleasant av and Huggins pike.
Eilering Richard, brick mnfr, s s Bethel av 2 e of Zwingley, h same.
Eilert Wm F, shoemkr, h 3 Hermann.
Eilhard Frederick H, mach opr The Indpls News, b 255 Fletcher av.
Eilhard Mary (wid Henry), h 255 Fletcher av.
Einatz Olive G (wid Anthony), h 45 Bloomington.
Eiremann Charles B, tel opr, b 80 S Brightwood av (B).
Eis Nellie (wid Charles), h 172 E Louisiana.
Eisele Emma, jeweler, 81 E Washington, h 465 N Senate av.
Eisele Wm J, mngr, h 465 N Senate av.
Eisenbarth Henry J, cabtmkr, h 8 Iowa.
Eisenbeis John F, polisher, h 318 S Illinois.
Eisenbeiss Erastus M, phys, 254½ W Washington, h same, tel 1230.
Eisenmann John J, switchman, h 27 Eastern av.
Eiser Engelbert J, carp, h 24 Singleton.
EITEL CHARLES A, Druggist, 184 Shelby, Tel 1381; h 66 Wallack.
Eitel George, clk, h 26½ N Senate av.
EITEL HENRY, Sec, Vice-Pres and Treas Union Trust Co, 68 E Market, Tel 1576; h 853 N Meridian.
Eitel John, foreman Indpls Brewing Co, h 31 Davis.
Eix Charles, cigarmkr, b rear 571 E Washington.
Eix Henry, express, h rear 571 E Washington.
Eix Henry C, instructor, b rear 571 E Washington.
Eklund John, b 58½ W Ohio.
Eklund Julia (wid Frank), h 58½ W Ohio.
Ekron Stewart J, carver, b 589 W Eugene (N I).
Ela Wm C, brakeman, h 106 Nordyke av (W I).
Elam Edwin M, vice-pres Elam Mnfg Co, broker, 89 S Meridian, h 1036 N Meridian.
Elam John B (Miller & Elam), h 300 Park av.
ELAM MANUFACTURING CO, George C Brinkmeyer Pres, Edwin M Elam Vice-Pres, Arba T Perry Sec and Treas, Mnfrs of Soap Powder, 26-30 W Georgia, Tel 406.

EQUITABLE LIFE ASSURANCE SOCIETY OF THE UNITED STATES.
RICHARDSON & McCREA
Managers for Central Indiana.
79 East Market St. Telephone 182.

Elam Percy, clk, r 5 Stewart pl.
Elam Richard L, student, b 300 Park av.
Elbert Frank J, baker, b 36 Bicking.
Elbert John, baker, b 36 Bicking.
Elbert John J, baker, b 36 Bicking.
Elbert Samuel A, phys, 104 Indiana av, h 760 N Capitol av.
Elbertson Griffith A, patternmkr, h 11 Madison av.
Elbertson Marie A, hairdresser, 11 Madison av, h same.
Elbrecht, see also Albrecht.
Elbrecht August, bkkpr, h 776 Madison av.
Elbreg Beatrice V, music teacher, 48 Ash, b same.
Elbreg Frederick J, lab, h 314 Spring.
Elbreg George W, notions, 26 English av, h 113 Pleasant.
Elbreg Henry H, h 48 Ash.
Elbreg Mary E, artist, 48 Ash, b same.
Elder Burr L, carp, h 55 Tremont av (H).
Elder Catherine E (wid Elijah S), h 39 Christian av.
Elder Edward C, sec Clay Shingle Co, b 150 N New Jersey.
Elder Eli A, b 134 Broadway.
Elder Frank, butcher, h w s Johnson 1 s of Judge Harding (W I).
Elder George M, engr, h 1646 N Capitol av.
Elder Hannah L (wid Wm W), teacher Public School No 33, h 341 Broadway.
Elder Harry T, b 433 Park av.
Elder James M (Indiana Elevator Gate Co), h 1205 N Illinois.
Elder James W, b w s Broadway 2 s of Fleet.
Elder James W, tinner, h 433 Park av.
Elder John J, clk M D T Co, r 81 E Vermont.
Elder John R, pres Clay Shingle Co, h 150 N New Jersey.
Elder Joseph I, contr, 110 S Judge Harding (W I), h same.
Elder Leonard M, feed, 368 E 7th, h w s Broadway 2 s of Fleet.
Elder Robert, foreman David I Scott & Co, h 148 Bellefontaine.
Elder Robert, carp, h 148 Bellefontaine.

STENOGRAPHERS FURNISHED.
EXPERIENCED OR BEGINNERS, PERMANENT OR TEMPORARY.
S. H. EAST, State Agent,
The Williams Typewriter,
55 THORPE BLOCK. 87 EAST MARKET ST.

ELLIS & HELFENBERGER { ENTERPRISE FOUNDRY & FENCE CO. 162-170 S. Senate Ave. Tel. 958.

THE HOGAN TRANSFER AND STORAGE COMP'Y
Household Goods and Pianos Moved—Packed—Stored...... Baggage and Package Express Machinery and Safes a Specialty Cor. Washington and Illinois Sts. TELEPHONE No. 675.

Hose, Belting, Packing, Clothing, Druggists' Sundries, Bicycle Tires, Cotton Hose, Etc. New York Belting & Packing Co., L't'd.
The Central Rubber & Supply Co. PHONE 922. 79 S. ILLINOIS ST., INDIANAPOLIS, IND.

A death rate below all other American Companies, and dividends from this source correspondingly larger.
The Provident Life and Trust Company
Of Philadelphia.
D. W. EDWARDS, General Agent,
508 Indiana Trust Building.

Elder Wm J, bkkpr Tanner & Sullivan, h 602 Park av.
ELDER WM L, Furniture, 43-45 S Meridian, Tel 805; h 16 E Michigan, Tel 497.
Elder Wm R, plumber, h 1372 N Capitol av.
Elders Charles, clk, b 8 Central av.
Elders Charles, lab, b 77 Park av.
Eldrick Herman, chairmkr, r 169 W Market.
Eldridge, see also Aldridge.
Eldridge Charles B, painter J K & H K English, h 941 Grove av.
Eldridge Edward H (E H Eldridge & Co), h 76 E Michigan.
Eldridge E H & Co (Edward H and George O Eldridge), planing mill, 174 S New Jersey.
Eldridge George O (E H Eldridge & Co), h 24 W 14th.
Eldridge Henry W B, harnessmkr, b n s 30th 4 e of Illinois (M).
Eldridge Isaac, condr, h 180 Dillon.
Eldridge Job, 2d hd goods, 275 Mass av, h same.
Eldridge Milton, clk, h 1053 E Michigan.
Eldridge Wm J, clk, b 76 E Michigan.
Electrical Constuction Co (Joseph C Stewart, Joseph T Lipps), 116 N Delaware.
Elff Frank, h 404 S East.
Elff Frank, h 273 S New Jersey.
Elff Frederick, bartndr, b 273 S New Jersey.
Elff Mary, clk, b 273 S New Jersey.
Elgin Maude R, stenog, b 123 Christian av.
Elgin Myra V (wid Gaddis), h 123 Christian av.
Eliason Charles, papermkr, h 167 E South.
Eliker Mary E, chiropodist, 4 Mass av, h same.
Eliker Wm H, produce, 39 E Mkt House, h 179 E New York.
ELITE CAFE, John L Booth Mngr, 120-122 N Illinois.
Elite Portrait and Frame Co, D L Belligheimer pres, E Niederman sec, 68½ E Market.

Julius C. Walk & Son,
Jewelers
Indianapolis.
12 EAST WASHINGTON ST.

Elixmann Charles H, coremkr, b 98 Tremont av (H).
Elixmann Frank G, tmstr, b 98 Tremont av (H).
Elixmann Wm C, molder, h 98 Tremont av (H).
Elkins Albert E, tmstr, h w s Webb 1 n of Raymond.
Elkins Edward L, clk, b 91 N Delaware.
Elkins George E, news agt, b 91 N Delaware.
Elkins Ida (wid John), h 761 Brooker's al.
Elkins John, waiter, h 516 N Senate av.
Elkins John A, engraver F H Smith, h 237 S East.
Elkins Nancy (wid Hiram), b 62 Bates.
Elkins Samuel, h 516 N Senate av.
Elkins Wm, painter, h 71 Maple.
Elkins Wm J, plastr, h 31 Columbia al.
Ellenwood Emma G (wid Cyrus), h 49 School.
Elier Catherine, h 43 Tecumseh.
Eller James E, trunkmkr, h 440 Michigan av.
Eller Sarah E (wid Harvey), h 43 Tecumseh.
Eller Wm H, lab, h 215 S Olive.
Ellerbrock Henry, clk, b 401 S Meridian.
Ellerbusch Charles, porter, h 77 Park av.
Ellerkamp Christian, saloon, 183 Prospect, h 177 same.
Ellerkamp Frederick, h s e cor Auburn and Bethel avs.
Ellerkamp Frederick, finisher, h 238 Dougherty.
Ellerman Samuel E, sec Big Four Bldg Assn, poutlry, 205 Ft Wayne av, h 312 N New Jersey.
Ellig Albert, carp, h 139 S East.
Ellig Bernard E, painter, 204 E Morris, h same.
Ellinger Fannie (wid Reuben), h 22 Spann av.
Ellinger Samuel S, printer Catholic Record, b 22 Spann av.
Ellington James, driver, h rear 27 Cornell av.
Ellington Sarah (wid Wm), h 472 Cornell av.
Ellington Wm H, tmstr, h 276 Alvord.
Elliott Albert (Elliott Bros), b 255 Keystone av.
Elliott Ann E (wid Evans), h 354 Talbott av.
Elliott Anna B (wid John M), h 381 S East.
Elliott Anna G, cashr, b 155 Meek.
Elliott Arthur, waiter, b 251 E Washington.
Elliott Bros (Albert and Wm C), grocers, 255 Keystone av.
Elliott Byron K (Elliott & Elliott), h 837 N Meridian.
Elliott Calvin R, brazier, h 155 Meek.
Elliott Charles N, clk, b 70 N East.
Elliott Charles V, student, r 96 N Alabama.
Elliott Chloe (wid Samuel), h 227 W Chesapeake.
Elliott Clifford K, mach hd, h 354 Cornell av.
Elliott Daniel D, hostler, h 319 W Market.
Elliott David M, finance clk P O, h 371 Talbott av.
Elliott Edward, barber, r 69 N Alabama.
Elliott Ella M, stenog, b 217 E Ohio.
Elliott Elton B, lumber, h 332 Cornell av.
Elliott Ernest E, lab, b 374 Cornell av.
Elliott Ernest M, clk P C C & St L Ry, h 946 N Alabama.
Elliott George, janitor, h 206 Middle.

OTTO GAS ENGINES | BUILDERS' EXCHANGE S. W. Cor. Ohio and Penn. Telephone 535.

Becker & Son Charles Becker Jacob Becker Jr. Merchant Tailors. 21 N. Penn. St. Tel. 934

SALISBURY & STANLEY OFFICE, STORE AND BANK FIXTURES. Contractors and Builders. Repairing of all kinds done on short notice. 177 Clinton St., Indianapolis, Ind. Telephone 999.

Elliott George B, clk Elliott & Butler, b 463 N Penn.
Elliott George W, clk, h 273 Bright.
Elliott Harry M, carp, b 1071 N Capitol av.
Elliott Henry, lineman, b rear 150 Madison av.
Elliott Henry H, janitor, h 126 Lynn av (W I).
Elliott Inez V, teacher Public School No 11, b 816 E Market.
Elliott James E, foreman, h 561 Ash.
Elliott Jeremiah N, lab, b 190 N East.
Elliott Joel T, carp, 89 Oliver av (W I) and drugs, 1201 Northwestern av, h 89 Oliver av (W I).
Elliott John (Elliott & Erganbright), h 134 Blackford.
Elliott John L, mer police, h 97 W 13th.
Elliott John T, condr, h 191 N Noble.
Elliott John W, carp, h 68 Lexington av.
Elliott Joseph T (Elliott & Butler), h 463 N Penn.
Elliott Joseph T jr, pres and mngr Reporter Pub Co, b 463 N Penn.
Elliott Larkin B, agt, h 690 N Capitol av.
Elliott Lee, fireman, b 124 English av.
Elliott Leon D, carp, h 100 Oliver av (W I).
Elliott Mahlon E, b 126 Lynn av (W I).
Elliott Maud S, treas The L A Kinsey Co, b 354 College av.
Elliott Melissa A, b 240½ E Washington.
Elliott Miller, supt Citizens' Street Railway Co, b Grand Hotel.
Elliott Nancy, h 172 W Georgia.
Elliott Nathan, lab, b e s Northwestern av 1 n of 30th.
Elliott Paul, brakeman, h 17 Dearborn.
Elliott Perry J, agt, h 374 Cornell av.
Elliott Robert, sec and treas The Standard Dry Kiln Co, h 506 Broadway.
Elliott Robert H, mach, h 816 E Market.
Elliott Robert J, bkkpr M Sells & Co, h 554 Park av.
Elliott Rose, teacher Public School No 10, b 374 Cornell av.
Elliott Samuel, lab, h n s Prospect 2 e of Belt R R.
Elliott Samuel, lab, b 185½ Indiana av.
Elliott Sarah M, teacher Public School No 5, b 816 E Market.
Elliott Sarah P (wid James S), b 4 Cornell av.
Elliott Thomas H, lab, h 17 Woodruff av.
Elliott Wallace C, mach hd, b 381 S East.
Elliott Wilber, janitor, h 11½ N Meridian.
Elliott Wm, h 77 Park av.
Elliott Wm, blksmith, h 205½ Virginia av.
Elliott Wm C (Elliott Bros), b 255 Keystone av.
Elliott Wm F (Elliott & Elliott), b 837 N Meridian.
Elliott Wm G, chief clk The Grand Hotel.
Elliott Wm M, actor, b 48 N East.
Elliott Wm O, clk, h 210 Hoyt av.
Elliott Wm P, asst ticket agt I U Ry Co, h 946 N Alabama.
Elliott Wm S, clk, b 169 N Noble.
ELLIOTT & BUTLER (Joseph T Elliott, Ovid D Butler), Abstracts of Title, 84 E Market.
ELLIOTT & ELLIOTT (Byron K and Wm F), Lawyers, 9-11 Fletcher's Bank Bldg, Tel 1534.
Elliott & Erganbright (John Elliott, Charles H Erganbright), vet surg, 83 E Wabash.
Ellis Albert, lab, b 507 E 11th.
Ellis Annie, dressmkr, 319 S Meridian, b same.

Henry H. Fay, 40½ E. Washington St., REAL ESTATE, AND LOAN BROKER.

Ellis Bartlett, janitor, h 85 Martindale av.
Ellis Boaz A, lab, h 477 Charles.
Ellis Brook B, molder, h 268 Alvord.
Ellis Charles, barber, h 313 E Miami.
Ellis Charles E, blksmith, r 193 W Washington.
Ellis Charles W, supt, h 466 S Meridian.
Ellis Clark J, lab, h 14 Sheldon.
Ellis Dangerfield, lab, b 12 Hadley.
Ellis David A, paperhngr, h 107 Hoyt av.
Ellis Decatur D, lab, b 193 W Ray.
Ellis Elzy J, bricklyr, b 24 Brookside av.
Ellis Eugene E, ins agt, h 123 E Michigan.
Ellis Flora E, teacher Public School No 38, b 668 College av.
Ellis Frank B, watchman, h 123 Yeiser.
Ellis Frank R, helper, b 40 Wilcox.
Ellis Frank W, molder, h 46 Barth av.
Ellis George B, lab, b 59 Orange.
Ellis George F, molder, b 37 Bradshaw.
Ellis George G, clk Paul H Krauss, r 74 Huron.
Ellis George R (Ellis & Helfenberger), h 1098 N Penn.
Ellis George W, finisher, h 312 S West.
Ellis Harris C, molder, h 584 Morris (W I).
Ellis Henry, lab, h 368 Olive.
Ellis Hiram R, contr, 16 Hamilton av, h same.
Ellis Horace R, molder, h 126 Oliver av (W I).
Ellis James, lab, b 683 N Senate av.
Ellis James, mnfrs' agt, 6 Indiana av, r same.
Ellis James A, soldier U S Arsenal.
Ellis James B, tmstr, b 83 N Rural.
Ellis James W, painter, h 221 S Reisner (W I).
Ellis John, lab, h 587 N Missouri.
Ellis John J, lab, h 53 Drake.
Ellis John L, electrician, b 304 Union.
Ellis John S, mach, h 40 Wilcox.
Ellis John W, clk, b 134 Broadway.
Ellis John W, lab, h 226 Ramsey av.
Ellis Joseph H, lab, h 219 S Reisner (W I).
Ellis Lewis, blksmith, h 208 W McCarty.
Ellis Lewis E, ice cream mkr, r 167 E Vermont.

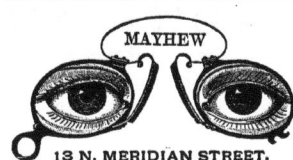

MAYHEW 13 N. MERIDIAN STREET.

LIME, CEMENT, PLASTER FIRE BRICK AND CLAY SEWER PIPE, ETC. BALKE & KRAUSS CO., Cor. Market and Missouri Streets.

C. FRIEDGEN HAS THE FINEST STOCK OF LADIES' PARTY SLIPPERS and SHOES 19 NORTH PENNSYLVANIA ST.

SAMUEL LAING ▸ TIN, SLATE AND STEEL ROOFING 72 AND 74 EAST COURT STREET.

M. B. WILSON, Pres. W. F. CHURCHMAN, Cash.
THE CAPITAL NATIONAL BANK,
INDIANAPOLIS, IND.
Pays Interest on Time Certificates of Deposit.
Buys and Sells Foreign Exchange at Low Rates.
Capital, - - $300,000
Surplus and Earnings, 50,000
No. 28 S. Meridian St., Cor. Pearl.

Ellis Mack, lab, h n e cor Indianapolis av and 16th.
Ellis Marshall D, lawyer, h 73 Stevens.
Ellis Mary J (wid Micajah), h 1172 N Illinois.
ELLIS MRS DR, Astrologist, r 190 N Capitol av.
Ellis Pearl, coremkr, h 66 Warren av (W I).
Ellis Robert, lab, b 31 Catherine.
Ellis Rose M, dressmkr, 463 Ash, h same.
Ellis Samuel, lab, h 432 W Chicago (N I).
Ellis Samuel B, lab, h 83 N Rural.
Ellis Samuel D, watchmkr James N Mayhew, r 132 N Capitol av.
Ellis Sarah (wid James), h 81 Margaret.
Ellis Sarah E (wid Edwin R), h 231 Yandes.
Ellis Simeon, tmstr, b 176 Douglass.
Ellis Simon, peddler, h 15 Willard.
Ellis Thomas, h 37 Bradshaw.
Ellis Wm A, lumber insp, b 110 Clifford av.
Ellis Wm H, blksmith, h 457 W 2d.
Ellis Wm T, watchman, h 117 Highland pl.
Ellis Wm T jr, asst foreman The Indpls News, b 117 Highland pl.
ELLIS & HELFENBERGER (George R Ellis, Wm Helfenberger), Proprs Enterprise Foundry and Fence Co, 162-168 S Senate av, 2 squares west of Union Station, Tel 958. (See right bottom lines.)
Ellison, see also Allison.
Ellison Daniel J Rev, pastor First Baptist Church, h 425 N Delaware.
Ellison Felix, lab, b 177 W 2d.
Ellison Frederick, claim agt, h 1185 N Illinois.
Ellison Jessie R, music teacher, b 140 W Vermont.
Ellison John W, bkkpr Schrader Bros, h 1121 N Penn.
Ellwanger Daniel F, gardener, h n s Grandview av 2 n of Tremont av (H).
Ellwanger Daniel F, trav agt, h 171 Elm.
Ellsworth Frank, lab, b 230 W 2d.
Ellsworth Wm H, waiter, r 39 N Illinois.
Elmendorf Lucius F, mngr Chicago Shoe Co, 68 E Washington, b 277 N Delaware.

TUTTLE & SEGUIN,
28 E. Market Street.
Fire Insurance,
Real Estate, Loan
and Rental Agents.
TELEPHONE 1168.

Elmendorf Will H, clk L E & W R R, h 10 Arch.
Elmer Harry H, bkkpr Hildebrand Hardware Co, h 106 High.
Elmer Harry L, printer The Indpls News, b 377 S Meridian.
Elmer John W, clk, h 192 E McCarty.
Elmer Margaret L (wid Orrin E), h 377 S Meridan.
Elmore John L, foreman, h 182 W 3d.
Elrod Charles R, mach, b 28 Dearborn.
Elrod James R, lab, h 28 Dearborn.
Elrod Jennie, bkkpr, r 155 N Illinois.
Elroy Pearl, h 280 E Court.
Elsasser Louis, tailor, h 243 S Alabama.
Elsasser Rudolph, barber, h 1095 W New York.
Elsasser Wm C, cutter P Gramling & Son, h 243 S Alabama.
Elsenheimer Carl A, brassmolder, h 67 Omer.
Elsenheimer Carl A jr, brassmolder, b 67 Omer.
Elser Andrew, butcher, b 399 S Delaware.
Elslager, see also Oelschlager.
Elslager Albert L, clk, b 156 Church.
Elslager Charles, lab, h s s 30th 1 e of Senate av (M).
Elslager Elizabeth (wid John B), h 156 Church.
Elslager Jacob L, driver, h 64 Park av.
Elsner August, clk, h 140 Dunlop.
Elsner Emil, lab, b 140 Dunlop.
Elster Albert C, h 1130 N Penn.
Elster Mary O, teacher Public School No 3, h 1130 N Penn.
Elstrod Frederick, bartndr, b 118 N Noble.
Elstrod Henry, mach, h 326 E Miami.
Elstrod Henry H, cabtmkr, h 118 N Noble.
Elstrod Mary, laundress Deaf and Dumb Inst.
Elstun Emma, grocer, 1027 E Washington, h same.
Elstun Frank M, ins, h e s Arlington av 2 n of Washington av (I).
Elstun Horace H (Merritt & Elstun), h 18 Newman.
Elstun John W, mngr Hide, Leather and Belting Co, h s w cor Fletcher and National avs (I).
Elstun Marion E, cashr H T Conde Implement Co, h 530 Park av.
Eltzroth Adelia A (wid Jacob), b 77 W 7th.
Eltzroth John W, baker, b 60 Fletcher av.
Elvin Gardner W, glasscutter, h 594 S East.
Elvin Louis F, bkkpr, Indiana National Bank, h 363 Talbott av.
Elvin Robert J, h 888 N Illinois.
Elvin Wm A, pres The Bowen-Merrill Co, b 888 N Illinois.
Elvis, see also Alvis.
Elvis Edith, clk, b 174 Madison av.
Elvis Margaret (wid Wm H), b 479 N New Jersey.
Elward James, condr, b 188 Maple.
Elward Joseph, distributer, b 188 Maple.
Elward Wm, flagman, h 188 Maple.
Elwarner Wm, grocer, 503 E 7th, h 338 Bellefontaine.
Elwell Mary E (wid Esdras), h 129 Woodlawn av.
Elwood Ella (wid John), h 54 S California.
Elwood Frank, lab, b 54 S California.
Ely Elmer H, ins agt, h 122 Highland pl.
Ely Frank J, messenger Am Ex Co, h 210½ S Meridian.
Ely James D, bkkpr The Sinker-Davis Co, h 40 W St Joseph.

SULLIVAN & MAHAN Manufacturers of all kinds of PAPER BOXES 41 W. Pearl St.

DIAMOND WALL PLASTER { Telephone 1410 BUILDERS' EXCHANGE.

Telephone 1769. 197 S. Illinois St.

Ely Jordan, lab, b 79 W Wabash.
Ely Lillie, dressmkr, 173 Mass av, h same.
Ely Rachel, h 432 Douglass.
Ely Robert, fireman, b 124 English av.
Elzea Andrew J, carp, h 37 Detroit.
Elzroth Wm, waiter, b 196 N Senate av.
Elzy Curran, lab, h 272 W 3d.
Elzy Harry, lab, h 348 Columbia av.
Elzy James, lab, h rear 648 N West.
Elza Marcellus Rev, pastor First Baptist Church (col) (W I), h 408 N Brookside av.
Emanuel Edward, clk, r 77½ S Illinois.
Embers Susan, h rear 631 N Senate av.
Embery Henry, molder, b 188 S Senate av.
Embree Francis, bkkpr, b 228 N Illinois.
Embree Frank N, trav agt, h 184 N Noble.
Embree Wm A, watchman, b 49 Helen.
Emden Jacob, clk, h 94 N East.
Emden Leo, clk, b 250 E Ohio.
Emden Michael, clk, h 250 E Ohio.
Emden Sophia, grocer, 250 E Ohio, h same.
Emden Wm, clk, b 250 E Ohio.
Emerine Charles, lab, h 134 Agnes.
Emerson Edward E, carp, h 23 Ellsworth.
Emerson Frank, brakeman, h 521 N Senate av.
Emerson John B, h 224 N West.
Emery, see also Emory and Emry.
Emery Anderson L, lab, h 511 W Addison (N I).
Emery Charles, lab, h 430 S Capitol av.
Emery Herbert T, student, b 10 E Michigan.
Emery Jordan A (Emery & Scott), r 12½ Indiana av.
Emery Kate (wid John B), b 10 E Michigan.
Emery & Scott (Jordan A Emery, Clarence C Scott), saloon, 33 Kentucky av.
Emhardt Adolph G, clk, b 772 S East.
Emhardt Charles D, bartndr, b 772 S East.
Emhardt John, saloon, 781 S East, h 772 same.
Emhardt Julius, driver, b 772 S East.
Emhardt Paul, waiter, b 772 S East.
Emhoff Jacob, plater, b 583 S East.
Emigholz Frederick, clk Pearson & Wetzel, h Churchman pike ½ mile s of Belt R R.
Eminger Elizabeth (wid Henry), b n w cor Morris and Tremont av (W I).
Eminger Ira D, notions, 652 Virginia av, res Pendleton, Ind.
Eminger Thomas, mer police, b 162 Columbia av.
Eminger Wm D, mngr, h 652 Virginia av.
Emmare & Gayler (Frank J Emmare, Louisville, Ky, George M Gayler), dyers, 8½ E Washington.
Emmelmann Alvin C, bricklyr, h 12 Draper.
Emmelmann Charles P, trav agt, h 23 Smithson.
Emmelmann Ernest E, bricklyr, h 241 S Spruce.
Emmelmann Frederick G, student, b 27 Smithson.
Emmelmann Henry, porter, h 27 Smithson.
Emmerich, see also Emrich.
Emmerich Adolph (J A Ehrensperger & Co), h 286 Broadway.
Emmerich Charles E, prin Industrial Training School, h 329 E New York.
Emmerich Johanna S (wid Henry), h 286 Broadway.
Emmerich Max P, clk Merchants' Natl Bank, b 329 E New York.
Emmett Robert F, h 76 W North.
Emminger Emil A, barber, b 67 N Noble.
Emminger Joseph, cabtmkr, h 96 Geisendorf.

FRANK NESSLER. WILL H. ROST.
FRANK NESSLER & CO.
Tailors
56 EAST MARKET ST. (Lemcke Building),
INDIANAPOLIS, IND.

EMMINGER JOSEPH, Saloon, 11 Monument Pl, Tel 1945; h 67 N Noble.
Emminger Mary U (wid Joseph), b 67 N Noble.
Emminger Otto A, packer, b 67 N Noble.
Emmons Benjamin F, lab, h 176 Meek.
Emmons Charles F, painter, b 176 Meek.
Emmons John W, carp, h 33 N Gale (B).
Emmons Willis J, fireman, b 33 N Gale (B).
Emory Smith, lab 182 N Meridian.
Empey George W (Empey & Loftin), h 951 N Senate av.
Empey & Loftin (George W Empey, Charles Loftin), real est, 37½ W Washington.
EMPIRE FAST FREIGHT LINE, Nathan H Kipp Agt, 67 W Maryland, Tel 365.
Empire Theater, Charles Zimmerman mngr, n w cor Delaware and Wabash.
Emrich, see also Emmerich.
Emrich Christine (wid Frank), h s e cor Lafayette and Crawfordsville rd.
Emrich Clarence, horseshoer, 25 S New Jersey, h 73 Belmont av.
Emrich Ellsworth, sander, h 40 Centennial (H).
Emrich Furniture Co The, Henry Emrich pres, George H Drechsel vice-pres, John H Emrich sec and treas, 190 W Morris.
Emrich Henry, pres The Emrich Furniture Co, h 480 S New Jersey.
Emrich Jacob A, trav agt, b 480 S New Jersey.
Emrich Jacob A, grocer, n e cor Lafayette and Crawfordsville rd, h same.
Emrich Jacob K, trav agt, b 480 S New Jersey.
Emrich John C, saloon, s e cor Lafayette and Crawfordsville rd, h same.
Emrich John H, sec and treas The Emrich Furniture Co, h 188 W Morris.
Emrich John W, sander, h e s Bismarck av 5 n of Emrich (H).
Emrich Wm F, clk, b 480 S New Jersey.
Emrick Emma J, h 506½ E Washington.
Emry Camillus V, car rep, h w s Station 1 n of Schofield (B).

ACORN STOVES AND RANGES
Haueisen & Hartmann
163-169 E. Washington St.
FURNITURE,
Carpets,
Household Goods,
Tin, Granite and China Wares, Oil Cloth and Shades

THE HOME LAUNDRY { WORK CALLED FOR AND DELIVERED.

THE WM. H. BLOCK CO. 7 AND 9 EAST WASHINGTON STREET. DRY GOODS, HOUSE FURNISHINGS AND CROCKERY.

London Guarantee and Accident Co. (Ltd.) Employers', Public and Teams' Liability, Workmen's Collective Insurance and Fidelity Bonds
GEORGE W. PANGBORN, General Agent, 704-706 Lemcke Bldg. Telephone 140.

FRANK K. SAWYER | Reliable Fire Insurance. Reasonable Rates.
74 E. MARKET STREET. Telephone 6.

JOSEPH GARDNER,
TIN, IRON, STEEL AND SLATE ROOFING,
GALVANIZED IRON CORNICES & SKYLIGHTS.
37, 39 & 41 KENTUCKY AVE. Telephone 322.

Emry Harry J, lineman, h 164 N Pine.
Emry James H, clk Natl Starch Mnfg Co, h 492 Park av.
Emry Oscar D, lineman, h 590 W Washington.
Ems Frederick W, saloon, 293 Bates, h same.
Enbody James W, barber, h 224 N New Jersey.
Enbogy Wm J, barber, h 205 E Ohio.
Enderberg Axel, clk, b 212 N Noble.
Enderberg Martin, tailor, h 212 N Noble.
ENDERS C F AUGUST (Enders & Kopp), Tin, Copper, Sheet and Galvanized Iron Work; Gas Fitting a Specialty; House and Job Work Promptly Attended to; Satisfaction Guaranteed; 506 E Washington, h same.
Enders Wm, lab, b 58 Jefferson.
Enders & Kopp (C F August Enders, Wm H Kopp), plumbers, 506 E Washington.
Endicott James, painter, b 104 S Illinois.
Endicott Mary (wid John), h 127 Columbia al.
Endicott Wm M, carp, h 62 S Belmont av (W I).
Ending John H, bkkpr, h w s Auburn av 9 s of English av.
Endly John A, painter, h 505 Broadway.
Endly Thomas E, h 568 Park av.
Ends Benjamin, painter, b 77 Hill.
Ends Wm, painter, h 77 Hill.
Endsley Esther (wid Josiah), b 247 S New Jersey.
Endsley George W, agt, h 247 S New Jersey.
Endsley John P, mach, b 39 Jefferson av.
Endsley Thomas J, engr, h 123 Walcott.
Enell Otto E, trav agt, h 429 Broadway.
Engdahl Charles, mach, h 504 S West.
Engdahl Charles A, mach, h 504 S West.
Engel Christian, lab, b 220 Belmont av (H).
Engel Wm F, blksmith, h 5 Eureka av.
Engelau Wm, gardener, h 884 Madison av.
Engelau Wm jr, gardener, b 884 Madison av.
Engelbach Herman, h 441½ Virginia av.
Engelke Edward, boxmkr, b 40 Maple.

J. S. FARRELL & CO.
STEAM AND HOT WATER HEATING AND PLUMBING CONTRACTORS
84 North Illinois Street. Telephone 382.

Engelke George W, driver, h 475 S Missouri.
Engelke John, baggage master, h 457 S Missouri.
Engelke John F, clk, b 475 S Missouri.
Engelke Mary (wid Frederick), h 1001 N Senate av.
Engelken Henry F, printer, h 76 Minerva.
Engelken Henry G, b 76 Minerva.
Engelken Wm, lab, h 63 Paca.
Engelking Charles, lab, h 291 W Morris.
Engelking Elizabeth (wid Charles), b 191 E South.
Engelking Frank A, clk Ward Bros Drug Co, h 405 Union.
Engelking Frederick, draughtsman, b 208 Union.
Engelking Frederick W, drayman, h 443 S Meridian.
Engelking Herman, lab, b 208 Union.
Engelking Louis C, trav agt McCoy-Howe Co, b 443 S Meridian.
Engelking Wm A, driver, h 208 Union.
Engelking Wm C, driver, h 480 E Georgia.
Engesser John, boarding 128 Blake.
Engesser Joseph, lab, h 159 Church.
Engilman Isaac M, cigar mnfr, 34 Hubbard blk, r same.
England George, carp, h 37 Helen.
England Harry, lab, h 43 Smith.
England Henry, poultry, h 206 Oliver av (W I).
England Wm N, porter, h rear 123 Broadway.
Engle Clara M, b 223½ W Washington.
Engle Daniel W, saloon, 101 S Illinois, h 49 Camp.
Engle Francis E (F E Engle & Son), h 490 Broadway.
Engle Francis S (F E Engle & Son), b 490 Broadway.
Engle Frank W, mach, h 56 Hope (B).
Engle F E & Son (Francis E and Francis S), printers, 16 N Delaware.
Engle George B, printer, b 490 Broadway.
Engle George B Rev, h 172 S Noble.
Engle John E, clk Supt of Police, h 463 Ash.
Engle Newton, foreman, b 28 N West.
Engle Reuben M, bricklyr, h 171 St Mary.
Engle Silas P, condr, h 54 Hope (B).
Engle Stephen S, b 172 S Noble.
Engle Theodore W, printer, b 490 Broadway.
Engle Walter C, student, b 54 Hope (B).
Engle Wm T, printer, b 490 Broadway.
Engle Willis D Rev, sec Ind Chil Home Soc, h 432 Talbott av.
Engledow Lester L, brakeman, h 442 E McCarty.
Engleman John, porter, r rear 175 N Penn.
Engler Wm, engr, r 12 N State av.
Englert Benjamin, coremkr, b 77 Wright.
Englert John M, foreman Evans Linseed Oil Wks, h 77 Wright.
Englert Patrick, coremkr, b 77 Wright.
Englert Wm, mach, h 952 W Vermont.
ENGLEWOOD CHRISTIAN CHURCH, Rev Asa L Orcutt Pastor, 40 N Rural.
English Adelia, b 45½ N Capitol av.
English Benjamin F, bricklyr, b 10 Beecher.
English Frank C, painter, b 1000 W Washington.
English Frank J, trav agt, h 299 Fletcher av.
English Frank M, bricklyr, h 270 Olive.
English Henry, lab, h 19 Cora.
English Henry, lab, b 191 Spann av.
English Henry K (J K and H K English), h 583 Broadway.

POLICIES IN UNITED STATES LIFE INSURANCE CO., offer indemnity against death, liberal cash surrender value or at option of policy-holder, fully paid-up life insurance or liberal life income.
E. B. SWIFT, M'g'r, 25 E. Market St.

WM. KOTTEMAN } WILL FURNISH YOUR HOUSE COMPLETE
89 & 91 E. Washington St. Telephone 1742

SHOW CASES || WILLIAM WIEGEL || 6 West Louisiana Street Opp. Union Station.

English James F, lab, h 133 Madison.
English John L, porter, h 191 Spann av.
English John M, bricklyr, h 45 Lord.
English Joseph, tmstr, h 284 Alvord.
English Joseph K (J K and H K English), h 889 College av.
ENGLISH J K & H K (Joseph K and Henry K), House and Sign Painters, 143½ N Delaware.
English Leeper N, butler 579 N Penn.
English Mary F (wid Elza C), h 39 Hosbrook.
English Opera House, w s Monument pl bet Market and Meridian.
English Will E, office 5 Hotel English, b same.
English Wm A, h 346 Bates.
Engs Mitchell, lab, h 64 Mankedick.
Enners Charles H, tinner, h 369 N Noble.
Enners Edward H, drugs, 150 N Noble, h 148 same.
Enners Henry, bricklyr, h 35 English av.
Enners Louis, tmstr, b 186 W 1st.
Euners Louis J, butcher, b 76 Cincinnati.
Ennes Lorenzo D, well driller, h rear 476 N Illinois.
Ennis Edward, h 277 Indiana av.
Ennis Elmer, riveter, b 12 Eldridge (N I).
Ennis George H, bartndr, h 247½ E Washington.
Ennis John W, salesman Emil Wulschner & Son, h 488 N Senate av.
Ennis Lotta, dressmkr, r 113 S Illinois, h same.
Ennis Louis, painter, b 184 W 1st.
Ennis Mary E (wid Abraham), b 875 N Penn.
Ennis Tillie A, dressmkr, 6½ E Washington, h same.
Ennis Willard W, motorman, h 1374 N Capitol av.
Enoch Charles A, showman, b 126 Windsor.
Enoch Theodore L, showman, b 126 Windsor.
Enoch Wm I, clk, b 126 Windsor.
Enoch Wm L, h 126 Windsor.
Enos Charles K, collr Lilly & Stalnaker, b 363 Bellefontaine.
Enos Trovillo H K (The Allison-Enos Co), h 363 Bellefontaine.
Enrdt Charles, lab, h 40 Parker.
Enright, Joseph J, plastr, h w s Concord 2 s of Clifford av.
Ensey Albert J, mach hd, b 154 N State av.
Ensey Charles W, letter carrier P O, h 121 St Mary.
Ensey Elizabeth (wid Samuel T), h 154 N State av.
ENSEY ORVIS B, Mnfr of Galvanized Iron Cornices and Metal Ceilings; also Slate and Tin Roofer, cor 6th and Illinois, Tel 1562; h 67 W 7th. (See left bottom cor cards.)
Ensey Walter, engr, b 154 N State av.
ENSIGN THE, A E Winters Editor, 33 Talbott Blk. (See adv opp classified Newspapers.)
Ensler Frederick, trunkmkr, r 9½ Madison av.
Ensley Andrew J, lab, h 68 Oliver av (W I).
Ensley Edward, lab, b 86 Oliver av (W I).
Ensley George, mach, h 39 Jefferson av.
Ensley Nicholas, sec Union Nat S and L Assn, h 816 N Meridian.
Ensley Oliver P, sec and treas Foster Lumber Co, h 168 N Meridian.

THOS. C. DAY & CO.
INVESTING AGENTS,
TOWN AND FARM LOANS,
Rooms 325 to 330 Lemcke Bldg.

Ensley Oscar J, clk Union Nat S and L Assn, b 816 N Meridian.
Ensley Wm A (Ziegner & Ensley), r 460 Virginia av.
Ensley Wm S, condr, b 68 Oliver av (W I).
Ensminger John, lab, h 321 E Wabash.
Ensworth Frank H, sol agt, b 933 N Illinois.
Ent Orion B, bricklyr, h 437 W Udell (N I).
ENTERPRISE FOUNDRY AND FENCE CO, Ellis & Helfenberger Proprs, 162-168 S Senate av, 2 squares west of Union Station, Tel 958. (See right bottom lines.)
ENTERPRISE HOTEL, Wm H Baker Propr, 78-88 Mass av, Tel 627.
ENTERPRISE ODORLESS VAULT AND SINK CLEANING CO, John L Major Propr, 200 Elizabeth, Tel 1675. (See adv in classified Vault Cleaners.)
Entwistle Frank B, lab, b 130 Bright.
Entwistle George W, beamer, h 130 Bright.
Entwistle James, car rep, b 51 Olwer av (W I).
Entwistle John, janitor, h 51 Oliver av (W I).
Eoff Samuel A, h 51 S Linden.
Eoff Wm D, paperhngr, h 334 Jackson.
EPITOMIST PUBLISHING CO, E Chubb Fuller Pres, Charles W Hackleman Sec and Treas, Publishers Agricultural Epitomist, 21½ W Washington.
Eppelin Theodore C, clk, r 80 E New York.
Epperson Alonzo D, driver, r 88 N New Jersey.
Eppert Frank M, bailiff Superior Court Room No 1, Court House, h 191 Buchanan.
Eppert Frederick W, bkkpr Krag-Reynolds Co, h 1661 N Penn.
Epps Joseph, hostler n s Oak av 2 e of Central av (I).
Epstein Dora (wid Moses), h 136 Eddy.
Epworth League Headquarters, Solomon M Hoff mngr, 19 Pembroke Arcade.
EQUITABLE LIFE ASSURANCE SOCIETY OF THE UNITED STATES THE, 600-603 Indiana Trust Bldg, Tel 1143.

EAT——
HITZ'S CRACKERS AND CAKES.
ASK YOUR GROCER FOR THEM.

Capital Steam Carpet Cleaning Works
M. D. PLUNKETT Proprietor, Telephone 818

BENJ. BOOTH PRACTICAL EXPERT ACCOUNTANT. Accounts of any description investigated and audited, and statements rendered. Room 18, 82½ E. Washington St., Indianapolis, Ind.

The Best Place in the City to Get a Good Meal THE SHERMAN RESTAURANT ❖❖❖❖ 18 and 20 S. Meridian Street KERSHNER BROS., Proprs.

ESTABLISHED 1876. TELEPHONE 168.
CHESTER BRADFORD,
SOLICITOR OF PATENTS,
AND COUNSEL IN PATENT CAUSES.
(See adv. page 6.)
Office:—Rooms 14 and 16 Hubbard Block, S.W. Cor. Washington and Meridian Streets, INDIANAPOLIS, INDIANA.

EQUITABLE LIFE ASSURANCE SOCIETY OF THE UNITED STATES, Richardson & McCrea Mngrs for Central Indiana, 79 E Market, Tel 182. (See right top cor cards.)
EQUITABLE MUTUAL LIFE ASSOCIATION OF WATERLOO, IOWA, W R and E H Scott, State Mngr, 66½ N Penn.
EQUITABLE SAVINGS AND LOAN ASSOCIATION, Wm F Barrows Pres, Gottlob C Krug Vice-Pres, Leonidas G Dynes Sec, Roswell S Hill Jr Treas, 245 E Washington, Tel 1388.
Equitable State Building and Loan Association of Indiana, J H Tomlin pres, Hervey D Vories sec and treas, 512 Indiana Trust bldg.
ERATH FRANK X, Dealer in Staple and Fancy Groceries, Fresh and Salt Meats, Live and Dressed Poultry, Butter and Eggs, 398 Bellefontaine, Tel 1653; h 477 E 8th.
Erb Solomon, mach, h 16 Carlos.
Erbe Henry, lab, b 304 E Ohio.
Erber Charles, engraver, b 277 Jefferson av.
Erber Frances, grocer, 81 Louise, h same.
Erber Frederick, stonecutter, b 277 Jefferson av.
Erber Gottlieb, cabtmkr, h 81 Louise.
Erber John, stonecutter, h 277 Jefferson av.
Erbrich August, grocer, 147 Fletcher av, h 12 Ketcham.
Erbrich August jr, clk, b 12 Ketcham.
Erby Henry, b 304 E Ohio.
ERDELMEYER FRANK, Druggist, 489 N New Jersey, h same.
Erdelmeyer Frank W, clk, b 489 N New Jersey.
Erdman Adolph, trav agt, h 269 E Ohio.
Erdman Arthur, bkkpr, b 269 E Ohio.
Erdman Bernhard, student, b 321 E Ohio.
Erdman David, tailor, 97 N Meridian, h 321 E Ohio.
Erdman Ernst I, clk, b 321 E Ohio.

O. B. Ensey
SLATE, STEEL, TIN AND IRON ROOFING.
Cor. 6th and Illinois Sts. Tel. 1562

Erdman Isaac, ins agt, b 269 E Ohio.
Erdman Joseph, clk, r 170 N West.
Erganbright Charles H (Elliott & Erganbright), r 173 W Ohio.
Erganbright Luther L (Durham & Erganbright), h 44 Cherry.
Erhard Charles S, clk, r 131 W Ohio.
Erhart, see also Earhart and Ehrhard.
Erhart Barbara (wid Albert), grocer, 681 Madison av, h same.
Erickson John E, carp, h rear 423 Virginia av.
ERIE DESPTACH, Great Western Division, Erie and Pacific Desptach Division South Shore Line, Joseph W Smith Agt, 46 W Washington, Tel 517.
ERIE RAILROAD CO, W H Tennis Genl Agt, A R Tennis Chief Clerk, 46 W Washington, Tel 517.
Erie Valentine, molder, h 20 S Delaware.
Erle, see also Earl.
Erle Frederick H, painter, h 104 Keystone av.
Erner Thomas, lab, h 11 Douglass.
Ernest Corwin J, porter Spencer House.
Ernest Herman, driver, h 141 Bates.
Ernestinoff Alexander, music teacher, 1119 N Meridian, h same.
Ernst Catherine (wid Nicholas L), h 1482 N Senate av.
Ernest Conrad, lab, h 291 Kentucky av.
Ernst Frederick, turner, b 1482 N Senate av.
Ernst Gustave, asst chief Fire Dept, b 137 Union.
Ernst Gustavus, sawyer, b 1482 N Senate av.
Ernst John, painter, h 135 N Liberty.
Ernst Joseph, contr, 1 Builders' Exchange, h 550 S New Jersey.
Ernst Salome (wid Frederick), h 137 Union.
Ernst Wm A, plastr, b 550 S New Jersey.
Ernstburger August, lab, h rear 65 Maxwell.
Ernsting Henry, lab, h 89 Quincy.
Ernsting Herman, lab, b 89 Quincy.
Ernsting Wm, bricklyr, b 89 Quincy.
ERTEL JOHN C, Propr Ertel Steam Laundry, h 71 Lockerbie.
Ertel Louis, sawmkr, h 26 Wisconsin.
Ertel Louis G, driver, h 55 Rockwood.
ERTEL STEAM LAUNDRY, John C Ertel Propr, 26-28 N Senate av, Tel 1089. (See right side lines.)
Erther John W, clk H P Wasson & Co, h 436 W 22d (W I).
ERVEN ISAAC G, Hotel, 78-80 W Maryland, h same.
Ervin Ola, lab, r 21 Riley blk.
Ervin Sarah J (wid Joseph L), h 540 W Washington.
Ervin Thomas, lab, h 135 River av (W I).
Erwin Charles L, driver, h 136 N Liberty.
Erwin Columbus G, carp, h 101 Keystone av.
Erwin Daniel P (D P Erwin & Co), pres Erwin Hotel Co, h 710 N Meridian.
ERWIN D P & CO (Daniel P Erwin, Louis P Goebel, Alvin S Lockard), Wholesale Dry Goods, 106-114 S Meridian and 5-13 McCrea, Tel 336.
ERWIN HOTEL CO, Daniel P Erwin Pres, Terry J Cullen Treas and Mngr, Proprs The Denison, s e cor Penn and Ohio, Tel 471.

TUTEWILER UNDERTAKER, No. 72 WEST MARKET STREET. TELEPHONE 216.

PROVIDENT LIFE AND TRUST CO. OF PHILADELPHIA. D. W. Edwards, G. A., 508 Indiana Trust Bldg. In form of policy; prompt settlement of death losses; equitable dealing with policy-holders; in strength of organization; and in everything which contributes to Security and Cheapness of life insurance, this company is unsurpassed.

THEODORE F. SMITHER

Erzinger Abraham, car rep, b 29 Peru av.
Erzinger Henry B, car rep, h 29 Peru av.
Erzinger Jacob, car insp, h 344 N Pine.
Erzinger John, car insp, b 344 N Pine.
Erzinger John E, car rep, b 29 Peru av.
Erzinger Mary A, dressmkr, 344 N Pine, h same.
Eschbach Marie (wid Jerome), h 102 High.
Eschbach Wm A (Vail Seed Co), b 315 S Delaware.
Eschbaugh Frederick C, painter, h 1159 Northwestern av.
Eschenbach Charles, tinner, h 844 Chestnut.
Eschenbach Joseph, tailor, b 605 Madison av.
Eschenbach Moritz, tinner, 605 Madison av, h same.
Eschenbrenner Wilhelmina (wid Wm), h 498 S East.
Escott Mary E (wid Matthew H), h 18 Wendell av.
Escott Walter A, molder, h 18 Wendell av.
Esebett Norah (wid Joseph), h 66 English av.
Esebett Wm L, collr, b 66 English av.
Eshleman Frank, cigarmkr, b 250 Douglass.
Eshleman Jane A (wid Adam), b 43 Henry.
Eshleman Theodore F, lab, h 250 Douglass.
Eskew Howell T, phys, 33 W Ohio, h same.
Eskew Wm O, lab, r 33 W Ohio.
Esky Conrad C, brakeman, b 43 Jefferson av.
Espey Charles B, student, b 1113 N Meridian.
Espey Henry, car insp, h 1 Dawson.
Espey Mary (wid Paul), h 1113 N Meridian.
Espey Wm F, tel opr, h 539 Broadway.
Espy Agnes J, nurse, 25 Walcott, b same.
Espy Charles L, driver, h 225 Virginia av.
Essex Bert, vice-pres The Indpls Millinery Co, h 136 E North.
Essex Hugh, clk Model Clothing Co, h 501 W McLene (N I).
Essex John I (Holland & Essex), h 405 W Udell (N I).
Essex Wells, farmer, h 4 S Morris (B).
Essick Charles P, blksmith, h 22 Bates.
Essick Woodford, lab, b 317 W North.
Essig Gustav, cigarmkr, b 7 Roseline.
Essig Thomas, grocer, 7 Roseline, h same.
Essigke Louis G, horseshoer, h 838 S Meridian.
Essigke Richard, h 764 S Meridian.
Essigke Wm F, grocer, 129 Hadley av (W I), h 66 Nordyke av (W I).
Essmann Gertrude (wid Wm), b Illinois House.
Essmann Harry, bartndr, b 54 Greer.
Essmann Louis S, saloon, 29 W Pearl, h 54 Greer.
Essmann Wm L, propr Illinois House, 181 S Illinois.
Estabrook, see also Eastabrook.
ESTABROOK GAY R, Lawyer, Rooms 8-9 Brandon Blk, 95 E Washington, h 449 Talbott av.
Estabrook Jane C, dressmkr, 433 Ash, h same.
Estabrook Wm C, music teacher, 447 Talbott av, h same.
Estabrook Wm W, shoemkr, 509 E 7th, h 433 Ash.
Estell Wm, lab, h 219 W 3d.
Esterbrook George S, foreman Indpls Daily Live Stock Journal, b 634 Marlowe av.
Esterline Charles W, boilermkr, h 47 Tacoma av.

THE WHEN IS A WORLD BEATER.

Estes Noah, coachman 616 N Meridian.
ESTEY-CAMP MUSIC HOUSE, Hendricks & Wood Proprs, Pianos, Organs and Musical Merchandise, 144 Mass av. (See adv in classified Pianos and Organs.)
Etherton Ida M, h 247 N Capitol av.
Etmire Elmer C, switchman, h 485 E Georgia.
Etris Mary (wid Stephen), h 599 W Udell (N I).
Etris Wilber P, painter, b 187 S Capitol av.
Etsom James, coachman 826 N Meridian.
Etter Charles F, constable, 88½ E Washington, h 211 Orange.
Etter George E, mach, h 47 Draper.
Etter Henry C, carp, b 404 Dillon.
Etter Isaac B, lab, b 212 Minnesota.
Etter Levi M, mach hd, h 34 Miley av.
Etter Mary E (wid George), h 404 Dillon.
Etter Michael, carp, h 116 Yeiser.
Etter Nancy U (wid Wm H), h 212 Minnesota.
Etter Wm J, fireman, b 738 E Washington.
Ettinger Charles G, elevator opr, b 295 Kentucky av.
Ettinger Gustav, switchman, h 295 Kentucky av.
Eubank, see also Ewbank.
Eubank Lucy A (wid Wm D), b 274 N New Jersey.
Eubanks Caroline (wid Benjamin), h 510 Superior.
Eubanks Joseph, lab, b 510 Superior.
Eudaly Zeralda C (wid Nathaniel), b 393 Bellefontaine.
Euell James A, lab, h 10 Hadley.
Eulass Wm A, glass cutter, h 74 E North.
Euler Frank P, insp, h 57 Talbott av.
Eurich Helen M, stenog N Y Life Ins Co, b 1094 N Penn.
Eurich Kate, forewoman, h 643 E Ohio.
Eurich Mary, bkkpr, b 643 E Ohio.
Eurich Mary C (wid Edward C), b 439 S State av.
Eurich Mary E (wid John L), h 1094 N Penn.
Eusey Andrew, mach hd, h 77 Centennial (H).

The A. Burdsal Co. CELEBRATED HOMESTEAD READY MIXED PAINT. WHOLESALE AND RETAIL. 34 AND 36 SOUTH MERIDIAN STREET.

COMPOSITION ROOFING MATERIALS. BEST IN THE MARKET. TELEPHONE 861. OFFICE, 151 WEST MARYLAND ST.

ELECTRIC SUPPLIES We Carry a full Stock. Prices Right. C. W. MEIKEL, Tel. 466. 96-98 E. New York St.

DALTON & MERRIFIELD {LUMBER South Noble St., near E. Washington

INDIANA ELECTROTYPE CO. : BEST WORK. LOWEST PRICES. 23 WEST PEARL ST., INDIANAPOLIS, IND. JOB WORK. BOOK PLATES. All Orders Promptly Filled. BEST PATENT BASE ON THE MARKET.

KIRKHOFF BROS.,
Electrical Contractors, Wiring and Construction.
102-104 SOUTH PENNSYLVANIA ST.
TELEPHONE 910.

Eusey Jacob, engr, h 102 Brookside av.
Eusey John, engr, h 691 Mass av.
Eusey John H, engr, h 36 N Station (B).
Eusey Katherine, h 580 E St Clair.
Eusey Samuel L, engr, b 580 E St Clair.
Evadinger Emil F, packer, b 61 Rockwood.
EVANS ADA P MME, Wholesale and Retail Hair Goods, Manicure, Massage and Hair Dressing Parlors, over 2½ W Washington, h 176 N Illinois. (See adv in classified Hair Goods.)
Evans Alfred D, local freight agt C H & D R R, r 524 N Capitol av.
Evans Alfred O, mach, h 338 Yandes.
Evans Alla A (wid Henry N), h 15 Leonard.
Evans Anna E (wid Robert), b 446 N East.
Evans Arthur L, carp, b 401 W 2d.
Evans Asher B, supt Evans Linseed Oil Wks, b 360 N Alabama.
Evans Benjamin F, brakeman, b 1092 E Washington.
Evans Charles H (Alloways & Co), h 964 N Delaware.
Evans Cheek P, dairy, n e cor Ritter av and Brookville rd (I), h same.
Evans, Clarence C, boilermkr, b 498 Madison av.
Evans Duzan C, sawyer, h 498 Madison av.
Evans Ebenezer E, blksmith, h 18 Warren av (W I).
Evans Edgar H, asst mngr, b 548 N Meridian.
Evans Edward D, asst mngr Evans Linseed Oil Wks, h 867 N Delaware.
Evans Edward E, engr, h 177 Lexington av.
Evans Edwin H, lab, h 30 Centennial (H).
Evans Elizabeth F (wid Elias), h 29 Rockwood.
Evans Elmer J, driver, h 29 Rockwood.
Evans Emma, hair dresser, h 29 Rockwood.
Evans Ernest, hostler, b 239 Douglass.
Evans Evander N, stairbuilder, h 29 Warren av (W I).
Evans Fannie B (wid John W), h 71 Cleaveland blk.
Evans Fannie L, dressmkr, 446 N East, b same.

THE W. G. WASSON CO.,
130 Indiana Ave. Tel. 989.
STEAM
COAL
Car Lots a Specialty. Prompt Delivery.
Brazil Block, Jackson and Anthracite.

Evans Frank, patternmkr, b 340 Blake.
Evans Frederick L, b 469 N Illinois..
Evans George, hostler, h 131 Columbia al.
Evans George H, sec and treas The Hay & Willits Mnfg Co, h 74 E St Clair.
Evans George R, lab, h 226 S Linden.
Evans George T, flour mills, 452 W Washington, h 548 N Meridian.
Evans Gibson, dairyman, h 86 Sullivan.
Evans Hannah (wid Charles), janitress, h 498 W Ontario (N I).
Evans Henry H, b 15 Leonard.
Evans Isabell E, grocer, n e cor Grandview and Belmont avs (H), h same.
Evans Jesse A, carpenter, 194 Oliver av (W I), h same.
Evans John, lab, b 277 S Penn.
Evans John, lab, h 169 Elizabeth.
Evans John L, barber, h 97 Locke.
Evans Joseph R, pres Commercial Electric Co and mngr Evans Linseed Oil Wks, h 360 N Alabama.
Evans Lester O, carp, h 32 Warren av (W I).
EVANS LINSEED OIL WORKS, Joseph R Evans Mngr, Edward D Evans Asst Mngr, Mnfrs of Linseed Oil and Oil Cake, 4 Ingalls Blk, Tel 431.
Evans Lizzie J, governess Blind Institute.
Evans Lucy (wid Clement), h 59 Agnes.
Evans Margaret A (wid Wm R), h 470 N Delaware.
Evans Marion, contr, 1079 Morris (W I), h same.
Evans Martin E, clk R M S, b 164 N Illinois.
Evans Mary (wid John J), h 254½ W Washington.
Evans Mary A (wid Thomas), h 43 Lockerbie.
Evans Mary C, drugs, 1299 N Meridian, h same.
Evans Mary E, b 23 Arbor av (W I).
Evans Meda, dressmkr, 410 N Penn, h same.
Evans Melvina (wid Thomas), b 422 Central av.
Evans Morgan H, carp, h 384 W 2d.
Evans Noah S, bricklyr, h 213 Mass av.
Evans Perry D, stenog, Wm L Elder, b 498 Madison av.
Evans Rebecca A (wid Jonathan), h 170 English av.
Evans Robert, lab, h 604 N West.
EVANS ROWLAND, Official Stenographer U S Courts, P O Bldg, Tel 112; b 744 N Alabama.
Evans Roy L, lab, b 217 S Illinois.
Evans Samuel A, h 191 Pleasant.
Evans Samuel J, sawyer, h 22 St Mary.
Evans Sanford A, collr, b 1299 N Meridian.
Evans Sarah E, b 176 Martindale av.
Evans Sophia (wid Wm F), b 53 Omer.
Evans Sophronia G (wid Robert A), h 144 N Pine.
Evans Susan (wid John), h 661 Charles.
Evans Thomas W L, music teacher, 90 Hoyt av, h same.
Evans Venning P, h rear 476 N Senate av.
Evans Wade H, b n e cor Grandview and Belmont avs (H).
Evans Walter E, salesman The Bowen-Merrill Co, h 947 N Alabama.
Evans Willard A, treas Commercial Electric Co, h 368 N Alabama.
Evans Wm, tinner, r 346 N Senate av.
Evans Wm C, helper, b 498 Madison av.
Evans Wm G, barber, 160 W 12th, h 17 Shriver av.

W. H. Messenger FURNITURE, CARPETS, STOVES, 101 EAST WASHINGTON ST. TEL. 491.

McNamara, Koster & Co. | Foundry and Pattern Shop, 212-218 S. PENN. ST. . . . PHONE 1593.

THE FRED DIETZ CO.

Evans Wm H, molder, h 149 High.
Evans Wm L, mach opr Indpls Journal, h 91 Keystone av.
Evans Wm L, stairbldr, b 401 W 2d.
Evans Wm M, carp, h 350 Bates.
Evans Wm R, clk, h 39 Greer.
Evans Wm R, stairbldr, h 401 W 2d.
Evans Wm W, trav agt, r 20 Franklin Life Ins bldg.
Evans Wm W, lab, b 170 English av.
Evard John E, watchmkr Julius C Walk & Son, h 27 Fletcher av.
Eveland James G, butcher, h 322 Lincoln av.
Eveland Thomas C, driver, h 352 Virginia av.
Everding Ernst, lab, h 531 S Meridian.
Everett Andrew J, carp, 38 Eastern av, h same.
Everett David T, blksmith, h 93 Division (W I).
Everett George A, contr, h 22 Thalman av.
Everett Harmon J, lawyer, 92½ E Washington, h n w cor Clifford and Lebanon avs.
Everett Jesse, driver, b 38 Eastern av.
Everett Jesse E, clk, b 1322 N Alabama.
Everett John E, chemist, h 109 Decatur.
Everett Lora A, dressmkr, b 38 Eastern av.
Everett Titus B, engr, h 500 Madison av.
Everhart George, clk, r 23 Ryan blk.
Everhart Willis, lab, h 30 Center.
Everingham Ray A, nurse, 242 E Vermont, r same.
Everingham Stella S, nurse, 242 E Vermont, r same.
Everitt James A, pres J A Everitt Seedsman, h 121 W Washington.

EVERITT J A SEEDSMAN, James A Everitt Pres, L J Everitt Sec and Treas, 121-123 W Washington and 50 N Delaware, Tel 1256.

Everitt Laura J, sec and treas J A Everitt Seedsman, h 121 W Washington.
Everling Amos D, lab, h 155 Locke.
Everling Edward, lab, b 155 Locke.
Everroad Benjamin F (Everroad & Prunk), h w s LaSalle 3 n of Indiana av (M P).
Everroad Jesse, tinner, h 366 N Senate av.

EVERROAD & PRUNK (Benjamin F Everroad, Frank H Prunk), Hardware, Furnaces and Pumps, 170 Indiana av, Tel 1188.

EVERTS CHARLES C, Dentist, 8½ N Penn, h 1134 N Meridian.

Evingston John, brakeman, b 176 S New Jersey.
Evison Harry, confr, 70 Indiana av, h 70½ same.
Eviston Henry U, basketmkr, h 178 Bates.
Ewadinger Barbara (wid Rudolph), h 61 Rockwood.
Ewadinger Emil, lab, h 61 Rockwood.
Ewadinger Leo, molder, h 61 Rockwood.
Ewadinger Rudolph, driver, h 61 Rockwood.
Ewald Henry, blksmith, b 163 Fulton.
Ewald Wm F, cigarmkr, b 163 Fulton.
Ewalt Louisa (wid John H), h 338 W 23d.
Ewan Albert O, h 393 Broadway.
Ewan Albert T, b 163 Hoyt av.
Ewan Hattie, h 12 Willard.
Ewart Mnfg Co, chain mnfrs, cor Michigan and Holmes av (H).
Ewbank, see also Eubank.
Ewbank George W, lab, h 409 W Udell (N I).

Henry H. Fay,
40½ E. Washington St.,
REAL ESTATE,
AND LOAN BROKER.

Ewbank Louis B (Ewbank & Watson), b 201 Lincoln av.

EWBANK & WATSON (Louis B Ewbank, Benjamin F Watson), Lawyers, 12 Brandon Blk, 95 E Washington.

Ewell Charles J, motorman, h 224½ W Washington.
Ewers Frank H, sec G F Wittmer Lumber Co, r 16 Fletcher av.
Ewert Robert, waiter, r 183½ W Washington.
Ewerz Sarah J (wid Frank), h 4 N Dorman.
Ewick Jesse, mach, h 87 Nordyke av (W I).
Ewick Lewis, plastr, b 125 W Maryland.
Ewing Andrew, lab, b 26 Holborn.
Ewing Bazil, janitor, h 1 Darwin.
Ewing Calvin K, phys, 24 E Ohio, h 138 N New Jersey.
Ewing Ellen (wid Wm), h 236 Spring.
Ewing Henry W, trunkmkr, h 216 N Noble.
Ewing Jacob D, b 216 N Noble.
Ewing James, lab, h 21 Bloomington.
Ewing John W, lab, h 29 Columbia al.
Ewing Mary E (wid Wm H), h 204 N Illinois.
Ewing Robert, lab, h 646 W Washington.
Ewing Robert E, waiter, r 183½ W Washington.
Ewing Rufus, plastr, b 17 Beacon.
Ewing Wesley, lab, h 29 Columbia al.
Ewing Wm, car rep, h 24 Everett.
Ewing Wm, lab, h 123 Bryan.
Ewing Wm H, clk L S Ayres & Co, b 204 N Illinois.
Ewing Wm J, driver, b 207 W Michigan.
Ewing Wm P, lab, h 593 W Washington.
Ewry Rose L, prin Liberty Street Free Kindergarten, b 82 E Vermont.
Excelsior Shirt Mnfg Co, Raphael Kirschbaum pres, Bernard W Kirschbaum sec and treas, 27 W Pearl.
Excelsior Steam Laundry, Major Taylor propr, 2-6 Masonic Temple, Capitol av.
Exchange Hotel, Henry Cavett propr, Union Stock Yards (W I).
Exler Catherine (wid John), h 75 Drake.
Exler Charles, insp, b 75 Drake.

UNIUN CASUALTY & SURETY CO.
OF ST. LOUIS, MO.
All lines of Personal Accident and Casualty Insurance, including Employers' and General Liability.
W. E. BARTON & CO., General Agents,
504 Indiana Trust Building.
LONG DISTANCE TELEPHONE 1918.

WOODEN PACKING BOXES MADE TO ORDER. FACTORY AND WAREHOUSE TRUCKS. 400 Madison Avenue. Telephone 654.

Indianapolis BUSINESS UNIVERSITY
Leading College of Business and Shorthand. Elevator day and night. Individual instruction. Large faculty. Terms easy. Enter now. See p. 4. When Block. E. J. HEEB, President.

Water Works Pumping Engines { HENRY R. WORTHINGTON, 64 SOUTH PENNSYLVANIA ST. Long Distance Telephone 284.

UNION CO-OPERATIVE LAUNDRY { (COMPOSED OF UNION LAUNDRY GIRLS.) NOS. 3, 40 AND 142 VIRGINIA AVENUE. — T. E. SOMERVILLE, MANAGER — TELEPHONE 1269. INDIANAPOLIS, IND.

HORACE M. HADLEY
REAL ESTATE AND INSURANCE
66 East Market Street, Basement
TELEPHONE 1540.

Exler Wm H, plumber, 22 Michigan (H), b 75 Drake.
Exon Wm, porter, r 232 W North.
Eyles Anton G, pianomkr, b 385 N New Jersey.
Eyles Otto, musician, b 385 N New Jersey.
Eymann George, clk, b 180 Blake.
Eymann John H, shoemkr, 33 Monument pl, h 180 Blake.
Eymann Mary E, bkkpr Brower & Love Bros, b 180 Blake.
EYSTER A M, Druggist, 602 N Senate av, h same, Tel 1019.
Eyster Elmer E, engr, h 16 Cornell av.
Ezekiel Clementine (wid Michael), b 191 N New Jersey.

F

Fabel Gustav, condr, h 28 N State av.
Faber George J, sawmkr, h 315 Union.
Faber John A, clk, b 60 Thomas.
Faber John W, lab, b 60 Thomas.
Faber Magdalena (wid Jacob J), h 196 Prospect.
Faber Samuel E, ins, 7 Ingalls blk, r 318 N Meridian.
Faber Sarah E, boarding 27 N New Jersey.
Fabian Joseph, baker, b 89 Coburn.
Fachmann Herman W, wireworks, 77 N Delaware, h 78 N Noble.
Fack Mary A (wid Frederick), h 119 Kennington.
Facker John, molder, r 104 Michigan (H).
Fackler Frank X, brewer, b 180 E McCarty.
Fadely Lewis W, trav agt Hildebrand Hardware Co, h 229 N Liberty.
Fagan George W, molder, b 105 Oliver av (W I).
Fagans Harry, waiter, r 10 Roanoke.
Fager Joseph C, porter, b 88 W Market.
Fahey John, butcher, h 223 Elizabeth.
Fahey Philip, lab, b 57 S California.
Fahey Thomas, lab, h 673 W Vermont.
Fahle August R, supt, h 449 Union.
Fahle Frank, collr, b 449 Union.
Fahle Marguerite, stenog George Wolf, b 449 Union.

PERSONAL AND PROMPT ATTENTION GIVEN TO COLLECTIONS.
Merchants' and Manufacturers' Exchange
J. E. TAKKEN, Manager,
19 Union Building, 73 West Maryland Street.

Fahle Laura (wid Henry), h 127 E Merrill.
Fahl Paul, solr Indpls Brewing Co, h 31 Newman.
Fahlsing Wm, clk, b 1049 N Capitol av.
Fahnley Carl, clk Fahnley & McCrea, b 200 N Meridian.
Fahnley Frederick (Fahnley & McCrea), h 200 N Meridian.
FAHNLEY & M'CREA (Frederick Fahnley, Rollin H McCrea), Wholesale Millinery, 140-142 S Meridian, 39-41 McCrea and 8 W Louisiana Tel 1010.
Fahner Jacob, lab, h e s Denny 4 n of Washington.
Fahrbach Andreas, carp, h 62 Gresham.
Fahrbach Andrew, packer, b 109 Coburn.
Fahrbach Andrew K, lab, h 56 Wallack.
Fahrbach Christina (wid Andrew), b 19 Ketcham.
Fahrbach George H, bookbndr, h 231 W 1st.
Fahrbach George H, varnisher, b 109 Coburn.
Fahrbach Joseph, baker, b 149 English av.
Fahrbach Katherine (wid George P), h 109 Coburn.
Fahrbach Valentine, bartndr, h 253 S Alabama.
Fahrion Christine, cabtmkr, h 130 Keystone av.
Fahrion Emil E, cashr, b 377 S Delaware.
Fahrion George H, carver, h n e cor Centennial and Coyner.
Fahrion J George, flour, 373 S Delaware, h 377 same.
Fahrner Henry J, clk, h 455 Charles.
Fahrnheim Wm, porter, b 37 S Delaware.
Failey Bruce F, b 585 N Delaware.
Failey Dennis, carp, b 110 Dunlop.
Failey James F (Blair & Failey), receiver O I H, 615 Indiana Trust bldg, h 585 N Delaware.
Failey John W, trav agt, h 72 Ft Wayne av.
FAILLES CHARLES, Ostrich Feathers, 28 S Illinois, h 140 N Senate av.
Fair David, saloon, 793 N Senate av and n w cor 30th and L N A & C Ry, h 780 N Senate av.
Fairall Charles J, clk, h 60 N Noble.
Fairbank George, clk, b 19 Ketcham.
Fairbank Hiram C, trav agt, h 218 Keystone av.
Fairbanks Charles W, lawyer, 37 Ingalls blk, h 410 Park av.
Fairbanks Crawford, office 411 Indiana Trust bldg, res Terre Haute, Ind.
FAIRBANKS, MORSE & CO, H H Child Mngr, Scales, 100 S Meridian, Tel 977.
Fairbanks Warren, student, b 410 Park av.
Fairchild Manford E, clk, h 74 Marion av (W I).
Faires Nancy (wid Wilson), b 182 Lexington av.
Fairhead Johanna (wid Robert), h 191 Virginia av.
Fairleigh John S, bkkpr, h 882 W Highland av (N I).
Faison Anthony E, lab, b 55 Wallack.
Faison George H, porter, h 178 Minerva.
Faison Green, lab, h 55 Wallack.
Fait, see also Fate.
Fait Frank S, tel opr, b 717 E Market.
Fait Mae A, teacher, b 717 E Market.
Fait Nenette E, teacher Public School No 20, b 717 E Market.

CLEMENS VONNEGUT
184, 186 and 192 E. Washington St.
FOUNDRY AND MACHINISTS' SUPPLIES. "NORTON" EMERY WHEELS AND GRINDING MACHINERY.

THE WM. H. BLOCK CO. DRY GOODS, MILLINERY, CLOAKS AND FURS.
7 AND 9 EAST WASHINGTON STREET.

Fait Wallace F, tel opr P C C & St L Ry, b 717 E Market.
Fait Walter L, milk, h 717 E Market.
Faith Edward C, student, b 176 Bright.
Falbe Allen R, steward, h 102 N Capitol av.
Falconbury John G, foreman, h 86 Nordyke av (W I).
Falconer Elizabeth D, b 268 Park av.
Falderman Barnett H, molder, h 74 Willow.
Falderman Frank G, lab, b 74 Willow.
Falender Julius (S Falender & Co), b 126 Maple.
Falender Louis, peddler, h 126 Maple.
Falender Simon (S Falender & Co), b 126 Maple.
Falender S & Co (Simon and Julius Falender), junk, 92 Eddy.
Falk Adam H, tmstr, b 509 N California.
Falk Edward, lab, h 406 W 2d.
FALK FREDERICK, Physician and Surgeon, Office Hours 1-3 and 7-8 P M, 47½ S Illinois, Tel 1529; h 682 N Illinois.
Falk Henry, h 509 N California.
FALK NANNIE P, Milliner, 47 S Illinois, h 682 N Illinois.
Falke Frederick W A, porter, b 133 E St Joseph.
Falkenstein Adolph A, scavenger, h rear 418 S Delaware.
Fallon Frank J, mach, b 450 Mass av.
Fallon John J, butcher, h 21 Helen.
Fallon Julia (wid Martin), h 51 Helen.
Fallon Martin, lab, h 344 W Pearl.
Fallon Peter J, clk U S Pension Agency, b 121 N Capitol av.
Falls Wm G, lab Deaf and Dumb Inst.
Faltings Edward, lab, h 137 Kennington.
Falvey John M, lab, b 346 E Morris.
Falvey Timothy C, stoker, h 346 E Morris.
Falvey Timothy P, metermkr, b 346 E Morris.
Family Dress Guide Co, Louise L Lawrence pres, Mary L Nicolai treas, 6, 156½ E Washington.
FAMOUS STOVE CO, A E Wells Mngr, Stoves and Ranges, 135 S Meridian, Tel 1326.
Fancher Charles W, lab, h 658 Charles.
Fancher George E, miller, b 72 Cypress.
Fanciers' Gazette, Fanciers' Gazette Co pubs, 49 Virginia av.
Fanciers' Gazette Co, Burt N Pierce pres, Beriah N Pierce vice-pres, Wm H Price sec and treas, pubs Fanciers' Gazette, 49 Virginia av.
Fanger Edward W, trav agt, r 176½ N Alabama.
Fanning John T, mach hd, h rear 226 E Washington.
Fanning John W, lineman Fire Dept, h 60 Minerva.
Fanning Joseph B, r 39 Talbott blk.
Fanning Joseph W, trav agt, b Grand Hotel.
Fanning Patrick E, lineman Fire Dept, h 875 N Senate av.
Fanning Peter P, molder, h 482 E Georgia.
Fansler Mary A (wid David), h 283 N Meridian.
Fansler Abraham E, butcher, h 136 Cornell av.
Fansler George W, plastr, h 268 Martindale av.
Fansler Joshua B, clk The Progress Clothing Co, h 179 N Penn.

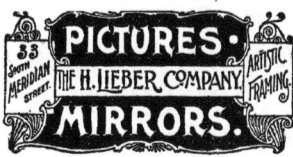

33 South Meridian Street. PICTURES. THE H. LIEBER COMPANY. ARTISTIC FRAMING. MIRRORS.

Fansler Samuel O, lab, h 270 Alvord.
Fansler Thomas H, blksmith, b 85 Trowbridge (W).
Fant Carrie R, b 397 Cornell av.
Fant Samuel, lab, h 182 Bismarck av (H).
Faradizer Co The, Turner D Bottome pres, Carl C Hartman sec, electrical apparatus, 513 Majestic bldg.
Farb Samuel, peddler, h 265 S Capitol av.
Farber Annie, notions, 115 E Mkt House, h rear 134 N Liberty.
Farber Conrad, porter, b 389 N West.
Farber John W, packer, b 125 W 6th.
Farber Peter F, lab, h 12 Sumner.
Farenbaugh Frank, lab, b 249 E Louisiana.
Fargo Chancellor O, clk Am Ex Co, b 916 N Delaware.
Fargo Fayette C, supt Am Ex Co, h 916 N Delaware.
Farhear Patrick, lab, h 91 Nordyke av (W I).
Faries Timothy C, dentist, 108 Hoyt av, h same.
Faries Werter W, engr, b 108 Hoyt av.
Faringer Dennis, lab, h 20 Martha (W I).
Faringer Edward, lab, b 20 Martha (W I).
Faris Frank H, letter carrier P O, h 641 Broadway.
Faris John D, undertaker, b 276 E Market.
Fariss Harry C, h 1212 N Illinois.
Farlee Thomas E, woodwkr, b 83 Quincy.
Farlee Wm B, mach hd, b 83 Quincy.
Farlee Wm H, car rep, h 83 Quincy.
Farley Benjamin, r 142 S East.
Farley Clinton D, motorman, b 489 College av.
Farley Elizabeth (wid Patrick), h 28 Deloss.
Farley John F, lab, h 98 Lee (W I).
Farley John T, engr, h 140 Fletcher av.
Farley Thomas, saw mnfr, 19 McNabb, h same.
Farley Wm B, bkkpr Miller Oil Co, h e s Charles 1 n of Carleton av (M).
Farley Wm M, barber and postmaster Mt Jackson, h 31 Harris av (M J).
Farlow David, lab, b 172 Bright.
Farlow James F, lab, b 172 Bright.
Farlow Mary C (wid John), h 172 Bright.
Farlow Silas E, lab, b 172 Bright.

GUIDO R. PRESSLER,
FRESCO PAINTER
Churches, Theaters, Public Buildings, Etc., A Specialty.
Residence, No. 325 North Liberty Street.
INDIANAPOLIS, IND.

INDIANAPOLIS STEEL ROOFING AND CORRUGATING WORKS, 23 and 25 East South Street. S. D. NOEL, Proprietor.

David S. McKernan REAL ESTATE AND LOANS. Exchanging real estate a specialty. A number of choice pieces for encumbered property. Rooms 2-5 Thorpe Block.

DIAMOND WALL PLASTER { Telephone 1410 BUILDERS' EXCHANGE.

UNION TRANSFER AND STORAGE CO. Cor. E. Ohio St. and C., C., C. & St. L. R'y Tracks. Storage of Household Goods and Pianos a Specialty.

W. McWORKMAN,
Galvanized Iron Cornice Works
TIN AND SLATE ROOFING.
930 WEST WASHINGTON STREET.
TELEPHONE 1118.

Farlow Wm H, lab, b 172 Bright.
Farman John H, stonecutter, h 415 S Capitol av.
Farmer Alexander, tmstr, b e s James 4 n of Sutherland (B).
Farmer Alice (wid George W), h 39 Benton.
Farmer Charles W, clk Francke & Schindler, h 75 Highland pl.
Farmer De Lotus, filer, b 39 Benton.
Farmer Edwin, music teacher, r 347 N Illinois.
Farmer Edwin G, bkkpr J S Cruse, b 103 Spann av.
Farmer Emily, housekpr 210 Hamilton av.
Farmer George E, brakeman, h 279 E North.
Farmer Hattie, h 222 W 8th.
Farmer James, lab, b 140 Hosbrook.
Farmer Jason, lab, b w s Rural 2 s of 17th.
Farmer Jason R, lab, h w s Rural 3 s of 17th.
Farmer James W F, lab, r 140 Hosbrook.
Farmer Joseph, lab, h 367 Newman.
Farmer Richard, mason, h rear 80 Yandes.
Farmer Samuel W, clk Capital House, h same.
Farmer Thomas E, clk Shaw & Vinson, b Roosevelt House.
Farmer Abraham, barber, 247 W South, h same.
Farnham Ella R, clk The Wm H Block Co, h 294 N Liberty.
Farnham Florence, stenog Levi P Harlan, b 294 N Liberty.
Farnham Jerusha (wid Edward K), dressmkr, h 75 W 5th.
Farnham Milton G, cigarmkr, h 189 Fulton.
Farnsworth Caroline F (wid Thomas D), b 1126 N Meridian.
Farnsworth Louis A, electrician, b 1126 N Meridian.
Farnsworth Theodore, b 155 N Capitol av.
Farnsworth Theodore W, phys, 11 Stewart pl, r same.
Farnsworth Theodore W jr, dentist, 11 Stewart pl, r same.
Farquhar Frances M (wid John H), h 477 N Penn.

SEALS,
STENCILS,
STAMPS, Etc.
GEO. J. MAYER
15 S. Meridian St.
TELEPHONE 1386.

Farquhar George T, opr W U Tel Co, b 652 College av.
Farra Annette L (wid Jesse B), h 46 Jefferson av.
Farra Robert G, brakeman, h 46 Jefferson av.
Farrabee Belt D, ins agt, b 1166 N Penn.
Farrabee Sanford D, ins agt, h 1166 N Penn.
Farrell Barnabas, lab, r 200½ W Washington.
Farrell Benjamin Rev, pastor Mt Zion Baptist Church, h 117 W 4th.
Farrell Charles B, bartndr, r 18 Shields blk.
Farrell Charles L, bkkpr The State Bank of Indiana, r 226 N Delaware.
Farrell Daniel E, barber, 80 W South, h rear 279 S West.
Farrell Elizabeth (wid Patrick K), h 299 S East.
Farrell Ella, h 140 E McCarty.
Farrell Frank W, brakeman, b 32 Warman av (H).
Farrell Harry E, foreman, b 170 N Dorman.
Farrell James, section boss, h 33 S Arsenal av.
Farrell Jeremiah, fireman, h 43 N Gillard av.
Farrell John S (J S Farrell & Co), h 438 College av.
Farrell John W, painter, b 26 S Senate av.
Farrell Joseph A, fireman, h 28 Roe.
FARRELL J S & CO (John S Farrell), Steam and Hot Water Heating, Plumbing Contractors and Gas Fitters, 84 N Illinois, Tel 382. (See left bottom cor cards.)
Farrell Maria (wid Patrick), h 407 W New York.
Farrell Martin F, car oiler, h 1207 Morris (W I).
Farrell Mary (wid John), h rear 169 Davidson.
Farrell Michael, lab, h 20 N Gillard av.
Farrell Michael H, marble dealer, 208 W Washington, h 242 Bright.
Farrell Patrick H, hostler, h 339 S East.
Farrell Robert E, plumber, h 100 Agnes.
Farrell Thomas, plumber, b 39 N Alabama.
Farrell Thomas H, tel opr P C C & St L Ry, h 46 Temple av.
Farrell Thomas T, boilermkr, h 434 Highland av.
Farrell Willis R, trav agt, r 169 W Market.
Farrer George A, lab, h 133 Locke.
Farrin James H, waiter, r 283 S Capitol av.
Farrington Wyatt L, saloon, 275 W Washington, h same.
Farris Charles, lab, h 1218 N Penn.
Farris Jennie R, nurse City Hospital.
Farris John, lab, h 52 Thomas.
Farris Robert L (O D Hardy & Co), b 240½ E Washington.
Farrow James, painter, h 40 Mill.
Farry Roland R, wireman Sanborn Electric Co, h 1007 N Illinois.
Farry Wm R, cashr The McElwaine-Richards Co), h 1005 N Illinois.
Farthing Wm A, b 74 Highland pl.
Fasey Wm, painter, h 53 Church.
Fassell Lydia (wid George), h rear 393 S East.
Fastleben Henry, clk, h 332 Fulton.
Fate, see also Fait.
Fate George, mngr Circle Park Barber Shop, 15 Monument pl, h 25 Tacoma av.

A. METZGER AGENCY ESTABLISHED 1863. L-O-A-N-S

LAMBERT GAS & GASOLINE ENGINE CO.
ANDERSON, IND. GAS ENGINES FOR ALL PURPOSES.

Fate Laura B, dressmkr, 21 S Alabama, h 25 Tacoma av.
Fate Wm, motorman, b 31 Beacon.
Fatout Ansel (M K Fatout & Son), b 233 N Illinois.
Fatout Arthur, clk, b 326 N Illinois.
Fatout Daniel H, contr, h 1084 W Washington.
FATOUT HERVEY B, Surveyor and Civil Engineer, Room 1, 30½ N Delaware, h 375 N Capitol av. (See adv in classified Civil Engineers.)
Fatout Joshua L, contr, h 326 N Illinois.
FATOUT J NOBLE, Sign Painter, 4 Cyclorama Pl, h 126 W 6th.
Fatout Marion T, mach hd, b 105 Wright.
Fatout Moses K (M K Fatout & Son), h 233 N Illinois.
FATOUT M K & SON (Moses K and Ansel), Planing Mill and Lumber, 443-463 E St Clair, Tel 677.
Fatout Nellie B, teacher, b 326 N Illinois.
Fatout Walter P, lineman, b 326 N Illinois.
Fatout Warren, contr, 28 Mass av, b Illinois House.
Fauch Charles H, polisher, h 894 S Meridian.
Faucett, see also Fausset.
Faucett Alpheus, carp, b 317 N California.
Faucett Charles E, city salesman Kingan & Co, b 317 N California.
Faucett Cicero F, lab, h 225 River av (W I).
Faucett Emmett J, clk, h 420 W Udell (N).
Faucett James E, agt, h 297 N California.
Faucett Joseph T, clk, r 27 N West.
Faucett LeRoy, lab, b 317 N California.
Faucett Nancy L (wid Benjamin F), h 317 N California.
Faught Abram E, carp, 26 Ruckle, h same.
Faught George W, clk, h 281 Bellefontaine.
Faught Oren H (Faught & Co), h 844 W Morris (W I).
Faught Willis H, lab, b 8 Minerva.
Faught & Co (Oren H Faught, Samuel L Douglass, August E Rahke), brokers, 18½ N Meridian.
Faulhaber John B, seatmkr, h 50 Morton.
Faulkconer Alvah J, blksmith, b 68 Buchanan.
Faulkconer James S, blksmith, h 68 Buchanan.
Faulkconer Joseph K, uphlr, b 68 Buchanan.
Faulkison Robert, tmstr, h 3 Clinton.
Faulkner Alice M (wid Oscar), boarding 342 S Meridian.
Faulkner Charles F (Faulkner & Webb), h 123 Ruckle.
Faulkner Claude H, clk, b 20 Wilcox.
Faulkner Cora A, bkkpr Faulkner & Webb, b 123 Ruckle.
Faulkner Edward, trav agt, b 321 W Market.
Faulkner George A, fireman, b 441 N California.
Faulkner Harriet (wid George), h 441 N California.
Faulkner James, lab, b 144 Elizabeth.
Faulkner Jeremiah E, lab, h rear 71 Indiana av.
Faulkner John J, bricklyr, h 144 Elizabeth.
Faulkner Joseph H, engr, h 20 Wilcox.
Faulkner Louis, lab, b 144 Elizabeth.
Faulkner Louis A, driver, h 21 Minnesota.
Faulkner Louis N, carver, b Illinois House.
Faulkner Rhoda, confr, 144 Elizabeth, h same.
Faulkner Wm, clk, b 376 Union.

THOS. C. DAY & CO.
INVESTING AGENTS,
TOWN AND FARM LOANS,
Rooms 325 to 330 Lemcke Bldg.

FAULKNER & WEBB (Charles F Faulkner, Homer C Webb), Proprs Indianapolis Pickling and Preserving Co, Pickles, Catsup, Mustards, Vinegar and Sauces, 200 S Penn, Tel 545.
Faulstich Louis, baker, h 59 Sanders.
Faulstitch Magdalen (wid John), b 103 Woodlawn av.
Fauple Henry, meats, 151 N Noble, b 167 same.
Faure Bert, r 199 S Illinois.
Fauser Frederick W, mach, h 189 Meek.
Fausset, see also Faucett.
Fausset Charles E, electrician, h 338 N Liberty.
Fausset Charles S, clk, h 31 Cornell av.
Fausset Elizabeth L (wid Robert), r 90½ Mass av.
Faust, see also Foust.
Faust Frank A, driver, h 60 Kansas.
Faust George H, foreman, h e s Sherman Drive, 2 s of Alexander av.
Faust George W, engr, h 60 N State av.
Faust Theodore L, blksmith, h 337 S New Jersey.
Fauver Anna (wid Joseph), b 16 Stevens pl.
Favors Josephine, dressmkr, 188 Meek, b same.
Favour Alonzo H, painter, h 150 Michigan av.
Fawcett Morton, clk Columbia Club, b 292 S East.
Fawkner Charles B, insp, h 38 W Michigan.
Fawkner Flora M, pianist, h 38 W Michigan.
Fay, see also Feyh.
Fay Florence, prin Public School No 21, h s s Lawrence 1 w of Hazel.
FAY HENRY H, Real Estate, Loans, Rental and Insurance Agt, 40½ E Washington, Tel 821; h 847 E Michigan. (See right top cor cards.)
Fay Louis, clk, r 185½ N Senate av.
Feadler Henry F, driver, h 154 Bates.
Feadler John A, shoemkr, b 154 Bates.
Fear Henry C, car rep, h 135 Newman.
Fearey John, contr, 477 N East, h same.

EAT
QUAKER BREAD
ASK YOUR GROCER FOR IT.
THE HITZ BAKING CO.

BICYCLES $5 DOWN. MONTHLY. Best Wheels. Best Terms. WHEELMEN'S CO. 31 W. OHIO ST. LONG DISTANCE TEL. 1855.

J. H. TECKENBROCK Grilles, Fretwork and Wood Carpets
94 EAST SOUTH STREET.

FIDELITY MUTUAL LIFE PHILADELPHIA, PA. A. H. COLLINS { General Agent, 52-53 Baldwin Block.

Edwards Mining 6. Rooms 42 and 43 When Building.
SUPERIOR BITUMINOUS COAL For Steam and Domestic . . Purposes . .

ESTABLISHED 1876. TELEPHONE 163.
CHESTER BRADFORD,
SOLICITOR OF PATENTS,
AND COUNSEL IN PATENT CAUSES.
(See adv. page 6.)
Office:—Rooms 14 and 16 Hubbard Block, S.W. Cor. Washington and Meridian Streets, INDIANAPOLIS, INDIANA.

Fearis Abbie J (wid George L), h 911 N Capitol av.
Fearnaught Albert, b 50 Elm.
Fearnaught Charles, sec and treas Western Furniture Co, h 58 Beaty.
Fearnaught Dora (wid Ernest), h 50 Elm.
Fearon James F, waiter, h 184 S Capitol av.
Fearrin Charles, lab, b 631 W 22d (N I).
Fearrin John, lab, b 631 W 22d (N I).
Fearrin Leander, farmer, h 631 W 22d (N I).
Fearrin Wm H, lab, b 631 W 22d (N I).
Feaster Daniel A, lab, h 225 Clinton.
Featheringill Anna C, teacher, b 36 N Station (B).
Featheringill Forrest, mach, b 46 Paw Paw.
Featherlin Harry, lab, b s s Brookville rd 1 w of Ritter av (I).
Featherlin Samuel, lab, h s s Brookville rd 1 w of Ritter av (I).
Featherston Harry B, lab, b n s Willow 2 w of Station (B).
Featherston Wm E, marketer, h 200 Bright.
Featherston Wm P, lab, h 172 Douglass.
Featherstone Anna (wid Darby), h 352 S Alabama.
Featherstone Daniel, watchman, h 402 S Delaware.
Featherstone Ellen, b 402 S Delaware.
Featherstone Wm W, mach, h 53 Malott av.
Fechtmann Daniel D, teacher, h 74 Buchanan.
Fechtmann Henry W, bkkpr The H Lieber Co, h 411 S New Jersey.
Fecker Joseph, driver, h rear 669 E Washington.
Federle Jacob, turner, h 218½ E Morris.
Federspill Henry, molder, h 29 Everett.
Federspill John, h 255½ E Washington.
FEDERSPILL MICHAEL, Choice Liquors and Cigars, 27 S Illinois, h 336 N Noble.
Fee James H, lab, h 479 W Eugene (N I).
Fee Oran G, filer, h 479 W Eugene (N I).
Feelemyer Joseph F (Wheeler Dressed Beef Co), acct Indpls Abattoir Co, h 447 Ash.
Feeney Catherine (wid Michael), h 103 Elm.
Feeney Furniture and Stove Co (George E Feeney, James Renihan), 76 W Washington.

HAY & WILLITS MFG CO.
76 N. PENNSYLVANIA ST.,
MAKERS
Outing BICYCLES
PHONE 598.

Feeney George E (Feeney Furniture and Stove Co), h 254 S Missouri.
Feeney James, lab, h 30 Haugh (H).
Feeney John, lab, b 52 Minerva.
Feeney John, lab, h 50 Tremont av (H).
Feeney Richard, lab, r 167 Muskingum al.
Feeny Peter J, h 190 Fayette.
Feeny Timothy, saloon, 252 W New York, h 254 same.
Feeser Charles J, harnessmkr, h 251 Bright.
Fegan Thomas A, agt, h 1717 N Illinois.
Fehlinger John A, carp, h 330 E Georgia.
Fehr Charles C, electrician The Wm H Block Co, h 234 W 2d.
Fehr Conrad, tailor, h 337 Coburn.
Fehr Henry, bookbndr, h 64 Highland pl.
Fehr John C, tinner, b 337 Coburn.
Fehrenbach John W, foreman Jacob Metzger & Co, h 40 Ashland (W I).
Fehrenbach Joseph F, clk Nathan Kahn, h 71 N Spruce.
Fehrenbach Louis H, clk Charles J Kuhn Co, b 335 S Meridian.
Fehrenbach Michael L, cellarman, h 177 Maple.
Fehrenbach Theresa (wid Joseph), h 335 S Meridian.
Feibleman Bert L, State agt North American Accident Assn, 35 W Market, b 226 E New York.
FEIBLEMAN CHARLES B, Lawyer, 90 E Court, h 180 N East.
Feibleman Dora (wid Leopold), h 226 E New York.
Feibleman Harry, clk, b 180 N East.
Feibleman Isidore, lawyer, 139 Commercial Club bldg, h 180 N East.
Feibleman Joseph L, trav agt Daniel Stewart Co, b 226 E New York.
Feicke Rudolph, h 185 Hadley av (W I).
Feigen John, engr, r 236 Lemcke bldg.
Feil Alphonso G, millwright, b 127 Hadley av (W I).
Feil John, h 127 Hadley av (W I).
Feiler Joseph, lab, h 620 S East.
Feiner Julius, lab, h 58 Downey.
Feiner Julius jr, jeweler, b 30 Gresham.
Feintuch Wm, rubber stamps, 134 Eddy, h same.
Feisel August H, butcher, h rear 100 Hoyt av.
Feist Andrew J, molder, h 9 Highland av (H).
Feit Modestus, lab, h 521 W Jones (N I).
Feitel Carl, mngr Slatts & Poe, b Spencer House.
Feld Clemens, lab, h 18 Vinton.
Feld Henry C, clk Parry Mnfg Co, b 18 Vinton.
Feld Oscar P, cigar mnfr, n e cor Michigan and canal, h 178 W Michigan.
Felder Eliza (wid Edmund), h 310 E Washington.
Feldkamp Reinhard W, whol liquors, 267 E Washington, h 135 Central av.
Feldmaier Charles, painter, h 666 Chestnut.
Feldman August, lithog, b 871 N Penn.
Feldman John H, clk, r 45½ N Capitol av.
Feldmann, see also Feltmann.
Feldmann Herman H, lab, h 30 Kansas.
Feldmann John H, printer, b 30 Kansas.
Feldpusch Conrad, driver, h 428 E Vermont.
Feldpusch John, h 403 E New York.
Feldt August F, mach hd, h 19 Alvord.
Feldt Carl J, mach hd, h 12 Hermann.
Feldt Ernest, drayman, b 439 E Ohio.
Felix Joseph F, printer, b 306 N Senate av.

ROOFING MATERIAL C. ZIMMERMAN & SONS, SLATE AND GRAVEL ROOFERS, 19 SOUTH EAST STREET.

DRIVEN WELLS And Second Water Wells and Pumps of all kinds at CHARLES KRAUSS', 42 S. PENN. ST., TEL. 465. REPAIRING NEATLY DONE.

If You are not Satisfied with Your Laundry Work Give Us a Trial. ERTEL STEAM LAUNDRY 26 and 28 N. Senate Avenue. Telephone 1089.

Felix Julia (wid John), b 908 N Alabama.
Felkner Isaac, ironwkr, b 23 Nordyke av (W I).
Fell Harry M, trav agt, h 66 The Blacherne.
Fella Margaret E, b 75 N State av.
Feller Caroline (wid Charles), h 263 W Pearl.
Feller John, grocer, 33 Harris av (M J), h same.
Feller Louis, jeweler, 218 E Washington, h 357 Central av.
Feller Margaret (wid George J), b 79 N New Jersey.
Fellows Lewis L, agt Midland Fast Freight Line, 26 S Illinois, h 4 The Chalfant.
Fells Harry J, horseshoer, 446 E Market, h 363 S Olive.
Fells Wm B, propr Indpls Church Furniture Co, h 136 Spann av.
Felske Louis, lab, h 80 Dunlop.
Felske Paul C, clk, b 80 Dunlop.
Felt Emma G, h 186½ Ft Wayne av.
Feltman Solomon, cigars, 586 W Washington, h same.
Feltmann, see also Feldmann.
Feltmann Herman, shoemkr, h 83 Palmer.
Felton Alexander, clk, h 382 Coburn.
Felton Charles S, clk, b 111 N Senate av.
Felton Grant, motorman, b 26 N Beville av.
Felton Leroy, driver, h 17 N Spruce.
Felton Mary E (wid Ransom H), h rear 70 Yandes.
Felton Mattie (wid Josephus), h 48 Sheffield (W I).
Felton Sylvander, grocer, 179 W 12th, h 111 N Senate av.
Feltz Ernestina (wid Philip), h 476 W New York.
Feltz John A, mach, b 476 W New York.
Feltz Joseph A, mach, b 476 W New York.
Feltz Philip J, cooper, b 476 W New York.
Feltz Wm J, mach, h 480 W New York.
Femyer Frank, painter, h 46 Arizona.
Femyer Jesse, mach hd, h 699 Chestnut.
Fender Frank, lab, h 219 Orange.
Fender Mary A (wid Jacob), b 68 Hoyt av.
Fender Nicholas, miller, h 34 Pansy.
Fendley Salathiel C, tanner, r Riley blk.
Fene George H, cook, h 20 Sumner.
Fenkbeiner Joseph Rev, pastor Second Evangelical Church, h 79 Kansas.
Fenley Addison C, condr, h 38 Division (W I).
Fenley Mary S, seamstress, h 68 Clifford av.
Fennell James T, lab, b 18 Henry.
Fennell John A, h 181 S New Jersey.
Fennell Retta, boarding 181 S New Jersey.
Fennell Wm T, lab, h 143 High.
FENNEMAN EDWARD W, Staple and Fancy Groceries and Meat Market, 299 N Senate av, h same.
Fenneman George W, tmstr, h 26 E Ray.
Fennessy John, mach, h 15 Tecumseh.
Fenter Frederick, b 9 W Sutherland (B).
Fenter Frederick jr, engr, 9 W Sutherland (B).
Fenter George F, tailor, h 24 King.
Fenter Margaret, clk, b 185 Hoyt av.
Fenter Wm G, engr, h 123 Fulton.
Fenton Arthur, condr, b 530 W Francis (N I).
Fenton Charles F, sawfiler, b 124 Christian av.
Fenton Ellsworth, foreman, h 1102 N Senate av.
Fenton George, car rep, b 162 Harrison.
Fenton John, mach, h 186 Columbia av.
Fenton John B J, bkkpr, r 131 W Ohio.

Richardson & McCrea, REPRESENTING BEST KNOWN FIRE INSURANCE COMPANIES. Fidelity and Casualty Insurance Company of New York Represented. Telephone 182. 79 East Market St.

Fenton John H, lab, h 26 N Judge Harding (W I).
Fenton Michael, lab, b 19 Oxford.
Fentz Chauncey D, brakeman, h 19 Lawn (B).
Fenwick Joseph B, stonecutter, h 155½ W Washington.
Ferger Charles, baker, h 68 Torbet.
FERGER CHARLES, Wholesale Flour, 45 Virginia av, Tel 1219, h 541 N Capitol av.
Ferger Charles jr, trav agt Charles Ferger, b 541 N Capitol av.
Ferger Edward, clk Bates House Pharmacy, b 541 N Capitol av.
Ferger Eliza (wid Louis), h 187½ E Washington.
Ferger John C, baker, h 85 Weghorst.
Ferger Louis H, clk, h 924 N New Jersey.
Ferger Wm L, hackman, b 187½ E Washington.
Ferguson, see also Furgason.
Ferguson Albert, tmstr, h 358 Fulton.
Ferguson Albert J, enameler, h 373 Fletcher av.
Ferguson Alfred P, chairmkr, b 124 W New York.
Ferguson Alonzo, trav agt J D Adams & Co, h 75 Ruckle.
Ferguson Anna A (M J & A A Ferguson), b 103 N Beville av.
Ferguson Caroline (wid Andrew), h 81 Columbia al.
Ferguson Charles E, supt City Hospital, n w cor Locke and Margaret, h 1102 N Penn.
Ferguson Clement A, h 49 W 7th.
Ferguson David, barber, h 21 Wood.
Ferguson David E, lab, b 475 E St Clair.
Ferguson Edgar, grinder, h 18 Edward (W I).
Ferguson Edward H, bricklayer, h 463 N Meridian.
Ferguson Ella, h 552 Virginia av.
FERGUSON FRANK C, Physician and Surgeon, Sanatorium for Diseases of Women and Abdominal Surgery, 208 N Alabama, h 487 Park av.
Ferguson George H, lab, h 37 Brett.

The Williams Typewriter Elegant Work, Visible Writing, Easy Operation, High Speed. S. H. EAST, State Agent, 55 Thorpe Block, 87 E. Market St.

ELLIS & HELFENBERGER Manufacturers of IRON and WIRE FENCES 162-170 S. SENATE AVE. TEL. 358.

THE HOGAN TRANSFER AND STORAGE COMP'Y
Household Goods and Pianos Moved—Packed—Stored...... Baggage and Package Express Machinery and Safes a Specialty Cor. Washington and Illinois Sts. TELEPHONE No. 675.

Hose, Belting, Packing, Clothing, Druggists' Sundries, Bicycle Tires, Cotton Hose, Etc. New York Belting & Packing Co., L't'd. The Central Rubber & Supply Co. 79 S. Illinois St., Indianapolis, Ind. Phone 8.

HIGHEST SECURITY
LOWEST COST OF INSURANCE.
The Provident Life and Trust Co.
Of Philadelphia.
D. W. EDWARDS, Gen. Agent,
508 Indiana Trust Building.

Ferguson George I, b 49 W 7th.
Ferguson Harold A, clk, b 373 Fletcher av.
Ferguson Henry C, clk, h 329 N East.
Ferguson Henry R, lab, h 35 Brett.
Ferguson Hill, lab, b 35 Willard.
Ferguson James, coachman, h rear 172 N West.
Ferguson James A, bookbndr, r 24½ Kentucky av.
Ferguson James B, musician, r 171 Mass av.
Ferguson James N, lab, h 645 S State av.
Ferguson Jane (wid Wm H), b 88 W 8th.
Ferguson Jennie M (wid Jesse), dressmkr 320 E Louisiana, b same.
Ferguson Jesse, lab, h 153 Harmon.
Ferguson John, supt Kingan & Co, (ltd), h 240 N West.
Ferguson John I, genl baggage agt Union Station, b 49 W 7th.
Ferguson John T, mach hd, h 124 W New York.
Ferguson Martha A (wid George), h 427 W Chicago (N I).
Ferguson Mary J (M J & A A Ferguson), b 103 N Beville av.
Ferguson Matilda, dressmkr, 131 Indiana av, h same.
Ferguson Mattie E (Union Co-Operative Laundry), b 475 E St Clair.
Ferguson M J & A A (Mary J and Anna A), dressmkrs, 103 N Beville av.
Ferguson Nicholas C, lab, h 138 Eureka av.
Ferguson Norval W, bkkpr, h 340 Clifford av.
Ferguson Oscar, tmstr, h 153 Harmon.
Ferguson Paul H, clk Edgar H Wilson, r 1 Bates.
Ferguson Rezin, h 1101 N Penn.
Ferguson Robert A, tinner, h 168 S Linden.
Ferguson Robert H, bricklyr, h 27 W Pratt.
Ferguson Robert M, painter, b 171½ E Washington.
Ferguson Samuel L, lab, h 475 E St Clair.
Ferguson Thomas M, b 138 Eureka av.
Ferguson Wm, h 103 N Beville av.
Ferguson Wm, lab, b 37 Brett.
Ferguson Wm, lab, b 80 W St Clair.
Ferguson Wm B, painter, h 28 Sinker.

Julius C. Walk & Son,
Jewelers
Indianapolis.
12 EAST WASHINGTON ST.

Ferguson Wm C, clk P C C & St L Ry, h 510 E Georgia.
Ferguson Wm N, lab, h e s Illinois 1 n of 30th (M).
Ferguson Wm O, lab, b 475 E St Clair.
Ferguson W Sinks, music teacher, 143 Dougherty, h same.
Fern Ethel (wid Frank), h 222½ E Washington.
Fern Frank, mach, h 395 N East.
Ferneding Henry F, cigarmkr, h 33 Elm.
Ferneding Herman H, cigarmkr, b 33 Elm.
Ferneding John C, mach, b 33 Elm.
Ferneding Josephine (wid Henry), b 33 Elm.
Fernkas John, barber, 195 Howard (W I), h same.
Ferns Arthur A, cashr Standard Oil Co, h s s Clifford av 2 e of Rural.
Ferracane Samuel, fruits, h 220 S East.
Ferrall Andrew, lab, b 241 Indiana av.
Ferrall Edward, solr, h 241 Indiana av.
Ferrall Joseph E, painter, h 497 W Francis (N I).
Ferrall Josephine, music teacher, 241 Indiana av, b same.
Ferrall Kate M, clk George J Marott, b 397 S Alabama.
Ferrall Mary E (wid Joseph K), r 133 E North.
Ferran Annie E, h 8 Springfield.
Ferran Frederick F, lab, b 8 Springfield.
Ferree, see also Ferry.
Ferree John C, bkkpr Holliday & Wyon, h 630 N Penn.
FERREE SHADRACH L, Physician and Surgeon, Office Hours 9-10 A M, 2-3 and 7-8 P M, 725 E Washington, h same, Tel 845.
Ferree V Morris, clk Railway Officials' and Employes' Accident Assn, h 490 N Alabama.
Ferree Wm, trav agt, h 96 Andrews.
Ferrell Alonzo, lab, b 509 W Eugene (N I).
Ferrell Charles E, mngr Schauroth & Co, b 128 W Ohio.
Ferrell David L, blksmith, b 573 W Udell (N I).
Ferrell George F, hostler, h 11 Lawn (B).
Ferrell Milton G, lab, b 509 W 22d (N I).
Ferrell Wayne, clk, h 616 W Udell (N I).
Ferrie Edward J, foreman, h 366 S Alabama.
Ferrin Chester, mach, h 446 Sheldon.
Ferringer Carrie R, dressmkr, 401 Blake, h same.
Ferris Arlen, carp, b 1552 Northwestern av (N I).
Ferris Charles H, condr, h 489 College av.
Ferris Ellsworth W, canmkr, b 558 Union.
Ferris Harry, carp, h 649 W 22d (N I).
Ferris Iradell V, lab Indiana Foundry, b 1365 W Washington (M J).
Ferris John, lab, h 9 Meikel.
Ferris John E, saloon, 90 W Washington, r Senate Hotel.
Ferris John S, clk I D & W Ry, h 301 E St Clair.
Ferris Martha (wid Hezekiah), b 124 E 25th.
Ferriter James, driver, b 56 Cook.
Ferry, see also Ferree.
Ferry Louis, stairbldr, h 49 Sinker.
Fertig Charles D, portraits, 326 Mass av, h same.
Fertig Emil (Fertig & Kevers), h 340 N Senate av.
Fertig Francis, painter, h 299 E Vermont.
Fertig Frank, h 470 N Senate av.

OTTO GAS ENGINES | BUILDERS' EXCHANGE S. W. Cor. Ohio and Penn. Telephone 535.

Becker & Son Charles Becker Jacob Becker Jr. Merchant Tailors, 21 N. Penn. St. Tel. 934

SALISBURY & STANLEY OFFICE, STORE AND BANK FIXTURES. Contractors and Builders. Repairing of all kinds done on short notice. 177 Clinton St., Indianapolis, Ind. Telephone 999.

Fertig Joseph L, hostler, h 434 Mulberry.
Fertig Louis, painter, h 168 Davidson.
FERTIG & KEVERS (Emil Fertig, Gustave W Kevers), Painters, 8 W Market, Tel 120. (See adv in classified Painters.)
Fertil Morris, lab, h 225 W Maryland.
Fesey Wm, lab, h rear 53 Church.
Feske Charles, bartndr H C Dippel, r 60 N Delaware.
Fesler Ellis C, live stock, b 74 Fletcher av.
FESLER JAMES W, Clerk Marion County, 24-29 Court House, Tel 230; h 74 Fletcher av.
Fesler John F, dep clk Marion County, h 10 Clay.
Fesler John R, clk, h 74 Fletcher av.
Fesler Oliver C, barber, b 53 Minerva.
Fesler Thomas, carp, h 31½ Virginia av.
Fesler Wm B, carp, 290 Union, h same.
Fesmire John C, lineman, b 95 N Meridian.
Fess George M, mer police, h 424 N California.
Fessler Ada B, dressmkr, b 1799 N Illinois.
Fessler Albert, cook The Denison.
Fessler David, saloon, 180 E McCarty, h same.
Fessler Frederick, carp, b 1799 N Illinois.
Fessler John, carp, h 1799 N Illinois.
Fetrow Charles S, lab, b 336 E Market.
Fetrow Edward, lab, b 234 E Louisiana.
Fetrow H Wm, lab, b 234 E Louisiana.
Fetrow John, yardman, h 72½ Yandes.
Fetrow Joseph, carp, b 336 E Market.
Fetrow Nellie A (wid Joseph), dressmkr, 234 E Louisiana, h same.
Fetsch Carl P, artist, 3 Williams, h same.
Fette Charles, tailor, b 221 S Alabama.
Fette Conrad F, tailor, 205 S Noble, h Shelby nr Belt R R.
Fette George H, clk, b 221 S Alabama.
Fette Nicholas H, miller, h 18 Wisconsin.
Fette Wilhelmina (wid George), h 221 S Alabama.
Fette Wm B, opr W U Tel Co, b 221 S Alabama.
Fetter Christian, fireman, b e s Brightwood av 7 s of Willow (B).
Fetters Charles B, bicycle rep, b 131 Cornell av.
Fetters Frank (Fetters & Smock), h 131 Cornell av.
FETTERS & SMOCK (Frank Fetters, Howard A Smock), Upholsterers and Furniture Repairers, 124 Mass av.
Fetty Arnold H, clk Holliday & Wyon, b 405 Blake.
Fetty David W, mach hd, h rear 19 Chadwick.
Fetty John C, harnessmkr, h w s Addison 1 s of Washington (M J).
Fetty Josephus, b rear 19 Chadwick.
Feucht Paul, baker, 28 King av (H), h same.
Feuchter Christian, meats, 51 E Mkt House, h 72 Oriole.
Fewell Howard, waiter, r 49 Hubbard blk.
Feyh, see also Fay.
Feyh George A, cementer, b 548 S New Jersey.
Feyh Henry, lab, h 548 S New Jersey.
Fichtner Wm, foreman Kingan & Co, h 279 S West.
Fick Delos W, polisher, h 313 E Georgia.
Fickenwirtch John, lab, h 6½ Wilcox.
Fickes Edward, billposter, h 38½ Kentucky av.

Henry H. Fay, 40½ E. WASHINGTON ST., AGENT FOR Insurance Co. of North America, Pennsylvania Fire Ins. Co.

Fickes Laura (wid Eugene B), r 38½ Kentucky av.
Fickinger David H, driver, h 203 Davidson.
Fickinger Gustav, clk, b 264 N California.
Fickinger Stephen H, lab, b 203 Davidson.
Fickinger Wm J, clk C C C & St L Ry, b 203 N Davidson.
Fickle Albert, patrolman, h 140 N East.
Fickle Elva E, lab, b 179 Meek.
Fickle Josephine, printer, b 80 Ft Wayne av.
Fickle Manington, fruit, h 80 Ft Wayne av.
Fiddler Henry, painter, h 268 Highland av.
FIDELITY BUILDING AND SAVINGS UNION, James B Patten Pres, Andrew M Sweeney Vice-Pres and Treas, Edward J Robison Sec, Jacob H Slater Actuary, Orin Z Hubbell Attorney, 81-83 W Market, Tel 1066.
FIDELITY MUTUAL LIFE INSURANCE CO OF PHILADELPHIA, A H Collins State Mngr, 52-53 Baldwin Blk. (See left top lines.)
Fidelity Saving and Loan Assn The, Charles A Webb pres, Thomas Smith vice-pres, Wm W Christy treas, A C Simms sec, 184 Indiana av.
FIDELITY AND DEPOSIT CO OF MARYLAND, George W Pangborn Genl Agt, 704-706 Lemcke Bldg, Tel 140. (See left top lines.)
Fidler Emma F (wid John H), b 119 Ramsey av.
Fidler Harry J, actor, b 342 N Missouri.
Fidler Harry L, engr, h 80 N Arsenal av.
Fieber Herbert E (Fieber & Reilly), b 273 E St Clair.
Fieber Josephine A (wid Wm), h 273 E St Clair.
FIEBER & REILLY (Herbert E Fieber, John J Reilly), Real Estate and Insurance, 84 E Market, Tel 878.
Fiedler Ida (wid Gottlieb C), h 126 Greer.
Fiel Augustus G, money delivery clk Am Ex Co, h 43 Madison av.

MAYHEW'S SPECTACLES THE BEST IN USE SOLD ONLY AT 13 N. MERIDIAN ST.

LUMBER Sash and Doors BALKE & KRAUSS CO., Corner Market and Missouri Sts.

Friedgen Has the BEST PATENT LEATHER SHOES AT LOWEST PRICES. 19 North Pennsylvania St.

SAMUEL LAING ! HOT AIR FURNACES 72 AND 74 EAST COURT STREET.

M. B. WILSON, Pres. W. F. CHURCHMAN, Cash.
The Capital National Bank,
INDIANAPOLIS, IND.
Banking business in all its branches. Bonds and Foreign Exchange bought and sold.
Interest paid on time deposits.
Checks and drafts on all Indiana and Illinois points handled at lowest rates.
No. 28 South Meridian Street, Cor. Pearl.

Fiel Charles, plumber E A Strong, b 43 Madison av.
Fiel John, carp, h 85 Wright.
Fiel Wm, clk Am Ex Co, b 43 Madison av.
Field Alfred G, clk, b 1541 N Illinois.
Field Augustus P, clk Claude Field, b 318 E St Clair.
Field Charles W, bkkpr Wm H Ballard, h 31 Hall pl.
FIELD CLAUDE, Druggist, 400 Bellefontaine, Tel 1653; h 318 E St Clair.
Field David, lab, h rear 53 Church.
Field Ella (wid John H), r 14 Church.
Field Frank W, trav agt Wyckoff, Seamans & Benedict, b 182 East Drive (W P).
Field George E, mngr Wyckoff, Seamans & Benedict, 34 E Market, h 182 East Drive (W P).
Field Greenberry, h 120 Ramsey av.
Field Henrietta (wid Lindsey), h 177 W 5th.
Field Jennie, h 53½ Russell av.
Field John W Rev, h 1261 E Washington.
Field Maria (wid George), h 293 Indiana av.
Field Martin H, phys, Broadway, h 318 E St Clair.
Field Omrie T, carp, 120 Ramsey av, h same.
Field Richard A, hotel, 35 W Georgia.
Field Sanford E, barber, 307 Mass av, h 51 Newman.
Fielder Edward G, meats, 48 E Mkt House, b Enterprise Hotel.
Fielding Roy D, city agt, h 360 Coburn.
Fields Alexander, lab, r 311½ W Pearl.
Fields Annie (wid James), h 537 Fremont (N I).
Fields Edward, lab, b 98 Maxwell.
Fields James M, shoemkr, rear 50 S West, h 35 same.
Fields John, lab, b 318 E Court.
Fields John B, foreman, b 296½ W Washington.
Fields John F, barber, 1555 N Illinois, h 230 Howard.
Fields Lemuel W, fireman, h 562 Jefferson av.
Fields Milton B, h 296½ W Washington.
Fields Oscar, lab, h 86 Kappus (W I).

Insure Against Accidents
WITH
TUTTLE & SEGUIN,
Agents for
Fidelity and Casualty Co., of New York.
$10,000 for $25. $5,000 for $12.50.
TEL. 1168. 28 E. MARKET ST.

Fields Uri, lab, h 46 Cushing.
Fien Caroline (wid Ferdinand), h rear 23 Palmer.
Fierce John J, cooper, h 20 N West.
Fierlein Baxter, trav agt, b 399 N Penn.
Fiesel August J, blksmith, h 187 Davidson.
Fiesel Charles E, boilermkr, b 187 Davidson.
Fiesel George A, clk, h 86 Benton.
Fiesel Wm H, blksmith, h 249 S Delaware.
Fiester Daniel, pdlr, h 271 N Noble.
Fife George W, bkkpr, b 461 N East.
Fife Wm, contr, 461 N East, h same.
Fifer Joseph H, paperhngr, h 453 W Wells.
Figg John T, h 134 E North.
Figg Mamie T, milliner, 42 N Illinois, h 134 E North.
Figg Maude E (wid Theodore M), b 294 N Penn.
Figg Millard F, painter, h 279 Jefferson av.
Figgs Oliver, lab, h 251 W 5th.
Fike Burley, candymkr, b 433 Dillon.
Fike Charles, lab, h 563 Shelby.
Fike George W, pdlr, b 561 Shelby.
Fike Herbert G, agt, b 89 N State.
Fike Jacob, blksmith, h 241 Virginia av.
Fike John W, farmer, h 561 Shelby.
Fike Wm W, mach, h 433 Dillon.
Filardo Gabriel, confr, 368 Mass av, h same.
Filbert Redford M, baker, h 25 Dougherty.
Filcer John H, foreman C C C & St L Ry, h 78 Cornell av.
Filer Rose, h 93 Middle Drive (W P).
Files Frank, lab, b 10 Michigan (H).
Fillion Charles C, marblecutter, b 229 W Washington.
Filz Frank, meats, 23 E Mkt House, h 67 Kansas.
Filz Frank H, pressfeeder, b 67 Kansas.
Finch Caroline (wid Samuel), h 6 Eckert.
Finch Fabius M (Finch & Finch), h 247 Park av.
Finch James, lab, b 6 Eckert.
Finch John A (Finch & Finch), h 247 Park av.
Finch Maria M (wid Heneage B), b 643 N Illinois.
FINCH & FINCH (Fabius M and John A), Lawyers, Law of Insurance a Specialty, 26, 28 and 30 Thorpe Blk, Tel 1152.
Fincker Charles D, driver, h 125 N West.
Finchum Isaiah H, paperhngr, h 26½ N Senate av.
Findlay George, boarding 165 S Alabama.
Findling Abraham, gas insp, r 169 W New York.
Findling Edward A, clk C C C & St L Ry, r 169 W New York.
Fine John B, molder, b 48 Torbet.
Fine John D, carp, h 48 Torbet.
Fine Samuel R, tmstr, b 48 Torbet.
Finegan John H, foreman, h 282 Highland av.
Finehout Curry H, plumber, b 218 Huron.
Finehout John H jr, pressman, b 218 Huron.
Finehout Lee R, detective, b 218 Huron.
Finehout Nellie L, teacher, b 218 Huron.
Fines Oliver, coachman 68 Talbott av.
Finfrock Walter W, bkkpr, Standard Oil Co, b 23 Tacoma av.
Fingerly Frank C, driver, b 1029 N Senate av.
Fingerly Henry, clk, h 7 Minkner.
Fenitzer John, saloon, 184 W 1st, h same.
Fink Frederick R, engr, h 539 S West.

WEDDING CAKE BOXES · SULLIVAN & MAHAN 41 W. Pearl St.

DIAMOND WALL PLASTER { Telephone 1410 BUILDERS' EXCHANGE.

Fink Henry, h s s Washington 3 e of Sherman Drive.
Fink Henry J, clk Hendricks & Cooper, h 51 E McCarty.
Fink John, fireman, b 673 W Washington.
Fink John H, lab, h 812 Chestnut.
Fink Margaret J (wid Wm H), b 651 Broadway.
Fink Mary K (wid John F W), h 51 E McCarty.
Fink Nicholas, storekpr The Denison.
Fink Wm H, lab, b 651 Broadway.
Finkbeiner Samuel H, huckster, h 25 Byram pl.
Finkbeiner Thomas Rev, pastor Second German Evangelical Church, b 79 Kansas.
Finkelstein Isaac, clk, b 351 S Penn.
Finkelstein Jacob, trav agt, b 351 S Penn.
Finkelstein Louis, clothing, 422 S Meridian, b same.
Finkelstein Louis, junk, h 53 Union.
Finkelstein Solomon, junk, 167 Madison av, h 351 S Penn.
Finley Alfred C, carp, h 622 N Senate av.
Finley Bartlett, lab, h 336 W North.
Finley Delia (wid James H), h 367 W Pearl.
Finley Doretha (wid Joseph), h e s Auburn av s of Bethel av.
Finley Edward, porter, b 336 W North.
Finley Ellen (wid John), h 162 Maple.
Finley Frank, dairy, e s Belmont 2 s of Johnson (W I), h same.
Finley Harriet E (wid Owen), h 45 Ellen.
Finley Ida D (wid Leighton), b 1030 N New Jersey.
Finley James D, baggageman, h 233 Hamilton av.
Finley John, lab, b 162 Maple.
Finley Maria (wid Samuel), h 174 Bismarck av (H).
Finley Morris, lab, b 162 Maple.
Finley Othello, janitor, h 399 W North.
Finley Richard (Matthews & Finley), r 28½ Indiana av.
Finley Sarah H (wid Newton N), h 374 Virginia av.
Finley Sarah J, milliner, 622 N Senate av, h same.
Finley Thomas M, lab, b 162 Maple.
Finley Timothy J, lab, b 14½ Bates.
Finley Wallace C, musician, h rear 7 Elizabeth.
Finley Wayland, lab, h e s Auburn av 5 s of Bethel av.
Finley Wm, porter, h 224 W Chesapeake.
Finley Wm R, lab, b 336 W North.
Finn Benjamin W, hostler, h 269 Dillon.
Finn Bridget (wid Wm), h 80 Maple.
Finn Chesterfield, lab, h 3 Wood.
Finn Daniel W, clk, b 92 Maple.
Finn Daniel W, grocer, 501 S Capitol av, h same.
Finn Elizabeth (wid John), h 126 Union.
Finn George W, porter, r rear 81 W North.
Finn James, milk pdlr, h 19 Holly av (W I).
Finn James F, engr, h 48 Chadwick.
Finn James P, driver, b 50 Bridge (W I).
Finn John, lab, b 27 Grant.
Finn John P, clk, b 209 Douglass.
Finn John W, clk, b 294 W Maryland.
Finn Martin, butcher, h 270 W Merrill.
Finn Mary (wid John), h 209 Douglass.
Finn Michael, saloon, 252 S West, h same.
Finn Patrick, lab, b 25 Chadwick.
Finn Philip J, roofer, h 294 W Maryland.
Finn Robert, lab, h 265 Lafayette.
Finn Thomas, lab, h 25 Chadwick.
Finn Thomas, lab, h 27 Grant.

FRANK NESSLER. WILL H. ROST.
FRANK NESSLER & CO.
Tailors
56 EAST MARKET ST. (Lemcke Building),
INDIANAPOLIS, IND.

Finn Thomas, lab, b 299 W Maryland.
Finn Thomas, lab, b 312 W Pearl.
Finn Timothy, lab, b 209 Douglass.
Finn Wm, ironwkr, b 11 E South.
Finn Wm J, clk, b 209 Douglass.
Finnegan Owen, b 166 English av.
Finnegan Wm, engr The Bates.
Finneran James, motorman, h 45 Vinton.
Finneran Kate (wid Patrick), h 23½ Chadwick.
Finneran Michael, lab, b 23½ Chadwick.
Finney, see also Phinney.
Finney Catherine (wid Mitchell), h 103 Elm.
Finney Charles E, dispatching clk P O, h 35 Elder av.
Finney David H, clk, b 61 Camp.
Finney Edwin, trav agt D P Erwin & Co, h 727 College av.
Finney Frank W, clk White Line, b 221 College av.
Finney Frederick E, printer, b 61 Camp.
Finney George E, jeweler, h 25 Harlon.
Finney Henry C, city agt, b 61 Camp.
Finney Jasper, clk, h 221 College av.
Finney John G, h 23 Nordyke av (W I).
Finney Joseph P, printer, b 61 Camp.
Finney Robert J, clk, b 35 Elder av.
Finney Wm A, bicycle rep, b 61 Camp.
Finney Wm P, mach, b 867 Bellefontaine.
Finnigan James, lab, b 473 S Capitol av.
Finnigan Luke, engr, r 195 N Delaware.
Finnigan Mary (wid John), h 473 S Capitol av.
Finnigan Michael, lab, b 473 S Capitol av.
Finucon Michael, bricklyr, b 252 E Washington.
Firebaugh Robert, carp, h n s Grandview 1 e of Merrit (H).
Firestine Jacob, lab, h 388 W Chicago (N I).
Firman Essig, lab, h 374 W 2d.
Firmin Brother, teacher, b cor Coburn and Short.
Firquin Charles E, clk, b 123 N Capitol av.
Firquin Wm, drugs, 50 N Senate av, h same.
Fisch Fredericka J H (wid John), h 462 E Georgia.
Fischer, see also Fisher.

Haueisen & Hartmann
163-169 E. Washington St.
FURNITURE,
Carpets,
Household Goods,
Tin, Granite and China Wares, Oil Cloth and Shades

Best Work. Prompt Delivery. } THE HOME LAUNDRY 197 S. ILLINOIS ST. TEL. 1769. } Collars and Cuffs a Specialty.

THE WM. H. BLOCK CO. 7 AND 9 EAST WASHINGTON STREET. DRY GOODS, HOUSE FURNISHINGS AND CROCKERY.

London Guarantee and Accident Co. (Ltd.) All forms of Liability Insurance, Workmen's Collective Insurance, Fidelity Bonds and Individual Accident Insurance.
Geo. W. Pangborn, Gen. Agent, 704-706 Lemcke Bldg. Telephone 140.

Prussian National Insurance Company OF STETTIN, GERMANY. ORGANIZED 1845. FRANK K. SAWYER, AGENT 74 East Market Street. Telephone 863.

JOSEPH GARDNER,
TIN, COPPER AND SHEET-IRON WORK AND
HOT AIR FURNACES.
37, 39 & 41 KENTUCKY AVE. Telephone 322

Fischer Adolph H, cabtmkr, h 121 Spring.
Fischer Anthony, carp, h 373 English av.
Fischer August, meats, 293 Coburn, b same.
Fischer Augusta, h 33 Kennington.
Fischer Blessing E, clk, b 17 McKim av.
Fischer Carl, lab, h w s Belmont av 1 n of Morris (W I).
Fischer Charles W, mach hd, h 455 Clifford av.
Fischer Elizabeth (wid Isaac), b 851 N Meridian.
Fischer Frank, lab, b 32 N Judge Harding (W I).
Fischer George, shoemkr, 100 Hill av, h same.
Fischer George C, lab, b 336½ E Washington.
Fischer Gustaf, carver, b 455 Clifford av.
Fischer Helena (wid Charles C), h 336½ E Washington.
Fischer Henry R, mach, h 225 Coburn.
Fischer Herman G, cabtmkr, b 100 Hill av.
Fischer John F, finisher, h 37 Kennington.
Fischer Joseph, cabtmkr, h 82 Dunlop.
Fischer Joseph, meats, 74 E Mkt House, h 293 Coburn.
Fischer Louis, carp, h 95 Weghorst.
Fischer Louisa, tailoress, b 670 S Meridian.
Fischer Mary E (wid Charles P), h 17 McKim av.
Fischer Salome (wid Adam), h 670 S Meridian.
Fischer Silas W, woodwkr, h 455 Clifford av.
Fiscus Andrew J, contr, 254 Alvord, h same.
Fiscus Elizabeth J (wid Thomas W), h 331 N Noble.
Fiscus George E, insp Central Traffic Assn, h 20 Vine.
Fiscus Georgia A (wid John R), b 1037 N Meridian.
Fiscus Harry A, clk, b 1037 N Meridian.
Fiscus Marion, h 402 E Market.
Fiscus Mary A, b 47 Andrews.
Fiscus Raymond C, clk L E & W R R, b 882 W Washington.
Fish Alta M, b 142 Hill av.
Fish Bert, r 116½ W New York.
Fish Frances, teacher Public School No. 6, b 52 English av.

J. S. FARRELL & CO.
STEAM AND HOT WATER HEATING FOR STORES, OFFICES, PUBLIC BUILDINGS, PRIVATE RESIDENCES, GREENHOUSES, ETC.
84 North Illinois St. Telephone 382.

Fish Frank O, clk Sentinel Printing Co, h 506 N New Jersey.
Fish George T, fireman, h 96 N Noble.
Fish James L, bkkpr Indiana National Bank, h 273 N New Jersey.
Fish Jesse, carp, r 116½ W New York.
Fish J Elliston, trav agt Indpls Fancy Grocery Co, h 24 Arch.
Fish Louis C, carp, n s Orange av 2 e of Ramsey av, h same.
Fish Robert, clk, b 48 W St Joseph.
Fish Walter E, packer, b 116½ W New York.
Fish Wm, carp, h 130½ Newman.
Fish Wm S, pres Sentinel Printing Co, h 36 The Blacherne.
Fishback Edward, lab, r 66 N Missouri.
Fishback Fannie S, b 869 N Delaware.
Fishback Frank S, mnfrs' agt, 32 S Meridian, h 319 Ash.
Fishback John, lab, r 182 W Market.
Fishback Mary, h 189 Patterson.
Fishback Matilda (wid Robert), h 284 Blackford.
Fishback Ora W, lab, b 200 Huron.
Fishback Robert M, acting sec Indiana Law School, h 733 N Delaware.
Fishback Samuel, cook, r 154 W North.
Fishback Sarah E (wid John), h 869 N Delaware.
Fishback Wm P (Fishback & Kappes), Master in Chancery U S Court, 631 Lemcke bldg, h 733 N Delaware.
FISHBACK & KAPPES (Wm P Fishback, Wm P Kappes), Lawyers, 631-633 Lemcke Bldg, Tel 997.
Fishbein Benjamin, trav agt, h 300 Blackford.
Fishbein Henry, b 143 Maple.
Fishel Charles S, sec Indpls Fancy Grocery Co, b 1232 N Penn.
Fisher, see also Fischer.
Fisher Absalom M, b 289 N New Jersey.
Fisher Ada E (wid Benjamin G), b 368 N New Jersey.
Fisher Albert, ballplayer, b 12 Henry.
Fisher Amos W, phys, 35 W Ohio, h 277 W Michigan.
Fisher Anthony, lab, b 33 Standard av (W I).
Fisher Arthur, mason, b 174 E Pearl.
Fisher Bern, porter, b 166 W 1st.
Fisher Bertha B, teacher Public School No 13, b 75 Central av.
Fisher Bettie (wid Isaac), b 851 N Meridian.
Fisher Carl G (C G Fisher & Co), h 48 W St Joseph.
Fisher Catherine (wid John), b 181 Meek.
Fisher Charles, flour, 306 Virginia av, h 133 Woodlawn av.
Fisher Charles, lab, r 264 Bates.
Fisher Charles, basketmkr, b 22 Bates.
Fisher Clyde G, clk, h 77 Martindale av.
FISHER C G & CO (Carl G Fisher), Bicycles, Wholesale and Retail, Agts for Stearns, Smalley and Grande Wheels, 64 N Penn, Tel 815.
Fisher Daniel (Fisher & Myers), h 71 W Michigan.
Fisher David J, packer, h 187 Keystone av.
Fisher David M, foreman, h 142 Newman.
Fisher David N, lab, h 78 Columbia av.
Fisher Edward, lab, h 137 Broadway.
Fisher Edward, lab, h rear 163 St Mary.
Fisher Elizabeth (wid Franklin), h 237 Buchanan.
Fisher Erastus, switchman, h 326 S East.

United States Life Insurance Co., of New York.
E. B. SWIFT. M'g'r. 25 E. Market St.

WM. KOTTEMAN 89 & 91 E. Washington St. Telephone 1742 RUGS MATTINGS WINDOW SHADES

WILLIAM WIEGEL MANUFACTURER OF SHOW CASES 6 W. Louisiana St. Opposite Union Station.

Fisher Estelle H, teacher Public School No 4, b 75 Central av.
Fisher Ezra M, bkkpr, b 368 N New Jersey.
Fisher Florence, stenog, h 478 N California.
Fisher George C, propr Fisher's Pharmacy, 402 College av, h 392 Broadway.
Fisher George P, grocer, 453 Central av, h 69 Ruckle.
Fisher George W, brakeman, r 4 Walcott.
Fisher Grant, lab, b 161 Alvord.
Fisher Harry C, clk L E & W R R, b 75 Central av.
Fisher Harry H, engr, h 98 Elm.
Fisher Harvey, carp, h 34 Hester.
Fisher Hattie, proofreader, b 237 Buchanan.
Fisher Henry, clk Indpls Dist Tel Co, h 478 N California.
Fisher Henry, driver, h 123 E Ohio.
Fisher Henry, lab, h 118 Dougherty.
Fisher Henry, lab, h 13 N Spruce.
Fisher Henry C, car insp, h 23 Decatur.
Fisher Henry H, engr, h 98 Elm.
Fisher Ida, b 48 W St Joseph.
Fisher Ira, lab, b 78 Columbia av.
Fisher Jacob P, molder, h 542 Broadway.
Fisher James E, carp, b 969 Grove av.
Fisher James H, lab, b 1059 W Vermont.
Fisher James W, grocer, 59 Beacon, h 276 Springfield.
Fisher Jennie, nurse, r 133 N Penn.
Fisher John, barber, 412 Virginia av, h 168 Fletcher av.
Fisher John, lab, b 194 W 2d.
Fisher John, hostler, b 237 W 3d.
Fisher John R, fireman, h 262 Springfield.
Fisher John W, engr, h 276 Springfield.
Fisher Joseph, blksmith, h 12 Henry.
Fisher Julia (wid David), h 105 Bismarck av (H).
Fisher Julia E, b 1162 N Penn.
Fisher Kendrick, shoemkr, h 540 W Udell (N I).
Fisher Levi, lab, r 4 Susquehanna.
Fisher Lee Rev, pastor Brightwood Baptist Church, h 20 S Stuart (B).
Fisher Louis, porter, r 193½ S Illinois.
Fisher Louisa W (wid Samuel), h 75 Central av.
Fisher Martha J (wid Joseph L), b 368 N New Jersey.
Fisher Martin, lab, h 234 Muskingum al.
Fisher Mary, h 160 W Maryland.
Fisher Mattie, h 230 W Vermont.
Fisher Mont R, painter, r 178½ E Washington.
Fisher Moses P, paper, 131 S Meridian, b 851 N Meridian.
Fisher Nancy (wid Charles), h 572 Broadway.
Fisher Noah, lab, h 60 Rhode Island.
Fisher Omer, attendant Insane Hospital.
Fisher Omer L, switchman, b 326 S East.
Fisher Oren D Rev, pastor People's Congregational Church, h 242 N West.
Fisher Osa (wid Henry J), b 300 W New York.
Fisher Otto, bricklyr, b 174 E Pearl.
Fisher Peter, lab, b 60 Rhode Island.

FISHER'S PHARMACY, George C Fisher Propr, 402 College av, cor 7th, Tel 1857.

Fisher Philip, blksmith, h 174 E Pearl.
Fisher Philip, lab, b s s Finley av 2 e of Shelby.
Fisher Robert D, reporter, h 916 N New Jersey.
Fisher Roland M, tmstr, b 133 Woodlawn av.

THOS. C. DAY & CO.
Financial Agents and Loans.
We have the experience, and claim to be reliable.
Rooms 325 to 330 Lemcke Bldg.

Fisher Russell H, piano tuner, h 564 W Eugene (N I).
Fisher Samuel, lab, b 67 S Noble.
Fisher Samuel A, trav agt Indpls Drug Co, h 238 Ash.
Fisher Thomas, lab, b 29 Downey.
Fisher Thomas G M, associate editor The Sun, h 54 West Drive (W P).
Fisher Toliver, lab, h 434 W Addison (N I).
Fisher Wm, lab, h 283½ S Capitol av.
Fisher Wm, trav agt, h 45 Hall pl.
Fisher Wm H, lab, h e s Sangster av 3 n of Belle.
Fisher Wm W, trav agt, b 75 Central av.
Fisher & Myers (Daniel Fisher, Wm C Myers), builders, 71 W Michigan.

FISHINGER CHARLES, Propr Reichwein's Hall, 349 E Market, h same.

Fishinger Kate (wid Wm G), h 52 Michigan av.
Fishinger W Edward, plumber, b 52 Michigan av.
Fisk Americus, h 100 Sycamore.
Fisk Edward L, lab, h 125 Harlan.
Fisk Ella Sosler, b 504 Central av.
Fisk Henry C (H C Fisk & Son), h 374 Talbott av.

FISK H C & SON (Henry C and Wm E), Carriage Repository, 12-14 Monument Pl, Tel 1018.

FISK J GUARD, Physician, Office Hours 8-11 A M, 1-5 and 7-10 P M (at Office All Night), cor 19th and Bellefontaine, Tel 1863; h 374 Talbott av.

Fisk Wallace M, millwright, h 100 Auburn av.
Fisk Wm E (H C Fisk & Son), h 1485 Northwestern av.
Fisk Wm H, b 293 Mass av.
Fisk Wm H, cashr, h 234 S Linden.
Fiske Charles H, real est, h 201 Lincoln av.
Fiske Helen, bkkpr George J Marott, b 178 E North.
Fislar George W, tel opr, b 659 E Market.
Fislar Napoleon B, mach, h 659 E Market.
Fisse John H (Bischoff & Fisse), h w s Rural 2 n of Bloyd av.

EAT
QUAKER BREAD
ASK YOUR GROCER FOR IT.
THE HITZ BAKING CO.

CARPETS AND RUGS RENOVATED.......... | CAPITAL STEAM CARPET CLEANING WORKS M. D. PLUNKETT, TELEPHONE No. 818

BENJ. BOOTH PRACTICAL EXPERT ACCOUNTANT. Complicated or disputed accounts investigated and adjusted. Room 18, 82½ E. Wash. St., Ind'p'l's, Ind.

18 and 20 South Meridian Street KERSHNER BROS., Proprs. THE SHERMAN RESTAURANT

ESTABLISHED 1876. TELEPHONE 168.
CHESTER BRADFORD,
SOLICITOR OF PATENTS,
AND COUNSEL IN PATENT CAUSES.
(See adv. page 6.)
Office:—Rooms 14 and 16 Hubbard Block, S.W. Cor. Washington and Meridian Streets, INDIANAPOLIS, INDIANA.

Fisse John H (Demaree & Fisse), r 41 Virginia av.
Fister Lovina (wid Jacob), b 321 W Market.
Fitch Asa M (A M Fitch & Co), h 439 N New Jersey.
Fitch A M & Co (Asa M Fitch), chewing gum mnfrs, 79 Ft Wayne av.
Fitch Barry W, sec Am Tribune Soldier Colony Co, h 221 E New York.
Fitch Charles, lab, r 204 W South.
Fitch David B, lab, h 1245 Schurman av (N I).
Fitch Frank M, clk, b 439 N New Jersey.
Fitch Harry M, clk The A Burdsal Co, h 614 W 22d (N I).
Fitch James M, collr, h w s Sheffield av 4 n of Clarke (H).
Fitch Luke, lab, h 1245 Schurman av (N I).
Fitch Marion, trav agt, h 28 Becker (M J).
FITCH MARY J MRS, Modiste, 2, 19½ N Meridian, h 383 Park av.
Fitch Samuel M, tmstr, b w s Sheffield av 4 n of Clarke (H).
Fitch Walter H, civil engr, h 1058 N Senate av.
Fitch Wm H, locksmith, 35 Indiana av, h 383 Park av.
Fitchet Jacob, cooper, h 94 Geisendorff.
Fitchey Charles E, carp, h 176 W 8th.
Fitchie Michael G, architect, h 868 N Senate av.
Fitchie Otis F, clk, b 868 N Senate av.
Fithian Gurdon H, b 1108 N Meridian.
Fithian Wm H, h 1108 N Meridian.
Fitzer John, shoemkr, h 276½ Coburn.
Fitzgerald Anna, h 169 Dougherty.
Fitzgerald Anna (wid Michael), grocer, 182 Meek, h same.
Fitzgerald Bartholomew, lab, b 165 W McCarty.
Fitzgerald Bert G, student, b 415 N Meridian.
Fitzgerald Catherine E (wid Edward D), h 816½ E Washington.
Fitzgerald Christopher C, asst engr m of w P & E Ry, r 348 N New Jersey.
Fitzgerald Cornelius, condr, h 204 Bellefontaine.

Matal Ceilings and all kinds of Copper, Tin and Sheet Iron work,
O. B. ENSEY,
TELEPHONE 1562.
CORNER 6TH AND ILLINOIS STS.

Fitzgerald Edward J, engr, b 816½ E Washington.
Fitzgerald Edward M, stonecutter, h 272 E Merrill.
Fitzgerald Edward P (P J Ryan & Co), h 650 N Capitol av.
Fitzgerald Ella M, clk T P Kean, b 816½ E Washington.
Fitzgerald Eva M, first asst State Librarian, r 430 The Shiel.
Fitzgerald Frank N (Fitzgerald & Ruckelshaus and Fitzgerald & Delp), h 1006 N Alabama.
Fitzgerald Helen (wid John), b 404 Highland av.
Fitzgerald James, lab, b 165 W McCarty.
Fitzgerald Johanna (wid James), b 34 Eastern av.
Fitzgerald John, lab, r 355 S Capitol av.
Fitzgerald John, lab, b 40 S West.
Fitzgerald John, lab, b 230 W Maryland.
Fitzgerald John, lab, b 333 W Maryland.
Fitzgerald Joseph, chairmkr, h 210 Blackford.
Fitzgerald Joseph E, lab, h 4 Douglass.
Fitzgerald Marcus, lab, h 44 Deloss.
Fitzgerald Margaret L (wid Wm), h 165 W McCarty.
Fitzgerald Michael N, mach, b 272 E Merrill.
Fitzgerald Patrick, lab, b 165 W McCarty.
Fitzgerald Patrick, porter 151 W Washington.
Fitzgerald Patrick J, lab, h 69 Fayette.
Fitzgerald Philander H, pres American Tribune Soldier Colony Co, pub and propr American Tribune and treas Indiana Mut Bldg and Loan Assn, h 415 N Meridian.
Fitzgerald Thomas F, boilermkr, b 816½ E Washington.
Fitzgerald Thomas J, molder, r 64½ N Illinois.
Fitzgerald Timothy, mach hd, h 38 Ludlow av.
Fitzgerald Walter J, tel opr C C C & St L Ry, h 157 E Ohio.
Fitzgerald Wm, lab, b 165 W McCarty.
Fitzgerald Wm L, boilermkr, b 816½ E Washington.
FITZGERALD & DELP (Frank N Fitzgerald, Otto Delp), Pension Attorneys, 47 Journal Bldg. (See adv in classified Pension Agts and Attorneys.)
Fitzgerald & Ruckelshaus (Frank N Fitzgerald, John C Ruckelshaus), lawyers, 73 Lombard bldg.
Fitzgibbon David, pres Blue Flame Oil Burner Co, h 296 E New York.
Fitzgibbon Edward, car rep, h 259 Howard (W I).
Fitzgibbon John, lab, h 230 W Maryland.
Fitzgibbon Wm M, clk H P Wasson & Co, b 296 E New York.
Fitzgibbons David, b 97 William (W I).
Fitzgibbons John, lab, b 194 Bates.
Fitzgibbons Thomas, driver, h 19 Birch av (W I).
Fitzgibbons Wm, lab, b 97 William (W I).
Fitzhugh Wm, lab, h rear n s Ohio 7 e of Rural.
Fitzjearl Harry, b 152 N Illinois.
Fitzjearl Helen T (wid James J), h 152 N Illinois.
Fitzpatrick Arthur, r 247 N Capitol av.
Fitzpatrick Emmet A, pressman, b 126 Talbott av.
Fitzpatrick Hugh L, shoemkr, 411 Indiana av, h same.

TUTEWILER UNDERTAKER, No. 72 WEST MARKET STREET. TELEPHONE 216.

The Provident Life and Trust Co. Dividends are paid in cash and are not withheld for a long period of years, subject to forfeiture in the event of death or the termination of policy.
D. W. EDWARDS, GENERAL AGENT, 508 INDIANA TRUST BUILDING.

THEODORE F. SMITHER • ROOFER
Competent and Responsible
Telephone 861. 151 W Maryland St

Fitzpatrick James, carp, h 619 W Vermont.
Fitzpatrick James P, clk Kingan & Co, b 619 W Vermont.
Fitzpatrick John, mach, b 619 W Vermont.
Fitzpatrick Joseph, clk Indpls Mnfrs' and Carps' Union, h 126 Talbott av.
Fitzpatrick Wm M, h 88 Indiana av.
Fitzsimmons Elmer E, driver, b 363 S Capitol av.
Fitzsimmons Frank, lab, b 363 S Capitol av.
Fitzsimmons James, lab, b 363 S Capitol av.
Fitzsimmons Robert, lab, b 363 S Capitol av.
Fitzsimmons Sarah A (wid Wm), h 363 S Capitol av.
Fivecoat Joseph, carp, b 233 Fletcher av.
Fivecoat Samuel F, condr, b 233 Fletcher av.
Fivecoats Archibald, lab, b e s Rembrant 1 n of Humboldt av (M P).
Fivecoats Sarah E (wid Michael), h e s Rembrant 1 n of Humboldt av (M P).
Flack, see also Fleck and Flick.
Flack Joseph F, propr Indpls Creamery, 52 Mass av, h 1140 W Washington (H).
Flackhammer Charles W, meats, 33 E Mkt House, h 36 Gatling.
Flager Edward, electrician, b 54 Poplar (B).
Flagg Wm E, mach, b 81 Springfield.
Flaherty Anna C, stenog Am Tin Plate Co, b 436 S New Jersey.
Flaherty Anna M (wid Thomas), b 483 S West.
Flaherty Edward, h 10 Oxford.
Flaherty Edward, lab, b 298 S Capitol av.
Flaherty Ella, laundress, b 30 Stevens.
Flaherty John, barn boss, h 267 W Ray.
Flaherty John, lab, b 284 W Maryland.
Flaherty John F, temperer, b 34 Grant.
Flaherty John O, lab, h 75 W 1st.
Flaherty Joseph, lab, h 34 Grant.
Flaherty Kate (wid Frederick), b 340 S West.
Flaherty Michael, contr, 120 W Ray, h same.
Flaherty Michael, lab, b 32 Helen.
Flaherty Michael O, grocer, 349 Fletcher av, h same.
Flaherty Thomas, trav agt, b 186 S Olive.
Flaherty Thomas F, clk, h 436 S New Jersey.
Flaherty Wm, lab, h 32 Helen.
Flaherty Wm, lab, h 20 Mulberry.
Flaherty Wm, lab, b 472 S Missouri.
Flaig Edmund H, carp, b 346 Fletcher av.
Flaig Jacob, lab, h 8 Belmont av (H).
Flaig Matthew V, mach hd, h 346 Fletcher av.
Flake Albert, blksmith, b 4 Morgan (W I).
Flake Gideon D, blksmith, h 4 Morgan (W I).
Flanagan James, sawmkr, h 116 Chadwick.
Flanagan John, tinner, h 140 Dougherty.
Flanagan Patrick, lab, h 108 Bates.
Flanagan Peter J, sawmkr, h 116 Chadwick.
Flanagan Thomas, watchman, h 326 Bates.
Flanagan Thomas J, lab, b 108 Bates.
Flanagan Wm, janitor, h rear 410 S Delaware.
Flanagen Daniel R, brakeman, h 1058 W Vermont.
Flanary Rose A (wid Dennis), h 95 Chadwick.
Flanary Thomas, mach, b 902 W Washington.
Flanedy David J, collr P F Collier, r 159 E Ohio.
Flanedy Patrick J, mngr P F Collier, 93 N Delaware, h 555 Ash.

THE WHEN IS A WORLD BEATER.

Flanigan Albert, mach hd, b 90 S Wheeler (B).
Flanigan Catherine, b 54 Columbia av.
Flanigan Thomas F, molder, b 230 W Maryland.
Flanigan Wm, lab, b 90 S Wheeler (B).
Flanner Frank B, stenog W J Holliday & Co, b 1009 N Penn.
Flanner Frank W (Flanner & Buchanan), h 1009 N Penn.
Flanner Orpha A (wid Henry), b 952 N Delaware.
FLANNER & BUCHANAN (Frank W Flanner, Charles J Buchanan), Funeral Directors, 172 N Illinois, Tel 641.
Flannery John, b 48 Miley av.
Flannery Mary E, dressmkr, 104½ Broadway, h same.
Flannery Philip H, lab, b 420 S East.
Flannery Thomas A, filer, h 104½ Broadway.
Flannery Thomas E, mach, b 420 S East.
Flannery Wm H, mach, h 133 S East.
FLASKAMP FRED, Grocer and Meat Market, 126 Hillside av, cor 8th, h 744 E 8th.
Flaskamp Henry G, clk, b 744 E 8th.
Flaskamp John, boilermkr, h 138 Newman.
Flaskey Wm, lab, b 324 W Maryland.
Flathers James B, carp, h e s Central av 2 n of 30th.
Flatley Margaret T, b 97 Camp.
Flatley Marie, b 3 Carlos.
Fleck, see also Flack and Flick.
Fleck Elizabeth M (wid George), h 159 Eureka av.
Fleck Frederick W, harnessmkr, h 23 N West.
Fleck Jacob T, condr, h 24 King.
Fleck John, b 116 Trowbridge (W).
Fleck John B (Indiana Electrotype Co), b 324 N Noble.
Fleck Joseph E (Indiana Electrotype Co), h 513 S Capitol av.
Fleck Michael A (Indiana Electrotype Co), h 513 S Capitol av.
Fleck Rosa A, dressmkr, 24 King, h same.

The A. Burdsal Co.
Manufacturers of
STEAMBOAT COLORS
BEST HOUSE PAINTS MADE.
Wholesale and Retail.
34 AND 36 SOUTH MERIDIAN STREET.

Electric Contractors | We are prepared to do any kind of Electric Contract Work.
C. W. MEIKEL. Telephone 466.
96-98 E. New York St.

DALTON & MERRIFIELD { LUMBER South Noble St., near E. Washington

INDIANA ELECTROTYPE CO. ••• BEST WORK. LOWEST PRICES.
23 WEST PEARL ST., INDIANAPOLIS, IND. JOB WORK. BOOK PLATES. All Orders Promptly Filled. BEST PATENT BASE ON THE MARKET.

KIRKHOFF BROS.,
Sanitary Plumbers
STEAM AND HOT WATER HEATING.
102-104 SOUTH PENNSYLVANIA ST.
TELEPHONE 910.

Fleckenstein John, driver, h 447 E Ohio.
Fleece James, lab, h 217 W 2d.
Fleece Silas F, genl agt D M Osborne & Co, h 90 Highland pl.
Fleehart James E (Baker & Fleehart), h 77 Oak.
FLEENER DANIEL F, Genl Agt United States Casualty Co of New York, 427-428 Lemcke Bldg, h 1034 N Meridian.
Fleischmann John L, shoes, 151 Prospect, h 36 S Spruce.
Fleischmann & Co, Robert H Bryson mngr, yeast, 213 S Illinois.
Fleitz Charles J, blksmith, h 487 S Meridian.
Fleitz Eugene S, blksmith, h 87 Keystone av.
Fleitz John C, lab, b 487 S Meridian.
Fleming Agnes, bkkpr, b 408 Union.
Fleming Andrew, fireman, b 772 E Washington.
Fleming Andrew, trav agt, h 522 Virginia av.
Fleming Arthur, h 341 E South.
Fleming Charles (Fryer & Fleming), h 882 N Senate av.
Fleming David, b 522 Virginia av.
Fleming Edward, waiter, b 287 N California.
Fleming Erin, bkkpr, b 408 Union.
Fleming Frank, driver, b 24 Keith.
Fleming George C, cook, b 223 River av (W I).
Fleming George H, h 51 The Plaza.
Fleming Harry M, glazier, b 882 N Senate av.
Fleming Henry E, packer, b 882 N Senate av.
Fleming Herman J, clk, b 24 Keith.
Fleming James, h 24 Keith.
Fleming James, clk, h 882 N Senate av.
Fleming James, insp, h 240 N California.
Fleming James A, engr, h 55 Mayhew.
Fleming James C, clk, b 882 N Senate av.
Fleming James D, lab, b 55 Mayhew.
Fleming John, kilnman, h 3 Sumner.
Fleming John C, carp, h 507 Broadway.
Fleming John S, h e s Sutherland av 1 n of 20th.

Lime, Lath, Cement,
THE W. G. WASSON CO.
130 INDIANA AVE. TEL. 989.
Sewer Pipe, Flue Linings, Fire Brick, Fire Clay.

Fleming Lettie, cashr State House Bldg Assns, b 341 E South.
Fleming Lincoln, switchman, h 21 Decatur.
Fleming Mary C (wid John), h 408 Union.
Fleming Neal, ship clk The Wm H Block Co, b 174 N Illinois.
Fleming Peter, h 772 E Washington.
Fleming Robert J, stonecutter, b 223 River av (W I).
Fleming Sarah A (wid George C), h 223 River av (W I).
Fleming Sophia (wid Henry), h 287 N California.
Fleming Taylor, mach, b 341 E South.
Fleming Thomas, h 178 N Senate av.
Fleming Thomas D, trav agt, h 20 Ruckle.
FLEMING THOMAS W, Merchant Tailor, 68 Indiana av, b 178 N Senate av.
Fleming Walter, elev opr, b 287 N California.
Fleming Warren D, h 226 N Delaware.
Fleming Wm A, lab, h 427 W Pratt.
Flemming Olive, forewoman, b 46 N Senate av.
Flesher Sarah J (wid Peter), r 21 Columbia blk.
Flesher Theodore G, motorman, h 5 Allfree av.
Fleshman Douglas W, mach, r 9 S Gale (B).
Fletcher Allen M (S A Fletcher & Co), h 250 N Meridian, tel 211.
Fletcher Anna (wid George), b 859 N Illinois.
Fletcher Anna E, dressmkr, 46 Hill av, h same.
Fletcher Calvin, farmer, h 423 Home av.
Fletcher Calvin F, mach, h 41 Carlos.
FLETCHER CALVIN I, Physician and Surgeon, Office Hours 9-10 A M, 2-4 and 7-8 P M, Sundays 9-10 A M, 369 S Meridian, Tel 907; h 585 N Penn, Tel 427.
Fletcher Charles, cutter, b 236 S Missouri.
Fletcher Charles B, capitalist, h 280 Clifford av.
FLETCHER CHARLES B & JESSE, Trustees, 252 Clifford av, Tel 717.
Fletcher Charles W, lab, b 665 Madison av.
Fletcher Claude D, mach, b 65 Hadley av (W I).
Fletcher David J, carp, h 228 Yandes.
Fletcher David M, h 260 Christian av.
Fletcher Edward C, sec Indpls Chain and Stamping Co, h 356 N East.
Fletcher Elmer E, clk, b 859 N Illinois.
Fletcher Frank, painter, b 76 Chapel.
Fletcher Gertrude E, stenog, b 46 Hill av.
Fletcher Grace, h 171½ W Washington.
Fletcher Harry R V, clk, b 65 Hadley av (W I).
Fletcher Henry D, cashr Frank Bird Transfer Co, b 410 N Penn.
Fletcher Henry F, bkkpr Indpls Chain and Stamping Co, h 356 N East.
Fletcher Homer E, clk, h 300 Columbia av.
FLETCHER HORACE H, Genl Contractor, 7 Lorraine Bldg, h 35 The Blacherne.
Fletcher James M, lab, h 168 Sheffield av (H).
Fletcher James O, bartndr, h 46 Harrison.
Fletcher Jesse, capitalist, res Millersville, Ind.

YOUR HOMES FURNISHED BY W. H. MESSENGER 101 East Washington St. Telephone 491.

McNamara, Koster & Co. Phone 1593. 212-218 S. PENN. ST. PATTERN MAKERS

THE FRED DIETZ CO. WOODEN PACKING BOXES MADE TO ORDER. FACTORY AND WAREHOUSE TRUCKS. 400 Madison Avenue. Telephone 654.

Fletcher John B, mach, h 65 Hadley av (W I).
Fletcher John W, boilermkr, h 42 Johnson av.
Fletcher Joseph H, distributer Vansyckle Advertising Co, b 41 Carlos.
Fletcher Lafayette W (Coffin, Fletcher & Co), h 344 N Capitol av.
Fletcher Lucinda (wid Richard), h 428 Fulton.
Fletcher Mabel C, opr Cent U Tel Co, b 260 Christian av.
Fletcher Margaret A (wid James), h 59 Superior.
Fletcher Marie Louise (wid Stoughton A), h 15 The Blacherne.
Fletcher Mary B (wid James L), b 178 Broadway.
Fletcher Mary F (wid Wm M), h 31 Elder av.
Fletcher Mary M, attendant Public Library, b 437 N Capitol av.
Fletcher Nora (wid John B), h rear 650 Virginia av.
Fletcher Robert N, r 437 N Capitol av.
FLETCHER SAFE DEPOSIT CO, Stoughton J and Allen M Fletcher Proprs, John S Tarkington Mngr, 30-34 E Washington, Tel 4.
Fletcher Samuel H (Coffin, Fletcher & Co), b 344 N Capitol av.
FLETCHER STEPHEN K (Successor to Fletcher & Thomas), Brick Machinery and Brickmakers' Supplies, 45 Ingalls Blk, h 437 N Capitol av.
Fletcher Stoughton J (S A Fletcher & Co), h 180 E Ohio, tel 205.
FLETCHER S A & CO (Stoughton J and Allen M Fletcher), Bankers, 30-34 E Washington, Tel 4.
Fletcher Warren, lab, b 65 Hadley av (W I).
FLETCHER WM B, Physician, Sanatorium 124 N Alabama, Tel 381; h 130 same.
Fletcher Wm H, trav agt, b 31 Elder av
Fletcher Wm T, insp, h 955 N Alabama.
Fleury Charlotte, bkkpr Krull & Schmidt, b 457 N Alabama.
Fleury Louis A, tailor, h 457 N Alabama.
Flick Gottlieb, carver, h 145 Greer.
Flick Jacob, meats, 846 W Washington, h same.
Flickinger Elmer E (Williams & Flickinger), h 1111 N Penn.
Flickinger Frederick W, baker, 32 Singleton, h same.
Flickinger Wendel, grocer, cor Sugar Grove and Miller avs (M P), h same.
Fliegeltaub Agnes (wid Isaac), b 129 Eddy.
Fliegenschmidt Carl, lab, h 158 Laurel.
Fligel Michael, reedwkr, b 47 Iowa.
Fling Mary (wid John), boarding 34 S West.
Flinn, see also Flynn.
Flinn John L, mach opr The Indpls Sentinel, h 15 Sinker.
Flinn Margaret A (wid John N), h 106 Meek.
Flinn Mary (wid John), b 34 S West.
Flint George, lab, r 119 Ft Wayne av.
Flisk Martin, lab, b 286 W Maryland.
Flisk Patrick, lab, b 40 S West.
Floder Mary A (wid Bernard), r 137½ Mass av.
Floerke Frederick W, lab, h 450 Mulberry.
Flood Sylvester, lab, b 32 Davis.

Henry H. Fay, 40½ E. WASHINGTON ST., FIRE INSURANCE, REAL ESTATE, LOANS AND RENTAL AGENT.

Flora George W, lab, b s s Jones 1 e of Schurman av (N I).
Flora Irvin M, clk, h 550 E 8th.
Flora James D, lab, h s s Jones 1 e of Schurman av (N I).
Flora Jasper E, lab, b 42 Smith.
Flora John, cigar mnfr, 35 Tecumseh, h same.
Flora Joseph M, janitor Public School No 37, h n e cor Baltimore av and 17th.
Flora Theodore, switchman, h 275 S Missouri.
Flora Wm M, lab, b n e cor Baltimore av and 17th.
Florea Joshua E (Florea & Seidensticker), h 735 College av.
FLOREA & SEIDENSTICKER (Joshua E Florea, George and Adolph Seidensticker), Lawyers, 27½ S Delaware, Tel 1772.
Florence Henry, waiter, r 398 Blackford.
Florence Margaret (wid Richard), h 398 Blackford.
Florinmond Brother, teacher, b 74 W Georgia.
Floros Peter, confr, 45 W Washington, r 17 Kentucky av.
Florsheim Milton S, shoes, 50 E Washington, res Chicago, Ill.
Flory Emanuel, tinner, h 535 W Washington.
Flory Lawrence, pdlr, h 535 W Washington.
Florye Margaret, h 32 Cushing.
Flowers Andrew, lab, b 33 Garden.
Flowers Benjamin, lab, b 33 Garden.
Flowers Jennie, h 60 S Noble.
Flowers Joel, belter, h 181½ S Meridian.
Flowers John W, mach, h 60 S Noble.
Flowers Samuel G W, harnessmkr, h 33 Garden.
Flowers Sanford, lab, h 148 Eddy.
Flowers Thomas J, carp, 333 Bates, h same.
Floyd Benjamin F, porter, h 40 Center.
Floyd Charles, foreman, h 189 Virginia av.
Floyd Charles H, city fireman, h 478 Blake.
Floyd Clarinda H (wid Mahlon H), h 496 Ash.

SURETY BONDS
American Bonding & Trust Co. OF BALTIMORE, MD.
Authorized to act as Sole Surety on all Bonds. Total Resources over $1,000,000.00.
W. E. BARTON & CO., General Agents, 504 INDIANA TRUST BUILDING. Long Distance Telephone 1918.

Business World Supplied with Help GRADUATES ASSISTED TO POSITIONS 10,000 NOW IN GOOD SITUATIONS. TEL. 499. E. J. HEEB, PRES. Indianapolis BUSINESS UNIVERSITY

Water and Oil Meters { HENRY R. WORTHINGTON, 64 S. PENNSYLVANIA ST. Long Distance Telephone 284.

UNION CO-OPERATIVE LAUNDRY { NOS. 8, 40 AND 42 VIRGINIA AVENUE. (COMPOSED OF UNION LAUNDRY GIRLS.) T. E. SOMERVILLE, MANAGER TELEPHONE 8. INDIANAPOLIS, IND.

HORACE M. HADLEY

Insurance, Real Estate, Loan and Rental Agent

66 EAST MARKET STREET,

Telephone 1540. Basement.

Floyd Frank E, salesman The Bowen-Merrill Co, h 496 Ash.
Floyd James L, clk McCormick H M Co, h 496 Ash.
Floyd Sarah, h 506 S Illinois.
Floyd Thomas J, porter, h 420 W Pratt.
Floyd Wm T, barber, 20 Indiana av, h 166 W 1st.
Flum Joseph, molder, h 60 Beacon.
Flum Julius, lab, h 34 Sanders.
Flynn, see also Flinn.
Flynn Annie, dressmkr, 338 N Noble, h same.
Flynn Bartholomew, molder, b 413 Union.
Flynn Charles L, molder, h 253 Union.
Flynn David, stoker, h 413 Union.
Flynn James, clk, b 80 S West.
Flynn John R, molder, b 413 Union.
Flynn John W, motorman, h 28 Edward (W I).
Flynn Joseph, lab, b 413 Union.
Flynn Margaret (wid Thomas), b 338 N Noble.
Flynn Marie A, stenog Nat Electric Headlight Co, b 345 N Alabama.
Flynn Michael, lab, h 45 Helen.
Flynn Thomas, driver, b St Vincent's Hospital.
Flynn Warren, student, r 181 N Delaware.
Flynn Wm, lab, h 209 Kentucky av.
Flynn Wm, mach, b 413 Union.
Flynn Wm, saloon, 114 W Ray, h same.
Flynn Wm O, tailor, r 11½ W Washington.
Fodrea Alfred H, hostler, h 121 E New York.
Fodrea Benjamin D, shoemkr, h 17 Greer.
Fodrea Emeline, boarding 121 E New York.
Foerster Adolph E, cigar mnfr, 759 S East, h same.
Foerster Charles, clk, h 363 W Michigan.
Foerster Herman, clk, b 363 W Michigan.
Foerster Wm, harnessmkr, b 759 S East.
Fogleman Albert P, lab, b 42 N William (W I).
Fogleman Arley W, lab, b 42 N William (W I).
Fogleman Charles A, fireman, h 39 N Beville av.
Fogleman James, filer, b 42 N William (W I).

Special Detailed Reports Promptly Furnished by Us.

MERCHANTS' AND MANUFACTURERS' EXCHANGE

J. E. TAKKEN, Manager,

19 Union Building, 73 West Maryland Street.

Fogleman Lawrence, carp, h 111 Patterson.
Fogleman Wm M, tmstr, h 42 N William (W I).
Foglesong Anna, clk, b 63 Lynn av (W I).
Foglesong George W, lab, b 63 Lynn av (W I).
Foglesong Sylvester, carp, h 63 Lynn av (W I).

FOHL BERNIE A, Florist, n w cor Senate av and 30th (M), h same.

Fohl John R, florist, 1149 N New Jersey, h same.
Foland Milton C, mach, h 73 Cushing.
Foland Valentine, mach, b 237 E South.
Folander Adolph V, millwright, b 810 Ash.
Folbath Charles, florist, b n e cor Senate av and 26th.
Folckemer Leonidas, clk, h 60 Brookside av.
Folckemer Lucy, dressmkr, 60 Brookside av, h same.
Foley Alice, h 25½ Mass av.
Foley Amanda, h 203 W 4th.
Foley Bridget (wid James), b 1329 N Delaware.
Foley Bros & Co (John C, Thomas W and Peter J Foley), plumbers, 84 Mass av.
Foley Daniel, contr, 52 English av, h same.
Foley Daniel, wiper, b 87 Leota.
Foley Dennis E, engr, h 87 Quincy.
Foley Emeline (wid Hugh), b 104 Walcott.
Foley James, brakeman, r 60 S Summitt.
Foley James J, h 111 Chadwick.
Foley James M, bkkpr, b 52 Lord.
Foley James W, clk P Gramling & Son, b 500 N Delaware.
Foley Jeremiah, h 17 Tacoma av.
Foley Jeremiah, fireman, b n w cor Michigan and State avs.
Foley Jeremiah foreman, h 43 Benton.
Foley Jeremiah, lab, b 85 Fayette.
Foley Jeremiah C, dep U S Marshal, h 552 College av.
Foley John, bricklyr, h 37 Jones.
Foley John, tel opr, h 185 W South.
Foley John C (Foley Bros & Co), h 477 N Illinois.
Foley John E, chief dep U S Marshal, 29½ N Penn, b 1329 N Delaware.
Foley Margareth, supervisoress Insane Hospital.
Foley Mary (wid John), h 197 Meek.
Foley Mary D (wid Dennis), b 1130 E Washington.
Foley Patrick, lab, h 85 Fayette.
Foley Patrick T, switchman, b 268 Fletcher av.
Foley Peter J (Foley Bros & Co), b 477 N Illinois.
Foley Thomas W (Foley Bros & Co), h 709 Ash.
Foley Wm, flagman, h 52 Lord.
Folger Emma J (wid Edwin H), b 99 Ash.
Folger Jessie E, dressmkr, 99 Ash, b same.
Folger John W, printer, h 99 Ash.
Folkening Ellis, clk, h s s Sturm av 2 w of N State av.
Folkening Louisa (wid Charles), h 196 Lincoln la.
Folkening Wm F, drayman, h 141 Lexington av.
Folkerth Birt, brakeman, b 30 Eastern av.
Folkerth Harry, clk, b 30 Eastern av.
Folkerth John M, photog, b 30 Eastern av.
Folkerth Lucy (wid Clay), h 30 Eastern av.
Follett George, helper, h 45 Wisconsin.
Follett John, mach, h 64 Lynn av (W I).
Follett Nathaniel, miller, h 129 Union.
Folsom Edson F, clk, b 332 Park av.

CLEMENS VONNEGUT 184, 186 and 192 E. Washington St. || CABINET HARDWARE CARVERS' TOOLS. Glues of all kinds.

THE WM. H. BLOCK CO. DRY GOODS, MILLINERY, CLOAKS AND FURS.
7 AND 9 EAST WASHINGTON STREET.

INDIANAPOLIS STEEL ROOFING AND CORRUGATING WORKS, 23 and 25 East South Street. S. D. NOEL, Proprietor.

FOLSOM EDWIN S, Genl Agt Phoenix Mutual Life Insurance Co, 34 Mass av, h 332 Park av.
Folsom Isaac N, painter, h 12 Sycamore.
Foltz, see also Fultz.
Foltz Alfred (Ready & Foltz), h 69 Bismarck (W I).
Foltz Alonzo H, molder, h 34 N Haugh (H).
Foltz Andrew, lab, h s s Colgrove 1 e of Galena.
Foltz Anthony, grocer, 38 S Reisner (W I), h same.
Foltz Charles E, cooper, b Jacob Foltz.
Foltz Christopher, b 1341 N Senate av.
Foltz Cyrus, finisher, b 205 E Market.
Foltz Herbert, waiter, b Jacob Foltz.
FOLTZ HERBERT W, Architect and Supt, 49-50 Ingalls Blk, s w cor Penn and E Washington, h 279 N Alabama, Tel 1833. (See adv in classified Architects.)
Foltz Howard M, cashr D H Baldwin & Co, h 279 N Alabama.
Foltz Jacob, cooper, h e s Lincoln av 2 s of Jackson (M J).
Foltz Jesse, carp, h 27 Harris av (M J).
Foltz John, carp, b 27 Harris av (M J).
Foltz Valentine, driver, b 73 Centennial.
Foltzenlogel John, mer police, h 417 Union.
Foltzenlogel Joseph, mach, h 45 Nebraska.
Foncannon Mary, b 96 Yandes.
Fontaine Flora, nurse City Hospital.
Fontaine Mary J W (wid Massena), h 75 N State av.
Fontaine Thomas P, clk Penna Lines, b 75 N State av.
Fontaine Willard M, carp, 60 Walcott, h same.
Foor Jesse, fencemkr, r 77½ S Illinois.
Foor Wm M, h 832 N Penn.
Foote Edward A, legal dept C C C & St L Ry, r 440 N Meridian.
Foote Mary E (wid Jacob), h 223 Cedar.
Foote Rhoda J (wid Henry H), h 70 Woodlawn av.
Foote Thomas, helper, h 188 Bates.
Foote Thomas J, hostler, r 180 E Wabash.
Foppiano John, fruits, 11 S Illinois, h 122 Buchanan.
Foppiano Joseph, lab, h 127 Church.
Forbeck Harry M, lab, h 280 Bates.
Foreberger Andrew J, cabtmkr, h 31 King.
Forbes Charles C, janitor, b 156 Minerva.
Forbes Charles C, salesman Carlin & Lennox, b 882 Cornell av.
Forbes Charles F, clk, r 183 N Capitol av.
Forbes Corydon A, clk, b 11 Ketcham.
Forbes Edwin C, recruiting sergeant U S Army, b 25½ N Illinois.
Forbes Frances (wid John F), h 11 Ketcham.
Forbes George D, lab, b 156 Minerva.
Forbes Joseph R, trav agt, h 42 Lexington av.
Forbes Lorenzo B, lumber, h 882 Cornell av.
Forbes Louisa (wid Henry), h 156 Minerva.
Forbis David M, b 101 Oliver av (W I).
Forbis Hugh, engr, h 142 Ft Wayne av.
Forbis Wm G, chairmkr, h 101 Oliver av (W I).
Forcht Charles E, hatter, b 79 Woodburn av (W I).
Ford Andrew, lab, h 63 Agnes.
Ford Anthony, lab, b 63 Agnes.
Ford Brown, lab, h 181 W 5th.
Ford Byron, blksmith, b 11 E South.

Ford Charles A, clk, b s s Washington av 1 e of Commercial av (I).
Ford Charles B, clk, h 823 College av.
Ford Charles F, millwright, h 875 LaSalle (M P).
Ford Clarence, painter, b 225 E Market.
Ford Edward, paperhngr, b 514 N West.
Ford Eliza T, teacher Public School No 27, h 868 N Penn.
Ford James, engr, b 13 Riley blk.
Ford James E, blksmith, b 875 LaSalle.
Ford Jane (wid John), b 441 Indiana av.
Ford John, lab, h 38 Agnes.
Ford John, lab, b 31 Blake.
Ford John, lab, b 29 Frazee (H).
Ford John F, clk County Recorder's Office, h 366 W 1st.
Ford Jonathan, h rear 80 Sheffield av (H).
Ford Joseph, lab, h 124 N Missouri.
Ford Laura F, teacher Pubic School No 32, b 868 N Penn.
Ford Leonidas, bkkpr, b 875 LaSalle (M P).
Ford Maria (wid Samuel), b n e cor Caroline av and 17th.
Ford Mary (wid Michael), h 362 W Maryland.
Ford Michael, lab, h 205 Fayette.
Ford Michael, lab, b 29 Frazee (H).
Ford Michael, lab, b 337 W Maryland.
Ford Michael, paperhngr, h 1559 Graceland av.
Ford Michael, saloon, 113 Agnes, h same.
Ford Michael, shoemkr, 71 Camp, h same.
Ford Michael J, finisher, h 505 N California.
Ford Nancy A (wid John E), h 192 English av.
Ford Oliver B, trav agt, b 224 W New York.
Ford Patrick, lab, h 29 Frazee (H).
Ford Peter, lab, b 29 Frazee (H).
Ford Robert, lab, h 31 N McLain (W I).
Ford Samuel, lab, h rear 127 E St Joseph.
Ford Simpson, janitor, h 357 Blake.
Ford Susan L, dressmkr, 357 Blake, h same.
Ford Thomas, lab, h 316 Clinton.
Ford Thomas, lab, h 37 Minerva.
Ford Thomas J, blksmith, b 103 W South.
Ford Thomas S, condr, r 28 Elder av.

GUIDO R. PRESSLER,
FRESCO PAINTER
Churches, Theaters, Public Buildings, Etc., A Specialty.
Residence, No. 325 North Liberty Street.
INDIANAPOLIS, IND.

David S. McKernan | REAL ESTATE AND LOANS
Houses, Lots, Farms and Western Lands for sale or trade.
ROOMS 2-5 THORPE BLOCK.

DIAMOND WALL PLASTER { Telephone 1410 BUILDERS' EXCHANGE.

UNION TRANSFER AND STORAGE CO. Cor. E. Ohio St. and C., C., C. & St. L. R'y Tracks. ISSUE NEGOTIABLE RECEIPTS ON MERCHANDISE AND HOUSEHOLD GOODS.

W. McWORKMAN,
ROOFING AND CORNICE WORKS,
930 W. Washington St. Tel. 1118.

Ford Walter, lab, b 29 Frazee (H).
Ford Walter A, molder, h 211 Fayette.
Ford Wm, lab, h 51 Blake.
Ford Wm A, boarding 224 W New York.
Ford Wm B, porter, b 422 N Senate av.
Forde Kate W (wid Richard), h 235 Indiana av.
Foreal Robert, carp, h 604 W North.
Foree Edward, lab, h 42 Guffin.
Foree George, cabtmkr, h 677 Wells (N I).
Foree Parthenia (wid Richard), h 32 Torbet.
Foree Preston, carp, b 677 Wells (N I).
Foree Thomas, cabtmkr, b 402 W Pratt.
Forelander Adolph, miller, b 810 Ash.
Foreman Charles T, clk, h 120 Bright.
Foreman George, mnfrs' agt, 34 W Maryland, h 161 Ft Wayne av.
Foreman George jr, clk, b 161 Ft Wayne av.
Foreman John M (J M Foreman & Co), h 218 Blackford.
Foreman J M & Co (John M Foreman), horseshoers, 285 W Washington.
Foreman Milton, blksmith, 345 Indiana av, h 380 same.
Foreman Warren, porter, r 236 W Wabash.
Forest Avenue Pharmacy, Lamberson & Hackleman proprs, Cornell av and 20th.
Forest Jane (wid Edward), h 58 Greer.
FOREST W E "FLUCTUATION SYSTEM," Thomas S S Kerr Genl Agt, 77½ E Market. (See adv p 9.)
Forestal Michael, boilermkr, h 77 Leota.
Forestal Robert, carp, h 604 W North.
Forgy Fannie, nurse, b 197 N Delaware.
Forkner Edna D, teacher Kindergarten No 7, b 469 W Francis (N I).
Forkner Samuel A, lawyer, 19 Baldwin blk, h 469 W Francis (N I).
Fornshell Charles H, coremkr, h 403 Jackson.
Forrest Edwin R, uphlr, h e s Lincoln av 1 s of C C C & St L Ry (M J).
Forrest George B, bkkpr Moore & Co, h 273 Huron.
Forrest Gertrude, stenog, b 736 E Washington.
Forrest James W (Forrest & Coolman), h 206 Blackford.

GEO. J. MAYER,
MANUFACTURER OF
SEALS
STENCILS, RUBBER STAMPS, CHECKS, BADGES, DOOR PLATES, ETC.
15 S. Meridian St., Ground Floor. TEL. 1386.

Forrest Joseph H, foreman, h 736 E Washington.
Forrest Samuel T, miller, b 319 S Meridian.
Forrest Thomas B, lab, b 48 Tremont av, (H).
Forrest & Coolman (James W Forrest, Charles Coolman), grocers, 353 W New York.
Forrester Edward F, lab, b 273 S West.
Forrester Frank, waiter, r 101 N New Jersey.
Forrester James C, clk, b 273 S West.
Forrester Mamie E, stenog Newark Machine Co, b 273 S West.
Forrester Richard, lab, h 273 S West.
Forrester Richard jr, horseshoer, b 273 S West.
Forrester Wilken, tmstr, h 372 Lincoln av.
Forsee Frederick, tinner, b 578 W Udell (N I).
Forsha Joseph, farmer, b 519 Jefferson av.
Forsha Louis, brakeman, b 1100 W Washington (H).
Forshee George W, blksmith, 222 Mass av, h 347½ N Noble.
Forshee George W jr, foreman Flanner & Buchanan, h 172 N Illinois.
Forshee Grant E, clk Otto Roemler, b 533 E 7th.
Forsinger Charles C, foreman, b s e cor Rural and Tinker.
Forsinger George C, mngr Indpls Paint and Roofing Co, h s e cor Rural and Tinker.
Forslund Peter A, bicycles, 417 Virginia av, h same.
Forson Isaac, tmstr, b 73 Norwood.
Forster, see also Foerster and Foster.
Forster Barbara (wid Philip), h 57 Beaty.
Forster John G, foreman, h 599 Marlowe av.
Forsyth Alice I, teacher Public School No 20, b 132 Fletcher av.
Forsyth Clarence, h e s Maxwell 2 n of Walnut av (I).
Forsyth Clarence J Rev, h 15 Hall pl.
Forsyth Elijah J jr, painter, b 132 Fletcher av.
Forsyth Elizabeth F, teacher Public School No 28, b 132 Fletcher av.
Forsyth Lucy H (wid John T), h e s Maxwell av 2 n of Walnut av (I).
Forsyth Mary M (wid Elijah J), b 132 Fletcher av.
Forsyth Wm, artist, 132 Fletcher av, h same.
Forsythe Andrew J, actor, b 1202 N Illinois.
Forsythe Wm G, clk R M S, h 56 Lord.
Fort Harry O, fireman, b 366 Cedar.
Fort James F, cook, r 186 W 3d.
Fort John H, janitor, h 520 W 22d (N I).
Fort John W, pres The Capital Live Stock Commission Co, h 470 Bellefontaine.
Fort Lydia V (wid Milton P), h 366 Cedar.
Fort Milton P, detective, 59 Baldwin blk, h 125 Ash.
Fort Richard D, helper, h 58 Ingraham.
Fort Wallace W, tmstr, h n w cor Wheeler and Bloyd av (B).
Forth Frank J, baker, h 536 S Meridian.
Fortner Alexander C, lab, h n s 30th 1 e of Northwestern av.
Fortner Josephine (wid Alfred J), b 469 N Illinois.
Fortner Sanford S, salesman Murphy, Hibben & Co, h 104 Ruckle.
Fortner Sarah A (wid Charles P), b 331 Spring.
Fortney Charles P, plastr, h 275 Alvord.
Fortune David H, molder, h 31 Frazee (H).

A. METZGER AGENCY ESTABLISHED 1863. REAL ESTATE

LAMBERT GAS & GASOLINE ENGINE CO.
ANDERSON, IND. GAS AND GASOLINE ENGINES, 2 TO 50 H. P.

Fortune Edward, molder, b 31 Frazee (H).
Fortune Mary (wid Wm), h 6 Wyandot blk.
Fortune May, clk, b 6 Wyandot blk.
Fortune Wm, pres Municipal Engineering Co, h 154 East Drive (W P).
Fosdick Edwin B, clk R M S, h 1146 N Alabama.
Fosdick Horace W C, clk Indiana National Bank, b 1146 N Alabama.
Fosdyke Arthur G, h 500 E 8th.
Foss Bros (Frank O and James H), grocers, Wells opp Big Four depot (N I).
Foss Frank O (Foss Bros), h Wells opp Big Four depot (N I).
Foss James H (Foss Bros), b 212 Douglass.
Foss Justin O, engr, h 212 Douglass.
Fossati John, fruits, 85 S Illinois, h same.
Fost George W, engr, h 60 N State av.
Foster, see also Forster.
Foster Alexander, molder, b 47 Elizabeth.
Foster Alonzo T, boltmkr, h 139 W Morris.
Foster Andrew A, painter, b 47 Elizabeth.
Foster Annie (wid Andrew T), b 361 W Pearl.
Foster Annie R, stenog Evan A Bonham, b 10 Union.
Foster Carrie A (wid Thomas), news agt, r 7, 249½ W Washington.
Foster Catherine (wid Thomas), b 29 Jefferson av.
Foster Chapin C, pres Foster Lumber Co, h 762 N Penn.
Foster Charles B, h 47 Woodlawn av.
Foster Charles B, bkkpr, h 184 Park av.
Foster Charles W, lab, b rear 276 S Meridian.
Foster Clarence M, trav agt, b 352 N New Jersey.
Foster David A, wagonmkr, h 399 N New Jersey.
Foster Dudley, motorman, h 18 Hadley.
Foster Edgar J, ins agt, 25 E Market, h 339 N Penn.
Foster Edward, lab, b rear 163 St Mary.
Foster Edward, tailor, 8 Monument pl, h 266 E St Clair.
Foster Edward jr, tailor, b 266 E St Clair.
Foster Edward L, bkkpr, h 29 Jefferson av.
Foster Elroy S, barber, h 617 Marlowe av.
Foster Ernest, lithog, b 47 Elizabeth.
Foster Florence (wid Andrew), h 389 Blackford.
Foster Frank M, clk Nordyke & Marmon Co, h 74 Nordyke av (W I).
FOSTER FRANK S, Lawyer, 536 Lemcke Bldg, h 702 N Alabama.
Foster Frederick E, polisher, b 37 Harris av (M J).
Foster George D, hostler 226 Randolph.
Foster George M, bleacher, h 628 Home av.
Foster Henry, lab, b rear 276 S Meridian.
Foster James, helper, h 47 Elizabeth.
Foster James B, h 161 St Mary.
Foster Jesse, engr, h 227 Hoyt av.
Foster John, porter, r 659½ Virginia av.
Foster John A, lab, b 47 Elizabeth.
Foster John B, switchman, h 37 Harris av (M J).
Foster John F, janitor, h rear 294 E Ohio.
Foster John H, plastr, h 542 W Udell (N I).
Foster John T, lab, b rear 276 S Meridian.
Foster Louisa (wid Leavitte E), h 106 Bates.
Foster Luceba A, ins agt, b 106 Bates.
Foster Lucy J (wid Wesley), b 192 W 1st.
FOSTER LUMBER CO, Chapin C Foster Pres, Alonzo P Hendrickson Vice-Pres, Oliver P Ensley Sec and Treas, n w cor St Clair and N Senate av, Tel 254. (See adv in classified Planing Mills.)

Farm and City Loans
25 Years' Successful Business.
THOS. C. DAY & CO,
Rooms 325 to 330 Lemcke Building.

Foster Luna L, printer, b 399 N New Jersey.
Foster Martha J (wid Albert), h 16 Fletcher av.
Foster Mary I (wid Abraham J), h 486 S State av.
Foster May A (wid John), b 5 River av (W I).
Foster Orin O, finisher, h 652 Chestnut.
Foster Reuben, lab, h rear 276 S Meridian
Foster Robert, lab, b rear 276 S Meridian.
FOSTER ROBERT M, Restaurant, 94-96 E Washington, h 878 N Delaware.
Foster Robert R, b 878 N Delaware.
Foster Robert S (R S Foster & Co), h 352 N New Jersey.
Foster Robert S jr, student, b 762 N Penn.
FOSTER R S & CO (Robert S Foster, Ellis Y Shartle), Grain and Commission, 47 Board of Trade Bldg, Tel 147.
Foster Samuel, lab, h 424 Muskingum al.
Foster Sarah A (wid Isaac), h 407 Coburn.
Foster Sarah W, teacher Public School No 1, b 339 N Penn.
Foster Thomas A, boltmkr, h e s Belmont av 1 n of Morris (W I).
Foster Thomas J, tailor, b 266 E St Clair.
Foster Wallace, clk Consumers' Gas Trust Co, h 1040 N Capitol av.
Foster Wm B, electrician, r 102 N Capitol av.
Foster Wm C, turner, b 100 N Alabama.
Foster Wm E, b 1040 N Capitol av.
Foster Wm M, tailor, b 266 E St Clair.
Foster Wm N, carp, b 60 Brookside av.
Fotheringham Mary (wid Thomas), b 130 N Belmont av (H).
Fouch Charles H, polisher, h 894 S Meridian.
Fouche Wilber F, lumberman, h 331 N New Jersey.
Foudray Edgar E, livery, 19 Bismarck av (H), h 20 same.
Foudray Ida M, b 215 N New Jersey.
Foudray Livingston D, bartndr, r 200½ W Washington.

EAT
HITZ'S CRACKERS AND CAKES.
ASK YOUR GROCER FOR THEM.

BICYCLES $5 DOWN. Best Wheels. Best Terms. WHEELMEN'S CO. 31 W. OHIO ST. LONG DISTANCE TEL. 1855.

J. H. TECKENBROCK Painter and Decorator, 94 EAST SOUTH STREET.

FIDELITY MUTUAL LIFE—PHILADELPHIA, PA.
MATCHLESS SECURITY At LOW COST. } A. H. COLLINS { General Agent Baldwin Block.

Edwardsport Coal and Mining Co. Miners and Shippers Steam and Domestic Coal. Rooms 42 and 43 WHEN BUILDING.

ESTABLISHED 1876. TELEPHONE 168.
CHESTER BRADFORD,
SOLICITOR OF PATENTS,
AND COUNSEL IN PATENT CAUSES.
(See adv. page 6.)
Office:—Rooms 14 and 16 Hubbard Block, S. W. Cor. Washington and Meridian Streets, INDIANAPOLIS, INDIANA.

Foudy Abram, lab, h 99 Oriole.
Foulks Anna, dyer, 299 Virginia av, h 83 Dugdale.
Foulks John W, lab, h 83 Dugdale.
Foullois Edward H, city fireman, h 162 Prospect.
Foullois Henry V, cabtmkr, h 36 Smithson.
Fountain Cyrus A, painter, h 28 N Reisner (W I).
Fountain John, lab, b 58 Smith.
Fountain Millie, h 119 Darnell.
Fountain Oscar, painter, b 223 Cornell av.
Fountain Robert, lab, b 119 Darnell.
Fountain Samuel, h 223 Cornell av.
Fountain Wm C, bkkpr David F Swain, h n e cor Penn and 7th.
Fournace John B, livery, 70 Kentucky av, saloon, 129 W Maryland, h 1581 N Capitol av.
Foust, see also Faust.
Foust Bert B, driver, b 168 Spring.
Foust Daniel W, painter, h 57 E Merrill.
Foust Jennie (wid Henry L), h 168 Spring.
Foust Sarah, h 387 Indiana av.
Foutch Wm, porter, h 886 N Capitol av.
Fouts Albert, b 237 Douglass.
Fouts Charles, peddler, h 27 S Gale (B).
Fouts John M, student, b 327 S New Jersey.
Fouts Louisa E (wid Alfred), b 237 Douglass.
Fouts Sarah A, b 578 W 22d (N I).
Fouty Abraham C, mer police, h rear 624 Madison av.
Foutz Grace, opr C U Tel Co, b 83 W St Clair.
Foutz John W, h 83 W St Clair.
Fowler Alden S, messenger, r 282 N Illinois.
Fowler Amanda (wid John W), b 85 Lexington av.
Fowler Anna J, grocer, 226 Howard, h same.
Fowler Benjamin F, carp, h 510 W McLene (N I).
Fowler Catherine, b 409 Talbott av.
Fowler Charles A, agt, r 30 Stewart pl.
Fowler David C, engr, h 283 English av.

Fowler Edward T, barber, h 85 Lexington av.
Fowler Ellen R (wid Collin), h 158 E 8th.
Fowler Fannie (wid Robert P), h 174 E Ohio.
Fowler Frank B, bkkpr K and L of H, b 16 Hall pl.
Fowler George, meats, 226 Howard, h same.
Fowler George I, painter, 904 N Delaware, b same.
Fowler Georgiana, b 560 Jefferson av.
Fowler Harry, photog, h 155 N New Jersey.
Fowler Henry, express, h 40 Springfield.
Fowler James P, carp, h 281 Huron.
Fowler John T, molder, h 37 State.
Fowler Lucinda B (wid Leroy Z), h 16 Hall pl.
Fowler Maria E, h 5, 502½ E Washington.
Fowler Merton, driver, b 194 E Washington.
Fowler Oscar W, filer, h 333½ Dillon.
Fowler Thomas B, tallyman C C C & St L Ry, h 188 Huron.
Fowler Wm, cook 139 N Meridian.
Fowley Jacob M, presser, b 12 N Gale (B).
Fowley James P, painter, b 12 N Gale (B).
Fowley Wm, presser, h 12 N Gale (B).
Fowley Wm F, carver, b 12 N Gale (B).
Fox, see also Fuchs.
Fox Adam F, filer, h 89 Maple.
Fox Albert T, condr, b rear 236 S Capitol av.
Fox Alexander P, sec and mngr Fox & Garhart Specialty Co, h 24 Home av.
Fox Andrew J, clk, b 80 S West.
Fox Arthur, dentist, 45 Holly av (W I), h same.
Fox Bolsar, clk George F Traub, h 179 Blake.
Fox Balser, condr, h 33 Yandes.
Fox Caroline, dry goods, 424 W North, h same.
Fox Casper G, mach, h 424 W North.
Fox Charles F, plumber, b 2 Quincy.
Fox Charles L, waiter, r 55 Empire blk.
Fox Christian J, engr, h 25 Nebraska.
Fox Elijah B (Central Rubber and Supply Co), h 74 W North.
Fox Everitt M, clk, b 294 Coburn.
Fox Frances H, stenog, b 551 Park av.
Fox Francis M, printer, b 318 N East.
Fox Frank J, electrician, b 929 N Meridian.
Fox Frederick L, stenog engr m of w C C C & St L Ry, b 46 Huron.
Fox George H, printer, b 318 N East.
Fox Harrold W, stenog, h 685 N Illinois.
Fox Helen (wid Michael), h 230 W Maryland.
Fox Henry A, foreman, h 179 Hadley av (W I).
Fox Henry J, clk, h 28 Prospect.
Fox Henry S, meats, 495 W 22d, h 465 W 23d (N I).
Fox Israel, clk, r 74 W North.
Fox Jacob, mngr The Singer Mnfg Co, h 929 N Meridian.
Fox Jacob, stock examiner Bureau of Animal Industry, h 274 E Merrill.
Fox Jacob F, bottler, b 274 E Merrill.
Fox Jacob J, engr, h 406 S Capitol av.
Fox James C, bkkpr Carlin & Lennox, h n w cor 26th and Superior.
Fox James E, tailor, r 180 W Michigan.
Fox John, condr, b 78 Springfield.
Fox John, molder, h 98 Agnes.
Fox John H, student, b 929 N Meridian.
Fox John P, capt Engine Co No 5, h 1192 N Illinois.
Fox John T, tel opr, b 7 Empire blk.

C. ZIMMERMAN & SONS | SLATE AND GRAVEL ROOFERS 19 South East Street.

DRIVEN WELLS And Second Water Wells and Pumps of all kinds at CHARLES KRAUSS', 42 S. PENN. ST. TELEPHONE 465.

ERTEL STEAM LAUNDRY LARGEST AND BEST IN THE STATE. PROMPT SERVICE. 26 and 28 N. 5th Ave. Telephone 1089.

Fox Joseph, finisher, h 631 Madison av.
Foy Joseph W, tailor, r 35½ E Washington.
Fox Lawrence P, grocer, 2 Carlos, h same.
Fox Louis M, lab, b 274 E Merrill.
Fox Martin, bartndr, h 631 Madison av.
Fox Mary, clk C C C & St L Ry, b 274 E Merrill.
Fox Mary L (wid Nicholas), h 76 Park av.
Fox Meta, cashr The Globe Clothing Co, b 293 E Market.
Fox Newton, trimmer, b 144 W New York.
Fox Nicholas, carp, b 76 Park av.
Fox Peter J, wagonmkr, h 179 Blake.
Fox Samuel (Dreyfoos & Co), h 293 E Market.
Fox Sarah F (wid Noah), h 294 Coburn.
Fox Stella R, teacher Public School No 15, b 149 N Penn.
Fox Thomas, driver, h 635 W Vermont.
Fox Thomas, lab, h 7 Empire.
Fox Wallace, cooper, b 294 Coburn.
Fox Wilhelmina (wid Casper), h 2 Quincy.
Fox Wm F, clk L E & W R R), h 551 Park av.
Fox & Garhart Specialty Co (Wm K Bellis pres, Nathan K Garhart vice-pres, Alexander P Fox sec and mngr), dental supplies, 88 N Penn.
Foxall Henry Y, mach, h 210 Yandes.
Foxlow Alois, shoemkr, h 32 Kansas.
Foxlow Benjamin F, uphlr, b 32 Kansas.
Foxworthy Frank W, student, r 106½ E New York.
Foxworthy Harry R, tel opr, h 738 E Ohio.
Foxworthy Landon B, fireman, b 709 E Market.
Foxworthy Samuel T, carp, h 709 E Market.
Foxworthy Wm B, painter, h 73 Hill av.
Foy Beatrice S, teacher Industrial School, h 94 Highland av.
Foy Charles A, clk, b 540 S Capitol av.
Foy George, carp, h 540 S Capitol av.
Foy Joseph W, tailor, b 94 Highland av.
Foy Marion F, fireman, b 310 E Wabash.
Foy Owen, mach, b 94 Highland av.
Foy Wm H, mach opr, b 14 S Senate av.
Foy Wm M, exp messenger, h 529 W 22d (N I).
Frady Charles C, trav agt, h 176 W Ohio.
Frailey Charles E, winder, b s e cor Moore av and Dearborn.
Frailey Joseph D, lab, b 288 W Washington.
Fraim Henry, agt, r 305 N Senate av.
Fraim John W, printer, h 301 S Penn.
Frakes Frank, elevator opr, b 12½ Indiana av.
Fraley Mollie E (wid James), boarding 227 S Senate av.
Framke Albert, lab, h 87 Nebraska.
France John W, driver, h 563 N West.
Frances Power Cobbe Refuge, 1130 N Penn.
Francis Bartlet, lab, b 580 N West.
Francis Benjamin, fireman, b n w cor Michigan and State av.
Francis Carrie B, teacher Public School No 38, b 107 E St Joseph.
Francis David T, carp, 437 E Vermont, h same.
Francis Dock, porter, h 83 Oregon.
Francis Dollson, lab, h 85 Howard.
Francis Edward, cook, h 348 W 2d.
Francis Edward, lab, b 392 E Michigan.
Francis Frederick C, lab, b 292 E Michigan.
Francis George E, butcher, b 145 Oliver av (W I).
Francis Harry H, electrician, h 275 S West.
Francis Isabel (wid John T), h 105 Prospect.

RICHARDSON & McCREA, MANAGERS FOR CENTRAL INDIANA. EQUITABLE LIFE ASSURANCE SOCIETY Of the United States. 79 EAST MARKET STREET. TELEPHONE 182.

Francis James, driver, h 328 Superior.
Francis James B, tinner, 392 E Michigan, h same.
Francis James M, lab, b 392 E Michigan.
Francis John, hostler, h 85 Howard.
Francis John, lab, h 543 Fremont (N I).
Francis John G, lab, h 23 Osgood (W I).
Francis John J, barber, b 105 Prospect.
Francis John L (Francis & Swails), h 183 N Belmont av (H).
Francis J Richard, sec and treas The J N Hurty Pharmacy Co, 102-104 N Penn, r 134 N Meridian.
Francis Louis E, trav agt, h 1115 N Meridian.
Francis Louis E jr, trav agt, h 1138 N Penn.
Francis Martha (wid Robert), b Exchange Hotel (W I).
Francis Mary (wid Hillman), h 85 Howard.
Francis Thomas, fireman, b 260 Bates.
Francis Thomas E, feed, 237 Blake, h 203 same.
Francis Wm, porter, h 325 Douglass.
Francis Wm H, lab, h 78 Holmes av (H).
Francis Wm H, tel opr P C C & St L Ry, b Enterprise Hotel.
Francis & Swails (John L Francis, James W Swails), blksmiths, s w cor Indiana av and Locke.
Francke Frederick (Francke & Schindler), h 984 N Meridian.
Francke Otto, butcher, b 207 W Michigan.
FRANCKE & SCHINDLER (Frederick Francke), Wholesale and Retail Hardware, 35 S Meridian, Tel 329.
Frank Abraham, clk, b 160 Indiana av.
Frank Abraham H, cigar mnfr, 340 W Washington, h 400 W New York.
Frank Adam, cabtmkr, h 504 Madison av.
Frank Barbara, h 176 E Walnut.
Frank Charles, molder, h 98 N Belmont av (H).
Frank Daniel W L, cementwkr, h 48 N East.
Frank George H, engr, h 780 E Market.
Frank Gustav, clk, b Stubbin's Hotel.
Frank Henry, h 644 N Illinois.
Frank Jacob F, clk Kingan & Co, h 9 Lynn.

Typewriter-Ribbons ALL COLORS FOR ALL MACHINES. THE BEST AND CHEAPEST. S. H. EAST, STATE AGENT. The Williams Typewriter.... 55 THORPE BLOCK, 87 E. MARKET ST.

ELLIS & HELFENBERGER Architectural Iron Work and Gray Iron Castings. 162-170 South Senate Ave. Tel. 958.

THE HOGAN TRANSFER AND STORAGE COMP'Y
Household Goods and Pianos Moved—Packed—Stored...... Baggage and Package Express Machinery and Safes a Specialty Cor. Washington and Illinois Sts. TELEPHONE No. 675.

The Central Rubber & Supply Co. ♦♦♦♦ Hose, Belting, Packing, Clothing, Druggists' Sundries, Bicycle Tires, Cotton Hose, Etc. New York Belting & Packing Co., L't'd. PHONE 922. 79 S. ILLINOIS ST., INDIANAPOLIS, IND.

The Provident Life and Trust Company Of Philadelphia.
Grants Certificates of Extension to Policyholders who are temporarily unable to pay their premiums
D. W. EDWARDS, Gen. Agt., 508 Indiana Trust Bldg.

Frank John (Co-Operative Carriage and Wagon Co), h 55 Gatling.
Frank Wm, uphlr, b 504 Madison av.
Frank Wm H, engr, h 162 Walcott.
Frank Albert F, lab, h 87 Nebraska.
Franke Andrew C (Frank & Seele), b 199 Prospect.
Franke Charles C, tmstr, h 78 N Gillard av.
Franke Harry F, mach, b 224 Cedar.
Franke Joseph, mach, h 38 Johnson av.

FRANKE & SEELE (Andrew C Franke, Christian J Seele), Hardware, s w cor Prospect and State av.

FRANKEL JACOB, State Agt Mutual Life Insurance Co of Kentucky, 90 Lombard Bldg, h 238 E Ohio.

Franken Isaac L, h 449 N Capitol av.
Franken Jonathan, h 249 N Illinois.
Frankfort Henry, clothing, 107 Mass av, h 77 Hudson.
Frankhouse Arthur, lab, h 5½ Cottage av (W I).
Franklin Adelaide (wid Wm), h 66 N Missouri.
Franklin Alexander C, clk, h 28 Johnson av.
Franklin Allen, coachman 496 College av.
Franklin Benjamin, carp, h 39 Samoa.
Franklin Benjamin, dep Recorder of Marion County, 44 Court House, h 221 Bellefontaine.
Franklin Bessie S, cashr Union Mutual Bldg and Loan Assn, b 713 N Capitol av.
Franklin Bettie (wid George G), b 469 N New Jersey.
Franklin Edward, mach, b 179 E New York.
Franklin Edward J, foreman, b 713 N Capitol av.
Franklin Felix, lab, h 39 Northwestern av.
Franklin Frederick G, clk, b 72 Oliver av (W I).
Franklin F Lafayette, plumber, r 468 Muskingum al.
Franklin G Thomas, lab, h 21 Rhode Island.
Franklin Henry, lab, h 5 Carter.
Franklin Henry, live stock, h 72 Oliver av (W I).

Julius C. Walk & Son, Jewelers Indianapolis.
12 EAST WASHINGTON ST.

Franklin James E, sec Union Mutual Bldg and Loan Assn, h 713 N Capitol av.
Franklin Jeremiah J (Moss & Franklin), r 53 Fayette.
Franklin John, lab, h 16 Mill.
Franklin John, lab, h 234 E Wabash.
Franklin John E, carp, h n s Washington 3 w of Crawfordsville rd (M J).
Franklin Joseph A, clk Robert Keller, h 567 S East.
Franklin Kate C (wid Wm), h 485 Lafayette.
Franklin Louis, waiter, r 232 W North.
Franklin Louisa A (wid Nicholas), h 76 Mayhew.
Franklin Moses, grocer, 301 Fayette, h same.
Franklin Philip, plumber, 468 Muskingum al, r same.
Franklin Priscilla (wid Urias), h 757 Brooker's al.
Franklin Robert, coachman 708 N Alabama.
Franklin Samuel, tinner, b 325 Bellefontaine.
Franklin Savings Assn, Wm A Rhodes sec, 72 E Market.
Franklin Walter D, clk C C C & St L Ry, h 387 Ash.
Franklin Wm, b n s Washington 3 w of Crawfordsville rd (M J).
Franklin Wm, brakeman, r 500 E Washington.
Franklin Wm, lab, h 74 Mayhew.
Franklin Wm, lab, b 39 Northwestern av.
Franklin Wm O, lab, h 113 Martindale av.
Frankmoelle Gertrude, milliner, 39 E Washington, b 224 Broadway.
Frankowich Frank, cabtmkr, b 175½ E Washington.
Franks Jay R, clk, r 87 E Market.
Franks John W, mach hd, h 19 Arthur.
Franson Charles F, draughtsman, r 74 W Walnut.
Frantz Harry A, brakeman, h 335 E Wabash.
Frantz John G, clk, b 169 Clinton.
Frantz Mary C (wid Jacob), h 169 Clinton.
Frantz Samuel J, bookbndr, b 169 Clinton.
Frantz Wm F, clk, b 169 Clinton.
Frantzreb Philip A K, carp, h 107 Weghorst.
Frantzreb Theresa (wid John), midwife, 11 Smithson av, h same.
Frantzreb Wm C, carp, h 446 Mulberry.
Franz Charles H, clk George C Morrison, b 106 Nebraska.
Franz George L, cigar mnfr, 395 N Brookside av, h same.
Franz Henry, phys, 275 E Ohio, h same.
Franz John A M, tallyman, h 106 Nebraska.
Franz John P, dep collr Internal Revenue, h 9 Atlas.
Franz Margaret (wid John P), h rear 31 Alvord.
Franz Wm, cigarmkr, 27 Yandes, h same.
Franzman Amelia (wid Adam), b 23 Tuxedo.
Franzman Peter, h 23 Tuxedo.
Frauzman Wm J, condr, h 217 Blake.
Fraser, see also Frazier.

FRASER BROS & VAN HOFF (Dwight, Selby P and Joshua G Fraser, Henry L Van Hoff), Lumber, Lath, Shingles, Sash, Doors and Blinds, 41 Michigan av, Tel 278.

Fraser Dwight (Fraser Bros & Van Hoff), h 768 N Penn.

OTTO GAS ENGINES | BUILDERS' EXCHANGE S. W. Cor. Ohio and Penn. Telephone 535.

Becker & Son Charles Becker Jacob Becker Jr. Merchant Tailors. 21 N. Penn. St. Tel. 934

SALISBURY & STANLEY, Contractors and Builders TELEPHONE 999. Office, Store and Bar Fixtures a Specialty. Repairing of all kinds done on short notice. 177 Clinton St. Indianapolis, Ind.

Fraser Henry S, genl agt C C C & St L Ry, cor Delaware and South, h 754 N Delaware.
Fraser Joshua G (Fraser Bros & Van Hoff), h 625 N Penn.
Fraser Selby P (Fraser Bros & Van Hoff), h 850 N Illinois.
FRATERNAL BUILDING-LOAN ASSOCIATIONS, James R Carnahan Pres, Robert W McBride Vice-Pres, George W Powell Sec, Frank Bowers Treas, McBride & Denny Attorneys, 51-52 Journal Bldg, Tel 1322.
Frauer Anna, pickles, 93 E Mkt House, h 178 N Pine.
Frauer Caroline A, housekpr 28 N East.
Frauer Gustave E, turner, b 28 N East.
Frauer Herman E (H E Frauer & Co), h 28 N East.
FRAUER H E & CO (Herman E Frauer, Herman E Thoms), Druggists, 246 E Washington, Tel 554.
Frauer May E (wid Edward E), boarding 24 Brookside av.
Frauer Rudolph E, produce, h 178 N Pine.
Fraul Julia, h 1129 E Washington.
Frazee Alva E, dairyman, h 178 Sheffield av (H).
Frazee Annetta D (wid Samuel), b 605 N Capitol av.
Frazee George W, carp, r 111 E Washington.
Frazee Joseph, creamery, rear 152 Lexington av, h 152 same.
Frazee Mary F (wid Clark), b 112 Lexington av.
Frazee Stephen J, cigars, 67 S Illinois, h 31 W Michigan.
Frazee Theodore T, lab, h 46 Arch.
Frazee Wm D, bkkpr State B and L Assn, b 269 E St Clair.
Frazer Robert, lab, h 6 Lafayette.
Frazeur Winfield S, mach, h 302 E Georgia.
Frazier, see also Fraser.
Frazier Arthur O, carp, h 448 W Shoemaker (N I).
Frazier Charles F, lab, h 481 W Addison (N I).
Frazier Charles H, brakeman, h 29½ N Beville av.
Frazier Charles L, trav agt McKee Shoe Co, b s s University av 2 w of Downey av (I).
Frazier Charles P, lab, h 481 W Addison (N I).
Frazier Ella, bkkpr, b s s University av 2 w of Downey av (I).
Frazier Frederick, clk, b 21 Walcott.
Frazier George H, engr, h 21 Walcott.
Frazier Giles, tmstr, h 451 S Illinois.
Frazier H Edwin, cashr Indiana Car and Foundry Co, h 29 Newman.
Frazier James, cook, h 266 Highland av.
Frazier James A, b 21 Walcott.
Frazier Josephine, h rear 25 Center.
Frazier Martha (wid John H), dressmkr, 281 N East, r same.
Frazier Orla F, baker Parrott & Taggart, b 119 Yeiser.
Frazier Simeon, sec Edwardsville Coal and Mining Co, h s s University av 2 w of Downey av (I).
Frazier Theodore, stone cutter, h 119 Yeiser.
Freaney Bros (Patrick J and Wm J), plumbers, 26 Virginia av.
Freaney Patrick J (Freaney Bros), h 158 E Michigan.

Henry H. Fay, 40½ E. Washington St., REAL ESTATE, AND LOAN BROKER.

Freaney Wm J (Freaney Bros), h 23 E North.
Fred Francis M, lab, h 49 S Austin (B).
Fred Francis O, lab, b 49 S Austin (B).
Frederick Edward, lab, h 396 Columbia av.
Frederick Herman T, clk, h 230 S Noble.
Frederick John W, supt E Rauh & Sons, h 867 S East.
Frederick Julius R, observer U S Weather Bureau, h 104 Middle Drive (W P).
Frederick Samantha C, h 27½ Mass av.
Fredericks Charles W, produce, b n s Brookside av 2 e of Orange av.
Fredericks Elizabeth (wid Paul M), h 174 Jefferson av.
Fredericks George W, cupola tndr, h 247 Shelby.
Fredericks John H, molder, b n s Brookside av 2 e of Orange av.
Fredericks Louis, pressfeeder, b 174 Jefferson av.
Fredericks Nancy A (wid Godfrey), h n s Brookside av 2 e of Orange av.
Fredericks Wm M, lab, h 253 S Senate av.
Frederickson Carrie (wid Hans F), b 99 N Arsenal av.
Free Addison D, mach, h 615 N West.
Free Charles D, millwright, h 355 Jefferson av.
Free Frederick, mach hd, h 51 Oriental.
Free Frederick C, turner, b 51 Oriental.
Free John W, cabtmkr, h 435 N Pine.
Free Oliver H, mach hd, b 1137 Northwestern av.
Freeberg, see also Freiberg.
Freeberg Caroline (wid Larson), b 110 Sycamore.
Freeberg John, watchman Indpls Gas Co, h 110 Sycamore.
Freeborn Eben E, ins agt, h 116 Highland pl.
Freehaver George W, trav agt, h 85 N Arsenal av.
Freeland Charles, lab, b 117 Kappus (W I).
Freeland Edward H, mach hd, r 292 N Illinois.
Freeland James A, contr, 96 Lee (W I), h same.
Freeman Alfred, car rep, h 146 Clark.
Freeman Anna, h 219 W North.

COAL AND LIME Cement, Hair, Sewer Pipe, etc. BALKE & KRAUSS CO. Cor. Missouri and Market Sts.

FRIEDGEN'S IS THE PLACE FOR THE NOBBIEST SHOES Ladies' and Gents' 19 North Pennsylvania St.

SAMUEL LAING || COPPER AND GALVANIZED IRON CORNICE MANUFACTURER
SKYLIGHTS AND VENTILATORS. 72 AND 74 E. COURT STREET.

M. B. WILSON, Pres. W. F. CHURCHMAN, Cash.
THE CAPITAL NATIONAL BANK,
INDIANAPOLIS, IND.
Our Specialty is handling all Country Checks and Drafts on Indiana and neighboring States at the very lowest rates. Call and see us.
Interest Paid on Time Deposits.
28 S. MERIDIAN ST., COR. PEARL.

Freeman Celia E (wid Joseph T), h 107 Hadley.
Freeman Charles, gardener, h s s Shearer pike 1 e of Belt R R (B).
Freeman Charles, lab, b n s 8th 2 w of canal.
Freeman Charles L, lab, h 20 Roanoke.
Freeman Clyde M, collr C E Coffin & Co, b 264 N Brookside av.
Freeman David H, watchman, h 24 Iowa.
Freeman Edwin N, condr, h w s Brightwood av 3 n of Willow (B).
Freeman Eliza (wid Nelson), h 519 Jefferson av.
Freeman Emery, lab, h 7 Concord (H).
Freeman Fannie, h 374 N Missouri.
Freeman Frank, lab, h 4 Concord (H).
Freeman Frank R, sawmkr, b 37½ W Market.
Freeman Guy S, salesman, b Exchange Hotel (W I).
Freeman Henry C, lab Deaf and Dumb Inst.
Freeman Henry C, mach, h 1020 E Washington.
Freeman John, blksmith, h 29 Elder av.
Freeman John, plumber, h 525 Jefferson av.
Freeman John S, porter C C C & St L Ry, h 99 Paca.
Freeman Jonathan B, engr, h 74 Columbia av.
Freeman Jordan, lab, h 291 Bright.
Freeman Laurens B, city pass agt Penna Lines, h 352 N Meridian.
Freeman Levi, lab, h 9 Brown.
Freeman Samuel, lab, b 1282 Northwestern av (N I).
Freeman Samuel, plastr, b 75 Margaret.
Freeman Susan B (wid Laurenz), b 685 Wells (N I).
FREEMAN THE, George L Knox Publisher and Propr, Elwood C Knox, Mngr, 57½ Indiana av.
Freeman Wm, lab, b 156 W Washington.
Freeman Wm A, mach, b 24 Iowa.
Freeman Wm E, lab, b 14 Willard.
Freeman Wm O L, driver, b 122½ Ft Wayne av.

TUTTLE & SEGUIN,
28 E. Market St. Ground Floor.
COLLECTING RENTS AND CARE OF PROPERTY A SPECIALTY.
Telephone 1168.

Freeman Winfield S, waiter, r 115 N New Jersey.
Freers Adolph, finisher, b 274 W Court.
Freers Frank, lab, b 274 W Court.
Freers Louis, musician, h 274 W Court.
Freers Otto, waiter, r 185½ W Washington.
Frees, see also Frese and Fries.
Frees George, finisher, h 60 E McCarty.
Freiberg, see also Freeberg.
Freiberg Henry, poultry, 121 E Mkt House, h 919 S Meridian.
Freiberg John (Techentin & Freiberg), h 1402 N Illinois.
Freije Alexander, pdlr, h 18 Willard.
Freis Charles T, architect, h 83 Park av.
Freismuth Franz B, foreman, h 29 Dickson.
Freitag Andrew H Rev, pastor German Baptist Church, h 306 Davidson.
Freitag John M, h 268 Spring.
Freitag Joseph, bottler, b 268 Spring.
Fremer Barbara (wid Peter), h 292 E Louisiana.
Frenary John W, engr, h 9 Crawford.
French Alice M, h 138 E North.
French Benjamin T, phys, 884 N Capitol av, h same.
French Calvin, lab, h 821 Mass av.
FRENCH CHEMICAL WORKS, Elso Keller Pres, Clare T Keller Vice-Pres, Elisha B Osborn Sec and Treas, Mnfrs of Keller's Kompound and Grocers' Specialties, 22 S Alabama.
French Ella (wid Charles), h 25 Alvord.
French Elmer, motorman, h 324 Lincoln av.
French Elmer I, window dresser, h 894 N Senate av.
French Elmer S, motorman, h 356 N Pine.
French Eugene R, grocer, n s Michigan av 4 e of Sharpe av (W), h same.
French George, lab, b 729 N Capitol av.
French George O, cook Marion County Work House, r 31 Garden.
French Henrietta I (wid Wm B), h 81 E Vermont.
French Henry, lab, h rear 97 Locke.
French Henry, lab, h rear 671 N Senate av.
French Ira A, finisher, b 821 Mass av.
French Isabella H (wid Howard H), h 352 Talbott av.
French Joseph C, h 20 Garfield pl.
French Levi E, painter, b 147 Madison.
French Lewis, h 110 Trowbridge (W).
French Lewis B, clk P C C & St L Ry, h 42 N Gillard av.
French Louise C (wid Shelby), b 501 S Meridian.
French Margaret (wid John), b 226 N Delaware.
French Martha J, phys, 113 Highland pl, h same.
French Oscar W, butcher, b 63 N Alabama.
French Samuel B, wireman Sanborn Electric Co, b 89 Indiana av.
French Samuel E, stenog, h 138 S Judge Harding (W I).
French Sylvester J, motorman, h 312 College av.
French Truman B, mngr Wm T Long, b 89 Indiana av.
French Wm L, lab, h 14 Smithson av.
Frenk George J, cutter Frenk & Birk, r 142 N Illinois.
Frenk Gertrude A (Frenk & Birk), h 148 W Michigan.
Frenk John G, brewer, h 123 Agnes.

PAPER BOXES : SULLIVAN & MAHAN 41 W. Pearl St.

DIAMOND WALL PLASTER { Telephone 1410 BUILDERS' EXCHANGE.

If your Laundry Work is not satisfactory, try THE HOME LAUNDRY 197 S. Illinois St. Telephone 1769.

FRENK & BIRK (Gertrude A Frenk, Otto E Birk), Merchant Tailors, 70 N Penn, Tel 394.
Frentz Charles W, fireman, b 878 Cornell av.
Frentz Elizabeth (wid Peter), h 878 Cornell av.
Frentz John B, fireman, b 878 Cornell av.
FRENZEL BROS (John P, Otto N and Oscar F), Dealers in Municipal Bonds, Loans and Investment Securities, Foreign Exchange and Steamship Agts, s w cor Washington and Meridian, Tel 565.
Frenzel Caroline P (wid John P), h 340 N East.
Frenzel George M, cor clk Merchants' Natl Bank, b 340 N East.
FRENZEL JOHN P (Frenzel Bros), Pres The Merchants' National Bank and The Indiana Trust Co, Sec Indianapolis Brewing Co, h 346 N East, Tel 1666.
Frenzel Oscar F (Frenzel Bros), asst cashr The Merchants' Natl Bank, h 290 E New York.
Frenzel Otto N (Frenzel Bros), vice-pres and cashr The Merchants' Natl Bank, treas Indpls Brewing Co, h 845 N Illinois, tel 1365.
Frenzel Wm, h 37 Leon.
Frenzel Wm F, elev opr, h 462 E Vermont.
Frese, see also Fries.
Frese Wm H, drop forgeman, h 394 N Brookside av.
Fretwell John L, coachman 302 N Capitol av.
Fretwell Mattie (wid Thomas), h 25 Athon.
Freund, see also Friend.
Freund Frederick C, mach, h 125 Yeiser.
Freund Matthew, carp, 508 N West, h same.
Freund Oscar, clk Robert Keller, b 547 S New Jersey.
Freund Ottilie, b 164 E Washington.
Freund Robert, clk Robert Keller, h 547 S New Jersey.
Frey, see also Fry.
Frey Adolph, notary public, 196 Elizabeth, h same.
Frey Adolph jr, painter, h 371 E Michigan.
Frey Barbara (wid Nicholas), b 449 N New Jersey.
Frey Benjamin, clk, h 996 N Penn.
Frey Bernhardt, city sanitary insp, h 458 S Illinois.
Frey Edward E, painter, h 338 Spring.
Frey Ephraim, fruits, E Mkt House, h 150 Eddy.
Frey Ernest, engraver, b 196 Elizabeth.
FREY F JOSEPH, Druggist, 752 E Washington, h 750½ same, Tel 1647.
Frey Harry, pdlr, b 150 Eddy.
Frey Herman, printer, r 262½ E Washington.
Frey J Fremont, stereotyper The Indpls Journal, h 204 Christian av.
Freyberger Lee, painter, r 33 Hendricks blk.
Freyen Frederick, cabtmkr, h 85 Bloomington.
Freyer Michael, lab, b 326 W Vermont.
Frick Charles, grocer, 752 N Senate av, h same.
FRICK CO THE, Webb Jay Genl Agt, Engines, Threshers and Saw Mills, 28 Kentucky av.

FRANK NESSLER. WILL H. ROST.
FRANK NESSLER & CO.
Tailors
56 EAST MARKET ST. (Lemcke Building),
INDIANAPOLIS, IND.

Frick Conaway, barber, b 63 Peru av.
Frick George, carp, b 23 W St Clair.
Frick Jacob, lab, h 610 N Senate av.
Frick John, r 301 Mass av.
Frick Julius, tinner, h 332 Orange.
Frick Lawrence, carp, h 49 Paca.
Frick Martin P, barber, h 205 E Ohio.
Frick Peter, solr The Home Brewing Co, h 362 Bellefontaine.
Frick Philip J, tinner, h 46 Sullivan.
Frick Philip J jr, foreman Christian Off & Co, h 219 W New York.
Fricker George C, hostler, b 116 Walcott.
Fricker John A, h 18 Quince.
Fricker Wm W, porter, h 347 Fletcher av.
Friddle Henry, lab, h 1191 Morris (W I).
Friddle James H, gearmkr, b 287 W Merrill.
Friddle Martha M (wid Emory A), b 15 Coble.
Friddle Sarah (wid Laban), b 900 Morris (W I).
Friderici Wm J, mach hd, b 186 W Merrill.
Fridley Wm K, glazier, r 127 W Michigan.
Friedendall John W, lab, b 166 Beacon.
Frieder Samuel, fruits, E Mkt House, h 12 Mulberry.
Friedgen Albert L, plumber, b 416 E Walnut.
Friedgen Charles H, electrician, h 416 E Walnut.
FRIEDGEN CORNELIUS, Boots and Shoes, 19 N Penn, h 287 N Delaware. (See left top lines.)
Friedgen Wilhelmina (wid Charles H), h 416 E Walnut.
Friedley Harmon H, ins adjuster, 11 Talbott blk, h 979 N Delaware.
Friedman Gustav, car rep, h s s Brookside av 1 e of Roseline.
Friedman Henry, city agt, h 139 Miller (W I).
Friedman Marquis, pdlr, h 79 Maple.
Friedman Martin J, bkkpr The Capitol National Bank, b Hotel English.
Friedman Nicholas, tinner, h 66 Highland pl.
Friedman Samuel, clk, h rear 20 Mulberry.
Friedrich Frederick, brewer, h 5 Hendricks.

ACORN STOVES AND RANGES
Haueisen & Hartmann
163-169 E. Washington St.
FURNITURE,
Carpets,
Household Goods,
Tin, Granite and China Wares, Oil Cloth and Shades

THE WM. H. BLOCK CO. 7 AND 9 EAST WASHINGTON STREET. DRY GOODS, MEN'S FURNISHINGS.

The Fidelity and Deposit Co. OF MARYLAND. Bonds signed for Administrators, Assignees, Executors, Guardians, Receivers, Trustees, and persons in every position of trust.
GEO. W. PANGBORN, General Agent, 704-706 Lemcke Building. Telephone 140.

INSURE YOUR PROPERTY WITH FRANK K. SAWYER

•JOSEPH GARDNER•
GALVANIZED IRON
CORNICES and SKYLIGHTS.
Metal Ceilings and Siding.
Tin, Iron, Steel and Slate Roofing.
37, 39 & 41 KENTUCKY AVE. Telephone 322

Friedrich John C, lab, h 673 Wells (N I).
Friedrich Max, saloon, 764 S East, h same.
Friedrichs Caroline (wid August), b 75 W McCarty.
Friedrichs Charles, clk, b 75 W McCarty.
Friedrichs Louis, grocer, 75 W McCarty, h same.
Friend, see also Freund.
Friend's Boarding Home for Young Ladies, Rachel E Clarke matron, 155 N Illinois.
Friend Kidder M, trav agt, h 1668 N Illinois.
Friendly Inn, Wm R Moore supt, 290 W Market.
Friero Vincenzo, scissors grinder, h 336½ E Washington.
Fries, see also Frese.
Fries Casper J, beltmkr, h 469 Union.
Fries Douglass, lab, h 14 Wisconsin.
Fries Edward G, lab, h 41 Wisconsin.
Fries Frank, lab, h 486 Union.
Fries John M, cigarmkr, h 18 King.
Fries John P, packer, h 92 Phipps.
Fries Michael, h 14 Wisconsin.
Fries Michael, lab, b 242 Fremont av (H).
Fries Paul, cigarmkr, b 18 King.
Fries Stephen A D, millwright, b 14 Wisconsin.
Fries Thomas E, lab, b 14 Wisconsin.
Friesner Samuel, cabtmkr, h 568 Jefferson av.
Frietzsche Anna M, stenog The Bates, b 203 N Arsenal av.
Frietzsche Ella E, teacher Public School No 15, b 203 N Arsenal av.
Frietzsche Ernest F, mngr Homeopathic Pharmacy, 62 E Ohio, h 203 N Arsenal av.
Frietzsche Frank F, plumber, b 203 N Arsenal av.
FRIETZSCHE JOHN U, Homeopathic Pharmacy, Ernest F Frietzsche Mngr, 62 E Ohio.
Frietzsche Margaret J (wid John U), h 203 N Arsenal av.
Frink Bertha M, b rear 472 E Washington.
Frink Charlotte M (wid Erastus), h 565 Highland av (N I).

J. S. FARRELL & CO.
Have Experienced Workmen and will Promptly Attend to your
PLUMBING
Repairs. 84 North Illinois Street. Telephone 382.

Frink Edward S (Mills & Frink), h 680 McLene (N I).
Frink George O, artist, h 565 Highland av (N I).
Frish John H, lab, h 8 Ethel (W I).
Fritch James, blksmith, r 247½ S Capitol av.
Fritch Margaret, bkkpr, b 175 E Market.
Fritche Emma, h 49 Oak.
Fritsch August F, cabtmkr, h 52 Michigan av.
Fritsch John N, clk, h 171 Bright.
Fritsch Joseph, grocer, 438 Clifford av, r same.
Fritsch Martin, saloon, 428 Clifford av, h same.
Fritts Daniel H, h 162 Pleasant.
Fritts Henry, bricklyr, h 214 Jefferson.
Fritz Adolph, butcher, b 70 Stevens.
Fritz George M, bkkpr, b 624 S East.
Fritz Gottlieb, mach, h 4 Quince.
Fritz Herman, clk, b 70 Stevens.
Fritz Jacob (Koss & Fritz), h 624 S East.
FRITZ JOHN P, Druggist and Chemist, Deutsche Apotheke, 355 Virginia av, Tel 1642, b 70 Stevens.
Fritz Joseph, student, b 122 Patterson.
Fritz Noah, lab, h 17 Columbia al.
Fritz Peter, stone contr, h 70 Stevens.
Fritz Sebastian, driver, b 529 S New Jersey.
Fritz Walter R, salesman, h 352 Prospect.
Frobenius Frederick, mach, h 345 W Michigan.
Frobenius Gustav E, engraver, b 345 W Michigan.
Frobenius Kunigunda, dressmkr, 345 W Michigan, h same.
Froehlich August E, cooper, h 72 W McCarty.
Froehlich George M, cooper, h 126 Patterson.
Froehlich John G, watchman, b 126 Patterson.
Froelich Henry, b 456 S East.
Frohliger Wm, mach, h 364 E Market.
Frohliger Wm S, boilermkr, h 292 E Louisiana.
Froi De Veaux Augustus A, collr Dyer & Rassmann, b 232 N Noble.
Froman Silas, lab, h 143 Harlan.
Fromeyer Joseph W, mngr Standard Oil Co, b Spencer House.
Fromhold Andrew, clk, b 277 S Delaware.
Fromhold Mary E (wid John), h 277 S Delaware.
FROMMEYER BROS (Henry Jr and Herman), China, Glass and Queensware, 24 S Meridian.
Frommeyer Henry, clk, h 134 N Senate av.
Frommeyer Henry jr (Frommeyer Bros), h 80 N Senate av.
Frommeyer Herman (Frommeyer Bros), h 1110 N Penn.
Fronefield Edith E, stenog Jenney Electric Motor Co, b 1871 E Washington.
Frosch Hilbert, butcher, h 204 S William (W I).
Froschauer Charles P, foreman Carlon & Hollenbeck, h 228 S New Jersey.
Fross George W, plastr, h 234 Cedar.
Frost Almira J (wid Jesse D), b 293 W Vermont.
Frost Edward, chief engr Insane Hospital.
Frost Frederick, brickmkr, h w s Merrit 2 s of Grandview av (H).
Frost George R, lab, b w s Merrit 2 s of Grandview av (H).
Frost Wm G, salesman, h 27 Lynn av (W I).

GUARANTEED INCOME POLICIES issued only by the United States Life Insurance Co.
E. B. SWIFT, Manager. 25 E. Market St.

Furniture Carpets } WM. KOTTEMAN { Stoves Ranges
89 and 91 East Washington Street. Telephone 1742.

WILLIAM WIEGEL } MANUFACTURER OF.... } SHOW CASES } 6 W. Louisiana St. Opposite Union Station.

Fry, see also Frey.
Fry Albert, lab, h 362 Douglass.
Fry Andrew J, janitor, h 205 W 4th.
Fry Ida (wid George), h 173 S Noble.
Fry James, huckster, b 71 Peru av.
Fry James M, h s e cor Shade and Willow (B).
Fry James R, poultry, 319 Virginia av, h same.
Fry James R, teacher, h w s Grand av 5 s of University av (I).
Fry John, condr, b 1139 N Illinois.
Fry Julia (wid Monroe), h 19 Cincinnati.
Fry Kate (wid Archibald), h 17 Fayette.
Fry Rebecca N, h 192 W Ohio.
Fry Sarah (wid Henry), b 508 College av.
Fry Wm H, h 96 Ruckle.
Fryberger Amanda J, h 1259 N Penn.
Fryberger Charles W, carp, 70 Temple av, h same.
Fryberger Christina (wid Frank), b 77 Ash.
Fryberger Edgar L, b 1259 N Penn.
Fryberger John, architect, h 68 Temple av.
Frye Annie E (wid Henry), h 55 Fletcher av.
Frye Carey, painter, h e s Commercial av 2 s of Washington av (I).
Frye Henry, chair mnfr, 1 Fayette, h same.
Frye Jessie, teacher Kindergarten No 7, b e s Commercial av 2 s of Washington av (I).
Frye Wm S, condr, b 55 Fletcher av.
Frye Woodson H, clk Penna Lines, b 55 Fletcher av.
Fryer David L (Fryer & Fleming), h 101 N State av.
Fryer & Fleming (David L Fryer, Charles Fleming), electric supplies, 27 Monument pl.
Fuchs, see also Fox.
Fuchs Charles F, driver, h 260 N Pine.
Fuchs Louis, mach hd, h s w cor Brookside av and Jupiter.
Fuchs Martin, bartndr, b 318 N East.
Fuchs Michael, hostler, h 27 Downey.
Fuchs Paulina (wid Peter), b 264 Bates.
Fudge Frederick C, painter, h 130 Elizabeth.
Fudge Henry M, lab, b 582 W 22d (N I).
Fudge Louis J, millwright, h 527 E 8th.
Fudge Thomas J, carp, h 130 Elizabeth.
Fuehring Bros (Frederick W and Wm H), street sprinkling contrs, 545 E Ohio.
Fuehring Emma A (Wiese & Fuehring), b 71 Leota.
Fuehring Ernest H W, carp, h 71 Leota.
Fuehring Frederick (Fuehring Bros), h 545 E Ohio.
Fuehring Wm H (Fuehring Bros), h 652 E Market.
Fuel Elizabeth, h 70 Oliver av (W I).
Fuerst August, tinner, h 154 Harmon.
Fuerst Charles J, grocer, 479 S New Jersey, h same.
Fuerst Joseph F, grocer, 573 S Meridian, h same.
Fuerst Paul, waiter, b 154 Harmon.
Fugate James L, clk Hildebrand Hardware Co, h 203 N Penn.
Fugate John T, lab, h 188 Madison av.
Fugate Walter L, trav agt Van Camp H and I Co, h 434 N Capitol av.
Fugate Willis T, clk, b 422 Park av.
Fulbright Pearl L, b 174 Broadway.
Fulford John, lab, h 618 N West.
Fulkerson Robert, lab, h rear 418 N East.
Fullen Charles, porter, h 37 Sullivan.
Fullen Charles H, clk Murphy, Hibben & Co, h 37 Sullivan.
Fullen John T, clk, h 408 N California.

We Buy Municipal ~ Bonds ~
THOS. C. DAY & CO,
Rooms 325 to 330 Lemcke Bldg.

Fullen Shelby D (Strouse & Fullen), h 74 Lockerbie.
Fullenwider John C (Webb & Co), b Hotel English.
Fuller Charles Hector, reporter The Indpls News, h 77 E 15th.
Fuller Edward P, boarding State Fair Grounds.
Fuller Emeline E (wid Philander), b 26 Hill.
Fuller Ephraim, salesman, h 855 N New Jersey.
Fuller E Chubb, pres Epitomist Pub Co, r 272 N Meridian.
Fuller Frank E, mngr American Wringer Co, 27 Indiana av, h 200 College av.
Fuller George F, opr W U Tel Co, h 195 Church.
Fuller George W (Jeffery, Fuller & Co), h 43 Hall pl.
Fuller Harvey, mach, b Ross House.
Fuller James C, teacher Blind Inst, h 26 Hill.
Fuller Lorenzo D, car insp, h 27 Carlos.
Fuller Wm H, lab, h 15 Grant.
Fuller Wm J, clk, h 43 Hall pl.
Fullerton Wm, lab, r 440 E Washington.
Fullgraff Adolph F, driver, b 9 Ketcham.
Fullgraff Elizabeth (wid Adolph), h 9 Ketcham.
Fullgraff Otto, uphlr, h 180 Spring.
Fullilove James H, butcher, b 572 W Shoemaker (N I).
Fullilove Julia A (wid James A), h 572 W Shoemaker (N I).
Fullington Thomas M, molder, h 71 King av (H).
Fulmer Charles H, mach, b 247 Bellefontaine.
Fulmer David P, mach, h 15 Brown.
Fulmer Edward P (E P Fulmer & Co), h 1103 N Senate av.
FULMER E P & CO (Edward P Fulmer, Joseph B Warne), Printers' Press work, 94 E Court.
Fulmer Harvey B, mach, 37 McNabb.
Fulmer Hattie M, stenog, b 63 English av.
Fulmer Herbert, clk, b 63 English av.

EAT
HITZ'S CRACKERS AND CAKES.
ASK YOUR GROCER FOR THEM.

TURKISH RUGS AND CARPETS RESTORED TO ORIGINAL COLORS LIKE NEW | Capital Steam Carpet Cleaning Works M. D. PLUNKETT, Telephone 818

BENJ. BOOTH PRACTICAL EXPERT ACCOUNTANT. Books Opened, Written Up, Posted and Balanced. Room 18, 82½ E. Washington St., Indianapolis, Ind.

THE SHERMAN RESTAURANT 18 and 20 S. MERIDIAN STREET
IF YOU WANT A GOOD MEAL AND HAVE IT NICELY SERVED GO TO

ESTABLISHED 1876. TELEPHONE 168.
CHESTER BRADFORD,
SOLICITOR OF PATENTS,
AND COUNSEL IN PATENT CAUSES.
(See adv. page 6.)
Office:—Rooms 14 and 16 Hubbard Block, S. W. Cor. Washington and Meridian Streets, INDIANAPOLIS, INDIANA.

Fulmer Leander A, pres Fulmer-Seibert Co, h 63 English av.
Fulmer Loretah B, stenog Central Union Tel Co, b 15 Brown.
Fulmer Marcus, lab, h 141 Excelsior av.
Fulmer Schuyler C Rev, h 292 Lincoln av.
Fulmer-Seibert Co (Leander A Fulmer pres, George W Seibert jr sec and treas, sewer contrs, 27-28 Baldwin blk.
Fulmer Thomas B, clk C E Coffin & Co, b 15 Brown.
Fulton Franklin P, bookbinder, b 457 Broadway.
Fulton Jane (wid Robert), h s w cor La Salle and Vorster av (M P).
Fulton John, switchman, b 1027 E Washington.
Fulton Joseph W, lab, h 38 Standard av (W I).
Fulton Martha A (wid Felix M), h 457 Broadway.
Fulton Robert, lab, r 32 N Senate av.
Fulton Robert G, lab, b s w cor LaSalle and Vorster av (M P).
Fulton Sarah C (wid Homer), h 39 Hall pl.
Fulton Simpson R, opr W U Tel Co, h 37 Hall pl.
Fulton Wm B, grocer, s w cor Cornell av and 22d, h same.
Fulton Wm F, patternmkr, b s w cor Cornell av and 22d.
Fulton Wm H, ins agt, h 435 S Brookside av.
Fultz, see also Foltz.
Fultz Edward, plater, h 123 Garden.
Fultz Frank A, painter, h 599 Mass av.
Fultz Jacob, mach hd, h 214 Yandes.
Fultz James, lab, b 741 Nevada.
Fultz James E, molder, h 18 Cleveland (H).
Fultz James G, lab, h 35 Hadley av (W I).
Fultz John, turner, h 99 Woodburn av (W I).
Fultz John W, gasfitter, h 102 Andrews.
Fultz Joseph, tmstr, h 205 Colgrove.
Fultz Mary (wid Timothy), h 103 Malott av.
Fultz Nina M, clk, b n w cor Andrews and 16th.
Fultz Wm H, foreman, h 959 Cornell av.
Fultz Zachariah A, carp, h 63½ Indiana av.

O. B. ENSEY
MANUFACTURER OF
GALVANIZED IRON CORNICE,
SKYLIGHTS AND WINDOW CAPS,
TELEPHONE 1562. Cor. 6th and Illinois Sts.

Fulwell George, steward The Bates.
Funck Emil, driver, b 51 Sanders.
Funck Frank, saloon, 71 Wyoming, h same.
Funk Amer J, lab, h 168 Church.
Funk Anthony, barber, b 630 S Meridian.
Funk Charles D, molder, h 48 Bismarck av (H).
Funk Charles H, mach, b 168 Church.
Funk Edgar A, meats, 85 E Mkt House, h s e cor Fletcher and Auvergne avs (I).
Funk Edward A, baker, h 158 Harmon.
Funk Frederick, lather, r 80 N New Jersey.
Funk James B, phys, 436 Talbott av, h same.
Funk James O, molder, h 22 Cleveland (H).
Funk John, butcher, r 80 N New Jersey.
Funk Joseph, baker Insane Hospital, h 60 Haugh (H).
Funk Susannah M (wid John H), b 48 Bismarck av (H).
Funke Anthony, barber, 586 S Meridian, b 630 same.
Funke Charles H, mach, h 127 Trowbridge (W).
Funke Frederick H, mach, b 93 Coburn.
Funke Hannah G (wid Gottlieb), h 129 Trowbridge (W).
Funke Henry W, lab, h 93 Coburn.
Funkhouser Cornelius, cooper, h 445 W Addison (N I).
Funkhouser Hugh C, salesman D H Baldwin & Co, h 15 S Gale (B).
Furches Abram, lab, h 16 Rhode Island.
Furgason, see also Ferguson.
Furgason Albert, filer, h 483 Virginia av.
Furgason Albert L, supt Ingalls blk, office 18 same, h 1145 N Meridian.
Furgason Carrie M (wid Leslie P), b 601 N Senate av
Furgason Charles, lab, b 334 W Washington.
Furgason Charles H, engr, h 121 English av.
Furgason C Cary, rate clk Big 4 Route, b 1145 N Meridian.
Furgason Daniel, lab, b 125 Ft Wayne av.
Furgason Francis M, feed, 636 N West, h 634 same.
Furgason Frank L, bkkpr Van Camp H and I Co, h 1021 N Penn.
Furgason Henry S, collr, h 31 William.
Furgason James W, lab, h 101 N Linden.
Furgason John A, grocer, 306 N Illinois, h 270 N Capitol av.
Furgason Leslie P, paperhngr, h 10 Maria.
Furgason Robert, clk, b 334 W Washington.
Furgason Virgil T, clk, b 634 N West.
Furgason Wm, lab, b 188 Alvord.
Furgason Wm C, bkkpr, h 925 N Alabama.
Furgason Wilson, clk, b 634 N West.
Furgerson James, lab, b 24 Blackford.
Furgerson Jennie, h 24 Blackford.
Furley Milton, carp, h 1074 W Vermont.
Furlong Anna (wid Patrick), b 83 John.
Furnas Arthur L, ins agt, h 369 Clifford av.
Furnas Charles W, clk, h 181 River av (W I).
Furnas Christopher L, r 15 Commercial blk.
Furnas Horace B, engr, r 93 N Alabama.
Furnas John, pres American Fruit Co, sec State Capital Investment Assn, treas Old Wayne Mutual Life Assn, h 374 Clifford av.
Furnas John H, mngr Indpls Street Cleaning Co, h 72 Middle Drive (W P).
Furnas Robert M, agt, h 102 Middle Drive (W P).

TUTEWILER UNDERTAKER, No. 72 WEST MARKET STREET. TELEPHONE 216.

PARTNERSHIP INSURANCE At low cost. By which provision is made against the pecuniary loss and embarrassment resulting from the death of a member of a firm.
Provident Life and Trust Co. of Philadelphia, D. W. EDWARDS, Gen'l Agt., 508 Indiana Trust Bldg.

THEODORE F. SMITHER - GRAVEL ROOFING MATERIALS
2 and 3-Ply Ready Roofing Building Paper, etc. B of Materials.
Telephone 86. 01 15 West Maryland St.

FURNAS ROBERT W, Creamery and Ice Cream Mnfr, 112-114 N Penn, h 268 Central av, Tel 1047.
Furnas Walter J, asst sec State Capital Investment Assn, b 374 Clifford av.
Furness Wm, mach, b 5 S Station (B).
Furniss Henry W, phys, 92 W New York, r 56 Orange.
Furniss Sumner A, phys, 92 W New York, r 56 Orange.
Furniss Wm H, canceling clk P O, r 56 Orange.
Furry Frank, motorman, h 620 E 10th.
Furry Margaret C, h 316 E Wabash.
Furry Quinton, waiter, b 316 E Wabash.
Fuss Ernest, cabtmkr, b 220 Columbia av.
Fussey Delia H (wid Edward C), h 26½ English av.
Fussner Adam, carp, b 409 Union.

G

Gabb Hannah (wid Wm), b 1126 N Delaware.
Gabbei August, lab, b 23 Thomas.
Gabbei Reinholt, lab, h 23 Thomas.
Gabe Harry E, phys, 539 Virginia av, h 1372 N Illinois.
Gabel Conrad, h 196 N Noble.
Gabert Mary C (wid Frederick), b 478 Stillwell.
Gable Charles, condr, r 190½ S Illinois.
Gable Clyde C, restaurant, 110 E Wabash, h same.
Gable George M, mach, h 1123 E Washington.
GABLE LEWIS A, Druggist, 828 N Illinois, tel 1028, h 824 N Penn.
Gable Joseph A, trav agt J L Kavanagh, b Circle Park Hotel.
Gabrie Elizabeth (wid Jacob), h 480 Lincoln av.
Gabriel Frederick, lab, b 83 Morton.
Gabriel Robert C, condr, h 101 Brookside av.
Gadd Anna E (wid Morrison N), dressmkr, 454 S Delaware, b same.
Gadd Bert S, sawyer, b 330 Prospect.
Gadd Espy M, harnessmkr, h 454 S Delaware.
Gadd George W, bkkpr The Indpls Stove Co, h 236 N East.
Gaddie John E, janitor, h 202 Martindale av.
Gaddie Wm H, hostler, r 29 Ellsworth.
Gaddis George P (Cloud & Co), h 67 Elm.
Gaddis Harry E, candymkr, b 67 Elm.
Gaddis Wm C, timekpr Parry Mnfg Co, r 40 S Capitol av.
Gaddy Alice, housekpr 274 College av.
Gaddy John, lab, h 18 Sumner.
Gaddy Martha (wid Henry), h rear 16 W North.
Gaddy Richard H, lab, r rear 626 Home av.
Gaebler Charles, driver, h 366 W New York.
Gaeth Frederick, caller, h 521 S Illinois.
Gaeth Henry C, bkkpr, b 521 S Illinois.
Gaeth Herman F, clk Hetherington & Berner Co, h 232 W South.
Gaff Thomas T, pres Cerealine Mnfg Co, res Cincinnati, O.
Gafkey Frank, lab, r 290 W Market.
Gage Elizabeth (wid Willard), b 250 N Meridian.
Gage Lyman H (Gage & Boyd), h 722 Broadway.

THE WHEN IS A WORLD BEATER.

Gage Matthew W, electrician, b 114 Prospect.
Gage Robert J, electrician, h 26 Laurel.
Gage Thomas H, electrician, h 161 Elm.
Gage & Boyd (Lyman H Gage, Thomas M Boyd), lumber, 336 Lemcke bldg.
Gagle Charles G, barber, 503 Bellefontaine, h same.
Gahen Henry, lab, b 300 W Maryland.
Gahm Lena (wid John), h 326 N West.
Gahr John, cabtmkr, h 227 Davidson.
Gahr Richard A, mach, b 227 Davidson.
Gahs Edward, baker Parrott & Taggart, r 90 Fletcher av.
Gail Charles H, weaver, b 116 Cornell av.
Gail John F, supt, h 106 Andrews.
Gaile Frank, hostler, r 120 E Pearl.
Gain James W, pdlr, h 610½ Virginia av.
Gaines Duke, lab, b 65 N Dorman.
Gaines Frank, waiter, h 237 W Michigan.
Gaines Frank E, clk, b 209 W New York.
Gaines George B, millwright, h 209 W New York.
Gaines Silas, brakeman, b 28 S Judge Harding (W I).
Gaines Tapley, lab The Bates.
Gainey Louis C, trav agt B B Dildine, h 350 N Illinois.
Gakstatter Charles, tailor, h 22 Ketcham.
Gakstatter Philip, shoemkr, 74 W 1st, h same.
Galbraith Harriet E, teacher Public School No 11, b 781 N Alabama.
Galbraith Harris H, clk, h 824 N Penn.
Galbraith James, lab, h 308 Blackford.
Galbraith Jane (wid Arthur N), h 781 N Alabama.
Galbraith Richard, b 149 Newman.
Galbraith Richard, shoemkr, 734 E 7th, h same.
Galbreath Edward, lab, r 13 Cleaveland blk.
Galbreath Freeman K, student, h 236 E Vermont.
Gale Charles F, bkkpr Christian Koepper, h 413 S New Jersey.
Gale Edward C, clk Christian Koepper, b 76 N East.
Gale Elizabeth R (wid Richard), b 257 N Senate av.

THE A. BURDSAL CO.
WINDOW AND PLATE
GLASS
Putty, Glazier Points, Diamonds.
Wholesale and Retail. 34 and 36 S. Meridian St.

ELECTRIC CONSTRUCTION Isolated Plants Installed. Electric Wiring and Fittings of all kinds. C. W. Meikel. Tel. 466. 96-98 E. New York St

DALTON & MERRIFIELD { LUMBER South Noble St., near E. Washington

INDIANA ELECTROTYPE CO. : BEST WORK LOWEST PRICES.
23 WEST PEARL ST., INDIANAPOLIS, IND. JOB WORK. BOOK PLATES. All Orders Promptly Filled. BEST PATENT BASE ON THE MARKET.

KIRKHOFF BROS.,
GAS AND ELECTRIC FIXTURES
THE LARGEST LINE IN THE CITY.
102-104 SOUTH PENNSYLVANIA ST.
TELEPHONE 910.

Gale Giles T, mach, b 14 Chadwick.
Gale Henry, janitor Public School No 12, h 14 Chadwick.
Gale Henry, lab, h 46 Birch av (W I).
Gale Jarvis, watchman, b 248 S East.
Gale Lewis C, trav agt Christian Koepper, h 154 S Noble.
Gale Mnfg Co, Hiram O Winter agt, farm impits, 117 W Washington.
Gale Nicholas, fireman, h 120 Lee (W I).
Gale Wm T, lab, h s s Walnut 1 e of Race.
Galiton Sarah (wid Albert), b 158 Howard.
Gall, see also Gaul and Goll.
GALL ALBERT, Carpets, Draperies and Wall Paper, 17-19 W Washington, Tel 386; h 300 N Illinois.
Gall Albert jr, mngr wall paper dept Albert Gall, b 374 N Illinois.
Gall Edmund F, clk Albert Gall, h 1009 N Illinois.
Gall Elizabeth (wid John), h rear 19 Russell av.
Gall Fred, student, b 300 N Illinois.
Gall John G, seat caner, b 122½ Ft Wayne av.
Gall Peter J, agt, h 45 Cornell av.
Gallagher Annie, b 372 S Missouri.
Gallagher Anthony E, coremkr, b 48 N Belmont av (H).
Gallagher Bernard, brakeman, r 32 S Gale (B).
Gallagher Charles S, h 378 Talbott av.
Gallagher Edward W, tel opr, b 85 Columbia av.
Gallagher Elizabeth (wid Thomas), b 119 Dougherty.
Gallagher Frank, lab, h 267 W Merrill.
Gallagher James H, b 704 Morris (W I).
Gallagher James J, plumber, b 372 S Missouri.
Gallagher James L, boilertndr, r Grand Opera House blk.
Gallagher John, bartndr, b 49 Yandes.
Gallagher John, coachman, b 262 Roanoke.
Gallagher John, lab, h 40 Holmes av (H).
Gallagher John, lab, b 179 W South.
Gallagher John F, lab, b 26 Clay.
Gallagher John F, lab, h rear 331 E Michigan.

COAL AND COKE
The W. G. Wasson Co.,
130 INDIANA AVE. TEL. 989
LIME AND LATH

Gallagher John J, clk P C C & St L Ry, b 838 E Market.
Gallagher Joseph, clk, h 250 Bright.
Gallagher Joseph P, lab, b 278 S West.
Gallagher Margaret (wid Francis), h 85 Columbia av.
Gallagher Michael, molder, h 22 Highland av (H).
Gallagher Michael J, messenger Am Ex Co, h 319 S Meridian.
Gallagher Michael W, lab, h 48 N Belmont av (H).
Gallagher Patrick, flagman, h 20 Chadwick.
Gallagher Patrick, lab, h 262 Roanoke.
Gallagher Patrick B, saloon, 195 W Washington, h 113 Bright.
Gallagher Patrick H, lab, h 278 S West.
Gallagher Peter, engr, h 331 W 2d.
Gallagher Peter, molder, h 159 Sheffield av (H).
Gallagher Thomas, mach, h 161 Harrison.
Gallagher Thomas, molder, h 10 Highland av (H).
Gallagher Thomas H, mach, b 20 Chadwick.
Gallahue Philip M, whol carpets, 40 W Market, h n s Oak av 2 s of Central (I).
Gallahue Phoenix M, mnfr's agt, 40 W Market, h s e cor Oak av and Central (I).
Gallahue Ralph L, musician, b 75 Hoyt av.
Gallahue Warren C, mnfr's agt, 40 W Market, h 75 Hoyt av.
Gallatin John, foreman, h 162½ Indiana av.
Gallatin Sarah (wid Albert), b 158 Howard.
Gallaway Lucy F (wid John A), b 25 W 1st.
Gallaway Mary (wid Wesley), h rear 21 Mill.
Gallimore Henry, carp, h 69 Thalman av.
Gallivan Catherine (wid Michael J), h 150 S Noble.
Gallivan John F, boilermkr, b 150 S Noble.
Gallivan Honora (wid Matthew), h 395 S Capitol av.
Gallivan Mary (wid Patrick), h 178 Deloss.
Gallivan Mortimer, foreman, h 327 Bates.
Gallivan Mortimer D, lab, h 91 Sanders.
Gallivan Edward J, steward, b 178 Deloss.
Galloway Alexander, supt C H & D R R, h 1081 N Illinois.
Galloway Charles, lab, r 480 W Lake (N I).
Galloway Clinton E, phys, 444 Central av, h same.
Galloway Edward, helper, h 193 W Merrill.
Galloway George E, meats, 290 E Washington, h same.
Galloway George W, lab, h 421 W Eugene (N I).
Galloway James H, bkkpr, h 195 Blake.
Galloway James W, butcher, h 63 Orange.
Galloway Samuel G, tilemkr, b 421 W Eugene (N I).
Galloway Walter S, mech engr, b 1081 N Illinois.
Galloway Zina B, city agt, b 421 Eugene (N I).
Galluzzo Guiseppe, pdlr, h 141 E Maryland.
Galluzzo Salvadore, shoemkr, b 159 S Alabama.
Gally Julius M, saloon, 149 Ft Wayne av, h same.
Galm Michael, saloon, 628 Virginia av, h same.
Galm Lena M (wid Martin), h 99 Broadway.
Galpin Wm R, clk H P Wasson & Co, b 618 Broadway.
Galt Harry S, lab, h 79 Germania av (H).
Galvin George W, lawyer, 18½ N Penn, h n w cor Downey and Omer avs (I).
Galvin James, lab, h 308 Blackford.

W. H. MESSENGER COMPLETE HOUSE FURNISHER 101 East Washington Street, Telephone 491

Foundry and Pattern Shop } McNamara, Koster & Co. { PHONE 1593 212-218 S. Penn. St.

THE FRED DIETZ CO. WOODEN PACKING BOXES MADE TO ORDER. FACTORY AND WAREHOUSE TRUCKS. 400 Madison Avenue. Telephone 654.

Galvin John, clk Kingan & Co (ltd), r 84 W Ohio.
Galvin John, harnessmkr, b 29 Madison av.
Galvin Patrick J, foreman, h 457 S Capitol av.
Gamble Wm G, nurse 102 N Alabama.
Gambold Charles B, clk, b 104 Ash.
Gambold John S, brakeman, b 336 E Market.
Gambold Levi S, carp, h 336 E Market.
Gambold Thomas E, agt, h 67 Madison av.
Gambold Wm H, brakeman, b 336 E Market.
Gamerdinger Charles, blksmith, h 121 Fulton.
Gamerdinger Frank W, clk The Aldag Paint and Varnish Co, b 559 E Washington.
Gamerdinger Jacob, h 559 E Washington.
Gamerdinger Jacob jr (Keller & Gamerdinger), h 453 E Market.
Gamman David, trav agt, h 60 Andrews.
Gamstetter Michael, carp, h 87 High.
Gandolfo Nicolo, confr, 214 E Washington, h same.
Gang Joseph, bartndr, h 74 Wisconsin.
Ganly James A, barber, b 107 W South.
Gann Aaron, janitor, h 388 W 2d.
Gann Charles R, coachman 952 N Delaware.
Gann James, plumber, b 388 W 2d.
Gannon Martin, stonecutter, h 46 Ash.
Gannon Wilbur N, bkkpr, h 312 Bellefontaine.
Gano Wm D, city fireman, b 428 N Capitol av.
Ganon George W, boilermkr, h 191 Douglass.
Ganon Henry F, h 41 Warren av (W I).
Ganote Edwin M, teas, 100 Mass av, h 96 N Alabama.
Gansberg Bros (Wm F and Frederick A), coal, 368 Shelby.
Gansberg, Charlotte (wid Frederick), h 51 Prospect.
Gansberg Frederick A (Gansberg Bros), b 51 Prospect.
Gansberg Wm F (Gansberg Bros), b 51 Prospect.
Gansberg Wm F, contr, 35 S Linden, h same.
Gant Alvey C, painter, h 103 Rhode Island.
Gant David W, clk, h 333 N Liberty.
Gant Ellen B, b 274 Blake.
Gant Jesse, carp, 547 E Michigan, h same.
Gant Joseph F, dentist, h 519 N West.
Gant Willard, driver, h 421 National rd.
Gant Wm A, dentist, 40½ E Washington, h 525 Talbott av.
Ganter Catherine (wid Cassian), h 150 N Pine.
Ganter Daniel C, mach, h 31½ Virginia av.
Gantley James A, coremkr, b 58 Kansas.
Gantley John P, lab, b 58 Kansas.
Gantley Michael, lab, h 58 Kansas.
Gantner Frances T, cashr, b 615 Charles.
Gantner Magdalene, cashr H H Lee, b 615 Charles.
Gantner Michael, custodian City Hall, 14 basement Court House, h 615 Charles.
Gantner Michael J, lab, b 615 Charles.
Gapen Philip M, b 430 Park av.
Gapen Samuel E, harnessmkr, h 901 N Delaware.
Garard Bertha E, stenog, b 117 Lexington av.
Garard Joseph T, carp, h w s Denny 3 n of Washington.
Garber Daniel H, lineman, b 227 Virginia av.

Henry H. Fay,
40½ E. WASHINGTON ST.,
AGENT FOR
Insurance Co. of North America,
Pennsylvania Fire Ins. Co.

Garber Gertrude E, clk, b 148 Brookside av.
Garber, Jacob K, millwright, h 227 Virginia av.
Garber Jesse M, millwright, b 227 Virginia av.
Garber Mathilda J, stenog, b 227 Virginia av.
Garber Max, lab, b 418 S Capitol av.
Garber Wm S (Garber & Carpenter), h 784 N Penn.
GARBER & CARPENTER (Wm S Garber, Walter N Carpenter), Official Reporters and Stenographers Marion Circuit Court and Superior Court Room 1, Office 51 Court House, Tel 547.
Garbison James, lab, h 2 Dakota.
Gard Edwin V, pdlr, h 335 W Ontario (N I).
Gard Lillian M, stenog, r 121 E Ohio.
Gard Samuretta V, music teacher, 121 E Ohio, r same.
Garder George A, fireman, b n w cor Michigan and State avs.
Gardiner John C, clk, h 110 Bates al.
Gardiner Mary (wid Samuel), h 45½ N Capitol av.
Gardiner Thomas, lab, h 336 Blake.
Gardner Allen, painter, b 244½ E Washington.
Gardner Anderson S, r 36 Waverly blk.
Gardner Anna M, midwife, 194 E Morris, h same.
Gardner Anson J, livery, 408 College av, h 1028 N Meridian.
Gardner Arthur U, clk L E & W R R, b 431 E Georgia.
Gardner Benjamin T, collr, h 65 N East.
Gardner Bros & Ross (John T and Edward G Gardner, Frederick T Ross), jewelers, 56 N Penn.
Gardner Charles A, mach hd, b 194 E Morris.
Gardner Charles C, filer, b 1028 N Meridian.
GARDNER CHARLES J, Wholesale and Retail Meats, Vandalia R R and River and 47 N Illinois, Tel 789; h 1058 W Washington.

Union Casualty & Surety Co.
of St. Louis, Mo.
Employers', Public, General, Teams and Elevator Liability; also Workmen's Collective, Steam Boiler, Plate Glass and Automatic Sprinkler Insurance.
W. E. BARTON & CO., General Agents,
504 Indiana Trust Building.
LONG DISTANCE TELEPHONE 1918.

Shorthand! BUSINESS UNIVERSITY. When Bl'k. Elevator day and night. Typewriting, Penmanship, Book-keeping, Office Training free. See page 4. Est. 1850. Tel. 499. E. J. HEEB, Proprietor.

HENRY R. WORTHINGTON JET and SURFACE CONDENSERS 64 S. PENN. ST. Long Distance Telephone 284.

UNION CO-OPERATIVE LAUNDRY (COMPOSED OF UNION LAUNDRY GIRLS.) NOS. 8, 40 AND 42 VIRGINIA AVENUE. T. E. SOMERVILLE, MANAGER. TELEPHONE 1269. INDIANAPOLIS, IND.

HORACE M. HADLEY
REAL ESTATE AND LOANS....
66 East Market Street
Telephone 1540. BASEMENT.

Gardner David S, printer, h 58 Huron.
Gardner Edward G (Gardner Bros & Ross), h 258 Davidson.
Gardner Eliza E (wid James P), r 40 Ash.
Gardner Emeline B (wid Samuel), b 377 W New York.
Gardner Frank, janitor, b 182 Muskingum al.
Gardner Frank, lab, h 119 Clarke.
Gardner Frederick, filer, h 251 Lincoln la.
Gardner Fred C, cashr E C Atkins & Co, h 292 Broadway.
Gardner George, lab, h 194 E Morris.
Gardner George E, lab, b 251 Lincoln la.
Gardner Henry, piano tuner, h 427 S East.
Gardner Jane M (wid Andrew), h 220 W 5th.
Gardner Jesse S, phys, 25 N Illinois, h 413 W Addison (N I).
Gardner John, b 227 S New Jersey.
Gardner John, butcher, h 30 Bloomington.
Gardner John, lab, h 823 Chestnut.
Gardner John, lab, b 323 W St Clair.
Gardner John F, hostler, h 222½ E Washington.
Gardner John G, saloon, 189 S Reisner (W I), h same.
Gardner John T (Gardner Bros & Ross), h 329 N Pine.
GARDNER JOSEPH, Tin, Copper and Sheet Iron Worker and Dealer in Hot-Air Furnaces, Roofing of All Kinds, 37, 39 and 41 Kentucky av, Tel 322; h 190 N West. (See left top cor cards.)
GARDNER JOSEPH C, with Joseph Gardner, h 639 E Ohio.
Gardner Kate A (wid Conrad), b 998 W Washington.
Gardner Laura (wid Samuel), h 166 Blake.
Gardner Lena (wid Henry), b 158 Spring.
Gardner Major, barber, h 35 Center.
Gardner Marshall F (Gardner & Proctor), h 139 Huron.
Gardner Martha (wid Thomas), b 14 Haugh (H).
Gardner Mary A (wid Robert J), b w s Central av 2 s of 24th.

Merchants' and Manufacturers Exchange
Make Collections and Commercial Reports......
J. E. TAKKEN, MANAGER,
19 Union Building, 73 West Maryland Street

Gardner Mary H (wid John), b 166 Howard.
Gardner Mary J, dressmkr, 273 E Court, h same.
Gardner Napoleon P, barber, 1 S Meridian, h 35 Center.
Gardner Parker I, farmer, b 316 E North.
Gardner Samuel M, driven wells, 72 E Court, h 112 Ash.
Gardner Stirling, printer, b 58 Huron.
Gardner Thomas, molder, b 14 Haugh (H).
Gardner Thomas P, molder, h 41 King av (H.)
Gardner Thomas W, watchmkr, h 316 E North.
Gardner Walter K, blksmith, h e s Rural 2d n of Bloyd av.
Gardner Warren O, mngr, h 423 N Senate av.
Gardner Wendel, h 341 N California.
Gardner Wm, clk, b 1058 W Washington.
Gardner Wm, farmer, h 14 Haugh (H).
Gardner Wm, pdlr, h 58 Huron.
Gardner Wm F, foreman Charles Krauss, r 127 E Washington.
Gardner Wm H, clk, b 322 Ft Wayne av.
Gardner Wm H, trav agt Van Camp H and I Co, r 568 E Washington.
Gardner & Proctor (Marshall F Gardner, Thomas Proctor), hardware, 13 Shelby.
Garey, see also Gary.
Garey George G, trav agt, h 481 N Alabama.
Garhart Nathan K, vice-pres Fox & Garhart Specialty Co, h 348 N New Jersey.
Garis Olive H (wid Wm F; Mythen & Garis), h 30 School.
Garitson James, lab, h w s Garfield av 5 n of Washington.
Garitson John W, driver, b James Garitson.
Garitson Otto, driver, b James Garitson.
Garland Ira, brakeman, h 763 E Washington.
Garland James, lab, b w s Samoa 1 s of Mass av.
Garland John, butcher, h 15 Wallace.
Garland Patrick, butcher, h 15 Wallace.
Garlock James F, lab, b 21 Reynolds av (H).
Garlock Wesley G, lab, h 21 Reynolds av (H).
Garman John E (Garman & Kane), r 17 Stewart pl.
Garman & Kane (John E Garman, Walter J Kane), pictures, 17 Stewart pl.
Garn Adam, collr, h 8 Brookland av.
Garner Dora (wid Robert), b 34 Athon.
Garner George W, lab, h 9 Geneva.
Garner Horatio S, foreman Wm B Burford, h 922 N Senate av.
Garnet Taylor, tmstr, h 486 W 1st.
Garnett Allen, lab, h 120 Rhode Island.
Garnett Charles, lab, h 209 W 6th.
Garnett Clara (wid Thomas), h 166 Woodlawn av.
Garnett Granville, tmstr, h 90 Locke.
Garr Benjamin T, orthopedist, 463 Central av, h 315 Alvord.
Garr Charles W, carp, h 15 Windsor.
Garr Joseph M, mach, b 315 Alvord.
Garr Thomas W, horseshoer, 463 Central av, b 315 Alvord.
Garr Wm B, clk, b 35 Division (W I).
Garrard, see also Gerard and Girard.
Garrard Charles A (T J Garrard & Son), b 225 Broadway.
Garrard Louise, curator Propylaeum, b 22 Home av.
Garrard Thomas J (T J Garrard & Son), h 95 Broadway.

CLEMENS VONNEGUT 184, 186 and 192 E. Washington St. | Wire Rope, Machinery, Lathes, Drills and Shapers

THE WM. H. BLOCK CO. DRY GOODS, DRAPERIES, RUGS. WINDOW SHADES.
7 AND 9 EAST WASHINGTON STREET.

Garrard J T & Son (Thomas J and Charles A), brokers, 21 W Maryland.
Garrett Benjamin B, bricklyr, b 529½ N Illinois.
Garrett Benjamin D, carp, h 861 N New Jersey.
Garrett Benjamin E, tile setter, b 861 N New Jersey.
Garrett Earl S, clk, b 78 Prospect.
Garrett Frank J, plumber, h 531½ N Illinois.
Garrett Frank P, plastr, b 861 N New Jersey.
Garrett James H, porter, h 118 Yandes.
Garrett John M, h 78 Prospect.
Garrett Lawrence, bridgewkr, b 350 S Alabama.
Garrett Mary (wid Richard), h 350 S Alabama.
Garrett Michael, driver, h 165 Harmon.
Garrett Owen, lab, h cor Sherman Drive and C C C & St L Ry.
Garrett Robert, waiter, b 174 Indiana av.
Garrett Vivian N, molder, b 324 W Pearl.
Garrett Wm, mason, h 142 Randolph.
Garrett Wm P, switchman, h 34 N Olive.
Garrettson Charles A F, lab, b s s Lambert 1 e of McLain (W I).
Garrettson George W, driver, h 77 Eastern av.
Garrettson George W, driver, h 127 S Reisner (W I).
Garrigan David, sawyer, r 70 English av.
Garringer Charles E, bartndr, h 1234 Franklin (N I).
Garringer John R, rollman, b 1234 Franklin (N I).
Garringer Joseph, farmer, h 1234 Franklin (N I).
Garringer Wm F, carp, b 1234 Franklin (N I).
Garriott Augustus F, trav agt Indpls Drug Co, h 32 E 24th.
Garriott Mary E (wid Samuel), b 32 E 24th.
Garris Uriah, clk, h 649 E Market.
Garrish Nathaniel W, bricklyr, b 4 Roseline.
Garrison Charles, painter, b 250 Huron.
Garrison Clinton, filer, h 75 S Noble.
Garrison Francis M, carp, h 12 Division (W I).
Garrison Frederick, agt, b 30 McGill.
Garrison James, yardman, h e s Chester av 1 n of E Washington.
Garrison, Landon, car rep, h 138 N Noble.
Garrison Lillian, stenog, b 342 N Illinois.
Garrison Stephen C, lab, r 234 E Wabash.
Garrison Wm C, bkkpr, h 51 The Blacherne.
Garrison Wm S, packer, h 783 N Senate av.
Garritson Arthur J, driver, b 99 Eastern av.
Garritson John, b 2 Water.
Garrity Andrew, lab, h 68 McGinnis.
Garrity James, lab, b 63 Fletcher av.
Garrity John, engr, b 853 Bellefontaine.
Garrity John, lab, h 179 W South.
Garrity Robert J, clk, b 552 S West.
Garry Patrick, fireman, h 21 N Gillard av.
Garshwiler Joseph F, lab, h 46 Thalman av.
GARSHWILER WM P, Physician, 4 Hill av, r same, Tel 617.
Garstang Ellen (wid Robert), b 890 N Penn.
Garstang Reginald W, phys, 142 Mass av, h 890 N Penn.
Garstang Wilfred R, abstract clk C C C & St L Ry, b 890 N Penn.
Garstang Wm, supt motive power C C C & St L Ry, n e cor Delaware and South, h 890 N Penn.

Garten George, lab, h 127 Rhode Island.
Garthus George W, uphlr, h 42 Hoyt av.
Gartin Clement, lab, b 291 Christian av.
Gartlein John F, cigar mnfr, 123 Windsor, h same.
Garver, see also Garber and Gerber.
Garver Bert L, mattressmkr, b 140 Mass av.
Garver Emma J (wid John), h rear 1030 W Washington.
Garver Frank L, checkman, h 126 S East.
Garver John H, letter carrier P O, r 77½ S Illinois.
GARVER JOHN J, Physician, 126 N Meridian, h 888 N Penn, Tels Office 480, Res 794.
Garver Mathias, vice-pres Artificial Ice and Cold Storage Co, h 729 N Capitol av.
Garver Uno E, artist, h 426 Talbott av.
Garver Wm R, phys, 426 Talbott av, h same.
Garvey Clarence J, timekpr, b 619 N Meridian.
Garvey Clayton H, vice-pres American Steel Co, h Anderson, Ind.
Garvey Clifford P, mngr American Steel Co, h 649 N Penn.
Garvey James, lab, h 346 W Maryland.
Garvey James C, bicyclemkr, r 292 E South.
Garvey Michael, lab, h 62 S California.
Garvey Michael, lab, b 346 W Maryland.
Garvey Patrick, lab, b 346 W Maryland.
Garvin Frank, janitor, r 30 Monument pl.
Garvin Hugh C, prof Butler College, h w s National av 2 s of Washington av (I).
Garvin John, lab, b 483 S West.
Garvin John M, porter, b 255 N West.
Garvin Louis H, b Hugh C Garvin.
Garvin Lulie (wid Newton S), h 24 Sheffield av (H).
Garvin Timothy, lab, b 309 S West.
Garvin Wm M, janitor, h 209 Belmont av (H).
Gary, see also Garey.
Gary Charles J, printer, h 266 W Michigan.
Gary Harry L, cabtmkr, h 462 Francis (N I).
Gary Melissa (wid Enos), h 462 W Francis (N I).
Gary Wm T, ins agt, r 28 W Vermont.

GUIDO R. PRESSLER,
FRESCO PAINTER
Churches, Theaters, Public Buildings, Etc., A Specialty.
Residence, No. 325 North Liberty Street
INDIANAPOLIS. IND.

INDIANAPOLIS STEEL ROOFING AND CORRUGATING WORKS, 23 and 25 East South Street. S. D. NOEL, Proprietor.

David S. McKernan, Rooms 2-5 Thorpe Block.
REAL ESTATE AND LOANS
A number of choice pieces for subdivision, or for manufacturers' sites, with good switch facilities.

DIAMOND WALL PLASTER { Telephone 1410 BUILDERS' EXCHANGE.

UNION TRANSFER AND STORAGE CO. Cor. E. Ohio St. and C., C., C. & St. L. R'y Tracks. BRICK WAREHOUSE; CLEANEST AND SAFEST STORAGE IN CITY FOR HOUSEHOLD GOODS AND MERCHANDISE.

W. McWORKMAN,

METAL CEILINGS,
ROLLING SHUTTERS,
DOORS AND PARTITIONS.

930 W. Washington St. Tel. 1118.

Gary Wm W, cabtmkr, h 462 W Francis (N I).
Gasaway Addison H, lab, h 530 S Illinois.
Gasaway Sarah (wid Thomas J), h 15 Haugh (H).
Gaseway Thomas O, phys, 369 Newman, h same.
Gashbach Margaret A (wid John H), b 31 Peru av.
Gaskell Wm, driver, h 15 Osgood (W I).
Gaskin Richard J, lab, h rear 121 N Senate av.
Gasper Charles C, patternmkr, b 397 N West.
Gasper Frank G, bkkpr, b 139 N Delaware.
Gasper Frank W, mngr, r 82½ E Washington.
Gasper George W, bartndr, r 82½ E Washington.
GASPER JOHN B, Saloon, 53 N Penn, h 111 Fayette.
Gasper John H, carp, h 457 W Eugene (N I).
Gasper Joseph, saloon, 68 Virginia av, h 143 Greer.
Gasper Joseph L (Horne & Gasper), h 221 E Vermont.
Gasper Matthew, bartndr, b 1349 N Capitol av.
Gasper Simon, patternmkr, h 397 N West.
Gass Andrew J, uphlr, h 154 E St Joseph.
Gass Louis H, clk, h 318 Cornell av.
Gassert Gottlieb, saloon, 464 S Delaware, h 462 same.
Gastineau Henri, phys, h 9 Ft Wayne av.
Gastineau Plummer E, condr, h 840 E Market.
Gastineau Senteney S, clk, b 9 Ft Wayne av.
Gaston George B, sec and treas Frank Bird Transfer Co, r 74 The Blacherne, tel 179.
Gaston Blucher N, condr, b 272 S Penn.
Gaston Charles, plumber, b 272 S Penn.
Gaston Delilah (wid Hiram R), h 268 N Alabama.
Gaston Edward, grocer and saloon, 53 Kentucky av and 84 W Maryland, h same.

SEALS,
STENCILS,
STAMPS, Etc.
GEO. J. MAYER
15 S. Meridian St.
TELEPHONE 1386.

Gaston George B, h 280 Clifford av.
Gaston James H, mach, b 272 S Penn.
Gaston James M, bkkpr, h 272 S Penn.
Gaston John M, phys, 147 N New Jersey, h same.
Gaston John R, yardman, h rear 121 N Senate av.
Gaston Minnie W (wid Wm), h 84 W Maryland.
Gaston Wm W, bkkpr Bockhoff Bros, h 121 E Ohio.
Gatch George L, trav agt, h 54 Andrews.
Gatchell Theodore, railroad sec Y M C A, h 19 Poplar (B).
Gaten Felix, clk, r 175 W North.
Gater Joseph J, ins agt, h 318 S East.
Gates Alfred B, pres Climax Baking Powder Co, h 826 N Meridian.
Gates Alfred B jr, salesman Krag-Reynolds Co, h 434 S New Jersey.
Gates Alfred D, clk, b 987 N Delaware.
Gates Alonzo, mer police, h 139 N Dorman.
Gates Aretus, clk Paul H Krauss, h 27 Williams.
Gates Arthur D, asst supt E C Atkins & Co, h 839 N Illinois.
Gates Austin B, horse dealer, h 75 Highland av.
Gates Cecil H, blksmith, w s Maple av 1 n of Washington av (I), b same.
Gates Charles, news agt, b 158 W McCarty.
Gates Charles A, lab, b s e cor Moore av and Rural.
Gates Edward E (Gates & Hume), b 826 N Meridian.
Gates Emma (wid Adam), h 136 N Dorman.
Gates Ernest M, clk Fahnley & McCrea, b 75 Highland av.
Gates Estella, r 171 Newman.
Gates Evert R, tel opr P C C & St L Ry (I), b w s Maple av 1 n of Washington av (I).
Gates Frank E, trav agt, b 413 N Illinois.
Gates Frank E, clk A Metzger Agency, h 334 Prospect.
Gates Frank L, foreman The Indpls Sentinel, h 375 N Capitol av.
Gates Frederick E, trav agt, b 338 W 1st.
Gates Frederick F, lab, b 136 N Dorman.
Gates Harry, clk P B Ault & Co, h 72 Jefferson.
Gates Harry B, sec Climax Baking Powder Co, h 651 N Penn.
Gates Herbert, b 839 N Illinois.
Gates Hiram J, molder, h 46 Wallack.
Gates James E, stonecutter, h 47 Torbet.
Gates James M, huckster, h 141 N Gillard av.
Gates Jeremiah K, h 18 Oriental.
Gates Joseph W, saloon, 687 E Washington, h 234 Blackford.
Gates Leonidas E, clk, b Stubbins Hotel.
Gates Oliver, collr, h 87 S Linden.
Gates Peter M (Blackwell & Gates), b 987 N Delaware.
Gates Peter M, mach hd, r 18 Catterson blk.
Gates Wesley, gasfitter, h w s Maple av 1 n of Washington av (I).
Gates Willard W, dentist, 1 Odd Fellows' blk, h 1159 N Penn.
Gates Wm, mach, b 269½ E Washington.
Gates Wm M, clk, b 180 N Illinois.
Gates Wm N, treas Climax Baking Powder Co, b 956 N Illinois.
Gates Wm W, clk Great Atlantic and Pacific Tea Co, b 129 N Illinois.
GATES & HUME (Edward E Gates, George E Hume), Lawyers, 301-302 Lemcke Bldg, Tel 1509.

A. METZGER AGENCY ESTABLISHED 1863. INSURANCE

LAMBERT GAS & GASOLINE ENGINE CO.
ANDERSON, IND. PORTABLE GASOLINE ENGINES. 2 TO 25 H. P.

Gatewood Charles, lab, h rear 163 St Mary.
Gatewood Charles, lab, h 592 E 10th.
Gatewood Ellison, watchman, h 87 Fountain.
Gatewood Jeremiah, lab, h 592 E 10th.
Gatewood Thomas, lab, h 125 Ft Wayne av.
Gatewood Wm A, lab, h 87 Fountain av.
Gaton Matthew, lab, b 40 Torbet.
Gatskill Charles, waiter The Denison.
Gattling Eliza (wid Philip), b 92 Prospect.
Gauchert Frederick, bath attendant, h 440 Talbott av.
Gauding Charles H, framemkr, h 376 Bellefontaine.
Gauding Elizabeth (wid Henry), h 434 Cornell av.
Gauding Wm J, framer, b 434 Cornell av.
Gaughan Anthony, fireman, h 38 McGinnis.
Gaughan Catherine (wid John), h 268 S West.
Gaughan Edward, lab, b 268 S West.
Gaughan James R, lab, h 526 S Capitol av.
Gaughan James, lab, b 268 S West.
Gaughan John, lab, b 268 S West.
Gaughan John F, lab, b 526 S Capitol av.
Gaughan Lackey, lab, h 86 McGinnis.
Gaughen Peter, lab, h e s Hope 1 s of Schofield (B).
Gaul, see also Gall and Goll.
Gaul Frederick W, saloon, 404 S West, h 507 same.
Gauld Adam A (A B Gauld & Bro), h 574 W Francis (N I).
Gauld Alexander B (A B Gauld & Bro), h 522 W McLene (N I).
GAULD A B & BRO (Alexander B and Adam A), Druggists, 499 W Addison, North Indianapolis, Tel 1594.
Gauld Gordon R, clk John D Gauld, b 229 N West.
GAULD JOHN D, Druggist, 201 Indiana av, Tel 1178; h 229 N West.
Gault Wm L, carp, h 48 S Reisner (W I).
Gaumer Apollo T, printer, r 93 N Alabama.
Gaumer Clarence, cigarmkr, h 393 S East.
Gaunt Charles D, clk, h 322 Spann av.
Gaupen Louisa, millinery, 617 Virginia av, h same.
Gaus Benjamin, filer, b 46 Russell av.
Gause Albert, brakeman, h 56 Church.
Gause David H, messenger Am Ex Co, h 24 Meikel.
GAUSEPOHL EDWARD J, Clerk L E Morrison, 4 N Meridian, and Loans, Room 4, 2½ W Washington, Tel 293; h 8 Fletcher av.
Gausepohl Frederick J, cabtmkr, h 164 S Noble.
Gausepohl George H (Hardy & Gausepohl), b 164 S Noble.
Gauss Caroline (wid Charles), h 439 Union.
Gauss Charles A, tinner, 67 Russell av, h 341 S Meridian.
Gauss Emil, bartndr B B Jearl, h 193 S East.
Gauss Eugene J, bkkpr, h 826 E Market.
Gauss Theodore L, asst bkkpr Charles Mayer & Co, b 826 E Market.
Gauthier Arthur J, barber, r 26 Stewart blk.
Gauthier David, stonecutter, b 75 Kentucky av.
Gauze Arthur, brakeman, h 56 Church.
Gavin Annie (wid Patrick), b 40 S West.
Gavin Bridget (wid Thomas), h 335 S Penn.
Gavin Bridget (wid Wm), h 78 Pleasant.
Gavin Charles R, asst treas Park Theater, b 261 S Penn.

Farm and City Loans
25 Years' Successful Business.
THOS. C. DAY & CO,
Rooms 325 to 330 Lemcke Building.

Gavin Frank E (Gavin & Davis), h 477 N Penn.
Gavin John, flagman, h 261 S Penn.
Gavin John jr, lab, b 335 S Penn.
Gavin John E, clk Hayes & Ready, b 78 Pleasant.
Gavin John P, lab, b 45 Chadwick.
Gavin Joseph H, genl treas Grand and English Opera Houses, h 169 Madison av.
Gavin Martin J, miller, h 55 Agnes.
Gavin Martin P, mach, b 78 Pleasant.
Gavin Michael, lab, h 40 S West.
Gavin Patrick, lab, h 45 Chadwick.
Gavin Thomas M, lab, b 45 Chadwick.
Gavin Timothy, saloon, 336 S West, h 309 same.
Gavin Wm L, mngr Park Theater, b 261 S Penn.
Gavin & Davis (Frank E Gavin, Theodore P Davis), lawyers, 903-904 Majestic bldg.
Gavisk Francis Henry Rev, rector St John's Catholic Church, h 76 W Georgia.
Gay Clarence E, painter, b 348 Indiana av.
Gay Elmer F, buyer N Y Store, h 715 College av.
Gay George A, genl mngr Pettis Dry Goods Co, 25-33 E Washington, tel 1530; h 836 N Meridian.
Gay George B, b s s Lambert 1 e of Belmont (W I).
Gay Henry E, carp, 248 Indiana av, h same.
Gay Leonard A, engr, b 248 Indiana av.
Gay Mary (wid Alfred), b 426 Douglass.
Gaylor John, molder, h 396 S West.
Gaylor Orin, attendant Insane Asylum.
Gaylord Edward S, treas Indpls Engine Co, h 378 College av.
Gaylord Francis B, trav agt, h 328 Bellefontaine.
Gaylord Harry G, phys, 19 Prospect, h same.
Gaylord Jesse B, supt, b 378 College av.
Gaynor John J, mach, h 204 Blake.
Gaynor Matthews, engr, h 497 S Capitol av.
Gaynor Michael, lab, h 181 Spann av.
Gaynor Silas C, fireman, b 181 Spann av.
Gaynor Stephen O, engr, h 21 Spann av.
Gaynor Thomas, checkman, b 349 S New Jersey.

EAT
QUAKER BREAD
ASK YOUR GROCER FOR IT.
THE HITZ BAKING CO.

BICYCLES $5 DOWN. MONTHLY. Best Wheels. Best Terms. WHEELMEN'S CO. 31 W. OHIO ST. LONG DISTANCE TEL. 1855.

J. H. TECKENBROCK House, Sign and Fresco Painter, 94 EAST SOUTH STREET.

FIDELITY MUTUAL LIFE PHILADELPHIA, PA. A. H. COLLINS, Gen. Agt. Baldwin Blk. } RATES REASONABLE. SOUND BEYOND QUESTION. BUSINESS-LIKE IN PRACTICE.

BITUMINOUS COAL ▸▸ Edwardsport Coal and Mining Company ROOMS 42 AND 43 WHEN BUILDING.

ESTABLISHED 1876. TELEPHONE 168.
CHESTER BRADFORD,
SOLICITOR OF PATENTS,
AND COUNSEL IN PATENT CAUSES.
(See adv. page 6.)
Office:—Rooms 14 and 16 Hubbard Block, S. W. Cor. Washington and Meridian Streets, INDIANAPOLIS, INDIANA.

Gaynor Timothy, janitor, h 349 S New Jersey.
Gaynor Timothy jr, mach, b 349 S New Jersey.
Gayton Abner, packer, b 40 Torbet.
Gear Clayton I, fireman, b 84 Michigan av.
Gearen Wm, painter, b 89 Deloss.
Gearhard, see also Gerhart.
GEARHARD CHARLES P, Real Estate, 66½ N Penn, h 144 Cornell av.
Gearhart Henry, mach, h 287 Hillside av.
Geary Ida B, teacher Public School No 11, r 455 N Capitol av.
Gebhardt Charles, finisher, b 47 Thomas.
Gebhardt Edward, bartndr, b 47 Thomas.
Gebhardt Frederick, ins agt, r 66 N East.
Gebhardt George J, sawfiler, h s w cor Excelsior and Commerce avs.
Gebhardt Henry, cigar mnfr, 353 E McCarty, h same.
Gebhardt Jacob, carp, h 648 Chestnut.
Gebhardt John N, uphlr, b 170 Harrison.
Gebhardt Mary (wid George M), h 47 Thomas.
Gebhardt Philip, cigarmkr, b 75 Gimbel.
Gebhart Andrew J, coachman, h n s Bedford av nr Park av.
Gebhart John, lab, b 14 McCauley.
Gebhart Kate (wid Abram P), cook, h 245 E Market.
Gebhart Raleigh, boilermkr, b 14 McCauley.
Geckler John F, pressman, h 437 Olive.
Geddes George, carp, h e s Rural 1 n of Brookside av.
Geddes Thomas, phys, 24 S Reisner (W I), b same.
Geddings Andrew, hostler, h 109 Hoyt av.
Geddis Robert, purchasing agt Indiana Bicycle Co, h 1030 N Alabama.
Gedig Anthony, sawyer, b 365 English av.
Gedig John, h 365 English av.
Gedig John, cabtmkr, h 57 Jefferson av.
Gedig Joseph, mach hd, b 365 English av.
GEE EDGAR F REV, Rector Grace Cathedral, Office Knickerbacker Hall, h 360 Central av.
Gee Frank, lab, b 230 W Vermont.

BUY THE BEST.
Outing BICYCLES $85
MADE BY
HAY & WILLITS MFG. CO.
76 N. PENN. ST. Phone 598.

Geeatus Louis, lab, h 38 Howard.
Geeting David M, State Supt of Public Instruction, 27 State House, h 542 Central av.
Gehbauer John C, lab, h 36 Bloomington.
Gehl Matthew, cigarmkr, b 349 E Market.
Gehle Frederick, gasfitter, 472 E Washington, h same.
Gehler John, molder, h 5 W Chesapeake.
Gehman Sylvester, bartndr, h 84 N Delaware.
Gehring Joseph T, trav agt F P Rush & Co, h 427 N East.
Gehring Lena (wid Conrad), b 112 Middle Drive (W P).
Gehring Scott L, printer, The Indpls News, b 427 N East.
Gehring Wm, lab, h 37 Everett.
Gehring Wm I, gasfitter, b 427 N East.
Gehrisch Joseph, shoemkr, h 678 Vorster av (M P).
Gehrke Christian F, shoemkr, 151 Mass av, b 364 Clifford av.
Gehrlein Andrew, butcher, h 506 S West.
Gehrlich Catherine M, stenog, b 21 Harlan.
Gehrlich Charles F, lab, h 414 Union.
Gehrlich Isadore, b 421 Union.
Gehrlich Jacob, carp, h 21 Harlan.
Geider August J, helper, b 176 Union.
Geider Charles G N (Saffell & Geider), h 176 Union.
Geiger, see also Giger.
Geiger Adam, helper, b 79 Wisconsin.
Geiger Alois, bkkpr P Lieber Branch Indpls Brewg Co, h 510 Madison av.
Geiger Frederick M, clk, b 116 E Pratt.
Geiger George W, trav agt D P Erwin & Co, h 116 E Pratt.
Geiger Gottlieb, shoemkr, 253 Highland av, h same.
Geiger Henry C (Cooney, Semer & Co), h 630 E New York.
Geiger John A, cabtmkr, h 76 Wisconsin.
Geiger John G, mach, h 79 Cincinnati.
Geiger John L, musician, b 116 E Pratt.
Geiger, John W, lab, b 79 Wisconsin.
Geiger Joseph, brewmaster C Maus Branch Indpls Brewing Co, h 20 Agnes.
Geiger Leonard F, confr, 348 Virginia av, h 85 Gimbel.
Geiger Melchior, artist, 91 Hoyt av, h same.
Geis Algernon F, checkman, h 221 Buchanan.
Geis Frank G, clk Wheelmen's Co, b 473 S East.
Geis Frank P, ruler, h n s Prospect 5 e of Belt R R.
Geis Henry J, butcher, b Jacob Geis.
Geis Henry M, clk Francke & Schindler, b 473 S East.
Geis Jacob, meats, 292 E Georgia, h e s Watts 2 n of Washington.
Geis Jacob J (Cella & Geis), b 74 N Illinois.
Geis John F, phys, 105 N New Jersey, r same.
Geis John G, foreman, h 39 Coburn.
Geis John H, butcher, b e s Watts 2 n of Washington.
Geis Lawrence A, clk Penna Lines, h 245 E Morris.
Geis Lawrence G, clk Wheelemen's Co, b 473 S East.
Geis Magdalena (wid John), h 473 S East.
Geisel Henry E, carp, h 267 Davidson.
Geisel Jennie, grocer, s e cor Clifford av and Rural, h e s Rural 1 s of Clifford av.
Geisel Mary (wid George), b 507 S West.
Geisel Wm J, clk Robertson & Nichols, h e s Rural 1 s of Clifford av.

ROOFING MATERIAL C. ZIMMERMAN & SONS, SLATE AND GRAVEL ROOFERS, 19 SOUTH EAST STREET.

PUMPS Chain Pumps, Driven Wells and Deep Water Wells. Repairing Neatly Done. Cisterns Built. CHARLES KRAUSS', 42 S. PENN. ST. TELEPHONE 465.

Collars and Cuffs Laundered in Best of Style. Domestic or High Gloss Finish.

Geisendorf Lydia (wid George W), b 222 N Illinois.
Geisendorff Albert T, foreman, b 328 W New York.
Geisendorff Christian E, h 328 W New York.
Geisendorff Claude E, clk, h 1263 E Washington.
Geisendorff C E & Co, S A Fletcher & Co proprs, wool dealers and mnfrs, 402-404 W Washington av.
Geisendorff George E, trav agt, b 328 W New York.
Geisendorff George T, mach hd, h 617 W Michigan.
Geisendorff Holland E, mach, h 65 Lynn av (W I).
Geisendorff Lee H, mach, h 101 Nordyke av (W I).
Geisendorff Louis R, clk, h 62 Minerva.
Geisendorff Lydia T (wid George W), b 222 N Illinois.
GEISER MNFG CO THE, Joseph A Van Camp Agt, Mnfrs of Engines, Threshers and Hullers, 73 W Maryland.
Geiss Johanna (wid Joseph), h 331 E Morris.
Geiss John L, bartndr, b 331 E Morris.
Gekeler Alvin G Rev, pastor Third (Immanuel) German Reformed Church, h 128 Coburn.
Gelbert George, trav agt, r 130 W Ohio.
Gelbert Martin, blksmith, cor 6th and Northwestern av, h Ben Davis, Ind.
Gelderman Edmund C, car rep, h n s Willow 1 w of Station (B).
Gelderman Frederick W, car rep, h 169 Spann av.
Geldermann Henry G, meats, 62 E Mkt House, h 64 Woodlawn av.
Gellert Paul, tailor, h 61 Dawson.
Gellhaus Frederick, porter, b 401 S Delaware.
Gelman, see also Gilman.
Gelman Adolph H, shoes, 126 Indiana av, h same.
Gelman Carl, photog, b 178 Indiana av.
Gelman Eli, gents' furngs, 227 W Washington, h same.
Gelman Samuel, clothing, 178 Indiana av, h same.
Geltmeier Henry, grocer, 200 Orange, h same.
Geltmeier Mary (wid Henry C), h 366 S Alabama.
Geltner Florence (wid Clarence), b 46 S Capitol av.
Geltner Reinhold, mach, b 215 S Alabama.
GEM GARMENT CO, Hanway, Bookwalter & Co Proprs, 17-23 W Pearl.
GEM STEAM LAUNDRY, Logan C Scholl Propr, 37-39 Indiana av, Tel 1671.
Gemmer Charles, huckster, h 32 Ramsey av.
Gemmer Conrad, h 141 Fulton.
Gemmer Gideon, meats, 461 Virginia av, h 48 Sullivan.
Gemmer Wesley, grocer, 37 E Mkt House, b 141 Fulton.
Gemmer Wm, fruits, E Mkt House, h 3 Dawson.
Genolin Thomas M, clk R M S, h 33 Tecumseh.
Gent Joseph F, vice-pres Cerealine Mnfg Co, h 167 N Alabama.
Gent Richard T, miller, h 960 Sugar Grove av (M P).
Gentile Arthur W, lab, h 160 Minerva.

Richardson & McCrea,
79 East Market Street,
FIRE INSURANCE,
REAL ESTATE, LOANS,
AND RENTAL AGENTS.
Telephone 182.

Gentile Benjamin, lab, b 160 Minerva.
Gentle James M, vice-pres The J N Hurty Pharmacy Co, b 381 N Illinois.
Gentle Luke M, phys, 19 W Ohio, r 540 Broadway.
Gentra Alpha, lab, b 285 S Capitol av.
Gentry Albert B, lab, b w s Hope 1 s of Schofield (B).
Gentry Charles, clk, b 10 Fletcher av.
Gentry Emory, clk, h 46 Osgood (W I).
Gentry Green, janitor, b 60 Howard.
Gentry Harry N, patternmkr, b 30 Belmont av (H).
Gentry Jeremiah, feed, 25 Marion av, h 44 Holly av (W I).
Gentry Joseph, carp, h 80 Martindale av.
Gentry Leslie, porter, h 41 Roanoke.
Gentry Milton, lab, h 184 W 2d.
Gentry Robert, draughtsman, b 30 Belmont av (H).
Gentry Roy, clk, r 84 E New York.
Gentry Wm E, clk, b 428 E 12th.
Gentry Wm H, painter, h 230½ W Washington.
Gentry Zachariah M, engr, h 30 Belmont av (H).
Genus Fannie (wid John), b 148 Elizabeth.
Genus Henry, lab, h 148 Elizabeth.
Genus Nebraska, porter, h 410 W North.
Genus Robert H, watchman, h 218 Columbia av.
George Angeline C, b 469 N New Jersey.
George Austin R, carp, h 188 W 3d.
George Benjamin F, carp, 297 E Market, h same.
George Charles A, feed, 1114 E Washington, h 42 Jefferson av.
George Charles L, cook, h 27 Rockwood.
GEORGE CO THE (Lawrence W and Henderson George), Books, Stationery, Periodicals, Typewriters and Supplies, 11 Mass av.
George Ellwood H, trav agt, h 462 N Alabama.
George Franklin E, clk, b 4 Ruckle.
George Harry, lab, h 151 W McCarty.
George Henderson (The George Co), h 517 College av.

SHORTHAND REPORTING......
CONVENTIONS, SPEECHES, SERMONS.
COPYING ON TYPEWRITER.
S. H. EAST, State Agent,
THE WILLIAMS TYPEWRITER
55 Thorpe Block, 87 East Market Street.

ERTEL STEAM LAUNDRY 26 and 28 N. Senate Ave. Telephone 1089.

ELLIS & HELFENBERGER Manufacturers of Iron Vases, Setees and Hitch Posts. 162-170 South Senate Ave. Tel. 958.

THE HOGAN TRANSFER AND STORAGE COMP'Y
Household Goods and Pianos Moved—Packed—Stored...... Baggage and Package Express Machinery and Safes a Specialty Cor. Washington and Illinois Sts. TELEPHONE No. 675.

The Provident Life and Trust Co. OF PHILADELPHIA.
Small Death Rate. Small Expense Rate. Safe Investments. Insurance in force $115,000,000
D. W. EDWARDS, General Agent, 508 Indiana Trust Building.

George Henry S, cigars, 33 McCrea, h 608 E Washington.
George Horace T, plumber, h 27 Rockwood.
George's Hotel, Richard J George propr, 201 E Washington and 120 S Illinois.
George Howard C, clk, b 1092 N Penn.
George Isaac L, grocer, 826 N Illinois, h 4 Ruckle.
George James F, clk, h 920 Morris (W I).
George James H, motorman, h 418 W Shoemaker (N I).
George James O, capt Engine Co No 1, h 535 Virginia av.
George Jesse, h 418 W Shoemaker (N I).
George John L, clk L N A & C Ry, h 267 E New York.
George Joseph H, dentist, 413 Lemcke bldg, h 902 N New Jersey.
George J DeWitt (George & George), h 367 Park av.
George Lawrence W (The George Co), b 517 College av.
George Louis P, asst, r 316 The Shiel.
George Matthias Rev, pastor Third German M E Church, h 164 W Morris.
George Monroe, clk, b 297 E Market.
George Nathaniel F, blksmith, h 418 W Shoemaker (N I).
George Otho G, h 330 Bellefontaine.
George Richard J, propr George's Hotel, 201 E Washington and 120 S Illinois.
George Robert, h 188 W 3d.
George Thomas A, motorman, h 418 W Shoemaker (N I).
George Wm E (George & George), h 1092 N Penn.
GEORGE & GEORGE (J DeWitt and Wm E), Physicians and Surgeons, Office Hours 8-11 A M, 2-5 and 7-8 P M, Rooms 1, 2, 3 and 4 Baldwin Blk, Tel 975.
Gephart Charles W, clk Paul H Krauss, b 168 Union.
Gephart John O, lab, h 169 Douglass.
Geraghty Patrick, press feeder, b 184 E Vermont.
Geran Daniel, lab, h 316 Bates.
Geran Daniel J, tel opr, b 72 Chadwick.

Julius C. Walk & Son, Jewelers Indianapolis.
12 EAST WASHINGTON ST.

Geran Mary (wid Jeremiah), h 72 Chadwick.
Geran Stephen W, bkkpr, b 72 Chadwick.
Gerard, see also Garrard and Girard.
Gerard David M, carp, b 458 Broadway.
Gerard Elizabeth P (wid Lewis H), nurse, 108 Cornell av, h same.
Gerard Fannie E, nurse, 108 Cornell av, b same.
Gerard Sarah J (wid Benjamin F), b 397 Central av.
GERARD "THE TICKETMAN" (Wesley M Gerard), s w cor Washington and Illinois, Tel 1603.
Gerard Wesley M (Gerard "The Ticketman"), h 458 Broadway.
Gerardy Anna, h 170 Olive.
Gerardy John H, varnisher, h 114 Laurel.
Gerardy Peter, mach, h 170 Olive.
Gerber Edwin C, clk L S Ayres & Co, h 276 E North.
Gerber Frank A, cigarmkr, h 102 Maple.
Gerber Nicholas, clk, b 139 W South.
Gerber Samuel S, patrolman, h 128 W North.
Gerber Valentine E, driver, b 276 E North.
Gerber Walter P, porter, b 276 E North.
Gerber Wm W, clk 184 Virginia av, b same.
Gerbiz Stephen, lab, b 107 Sheffield av (H).
Gercke John H, baker, r 10 N Delaware.
Gerdgrottrup George, h 707 Chestnut.
Gerdts Frederick G, clk, h 909 Madison av.
Gerdts Harry A, porter, b 442 S New Jersey.
Gerdts John B, watchman, h 442 S New Jersey.
Gerdts John H, driver, b 442 S New Jersey.
Gerdts Wm H, clk P O, h 667 Virginia av.
Gerhard Edward, mach, b 201 E Washington.
Gerhard Irwin, trav agt, b 34 Larch.
Gerhardt Christian A, cigarmkr, h 18 Carlos.
Gerhart, see also Gearhard.
Gerhart Albert H (Gerhart & Co), h 248 Blake.
Gerhart Edward M, huckster, h 210 Fayette.
Gerhart & Co (Clifton A Parker, Albert H Gerhart), produce, 3 E Mkt House.
Gerkin John, tinner, 1547 N Illinois, h 1663 N Capitol av.
Gerlach Amelia G (wid Philip), h 172 Blake.
Gerlach Charles F, clk, h 325 N West.
Gerlach Frank H, lab, b 261 Davidson.
Gerlach John L, butcher, h 516½ E Washington.
Gerlach Lawrence, lab, h 261 Davidson.
Gerlach Martin W, baker, b 261 Davidson.
Gerlach Wm P, clk, b 172 Blake.
Gerland Wm F, fireman, b 162 Harrison.
Germain Charles, b California House.
GERMAN AMERICAN BUILDING ASSOCIATION OF INDIANA, Otto Stechhan Pres, Fred Knefler Vice-Pres, George W Brown Sec, Albert Sahm Treas, Christian G Weiss Genl Agt, 100 N Delaware, Tel 1719.
German-American Savings Life Assn, James W Hess pres, Austin T Quick sec, J R Henry treas, 718 Lemke bldg.
German Evangelical Lutheran Orphans' Home, Wm C Jaeger supt, n e cor Washington and Watts.
GERMAN FIRE INSURANCE CO OF INDIANA, Theodore Stein Pres, Lorenz Schmidt Sec, Theodore Reyer Treas, 27-33 S Delaware, Tel 1237.

OTTO GAS ENGINES | BUILDERS' EXCHANGE S. W. Cor. Ohio and Penn. Telephone 535.

The Central Rubber & Supply Co. PHONE 8. 79 S. ILLINOIS ST., INDIANAPOLIS, IND. Hose, Belting, Packing, Clothing, Druggists' Sundries, Bicycle Tires, Cotton Hose, Etc. New York Belting & Packing Co., L't'd.

Becker & Son Charles Becker Jacob Becker Jr. Merchant Tailors. 21 N. Penn. St. Tel. 934

SALISBURY & STANLEY • Office, Store and Yard 177 Clinton St. Indianapolis, Ind. Repairing of all kinds done on short notice a Specialty. • Contractors and Builders TELEPHONE 999.

German Harry B, agt, b 96 Eddy.
German General Protestant Orphan Asylum, State av opp Sycamore, Henry F Roesener supt.
German Hyman, agt, b 96 Eddy.
German John, lab, h 35 Wyoming.
German Michael, finisher, b 35 Wyoming.
GERMAN TELEGRAPH THE (Daily), Gutenberg Co Publishers, 27 S Delaware, Tel 269.
German Wm H, h 166 S Linden.
GERMANIA HOUSE, Charles F Weeber Propr, 200 S Meridian.
GERMANIA LIFE INSURANCE CO OF NEW YORK, W H Coburn State Mngr, Room 4 Odd Fellows' Blk.
Germania Mutual Benefit Society, Henry Kranz, mngr, 73 Lombard bldg.
Germann Mollie, h 235 E Wabash.
Gerold Ignatz, baker, 29 Meek, h same.
Gerrard Edward, bkkpr The Standard Dry Kiln Co, h 15 Ketcham.
Gerrish James, electrotype finisher, b 85 Ft Wayne av.
Gerson Ellis R, clk, r 197 N Illinois.
Gerstner Anthony J, tailor, 171 E Washington, h 246 Park av.
Gerstner Christian J, clk, h 124 Davidson.
Gertig Frederick, lab, h 105 Malott av.
Gerwig Wm, baggage master, h 231 Hamilton av.
Gespaj Antonio, lab, h 73 Harmon.
Gessert Frank W, cigar mnfr, 429 S State av, h same.
Gessert Frederick, wagonmkr, h s s Ohio 1 e of Watts.
Gessert John E, boxmkr, b s s Ohio 1 e of Watts.
Gessler Jacob, restaurant, 128 E Wabash, h 123 E Ohio.
Gest Clarence O (George I Gest & Sons), b 328 Hillside av.
Gest Claude A (George I Gest & Sons), b 328 Hillside av.
Gest George I (George I Gest & Sons), h 328 Hillside av.
GEST GEORGE I & SONS (George I, Claude A and Clarence O), Mnfrs of Cigars and Tobacco, 328 Hillside av.
Getchell Clara A (wid Edwin S), h 121 N Illinois.
Gettier Wm J, boxmkr, h 24 Arizona.
Geyer Albert E, driver, b 46 Elizabeth.
Geyer Jacob B, framemkr, h 1679 Graceland av.
Geyer Mary (wid Samuel), b 499 Bellefontaine.
Geyer Milton H, b 1526 N Capitol av.
Geyer Samuel, feed, 177 Indiana av, h 198 W 5th.
Geyer Samuel B, driver, h 39 Hendricks.
Geyer Wm, brewer, h 117 Downey.
Geyer Wm B, tmstr, b 681 Madison av.
Geyer Wm L, uphlr, b 75 Kansas.
Geyer & Haehl (Jacob B Geyer, John C Haehl), lounge mnfrs, 682 Charles.
Ghabour John H, painter, h 110 N Dorman.
Gheurm Desdemona, milliner, b 1595 W Illinois.
Gheurm John D, clk, b 1595 N Illinois.
Gianakos Harry, candy, b 332 E Washington.
Giardnia Paulo, pdlr, h 70 E Maryland.
Giardnia Philip, pdlr, b 70 E Maryland.
Giardina Vincluso, fruits, h 121 Duncan.
Gibbany Charles F, chairmkr, r 130 N Senate av.

Henry H. Fay,
40½ E. WASHINGTON ST.,
FIRE INSURANCE, REAL ESTATE,
LOANS AND RENTAL AGENT.

GIBBONS CHARLES W, Grocer, 499 W McLene (N I), h same.
Gibbons Frank, clk Wyckoff, Seamans & Benedict, r 370 N Meridian.
Gibbons James, grocer, 241 W McCarty, h same.
Gibbons James T, trav agt, r 276 N Alabama.
Gibbons John, engr, h 163 Huron.
Gibbons John A, student, b 327 S New Jersey.
Gibbons Wm, clk The Wm H Block Co, b 61 Fletcher av.
Gibbons Wm E, lab, h 224 W 8th.
Gibbs Charles, coachman 790 N Meridian.
Gibbs Charles E, hostler, b 748 N West.
Gibbs Charles H, lab, h 107 W 10th.
Gibbs Cushioned Horseshoe Co, Hiram H Gibbs pres, Frank T Melcher treas, John L McFarland sec, 67 N Capitol av.
Gibbs Deborah M, b e s Addison 1 s of Washington (M J).
Gibbs Eliza J (wid Duncan), h 748 N West.
Gibbs Ellis, cook, b 180 E Ohio.
Gibbs Frances P, h 155½ Indiana av.
Gibbs Hiram C, clk, b 1029 N Alabama.
Gibbs Hiram H, pres Gibbs Cushioned Horseshoe Co, h 1029 N Alabama.
Gibbs James, waiter, r 370 N Senate av.
Gibbs Jane (wid Joseph), h 391 Blackford.
Gibbs Joshua, lab, b 391 Blackford.
Gibbs Thomas T, lab, b 391 Blackford.
Giberson Lewis W, grocer, 951 W Michigan, h same.
Giblin David, lab, b 129 Bates.
Giblin David, lab, b 27 Helen.
Giblin Elizabeth J, cigars, 200 W Chesapeake, h same.
Giblin Frank, patrolman, h 129 Bates.
Giblin James H, lab, b 272 W Maryland.
Giblin Wm, lab, b 40 S West.
Gibney John H, bkkpr The McElwaine-Richards Co, h 27 Home av.
Gibs Max, notions, E Mkt House, h 328 E Market.
Gibson Alfred M, clk Fitzgerald & Delp, h 124 Pleasant.
Gibson Amos A, lab, h 355 Spring.

JAS. N. MAYHEW,
MANUFACTURING
OPTICIAN
LENSES AND FRAMES A SPECIALTY.
No. 13 North Meridian St., Indianapolis.

LUMBER | Sash, Door and Planing Mill Work. | Balke & Krauss Co. Cor. Market and Missouri Streets.

FRIEDGEN'S TAN SHOES are the Newest Shades Prices the Lowest. 19 North Pennsylvania St.

SAMUEL LAING 72 AND 74 E. COURT STREET. General Job Work in Sheet Metal of all Kinds

M. B. WILSON, Pres. W. F. CHURCHMAN, Cash.
THE CAPITAL NATIONAL BANK,
INDIANAPOLIS, IND.
Make collections on all points in the States of Indiana and Illinois on the most favorable rates.
Capital, - - $300,000
Surplus and Earnings, 50,000
No. 28 S. Meridian St., Cor. Pearl.

Gibson Boston, lab, h w s Arlington av 2 n of Walnut av (I).
Gibson Calvin, lab, b 1000 W Washington.
Gibson Charles, mounter, h 574 S West.
Gibson Charles C, lab, h 35 Blake.
Gibson David, draughtsman L H Gibson, h 909 N Delaware.
Gibson Dora B, teacher Public School No 12, b 296 E New York.
Gibson Elizabeth (wid Emmett), h 105 N Penn.
Gibson Elizabeth (wid John), h 73 Maxwell.
Gibson Florence, b 285 W North.
Gibson Frederick E, cook, h 285 W Pearl.
Gibson George, barber, r 104 S Noble.
Gibson George W, carp, h 591 Mass av.
Gibson James, stonecutter, r 90 N Senate av.
Gibson James A, engr, h 318 S Alabama.
Gibson James H, lab, b 138 N Pine.
Gibson James W, h 129 Yandes.
Gibson James W, butcher, h 190 Columbia av.
Gibson James W, grocer, 656 N West, h same.
Gibson Jasper N, carp, h Thalman av.
Gibson John, tinner, h 227 W Merrill.
Gibson John, lab, h 98 Maxwell.
Gibson John F, lab, b 36 Fayette.
Gibson John R, insp City Civil Engineer's Office, h 282 Prospect.
Gibson Joseph A, printer, b 36 Fayette.
Gibson Laura (wid Frank), b 62 Yandes.
Gibson Louis H, architect, 84 E Market, h 830 N Penn.
Gibson Lucinda (wid John), dressmkr, 105 Minerva, h same.
Gibson Margaret (wid James), h 36 Fayette.
Gibson Mary D (wid David), h 909 N Delaware.
Gibson Miles, engr, h 37 Bloomington.
Gibson Robert H, lab, h 2 Center.
Gibson Robert H, polisher, r 59 Columbia av.
Gibson Samuel D, carp, h w s Denny 5 n of Washington.
Gibson Thomas F, clk, h 113 Oak.
Gibson Thomas H, finisher, h 285 W Pearl.
Gibson Thomas J, miller, h 746 N Senate av.

MONEY
Loaned on Short Notice at Lowest Rates.
TUTTLE & SEGUIN,
Tel. 1168. 28 E. Market St.

Gibson Thomas T, mach hd, b 36 Fayette.
Gibson Tyce W (wid Thomas M), h 284 N Capitol av.
Gibson Wm, roll hd, r 78 W Georgia.
Gibson Wm E, mach hd, b 36 Fayette.
Gibson Wm E, porter, h 439 W Chicago (N I).
Gibson Wm S, carp, h s s Ohio 4 e of Watts.
Gideon Wm, mach hd, h 365 W Pearl.
Gielow Frederick W, clk Hendricks & Cooper, b 736 E Ohio.
Gielow Wm, clk Hendricks & Cooper, b 736 E Ohio.
Gierke Wm F A, bookbndr, 408½ S East, h same.
Gierke Wm F A jr, bookbndr, b 408½ S East.
Giese Charles W Rev, pastor German Evangelical Lutheran St Peter's Church, h s s Brookside av 2 e of Jupiter.
Gieseking Frederick, mach, b 513 E Georgia.
Gieseking Gottlieb, produce, 11 E Mkt House, h 288 E Michigan.
Gieseking Henry, lab, h 513 E Georgia.
Giesking Christian F, carp, h 242 Dougherty.
Giesking Wm F, driver, h 49 Jefferson.
Giesler Gottlieb, mach, b 142 Woodlawn av.
Giesler Mathias, condr, r 888 W Washington.
Giezendanner Charles jr, clk Lewis A Gable, b 148 W Vermont.
Giezendanner Harry F, clk, b 148 W Vermont.
Giezendanner J George, baker, h 389 Indiana av.
Giezendanner Nicholas, baker, b 44 Pendleton av (B).
Giezendanner Rudolph, lab, b 148½ W Vermont.
Giezendanner Wm, baker, n e cor Schurman and Vorster avs, h same.
Giezendanner Wm jr, baker, 104 Yandes, h same.
Giffin James E, mngr Theodore Marceau, b Hotel English.
Giffin Martha J (wid Wm F), b 509 N West.
Gifford Charles C, bartndr, h 170 Blake.
Gifford Joseph S, clk, h 107 Martindale av.
Gifford Letitia (wid John T), h 34 S Capitol av.
Gifford Ollie (wid Samuel), b 143 N Alabama.
Gifford Samuel, tmstr, b w s Miami 6 s of Prospect.
Gift Benjamin F, shoes, 442 Mass av, h 427 College av.
Gift Charles R, clk, b 427 College av.
Giger, see also Geiger.
Giger Henry J, florist, b w s Senate av 2 n of 30th (M).
Gilbert Amelia Q (wid John W), h 1037 N Meridian.
Gilbert Charles M, b Enterprise Hotel.
Gilbert Charles R, blksmith, e s Lancaster av 2 n of Clifford av, h same.
Gilbert Edward, ins, 44½ N Penn, h 305 Indiana av.
Gilbert Edward O, lab, b 416 Clifford av.
Gilbert Eliza (wid Caleb), b 327 S Delaware.
Gilbert Esther M (wid Edmund A), dressmkr, rear 161 St Mary, h same.
Gilbert Euphemia, h 151 Meek.
Gilbert Frank C, barber, r 15 E New York.
Gilbert James, pdlr, b s w cor Elwood and Elizabeth.
Gilbert James J, mach, r 2 Spann av.
Gilbert John, driver, h 587 Virginia av.
Gilbert Lida E, teacher Butler College, b w end University av (I).

PAPER BOXES, MANUFACTURED BY SULLIVAN & MAHAN 41 W. PEARL STREET.

DIAMOND WALL PLASTER { Telephone 1410 BUILDERS' EXCHANGE.

Fine Laundry Work or Specialty. Collars and Cuffs our Hobby.

Gilbert Martha M (wid Austin L), h 448 College av.
Gilbert Mary (wid Jacob), h 35 Henry.
Gilbert Omer T, baggageman, h 178 S East.
Gilbert Samuel, lab, h 331 Olive.
Gilbert Stephen W, teacher Deaf and Dumb Inst, b 29 N State av.
Gilbert Wm H, filer, h 193 W Maryland.
Gilbert Zoe, bkkpr O S Runnels, b 448 College av.
Gilbreath, see also Galbraith.
Gilbreath Frank M, tmstr, h 344½ E St Clair.
Gilbreath Harry A, piano tuner, b 130 Christian av.
Gilbreath John S, livery, 130 Christian av, h same.
Gilbreath Joseph F, condr, h 921 Bellefontaine.
Gilbreath Victor G, student, b 921 Bellefontaine.
Gilby John, carp, h 81 Warren av (W I).
Gilby John F, filecutter, b 81 Warren av (W I).
Gilby James T, helper, b 81 Warren av (W I).
Gilchrist Frank N, driller, b 1 Allfree.
Gilchrist George E, tmstr, h 14 S Station (B).
Gilchrist Job J, presser, h 22 S Austin (B).
Gilchrist Lizzie B, h 261 N West.
Gilchrist Minerva M, restaurant, 33 S Station (B), h 14 same.
Giles John, lab Insane Hospital.
Gilgour Catherine (wid John), h 59 Clifford av.
Gilgour James D, plastr, h 27 Camp.
Gilgour Jennie, bkkpr, b 122 Ruckle.
Gilgour John, clk, b 122 Ruckle.
Gilgour Robert, lab, b 122 Ruckle.
Gilgour Wm, blksmith, h 122 Ruckle.
Gilkey Adaline (wid Joseph A), h 244½ E Washington.
Gilkey Oliver B, carp, 248 Virginia av, h 19 Pleasant.
Gilkey Samuel T, lab, h e s Denny 6 n of Washington.
Gilkison Mary Z, teacher Public School No 11, b 610 Broadway.
Gilkison Wm F, h 610 Broadway.
Gill Bridget (wid Patrick), grocer, 202 W South, h same.
Gill Benjamin F, lab, h 91 S Reisner (W I).
Gill Dennis, r 267 N New Jersey.
Gill Edward N, clk, h 63 Tacoma av.
Gill Elliott A, tel opr, h 179 Jefferson av.
Gill Eugene G, huckster, h 144 S William (W I).
Gill Frank L, sawmkr, b 144 Williams (W I).
Gill Frederick, paperhngr, b 379 N West.
Gill James D, painter, 174 Lexington av, h same.
Gill John, bartndr, b 57 S California.
Gill John, lab, r 81 Muskingum al.
Gill John L, lab, b 63 Tacoma av.
Gill Joseph P, mach, h 49 Temple av.
Gill Joseph R, carp, r 190 E Market.
Gill Louis C, carriagemkr, h 1100 E Ohio.
Gill Louis C jr, mach, b 1100 E Ohio.
Gill Mary A (wid James), h 174 Lexington av.
Gill Michael F, foreman, h 36 Temple av.
Gill Philip, cook, r 81 Muskingum al.
Gill Raymond E, varnisher, h 180 Elizabeth.
Gill Richard, clk, b 202 W South.
Gill Sarah C (wid Caleb B), b 75 E New York.

FRANK NESSLER. WILL H. ROST.
FRANK NESSLER & CO.
Tailors
56 EAST MARKET ST. (Lemcke Building),
INDIANAPOLIS, IND.

Gill Thomas A, brakeman, h 63 Tacoma av.
Gill Wm, butcher, b 57 S California.
Gill Wm, uphlr, b 80 Lexington av.
Gill Wm A, foreman, r 29 Commercial blk.
Gill Wm A, clk M M Cummings, r 53½ W Washington.
Gill Wm H, b 100 Yeiser.
Gill Wm H, fireman, h 64 Temple av.
Gill Wm H, sawmkr, h 16 Garland (W I).
Gillaspie Edward, lab, r 199 S Capitol av.
Gillaspie Thaddeus J, ironwkr, h 317 S Alabama.
Gillaspy George W, attendant Insane Hospital.
Gillaspy John W, tinner, b 501 N California.
Gillaspy Rachel (wid Andrew J), h 450 W Wells (N I).
Gilleland Charles H, plastr, h 235 Columbia av.
Gilleland Raymond I, clk, b 45 Edward (W I).
Gilleland Theodore R, agt, h 45 Edward (W I).
Gillespie Bryant W (Stockton, Gillespie & Co), h 61 S Reisner (W I).
Gillespie Celia, h 91 Cornell av.
Gillespie Charles, lab, h 124 Minerva.
Gillespie Edward, lab, b 199 S Capitol av.
Gillespie Gilbert H, plastr, h s w cor Ethel av and 17th.
Gillespie James E, carp, h 25½ Kentucky av.
Gillespie John A, plastr, h 25 Arbor av (W I).
Gillespie John S, farmer, h s w cor Ethel av and 17th.
Gillespie Samuel, lab, r 264 Bates.
Gillespie Wm F, carp, h 98 Oliver av (W I).
Gillespie Wm J, sec and treas Indiana and Chicago Coal Co, b 593 N Penn.
Gillet Arthur, mngr Acme Milling Co, h 222 Randolph.
Gillet Harriet M (wid Horace S), h 222 Randolph.
Gillett Anna B (wid Augustus B), h 265 N Illinois.
Gillett Welby H, mnfrs' agt, 333 Lemcke bldg, r 30 Hendricks blk.

ACORN STOVES AND RANGES
Haueisen & Hartmann
163-169 E. Washington St.
FURNITURE,
Carpets,
Household Goods,
Tin, Granite and China Wares, Oil Cloth and Shades

THE HOME LAUNDRY
197 S. Illinois St. Telephone 1769.

THE WM. H. BLOCK CO. 7 AND 9 EAST WASHINGTON STREET. DRY GOODS, MEN'S FURNISHINGS.

Fidelity and Deposit Co. of Maryland. BONDS SIGNED.—LOCAL BOARD John B. Elam, Albert Sahm, Smiley N. Chambers, John M. Spann.
GEORGE W. PANGBORN, General Agent, 704-706 Lemcke Building. Telephone 140.

Insure Your Property With FRANK K. SAWYER || 74 EAST MARKET STREET Telephone 8.

JOSEPH GARDNER,
Hot Air Furnaces
With Combination Gas Burners for Burning Gas and Other Fuel at the Same Time.
37, 39 & 41 KENTUCKY AVE. Telephone 322.

Gillette Arthur J, lumber, h 170 Bellefontaine.
Gillette Charles H, woodwkr, h 45 Broadway.
Gillette Ebenezer F, com, h 66 Beaty.
Gillette Edward N, mngr, h 227 E 7th.
Gillette Frederick E, foreman, b 282 Central av.
Gillette Howard P, woodwkr, b 45 Broadway.
Gillette Mary A (wid Henry R), h 81 W Michigan.
Gillette Oscar S, bentwood wks, s w cor Bloyd av and Morris (B), h 282 Central av.
Gilliam Edward L Rev, presiding elder Indiana Distruct A M E Church, h 473 W Eugene (N I).
Gilliam John T, clk W H Roll's Sons, h 239 E Louisiana.
Gilliam Wm H, b 473 W Eugene (N I).
Gilliard Peter M, lab, b 44 Prospect.
Gilliland David, driver, h 147 Ludlow av.
Gilliland Edward, plumber, b 330 W Vermont.
Gilliland Edward W, bicycle rep, b 147 Ludlow av.
Gilliland Elmer G, horseshoer, b 363 Talbott av.
Gilliland Wm H, wagonmkr, h 330 W Vermont.
Gillispie John, saloon, 291 W Maryland, b 57 S California.
Gillispie Mary J (wid Garrett), b 399 Ash.
Gillman Eli, gents furngs, 227 W Washington, h same.
Gillman George E, cabtmkr, h 174 Excelsior av.
Gillmore Lewis R, train dispatcher P & E Ry, r 37½ W Washington.
Gillum Granville N, grocer, w s Denny 1 n of Washington, h same.
Gillum Lee A, carp, h w s Chester av 3 n of Washington.
Gilman, see also Gelman.
Gilman Benjamin, grocer, 276 S Illinois, h same.
Gilman Charles H, printer, h 1376 N Senate av.

J. S. FARRELL & CO.
Plumbing
Natural and Artificial Gas Fitting.
84 N. ILLINOIS STREET.
TELEPHONE 382.

Gilman Frank L, dentist, 653½ N Senate av, h same.
Gilman Grace M, teacher Girls' Classical School, b 27 E Pratt.
Gilman John C F, clk, b 323 Home av.
Gilman Lydia D (wid Henry F), h 323 Home av.
Gilman Samuel C, printer, b 323 Home av.
Gilmartin John F, fireman, b 280 W Maryland.
Gilmartin Joseph H, printer, b 280 W Maryland.
Gilmartin Susan (wid John), h 280 W Maryland.
Gilmer George C, driver, h 209 LeGrand av.
Gilmer Silas, porter, h 136 Patterson.
Gilmore Albert M, clk L E & W R R, b 143 N Alabama.
Gilmore Charles C, clk, h 147 W South.
Gilmore Charles C, r r agt, b 116 Cornell av.
Gilmore Charles C, sec Old Wayne Mutual Life Assn, h 1239 N Illinois.
Gilmore Eliza (wid Thomas), b 574 N Penn.
Gilmore Elizabeth W (wid Abel C), h 75 Sheldon.
Gilmore John E, boilermkr, h 44 N Gale (B).
Gilmore Lawrence, fireman, b 882 W Washington.
Gilmore Maria (wid James), h 219 W 3d.
Gilmore Mary A (Wm H Gresh & Co), b 75 Sheldon.
Gilmore Russell H, printer, b 251 S New Jersey.
Gilmore Thomas H, pressman, h 251 S New Jersey.
Gilmore Wm, lab, b 41 Hiawatha.
Gilpatrick George H, ins, 54 When bldg, h 245 N Delaware.
Gilpin David R, baker, h w s Oakland av 2 n of Clifford av.
Gilpin Israel, lab, h e s Brookville rd 3 s of Washington.
Gilpin James E, musician, b e s Brookville rd 3 s of Washington.
Gilpin Job B, baker, 385 Clifford av, h 404 same.
Gilpin Leda I (wid Thomas), h 240 Dougherty.
Gilpin Thomas L, trav agt, h 240 Dougherty.
Gilray Wm J, trav agt, h 55 Woodlawn av.
Giltner Bernard, carp, h 133 Clinton.
Giltner Herbert E, helper, b 133 Clinton.
Gilyard James, lab, r 3 Wood.
Gimbel Edward J, brazier, b 268 Spring.
Gimbel Frank G, printer, b 268 Spring.
Gimbel George F, lab, h 28 Fenneman.
Gimbel Henry K, packer, h 21 Stevens.
Gimbel Katherine (wid George M), dressmkr, 20 Morton, h same.
Gimbel Martin, lab, b 355 S East.
Gimbel Michael H, h 355 S East.
Gimbel Wm H, clk, h 19 Stevens.
Ginfitto Benardo, fruits, h 155 Harmon.
Ginfitto Frank, fruits, h 157 Harmon.
Ginfitto Louinno, fruits, b 157 Harmon.
Ging Benjamin F, feed e s National av 5 s of Washington av (I), h same.
Ging Virgil B, student, b e s National av 5 e of Washington av (I).
Gingerrich Daniel, carp, h 29 Barth av.
Ginkel Sophia (wid George), b 519 S West.
Ginkel Valentine, beltmkr, b 519 S West.
Ginn Henry, farmer, h w s Central av 1 n of 24th.
Ginn John, h 318 Indiana av.

IF CONTINUED to the end of its dividend period, policies of the UNITED STATES LIFE INSURANCE CO., will equal or excel any investment policy ever offered to the public. | E. B. SWIFT, Manager, 25 E. Market St.

Wm.Kotteman 89 & 91 E. Washington St. TELEPHONE 1742 Furniture

SHOW CASES WILLIAM WIEGEL 6 West Louisiana Street Opp. Union Station.

Ginn John T, watchmkr, 260 W Washington, h same.
Ginsberg Charles J, cabtmkr, h 91 Belmont av.
Gintner Emma, clk, b 630 S Meridian.
Ginz Albert, stenog Parry Mnfg Co, b 443 N East.
Ginz Emma (wid Michael), h 443 N East.
Ginz George D, mach, b 443 N East.
Ginz George D, toolmkr, h 502 Eugene (N I).
Ginz Otto W, cutter, b 443 N East.
Gioscio John, painter, 170 N Alabama, r 83½ Mass av.
Gioscio Marcelo, r 7, 83½ Mass av.
Gipe Francis M, h 496 Broadway.
Gipe Sylvester H, engr, h 162 Johnson av.
Gipe Unia E, clk New York Store, b 24 S Pine.
Gipe Warren T, engr, h 41 Jefferson av.
Gipe Wm F, flagman, h 24 S Pine.
Gipson John S, lab, h 32 Hadley.
Girard, see also Garrard and Gerard.
Girard Reuben, cabtmkr, h 413 W Eugene (N I).
Girick Isaac, wrapper mnfr, 53 Russell av, h same.
Girls' Classical School, May Wright Sewall prin, 426 N Penn.
Girton Charles, livery, 187 Indiana av, h 45 Fayette.
Girton James, coachman, h 221 W 3d.
Girton John, lab, h 170 Lafayette.
Girton Mary A (wid Samuel), h 378 Lafayette.
Girton Robert, lab, h 1281 Morris (W I).
Girvasi Antoni, lab, h 124 Duncan.
Gish Abraham G (Middlesworth, Benson, Nave & Co), h 180 S Missouri.
Gish David J, clk, h 105 S Reisner (W I).
Gisler Conrad, meat mkt, 812 S East, h 814 same.
Gisler Frank, saloon, 185 E Washington, h 78 Lockerbie.
Gisler George H, shoes, 650 Virginia av, h 31 Prospect.
Gisler Gottlieb, mach, b 142 Woodlawn av.
Gisler John U, carp, 114 Greer, h same.
Gisler Valentine, cooper, h 570 S West.
Gist Lee, lab, h rear 138 E St Joseph.
Gist Theodore H, real est, h s s Washington av 1 e of Cherry av (I).
Gist Wm T, lab, h 42 Northwestern av.
Githens Charles D, tailor, b 87 E Michigan.
Githens Charles H, mach, h 656 W Washington.
Githens Charles O, lab, b 11 Concordia.
Githens Franklin A, lab, h 34 State.
Githens Harry T, mach hd, h 28 Brett.
Githens Joseph O, lab, r 249½ W Washington.
Githens Leonidas M, engr, b 11 Concordia.
Githens Martha E (wid Jesse), r 23 Wyandot blk.
Giuliano Antonio, confr, 287 E Washington, h same.
Giuliano Joseph (F Mascari, Bros & Co), h 127 Duncan.
Giuliano Michael, clk, b 287 E Washington.
Givan Benjamin F, mach, h 124 Columbia av.
Givan Mary E, dressmkr, 124 Columbia av, h same.
Given George A, musician, b 1165 N Penn.
Given George A jr, musician, b 705 N Senate av.
Given George W, mach, h 99 N State av.
Given John A, grocer, 30 Indiana av, h 705 N Senate av.

We Buy Municipal
~ Bonds ~
THOS. C. DAY & CO,
Rooms 325 to 330 Lemcke Bldg.

Given John B, clk, b 705 N Senate av.
Given Kirk, condr, h 888 W Washington.
Givens Albert S, stonecutter, h 408 E Pearl.
GIVENS CHARLES W, Druggist, 27 Clifford av, r same.
Givens Eva, h 221 W Michigan.
Givens James D, photog, r 4 Mass av.
Givens John, waiter, r 175 W North.
Givens Lemuel D, lab, h 88 Division (W I).
Givens Mack, waiter, r 175 W North.
Givens Nancy (wid Frank), b 574 E St Clair.
Givens Robert, h 400 Blackford.
Givens Robert, porter, h 140 Indiana av.
Givens Samuel G, barber, 46 Virginia av, h 225 Fayette.
Givens Wm E, barber, 517 Virginia av, h 107 Shelby.
Glaab George, boxmkr, h 59 Wisconsin.
Glaab Michael, lab, b 59 Wisconsin.
Gladden Alfred H (Gladden Lumber Co), h 392 Park av.
Gladden Alva, clk, h 314 N West.
Gladden Charles S (Gladden Lumber Co), res Memphis, Tenn.
Gladden George W, clk, b 314 N West.
Gladden Lumber Co (Alfred H, Charles S, Otis W and Oscar P Gladden), lumber, 133 Commercial Club bldg.
Gladden Oscar P (Gladden Lumber Co), b 392 Park av.
Gladden Otis W (Gladden Lumber Co), h 853 N New Jersey.
Gladden Wm A, clk, b 314 N West.
Glading George M, lather, b 114 Clinton.
Gladish Samuel M, clk, b Exchange Hotel (W I).
Gladish Willis L Rev, pastor New Church Chapel, h 905 N Delaware.
Glaescher Frederick, tailor, 159 Virginia av, h 207 Fletcher av.
Glander Benjamin, agt, b 125½ Hadley av (W I).
Glascock Charlotte E (wid James), nurse, 29 College av, h same.
Glascock Nathan C, stable foreman U S Express Co, b 135 N Illinois.

EAT
QUAKER BREAD
ASK YOUR GROCER FOR IT.
THE HITZ BAKING CO.

CARPETS CLEANED LIKE NEW. TELEPHONE 818
CAPITAL STEAM CARPET CLEANING WORKS

BENJ. BOOTH PRACTICAL EXPERT ACCOUNTANT. Thirty years' experience. First-class credentials. Room 18, 82½ E. Washington St. Indianapolis, Ind.

18 and 20 S. Meridian St. Established 8. The Old Re ... le Sherman European Restaurant

ESTABLISHED 1876. TELEPHONE 168.
CHESTER BRADFORD,
SOLICITOR OF PATENTS,
AND COUNSEL IN PATENT CAUSES.
(See adv. page 6.)
Office:—Rooms 14 and 16 Hubbard Block, S.W. Cor. Washington and Meridian Streets,
INDIANAPOLIS, INDIANA.

Glascock Wm C, mach, h 29 College av.
GLASCOCK WM H, Supt Indiana Institution for the Education of the Blind, n s North bet Meridian and Penn, h. same, Tel 1335.
Glaser Adam, driver, h 30 Deloss.
Glaser Alfred, miter cutter, h w s Shade 8 s of Pendleton av (B).
Glasgow Wm H, mngr, r 203 N Illinois.
Glasing Charles, painter, h 55 N Judge Harding (W I).
Glass Christopher C, b 173 Hadley av (W I).
Glass Edward, horseshoer, b 243 W Washington.
Glass Frank L, constable, 91½ E Court, h 37 Hoyt av.
Glass James J, lab, h 15 Lennox.
Glass Robert, engr, h 384 Olive.
Glassburn Joseph H, lab, h 1280 Morris (W I).
Glasscock Bert, polisher, b 49 School.
Glasscock Charles W, carp, h 49 School.
Glasser Edward, pdlr, h 93 Douglass.
Glassman Simon (Glassman & Sattinger), h 418 S Capitol av.
Glassman & Sattinger (Simon Glassman, Jacob Sattinger), meats, 37 Russell av.
Glasspool Walter, plastr, b 12 S Senate av.
GLATTFELDER HENRY, Genl Blacksmith and Horseshoer, 477 S Delaware, h 91 Coburn. (See adv in classified Carriage and Wagonmakers.)
Glauber Barbara (wid Nicholas), b 89 Wilson.
Glaubke Wm A, florist, w s Carter 1 s of 30th, h same.
Glaus Peter, tmstr, h 329 W 2d.
Glavin Edward, lab, h 410 S Delaware.
Glavin John, lab, h 352 S Alabama.
Glavin Patrick F, lab, b 410 S Delaware.
Glaze Frank, h 326 W Court.
Glaze Wm T, scale rep, h 960 W Vermont.
Glazebrook Anthony, lab, h 120 Earhart (N).
Glazebrook Charles, tailor, b 121 W Vermont.

CORRUGATED IRON CEILINGS AND SIDING.
ALL KINDS OF REPAIRING.
O. B. ENSEY,
TELEPHONE 1562.
COR. 6TH AND ILLINOIS STREETS.

Glazier Albert J, foreman Journal Job Printing Co, h 42 Ashland (W I).
Glazier Francis H, h 151 Hadley av (W I).
Glazier Frank F, pressfeeder, b 139 E South.
Glazier Franklin T, elev opr Court House, b 139 E South.
Glazier Harvey D, city fireman, h 359 S East.
Glazier John P, clk, b 139 E South.
Glazier John T, city fireman, h 139 E South.
Glazier Louis A, engr, h 56 River av (W I).
Glazier Lydia (wid Charles), b 41 Hoyt av.
Glazier Peter F, collr Indpls Gas Co, h 151 Hadley av (W I).
Glazier Strawder G, capt Engine Co No 15, h 254 S Olive.
Gleason Bridget (wid Edward), h 23 Grant.
Gleason Charles, agt, b 86 E Ohio.
Gleason David, lab, h 431 Mulberry.
Gleason Major K, baker, 947 Ash, h same.
Gleason Wm, h 547 N West.
Gleason Wm E, ins agt, 11 Talbott blk, h 1446 N Illinois.
Gleeson Michael, lab, b 63 Fletcher av.
Gleeson Thomas, lab, b 26 Rose.
Glenn Amanda A (wid John), b 58 College av.
Glenn Anna (wid Michael), b 55 E McCarty.
Glenn Annie (wid James), b 5 Frazee (H).
Glenn Charles, lab, b 58 College av.
Glenn Elwood, clk, b Roosevelt House.
Glenn Emily (wid John), h 54 Rhode Island.
Glenn Ernest, porter, r 278 E Court.
Glenn Eveline (wid Liberty), h 54 Rhode Island.
Glenn Fannie L, teacher, b 862 E Washington.
Glenn Harry, cabtmkr, r 237½ Mass av.
Glenn James C, lab, h 53 Torbet.
Glenn John, engr, b 772 E Washington.
Glenn John, lab, b 54 Rhode Island.
Glenn Mabel, dressmkr, r 90½ Mass av.
Glenn Mary J, h 200 E St Joseph.
Glenn Michael D, bartndr, h 205½ W Ohio.
Glenn Nathan, lab, h 12 Hiawatha.
Glenn Patrick, lab, b 52 Minerva.
Glenn Peter, waiter, r 320 E Court.
Glenn Robert T, city ticket agt Penna Lines, 46 Jackson pl, b 862 E Washington.
Glenn Samuel, lab, b 54 Rhode Island.
Glenn Sherman, plastr, b 1373 W Washington (M J).
Glenn Thomas, lab, h 240 N Capitol av.
Glenn Thomas M, molder, b 55 E McCarty.
Glenn Thomas T, lab, h 467 W Chicago (N I).
Glenn Wm, h 862 E Washington.
Glenn Wm, lab, b 17 Howard.
Glenn Wm, molder, b 52 Minerva.
Glenn Wm L, steamfitter, b 862 E Washington.
Glenn Wm N, lab, h 565 N Senate av.
Glenn Winifred (wid John), h 52 Minerva.
Glennen Edward R, asst engr The Blacherne, h 144 N Capitol av.
Glennon Maurice, bricklyr, b 252 E Washington.
Glenny Wm P, buyer N Y Store, b 400 N Illinois.
Glenroy James R, musician, b Hotel English.
GLENS FALLS INSURANCE CO, Carroll L De Witt Special Agt, Harvey B Martin Local Agt, 311-312 Lemcke Bldg, Tel 1740.
Glessing Carl, painter, h 55 Harding (W I).
Glessing Louise (wid Thomas B), h 237 W New York.

TUTEWILER UNDERTAKER, No. 72 WEST MARKET STREET. TELEPHONE 216.

THE PROVIDENT LIFE AND TRUST CO. OF PHILADELPHIA. Endowment Insurance presents the double attraction of relieving manhood and middle age from anxiety and old age from want.
For particulars apply to D. W. EDWARDS, General Agent, 508 Indiana Trust Building.

THEODORE F. SMITHER, AGENT FOR WARREN'S ANCHOR BRAND ASPHALT ROOFING OFFICE, 151 WEST MARYLAND ST. TEL. 861.

Glessing Rudolph, brewer, b 180 E McCarty.
Glessner George W, constable, 91½ E Court, h 145 Yandes.
Glessner Taylor, carp, b 99 Columbia av.
Glick Adolph, dry goods, 211 W Washington, h same.
Glick Albert B, clk Adams Ex Co, h 33 N Reisner (W I).
Glick Elias, tailor, h 515 S New Jersey.
Glick George H, farmer, h 33 N Reisner (W I).
Glick Henry, dry goods, 254 W Washington, h same.
Glick Henry, fruits, 47 E Mkt House and 292 Virginia av, h 290 same.
Glick John, lab, h 46 Geisendorff.
Glick Mary M (wid Solomon M), b 33 N Reisner (W I).
Glick Samuel, clk, b 211 W Washington.
Glick Solomon, porter, b 33 N Reisner (W I).
Glickert Charles A, electrician, b 306 S West.
Glickert John, shoes, 306 S West, h same.
Glickert John E, mach, b 306 S West.
Glidden Jeannette (wid Seth D), r 28½ Indiana av.
Glidewell Albert G, tinner, h 32 Lynn av (W I).
Glidewell Robert F, boilertester, b 80 Yandes.
Glidewell Therod N, farmer, h s e cor Schurman and Floral avs (M P).
Glidewell Thomas J, h 80 Yandes.
Glidewell Thomas S, lab, b 80 Yandes.
Glines Grace G, stenog Indpls Rubber Co, b 68 W New York.
Glines Ida M (wid James S), h 68 W New York.
Glisson Catherine (wid Joseph), b 8 Cleveland (H).
Glitzeirstein Charles, saloon, 286 W Washington, h same.
GLOBE ACCIDENT INSURANCE CO, Albert Sahm Pres, Wm A Walker Sec, Union Trust Co Treas, Charles F Coffin Genl Counsel, 15-19 Aetna Bldg, 19½ N Penn, Tel 1161. (See adv back cover.)
GLOBE ADVERTISING CO, Ernest H Youel Mngr, 303 Indiana Trust Bldg.
GLOBE CLOTHING CO THE, Dreyfoos & Co Proprs, 97-99 E Washington.
Globe Excelsior Works, Josh Zimmerman propr, 19 S East.
GLOBE MACHINE WORKS, A G Cox Pres, C A McConnell Sec, C B Wanamaker Supt, Machinery for All Purposes Made and Repaired, 72-74 W Court, Tel 1811.
Glode Frederick, driver, h 39 Arizona.
Gloger Otto, lab, h rear 31 Wisconsin.
Glogower Alexander, clk, b 156 N Liberty.
Glore Edward M, condr, h 20 Bloomington.
Glossbrenner Alfred M, mngr Levey Bros & Co, h 1666 N Illinois.
Glossbrenner John E, clk Levey Bros & Co, b 1335 N Delaware.
Glossbrenner Wm J, clk R M S, h 1335 N Delaware.
Glover Charles M, bkkpr, h 4 Hillside av.
Glover James W, foreman Indiana Newspaper Union, h 16 Shover (W I).
Glover John, porter, b 154 W Washington.
Glover John B (Wildman & Glover), h 274 Keystone av.

THE WHEN IS A WORLD BEATER.

Glover John E, lab, r 167 N Capitol av.
Glover Wm, porter, h 39 Center.
Gluck Anna (wid Frederick), b 66 Birch av (W I).
Glunt Martha (wid John), b 292 Howard (W I).
Glunt Ora A, lab, b 173 N Pine.
Gmeiner Casper, baker, h 619 Madison av.
Goatley James, porter, r 226 Roanoke.
Gobin Frederick C, trav agt Emil Wulschner & Son, b 430 Broadway.
Gobin Mary F, dressmkr, 430 Broadway, h same.
Goble Bertha M, stenog, b 233 Mass av.
Gochem Charles, varnisher, b 114 Laurel.
Gochem John, b 114 Laurel.
Gochnat Charles, b 226 E Merrill.
Goddard Albert, clk, b 332 E New York.
Goddard Clark P, boilermkr, h 212 Fletcher av.
Goddard Eliza (wid Clark), h 212 Fletcher av.
Goddard Frank, boilermkr, h 212 Fletcher av.
Goddard Joseph N, brakeman, h 35 Wilcox.
Goddard Samuel, contr, h 181 Blackford.
Godfrey Adelia (wid Thomas), h 459 S Capitol av.
Godfrey Bridget (wid Thomas), h 459 S Capitol av.
Godfrey Daniel, lab, b 107 W South.
Godfrey Harry A, tel opr W U Tel Co, h n e cor Ramsey and Orange avs.
Godfrey John T, bkkpr Fertig & Kevers, b 459 S Capitol av.
Godfrey Thomas J, foreman, h 222 S Missouri.
Godley Mary T, dressmkr, 395 Ash, h same.
Godly Patrick, lab, h 31 Brett.
Godly Thomas J, lab, b 31 Brett.
Godown John M, clk Knight & Jillson, h 71 W 1st.
Godwin, see Goodwin.
Godwin George O, foreman, h 13 New.
Goe Herbert, clk, b n w cor Ritter av and P C C & St L Ry (I).
Goe Hezekiah N, clk, h n w cor Ritter av and P C C & St L Ry (I).
Goe Horace S, clk, b 31 Yandes.

THE A. BURDSAL CO.
Manufacturers of
Paints and Colors
VARNISHES,
Brushes, Painters' and Paper Hangers' Supplies.
34 AND 36 SOUTH MERIDIAN STREET.

ELECTRICIANS | DON'T FORGET US. ALL WORK GUARANTEED. C. W. MEIKEL, Tel. 466. 96-98 E. New York St.

DALTON & MERRIFIELD { LUMBER South Noble St., near E. Washington

INDIANA ELECTROTYPE CO. :: BEST WORK LOWEST PRICES. 23 WEST PEARL ST., INDIANAPOLIS, IND. JOB WORK. BOOK PLATES. BEST PATENT BASE ON THE MARKET. All Orders Promptly Filled.

KIRKHOFF BROS.
Steam and Hot Water Heating Apparatus,
Plumbing and Gas Fitting.
102-104 SOUTH PENNSYLVANIA ST.
TELEPHONE 910.

Goe Margaretta C, grocer, n w cor Central av and P C C & St L Ry (I), h n w cor Ritter av and P C C & St L Ry (I).
Goe Robert M, produce, b 31 Yandes.
Goe Sarah J (wid John), h 31 Yandes.
Goebel A Wm, painter, h 325 E Morris.
Goebel Emanuel M, market master, E Mkt House, b 24 Sterling.
Goebel Joseph, lab, b 22 Maple.
Goebel Louis P (D P Erwin & Co), h 385 College av.
Goebel Theresa (wid Jacob), h 24 Sterling.
Goebes Sebastian, carp, b 419 S Delaware.
Goebes Wm, carp, h 744 S East.
Goebler Adam, tailor, h 24 Laurel.
Goebler Charles H, mach, h 88 Laurel.
Goebler Henry, tinner, h 178 W 9th.
Goebler John A, mach, b 24 Laurel.
Goebler Ora, clk, h 87 W McCarty.
Goebler Wm F, lab, b 24 Laurel.
Goede August, mason, h 427 E Georgia.
Goeller Caroline (wid Louis), b 362 Broadway.
Goeltner Reinhold, mach, b 213 S Alabama.
Goens Alice (wid James), h rear 418 N East.
Goepper Albert H, sec Consolidated Coal and Lime Co, h 122 W North.
Goepper Charles, storekpr The Bates.
Goepper Emma, teacher Public School No 32, b 371 Park av.
Goepper Frederick, coal, n s Jackson 2 w of Harris av (M J), h 1367 W Washington (M J).
Goepper Frederick J (Indpls Tool and Mnfg Co), h 371 Park av.
Goepper Frederick J jr, mach, b 371 Park av.
Goepper Susannah (wid Frederick), h 371 Park av.
Goettling Charles F, molder, b 50 Singleton.
Goettling Gottlieb, lab, h 129 Weghorst.
Goettling Julius A, bartndr, h 283 S West.
Goettsche Frederick, molder, h 26 Holmes av (H).
Goetz Anna T, dressmkr, 350 Indiana av, b same.
Goetz Charles A, h 331 E Market.
Goetz Cora H, bkkpr R F Catterson & Son, b 331 E Market.

LIME
BUILDING SUPPLIES,
Hair, Plaster, Flue Linings,
The W. G. Wasson Co.
130 INDIANA AVE. Tel. 989.

Goetz Frederick, mach hd, h 94 Walcott.
Goetz George J, packer, h 331 W Vermont.
Goetz Herman, b 380 W 1st.
Goetz John H, baker, h 350 Indiana av.
Goetz Kate C (wid John A C), h 380 W 1st.
Goetz Louis J, laundryman, h 98 Greer.
Goetz Michael, bartndr, h 420 E St Clair.
Goetz Philip, sec and treas Indiana Bicycle Co, 67-99 S East, h n w cor Delaware and 7th.
Goff Amos, h 421 E 17th.
Goff Burwell, printer, b 344 W Pearl.
Goff Eliza A (wid Samuel), h 213 N West.
Goff Otis L, fitter, b 81 Burch av (W I).
Goff Walter D, baker, b 344 Pearl.
Gogen Calvin L, clk, b 573 N West.
Gogen James, printer, h 573 N West.
Goger Joseph, basketmkr, h 897 Madison av.
Goggin Anna E, stenog C C C & St L Ry, h 530 S East.
Goggin Thomas F, carver, b 530 S East.
Gogin Charles L, porter, h 573 N West.
Gohagan, see also Kohagan.
Gohagan Melvin, tmstr, h 10 Catharine.
Goheen Frank H, bkkpr Hide, Leather and Belting Co, h 348 Coburn.
Gohen James A, master painter C C C & St L Ry, h 1224 N Illinois.
Gohl Frederick, printer, b 29 Dickson.
Gohmann Edward B, driver, b 24 English av.
Gohmann Otto E, clk, b 24 English av.
Goines Charles, hostler, b 156 N West.
Goings Cassie, h 21 Columbia al.
Goings Norman A, clk R M S, h 251 Cornell av.
Goins Cary T, bartndr, r 167½ Indiana av.
Goins Eugene, lab, h 223 W Vermont.
Goins George H, barber, h 53 Mayhew.
Goins Henry, barber, h 85 Eddy.
Goins James H, porter, b rear 958 N Meridian.
Goins John F, painter, h 51 Mayhew.
Goins Lafayette L, lab, h 408 W 1st.
Goins Mahala (wid Samuel), h 49 Mayhew.
Goins Manson S, barber, h 49 Mayhew.
Goins Thomas, barber, r 19 N Noble.
Goins Wm N, lab, h 80 Bloomington.
Golay Annie E (wid Lafayette), b 292 W Market.
Golay George C, patternmkr, b 511 Bellefontaine.
Gold, see also Gould.
Gold Elizabeth R (wid James), h 824 Rembrant (M P).
Gold James N, mach, h 824 Rembrant (M P).
Gold Lyman, foreman, h 826 Rembrant (M P).
Gold Norwood, mach, b 824 Rembrant (M P).
Gold Patrick, huckster, b 336½ E Washington.
Gold Simon (Gold & Adler), b 119 Maple.
Gold Samuel N (S N Gold & Co), h 164 Broadway.
Gold S N & Co (Samuel N Gold), com mers, 49 S Delaware.
Gold & Adler (Simon Gold, Wolf Adler), opticians, 61 S Illinois.
GOLDBERG ABE H, Railroad Ticket Broker; Cheap Rates Everywhere; 112 S Illinois, Tel 1227; b 52 Maple.
Goldberg Abraham, pdlr, b 466 S Capitol av.
Goldberg Bennett, 2d hd goods, 217 E Washington, h 52 Maple.
Goldberg Bert, collr, b 466 S Capitol av.

Parlor, Bed Room, Dining Room, Kitchen, Furniture W. H. MESSENGER, 101 E. Wash. St., Tel. 491.

ALL KINDS OF HEAVY AND LIGHT GRAY IRON CASTINGS } McNamara, Koster & Co. { Foundry and Pattern Shop
Phone 1593. 212-218 S. Penn. St.

THE FRED DIETZ CO. WOODEN PACKING BOXES MADE TO ORDER FACTORY AND WAREHOUSE TRUCKS. 40 Madison Avenue. Telephone 69.

Goldberg Gustav, clk, b 52 Maple.
Goldberg Henry H, shoemkr, b 283 E Washington.
Goldberg Lottie (wid Abraham), b 370 S Missouri.
Goldberg Mendel, cooper, h 466 S Capitol av.
Goldberg Meyer, clk, b 52 Maple.
Goldberger Joseph, clothing, 117 Mass. av, h same.
Golden Charles E, lab, h w s Madeira 1 s of Prospect.
Golden Dennis F, clk Indpls Gas Co, b 397 Virginia av.
Golden Ella, clk, b rear 448 S East.
Golden Isaac, h 84 S Wheeler (B).
Golden James H, lab, b 84 S Wheeler (B).
Golden Margaret J, music teacher, b rear 448 S East.
Golden Mary (wid Michael), h rear 448 S East.
Golder Alonzo H, driver, h 26 Springfield.
Golder Francis, lab, h 62 Bismarck (W I).
Golder George L, mach, b 15 Bridge (W I).
Golder Wm A, lab, b 15 Bridge (W I).
Golding, see also Goulding.
Golding Andrew J, lab, b 159 W 8th.
Golding Charles W, huckster, h n w cor Paris av and 20th.
Golding Jennie (wid Andrew J), h 159 W 8th.
Golding Mary (wid Levi), h 20 N West.
Golding Richard G, lab, b 159 W 8th.
Goldman Abraham, junk, b 517 S Capitol av.
Goldman Benjamin, pdlr, h 108 Eddy.
Goldman David, notions, 98 E Mkt House, grocer, 350 S Meridian and 282 S Illinois, h 350 S Meridan.
Goldman George, trav agt, b 185 N Delaware.
Goldman Hyman, lab, b 108 Eddy.
Goldman Isaac, baker, b 412 S Meridian.
Goldman Jacob, b 156 N Liberty.
Goldman Nathan, clk, b 517 S Capitol av.
Goldman Simon, h 517 S Capitol av.
Goldmeyer Henry, mach hd, b 799 S East.
Goldmeyer Henry W, b 242 Minnesota.
Goldner Reinhart, mach, b 213 S Alabama.
Goldrick Wm O, contr, h 1 Allfree.
Goldsberry Bertha, teacher Public School No 28, b 259 Virginia av.
Goldsberry Carey W, barber, b 101 Hoyt av.
Goldsberry G Hamer, trav agt, h 158 N New Jersey.
Goldsberry Samuel S, mach Indpls Pattern Wks, h 259 Virginia av.
Goldsmith Elias, clk, b Illinois House.
Goldsmith Simon, clk, h 279 W Michigan.
Goldstein Abraham H, bkkpr, b 124 Maple.
Goldstein Albert S, bkkpr, b 124 Maple.
Goldstein Joseph, clothing, 115 Mass av, h same.
Goldstein Morris, pdlr, h 121 Eddy.
Goldstein Morris, pdlr, h 124 Maple.
Goldstine Mary E (wid Edward), mngr Montezuma Mill Co, h 1052 W Washington.
Goley John, cooper, h 69 S California.
Goliah Sampson, lab, h 175 Ludlow av.
Golibart Francis L, bkkpr Syerup & Co, h 603 Park av.
Goll, see also Gall and Gaul.
Goll Adolph, collr, b 375 Blake.
Goll Charles F, driver, h 235 S Olive.
Goll Christian, meats, 377 Blake, h 375 same.
Goll John, tailor, b 375 Blake.
Goll Otto C, collr, b 375 Blake.
Golladay Alta, opr C U Tel Co, b 282 N Illinins.

Henry H. Fay,
40½ E. WASHINGTON ST.,
FIRE INSURANCE, REAL ESTATE,
LOANS AND RENTAL AGENT.

Golladay Anna (wid Charles), r 116½ W New York.
Golladay Clifford, fitter, h 116½ W New York.
Golladay Lewis, waiter, r 70 Davidson.
Golladay Mary A (wid James G), h 282 N Illinois.
Gollnisch Charles P, uphlr, h 352 S Olive.
Gollnisch Otto, sawyer, h 352 S Olive.
Gollnisch Otto jr, lab, b 352 S Olive.
Golly Julius, bartndr, b 611 Mass av.
Golt Walter F C, chief clk receiver Indpls National Bank, 607-609 Indiana Trust bldg, h n e cor 30th and Senate av.
Goltra Wm F, sec to genl mngr and chief clk to chief engr and pur agt L E & W R R, h 302 E New York.
Gommel Wm E, lab, h 212 Coburn.
Gompers Samuel, pres Am Federation of Labor, r 271 E Ohio.
Gompf Christopher, h 299 E Market.
Gompf Frederick (Home Lumber Co), h 633 Marlowe.
Gompf Harry, bkkpr Emil Wulschner & Son, b 299 E Market.
Good Alonzo J, butcher, h 65 Woodburn av (W I).
Good Bryant, lab, h 225 Howard.
Good Bryant C, driver, b 225 Howard.
Good Charles, clk, b 998 N Meridian.
Good George, lab, h 69 N Dorman.
Good George W, painter, b 96 Harrison.
Good James, butcher, h 37 Nordyke av (W I).
Good James, lab, b 69 N Dorman.
Good John L, lab, b 96 Harrison.
Good John S, flagman, h 96 Harrison.
Good Joseph, student, b 415 N Meridian.
Good Lewis K, painter, b 96 Harrison.
Good Manufacturing Co, Constantine Riegger pres, Arnold F Riegger sec and treas, 28 Monument pl.
Goodale Alfred W, tinner, h 95 Malott av.
Goodale Frank P, coppersmith, h 22 Mayhew.
Goodale George W, policeman Union Station, h 140 John.
Goodall Abraham, janitor, b 168 Bird.
Goodall George F, clk, b 1350 W Senate av.

WILL GO ON YOUR BOND
American Bonding & Trust Co.
Of Baltimore, Md. Approved as sole surety by the United States Government and the different States as Sole Surety on all Forms of Bonds.
W. E. BARTON & CO., General Agents,
504 Indiana Trust Building.
LONG DISTANCE TELEPHONE 1918.

BUSINESS EDUCATION A NECESSITY. TIME SHORT. DAY AND NIGHT SCHOOL. SUCCESS CERTAIN AT THE PERMANENT, RELIABLE Indianapolis BUSINESS UNIVERSITY

NEW YORK FILTER MFG. CO. Filters for Water-Works, Boiler Plants, Laundries, Hotels, Private Residences, Etc. | Henry R. Worthington, 64 S. Pennsylvania St. Long Distance Telephone 284.

UNION CO-OPERATIVE LAUNDRY (OWNED AND OPERATED BY UNION LAUNDRY GIRLS.) 38, 40 AND 42 VIRGINIA AVENUE. T. E. SOMERVILLE, MANAGER. TELEPHONE 1269. INDIANAPOLIS, IND.

HORACE M. HADLEY
INSURANCE AND LOANS
66 E. Market Street, Basement
TELEPHONE 1540.

Goodall John, h 1350 W Senate av.
Goodall John L, janitor, b 168 Bird.
Goodall Mines, janitor, h 168 Bird.
Goodall Walter, waiter The Denison.
Goodall Walter J (W J Holliday & Co), h 1005 N Penn.
Goode Elizabeth A (wid Richard), h 250 Keystone av.
Goode James, lab, h 33 Thomas.
Goode John S, carp, b 250 Keystone av.
Goode Landers M, trav agt, h 621 E Market.
Goode Lee, lab, b 160 W Maryland.
Goode Lucy B, h 14 The Blacherne.
Goode Solon L, h 998 N Meridian.
Goode Thomas J, carp, b 160 W Maryland.
Goode Wm D, lab, b 250 Keystone av.
Goodell Hannah (wid Asa A), h 594 W Udell (N I).
Gooden Beverly, lab, r 9 W Chesapeake.
Gooden John, lab, h 202 W 6th.
Gooden Wm H, lab, h 3 Brookers al.
GOODHART BENJAMIN F, Mngr Real Estate Dept A Metzger Agency, 5 Odd Fellows' Hall, h 476 Broadway.
Goodhart Caroline, teacher Public School No 15, b 476 Broadway.
Goodin Alvin M (Goodin & Davenport), h 318 E New York.
Goodin Harry A, lab, b 129 King av (H).
Goodin Harvey, molder, b 129 King av (H).
Goodin Maud, dressmkr, 108½ Mass av, h same.
Goodin & Davenport (Alvin M Goodin, Jerome B Davenport), livery, 137 Hudson.
GOODING DAVID S, Lawyer, 47 Thorpe Blk, Res Greenfield, Ind.
Goodknight Florence (wid John), h 171 E South.
Goodknight Florence A, h 163 N New Jersey.
Goodlet Martha (wid James), h e s Tibbs av 1 n of Michigan (H).
Goodet Robert G, mach, h 92 Bismarck av (H).
Goodloe Thomas M, mngr Indpls Fire Inspection Bureau, h 75 The Blacherne.
Goodlow Frank, butler 699 N Meridian.

COLLECTIONS
MERCHANTS' AND MANUFACTURERS' EXCHANGE
Will give you good service.
J. E. TAKKEN, Manager,
Union Building, over U. S. Pension Office.
73 West Maryland Street.

Goodman Abram, tailor, h 80 Garden.
Goodman Charles, cabtmkr, h 275 W Market.
Goodman Frank S, mach opr Indpls Journal, h 97 Dougherty.
Goodman George N, bricklyr, h 250 Michigan (H).
Goodman John, lab, r 20 Columbia blk.
Goodman Judson E, lab, b 155 Shelby.
Goodman Michael, butcher, b 398 S Illinois.
Goodman Nicholas H, lab, h 507 W Washington.
Goodman Sarah J, h 11 W Chesapeake.
Goodnecht John, painter, b 203 Columbia av.
Goodnecht John H, painter, h 203 Columbia av.
Goodnecht Wm A, clk H P Wasson & Co, h 223 E St Clair.
Goodner Jackson, lab, b 67 S Noble.
Goodner John, bicyclemkr, b 131 S East.
Goodnight John W, lab, h 130 Geisendorff.
Goodnoe Ellen (wid Jonas D), matron Union Station, b 355 S Meridian.
Goodnoe Walter D, lab, b 355 S Meridian.
Goodnough Franklin, waiter, h 117 Anderson.
Goodnow Lela M, b 181 Newman.
Goodnow Mary J (wid Charles), b 938 Gent (M P).
Goodnow Wm E, printer, h 938 Gent (M P).
Goodperle Edward, finisher, h rear n s Michigan 1 e of Belt R R.
Goodperle George, clk, b s e cor Lebanon and Waverly avs.
Goodperle John, finisher, h e s Brookland av 2 n of Brookside av.
Goodperle Peter, h s e cor Lebanon and Pope avs.
Goodrich German, hostler, r 45 N Alabama.
Goodrich James M, lab, h 526 W Ontario (N I).
Goodridge Frederick R, reporter The Indpls Sentinel, r 68½ Mass av.
Goodspeed Benjamin F, wheelfinisher, h 50 Hadley av (W I).
Goodspeed Lena L (wid Silas E), h 55 Davidson.
Goodspeed Wm B, driver, b 55 Davidson.
Goodwin, see also Godwin.
Goodwin David, foreman, h 84 N New Jersey.
Goodwin Elizabeth (wid John H), h 139 S Summit.
Goodwin Frank, printer, h 97 Dougherty.
Goodwin Harry, baggageman, h 146 Spann av.
Goodwin Henry E, preserves, 214 Blackford, h same.
Goodwin Hugh, lab, h 21 Douglass.
Goodwin James H, lab, h 36 Holmes av (H).
Goodwin James H, mach, h 128 Nordyke av (W I).
Goodwin Jesse, elev opr The Denison.
Goodwin John, bartndr, b Floral av 1 n of 9th.
Goodwin Mary (wid Hugh), b 138 Blackford.
Goodwin Mitchell L, boilermkr, b 139 S Summit.
Goodwin Samuel G, b 232 College av.
Goodwin Thomas, lab, 74 W Michigan.
Goodwin Thomas A, h 232 College av.
Goodwin Wm M, brakeman, h 60 Spann av.
Goodyear John W, paperhngr, h 22 Dearborn.
Goodykoontz Harvey W, paperhngr, h 43 Tremont av (H).

CLEMENS VONNEGUT 184, 186 and 192 E. Washington St. | BUILDERS' HARDWARE, Building Paper. Duplex Joist Hangers

THE WM. H. BLOCK CO. DRY GOODS, DRAPERIES, RUGS, WINDOW SHADES.
7 AND 9 EAST WASHINGTON STREET.

Gookin George F, mnfrs' agt, 59 Commercial Club bldg, h 236 Central av.
Goory Christopher C, h 14 Church.
Goory Wm J, clk, b 14 Church.
Gorden Margaret D (wid George N), h 77 Indiana av.
Gordenhill George, photog, b 742 N Senate av.
Gordon Addie, r 6 Columbia blk.
Gordon Albert E, barber, 179 S Illinois, h 598 Morris (W I).
Gordon Belle G (wid Benjamin G), b 28 W New York.
Gordon Benjamin F, h 83 Indiana av.
Gordon Bernard, mach, h 104 Hosbrook.
Gordon Carey B, brakeman, b 28 W New York.
Gordon Cary W, clk N Y Store, h 483 N Illinois.
Gordon Charles F, driver wells, 205 E Washington, h 190 N East.
Gordon Charles U, mail driver, h 125 Bicking.
Gordon Daniel, mach, h 4 Hadley.
Gordon Edward, lab, h s w cor Washington and Lake avs (I).
Gordon Edward R, grocer, 852 LaSalle, h same.
Gordon Elizabeth A (wid Rev John M), b 44 Windsor.
Gordon Elmer A, carp, r 39 W Pratt.
Gordon George, steelwkr, b 46 S Capitol av.
Gordon Henry, lab, h 30 John.
Gordon Herbert D, clk, r 142 N Illinois.
Gordon Herman A, lab, b 393 W 2d.
Gordon Howard H, clk, h 20 W Michigan.
Gordon Irving S, pres The Gordon-Kurtz Co, h 20 W Michigan.
Gordon James, lab, h 126 W Pearl.
Gordon James E, clk Model Clothing Co, b 104 Hosbrook.
Gordon John, lab, b 50 S California.
Gordon John, lab, b 299 W Maryland.
Gordon John M, master mechanic I U Ry Co, h 180 Nordyke av (W I).

GORDON-KURTZ CO THE, Irving S Gordon Pres, Edwin A Wert Vice-Pres, Wm E Kurtz Sec and Treas, Saddlery, Hardware and Horse Clothing, 141-143 S Meridian, Tel 41.

Gordon Louis O, hatter, r 6 Columbia blk.
Gordon Malachi, lab, b 299 W Maryland.
Gordon Margaret D (wid George N), h 77 Indiana av.
Gordon Mary, dressmkr, 4 Hadley, b same.
Gordon Mary E (wid John), b 13 Belmont av.
Gordon Milton S, news agt, h 392 W 1st.
Gordon Nathan, teacher, h 98 Eddy.
Gordon Robert, photog, h 34 Eastern av.
Gordon Robert B, printer The Indpls Sentinel, h 34 Tecumseh.
Gordon Samuel, tailor, h 189 S New Jersey.
Gordon Sarah C (wid Ross), h 5 West Drive (W P).
Gordon Sarah E (wid John), h 473 College av.
Gordon Thomas, fireman, b 889 Morris (W I).
Gordon Willard G, driver, h 225 Bright.
Gordon Wm, real est, 219 Lemcke bldg, h 1033 N Alabama.
Gordon Wm H (Gordon & Harmon), r 151 N Alabama.
Gordon Wm H, stripper, h 121½ Ft Wayne av.
Gordon Wm S, ins agt, h 189 Brookside av.

THE H. LIEBER COMPANY. ART EMPORIUM 33 SOUTH MERIDIAN ST. VISITORS WELCOME.

GORDON & HARMON (Wm H Gordon, Willard Harmon), Agricultural Implements, 75-77 W Washington, Tel 1004.

Gore Eliza (wid Louis), h 683 N Senate av.
Gore James V, tmstr, h 25 Highland av (H).
Gorham Charles P, lab, h 66 Arbor av (W I).
Gorham Henry K, engr, h 35 Belmont av.
Gorham Wm O, motorman, h 216 Blake.
Goring Arthur, lab, r 32 N Senate av.
Goring Jane, h 268 Mass av.
Goritz Christian, lab, h 49 Arizona.
Gorius Anna J (wid Adam), nurse, 185 E Morris, h same.
Gorius Frederick, clk, b 505 Madison av.
Gorius Louis C, clk Indpls Brewg Co, b 185 E Morris.
Gorman, see also O'Gorman.
Gorman Bridget (wid Thomas), h 383 N Illinois.
Gorman Frank, saloon, 175 S Illinois, h 82 Walcott.
Gorman Frank S, harnessmkr, h 1306 N Delaware.
Gorman Harry M, printer, b 331 N Pine.
Gorman James, lab, h rear 117 Bright.
Gorman James, lab, b 17 Springfield.
Gorman James, watchman, h 331 N Pine.
Gorman John, b 82 Walcott.
Gorman John, artist, b 74 W New York.
Gorman Patrick J (Perrott & Gorman), b 383 N Illinois.
Gorman Wm J, clk, b 331 N Pine.
Gorris Christian, lab, b 49 Arizona.
Gorsuch Carey E, clk George J Marott, h w s National av 2 s of P C C & St L Ry (I).

GORSUCH CHARLES W, Real Estate and Loans, 305 Indiana Trust Bldg, h 270 E South, Tel 508.

Gorsuch John T, driver, h 180 E North.
Gort Stephen, lab, b 271 W McCarty.
Gosney Boone M, oil, b 298 Bellefontaine.
Gosney Elizabeth S (wid Robert), h 408 Cornell av.
Gosney Jesse F, teacher Public School No 9, b 408 Cornell av.

GUIDO R. PRESSLER,
FRESCO PAINTER
Churches, Theaters, Public Buildings, Etc., A Specialty.
Residence, No. 325 North Liberty Street.
INDIANAPOLIS, IND.

INDIANAPOLIS STEEL ROOFING AND CORRUGATING WORKS, 23 and 25 East South Street. S. D. NOEL, Proprietor.

David S. McKernan, Rooms 2-5 Thorpe Block.
REAL ESTATE AND LOANS Money to loan on real estate. Special inducements offered those having money to loan. It will pay you to investigate.

DIAMOND WALL PLASTER { Telephone 1410 BUILDERS' EXCHANGE.

UNION TRANSFER AND STORAGE CO. Cor. E. Ohio St. and C., C., C. & St. L. R'y Tracks. BEST FACILITIES FOR STORING AND TRANSFERRING MACHINERY AND MERCHANDISE.

W. McWORKMAN

FIRE SHUTTERS,
FIRE DOORS,
METAL CEILINGS.

930 W. Washington St. Tel. 1118.

Gosney Oscar, clk Chandler & Taylor Co, h 138 Agnes.
Gosney Wm S. oil, h 298 Lincoln av.
Goss Clark, phys, b 614 E Washington.
Goss David K, supt Public Schools, h 153 N East.
Goss Frederick, news agt, r 193½ S Illinois.
Goss James L, engr, h 32 Jefferson av.
Goss Joseph E, bill clk Charles Mayer & Co, b 991 N Penn.
Gossett Clarence W, packer, h 887 Milburn (M P).
Gossett Katherine, teacher Public School No 11, b 390 College av.
Gossett Sibba O, clk, b 248 N East.
Gossman John F, clk The Wm H Block Co, h 441 S Meridian.
Gossom Amanda (wid Wm H), b 113 Talbott av.
Gossom Hayden F, bkkpr Elmer E Nichols Co, h 1310 N Delaware.
Gostarnd Edward J, varnisher, b 180 Columbia av.
Gostarnd Herman H, lab, b 180 Columbia av.
Goth Benjamin F, driver, b 128 N Liberty.
Goth Charles A (Goth & Co), h 119 Ruckle.
Goth Charles L, trav agt, h 156 Davidson.
Goth George, lab, h 166 Elm.
GOTH HERMAN A, Plumber and Gas Fitter, 487 N New Jersey, Tel 962; b 453 same.
Goth Jeannette E (wid Valentine), h 128 N Liberty.
Goth John L (Goth & Co), b 453 N New Jersey.
Goth John W, lab, h 128 N Liberty.
Goth Peter, h 453 N New Jersey.
Goth Wm, foreman, h 128 N Liberty.
Goth & Co (Charles A and John L Goth), monuments, 157 Mass av.
Gotsch George Rev, pastor German Evangelical Lutheran St John's Church, h 123 Bismarck av (H).
Gottchalkson Selmar, mngr, h 280 N East.
Gottwalles Joseph M, grocer, 122 Patterson, h same.
Goudy Anna B (wid James W), h 350 N Alabama.

GEO. J. MAYER,
MANUFACTURER OF
SEALS
STENCILS, RUBBER STAMPS, CHECKS, BADGES, DOOR PLATES, ETC.
.. S. Meridian St., Ground Floor. TEL. 1386

Goudy Frank D, timekpr Indiana Bicycle Co, h 59 Tacoma av.
Goudy Hugh, agt, h 160 Dougherty.
Gough, see also Goff.
Gough Alfred B, clk Parry Mnfg Co, h 344 S Alabama.
Gough Elizabeth I, music teacher, 72 E Maryland, b same.
Gough Hannah (wid John B), h 72 E Maryland.
Gough Margaret E (wid Charles M), h 327 E Michigan.
Goul Sadie J, dressmkr, 68 Huron, h same.
Gould, see also Gold.
Gould Ambrose E, messenger Am Ex Co, b 246 Blackford.
Gould Anna M, prin Kindergarten No 1, b 246 Blackford.
Gould Charles A, clk, b 390 N Delaware.
Gould Edwin F, pub, h 77 Sanders.
Gould Homer S, messenger Am Ex Co, h 246 Blackford.
GOULD RICHARD H, Propr Fine Livery Stables, 130-132 E St Clair, h 390 N Delaware, Tel 498.
Gould Steel Co, W E Kurtz sec and mngr, 143½ S Meridian.
Gould Sylvester, carp, h 258 River av (W I).
Gould Thomas C, tel opr, b 246 Blackford.
Gould Wm M, mach, h 520 Park av.
Goulding, see also Golding.
Goulding John A, trav agt, h 430 Park av.
Goulding Samuel W, clk, h 11 Morrison.
Gove Albert H, express, b 109 Orange.
GOVERNMENT BUILDING AND LOAN INSTITUTION THE, Thomas L Sullivan Pres, Hiram E Rose Sec, 31 Journal Bldg, Tel 372.
GOVERNOR OF STATE'S OFFICE, James A Mount Governor, Room 6 State House.
Govey Joseph, lab, b 63 S California.
Gowdy, John K, b The Denison.
Gowdy Lincoln, houseman The Bates.
Gowdy Silas, driver, h 36 Rhode Island.
Gowdy Wm, coachman, h 27 W 1st.
Gower Emerson L, h n w cor 10th and Atlas.
Goyns Charles W, printer, b 62 Chapel.
Goza Alonzo F, baker, h 85 N Noble.
Goza Augusta S (wid Zeno A), h 410 E Pearl.
Goza Frederick, finisher, b 410 E Pearl.
Graber Frederick, trav agt, h 60 Yeiser.
Graber Frederick W H, clk Indpls Coffin Co, b 60 Yeiser
GRACE CATHEDRAL, Rev Edgar F Gee Rector, s e cor Central av and 7th.
Grace Harry, stage mngr, h 464 N Senate av.
Grace Jessie, b 516 N West.
Grace John, carp, h 434 W 1st.
Graderlein Ernest, shoemkr, 315 Shelby, h same.
Grady Aaron, carp, h 581 S State av.
Grady Charles F, electrician, b 50 Laurel.
Grady Hugh H A, contr, h 50 Laurel.
Grady Jeremiah, fireman, h 289 Bates.
Grady Jeremiah, lab, b 43 Benton.
Grady Jeremiah, lab, h 14 Root.
Grady John, lab, b 43 Benton.
Grady John E, clk, b 405 W 2d.
Grady John W, engr, h 40 Sanders.
Grady Lawrence P, chief special agt C C C & St L Ry, h 265 Keystone av.

A. METZGER AGENCY ESTABLISHED 1863. REAL ESTATE

LAMBERT GAS & GASOLINE ENGINE CO.
ANDERSON, IND. NATURAL GAS ENGINES.

Grady Martin J, lab, b 150 Agnes.
Grady Martin P, clk Bureau of Animal Industry, h 13 Blackford.
Grady Mary (wid John), h 7 Carlos.
Grady Michael, engr, h 25 Fletcher av.
Grady Solomon, coachman 956 N Illinois.
Grady Wm, lab, b 7 Carlos.
Grady Wilton A, carp, b 50 Laurel.
Graebner John, saloon, 307 Shelby, h same.
Graebner Marie, housekpr 407 Broadway.
Graener Herman J, harnessmkr, h 104 Torbet.
Graeter Elizabeth (wid Ernest C), b 208 Fletcher av.
Graeter Frederick O, agt, h 493 Sheldon.
Graeter Louis V, pictures, 13 Madison av, h 208 Fletcher av.
Graf Charles, lab, r 685 Mass av.
Graf Gottfried, grocer, 228 E Morris, h same.
Graf John, mach, h w s Hampton 1 s of Clifford av.
Graff, see also Groff.
Graff Charles J, framemkr, h 131 Newman.
Graff John, butcher, b 23 Russell av.
Graff Philip, clk, h 106 Hosbrook.
Grafford Leonard, barber, 35 Kentucky av, r same.
Grafftey Alfred H (Grafftey, Ault & Co), h 223 N West.
Grafftey, Ault & Co (Alfred H Grafftey, Percy B Ault, Garrett A Archibald), shirtmkrs, 38 E Washington.
Grafftey Eliza M (wid James), b 17 Hoyt av.
Grafftey Harry, clk P B Ault & Co, b 223 N West.
Grafftey James F, trav agt, h 310 Ash.
Grafftey Lawrence G, oil, b 31 N Spruce.
Graft Gottlieb, lab, b Marion Park Hotel (M P).
Grah Charles G, barbers' supplies, 64 S Illinois, h 77 Dearborn.
Graham Albert H, foreman Van Camp Packing Co, h 181 Hill av.
Graham Alois B, phys, 107 N Alabama, r 305 The Shiel.
Graham Alonzo, filer, h 144 Meek.
Graham Andrew J Rev, pastor Christ's Episcopal Church, h 30 Christian av.
Graham Charles, painter, h 58½ W Ohio.
Graham Charles H, clk, b 180 Maple.
Graham Charles L, painter, h 58½ W Ohio.
Graham Daniel A, lab, h 49 Jones.
Graham David A Rev, pastor Bethel A M E Church, h 214 W Vermont.
Graham Della (wid Daniel B), b 189 E Ohio.
Graham Edward B, plumber, b 299 N Liberty.
Graham Edward F, cashr, h 585 Park av.
Graham Elizabeth C (wid Wm), b 48 Eastern av.
Graham Frank, painter, b 29 Shover (W I).
Graham Frank D, clk, h 110 S Linden.
Graham Frank W, watchman Court House Tower, h 292 Highland av.
Graham George R, gardener Blind Inst, h 514 College av.
Graham Harry J, asst genl freight agt L E & W R R, b 30 E Pratt.
Graham Harry T, driver, h w s Gladstone av 2 n of Washington.
Graham Harry W, waiter, r 8 Eden pl.
Graham Isaac, tmstr, h w s Earhart 7 s of Prospect.
Graham James C, plastr, h 22 Athon.
Graham James M, hostler, h 114 Bright.
Graham Jenny A, teacher Public School No 3, b 514 College av.

THOS. C. DAY & CO.
Financial Agents and Loans.
We have the experience, and claim to be reliable.
Rooms 325 to 330 Lemcke Bldg.

Graham Jesse H, brakeman, b 92 Michigan av.
Graham John, b 240 N Capitol av.
Graham John, condr, h 79 W Michigan.
Graham John, saloon, 151 Elizabeth, h same.
Graham John E, tmstr, h w s Perkins pike 1 s of Big 4 R R.
Graham John R, finisher, b 1595 N Illinois.
Graham Lyman A, clk, b 585 Park av.
Graham Margaret A (wid Benjamin F), h 585 Park av.
Graham Mary A (wid George), h 180 Maple.
Graham Mary B (Indpls Suspender Co), dressmkr, 25½ W Washington, h 74 W Vermont.
Graham Nancy (wid John), boarding 159 W Merrill.
Graham Oliver F, carp, h 567½ Virginia av.
Graham Oliver F, lab, h w s canal 2 s of 7th.
Graham Rebecca J (wid Wm A), h 270 Jefferson av.
Graham Robert D, h 80 S Linden.
Graham Samuel J, condr, h 299 N Liberty.
Graham Sarah E, dressmkr, 246 S East, h same.
Graham Summerfield F, lather, h 25 Deloss.
Graham Thomas K, motorman, b 1063 N Capitol av.
Graham Thomas W, fireman, b 53 S Linden.
Graham Washington F, farmer, b s w cor 22d and Sangster av.
Graham Wm, attendant Insane Asylum.
Graham Wm, lab, h rear 13 McCauley.
Graham Wm E, restaurant, 185 W Washington, h 183½ same.
Graham Wm H H (Charles W Brouse & Co), h n s University av 2 w of Ritter (I).
Graham Wm M, h 53 S Linden.
Graham Wm R, grocer, 106 S Linden, h 53 same.
Graham Wm S, lab, h 148 Meek.
Graham Wm U, clk Township Assessor's Office, h 268 W Maryland.
Grahn Edward G, drugs, 143 Cornell av, h 165 same.
Grahn Gustav E, clk, b 165 Cornell av.
Grahn Harry H, gilder, b 165 Cornell av.

EAT HITZ'S CRACKERS AND CAKES.
ASK YOUR GROCER FOR THEM.

BICYCLES $5
Best Wheels. Best Terms.
WHEELMEN'S CO. 31 W. OHIO ST. LONG DISTANCE TEL. 1855.

J. H. TECKENBROCK General House Painter, 94 EAST SOUTH STREET.

FIDELITY MUTUAL LIFE—PHILADELPHIA, PA.
$75,000,000, Insurance In Force. $3,500,000, Death Losses Paid. $1,500,090, Surplus. A. H. COLLINS {General Agent, Baldwin Block.

Edwardsport Coal & Mining Co. ●●●●● BITUMINOUS COAL IN CAR LOADS TO DEALERS AND MANUFACTURERS. ROOMS 42 AND 43 WHEN BUILDING.

ESTABLISHED 1876. TELEPHONE 168.
CHESTER BRADFORD,
SOLICITOR OF PATENTS,
AND COUNSEL IN PATENT CAUSES.
(See adv. page 6.)
Office:—Rooms 14 and 16 Hubbard Block, S. W. Cor. Washington and Meridian Streets, INDIANAPOLIS, INDIANA.

Grambley Marion H, teamster, r 49 Bellefontaine.
Gramby, Alfred E, barber, h 961 N New Jersey.
Gramling Anton, clk P Gramling & Son, b 42 Union.
Gramling Caroline M, (wid Peter), h 500 N Delaware.
Gramling Eugene C (P Gramling & Son), h 646 N Penn.
Gramling Eugene E, tailor, b 42 Union.
Gramling Henry A, cutter P Gramling & Son, h 704 N Alabama.
Gramling John, h 490 N Delaware.
Gramling John, h 42 Union.
Gramling Simeon A, b 500 N Delaware.
GRAMLING P & SON (Eugene C Gramling), Merchant Tailors, Clothiers and Gents' Furnishings, 35 E Washington.
Gramling Wilhelmina C, h 42 Union.
Gramling Wm C, tailor, 96 N Illinois, b 42 Union.
Gramling Wm H, tailor, b 42 Union.
Gramse Henry, paperhngr, b 115 Maxwell.
Grand Army of the Republic, Dept of Indiana, 25 State House.
GRAND HOTEL THE, The Grand Hotel Co Proprs, s e cor Illinois and Maryland, Tel 240.
Grand Hotel Co The, Thomas Taggart pres, Albert Sahm sec, Sterling R Holt treas, proprs The Grand Hotel, s e cor Illinois and Maryland.
Grand Opera House, Dickson & Talbott proprs, 73 N Penn.
GRAND OPERA HOUSE LIVERY STABLES, John H Spahr Agt, 75 E Wabash, Tel 102. (See adv in classified Livery.)
Grande John, florist, 322 Shelby, h 22 Gatling.
Grandee Augustus, barber, h 117 Mill.
Granderson Nelson, lab, r 20 Sheffield av (H).
Granderson Ollie S J Rev, pastor Freewill Baptist Church, b 121 Darnell.

Outing BICYCLES
..MADE BY..
HAY & WILLITS MFG. CO.
76 N. Pennsylvania St. Phone 598.

Grandjean Frank, barber, 439 Virginia av, r same.
Grandstaff Emma, tailoress, h 668 S Meridian.
Grandy Carlton D, lab, b 42 Ingraham.
Grandy Ora B Rev, h 42 Ingraham.
Grandy Lucius R, painter, b 42 Ingraham.
Grandy Max G, lab, b 42 Ingraham.
Graney, see also Greany.
Graney Margaret, clk C C C & St L Ry, b 30 Stevens.
Graney Patrick, engr, r 23 Johnson av.
Graney Patrick, mach, b 61 E South.
Graney Patrick, stoker, h 28 Spann av.
Graney Wm, lab, h 57 Paca.
Granger Carah N, brakeman, h 75 Johnson av.
Granger Carl, coachman 900 N Meridian.
Granger Colbert, lab, h 17 Mill.
Granger Colbert jr, lab, h 17 Mill.
Granger James, millwright, r 58 Nordyke av (W I).
Granger Riley, coachman 950 N Meridian.
Granger Robert, waiter The Bates.
Granland Charles, fireman, r 832 Grandview av.
Grannemann Frederick, gardener, h 1000 Madison av.
Grannis Edward, ins agt, r 101 N New Jersey.
Grant Allen, harnessmkr, h 172 Elm.
Grant Amandus N, lawyer, 419 Lemcke bldg, h 490 N Illinois.
Grant Benjamin F, contr, 50 Arbor av (W I), h same.
Grant Blanche, teacher Public School No 29, b 766 N Penn.
Grant Charles, porter, h 211 Northwestern av.
Grant George, lab, h 8 Vine.
Grant James L, janitor, h 289 Indiana av.
Grant John M, musician, h 49 Yandes.
Grant Joseph E, molder, b 50 Arbor av (W I).
Grant Lewis N, fireman, b 135 Michigan av.
Grant Nellie, dressmkr, h 389 E Market.
Grant Wm, nurse, h rear 232 N Noble.
Grant Wm C, clk P O, b 888 W Washington.
Granus Ida, h 265 E Court.
Grape Helen, teacher German Public School No 22, b 394 N Delaware.
Graper Wm J, lab, h 62 Holmes av (H).
Grappy Catherine, b 92 River av (W I).
Grasges Michael, molder, h 158 Belmont av (H).
Grass Samuel, carp, h 596 E Vermont.
Grass Wm A, carp, h 331 W Michigan.
Grassman Charles W, cementwkr, h 145 E Merrill.
Grassow August C, paperhngr, h 264 Highland av.
Grassow Caroline (wid John F), b 428 E McCarty.
Grassow Catherine (wid Wm A), b 530 E Ohio.
Grassow Edward F, carver, h 48 Preston.
Grassow Gustavus A, clk Charles Mayer & Co, h 53 Beaty.
Grassow Henry E, bkkpr, h 428 E McCarty.
Grassow John W, watchmkr, b 428 E McCarty.
Grau Alexander (Grau Bros), h 364 Blake.
Grau August, bartndr, r 76 S Delaware.
Grau Bros (Alexander and Julius), saloon, 364 Blake.
Grau Julius (Grau Bros), b 364 Blake.
Grau Julius jr, cigars, 366 Blake, h same.
Graubmann Joachim, lab, h 97 Coburn.

C. ZIMMERMAN & SONS | SLATE AND GRAVEL ROOFERS 19 South East Street.

DRIVEN WELLS And Second Water Wells and Pumps of all kinds at CHARLES KRAUSS', 42 S. PENN. ST., Telephone 465.

Grauel Conrad J, clk Charles Mayer & Co, b Rev Julius Grauel.
Grauel Julius Rev, h e s Rural 2 s of Clifford av.
Grauel Armin C, clk, b 66 Woodruff av.
Grauman Essie C, b 226 E New York.
Grautman George C, lab, h 21 Carlos.
Grave Alonzo L, brakeman, b 39 Temple av.
Grave Charles, mach, h 572 Shelby.
Grave Dora, ice cream, 572 Shelby, h same.
Grave John, carp, b 572 Shelby.
Grave John L, cabtmkr, h 10 Pleasant av.
Grave Joseph J, painter, b 572 Shelby.
Grave Oliver S, clk R M S, b 39 Temple av.
Grave Perilee (wid Jesse), h 39 Temple av.
Grave Theodore, lab, b 572 Shelby.
Graves Albert, cooper, b 104 Blackford.
Graves Alfred, lab, h 28 S William (W I).
Graves America (wid Wm), h e s Race 2 s of Raymond.
Graves Calvin, tmstr, b 23 S William (W I).
Graves Carleton, hostler, h 12 Detroit.
Graves Charles, waiter, h 167 E St Joseph.
Graves Edward M, civil engr, b 317 N New Jersey.
Graves Frances, h 253 N West.
Graves George, coachman 284 W Vermont.
Graves George, stenog, b 249 W New York.
Graves George H, supt I D & W Ry, h 74 W Walnut.
Graves George S, tel opr Union Stock Yards (W I), b 23 Tacoma av.
GRAVES GILBERT H, Druggist, 630 N West. h same.
Graves James R, coachman, h 482 Superior.
Graves John, carp, h 848 Rembrant (M P).
Graves John H, millwright, b 198 Woodlawn av.
Graves Martha (wid Eber L), b 97 Dearborn.
Graves Owen, porter, b 92 Torbet.
Graves Samuel L, b 121 Walcott.
Graves Sarah B (wid Abraham), h 23 Tacoma av.
Graves Solomon, waiter The Bates.
Graves Thomas, grocer, 524 S Brookside av, h same.
Graves T Smith (M Sells & Co), h 317 N New Jersey.
Graves Wm A, cooper, b 104 Blackford.
Graves Wm, waiter, r 57 Church.
Graves Wm J, clk Great Atlantic and Pacific Tea Co, b 140 N East.
Graves Willis Y, supt, h 321 N New Jersey.
Gray, see also Grey.
Gray Albert J, student, b 395 N West.
Gray Albert R (Gray & Gribben), h 1206 N Illinois.
Gray Alma (wid Charles), h 45 Benton.
Gray Andrew, lab, h 906 Morris (W I).
Gray Anna, h 6 Howard.
Gray Anna B, sec Christian Woman's Board of Missions, h 597 N Capitol av.
Gray Asher Wm, collr, h 264 W Michigan.
Gray Bayard, b 661 N Penn.
Gray Bell A, b 137 Gillard av.
Gray Calvin, lab, h 18 Holborn.
Gray Charles B, lab, b 233 Michigan (H).
Gray Charles T, bricklyr, h e s Baltimore av 2 s of 17th.
Gray Cyrus E, grocer, 201 English av, b same.
Gray Daniel P, carp, h 620 Bellefontaine.
Gray Edgar B, trav agt, h 468 College av.
Gray Edward, lab, b 91 Birch av (W I).
Gray Edward, lab, b 138 Elizabeth.

EQUITABLE LIFE ASSURANCE SOCIETY OF THE UNITED STATES.
RICHARDSON & McCREA
Managers for Central Indiana,
79 East Market St. Telephone 182.

Gray Eliza J (wid Isaac P), h 661 N Penn.
Gray Ernest S, clk, b 478 N Capitol av.
Gray Ethel G, clk, b n s 30th 4 e of Illinois (M).
Gray Fannie (wid Oliver), h 33 Columbia av.
Gray Fannie, stenog, b 83 Ash.
Gray Flavius H, foreman Hitz Baking Co, h 224 E Merrill.
Gray Frank, tanner, S Belmont av s of Johnson (W I), h 91 Birch av (W I).
Gray Frank, wheelmkr, b 22 Shelby.
Gray Frank E, hostler, r 440 E Washington.
Gray Frederick, driver, h 121 W 5th.
Gray George, h w s Central av 3 s of Grand av (I).
Gray George, lab, b 17 Athon.
Gray George, lab 348 N Capitol av.
Gray George T, bricklyr, h 40 N Dorman.
Gray George W, lab, h 138 Columbia al.
Gray Harry, mach, h 20 N Brightwood av (B).
Gray Harry C, gilder, h n s 30th 4 e of Illinois (M).
Gray Harry H, ck P C C & St L Ry, b 597 N Capitol av.
Gray Henrietta (wid Isaac), h 191 W 4th.
Gray Henry, mach, h 20 N Brightwood av (B).
Gray Isaac N, carp, h 98 Pierce.
Gray James, foreman, h e s Manlove av 1 n of Blackmore.
Gray James, lab, b 341 W Market.
Gray James A, stenog Van Camp H and I Co, r 84 W Vermont.
Gray James B, mach, h 263 Yandes.
Gray James G, lab, b 1083 W Michigan.
Gray James H, bricklyr, h 279 S Olive.
Gray Jane, h 263 Yandes.
Gray Jesse A, bricklyr, b 54 Sheldon.
Gray John, bricklyr, b 54 Sheldon.
Gray John, hostler, r 8 E Court.
Gray John, ironwkr, b e s Manlove av 1 n of Blackmore.
Gray John, lab, b 372 S Capitol av.
Gray John, lab, h 85 W McCarty.
Gray John C, plumber, h 205½ W Ohio.

STENOGRAPHERS FURNISHED.
EXPERIENCED OR BEGINNERS, PERMANENT OR TEMPORARY.
S. H. EAST, State Agent,
The Williams Typewriter,
55 THORPE BLOCK. 87 EAST MARKET ST.

E R ELSTEAM LAUNDRY 26 & 28 N. Senate Avenue. Tel. 1018
WE WILL CALL FOR AND DELIVER YOUR WORK. SATISFACTION GUARANTEED.

ELLIS & HELFENBERGER { ENTERPRISE FOUNDRY & FENCE CO. 162-170 S. Senate Ave. Tel. 958.

THE HOGAN TRANSFER AND STORAGE COMP'Y
Household Goods and Pianos Moved—Packed—Stored...... Baggage and Package Express Machinery and Safes a Specialty Cor. Washington and Illinois Sts. TELEPHONE No. 675.

Hose, Belting, Packing, Clothing, Druggists' Sundries, Bicycle Tires, Cotton Hose, Etc. New York Belting & Packing Co., L't'd.

A death rate below all other American Companies, and dividends from this source correspondingly larger.
The Provident Life and Trust Company
Of Philadelphia.
D. W. EDWARDS, General Agent,
508 Indiana Trust Building.

Gray John E, well driver, 57 Maxwell, h same.
Gray John R, bkkpr F P Rush & Co, b w s Central av 3 s of Grand av (I).
Gray Jonathan, bricklyr, h 54 Sheldon.
Gray J Walter, photog, b 258 N Penn.
Gray Leonard N, lab, h 1083 W Michigan.
Gray Louis, driver, h 372 Coburn.
Gray Louis M, cutter A J Treat & Son, r 425 N Penn.
Gray Lucian A, lab, r 116½ W New York.
Gray Maggie R (Union Co-Operative Laundry), b 28 Lord.
Gray Margaret, seamstress, b 294 N Liberty.
Gray Martin L, lab, h 2 Brown av (H).
Gray Mary C (wid James W), uphlr, 149 N Delaware, h 258 N Penn.
Gray Mary I (wid Henry C), h n s 30th 4 e of Illinois.
Gray Mary J (wid James), h 419 W New York.
Gray Michael, lab, b 91 Birch av (W I).
Gray Ogden H, clk, b 468 College av.
Gray Oscar L, hostler, r 413 E Washington.
Gray Parker G, bricklyr, h 279 S Olive.
Gray Patrick, lab, b 327 Bates.
GRAY PIERRE, Lawyer, 35-39 Thorpe Blk, Tel 110; h 661 N Penn.
Gray Robert, carp, 78 E St Clair, h same.
Gray Robert, coachman 644 N Penn.
Gray Robert, ironwkr, b n e cor Harrison av and Blackmore.
Gray Robert, trav agt Daggett & Co, b 136 W Maryland.
Gray Robert L, engr, h 28 Lord.
Gray Samuel, barber, r 175 W North.
Gray Samuel E, barber, h 126 E 9th.
Gray Samuel F, div freight agt P C C & St L Ry, 28 Commercial Club bldg, h 597 N Capitol av.
Gray Stephen, cutter Kahn Tailoring Co, h 478 N Capitol av.
Gray Thomas (Gray & Lodge), h 128 Cornell av.
Gray Wallace M, clk Van Camp H and I Co, b 78 E St Clair.
Gray Wm, coachman 1009 N Penn.

Julius C. Walk & Son,
Jewelers
Indianapolis.
12 EAST WASHINGTON ST.

The Central Rubber & Supply Co. PHONES. 79 S. ILLINOIS ST., INDIANAPOLIS, IND.

Gray Wm, engr, h 105 Cherry.
Gray Wm, lab, b 224 E Merrill.
Gray Wm, lab, b 619 W Pearl.
Gray Wm, phys, 50½ S Illinois, r same.
Gray Wm H, condr, h 83 Ash.
Gray Wm J, baggagemaster, h 345 S Olive.
Gray Wm O, clk, h 233 Michigan (H).
Gray Wm R, clk, b w s Central av 3 s of Grand av (I).
Gray Wiltshire S, clk, h 477 W 22d (N I).
GRAY & GRIBBEN (Albert R Gray, David S Gribben), Jewelry, Watches and Diamonds, 92 N Illinois.
GRAY & LODGE (Thomas Gray, Laban L Lodge), Wholesale Leaf Tobacco, 25-27 W Pearl.
GRAYBILL HARRY C, Traffic Mngr Belt R R and Stock Yards Co, b Grand Hotel.
Graybill Howard, miller, h 214 Douglass.
Graydon Alexander, b 740 N Alabama.
Graydon Alice B, b 740 N Alabama.
Graydon Andrew, chief clk div frt office P C C & St L Ry, h 740 N Alabama.
Graydon Ellen D, teacher Public School No 10, b 288 Central av.
Graydon Jane M, teacher Public School No 2, b 288 Central av.
Graydon Mary M, h 288 Central av.
Graydon Wm M, b 986 N Penn.
Graydon Wm M jr, lumber, h 288 Central av.
Grayson Edward, coachman, b 232 W 5th.
Grayson John T, lab, h e s Sheffield 2 n of Morris (W I).
Grayson Joseph, lab, h 232 W 5th.
Grayson Lydia B (wid Sanford W), b 215 N Illinois.
Grayson Minnie, h 90 S Senate av.
Grayson Sanford, lab, r 189 W 4th.
Grayville John, r 26 Talbott blk.
Grealish Mary (wid Luke), b 29 Frazee (H).
Greany, see also Graney.
Greany John F, mach, b 175 Meek.
Greany Mary (wid Dennis), h 175 Meek.
Greany Thomas, engr, h 160 Spann av.
GREAT ATLANTIC AND PACIFIC TEA CO THE, Edward Newton Mngr, 20 W Washington and 152 E Washington, Tel 748.
Great Northern Express Co, 5 E Washington and 145 S Meridian.
Greathouse Archibald, saloon, 10 Indiana av, h 202 Yandes.
Grebe Charles, r 85 N Delaware.
Gredhlein Ernst, shoemkr, h 315 Shelby.
Greegor James B, h 460 Bellefontaine.
Greegor Jeremiah W, foreman C C C & St L Ry, b 460 Bellefontaine.
Greek Albert, lab, h 275 N Noble.
Greek Benjamin F, tilesetter, b 25 S West.
Greek Benjamin F jr, tilesetter, h 83 Cornell av.
Greek Elmer, floorman, h 1097 W Washington.
Greek Wm H, tilesetter, h 320 Cornell av.
Greeley Mamie B, bkkpr Star Store, b 52 Elm.
Greeley Michael, plastr, h 52 Elm.
Greeley Patrick, lab, h 214 Deloss.
Greelish Wm, lab, h rear 224 Blake.
Greely Almira (wid Seth B), h 45 Park av.
Greely Flora B, opr W U Tel Co, h 45 Park av.
Greely Laura, stenog Board of State Charities, b 45 Park av.

OTTO GAS ENGINES | BUILDERS' EXCHANGE S. W. Cor. Ohio and Penn. Telephone 535.

Becker & Son Charles Becker Jacob Becker Jr. Merchant Tailors. 21 N. Penn. St. Tel. 934

SALISBURY & STANLEY

O FFICE, STORE AND BANK FIXTURES.

Contractors and Builders. Repairing of all kinds done on short notice. 177 Clinton St., Indianapolis, Ind. Telephone 999.

Greely Mattie P, opr W U Tel Co, b 45 Park av.
Green Agnes H, dry goods, 692 N Senate av, h 700 same.
Green Albert, mach, b 119 Roanoke.
Green Alexander G, blksmith, b 1157 N Meridian.
Green Alonzo P, mach, b 70 McLain (W I).
Green Amanda (wid Thomas), h 18 Bates.
Green Americus V, driver, h 6 Edward (W I).
Green Anna, trimmer, b 12 Prospect.
Green Anna E (wid Edward), b 167 Muskingum al.
Green Arthur, packer, b 46 Russell av.
Green Beecher, hostler, r 65 N New Jersey.
Green Benjamin, driver, h 33 Iowa.
Green Charles, coachman 675 N Penn.
Green Charles, lab, h 35 Alvord.
Green Charles, lab, b 126 Downey.
Green Charles, lab, h 105 Kappus (W I).
Green Charles, sander, b 124 W New York.
Green Charles A, coachman 443 N New Jersey.
Green Charles D, designer U S Encaustic Tile Wks, b 780 Ash.
Green Charles E, h 12 W Chesapeake.
Green Charles E, student, h 446 W Addison (N I).
Green Charles H, dentist, propr Green Dental Rooms, s e cor Illinois and Ohio, h same.
Green Charlotta (wid Hiram), h 134 Downey.
Green Cornelius, carp, h 325 E Michigan.
Green Cyrus, lab, h 311½ E Washington.

GREEN DENTAL ROOMS, Charles H Green Propr, Stewart Pl, s e cor Illinois and Ohio, Tel 1099.

Green Eden H, lab, h 129 S Reisner (W I).
Green Elijah, lab, b 156 Hosbrook.
Green Elijah, lab, h 105 Kappus (W I).
Green Eliza A (wid Jacob), h 143 Lynn av (W I).
Green Elmer, lab, h 266 Lincoln la.
Green Emanuel, lab, b 119 W 4th.
Green Frank, h 773 Ash.
Green Frank, lab, b 297 E Court.
Green Frank, lab, b 419 Bellefontaine.
Green George, city agt, h 132 W Ohio.
Green George A, clk, b 700 N Senate av.
Green George F, carp, h 823 S East.
Green George H, lab, b 325 E Michigan.
Green George M, carp, h 85 Dougherty.
Green George W, carpetlyr, h 277 Olive.
Green Grace (wid Bowling), h 385 Lafayette.
Green Harry, clk, h 114 Keystone av.
Green Henry, cabtmkr, h 271 Davidson.
Green Henry, cabtmkr, b 10 Oxford.
Green Henry C, plumber, h 1779 N Senate av.
Green Henry T, trav agt, h 502 Central av.
Green Herbert C, mach, b 325 E Michigan.

GREEN HERBERT W, "Tuxedo," 67 N Penn, h 363 Talbott av.

Green Hugh M, clk H P Wasson & Co, h 857 N Meridian.
Green Isaac, carp, 60 N New Jersey, r 190 E Market.
Green Isaac A, milk, 747 N Capitol av, res Carmel, Ind.
Green James, elevator opr, b 289 River av (W. I).
Green James, lab, r 225 W Ohio.
Green James A, engr, b 124 English av.

Henry H. Fay,
40½ E. Washington St.,
REAL ESTATE,
AND LOAN BROKER.

Green James A, vice-pres Union Transfer and Storage Co, res Detroit, Mich.
Green James B, shoes, 178 Virginia av, h same.
Green James E, laddermkr, h 594 W Shoemaker (N I).
Green James F, mach, h e s Concord 3 s of Michigan.
Green James O, driver, h 271 Spring.
Green James P (Green & Co), res Danville, Ill.
Green James R, clk, b 289 River av (W I).
Green Jane (wid Benjamin), h 12 S Linden.
Green Jasper C, boxmkr, b 85 Dougherty.
Green John, b 700 N Senate av.
Green John, lab, h 426 W 2d.
Green John, lab, b n e cor 7th and Lennox.
Green John, lab, h 25 Springfield.
Green John, mach hd, b 777 N Senate av.
Green John, sec Sun Building, Loan and Investment Co, 12½ N Delaware, r same.
Green John B, shoes, 680 N Senate av, h 684 same.
Green John C, lawyer, attorney Mutual Life Ins Co of Ind, h n w cor Washington and Gladstone av.
Green John J, checkman, r 67 N New Jersey.
Green John L, salesman, h 1157 N Illinois.
Green John P, gearmkr, h 425 S Capitol av.
Green John S, barber, 81 E Wabash, r 30 Roanoke.
Green John T, lab, h 316 Shelby.
Green John W, lab, h 22 Springfield.
Green John W, lab, h 113 W 10th.
Green Joseph, lab, h rear 346 S Alabama.
Green Kate, h 88 Columbia al.
Green Lizzie J, tailoress Model Clothing Co, r 133½ Virginia av.
Green Lucien L, clk Frank M Millikan, b 248 S East.
Green Margaret A (wid John), h 14 Deloss.
Green Marion E, dynamo tender, r 8 Grand Opera House blk.
Green Martha J, h n s University av 3 w of Central av (I).
Green Mary, h 311 E Washington.
Green Mary A (wid George), h 700 N Senate av.

LIME, CEMENT, PLASTER FIRE BRICK AND CLAY SEWER PIPE, ETC. BALKE & KRAUSS CO., Cor. Market and Missouri Streets.

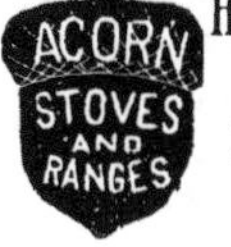

C. FRIEDGEN HAS THE FINEST STOCK OF LADIES' PARTY SLIPPERS and SHOES 19 NORTH PENNSYLVANIA ST.

SAMUEL LAING ▸ TIN, SLATE AND STEEL ROOFING, 72 AND 74 EAST COURT STREET.

M. B. WILSON, Pres. W. F. CHURCHMAN, Cash.
THE CAPITAL NATIONAL BANK,
INDIANAPOLIS, IND.
Pays Interest on Time Certificates of Deposit.
Buys and Sells Foreign Exchange at Low Rates.
Capital, - - $300,000
Surplus and Earnings, 50,000
No. 28 S. Meridian St., Cor. Pearl.

Green Mary E (wid Davis J), h 481 Union.
Green Mattie, dressmkr, 35 Alvord, h same.
Green Minday (wid Thomas), h 18 Bates.
Green Minnie (wid John), h 16 Mill.
Green Minnie, dressmkr, 18 Commercial blk, r same.
Green Nancy A (wid Albert B), h 379 N Alabama.
Green Nancy J (wid Alpheus), b 100 Ruckle.
Green Needham, lab, h s s Colgrove 2 w of Mattie av.
Green Nettie B, trimmer, b 12 S Linden.
Green Oliver P, driver, h 116 Dougherty.
Green Otis W, clk, h 568 Central av.
Green Perry D, clk W U Tel Co, b 1157 N Illinois.
Green Peter, hostler, b 311½ E Washington.
Green Porter, lab 496 N Meridian.
Green Richard, car insp, h 46 Sheffield av (H).
Green Richard, hostler, h 311 E Washington.
Green Samuel, r 127 Dearborn.
Green Samuel, painter, h 335 Bates.
Green Samuel S, cook, h 187 W 9th.
Green Sophia (wid Christopher), h 126 Downey.
Green Theodore, helper, h 46 Sheffield av (H).
Green Theresa (wid Bernard), h 97 Bates.
Green Thomas C, lab, h 50 Bluff rd.
Green Thomas H, driver, b 385 Lafayette.
Green Thomas L, mach, 331 Mass av, b 325 E Michigan.
Green Tompkins, hostler, h 121½ Ft Wayne av.
Green Walter, lab, b 823 S East.
Green Walter B, bkkpr, b 289 River av (W I).
Green Walter J, sawyer, b 823 S East.
Green Wm, dairy, 30th and L N A & C Ry, h same.
Green Wm, express, r 24 N West.
Green Wm, lab, r 151 Indiana av.
Green Wm, lab, h 22 Koerner.
Green Wm, lab, r 66 N Missouri.
Green Wm A, foreman Meridian Stables, r 114 N Meridian.

TUTTLE & SEGUIN,
28 E. Market Street.
Fire Insurance,
Real Estate, Loan
and Rental Agents.
TELEPHONE 1168.

Green Wm A, messenger Am Ex Co, h 773 Ash.
Green Wm A, waiter, b 88 W Market.
Green Wm N W, wagonmkr, h 289 River av (W I).
Green Wm J, coachman, h 29 W 1st.
Green Zulu M, stenog V H Lockwood, b 956 N Capitol av.
GREEN & CO (James P Green, A W Heinly), Transfer, Livery, Hacks and Coupes, 63-69 W Market, Tel 1036.
Greenbaum Abraham, clothing, 182 Indiana av, h same.
Greene Albert B, printer, b 360 S New Jersey.
Greene Andrew S, boilermaker, h e s Concord 2 s of Michigan (H).
Greene Barbara (wid John), h 590 S East.
Greene Bernard, lab, b 185 Hadley av (W I).
Greene Charles P, genl agt Connecticut Mut Life Ins Co, h 25 W Walnut.
Greene Charles W, printer, h 360 S New Jersey.
Greene Daniel, lab, h 60 Traub av.
Greene David W, oiler, b 215 Huron.
GREENE DAVIES M (James Greene & Co), h 364 N Meridian.
Greene Edward P, stenog, b 172 N New Jersey.
Greene Emanuel, lab, b 119 W 4th.
Greene Frank W, mach hd, h 288 Howard (W I).
Greene Grosvenor L, clk L E & W R R, b 1052 E Michigan.
GREENE JAMES & CO (Davies M Greene), Real Estate and Rental Agts, Stock and Investment Brokers, 227-228 Lemcke Bldg.
Greene John N, local agt The Indpls News, b 590 S East.
Greene Lewis W (Williams & Greene), r rear 685 N Delaware.
Greene Mary B (wid James), h 364 N Meridian.
Greene Mary W, teacher Knickerbacker Hall, b e s Central av near 7th.
Greene Michael F, mach opr The Indpls News, h 504 S New Jersey.
Greene Samuel E, trav agt, h 325 Orange.
Greene S Ashley, clk L E & W R R, b 325 Orange.
Greene Thomas A, local agt The Indpls News, h 76 High.
Greene Wm A, mach opr Indpls Journal, b 590 S East.
Greene Wm D, h 141 Park av.
Greenebaum Max A, cigarmkr, b 183 N Pine.
Greenen Alfred C, fireman, b 34 N Arsenal av.
Greenen Charles P (J W Greenen & Son), b 34 N Arsenal av.
Greenen Francis M, fireman, b 128 S Noble.
Greenen Joseph J, fireman, b 34 N Arsenal av.
GREENEN JOSEPH W (J W Greenen & Son), Trainmaster Indianapolis Division P C C & St L Ry, h 34 N Arsenal av, Tel 1058.
Greenen J W & Son (Joseph W and Charles P), coal, 825 E Washington.
Greenen Michael H, engr, h 128 S Noble.
Greenen Thomas W, clk W U Tel Co, b 34 N Arsenal av.
Greener Andrew, engr, h 139 E Morris.
Greengrass Henry, lab, h 421 E Michigan.

SULLIVAN & MAHAN Manufacturers of all kinds of PAPER BOXES 41 W. Pearl St.

DIAMOND WALL PLASTER { Telephone 1410 BUILDERS' EXCHANGE.

Tel phone 1769. 1 1/2 S. Illinois St. } THE HOME LAUNDRY } WORK CALLED FOR AND DELIVERED.

Greening Henry C, blksmith, 42 Paw Paw, h same.
Greenland Frederick G, mach, h 30 Wiley av.
Greenland George, engr, b n w cor Michigan and State avs.
Greenleaf Clement A, mach, h 51 Paw Paw.
Greenleaf Edward T, draughtsman Consumers' Gas Trust Co, h 905 N New Jersey.
Greenlee Wm B, printer, h 217 S New Jersey.
Greenman Jacob, saloon, 109 Mass av, h 101 same.
Greenough Clarence F, clk, b 132 N New Jersey.
Greenough Estella E (wid Henry), h 132 N New Jersey.
Greenstreet Charles J, chemist, b 565 N Capitol av.
Greenstreet Jason H, pur agt Kingan & Co, h 565 N Capitol av.
Greenwald Henry, carp, h e s Euclid av 1 n of Washington.
Greenwell Charles H, blksmith, s e cor College av and 9th, h 490 Ash.
Greenwell Wm F, bartndr, b 813 N Capitol av.
Greenwood David, patternmkr, b 230 Excelsior av.
Greenwood Deloss A, lineman, h w s St Paul 1 s of Stanton av.
Greenwood Frank E, lineman, b e s St Paul 1 s of Stanton av.
Greenwood Harry E, mach, b 230 Excelsior av.
Greenwood Ira T, mach, b 230 Excelsior av.
Greenwood James P, lab, b 57 Harrison.
Greenwood Joseph, h 175½ W Washington.
Greenwood Lemuel R, carp, h 320½ E Washington.
Greenwood Missouri H (wid Joseph), b w s St Paul 1 s of Stanton av.
Greenwood Wm J, teacher High School, h 225 N Delaware.
Greer Anna (wid Alexander), milliner, 42 S Illinois, r 4 Wyandot blk.
Greer Harry, clk, b 285 Kentucky av.
Greer James, cabtmkr, 248 S Senate av, b 266 same.
Greer James E, Commissioner Marion County, 43 Court House, h w s Commercial av 1 s of Washington av (I).
Greer Martin S, janitor, h 174 Buchanan.
Greer Squire R (Greer-Wilkinson Co), h 178 N Penn.
Greer Thomas H, watchman, h 143 N State av.
Greer-Wilkinson Co (Squire R Greer, Allen A Wilkinson), lumber, 477 E Michigan.
Greer Wm E, clk, b 199 S Illinois.
Greeson Albert C, lab, b w s N Illinois 3 n of 28th.
Greeson Alonzo E, lab, r 170 W Market.
Greeson John B, carp, h 252½ W Washington.
Gregg Adaline E (wid Clark), b 100 Camp.
Gregg Elizabeth (wid Andrew W), h 241 Shelby.
Gregg Fidelia J (wid Wm S), h 103 Germania av (H).
Gregg Frederick C, clk, b 74 Huron.
Gregg George R, timekpr, b 241 Shelby.
Gregg James F, storekpr, h 26 Tuxedo.
Gregg James F, tmstr, h 151 King av (H).
Gregg James M, trav agt, h 74 Huron.
Gregg John, lab, b 334 Douglass.
Gregg John E, lab, h rear 173 Bright.
Gregg Lincoln H, mach, b 320 W 1st.

FRANK NESSLER, WILL H. ROST.
FRANK NESSLER & CO.
Tailors
56 EAST MARKET ST. (Lemcke Building),
INDIANAPOLIS, IND.

Gregg Thomas F, lab, b 241 Shelby.
Gregoire Ella T (wid Lewis), nurse, 1025 N Penn, b same.
Gregori Mansuel, fruits, 76 S Illinois, h 125 Duncan.
Gregory Alonzo C, clk, b 139 N Delaware.
Gregory Alonzo H, driver, h 344 Union.
Gregory Augustus C, trav agt, h 302 N Delaware.
Gregory Caroline (wid John W), h 556 W North.
Gregory Daniel, tmstr, h 3 Brooks.
Gregory Edward, lab, h e s Earl 1 s of Belt R R.
Gregory Fred A (Gregory & Appel), h 935 N Meridian.
Gregory Harry W, clk, b 72 W New York.
Gregory John, lab, b 28 Journal bldg.
Gregory John W, engr, h n s Sutherland 2 w of Gale (B).
Gregory J Frank, bkkpr, b 72 W New York.
Gregory Lorenz, soldier U S Arsenal, b 684 E St Clair.
Gregory Lucy A (wid Noble), b n s Sutherland 2 w of Gale (B).
Gregory Madge (wid Mason), r 40 S Capitol av.
Gregory Marshall O, tmstr, b 556 W North.
Gregory Martha M (wid Albert), b 935 N Meridian.
Gregory Otto, lab, h 18 Elliott.
Gregory Robert, lab, b 428 W Chicago (N I).
Gregory Walter, sawmkr, b 319 S Meridian.
Gregory Walter W, r 267 N New Jersey.
Gregory Wm C, lab, h 34 Rhode Island.
Gregory Wm H, tmstr, h 556 W North.
GREGORY & APPEL (Fred A Gregory, John J Appel), Real Estate, Loans, Rentals and Insurance, 96 E Market, Tel 995.
Greig Alexander (Dynes & Greig), b 158 S Olive.
Greig Alexander, bkkpr F H Smith, b 158 S Olive.
Greig Alfred H, designer, b 58 Kansas.
Greig John, h 158 S Olive.
Greig Walter A, clk, b 158 S Olive.

Haueisen & Hartmann
163-169 E. Washington St.
FURNITURE,
Carpets,
Household Goods,
Tin, Granite and China Wares, Oil Cloth and Shades

THE WM. H. BLOCK CO. 7 AND 9 EAST WASHINGTON STREET. DRY GOODS, HOUSE FURNISHINGS AND CROCKERY.

London Guarantee and Accident Co. (Ltd.) Employers', Public and Teams' Liability. Workmen's Collective Insurance and Fidelity Bonds
GEORGE W. PANGBORN, General Agent, 704-706 Lemcke Bldg. Telephone 140.

FRANK K. SAWYER || Reliable Fire Insurance. || Reasonable Rates.
74 E. MARKET STREET. Telephone 4.

JOSEPH GARDNER,
TIN, IRON, STEEL AND SLATE ROOFING,
GALVANIZED IRON CORNICES & SKYLIGHTS.
37, 39 & 41 KENTUCKY AVE. Telephone 322.

Greiger Wm, lab, h 117 Downey.
Greilich Albert E, helper, b 159 John.
Greilich John, foreman C C C & St L Ry, h 159 John.
Greilich Wm J, mach, b 159 John.
Grein Charles H, baker, b 50 N State av.
Grein John, h 50 N State av.
Greiner Christian F, h 126 Douglass.
Greiner Christian F jr, molder, b 126 Douglass.
Greiner Christian W, coremkr, h 101 Minerva.
Greiner Emma M, h 244½ E Washington.
Greiner Edward L, clk, b 224 Prospect.
Greiner Henry, foreman, h 61 Columbia av.
Greiner John, brewer, h 93 Oriole.
Greiner John, shoemkr, 226 Prospect, h 224 same.
Greiner John F, mach, h 130 Douglass.
Greiner Joseph M, asst L A Greiner, b 613 E Vermont.
GREINER LOUIS A, Veterinary Surgeon and Propr Indianapolis Veterinary Infirmary, 18-24 S East, Tel 905; h 613 E Vermont, Tel 1798. (See adv in classified Veterinary Surgeons.)
Greiner Margaret (wid Louis), h 246 Bright.
Greiner Wm J, lab, h 7 Highland av (H).
Greist Louis T, legal dept C C C & St L Ry, h 27 Garfield pl.
Greist Rebecca G (wid Alva C), h 262 Lincoln av.
Greist Walter C, bkkpr, b 262 Lincoln av.
Greistow Frederick, carp, h 30 Windsor.
Greive James G, mach, b 66 King av (H).
Greive James L, engr, h 66 King av (H).
Grenberg Matilda, housekpr 298 Park av.
Grenwald Sam, cigar mnfr, rear 333 Jefferson av, h 329 Jefferson av.
Gresh Benneville F, dancing academy, 181 E Washington, h 177 E Ohio.
Gresh David A, city fireman, h 78 Fayette.
Gresh John B, driver, h 93 Malott av.
Gresh Otis, painter, h 488 W Francis (N I).
Gresh Wm H, mngr, h 126 Clifford av.
Gresh Wm H & Co (Mary A Gilmore), coal, s e cor Peru and Mass avs.

J. S. FARRELL & CO.
STEAM AND HOT WATER HEATING AND PLUMBING CONTRACTORS
84 North Illinois Street. Telephone 382.

Gresham Albert G, h 187 N Penn.
Gresham Girdy C, candymkr, b 40 Kansas.
Gresham John, lab, h 255 W 5th.
Gresham Samuel C, lab, h 40 Kansas.
Gress Frank, yardmstr L E & W R R, h 94 Fulton.
Greulich Adam G, lab, b 149 Columbia av.
Greuling Reinholdt, cabtmkr, h 412 Excelsior av.
Grey, see also Gray.
Grey Edward P, driver, h 398 Rembrant (M P).
Grey Francis S, clk Kingan & Co (ltd), r 455 N Capitol av.
Grey John, fireman, r 34 S State av.
Grey Wm T, rollman, h n e cor Vorster and Sugar Grove av (M P).
Gribben David S (Gray & Gribben), h 207 N Pine.
Griblinghof Mattie, housekpr The Grand Hotel.
Grider Benjamin, driver, h 320 Lincoln av.
Grider George R, lab, h rear 834½ S Meridian.
Grider Hiram, lab, h n s Minnesota 1 w of Meridian.
Grider Warren H, tmstr, h 31 Carson.
Grider Welby, porter, b 320 Lincoln av.
Grider Wm T, lab, h 20 Sheffield av (H).
Gridley Wm F, lab, h 563 Union.
Grieb Christina (wid Gottlieb), h 340 Fulton.
Grieb George V, clk A Kiefer Drug Co, h 218 N Pine.
Grieb John, uphlr, h 205 N Pine.
Grieb John B, lab, h rear 236 N Pine.
Grieb John H, lab, b 340 Fulton.
Grieb Wm C F, uphlr, h 327 E Walnut.
Griebelbaur Wm, finisher, h 654 S Illinois.
Griepenstorh August, horseshoer, b 62 Sanders.
Grieser John, lab, r 70 Bicking.
Grieshaber Albert, clk Murphy, Hibben & Co, b 1 Water.
Grieshaber Frank J, mach, h 445 Ash.
Griesmann Edward P, mach hd, b 354 Highland av.
Griesmann George H, mach hd, b 354 Highland av.
Griesmann Mary H (wid Philip), b 354 Highland av.
Griewe Wm F Rev, pastor First German M E Church, h 185 E New York.
Griffey John B, trav agt G W Stout, h n s 11th 3 e of College av.
Griffey John W, lab, h 181½ S Meridian.
Griffey Owen, shoemkr, b 181½ S Meridian.
Griffey Pleasant B, clk G W Stout, h John B Griffey.
Griffey Wm, junk, 18 Wright, h same.
Griffie Jesse J, photog, h n e cor Northwestern av and 9th (H).
Griffin Albert, tmstr, b 7 Lexington av.
Griffin Archer, lab, h 77 Adams.
Griffin Bartholomew, farmer, h w s Warren 1 e of Line (I).
Griffin Charles F, pres Union Natl S and L Assn, res Hammond, Ind.
Griffin Claude, adv agt, h 222 Clinton.
Griffin Cora B, b 35 Helen.
Griffin Cornelius, lab, h 458 S Capitol av.
Griffin David E, lab, b 378 N Missouri.
Griffin David J, driver, b 27 Fayette.
Griffin David H, barber, h 74 Spruce.
Griffin Dudley S, plumber, h 267 Fayette.
Griffin Edward, foreman Kingan & Co (ltd), h 234 Bright.
Griffin Ellen (wid Martin), h 370 W 1st.
Griffin Forrest P, clk, b 267 N West.

POLICIES IN UNITED STATES LIFE INSURANCE CO., offer indemnity against death, liberal cash surrender value or at option of policy-holder, fully paid-up life insurance or liberal life income. E. B. SWIFT, M'g'r, 25 E. Market St.

WM. KOTTEMAN WILL FURNISH YOUR HOUSE COMPLETE
89 & 91 E. Washington St. Telephone 1742

SHOW CASES | WILLIAM WIEGEL | 6 West Louisiana St. Opp. Union Station.

Griffin Frank, lab, b 7 Wilcox.
Griffin Gabriel, janitor, h 470 Cornell av.
Griffin George A, cook, h 267½ Fayette.
Griffin George G (Schnull & Co), b 273 N Capitol av, tel 1102.
Griffin George P, mach, b 258 Bates.
Griffin Harry L, insp, h 206 E Morris.
Griffin Henry, lab, r 177½ Muskingum al.
Griffin Henry, lab, h 490 W 2d.
Griffin Henry M, barber, 140 Howard (W I), h 78 S Judge Harding (W I).
Griffin Isaac E, carp, b rear 25 Cornell av.
Griffin Isom, furniture, 180 Indiana av, h 267 N West.
Griffin James, lab, h 20 Sand.
Griffin James, insp Indpls Gas Co, b 25 Fletcher av.
Griffin Jeremiah, real est, b 146 Meek.
Griffin Jeremiah A, awnings, 175 Clinton, h same.
Griffin John, h 79 Fayette.
Griffin John, b 267 W Ray.
Griffin John, farmer, h n s Warren 1 e of Line (I).
Griffin John, lab, h 287 Indiana av.
Griffin John, lab, b 26 Roe.
Griffin John, lab, b 21 Hoyt av.
Griffin John A, bartndr, b 17 Maple.
Griffin John D, plumber, b 180 N Dorman.
Griffin John E, lab, b 370 W 1st.
Griffin John F, clk, h 211 W McCarty.
Griffin John F, foreman, h 443 N California.
Griffin John J, lab, b 79 Fayette.
Griffin John M, mach hd, b 258 Bates.
Griffin John T, b 78 S Judge Harding (W I).
Griffin John T, lab, h 16 McGinnis.
Griffin Josephine, stenog J S Farrell & Co, b 180 N Dorman.
Griffin Kate E, teacher Public School No 6, b 146 Union.
Griffin Kathleen G, stenog Glens Falls Ins Co, b 318 S West.
Griffin Margaret (wid George), h 17 Maple.
Griffin Martha M (wid George), h 273 N Capitol av.
Griffin Mary (wid Thomas), h 142 S Noble.
Griffin Mary, dressmkr, 49½ N Illinois, h 325 S Alabama.
Griffin Maude I, bill clk, b 257 Bellefontaine.
Griffin May M, grocer, 211 W McCarty, h same.
Griffin Michael, boilermkr, h 214 English av.
Griffin Michael, foreman, h 180 N Dorman.
Griffin Michael, stoker, h 124 Meek.
Griffin Michael F, teamster, h 12 Douglass.
Griffin Michael L, stenog C C C & St L Ry, b 34 Union.
Griffin Michael S, cashr Schnull & Co, b 273 N Capitol av.
Griffin Patrick, clk The Bowen-Merrill Co, h 278 N Missouri.
Griffin Patrick, lab, h 258 Bates.
Griffin Patrick F, packer, b 378 N Missouri.
Griffin Patrick J, h 13 Chadwick.
Griffin Patrick J, fireman, h 21 Hoyt av.
Griffin Patrick J, flagman, h 74 S Spruce.
Griffin Ransom, broker, 21 W Maryland, r 316 N Meridian.
Griffin Richard, lab, h 121 Douglass.
Griffin Robert, mach, h 126 Greer.
Griffin Robert, lab, b n s Warren 1 e of Line (I).
Griffin Samuel, journalist, h 383 Ash.
Griffin Sarah A (wid James), h 833 S Meridian.
Griffin Thomas, h 78 W McCarty.
Griffin Thomas, lab, h 76 Chadwick.

THOS. C. DAY & CO.
INVESTING AGENTS,
TOWN AND FARM LOANS,
Rooms 325 to 330 Lemcke Bldg.

Griffin Thomas, watchman, b 201 E Washington.
Griffin Thomas F, foreman, b 142 S Noble.
Griffin Timothy, clk, b n s Warren 1 e of Line (I).
GRIFFIN TIMOTHY, Custodian State House, Room 45 State House, Tel 1057; h 146 Union.
Griffin Timothy, stoker, h 318 S West.
Griffin Wm, barber, 42 Indiana av, r same.
Griffin Wm D, engr, h 257 Bellefontaine.
Griffin Wm F, boilermkr, b 180 N Dorman.
Griffin Wm H, engr Butler College, h w end Lena (I).
Griffin Wm H, shoemkr, 152 W North, r same.
Griffin Wm H, trav agt, h 80 S Judge Harding (W I).
Griffin Wm J (Schnull & Co), h 984 N Penn, tel 1483.
Griffis James A, brakeman, h 47 N State av.
Griffith Alice B, teacher Public School No 29, b 918 Ash.
Griffith Andrew J, cashr, h 475 E Market.
Griffith Anna J, teacher Industrial School, b 918 Ash.
GRIFFITH BROS (Theodore E, Wm H and Claude T), Wholesale Milliners, 132 S Meridian, Tel 1037.
Griffith Carl V, with Griffith Bros, b 446 N Capitol av.
Griffith Charles R, messenger, b 197 N East.
Griffith Claude T (Griffith Bros), h 316 Broadway.
Griffith DeWitt C, trav agt, h 286 Central av.
Griffith Edward J, mach, h 10 N Brightwood av (B).
Griffith Elenora L (wid Wm C), h 415 Broadway.
Griffith Elizabeth B, stenog Chambers, Pickens & Moores, b 918 Ash.
Griffith Emelie (wid James D), b 5 Jefferson.
Griffith Etta M, bkkpr Com Trav Mut Acc Assn, b 197 N East.

EAT
HITZ'S CRACKERS AND CAKES.
ASK YOUR GROCER FOR THEM.

Capital Steam Carpet Cleaning Works
M. D. PLUNKETT Proprietor, Telephone 818

BENJ. BOOTH PRACTICAL EXPERT ACCOUNTANT. Accounts of any description investigated and audited, and statements rendered. Room 18, 82½ E. Washington St., Indianapolis, Ind.

The Best Place in the City to Get a Good Meal THE SHERMAN RESTAURANT 18 and 20 S. Meridian Street KERSHNER BROS., Proprs.

ESTABLISHED 1876. TELEPHONE 168.
CHESTER BRADFORD,
SOLICITOR OF PATENTS,
AND COUNSEL IN PATENT CAUSES.
(See adv. page 6.)
Office:—Rooms 14 and 16 Hubbard Block, S.W. Cor. Washington and Meridian Streets, INDIANAPOLIS, INDIANA.

Griffith Frank L, student, b 415 Broadway.
Griffith Frank R, truckman, h 226 Buchanan.
Griffith Frank X, trav agt Jacob Metzger & Co, h 170 Cornell av.
Griffith George M, billposter, h 72 Clifford av.
Griffith Harriet L (wid Thomas), h 991 N Meridian.
Griffith Harry, clk, h 68½ N East.
Griffith Harry E, billposter, h 34 Garfield pl.
Griffith Harry W, student, b 415 Broadway.
Griffith Henry, clk, b 200 N West.
Griffith Jennie M (wid Orlando P), h 429 N Penn.
Griffith John, farmer, h n s Walnut 1 w of Arlington av (I).
Griffith John W, h 918 Ash.
Griffith Lena (wid John W), r 116½ W New York.
Griffith Louis L, stonecutter, h 197 N East.
Griffith Martha L, teacher Public School No 9, b 918 Ash.
Griffith Perry, barber, r Halcyon blk.
Griffith Pleasant H, b 612 N Illinois.
Griffith Richard B, miller, h 243 W New York.
Griffith Robert W, mnfr bakers' machinery, 86 E Georgia, h 126 Greer.
Griffith St Clair, foreman, b 429 N Penn.
Griffith Seth T, foreman Nordyke & Marmon Co, h 126 Cornell av.
Griffith Theodore E (Griffith Bros), b 446 N Capitol av.
Griffith Thomas, mach, h n s Willow 4 w of Brightwood av (B).
Griffith Thomas J, molder, h 242 Oliver av (W I).
Griffith Thomas S, lab, h 121 E Reisner (W I).
Griffith Wm, lab, b 29 Eastern av.
Griffith Wm C, motorman, h 41½ State.
Griffith Wm E, condr, h 197 N East.
Griffith Wm G, sales agt National Malleable Castings Co, r 307 N Delaware.
Griffith Wm H, h 252½ W Washington.
Griffith Wm H (Griffith Bros), h 534 N Delaware.

O. B. Ensey
SLATE, STEEL, TIN AND IRON ROOFING.
Cor. 6th and Illinois Sts. Tel. 1562

Griffith Henry, vice-pres Balke & Krauss Co, h 200 N West.
Griffiths James, shoemkr, h 188 Meek.
Griffiths John L (Griffiths & Potts), h 566 N Delaware.
Griffiths Wm R, bkkpr, h 9 English av.
GRIFFITHS & POTTS (John L Griffiths, Alfred F Potts), Lawyers, 713-719 Lemcke Bldg, Tel 827.
Griffy Theodore S, brakeman, h 852½ E Washington.
Griggs Francis W (Griggs & Tyler), b 21 Cherry.
Griggs Joseph E, boiler compound mnfr, 22 Ingalls blk, b s w cor National and English avs (I).
GRIGGS & TYLER (Francis W Griggs, Lambert D Tyler), Home Furnishings, 118 N Meridian.
Griggsby James M, driver, h 242 Huron.
Grigsby George W, cooper, b n w cor Michigan and State avs.
Grigsby Harry, lab, h 15 S Rural.
Grigsby Harry L, engr, h 186 Hoyt av.
Grigsby Henry E, janitor, h 50½ Monument pl.
Grigsby James, h 114 Michigan av.
Grigsby James, car rep, h 67 Leota.
Grigsby Jesse, car rep, h 36 N State av.
Grigsby Wm, lab, b rear 606 N West.
Grilich Wm F, mach, h 13 Traub av.
Grill Lizzie, clk Treasurer of State, b 789 N Penn.
Grim John H, ballplyr, h 132 Shelby.
Grim Louis, custodian The Limited Gun Club, h w s L N A & C Ry 1 s of 30th.
Grim Manoah W (M W Grim & Sons), h 171 Coburn.
Grim M W & Sons (Manoah W, Ulysses S and Wm H), com mers, 17 S Alabama.
Grim Ulysses S (M W Grim & Sons), b 171 Coburn.
Grim Wm H (M W Grim & Sons), b 171 Coburn.
Grimes Aaron R, shoemkr, 27½ Monument pl, h same.
Grimes Charles E, cook, h 227 S East.
Grimes Edward, truckman, h 447 S East.
Grimes Harry R, collr Balke & Krauss Co, h 325 N West.
Grimes Joseph N, carp, h 33 Cornell av.
Grimes Marcus A, lab, h 28 Excelsior av.
Grimes Samuel, clk, b 549 W Udell (N I).
Grimes Thomas, b 542 S East.
Grimes Union, trav agt, h 678 Broadway.
Grimes Van P, policeman, h 549 W Udell (N I).
Grimes Wm H, mach hd, h 325 N West.
Grimm Alice S, h 209 W Ohio.
Grimm Charles, mach, b 14 Morton.
Grimm Charles H, clk Albert Gall, b 50 Brand.
Grimm Cornelius, lab, h 14 Morton.
Grimm Frederick J, mounter, r 132 N Capitol av.
Grimm John, lab, b 300 Kentucky av.
Grimn Lambert, canmkr, b 14 Morton.
Grimsley Felix, lab, h s s Michigan av 2 e of Auburn av.
Grinstead Thomas A, condr, h 88 Warren av.
GRINSTEINER BROS (George and Wm H), Funeral Directors, 276 E Market, Tel 908.
Grinsteiner George (Grinsteiner Bros), h 276 E Market.
Grinsteiner George C, clk, b 235 Davidson.

TUTEWILER UNDERTAKER, No. 72 WEST MARKET STREET. TELEPHONE 216.

PROVIDENT LIFE AND TRUST CO. OF PHILADELPHIA. D. W. Edwards, G. A., 508 Indiana Trust Bldg. In form of policy; prompt settlement of death losses; equitable dealing with policy-holders; in strength of organization; and in everything which contributes to Security and Cheapness of life insurance, this company is unsurpassed.

THEODORE F. SMITHER ROOFER

Grinsteiner Joseph, undertaker, h 235 Davidson.
Grinsteiner Joseph J, clk, b 235 Davidson.
Grinsteiner Mary A (wid George), h 87 N Noble.
Grinsteiner Wm (Grinsteiner Bros), b 87 N Noble.
Griser Victor L, clk The Wm H Block Co, b 518 Talbott av.
Grissell Patrick, bartndr, b 151 W Washington.
Grissom Wm, lab, b 115 Martindale av.
Grist Jeremiah A, barber, 13 S Illinois, h 518 E Ohio.
Grist Wm M, lab, h 366 Olive.
Griswold George W, engr, h 10 Wallace.
Griswold George W, tel opr I U Ry Co, h 27 Sinker.
Griswold Patrick, bartndr, h 274 N West.
Griswold Tillie (wid John), h 296 E South.
Grizzle Bragg, lab, b 71 Yandes.
GROCERS' MANUFACTURING CO THE (Anson B Conkle, Charles A Ross, Horace E Hadley, John A Black), Importers and Dealers in Fine Teas, Mnfrs of Pure Baking Powder, Vinegar, Extracts and Grocers' Specialties, 80 S Penn, Tel 660.
Grodnick Max, ins agt, r 101 N New Jersey.
Groendyke Frank, trav agt, r 168 Union.
Groener Herman J, harnessmkr, h 104 Torbet.
Groennert Henry C, drayman, h 35 W Morris.
Groenwoldt Albert J (Groenwoldt & Behringer), h 146 Bates.
Groenwoldt Edwin J, clk, b 146 Bates.
Groenwoldt Frank J, bkkpr, h 1128 N Penn.
Groenwoldt Wm J, bkkpr The Capitol National Bank, b 146 Bates.
Groenwoldt & Behringer (Albert J Groenwoldt, Joseph Behringer), whol liquors, 84 S Delaware.
Groeschel August, tailor, h 547 S East.
Groeschel Christina (wid Charles), b 81 W 19th.
Groeschel John H, lab, h 81 W 19th.
Groff Elmer, cement wkr, r 177½ W Washington.
Groff Frank, lab, h 42 Centennial (H).
Groff Harry A (N B Groff & Son), butter, 142 E Mkt House, b 184 Talbott av.
Groff John W, car insp, h 286 Indiana av.
Groff Nathaniel B (N B Groff & Son), h 184 Talbott av.
Groff N B & Son (Nathaniel B and Harry A), butter, 97 N Delaware and 43 E Mkt House.
Groff Otto, barber, b n e cor Brightwood av and C C C & St L Ry (B).
Groff Robert E, clk When Clothing Store, h 232 N East.
Groff Robert I, b 232 N East.
Groff Wm H, mngr Am Coll and Rep Assn, b 124 Christian av.
Grohs Isadore, trav agt, h 282 E New York.
Gronauer Frank, baker Parrott & Taggart, h 121 Eureka av.
Groninger Frank C (Groninger & Moore), r 81 W Vermont.
GRONINGER & MOORE (Frank C Groninger, Jesse C Moore), Lawyers, 323-325 Indiana Trust Bldg.
Grooms Wm E, lithog, h 428 N Capitol av.
Grosch John, h 281 E New York.
Grosch Justus, b 236 Lincoln la.
Grose Caroline (wid Charles), b 12 Brookside av.

THE WHEN IS A WORLD BEATER.

Grose Charles, engr, h 14 Brookside av.
Grose John T, painter, h 96 N Judge Harding (W I).
Grose Madison, engr, h 867 Bellefontaine.
Grose Sidney, tel opr, b 12 Brookside av.
Grose Wm C, engr, h 12 Brookside av.
Grose Wm F, mach hd, h 654 W Wells (N I).
Gross Andrew L, barber, 289 W Maryland, h same.
Gross Catherine (wid Peter), h 149 Hosbrook.
Gross Edwin E, undertaker George Herrmann, h 50 Oriole.
Gross Elizabeth (wid Charles), h 118 N Liberty.
Gross Elwood, painter, r 289½ Mass av.
Gross Frederick G (Gross & Co), b 359 N Noble.
Gross Herbert S, clk, b 32 Hendricks.
Gross John, b 259 Bates.
Gross John T, lab, b 37 N Judge Harding (W I).
Gross Joseph, lab, h 323 E Wabash.
Gross Joseph, lab, h 768 Charles.
Gross Lemuel C, carp, h 74 Wright.
Gross Martin R, trav agt, h 32 Hendricks.
Gross Orville, engine disp C C C & St L Ry, h 163 Cornell av.
Gross Peter, lab, h 20 Church.
Gross Philip E, printer, h 168 Douglass.
Gross Philip J (Gross & Co), h 359 N Noble.
Gross Phoebe M, artist, 149 Hosbrook, h same.
Gross Sidney W, opr W U Tel Co, b 12 Brookside av.
Gross Wm, clk, b 118 N Liberty.
Gross Wm, mach hd, h 654 Wells (N I).
Gross & Co (Philip J and Frank G Gross), grocers, 243 Mass av.
Grossart Frederick C, mngr C Maus Branch Indpls Brewing Co, h 324 E South.
Grosse Wm F, mach hd, h 654 Wells (N I).
Grosskopf Adam (Nutz & Grosskopf), h 110 Wright.
Grosskopf Charles, mach hd, b 108 Wright.
Grosskopf Michael, lab, h 108 Wright.
Grossman Louis, clk, b 134 Eddy.

GRAVEL AND OTT COMPOSITION 151 W. Maryland St. Office, 151 W. Maryland St. Telephone 86

The A. Burdsal Co. CELEBRATED HOMESTEAD READY MIXED PAINT. WHOLESALE AND RETAIL. 34 AND 36 SOUTH MERIDIAN STREET.

ELECTRIC SUPPLIES We Carry a full Stock. Prices Right. C. W. MEIKEL, Tel. 466. 96-98 E. New York St.

DALTON & MERRIFIELD { LUMBER South Noble St., near E. Washington

INDIANA ELECTROTYPE CO. : BEST WORK. LOWEST PRICES.
23 WEST PEARL ST., INDIANAPOLIS, IND. JOB WORK. BOOK PLATES. BEST PATENT BASE ON THE MARKET. All Orders Promptly Filled.

KIRKHOFF BROS.,
Electrical Contractors, Wiring and Construction.
102-104 SOUTH PENNSYLVANIA ST.
TELEPHONE 910.

Grossman Simon, pdlr, h 464 S Capitol av.
Grossman Wm, waiter, r 253 S New Jersey.
Grosvenor Samuel, mach hd, h e s Rural 4 n of Brookside av.
Grote August F, candymkr, b 172 Meek.
Grothaus Caroline R, milliner, 229 E Morris, b same.
Grothaus Elizabeth (wid Edward C), h 132 Downey.
Grothaus George W, uphlr, h 44 Hoyt av.
Grothaus Henry D, clk, h 119 Sanders.
Grothaus Henry J, h 229 E Morris.
Grothaus Theodore A, cabtmkr, h 229 E Morris.
Grothe Charles, lab, b 15 Ellsworth.
Grothe Florence, tailoress, h 1 Cleaveland blk.
Grothe Frank J, clk A Kiefer Drug Co, h 259 S Delaware.
Grothe Henry (Grothe & Son), h 396 E Market.
Grothe Henry, lab, b 15 Ellsworth.
Grothe Henry H, chairmkr, h 29 Buchanan.
Grothe Joseph (Grothe & Son), b 396 E Market.
Grothe Lulu, h 181 Harmon.
Grothe & Son (Henry and Joseph), livery, 40 E Maryland.
Grottendick Mina K (wid Henry H), h 199 N Liberty.
Grottendick Rose, stenog Reserve Fund S and L Assn, b 199 N Liberty.
Grottrup John, truckman, h 113 Lincoln la.
Grout Charles S, genl sec Charity Organization Society, 1 Plymouth bldg, b 170 Christian av.
Grove Albert H, painter, 94 E Market, b 530 Dillon.
Grove Andrew W, cigarmkr, h 530 Dillon.
Grove Anna M (wid Samuel A), h rear 421 N East.
Grove Arthur A, clk, b rear 421 N East.
Grove Benjamin, b 1398 N Senate av.
Grove Claude E Rev, pastor Brightwood Congregational Church, r 26 S Stuart (B).
Grove Daniel L, carp, h 1316 N Capitol av.
Grove Eunice E (wid Benjamin F), h 248 W 12th.
Grove Lula, clk Kershner Bros, b 223 E Ohio.

THE W. C. WASSON CO.,
130 Indiana Ave. Tel. 989.
STEAM
COAL
Car Lots a Specialty. Prompt Delivery.
Brazil Block, Jackson and Anthracite.

Grove Lulu C, teacher Public School No 2, b 138 E North.
Grove Mary E (wid Thomas M), h 212 E Ohio.
Grove Myrtle (wid Jacob D), b 293 W Morris.
Grove Peter, lab, h 20 Church.
Grove Samuel, painter, h 91 Yandes.
Grove Wm M, trav agt, r 138 E North.
Grove Wm R, plastr, 947 Morris (W I), h same.
Grove Zepha (wid Wm), b 140 W Vermont.
Grovenbery Wm P, painter, r 40 N East.
Grover Albert, plumber, b 89 Indiana av.
Grover Arthur B, real est, 436 Lemcke bldg, r 282 N Penn.
GROVER DRUG CO, Ira D Grover Mngr, 199 S Illinois.
Grover Elizabeth A (wid Joseph), h 180 Sheldon.
Grover Frederick, clk The H Lieber Co, b 50 Dawson.
Grover Gardner H, clk, b w s James 3 n of Bloyd av (B).
Grover George C, lab, b 180 Sheldon.
Grover Ira D, mngr Grover Drug Co, h 282 N Penn.
Grover Martha A, cashr The Bates, r 225 N New Jersey.
GROVER R B & CO, Proprs Emerson Shoe Store, Lewis A Harmeyer Mngr, 40 E Washington.
Grover Wm, painter, 50 Dawson, h same.
Groves David F, carp, 131 Madison, b same.
Groves Edward, barber, rear 586 Morris, h 95 Hadley av (W I).
Groves Helen J M, dry goods, 378 E 9th, h 397 same.
Groves Lafayette, nurseryman, h 1350 N Alabama.
Groves Marshall J, gas inspr, h 376 E 9th.
Groves Martin, student, b 193 N West.
Groves Virginia, milliner, 378 E 9th, h 376 same.
Grow Arthur D, condr, b 150 Cornell av.
Grow Eva M (wid Norman), h 168 Union.
Grubb Elmer, polisher, h 20 Hillside av.
Grubb James M, r 20 E Pratt.
Grubb Mary V L, r 20 E Pratt.
Grubb Norval D, grocer, 118 Oliver av, h 40 Marion av (W I).
Grubb Oliver J, farmer, h w s Downey av 2 s of University av (I).
Grubb Sarah P (wid Wm P), h 124 E Vermont.
Grubb Theodore, patrolman, h 495 Virginia av.
Grubb Walter D, clk Knight & Jillson, r 10½ N Delaware.
Grubbs Benjamin F, lab, h 632 W Udell (N I).
Grubbs Clarence J, waiter, r 163 Bird.
Grubbs Daniel W, lawyer, 9 Cyclorama pl, r 408 N Illinois.
Grubbs Deborah A, dressmkr, 1 Jefferson, h same.
Grubbs Donald R, clk, b 220 N Capitol av.
Grubbs Frank I, mngr American Press Assn, h 30 The Chalfant.
Grubbs Robert H, printer, r 62 College av.
Grube Aaron, carp, h 127 Eureka av.
Grube George M, driver, b 321 S Delaware.
Grube John H, carp, 296 S Illinois, h same.
Grube Samuel R, h 321 S Delaware.
Grube Simon H, framemkr, h 168 Hoyt av.
Grueb Gottlieb, adv agt Indiana Tribune, h 47 Rockwood.
Gruell Benjamin N, driver, h 129 Huron.

W. H. Messenger FURNITURE, CARPETS, STOVES, 101 EAST WASHINGTON ST. TEL. 491.

McNamara, Koster & Co. | Foundry and Pattern Shop, 212-218 S. PENN. ST. • • • PHONE 1593.

Gruelle Emma H (wid Wallace N), b 63 Sanders.
Gruelle George D P, painter, b 20 Spann av.
Gruelle Richard B, artist, 35 Coffin blk, h 29 Eureka av.
Gruelle Thomas M, printer, h 63 Sanders.
Gruelle Wallace, bookbndr, b 63 Sanders.
Gruenert Catherine (wid Herman), h 490 W New York.
Gruenert George L, lab, b 490 W New York.
GRUENERT J HENRY, Propr Jefferson House, 59-63 E South.
Gruenert Rosa (wid Henry), h 593 S Meridian.
Gruenert Wm F, candymkr, b 490 W New York.
Gruenfeld Casper, modeler, b 28 Broadway.
Gruenke Albert, lab, b 334 Columbia av.
Gruenke Herman, lab, h 334 Columbia av.
Gruenke John F, b 334 Columbia av.
Grummann Albert G, packer, h 237 S Noble.
Grummann Alfred C, clk Clemens Vonnegut, b 262 N Noble.
Grummann Henry A, clk A Metzger Agency, b 262 N Noble.
Grummann Julius, janitor, h 262 N Noble.
Grummann Mary L, dressmkr, 237 S Noble, b same.
Grummann Paul H, teacher Industrial School, h 322 S Alabama.
Grund George W, cigarmkr, 636 Virginia av, h 26 S Linden.
Grund Johanna (wid George), h 51 Weghorst.
Grund Wm, confr, 427 N Illinois; meats, 18 E Mkt House, h 427 N Illinois.
Gruner Edward, molder, b 61 Bicking.
Gruner George G, clk, b 61 Bicking.
Gruner Joseph P, mach, b 61 Bicking.
Gruner Michael, foreman, h 61 Bicking.
Gruner Peter, finisher, h 41 Wyoming.
Grunwald Joseph, saloon, 428 Mass av, h same.
Gruzard John L, bkkpr, r 321 N New Jersey.
Grysell John H, lab, h 255 W 5th.
GUARANTEE ROOFING COMPANY (George E Plant, Alfred E Dochez), 82 Mass av, Tel 1345. (See adv in classified Roofers.)
Guarantee Savings and Investment Assn, Charles E Merrifield pres, Samuel D La-Fuze sec, Francis M Helms treas, 68 Lombard bldg.
GUARANTEE SHOE STORE THE, Charles A Volz Mngr, 50 N Illinois.
GUARANTORS' LIABILITY INDEMNITY CO OF PENNSYLVANIA, Wm H Price Genl Agt, 93 Lombard Bldg.
GUARDIAN SAVINGS AND LOAN ASSOCIATION, Preston C Trusler Pres, John W Schmidt Vice-Pres, Wm H Hobbs Sec, Frank D Stalnaker Treas, 70 E Market.
Gubler George, horse dealer, r 1 Susquehanna.
Gudgel Mary A (wid Amos), h 751 N Capitol av.
Gue Alonzo, asst propertyman Empire Theater, h 502 N Alabama.
Gue Alonzo T, lab, h 536 W Wells (N I).
Gue Clinton E, foreman, h 105½ Broadway.
Gue Clyde, lab, b 542 W Shoemaker (N I).
Gue Edward, h 502 N Alabama.
Gue Napoleon, lab, h 542 W Shoemaker (N I).

Henry H. Fay, 40½ E. Washington St., REAL ESTATE, AND LOAN BROKER.

Gue Robert H, h 413 Coburn.
Guedel Charles F, sawfiler, h 281 Olive.
Guedel John, filer, h 176 E Morris.
Guedel Kate, dressmkr, 176 E Morris, b same.
Guedel Louis A, mach, b 176 E Morris.
Guedelhoefer August, foreman, h 257 S Senate av.
Guedelhoefer Bernard J, bkkpr, b 370 S Illinois.
Guedelhoefer John, carriage mnfr, 102 Kentucky av, h 370 S Illinois.
Guedelhoefer Otto C, cutter Paul H Krauss, b 370 S Illinois.
Guelding Joseph, tinner, b 56 Wyoming.
Guenther Anna K, cashr The H Lieber Co, r 139 N Meridian.
Guenther Casimir, shoemkr, 696 N Capitol av, h same.
Guenther Charles I, night turnkey County Jail, h 193 Bates.
Guenther Julius H F, driver, h 730 S Meridian.
Guenzer Paul, butcher, b 401 S Meridian.
Guercio Caesar, barber, rear 249 English av, h 257 same.
Guerrieri Angelo, pdlr, h 19 S Liberty.
Guess George, condr, r 16 Fair blk.
Guetig Henry, barber, 347 E Market, h 326 same.
Guffin Andrew J, h 225 S New Jersey.
Guffin Henry H, produce, b 225 S New Jersey.
Guffin Leroy C, clk C C C & St L Ry, b 225 S New Jersey.
Guffin Wm D, agt, b 225 S New Jersey.
Guinan Matthew, painter, 477 S Capitol av, h same.
Guinea Sadie A (wid Wm), dressmkr, 440 Blake, h same.
Guion Wm H, farmer h 487 Highland (N I).
Guliano Mercurio, porter, h 45½ Virginia av.
Gulick John F, h 477 Charles.
Gulick Wm W, clk, h 965 N Senate av.
Gulley Alva W, clk P O, h n s Washington 2 w of Crawfordsville rd (M J).
Gulley Wade, lab, b rear 432 E St Clair.

UNION CASUALTY & SURETY CO. OF ST. LOUIS, MO. All lines of Personal Accident and Casualty Insurance, including Employers' and General Liability. W. E. BARTON & CO., General Agents, 504 Indiana Trust Building. LONG DISTANCE TELEPHONE 1918.

THE FRED DIETZ CO. WOODEN PACKING BOXES MADE TO ORDER FACTORY AND WAREHOUSE TRUCKS. 400 Madison Avenue. Telephone 654.

Indianapolis BUSINESS UNIVERSITY Leading College of Business and Shorthand. Elevator day and night. Individual instruction. Large faculty. Terms easy. Enter now. See p. 4. When Block. E. J. HEEB, President.

Steam Pumping Machinery { HENRY R. WORTHINGTON, 64 S. PENNSYLVANIA ST. Long Distance Telephone 284.

UNION CO-OPERATIVE LAUNDRY { NOS. 3, 40 AND 42 VIRGINIA AVENUE. (COMPOSED OF UNION LAUNDRY GIRLS.) T. E. SOMERVILLE, MANAGER — TELEPHONE 1269. INDIANAPOLIS, IND.

HORACE M. HADLEY
REAL ESTATE AND INSURANCE
66 East Market Street, Basement
TELEPHONE 1540.

Gulley Wm, driver, b w s McPherson 2 n of English av (S).
Gullion George, lab, b w s Caroline av 4 n of 17th.
Gullion George W, agt, h rear 83 Cornell av.
Gullion Mary (wid James), b e s Warren 2 s of Washington av (I).
Gullion Thomas, h 533 Yandes.
Gulliver Wm, h 167 Muskingum al.
Gully Thomas J, h 5 McCormick.
Gumbinsky Bernard, pdlr, h 354 S Illinois.
Gumbinsky Jacob, shoes, 153 W Washington, h 434 S Illinois.
Gumnoe James A, lab, h 75 Germania av (H).
Gump Benjamin F, carpetlyr, h 112 Brookside av.
Gumpf May, h 48½ Virginia av.
Gun Charles, laundry, 565 Virginia av, b same.
Gunckel Carl, clk Francke & Schindler, h 267 Michigan av.
Gund John J, trav agt, h 534 E 7th.
Gundelfinger Benjamin clothing, 72 W Washington, h 296 N Alabama.
Gundelfinger Benno, plumber, 461 Central av, h 428 Bellefontaine.
Gundelfinger Max, real est, h 570 N Delaware.
Gunder George R, student, b 111 N New Jersey.
Gunder Jasper N, h 529 W Francis (N I).
Gundlach Henry, lab, h 3 Sterling blk.
Gundlach Henry, trucker, h 142 E McCarty.
Gundlach Mary (wid Henry), h 81 Kansas.
Gundrun Lot E, driver, r 167 E Vermont.
Guning Daniel, lab, b 169 S Reisner (W I)
Gunkle Anthony W, h e s Auburn av 1 n of English.
Gunkle Milton, driver, b 445 S East.
Gunn Bridget, h 7 Minerva.
Gunn Elizabeth, seamstress, b 332 E Louisiana.
Gunn Jean, farm hd Insane Hospital.
Gunn John, carver, h 103 S Linden.
Gunn John F, molder, h 639 S State av.
Gunn John F, plumber, h 114 S Linden.
Gunn Wm, plumber, 23 S Alabama, h 103 S Linden.

PERSONAL AND PROMPT ATTENTION GIVEN TO COLLECTIONS.
Merchants' and Manufacturers' Exchange
J. E. TAKKEN, Manager,
19 Union Building, 73 West Maryland Street.

Gunnemann Henry, carp, h 573 E St Clair.
Gunnip George, h 680 N Illinois.
Gunsolus Frederick W, patrolman, h 302 Blake.
Gunsser Paul H, butcher, b 401 S Meridian.
Gunstler Jacob, lab, r 428 Mass av.
Gunter George T, clk, b w s Maxwell av 2 n of Walnut av (I).
Gunter Michael, liquors, h 398 W New York.
Gunter Moses, mngr Thomas Markey, h 398 W New York.
Gunter Wm M, grocer, s w cor Washington and Lake avs (I), h w s Maxwell av 2 n of Walnut av (I).
Guntermann Joseph, music teacher, 34 School, h same.
Gunther Albert J, mach, h 10 Ethel (W I).
Gunther Charles W, umbrellas, 21 Pembroke Arcade and 56 Mass av, r same.
Gunther James R, condr, h 225 N Liberty.
Guntz Frederick, mach hd, h 24 Yeiser.
Guntz George, mach hd, b 24 Yeiser.
Guntz Simon J, patrolman, h 535 S Capitol av.
Gunvey George, molder, b 41 Madison av.
Gupton James V, painter, h 526 W Wells (N I).
Gurdon James, lab, h 221 W 3d.
Gurley Charles E, lab, b 38 Oliver av (W I).
Gurley Francis T, road supervisor I U Ry Co, h 186 S Lee (W I).
GURLEY SCHUYLER C, Sheet Metal Worker; Bar Drainers, Coffee and Water Urns a Specialty, 67½ W Georgia, h 165 Woodlawn av.
Gurley Thaddeus S, carp, h 20 Hester.
Gurley Thomas C, carp, h 43 Frank.
Gurnell Amelia (wid Isaac), b 32 Torbet.
Gurnell Roland, driver, h 476 Cornell av.
Gurt Stephen, lab, h 271 W McCarty.
Gussell Wm L, bookbndr, b 157 Fayette.
Gustetter Clara, b 835 N Illinois.
Gustin Esom B, h 182 Huron.
Gustin John B, cooper, h 104 Blackford.
Gustin Lewis Q, trav agt Standard Oil Co, h 137 Prospect.
Gustin Rebecca (wid John), h 91 Pleasant.
Gustin Robert H, mach, h 43 Clifford av.
Gustin Theodore H, brakeman, h 225 Michigan av.
Gustin Wm J, painter, 26 Water, h same.
GUTENBERG CO THE, Harry O Thudium Pres, Frederick J Striebeck Sec, Publishers German Telegraph (Daily Except Sunday), Volksblatt (Weekly), Spottvogel (Sunday); also English and German Book and Job Printers, 27 S Delaware and 113-115 E Pearl, Tel 269.
Gutfleisch George O, meats, 1 Paca, h same.
Guth Emelia (wid Edward), h 101 Downey.
Guth F Adolph, bkkpr, b 819 S East.
Guth Rudolph, clk McCune & Co, h 819 S East.
Guthrie Charles, lab, h 129 Columbia al.
Guthrie George L, student, b 150 N Illinois.
Guthrie J Augustus, bkkpr, h 285 N Noble.
Guthrie Thomas S Rev, pastor Central Universalist Church, h 162 E 6th.
Guthrie Wm A, timber, b 150 N Illinois.
Gutknecht Albert, mach, h 236 Hoyt av.
Gutknecht Anna, h 157 Ft Wayne av.
Gutknecht Charles E, lab, b 157 Ft Wayne av.
Gutman George M, mason, h 250 W Michigan (H).
Gutzwiller Carl, clk, b 330 E Morris.
Gutzwiller Paul M, clk, h 330 E Morris.

CLEMENS VONNEGUT
184, 186 and 192 E. Washington St.
FOUNDRY AND MACHINISTS' SUPPLIES. "NORTON" EMERY WHEELS AND GRINDING MACHINERY.

THE WM. H. BLOCK CO. DRY GOODS, MILLINERY, CLOAKS AND FURS.
7 AND 9 EAST WASHINGTON STREET.

Gutzwiller Rosa (wid Theophilus), h s w cor Edgewood and Downey.
Gutzwiller Theophilus, plumber, h s w cor Birkenmeyer and Edgewood.
Guy James C, confr, 269 Mass av, h same.
Guy Wm H, barber, 340 W Washington, r same.
Guy Wm H, chairmkr, h 888 Milburn.
Guy Wm H, lab, h 137 Downey.
Guyer Amos M, tmstr, h 129 Virginia av.
Guyer Anna N, teacher Kindergarten No 7, b 155 N Illinois.
Guyer Charles B (Wm Guyer & Sons), h 1096 E Washington.
Guyer John A (Wm Guyer & Sons), h 1096 E Washington.
Guyer Mary A (wid Samuel), b 499 Bellefontaine.
Guyer Wm (Wm Guyer & Sons), res Antrim, Ind.
Guyer Wm & Sons (Wm, John A and Charles B), creamery, 1096 E Washington.
Guymon Jemima (wid Presley), h 227 N West.
Guymon John A, trav agt, b 216 E Market.
Guyton Jesse D, foreman L E & W R R, h 116 N Noble.
Guyton Omer J, stenog, r 282 N Senate av.
Gwick Henry, carp, h 42 Tacoma av.
Gwin Elmer D, condr, h 43 Lynn.
Gwin Emory, clk, b 59 Beaty.
Gwin John E, condr, h 167 Sharpe av (W).
Gwin John W, clk, h 59 Beaty.
Gwin Joseph B, trav agt, h 1123 N Penn.
Gwin Margaret (wid Wm R), b 41 Lynn.
Gwin Robert B, oiler, h 41 Lynn.
Gwin Robert E, clk, h 43 Atlas.
Gwin T Everett, driver, r 39 W Pratt.
Gwinn Alfred D, waiter, h 281 S Capitol av.
Gwinn Alexander, mach, h 146 Eureka av.
Gwinn Sylvester A, carp, h 11 Harvey.
Gwinn Wm, mach, h 131 Forest av.
Gwinnup Arthur, printer, b 216 Huron.
Gwinnup Charles W, lather, h e s Indianapolis av 2 s of 16th.
Gwinnup Ira G, printer, h 37½ W Market.
Gwinup Clayton S, harnessmkr, b 216 Huron.
Gwinup Mason S, harnessmkr, b 216 Huron.
Gwyn Martin, butcher, b 75 Patterson.
Gwynn Charles E, waiter, r 183½ W Washington.
Gwynn Ery L, yardmaster Belt R R, h 6 Traub av.
Gwynne Mae M (wid Wm F), stenog The Viavi Co, h 413 N Alabama.

H

Haag, see also Haug.
Haag Anthony A, shoes, 186 Indiana av, h 454 N West.
Haag Bros (John T and James A), oysters, 168 Indiana av.
Haag Charles G, clk, b 31 Broadway.
Haag Emil A, phys, 138 Park av, h same.
Haag Frank J, bookbndr, b 454 N West.
Hagg James A (Haag Bros), b 454 N West.
Haag John F (Haag Bros), b 454 N West.
HAAG JULIUS A, Druggist, 87 N Penn, b 31 Broadway, Tel 1906.
Haag Leon C, trav agt, b 31 Broadway.
HAAG LOUIS E, Druggist, 302 Mass av, cor of College av, Tel 1030; b 31 Broadway.
Haag Louisa (wid Charles), h 31 Broadway.

Haag Melissa B (wid Wm M), h 298 N New Jersey.
Håar Helena (wid John), b 10 Water.
Haas Charles, lab, b 115 Agnes.
Haas Charles, varnisher, b 223 S Capitol av.
Haas Frank E, carriage hngr, h [illegible] Bridge (W I).
Haas George J, clk, h 255 N Liberty.
Haas Henry, driver, b 61 Maxwell.
Haas Jonas, pdlr, h 421 S Capitol av.
Haas Joseph, medicines, 56 S Penn, h 291 N Alabama.
Haas Joseph, pdlr, h 61 Maxwell.
Haas Leon, clk, b 291 N Alabama.
Haas Mary (wid John), dressmkr, 223 S Capitol av, h same.
HAAS SCHUYLER A, Lawyer, 531-533 Lemcke Bldg, Tel 1163; r 81 W Vermont.
Haas Wm A, foreman Kingan & Co, h 157 W New York.
Haase, see also Hasse.
Haase Christian T, driver, h 232 Minnesota.
Haase Francis P Very Rev, rector Sacred Heart Church, h n w cor Palmer and Union.
Haase Frederick, truckman, h 236 Minnesota.
Haase Jarvis, lab, h 510 W Maryland.
Haase Jefferson, junk, h s w cor Prospect and Miami.
Haase Jefferson J, driver, h 256 Springfield.
Haase John J, tmstr, h 421 S Capitol av.
Haase Louis, mngr Mamie Haase, h 405 W New Jersey.
Haase Mamie, jeweler, 17½ S Meridian, h 405 N New Jersey.
Haase Maria (wid Christian), b 232 Minnesota.
Haase Newman, clk Mamie Haase, b 405 N New Jersey.
Haase Robert, electrician, h 419 S Capitol av.
Haase Sherman, mach, b 510 W Maryland.
Haase Thomas J, tmstr, h 553 Union.

GUIDO R. PRESSLER,
FRESCO PAINTER
Churches, Theaters, Public Buildings, Etc., A Specialty.
Residence, No. 325 North Liberty Street.
INDIANAPOLIS, IND.

INDIANAPOLIS STEEL ROOFING AND CORRUGATING WORKS, 23 and 25 East South Street. S. D. NOEL, Proprietor.

David S. McKernan REAL ESTATE AND LOANS. Exchanging real estate a specialty. A number of choice pieces for encumbered property. Rooms 2-5 Thorpe Block.

DIAMOND WALL PLASTER { Telephone 1410 BUILDERS' EXCHANGE.

Cor. E. Ohio St. and C., C., C. & St. L. R'y Tracks. Storage of Household Goods and Pianos a Specialty.

W. McWORKMAN,
Galvanized Iron Cornice Works
TIN AND SLATE ROOFING.
930 WEST WASHINGTON STREET.
TELEPHONE 1118.

HABBE JOHN F, Mngr Massachusetts Mutual Life Insurance Co, Rooms 1002 Majestic Bldg, Tel 839.
Habeney Christina (wid Henry), b 120 S East.
Habeney Henry F (Brinker & Habeney), h 120 S East.
Haberer Matthias, produce, E Mkt House; h n w cor Brookside av and Atlas.
Haberern Michael, saloon, 504 N West, h same.
Haberkamp Wm, clk, b 50 Prospect.
Haberle Kate, seamstress, r 106½ N Meridian.
Habermann Gustav A, shoes, 1095 E Washington, h same.
Habermann Joseph, driver, h 210 S Linden.
Habich Albert C, gilder The H Lieber Co, h 221 Hamilton av.
Habich Carl, justice of peace, 96 E Court, h 269 N California.
Habich Carl jr, pres The C Habich Co, h 336 W Vermont.
Habich C Co The, Carl Habich jr pres, Frank A Maus vice-pres, Joseph C Schaf sec and treas, bottlers, 187 W Ohio.
Habich Frank, bottler, h 269 N California.
Habich Gustave, gunsmith, 62 W Market, h 630 E Market.
Habich Herman, bkkpr, b 269 N California.
Habig Charles, mason, h 17 E McCarty.
Habig Charles jr, trimmer, b 17 E McCarty.
Habig Edward H, bkkpr Parry Mnfg Co, h 1588 Kenwood av.
Habig Michael, lab, h 30 Asbury.
Habig Wm H, trimmer, b 17 E McCarty.
Habing Bernard G, agt, h 161 N New Jersey.
Habing John G, clk, b 161 N New Jersey.
Hack Wm F, finisher, b 90 S East.
Hackedorn Hillis F, sec State House Bldg Assns and State House Dime Assn, h 220 Clifford av.
HACKEDORN WM E, Genl Solicitor L E & W R R, s w cor Washington and Noble, Tel 1472; h 394 N Delaware.
Hackemeyer Wm, gardener, h n s Howland av 2 w of Orchard.

SEALS,
STENCILS,
STAMPS, Etc.
GEO. J. MAYER
15 S. Meridian St.
TELEPHONE 1386.

Hacker, see also Hecker.
Hacker Asby P, h 465 E Georgia.
Hacker Charles, baker Kershner Bros, h 34 S Dorman.
Hacker Charles jr, clk, b 34 S Dorman.
Hacker Charles H, condr, h 515 W 22d (N I).
Hacker Daniel, lab, h 111 Hoyt av.
Hacker David G, insp, b 538 Chestnut.
Hacker Edmond H, watchman, b 538 Chestnut.
Hacker Eliza A (wid James V), 135½ Cornell av.
Hacker James, filer, b 121 Dougherty.
Hacker John F, planer, h 341 Fletcher av.
Hacker Malinda C (wid David F), h 538 Chestnut.
Hacker Samuel G, trav agt, h 299 N Pine.
Hacker Thomas S, dentist, 28½ E Ohio, h 17 West Drive (W P).
Hacker Wm R, saddler, 1 34 S Dorman.
Hacker Winfred E, riveter, b 538 Chestnut.
Hackett Cornelia, bkkpr, r 203 The Shiel.
Hackett Snowden S, clk R M S, r 29½ E Market.
Hackleman Benjamin M, carp, h 588 Morris (W I).
Hackleman Charles W (Lamberson & Hackleman), sec and treas Epitomist Pub Co, h 575 Park av.
Hackley Ann (wid Joel), h 21 Centennial (H).
Hackley Bros (Robert M and Napoleon B), barbers, 29 Monument pl.
Hackley John H, chief clk yard office L E & W R R, h 15 Harrison.
Hackley Lavant R, mach, h 51 Sullivan.
Hackley Mary (wid Wade), h rear 432 Douglass.
Hackley Napoleon B (Hackley Bros), h 97 Gillard av.
Hackley Oliver M, barber, 858 Morris (W I), h same.
Hackley Robert M (Hackley Bros), h 21 Shover (W I).
Hackney Frederick W, clk R M S, h 118 Woodlawn av.
Hackney James C, lab, h 32 N Senate av.
Hackney Kate (wid Leonard J), h 81 W 11th.
Hackney Leonard J, Chief Justice Supreme Court of Indiana, 75 State House, res Shelbyville, Ind.
Hackstein Christina L (wid Christian J), h 166 Union.
Hackstein Christopher W, checkman, b 166 Union.
Hackstein Frederick W, clk Consumers' Gas Trust Co, h 455 S East.
Hadden Oliver H, carp, h 131 Cornell av.
Hadden Sarah (wid James), h rear 306 Blake.
Hadden Thomas L, brakeman, h 86 Warren av (W I).
Haddex George W, lab, b 24 Koerner.
Haddex Samuel, lab, r 66 N Missouri.
Haddex Washington, lab, h 24 Koerner.
Haden, see also Hayden.
Haden Charles M, blksmith, h 322 Hillside av.
Hadley Alonzo M, lawyer, 62½ E Washington, r 124 E Ohio.
Hadley Alonzo W, collr, h 80 Wallack.
Hadley Artemus N, mech engr, 23 Talbott blk, h 592 Ash.
Hadley Brewer M, printer, b 1325 N New Jersey.
Hadley Bros (John W Hadley), drugs, 317 Indiana av.

UNION TRANSFER AND STORAGE CO.

A. METZGER AGENCY ESTABLISHED 1863. L-O-A-N-S

LAMBERT GAS & GASOLINE ENGINE CO.
ANDERSON, IND. GAS ENGINES FOR ALL PURPOSES.

Hadley Cassius C, lawyer, 712 Lemcke bldg, h 175 N Penn.
Hadley Chalmers R, b 270 N Delaware.
Hadley Charles E, mechanical expert Indiana Bicycle Co, b 354 N Illinois.
Hadley Edgar, student, h 395 N West.
Hadley Evan, phys, 136 N Penn, h 270 N Delaware.
Hadley George W, solr Kingan & Co (ltd), b 276 N New Jersey.
Hadley Hannah T (wid Wm), b 545 Bellefontaine.
Hadley Henry, lab, h 3 LeGrand av.
Hadley Herbert H, bkkpr Wm L Elder, h 1008 N Penn.
Hadley Horace E (The Grocers' Mnfg Co), r 268 College av.

HADLEY HORACE M, Real Estate, Loans and Insurance, 66 E Market, Tel 1540; h 613 Broadway. (See left top cor cards.)

Hadley Hugh H, lawyer, 44 Lorraine bldg, r 173 E Walnut.
Hadley Ira, mer police, h 522 E Ohio.
Hadley Ivy C, florist, b 1799 N Capitol av.
Hadley Jabin L, driver, h 1799 N Capitol av.
Hadley Joel W, sec and treas The J B Allfree Mnfg Co, h 160 Park av.
Hadley John, cook, b 117 Cornell av.
Hadley John S, condr, h 1325 N New Jersey.
Hadley John W (Hadley Bros), h 416 N West.
Hadley Levi W E, broommkr, h 294½ Mass av.
Hadley Matilda, h 89½ N Delaware.
Hadley Robert M, trav agt, h 189 Ramsey av.
Hadley S Lee, sec Commercial Electric Co, h 486 College av.
Hadley Theresa (wid Job), b 1023 N New Jersey.
Hadley Thomas E, millwright, h 76 W 5th.
Hadley Wm S, driver, r 31½ Indiana av.
Hadlock Alvah R, b 165 E Merrill.
Hadlock Frank W, agt Wagner Palace Car Co, Union Station, r 329 N Illinois.
Hadlock Melissa C (wid John C), b 329 N Illinois.
Hadsell Ray W, stenog, b 436 Talbott av.
Hadsell Warren R, stenog, b 436 Talbott av.
Haeberle Amelia (wid Frederick), b 184 Park av.
Haeberle Gottlieb, b n w cor Brookside av and Jupiter.
Haeberle Wm A, grocer, n w cor Brookside av and Jupiter, h same.
Haefner Adam, lab, h rear 319 S Alabama.
Haehl Cornelius, cigar mnfr, 128 Orange av, h same.
Haehl Edward B, carver, b 668½ S Meridian.
Haehl Emma (wid Jesse), clk Robert Keller, h 48 Davis.
Haehl Herbert G, blksmith, b 668½ S Meridian.
Haehl John C (Geyer & Haehl), h 1675 Graceland av.
Haehl John F, bartndr, h 512 S New Jersey.
Haehl Margaret (wid Jacob), h 668½ S Meridian.
Haehl Wm A, candymkr, h 157 S William (W I).
Haehner Mary A, stenog Gates & Hume, b 21 Sylvan.
Haehner Wilhelmina (wid Wm), h 21 Sylvan.

THOS. C. DAY & CO.
INVESTING AGENTS,
TOWN AND FARM LOANS,
Rooms 325 to 330 Lemcke Bldg.

Haenggi Katherine (wid John), b 628 E New York.
Haenggi Theophilus (Wernsing & Haenggi), h e s Sherman Drive 5 s of Washington.
Haensel E Robert, feed stable, 189 E Wabash, h 32 McCrea.
Haerle George, h 775 N Penn.
Haerle George C, clk, b 854 N Meridian.

HAERLE WM, Ladies' Furnishing Goods, 4 W Washington, h 854 N Meridian, Tel 192.

Haerle Wm jr, clk, b 854 N Meridian.
Haffield Elijah G, tmstr, h nr cor Park av and 16th.
Haffield Homer C, driver, b n s Fountain 1 w of Floral av.
Haffield Joseph, b nr cor Park av and 16th.
Haffield Robert A, watchman, h n s Fountain 1 w of Floral av.
Haffield Wm N, farmer, h s e cor Western and Park avs.
Haffner Adam, bottler, h 457 Charles.
Haffner Fannie E (wid Theodore C), r 234 Ash.
Haffner Harry, asst bkkpr Postal Tel Cable Co, b 234 Ash.
Hafford James M, lab, h 1 Susquehanna.
Hafner August H, saloon, 323 W Washington, h same.
Hafner Bertha, bkkpr Noblesville Milling Co, b 319 W Washington.
Hafner John E, bkkpr, b 1246 E Washington.
Hafner John V, saloon, 1246 E Washington, h same.
Hafner Katherina (wid August), h 319 W Washington.
Hagaman Edgar M, lab, h 206 Spring.
Hagaman Wm D, lab, h 151 Locke.
Hagan, see also Hagen and Hogan.
Hagan Alfred M, clk Van Camp H and I Co, h 67 Sanders.
Hagan John M, clk, b 67 Sanders.
Hagan Mary E (wid James L), h 67 Sanders.
Hagan Oscar, driver, r 71 W Market.
Hagedon Charles, harness, 53 Mass av, h 190 Davidson.

EAT
QUAKER BREAD
ASK YOUR GROCER FOR IT.
THE HITZ BAKING CO.

BICYCLES $5 DOWN. MONTHLY. Best Wheels. Best Terms. WHEELMEN'S CO. 31 W. OHIO ST. LONG DISTANCE TEL. 1855.

J. H. TECKENBROCK | Grilles, Fretwork and Wood Carpets
94 EAST SOUTH STREET.

FIDELITY MUTUAL LIFE PHILADELPHIA, PA.
A. H. COLLINS { General Agent, 52-53 Baldwin Block.

Edwardsport Coal & Mining Co. Rooms 42 and 43 When Building.

ESTABLISHED 1876. TELEPHONE 168.
CHESTER BRADFORD,
SOLICITOR OF PATENTS,
AND COUNSEL IN PATENT CAUSES.
(See adv. page 6.)
Office:—Rooms 14 and 16 Hubbard Block, S.W. Cor. Washington and Meridian Streets, INDIANAPOLIS, INDIANA.

Hagedon Edward N, cabtmkr, h 544 S Capitol av.
Hagedorn George W, clk, b 564 Morris (W I).
Hagedorn Henry, grocer, 564 Morris, h same.
Hagedorn Herman, lab, h 25 Coburn.
Hagedorn Wm, watchman, h e s Rembrant av 2 n of Indiana av.
Hagedorn Wm L, pres Western Furniture Co, h 84 Greer.
Hagelskamp Benjamin, lab, h 127 Shelby.
Hagelskamp George, grocer, 50 Prospect, h same.
Hagelskamp Richard, lab, h 45 Evison.
Hagen Andrew, sec and treas The Home Brewing Co, h 492 E Market.
Hagen Frederick G, bkkpr The Home Brewing Co, b 492 E Market.
Hagen Louis G, stenog, h 116 Fayette.
Hagenmeier Jeremiah, baker, b 135 E Washington.
Hager Carl F, blksmith, b 107 E Morris.
Hager Frank M, engr, h 83 Maple.
Hager Frank M jr, sawmkr, b 83 Maple.
Hager Orrin, engr, b 83 Maple.
Hager Wm, car insp, b 167 E Morris.
Hagerhorst Clara M (Union Co-Operative Laundry), b 244 S Capitol av.
Hagerhorst Harry C, trav agt John Rauch, b 434 Talbott av.
Hagerhorst Wm H, h 434 Talbott av.
Hagerhorst Wm L, clk, b 434 Talbott av.
Hagerman Green, patrolman, h w s Sugar Grove av 4 s of Miller av (M P).
Hagerman John, lab, b 67 Minerva.
Hagerty, see also Hegarty.
Hagerty Catherine (wid Martin), h 31 English av.
Hagerty Charles T, tmstr, b 261 S Capitol av.
Hagerty Cornelius, lab, h 339 W Maryland.
Hagerty Edward H, bartndr, h 294 Columbia av.
Hagerty Frank B, lab, b 339 W Merrill.
Hagerty Frank H, saloon, 250 Columbia av, h same.
Hagerty James, lab, h 195 River av (W I).
Hagerty James, tmstr, b 261 S Capitol av.

76 N. PENNSYLVANIA ST.,
MAKERS

PHONE 598.

Hagerty James D, bartndr, h 473 N New Jersey.
Hagerty John, lab, h 191 River av (W I).
Hagerty John jr, lab, b 191 River av (W I).
Hagerty Margaret (wid Wm), b 273 Huron.
Hagerty Patrick B, lab, r 113 Bright.
Hagerty Patrick, tmstr, h 261 S Capitol av.
Hagerty Robert, lab, b 191 River av (W I).
Haggard Elcena (wid Martin), h 361 E Market.
Haggard Ernest M, phys, 95 Mass av, h 146 Bellefontaine.
Haggard Esther I, carpet weaver, 79 Shepard (W I), h same.
Haggard James W, mach, h 12 Shelby.
Haggard John N, carp, b 79 Shepard (W I).
Haggard Laura B, dressmkr, 361 E Market, b same.
Haggard Thomas A, lab, b 79 Shepard (W I).
Haggard Wm A, lab, h 79 Shepard (W I).
Haggard Wm S, Lieut Governor State of Indiana, room 83 State House, res Lafayette, Ind.
Haggins Mary J, r 364 N Senate av.
Hagood Louis M, phys, 135 W 6th, h 749 N Senate av.
Hague Henry, b 434 W Washington.
Hague Joseph F, shoemkr, 184 Blake, h same.
Hague Wm A, clk, h 434 W Washington.
Hahle Wm, mach, b 2 Quincy.
Hahn, see also Hann.
Hahn Adam, grocer, 113 S William (W I), h same.
Hahn Adolf R, printer, h 87 Weghorst.
Hahn Anna (wid Henry), h 867 N New Jersey.
Hahn Bert, lab, b 122 Bright.
HAHN CHARLES C, Druggist, n e cor Hadley av and Morris, Tel 897; h 143 Hadley av (W I).
Hahn Charles F, clk, b 151 River av (W I).
Hahn Edward A, uphlr, h 120 Ruckle.
Hahn Ella (wid Jacob), h 29 McCauley.
Hahn Frederick, cupola tndr, h 13 Chadwick.
Hahn Henrietta (wid Dettlop), b 214 Union.
Hahn Jacob, baker, 409 S Delaware, h same.
Hahn Jacob, meats, 909 Morris (W I), h same.
Hahn Jennie (wid Jacob), h 122 Bright.
Hahn John, h 28 Carlos.
Hahn John, butcher, r 166½ W Washington.
Hahn John, clk, b 113 S William (W I).
Hahn John F, lab, h 117 Bright.
Hahn John L, butcher, b 429½ S Meridian.
Hahn Joseph, molder, h 404 N Pine.
Hahn Josephine, h 45½ N Capitol av.
Hahn Josephine B, artist, 409 S Delaware, h same.
Hahn Louis, butcher, h 305 S West.
Hahn Margaret (wid Jacob), tailor, 264 S Illinois, h same.
Hahn Orville L, dry goods, 31 S Station (B), h 7 same.
Hahn Queena J, artist, w s Denny 1 n of Ohio, h same.
Hahn Samuel, clk, b 461 N Capitol av.
Hahn Wm L, cigarmkr, b 281 S West.
Haifley Charles E, clk, b 1137 Northwestern av.
Haile Arthur, molder, h 367 S Olive.
Haile Rachel (wid Mason W), b 387 N New Jersey.
Hailman George F, carp, b e s Bradley 5 n of Ohio.

SUPERIOR BITUMINOUS COAL For Steam and Domestic . . Purposes . .

ROOFING MATERIAL C. ZIMMERMAN & SONS, SLATE AND GRAVEL ROOFERS, 19 SOUTH EAST STREET.

DRIVEN WELLS And Second Water Wells and Pumps of all kinds at CHARLES KRAUSS', 42 S. PENN. ST., TEL. 465. REPAIRING NEATLY DONE.

If You are not Satisfied with Your Laundry Work Give Us a Trial . . . ERTEL STEAM LAUNDRY 26 and 28 N. Senate Avenue. Telephone 19.

Hailman Rufus A, candymkr, b e s Bradley 5 n of Ohio.
Haine Wm E, sawyer, h 480 W Francis (N I).
Hainen Samuel R, mach, h 168 Chestnut.
Haines, see also Haynes.
Haines Abel S, lumber, h 1135 N Penn.
Haines Alvin E, carp, h 206 W Raymond.
Haines Amos H, mach hd, h 34 Water.
Haines Arthur R, clk, b 34 Water.
Haines Benjamin A, mach, b 92 Highland pl.
Haines Charles B, plumber, h 259 N California.
Haines Charles F, bkkpr Bassett & Co, h 103 Middle Drive (W P).
Haines Edward M, trav agt Milwaukee Harvester Co, h 92 Highland pl.
Haines Frank H, clk, h 391 Bellefontaine.
Haines Gardner, trav agt, h 1226 N Illinois.
Haines Hortense C (wid Elwood), h 235 Mass av.
Haines Jerome K, brakeman, r 102 S Illinois.
Haines Jesse A, carp, h 351 Lexington av.
Haines Matilda R (wid George), b 427 Highland av.
Haines Matthias L, pastor First Presbyterian Church, h 485 N Meridian.
Haines Morris, student, b 103 Middle Drive (W P).
Haines Samuel A, pres The S A Haines Co, h 68 E Pratt.
HAINES S A CO THE, S A Haines Pres, Horatio C Newcomb Sec, Dealers in High and Medium Grade Bicycles and Bicycle Sundries, 44 N Penn, Tel 1014.
Haines Wm, clk Indpls Dist Tel Co, b 235 Mass av.
Hainsworth John J, engr, h 217 Virginia av.
Hair Charles H, hostler, h 26 Cincinnati.
Haisley Wm E, student, h 72 E Vermont.
Haislup Alva R, stenog The Western Paving and Supply Co, h Flackville, Ind.
Hake Charles A, painter, h 554 Mulberry.
Hake Martha, h 14 Ketcham.
Halbing Anna, notions, 290 W Morris, h same.
Halbing Henry M, h 110 S William (W I).
Halbing Lother, painter, h 290 W Morris.
Halbing Lucas N, cigarmkr, h 29 Jones.
Halbleib Charles, chairmkr, h 66 Elm.
Halcott George, paperhngr, b 85 Yandes.
Halcott Sarah A (wid John S), h 85 Yandes.
Haldeman Harry M, trav agt The McElwaine-Richards Co, b 1140 W Washington (H).
Haldeman Kinsey E, condr, b 508 E 11th.
Haldeman Mary C (wid Jacob C), h 508 E 11th.
Haldman Melville O, see The McElwaine-Richards Co, h 241 N Delaware.
Haldeman Wm P, motorman, h 504½ College av.
Haldy Catherine, b 48 Kansas.
Haldy Henry C, plumber, b 48 Kansas.
Haldy Wilhelmina (wid Conrad), h 48 Kansas.
Hale Addison H, packer, b 60 Bates.
Hale Alexandra, clk, b 124 E 6th.
Hale Arthur, lab, h 367 S Olive.
Hale Aurelia R (wid Francis E), h 124 E 6th.
Hale Bernard, b 325 E Ohio.
Hale Charles W, bkkpr W D Allison Co, h 495 N East.
Hale Edward C, carp, b 194 Oliver av (W I).

Richardson & McCrea, REPRESENTING BEST KNOWN FIRE INSURANCE COMPANIES. Fidelity and Casualty Insurance Company of New York Represented. Telephone 182. 79 East Market St.

Hale Edward T, mach hd, b 60 Bates.
Hale Frank, driver, b 227 W New York.
Hale Frank R, printer, 32½ Clifford av, h 103 Malott av.
Hale Frederick P, trav agt, h 111 Broadway.
Hale James, lumber, 136 S Illinois, h n w cor Meridian and 29th.
Hale James W, lumber insp, b n w cor Meridian and 29th.
Hale James E, finisher, h 35 Valley Drive.
Hale Joel E, engr, h 60 Bates.
Hale John, lab, h 28 Sheffield (W I).
Hale Julius, lab, h 302 Fayette.
Hale Martin, lab, h 84 W 8th.
Hale Matilda L, nurse, h 133 N Penn.
Hale Stephen F, condr, b 792 W Washington.
Hale Stephen J, packer, h 496 Jackson.
Hale Wm A, cook, h 157 S William (W I).
Haley, see also Healey.
Haley Anna (wid Thomas), h 288 W Maryland.
Haley Ashley, lab, h 328 W 2d.
Haley Bartholomew, mason, b 214 Coburn.
Haley Cary, lab, b 2[illegible] W Maryland.
Haley Daniel F, patrolman, h 80 John.
Haley Edward, lab, h 14 Bates al.
Haley Edward L, gasfitter, h 73 Johnson av.
Haley Frank F, mach, b 758 S East.
Haley George, polisher, h 27 Everett.
Haley Harrison, lab, b 158 Hosbrook.
Haley Henry, lab, h 131 Maple.
Haley Henry, lab, h rear 218 Charles.
Haley James F, lab, b 23 Carlos.
Haley Jeremiah, lab, h 214 Coburn.
Haley John F, switchman, h 758 S East.
Haley Joseph G, blksmith, h 92 River av (W I).
Haley Margaret, tel opr, b 214 Coburn.
Haley Martin F, lab, h 23 Carlos.
Haley Mary (wid Lawrence), h 50 Martin.
Haley Perry, lab, b 288 W Maryland.
Haley Wm, engr, h 144 S Summit.
Halffin Edwin V, lab, r 83 N Capitol av.
Halffin Elizabeth A (wid Edward V), boarding 310 E Wabash.
Hall Albert B, chemist, h 89 W Walnut.
Hall Albert B, machinery, 126 W Maryland, h 429 N Senate av.

The Williams Typewriter. Elegant Work, Visible Writing, Easy Operation, High Speed. S. H. EAST, State Agent, 55 Thorpe Block, 87 E. Market St.

ELLIS & HELFENBERGER Manufacturers of IRON and WIRE FENCES 162-170 S. SENATE AVE. TEL. 958.

THE HOGAN TRANSFER AND STORAGE COMP'Y
Household Goods and Pianos Moved—Packed—Stored...... Baggage and Package Express Machinery and Safes a Specialty Cor. Washington and Illinois Sts. TELEPHONE No. 675.

Hose, Belting, Packing, Clothing, Druggists' Sundries, Bicycle Tires, Cotton Hose, Etc. New York Belting & Packing Co., L't'd.
The Central Rubber & Supply Co. PHONE 8. 79 S. ILLINOIS ST., INDIANAPOLIS, IND.

HIGHEST SECURITY
LOWEST COST OF INSURANCE.
The Provident Life and Trust Co.
Of Philadelphia.
D. W. EDWARDS, Gen. Agent,
508 Indiana Trust Building.

Hall Albert F, bill clk Kothe, Wells & Bauer, b 525 College av.
Hall Albert N, b 667 Virginia av.
HALL ALBERT W, Vice-Pres The McGilliard Agency Co, 83-85 E Market, Tel 479; h 1518 N Meridian.
Hall Alonzo C, lab, h 21 Meikel.
Hall Anna E, h 49 Elizabeth.
Hall Archibald, mach, b 200 Bates.
Hall Archibald M, A M prof Butler College, r s s University av 2 w of Downey av (I).
Hall Arthur F, cashr The Indpls Journal, sec and treas Reporter Pub Co, h 55 The Blacherne.
Hall Benjamin F, painter, b 439 N Illinois.
Hall Caroline (wid Hugh H), b s s E Washington 5 e of Belt R R.
Hall Charles, lab, h 235 S Noble.
Hall Charles D, clk R M S, b 240 Central av.
Hall Charles E, receiving teller The State Bank of Indiana, r 275 N Meridian.
Hall Charles G, driver, b 141 Locke.
Hall Charles M, gasfitter, h 66 John.
Hall Charles N, chairmkr, h 22 Douglass.
Hall Charles N, lab, h 305 Columbia av.
Hall Chester F, State Supervisor of Oil Inspection, room 92 State House, res Danville, Ind.
Hall Clayton A, barber, r 127 E Washington.
Hall Clinton E, genl agt John Hancock Mut Life Ins Co, r 24 Mass av.
Hall Don K, bkkpr E C Atkins & Co, h 627 Park av.
Hall Earl S, ins agt, h 101 Highland pl.
Hall Edward, ins agt, h 240 Central av.
Hall Elisha H, sec U S Saving Fund and Investment Co, h 525 College av.
Hall Elizabeth (wid Wm), h 247½ S Capitol av.
Hall Elizabeth A, teacher, b 82 S Reisner (W I).
Hall Ellen, cook, r 315 E Washington.
Hall Elmer F, driver, h 116 Christian av.
Hallt Emma A (wid Lewis), b 89 W Walnu .

Julius C. Walk & Son,
Jewelers
Indianapolis.
12 EAST WASHINGTON ST.

Hall Emmanuel, lab, h w s Indianapolis av 3 n of Fall creek.
Hall Esther P (wid Grant), b 2 Lafayette.
Hall Frank, h 182 Talbott av.
Hall Frank, carp, h 185 River av (W I).
Hall Frank, brakeman, h 211½ E Washington.
Hall Frank A, drugs, 901 Morris (W I), h 20 Lee (W I).
Hall George, lab, h 260 W 5th.
Hall George, lab, r 37½ Kentucky av.
Hall George, waiter, r 409 W North.
Hall George B, single tree mnfr, cor Judge Harding and Vandalia R R (W I), h 67 Highland pl.
Hall George W, trav agt, h 412 N Brookside av.
Hall Grace, b 1324 N Senate av.
Hall Halden, lab, b 728 N Senate av.
Hall Halstead, printer, b 139 N Delaware.
Hall Hannibal, lab, h rear 115 Newman.
Hall Harley A, dep State Supervisor of Oil Inspection, r 92 State House.
Hall Harriet B (wid Truman W), h 3 The Blacherne.
Hall Harry A, lab, b 132 Oliver av (W I).
Hall Harry C, tinner, h 441 Union.
Hall Harry H, trav agt, b 116 Christian av.
Hall Harvey, driver, b 265 Howard.
Hall Haywood, lab, h w s Indianapolis av 2 n of Fall creek.
Hall Hiram H, carp, h e s Commercial av 6 s of Washington av (I).
Hall Hugh B, painter, b 25½ Kentucky av.
Hall Hugh H, boilermkr, h s s E Washington 5 e of Belt R R.
Hall Ida B, teacher Public School No 23, b 289 Bright.
Hall Isaac N, bkkpr U S Encaustic Tile Wks, h 132 N Senate av.
Hall Isom C (Circle Transfer Co), r rear 490 N Illinois.
Hall James, hostler, h 249 E Louisiana.
Hall James, lab, h 71 Yandes.
Hall Jerry S, propr Hotel English, w s Monument pl, bet Market and Meridian, tel 834.
Hall Jesse D, huckster, h 35 Valley Drive.
Hall John, agt, h 23 Garfield pl.
Hall John, bellboy The Bates.
Hall John, lab, h w s Indianapolis av 3 s of 16th.
Hall John, lab, r 154 W Washington.
Hall John C (Cripe, Harris & Co), h 7 Morrison.
Hall John S, ice, 70 Elizabeth, h same.
Hall John W, fireman, h 16 Poplar (B).
Hall John W, sec Washington S and L Assn, 19½ N Penn, h 446 Talbott av.
Hall Joseph, foreman, h 59 Division (W I).
Hall Joseph R, office 75 W Washington, h 275 N Meridian.
Hall Judson B, musician, b 439 N Illinois.
Hall Laura (wid Thomas W), b 627 Park av.
Hall Lavenia A, teacher Public School No 26, h 23 Garfield pl.
Hall Lee R, finisher, h 80 Temple av.
Hall Lena R (wid Frederick H), h 116 Christian av.
Hall Lewis E, stripper, h 1 Susquehanna.
Hall Margaret, janitress Coffin blk, r same.
Hall Marion G, b 141 Locke.
Hall Martin B, stenog, h 146 Newman.
Hall Mary (wid David), h 882 W Washington.
Hall Mary (wid Franklin), h 141 Locke.
Hall Matilda C (wid Joseph), h 175 W McCarty.

OTTO GAS ENGINES
BUILDERS' EXCHANGE
S. W. Cor. Ohio and Penn.
Telephone 585.

Becker & Son Charles Becker, Jacob Becker Jr. Merchant Tailors. 21 N. Penn. St. Tel. 934

SALISBURY & STANLEY

Hall Nancy E (wid Wm), b 338 Hillside av.
Hall Nettie M, stenog, b 87 Woodruff pl.
Hall Peter, lab, h 449 W 2d.
Hall Ralph H, trav agt, b 526 N Illinois.
Hall Rebecca F (wid George T), b 66 John.
Hall Reginald H Mrs, h 210 N Meridian.
Hall Reuben, printer, b 139 N Delaware.
Hall Richard E, clk, b 80 Temple av.
Hall Robert H, driver, h rear 359 Blake.
Hall Robert Rev A M, prof Butler College, b s s University av 3 w of Downey av (I).
Hall Samuel, lab, h 99 Talbott av.
Hall Samuel, lab, h 424 W 2d.
Hall Sarsfield P, trimmer, h 7 Hosbrook.
Hall Silas, houseman 777 N Meridian.
Hall Stephen E, trav agt, b 174 N Illinois.
Hall Susan E (wid John), r 315 E Washington.
Hall Thomas L, paperhanger, b 49 Elizabeth.
Hall Walter M, waiter, r 289 Bright.
Hall Walter V, lab, b 256 S Meridian.
Hall Wesley, hostler, b 321 E Court.
Hall Wesley J, lab, b 338 Tremont.
Hall Wm, h 200 Bates.
Hall Wm, carp, h 289 Bright.
Hall Wm, carp, h 110 Sycamore.
Hall Wm, lab, h 126 Allegheny.
Hall Wm, lab, h 296 S East.
Hall Wm, porter, r 369 W New York.
Hall Wm C, lab, h 52 King av (H).
Hall Wm C, pres Indiana Underwriters' Ins Co, h 526 N Illinois.
Hall Wm C, watchman, h 151 Sheffield (B).
Hall Wm H, clk Clemens Vonnegut, h 80 Temple av.
Hall Wm H, clk The McGilliard Agency Co, b 526 N Illinois.
Hall Wm H, engr Hotel English.
Hall Wm P, musician, h 439 N Illinois.
Hall Wm L, clk, b 240 Central av.
Hall Wm T, brakeman, h 102 S State av.
Hall Wm W, lab, b 256 S Meridian.
Hall Wm W, letter carrier P O, h 131 W 5th.
Hall Zoe, milliner, b 1324 N Senate av.
Hallard Frances (wid Alexander R), cook 801 E Washington.
Hallcross Wm E, helper, h 226 Christian av.
Hallen May E, h 124 N Liberty.
Haller David, asst florist Insane Hospital, h 39 Cleveland (H).
Haller Gottlieb J, bottler, b 71 Bicking.
Haller Gustav A, furnacemkr, h 137 Douglass.
Haller Henry, uphlr, b 71 Bicking.
Haller Hubbard G, engr, h 52 Spann av.
Haller Jacob, packer, h 71 Bicking.
Hallett Andrew J, fruits, 55 E Mkt House, h 1143 N Penn.
Hallick Jasper N, baggageman, h 351 Fletcher av.
Halliday James, presser, h s e cor Harriet and Sutherland (B).
Halliday Robert H, mngr Nelson Morris & Co, h 42 Henry.
Hallinin Martin J, steamer, b 127 Coburn.
Hallinin Thomas, lab, h 127 Coburn.
Hallinin Thomas F, clk, b 127 Coburn.
Hallock Samuel D, painter, 71½ Lockerbie, h same.
Hallowell David H, engr, h 112 Brookside av.

HALLS THOMAS E, Genl Mngr Indianapolis Bureau of Inquiry and Investigation, Rooms 68-69 Ingalls Blk, b 181 N Alabama.

Halmbacher Otto, plater, b 669 Mass av.
Halpern Adolph, cabtmkr, h 119 Maple.

Henry H. Fay,
40½ E. WASHINGTON ST.,
AGENT FOR
Insurance Co. of North America,
Pennsylvania Fire Ins. Co.

Halpin Martin H, printer Indpls Journal, h 325 W North.
Halstead Charles H, carp, h 129 Martndale av.
Halstead Charles M, Co-Operative Carriage and Wagon Co, h 158 Maple.
Halstead Everett C, waiter, h 40 N New Jersey.
Halstead Henry C, lab, h 116½ Oliver av.
Halstead James H, grocer, 133 Martindale av, h same.
Halstead Rollo H, trimmer, b 158 Maple.
Halter George L, lab, b 243 N West.
Haltmeyer Charles A, carp, b 69 Yeiser.
Haltmeyer Christian, cabtmkr, h 293 N Pine.
Haltmeyer Christian jr, clk Penna Lines, b 293 N Pine.
Haltmeyer Mary (wid Charles), h 69 Yeiser.
Halton Samuel, lab, h 17 Lafayette.
Haltzlow John, clk, b 236 N Illinois.
Ham, see also Hamm.
Ham Hardy, lab, b 594 W North.
Ham Joseph M, carp, 446 Olive, h same.
Ham Matilda (wid Henry A), h 594 W North.
Ham Simeon, plumber, b 446 Olive.
Ham Thomas R, harnessmkr, r 79 W Ohio.
Hamar Wm J, foreman, h 70 Spruce.
Hambley David, chairmkr, h 69½ Indiana av.
Hamens Wm W, trunkmkr, h 31½ Indiana av.
Hamerly Frank, lab, r 90 N Senate av.
Hamill John S, live stock, b 403 S Olive.
Hamill Joseph, lab, b 359 S Illinois.
Hamill Kate E, dressmkr, 403 S Olive, h same.
Hamill Michael, live stock, h 403 S Olive.
Hamill Patrick, saloon, 404 W Washington, b 240 N California.
Hamilton Andrew, h 77 Oak.
Hamilton Anna (wid James), h 345 S Alabama.
Hamilton Armenta (wid Henry), h 124½ Ft Wayne av.
Hamilton Arthur G, tel opr, b 345 S Alabama.

MAYHEW'S
SPECTACLES
THE BEST IN USE
SOLD ONLY AT 13 N. MERIDIAN ST.

OFFICE, STORE AND BANK FIXTURES.
Contractors and Builders. Repairing of all kinds done on short notice. 177 Clinton St. Indianapolis, Ind. Telephone 999.

LUMBER Sash and Doors | BALKE & KRAUSS CO., Corner Market and Missouri Sts.

Friedgen Has the BEST PATENT LEATHER SHOES AT LOWEST PRICES. 19 North Pennsylvania St.

SAMUEL LAING: HOT AIR FURNACES 72 AND 74 EAST COURT STREET.

M. B. WILSON, Pres. W. F. CHURCHMAN, Cash.
The Capital National Bank,
INDIANAPOLIS, IND.
Banking business in all its branches. Bonds and Foreign Exchange bought and sold. Interest paid on time deposits. Checks and drafts on all Indiana and Illinois points handled at lowest rates.
No. 28 South Meridian Street, Cor. Pearl.

Hamilton Calvin C, mach hd, h 1261 E Washington.
Hamilton Charles, watchman, h 140 Cornell av.
Hamilton Charles E, painter, h 50½ Clifford av.
Hamilton Charles L, carp, 119 Spann av, h same.
Hamilton Cicero, h 745 Nevada.
Hamilton Clarence M, clk N Y Store, b 551 E Market.
Hamilton Clay C, tmstr, b 30 School.
Hamilton Daniel L, carp, b Ross House.
Hamilton Edwin F, fireman, h 30 School.
Hamilton Elizabeth (wid John), h 73 S Capitol av.
Hamilton Elizabeth (wid Samuel), h 250 S East.
Hamilton Exie E, matron Indiana Reformatory.
Hamilton Ezra, city fireman, b 77 W 6th.
Hamilton Foley, plastr, b 72 Bismarck (W I).
Hamilton Francis W, real est, 31 Lombard bldg, h 125 Park av.
Hamilton Frank A, dentist, 23-24 Marion blk, b 199 Bellefontaine.
Hamilton Frank S, bkkpr, b 188 Dougherty.
Hamilton George B, lab, b 745 Nevada.
Hamilton George E, driver, h 53 Oriental.
Hamilton George T, hostler, b 486 Central av.
Hamilton Harry E, mach, b 60 Fountain.
Hamilton Harry E, glass, 18 Pembroke Arcade, h 134 W Michigan.
Hamilton Haywood, wirewkr, h 75 Columbia al.
Hamilton Henry, blksmith, h 161 E Ohio.
Hamilton Henry, engr, h 364 Union.
Hamilton Henry D, paying teller The State Bank of Indiana, h 126 E Pratt.
Hamilton Isaac, lab, r 102 N Capitol av.
Hamilton James, brakeman, r 205½ W Ohio.
Hamilton James, tmstr, h e s Madeira 6 s of Prospect.
Hamilton James A, sec and treas Indpls Lounge Co, h 199 Bellefontaine.
Hamilton James G, electrician, b 30 S Summit.

Insure Against Accidents
WITH
TUTTLE & SEGUIN,
Agents for
Fidelity and Casualty Co., of New York.
$10,000 for $25. $5,000 for $12.50.
TEL. 1168. 28 E. MARKET ST.

Hamilton James H, carp, h 551 E Market.
Hamilton James H, hackdriver, h 122 N Senate av.
Hamilton James R, meats, 1 E Mkt House, h 564 W Shoemaker (N I).
Hamilton James W, plastr, 218 E South, h same.
Hamilton Jessie, teacher Blind Institute.
Hamilton John B, molder, b 345 S Alabama.
Hamilton John C, pres American Medical College, h 1742 N Capitol av.
Hamilton John E, lab, h 745 Nevada.
Hamilton John J (T J Hamilton & Co), h 98 Bright.
Hamilton John M, grocer, 60 Fountain, h same.
Hamilton John W, bkkpr S A Fletcher & Co, h 679 Broadway.
Hamilton John W, painter, 34½ S Penn, h 115 S Belmont av (W I).
Hamilton Joseph, real est, h 25 S Linden.
Hamilton Judge, tmstr, b 50 Draper.
Hamilton Julia, restaurant, 186 W 3d, h same.
Hamilton Kate, teacher Public School No 13, b 188 Dougherty.
Hamilton Kate M, stenog C H McDowell, b 1703 N Penn.
Hamilton Linda E (wid John), b 1088 N Senate av.
Hamilton Margaret, prin Public School No 2, h 160 Park av.
Hamilton Margaret, stenog, b n e cor Walnut and Maxwell avs (I).
Hamilton Margaret E, h 503 N Penn.
Hamilton Marion, barber, r 69 N Alabama.
Hamilton Martha, h 170½ W Washington.
Hamilton Mary (wid Henry), h 172 N Missouri.
Hamilton Mary (wid Lewis), h 283 Fayette.
Hamilton Mary, forelady, b 345 S Alabama.
Hamilton Mary, laundress, h 236 E Wabash.
Hamilton Mary A (wid Charles), r 2 Ryan blk.
Hamilton Mary E, dressmkr, 161 E Ohio, b same.
Hamilton Mary F, music teacher, 1261 E Washington, h same.
Hamilton Mary W, elocution teacher, 142 N Illinois, h same.
Hamilton Minnie (wid George T), h 124 E 9th.
Hamilton Minta (wid Harry), h 122½ Ft Wayne av.
Hamilton Nancy J (wid Emsley), b 551 Bellefontaine.
Hamilton Rachel (wid Robert), h 94 Lexington av.
Hamilton Robert A, salesman Regal Mnfg Co, h 188 Dougherty.
Hamilton Roxana A, h 117 Minerva.
Hamilton Samuel A, h 142 N Illinois.
Hamilton Samuel A (S Hamilton & Co), h 30 S Summit.
HAMILTON SANFORD P, Storage and Moving, 11 S Alabama, h 486 Central av, Tel 768.
Hamilton Sophia, b 73 S Capitol av.
Hamilton Susan A (wid James W), dressmkr, 564 W Shoemaker (N I), h same.
Hamilton S & Co (Samuel A Hamilton, Mary F McDougall), grocers, 9 Lynn.
Hamilton Thomas, fresco painter, b 478 Bellefontaine.
Hamilton Thomas D, notions, E Mkt House, r 205 E Ohio.
Hamilton Thomas J (T J Hamilton & Co), h 73 S Capitol av.

WEDDING CAKE BOXES · SULLIVAN & MAHAN 41 W. Pearl St.

DIAMOND WALL PLASTER { Telephone 1410 BUILDERS' EXCHANGE.

Best Work. Prompt Delivery. } THE HOME LAUNDRY 197 S. ILLINOIS ST. TEL. 1759. { Collars and Cuffs a Specialty.

HAMILTON T J & CO (Thomas J and John J Hamilton and Rinehart Weber), Cigar Mnfrs, 43 Kentucky av and 177-179 W Maryland, Tel 1492.

Hamilton Wm, lab, r 77 Kentucky av.
Hamilton Wm, motorman, b 193 S Illinois.

HAMILTON WM A, Dealer in Lumber, Lath, Shingles, Doors, Sash, Blinds, Frames, Etc; Estimates Furnished on Application; 143 Dillon, h 53 Jefferson, Tel 779.

Hamilton Wm E, printer, Wm B Burford, r 48½ S Capitol av.
Hamilton Wm F, motorman, h 63 S McLain (W I).
Hamilton Wm H A, foreman Wm B Burford, h 117 Park av.
Hamilton Wm J, lab, b 889 Morris (W I).
Hamilton Wm L, h n e cor Walnut and Maxwell avs (I).
Hamlen Frances H, clk C C C & St L Ry, r 100 Fletcher av.
Hamlet John H, trav agt, h 1022 N New Jersey.
Hamley George, lab, h 40 Osage.
Hamlin Carlin, propr Capital House, 193 W Washington.
Hamlin Charles E, mach hd, h 410 Bates.
Hamlin Florence E, clk, b 28 Ft Wayne av.
Hamlin Frederick, hostler, b 264 Springfield.
Hamlin Frederick E, tel opr Associated Press, h w s Kenwood av bet 27th and 28th.
Hamlin James D, saloon, 312 Blake, h 316 same.
Hamlin Louisa, b w s Kenwood av bet 27th and 28th.
Hamlin Nellie I, clk, b 28 Ft Wayne av.
Hamlin Wm H, coachman, h 119 W 4th.
Hamm, see also Ham.
Hamm Henry C, attendant Insane Hospital.
Hamm John J, insp City Engineer, b 185 Madison av.
Hamm Joseph, lab, b 334 E Michigan.
Hamm Joseph P, lab, h 19 Douglass.
Hamm Robert L, poultry, 440 Mass av, h 63 Clifford av.
Hamm Stephen, lab, b 334 E Michigan.
Hammacher Henry, varinsher, b 754 S East.
Hammall John, lab, h 515 W Maryland.

HAMMEL GEORGE J, Grocery and Meat Market, 110-112 Mass av and 215-217 N Alabama, h 214 N Alabama, Tel 755.

Hammel George J jr, bkkpr, b 214 N Alabama.
Hammel Peter, engr, b 83 English av.
Hammel Peter H, blksmith, h 528 W 22d (N I).
Hammel Theodore, trav agt Indpls Brewing Co, b 355 N West.
Hammel Wm W, sec The Perry Broom Co, b 214 N Alabama.
Hammer Charles L, grain broker, 68 E Wabash, h 385 E Market.
Hammer Christian, grocer, 251 Yandes, h same.
Hammer Emmett J, printer, 124 E New York, h 321 N Illinois.
Hammer Frank E, artist, 77¼ S Illinois, h 516 Talbott av.
Hammer Herman H, clk, b 251 Yandes.
Hammer Nathan L, phys, 277 Douglass, b 2 Arch.

FRANK NESSLER. WILL H. ROST.
FRANK NESSLER & CO.
Tailors
56 EAST MARKET ST. (Lemcke Building),
INDIANAPOLIS, IND.

HAMMER ROYAL C, Agt Gulf Coast Artificial Ice Co, 30 N Liberty, h same.

Hammer Sabina H (wid Godfrey S), h 30 N Liberty.
Hammerle Peter G, baker, h 24 Lord.
Hammerly Samuel K, clk, b 1733 N Illinois.
Hammerly Theresa (wid Valentine), h 1733 N Illinois.
Hammermann Benjamin, pdlr, h 153 Maple.
Hammermann Wm, lab, h 108 Torbet.
Hammermann Wm F, printer, b 108 Torbet.
Hammerschlag Jacob, lab, h 112 Minerva.
Hammersmith Martin, mach, b 170 E Morris.
Hammersmith Minnie (wid Philip), h 170 E Morris.
Hammett James P, painter, h 361 English av.
Hammon Antonia (wid George), h 45 Martin.
Hammond Charles M (Hammond & Pasquier), h 64 Beaty.
Hammond Harry L, motorman, b 1028 W Washington.
Hammond James, cook, Exchange Hotel (W I).
Hammond Martha F, h 177 Park av.
Hammond Nancy (wid Francis J), h 627 N Illinois.
Hammond Ormond H, student, b 864 Bellefontaine.
Hammond Rezin R, h 32 Cherry.
Hammond Robert F, h 137 Madison.
Hammond Thomas C, farmer, h 864 Bellefontaine.
Hammond Thomas D, student, b 864 Bellefontaine.
Hammond Upton, driver, b 427 N Illinois.
Hammond Upton J (Hammond & Rogers), h 90 E Pratt.
Hammond Walter P, molder, h 111 Frazee (H).
Hammond & Pasquier (Charles M Hammond, John Pasquier), grocers, 316 Virginia av.

HAMMOND & ROGERS (Upton J Hammond, Edwin St George Rogers), Lawyers, 17-18 Fletcher's Bank Bldg, Tel 1242.

Haueisen & Hartmann
163-169 E. Washington St.
FURNITURE,
Carpets,
Household Goods,
Tin, Granite and China Wares, Oil Cloth and Shades

THE WM. H. BLOCK CO. 7 AND 9 EAST WASHINGTON STREET. DRY GOODS, HOUSE FURNISHINGS AND CROCKERY.

London Guarantee and Accident Co. (Ltd.) All forms of Liability Insurance, Workmen's Collective Insurance, Fidelity Bonds and Individual Accident Insurance.
Geo. W. Pangborn, Gen. Agent, 704-706 Lemcke Bldg. Telephone 140.

FRANK K. SAWYER, AGENT 74 East Market Street. Telephone 8.
Prussian National Insurance Company OF STETTIN, GERMANY. ORGANIZED 1845.

JOSEPH GARDNER,
TIN, COPPER AND SHEET-IRON WORK AND
HOT AIR FURNACES.
37, 39 & 41 KENTUCKY AVE. Telephone 322.

Hammonds Nellie (wid John), h 258 W Pearl.
Hammons John L, foreman, h 227 Hoyt av.
Hammons Rufus, hostler, h w s Good av 5 s of Railroad (I).
Hammons Wm, lab, h w s Good av 6 s of Railroad (I).
Hammons Wm H, real est, 24 Thorpe blk, r same.
Hamonds Henry, lab, h 529 Roanoke.
Hampton Albert S, engr, h 340 W Vermont.
Hampton Alonzo, lab, r 230 W Market.
Hampton Alvin W, carp, b 220½ W Washington.
Hampton Carl, collr, b 286 N Alabama.
Hampton Carrie (wid Washington), h 220½ W Washington.
Hampton David B, car rep, b 44 N Station (B).
Hampton Eli, fireman, h 133 S Reisner (W I).
Hampton Fletcher, barber, b 220½ W Washington.
Hampton James, porter, h 13 Ellsworth.
Hampton Jehiel B, carriage body mnfr, 112 S East, h same.
Hampton John, trav agt, h 250 Union.
Hampton John E (John E & Wm W Hampton), h 277 E Merrill.
Hampton John E & Wm W, printers, 67½ W Georgia.
Hampton Matilda M (wid Wade), b 529 Park av.
Hampton Phineas, bell boy, b 13 Ellsworth.
HAMPTON RUFUS C, Drugs, Paints, Oils and Glass, 2 Hill av, cor Columbia av, h same, Tel 617.
Hampton Wm W (John E & Wm W Hampton), b 286 N Alabama.
Hamrick Jesse D, lawyer, 35½ E Washington, h 1564 N Meridian.
Hamrick John F, trav agt, b 243 Douglass.
Han James, repairman Insane Hospital.
Han Michael, uphlr, r 143 Ft Wayne av.
Hanable Charles A, phys, 624 Central av, h same.
Hanahan Edward P, contr, b 43 Elm.
Hanahan James C, engr, h 30 Tacoma av.

J. S. FARRELL & CO.
STEAM AND HOT WATER
HEATING FOR STORES, OFFICES,
PUBLIC BUILDINGS,
PRIVATE RESIDENCES,
GREENHOUSES, ETC.
84 North Illinois St. Telephone 382.

Hanch Charles C, creditman Nordyke & Marmon Co, b 418 Park av.
Henckel Henry S, solr John S Spann & Co, h 175 N New Jersey.
Hancock Charles E, wines, 82 Monument pl, h 298 E St Clair.
Hancock Ellen (wid Benjamin F), h 506 N Delaware.
Hancock Frank, h 506 N Delaware.
Hancock George W, mer police, b 702 N Capitol av.
Hancock Harrison, lab, b s s Brookville rd 2 w of Ritter av (I).
Hancock James, h 951 Mass av.
Hancock Jessie L, teacher Public School No 2, b 466 Broadway.
Hancock John E, motorman, b 29 Cornell av.
Hancock John W, h s s Prospect 2 w of Miami.
Hancock John W, condr, h 269 Dougherty.
Hancock Joseph, sawmkr, b 319 S Meridian.
Hancock Martha (wid Cread), h w s Perkins pike 5 n of Bethel av.
Hancock Mary A, prin Public School No 38, b 466 Broadway.
Hancock Mary J (wid Henry J), h 29 Cornell av.
Hancock Owen, lab, h 26 Abbott.
Hancock Richard B, sawyer, h 310 Cornell av.
Hancock Robert, lab, h 23 Athon.
Hancock Will R, mngr Security Mortgage Loan Co, h 471 Bellefontaine.
Hancock Wm, h 466 Broadway.
Hancock Wm, lab, b 23 Athon.
Hand Adolphus C, bricklyr, b 482 Chestnut.
Hand Casper, engr, h 149 Huron.
Hand Charlotte (wid Wm), b 121 Woodlawn av.
Hand Elsie (wid Wm J), h 235 W South.
Hand Harry E, clk Am Ex Co, h 80 Hoyt av.
Hand Harvey S, hatter, b 347 Coburn.
Hand Laura (wid Harvey T), b 58 S Belmont (W I).
Hand Levi S, h 121 Woodlawn av.
Hand Samuel, paperhngr, h 347 Coburn.
Handel Frederick C, printer, b 79 Shepard (W I).
Handey Albert, clk Am Ex Co, b 231 E South.
Handle-Hoop Tub Co, Evert M Thompson pres and treas, s w cor St Clair and C C C & St L Ry.
Handley Frederick L, driver, b 179 Elizabeth.
Handley Nicholas, foreman, h 420 N Pine.
Handlin Daniel J, condr, h 271 Fletcher av.
Handlon Catherine, dry goods, 376 Blake, h same.
Handlon Richard, carp, h 376 Blake.
Handrich Albert, shoemkr, w s Rural 6 n of of Brookside av, h same.
Handrich Robert, lab, h w s Rural 5 n of Brookside av.
Handy George, lab, h 145 Winchester.
Handy Harvey, watchman, h 35 Gatling.
Handy Wm, waiter, r 111 Indiana av.
Handy Wm J, cashr Michigan Mutual Life Ins Co, h 52 The Blacherne.
Handy Wilson T, condr, h 44 Tacoma av.
Haneman Frederick W, driver, b 705 Mass av.
Haneman John F, grocer, 186 Hillside av, h 705 Mass av.
Haneman Ralph E, clk, b 705 Mass av.
Hanes, see also Haines and Haynes.
Hanes Cyrus M, lab, h 114 Trowbridge (W).

United States Life Insurance Co., of New York.
E. B. SWIFT M'g'r. 25 E. Market St.

WM. KOTTEMAN } 89 & 91 E. Washington St. Telephone 1742 { RUGS MATTINGS WINDOW SHADES

WILLIAM WIEGEL } MANUFACTURER OF..... } SHOW CASES } 6 W. Louisiana St. Opposite Union Station.

HANES GEORGE T, Supt Life Insurance Co of Virginia, 45-46 Lorraine Bldg, h 221 N Capitol av.
Hanes James S, tmstr, h 331 S Delaware.
Haney Mary A (wid John), r 235 Mass av.
Haney Michael, h s s Walnut 3 w of Sherman Drive.
Haney Scott, livery and feed, n w cor Missouri and Court, h 10 Emerson pl.
Haney Thomas P, mech engr, 10 Union, b same.
Hanf Henry, lab, h 546 S New Jersey.
Hanf Henry F, uphlr N Y Store, h 62 Dougherty.
Hanf Valentine, bartndr, h rear 176 N Pine.
Hanford Charles L, trav agt, h 71 W 3d.
Hanger Albert, plastr, b 25 Decatur.
Hanger James A, attendant, h 25 Decatur.
Hankemeier Ernest J, trav agt, b 452 N Senate av.
Hankemeier Henry, solicitor, b 452 N Senate av.
Hankemeier Wm F, trav agt, h 452 N Senate av.
Hankins Alfred L, brakeman, h 272 English av.
Hankins Anthony M, trav agt, r 272 N Meridian.
Hankins Calvin, lab, b 33 Malott av.
Hankins Charles L, driver, h 185 Dearborn.
Hankins Edgar E, lab, h 118 Sheffield av (H).
Hankins Frank, mason, h 164 Keystone av.
Hankins Ira, coachman, 770 N Meridian.
Hankins John B, h 438 S East.
Hankins John W, lab, h 94 S Noble.
Hankins Keelin, lab, b 14 Barrows.
Hankins Lorenzo D, teacher, h 19 Dunlop.
Hankins Mary A (wid Prior), h 33 Malott av.
Hankins Thomas J, plastr, h 38 Centennial (H).
Hanley, see also Henley.
Hanley Andrew, lab, r 117 Minerva.
Hanley Catherine, b 297 S East.
Hanley Cornelius, foreman, h 420 N Pine.
Hanley Edward, lab, b 68 Maple.
Hanley Frederick L, clk, b 179 Elizabeth.
Hanley George, carp, h 338 Coburn.
Hanley John, lab, h 9 Warren.
Hanley John C, plastr, h 361 Virginia av.
Hanley Michael, tallyman C C C & St L Ry, h 297 S East.
Hanley Michael J, engr, h 184 Keystone av.
Hanley Richard, bartndr, h 32 Buchanan.
Hanley Wm, lab, h 199 S Pine.
Hanley Wm M, clk, h 179 Elizabeth.
Hanlon Lawrence, patrolman, h 247 S West.
Hanlon Malachi G, clk, b 221 N Capitol av.
Hanlon Patrick, lab, h 47 Blake.
Hann, see also Hahn.
Hann Andrew M, carp, h 428 Columbia av.
Hann Frank C, lab, h 340 Columbia av.
Hann George, harnessmkr, b 103 S Reisner (W I).
Hann Harry B, tinner, b 161 Buchanan.
Hann John B, loans, 324 Lemke bldg, h 649 College av.
Hann Otis C (Shingler, Hann & Co), h 901½ Cornell av.
Hann Sarah A (wid Thomas R), artist, 178 N Alabama, r same.
Hanna Albert C, produce, b 290 S East.
Hanna Anna R, notions, 452 S Meridian, h same.
Hanna Cecelia (wid Madison), b 483 N Illinois.
Hanna Charles T, student, b 249 Hamilton av.

THOS. C. DAY & CO.
Financial Agents and Loans.
We have the experience, and claim to be reliable.
Rooms 325 to 330 Lemcke Bldg.

Hanna Edwin S, foreman I D & W Ry, h 235 S East.
Hanna Eldron B, engr, h 24 S Gale (B).
Hanna Garrett P, h 290 S East.
Hanna George L, clk Indiana National Bank, b 913 N New Jersey.
Hanna Gertrude, notary public and stenog, 18½ N Penn, b 432 same.
Hanna Hiram C, soldier U S Arsenal.
Hanna Hotel, Martin M Power propr, 63 N Alabama.
Hanna Hugh H, pres Atlas Engine Works, h 786 N Penn.
Hanna Hugh H jr, clk Atlas Engine Works, b 786 N Penn.
Hanna Isabella A (wid Samuel), h 447 E Ohio.
Hanna John A (Judson & Hanna), h 85 Broadway.
Hanna John L, student, b 84 E New York.
Hanna Laura E, teacher Public School No 33, b 913 N New Jersey.
Hanna Lillie M, clk Rockwood Mnfg Co, b 290 S East.
Hanna Samuel C, h 913 N New Jersey.
Hanna Theodore P, checkman, b 290 S East.
HANNA THOMAS, Lawyer, Rooms 5-6 Rialto Blk, 18½ N Penn, Tel 1586, h same.
Hanna Walter P, mailing clk P O, h 1321 N Alabama.
Hannafin Catherine (wid John), h 185 Jefferson av.
Hannafin John, plumber, b rear 262 S Missouri.
Hannafin Timothy, switchman, h 282 S Capitol av.
Hannah Archibald A, b s w cor Washington and National avs (I).
Hannah Clyde E, b 23 W St Clair.
Hannah Laura, dressmkr, 23 W St Clair, h same.
Hannah Mary E (wid Archibald A), b s w cor Washington and National avs (I).
Hannan Edward J, lab, h 97 High.
Hannan James J, drayman, b 97 High.
Hannan John B, clk C C C & St L Ry, h 1129 E Michigan.

EAT
QUAKER BREAD
ASK YOUR GROCER FOR IT.
THE HITZ BAKING CO.

CARPETS AND RUGS RENOVATED.......... | CAPITAL STEAM CARPET CLEANING WORKS M. D. PLUNKETT, TELEPHONE No. 818

BENJ. BOOTH PRACTICAL EXPERT ACCOUNTANT. Complicated or disputed accounts investigated and adjusted. Room 18, 82½ E. Wash. St., Ind'p'l's, Ind.

THE SHERMAN RESTAURANT || 18 and 20 South Meridian Street KERSHNER BROS., Proprs.

ESTABLISHED 1876. TELEPHONE 168.
CHESTER BRADFORD,
SOLICITOR OF PATENTS,
AND COUNSEL IN PATENT CAUSES.
(See adv. page 6.)
Office:—Rooms 14 and 16 Hubbard Block, S.W. Cor. Washington and Meridian Streets, INDIANAPOLIS, INDIANA.

Hannan Patrick, lab, b 272 W Maryland.
Hannegan John P, editor Indiana Labor Leader, r s s Michigan 2 w of Delaware.
Hannemann Albert, sawdust, h 329 N Alabama.
Hanney Michael E, mach hd, b 22 Wyoming.
Hanney Wm J, tallyman, h 128 Meek.
Hanninger, see also Henninger.
Hannold Ira, carp, b 255 N Liberty.
Hannon Dennis, treas Empire Theater, r same.
Hanovan Martin, lab, r 157 E Ohio.
Hanrahan Anna (wid Frank), h 431 S Missouri.
Hanrahan Catherine, matron City Dispensary, r 35 Wyandot blk.
Hanrahan Ellen G (K & E Hanrahan), b 209 W South.
Hanrahan Frank, engr The Bates.
Hanrahan John F, mach, b 13 Henry.
Hanrahan John W, engr, h 315 S Penn.
Hanrahan Kate A (K & E Hanrahan), b 209 W South.
Hanrahan K & E (Kate A and Ellen G), dressmkrs, 19 Commercial blk.
Hanrahan Lawrence, h 60 Pendleton av (B).
Hanrahan Michael J, molder, h 13 Henry.
Hanrahan Nellie, dressmkr, h 431 S Missouri.
Hanrahan Nellie (wid John F), confr, 59 E South, h same.
Hanrahan Thomas P, molder, h 277 W Maryland.
Hanrahan Wm M, mach, b 13 Henry.
Hansbery Meriman, lab, h 169 Minerva.
Hansel Arthur, lab, b 14 McCauley.
Hanselmann Elizabeth (wid Jacob), h 381 S State av.
Hanselmann Joseph J, blksmith, h 425 S State av.
Hanselmann Otto F, driver, b 381 S State av.
Hansen, see also Hanson and Henson.
Hansen Andrew, clk Daniel Stewart, b 37 Nebraska.
Hansen Christian H, clk A Kiefer Drug Co, h 24 Sanders.

Metal Ceilings and all kinds of Copper, Tin and Sheet Iron work.
O. B. ENSEY,
TELEPHONE 1562.
CORNER 6TH AND ILLINOIS STS.

Hansen Hans, lab, h n s Orient 1 e of C C C & St L Ry (N I).
Hansen Hans C, painter, h 36 Carlos.
Hansen Hans P, lab, b 28 Sanders.
Hansen Hemming W, patternmkr, h 66 Barth av.
Hansen Jacob, grocer, 150 Spann av, h same.
Hansen Joseph A, lab, b 143 E Washington.
Hansen Lawrence, bottler, b 116 Wright.
Hansen Louis P, cabtmkr, h 116 Wright.
Hansen Martin A, drayman, h 37 Nebraska.
Hansen Minnie (wid Charles), h 32 Water.
Hansen Morris, student, b 43 Beaty.
Hansen Morris J T, student, b 150 Spann av.
Hansen Niels C, hostler, b n s Orient 1 e of C C C & St L Ry (N I).
Hansen Ole, veneerer, h 54 Wallack.
Hansen Peter, grocer, 258 E McCarty, h 444 S East.
Hansen Peter, lab, b 465 Union.
Hansen Peter C, painter, h 66 Tremont av (H).
Hansen Rasmus, driver, h 104 High.
Hansen Soren, drayman, h 47 Beaty.
Hansen Soren, grocer, 768 S East, h same.
Hansen Thomas, drayman, b 37 Nebraska.
Hansen Wm J P, pressman, b 37 Nebraska.
Hanser Joseph L, painter, h 84 Michigan av.
Hansford Isham, lab, r rear 18 W Michigan.
Hansford Robert, lab, r 4 Susquehanna.
Hanshaw, see also Henshaw.
Hanshaw Elizabeth (wid John), h 232 W Chesapeake.
Hanshaw Lee D, cook, h 90 N Senate av.
Hansing Christian, bricklyr, h 137 Shelby.
Hansing Christian, lab, b 774 S East.
Hansing Christian, lab, h n s Orient 2 e of C C C & St L Ry (N I).
Hansing Christian, mer police, h 174 Shelby.
Hansing Christian W, driver, h 774 S East.
Hansing Frederick J, carp, h 78 Harmon.
Hansing Wm, uphlr, b 78 Harmon.
Hansom Mary E (wid Joseph), b 101 Elm.
Hanson, see also Hansen and Henson.
Hanson Alice M (Hardy & Hanson), r 502 Lemcke bldg.
Hanson Alice M, seamstress, b 574 Morris (W I).
Hanson Alpha B, clk, b 33 W St Joseph.
Hanson Anna C (wid Nicholas), h rear 209 N Pine.
Hanson Carrie (wid Frederick), b 99 N Arsenal av.
Hanson Charles F, musician, h 222 N Illinois.
Hanson Charles W, painter, h 33 W St Joseph.
Hanson Emma, clk Nathan Kahn, b 42 Davis.
Hanson Frank W, motorman, h 164½ E Washington.
Hanson Frederic W, bkkpr Geo W Stout, h 555 N Illinois.
Hanson John, clk Robert Keller, h 129 Dougherty.
Hanson John, molder, h 1067 W Michigan.
Hanson Josephine L, seamstress, b 574 Morris (W I).
Hanson Julius A, h 600 N Delaware.
Hanson Matthew, h 42 Davis.
Hanson Walter F, carp, h 506 E 11th.
Hanson Walter T, painter, b 33 W St Joseph.
Hanson Wm, engr, h 139 English av.

TUTEWILER ▲ UNDERTAKER, No. 72 WEST MARKET STREET. TELEPHONE 216.

The Provident Life and Trust Co. Dividends are paid in cash and are not withheld for a long period of years, subject to forfeiture in the event of death or the termination of policy.
D. W. EDWARDS, GENERAL AGENT, 508 INDIANA TRUST BUILDING.

THEODORE F. SMITHER COMPOSITION ROOFING MATERIALS. BEST IN THE MARKET. TELEPHONE 861. OFFICE, 151 WEST MARYLAND ST.

Hanson Wm M F, painter, h 138½ N Dorman.
Hanthorn Nancy H (wid Wm), h 93 Brookside av.
Hanvey Albert, clk Am Ex Co, b 231 E South.
Hanvey Alexander, shoemkr, 12 Ft Wayne av, h 231 E South.
Hanvey George, clk R M S, h 580 Broadway.
Hanway Amos Rev, h 331 S New Jersey.
Hanway, Bookwalter & Co (Samuel Hanway, Charles A Bookwalter, Frank J Noll), proprs Gem Garment Co, 17-23 W Pearl.
Hanway Samuel (Hanway, Bookwalter & Co), h w s Central av 1 n of 26th.
Hanway Thomas, mason, e s Senate av 1 s of 28th, h same.
Happersberger Frank, watchmkr, Julius C Walk & Son, h 308 E New York.
Harbick Stephen, lab, h 120 Sheffield av (H).
Harbison Alexander, mngr Indpls Bill Posting Co, 61½ N Penn, h 77 Ash.
Harbison Joseph E, foreman Natl Malleable Castings Co, h 69 King av (H).
Hardacre Edgar E, actor, b 9 Cornell av.
Hardacre John, contr, h 9 Cornell av.
Hardacre Napoleon B, lather, h 324 Yandes.
Hardacre Wm B, carp, b 9 Cornell av.
Hardaway George B, coachman, b 208 Middle.
Hardaway Martha E (wid John), b 208 Middle.
Hardee John A, trav agt, h 144 N Illinois.
Hardee John S, trav agt, r 132 The Shiel.
Hardee Wm A, carp, h 228 Michigan (H).
Hardegen Emil C, mach, h 32 Camp.
Hardegen Otto, lab, h 48 S Judge Harding (W I).
Harden, see also Hardin.
Harden Elizabeth (wid Peyton), h 237 W Vermont.
Harden James M, waiter, r 335 E Miami.
Harden Richard, barber, 270 W Washington, h same.
Harden Robert, lab, r 200½ W Washington.
Harden Thomas, lab, h 167 W McCarty.
Harden Thomas J, cabtmkr, h 196 W 2d.
HARDEN TYRE N, Genl Agt Northwestern Mutual Life Insurance Co of Milwaukee, 125 E Walnut, h 347 N Alabama.
Harden Wm E, ins, h 125 E Walnut.
Harder Henry A, packer Charles Mayer & Co, h 325 E New York.
Harder Joseph C, collr, r 77½ E Market.
Hardern Andrew, lab, h 650 W Washington.
Hardesty Alvin E, bartndr, b 186 S Illinois.
Hardesty Erastus J, engr, h 1359 N Illinois.
Hardesty George W, brakeman, h 138 Fletcher av.
Hardesty George W, trav agt, h 368 N Senate av.
Hardesty Lafayette, lab, 338 Superior.
Hardey Jerome F (Hardey & Gausepohl), b 164 S Noble.
Hardey Sophronia (wid Frank H), h 218 N Alabama.
Hardey & Gausepohl (Jerome F Hardey, George H Gausepohl), grocers, 150 Madison av.
Hardie, see also Hardy.
Hardie Harry B, bkkpr, b 790 E Washington.
Hardie Wm, bkkpr John S Spann & Co, h 790 E Washington.

THE WHEN IS A WORLD BEATER.

Hardie Wm, mason, h 22 Lexington av.
Hardin, see also Harden.
Hardin Albert G, adv clk The Indpls Journal, h 140 Cornell av.
Hardin Augustus, b 118 Ash.
Hardin Benjamin, lab, h e s Tremont av 1 s of Clarke (H).
Hardin Charles, lab, h 6 Lafayette.
Hardin Charles, lab, b 391 W 2d.
Hardin David, lab, h 7 Willard.
Hardin Ella L, b 282 Fulton.
Hardin Ethel, bkkpr, b 226 E 7th.
Hardin Ezra A, copy holder, b 140 Cornell av.
Hardin John G, express, h 104 Laurel.
Hardin Lee A, carp, b 593 W 22d (N I).
Hardin Many, janitress 77½ S Illinois, r same.
Hardin Newton, clk C M Warner & Co, h 66 The Windsor.
Hardin Rebecca (wid Stephen NJ), b 104 Laurel.
Hardin Richard E, carp, h 593 W 22d (N I).
Hardin Samuel, painter, b 593 W 22d (N I).
Hardin Thomas, lab, b 118 Ash.
Harding Albert G, switchman, h Morris w of Eagle Creek (W I).
Harding Alice, stenog The State Bank of Indiana, b 359 N New Jersey.
Harding Altus M, shirt mnfr, 18½ N Meridian, h 359 N New Jersey.
Harding Bates W, clk, b 144 N Senate av.
Harding Bettie, h 115 Columbia al.
Harding Charles W, h 1134 N Delaware.
Harding Edwin S, printer, h e s Chester av 2 n of Washington.
Harding George W, lab, h n s Glen Drive 3 w of Station (B).
Harding Henry L, Commissioner Marion County, 43 Court House, h Haughville.
Harding Jacob O, proof reader Indpls Journal, r 18 W Michigan.
Harding John, mach, b 340 E Market.
Harding John A, lab, h 111 W Sutherland (B).
Harding John F, mach opr Indpls Journal, h 40 Hall pl.
Harding John I, b n s Glen Drive 3 w of Station (B).

The A. Burdsal Co.
Manufacturers of
STEAMBOAT COLORS
BEST HOUSE PAINTS MADE.
Wholesale and Retail.
34 AND 36 SOUTH MERIDIAN STREET.

Electric Contractors We are prepared to do any kind of Electric Contract Work. C. W. MEIKEL. Telephone 466. 96-98 E. New York St.

DALTON & MERRIFIELD { LUMBER South Noble St., near E. Washington

INDIANA ELECTROTYPE CO. ••• BEST WORK. LOWEST PRICES.
23 WEST PEARL ST., INDIANAPOLIS, IND. JOB WORK. BOOK PLATES. BEST PATENT BASE ON THE MARKET.
All Orders Promptly Filled.

KIRKHOFF BROS.,
Sanitary Plumbers
STEAM AND HOT WATER HEATING.
102-104 SOUTH PENNSYLVANIA ST.
TELEPHONE 910.

Harding John L, shoemaker, 139 Oliver av (W I), h same.
Harding Joseph H, condr, h 742 E Ohio.
Harding Julia C (wid George), b 40 Hall pl.
Harding Mary T (wid Wm), h 460 E North.
Harding Maud M C V, cashr Marceau & Bassett, b 124 N Capitol av.
Harding Michael, waiter, r 102 N Capitol av.
Harding Wm, car rep, h 1044 W Vermont.
Harding Wm N (Harding & Hovey), h 824 N Meridian.
HARDING & HOVEY (Wm N Harding, Alfred R Hovey), Lawyers, 51-54 Lombard Bldg, Tel 457.
Hardison Melton, lab, b 264 Lafayette.
Hardison Wm, lab, h 264 Lafayette.
Hardman John S, filer, b 412 S Delaware.
Hardman Wm, lab, b 36 Rhode Island.
Hardwick Alexander, carp, h 125 N Senate av.
Hardwick George W, honey, E Mkt House, h 228 E Market.
Hardy, see also Hardie.
Hardy Addie L (Hardy & Hanson), b 31 W Vermont.
Hardy Albert E, clk, b 891 Mass av.
Hardy Alexander, whitewasher, h rear 472 E Washington.
Hardy Bailey B, lab, h 468 W Chicago (N I).
Hardy Charles T, tobacco mnfr, 480 E Washington, b 25½ Jefferson av.
Hardy Earl W, typewriter, h 31 W Vermont.
Hardy Edward S, tel opr, b 93 S Reisner (N I).
Hardy George W, mach, b 320 E New York.
Hardy Henry, brakeman, b 99 Lexington av.
Hardy Henry, lab, h 274 Alvord.
Hardy Ida, h 239 W McCart.
Hardy James B, clk AlbertyGall, h 30 W St Joseph.
Hardy James D, carp, b 38 Sullivan.
Hardy James E, checkman Frank Bird Transfer Co, h rear 31 E McCarty.
Hardy James O, mngr, h 25½ Jefferson av.
Hardy Joseph A, driver, h 422 E St Clair.

Lime, Lath, Cement,
THE W. G. WASSON CO.
130 INDIANA AVE. TEL. 989.
Sewer Pipe, Flue Linings, Fire Brick, Fire Clay.

Hardy Lawrence B, lab, h 468 W Chicago (N I).
Hardy Lucinda (wid Joseph P), b 179 S William (W I).
Hardy Margaret E (wid Wm), h 25½ Jefferson av.
Hardy Martha E (wid Charles), h 172½ E Washington.
Hardy Nathaniel, flagman, h 93 S Reisner (W I).
Hardy Niles, grocer, 296 Howard (W I), h same.
Hardy Ole D (O D Hardy & Co), h 240½ E Washington.
Hardy O D & Co (Ole D Hardy, Artemus G Simmons, Robert L Farris), portraits, 240½ E Washington.
Hardy Samuel E, grocer, 891 Mass av, h same.
Hardy Solomon G, tel opr, b 93 S Reisner (W I).
Hardy Wm, lab, h 252 Hamilton av.
Hardy Wm jr, lab, b 252 Hamilton av.
Hardy Wm F, clk Model Clothing Co, b 38 Sullivan.
Hardy Wm F, mach, b 93 S Reisner (W I).
HARDY & HANSON (Addie L Hardy, Alice M Hanson), Stenographers, 501 Lemcke Bldg, Tel 900.
Hare Adam N, electrician, b 503 S West.
Hare Albert W, mach, h 42 Catherine.
Hare Amos G, winder, b 503 S West.
Hare Calvin A Rev, pastor College Avenue Baptist Church, h 421 Park av.
Hare Clinton L, cashr County Clerk, h 787 N Meridian.
Hare George, condr, b 78 Springfield.
Hare Henry F, brakeman, h 116 Wright.
Hare Marcus L, stock farm, h 500 N Penn.
Hare Mary A (wid Michael), h 503 S West.
Hare Sarah, h 62 Geisendorff.
Hare Serena T, h 70 Christian av.
Haren Daniel, lab, h 418 Newman.
Harges Paul C, b 1 Madison av.
Hargraves Wm B, lab, h 430 Superior.
Hargreaves Clarissa V, b 1285 N Meridian.
Hargreaves John A, foreman The H Lieber Co, h 393 Central av.
Hargrove Romeo, brakeman, b 714 E Washington.
Harity Patrick, umbrellas, 43 Virginia av, h 279 W Vermont.
Harker David T, lab, h 59 New.
Harker Jefferson, stairbldr, b 201 E Washington.
Harker Samuel A, teacher, h n s University av 5 w of Central av (I).
Harker Wm, brakeman, r 852½ E Washington.
Harkins George, lab, b 1169 E Washington.
Harkins Richard E, fitter, b 1169 E Washington.
Harkness John, h 1066 N Illinois.
Harlan A E, sec Western Horseman Co, 49 Monument pl, res Alexandria, Ind.
Harlan Frances (wid George), b 65½ Beaty.
Harlan George, foreman, h 65½ Beaty.
Harlan Henry, lab, h 115 S Spruce.
Harlan Hiempsal L, medicine mnfr, 477 N Meridian, h same.
HARLAN ISAAC N, Recording Agt Agricultural Insurance Co of Watertown, N Y, Concordia Insurance Co of Milwaukee, Wis, 36 N Delaware, Tel 1210; h 19 Vine.
Harlan Jacob N, molder, h 131 King (H).

YOUR HOMES FURNISHED BY W. H. MESSENGER 101 East Washington St. Telephone 491.

McNamara, Koster & Co. Phone 1593. 212-218 S. PENN. ST. PATTERN MAKERS

Harlan James A, foreman, h 30 Wyoming.
Harlan Julia C (wid John J), b 23 Keith.
HARLAN LEVI P, Lawyer, 62½ E Washington, Tel 1491; h National pike 5 miles east of city limits.
Harlan Maria L, h 252½ Mass av.
Harlan Marion H, carp, h 197 W Maryland.
Harlan Samuel A, trav agt Elmer E Nichols & Co, h 1750 N Penn.
Harlan Susan (wid George W), h 136 N Capitol av.
Harley James R, cabtmkr, h 32 Holmes av (H).
Harman, see also Harmon, Herman and Hermann.
Harman Amos W, clk Charles Mayer & Co, h 1111 N Meridian.
Harman Edward A, clk Indiana Bicycle Co, b 1111 N Meridian.
Harman Entha M, bkkpr The Indpls Sentinel, b 1325 N Alabama.
Harman Hale, carp, h 94 Sheffield av (H).
Harman Howard H, finisher, b 178 Columbia av.
Harman John H, express, h 178 Columbia av.
Harmann Willis, molder, h 66 Holmes.
Harmanni Margaret, b 54 Downey.
Harmening Amelia, h 136 Eureka av.
Harmening Charles A, car rep, h 28 S Spruce.
Harmening Charles C, farmer, h n s St Marie 1 n of Walker av.
Harmening Charles H, mach, h 273 S Delaware.
Harmening Christian H, saloon, 12 N Delaware, h 524 E Ohio.
Harmening Christian H, lab, b w s Auburn av 2 s of Belt R R.
Harmening Edward A, foreman, h 204 W Vermont.
Harmening Edward H, clk, h 333 N Liberty.
Harmening Frank, lab, b w s Auburn av 2 s of Belt R R.
Harmening Henry C, farmer, b n s St Marie 1 n of Walker av.
Harmening Henry F, farmer, h n s St Marie 1 n of Walker av.
Harmening Henry F, condr, h 398½ College av.
Harmening Wm H, dairy, w s Auburn av 2 s of Belt R R, h same.
Harmeson Wm J, turner, b 55 S California.
Harmeyer Lewis A, mngr R B Grover & Co, h 309 E New York.
Harmon, see also Harman, Herman and Herrmann.
Harmon Charles, bartndr, b 23 Springfield.
Harmon George H, bartndr, b s s Sutherland 2 w of Gale (B).
Harmon Eleanor, teacher, r 140 N Alabama.
Harmon Lucia, teacher, r 140 N Alabama.
Harmon Louella (wid Wm H), h 258 W Pearl.
HARMON MATTHEW H, Propr Haughville Mineral Well and Bath House, w s Holmes av 1 s of Michigan (H), h 24 Holmes av (H). (See adv in classified Baths.)
Harmon Rudolph, cabtmkr, h 515 S West.
Harmon Wesley, lab, b rear 1 Rathbone.
Harmon Willard (Gordon & Harmon), h 1195 N Illinois.
Harmon Wm R, lab, h 336 S Alabama.
Harms Arthur E, cigar mnfr, 507 Broadway, h same.
Harms August, printer, b 174 W New York.

Henry H. Fay, 40½ E. WASHINGTON ST., FIRE INSURANCE, REAL ESTATE, LOANS AND RENTAL AGENT.

Harms August C, cigar mnfr, 534 Broadway, h same.
Harms Edward H, lab, b 44 Jones.
Harms Henry, lab, h 44 Jones.
Harms Herman P, cigar mnfr, 292 E Washington, b 70 N East.
Harms Martha (wid Theodore F), cigar mnfr, 77 W Walnut, h same.
Harms Otto W, cigarmkr, b 507 Broadway.
Harms Sophie E (wid August), b 375 E 9th.
Harmuth Kate (wid August), nurse, 529½ N Illinois, h same.
Harness Edward M, bkkpr Peter F Bryce, h 13 E South.
Harness George C, collr R F Catterson & Son, b 145 Cottage av.
Harness George L, clk Van Camp H and I Co, h 91 Chadwick.
Harness Wm W, supt, h 167 Douglass.
Harney Amos, lab, b 44 Athon.
Harold, see also Harrold.
Harold Adolphus, salesman, b 594 Morris (W I).
Harold Arthur O, clk, b 453 College av.
Harold Cyrus N, phys, 451 College av, h 453 same.
Harold Henry E, student, r 367 N Alabama.
Harold Marion M, painter, h 69 Elizabeth.
Harold Milton L, carp, h 99 Greencastle av.
Harper Charles S, porter, h 81 Camp.
Harper Elva F, attendant Insane Hospital.
Harper Enos L, carp, h 4 Race.
Harper Frank A, engr, h 262 Lincoln la.
Harper Frank C, shoemkr, 53 N Illinois, h 445 N New Jersey.
Harper George, lab, b 4 Race.
Harper Henry, driver, h 136 Columbia al.
Harper Henry L, barber, b 496 Newman.
Harper James A, pdlr, h 667 Madison av.
Harper James H, painter, h 197 W Maryland.
Harper James W, lawyer, 212 Indiana Trust bldg, h 824 N Delaware.
Harper Jemima (wid James), b 123 W 4th.
Harper John W, cigarmkr, h 859 Mass av.
Harper Joseph, lab 654 N Meridian.
Harper Joseph P, clk, b 21 Hall pl.
Harper Joseph T, shoemaker, h 445 N New Jersey.

SURETY BONDS
American Bonding & Trust Co. OF BALTIMORE, MD.
Authorized to act as Sole Surety on all Bonds. Total Resources over $1,000,000.00.
W. E. BARTON & CO., General Agents, 504 INDIANA TRUST BUILDING.
Long Distance Telephone 1918.

THE FRED DIETZ CO. WOODEN PACKING BOXES MADE TO ORDER. FACTORY AND WAREHOUSE TRUCKS. 400 Madison Avenue. Telephone 654.

Business World Supplied with Help. GRADUATES ASSISTED TO POSITIONS. 10,000 NOW IN GOOD SITUATIONS. TEL. 499. E. J. HEEB, PRES. Indianapolis BUSINESS UNIVERSITY

Water Works Pumping Engines { HENRY R. WORTHINGTON, 64 SOUTH PENNSYLVANIA ST. Long Distance Telephone 284.

UNION CO-OPERATIVE LAUNDRY { (COMPOSED OF UNION LAUNDRY GIRLS.) NOS. 38, 40 AND 42 VIRGINIA AVENUE. T. E. SOMERVILLE, MANAGER — TELEPHONE 1 — INDIANAPOLIS, IND.

HORACE M. HADLEY
Insurance, Real Estate, Loan and Rental Agent
66 EAST MARKET STREET,
Telephone 1540. Basement.

Harper Martha (wid Wm), b 27 Spann av.
Harper Mary J (wid Charles A), h 21 Hall pl.
Harper Samuel, h e s Baltimore av 5 n of 22d.
Harper Samuel B, barber, r 226 Roanoke.
Harper Thaddeus S, clk, b 21 Hall pl.
Harper Walter S, trav agt, h 560 Bellefontaine.
Harper Wm, lab, b 23 Mill.
Harper Winfield S, pressman, h 86 Oliver av (W I).
Harr Adolph, violinmkr, b 274 N Liberty.
Harr Charles G, shoemkr, b 274 N Liberty.
Harr John G, h 274 N Liberty.
Harrah Thomas C, grocer, 98 Kappus (W I), h same.
Harrell Adolph, carp, 105 Patterson, h same.
Harrell Charles O, switchman, h 502½ E Washington.
Harrell Isaac B, lab, h 19 Sinker.
Harrell John B (Tolin, Totten, Tibbs & Co), res Fairland, Ind.
Harrell Lewis R, butcher, h 35 Maxwell.
Harrell Ora C, fireman, b 139 English av.
Harrell Wm D, condr, h 11 Shriver av.
Harrigan Cornelius A, grocer, 457 E Georgia, h same.
Harrington, see also Herrington.
Harrington Abraham, plastr, h 5 Everett.
Harrington Belle (wid Wm), h 190½ Indiana av.
Harrington Charles (Harrington & Carlon), h 259 Bellefontaine.
Harrington Charles W, motorman, h 474 E 8th.
Harrington Daniel J, clk, h 197 W Merrill.
Harrington Dennis, boilermkr, h 46 Keystone av.
Harrington Dennis, mach, b 454 Ash.
Harrington Edward H, condr, h 80 Cypress.
Harrington Frederick, stenog Murphy, Hibben & Co, r 76 N East.
Harrington Gibson H, tmstr, h 422 S West.
Harrington Henderson, lab, b 126 N Senate av.
Harrington Humphrey, supt Indpls Chain and Stamping Co, b 454 Ash.

Special Detailed Reports Promptly Furnished by Us.
MERCHANTS' AND MANUFACTURERS' EXCHANGE
J. E. TAKKEN, Manager,
19 Union Building, 73 West Maryland Street.

Harrington James, clk The Indpls Book and Stationery Co, b 454 Ash.
Harrington Johanna (wid Dennis), h 454 Ash.
Harrington John, lab, b 197 W Merrill.
Harrington John, lab, h 264 W 7th.
Harrington John F, lab, b 368 S Missouri.
Harrington Malinda (wid Edward), h 219 Dillon.
Harrington Patrick, h 368 S Missouri.
Harrington Rinaldo, varnisher, h 80 Cypress.
Harrington Rose (wid Charles B), h 11 Margaret.
Harrington Thomas, electrician, r 81 W Georgia.
Harrington Thomas, lab, h 126 N Senate av.
Harrington Thomas, mach hd, h 19 Grant.
Harrington Thomas F, trav agt, h 408 N New Jersey.
Harrington Thomas J, engr, h 62 Woodruff av.
Harrington Timothy, proofreader, b 454 Ash.
Harrington Wm J, saloon, 199 S Capitol av, h same.
Harrington Wilson, janitor, b 230 E Wabash.
HARRINGTON & CARLON (Charles Harrington, Patrick J Carlon), Lawyers, 515-517 Indiana Trust Bldg, Tel 1480.
Harris Ada B, teacher, b 535 W North.
HARRIS ADDISON C, Lawyer, Rooms 1, 2 and 3, Fletcher's Bank Bldg, Tel 134; h 744 N Meridian.
Harris Albert, lab, h 319 Clinton.
Harris Albert E, lab, h 275 S Capitol av.
Harris Anna M (wid Henry C), h 223 N Alabama.
Harris A Myrtle, printer, b 173 W North.
Harris Benjamin F, lab, b 66 N Missouri.
Harris Bert H, train desp I & V Ry, h 1020 N Senate av.
Harris Beverley, barber, 261½ Mass av, h same.
Harris Catherine, h 380 S Delaware.
Harris Charles, r 28½ Mass av.
Harris Charles, porter, r 232 W North.
Harris Charles, scalemkr, b 223 E Market.
Harris Charles A, b 81 Columbia al.
Harris Charles D, carp, b 523 Park av.
Harris Charles H, trav agt, h 47 Ash.
Harris Charles E, carp, 122 Wright, h same.
Harris Charles M, carp, b 72 Pleasant.
Harris Charles O, weigher, h 89 Sanders.
Harris Curtis, porter, r 3 Wood.
Harris David, b 74 Spann av.
Harris David, h 618 W Vermont.
Harris Edward (Harris & Puryear), h 45 Hiawatha.
Harris Edward, bell boy The Bates.
Harris Edward J, lab, b 33 Everett.
Harris Edward, patrolman, h 44 Prospect.
Harris Eli J, mach hd, h 361 Indiana av.
Harris Eliza (wid Charles H), h 341 Cornell av.
Harris Eliza, dressmkr, 191½ Indiana av, h same.
Harris Elizabeth (wid Wm), h 201 W 2d.
Harris Ellsworth B, chemist, b 445 Broadway.
HARRIS EMMA P (Cripe, Harris & Co), Real Estate, 82 Baldwin Blk, h 374 College av.
Harris Eugene F, ins, h 908 N Delaware.

CLEMENS VONNEGUT | CABINET HARDWARE
184, 186 and 192 E. Washington St. | CARVERS' TOOLS. Glues of all kinds.

THE WM. H. BLOCK CO. DRY GOODS, MILLINERY, CLOAKS AND FURS.
7 AND 9 EAST WASHINGTON STREET.

Harris Flora, h 235 W Vermont.
Harris Frank, clk, b 445 Broadway.
Harris Frederick B, lab, b 211 W 2d.
Harris Fremont, lab, h 28 Tacoma av.
Harris George, lab, b 223 E Market.
Harris George, lab, b 338 Martindale av.
Harris George B, painter, b 211 S McLain (W I).
Harris George F, architect, b 445 Broadway
Harris George W, boarding 66 N Missouri, h same.
Harris George W, carp, 70 Pleasant, h same.
Harris Gilbert, bicycle rep, b 53 Holly av (W I).
Harris Harry, lab, h 6 Lafayette.
Harris Harvey T, molder, h 17 Wilcox.
Harris Henry, lab, h 239 W 7th.
Harris Henry J, carp, h 85 Clifford av.
Harris Henry W, shirt mnfr, 277 N East, h same.
Harris Hiram D, foreman, h 74 Spann av.
Harris Isham H, barber, 14 Michigan (H), h 8 Reynolds av (H).
Harris Jacob, shoemkr, 283 E Washington, h same.
Harris James, barber, b 81 Columbia al.
Harris James, porter, b 186 S Illinois.
Harris Jefferson, lab, h 33 Everett.
Harris Jennie (wid Henry C), h 49 Rhode Island.
Harris Jesse, carp, 240 Oliver av (W I), b same.
Harris John C, carp, h 21 Lynn av (W I).
Harris John D, clk, h w s Garfield av 1 n of Washington.
Harris John H, miller, h 75 Miller (W I).
Harris John L, trav agt, r 90½ Mass av.
Harris John M, clk Parry Mnfg Co, b Sherman House.
Harris John T, plastr, h 266 W St Clair.
Harris John W, mason, h w s Brookland av 1 s of Pope av.
Harris Joseph E, contracting agt Union Line, r 79 E Michigan.
Harris Joseph W, casnr N Y Life Ins Co, r 47 The Chalfant.
Harris Joshua F, porter, h 76 Church.
Harris Josiah G, carp, h 634 N Senate av.
Harris Katherine, h 222 W Ohio.
Harris Lee, shoemkr, 193 Mass av, b 520 N New Jersey.
Harris Lewis, hackman, h 223 E Market.
Harris Lou, restaurant, 180 Indiana av, h same.
Harris Louis B, bartndr, h 186 W 2d.
Harris Margaret (wid Wm), h 211 W 2d.
Harris Martin, lab, h 162½ Indiana av.
Harris Mary (wid John), b 200 N West.
Harris Mary A (wid James H), h 200 Oliver av (W I).
Harris Matthew, millwright, h 238 Fayette.
Harris Maxwell G, mach, h 25 King av (H).
Harris Moses, lab, b 162½ Indiana av.
Harris Moses O, carp, h 34 N Brightwood av (B).
Harris Murray P, painter, h 66 Oscar.
Harris Nancy, b 37 Lockerbie.
Harris Nellie H, bkkpr, b 612 College av.
Harris Noah, inventor, h 520 N New Jersey.
Harris Noah L, shoemkr, b 520 N New Jersey.
Harris Oscar C, sawmkr, h 18 Edgewood.
Harris Otto E, pumpmkr, h 406 Martindale av.
Harris Perry S, carp, b 52 S Belmont (W I).
Harris Radford, engr, h 236 W 3d.
Harris Robert, lab, r 1½ Wood.

HEADQUARTERS PHOTOGRAPHIC OUTFITS AMATEUR OR PROFESSIONAL
THE H. LIEBER COMPANY, 33 S. MERIDIAN ST.

Harris Robert, lab, r rear 33 S Alabama.
Harris Robert C, lab, b 49 Rhode Island.
HARRIS ROLLA, Agt Mills & Gibb, Dry Goods, 35 W Pearl and New York City, h 61 Highland Pl.
Harris Samuel P, h 284 E Ohio.
Harris Susannah (wid Matthew J), h 314 Clinton.
Harris Susan J (wid Wm), h 123 Allegheny
Harris Sylvester S, carp, h 72 Pleasant.
Harris Sylvester W, cook Occidental Hotel.
Harris Thomas, plumber, h 216 W 6th.
Harris Thomas J, trav agt, b 105 Andrews.
Harris Thomas M, plumber, h 220 W 6th.
Harris Thomas W, plastr, h 1148 E Ohio.
Harris Wallace, lab, b 162½ Indiana av.
Harris Wallace, lab, h 183 Indiana av.
Harris Walter B, plumber, 1547 N Illinois, h 870 Cornell av.
Harris Warren, lab, h 232 E Wabash.
Harris Wesley, painter, b 284 E Ohio.
Harris Wm, driver, b 223 E Market.
Harris Wm, lab, b 118 S Judge Harding (W I).
Harris Wm A, lab, b 211 S McLain (W I).
Harris Wm B, shoes, 51 W Washington, h 445 Broadway.
Harris Wm H, lab, h 211 W 2d.
Harris Wm H, trav agt, h 552 Broadway.
Harris Wm J, carp, h 191½ Indiana av.
Harris Wm J, casnr Parry Mnfg Co, r 152 N Senate av.
Harris Wm L, engr, h 211 S McLain (W I).
Harris Wm R, plastr, b 1148 E Ohio.
HARRIS & PURYEAR (Edward Harris, John A Puryear), Transfer of Furniture, Pianos, Safes, Etc; also First-Class Storage; 76-78 W New York, Tel 561.
Harrison Albert H, trav agt, h 1213 Northwestern av.
Harrison Allison C, fireman, h 42 N Station (B).
Harrison Benjamin, lab 1036 N Alabama.
Harrison Benjamin, lawyer, 24, 68½ E Market, h 674 N Delaware.
Harrison Benjamin, painter, h 99 Oliver av (W I).

GUIDO R. PRESSLER,
FRESCO PAINTER
Churches, Theaters, Public Buildings, Etc., A Specialty.
Residence, No. 325 North Liberty Street.
INDIANAPOLIS, IND.

INDIANAPOLIS STEEL ROOFING AND CORRUGATING WORKS, 23 and 25 East South Street. S. D. NOEL, Proprietor.

David S. McKernan | REAL ESTATE AND LOANS
Houses, Lots, Farms and Western Lands for sale or trade.
ROOMS 2-5 THORPE BLOCK.

DIAMOND WALL PLASTER { Telephone 1410 BUILDERS' EXCHANGE.

Cor. E. Ohio St. and C., C., C. & St. L. R'y Tracks.
UNION TRANSFER AND STORAGE CO.
ISSUE NEGOTIABLE RECEIPTS ON MERCHANDISE AND H USDH LD GOODS.

W. McWORKMAN,
ROOFING AND CORNICE WORKS,
930 W. Washington St. Tel. 1118.

Harrison Benjamin T, driver, h 252 Fayette.
Harrison Catherine, h 390 N California.
Harrison Catherine (wid Wm C), notions, 144 Blake, h same.
Harrison Charles, lab, h 620 W Udell (N I).
Harrison Charles A (Tobin & Harrison), h 650 N Senate av.
Harrison Charles A, gasfitter, h 234 W 23d.
Harrison Charles B, packer, b 99 Buchanan.
Harrison Charles W, bricklyr, h 22 John.
Harrison Collier, tmstr, h w s James 5 n of Sutherland (B).
Harrison Cornelius, painter, h 167 Virginia av.
Harrison Eliza, h e s Lancaster av 1 n of Clifford av.
Harrison Elizabeth V, stenog Lawyers' Loan and Trust Co, h 501 W 22d.
Harrison George A, molder, h 175 W Michigan.
Harrison George B, waiter Occidental Hotel.
Harrison George W, shoemkr N Y Store, h 204 E Market.
Harrison Hannibal, lab, b e s Lancaster av 1 n of Clifford av.
Harrison Harvey A, motorman, h 6 Allfree av.
Harrison Henry, lab, h 217 N West.
Harrison Jackson, lab, h 37 Rhode Island.
Harrison James (White & Harrison), h 109 John.
Harrison James C Rev, pastor Mt Pilgrim Baptist Church, h 4 Hill.
Harrison James T, carp, h 501 W 22d (N I).
Harrison John G, blksmith, 236 E Michigan, h 341 Columbia av.
Harrison John H, lab, h 4 N Sheffield (W I).
Harrison John H, press agt, b 180 East Drive (W P).
Harrison John J, h 579 N Penn.
Harrison John T, clk, b 143 E Washington.
Harrison John W, barber, b 806 W Washington.
Harrison John W, foreman, h 551 Highland av (N I).
Harrison Katherine, stenog Ry Officials' and Employes' Accident Assn, b 338 N New Jersey.

GEO. J. MAYER,
MANUFACTURER OF
SEALS
STENCILS, RUBBER STAMPS, CHECKS, BADGES, DOOR PLATES, ETC.
15 S. Meridian St., Ground Floor. TEL. 1386.

Harrison Louisa E (wid Thomas J), housekpr 759 N Penn.
Harrison Lucinda (wid James), b 428 W Chicago (N I).
Harrison Lydia B (wid Alfred), h 252 N Meridian.
Harrison Major P, clk, h 78 E Pratt.
Harrison Mary L (wid Francis P), h 382 Indiana av.
Harrison Mary L (wid Walter S), h 126 E Walnut.
Harrison Mertie M, music teacher, h 501 W 22d (N I).
Harrison Minta H (wid Thomas H), b 180 East Drive (W P).
Harrison Nicholas M, trav agt, r 28 The Chalfant.
Harrison Orval D, clk, b 501 W 22d (N I).
Harrison Parker, clk Exchange Hotel (W I).
Harrison Robert, lab, r 66 N Missouri.
Harrison Samuel, lab, h 428 Lafayette.
Harrison Sarah C (wid Alvin C), h w s Maderia 3 s of Prospect.
Harrison Snyder, tmstr, b 290 E Morris.
Harrison Theodore F, real est, h 1598 N Illinois.
Harrison Thomas G, printer and publr Indpls Bulletin, 84 E Court, h 129 Cornell av.
Harrison Tillman W, lab, b 2220 N Illinois.
Harrison Turner, porter, b 390 N California.
Harrison Walter D, painter, h College av nr 21st.
Harrison Wm, lab, h 442 W North.
Harrison Wm, mach hd, h 551 Highland av (N I).
Harrison Wm, tel opr, b 71 Minerva.
Harrison Wm H, janitor, h 316 E Court.
Harirson Wm H, janitor Township Trustee's Office, h 108½ Mass av.
Harritt Herbert T, clk, b n e cor Meridian and 24th.
Harritt Rolla F, florist, E Mkt House, h n e cor Meridian and 24th.
Harrod, see also Herod.
Harrod Clay, clk U S Pension Agency, b 121 E New York.
Harrod George W, engr, b 220 N Missouri.
Harrod Joel E, photog, 62½ Virginia av, h 14 Temple av.
Harrod Sanford L, waiter, r 31 Grand Opera House blk.
Harrod Susan E (wid George), h 27 W Beville av.
Harrold, see also Harold.
Harrold Dennis, flagman, h 32 S McLain (W I).
Harrold Margaret, stenog, b 32 S McLain (W I).
Harrold Patrick J, h 225 S West.
Harrold Thomas F, weighmaster City Hay Market, cor Pine and Washington, b 225 S West.
Harrold Walter L, car rep, b 1 E Sutherland (B).
Harry Charles A, cabtmkr, b 17 Brett.
Harry Thomas J, tmstr, h 17 Brett.
Harry Wm F, cigarmkr, b 17 Brett.
Harryman Emily (wid Elijah), b n w cor Baltimore av and Blackmore.
Harryman Robert M, lab, h 17 Central av.
Harryman Wm P, lab, h 7 Douglass.
Harsch Frederick, h 196 W 22d.
Harsch Frederick jr, gardener, b 196 W 22d.
Harseim Adolph R, trav agt, h 309 S Penn.
Harseim Robert G, overall mnfr, 202 S Meridian, h 590 N Illinois.
Harshman Albert T, condr, h 318 Union.

A. METZGER AGENCY ESTABLISHED 1863. REAL ESTATE

LAMBERT GAS & GASOLINE ENGINE CO.
ANDERSON, IND. GAS AND GASOLINE ENGINES. 2 TO 50 H. P.

Harshman Martin C, lab, b 48 Athon.
Harshman Wm, lab, h 48 Athon.
Harsin Charles, carp, b rear 306 E Louisiana.
Harsin George, carp, h 137 Berlin av.
Harson Charles, carp, b 75 McGinnis.
Harston Albert, instmkr, b 241 S Senate av.
Hart Abigail, teacher Public School No 17, b 188 Douglass.
Hart Alva T, clk, h 682 E Market.
Hart Andrew, bartndr, b 349 E Market.
Hart Andrew T, crier U S Courts, P O bldg, h 401½ N Alabama.
Hart Catherine (wid Thomas D), h 224 S Senate av.
Hart Charles, lab, b 889 Morris (W I).
Hart Charles, lab, h 123½ Oliver av (W I).
Hart Charles H (C H Hart & Co), fruits, 49 E Mkt House, h 294 N California.
Hart Charles R, driver, b 74 Margaret.
Hart Clara J, cook, h 291 E New York.
Hart C H & Co (Charles H Hart, Francis M Ravencraft), butter, 44 E Mkt House.
Hart David, lab, b 150 Madison.
Hart Edward, lab, b 236 N Senate av.
Hart Edward F, driver, h 188 Douglass.
Hart Edward F, pressman, b 224 S Senate av.
Hart Elizabeth (wid Plato), h 42 Mill.
Hart Ella (wid Tubal), h 740 N West.
Hart Ellsworth, lab, b 74 Margaret.
Hart Emanuel, lab, h 251 W 6th.
Hart Emma I, clk, b 282 Lincoln av.
Hart Espanola, stenog, b 682 E Market.
Hart George, foreman, b 342 S Meridian.
Hart George, pdlr, r 149½ Oliver av (W I).
Hart George W, boxmkr, h 193½ S Illinois.
Hart Harry H, lab, b 510 Talbott av.
Hart Harry H, printer, b 110 Bates.
Hart Henry V, musician, h 623 N Capitol av.
Hart Hillie M, lab, b rear 163 St Mary.
Hart Ira, lineman, b 282 W Michigan.
Hart James E, student, b 188 Douglass.
Hart James H, brakeman, b 43 N State av.
Hart James L, lab, b 74 Margaret.
Hart John, packer, h 103 Woodlawn av.
Hart John, well driver, h 510 Talbott av.
Hart John C, shoes, 10 N Penn, h 69 Vine.
Hart John J, well driver, b 510 Talbott av.
Hart John P, bkkpr L E & W R R auditor's office, h 5 West Drive (W P).
Hart John R, bricklyr, h e s Western av 3 n of 22d.
Hart John W (Hart & Schlosser), h 108 College av.
Hart Joseph A, blksmith, h w s Harris av 3 s of C C C & St L Ry (M J).
Hart Lawrence, lineman, h 70 Hosbrook.
Hart Levi, electrician, h 121 Hosbrook.
Hart Lewis, lab, h 345 Jefferson av.
Hart Louisa J (wid P Henry), h 639 E Wabash.
Hart Mary A (wid James T), h 74 Margaret.
Hart Mary A (wid Thomas J), h 27 W 22d.
Hart Matilda (wid Charles), b 377 N West.
HART MILLARD M, Physician, 1550 N Illinois, h same, Tel 1948.
Hart Nellie, b 568 Ash.
Hart Nola, stenog, b 682 E Market.
Hart Oliver S, lab, h 110 Bates.
Hart Patsy A (wid Wm), h 289½ W North.
Hart Samuel T, spl police, h 338 Fletcher av.
Hart Sarah E, dressmkr, 682 E Market, h same.
Hart Simpson T, patrolman, h 297 Indiana av.

Farm and City Loans
25 Years' Successful Business.
THOS. C. DAY & CO,
Rooms 325 to 330 Lemcke Building.

Hart Smith, lab, b 183 Indiana av.
Hart Thomas, h 268 Fletcher av.
Hart Thomas J, plumber, b 224 S Senate av.
Hart Wm, shoes, 460 S Meridian, h same.
Hart Wm F, condr, h 90 Bright.
Hart Wm H, dep Auditor State of Indiana and sec State Board of Tax Commissioners, 38 State House, b The Denison.
Hart W Riley, mngr Occidental Veterinary Remedy Co, 15-17 McNabb, r 28 W New York.
Hart & Schlosser (John W Hart, John Schlosser), shoes, 39 W Washington.
Hartbeck Emma (Baker & Hartbeck), b 140 N Summit.
Hartelt John, lab, b 136 S Summit.
Hartenstein Frederick, mach hd, b 237 E Morris.
Hartenstein Geor e, lab, b 237 E Morris.
Hartenstein Johng lab, h 237 E Morris.
Hartenstein John jr, lab, b 237 E Morris.
Hartenstein Mathias, lab, b 237 E Morris.
Hartenstein Wm, lab, b 237 E Morris.
Harter Andrew, lab, b 70 Downey.
Harter Frederick, driver, r 316½ Virginia av.
Harter James B (Powell & Harter), r 197 N Illinois.
Harter John J, stage hd, r 5 Bates al.
Harter Joseph G, clk W U Tel Co, r 152 N Senate av.
Harter Mary (wid Andrew), h 70 Downey.
Harter Samuel W, motorman, h 950 N New Jersey.
Harter Stephen H, engr, h 80 Springfield.
Hartgen John, mach hd, h 310 S Penn.
Harth Matilda (wid Charles), b 377 N West.
Harting, see also Hartung.
Harting Elizabeth, housekpr, b 1040 N Capitol av.
Harting Engel (wid Frederick), h 62 Russell av.
Harting Ernest, lab, h 145 Harmon.
Harting Frederick H, clk, b 62 Russell av.
Harting Henry, h 363 S Illinois.
Harting John H, mach hd, h 432 W Ontario (N I).

EAT—
HITZ'S CRACKERS
AND CAKES.
ASK YOUR GROCER FOR THEM.

BICYCLES $5 DOWN. $ at Wheels. $ at Terms. MONTHLY. WHEELMEN'S CO. 31 W. OHIO ST. LONG DISTANCE TEL. 1855.

J. H. TECKENBROCK Painter and Decorator, 94 EAST SOUTH STREET.

FIDELITY MUTUAL LIFE—PHILADELPHIA, PA.
MATCHLESS SECURITY At LOW COST. A. H. COLLINS General Agent Baldwin Block.

Rooms 42 and 43 WHEN BUILDING. Miners and Shippers Steam and Domestic Coal. Edwardsport 81 and Mining Co.

ESTABLISHED 1876. TELEPHONE 168.
CHESTER BRADFORD,
SOLICITOR OF PATENTS,
AND COUNSEL IN PATENT CAUSES.
(See adv. page 6.)
Office:—Rooms 14 and 16 Hubbard Block, S. W. Cor. Washington and Meridian Streets,
INDIANAPOLIS, INDIANA.

Hartje John, florist, 1633 N Illinois, b 2 Hanway.
Hartlage Casper, molder, b 39 Vinton.
Hartlage Henry H, molder, h 39 Vinton.
Hartlauf Aloysius, molder, h 98 W Ohio.
Hartlauf John, molder, b 98 W Ohio.
Hartley Benjamin W, bricklyr, h 231 Lincoln la.
Hartley Egbert J, engr, h 43 Helen.
Hartley Frank A, clk, h 65 Harrison.
Hartley James, lab, b 73 Lee (W I).
Hartley James L, carp, h w s Garfield av 2 n of Washington.
Hartley Lovina, h 82 Yandes.
Hartley Thomas S, shoemkr, 107 Harrison, h same.
Hartley Walter N, carp, b w s Garfield av 2 n of Washington.
Hartley Wm B, ins, h 30 N Reisner (W I).
Hartley Wm J, gardener, h rear w s Brightwood av 2 s of Wolf pike (B).
Hartman Albert H, porter, h 46 N State av.
Hartman Ambrose R, tel opr, h 384 Columbia av.
Hartman Anton, carp, h e s Jones 2 s of Central av (I).
Hartman Carl C, sec The Faradizer Co, b 741 E Washington.
Hartman Charles, farmer, h n s Brookville rd 2 w of Line (I).
Hartman Charles C, lab, h 40 Beaty.
Hartman Charles H F, uphlr, h 119 Coburn.
Hartman Christian F, truckman, h 279 E Ohio.
Hartman Christian F W, switchman, h 245½ E Washington.
Hartman Daisy, stenog H E Kinney, b 83 Quincy.
Hartman Edward A, clk, b 279 E Ohio.
Hartman Edwin C, h 429 Park av.
Hartman Edwin M, cigarmkr, b 56 Bradshaw.
Hartman Elmer E, salesman, h 376 Union.
Hartman Frank, canmkr, b 863 S Meridian.
Hartman Frederick (Hartman & Bulmahn), h 479 E Georgia.
Hartman Frederick H, clk The H Lieber Co, b 76 Stevens.

Outing BICYCLES
$85.00.
MADE AND SOLD BY
HAY & WILLITS MFG. CO.
76 N. PENNSYLVANIA ST. PHONE 598.

Hartman Frederick W (Yule & Hartman), h 279 E Ohio.
Hartman George, b 524 S East.
Hartman Harry, checkman, h 62 Lexington av.
Hartman Henry C, dairy, w s LaSalle 1 s of P C C & St L Ry, h same.
Hartman Herman C, city agt Kothe, Wells & Bauer, h 741 E Washington.
Hartman Herman J, bartndr, b 123 N Capitol av.
Hartman James L, carp, h 462½ S Meridian.
Hartman John, lab, h 162½ Indiana av.
Hartman John C, carp, h 353 Coburn.
Hartman John C, clk, h 76 Stevens.
Hartman Mamie L, stenog Am Press Assn, b 56 Bradshaw.
Hartman Margaret (wid Daniel C), h 56 Bradshaw.
Hartman Mary (wid Carl), b 90 Union.
Hartman Nettie (wid Charles), b 1523 N Meridian.
Hartman Patrick, lab, h 66 Park av.
Hartman Peter B, collr H Seyfried, h 182 E Morris.
Hartman Rebecca (wid Matthew), h 233 E Michigan.
Hartman Walter, harnessmkr, h 175 Spring.
Hartman Wm, bartndr, h 431 Charles.
Hartman Wm jr, mach hd, b 431 Charles.
Hartman Wm, farmer, h n w cor Line and Brookville rd (I).
Hartman Wm, motorman, b 69½ W Market.
Hartman Wm C, clk Krull & Schmidt, b w s LaSalle s of P C C & St L Ry.
Hartman Wm H, salesman, h 127 E McCarty.
Hartman Wm J, airbrake instructor, b 230 E North.
Hartman & Bulmahn (Frederick Hartman, Charles Bulmahn), wagonmkrs, 220 E South.
Hartmann August, grocer, 412 N West, h same.
Hartmann Charles, h 196 Coburn.
Hartmann Charles, carp, h 123 Kansas.
Hartmann Charles C L, b n w cor Ohio and Sherman Drive.
Hartmann Charles L (Haueisen & Hartmann), h n w cor Ohio and Sherman Drive.
Hartmann Frank, driver, b 476 E Washington.
Hartmann George, huckster, b 110 Nebraska.
Hartmann George H, clk Bertermann Bros, b n w cor Ohio and Sherman Drive.
Hartmann Joseph F, carp, h 100 Highland av.
Hartmann Oswald, shoemkr, 250 Davidson, b 256 N Pine.
Hartmann Wm F, mach, b 110 Nebraska.
Hartmann Wm V, clk Standard Oil Co, h 8 Lincoln av.
Hartmeyer Charles, carp, b 69 Yeiser.
Hartness Louisa C A, b 134 Union.
Hartnett Edward L, molder, b 284 Blake.
Hartnett Ellen (wid Patrick), h 284 Blake.
Hartpence Alice S (wid George C), h 202 Fayette.
Hartpence Charles W, mach hd, b 202 Fayette.
Hartpence Robert M, car insp, h 68 Fremont av (H).
Hartpence Walter, agt, b 139 N Delaware.
Hartsock Samuel W, plumber, b 45 Cornell av.

C. ZIMMERMAN & SONS SLATE AND GRAVEL ROOFERS 19 South East Street.

DRIVEN WELLS And Second Water Wells and Pumps of all kinds at CHARLES KRAUSS', 42 S. PENN. ST. TELEPHONE 465.

ERTEL STEAM LAUNDRY LARGEST AND BEST IN THE STATE. PROMPT SERVICE. 26 and 28 N. Senate Ave. Telephone 1089.

Hartung, see also Harting.
Hartung Charles E, sawmkr, b 41 Fayette.
Hartung Edward C, electrician, 5 Cyclorama pl, h 476 W Addison (N I).
Hartung Frederica (wid Edward), h 41 Fayette.
Hartub Charles W, lab, h 630 W Eugene (N I).
Hartwell Charles A, agt, h 353 N Illinois.
Hartwig Catherine (wid Henry), h 128 Davidson.
Hartwig George, driver, b 128 Davidson.
Hartwig John, welldriver, h 81 Stevens.
Hartwig John H (Neiger & Hartwig), h 81 Stevens.
Hartwig Wm F, driver, h 162 Fulton.
Hartwig Wm H, lab, h 100 High.
Harty John, mach, r 617 W Francis (N I).
Hartz Joseph F, carver, b 144 N Senate av.
Hartzell Owen F, painter, h 92 Bradshaw.
Hartzell Roger E, mach hd, b 92 Bradshaw.
Hartzog Charles E, paperhngr, h 411 W 22d.
Hartzog Henry S, paperhngr, h 172 E North.
Hartzog John, painter, h 242 W Maryland.
Hartzog Samuel C, h 799 N Capitol av.
Harves Bros (Samuel and Charles), shoemkrs, 235 W Washington.
Harves Charles (Harves Bros), h 432 S Capitol av.
Harves Samuel (Harves Bros), h 434 S Capitol av.
Harvey, see also Hervey.
Harvey Andrew M, carp, h 20 Orange av.
Harvey Annie (wid Wm), h 260 W Washington.
Harvey Carl, lab, b 260 W Washington.
Harvey Carrol, lab, h 445 Columbia av.
Harvey Charles A, mach, b 90 Laurel.
Harvey Charles C, switchman, b 275 Fletcher av.
Harvey Charles W, supreme sec Knights and Ladies of Honor, h 7 Hunter av (I).
Harvey Clara M (wid Wm), b 742 N Senate av.
Harvey Delitha B (wid Thomas B), b 1576 N Meridian.
Harvey Edward Y, mach, h 822 Cornell av.
Harvey Elizabeth (wid Robert), b 24 W 1st.
Harvey Esther, clk, b 369 S Meridian.
Harvey Flora, prin Public School No 35, b 1069 E Michigan.
Harvey Foster W, b e s Shade 2 s of Willow (B).
Harvey Frank C, packer, h 284 Howard.
Harvey Franklin M, driver, h 596 E St Clair.
Harvey George H, mach, h 90 Laurel.
Harvey Harry, lab, h 1129 E Washington.
Harvey Henry, h 890 W Washington.
Harvey Henry H, reg clk P O depot branch, h 150 Hoyt av.
Harvey Horace G, phys, h e s Shade 2 s of Willow (B).
Harvey Irvin A, lab, b 1710 N Meridian.
Harvey Isaac, hostler, h rear 130 E St Joseph.
Harvey James B, trimmer, r 184 Indiana av.
Harvey James T, photog, h 146 Buchanan.
Harvey Jesse B, phys, 152 W 12th, h 1109 N Penn.
Harvey John S, brakeman, h 94 Tremont av (H).
Harvey John W, lab, h 1120 N Delaware.
Harvey John W, lab, h 526 W Maryland.
Harvey John W, trav agt Nichols & Shepard Co, h 53 Oak.
Harvey Lawson M, judge Superior Court, room 2 Court House, h 395 N Alabama.

RICHARDSON & McCREA,
MANAGERS FOR CENTRAL INDIANA.
EQUITABLE LIFE ASSURANCE SOCIETY
Of the United States.
79 EAST MARKET STREET,
TELEPHONE 182.

Harvey Leander, fireman, b 53 Pierce.
Harvey Louis L, lab, b 1710 N Meridian.
Harvey Marcus, gardener, b e s Carter 1 s of 30th.
Harvey Martha (wid Moses B), h 1069 E Michigan.
Harvey Nancy A (wid Wm), r 20 Columbia blk.
Harvey Nancy (wid Marcus P), h 474 W Chicago (N I).
Harvey Other P, r 20 Columbia blk.
Harvey Pauline, h 31 Meek.
Harvey Preston, lab, h 1710 N Meridian.
Harvey Richard, lab, r 33 Cleaveland blk.
Harvey Samuel, lab, h 354 W 22d.
Harvey Samuel E, tmstr, b 354 W 22d.
Harvey Silas L, clk, r 91½ E Court.
Harvey Sophronia (wid Joseph P), b 890 W Washington.
Harvey Thomas, waiter, r 203 N Illinois.
Harvey Thomas H, lab, b 125 Hillside av.
Harvey Thomas H, lab, h 198 Middle.
Harvey Thompson, carp, h 54 N William (W I).
Harvey Wm, h 1129½ E Washington.
Harvey Wm, janitor, r 128 W Vermont.
Harvey Wm A, storekpr P C C & St L Ry, h 53 N State av.
Harvey Wm D, trav agt, h 1247 N Penn.
Harvey Wm L, driver, b 133 Union.
Harvey Wm N, engr, h 52 Rockwood.
Harvie Andrew M, carriagemkr, h e s James 1 s of Sutherland (B).
Harvie George W, clk, h 20 Leonard.
Harwood Emeline L (wid Irvin M), h 76 N Noble.
Harwood Harry C, carp, b 256 Coburn.
Harwood James W, grocer, 2 Howard, h same.
Harwood Wm H, mer police, b 76 N Noble.
Harz Ludwig J, mach hd, h 87 Wisconsin.
Hasely Charles R, lawyer, 15½ Virginia av, r same.
Hasely John G, miller, b 501 S New Jersey.
Hasely Joseph, clk, b 550 S Meridian.
Hasely Minnie E, stenog Indpls Harness Co, b 78 S Linden.

Typewriter-Ribbons
ALL COLORS FOR ALL MACHINES.
THE BEST AND CHEAPEST.
S. H. EAST, STATE AGENT,
The Williams Typewriter....
55 THORPE BLOCK, 87 E. MARKET ST.

ELLIS & HELFENBERGER Architectural Iron Work and Gray Iron Castings. 162-170 South Senate Ave. Tel. 958.

THE HOGAN TRANSFER AND STORAGE COMP'Y
Household Goods and Pianos Moved—Packed—Stored...... Baggage and Package Express Machinery and Safes a Specialty Cor. Washington and Illinois Sts. TELEPHONE No. 675.

The Central Rubber & Supply Co. ◆◆◆◆ Hose, Belting, Packing, Clothing, Druggists' Sundries, Bicycle Tires, Cotton Hose, Etc. New York Belting & Packing Co., L't'd. PHONE 922. 79 S. ILLINOIS ST., INDIANAPOLIS IND.

The Provident Life and Trust Company
Of Philadelphia.
Grants Certificates of Extension to Policyholders who are temporarily unable to pay their premiums
D. W. EDWARDS, Gen. Agt., 508 Indiana Trust Bldg.

Hasenstab Alois, shoemkr, 33 Kennington, b same.
Haskell Joseph E, broker, 19½ N Meridian, h 568 Park av.
Haskell Raymond, student, b 568 Park av.
Haskerl Charles H, shoemkr, 181 Madison av, h same.
Hasket Elijah, pumpmkr, rear 80 S Delaware, h 80½ same.
Haskett Wm, lab, h 417 Columbia av.
Haskins Benjamin, lab, h 2 Darwin.
Haskins Elizabeth (wid Henry J), b 407 Madison av.
Haskins Jennie (wid Simon), h 173 W Wabash.
Haskinson Amy, phys, 138 Mass av, h same.
Haskitt Artemus E, gasfitter, h 16 Sullivan.
Haskitt Charles T, lab, b 83 N Pine.
Haskitt Harry A, lab, b 83 N Pine.
Haskitt Pharrie, stenog, b 66½ N Delaware.
Haskitt Wm W, lab, h 83 N Pine.
Haslep Carrie (wid Henry), h 900 W Washington.
Haslep Marie, phys, 16 The Windsor, h same.
Haslet Josie, printer, r 87 The Windsor.
Haslett Eliza (wid Wm B), b 837 N Capitol av.
Haslinger John B, clk Frederick Riebel, h 186 Clifford av.
Haslinger Joseph F, plumber, 73 Mass av, h 47 Johnson av.
Haslinger Leonard, h 528 E Washington.
Haslop Anna, r 106½ N Meridian.
Haspel Emil G, clk, b 110 Clinton.
Haspel Joseph G, mach, b 110 Clinton.
Haspel Mary (wid Andrew), h 110 Clinton.
Hasse, see also Haase.
Hasse Ferdinand, tailor, h w s James 2 s of Sutherland (B).
Hasse Herman, lab, h e s Rural 4 s of Sutherland (B).
Hasse Reinhold, lab, h 24 Keystone av.
Hasse Theodore, baker, h 286 W Morris.
Hasselberg Henry, huckster, h 28 Springfield.
Hasseld Bettie E, (wid Adelbert), b 204 Fletcher av.

Julius C. Walk & Son, Jewelers Indianapolis. 12 EAST WASHINGTON ST.

Hasseld Jacob J, clk, h rear 31 Clifford av.
Hassell Jennie, h 271 Lafayette.
Hasselman Lewis W, b 100 E Michigan.
Hasselman Otto H, pres Hasselman Printing Co and propr Journal Job Printing Co, 126-130 W Maryland, h 100 E Michigan.
HASSELMAN PRINTING CO, Otto B Hasselman Pres, Printers, Engravers and Etchers, 126-130 W Maryland, Tel 490.
Hasselman Watson J, mach, h e s Central av 2 n of 26th.
Hassey Charles T, paperhngr, h 3 Grove.
Hassler Avery H, bkkpr J M Lilly, h 430 N Capitol av.
Hassler Charles N, bkkpr, h 126 Butler.
Hassler Edward E, polisher, h 329 S Olive.
Hassler Elizabeth (wid David), b 430 N Capitol av.
Hastie Adam, lab, r 77½ S Illinois.
Hastings Annie M (wid Wm), h 125 Lawrence.
Hastings Clara W (wid Lewis), hair goods, 37½ W Washington, h 1315 N New Jersey.
Hastings Ellen C (wid Edwin L), h 550 N Illinois.
Hastings Paul E, clk, b 1315 N New Jersey.
Hastings Robert, meats, 45 E Mkt House, h n s E Ohio nr city limits.
HASTINGS SAMUEL A, Architect, 33 W Market, h 380 E Michigan. (See adv in classified Architects.)
Hastings Wm W, glassblower, b 260 E South.
HASTY GEORGE, Physician; also Editor and Publisher Physio-Medical Journal, 35 W Ohio, h 291 W Michigan.
Hasty George L, attendant Haughville Baths, b 13 Haugh (H).
Hasty Harry M, mach, b rear 347 S Alabama.
Hasty John A, car insp, h 49 Miley av.
Hasty John A, electrician, h rear 347 S Alabama.
HATCH ARETAS W, Lawyer, 14 Talbott Blk, h 84 W 2d.
Hatch George, lab, h 308 W Court.
Hatch Norris R, lab, b 238 W Wabash.
Hatfield Abraham, h 66 Germania av (H).
Hatfield Anna E, teacher, b 33 Broadway.
Hatfield Benjamin, tmstr, h rear 512 W Maryland.
Hatfield Charles C, pres The Indpls District Tel Co, h 435 N Capitol av.
Hatfield Edward E, condr, h e s Denny 2 n of Washington.
Hatfield Emma, dressmkr, h 1 Miller blk.
Hatfield John J B, supt U S Arsenal grounds, h 189 N Arsenal av.
Hatfield John, waiter, r 222 W Maryland.
Hatfield Joseph B, clk, h 33 Broadway.
Hatfield Millard F, truckman, h 360 N Pine.
Hatfield Theodore B, cashr Syerup & Co, b 435 N Capitol av.
Hatfield Wm F, supt letter carriers P O, r 75½ Mass av.
Hathaway Charles A, clk Kingan & Co (ltd), b 50½ N Senate av.
Hathaway Enos W, painter, h 146 Newman.
Hathaway George, porter, b 99 Paca.
Hathaway Harry, bartndr, b 322 E Market.
Hathaway Katie, b 138 Fayette.

OTTO GAS ENGINES | BUILDERS' EXCHANGE S. W. Cor. Ohio and Penn. Telephone 535.

Becker & Son Charles Becker Jacob Becker Jr. Merchant Tailors. 21 N. Penn. St. Tel. 934

SALISBURY & STANLEY • Office, Store and Bank Fixtures a Specialty. Repairing of all kinds done on short notice. 177 Clinton Street, Indianapolis, Ind. • Contractors and Builders TELEPHONE 999.

Hathaway Sol P, propr The Independent, 19 Miller blk, h 89 Highland pl.
Hathaway Wm, painter, h 2 Douglass.
Hathaway Wm H, painter, b 279 W Washington.
Hatler Fred M, lab, h 95 Bismarck av (H).
Hatley Lafayette, painter, h 14 Maria.
Hatley Wm H, lab, h 187 College av.
Hattel Wm, mach, 433 N Illinois.
Hatten Sarah J (wid Thomas H), b 198 Cornell av.
Hattendorf Christian, bricklyr, b 143 Meek.
Hattendorf Henry C, h 61 S Noble.
Hattendorf Walter J, insp, b 61 S Noble.
Hattery Annie (wid Rufus), r 4 Miller blk.
Hatton Abe B, waiter, r 92 W Ohio.
Hatton Benjamin, b n w cor LaSalle and Indiana av (M P).
Hatton Courtney M, finisher, h 393 Mass av.
Hatton Elmaza, h 42½ Mass av.
Hatton George W, grocer, 179 Elm, h same.
Hatton George W jr, patternmkr Indpls Pattern Wks, b 179 Elm.
Hatton John M, real est, h 596 Ash.
Hatton Thomas F, artist, 19 Greer, h same.
Hatton Wade, driver, r 156 W North.
Hatwood Amanda, h 236 W Market.
Haubold Nicholas, bartndr, r 71½ N Illinois.
Haubold Wm E, mngr Hotel Oneida, 114-116 S Illinois.
Haubrich Adam, saloon, 64 N Delaware, h 291 N Noble.
Haubrich Wm C, foreman Levey Bros, b 291 N Noble.
Hauck Albert, baker, b 155 Cornell av.
Hauck August, clk, h 157½ E Washington.
Hauck Edward L, grocer, 441 N Illinois, b 373 N East.
Hauck Frederick H, driver Home Bwg Co, h 83 Harmon.
Hauck John, clk h 373 N East.
Hauck John, stenog, b 155 Cornell av.
Hauck Julius, barber, h 225 Virginia av.
Hauck Lee, tinner, 155 Cornell av.
Hauck Louis, driver, h 297 S Delaware.
Hauck Philip, car rep, h 155 Cornell av.
HAUEISEN WM, Capitalist, Office 167 E Washington, h 297 N Capitol av.
Haueisen Wm C (Haueisen & Co), h 785 N Meridian.
HAUEISEN & HARTMANN (Wm C Haueisen, Charles L Hartmann), Furniture, Carpets, Stoves, Household Goods, Toys and Baby Carriages, 163-169 E Washington, Tel 1724. (See right bottom cor cards.)
Hauenschild Rachel (wid Henry), h 431 Blake.
Haufe Oscar, lab, b 251 W Morris.
Haufe Theodore F, driver, h 49 Elizabeth.
Haufe Walter, baker, b 49 Elizabeth.
Haufler John S, cabtmkr, h 452 Indiana av.
Haufler Wesley, mach, b 226 Fayette.
Haufler Wm F, turner, h 450 Indiana av.
Haug, see also Haag.
Haug August, baker, 421 S Meridian and 135 E Mkt House, h 421 S Meridian.
Haug Catherine (wid Michael G), b 1007 N Capitol av.
Haug Charles G, shoemkr, 102 Ft Wayne av, h 426 E St Clair.
Haug John M Rev, h 140 N Summit.
Haug Rudolph, foreman P Lieber Bwg Co, h 483 Madison av.
Hauger Anna (wid Andrew), b 80 N Senate av.

Henry H. Fay, 40½ E. Washington St., REAL ESTATE, AND LOAN BROKER.

Haugh Alexander W, h 406 S Illinois.
Haugh Benjamin F, vice-pres Haugh-Noelke Iron Wks, res Anderson, Ind.
Haugh Charles E, vice-pres Sentinel Printing Co, b 244 E Vermont.
Haugh Emanuel, h 244 E Vermont.
Haugh Emma, h 77 Kentucky av.
Haugh George W, molder, h 300 Michigan (H).
Haugh J Guy, trav agt Paul H Krauss, r 136 E New York.
Haugh Lawrence, mach, b 68 Miley av.
Haugh-Noelke Iron Works, Frederick Noelke pres, Benjamin F Haugh vice-pres, Christian F H Waterman sec and treas, founders, cor Palmer and J M & I R R.
Haugh Wm, bookbndr, b 244 E Vermont.
Haughey Hannah C, h n e cor Senate av and 30th (M).
Haughey James W (Haughey & Coleman), b 68 N Liberty.
Haughey Joseph, lab, h 430 Muskingum al.
HAUGHEY & COLEMAN (James W Haughey, Richard M Coleman), Lawyers, 48 Thorpe Blk.
Haught Frank E, engr, h 1732 Graceland av.
Haught James H, engr Wm B Burford, h 63 Pleasant.
Haught John M, b 1738 Graceland av.
HAUGHVILLE MINERAL WELL AND BATH HOUSE, Matthew H Harmon Propr, w s Holmes av 1 s of Michigan (H). (See adv in classified Baths.)
Hauhn Clyde T, condr, b 87 Cornell av.
Hauhn Frank J, carp, h 87 Cornell av.
Hauk, see also Hawk and Houk.
Hauk Charles A, driver, b 289 Virginia av.
Hauk John, roller, b 187 S Capitol av.
Hauk John A, carp, h 873 Cornell av.
Hauk Mary A, b 477 Ash.
Hauk Ralph F, insp, h 597 W Shoemaker (N I).
Hauk Wm B, trav agt, h 664 Broadway.
Haulter August, butcher, h 243 N West.

MAYHEW'S
SPECTACLES
THE BEST IN USE
SOLD ONLY AT 13 N. MERIDIAN ST.

COAL AND LIME Cement, Hair, Sewer Pipe, etc. BALKE & KRAUSS CO. Cor. Missouri and Market Sts.

FRIEDGEN'S IS THE PLACE FOR THE NOBBIEST SHOES
Ladies' and Gents' 19 North Pennsylvania St.

SAMUEL LAING | COPPER AND GALVANIZED IRON CORNICE MANUFACTURER
72 AND 74 E. COURT STREET. SKYLIGHTS AND VENTILATORS.

M. B. WILSON, Pres. W. F. CHURCHMAN, Cash.
THE CAPITAL NATIONAL BANK,
INDIANAPOLIS, IND.
Our Specialty is handling all Country Checks and Drafts on Indiana and neighboring States at the very lowest rates. Call and see us.
Interest Paid on Time Deposits.
28 S. MERIDIAN ST., COR. PEARL.

Haulter George A, b 243 N West.
Haunss Frederick, baker, 363 Shelby, h same.
Haupt Karl, sec Indpls Planing Mill Co, h 75 Oriole.
Haus Ann (wid Gustav), b 104 Davidson.
Hauschild Charles, printer, b 415 S West.
Hausdorfer Paul B, mach, h 174 S Noble.
Hause James C, porter, h 465 Mulberry.
Hause Joshua F, lab, h 115 Sharpe av (W).
Hause Wm A, tmstr, h 296 S East.
Hauser, see also Houser.
Hauser Albert, gardener, h 168 Bismarck av (H).
Hauser Albert jr, clk, b 168 Bismarck av (H).
Hauser Anna (wid Gustav), h 114 Buchanan.
Hauser Benjamin, lab, b 168 Bismarck av (H).
Hauser Conrad, patrolman, h 300 Wright.
Hauser Frank, stairbuilder, h 124 E Merrill.
Hauser Frank S, lab, b 168 Bismarck av (H).
Hauser Frederick, packer, h 538 S New Jersey.
Hauser George, molder, h 965 S East.
Hauser Jacob, lab, h 58 W Raymond.
Hauser Kate (wid James C), h 184 Meek.
Hauser Ora C, cooper, b 184 Meek.
Hauser Romeo, clk, b 124 E Merrill.
Hauser Scott S, driver, b 184 Meek.
Hauser Wm, lab, b 168 Bismarck av (H).
Hauss Philip J, h 481 N Senate av.
Hausser Charles, h 185 Spann av.
Hausser Charles, tinner, h 167 S Olive.
Havekotte George, carp, h 15 Cincinnati.
Havelick Pearl A (F M Snyder & Co), sec John C Wright, h 892 N Penn.
Havens Frank M, condr, h 623 N Illinois.
Havens Henry, coachman 134 N Meridian.
Havens John, lab, h 55 Elm.
Havens Sophie L (wid George W), b 497 Mulberry.
Haverfield Charles K, train desp P & E Ry, r 151 N Alabama.
Haverkamp Benjamin, clk, b 129 N Dorman.

TUTTLE & SEGUIN,
28 E. Market St. Ground Floor.
COLLECTING RENTS AND CARE OF PROPERTY
A SPECIALTY.
Telephone 1168.

Haverstick Charles, carp, h 156 Clarke.
Haverstick Charles N, lab, h 111 S Reisner (W I).
Haverstick George E, bookbndr Wm B Burford, h 114 Clifford av.
Haverstick George T, lab, h 347 N Noble.
Haverstick George W, lab, b 21 Lynn av (W I).
Haverstick Jackson H, car rep, h 96 Kappus (W I).
Haverstick James M, carver, b 347 N Noble.
Haverstick James M, paperhanger, b 156 Clarke.
Haverstick Robert L, condr, h 254 Howard (W I).
Haverstick Wm F, bookbndr Wm B Burford, b 347 N Noble.
Havey Wm J, foreman Am Press Assn, h 240 S Missouri.
Havice James B, opr W U Tel Co, b 174 N Illinois.
Havlin Carl E, coremkr, b 19 Bridge (W I).
Havlin Joseph F, molder, h 19 Bridge (W I).
Hawekotte George H, clk Francke & Schindler, h 485 S Illinois.
Hawekotte Harry G (Potter & Hawekotte), h 127 Union.
Hawes Charles L, grocer, 115 Birch av (W I), h same.
Hawes John, lab, b 65 N Dorman.
Hawes Judson S, yeast, 11 N Alabama, h 515 Ash.
Hawes Martha (wid Edward), h 65 N Dorman.
Hawk Clark J, carp, h 611 Bellefontaine.
Hawk Frank B, driver, b 206 W Walnut.
Hawk Frederick A, switchman, b 90 S East.
Hawk James S, driver, h 294 W St Clair.
Hawk Kate (wid George), h 90 S East.
Hawk Wm, lab, h 330 S Missouri.
Hawk Wm, wagonmkr, h 206 W Walnut.
Hawk Wm F, b 90 S East.
Hawke Joseph E, millwright, h 86 Nordyke av (W I).
Hawkey Stanton W, contr, h 1181 N Illinois.
Hawkins Caroline (wid Reason), b 27 Centennial.
Hawkins Charles N, bkkpr D H Baldwin & Co, b 258 N East.
Hawkins David, cook The Denison.
Hawkins David A, oils, h 390 E Market.
Hawkins Dillard, lab, b 27 S Dorman.
Hawkins Donald, student, b 374 Broadway.
Hawkins Edward, cook The Denison.
Hawkins Edward, lab, b 388 Clinton.
HAWKINS EDWARD, Treas and Genl Mngr Indiana School Book Co and Receiver Indianapolis National Bank, 605-607 Indiana Trust Bldg, Tel 35; h 374 Broadway.
Hawkins Edward W, tmstr, h 115 Martindale av.
Hawkins Edward W jr, pdlr, b 115 Martindale av.
Hawkins Ella, h 262 N East.
Hawkins Elmer D, attendant Insane Hospital.
Hawkins Elvina, dressmkr, 390 E Market, h same.
Hawkins Epha A (wid John S), h 50 Eureka av.
Hawkins Frank L, foreman, h 28 W 22d.
Hawkins Frank M, carp, h 258 N East.
Hawkins George E, molder, b 117 Blake.
Hawkins George M, broker, 308 Lemcke bldg, h 1010 N Penn.
Hawkins George S, engr Brinker & Habeney, h 199 N East.

PAPER BOXES SULLIVAN & MAHAN 41 W. Pearl St.

DIAMOND WALL PLASTER { Telephone 1410 BUILDERS' EXCHANGE.

If your Laundry Work is not satisfactory, try THE HOME LAUNDRY 197 S. Illinois St. Phone 1769.

Hawkins Harry L, tinner, h 356 E Market.
Hawkins Harry R, lather, b 50 S Belmont (W I).
Hawkins Harry W, broommkr, b 262 N East.
Hawkins Harry W, nurse, b 258 N East.
Hawkins Isaiah, lab, h rear 738 N West.
Hawkins James H, engr, h 80 Highland pl.
Hawkins Jennie E, dressmkr 199 N East, b same.
Hawkins Jesse F, grocer, 50 S Belmont av (W I). h same.
Hawkins Jessie L, b 258 N East.
Hawkins John, lab, b 334 W Court.
Hawkins John, lab, h 125 Ft Wayne av.
Hawkins John, roofer, b 328 W Pearl.
Hawkins Joseph, h 199 N East.
Hawkins Joseph E, pressman, b 909 N New Jersey.
Hawkins Lillie M (wid Thomas S), h 54 Eureka av.
Hawkins Lloyd L, carpetlyr, r 127½ E Washington.
Hawkins Mary A (wid Willis), b 17 Howard.
Hawkins Matilda M (wid Henry), h 452 S Meridian.
Hawkins Nancy (wid John), b 83 E Michigan.
Hawkins Nora O, stenog I D & W Ry, b 390 E Market.
Hawkins Reuben L, millwright, b 125 Woodlawn av.
Hawkins Robert, mngr Compton, Ault & Co, 82 S Penn, h 119 Dougherty.
Hawkins Rollin, tinner, h 34 Ramsey av.
Hawkins Roscoe O (Hawkins & Smith), h 376 N Capitol av, tel 1084.
Hawkins Samuel, blksmith, 185 Prospect, h 480 Virginia av.
Hawkins Sarah C, h rear 624 Home av.
Hawkins Susan J (wid Alexander S), h 190 Prospect.
Hawkins Theron G, clk Indpls Gas Co, r 376 N Capitol av.
Hawkins Thomas E, blksmith, h 213 Douglass.
Hawkins Wm H, lab, h 102 Drake.
Hawkins Wm H, U S Marshal, 29½ N Penn, h 322 N New Jersey.
Hawkins Wm M (Hawkins & Shaw), h Sherman House.
HAWKINS & SHAW (Wm M Hawkins, Alphonso Shaw), Proprs Sherman House, n e cor Louisiana and McCrea, Tel 1900.
HAWKINS & SMITH (Roscoe O Hawkins, Horace E Smith), Lawyers, 303-308 Lemcke Bldg, Tel 39.
Hawley Chauncey H, tmstr, h 135 S Summit.
Hawley Fred, lab, b 15 Sample (W I).
Hawley Mary, h 37 Oriental.
Hawley Mittie N (wid Austin S), b 68 E Pratt.
Hawn Albert C, engr, h 69 N Olive.
Hawn Cynthia J, h 195 College av.
Haworth Albert C, butter, 38 E Mkt House, h 165 N Alabama.
Haworth Nancy (wid Edward), b 123 Hill av.
Hawthorn Charles E, h 58½ W Ohio.
Hawthorne John W, clk Lay & McCaffrey, b s s Washington 5 w of Harris av (M J).
Hay Campbell C, ins, b 324 Park av.
Hay Charles L, trav agt, h 604 E Washington.
Hay Frank G, supt mail dept The Indpls News, h 795 College av.

FRANK NESSLER. WILL H. ROST.
FRANK NESSLER & CO.
Tailors
56 EAST MARKET ST. (Lemcke Building),
INDIANAPOLIS, IND.

HAY FRANK M, Justice of the Peace, 80½ E Market, Tel 169; h 79 Woodlawn av.
Hay George, clk, b 27 W 2d.
Hay James, lab, h 259 Lincoln la.
HAY LINN D, Lawyer, 307-309 Indiana Trust Bldg, r 251 N Meridian.
Hay Pliny, lab, b s s E Washington 4 e of Belt R R.
Hay Thomas J, pres The Hay & Willits Mnfg Co, b 79 Woodlawn av.
Hay Varo E, lab, h 541 S State av.
Hay Wm H, clk Hildebrand Hardware Co, h 27 W 2d.
Hay Wm H jr, clk, b 27 W 2d.
HAY & WILLITS MANUFACTURING CO THE, Thomas J Hay Pres, George H Evans Sec and Treas, V Burton Willits Mngr, Bicycle Mnfrs and Dealers in Bicycle Sundries and Sporting Goods, Office and Sales Room 76 N Penn, Tel 598; Factory cor Vorster av and Belt R R, Tel 1766. (See left bottom cor cards.)
Hayden, see also Haden and Heydon.
Hayden Ambrose, lab, h 9 Church.
Hayden Anna, r 249½ W Washington.
Hayden Benjamin F, h 185 Newman.
Hayden Capitola C (wid John F), h 140 Agnes.
Hayden Charles H (Hayden & Spann), b 182 S New Jersey.
Hayden Emma L (wid John C), boarding 182 S New Jersey.
Hayden Harry, driver, b 191 Bell.
Hayden Lucinda, teacher Public School No 40, h 199 Martindale av.
Hayden Martha E, h 184 Newman.
Hayden Moses, lab, h 400 E Georgia.
Hayden Richard, lab, r 182 W Market.
Hayden Wm, lab, h 199 Martindale av.
Hayden & Spann (Charles H Hayden, Charles B Spann), proprs North Side Furniture Co, 72 Indiana av.
Haydon Elizabeth A (wid Benjamin), h 277½ Mass av.

Haueisen & Hartmann
163-169 E. Washington St.
FURNITURE,
Carpets,
Household Goods,
Tin, Granite and China Wares, Oil Cloth and Shades

THE WM. H. BLOCK CO. DRY GOODS, MEN'S FURNISHINGS.
7 AND 9 EAST WASHINGTON STREET.

The Fidelity and Deposit Co. OF MARYLAND. Bonds signed for Administrators, Assignees, Executors, Guardians, Receivers, Trustees, and persons in every position of trust.
GEO. W. PANGBORN, General Agent, 704-706 Lemcke Building. Telephone 140.

INSURE YOUR PROPERTY WITH FRANK K. SAWYER

•JOSEPH GARDNER•
GALVANIZED IRON
CORNICES and SKYLIGHTS.
Metal Ceilings and Siding.
Tin, Iron, Steel and Slate Roofing.
37, 39 & 41 KENTUCKY AVE. Telephone 322.

Haydon Leonidas M, express, h 9 Valley Drive.
Hayes, see also Hays.
Hayes Aaron, mach, h 3 Lynn.
Hayes Abiah, polisher, b 268 W Court.
Hayes Amanda (wid Philip), h 1381 N Senate av.
Hayes Anna, b 1381 N Senate av.
Hayes Austin B, draughtsman Nordyke & Marmon Co, h 48 N William (W I).
Hayes Clinton T, plumber, h 436 W North.
Hayes Cornelius A, bkkpr Nelson Morris & Co, b 240 Virginia av.
Hayes Daniel R, lab, h 11 Langley av.
Hayes Frank J, steamfitter, h 348 Douglass.
Hayes Frederick, gilder, b 70 Bicking.
Hayes George C, tmstr, h 1358 N Senate av.
Hayes George W, mach, h 8 Crawford.
Hayes Gertrude E, b 923 Shelby.
Hayes Gibbie, lab, b 159 W Merrill.
Hayes Herbert P, clk, r 76 W Walnut.
Hayes Hiram, lab, h 258 Alvord.
Hayes Horace, hostler, h 102 N Missouri.
Hayes James W, brakeman, b 5 S Station (B).
Hayes John, cook The Denison.
Hayes John, mach, b 103 English av.
Hayes John, lab, b 63 Fletcher av.
Hayes John, lab, h 11 Meikel.
Hayes John, lab, h 166 Osage.
Hayes Joseph, clk, b rear 236 S Missouri.
Hayes Joseph H, tinner, h rear 136 N Liberty.
Hayes Joseph H, h 286 W Court.
Hayes Joseph R, condr, h 276 W New York.
Hayes Leona D, stenog, b 276 W New York.
Hayes Lewis C, drugs, 152 Indiana av, h same.
Hayes Margaret (wid Patrick), b 12 Henry.
Hayes Michael, lab, h rear 236 S Missouri.
Hayes Oliver, sawmkr, h 41 Benton.
Hayes Orison H, student, b 276 W New York.
Hayes Patrick, lab, h 76 Bates.
Hayes Robert, lab, h 158 English av.
Hayes Sallie T, nurse, b 28 S Reisner (W I).
Hayes Thomas (Hayes & Ready), h w s Shelby 1 mile s of Belt R R, tel 592.

J. S. FARRELL & CO.
Have Experienced Workmen and will Promptly Attend to your
PLUMBING
Repairs. 84 North Illinois Street. Telephone 382.

Hayes Wm, artist, b 88 W Ohio.
Hayes Wm, lab, h 1036 S Meridian.
Hayes Wm A, gilder, h w s Rural 6 n of S Brookside av.
Hayes Wm A, trav agt Van Camp H and I Co, h 63 The Blacherne.
Hayes Wm W, driver J M Lilly, b 268 W Court.
HAYES & READY (Thomas Hayes, Michael J Ready), Wholesale Liquors, 123 S Meridian, Tel 421.
HAYLER GEORGE W, District Pass Agt C H & D R R and L N A & C Ry, 2 W Washington, Tel 737; h 244 N Alabama.
Haymaker Ira P, trav agt, b 158 S Judge Harding (W I).
Haymaker Robert L, lab, h 185 Minnesota.
Haymond Frederick, mach hd, h 223 English av.
Haymond George L, h 533 Ash.
Haymond Harry, millwright, h 177 Spann av.
Haymond Henry D, clk, h 21 Ketcham.
Haymond Norman, student, b 21 Ketcham.
Haynes, see also Haines.
Haynes Aurelia K (wid Washington), b 242 Central av.
Haynes Charles, mach hd, h 820 Chestnut.
Haynes Charles H, mach hd, b 128 Dougherty.
Haynes Cyrus, porter, h 114 Trowbridge.
Haynes Edward J, lab, h 460 Union.
Haynes Frederick E, lineman, b 214 Blake.
Haynes George T, ins, r 221 N Capitol av.
Haynes George W, huckster, h 30 Evison.
HAYNES HORACE F, Restaurant, 62 N Penn and 72 N Delaware, h 222 N Delaware.
Haynes James, lab, h 22 Shelby.
Haynes James F, nailer, b 128 Dougherty.
Haynes Jefferson, porter, h 173 Patterson.
Haynes John R, phys, 264 N Illinois, h same.
Haynes Milton P, mach hd, h 78 Dugdale.
Haynes Robert, h 62 Spann av.
Haynes Thomas H, clk, h 214 Blake.
Haynes Wm A, welldriver, h 20 N West.
Haynes Wm H, phys, 2 Chislett blk, h 48 Hall pl.
Haynes Zachariah, lab, h 128 Dougherty.
Hays, see also Hayes.
Hays Anna L (wid Wm L), clk Julius C Walk & Son, h 238 N Delaware.
Hays Arthur D, bricklyr, b 36 S Capitol av.
Hays Benjamin F, carp, h 123 S Reisner (W I).
Hays Carl J, clk, b 16 Stevens pl.
Hays Charles A, electrician, b 223½ E North.
Hays Charles S, lunch counter, 178 S Illinois, h 23 Roanoke.
Hays Elsie C, h 273 W Market.
Hays Flora, agt, b 56 William (W I).
Hays Flora (wid Wiley G), b 516 N Senate av.
HAYS FRANKLIN W, Physician, Office Hours 9-10 A M and 12-1 P M, Sundays 12-1 P M, 19 E Ohio, h same, Tel 44.
Hays George E, doorkpr Park Theater, h 456 Indiana av.
Hays Hayden, porter, r 63 Drake.
Hays Isaac C, ins, h 340 N Alabama.
Hays James, lab, h w s Earhart 5 s of Prospect.
Hays Jane (wid Allen), h 252 Howard (W I).

GUARANTEED INCOME POLICIES issued only by the United States Life Insurance Co.
E. B. SWIFT, Manager. 25 E. Market St.

Furniture Carpets } WM. KOTTEMAN { Stoves Ranges
89 and 91 East Washington Street. Telephone 1742.

Hays John, lab, r rear 175 N Penn.
Hays John, lab, r 169 W Wabash.
Hays Leslie, porter, h 41 Roanoke.
Hays Lewis O, lab, h rear 569 E Washington.
Hays Louella, dresmkr, 16 Stevens pl, b same.
Hays Mary H (wid Simeon B), h 16 Stevens pl.
Hays Minnie W, nurse, 223½ E North, b same.
Hays Robert H, clk, b 275 E Walnut.
Hays Philonides, trav agt, h 432 W Ontario (N I).
Hays Roxanna (wid John), b 20 LaSalle.
Hays Solomon, h 1122 N Meridian.
Hays Tabitha (wid Simeon B), b 6 Emerson pl.
Hays Walter, asst mngr Model Clothing Co, b 1122 N Meridian.
Hays Walter W, teacher, b 143 N Alabama.
Hays Wm M, car rep, b 252 Howard (W I).
Hays Wm O, clk County Auditor, b 238 N Delaware.
Hays Zachariah, lab, h 258 Howard (W I).
Hayward James E, lab, b 336½ E Washington.
Hayward James L, hostler, h 336½ E Washington.
Haywood Alfred, artificial limbs, 61 S Illinois, h 310 E New York.
Haywood Augustus, lab, h 319 Clinton.
Haywood Bennett, lab, h 184 Bismarck av (H).
Haywood David A, contr, 302 Park av, b same.
Haywood Henry B, spl agt Hartford Fire Ins Co, b The Dennison.
Haywood Shepard, lab, h 270 Yandes.
Haywood Wm A, porter, h 319 Clinton.
Hayworth Jacob L, tilemkr, h 247 W 7th.
Hayworth Lindley, lab, h 245 W 7th.
Hayworth Milton D, clk The Progress Clothing Co, r 31½ Indiana av.
Hayworth Wm, brakeman, b 23 Poplar (B).
Hayworth Wm, lab, b 106 Bates.
Hayworth Wm E, lab, b 245 W 7th.
Hazell Margaret E, h 104 Geisendorff.
Hazelrigg Albert W, clk Cerealine Mnfg Co, h 642 E Ohio.
Hazelrigg Anna D (wid Wm N), h e s Central av 1 n of 30th.
Hazelrigg Charles, brakeman, h 1 Traub av.
Hazelrigg Ida M, b 263 S Penn.
Hazelrigg James M, condr, h 475 E 8th.
Hazelrigg Thomas H, supt of agts Home Savings Assn, h 483 W 31st.
Hazelrigg Wm, h 264 Springfield.
Hazelrigg Wm, condr, h 255 Springfield.
Hazelwood Charles H, lab, h rear 1379 N Senate av.
Hazen Annie T (wid George), h 1507 N Illinois.

HAZEN CO THE, John F Hazen Pres, Steel and Iron Factors, 807 Majestic Bldg, Tel 73.

Hazen George W, motorman, h 78 W 12th.
Hazen John F, vice-pres The American Tin Plate Co and pres The Hazen Co, b The Denison.
Hazleton Elizabeth E, phys, 4 Ash, h same.
Hazleton Frederick Q, phys, 4 Ash, h same.
Hazlett America, b 4 Ruckle.
Hazlett Douglass, tel opr, b 174 N Illinois.
Hazlett John D, mach, b 139 N Delaware.
Hazlett Josephine, milliner, r 103 The Shiel.

We Buy Municipal
~ Bonds ~
THOS. C. DAY & CO,
Rooms 325 to 330 Lemcke Bldg.

Hazlewood Susan (wid John), h 680 W Vermont.
Hazley George, lab, b 501 S New Jersey.
Hazzard Belle (wid Wesley), h 574 N Senate av.
Head Clarence, lab, b 254 W 5th.
Head Cloyd J, trav agt, h 434 Central av.
Head Johanna (wid John), b 218 W 8th.
Head John E, lab, h 218 W 8th.
Head Mary (wid Elias), h 97 Yandes.
Head Wm E, lab, b 218 W 8th.
Headen Charles M, blksmith, h 322 Hillside av.
Headley James R, molder, h 225 Summit (H).
Headley Joseph E, bkkpr, r 16 W Michigan.
Headspeth John, tmstr, h 26 Hiawatha.
Heady James M, clk N Y Store, r 265 N Illinois.
Heady Joseph P, lab, b 328 E Washington.
Heady Nancy, h 121 W Maryland.
Heagan Joel W, lab, b 316 E Court.
Heagan Samuel S, lab, b 316 E Court.
Heagy Charles F, designer, b 803 E Washington.
Heagy Stephen J, painter, b 233 N Beville av.
Heal Daniel, pedlr, r 76 S Missouri.
Heal Wm C, modelmkr, h 438 E St Clair.
Healey, see also Haley.
Healey Daniel J, pressman, b 194 Dougherty.
Healey James, city fireman, h 481 S Capitol av.
Healey James H, mach, h 345 N Pine.
Healey James J, condr, b 267 S Senate av.
Healey John, lab, b 18 Meikel.
Healey John E, barber, b 194 Dougherty.
Healey John T, lab, h 40 Geisendorff.
Healey Joseph J, condr, h 239 W South.
Healey Margaret (wid Dennis), h 267 S Senate av.
Healey Martin W, letter carirer P O, h 73 W 2d.
Healey Mary (wid Oliver), h 194 Dougherty.
Healey Mary (wid Thomas), b 481 S Capitol av.
Healey Maurice, porter, h 219 Dougherty.

EAT
HITZ'S
CRACKERS
AND CAKES.
ASK YOUR GROCER FOR THEM.

WILLIAM WIEGEL } MANUFACTURER OF.... } SHOW CASES { 6 W. Louisiana St. Opposite Union Station.

TURKISH RUGS AND CARPETS RESTORED TO ORIGINAL COLORS LIKE NEW | Capital Steam Carpet Cleaning Works M. D. PLUNKETT, Telephone 818

BENJ. BOOTH PRACTICAL EXPERT ACCOUNTANT. Books Opened, Written Up, Posted and Balanced. Room 18, 82½ E. Washington St., Indianapolis, Ind.

18 and 20 S. MERIDIAN STREET

ESTABLISHED 1876. TELEPHONE 168.
CHESTER BRADFORD,
SOLICITOR OF PATENTS,
AND COUNSEL IN PATENT CAUSES.
(See adv. page 6.)
Office:—Rooms 14 and 16 Hubbard Block, S. W. Cor. Washington and Meridian Streets, INDIANAPOLIS, INDIANA.

Healey Maurice F, bookbndr, b 194 Dougherty.
Healey Maurice F, city fireman, b 219 Dougherty.
Healey Oliver P, bookbndr, h 154 Dougherty.
Healey Thomas, fireman, b 481 S Capitol av.
Healey Wm A, clk Hayes & Ready, b 267 S Senate av.
Healy Allen, cigarmkr, h 100 Spring.
Healy Alonzo F, lab, b 100 Spring.
Healy Anna (wid James), h 288 W Maryland.
Healy Cornelius, lab, b 72 English av.
Healy Edward, engr, b 451 E Georgia.
Healy James M (Healy & O'Brien), h 439 Central av.
Healy James P, lab, b 288 W Maryland.
Healy Thomas, bricklyr, b 251 W Morris.
Healy Wm, engr, h 144 S Summit.
Healy Wm, porter, h 359 N Pine.
Healy Wm M, agt, h 539 Madison av.
Healy & O'Brien (James M Healy, Michael O'Brien), plumbers, 57 W Maryland.
Heard Charles R, porter, b 924 Morris (W I).
Heard John, real est, 924 Morris (W I), h same.
Heard Robert, carriage trimmer, r 285 S Illinois.
Heard Wm, driver, b 74 Willow.
Hearden Thomas, h 237 W Vermont.
Hearne Charles, barber, h 533½ Virginia av.
Hearne Edward L, masseur, h 860 LaSalle.
Hearne Elizabeth (wid John), b 277 S Penn.
Hearne Harry S, brakeman, h 41 English av.
Hearne Oscar S, brakeman, b 44 Lord.
Hearne Wm H, clk, h 13 Minerva.
Hearsey Henry T (H T Hearsey Cycle Co), h 1179 N Illinois.
HEARSEY H T CYCLE CO (Henry T Hearsey), 116-118 N Penn, Tel 1610.
Heart Henry, barber, 100 E Market, h 42 N New Jersey.
Heart Sarah, boarding 42 N New Jersey.
Heater David P, waiter, r 283 Chapel.

O. B. ENSEY
MANUFACTURER OF
GALVANIZED IRON CORNICE, SKYLIGHTS AND WINDOW CAPS.
TELEPHONE 1562. Cor. 6th and Illinois Sts.

Heath Amos R, carp, h 68 Ludlow av.
Heath Benjamin F, carp, h 220 Hoyt av.
Heath Charles, lab, r 219 Mass av.
Heath Corydon A, mdse broker, 37 E Maryland, h 177 Christian av.
Heath Elizabeth (wid Lorraine B), h 100 Wright.
Heath Frank B, carp, h 529 W Eugene (N I).
HEATH FREDERICK C, Physician (Eye and Ear), 19 W Ohio, h 78 W 3d.
Heath Jasper H, carp, h 3 Sylvan.
HEATH SAMUEL, Laundry, 147 Mass av, h 506 Bellefontaine.
Heath Sarah C, h 177 Christian av.
Heath Wilfred J, clk, b 61 Minerva.
Heath Wm A, butter, 29 S Delaware, b 635 College av.
Heath Wm H, b 310 E New York.
Heath Wm R, tmstr, h 1052 S Meridian.
Heathco Emanuel F, carp, h 1530 N Capitol av.
Heathcote Eleanor (wid George), h 177 Columbia av.
Heaton Daniel W, r 115 Hosbrook.
Heaton Ebenezer H, engr, h 126 Dougherty.
Heaton Emily (wid John), b s e cor Keystone and S Brookside avs.
Heaton Esther A (wid Edgar R), h 292 E Michigan.
Heaton John M, condr, h 48 Temple av.
Heaton Robert S, clk, h 24 Ft Wayne av.
Heaton Sarah J (wid David), b 184 Blackford.
Heaton, Sims & Co (Wait M Heaton, John M Sims), whol jewelers, 17 W Maryland.
Heaton Wait M (Heaton, Sims & Co), res Knightstown, Ind.
Heave Frank, teacher, r 70 W Walnut.
Hebble Catherine (wid Musser B), h 92 E South.
Hebble Christian G, bottler, b 92 E South.
Hebble Frank W, meats, 252 Indiana av, h 398 N California.
Hebble George M, music teacher, 398 N California, b same.
Hebble Hannah (wid John W), h 398 N California.
Heber Elizabeth, teacher Public School No 4, b 59 Woodlawn av.
Heber Julia (wid Oscar), h 182 Harmon.
Heber Mary B (wid Jedidiah), h 67 Middle Drive (W P).
Hebert Octave, tailor, r 262 N Alabama.
Hebron Ellen (wid Patrick), h 60 Columbia av.
Hebron Patrick F, yardman, b 60 Columbia av.
Hecathorn Seymour S, lab, h 579 W 22d (W I).
Hechinger Joseph, butcher, b 73 Kansas.
Hechinger Louis, lab, b 279 S West.
Hechinger Michael, carp, h 73 Kansas.
Hecht Albert, lab, b 313 E Washington.
Hecht Wolff, solr N Y Life Ins Co, h 401 N New Jersey.
Hechtmann Gustav, baker, b 135 E Washington.
Heck Charles E, lab, h 69 Rockwood.
Heck Charles J, waiter, b 50 Pendleton av (B).
Heck Harry, h 69 Rockwood.
Heck John A, lab, r 193 S Alabama.
Heck John P, flagman, h 48 S Brightwood av (B).

THE SHERMAN RESTAURANT
IF YOU WANT A GOOD MEAL AND HAVE IT NICELY SERVED GO TO

TUTEWILER UNDERTAKER, NO. 72 WEST MARKET STREET. TELEPHONE 216.

PARTNERSHIP INSURANCE At low cost. By which provision is made against the pecuniary loss and embarrassment resulting from the death of a member of a firm.
Provident Life and Trust Co. of Philadelphia, D. W. EDWARDS, Gen'l Agt., 508 Indiana Trust Bldg.

THEODORE F. SMITHER ROOFER Competent and Responsible Telephone 86 Office, 51 West Maryland St.

Heckard Wm A, dentist, 14 W Ohio, h 134 N Meridian.
Hecker, see also Hacker.
Hecker Charles M, foreman Deaf and Dumb Inst.
Hecker Edward J, teacher Deaf and Dumb Institute, h 53 Walcott.
Hecker Wm, h 600 E St Clair.
Heckman Albert L, butcher, b 464 Stillwell.
Heckman Amelia (wid George), b 534 E Ohio.
Heckman Christian F, cabtmkr, h 85 Oak.
Heckman Christopher, supt fire hydrants Indpls Water Co, r 75 Monument pl.
Heckman David P (D P Heckman & Sons), h 549 W 22d (N I).
Heckman D P & Sons (David P, John A and Nelson D), meats, 4 E Mkt House and 549 W 22d (N I).
Heckman George M, motorman, h 477 W Francis (N I).
Heckman Harry H, clk, b 85 Oak.
Heckman John, brakeman, h 40 Temple av.
Heckman John A (D P Heckman & Sons), h 595 W 22d (N I).
Heckman John F, butcher, h 324 Blake.
Heckman Kate, housekpr 654 E Washington.
Heckman Maria C (wid Gerhard H), h 21 King.
Heckman Nellie, b 324 Blake.
Heckman Nelson D (D P Heckman & Sons), h 566 W Eugene (N I).
Heckman Wm, lab, h 54 Iowa.
Heckman Wm H, packer, b 21 King.
Heckmann Andrew, mach, h 54 W Raymond.
Heckmann Charles, mach hd, h 55 E Morris.
Heckmann Frederick, mach, b 307 Union.
Heckmann Edward C, finisher, b 55 E Morris.
Heckmann Henry, car insp, h 70 W Raymond.
Heckmann Louis, dairy, 149 Wisconsin, h same.
Heckmann Wm D, h 307 Union.
Hecla Consolidated Mining Co, John Thomas pres, John C McCutcheon sec, John C Wright treas, Henry Knippenberg gen mngr, 25, 68½ E Market.
Hecock Amos T, live stock, h 141 Walcott.
Hedden Edwin C, clk, h 68 Talbott av.
Hedden Harry J, barber, rear 501 College av, h 36 Cornell av.
Hedderich Arthur G, bkkpr, b 229 N Noble.
Hedderich Bertha, stenog, b 229 N Noble.
Hedderich Charles C, carver, h 229 N Noble.
Hedderich Henry, printer, h 311 Spring.
Hedderich Peter, h 229 N Noble.
Hedderich Sophia (wid John C), h 82 Columbia av.
Hedderich Wm H, bridgebldr, b 82 Columbia av.
Hedegaard Laurits N, sergt U S Arsenal, h 460 Highland av.
Hedge Alanson, flagman, h 408 W Pratt.
Hedge Clarence A, barber, 105 Harrison, b 95 Hoyt av.
Hedge George, lab, b 21 Meikel.
Hedge Sarah E (wid Clarence), h 260 E South.
Hedge Wm G, barber, r 112 Blackford.
Hedgepath Charles, porter, h 23½ Harris.
Hedgepath Charles, porter, b 227 W 2d.
Hedges Charles J, tailor, b 1061 W Washington.
Hedges Charles W, janitor, h 131 Lynn av (W I).

THE WHEN IS A WORLD BEATER.

Hedges Cynthia A, h 140 N Capitol av.
Hedges Elijah, doorkpr Empire Theater, h 83 N Noble.
Hedges Elizabeth, b 75 Davidson.
Hedges Francis M, lab, h 2 W Chesapeake.
Hedges George B, h 1061 W Washington.
Hedges George C, driver, b 1061 W Washington.
Hedges Harry C, city agt C F Adams & Co, h 104 Ramsey av.
Hedges Harry H, billposter, b 230 Ash.
Hedges Hiram C, lab, b 301 W Pearl.
Hedges Isaac L, h 230 Ash.
Hedges James, lab, b 4 Coe.
Hedges John T, mailing clk P O, h 357 Talbott av.
Hedges Jonas, lab, b 4 Coe.
Hedges Ralph M, clk, b 230 Ash.
Hedges Ruth, h 140 N Capitol av.
Hedges Ruth A (wid Moses T), h 37 E South.
Hedges Samuel, finisher, h 117 S Summit.
Hedges Sarah A (wid Wm A), boarding 83 N Capitol av.
Hedges Wm E, mach opr The Indpls News, b 19 Edwards (W I).
Hedges Wm H, grocer, 1061 W Washington, h same.
Hedges Wm H, shoemkr, 48 S Illinois, h 19 Edward (W I).
Hedges Wm M, h 4 Coe.
Hedian Thomas G, supt sta 1 P O, r 113 S Illinois.
Hedlund John W, carp, rear 21 Kentucky av, h 20 Elliott.
Hedrick Frank W, signwriter, b 406 E Michigan.
Hedrick George H, carp, h 430 Columbia av.
Hedrick George W, grocer, 199 Shelby, h 18 Linden.
Hedrick Henry, h 52½ Mass av.
Hedrick Mary E, housekpr 334 N New Jersey.
Hedrick Robert G, trav agt Frank G Kamps, h 406 E Michigan.
Hedrick Sophia, h 82 Columbia av.

THE A. BURDSAL CO.
WINDOW AND PLATE
GLASS
Putty, Glazier Points, Diamonds.
Wholesale and Retail. 34 and 36 S. Meridian St.

ELECTRIC CONSTRUCTION Isolated Plants Installed. Electric Wiring and Fittings of all kinds. C. W. Meikel. Tel. 466. 96-98 E. New York St

DALTON & MERRIFIELD { LUMBER South Noble St., near E. Washington

INDIANA ELECTROTYPE CO. : BEST WORK. LOWEST PRICES. 23 WEST PEARL ST., INDIANAPOLIS, IND. JOB WORK. BOOK PLATES. All Orders Promptly Filled. BEST PATENT BASE ON THE MARKET.

KIRKHOFF BROS.,
GAS AND ELECTRIC FIXTURES
THE LARGEST LINE IN THE CITY.
102-104 SOUTH PENNSYLVANIA ST.
TELEPHONE 910.

HEEB EMMETT J, Propr Indianapolis Business University, When Bldg, N Penn (Bryant & Stratton and Indianapolis Business Colleges Consolidated), Tel 499; Pres Heeb Publishing Co, h 813 N Delaware. (See front cover, right bottom lines and p 4.)
HEEB FREDERICK C, Executive Staff Indianapolis Business University and Mngr Heeb Publishing Co, 81 When Bldg, Tel 499; r 70 W Walnut.
HEEB PUBLISHING CO, Emmett J Heeb Pres, Frederick C Heeb Mngr, Publishers Subscription and Commercial Text Books, 81 When Bldg, Tel 499.
Heede August R, carp, b 254 Bates.
Heede George W H, boxmkr, b 254 Bates.
Heede Henry, cigarmkr, 254 Bates, h same.
Heede Wm E, carp, b 254 Bates.
Heeg Charles A, cigarmkr, b 208 E Morris.
Heeg Charlotte (wid Adam), cigarmfr, 208 E Morris, h same.
Heekin James & Co, Robert W Moore agt, coffees, 25 W Georgia.
Heenan Wm, fireman, h 22 Poplar (B).
Heer Frederick C, trav agt, h 273 E Walnut.
Heerting Wm, car rep, h 1044 W Vermont.
Heess Conrad, saloon, 330 Mass av, h same.
Heever Edward, bartndr, b 76 S Delaware.
Heffernan Thomas J, saloon, 84 W Market, h 149 W 12th.
Heflin Henry E, tinner, h 165 N Senate av.
Hefner Elmer O, lab, h 32 Tacoma av.
Hefty Casper, printer, b 183 Madison av.
Hefty Charlotte, bkkpr, b 183 Madison av.
Hefty John J, painter, h 183 Madison av.
Hegarty, see also Hagerty.
Hegarty James H, saloon, 438 National rd, h same.
Hegarty Patrick, bartndr, b 438 National rd.
Hege Enos, contr, h 455 N Meridian.
Heger Frederick, lab, b 1087 E Michigan.
Heger Henry, lab, h 77 Dugdale.
Hehr Gottlieb, polisher, b 232 E Morris.
Hehr Otto, instmkr, h 232 E Morris.

COAL AND COKE
The W. G. Wasson Co.,
130 INDIANA AVE. TEL. 989
LIME AND LATH

Heibernick John, lab, h 60 Holmes av (H).
Heibner August, lab, h 278 E Georgia.
Heicher Barbara, cook, b n e cor Washington and Watts.
Heid, see also Heidt.
Heid Edward, molder, b 326 Hudson.
Heid Frank, lab, h 1199 Morris (W I).
Heid George, cooper, h 1187 Morris (W I).
Heid George P, packer, b 326 Hudson.
Heid Henry G, lab, h 315 Howard (W I).
Heid Jacob, saloon, 403 Clifford av, h 401 same.
Heid John, bartndr, h 1195 Morris (W I).
Heid John, butcher, b 332 E Michigan.
Heid John F, meats, 1017 S Meridian and 6 E Mkt House, h 1017 S Meridian.
Heid Joseph, h 326 Hudson.
Heid Joseph X, printer, b 326 Hudson.
Heid Louis C, engr, b 180 E McCarty.
Heid Philip, lab, b n s Ohio 2 e of Rural.
Heid Thomas, bedmkr, b 326 Hudson.
Heide Otto T A H, bracemkr, h 165 Newman.
Heidelberger Albert, lab, b 704 Morris (W I).
Heidelberger Jacob, mach, h 704 Morris (W I).
Heidelman Henry O, h 382 S Delaware.
Heidelman Joseph, mach, b 382 S Delaware.
Heidelman Mary R, teacher, b 382 S Delaware.
Heiden Frederick, lab, h 42 Fenneman.
Heidenreich Andrew, brewer, h 41 Nebraska.
Heidenreich Edward, shoemkr, 583 Morris (W I), r same.
Heidenreich Frank W, clk, b 23 N Gillard av.
Heidenreich Frederick C, mach, b 145 Locke.
Heidenreich John J, florist, s w cor Applegate and Morton, h same.
Heidenreich John J, tailor, 20 Commercial blk, r same.
Heidenreich Rena, dressmkr, 69 N East, h same.
Heidenreich Wm, printer, h 145 Locke.
Heider Oscar, trav agt Krull & Schmidt, h 857 Bellefontaine.
Heidergott Wm, farmer, h e s School 3 n of Schofield (B).
Heidergott Wm F, blksmith, b e s School 3 n of Schofield (B).
Heidlinger John A jr, clk, h 809 N New Jersey.
Heidrick Frank A, bartndr H W Green, h 683 E Washington.
Heidt, see also Heid.
Heidt Albert W, lab, b 166 Howard.
Heidt George, grocer, 442 Indiana av, h same.
Heier Charles, lab, h 329 S Penn.
Heier Daniel J, grinder, h 314 E Georgia.
HEIER FRED F, Sample Room; Imported and Domestic Wines, Liquors and Cigars; 18-20 S New Jersey, h same, Tel 1526.
Heier Herman, engr, b 325 W Market.
Heier John H, bartndr, h 22½ S New Jersey.
Heil Charles P, brakeman, b 251½ E Washington.
Heil Henry, carp, h 56 School (B).
Heil Henry V, foreman, h 6 Lexington av.
Heil Wm, painter, h 56 Foundry (B).
Heilman Frederick, shoemkr, 94 Russell av, h same.
Heilmann Adam, cabtmkr, h 123 Chadwick.
Heim Charlotte, h 503 E Washington.

W. H. MESSENGER COMPLETE HOUSE FURNISHER 101 East Washington Street, Telephone 491

Foundry and Pattern Shop } McNamara, Koster & Co. { PHONE 1593 212-218 S. Penn. St.

THE FRED DIETZ CO. || WOODEN PACKING BOXES MADE TO ORDER FACTORY AND WAREHOUSE TRUCKS. 400 Madison Avenue. Telephone 64.

Heim George T, molder, b 257½ Mass av.
Heim John R, piano tunter, 559 E St Clair, b same.
Heim Wm H, restaurant, 257 Mass av, h same.
Heim Wm J, printer The Indpls News, b 257 Mass av.
Heim Wm S, tmstr, h 360 Virginia av.
Heimann Therese (wid John), h 13 Gresham.
Heimbach Edward J, lab, b 33 N Liberty.
Heimbach John, meats, 1348 N Capitol av, h same.
Heimbaugh Wm, b 187 S Capitol av.
Heimbo Henry, lab, b 110 Blackford.
Heimbo John, clk, h 208 Bright.
Heimbo Joseph, lab, b 110 Blackford.
Heimbo Michael butcher, h 106 Blackford.
Heimbo Philip, lab, h 83 Geisendorff.
Heimbow George, mach hd, r 188 W Ohio.
Heimbuch George, mach hd, r 11 S Senate av.
Heims Isaac N, drugs, 51 N Illinois, h 74 W North.
Heims Rosa (wid Simon), h 302 E Market.
Heims Sarah C, b 302 E Market.
Hein Charles, cabtmkr, h 2 Orchard av.
Hein Charles A, h 162 N Liberty.
Hein Otto E, varnisher, r 563 Madison av.
Heinbuch George H, mach hd, h 354 Highland av.
Heinbuch Henry L, mach hd, b 279 Highland av.
Heince Gustav, mach, h 420 E Maryland.
Heine Charles C, bottler, h 36 Bismarck.
Heine Christian H, shoes, 479 Virginia av, h same.
Heine Henry, h 54 Elm.
Heine Henry, lab, b 175 Madison av.
Heine Hubert E, bkkpr Hollweg & Reese, h 233 Excelsior av.
Heinemann Thomas, mach, h n s Michigan 5 e of Sherman Drive.
Heiner Doretta S, h 193½ E Washington.
Heimer Frederick A, engr, h 249 N Pine.
Heiner John, tmstr, h 36 Thomas.
Heiner John M, grain insp, h 163 Buchanan.
Heiner Melville E, trav agt, r 222 N Illinois.
Heiner Sophia (wid Andrew), b 114 Walcott.
Heininger James F, mach, h 454 Charles.
Heinlein Andrew, lab, h 115 Agnes.
Heinlein John, saloon, 199 Indiana av, h same.
Heinlein John jr, fish, 193 Indiana av, b 199 same.
Heinly A W (Green & Co), res Danville, Ill.
Heinrich Carl A, clk, h 576 N Senate av.
Heinrich Christian F, meats, 576 N Senate av, h same.
Heinrichs Charles E, carp, h 360 S Alabama.
Heinrichs John H, stenog, h 480 Ash.
HEINRICHS WM F, Lawyer, 15 Ingalls Blk, h 365 Ash.
Heinricke Carrie (wid August), h 138 Davidson.
Heintz Valentine, mason, h 1 Hermann.
Heinz H J Co, Charles T Patterson mngr, whol pickles, 33 S Delaware.
Heinz Peter, engr, h 155 Hendricks.
Heinzerling Henry G, clk, r 187 Lexington av.
Heipel Arthur, bartndr, b 53 River av (W I).
Heirman Rudolph, cabtmkr, h 513 S West.
Heirman Wm, mach hd, b 513 S West.
Heise Henry, lab, b 112 Reynolds av (H).
Heise John, mach, h 39 Omer.
Heiser Alonzo, lab, h 133 Indiana av.

Henry H. Fay,
40½ E. WASHINGTON ST.,
AGENT FOR
Insurance Co. of North America,
Pennsylvania Fire Ins. Co.

Heiser Casper, lab, b 1000 W Washington.
Heise Charles F, blksmith, h 97 Tremont (H).r
Heiser Conrad, foreman, h 118 Davidson.
Heiser Henry, plastr, h 670 Home av.
Heiser John, bartndr, b 286 W Washington.
Heiser John, mason, h 664 Chestnut.
Heiser Wm, lab, b 330 Indiana av.
Heiskell Arthur R, mngr coll dept McCormick H M Co, b 331 Central av.
Heiskell Frank W, clk McCormick H M Co, b 331 Central av.
Heiskell Lucy E, collr Mas Mut Ben Soc, b 918 N New Jersey.
Heiskell Margaret (wid Robert), h 918 N New Jersey.
Heiskell Walter W, trav agt The Indpls News, b 331 Central av.
Heiskell Wm L, dentist, 76½ E Market, h 331 Central av.
Heisler Jacob, flagman, h 258 Highland av.
Heissenberg August, stone cutter, h 92 Nebraska.
Heissenberg Louis, baker, b 92 Nebraska.
Heissenberg Oscar, mach hd, b 92 Nebraska.
Heitkam Edward H, cigarmkr, h 19 S Rural.
Heitkam Henry J, meats, 350 Virginia av, h same.
Heitkam John, asst supt Indpls Cabinetmakers' Union, h 92 Hanna.
Heitkam John W, saloon, 184 W 7th, h same.
Heitkam Martin, lab, b 232 Dougherty.
Heitkam Walter, clk The H Lieber Co, b 92 Hanna.
Heitkam Wm, clk Charles Mayer & Co, b 92 Hanna.
Heitman Anna (wid Bernard), b 81 Meikel.
Heitman John H, carp, h 18 Coffey (W I).
Heitman Wm F, artist, b 81 Meikel.
Heitman Henrietta (wid Wm), b 31 E McCarty.
Heitz Magdalen (wid Louis), b 22 Weghorst.
Heitz Mary A, housekpr 44 Pendleton av.
Heizer Aaron, lab, h 110 Shepard (W I).
Heizer Arthur S, salesman Clark, Wysong & Voris, h 87 S McLain (W I).

Union Casualty & Surety Co.
of St. Louis, Mo.
Employers', Public, General, Teams and Elevator Liability; also Workmen's Collective, Steam Boiler, Plate Glass and Automatic Sprinkler Insurance.
W. E. BARTON & CO., General Agents,
504 Indiana Trust Building.
LONG DISTANCE TELEPHONE 1918.

Shorthand! BUSINESS UNIVERSITY. When Bl'k. Elevator day and night. Typewriting, Penmanship, Book-keeping, Office Training free. See page 4. Est. 1850. Tel. 499. E. J. HEEB, Proprietor.

Water and Oil Meters { HENRY R. WORTHINGTON, 64 S. PENNSYLVANIA ST. Long Distance Telephone 284.

UNION CO-OPERATIVE LAUNDRY { NOS. 138, 140 AND 142 VIRGINIA AVENUE (COMPOSED OF UNION LAUNDRY GIRLS.) T. E. SOMERVILLE, MANAGER — TELEPHONE 1269. INDIANAPOLIS, IND.

HORACE M. HADLEY
REAL ESTATE AND LOANS....
66 East Market Street
Telephone 1540. BASEMENT.

Heizer Cyrus C, h 264 Bellefontaine.
Heizer Cyrus E, pressman The Indpls News, h 282 E Merrill.
Heizer David F, engr The Indpls News, h 282 E Merrill.
Heizer Eva B, teacher Deaf and Dumb Inst, b 264 Bellefontaine.
Heizer George, lab, h 127 Maple.
Heizer George S, helper, h 105 Malott av.
Heizer Jesse E, lab, h 642 E 8th.
Heizer Mary A (wid James M), b 1387 N Capitol av.
Heizer Wm, lab, b 127 Maple.
Heizer Wm J, helper, h 79 Columbia av.
Helbert Hiram, carp, b 50 S Judge Harding (W I).
Helbert Theresa (wid Wm), h 50 S Judge Harding (W I).
Helbing Charles, lab, b 135 E Washington.
Helbing Gustav, carp, b 228 N Capitol av.
Helbing John, lab, b 150 Nordyke av (W I).
Helcher Charles A, waiter, h 88 W McCarty.
Helcher Frederick A, car insp, h 239 Lincoln la.
Helcher Wm J, finisher, h 30 McGinnis.
Held Amelia A, h 469 Blake.
Held Charles H, printer, b 561 S Illinois.
Held Frederick W, printer, b 561 S Illinois.
Held Louis, mach, h 561 S Illinois.
Held Louis C, printer, b 561 S Illinois.
Heldt Johanna, h 51 Thomas.
Heldt Rudolph, lab, b 51 Thomas.
Helfenberger Charles, ironwkr, b 44 Union.
Helfenberger Frederick, trav agt, b 44 Union.
Helfenberger Sabina (wid Julius), h 44 Union.
Helfenberger Wm (Ellis & Helfenberger), h 1159 N Meridian.
Helfer Charles A, trav agt, h 125 W 7th.
Helfer Clarissa T (wid Andrew A), h 223 E New York.
HELFER EDWARD T, Carriage Mnfr, 37-41 N Capitol av, h 364 N New Jersey, Tel 313.
Helfer Sarah S (wid Andrew A), h 123 W 7th.

Merchants' and Manufacturers' Exchange
Make Collections and Commercial Reports......
J. E. TAKKEN, MANAGER,
19 Union Building, 73 West Maryland Street

Helfert John, mach hd, h 326 W Maryland.
Helfrich Adam H, wagonmkr, 380 W Washington, h 102 Blackford.
Helfrich Albert B, foreman, h 389 N California.
Helfrich John, lab, b 389 N California.
Helfrich John W, uphlr, h 82 Lexington av.
Helfrich Samuel G, switchman, b 102 Blackford.
Hellekamp Wm, pressman, h 19 Gatling.
Hellekson John H, ins adjuster, 11 Talbott blk, h 996 N Alabama.
Hellor, see also Hiller.
Heller Annie R (wid James E), h 1008 N Capitol av.
Heller C May, teacher, b 17 Lexington av.
Heller Earl, messenger, b 17 Lexington av.
Heller Earl W, clk, b 1008 N Capitol av.
Heller Ellsworth E (Buddenbaum & Heller), h 121 Pleasant.
Heller Henry B, student, b 121 E New York.
Heller Herbert M, b 1008 N Capitol av.
Heller James M, carp, h 17 Lexington av.
Heller James M, sec Ind All B and L Assn, h 391 Ash.
Heller Jennie E, teacher Public School No 13, b 17 Lexington av.
Heller John H, student, b 121 E New York.
Heller John T, engr, h 12 Traub av.
Heller Mabel, cashr Danbury Hat Co, b 49 Vine.
Heller Marie M, dressmkr, 105 N Meridian, b 185 Coburn.
Heller Orville J, clk, b 17 Lexington av.
Heller Robert J, lumber, h 49 Vine.
Heller Wm, clk, r 74 W Ohio.
Heller Wm J, grocer, 149 Oliver av (W I), h 44 Division (W I).
Hellmann, see also Hillmann.
Hellmann Carl, mach, b 166 Agnes.
Hellmann Charles, h 259 Bates.
Hellmann Grace (wid Peter), b 34 Dawson.
Hellmann Louis, blksmith, h 166 Agnes.
Hellmann Peter L, blksmith, 576 W Michigan, h 153 Minerva.
Hellmer Elizabeth (wid Henry), h 704 N Illinois.
Hellmer Victor H, springmkr, h 96 Columbia av.
HELLSTERN AUGUST A, Stove Repair House; Odd Pieces Furnished, 289 E Washington, Tel 1812; h 841 Chestnut.
Helm Adam, carp, 283 E North, h same.
Helm Andrew G, cabtmkr, h 34 Harlan.
Helm Clara D, stenog M W Hopkins, b 34 Harlan.
Helm Clifford L, jeweler, b 353½ W New York.
Helm Daniel J, lab, h 179 W New York.
Helm Dorothy (wid Lawrence), b 34 Harlan.
Helm Edward, lab, b 105 N Rural (B).
Helm Edward P, diesinker, b 272 N Pine.
Helm Ellen (wid Mack), h 113 Ft Wayne av.
Helm Fred W, musician, r 11 Ellsworth.
Helm George E, carp, h 271 Jefferson av.
Helm Henry A, h 627 E Washington.
Helm Henry W, clk A Kiefer Drug Co, b 227 N Pine.
Helm Iva A, dressmkr, 133½ Martindale av, h same.
Helm John, h 272 N Pine.
Helm John C, patrolman, h 167 N Noble.
Helm John H, carp, h 278 Jefferson av.
Helm Joseph H, carp, h 1126 N Delaware.

CLEMENS VONNEGUT
184, 186 and 192 E. Washington St.
Wire Rope, Machinery, Lathes, Drills and Shapers

THE WM. H. BLOCK CO. DRY GOODS, DRAPERIES, RUGS, WINDOW SHADES.
7 AND 9 EAST WASHINGTON STREET.

Helm Joseph W, b 382 Bellefontaine.
Helm Lester, waiter, r 1½ Wood.
Helm Mortimer F, painter, h 133½ Martindale av.
Helm Ralph H, clk Natl Malleable Castings Co, b 627 E Washington.
Helm Robert F, treas The Capital Live Stock Commission Co, b The Denison.
Helm Samuel S, trav agt, h 382 Bellefontaine.
Helm Valentine J, h 353½ W New York.
Helm Verling W, asst state sec Indiana Y M C A, b 1155 N Penn.
Helmick John M, lab, h 432 W Eugene (N I).
Helming Bertha K, teacher, b 606 S East.
Helming Herman F, phys, 606 S East, b same.
Helming Theodore W, phys, 606 S East, h same.
Helms Allen, attendant Insane Hospital.
Helms Allen E, barber, h 649½ Virginia av.
Helms Amos, lab, h 245 W 3d.
Helms August, saloon, 2 Lexington av, h same.
Helms August jr, bartndr, b 2 Lexington av.
Helms Carl A, barber, 347 Madison av, h same.
Helms Ella, h 24½ Indiana av.
Helms Francis M, treas Guarantee Sav and Inv Assn, h 91 Shelby.
Helms Frederick, clk C C C & St L Ry, b 364 N Pine.
Helms Henry, carp, 364 N Pine, h same.
Helms Louis A, dentist, 37½ W Washington, h 430 N Alabama.
Helms Mary (wid Philip), h 38 Oliver av (W I).
Helms Robert, lab, h 115 Columbia al.
Helms Samuel S, trav agt H T Conde Implement Co, h 382 Bellefontaine.
Helms Thomas, hostler, r 1128 N Meridian.
Helms Thomas M, chairmkr, h 495 E 9th.
Helmstetter Louise, clk, b 426 N New Jersey.
Helmstetter Margaret (wid John), b 426 N New Jersey.
Helmuth Anna M (wid Henry), h 147 Locke.
Helpling Charles A, tel opr L E & W R R, b George's Hotel.
Helpman Mary E, drygoods, 211 Prospect, b 180 S Olive.
Helstein Ira I, clk, b 1008 N Meridian.
Helstein Simon F, furs, 25 W Washington, h 1008 N Meridian.
Helt Frederick W (Helt & Trotter), b 151 River av (W I).
Helt & Trotter (Frederick W Helt, Oscar Trotter), grocers, 153 River av (W I).
Helton Frank M, motorman, h 329 Virginia av.
Heltzel Amos C, engr Blind Inst, h 42 Highland pl.
Helvie Charles E, mnfrs' agt, 92 S Illinois, r 180 Christian av.
Helwagen Minnie D (wid James F), h 563 W Francis (N I).
Helwig Frank E, supt Indpls Chair Mnfg Co, n w cor New York and Ellsworth, h 94 W Walnut.
Helwig Jacob, shoemkr, 849 E Michigan, h 171 Benton.
Helwig Minnie J, stenog, b 171 Benton.
Hemerly Frank A, b 623 N Senate av.
Hemerly Isadore G, tinner, h 623 N Senate av.
Hemmelgarn Herman, collr Charles Willig, h 26 Ingram.

Hemmelgarn John, uphlr, b 26 Ingram.
Hamphill George W, cook, h 214 E Wabash.
Hemphill Harry E, driver, b 41 Elm.
Hempleman Isaac L, jeweler, 563 S Meridian, h 561 same.
Hempleman Laura B, milliner, 563 S Meridian, b 561 same.
Hemritte Monroe, lab, h 68 Cincinnati.
Henchman Mary L, nurse, 10 Wyandot blk, r same.
Hendershot Charles McC, carp, h 725 E 7th.
Hendershot Isaac H, mngr U S Wringer Co, 19 Indiana av, h 1504 Kenwood av.
Hendershot John, bartndr, b 30th n w cor L N A & C Ry.
Hendershot Marion F, clk, r 271 Mass av.
Hendershott Daniel J, carp, h w s Colorado av 4 n of Ohio.
Henderson Agnes (wid James), b 961 N Senate av.
Henderson Albert H, porter R M S, h 239 N California.
Henderson Alexander C, butcher, h 75 Minerva.
Henderson Amanda (wid Warren), b 217 W 3d.
Henderson Benjamin, lab, h 411 Coburn.
Henderson Catharine A (wid James J), b 89 Division (W I).
Henderson Charles, lab, h 81 Sheldon.
Henderson Charles C, condr, h 96 W 7th.
Henderson Charles K, clk, h 397 Central av.
Henderson Cynthia A (wid James H), h 414 S West.
Henderson Edwin, cooper, b 229 W Washington.
Henderson Frank, painter, b 211 W Market.
Henderson George, coachman 373 Broadway.
Henderson George M, painter, b 439 Broadway.
Henderson George W, carp, h 35 Rhode Island.
Henderson Harry L Rev, b 192 Hillside av.
Henderson Harry R, clk Adams Ex Co, h n s 32d 2 e of Charles (M).
Henderson Harvey, r 165 N Capitol av.
Henderson Henry, condr, b 230 English av.

GUIDO R. PRESSLER,
FRESCO PAINTER
Churches, Theaters, Public Buildings, Etc., A Specialty.
Residence, No. 325 North Liberty Street
INDIANAPOLIS, IND.

INDIANAPOLIS STEEL ROOFING AND CORRUGATING WORKS, 23 and 25 East South Street. S. D. NOEL, Proprietor.

David S. McKernan, Rooms 2-5 Thorpe Block.
REAL ESTATE AND LOANS
A number of choice pieces for subdivision, or for manufacturers' sites, with good switch facilities.

DIAMOND WALL PLASTER { Telephone 1410 BUILDERS' EXCHANGE.

UNION TRANSFER AND STORAGE CO. Cor. E. Ohio St. and C., C., C. & St. L. R'y Tracks. BRICK WAREHOUSE; CLEANEST AND SAFEST STORAGE IN CITY FOR HOUSEHOLD GOODS AND MERCHANDISE.

W. McWORKMAN,

METAL CEILINGS,
ROLLING SHUTTERS,
DOORS AND PARTITIONS.
930 W. Washington St. Tel. 1118.

Henderson Isaac C, lab, b w s Northwestern av 1 n of Grand av (N I).
Henderson James, waiter The Denison.
Henderson James, clk, b 102 Meek.
Henderson James, lab, h s e cor Sangster av and 17th.
Henderson James B, lab, h w s Northwestern av 1 n of Grand av (N I).
Henderson Jerome, lab, b 942 Gent (M P).
Henderson Jesse C, carp, h w s Linwood av 4 n of Ohio.
Henderson John, cook, b Enterprise Hotel.
HENDERSON JOHN J, Agt Adams, Southern and Texas Express Cos, 25 S Meridian, Tel 101; h 780 N Alabama, Tel 837.
Henderson John O, sec The Holt Ice and Cold Storage Co, h 846 N Penn.
Henderson John R, barber, b 214 Bellefontaine.
Henderson John R, tmstr, h n s Oakwood 1 e of Hillside av.
Henderson John T, lab, h 741 Nevada.
Henderson Joseph S, h 4 Gimbel.
Henderson Letitia, h 143 Harmon.
Henderson Margaret, r 199½ Mass av.
Henderson Martin L, condr, b 28 S State av.
Henderson Mary D, grocer, 143 E 7th, b 78 Woodlawn av.
Henderson May (wid Charles), dressmkr, 330½ E Washington, h same.
Henderson Milton R, lab, h 29 Ludlow av.
Henderson Morris, clk, b 1210 N Illinois.
Henderson Nellie E, h 168½ E Washington.
Henderson Orin S, boilermkr, h 143 E Merrill.
Henderson Oscar B, supt agencies The Hay & Willits Mnfg Co, h 112 Hoyt av.
Henderson Peter, cook, r 32 N Senate av.
Henderson Robert B, clk, h 75 Minerva.
Henderson Sarah (wid Robert), h 214 Bellefontaine.
Henderson Sarah E (wid Alexander), b 347 W Michigan.
Henderson Simeon, driver, h 301½ E Washington.
Henderson Susan (wid Wm), b 22 Lexington av.
Henderson Walker P, lab, h 58 Maple.

SEALS,
STENCILS,
STAMPS, Etc.
GEO. J. MAYER
15 S. Meridian St.
TELEPHONE 1386.

Henderson Wm, foreman, b 230 Dillon.
Henderson Wm A, lab, b w s Northwestern av 1 n of Grand av (N I).
Henderson Wm F, lab, h 186 Patterson.
Henderson Wm H, mach, b 214 Bellefontaine.
Hendricks, see also Henricks.
Hendricks Allen W, b 74 Middle Drive (W P).
Hendricks Anna, teacher Deaf and Dumb Inst, b 611 N Meridian.
Hendricks Anna B (wid Abram T), b 611 N Meridian.
Hendricks Caroline B, lawyer, 501 Indiana Trust bldg, b 74 Middle Drive (W P).
Hendricks Charles M, lab, 144 East Drive (W P).
Hendricks Christopher, lab, r 175 S Illinois.
Hendricks Claude L, uphlr, b 836 E 9th.
Hendricks Club, 19½ N Meridian.
Hendricks Eli J, carp, h 43 Smithson.
Hendricks Eliza C (wid Thomas A), h 81 N Capitol av.
Hendricks Emma, h 72 S West.
Hendricks Ezra R, clk Krag-Reynolds Co, b 74 Middle Drive (W P).
Hendricks Flora A, b 45 Holly av (W I).
Hendricks Frederick A, mach, h 834 E 9th.
Hendricks George W, clk, h 738 S East.
Hendricks Hannah K (wid John), b 146 East Drive (W P).
Hendricks John, porter, r 165 Indiana av.
Hendricks John D, clk, r 449 Central av.
Hendricks Joseph S, lab, h 35 Gatling.
Hendricks Josephine C, dressmkr, 362 Talbott av, b same.
Hendricks Louisa, h 904 N Senate av.
Hendricks Mary A, supt Katharine Home, n e cor Capitol av and 11th.
Hendricks Omri L, mach, h 343 Yandes.
Hendricks Sarah B (wid Abram W), h 74 Middle Drive (W P).
Hendricks Sarah H (wid James C), h 362 Talbott av.
Hendricks Thomas A, clk Daniel Stewart Co, h 82 E Vermont.
Hendricks Victor K (Hendricks & Cooper), h 611 N Meridian.
Hendricks Wm G, printer, 37 W Market, h 274 W Michigan.
Hendricks Wm H (Hendricks & Wood), cement, street and cellar contr, h 922 N Senate av.
HENDRICKS & COOPER (Victor K Hendricks, Wm D Cooper), Wholesale Boots and Shoes, 85-87 S Meridian, Tel 862.
HENDRICKS & WOOD (Wm H Hendricks, George W Wood), Proprs Estey-Camp Music House, 144 Mass av. (See adv in classified Pianos and Organs.)
Hendrickson Alonzo P (Hendrickson, Lefler & Co), h 800 N Meridian.
Hendrickson Edward G, stenog McBride & Denny, b 298 E Market.
Hendrickson Edwin A (Indpls Harness Co), h 999 N Penn.
Hendrickson George A, lab, b 423 Chestnut.
Hendrickson Harry C, clk I & V Ry, b 578 Broadway.
HENDRICKSON HENRY C, Architect, Room 10, 68½ E Market, h 578 Broadway.
Hendrickson John A, clk, b 578 Broadway.

A. METZGER AGENCY ESTABLISHED 1863. INSURANCE

LAMBERT GAS & GASOLINE ENGINE CO.
ANDERSON, IND. PORTABLE GASOLINE ENGINES. 2 TO 25 H. P.

HENDRICKSON, LEFLER & CO (Alonzo P Hendrickson, Charles W Lefler), Wholesale Hats and Furs, 89 S Meridian, Tel 1537.
Hendrickson Sarah J (wid Samuel D), h 229 Madison av.
Hendrickson Thomas, finisher, h 44 Lee (W I).
Hendrickson Thomas, mach, b 494 S West.
Hendrickson Wm A Rev, pastor Twelfth Presbyterian Church, r 194 N Illinois.
Hendrickson Wm H, bottler, h 307 Union.
Hendrickson Wm T, watchman, b 494 S West.
Hendrix Alexander, trimmer, h 1258 N Penn.
Hendrix Lemuel, switchman, h 51 N Brightwood av (B).
Hendrixson Charles W, clk, b 36 Ludlow av.
Hendrixson Edward L, carp, b rear 265 Mass av
Hendrixson George K, waiter, h rear 265 Mass av.
Hendrixson James R, carp, h 36 Ludlow av.
Hendryx Aylmer E, student, b 131 E North.
Hendryx Warren B Rev, h 131 E North.
Heney Cornelius, lab, 702 N Meridian.
Hengen Peter, paperhngr, h 47 Bates.
Heninger, see Henninger.
Henkle, see also Hinkle.
Henkle Charles B, clk, h 38 Temple av.
Henkle Frank G, clk, h 37 Windsor.
Henley, see also Hanley.
Henley Albert, engr, h 265 W Vermont.
Henley, Eaton & Co (Wm F Henley, Ezra F Eaton), hats, 58 S Meridian.
Henley Edward, lab, h 16 Douglass.
Henley Frank D, plastr, h 267 Alvord.
Henley Wm, mach, h 267 Alvord.
Henley Wm F (Henley, Eaton & Co), h 308 College av.
Henley Wm J, judge Appellate Court of Indiana, 115 State House.
Henley Wm O, molder, h 325 Cornell av.
Henly Minnie, phys, r 136 N Penn.
Henn Alois, saloon, 627 Madison, h same.
Henn Benedict, molder, h 324 E Michigan.
Henn Charles K, artist, b 324 E Michigan.
Henn Frank B, painter, b 324 E Michigan.
Henn John, driver, h 627 Madison av.
Henn John jr, lab, b 627 Madison av.
Henn Louis B, lab, b 233 Buchanan.
Henn Oscar, clk The Gordon-Kurtz Co, r 124 E Ohio.
Hennan John B, ins agt, h 120 S Noble.
Henneberger Frank, r 42 S Capitol av.
Henneke Henry, driver, b 2220 N Illinois.
Hennessey John F, agt, h 127 E St Joseph.
Hennessey Wm, lab, b 272 W Maryland.
Hennessy Daniel, lab, h 276 S Alabama.
Hennessy Elizabeth (wid David), boarding 171 S New Jersey.
Hennessy Hannah (wid John), h 125 E Merrill.
Hennessy James F, condr, h 331 Fletcher av.
Hennessy Mary (wid Patrick), h 260 Union.
Hennessy Michael E, clk, h 125 E Merrill.
Hennessy Thomas G, clk, b 125 E Merrill.
Hennessy Timothy P, boilermkr, h 276 S Alabama.
Hennessy Wm, gas insp, b 260 Union.
Henney George, lab, h 357 Cornell av.
Hennigar John W, engr, h n end Decatur.
Hennigar Oscar A, mach, h 32 Everett.
Henning Albert C, paperhanger, b 357 E Market.
Henning Albert G, printer, h 368 Fulton.

Farm and City Loans
25 Years' Successful Business.
THOS. C. DAY & CO,
Rooms 325 to 330 Lemcke Building.

Henning Charles, cigarmkr, r 173 E Washington.
Henning Dora (wid Gottlieb), b 368 Fulton.
Henning Frank H, mngr Peoria Athletic Co, 58-60 N Penn, b The Denison.
Henning Henry R, h 357 E Market.
Henning Joseph P, mason, h s s Michigan av 1 e of State av.
Henning Oscar H, clk Penna Lines, b 357 E Market.
Henning Patrick, driver, h 313 S Olive.
Henning Paul G, clk Penna Lines, b 357 E Market.
Henning Rudolph H, printer, h 10 Jupiter.
Henninger Arthur E, mach, b 37 S Wheeler (B).
Henninger Edward (G & E Henninger), h 353 S New Jersey.
Henninger Frederick W, tailor, 336 E Market, r same.
Henninger Gustav (G & E Henninger), b 353 S New Jersey.
Henninger G & E (Gustav and Edward), musical insts, 35 Virginia av.
Henninger Herman J, lab, h 56 Morton.
Henninger John F, constable, 34 N Delaware, h 37 S Wheeler (B).
Henninger Richard, plumber, b 353 S New Jersey.
Henninger Sanford F, lab, r 232 S Capitol av.
Henricks, see also Hendricks.
Henricks Reuben, carp, h 10 Hill.
Henricks Stephen S, carp, h 6 Hill.
Henricks Wm A, tinner, h 78 Cypress.
Henry Amanda (wid Robert B), b 58 Tremont av (H).
Henry Anna (wid Enoch), b 884 Bellefontaine.
Henry Barnett G, molder, h 58 Tremont av (H).
Henry Benjamin F, lab, b 58 Tremont av (H).
Henry Caroline, boarding 252 E Washington.
Henry Charles G, clk, b 224 Davidson.
Henry Christopher E, patternmkr, b 38 Bismarck av (H).

EAT
QUAKER BREAD
ASK YOUR GROCER FOR IT.
THE HITZ BAKING CO.

BICYCLES $5 DOWN. MONTHLY. Best Terms. 86 Wheels. WHEELMEN'S CO. 31 W. OHIO ST. LONG DISTANCE TEL. 1855.

J. H. TECKENBROCK House, Sign and Fresco Painter, 94 EAST SOUTH STREET.

FIDELITY MUTUAL LIFE PHILADELPHIA, PA. A. H. COLLINS, Gen. Agt. Baldwin Blk. RATES REASONABLE. SOUND BEYOND QUESTION. BUSINESS-LIKE IN PRACTICE.

BITUMINOUS COAL ▸▸ Edwardsport Coal and Mining Company ROOMS 42 AND 43 WHEN BUILDING.

ESTABLISHED 1876. TELEPHONE 168.
CHESTER BRADFORD,
SOLICITOR OF PATENTS,
AND COUNSEL IN PATENT CAUSES.
(See adv. page 6.)
Office:—Rooms 14 and 16 Hubbard Block, S. W. Cor. Washington and Meridian Streets, INDIANAPOLIS, INDIANA.

Henry David S, molder, b 58 Tremont av (H).
Henry Elizabeth J (wid Martin V), h 189 N Noble.
Henry Ella B (wid Wm), h 221 N Noble.
Henry Frank F, steward Grand Hotel.
Henry Frank M, private U S Army, b 25½ N Illinois.
Henry George A, saloon, 296 E Georgia, h 282 same.
Henry George S, carp, h 613 W 22d (N I).
Henry George W, ballplayer, h 261 E Market.
Henry Jackson, mach, b 334 N Illinois.
Henry Jacob, carp, h 172 Blake.
Henry Jacob B, saloon, 176 E Washington, h 185 Davidson.
Henry James B, lab, b 58 Tremont av (H).
Henry James R, cashr State Bank of Indiana, b 469 N Meridian.
Henry Jessie, h 187 W Court.
Henry John, brakeman, b 1082 W New York.
Henry John, waiter, b 25 S West.
Henry Joseph, lab, b 359 S Illinois.
Henry Joseph J, lab, h 38 Bismarck av (H).
Henry Lillie, h 212 W Court.
Henry Louis S, molder, h 24 Bismarck av (H).
Henry Mary (wid Lawrence), b 92 Bates.
Henry Mary E (wid Jonas), dressmkr, 602½ N West, h same.
Henry Monroe, lab, r 10 Roanoke.
Henry Morris C, driver, h 394 W Pratt.
Henry Oliver A, fireman, b 882 W Washington.
Henry Oliver M, engr, h 327 W Maryland.
Henry Oliver M, trav agt Holliday & Wyon, h 34 Bellefontaine.
Henry Omer T, engr, h 48 Huron.
Henry Oscar, lab, r 10 Roanoke.
Henry Reliance T (wid John T), b 394 W Pratt.
Henry Richard A, clk, h 484 Shoemaker (N I).
Henry Samuel C, clk R M S, h 545 N Alabama.
Henry Theodore L (T L Henry & Co), r 25 W Walnut.

BUY THE BEST.
Outing BICYCLES $85
MADE BY
HAY & WILLITS MFG CO.
76 N. PENN. ST. Phone 598.

Henry T L & Co (Theodore L Henry), canning factory, n w cor W St Clair and C C C & St L Ry.
Henry Wm, road master, h 224 Davidson.
Henry Wm (Henry & Son), h 252 E Washington.
Henry Wm O (Henry & Son), b 252 E Washington.
Henry Wm O, foreman Dugdale Can Co, h s w cor Madison av and Hoefgen la.
Henry & Son (Wm and Wm O), livery, 240 W Pearl.
Henschall Mary (wid Charles), h 75 Adams.
Henschel August, lab, h 57 New.
Henschel Frank, lab, h rear 31 Wisconsin.
Henschen Adam H, shoes, 526 S Meridian, h 373 Union.
Henschen Elilzabeth (wid Frank H), b 373 Union.
Henschen Frederick W, mach, b 472 Union.
Henschen Harry C, carp, b 259 S East.
Henschen John W, tinner, b 259 S East.
Henschen Wm H, carp, 259 S East, h same.
Hensel John H, candymkr, h 85 S Belmont av (W I).
Hensel Julia A (wid Samuel T), h 183 Dearborn.
Henshaw, see also Hanshaw.
Henshaw Hannah (wid Wm B), h 20 N State av.
Henshaw Thomas J, trav agt, r 28 W New York.
Henshen John F, mach, h 54 Hadley av (W I).
Henshen Wm H, lab, b 54 Hadley av (W I).
Hensler John, lab, b 294 Columbia av.
Hensley, see also Hinesley.
Hensley Charles, polisher, h 563 W Addison (N I).
Hensley Harry B, driver, b 476 N California.
Hensley Harry E, miller, h 292 Blake.
Hensley Isaac N, car insp, h 101 Decatur.
Hensley James W, trav agt, h 41 Hall pl.
Hensley John, r 271 Indiana av.
Hensley John, lab, b 434 Douglass.
Hensley John, watchman, b 174 Martindale av.
Hensley John M, driver, h 118 Fulton.
Hensley Kate, seamstress, b 625 S Meridian.
Hensley Martha A (wid Wilburn J), h 53 Tremont av (H).
Hensley Nancy J (wid John T), h 476 N California.
Hensley Samuel, brakeman, b 187 Hoyt av.
Hensley Thomas F, carp, h 434 Douglass.
Hensley Vina (wid Jacob), dressmkr, 247 N West, h same.
Hens e Wm H, express, b 53 Tremont av (H)l y
Hensmann Wm, lab, h 108 Torbet.
Henson, see also Hansen and Hanson.
Henson Charles S, furnacesetter, h 322 E Wabash.
Henson Charles S jr, mach, b 322 E Wabash.
Henson Frank W, lab, h rear 258 S Meridian.
Henson Robert, waiter, h 123 W Vermont.
Henthorne Johanna C (wid Leroy S), h 735 N Senate av.
Henze Harry G, clk, h 84 Hadley av (W I).
Henzie Adolphus, condr, h 578 Morris (W I).
Hepler Alfred R, stonecutter, h 179 Mass av.
Hepler Thomas D, lab, b 179 Mass av.
Hepp Augustus A, mach, h 108 Cherry.
Hepp John K, carp, h 153 Excelsior av.
Henstein Isaac, pdlr, h 120 Maple.
HERANCOURT BREWING CO THE, Joe G Tilly Mngr, 61-63 S Liberty, Tel 712.

ROOFING MATERIAL C. ZIMMERMAN & SONS, SLATE AND GRAVEL ROOFERS, 19 SOUTH EAST STREET.

PUMPS Chain Pumps, Driven Wells and Deep Water Wells. Repairing Neatly Done. Cisterns Built. CHARLES KRAUSS', 42 S. PENN. ST. TELEPHONE 465.

Collars and Cuffs Laundered in Best of Style. Domestic or High Gloss Finish. ERTEL STEAM LAUNDRY 26 and 28 N. Senate Ave. Telephone 1089.

Herbert Albert, condr, h 93 Oliver av (W I).
Herbert Joseph O, tailor, r 56 Hendricks blk.
Herbertz Nicholas, lab, b 28 Lee (W I).
Herbic Michael, lab, b 49 Holmes av (H).
Herbine Daniel B, clk N Y Store, h 1195 N Capitol av.
Herbine Lottie G, clk N Y Store, h 1195 N Capitol av.
Herboldsheimer Frederick, lab, h 68 Oscar.
Herbsbreith Charles, baker, b 135 E Washington.
Herbst Lewis C, molder, h 174 Germania av (H).
Hercules Powder Co, Charles W Meeker agt, 21½ W Maryland.
Herd, see also Hurd.
Herd Charles E, bkkpr, h 423 Central av.
Herd Henry J, toolmkr, h 383 E Michigan.
Herd John T, beltmkr, h 313 Union.
Herder George P, mach, h 428 Cornell av.
Herder John H, switchman, h 277 S West.
Herder John M, cabtmkr, h 19 Lord.
Herder Louis R, bartndr, h 281 Bates.
Herdman Carrie M, hardware, 418 W Michigan, h same.
Herdman Wm, clk, h 418 W Michigan.
Herdrich Charles, pres The Herdrich-Woollen Machine Co, h 174 Hamilton av.
Herdrich-Woollen Machine Co The, Charles Herdrich pres, Harry Woollen sec and treas, 329 Mass av.
Hereth, see also Hoereth.
Hereth Ad, office 82½ E Washington, h 126 E Michigan.
Hereth Edward G, bkkpr D H Baldwin & Co, b 769 N New Jersey.
Hereth Frank S, b 355 N Noble.
Hereth George L, notions, 508 N West, h same.
Hereth George E, paperhngr, b 252½ Mass av.
Hereth George P, carp, h 374 Coburn.
Hereth Gertrude E, dressmkr, 160 Davidson, b same.
Hereth Guy W, clk, b 160 Davidson.
Hereth Henry J, carp, h 85 Clifford av.
Hereth John C, harness cutter, h 769 N New Jersey.
Hereth Oliver T, harnessmkr, b 769 N New Jersey.
Hereth Peter P, carp, 501 Broadway, b 523 Park av.
Hereth Philip, harnessmkr, h 160 Davidson.
Hereth Wm L, paying teller Indiana National Bank, h 848 N New Jersey.
Hergenroether Leopold, lab, h 276 Coburn.
Hergt Charles A, meats, 834 E Washington, h 819 E Market.
Hergt Frederick L, h 826 E Washington.
Hergt Frederick W, grocer, 119 Prospect, h 179 S Olive.
Herider John M, foreman Sinker-Davis Co, h 178 Fletcher av.
Herider Wm C, millwright, h 69 Hoyt av.
Herig John E, lab, b 134 River av (W I).
Herig John H, justice of peace, h 134 River av (W I).
Heringe John P, h 306 Michigan (H).
Heringe Thomas W, lab, b 306 Michigan (H).
Herman, see also Harman, Harmon and Herrmann.
Herman Annie M (wid John), h 133 N Liberty.
Herman Benjamin H (B H Herman & Co), b 43 The Blacherne.
HERMAN B H & CO (Benjamin H Herman), Pictures and Picture Frames, 66 N Penn.

Richardson & McCrea, 79 East Market Street, FIRE INSURANCE, REAL ESTATE, LOANS, AND RENTAL AGENTS. Telephone 182.

Herman Catherine (wid Wm), h 962 S Meridian.
Herman Christopher B, trav agt, h 122 Hosbrook.
Herman Cinderella (wid Charles), h 40 Drake.
Herman George, lab, b 150 Randolph.
Herman George H, mach, b 133 N Liberty.
Herman Henry, motorman, r 330 E Georgia.
Herman Henry L, mince meat mnfr, 80 E Maryland, h 241 N Liberty.
Herman Henry S, grocer, 59 W Morris, h 550 S Capitol av.
Herman Samuel, fruits, 215 W Washington, h same.
Herman Valentine, lab, h 873 Mass av.
Herman Wiley, cook The Denison.
Herman Wm L, driver, b 166 W 2d.
Hermann Albert A, bkkpr Robert Keller, b 607 S Meridian.
Hermann Edward, mach, h 153 John.
Hermann Edward A, bkkpr Robert Keller, b 607 S Meridian.
Hermann Frederick, mach, h 5 Frazee (H).
Hermann Henry R, driver, h 219 English av.
Hermann Ida M, stenog, b 277 N Pine.
Hermann Ignatz, watchman, h 607 S Meridian.
Hermann Jacob, carp, h 277 N Pine.
Hermann Jacob, lab, h 77 Agnes.
Hermann Nicholas J, watchman, h 1 Merrit (H).
Hermann Oscar, plumber, 376 E 7th, h 445 Bellefontaine.
Hermann Wm, carver, h 427 Union.
Hermanny Andrew, grocer, 150 Blake, h 420 W New York.
Hermanny George, b 420 W New York.
Hermanny Louisa (wid Wm), h 556 Union.
Hermantz George, waiter, r 1 Hutchings blk.
Hern Ryman, lab, b w s canal 1 s of 7th.
Herndon Lucy J (wid Wm M), b 14 Hoyt av.
Herner Mary, boxmkr, b 497 Union.
Herner Peter H, foreman, h 497 Union.
Hernly Amos B, boarding 166 N Delaware.

SHORTHAND REPORTING...... CONVENTIONS, SPEECHES, SERMONS. COPYING ON TYPEWRITER. S. H. EAST, State Agent, THE WILLIAMS TYPEWRITER 55 Thorpe Block, 87 East Market Street.

ELLIS & HELFENBERGER Manufacturers of Iron Vases, Setees and Hitch Posts. 162-170 South Senate Ave. Tel. 958.

THE HOGAN TRANSFER AND STORAGE COMP'Y
Household Goods and Pianos Moved—Packed—Stored...... Baggage and Package Express Machinery and Safes a Specialty Cor. Washington and Illinois Sts. TELEPHONE No. 675.

The Central Rubber & Supply Co. ♦♦♦ Hose, Belting, Packing, Clothing, Druggists' Sundries, Bicycle Tires, Cotton Hose, Etc. New York Belting & Packing Co., L't'd. PHONE 822. 79 S. ILLINOIS ST., INDIANAPOLIS, IND.

The Provident Life and Trust Co.
Small Death Rate. Small Expense Rate. Safe Investments. OF PHILADELPHIA. Insurance in force
D. W. EDWARDS, $115,000,000
General Agent, 508 Indiana Trust Building.

Herntschier Anton, shoemkr, 3 Cherry, h 167 Ft Wayne av.
Herod, see also Harrod.
Herod Wm P (Herod & Herod), patent attorneys, 14-17 Fletcher's Bank bldg, h 661 N Meridian, tel 1571.
Herod Wm W (Herod & Herod), h 731 N Meridian.
HEROD & HEROD (Wm W and Wm P), Lawyers, 14, 15, 16 and 17 Fletcher's Bank Bldg, Tel 692.
Herold Peter J, tailor, h 10 Ketcham.
Heron Alexander, h 642 N Illinois.
Heron Claude, barber, r 321 W North.
Herpick George H, foreman street repairs, 14 basement Court House, tel 1638, h 42 Camp.
Herpick John, foreman, h 149 Trowbridge (W).
Herr Ida B, dressmkr, 113 E St Joseph, h same.
Herr John M, clk, h 374 Bellefontaine.
Herr Joseph, clk, b 163 Clinton.
Herr Mary M (wid Abraham), h 113 E St Joseph.
Herr Milton F, harnessmkr, b 113 E St Joseph.
Herr Rebecca A (wid John P), h 267 Huron.
Herr Wm H, mach hd, b 267 Huron.
Herre Henry, butcher, h 369 S Missouri.
Herrell Garrett, lab, h 21 Springfield.
Herrick Clara W, bkkpr Smith, Day & Co, h 84 Shelby.
HERRICK RICHARD C, Sec Board of Public Safety, Room 2 Basement Court House, Tel 1390; h 124 Cornell av.
Herrick Wm, watchman, h 579 Mass av.
Herriman Ira, pdlr, h 352 N Pine.
Herriman Sarah A (wid George W), b 266 W Vermont.
Herrin Charles W, barber, 541 Shelby, h same.
Herrin Daniel M, h 461 Bellefontaine.
Herring Charles A, uphlr, b 93 Greencastle av.
Herring Charles H, collr, h 335 Spring.

Julius C. Walk & Son,
Jewelers
Indianapolis.
12 EAST WASHINGTON ST.

Herring John W, tmstr, h 38 Sheffield (W I).
Herring Samuel, clk, r 171 W Ohio.
Herring Wm, bartndr, r 77 Kentucky av.
Herrington, see also Harrington.
Herrington Edward J, clk, h 425 College av.
HERRINGTON FRANK L (Successor to I H Herrington & Son), Mnfr and Dealer in Fine Harness, Saddles, Etc, 81 E Market, h 597 Bellefontaine. (See adv opp.)
Herrington Isaac H, h 425 College av.
Herrington James S, porter, r 354 Douglass.
Herrington Samuel P, mnfr, h 472 Park av.
Herrington Wilson J, clk When Clothing Store, b 472 Park av.
Herriott Ephraim M, lab, b 863 S Meridian.
Herriott Juliet I (wid Wm), dental depot, 110 N Penn, h 76 The Blacherne.
Herriott Wm M, h 609 N Capitol av.
Herrlich Herman F, filer, h 14 Eckert.
Herrmann, see also Harman, Harmon and Herman.
Herrmann Ernest A, watchmkr, h 78 N Liberty.
Herrmann George, supt Western Furniture Co, h 191 Minnesota.
HERRMANN GEORGE, Undertaker, Livery and Boarding Stables, Carriages for Wedding Parties, Day and Night, Office 26 S Delaware, Stables 120-128 E Pearl, Tel 911; h 326 N New Jersey.
Herrmann George H, baker, 285 E Washington, h same.
Herrmann George O, toolmkr, h 424 Bellefontaine.
Herrmann Gustav L, h 530 E Ohio.
Herrmann Henry, lumber, 213 S Penn, res New York City.
Herrmann John, h 478 E Market.
Herrmann Magdalena (wid Jacob), b 326 N New Jersey.
Herrmann Philip, undertaker George Herrmann, b 326 N New Jersey.
Herron, see also Hearne and Heron.
Herron Alexander P, dentist, 95½ N Delaware, h 456 same.
Herron Charles F, h w s Milburn 1 n of Indiana av (M P).
HERRON FREDERICK M, Jeweler, 4 E Washington, h 700 N Alabama.
Herron Frederick P, watchmkr Frederick M Herron, h 1127 N Penn.
Herron Josephine B, teacher Public School No 11, b 700 N Alabama.
Herron Samuel F, sewer contr, 265 W 6th, h same.
Herron Walter W, trav agt Parrott-Taggart Bakery, r 425 N Penn.
Hersey Henry A, trav agt, b 30 E Pratt.
Hersh Jacob, tinner, 278 W Washington, r 120 Indiana av.
Hershey Charles, clk, b 297 N Senate av.
Hershey John W, piano tuner, b 464 N Senate av.
Hershey John W jr, stage hd, b 464 N Senate av.
Herskovitz Benjamin, bartndr, h 119 Mass av.
Hert, see also Hurt.
Hert Albert, sawmkr, h 266 N Noble.
Hert Albert J, sawmkr, b 266 N Noble.
Hert Elizabeth (wid Wm), h 383 E Michigan.
Hert Henry J, toolmkr, b 383 E Michigan.

OTTO GAS ENGINES | BUILDERS' EXCHANGE S. W. Cor. Ohio and Penn. Telephone 535.

F. L. HERRINGTON

Successor to I. H. HERRINGTON & SON.

. . . FULL LINE OF . . .

Fine Harness Turf Goods, Etc.

"Agent for Celebrated Whitman Saddle."

81 East Market Street, Indianapolis.

REPAIRING OF ALL KINDS DONE PROMPTLY.

Hesner Joseph, tinner, h 121 Maple.
Hespelt Charles D, baker, 372 Virginia av, h same.
Hess Albert, clk, r 151 N Alabama.

HESS ALEXANDER, Clerk Indiana Supreme and Appellate Courts, Room 17 State House, h 185 N Illinois.

Hess Anna, music teacher, 173 E South, h same.

HESS CASPER, Grocer and Saloon, 507 Madison av, h same.

Hess Catherine (wid John), h 131 Locke.
Hess Charles, carp, h 126 W New York.
Hess Charles F, carp, h 75 E Walnut.
Hess Charles W, fruits, E Mkt House, h 90 S Judge Harding (W I).
Hess Fay, lithog, b 25 Camp.
Hess Frederica (wid Frederick), b 857 N Meridian.
Hess Frederick C, clk, b 507 Madison av.
Hess Frederick G, brewer, h 33 Gresham.
Hess Frederick W, clk Clemens Vonnegut, h 375 Talbott av.
Hess George G, mach hd, h 281 E Georgia.
Hess Gustav, lab, h 36 Center.
Hess Gustav J, foreman, h 320 E Vermont.
Hess Henry H, polisher, b 131 Locke.
Hess Harry W, sawmkr, b 499 S Capitol av.
Hess Herman, mach, h 4 Andrews.
Hess Jacob, cabtmkr, h w s Lincoln av 4 s of Jackson (M J).
Hess Jacob, bartndr, r 499 N Senate av.
Hess James W, pres Indpls Lounge Co, h 555 N Alabama.
Hess John, carp. h 527 Madison av.
Hess John, cigarmkr, h 423 E Michigan.

Hessling Theophilus B, bartndr, h 62 Fulton.
Hessong J Wm, blksmith, s e cor Meridian and 30th, res Broad Ripple, Ind.
Hesten Charles R, engr, h 15 Russell av.
Hesten Wm, waiter, r 88 W Market.
Hester Albert, lab, h 444 Superior.
Hester Frank D, steog State Supt of Public Instruction, b 148 N Illinois.
Hester Frank O, teacher Industrial School, r 76 W North.
Hester Newton H, h 70 Marion av (W I).
Hester Samuel, lab, r 102 S Illinois.
Hester Timothy, hostler, b 28 Columbia al.
Hester Wm, agt, b 287 S New Jersey.
Hester Wm M, lab, h 513 S West.
Heston Daniel W Rev, h 227 Columbia av.
Heston Horace, foreman, h 355 Blake.
Heston Hugh R, coremkr, b 355 Blake.
Heston Patrick, lab, h 462 S Missouri.
Heston Thomas, b 355 Blake.
Heston Thomas, lab, h 38 Holmes av (H).
Hetherington Benjamin F, pres Hetherington & Berner Co, h 846 N New Jersey.

JAS. N. MAYHEW,
MANUFACTURING
OPTICIAN
LENSES AND FRAMES A SPECIALTY.
No. 13 North Meridian St., Indianapolis.

Bank Fixtures a Specialty. Kinds done on short notice.
Street, Indianapolis, Ind.
Contractors and Builders
TELEPHONE 999.

LUMBER | **Sash, Door and Planing . Mill Work .** | **Balke & Krauss Co.** Cor. Market and Missouri Streets.

THE HO
Household Good
Moved—Packed—

The Provid
Small Death
Small Expens
Safe Investme
D. W. EDWA
General

Hose, Belting, Packing, Clothing, Druggists' Sundries, Bicycle Tires, Cotton Hose, Etc.
New York Belting & Packing Co., L't'd.
The Central Rubber & Supply Co.
79 S. ILLINOIS ST., INDIANAPOLIS, IND.
PHONE 8.

Herntschler A
167 Ft Wayne
Herod, see also
Herod Wm P
torneys, 14-17
N Meridian,
Herod Wm W
Meridian.
**HEROD & HE
Lawyers, 14
Bank Bldg,**
Herold Peter J
Heron Alexand
Heron Claude,
Herpick George
14 basement
Camp.
Herpick John,
(W).
Herr Ida B, d
same.
Herr John M,
Herr Joseph, c
Herr Mary M (
seph.
Herr Milton F, harnessmkr, b 113 E St Joseph.
Herr Rebecca A (wid John P), h 267 Huron.
Herr Wm H, mach hd, b 267 Huron.
Herre Henry, butcher, h 369 S Missouri.
Herrell Garrott, lab, h 21 Springfield.
Herrick Clara W, bkkpr Smith, Day & Co, h 84 Shelby.
HERRICK RICHARD C, Sec Board of Public Safety, Room 2 Basement Court House, Tel 1390; h 124 Cornell av.
Herrick Wm, watchman, h 579 Mass av.
Herriman Ira, pdlr, h 352 N Pine.
Herriman Sarah A (wid George W), b 266 W Vermont.
Herrin Charles W, barber, 541 Shelby, h same.
Herrin Daniel M, h 461 Bellefontaine.
Herring Charles A, uphlr, b 93 Greencastle av.
Herring Charles H, collr, h 335 Spring.

Julius C. Walk & Son,
Jewelers
Indianapolis.
12 EAST WASHINGTON ST.

New
Herrm , 478 E Market.
Herrma M alena (wid Jacob), b 2[illegible] N New y
Herrm undertaker George H man, ew Jersey.
Herron Hearne and Heron.
Herron xander P, dentist, 5[illegible] N Delaware, h same.
Herron rles F, h w s Millborn 1 n of Indiana M P).
HERRO FREDERICK M, Jeweler, 4 E Washington, h 700 N Alabama.
Herron deri k P, watchmkr Frederick M Herr h 1[illegible] N Penn.
Herron J phin teacher Public School No 11. [illegible]0 N Alabama.
Herron S u l F, sewer contr, 2[illegible] W 6th, h san
Herron r W, trav agt Parrott-Taggart r 4[illegible] N Penn.
Hersey A trav agt, b 30 E Pratt.
Hersh J [illegible]r, 2[illegible] W Washington, r 120 Ind a.
Hershey k, b 297 N Senate av.
Hershey W piano tuner, b 464 N Senate av.
Hershey W r, stage hd, b 464 N Senate av.
Herskovi min, bartndr, h 119 Mass
Hert, see Hurt.
Hert Alb sawmkr, h 266 N Noble.
Hert Alb J sawmkr, b 266 N Noble.
Hert Eliz th (wid Wm), h 353 E Michigan.
Hert Henr kr, b 353 E Michigan.

OTTO GAS ENGINES
BUILDERS' EXCHANGE
S W. Cor. Ohio and Penn.
Telephone 535.

L ... Merchant Tailors. 21 N. Penn. St. Tel. 934

SALISBURY & STANLEY • Office, Store and Repairing of all kinds done on short notice 177 Clint or Street, Indianapolis, Ind. • Contractors and Builders TELEPHONE 999.

Henry H. Fay,
40½ E. WASHINGTON ST.,
FIRE INSURANCE, REAL ESTATE,
LOANS AND RENTAL AGENT.

81 East

Hesner Joseph, ...
Hespelt Charles D, ... av, h same.
Hess Albert, clk, r ... N A...
HESS ALEXANDER, Clerk ... Supreme and Appellate Cou... Room 17 State House, h 185 N Ill...s.
Hess Anna, music teacher ... same.
HESS CASPER, Grocer and ...on, 507 Madison av, h same.
Hess Catherine (wid J...
Hess Charles, carp, h ...
Hess Charles F, carp, h ...
Hess Charles W, fruit... h 90 S Judge Harding (W I).
Hess Fay, lithog, b 25 ...
Hess Frederica (wid Fr... N Meridian.
Hess Frederick C, clk, ...av.
Hess Frederick G, brew...
Hess Frederick W, ck ... Vonne-gut, h 375 Talbott av.
Hess George G, mach h ... Georgia.
Hess Gustav, lab, h 36 ...
Hess Gustav J, foreman ... Vermont.
Hess Henry H, polisher, ...
Hess Harry W, sawmkr, ...tol av.
Hess Herman, mach, h 4 ...
Hess Jacob, cabtmkr, h w s ... av 4 s of Jackson (M J).
Hess Jacob, bartndr, r 4 ... N ... av.
Hess James W, pres In... Co, h 555 N Alabama.
Hess John, carp h 527 M...
Hess John, cigarmkr, h ...gan.

Hess Lenna, milliner, h 173 E South.
Hess Martha D (wid John H), b 820 N Alabama.
Hess Oliver, wheelmkr, b 499 S Capitol av.
Hess Rosa, h 272½ S Noble.
Hess Sarah (wid Calvin), h 25 Camp.
Hess Theresa (wid Christian), h 70 Bicking.
Hess Thomas D, lab, h 187 Trowbridge (W).
Hess Walter H, lab, h 499 S Capitol av.
Hess Walter S, carp, h n s Michigan av 5 e of Sharpe av (W).
Hess Wm M, grinder, h 71 Oliver av (W I).
Hesse Frances (wid Henry), b 168 W Morris.
Hesse Frank H, mach hd, h 75 Lockerbie.
Hesse Henry D, trav agt, h 184 Ash.
Hesse Robert G, mach The Indpls News, h 7 English av.
Hesseldenz Henry J, clk Singer Mufg Co, b 430 W New York.
Hession Dennis, lab, h 37 S West.
Hession John, lab, h 37 S West.
Hessler Edward, polisher, h 329 S Olive.
Hessling Bernard, tailor, h 76 Hanna.
Hessling Theophilus B, bartndr, h 62 Fulton.
Hessong J Wm, blksmith, s e cor Meridian and 30th, res Broad Ripple, Ind.
Hesten Charles R, engr, h 15 Russell av.
Hesten Wm, waiter, r 88 W Market.
Hester Albert, lab, h 444 Superior.
Hester Frank D, stenog State Supt of Public Instruction, b 148 N Illinois.
Hester Frank O, teacher Industrial School, r 76 W North.
Hester Newton H, h 70 Marion av (W I).
Hester Samuel, lab, r 102 S Illinois.
Hester Timothy, hostler, b 28 Columbia al.
Hester Wm, agt, b 287 S New Jersey.
Hester Wm M, lab, h 513 S West.
Heston Daniel W Rev, h 227 Columbia av.
Heston Horace, foreman, h 355 Blake.
Heston Hugh R, coremkr, h 355 Blake.
Heston Patrick, lab, h 462 S Missouri.
Heston Thomas, b 355 Blake.
Heston Thomas, lab, h 38 Holmes av (H).
Hetherington Benjamin F, pres Hetherington & Berner Co, h 846 N New Jersey.

JAS. N. MAYHEW,
MANUFACTURING
OPTICIAN
LENSES AND FRAMES A SPECIALTY.
No. 13 North Meridian St., Indianapolis.

LUMBER | Sash, Door and Planing Mill Work. | Balke & Krauss Co. Cor. Market and Missouri Streets.

Joseph.

Herr Rebecca A (wid John P), h 267 Huron.

Herr Wm H, mach hd, b 267 Huron.

Herre Henry, butcher, h 369 S Missouri.

Herrell Garrott, lab, h 21 Springfield.

Herrick Clara W, bkkpr Smith, Day & Co, h 84 Shelby.

HERRICK RICHARD C, Sec Board of Public Safety, Room 2 Basement Court House, Tel 1390; h 124 Cornell av.

Herrick Wm, watchman, h 579 Mass av.

Herriman Ira, pdlr, h 352 N Pine.

Herriman Sarah A (wid George W), b 266 W Vermont.

Herrin Charles W, barber, 541 Shelby, h same.

Herrin Daniel M, h 461 Bellefontaine.

Herring Charles A, uphlr, b 93 Greencastle av.

Herring Charles H, collr, h 335 Spring.

Julius C. Walk & Son,
Jewelers
Indianapolis.
12 EAST WASHINGTON ST.

New York City.

Herrmann John, h 478 E Market.

Herrmann Magdalena (wid Jacob), b 326 N New Jersey.

Herrmann Philip, undertaker George Herrmann, b 326 N New Jersey.

Herron, see also Hearne and Heron.

Herron Alexander P, dentist, 95½ N Delaware, h 456 same.

Herron Charles F, h w s Milburn 1 n of Indiana av (M P).

HERRON FREDERICK M, Jeweler, 4 E Washington, h 700 N Alabama.

Herron Frederick P, watchmkr Frederick M Herron, h 1127 N Penn.

Herron Josephine B, teacher Public School No 11, b 700 N Alabama.

Herron Samuel F, sewer contr, 265 W 6th, h same.

Herron Walter W, trav agt Parrott-Taggart Bakery, r 425 N Penn.

Hersey Henry A, trav agt, b 30 E Pratt.

Hersh Jacob, tinner, 278 W Washington, r 120 Indiana av.

Hershey Charles, clk, b 297 N Senate av.

Hershey John W, piano tuner, b 464 N Senate av.

Hershey John W jr, stage hd, b 464 N Senate av.

Herskovitz Benjamin, bartndr, h 119 Mass av.

Hert, see also Hurt.

Hert Albert, sawmkr, h 266 N Noble.

Hert Albert J, sawmkr, b 266 N Noble.

Hert Elizabeth (wid Wm), h 383 E Michigan.

Hert Henry J, toolmkr, b 383 E Michigan.

The Central Rubber & Supply Co
PHONES. 79 S. ILLINOIS ST., INDIANAPOLIS, IND.

OTTO GAS ENGINES | BUILDERS' EXCHANGE S. W. Cor. Ohio and Penn. Telephone 535.

Becker & Son Charles Becker Jacob Becker Jr. Merchant Tailors, 21 N. Penn. St. Tel. 934

Hert Kiah O, trav agt Sentinel Printing Co, r 75 W Market.
Hert Vincent B, mach, b 383 E Michigan.
Hert Wm A, printer, h 324 Fulton.
Hert Wm H, lab, b 266 N Noble.
Hertweck Albert F, uphlr, h 118 Blackford.
Hertweck Philip J, sawmkr, h 106 Chadwick.
Hertz Frank M, saloon, 251 English av, b 213 Hoyt av.
Hertz Magdaline, notions, 15 E Mkt House, h 133 Hosbrook.
Hertz Martin, carp, 213 Hoyt av, h same.
Hertzberg Adolph, pdlr, h 104 Maple.
Hertzberger George J, cabtmkr, h s s Bloyd av 4 w of Shade (B).
Hertzler Elias M, carp, b 1123 E Michigan.
Hervey, see also Harvey.
Hervey Carey F, teacher, b 533 W Addison (N I).
Hervey Charlotte B (wid Lambertine B), b 568 Shelby.
Hervey Edwin V, phys, 744 Shelby, b same.
Hervey Elizabeth, notary public and stenog A J Beveridge, b 124 Broadway.
Hervey Gilford P, grocer, 533 W Addison (N I), h same.
Hervey James R, cigarmkr, h 75 Madison av.
Hervey James W, phys, 744 Shelby, h same.
Hervey Sarah A (wid Worthington W), h 124 Broadway.
Hervey Taylor M (T M Hervey & Co), b 75 Madison av.
Hervey T M & Co (Taylor M Hervey, John C Myers), ticket brokers, 15 S Illinois.
Hervey Walter J, clk, b 75 Madison av.
Herzig Charles, baker, h 91 Benton.
Herzsch August F, vice-pres The Indpls Book and Stationery Co, h 465 Broadway.
Hesley Daniel H, mach, h 43 Church.
Hesner Joseph, tinner, h 121 Maple.
Hespelt Charles D, baker, 372 Virginia av, h same.
Hess Albert, clk, r 151 N Alabama.

HESS ALEXANDER, Clerk Indiana Supreme and Appellate Courts, Room 17 State House, h 185 N Illinois.

Hess Anna, music teacher, 173 E South, h same.

HESS CASPER, Grocer and Saloon, 507 Madison av, h same.

Hess Catherine (wid John), h 131 Locke.
Hess Charles, carp, h 126 W New York.
Hess Charles F, carp, h 75 E Walnut.
Hess Charles W, fruits, E Mkt House, h 90 S Judge Harding (W I).
Hess Fay, lithog, b 25 Camp.
Hess Frederica (wid Frederick), b 857 N Meridian.
Hess Frederick C, clk, b 507 Madison av.
Hess Frederick G, brewer, h 33 Gresham.
Hess Frederick W, clk Clemens Vonnegut, h 375 Talbott av.
Hess George G, mach hd, h 281 E Georgia.
Hess Gustav, lab, h 36 Center.
Hess Gustav J, foreman, h 320 E Vermont.
Hess Henry H, polisher, b 131 Locke.
Hess Harry W, sawmkr, b 499 S Capitol av.
Hess Herman, mach, h 4 Andrews.
Hess Jacob, cabtmkr, h w s Lincoln av 4 s of Jackson (M J).
Hess Jacob, bartndr, r 499 N Senate av.
Hess James W, pres Indpls Lounge Co, h 555 N Alabama.
Hess John, carp, h 527 Madison av.
Hess John, cigarmkr, h 423 E Michigan.

Henry H. Fay,
40½ E. WASHINGTON ST.,
FIRE INSURANCE, REAL ESTATE,
LOANS AND RENTAL AGENT.

Hess Lenna, milliner, h 173 E South.
Hess Martha D (wid John H), b 820 N Alabama.
Hess Oliver, wheelmkr, b 499 S Capitol av.
Hess Rosa, h 272½ S Noble.
Hess Sarah (wid Calvin), h 25 Camp.
Hess Theresa (wid Christian), h 70 Bicking.
Hess Thomas D, lab, h 187 Trowbridge (W).
Hess Walter H, lab, h 499 S Capitol av.
Hess Walter S, carp, h n s Michigan av 5 e of Sharpe av (W).
Hess Wm M, grinder, h 71 Oliver av (W I).
Hesse Frances (wid Henry), b 168 W Morris.
Hesse Frank H, mach hd, h 75 Lockerbie.
Hesse Henry D, trav agt, h 184 Ash.
Hesse Robert G, mach The Indpls News, h 7 English av.
Hesseldenz Henry J, clk Singer Mnfg Co, b 420 W New York.
Hession Dennis, lab, b 37 S West.
Hession John, lab, h 37 S West.
Hessler Edward, polisher, h 329 S Olive.
Hessling Bernard, tailor, h 76 Hanna.
Hessling Theophilus B, bartndr, h 62 Fulton.
Hessong J Wm, blksmith, s e cor Meridian and 30th, res Broad Ripple, Ind.
Hesten Charles R, engr, h 15 Russell av.
Hesten Wm, waiter, r 88 W Market.
Hester Albert, lab, h 444 Superior.
Hester Frank D, steog State Supt of Public Instruction, b 148 N Illinois.
Hester Frank O, teacher Industrial School, r 76 W North.
Hester Newton H, h 70 Marion av (W I).
Hester Samuel, lab, r 102 S Illinois.
Hester Timothy, hostler, b 28 Columbia al.
Hester Wm, agt, b 287 S New Jersey.
Hester Wm M, lab, h 513 S West.
Heston Daniel W Rev, h 227 Columbia av.
Heston Horace, foreman, h 355 Blake.
Heston Hugh R, coremkr, b 355 Blake.
Heston Patrick, lab, h 462 S Missouri.
Heston Thomas, b 355 Blake.
Heston Thomas, lab, h 38 Holmes av (H).
Hetherington Benjamin F, pres Hetherington & Berner Co, h 846 N New Jersey.

JAS. N. MAYHEW,
MANUFACTURING
OPTICIAN
LENSES AND FRAMES A SPECIALTY.
No. 13 North Meridian St., Indianapolis.

SALISBURY & STANLEY • Office, Store and Bar Fixtures a Specialty. Repairing of all kinds done on short notice. 177 Clint or Set. Indpls, Ind. • Contractors and Builders TELEPHONE 999.

LUMBER | Sash, Door and Planing . Mill Work . | Balke & Krauss Co. Cor. Market and Missouri Streets.

FRIEDGEN'S TAN SHOES are the Newest Shades
Prices the Lowest. 19 North Pennsylvania St.

SAMUEL LAING General Job Work in Sheet Metal of all Kinds
72 AND 74 E. COURT STREET.

M. B. WILSON, Pres. W. F. CHURCHMAN, Cash.
THE CAPITAL NATIONAL BANK,
INDIANAPOLIS, IND.
Make collections on all points in the States of Indiana and Illinois on the most favorable rates.
Capital, - - $300,000
Surplus and Earnings, 50,000
No. 28 S. Meridian St., Cor. Pearl.

Hetherington Christopher J, lab, h 7 Geneva (W).
Hetherington Frederick A, sec Hetherington & Berner Co, h 989 N Alabama.
HETHERINGTON & BERNER CO, Benjamin F Hetherington Pres, Frederick Berner Vice-Pres, Frederick A Hetherington Sec, Frederick Berner Jr Treas, Architectural Iron Works and Mnfrs of Structural Steel and Asphalt Plants, 19-27 W South, Tel 419.
Hett John M, saloon, 342 National rd, h 41 State.
Hett Michael, bartendr, b 41 State.
Hettinger Alice, h 18 S Senate av.
Hettinger Charles B, collr, b 63 E 26th.
Hettinger Iby B, phys, h 63 E 26th.
Hettwer John, clk Circle Park Hotel.
Hetz Frederick, confr, 68 N Penn, h 66½ same.
Hetzel Albert, brewer, h 717 Charles.
Hetzel Edgar B, supt J B Allfree Mnfg Co, b 137 Highland pl.
Hetzler Frank M, brakeman, r 15 N State av.
Heupel Arthur J, bartndr, b 53 River av (W I).
Heure Henry, lab, h 369 S Missouri.
Heurlin John, tailor, r 55 Dearborn.
Heuser Catherine (wid Wm L), h 185 Elizabeth.
Heuser Christian E, coremkr, b 185 Elizabeth.
Heuser Henry W, molder, b 185 Elizabeth.
Heuser Wm, uphlr, h 30 Wisconsin.
Heuser Wm L, driver, h 64 Maxwell.
HEUSS FREDERICK A, Propr Indianapolis Lithographic Co, 95 E South, h 118 Kennington.
Heustis Lou (wid John B), r 34 E Vermont.
Hewes George E, engr, h 13 W Sutherland (B).
Hewett Mollie E, milliner, r 124 E Ohio.
Hewitt Edward, lab, h 593 W Washington.
Hewitt Horace B, bkkpr, b 182 College av.

MONEY
Loaned on Short Notice at Lowest Rates.
TUTTLE & SEGUIN,
Tel. 1168. 28 E. Market St.

Hewitt Horace L, sec and treas Mohawk Cycle Co and propr North Indianapolis Cradle Works, h 182 College av.
Hewitt James W, trav auditor C C C & St L Ry, h 127 E Pratt.
Hewitt Mary A (wid George), b 182 College av.
Hewitt Orin, lab, b 100 Lee (W I).
Hewitt Robert A, lab, h 39 S Reisner (W I).
Hews Joseph, b 107 Sharpe av (W).
Hewson Edwin C, cooper, h 135 Tacoma av.
Hewson Elliott D, b 223 Elm.
Hewson John E, clk, h 53 Laurel.
Hey Edward, clk R M S, r 12 Union.
Hey Jacob R, cabtmkr, b 42 Sullivan.
Hey John, lab, h 107 Wisconsin.
Hey Peter J, mach opr The Indpls Sentinel, h 42 Sullivan.
Hey Scioto (wid Jacob), b 42 Sullivan.
Hey Valentine S, printer, h 255 Coburn.
Heyden John, clk, h 107 Wisconsin.
Heyer, see also Heier.
Heyer Oscar, dry goods, 698 Home av, h 66 Woodruff av.
Heyer Wm A, barber, 161 W Washington, h 221 Blake.
Heyob Jacob, lab, h 447 S West.
Heywood Amanda M, h 146 S East.
Heywood Augustus, lab, h 319 Clinton.
Heywood Frank W, trav agt McCormick H M Co, h 578 Park av.
HEYWOOD JAMES B, Genl Agt McCormick Harvesting Machine Co, 67-69 S Penn, Tel 781; h 639 College av, Tel 1024.
Hiatt, see also Hyatt.
Hiatt Albert, carp, h 21 S Rural.
Hiatt Alonzo, cigarmkr, h 191 W South.
Hiatt Augusta, bkkpr, b 31 Cornell av.
Hiatt Eli W, mason, h 502 Highland av (N I).
Hiatt Francis H, foreman, h 224 E New York.
Hiatt Frederick C, cigarmkr, b 102 Cook.
Hiatt George E, asst sec Railroad Y M C A, h n e cor Brightwood av and C C C & St L Ry (B).
Hiatt Harvey, brakeman, b 28 S State av.
Hiatt Henry, fireman, b 162 Harrison.
Hiatt Henry F, foreman, h 224 E New York.
Hiatt John, helper, b 149 S Noble.
Hiatt John, farmer, h s s P C C & St L Ry 1 e of Line (I).
Hiatt Lawrence M, cigarmkr, b 102 Cook.
Hiatt Martin D, lab, r 32 N Senate av.
Hiatt Martin S, driver, h 146 Ft Wayne av.
Hiatt Mary (wid John), h s s Lambert 1 e of Belmont (W I).
Hiatt Mary E (wid James M), h 104 Michigan (H).
Hiatt May E, school teacher, b 512 Bellefontaine.
Hiatt Otis, collr Nelson Morris & Co, b 191 W South.
Hiatt Otis S, reedwkr, b 102 Cook.
Hiatt Otto H, b 104 Michigan (H).
Hiatt Richard, driver, b 102 Cook.
Hiatt Sarah E, h 102 Cook.
Hibaugh David, lab, h 218 W Wabash.
Hibben Benjamin, h 424 E Maryland.
Hibben Benjamin M, express, h 626 Madison av.
Hibben Harold B (Murphy, Hibben & Co), h 743 N Delaware.
Hibben Henry B, switchman, b 38 S State av.
Hibben Sarah A (wid James S), b 737 N Delaware.

PAPER BOXES, MANUFACTURED BY SULLIVAN & MAHAN 41 W. PEARL STREET.

DIAMOND WALL PLASTER { Telephone 1410
BUILDERS' EXCHANGE.

Fine Laundry Work or Special ty
Collars and Cuffs our Hobby.
THE HOME LAUNDRY
197 S. Illinois St.
Telephone 1769.

Hibben Thomas E, buyer Murphy, Hibben & Co, h 750 College av.
Hibbits Sarah (wid Frank), b 113 W 4th.
Hibbitts Samuel, driver, h 267 W 5th.
Hibbs Clarence E, sub letter carrier P O, b 46 Hoyt av.
Hibbs Elmer E, clk, b 46 Hoyt av.
Hibbs James I, phys, 46 Hoyt av, b same.
Hibbs Melvina M, h 46 Hoyt av.
Hibler Daniel, carp, h 191 Belmont av (H).
Hibler Henry K, mach hd, h 643 Mass av.
Hibler John C, carp, h 653 E 7th.
Hibler Wm R, mach hd, b 653 E 7th.
Hibner, see also Huebner.
Hibner Charles F, mach, h 22 Quincy.
Hibner Otto, lab, h 40 Jones.
Hice Samuel, mer police, h 91 Maple.
Hice Samuel M, ticket agt C C C & St L Ry, 36 Jackson pl, h 68 Prospect.
Hickerson Frank, driver, h 12 Parker.
Hickey Ellen (wid John), h 85 McGinnis.
Hickey Harry H, salesman Pearson's Music House, h 735 N Illinois.
Hickey Helen, principal Public School No 31, r 381 N Delaware.
Hickey James A, clk, h 180 English av.
Hickey John, lab, b 85 McGinnis.
Hickey John F, flagman, h 100 Bates.
Hickey John J, huckster, h 52 Bates.
Hickey John J, lab, h 39 N Dorman.
Hickey Joseph C, stonecutter, h 30 Grant.
Hickey Lawrence, lab, b 252 E Washington.
Hickey Michael F, uphlr, b 85 McGinnis.
Hickey Patrick J, engr, h 311 Fletcher av.
Hicklin Eber K, adv agt, b 12 Lynn av (W I).
Hickman Wm M, stock examiner Bureau Animal Industry, h 12 Lynn av (W I).
Hickman, see also Heckman.
Hickman Albert, tmstr, b 258 S Capitol av.
Hickman Alonzo, mach hd, b 130 Pleasant.
Hickman Benjamin, bartndr, h 120 Vincennes (W I).
Hickman Charles A, lab, h 258 S Capitol av.
Hickman George A M, tmstr, h 114 Harrison.
Hickman Jonathan B, carp, h 130 Pleasant.
Hickman Martha, laundress, h 230 E Wabash.
Hickman Mary (wid George), boarding 230 S Penn.
Hickman Ora, engr, b 130 Pleasant.
Hickman Royal B, lab, h 80 Marion av (W I).
Hickman Wm, lab The Bates.
Hickner Joseph, lab, b 298 W Morris.
Hickok George E, tmstr, h 62 Poplar (B).
Hickok Horace F, b 62 Poplar (B).
Hicks Adelbert F, h 66 S Noble.
Hicks Alfred, lab, h 462 W Chicago (N I).
Hicks Allison M, lab, h 60 Bismarck (W I).
Hicks Celia (wid Aaron), h 88 Torbet.
Hicks Daniel, lab, h 16 Lafayette.
Hicks Edgar J, mach, h 961 Cornell av.
Hicks Edward, lab, r 275 W Market.
Hicks Edward A, lab, b 29 W Market.
Hicks Edward B, mach, r 166½ W Washington.
Hicks Edward L, porter, r 9 Fayette.
Hicks Edwin N, trav pass agt L E & W R R, h 405 Ash.
Hicks Emmazetta (wid Jeremiah), h 476 Ash.
Hicks Frances A (wid Mortimer W), h 376 S Missouri.
Hicks Frank lab, h 35 Everett.
Hicks Frederick, lab, h w s Dayton av 2 s of English av (I).

FRANK NESSLER. WILL H. ROST.
FRANK NESSLER & CO.
Tailors
56 EAST MARKET ST. (Lemcke Building),
INDIANAPOLIS, IND.

Hicks George, trav agt, b Circle Park Hotel.
Hicks George H, lab, b 88 Torbet.
Hicks Grant, mach hd, b 287 E Georgia.
Hicks Harry L, switchman, b 103 Prospect.
Hicks Harry S, treas Ind Dental College, b The Denison.
Hicks Henry, foreman, b 300 W Maryland.
Hicks Horatio, lab, b 91 Patterson.
Hicks James, polisher, h 17 S Senate av.
Hicks James L, carp, h 91 Patterson.
Hicks James S, carp, h 451½ N New Jersey.
Hicks John, lab, b 125 N West.
Hicks John, lab, r 275 W Market.
Hicks John, polisher, h 579 W Michigan.
Hicks John A, lab, b 88 Torbet.
Hicks John P, lab, h 135 Lexington av.
Hicks John Q, genl yardmaster C C C & St L Ry, h 103 Prospect.
Hicks John R, student, b 476 Ash.
Hicks Jonathan, lab, b 107 Minerva.
Hicks Joseph, cooper, b 326 W Maryland.
Hicks Joseph M, phys, 171 E Washington, h e s Watts 1 s of Clifford av.
Hicks LeRoy, filer, b 66 S Noble.
Hicks Lydia, h 245 E Market.
Hicks Martha (wid Wm H), b 216 Alvord.
Hicks Mary (wid Jonathan P), b 107 Minerva.
Hicks Mary S, h 280 College av.
Hicks Michael, hostler, b 125 E Washington.
Hicks Otis V, cashr I D & W Ry, b 268 S Meridian.
Hicks Richard L, news dealer, 127 W Washington, h same.
Hicks Sabina (wid Simeon), h 570 W Michigan.
Hicks Sarah A (wid Charles), b 206 Blackford.
Hicks Uriah G, mach hd, h 287 E Georgia.
Hicks Wm, carp, r rear 226 E Washington.
Hicks Wm, cooper, b 261 S West.
Hicks Wm H, lab, h 197 Pleasant.
Hicks Wm W, carp, 221 Buchanan, h same.
Hickson Mary A (wid Harry), b 240 N Noble.
Hicky Addie, h 23 W Ohio.

Haueisen & Hartmann
163-169 E. Washington St.
FURNITURE,
Carpets,
Household Goods,
Tin, Granite and China Wares, Oil Cloth and Shades

THE WM. H. BLOCK CO. DRY GOODS,
7 AND 9 EAST WASHINGTON STREET. MEN'S FURNISHINGS.

Fidelity and Deposit Co. of Maryland. BONDS SIGNED.—LOCAL BOARD John B. Elam, Albert Sahm, Smiley N. Chambers, John M. Spann.
GEORGE W. PANGBORN, General Agent, 704-706 Lemcke Building. Telephone 140.

74 EAST MARKET STREET Telephone 863.
Insure Your Property With FRANK K. SAWYER

JOSEPH GARDNER,
Hot Air Furnaces
With Combination Gas Burners for Burning Gas and Other Fuel at the Same Time.
37, 39 & 41 KENTUCKY AVE. Telephone 322

Hicky Joseph C, stonecutter, h 401 Cornell av.
Hiday Charles M, condr, h 34 Depot (B).
Hiddinger Peter J, condr, h 141 Spann av.
Hide Charles, lab, b 217 E Wabash.
HIDE, LEATHER AND BELTING CO, George W Snyder Propr, John W Elstun Mngr, Leather and Belting, 125 S Meridian, Tel 428.
Hiden George A, fireman, b 6 Detroit.
Hider George W, lab, h e s Sherman Drive 5 n of Washington.
Hieatt Mary (wid Richard A), b 445 Bellefontaine.
Hiens John F, barber, 323 Clifford av, h same.
Hiers Oliver T, driver, h 474 E Washington.
Hiese Henry, molder, h 12 Reynolds av (H).
Higbee Wm R, shoemkr, h 8 Warren av (W I).
Higdon Clara M, asst R I Blakeman, b 12 Wendell av.
Higdon John E, teacher High School, b 65 Ruckle.
Higdon Sadie (wid Edward D), h 12 Wendell av.
Higgins Abraham, lab, h 4 Susquehanna.
Higgins Arthur D, h 225 E St Clair.
Higgins Cassius E, switchman, h 48 Chase (W I).
Higgins Catherine (wid John), h 446 Cornell av.
Higgins Clement, driver, r 120 Roanoke.
Higgins Edward B, porter, h 135 Ft Wayne av.
Higgins Ella (wid Wm A), h 250 W 12th.
Higgins Ella F, h 191 N Liberty.
Higgins George B, carp, h 466 W Udell (N I).
Higgins James B, carp, h 646 Herbert (M P).
Higgins James H, butcher, h 12 Eden pl.
Higgins Johanna (wid Charles D), h 6 S Gale (B).
Higgins John M, drayman, h 3 Carlos.
Higgins John W, carp, h 1401 Rader (N I).
Higgins Jonathan J, b 126 Highland pl.
Higgins Joseph B, carp, h 470 W Shoemaker (N I).

J. S. FARRELL & CO.
Plumbing
Natural and Artificial Gas Fitting.
84 N. ILLINOIS STREET.
TELEPHONE 382.

Higgins Julius J, real est, h 242 Broadway.
Higgins Leslie C, fireman, b 6 S Gale (B).
Higgins Margaret E, boarding 646 Herbert (M P).
Higgins Michael, drayman, h 1 Carlos.
Higgins Peter K, chief insp Cent U Tel Co, h 866 N Senate av.
Higgins Robert A, lab, h 88 Meikel.
Higgins Thomas F, driver, h 45 Fenneman.
Higgins Walter, lab, h 237 Douglass.
Higgins Webster R, mach, h 75 Dearborn.
Higgins Wm, bkkpr, b 334 N Illinois.
Higgins Wm, lab, h 66 Geisendorff.
Higgins Wm, lab, h 320 Highland av.
Higgins Wm, lab, h 955 S Meridian.
Higgins Wm, lab, b 551 W Washington.
Higgins Wm A, teacher, h 1401 Rader (N I).
Higgins Wm G, coachman, h rear 175 St Mary.
Higgins Wm H, r 242 E Vermont.
Higgins Wm L, vice-pres Metallic Mnfg Co, b 483 N Meridian.
Higginson Andrew J, b 368 N New Jersey.
Higgs David, lab, h 50 Geisendorff.
Higgs Georgiana (wid Wm H), h 233 Cedar.
Higgs Jeremiah, lab, b 50 Geisendorff.
Higgs Mary (wid David), h 551 W Washington.
Higgs Pearl Z (wid George N), h 101 Elm.
Higgs Wm B, waiter, r 9 Fayette.
Higgs Wm H, engr, h 50 Spann av.
High John, b 155 Shelby.
High Wm K, foreman C C C & St L Ry, h 57 Bellefontaine.
Higham Thomas H, h 168 Cornell av.
Highbaugh Burton, lab, h rear s s Washington 3 e of Line (I).
Highbaugh Clark, lab, b rear s s Washington 3 e of Line (I).
Highbaugh Harriet (wid Scipio), h w s Arlington av 3 n of Walnut av (I).
Highland, see also Hyland.
Highland Charles, mach, h 115 Buchanan.
Highland Elmer, agt, r 117 N Senate av.
Highland John W, auctioneer, h 619 Bellefontaine.
Highstreet Charles, miller, h 51 Davis.
Highstreet Cornelius, lab, h 75 Miller (W I).
Highstreet George J, lab, b 628 Madison av.
Highstreet Jacob J, mach hd, h 96 Hendricks.
Highstreet Jacob L, mach hd, h 115 Dunlop.
Highstreet John, butcher, h 628 Madison av.
Highstreet Mary (wid Harry), b 26 Mulberry.
Hightower James H, janitor, h 175 N Penn.
Hightower Oscar, b 276 Chapel.
Hightower Sarah, h 276 Chapel.
Hightower Wm, waiter, b 276 Chapel.
Hightower Wm D, porter 277 N Delaware.
Hightshoe David, b 91 Laurel.
Hightshoe David W, carp, h 60 Sheffield (W I).
Highwarden Wm, lab, b 115 Douglass.
Higinbotham Frank, stereotyper, b 130 E New York.
Higinbotham George D, wood polisher, b 130 E New York.
Higinbotham Ida B (wid Jacob), b 239 W McCarty.
Higinbotham Sarah F (wid Charles P), h 130 E New York.
Higinbotham Thomas, tmstr, h 413 S West.
Higinbotham Wm, cook, r 319 E Washington.
Hignight James R, saloon, 598 Virginia av, h 479 Dillon.
Hilands Charles A, civ engr, r 151 Ft Wayne av.

IF CONTINUED to the end of its dividend period, policies of the UNITED STATES LIFE INSURANCE CO., will equal or excel any investment policy ever offered to the public. | E. B. SWIFT, Manager, 25 E. Market St.

Wm. Kotteman 89 & 91 E. Washington St. TELEPHONE 1742 Furniture

Hild Ferdinand C J, janitor, h 445 S Illinois.
HILD WM, Sample Room, n w cor Blake and New York, h same.
Hildebrand Caroline M (wid Henry W), h 308 N Delaware.
Hildebrand Charles F, car rep, h 68 Orange av.
Hildebrand Clayton S, clk Hildebrand Hardware Co, h 188 N Capitol av.
Hildebrand George B, car rep, h 32 Larch.
HILDEBRAND HARDWARE CO, Philip M Hildebrand Mngr, Wholesale and Retail Hardware, 52-54 S Meridian, Tel 323.
Hildebrand Harry F, bkkpr, b 308 N Delaware.
Hildebrand Jacob S, clk Hildebrand Hardware Co, h 51 Madison av.
Hildebrand Louis H, foreman, r 720 E Ohio.
Hildebrand Philip M, mngr Hildebrand Hardware Co, h 937 N Meridian.
Hildebrand Rosa (wid Charles), h 467 S Delaware.
Hildebrandt John, carp, h e s Rural 2 n of Clifford av.
Hildreth Theodore A, genl sec Y M C A, h 62 Andrews.
Hiles Charles O, wheelmkr, h 879 Milburn (M P).
Hiles George F, mach, h rear 170 Beacon.
Hiles Mary (wid Aaron), b 40 Martin.
Hilgemeier August G, butcher, b 56 Gatling.
Hilgemeier Bros (George A and Frank F), meats, 60 E Mkt House and n e cor Raymond and Applegate.
Hilgemeier Christian H, grocer, 360 Shelby, h same.
Hilgemeier Frank F (Hilgemeier Bros), b 56 Gatling.
Hilgemeier George A (Hilgemeier Bros), b 56 Gatling.
Hilgemeier Mary E (wid Christian), h 56 Gatling.
Hilgenberg Catherine (wid Christopher), h 45 Martin.
Hilgenberg Christian A, real est, 27 W Ohio, h 346 W 1st.
Hilgenberg John J, clk, h 45 Martin.
Hilgert Peter, lab, h 38 Gatling.
Hilkenbach Edward D, clk Kingan & Co (ltd), h 180 Douglass.
Hilkene Jacob H, foreman, h 736 Chestnut.
Hill Adeline (wid Benjamin F), h 103 Columbia av.
Hill Albert, phys, b 46 S Capitol av.
Hill Albert A, b 448 W McLene (N I).
Hill Alice J, teacher Industrial School, b 453 Ash.
Hill Benjamin F, creamery, 291 Mass av, h 260 Keystone av.
Hill Benjamin F, lab, b 103 Columbia av.
Hill Bird, painter, r 94 E South.
Hill Caleb E, b 418 Park av.
Hill Carmel, horseshoer, h 65 Lynn av (W I).
Hill Caroline (wid John), h 52 Hosbrook.
Hill Charles A (G W Hill & Son), b 110 S East.
Hill Charles L, lab, b 325 E Ohio.
Hill Charles L, clk, r 57½ W Maryland.
Hill Charles M, engr, h 865 Bellefontaine.
Hill Charles W, lab, h 395 S Capitol av.
Hill Clara L, music teacher, 5 Ruckle, b same.

We Buy Municipal ~ Bonds ~
THOS. C. DAY & CO,
Rooms 325 to 330 Lemcke Bldg.

Hill Collins F, foreman Sinker-Davis Co, h 78 S Linden.
Hill Conrad (Stark & Hill), h 31 Clarke.
Hill Corydon T, ironwkr, h 166 S William (W I).
Hill Daniel W, canmkr, h 12 Minnesota.
Hill David B, engr, b 173 E Market.
Hill David S, gen supt L E & W R R, s w cor Washington and Noble, b The Bates.
Hill Edgar, lab, b 171 W Wabash.
Hill Edward, insp City Engineer, h 546 N Senate av.
Hill Edward, porter, h rear 163 St Mary.
HILL EDWIN, Sec The McGilliard Agency Co, 83-85 E Market, Tel 479; h 38 Ruckle.
Hill Elmer P, mach, b 453 Ash.
Hill Ezra D, supt Western Paving and Supply Co, h 347 N Delaware.
Hill Frances A (wid Asbury), h 121 Yandes.
Hill Francis, cooper, h 54 Lord.
Hill Frank, driver, b 227 W New York.
Hill Frank, lab, b 404 Blackford.
Hill Frank, lab, b 171 W Wabash.
Hill Frank, solicitor, h 493 Madison av.
Hill Frank, waiter, r 170 Bird.
Hill Frank B, mach, b 435 W Eugene (N I).
Hill Frank M, mason, b 865 Bellefontaine.
Hill George E Rev, h 123 E 6th.
Hill George E, condr, h 1151 Northwestern av.
Hill George G, photog, b 742 N Senate av.
Hill George H, clk L E & W R R, b Hotel English.
Hill George R, attendant Insane Hospital.
Hill George R, lab, b 435 W Eugene (N I).
Hill George W (G W Hill & Son), h 110 S East.
Hill G W & Son (George W and Charles A), coopers, 110 S East.
Hill Harley B, paperhngr, b 103 Columbia av.
Hill Harrison C, tmstr, h 98 Martindale av.
Hill Harry, lab, b 171 W Wabash.
Hill Henrietta, confr, 221 W Ohio, h 219 same.
Hill Henry, mach, r 19 N Arsenal av.

EAT
QUAKER BREAD
ASK YOUR GROCER FOR IT.
THE HITZ BAKING CO.

SHOW CASES || WILLIAM WIEGEL || 6 West Louisiana Street Opp. Union Station.

CARPETS CLEANED LIKE NEW. TELEPHONE 818
CAPITAL STEAM CARPET CLEANING WORKS

BENJ. BOOTH PRACTICAL EXPERT ACCOUNTANT. Thirty years' experience. First-class credentials. Room 18, 82½ E. Washington St. Indianapolis, Ind.

18 and 20 S. Meridian St. Established 8. The Old Red Ye Sherman European Restaurant

ESTABLISHED 1876. TELEPHONE 168.
CHESTER BRADFORD,
SOLICITOR OF PATENTS,
AND COUNSEL IN PATENT CAUSES.
(See adv. page 6.)
Office:—Rooms 14 and 16 Hubbard Block, S.W. Cor. Washington and Meridian Streets, INDIANAPOLIS, INDIANA.

Hill Henry, shoemkr, 34 Monument pl, h 227 W 2d.
Hill Henry, wagonmkr, b 90 S West.
Hill Henry B, bartndr, h 127 E Ohio.
Hill Henry C, horseshoer, 297 W Washington, b 221 W Pearl.
Hill Hillard, tinner, h 415 W Addison (N I).
Hill Holman T, baker, w s Watts 1 n of Michigan, h same.
Hill Ida M, dressmkr, 453 Ash, h same.
Hill Isaiah, coachman 467 N Delaware.
Hill Jacob P, blksmith, h 448 W McLene (N I).
Hill James F, lab, h 146 Patterson.
Hill James L, barber, h 285 Indiana av.
Hill James T, lawyer, 10½ N Delaware, h 112 Martindale av.
Hill Jane, h 404 Blackford.
Hill Jeannette (wid George W), b 26 School.
Hill John C, policeman, h 167 N Noble.
Hill John G, lab, b 448 W McLene (N I).
Hill John H, lab, h 67 Ruth (M J).
Hill John J, mach hd, b 16 Biddle.
Hill Joseph, lab, h 22 S Harriet (B).
Hill Joseph, porter, b 285 Christian av.
Hill Laura E, teacher Blind Institute.
Hill Lawrence S, city agt, h 31 Bradshaw.
Hill Lillian A, teacher Public School No 40, b 108 Sherman Drive (S).
Hill Louisa (wid Hanshaw), h 171 W Wabash.
Hill Margaret (wid John), h 54 Chadwick.
Hill Margaret M (wid Chalmer C), h 1325 N Alabama.
Hill Marion, lab, b 111 Hoyt av.
Hill Mary C (wid George E), h 453 Ash.
Hill Murray F, mach, h 27 Gattling.
Hill Nathaniel M, janitor, h 158 Yandes.
Hill Olive (wid Nathaniel), dressmkr, 123 Cornell av, h same.
Hill Paul C, shoes, 204 W Washington, h 14 Michigan (H).
Hill Ralph (Lamb & Hill), h 220 E New York.
Hill Ralph E, student, b 220 E New York.
Hill Roswell S, h 418 Park av.
Hill Roswell S jr, treas Equitable Savings and Loan Assn, b 418 Park av.

CORRUGATED IRON CEILINGS AND SIDING.
ALL KINDS OF REPAIRING.
O. B. ENSEY,
TELEPHONE 1562.
COR. 6TH AND ILLINOIS STREETS.

Hill Sadie E, teacher Public School No 40, h 112 Martindale av.
Hill Samuel, lab, h rear 671 N Senate av.
Hill Sarah J (wid Oliver W), h 150 N Illinois.
Hill Sarah L, dressmkr, 529 E Washington, h same.
Hill Selwyn B, painter, h 48 Thalman av.
Hill Tillie, h 31 Clinton.
Hill Turner, mach hd, h 448 W McLene (N I).
Hill Ulysses B, clk, h 435 W Eugene (N I).
Hill Wade, saloon, 223 W Ohio, b 219 same.
HILL WALTER L, Local Mngr Central Union Telephone Co, Tels 1 and 319; h 175 N Penn, Tel 2.
Hill Wm, plastr, h 549 W Udell (N I).
Hill Wm A, paperhngr, h 108 Sherman Drive (S).
Hill Wm M, carp, h 627 E 7th.
Hill Wm M, blksmith, h 146 N Dorman.
Hill Wm P, printer, r 167 N Capitol av.
Hill Wm T, printer, h 35 Bridge (W I).
Hill Wm T, tmstr, h 867 S Meridian.
Hilleary Ridgely B, clk Indpls Foundry, b 1088 N Illinois.
Hiller, see also Heller.
Hiller Conrad, baker, b 231 W Michigan.
Hiller Erasmus W, engr, b 1004 N Senate av.
Hiller John J, clk Frank E Janes, b 793 S East.
Hiller Katie A, clk Keller & Gamerdinger, b 793 S East.
Hiller Louisa (wid Rev Christian G), h 793 S East.
Hilliard Alva M, mach, b 12 Brookside av.
Hilliard Caroline (wid Charles), b 12 Brookside av.
Hilliard George W, clk R M S, b 39 Alvord.
Hilliard George W, engr, h 490 N California.
Hilliard Harry S, clk, b 12 Brookside av.
Hilliard James, lab, b 39 Alvord.
Hilliard Lucy (wid Washington), h 39 Alvord.
Hilliard Stephen E, carp, h 370 Martindale av.
Hilligoss Erastus A, clk, h 251 Howard (W I).
Hilligoss Frank L, agt, h 93 Chadwick.
Hilligoss Sullivan M, dep County Clerk, h n s University av 2 w of Ritter av (I).
Hilligoss Wm P, mach, b 251 Howard (W I).
Hilligoss Wilmer, barber, h 54 Sinker.
Hilliker Alpha W, restaurant, 46 N Penn, r 21 Wyandot blk.
Hillman, see also Hellmann.
Hillman Charles T, insp, h 238 Union.
Hillman Cynthia J (wid John I), h 245 W Ohio.
Hillman Frank W, lab, h 607 W Pearl.
Hillman Fredrica (wid Charles), h 523 S Illinois.
Hillman Frederica L (wid John), b 238 Union.
Hillman Frederick, painter, b 523 S Illinois.
Hillman Frederick W, clk, h 409 S New Jersey.
Hillman George, waiter, b 245 W Ohio.
Hillman George H, carp, h 18 Dawson.
Hillman John W, lab, b 229 W Washington.
Hillman Joseph W, draughtsman Nordyke & Marmon Co, h 575 Bellefontaine.
Hillman LeRoy T, student, b 575 Bellefontaine.
Hillman Lewis C, blksmith, h 595 S East.
Hillman Louis, finisher, b 130 Harlan.

TUTEWILER UNDERTAKER, NO. 72 WEST MARKET STREET. TELEPHONE 216.

THE PROVIDENT LIFE AND TRUST CO. OF PHILADELPHIA. Endowment Insurance presents the double attraction of relieving manhood and middle age from anxiety and old age from want.
For particulars apply to D. W. EDWARDS, General Agent, 508 Indiana Trust Building.

Hillman Wm, b 523 Madison av.
Hillman Wm, mer police, h 527 S Meridian.
Hillman Wm A, flagman, b 157 Bates.
Hillman Wm F, salesman Schnull & Co, h 164 Church.
Hillman Wm P, clk, b 527 S Meridian.
Hillmann Charles, patternmkr, h 30 Water.
Hillmer Frederick J, painter, h 47 Kansas.
Hillock Ira C, steelwkr, h 232 S Missouri.
Hillock Wm E, foreman, h 24 Minnesota.
Hillrige Wm, express, h cor St Peter and C C C & St L Ry.
Hillyer James H, lab, h 43 Lee (W I).
Hillyer John E, packer, h 145 Yandes.
Hilpert F Rudolph, finisher, h 450 Charles.
Hilpert Rudolph W, baker, 473 S Meridian, h same.
Hilsabeck Judson A, painter, 213 Yandes, h same.
Hilsabeck Wm A, painter, 52 S Belmont av (W I), h same.
Hilt Ann E (wid Franklin), b 590 N Senate av.
Hilt John Lake Ice Co, Volney T Malott pres, Indiana Natl Bank bldg.
Hiltenbaugh Edward, lab, b 383 W New York.
Hilton Emanuel H, lab, h Fairview park.
Hilton Frederick H, tailor, h 44 Sycamore.
Hilton Horatio S Rev, supt Indpls Children's Home Society, h 382 N East.
Hilton Jefferson B, lab, b 1775 N Senate av.
Hilton Mary F (wid Harry H), h 212½ S Meridian.
Hina Mary L, h 134 N Penn.
Hinchman Carl E, clk L E & W R R, b 464 N East.
Hinchman George F, motorman, b 6 Cornell av.
Hinchman Ernest G, checkman, b 286 S East.
Hinchman Ira G, monument police, h 286 S East.
Hinchman Joseph C, insp, h 131 Keystone av.
Hinchman Leonidas C, clk, r 344 E Washington.
Hinchman Madison, b 534 College av.
Hinchman Omer, polisher, b 286 S East.
Hinchman Rufus E, carp, h e s Rural 3 n of Progress av.
Hinchman Wm M, trav agt, h 464 N East.
Hinckley Jacob C, lab, h 30 S Rural.
Hinckley Wm H, trav agt, h 243 E South.
Hindel Rosa (wid Wm), h 377 N West.
Hindman Frank, musician, r 5 Grand Opera House blk.
Hindman Frank M, condr, h 74 W 7th.
Hinds Catherine (wid Solomon), b 501 Highland av (N I).
Hinds Harry L, brakeman, h 118 Pleasant.
Hinds John, condr, h 294½ Mass av.
Hine Benjamin F, huckster, h 73 Davidson.
Hine Charles A, lab, h 248 S Pine.
Hine Elizabeth (wid Charles H), b 248 S Pine.
Hiner Andrew, lab, b 658½ N West.
Hiner Charles, lab, b 658½ N West.
Hiner John, lab, h 36 Thomas.
Hiner Lorinda (wid Henry), h 658½ N West.
Hiner Melville E, trav agt, b 222 N Illinois.
Hines Andrew, produce, 122 E Mkt House, h 321 Davidson.
Hines Andrew jr, produce, E Mkt House, b 321 Davidson.
Hines Benjamin T, lab, b 447 Howard (W I).
Hines Cornelius, motorman, b 102 Harrison.

THE WHEN IS A WORLD BEATER.

Hines Fletcher S, lawyer, 4 Franklin Fire Ins bldg, 25 E Market, h Washington twp.
Hines Francis, lab, h 447 Howard (W I).
Hines Henry, driver, h 515 N Senate av.
Hines John, clk Am Ex Co, h 52 Ruckle.
Hines John, lab, b 43 Ruckle.
Hines John, lab, h 54 Pierce.
Hines John, lab, b 43 Blake.
Hines John F, barber, 323 Clifford av, h same.
Hines Mary A (wid George), b 17 Howard.
Hines Norah (wid Patrick), b 102 Harrison.
Hines Perry, packer, b Marion Park Hotel (M P).
Hines Robert H, mach hd, h 59 Bicking.
Hines Thomas, brakeman, h 44 English av.
Hinesley, see also Hensley.
Hinesley Andrew J, gasfitter, h 1536 N Delaware.
Hinesley Charles E, dairy, w s Illinois 1 n of 29th, h same.
Hinesley Eliza (wid Andrew J), h 441 N Senate av.
Hinesley Harry M, stenog, h 854 Milburn.
Hinesley John U, lab, h 417 W Udell (N I).
Hinesley Wm A, city fireman, b 441 N Senate av.
Hiney George W, driver, h 274 W 9th.
Hinkle, see also Henkle.
Hinkle Charles E, tel opr, h 25 Tompkins.
Hinkle Harvey, cooper, b 95 S West.
Hinkle Henry, lab, h 75 Davidson.
Hinkle Henry, lab, h 401 Pleasant.
Hinkle Henry H, blksmith, h 143 Patterson.
Hinkle Jesse A, cooper, b 95 S West.
Hinkle John, lab, b 95 S West.
Hinkle Leonard, soap mnfr, 174 W Market, h 61 N New Jersey.
Hinkle Morris, tmstr, b Marion Park Hotel (M P).
Hinkle Wm, molder, h 313 W Merrill.
Hinkley George W, barber, b 601 N Senate av.
Hinkley Mary C (wid Wm B), h 601 N Senate av.
Hinkley Thomas B, painter, r 132 W Vermont.
Hinman Jack J, trav agt Griffith Bros, h 527 N Delaware.

THE A. BURDSAL CO.
Manufacturers of
Paints and Colors
VARNISHES,
Brushes, Painters' and Paper Hangers' Supplies.
34 AND 36 SOUTH MERIDIAN STREET.

THEODORE F. SMITHER ~ Roofing Materials
2 and 3-Ply Ready Roofing, Building Paper, etc. Office, 151 W. Maryland St.

ELECTRICIANS | DON'T FORGET US. ALL WORK GUARANTEED. C. W. MEIKEL, Tel. 466. 96-98 E. New York St.

DALTON & MERRIFIELD { LUMBER South Noble St., near E. Washington

INDIANA ELECTROTYPE CO. :: BEST WORK. LOWEST PRICES.
23 WEST PEARL ST., INDIANAPOLIS, IND. JOB WORK. BOOK PLATES. All Orders Promptly Filled. BEST PATENT BASE ON THE MARKET.

KIRKHOFF BROS.
Steam and Hot Water Heating Apparatus,
Plumbing and Gas Fitting.
102-104 SOUTH PENNSYLVANIA ST.
TELEPHONE 910.

Hinman Lorenzo D, clk, b 64 Fountain av.
Hinnenkamp Frederick H, saloon, 149 N Noble, h same.
Hinners Christian M, grocer, 301 N Pine, h same.
Hinnig Marcus, lab, h 94 Nebraska.
Hinsch Louis E, boilermkr, h 54 N Station (B).
Hinsch Maria (wid Frederick), b 54 N Station (B).
Hinsch M Elizabeth, asst postmaster (B), b 54 N Station (B).
Hinsching Herman F, musician, h 192 Clifford av.
Hinsching Julius, musician, h 457 S Missouri.
Hinsdale Frank W, sec and treas The N C Hinsdale's Sons' Granite Co, h 76 W 10th.
Hinsdale Nehemiah C, pres N C Hinsdale's Sons' Granite Co, res Detroit, Mich.
HINSDALE'S N C SONS' GRANITE CO THE, Nehemiah C Hinsdale Pres and Genl Mngr, Frank W Hinsdale Sec and Treas, 709-710 Lemcke Bldg.
Hinshaw Catherine F (wid Frederick B), grocer, 510 S West, h same.
Hinshaw Hannah (wid Wm B), h 20 N State av.
Hinshaw John C (Hinshaw & Baker), h 142 Broadway.
Hinshaw Thomas M, phys, 37½ W Market, b 142 Broadway.
HINSHAW & BAKER (John C Hinshaw, Alden H Baker), Bakers and Mnfrs of Bread and Cakes, Ice Cream and Fruit Ices, Wholesale and Retail, 142 Broadway, cor Christian av, Tel 1035.
Hinson Charles, molder, h 46 Tremont av (H).
Hinson Marshall, lab, b 122 Agnes.
Hinson Wm C, clk When Clothing Store, h 355 N Illinois.
Hinton Alonzo, lab, b 34 Howard.
Hinton John M, car rep, b 8 N Brightwood av (B).

LIME
BUILDING SUPPLIES,
Hair, Plaster, Flue Linings,
The W. G. Wasson Co.
130 INDIANA AVE. Tel. 989.

Hinton Mary E (wid Henry), h 89 N Delaware.
Hinton Wm T, lab, h 193 Middle.
Hinz Jacob, b 47 Hendricks.
Hinz Michael, lab, h 78 Morton.
Hinz Peter, lab, h 47 Hendricks.
Hipp Flora M, b 622 Central av.
Hipple Frank C, clk C C C & St L Ry, r 135 E New York.
Hipple Frank S, salesman, h 221 Michigan av.
Hipwell Wm J, mach, h 594 Chestnut.
Hires Oliver T, driver, h rear 472 E Washington.
Hirlinger Frank H, ironwkr, b 344 N Pine.
Hirsch Anton V, molder, h 19 Harlan.
Hirsch Bell, h 184 W Market.
Hirsch Louis, clk, b 221 E Ohio.
Hirschauer Wm P, embalmer, h 497 Virginia av.
Hirschman Conrad, foreman J C Hirschman, h 550 E Market.
Hirschman Frank H, bkkpr J C Hirschman, b 654 E Washington.
HIRSCHMAN JACOB C ESTATE OF, Mattress Mnfr and Feathers, 69-71 N New Jersey, Tel 146.
Hirschman Mary A (wid Jacob C), h 654 E Washington.
Hirshkowitz Benjamin, bartndr, r 119 Mass av.
Hirst Charles D, ins agt, b 84 W Vermont.
Hirt Jacob, hostler, h 433½ National rd.
Hirth Bridget (wid Leo), grocer, 1020 W Washington, h same.
Hirth Frank, fireman, h 218 S Reisner (W I).
Hirth Frederick, boilermkr, h 139 Sharpe av (W).
Hirwatz Charles, grocer, 432 S Capitol av, h same.
Hirwatz Samuel, shirtmkr, h 434 S Capitol av.
Hise Harry E, molder, b 275 W Washington.
Hise Wm, produce, h 416 S Olive.
Hiser, see also Heiser and Heizer.
Hiser Benjamin H, teacher, b 84 S Reisner (W I).
Hiser John H, clk, b 399½ Bellefontaine.
Hiser Joseph W, engr, h 21 Beacon.
Hiser Samuel, porter, h 409 W North.
Hiserodt Samuel W, engr, h 1029 W Washington.
Hisey Allen, carp, h 373 W New York.
Hisey Edwin R, clk L E & W R R, b 373 W New York.
Hisey Nettie M, clk, b 373 W New York.
Hislop John M, clk J B Allfree Mnfg Co, h 65 Highland pl.
Hislop Thomas, lab, h 22 Detroit av.
Hission Eleanor (wid David), h 466 College av.
Hission James H, trav agt Indpls Brwg Co, r 253 N Senate av.
Hission John T, uphlr, b 466 College av.
Hission Mary E, stenog The Sinker-Davis Co, b 466 College av.
Hission Michael W, trav agt, b 466 College av.
Histed Howard L, baggageman, h 30 Brookside av.
Hitchcock Benjamin F, carp, h 248 Yandes.
Hitchcock Charles, plumber, b 122 College av.
Hitchcock Henry H, mach, b 678 W Washington.

Parlor, Bed Room, Dining Room, Kitchen, Furniture W. H. MESSENGER, 101 E. Wash. St., Tel. 491.

ALL KINDS OF HEAVY AND LIGHT GRAY IRON CASTINGS } McNamara, Koster & Co. Phone 1593. 212-218 S. Penn. St. { Foundry and Pattern Shop

Hitchcock Jesse S, tmstr, b 150 River av (W I).
Hitchcock Julius M, salesman, h 123 N Noble.
Hitchcock Mary L, bkkpr b 166 N Alabama.
Hitchcock Rachel P (wid Alexander), h 186 E St Joseph.
Hitchcock Samuel S, mach hd, h 541 W Francis (N I).
Hitchcock Wm, lab, b 6 Coble.
Hitchcock Wm E, mach hd, b 541 W Francis (N I).
Hitchens Clement, driver, b 120 Roanoke.
Hitchens Robert, lab, h 725 E 8th.
Hitchens Wm, houseman, r 102 N Capitol av.
Hite Samuel M, ticket agt, h 68 Prospect.
Hite Wm D, patrolman, h 30 Keystone av.
Hiteshue Fannie A (wid Theodore G), boarding 183 E Ohio.
Hiteshew Schuyler C, condr, b 304 E Market.
Hitt Daniel C (D C & J B Hitt), h 169 Broadway.
Hitt D C & J B (Daniel C and James B), cigars, 32 S Meridian.
Hitt George C, sec, treas and business mngr Indpls Journal Newspaper Co, h 648 N Alabama, tel 772.
Hitt James B (D C & J B Hitt), res Urbana, O.
Hitt Wilbur F, clk R M S, h 408 N Illinois.
Hittle Benjamin F, decorator, h 132 E Walnut.
Hittle Homer E, mach, h 59 Laurel.
Hittle Kate, b 636 Home av.
Hittle Lulu G, boarding 132 E Walnut.
Hitz Alfred D, bkkpr George Hitz & Co, b 160 Elm.
HITZ BAKING CO-THE (Capital $60,-000), George Hitz Pres, Benjamin F Hitz Vice-Pres, Charles F Igelmann Sec and Treas, Bakers of the Celebrated "Quaker Bread," 68-70 S Delaware, Tel 1129. (See right bottom cor cards.)
Hitz Benjamin F (George Hitz & Co), vice-pres The Hitz Baking Co, h 175 N Penn.
Hitz B Graham, cashr The Hitz Baking Co, b 1120 N Meridian.
Hitz George (George Hitz & Co), pres The Hitz Baking Co, h 160 Elm.
HITZ GEORGE & CO (George, Benjamin F, Stephen T and Joseph Hitz), Commission Merchants and Fruit Dealers and Vegetable and Fruit Packers, Office 30-32 and 68-70 S Delaware, Tel 63.
Hitz Jesse E, feed, 78 S Delaware, h 1317 N Delaware.
Hitz Joseph (George Hitz & Co), res Madison, Ind.
Hitz Stephen T (George Hitz & Co), h 1120 N Meridian.
Hitz Walter H, salesman George Hitz & Co, b 160 Elm.
HITZELBERGER ALBERT, Wine Mnfr and Saloon; My Own Make of Wine a Specialty; W McLene and canal, North Indianapolis, h same.
Hitzelberger George, clk George R Popp, b 598 McLene (N I).
Hitzelberger Louis, sec and treas The Home Stove Co, h 281 Virginia av.
Hitzeman Gottlieb C, car rep, h 27 Leota.
Hitzke Albert, mach hd, b 96 Kansas.

Henry H. Fay,
40½ E. WASHINGTON ST.,
FIRE INSURANCE, REAL ESTATE,
LOANS AND RENTAL AGENT.

Hitzke Robert, uphlr, h 152 Carlos.
Hitzke Wilhelmina A (wid Albert W), h 96 Kansas.
Hitzkin Edward H, paperhngr, h 188 W Pearl.
Hix George W, carp, b 597 Central av.
Hixon Orion B, trav agt, h 152 Randolph.
Hixson, see also Hickson.
Hixson Leroy T, bkkpr, b 190 Keystone av.
Hixson Maude, stenog, b 190 Keystone av.
Hixson Walter B, grain, 49 Board of Trade bldg, h 190 Keystone av.
Hizel Albert, brewer, h 717 Charles.
Hizer Alonzo, lab, h 330 Indiana av.
Hizer Daniel, lab, b 332 Indiana av.
Hizer George, lab, h 332 Indiana av.
Hizer Nancy (wid Joseph), h 332 Indiana av.
Hoadley Cyrus, die cutter, h 337 N Liberty.
Hoag Jedidiah, b e s Central av 1 s of Beechwood av (I).
Hoagland, see also Hogeland.
Hoagland Charles, brakeman, b 51 Traub av.
Hoagland George W, scavenger, h 527 W Maryland.
Hoagland Jessie R, stenog Parry Mnfg Co, b 50 Hillside av.
Hoagland Joseph, watchman, b 527 W Maryland.
Hoagland Minnie E (wid Thomas), h 50 Hillside av.
Hoagland Sarah (wid Wm), b 47 N Judge Harding (W I).
Hoagland Wm A, express, h 51 Traub av.
Hoagland Wm D, blksmith, h 47 N Judge Harding (W I).
Hoar John H, music teacher, 121 Chadwick, h same.
Hoar Michael, cabtmkr, b 119 N Gillard av.
Hoard James M, lab, b 162 Harrison.
Hoare Alfred R, butcher, h 462 Highland av.
Hoban Hopkins E, grocer, 384 Dillon, h same.
Hobart Charles F, paperhngr, b 166 Lexington av.
Hobart Edward S, photo engraver H C Bauer Engraving Co, b 205 Prospect.

WILL GO ON YOUR BOND
American Bonding & Trust Co.
Of Baltimore, Md. Approved as sole surety by the United States Government and the different States as Sole Surety on all Forms of Bonds.
W. E. BARTON & CO., General Agents,
504 Indiana Trust Building.
LONG DISTANCE TELEPHONE 1918.

THE FRED DIETZ CO. WOODEN PACKING BOXES MADE TO ORDER FACTORY AND WAREHOUSE TRUCKS. 40 Madison Avenue. Telephone 68.

BUSINESS EDUCATION A NECESSITY. TIME SHORT. DAY AND NIGHT SCHOOL. SUCCESS CERTAIN AT THE PERMANENT, RELIABLE Indianapolis BUSINESS UNIVERSITY

NEW YORK FILTER MFG. CO. Filters for Water-Works, Boiler Plants, Laundries, Hotels, Private Residences, Etc. | Henry R. Worthington, 64 S. Pennsylvania St. Long Distance Telephone 284.

UNION CO-OPERATIVE LAUNDRY (COMPOSED OF UNION LAUNDRY GIRLS.) NOS. 138, 140 AND 142 VIRGINIA AVENUE. T. E. SOMERVILLE, MANAGER—TELEPHONE 1269. INDIANAPOLIS, IND.

HORACE M. HADLEY
INSURANCE AND LOANS
66 E. Market Street, Basement
TELEPHONE 1540.

Hobart Wm, drugs, 327 Dillon, h 166 Lexington av.
Hobbs Alice L, phys, 199 N Illinois, h same.
Hobbs Anselm, sec and treas Indpls Tobacco Works, h 1183 N Illinois.
Hobbs Bert L, clk Rouse Bros, b 277 Indiana av.
Hobbs John N, letter carrier P O, h 184 Highland av.
Hobbs Lindsey, porter, h 30 Cincinnati.
Hobbs Martha A (wid Solomon), b 9 Ruckle.
Hobbs Minerva (wid Pliny F), milliner, b 229 Michigan av.
Hobbs Oliver P, carp, h 58 Tacoma av.
Hobbs Riley P, mach, h 199 N Illinois.
HOBBS ROBERT D, Lawyer, 58-59 Baldwin Blk, h 283 N East.
Hobbs Robert W, student, b 80 Ash.
Hobbs Ruth D (wid John), h 165 Hoyt av.
Hobbs Sarah E, dressmkr, 165 Hoyt av, h same.
Hobbs Walton C, agt Kanawha Despatch, n e cor Delaware and South, h 80 Ash.
HOBBS WM H, Real Estate and Insurance, 70 E Market, h 715 N Alabama, Tel 1009.
Hobbs Wm L, barber, 151½ Michigan (H), h 157 same.
Hobbs Wm V, lab, b 58 Tacoma av.
Hoben Lucie, lecturer, h 45 Paca.
Hoben Thomas, pdlr, h 45 Paca.
Hoberg Alfred, b 209 N Penn.
Hoblit Walter B, trav agt, h 799 N Capitol av.
Hobson Franklin D, student, h 132 Trowbridge (W).
Hobson John, lab, h 26 Hadley.
Hobson Joseph C, trav agt Griffith Bros, h 487 W Walnut av (N I).
Hobson Ola J, teacher Public School No 21, h 132 Trowbridge (W).
Hoch Albert, lab, b 59 Yeiser.
Hoch John H, pdlr, h 404½ W Washington.
Hoch Joseph, carp, h 59 Yeiser.
Hoch Walter, mach, b 548 S New Jersey.
Hoch Wm, b 59 Yeiser.
Hoch Wm, blksmith, b 404½ W Washington.

COLLECTIONS
MERCHANTS' AND MANUFACTURERS' EXCHANGE
Will give you good service.
J. E. TAKKEN, Manager,
Union Building, over U. S. Pension Office.
73 West Maryland Street.

Hochstetter George M, trav agt Tanner & Sullivan, b 99 Greer.
Hockaday Gipson, coachman, h 9 Ellworth.
HOCKENSMITH HARRY E, Wholesale and Retail Flour and Feed at Cut Rates, 478 E Washington, h 521 same, Tel 1123.
Hocker Frances C, b 56 Martindale av.
Hocker Jacob H, vet surg, h 171 Douglass.
Hocker Sarah E (wid Nicholas), b 488 N Missouri.
Hockersmith Henry, mach, b 384 Bellefontaine.
Hockersmith Judiah D, carp, h 38 N Dorman.
Hockersmith Terry, clk, b 38 N Dorman.
Hockett Benjamin, huckster, h 46 Leon.
Hockett Frank M, paperhngr, b 46 Leon.
Hockett Fred, plumber, b 156 W Washington.
Hockett George M, tinner, h 296 Cornell av.
Hockett Walter E, mach, h 54 Arbor av (W I).
Hockett Wm L, clk, h 3 Orange av.
Hocky Emma, b rear 71 River av (W I).
Hoctor Joseph W, lab, h 176 Chestnut.
Hoctor Thomas E, collarmkr, h 434 S Meridian.
Hoctor Wm J, h 176 Chestnut.
Hoctor Wm J jr, lab, b 176 Chestnut.
Hodde Wm H, mach hd, h 62 Sanders.
Hodge Frank R, lab, b 37 Warren av (W I).
Hodge Frederick, bellboy, b 238 W 3d.
Hodge George W, lab, b 15 N New Jersey.
Hodge London, lab, h 298 Highland av.
Hodge Samuel, engr Indpls Water Co, h 37 Warren av (W I).
Hodge Walter, porter, h 238 W 3d.
Hodges Caroline (wid Peter), h 432 Douglass.
Hodges Daniel W, lab, b rear 133 S Reisner (W I).
Hodges Edward F, phys, 2 W New York, h 152 N Meridian.
Hodges Edward R, adv agt, 29½ W Ohio, r same.
Hodges Elizabeth, h 367 W North.
Hodges Gilbert T, molder, h 135 Lambert (W I).
Hodges James W, engr, h rear 117 Birch av (W I).
Hodges John T, lab, h 109 Shepard (W I).
Hodges Lizzie, h 367 W North.
Hodges Maria (wid Nelson), r 180 W Michigan.
Hodges Reynolds, lab, r 205 W North.
Hodges Theodore, lab, h 59 S Reisner (W I).
Hodges Theresa (wid Graham), h rear 133 S Reisner (W I).
Hodgin Edward E, phys, n s 20th 1 e of Cornell av, h 864 Cornell av.
Hodgin Francis T, driver, h 217 Ramsey av.
Hodgin Leonard A, mach, h 13 N Gale (B).
Hodgin Myrtilla, governess Asylum for Friendless Colored Children.
Hodgin Samuel A, h 115 Highland pl.
Hodgkinson George A, trav agt, h 367 Ash.
Hodgson Edgar J, architect, h 468 N Alabama.
Hodle Samuel, wagonmkr, r 190 E Market.
Hodson Alonzo, carp, h 431 Martindale av.
Hodson Benjamin A, carp, h 92 S Liberty.
Hodson Frank, lab, b 92 S Liberty.
Hodson Harry W, clk, h 463 E Georgia.
Hodson Henry A, foreman C C C & St L Ry, h 44 N Station (B).
Hodson James, lab, h 435 Martindale av.
Hodson Joseph, grocer, 452 Newman, h same.

CLEMENS VONNEGUT 184, 186 and 192 E. Washington St. | BUILDERS' HARDWARE, Building Paper. Duplex Joist Hangers

THE WM. H. BLOCK CO. DRY GOODS, DRAPERIES, RUGS, WINDOW SHADES.
7 AND 9 EAST WASHINGTON STREET.

Hodson Joseph, lab, b 92 S Liberty.
Hodson Martin L, fireman, b 44 N Station (B).
Hodson Oscar A, clk Schnull & Co, h 466 E Georgia.
Hodson Wm S, foreman, h n s Willow 3 w of Brightwood av (B).
Hoeffner, see Hoffner.
Hoefgen Benjamin F, lab, h 612 S Meridian.
Hoefgen Emanuel G W, watchman, h 48 Drake.
Hoefgen Eva M, b 612 S Meridian.
Hoefgen Henrietta, b 927 S Meridian.
Hoefgen John V, farmer, h 927 S Meridian.
Hoefgen Leslie, bkkpr, b 48 Drake.
Hoefgen Wm H, b 89 N State av.
Hoefler Gustavus A R, piano tuner, h 456 S Alabama.
Hoehaver Felix, b 189 S Illinois.
Hoelscher Henry W, car insp, h 225 Michigan av.
Hoeltke Anna S C, confr, 328 Mass av, h same.
Hoeltke Charles, gardener, h rear 1040 Madison av.
Hoeltke Wm C F, collr, h 328 Mass av.
Hoeltkemeyer Henry C, cabtmkr, h 99 Weghorst.
Hoelzer Lawrence, lab, h 33 Agnes.
Hoenig, see also Hennig.
Hoenig Carl, organist, b 88 W Ohio.
Hoenig Herman H, coll clk Merchants' Natl Bank, b 458 S Meridian.
Hoenig Margaretha (wid Sebastian), drygoods, 458 S Meridian, h same.
Hoeping Anton, h 26 Fenneman.
Hoereth, see also Hereth.
Hoereth Adam, h 35 Pleasant.
Hoereth Conrad, saloon, 600 S West, h same.
Hoereth John G, carp, 263 N East, h same.
Hoerger Eliza (wid Jacob H), h 92 Bloomington.
Hoerhammer Michael, molder, h 100 Tremont av (H).
Hoermann Frederick, mach, r 770 E Market.
Hoey Patrick, gasfitter, b 272 W Maryland.
Hofacker Charles H, barber, b 385 Coburn.
Hofacker Gottlob, grocer, 73 N Liberty, h same.
Hofacker Henrietta (wid Charles), h 385 Coburn.
Hofacker John E, butcher, h 351 Coburn.
Hofacker Wm, barber, b 73 N Liberty.
Hofer Charles M, mach hd, h 10 Iowa.
Hofer Clarence, sawyer, h 3 Singleton.
Hofer Edward G, shoemkr, 155 Virginia av, b 185 Elm.
Hofer George H, shoemkr, h 141 Elm.
Hofer Jacob H, lab, h 63 Harrison.
Hofer Otto A, clk, b 141 Elm.
Hoff, see also Hough and Huff.
Hoff Annie, h 211 Indiana av.
Hoff Charles C, lab, h 144 N Rural.
Hoff Eleanor (wid Anton), h 181 Pleasant.
Hoff Herman, lab, b 22 Carlos.
Hoff Solomon M, mngr Epworth League Headquarters, b 72 W New York.
Hoff Wm, carp, b 181 Pleasant.
Hoff Xavier, wheelmkr, h 145 River av (W I).
Hoffbauer Joseph G, saloon, 1 Orange av, h 2 same.
Hoffbauer Nicholas J, patrolman, h 117 Hill av.
Hoffbauer Philip J, saloon, 107 Hill av, h 109 same.

Hoffert Andrew J, car rep, h 388 Highland av.
Hoffert Daniel S, carp, 394 Highland av, h same.
Hoffman, see also Hofmann and Huffman.
Hoffman Albert, watchman, h 67 Wisconsin.
Hoffman Alva R, grocer, 211 Christian av, h 534 Ash.
Hoffman Amanda, h 71 N East.
Hoffman Arthur L, mach hd, b 19 Minerva.
Hoffman August, lab, r 454 E Ohio.
Hoffman August, molder, h 26 Everett.
Hoffman August A, lab, h 96 River av (W I).
Hoffman Caroline (wid Frederick), b 26 Everett.
Hoffman Casper, lab, h 297 E 10th.
Hoffman Charles, cook, h 434 Chestnut.
Hoffman Charles, painter, b 43 Haugh (H).
Hoffman Charles D (C D Hoffman & Co), h 116 Greer.
Hoffman Charles H, carp, h 47 Christian av.
Hoffman Charles M, mach, h 196 N Beville av.
Hoffman Christopher, molder, b 1 Taylor av.
Hoffman Christian G, cook, r 49 N Alabama.
Hoffman Conrad, butcher, h 360 Spring.
HOFFMAN C D & CO (Charles D Hoffman), Proprs Indianapolis Elevator and Millwright Shop, 29 Kentucky av. (See adv in classified Elevators.)
Hoffman Edward W, instructor Indiana Bicycle Co, h 225 S Alabama.
Hoffman Eugene J, watchmkr, h 161 Union.
Hoffman Frank (Indpls Pulley Mnfg Co), b 121 E Pratt.
Hoffman George, clk Charles Mayer & Co, b 67 Wisconsin.
Hoffman George J, lab, b 22 Vinton.
Hoffman George W, barber, 52 E Washington, h 48 Eastern av.
Hoffman George W, polish mnfr, 295 E Washington, h 328 N Alabama.

GUIDO R. PRESSLER,
FRESCO PAINTER
Churches, Theaters, Public Buildings, Etc., A Specialty.
Residence, No. 325 North Liberty Street.
INDIANAPOLIS, IND.

INDIANAPOLIS STEEL ROOFING AND CORRUGATING WORKS, 23 and 25 East South Street. S. D. NOEL, Proprietor.

David S. McKernan, REAL ESTATE AND LOANS
Rooms 2-5 Thorpe Block.
Money to loan on real estate. Special inducements offered those having money to loan. It will pay you to investigate.

DIAMOND WALL PLASTER { Telephone 1410 BUILDERS' EXCHANGE.

UNION TRANSFER AND STORAGE CO. Cor. E. Ohio St. and C., C., C. & St. L. R'y Tracks. BEST FACILITIES FOR STORING AND TRANSFERRING MACHINERY AND MERCHANDISE.

W. McWORKMAN

FIRE SHUTTERS,
FIRE DOORS,
METAL CEILINGS.

930 W. Washington St. Tel. 1118.

Hoffman Henry A, ins agt, h 198 Blake.
Hoffman Henry V, chief train desp C H & D R R, b 126 S East.
Hoffman Irenius M, bell mnfr, w s Watts 2 n of Michigan, h same.
Hoffman Jennie, h 150½ College av.
Hoffman John, coremkr, h 43 Ketcham (H).
Hoffman John, porter Charles Mayer & Co, h 118 Yeiser.
Hoffman John A, M O clk P O, h 225 S Alabama.
Hoffman John P, barber, r 12½ N Delaware.
Hoffman Louis F, insp, h 844 Park av.
Hoffman Mary J, h 71 N East.
Hoffman Mathilde (wid John), r 5½ Shelby.
Hoffman Peter, vet surg, h 32 Sheffield (W I).
Hoffman Robert C, clk, b 47 Christian av.
Hoffman Wm C, oiler, h 19 Minerva.
Hoffman Wm C, bailiff Commissioners' Court, res Valley Mills, Ind.
Hoffman Wm H, driver, b 197 E Morris.
Hoffman Wm H, grocer, 1650 N Capitol av, h same.
Hoffman Wolf, pdlr, h 64 Church.
Hoffmann August, clk, b 151 E Ohio.
Hoffmann Catherine (wid John H), h 121 E Pratt.
Hoffmann Elizabeth K (wid Jacob), tailoress, b 546 S New Jersey.
Hoffmann Franz S, tinner, b 108½ Mass av.
Hoffmann George, bookbndr, h 508 N Alabama.
Hoffmann George I, paperhanger, b 177 S Alabama.
Hoffmann George J, bkkpr Fahnley & McCrea, h 249 Union.
Hoffmann Harvey J, driver, h 177 S Alabama.
Hoffmann Henry, finisher, h 6 Quince.
Hoffmann Henry, shoemkr, 23½ S Delaware, h same.
Hoffmann John H, foreman E H Eldridge & Co, h 197 E Morris.
Hoffmann Joseph, driver, b 531 E Ohio.
Hoffmann Louis A, mach, b 249 Union.
Hoffmann Mary (wid Caspar), h 508 N Alabama.

GEO. J. MAYER,
MANUFACTURER OF
SEALS
STENCILS, RUBBER STAMPS, CHECKS, BADGES, DOOR PLATES, ETC.
.. S. Meridian St., Ground Floor. TEL. 1386.

Hoffmann Pearl E (wid Max F A), h 108½ Mass av.
Hoffmann Percy M, lithog, b 108½ Mass av.
Hoffmann Philip M, tailor, b 531 E Ohio.
Hoffmann Theodore C, collection teller Merchants' Natl Bank, h 76 Highland pl.
Hoffmann Valentine, porter, h 41 Dunlop.
Hoffmann Wm, brewer, h 41 Dunlop.
Hoffmann Wm H, clk, b 197 E Morris.
Hoffmann Wm L, pressman, b 177 S Alabama.
Hoffmark John H, mach, h 105 Gray.
Hoffmark Simon, grocer, 473 E St Clair, h same.
Hoffmark Wm G, mach, b 453 E St Clair.
Hoffmeister, see also Hofmeister.
Hoffmeister Caroline (wid Charles), h 182 Blackford.
Hoffmeister Wm O, tinner, b 114 Buchanan.
Hoffmeyer Albert H, electrician, b 376 E New York.
Hoffmeyer Christina L (wid Wm F), h 376 E New York.
Hoffmeyer Edward, clk, b 376 E New York.
Hoffmeyer Elmer F, plumber, h 402 Highland av.
Hoffmeyer Frederick J, mach, b 372 Highland av.
Hoffmeyer George F, clk, b 376 E New York.
Hoffmeyer Henry, tailor, h 195 N Liberty.
Hoffmeyer Henry W, yardmaster, h 368 Highland av.
Hoffmeyer James B, turner, h 484 Highland av.
Hoffmeyer Rebecca (wid Frederick W), h 372 Highland av.
Hoffmeyer Wm H, tailor, h 122 N Pine.
Hoffner Jacob H, fireman, b 7 Detroit.
Hoffner Luke A, clk, h 7 Detroit.
Hoffstedt Martin, salesman, r 220 N Capitol av.
Hofft Anna L, teacher, b 134 E St Joseph.
Hofft Frederick B, clk, b 134 E St Joseph.
Hofft Louisa E (wid Barnard), h 134 E St Joseph.
Hofherr Caroline (wid Louis), h 505 Madison av.

HOFHERR FREDERICK C, Fancy and Staple Groceries, Saloon, Cigars and Tobacco, 505 Madison av, h same.

Hofman George, b 675 Madison av.
Hofmann, see also Hoffman and Huffman.
Hofmann Adeline (wid Michael), b 912 S Meridian.
Hofmann August F, clk, h 77 Downey.
Hofmann Benjamin W, clk engr m of w C C C & St L Ry, b 108 Ash.
Hofmann Carl W, printer, b 419 Madison av.
Hofmann Charles, painter, 419 Madison av, h same.
Hofmann George, driver, h 912 S Meridian.
Hofmann George J, carp, h 196 Nebraska.
Hofmann Jacob, clk, h 108 Ash.
Hofmann John P, porter, h 429 S West.
Hofmann Margaret C (wid Albert), h 508 S Capitol av.
Hofmann Otto, saloon, 470 S Meridian, h same.
Hofmann Philip H, grocer, n w cor Lawrence and Rural, h same.
Hofmann Valentine, foreman German Telegraph, h 18 Sinker.
Hofmeister, see also Hoffmeister.
Hofmeister Adelaide (wid Nicholas), h 312 N Liberty.

A. METZGER AGENCY ESTABLISHED 1863. REAL ESTATE

LAMBERT GAS & GASOLINE ENGINE CO.
ANDERSON, IND. NATURAL GAS ENGINES.

Hofmeister Henry, grocer, 75 Hill av, h 21 Ingraham.
Hofmeister Joseph, bartndr, b 312 N Liberty.
Hofstetter Joseph P, carp, h 230 Madison av.
Hogan Alexander T, b 36 Elder av.
Hogan Anson O, plastr, h n e cor Eugene and Elmira (N I).
Hogan Bridget, h 267 W Maryland.
Hogan Charles L, brakeman, h 36 Elder av.
Hogan Cornelius, lab, b 37 Williams.
Hogan Daniel, h 1496 N Senate av.
Hogan Daniel, waiter, h 127½ Indiana av.
Hogan David W, trav agt, h 60 Woodruff av.
Hogan Dennis, lab, b 169 Michigan (H).
Hogan Ellen (wid James), b 350 S West.
Hogan Harry G, lab, b 314 E Miami.
Hogan Helen (wid Wm), h 340 S West.
Hogan Jeremiah, lab, h 200 Newman.
Hogan Jeremiah A, opr W U Tel Co, b 42 McKim av.
Hogan John, lab, h 156 Bates.
Hogan John D (The Hogan Transfer and Storage Co), h 377 N Delaware.
Hogan John J, clk, r 100 N Senate av.
Hogan John J, lab, h 37 Williams.
Hogan John S, lab, h 1383 N Senate av.
Hogan John V, tel opr, b 42 McKim av.
Hogan John W (The Hogan Transfer and Storage Co), h 224 E St Clair.
Hogan Justus M, engr, h 314 E Miami.
Hogan Mary (wid John), b 93 Hadley av (W I).
Hogan Mary, milliner, b 377 N Delaware.
Hogan Michael D, h 42 McKim av.
Hogan Oliver O, ins, h 54 Tacoma av.
Hogan Sarah J (wid Thomas), b 162 Spring.
Hogan Thomas, watchman, h 528 S West.
HOGAN TRANSFER AND STORAGE CO THE (John D, Wm J and John W Hogan), Office s w cor Washington and Illinois, Stables Delaware and Georgia, Tel 675. (See left top lines and adv in classified Transfer Cos.)
Hogan Wm, lab, b 196 Newman.
Hogan Wm A, lab, h 134 Martindale av.
Hogan Wm J (The Hogan Transfer and Storage Co), b 377 N Delaware.
Hogarth Sarah J (wid Edwin P), h 361 Broadway.
Hogarty, see Haggerty.
Hogeland, see also Hoagland and Hoogland.
Hogeland Harry, printer, b 255 S East.
Hogeland Wm J, tel opr W U Tel Co, h 255 S East.
Hogg John J, carp, h 22 Villa av.
Hogland John D, b n w cor Wheeler and Park (B).
Hogland Joseph R, lab, h 44 Gresham.
Hogland Samuel, flagman, h 76 E Wilkins.
Hogle Cassius L, h 14 Bedford av.
Hogle Samuel M, carp, r 190 E Market.
Hogreiver George, ballplayer, h 24 Randolph.
Hogue Henry H, carp, w s Rural 2 n of Orchard av, h same.
Hogue Joseph L, insp, h 563 W 22d (N I).
Hogue Samuel A, live stock, h 84 S Reisner (W I).
Hoheisel Albert, baker, h 136 S Summit.
Hoheisen August, hostler, h 231 E Morris.
Hohl Albert C, clk, b 12 Park av.
Hohl Charles F, dentist, 12 Park av, h same.
Hohl Elizabeth (wid Christopher G), b 12 Park av.

THOS. C. DAY & CO.
Financial Agents and Loans.
We have the experience, and claim to be reliable.
Rooms 325 to 330 Lemcke Bldg.

Hohlt Frederick W, dry goods, 133 Hadley av (W I), h 163 W Morris.
Hohlt Wm, gardener, h 1372 Sherman av (N I).
Hohlt Wm H, driver, h 470 S East.
Hohn George, b 451 W Walnut av (N I).
Hohn John, brick mnfr, h 451 W Walnut av (N I).
Hohnstedt Philip L, florist, b 1542 N Senate av.
Holbrook Wm H, h 1668 Graceland av.
Holcomb John Z, attendant Insane Hospital.
Holcomb Sarah, dressmkr, 239 Blackford, b same.
Holdeman Eugene, student, b 676 E St Clair.
Holden Albert J, clk, b 49 Andrews.
Holden Charles L, foreman Knight & Jillson, h 49 Andrews.
Holden Frank A, lab, b n s Washington 1 e of Linwood av.
Holden Joseph, janitor, h 191 W Vermont.
Holden Pearl, opr Cent U Tel Co, b 191 W Vermont.
Holden Robert, bartndr, h 618 W Vermont.
Holden Wm J, lab, h 475 Virginia av.
Holder James T, lab, h rear 716 Morris (W I).
Holder Wm, lab, b 172 Bismarck av (H).
Holderman George H, supt fire alarm tel, h 414 Bellefontaine.
Holderman James H, barber, 490 S Illinois, h 24 W McCarty.
Holding Barnes, switchman, b 74 S West.
Holding Lorenzo, clk, b 74 S West.
Holding Oscar, lab, h 104 Hoyt av.
Holding Samuel, sawyer, h 74 S West.
Holdman George, porter, r 12½ Indiana av.
Holdreith Frank, clk, b 102 Prospect.
Hole Albert T, produce, E Mkt House, b 407 Madison av.
Hole Mary (wid Thomas G), h 407 Madison av.
Hole Wilson J, prin Public School No 2 (H), h 160 Sheffield av (H).
Hole Thomas R (mach hd), h 3 Morgan (W I).

EAT
HITZ'S CRACKERS
AND CAKES.
ASK YOUR GROCER FOR THEM.

BICYCLES $5 DOWN. MONTHLY. Terms. WHEELMEN'S CO. 31 W. OHIO ST. LONG DISTANCE TEL. 1855.

J. H. TECKENBROCK General House Painter, 94 EAST SOUTH STREET.

FIDELITY MUTUAL LIFE—PHILADELPHIA, PA.
$75,000,000, Insurance In Force. $3,500,000, Death Losses Paid. $1,500,090, Surplus. } A. H. COLLINS {General Agent, Baldwin Block.

BITUMINOUS COAL IN CAR LOADS TO DEALERS AND MANUFACTURERS. ROOMS 42 AND 43 WHEN BUILDING. Edwardsport Coal & Mining Co.

ESTABLISHED 1876. TELEPHONE 168.
CHESTER BRADFORD,
SOLICITOR OF PATENTS,
AND COUNSEL IN PATENT CAUSES.
(See adv. page 6.)
Office:—Rooms 14 and 16 Hubbard Block, S. W. Cor. Washington and Meridian Streets,
INDIANAPOLIS, INDIANA.

Holipeter Charles, mach hd, r 328 E Washington.
Holl Benjamin, clk, b 211 S Penn.
Holl Burnett L, baker, b 376 E Wabash.
Holl Charles W, clk Emil Wulschner & Son, h 84 Prospect.
Holl Edward H, agt, h 211 S Penn.
Holl Matilda (wid Henry), b 91 Brookside av.
Holl Wm H, insp City Engineer, h 345 Cornell av.
Hollabaugh Milton A, office sec Indiana Y M C A, b 27 E Pratt.
Holladay Arthur, asst bkkpr Merchants' Natl Bank, h 426½ Mass av.
Hollahan, see also Hollihan and Houlihan.
Hollahan, Catherine (wid Patrick), h 424 S Capitol av.
Hollahan Daniel J, mach, b 424 S Capitol av.
Hollahan James, lab, h 2 Brooks.
Hollahan Jeremiah A, patrolman, h 82 Church.
Hollahan Patrick E, lab, b 424 S Capitol av.
Holland Calvin R, custodian Pythian Hall, r 144 N Pine.
Holland Charles A, ins, h 573 Park av.
Holland Dennis, h 296 Blackford.
Holland Edward (Holland & Donahue), grocer, 428 S West, h same.
Holland Edward T, painter, b 869 Milburn (M P).
Holland Fannie (wid Wm), b 124½ Ft Wayne av.
Holland Frank H, horse dealer, h 404 E Michigan.
Holland George, tmstr, h 72 Holmes av (H).
Holland George F, clk, b 252 N California.
Holland Harris F, salesman, h 908 N New Jersey.
Holland Hester (wid Joseph), b 14 Lafayette.
Holland James, lab, h 113 W Ray.
Holland John A, clk Vandalia Line, h 128 Duncan.
Holland John H, supt, h 78 Nordyke av (W I).
Holland John H, trav agt, h 370 Home av.
Holland John J, cook, b 296 Blackford.

Outing BICYCLES
..MADE BY..
HAY & WILLITS MFG CO.
76 N. Pennsylvania St. Phone 598.

Holland John M, clk George J Marott, h 84 The Windsor.
Holland Joseph, gasfitter, r 255 N West.
Holland Julia, school teacher, b 158 Bellefontaine.
Holland Melvina B, h 869 Milburn (M P).
Holland Martin O, lab, h 28 Grant.
Holland Mary (wid John), h 305 S Delaware.
Holland Mary A (wid Jasper), h 149 N Penn.
Holland Mary E (wid James), h 312 Coburn.
Holland Michael, lab, h 104 S Linden.
Holland Patrick, bartndr, h 31 S West.
Holland Richard, lab, r 592 Morris (W I).
Holland Susan J (wid Wm), h 233 W South.
Holland Theodore F, broker, 74-76 S Meridian, h 158 Bellefontaine.
Holland Timothy J, lab, h 305 S Delaware.
Holland Wallace C, bkkpr Tuttle & Seguin, b 573 Park av.
Holland Wm, driver, h 347 N California.
Holland Wm G (Holland & Essex), h 915 N Capitol av.
Holland Wm H, upfitter, h 284 Christian av.
Holland Wm M, bill clk C C C & St L Ry, b 305 S Delaware.
Holland & Donahue (Edward Holland, Jeremiah Donahue), baking powder mnfrs, 135 Church.
Holland & Essex (Wm G Holland, John I Essex), mnfrs' agts, 198 S Meridian, tel 783.
Holle, see also Holly.
Holle Albert, lab, b 472 Mulberry.
Holle August, lab, b 26 Yeiser.
Holle Bertha L C, teacher Public School No 13, b 343 E Market.
Holle Charles J, driver, h 31 Applegate.
Holle Christina (wid Gottlieb), h 472 Mulberry.
Holle Conrad F, clk Hollweg & Reese, h 310 Spann av.
Holle Frederick W, truckman, h 128 Greer.
Holle Frederick W, weaver, b 126 Patterson.
Holle Henry F, cabtmkr, b 535 S Capitol av.
Holle Herman C, contr, 343 E Market, h same.
Holle Margaret (wid August), h 26 Yeiser.
Hollenbach Ernest, baker, h 394 S West.
Hollenbach Wm M, carp, h 278 Springfield.
Hollenbeck Charles D, collr, r 217 N Senate av.
Hollenbeck Charles E (Carlon & Hollenbeck), h 957 N Meridian.
Hollenbeck Frank, cigars, Stubbins Hotel, b Senate Hotel.
Hollenbeck George W (T P Hollenbeck & Son), h 217 N Senate av.
Hollenbeck Jacob G, passenger agt I D & W Ry, 134 S Illinois, b 322 N Illinois.
Hollenbeck Jacob W, U S gauger P O bldg, h 322 N Illinois.
Hollenbeck James, clk, b Senate Hotel.
Hollenbeck Theodore P (T P Hollenbeck & Son), h Clifford av e of Belt R R.
Hollenbeck Thomas W, clk Krag-Reynolds Co, b 322 N Illinois.
Hollenbeck T P & Son (Theodore P and George W), wire goods, 32 S Meridian.
Hollenberry Ella D (wid Jacob M), h 380 College av.
Holler Augusta (wid Philip H), b 352 Spring.
Holler Philip W (Sherfey & Holler), h 352 Spring.
Holler Reinhardt, baker, h 258 Davidson.
Hollern Mary (wid Thomas), h 160 Meek.

C. ZIMMERMAN & SONS | SLATE AND GRAVEL ROOFERS 19 South East Street.

DRIVEN WELLS And Second Water Wells and Pumps of all kinds at CHARLES KRAUSS', 42 S. PENN. ST., Telephone 465.

ERTEL STEAM LAUNDRY 26 and 28 N. Senate Avenue. 'Phone 19 WE WILL CALL FOR AND DELIVER YOUR WORK. SATISFACTION GUARANTEED.

Hollern Wm, lab, b 160 Meek.
Hollett Catherine (wid John M), b 368 E Morris.
Hollett John E, lawyer, 502 Indiana Trust bldg, b 75 E Walnut.
Hollett Wm G, plumber, b 54 Belmont av (H).
Hollett Woodard, h 49 Warren av (W I).
Hollette Mark H, h 322 N Senate av.
Hollette Thomas A, jeweler, b 322 N Senate av.
Holley, see Holle and Holly.
Holliday Charles A, cooper, h 25 Blake.
Holliday Edward J, clk Holliday & Wyon, b 11 Morrison.
Holliday Francis T, treas The Indpls News, h 93 Middle Drive (W P).
Holliday Frank, lab, h 637 W Vermont.
Holliday Henry C, cooper, h 120 Blackford.
Holliday Jacquelin S (W J Holliday & Co), h 739 N Delaware.
Holliday John D (Holliday & Wyon), h 11 Morrison.
HOLLIDAY JOHN H, Pres Union Trust Co and Sec Belt R R and Stock Yards Co, h 601 N Meridian.
Holliday Wilbur F, h 45 Bellefontaine.
Holliday Wm J (W J Holliday & Co), h 241 N Meridian.
HOLLIDAY W J & Co (Wm J and Jacquelin S Holliday, Walter J Goodall), Wholesale Hardware, 59-61 S Meridian, Tel 462.
HOLLIDAY & WYON (John D Holliday, Albert F Wyon), Wholesale Harness and Collar Mnfrs and Dealers in Leather and Shoe Findings, 96-100 S Penn, Tel 506.
Hollihan, see also Hallihan and Houlihan.
Hollihan Bridget (wid Jeremiah), h 44 Elizabeth.
Hollihan Daniel, h 417 Highland av.
Hollihan Jeremiah, customs warehouseman, h 173 N Capitol av.
Hollinger Robert T, clk Illinois House, h 121 Minerva.
Hollingsworth Benjamin G, carp, h 622 W Eugene (N I).
Hollingsworth Charles, carp, h 31 Cincinnati.
Hollingsworth Charles, turner, b 50 Standard av (W I).
Hollingsworth Charles P, draughtsman J B Allfree Mnfg Co, h 545 Bellefontaine.
Hollingsworth Clarence, molder, h 467 W Eugene (N I).
Hollingsworth Curtis, clk, b 141 Highland pl.
Hollingsworth Daniel, h 499 Highland av (N I).
Hollingsworth Dorotha, b 438 E Georgia.
Hollingsworth Earl J, engr, b 265 W Vermont.
Hollingsworth Elizabeth A (wid Jeremiah), h 314 N Alabama.
Hollingsworth Harvey, soldier U S Arsenal.
Hollingsworth James E, lab, h 388 W Shoemaker (N I).
Hollingsworth John, lab, h 554 W Addison (N I).
Hollingsworth John M, engr, h 124 Hill av.
Hollingsworth John S, phys, 92 Oliver av (W I), h same.
Hollingsworth Joseph, driver, b 645 Mass av.
Hollingsworth Joseph X, clk, b Enterprise Hotel.

EQUITABLE LIFE ASSURANCE SOCIETY OF THE UNITED STATES.
RICHARDSON & McCREA
Managers for Central Indiana,
79 East Market St. Telephone 182.

Hollingsworth Lucinda, boarding 144 N Senate av.
Hollingsworth Mary F (wid Valentine), h 100 Stoughton av.
Hollingsworth Minnie, stenog A Burdsal Co, b 100 Stoughton av.
Hollingsworth Oral T, lab, h 433 W Addison (N I).
Hollingsworth Samuel, cooper, h 62 Ingraham.
Hollingsworth Sarah D, h 164½ E Washington.
Hollingsworth Sylvanus, clk Gordon & Harmon, h 484 W Eugene (N I).
Hollingsworth Wallace, ballplayer, r 112 Ramsey av.
Hollingsworth Wm F, tmstr, h 116 Colgrove.
Hollingsworth Wm N, carp, h 141 Highland pl.
Hollingsworth Zeph, livery, 167 W Pearl, h 126 Highland pl.
Hollins George, sawmkr, h 135 Oliver av (W I).
Hollins George jr, lab, b 135 Oliver av (W I).
Hollis Charles C, collr Frank Bird Transfer Co, h 103 N Noble.
Hollis Chester H, h 292 Cornell av.
Hollis Earl H, b 292 Cornell av.
Hollis Joseph D, polisher, b 46 Fletcher av.
Hollis Louis A, condr, h 103 Spann av.
Hollis Margaret C (wid George W), h 46 Fletcher av.
Hollis Milton A, switchman, h 46 Fletcher av.
Hollis Ora B, b 518 W Maryland.
Hollis Wm H, condr, h 1028 W Washington.
Hollister Albert M, clk, b 139 N Penn.
Hollister James L, plater, b 139 N Penn.
Hollister Owen P S, h 272 N Senate av.
Holloran Edward P, lab, b 426 S West.
Holloran James, lab, h 118 W Ray.
Holloran Martin O, lab, h 28 Grant.
Holloran Patrick, bartndr, b 31 S West.
Holloran Patrick, lab, h 426 S West.
Holloway Armstead, h 217 E Ohio.
Holloway Charles E (C E Coffin & Co), sec Ind Savings and Inv Co, h 844 N Penn.

STENOGRAPHERS FURNISHED.
EXPERIENCED OR BEGINNERS, PERMANENT OR TEMPORARY.
S. H. EAST, State Agent,
The Williams Typewriter,
55 THORPE BLOCK. 87 EAST MARKET ST.

ELLIS & HELFENBERGER { ENTERPRISE FOUNDRY & FENCE CO. 162-170 S. Senate Ave. Tel. 958.

THE HOGAN TRANSFER AND STORAGE COMP'Y
Household Goods and Pianos Moved—Packed—Stored...... Baggage and Package Express Machinery and Safes a Specialty Cor. Washington and Illinois Sts. TELEPHONE No. 675.

The Central Rubber & Supply Co. PHONE 922. 79 S. ILLINOIS ST., INDIANAPOLIS, IND. Hose, Belting, Packing, Clothing, Druggists' Sundries, Bicycle Tires, Cotton Hose, Etc. New York Belting & Packing Co., L't'd.

A death rate below all other American Companies, and dividends from this source correspondingly larger.
The Provident Life and Trust Company
Of Philadelphia.
D. W. EDWARDS, General Agent,
508 Indiana Trust Building.

Holloway Chester C, fireman, h n w cor Eureka and Progress avs.
Holloway Cornelius B, livery, 22 Cherry, h 22 Home av.
Holloway David A, cupola tender, h 65 Maple.
Holloway Elisha B, real est, h 781 N Delaware.
Holloway Eliza A (wid Cornelius), h 22 Home av.
Holloway Elmer E, tuner Emil Wulschner & Son, h 53 Central av.
Holloway Frank E, clk, r 451 N Capitol av.
Holoway Harry H, foreman Ertel Steam Laundry, h 387 N Illinois.
Holloway Henry, b 387 N Illinois.
Holloway Horace B, clk John S Spann & Co, b 141 St Mary.
Holloway Ithamar W, supt Gem Laundry, h 387 N Illinois.
Holloway Jennie A, cashr Wm T Marcy, b 270 N Capitol av.
Holloway Lewis W, lumber, h 409 Ash.
Holloway Matthew, porter, h 548 N Missouri.
Holloway Maxie L, b 409 Ash.
Holloway Mary, b 165 W Morris.
Holloway Otis D, h 27 Ft Wayne av.
Holloway Pearl L, stenog, b 217 E Ohio.
Holloway Wm H, engr, h 165 W Morris.
Holloway Wm R, sec Dept Public Parks, 619 Indiana Trust bldg, r 8 Halcyon blk.
Hollowell Amos K, pres Jenney Electric Motor Co and Ind Lumber and Veneer Co, and treas Nordyke & Marmon Co, h 803 College av.
Hollowell Calvin L, grocer, 603 E Washington, h 626 E Market.
Hollowell Charles, nailer, h 549 E Michigan.
Hollowell Joseph A, painter, b 73 Torbet.
Hollowell Lynn P, treas Indiana Lumber and Veneer Co, h 454 Talbott av.
Hollowell Matilda (wid Edward), b 626 E Market.
Hollowell Wm, cook Deaf and Dumb Inst.
Hollowitz Harris, pdlr, h 140 Eddy.
Hollweg Ferdinand L, salesman Hollweg & Reese, b 505 N Meridian.

Julius C. Walk & Son,
Jewelers
Indianapolis.
12 EAST WASHINGTON ST.

Hollweg Louis (Hollweg & Reese; Murphy, Hibben & Co), h 505 N Meridian.
HOLLWEG & REESE (Louis Hollweg), Wholesale Glassware and Crockery, 82-98 S Meridian, Tel 71.
Holly, see also Holle.
Holly James, lab, b 46 Standard av (W I).
Hollywood Richard H, trav agt Odd Fellows' Talisman, b 287 N Alabama.
Holman Aaron, h 334 N Illinois.
Holman Charles C, phys, 124 Oliver av (W I), h same.
Holman Daniel B, real est, h 550 Chestnut.
Holman Edward B, carp, b 1335 N Senate av.
Holman Edward J, molder, b 550 Chestnut.
Holman George W, broommkr, h 163 Agnes.
Holman Helen B (wid John A), b 44 W North.
Holman Hiram, agt, h 275 W 1st.
Holman James H, trav agt Eli Lilly & Co, h 1011 N Illinois.
Holman John, lab, h 12 Columbia al.
Holman John B, lumber, b 371 Talbott av.
Holman John H, carp, h 1363 N Capitol av.
Holman John H, lab, h 855 Milburn (M P).
Holman Nelson, lab, b 102 Torbet.
Holman Wm, express, b 102 Torbet.
Holmes Albert K, clk, b 389 Clifford av.
Holmes Alfred B, mitrecutter, h s s Shearer pike 1 mile e of Brightwood.
Holmes Catherine J (wid Canada), h 78 W North.
Holmes Charles, agt, h 886 N Penn.
Holmes Charles, lab, b 415 N East.
Holmes David, lab, r 222 W Maryland.
Holmes David J (Wamsley & Holmes), b 453 N West.
Holmes Edgar, coachman, h 183 W 2d.
Holmes Edward, painter A H Grove, b 129 Tacoma av.
Holmes Edward G, clk Natl Malleable Castings Co, h 1309 N Delaware.
Holmes Emma A, asst matron Indiana Reformatory.
Holmes E Eugene (Holmes & Co), h 264 Talbott av.
Holmes Harry W, engr, h 852 LaSalle.
Holmes Henry, lab, h 85 Oregon.
Holmes Ira M, salesman, b 123 Cornell av.
Holmes James, carp, h 38 N Station (B).
Holmes James H, phys, h 129 Tacoma av.
Holmes Johanna F (wid Henry), h 453 N West.
Holmes John C (Holmes & Carey), b 453 N West.
Holmes Johnson C, cashr Polar Ice Co, h 150 N Noble.
Holmes Leslie, painter, h 29 College av.
Holmes Lewis W (L W Holmes & Co), h 352 Clifford av.
Holmes Louisa (wid Charles), h 217 S New Jersey.
Holmes L W & Co (Lewis W and Wm F Holmes), druggists, 352 Clifford av.
Holmes Marion S, mach hd, b 283 E Georgia.
Holmes Mary A, dressmkr, 223 W Maryland, h same.
Holmes Matthew W, foreman, b 19 N Arsenal av.
Holmes Thomas J, saloon, 75 S West, b 453 N West.
Holmes Wm A, paperhngr, h 165 Columbia av.
Holmes Wm F (L W Holmes & Co), b 352 Clifford av.
Holmes Wm H, clk, b 453 N West.

OTTO GAS ENGINES | BUILDERS' EXCHANGE S. W. Cor. Ohio and Penn. Telephone 535.

Becker & Son Charles Becker Jacob Becker Jr. Merchant Tailors. 21 N. Penn. St. Tel. 934

SALISBURY & STANLEY OFFICE, STORE AND BANK FIXTURES.

Holmes Wm M, waiter The Bates.
Holmes & Carey (John C Holmes, Wm J Carey), horseshoers, 82 W Wabash.
HOLMES & CO (E Eugene Holmes, George E Coburn), Experienced Gas Fitters and Plumbers, 92 E Market.
Holschultz Sarah, clk, b 996 N Penn.
Holsey Lyman G, agt, r 491 E Market.
Holsinger John T, cashr Nederland Life Ins Co (ltd), b Hotel English.
Holsker Caroline (wid Benjamin), h 36 Helen.
Holsker George, lab, b 36 Helen.
Holsker Henry, carbldr, h 137 Lynn av (W I).
HOLSTEIN, BARRETT & HUBBARD (Charles L Holstein, Charles E Barrett, Wm B Hubbard), Lawyers, 7-12 Hartford Blk, 84 E Market, Tel 417.
Holstein Charles L (Holstein, Barrett & Hubbard), h 26 Lockerbie.
Holston Lee, coachman 743 N Delaware.
Holston Rebecca B (wid Joshua), b 345 Talbott av.
Holt Allen E, clk, b 153 Park av.
Holt Clara A, h 159 E Ohio.
Holt Eugene, clk Kingan & Co (ltd), b 174 N Illinois.
Holt Fannie, h 176 Agnes.
Holt Frank, lab, h 192 Huron.
Holt Frank H, sec and mngr Metallic Mnfg Co, h 98 Ruckle.
Holt Henry, agt, 77½ E Market, h 551 same.
Holt Henry, lab, h 63 Columbia av.
Holt Henry, lab, b 339 W Market.
Holt Henry W, tmstr, h 15 Valley Drive.
Holt Hiram S, grocer, 430 National rd, h same.
Holt Ice and Cold Storage Co The, Sterling R Holt pres, Michael Downing vice-pres, John O Henderson, sec, James L Keach treas, n e cor North and canal.
Holt John F, clk, b 508 College av.
Holt Peter, porter, r 193 W Washington.
Holt Robert, porter, h 162 Bird.
Holt Samantha (wid Andrew J), h 508 College av.
Holt Samuel H, lab, h 43½ Brookside av.
Holt Sterling R, pres Artificial Ice and Cold Storage Co and Holt Ice and Cold Storage Co and treas Grand Hotel Co.
Holt Wm, gardener, h 1372 Schurman av (N I).
Holt Wm A, clk The Bates, h 41 Highland pl.
Holtgen F August, h 197 Blake.
Holtmann August H, lab, h 22 Eureka av.
Holtmann Charles, plumber, 348 E New York, b 84 N Arsenal av.
Holtmann Charles F, clk, h 225 N Beville av.
Holtmann Charles H, mach hd, b 142 Excelsior av.
Holtmann Henry, carp, h 23 Excelsior av.
Holtmann Henry F, cabtmkr, b 1130 E Michigan.
Holtmann Herman H, h 142 Excelsior av.
Holtmann Herman H jr, lab, b 142 Excelsior av.
Holtmann John, lab, h 84 N Arsenal av.
Holtmann John H, car insp, h 335 N Noble.
Holtmann Wm, mach hd, b 335 N Noble.
Holtmann Wm, carp, h 1130 E Michigan.
Holtmann Wm, plumber, b 84 N Arsenal av.
Holton Flora M, stenog The Universal Credit Agency, b 38 Garfield pl.

Henry H. Fay,
40½ E. Washington St.,
REAL ESTATE,
AND LOAN BROKER.

Holton Frank E, clk, r 262 E Washington.
Holton Harry S, pres and mngr The Universal Credit Agency, h 331 Bellefontaine.
Holton Henry H, bricklyr, h 452 Central av.
Holton Hiram S, vice-pres W B Holton Mnfg Co, h 38 Garfield pl.
Holton Winfred B, pres W B Holton Mnfg Co and treas Reserve Fund Savings and L Assn, h 769 N Alabama.
HOLTON W B MANUFACTURING CO, Winfred B Holton Pres, Hiram S Holton Vice-Pres, George J Macy Sec and Treas, Agricultural Implements, 177 E Washington.
Holtsclaw Alexander B, tmstr, h 271 S Illinois.
Holtsclaw John B, clk The Bowen-Merrill Co, b 236 N Illinois.
Holtsclaw Newton F, clk, b 3 Vine.
Holtsclaw Wm C (John Baughman & Co), h 3 Vine.
Holtz August C, porter The Indpls Book and Stationery Co, h 42 Sanders.
Holtz Charles F, pressman, h 175 Wright.
Holtz Daniel A, truckman, h 562 S East.
Holtz John, lab, h 562 S East.
Holtz John B, attendant Insane Hospital.
Holtz Louis C, asst ticket agt I U Ry Co, h 99 Fulton.
Holtz Wm A, patrolman, h 562 S East.
Holtzhausen Charles, driver, h 42 W 4th.
Holtzman Henry A, grocer, 168 Shelby, h 235 Cottage av.
Holtzman John W (Holtzman & Leathers), h 33 The Blacherne.
Holtzman Lee, h 835 N Capitol av.
HOLTZMAN & LEATHERS (John W Holtzman, James M Leathers), Lawyers, 34-35 Journal Bldg, Tel 1339.
Holy Joseph, tailor, h 27½ Monument pl.
Holy Joseph M, condr, h 78 Springfield.
Holzer Peter J, carp, h 32 Leonard.
Holzworth Albert, carver, h 55 Kansas.
Holzworth Catherine (wid Gottlob), h 74 Oriole.
Holzworth Gottlob, lab, h w s Minnesota 1 w of Meridian.

Contractors and Builders. Repairing of all kinds done on short notice. 177 Clinton St., Indianapolis, Ind. Telephone 99.

LIME, CEMENT, PLASTER FIRE BRICK AND CLAY SEWER PIPE, ETC. BALKE & KRAUSS CO., Cor. Market and Missouri Streets.

C. FRIEDGEN HAS THE FINEST STOCK OF LADIES' PARTY SLIPPERS and SHOES 19 NORTH PENNSYLVANIA ST.

SAMUEL LAING ▸ TIN, SLATE AND STEEL ROOFING 72 AND 74 EAST COURT STREET.

M. B. WILSON, Pres. W. F. CHURCHMAN, Cash.
THE CAPITAL NATIONAL BANK,
INDIANAPOLIS, IND.
Pays Interest on Time Certificates of Deposit.
Buys and Sells Foreign Exchange at Low Rates.
Capital, - - $300,000
Surplus and Earnings, 50,000
No. 28 S. Meridian St., Cor. Pearl.

Holzworth Louisa, stenog Atlas Engine Wks, b 74 Oriole.
Homan Charlotte T, h 227 E South.
Homan Emma, h 391½ Indiana av.
Homan Frank J, clk, b 171 Olive.
Homan John, lab, h 12 Columbia al.
Homan Wm J, gasfitter, h 75 E McCarty.
Homburg Henry F, cook, h 292 E Merrill.
Homburg John J, paperhngr, h 20 Bell.
Homburg Mary (wid Wm), h 13 Paca.
Home Benefit Assn The, Louis S Smith pres, Joseph B Classick vice-pres, Samuel L Marrow sec and treas, 67 Ingalls blk.
HOME BREWING CO OF INDIANAPOLIS THE, Wm P Jungclaus Pres, Andrew Hagen Sec and Treas, cor Cruse and Wilson, Tel 1050.
HOME CRACKER CO, John H Plum Mngr, 192-194 S Meridian, Tel 1076.
Home for Aged Poor, conducted by Little Sisters of the Poor, n s Vermont near East.
HOME LAUNDRY THE, Charles F Roesener Mngr, 197 S Illinois, Tel 1769. (See right side lines.)
HOME LUMBER CO (Henry C Prange, Frederick Gompf), 460-474 E Michigan, Tel 1046.
Home of the Good Shepherd, 57 W Raymond.
HOME SAVINGS ASSOCIATION, C H McDowell Pres, C J Buchanan Vice-Pres, Alice V Mendenhall Sec, 627-629 Lemcke Bldg.
HOME SECURITY LIFE ASSOCIATION OF SAGINAW, MICH, George B McGill State Mngr, Rooms 334-335 Lemcke Bldg.
HOME STOVE CO THE, George Alig Pres, Louis Hitzelberger Sec and Treas, Mnfrs of Stoves, Ranges and Hollow Ware, 79 S Meridian, Tel 1273.
Homeier Wm, car rep, h 22 Gatling.
Homer Henry, engr, r 149 Huron.

TUTTLE & SEGUIN,
28 E. Market Street.
Fire Insurance,
Real Estate, Loan
and Rental Agents.
TELEPHONE 1168.

Homer Henry S, clk, h 44 Birch av (W I).
Hommown John, boarding stable, 30 Roanoke, h 129 N Senate av.
Homuth Edward, grocer, 564 E St Clair, h 566 same.
Homuth Frederick, b 566 E St Clair.
Honecker Henry, cabtmkr, h 19 Clay.
Honecker John, cabtmkr, h 23 Bridge (W I).
Honecker Louis C, carp, h 20 Rock.
Honeycutt Hiram H, driver, h 488 N Missouri.
Honickman Johanna (wid Hirsh), h 412 S Meridian.
Honnold James L, b 792 N Senate av.
Hood Arthur M (H P Hood & Son), h 316 Cornell av.
Hood Benjamin T, lab, h rear 671 N Senate av.
Hood, Foulkrod & Co, whol dry goods, 17½ McCrea.
Hood Frank C Rev, pastor East Washington Street Presbyterian Church, h 63 N Arsenal av.
Hood Harrison P (H P Hood & Son), h 125 E Michigan.
Hood Harry H, fireman, h 239 Dillon.
Hood Henry, lab, b 444 E 7th.
HOOD H P & SON (Harrison P and Arthur M), Patent Attorneys and Consulting Experts in Infringement Suits, 29-30 Wright's Blk, 68½ E Market. (See adv in classified Patent Attorneys.)
Hood Julia E (wid James), h 464 N Alabama.
Hood Nicholas, tmstr, h 112 Colgrove.
Hood Redick, lab, h 565 Shelby.
Hood Thomas M, lab, h rear 52 Osgood (W I).
Hood Thomas W, tree agt, h 523 E 8th.
Hood Wm, tmstr, h e s Temperance 1 s of English av (I).
Hood Wm B, baker, h 273 Indiana av.
Hood Wm S, bkkpr C F Hunt Co, b 39½ Indiana av.
Hoogland, see also Hoagland and Hogeland.
Hoogland Herman A, driver, h 115 College av.
Hook August, supt Home Brewing Co, h 71 N Noble.
Hook Elam, helper, h 123 Sharpe av (W).
Hook Ferdinand J, clk Francke & Schindler, b 71 N Noble.
Hook Frank M, pass clk C C C & St L Ry, r 176 E New York.
Hook Jacob, brewer, h 167 Meek.
Hook James K Rev, h 147 Sharpe av (W).
Hook Otto G, lab, b 147 Sharpe av (W).
Hooker Frank R, h 251 S East.
Hooker Franklin, painter, h 1103 E Ohio.
Hooker George B, mach, h 236 E Market.
Hooker Henry, pdlr, h n s Miller 1 w of Belmont av (W I).
Hooker Henry S, bkkpr U S Lounge Mnfg Co, h 21 West Drive (W P).
Hooker James, trav agt, h 408 Talbott av.
Hooker James H, pres The Sinker-Davis Co and Hoosier Canning Machinery Co, h 21 West Drive (W P).
Hooker John, lab, r 152 W Washington.
Hooker John I, lab, h rear 775 N Senate av.
Hooker Rebecca S (wid James), h 21 West Drive (W P).
Hooks Daniel C, cooper, h 88 S West.
Hoop Abner, blksmith, h 5 Wilson.
Hoop Austin, nurse, 102 N Alabama.
Hoop Bell, r 28 Ryan blk.

SULLIVAN & MAHAN Manufacturers of all kinds of PAPER BOXES 41 W. Pearl St.

DIAMOND WALL PLASTER { Telephone 1410 BUILDERS' EXCHANGE.

Telephone 1769. 197 S. Illinois St. } THE HOME LAUNDRY { WORK CALLED FOR AND DELIVERED.

Hoop Harry, barber, b 5 Wilson.
Hoop Lee H, driver, r Ryan blk.
Hooper Charles A, clk, h 243 W McCarty.
Hooper Henry H, salesman Emil Wulschner & Son, b 138 E Pratt.
HOOSAC TUNNEL FAST FREIGHT LINE, Wm H Parmelee Agt, Harry F Parmelee Contracting Agt, 15 Union Bldg, 69 W Maryland, Tel 711.
Hoosier Canning Machinery Co, James H Hooker pres, Orra Hubbell sec, Henry R Bliss treas, 50 McGill.
Hoosier Construction Co, Clarence A Kenyon pres and treas, Frank H Kenyon sec, 301 Indiana Trust bldg.
Hoosier Lecture Bureau, 629 Lemcke bldg.
HOOSIER MANUFACTURING COMPANY, W R Wands Mngr, Mnfrs of Hoosier Journal and Axle Lubricants, Elevator Grease, Harness Dressing, Wool Scouring and Steam Laundry Soaps; Agts Traders' Oil Co, Cylinder and Lubricating Oils, 192 S Illinois, Tel 1463.
Hoosier Packing Co, Francis R Jennings pres, Matte E Scudder sec, fruit butter, 183 W Pearl.
Hoosier Sweat Collar Co The (John C Mendenhall, Wm F Williams), horse collar mnfrs, s w cor Alvord and 8th.
Hoover Abraham L, clk Cornelius Friedgen, h 639 Park av.
Hoover Albertine (wid Fremont), b 218 N Alabama.
Hoover Alonzo W, teacher, h 47 College av.
Hoover Andrew, timekpr, h 389 N Senate av.
Hoover Andrew L, b 185 N Belmont av (H).
Hoover Charles F, mach hd, h 110 Deloss.
Hoover Charles N, collr, h 16 S Senate av.
Hoover Charles P, clk When Clothing Store, h 423 E 15th.
Hoover Charles V, letter carrier P O, h 132 Walcott.
Hoover Conrad D, mach, b 30 Johnson av.
Hoover Elgin J, clk, b 408 Indiana av.
Hoover Enos W (E W Hoover & Co), b 171 N Capitol av.
Hoover E W & Co (Enos W Hoover, Austin T Quick), ins, 718 Lemcke bldg.
Hoover Forest G, dairyman, n e cor Broadway and 22d, b same.
Hoover Frances C (wid Jacob B), h n e cor Broadway av and 22d.
Hoover George F, well digger, h w s Central av 4 s of Railroad (I).
Hoover George G, clk U S Pension Agency, r 230 The Shiel.
Hoover George W, lab, h 1182 N Capitol av.
Hoover Harry F, clk I D & W Ry, b 146 Pleasant.
Hoover Henry, h 213 LeGrand av.
Hoover James A, molder, h 96 N Belmont av (H).
Hoover John D, h 350 W 1st.
Hoover John E, phys, 541 E Washington, h 76 Fletcher av.
Hoover John J (J J Hoover & Son), h 33 Davis.
Hoover John O, electrician, b 33 Davis.
Hoover John S, lab, h 5 Hill.
Hoover John W, lab, b 2 Florence (H).
Hoover Joseph S, truckman, h 30 Johnson av.
Hoover J J & Son (John J and Ralph P), tinners, 485 S Delaware.

FRANK NESSLER. WILL H. ROST.
FRANK NESSLER & CO.
Tailors
56 EAST MARKET ST. (Lemcke Building),
INDIANAPOLIS, IND.

Hoover Leander W, h 72½ N Delaware.
Hoover Lewis, bkkpr Commercial Club, h 260 Eureka av.
Hoover Mary A, h 73 Lee (W I).
Hoover Mary A (wid Jacob W), h 64 N State av.
Hoover Melinda (wid Alexander), b 795 N Penn.
Hoover Miles H, b 146 Pleasant.
Hoover Orlando S, gardener, h s e cor Grove av and 22d.
Hoover Perry, grocer, 235 Cornell av, h same.
Hoover Ralph P (J J Hoover & Son), h 739 Chestnut.
Hoover Samuel C, foreman C C C & St L Ry, h 124 Greer.
Hoover Thomas A, engr, h 185 N Belmont av (H).
Hoover Wm, lab, h 2 Florence (H).
Hoover Wm H, real est, 146 Pleasant, h same.
Hoover Wm M, clk, b 408 Indiana av.
Hoover Wm W, grocer, 408 Indiana av, h same.
Hope Mary E (wid Frederick J), b 654 Wells (N I).
Hopfinger Frank, brewer, h 92 Lincoln la.
Hopfinger John, brewer, h 155 Carlos.
Hopkins Alfred W, student, b 272 N Senate av.
Hopkins Charles H, carp, 210 Fletcher av, h same.
Hopkins Eliza M (wid John O), prin Public School No 16, h 481 Ash.
Hopkins Henry, waiter The Bates.
Hopkins Homer D, pharmacist H C Pomeroy, h 73 E St Clair.
Hopkins Irwin, coachman, r rear 70 Yandes.
Hopkins James W, trav agt Elmer E Nichols Co, h 427 Central av.
Hopkins Jennie, b 521 N West.
Hopkins John, waiter, h 147½ Eddy.
Hopkins John E, r 272 N Senate av.
Hopkins John S, steelwkr, b 52 McGinnis.
HOPKINS LINN B, Mantels, Grates and Tile Work, 145 N Delaware, h 255 S Olive.

ACORN STOVES AND RANGES
Haueisen & Hartmann
163-169 E. Washington St.
FURNITURE,
Carpets,
Household Goods,
Tin, Granite and China Wares, Oil Cloth and Shades

THE WM. H. BLOCK CO. 7 AND 9 EAST WASHINGTON STREET. DRY GOODS, HOUSE FURNISHINGS AND CROCKERY.

London Guarantee and Accident Co. (Ltd.) Employers', Public and Teams' Liability. Workmen's Collective Insurance and Fidelity Bonds
GEORGE W. PANGBORN, General Agent, 704-706 Lemcke Bldg. Telephone 140.

FRANK K. SAWYER || Reliable Fire Insurance. Reasonable Rates. 74 E. MARKET STREET. Telephone 8.

JOSEPH GARDNER,
TIN, IRON, STEEL AND SLATE ROOFING,
GALVANIZED IRON CORNICES & SKYLIGHTS.
37, 39 & 41 KENTUCKY AVE. Telephone 322.

Hopkins Mary, b 116 Yandes.
Hopkins Mary (wid John W), h 178½ Indiana av.
Hopkins Milton I, student, b 481 Ash.
HOPKINS MURAT W, Lawyer, 20-21 Fletcher's Bank Bldg, h 612 Broadway, Tel 1242.
Hopkins Phylena (wid Moses), b 956 N Delaware.
Hopkins Rufus E, switchman, h 60 Fletcher av.
Hopkins Samuel S, carp, h w s Gale 2 n of Willow (B).
Hopkins Thomas, lab, h 45 Guffin.
Hopkins Wm A, mach, h 103 Columbia av.
Hopkins Willis, lab, h 14 Lafayette.
Hoppe John G, cigarmkr, b 147 Hosbrook.
Hoppe John W, tinner, h 147 Hosbrook.
Hopper Charles A, clk, b 243 W McCarty.
Hopper Edwin C, bartndr, h 255 S Senate av.
Hopper Elijah K, barber, 50 S West, h same.
Hopper Oliver S, cooper, h 32 Ashland (W I).
Hopper Robert S, mach hd, h 45 Yandes.
Hopper Wm O, fireman, h 111 N Beville av.
Hopping Charles, dentist, h 539 E Market.
Hopping James A, crater, h 160 Hoyt av.
Hopping John H, clk, b 159 N Illinois.
Hoppins Edmund J, trav agt, h 138 12th.
Hoppins Frank H, mach, b 527 Park av.
Hopson Calvin, carp, h 13 St Charles.
Hopson Isaac P, detective, 88 Baldwin blk, r same.
Hopwood Clarence M, mach, b 131 W McCarty.
Hopwood Daniel, coremkr, b 131 W McCarty.
Hopwood Elijah M, carp, h 131 W McCarty.
Hopwood Frank, driver, b 145 W North.
Hopwood John B, collr, h 219 River av (W I).
Hopwood Mary (wid Newton), h Miller blk.
Hopwood Moses K, carp, h 59 Church.
Hopwood Wm M, lab, b 131 W McCarty.
Horan James, fireman, b 22 S State av.
Horan James D, ins agt, r 612 E Washington.

J. S. FARRELL & CO.
STEAM AND HOT WATER HEATING AND PLUMBING CONTRACTORS
84 North Illinois Street. Telephone 382.

Horan John, b 253 Springfield.
Horan Michael (Moore & Horan), h 253 Springfield.
Horan Patrick, brakeman, b 253 Springfield.
Horan Wm W, mach, h 17 Maple.
Horat Joseph, toolmkr, h 447 W Eugene (N I).
Hord Emma B (wid Francis T), h 50 West Drive (W P).
Hord Francis T (Hord & Perkins), h 24 The Blacherne.
Horn Harry J, clk, h 736 S Meridian.
Hord Horace B, lawyer, 431 Lemcke bldg, b 50 West Drive (W P).
HORD & PERKINS (Francis T Hord, Lafayette Perkins), Attorneys, 504, 505 and 506 Lemcke Bldg, Tel 1731.
Horine Samuel M, plastr, b 89 Oliver av (W I).
Hornell Wm H, lather, h 368 S East.
Horn Byron J, grainer, b 35 Louise.
Horn Charles W, painter, 65 Mass av, h 213 Hoyt av.
Horn Hardy, carp, h 261 W 3d.
Horn Henry J, clk, h 736 S Meridian.
Horn Herman, b 124 Walcott.
Horn Hosea B, painter, h 211 Newman.
Horn James H, painter, h 259 Alvord.
Horn Lawrence, lab, b 286 W Washington.
Horn Louis E, painter, b 35 Louise.
Horn Mildred M, teacher Industrial School, b 736 S Meridian.
Horn Sarah (wid George), b 266 Bright.
Horn Turner B, woodwkr, h 35 Louise.
Horn Wm, lab, h 17 Maple.
Hornaday Alonzo E, brazier, b 272 E North.
Hornaday Frederick W, clk W U Tel Co, b 254 College av.
Hornaday Harry B, polisher, b 949 N New Jersey.
Hornaday Henderson F, collr, h 82 Willow.
Hornaday James P, asst city editor The Indpls News, h 1157 N Penn, tel 1504.
Hornaday Martha J (wid John), h 41 Omer.
Hornaday May K (wid Grant M), b 1213 N Capitol av.
Hornaday Miles Grant, chief clk City Engineer, r 116 N Meridian.
Hornaday Sanford, foreman, b 249 E Louisiana.
Hornaday Thomas B, driver, h 949 N New Jersey.
Hornberger Andrew, butcher, h 385 Indiana av.
Hornberger Charles J, lab, b 385 Indiana av.
Hornberger Christian, stairbldr, h 70 Gregg.
Hornberger George, pressfeeder, b 464 Union.
Hornberger George F, clk Rich & McVey, b 70 Gregg.
Hornberger John A, clk, b 70 Gregg.
Hornberger John G, pressman, h 488 Union.
Hornberger Louis P, finisher, b 385 Indiana av.
Hornberger Peter, lab, h 464 Union.
Hornberger Peter, pressman, h 43 Palmer.
Hornbrook Elizabeth, bkkpr Charles L Wayne & Co, b 217 Davidson.
Hornbrook Henry H (Duncan, Smith & Hornbrook), h 381 N Capitol av.
Hornbrook Henry H, trav agt, h 217 Davidson.
Hornbrook Martha (wid Wm P), b 217 Davidson.
Horne Charles E, stenog Horne & Gasper, b 1044 N Illinois.
Horne John, brakeman, h 37 Wilcox.

POLICIES IN UNITED STATES LIFE INSURANCE CO., offer indemnity against death, liberal cash surrender value or at option of policy-holder, fully paid-up life insurance or liberal life income. E. B. SWIFT, M'g'r, 25 E. Market St.

WM. KOTTEMAN } WILL FURNISH YOUR HOUSE COMPLETE
89 & 91 E. Washington St. Telephone 1742

SHOW CASES | WILLIAM WIEGEL | 6 West Louisiana Street Opp. Union Station.

Horne Wilbur F, condr, h 222 Blake.
Horne Wm L jr (Horne & Gasper), b 1044 N Illinois.
HORNE & GASPER (Wm L Horne Jr, Joseph L Gasper), Genl Agts New England Mutual Life Insurance Co, 400 Indiana Trust Bldg, Tel 1040.
Hornefius Benjamin F (Wm E Jones & Co), b 797 N Illinois.
Horner Alice S, h 1001 E Washington.
Horner Benjamin F, engr, h 444 W Washington.
Horner David H, carp, h 328 Cornell av.
Horner Ida M, h 1001 E Washington.
Horner Jane I (wid Jacob), b 397 Central av.
Horner Samuel I, draughtsman, b 328 Cornell av.
Horney Clarence, baker, b 56 Columbia av.
Horney Harry C, mach, b 131 S East.
Horney Isaac, lab, h 184 Minerva.
Horney Reuben, lab, h 41 Smith.
Horney Solomon C M, mngr Indpls branch Noblesville Milling Co, h 1351 N Illinois, tel 695.
Horning Charles J, condr, h 18 N Brightwood av (B).
Horning Charles L, condr, b 707 E Washington.
Horning Frank J, city agt Louis G Deschler, b 118 E Pratt.
Horning George, brakeman, b e s Brightwood av 7 s of Willow (B).
Horning Jacob F, lab, h 272 Martindale av.
Horning Valentine W, shoemkr, h 19 S Stuart (B).
Hornish Harry C, vice-pres and mngr Blue Flame Oil Burner Co, h 459 Ash.
Hornshu Charles F, condr, h 417 College av.
Hornshu Theresa (wid Frederick), b 417 College av.
Hornung Christina B (wid John C), h 23 Wyoming.
Hornung Frederica (wid Jacob H), h 276 N Noble.
Hornung John G, pressman, b 23 Wyoming.
Horr Frank T, finisher, h 41 Jones.
Horsch John T, mach hd, h 455 Madison av.
Horshoff Israel, pdlr, h 119 Maple.
Horst Caroline (wid Henry), h 16 Warren.
Horst Edmund C, trav agt Hollweg & Reese, h 130 W North.
Horst George W, bkkpr Murphy, Hibben & Co, b 16 Warren.
Horstman Elizabeth (wid Charles), h 336 Martindale av.
Horstman Henry, lab, h 336 Martindale av.
Horstman John, lab, h 336 Martindale av.
Horstman Louis, porter, b 18 S New Jersey.
Horstman Richard, mach, r 292 E South.
Horstmann Clara, stenog Baker & Thornton, b 187 Woodlawn av.
Horstmann Henry C, drayman, h 187 Woodlawn av.
Horstmann John H, clk, b 187 Woodlawn av.
Horton Bertram, printer, b 171 Douglass.
Horton Charles W, carp, h 51 Brookside av.
Horton Edwin J, painter, b 436 Chestnut.
Horton Elsa A, blksmith, h 172 Duncan.
Horton Eva M, b 1815 N Senate av.
Horton James, master mechanic, b Spencer House.
Horton John, uphlr, b 309 E McCarty.
Horton Joseph H, b 193 S Alabama.
Horton Lewis V, sec Wooton Office Desk Co, b 298 N Delaware.

THOS. C. DAY & CO.
INVESTING AGENTS,
TOWN AND FARM LOANS,
Rooms 325 to 330 Lemcke Bldg.

Horton Lewis B, ins agt, b 282 N Illinois.
Horton Minnie, boarding 193 S Alabama.
Horton Olister, lab, b 171 E Walnut.
Horton Oscar, carp, h 56 Gresham.
Horton Theodore R, tmstr, b 12 S Judge Harding (W I).
Horton Thomas E, carp, h 69 Hill av.
Horton Thomas S, pdlr, h 31 Hiatt (W I).
Horton Wm, student, b 395 N West.
Horuff Albert N (Horuff & Sons), b 305 E South.
Horuff Clara E, h 305 E South.
Horuff Frank J (Horuff & Sons), b 305 E South.
Horuff Mary (Horuff & Sons), h 305 E South.
Horuff Wm, h 305 E South.
HORUFF & SONS (Mary, Albert N and Frank J), Fine Shoes, 188-190 Virginia av.
Horwitz Samuel, shoemkr, h 117 Eddy.
Hosbrook Daniel B, civil engr, h 91 Laurel.
HOSBROOK FRANK, Fancy and Staple Groceries; Prompt Delivery, 202 Prospect, cor S State av, h 141 Prospect.
Hosbrook Harvey, b 915 N New Jersey.
Hosbrook Mary A (wid John L), h 479 N Illinois.
Hosea Anna, stenog State Geologist, b 68 W Vermont.
Hosea Elizabeth V (wid John), h 68 W Vermont.
HOSHOUR ED S, Druggist, 650 College av, cor 12th, h 568 Broadway, Tel 1625.
Hoskins Charity A (wid Allen), b 355 Spring.
Hoskins Charles, clk, h 335 Blake.
Hoskins Eliza A (wid Rowland G), h 122 Irwin.
Hoskins Horace R, clk, b 122 Irwin.
Hoskins John, hostler, r 174 N Dorman.
Hoskins John R, ins agt, b Stubbins Hotel.

EAT
HITZ'S
CRACKERS
AND CAKES.
ASK YOUR GROCER FOR THEM.

Capital Steam Carpet Cleaning Works
M. D. PLUNKETT Proprietor, Telephone 818

BENJ. BOOTH PRACTICAL EXPERT ACCOUNTANT. Accounts of any description investigated and audited, and statements rendered. Room 18, 82½ E. Washington St., Indianapolis, Ind.

The Best Place in the City to Get a Good Meal THE SHERMAN RESTAURANT 18 and 20 S. Meridian Street KERSHNER BROS., Proprs.

ESTABLISHED 1876. TELEPHONE 168.
CHESTER BRADFORD,
SOLICITOR OF PATENTS,
AND COUNSEL IN PATENT CAUSES.
(See adv. page 6.)
Office:—Rooms 14 and 16 Hubbard Block, S.W. Cor. Washington and Meridian Streets, INDIANAPOLIS, INDIANA.

HOSKINS WALTER D, Physician, 186½ Ft Wayne av, h 122 Irwin; Tels, Office 195, Res 1051.
Hoskinson Amanda (wid Wm), h w s Auburn av 2 s of Bethel av.
Hoskinson John, hostler, b 14 Concordia.
Hoskinson John A, clk, b 156 N Pine.
Hosman Frederick L, student, b 191 Ramsey av.
Hosman John W, clk, h 191 Ramsey av.
Hosmer Edwin S, engr, h 68 W 19th.
Hosmore Elizabeth (wid Richard), b 84 S Senate av.
Hoss Anton C, farmer, h e s School 2 n of Schofield (B).
Hoss David, driver, h rear 483 Virginia av.
Hoss Jacob D A, contr, 92 Baldwin blk, h 30 Oak.
Hoss Jacob V, drugs, n e cor Glen Drive and Gale (B), h 70 Arch.
Hoss James J, b 175 E South.
Hoss John C, real est, h n w cor Orchard av and Crown.
Hoss Marie J, tailoress, b 175 E South.
Hoss Nelson, clk, r Three Notch rd 2 miles s of city limits.
Hoss Walter S, hardware, 860 Morris (W I), h 21 N William (W I).
Hossler Cartherine (wid Quincy), b 622 Central av.
Hossmann John, lab,h 16 Roe.
Hoster James P, salesman J C Perry & Co, b 796 Broadway.
Hoster Samuel, gardener, h 796 Broadway.
Hostetler Charlton E, plumber, b 328 Blake.
Hostetler John A, student, b 26 Standard av (W I).
Hostetler John V, mach hd, h 328 Blake.
Hoswell Milton H, tailor, b 135 E Washington.
HOTEL ENGLISH, Jerry S Hall Propr, w s Monument Pl bet Market and Meridian, Tel 834.
HOTEL ONEIDA, Mrs N E Miles Propr, 108-118 S Illinois.
Hottell Emma B (wid Wm), b s s Prospect 3 e of Madeira.

O. B. Ensey
SLATE, STEEL, TIN AND IRON ROOFING.
Cor. 6th and Illinois Sts. Tel. 1562

Hottes John W, clk McElwaine-Richards Co, b 121 Kennington.
Hottmann George J, cook, h 23 Madison av.
Hotz Elizabeth (wid George), h 384 Ash.
HOTZ GEORGE, Merchant Tailor, 124 S Illinois, b 384 Ash.
Hotz John, meats, 796 N Senate av, h same.
Hotz Wm F, meats, 502 Bellefontaine, b 796 N Senate av.
Hotze Anna (wid Eugene), b 538 E Ohio.
Houchin Bert M, clk Guarantee Shoe Store, r 121 N Capitol av.
Hough, see also Hoff and Huff.
Hough Courtland C, b 507 Central av.
Hough George O, clk Sentinel Printing Co, h 511 W Eugene.
Hough Harry G, trav agt Sentinel Printing Co, b 507 Central av.
Hough Jesse D, b 507 Central av.
Hough Lewis G, h 236 N Illinois.
Hough Martha R (wid Almorn V), h 507 Central av.
Hough Ora B, employment office, 95½ N Delaware, h 246 N Illinois.
Hough Willard D, candymkr, h 51 Walcott.
Houghes Ada, h 228½ Muskingum al.
Houghland George E, pdlr, b 264 E Miami.
HOUGHTON ALFRED, Teacher of Music and Director Second Regiment Infantry Indiana Legion Band and Orchestra; Music Furnished for Concerts, Balls and Parties on Short Notice, 383 E New York, h same. (See adv in classified Bands of Music.)
Hougland Sadie E (wid Edward A), b 375 Central av.
Houk Newton J, wheelmkr, h 252 S Delaware.
Houk Otis H, clk, b 252 S Delaware.
Houlihan Dennis J, lab, b 14 Davis.
Houlihan Timothy, lab, h 14 Davis.
Houppert Albert, waiter, b 103 Meek.
Houppert Anna, music teacher, 103 Meek, b same.
Houppert Frank, grocer, 101 Meek, h 103 same.
Houppert George, lab, b 103 Meek.
Houppert Henry J, clk, b 103 Meek.
Houppert Wm C, clk, b 103 Meek.
Houpt Thomas J, bailiff, b 276 N New Jersey.
Hourigan Martin, b 19 Agnes.
Housand Noah, b 215 S Olive.
House David A, dentist, 28½ E Ohio, h 1117 N Penn.
House Ernest L, grocer, 201 Columbia av, h same.
House George H F, phys, 1563 N Illinois, h same.
House Leslie F, tel opr, b 691 Chestnut.
House Louella (wid George A), h 761 E Washington.
House Mary A (wid Benjamin D), h 152 N Senate av.
House Minnie (wid Charles E), h 444 W Washington.
House Theodore L, mach hd, b 115 Auburn av.
House Wm A, lab, b 304 W Maryland.
HOUSEHOLD LOAN ASSOCIATION, Robert R Bennett Pres, Esther R Bell Sec, 44 Lombard Bldg.
Householder Charles E, lab, b 96 Prospect.
Householder John F, h 96 Prospect.
Householder Lela A (wid Emory), b 242 Indiana av.

TUTEWILER UNDERTAKER, No. 72 WEST MARKET STREET. TELEPHONE 216.

PROVIDENT LIFE AND TRUST CO. OF PHILADELPHIA. D. W. Edwards, G. A., 508 Indiana Trust Bldg. In form of policy; prompt settlement of death losses; equitable dealing with policy-holders; in strength of organization; and in everything which contributes to Security and Cheapness of life insurance, this company is unsurpassed.

Housel Thomas, news dealer, 71 Mass av, h 195 N Alabama.
Houser, see also Hauser.
Houser Calvin P, agt, h 328 E New York.
Houser James A (J A & S K Houser), h 604 N Alabama.
Houser John H, engraver, b 224 W New York.
Houser J A & S K (James A and Solon K), phys, 21½ W Maryland.
Houser Samuel R, condr, h 734 College av.
Houser Solon K (J A & S K Houser), h 13 Park av.
Houser Virgil E, clk, b 43 Park av.
Housley Maria (wid George), h 197 W 4th.
Housley Murray P, nurse, h 18 Roanoke.
Houston, see also Huston.
Houston Carrie, b 23 Willard.
Houston Charles D, foreman Polar Ice Co, h 178 E Michigan.
Houston James M, carp, h e s Fairview 1 s of Lake (N I).
Houston John R, tinner, b 257 Mass av.
Houston Minnie, h 326 E Washington.
Houston Samuel L, supt claims Ry Officials' and Employes' Accident Assn, h 584 N Alabama.
Houston Thaddeus, bkkpr Knight & Jillson, b 267 N Alabama.
Houston Wm, filemkr, h 89 N Delaware.
Hout Wm, tmstr, h 446 W Washington.
Houtman Berendina R (wid John T), b 901 Broadway.
Houton John W (Houton & Noe), res Paris, Ill.
Houton & Noe (John W Houton, John B Noe), feed, n w cor Pine and Noble.
Hover Blanche, nurse, 357 S Alabama, b same.
Hovey Alfred R (Harding & Hovey), h 855 N Illinois.
Hovey Alvin J, dentist, 509-510 Lemcke bldg, b 50 W St Joseph.
Hovey Frank H, sec and treas State B and L Assn, 31 S Penn, h 645 Park av.
Hovey Oliver H, supt Agents' State Capitol Inv Assn, h 649 Park av.
Howard Ann (wid Michael), b 84 S Noble.
Howard Anna (wid Adam), b 334 Hillside av.
Howard Asher P, lab, h 143 Trowbridge (W).
Howard Benjamin, sec and treas Crescent Oil Co, h 801 N Illinois.
Howard Beverly, lab, b 83 Martindale av.
Howard Catherine (wid Beverly), h 83 Martindale av.
Howard Charles B, clk N Y Store, b 450 W Eugene (N I).
Howard Charles W, carp, h 69 S Summit.
Howard Edward, phys, 223 N Illinois, h same.
Howard Edward M, clk, h 163 Clinton.
Howard Edward W, clk N Y Store, b 180 S Senate av.
Howard Eliza (wid Thomas), h rear 77 Cornell av.
Howard Eliza A (wid Stephen), h 60 Hosbrook.
Howard Eliza P (wid Nelson K), b 56 Bellefontaine.
Howard Ellen (wid Michael), h 27 Roe.
Howard Emma (wid Patrick L), h 47 Jefferson av.
Howard Finley W, carp, h 88 Harrison.
Howard Frank O, poultry, 196 W Maryland, h 230 N Capitol av.
Howard Franklin M, engr, h 280 E Georgia.

THE WHEN IS A WORLD BEATER.

Howard George, bartndr, r 219 W Ohio.
Howard George, lab, b 83 Martindale av.
Howard George R, h 31 Peru av.
Howard Henry, tmstr, h 111 Colgrove.
Howard Jackson, cook, r 320 E Court.
Howard James, bartndr, r 14 E Michigan.
Howard James, lab, h 87 Decatur.
Howard James P, shoemkr, 207 S Noble, r same.
Howard James R, porter, r 28 Muskingum al.
Howard John, b 106 Newman.
Howard John, engr, r 166½ W Washington.
Howard John, sawmkr, h 180 S Senate av.
Howard John F, engr, h 109 Blake.
Howard John J, yardmaster, h 44 Greer.
Howard Josephine (wid Samuel), h 792 N Senate av.
Howard Kate (wid Frank), artist, 116½ N Meridian, h same.
Howard Lewis, porter, b 165 Indiana av.
Howard Lewis N, phys, 62½ S Illinois, h 265 N Senate av.
Howard Liberty, carpet cleaner, n w cor St Clair and canal, h 26 Gregg.
Howard Louis J, lab, b 328 E Washington.
Howard Louisa (wid Jeremiah K), r 164 W Maryland.
Howard Louise (wid Langham), h 391 Roanoke.
Howard Mary (wid Nicholas), h 216 W Merrill.
Howard Mary D, teacher Public School No 3, h 77 The Blacherne.
Howard Michael E, machinery, 174 S Senate av, h 27 Roe.
Howard Nancy B (wid Joseph), h 253 N Alabama.
Howard Nancy F (wid John W), h 325 S Olive.
Howard Ollie F (wid John), h 13 Athon.
Howard Robert, janitor John S Spann & Co, h 29 Howard.
Howard Robert, lab, r 391 Roanoke.
Howard Samuel A, real est, h 454 W Shoemaker (N I).
Howard Sarah (wid Robert), h rear 195 Agnes.

The A. Burdsal Co. CELEBRATED HOMESTEAD READY MIXED PAINT. WHOLESALE AND RETAIL. 34 AND 36 SOUTH MERIDIAN STREET.

THEODORE F. SMITHER, AGENT FOR WARREN'S ANCHOR BRAND ASPHALT ROOFING OFFICE, 151 WEST MARYLAND ST. TEL. 861.

ELECTRIC SUPPLIES We Carry a full Stock. Prices Right. C. W. MEIKEL, Tel. 466. 96-98 E. New York St.

DALTON & MERRIFIELD { LUMBER South Noble St., near E. Washington

INDIANA ELECTROTYPE CO. : BEST WORK LOWEST PRICES. 23 WEST PEARL ST., INDIANAPOLIS, IND. JOB WORK. BOOK PLATES. All Orders Promptly Filled. BEST PATENT BASE ON THE MARKET.

KIRKHOFF BROS.,
Electrical Contractors, Wiring and Construction.
102-104 SOUTH PENNSYLVANIA ST.
TELEPHONE 910.

Howard Simeon, lab, h 9 Elizabeth.
Howard Thomas, capt Hose Co No 16, h 247 Cornell av.
Howard Thomas, lab, b 180 S Senate av.
Howard Thomas A, carp, r 80½ S Delaware.
Howard Thomas T, lab, r 458 N California.
Howard Timothy E, associate justice Supreme Court of Indiana, 69 State House, res South Bend, Ind.
Howard Truviller E, molder, h 450 W Eugene (N I).
Howard Wallace E, molder, h 253 Sheffield av (H).
Howard Washington, lab, h 767 E 10th.
Howard Wm, coachman 344 N Capitol av.
Howard Wm, coachman 865 N Meridian.
Howard Wm, lab, b 9 Elizabeth.
Howard Wm, lab, r 374 N Missouri.
Howard Wm, lab, b 391 Roanoke.
Howard Wm, porter Sherman House.
Howard Wm A, baggageman, h 355 S Delaware.
Howard Wm B, stairbldr, h 314 Alvord.
Howard Wm G, clk, b 314 Cedar.
Howard Wm H (Howard & Davidson), b 56 Bellefontaine.
Howard Willis, lab, b 482 Chapel.
Howard & Davidson (Wm H Howard, Alexander D Davidson), feed, 502 E Washington.
Howden Alice J (wid Wm), dressmkr, 373 E Ohio, h same.
Howden Frederick E, horseshoer, b 373 E Ohio.
Howe Aaron B, vice-pres McCoy-Howe Co, h 454 N New Jersey.
Howe Benjamin J C, h 283 Hillside av.
Howe Charles H, clk, b 63 Barth av.
HOWE DANIEL WAIT, Lawyer, 5-9 Hubbard Blk, Tel 1645; h 509 N New Jersey.
Howe Edward M, mach, b 189 S Capitol av.
Howe Elbert T, mngr Union Publishing Co, h n e cor Windsor and Stoughton av.
Howe Elizabeth E (wid Robert L), h e s Central av 1 s of Oak av (I).
Howe Elizabeth (wid Alonzo W), h 93 N New Jersey.

THE W. G. WASSON CO.,
130 Indiana Ave. Tel. 989.
STEAM
COAL
Car Lots a Specialty. Prompt Delivery.
Brazil Block, Jackson and Anthracite.

Howe Florence A, sec Indpls Engine Co, b 283 Hillside av.
Howe Frederick, drayman, h 42 Smithson.
Howe Frederick H L, clk, b 63 Barth av.
Howe George O, roofer, h 419 W Eugene (N I).
Howe George W, mach, h 86 Sheffield av (H).
Howe Glenn G, pres Metallic Mnfg Co and supt Ewart Mnfg Co, b 30 E Pratt.
Howe Harry H, lab, b 515 Bellefontaine.
Howe Henry L, h 63 Barth av.
Howe Herbert K, trav agt, b 283 Hillside av.
Howe James L, clk, h 37 English av.
Howe Lewis M, pres Indpls Engine Co, h 283 Hillside av.
Howe Lewis W, pdlr, h 24 Marion av (W I).
Howe Lou, mngr, b 751 N Capitol av.
Howe Louis C, brass founder, s e cor Michigan and Warman av (H), b 1095 W Michigan.
Howe Mary (wid Samuel M), housekpr 238 Fayette.
Howe Perley G, trav agt, b 283 Hillside av.
Howe Sarah, teacher, b 1395 N Capitol av.
Howe Thomas C, prof Butler College, b e s Central av 1 s of Oak av (I).
Howe Walter L, genl agt State Life Ins Co, h s s University 4 w of Downey av (I).
Howe Wm D, prof Butler College, b e s Central av 1 s of Oak av (I).
Howe Wm F, phys, 168 Bellefontaine, h same.
Howe Wm M, confr, 147 E 7th, h 796 N Alabama.
Howel Wm E, lab, b 792 W Washington.
Howell Benjamin F, lab, b 64 Columbia av.
Howell Charles D, cabtmkr, h 290 W Vermont.
Howell Charles E (Mendenhall, Howell & Trotter), h 567 Central av.
Howell Clara S, stenog, b 295 Fletcher av.
Howell Edward W, trav agt, h 295 Fletcher av.
Howell Elva (wid Charles), h 145½ Oliver av (W I).
Howell George E, condr, h 127 Spann av.
Howell Grant, lab, h 295 Columbia av.
Howell Harry E, coremkr, b 295 Fletcher av.
Howell Horace F, polisher, h 326 Spann av.
Howell James, lab, h 776 W Washington.
Howell James S, bricklyr, h 64 Columbia av.
Howell John O, printer, b 56 River av (W I).
Howell Liberty S, tel opr, b 326 Spann av.
Howell Susan B (wid Nathaniel B), h 1123 N Delaware.
Howell Thomas F, meats, 152 English av, h 161 same.
Howell Thomas H, painter, b 295 Fletcher av.
Howell Wm, cook, h 11½ W Washington.
Howell Wm H, barber, b 129 Columbia.
Howell Wm I, carp, h 17 Pleasant.
Hower Laura C (wid Charles), h 342 N Illinois.
Howes Charles A, meats, 154 Blake, h 171 same.
Howes Charles A jr, chainman City Engineer, h 94 N Senate av.
Howes Henry L, carp, h 29 Camp.
Howes Joseph H, gen delivery clk P O, b 171 Blake.
Howie Wm P, dentist, b 160 Cornell av.

W. H. Messenger FURNITURE, CARPETS, STOVES, 101 EAST WASHINGTON ST. TEL. 491.

McNamara, Koster & Co. | Foundry and Pattern Shop, 212-218 S. PENN. ST. . . . PHONE 1593.

Howie Wm W, mach, h 160 Cornell av.
Howland Charles B, trav agt, h 591 Park av.
Howland Desdemona H (wid John D), h 627 N Penn.
Howland Elisha J, farmer, h n e cor Howland av and Fall creek rd.
Howland Hewitt H (H H Howland & Co), b 826 N Meridian.
Howland H H & Co (Hewitt H Howland), mdse brokers, 36 Commercial Club bldg.
Howland Ida (wid Livingston), h 25 E St Joseph.
Howland Louis, editorial writer The Indpls News, h 627 N Penn.
Howland Ralph P, clk, b 181 Fletcher av.
Howland Sarah E, h 224 E Court.
Howland Thomas P, condr, h 181 Fletcher av.
Howlett Wm, farmer, h e s Line 1 s of P C C & St L Ry (I).
Howlett Wm F, plumber, b 87 N Belmont av.
Howrey Louis W, plumber, h 5 Douglass.
Howson Wm, b 7 Beacon.
Hoy Albert H, baggageman, h 413 E St Clair.
Hoy Asa R, mach, h 218 N Noble.
Hoy Benjamin, tmstr, h 204 Elizabeth.
Hoy Henry, engr, b 122 Mass av.
Hoy Joseph, janitor W U Tel Co, r 431 Muskingum al.
Hoy Joseph, sec Blake Street Savings and Loan Assn, grocer, 368 Blake, h same.
Hoy Mary J (wid John), b 122 Mass av.
Hoy Wm L, clk, b 368 Blake.
Hoy Zella A, dressmkr, 122 Mass av, h same.
Hoyl Simeon C, capt Hose Co No 12, h 546½ E Ohio.
Hoyle Clinton, carp, b 43 Helen.
Hoyle John H, polisher, b 174 Dillon.
Hoyt Addie, artist, 178 Huron, h same.
Hoyt Asenath (wid Lyman), h 334 Ash.
Hoyt David B, painter, h 522 Chestnut.
Hoyt Harriet (wid Benijah), b s s Washington 5 e of Sherman Drive.
Hoyt Henry B, driver, h 178 Huron.
Hoyt John, clk R M S, r 176½ N Alabama.
Hoyt Lois L, teacher Public School No 26, b 334 Ash.
Hoyt Mary (wid John), h 294½ Mass av.
Hoyt Ralph W, capt U S Army, recruiting office 25½ N Illinois, h 479 N Penn.
Hoyt Walter D, engr, b Enterprise Hotel.
Hoyt Wm H, painter, h 84 Paca.
Hoyt Wm T, cooper, h 53 S Reisner (W I).
Hrowitz Corinne B, stenog, b 302 E Market.
Hrowitz Ella, b 302 E Market.
Hubbard Alfred, lawyer, h 855 N Illinois.
Hubbard Beaufort, lab, h 44 Paca.
Hubbard Carrie M, dressmkr, r 155 N Illinois.
Hubbard Charles, janitor, h 199 Yandes.
Hubbard Edward P, tinner, b 144 E New York.
Hubbard Florence M, b 61 Central av.
Hubbard Franklin D, tmstr, h 118½ Woodlawn av.
Hubbard George, bill poster, b 144 E New York.
Hubbard George M, guitarmkr, h 144 E New York.
Hubbard Harold E, tel opr, b 31 S Summit.
Hubbard Harry C, tinner, h 37 Draper.
Hubbard Harvey H, lab, h 464 Jackson.
Hubbard Jennie, h 323 W St Clair.
Hubbard Jesse L, lab, b 118½ Woodlawn av.
Hubbard John, engr, h 524 N Senate av.

Henry H. Fay,
40½ E. Washington St.,
REAL ESTATE,
AND LOAN BROKER.

Hubbard John, lab, b 183 Patterson.
Hubbard John, switchman, h 1086 W New York.
Hubbard John H, lab, h 44 Paca.
Hubbard Lucy E (wid Seth), b 172 S Noble.
Hubbard Monroe, patternmkr I D & W Ry.
Hubbard Thomas, mach, h n w cor Bruce and Jackson.
Hubbard Thomas F, switchman, h 50 Martin.
Hubbard Walter J, loans, 212 Lemcke bldg, h 44 The Blacherne.
Hubbard Walter, city salesman Shellhouse & Co, h 31 S Summit.
Hubbard Willard W, sec Island Coal Co, h 532 N Delaware.
Hubbard Wm, lab, h 172 Keystone av.
Hubbard Wm B (Holstein, Barrett & Hubbard), h 444 Bellefontaine.
Hubbard Wm H, treas Commonwealth L and S Assn of Ind, broker, 3 Hubbard blk, h 577 N Illinois.
HUBBARD WM S, Office 3 Hubbard Blk, h 577 N Illinois.
Hubbartt Sarah (wid George E), b 172 E Louisiana.
Hubbartt Wm F, carp, h e s Ilinois 2 n of 30th (M).
Hubbell Clemens, lab, h 81 N Rural.
Hubbell Frank J, polisher, h 81 N Rural.
Hubbell Orra, Hoosier Canning Machinery Co, h 231 N Senate av.
Hubbell Orrin Z, attorney Fidelity Building and Savings Union, res Elkhart, Ind.
Hubbell Samuel R, polisher, h 200 W South.
Hubble Fountain, lab, h 156 Maple.
Huber, see also Hueber.
Huber August, butcher, h 222 S Reisner (W I).
Huber Catherine, stenog, b w s Ritter av 10 n of Washington av (I).
Huber Charles J, lab, h 192 N Beville av.
Huber George W, clk, b 835 N Illinois.
Huber Gottlieb, lab, h 3 Hendricks.
Huber Henry, carver August Diener, h 254 W 7th.
Huber John F, waiter, r 44 N Senate av.
Huber Jonas F, farmer, h w s Ritter av 10 n of Washington av (I).

UNION CASUALTY & SURETY CO.
OF ST. LOUIS, MO.
All lines of Personal Accident and Casualty Insurance, including Employers' and General Liability.
W. E. BARTON & CO., General Agents,
504 Indiana Trust Building.
LONG DISTANCE TELEPHONE 1918.

THE FRED DIETZ CO.
WOODEN PACKING BOXES MADE TO ORDER. FACTORY AND WAREHOUSE TRUCKS.
40 Madison Avenue. Telephone 654.

Indianapolis BUSINESS UNIVERSITY
Leading College of Business and Shorthand. Elevator day and night. Individual instruction. Large faculty. Terms easy. Enter now. See p. 4. When Block. E. J. HEEB, President.

HENRY R. WORTHINGTON JET and SURFACE CONDENSERS 64 S. PENN. ST. Long Distance Telephone 284.

UNION CO-OPERATIVE LAUNDRY (COMPOSED OF UNION LAUNDRY GIRLS.) NOS. 3, 40 AND 142 VIRGINIA AVENUE. INDIANAPOLIS, IND. TELEPHONE 8. T. E. SOMERVILLE, MANAGER

HORACE M. HADLEY
REAL ESTATE AND INSURANCE
66 East Market Street, Basement
TELEPHONE 1540.

Huber Joseph, marble cutter, h 254 W 7th.
Huber Joseph M, stonecutter, h 37 Brett.
Huber Louise M (wid John J), h 835 N Illinois.
HUBER MANUFACTURING CO THE, Henry A Davis Mngr, Engines and Threshers, 40 Kentucky av, Tel 1312.
Huber Mary C (wid John M), h e s Commercial av 9 s of Washington av (I).
Huber Theodore, clk Holliday & Wyon, h 299 S New Jersey.
Huber Wm, clk Charles Mayer & Co, r 41 Wyoming.
Huber Wm G, collr Original Eagle, b 835 N Illinois.
Hubert George, butcher, b 527 S Capitol av.
Hubert George C, grocer, 152 Martindale av, h same.
Hubert John B, condr, h 424 College av.
Hubert Michael, meats, 527 S Capitol av, h same.
Hubke, see Hupke.
Huckemeyer Charles H, boilermkr, h 40 Eastern av.
Huckemeyer George A, bartndr, b 41 Eastern av.
Huddleston Alvah W, lab, b 20 Germania av (H).
Huddleston Carl, blksmith, h 64 E McCarty.
Huddleston Charles W, lab, h 127 King av (H).
Huddleston Elizabeth (wid Hiram), h 20 Germania av (H).
Huddleston Ida, stenog, b 311 N Delaware.
Huddleston Robert, waiter, b 219 N West.
Hudelson Jennie M, h 297 N Capitol av.
Hudelson Lee L, trav agt, b 482 Broadway.
Hudelson Rufus I, b 279 N Capitol av.
Hudelson Sallie B, b 279 N Capitol av.
Hudelson Wm, h 482 Broadway.
Huder Henry J, drugs, 52 E Washington, h 529 Ash.
Huder Louisa, dressmkr, 529 Ash, h same.
Huder Magdalene (wid Henry), h 529 Ash.
Hudson Albert, lab, h 496 W Udell (N I).
Hudson Alonzo, motorman, h s e cor Lincoln av and Jackson (M J).

PERSONAL AND PROMPT ATTENTION GIVEN TO COLLECTIONS.
Merchants' and Manufacturers' Exchange
J. E. TAKKEN, Manager,
19 Union Building, 73 West Maryland Street.

Hudson Caroline (wid John), h 180 W Vermont.
Hudson Charles L, carp, h rear 122 Ruckle.
Hudson Clinton, lab, h rear 671 N Senate av.
Hudson Dana, lab, b 892 W Washington.
Hudson Daniel B, carp, h 17 Cincinnati.
Hudson David H, tankman, h 409½ E Pearl.
Hudson Edward J, carp, h 83 Cincinnati.
Hudson Emma (wid Clarence), h 3 Bell.
Hudson Henry, lab, b w s Indianapolis av 2 n of Fall creek.
Hudson Henry T, plumber, 435 Madison av, h same.
Hudson James K, clk, h 27 S McLain (W I).
Hudson James L, lab, h 173 W 3d.
Hudson James W, contr, 319 Union, h same.
Hudson John E, carp, h 83 Cincinnati.
Hudson Josephine, h 90 N East.
Hudson Josephine, r 164½ S East.
Hudson Leven, mach hd, h 66 Yandes.
Hudson Margaret A, cashr The Denison, b 330 N New Jersey.
Hudson Pearl, bkkpr, b 172 N East.
Hudson Simeon T, uphlr, 135 Mass av, h 172 N East.
Hudson Thomas J, clk Bureau of Assessments, h 54 Orange.
Hudson Wm, b 182 Muskingum al.
Hudson Wm, driver, r 279 Chapel.
Hudson Wm, lab, h 30 Hosbrook.
Hudson Wm, lab, h 326 W Vermont.
Hudson Wm H, waiter The Denison.
Hueber, see also Huber.
Hueber Albert J, bkkpr Gregory & Appel, b 241 Union.
Hueber Benjamin N, trav agt Daggett & Co, h 509 Bellefontaine.
Hueber Francis J, mach, h 92 Michigan av.
Hueber Frank, clk, b 92 Michigan av.
Hueber Frank M, sec Advance Saving and Loan Assn, 103½ E Washington, h 18 Minnesota.
Hueber George V, varnisher, b 241 Union.
Hueber Joseph F, mach, h 92 S Eastern av.
Hueber Nicholas, mach hd, h 241 Union.
Hueber Walter, plumber, b 92 Michigan av.
Hueber Wm, cigarmkr, b 92 Michigan av.
Hueber Wm J, shoemkr, h 542 Charles.
Huebner, see also Hebner.
Huebner Amelia, printer, b 514 S New Jersey.
Huebner Augusta S, school teacher, b 514 S New Jersey.
Huebner Charles H, car repairer, h 483 E Georgia.
Huebner Gertrude, shader, b 514 S New Jersey.
Huebner Maria (wid Henry R), h 514 S New Jersey.
Huebner Wm, lab, h 39 Meek.
Huebschmann John, brewer, h 31 Deloss.
Huechtker Frederick W, cabtmkr, h 508 E Georgia.
Huegele Edward J, chief engr Indpls Brewing Co, h 246 E McCarty.
Huegele Frank, fireman, h 54 Dougherty.
HUEGELE JOHN, Saloon and Restaurant, 60 E Washington, h 507 N Alabama, Tel 1489.
Huegele Joseph A, mach hd, h 309½ S Penn.
Huendling Meinhardt, packer, h 110 Gray.
Huenefeld George, lab, h 104 Downey.
Huenefeld Harry, clk, b 104 Downey.
Huerel Louise (wid Benjamin), b 176 Sheffield av (H).
Huettig Arno R, piano tuner, h 72 S Noble.
Huey, see also Hughey.
Huey David N, gas insp, h 461 Cornell av.
Huey Harry A, artist, b 461 Cornell av.

CLEMENS VONNEGUT 184, 186 and 192 E. Washington St. FOUNDRY AND MACHINISTS' SUPPLIES. "NORTON" EMERY WHEELS AND GRINDING MACHINERY.

THE WM. H. BLOCK CO. DRY GOODS, MILLINERY, CLOAKS AND FURS.
7 AND 9 EAST WASHINGTON STREET.

Huey Harry H, photog, h 522 Talbott av.
Huey Jesse C, printer, b 522 Talbott av.
Huey John, foreman, b 99 Lexington av.
Huey John A, mach, b 522 Talbott av.
Huey Milton S (M S Huey & Son), h 90 Middle Drive (W P).
HUEY M S & SON (Milton S and Oscar L), Mnfrs and Dealers Wood Mantels and Grates, 551 Mass av, Tel 416. (See page 5.)
Huey Oscar L (M S Huey & Son), h 116 Middle Drive (W P).
Huey Perry K, mach hd, h 39 N Rural.
Huey Wm E, photog, b 522 Talbott av.
Huff, see also Hoff and Hough.
Huff Albert, condr, b 678 W Washington.
Huff Andrew L, billiards, 40 Pendleton av (B), h 33 Lawn (B).
Huff Clinton C, clk, h 118 N Dorman.
Huff Edward, lab, h e s Bond 1 s of Chicago (N I).
Huff Eva, h 325 Bellefontaine.
Huff John E, engr, b 33 Lawn (B).
Huff Lewis E, fireman, b 33 Lawn (B).
Huff Martha J (wid Armstead M), b 325 Bellefontaine.
Huff Martha J (wid Harden), b 1147½ N Illinois.
Huff Romeo A, farmer, h 575 W Francis (N I).
Huff Wm, lab, h e s Bond 1 s of Chicago (N I).
Huff Wm B (Pfaff & Co), h 45 Malott av.
Huff Wm M, lab, h 293 Yandes.
Huffer Albert T, carp, h 199½ E Washington.
Huffer Caroline M (wid James), b 429 N Capitol av.
Huffer Dellie D, painter, b 199½ E Washington.
Huffer Edward, baker, b 18 Hosbrook.
Huffer Frank D, harnessmkr, h 18 Hosbrook.
Huffer John M, driver, b 18 Hosbrook.
Huffines Newton, tmstr, b n w cor Washington and Quincy.
Huffington Agnes M (wid John B), b 25 Jefferson av.
Huffington Harry C, clk Great Atlantic and Pacific Tea Co, h 25 Jefferson av.
Huffington Nancy E (wid Abel C), b 134 Hoyt av.
Huffman, see also Hoffman and Hofmann.
Huffman Andrew M, lab, b 36 Depot (B).
Huffman Burton B, plumber, h w s Foundry 3 s of Schofield (B).
Huffman Charles W, grocer, 1 Hillside av, h same.
Huffman Charles W, lab, h 282 Columbia av.
Huffman Daniel C, engr, h n s Willow 1 e of Brightwood av (B).
Huffman David W, lab, h 51 Leota.
Huffman Edward, presser, b 36 Depot (B).
Huffman Edward E, planer, b 102 S State av.
Huffman Ella (wid John), h 209 Alvord.
Huffman James, brakeman, h 15 Lawn (B).
Huffman John, lab, h 572 S West.
Huffman Robert E, brakeman, b n s Willow 1 e of Brightwood av (B).
Huffman Sarah A (wid Wm), h 36 Depot (B).
Huffman Simeon, clk U S Pension Office, r 265 N Illinois.
Huffman Wm D, vinegar mnfr, 24 Dunlop, r 257 N Illinois.

PICTURES · MIRRORS.
THE H. LIEBER COMPANY
33 South Meridian Street.
ARTISTIC FRAMING.

Huffman Wm M, condr, h 102 S State av.
Huffman Wm M, lab, b 607 W Pearl.
Huffmeister, see Hoffmeister.
Hufford Clarence D, b 223 Park av.
Hufford George W, prin High School, h 223 Park av.
Hufford Lois G, teacher High School, h 223 Park av.
Hufford Wm J, letter carrier P O, h 82 Holmes av (H).
Hufnall John A, foreman Levey Bros, h 63 Highland pl.
Hug George A, bkkpr, r 105 N Meridian.
Hugely Charles, lab, h 298 Alvord.
Hugg John A, dep County Clerk, h 107 Spring.
Hugg Martin M (Kealing & Hugg), h 107 Spring.
Huggins Edward E, lab, h 71 Newman.
Huggins George A, clk County Treasurer, h s s Huggins pike nr Sherman Drive.
Huggins George T, lab, h w s Waverly av 4 n of Clifford av.
Huggins Harwood T, h 82 Prospect.
Huggins James, lab, h w s Waverly 3 n of Clifford av.
Huggins John H, lab, h w s Waverly av 2 s of Pope av.
Huggins Mary (wid Wm H), b w s Waverly 2 s of Pope av.
Huggins Robert C, farmer, h 251 Pleasant av.
Huggins Wm S, lab, h 108 Eureka av.
Huggler John W, dairy, n w cor Watts and Clifford av, h same.
Hughbanks, see also Eubanks.
Hughbanks Edward, lab, b 20 Ethel (W I).
Hughes Alexander T, collr, h 215 N Senate av.
Hughes Andrew, barber, 17 Pembroke Arcade, h 12 Ashland (W I).
Hughes Anna (wid Randolph), b 251 N West.
Hughes Charles L, clk Copeland & McIntire, b 1108 N Alabama.
Hughes Charles P, clk, b 937 Mass av.
Hughes Charles W, cook, h 56 Carson.
Hughes Charles W, driver, h rear 393 S East.

GUIDO R. PRESSLER,
FRESCO PAINTER
Churches, Theaters, Public Buildings, Etc., A Specialty.
Residence, No. 325 North Liberty Street.
INDIANAPOLIS, IND.

INDIANAPOLIS STEEL ROOFING AND CORRUGATING WORKS, 23 and 25 East South Street. S. D. NOEL, Proprietor.

David S. McKernan REAL ESTATE AND LOANS. Exchanging real estate a specialty. A number of choice pieces for encumbered property. Rooms 2-5 Thorpe Block.

HENRY R. WORTHINGTON JET and SURFACE CONDENSERS 64 S. PENN. ST. Long Distance Telephone 284.

UNION CO-OPERATIVE LAUNDRY (COMPOSED OF UNION LAUNDRY GIRLS.) NOS. 38, 40 AND 42 VIRGINIA AVENUE. T. E. SOMERVILLE, MANAGER TELEPHONE 12. INDIANAPOLIS, IND.

HORACE M. HADLEY
REAL ESTATE AND INSURANCE
66 East Market Street, Basement
TELEPHONE 1540.

Huber Joseph, marble cutter, h 254 W 7th.
Huber Joseph M, stonecutter, h 37 Brett.
Huber Louise M (wid John J), h 835 N Illinois.
HUBER MANUFACTURING CO THE, Henry A Davis Mngr, Engines and Threshers, 40 Kentucky av, Tel 1312.
Huber Mary C (wid John M), h e s Commercial av 9 s of Washington av (I).
Huber Theodore, clk Holliday & Wyon, h 299 S New Jersey.
Huber Wm, clk Charles Mayer & Co, r 41 Wyoming.
Huber Wm G, collr Original Eagle, b 835 N Illinois.
Hubert George, butcher, b 527 S Capitol av.
Hubert George C, grocer, 152 Martindale av, h same.
Hubert John B, condr, h 424 College av.
Hubert Michael, meats, 527 S Capitol av, h same.
Hubke, see Hupke.
Huckemeyer Charles H, boilermkr, h 40 Eastern av.
Huckemeyer George A, bartndr, b 41 Eastern av.
Huddleston Alvah W, lab, b 20 Germania av (H).
Huddleston Carl, blksmith, h 64 E McCarty.
Huddleston Charles W, lab, h 127 King av (H).
Huddleston Elizabeth (wid Hiram), h 20 Germania av (H).
Huddleston Ida, stenog, b 311 N Delaware.
Huddleston Robert, waiter, b 219 N West.
Hudelson Jennie M, h 297 N Capitol av.
Hudelson Lee L, trav agt, b 482 Broadway.
Hudelson Rufus I, b 279 N Capitol av.
Hudelson Sallie B, b 279 N Capitol av.
Hudelson Wm, h 482 Broadway.
Huder Henry J, drugs, 52 E Washington, h 529 Ash.
Huder Louisa, dressmkr, 529 Ash, h same.
Huder Magdalene (wid Henry), h 529 Ash.
Hudson Albert, lab, h 496 W Udell (N I).
Hudson Alonzo, motorman, h s e cor Lincoln av and Jackson (M J).

PERSONAL AND PROMPT ATTENTION GIVEN TO COLLECTIONS.
Merchants' and Manufacturers' Exchange
J. E. TAKKEN, Manager,
19 Union Building, 73 West Maryland Street.

Hudson Caroline (wid John), h 180 W Vermont.
Hudson Charles L, carp, h rear 122 Ruckle.
Hudson Clinton, lab, h rear 671 N Senate av.
Hudson Dana, lab, b 892 W Washington.
Hudson Daniel B, carp, h 17 Cincinnati.
Hudson David H, tankman, h 409½ E Pearl.
Hudson Edward J, carp, h 83 Cincinnati.
Hudson Emma (wid Clarence), h 3 Bell.
Hudson Henry, lab, b w s Indianapolis av 2 n of Fall creek.
Hudson Henry T, plumber, 435 Madison av, h same.
Hudson James K, clk, h 27 S McLain (W I).
Hudson James L, lab, h 173 W 3d.
Hudson James W, contr, 319 Union, h same.
Hudson John E, carp, h 83 Cincinnati.
Hudson Josephine, h 90 N East.
Hudson Josephine, r 164½ S East.
Hudson Leven, mach hd, h 66 Yandes.
Hudson Margaret A, cashr The Denison, b 330 N New Jersey.
Hudson Pearl, bkkpr, b 172 N East.
Hudson Simeon T, uphlr, 135 Mass av, h 172 N East.
Hudson Thomas J, clk Bureau of Assessments, h 54 Orange.
Hudson Wm, b 182 Muskingum al.
Hudson Wm, driver, r 279 Chapel.
Hudson Wm, lab, h 30 Hosbrook.
Hudson Wm, lab, h 326 W Vermont.
Hudson Wm H, waiter The Denison.
Hueber, see also Huber.
Hueber Albert J, bkkpr Gregory & Appel, b 241 Union.
Hueber Benjamin N, trav agt Daggett & Co, h 509 Bellefontaine.
Hueber Francis J, mach, h 92 Michigan av.
Hueber Frank, clk, b 92 Michigan av.
Hueber Frank M, sec Advance Saving and Loan Assn, 103½ E Washington, h 18 Minnesota.
Hueber George V, varnisher, b 241 Union.
Hueber Joseph F, mach, h 92 S Eastern av.
Hueber Nicholas, mach hd, h 241 Union.
Hueber Walter, plumber, b 92 Michigan av.
Hueber Wm, cigarmkr, b 92 Michigan av.
Hueber Wm J, shoemkr, h 542 Charles.
Huebner, see also Hebner.
Huebner Amelia, printer, b 514 S New Jersey.
Huebner Augusta S, school teacher, b 514 S New Jersey.
Huebner Charles H, car repairer, h 483 E Georgia.
Huebner Gertrude, shader, b 514 S New Jersey.
Huebner Maria (wid Henry R), h 514 S New Jersey.
Huebner Wm, lab, h 39 Meek.
Huebschmann John, brewer, h 31 Deloss.
Huechtker Frederick W, cabtmkr, h 508 E Georgia.
Huegele Edward J, chief engr Indpls Brewing Co, h 246 E McCarty.
Huegele Frank, fireman, h 54 Dougherty.
HUEGELE JOHN, Saloon and Restaurant, 60 E Washington, h 507 N Alabama, Tel 1489.
Huegele Joseph A, mach hd, h 309½ S Penn.
Huendling Meinhardt, packer, h 110 Gray.
Huenefeld George, lab, h 104 Downey.
Huenefeld Harry, clk, b 104 Downey.
Huerel Louise (wid Benjamin), b 176 Sheffield av (H).
Huettig Arno R, piano tuner, h 72 S Noble.
Huey, see also Hughey.
Huey David N, gas insp, h 461 Cornell av.
Huey Harry A, artist, b 461 Cornell av.

CLEMENS VONNEGUT 184, 186 and 192 E. Washington St. FOUNDRY AND MACHINISTS' SUPPLIES. "NORTON" EMERY WHEELS AND GRINDING MACHINERY.

THE WM. H. BLOCK CO. DRY GOODS, MILLINERY, CLOAKS AND FURS.
7 AND 9 EAST WASHINGTON STREET.

Huey Harry H, photog, h 522 Talbott av.
Huey Jesse C, printer, b 522 Talbott av.
Huey John, foreman, b 99 Lexington av.
Huey John A, mach, b 522 Talbott av.
Huey Milton S (M S Huey & Son), h 90 Middle Drive (W P).
HUEY M S & SON (Milton S and Oscar L), Mnfrs and Dealers Wood Mantels and Grates, 551 Mass av, Tel 416. (See page 5.)
Huey Oscar L (M S Huey & Son), h 116 Middle Drive (W P).
Huey Perry K, mach hd, h 39 N Rural.
Huey Wm E, photog, b 522 Talbott av.
Huff, see also Hoff and Hough.
Huff Albert, condr, b 678 W Washington.
Huff Andrew L, billiards, 40 Pendleton av (B), h 33 Lawn (B).
Huff Clinton C, clk, h 118 N Dorman.
Huff Edward, lab, h e s Bond 1 s of Chicago (N I).
Huff Eva, h 325 Bellefontaine.
Huff John E, engr, b 33 Lawn (B).
Huff Lewis E, fireman, b 33 Lawn (B).
Huff Martha J (wid Armstead M), b 325 Bellefontaine.
Huff Martha J (wid Harden), b 1147½ N Illinois.
Huff Romeo A, farmer, h 575 W Francis (N I).
Huff Wm, lab, h e s Bond 1 s of Chicago (N I).
Huff Wm B (Pfaff & Co), h 45 Malott av.
Huff Wm M, lab, h 393 Yandes.
Huffer Albert T, carp, h 199½ E Washington.
Huffer Caroline M (wid James), b 429 N Capitol av.
Huffer Dellie D, painter, b 199½ E Washington.
Huffer Edward, baker, b 18 Hosbrook.
Huffer Frank D, harnessmkr, h 18 Hosbrook.
Huffer John M, driver, b 18 Hosbrook.
Huffines Newton, tmstr, b n w cor Washington and Quincy.
Huffington Agnes M (wid John B), b 25 Jefferson av.
Huffington Harry C, clk Great Atlantic and Pacific Tea Co, h 25 Jefferson av.
Huffington Nancy E (wid Abel C), b 134 Hoyt av.
Huffman, see also Hoffman and Hofmann.
Huffman Andrew M, lab, b 36 Depot (B).
Huffman Burton B, plumber, h w s Foundry 3 s of Schofield (B).
Huffman Charles W, grocer, 1 Hillside av, h same.
Huffman Charles W, lab, h 282 Columbia av.
Huffman Daniel C, engr, h n s Willow 1 e of Brightwood av (B).
Huffman David W, lab, h 51 Leota.
Huffman Edward, presser, b 36 Depot (B).
Huffman Edward E, planer, b 102 S State av.
Huffman Ella (wid John), h 209 Alvord.
Huffman James, brakeman, h 15 Lawn (B).
Huffman John, lab, h 572 S West.
Huffman Robert E, brakeman, b n s Willow 1 e of Brightwood av (B).
Huffman Sarah A (wid Wm), h 36 Depot (B).
Huffman Simeon, clk U S Pension Office, r 265 N Illinois.
Huffman Wm D, vinegar mnfr, 24 Dunlop, r 257 N Illinois.

Huffman Wm M, condr, h 102 S State av.
Huffman Wm M, lab, b 607 W Pearl.
Huffmeister, see Hoffmeister.
Hufford Clarence D, b 223 Park av.
Hufford George W, prin High School, h 223 Park av.
Hufford Lois G, teacher High School, h 223 Park av.
Hufford Wm J, letter carrier P O, h 82 Holmes av (H).
Hufnall John A, foreman Levey Bros, h 63 Highland pl.
Hug George A, bkkpr, r 105 N Meridian.
Hugely Charles, lab, h 298 Alvord.
Hugg John A, dep County Clerk, h 107 Spring.
Hugg Martin M (Kealing & Hugg), h 107 Spring.
Huggins Edward E, lab, h 71 Newman.
Huggins George A, clk County Treasurer, h s s Huggins pike nr Sherman Drive.
Huggins George T, lab, h w s Waverly av 4 n of Clifford av.
Huggins Harwood T, h 82 Prospect.
Huggins James, lab, h w s Waverly 3 n of Clifford av.
Huggins John H, lab, h w s Waverly av 2 s of Pope av.
Huggins Mary (wid Wm H), b w s Waverly 2 s of Pope av.
Huggins Robert C, farmer, h 251 Pleasant av.
Huggins Wm S, lab, h 108 Eureka av.
Huggler John W, dairy, n w cor Watts and Clifford av, h same.
Hughbanks, see also Eubanks.
Hughbanks Edward, lab, b 20 Ethel (W I).
Hughes Alexander T, collr, h 215 N Senate av.
Hughes Andrew, barber, 17 Pembroke Arcade, h 12 Ashland (W I).
Hughes Anna (wid Randolph), b 251 N West.
Hughes Charles L, clk Copeland & McIntire, b 1108 N Alabama.
Hughes Charles P, clk, b 937 Mass av.
Hughes Charles W, cook, h 56 Carson.
Hughes Charles W, driver, h rear 393 S East.

GUIDO R. PRESSLER,
FRESCO PAINTER
Churches, Theaters, Public Buildings, Etc., A Specialty.
Residence, No. 325 North Liberty Street.
INDIANAPOLIS, IND.

INDIANAPOLIS STEEL ROOFING AND CORRUGATING WORKS, 23 and 25 East South Street. S. D. NOEL, Proprietor.

David S. McKernan REAL ESTATE AND LOANS. Exchanging real estate a specialty. A number of choice pieces for encumbered property. Rooms 2-5 Thorpe Block.

DIAMOND WALL PLASTER { Telephone 1410 BUILDERS' EXCHANGE.

UNION TRANSFER AND STORAGE CO. Cor. E. Ohio St. and C., C., C. & St. L. R'y Tracks. Storage of Household Goods and Pianos a Specialty.

W. McWORKMAN,
Galvanized Iron Cornice Works
TIN AND SLATE ROOFING.
930 WEST WASHINGTON STREET.
TELEPHONE 1118.

Hughes David C, clk The Bates, h 311 E St Clair.
Hughes Edward, lab, h 28 Church.
Hughes Edward jr, lab, b 28 Church.
Hughes Elizabeth (wid Elmore), h 128 Columbia al.
Hughes Elizabeth (wid Frank M), h 733 Shelby.
Hughes Elizabeth G, teacher Girls' Classical School, b 979 N Delaware.
Hughes Elmer, lab, b 215 Elm.
Hughes Frank D, lab, b 184 Elm.
Hughes Frank E, wheelmkr, h 5 Division (W I).
Hughes Frank J, carp, h 393 Martindale av.
Hughes Frank L, fireman, b 41 Walcott.
Hughes Freeman, carp, h 24 Birch av (W I).
Hughes George, engr, h Brightwood.
Hughes George, lab, b 18 Seibert.
Hughes George, lab, h 11 Willard.
Hughes George A, janitor, h 215½ E Washington.
Hughes George W, waiter, h 81 Harmon.
Hughes Harry H, hostler, r 70 W Maryland.
Hughes Henry, lab, h 196 W Ray.
Hughes Homer D, paperhngr, b 135 Martindale av.
Hughes Ida M, h 227 Huron.
Hughes Isaac H, lab, h 196 W Ray.
Hughes Isham, engr, h 673 E Market.
Hughes James, lab, h 159 W McCarty.
Hughes James, policeman (W I), h 127 S Lee (W I).
Hughes James R, lab, h 169 W 6th.
Hughes James W, lab, h rear 135 Martindale av.
Hughes John, saloon, 122 Michigan (H), h same.
Hughes John A, grocer, 939 Mass av, h 937 same.
Hughes John W, h 63 S California.
Hughes John W jr, lab, b 63 S California.
Hughes Joseph, pdlr, h 733 Shelby.
Hughes Joseph A, carp, 45 S Wheeler (B), h same.
Hughes Joshua, lab, h 89 Nebraska.
Hughes Joshua W, bkkpr, r 183 N Capitol av.

SEALS,
STENCILS,
STAMPS, Etc.
GEO. J. MAYER
15 S. Meridian St.
TELEPHONE 1386.

Hughes Margaret, r rear 1379 N Senate av.
Hughes Margaret, seamstress, b 46 N Senate av.
Hughes Nelson R, pumps, 27 N Capitol av, h 29 Gatling.
Hughes Ottis, mach, h 499 E 11th.
Hughes Oliver, tmstr, h 121 Trowbridge (W).
Hughes Rachel A (wid Edward), h 41 Walcott.
HUGHES RICHARD D, Supt Metropolitan Life Insurance Co of New York, 75-76-77-80 Baldwin Blk, h 355 N Senate av.
Hughes Samuel, bricklyr, h 137 Downey.
Hughes Stephen, gasfitter, h 27 Sullivan.
Hughes Stephen C, fireman, h 36 Oliver av (W I).
Hughes Thomas, junk, rear 131 E Washington, b 733 Shelby.
Hughes Thomas S, baggageman, h 184 Elm.
Hughes Wm, butcher, b 28 Church.
HUGHES WM A, Chief Clerk Bureau of Assessments, Room 12 Basement Court House, h 329 Park av.
Hughey, see also Huey.
Hughey Frank, carp, h 586 S Illinois.
Hughey George W, wheelmkr, h 338 N West.
Hughey Joseph L, cabtmkr, h 20 Wisconsin.
Hughey Leonard S, foreman, h 176 W Morris.
Hugle Lucy E (wid Louis A), employment office, 23 W Ohio, h 139 Ynnn av (W I).
Hugle Maude M, cashr, b 139 Lynn av (W I).
Hugle Samuel, lab, b 320 E Court.
Hugley Anna (wid Sanford), b 32 Torbet.
Hugley Charles, lab, h 298 Alvord.
Hugo Adeline (wid Herman), b 280 S West.
Hugo Catherine M (wid Henry A), h 113 S Pine.
Hugo Elizabeth (wid Wm), h 230 S New Jersey.
Hugo Wm C, fireman, h 230 S New Jersey.
Hugo Wm J, solr Consumers' Gas Trust Co, b 45 Ruckle.
Huhn Peter, wiper, h 10 Deloss.
Hukriede Ernst (Hukriede & Sons), h 499 S State av.
Hukriede Frederick R (Hukriede & Son), b 499 S State av.
Hukriede Rudolph H, lab, h 26 Vinton.
Hukriede & Son (Ernst and Frederick R), florists, 495 S State av and 528 Virginia av.
Hula Joseph, lab, b 361 W Vermont.
Hulan Walter, lab, b 19 Grant.
Hulbusch Wm, h 158 Laurel.
Hulce George H, printer, h 52 Broadway.
Hulen Willard, porter, h 149 Sharpe av (W).
Hulin Aaron, lab, b 42 S Belmont av (W I).
Hulings Martha (wid George), h 342 E New York.
Hull Albert C, h 2 Wendell av.
Hull Albert C, condr, b 738 E 7th.
Hull Andrew J (A J Hull Medical Co), h 121 Cottage av.
Hull Andrew J jr (A J Hull Medical Co), b 121 Cottage av.
Hull Armstrong, lab, h 717 N Capitol av.
Hull A J Medical Co (Andrew J, James W and Andrew J Hull jr), medicine mnfrs, 481 Virginia av.
Hull Bertha, stenog, b 84 E New York.
Hull Charles C, asst supt Parry Mnfg Co, h 1097 N Penn.

A. METZGER AGENCY ESTABLISHED 1863. L-O-A-N-S

LAMBERT GAS & GASOLINE ENGINE CO.
ANDERSON, IND. GAS ENGINES FOR ALL PURPOSES.

BICYCLES $5 DOWN. MONTHLY. Best Wheels. Best Terms. WHEELMEN'S CO 31 W. OHIO ST. LONG DISTANCE TEL. 1855.

Hull Charles H, bkkpr Indiana National Bank, b 914 N Alabama.
Hull Emanuel G, molder, h w s Merrit 2 n of Summit (H).
Hull Frank W, clk, b w s Talbott av 2 s of 22d.
Hull George, fireman, h 78 Bloomington.
Hull George, mach, h 88 N Belmont av (H).
Hull James W (A J Hull Medical Co), h 568 Shelby.
Hull John, city fireman, h 20 Grace.
Hull Joseph, lab, b 613 Miller av (M P).
Hull Justinian H, cashr Consumers' Gas Trust Co, h 914 N Alabama.
Hull Lillian M, asst cashr Consumers' Gas Trust Co, b 914 N Alabama.
Hull Missouri A, h 37½ Kentucky av.
Hull M Robert, ship clk Parry Mnfg Co, h 926 Cornell av.
Hull Royal C, bkkpr Indiana Mutual B and Loan Assn, h 72 W 1st.
Hull Wade, lab, b 266 Michigan (H).
Hull Wiley G, blksmith, h 266 Michigan (H).
Hull Wm, fireman, h 140 Naomi.
Hull Wm H, trav agt, h 128 W 1st.
Hull Wm H, yardmaster, h w s Talbott av 2 s of 22d.
Hull Wm H jr, yardmaster, b w s Talbott av 2 s of 22d.
Huller Ernest T, bkkpr, b 64 N Noble.
Huller Louisa R E (wid Theodore), clk, h 64 N Noble.
Huls Charles, packer, b 320 S Illinois.
Huls Harrison F, lab, h 221 Bismarck av (H).
Huls Joseph, b 221 Bismarck av (H).
Huls Mary I (wid Alfred D), h 229 Mass av.
Huls Wesley G, packer, b 320 S Illinois.
Hulse Amos, lab, h 340 Yandes.
Hulse Micajah C, carp, h s e cor Rural and Sutherland (B).
Hulse Wm C, poultry, E Mkt House, h e s Rural 2 s of Sutherland (B).
Hulsizer Thomas, plastr, h 252½ Mass av.
Hulskamp Anna M (wid Henry), h 4 Madeira.
Hulsker, see also Holsker.
Hulsker Caroline, h 15 Grant.
Hulsman Paul E, clk, r 72 E Vermont.
Hulsmann Charles W, uphlr, b 41 W Morris.
Hulsmann Clara (wid Charles), h 41 W Morris.
Hulsmann Frank H, mach, b 41 W Morris.
Hulsmann Joseph H, cutter, b 41 W Morris.
Hulsopple John F, porter, h e s Lincoln av 3 s of C C C & St L Ry (M J).
Humann Albert E, clk, b w s Commercial av 3 s of Washington av (I).
Humann John F, clk, b w s Commercial av 3 s of Washington av (I).
Humann John H, piano tuner, w s Commercial av 3 s of Washington (I), h same.
Humbert Brother, teacher, b cor Coburn and Short.
Humbert Bruce L, bkkpr, r 247 N Capitol av.
Humble Charles, porter, r 311 Indiana av.
Hume Charles W, music teacher, 136 E St Joseph, h same.
Hume Charles W, music teacher, 136 E St Joseph, h same.
Hume Clay A B, music teacher, 136 E St Joseph, h same.
Hume Eliza (wid Madison), h 784 N Illinois.

THOS. C. DAY & CO.
INVESTING AGENTS,
TOWN AND FARM LOANS,
Rooms 325 to 330 Lemcke Bldg.

Hume Elizabeth (wid David M), b 116 Highland pl.
Hume Frederick, lab, b 325 W Morris.
Hume Elizabeth, stenog, b 130 Prospect.
Hume George E (Gates & Hume), h n e cor Illinois and 24th.
Hume Harry C, painter, h 137 E Vermont.
Hume Isaac N, farmer, h 130 Prospect.
Hume James A, carp, h 265 Bates.
Hume James M, h n e cor N Illinois and 24th.
Hume Rice, lab, h 59 Orange.
Hume Thomas, watchman, h 36 McIntyre.
Hume Wm H, clk, h 40 Tecumseh.
Humer Wm A, driver, h rear 298 Chestnut.
Humerson Mary E (wid Samuel), h 105½ Broadway.
Humerson Samuel W, carriage trimmer, b 105½ Broadway.
Humes Eliza (wid Madison), h 784 N Illinois.
Humes Wm, driver, r 120 E Wabash.
Hummel Albert P, electrician, b 771 E Washington.
Hummel Charles F, lab, b 167 Michigan (H).
Hummel George J, clk Jenney Electric Motor Co, h 165 Dougherty.
Hummel George W, bartndr, b 167 Michigan (H).
Hummel Zennia M, instructor Indpls Business University, When bldg, b 195 N Alabama.
Hummons Caroline, h 202 W 5th.
Humphreville Griffith, steelwkr, h 83 Church.
Humphrey Charles A, trav agt Daniel Stewart Co, h 433 Broadway.
Humphrey Charles B, plastr, 82 Paca, h same.
Humphrey Frank, lab, b 90 N Delaware.
Humphrey Frederick, lab, b 201 E Washington.
Humphrey Hervey S, electrician, b 433 Broadway.
Humphrey Isaac, lab, h rear 671 N Senate av.

EAT
QUAKER BREAD
ASK YOUR GROCER FOR IT.
THE HITZ BAKING CO.

J. H. TECKENBROCK | Grilles, Fretwork and Wood Carpets
94 EAST SOUTH STREET.

FIDELITY MUTUAL LIFE PHILADELPHIA, PA. A. H. COLLINS { General Agent, 52-53 Baldwin Block.

SUPERIOR BITUMINOUS COAL For Steam and Domestic . . Purposes . . Edwardsport Coal & Mining C. Rooms 42 and 43 When Building.

ESTABLISHED 1876. TELEPHONE 168.
CHESTER BRADFORD,
SOLICITOR OF PATENTS,
AND COUNSEL IN PATENT CAUSES.
(See adv. page 6.)
Office:—Rooms 14 and 16 Hubbard Block, S.W. Cor. Washington and Meridian Streets, INDIANAPOLIS, INDIANA.

Humphrey James R, mason, h 90 N Delaware.
Humphrey John W, grocer, 314 Indiana av, h same.
Humphrey Kate (wid Charles B), h 155 Cornell av.
Humphrey Robert (Humphrey & Jelf), r 45 Indiana av.
Humphrey & Jelf (Robert Humphrey, Shelton H Jelf), barbers, 9 Indiana av.
Humphreys David, tinner, h 119 S East.
Humphreys Eula, bkkpr Taylor & Taylor, b 119 S East.
Humphreys George H, adv agt, 31 Lombard bldg, h 215 Douglass.
Humphreys Harry G, baggagemaster, h 202 Christian av.
Humphreys Hugh (M E Humphreys & Co), res Fair Heaven, Vt.
Humphreys John (M E Humphreys & Co), r 36 Wyandot blk.
Humphreys Josepn A, clk, h 908 N Alabama.
Humphreys Martha E (M E Humphreys & Co), h 118 S East.
HUMPHREYS M E & CO (Martha E, John, Hugh, Wm and Robert T Humphreys, Albert B Sargent), Galvanized Iron Cornice, Slate and Tin Roofers, rear 119 S East, Tel 1144.
Humphreys Reuben M, lab, h 43 Athon.
Humphreys Robert T (M E Humphreys & Co), h 195 Walcott.
Humphreys Wm (M E Humphreys & Co), h 255 S New Jersey.
Humphries Estella I, teacher, b 15 E Sutherland (B).
Hundley John A, foreman, h 1 E Sutherland (B).
Hundling Carolina (wid Dirk), b n e cor Bluff rd and Raymond.
Hunefelder George, lab, h 24 Downey.
Hungate Peter H, lab, h 156 N Belmont av (H).
Hunsucker Samuel W, mach, h 17 Bismarck av (H).
Hunt Ann (wid John), h 335 S Missouri.
Hunt Caroline (wid Michael G), b 92 Hoyt av.

HAY & WILLITS MFG. CO.
76 N. PENNSYLVANIA ST.,
MAKERS
Outing BICYCLES
PHONE 598.

Hunt Charles A, driver U S Ex, h 151 Shelby.
Hunt Charles E, lab, b 282 W Maryland.
Hunt Charles E, paperhngr, h 367 Virginia av.
Hunt Charles E, printer Indpls News, b 1079 N Capitol av.
Hunt Charles F, mngr C F Hunt Co, h 332 N Alabama.
Hunt Charles L, ins agt, h n s Michigan 1 e of Chester av.
HUNT C F CO, Charles F Hunt Mngr, Bridge Builders and Dealers in Stone Crushers, Road Machinery, Street Sweepers, Sewer and Cast Iron Pipe, 92 S Illinois, Tel 1169.
Hunt Daniel, coachman, h rear 635 N Senate av.
Hunt David L, h 10 Lafayette.
Hunt Delilah (wid Robert R), h 553 N West.
Hunt Edgar A, barber, 147 W Washington, h same.
Hunt Edward, ironwkr, b 282 W Maryland.
Hunt Edward A, mnfrs' agt, 503 Lemcke bldg, b 82 E North.
Hunt Edward L, barber, h 6 Carter.
Hunt Eldon B, foreman, h 142 Spann av.
Hunt Eliza J (wid Wm A), b 36 Tecumseh.
Hunt Elmer E, clk, h 13 Ryan blk.
Hunt Entis, b 402 W New York.
Hunt Fairfax, carp, h 75 Jones.
Hunt Frank, lab, h 251 S Capitol av.
Hunt Frank, molder, b 55 King av (H).
Hunt Frank C, pressman, b 1079 N Capitol av.
Hunt Frank M, lineman, b 95 N Meridian.
Hunt Frederick, lab, b 341 Bates.
Hunt Fremont, molder, h 55 King av (H).
Hunt George E, sec Indiana Dental College, h 199 N Penn.
Hunt Henrietta (wid Daniel), h 564 N Senate av.
Hunt Henry, b 1674 N Penn.
Hunt Henry C, millwright, b 29 Belmont av.
Hunt Henry M, mach, b 135 Central av.
Hunt Herbert, city editor The Sun, b w s Central av 1 s of 22d.
Hunt Hiram W, lab, b 516 S Illinois.
Hunt James, lab, h 282 W Maryland.
Hunt James W, lab, b 282 W Maryland.
Hunt John T, city fireman, b 335 S Missouri.
Hunt John W, mach, h 516 S Illinois.
Hunt Joseph, bartndr, r 39½ W Market.
Hunt Julian T, printer Wm B Burford, h 629 Marlowe av.
Hunt Louella, b 654 College av.
Hunt Lucinda (wid James E), h 6 Carter.
Hunt Martin W, trav agt Nordyke & Marmon Co, h 810 Ash.
Hunt Mary (wid John), h 516 S Illinois.
Hunt Mary A (wid James), b 1178 N Illinois.
Hunt Mary C (Williams & Hunt), h 701 S West.
Hunt Mary E (wid John R), b 553 N West.
Hunt Mary J (wid Erastus F), dressmkr, 499 N West, h same.
Hunt Melissa E, h 101 N New Jersey.
Hunt Milton, lab, h 1277 Morris (W I).
Hunt Olive E, housekpr 316 College av.
Hunt Ora, lab, b 43 S West.
Hunt Otto W, printer, h 49 King.
Hunt Patrick E, weighmaster, b 335 S Missouri.
Hunt Philip S, bartndr, r 13 Stewart pl.
Hunt Roy, live stock, b 1277 Morris (W I).
Hunt Reuben V, carp, h 8 Lord.
Hunt Sarah C (wid Lemuel C), h 1079 N Capitol av.

ROOFING MATERIAL C. ZIMMERMAN & SONS, SLATE AND GRAVEL ROOFERS, 19 SOUTH EAST STREET.

DRIVEN WELLS And Second Water Wells and Pumps of all kinds at CHARLES KRAUSS', 42 S. PENN. ST., TEL. 466. REPAIRING NEATLY DONE.

Hunt Susan, stenog C C C & St L Ry, b 1674 N Penn.
Hunt Wm, coachman 373 Ash.
Hunt Wm A, express, h 189 Columbia av.
Hunt Wm H (Pfeffer & Hunt), b 85 W Michigan.
Hunt Wm H, musician, b 1 Carter.
Hunt Wm M, marble cutter, h 341 Bates.
Hunt Willis C, canmkr, b 553 N West.
Hunter Albert A, clk Great Atlantic and Pacific Tea Co, h 146 Blackford.
Hunter Albert B, lab, b 216 W Chesapeake.
Hunter Allie, lab, h e s National av 1 s of C H & D R R (I).
Hunter Bessie, boarding 132 N Capitol av.
Hunter Blanche, b 293 E Court.
Hunter Burton, waiter, r 235½ Mass av.
Hunter Charles, lab, h rear 163 St Mary.
Hunter Charles W, clk, b 132 N Capitol av.
Hunter Daniel D, printer, h 65 Martindale av.
Hunter Dickson, express, h 3 Peck.
Hunter Edgar O, draughtsman Vonnegut & Bohn, b 159 N East.
Hunter Edwin G Rev, rector Holy Innocents' Church, h 175 Cedar.
Hunter Eliza (wid Hugh), h 95½ Chadwick.
Hunter Elizabeth (wid Thomas), b 363 Ash.
Hunter Ellis F, clk, b 409 N Delaware.
Hunter Flora M, vice-pres and treas Metropolitan School of Music, h 409 N Delaware.
Hunter Frank P, barber, 175 Virginia av, h 45 Buchanan.
Hunter George, watchman, h 51 Hendricks blk.
Hunter George W, plumber, h 129 Ft Wayne av.
Hunter Gilbert, lab, h 31 Athon.
Hunter Harry S, trav agt Wm B Burford, h 485 N Senate av.
Hunter Henry C, hostler, h 28 W 1st.
Hunter James T, restaurant, 229 W Washington, h 194 Bright.
Hunter John E, lab, h 128 Chadwick.
Hunter John H, trav agt, h 159 N East.
Hunter John W, barber, 161 Indiana av, h same.
Hunter Joseph G, lab, h n s Sample near Belt R R (W I).
Hunter Joseph L, farmer, h e s Ritter av 2 n of Washington av (I).
Hunter Lucy, restaurant, 119 Ft Wayne av, h same.
Hunter Maggie M, h 21 Fayette.
Hunter Mark P, lab, h 563 W Addison (N I).
Hunter Martin, lab, h 211 Agnes.
Hunter Mary, nurse, 66 Hill av, b same.
Hunter Mary E (wid Daniel), h 138 Martindale av.
Hunter Mary E (wid John M), h 276 N California.
Hunter Mary J (wid Cicero), h 319 Clinton.
Hunter Mary J (wid Ralph), h 66 Hill av.
Hunter May F (wid John A), baker, 293 Mass av, h same.
Hunter Melvin R, painter, b 12 Floral av.
Hunter Perry, clk, b 132 N Capitol av.
Hunter Rice V, pastor Seventh Presbyterian Church, h 240 Virginia av.
Hunter Robert, lab, b 211 Agnes.
Hunter Robert M, fireman, h 211 Agnes.
Hunter Samuel, lab, b 31 Alvord.
Hunter Samuel, lab, h n s Sample nr Belt R R (W I).
Hunter Silas W, restaurant, 104 S Illinois h 132 N Capitol av.
Hunter Wesley, lab, b rear 163 St Mary.

Richardson & McCrea,
REPRESENTING BEST KNOWN
FIRE INSURANCE COMPANIES.
Fidelity and Casualty Insurance Company of New York Represented.
Telephone 182. 79 East Market St.

Hunter Wm G, chief clk, h 409 N Delaware.
Hunter Wm H, lab, h 31 Alvord.
Huntington Angelina C (wid James N), h 217 Bellefontaine.
Huntington Harry, cook, r 100 N Alabama.
Huntington Hector, waiter, r 100 N Alabama.
Huntington John C, tmstr, h 541 W Shoemaker (N I).
Huntington John T (Huntington & Page), h 342 S New Jersey.
Huntington Martha D (wid Forrest C), clk Keller & Gamerdinger, b 559 E Washington.
Huntington Nettie N, clk, b 217 Bellefontaine.
Huntington Ora, driver, b 180 E Washington.
Huntington Oran, r 100 N Alabama.
Huntington Pearl, stenog Huntington & Page, b 217 Bellefontaine.
HUNTINGTON & PAGE (John T Huntington, Thomas V Page), Seedsmen, Flour and Feed, 78 E Market, Tel 129. (See page 5.)
Huntsinger Abigail (wid Wm), b 7 Fay (W I).
Huntsinger Wm M, millwright, h 596 W 22d (N I).
Hunzinger Herman A, bartendr, h 441 S Delaware.
Hupke August O, lab, h 51 Arizona.
Hupke Ferdinand, lab, h 73 Wisconsin.
Hupp George W, sawyer, h 225 N Pine.
Hupp George W jr, clk The Progress Clothing Co, b 225 N Pine.
Hupp Sebren, carp, h 20 Haugh (H).
Hurd, see also Herd.
Hurd James E, carp, 577 W Addison (N I), h same.
Hurd James H, lab, r 318 W Court.
Hurd Wm A, tmstr, h 74 Willow.
Hurford Frank, chemist, b 46 S Capitol av.
Hurlbert Lewis G, trav agt, b 27 E 2d.
Hurlbut Isaac H, blksmith, h 570 W Udell (N I).
Hurlbut Jeremiah P, lab, b 570 W Udell (W I).

The Williams Typewriter
Elegant Work, Visible Writing, Easy Operation, High Speed.
S. H. EAST, State Agent,
55 Thorpe Block, 87 E. Market St.

If You are not Satisfied with Your Laundry Work Give Us a Trial . . ERTEL STEAM LAUNDRY 26 and 28 N. Senate Avenue. Telephone 18.

ELLIS & HELFENBERGER Manufacturers of IRON and WIRE FENCES 162-170 S. SENATE AVE. TEL. 758.

THE HOGAN TRANSFER AND STORAGE COMP'Y
Household Goods and Pianos Moved—Packed—Stored...... Baggage and Package Express Machinery and Safes a Specialty Cor. Washington and Illinois Sts. TELEPHONE No. 675.

The Central Rubber & Supply Co. ◆◆◆ Hose, Belting, Packing, Clothing, Druggists' Sundries, Bicycle Tires, Cotton Hose, Etc. New York Belting & Packing Co., L't'd. PHONE 922. 79 S. ILLINOIS ST., INDIANAPOLIS, IND.

HIGHEST SECURITY
LOWEST COST OF INSURANCE.
The Provident Life and Trust Co.
Of Philadelphia.
D. W. EDWARDS, Gen. Agent,
508 Indiana Trust Building.

Hurlbut Wm R, lab, b 21 Agnes.
Hurley Augustus A, brakeman, h 164 Deloss.
Hurley Charles H, saloon, 33 Kentucky av, h same.
Hurley Daniel, engr, h 60 Lexington av.
Hurley James, plumber, b 17 Ellen.
Hurley Jeremiah, cook, b 17 Ellen.
Hurley John, painter, b 477 N California.
Hurley John E, packer H P Wasson & Co, b 17 Ellen.
Hurley John F, condr, h 199 W Merrill.
Hurley Joseph F, lab, h 71 McGinnis.
Hurley Louise, b 1027 N New Jersey.
Hurley Margaret (wid John), h 17 Springfield.
Hurley Mary A (wid Patrick), h 477 N California.
Hurley Michael, engr, b 60 Lexington av.
Hurley Michael, tmstr, h 17 Ellen.
Hurley Patrick H, painter, b 477 N California.
Hurley Sarah, h 259 W Ray.
Hurley Thomas C, mach, h 552 Jefferson av.
Hurley Timothy, saloon, 102 S Illinois, h 455 N West.
Hurley Wm H, carp, 579 E St Clair, h same.
Hurley Wm H, condr, h 72 Bismarck (W I).
Huron Enos T, h 208 S Pine.
Hurrle Casimir J, cutter, b 63 N Noble.
Hurrle Ignatz, tailor, 4 Pembroke Arcade, h 63 N Noble.
Hurrle Sebastian (Kramer & Hurrle), h 287 S Delaware.
Hursh Homer W, bartndr, h 38 Warren av (W I).
Hurst Charles F, driver, h 516 E 9th.
Hurst Cleon H, condr, h 113 Germania av (H).
Hurst Erastimus S, coremkr, b 229 Michigan (H).
Hurst Ernest G (Schuck & Hurst), b 229 Michigan (H).
Hurst John L, tel opr, b 229 Michigan (H).
Hurst Lawrence T, collr, h n s Beechwood av 1 e of Central av (I).
Hurst Monroe E, mach, b 60 Brookside av.
Hurt, see also Hert.
Hurt Conrad, lab, b 8 Hiawatha.

Julius C. Walk & Son,
Jewelers
Indianapolis.
12 EAST WASHINGTON ST.

Hurt Essie F, dressmkr, 362 Douglass, b same.
Hurt Frank, lab, h e s Bismarck av 2 n of Emrich (H).
Hurt Frederick C, student, r 106½ E New York.
Hurt Harry, h 247 N Capitol av.
Hurt James C, porter, b 162 Elizabeth.
Hurt James F, saloon, 185 Tremont av (H), h 162 Elizabeth.
Hurt John, bicycle rep, h 162 Elizabeth.
Hurt Joseph H, porter, b 162 Elizabeth.
Hurt Joseph H, lab, b 362 Douglass.
Hurt Reuben, porter, h 232 E Wabash.
Hurt Webster, lab, b 162 Elizabeth.
Hurt Wm, lab, b 20 Sheffield av (H).
Hurt Wm E, tmstr, h 29 Hiawatha.
Hurty John N, pres The J N Hurty Pharmacy Co, sec State Board of Health, 24 State House, analytical chemist, 8 Hutchings blk, h 29 E 2d.
HURTY J N PHARMACY CO THE, John N Hurty Pres, James M Gentle Vice-Pres, J Richard Francis Sec and Treas, 102-104 N Penn, Tel 1029.
Husband Nancy (wid Lindsey), b 220 Indiana av.
Husbands Wm M, trav agt Tanner & Sullivan, h 64 Talbott av.
Huselager Wm, lab, h rear 36 S Spruce.
Huskey James H, finisher, h 268 Fulton.
Husselman Wesley E, salesman D H Baldwin & Co, h 450 W Shoemaker (N I).
Hussey Edward, h 356½ S West.
Hussey Edward J, clk, b 356½ S West.
Hussey Frank S, trav agt Syfers, McBride & Co, h 490 College av.
Hussey Jesse H, stenog, h 29 N Beville av.
Hussey John R, sec and treas Capital Lumber Co, h 30 West Drive (W P).
Hussey Lawrence, b 356½ S West.
Hussey Lutellus (Hussey & Baker), res Lockland, O.
Hussey Michael J, plastr, h 191 Yandes.
Hussey Peter, lab, b 356½ S West.
Hussey Wm P, vice-pres The Standard Dry Kiln Co, res Chicago, Ill.
HUSSEY & BAKER (Lutellus Hussey, John M Baker), Plumbers, 116 N Delaware. (See adv in classified Plumbers.)
Hust George C, h 512 E Washington.
Husted Ann A (wid Thomas A), b 68 Middle Drive (W P).
Husted Margaret A, clk, b 157 Walcott.
Huster Henry, condr, h 1005 N Senate av.
Huston, see also Houston.
Huston Cephas B, h 489 N Illinois.
Huston John, lab, h 205 W North.
Huston John A, printer Wm B Burford, h 195 N East.
Huston Milo, lab, h 96 Lincoln la.
Huston Octavia (wid Fieldon), h 371 W North.
Huston Rufus, waiter, b 88 W Market.
Huston Samuel, lab, h 59 Rhode Island.
Huston Wm H, constable, 34 N Delaware, h 15 Cornell av.
Hutchason Ella, milliner, 10 W Market, b 654 N Alabama.
Hutchason Willis E, mngr O H & F E Taft, h 653 E Market.
Hutchens Allie, b 568 E Washington.
Hutchens Edward O, engr, h 49 S Spruce.
Hutchings Dalphon, h 600 Broadway.
Hutchingson Charles E, painter, h 127 W McCarty.

OTTO GAS ENGINES | BUILDERS' EXCHANGE S. W. Cor. Ohio and Penn. Telephone 535.

Becker & Son Charles Becker Jacob Becker Jr. Merchant Tailors. 21 N. Penn St. Tel. 934

SALISBURY & STANLEY Co and Builders. Repairing of all kinds done on short notice. 177 ... St. Indianapolis, Ind. Telephone 99 O ... FIXTURES, STORE AND BANK FIXTURES.

Hutchingson Charles I, painter, h 72 S West.
Hutchins Frank F, phys, 409 N Alabama, b same.
Hutchins George A, shoemkr, 10½ Prospect, h 44 Barth av.
Hutchins Henry H, h 574 E Market.
Hutchins Luther, stenog, r 328 E New York.
Hutchins Mary E (wid Hezekiah S), h 409 N Alabama.
Hutchinson Albert, furniture, 178 E Washington, h 510 S Illinois.
Hutchinson Byron, trav agt, h 550 N Capitol av.
Hutchinson Carrie E, stenog C C C & St L Ry, b 202 E McCarty.
Hutchinson Charles, driver, b 737 N Capitol av.
Hutchinson Charles, lab, h 781 E Market.
Hutchinson Charles, switchman, h 31 Miley av.
Hutchinson Charles, helper, h 73 N Beville av.
Hutchinson Charles L, real est, 178 E Washington, h 412 N East.
Hutchinson Charles P, printer, b 737 N Capitol av.
Hutchinson Charlotte, stenog, b 202 E McCarty.
Hutchinson Edward B, genl claim agt P C C & St L Ry, h 733 N Meridian.
Hutchinson George, salesman, h 686 E St Clair.
Hutchinson Harry H, clk, b 202 E McCarty.
Hutchinson John L, carpet layer, h 441 W 2d.
Hutchinson Lotta, stenog Indpls Union Ry Co, b 202 E McCarty.
Hutchinson Ruth (wid David), b 202 E McCarty.
Hutchinson Walter, lab, b 433 E Vermont.
Hutchison Aaron W, carp, h 57 Lexington av.
Hutchison Alexander, lab, h rear 136 W 1st.
Hutchison Bert, lab, r 66 N Missouri.
Hutchison Ella L (wid John), h 40 Grant.
Hutchison Elon W, clk, b 57 Lexington av.
Hutchison Frank, tmstr, h 26 Parker.
Hutchison George W, tmstr, h 58 Hazel.
Hutchison John, engr, b 788 E Market.
Hutchison Knox L, collr National Collection Agency, b 121 Christian av.
Hutchison Leonora, stenog, b 121 Christian av.
Hutchison Oren N, shoemkr, h 44 Ash.
Hutchison Robert G, caller, h 20 Oriental.
Huter Frank S, carp, h 56 S Morris (B).
Huter Frank B, mach hd, b 56 S Morris (B).
Huter Oliver, lab, b 56 S Morris (B).
Huth John F, brakeman, r 117 Lexington av.
Hutsebout Frank, cigarmkr, r 353 E St Clair.
Hutsel Catherine R (wid Isaac), h 589 W Udell (N I).
Hutsel George O, veneerer, b 589 W Udell (N I).
Hutsell Charles E, boxmkr, b 188 Coburn.
Hutsell Fannie (wid John W), h 188 Coburn.
Hutsell Jesse K, nailer, b 188 Coburn.
Hutsell John W, carp, b 164 Prospect.
Hutsell Wm C, jeweler, h 188 Coburn.
Hutson Albert W, plastr, h 151 Clarke.
Hutson George W, chiropodist, r 18 N Illinois.
Hutson Robert W, plastr, h 11 Valley Drive.
Hutton Benjamin, lab, b 734 Shelby.
Hutton Edward M, tel opr, b 61 Johnson av.
Hutton Eliza J (wid Wm), h 34 Samoa.

Henry H. Fay,
40½ E. WASHINGTON ST.,
AGENT FOR
Insurance Co. of North America,
Pennsylvania Fire Ins. Co.

Hutton Jacob, painter, b 111 E Washington.
Hutton John H, engr, h 111 N Gillard av.
Hutton John N, baggageman, h 61 Johnson av.
Hutton John Harvey, mngr Indiana Electrotpye Co, b 913 N Delaware.
Hutton Mary A (wid Nicholas R), h 913 N Delaware.
Hutton Weeber W, clk K and L of H, b 913 N Delaware.
Hutton Wm, carp, b w s James 1 n of Sutherland (B).
Hutton Wm D, hostler, h 223 Elm.
Hutton Wm M, b 32 S Senate av.
Huxley Joseph, painter, 17½ Virginia av, h 74 N Olive.
Hyatt, see also Hiatt.
Hyatt Carrie A, music teacher, 6 Lincoln av, b same.
Hyatt Charles F, livery, 26 W Merrill, h 300½ S Penn.
Hyatt Charles L, clk, b 842 Morris (W I).
Hyatt Fielding A, agt P P Mast & Co, 100 S Capitol av, h 6 Lincoln av.
Hyatt Frank A, agt, h 6 Lincoln av.
Hyatt James W, carp, h 78 S Belmont av (W I).
Hyatt John W, grinder, b 249 S Penn.
Hyatt Mort, hostler, h 399 S Illinois.
Hyatt Oscar O, lab, h 842 Morris (W I).
Hyatt Wm H, painter, h 45½ Virginia av.
Hyatt Wm L, packer, h 262 River av (W I).
Hyde Henry, lab, b 234 Clinton.
Hyde Isaac, lab, r 117 W 4th.
Hyde Isaac, lab, r 140 W 6th.
Hyde Lorin A, student, b 264 Bellefontaine.
Hyde Nathaniel A Rev, h 710 N Delaware.
Hyde Nelson J, restaurant, 59 S Illinois, h 960 N Capitol av.
Hyde Noah, lab, b 265 Spring.
Hyde Park Drug Store, Frank Keegan propr, cor Illinois and 22d.
Hyde Wm, mason, b 90 Bradshaw.
Hyder Charles, clk, b 347 Cornell av.
Hyder Charles W, photog, h 347 Cornell av.

MAYHEW'S
SPECTACLES
THE BEST IN USE
SOLD ONLY AT 13 N. MERIDIAN ST.

LUMBER Sash and Doors BALKE & KRAUSS CO., Corner Market and Missouri Sts.

Friedgen Has the BEST PATENT LEATHER SHOES AT LOWEST PRICES. 19 North Pennsylvania St.

SAMUEL LAING ! HOT AIR FURNACES 72 AND 74 EAST COURT STREET.

M. B. Wilson, Pres. W. F. Churchman, Cash.
The Capital National Bank,
INDIANAPOLIS, IND.
Banking business in all its branches. Bonds and Foreign Exchange bought and sold.
Interest paid on time deposits.
Checks and drafts on all Indiana and Illinois points handled at lowest rates.
No. 28 South Meridian Street, Cor. Pearl.

Hyer Clifford A, helper, b 158 Randolph.
Hyer Mary E (wid Joshua), h 158 Randolph.
Hyer Orville T, brakeman, b 158 Randolph.
Hyland, see also Highland.
Hyland Anna (wid Richard), h 347 S Missouri.
Hyland James, brushmkr, h 6 Springfield.
Hyland John, lab, b 46 Ash.
Hyland John C, clk M O'Connor & Co, b 673 N Illinois.
Hyland John M, bricklyr, h 630 N Senate av.
Hyland John P, carp, b 347 S Missouri.
Hyland Kate (wid Michael), h 673 N Illinois.
Hyland Martin J, sergt of police, h 204 N Noble.
Hyland Mary (wid Thomas), h 46 Ash.
Hyland Mitchell M, bricklyr, h 203 W 1st.
Hyland Thomas, mach, b 119 Bright.
Hyland Wm F, bricklyr, h 180 W 8th.
Hyland Wm J, b 347 S Missouri.
Hyle John, lab, b w s Auburn av 1 n of C C C & St L Ry.
Hylton Augustus, lab, b 119 Tremont av (H).
Hylton Silas W, mach, h 119 Tremont av (H).
Hyman Helena (wid Robert), b 149 Bellefontaine.
Hyman Louis, junk, 428 W Washington, h 457 S Illinois.
Hyman Louis S, pdlr, r 96 N Alabama.
Hyman Max R, pub, 78 Broadway, h same.
Hymer James I, printer, b 177 N Penn.
Hynes Amos P, lawyer, 5 Brandon blk, b 25 Stoughton av.
Hynes McKee D, clk The Bowen-Merrill Co, b 25 Stoughton av.
Hynes Paul H, insp, b 25 Stoughton av.
Hynes Wm D, clk R M S, h 25 Stoughton av.
Hynson George W, h 84 W 2d.
Hyser Clyde R, b 363 Ash.
Hyslop John, fireman, b 678 W Washington.
Hysung Jacob P, h 1110 N Senate av.

Insure Against Accidents
WITH
TUTTLE & SEGUIN,
Agents for
Fidelity and Casualty Co., of New York.
$10,000 for $25. $5,000 for $12.50.
TEL. 1168. 28 E. MARKET ST.

I

Icenbarger George W, patternmkr, h s e cor Alabama and St Joseph.
Iddings Edward S, millwright, h 112 Deloss.
Iddings Elizabeth A (wid Wilmer), h 297 Fletcher av.
Iddings Hannah J (wid Wm H), h 107 Woodlawn av.
Iddings Joseph, mach, b 79 N Olive.
Iddings Joseph F, mach, b 297 Fletcher av.
Iddings Margaret E, nurse, 33 Wyandot blk, b 297 Fletcher av.
Iddings Wm B, gasfitter, b 297 Fletcher av.
Iden Thomas M, prof Butler College, h n e cor Downey and University avs (I).
Iden Wm M, farmer, h s w cor Cherry and Houston avs (I).
Idler Clinton D, foreman, h 171 W South.
Idler Rudolph W, clk, h 418 S Illinois.
Igelmann Charles F, sec and treas The Hitz Baking Co, b 142 Woodlawn av.
Igelmann Edwin O, bkkpr Emil Wulschner & Son, b 142 Woodlawn av.
Igelmann Herman H, solr, h 142 Woodlawn av.
Iglick Rose, h 298 S West.
Igoe Stanley C, bkkpr A J Treat & Son, h 947 N Penn.
Igoe Trustin K, h 28 Lockerbie.
Ihndris Charles, mach, h 156 Martindale av.
Ihndris Dorothea (wid John), h 441 N East.
Ihndris Neatha, confr, 156 Martindale av, h same.
Ihrig John F, baker Parrott & Taggart, h 530 E Washington.
Ihsleib Christian O, brewer, h 22 Deloss.
Ijams Addie (wid John S), b 277 E Georgia.
Ijams Wm P, pres Belt R R and Stock Yards Co and treas Indpls Packing and Rendering Co, h Terre Haute, Ind.
Ike John H, flagman, h 101 S New Jersey.
Iles Gustava, instructor Indpls Business University, When bldg, r 37 W Vermont.
Iles Marshall L, bkkpr McCormick H M Co, h 385 N East.
Iles Orlando B, lawyer, 35 Lombard bldg, r 366 N Alabama.
Ilg Frederick, saloon, 23 Virginia av, h 309 E Merrill.
Ilg Matthew, cooper, h 20 Carlos.
Ilg Walter J, chief's clk City Fire Dept, h 279 E Merrill.
Iliff Charles E, clk, r 220 The Shiel.
Iliff Charles W, cashr Anheuser-Busch Brewing Assn, b 801 E Washington.
Iliff James A, clk The Progress Clothing Co, h 801 E Washington.
Iliff Lewis E, bkkpr Anheuser-Busch Brewing Assn, b 801 E Washington.
Iliff Louis S, trav agt, r 292 N Illinois.
Iliff Walter W, framemkr, r 259 N Illinois.
Iliff Wm H, molder, h rear 279 Springfield.
Illinois Central R R, land office, Leo A Bond district agt, Union Station.
Illinois House, Wm L Essmann propr, 181 S Illinois.
Illyes Levi R, student, b 41 Madison av.
Immell John F, mach, h 26 S Gale (B).
Imperial Savings and Loan Association of Indiana, Milton S Huey pres, James H Webber sec, Medford B Wilson treas, 91 E Market.
Independent The, Sol P Hathaway propr, 19 Miller blk.
Independent Hair Co The, Samuel E Rauh pres, Henry Rauh sec and treas, 219 S Penn.

WEDDING CAKE BOXES · SULLIVAN & MAHAN 41 W. Pearl St.

DIAMOND WALL PLASTER { Telephone 1410 BUILDERS' EXCHANGE.

Best Work. Prompt Delivery. } THE HOME LAUNDRY 197 S. ILLINOIS ST. TEL. 1769. { Collars and Cuffs our Specialty.

Indiana Association of Underwriters, John B Cromer pres, J Irving Riddle vice-pres, Isaac C Hays sec and treas, 4 Hartford blk, 84 E Market.

Indiana Baptist The, Indiana Baptist Publishing Co pubs, 68 Baldwin blk.

Indiana Baptist Publishing Co, W T Stott pres, Uriah M Chaille treas, 68 Baldwin blk.

INDIANA BERMUDEZ ASPHALT CO, John W Cooper Pres, Allen W Conduitt Sec and Treas, Rooms 25 and 26 Baldwin Blk, Tel 1330; Yards cor E Vermont and Big Four Tracks, Tel 1298.

INDIANA BICYCLE CO, CHARLES F Smith Pres, Philip Goetz Sec and Treas, Mnfrs of Bicycles, 67-99 S East, Tel 49.

INDIANA BICYCLE CO, Retail Dept, Frank Staley Mngr, 100 N Penn, Tel 1654.

Indiana Bond Co, 85 Baldwin blk.

INDIANA BOSTON SCHOOL OF ELOCUTION AND EXPRESSION OF INDIANAPOLIS, Mrs Harriet A Prunk Principal, 368 W New York. (See adv in Miscellaneous Directory.)

Indiana Car Service Association, Duncan T Bacon mngr, Union Station.

Indiana Car and Foundry Co, Major Collins pres, Charles Judah sec, Hadley av s of Belt R R (W I).

INDIANA CHAIN CO, Samuel L Pattison Pres, Frank W Wood Mngr, Mnfrs of Bicycle Chains, cor 15th and Belt Railway, Tel 1852.

Indiana Children's Home Society, Wm A Wood pres, Rev Willis D Engle sec, Charles Z Coffin treas, Rev Horatio S Hilton D D supt, 46 Coffin blk.

INDIANA COLLECTION BUREAU, Ernest H Youel Sec, 303 Indiana Trust Bldg.

Indiana Construction Co, Derk DeRuiter pres, Preston C Trusler sec and treas, 103½ E Washington.

Indiana Cooperage Co, E P McDonald mngr, 315 Bates.

INDIANA, DECATUR & WESTERN RY CO, M D Woodford Pres, R B F Peirce Genl Mngr, George H Graves Supt, John S Lazarus Genl Freight and Pass Agt, George W Lishawa Auditor, F H Short Treas, George W Balch Purchasing Agt, Commercial Club Bldg, Tel 377.

Indiana Dental College, John N Hurty pres, George E Hunt sec, Harry S Hicks treas, 89 E Ohio.

Indiana Dry Goods Co The, Wm F Piel pres, Edward Prange sec, Frank H Sudbrock treas, 158 E Washington.

INDIANA ELECTROTYPE CO (Wm Wands, Joseph E, Michael A and John B Fleck), Electrotype Foundry, 23 W Pearl, Tel 1270. (See left side lines.)

INDIANA ELEVATOR GATE CO (James M Elder), Mnfrs of Automatic Safety Elevator Gates, 1205 N Illinois.

FRANK NESSLER. WILL H. ROST.
FRANK NESSLER & CO.
Tailors
56 EAST MARKET ST. (Lemcke Building),
INDIANAPOLIS, IND.

Indiana Farmer The, Indiana Farmer Co pub, 30½ N Delaware.

INDIANA FARMER CO, John B Conner Pres, Wm F Barrows Vice-Pres, James G Kingsbury Sec, James L Kingsbury Treas, Publishers The Indiana Farmer, 30½ N Delaware, Tel 337.

Indiana Fruit Co, Daniel Chenoweth pres, A D Titsworth sec, Andrew Harmon treas, 66 E Market.

INDIANA GRAPHOPHONE CO, Spear & Co Genl Agts, 50, 51 and 52 When Bldg. (See adv in classified Talking Machines.)

Indiana Home and Savings Association, Rufus J Stukey pres, Clinton E Galloway sec, Martin V McGilliard treas, 94 E Market.

Indiana Horticultural Society, 11 State House.

INDIANA HOSPITAL FOR INSANE (Central), George F Edenharter, M D, Supt, National Road 3 miles west of City, Tel 389.

Indiana Humane Society, Horace McKay pres, 29½ N Penn.

INDIANA ILLUSTRATING CO, E E Stafford Propr, Zinc Etchings, Half-Tone Engravings, Newspaper Illustrating and Designing, s e cor Market and Illinois, Tel 1077. (See adv opp classified Engravers.)

Indiana Indemnity Co, Samuel Heath sec, 147 Mass av.

INDIANA INSTITUTE FOR THE EDUCATION OF THE BLIND, Wm H Glascock Supt, n s North bet Meridian and Penn, Tel 1335.

INDIANA INSTITUTION FOR THE EDUCATION OF THE DEAF AND DUMB, Richard O Johnson Supt, s e cor Washington and State av, Tel 104.

Haueisen & Hartmann
163-169 E. Washington St.
FURNITURE,
Carpets,
Household Goods,
Tin, Granite and China Wares, Oil Cloth and Shades

THE WM. H. BLOCK CO. 7 AND 9 EAST WASHINGTON STREET. DRY GOODS, HOUSE FURNISHINGS AND CROCKERY.

London Guarantee and Accident Co. (Ltd.) All forms of Liability Insurance, Workmen's Collective Insurance, Fidelity Bonds and Individual Accident Insurance.
Geo. W. Pangborn, Gen. Agent, 704-706 Lemcke Bldg. Telephone 140.

Prussian National Insurance Company OF STETTIN, GERMANY. ORGANIZED 1845. **FRANK K. SAWYER, AGENT** 74 East Market Street. Telephone 863.

JOSEPH GARDNER,
TIN, COPPER AND SHEET-IRON WORK AND HOT AIR FURNACES.
37, 39 & 41 KENTUCKY AVE. Telephone 322

INDIANA INSURANCE CO OF INDIANAPOLIS, Martin V McGilliard Pres, Charles Schurmann Vice-Pres, J Kirk Wright Sec, Edward G Cornelius Treas, Fire and Cyclone Insurance, The McGilliard Agency Co Genl Agts, 83-85 E Market, Tel 479.

Indiana Journal of Commerce, Wm H Drapier propr, 78½ S Delaware.

Indiana Labor Leader, Hannegan & White pubs, 25 S Delaware.

Indiana Land Co, David C Bryan pres, 236 Lemcke bldg.

Indiana Law School, Byron K Elliott pres, Wm P Fishback dean, Wm C Bobbs treas, Robert M Fishback acting sec, 71 W Market.

Indiana Law Student, George C Calvert pub, 18½ N Penn.

INDIANA LUMBER AND VENEER CO, Amos K Hollowell Pres, Oran M Pruitt Sec, Lynn P Hollowell Treas, Wm M Dickerson Supt, cor 15th and L E & W R R, Tel 1450.

Indiana League of Fire Underwriters, Daniel A Rudy pres, John R Engle sec and treas, Spencer House.

INDIANA MANUFACTURING CO THE, Arthur A McKain Pres, Joseph K Sharpe Jr Sec and Treas, Mnfrs of Farmers' Friend Straw Stackers, 401-405 Indiana Trust Bldg, Tel 64.

Indiana Medical Journal, Indiana Medical Journal Publishing Co proprs, 18 W Ohio.

Indiana Medical Journal Publishing Co, Lehman H Dunning pres, Hugh M Lash sec, George J Cook treas and genl mngr, 18 W Ohio.

INDIANA MILLERS' MUTUAL FIRE INSURANCE CO, M S Blish Pres, W L Kidder Vice-Pres, E E Perry Sec and Treas, J W Hahn Genl Agt and Inspector, 32 Board of Trade Bldg.

Indiana Mortgage Loan Co, Aufderheide & Zumpfe mngrs, 4 Lombard bldg.

J. S. FARRELL & CO.
STEAM AND HOT WATER HEATING FOR STORES, OFFICES, PUBLIC BUILDINGS, PRIVATE RESIDENCES, GREENHOUSES, ETC.
84 North Illinois St. Telephone 382.

INDIANA MUTUAL BUILDING AND LOAN ASSOCIATION, Edward G Cornelius Pres, John C Ingram Vice-Pres, Charles Kahlo Sec, Philander H Fitzgerald Treas, McBride & Denny Genl Attorneys, 32 E Market, Tel 1239.

INDIANA NATIONAL BANK, Volney T Malott Pres, George B Yandes Vice-Pres, Edward B Porter Cashier, Macy W Malott Asst Cashier, Indiana National Bank Bldg, s e cor Virginia av and Penn, Tel 31.

Indiana Natural and Illuminating Gas Co, Charles F Dieterich pres, Samuel D Pray sec, John H Dilks genl mngr, 49 S Penn, tel 678.

Indiana Newspaper Record, Indiana Newspaper Union pubs, 32 W Court.

INDIANA NEWSPAPER UNION, W D Pratt Propr, Newspaper Publishers, News Bldg, 32 W Court, Tel 1407.

Indiana Oil Tank Line, Mortimer A Daugherty mngr, cor Oliver av and N Judge Harding (W I).

INDIANA PAINT AND ROOFING CO, Rubber, Cement, Pitch and Gravel Roofing, Slate Paint, Building Paper and Roofing Felt, 27-29 Muskingum.

Indiana Paper Co, Charles E Coffin treas, paper mnfrs, 27 E Maryland.

Indiana Paving Brick Co, 46½ N Penn.

Indiana Phalanx, Wm F and Wm F Clark jr pubs, 25 Cyclorama pl.

Indiana Pharmacist, Russell C Kelsey, M D, editor and propr, 107 E Ohio.

Indiana Pharmacist Publishing Co, Russell C Kelsey, M D, propr, 107 E Ohio.

INDIANA REFORM SCHOOL FOR GIRLS AND WOMAN'S PRISON, Sarah F Keely Supt, s e cor Michigan and Randolph, Tel 674.

Indiana Retail Merchants' Assn The, Frederick Buddenbaum pres, Wm F Buschman treas, W Marshall Thomas sec and genl mngr, 46 Board of Trade bldg.

INDIANA RUBBER CO (Hughes Mason, Winfield S Johnson), Wholesale Dealers in Rubber Clothing, Boots and Shoes, 127 S Meridian, Tel 1800.

INDIANA SAVINGS AND INVESTMENT CO OF INDIANAPOLIS THE (Capital Stock $1,000,000), Charles E Coffin Pres, Lorenzo D Moody Vice-Pres, Charles E Holloway Sec, 90 E Market, Tel 518.

INDIANA SCHOOL BOOK CO, Edward Hawkins Treas and Genl Mngr, Publishers and Contractors of Indiana State Series School Text Books, Room 605 Indiana Trust Bldg, Tel 35.

Indiana School Journal, Wm A Bell pub, 66½ N Penn.

Indiana School of Art, Hilton U Brown pres, Carl H Lieber sec, Charles E Hollenbeck treas, n w cor Monument pl and Market.

Indiana School of Nursing, n w cor Locke and Margaret.

INDIANA SCREEN FACTORY, W A Scott & Sons Proprs, Door and Window Screens, 591-593 Central av near 14th, Tel 1128. (See front cover.)

United States Life Insurance Co., of New York.
E. B. SWIFT, M'g'r. 25 E. Market St.

Indiana Trust Company.

TRUST DEPARTMENT.

AUTHORIZED BY LAW TO ACT AS

Executor, Guardian,
Administrator, Receiver,
Trustee, Assignee,
Agent.

REGISTERS AND TRANSFERS BONDS AND STOCKS.

Safety Vault Department.

Boxes for rent from **$5.00 PER ANNUM AND UPWARDS,** in an absolutely fire and burglar proof vault, for the safe keeping of bonds, stocks, valuable papers, jewelry, keepsakes, etc. Special fire and burglar proof vault for the storage of silverware, sealskin coats, and treasures of all kinds.

Separate apartments for women.

Bond and Loan Department.

High-grade municipal and county bonds bought and sold. Securities suitable for trust funds and the most conservative investors always on hand.

Loans made on first mortgage and collateral security, upon the most favorable terms as to time, rate and payments.

Real Estate and Insurance Department.

Acts as general or special agent in taking care of real estate. Attends to the collection of rents, the payment of taxes, and the keeping up of repairs. **WRITES FIRE INSURANCE.**

OFFICES IN COMPANY'S BUILDING,

Long Distance Telephone No. 36.

INDIANA TRUST COMPANY

CAPITAL, $1,000,000.00.

INDIANAPOLIS.

OFFICES: INDIANA TRUST BLDG.

GENERAL AGENT AND ADVISER IN ALL BUSINESS MATTERS.

UNDERTAKES ALL FORMS OF TRUSTEESHIP.

SAFETY VAULT DEPARTMENT.

The Liabilities of the Stockholders of this Company, added to its Capital, make a sum of $2,000,000 pledged for the faithful discharge of its obligations.

J. P. FRENZEL, President. E. G. CORNELIUS, Second Vice-Pres't.
FREDERICK FAHNLEY, First Vice-Pres't. JOHN A. BUTLER, Secretary.
CHRISTIAN BRINK, Trust Officer.

DIRECTORS.

FREDERICK FAHNLEY. EDWARD HAWKINS.
ALBERT LIEBER. E. G. CORNELIUS.
JAMES F. FAILEY. H. W. LAWRENCE.
O. N. FRENZEL. CHARLES B. STUART.
F. G. DARLINGTON. WM. F. PIEL.
J. P. FRENZEL.

WM. KOTTEMAN } 89 & 91 E. Washington St. Telephone 1742 { RUGS MATTINGS WINDOW SHADES

WILLIAM WIEGEL { MANUFACTURER OF.... } SHOW CASES { 6 W. Louisiana St. Opposite Union Station.

INDIANA SHORTHAND COLLEGE, Consolidated Indianapolis Business University, When Bldg, N Penn, Tel 499; E J Heeb Propr. (See front cover, right bottom lines and p 4.)

INDIANA SOCIETY FOR SAVINGS, Charles E Thornton Pres, Charles A Bookwalter Sec and Treas, 214-218 Lemcke Bldg, Tel 1517.

Indiana State Attorney General's Office, Wm A Ketcham atty genl, 19 State House.

Indiana State Board of Agriculture, Charles F Kennedy sec, 14 State House.

Indiana State Board of Charities, Ernest Bicknell sec, 52 State House.

Indiana State Board of Health, John N Hurty sec, 24 State House.

Indiana State Board of Tax Commissioners, 35 State House.

Indiana State Board of Public Printing, Binding and Stationery, 3 State House.

Indiana State Bureau of Statistics, Simeon J Thompson chief, 33 State House.

Indiana State Gas Inspector's Office, 89 State House.

INDIANA STATE GAZETTEER AND BUSINESS DIRECTORY, R L Polk & Co Publishers, Rooms 23-24 Journal Bldg; Directories of all the Principal Cities on File for Reference. (See adv back fly leaf.)

Indiana State Geological Museum, 126 State House.

Indiana State Geologist's Office, 89 State House.

Indiana State Inspector of Mines Office, 89 State House.

Indiana State Inspector of Oils Office, 92 State House.

Indiana State Law Library, John C McNutt librarian, room 64 State House.

Indiana State Library, 47 State House.

INDIANA STATE JOURNAL THE (Republican, Weekly), The Indianapolis Journal Newspaper Co Publishers, n e cor Monument Pl and Market, Tel 238; Editorial Rooms Tel 86.

INDIANA STATE SENTINEL (Democratic, Weekly), The Indianapolis Sentinel Co Publishers, 21 and 23 N Illinois, Tels, Office 164; Editorial Rooms 69.

Indiana State Soldiers' and Sailors' Monument Regents, 93 State House.

Indiana Tract Society, John W Moore sec, 175 Central av.

Indiana Tribune (German), Philip Rappaport editor, 18 S Alabama.

INDIANA TRUST CO THE, John P Frenzel Pres, Frederick Fahnley 1st Vice-Pres, E G Cornelius 2d Vice-Pres, John A Butler Sec, Christian Brink Trust Officer, John G Prinz Mngr Insurance Dept, P S Cornelius Mngr Safety Vault Dept, Mrs Mary McKenzie Mngr Woman's Dept Safety Vault, Indiana Trust Bldg, s e cor Washington and Virginia av, Long Distance Tel 36. (See adv front cover and opp.)

INDIANA UNDERWRITERS' INSURANCE CO, Wm C Hall Pres, M V McGilliard Sec, Medford B Wilson Treas, The McGilliard Agency Co Genl Agts, 83-85 E Market, Tel 479. (See backbone.)

THOS. C. DAY & CO.
Financial Agents and Loans.
We have the experience, and claim to be reliable.
Rooms 325 to 330 Lemcke Bldg.

INDIANA VETERINARY COLLEGE, Louis A Greiner, V S, Sec, 18-24 S East, (See adv in classified Veterinary Surgeons.)

INDIANA WALL PAPER CO (Hervey E Paramore, Marcus G Adkins), Wall Paper, 82-84 Virginia av.

Indiana Warp Mills, Brower and Love Bros props, e bank White river n of National rd.

INDIANA WIRE WORKS, Lewis C Walter Propr, 70½ W Court, Tel 696.

INDIANA WOMAN THE, Earl E Stafford Publisher, 49½ N Illinois.

Indiana & Chicago Coal Co, John McFadyen pres, Wm J Gillespie sec and treas, 8 Fair blk.

INDIANAPOLIS ABATTOIR CO, Joseph Allerdice Pres, Wm G Axt Sec, Wm A Mooney Treas, Works cor Morris and White River (W I), Tel 96.

Indianapolis Academy for Boys, 498 N Penn.

Indianapolis Bar Association Library, 57 Court House.

Indianapolis Baseball Club, 13 When blk.

Indianapolis Basket Co, Isaac Springer pres, Frank M Talbott vice-pres, 482 E New York.

Indianapolis Bill Posting Co, Alexander Harbison mngr, 61½ N Penn.

Indianapolis Bleaching Co, Stephen A Bemis pres, Hugh M Love vice-pres, John R Love sec and treas, e bank of White river n of National rd.

INDIANAPOLIS BOARD OF TRADE THE, Justus C Adams Pres, H E Kinney Vice-Pres, John Osterman Treas, Jacob W Smith Sec, Hugh S Byrkit Asst Sec, Office 38 Board of Trade Bldg, Tel 340.

INDIANAPOLIS BOLT AND MACHINE WORKS, Parkhurst Bros & Co Proprs, 122-128 Kentucky av and 177-201 W Georgia, Tel 306. (See adv in classified Elevator Mnfrs.)

EAT
QUAKER BREAD
ASK YOUR GROCER FOR IT.
THE HITZ BAKING CO.

CARPETS AND RUGS RENOVATED.......... | CAPITAL STEAM CARPET CLEANING WORKS M. D. PLUNKETT, TELEPHONE No. 818

BENJ. BOOTH PRACTICAL EXPERT ACCOUNTANT. Complicated or disputed accounts investigated and adjusted. Room 18, 82½ E. Wash. St., Ind'p'l's, Ind.

18 and 20 South Meridian Street KERSHNER BROS., Proprs. THE SHERMAN RESTAURANT

ESTABLISHED 1876. TELEPHONE 168.
CHESTER BRADFORD,
SOLICITOR OF PATENTS,
AND COUNSEL IN PATENT CAUSES.
(See adv. page 6.)
Office:—Rooms 14 and 16 Hubbard Block, S.W. Cor. Washington and Meridian Streets, INDIANAPOLIS, INDIANA.

INDIANAPOLIS BOOK AND STATIONERY CO THE, Richard H Barnes Pres, August F Herzsch Vice-Pres, Wm M Cronyn Treas, James H Wilson Sec, Wholesale Booksellers and Stationers, 75 S Meridian, Tel 978.

INDIANAPOLIS BOX FACTORY. See The Fred Dietz Co.

INDIANAPOLIS BREWING CO (Capital $300,000), Comprising the C F Schmidt, C Maus and P Lieber Breweries, Albert Lieber Pres and Genl Mngr, John P Frenzel Sec, Otto N Frenzel Treas, Office 25 High, Tel 432.

Indianapolis Brush Electric Light and Power Co. See Indianapolis Light and Power Co.

Indianapolis Brush Mnfg Co, rear 736 W Washington.

Indianapolis Buggy Top Co (Anthony and Joseph A Marshall), 119 N Alabama.

Indianapolis Building and Loan Assn, Wm A Rhodes sec. 72 E Market.

Indianapolis Bulletin The, T G Harrison pub, 84 E Court.

INDIANAPOLIS BUREAU OF INQUIRY AND INVESTIGATION, Thomas E Halls Genl Mngr, Jesse R Moores Chief Inspector, Rooms 68-69 Ingalls Blk. (See adv under classified Detective Agencies.)

INDIANAPOLIS BUSINESS COLLEGE, Consolidated Indianapolis Business University, When Bldg, N Penn, E J Heeb Propr, Tel 499. (See front cover, right bottom lines and p 4.)

INDIANAPOLIS BUSINESS UNIVERSITY, When Bldg, N Penn (Bryant & Stratton and Indianapolis Business Colleges, Consolidated 1885), E J Heeb Propr, Tel 499. (See front cover, right bottom lines and p 4.)

Matal Ceilings and all kinds of Copper, Tin and Sheet Iron work.
O. B. ENSEY,
TELEPHONE 1562.
CORNER 6TH AND ILLINOIS STS.

Indianapolis Cabinet Works, John T Dickson pres, Charles Krauss sec, Henry Rauh treas, desk mnfrs, cor Malott and Columbia avs.

INDIANAPOLIS CABINETMAKERS' UNION, Henry Bauer Pres, Gustav G Stark Sec, George A Albrecht Treas, Henry H Tapking Supt, John Heitkam Asst Supt, Wm C Reger Foreman, n w cor Market and Pine.

INDIANAPOLIS CALCIUM LIGHT CO, James L Bishop Mngr, Mnfrs and Dealers in Calcium Light Supplies, Rear 126 W Maryland and 127 W Pearl.

Indianapolis Caledonian Quoiting Club, 36½ W Washington.

INDIANAPOLIS CHAIN AND STAMPING CO, Charles E Test Pres, Edward C Fletcher Sec, Arthur C Newby Treas, s e cor Senate av and Georgia, Tel 653.

Indianapolis Chair Manufacturing Co, Edward G Cornelius pres, Norman S Byram vice-pres, Frank E Helwig supt, n w cor New York and Ellsworth.

Indianapolis Chemical Co, Emil A Martin pres, 543 Madison av.

INDIANAPOLIS CITY DIRECTORY, R L Polk & Co Publishers, Rooms 23-24 Journal Bldg; Directories of All States and Principal Cities on File for Reference. (See adv back fly leaf.)

Indianapolis Church Furniture Co, Wm B Fells propr, s e cor Shelby and Martin.

INDIANAPOLIS CLEARING HOUSE ASSOCIATION, Frederick Baggs Mngr, S Fletcher's Bank Bldg, Tel 264.

INDIANAPOLIS COAL AND FEED CO, Coal and Feed, cor Kentucky av and Merrill.

INDIANAPOLIS COFFIN CO THE, Carl Von Hake Pres, Franklin Vonnegut Vice-Pres, Clemens Vonnegut Jr Sec and Treas, 188 E Washington, Tel 777.

Indianapolis College of Music, James M Dungan mngr, n w cor Monument pl and Market.

INDIANAPOLIS CREAMERY, Joseph F Flack Propr, Daniel W Jackson Mngr, 52 Mass av, Tel 1532.

Indianapolis Cycle Club, James Comstock sec, 84 N Delaware.

Indianapolis Daily Live Stock Journal, Indianapolis Live Stock Journal and Printing Co proprs, Union Stock Yards (W I).

Indianapolis Desiccating Co, Frederick M Bachman pres, August Elbrecht sec and treas, s e cor Madison av and Lincoln la.

INDIANAPOLIS DESK FILE AND PAPER BOX MANUFACTORY, Frank F McCrea Propr, 143½-145 S Meridian, Tel 1327.

INDIANAPOLIS DISTRICT TELEGRAPH CO THE, Charles C Hatfield Pres, Thomas Taggart Sec, Jacob E Bombarger Mngr, 15 S Meridian, Tel 123. (See adv in classified Electrical Supplies.)

Indianapolis Drop Forging Co, Frank P Bates pres, Otto Stechhan sec and treas, s w cor Hanway and Madison av.

TUTEWILER UNDERTAKER, NO. 72 WEST MARKET STREET. TELEPHONE 216.

Indianapolis Collecting

. . . . AND . . . .

Reporting Agency

39-40 JOURNAL BUILDING.

WE CHARGE NO MEMBERSHIP FEE

Having an attorney in every county seat in the State of Indiana, we are especially prepared to handle claims and to make adjustments and settlements promptly and without delay.

SMALL COMMISSION ON MONEY COLLECTED.

We refer to the following:

Parry Manufacturing Co.
Van Camp Packing Co.
D. M. Parry.
Merchant's National Bank.
P. H. Fitzgerald, Etc.

Local Attorneys

FITZGERALD & RUCKELSHAUS

39-40 Journal Building.

itol av and 11th, tel 1132.

INDIANAPOLIS HOMINY MILLS, Hervey Bates Pres, Hervey Bates Jr Sec and Treas, Hominy Mnfrs, cor Madison av and Palmer, Tel 50.

INDIANAPOLIS INFIRMARY, Quincy Van Hummell, M D, Medical Director, 60 Monument Pl, Tel 1434. (See adv in classified Surgical Institutes.)

Manufacturers of

STEAMBOAT COLORS

BEST HOUSE PAINTS MADE.

Wholesale and Retail.

34 AND 36 SOUTH MERIDIAN STREET.

OOFER

Electric Contractors

We are prepared to do any kind of Electric Contract Work.
C. W. MEIKEL, Telephone 466.
96-98 E. New York St.

BENJ. BOOTH PRACTICAL EXPERT ACCOUNTANT. Complicated or disputed accounts investigated and adjusted. Room 18, 82½ E. Wash. St., Ind'p'l's, Ind.

120 South Meridian Street
KERSHNER BROS., Proprs.

ESTABLISHED 1876. TELEPHONE 168.
CHESTER BRADFORD,
SOLICITOR OF PATENTS,
AND COUNSEL IN PATENT CAUSES.
(See adv. page 6.)
Office:—Rooms 14 and 16 Hubbard Block, S.W. Cor. Washington and Meridian Streets,
INDIANAPOLIS, INDIANA.

Indianapolis Cabinet Works, John T Dickson pres, Charles Krauss sec, Henry Rauh treas, desk mnfrs, cor Malott and Columbia avs.

INDIANAPOLIS CABINETMAKERS' UNION, Henry Bauer Pres, Gustav G Stark Sec, George A Albrecht Treas, Henry H Tapking Supt, John Heitkam Asst Supt, Wm C Reger Foreman, n w cor Market and Pine.

INDIANAPOLIS CALCIUM LIGHT CO, James L Bishop Mngr, Mnfrs and Dealers in Calcium Light Supplies,

Tel 1327.

INDIANAPOLIS DISTRICT TELEGRAPH CO THE, Charles C Hatfield Pres, Thomas Taggart Sec, Jacob E Bombarger Mngr, 15 S Meridian, Tel 123. (See adv in classified Electrical Supplies.)

Indianapolis Drop Forging Co, Frank P Bates pres, Otto Stechhan sec and treas, s w cor Hanway and Madison av.

THE S

Tin and Sheet Iron Work.
O. B. ENSEY,
TELEPHONE 1562.
CORNER 6TH AND ILLINOIS STS.

TUTEWILER UNDERTAKER, NO. 72 WEST MARKET STREET. TELEPHONE 216.

The Provident Life and Trust Co. Dividends are paid in cash and are not withheld for a long period of years, subject to forfeiture in the event of death or the termination of policy.
D. W. EDWARDS, GENERAL AGENT, 508 INDIANA TRUST BUILDING.

INDIANAPOLIS DRUG CO (J George Mueller, Herman Pink, John R Miller), Wholesale Druggists, 21-25 E Maryland, Tel 1315.

INDIANAPOLIS ELECTROTYPE FOUNDRY, George F Reeves pres, George L Davis Vice-Pres, Albert W Marshall Treas, David G Wiley Sec, 17-25 W Georgia, Tel 474.

Indianapolis Elevator Co, James H Baldwin pres, George S Warren sec, John C Wright treas, 11 Board of Trade bldg.

INDIANAPOLIS ELEVATOR AND MILLWRIGHT SHOP, C D Hoffman & Co Proprs, 29 Kentucky av. (See adv in classified Elevators.)

INDIANAPOLIS ENGINE CO, Lewis M Howe Pres, Edward A Sheldon Vice-Pres, Edward S Gaylord Treas, Florence A Howe Sec, Pump and Engine Mnfrs, n e cor Bloyd and Hillside avs, Tel 1257.

INDIANAPOLIS FANCY GROCERY CO, Henry S Rominger Pres, Samuel Denny Vice-Pres, Charles S Fishel Sec, John C Smith Treas, 60 S Penn, Tel 1146.

INDIANAPOLIS FENCE CO, Henry G Byram Mngr, 15 Thorpe Blk.

INDIANAPOLIS FIRE INSPECTION BUREAU, Thornton M Goodloe Mngr, 18-20 Journal Bldg, Tel 1225.

INDIANAPOLIS FOUNDRY CO, Frank W Lewis Pres, James I Dissette Sec and Treas, Mnfrs of Heavy and Light Castings, Judge Harding s of Washington, Tel 856.

INDIANAPOLIS GAS CO THE, Charles F Dieterich Pres, John R Pearson Asst to Pres, E C Benedict Vice-Pres, Samuel D Pray Sec, Arthur B Proal Treas, James Somerville Supt, Artificial Gas, Genl Offices Majestic Bldg, n e cor Penn and Maryland, Tels 82 and 678.

INDIANAPOLIS GERMAN MUTUAL FIRE INSURANCE CO, Frank A Maus Pres, Gottlob C Krug Vice-Pres, Albert H Krull Treas, Charlotte Dinkelaker Sec, Room 7, 156½ E Washington, Tel 1038.

Indianapolis, Greenwood & Franklin Railroad, John A Polk pres, Henry L Smith genl mngr, 731 Lemcke bldg.

INDIANAPOLIS HARNESS CO (John M Dalrymple, Edwin A Hendrickson), Wholesale Mnfrs of Harness, Saddlery and Collars, 10-16 McCrea and 38 E South, Tel 1397.

Indianapolis Home for Friendless Women, Gertrude T Marquess matron, s e cor Capitol av and 11th, tel 1132.

INDIANAPOLIS HOMINY MILLS, Hervey Bates Pres, Hervey Bates Jr Sec and Treas, Hominy Mnfrs, cor Madison av and Palmer, Tel 50.

INDIANAPOLIS INFIRMARY, Quincy Van Hummell, M D, Medical Director, 60 Monument Pl, Tel 1434. (See adv in classified Surgical Institutes.)

THE
WHEN
IS A WORLD BEATER.

INDIANAPOLIS JOURNAL NEWSPAPER CO THE, John C New Pres, Harry S New Vice-Pres, George C Hitt Sec, Treas and Business Mngr, Publishers The Indianapolis Journal (Daily and Sunday) and Indiana State Journal (Weekly), n e cor Monument Pl and Market, Tel 238; Editorial Rooms Tel 86.

INDIANAPOLIS JOURNAL THE (Daily and Sunday), The Indianapolis Journal Newspaper Co Publishers, n e cor Monument Pl and Market, Tel 238; Editorial Rooms Tel 86.

INDIANAPOLIS LEAF TOBACCO CO, Albert G Rice Mngr, 71 E Court.

INDIANAPOLIS LIGHT AND POWER CO, Daniel W Marmon Pres, John Caven Vice-Pres, Charles C Perry Sec and Treas, Thomas A Wynne Supt, 24 Monument Pl, Tel 477.

INDIANAPOLIS LITHOGRAPHIC CO, Frederick A Heuss Propr, Checks, Drafts, Letter and Bill Heads, Cards, Invitations, Labels, Plats, Etc, 95 E South.

INDIANAPOLIS LIVE STOCK JOURNAL AND PRINTING CO, Charles A Uhl Pres, Wm A Cowan Vice-Pres, Martin Mann Sec, Proprs Indianapolis Daily Live Stock Journal, Union Stock Yards (W I).

Indianapolis Lounge Co, James W Hess pres, James A Hamilton sec and treas, cor Hanway and J M & I R R.

INDIANAPOLIS MALLEABLE IRON WORKS. See National Malleable Castings Co.

INDIANAPOLIS MANUFACTURERS' AND CARPENTERS' UNION, Valentine Schaaf Pres and Supt, Frederick Schmid Sec and Treas, Planing Mill and Mnfrs of Sash, Doors and Blinds; also Dealers in Hardwood and Pine Lumber, 38-42 S New Jersey, Tel 590. (See adv p 2.)

The A. Burdsal Co.
Manufacturers of
STEAMBOAT COLORS
BEST HOUSE PAINTS MADE.
Wholesale and Retail.
34 AND 36 SOUTH MERIDIAN STREET.

THEODORE F. SMITHER ROOFER
GRAVEL AND OTHER COMPOSITION
Yard, 19 W. Maryland St. Telephone 86
Off 15 W. Maryland St.

Electric Contractors We are prepared to do any kind of Electric Contract Work.
C. W. MEIKEL. Telephone 466.
96-98 E. New York St.

DALTON & MERRIFIELD { LUMBER South Noble St., near E. Washington

INDIANA ELECTROTYPE CO. : BEST WORK LOWEST PRICES. 23 WEST PEARL ST., INDIANAPOLIS, IND. JOB WORK. BOOK PLATES. All Orders Promptly Filled. BEST PATENT BASE ON THE MARKET.

KIRKHOFF BROS.,
Sanitary Plumbers
STEAM AND HOT WATER HEATING.
102-104 SOUTH PENNSYLVANIA ST.
TELEPHONE 910.

Indianapolis Manufacturing Co The, James A Landers pres, Edward Kettenbach sec, Charles F Piel treas, baby carriage mnfrs, s w cor Madison av and Ray.

INDIANAPOLIS MEDICAL AND SURGICAL INSTITUTE, Quincy Van Hummell, M D, Pres, 60 Monument Pl, Tel 1434. (See adv in classified Surgical Institutes.)

INDIANAPOLIS MILLINERY CO THE, J C Norris Pres, Bert Essex Vice-Pres, W B Judah Sec, James L D Chandler Treas and Mngr, 15, 17 and 19 McCrea, Tel 387.

Indianapolis Military Band, Joseph Cameron leader, 72 E Court.

INDIANAPOLIS MORTGAGE LOAN CO, Frank P Archer Mngr, 10 Thorpe Blk, 87 E Market.

INDIANAPOLIS NATIONAL BANK, Edward Hawkins Receiver, Rooms 607-609 Indiana Trust Bldg, Tel 35.

INDIANAPOLIS NEWS CO THE (Wm J Richards, Charles R Williams), Proprs The Indianapolis News, News Bldg, 32 W Washington, Tel 161; Mechanical and Editorial Depts in rear on W Court, Tel 673.

INDIANAPOLIS NEWS THE (Daily Except Sunday), The Indianapolis News Co Proprs, Charles R Williams Editor, Tel 673, Wm J Richards Mngr, Tel 161, News Bldg, 32 W Washington; Mechanical and Editorial Depts in rear on W Court.

Indianapolis Orphan Asylum, n e cor College and Home avs.

Indianapolis Packing and Rendering Co, Michael Sells pres, Wm P Ijams treas, Harry D Lane, sec, Union Stock Yards (W I).

INDIANAPOLIS PAINT AND COLOR CO, Leonard S Sargent Pres, Wm H Baumgartner Vice-Pres, Edward J Mahoney Sec, Paint Mnfrs, 40, 42, 44, 46 and 48 Mass av, Tel 1770. (See adv in classified Paints and Oils.)

Lime, Lath, Cement,
THE W. G. WASSON CO.
130 INDIANA AVE. TEL. 989.
Sewer Pipe, Flue Linings, Fire Brick, Fire Clay.

INDIANAPOLIS PASSENGER ASSOCIATION, John S Lazarus Chairman, Robison M Case Sec, s w cor Washington and Noble, Tel 1472.

INDIANAPOLIS PATTERN WORKS, Scullin & Myers Proprs, Models and Experimental Work, 101 S Penn.

Indianapolis Pickling and Preserving Co, Faulkner & Webb proprs, 200 S Penn.

Indianapolis Planing Mill Co, Diedrick Mussmann pres and treas, Karl Haupt sec, s w cor Meridian and Wilkins.

INDIANAPOLIS PLUMBING CO, Wm F Koepper Propr, 9 Mass av, Tel 1321.

INDIANAPOLIS PRINTING CO, P J Kelley Mngr, 37-39 Virginia av, Tel 1220.

Indianapolis Propylaeum Association, Mrs May Wright Sewall pres, Mrs Elizabeth V Pierce treas, 25 E North.

INDIANAPOLIS PUBLIC LIBRARY, Eliza G Browning Librarian and Sec, s w cor Meridian and Ohio, Branch 528 S Meridian.

INDIANAPOLIS PULLEY MNFG CO (Frank Hoffman, Wm C Spiegel), Mnfrs Wood Split Pulleys, 372-374 E Michigan, Tel 1626. (See adv in classified Pulley Mnfrs.)

INDIANAPOLIS RUBBER CO. John Ed Smith Pres, Harold O Smith Sec and Treas, 301-309 E Georgia, Tel 1482.

INDIANAPOLIS SAVINGS AND INVESTMENT CO, Aquilla Q Jones Pres, Joseph T Elliott Vice-Pres, Wm F Churchman Treas, George L Raschig Sec, 36 Monument Pl.

INDIANAPOLIS SENTINEL CO THE, Samuel E Morss Pres, Bart McCarthy Sec and Treas, Publishers and Proprs The Indianapolis Sentinel (Daily and Sunday), and Indiana State Sentinel (Weekly), 21-23 N Illinois, Tels Office 164, Editorial Rooms 69.

INDIANAPOLIS SENTINEL THE (Daily), The Indianapolis Sentinel Co Publishers and Proprs, 21-23 N Illinois, Tels Office 164, Editorial Rooms 69.

INDIANAPOLIS STEEL ROOFING AND CORRUGATING WORKS, Sylvester D Noel Propr, Office and Factory 23-25 E South, Tel 832. (See right side lines.)

INDIANAPOLIS STORAGE AND TRANSFER COMPANY, M Seyfried Sec and Mngr, Registered Public Warehouses 370-372 S Delaware, Tel 1049. (See adv back cover.)

INDIANAPOLIS STOVE CO THE, Henry W Bennett Pres, Wm J Brown Vice-Pres, Wm H Bennett Sec and Treas, Mnfrs of Stoves and Ranges, 71-73 S Meridian, Tel 455; Foundry 20 Sharpe, Tel 1445.

Indianapolis Street Cleaning Co, Robert W Furnas pres, Jesse Kellum sec, John H Furnas mngr, 112 N Penn.

INDIANAPOLIS SUSPENDER CO (Jedidiah W Burns, Mary B Graham), Mnfrs of Fine Suspenders, Shoulder Braces, Hose Suspenders and Arm Bands, 144-150 S Meridian.

YOUR HOMES FURNISHED BY W. H. MESSENGER 101 East Washington St. Telephone 491.

McNamara, Koster & Co. Phone 1593. ◆ 212-218 S. PENN. ST. PATTERN MAKERS

Indianapolis Switch and Frog Co, Elias Jacoby pres, 37 Ingalls blk.

INDIANAPOLIS TENT AND AWNING CO, Ed Rosenberg Mngr, 20 S Alabama, Tel 1122.

Indianapolis Terra Cotta Co, Benjamin D Walcott pres and treas, Wm F Stilz vice-pres, Joseph Joiner sec, s e cor Bloyd av and Shade (B).

Indianapolis Tobacco Works, Wm D Beeson pres, Anselm Hobbs sec and treas, tobacco mnfrs, 35 S Alabama.

INDIANAPOLIS TOOL AND MANUFACTURING CO (James A McCrossan, Frederick J Goepper), Special Tools and Machinery and Bicycle Specialties, 15-17 McNabb, opp Union Station.

INDIANAPOLIS TRADE JOURNAL THE, Wm H Robson Publisher, Rooms 35-36 Commercial Club Bldg, Tel 1284.

INDIANAPOLIS UNION RAILWAY CO, James McCrea Pres, E F Osborn Vice-Pres, Wm N Jackson Sec, Wm T Cannon Treas and Purchasing Agt, Charles A Vinnedge Auditor, Alonzo A Zion Supt, Genl Offices Union Station, Tel 314.

INDIANAPOLIS VARNISH CO, John Ebner Pres, Emil Ebner Vice-Pres, Bertha E Ebner Sec and Treas, Mnfrs Fine Varnishes and Japans, s e cor Ohio and Pine, Tel 567.

INDIANAPOLIS VETERINARY INFIRMARY, Louis A Greiner, V S, Propr, 18-24 S East, Tel 905. (See adv in classified Veterinary Surgeons.)

Indianapolis Warehouse Co, Wm E Kurtz pres, Frederick V Chislett vice-pres and treas, Harry A Crossland sec, 265 S Penn.

INDIANAPOLIS WATER CO, Thomas A Morris Pres, Frederick A W Davis Vice-Pres and Treas, Milton A Morris Sec, 75 Monument Pl, Tel 510.

Indianapolis Women's Club, The Propylaeum, 25 W North.

Indianapolis World, A E Manning pub, 38½ S Illinois.

Indianapolis Wrench and Stamping Co, H E Reeves sec and treas, 96 S Delaware.

INDIANAPOLIS AND BROAD RIPPLE RAPID TRANSIT CO, Robert C Light Pres and Genl Mngr, 1-2 Lombard Bldg, Tel 1657.

Industrial Alliance B and L Assn, Granville M Ballard pres, James M Heller sec, 35 Baldwin blk.

INDUSTRIAL LIFE ASSOCIATION OF INDIANAPOLIS, IND, John O Cooper Pres, James W Morris Sec and Treas, John O Copeland Genl Supt, Rooms 1, 2 and 3 Hartford Blk, 84 E Market.

Industrial Training School, n e cor Meridian and Merrill.

Ingalls Frances (wid C Perry), dressmkr, 519 N Alabama, h same.

Ingalls Land Co, Arthur B Grover pres, John G Thurtle sec, 436 Lemcke bldg.

Ingalls Lime Co, Arthur B Grover mngr, 436 Lemcke bldg.

Ingalls Perry C, clk, h 517 N Alabama.

Henry H. Fay,
40½ E. WASHINGTON ST.,
FIRE INSURANCE, REAL ESTATE,
LOANS AND RENTAL AGENT.

Ingersoll Albert E (Pierce & Ingersoll), h n w cor Garfield av and Washington.

Ingersoll Arnold S, driver, h 200 N Capitol av.

Ingersoll Edward R, city ticket agt C H & D R R, b 521 N New Jersey.

Ingersoll Harrison P, clk, h 1112 N Senate av.

Ingersoll Helen, teacher, b 1155 N Penn.

Ingersoll Henrie, teacher Industrial School, h 114 Fletcher av.

Ingersoll Isabel (wid Franklin B), h 1155 N Penn.

Ingersoll Jessie, teacher Public School No 36, b 1155 N Penn.

Ingersoll Mary H, teacher Public School No 12, h 114 Fletcher av.

Ingersoll M Selma, teacher Public School No 3, h 114 Fletcher av.

Inglam Albert, lab, h 150 Harlan.

Ingle Hattie C, bookbinder, h 305 N Senate av.

Ingle Tobias, watchman, h 101 Malott av.

Inglis Alexander, mach, h 10 Lexington av.

Ingold Adelaide J, mngr, b 333 N Illinois.

Ingraham Charles B, h 265 N Capitol av.

Ingraham Ellen M, artist, 265 N Capitol av, h same.

Ingram Catherine A (wid Wm), h 54 Vine.

Ingram Eli S, cooper, h 47 Deloss.

Ingram Harry S, filer, h 97 Deloss.

Ingram Isaac K, lab, h 768 E 10th.

Ingram James F, lab, h 260 Columbia av.

INGRAM JOHN C, Special Agt Liverpool and London and Globe Insurance Co, 345 Park av, h same.

Ingram Lewis, lab, h 48 Rhode Island.

Ingram Lytle E, carp, h 152 Bloyd av.

Ingram Martha (wid Thomas), h 105 Fountain av.

Ingram Pingston H, lab, h 237 Elizabeth.

Ingram Wm, lab, b rear 124 Broadway.

Ingram Willis H, clk, b 54 Vine.

Inhault Henry, lab, b 58 S Gale (B).

INLAND CHEMICAL CO (Edward H Schmidt), Pharmaceutical Specialties, 126-130 W Maryland.

SURETY BONDS
American Bonding & Trust Co.
OF BALTIMORE, MD.
Authorized to act as Sole Surety on all Bonds.
Total Resources over $1,000,000.00.
W. E. BARTON & CO., General Agents,
504 Indiana Trust Building.
Long Distance Telephone 1918.

THE FRED DIETZ CO. WOODEN PACKING BOXES MADE TO ORDER FACTORY AND WAREHOUSE TRUCKS. 400 Madison Avenue. Telephone 69.

Business World Supplied with Help
GRADUATES ASSISTED TO POSITIONS
10,000 NOW IN GOOD SITUATIONS. TEL. 499. E. J. HEEB, PRES.
Indianapolis BUSINESS UNIVERSITY

Steam Pumping Machinery { HENRY R. WORTHINGTON, 64 S. PENNSYLVANIA ST. Long Distance Telephone 284.

UNION CO-OPERATIVE LAUNDRY { (COMPOSED OF UNION LAUNDRY GIRLS.) NOS. 3, 40 AND 42 VIRGINIA AVENUE. T. E. SOMERVILLE, MANAGER — TELEPHONE 8. INDIANAPOLIS, IND.

HORACE M. HADLEY

Insurance, Real Estate, Loan and Rental Agent

66 EAST MARKET STREET,

Telephone 1540. Basement.

Inlow Charles, carp, b 21 Tuxedo.
Inlow James, b 11 Quince.
Inlow John W, clk The Wm H Block Co, h 99 College av.
Inlow Wm E, collr, b 21 Tuxedo.
Inman Catherine (wid Brazie), b 144 N Capitol av.
Inman Clifford L, ins agt, h 12 Sharpe.
Inman Edmund F, condr, h 98 Columbia av.
Inman Martha, h 15 Wood.
Inman Mary, h 311 W Pearl.
Inman Nelson G, horseshoer, h 45 Brookside av.
Inman Valentine H, fireman, b McKeehan Hotel.
Inman Wm, cooper, b 311 W Washington.
Inman Wm, plastr, h 306 Columbia av.
INTERIOR HARDWOOD CO THE, Charles Latham Pres, Charles H Comstock Vice-Pres and Mngr, Henry Latham Sec and Treas, 317 Mass av, Tel 576.
Internal Revenue Office, see United States Deputy Revenue Office.
INTERNATIONAL BUILDING AND LOAN ASSOCIATION, James T Layman Pres, Charles Schurmann Sec, Norman S Byram Treas, 83 E Market, Tel 1683.
International Typographical Union, Wm B Prescott pres, J W Bramwood sec and treas, 29½ E Market.
INTERSTATE ART GLASS CO, Henry W Rudolf Genl Mngr, Designers and Mnfrs of Ornamental Glass and Mirrors, 77-81 N Delaware.
Interstate and Indiana Official Railway Guide, Journal Job Printing Co pub, 126 W Maryland.
Inter-Synod The, Union Pub Co proprs, 36 When bldg.
INVESTOR PRINTING AND PUBLISHING CO, Jay E Cowgill Mngr, 537 Lemcke Bldg.
Ioor Charles J, shoes, 162 W Washington, h 283 S East.

Special Detailed Reports Promptly Furnished by Us.

MERCHANTS' AND MANUFACTURERS' EXCHANGE

J. E. TAKKEN, Manager,

19 Union Building, 73 West Maryland Street.

Ireland Edgar L, harnessmkr, h 377 English av.
Ireland Henry J, lab, h rear 186 Howard.
Ireland John T, cashr, b 111 E Washington.
Ireland May, clairvoyant, h 377 English av.
Ireland Wm H, fireman, b 162 Harrison.
Irey Volney K, engr, h Golden Hill.
Irick Ella (wid John W), b 350 N West.
Irick Etta, stenog C C C & St L Ry, b 425 Central av.
Irick George W, phys, 40½ Kentucky av, h 645 S Meridian.
Irick Harry B, mach hd, h 30 Water.
Irick Julia A (wid Wm H), b 425 Central av.
Irick Wm C, bricklyr, h 425 Central av.
Irie Matthew (Kerr & Irie), r 6 Franklin Life Ins bldg.
Irish Charles, lab, h 25 Hendricks.
Irish Charles L, lab, h 38 Gatling.
Irish David, tmstr, h 261 Shelby.
Irish Frank M, lab, h 38 Gatling.
Irish John H, lab, h 52 Gatling.
Irish John R, carp, h 40 Gatling.
Irish Richard W, lab, h 39 Wallack.
Irish Samuel F, patrolman, h 169 Olive.
Irmer Ernst, trav agt Indpls Brewing Co, h 321 E Michigan.
Irmer Louisa M, stenog E Rauh & Sons, h 321 E Michigan.
Irons Ira J, lab, h 113 Sharpe av (W).
Irrgang Christian, lab, h 112 Brookland av.
Irrgang Roderick H, mach, h 444 S Delaware.
Irrgang Wm, bricklyr, h 93 W Morris.
Irvin Albert (Irvin & Adams), h 1158 N Penn.
Irvin Benjamin B, showman, h rear 549 W Washington.
Irvin Benjamin F, lab, h rear 549 W Washington.
Irvin Davis H, painter, h 154 Trowbridge (W).
Irvin Frank B, h 595 W Pearl.
Irvin George, lab, h 372 N New Jersey.
Irvin George W, lab, h 9 Henry.
Irvin Hamilton, grinder, b 611 W Michigan.
Irvin James D, b 301 River av (W I).
Irvin Jane (wid George), h 611 W Michigan.
Irvin John A, tel opr P C C & St L Ry, h 296 E Market.
Irvin Pelton B, student, b 38 N Reisner (W I).
Irvin Susan (wid Perry), b 516 W Shoemaker (N I).
Irvin Wasington C, agt, h 125 Susquehanna.
Irvin Wm, lawyer, 69 When bldg, h 902 Broadway.
IRVIN & ADAMS (Albert Irvin, Will H Adams), Undertakers, 97 N Illinois and 37 W Ohio, Tel 1154.
Irvine Hamilton P, grinder, b 611 W Michigan.
Irvine Jane (wid George), h 611 W Michigan.
Irving Avis (wid John), b 393 Central av.
Irving Benjamin, plastr, b rear 79 W North.
Irving Ellis L, trav agt, b 39 Morrison.
Irving Jacob R, trav agt, h 39 Morrison.
Irving James F, tmstr, h 109 Brookside av.
Irving Joseph L, baker, 503 College av, h same.
Irving Lewis L, trav agt J C Perry & Co, b 39 Morrison.
Irving Nelson, h 218 W Michigan.
Irving Thomas, lab, b 272 W Maryland.
Irwin Alice H (wid Joseph D), h 144 Bellefontaine.
Irwin Amory T, reporter The Sun, b 678 N Delaware.

CLEMENS VONNEGUT 184, 186 and 192 E. Washington St. | CABINET HARDWARE CARVERS' TOOLS. Glues of all kinds.

THE WM. H. BLOCK CO. DRY GOODS, MILLINERY, CLOAKS AND FURS.
7 AND 9 EAST WASHINGTON STREET.

Irwin Bernice J, stenog D H Baldwin & Co, b 144 Bellefontaine.
Irwin Charles, driver, h 172½ E Washington.
Irwin Charles M, engr, r 228 W New York.
Irwin Cyrus C, carp, h 452 W Francis (N I).
Irwin Edward L, marble polisher August Diener, b George's Hotel.
Irwin Helen M, teacher Public School No 12, h 393 Bellefontaine.
Irwin Hugh C, clk, h 393 Bellefontaine.
Irwin John D, b 144 Bellefontaine.
Irwin Joseph M, printer, b 144 Bellefontaine.
Irwin Margaret A, janitor, h 103 Eddy.
Irwin Oliver C, salesman George Hitz & Co, h 1067 N Illinois.
Irwin Ora J, b 20 S Judge Harding (W I).
Irwin Orfila C, electrician, h 2117 S Olive.
Irwin Ralph, student, b 154 Union.
Irwin Robert M, stenog, r 502 W Addison (N I).
Irwin Rollin C, printer, h 30 Hoyt av.
Irwin Sherman W, condr, h 585 E Washington.
Irwin Thomas H, foreman, b 255 N Liberty.
Isaacs George A, clk, b 126 Spring.
Isaacs Samuel, clk, h 127 Home av.
Isaacs James G, lab, r 180 Muskingum al.
Isack Philip, lab, h 663 Union.
Isemann Charles F, carp, h 61 Yeiser.
Isemann Henry, cabtmkr, h 213 Virginia av.
Isemann Mary C (wid Joseph), b 127 Wegħorst.
Isenflamm Edward, meats, 258 S Alabama, h same.
Isenhour Daniel V, lab, b 427 W Pratt.
Isensee Albert F W, locksmith, r 31 Commercial blk.
ISENSEE ALBERT T, Locksmith, Bellhanger and Safe Expert, 31 Monument Pl, h 37 W St Joseph. (See adv in classified Locksmiths and Safe Experts.)
Isensee Clara A, music teacher, 37 W St Joseph, b same.
Isensee John F Rev, h 228 N California.
Isensee Thirza O, music teacher, 228 N California, b same.
Isenthal Otto G, shoemkr, h 551 S West.
Isgrigg Alexander I, lumber, b 75 W 10th.
Isgrigg David M, bkkpr, h 1034 N Capitol av.
Isgrigg James A, lumber, n w cor Senate av and 5th, h 75 W 10th.
Isgrigg Jeremiah T, lab, h 33 Kansas.
Isgrigg John G, finisher, b 678 S Meridian.
Isgrigg Wm H, carp, h 678 S Meridian.
Isgrigg Wm H jr, molder, h 26 Cleveland (H).
Isherwood Claude H, clk, b 64 Marion av (W I).
Isherwood Mahlon W, meats, 54 Marion av, h 64 same.
Ishmaelite The, published by Mount Nebo Press, 36 Commercial Club bldg.
Ishmal Andrew, lab, h 458 W 2d.
Ishmal Frank, lab, b 458 W 2d.
Ishmal George, tmstr, h 121 Maxwell.
Ishmal Henry, lab, b 458 W 2d.
Iske Albert, clk, h 188 Buchanan.
ISKE BROS (Frank C, Charles F and George C), Furniture and Upholsterers, 105 E Washington, Tel 1223.
Iske Charles F (Iske Bros), h 74 Prospect.
Iske Christian J, b 487 Virginia av.
Iske Frank C (Iske Bros), h 174 Prospect.

HEADQUARTERS PHOTOGRAPHIC OUTFITS AMATEUR OR PROFESSIONAL. THE H. LIEBER COMPANY 33 S. MERIDIAN ST.

Iske Frederick C, books, 329 S New Jersey, h same.
Iske George C (Iske Bros), h 176 Prospect.
Iske Wm F, clk, h 485 Virginia av.
Island Coal Co, Alfred L Ogle pres, Willard W Hubbard sec, 5 Hartford blk.
Isleib Christian O, brewer, h 22 Deloss.
Isler Harmon, lab, h 761 Mass av.
Isom Robert, lab, r 167 Muskingum al.
Isphording Richard C, brass engraver, h 579 Shelby.
Israel Albert F, painter, h 177 S William (W I).
Israel James N, painter, 20 Douglass, h same.
Israel Wesley, porter, b 26 Roanoke.
Issler Silas, lab, h s s Colgrove 4 w of Mattie av.
Iten Frank, propr Philadelphia Dye House, 6 W Market, dyer, 21 Monument pl, h 430 Talbott av.
Itskin H Edward, paperhngr, b 188 W Pearl.
Ittenbach Frank (G Ittenbach & Co), h 152 Harrison.
Ittenbach Gerhard J, h 330 E South.
Ittenbach Gerhard J, bookbndr, h 57 Sanders.
Ittenbach Gerhard L (G Ittenbach & Co), h 631 E Washington.
ITTENBACH G & CO (Frank, John B and Gerhard L Ittenbach, Michael Schumacher), Steam Stone Works and Cut Stone Contractors, 150 Harrison, Tel 1065.
Ittenbach Helena (wid John), b 235 S Alabama.
Ittenbach John B (G Ittenbach & Co), sec Polar Ice Co, h 74 English av.
Ittenbach Mary A, boarding 235 S Alabama, b same.
Iula Frederick, cook, h 271 E Merrill.
Iuppenlatz Louis N, train disp I D & W Ry, b n e cor Washington and Colorado av.
Iuvoni Gaetano, music teacher, h 112 Clinton.
Iversen Christian, confr, 309 N West, h same.
Ivec Edward C, barber, r 18 Ryan blk.

GUIDO R. PRESSLER,
FRESCO PAINTER
Churches, Theaters, Public Buildings, Etc., A Specialty.
Residence, No. 325 North Liberty Street.
INDIANAPOLIS, IND.

INDIANAPOLIS STEEL ROOFING AND CORRUGATING WORKS, 23 and 25 East South Street. S. D. NOEL, Proprietor.

David S. McKernan REAL ESTATE AND LOANS
Houses, Lots, Farms and Western Lands for sale or trade.
ROOMS 2-5 THORPE BLOCK.

DIAMOND WALL PLASTER { Telephone 1410 BUILDERS' EXCHANGE.

Cor. E. Ohio St. and C., C., C. & St. L. R'y Tracks.
UNION TRANSFER AND STORAGE CO.
ISSUE NEGOTIABLE RECEIPTS ON MERCHANDISE AND HOUSEHOLD GOODS.

W. McWORKMAN,
ROOFING AND CORNICE WORKS,
930 W. Washington St. Tel. 1118.

Ivory Joseph, clk, b 56 Grant.
Ivory Peter, bartndr, b 56 Grant.
Ivory Thomas, lab, h 56 Grant.
Izor Albert (Izor Bros), pres Brown Straw Binder Co, h 275 N Pine.
Izor Benton H (Izor Bros), h 196 N California.
Izor Bros (Albert and Benton H), druggists, 259 W Washington.
Izor Frank S, horseshoer, 1 Susquehanna, h 448 Talbott av.
Izor Ira, ins, h 1142 N Penn.
Izzard Nelson, lab, h 846 S Meridian.

J

Jablonski Benno, h 82 N Liberty.
Jachman Gertrude, stenog, b 74 Sheffield av (H).
Jachman Robert H, paperhngr, h 74 Sheffield av (H).
Jachmann Augusta (wid Herman), notions, 131 E Mkt House, h 413 E Washington.
Jachmann Wm F, paperhngr, 413 E Washington, h same.
Jack George B, clk L E & W R R, r 28½ Mass av.
Jack Mary E, stenog The Interior Hardware Co, b 82 Bellefontaine.
Jackman James B, engr, h 36 McKim av.
Jackman Wm W, bricklyr, h n s Jackson 3 w of Lincoln av (M J).
Jacks Alva R, mason, h 249 Fletcher av.
Jacks Charles M, bricklyr, b 143 Tacoma av.
Jacks John, lab, r 289½ Mass av.
Jacks Mary L (wid Isaac N), h 48½ S Capitol av.
Jacks Richard F, mason, h 143 Tacoma av.
Jacks Rose C, dressmkr, 11 Paca, h same.
Jackson Albert, lab, h 61 Paw Paw.
Jackson Albert, waiter, r 40 W 1st.
Jackson Alexander, lab, b 207 W North.
Jackson Alexander A, lab, h 329 Clinton.
Jackson Alfred, lab, h 29 Bates al.
Jackson Allen, porter, h 232 Muskingum al.
Jackson Andrew, lab, h 772 E 10th.
Jackson Andrew, tmstr, h 276 W North.
Jackson Andrew, watchman, h 461 N Senate av.

GEO. J. MAYER,
MANUFACTURER OF
SEALS
STENCILS, RUBBER STAMPS, CHECKS, BADGES, DOOR PLATES, ETC.
15 S. Meridian St., Ground Floor. TEL. 1386.

Jackson Andrew M, lumber, 47½ N Illinois, h 699 N Capitol av.
Jackson Arthur, coachman 666 N Meridian.
Jackson Arthur W, cabtmkr, b 51 Stevens.
Jackson Belle, h 649½ Virginia av.
Jackson Belle V (wid John W), h 237 W 3d.
Jackson Benjamin F, h 279 Blake.
Jackson Benjamin F (B F Jackson & Co), b 36 Bellefontaine.
Jackson Benton H, condr, b 35 Garfield pl.
Jackson Bessie B, teacher, b 288 N Penn.
Jackson Bloom, lab, h 171 Alvord.
Jackson B F & Co (Benjamin F and Wm S Jackson), chemists, rear 71 Ash.
Jackson Celia (wid John), h 18 Church.
Jackson Charles, yardmaster, h 673 Madison av.
Jackson Charles, lab, b 333 S Meridian.
Jackson Charles, porter, h 254 W 3d.
Jackson Charles, turner, h 1018 E Washington.
Jackson Charles, waiter, r 113 Indiana av.
Jackson Charles A, lab, b 464 Chestnut.
Jackson Charles B, designer H C Bauer Engraving Co, b 57 N Dorman.
Jackson Charles C, lab, b n w cor Yandes and Davidge.
Jackson Charles H, lab, h 226 W Wabash.
Jackson Charles R, student, r 367 N Alabama.
Jackson Charles W, saloon, 338 Indiana av, h same.
Jackson Clarence, lab, h n w cor Bird and Allegheny.
Jackson Clinton M, condr, h 1399 N Illinois.
Jackson Cora B, teacher Public School No 23, b 48 Elizabeth.
Jackson Cyrus W, photog, h w s Oakland av 1 n of Clifford av.
Jackson Daniel W (E B & D W Jackson), mngr Indpls Creamery, h 52½ Mass av.
Jackson David, lab, h 129 Rhode Island.
Jackson David M, brakeman, b 1092 E Washington.
Jackson Earl, clk, b 19 Cherry.
Jackson Eckert, miller, b 26 Iowa.
Jackson Edith M, stenog, b 84 E North.
Jackson Elgernon, student, r 239 N California.
Jackson Eli, lab, r 130 W Vermont.
Jackson Elijah T, waiter, r 90 Columbia al.
Jackson Elizabeth, b 446 W North.
Jackson Ellis B (E B & D W Jackson), h 169 Cornell av.
Jackson Emily J, stenog, b w s Illinois 2 n of 30th (M).
Jackson Enoch E, trav agt, h 94 Huron.
Jackson E B & D W (Ellis B and Daniel W), toilet goods, 2½ W Washington.
Jackson Frank, clk, h 809 LaSalle.
Jackson Frank, janitor, h 540 Superior.
Jackson Gaylord M, harnessmkr, h 19 Cherry.
Jackson George, porter, r 18½ Indiana av.
Jackson George, stable fastener mnfr, h w s Illinois 2 n of 30th (M).
Jackson George F, attendant Insane Asylum.
Jackson George W, h 317 W North.
Jackson George W, engr, h 34 N East.
Jackson Grace A, stenog A H Sturtevant, b 84 E North.
Jackson Harriet K (wid Luther M), h rear 179 N California.
Jackson Harry, lab, h 151 W 8th.
Jackson Harry E, dentist, h 332 Bellefontaine.

A. METZGER AGENCY ESTABLISHED 1863. REAL ESTATE

LAMBERT GAS & GASOLINE ENGINE CO.
ANDERSON, IND. GAS AND GASOLINE ENGINES, 2 TO 50 H. P.

Jackson Harry H, engr, h 69 Torbet.
Jackson Harry V, trav agt, h 448 Central av.
Jackson Henry, coachman 569 N Penn.
Jackson Henry, cook, r 12½ Indiana av.
Jackson Henry, lab, b 228 E St Clair.
Jackson Henry, waiter, h 95 Columbia al.
Jackson Herbert F, clk R M S, b 251 Virginia av.
Jackson Homer, clk C Friedgen, b 82 E North.
Jackson Horace F, trav agt Nichols & Shepard Co, h 105 Ft Wayne av.
Jackson Isabella V, h 194 W 2d.
Jackson James, clk, b 334 N Illinois.
Jackson James, collr W G Wasson Co, h 194 W Vermont.
Jackson James, express, h 265 Fayette.
Jackson James, flagman, h 2 Iowa.
Jackson James, lab, b 79 Elizabeth.
Jackson James, lab, b 765 E 10th.
Jackson James, lab, h 248 Fayette.
Jackson James A, contr, h 84 E North.
Jackson James F, packer, h 243 Douglass.
Jackson James H, artist, 382 College av, b same.
Jackson James H, lineman, h 180 W 3d.
Jackson James L, trav agt, h 73 Adams.
Jackson James M, mach, h 250 English av.
Jackson James R, lab, h 172 Bismarck av (H).
Jackson James W, coachman, h 44 Drake.
Jackson James W, engr, b 1035 W Washington.
Jackson Jason, condr, b 75 W 13th.
Jackson Jennie J (wid Benjamin F), h 107 Park av.
Jackson Jeremiah, student, b 228 W Vermont.
Jackson Jessie B, h 127 Columbia al.
Jackson John, lab, h 460 Dillon.
Jackson John, lab, r 325 E Wabash.
Jackson John, lab, h 56 Mayhew.
Jackson John, lab, b 90 Newman.
Jackson John C, condr, h 832 E 9th.
Jackson John F, waiter, b 269 N West.
Jackson John M, woodwkr, h 137 Oliver av (W I).
Jackson John N, trav agt, h 775 E Washington.
Jackson John R, foreman, h 55 Palmer.
Jackson John W, porter, h 514 Superior.
Jackson Jonathan B, cooper, h 56 Newman.
Jackson Joseph, cook, h 207 Middle.
Jackson Joseph D, mngr George J Marott, h 410 Bellefontaine.
Jackson Joseph W, lawyer, h 23 Park.
Jackson Judah (wid George), b 18 Roanoke.
Jackson J Clarence, civil engr, b 288 N Penn.
Jackson J Harry, printer, r 18½ Indiana av.
Jackson Lee, lab, b 390 N California.
Jackson Louisa (wid Moses), h n w cor Yandes and Davidge.
Jackson Louise L, Free Industrial School and pres Family Dress Guide Co, h 1875 E Washington.
Jackson Major, trav agt, b 243 Douglass.
Jackson Margaret (wid George), b 479 Lafayette.
Jackson Margaret E (wid George P), b 808 Park av.
Jackson Martha, dressmkr, 34 N East, h same.
Jackson Mary B (wid John T), h 747 N Illinois.
Jackson Mary E, h 215 Elm.
Jackson Mary O (wid David T), dressmkr, 395 S Capitol av, h same.

Farm and City Loans
25 Years' Successful Business.
THOS. C. DAY & CO,
Rooms 325 to 330 Lemcke Building.

Jackson Mason L, lab, h 312 Martindale av.
Jackson Matthew, lab, h rear 258 Alvord.
Jackson Matthew E, engr, h 51 Stevens.
Jackson Maud, grocer, 231 S Delaware, b same.
Jackson Mildred, h 226 Roanoke.
Jackson Milton E, lab, b 51 Stevens.
Jackson Napoleon B, lab, h 194 W Ray.
Jackson Nelson, cook, r 180 W Michigan.
Jackson Nelson H, condr, h 23 Temple av.
Jackson Newton, patrolman, h 231½ S Delaware.
Jackson Orren W, lab, h 478 N Brookside av.
Jackson Owen H, master mechanic, h 1035 W Washington.
Jackson Palmer, lab, h 230 E Wabash.
Jackson Perry, lab, h n w cor Reisner and Johnson (W I).
Jackson Richard, porter, b 446 W North.
Jackson Richard R, lawyer, b 21 Willard.
Jackson Robert, lab, b 546 Superior.
Jackson Rosa (wid Arthur), b 441½ Virginia av.
Jackson Russell, lab, b 358 Fulton.
Jackson Samuel, car insp, h 26 Iowa.
Jackson Samuel, lab, h 586 N Missouri.
Jackson Samuel M, agt National Wall Paper Co, 136 S Illinois, h 488 N Capitol av.
Jackson Silas, cook, r 374 N Missouri.
Jackson Sylvester C, electrotyper, b 478 N Brookside av.
Jackson Tanner, lab, b rear 70 Yandes.
Jackson Taylor, lab, b n w cor Yandes and Davidge.
Jackson Thomas, lab, b 18 Church.
Jackson Thomas B, clk, h 1507 N Meridian.
Jackson Thomas F, clk, h 809 LaSalle (M P).
Jackson Walter H, engr, b 327 S Delaware.
Jackson Wesley, janitor, h 59 The Chalfant.
Jackson Wm, lab, h 319 Columbia av.
Jackson Wm, b 58 Sheffield (W I).
Jackson Wm, lab, b 514 Superior.
Jackson Wm, scavenger, h 464 Chestnut.
Jackson Wm, supt, r 70 W Vermont.
Jackson Wm E, lab, b 19 Cherry.

EAT
HITZ'S
CRACKERS
AND CAKES.
ASK YOUR GROCER FOR THEM.

BICYCLES $5 DOWN. Best Wheels. Best Terms. WHEELMEN'S CO. 31 W. OHIO ST. LONG DISTANCE TEL. 855.

J. H. TECKENBROCK Painter and Decorator, 94 EAST SOUTH STREET.

FIDELITY MUTUAL LIFE—PHILADELPHIA, PA.
MATCHLESS SECURITY At LOW COST. } A. H. COLLINS { General Agent Baldwin Block.

Rooms 42 and 43 WHEN BUILDING.

Edwardsport Bl and Mining Co. Miners and Shippers Steam and Domestic Coal.

ESTABLISHED 1876. TELEPHONE 168.
CHESTER BRADFORD,
SOLICITOR OF PATENTS,
AND COUNSEL IN PATENT CAUSES.
(See adv. page 6.)
Office:—Rooms 14 and 16 Hubbard Block, S. W. Cor. Washington and Meridian Streets, INDIANAPOLIS, INDIANA.

Jackson Wm H, barber, 196 Prospect, h 373 Orange.
Jackson Wm H, clk County Auditor, r 128 W Vermont.
Jackson Wm H, janitor Public School No 18, h 569 E 7th.
Jackson Wm H, trimmer, r 183½ W Washington.
Jackson Wm J, salesman Lewis Meier & Co, r 272 N Senate av.
Jackson Wm M, lab, b 312 Martindale av.
Jackson Wm N, sec Indpls Union Ry Co, Union Station, h 210 N Meridian.
Jackson Wm R, waiter, h 358 Douglass.
Jackson Wm S (B F Jackson & Co), b 36 Bellefontaine.
Jackson Wm W, box clk P O, h 556 Jefferson av.
Jackson Winifred, stenog, b 288 N Penn.
Jacob Christian J, brewer, h 38 Sanders.
JACOB FRANK A (Jacob & Co), h 320 N Senate av. (See adv opp classified Pattern and Modelmakers.)
Jacob Michael A, carp, b 147 E Washington.
JACOB THEODORE P (Jacob & Co), b 320 N Senate av. (See adv opp classified Pattern and Modelmakers.)
Jacob Wm, lab, r 186½ W Washington.
JACOB & CO (Frank A and Theodore P Jacob), Pattern and Modelmakers, s w cor Georgia and Penn. (See adv opp classified Pattern and Modelmakers).
Jacobi, see also Jacoby.
Jacobi Anna (wid Frederick), b 471 S Delaware.
Jacobi August R (Jacobi & Maass), h 399 S Delaware.
Jacobi John P, cabtmkr, h 108 Columbia av.
Jacobi & Maass (August R Jacobi, George J Maass), grocers, 397 S Delaware.
Jacobs Abraham, saloon, 270 S Illinois, h same.
Jacobs Amanda S (wid Charles P), h 601 N Delaware.
Jacobs Bennett E, salesman The Geo D Campbell Co, b 563 E Market.

Outing BICYCLES
$85.00.
MADE AND SOLD BY
HAY & WILLITS MFG. CO.
76 N. PENNSYLVANIA ST. PHONE 598.

Jacobs Charles, barber, 188 Madison av, b same.
Jacobs Frank, lab, h 7 Lynn.
JACOBS FRANK F, Practical Horseshoer; Prompt Attention and Satisfaction Guaranteed; Horses Called for and Returned, 86 E St Clair, Tel 1216; h same. (See adv in classified Horseshoers.)
Jacobs Hannah E (wid David), h 104 Cherry.
Jacobs James, lab, b 128 N Liberty.
Jacobs James, lab, h 142 S Judge Harding (W I).
Jacobs James D, clk Lilly & Stalnaker, b 104 Cherry.
Jacobs James M, horsedealer, h 24 W Pratt.
Jacobs James R, insp, h n e cor 15th and Cornell av.
Jacobs James W, barber, b 188 Madison av.
Jacobs John, b 146 Church.
Jacobs John, h rear 186 Shelby.
Jacobs John, roofer, b 328 W Pearl.
Jacobs John jr, foreman L E & W R R, h 146 Church.
Jacobs John W, boxmkr, h 402 Madison av.
Jacobs John W, carp, h 378 N West.
Jacobs Martin A, horseshoer, b 84 E St Clair.
Jacobs Milton C, gasfitter, 118 N East, b same.
Jacobs Nancy A (wid Henry), h 256 Douglass.
Jacobs Parmenas C, livery, s e cor Washington and Lake avs (I), h w s Commercial av 6 s of Washington av (I).
Jacobs Piety, grocer, 76 Oliver av, h 14 Cornell av (W I).
Jacobs Todd, butcher, b 95 S William (W I).
Jacobs Wm, carp, h 63 Dunlop.
Jacobs Wm L, printer, h 1113 N Penn.
Jacobs Wm P, lab, b 330 E Georgia.
Jacobsen Charles P, trav agt, h 121 W 3d.
Jacobsen Hans J, porter, h 54 Bicking.
Jacobsen Niels J, florist, b n e cor Senate av and 27th.
Jacobson Sofus, lab, b w s Schurman 1 n of Vorster av (M P).
Jacoby, see also Jacobi.
Jacoby Edward T, wall paper, 27 Mass av, h 1207 E Washington.
Jacoby Elias, lawyer and pres Indpls Switch and Frog Co, 37 Ingalls blk, h 90 W Walnut.
Jacoby Sophia (wid David), b 1207 E Washington.
Jacoby Thomas E, clk, b 110 N Beville av.
Jacoby Wm A, steamfitter, h 534 N Wells (N I).
Jacquemin Joseph F, sec The W G Wasson Co, b 180 Union.
Jacquemin Odilia (wid Frank), h 180 Union.
Jaeger Alfred S, b 206 N Noble.
Jaeger Catherine (wid Charles), h 44 Iowa.
Jaeger Clara J, matron German Evangelical Lutheran Orphans' Home, h n e cor Washington and Watts.
Jaeger Emil, lab, b 44 Iowa.
Jaeger Joseph H, jeweler, h 20 King.
Jaeger Minnie I, music teacher, 20 King, h same.
Jaeger Wm C, supt German Evangelical Lutheran Orphans' Home, h n e cor Washington and Watts.
Jaehnke Bruno E, clk, b 646 S Meridian.
Jaehnke Edward, baker, 642 S Meridian, h 646 same.
Jaffe Aaron, bartndr, b 565 S Capitol av.

C. ZIMMERMAN & SONS | SLATE AND GRAVEL ROOFERS 19 South East Street.

DRIVEN WELLS And Second Water Wells and Pumps of all kinds at CHARLES KRAUSS', 42 S. PENN. ST. TELEPHONE 465.

Jaffe Berthold, optician, h 293 E New York.
Jaffe Louis, pdlr, h 531 S Capitol av.
Jaffe Isaac, meats, 221½ W Washington, h 262 W Pearl.
Jahn, see also John.
Jahn Charles F, teacher, r 389 S New Jersey.
Jaillet Adelaide C, music teacher, 222 Keystone av, h same.
Jaillet Arthur D F, teacher of languages, 222 Keystone av, h same.
Jaleski Albert C, mach, b 127 W 9th.
Jaleski Christina L (wid Carl), h 127 W 9th.
James Alice M (wid Frank), h 8 Elliott.
James Andrew, lab, h 400½ E Georgia.
James Annie (wid Thomas), boarding 39 N Alabama.
James Charles, condr, b 253 N Alabama.
James Charles L, vice-pres and supt Capitol Paving and Construction Co, 1 Hubbard blk, r 253 N Alabama.
James Charles S, city fireman, h 46 Johnson av.
James David J, engr, h 100 Nordyke av (W I).
James David L (James & McLain), h 537 E Ohio.
James Edgar M, foreman Standard Oil Co, h 74 Beaty.
James Edward E, engr, b 564 W Washington.
James Edward L, barber, r 188 N Missouri.
James Elijah, coachman 300 Park av.
James Harriet E (wid Elwood E), b 168 E North.
James Harry, bicycle rep, b 168 E North.
James Helen, housekpr s e cor Senate av and 29th.
James Henry H, bkkpr U S Wringer Co, b 227 E New York.
James House, 39 N Alabama.
James James P, fireman Indpls Water Co, h 13 Warren av (W I).
James Jessie A, stenog Natl Coll Agency, b 327 N Alabama.
James John, lab, r 66 N Missouri.
James John M, fireman, r 15 Fair blk.
James John T, painter, h e s Colorado av 4 n of Ohio.
James John W, barber, b 8 Elliott.
James Joseph, painter, h 310 W Pearl.
James Juliet E, stenog D H Baldwin & Co, b 327 N Alabama.
James Lucinda, h 65 N New Jersey.
James Margaret (wid Caesar), b 344 Yandes.
James Martha M (wid Milton M), h 1135 N Meridian.
James Mary, h 170 W Chesapeake.
James Oliver H, plastr, h 921 N Senate av.
James Orville S, mach, b 537 E Ohio.
James Otto, bicycle rep, b 168 E North.
James Preston, coachman 573 N Meridian.
James Reed C, lab, b 537 E Ohio.
James Robert, driver, h 155½ Indiana av.
James Samuel, watchman Court House Tower, h 46 Johnson av.
James Sarah (wid Elisha), h n w cor Humboldt and Rembrant avs.
James Sarah A (wid John H), b 46 Johnson av.
James Wilbur H, lab, h 334 E Ohio.
James Wm, engr, h 241 Kentucky av.
James Wm A, waiter, r 141 W Washington.
James Wm C, mach, r 19 N Arsenal av.
James Wm E (Springsteen & James), h 929 N Senate av.
James Wm H, molder, h 143½ E Washington.
James & McLain (David L James, Charles

RICHARDSON & McCREA,
MANAGERS FOR CENTRAL INDIANA.
EQUITABLE LIFE ASSURANCE SOCIETY
Of the United States.
79 EAST MARKET STREET,
TELEPHONE 182.

McLain), grocers, 537 E Ohio.
Jameson, see also Jamison.
Jameson Alexander, dentist, 20 W Ohio, h 767 N New Jersey.
Jameson Alexander W, driver, r 201 E Washington.
Jameson Benjamin W, gasfitter, r 4 Clifford av.
Jameson Bertha, stenog, b 1200 Madison av.
Jameson Edmund, lab, h 219 W Merrill.
Jameson Elizabeth K (wid Love H), h 413 Ash.
Jameson Elizabeth M, artist, 413 Ash, h same.
Jameson Frank, coachman 1165 N Penn.
Jameson Frank, lab, r 17 Center.
JAMESON HENRY, Physician, 28 E Ohio, Tel 105; h 228 N Delaware, Tel 251.
Jameson James, lab, b 80 W 8th.
Jameson James M, h 458 Ash.
Jameson Jeremiah, housemover, b 167 John.
Jameson Levi, lab, h 297 S Capitol av.
Jameson Lucy, b 330 Broadway.
Jameson Mame, seamstress, b 338 N Delaware.
Jameson Martha (wid Benjamin), janitor Public School No 35, h 1200 Madison av.
Jameson Martha (wid George), b 164 John.
Jameson Oliver, lab, b 254 W 5th.
Jameson Ovid B (Jameson & Joss), h 515 N Penn.
JAMESON PATRICK H, Physician, 28 E Ohio, Tel 105; h 330 Broadway, Tel 268.
Jameson Robin, lab, h 1256 Morris (W I).
Jameson Statham, bond clk County Treasurer's Office, h 942 Ash.
Jameson Thomas, driver, h 23 Center.
Jameson Thomas H, carp, Builders' Exchange, b 1270 Morris (W I).
Jameson Thomas J, b 1365 W Washington (M J).
Jameson Walter, supt The Webb-Jameson Co, h 164 John.
Jameson Wm H, messenger Am Ex Co, b 235 S Alabama.

Typewriter-Ribbons
ALL COLORS FOR ALL MACHINES.
THE BEST AND CHEAPEST.
S. H. EAST, STATE AGENT.
The Williams Typewriter....
55 THORPE BLOCK, 87 E. MARKET ST.

ERTEL STEAM LAUNDRY | LARGEST AND BEST IN THE STATE. PROMPT SERVICE. 26 and 28 N. Senate Ave. Tel 18

ELLIS & HELFENBERGER Architectural Iron Work and Gray Iron Castings. 162-170 South Senate Ave. Tel. 958.

THE HOGAN TRANSFER AND STORAGE COMP'Y
Household Goods and Pianos Moved—Packed—Stored..... Baggage and Package Express Machinery and Safes a Specialty Cor. Washington and Illinois Sts. TELEPHONE No. 675.

The Central Rubber & Supply Co. PHONE 922. 79 S. ILLINOIS ST., INDIANAPOLIS, IND. Hose, Belting, Packing, Clothing, Druggists' Sundries, Bicycle Tires, Cotton Hose, Etc. New York Belting & Packing Co., L't'd.

The Provident Life and Trust Company
Of Philadelphia.
Grants Certificates of Extension to Policyholders who are temporarily unable to pay their premiums
D. W. EDWARDS, Gen. Agt., 508 Indiana Trust Bldg.

JAMESON & JOSS (Ovid B Jameson, Frederick A Joss), Lawyers, Rooms 5 and 7 Brandon Blk, 95 E Washington, Tel 1142.
Jamieson Jessie (wid John), h n w cor Yandes and Bruce.
Jamieson Joseph L, mach hd, h 313 E Georgia.
Jamieson Wm, lab, b 313 E Georgia.
Jamison Isaac, lab, h 39 Hadley.
Jamison James C, druggist Insane Hospital.
Jamison Jennie, h 46 N California.
Jamison Louisa (wid Frank), h 469 Charles.
Janeck Augusta, b 35 W Morris.
Janeck Carolina (wid John), b 35 W Morris.
Janert Albert, butcher, h 419 Union.
Janes Albert, poultry, 1½ E Mkt House, h 80 Dugdale.
JANES FRANK E, Wholesale and Retail Dealer in Flour, Grain, Hay, Fancy Groceries and Breakfast Cereals; Recleaned Oats a Specialty, 107-113 N Delaware, Tel 396; h 869 N Delaware.
Janesville Machine Co, Robert C Craig agt, farm implements, 75 W Washington.
Janicke Wm M, carriage trimmer, b 187 S Capitol av.
Janitz Charles F, truckman, h 183 English av.
Janitz Frederick A, plumber, b 285 English av.
Janitz Julius G, lab, h 285 English av.
Janke, see also Yanke.
Janke Arthur C, polisher, h 65 Rockwood.
Janke Frank A, clk, h 65 Rockwood.
Janke Frederick, tallyman C C C & St L Ry, h 111 Spann av.
Janke Paul F, circulator Indiana Tribune, h 65 Rockwood.
Janke Wm H, tmstr, h 766 Chestnut.
Jankin John R, tinner, r 115 N Illinois.
Janneaux John M, h 280 E New York.
Janneaux L Marie, bkkpr Mutual Life Ins Co of Newark, b 280 E New York.
Janney Mary, h 64 William.
Jansen, see also Jenson and Johnson.

Julius C. Walk & Son, Jewelers Indianapolis.
12 EAST WASHINGTON ST.

Jansen Emil F, clk Clemens Vonnegut, b 8 Hermann.
Jansen John W F, shoemkr, h 112 Douglass.
Jaques Ira A, draughtsman P C C & St L Ry, r 31 W Vermont.
Jaqueth Burnham G, painter, 185 W New York, h same.
Jaquith Cyrus V, law clk John T Dye, h 2 Pressley Flats.
Jarboe R Fuller, musician, h 126 W 5th.
Jardini Frank, fruit, h 70 E Maryland.
Jardini Michael, pdlr, b 70 E Maryland.
Jardini Paul, fruits, 38 E Mkt House, h 41 Virginia av.
Jardini Vincent, produce, E Mkt House, h 121 Duncan.
Jared Frank S, bottler, h 121 N Gillard av.
Jared Millard F, engr, h 1052 E Michigan.
Jarrell Harry L, painter, b 318 E Wabash.
Jarrell Henry, painter, h 318 E Wabash.
Jarrell John, wagonmkr, b e s Lancaster av 2 n of Clifford av.
Jarrell Wm T, baggageman, h 37 N Arsenal av.
Jarrett Alonzo M, clk, h 109 Naomi.
Jarver John, lab, b 20 Sheffield av (H).
Jarvis George A, bartndr, r 67 N Alabama.
Jarvis Richard, varnisher, h 53 Kansas.
Jarvis Thomas E, condr, r 31½ Indiana av.
Jarvis Walter C, architect, h 373 E 15th.
Jaschka John, lab, h 405 W New York.
Jaschka John jr, clk The J N Hurty Pharmacy Co, b 405 W New York.
Jasper Aldrich, lab, h 208 W 2d.
Jasper Aldrich jr, lab, b 208 W 2d.
Jasper Ernest H, carp, h 457 S East.
Jasper Frederick W, brakeman, h 109 Shelby.
Jasper Levi, lab, h 215 W 3d.
Jasper Mary (wid Herman W), h 525 S New Jersey.
Jasper Robert, lab, b 208 W 2d.
Jasper Rudolph W, collr Jacob Bos, h 344 E Morris.
Jasper Wm, lab, h 395 W 2d.
Jasper Wm C (Loucks & Jasper), h 201 Fletcher av.
Jasper Wm H, molder, h 113 Downey.
Jauch Jacob, turner, h 9 Harvey.
Jaus Wm, meats, 902 S Meridian, h same.
Jaus Wm jr, butcher, b 575 Madison av.
Jay Elijah, h 77 Shepard (W I).
Jay Fannie (wid John W), b 41 Indiana av.
Jay Harry, lab, b 82 Nordyke av (W I).
Jay James E, saloon, 45 W Pearl, b 124 W 5th.
Jay Leslie B, b 163 Jefferson av.
Jay Lorenzo A, mach, h 692 W Shoemaker (N I).
Jay Mattie, stenog Avery Planter Co, b 2 Allfree.
Jay Moses C, trav agt, h 26 Jefferson av.
Jay Thomas C, mach, h 235 W South.
JAY WEBB, Genl Agt Frick Co, 28 Kentucky av, h 42 Bellefontaine.
Jaycox Louisa, h 2 Riley blk.
Jayne Alvin L, clk McKeehan Hotel, h 223 Hadley av (W I).
Jayne Morris, h 306 E North.
Jaynes Zerua J P, matron Rescue Mission Home, h 49 E South.
Jean Melvin, attendant Insane Hospital.
Jeannette Albert, actor, h 269 Fayette.
JEARL BEN B, Saloon, 58 N Delaware, h same.
Jebb Richard, finisher, h 1388 Northwestern av (N I).

OTTO GAS ENGINES | BUILDERS' EXCHANGE S. W. Cor. Ohio and Penn. Telephone 535.

Becker & Son Charles Becker Jacob Becker Jr. Merchant Tailors. 21 N. Penn. St. Tel. 934

SALIS RY & STANLEY • 177 Office, Store and Bk Fixtures a Rg of all kinds done on short n. Sq. Indianapolis, Ind. • Contractors and Builders TELEPHONE 999.

Jeffers Charles F, grocer, 2 S Belmont av (W I), h same.
Jeffers James T, sergeant U S Arsenal.
Jeffers John W, tmstr, h 57 Hazel.
Jefferson Agnes (wid Wm), h 15 Guffin.
Jefferson Ezra, lab, b 312 Clinton.
Jefferson Harriet E (wid Bartlett), h 276 Fayette.
Jefferson Henry, waiter, r 182 W Michigan.
Jefferson House, J Henry Gruenert propr, 59-63 E South.
Jefferson James, coal, 259 E Washington, h same.
Jefferson James W, clk Indpls Gas Co, h 444 E McCarty.
Jefferson John P, lab, h 233 N Beville av.
Jefferson Lafayette M, huckster, h 276 Fayette.
Jefferson Martin, lab, h 312 Clinton.
Jefferson Michael L, dep Township Assessor, 35 Court House, h 18 Greer.
Jefferson Thomas E, lab, b 276 Fayette.
Jeffersonville, Madison and Indianapolis R R. See Penna Lines.
Jeffery Cecil, clk Kingan & Co, b 117 N West.
Jeffery Charles, broker, h 117 N West.
Jeffery Franklin E Rev, pastor Southside Congregational Church, h 137 Pleasant.
Jeffery, Fuller & Co (Thomas A Jeffery, George W Fuller, Frank F Churchman), live stock com, Union Stock Yards (W I).
Jeffery Julian F, cigar mnfr, 122 Ft Wayne av, b 220 E Walnut.
Jeffery Mary E (wid Reuben E), h 30 E Pratt.
Jeffery Thomas A (Jeffery, Fuller & Co), res Southport, Ind.
Jeffries Charles A, bricklyr, h 271 E Miami.
Jeffries Earl, clk, b 39 W St Joseph.
Jeffries Elsie M (wid Wm H), h 615 N Capitol av.
Jeffries Evelyn, music teacher, s s University av 3 w of Downey av (I), b same.
Jeffries Frank R, mach hd, b 293 Davidson.
Jeffries George L, molder, h 34 Hendricks.
Jeffries Harry A, clk Kingan & Co, b 615 N Capitol av.
Jeffries Homer, clk R M S, h 39 W St Joseph.
Jeffries James D, presser, h 228 W New York.
Jeffries James S, carp, 293 Davidson, h same.
Jeffries Jennie (wid Wm H), h s s University av 3 w of Downey av (I).
Jeffries Joseph M, trav agt, r 90½ Mass av.
Jeffries Leonidas, mach, b 317 Jefferson av.
Jeffries Lloyd, driver, b 37 Buchanan.
Jeffries Marcus L, h 394 Cornell av.

JEFFRIES WM E, Physician, Office Hours 8-9 A M, 1-3 and 7-8 P M, 456 Virginia av, h same, Tel 1634.

Jeffries Willis O, trav agt, h 57 English av.
Jeffries Wilson, lab, h 317 Jefferson av.
Jelf Armstead, blksmith, b 8 Cornell av.
Jelf Isaac L, grocer, 151 Martindale av, h same.
Jelf Shelton A (Humphrey & Jelf), h 1771 N Senate av.
Jelgerhuis Bernard, produce, h w s Auburn av 1 n of Prospect.
Jelgerhuis Mary, b 29 Standard av (W I).
Jelgerhuis Wybe L, cook 262 N Meridian.
Jelleff Charles E, clk The Grand Hotel, h 248 N East.
Jelleff Frank R, advertiser N Y Store, b 248 N East.

Henry H. Fay,
40½ E. Washington St.,
REAL ESTATE,
AND LOAN BROKER.

Jelleff James F, bkkpr, r 79 W Michigan.
Jelleff John M, clk Paul H Krauss, b 79 W Michigan.
Jemison, see also Jameson.
Jemison Morton L, butter, h 176 Lexington av.
Jemison Zephaniah P, drayman, h 69 Spann av.
Jenckes Joseph S Rev, h 1044 N Illinois.
Jenkins Abigail (wid Charles), h 295 E 10th.
Jenkins Agnes M (wid Jesse W), h 490 E 10th.
Jenkins Alfred, carp, h 334 Cornell av.
Jenkins Amanda F, h 501 N West.
Jenkins Arthur B, printer, h 199 Fayette.
Jenkins Burris A Rev, pastor Third Christian Church, h 27 Lincoln av.
Jenkins Carrie A, teacher, b 346 Columbia av.
Jenkins Carroll, porter, b 178 W 10th.
Jenkins Cassius C, engr, h 729 E Market.
Jenkins Charles, lab, h 433 W Ontario (N I).
Jenkins Charles W, foreman Penna Lines, h 766 N Penn.
Jenkins Cyrus H, driver, h 27 College av.
Jenkins Daniel L, carp, h 83 Camp.
Jenkins David A, shoemkr, 521 E 9th, h 502 E 11th.
Jenkins Dennis H, pub Jersey Bulletin, 76 S Illinois, h 20 West Drive (W P).
Jenkins Dora A (wid Jesse W), dressmkr, 490 E 10th, h same.
Jenkins Edward, fireman, r 486½ Virginia av.
Jenkins Edward E, painter, r 161 E Ohio.
Jenkins Ethelbert W, clk, b 502 E 11th.
Jenkins Frank, foreman, h 522 W Francis (N I).
Jenkins Frederick H, electrician, b 490 E 10th.
Jenkins George F, carp, h 991 Cornell av.
Jenkins Granville R, carp, h 196 S William (W I).
Jenkins Harry D, printer, b 1160 N Penn.
Jenkins Harry E, student, b 991 Cornell av.
Jenkins Henry L, carp, h 441½ N Illinois.
Jenkins Henry P, mach hd, h 122 Fayette.
Jenkins Horace A, collr, h 65 Arch.

MAYHEW'S SPECTACLES
THE BEST IN USE
SOLD ONLY AT 13 N. MERIDIAN ST.

COAL AND LIME Cement, Hair, Sewer Pipe, etc. BALKE & KRAUSS CO. Cor. Missouri and Market Sts.

FRIEDGEN'S IS THE PLACE FOR THE NOBBIEST SHOES Ladies' and Gents' 19 North Pennsylvania St.

SAMUEL LAING | COPPER AND GALVANIZED IRON CORNICE MANUFACTURER
72 AND 74 E. COURT STREET. SKYLIGHTS AND VENTILATORS.

M. B. WILSON, Pres. W. F. CHURCHMAN, Cash.
THE CAPITAL NATIONAL BANK,
INDIANAPOLIS, IND.
Our Specialty is handling all Country Checks and Drafts on Indiana and neighboring States at the very lowest rates. Call and see us.
Interest Paid on Time Deposits.
28 S. MERIDIAN ST., COR. PEARL.

Jenkins James (Mansfield & Jenkins), h 511½ N West.
Jenkins James, lab, h 76 Kappus (W I).
Jenkins James H, lab, b 204 Oliver av (W I).
Jenkins James L, tinner, h 543 E Vermont.
Jenkins John, lab, h 204 Martindale av.
Jenkins John C, lawyer, 18½ N Penn, b 501 N West.
Jenkins John D, M D, The H R Allen National Surgical Institute, n w cor Ohio and Capitol av, h same.
JENKINS JOHN H, Collector, h 488 N West.
Jenkins John J, transfer, 11 N Alabama, h 457 Ash.
Jenkins John R, tinner, b 39 N Alabama.
Jenkins John W, tmstr, h 176 W 1st.
Jenkins Joseph F, millwright, h 48 Lee (W I).
Jenkins Lawrence E, clk R M S, h 529 Park av.
Jenkins Lewis C, barber, r 11 Russell av.
Jenkins Lydia T (wid Andrew), b 222 N Illinois.
Jenkins Maria L, b 59 College av.
Jenkins Mary, b 4 Willard.
Jenkins Mary G, h 1160 N Penn.
Jenkins Nancy J, artist, r 66½ N Penn.
Jenkins Nelson, porter, r 119 W Vermont.
Jenkins Oran, carp, h 330 E Michigan.
Jenkins Oscar D, clk Outing Bicycle Co, h 314 Bellefontaine.
Jenkins Otto M, contr, b 991 Cornell av.
Jenkins Rebecca (wid Joseph C), b 75 Germania av (H).
Jenkins Richard E, mngr, b 439 College av.
Jenkins Robert, barber, h 122 Agnes.
Jenkins Robert J Rev, h 122 Agnes.
Jenkins Samuel, fireman, b 142 Bates.
Jenkins Susan A, b 177 Buchanan.
Jenkins Thomas A, agt, b 111 N New Jersey.
Jenkins Thomas J (Jenkins & Co), b 166 Prospect.
Jenkins Walter F, uphlr, h 390 Columbia av.
Jenkins Wm (Jenkins & Co), h 166 Prospect.
Jenkins Wm, baker, b 488 N West.
Jenkins Wm, lab, b 204 Oliver av (W I).

TUTTLE & SEGUIN,
28 E. Market St. Ground Floor.
COLLECTING RENTS AND CARE OF PROPERTY A SPECIALTY.
Telephone 1168.

Jenkins Wm A (Jenkins & Co), b 166 Prospect.
Jenkins Wm A, barber, h 129 N Illinois.
Jenkins Wm F, h 338 W New York.
Jenkins Wm M, lab, h 18 Lennox.
Jenkins & Co (Wm A and Thomas J Jenkins), whol confrs, 84 E Georgia and 98 Mass av.
Jenks George W, b 194 N Illinois.
Jenks Rolla M, bill clk C C C & St L Ry, b 194 N Illinois.
Jenne Charles H, trav agt, h 122 Cornell av.
Jenne Clara A, seamstress, b 122 Cornell av.
Jenner Leopold A, awnings, 89 N Delaware, h same.
Jenney Arthur E, electrician, h w s Ritter av 2 s of Railroad (I).
Jenney Charles D, vice-pres Jenney Electric Motor Co, h 1871 E Washington.
Jenney Edwin W, sec and treas Jenney Electric Motor Co, h n s Walnut av 2 w of Arlington av (I).
Jenney Electric Motor Co, Amos K Hollowell pres, Charles D Jenney vice-pres, Edwin W Jenney sec and treas, Belt R R and Pan Handle crossing (Englewood).
Jennings Albert, h 294½ Mass av.
Jennings Alonzo J, ins agt, h s w cor Waverly and Pope avs.
Jennings Augustus, bkkpr C E Coffin & Co, h 29 W Vermont.
Jennings Benjamin V, mach hd, b 471 W Francis (N I).
Jennings Daniel D, mach, b 127 E Ohio.
Jennings Edwin, mach, h 88 Clarke.
Jennings Francis R, pres Hoosier Packing Co, broker, 66½ W Maryland, livery, 70 same, h 810 N Meridian.
Jennings George R, h 45 Fletcher av.
Jennings Daniel D, mach, b 127 E Ohio.
Jennings Jesse, lab, b 297 River av (W I).
Jennings John, finisher, b 177 Elizabeth.
Jennings John R, lab, h rear 488 S Meridian.
Jennings John Q A, boarding 301 River av (W I).
Jennings Joseph, lab, h 60 Chapel.
Jennings LeRoy H, clk, b 45 Fletcher av.
Jennings Margaret (wid Arthur), h 50 Locke.
Jennings Matthew, lab, b 177 Elizabeth.
JENNINGS MILTON, Agt Boiler Cleansing Compound, Lord's Patent Improved, 177 S Illinois, h 122 E Merrill.
Jennings Pearl, lab, h 265 E Wabash.
Jennings Preston, carp, h 177 Elizabeth.
Jennings Rufus D, mach, h 147 Kansas.
Jennings Theodore H, cigar mnfr, rear 56 Newman, h 58 same.
Jennings Thomas J, boarding 46 Standard av (W I).
Jennings W J, dispatching clk P O, h 186 Shelby.
Jensen, see also Jansen and Johnson.
Jensen Andrew, furniture, 567 Virginia av, h same.
Jensen Charles, lab, h 164 Trowbridge (W).
Jensen Henry C, lab, b 229 W Washington.
Jensen Martin, painter, h 1200 S Meridian.
Jensen Niels, letter carrier P O, h Delaware 1 n of 35th.
Jenson Andrew, brickmkr, b 653 Union.
Jenson August, lab, h 653 Union.
Jenson August jr, lab, b 653 Union.
Jenson Christian, carp, h 26 Rock.
Jenson Frederick, welldriver, b 660 Chestnut.

PAPER BOXES SULLIVAN & MAHAN 41 W. Pearl St.

DIAMOND WALL PLASTER { Telephone 1410 BUILDERS' EXCHANGE.

If your Laundry Work is not satisfactory, try THE HOME LAUNDRY 197 S. Illinois St. Telephone 1769.

Jenson Jacob, shoemkr, 951 S Meridian, h same.
Jenson John, carp, h 253 Fayette.
Jenson Wm, cutter, r 223 E New York.
Jenson Wm, mach hd, b 253 Fayette.
Jereissati Bros (Rasheed N and Salem M), Japanese goods, 48 N Illinois.
Jereissati Rasheed M (Jereissati Bros), r 191 N Delaware.
Jereissati Salem M (Jereissati Bros), r 191 N Delaware.
Jerman Edward C, electrician, h 242 Indiana av.
Jerman James, carp, h w s Centennial 1 s of Michigan (H).
Jerome Wm E, clk, r 84 E North.
Jerrell Frank, lab, h rear 407 S Delaware.
Jersey Bulletin, Dennis H Jenkins pub, 76 S Illinois.
Jerusalem Albert H, bookbndr, b 159 Spring.
Jerusalem Robert B, jeweler, 236 W Washington, h 409 Talbott av.
Jerusalem Robert J, lab, h 159 Spring.
Jeslop Riley C, lab, h 153 N Gillard av.
Jesse Edward N, clk Adams Ex Co, r 210½ S Meridian.
Jessen Julius E, cabtmkr, h 17 Columbia av.
Jessop Elizabeth K (wid Samuel S), h 91 Highland pl.
Jessup Ann (wid John W), h 452 S West.
Jessup Lydia A, dressmkr, 50 Division (W I) b same.
Jessup Nathan, real est, h 50 Division (W I).
Jessup Roscoe C, foreman R W Furnas, h 601 E New York.
Jessup Sarah A, dressmkr, b 50 Division (W I).
JessupWm, painter, h 53½ Russell av.
Jester Charles M, painter, h 10 Drake.
Jester Owen E, packer, h 623 W Vermont.
Jeter Frank, phys, 52 Michigan (H), h same.
Jetter Magdalena (wid Gottlieb), h 618 S East.
JEUP BERNARD J T, City Civil Engineer, Rooms 13-15 Basement Court House, Tel 512; h 97 Highland av.
Jeup Elizabeth, clk M O div P O, b 119 Walcott.
Jeup John B, editor The German Telegraph, h 119 Walcott.
Jewar Joseph F, trav agt Tanner & Sullivan, h 315 Broadway.
Jewell Charles A, clk Robertson & Nichols, h 286 N Senate av.
Jewell Sarah, h 163 Bird.
Jewell Silas C, salesman, h 78 Wright.
Jewett Henry T, lab, b 30 Columbia al.
Jillson Louise M, h 737 N Alabama.
Jillson Marcus A, treas Meridian L and T Co, 432 Lemcke bldg.
Jillson Murray E, lab, h 18 Reynolds av (H).
Jillson Wm M (Knight & Jillson), h 756 N Delaware, tel 1796.
Jimeson Mary J (wid Rev Allen A), b 92 Eureka av.
Jimison Elizabeth, h 219 W Merrill.
Jines Charles E, finisher, b 188 W Vermont.
Jines Franklin, waiter, b 73 N Alabama.
Jines Jasper N, molder, h 42 Tremont av (H).
Jines John R, woodwkr, h 188 W Vermont.
Jines Walker, lab, b 42 Tremont av (H).
Jines Wm E, finisher, b 188 W Vermont.
Jiuffre August, shoemkr, b 141 E Maryland.

FRANK NESSLER. WILL H. ROST.
FRANK NESSLER & CO.
Tailors
56 EAST MARKET ST. (Lemcke Building),
INDIANAPOLIS, IND.

Joachim Julius, florist, h rear 1374 E Washington.
Job Olivia (wid Alzire), h 641 Virginia av.
Jobe Hiram, ironwkr, r 174 E Washington.
Jobes George O, drugs, 417 Indiana av, h same.
Jobes Norman E, student, b 417 Indiana av.
Jochem Charles, finisher, b 114 Laurel.
Jochem Kate (wid John), b 114 Laurel.
Jockers Joseph, clk Henry C Maass, b 451 S Delaware.
Joerg Catherine (wid Peter), b 31 Deloss.
Joerg Henry, lab, b 31 Deloss.
Johannes Anna (wid Peter), h 23 Minnesota.
Johannes George, stonecutter, h 716 S East.
Johannes John, shoemkr, 27 Minnesota, b 23 same.
Johannes Mary, b 23 Minnesota.
Johannes Matthias, packer, h 206 Minnesota.
Johannes Peter, mach hd, b n s Cottage av 1 e of Wright (W I).
Johanning Wm, clk, h 189 Pleasant.
Johanson Wm A, lab Deaf and Dumb Inst.
Johantgen Charles W, gilder, h 830 S Meridian.
Johantgen Christina (wid Matthias), h 675 Union.
Johantgen George J, h 51 Hope (B).
Johantgen Henry W, barber, 853 S Meridian, b 830 same.
Johantgen John, tinner, b 830 S Meridian.
Johantgen Leo, lab, b 830 S Meridian.
Johantgen Nicholas, engr, h 830 S Meridian.
Johantgen Stephen, carp, h 94 Lincoln la.
Johantges Frank J, mach, b 996 S Meridian.
Johantges Jacob, lab, h 533 Madison av.
Johantges Joseph, blksmith, h 996 S Meridian.
John, see also Jahn.
John Alfred H, clk, b 123 W Michigan.
John Bertha (wid Wm), h 547 S West.
John Charles, h 273 N Senate av.
John Edward B, jeweler, b 62 Park av.
John Eleanor M, teacher Public School No 15, b 645 E Ohio.
John Henry, lab, h 660 N Meridian.
John Henry B, brakeman, h 645 E Ohio.

Haueisen & Hartmann
163-169 E. Washington St.
FURNITURE,
Carpets,
Household Goods,
Tin, Granite and China Wares, Oil Cloth and Shades

THE WM. H. BLOCK CO. 7 AND 9 EAST WASHINGTON STREET. DRY GOODS, MEN'S FURNISHINGS.

The Fidelity and Deposit Co. OF MARYLAND. Bonds signed for Administrators, Assignees, Executors, Guardians, Receivers, Trustees, and persons in every position of trust.
GEO. W. PANGBORN, General Agent, 704-706 Lemcke Building. Telephone 140.

INSURE YOUR PROPERTY WITH FRANK K. SAWYER

•JOSEPH GARDNER•
GALVANIZED IRON
CORNICES and SKYLIGHTS.
Metal Ceilings and Siding.
Tin, Iron, Steel and Slate Roofing.
37, 39 & 41 KENTUCKY AVE. Telephone 322.

John Henry B jr, clk, b 645 E Ohio.
John Paul R, grocer, 547 S West, b same.
John Virginia (wid Washington D), h 173 E Washington.
John Wm L, agt, b 203 N Illinois.
John Wm S, plastr, r 141 W Washington.
Johns Allen, lab, h 77 Germania (H).
Johns Anna, nurse, 294½ Mass av, h same.
Johns Frank R, engraver, h 21 E North.
Johns Hiram A, lab, h 77 Germania av (H).
Johns John T, lab, b 14 Detroit.
Johns Lester E, clk Hardey & Gausepohl, b 67 Madison av.
Johns Samuel E, bookbndr, h 62 Park av.
Johns Wm T, nurseryman, h 164½ E Washington.
Johnson, see also Jansen and Jensen.
Johnson Ada, h 10 W Chesapeake.
Johnson Adam J, h 22 E St Joseph.
Johnson Addie (wid Amos), h rear 224 E Merrill.
Johnson Addie B (wid Wm F), b 1137 N Meridian.
Johnson Albert, farmer, h s s 28th 1 e of Central av.
Johnson Albert, lab, h 119 Bismarck av (H).
Johnson Albert, h e s Downey av 1 s of P C C & St L Ry (I).
Johnson Albert D, sec and treas Central Cycle Mnfg Co, h 778 N New Jersey.
Johnson Albert E, clk, h 79 Torbet.
Johnson Albert H, bkkpr, h 981 N Illinois.
Johnson Albert H, lab, h 482 Chestnut.
Johnson Albert M, trav agt, r 85½ W Market.
Johnson Alfred D, tailor, r 30 Hutchings blk.
Johnson Alfred H, clk Custom House, h 123 W Michigan.
Johnson Alice, printer, b 599 S East.
Johnson Alice (wid Robert), restaurant, 223 W Ohio, h 225 same.
Johnson Alice R (wid Edwin), h 699 N Alabama.
Johnson Almon, lab, h 63 Smith.
Johnson Alvin, agt, h n s Beechwood av 1 e of Central av (I).
Johnson Alvin H, oil, h 381 Bellefontaine.

J. S. FARRELL & CO.
Have Experienced Workmen and will Promptly Attend to your
PLUMBING
Repairs. 84 North Illinois Street. Telephone 382.

Johnson Alvin H jr, molder, b 381 Bellefontaine.
Johnson America (wid John), h 185 E Court.
Johnson Andrew, lab, r 62 E Washington.
Johnson Andrew, lab, h 95 Hiatt (W I).
Johnson Andrew C, mach hd, h 20 Ketcham (H).
Johnson Andrew J, lab, h 25 Oriental.
Johnson Andrew P, mach, b 250 N Liberty.
Johnson Annie (wid Perry), h 333 Lafayette.
Johnson Anton, bricklayer, b 292 W Morris.
Johnson Armstead, lab, b 230 N New Jersey.
Johnson Arthur, b 179 E St Clair.
Johnson Arthur, carp, h 619 W Vermont.
Johnson Arthur A, student, b e s Downey av 1 s of P C C & St L Ry (I).
Johnson Arthur R, mach hd, h 312 Clifford av.
Johnson Arthur T, tinner Van Camp H and I Co, b 715 Mass av.
Johnson Arthur W, attendant Insane Asylum.
Johnson Asbury G, molder, h 133 King av (H).
Johnson Ashley, driver, h 39 College av.
Johnson Augustus, lab, r 364 W North.
Johnson Augustus A, cabtmkr, h 435 W Udell (N I).
Johnson Benjamin, lab, h 40 Torbet.
Johnson Benjamin C, clk, b 469 W Francis (N I).
Johnson Benjamin F, lab, h 240 S West.
Johnson Beverly, lab, h w s Caroline av 4 n of 17th.
Johnson Caleb R, livery, rear 1 Fayette, h 211 W Market.
Johnson Callie V (wid Oscar), b 203 Alvord.
Johnson Carrie (wid Jeremiah), h 260 W Washington.
Johnson Carrie H (wid George W), b 507 Park av.
Johnson Carrie L, asst bkkpr N Y Store, r 40 Huron.
Johnson Cassie, h 179½ Muskingum al.
Johnson Catherine (wid Matthew), h 230 N New Jersey.
Johnson Catherine C (wid David F), h 141 Bellefontaine.
Johnson Catherine J (wid Albert), b 186 Deloss.
Johnson Charles, b 349 Michigan (H).
Johnson Charles, clk Am Ex Co, h 319 S Meridian.
Johnson Charles, ironwkr, r 164 W Maryland.
Johnson Charles, molder, h 8 Haugh (H).
Johnson Charles A, clk, b 304 W Maryland.
Johnson Charles A, plumber, 35 W Market, h 227 Bright.
Johnson Charles D (Johnson & Metcalf), h 363 Park av.
Johnson Charles E, condr, h 61 Holmes av (H).
Johnson Charles E, opr W U Tel Co, h n w cor Harris av and Jackson (M J).
Johnson Charles H (C H Johnson & Co), res Rushville, Ind.
Johnson Charles H, clk, b Senate Hotel.
Johnson Charles J, bottler, b 223 Blake.
Johnson Charles J, lab, b 160 W Michigan (H).
Johnson Charles L, r 59½ N Illinois.
Johnson Charles M, mach, h 34 Ludlow av.
Johnson Charles O, battervman, b 116 N Dorman.

GUARANTEED INCOME POLICIES issued only by the United States Life Insurance Co.
E. B. SWIFT, Manager. 25 E. Market St.

Furniture Carpets } WM. KOTTEMAN { Stoves Ranges
89 and 91 East Washington Street. Telephone 1742.

WILLIAM WIEGEL { MANUFACTURER OF.... } SHOW CASES { 6 W. Louisiana St. Opposite Union Station.

Johnson Christiana A, r 31 Stewart pl.
Johnson Christopher, janitor, b 218 E Wabash.
Johnson Clarence, painter, h 148 Michigan av.
Johnson Clark A, janitor, b 130 Columbia al.
Johnson Claude M, clk, b 270 W Vermont.
Johnson Clement, lab, b 148 Lennox.
Johnson Crawford, lab, h 108½ Mass av.
Johnson Cynthia A (wid Robert), h 476 W North.
Johnson C H & Co (C H Johnson, G Bridenbucker), com mer, 16 Board of Trade bldg.
Johnson Daniel W, h 433 S Olive.
Johnson David, farmer, h 161 S Belmont av (W I).
Johnson David C, lab, h 82 Bradshaw.
Johnson David K, bartndr, h 602½ N West.
Johnson Delia L, stenog, b 778 N New Jersey.
Johnson Donah, b 36 St Paul.
Johnson Dover C, porter, h 47 Tecumseh.
Johnson Edgar, mach, b 249 Alvord.
Johnson Edgar K, sawmkr, h 392 S Delaware.
Johnson Edward, r 47 Cleaveland blk.
Johnson Edward, lab, b 160 W Maryland.
Johnson Edward, lab, h 17 Poplar (B).
Johnson Edward, mach hd, r 129 Virginia av.
Johnson Edward B, city fireman, h 77 Birch av (W I).
Johnson Edward D, watchmkr, r 131 S East.
Johnson Edward M, painter, h 724 Ash.
Johnson Elhanon, grocer, 502 W Addison (N I), h same.
Johnson Eli M, trav agt The Indpls Millinery Co, h 516 College av.
Johnson Elias V, clk, h 270 W Vermont.
Johnson Elijah S, lab, h s e cor Jackson and Clyde.
Johnson Elizabeth (wid Albert), h 151½ W McCarty.
Johnson Elizabeth (wid Benjamin), b 564 E Vermont.
Johnson Ella O (wid Charles W), h 799 N Capitol av.
Johnson Ellsworth, lab, h 240 Brookside av.
Johnson Epha M (wid Wm L), teacher Public School No 2, h 85 Shepard (W I).
Johnson Ephraim, lab, h 43 Harris.
Johnson Ernest J, lab, h 1656 Graceland av.
Johnson Ernest B, stenog A W Wishard, b 22 E St Joseph.
Johnson Erwin, h 179 E St Clair.
JOHNSON EUDORUS M, City Comptroller, Room 1 Basement Court House, Tel 1890; h 817 N Meridian.
Johnson Eugene H, clk, b 586 Park av.
Johnson Eva A, h 37 College av.
Johnson Florence, teacher Public School No 20, b 347 S State av.
Johnson Francis G, watchman, h 242 River av (W I).
Johnson Frank, brakeman, b 46 Windsor.
Johnson Frank, lab, h 139 Geisendorff.
Johnson Frank, mach, h 65 Huron.
Johnson Frank, motorman, b 1139 N Illinois.
Johnson Frank, uphlr, b 664 S Meridian.
Johnson Frank B, trav agt, h 133 N Senate av.
Johnson Frank E, printer, h 177 E Merrill.

We Buy Municipal ~ Bonds ~
THOS. C. DAY & CO,
Rooms 325 to 330 Lemcke Bldg.

Johnson Frank G, clk, h 545 Ash.
Johnson Frank H, boarding 156 N Illinois.
Johnson Frank H, lab, b 210 Elm.
Johnson Frank M, brakeman, h 191 Elm.
Johnson Frank M, meats, 57 E Mkt House, h 230 E Morris.
Johnson Frank O, restaurant, 16-18 Monument pl, r 20 The Plaza.
Johnson Frank P, farmer, h 30th and L E & W R R.
Johnson Frederick, barber, r 147 W Washington.
Johnson Frederick, porter Stubbins Hotel.
Johnson Frederick C, mach hd, b n s Clifford 3 e of Brightwood av.
Johnson Frederick T, collr Gregory & Appel, b 586 Park av.
Johnson F Tom, solr, h 156 Fayette.
Johnson Gabriel, lab, h 153 W Merrill.
Johnson Gabriella, cook, h rear 310 E Washington.
Johnson Gens, lab, b w s Schurman 1 n of Vorster av (M P).
Johnson George, lab, h 1164 Northwestern av (N I).
Johnson George A, butcher, h 261 W Morris.
Johnson George B, mach hd, b rear 192 W Merrill.
Johnson George C, lab, b 134 Columbia av.
Johnson George D, barber, 42 W 13th, h 232 Howard.
Johnson George F, mach hd, b 44 Wallack.
Johnson George O, painter, h 244 N Judge Harding (W I).
Johnson George W, porter, h 23 N New Jersey.
Johnson Grant, lab, h 596 W North.
Johnson Harry, r 282 N Illinois.
Johnson Harry, lab, b 136 Columbia av.
Johnson Harry C, cigarmkr, b 15 E New York.
Johnson Harry D, lab, b 260 W Washington.
Johnson Harry H, baggageman, h 116 Union.
Johnson Harry H, bicycle rep, h 18 Cornell av.
Johnson Harry O, painter, 175½ S East, b same.

EAT
HITZ'S CRACKERS AND CAKES.
ASK YOUR GROCER FOR THEM.

TURKISH RUGS AND CARPETS RESTORED TO ORIGINAL COLORS LIKE NEW | Capital Steam Carpet Cleaning Works M. D. PLUNKETT, Telephone 818

BENJ. BOOTH PRACTICAL EXPERT ACCOUNTANT. Books Opened, Written Up, Posted and Balanced. Room 18, 82½ E. Washington St., Indianapolis, Ind.

ESTABLISHED 1876. TELEPHONE 168.
CHESTER BRADFORD,
SOLICITOR OF PATENTS,
AND COUNSEL IN PATENT CAUSES.
(See adv. page 6.)
Office:—Rooms 14 and 16 Hubbard Block, S. W. Cor. Washington and Meridian Streets, INDIANAPOLIS, INDIANA.

Johnson Harvey M, lab, h s e cor Jackson and Clyde.
Johnson Hattie (wid Philip), h 412 S State av.
Johnson Hattie E, boarding 184 N Capitol av.
Johnson Henry, clk, r 211 N Illinois.
Johnson Henry, driver, b 285 S Penn.
Johnson Henry, lab, r 163 Bird.
Johnson Henry, lab, h e s National av 1 s of C H & D R R (I).
Johnson Henry, lab, h 182 Tremont av (H).
Johnson Henry, lab, h 484 W North.
Johnson Henry, switchman, h 597 W Pearl.
Johnson Henry C, weigher, h 239 Fletcher av.
Johnson Henry F, lab, h 7 N Gillard av.
Johnson Herbert E, draughtsman, r 438 N Meridian.
Johnson Herschel V, insp Indiana Car Service Assn, h 269 W Vermont.
Johnson Hiram, lab, r 166½ W Washington.
Johnson Hiram G, carp, b 438 E Georgia.
Johnson Horace, jeweler, 23 Mass av, h same.
Johnson Howard A, salesman, h 586 Park av.
Johnson Hubbard, lab, h rear e s Arlington av 3 n of Walnut av (I).
Johnson Ira, tmstr, h 111 Minerva.
Johnson Isaac, gardener, h 52 S William (W I).
Johnson Isaac B, barber, h 450 W 1st.
Johnson Isaac P, porter, h 567 E 7th.
Johnson Isham, h 253 W 5th.
Johnson Jacob, porter, h 27 N Spruce.
Johnson James, h 116 Columbia av.
Johnson James, carp, h 49 Yandes.
Johnson James, janitor, h 210 Elm.
Johnson James, lab, r 319 E Washington.
Johnson James, lab, h 1166 Northwestern av (N I).
Johnson James, lab, b 230 N New Jersey.
Johnson James, real est, h 254 College av.
Johnson James, tmstr, h 1375 W Washington (M J).
Johnson James A, carp, 170 Woodlawn av, h same.
Johnson James A, mach hd, b 83 Fletcher av.

O. B. ENSEY
MANUFACTURER OF
GALVANIZED IRON CORNICE,
SKYLIGHTS AND WINDOW CAPS,
TELEPHONE 1562. Cor. 6th and Illinois Sts.

Johnson James B, painter, b 12 Grace.
Johnson James C, foreman Ballweg & Co, h 115 Coburn.
Johnson James G, waiter, r 321 W North.
Johnson James H, clk, b 247 N East.
Johnson James H, clk, h 456 N West.
Johnson James H, clk R M S, h 624 Park av.
Johnson James H, fireman, b 465 College av.
Johnson James M, foreman Henry Coburn, h 348 S Missouri.
Johnson James O, barber, 1111 E Michigan, b 233 N Beville av.
Johnson James W, lab, h e s Bismarck av 4 n of Emrich (H).
Johnson Jefferson, lab, r 301 N California.
Johnson Jerome B, barber, b 525 N Senate av.
Johnson Jesse, r 128 W Ohio.
Johnson Jesse, lab, b 23 Bloomington.
Johnson Jesse B, excelsior mnfr, 366 W Market, h 349 W Vermont.
Johnson Jesse T, draughtsman, b 381 Bellefontaine.
Johnson John, h 184 N Capitol av.
Johnson John, barber, h 91 Nebraska.
Johnson John, lab, b 310 E Court.
Johnson John, lab, b 23 N New Jersey.
Johnson John, lab, h 559 N West.
Johnson John, lab, h w s Rural 1 s of 17th.
Johnson John, lab, r 298 Virginia av.
Johnson John, pdlr, b 93 Douglass.
Johnson John, waiter, r 232 W North.
Johnson John A, trav agt, h 46 Windsor.
Johnson John C, finisher, h 44 Wallack.
Johnson John C, mer police, h 204 E McCarty.
Johnson John C, painter, h 415 Chestnut.
Johnson John C, gas inspr, h 116 Yeiser.
Johnson John D Rev, h 33 Brett.
Johnson John F, janitor, h 186½ W Washington.
Johnson John H, lab, h 32 Bismarck.
Johnson John H, mach hd, b 599 S East.
Johnson John J, blksmith, h 50 School (B).
Johnson John J, brick mnfr, s e cor Mass and Peru avs, res Castleton, Ind.
Johnson John J, condr, h 100 Walcott.
Johnson John J, lab, h 554 W North.
Johnson John J, shoemkr, h s e cor Morris and McKernan.
Johnson John K, painter, h 40 Atlas.
Johnson John W, clk, h 164 Randolph.
Johnson John W, trav agt, h 597 Central av.
JOHNSON JONAS F, Agt Seasongood, Stix, Krouse & Co of Cincinnati, O, Clothing, 146 S Meridian, h 467 N Delaware.
Johnson Joseph, lab, b 1164 Northwestern av (N I).
Johnson Joseph H, h 599 S East.
Johnson Joseph M, clk W B Holton Mnfg Co, r 177 E Washington.
Johnson Joseph R (Johnson & Reichardt), h 423 N East.
Johnson Joseph R, engr, h 436 W Washington.
Johnson Josiah T, b 236 S Capitol av.
Johnson Julia, bkkpr The Webb-Jameson Co, b 473 Bellefontaine.
Johnson Julia E, dressmkr, 317 N Alabama, h same.
Johnson Julius, molder, b 181 Blake.
Johnson Kinney, clk, b 85 Yandes.
Johnson Laura, b 45 Benton.
Johnson Lemuel S, janitor, h 130 Columbia al.

TUTEWILER UNDERTAKER, NO. 72 WEST MARKET STREET. TELEPHONE 216.

IF YOU WANT A GOOD MEAL AND HAVE IT NICELY SERVED GO TO THE SHERMAN RESTAURANT 18 and 20 S. MERIDIAN STREET

PARTNERSHIP INSURANCE At low cost. By which provision is made against the pecuniary loss and embarrassment resulting from the death of a member of a firm.
Provident Life and Trust Co. of Philadelphia, D. W. EDWARDS, Gen'l Agt., 508 Indiana Trust Bldg.

THEODORE F. SMITHER
COMPOSITION ROOFING MATERIALS. BEST IN THE MARKET. TELEPHONE 861. OFFICE, 151 WEST MARYLAND ST.

Johnson Leonard, h 244½ E Washington.
Johnson Letha M (wid Hamilton), b 534 College av.
Johnson Lillian, prin Free Kindergarten School No 2, b 910 N Alabama.
Johnson Lincoln C, collr, b 62 Highland pl.
Johnson Logan, musician, h 45 Benton.
Johnson Louis, lab, b 44 Wallack.
Johnson Louisa, h 134 N Penn.
Johnson Lucy (wid George), b 67 Martindale av.
Johnson Lucy J (wid Robert), b 1092 N Penn.
Johnson Mabel, hairdresser, b 450 W 1st.
Johnson Mack, lab, b 183 Blake.
Johnson Mahlon M, turner, h 77 Buchanan.
Johnson Marion, carp, h 90 Sheffield av (H).
Johnson Marquis L, lawyer, 10½ N Delaware, h 1302 E Washington.
Johnson Marshall M, mach hd, h rear 161 Jefferson av.
Johnson Martha J (wid Wm), b 630 N Senate av.
Johnson Martha J, dressmkr, 139 St Mary, h same.
Johnson Mary (wid Andrew), h 186 Howard.
Johnson Mary (wid Samuel), cook McKeehan Hotel.
Johnson Mary A, h 274 N West.
Johnson Mary C (wid James A), h 62 Highland pl.
Johnson Mary E (wid George H), b 761 N Senate av.
Johnson Mary E (wid Isaac B), h 465 College av.
Johnson Mary E (wid Joel M), b 46 Paw Paw.
Johnson Mary F, teacher, b 347 S State av.
Johnson Mary H (wid Wm), h 184 Mass av.
Johnson Mary L (wid Henry), b 224 N West.
Johnson Mary M (wid Jesse), b 15 Bismarck av (H).
Johnson Mary M (wid Wm J), h 194 Davidson.
Johnson Matthew, lab, b 295 Indiana av.
Johnson Matthew S Rev, h 299 Fayette.
Johnson Melinda (wid John W), h 5 Henry.
Johnson Melville, driver, h 554 W North.
Johnson Melville E, b 572 N Penn.
Johnson Melvin, lab, b 554 W North.
Johnson Millard F, brakeman, h 236 S Capitol av.
Johnson Nancy (wid George), b 134 Columbia av.
Johnson Nathan, waiter, h 27 Roanoke.
Johnson Oliver J, trav agt Hoosier Canning Machine Co, b Enterprise Hotel.
Johnson Oliver R, tel editor The Indpls News, b Columbia Club.
Johnson Omie, barber, h 212 W New York.
Johnson Ora A, housekpr 40 Atlas.
Johnson Oscar, coachman 200 N Meridian.
Johnson Oscar, lab, h 257 W 6th.
Johnson Oscar B, foreman M S Huey & Son, h 596 Bellefontaine.
Johnson Otto W, clk Cerealine Mnfg Co, h 153 N State av.
Johnson Overton A, salesman Murphy, Hibben & Co, h 179 E St Clair.
Johnson Owen, lab, h 491 W Wells (N I).
Johnson Pearl, h 161 W Maryland.
Johnson Percy E, salesman M Sells & Co, b 349 Michigan (H).
Johnson Ralph, fireman, r 810 Cornell av.
Johnson Rebecca (wid Benjamin), h 231 N Beville av.
Johnson Reddin, barber, 497½ S West, h 45 Thomas.

THE WHEN IS A WORLD BEATER.

Johnson Richard, lab, h 278 Alvord.
Johnson Richard A, lab, h 34 Drake.
Johnson Richard H, foreman Badger Furniture Co, h 39 Tacoma av.
JOHNSON RICHARD O, Supt Indiana Institution for the Education of the Deaf and Dumb, s e cor Washington and State av, Tel 104.
Johnson Robert, barber, b 252 Fayette.
Johnson Robert, lab, h 29 Reynolds av (H).
Johnson Robert H, uphlr, h 39 Tacoma av.
Johnson Rollo E, civil engr, b 981 N Illinois.
Johnson Rose, h 93 Darnell.
Johnson Ross F, lab, b 186½ W Washington.
Johnson Samuel, h 45 Clifford av.
Johnson Samuel, hotel runner, b California House.
Johnson Samuel, lab, h 218 W 2d.
Johnson Samuel, lab, b 412 W 2d.
Johnson Samuel, lab, h rear 3 Wilcox.
Johnson Samuel L, printer, h 469 W Francis (N I).
Johnson Samuel O, janitor, h 226 Muskingum al.
Johnson Samuel P, switchman, h 887 Morris (W I).
Johnson Sarah, h 43 Ellen.
Johnson Seaton, lab, r rear 234 E Wabash.
Johnson Sidney H, plastr, h 16 Lennox.
Johnson Sina (wid Morris), h 31 Yeiser.
Johnson Smith, porter, r 50 S Illinois.
Johnson Stephen, lab, b 119 Bismarck av (H).
Johnson Stuart R, clk, h 392 S Delaware.
Johnson Susan (wid Clemence), h 260 W 6th.
Johnson Sylvester, pres Am Union Savings Assn, h w s Central av 1 s of Washington av (I).
Johnson Sylvia, b 93 Columbia al.
Johnson Tarlton L, barber, 181 S Meridian, r 65 Huron.
Johnson Thaddeus, brakeman, r 62½ S Illinois.
Johnson Thaddeus, lab, h 473 Bellefontaine.
Johnson Thomas, lab, h 593 W Maryland.
Johnson Thomas, lab, b 109 Yeiser.

THE A. BURDSAL CO.
WINDOW AND PLATE GLASS
Putty, Glazier Points, Diamonds.
Wholesale and Retail. 34 and 36 S. Meridian St.

ELECTRIC CONSTRUCTION Isolated Plants Installed. Electric Wiring and Fittings of all kinds. C. W. Meikel. Tel. 466. 96-98 E. New York St

DALTON & MERRIFIELD { LUMBER South Noble St., near E. Washington

INDIANA ELECTROTYPE CO. : BEST WORK. LOWEST PRICES.
23 WEST PEARL ST., INDIANAPOLIS, IND. JOB WORK. BOOK PLATES. All Orders Promptly Filled. BEST PATENT BASE ON THE MARKET.

KIRKHOFF BROS.,
GAS AND ELECTRIC FIXTURES
THE LARGEST LINE IN THE CITY.
102-104 SOUTH PENNSYLVANIA ST.
TELEPHONE 910.

Johnson Thomas E, lawyer, 35½ E Washington, h 139 St Mary.
Johnson Thomas H, porter, h 7 Stoughton av.
Johnson Thomas J, mach opr Indpls Journal, b 128 Cornell av.
Johnson Thomas R, condr, h 26 Lexington av.
Johnson Tillman A H, real est, h 586 Park av.
Johnson Ulysses A, mach hd, 312 Clifford av.
Johnson Vida, clk, h 37 College av.
Johnson Virgil H, grocer, 109 E Mkt House, b 39 College av.
Johnson Virginia (wid Charles G), b 250 Howard.
Johnson Walker E, janitor, h 441 Lincoln av.
Johnson Wallace E, lab, h 223 Blake.
Johnson Walter, clk U S Pension Agency, h 164 Randolph.
Johnson Walter, lab, h 135 S Reisner (W I).
Johnson Walter C, ladies' tailor, 18½ N Meridian, h same.
Johnson Walter J, h 31 Rockwood.
Johnson Webb M, engr, h 469 Lincoln av.
Johnson Will E, collr The Indpls News, b 22 E St Joseph.
Johnson Wm, bricklyr, b 695 N Senate av.
Johnson Wm, broommkr, b 341 Tremont.
Johnson Wm, butcher, h 375 Lincoln av.
Johnson Wm, driver, h 29 Harris av (M J).
Johnson Wm, electrotype finisher, h 298 E North.
Johnson Wm, engr, b 136 Columbia av.
Johnson Wm, lab, h 115 Douglass.
Johnson Wm, lab, h 44 Locke.
Johnson Wm, lab, b 19 N Noble.
Johnson Wm, lab, h 2 Susquehanna.
Johnson Wm, lab, h rear 518 Virginia av.
Johnson Wm, lab, h 170 S William (W I).
Johnson Wm A, lab, h 11 Lafayette.
Johnson Wm A, painter, h 545 Ash.
Johnson Wm A, trav agt, h 26 N Reisner (W I).
Johnson Wm C, carp, h 185 Elm.
Johnson Wm C, hardware, 249 W Washington, h 276 N West.

COAL AND COKE
The W. G. Wasson Co.,
130 INDIANA AVE. TEL. 989
LIME AND LATH

Johnson Wm D, checkman, h w s Talbott av 2 s of 22d.
Johnson Wm D, mach hd, h w s Garfield av 6 n of Washington.
Johnson Wm D, tentmkr, b 634 N Senate av.
Johnson Wm F, b 184 Mass av.
Johnson Wm F, h 22 N William (W I).
Johnson Wm G, foreman, b 624 Park av.
Johnson Wm H, barber, r 318 W North.
Johnson Wm H, druggist and phys, 30 S Station (B), h 20 Depot (B).
Johnson Wm H, lab, h 138½ Agnes.
Johnson Wm H, lab, h 309 E McCarty.
Johnson Wm H, lab, h 715 Mass av.
Johnson Wm H, pressman, h 135 S Olive.
Johnson Wm H, trav agt, h 35 Newman.
Johnson Wm H, waiter, b 130 Columbia al.
Johnson Wm J (Johnson & Stewart), h 409 W 22d (N I).
Johnson Wm J, filer, h rear 192 W Merrill.
Johnson Wm M (Booth & Johnson), h s s Oak av 1 e of Grand av (I).
Johnson Wm M, electrotyper, h 62 Ash.
Johnson Wm O, foreman, h 104 King.
Johnson Wm O, gardener, h 297 Miller (W I).
Johnson Wm S, drayman, h 1363 W Washington (M J).
Johnson Wm S, foreman, h 476 E Georgia.
Johnson Wm S, lab, b 473 Bellefontaine.
Johnson Wm W, lab, h 19 N Noble.
Johnson Winfield S (Indiana Rubber Co), h 640 College av.
Johnson W Frank, grocer, 145 Buchanan, h 135 same.
Johnson Yancy T, lab, b 314 E Court.
Johnson Zachariah, lab, h rear 738 N West.
JOHNSON & METCALF (Charles D Johnson, Alberti C Metcalf), Official Court Reporters, 81 Court House, Tel 398.
Johnson & Reichardt (Joseph R Johnson, Charles F Reichardt), grocers, 421 N East.
Johnson & Stewart (Wm J Johnson, Elmer E Stewart), blksmiths, 1438 Northwestern av (N I).
Johnston Alexander A, dep assessor Marion County, 35 Court House, h 190 Fletcher av.
Johnston Alexander W, h 718 N Capitol av.
Johnston Amanda, stenog Kealing & Hugg, b 1101 N Senate av.
Johnston Anna (wid Arthur), h 98 Bates.
Johnston Catherine B (wid Hamilton R), r 390 N Senate av.
Johnston Chapman D, carp, b 73 Columbia av.
Johnston Charles, lab, h 38 Haugh (H).
Johnston Charles E, clk, b 447 N New Jersey.
Johnston Charles E, phys, 95 Mass av, h 169 E St Joseph.
Johnston Charles G, porter, b 319 S Meridian.
Johnston Charles L, mach, h 136 Lexington av.
Johnston Charles M, clk Levey Bros, b 718 N Capitol av.
Johnston Charles W, lab, h 85 Spring.
Johnston Clyde, lab cor Wallace and McGarry.
Johnston Dennis F, harnessmkr, r 15 S Senate av.
Johnston DeWitt C, bkkpr, h 664 N Capitol av.

W. H. MESSENGER COMPLETE HOUSE FURNISHER 101 East Washington Street, Telephone 491

Foundry and Pattern Shop } McNamara, Koster & Co. { PHONE 1593 212-218 S. Penn. St.

Johnston Edgar, brakeman, b 66 English av.
Johnston Elizabeth (wid Milton C), h w s Madeira 6 s of Prospect.
Johnston Elizabeth, milliner, 484 Virginia av, h same.
Johnston Elizabeth E, h 2 Cornell av.
Johnston Elliott A, lab, b 1000 W Washington.
Johnston Ennius E, salesman Fahnley & McCrea, b 190 Fletcher av.
Johnston Fanny L (wid John), h 714 E Washington.
Johnston Frank D, student, h 471 Union.
Johnston Frank M, brakeman, b 173 S East.
Johnston George F, molder, h 22 Lynn.
Johnston Guy P, timekpr, h 465 Stillwell.
Johnston Hannah (wid John M), h e s Good av 3 s of Railroad (I).
Johnston Harry B, truckmaan, b 128 Lexington av.
Johnston Helen N (wid Thomas D), h 948 N Penn.
Johnston Henry E, baker, b e s Ritter av 4 n of Washington av (I).
Johnston Henry W, lab, r 200½ W Washington.
Johnston Hugh, clk Daniel Stewart Co, h 19 Carlos.
Johnston Isaac N, lab, h 563 S West.
Johnston James, lab, h 155 Hillside av.
Johnston James B, motorman, h 30 Byram pl.
Johnston James C, real est, h 297 Union.
Johnston James L, lab, b 74 Maxwell.
Johnston Jesse B, lab, b 23 Bloomington.
Johnston John C, clk, h e s Good av 3 s of Railroad (I).
Johnston John D, chief clk telegraph L E & W R R, telegraph and electrical school, 19, 156½ E Washington, h w s Lake av 4 s of Washington av (I).
Johnston John E, filer, h 133 Lynn av (W I).
Johnston John F, carp, h 398½ College av.
Johnston John F, drugs, 401 N Illinois, h 388 same.
Johnston John H, h 484 Virginia av.
Johnston John F, helper, h 7 Taylor av.
Johnston Joseph C, clk, h 128 Lexington av.
Johnston Joseph F, h 70 Omer.
Johnston Josiah, lab, b 565 S West.
Johnston Josiah T, b 5 Taylor av.
Johnston Lucy E, h 403 W 2d.
Johnston Margaret L, b 173 S East.
Johnston Marshall C, clk, b 718 N Capitol av.
Johnston Marshall E, condr, h s s 30th 1 e of Capitol av.
Johnston Mary (wid Thomas), h 447 N New Jersey.
Johnston Millard F, brakeman, h 5 Taylor av.
Johnston Noble, waiter, r 318 N California.
Johnston Norman R, mach hd, b 297 Union.
Johnston Oliver T, condr, h 94 Spann av.
Johnston Rachel (wid James), b 565 S West.
Johnston Richard, switchman, h 117 Chadwick.
Johnston Samuel A, floorwalker H P Wasson & Co, h 626 N Penn.
Johnston Sterling F, carp, h 139½ E Washington.
Johnston Ulysses S G, switchman, h 86 Eureka av.
Johnston Wiley W, trav agt, b w s Lake av 4 s of Washington av (I).
Johnston Wm, engr, h 565 S West.
Johnston Wm H, lab, h 74 Maxwell.

Henry H. Fay,
40½ E. WASHINGTON ST.,
AGENT FOR
Insurance Co. of North America,
Pennsylvania Fire Ins. Co.

Johnston Wm M, mngr The Capital Live Stock Commission Co, h 570 N Alabama.
Johnston Wm N, teller Indiana National Bank, b 258 N Penn.
Johnston Wm P, broker, h 849 N Penn.
JOHR AUGUSTUS J, Carriage Dealer, 154 E Ohio, h same.
Joiner Ernest, porter, r 321 W North.
Joiner Ernest A L, student, b 414 Talbott av.
Joiner Gerald, collr Emil Wulschner & Son, b 414 Talbott av.
Joiner Herbert, clk, h 350 N Illinois.
Joiner Joseph, mngr Indpls Terra Cotta Co, h 414 Talbott av.
Joiner Joseph H B, clk Emil Wulschner & Son, b 414 Talbott av.
Joiner Martha E, music teacher, 414 Talbott av, h same.
Joint Rate Association, John B Eckman sec, 42 Board of Trade bldg.
Jolly Charles W, driver, h 373 Coburn.
Jolly Wm P, watchman, h 91 Harmon.
Jolliffe Anna, b 52 Bates.
Jolliffe James S, tree trimmer, h 156 Meek.
Jolliffe John E, engr, h 37 Bates.
Jolliffe John W, mach, b rear 88 S Noble.
Jolliffe McClelland, plastr, b 156 Meek.
Jolliffe Mary E (wid Wm B), h rear 88 S Noble.
Jolliffe Wm O, lab, h 27 Osgood (W I).
Jolly Charles, contr, b Marion Park Hotel (M P).
Jolly Florence E, h 189 W Maryland.
Jolly George, mach opr Indpls Journal, h 638 W Vermont.
Jolly James, flagman, h 523 N Senate av.
Jolly James A, b 523 N Senate av.
Jolly James C, lab, h 80 Ludlow av.
Jolly Jessie E, stenog, b 523 N Senate av.
Jolly John R, shoemkr, 287 Howard (W I), b 34 N Sheffield (W I).
Jolly Robert R, mach hd, h 393 E New York.
Jolly Wm G, messenger Am Ex Co, h 263 S Penn.
Jomuck John, lab, h 35 Parker.
Jonas Alexander C, carp, h 81 Chadwick.

Union Casualty & Surety Co.
of St. Louis, Mo.
Employers', Public, General, Teams and Elevator Liability; also Workmen's Collective, Steam Boiler, Plate Glass and Automatic Sprinkler Insurance.
W. E. BARTON & CO., General Agents,
504 Indiana Trust Building.
LONG DISTANCE TELEPHONE 1918.

THE FRED DIETZ CO.
WOODEN PACKING BOXES MADE TO ORDER. FACTORY AND WAREHOUSE TRUCKS. 400 Madison Avenue. Telephone 654.

Shorthand! BUSINESS UNIVERSITY. When Bl'k. Elevator day and night. Typewriting, Penmanship, Book-keeping, Office Training free. See page 4. Est. 1850. Tel. 499. E. J. HEEB, Proprietor.

Water Works Pumping Engines { HENRY R. WORTHINGTON, 64 SOUTH PENNSYLVANIA ST. Long Distance Telephone 284.

UNION CO-OPERATIVE LAUNDRY { (COMPOSED OF UNION LAUNDRY GIRLS.) NOS. 138, 40 AND 42 VIRGINIA AVENUE — T. E. SOMERVILLE, MANAGER — TELEPHONE 189 INDIANAPOLIS, IND.

HORACE M. HADLEY
REAL ESTATE AND LOANS....
66 East Market Street
Telephone 1540. BASEMENT.

Jonas Godfrey, lab, h rear 71 Ash.
Jonas Gustave C, packer, h 57 Chadwick.
Jonas Wilhelmina (wid Charles), h 49 Chadwick.
Jonas Wm F, cigar mnfr, 549 S West, h same.
Jonas Wm F, lab, h 497 S Missouri.
Jones Ada, printer, b 173 E Vermont.
Jones Adelaide E, stenog, 702 Lemcke bldg, b N Capitol av nr 30th.
Jones Albert, lab, b 529½ N Illinois.
Jones Albert, lab, h 305 W Pearl.
Jones Albert R, bkkpr Am Steel Co, b Stubbins Hotel.
Jones Alexander, h 72½ E Washington.
Jones Alexander, janitor, h 209 Elm.
Jones Alice J, ins, h 62½ S Illinois.
Jones Ambrose, lab, h 648 N West.
Jones Anderson, carp, h e s Concord 1 s of Michigan (H).
Jones Andrew D, lab, h rear 68 S State av.
Jones Ann M (wid Edward M), h 33 Ellen.
Jones Anna H, h 81 W North.
Jones Annie, h 297 W St Clair.
Jones Annie (wid Isaac), h 314 E Court.
JONES AQUILLA Q (Ayres & Jones), Pres Indianapolis Savings and Investment Co, h 1038 N Illinois.
Jones Augustus, waiter, h 326 Muskingum al.
Jones Austin, lab, b w s Denny 1 n of Washington.
Jones A Cary, ins agt, 234 Lemcke bldg, h 284 E Ohio.
Jones Belle, h 234 Clinton.
Jones Benjamin F, patrolman, h 15 Coble.
Jones Benjamin F, trav agt, b 785 N Penn.
Jones Caleb (C Jones & Son), res St Paris, O.
Jones Carl, mach, b 1071 E Michigan.
Jones Caroline F (wid Curtis), b 124 W North.
Jones Carter, lab, h 8 Arthur.
Jones Cassius M C, uphlr, 287 Christian av, h 117 Cornell av.
Jones Catherine (wid Henry L), b 297 N Delaware.
Jones Charles, r 9 S Senate av.

Merchants' and Manufacturers Exchange
Make Collections and Commercial Reports......
J. E. TAKKEN, MANAGER,
19 Union Building, 73 West Maryland Street

Jones Charles (John W Jones & Co), h 68 W 4th.
Jones Charles, clk, b 89 Indiana av.
Jones Charles, lab, r 236 W Wabash.
Jones Charles, porter, h 392 Clinton.
Jones Charles E, printer The Indpls News, h 80 W 18th.
Jones Charles L, carp, h e s Brightwood av 1 n of Schofield (B).
Jones Charles L, lab, h 151 Maple.
Jones Charles Q, bkkpr Singer Mnfg Co, b 68 W 4th.
Jones Charles R, supreme counsellor Order of Equity, 7, 30 Monument pl, tel 774, h 1056 E Michigan.
Jones Charles W, produce, 61 E Mkt House, h 324 E Ohio.
Jones Charlotte (wid Albert), h 276 Lafayette.
Jones Claude G, lab, b 217 S Olive.
Jones Claudius C, trav agt, h 1136 N Meridian.
Jones Clayton, janitor, h 230 Northwestern av.
Jones Clinton, lab, b 102 Martindale av.
Jones Clinton W (Jones & Son), meats, 96 E Mkt House, h 194 Prospect.
Jones Conrad R, lab, h 56 Birch av (W I).
Jones Curtis M, lab, h 219 W 1st.
Jones C & Son (Caleb and Xerxes A), drugs, 101 N Delaware.
Jones Daniel, brakeman, b 30 Crawford.
Jones Daniel, lab, h rear 50 Warren av (W I).
Jones Daniel D, lab, b 5 Willard.
Jones Daniel G, lab, h 231 Michigan (H).
Jones Dennis G, grocer, 1200 Northwestern av, h s Myrtis 1 e of Northwestern av (N I).
Jones DeWitt C, trav agt, h 620 E Washington.
Jones Dudley D, lab, h 48 King av (H).
Jones Dwight L, ins insp, 10 Talbott blk, h 517 Highland av (N I).
Jones Earle C, artist, b 620 E Washington.
Jones Edward, lab, r 15 Rhode Island.
Jones Edward A, ins agt, b 298 E Market.
Jones Edward B, engr, h 118 John.
Jones Edward E, clk, b 172 E St Clair.
Jones Edward F, messenger, b 195 W North.
Jones Edward L, saloon, 105 Mass av, h 1129 N Penn.
Jones Edward M, lab, h 3 N Dorman.
Jones Edward S, barber, s s Washington 20 w of Harris av (M J), h same.
Jones Edwin, driver, h e s Western av 6 n of 22d.
Jones Elias, shoemkr, 103 Oliver av, h 243 River av (W I).
Jones Elijah, grocer, 21 Sheffield av (H), h same.
Jones Eliza J (wid Wm H), h 811 N Meridian.
Jones Elizabeth (wid Wm), h 176 Muskingum al.
Jones Elizabeth W (wid Charles T), b 163 Prospect.
Jones Ella (wid John H), h 52 Lexington av.
Jones Ella (wid Wm), b 171 W 5th.
Jones Ella, dressmkr, 87 Coburn, b same.
Jones Ellen, h 475 E Market.
Jones Elmer E, clk R M S, h 12 Grace.
Jones Emma L, milliner, 1071 E Michigan, h same.
Jones Evan C, b 416 Excelsior av.
Jones Flora C (wid Aquilla), h 467 N Penn.
Jones Florence, h 176½ Muskingum al.
Jones Frances J, dressmkr, b 13 Ketcham.

CLEMENS VONNEGUT || Wire Rope, Machinery, Lathes, Drills and Shapers
184, 186 and 192 E. Washington St.

THE WM. H. BLOCK CO. DRY GOODS, DRAPERIES, RUGS, WINDOW SHADES.
7 AND 9 EAST WASHINGTON STREET.

Jones Frank, engr, h e s Sherman Drive 2 n of Washington.
Jones Frank, lab, b 364 Colburn.
Jones Frank, lab, h 419 S West.
Jones Frank, tmstr, h 140 E McCarty.
Jones Frank B, florist, h Fairview Park.
Jones Frank C, barber, b 112 Blackford.
Jones Frank D, twistmkr, b 327 Jefferson av.
Jones Frederick E, timekpr C C C & St L Ry, b 263 Huron.
Jones Frederick K, h 29 Lincoln av.
Jones Gabriel L, clk County Recorder's Office, h 282 Fayette.
Jones George, h e s Lincoln av 7 s of C C C & St L Ry (M J).
Jones George, lab, r 122 Agnes.
Jones George, fireman, b 22 S State av.
Jones George D (George D Jones & Co), b 439 S Illinois.
Jones George D & Co (George D Jones, Elizabeth M Berry), grocers and meats, 41-43 E North.
Jones George E, clk, h 95 Hoyt av.
Jones George F, pressman, h 444 W Shoemaker (N I).
Jones George J, bkkpr Kirkhoff Bros, h 490 Francis (N I).
Jones George W, carp, h 797 N Illinois.
Jones George W, clk, b 34 Oliver av (W I).
Jones George W, lab, b 87 Coburn.
Jones George W, lab, h 5 Willard.
Jones George W, porter Charles Mayer & Co, h 73 Paca.
Jones George W, tmstr, h 1096 W Vermont.
Jones Gilderoy H, trav agt, h 969 N Delaware.
Jones Halbert H, bkkpr, b 126 Park.
Jones Hannibal F, carp, h 944 Morris (W I).
Jones Harriet, clk, b 13 Ketcham.
Jones Harriet D (wid George F), h 175 W North.
Jones Harriet S (wid Adam), h 13 Ketcham.
Jones Harry, adv agt, b 430 N Senate av.
Jones Harry, butler, 606 N Delaware.
Jones Harry, hostler, h 215½ E Washington.
Jones Harry, porter, h 512 E 7th.
Jones Harry B, bkkpr F Mascari Bros & Co, r 47 S Delaware.
Jones Harry C, driver, h 290 Howard (W I).
Jones Harry E, lather, b 34 Samoa.
Jones Harry W, elev opr, b 28 Journal bldg.
Jones Harvey T, draper, b 118 John.
Jones Henderson J, waiter, h 372 Muskingum al.
Jones Henry, lab, r 130 Allegheny.
Jones Henry, lab, b 648 N West.
Jones Henry, waiter, b 197 W 4th.
Jones Henry C, bartndr, b 140 Columbia av.
Jones Henry E, sawyer, b 585 N Senate av.
Jones Henry W, lab, h 37 Cleveland (H).
Jones Herbert C, uphlr, b 117 Cornell av.
Jones Herbert S, cabtmkr, b 89 Columbia av.
Jones Hester C, grocer, 812 W Washington, h 86 Springfield.
Jones Homer, lab, b 171 S New Jersey.
JONES HOMER I, Physician, 58 E Ohio, Tel 1628; h 247½ N Noble, Tel 967.
JONES HORACE B, Mechanical Engineer and Draughtsman, 415-418 Lemcke Bldg, Long Distance Tel 1103; r 544 Ash. (See adv under classified Mechanical Engineers.)
Jones Horatio S, switchman, b 30 Crawford.

THE H. LIEBER COMPANY
IMPORTERS
Fine Brushes, Canvas, Colors
STUDIES
33 S. MERIDIAN ST.
ARTISTS MATERIALS

Jones Howard L, salesman The Hay & Willits Mnfg Co, b 1136 N Meridian.
Jones Hugh, bricklyr, h 35 Mayhew.
Jones H Guy, clk N Y Store, b 117 Cornell av.
Jones Ira A, trav agt Hollweg & Reese, h 30 Morrison.
Jones Irvin, lab, b 11 E South.
Jones Isaac M, ins agt, h 1178 N Illinois.
Jones Isom, lab, h 76 Columbia al.
Jones Jacob, lab, b 25 W 7th.
Jones James, h 126 Park av.
Jones James, coachman 750 N Delaware.
Jones James, lab, b 244 W 3d.
Jones James B, carp, h 81 S McLain (W I).
Jones James H, lab, b 221 Howard.
Jones James M, hackman, h 24 Roe.
Jones James W, lab, h e s Western av 6 n of 22d.
Jones James W, solr, h 470 W Shoemaker (N I).
Jones Jesse, lab, h 73½ Meikel.
Jones Jesse E, foreman, h 411 N Brookside av.
Jones Jewett W, contr, 12 Arbor av (W I), h same.
Jones John, boilermkr, h 20 Lynn.
Jones John, clk, h 86 Springfield.
Jones John, coachman 515 N Penn.
Jones John, farmer, h 428 W Chicago (N I).
Jones John, lab, h 121½ Ft Wayne av.
Jones John, lab, b 1 Peck.
Jones John B, shoemkr, 176 Indiana av, h same.
Jones John H, engr, h s s Lily 1 w of Rural.
Jones John H, lab, r 5 Susquehanna.
Jones John H, mach hd, h 327 Jefferson av.
Jones John H, painter, b 173 E Market.
Jones John J, carp, h 21 Minkner.
Jones John K, h 124 Park av.
Jones John L, carriagemkr, h 109 Columbia av.
Jones John L, messenger, h 221 N Illinois.
Jones John R, painter, h 21 Sullivan.
Jones John W (John W Jones & Co), h 172 E St Clair.
Jones John W, blksmith, h 108 Keystone av.
Jones John W, cashr, h 79 Bradshaw.

GUIDO R. PRESSLER,
FRESCO PAINTER
Churches, Theaters, Public Buildings, Etc., A Specialty.
Residence, No. 325 North Liberty Street
INDIANAPOLIS, IND.

INDIANAPOLIS STEEL ROOFING AND CORRUGATING WORKS, 23 and 25 East South Street. S. D. NOEL, Proprietor.

David S. McKernan, Rooms 2-5 Thorpe Block.
REAL ESTATE AND LOANS
A number of choice pieces for subdivision, or for manufacturers' sites, with good switch facilities.

DIAMOND WALL PLASTER { Telephone 1410 BUILDERS' EXCHANGE.

UNION TRANSFER AND STORAGE CO., Cor. E. Ohio St. and C., C., C. & St. L. R'y Tracks. BRICK WAREHOUSE; CLEANEST AND SAFEST STORAGE IN CITY FOR HOUSEHOLD GOODS AND MERCHANDISE.

W. McWORKMAN,

METAL CEILINGS,
ROLLING SHUTTERS,
DOORS AND PARTITIONS.
930 W. Washington St. Tel. 1118.

Jones John W, lab, h 84 Ludlow av.
Jones John W, lab, h 456 W Chicago (N I).
Jones John W, molder, b 118 S Judge Harding (W I).
Jones John W & Co (John W and Charles Jones), sugar brokers, 200 S Capitol av.
Jones Joseph, blksmith, b 190 N Missouri.
Jones Joseph F G, hatter, b 117½ W Washington.
Jones Joseph J, blksmith, h 365 Coburn.
Jones Jacob J, hostler, r 189 E Wabash.
Jones Julia (wid Isaac), h 197 W 4th.
Jones Julius, carp, h 1132 N Penn.
Jones Junius, lab, b 85 Camp.
Jones J Lyman, lawyer, 701 Lemcke bldg, h e s N Capitol av 3 s of 30th.
Jones LaMonte E, clk, b 620 E Washington.
Jones Lars, lab, h 423 Lafayette.
Jones Laura B, music teacher, 430 N Senate av, b same.
Jones Lawrence Rev, h s s University av 1 w of Ritter av (I).
Jones Leander W, station agt Consumers' Gas Trust Co, h 1695 Graceland av.
Jones Lee, lab, h 162½ W McCarty.
Jones Lee E, lineman, h 610 W Washington.
Jones Leslie I, spring bed mkr, h 426 W 2d.
Jones Lester E, clk, b 67 Madison av.
Jones Lewis L (Stowers & Jones), h 420 S State av.
Jones Lewis M, clk Charles J Kuhn Co, b 10 Huron.
Jones Lida, stenog, b 24 W New York.
Jones Lillie, cook, b rear 339 S Delaware.
Jones Lillian V, teacher Public School No 19, b 182 Sheldon.
Jones Lilly (wid John), h 1 Peck.
Jones Louis S (Sawyer & Jones), b 126 Park av.
Jones Luke, lab, h 177 W 2d.
Jones Luther, pdlr, b 9 Minerva.
Jones Margaret (wid John), h 336 W Court.
Jones Margaret F (wid John D), h 430 N Senate av.
Jones Maria E, h 406 W Pratt.
Jones Martha A (wid Jasper), h 480 W Lake (N I).
Jones Mary, solr, h 80 Clifford av.
Jones Maude, bkkpr, b 57 Eureka av.

SEALS,
STENCILS,
STAMPS, Etc.
GEO. J. MAYER
15 S. Meridian St.
TELEPHONE 1386.

Jones Milton, lab, h 119 Indiana av.
Jones Moses, lab, h 329 Tremont.
Jones Nancy (wid James), h rear 339 S Delaware.
Jones Nancy (wid John), h 108½ Mass av.
Jones Nimrod, expressman, h 221 Howard.
Jones Noah, h 227 Mass av.
Jones Norman, painter, h 141 Harlan.
Jones Norman H, cooper, b 99 Lily.
Jones Oscar, clk Robert Zener & Co, b 585 N Senate av.
Jones Otto M, lab, b 21 Minkner.
Jones Paul D, asst engr P C C & St L Ry, h 247 N Delaware.
Jones Pearl O, switchman, b 119 Trowbridge (W).
Jones Philip H, boxmkr, h rear 453 S Missouri.
Jones Pleasant P, lab, h 139½ E Washington.
Jones Ralph H, baker, e s Capitol av 3 s of 30th, h same.
Jones Reuben A (Jones & Son), b 194 Prospect.
Jones Richard, barber, 694 N Capitol av, b 424 W 2d.
Jones Richard, lab, h 412 W 2d.
Jones Richard G, lab, h 252 Lafayette av.
Jones Robert, driver, h 18 Mill.
Jones Robert, lab, h 44 Cora.
Jones Robert J, sawyer, h 585 N Senate av.
Jones Robert O, b 30 Belmont av (H).
Jones Robert S, watchman, h 140 Columbia av.
Jones Rose E (wid Charles), b 407 Broadway.
Jones Ross T, lab, h 402½ College av.
Jones Sarah (wid Alexander), h 520 N West.
Jones Sarah A (wid Lewis), b 274 E Walnut.
Jones Sarah E (wid Robert A), b 211 Cornell av.
Jones Sidney M, steward The Bates.
Jones Stanton T, lab, h 102 Martindale av.
Jones Stephen, finisher, b 73 Columbia av.
Jones Stephen, foreman, b 18 Columbia av.
Jones Stephen G, carp, h 64 Frank.
Jones Stephen L, h 142 S East.
Jones Susan (wid Marion), h 43 Cleaveland blk.
Jones Susan (wid Zachariah), b 191 W 9th.
Jones Susan A (wid Wm), h 34 Oliver av (W I).
Jones Taylor Z, miller, h 269 S West.
Jones Thomas, lab, h 61 Dunlop.
Jones Thomas, lab, h 197 W 2d.
Jones Thomas, painter, r 164½ E Washington.
Jones Thomas, tinner, h 127 E Ohio.
Jones Thomas A, molder, h 20 Michigan (H).
Jones Thomas A L, lab, h 413 S Olive.
Jones Thomas E, grocer, 43 Torbet, h 444 W Shoemaker (N I).
Jones Thomas H, lab, h 69 Langley av.
Jones Thomas J, h 244 S East.
Jones Thomas M, boxmkr, b 329 E Georgia.
Jones Thomas M, lab, h 416 W 2d.
Jones Thomas W, lab, h 134 Columbia al.
Jones Vincent C, tmstr, h rear 84 Wallack.
Jones Walter, clk, b 182 E St Clair.
Jones Walter B, bkkpr, h 297 Bellefontaine.
Jones Walter D, salesman, b 399 N New Jersey.
Jones Walter E, engr, b 13 Ketcham.
Jones Walter R, mach, b 118 John.
Jones Wayne C, bkkpr Eli Lilly & Co, h 315 Ash.
Jones Wm, driver, b 27 Hudson.

A. METZGER AGENCY ESTABLISHED 1863. INSURANCE

LAMBERT GAS & GASOLINE ENGINE CO.
ANDERSON, IND. PORTABLE GASOLINE ENGINES. 2 TO 25 H. P.

Jones Wm, driver, b 224 Muskingum al.
Jones Wm, ins agt, r 135 N Delaware.
Jones Wm, janitor, h 234 Fayette.
Jones Wm, lab, h 184 Anderson.
Jones Wm, lab, h 113 W 4th.
Jones Wm, lab, h rear 398 Mass av.
Jones Wm, lab, h rear 72 S Noble.
Jones Wm, lab, b 73 Paca.
Jones Wm, mach hd, h 446 Shoemaker (N I).
Jones Wm A, pres Red Clay Orchard Co, b 116 Huron.
Jones Wm D, lab, h rear 53 Ash.
Jones Wm E (Wm E Jones & Co), b 797 N Illinois.
Jones Wm E, driver, h 26½ N Senate av.
Jones Wm E, lab, h 162 W McCarty.
Jones Wm E, letter carrier P O, h 116 Huron.
Jones Wm E & Co (Wm E Jones, Benjamin F Hornefius), grocers, 52 Marion av (W I).
Jones Wm G, h 60 W 12th.
Jones Wm H, clk, h 31 N Beville av.
Jones Wm H, porter, h 74 Dugdale.
Jones Wm J, mach hd, h 446 W Shoemaker (N I).
Jones Wm L, h 81 Highland pl.
Jones Wm L, motorman, r 172 E North.
Jones Wm M, clk R M S, h 23 Ft Wayne av.
Jones Wm M, lab The Bates.
Jones Wm O, driver, h 26½ N Senate av.
Jones Wm O, lab, h 48 King av (H).
Jones Wm P, lab, h 20 Haugh (H).
Jones Wm R, lab, h 950 N New Jersey.
Jones Wm T, crater, h 126 Union.
Jones Wm U, blksmith, h s e cor Rural and Pope av.
Jones Wm W, clk H P Wasson & Co, b 969 N Delaware.
Jones W Franklin (Brown & Jones), h 310 E Market.
Jones Willis, molder, h 32 Wilcox.
Jones Willis A, lab, b 48 King av (H).
Jones Wyley D, lab, h 24 Lynn.
Jones Xerxes A (C Jones & Son), r 122 E Ohio.
Jones Zachary T, miller, h 269 S West.
Jones & Son (Reuben A and Clinton W), meats, 106 Prospect.
Jontz John A (Dwinnell & Jontz), h 401 W Shoemaker (N I).
Jordan, see also Jourdan.
Jordan Albert C, engr, h 23 Miley av.
Jordan Alice, bkkpr Power & Drake, b 281 S East.
Jordan Amanda (wid Joseph), h 137 Downey.
Jordan Amita, brakeman, r 102 S Illinois.
Jordan Arthur, pres Arthur Jordan Co, h 729 N Meridian
Jordan Arthur Co, Arthur Jordan pres, Milton A Woollen vice-pres, Charles W Sutton sec and treas, produce, s w cor Delaware and Maryland.
Jordan Barclay R, carp, b 51 Andrews.
Jordan Celia L (wid Rev Wm R), h 388 Central av.
Jordan Charles A, porter L E & W R R, cor Washington and Noble.
Jordan Charles C, temperer, h 541 S Capitol av.
Jordan Charles E, driver, h 15 Cooper.
Jordan Charles R, clk, h 297 E New York.
Jordan Charles R, mach, b 23 Miley av.
Jordan Charles T, huckster, h 3 Atlas.
Jordan Christina, nurse 194 E Michigan.
Jordan Daniel S, b 75 Hoyt av.
Jordan Edward, lab, h 49 Henry.
Jordan Edward P, crater, h 445 Martindale av.

Farm and City Loans
25 Years' Successful Business.
THOS. C. DAY & CO,
Rooms 325 to 330 Lemcke Building.

Jordan Edwin M, lab, b 23 Miley av.
Jordan Emons, lab, b 35 Garden.
Jordan Ezra C, switchman, h 398 Martindale av.
Jordan Frank C, clk Indpls Water Co, h 388 Central av.
Jordan Frank C, lab, b 373 W North.
Jordan George, lab, h 15 Cooper.
Jordan Gilmore, bkkpr, h 186 N Capitol av.
Jordan Harrison, lab, h 239 Elizabeth.
Jordan Harry H, porter, b 137 Downey.
Jordan Henry C, lawyer, 713 Lemcke bldg, h 548 Highland av (N I).
Jordan Henry H, contr, h 26 Ludlow av.
Jordan Henry T, clk Adams Ex Co, r 297 E New York.
Jordan James, carp, b 1683 N Senate av.
Jordan James G, painter, b 548 Highland av (N I).
Jordan James H, Associate Justice Supreme Court of Indiana, 61 State House, res Martinsville, Ind.
Jordan John, plastr, b 171 E Court.
Jordan John L, carp, b 346 N Senate av.
Jordan John S, phys, 36 W Washington, h 1118 N Penn.
Jordan Louisa (wid Peter), h 214 Fulton.
Jordan Minnie (wid Joseph), b 135 Forest av.
Jordan Monford M, lab, h 20 Nordyke av (W I).
Jordan Mordecai E, weigher, h 3 Traub av.
Jordan Morton W, lab, b 204 Lexington av.
Jordan Orlando, varnisher, b 223 Ramsey av.
Jordan Orville M, painter, b 23 Miley av.
Jordan Otto A, carpet cutter, h 139 Olive.
Jordan Perry E, lab, h 444 Martindale av.
Jordan Phineas G, insp, h 120 Park av.
Jordan Rachel (wid Wesley), h 173 W 6th.
Jordan Robert H, patrolman, h 25 Lord.
Jordan Robert W, bkkpr Kingan & Co (ltd), h 619 W Eugene (N I).
Jordan Roy, lab, b 23 Miley av.
Jordan Samuel S, carp, h 51 Andrews.
Jordan Sidney T (The A Burdsal Co), h e s Illinois 1 n of 29th.
Jordan Theodore, watchman, b 346 N Senate av.

EAT
QUAKER BREAD
ASK YOUR GROCER FOR IT.
THE HITZ BAKING CO.

BICYCLES $5 DOWN. MONTHLY. Best Wheels. Best Terms. WHEELMEN'S CO. 31 W. OHIO ST. LONG DISTANCE TEL. 1855.

J. H. TECKENBROCK House, Sign and Fresco Painter, 94 EAST SOUTH STREET.

FIDELITY MUTUAL LIFE PHILADELPHIA, PA. A. H. COLLINS, Gen. Agt. Baldwin Blk. RATES REASONABLE. SOUND BEYOND QUESTION. BUSINESS-LIKE IN PRACTICE.

BITUMINOUS COAL ▸▸ Edwardsport Coal and Mining Company ROOMS 42 AND 43 WHEN BUILDING.

ESTABLISHED 1876. TELEPHONE 168.
CHESTER BRADFORD,
SOLICITOR OF PATENTS,
AND COUNSEL IN PATENT CAUSES.
(See adv. page 6.)
Office:—Rooms 14 and 16 Hubbard Block, S. W. Cor. Washington and Meridian Streets, INDIANAPOLIS, INDIANA.

Jordan Thomas, lab, b n s Orchard av 1 e of Rural.
Jordan Thomas, phys, 99 Bates, b same.
Jordan Thomas Q, caller, h 35 Peru av.
Jordan West, lab, h 31½ Columbia al.
Jordan Wilbur S, tel opr, b 25 Lord.
Jordan Will P, collr When Clothing Store, b 548 Highland av (N I).
Jordan Wm, porter, r 390 W 1st.
Jordan Wm A, clk, b 764 Broadway.
Jordan Wm D, clk, b 388 Central av.
Jordan Wm H, druggist, b 600 Central av.
Jordan Wm H, lawyer, 211 Lemcke bldg, h 1256 N Penn.
Jordan Wirt, packer, h 223 Ramsey av.
Jordan Wright S, trav pass agt C C C & St L Ry, 1 E Washington, h 1176 N Illinois.
Jorgensen Lars C, janitor A Kiefer Drug Co, h 3 Beecher.
Jorgensen Mads, h 64 Nebraska.
Jorion Nicholas, carp, h 317 Davidson.
Jorker Robert, butcher, b 754 E Washington.
Jorman John, lab, h 119 Darnell.
Jose Gustav C, ins agt, h 324 Orange.
Jose Herman C, glazier Wm Wiegel, h 335 Orange.
Jose Nicholas, com mer, h 350 Orange.
Jose Oscar, clk, b 350 Orange.
Jose Victor R, com mer, 41 S Delaware, h 333 Orange.
Josefsberg Abraham, clothing, 54 Indiana av, h same.
Joseph Frank, bookbndr, b 454 N West.
Joseph Gustav, trav agt, h 336 S Illinois.
Joseph Jacob, pdlr, h 2 Willard.
Joseph Moses, pdlr, b 51 Russell av.
Joseph Lipman, pdlr, h 144 Eddy.
Joseph Philip, driver, r 166½ W Washington.
Joseph Wm, driver, h 27 S Dorman.
Joslin Frederick F, painter, b 170 Maple.
Joslin Harry E, condr, b 210 Highland av.
Joslin Margaret S (wid Edward H), h 170 Maple.
Joslin Nannie, h 24 N West.
Joslin Sylvanus, carp, 210 Highland av, h same.
Joslin Wm C, condr, h 619 E Vermont.

BUY THE BEST.
Outing BICYCLES $85
MADE BY
HAY & WILLITS MFG. CO.
76 N. PENN. ST. Phone 598.

Joss Albert C, trav agt, b 467 N California.
Joss Frederick A (Jameson & Joss), h 134 St Mary.
Joss George N, cigars, 82 Indiana av, h same.
Joss Mary E, milliner, 80 Indiana av h same.
Joss Wm L, driver, h 26 N Gillard av.
Josse Peter A, barber, 347 Madison av, h same.
Josse Wm C F, harnessmkr, b 366 N Brookside av.
Jostarnd Edward J, finisher, b 180 Columbia av.
Jourdan Bailey D, baggagemaster, b 361 Broadway.
JOURNAL JOB PRINTING CO, Otto H Hasselman Propr, Printers, Publishers of Interstate and Indiana Official Railway Guide, 126-130 W Maryland, Tel 490.
Jowitt Richard, mach, h 329 Bates.
Joyce Franklin P, car rep, b 28 Marion av (W I).
Joyce Frederick, butcher, b 276 W McCarty.
Joyce Hallie A, dep County Clerk, b 186 Fletcher av.
Joyce Helen M, dep County Clerk, b 186 Fletcher av.
Joyce John L, car rep, h 15 Wilcox.
Joyce John T, lab, h 285 W Merrill.
Joyce Josie C, bkkpr Gem Laundry, b 45 Minerva.
Joyce Lynn, lab, h 20 N West.
Joyce Maurice, mach hd, b 45 Minerva.
Joyce Nannie E (wid Aurelius J), h 186 Fletcher av.
Joyce Patrick J, molder, h 193 Michigan (H).
Joyce Thomas, shoemkr, 171 Virginia av, h same.
Joyce Wm, lab, b 84 Cleaveland blk.
Joyce Wm A, officer Board of Children's Guardians, h 335 Jefferson av.
Joyner Henry, lab, h 6 Reynolds av (H).
Judah Charles, sec Indiana Car and Foundry Co, res Cincinnati, O.
Judah Parker, salesman The Indpls Millinery Co, b 350 N New Jersey.
Judah Wm B, sec Indpls Millinery Co, h 350 N New Jersey.
Juday, see also Judy.
Juday Maurice W, clk County Auditor's Office, h 514 Ash.
Juday Susan W (wid Christian W), h 514 Ash.
Judd Albert, bricklyr, h 279 Yandes.
Judd Albert A, plater, h 224 Douglass.
Judd Dill, h 255½ S Delaware.
Judd Frederick J, weaver, h 215 Blake.
Judd Henry T, lab, b 16 Columbia al.
Judd Richard, lab, h 125 Maxwell.
Judd Thomas, miller, h 88 Patterson.
Judd Walter H, stenog, b 215 Blake.
Judd Wm F (Wilcox & Judd), h 264 Douglass.
Judge Anna, h 461 S East.
Judge Catherine (wid James), h 41 Buchanan.
Judge Ellen (wid James), b 42 Barth av.
Judge Martin P, fireman, h 18 Grant.
Judge Martin T, clk, b rear 460 S Meridian.
Judge Mary (wid James), b 18 Grant.
Judge Thomas, lab, h rear 460 S Meridian.
Judkins Charles V, carp, b n s Rawles av 2 w of Line (I).

ROOFING MATERIAL C. ZIMMERMAN & SONS, SLATE AND GRAVEL ROOFERS, 19 SOUTH EAST STREET.

PUMPS Chain Pumps, Driven Wells and Deep Water Wells. Repairing Neatly Done. Cisterns Built. CHARLES KRAUSS', 42 S. PENN. ST. TELEPHONE 465.

Collars and Cuffs Laundered in Best of Style. Domestic or High Gloss Finish. ERTEL STEAM LAUNDRY 26 and 28 N. Senate Ave. Telephone 1089.

Judkins Frederick O, b n s Rawles av 2 w of Line (I).
Judkins Jefferson, lab, h n s Rawles av 2 w of Line (I).
Judkins John W, brakeman, b 64 S State av.
Judkins Wm M, shoemkr, rear 251 English av, h 271 Prospect.
Judkins Wm R jr, collr, h 12 Dawson.
Judson Abby V (wid Charles E), h 407 N Capitol av.
Judson Adoniram B, trav agt, b 799 N Capitol av.
Judson Charles E (Judson & Hanna), h 850 N Illinois.
Judson Dolly A, artist, b 799 N Capitol av.
Judson Frederick, h 23 W 12th.
Judson James M, bkkpr Kingan & Co (ltd), b 23 W 12th.
Judson Mary J, treas Christian Woman's Board of Missions, r e s Delaware 2 n of New York.
Judson Willet A, salesman Baker & Thornton, h 81 Lockerbie.
Judson & Hanna (Charles E Judson, John A Hanna), whol cigars, 21 W Maryland.
Judy, see also Juday.
Judy Emma (wid Raymond), h 48 N California.
Judy India, lab, r rear 478 N Penn.
Julian Allen, lab, h 586 Chestnut.
Julian Bowen F, mer police, h 75 Hudson.
Julian George O, carriagemkr, h 178 Maple.
Julian George W, h e s Central av 2 s of Washington av (I).
Julian Harry E, lab, b 264 Springfield.
Julian Jacob B (Julian & Julian), h s s Railroad 2 e of Central av (I).
Julian John F (Julian & Julian), h s s Railroad 2 e of Central av (I).
Julian John S, mach, b 586 Chestnut.
Julian Marcee L, lab, h 233 N Beville av.
Julian Paul, civil engr, r 82½ E Washington.
Julian Wm A, lab, b 586 Chestnut.
Julian & Julian (Jacob B and John F), lawyers, 12½ N Delaware.
Julian Antonio, confr, 287 E Washington, h same.
Juliano Joseph, porter, h 127 Duncan.
Juliano Michael, clk, h 45½ Virginia av.
Julien Anna L (wid Wm H), seamstress The J B Allfree Mnfg Co.
Julien Isaac N, lab, h 374 Union.
Julien James B, miller, h 234 Lincoln la
Julier Charles W, messenger Am Ex Co, h 407 N Alabama.
Julier Benjamin R, clk, b 407 N Alabama.
Julius Frank, lab, b 776 S East.
Jumper Alpha W, lab, b 84 Bradshaw.
Jumper Wm T, lab, h 84 Bradshaw.
June Homer H, r 84½ N Illinois.
June Wm H, h 906 N Senate av.
Junemann Frederick, foreman, b w s Sugar Grove av 5 s of Miller av (M P).
Jung, see also Young and Yung.
JUNG BREWING CO OF CINCINNATI, O, AND AURORA, IND, THE, Jacob Reuter Agt, cor Dillon and Big Four Ry, Tel 1032.
Jung John, uphlr, h 80 Lexington av.
Jung Joseph, baker, h 176½ E Washington.
Jung Louis, meats, 340 Mass av, h same.
Jungclaus Frederick W, sec The Wm P Jungclaus Co, b 398 N East.
Jungclaus Wm P, pres The Wm P Jungclaus Co, The Home Brewing Co and Polar Ice Co, h 398 N East.

Richardson & McCrea, 79 East Market Street, FIRE INSURANCE, REAL ESTATE, LOANS, AND RENTAL AGENTS. Telephone 182.

JUNGCLAUS WM P CO THE, Wm P Jungclaus Pres, Frederick W Jungclaus Sec, Matthew Roth Supt, Contractors and Builders, Planing Mill and Lumber Yards, 317 Mass av, Branch Office 7 Pembroke Arcade, Tel 62.
Junge Herman (Junge & Sonnenschmidt), h s s Brookville rd 1 w of P C C & St L Ry (S).
Junge & Sonnenschmidt (Herman Junge, Carl Sonnenschmidt), florists s s Brookville rd 1 w of P C C & St L Ry (S).
Junghans Gustav C, plastr, 241 Eureka av, h same.
Junghans Oscar G, uphlr, b 241 Eureka av.
Junker John B, bricklyr, h 413 W Shoemaker (N I).
Just Gustav, h 44 S Pine.
Justice Edward W, brakeman, r 220½ S Meridian.
Justice John Q (Justice & Warren), h 1015 N Penn.
JUSTICE & WARREN (John Q Justice, Charles E Warren), Grocers, 1547-1549 N Illinois.
Justus Everett M, bricklyr, h 1687 Kenwood av.
Justus Henry, lab, h 28 Parker.
Justus Henry L, tmstr, h 182 Newman.
Justus Jesse G, cooper, h 249½ W Maryland.
Justus John B, hostler, h 249½ W Maryland.
Justus M Ella, h 425 S Meridian.
Jutt August, teacher Deaf and Dumb Inst, h s s Washington av 1 e of Downey av (I).
Jutte Andrew, gardener, b 886 S Meridian.
Jutte Caroline (wid Matthias), h 886 S Meridian.
Jutzi Henry, cabtmkr, r 158 N New Jersey.
Jutzi Louisa J, clk, h 37 College av.
Jutzi Paul, cabtmkr, h 65 Beaty.
Jux, see Yux.

K

Kabelle Dorothea (wid Albert), b 213 S Alabama.

SHORTHAND REPORTING...... CONVENTIONS, SPEECHES, SERMONS. COPYING ON TYPEWRITER. S. H. EAST, State Agent, THE WILLIAMS TYPEWRITER 55 Thorpe Block, 87 East Market Street.

ELLIS & HELFENBERGER Manufacturers of Iron Vases, Setees and Hitch Posts. 162-170 South Senate Ave. Tel. 958.

THE HOGAN TRANSFER AND STORAGE COMP'Y
Household Goods and Pianos Moved—Packed—Stored...... Baggage and Package Express Machinery and Safes a Specialty Cor. Washington and Illinois Sts. TELEPHONE No. 675.

The Central Rubber & Supply Co. PHONE 2. 79 S. ILLINOIS ST., INDIANAPOLIS, IND. Hose, Belting, Packing, Clothing, Druggists' Sundries, Bicycle Tires, Cotton Hose, Etc. New York Belting & Packing Co., L't'd.

The Provident Life and Trust Co.
Small Death Rate. Small Expense Rate. Safe Investments. OF PHILADELPHIA. Insurance in force $115,000,000
D. W. EDWARDS, General Agent, 508 Indiana Trust Building.

Kackley Thomas R, pur agt Atlas Engine Wks, b 20 Garfield pl.
Kader Wm G, flagman, b 121 Agnes.
Kaehn Henry, molder, b 306 S Penn.
Kaehn John G, detective, h 306 S Penn.
Kaehn Michael J, ironwkr, h 149 Agnes.
Kaempl Louis, lab, b 82 S Delaware.
Kaesberg Mathias, grocer, 70 High, h same.
Kafader Joseph, polisher, h 191 Harrison.
Kafader Otto, engr, b 1861 Michigan av.
Kahan Morris, grocer, 231 W Washington, h 233 same.
Kahl, see also Cole and Kohl.
Kahl Charles, grocer, 373 W Michigan, h same.
Kahl Charles F, clk, b 373 W Michigan.
Kahl Claus, drayman, h 174 Harrison.
Kahl Mary (wid Peter), b 373 W Michigan.
Kahle Frederick C, grocer, 607 W Michigan, and produce, E Mkt House, h 108 Agnes.
Kahler Charles E, phys, 720 E Ohio, b same.
Kahler Frederick, r 25½ S Alabama.
Kahler Wm S, baggagemstr, h 57 Woodruff av.
Kahley James H, fireman, h 856 Bellefontaine.
Kahlo Charles, sec Indiana Mutual B and L Assn, h 475 N Meridian.
Kahlo George D, phys, 60 Journal bldg, h 36 W 2d.
Kahlo Harry C, dentist, 60 Journal bldg, b 475 N Meridian.
Kahn, see also Cahn.
Kahn Abraham (A Kahn & Son), h 362 E New York.
Kahn Adolph, h 128 N East.
Kahn Alexander, brewer, h 54 Dunlop.
Kahn A & Son (Abraham and Harry A), live stock com, Union Stock Yards (W I).
Kahn Bertha, bkkpr, b 127 Home av.
Kahn Caroline (wid Levi), h 127 Home av.
Kahn David (David Kahn & Co), h 851 N Meridian.
Kahn David & Co (David Kahn, Raphael Kirschbaum), brokers, 131 Commercial Club bldg.
Kahn David A, clk, b 362 E New York.

Julius C. Walk & Son, Jewelers Indianapolis.
12 EAST WASHINGTON ST.

Kahn David L, phys, 867 N Meridian, h same.
Kahn Edward A, clk People's Outfitting Co, b 362 E New York.
Kahn Eli (Brunswick & Kahn), b 128 N East.
Kahn Emma E, b 33 Davis.
Kahn Gertrude (wid Samuel), b 283 E Market.
Kahn Harry A (A Kahn & Son), b 362 E New York.
Kahn Henry, mngr Kahn Tailoring Co, h 950 N Penn.
Kahn Isaac, clk, b 127 Home av.
Kahn Jacob, real est, h 400 N East.
Kahn Lee R, bkkpr, h 300 E Market.
Kahn Leon, h 164 N East.
Kahn Louis, lab, b 335 S Meridian.
Kahn Max, clk, b 127 Home av.
KAHN NATHAN, Dry Goods, Clothing, Boots and Shoes, 580-582 S East, h same.
Kahn Nathan A, clk, b 362 E New York.
Kahn Otto, h 128 N East.
Kahn Robert J, butcher, h 456 S Delaware.
KAHN SYLVAN W, Lawyer, 90-92 Baldwin Blk, b 164 N East, Tel 740.
KAHN TAILORING CO, Henry Kahn Mngr, 22-24 E Washington, Tel 1031.
Kahn Walter, clk, b 128 N East.
Kaiser, see also Kaser and Kiser.
Kaiser August, painter, 459 Sheldon, b same.
Kaiser Elizabeth (wid Charles), b 18 Minnesota.
Kaiser Emile, brewer Indpls Brewing Co, h 497 S New Jersey.
Kaiser Henry D, clk U S Pension Agency, h 58 Cherry.
Kaiser Laura (wid Adam), b 421 S Illinois.
Kaiser Otto, engr, b 390 S East.
Kaiser Theresa (wid Joseph), b 497 S New Jersey.
Kaiser Wm, sew machs, 654 Virginia av, h 252 S Olive.
Kaiser Wm, tmstr, h 82 N State av.
Kalb, see also Kolb.
Kalb Eleanor A, teacher Public School No 29, b 549 Bellefontaine.
Kalb Frank J, clk Indpls Gas Co, b 164 E St Joseph.
Kalb Frederick W, plumber, b 164 E St Joseph.
Kalb George P, driver, h 755 N Illinois.
Kalb Henry, h 164 E St Joseph.
Kalb John, tinner, 751 N Illinois, h 549 Bellefontaine.
Kalb Louis J, clk, b 549 Bellefontaine.
Kalb Wm C, watchmkr Wm T Marcy, h 876 N Alabama.
Kalbfleisch Frederick Rev, pastor Fourth German Reform Church, h 79 N Belmont av (H).
Kaler, see also Caylor, Kaylor, Keeler, Keller, Koehler and Kuhler.
Kaler Emory E, condr, h 721 N Capitol av.
Kaler Jacob E, shoemkr, 743 N Capitol av, h 724 same.
Kaler Louis, clk, b 421 S West.
Kaler Louis J, clk, b 724 N Capitol av.
Kaler Wm E, driver, b 724 N Capitol av.
Kaley Elmer B, watchmkr, b 58 Brookside av.
Kaley Henry L, painter, 58 Brookside av, h same.
Kalff Anna (wid Herman), h 177 Johnson av.

OTTO GAS ENGINES | BUILDERS' EXCHANGE S. W. Cor. Ohio and Penn. Telephone 535.

Becker & Son Charles Becker Jacob Becker Jr. Merchant Tailors. 21 N. Penn. St. Tel. 934

Kaltenbrum James, trav agt, b 150 N Illinois.
Kaltenbrunner John, car rep, h 46 Hope (B).
Kalter Albert E, fertilizers, 418 W Washington, h 428 Park av.
Kamber Amadee, engraver, 11½ N Meridian, h 72 Wisconsin.
Kaminsky Clarence, trav agt, h 414 S Illinois.
Kaminsky Emma, stenog W J Beckett, b 414 S Illinois.
Kaminsky Henry, pdlr, b 39 Russell av.
Kaminsky Isaac L, pdlr, h 39 Russell av.
Kaminsky Julius M, clk Original Eagle, b 39 Russell av.
Kaminsky Louis, pdlr, b 39 Russell av.
Kamm Gottlieb, lab, h 539 S New Jersey.
Kamm Wm, lab, b 539 S New Jersey.
Kammacher Henry, varnisher, b 754 S East.
Kamman George H, blksmith, h 371 English av.
Kamp, see also Camp and Kemp.
Kamp David, condr, h 58 Russell av.
Kamp Edward, student, b 58 Russell av.
Kamp Mollie, h 86 Columbia al.
Kampman Henry, carver, h 280 Brookside av.
Kampman Henry W, saloon, 124 E Wabash, h 219 E Market.
Kampmann Albert F, carp, b 309 Alvord.
Kampmann Alexander, b 70 Lockerbie.
Kampmann August, lab, h 309 Alvord.
Kampmann Frederick W, lab, b 70 Lockerbie.
Kampmann Louis, carp, 117 Fulton, b same.
Kampmann Wm, driver, h 117 Fulton.
Kamps Bernard G, printer, b 11 Cincinnati.
Kamps Caroline (wid Bernard), b 11 Cincinnati.
KAMPS FRANK G, Oysters, Fish and Game, 40 Virginia av and 37 E Market House, Tel 610; h 333 Clifford av.
Kanawha Despatch, Walton C Hobbs agt, n e cor Delaware and South.
Kane, see also Cain, Kaehn, Kahn and O'Cain.
Kane Andrew J, lab, h 592 Morris (W I).
Kane Ella L, dressmkr, h 74 Nebraska.
Kane Henry, baker, 63 E Mkt House, h 907 N Capitol av.
Kane James B, mach, h 83 Buchanan.
Kane Mary A, tailoress, h 74 Nebraska.
Kane Thomas, gasfitter, b 334 E Michigan.
Kane Thomas C, trav agt, r 81 E Michigan.
Kane Thomas E, condr, h 812 E Market.
Kane Walter J (Gorman & Kane), r 69 Mass av.
Kanouse Francis, paperhngr, h e s Good av 1 s of Railroad (I).
Kantmann Frances (wid Mathias), b 79 N East.
Kantrowitz Bros (Isaac M and Henry J), clothing, 10 W Washington.
Kantrowitz Henry J (Kantrowitz Bros), h 819 N Meridian.
Kantrowitz Isaac M (Kantrowitz Bros), h 947 N Meridian.
Kapfmeyer Wm, driver, b 228 E Morris.
Kappeler Anthony E, shoemkr, 103 Ash, h same.
Kappeler Edward J, jeweler, b 103 Ash.
Kappeler Wm C, clk, b 103 Ash.
Kappes Edward H, press feeder, r 335 E Wabash.
Kappes Wm, printer, r 335 E Wabash.
Kappes Wm P (Fishback & Kappes), h 750 N Alabama.
Kappler Benjamin N, clk C C C & St L Ry, cor Delaware and South.

Henry H. Fay,
40½ E. WASHINGTON ST.,
FIRE INSURANCE, REAL ESTATE,
LOANS AND RENTAL AGENT.

Kappler Ernest J, clk C C C & St L Ry, cor Delaware and South.
Kappus Charles, mach, b 65 Chadwick.
Kappus John, packer, h 65 Chadwick.
Kappus John jr, lab, b 65 Chadwick.
Kappus Wm, lab, b 65 Chadwick.
Karch Ernest J, h n w cor Garfield av and Michigan.
Karch Paul A, printer, b n w cor Garfield av and Michigan.
Karcher Joseph, engr, h 1043 S Meridian.
Karcher Wm, lab, h 831 S Meridian.
Kares Anna, teacher Public School No 20, b 163 Spann av.
Kares Edward W, bartndr, b 109 Davidson.
Kares Harvey L, clk, b 109 Davidson.
Kares Joseph, h 109 Davidson.
Kares Robert L, driver, b 109 Davidson.
Kares Wm A R, fireman, h 163 Spann av.
Karibo Edmund, mach, h 63 N Brightwood av (B).
Karibo Frederick, grocer, 63 N Brightwood av (B), b same.
Karle, see also Carle.
Karle Christian, h 356 Central av.
Karle Joseph C, shoes, 73 E Washington, h 859 N New Jersey.
Karn Irwin, tiremkr, h 27 Bates.
Karn Nathan, huckster, h 96 N Alabama.
Karnatz Herman, cook, h 336 N Liberty.
Karnatz Jesse F (Cassell & Karnatz), h 52½ S Illinois.
Karnatz John C, clk, h 395 Cornell av.
Karnes Celia, buyer N Y Store, b 316 N Meridian.
Karrer Charles T, carp, h 54 Martindale av.
Karrer Frederick, car rep, h 105 Yandes.
Karrer George, blksmith, 120 Hill av, h 122 same.
Karrer Henry A, bricklyr, b 54 Martindale av.
Karrer Wm E, blksmith, 368 Lincoln av, b 105 Yandes.
Karrmann Julius, bkkpr, h 888 N Capitol av.
Karst E Frank, shoes, 360 Mass av, h 98 Park av.
Karstetter Emma H, propr Senate Hotel, 50½ N Senate av.

JAS. N. MAYHEW,
MANUFACTURING
OPTICIAN
LENSES AND FRAMES A SPECIALTY.
No. 13 North Meridian St., Indianapolis.

SALIS & STANLEY. Contractors and Builders. Office, 177 Clinton St. Indianapolis, Ind. Gas and Electric Fixtures a Specialty. Repairing of all kinds done on short notice. TELEPHONE 999.

LUMBER | Sash, Door and Planing Mill Work. | Balke & Krauss Co. Cor. Market and Missouri Streets.

FRIEDGEN'S TAN SHOES are the Newest Shades Prices the Lowest. 19 North Pennsylvania St.

SAMUEL LAING General Job Work in Sheet Metal of all Kinds 72 AND 74 E. COURT STREET.

M. B. WILSON, Pres. W. F. CHURCHMAN, Cash.
THE CAPITAL NATIONAL BANK,
INDIANAPOLIS, IND.
Make collections on all points in the States of Indiana and Illinois on the most favorable rates.
Capital, - - $300,000
Surplus and Earnings, 50,000
No. 28 S. Meridian St., Cor. Pearl.

KARSTETTER WM B, Physician, 471 W 22d (N I), h same, Tel 1033.
Karweik Albert L, wiper, h e s Rural 2 n of Michigan.
Kasberg Joseph, bookbndr, h 295 S Alabama.
Kasberg Wm J, bkkpr A Metzger Agency, b 295 S Alabama.
Kaschenreuter Frank, carp, h 32 Lee (W I).
Kaser, see also Kaiser and Kiser.
Kaser Albert C, clk, b 494 W North.
Kaser David G, grocer, 494 W North, h same.
Kaser Edward H, shoemkr, 310 E Washington, h 36 N East.
Kashman George J, lab, h 291 W Merrill.
Kashmeyer Christian, car rep, h 27 Deloss.
Kashner Alonzo R, grocer, 578 E 7th, h same.
Kassebaum Frederick W, b 1012 N Capitol av.
Kassebaum Wm F (Probst & Kassebaum), h 162 Bellefontaine.
Kassing Edmund H, clk Paul H Krauss, b 228 N Pine.
Kassing Wm, clk Charles Mayer & Co, h 228 N Pine.
Kassulke Ernst H, helper, h 87 Spann av.
Kast George, beveler, h 197 Wright.
Kasting Herman H, driver, b 209 Lincoln la.
Kastner Charles F, foreman George Merrill & Co, h 19 Maxwell.
Kastner Claude A, fuller, b 19 Maxwell.
Katharine Home for Aged Women, Mary A Hendricks supt, n e cor Capitol av and 11th, tel 1145.
Kathmann Bernard, shoemkr, 5 Indiana av, h same.
Kaths Ferdinand C, b 17 E North.
Katins Christopher, car rep, h 125 Eureka av.
Kattau Herman H, bkkpr, b 151 Harrison.
KATTAU WM H, Genl Contractor and Builder; also Planing Mill, 151 Harrison, h same, Tel 1272.
Kattmann Ernst, h 555 S New Jersey.
Katzenbach Marie, dressmkr, r 214 The Shiel.

MONEY
Loaned on Short Notice at Lowest Rates.
TUTTLE & SEGUIN,
Tel. 1168. 28 E. Market St.

Katzenbach Rebecca B, dressmkr, 58 Ingalls blk, h 214 The Shiel.
Katzenberger John G, lab, h 176 Keystone av.
Katzenberger Wm L, cabtmkr, h 195 Ramsey av.
Kauffman, see also Coffman.
Kauffman Benjamin K, lab, h 94½ E South.
Kauffman Frank, lab, h 520 Shelby.
Kauffman Louis H, clothing, 158 E Washington, h 120 W New York.
Kauffman Max, clothing, 158 Indiana av, h same.
Kauffmann Simon, lab, b 553 N West.
Kauffmann Joseph A, bartndr, h 147 S Spruce.
Kaufman Abraham G (S Kaufman & Sons), h 669 N Penn.
Kaufman Adam, bartndr, h 39 N Illinois.
Kaufman Adam, molder, h 47 Tremont av (H).
Kaufman Albert, bartndr, b 299 S Delaware.
Kaufman Andrew, butcher, h 117 E Merrill.
Kaufman Babette (wid Hassinger), h 432 Bellefontaine.
Kaufman Bernard (B Kaufman & Son), h 221 E Ohio.
KAUFMAN B & SON (Bernard and Eli B), Wholesale and Retail Liquors, Jobbers in Cigars and Tobacco, 168 W Washington.
Kaufman Caroline (wid Samuel), b 303 E Market.
Kaufman Charles, furrier, b 432 Bellefontaine.
Kaufman Eli B (B Kaufman & Son), b 221 E Ohio.
Kaufman Fannie (wid Simon), b 440 N New Jersey.
Kaufman Herbert L (S Kaufman & Sons), b 669 N Penn.
Kaufman Jacob B, clk, b 221 E Ohio.
Kaufman Lulu J (wid Louis J), h 21 Tuxedo.
Kaufman Morris, h 307 N West.
Kaufman Morris D, crockery, 173 W Washington, h 440 N New Jersey.
Kaufman Moses, h 669 N Penn.
Kaufman Peter T, painter, r 298 N Capitol av.
Kaufman Richard A, butcher, h 75 N Judge Harding (W I).
Kaufman Samuel, lab, h 28 Dougherty.
Kaufman Solomon, furs, 21½ W Washington, b 432 Bellefontaine.
Kaufman Sophia (S Kaufman & Sons), h 669 N Penn.
Kaufman S & Sons (Sophia, Abraham G and Herbert L), fertilizers, 1½ E Washington.
Kaulla Hermann, bkkpr Murphy, Hibben & Co, b 401 S Meridian.
Kautsky Alexander (Wenzel Kautsky), b 179 Coburn.
Kautsky Edward (Wenzel Kautsky), h 179 Coburn.
Kautsky Frank, lab, h 69 Oriole.
Kautsky Joseph (Wenzel Kautsky), h 181 Coburn.
Kautsky Joseph jr, mach hd, b 179 Coburn.
Kautsky Wenzel (Edward, Joseph and Alexander Kautsky), molding mnfrs, 128 E Morris.
Kautsky Wenzel, gilder, h 331 Coburn.
Kautz F Rollin, clk The Bowen-Merrill Co, h e s Downey av 2 s of Houston av (I).
Kavanagh, see also Cavanagh.

PAPER BOXES, MANUFACTURED BY SULLIVAN & MAHAN 41 W. PEARL STREET.

DIAMOND WALL PLASTER { Telephone 1410 BUILDERS' EXCHANGE

Kavanagh James P, leaf tobacco, 54 S Penn, b The Bates.
Kavanagh Wm T, clk R M S, h 65 W 12th.
Kavanaugh Edward L, engr E Mkt House, h 81 High.
Kavaska Bruno, butcher, b 72 English av.
Kay George, wheelmkr, h 40 Davis.
Kay James, lab, b 40 Davis.
Kay Joseph, lab, b 41 Mayhew.
Kaylor, see also Caylor, Kaler, Keylor and Koehler.
Kaylor Albert J, patternmkr, b 350 Columbia av.
Kaylor Elizabeth J (wid Adam), h 350 Columbia av.
Kaylor Robert L, clk, b 54 Johnson av.
Kaylor Thomas H, genl bkkpr Indiana Natl Bank, h 54 Johnson av.
Kaylor Wm H, tel editor The Indpls Journal, h 34 Fletcher av.
Kaylor Wm S, h 54 Johnson av.
Kayne Jennie A (wid Henry), phys, e s Waverly 1 s of Sutherland (B), h same.
Keach James L, treas The Holt Ice and Cold Storage Co, and produce, 62 S Delaware, h 8 Huron.
Keach Mary (wid Leroy C), b 8 Huron.
Kealing Edward, clk, b 322 Cornell av.
Kealing Harry D, student, b 518 N Capitol av.
Kealing James A, blksmith, 1440 E Washington, h same.
Kealing John W, lawyer, 46 Lombard bldg, h 1440 E Washington.
Kealing Joseph B (Kealing & Hugg), h 714 N Alabama.
Kealing Peter, h n s E Washington 4 e of Belt R R.
KEALING SAMUEL, Creamery, 531-533 N Illinois, Tel 1399; h 518 N Capitol av.
KEALING & HUGG (Joseph B Kealing, Martin M Hugg), Lawyers, Rooms 1-2 Brandon Blk, 95 E Washington, Tel 1436.
Kean Eugene, truckman, h 202 English av.
KEAN THOMAS P, Dry Goods, Clothing, Fine Shoes, Hats and Caps, Gloves, Jewelry, Etc, 816 E Washington, h same.
Keaney Patrick, lab, h 88 Bright.
Kearney Thomas, insp City Engineer, r 14 Catterson blk.
Kearns Franklin W, waiter, h 81 N Liberty.
Kearns George, photog, b 1093 N Penn.
Kearns Horace M, condr, h 1093 N Penn.
Kease Hiram, engr, h 288 S East.
Keasley August, lab, h 264 W Merrill.
Keath James A, carp, h 392 N West.
Keating Bessie (wid Michael), h 35 Foundry (B).
Keating James, lab, b 153 Bates.
Keating John, h 166½ W Washington.
Keating John, capt Engine Co No 4, h 170 Church.
Keating John, insp Indpls Gas Co, h 226 E Merrill.
Keating John, lab, h 176 Harrison.
Keating John, lab, b 145 E Washington.
Keating John J, mach, b 322 Cornell av.
Keating Joseph F, saloon, 132 Michigan (H), h same.
Keating Katherine (wid Jeffrey), h 170 Church.
Keating Thomas, trav agt Hayes & Ready, h 20 Ketcham.
Keating Wm, caller, b 35 Foundry (B).

FRANK NESSLER. WILL H. ROST.
FRANK NESSLER & CO.
Tailors
56 EAST MARKET ST. (Lemcke Building),
INDIANAPOLIS. IND.

Keating Wm J, weaver, b 20 Ketcham.
Keatley Alice, teacher Public School No 16, b 33 Garfield pl.
Keatley Wm W, real est, h 33 Garfield pl.
Keaton Virgil D, express, h 175 S Linden.
Keay Anna B, teacher Public School No 2, b 378 N East.
Keay Mary (wid Wm), b 378 N East.
Keay Wm F, transfer clk County Auditor, h 442 N East.
Kehler Carrie, stenog R G Dun & Co, b 670 E Washington.
Kebler Joseph A, mngr R G Dun & Co and pres Y M S and L Assn, h 670 E Washington.
Keck Lewis J, mngr retail dept Central Cycle Mnfg Co, 52 N Penn, r 19 The Chalfant.
Keck Wm, clk, b 90 Kansas.
Keeble George L, barber, h 130 W 4th.
Keeble George L jr, barber, b 130 W 4th.
Keeble Sampson P, clk P O, b 130 W 4th.
Keefe, see also O'Keefe.
Keefe Edward F, steamfitter, b 95 English av.
Keefe Francis, h 268 S Capitol av.
Keefe Frank, lab, b 43 Harrison.
Keefe Harry C, brakeman, b 268 Huron.
Keefe James, lab, b 37 Sinker.
Keefe John, flagman, b 43 Harrison.
Keefe John, lab, h 52 Deloss.
Keefe John B, condr, h 268 Huron.
Keefe Joseph, lab, b 43 Harrison.
Keefe Margaret (wid Michael), h 37 Sinker.
Keefe Michael A, printer Indpls Journal, h 43 Harrison.
Keefer Horace, bartndr, h 21 Ft Wayne av.
Keegan Daniel P, engr, b 124 English av.
KEEGAN FRANK, Propr Hyde Park Drug Store, cor Illinois and 22d, Tel 1948; h s w cor Illinois and 21st.
Keehan Wm, lab, h 28 Keystone av.
Keehn Albert, lineman, b 594 Chestnut.
Keehn Clarence H, cashr Kingan & Co (ltd), b 510 N West.
Keehn Elizabeth (wid Ernest), h 185 Bright.
Keehn Hiram W, preserves, 99 E Mkt House, h 510 N West.

Haueisen & Hartmann
163-169 E. Washington St.
FURNITURE,
Carpets,
Household Goods,
Tin, Granite and China Wares, Oil Cloth and Shades

Fine Laundry Work our Specialty. Collars and Cuffs our Hobby. THE HOME LAUNDRY 197 S. Illinois St. Telephone 1769.

THE WM. H. BLOCK CO. 7 AND 9 EAST WASHINGTON STREET. DRY GOODS, MEN'S FURNISHINGS.

Fidelity and Deposit Co. of Maryland. BONDS SIGNED.—LOCAL BOARD John B. Elam, Albert Sahm, Smiley N. Chambers, John M. Spann.
GEORGE W. PANGBORN, General Agent, 704-706 Lemcke Building. Telephone 140.

Insure Your Property With FRANK K. SAWYER ‖ 74 EAST MARKET STREET Telephone 8.

JOSEPH GARDNER,
Hot Air Furnaces
With Combination Gas Burners for Burning Gas and Other Fuel at the Same Time.
37, 39 & 41 KENTUCKY AVE. Telephone 322.

Keehn Maria C, teacher Public School No 12, b 510 N West.
Keehn Wm, lab, h 185 Bright.
Keehn Wm E, bartndr, b 185 Bright.
Keeler, see also Caylor, Kaler, Keyler, Koehler and Kuhler.
Keeler Cary A, molder, b 58 Spann av.
Keeler Charles B, broommkr, h 31 E Wilkins.
Keeler Eben W, clk R M S, r 173 Broadway.
Keeler Edward W, trav agt, r 312 N New Jersey.
Keeler Elmer L, barber, b 53 Dougherty.
Keeler Emma B (wid George W), h 292 Bright.
Keeler Frank F, packer, h 39 Standard av (W I).
Keeler Frank W, car rep, h 272 Blake.
Keeler Harry W, mach hd, b 58 Spann av.
Keeler Ira G, candymkr, b 58 Spann av.
Keeler James O, printer, h 213 E Morris.
Keeler John I, carp, h 53 Dougherty.
Keeler Joseph K, carp, h 58 Spann av.
Keeler Lulu, teacher, b 292 Bright.
KEELEY INSTITUTE, Charles F Odell Mngr, Plainfield, Ind.
Keeley John S, b 118 N East.
Keeling Anna, h 171½ E Washington.
Keeling Edward A, electrician, b 229 Mass av.
Keeling George R, lab, b 126 Meek.
Keeling Joseph, trucker, b 146 Meek.
Keely Daniel C, mason, h rear s s Brookville rd 2 w of P C C & St L Ry (S).
Keely Daniel W, b rear s s Brookville rd 2 w of P C C & St L Ry (S).
Keely Frank S, clk Robert Keller, b 567 S East.
Keely George L, bricklyr, b 29 Centennial.
Keely Henry, carp, h 353 Mass av.
Keely Henry S, insp City Engineer, h 438 Central av.
Keely Isaac I, watchman, r 131 W Washington.
Keely James F, foreman, h 404 Highland av.
Keely John B, bricklyr, b 309 E Ohio.

J. S. FARRELL & CO.
Plumbing
Natural and Artificial Gas Fitting.
84 N. ILLINOIS STREET.
TELEPHONE 382.

Keely John E, coremkr, b 246 Tremont av (H).
Keely Joseph E, bricklyr, h 76 Cincinnati.
Keely Josiah L, coremkr, h 240 N Brookside av.
Keely Lafayette, coremkr, h 240 N Brookside av.
Keely Martha J, h 438 Central av.
Keely Oliver A, M O clk P O, b 438 Central av.
Keely Oscar P, mason, h w s Denny 6 n of Washington.
Keely Samuel W, mason, h 10 Bismarck.
KEELY SARAH F, Supt Indiana Reform School for Girls and Woman's Prison, s e cor Michigan and Randolph, Tel 674.
Keely Wm H, h 309 E Ohio.
Keely Wm H, carp, h 353 Mass av.
Keen Elias C, butcher, h 88½ Tremont av (H).
Keen Ellen, nurse City Hospital.
Keen Frederick J, bookbndr, h 299 S Alabama.
Keen Mildred (wid George), h 65 Ludlow av.
Keen Minnie (wid John), h 271 Indiana av.
Keen Wm H, lab, h 65 Ludlow av.
Keen Wm P, barber, 618 N Senate av, h same.
Keen W Witcher, ins, 319 Indiana Trust bldg, r 294 N Meridian.
Keenan Felix, h 319 N Capitol av.
Keenan James, painter, h 359 English av.
Keenan James H, drugs, 151 Michigan (H), h 278 W New York.
Keenan John W, tmstr, h 197 Bates.
Keenan Kate, h 116 Laurel.
Keenan Marcus, foreman, h 4 Dawson.
Keenaugh Thomas C, policeman, h s w cor Humbolt and Rembrant avs.
Keene Annabelle, dressmkr, 383 Fletcher av, b same.
Keene Bernard, clk, b 282 Prospect.
Keene Ella H, nurse, 10 Wyandot blk, r same.
Keene Lorenzo D, carp, h 383 Fletcher av.
Keep George H, clk, b 84 W 2d.
Keepers Elisha M, switchman, h 13 Eureka av.
Keepers Irene (wid John B), h 223 N Beville av.
Keepers Penuel M, clk, h 213 W Maryland.
Keers Albert C, lab, h 175 Douglass.
Keers David, lab, r 175 Douglass.
Keers George W, grocer, 532 W North, h same.
Keers Mary (wid Wm), b 175 Douglass.
Kees Hiram, engr, h 288 S East.
Keesee Margaret, h 31 Helen.
Keesee Martha J (wid George L), b 16 Springfield.
Keesee Theodore W, lab, h 16 Springfield.
Keesey Elias G, carp, h 75 Hamilton av.
Keesling Orus H, teacher Industrial School, b w s Central av 1 n of 21st.
Keeter Joseph P, photog, 214 W Washington, h 238½ same.
Keeter Rufus G, photog, 6½ E Washington, h 195 N West.
Keeter Susan (wid James), b 175 N West.
Keeton Martha B (wid James M), h 111 Locke.
Keever Elizabeth (wid Martin), b 71 Maxwell.
Keever Horace C, bartndr, h 21 Ft Wayne av.
Kegel Wm C, molder, h 93 Weghorst.

IF CONTINUED to the end of its dividend period, policies of the UNITED STATES LIFE INSURANCE CO., will equal or excel any investment policy ever offered to the public. | E. B. SWIFT, Manager, 25 E. Market St.

Wm. Kotteman 89 & 91 E. Washington St. TELEPHONE 1742 Furniture

Kegereis Joseph, butcher, h 853½ S Meridian.
Kegley Emma B (wid Fernando C), boarding 862 Cornell av.
Kegley Wm H, clk, h 1741 Graceland av.
Kehl Bernard T, brakeman, h 319 Fletcher av.
Kehl Frederick J, mason, h 29 Bates.
Kehl Roland T, brakeman, b 29 Bates.
Kehl Valentine E, carp, h 9 Bates al.
Kehlbeck Herman F, grocer, 195 E South, h 153 Huron.
Kehling Wm A, butcher, h 58 Yandes.
Kehling Wm A jr, clk, b 58 Yandes.
Kehoe Michael A, painter, b 93 Hiatt (W I).
Kehr Charles F, baker, h 122 Greer.
Kehr Lawrence, music teacher, b 181 W Vermont.
Kehrein Philip F, stairbldr, b 18 E Michigan.
Kehrer Charles, foreman, h 17 Biddle.
Kehrman Charles, lab, h 13 Iowa.
Keifer Andrew C, vice-pres and treas Sun Pub Co, h 167 E St Joseph.
Keigan Thomas F, lab, h 312 S Missouri.
Keil, see also Kiel and Kyle.
Keil August, cabtmkr, h 42 Arizona.
Keil August, lab, b 424 E St Clair.
Keil Conrad, h 424 E St Clair.
Keil Mary (wid John C), h 50 W Raymond.
Keirtsey Charles, lab, h s e cor Gatling and Beecher.
Keiser Charles, clk, h 512 S West.
Keiser Charles G, cancelling clk P O, h 58 Omer.
Keiser Joseph M, attendant Insane Hospital.
Keister Newton H, clk R M S, r 366 N Alabama.
Keitch John, lab, b 27 Hosbrook.
Keith Christiana (wid Henry), h 533 W Maryland.
KEITH ERNEST R, Lawyer, Rooms 1-3, 38½ E Washington, Tel 341; h 826 N Penn.
Keith Gustavus S, candymkr, b 253 E Washington.
Keith Henry C, lab, b 533 W Maryland.
Keith James A, carp, h 392 N West.
Keith John, bricklyr, h 319 N Noble.
Keith John A, lab, h 275 S Noble.
Keith John O, lab, h 486 Ontario (N I).
Keith John O, engr, h 150 S William (W I).
Keith Mary, confr, 150 S William (W I), h same.
Keith Mary H (wid Frank A), h 367 N Alabama.
Keith Robert B, lawyer, 68½ E Market, r 91 The Windsor.
Keithley Emma R (wid Jesse W), h 223½ E North.
Keithley Wm W, coremkr, b 112 Oliver av (W I).
Kelch Stuart, gilder, h 28 Henry.
Kellehan Lyman K, collr, h 10 Shriver av.
Kelleher Jane (wid Michael), h 79 Davidson.
Kelleher John, huckster, b 79 Davidson.
Kelleher John, checkman, h 176 English av.
Kelleher Michael, driver, b 79 Davidson.
Kelleher Patrick J, trav agt, h 317 S Meridian.
Kellenberger Peter B, confr, 33 Mass av, h 559 Ash.
Keller, see also Caylor, Kaler, Kaylor, Keeler, Koehler, Koller and Kuhler.
Keller Amelia R, phys, 352 S Meridian, b 218 Union.

We Buy Municipal ~ Bonds ~
THOS. C. DAY & CO,
Rooms 325 to 330 Lemcke Bldg.

Keller Andrew, cigar mnfr, 86 Stevens, h same.
Keller Anton, cigarmnfr, 86 Stevens, h same.
Keller August K, clk Robert Keller, b 401 Madison av.
Keller August P, barber, b 47 Buchanan.
Keller Burt, b 437 N East.
Keller Charles H, clk, b 175 St Mary.
Keller Charles W, lab, h 66 Brookside av.
KELLER CONRAD, Druggist, 680 S Meridian, b 218 Union, Tel 864.
Keller Eliza J, forewoman, b 476 W Francis (N I).
Keller Elizabeth (wid Frederick), h 218 Union.
Keller Elso, pres French Chemical Works, h 643 Marlowe av.
Keller Ernst, credits N Y Store, h 11 Ruckle.
Keller Frances (wid Wm), h 27 Wyoming.
Keller Frank, b 563 S East.
Keller Frank, foreman, h 410 Union.
Keller Frank H, dept mngr Robert Keller, b 401 Madison av.
Keller Frank J, lab, h 7 S Beville av.
Keller Frederick B, bkkpr, b 124 S East.
Keller Fred C, trav agt Charles Mayer & Co, h 115 Middle Drive (W P).
Keller George, driver, h 89 Torbet.
Keller George C, tinner, b 396 S Alabama.
Keller George J, saloon, 243 Hadley av (W I), h 115 Nordyke av (W I).
Keller Gustav, treas Indiana Paint and Roofing Co, h 904 S Meridian.
Keller Harry F, plumber, b 147 W South.
Keller Henry, clk Clemens Vonnegut, h 289 Fletcher av.
Keller Henry, lab, h 175 St Mary.
Keller Hieronymus, engraver, h 495 W Highland av (N I).
Keller John F, blksmith, h 54 Foundry (B).
Keller John V, butcher, h 163 Spring.
Keller Jonathan, express, h 297 N Pine.
Keller Joseph, hostler, b 508 E Market.
Keller Joseph H (Keller & Gamerdinger), h 199 Coburn.
Keller Josie, b 91 Harmon.

EAT
QUAKER BREAD
ASK YOUR GROCER FOR IT.
THE HITZ BAKING CO.

SHOW CASES WILLIAM WIEGEL 6 West Louisiana Street Opp. Union Station.

CARPETS CLEANED LIKE NEW. TELEPHONE 818
CAPITAL STEAM CARPET CLEANING WORKS

BENJ. BOOTH PRACTICAL EXPERT ACCOUNTANT. Thirty years' experience. First-class credentials. Room 18, 82½ E. Washington St. Indianapolis, Ind.

18 and 20 S. Meridian St. Established 1880. The Old Reliable Sherman European Restaurant

ESTABLISHED 1876. TELEPHONE 168.
CHESTER BRADFORD,
SOLICITOR OF PATENTS,
AND COUNSEL IN PATENT CAUSES.
(See adv. page 6.)
Office:—Rooms 14 and 16 Hubbard Block, S.W. Cor. Washington and Meridian Streets, INDIANAPOLIS, INDIANA.

KELLER JULIUS, Propr Arcade Kneipe, 38 Virginia av, and Contractor Cement Work, 7 Pembroke Arcade, Tel 1802; h 437 N East, Tel 1073.
Keller Julius jr, clk Albert Gall, b 410 Union.
Keller J Edward, bkkpr Merchants' Natl Bank, b 199 Park av.
Keller Lee W, ins, h 52 Buchanan.
Keller Lena (wid Lewis), domestic 233 E New York.
Keller Louisa, h 115 N New Jersey.
Keller Martha (wid Alonzo), h 174 W New York.
Keller Mary, h 181½ Indiana av.
Keller Mary (wid Thomas), h 35 Leon.
Keller Mary E, h 476 W Francis (N I).
Keller Mary E (wid Taylor), h 415 E Washington.
Keller Ottmar, saloon, 113 E Washington, h 120 Wright.
Keller Otto, clk Charles Mayer & Co, b 218 Union.
KELLER ROBERT, Dry Goods, Clothing, Millinery, Boots and Shoes, Groceries and Feed, also Meat Market, 570-578 S East, n w cor Coburn, Tel 735; h 401 Madison av.
Keller Robert H, b 122 College av.
Keller Thomas, chainmkr, b 35 Leon.
Keller Thomas, lab, h 284 Fulton.
Keller Vincent, glasswkr, b 495 Highland av (N I).
Keller Wm, driver, r 115 N East.
Keller Wm A, foreman, h 142 Pleasant.
Keller Wm E, clk R M S, h 22 Shriver.
Keller Wm F, clk Kingan & Co (ltd), b 144 N Senate av.
Keller Wm H, veneerer, h 135 Cornell av.
Keller Wm J, clk County Treasurer, h 1A Orange.
Keller Zachariah P, mach, h 89 Fletcher av.
KELLER & GAMERDINGER (Joseph H Keller, Jacob Gamerdinger Jr), Dry Goods, Notions, Millinery, Etc, 248-250 E Washington.

CORRUGATED IRON CEILINGS AND SIDING.
ALL KINDS OF REPAIRING.
O. B. ENSEY,
TELEPHONE 1562.
COR. 6TH AND ILLINOIS STREETS.

Kellermeier August C, clk, h 110 Pleasant.
Kellermeier Christian C, mach, h 225 Michigan av.
Kellermeier Christian T, car rep, h 623 Marlowe av.
Kellermeier Edwin H, car rep, h 74 William.
Kellermeier Henry, flagman, h 241 S Alabama.
Kellermeier Henry F, lab, b 241 S Alabama.
Kellermeier Julius H, packer, h 14 Lexington av.
Kellermyer Andrew, confr, h 270 Coburn.
Kellermyer Edward A, mach hd, b 270 Coburn.
Kellermyer Harry H, mach, b 248 Coburn.
Kellermyer Henry W, packer, h 270 Coburn.
Kellermyer Mary, h 270 Coburn.
Kellermyer Wm F A, motorman, h 248 Coburn.
Kelley, see also Kelly.
Kelley Bernard, lab, h 21 Grant.
Kelley Bernard, waiter, h 273 Douglass.
Kelley Bert, molder, b 312 W Pearl.
Kelley Catherine, teacher, b 296 Clifford av.
Kelley Catherine (wid Patrick), b 28 Buchanan.
Kelley Catharine (wid Wm), b 787 E Market.
Kelley Cornelius, lab, b 240 S Missouri.
Kelley Daniel, coal, h 345 N Senate av.
Kelley Daniel, driver Union Co-Operative Laundry, b 339 S Missouri.
Kelley Daniel, lab, h 424 Highland av.
Kelley Daniel jr, helper, b 424 Highland av.
Kelley David E, carp, h 131 W 2d.
Kelley David E, lab, h 421 N Pine.
Kelley Dennis, lab, b 55 Pierce.
Kelley Ebenezer P, oils, h 389 Bellefontaine.
Kelley Elisha C, carp, h 448 W 1st.
Kelley Elizabeth (wid Thomas), h 1725 N Illinois.
Kelley Genevieve, milliner, r 303 The Shiel.
Kelley Ileane E, confr, h e s Capitol av 3 s of Ray.
Kelley James, lab, h 413 Columbia av.
Kelley James, plumber, b 421 N Pine.
Kelley James, b 39 N Alabama.
Kelley James A, porter, h 207 W 3d.
Kelley James B, bkkpr W B Barry Saw and Supply Co, b 131 W 2d.
Kelley James L, molder, h 28 Grove.
Kelley Jeremiah A, driver, b 534 S Illinois.
Kelley John, basketmkr, b 424 Highland av.
Kelley John, lab, h 439 S West.
Kelley John, molder, h 91 Wright.
Kelley John E, furnacemkr, b 1012 E Washington.
Kelley John F, lab, h 342 S West.
Kelley John J, insp, b 290 W Maryland.
Kelley John W, plumber, h 13 Quince.
Kelley Julia, bkkpr Feeney Furniture and Stove Co, b 534 S Illinois.
Kelley Kate, teacher Public School No 4, r 195 N Alabama.
Kelley Leander O, condr, h 203 Fletcher av.
Kelley Manus, lab, h 29 Ketcham (H).
Kelley Mary, cook Deaf and Dumb Inst.
Kelley Mary, housekpr 299 W Maryland.
Kelley Mary (wid John), h 534 S Illinois.
Kelley Mary F (wid James), nurse, 303 The Shiel, r same.
Kelley Mary L, chief laundress Insane Hospital.
Kelley Mary T (wid Joshua R), h 296 Clifford av.
Kelley Matthew, lab, h 290 W Maryland.

TUTEWILER UNDERTAKER, No. 72 WEST MARKET STREET. TELEPHONE 216.

THE PROVIDENT LIFE AND TRUST CO. OF PHILADELPHIA. Endowment Insurance presents the double attraction of relieving manhood and middle age from anxiety and old age from want. For particulars apply to D. W. EDWARDS, General Agent, 508 Indiana Trust Building.

THEODORE F. SMITHER Competent and Responsible ROOFER Office, 151 West Maryland St. Telephone 86

Kelley Michael, lab, b 290 W Maryland.
Kelley Michael, lab, b 223 S West.
Kelley Michael C, bartndr, b 100 S Illinois.
Kelley Michael F, brakeman, h 518 S Capitol av.
Kelley Michael F, clk Occidental Hotel, b same.
Kelley Michael T, lab, h 337 S Missouri.
Kelley Patrick, lab, h 14 Sharpe.
Kelley Patrick C, driver, b 92 Greer.
Kelley Patrick J, farmer, b 55 Pierce.
Kelley Peter, huckster, b 72 English av.
KELLEY P J, Mngr Indianapolis Printing Co, 37 Virginia av, h 28 Buchanan.
Kelley Rose, attendant Public Library, b 787 E Market.
Kelley Samuel B, printer, b 165 Pleasant.
Kelley Thomas, flagman, h 55 Pierce.
Kelley Timothy, huckster, b 72 English av.
Kelley Timothy J, tmstr, b 252 E Washington.
Kelley Walter, lab The Bates.
Kelley Wm E, condr, h 355 Coburn.
Kelley Wm H (Vail Seed Co), h 296 Clifford av.
Kelley Winnifred, clk, r 205 The Shiel.
Kellish Adeline (wid Martin), b 74 Prospect.
Kellogg Charles N, lumber, h 202 Ash.
Kellogg Edwin P, lumber, h 202 Ash.
Kellogg Henry C, real est, 67 S Penn, r same.
Kellogg Justin A, lawyer, b 76 W 2d.
Kellogg Mary (wid Wm), h 144 N Capitol av.
Kellogg Newton, h 47 N West.
Kellogg Norman P, h 202 Ash.
Kellogg Wm J, watchman, h 126 S Pine.
Kellogg Wm L, mach, b 52½ W 7th.
Kellogg Wm R, mach b 52½ W 7th.
Kellum Jesse, sec Indpls Street Cleaning Co, h 360 N East.
Kellum Orpha L, bkkpr, b 72 Center Drive (W P).
Kelly, see also Kelley.
Kelly Alexander, lab, b 64 Mankedick.
Kelly Alfred S, uphlr, h 110 Ft Wayne av.
Kelly Anna F, teacher Public School No 17, b 424 W New York.
Kelly Anthony, tailor, b 215 Dougherty.
Kelly Arthur E, clk, b 286 Bellefontaine.
Kelly Bartholomew, lab, h 242 W Market.
Kelly Bartholomew, waiter The Denison.
Kelly Bernard E, h 29 Dougherty.
Kelly Charles, lab, h 700 Madison av.
Kelly Charles J, tailor, b 58 Dougherty.
Kelly Charles R, musician, h 25 S Summit.
Kelly Cornelius, painter, h 424 W New York.
Kelly Delilah J (wid Ellis), h 165 Pleasant.
Kelly Dennis P, enameler, h 78 Cypress.
Kelly Ella B (wid Capron C), h 32 S Arsenal av.
Kelly Emma R, dressmkr, 25 S Summit, h same.
Kelly Frank M, fantndr, b 424 W New York.
Kelly Harriet M (wid Moses T), h 14 Shriver av.
Kelly Harry C, fireman, b 860 E Washington.
Kelly Henry, paperhngr, h 28 Drake.
Kelly Hugh, lab, h 144 Randolph.
Kelly James, molder, b 439 N Alabama.
Kelly James, tmstr, h 19 Willard.
Kelly James H, brakeman, h 86 Temple av.
Kelly James M, grocer, 201 Bellefontaine, h 286 same.

THE WHEN IS A WORLD BEATER.

Kelly James W, enameler, h 14 Gatling.
Kelly John, drayman, h 613 W Vermont.
Kelly John, lab, h 22 Center.
Kelly John, lab, b 310 E Court.
Kelly John, lab, r 191½ Indiana av.
Kelly John, lab, h 402 W Shoemaker (N I).
Kelly John E, filer, h 386 W Shoemaker (N I).
Kelly John J, artist, r 23 Stewart pl.
Kelly John J, saloon, 151 English av, h 82 Fletcher av.
Kelly John J, tailor, r 8 Warren.
Kelly John T, lab, h 14 Gatling.
Kelly John T, trav agt, h 177 E Louisiana.
Kelly John W, lab, h 247 Fayette.
Kelly Joseph, driver, r 175 W Ohio.
Kelly Joseph P, clk, b 144 Randolph.
Kelly Karl B, clk, b 32 S Arsenal av.
Kelly Kate, dressmkr, 113 S Illinois, b Circle Park Hotel.
Kelly Lizzie (wid John T), r 9½ Madison av.
Kelly Louise M, teacher Public School No 6, b 439 N Alabama.
Kelly Malachi L, saloon, 246 W Washington, h same.
Kelly Martin, bartndr, r 251 W Washington.
Kelly Mary (wid Thomas), h 435 Union.
Kelly Mary A (wid John), h 87 High.
Kelly Michael, lab, h 439 N Alabama.
Kelly Michael, lab, h 64 Deloss.
Kelly Michael, mach, b 89 Indiana av.
Kelly Michael L, mach, b 439 N Alabama.
Kelly Patrick J, tailor, 1098 E Washington, h 58 Dougherty.
Kelly Philip E, clk People's Outfitting Co, h 118 Fayette.
Kelly Robert H, agt The Indpls News, r 77 E Walnut.
Kelly Samuel A, engr, h 50½ Clifford av.
Kelly Stephen, mach, h 679 Mass av.
Kelly Thomas, driver, b 313 S Olive.
Kelly Thomas A, pressman, h 518 Shelby.
Kelly Thomas C, clk P O, b 424 W New York.
Kelly Thomas J, lab, h 402 W Shoemaker (N I).
Kelly Thomas J, lab, h 435 Union.

THE A. BURDSAL CO.
Manufacturers of
Paints and Colors
VARNISHES,
Brushes, Painters' and Paper Hangers' Supplies.
34 and 36 South Meridian Street.

ELECTRICIANS DON'T FORGET US. ALL WORK GUARANTEED. C. W. MEIKEL, Tel. 466. 96-98 E. New York St.

DALTON & MERRIFIELD { LUMBER South Noble St., near E. Washington

KIRKHOFF BROS.
Steam and Hot Water Heating Apparatus,
Plumbing and Gas Fitting.
102-104 SOUTH PENNSYLVANIA ST.
TELEPHONE 910.

Kelly Timothy M, steward, h 340 Indiana av.
Kelly Wm, h 3 Kauffmann pl.
Kelly Wm, lab, b 88 Greer.
Kelly Wm, lab, h 402 W Shoemaker (N I).
Kelly Wm G, mach, h 26 N California.
Kelly Wm G, tel opr P C C & St L Ry, h 297 N Alabama.
Kelpin John, foreman, b 263 Hadley av (W I).
Kelpin Louisa (wid Charles), h 590 Morris (W I).
Kelpin Otto C, b 590 Morris (W I).
Kelsey Asa I, student, h 242 Indiana av.
Kelsey Benjamin, ins adjuster, 300 Indiana Trust bldg, h 360 College av.
Kelsey Benjamin C, city ticket agt C C C & St L Ry, 1 E Washington, b 360 College av.
Kelsey Russell C, phys and sec Am Medical College, 105 E Ohio, tel 1500, h same.
Kelshaw George M, ticket agt North Street Station, h s s Howland 1 w of Nicholas.
Kelshaw John, b s s Wolf pike 2 e of Baltimore av.
Kelso Fayette E, lab, h 426 Newman.
Kelso Ira E, tmstr, b 253 Lincoln la.
Kelso Jamison, farmer, h w s Bluff rd 1 s of Raymond.
Kelso John W, tmstr, b w s Bluff rd 1 s of Raymond.
Kelso Margaret S (wid Isaac), h n s 17th 1 e of Hillside av.
Kelso Orin, tmstr, h w s Bluff rd 1 s of Raymond.
Kelso Reuben E (Oeth & Kelso), jewelers, 820 N Illinois, h same.
Keltenbrun James J, mufrs' agt, 333 Lemcke bldg, b 150 N Illinois.
Keltenich Frederick W H, draughtsman D A Bohlen & Son, b 50½ N Senate av.
Kelvie John B, supt, r 143 N Alabama.
Kemker Sophia (wid Charles), h 1102 N Alabama.
Kemker Wm C, h 921 Cornell av.
Kemmet George, lab, h rear 12 Mulberry.
Kemnitz Charles F, insp, h 46 Michigan av.
Kemnitz Henrietta, dressmkr, 46 Michigan av, h same.

LIME
BUILDING SUPPLIES,
Hair, Plaster, Flue Linings,
The W. G. Wasson Co.
130 INDIANA AVE. Tel. 989.

Kemnitz Wm, lab, h w s Webb 3 n of Raymond.
Kemp, see also Camp.
Kemp Alice, h 404 W 1st.
Kemp Colonel H, lab, h 352 W North.
Kemp Curtis H, painter, b 69 N Alabama.
Kemp George, painter, h 244 Yandes.
Kemp John V, driver, h 365 W Francis (N I).
Kemp Louis, lab, b 221 S West.
Kemp Phoenicia J, restaurant, 69 N Alabama, h same.
Kemp Wm A, lab, b 24 Ellsworth.
Kemp Wm S, fireman, h 38 N William (W I).
Kempe Charles, blksmith, h 161 Gresham.
Kempe Johanna (wid Charles), h s w cor Applegate and Morton.
Kempe Paul, blksmith, h 133 Wegborst.
Kempe Wm, mach, b s w cor Applegate and Morton.
Kemper Albert H, hostler, h 30 N Station (B).
Kemper George S, coppersmith, h 233 S Spruce.
Kemper Jesse M, drayman, h 50 Pleasant.
Kemper Joseph W, carp, h 202 Fletcher av.
Kemper Leland J, carp, h 211 Hoyt av.
Kemper Marion B, poultry, 65 E Mkt House, b 211 Hoyt av.
Kemper Robert J, mach, b 30 N Station (B).
Kemper Roy, clk, b 211 Hoyt av.
Kemper Samuel N, carp, h 86 N Olive.
Kemper Sylvester P, lab, b 86 N Olive.
Kemper Talbot B, foreman Foster Lumber Co, h 512 N West.
Kemper Walter, h 337 S Alabama.
Kemper Wm, lab, b 6 Lafayette.
Kemper Wm E, lab, b 512 N West.
Kemper Wm O, painter, h 332 E Michigan.
Kempf August, mach hd, h 338 N Pine.
Kempf Frank C, harnessmkr, b 618½ S Meridian.
Kempf Robert, h 618½ S Meridian.
Kempf Theodore, checkman, b 618½ S Meridian.
Kempfer Otto P H, cabtmkr, h 35 Smithson.
Kemphfer Charles R, baggageman, h 107 Fletcher av.
Kempter Paul, lab, h 57 N Judge Harding (W I).
Kendall Albert G, fireman, b 678 W Washington.
Kendall Anna, h 133½ E Washington.
Kendall Bladen A, carp, h 490 W Shoemaker (N I).
Kendall Charles, tailor, h 83 Lockerbie.
Kendall Edward L, clk R M S, h 75 W McCarty.
Kendall Ella M, dressmkr, h 19½ N Meridian.
Kendall Frederick C, teacher High School, b 84 E New York.
Kendall Hannah A (wid James N), b 412 S West.
Kendall Harry J, painter, b 80 Oliver av (W I).
Kendall Ira C, clk, b 15 Greer.
Kendall Jesse G, condr, h 182 N Missouri.
Kendall John A, dyer, 43 Mass av, h 210 N Noble.
Kendall Levi, farmer, h 80 Oliver av (W I).
Kendall Lizzie (wid John), h 139 E South.
Kendall Martha E (wid Walter R), h 84 E New York.
Kendall Martha W (wid Sylvester W), h 176 E New York.
Kendall Mary (wid John), dyer, 25 Mass av, b 120 same.

Parlor, Bed Room, Dining Room, Kitchen, Furniture W. H. MESSENGER, 101 E. Wash. St., Tel. 491.

INDIANA ELECTROTYPE E CO. :: BEST WORK. LOWEST PRICES.
23 WEST PEARL ST., INDIANAPOLIS, IND. JOB WORK. BOOK PLATES. BEST PATENT BASE ON THE MARKET. All Orders Promptly Filled.

ALL KINDS OF HEAVY AND LIGHT GRAY IRON CASTINGS | McNamara, Koster & Co. Phone 1593. 212-218 S. Penn. St. | Foundry and Pattern Shop

Kendall Pearl M. clk. b 29½ N Meridian.
Kendall Philip, clk. b 4 Miller blk.
Kendall Schuyler T. [illegible] b 14 E New York.
Kendall Victor C. [illegible] L S Ayres & Co. b 469 N Alabama.
Kendall Wm. [illegible] Gas Co. b 128 [illegible].
Kendrick John, [illegible] r 259 S Senate av.
Kendrick Robert, b 46½ Mass av.
Kendrick Robert L. [illegible] b 265 River av (W I).
Kendrick Wm. H. [illegible] N East, b same.
Kenge James M. [illegible] b same.
Kenley Charles W. [illegible] b 42 N Beville av.
Kennard Howard, lab. b 26 W Ray.
Kennard Jesse A. lab. b 89 W Udell (N I).
Kennaugh Thomas C. patrolman, b 93 [illegible].
Kennedy Benjamin, carp. b 410 W Udell (N I).
Kennedy Bernard F. student, b 17 West Drive (W P).
Kennedy Byron L. [illegible] b 241 Shelby.
Kennedy Charles H. carp. b 317 Cornell av.
Kennedy Catherine, b 236 W St. Clair.
Kennedy Charles F. secretary State Board of Agriculture, 14 State House, b 295 Bellefontaine.
Kennedy Charles M. [illegible] b 213 Virginia av.
Kennedy Cornelius, lab. b 173 Meek.
Kennedy Daniel, b 29 S Beville av.
Kennedy Daniel, lab. b 797 Bismarck av (H).
Kennedy Daniel, switchman, b 16 N Gale (B).
Kennedy Daniel F. stonecutter, b 279 Dearborn.
Kennedy Edward F. lab. b 172 Meek.
Kennedy Francis M. [illegible] b 307 S Alabama.
Kennedy Frank, [illegible] b 39 N Belmont av (H).
Kennedy Frederick E. clk. b 172 Fayette.
Kennedy George W. clk. r 129½ N Delaware.
Kennedy George B. mach. hd. b 122 W Maryland.
Kennedy George E. attendant [illegible] Hospital.
Kennedy Harry L. [illegible] b 26 N Mary.
Kennedy Jackson, lab. b 18 Asbury.
Kennedy James, lab. b 46 N Belmont av (H).
Kennedy James, lab. b 173 Meek.
Kennedy James, mach. b 1 S Station (B).
Kennedy James, switchman, b 173 E South.
Kennedy James F. mach. b 36 W 1st.
Kennedy James M. [illegible] b s e cor W North and Elwood.
Kennedy Jeremiah, lab. b 451 Mass av.
Kennedy Jessie E. [illegible] Clifford, Bowser & Moffett, b 122 Fayette.
Kennedy John, drayman, b 125 Bright.
Kennedy John, lab. b 27 Patterson.
Kennedy John, lab. b 312 Baker.
Kennedy John, lab. r 135½ W Washington.
Kennedy John H. [illegible] Walter A. Wood Harvester Co. b 458 Broadway.
Kennedy John R. [illegible] b 26 St. Mary.
Kennedy John T. lab. b w s Calvin 2 s of Bethel av.
Kennedy John W. lab. b 28 S Stuart (B).
Kennedy John T. phys. 104 N East, b same.
Kennedy Joshua, lab. b 4 Concord (H).

Henry H. Fay,
40½ E. WASHINGTON ST.,
FIRE INSURANCE, REAL ESTATE,
LOANS AND RENTAL AGENT.

Kennedy Joseph J. Rev. pastor Lovely Lane A M E Zion Church, b 150 W Michigan.
Kennedy Lafayette, lab. b 322 S [illegible].
Kennedy Levi, see Commercial B and L Assn. b 18 Hammond pl.
Kennedy Lydia E. (wid James H.) b 421 N East.
Kennedy Mary (wid James) b 237 Hartman.
Kennedy Michael, [illegible] b 19 S [illegible] av.
Kennedy Michael R. saloon, 40 S West, b same.
Kennedy Odin, tailor, b 122 Spann av.
Kennedy Patrick, lab. b 39 N Belmont av (H).
Kennedy Patrick, lab. b 133 S West.
Kennedy Patrick J. helper, b 167 English av.
Kennedy Patrick W. (Kennedy & Connaughton), b 208 S Pine.
Kennedy Perry, [illegible] b 154 Davidson.
Kennedy Richard, [illegible] b 215 LeGrand av.
Kennedy Richmond, lab. b 540 Harlan.
Kennedy Robert J. lab. b 344 Blake.
Kennedy Robert N. carp. b 167 W Alabama.
Kennedy Roland, lab. b 34 Hill.
Kennedy Samuel, r 129½ N Delaware.
Kennedy Samuel A. phys. 120 Fayette, b same.
Kennedy Samuel G. painter, b 122 Fayette.
Kennedy Thomas, driller, b 43 Tecumseh.
Kennedy Thomas, lab. b 31 Temple av.
Kennedy Thomas, [illegible] b 192 Wright.
Kennedy Warren J. [illegible] b 421 E North.
Kennedy Wm. [illegible] b s e cor Brightwood av and C C C & St L Ry (B).
Kennedy Wm. lab. r 135½ W Washington.
Kennedy Wm. D. [illegible] b 122 Spann av.
Kennedy Wm. E. mach. hd. b 27 Patterson.
Kennedy Wm. G. r 294½ Mass av.
Kennedy Wm. M. [illegible] b 18 Everett.
Kennedy Wm. T. mach. hd. b 32 Holloway av.
Kennedy Wm. W. lab. b 412 W Udell.

WILL GO ON YOUR BOND
American Bonding & Trust Co.
of Baltimore, Md. Approved as sole surety by the United States Government and the different States as Sole Surety on all Forms of Bonds.
W. E. BARTON & CO., General Agents,
504 Indiana Trust Building.
Long Distance Telephone 1918.

THE FRED DIETZ CO. WOODEN PACKING BOXES MADE TO ORDER. FACTORY AND WAREHOUSE TRUCKS. 400 Madison Avenue. Telephone 654.

BUSINESS EDUCATION A NECESSITY. TIME SHORT. DAY AND NIGHT SCHOOL. SUCCESS CERTAIN AT THE PERMANENT, RELIABLE Indianapolis BUSINESS UNIVERSITY

DALTON & MERRIFIELD { LUMBER South Noble St., near E. Washington

INDIANA ELECTROTYPE CO. : BEST WORK LOWEST PRICES. 23 WEST PEARL ST., INDIANAPOLIS, IND. JOB WORK. BOOK PLATES. All Orders Promptly Filled. BEST PATENT BASE ON THE MARKET.

KIRKHOFF BROS.
Steam and Hot Water Heating Apparatus,
Plumbing and Gas Fitting.
102-104 SOUTH PENNSYLVANIA ST.
TELEPHONE 910.

Kelly Timothy M, steward, h 340 Indiana av.
Kelly Wm, h 3 Kauffmann pl.
Kelly Wm, lab, b 88 Greer.
Kelly Wm, lab, h 402 W Shoemaker (N I).
Kelly Wm G, mach, h 26 N California.
Kelly Wm G, tel opr P C C & St L Ry, h 297 N Alabama.
Kelpin John, foreman, b 263 Hadley av (W I).
Kelpin Louisa (wid Charles), h 590 Morris (W I).
Kelpin Otto C, b 590 Morris (W I).
Kelsey Asa I, student, h 242 Indiana av.
Kelsey Benjamin, ins adjuster, 300 Indiana Trust bldg, h 360 College av.
Kelsey Benjamin C, city ticket agt C C C & St L Ry, 1 E Washington, b 360 College av.
Kelsey Russell C, phys and sec Am Medical College, 105 E Ohio, tel 1500, h same.
Kelshaw George M, ticket agt North Street Station, h s s Howland 1 w of Nicholas.
Kelshaw John, b s s Wolf pike 2 e of Baltimore av.
Kelso Fayette E, lab, h 426 Newman.
Kelso Ira E, tmstr, b 253 Lincoln la.
Kelso Jamison, farmer, h w s Bluff rd 1 s of Raymond.
Kelso John W, tmstr, b w s Bluff rd 1 s of Raymond.
Kelso Margaret S (wid Isaac), h n s 17th 1 e of Hillside av.
Kelso Orin, tmstr, h w s Bluff rd 1 s of Raymond.
Kelso Reuben E (Oeth & Kelso), jewelers, 820 N Illinois, h same.
Keltenbrun James J, mnfrs' agt, 333 Lemcke bldg, b 150 N Illinois.
Keltenich Frederick W H, draughtsman D A Bohlen & Son, b 50½ N Senate av.
Kelvie John B, supt, r 143 N Alabama.
Kemker Sophia (wid Charles), h 1102 N Alabama.
Kemker Wm C, h 921 Cornell av.
Kemmet George, lab, h rear 12 Mulberry.
Kemnitz Charles F, insp, h 46 Michigan av.
Kemnitz Henrietta, dressmkr, 46 Michigan av, h same.

LIME
BUILDING SUPPLIES,
Hair, Plaster, Flue Linings,
The W. G. Wasson Co.
130 INDIANA AVE. Tel. 989.

Kemnitz Wm, lab, h w s Webb 3 n of Raymond.
Kemp, see also Camp.
Kemp Alice, h 404 W 1st.
Kemp Colonel H, lab, h 352 W North.
Kemp Curtis H, painter, b 69 N Alabama.
Kemp George, painter, h 244 Yandes.
Kemp John V, driver, h 565 W Francis (N I).
Kemp Louis, lab, b 221 S West.
Kemp Phoenicia J, restaurant, 69 N Alabama, h same.
Kemp Wm A, lab, b 24 Ellsworth.
Kemp Wm S, fireman, h 38 N William (W I).
Kempe Charles, blksmith, h 161 Gresham.
Kempe Johanna (wid Charles), h s w cor Applegate and Morton.
Kempe Paul, blksmith, h 133 Weghorst.
Kempe Wm, mach, b s w cor Applegate and Morton.
Kemper Albert H, hostler, h 30 N Station (B).
Kemper George S, coppersmith, h 233 S Spruce.
Kemper Jesse M, drayman, h 50 Pleasant.
Kemper Joseph W, carp, h 202 Fletcher av.
Kemper Leland J, carp, h 211 Hoyt av.
Kemper Marion B, poultry, 65 E Mkt House, b 211 Hoyt av.
Kemper Robert J, mach, b 30 N Station (B).
Kemper Roy, clk, b 211 Hoyt av.
Kemper Samuel N, carp, h 86 N Olive.
Kemper Sylvester P, lab, b 86 N Olive.
Kemper Talbot B, foreman Foster Lumber Co, h 512 N West.
Kemper Walter, h 337 S Alabama.
Kemper Wm, lab, b 6 Lafayette.
Kemper Wm E, lab, b 512 N West.
Kemper Wm O, painter, h 332 E Michigan.
Kempf August, mach hd, h 338 N Pine.
Kempf Frank C, harnessmkr, b 618½ S Meridian.
Kempf Robert, h 618½ S Meridian.
Kempf Theodore, checkman, b 618½ S Meridian.
Kempfer Otto P H, cabtmkr, h 35 Smithson.
Kemphfer Charles R, baggageman, h 107 Fletcher av.
Kempter Paul, lab, h 57 N Judge Harding (W I).
Kendall Albert G, fireman, b 678 W Washington.
Kendall Anna, h 133½ E Washington.
Kendall Bladen A, carp, h 480 W Shoemaker (N I).
Kendall Charles, tailor, h 83 Lockerbie.
Kendall Edward L, clk R M S, h 75 W McCarty.
Kendall Ella M, dressmkr, h 19½ N Meridian.
Kendall Frederick C, teacher High School, b 84 E New York.
Kendall Hannah A (wid James N), b 412 S West.
Kendall Harry J, painter, b 80 Oliver av (W I).
Kendall Ira C, clk, b 15 Greer.
Kendall Jesse G, condr, h 182 N Missouri.
Kendall John A, dyer, 43 Mass av, h 210 N Noble.
Kendall Levi, farmer, h 80 Oliver av (W I).
Kendall Lizzie (wid John), h 139 E South.
Kendall Martha E (wid Walter R), h 84 E New York.
Kendall Martha W (wid Sylvester W), h 176 E New York.
Kendall Mary (wid John), dyer, 25 Mass av, b 120 same.

Parlor, Bed Room, Dining Room, Kitchen, Furniture W. H. MESSENGER, 101 E. Wash. St., Tel. 491.

ALL KINDS OF HEAVY AND LIGHT GRAY IRON CASTINGS | McNamara, Koster & Co. Phone 1593. 212-218 S. Penn. St. | Foundry and Pattern Shop

Kendall Pearl M, clk, b 19½ N Meridian.
Kendall Philip, clk, h 8 Miller blk.
Kendall Schuyler T, bkkpr, b 84 E New York.
Kendall Victor C, bkkpr L S Ayres & Co, b 699 N Alabama.
Kendall Wm, insp Indpls Gas Co, h 124 Weghorst.
Kendrick John, boilermkr, r 188 S Senate av.
Kendrick Robert, b 444½ Mass av.
Kendrick Robert L, horse dealer, b 243 River av (W I).
Kendrick Wm H, phys, 73 N East, h same.
Kenipe James M, feed, 90 E South, h same.
Kenley Charles W, condr, h 62 N Beville av.
Kennard Howard, lab, h 195 W Ray.
Kennard Jesse A, lab, h 630 W Udell (N I).
Kennaugh Thomas C, patrolman, h 870 Rembrant.
Kennedy Benjamin, carp, h 610 W Udell (N I).
Kennedy Bernard F, student, b 17 West Drive (W P).
Kennedy Byron D, pdlr, h 293 Shelby.
Kennedy Cassius R, carp, h 297 Cornell av.
Kennedy Catherine, h 295 W St Clair.
Kennedy Charles F, secretary State Board of Agriculture, 14 State House, h 285 Bellefontaine.
Kennedy Charles M, cooper, h 233 Virginia av.
Kennedy Cornelius, lab, h 173 Meek.
Kennedy Daniel, b 20 S Beville av.
Kennedy Daniel, lab, h 180 Bismarck av (H).
Kennedy Daniel, switchman, h 18 N Gale (B).
Kennedy Daniel F, stonecutter, h 179 Dearborn.
Kennedy Edward F, lab, b 173 Meek.
Kennedy Francis M, mailer, b 167 S Alabama.
Kennedy Frank, coremkr, b 20 N Belmont av (H).
Kennedy Frederick E, clk, b 133 Fayette.
Kennedy George W, clk, r 12½ N Delaware.
Kennedy George B, mach hd, h 522 W Maryland.
Kennedy George E, attendant Insane Hospital.
Kennedy Harry L, metermkr, b 185 St Mary.
Kennedy Jackson, lab, h 24 Asbury.
Kennedy James, lab, h 80 N Belmont av (H).
Kennedy James, lab, b 173 Meek.
Kennedy James, mach, b 5 S Station (B).
Kennedy James, switchman, h 179 E South.
Kennedy James F, mach, b 390 W 1st.
Kennedy James M, huckster, h n e cor W North and Elwood.
Kennedy Jeremiah, lab, b 450 Mass av.
Kennedy Jessie B, stenog Clifford Browder & Moffett, b 133 Fayette.
Kennedy John, drayman, h 125 Bright.
Kennedy John, lab, h 27 Patterson.
Kennedy John, lab, h 283 Bates.
Kennedy John, lab, r 155½ W Washington.
Kennedy John B, mngr Walter A Wood Harvester Co, h 618 Broadway.
Kennedy John E, metermkr, h 185 St Mary.
Kennedy John T, lab, h w s Calvin 2 s of Bethel av.
Kennedy John W, lab, b 38 S Stuart (B).
Kennedy John Y, phys, 194 N East, h same.
Kennedy Joshua, lab, h 6 Concord (H).

Henry H. Fay,
40½ E. WASHINGTON ST.,
FIRE INSURANCE, REAL ESTATE,
LOANS AND RENTAL AGENT.

Kennedy Junius J Rev, pastor Lovely Lane A M E Zion Church, h 240 W Michigan.
Kennedy Lafayette, lab, h 553 E 7th.
Kennedy Levi, sec Commercial B and L Assn, h 48 Highland pl.
Kennedy Lydia E (wid James H), b 473 N East.
Kennedy Mary (wid James), b 137 Harrison.
Kennedy Michael, brakeman, h 20 S Beville av.
Kennedy Michael R, saloon, 49 S West, h same.
Kennedy Odel, caller, b 123 Spann av.
Kennedy Patrick, lab, h 20 N Belmont av (H).
Kennedy Patrick, lab, b 319 S West.
Kennedy Patrick J, helper, h 267 English av.
Kennedy Patrick W (Kennedy & Connaughton), h 209 S Pine.
Kennedy Perry, foreman, h 164 Davidson.
Kennedy Richard, driver, h 215 LeGrand av.
Kennedy Richmond, lab, h 145 Harlan.
Kennedy Robert J, lab, h 386 Blake.
Kennedy Robert N, carp, h 167 S Alabama.
Kennedy Roland, lab, h 28 Hill.
Kennedy Samuel, r 12½ N Delaware.
Kennedy Samuel A, phys, 133 Fayette, h same.
Kennedy Samuel O, painter, b 133 Fayette.
Kennedy Thomas, driller, b 43 Tecumseh.
Kennedy Thomas, lab, b 36 Temple av.
Kennedy Thomas, opr, h 102 Wright.
Kennedy Warren J, meat cutter, h 426 E North.
Kennedy Wm, janitor, b n e cor Brightwood av and C C C & St L Ry (B).
Kennedy Wm, lab, r 155½ W Washington.
Kennedy Wm D, condr, h 123 Spann av.
Kennedy Wm E, mach hd, b 27 Patterson.
Kennedy Wm G, r 234½ Mass av.
Kennedy Wm M, motorman, h 36 Everett.
Kennedy Wm T, mach hd, h 52 Holloway av.
Kennedy Wm W, lab, h 612 W Udell.

WILL GO ON YOUR BOND
American Bonding & Trust Co.
Of Baltimore, Md. Approved as sole surety by the United States Government and the different States as Sole Surety on all Forms of Bonds.
W. E. BARTON & CO., General Agents,
504 Indiana Trust Building.
LONG DISTANCE TELEPHONE 1918.

THE FRED DIETZ CO. — WOODEN PACKING BOXES MADE TO ORDER. FACTORY AND WAREHOUSE TRUCKS. 40 Madison Avenue. Telephone 619.

BUSINESS EDUCATION A NECESSITY. TIME SHORT. DAY AND NIGHT SCHOOL. SUCCESS CERTAIN AT THE PERMANENT, RELIABLE
Indianapolis BUSINESS UNIVERSITY

Water and Oil Meters { HENRY R. WORTHINGTON, 64 S. PENNSYLVANIA ST. Long Distance Telephone 284.

UNION CO-OPERATIVE LAUNDRY { (COMPOSED OF UNION LAUNDRY GIRLS.) NOS. 3, 40 AND 42 VIRGINIA AVENUE. } T. E. SOMERVILLE, MANAGER — TELEPHONES. INDIANAPOLIS, IND.

HORACE M. HADLEY
INSURANCE AND LOANS
66 E. Market Street, Basement
TELEPHONE 1540.

KENNEDY & CONNAUGHTON (Patrick W Kennedy, John F Connaughton), Proprs Capital City Steam Boiler and Sheet Iron Works, 207-209 S Illinois, Tel 1748. (See adv in classified Boilermakers.)
Kennelley George J, cabtmkr, b 144 N Senate av.
Kennelly Dennis, engr, h 61 Omer.
Kennelly John W, clk C C C & St L Ry, b 63 Omer.
Kennelly Martin, lab, b 72 English av.
Kennelly Michael, porter, b 83 W Michigan.
Kennelly Wm T, carp, h 163 Beacon.
Kenner Ida M (wid Charles A), h 651½ N Senate av.
Kennett Ernest, motorman, r 423 N Senate av.
Kennett Ira W, broker, b 595 Broadway.
Kennett Mary M, shirtmkr, r 3, 137½ Virginia av.
Kenney, see also Kinney.
Kenney Catherine C (wid Minot), b 162 Huron.
Kenney Edward (Kenney & Sullivan), gen agt The Aultman Co, h 55 West Drive (W P).
Kenney George A, lab, b 162 Huron.
Kenney John, lab, b 489 S West.
Kenney Michael, butcher, b 111 W South.
Kenney Sarah (wid Michael), h 489 S West.
Kenney Thomas J, bartndr, h 173 W Ohio.
Kenney & Sullivan (Edward T Kenney, Daniel B Sullivan), farm implements, 3 Board of Trade bldg.
Kennington Albert R, sawmkr, b 288 S Alabama.
Kennington Bros (Frank R and John R), coutrs, 455 S Delaware.
Kennington Frank R (Kennington Bros), b 455 S Delaware.
Kennington Harry, mach, b 288 S Alabama.
Kennington Harry H, brakeman, h 302 Bates.
Kennington James B, molder, b 288 S Alabama.
Kennington John, h 288 S Alabama.

COLLECTIONS
MERCHANTS' AND MANUFACTURERS' EXCHANGE
Will give you good service.
J. E. TAKKEN, Manager,
Union Building, over U. S. Pension Office.
73 West Maryland Street.

Kennington John jr, molder, b 288 S Alabama.
Kennington John H, mach hd, h 206 Deloss.
Kennington John R (Kennington Bros), h 51 Bicking.
Kennington Mary (wid Moses), b 140 Lexington av.
Kennington Moses J, fireman, h 140 Lexington av.
Kennington Ralph E, yard foreman C C C & St L Ry, h 1175 E Washington.
Kennington Richard, draughtsman, b 288 S Alabama.
Kennington Richard, brakeman, b 115 Meek.
Kennington Robert, h 455 S Delaware.
Kennington Robert H, blksmith, b 206 Deloss.
Kenny Charles C, trunkmkr, h 63 Hazel.
Kenny Frank W, chief insp Consumers' Gas Trust Co, h 310 N Noble.
Kenny Jane (wid Richard), b 122 W Michigan.
Kenny Wm A, mach hd, h 96 N Gillard av.
Keno George, lab, h 602½ N West.
Kenoyer Aaron, h 49 Brett.
Kensler John, h 154 E New York.
Kent Carroll R, mach hd, b 623 W Eugene (N I).
Kent Charles, sander, b 623 W Eugene (N I).
Kent Charles C, foreman, b 106 Minerva.
Kent Edward T, mach, h 45 Wright.
Kent Ella S (wid Chester F), h 20 N Spruce.
Kent Harry E, lab, b 623 W Eugene (N I).
Kent Henry C, carp Insane Hospital.
Kent John, h 49 Hope (B).
Kent John, bartndr, h 216 Springfield.
Kent John C, watchman, h 623 W Eugene (N I).
Kent Joseph, lab, r 148 W Maryland.
Kenton James (Kurts & Kenton), b 23 Center.
Kenton John R, student, b 253 E Washington.
Kenton Wm T, paperhngr, b 253 E Washington.
Kenworthy Isaac C, h 84 N Rural.
Kenworthy Thomas G, basketmkr, b 84 N Rural.
Kenworthy Wm H, messenger Am Ex Co, h 78 E North.
Kenyon Albert A, trav agt, h 67 Ruckle.
Kenyon Albert M, city fireman, h 748 N New Jersey.
Kenyon Clarence A, pres Hoosier Construction Co, h 125 E Pratt.
Kenyon Frank H, sec Hoosier Construction Co, h 780 N Illinois.
Kenyon Hannah E (wid Addison G), h 535 Central av.
Kenyon Lewis, hostler, r 175 E Michigan.
Kenyon Lukins S, driver, b rear 353 E Market.
Keogh Anna (wid John E), dressmkr, 291 S East, h same.
Keogh James W, agt Deering Harvester Co, 192 W Market, h 297 Excelsior av.
Keogh Mary (wid Thomas), b 297 Excelsior av.
Kephart Edgar T, condr, h 297½ S Illinois.
Keplinger John, real est, h 836 E 9th.
Kepner Albert L, brakeman, b 97 Walcott.
Kepner Charles A, clk The Bates.
Kepner Charles F, mason, h 52 Hadley av (W I).
Kepner Harry R, clk N Y Store, b 97 Walcott.

CLEMENS VONNEGUT 184, 186 and 192 E. Washington St. | BUILDERS' HARDWARE, Building Paper, Duplex Joist Hangers

THE WM. H. BLOCK CO. DRY GOODS, DRAPERIES, RUGS, WINDOW SHADES.
7 AND 9 EAST WASHINGTON STREET.

Kepner Martin L, barber, 504 N West, h 339 W 2d.
Kepner Samuel A, h 97 Walcott.
Keppel Amer J, mach, h 163 Chruch.
Keppel Anna E, nurse, b 163 Church.
Keppel Harvey E, ins agt, h 14 Ruckle.
Keppel Henry, lab, h 174 Church.
Keppel Mahlon T, custodian Greenlawn Cemetery, h 294 W Morris.
Keppel Mary (wid Martin), b 14 Ruckle.
Keppel Wm, ins, h 1717 Graceland av.
Keppler James, blksmith, s e cor Washington and National avs (I), b w end of Church (I).
Keppler Marcus, lab, h 43 Fenneman.
Ker John, buyer N Y Store, h 459 N Alabama.
Kerbox Charles E, tmstr, h 396 Yandes.
Kerbox George, lab, h 12 Wallace.
Kercheval Columbia I, h 159 Christian av.
Kerein Philip H, stairbldr, b 18 E Michigan.
Kerfoot George B, clk Pearson & Wetzel, h 473 E Georgia.
Kerfoot John B, clk, b 473 E Georgia.
Kerfoot Margaret L (wid Leland B), b 620 Central av.
Kerfoot Wm P, clk, b 473 E Georgia.
Kerins Anna C, dressmkr, 137 Harrison, b same.
Kerins James P, lab, h 106 Church.
Kerins Jeremiah M, boilermkr, h 137 Harrison.
Kerins Kate, teacher Public School No 16, b 106 Church.
Kerkhoff, see also Kirkhoff.
Kerkhoff Charles F, car rep, h 342 Fletcher av.
Kerkhoff Frederick W, lab, h 74 Harlan.
Kerkhoff Mary J (wid Charles F), h 225 Naomi.
Kerlin Edward J, clk Penna Lines, h 585 E Washington.
Kern, see also Curran.
Kern Barbara M, h 245 Davidson.
Kern Bridget M (wid Michael), h 278 Bates.
Kern David G, h 454 E Michigan.
Kern George, engr, r 233 Cedar.
Kern George L, bkkpr, b 405 N Delaware.
Kern George P, engr, h 106 Dunlop.
Kern George S, watchmkr Wm T Marcy, h 6 Eden pl.
Kern John W (Kern & Bailey), h 880 N Penn.
Kern Julius, clk, b 173 S Linden.
Kern Louis, clk R M S, h 405 N Delaware.
Kern Louis, well driver, h 335 S Meridian.
Kern Michael B, lab, b 278 Bates.
Kern Rosa (wid Jacob), b 607 E New York.
Kern Walter H, drugs, 452 E Michigan, h 454 same.
Kern Wm, packer, h 173 S Linden.
Kern Wm G, paperhngr, h 405 S Olive.
KERN & BAILEY (John W Kern, Leon O Bailey), Lawyers, Rooms 1, 2, 3, 4 and 7, 8½ N Penn, Tel 1338.
Kernan Patrick W, bartndr, b 199 Indiana av.
Kernel Frank J, fish, 410 S Meridian, h same.
Kernel Joseph, carp, h 192 W Ray.
Kernel Joseph, lab, h 472 Chestnut
Kernel Nicholas, lab, h 31 Poplar.
Kerner Charles E, mach, h 84 Huron.
Kerney Charles, teacher, r 292 N Illinois.
Kernodell Horace G, genl yardmaster L E & W R R, h 610 Bellefontaine.
Kernodle Harry, glasswkr, b 129 N Illinois.
Kerns James, carp, h 273 W North.

Kerper John M, chief clk Consumers' Gas Trust Co, h 75 Middle Drive (W P).
Kerr Albert L, guard Work House, h 108 Blackford.
Kerr Ambrose M, polisher, b 320 W 1st.
Kerr Artemus P, r 32 W Court.
Kerr Charles G, clk McCormick H M Co, h 491 Bellefontaine.
Kerr Clifford C, bkkpr U S Pension Agency, r 140 N Alabama.
Kerr Flora S, h 1235 N Illinois.
Kerr George S, motorman, h 133 Oliver av (W I).
Kerr George W, lab, b 182 Yandes.
Kerr Guilford T, saloon, 81 S Illinois, h 175 Hadley av (W I).
Kerr Harriet (wid Wm), h 201 N Belmont av (H).
Kerr Henry E, watchman, h 259 S Senate av.
Kerr Hugh, clk N Y Store, h 145 Highland pl.
Kerr James A, agt, r 28½ Indiana av.
Kerr James H (Kerr & Irie), h 63 N Senate av.
Kerr John, helper, h 145 Highland pl.
Kerr John A, lab, h 76 Cypress.
Kerr John E, farmer, h 896 N Senate av.
Kerr John F (Lineback & Kerr), grocer, 98 Woodlawn av, h same.
Kerr John M L, butter, 17 E Mkt House, b 297 N Capitol av.
Kerr John W, printer, h 111 Davidson.
Kerr Thomas, h 412 N New Jersey.
KERR THOMAS S S, Genl Agt W E Forrest "Fluctuation System," 77½ E Market, r same. (See adv p 9.)
Kerr Warren D, butcher, h 37 Omer.
Kerr Wm A, city agt, h 111 Oak.
Kerr Wm M, horsedealer, r 82½ W Washington.
Kerr Wm W, trav agt, b 412 N New Jersey.
Kerr & Irie (James H Kerr, Matthew Irie), saloon, 88 W Washington and 82 N Delaware.
Kers John, b 179 Blake.
Kersey Charles E, cabtmkr, h 222 S Noble.
Kersey Emma, dressmkr, 1261 W Washington (M J), h same.

GUIDO R. PRESSLER,
FRESCO PAINTER
Churches, Theaters, Public Buildings, Etc., A Specialty.
Residence, No. 325 North Liberty Street.
INDIANAPOLIS, IND.

INDIANAPOLIS STEEL ROOFING AND CORRUGATING WORKS, 23 and 25 East South Street. S. D. NOEL, Proprietor.

David S. McKernan, Rooms 2-5 Thorpe Block.
REAL ESTATE AND LOANS
Money to loan on real estate. Special inducements offered those having money to loan. It will pay you to investigate.

Water and Oil Meters { HENRY R. WORTHINGTON, 64 S. PENNSYLVANIA ST. Long Distance Telephone 284.

UNION CO-OPERATIVE LAUNDRY } (COMPOSED OF UNION LAUNDRY GIRLS.) NOS. 3, 40 AND 42 VIRGINIA AVENUE. T. E. SOMERVILLE, MANAGER. TELEPHONE 16. INDIANAPOLIS, IND.

HORACE M. HADLEY
INSURANCE AND LOANS
66 E. Market Street, Basement
TELEPHONE 1540.

KENNEDY & CONNAUGHTON (Patrick W Kennedy, John F Connaughton), Proprs Capital City Steam Boiler and Sheet Iron Works, 207-209 S Illinois, Tel 1748. (See adv in classified Boilermakers.)
Kennelley George J, cabtmkr, b 144 N Senate av.
Kennelly Dennis, engr, h 61 Omer.
Kennelly John W, clk C C C & St L Ry, b 63 Omer.
Kennelly Martin, lab, b 72 English av.
Kennelly Michael, porter, b 83 W Michigan.
Kennelly Wm T, carp, h 163 Beacon.
Kenner Ida M (wid Charles A), h 651½ N Senate av.
Kennett Ernest, motorman, r 423 N Senate av.
Kennett Ira W, broker, b 595 Broadway.
Kennett Mary M, shirtmkr, r 3, 137½ Virginia av.
Kenney, see also Kinney.
Kenney Catherine C (wid Minot), b 162 Huron.
Kenney Edward (Kenney & Sullivan), gen agt The Aultman Co, h 55 West Drive (W P).
Kenney George A, lab, b 162 Huron.
Kenney John, lab, b 489 S West.
Kenney Michael, butcher, b 111 W South.
Kenney Sarah (wid Michael), h 489 S West.
Kenney Thomas J, bartndr, h 173 W Ohio.
Kenney & Sullivan (Edward T Kenney, Daniel B Sullivan), farm implements, 3 Board of Trade bldg.
Kennington Albert R, sawmkr, b 288 S Alabama.
Kennington Bros (Frank R and John R), coutrs, 455 S Delaware.
Kennington Frank R (Kennington Bros), b 455 S Delaware.
Kennington Harry, mach, b 288 S Alabama.
Kennington Harry H, brakeman, h 302 Bates.
Kennington James B, molder, b 288 S Alabama.
Kennington John, h 288 S Alabama.

COLLECTIONS
MERCHANTS' AND MANUFACTURERS' EXCHANGE
Will give you good service.
J. E. TAKKEN, Manager,
Union Building, over U. S. Pension Office.
73 West Maryland Street.

Kennington John jr, molder, b 288 S Alabama.
Kennington John H, mach hd, h 206 Deloss.
Kennington John R (Kennington Bros), h 51 Bicking.
Kennington Mary (wid Moses), b 140 Lexington av.
Kennington Moses J, fireman, h 140 Lexington av.
Kennington Ralph E, yard foreman C C C & St L Ry, h 1175 E Washington.
Kennington Richard, draughtsman, b 288 S Alabama.
Kennington Richard, brakeman, b 115 Meek.
Kennington Robert, h 455 S Delaware.
Kennington Robert H, blksmith, b 206 Deloss.
Kenny Charles C, trunkmkr, h 63 Hazel.
Kenny Frank W, chief insp Consumers' Gas Trust Co, h 310 N Noble.
Kenny Jane (wid Richard), b 122 W Michigan.
Kenny Wm A, mach hd, h 96 N Gillard av.
Keno George, lab, h 602½ N West.
Kenoyer Aaron, h 49 Brett.
Kensler John, h 154 E New York.
Kent Carroll R, mach hd, b 623 W Eugene (N I).
Kent Charles, sander, b 623 W Eugene (N I).
Kent Charles C, foreman, b 106 Minerva.
Kent Edward T, mach, h 45 Wright.
Kent Ella S (wid Chester F), h 20 N Spruce.
Kent Harry E, lab, b 623 W Eugene (N I).
Kent Henry C, carp Insane Hospital.
Kent John, h 49 Hope (B).
Kent John, bartndr, h 216 Springfield.
Kent John C, watchman, h 623 W Eugene (N I).
Kent Joseph, lab, r 148 W Maryland.
Kenton James (Kurts & Kenton), b 28 Center.
Kenton John R, student, b 253 E Washington.
Kenton Wm T, paperhngr, b 253 E Washington.
Kenworthy Isaac C, h 84 N Rural.
Kenworthy Thomas G, basketmkr, b 84 N Rural.
Kenworthy Wm H, messenger Am Ex Co, h 78 E North.
Kenyon Albert A, trav agt, h 67 Ruckle.
Kenyon Albert M, city fireman, h 748 N New Jersey.
Kenyon Clarence A, pres Hoosier Construction Co, h 125 E Pratt.
Kenyon Frank H, sec Hoosier Construction Co, h 780 N Illinois.
Kenyon Hannah E (wid Addison G), h 535 Central av.
Kenyon Lewis, hostler, r 175 E Michigan.
Kenyon Lukins S, driver, b rear 353 E Market.
Keogh Anna (wid John E), dressmkr, 291 S East, h same.
Keogh James W, agt Deering Harvester Co, 192 W Market, h 297 Excelsior av.
Keogh Mary (wid Thomas), b 297 Excelsior av.
Kephart Edgar T, condr, h 297½ S Illinois.
Keplinger John, real est, h 836 E 9th.
Kepner Albert L, brakeman, b 97 Walcott.
Kepner Charles A, clk The Bates.
Kepner Charles F, mason, h 52 Hadley av (W I).
Kepner Harry R, clk N Y Store, b 97 Walcott.

CLEMENS VONNEGUT
184, 186 and 192 E. Washington St.
BUILDERS' HARDWARE,
Building Paper, Duplex Joist Hangers.

THE WM. H. BLOCK CO. DRY GOODS, DRAPERIES, RUGS, WINDOW SHADES.
7 AND 9 EAST WASHINGTON STREET.

Kepner Martin L, barber, 504 N West, h 339 W 2d.
Kepner Samuel A, h 97 Walcott.
Keppel Amer J, mach, h 163 Chruch.
Keppel Anna E, nurse, b 163 Church.
Keppel Harvey E, ins agt, h 14 Ruckle.
Keppel Henry, lab, h 174 Church.
Keppel Mahlon T, custodian Greenlawn Cemetery, h 294 W Morris.
Keppel Mary (wid Martin), b 14 Ruckle.
Keppel Wm, ins, h 1717 Graceland av.
Keppler James, blksmith, s e cor Washington and National avs (I), b w end of Church (I).
Keppler Marcus, lab, h 43 Fenneman.
Ker John, buyer N Y Store, h 359 N Alabama.
Kerbox Charles E, tmstr, h 396 Yandes.
Kerbox George, lab, h 12 Wallace.
Kercheval Columbia I, h 159 Christian av.
Kerein Philip H, stairbldr, b 18 E Michigan.
Kerfoot George B, clk Pearson & Wetzel, h 473 E Georgia.
Kerfoot John B, clk, b 473 E Georgia.
Kerfoot Margaret L (wid Leland B), b 620 Central av.
Kerfoot Wm P, clk, b 473 E Georgia.
Kerins Anna C, dressmkr, 137 Harrison, b same.
Kerins James P, lab, h 106 Church.
Kerins Jeremiah M, boilermkr, h 137 Harrison.
Kerins Kate, teacher Public School No 16, b 106 Church.
Kerkhoff, see also Kirkhoff.
Kerkhoff Charles F, car rep, h 342 Fletcher av.
Kerkhoff Frederick W, lab, h 74 Harlan.
Kerkhoff Mary J (wid Charles F), h 225 Naomi.
Kerlin Edward J, clk Penna Lines, h 585 E Washington.
Kern, see also Curran.
Kern Barbara M, h 245 Davidson.
Kern Bridget M (wid Michael), h 278 Bates.
Kern David G, h 454 E Michigan.
Kern George, engr, r 233 Cedar.
Kern George L, bkkpr, b 405 N Delaware.
Kern George P, engr, h 106 Dunlop.
Kern George S, watchmkr Wm T Marcy, h 6 Eden pl.
Kern John W (Kern & Bailey), h 880 N Penn.
Kern Julius, clk, b 173 S Linden.
Kern Louis, clk R M S, h 405 N Delaware.
Kern Louis, well driver, h 335 S Meridian.
Kern Michael B, lab, b 278 Bates.
Kern Rosa (wid Jacob), b 607 E New York.
Kern Walter H, drugs, 452 E Michigan, h 454 same.
Kern Wm, packer, h 173 S Linden.
Kern Wm G, paperhngr, h 405 S Olive.
KERN & BAILEY (John W Kern, Leon O Bailey), Lawyers, Rooms 1, 2, 3, 4 and 7, 8½ N Penn, Tel 1338.
Kernan Patrick W, bartndr, b 199 Indiana av.
Kernel Frank J, fish, 410 S Meridian, h same.
Kernel Joseph, carp, h 192 W Ray.
Kernel Joseph, lab, h 472 Chestnut.
Kernel Nicholas, lab, h 31 Poplar.
Kerner Charles E, mach, h 84 Huron.
Kerney Charles, teacher, r 292 N Illinois.
Kernodell Horace G, genl yardmaster L E & W R R, h 610 Bellefontaine.
Kernodle Harry, glasswkr, b 129 N Illinois.
Kerns James, carp, h 273 W North.

THE H. LIEBER COMPANY. ART EMPORIUM 33 South Meridian St. Visitors Welcome.

Kerper John M, chief clk Consumers' Gas Trust Co, h 75 Middle Drive (W P).
Kerr Albert L, guard Work House, h 108 Blackford.
Kerr Ambrose M, polisher, b 320 W 1st.
Kerr Artemus P, r 32 W Court.
Kerr Charles G, clk McCormick H M Co, h 491 Bellefontaine.
Kerr Clifford C, bkkpr U S Pension Agency, r 140 N Alabama.
Kerr Flora S, h 1235 N Illinois.
Kerr George S, motorman, h 133 Oliver av (W I).
Kerr George W, lab, b 182 Yandes.
Kerr Guilford T, saloon, 81 S Illinois, h 175 Hadley av (W I).
Kerr Harriet (wid Wm), h 201 N Belmont av (H).
Kerr Henry E, watchman, h 259 S Senate av.
Kerr Hugh, clk N Y Store, h 145 Highland pl.
Kerr James A, agt, r 28½ Indiana av.
Kerr James H (Kerr & Irie), h 68 N Senate av.
Kerr John, helper, h 145 Highland pl.
Kerr John A, lab, h 76 Cypress.
Kerr John E, farmer, h 896 N Senate av.
Kerr John F (Lineback & Kerr), grocer, 98 Woodlawn av, h same.
Kerr John M L, butter, 17 E Mkt House, b 297 N Capitol av.
Kerr John W, printer, h 111 Davidson.
Kerr Thomas, h 412 N New Jersey.
KERR THOMAS S S, Genl Agt W E Forrest "Fluctuation System," 77½ E Market, r same. (See adv p 9.)
Kerr Warren D, butcher, h 37 Omer.
Kerr Wm A, city agt, h 111 Oak.
Kerr Wm M, horsedealer, r 82½ W Washington.
Kerr Wm W, trav agt, b 412 N New Jersey.
Kerr & Irie (James H Kerr, Matthew Irie), saloon, 88 W Washington and 82 N Delaware.
Kers John, b 179 Blake.
Kersey Charles E, cabtmkr, h 222 S Noble.
Kersey Emma, dressmkr, 1261 W Washington (M J), h same.

GUIDO R. PRESSLER,
FRESCO PAINTER
Churches, Theaters, Public Buildings, Etc., A Specialty.
Residence, No. 325 North Liberty Street.
INDIANAPOLIS, IND.

INDIANAPOLIS STEEL ROOFING AND CORRUGATING WORKS, 23 and 25 East South Street. S. D. NOEL, Proprietor.

David S. McKernan, Rooms 2-5 Thorpe Block. REAL ESTATE AND LOANS Money to loan on real estate. Special inducements offered those having money to loan. It will pay you to investigate.

DIAMOND WALL PLASTER { Telephone 1410 BUILDERS' EXCHANGE.

Cor. E. Ohio St. and C., C., C. & St. L. R'y Tracks. BEST FACILITIES FOR STORING AND TRANSFERRING MACHINERY AND MERCHANDISE.

UNION TRANSFER AND STORAGE CO.

W. McWORKMAN

FIRE SHUTTERS,
FIRE DOORS,
METAL CEILINGS.

930 W. Washington St. Tel. 1118.

Kersey Henry C, printer, h 412 S Pine.
Kersey Oliver, h rear 224 E Merrill.
Kersey Priscilla, dressmkr, 182 Fulton, h same.
Kersey Sarah J (wid James W), b 1261 W Washington (M J).
Kersey Simmons, barber, h 40 Mill.
Kersey Walter, lab, h 167 Minerva.
Kersey Wm H, foreman, h 381 E Georgia.
Kersey Wm S, paperhngr, h 15 Margaret.
Kersey Willis A, barber, 814 N Illinois, h 201 W 6th.
Kershaw Robert H, foreman, h 277½ W Michigan.
KERSHNER BROS (Charles E and Wm H), Proprs Sherman's Restaurant, 18-20 S Meridian, Tel 197. (See left side lines.)
Kershner Charles E (Kershner Bros), h 473½ N Illinois.
Kershner Robert B, ins agt, r 28½ Mass av.
Kershner Wm H (Kershner Bros), r 226 N Delaware.
Kersting Benjamin, saloon, 288 W Washington, h 202 E Morris.
Kersting Edward, bartndr, b 202 E Morris.
Kersting Elizabeth, stenog, b 202 E Morris.
Kersting Wm M, finisher, h 457 E North.
Kersting Wm, finisher, h 250 E Vermont.
Kertner Jacob, tmstr, h rear 472 E Washington.
Kervan John, clk, b 151 Dougherty.
Kervan Mary (wid John), h 151 Dougherty.
Kerwood Wayne H, b 199 College av.
Kerwood Wm R, h 199 College av.
Kerz Nikolaus, grocer, 591 W Michigan, h same.
Kerz Philip G, patternmkr, b 591 W Michigan.
Keske Ernst W, lab, h 73 Spann av.
Kesler Sarah E (wid Jacob), h 19 Madison av.
Kesler Stephen D, sawmkr, h 108 Douglass.
Kessener Herman, clk, h 128 E Market.
Kessing Clement R, bkkpr Albert Gall, r 311 N Delaware.
Kessing Frank, contr, r 311 N Delaware.
Kessing Herman, lab, h 118 Buchanan.

GEO. J. MAYER,
MANUFACTURER OF
SEALS
STENCILS, RUBBER STAMPS, CHECKS, BADGES, DOOR PLATES, ETC.
5 S. Meridian St., Ground Floor. TEL. 1386.

Kessler Aaron, gasfitter, h w s Senate av 4 s of Lynn (M).
Kessler Aaron, mach, h 223 Clinton.
Kessler Alonzo W, carp, h 322 Yandes.
Kessler Charles H, mach, h 339 Yandes.
Kessler Christian, supt Hitz Baking Co, h 113 High.
Kessler Clarence A, mach hd, b 336 E New York.
Kessler Eliza (wid Henry), b 62 W 13th.
Kessler Frank, gardener, h 71 Lily.
Kessler George, livery, 200 W Pearl, h 1252 Northwestern av.
Kessler Herman, clk, r 218 E Market.
Kessler Isadore, stenog McCoy-Howe Co, b 400 N Illinois.
Kessler Leroy, lab, b 322 Yandes.
Kessler Mary A (wid Frederick), h 345 S New Jersey.
Kessler Richard, carp, r 175½ W Washington.
Kessler Thomas A, mach hd, h 1679 N Senate av.
Kessler Walter, mngr Romona Oolitic Stone Co, h 2 College av.
Kessler Walter W, mach hd, b 1679 N Senate av.
Kester Newton I, painter, h 487 E 9th.
Kester Omer F, plumber, r 275 W Market.
Kester Samuel M, grainer, h 116 Clifford av.
Ketcham Donald, clk Brown-Ketcham Iron Wks, b 216 N Delaware.
Ketcham Frank M, sec The L A Kinsey Co, h 23 Tecumseh.
Ketcham Jane M (wid John L), h 2222 N Illinois.
Ketcham John L, sec and treas Brown-Ketcham Iron Wks, h 216 N Delaware.
Ketcham John L jr, b 216 N Delaware.
KETCHAM WM A, Lawyer, 26 Fletcher's Bank Bldg, Tel 966, and Attorney-General State of Indiana, Rooms 19-21 State House, Tel 1300; h 2222 N Illinois, Tel 1166.
Ketrick Thomas, lab, b 301 River av (W I).
Ketrow Charles S, brushmkr, r 37 Harris av (M J).
Ketrow Verda, cook, r 244½ E Washington.
Kettelhut Henry, driver, r 393 N West.
Kettenbach Edward, sec Indpls Mnfg Co, h s w cor Washington and Downey avs (I).
Kettenbach Elizabeth, h 279 Mass av.
Ketter Jacob, uphlr, h 113 Chadwick.
Ketterheinrich Frederick W, porter, h 23 Iowa.
Ketterheinrich Wm H, b 20 Nevada.
Ketterhenry Edward H, mach hd, h 692 Madison av.
Kettler Henry W, shoemkr, 317 Clifford av, h same.
Kettler Herman L, mach, b 45 Tecumseh.
Kettler John H, painter, h 45 Tecumseh.
Kettler Wm J, mach, h 586 Jefferson av.
Kettlewell John, mach, h 160 S Noble.
Kettlewell John F, mach, b 160 S Noble.
Kettrel Tuss, coachman 753 N Penn.
Keusink Garrett, fireman, h 18 Traub av.
Kevers Gustave W (Fertig & Kevers), h 128 W Pratt.
Kevil Robert L, tinner, h 331 E Ohio.
Kewen Edward J, plastr, h 417 Excelsior av.
Key Sarah E (wid Matthew), housekpr, s e cor Shade and Willow (B).
Keyes Margaret (wid Harry), h 294½ Mass av.
Keyes Wm S, trav agt, b 294½ Mass av.

A. METZGER AGENCY ESTABLISHED 1863. REAL ESTATE

LAMBERT GAS & GASOLINE ENGINE CO.
ANDERSON, IND. NATURAL GAS ENGINES.

BICYCLES $5 DN. Best Wheels. Best Terms. WHEELMEN'S CO. 31 W. OHIO ST. LONG DISTANCE TEL. 1855.

Keyler George B, bookbndr, r 197½ E Washington.
Keyless Lock Co, Arthur Jordan pres, George L Barney mngr, 81 Newman.
Keylor John, insp Kingan & Co (ltd), h 91 Bright.
Keys Ida B (Union Co-Operative Laundry), b 169 Woodlawn av.
Keys John H, tmstr, h 169 Woodlawn av.
Keys John T, machinery, 110 W Maryland, h same.
Keys Joseph A, city fireman, b 169 Woodlawn av.
KEYSER GEORGE W, Plumber, Gas and Steam Fitter, 91 N Illinois, Tel 947; h 4 Hall Pl.
KEYSTONE CO (Wm H and Oscar J Mansfield), Merchant Tailors and Dye Works, 17 Mass av.
Kibbe George P, bkkpr Indpls Drug Co, h 79 Hudson.
Kibbie James, lab, b 430 Blake.
Kidd Alvin, condr, b 1139 N Illinois.
Kidd John C, mach, b 3 Holmes av (H).
Kidd John D, grocer, 3 Holmes av (H), h same.
Kidney George F, flagman, h 138 Mass av.
Kidwell John W, carp, h 265 W Maryland.
Kidwell Thomas, lab, h 50 Nebraska.
Kidwell Thomas B, engr, h 198 Hoyt av.
Kidwell Wm T, lab, h 50 Nebraska.
Kiefer Adam, mach hd, b 73 Pleasant.
Kiefer Albert, bricklyr, b 79 W Morris.
Kiefer Albert, stonecutter, r 181½ S Meridian.
Kiefer Andrew, mach hd, h 64 Jefferson.
Kiefer Anna (wid Charles), h 417 E Pearl.
Kiefer Augustus, pres A Kiefer Drug Co, h 490 N Meridian.
KIEFER A DRUG CO, Augustus Kiefer Pres, Charles Mayer Vice-Pres, Charles S McBride Sec and Treas, Wholesale Druggists, 101-105 S Meridian, Tels 27 and 275.
Kiefer Calvin W, lab, h 563 W McLene (N I).
Kiefer Catherine L (wid Jacob), h 79 W Morris.
Kiefer Charles F, cigarmkr, b s w cor Belmont av and Emrich (H).
Kiefer Charles J, watchmkr, b 463 N Delaware.
Kiefer Edward A, trav agt, h 102 River av (W I).
Kiefer Frank L, collr, b 21 W Pratt.
Kiefer Henry, bartndr, b 764 S East.
Kiefer James, gilder, b 29 Nebraska.
Kiefer John, clk, h 173 Spann av.
Kiefer Louis, mach hd, h 7 Hester.
Kiefer Louis, mach, b n w cor Brookside av and Jupiter.
Kiefer Louis A (L F Kiefer & Son), b 463 N Delaware.
Kiefer L F & Son (Louis A Kiefer), jewelers, 86 N Penn.
Kiefer Major J, clk, b 237 Fayette.
Kiefer Margaret (wid John), h 34 Bismarck.
Kiefer Martha E (wid Ephraim), h 21 W Pratt.
Kiefer Martin A, h 425 E Georgia.
Kiefer Mary (wid Louis F), h 463 N Delaware.
Kiefer Maurice M, wire chief C U Tel Co, h 21 W Pratt.
Kiefer Max, bartndr, h 363 Indiana av.
Kiefer Norman E, clk, b 237 Fayette.

THOS. C. DAY & CO.
Financial Agents and Loans.
We have the experience, and claim to be reliable.
Rooms 325 to 330 Lemcke Bldg.

Kiefer Philip E, lithog, h 237 Fayette.
Kiefer Robert C, b 21 W Pratt.
Kiefer Rudolph C, cigar mnfr, 102 Michigan (H), h s w cor Belmont av and Emrich (H).
Kiefer Valentine, grocer, 191 Indiana av, h 254 W Michigan.
Kiehl Charles, painter, h 60 Mayhew.
Kiel, see also Keil and Kyle.
Kiel Charles L, car insp, h 349 S State av.
Kiel Edward F, carp, 361 N Noble, h same.
Kiel George H, cabtmkr, h 118 N Dorman.
Kiel Henry C, carp, 168 Prospect, h same.
Kiel Henry H, poultry, 638 Virginia av, h same.
Kiel Hugo, lab, b 272 E St Clair.
Kiel Ida, dressmkr, 168 Prospect, b same.
Kiemeyer Wm, cigar mnfr, 76 E Washington, h 199 S New Jersey.
Kienle Henry, tinner, r 12 Union.
Kienzle Gustav, mach, h 119 Clinton.
Kiesel George, baker, b 507 N West.
Kiesel John, baker, 507 N West, h same.
Kiesel Wm, bartndr, b 507 N West.
Kieser Frank A, blksmith, 643 Shelby, h same.
Kiesle Wm F, sub letter carrier P O, h 480 Union.
Kiess Clara, h 86 Newman.
Kiess Edward V, lab, b 86 Newman.
Kiewit Dietrich, lab, h 82 Weghorst.
Kiewit Edward D, finisher, b 82 Weghorst.
Kiewit John, finisher, b 82 Weghorst.
Kiger Charles W, condr, h 67 Lexington av.
Kight Alpheus, horseshoer, b 373 E Ohio.
Kight David W, horseshoer, h 481 Martindale av.
Kight John F, ins agt, h 639 N Illinois.
Kiker John C, well driver, 32 N Delaware, b 35 Hoyt av.
Kilcannon Catherine E, housekpr 112 Park av.
Kilchenmann Gottlieb, foreman, h 38 Cleveland (H).
Kilchenmann Jacob W, molder, b 38 Cleveland (H).
Kile Dawson C, ins agt, b 1102 N Delaware.
Kile Philip H, city fireman, r 306 E North.

EAT
HITZ'S CRACKERS
AND CAKES.
ASK YOUR GROCER FOR THEM.

J. H. TECKENBROCK  General House Painter, 94 EAST SOUTH STREET.

FIDELITY MUTUAL LIFE—PHILADELPHIA, PA.
$75,000,000, Insurance In Force. $3,500,000, Death Losses Paid. $1,500,090, Surplus. A. H. COLLINS {General Agent, Baldwin Block.

Edwardsport Coal & Mining Co. ●.... BITUMINOUS COAL IN CAR LOADS TO DEALERS AND MANUFACTURERS. ROOMS 42 AND 43 WHEN BUILDING.

ESTABLISHED 1876. TELEPHONE 168.
CHESTER BRADFORD,
SOLICITOR OF PATENTS,
AND COUNSEL IN PATENT CAUSES.
(See adv. page 6.)
Office:—Rooms 14 and 16 Hubbard Block, S. W. Cor. Washington and Meridian Streets, INDIANAPOLIS, INDIANA.

Kile Sherman C, clk R M S, h 1102 N Delaware.
Kiler Albert, armature winder, b 485 Central av.
Kiler Charles M, lab, h 67 Pleasant.
Kiler Edward, engr, h 247 Bellefontaine.
Kiler John N, engr, h 485 Central av.
Kiley Daniel T, mach, b 159 Columbia av.
Kiley James T, lab, h 159 Columbia av.
Kiley John, custodian Tomlinson Hall, h 266 S Delaware.
Kiley John M, salesman M O'Connor & Co, b 450 Mass av.
Kiley Philip, saloon, 450 Mass av, h same.
Kiley Philip J, ins agt, r 320 N Alabama.
Kiley Rebecca J (wid Philip), h 44½ N Penn.
Kiley Thomas E, bartndr, r 322 Clifford av.
Kiley Wm F, clk, b 450 Mass av.
Kilganon Wm, switchman, h 536 E Georgia.
Kilganon Wm E, helper, b 536 E Georgia.
Kilgore Rufus B, carp, b 14 Coffey (W I).
Killala John, car insp, h 287 Highland av.
Killala Lawrence, car insp, h 224 N Pine.
Killala Mark, lab, b 300 W Maryland.
Killalea James M, bricklyr, b 186 Meek.
Killalea Matthew, lab, h 186 Meek.
Killalea Wm, lab, b 186 Meek.
Killian Oscar L, mach, b 139 Oliver av (W I).
Killian Patrick, tagger Bureau of Animal Industry, h 205 Douglass.
Killian Samuel, lab, h 753 N Senate av.
Killian Wm E, lineman, h 409 E Pearl.
Killian Wm M, usher Insane Hospital, h 545 E Ohio.
Killie James H, mach, h 343 Cornell av.
Killie John H, lab, h 350 Cornell av.
Killie Vincent E, lab, b 350 Cornell av.
Killila James K, tailor, b 21 Chadwick.
Killila Patrick, lab, h 21 Chadwick.
Killila Thomas E, lab, r 43 S West.
Killinger Albert T, cabtmkr, h 311 W Washington.
KILLINGER GEORGE W, Mnfr of Bar Fixtures, Store and Office Furniture, s w cor Market and Missouri, Warerooms 141 Virginia av, h 230 N California. (See adv in classified Saloons.)

Outing BICYCLES
..MADE BY..
HAY & WILLITS MFG. CO.
76 N. Pennsylvania St. Phone 598.

Killinger John C, cabtmkr, b 230 N California.
Kilroy John T, painter, b 376 Blake.
Kimball, see also Kimble.
Kimball Edward T, clk Indpls Water Co, h 18 W New York.
Kimball Elmer F, tinner, h 248 Cornell av.
Kimball Ephraim F, trav agt, h 34 The Blacherne.
Kimball Frederick, lab, h 175 Patterson.
Kimball George, lab, b 130 Minerva.
Kimball Henry W, bkkpr, b 182 College av.
Kimball Howard, sec Aetna and Royal Savings and Loan Assns, 89 E Market, tel 1494, h n s Bedford av 2 e of Central av.
Kimball James H, carp, h 178 Mass av.
Kimball Jesse F, tinner, h 246 Cornell av.
Kimball Wm B, train disp P C C & St L Ry, h 121 N Senate av.
Kimbaugh Adam, lab, h rear 140 Agnes.
Kimbaugh John, lab, b rear 140 Agnes.
Kimber Abraham, trav agt, h 3 Stoughton av.
Kimber Arthur S, clk George J Marott, b 202 Bellefontaine.
Kimber Oscar A, clk, r 565 Ash.
Kimberlin Abigail (wid Wm H), h w s Illinois 2 s of 30th.
Kimberlin Albert C, phys, 136 N Penn, h 240 Park av.
Kimberlin Elsworth, lab, b 229 Keystone av.
Kimberlin Fletcher L, lab, b 337 N Pine.
Kimberlin Harry, clk, h 90 Indiana av.
Kimberlin Harvey O, lab, b 337 N Pine.
Kimberlin Jacob R, produce, 82 E Mkt House, h 28 Ludlow av.
Kimberlin James H, clk H T Conde Implement Co, h 90 Indiana av.
Kimberlin Lemuel E, cashr Knight & Jillson, h 656 Park av.
Kimberlin Thomas A, dentist, 136 N Penn, b 1099 N Penn.
Kimberlin Thomas P, basketmkr, h 337 N Pine.
Kimberlin Wm O, clk, b w s Illinois 2 s of 30th.
Kimberly Samuel S, trav agt, r 334 N Illinois.
Kimble, see also Kimball.
Kimble Adam, lab, b 98 Maxwell.
Kimble Charles E, millwright, h 814 La-Salle (M P).
Kimble Emma L (wid Thomas V), h 128 W Ohio.
Kimble Frank, driver, h 676 W Vermont.
Kimble Frank C, solr, b 128 W Ohio.
Kimble Georgia A (wid Wm H), h 573 W 22d.
Kimble John, lab, b 98 Maxwell.
Kimble John H, mach, b 564 S East.
Kimble Joseph, lab, h 22 N Belmont av (H).
Kimble Samuel J, sawyer, h 92 Greer.
Kimbrough Arthur W, lab, h e s James 2 s of Sutherland (B).
Kimbrough Frank, driver, b 175 Patterson.
Kimbrough Frederick, lab, b 175 Patterson.
Kimbrough Isaac, tmstr, h w s James 4 s of Sutherland (B).
Kimbrough Isaac N Rev, h s s Sutherland 2 w of James (B).
Kimbrough Jesse, bellman, b 90 Torbet.
Kimbrough Lucy E (wid Nicholas), b 179 Hill av.
Kimbrough Noah, b w s James 4 s of Sutherland (B).
Kimbrough Sanford, driver, h 175 Patterson.
Kimes Amza L, mach, h 130 Bates.

C. ZIMMERMAN & SONS | SLATE AND GRAVEL ROOFERS 19 South East Street.

DRIVEN WELLS And Second Water Wells and Pumps of all kinds at CHARLES KRAUSS', 42 S. PENN. ST., Telephone 465.

ERTEL STEAM LAUNDRY 26 and 28 N. Senate Avenue. Telephone 1089. WE WILL CALL FOR AND DELIVER YOUR WORK. SATISFACTION GUARANTEED.

Kimmel Albert A, grocer, 307 E 8th, h 374 same.
Kimmel Charles A, mach, h 81 Dugdale.
Kimmel Joseph F, finisher, b 81 Dugdale.
Kimmel Martin, butcher, h 262 Douglass.
Kimmel Wm G, cigarmkr, b 656 Chestnut.
Kimmich Christian F, lab, b n e cor Gale and Willow (B).
Kimmich Maria (wid Christian), b 50 Paw Paw.
Kimmons James M, trav agt, h 198 Bright.
Kimpel Henry, driver, h 24 Jefferson av.
Kimpel John N, patrolman, h 108 Hosbrook.
Kimpel Nicholas G, mach hd, h Madison av 1 mile s of Belt R R.
Kinander Charles, saloon, 510 E 9th, h 204 Alvord.
Kincaid Albert, plumber, b n e cor Cherry and Ritter avs (I).
Kincaid Anderson, lab, b 29 Willow.
Kincaid Anderson jr, brickmkr, h 29 Willow.
Kincaid Benjamin F, varnisher, h 92 Paca.
Kincaid Charles, coachman 67 Central av.
Kincaid Elizabeth (wid John), b 34 Dearborn.
Kincaid Margaret J (wid John E), b 66 Highland pl.
Kincaid Orestes, tmstr, b 50 Bradshaw.
Kincaid Samuel, lab, h 1012 S Meridian.
Kincaid Samuel, real est, b n e cor Cherry and Ritter avs (I).
Kincaid Thomas, bkkpr, h 274 E Walnut.
Kincaid Wendell P, carp, h 34 Cooper.
Kincaid Wm W, h n e cor Cherry and Ritter avs (I).
Kinchen Amanda (wid Sanco), b 210 Agnes.
Kinchen John S, lab, h 208 Agnes.
Kinchlow Carrie (wid George), h 440 Douglass.
Kinchlow Clarence, lab, b n s Prospect 2 e of Belt R R (N).
Kinchlow George W, clk, b 440 Douglass.
Kinchlow John, lab, r 155½ Indiana av.
Kindel Wm M, gas insp, h 124 Weghorst.
Kinder Adeline, dressmkr, 180 Mass av, b same.
Kinder Alonzo, mach hd, h 412 W Shoemaker (N I).
Kinder David, mach, h 582 W Addison (N I).
Kinder John W, driver, r 179 N Alabama.
Kinder Walter, driver, r 77 N Alabama.
Kinder Wesley M, mach hd, h 412 W Shoemaker (N I).
Kinder Wm S, mach hd, h 463 W Ontario (N I).
Kindle Lee, tmstr, b 306 E South.
KINDLEBERGER WM H, Physician, 18 W Ohio, h 881 N Delaware.
Kindler Albert E, mach, b 118 Columbia av.
Kindley Joseph J, tooldresser, h 1370 Indianapolis av.
Kindrick John, lab, h n s Lake 6 e of C C C & St L Ry (N I).
King Aaron, clk, h 413 W New York.
King Amanda E, teacher High School (B), b 1707 N Penn.
King Amy K, cashr, b 100 Cherry.
King Arthur T M, painter, b 914 Broadway.
King Bernard, grocer, 168 Elizabeth, h same.
King Catherine (wid John H), h 51 Peru av.
King C Bird, genl agt Kingan & Co (ltd), h 1220 N Penn.
King David, carp, h 12 Roanoke.
King David S, tmstr, h 31 McGill.
King Della (wid Wm), b 29 Biddle.

EQUITABLE LIFE ASSURANCE SOCIETY OF THE UNITED STATES. RICHARDSON & McCREA Managers for Central Indiana, 79 East Market St. Telephone 182.

King Dora, lab, b w s Baltimore av 2 n of 17th.
King Edward S, barber, 446 Mass av, h 65 John.
King Eli, painter, 259 Keystone av, h same.
King Elias F, sawyer, h 463 E Walnut.
King Eliza J (wid Wm A), b 1626 N Meridian.
King Eliza T, teacher Public School No 14, b 350 N Pine.
King Emeline A (wid George), b 60 W Walnut.
King Emma B, artist, 188 N Illinois, b same.
King Etta M, stenog, b 286 Jefferson av.
King Flora (wid Wm W), h 235 E Court.
King Forrest E, bookbndr, b 51 Peru av.
King Francis E, clk, h 1146 E Washington.
King Frank, finisher, h 35 Valley Drive.
King Frank C, tel opr, b 70 W Walnut.
King Frank W, lab, h 77 Chadwick.
King Frost, stenog Hord & Perkins, b 1626 N Meridian.
King Gains, lab, b 512 S West.
King George, engr, b 93 Spann av.
King George, porter, r 18½ Indiana av.
King George T, painter, h 127 Lynn av (W I).
King George W, baker, b 51 Peru av.
King Grace H, stenog Tanner & Sullivan, b 914 Broadway.
King Hampton D, bricklyr, h 269 Dillon.
King Hannah (wid Wm), h 468 N New Jersey.
King Hickman N Rev, pastor Grace M E Church, h 573 E Market.
King Harry, painter, h 226 Excelsior av.
King Harry J, condr, r 2 Halcyon blk.
King Harry N, tel opr, b 350 N Pine.
King Herbert H, waiter, r 211 N Illinois.
King Hezekiah, carriagemkr, h 143½ Virginia av.
King Homer B, printer, b 286 Jefferson av.
King Howard, attendant Insane Hospital.
King Indiana (wid Cornelius), h 450 Clifford av.
King Isaac (King & Knight), h 46 Huron.
King Isaac, lab, h 161 Alvord.
King James, coremkr, b 168 Elizabeth.

STENOGRAPHERS FURNISHED. EXPERIENCED OR BEGINNERS, PERMANENT OR TEMPORARY. S. H. EAST, State Agent, The Williams Typewriter, 55 THORPE BLOCK, 87 EAST MARKET ST.

ELLIS & HELFENBERGER { ENTERPRISE FOUNDRY & FENCE CO. 162-170 S. Senate Ave. Tel. 958.

THE HOGAN TRANSFER AND STORAGE COMP'Y
Household Goods and Pianos Moved—Packed—Stored...... Baggage and Package Express Machinery and Safes a Specialty Cor. Washington and Illinois Sts. TELEPHONE No. 675.

The Central Rubber & Supply Co. ◆◆◆ Hose, Belting, Packing, Clothing, Druggists' Sundries, Bicycle Tires, Cotton Hose, Etc. New York Belting & Packing Co., L't'd. PHONE 922. 79 S. ILLINOIS ST., INDIANAPOLIS, IND.

A death rate below all other American Companies, and dividends from this source correspondingly larger.
The Provident Life and Trust Company
Of Philadelphia.
D. W. EDWARDS, General Agent,
508 Indiana Trust Building.

King James, harnessmkr, 256 Mass av, h 350 N Pine.
King James K, painter, h 106 Hill av.
King James O, lab, b 207 Ash.
King James W, bkkpr Blind Institute, h 678 N New Jersey.
King James W jr, real est, b 678 N New Jersey.
King John, cigars, 215½ W Washington, h rear 162 same.
King John, contr, h 40 Sheffield av (H).
King John, mach, h 70 W Walnut.
King John, watchman Court House tower, h 511 W 22d (N I).
King John A, trav agt, h 448 N Alabama.
King John B, printer, 268 Jefferson av, b same.
King John H, blksmith, b 16 Lawn (B).
King John H, bkkpr Syerup & Co, h 207 Ash.
King John M, barber, b 369 English av.
King John M, ins agt, h 110 Cherry.
King John R, lab, h 26 Willard.
King John W, saloon, 37 N Alabama, h 103 Fletcher av.
King Joseph W, tel opr, b 20 Traub av.
King Katharina (wid Philip), b 15 Russell av.
King Letitia, h 235 E Court.
King Marian, tel opr, b 121 W South.
King Mary, b 109 Ruckle.
King Mary A (wid Jonathan L), h 286 Jefferson av.
King Mary C, dressmkr, 463 E Walnut, h same.
King Mary E (wid Wm), h 100 Prospect.
King Milo, h 29 Oxford.
King Mollie, music teacher, 251 N Liberty, b same.
King Moses, tailor, h 519 S Capitol av.
King Myron D, h 129 Home av.
King Nelson, lab, b rear 434 E St Clair.
King Nettie L (wid James M), h 914 Broadway.
King Orris, lab, b 26 Willard.
King Patrick, molder, b 3 N Haugh (H).
King Patrick H, janitor, h 11 Bates.
King Pet (wid Samuel), b 74 W New York.
King Peter, blksmith, h 15 Russell av.

Julius C. Walk & Son,
Jewelers
Indianapolis.
12 EAST WASHINGTON ST.

King Philip, packer, h w s Sugar Grove av 2 s of Miller av (M P).
King Ransom, stairbldr, h 1526 N Penn.
King Rebecca J (wid Edward), h 188 N Illinois.
King Richard, lab, h w s Indianapolis av 1 n of Fall Creek.
King Robert, foreman, h w s Indianapolis av 1 n of Fall Creek.
King Robert M, teacher, b 274 College av.
King Roderick A, clk S A Fletcher & Co, b 188 N Illinois.
King Russell G, clk A C Harris, b 1626 N Meridian.
King Samuel, produce, 79 E Mkt House, h 251 N Liberty.
King Samuel L, tmstr, h rear 434 E St Clair.
King Smith, trav agt The Indpls Journal, h 1626 N Meridian.
King Steward, motorman, h 258 W Michigan.
King Thomas B, cook, h 301 Indiana av.
King Vincent, janitor, h 168 Agnes.
King Warren, grocer, 495 W Addison (N I), h 486 same.
King Wesley R, lab, h 154 John.
King Wiley P, condr, h 44 Brookside av.
King Wm, clk, b 70 W Walnut.
King Wm, coachman 700 N Meridian.
King Wm, lab, h 413 Clinton.
King Wm, lab, h 191 Middle.
King Wm, lab, h rear 421 N New Jersey.
King Wm, lab, h 106 Roanoke.
King Wm, motorman, b 587 Park av.
King Wm B, carp, h 58 S Belmont (W I).
King Wm E, engr, h 36 N California.
King Wm F, bkkpr, h 70 E 25th.
King Wm G, lab, b 463 E Walnut.
King Wm H, blksmith, h rear 176 E Washington.
King Wm L, brakeman, h 16 Lawn (B).
King Wm L, city agt Standard Oil Co, h 86 English av.
King Wm M, h 1707 N Penn.
King Wm M, lab, h 369 English av.
King Wm W, engr, h 235 E Court.
King Winfield S, asst supt Prud Life Ins Co, b 167 E Vermont.
King Young, lab, h w s Baltimore av 2 n of 17th.
King & Knight (Isaac King, Wm W Knight), horseshoers, 60 Virginia av.
KINGAN & CO (Limited), Pork Packers, West End of Maryland, Tels 91 and 1899.
Kingen Wm R, janitor Public School No 15, h 1100 E Michigan.
Kingery George W, lab, h 522 Chestnut.
Kingham Albert, clk, b 253 Mass av.
Kingham Albert A, clk, b 22 Sheldon.
Kingham Eden W, pressman, h 441 Olive.
Kingham John A, contr, 22 Sheldon, h same.
Kingham Joseph, nurse, 253 Mass av, h same.
Kingman Ellen A, h e s Grand av 3 s of University av (I).
Kingman John R, b e s Grand av 3 s of University av (I).
Kingsbury Charles G, student, b n e cor Maple and Walnut avs (I).
Kingsbury Edward D (Dockweiler & Kingsbury), h 284 Lincoln av.
Kingsbury Frank E, electrician, h e s Graham 1 n of Walnut av (I).
Kingsbury James G, sec Indiana Farmer Co, h n e cor Maple and Walnut avs (I).

OTTO GAS ENGINES | BUILDERS' EXCHANGE S. W. Cor. Ohio and Penn. Telephone 535.

Becker & Son Charles Becker Jacob Becker Jr. Merchant Tailors. 21 N. Penn St. Tel. 934

SALISBURY & STANLEY OF FICE, STORE AND BANK FIXTURES. Contractors and Builders. Repairing of all kinds done on short notice. 177 Clinton St., Indianapolis, Ind. Telephone 999.

Kingsbury James L, treas Indiana Farmer Co, h s w cor Chambers and Layman av (I).
Kingsbury John H (Spahr & Kingsbury), b 544 E Ohio.
Kingsbury Nancy (wid John), h 544 E Ohio.
Kingsbury Robert J, insp City Engineer, b 544 E Ohio.
Kingsbury Robert M, janitor Public School No 29, h n s 11th 2 e of College av.
Kingsbury Thomas C, clk, b 544 E Ohio.
Kingsbury Thomas M, mer police, h 540 E Market.
Kingsley Adriel S, h 267 W Washington.
Kingsley Frank E, sawmkr, h 227 S New Jersey.
Kingsley Frank J, clk, b 5 N Station (B).
Kingsley James, shoemkr, 63 E Sutherland (B), h 5 N Station (B).
Kingsley Mary L (wid Charles), retoucher, r 89 The Windsor.
Kingsley Royal S, creamery, 267 W Washington, b 298 Bellefontaine.
Kingsley Wm W, r 181½ S Meridian.
Kingston Bernard B W, teacher, h 5 N Dorman.
Kingston Frederick A, clk Model Clothing Co, h 192 Virginia av.
Kingston John R, fireman, h 43 Elder av.
Kingston Samuel, dry goods, 192 Virginia av, h same.
Kingston Samuel H, dry goods, 786 S East, h same.
Kingston Wm N, clk, b 192 Virginia av.
Kinister Wm H, grocer, 100 Paca, h same.
Kinkaid Samuel, lab, b 275 E Ohio.
KINKLIN RICHARD, Costumer and Wig Maker, 240-242 E Washington, h same. (See adv in classified Costumers.)
Kinley Albert H, pdlr, h 509 W Maryland.
Kinley David, cooper, h 5 Astor.
Kinley Frederick, pdlr, b 279 W Washington.
Kinley James M, lab, h 279 W Washington.
Kinley James W, mach, h n s Washington av 1 e of Ritter av (I).
Kinley Wm T, lab, b 5 Astor.
Kinnaman James M, carp, h 571 W 22d (N I).
Kinnan Frederick, finisher, h 232 Dougherty.
Kinnan Harry J, clk, b 776 N Senate av.
Kinnan Leonidas R; farmer, h 1004 N Capitol av.
Kinnan Thomas B, h 776 N Senate av.
Kinnear Aurelius S, carp, b 173 English av.
Kinnett Birt W, mach hd, b 64 Fountain av.
Kinnett George L, lab, h 64 Fountain av.
Kinnett Jesse T, clk, b 64 Fountain av.
Kinney, see also Kenney.
Kinney Alexander, lab, r 181½ S Meridian.
Kinney Andrew J, lab, h 122 Downey.
Kinney Charles P, lab, h 120 Spring.
Kinney Cornelius, lab, h 270 W St Clair.
Kinney Collie E, lawyer, 55 N Illinois, h 72 S Summit.
Kinney Daniel, brakeman, b 379 E Georgia.
Kinney David, cooper, h 27 Blackford.
Kinney Dillard, lab, b 65 S California.
Kinney Frank, cooper, h 102 Geisendorff.
Kinney George W, cooper, b 65 S California.
Kinney Henry J, patternmkr, h 89 Weghorst.
KINNEY HORACE E, Grain, Mill Feed and Hay, 20-22 Board of Trade Bldg, Tel 18; h 337 N Capitol av, Tel 752.

Henry H. Fay, 40½ E. Washington St., REAL ESTATE, AND LOAN BROKER.

Kinney James L, plumber, h 516 N California.
Kinney Jeremiah E, detective, h 57 Elizabeth.
Kinney Jeremiah F, shoemkr, h 202 Lexington av.
Kinney Jeremiah M, cooper, h 65 S California.
Kinney John, huckster, r 193½ S Illinois.
Kinney John H, clk, b 173 W Vermont.
Kinney John P, mach hd, h 35 Grove.
Kinney Kate, h 215 W Court.
Kinney Margaret, boarding 79 E Vermont.
Kinney Martin, lab, b 40 S West.
Kinney Otto, grocer, 287 Coburn, h 285 same.
Kinney Patrick, lab, h 379 E Georgia.
Kinney P Henry, clk Cerealine Mnfg Co, h 79 E Vermont.
Kinney Ray L, livery, 440 E Washington, h 54 Michigan av.
Kinney Samuel, driver, h 369 S Capitol av.
Kinney Stephen M, cabtmkr, b 379 E Georgia.
Kinney Stephen P, upfitter, b 379 E Georgia.
Kinney Thomas P, engr, h 38 Concordia.
Kinney Van, lab, h 154 S Judge Harding (W I).
Kinney Wm, lab, b 215 W Court.
Kinney Wm, lab, h 48 Pierce.
Kinney Wm D, gasfitter, h 25 S West.
Kinney Wm F, clk W U Tel Co, h 270 W St Clair.
Kinney Wm T, lab, b 27 Blackford.
Kinnick James W, carp, h 159 Woodlawn av.
Kinnick Samuel E, driver, h 45 Barth av.
Kinsel George, lab, r 404 S West.
Kinsella John, lab, h 424 S West.
Kinselle Hattie (wid Louis), h 110 W Vermont.
Kinsey Henry, motorman, h 324 W Vermont.
Kinsey Julia A (wid David), h 400 N New Jersey.
Kinsey Louis A, pres The L A Kinsey Co, h 354 College av, tel 1592.

LIME, CEMENT, PLASTER FIRE BRICK AND CLAY SEWER PIPE, ETC. BALKE & KRAUSS CO., Cor. Market and Missouri Streets.

C. FRIEDGEN HAS THE FINEST STOCK OF LADIES' PARTY SLIPPERS and SHOES 19 NORTH PENNSYLVANIA ST.

SAMUEL LAING ▸ TIN, SLATE AND STEEL ROOFING, 72 AND 74 EAST COURT STREET.

M. B. WILSON, Pres. W. F. CHURCHMAN, Cash.
THE CAPITAL NATIONAL BANK,
INDIANAPOLIS, IND.
Pays Interest on Time Certificates of Deposit.
Buys and Sells Foreign Exchange at Low Rates.
Capital, - - $300,000
Surplus and Earnings, 50,000
No. 28 S. Meridian St., Cor. Pearl.

KINSEY L A CO THE, Louis A Kinsey Pres, Frank M Ketcham Sec, M S Elliott Treas, Stock and Grain Brokers, Commercial Club Bldg, Tel 1375.
Kinsey Robert W, clk, h 539 Central av.
Kinsler Frederick, brewer, h 113 Kennington.
Kinsler Peter F, helper, h 512 Chestnut.
Kinsley Ida B, teacher Deaf and Dumb Inst, r 42 S Arsenal av.
Kinst Robert, sawmkr, b 12 Bates al.
Kinz Adam, hostler, h 218 Coburn.
Kinz Edward, janitor, b 530 S New Jersey.
Kinz George A, clk, b 218 Coburn.
Kinzly Herman H, hair goods, 46 N Illinois, r 207 The Shiel.
Kiplinger Charles L, clk Albert Gall, h 541 Broadway.
Kipp Albrecht, pres Kipp Bros Co, h 136 N New Jersey.
Kipp Alfred R, mech engr, b 192 Park av.
KIPP BROS CO, Albrecht Kipp Pres, Robert Kipp Sec and Treas, Wholesale Fancy Goods, 37-39 S Meridian, Tel 525.
Kipp Nathan H, agt Empire Fast Freight Line, 67 W Maryland, tel 365, h 192 Park av.
Kipp Otto L, clk, b 136 N New Jersey.
Kipp Robert, sec and treas Kipp Bros Co, h 288 E New York.
Kipp Wm C, clk, b 288 E New York.
Kipper August, h 425 E Georgia.
Kipper John P, patternmkr, b 73 Leota.
Kirby Alexander, mach hd, h 50 Chase (W I).
Kirby Anna D, proof reader The Sun, b 87 W 8th.
Kirby Catherine (wid Martin), h 75 Wilson.
Kirby Dennis M, lab, h 87 W 8th.
Kirby Eleanor D, teacher, b 27 W 2d.
Kirby Elizabeth (wid Nahum W), b 309 Brookside av.
Kirby Richard B, clk, h 90 Paca.
Kirby Thomas, driver, b 75 Wilson.
Kirby Timothy R, tilewkr, b 87 W 8th.

TUTTLE & SEGUIN,
28 E. Market Street.
Fire Insurance, Real Estate, Loan and Rental Agents.
TELEPHONE 1168.

Kirby Wm L, saleman Fahnley & McCrea, b 27 W 2d.
Kirch George, lab, h 90 Bismarck av (H).
Kirch Jacob, contr, 26 Sanders, h same.
Kirch Matthew, carp, b 419 S Delaware.
Kirch Nicholas, carp, h 56 Sanders.
Kirchner, see also Kirschner.
Kirchner Frank J J, barber, h 399 Virginia av.
Kirchner Walter S, baker, h 214 Keystone av.
Kirchoff Christian F, carp, h 99 New.
Kirchoff Ellen (wid Gottlieb), b 227 Lincoln la.
Kirk Amelia (wid John), h 394 Virginia av.
Kirk Daniel A, turner, h 131 Meek.
Kirk Edward P, mach, b 17 N Station (B).
Kirk John, b 187 S Capitol av.
Kirk John, lab, h 41 Minerva.
Kirk John A, clk, b 394 Virginia av.
Kirk John F, clk J C Perry & Co, r 130 N Senate av.
Kirk John M, clk, b 166 Yandes.
Kirk Joseph H, grocer, 448 W North, h same.
Kirk Lester A, blksmith, h 1123 E Michigan.
Kirk Lovell, barber, 548 W Addison (N I), b 542 same.
Kirk Margaret (wid Patrick), b 521 S West.
Kirk Mary, h 118 W Maryland.
Kirk Patrick, lab, b 324 W Maryland.
Kirk Richard, lab, h 8 Poplar (B).
Kirk Robert, carp, b 506 N California.
Kirk Robert, lab, b 297 N Capitol av.
Kirk Robert jr, driver, h 9 Lafayette.
Kirk Robert A, lab, b 448 W North.
Kirk Ruby, h 77 S Senate av.
Kirk Thomas, lab, b 521 S West.
Kirk Walter, lab, b 337 W Maryland.
Kirk Wm, foreman, h 17 S Station (B).
Kirk Wm, lab, h 17 Riley blk.
Kirk Wm, lab, b 205 Yandes.
Kirk Wm T, cook, b 50 Pendleton av (B).
Kirk Wm T, lab, b 31 New.
Kirkendall Hugh, switchman, h 115 Chadwick.
Kirkendall John, lab, b 13 Ellsworth.
Kirkendall Philip H, lab, b 197 W 2d.
Kirkendall Rufus, lab, b 210 N Meridian.
Kirkhoff, see also Kerkhoff.
KIRKHOFF BROS (J Herman, George F and Charles F), Plumbers, Steam and Hot Water Heating, Electrical Construction, Etc, 102-104 S Penn, Tel 910. (See left top corner cards and classified Plumbers.)
Kirkhoff Charles F (Kirkhoff Bros), h 87 Walcott.
Kirkhoff Charles S, carp, h 941 S East.
Kirkhoff Frank H, steamfitter, h 149 N State av.
Kirkhoff George F (Kirkhoff Bros), h 34 Oriental.
Kirkhoff Henry J, plumber, b 38 Oriental.
Kirkhoff Herman H, driver, h 38 Oriental.
Kirkhoff J Herman (Kirkhoff Bros), h 169 E Merrill.
Kirkman Eliza (wid Alexander), h 23 N Noble.
Kirkpatrick Annie E, laundress, h 34 Detroit.
Kirkpatrick Edward, supt, h 104 Highland pl.
Kirkpatrick Jacob M, live stock, h cor College av and 20th.
Kirkpatrick Robert jr, driver, h 9 Lafayette.
Kirkwood Adam, hostler, h 470 E Georgia.

SULLIVAN & MAHAN Manufacturers of all kinds of PAPER BOXES 41 W. Pearl St.

DIAMOND WALL PLASTER { Telephone 1410 BUILDERS' EXCHANGE.

197 S. Illinois St. { Tel. 1769. } THE HOME LAUNDRY { WORK CALLED FOR AND DELIVERED.

Kirkwood David H, motorman, b 533 E Washington.
Kirkwood George A, clk Kingan & Co (ltd), b 470 E Gerogia.
Kirkwood John A, clk, b 220 Fletcher av.
Kirkwood John G, clk Model Clothing Co, h 878 N Penn.
Kirkwood Mary (wid John), h 220 Fletcher av.
Kirland Charles, h 1042 W Washington.
Kirland John F, clk Hayes & Ready, h 26 Ketcham.
Kirlin John B, cashr freight office Penna Lines, h 405 Central av.
Kirlin Mary J, b 60 Talbott av.
Kirlin Sarah L, teacher Public School No 20, b 60 Talbott av.
Kirn Jacob, carp, h 760 S East.
Kirn Joseph E, bricklyr, b 760 S East.
Kirsch Adam, lab, h 59 John.
Kirsch Alice, h 589½ S Meridian.
Kirsch Andrew L, baker, b 298 Union.
Kirsch Balser, motorman, h 111 Ft Wayne av.
Kirsch Elizabeth (wid Adam), h 63 Spring.
Kirsch George W, lithog, b 63 Spring.
Kirsch John, bricklyr, b 187 S Capitol av.
Kirsch John, turner, h 298 Union.
Kirsch Magdalena M (wid John N), dairy, 31 New, h same.
Kirsch Nicholas, lab, h 313 Cornell av.
Kirsch Nicholas, carp The Denison.
Kirsch Peter, trav agt, h 54 Sanders.
Kirschbaum Bernard W, sec and treas Excelsior Shirt Mnfg Co, b 900 N Meridian.
Kirschbaum George F, carp, h 194 Highland av.
Kirschbaum Raphael (David Kahn & Co), pres Excelsior Shirt Mnfg Co, h 900 N Meridian.
Kirschman Catherine (wid Martin), h 293 W Merrill.
Kirschmeier Wm, letter carrier P O, r 13 Hutchings blk.
Kirschner, see also Kirchner.
Kirschner Arthur W, bottler, b 689 S Meridian.
Kirschner Catherine (wid Frederick), h 689 S Meridian.
Kirschner Charles W, mach hd, h 681 Charles.
Kirschner Jacob, finisher, b 689 S Meridian.
Kirschner John B, driver, h 722 S East.
Kirsh John C, ironwkr, r 81 W Georgia.
Kirst Charles, janitor, h 45½ N Capitol av.
Kirst Robert, lab, h 12 Bates al.
Kirtley George, porter The Bates.
Kirtley Robert, lab, h 498 W Ontario (N I).
Kise Elisha S, tmstr, h 28 Camp.
Kise Samuel S, patternmkr, h 195 Michigan (H).
Kiser, see also Kaiser, Kaser and Keyser.
Kiser Charles L, printer, 280 River av, h 67 S McLain (W I).
Kiser George A, ins, b 125½ Hadley av (W I).
Kiser Gottlieb, meats, 150 N East, h 152 same.
Kiser Harter, grocer, 150 N East, b 152 same.
Kiser Simon L, trav agt Indpls Brewg Co, h 226 E Walnut.
Kiser Solomon S (Meyer & Kiser), h 168 N East.
Kiser Wm S, acct, r Stubbins Hotel.
Kismier Christian, car rep, h 27 Deloss.

FRANK NESSLER. WILL H. ROST.
FRANK NESSLER & CO.
Tailors
56 EAST MARKET ST. (Lemcke Building),
INDIANAPOLIS, IND.

KISSEL C FRED, Propr Kissel's Garden, cor Capitol av and 18th, Tel 1950, and Capital City Club House, 30th and Main Entrance to State Fair Grounds, Tel 1949; h s e cor Capitol av and 18th.
Kissel Henry J, bartndr, h 100 Chadwick.
Kissel Horace E, trav agt Hildebrand Hardware Co, h 170 E St Joseph.
Kissel Mary F (wid Frederick), h 1324 N Capitol av.
Kissel Wm, watchman, h 370 S West.
Kissel Wm F, ins agt, b Senate Hotel.
Kissell Frederick A, clk L E & W R R, h 126 S Noble.
Kissell Wallace B, bookbndr, h 6 Carlos.
Kissinger Wm H, painter, h 162 Columbia av.
Kissling Charles F, watchman Deaf and Dumb Inst.
Kistler Robert M, student, h 179 Meek.
Kistner Amelia H (wid John), h 232 N California.
Kistner Charles C, shoes, 83 S Illinois, h 561 Broadway.
Kistner Charles J, lab, h 52 Davis.
Kistner David, car insp, h 185 Bane.
Kistner Frank B, attendant Public Library, r 128 W Ohio.
Kistner Henry, printer, b 112 Highland pl.
Kistner Henry, shoemkr, 460 S Delaware, b 71 Yeiser.
Kistner Henry jr, cigar mnfr, 71 Yeiser, h same.
Kistner John, saloon, 198 W Washington, h same.
Kistner John, b 185 Bane.
Kistner John G, broker, b 232 N California.
Kistner Joseph, painter, h 55 Church.
Kistner Joseph, blksmith, b 185 Bane.
Kistner Rosina (wid John G), h 518 College av.
Kistner Wm, brewer, h s s Ohio 4 e of Rural.
Kitchell Alonzo R, bartndr, h 230 N East.
Kitchell Charles E, tinner, h 55 Oak.
Kitchell Henrietta S (wid Joseph S), b 305 Broadway.

Haueisen & Hartmann
163-169 E. Washington St.
FURNITURE,
Carpets,
Household Goods,
Tin, Granite and China Wares, Oil Cloth and Shades

THE WM. H. BLOCK CO. 7 AND 9 EAST WASHINGTON STREET. DRY GOODS, HOUSE FURNISHINGS AND CROCKERY.

London Guarantee and Accident Co. (Ltd.) Employers', Public and Teams' Liability, Workmen's Collective Insurance and Fidelity Bonds
GEORGE W. PANGBORN, General Agent, 704-706 Lemcke Bldg. Telephone 140.

FRANK K. SAWYER || Reliable Fire Insurance. Reasonable Rates.
74 E. MARKET STREET. Telephone 8.

JOSEPH GARDNER,
TIN, IRON, STEEL AND SLATE ROOFING,
GALVANIZED IRON CORNICES & SKYLIGHTS.
37, 39 & 41 KENTUCKY AVE. Telephone 322.

Kitchen Howard, carriagemkr, h 274 E Washington.
Kitchen John M, phys, 44½ N Penn, h 145 same.
Kittle John F, car rep, h 75 N Gillard av.
Kittle John S, trav agt, h 288 Lincoln av.
Kittle Thomas S, car rep, h 73 N Gillard av.
Kittle Walker, insp, b 75 N Gillard av.
Kittley Ottilie H, dressmkr, 289 W Michigan, r same.
Kittrick Nora (wid Michael), b 176 Madison av.
Kitz Ernest, b Circle Park Hotel.
Kitzing Charles R, barber, b 134 N Penn.
Kitzing Julius J, custodian, h 138 Scioto.
Kitzmiller Emily (wid Wm), h 451 Wells (N I).
Kitzmiller John C, patrolman, h 451 Wells (N I).
Kitzmiller Thomas W, lab, h 316 W Maryland.
Kitzmiller Wm, painter, r 174 E Washington.
Kizer Lucy (wid Robert), h e s Warren 2 s of Washington av (I).
Kizer Wm H, carp, h 571 Highland av (N I).
Klaesing Frederica (wid Charles), h n e cor Pleasant av and Huggins pike.
Klaisler Jacob J, lab, h 385 Fletcher av.
Klanke August, painter, 275 Coburn, h same.
Klanke Henry, clk Consumers' Gas Trust Co, h 432 Central av.
Klanke Henry W, painter, b 38 S Spruce.
Klanke Mary, clk Theodore Stein, b 275 Coburn.
Klanke Wm A, h 517 S New Jersey.
Klanke Wm F, clk, h s w cor Illinois and 30th.
Klann August, lab, h 202 Minnesota.
Klare Wm, molder, b 662 S Meridian.
Klare Wm F, cigarmkr, h 181 Church.
Klark Wm C, lab, h 308 E Georgia.
Klasing Frederick A, truckman, h 215 Naomi.
Klasing Henry C F, clk, b 215 Naomi.
Klass Charles, student, b 746 Chestnut.
Klass John, tailor, 746 Chestnut, h same.
Klass Otto, paperhngr, b 746 Chestnut.
Klausmann Henry, cabtmkr, h 10 Jupiter.

J. S. FARRELL & CO.
STEAM AND HOT WATER
HEATING AND PLUMBING
CONTRACTORS
84 North Illinois Street. Telephone 382.

Klausmann Henry W, rodman County Surveyor, h 1 Orchard av.
Klee Alfred P, trav agt Klee & Coleman, h 163 Coburn.
Klee Frederick, cooper, h 25 Grant.
Klee John (Klee & Coleman), res Dayton, O.
Klee John F, engr, h 11 Minnesota.
Klee Joseph, boxmkr, b 25 Grant.
KLEE & COLEMAN (John Klee and Henry Coleman, of Dayton O), Wm H Miller Mngr, Bottlers of All Kinds of Carbonated Beverages, 227-229 S Delaware, Tel 730.
Klefker Edward W, b 284 N Liberty.
Klefker Frank, lab, b 284 N Liberty.
Klefker Frederick, checkman Penna Lines, h 62 Buchanan.
Klefker Henry F, driver, b 284 N Liberty.
Klefker Sophie (wid Henry), h 284 N Liberty.
Klefker Wm F, uphlr, b 284 N Liberty.
Kleifgen Casper (The Wood Ornament Co), h 452 N California.
Kleimann John H, drayman, h 439 E Ohio.
Klein, see also Clineyand Kline.
Klein Abraham, bartndr, h 65 N Liberty.
Klein Albert, mach, b 5 English av.
Klein Albert F, clk Charles Mayer & Co, h 354 S New Jersey.
Klein Charles, asst mngr Indpls Brewing Co, h 210 Union.
Klein Charles J, helper, b 177 Meek.
Klein Elias, rabbi Hungarian Hebrew Ohew Zedeck Congregation, h 427 S Illinois.
Klein Engel (wid Frederick), h 522 S Meridian.
Klein Frank C, tailor, b 117 S Spruce.
Klein Frederick L P, watchmkr, h 103 Excelsior av.
Klein Harry, bartndr, b 65 N Liberty.
Klein Henry, clothing, 189 E Washington, h same.
Klein Henry, lab, b 177 Meek.
Klein Henry, pdlr, h 433 S Capitol av.
Klein Jacob, grocer, 130 Davidson, h same.
Klein John, bartndr, h 5 English av.
Klein John, shoemkr, 275 E Georgia, b same.
Klein John, cabtmkr, b 177 Meek.
Klein John M, helper, b 177 Meek.
Klein Louis F, uphlr, b 117 S Spruce.
Klein Magdalena (wid Frank C), h 117 S Spruce.
Klein Matthew, mach, h 275 E Georgia.
Klein Michael, butcher, b 275 E Georgia.
Klein Michael, cabtmkr, h 177 Meek.
Klein Nathan, butcher, b 51 Russell av.
Klein Nicholas, lab, b 275 E Georgia.
Klein Paul F, carp, b 72 E Wilkins.
Klein Peter, bartndr, b 680 W Washington.
Klein Philip, clk, h 83 Kansas.
Klein Wm H, baker Parrott-Taggart, h 111 Spring.
Kleine Frederick, collr Polar Ice Co, b 193 English av.
Kleine Henry, propr Diamond Sample Room, h 265 Mass av.
Kleine Wm C, foreman, h 315 E New York.
Kleiner John F, motorman, h 605 W Michigan.
Kleinfelter Jacob, sawmkr, h 132 Weghorst.
Kleinman Jacob, finisher, h 36 Iowa.
Kleinschmidt Anthony F (Shellhouse & Co), h 751 N Alabama.
Kleinschmidt Elizabeth (wid Henry), h 192 Indiana av.
Kleinschmidt Frederick, h 751 N Alabama.

POLICIES IN UNITED STATES LIFE INSURANCE CO., offer indemnity against death, liberal cash surrender value or at option of policy-holder, fully paid-up life insurance or liberal life income. E. B. SWIFT, M'g'r, 25 E. Market St.

WM. KOTTEMAN } WILL FURNISH YOUR HOUSE COMPLETE
89 & 91 E. Washington St. Telephone 1742

Kleinschmidt Frederick, tailor, 442 E Georgia, h same.
Kleinschmidt Frederick D, driver, h 44 Maple.
Kleinschmidt George, lab, b 44 Maple.
Kleinschmidt Minnie L, clk, b 44 Maple.
Kleinsmith Anna (wid Christian), h 86 Willow.
Kleinsmith Clara, dressmkr, 294 E Ohio, b same.
Kleinsmith Harry, clk, b 86 Willow.
Kleinsmith Pamelia K (wid Christian), h 294 E Ohio.
Kleinsmith Wm E, hats, 23 W Washington, b 294 E Ohio.
Kleis Charles, lab, h 130 Agnes.
Kleis Frederick, h 372 S Alabama.
Kleis Henry, switchman, b 372 S Alabama.
Kleis Wm F, collr, h 481 Madison av.
Klemm Charles, baker, h 44 Elizabeth.
Klene Bernard, cabtmkr, h 183 Harrison.
Klene Harry W, mach, b 183 Harrison.
Klene Wm, cabtmkr, b 183 Harrison.
Klene Wm jr, b 183 Harrison.
Klepfer Aletha E (wid Alva), b w s Hope 1 s of Schofield (B).
Klepfer Emanuel, lab, h 111 Harrison.
Klepfer Ammon, porter, r 77 N Alabama.
Klepfer Jesse, h 19 Deloss.
Klepfer Joseph H, blksmith, h 398 Martindale av.
Klepfer Rosana (wid Andrew J), b 591 E Washington.
Klepfer Solomon, trav agt, h 427 Park av.
Klepfer Walter V, tmstr, b 19 Deloss.
Klepker Henry, clk, Frank E Janes, b 284 N Liberty.
Klepp Ferdinand, uphlr, b 754 S East.
Kleppe Charles F, brewer, h 425 S Delaware.
Klepper Charles F, birds, 133 Mass av, h 286 N Pine.
Klepper Charles L, mach, b 317 N Pine.
Klepper Frederick H, driver, b 46 Sanders.
Klepper Henry C, clk, b 864 Cornell av.
Klepper Henry E, cabtmkr, h 317 N Pine.
Klepper Wm H, drugs, 100 Mass av, h 331 N Liberty.
Klewe Frederick, truckman, h 25 Iowa.
Klier Thomas, baker Parrott & Taggart, h 121 Yeiser.
Klinck Christina (wid Matthew), b 181 N Pine.
Klinck Louis (Klinck & Matthews), h 197 Spann av.
Klinck Louis J, stonecutter, b 197 Spann av.
Klinck & Matthews (Louis Klinck, Wm Matthews), stone yard, Kentucky av and White river.
Kline, see also Cline and Klein.
Kline Arthur A, barber, h 26 Cherry.
Kline Charles F, engr, h s w cor Fleet and Broadway.
Kline Edwin J, carp, h 631 N West.
Kline Frank B, clk, b 464 Bellefontaine.
Kline Fred, lab, b 45 Beacon.
Kline Frederick, gas insp, h 530 E Georgia.
Kline Frederick G, condr, h 40 Elder av.
Kline George, baggageman, h 36 Hendricks.
Kline George J, carp, h 522 Bellefontaine.
Kline George W, mach, h 1081 W Michigan.
Kline Henry F, sanitary insp, h 463 N Alabama.
Kline John G, barber, 55 Mass av, h 240 N Noble.
Kline Leo, ladies' tailor, 59 Ingalls blk, h 264 S Penn.
Kline Louis E, rodman, h 170 Excelsior av.

THOS. C. DAY & CO.
INVESTING AGENTS,
TOWN AND FARM LOANS,
Rooms 325 to 330 Lemcke Bldg.

Kline Thomas E, engr, h 832 Bellefontaine.
Kline Wm H, cabtmkr, h 361 Spring.
Kling John, soapmkr, b 701 S West.
Klinge Ernest, lab, b 540 S New Jersey.
Klinge Ernest, bottler, b 32 Sanders.
Klinge Wm F, hostler, h w s Hester 1 s of Lexington av.
Klingelhoffer Emma (wid Leonard), h 47½ Brookside av.
Klingelhoffer Jesse, driver, b 47½ Brookside av.
Klingensmith Alonzo A, lab, h 22 Minerva.
Klingensmith Armeda (wid Joseph), b 537 Jones (N I).
Klingensmith Charles F, blksmith, h 169 Benton.
Klingensmith Edward A, weaver, h 83 Patterson.
Klingensmith Elias, carp, h 110 Ruckle.
Klingensmith Isaiah L, drugs, 502 College av, h 478 Broadway.
Klingensmith Nathan G, condr, h 129 Pleasant.
Klingensmith Reuben, grocer, 182 Sheffield av (H), h same.
Klingensmith Susan (wid Jacob), b 7 Minkner.
Klingensmith Wm H, carder, h 495 W New York.
Klinger James S, trav agt, r 321 N Liberty.
Klinger Wm, hostler, h w s Harlan bet Lexington av and Jefferson.
Klingstein Ewald, carp, h 320 Clifford av.
Klingstein Hugo J, cabtmkr, h 17 Wyoming.
Klingstein Otto H, poultry, 53½ Prospect, h 30 Laurel.
Klingstein Paul G, finisher, h 18 Sheldon.
Klingstein Paulina (wid Julius), h 319 Spring.
Klink Christiana (wid Mathew), h 181 N Pine.
Klink Elizabeth, dressmkr, 233 E Morris, b same.
Klink Wm C, watchman, h 233 E Morris.
Klintwort Henry A, mach, h 115 Bismarck av (H).
Klippel Gustav, trav agt Indpls Chair Mnfg Co, h 257 Talbott av.

EAT
HITZ'S
CRACKERS
AND CAKES.
ASK YOUR GROCER FOR THEM.

SHOW CASES — WILLIAM WIEGEL — 6 West Louisiana Street Opp. Union Station.

Capital Steam Carpet Cleaning Works
M. D. PLUNKETT Proprietor, Telephone 818

BENJ. BOOTH PRACTICAL EXPERT ACCOUNTANT. Accounts of any description investigated and audited, and statements rendered. Room 18, 82½ E. Washington St., Indianapolis, Ind.

The Best Place in the City to Get a Good Meal THE SHERMAN RESTAURANT ♦♦♦ 18 and 20 S. Meridian Street KERSHNER BROS., Proprs.

ESTABLISHED 1876. TELEPHONE 168.
CHESTER BRADFORD,
SOLICITOR OF PATENTS,
AND COUNSEL IN PATENT CAUSES.
(See adv. page 6.)
Office:—Rooms 14 and 16 Hubbard Block, S.W. Cor. Washington and Meridian Streets, INDIANAPOLIS, INDIANA.

Klobb John, lab, h 197½ E Washington.
Klodfelter John, molder, h 44 S Reisner (W I).
Kloepper Charles C, driver, h 208 Minnesota.
Kloetzke Ferdinand, cabtmkr, h 90 Nebraska.
Klostermeier Charles W, painter, h 8 Harvey.
Kloth Rudolph D, druggist, 100 Prospect, h same.
Klotz Anna (wid John), h 413 S Illinois.
Klotz August W, sawyer, b 615 S Meridian.
Klotz Charles W, candymkr, b 615 S Meridian.
Klotz Carl F A, mach hd, h 615 S Meridian.
Kluge Gustav, cigar mnfr, 425 S Delaware, h same.
Kluge Herman W, drugs, 202 Hoyt av, h same.
Klugel Oscar G, clk, h 278 Blackford.
Kluger Maximilian, jeweler, b 145 E Merrill.
KLUM ROBERT L, State Agt German American Insurance Co of New York, 19½ N Penn, h 743 N New Jersey, Tel 295.
Klumpp Charles D, engr, h 175 Lexington av.
Klumpp Frederick, mach hd, h 48 Minerva.
Klumpp Sarah A (wid Frederick A D), h 140 Scioto.
Klusmann Caroline (wid Louis), h 123 St Mary.
Klusmann Charles L, uphlr, h 44 Sterling.
Klusmann Frederick, b 123 St Mary.
Klusmann Louis, trav agt Schrader Bros, h 449 Bellefontaine.
Knannlien Adam G, carp, h 50 Sullivan.
Knannlien Andrew, lab, b 38 Lexington av.
Knannlien Anna (wid George), h 38 Lexington av.
Knannlien John, lab, b 38 Lexington av.
Knapp Arthur J, clk, b 20 Pleasant.
Knapp Charles, lab, h 590 W Udell (N I).
Knapp Elijah W, h w s Grand av 2 s of University av (I).
Knapp Herman C, mach hd, h 141 Meek.
Knapp Jerome B, h 242 E Vermont.

O. B. Ensey
SLATE, STEEL, TIN AND IRON ROOFING.
Cor. 6th and Illinois Sts. Tel. 1562

Knapp Joseph A, fireman, h 20 Pleasant.
Knapp Joshua N, blksmith, h 35 S Linden.
Knapp Laura M, bkkpr, b w s Grand av 2 s of University av (I).
Knapp Wm W, abstracts, 8 Baldwin blk, h o s Downey av 1 n of P C C & St L Ry (I).
Knappe Matthew C, city agt, b 195 Fayette.
Knapton Thomas J, stonecutter, h 17 Jefferson av.
Knarr Louis, lab, b Muller's Hotel.
Knarzer Charles P, butcher, b 235 N California.
Knarzer George, saloon, 60 S Delaware, h e s Meridian 7 s of Pleasant run.
Knauer Charles, lab, b 128 Blake.
Knauer Wm, carp, h n s Washington 4 w of Insane Hospital (M J).
Knauss Christian G, patrolman, h 70 Smith.
Knauss Johanna (wid Christian), h 70 Smith.
Knauss John, clk Charles Mayer & Co, b 25 Dickson.
Knauss John D, turner, h 886 LaSalle.
Knauss Louis P, polisher, h 6 Margaret.
Knauss Samuel, polisher, b 70 Smith.
Knaut Martin, mach, r 19 N Arsenal av.
Kneale Wm C, foreman Natl Malleable Castings Co, h 70 King (H).
Kneckler Jacob, lab, h 60 Michigan av.
Knee Edgar, clk R M S, r 90 N Senate av.
Knee Elmer E, condr, h 70 Spann av.
Kneer Charles J, meats, rear 150 Spann av, b same.
Kneer Mary (wid Henry C), h 45 Depot (B).
Knefler Charles, bkkpr, r 11½ N Meridian.
Knefler Ernest F, clk Cerealine Mnfg Co, b 630 E Washington.
Knefler Frederick (Knefler & Berryhill), pres and supt Board of Regents State Soldiers' and Sailors' Monument, 93 State House, h 630 E Washington.
KNEFLER & BERRYHILL (Frederick Knefler, John S Berryhill), Lawyers, Rooms 5-6, 82½ E Washington, Tel 587.
Kneip Benjamin F, carver, b 19 Morrison.
Kneip Josephine, b 19 Morrison.
Kneph Wm D, waiter, h 132 N Liberty.
Knepper Abraham L, weighmaster, h 102 Bright.
Knerr Charles B, phys, 858 E Washington, h same.
Knetemeier Charles W, letter carrier P O, h 128 Spann av.
Knickerbacker Hall (The Diocesan School for Girls), cor 7th and Central av.
Knickerbocker Charles, lab, h 380 Talbott av.
Knickerbocker James B, window shades, 40½ Kentucky av, r 34 S Capitol av.
Knight America J (wid Ira), b 65 Malott av.
Knight Charles K, trav agt, b 129 N Illinois.
Knight Edward, lab, r 182 Muskingum al.
Knight John (Knight & Jillson), h 276 N Delaware.
Knight Joseph, porter Sherman House.
Knight Joseph A, carp, h 33 Division (W I).
Knight Jasper N, dry goods, s w cor Illinois and 30th, h same.
Knight Mary, baker, 140 E Mkt House, b 162 E St Clair.
Knight Mattie J, h 401½ N Alabama.
Knight Stanton P, mnfr, b 270 Central av.
Knight Wm E, paperhngr, h 65 Malott av.
Knight Wm H, carp, h 771 E Washington.
Knight Wm W (King & Knight), h 15 Pleasant av.
Knight Wm W (W W Knight & Co), r 329 Broadway.

TUTEWILER ▲ UNDERTAKER, No. 72 WEST MARKET STREET. TELEPHONE 216.

PROVIDENT LIFE AND TRUST CO. OF PHILADELPHIA. D. W. Edwards, G. A., 508 Indiana Trust Bldg. In form of policy; prompt settlement of death losses; equitable dealing with policy-holders; in strength of organization; and in everything which contributes to Security and Cheapness of life insurance, this company is unsurpassed.

THEODORE F. SMITHER ~ G & R MATERIALS
2 and 3-Ply Building Paper, etc. Best of Materials.
Telephone 861. Office, 151 West Maryland St.

KNIGHT W W & CO (Wm W Knight), Wholesale Lumber, 84 E Market.
KNIGHT & JILLSON (John Knight, Wm M Jillson), Steam, Water and Gas Supplies, 75 S Penn, Tel 68.
KNIGHTS AND LADIES OF HONOR, Charles W Harvey Supreme Sec, Charles F Dudley Supreme Treas, 601-624 Lemcke Bldg.
Knights of Pythias Castle Hall Assn, Frank L Dougherty sec, 49 Journal bldg.
Knipp Julius W (Atkinson & Knipp), h 576 Central av.
Knippenberg Henry, genl mngr Hecla Consolidated Mining Co, h 622 N Meridian.
Kniselle David, paperhngr, h 184 N Capitol av.
Kniselle Hattie (wid Lewis), b 184 N Capitol av.
Knittel Gottlieb C, blksmith, h 488 Chestnut.
Knittel Gottlob, mason, h 417 S Delaware.
Knittel Henry, lab, b 626 Chestnut.
Knittel Thekla (wid Carl), b 626 Chestnut.
Knittel Wm C, helper, b 626 Chestnut.
Knobe Anna E (wid Sebastian), b 453 E Market.
Knobe Lizzie A, h 474 E 8th.
Knode Henry C (J R Ross & Co), h 976 N Alabama.
Knode Wm P, trav agt McKee Shoe Co, h 1012 N Delaware.
Knodel Albert D, clk Indianapolis Brewing Co, b 80 Russell av.
Knodel Ernst, clk, b 80 Russell av.
Knodel Ernst F, clk, h 80 Russell av.
Knodel John, harnessmkr, h 63 Stevens.
Knodle Anna M, b 395 Central av.
Knodle Frederick S, artist The Sun, b 395 Central av.
Knodle George, clk U S Ex Co, h 395 Central av.
Knodle George W, clk R B Grover & Co, h 178 Talbott av.
Knoebel Jacob, car rep, h 18 Douglass.
Knoke Frank C, lab, b 23 N Gillard av.
Knoke John H, carp, h 23 N Gillard av.
Knoll Charles, polisher, b 329 S Olive.
Knoop George J, lab, h 88 N Gillard av.
Knop Charles, lab, b 83 N Dorman.
Knop Ernst, mach, b n w cor Lawrence and Rural.
Knop Minnie J (wid Wm H), h 83 N Dorman.
Knop Wm E, car rep, h e s Gale 1 n of Schofield (B).
Knopf Edward, clk, r 71 Madison av.
Knopf Henry, brewer, h rear 39 Davis.
Knopp Herman C, mach hd, h 141 Meek.
Knott Archibald J, sawmkr, b 84 McGinnis.
Knott Joseph A, lab, h 84 McGinnis.
Knotts Albert E, asst D Kregelo & Son, r 69 N Illinois.
Knotts Alonzo O, mach, h 19 Sullivan.
Knotts Alvah W, student, h 258 S Meridian.
Knotts David C, lab, h 458 Indiana av.
Knotts Edgar E, painter, h 412 E Walnut.
Knowles Harry W, condr, h 382½ E 9th.
Knowles Harvey, yardmaster, h 322 E Louisiana.
Knowles Walter L, flagman, b 322 E Louisiana.
Knowles Wm, clk Am Ex Co, b 322 E Louisiana.
Knowlton Amy, stenog German-American Sav Life Assn, b 26 Ashland (W I).
Knowlton Hiram, rimmer, h 26 Ashland (W I).

THE WHEN IS A WORLD BEATER.

Knowlton Martha (wid Aaron), b 311 N Alabama.
Knowlton Mary B (wid Orlando), prin Public School No 26, b 516 Ash.
Knox Elwood C, mngr The Freeman, b 128 W Vermont.
Knox Edwin S, phys, 323 S State av, r same.
Knox George, barber, r 66 N Missouri.
Knox George L, pub The Freeman, barber, 18-20 N Illinois, tel 244, h 128 W Vermont.
Knox John A, lab, r 66 N Missouri.
Knox Melville C, painter, h 581 Charles.
Knox S H & Co, Gardner T White mngr, notions, 24 W Washington.
Knubbe Anna F, artist, b 154 East Drive (W P).
Knubbe Jerusha (wid Frederick), b 154 East Drive (W P).
Knurr John, lab, h 21 Palmer.
Knurr John, lab, b 128 Blake.
Knurr John, salesman Pearson's Music House, h 119 Cornell av.
Knuth Albert, mach hd, b 320 Columbia av.
Knuth Frank H, cigarmkr, h 324 Columbia av.
Knuth Henry, lab, h 320 Martindale av.
Knuth Hermann, lab, h 320 Columbia av.
Knuth Wm, mach, b 320 Martindale av.
Kobler August, polisher, h 286 E Louisiana.
Koch, see also Cook.
Koch Albert F, lab, h 70 Arizona.
Koch Alice H (wid Charles), phys, 758 N Senate av, h same.
Koch Amelia, nurse, b 118 N Senate av.
Koch Anna M (wid John H), b 17 McKim av.
Koch Carl, trav agt, h 758 N Senate av.
Koch Carl I, clk, b 707 E Washington.
Koch Charles M, butcher, h 51 Sinker.
Koch Charles W, lab, b 68 Wisconsin.
Koch Charles W J, gardener, b 70 Arlington.
Koch Christian, furniture, 198 E Washington, h 25 Ashland (W I).
Koch Christian F, driver, h 41 Oriental.
Koch Christina (wid Thomas), h 16 Lockerbie.

The A. Burdsal Co.
CELEBRATED
HOMESTEAD
READY MIXED PAINT.
WHOLESALE AND RETAIL.
34 AND 36 SOUTH MERIDIAN STREET.

ELECTRIC SUPPLIES We Carry a full Stock. Prices Right. C. W. MEIKEL, Tel. 466. 96-98 E. New York St.

DALTON & MERRIFIELD { LUMBER South Noble St., near E. Washington

INDIANA ELECTROTYPE CO. :: BEST WORK LOWEST PRICES. 23 WEST PEARL ST., INDIANAPOLIS, IND. JOB WORK. BOOK PLATES. BEST PATENT BASE ON THE MARKET. All Orders Promptly Filled.

KIRKHOFF BROS.,
Electrical Contractors, Wiring and Construction.
102-104 SOUTH PENNSYLVANIA ST.
TELEPHONE 910.

Koch Frederick W, brickmkr, b 70 Arlington.
Koch George, shoemkr, 329 S East, h same.
Koch Henry F, brickmkr, b 70 Arlington.
Koch Herman H, h 35 Fletcher av.
Koch John, furniture, 464 Virginia av, h 56 Prospect.
Koch John A, brewer, h 139 Meek.
Koch John G, carp, h 474 Mulberry.
Koch Kate (wid Henry), h 606 S Meridian.
Koch Louisa M (wid Henry S), h 70 Arlington.
Koch Simon, lab, h n s Michigan 1 e of Rural.
Koch Wm C S, gardener, b 70 Arlington.
Koch Wm J C, clk, h 707 E Washington.
Koch Wm T, lab, b 68 Wisconsin.
Kochlin Carl, sec H H Symmes Co, b 268½ W Washington.
Koeckert Max P, shoes, 345 S Delaware, h same.
Koehl Amelia, bkkpr, b 525 W Maryland.
Koehl Catherine, bkkpr, b 525 W Maryland.
Koehl Mary (wid Peter), h 525 W Maryland.
Koehler, see also Caylor, Kaler, Keeler, Keller, Koller and Kuhler.
Koehler Albert, restrurant, 128 E Wabash, h 19 Tuxedo.
Koehler Charles W, lab, h e s Brookland av 3 n of Clifford av.
Koehler Edward, photog, b 77 Lockerbie.
Koehler Emil W (Craft & Koehler), h 1134 N Penn.
Koehler Frank, watchman, h 67 Buchanan.
Koehler Frederick W, packer, b 79 N Pine.
Koehler Gottfried (Koehler & Bishop), h 77 Lockerbie.
Koehler Henry C, cabtmkr, h 151 N Gillard av.
Koehler Jacob, cabtmkr, h 17 McRae.
Koehler John F, cigarmkr, 214 Hamilton av, h same.
Koehler Joseph (Co-Operative Carriage and Wagon Co), h 112 S East.
Koehler Louis C, grocer, 138 Buchanan, h 140 same.

THE W. G. WASSON CO.,
130 Indiana Ave. Tel. 989.
STEAM
COAL
Car Lots a Specialty. Prompt Delivery.
Brazil Block, Jackson and Anthracite.

Koehler Roderick, tmstr, b w s Brookland av 3 n of Clifford av.
Koehler Wm, lab, h 107 Fulton.
Koehler Wm F, grocer, 346 Clifford av, h 536 Jefferson av.
Koehler Wm H, plumber Insane Hospital.
KOEHLER & BISHOP (Gottfried Koehler, Charles T Bishop), Photographers; Special Attention Given to Amateur Work; 62½ E Washington.
Koehne Armin C, broker, h 227 Park av.
KOEHNE GEORGE W, Propr The Normandie European Hotel and Agt for B F Goodrich Co's Rubber Hose, and New Jersey Car Spring and Rubber Co's Cotton Fire Hose, 101-109 S Illinois, Tel 734.
Koehne Louis A, clk Daniel Stewart Co, b 548 N Capitol av.
Koehne Matthew, lab, h 14 Yandes.
Koehring Bernhard (B Koehring & Son), cooper, 38 Cincinnati, h 287 N Liberty.
KOEHRING B & SON (Bernhard and Charles), Hardware, 530 Virginia av, Tel 852.
Koehring Charles (B Koehring & Son), h 93 Fletcher av.
Koehring Edward, clk, r 532 Virginia av.
Koehring George, clk, r 532 Virginia av.
Koehring Theodore, clk, r 532 Virginia av.
Koehrn Frederick C, driver, h 351 Union.
Koelling, see also Kolling.
Koelling Charles C F (Schildmeier & Koelling), h 80 Fulton.
Koelling Charles F C, tailor, b 80 Fulton.
Koelling Wm C F, lab, h 33 Beacon.
Koenig Anna, h 336 N East.
Koenig Charles, shoemkr, 476 S East, h same.
Koenig Frank, lab, h 15 Geneva.
Koenig John, carp, h 116 S Summit.
Koenig John, printer b 368 W New York.
Koenig Maurice, tailor, 81 N Delaware, h 519 S Capitol av.
Koeniger George, h 491 Mulberry.
Koeniger George J, cigarmnfr, 124 Kennington, h same.
Koeniger John M, bartndr, r 167½ E Washington.
Koepke Ferdinand, h 118 Buchanan.
Koepke Frederick, express, h 504 Chestnut.
Koepke Frederick J, cigarmkr, b 504 Chestnut.
Koepke Wm C, cigarmkr, b 504 Chestnut.
Koeppen Frederick, porter, h 320 Raymond.
Koeppen John G, clk Moore & Co, b 263 Hadley av (W I).
Koeppen John R, lab, b 326 W Maryland.
Koepper Christian, liquors, 35 E Maryland, h 230 Union.
Koepper Christina (wid Frederick), h 465 Union.
Koepper Lucy A, music teacher, 25 Leota, h same.
Koepper Wm F, propr Indpls Plumbing Co, h 25 Leota.
Koepper Wm H, lab, h 45 Leota.
Koerner, see also Kerner.
Koerner Andrew, lab, b 113 Elm.
Koerner Andrew A, bottler, h 113 Elm.
Koerner Anna, music teacher, 30 Hall pl, h same.
Koerner Antoinette (wid Conrad C), h 951 N Meridian.
Koerner Carl, h 369½ S Delaware.
Koerner Charles H, agt, h 171 Germania av (H).

W. H. Messenger FURNITURE, CARPETS, STOVES, 101 EAST WASHINGTON ST. TEL. 491.

McNamara, Koster & Co. | Foundry and Pattern Shop, 212-218 S. PENN. ST. · · · PHONE 1593·

THE FRED DIETZ CO. WOODEN PACKING BOXES MADE TO ORDER. FAN AND WAREHOUSE TRUCKS. 40 Madison Avenue. Telephone 654.

Koerner Henry, fireman, b 951 N Meridian.
Koerner Henry, lab, b 285 S Capitol av.
Koerner John G, nurse, 59 Oak, h same.
Koerner Joseph, lab, b 113 Elm.
Koerner Waldemar, collr Pearson's music House, b 951 N Meridian.
Koerner Louis, bartndr, b 1050 S Meridian.
Koerner Valentine, saloon, 1050 S Meridian, h same.
Koers George H, drayman, h 38 Spann av.
Koers Herman B, hostler, h 44 Spann av.
Koester Sophie (wid Dietrich), b 371 Union.
Koesters Charles G, furniture, 456 S Meridian, h same.
Koesters Frank J, trimmer, h 632 Charles.
Koestle Frank J, chairmkr, h 274 Bright.
Kofahl Carl, mach, h 99 Chadwick.
Koffel John W, lab, h 159 Lexington av.
Kohagen, see also Gohagan.
Kohagen Carl, lab, b 647 S Meridian.
Kohl Gottfried, lab, h 92 High.
Kohlbauer John G, grinder, h 525 S Capitol av.
Kohler George, car rep, h 166 Spann av.
Kohler Henry, engr, h 96 N State av.
Kohler John, lab, b 446 Mulberry.
Kohlman Adam Rev, asst rector St Mary's Catholic Church, h 75 E Maryland.
Kohlstaedt George, foreman, h 426 S Delaware.
Kohlstaedt Wm, gardener, h 1008 S Meridian.
Kohn Benjamin, trav agt, b 226 E New York.
Kohn Elizabeth (wid Frederick), b 40 Davis.
Kohn Frederick J, blksmith, b 40 Davis.
Kohn Joseph, portraits, 44½ N Penn, h 322 N Senate av.
Kohne Benjamin F, ins agt, 118 N Illinois, h same.
Kohnle Charles R, clk, b 253 N Senate av.
Kohnle George F, butter, 61 Indiana av, h 253 N Senate av.
Kohnle Harry E, clk, h 253 N Senate av.
Kohnle Wm H, trav agt, h 701 N Alabama.
Kohns Wm, lab, h 59 N Judge Harding (W I).
Kokemiller Flora H, teacher Public School No 6, b 42 Carlos.
Kokemiller Frank C, boilermkr, b 42 Carlos.
Kokemiller Howard L, mach, h w s Utah 1 s of Kansas.
Kokemiller Malinda (wid Frederick), h 42 Carlos.
Kokemiller Wm C, driver, h e s Medeira 3 s of Prospect.
Koker Frank J, lab, b 370 W Maryland.
Koker Martha E (wid Charles), h 370 W Maryland.
Koker Noah F, lab, b 370 W Maryland.
Kolb, see also Kalb.
Kolb Frederick W, saloon, 21 Kentucky av, b 151 Davidson.
Kolb Wm F, grocer, 151 Davidson, h same.
Kolcheck George, saloon, 813 N Capitol av, h same.
Kolcheck Wm H, bartndr, b 813 N Capitol av.
Koldin Anton, lab, h 261 W Vermont.
Kolhoff Walter G, clk, b Lorraine bldg.
Kolker Henry A, saloon, 451 E Washington, h same.
Koller Charles F, carp, h 148 N State av.
Koller George J, car rep, h 166 Spann av.
Koller Henry C, electrician, h 69 N State av.
Koller Mary (wid Ernest E), h 112 N State av.

Henry H. Fay,
40½ E. Washington St.,
REAL ESTATE,
AND LOAN BROKER.

Kolling, see also Koelling.

KOLLING CHARLES F, Pharmacist; Best of Everything in Drug and Toilet Articles; Lowest Prices; Deutsche Apotheke, 205 Prospect, h same, Tel 1611.

Kolling Christina L (wid Wm F), h 439 S State av.
Kolling Wm F, finisher, b 439 S State av.
Kollinger John, helper, b 133 E Merrill.
Kollinger Peter, h 133 E Merrill.
Kollinger Wm H, lab, b 133 E Merrill.
Kollmer Henry C, maltster, r rear 407 S Delaware.
Kolmer John, phys, 203 N Illinois, r same.
Kolthof Frederick, boilermkr, b 75 Union.
Kolthof Henry E, harnessmkr, b 75 Union.
Kolthof Marguerite, b 75 Union.
Kolwes Mary A (wid George W), h n s 30th 1 w of Illinois (M).
Koning Wm K, foreman, h 332 Prospect.
Konnersman John H, printer, h 22 Cooper.
Konrad John, carp, h 98 S Reisner (W I).
Kontny John, shoemkr, h 119 Kennington.
Konz Jacob, tailor, h 258 W 7th.
Kooistra Charles, lab, b e s Perkins pike 2 n of Bethel av.
Koons, see also Coons.
Koons Carl, engr, b 44 Edward (W I).
Koons George B, patrolman, h 107 English av.
Koons John, packer, b 44 Edward (W I).
Koons Sarah (wid Samuel), h 44 Edward (W I).
Koons Wesley, baler, b 44 Edward (W I).
Koons Wm A, lab, h 274 W Pearl.
Koons Wm H, real est, h 226 N Beville av.
Koontz David, bartndr, b 109 N West.
Koontz George W, stock examiner Bureau of Animal Industry, h 288 N Senate av.
Koor Samuel, pdlr, h 100 Maple.
Koors Bernard A, engr, h 148 Kansas.
Koors John F, mach hd, b 148 Kansas.
Kopf Joseph, reedwkr, b 249 Union.
Koplan Solomon, grocer, 143 Eddy, h same.
Kopp Albert, clk Murphy, Hibben & Co, b 299 Park av.
Kopp Elise (wid Albert F), h 299 Park av.

UNION CASUALTY & SURETY CO.
OF ST. LOUIS, MO.
All lines of Personal Accident and Casualty Insurance, including Employers' and General Liability.
W. E. BARTON & CO., General Agents,
504 Indiana Trust Building.
LONG DISTANCE TELEPHONE 1918.

Indianapolis BUSINESS UNIVERSITY Leading College of Business and Shorthand. Elevator day and night. Individual instruction. Large faculty. Terms easy. Enter now. See p. 4. When Block. E. J. HEEB, President.

NEW YORK FILTER MFG. CO. Filters for Water-Works, Boiler Plants, Laundries, Hotels, Private Residences, Etc. | Henry R. Worthington, 64 S. Pennsylvania St. Long Distance Telephone 284.

UNION CO-OPERATIVE LAUNDRY (COMPOSED OF UNION LAUNDRY GIRLS.) NOS. 138, 40 AND 42 VIRGINIA AVENUE. T. E. SOMERVILLE, MANAGER—TELEPHONE 1269. INDIANAPOLIS, IND.

HORACE M. HADLEY
REAL ESTATE AND INSURANCE
66 East Market Street, Basement
TELEPHONE 1540.

Kopp Ernestine (wid Gotthold), baker, 351 E Market, h same.
Kopp Wm H (Enders & Kopp), h 641 E Ohio.
Korbly Bernard P, stenog Smith & Korbly, b 123 E North.
Korbly Charles A (Smith & Korbly), h 123 E North.
Korbly Charles A jr, notary public, 604 Indiana Trust bldg, b 123 E North.
Kord Caroline (wid Frederick), h 473 W Michigan.
Kord Charles F, lab, b 475 W Michigan.
Kord Frederick G, driver, h 475 W Michigan.
Kording Frederick A, watchman, h 74 Minnesota.
Korn Edward C, clk, b 128 Irwin.
Korn Elizabeth (wid Martin), b 814 S East.
Korn John W, clk Eli Lilly & Co, h 128 Irwin.
Kornet Frederick W, cabtmkr, h 575 W Addison (N I).
Kornfeld Henry, cigar mnfr, h 208 N Pine.
Kornfeld Henry and Lena, cigar mnfrs, 208 N Pine.
Kornfeld Lena, cigar mnfr, h 208 N Pine.
Kors Carrie M C, b 332 E Wabash.
Kors Henry J, teacher German Lutheran School, h 332 E Wabash.
Korte Henry, truckman, h Madison av s of Belt R R.
Kortepeter Edward, sawyer, h 28 Beecher.
Kortepeter Frank M, helper, b 19 Short.
Kortepeter Louisa (wid Wm), h 19 Short.
Kortepeter Wm H, drayman, h 42 Spann av.
Kortlitzky Catherine (wid Henry), h 181 Madison av.
Kortlitzky Henry, painter, h 181 Madison av.
Koschmider Charles, lab, h 1002 S Meridian.
Koschmider Frank, mach hd, h 298 Charles.
Koschmider Paul, lab, h 1002 S Meridian.
Koser George, mach, b 428 S Delaware.
Koser John, filer, h 428 S Delaware.
Koser John M, sawmkr, b 428 S Delaware.
Kosfeld Louis, porter, h 623 S Meridian.

PERSONAL AND PROMPT ATTENTION GIVEN TO COLLECTIONS.
Merchants' and Manufacturers' Exchange
J. E. TAKKEN, Manager,
19 Union Building, 73 West Maryland Street.

Koss Charles W, collr Polar Ice Co, b 32 Greer.
Koss Charles W, dry goods, 403 S Delaware, h 22 Bicking.
Koss Frank, lab, h 83 Nebraska.
Koss Ida, stenog, b 32 Greer.
Koss Louis, mach, 254 S Penn, h 22 Sullivan.
Koss Mary (wid Louis), h 329 Davidson.
Koss Wm, clk, b 443 S State av.
Koss Wm C, uphlr, h 127 Irwin.
Koss Wm F (Koss & Fritz), h 32 Greer.
Koss Wm T C, clk, h 121 Garden.
Koss & Fritz (Wm F Koss, Jacob Fritz), contrs, 1 Builders' Exchange.
Kossmann Andrew, butcher, b 477 S New Jersey.
Kossmann Frederick G, butcher, h 299 W Morris.
Kossmann John, butcher, h 42 Jones.
Kost Jacob, janitor, b 101 N Illinois.
Kostenbader Charles L, clk Model Clothing Co, b 9 Lexington av.
Kostenbader Charles R, stonecutter, h 9 Lexington av.
Kostenbader Wm J, lab, b 9 Lexington av.
Koster, see also Koester, Kuester and Kuster.
Koster Charles P, pressman, b 908 N Senate av.
Koster Frank, trimmer, h 617 S Meridian.
Koster Joseph F, sign writer, h 104½ Indiana av.
Koster Kate (wid Charles), b 237 Blackford.
Koster Kate (wid Joseph F), h 908 N Senate av.
Koster Louis J (McNamara, Koster & Co), h 607 E New York.
Koster Oscar (Oval & Koster), b 237 Blackford.
Koster Otto, b 908 N Senate av.
Koster Rudolph, music teacher, b 908 N Senate av.
Kothe George (Kothe, Wells & Bauer), h 362 Broadway.
Kothe Gustav, clk, h 471 S Delaware.
Kothe Henry, 2d vice-pres and treas Marion Trust Co, h 305 N Capitol av.
KOTHE, WELLS & BAUER (George Kothe, Wm Kothe, Charles W Wells, George Bauer), Wholesale Grocers, 128-130 S Meridian, Tel 30.
Kothe Wm (Kothe, Wells & Bauer), h 496 E Market.
Kottek Frank, mach, h 50 S Linden.
Kotteman Charles, bkkpr Wm Kotteman, r 263 N East.
Kotteman Frank, clk Wm Kotteman, r 263 N East.
KOTTEMAN WM, Furniture, Carpets, Stoves and House Furnishing Goods, 89-91 E Washington, Tel 1742; h 244½ E Washington. (See adv right top lines.)
Kottkamp Frederick W, tmstr, h 399 Union.
Kottkamp Wm F A, carp, b 399 Union.
Kottlowski Charles F, clk Charles Mayer & Co, h 393 E Georgia.
Kottlowski Charles T, contr, 220 S Noble, h same.
Kottlowski Ernest, carp, b 220 S Noble.
Kottlowski Frederica (wid Ernst), b 39 Sullivan.
Kougel Charles P, tailor When Clothing Store, b 141 Pleasant.
Koul Frank, lab, h 37 S Reisner (W I).
Kouns John W, tmstr, h 147 Geisendorff.
Kouns Wm A, lab, h 274 W Pearl.

CLEMENS VONNEGUT 184, 186 and 192 E. Washington St. | FOUNDRY AND MACHINISTS' SUPPLIES. "NORTON" EMERY WHEELS AND GRINDING MACHINERY.

THE WM. H. BLOCK CO. DRY GOODS, MILLINERY, CLOAKS AND FURS.
7 AND 9 EAST WASHINGTON STREET.

INDIANAPOLIS STEEL ROOFING AND CORRUGATING WORKS, 23 and 25 East South Street. S. D. NOEL, Proprietor.

Kraas Wilhelmina (wid Frederick), b 209 E Morris.
Kraas Wm, carp, 209 E Morris, h same.
Kraatz John E, cabtmkr, h 74 Woodlawn av.
Kraatz Wm O, mach, b 74 Woodlawn av.
Krabbe John, lab, h 97 N Dorman.
Krabbe John H, lab, b 97 N Dorman.
Frachenfels Erhard, carp, h 150 N Dorman.
Krachenfels Herman A, blksmith, b 150 N Dorman.
Krachenfels John F, clk, b 152 N Dorman.
Krackenberger Henry, lab, h 22 Nebraska.
Kraemer Jacob H, butcher, h 152 Minerva.
Kraf John, boilermkr, b 192 Indiana av.
Kraft Ernest L, div opr I & V Ry, h 124 Walcott.
Kraft, see also Craft.
Kraft Anna B (wid John F), h 408 N West.
Kraft Babette, dressmkr, 196 Elizabeth, b same.
Kraft Charles G, cigarmkr, b 42 Drake.
Kraft Eva (wid Frederick), h 138 Kennington.
Kraft Frederick D, tile setter, b 42 Drake.
Kraft George, lab, b 661 S Meridian.
Kraft John, lab, h 37 Palmer.
Kraft Louis, lab, h 42 Drake.
Kraft Nanette (wid George), h 194 Elizabeth.
Kraft Wm H, cigarmkr, b 42 Drake.
KRAG-REYNOLDS COMPANY (Charles M Reynolds Pres and Treas, Wm A Krag Vice-Pres and Genl Mngr, Wm Wallace Krag Sec, Wholesale Grocers, Coffee and Spices, 31-33 E Maryland, Tel 635.
Krag Wm A, vice-pres and gen mngr Krag-Reynolds Co, h 621 N Penn.
Krag Wm Wallace, sec Krag-Reynolds Co, b 621 N Penn.
Kragh Christian W, draughtsman, h 1699 Graceland av.
Krahler Mary (wid Valentine), h 5 Hendricks.
Kraig John F, carp, h n e cor 8th and Lennox.
Krakinski Joseph, lab, h 94 Maple.
Kramer, see also Cramer and Kraemer.
Kramer Andrew J, pres Kramer Mnfg Co, h 323 E New York.
Kramer Carl (Kramer & Hurrle), b 287 S Delaware.
Kramer Caroline (wid Moses), h rear 57 N East.
Kramer Charles, lab, b 191 W South.
Kramer Charles, tinner, b 172 Coburn.
Kramer Charles E, clk, b 605 W Michigan.
Kramer Charles N, tinner, b 932 Gent (M P).
Kramer Charles T, loans, 723 Lemcke bldg, h 96 Cherry.
Kramer Christopher H, butcher, b 547 N Senate av.
Kramer Edward F, driver, b 105 Agnes.
Kramer Edward F, sec Kramer Mnfg Co, h 324 S New Jersey.
Kramer Frederick, student, b 41 Madison av.
Kramer George, gilder, b 664 Chestnut.
Kramer George B, uphlr, b 172 Coburn.
Kramer Harry E, trimmer, b 109 Fulton.
Kramer Henry J, butcher, h 547 N Senate av.
Kramer Jacob H, h 612 W Michigan.

KRAMER JACOB J, Mnfr and Dealer in Carriages, Buggies, Wagons, Pony Carts, Etc; Repairing, Repainting and Horseshoeing, 213-215 E Market, h 109 Fulton.
Kramer Joseph, lab, h 31 New.
Kramer Lizzie (wid Willis), b 77 Drake.
Kramer Louis H, cook, h 33 McGinnis.
Kramer Mnfg Co, Andrew J Kramer pres, Edward F Kramer sec and treas, furniture, s e cor Merrill and New Jersey.
Kramer Paul, ironwkr, b 217 S Illinois.
Kramer Rebecca E (wid Wm), h 172 Coburn.
Kramer Walter S, messenger Am Ex Co, h 70 Ft Wayne av.
Kramer Wm H, h 352 Prospect.
Kramer & Hurrle (Carl Kramer and Sebastian Hurrle), meat market, 287 S Delaware.
Kramp Adolph, packer, h 157 N Pine.
Kramp Paul, carp, b 157 N Pine.
Kramp Theodore F, lab, h s s Ohio 1 e of Rural.
Krampl Joseph, carver, h rear 82 S Delaware.
Krampl Louis, carver, b rear 82 S Delaware.
Krantler Herman, lab, h 136 Elm.
Krantzus Frederick, b 75 Wisconsin.
Kranz Henry, mngr Ger Mut Ben Soc, 37 S Delaware.
Kranzuch August, lab, h 39 Iowa.
Krass Anthony J, lab, h 494 W New York.
Krass Elizabeth (wid Anthony), h 401 Blake.
Kraus Christian, carp, h 161 Minnesota.
Kraus Edward H, sawmkr, h 427 S State av.
Kraus Harry, tmstr, b 107 Prospect.
Kraus John, butcher, h 661 Charles.
Krause, see also Crouse, Cruse and Kruse.
Krause Carl L W, clk, h 61 Central av.
Krause Charles, b 80 Lockerbie.
Krause Charles H, bkkpr Clemens Vonnegut, h 119 N Liberty.
Krause Frank J, clk, h 5 Hermann.
Krause George E, insp, h 105 N Arsenal av.

GUIDO R. PRESSLER,
FRESCO PAINTER
Churches, Theaters, Public Buildings, Etc., A Specialty.
Residence, No. 325 North Liberty Street.
INDIANAPOLIS, IND.

David S. McKernan REAL ESTATE AND LOANS. Exchanging real estate a specialty. A number of choice pieces for encumbered property. Rooms 2-5 Thorpe Block.

DIAMOND WALL PLASTER { Telephone 1410 BUILDERS' EXCHANGE.

UNION TRANSFER AND STORAGE CO. Cor. E. Ohio St. and C., C., C. & St. L. R'y Tracks. Storage of Household Goods and Pianos a Specialty.

W. McWORKMAN,
Galvanized Iron Cornice Works
TIN AND SLATE ROOFING.
930 WEST WASHINGTON STREET.
TELEPHONE 1118.

Krause Harry, foreman The J B Allfree Mnfg Co.
Krause Harry C, mach, h 125 Excelsior av.
Krause Harry W, gents' furngs, 285 Mass av, b 134 N East.
Krause Henry, h 103 Excelsior av.
Krause J Edward, correspondent Indiana Bicycle Co, b 134 N East.
Krause Reinhold, gents' furngs, 127 E Washington, h 134 N East.
Krauss Catherine E (wid Jacob), h 214 Springfield.
KRAUSS CHARLES, Driven Wells, Cisterns and Pumps, 42 S Penn, Tel 465; h 393 N Penn. (See right top lines.)
Krauss Christian, h 528 E Ohio.
Krauss Emma C (wid Wm G), h 391 N Penn.
Krauss Frederick C, cutter Paul H Krauss, b 172 Park av.
Krauss Henry G, foreman, b 340 E Morris.
Krauss Jacob, watchman, b 74 S Delaware.
Krauss Ludwig, carp, h 10 Cincinnati.
Krauss Moses, gents' furngs, 604 N Senate av, h same.
KRAUSS PAUL H, Men's Furnishings, Shirt Mnfr and Laundry, 44-46 E Washington, Tel 741; h 172 Park av.
Krauss Rosa (wid Carl), b 354 S New Jersey.
Krauth Michael, lab, h 25 Wisconsin.
Kraylor Christina M (wid Wm T), b 604 Central av.
Kreber Clara, stenog, b 62 Fayette.
Kreber Jacob, mach hd, h 120 Fayette.
Kreber John C, mach hd, b 62 Fayette.
KREBER JOSEPH J, Real Estate, Insurance and Investment Broker, 434 Lemcke Bldg, b 62 Fayette.
Kreber Mary K, stenog, b 62 Fayette.
Kreber Veronica (wid Matthias), h 62 Fayette.
Kreber Wm A, clk H T Conde Implement Co, b 120 Fayette.
Krebs Edward J, tailor, b Illinois House.
Krebs Frank G, butcher, b 137 S Summit.
Krebs Reinhard, maltster, h 92 Laurel.

SEALS, STENCILS, STAMPS, Etc.
GEO. J. MAYER
15 S. Meridian St.
TELEPHONE 1386.

Krebs Wm, asst supt Prud Ins Co, r 612 E Washington.
Krebs Wm R, brakeman, b 50 Marion av (W I).
Kreft Henry, carp, b 180 Fulton.
Kregelo David (D Kregelo & Son), h 228 N West.
KREGELO D & SON (David and John L), Undertakers, 69 N Illinois, Tel 250.
Kregelo John L (D Kregelo & Son), h 367 Bellefontaine.
Kreglo Joseph, polisher, h 497 E Walnut.
Kreglo Lulu M, bkkpr, b 363 Jefferson av.
Kreglo Wm J C, clk, h 363 Jefferson av.
Kreglo Mary A (wid Jacob), b 367 N New Jersey.
Krego George L, driver, b 421 Pine.
Kreider Thomas, plastr, b 863 S Meridian.
Kreienbaum George H, cutter, h 14 Tecumseh.
Kreienbaum Henry, cutter, h 6 Yandes.
Kreis Anna M (wid Phillip), b 12 Park av.
Kreis Carl, clk T C Whitcomb, b 260 Blackford.
Kreis Peter, turner, h 260 Blackford.
Kreis Wm, patternmkr, b 260 Blackford.
Kreitlein Andrew G, clk, h 454 N Meridian.
Kreitlein Charles, clk, h 135 W Pratt.
Kreitlein George F, grocer, 250 W Washington, h 26 N West.
Kreitlein John, clk, r 77½ S Illinois.
Kremer James L, driver, b 560 E 8th.
Kremer John, shoemkr, rear 501 College av, h 560 E 8th.
Kremer Nicholas L, barber, rear 501 College av, b 560 E 8th.
Kremiller Caroline (wid Wm), h 112 Cornell av.
Kremiller Kate, stenog, b 112 Cornell av.
Kremiller Wm H, clk Wm Buschmann & Co, h 196½ Ft Wayne av.
Kremm Mathias, instrumentmkr, h 173 Michigan av.
Kremp Frederick, saloon, 49 N Alabama, h 232 N Liberty.
Krempe Elias, sexton, h rear 82 S Delaware.
Krentler Frederick C, clk Original Eagle, h 45 Dunlop.
Krentler Herman W, lab, h 136 Elm.
Krenzer Joseph, baker, b 191 Lincoln la.
Krenzer Joseph, lab, h rear 349 Yandes.
Kress Andrew, brewer, h 525 S New Jersey.
Kress John, brewer, h 196 Meek.
Kretsch, see also Kritsch.
Kretsch Anna M (wid Peter), boarding 179 S Alabama.
Kretsch Cassius, clk, b 179 S Alabama.
Kretsch Charles P, cigarmnfr, 221 S Alabama, h 356 Virginia av.
Kretsch Harry, caller, b 179 S Alabama.
Kretsch Peter, cigarmkr, 9 Gresham, h same.
Kretzer Nicholas J A, mach, h 487 S East.
Kretzer Peter, mach, h 241 E Morris.
Kretzschmar Maria, h 448 S East.
Kreuer Jacob, tailor, h 120 Dunlop.
Kreutzberger Henry, lab, r 174 E Pearl.
Kreutzer John, h 658 N Capitol av.
Krewson Amos D, h 90 N East.
Kribs Edward J, tailor, 177 S Illinois, b Illinois House.
Kribs Jacob, tailor, 181½ S Meridian, h 234 S Alabama.
Kribs John H, tailor, b 234 S Alabama.
KRICK JOHN W, Sec Capitol Life Insurance Co of Indiana, 29 N Penn, h 356 Sheldon.

A. METZGER AGENCY ESTABLISHED 1863. L-O-A-N-S

LAMBERT GAS & GASOLINE ENGINE CO.
ANDERSON, IND. GAS ENGINES FOR ALL PURPOSES.

Kriech Anthony, lab, h 82 Palmer.
Kriech Anthony I, finisher, b 82 Palmer.
Kriech Jacob, lab, h 390 Union.
Krieg August F, collr, b 517 S Meridian.
Krieg Bros (Louis W and Leopold), books, 62 S Illinois.
Krieg Felix J, printer, b 306 N Senate av.
Krieg George M, clk, h 8 Bates al.
Krieg Joseph M, engr, h 306 N Senate av.
Krieg Josephine (wid Wm), h 517 S Meridian.
Krieg Katharine C, clk, b 517 S Meridian.
Krieg Leopold (Krieg Bros), h 80 Oak.
Krieg Louis W (Krieg Bros), b 517 S Meridian.
Krieg Margaret (wid Levi), b 472 Stillwell.
Krieg Paulina L, bkkpr, b 517 S Meridian.
Krieger, see also Cruger, Krueger and Kruger.
Krieger Alberta (wid Wm), h 439 W Francis (N I).
Krieger Andrew, sawmkr, h 278 S Meridian.
Krieger Charles, roofer, h 6 Coble.
Krieger Ernestine (wid Henry), h 359 E New York.
Krieger Frank H, painter, b 359 E New York.
Krieger Gustav, janitor Public School No 4, h 291 Blackford.
Krieger Henry O, bricklyr, h 23 Warman av (H).
Krieger Henry W, uphlr, h n w cor Beech and Hope (B).
Krieger Himan H, carp, h 125 Kennington.
Krieger Louisa E (wid John H), h 359 E New York.
Krieger Richard, finisher, h 439 W Francis (N I).
Krieger Wm E, clk, b 362 Blake.
Kriel Wm, butcher, b 20 Blackford.
Kriel Wm C, cigars, Grand Hotel, h 898 N Illinois.
Kriese Albert, lab, h 45 Weghorst.
Krinei Lucinda (wid John S), b 48 Athon.
Kring John L, foreman M S Huey & Son, h 425 Bellefontaine.
Kringe Ernest W, bottler, b 32 Sanders.
Kringle Richard P, cabtmkr, b 471 W Francis (N I).
Kritsch, see also Kretsch.
Kritsch Charles F, lab, h 80 Morton.
Kritsch Charles F, uphlr, h 44 Randolph.
Kritsch Frank, lab, [illegible] Chestnut.
Kritsch Frank C, packer, b 698 Chestnut.
Kritsch Frederick W, lab, h 122 Downey.
Kritsch Louis, lab, h 698 Chestnut.
Kritsch Wm, lab, h 1 Oriole.
Kritsch Wm C, chairmkr, h w s Sherman Drive 1 n of Washington.
Kroeckel Frederick, saloon, 590 S Meridian, h same.
Kroeckel Frederick jr, bill poster, h 124 N Delaware.
Kroeger Nellie E (wid Joachim H), h 168½ E Washington.
Kroesing Paul G, tel editor The German Telegraph, h 211 N Pine.
Krokenfels John F, clk C C C & St L Ry, b 150 Dorman.
Krokinsky George, lab, h 94 Maple.
Kroll Amelia E, confr, 468 Indiana av, h same.
Kroll Edward W, driver, b 468 Indiana av.
Kroll John A, wagonmkr, h 468 Indiana av.
Kroll Louis, lab, h 442 W 1st.
Kroll Wm E (Solge & Kroll), b 468 Indiana av.
Krome Adolph, clk, h 216 Buchanan.

THOS. C. DAY & CO.
INVESTING AGENTS,
TOWN AND FARM LOANS,
Rooms 325 to 330 Lemcke Bldg.

Krome August, grocer, n e cor Market and Delaware, h 258 Excelsior av.
Krome Frederick, b 258 Excelsior av.
Krome Frederick, b 256 Bates.
Krome Frederick jr, lab, b 256 Bates.
Kron Harry J, printer, b 86 W Market.
Kronovsek Kancian, shoemkr, 355 S Capitol av, h same.
Kropp, see also Krupp.
Kropp August, tmstr, h 75 Wisconsin.
Kropp Franz W, lab, h 267 Bates.
Kropp Jacob, real est, 12½ N Delaware, h 181 E Morris.
Kropp Wm H, bkkpr Indiana Bicycle Co, h 233 Union.
Krotts Edward D, molder, h 24 Nordyke av (W I).
Kruckemeyer Frederick, lab, h 671 S East.
Krueger, see also Krieger and Kruger.
Krueger August J, mach, b 278 N Pine.
Krueger Charles H, tailor, h 278 N Pine.
Krueger Charles W, finisher, b 17 Iowa.
Krueger Henry C, lab, h 575 Charles.
Krueger Henry F, lab, h 17 Iowa.
Krueger Henry R, tailor, b 278 N Pine.
Krueger Louis H, lab, h 3 Sylvan.
Krueger Minnie, school teacher, b 189 N East.
Krueger Robert C, tailor, b 278 N Pine.
Krug Frank F, clk Robert Keller, h 175 S Olive.
Krug Frederick B, shoemkr, rear 115 Agnes, r same.
Krug Gottlob C, vice-pres Indpls German Mutl Fire Ins Co and Equitable Savings and Loan Assn, b 805 N Alabama.
Krug Hannah (wid George G), laundress, h 419 Mulberry.
Krug Henry E, butcher, h 145 W Michigan.
Krug H Stewart, M D, The H R Allen National Surgical Institute, n w cor Ohio and Capitol av.
Krug Karl, shoemkr, 48 Virginia av, h 30 Frank.
Krug Theodore, lineman, r 145 W Michigan.
Kruger, see also Krieger and Krueger.
Kruger Charles D, com mer, b 1141 N Meridian.

EAT
QUAKER BREAD
ASK YOUR GROCER FOR IT.
THE HITZ BAKING CO.

BICYCLES $5 DOWN. MONTHLY. Best Wheels. Best Terms. WHEELMEN'S CO. 31 W. OHIO ST. LONG DISTANCE TEL. 1855.

J. H. TECKENBROCK Grilles, Fretwork and Wood Carpets 94 EAST SOUTH STREET.

FIDELITY MUTUAL LIFE PHILADELPHIA, PA. A. H. COLLINS { General Agent, 52-53 Baldwin Block.

Edwardsport Coal & Mining Co. Rooms 42 and 43 When Building.

SUPERIOR BITUMINOUS COAL For Steam and Domestic . . Purposes . .

ESTABLISHED 1876. TELEPHONE 168.
CHESTER BRADFORD,
SOLICITOR OF PATENTS,
AND COUNSEL IN PATENT CAUSES.
(See adv. page 6.)
Office:—Rooms 14 and 16 Hubbard Block, S.W. Cor. Washington and Meridian Streets, INDIANAPOLIS, INDIANA.

Kruger Christian C L, police sergeant, h 74 E Wilkins.
Kruger Emma (wid Edward), h 67 Buchanan.
Kruger Ferdinand J, candymkr, h 594 W Udell (N I).
Kruger Frederick, flagman, h 430 S Delaware.
Kruger George C, clk, b 258 S East.
Kruger John H, lab, h 6 Sylvan.
Kruger Joseph E, gas fitter, h 218 Highland av.
Kruger Louis, lab, b 6 Sylvan.
Kruger Mathilde, confr, 99 Madison av, h 430 S Delaware.
Kruger Wm G, brakeman, h 34 Jefferson av.
Krugmann Ida, music teacher, 200 N West, b same.
Krukansky Barnet, pdlr, h 441 S Illinois.
Krull, see also Crull.
Krull Albert H (Krull & Schmidt), treas Indpls German Mutl Fire Ins Co, h 478 Park av.
Krull & Schmidt (Albert H Krull, Charles J Schmidt), whol confrs, 52 S Penn.
KRUMHOLZ LAMBERT, Propr Sanitary Odorless Co, 36 N Delaware, h 177 Union. (See adv in classified Vault and Sink Cleaners.)
Krummel Barbara (wid Philip), b 377 N Senate av.
Krump Charles O, lab, h 1340 E Ohio.
Krumrine George C, checkman, h 328 S New Jersey.
Krumshield Louis P, monuments, 112 E Ohio, h 27 Rhode Island.
Krupp, see also Kropp.
Krupp John, saloon, 341 S Penn, h 339 same.
Kruse, see also Crouse, Cruse and Kraus.
Kruse Charles C, clk, h 122 N Dorman.
Kruse Christian, produce, 86 E Mkt House, res Cumberland, Ind.
Kruse Christian F, h 15 E McCarty.
Kruse Christian G H, carp, h 67 Oriole.
Kruse Henry, watchman, r 1370 E Washington.

HAY & WILLITS MFG CO.
76 N. PENNSYLVANIA ST.,
MAKERS
Outing BICYCLES
PHONE 598.

Kruse Henry F, hostler, b 15 E McCarty.
Kruse Henry W, h 558 S East.
Kruse John H, mach, b 30 Standard av.
Kruse Louis C A, carp, h 10 Hutchings blk.
Kruse Theodore (Kruse & Dewenter), h 321 N Penn.
Kruse Wm C, driver, h 188 S Senate av.
KRUSE & DEWENTER (Theodore Kruse, Herman C Dewenter), Furnace Mnfrs, 223-225 E Washington, Tel. 1670.
Krutsch Charles A (Krutsch & Laycock), h 62 Omer.
Krutsch & Laycock (Charles A Krutsch, Joseph Laycock), architects, 25½ W Washington.
Krutz Margaret M (wid Charles G), h 324 Bellefontaine.
Kryl Bohumir, sculptor, b 82 Vine.
Kryter Charles A, mach, h 487 Virginia av.
Kryter Charles C, trav agt The Bowen-Merrill Co, b 487 Virginia av.
Kuback Wm, lab, b 72 English av.
Kubitz Albert H, mach, b 805 Mass av.
Kubitz Charles, mach, b 322 Cornell av.
Kubitz Gustave, lab, h 259 Yandes.
Kubitz Herman W, lab, h 805 Mass av.
Kubler Harry V, carver, h 104 W Vermont.
Kuchler Balthasar, basketmkr, h 224 E Morris.
Kuchler Michael, cement finisher, b 224 E Morris.
Kuchler Peter, cement layer, b 224 E Morris.
Kuechler Frederick, cigarmkr, b 8 Detroit.
Kuechler Isaac, lab, h 663 S Meridian.
Kuechler Jacob, lab, h 8 Detroit.
Kuechler John, lab, h 424 S West.
Kuechler John, saloon, 514 E Washington, h same.
Kuechler Julius, bkkpr Jacob Bos, b 349 Orange.
Kuechler Louis, insp, h 349 Orange.
Kuehn Charles, molder, h 175 Germania av (H).
Kuehn Henry, molder, h 271 Yandes.
Kuehn Wm L, clk, b 140 Highland pl.
Kuehrman Charles, porter, b 365 Union.
Kuehrmann Martin, packer, h 474 S New Jersey.
Kuerst Albert H, clk, b 182 Madison av.
Kuerst August F, turner, h 51 Beaty.
Kuerst Alvina, dressmkr, 51 Beaty, h same.
Kuerst Edith M, clk, b 51 Beaty.
Kuerst Ella, clk, b 51 Beaty.
Kuerst Henry, carp, h 182 Madison av.
Kuerst Margaret, clk, b 182 Madison av.
Kuerst Wm C, clk Hollweg & Reese, b 182 Madison av.
Kuester Ernest, mach hd, h 63 Buchanan.
Kuetemeier Charles, carp, h 317 E Market.
Kuetemeier Charles W, letter carrier, h 128 Spann av.
Kuetemeier Oscar C, mach, h 1508 N New Jersey.
Kugelman George E, molder, h 90 Bismarck av (H).
Kugelman Henry P, clk, h 160 Fayette
Kugelman Wm, lab, h 605 W Pearl.
Kugiman Margaret E (wid Wm), h 169½ E Washington.
Kuhl Charles, painter The Denison.
Kuhlemann Conrad F W, clk, b 399 S Delaware.
Kuhler Charles, cigarmkr, h 1058 E Michigan.
Kuhler George G, carver, b 223 Hamilton av.

ROOFING MATERIAL C. ZIMMERMAN & SONS, SLATE AND GRAVEL ROOFERS, 19 SOUTH EAST STREET.

DRIVEN WELLS And Second Water Wells and Pumps of all kinds at CHARLES KRAUSS', 42 S. PENN. ST., TEL. 465. REPAIRING NEATLY DONE.

Kuhler Mary (wid Jasper), b 1058 E Michigan.
Kuhler Mary (wid John), h 223 Hamilton av.
Kuhlman, see also Coleman and Culman.
Kuhlman Charles A, grocer, 72 Newman, h same.
Kuhlman Christina (wid Henry), h 250 Union.
Kuhlman Harry A, foreman, h 33 Temple av.
Kuhlman Walter M, mach, h 359 Jefferson av.
Kuhlman Wm C, finisher, h 68 Newman.
Kuhlmann Ernest H, gardener, h 321 Shelby.
Kuhlmann George E, gardener, b 321 Shelby.
Kuhlmann Henry F, millwright, h 50 Sanders.
Kuhn Annetta (wid Wm F), h 378 Broadway.
Kuhn Anton, finisher, b 102 High.
Kuhn August, finisher, h 172 E Washington.
Kuhn August M, pres Consolidated Coal and Lime Co, h 302 N Capitol av.
Kuhn Calvin L, meats, 100 E Mkt House, h n s Washington av 2 e of Line (I).
Kuhn Charles, stage carp, b 27½ College av.
Kuhn Charles A, brewer, h 120 High.
Kuhn Charles C, bkkpr Merchants' Natl Bank, h 78 Highland pl.
Kuhn Charles J, pres Charles J Kuhn Co, b 378 Broadway.
KUHN CHARLES J CO, Charles J Kuhn Pres, Gustave A Pfeiffer Sec and Treas, Grocers, 49 N Illinois, Tel 602.
Kuhn Francois X, lab, b 102 High.
Kuhn Frederick, blksmith, h 282 Yandes.
Kuhn Fredericka (wid Charles J), h 213 W Michigan.
Kuhn George F, bkkpr, b 84 Benton.
Kuhn Giulielma (wid Solomon), b n e cor Washington av and Line (I).
Kuhn John, lab, b 27½ College av.
Kuhn John, saw tester, h 155 Orange.
Kuhn John A, bkkpr, b 213 W Michigan.
Kuhn Morris, b 141 Mass av.
Kuhn Nanatta (wid Wm F), h 378 Broadway.
Kuhn Ora, lab, b n s Washington av 2 e of Line (I).
Kuhn Philip, blksmith, h 27½ College av.
Kuhn Philip, finisher, h 25 Arch.
Kuhn Wm, lab, h 28 Keystone av.
Kuhn Wm F, butcher, b 207 W Michigan.
Kuhn Wm F, pres L W Ott Mnfg Co, h 302 Broadway.
Kuhner Charles, finisher, h 173 Benton.
Kuhner Engelbert, car rep, h 333 Davidson.
Kuhns Benjamin F, produce, 78 E Mkt House, h e s Brightwood av 3 n of Schofield (B).
Kuhns Carey M, bkkpr S A Fletcher & Co, h 318 Coburn.
Kuhns Edward, mach, b 84 Prospect.
Kuhns Edward E, painter, h 554 Broadway.
Kuhrman Charles, lab, h 13 Iowa.
Kuhrmann Martin, porter, h 474 S New Jersey.
Kuhrmann Otto A, caller, b 474 S New Jersey.
Kull August F, car insp, h 200 Walcott.
Kull Charles, tinner, h 10 Detroit.
Kull Frank J, boilermkr, b 200 Walcott.
Kull John C, tinner, h 200 Walcott.
Kulp Robert C, gasfitter, h 283 Mass av.
Kulpe Emil, painter, h 23 Barth av.

Richardson & McCrea, REPRESENTING BEST KNOWN FIRE INSURANCE COMPANIES. Fidelity and Casualty Insurance Company of New York Represented. Telephone 182. 79 East Market St.

Kulpe Emil F, tailor, h 48 Pleasant.
Kumler Clarence D, trav agt, h 932 N Meridian.
Kumler Noah W, trav agt Daniel Stewart Co, h 932 N Meridian.
Kunert Henry, lab, h 125 Downey.
Kunkel Charles, lab, r 249½ W Washington.
Kunkel Charles, waiter, b 492 S East.
Kunkel Elizabeth (wid Bernard), h 890 S Meridian.
Kunkel George F, waiter, b 492 S East.
Kunkel Helena, printer, b 890 S Meridian.
Kunkel Henry, motorman, h 492 S East.
Kunkel Henry M, uphlr, b 890 S Meridian.
Kunkel Jacob, beltmkr, h 236 S Linden.
Kunkel John, carp, r 26 S Missouri.
Kunkel Magdalena (wid Michael), b 57 Newman.
Kunkel Mary (wid Carl), h 172 E Morris.
Kunkel Wm H, finisher, h 156 Brookside av.
KUNKEL WM M, Dentist, 52 Clifford av, b 156 Brookside av.
Kunkle Bernard, lather, h 12 W Chesapeake.
Kunkle Joseph, carp, b 52 Warren av (W I).
Kunkle Wm, r 154 W Washington.
Kunn John, lab, h 827 S Meridian.
Kuntz Henry, brewer, h 125 Weghorst.
Kuntz John, bartndr, b 219 E Washington.
Kuntz John, lab, h 274 W Pearl.
Kuntz Martin C, meats, 610 N Senate av, h 609 same.
Kunz Adam, hostler, h 218 Coburn.
Kunz Emelie (wid Jacob), b 27 Lord.
Kunz Helena, music teacher, 339 E McCarty, b same.
Kunz John G Rev, h 339 E McCarty.
Kunz Joseph F, tailor, 489 S Meridian, h same.
Kunzler Frederick, lab, b 410 S Meridian.
Kuppler Martin J, baker, b 36 Bicking.
Kurfiss John F, bkkpr The Capital National Bank, r 74 W Vermont.
Kurman Will A, bkkpr Jacob Metzger & Co, b 32 Laurel.
Kurman Wm H, clk The Indpls Stove Co, h 32 Laurel.

The Williams Typewriter Elegant Work, Visible Writing, Easy Operation, High Speed. S. H. EAST, State Agent, 55 Thorpe Block, 87 E. Market St.

If You are not Satisfied with Your Laundry Work Give Us a Trial. ERTEL STEAM LAUNDRY 26 and 28 N. Sen Avenue. Telephone 19.

ELLIS & HELFENBERGER Manufacturers of IRON and WIRE FENCES 162-170 S. SENATE AVE. TEL. 358.

THE HOGAN TRANSFER AND STORAGE COMP'Y
Household Goods and Pianos Moved—Packed—Stored...... Baggage and Package Express Machinery and Safes a Specialty Cor. Washington and Illinois Sts. TELEPHONE No. 675.

Hose, Belting, Packing, Clothing, Druggists' Sundries, Bicycle Tires, Cotton Hose, Etc. New York Belting & Packing Co., L't'd.
The Central Rubber & Supply Co. PHONE 8. 79 S. ILLINOIS ST., INDIANAPOLIS, IND.

HIGHEST SECURITY
LOWEST COST OF INSURANCE.
The Provident Life and Trust Co.
Of Philadelphia.
D. W. EDWARDS, Gen. Agent,
508 Indiana Trust Building.

Kurrasch Herman, lab, h 39 Parker.
Kurth Paul, harnessmkr, h 51 Thomas.
Kurth Wm H, clk Am Ex Co, h 309 E St Clair.
Kurts Hilpat (Kurts & Kenton), h 143 Locke.
Kurts & Kenton (Hilpat Kurts, James Kenton), blksmiths, 442 Douglass.
Kurtz Charles A, solr, h 223 Davidson.
Kurtz Charles C, fireman, h 97 N Beville av.
Kurtz Charles H, ship clk Central Cycle Mnfg Co, b 233 E Michigan.
Kurtz Frank A, lab, h 56 Martha (W I).
Kurtz Frank G, bartndr, b 230 S Penn.
Kurtz Henry, bartndr, h 233 S Delaware.
Kurtz Jacob D, patrolman, h 405 W New York.
Kurtz John A, pres Vanguard Cycle Co and mnfrs' agt, 143½ S Meridian, h 671 College av.
Kurtz John F, bailiff police court, h 28 Agnes.
Kurtz John G, shoemkr, 47 Kentucky av, h 43 same.
Kurtz Lew K, asst cashr Penna Lines, b 233 E Michigan.
Kurtz Luther, lab, h 272 W 7th.
Kurtz Sydney G, stenog, b 183 E Ohio.
Kurtz Wm E, pres Indpls Warehouse Co, sec Gould Steel Co, sec and treas The Gordon-Kurtz Co, h 613 N Illinois.
Kurtze Charles A, trav agt Indiana Farmer Co, h 78 N Noble.
Kurtze Sophia J (wid Charles A), b 78 N Noble.
Kurz Frederick, mach, h 315 Coburn.
Kurz Frederick C, opr W U Tel Co, h 370 E Morris.
Kussman John, foreman Kingan & Co, h 42 Jones.
Kuster Wm F, bkkpr, h 222 N Pine.
Kutsch John A, harnessmkr, 263 Mass av, h 264½ same.
Kutsch Loise M, stenog Wm H Hobbs, b 123 Hoyt av.
Kutzner August J, h 264 Bates.
Kutzner Augusta (wid Robert), b 261 Bates.

Julius C. Walk & Son,
Jewelers
Indianapolis.
12 EAST WASHINGTON ST.

Kutzner Frederick, bartndr, h 247½ S Capitol av.
Kutzner Robert H, lab, h 261 Bates.
Kuykendall John H, janitor Parry Mnfg Co, b 13 Ellsworth.
Kydna George F, fireman, h 138 Mass av.
Kydna Rose, boarding 138 Mass av.
Kyle, see also Keil and Kiel.
Kyle Daniel, lab, h 480 N California.
Kyle James, mach, h 67 Nordyke av (W I).
Kyle Lawrence M, mach hd, b 164 Clinton.
Kyle Mary (wid Isaac M), b 164 Clinton.
Kyle Mary E (wid John W), h 50 W Raymond.
Kyle Wm, lab, b 249 W South.
Kyte James L, b 207 W Ohio.

L

Laakmann Frederick (Laakmann & Sherer), h 280 W St Clair.
Laakmann & Sherer (Frederick Laakmann, Edward Sherer), cement paving, Builders' Exchange.
Laatz, see also Lotz.
Laatz Henry, grocer, 94 Dougherty, h same.
Laatz Jacob, foreman Green & Co, b 94 Dougherty.
Lababera Salvatore, fruits, b 268 S East.
Labadie Louis P, blueing mnfr, 1 Cress, h same.
LaBarth Charles, h 250 Fayette.
LaBelle Harry W, clk, h 27½ Clifford av.
LaBoyteaux Carl, clk, b 141 Prospect.
LaBoyteaux Thomas, condr, b 310 E Wabash.
Lace Albert F, lab, b 70 Germania av (H).
Lacey, see also Lacy.
Lacey Alfred, lab, h rear 7 Elizabeth.
Lacey Frank M, photog, 126 Mass av, r 29½ W Ohio.
Lacey George H, supt Indpls Terra Cotta Co, h 311 Park av.
Lacey George J, papermkr, b 38 Nordyke av (W I).
Lacey Grant, steelwkr, b 46 S Capitol av.
Lacey Henry, pdlr, r 186½ W Washington.
Lacey Lorenzo B, printer, h 302 N Delaware.
Lacey Lucy (wid Jacob), b 258 Alvord.
Lacey Nancy A (wid Addison), h 423 S Olive.
Lacey Wm civil engr, r 70 W Vermont.
Lachmann Anthony, cutter, h 564½ Virginia av.
Lachmann Lachmann, pdlr, h 436 S Capitol av.
Lachmann Marcus, pdlr, b 436 S Capitol av.
LACKAWANNA FAST FREIGHT LINE, Wm D Wilson Agt, 71 W Maryland, Tel 756.
Lackey, see also Leckey.
Lackey Charles A, asst Irvin & Adams, r 18 Stewart pl.
Lackey Enoch, sprinkler, b 108 Randolph.
Lackey Enos, farmer, b 555 Highland av (N I).
Lackey Frank E, street contr, 15 Elliott, h same.
Lackey James E, dispatching clk P O, h 53 Catherine.
Lackey Joseph, tmstr, h 60 Martindale av.
Lackey Lilly M (wid Charles), b 18 S Linden.
Lackey Mary (wid Green), h 84 Yandes.
Lackey Richard, h 108 Randolph.
Lacy, see also Lacey.

OTTO GAS ENGINES | BUILDERS' EXCHANGE S. W. Cor. Ohio and Penn. Telephone 535.

Lake Erie & Western R. R. Co.

Ft. Wayne, Cincinnati & Louisville R. R.
Northern Ohio Railway Co.

NATURAL GAS ROUTE

THE POPULAR SHORT LINE

..........BETWEEN..........

Peoria, Bloomington, Chicago, St. Louis, Springfield, Lafayette, Frankfort, Muncie, Portland, Lima, Findlay, Fostoria, Fremont, Sandusky, Akron, Indianapolis, Kokomo, Peru, Rochester, Plymouth, LaPorte, Michigan City, Ft. Wayne, Hartford, Bluffton, Connersville and Cincinnati, making direct connections for all points

EAST, WEST, NORTH & SOUTH.

THE ONLY LINE TRAVERSING THE

GREAT NATURAL GAS and OIL FIELDS

Of Ohio and Indiana, giving the patrons of this POPULAR ROUTE an opportunity to witness the grand sight from the train as they pass through. Great fields covered with tanks, in which are stored millions of gallons of Oil, NATURAL GAS wells shooting their flames high in the air, and the most beautiful cities, fairly alive with Glass and all kinds of factories.

We furnish our patrons with Elegant Reclining Chair Cars FREE on day trains, and L. E. & W. Palace Sleeping and Parlor Cars on night trains, at very reasonable rates.

Direct connections to and from Cleveland, Buffalo, New York, Boston, Philadelphia, Baltimore, Pittsburg, Washington, Kansas City, Denver, Omaha, Portland and San Francisco, and all points in the United States and Canada.

This is the popular route with the ladies on account of its courteous and accommodating train officials, and with the commercial traveler and general public for its comforts, quick time and sure connections. For any further particulars call on or address any ticket agent.

GEO. L. BRADBURY, Vice-President and General Manager.
CHAS. F. DALY, General Passenger and Ticket Agent.
INDIANAPOLIS, INDIANA.

Becker & Son Charles Becker Jacob Becker Jr. Merchant Tailors. 21 N. Penn. St. Tel. 934

SALISBURY & STANLEY OFFICE, STORE AND BANK FIXTURES.

Lacy Charles, live stock, h 180 Oliver av (W I).
Lacy Everett F, plastr, r 257 Mass av.
Lacy Fannie (wid Thomas), b e s Sangster av 5 n of Belle.
Lacy Frank D, plastr, r 257 Mass av
Lacy Lindsey, waiter, b 272 Fulton.
Lacy Lou J, dressmkr, 195 W Vermont, b same.
LaDana Burtis, switchman, h 213 N Noble.
Ladarack Mary (wid Frederick), h 39 Oliver av (W I).
Lafferty Frederick, clk The Wm H Block Co, b 181 N Delaware.
Laffey John, lab, b 299 W Maryland.
Laffey Miles, molder, h 92 N Belmont av (H).
Laffey Thomas, lab, h 95 Agnes.
Laffey Wm, lab, b 300 W Maryland.
Lafflin Edward, mach hd, h 191 Hillside av.
Lafkin John H, barber, h 210 E Morris.
Laflan Missouri C (wid Wm P), h 119 W 5th.
LaFleur Charles V, barber, h 143 Fayette.
Laflin George, lab, b 188 Elizabeth.
Laflin Lester L, driver, h 156 Pleasant.
Laflin Torsa C, barber, h 327 E New York.
La Follette Ellen (wid James T), dressmkr, h 56 Johnson av.
La Follette Harry C, editor Indiana Journal of Commerce, 12½ N Delaware, b 203 N Penn.
La Follette Solomon, well driver, h 14 N Noble.
La Fontaine Charles E, mach, b 199½ Mass av.
La Fontaine George, mach, h 34 Leon.
La Force David E, clk, b 145 Spann av.
La Forge Edward D, varnisher, h 525 S Illinois.
La Forge George B, painter, h 219 Union.
La Forge Mary E, h 226 E McCarty.
La Fuze Samuel D, lawyer, 68 Lombard bldg, h 57 Pleasant.
Lagler Charles J, grinder, h 248 Bates.
Lahey Anna (wid Michael), h 89 McGinnis.
Lahey Edward, trav agt, r 5, 113 S Illinois.
Lahey Michael F, clk Assessment Bureau, h 497 E Georgia.
Lahey Thomas, lab, b 493 E Georgia.
Lahey Thomas, lab, b 673 W Vermont.
Lahey Timothy, h 493 E Georgia.
Lahey Timothy, lab, b 89 McGinnis.
Lahey Timothy jr, lab, b 493 E Georgia.
Lahman August, grocer 505 N West, h same.
Lahman Corinne B (wid Roscoe D), h 153 Park av.
Lahmann Edward, driver, b 533 S Illinois.
Lahmann Frank W F, driver, h 150 Nordyke av (W I).
Lahmann Frederick H, cigarmkr, h 394 Coburn.
Lahmann George, painter, b 533 S Illinois.
Lahmann Henry E, clk, b 533 S Illinois.
Lahmann John W, lab, h 2 Race.
Lahmann Wm, h 533 S Illinois.
Lahr Frank J (Noel & Lahr), b 197 N Illinois.
Lail George H, real est, 38 When bldg, h 876 Cornell av.
Lail George S, chain tester, b 876 Cornell av.
Lail James M, engr, h 567 W Eugene (N I).
Lail James M, icemkr, h 557 W Eugene (N I).
Lail Wm S, clk, b 876 Cornell av.
Laing David V, trav agt, b 84 Prospect.

Henry H. Fay,
40½ E. WASHINGTON ST.,
AGENT FOR
Insurance Co. of North America,
Pennsylvania Fire Ins. Co.

LAING SAMUEL, Tinner and Sheet Metal Worker, 72-74 E Court, h 281 S Missouri, Tel 1428. (See left side lines.)
Laird Charles P, solr Rehm & Van Deinse, h 262 Indiana av.
Laird George, painter, h 517 E Georgia.
Laird James H, salesman Murphy, Hibben & Co, h 437 Bellefontaine.
Laird John, janitor, h e s Sherman Drive 3 n of Ohio.
Laird Mary M (wid James H), h 333 S Alabama.
Laird Wm H, h 554 N Illinois.
Laird Wm H jr, bkkpr A Kiefer Drug Co, b 554 N Illinois.
Laitner Louis, brushmkr, 27 Cleveland (H), h same.
Lake Ansel J, mach, b 121 Cherry.
Lake Charles N, paints, 208 S Meridian, h 36 N Olive.
Lake Emma, b 190½ S Illinois.
LAKE ERIE & WESTERN RAILROAD, George L Bradbury Vice-Pres and Genl Mngr, Samuel B Sweet Genl Freight Agt, Charles F Daly Genl Pass Agt, David S Hill Genl Supt, H F Bickell Asst Genl Supt, Thomas H Perry Purchasing Agt and Chief Engineer, Wm A Wildhack Auditor, Albert D Thomas Asst Treas, Wm E Hackedorn Genl Solicitor, John B Cockrum Genl Attorney; Local Freight Office 53 S Alabama, Marvin R Maxwell Local Freight Agt, Tel 155; Genl Offices s w cor Noble and Washington, Tels 838 and 1472. (See opp inside back cover.)
LAKE ERIE & WESTERN RAILROAD, Albert H Sellars City Pass and Ticket Agt, 26 S Illinois, Tel 1091.
Lake Hannah A (wid Ellis R), h 565 S Meridian.
Lake Harriet (wid Daniel), b 61 S Belmont av (W I).
Lake Isaac N, buyer Adams & Williamson, h 133 Meek.

MAYHEW'S SPECTACLES THE BEST IN USE SOLD ONLY AT 13 N. MERIDIAN ST.

Co and Builders. Repairing of all kinds done on short 177 Clinton St. Indianapolis, Ind. Telephone 99

LUMBER Sash and Doors | BALKE & KRAUSS CO., Corner Market and Missouri Sts.

Friedgen Has the BEST PATENT LEATHER SHOES AT LOWEST PRICES. 19 North Pennsylvania St.

SAMUEL LAING ! HOT AIR FURNACES 72 AND 74 EAST COURT STREET.

M. B. WILSON, Pres. W. F. CHURCHMAN, Cash.
The Capital National Bank,
INDIANAPOLIS, IND.
Banking business in all its branches. Bonds and Foreign Exchange bought and sold. Interest paid on time deposits. Checks and drafts on all Indiana and Illinois points handled at lowest rates.
No. 28 South Meridian Street, Cor. Pearl.

Lake Joseph, plumber, b 79 N Alabama.
Lake Joseph P, supt, h 121 Cherry.
Lake Martha (wid John), h 630 S Meridian.
Lake M Elizabeth, phys, 276 N Alabama, h same.
Lake Richard, detective American Detective Agency, r 96½ E Market.
Lake Shore, Lehigh Valley Route, Wm H Boyd agt, n e cor Delaware and South.
Lake Wm M, h 341 Blake.
Laker Henry, lab, h n w cor Harriet and Bloyd av (B).
Laker John, sawyer, b 24 Brookside av.
Laker Mae, clk Artificial Ice and Cold Storage Co, r 94 N Senate av.
Laker Mary, h 331 W 1st.
Lakin Edward J, carp, 75 Lily, h same.
Lakin James S, bkkpr, h 437 College av.
Lakin John H, driver, h 7 Bell.
Lakin J Harry, carp, b 75 Lily.
LALLEY BROS (Frank T and Wm D), Merchant Tailors, 5 N Meridian.
Lalley Catherine (wid Thomas), h 229 W South.
Lalley Charles H, b 229 W South
Lalley Frank T (Lalley Bros), b 229 W South.
Lalley John A, tailor, 437 Virginia av, h 364 E McCarty.
Lalley Luella C, teacher Public School No 4, b 73 W 2d.
Lalley Wm D (Lalley Bros), b 73 W 2d.
Lally Patrick D, car rep, h 251 S Missouri.
Lamar Morton E, carp, b 31 Bismarck.
Lamaster Wm H, lumber, h 88½ Ft Wayne av.
Lamay John, teacher High School, r 282 N Penn.
Lamb Agnes H, cashr Robert Keller, b 268 Bates.
Lamb Clara M, milliner Keller & Gamerdinger, b 268 Bates.
Lamb Everett R, well driver, h 1767 N Capitol av.
Lamb George, engr, h 57 Fletcher av.
Lamb Harry, helper, b 17 Eureka av.
Lamb Henry H, trav agt, h 787 N Delaware.
Lamb James, lab, h 435 National rd.

Insure Against Accidents
WITH
TUTTLE & SEGUIN,
Agents for
Fidelity and Casualty Co., of New York.
$10,000 for $25. $5,000 for $12.50.
TEL. 1168. 28 E. MARKET ST.

Lamb James F, clk Indpls Dist Tel Co, b 17 Eureka av.
Lamb James H, lab, h 268 Bates.
Lamb Job, lab, h 532 W Wells (N I).
Lamb Manley J, carp, h 13 Belmont av (H).
Lamb Robert N (Lamb & Hill), pres Consumers' Gas Trust Co, h 209 Central av.
Lamb Thomas F, lab, h 14 Brett.
Lamb Wm C, lawyer, h 219 E South.
Lamb Wm E, bkkpr, h w s Hanna 3 n of E Michigan.
Lamb Wm P, clk C C C & St L Ry, b 57 Fletcher av.
LAMB & HILL (Robert N Lamb, Ralph Hill), Lawyers, 507-513 Indiana Trust Bldg, Tel 174.
Lamberger Michael, lab, h 34 Osgood (W I).
Lamberson Ella, b 575 Park av.
Lamberson Frank O (Lamberson & Hackleman), b 575 Park av.
LAMBERSON & HACKLEMAN (Frank O Lamberson, Charles W Hackleman), Proprs Forest Avenue Pharmacy, Forest and 20th (old).
Lambert Cass, carp, h 404 S Olive.
Lambert Charles, carp, r 169 W Market.
Lambert Charles W, drugs, 448 W Michigan, h same.
Lambert David M, farmer, h n s Beechwood av 3 e of Central av (I).
LAMBERT GAS AND GASOLINE ENGINE CO, Genl Offices Anderson, Ind. (See right top lines.)
Lambert James E, wireman Sanborn Electric Co, h 117 Fayette.
Lambert James R, clk, h 1132 E Washington.
LAMBERT JOHN A, Physician, 146 E 7th, h 911 N Delaware, Tel 606.
Lambert John S, ins agt, 11 When bldg, b The Denison.
Lambert Lucretia, h 4 W Chesapeake.
Lambert Luther F, barber, b 197 W Vermont.
Lambert Mary, dressmkr, b 102 Hill av.
Lambert Minerva, drugs, 1132 E Washington, h same.
Lambert Thomas, molder, h 3 Walker (H).
Lambert Wm, bill poster, b 4 W Chesapeake.
Lambert Wm P, lab, h 8 Willard.
Lambur Anna J (wid Charles), h 1996 N Meridian.
Lamdon Susannah (wid John), h 23 Blake.
Lame Charles, lab, h 50 Bluff rd.
Lame John, policeman Union Station, h 945 Ash.
Lamkin James, molder, b 106 Oliver av (W I).
Lamkin James W, porter, h 115 Oliver av (W I).
Lamm Edgar R, woodwkr, h 209 Ramsey av.
Lamm Ozro, painter, h 1082 W Vermont.
Lamme Albert, fireman, r 219 Fletcher av.
Lamme Burton, engr, b 270 Fletcher av.
Lamme Susan H (wid Henry), b 33 N Spruce.
Lammert Frederick, carp, h 96 Stoughton av.
Lammert Henry F, cabtmkr, b 12 Jupiter.
Lammert Louise (wid Henry), h 12 Jupiter.
Lamont Wm, barber, r 230 W 2d.
Lamotte Elizabeth (wid Charles F), b 227 S East.

WEDDING CAKE BOXES · SULLIVAN & MAHAN 41 W. Pearl St.

DIAMOND WALL PLASTER { Telephone 1410 BUILDERS' EXCHANGE.

Best Work. Prompt Delivery. } THE HOME LAUNDRY 197 S. ILLINOIS ST. TEL. 1 { Collars and Cuffs our Specialty.

Lamoureux Camille W, plater, h 426 S Capitol av.
Lamoureu Napoleon, polisher, h 9 Carlos.
Lampert Wm, armature winder, h 113 Tremont av (H).
Lamphier Frederick F, bkkpr, b 122 N Noble.
Lamphier Jared, engr, h 122 N Noble.
LAMSON CONSOLIDATED STORE SERVICE CO, Fred R Taisey Dept Agt, Cash and Parcel Carrying Devices, 31½ Virginia av. (See adv under classified Cash Carriers.)
Lanahan Daniel J, saloon, 44 S West, h 241 N West.
Lanahan Henry, lab, h 43 Birch av (W I).
Lanahan Jeremiah, mach, b 15 Benton.
Lanahan Mary, dressmkr, 15 Benton, h same.
Lanahan Thomas, lab, h 15 Benton.
Lancaster Charles, lab, h 23 Cooper.
Lancaster Charles D, dairy, s s E Washington 4 e of Belt R R, h same.
Lancaster Christopher C, driver, h 272 Mass av.
Lancaster David R, patrolman, b 18 Ludlow av.
Lancaster Francis H, lab, h 18 Ludlow av.
Lancaster George W, h s w cor Meridian and 30th.
Lancaster H Vorhis, polisher, h 68 Meek.
Lancaster John T, lab, h 174 Yandes.
Lancaster Robert H (Lancaster & Orlopp), h 123 E Walnut.
Lancaster & Orlopp (Robert H Lancaster, Bertram G Orlopp), horseshoers, 106 S Delaware.
Lance George W, condr, h 173 Broadway.
Lance Jackson L, clk, b Hotel English.
Lance Lee, lab, h 42 Northwestern av.
Land Alexander B, lab, h 32 Cleveland (H).
Land Ertley, lab, b 32 Cleveland (H).
Land George W, molder, h 70 Sheffield av (H).
Land John, agt, b 235 W South.
Land Lulu B (wid Miller R), dressmkr, r 91 N Delaware.
Land Rebecca (wid Levi), b 144 Walker (H).
Land Robert H, molder, h 144 Walker (H).
Land Robert M, barber, h 91½ N Delaware.
Lander Francis C, student, b 110 Broadway.
Lander Frederick A, chief clk Order of Equity, b 39 Morrison.
LANDER WM F, Supreme Sec Order of Equity, Room 7, 30 Monument Pl, Tel 774; h 110 Broadway.
Landers Bartholomew F, boilermkr, b 22 Davis.
Landers Catherine, b 458 S West.
Landers Dwight C, farmer, b 402 N Penn.
Landers Edward, stoker, b 211½ E Washington.
Landlers Franklin, farmer, h 402 N Penn.
Landers Henry J, lab, h 294½ Mass av.
Landers Hicklin J (Landers & Donnelly), b 379 N Penn.
Landers Honora (wid John), b 35 Foundry (B).
Landers Jackson, vice-pres U S Encaustic Tile Wks, h 622 N Penn.
Landers James, trainmaster, h 774 E Washington.
Landers James A, pres and mngr Indpls Mnfg Co, h 321 Union.
Landers John, farmer, h 379 N Penn.
Landers John, watchman, h 340 S Illinois.

FRANK NESSLER. WILL H. ROST.
FRANK NESSLER & CO.
Tailors
56 EAST MARKET ST. (Lemcke Building),
INDIANAPOLIS, IND.

Landers Mamie C, stenog I & V R R, b 774 E Washington.
Landers Margaret, b 458 S West.
Landers Nellie C (Union Co-operative Laundry), h 458 S West.
Landers Philip, stoker, b 181 S New Jersey.
Landers Pierce J, civil engr I & V R R, Union Station, b 774 E Washington.
Landers Robert H, paperhngr, b 164½ E Washington.
Landers Thomas, h 22 Davis.
Landers Thomas J, printer, b 340 S Illinois.
Landers Timothy, tel opr, b 340 S Illinois.
Landers Wm, coachman 958 N Meridian.
Landers Wm C, lab, b 340 S Illinois.
Landers Wm F, supt U S Encaustic Tile Works, b 622 N Penn.
Landers Zachary T, engr, h 485 S Delaware.
Landers & Donnelly (Hicklin J Landers, Maurice Donnelly), hardwood lumber 148 S West.
Landerville Henry, stonecutter, r 141 W Washington.
Landers Harry K, motorman, h 793 N Capitol av.
Landes Wm F, supervising prin Center Township Schools, h 536 W Udell (N I).
Landfair Melvin, lab, h 96 Nebraska.
Landgraf George W, cutter Kahn Tailoring Co, h 86 Highland pl.
LANDGRAF NORBERT, Merchant Tailor, The Denison Blk, 83 N Penn, h Pressley Flats, 175 N Penn.
Landis Daniel, switchtndr, h 55 Bellefontaine.
Landis Harry C, foreman, b 870 N Alabama.
Landis Hiram F, ins agt, 135 Virginia av, h 274 S Olive.
Landis John F, driver, h 71 Meek.
Landis John J, correspondent Indiana Bicycle Co, h 67 Fletcher av.
Landis Virginia M (wid Milton M), h 870 N Alabama.
Landis Wm H, pressman, b 55 Bellefontaine.
Landmeier Henry, lab, h 933 Madison av.
Landmeier Henry W, drayman, h 225 Prospect.

Haueisen & Hartmann
163-169 E. Washington St.
FURNITURE,
Carpets,
Household Goods,
Tin, Granite and China Wares, Oil Cloth and Shades

THE WM. H. BLOCK CO. 7 AND 9 EAST WASHINGTON STREET. DRY GOODS, HOUSE FURNISHINGS AND CROCKERY.

London Guarantee and Accident Co. (Ltd.) All forms of Liability Insurance, Workmen's Collective Insurance, Fidelity Bonds and Individual Accident Insurance.
Geo. W. Pangborn, Gen. Agent, 704-706 Lemcke Bldg. Telephone 140.

Prussian National Insurance Comp'y of Stettin, Germany. Organized 1845. FRANK K. SAWYER, AGENT 74 East Market Street. Telephone 863.

JOSEPH GARDNER,
TIN, COPPER AND SHEET-IRON WORK AND
HOT AIR FURNACES.
37, 39 & 41 KENTUCKY AVE. Telephone 322.

Landmeier Wm H, h 774 Chestnut.
Lando Leo, optician, 93 N Penn, h 948 N Senate av.
Landon Hugh McK, sec Mnfrs' Natural Gas Co, b 677 N Alabama.
Landry Sylvester, h 285 S Illinois.
Landwehr Gustave A, barber, 403 S Meridian, r 16 Union.
Landwerlen Louis, beltmkr, h 445 Union.
Lane Arthur, polisher, b 56 Sheffield (W I).
Lane Charles, lab, b 206 St Mary.
Lane Charles, mach, b 342 S Meridian.
Lane Charles J, clk, h 302 Clifford av.
Lane Charles R, reporter The Indpls News, h 691 N Capitol av.
Lane Dora G, mach hd, h 430 S Olive.
Lane Eleanor R (wid Henry P), h 48 Cornell av.
Lane Frank D, clk, b 48 Cornell av.
Lane Frederick W, driver, b 50 Bicking.
Lane George L, stable boss, h 299 Cornell av.
Lane Harry, clk, r 410 N Penn.
Lane Harry D, auditor Belt R R and Stock Yards Co, h 26 W Pratt.
Lane Harry T, clk N Y Store, b 302 Clifford av.
Lane Henry J (Taylor & Lane), h cor Sheffield av and Clark (H).
Lane Henry S, condr, h 107 Wright.
Lane James L, trav agt, r 125 E New York.
Lane John, lab, b 125 E Washington.
Lane John A, clk city div P O, h 378 N East.
Lane John W, trimmer, h 627 S East
Lane Joseph, lab, h 339 Columbia av.
Lane Margaret, clk, b 97 S Noble.
Lane Martha J (wid Milroy), h 26 W Pratt.
Lane Michael, lab, b 359 S Illinois.
Lane Myron L, finisher, h 752 N Illinois.
Lane Nancy (wid Josiah), r 139 N Penn.
Lane Oliver P, lab, b 107 Wright.
Lane Patrick D, clk, h 219 N Capitol av.
Lane Richard T, polisher, h 56 Sheffield (W I).
Lane Sarah, h 247½ S Capitol av.
Lane Wm B, letter file mnfr, 160 Bane, h 135 Highland av.
Lane Wm E, condr, h 517 W 22d (N I).
Laney Charles, lab, r 206 St Mary.

J. S. FARRELL & CO.
STEAM AND HOT WATER
HEATING FOR STORES, OFFICES,
PUBLIC BUILDINGS,
PRIVATE RESIDENCES,
GREENHOUSES, ETC.
84 North Illinois St. Telephone 382.

Laney James F, lab, h 308 Yandes.
Lang, see also Lange and Long.
Lang Abraham, ins, b 950 N Penn.
Lang Albert, lab, h 76 Kennington.
Lang Charles, foreman, h 1149 E Washington.
Lang Charles W, car rep, b 191 N East.
Lang Charlotta (wid John), h 137 Downey.
Lang Daniel, pdlr, b 424 S Meridian.
Lang Emile, agt The Brunswick-Balke-Collender Co, 138 S Illinois, h 786 N Illinois.
Lang Frank C, switchman, h w s Sherman Drive 4 s of Brookville rd (S).
Lang Frederick P, mach, h 795 S East.
Lang George, brewer, h 475 S East.
Lang George, molder, h 30 Morton.
Lang George, waiter The Bates.
Lang George jr, tankman, b 475 S East.
Lang George P, barber, 447 E Washington, h same.
Lang Grace (wid Daniel), b 1538 N Illinois.
Lang Grace, b 503 S Meridian.
Lang Helen R, prin Public School No 39, b 874 N Delaware.
Lang Herman, restaurant, 240 W Washington and 107 S Illinois and livery 170 E Court, r 194 E Washington.
Lang John A, real est, h 691 S Meridian.
Lang Samuel, billiard hall, 140 S Illinois, b 786 N Illinois.
Lang Thomas, packer, b 227 E South.
Langbein Amelia (wid Joseph), h 511 College av.
Langbein Mary (wid Charles E), dressmkr, 511 College av, h same.
Langbein Theodore, draughtsman R P Daggett & Co, h 132 Cornell av.
Langdon Charles A, lab, h 180 Keystone av.
Langdon Eugene, driver, r 212 N Senate av.
Langdon Harry C, bkkpr Indiana Bicycle Co, b 1028 N Alabama.
Langdon Harry K, student, r 1 Ft Wayne av.
Langdon John H, surveyor Indpls Water Co, h 386 College av.
Langdon John J, clk Belt R R and Stock Yards Co, h 1028 N Alabama.
Langdon John P, b 386 College av.
Langdon Lewis A, trav agt, b 386 College av.
Lange Alexander J, mach, b 472 Union.
Lange Edward F (Bisig & Lange), h e s Sherman Drive 1 s of Brookville rd (S).
Lange Frank, blksmith, h 620 S West.
Lange Frank, clk, b 104 Bismarck av (H).
Lange Frank A, dentist, 155 Mass av, h 274 N New Jersey.
Lange Gustav C (Lange & Son), h 1044 S Meridian.
Lange Henrietta (wid Frederick), h e s Rural 1 n of Michigan.
Lange Henry, lab, h 126 N Gillard av.
Lange Leonard (Lange & Son), h 104 Bismarck av (H).
Lange Leonard jr (Lange & Son), b 104 Bismack av (H).
Lange Louis L, painter, 472 Union, h same.
Lange Otto T (Lange & Son), b 1044 S Meridian.
Lange Theresa (wid Albert), milliner, 187 Mass av, h same.
Lange Wm H, car rep, h 134 Temple av.
Lange & Son (Gustav C and Otto T), florists, 1044 S Meridian.
Lange & Son (Leonard and Leonard jr), grocers, 104 Bismarck av (H).
Langenbacher Engelbert, engraver H C Bauer Engraving Co, b 3 Wilson.

United States Life Insurance Co., of New York.
E. B. SWIFT, M'g'r. 25 E. Market St.

WM. KOTTEMAN } 89 & 91 E. Washington St. Telephone 1742 { RUGS MATTINGS WINDOW SHADES

WILLIAM WIEGEL { MANUFACTURER OF..... } SHOW CASES { 6 W. Louisiana St. Opposite Union Station.

Langenbacher Mary L (wid John N), h 3 Wilson.
Langenberg Henry W, saloon, 22 N Delaware, h 175 Walcott.
Langer Charles, shoemkr, 268 Bates, h 31 Hendricks.
Langere Herman, carp, 50 Barth av.
Langhorne Barbara A, stenog Eli Lilly & Co, b 184 E South.
Langhorne Barbara E (wid Albertus T), h 184 E South.
Langhorne Lucile A, trimmer, b 184 E South.
Langley Alvin L, foreman, h 53 Hoyt av.
Langley Arthur E, checkman, h 71 N Olive.
Langley Edwin S, cigarmkr, b 53 Paca.
Langley Willis H, tinner, h 53 Paca.
Langlund Peter, cigarmkr, h 390 E Michigan.
Langridge John, clk Kingan & Co (ltd), h 347 Blake.
Langridge Wm L, clk, r 49 S Illinois.
Langsdale Annetta, bkkpr Polar Ice Co, b 225 E Ohio.
Langsdale Frank C, trav agt, b 225 E Ohio.
Langsdale George J, editor American Tribune, h 129 E Pratt.
Langsdale James K, b 225 E Ohio.
Langsdale Joshua, bkkpr Armstrong Laundry, h 90 Lexington av.
Langsdale Mary R, teacher Public School No 6, b 129 E Pratt.
Langsdale Rebecca A, grocer, 295 E Georgia, h same.
Langsdale Richard W, collr, h 320 N East.
Langsdale Robert, grocer, 295 E Georgia, h same.
Langsdale Robert A, h 295 E Georgia.
Langsdale Thomas, b 22 S West.
Langsdale Violet (wid Joshua M W), h 225 E Ohio.
LANGSENKAMP BROS' BRASS WORKS (Henry J and Wm Langsenkamp Jr), Brass Founders and Finishers, 90-92 E Georgia, Tel 121. (See adv p 7.)
Langsenkamp Frank H, clk, b 244 Virginia av.
Langsenkamp Henry J (Langsenkamp Bros' Brass Wks), b 244 Virginia av.
LANGSENKAMP WM, Coppersmith, n w cor Delaware and Georgia, Tel 121; h 244 Virginia av. (See adv p 7.)
Langsenkamp Wm jr (Langsenkamp Bros' Brass Wks), b 244 Virginia av.
Langstaff Ida, clk W H Block Co, b 148 N Illinois.
Langstaff Wm, florist, h 605 E Washington.
Langston Charles H, barber, r 8½ N Penn.
Langston George A, painter, h 404 N Brookside av.
Langston Grace, stenog, b 56 S Summit.
Langston Thomas W, clk R M S, h 69 Highland pl.
Langtry James H, clk, h 289 Jefferson av.
Lanham George A, tile setter, b 191 E Market.
Lanham James, foreman, h 115 Walcott.
Lanham Oliver M, h 64 N Beville av.
Lanham Sarah (wid Samuel), h 191 E Market.
Lanham Susan E, nurse, 18 Wyandot blk, r same.
Lanham Wm F, trav agt Comstock & Coonse Co, h 65 Cornell av.
Lanier Charles H (Lanier & Moore), h 1371 N Capitol av.
Lanier George W, lab, r 81 W Georgia.

THOS. C. DAY & CO.
Financial Agents and Loans.
We have the experience, and claim to be reliable.
Rooms 325 to 330 Lemcke Bldg.

Lanier Rachel, h 21 Church.
Lanier Stella L (wid Alexander), b 512 N Meridian.
Lanier & Moore (Charles H Lanier, Henry Moore), barbers, 91 N Penn.
Lanigan Edward M, clk, r 28 W Vermont.
Lanigan Maurice, boilermkr, h 36 Eastern av.
Lanihan Michael, lab, h 2 Chadwick.
Lankford James, painter, b s s Bloyd av 2 w of Shade (B).
Lankford Samuel, lab, r 34 Roanoke.
Lanktree Barnabas T, carp, b 1156 N Delaware.
Lanktree James W, vault cleaner, 18 Baldwin blk, h 1156 N Delaware.
Lannen Michael, lab, h 276 E Georgia.
Lannert George J Rev, asst rector St Joseph's Church, b 323 E North.
Lannes Christiana M (wid Lewis), b 195 Miller (W I).
Lanphier Wm, bartndr, h 36 Kansas.
Lans P Maxwell, electrician, r 196 W Ohio.
Lansberry James W, carp, r 235½ Mass av.
Lansbery James, paperhngr, h 501½ W Washington.
Lansdale, see Langsdale.
Lansing John H, cooper, h 608 W Vermont.
Lantrey Theodore, pantryman, r 26 S West.
Lantry George, engr Kingan & Co (ltd).
Lantry James C, mach hd, h 89 Nordyke av (W I).
Lantry John, molder, b 3 Beacon.
Lantry Michael, lab, b 232 W Market.
Lantz, see also Lentz.
Lantz Benjamin J, letter carrier P O, h 58 Holloway av.
Lantz Frank S, brakeman, h 6 Depot (B).
Lapham Samuel H, tmstr, h w s Rural 2 n of Pope av.
La Porte Guy D (La Porte & Votaw), b 732 E Ohio.
La Porte Isaac R, engr, h 25 Eastern av.
La Porte James W, carp, h 173 Ash.
La Porte Miller J, police sergeant, h 732 E Ohio.
La Porte Wm S, plastr, 33 Johnson av, h same.

EAT
QUAKER BREAD
ASK YOUR GROCER FOR IT.
THE HITZ BAKING CO.

CARPETS AND RUGS RENOVATED.......... | CAPITAL STEAM CARPET CLEANING WORKS M. D. PLUNKETT, TELEPHONE No. 818

BENJ. BOOTH PRACTICAL EXPERT ACCOUNTANT. Complicated or disputed accounts investigated and adjusted. Room 18, 82½ E. Wash. St., Ind'p'l's, Ind.

18 and 20 South Meridian Street KERSHNER BROS., Proprs. THE SHERMAN RESTAURANT

ESTABLISHED 1876. TELEPHONE 168.
CHESTER BRADFORD,
SOLICITOR OF PATENTS,
AND COUNSEL IN PATENT CAUSES.
(See adv. page 6.)
Office:—Rooms 14 and 16 Hubbard Block, S.W. Cor. Washington and Meridian Streets, INDIANAPOLIS, INDIANA.

La Porte & Votaw (Guy D La Porte, Herman O Votaw), barbers, 354 Indiana av.
Laraja Anthony, cook, h 21 S Liberty.
Lardie Albert, lab, b 542 S West.
Lardie Peter L, lab, h 542 S West.
Large John W, lab, h 21 Leon.
Largent Benjamin P, clk, r 101 N Delaware.
Larger Felix C (Larger & Pryor), h 64 Nordyke av (W I).
Larger James E, salesman, h 553 E Washington.
Larger & Pryor (Felix C Larger, Harry A Pryor), machinists, 79 S Senate av.
Larick Wm, h 294½ Mass av.
Larimer Elizabeth (wid Robert C), h 78 W South.
Larimer Hugh E, trav agt, h 270 S Penn.
Larimore Albert S, mach, h 23½ S East.
Larimore Charles A, tmstr, h rear w s Rural 3 n of Brookside av.
Larimore Cornelius J, gardener, h s end of Hubbard.
Larimore Daniel M, lab, h 46 Catherine.
Larimore George, lab, b 46 Catherine.
Larimore P Otto, clk A Kiefer Drug Co, h w s Rural 3 n of S Brookside av.
Larimore Wm, lab, h 26 Abbott.
Larimore Wm W, lab, h 519 English av.
Larison John H, brick contr, 222 Prospect, h same.
Larkey David E, carp, h 1775 N Senate av.
Larkin Albert L, clk, h 166 S East.
Larkin George, lab, h 50 N California.
Larkin John, expressman, h 21 Ellen.
Larkin Thomas F, clk H P Wasson & Co, h 116 Lincoln av.
Larkins Landers, waiter The Bates.
Larned Chester C, musician, b 183 E Vermont.
Larned James M, janitor Public School No 1, h 183 E Vermont.
Larner Thomas, lab, h 323 W Maryland.
La Roche Emma (wid Charles), h 105 Fountain av.
La Roche Herman, lab, h rear 1370 E Washington.
La Roche Mary F (wid John A F), h 107 Fountain av.

Matal Ceilings and all kinds of Copper, Tin and Sheet Iron work.
O. B. ENSEY,
TELEPHONE 1562.
CORNER 6TH AND ILLINOIS STS.

Larosa Antonio, pdlr, h 160 Virginia av.
Larosa Joseph, pdlr, h 160 Virginia av.
La Rossa Frank, fruits, 67 E Mkt House, and com mer, 116 E Maryland, h same.
Larr George R, paperhngr, b 198 N Beville av.
Larr George W, h 198 N Beville av.
Larrabee Henry, canmkr, b 48 N West.
Larrabee Wm H, student, b 327 S New Jersey.
Larrimer Hugh E, agt J F Seiberling & Co, h 378 S Penn.
Larsen Anders, tailor, h 963 N Alabama.
Larsen Hans, molder, r 13 Ketcham (H).
Larsen James, molder, h 326 W Vermont.
Larsen John, molder, h 133 Sheffield av (H).
Larsen Louis C, notions, 556 W Udell (N I), h same.
Larsen Martin, molder, h 106 Woodburn av (W I).
Larsen Mary J (wid Jens), florist, E Mkt House and 328 W 23d, h same.
Larsen Tycho L, bkkpr Hetherington & Berner Co, b 963 N Alabama.
Larsh Arthur E, bkkpr, h 376 Talbott av.
Larsh A Homer, attendant Insane Hospital.
Larsh Carl L (Larsh & Meginniss), h 353 E St Clair.
Larsh Herschel D, b 22 Osgood (W I).
Larsh Jonas, car rep, h 44 S Gale (B).
Larsh Wm A, clk Van Camp H and I Co, h 22 Osgood (W I).
Larsh Wm W, clk, h 109 Oliver av (W I).
LARSH & MEGINNISS (Carl L Larsh, Thomas J Meginniss), Cigar Mnfrs; Make the Celebrated Cuban Twist and American Star Cigars, 353 E St Clair.
Larson Sophia, cook, b 1051 N Capitol av.
Larter Malcolm, bartndr, b 186 Minerva.
La Rue Caroline V, b 824 Ash.
La Rue Clarence L, painter, 302 Excelsior av, h same.
La Rue David B, bkkpr, h 510 E 8th.
La Rue Edward, clk, h 559 College av.
La Rue Edwin H, tel opr L N A & C Ry, h 853 Cornell av.
La Rue Gordon A, meats, 550 Bellefontaine, h 134 Cornell av.
La Rue Kate (wid Charles), b 4 Peck.
La Rue Leslie M, mach, h 50 Brookside av.
La Rue Matilda L (wid Isaac), h w s Excelsior av 2 s of Pope av.
La Rue Ralph, lab, h 117 N Missouri.
La Rue Roy, foreman, b 302 Excelsior av.
La Rue Warren, lather, b 432 Douglass.
La Rue Willis E, painter, 70½ E Court, h 310 Excelsior av.
La Rue Willis I, custodian, h 38 The Chalfant.
Lary Richard, lab, b s s Colgrove 4 w of Mattie av.
Lasater Jennie, b 491 Broadway.
Laser Charles F, brazier, h 84 Bates.
Lash Alexander, lab, h 138 Geisendorff.
Lash Augustus, lab, h e s Sangster av 5 n of Belle.
LASH HUGH M, Physician, Sec Indiana Medical Journal Publishing Co, 18 E Ohio, Tel 1231; h 395 Park av, Tel 1420.
Lash John A, steelwkr, h 52 McGinnis.
Lash Marshall E, brickmason, h 31 Brett.
Lash M Rice, wireman Sanborn Electric Co, b 410 E Walnut.
Lash Phoebe (wid Alexander), b 138 Geisendorff.
Lasher Clinton D, molder, h 948 N Penn.

TUTEWILER UNDERTAKER, No. 72 WEST MARKET STREET. TELEPHONE 216.

The Provident Life and Trust Co. Dividends are paid in cash and are not withheld for a long period of years, subject to forfeiture in the event of death or the termination of policy.
D. W. EDWARDS, GENERAL AGENT, 508 INDIANA TRUST BUILDING.

Lasher George, painter, b 700 E 9th.
Lashley Benjamin T, weighmaster, b 62 Temple av.
Lashley Robert J, condr, h 62 Temple av.
Lasley Benjamin W, carp, h 166 Hillside av.
Lasley Clarence, lab, h w s Miami 2 s of Prospect.
Lasley Henry, lab, h e s Miami 8 s of Prospect.
Lasley Wm, lab, b 29 Brett.
Lasley Wm, lab, h 446½ W Washington.
Lasley Wm T, lab, h w s Harriet 1 s of Division (B).
Lasman Emma, b 52 Beaty.
Lassen John, mach, b 125 E McCarty.
Lassen John N, drayman, h 448 S Meridian.
Lassen Katharina (wid Peter), h 125 E McCarty.
Laster Julia (wid Philip), h 36 Roanoke.
Laster Wylie, lab, b 20 Mill.
Laswell George L, lab, b 2 Edgewood.
Latham Charles, pres The Interior Hardwood Co, cashr S A Fletcher & Co, b 582 E Washington.
Latham Harry, chemist, b 4 Camp.
Latham Henry, sec and treas The Interior Hardwood Co, h 497 N Meridian.
Latham Sallie D (wid Robert T), h 4 Camp.
Latham Walter D, driver, b 4 Camp.
Latham Wm H, teacher Deaf and Dumb Inst, h 582 E Washington.
Lather John, carp, h w s Northwestern av 1 s of 30th (N I).
Lather Wm, carp, b w s Northwestern av 1 s of 30th (N I).
Lathrop Elmer E, mach, b 419 Bellefontaine.
Lathrop Esther M (wid Andrew), b 388 Central av.
Lathrop Homer S, painter, h 419 Bellefontaine.
Latsbaugh John C, bkkpr Union Mutl Bldg and Loan Assn, h 188 Dearborn.
Latta Wm H (Mason & Latta), b 462 Broadway.
Lattimore Charles, porter, r 74 N Delaware.
Lattimore John, lab, r 66 Missouri.
Lattipe George, lab, h rear 80 Yandes.
Lattipe Harry, lab, b rear 624 Home av.
Laube Julius P, clk Indpls Drug Co, h 17 Gatling.
Laubert Henry G, brewer, h 52 Downey.
Lauck Anthony H, clk, h 362 Union.
Lauck John, hardware, 496 S Meridian, h 500 same.
Lauck Peter W, finisher, h 827 Chestnut.
Laue Frederick, driver, b 50 Bicking.
Laue Henrietta (wid Wm), b 480 Lincoln av.
Laue Wm, driver, h 50 Bicking.
Lauer Charles, finisher, b 152 Michigan (H).
Lauer Charles W, trav agt, h 543 College av.
Lauer Wm, bartndr, b 349 E Market.
Laughlin, see also Loughlin and McLaughlin.
Laughlin Allen, engr, h 377 W North.
Laughlin Caroline (wid David J), h 68 Yeiser.
Laughlin Dennis, feed, 318 Indiana av, h 2 Center.
Laughlin Eleanor R, h 13 Wood.
Laughlin Frank A, clk, b 369 S Meridian.
Laughlin Lester L, driver, h 156 Pleasant.
Laughlin Martin, lab, b 323 W Pearl.
Laughlin Selena A (wid John), h 369 S Meridian.
Laughner George A, clk, b 133 W New York.

THE
WHEN
IS A WORLD BEATER.

Laughner John H, city agt, h 30 S Beville av.
Laughner Wm J, confr, 72 N Illinois, h 133 W New York.
Lauler Joseph, baker, 230 W McCarty, h same.
Laum Wm A, molder, h 7 Frazee (H).
Laun Theodore T, instrumentmkr, b 262½ E Washington.
Laupheimer John A, mach, h 498 S Capitol av.
Laurence Mary I, h 512 Broadway.
Laurie David, cigarmkr, b 435 E Washington.
Laurie Forbes M, turner, b 187 S Capitol av.
Laurie Frank, mill hd, r 76 W South.
Laurie John, bartndr, b 435 E Washington.
Laurie Wm (Wm Laurie & Co), h n s Bedford av nr Park av.
LAURIE WM & CO (Wm Laurie, James Proctor, Wm H Avant), Dry Goods, 15, 17 and 19 N Meridian.
Lausmann Charles, painter, h 141 Michigan av.
Laut Charles W, clk, b 170 S Noble.
Laut Henry W (H W Laut & Co), h 170 S Noble.
Laut Henry W jr, tinner, b 170 S Noble.
Laut H W & Co (Henry W Laut), tinners, 350 E South.
Laut Wm F, tinner, b 170 S Noble.
Lauter Alfred, clk, b 322 Home av.
Lauter Herman, furniture mnfr, Washington and N Judge Harding (W I), h 322 Home av.
Lauterbach Louisa (wid Carl), b 13 Carlos.
Lauth Wm, gilder, h 406 Madison av.
Laval Jesse, lab, r 121½ Ft Wayne av.
Lavanchy Robert C, clk R M S, h 84 Springfield.
Lavelle Catherine, h 140 St Mary.
Lavelle Mary, h 140 St Mary.
Lavelle Patrick C, mach, h 17 Depot (B).
Lavelle Wm, clk, r 112 S East.
Lavender Edward, switchman, b s s Sutherland 3 e of Shade (B).
Lavercomb Richard H, clk, h 134 S Linden.
Lavery Charles, clk John A McGaw, h 134 S Noble.

The A. Burdsal Co.
Manufacturers of
STEAMBOAT COLORS
BEST HOUSE PAINTS MADE.
Wholesale and Retail.
34 AND 36 SOUTH MERIDIAN STREET.

THEODORE F. SMITHER, AGENT FOR WARREN'S ANCHOR BRAND ASPHALT ROOFING. OFFICE, 151 WEST MARYLAND ST. TEL. 861.

Electric Contractors We are prepared to do any kind of Electric Contract Work. C. W. MEIKEL, Telephone 466. 96-98 E. New York St.

DALTON & MERRIFIELD { LUMBER South Noble St., near E. Washington

LOWEST PRICES. BEST PATENT BASE ON THE MARKET. All Orders Promptly Filled. BEST WORK. BOOK PLATES. INDIANA ELECTROTYPE CO. JOB WORK. 23 WEST PEARL ST., INDIANAPOLIS, IND.

KIRKHOFF BROS.,
Sanitary Plumbers
STEAM AND HOT WATER HEATING.
102-104 SOUTH PENNSYLVANIA ST.
TELEPHONE 910.

Lavery John, uphlr, b 375 S Meridian.
Lavery John F, clk Hollweg & Reese, h 375 S Meridian.
Lavigne Prosper, finisher, h 34 Cleveland (H).
Laville John, molder, h 47 Bismarck av (H).
Lavin Edward, switchman, b 14 E Sutherland (B).
Lavin Mary (wid Owen), h rear 319 W Washington.
Lavin Thomas O'D, frt receiver C C C & St L Ry, b 63 Fletcher av.
Lavrenz August W, finisher, h 131 Gresham.
Lavrenz Charles F, finisher, h 12 Gresham.
Law Benjamin A, fireman, h 299 Bates.
Law John H, lab, h 123 Huron.
Law Willis W, electrician, h 356 S West.
Lawanier Catherine W (wid Leopold), h 42 Thomas.
Lawe Mary E (wid Thomas B), h 12 Roanoke.
Lawhorn Elisha, lab, h 378 S West.
Lawhorn Ira, lab, h 91 Lord.
Lawhun Alice W (wid John B), h 290 W Vermont.
Lawhun Stephen G, tinner, b 290 W Vermont.
Lawler Esther (wid Leonard), b w s Illinois 2 n of 29th.
Lawler Francis M, master mech C C C & St L Ry, h 234 Bellefontaine.
Lawler Joseph S, clk C C C & St L Ry, b 289 S East.
Lawler Maggie, housekpr 45 N William (W I).
Lawler Margaret (wid John), h 237 W Maryland.
Lawler Patrick E, clk, h 136 Douglass.
Lawler Wm, h 289 S East.
Lawler Wm A, waiter, h 127 Osage al.
Lawler Wm H, mach, b 234 Bellefontaine.
Lawler Wm R, fireman, b 63 Church.
Lawless James, watchman, h 24 Deloss.
Lawless John, lab, b 24 Deloss.
Lawless Michael, h 136 S Noble.
Lawlor Diana M (wid Patrick), h 316 Spring.
Lawlor Michael D, h 432 S Delaware.

Lime, Lath, Cement,
THE W. G. WASSON CO.
130 INDIANA AVE. TEL. 989.
Sewer Pipe, Flue Linings, Fire Brick, Fire Clay.

Lawlor Patrick J, molder, h 92 Decatur.
Lawlor Thomas, condr, h 775 Ash.
Lawn Charles, lab, h 90 W McCarty.
Lawn Edward, janitor Public School No 16, h s w cor Bloomington and Everett.
Lawn John, lab, h 440 S Missouri.
Lawrence, see also Lorentz.
Lawrence Arthur V, grocer, 175 Howard, h 179 same.
Lawrence Arthur V jr, salesman, b s e cor Rural and Tinker.
Lawrence Belle, forewoman, b 512 Broadway.
Lawrence Charles, clk, h 170 Fayette.
Lawrence Charles P, cook, h 68½ Mass av.
Lawrence Charles, painter, h 174 Nordyke av (W I).
Lawrence Christian, molder, r 51 Tremont av (H).
Lawrence Cyrus W, news stand Hotel English, b 1323 N New Jersey.
Lawrence Edgar P, engr, h 40 Hill av.
Lawrence Edward, tailor A J Treat & Son, h 149 Fulton.
Lawrence Ellis (Lawrence & Thompson), h 1323 N New Jersey.
Lawrence George R, carp, h 19 McGinnis.
Lawrence Harry, trav agt, r 259 E New York.
Lawrence Henry O, lab, b 163 W South.
Lawrence Henry W, propr Spencer House, n w cor Illinois and Louisiana.
Lawrence Isaac J, mine-owner, h 86 Fletcher av.
Lawrence James E, janitor, r 37 Commercial Club bldg.
Lawrence James H, janitor, h s e cor Washington and Lake avs (I).
Lawrence James M, express, h 447 S Olive.
Lawrence John A, trav agt, b 179 Howard.
Lawrence Katherine R (wid Wm H), h n w cor Willow and Brightwood av (B).
Lawrence Leander A, artist, b Spencer House.
Lawrence Louis, lab, h 620 E 9th.
Lawrence Louise L, pres Women's Industrial Assn and pres Family Dress Guide Co, h 1875 E Washington.
Lawrence Martha J (wid John R), h 306 Cornell av.
Lawrence Mary A (wid Thomas R), nurse, h 465½ S Meridian.
Lawrence Morton P, lab, h s s Perkins pike 1 e of Golay.
Lawrence Nannie, clk Lawrence & Thompson, b 1323 N New Jersey.
Lawrence Nelson, lab, h 344 N Missouri.
Lawrence Samuel, brakeman, h 365 Fletcher av.
Lawrence Wm, clk, b 179 Howard.
Lawrence Wm, lab, h n s Finley av 4 e of Shelby.
Lawrence Wm, lab, b 86 W 8th.
Lawrence Wm H, engraver, b 135 N Illinois.
LAWRENCE & THOMPSON (Ellis Lawrence, James S Thompson), Fire Insurance, 62 E Market, Tel 1680.
Lawrie, see also Laurie and Lowry.
Lawrie Allan, bkkpr, b 384 N Capitol av.
Lawrie David, bartndr, h 621 E Washington.
Lawrie John C (Lawrie & Robson), h 384 N Capitol av.
Lawrie Joseph T, clk, b 384 N Capitol av.
Laws Caleb, lab, b 41 Harris.
Laws Emma (wid Henry), h 247 W 3d.
Laws Harrison, porter, b 247 W 3d.
Laws Wm J, motorman, h 89 W 14th.

YOUR HOMES FURNISHED BY W. H. MESSENGER 101 East Washington St. Telephone 491.

OFFICERS AND DIRECTORS.

W. F. CHURCHMAN, President.
H. F. STEVENSON, Secretary.
W. T. COX, General Counsel.
W. E. STEVENSON, Treasurer.
CLARENCE K. DAVIS, Actuary.

Cable Address, "Star" Indianapolis

Lawyers' Loan and Trust Co.

Capital, $300,000.00

This Company, under its trustee and agency powers, acts as register or transfer agent of stocks and bonds; as trustee for railroads and other mortgages; as attorney-in-fact for the collection of rents and incomes, and the management of the estates of married women and other persons; as trustee for corporations, alone or jointly with others; as agent or attorney-in-fact for inexperienced persons holding positions of trust, and, in other words, fills every position of trust that can be held by an individual (except what is known as court business).

It is also prepared and authorized under its charter to negotiate loans, deal in real estate paper and other securities, make desirable investments for persons and corporations, or to buy and sell shares in building, savings and loan associations.

68½ EAST MARKET STREET,

INDIANAPOLIS, INDIANA

McNamara, Koster & Co. Phone 1593. 212-218 S. PENN. ST. PATTERN MAKERS

Lawson Alonzo R, tmstr, b 50 Michigan av.
Lawson Alva, driver, r 277 W Washington.
Lawson Chesley, b 42 N State av.
Lawson Edward, miller, h 436 Douglass.
Lawson Edward G, condr, h 328 Fulton.
Lawson Elijah L, foreman, h 192 Blackford.
Lawson Ellen (wid John A), h 773 N Senate av.
Lawson Frank, tile setter, h 250 Cornell av.
Lawson Harvey J, clk, b 477 Indiana av.
Lawson Henry, lab, h 284 Yandes.
Lawson Hezekiah K, barber, 42 Indiana av, r 52 same.
Lawson Isaac N, b 773 N Senate av.
Lawson Jacob, lab, b 50 Springfield.
Lawson Jesse F, lab, b 423 E St Clair.
Lawson John, lab, b 50 W Springfield.
Lawson John W, engr, h 214 W McCarty.
Lawson Joseph F, bicycle rep, 255 W Washington, h 477 Indiana av.
Lawson Joseph H, lab, h 83 N Capitol av.
Lawson Louis, presser, b 269½ E Washington.
Lawson Martha J (wid Milton T), h 282 S East.
Lawson Nora, b 226 W Vermont.
Lawson Otis, lab, b 773 N Senate av.
Lawson Robert L, condr, h 874 N Senate av.
Lawson Sarah J, h 50 Michigan av.
Lawson Scott, second-hand goods, 289 Christian av, r same.
Lawson Thomas M, driver, b 50 Michigan av.
Lawson Wm S, city agt, h 265 W Morris.
Lawton Harry S, hatter, h 79 Woodburn av (W I).
Lawton John J, engr, h 73 Eastern av.
Lawyer Amy D (wid Lewis), dressmkr, 400½ N Senate av, h same.
LAWYERS' LOAN AND TRUST CO, Wm F Churchman Pres, Henry F Stevenson Sec, Wm E Stevenson Treas, Clarence K Davis Actuary, Genl Offices Wright's Market Street Blk, 68½ E Market. (See top edge and adv opp.)
Laxen Frank, carp, h w s Waverly av 3 s of Pope av.
Laxen Frederick, car rep, h w s Lebanon av 1 n of Pope av.
Lay Charles F (Lay & McCaffrey), h 62 S West.
Lay Frank F, mach, b 19 Tompkins.
Lay George F, mach hd, h 19 Tompkins.
Lay George J, foreman, h 29 Nordyke av (W I).
Lay John, waiter, r 327 W North.
Lay Louis G, plumber, b 62 S West.
Lay Mary M (wid Frederick), h 62 S West.
Lay Wm F, finisher, h 467 W New York.
LAY & McCAFFREY (Charles F Lay, James B McCaffrey), Dealers in Fine Drugs, Cigars and Toilet Articles, 186 W Washington, Tel 1136.
Laycock Charles F, carp contr, 401 E McCarty, h same.
Laycock Edward L, mach hd, b 401 E McCarty.
Laycock George W, filer, h 78 Bradshaw.
Laycock Joseph (Krutsch & Laycock), h 66 Omer.
Laycock Mary Y (wid Oliver), b 107 Ruckle.
Laycock Reuben T, phys, 107 Bates, h same.
Laycock Robert A, stenog, b 401 E McCarty.

Henry H. Fay, 40½ E. WASHINGTON ST., FIRE INSURANCE, REAL ESTATE, LOANS AND RENTAL AGENT.

Laycock Thomas B, sec and treas T B Laycock Mnfg Co, h 982 N Delaware.
LAYCOCK T B MANUFACTURING CO, Wm H Laycock Pres, John H Lytle Vice-Pres, Thomas B Laycock Sec and Treas, Spring Bed and Furniture Mnfrs, n w cor 1st and canal, Tel 835.
Laycock Wm F, clk L E & W R R, h 290 Fletcher av.
Laycock Wm H, pres T B Laycock Mnfg Co, b 431 N Senate av.
Layden Ollie J (wid Clinton), boarding 263 S Penn.
Layden Wm H, lab, h e s James 3 n of Sutherland (B).
Layer Jacob, brakeman, h 100 Harrison.
Layman Charles, blower, r 204 W South.
Layman Charles A, h 34 West Drive (W P).
Layman Daniel W, student, b s e cor Central and Washington avs (I).
Layman David M, lab, b 1558 N Meridian.
Layman James A, trav agt, h 414 Clifford av.
Layman James T (Layman & Carey Co), h s e cor Washington and Central avs (I).
Layman James T jr, trav agt, b s e cor Central and Washington avs (I).
Layman Louisa C (wid Theodore D), h 284 Lincoln av.
Layman Theodore D, clk, b s e cor Central and Washington avs (I).
Layman & Carey Co (James T Layman, Simeon B and Samuel C Carey), hardware, 63 S Meridian.
Layne George T, lab, b 46 Johnson av.
Layne Logan A, trav agt, h 137½ Virginia av.
Layton Arthur D, trav agt, h 1773 Graceland av.
Layton Frank, plumber, h 184 Walcott.
Layton Harry, clk, b 66 Hazel.
Layton John C, carp, h 191 Fletcher av.
Layton Robert M, clk Van Camp H and I Co, h 28 Osgood (W I).
Layton Timothy M, agt Pullman Palace Car Co, Union Station, r 115 The Shiel.
Layton Washington, lab, b 14 Smithson av.

SURETY BONDS
American Bonding & Trust Co. OF BALTIMORE, MD.
Authorized to act as Sole Surety on all Bonds. Total Resources over $1,000,000.00.
W. E. BARTON & CO., General Agents, 504 INDIANA TRUST BUILDING.
Long Distance Telephone 1918.

THE FRED DIETZ CO. WOODEN PACKING BOXES MADE TO ORDER. FACTORY AND WAREHOUSE TRUCKS. 400 Madison Avenue. Telephone 654.

Business World Supplied with Help GRADUATES ASSISTED TO POSITIONS 10,000 NOW IN GOOD SITUATIONS. TEL. 499. E. J. HEEB, PRES. Indianapolis BUSINESS UNIVERSITY

HENRY R. WORTHINGTON JET and SURFACE CONDENSERS 64 S. PENN. ST. Long Distance Telephone 284.

UNION CO-OPERATIVE LAUNDRY (COMPOSED OF UNION LAUNDRY GIRLS.) NOS. 38, 40 AND 142 VIRGINIA AVENUE. T. E. SOMERVILLE, MANAGER—TELEPHONE 1269. INDIANAPOLIS, IND.

HORACE M. HADLEY
Insurance, Real Estate, Loan and Rental Agent
66 EAST MARKET STREET,
Telephone 1540. Basement.

Lazarus George M (Lazarus & Ludwig), b 1000 N Meridian.
Lazarus John S, genl freight and passenger agt I D & W Ry, h 1000 N Meridian.
Lazarus Lazar, furrier, h 312 S Illinois.
LAZARUS & LUDWIG (George M Lazarus, Wm H Ludwig), Lawyers, 303 Indiana Trust Bldg.
Lazenby Charles B, lab, b 107 Spann av.
Lazenby Edwin, engr, h 102 Spann av.
Lazenby George R, fireman, h 107 Spann av.
Lea Mary C, laundress, h 274 Union.
Leabo Edward, lab, h 23 Centennial (H).
Leach, see also Leech.
Leach Albert A, carp, h 5 Barth av.
Leach David A (Leach & Odle), h 42 Huron.
Leach David S, elev opr Monument, h 48 Russell av.
Leach Ebenezer R, city fireman, h 9 Stoughton av.
Leach Eliza (wid David J), h rear 150 Madison av.
Leach Harry J, lab, b 92 River av (W I).
Leach James M, carp, h 21 Depot (B).
Leach Jesse C, farmer, b 21 Depot (B).
Leach John, trav agt, h 245 E Merrill.
Leach Joseph, agt, h 27 Athon.
Leach J C, State Supervisor of Natural Gas Inspection, 89 State House, res Kokomo, Ind.
Leach Leon T, stenog, b 492 N Capitol av.
Leach Lou (wid Ambrose), custodian Grand and English's Opera Houses, h 61½ N Penn.
Leach Silva P, filer, h 264 S Senate av.
Leach Wm, lab, h 231 Elizabeth.
Leach Wm E, teacher, h s e cor Jones and Central av (I).
LEACH & ODLE (David A Leach, Ernest R Odle), Lawyers, 13-14 Lombard Bldg.
Leachman Edith W, stenog, b 73 E Maryland.
Leachman Eliza (wid Bernard), b 135½ Cornell av.
Leachman Elizabeth (wid James), h 42 Bismarck.

Special Detailed Reports Promptly Furnished by Us.
MERCHANTS' AND MANUFACTURERS' EXCHANGE
J. E. TAKKEN, Manager,
19 Union Building, 73 West Maryland Street.

Leachman George S, salesman Murphy, Hibben & Co, h 54 Division (W I).
Leachman Mary J (wid Francis M), b 668 College av.
Leachman Virginia A (wid John T), h 134 Hoyt av.
Leacock John H, printer, h 175 Spann av.
Leamman John S, carp, h 238 S West.
Leane Patrick D, clk, b 219 N Capitol av.
Leap Albert, clk Indpls Gas Co, h 336 W New York.
Leap John W, lab, h 81 Holmes av (H).
Leap Samuel, motorman, b 1139 N Illinois.
Leary, see also O'Leary.
Leary Daniel F, mach, b 283 S Olive.
Leary Frank, porter The Bates.
Leary Honora (wid Timothy), b 117 Benton.
Leary James, letter carrier P O, h 117 Benton.
Leary Michael M, mach, h 283 S Olive.
Leary Patrick, lab, h 250 Bates.
Leas Clara C (wid Levi P), h 117 John.
Lease Jacob H, fruit grower, h e s Illinois 2 s of 38th.
Lease John T, finisher, h 430 W Addison (N I).
Leasure George, lab, h 26 Chadwick.
Leatherman Aaron (Styer & Leatherman), h n s Wolf pike 1 w of School (B).
Leatherman A Lincoln, phys, 132 N Alabama, h same.
Leathers David J, clk, h 74 Park av.
Leathers Douglass A, phys, 125 College av, h same.
Leathers James M (Holtzman & Leathers), h 1025 N Alabama.
Leauty, see also Liautey.
Leauty August, guns, 81 W Washington, h 139 W South.
Leavitt John B, clk, h 423 Cornell av.
Leavitt Oscar L, lab, h rear 470 E Washington.
Leavitt Roscoe C, printer, b 7 Frazee (H).
Lecher Sophia (wid Jacob), h 10 Peck.
Lechner Robert H, paperhngr, h 466 S Missouri.
Leck David B, clk, b 901 N Capitol av.
Leck George W, clk, b 901 N Capitol av.
Leck Robert M (Leck & Co), h 901 N Capitol av.
Leck Robert M jr, b 901 N Capitol av.
Leck & Co (Robert M Leck), grocers, 54 W 7th.
Leckey, see also Lackey.
Leckey Clara R (wid John A), b 443 Charles.
Lecklider John T, lawyer, 11½ N Meridian, h 18 E Vermont.
Leckner Max, music teacher, 359 N Penn, h same.
Ledermann John, barber, h 7 Paca.
Ledford Jesse S, engr, h 300 E Georgia.
Ledgerwood James, b 366 Bellefontaine.
Ledig Albert, painter, h 106 Wisconsin.
Ledig Helena (wid Julius), h 73 Oriole.
Ledig Julius E, printer, b 73 Oriole.
Ledig Rudolph, carp, b 73 Oriole.
Lee Alexander H, barber, b 34 N Reisner (W I).
Lee Alonzo, lab, h 291 Blake.
Lee Amanda M (wid Silas A), h 200 Park av.
Lee Andrew, shoemkr, 33 Camp, b same.
Lee Anthony J, bottler, h 66 Wisconsin.
Lee Arthur, lab, b 241 W Washington.
Lee Arthur, packer, b 261 N West.
Lee Benjamin, lab, h 217 W 6th.
Lee Benjamin J, clk N Y Store, h 276 E Miami.

CLEMENS VONNEGUT 184, 186 and 192 E. Washington St. | CABINET HARDWARE CARVERS' TOOLS. Glues of all kinds.

THE WM. H. BLOCK CO. DRY GOODS, MILLINERY, CLOAKS AND FURS.
7 AND 9 EAST WASHINGTON STREET.

Lee Carey O, clk Knight & Jillson, b 144 Cypress.
Lee Caroline M (wid Jeremiah), b 210 Columbia av.
Lee Charles, tailor, h 227 E Market.
Lee Charles, painter, b 53 High.
Lee Charles, tmstr, h e s Indianapolis av 1 s of 16th.
Lee Charles E, seeds, 145 E Mkt House, h 315 S Delaware.
Lee Charles H, clk R M S, r 228 College av.
Lee Charles N, h 200 Blackford.
Lee Charles P, phys, s e cor Senate av and 12th, b 1071 N Capitol av.
Lee Charles T, insp, b 200 Park av.
Lee Cyrene J (wid John R), b 300 Park av.
Lee Daniel, lab, h e s Line 4 s of Washington av (I).
Lee David F, painter, b 151 Walcott.
Lee Delmon L, express, h 94 S William (W I).
Lee Emanuel, lab, b 94 S William (W I).
Lee Fanny (wid Charles), b 185 Orange.
Lee Fielding T, clk N Y Store, h 555 Park av.
Lee Francis M, messenger Am Ex Co, b 109 S Illinois.
Lee Frank, lab, b 793 E Market.
Lee Frank J (Carter, Lee & Co), b 200 Park av.
Lee Frank W, agt, h 185 N Delaware.
Lee George, lab, b 391 W 2d.
Lee George, lab, r 230 W Vermont.
Lee George D, lab, b 94 S William (W I).
Lee George W, lineman, b 376 Lafayette.
Lee Granville, lab, h 753 Brookers al.
Lee Harry, restaurant, 210 W Washington, h same.
Lee Harry C, clk, b 200 Park av.
Lee Harry H, waiter, b 509 N Capitol av.
Lee Harvey (Craig & Co), h 36 Division (W I).
Lee Henry, printer, r 28 Ryan blk.

LEE HENRY H, Wholesale and Retail Dealer in Coffees, Teas and Fine Groceries, 34 W Washington, Tel 688; 250 Virginia av, 7-9 N Penn and 1 Madison av, h 187 N Illinois.

Lee Hop, laundry, 12 Indiana av, h same.
Lee Hop, laundry, 189 Indiana av, h same.
Lee Jacob W, lab, h 480 W Addison (N I).
Lee James, lab, b 36 Bright.
Lee James B, lab, b 105 Geisendorff.
Lee James F, condr, h 34 N Reisner (W I).
Lee James H, lab, h 204 W 2d.
Lee James O, lab, b 36 Division (W I).
Lee James R, lab, h 376 Lafayette.
Lee James W, waiter, h 306½ E Washington.
Lee Jennie, b 189 S Illinois.
Lee Jim, laundry, 241 W Washington, h same.
Lee John, huckster, h 64 Arizona.
Lee John, lab, b rear 228 S Missouri.
Lee John H, clk, h 240 N Alabama.
Lee John H, coachman, b 143 N Alabama.
Lee John J, farmer, h 1393 N Senate av.
Lee John M, trav agt, h 75 W North.
Lee John W, carp, h 557 W 22d (N I).
Lee John W, lab, h rear 474 N California.
Lee John W, lab, h 132 Newman.
Lee Joseph A, condr, b 69 W 13th.
Lee Leander, porter, b 185 W 5th.
Lee Lot, agt Associated Press, News bldg, h 444 Park av.
Lee Luvisa A (wid James W), h 151 Walcott.
Lee Mary A (wid Lloyd), h 27 Bicking.

HEADQUARTERS
PHOTOGRAPHIC OUTFITS
AMATEUR OR PROFESSIONAL
THE H. LIEBER COMPANY
33 S. MERIDIAN ST.

Lee Mary E, dressmkr, 151 Walcott, h same.
Lee Mary L (wid James W), h 243 Buchanan.
Lee Michael, lab, h 105 Geisendorff.
Lee Monroe D, bartndr, h 16 Eckert.
Lee Mordecai B, agt, h 56 Marion av (W I).
Lee Nora, nurse, b 444 N New Jersey.
Lee Orison P, tailor, h 587 W 22d (N I).
Lee Oscar, collr, b 83 Benton.
Lee Oscar E, stenog, h 495 S Illinois.
Lee Patrick, lab, h 29 Blake.
Lee Patrick, lab, b 105 Geisendorff.
Lee Quong, laundry, 118 N Delaware, r same.
Lee Quong Sing, laundry, 66 Indiana av, h same.
Lee Rebecca (wid Francis), b 222 Clinton.
Lee Rose, h 68 S Senate av.
Lee Sarah W (wid Alfred), h 114 S East.
Lee Sing, laundry, 226 E Washington, h same.
Lee Solon E, chief clk L E & W R R, h s e cor Washington and Laura (M J).
Lee Susan R, h 252½ Mass av.
Lee Thomas G, clk, h 620 Central av.
Lee Timothy, lab, h 86 Bright.
Lee Timothy C, lab, b 11 Astor.
Lee Virginia J (wid Greenup), b 620 Central av.
Lee Warren W, clk Murphy, Hibben & Co, h 34 Cherry.
Lee Wm, brakeman, r 242 W Maryland.
Lee Wm, fireman, h 8 Parker.
Lee Wm, lab, r 205½ W Ohio.
Lee Wm, lab, b 254 W Ray.
Lee Wm, waiter, h 147½ Eddy.
Lee Wm E, carp, b 36 Division (W I).
Lee Wm E, clk Navin's Pharmacy No 3, r 292 N Illinois.
Lee Wm E, h 686 N Illinois.
Lee Wm H, collr W H Messenger, h 26 W 22d.
Lee Wm H, lab, h 575 Highland av (N I).
Lee Wm H, lab, h 376 Lafayette.
Lee Wm J, b 226 S Linden.
Lee W Jesse, clk, r 16 Hendricks blk.
Leeb J John, painter, h 453 N Brookside av.
Leech, see also Leach.

GUIDO R. PRESSLER,
FRESCO PAINTER
Churches, Theaters, Public Buildings, Etc., A Specialty.
Residence, No. 325 North Liberty Street.
INDIANAPOLIS, IND.

INDIANAPOLIS STEEL ROOFING AND CORRUGATING WORKS, 23 and 25 East South Street. S. D. NOEL, Proprietor.

David S. McKernan REAL ESTATE AND LOANS
Houses, Lots, Farms and Western Lands for sale or trade.
ROOMS 2-5 THORPE BLOCK.

HENRY R. WOR

UNION CO-OPERATIVE LAUNDRY (COMPOSED OF UNION LAUNDRY GIRLS.) NOS. 138, 140 AND 142 VIRGINIA AVENUE. TELEPHONE 1269. INDIANAPOLIS, IND. T. E. SOMERVILLE, MANAGER

HORACE M. HAILEY

Insurance, Real Estate, [illegible] and Rental Agent

66 EAST MARKET ST[illegible]T.

Telephone 1840.

Lazarus George M [illegible] 1000 N Merid[illegible]
Lazarus John S [illegible] ngt I D & W R [illegible]
Lazarus Lazar, [illegible]

LAZARUS & LUDWIG (George [illegible] rus, Wm H Ludwig), [illegible] Indiana Trust Bldg.

Lazenby Charles [illegible]
Lazenby Edwin [illegible]
Lazenby George R [illegible]
Lea Mary C, [illegible]
Leabo Edward [illegible]
Leach, [illegible]
Leach Albert A [illegible]
Leach David A [illegible]
Leach David S [illegible] Russell av
Leach Ebenezer R [illegible] Stoughton [illegible]
Leach Eliza (wid [illegible]) [illegible]son av
Leach Harry J [illegible]
Leach James M [illegible]
Leach Jesse C, [illegible]
Leach John [illegible]
Leach Joseph [illegible]
Leach J C, State S[illegible] Inspection, [illegible] Ind.
Leach Leon T [illegible]
Leach Lou (wid A[illegible]) and English's Op[illegible] Penn.
Leach Silva P [illegible]
Leach Wm [illegible]
Leach Wm E, [illegible] Central av (I)

LEACH & ODLE (David A Le[illegible], Ernest R Odle), Lawyers, [illegible] Bldg.

Leachman Edith W [illegible] land.
Leachman Eliza (w [illegible]) [illegible]nell av.
Leachman Elizabeth [illegible] marck.

Special Detailed Reports Promptly Furnished [illegible] Us.

MERCHANTS' AND MANUFACTURERS' EXCHANGE

J. E. TAKKEN, Manager

19 Union Building, 73 West M[illegible]

CLEMENS VONNEGUT

184, 186 and 192 E. Washington St.

CABI[illegible]

THE WM. H. BLOCK

DRY GOODS,
MILLINERY, CLOAKS
AND FURS

Lee Carey O. clk [illegible] h [illegible] Cypress.
Lee Caroline [illegible] (wid Jeremiah) [illegible] Columbia av.
Lee Charles, [illegible] E Market.
Lee Charles, [illegible] E [illegible]
Lee Charles, [illegible] Indianapolis [illegible] 1 s of 30th.
Lee Charles E, [illegible] 215 S Delaware.
Lee Charles H, clk [illegible]
Lee Charles N, h [illegible] Rockford.
Lee Charles P, [illegible] 12th, b [illegible] N Capitol av.
Lee Charles T, [illegible] Park av.
Lee Cyrene J (wid John R.) h [illegible]
Lee Daniel, lab, h [illegible] of Washington av (I).
Lee David F, [illegible]
Lee Delmon L, [illegible] h [illegible] S William (W I).
Lee Emanuel, lab, h [illegible] S William (W I).
Lee Fanny (wid Charles) h [illegible]
Lee Fielding T, clk N Y Store, h [illegible]

Lee Francis M, [illegible] 109 S Illinois.
Lee Frank, [illegible] E Market.
Lee Frank J [illegible] Lee & Co [illegible]
Lee Frank W, [illegible] N Delaware.
Lee George, [illegible]
Lee George, [illegible]
Lee George [illegible]
Lee George [illegible]
Lee Granville [illegible]
Lee Harry [illegible]
Lee Harry [illegible]
Lee Harry [illegible]
Lee [illegible] (W I).
Lee [illegible]
LEE [illegible]
Dealer [illegible]
[illegible]

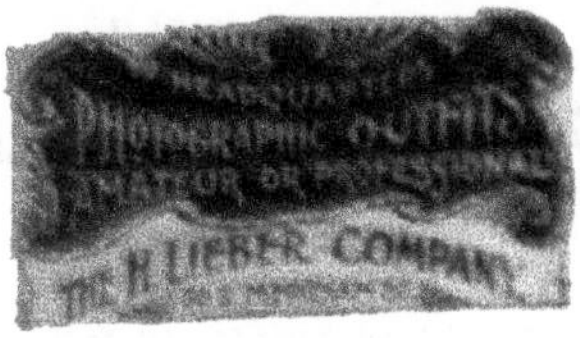

INDIANAPOLIS STEEL R[illegible] ING WORKS.

[illegible] THE H. LIEBER COMPANY.

DIAMOND WALL PLASTER | Telephone 1410 BUILDERS' EXCHANGE.

W. McWORKMAN,
ROOFING AND CORNICE WORKS,
930 W. Washington St. Tel. 1118.

Leech Ebenezer, city fireman, r Engine House No 2.
Leech Herbert E, printer, 95½ E South, b 1107 N Alabama.
Leech Hugh R, trav agt, h 1107 N Alabama.
Leeds Charles A, enameler, b 395 Mass av.
Leeds George, confr, 27 E Mkt House, h 157 N Senate av.
Leeds Learner B, mach hd, h 395 Mass av.
Leeds Learner B jr, clk, b 395 Mass av.
Leeds Wm B, pres The Am Tin Plate Co, h 675 N Delaware.
Leedy Ulysses G, musician, h 72 E Ohio.
Leedy Wm H, Grand Sec Grand Lodge and Grand Scribe Grand Encampment I O O F of Indiana, office Odd Fellows' Hall, h 165 E Merrill.
Leehey Timothy J, trav agt Hayes & Ready, r 7 Fair blk.
Leek Jeremiah, carp, h 461 Highland av.
Leeman Bert, mach, h 140 Union.
Leeman Enoch C, mach, b 325 E Ohio.
Leeman Frank, lab, b 140 Union.
Leeman Wm, filer, b 325 E Ohio.
Leen Patrick, lab, h 584 E St Clair.
Leerkamp Bernard F, bartndr, b 132 Michigan (H).
Lees John, toolmkr, h 57 Spann av.
Leeson Henry C, agt, h 552 E 8th.
Leet Callahan M, bkkpr Brown-Ketcham Iron Wks, h 18 Garfield pl.
Leet Ira L, patrolman, h 144 Madison av.
Leeth M Cortez, phys, 53½ W Washington, h 335 S West.
Le Feber Alonzo L, carp, h n w cor Ohio and Rural.
Le Feber Benton R, carp, h 646 W Vermont.
Le Feber Daniel L, carp, h 42 N Rural.
Le Feber John A, carp, h 1331 Isabella (N I).
Le Feber Myrtle, teacher Public School No 4, b 646 W Vermont.
Le Feber Vernon, carp, h 22 Ingram.
Le Fever Nellie (wid Samuel), h 295 E New York.
Leffingwell Artemus, carp, h 515 Bellefontaine.
L[illegible]well John, carp, b 515 Bellefontaine.

[illegible]. J. MAYER,
MANUFACTURER OF
SEALS
[illegible]S, RUBBER STAMPS, CHECKS, [illegible]DGES, DOOR PLATES, ETC.
[illegible] St., Ground Floor. TEL. 1886.

Leffingwell John L [illegible] mngr T[illegible] Indpls Sentinel, h 7[illegible] W 1[illegible]
Leffingwell Sam[illegible] printer h 7[illegible] W 13th.
Lefforge Amos, bar[illegible]r, h 115 Clarke.
Lefkowitz Bernar[illegible]k h 26 Co[illegible]umbia al.
Lefkowitz Jacob, [illegible] 19 E Washington, h same.
Lefler Charles W [illegible] Lefler & Co), h 374 College
Lefler Curtis H, [illegible] Lefler & Co, b 374 College
Lefler Otto, stu[illegible] 374 College av.
Lefler Wm, h 1[illegible] Pratt.
Leftwich Addi[illegible] k C C C & St L Ry, h 9 S Station (B)
Leftwich Calvin [illegible], h [illegible] N Alabama.
Leftwich Edgar [illegible] S Station (B).
Leftwich Harry [illegible] mist, b 9 S Station (B).
Leftwich Perry [illegible] Gem Laundry, b 9 S Station (B).
Legg Edward [illegible] S Virginia av.
Legg George [illegible] 7[illegible] [illegible] (W I).
Legg Howard [illegible] h 17 Wendell av.
Legg Nancy J [illegible] h 17 Wendell av.
Legg Walter W [illegible]
Leggo Helen L [illegible] Public School No 27, b 79 W [illegible]
Leggo Richard, h [illegible]
Lehman Andrew [illegible] ttmkr r [illegible] Kentucky av.
Lehman Francis [illegible] h 2063 N Senate av.
Lehman Henry [illegible] E [illegible]
Lehman Henry, [illegible] Marion av (W I).
Lehman Jennie [illegible] h [illegible] E New York.
Lehman Samuel [illegible] W Washington.
Lehman Simon, [illegible] Sipe, h 469 S East.

LEHMAN'S TRANS[illegible] OFFICE, Wm J Lehman Mngr, 19 [illegible]onument Pl, Tel 502.

Lehman Wm J, m[illegible] Lehman's Transfer Office, 19 Monument [illegible] h 734 W Market.
Lehmann Christin[illegible] wid Frederick), b 554 Chestnut.
Lehmann John, l[illegible] b [illegible] Gresham.
Lehmann Michael [illegible] h [illegible] S Meridian.
Lehnert John, tailor [illegible] N Senate av.
Lehr, see also Leehr
Lehr Albert, lab, h [illegible] Bismarck av (H).
Lehr Charles B, tr[illegible] [illegible] S State av.
Lehr Christian, agt [illegible] S State av.
Lehr Clara, h 6[illegible]1 Chestnut
Lehr Frederick, lab [illegible] 9 Catharine.
Lehr George, cigarmk h s e cor Addison and Burton av (N I)
Lehr George J, lab, h [illegible] Bismarck av 1 s of Emrich (H).
Lehr Harry, lab, r [illegible] Washington.
Lehr Henry, carp, h s Clifford av 2 e of Concord.
Lehr Henry, cigarmkr [illegible] s s Burton av 3 s of Addison (N I).
Lehr Henry J, clk C [illegible] & St L Ry, b 176 S New Jersey.
Lehr John E, dairy, [illegible] Clifford av 1 w of Watts, h same.
Lehr John G, chief clk [illegible] P & E Ry, h 1740 N Penn.
Lehr Julius, lab, b 20 [illegible]
Lehr Louis, grocer, 4[illegible] Illinois, h same.
Lehr Louis jr, sawmkr, 473 S Illinois.

Cor. E. Ohio St. and C., C., C. & St. L. R'y Tracks.
[illegible]AND STORAGE CO.
ISSUE NEW [illegible] RECEIPTS ON MERCHANDISE AND H[illegible] GOODS.

[illegible]ETZGER AGENCY ESTABLISHD 1863. REAL ESTATE

LAMBERT GAS & GASOLINE ENGINE CO.
ANDERSON, IND. GAS AND GASOLINE ENGINES, 2 TO 50 H. P.

BICYCLES $5 DOWN. MONTHLY. Best Wheels. Best Terms. WHEELMEN'S CO. 31 W. OHIO ST.

Lehr Margaret (wid ...
Lehr Maria (wid J ... Delaware b same
Lehr Martin J lab ... Burton av (N I
Lehr ...
Lehr Philip ...
Lehr Philip carp
Lehr Philip ...
Lehr Theodore ...
Lehr Wm F bartndr
Lehritter Adolph J ... av.
Lehritter Conrad, h same
LEHRRITTER HUGO H Drug ... Fletcher av, cor Grove ... 66 ... av.
Lehritter Ida, ...
Lehritter Martin J
Lehritter Otto bar
Lehritter ... av
Leib Edward H ... 1205 N North
Leib Sarah (wid ...
Leib Thomas ...
Leibhardt Char... ferson av
Leible Andrew ...
Leible ...
Leible George ...
[illegible]

Farm and City Loans
25 Years' Successful Business.
THOS. C. DAY & CO.
Rooms 325 to 330 Lemcke Building.

... R M S ... 112 Tremont
... W North
... Fletchers
... W North
... W North
... Davids...
... h 97
... New York
... New York

EAT
HITZ'S CRACKERS AND CAKES.
ASK YOUR GROCER FOR THEM.

BRICK Painter and Decorator, 94 EAST SOUTH STREET.

DIAMOND WALL PLASTER { Telephone 1410 BUILDERS' EXCHANGE.

UNION TRANSFER AND STORAGE CO. Cor. E. Ohio St. and C., C., C. & St. L. R'y Tracks.
ISSUE NEGOTIABLE RECEIPTS ON MERCHANDISE AND H USDH LD GOODS.

W. McWORKMAN,
ROOFING AND CORNICE WORKS,
930 W. Washington St. Tel. 1118.

Leech Ebenezer, city fireman, r Engine House No 2.
Leech Herbert E, printer, 95½ E South, b 1107 N Alabama.
Leech Hugh R, trav agt, h 1107 N Alabama.
Leeds Charles A, enameler, b 395 Mass av.
Leeds George, confr, 27 E Mkt House, h 157 N Senate av.
Leeds Learner B, mach hd, h 395 Mass av.
Leeds Learner B jr, clk, b 395 Mass av.
Leeds Wm B, pres The Am Tin Plate Co, h 675 N Delaware.
Leedy Ulysses G, musician, h 72 E Ohio.
Leedy Wm H, Grand Sec Grand Lodge and Grand Scribe Grand Encampment I O O F of Indiana, office Odd Fellows' Hall, h 165 E Merrill.
Leehey Timothy J, trav agt Hayes & Ready, r 7 Fair blk.
Leek Jeremiah, carp, h 461 Highland av.
Leeman Bert, mach, h 140 Union.
Leeman Enoch C, mach, b 325 E Ohio.
Leeman Frank, lab, b 140 Union.
Leeman Wm, filer, b 325 E Ohio.
Leen Patrick, lab, h 584 E St Clair.
Leerkamp Bernard F, bartndr, b 132 Michigan (H).
Lees John, toolmkr, h 57 Spann av.
Leeson Henry C, agt, h 552 E 8th.
Leet Callahan M, bkkpr Brown-Ketcham Iron Wks, h 18 Garfield pl.
Leet Ira L, patrolman, h 144 Madison av.
Leeth M Cortez, phys, 53½ W Washington, h 335 S West.
Le Feber Alonzo L, carp, h n w cor Ohio and Rural.
Le Feber Benton R, carp, h 646 W Vermont.
Le Feber Daniel L, carp, h 42 N Rural.
Le Feber John A, carp, h 1331 Isabella (N I).
Le Feber Myrtle, teacher Public School No 4, b 646 W Vermont.
Le Feber Vernon, carp, h 22 Ingram.
Le Fever Nellie (wid Samuel), h 295 E New York.
Leffingwell Artemus, carp, h 515 Bellefontaine.
Leffingwell John, carp, b 515 Bellefontaine.

GEO. J. MAYER,
MANUFACTURER OF
SEALS
STENCILS, RUBBER STAMPS, CHECKS, BADGES, DOOR PLATES, ETC.
15 S. Meridian St., Ground Floor. TEL. 1386.

Leffingwell John L, mach opr The Indpls Sentinel, h 78 W 18th.
Leffingwell Samuel L, printer, h 76 W 18th.
Lefforge Amos, bartndr, h 125 Clarke.
Lefkowitz Bernard, clk, h 26 Columbia al.
Lefkowitz Jacob, furng goods, 166 E Washington, h same.
Lefler Charles W (Hendrickson, Lefler & Co), h 374 College av.
Lefler Curtis H, clk Hendrickson, Lefler & Co, b 374 College av.
Lefler Otto, student, b 374 College av.
Lefler Wm, h 125 W Pratt.
Leftwich Addison W, clk C C C & St L Ry, h 9 S Station (B).
Leftwich Calvin S, agt, h 397 N Alabama.
Leftwich Edgar A, clk, b 9 S Station (B).
Leftwich Harry P, asst chemist, b 9 S Station (B).
Leftwich Perry C, bkkpr Gem Laundry, b 9 S Station (B).
Legg Edward, lab, h 275 Virginia av.
Legg George, tmstr, h 72 Lee (W I).
Legg Howard E, mach hd, b 17 Wendell av.
Legg Nancy J (wid George W), h 17 Wendell av.
Legg Walter W, b 17 Wendell av.
Leggo Helen L, teacher Public School No 27, b 79 W 20th.
Leggo Richard, h 79 W 20th.
Lehman Andrew D, cabtmkr, r 37½ Kentucky av.
Lehman Francis E, miller, h 1063 N Senate av.
Lehman Henry, b 469 S East.
Lehman Henry, electrician, h 94 Marion av (W I).
Lehman Jennie (wid Joseph), h 230 E New York.
Lehman Samuel, finisher, r 183½ W Washington.
Lehman Simon, salesman Jacob C Sipe, h 469 S East.
LEHMAN'S TRANSFER OFFICE, Wm J Lehman Mngr, 19 Monument Pl, Tel 502.
Lehman Wm J, mngr Lehman's Transfer Office, 19 Monument pl, h 37½ W Market.
Lehmann Christina S (wid Frederick), b 554 Chestnut.
Lehmann John, lab, h 13 Gresham.
Lehmann Michael, carp, h 737 S Meridian.
Lehnert John, tailor, b 777 N Senate av.
Lehr, see also Leehr.
Lehr Albert, lab, h 310 Bismarck av (H).
Lehr Charles B, tinner, h 427 S State av.
Lehr Christian, agt, b 427 S State av.
Lehr Clara, h 691 Chestnut.
Lehr Frederick, lab, h 39 Catharine.
Lehr George, cigarmkr, h s e cor Addison and Burton av (N I).
Lehr George J, lab, h e s Bismarck av 1 s of Emrich (H).
Lehr Harry, lab, r 812 W Washington.
Lehr Henry, carp, h s s Clifford av 2 e of Concord.
Lehr Henry, cigarmkr, h s s Burton av 3 s of Addison (N I).
Lehr Henry J, clk C C C & St L Ry, b 176 S New Jersey.
Lehr John E, dairy, s s Clifford av 1 w of Watts, h same.
Lehr John G, chief clk supt P & E Ry, h 1740 N Penn.
Lehr Julius, lab, b 20 Jones.
Lehr Louis, grocer, 475 S Illinois, h same.
Lehr Louis jr, sawmkr, b 475 S Illinois.

A. METZGER AGENCY ESTABLISHED 1863. REAL ESTATE

LAMBERT GAS & GASOLINE ENGINE CO.
ANDERSON, IND. GAS AND GASOLINE ENGINES, 2 TO 50 H. P.

Lehr Margaret (wid Christian), h 691 Chestnut.
Lehr Maria (wid John H), dressmkr, 442 S Delaware, b same.
Lehr Martin J, lab, h s e cor Addison and Burton av (N I).
Lehr Otto, uphlr, b 20 Jones
Lehr Philip, h s e cor Addison and Burton av (N I).
Lehr Philip, carp, 367 N Noble, h same.
Lehr Philip jr, finisher, b 367 N Noble.
Lehr Theodore, lab, h 20 Jones.
Lehr Wm F, bartndr, h 353 N Noble.
Lehrritter Adolph J, bartndr, b 349 Indiana av.
Lehrritter Conrad, saloon, 349 Indiana av, h same.
LEHRRITTER HUGO H, Druggist, 149 Fletcher av, cor Grove, Tel 1548; h 46 Spann av.
Lehritter Ida, clk, b 59 Spann av.
Lehrritter Martin J, h 201½ English av.
Lehrritter Otto, bartndr, r 77½ S Illinois.
Lehrritter Sibylla (wid George), h 59 Spann av.
Leib Edward H, broker, 76 S Meridian, r 116½ N Meridian.
Leib Sarah (wid Peter), h 36 Huron.
Leib Thomas I, r 116 N Meridian.
Leibhardt Charles W, mach hd, b 154 Jefferson av.
Leible Andrew, farmer, b 270 Howard (W I).
Leible August A, insp, h 32 Becker (M J).
Leible Edward C, bkkpr Indpls Water Co, h 966 N Delaware.
Leible George, shoemkr, h 69 Wisconsin.
Leible Herman, saloon, 270 Howard (W I), h same.
Leibold Frank J, clk Peoples' Outfitting Co, h 171 Fayette.
Leider Jacob, sign writer, r 96 N Alabama.
Leigeber John J, cement wkr, h 261 W 23d.
Leigh Wm F, ins agt, 60 Baldwin blk, h 615 E Vermont.
Leighton Margaret E (wid David G), h 31 Jefferson av.
Leihan Joseph J, finisher, b 456 Charles.
Leinberger George, lab, b 34 Osgood (W I).
Leinberger Michael, lab, h 34 Osgood (W I).
Leingruber Wm, finisher, b 322 Lincoln av.
Leiper Arthur W, bookbndr, b 200 Huron.
Leiper Mary J (wid Wm B), h 200 Huron.
Leiper Sarene T (wid Samuel W), h 435 Howard (W I).
Leisemann John H, cabtmkr, b 326 Highland av.
Leisemann Wm, lab, h 326 Highland av.
Leisemann Wm jr, pdlr, b 326 Highland av.
Leiss Charles F, driver, h 4 Weghorst.
Leist Jacob L, clk, h 76 King av (H).
Leitch Andrew, bkkpr Hotel Oneida, h 96 Walcott.
Leive Henry L, mach hd, h 77 Tacoma av.
Lekowitz Goldie (wid Lewis), h 26 Columbia al.
Lemaire Antoinette, rugs, 305 Bright, h 303 same.
Lemaire Nestor, teacher, h 303 Bright.
LeMasters Chester, clk, b 169 N Illinois.
LeMasters Harlen, student, b 166 Clinton.
LeMasters Louis C, hostler, h 113 Hoyt av.
Lemcke Julius A, office 231 Lemcke bldg, h 230 N Penn.
Lemen Charles D, brakeman, h 297 Bates.
Lemen Jennie, teacher Public School No 1 (H), b 112 Tremont av (H).
Lemen Oliver M, condr, h 295 N Alabama.

Farm and City Loans
25 Years' Successful Business.
THOS. C. DAY & CO,
Rooms 325 to 330 Lemcke Building.

Lemen Wm E, clk R M S, h 112 Tremont av (H).
Lemly Aaron, lab, h 218 Indiana av.
Lemmen Ella, dressmkr, b 34 W North.
Lemmen Emily, dressmkr, 22 Fletcher's Bank bldg, b 34 W North.
Lemmen Inez, dressmkr, b 34 W North.
Lemmen Mary (wid James), h 34 W North.
Lemmon Charles L, express, h 184 Davidson.
Lemmon James S, clk, h 34 Bellefontaine.
Lemmon Warren J, mach hd, b 73 Yandes.
Lemoine Josephine (wid Louis), h 150 Dougherty.
Lemon Albert E (Coval & Lemon), h 92 Hoyt av.
Lemon Arthur W, lab, b 668 Park av.
Lemon Charles E, ins, h 35 W 4th.
Lemon Daniel A, real est, 55 N Illinois, h 196 N Capitol av.
Lemon Isaac, h 74 Bradshaw.
Lemon Lucy A, teacher Public School No 12, h 165 St Mary.
Lemon Martha P (wid James A), h 668 Park av.
Lemon Mary R (wid Maxwell), h 165 St Mary.
Lemons Robert, butler 674 N Delaware.
Lemontree Frank, confr, 424 S Meridian, h same.
Lemontree Hyman, pdlr, b 424 S Meridian.
Lemontree Isaac, pdlr, r 23 N West.
Le Moyne Frank J, sec and treas H H Sprague Co, res Chicago, Ill.
Lenaghan Anthony F, city fireman, h 553 S West.
Lenaghan John N, saloon, 453 S West, h same.
Lenaghan Mary (wid Cornelius), b 453 S West.
Lenaghan Neal E, saloon, 100 S Illinois, h 39 Maple.
Lenahan James F, horseshoer, b 196 Douglass.
Lenahan John, driver, h 484 W New York.
Lenahan Michael, lab, h 2 Chadwick.
Lenahan Michael, lab, b 196 Douglass.
Lenahan Patrick jr, lab, b 484 W New York.
Lender Gustav, drugs, 254 N Noble, h 306 same.

EAT
HITZ'S CRACKERS
AND CAKES.
ASK YOUR GROCER FOR THEM.

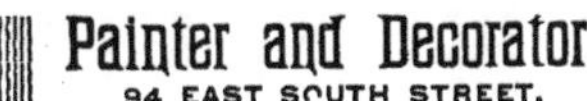

BICYCLES $5 DOWN. MONTHLY. Best Wheels. Best Terms. WHEELMEN'S CO. 31 W. OHIO ST. LONG DISTANCE TEL. 1555.

J. H. TECKENBROCK Painter and Decorator, 94 EAST SOUTH STREET.

DIAMOND WALL PLASTER { Telephone 1410 BUILDERS' EXCHANGE.

UNION TRANSFER AND STORAGE CO. Cor. E. Ohio St. and C., C., C. & St. L. R'y Tracks. ISSUE NEGOTIABLE RECEIPTS ON MERCHANDISE AND H USEH L D GOODS.

W. McWORKMAN,
ROOFING AND CORNICE WORKS,
930 W. Washington St. Tel. 1118.

Leech Ebenezer, city fireman, r Engine House No 2.
Leech Herbert E, printer, 95½ E South, b 1107 N Alabama.
Leech Hugh R, trav agt, h 1107 N Alabama.
Leeds Charles A, enameler, b 395 Mass av.
Leeds George, confr, 27 E Mkt House, h 157 N Senate av.
Leeds Learner B, mach hd, h 395 Mass av.
Leeds Learner B jr, clk, b 395 Mass av.
Leeds Wm B, pres The Am Tin Plate Co, h 675 N Delaware.
Leedy Ulysses G, musician, h 72 E Ohio.
Leedy Wm H, Grand Sec Grand Lodge and Grand Scribe Grand Encampment I O O F of Indiana, office Odd Fellows' Hall, h 165 E Merrill.
Leehey Timothy J, trav agt Hayes & Ready, r 7 Fair blk.
Leek Jeremiah, carp, h 461 Highland av.
Leeman Bert, mach, h 140 Union.
Leeman Enoch C, mach, b 325 E Ohio.
Leeman Frank, lab, b 140 Union.
Leeman Wm, filer, b 325 E Ohio.
Leen Patrick, lab, h 584 E St Clair.
Leerkamp Bernard F, bartndr, b 132 Michigan (H).
Lees John, toolmkr, h 57 Spann av.
Leeson Henry C, agt, h 552 E 8th.
Leet Callahan M, bkkpr Brown-Ketcham Iron Wks, h 18 Garfield pl.
Leet Ira L, patrolman, h 144 Madison av.
Leeth M Cortez, phys, 53½ W Washington, h 335 S West.
Le Feber Alonzo L, carp, h n w cor Ohio and Rural.
Le Feber Benton R, carp, h 646 W Vermont.
Le Feber Daniel L, carp, h 42 N Rural.
Le Feber John A, carp, h 1331 Isabella (N I).
Le Feber Myrtle, teacher Public School No 4, b 646 W Vermont.
Le Feber Vernon, carp, h 22 Ingram.
Le Fever Nellie (wid Samuel), h 295 E New York.
Leffingwell Artemus, carp, h 515 Bellefontaine.
Leffingwell John, carp, b 515 Bellefontaine.

GEO. J. MAYER,
MANUFACTURER OF
SEALS
STENCILS, RUBBER STAMPS, CHECKS, BADGES, DOOR PLATES, ETC.
15 S. Meridian St., Ground Floor. TEL. 1386.

Leffingwell John L, mach opr The Indpls Sentinel, h 78 W 18th.
Leffingwell Samuel L, printer, h 76 W 18th.
Lefforge Amos, bartndr, h 125 Clarke.
Lefkowitz Bernard, clk, h 26 Columbia al.
Lefkowitz Jacob, furng goods, 166 E Washington, h same.
Lefler Charles W (Hendrickson, Lefler & Co), h 374 College av.
Lefler Curtis H, clk Hendrickson, Lefler & Co, b 374 College av.
Lefler Otto, student, b 374 College av.
Lefler Wm, h 125 W Pratt.
Leftwich Addison W, clk C C C & St L Ry, h 9 S Station (B).
Leftwich Calvin S, agt, h 397 N Alabama.
Leftwich Edgar A, clk, b 9 S Station (B).
Leftwich Harry P, asst chemist, b 9 S Station (B).
Leftwich Perry C, bkkpr Gem Laundry, b 9 S Station (B).
Legg Edward, lab, h 275 Virginia av.
Legg George, tmstr, h 72 Lee (W I).
Legg Howard E, mach hd, b 17 Wendell av.
Legg Nancy J (wid George W), h 17 Wendell av.
Legg Walter W, b 17 Wendell av.
Leggo Helen L, teacher Public School No 27, b 79 W 20th.
Leggo Richard, h 79 W 20th.
Lehman Andrew D, cabtmkr, r 37½ Kentucky av.
Lehman Francis E, miller, h 1063 N Senate av.
Lehman Henry, b 469 S East.
Lehman Henry, electrician, h 94 Marion av (W I).
Lehman Jennie (wid Joseph), h 230 E New York.
Lehman Samuel, finisher, r 183½ W Washington.
Lehman Simon, salesman Jacob C Sipe, h 469 S East.
LEHMAN'S TRANSFER OFFICE, Wm J Lehman Mngr, 19 Monument Pl, Tel 502.
Lehman Wm J, mngr Lehman's Transfer Office, 19 Monument pl, h 37½ W Market.
Lehmann Christina S (wid Frederick), b 554 Chestnut.
Lehmann John, lab, h 13 Gresham.
Lehmann Michael, carp, h 737 S Meridian.
Lehnert John, tailor, b 777 N Senate av.
Lehr, see also Leehr.
Lehr Albert, lab, h 310 Bismarck av (H).
Lehr Charles B, tinner, h 427 S State av.
Lehr Christian, agt, b 427 S State av.
Lehr Clara, h 691 Chestnut.
Lehr Frederick, lab, h 39 Catharine.
Lehr George, cigarmkr, h s e cor Addison and Burton av (N I).
Lehr George J, lab, h e s Bismarck av 1 s of Emrich (H).
Lehr Harry, lab, r 812 W Washington.
Lehr Henry, carp, h s s Clifford av 2 e of Concord.
Lehr Henry, cigarmkr, h s s Burton av 3 s of Addison (N I).
Lehr Henry J, clk C C C & St L Ry, b 176 S New Jersey.
Lehr John E, dairy, s s Clifford av 1 w of Watts, h same.
Lehr John G, chief clk supt P & E Ry, h 1740 N Penn.
Lehr Julius, lab, b 20 Jones.
Lehr Louis, grocer, 475 S Illinois, h same.
Lehr Louis jr, sawmkr, b 475 S Illinois.

A. METZGER AGENCY ESTABLISHED 1863. REAL ESTATE

LAMBERT GAS & GASOLINE ENGINE CO.
ANDERSON, IND. GAS AND GASOLINE ENGINES, 2 TO 50 H. P.

Lehr Margaret (wid Christian), h 691 Chestnut.
Lehr Maria (wid John H), dressmkr, 442 S Delaware, b same.
Lehr Martin J, lab, h s e cor Addison and Burton av (N I).
Lehr Otto, uphlr, b 20 Jones
Lehr Philip, h s e cor Addison and Burton av (N I).
Lehr Philip, carp, 367 N Noble, h same.
Lehr Philip jr, finisher, b 367 N Noble.
Lehr Theodore, lab, h 20 Jones.
Lehr Wm F, bartndr, h 353 N Noble.
Lehrritter Adolph J, bartndr, b 349 Indiana av.
Lehrritter Conrad, saloon, 349 Indiana av, h same.
LEHRRITTER HUGO H, Druggist, 149 Fletcher av, cor Grove, Tel 1548; h 46 Spann av.
Lehritter Ida, clk, b 59 Spann av.
Lehrritter Martin J, h 201½ English av.
Lehrritter Otto, bartndr, r 77½ S Illinois.
Lehrritter Sibylla (wid George), h 59 Spann av.
Leib Edward H, broker, 76 S Meridian, r 116½ N Meridian.
Leib Sarah (wid Peter), h 36 Huron.
Leib Thomas I, r 116 N Meridian.
Leibhardt Charles W, mach hd, b 154 Jefferson av.
Leible Andrew, farmer, b 270 Howard (W I).
Leible August A, insp, h 32 Becker (M J).
Leible Edward C, bkkpr Indpls Water Co, h 966 N Delaware.
Leible George, shoemkr, h 69 Wisconsin.
Leible Herman, saloon, 270 Howard (W I), h same.
Leibold Frank J, clk Peoples' Outfitting Co, h 171 Fayette.
Leider Jacob, sign writer, r 96 N Alabama.
Leigeber John J, cement wkr, h 261 W 23d.
Leigh Wm F, ins agt, 60 Baldwin blk, h 615 E Vermont.
Leighton Margaret E (wid David G), h 31 Jefferson av.
Leihan Joseph J, finisher, b 456 Charles.
Leinberger George, lab, b 34 Osgood (W I).
Leinberger Michael, lab, h 34 Osgood (W I).
Leingruber Wm, finisher, b 322 Lincoln av.
Leiper Arthur W, bookbndr, b 200 Huron.
Leiper Mary J (wid Wm B), h 200 Huron.
Leiper Sarene T (wid Samuel W), h 435 Howard (W I).
Leisemann John H, cabtmkr, b 326 Highland av.
Leisemann Wm, lab, h 326 Highland av.
Leisemann Wm jr, pdlr, b 326 Highland av.
Leiss Charles F, driver, h 4 Weghorst.
Leist Jacob L, clk, h 76 King av (H).
Leitch Andrew, bkkpr Hotel Oneida, h 96 Walcott.
Leive Henry L, mach hd, h 77 Tacoma av.
Lekowitz Goldie (wid Lewis), h 26 Columbia al.
Lemaire Antoinette, rugs, 305 Bright, h 303 same.
Lemaire Nestor, teacher, h 303 Bright.
LeMasters Chester, clk, b 169 N Illinois.
LeMasters Harlen, student, b 166 Clinton.
LeMasters Louis C, hostler, h 113 Hoyt av.
Lemcke Julius A, office 231 Lemcke bldg, h 230 N Penn.
Lemen Charles D, brakeman, h 297 Bates.
Lemen Jennie, teacher Public School No 1 (H), b 112 Tremont av (H).
Lemen Oliver M, condr, h 295 N Alabama.

Farm and City Loans
25 Years' Successful Business.
THOS. C. DAY & CO,
Rooms 325 to 330 Lemcke Building.

Lemen Wm E, clk R M S, h 112 Tremont av (H).
Lemly Aaron, lab, h 218 Indiana av.
Lemmen Ella, dressmkr, b 34 W North.
Lemmen Emily, dressmkr, 22 Fletcher's Bank bldg, b 34 W North.
Lemmen Inez, dressmkr, b 34 W North.
Lemmen Mary (wid James), h 34 W North.
Lemmon Charles L, express, h 184 Davidson.
Lemmon James S, clk, h 34 Bellefontaine.
Lemmon Warren J, mach hd, b 73 Yandes.
Lemoine Josephine (wid Louis), h 150 Dougherty.
Lemon Albert E (Coval & Lemon), h 92 Hoyt av.
Lemon Arthur W, lab, b 668 Park av.
Lemon Charles E, ins, h 35 W 4th.
Lemon Daniel A, real est, 55 N Illinois, h 196 N Capitol av.
Lemon Isaac, h 74 Bradshaw.
Lemon Lucy A, teacher Public School No 12, h 165 St Mary.
Lemon Martha P (wid James A), h 668 Park av.
Lemon Mary R (wid Maxwell), h 165 St Mary.
Lemons Robert, butler 674 N Delaware.
Lemontree Frank, confr, 424 S Meridian, h same.
Lemontree Hyman, pdlr, b 424 S Meridian.
Lemontree Isaac, pdlr, r 23 N West.
Le Moyne Frank J, sec and treas H H Sprague Co, res Chicago, Ill.
Lenaghan Anthony F, city fireman, h 553 S West.
Lenaghan John N, saloon, 453 S West, h same.
Lenaghan Mary (wid Cornelius), b 453 S West.
Lenaghan Neal E, saloon, 100 S Illinois, h 39 Maple.
Lenahan James F, horseshoer, b 196 Douglass.
Lenahan John, driver, h 484 W New York.
Lenahan Michael, lab, h 2 Chadwick.
Lenahan Michael, lab, b 196 Douglass.
Lenahan Patrick jr, lab, b 484 W New York.
Lender Gustav, drugs, 254 N Noble, h 305 same.

EAT
HITZ'S CRACKERS
AND CAKES.
ASK YOUR GROCER FOR THEM.

BICYCLES $5 DOWN. MONTHLY. Best Wheels. B st Ts. WHEELMEN'S CO. 31 W. OHIO ST. LONG DISTANCE TEL. 1555.

J. H. TECKENBROCK  Painter and Decorator,
94 EAST SOUTH STREET.

FIDELITY MUTUAL LIFE—PHILADELPHIA, PA.
MATCHLESS SECURITY At LOW COST. } A. H. COLLINS { General Agent Baldwin Block.

Rooms 42 and 43 WHEN BUILDING.

ESTABLISHED 1876. TELEPHONE 168.
CHESTER BRADFORD,
SOLICITOR OF PATENTS,
AND COUNSEL IN PATENT CAUSES.
(See adv. page 6.)
Office:—Rooms 14 and 16 Hubbard Block, S. W. Cor. Washington and Meridian Streets,
INDIANAPOLIS, INDIANA.

Edwardsport Coal and Mining Co. Miners and Shippers Steam and Domestic Coal.

Lendormi Ellen (wid Joseph), b 21 Concordia.
Lendormi Paul, lab, h 266 Davidson.
Lendormi Philip S, uphlr, b 1024 N Senate av.
Lendrigan Catherine (wid Philip), b 28 Chadwick.
Lendrigan Wm E, mach, h 28 Chadwick.
Lengel John J, engr, h 68 Hoyt av.
Lenhert John, tailor, b 777 N Senate av.
Lenihan Patrick, bricklyr, h 661 W Vermont.
Lenker John, blksmith, h 121 Excelsior av.
Lenker Michael, clk, h 18 Tacoma av.
Lennig Anna, bkkpr, b 271 E Vermont.
Lennig Delta, clk, b 271 E Vermont.
Lennig Wm F, clk, h 271 E Vermont.
Lennon John B, treas Am Federation of Labor, res Bloomington, Ill.
Lennox Edwin L (Carlin & Lennox), h 174 Broadway.
Lennox Richard F, trav agt, h 1203 N Capitol av.
Lensmann Henry J, grocer, 562 Shelby, h same.
Lensmann Henry J jr, carp, b 562 Shelby.
Lentz, see also Lantz and Lintz.
Lentz Albert C, bartndr, b 50 N Noble.
Lentz August, lab, b 236 S Missouri.
Lentz Charles R, cabtmkr, b 189 Shelby.
Lentz Christian, gardener, h 99 N Belmont av.
Lentz Edward M, clk, b 31 Water.
Lentz Eugene F, gardener, h 1052 W Vermont.
Lentz Frank, lab, h 151 Harmon.
Lentz Frank, waiter, h 144 S Alabama.
Lentz Frank W, clk Pearson & Wetzel, b 31 Water.
Lentz Frederick J, h 145 W Morris.
Lentz Frederica (wid Adolph), b 50 N Noble.
Lentz George W, die cutter, h 448 Dillon.
Lentz Herman, saloon, 390 W North, h same.
Lentz Minnie, b 491 Mulberry.
Lentz Philip, lab, b 181 S New Jersey.
Lentz Wm, lab, h 298 W Morris.
Lentz Wm F, packer, h 31 Water.

Outing BICYCLES
$85.00.
MADE AND SOLD BY
HAY & WILLITS MFG. CO.
76 N. PENNSYLVANIA ST. PHONE 598.

Lentz Wm M, florist, b 355 S East.
Lenz Frederick W, mach hd, h 25 Catharine.
Lenz George A, lab, b 25 Catharine.
Lenze Wm, printer, b 333 S Penn.
Lenzen Marie B, cashr Emil Wulschner & Son, b 57 Wyoming.
Lenzen Wm S, saloon, 120 E Maryland, h 57 Wyoming.
Leon Boyer, lab, b 54 Hosbrook.
Leonard Allen, lab, b rear 198 River av (W I).
Leonard Alvin M, carp, h 164 Newman.
Leonard Brother, teacher, b cor Coburn and Short.
Leonard Charles M (Leonard & Dyer), h 47 Barth av.
Leonard Charles W, collr, r 37½ E Washington.
Leonard Clarence E, painter, h 33 College av.
Leonard Daniel J, fireman, b 14½ Bates.
Leonard Edith L (E L Leonard & Co), r 3 Wyandot blk.
Leonard Edmund J, engr, h 591 E Washington.
Leonard Enos E, milk dealer, b 1511 N Capitol av.
Leonard E L & Co (Edith L Leonard), men's furngs, 69 S Illinois.
Leonard Francis A, lab, h rear 198 River av (W I).
Leonard James F, mach hd, h 433 W Addison (N I).
Leonard James J, lab, b 29 Blake.
Leonard John, carp, h 431 W McLene (N I).
Leonard John, tailor, b n e cor 7th and Lennox.
Leonard John P, cook, b 131 W Washington.
Leonard John W, teacher, h w s Capitol av 4 s of 30th.
Leonard Joseph A, farmer, h 240 Bismarck av (H).
Leonard Lewis B, carp, h e s Charles bet 31st and 32d (M).
Leonard Marcus A, b 16 Stevens pl.
Leonard Minnie E (wid Merritt), boarding 6 Cornell av.
Leonard Morton, lab, h 355 S Capitol av.
Leonard Robert D, porter, h 61 Orange.
Leonard Samuel, plastr, r 156 W Washington.
Leonard Sarah E (wid Sylvanus), h 214 Fulton.
Leonard Sarah J (wid Cain), b w s James 3 s of Sutherland (B).
Leonard Shepherd V (Leonard & Sloan), h 245 Buchanan.
Leonard Stoughton G (Leonard & Simmonds), h 56 Barth av.
Leonard Theodore E, carp, h 229 Michigan av.
Leonard Thomas, lab, b 95 Agnes.
Leonard Thomas A, trav agt, b 269½ E Washington.
Leonard Walter B (Leonard & Thomas), h 71 Sheffield av (H).
Leonard Walter N, letter carrier P O, h 16 Holloway av.
Leonard Wm, lab, h 61 Minerva.
Leonard Wm, salesman, r 17½ S Alabama.
Leonard Wm F, engr, h 860 E Washington.
Leonard Wm H, carp, h 20 Holloway av.
Leonard Wm L, driver, h 25½ S Alabama.
Leonard & Dyer (Charles M Leonard, Wm B Dyer), machinery, 18½ N Meridian.
Leonard & Simmonds (Stoughton G Leonard, Fernandez M Simmonds), carriage mnfrs, cor Oliver av and Judge Harding (W I).

C. ZIMMERMAN & SONS | SLATE AND GRAVEL ROOFERS 19 South East Street.

THE art of printing—Good Printing—is simple enough when equipped with modern materials and machinery, and employ workmen whose experience has taught them how to produce an up-to-date arrangement of the ever-changing styles of Type, Borders and Color effects in .. ..

Printi g,
Lith graphing,
and **Bla k B oks.**

We do all this and more too.

Everything that we manufacture, print or design, we endeavor to make THE BEST, and for the reason that we have a modern plant in every sense of the word, you may rely upon getting what you want. .. ..

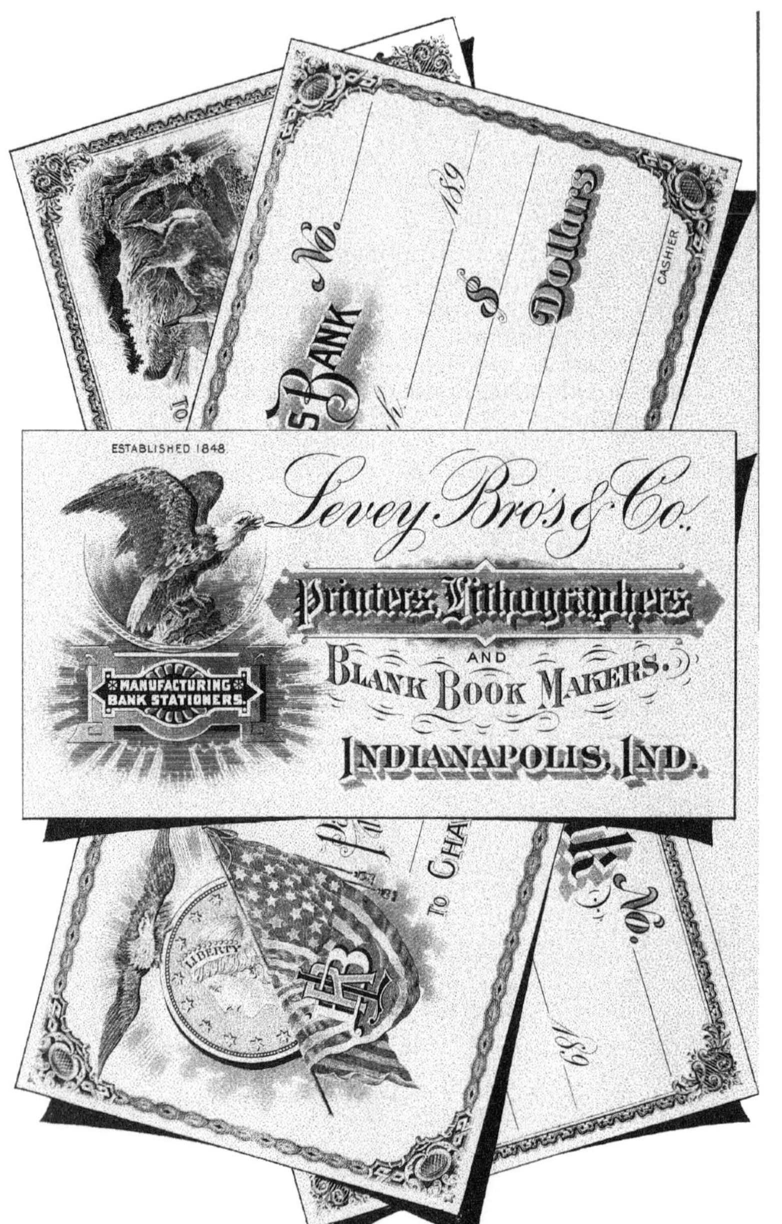

ESTABLISHED 1848.
Levey Bro's & Co.
Printers, Lithographers
AND
Blank Book Makers.
Indianapolis, Ind.
MANUFACTURING
BANK STATIONERS.

DRIVEN WELLS And Second Water Wells and Pumps of all kinds at CHARLES KRAUSS', 42 S. PENN. ST. TELEPHONE 465.

ERTEL STEAM LAUNDRY LARGEST AND BEST IN THE STATE. PROMPT SERVICE. 26 and 28 N. Senate Ave. Tel 1618

Leonard & Sloan (Shepherd V Leonard, Robert R Sloan), livery, 541 Virginia av.
Leonard & Thomas (Walter B Leonard, James A Thomas), founders, 171 River av (W I).
Leonhardt Herman E, watchman, h 56 Minerva.
Leonhardt Otto, tailor, b 56 Minerva.
Leonie Lawrence D, bartndr, h 14 E Michigan.
Leopold Arthur, clk Elliott & Butler, b 156 N Liberty.
Leopold Eliza (wid Solomon), h 156 N Liberty.
Le Page John P, monuments, 1552 Northwestern av (N I), h same.
Le Page Maude (wid Samuel), h 47 Rhode Island.
Lepine John M, molder, h 30 Cleveland (H).
Lepper Christina, h s s Orchard av 2 e of Rural.
Lepper Ezra L, boilermkr, h 8 Depot (B).
Lepper Henry, plastr, h 362 Spring.
Lepper Henry P, lab, h 150 Lily.
Lepper Philip, lab, b s s Orchard av 2 e of Rural.
Leppert George J, mach, b rear 292 E Louisiana.
Leppert Gotthard, teacher, h 630 Chestnut.
Leppert John S, cigarmkr, b 23 Lord.
Leppert Leopold, tailor, 79 E Washington, h 785 N Alabama.
Leppert Mary T (wid Nicholas), h 23 Lord.
Leppert Otto, tailor, b 140 River av (W I).
Leppert Samuel, patrolman, h 162 Minkner.
Leppert Wm, tailor, h 821 Chestnut.
Leppert Wm C, cutter, b 785 N Alabama.
Leppert Wm T, opr W U Tel Co, b 23 Lord.
Leser John jr, grocer, 331 W Morris, h 297 same.
Leser Peter C, insp, h 63 S Belmont av (W I).
Lesh Charles P (C P Lesh Paper Co), h 489 Central av.
LESH C P PAPER CO, Wholesale Paper, 85 W Market, Tel 1559.
Lesh Daniel, b 489 Central av.
Lesh Frank J, carp, b 29 Madison av.
LESLEY DANIEL, Agt The Toledo Bridge Co, Pres Edwardsville Coal Mining Co, Room 42 When Blk, Tel 1916; h n w cor Maxwell and Walnut avs (I). (See adv in classified Bridge Contractors.)
Lesley Wm A, lab, r rear 131 E Washington.
Leslie Hayden, lab, h 27 Cincinnati.
Leslie Margaret J, h s s Railroad 3 w of Central av (I).
Leslie Mary J, h 11 Morgan (W I).
Leslie Sophia (wid Wm), h 191½ Indiana av.
Lesman Charles, lab, h 256 Bates.
Lesser Edward B, mach, h 120 Harmon.
Lessing Anna, tailoress, b 413 S Illinois.
Lester Carlton, driver, b 315 E Miami.
Lester Edward M, well digger, b w s Caldwell 2 n of W North.
Lester Jacob W, mach, r 22 Catterson blk.
Lester John H, engr, h 315 E Miami.
Lester Robert T, pdlr, b 315 E Miami.
Lester Wm H, clk, h 226 N Delaware.
Lester Wm H, lab, h 403 Pleasant.
Lester Wm J, lab, h w s Caldwell 2 n of W North.
Letcher James W, porter, b 281 E Court.
Letcher Martha J (wid Jesse), h 281 E Court.

RICHARDSON & McCREA, MANAGERS FOR CENTRAL INDIANA. EQUITABLE LIFE ASSURANCE SOCIETY Of the United States. 79 EAST MARKET STREET, TELEPHONE 182.

Lethermon Araminta, seamstress, b 6 Hermann.
Leucht John J, lab, h 47 Wyoming.
Leukhardt August H, mach, h 167 Ramsey av.
Leukhardt Christian W, mach, h 8 Lawn (B).
Leukhardt Frederick I, carp, h 149 Eureka av.
Leukhardt Gottlieb, saloon, 102 N Noble, h same.
Leukhardt Wm C, carp, h 23 Peru av.
Leupen Herman, clk L S Ayres & Co, b 992 S Meridian.
Leupen John, h 992 S Meridian.
Leupen Linda, bkkpr, b 992 S Meridian.
Leupen Louis, uphlr, b 992 S Meridian.
Leupp John, tmstr, h 328 N Noble.
Leuthy Wm, lab, h 543 Jones (N I).
Levee Ida M, b 164 Broadway.
Level Lee, waiter, r rear 175 N Penn.
Levens Mary T, cook, h 108½ Mass av.
Lever Daniel V, plumber, b Germania House.
Levey Anne M (wid Wm M), h 753 N Penn.
Levey Anna R, clothing, 279 E Washington, h same.
Levey Benjamin, trav agt, h 279 E Washington.
LEVEY BROS & CO (Louis H Levey), Printers, Stationers, Binders and Blank Book Mnfrs, 19 W Maryland, Tel 1064. (See adv opp.)
Levey Dunn, printer, b 753 N Penn.
Levey Jacob I, clk, b 279 E Washington.
Levey Louis H (Levey Bros & Co), h 834 N Meridian.
Levey Marshall T, clk Levey Bros, h 753 N Penn.
Levi Harris, shoemkr, 191 S Illinois, b 189 same.
Levi Henry, tinner, b 121 Maple.
Levi Hyman, pdlr, b 423 S Capitol av.
Levi Philip, junk, h 512 S Capitol av.
Levihu Henry M, blksmith, h 20 Nevada.
Levin Lizzie, r 138 S East.
Levings Esther S (wid Calvin W), b 143 St Mary.

Typewriter-Ribbons ALL COLORS FOR ALL MACHINES. THE BEST AND CHEAPEST. S. H. EAST, STATE AGENT, The Williams Typewriter.... 55 THORPE BLOCK, 87 E. MARKET ST.

ELLIS & HELFENBERGER Architectural Iron Work and Gray Iron Castings. 162-170 South Senate Ave. Tel. 958.

THE HOGAN TRANSFER AND STORAGE COMP'Y
Household Goods and Pianos Moved—Packed—Stored...... Baggage and Package Express Machinery and Safes a Specialty Cor. Washington and Illinois Sts. TELEPHONE No. 675.

The Provident Life and Trust Company
Of Philadelphia.
Grants Certificates of Extension to Policyholders who are temporarily unable to pay their premiums
D. W. EDWARDS, Gen. Agt., 508 Indiana Trust Bldg.

Levings Wm A, foreman, b 136 W 1st.
Levinson Abraham, pdlr, h 79 Maple.
Levinston Perry H, bkkpr, h 224 E New York.
Levinston Harry S, clk, b 224 E New York.
Levis Dell T Rev, h 207½ Indiana av.
Levison Otto, salesman, r 191 N Delaware.
Levy Abraham, cook, h 108 Eddy.
Levy Harry, clk, r 271 E Ohio.
Levy Irene (wid Abram F), h 192 N East.
Levy Isaac, tailor, h 90 Huron.
Levy Maurice, stenog Coe & Roache, b 545 N Alabama.
Levy Myer, saloon, 220 W Washington, h 325 W Michigan.
Levy Myron, trav agt, b 545 N Alabama.
Levy Norman, mngr Percival Levy, b 180 N East.
Levy Percival, leaf tobacco, 81 E Court, b 180 N East.
Levy Rudolph, adv agt, h 86 N New Jersey.
Levy Theresa (wid Reuben), h 545 N Alabama.
Lewark Amanda C (wid Edwin), h 28 Warren av (W I).
Lewark Harry B, lab, h 613 W Pearl.
Lewark James H, h 82 S Linden.
Lewellen, see also Llewellyn.
Lewellen Harry P, opr Postal Tel Cable Co, b 215 W South.
Lewellen Wm H, butter, 24½ E Mkt House, h 107 N Beville av.
Lewellyn Richard L, carp, h 10 S Linden.
Lewis, see also Louis.
Lewis Abner (A Lewis & Co), h 477 N Alabama.
Lewis Abram T, dyer, 127 Indiana av, h 487 S Capitol av.
Lewis Agnes F, laundress, b 351 S Delaware.
Lewis Albert, clk, h 246 Fayette.
Lewis Albert, coachman 374 N Illinois.
Lewis Albert, lab, h 184 Howard.
Lewis Albert J, opr W U Tel Co, b 397 N Alabama.
Lewis Albert L, elev opr The Denison.
Lewis Alda J, dentist, h 220 E Walnut.
Lewis Amanda R (wid Robert M), b 572 S West.

Julius C. Walk & Son,
Jewelers
Indianapolis.
12 EAST WASHINGTON ST.

Lewis Anderson (O'Brien & Lewis), h 167 Talbott av.
Lewis Andrew R, station master Union Station, h 249 Cornell av.
Lewis Angeline M (wid Levin B), b 645 Park av.
Lewis Anna (wid Preston), h rear 163 E St Joseph.
Lewis Anna E, b 327 W North.
Lewis Annie A, bkkpr German Am Bldg Assn, b 729 College av.
Lewis Archibald, lab, h rear 130 E St Joseph.
Lewis Arthur T, molder, b 173 Germania av (H).
Lewis A & Co (Abner Lewis), grocers, 401 N Alabama.
Lewis Benjamin, farmer, h 35 Standard av (W I).
Lewis Benjamin F, harnessmkr, h 35 Garfield pl.
Lewis Casper, confr, 126 Oliver (W I), h same.
Lewis Catharine M (wid Tompkins A), h 528 N Meridian.
Lewis Charles, lab, h 20 Reynolds av (H).
Lewis Charles, lab, b 444 Superior.
Lewis Charles, molder, b 1093 W Michigan.
Lewis Charles, paperhngr, b 20 Bell.
Lewis Charles, porter, b 132 Michigan (H).
Lewis Charles, porter, b 212 W Vermont.
Lewis Charles A, b 528 N Meridian.
Lewis Charles A, painter, b 76 Michigan (H).
Lewis Charles A, paperhngr, b 57 N Dorman.
Lewis Charles H, mach, h 160 N Belmont av (H).
Lewis Charles K, lab, b 128 Blake.
Lewis Charles M, student, b 174 Mass av.
Lewis Charles S, sec and treas Wagner Car Door Co, h 600 N Illinois.
Lewis Charles W, carriage painter, 216 W North, b 167 Talbott av.
Lewis Charlotte (wid John L), h 52 Warren av (W I).
Lewis David P, carp, h 439 W Eugene (N I).
Lewis Earl P, clk, b 35 Garfield pl.
Lewis Edward, contr, 306 E South, h same.
Lewis Edward, lab, b 280 Fayette.
Lewis Edward L, printer, r 77 W Ohio.
Lewis Edward T, mach, h 16 Spann av.
LEWIS EDWIN R, Physician (Throat and Nose), 131 N Meridian, h 385 N Penn.
Lewis Elijah, lab, h 22 Willard.
Lewis Elizabeth C (wid Cyrus), h 288 Bright.
Lewis Flora B, officer Indiana Reformatory.
Lewis Florence (wid John R), h 26 S West.
Lewis Frank, fireman, h 130 Cornell av.
Lewis Frank S, painter, h 176 Madison av.
Lewis Frank W, pres Indpls Foundry Co, h 296 N Illinois
Lewis Frederick, lab, h 259 W 3d.
Lewis Frederick K, molder, h 47 Bismarck (W I).
Lewis George, condr, b 11 Emerson pl.
Lewis George, lab, h rear 29 W Michigan.
Lewis George jr, lab, b 280 Fayette.
Lewis George C, patternmkr, b 35 Garfield pl.
LEWIS GEORGE S, Cigars and Tobacco, 102 Mass av, h 108½ same.
Lewis George W, driver, h 280 Fayette.

The Central Rubber & Supply Co. Hose, Belting, Packing, Clothing, Druggists' Sundries, Bicycle Tires, Cotton Hose, Etc. New York Belting & Packing Co., L't'd.
PHONE 922. 79 S. ILLINOIS ST., INDIANAPOLIS, IND.

OTTO GAS ENGINES
BUILDERS' EXCHANGE
S. W. Cor. Ohio and Penn.
Telephone 535.

Becker & Son Charles Becker Jacob Becker Jr. Merchant Tailors. 21 N. Penn St. Tel. 934

SALISBURY & STANLEY • Office, Store and Bar Fixtures a Specialty. Repairing of all kinds done on short notice. 177 Cherry St., Indianapolis, Ind. • Contractors and Builders TELEPHONE 999.

Lewis George W, lab, h 65 Quince.
Lewis Gertrude E, bookbndr, b 353 N Noble.
Lewis Harrison E, sec The Capital Live Stock Commission Co, h 462 N Penn.
Lewis Harry A, lab, b 72 Nebraska.
Lewis Harry E, bkkpr, r 425 N Penn.
Lewis Harry E, engr, b 35 Garfield pl.
Lewis Harry S E, artist, 18½ N Meridian, r 212 E Ohio.
Lewis Helen N (wid Wm), h 557 N Senate av.
Lewis Henry M, clk, r 53 The Windsor.
Lewis Henry M, sergeant U S Army, b 25½ N Illinois.
Lewis Howard, lab, h e s Tremont av 3 s of Clark (H).
Lewis Irving, carp, b 217 S Illinois.
Lewis James, lab, b 525 Roanoke.
Lewis James, lab, h 16 Spann av.
Lewis James C D, phys, 215 Cornell av h same.
Lewis James F, lab, h 644 E 8th.
Lewis Jennie A (wid Lloyd), h rear 258 Alvord.
Lewis Jeremiah, trimmer, h 954 Wilcox.
Lewis Jocelyn E E, stenog The Smith Premeir Typewriter Co, b 215 Cornell av.
Lewis Joel, lab, h 22 Willard.
Lewis John, cook, r 232 W North.
Lewis John, porter, h 54 Davis.
Lewis John, porter, b 13 Fayette.
Lewis John, watchman, r 36 W Ohio.
Lewis John F, b 44 Bismarck (W I).
Lewis John H, insp City Civil Engineer's Office, b 567 Ash.
Lewis John O, motorman, h 19 Hall pl.
Lewis John T, lab, h rear 124 Broadway.
Lewis John W, elev opr, r 19 N Noble.
Lewis John W, lab, b 122 Ash.
Lewis John W, lab, b 556 Dillon.
Lewis Joseph, cook 731 N Meridian.
Lewis Joseph, lab 564 N Meridian.
Lewis Joseph, lab, b 783 N Senate av.
Lewis Joseph E, clk, b 477 N Alabama.
Lewis Joseph H, h 5½ Blackford.
Lewis Joseph M, lab, h 370 S Alabama.
Lewis Joseph W, waiter, h 261 W St Clair.
Lewis Julia, h 21 Howard.
Lewis Lavina (wid Henry J), h 556 Dillon.
Lewis Lawrence, cook, h 30 Depot (B).
Lewis Leonard E, lab, b 52 Warren av (W I).
Lewis Luna A, elocutionist, b 368 W New York.
Lewis Mamie, laundress, b 71 Peru av.
Lewis Marcus F, porter, h 40 W 1st.
Lewis Mary (wid Dallis), b 55 Clifford av.
Lewis Mary (wid John), h 206 Elm.
Lewis Matthew, molder, h 1093 W Michigan.
Lewis Matthew H, lab, r 40 W 1st
Lewis Minerva (wid Ezekiel), b 477 N Alabama.
Lewis Morris Rev, h 502 N California.
Lewis Newton, coachman 836 N Meridian.
Lewis Nimrod, lab, h 100 W 10th.
Lewis Oliver P, carp, h 136 Sheffield av (H).
Lewis Oliver P, harnessmkr, h 51 Chadwick.
Lewis Orlando V A, painter, h 10 Parker av.
Lewis Preston J, cistern builder, 237 W 7th, h same.
Lewis Prudence, critic Public School No 32, b 729 College av.
Lewis Rankin E, b 76 E New York.
Lewis Richard, driver, b 556 Dillon.

Henry H. Fay,
40½ E. Washington St.,
REAL ESTATE,
AND LOAN BROKER.

Lewis Richard P, mach hd, b 35 Garfield pl.
Lewis Robert, lab, b 140 Maple.
Lewis Rufus T, waiter, h 283 Fayette.
Lewis Sallie, housekpr 401 W 2d.
Lewis Samantha A (wid John H), h 80 Greer.
Lewis Sarah J (wid George W), h 286 Christian av.
Lewis Seibert R B, clk Laz Noble & Co, b 215 Cornell av.
Lewis Solomon H, chiropodist, 235 Mass av, r same.
Lewis Stephen L, lab, h 100 Sharpe av (W).
Lewis Temperance (wid Michael), h 69 S California.
Lewis Thomas, waiter, r 197 W 3d.
Lewis Thomas B, huckster, h 452 W McLene (N I).
Lewis Thomas R (Burnet & Lewis), h 113 Sanders.
Lewis Thomas W, driver, h 324 Hudson.
Lewis Walter W, molder, h 173 Germania av (H).
Lewis Washington, lab, h 2 Mankedick.
Lewis Wesley, driver, h 176 W 7th.
Lewis Wesley, lab, h 130 Ash.
Lewis Wm, coachman, b 29 W 1st.
Lewis Wm, coremkr, b 1093 W Michigan.
Lewis Wm, lab, b n s 23d 2 e of Northwestern av.
Lewis Wm, porter, b 219 W North.
Lewis Wm A, cooper, h 44 Bismarck av (W I).
Lewis Wm B, carpetlyr, h 57 N Dorman.
Lewis Wm B jr, clk, b 57 N Dorman.
Lewis Wm H, grocer, 203 Bellefontaine, h 286 same.
Lewis Wm J, clk L E & W R R, b 220 E Walnut.
Lewis Wm M, prin Public School No 42, h 296 Yandes.
Lewis Wm T, asst supt Citizens' St R R, h 567 Ash.
Lewis Zimri C, painter, h 1320 N Capitol av.
Lewitt Wm H, b s s Washington av 1 e of Maple av (I).
Lex Jacob L, pressman, h 112 Spring.
Lexon Frank, car rep, h s w cor S Brookside and Waverly avs.

MAYHEW'S SPECTACLES THE BEST IN USE SOLD ONLY AT 13 N. MERIDIAN ST.

COAL AND LIME Cement, Hair, Sewer Pipe, etc. BALKE & KRAUSS CO. Cor. Missouri and Market Sts.

FRIEDGEN'S IS THE PLACE FOR THE NOBBIEST SHOES Ladies' and Gents' 19 North Pennsylvania St.

M. B. WILSON, Pres. W. F. CHURCHMAN, Cash.
THE CAPITAL NATIONAL BANK,
INDIANAPOLIS, IND.
Our Specialty is handling all Country Checks and Drafts on Indiana and neighboring States at the very lowest rates. Call and see us.
Interest Paid on Time Deposits.
28 S. MERIDIAN ST., COR. PEARL.

Lexsow Charles, lab, h 65 Barth av.
Lexsow Charles H, finisher, b 65 Barth av.
Lexsow Frederick L, bottler, b 65 Barth av.
Leyendecker Charlotte (wid Henry), b 166 Columbia av.
Leyendecker John P (Leyendecker & Waters), h 166 Columbia av.
LEYENDECKER & WATERS (John P Leyendecker, Samuel R Waters), Lawyers, 308-310 Indiana Trust Bldg.
L'Heureux Rodolphe P, marble setter, b 850 N New Jersey.
Liautey, see also Leauty.
Liautey Amos, mach hd, h 447 Union.
Liautey John B, clk, h 47 Buchanan.
Libean Charles H, clk, h 334 Bellefontaine.
Libking Edward C, cutter, h 167 Spann av.
Libking Louis A, city agt, b 167 Spann av.
Libowitz Abraham, clothing, 207 E Washington, h 390 S Delaware.
Libowitz Jacob, trav agt, h 390 S Delaware.
Libowitz Samuel, clk, h 390 S Delaware.
Lich Albert F, jeweler, h 491 S Illinois.
Lichlyter George E, lab, b 479 Dillon.
Lichtenauer Frederick, grocer, 609 W Washington, h same.
Lichtenauer Simon, fireman, h 78 Torbet.
Lichtenberg Charles, watchman, h 82 N Beville av.
Lichtenberg Christian F, meats, 201 Shelby, h same.
Lichtenberg Henry, chairmkr, b 552 S Capitol av.
Lichtenberg John, grocer, 552 S Capitol av, h same.
Lichtenberg Wm E, grocer, 300 E Ohio, h same.
Lichtenfels Frederick, buffer, b 10 Hendricks.
Lichtenfels George, lab, h 10 Hendricks.
Lichtenfels George jr, lab, b 10 Hendricks.
Lichtenstetter Joseph S, cook, h 272 S East.
Lichtsinn Wm F, driver, h 183 Spann av.
Lichty Aaron, h 426 Talbott av.
Lichty Mary, drugs, 398 Talbott av, h 426 same.
Liddy Jeremiah J, brakeman, b 48 N State av.
Lidle Wm H, lab, b 228 N Missouri.

TUTTLE & SEGUIN,
28 E. Market St. Ground Floor.
COLLECTING RENTS AND CARE OF PROPERTY A SPECIALTY.
Telephone 1168.

Lieber Albert, pres and gen mngr Indpls Brewing Co, h 558 Madison av, tel 1542.
Lieber Carl H (The H Lieber Co), h 221 N New Jersey.
Lieber Herman, pres The H Lieber Co, h 250 N Alabama.
Lieber Herman P, trav agt The H Lieber Co, b 250 N Alabama.
LIEBER H CO THE, Herman Lieber Pres, Otto R Lieber Vice-Pres, Wm Wellmann Sec, Art Emporium, 33 S Meridian, Tel 500; Factory 590-620 Madison av, Tel 771. (See right top cor cards.)
Lieber Otto R, vice-pres The H Lieber Co, b 250 N Alabama.
LIEBER P BRANCH INDIANAPOLIS BREWING CO, 514 Madison av, Tel 424.
LIEBER RICH & CO (Richard Lieber, Gustave Oberlaender), Bottlers of High Grade Soda, Mineral and Medicinal Waters; also Distilled Water, cor New York and Agnes streets, Tel 1263.
Lieber Richard (Richard Lieber & Co), city editor Indiana Tribune, b 603 N Alabama.
Lieber Robert (The H Lieber Co), b 250 N Alabama.
Lieberherr Christina (wid Henry), b 644 W Washington.
Lieberherr George F, lab, h 628 W Eugene (N I).
Lieberherr Henry W, lab, b 551 W Washington.
Liebert Charles G S, mnfrs' agt, 143½ S Meridian, h 853 N Penn.
Liebert Joseph D, trav agt, b 27 E Pratt.
Liebrich George J, porter, h 322 W North.
Liebrich John F, mach, h 330 W North.
Liebtag Charles E, barber, b 549 W Addison (N I).
Liebtag Frederick, finisher, h 549 W Addison (N I).
Liebtag Wm G, barber, 545 W Udell, b 549 W Addison (N I).
Liedrich Lena (wid Louis J), b 626 N Capitol av.
Liehr, see also Lehr.
Liehr Peter, meats, 247 Davidson, h same.
Liehr Peter jr, lab, b 247 Davidson.
Liehr Philip, gateman, h 149 Yandes.
Liening Anton, grocer, 160 Keystone av, h same.
Liese August, mach hd, h 1165 E Washington.
Lieske Erdmann, lab, h 3 Brown av (H).
Lieske Gustav, molder, b 3 Brown av (H).
Lieutey Elizabeth (wid Charles), h 49 Empire.
Lifschitz Herman (Lifschitz & Mazo), b 431 S Capitol av.
Lifschitz Moses, pdlr, h 60 W Merrill.
Lifschitz & Mazo (Herman Lifschitz, Benjamin Mazo), feed, 92 Russell av.
Liggens Sarah, h 34 Hadley.
Light Arthur F, carp, h 522 Talbott av.
Light Carl F, carp, b 79 Columbia av.
Light Elizabeth L (wid John A), dressmkr, 5½ Indiana av, h same.
Light Milton C, wheelmkr, h 75 Division (W I).
Light Robert C, pres Indpls & Broad Ripple Rapid Transit Co, res Broad Ripple, Ind.
Light Theodore G, carp, h 64 Jefferson av.
Lighter Mattie E (wid Henry F), h 75 N Olive.

SAMUEL LAING || COPPER AND GALVANIZED IRON CORNICE MANUFACTURER
SKYLIGHTS AND VENTILATORS. 72 AND 74 E. COURT STREET.

PAPER BOXES SULLIVAN & MAHAN 41 W. Pearl St.

DIAMOND WALL PLASTER { Telephone 1410
BUILDERS' EXCHANGE.

If your Laundry Work is not satisfactory, try THE HOME LAUNDRY 197 S. Illinois St. Telephone 1769.

Lighter Wm V, trav agt, b 75 N Olive.
Lightfoot Thomas, lab, h 182 W Michigan.
Lightford James G, mech engr, h 203 Union.
Lightford Wm L, patternmkr, b 203 Union.
Lightner Charles, lab, b 433 Blake.
Liken John H, lab, b 275 S Capitol av.
Lilley James R, treas Indiana Paper Co, h 26 E 2d.
Lilley Roswell H, huckster, h 73 Maxwell.
Lilley Wm M, insp, h 44 Ashland (W I).
Lilliard Joseph, lab, b 333 Lafayette.
Lillie Albert M, lab, h 180 Meek.
Lilly Bros (Wm A and Herbert G), florists, 682 N Senate av.
Lilly Charles, pres Lilly Varnish Co, h 1053 N Illinois.
Lilly Eli, pres Eli Lilly & Co, h 720 N Meridian, tel 697.
LILLY ELI & CO, Eli Lilly Pres, James E Lilly Vice-Pres, Evan F Lilly Sec and Treas, Josiah K Lilly Supt, Mnfrs of Pharmaceutical Chemicals, 132-140 E McCarty, Tel 395.
Lilly Evan F, sec and treas Eli Lilly & Co, h 700 N Delaware.
Lilly Gustavus, chemist Eli Lilly & Co, h 38 Greer.
Lilly Henry, lab, h 213 W 3d.
Lilly Herbert G (Lilly Bros), h 682 N Senate av.
Lilly James E, vice-pres Eli Lilly & Co, h 996 N Illinois.
Lilly James W (Lilly & Stalnaker), h 600 N Capitol av.
Lilly John D, coremkr, b 165 Newman.
LILLY JOHN M, Hardwood Mantels, Grates and Tiles, 78-80 Mass av, Tel 207; h 510 N Delaware. (See adv p 8.)
Lilly Josiah K, supt Eli Lilly & Co, h 675 N Penn.
Lilly Mary P (wid Thomas J), b 88 S William (W I).
Lilly Samuel, b 280 Fayette.
Lilly Silas J, cooper, h 88 S William (W I).
Lilly Thomas, tmstr, h n e cor Nicholas and English.
Lilly Varnish Co, Charles Lilly pres, John M Lilly sec and treas, varnish mnfrs, 10 Rose.
Lilly Wm A (Lilly Bros), h 682 N Senate av.
LILLY & STALNAKER (James W Lilly, Frank D Stalnaker), Hardware, 64 E Washington, Tel 509.
Limbert Charles A, brakeman, r 61 S Summit.
Limle Charles H, painter, b 41 Madison av.
Lincoln Charles H, clk, h 31 W Pratt.
Lincoln Wm E, mach opr The Indpls Sentinel, b 31 W Pratt.
Lingburg Anna M (wid Clausen), r 5½ Shelby.
Lindell John, gardener, h s s Brookville rd 1 e of P C C & St L Ry (S).
Lindemann Charles, brazier, h 109 Benton.
Lindemann Elizabeth (wid Wm), b 109 Benton.
Lindemann Frank, grocer, 210 E Washington, h same.
Lindemann Frederick, lab, h 119 Dunlop.
Lindemann Frederick jr, carp, h 119 Dunlop.
Lindemann Frederick W, clk, h 99 Walcott.
Lindemann Harry A, clk, b 109 Benton.
Lindemann Henry L, engr, h 170 Walcott.
Lindemann Wm, carp, h 499 S Missouri.

FRANK NESSLER. WILL H. ROST.
FRANK NESSLER & CO.
Tailors
56 EAST MARKET ST. (Lemcke Building),
INDIANAPOLIS, IND.

Lindemann Wm M, lab, h 205 Meek.
Linden Joseph, porter 95 N Meridian.
Lindenberg Herman A, sculptor, 49 S Shade (B), h same.
Lindenschmidt Charles A, mach, h 39 Kennington.
Linder Charles, janitor Public School No 22, h 684 Chestnut.
Linder Frank C, mach, h 205 Newman.
Linder Henry, lab, h 186 Bismarck av (H).
Linder John L, lab, h 457 S West.
Linder John N, bartndr, h 728 S East.
Linder Nicholas J, carp, h 111 Gray.
Linder Wm, b 1044 N Illinois.
Linderman Willard W, actor, b 741 Nevada.
Lindley Ethel, teacher Public School No 26, b 33 Broadway.
Lindley James F, bkkpr, h 441 Central av.
Lindley Lucy (wid John A), b 33 Broadway.
Lindner Charles, lab, b 335 Jefferson av.
Lindner Charles C, train disp P & E Ry, h 375 E 15th.
Lindon Joseph, lab, b 78 W Maryland.
Lindsay Howard, switchman, h 575 W Udell (N I).
Lindsay James, lab, b 183 W South.
Lindsay John W, clk R M S, h 14 Dawson.
Lindsay Martin, tinner, b 197 W Maryland.
Lindsay Patrick, lab, b 293 Indiana av.
Lindsay Warren, tel opr, h 550 W Udell (N I).
Lindsey Adrian A, farmer, b 262 River av (W I).
Lindsey George, h 234 E Pearl.
Lindsey Henry H, carp, h 4 Highland av (H).
Lindsey John, hostler, r 26 W Merrill.
Lindsey John F, carp, h 1369 London av.
Lindsey Joseph, porter, h 161 Agnes.
Lindsey Mamie M, stenog, r 265 N Illinois.
Lindsey Nancy (wid George), b 198 Bright.
Lindsey Thomas, lab, h 234 E Pearl.
Lindsey Wm, bellboy Hotel English.
Lindstaedt Herman, mach, b 90 Kansas.
Lindstaedt Otto R, clk Haueisen & Hartmann, h s e cor Ohio and Sherman Drive.
Lindstaedt Theodore F, cabtmkr, h 94 Kansas.

Haueisen & Hartmann
163-169 E. Washington St.
FURNITURE,
Carpets,
Household Goods,
Tin, Granite and China Wares, Oil Cloth and Shades

THE WM. H. BLOCK CO.
7 AND 9 EAST WASHINGTON STREET.
DRY GOODS,
MEN'S
FURNISHINGS.

The Fidelity and Deposit Co. OF MARYLAND. Bonds signed for Administrators, Assignees, Executors, Guardians, Receivers, Trustees, and persons in every position of trust.
GEO. W. PANGBORN, General Agent, 704-706 Lemcke Building. Telephone 140.

INSURE YOUR PROPERTY WITH FRANK K. SAWYER

• JOSEPH GARDNER •
GALVANIZED IRON
CORNICES and SKYLIGHTS.
Metal Ceilings and Siding.
Tin, Iron, Steel and Slate Roofing.
37, 39 & 41 KENTUCKY AVE. Telephone 322.

Lindstrom Charles, molder, h 432 S State av.
Lindstrom Charles H, folder, b 432 S State av.
Lindstrom Edward E, clk, b 432 S State av.
Lindstrom Gustav G, printer, b 432 S State av.
Line Isaac N, bricklyr, b Enterprise Hotel.
Lineback Charles B (Lineback & Kerr), barber, 166½ W Washington, h 31 N New Jersey.
Lineback Harry, lab, b 325 Jefferson av.
Lineback Howard, b 325 Jefferson av.
Lineback Mary E (wid John A), b 325 Jefferson av.
Lineback Stephen, lab, h 576 W McLene (N I).
Lineback Stephen A, tmstr, b 325 Jefferson av.
Lineback & Kerr (Charles B Lineback, John F Kerr), barbers, 46 N Delaware.
Lineberry Wm W Rev, h 62 N Linden.
Linegar John T, mach, b 107 Cornell av.
Linegar Thomas F, baking powder, 31 W South, h 307 Cornell av.
Linegar Thomas S, carp, h 107 Cornell av.
Linehan Jennie (wid Richard P), r 81 W Michigan.
Linehan Nellie M, opr W U Tel Co, r 81 W Michigan.
Lines Amos G, filer, h 20 Cornell av.
Lines Charles, coachman 240 Park av.
Lines Cornelia (wid John), b 184 N Capitol av.
Lines Samuel, h 50 Lafayette av.
Lines Samuel M, butcher, h 222 N Capitol av.
Lingenfelter Albert H, switchman, h 326 E Georgia.
Lingenfelter Almorine P, fireman, h 56 N Gale (B).
Lingenfelter Arthur B, packer, h 32 Bradshaw.
Lingenfelter Calvin F, lab, h w s Morris 5 s of Division (B).
Lingenfelter Elmer G, engr, h 492 Stillwell.
Lingenfelter Frank C, contr, 12 Pleasant, h same.
Lingenfelter Halbert, driver, h 50 Oak.

J. S. FARRELL & CO.
Have Experienced Workmen and will Promptly Attend to your
PLUMBING
Repairs. 84 North Illinois Street. Telephone 382.

Lingenfelter Jefferson, carp, r 77½ E Market.
Lingenfelter Mary A (wid John J), h 261 Howard.
Lingenfelter Mary P (wid Archibald), b 492 Stillwell.
Lingenfelter Robert F, elev opr, b 261 Howard.
Lingenfelter Wm H, mach, h 26 King.
Lingham K Fletcher, actress, b 237 W New York.
Lingham Thomas G, actor, b 237 W New York.
Lingle John, brakeman, h 92 Marion av (W I).
Lingle Wm S, car rep, h e s Brightwood av 9 s of Willow (B).
Lingo Horace A, clk, r 102 N Capitol av.
Link Frank L, trav agt The Gordon-Kurtz Co, r 33 The Chalfant.
Link George, lab, h 207 Kentucky av.
Link Jacob P, varnisher, h 626 Chestnut.
Link John B, motorman, h 95 Oliver av (W I).
Link Wm F, clk F X Erath, h 402 Bellefontaine.
LINKE HERMANN, Razor Mnfr, Barbers' Supplies, Surgical Instruments, Cutler and Grinder, 197 S Meridian, h 472 Charles.
Linkenfelts Frederick, polisher, b 10 Hendricks.
Linlau Charles W, driver, h 154 Johnson av.
Linn, see also Lynn.
Linn Blanche E, b 131 Yandes.
Linn Charles F, mach, h 51 Laurel.
Linn Cicero H, clk Consumers' Gas Trust Co, b n s Orange av 2 w of Keystone av.
Linn Louis, b 175 S Capitol av.
Linn Samuel, tailor, h 331 S Meridian.
LINN THOMAS B, Supreme Recorder Order of Chosen Friends, 54 Commercial Club Bldg, h n s Orange av 2 w of Keystone av.
Linn Wm, dyer, b Senate Hotel.
Linn Wm C, mach, h 43 Wright.
Linna Henry, bricklyr, h 149 N Summit.
Linnamanu Anton, lab, h 62 Yandes.
Linnamann Elizabeth M (wid Frederick), h 111 N Rural (B).
Linnamann John, meats, n s Bloyd av 2 w of Harriet (B), h w s Rural 1 n of Bloyd av.
Linnamann John C, lab, b 141 Lambert (W I).
Linnamann Joseph, butcher, b 111 N Rural (B).
Linnell Edward, blksmith, h 410 Columbia av.
Linscott Charles, solr, h 156 N West.
Linskey Bernard, lab, b 286 W Washington.
Linskey John, lab, h 59 Minerva.
Linskey John J, butcher, h 93 Chadwick.
Linskey Malachi F, butcher, b 59 Minerva.
Linting Marie L, dressmkr, b 58 Russell av.
Lintner Albert, b 1377 Berlin av.
Lintner Amos W, b 1377 Berlin av.
Lintner Anna E (wid Christian), b 940 N Penn.
Lintner Melinda C (wid Amos H), h 1377 Berlin av.
Linton Cecil H, driver, h 240 N Senate av.
Linton Charles J, buyer, h 894 Morris (W I).
Linton Frederick, lab, b 240 N Senate av.
Linton George W (Linton & Co), b 1667 N Capitol av.
Linton Jonathan, lab, b 889 Morris (W I).
Linton Samuel, lab, r 127 Columbia al.

GUARANTEED INCOME POLICIES issued only by the United States Life Insurance Co.
E. B. SWIFT, Manager. 25 E. Market St.

Furniture Carpets } WM. KOTTEMAN { Stoves Ranges
89 and 91 East Washington Street. Telephone 1742.

Linton Supply Co, Willard W Hubbard pres, Alfred M Ogle treas, 5 Hartford blk.
Linton & Co (George W Linton, Albert C Austermuhle), grocers, 1551 N Illinois.
Lintz, see also Lantz and Lentz.
Lintz Julia (wid Benjamin), h 165 Meek.
Linus Daniel A, fish, 63 Mass av and 92 E Mkt House, h 176 Mass av.
Linus James H, b 89 Paca.
Linzy Walter M, waiter, r 293 Indiana av.
Lion Mantel and Grate House, Percy R Chevalier propr, 114 N Delaware.
Lipferd August, coremkr, h 146 Kansas.
Lipferd Frank, mach, b 146 Kansas.
Lipferd Herman, mach, h 133 Wright.
Lipferd Wilhelmina (wid Charles), b 178 Harrison.
Lipkins Julius, lab, h rear 671 N Senate av.
Lipknight Mary A, h 140 Geisendorff.
Lipman Freida J, stenog Thurman & Silvius, b 129 N Noble.
Lipman John, solr German Telegraph, h 129 N Noble.
Lipp Charles W, baker, h 23 Gresham.
Lipp George J, uphlr, h 189 Spann av.
Lipp Gustav, molder, h 5 Atlas.
Lipp Mary A (wid Henry), h 33 Yeiser.
Lipp Peter, engr, h 45 Iowa.
Lipp Wm, lab, b 1640 N Illinois.
Lippert, see also Leppert.
Lippert Andrew C, bookbndr, b 301 S East.
Lippert Joseph J, clk C C C & St L Ry, b 301 S East.
Lippert Margaret (wid John C), grocer, 301 S East, h same.
Lipps Anna M, dressmkr, 496½ S Meridian, b same.
Lipps Elizabeth (wid Wm), h 496½ S Meridian.
Lipps Henry N, bkkpr, h 34 Carlos.
Lipps John H, printer, b 496½ S Meridian.
Lipps Joseph T (Electrical Construction Co), b 496½ S Meridian.
Lipps Wm A, cooper, b 496½ S Meridian.
Lippy Edward, lab, h 10½ Clifford av.
Lipsey Hubert J, mach, b 26 Eastern av.
Lisle Henry, lab, h 171 Tremont av (H).
List George V, foreman, h n s Ohio av 2 w of Elm av (I).
List Henry, riding bailiff Sheriff's Office, res Perry twp.
List Herman V, cook, r 102 N Capitol av.
List Jane, b 629 Charles.
List Joseph H, driver, h 447 S Delaware.
List Malinda A (wid Darrah), h 629 Charles.
List Theodore, car rep, h 622 Chestnut.
List Wm, motorman, h 578 W Washington.
Lister Harry E, baggageman, b 467 Broadway.
Lister Mary, b 467 Broadway.
Lister Mary E (wid Roll), h 483 College av.
Lister Mattie, cashr George J Marott, b 483 College av.
Lister Wm J, foreman Green & Co, h 467 Broadway.
Litel John W, gardener, b e s Illinois 1 s of 38th.
Litel Joseph, gardener, h e s Illinois 1 s of 38th.
Litel Wm R, meats, 1 E Mkt House, h 84 Fayette.
Liter James A, lab, h 238 S Linden.
Littell Earl M, barber, b 563 Bellefontaine.
Littell Henry T, painter, b 58 Columbia av.
Littell Hubert L, painter b 58 Columbia av.
Littell John W, lab, h 192 Trowbridge (W).
Littell Joseph Rev, pastor First United Presbyterian Church, h 265 E Vermont.

We Buy Municipal ~ Bonds ~
THOS. C. DAY & CO,
Rooms 325 to 330 Lemcke Bldg.

Littell Wm B, carp, h 58 Columbia av.
Littell Wm T, bricklyr, h 563 Bellefontaine.
Litterer Burt C, filer, h 47 Russell av.
Little, see also Lytle.
Little Bros (Edward W and John W), grocers, 1202 E Washington.
Little Edward, paperhngr, h 395 S Missouri.
Little Edward W (Little Bros), h 1202 E Washington.
Little Edward W, tel opr, h 23 Eastern av.
Little Elisha R, lab, h 405½ S Delaware.
Little Emma, stenog Comstock & Coonse Co, b 228 Randolph.
Little Frank W, lab, r rear 130 N Penn.
Little Horace S, brakeman, b 251 E Washington.
Little James A, tailor, h 218 Walcott.
Little John W (Little Bros), res Cumberland, Ind.
Little Joseph C, lab, h 67 Norwood.
Little Joseph F, farmer, h e s Line 1 n of Grand av (I).
Little Mary E (wid Frank), h 392 Yandes.
Little Peter, pdlr, b 411 E Washington.
Little Sisters of the Poor, n s Vermont nr East.
Littlejohn Frank B, clk, b 58 Hendricks blk.
Littlejohn Frank S, mer police, h rear 1020 W Washington.
Littlejohn Hannah (wid Stephen B), h 58 Hendricks blk.
Littlejohn Harry, gasfitter, b rear 1020 W Washington.
Littleton Albert M, clk, h Buchanan nr Greer.
Littleton Frank L, lawyer, 9 Fletcher's Bank bldg, r 79 E Michigan.
Littleton Roy J, clk P & E Ry, b Buchanan nr Greer.
Litton Fulton R, carp, h w s Gladstone av 1 n of Ohio.
Litton Margaret (wid Preston), h 139 N Penn.
Littrell Andrew B, mach, h 278 Fulton.
Litz Frank, mach, b 1058 E Michigan.
Litz Herman J, lab, h n s Lily 2 e of Rural.
Lively Oscar, metermkr, r 72 W Ohio.
Livengood Wm L, foreman, h 384 S State av.

EAT
HITZ'S CRACKERS
AND CAKES.
ASK YOUR GROCER FOR THEM.

WILLIAM WIEGEL } MANUFACTURER OF.... } SHOW CASES } 6 W. Louisiana St. Opposite Union Station.

TURKISH RUGS AND CARPETS RESTORED TO ORIGINAL COLORS LIKE NEW | Capital Steam Carpet Cleaning Works M. D. PLUNKETT, Telephone 818

BENJ. BOOTH PRACTICAL EXPERT ACCOUNTANT. Books Opened, Written Up, Posted and Balanced. Room 18, 82½ E. Washington St., Indianapolis, Ind.

18 and 20 S. MERIDIAN STREET

ESTABLISHED 1876. TELEPHONE 168.
CHESTER BRADFORD,
SOLICITOR OF PATENTS,
AND COUNSEL IN PATENT CAUSES.
(See adv. page 6.)
Office:—Rooms 14 and 16 Hubbard Block, S. W. Cor. Washington and Meridian Streets, INDIANAPOLIS, INDIANA.

Livezey Caroline (wid Nathan), b 1740 N Capitol av.
Livingston Albert T, patternmkr, h 383 S State av.
Livingston Andrew, driver, b 131 River av (W I).
Livingston Charles, lab Insane Hospital.
Livingston Henry L, lab, h 88 W 8th.
Livingston Josephine (wid Halsy), b 294 N Penn.
Livingstone Arabelle (wid Stephen), h 44 S Summit.
Livingstone Carroll C L, fireman, b 44 S Summit.
Lizius Augusta (wid Carl B), dry goods, 1156 E Washington, h same.
Lizius Bernard J W, clk Murphy, Hibben & Co, b 513 College av.
Lizius James B (R P Daggett & Co), h 513 College av.
Llewellyn, see also Lewellen.
Llewellyn Arthur, lab, h 41 Peru av.
Llewellyn John, watchman, h 121 Bright.
Llewellyn Wheeler, lab, b 41 Peru av.
Lloyd, see also Loyd.
Lloyd Alphonso H, buyer, r 200 N Illinois.
Lloyd Cecil, b 477 E 9th.
Lloyd Charles, condr, h 162 E St Joseph.
Lloyd Charles E, molder, b 71 Holmes av (H).
Lloyd Charles W, blksmith, h 20 S William (W I).
Lloyd Charles Z, insp, r 90 Cherry.
Lloyd Evan, lab, h 82 Dugdale.
Lloyd Experience T (wid Allen), h 180 E 7th.
Lloyd George H, packer, b 256 Douglass.
Lloyd Harry S, mach, b 1 N Gale (B).
Lloyd Irvin A, coremkr, b 71 Holmes av (H).
Lloyd Israel S, polisher, h 24 Cushing.
Lloyd John H, car rep, h 182 Deloss.
Lloyd Martha C (wid Thomas C), h 71 Holmes av (H).
Lloyd Mary C, dentist, 19 Fletcher's Bank bldg, h 72 Talbott av.
Lloyd M Libbie, clk Nicholas McCarty, b 180 E 7th.
Lloyd Perry G, lab, h 201 Bismarck av (H).
Lloyd Radford, driver, h 336 S Alabama.

O. B. ENSEY
MANUFACTURER OF
GALVANIZED IRON CORNICE,
SKYLIGHTS AND WINDOW CAPS.
TELEPHONE 1562. Cor. 6th and Illinois Sts.

Lloyd Rebecca A, sec and treas Capitol Paving and Construction Co, h 180 E 7th.
Lloyd Spencer C, h 72 Talbott av.
Lloyd Wm C, tinner, h 4 Hendricks.
Lloyd W Durbin, clk, h 78 Dougherty.
Loback Albert C, condr, b 1156 N Capitol av.
Lobraico Joseph, confr, 90 N Illinois, h 39 Roanoke.
Loch Charles W, pressman, b 356 E Market.
Loch Joseph V, uphlr, b 356 E Market.
Loch Lena (Loch Sisters), b 356 E Market.
Loch Margaret (Loch Sisters), b 356 E Market.
Loch Mary A (wid Francis X), h 356 E Market.
Loch Sisters (Margaret and Lena), dressmkrs, 356 E Market.
Lock Clementina M (wid Hensley R), b 154½ Martindale av.
Lock Lizzie, h 172 W Morris.
Lockard Alvin S (D P Erwin & Co), h 729 N Delaware.
Lockard Cordelia B (wid Charles O), h 729 N Delaware.
Lockard Samuel, polisher, b 77 S Liberty.
Locke Benjamin, cooper, h 3 Minerva.
Locke Harry N, brakeman, h 43 Tacoma av.
Locke Charles F, pdlr, h 296 W St Clair.
Locke Marshall, r 297 E Market.
Locke Mary (wid James), b 261 Lafayette.
Locke Melissa (wid Amos), r 144 S East.
Locke Stephen S, painter, h 444 S Illinois.
Locke Wm M, h 1005 N Illinois.
Locke Wm T, shoemkr, 1547 N Illinois, res Broad Ripple, Ind.
Lockhart Anna M, bkkpr Indpls Brewing Co, b rear 274 S Meridian.
Lockhart Belle (wid Virgil M), h rear 274 S Meridian.
Lockhart Charles B, clk State Auditor, h 504 N New Jersey.
Lockhart Jennie, clk, b Roosevelt House.
Lockhart Louise, milliner, b Roosevelt House.
Lockhart Thomas R, brakeman, h 12 Warren.
Locklear Andrew, dyer, h 360 Douglass.
Locklear Arthur, driver, b 200 Middle.
Locklear Benjamin, lab, h 580 N West.
Locklear Israel, lab, b 580 N West.
Locklear James R, driver, h 206 Agnes.
Locklear Jennie (wid Arthur), b 166 Howard.
Lockman Anna E (wid Wm S), h 348 Clifford av.
Lockman Anthony, cutter, h 564½ Virginia av.
Lockman Charles D, bookbndr, h 32 Oak.
Lockman Charlotte, prin Center Township Public School No 1, b 348 Clifford av.
Lockman Mary (wid James R), h 273 Indiana av.
Lockman Milton, porter, b 273 Indiana av.
LOCKMAN WM S, Justice of the Peace, 34 N Delaware, Tel 1210; h 900 Broadway.
Lockridge Andrew L, propr Putnam County Milk Co, 14 N East, h 771 N Alabama.
Lockridge John E, phys, 37½ W Washington, r same.
Lockstand Mary E, notions, 750 N West, h same.
Lockstand Wm F, lab, h 750 N West.
Lockwood Albert, huckster, h 84 Woodlawn av.
Lockwood Charles W, foreman, h 23 Garland (W I).

IF YOU WANT A GOOD MEAL AND HAVE IT NICELY SERVED GO TO THE SHERMAN RESTAURANT

TUTEWILER UNDERTAKER, NO. 72 WEST MARKET STREET. TELEPHONE 216.

PARTNERSHIP INSURANCE At low cost. By which provision is made against the pecuniary loss and embarrassment resulting from the death of a member of a firm.
Provident Life and Trust Co. of Philadelphia, D. W. EDWARDS, Gen'l Agt., 508 Indiana Trust Bldg.

THEODORE F. SMITHER GRAVEL AND OTHER COMPOSITION ROOFER
Yard, 19 W. Maryland St. Office, 15 W. Maryland St. TEL 86

Lockwood David, carp, b 40 Arbor av (W I).
Lockwood Edward, lab, r 131½ E Washington.
Lockwood Frank E, lab, h 299 W Ray.
Lockwood Harry, driver, b 441½ Virginia av.
Lockwood John N, cooper, h 256 Indiana av.
Lockwood Lafayette, huckster, h 225 S Linden.
Lockwood Marie Louise, clk Order of Chosen Friends, b 316 N New Jersey.
Lockwood Mary A, h 316 N New Jersey.
Lockwood Mary F (wid Wm G), b 12 West Drive (W P).
Lockwood Matthew A, letter carrier P O, h 234 Ash.
Lockwood Simeon, huckster, b 225 S Linden.
LOCKWOOD VIRGIL H, Patent Lawyer, Counsel in Patent Cases, Rooms 415-418 Lemcke Bldg, Tel 1103; h 23 E St Joseph. (See adv in classified Patents.)
Lockwood Wm A, molder, h 40 King av (H).
Lockwood Youngs, pdlr, h 41 Stevens.
Loder Anna E, toilet articles, 123 Butler, b same.
Loder Hannah A (wid John W), h 123 Butler.
Loder Lucille M, bkkpr, b 123 Butler.
Loder Myrta O, teacher Public School No 41, b 123 Butler.
Lodge Caleb N, lawyer, sec U S B and L Inst, 719 Lemcke bldg, b 433 N Penn.
Lodge Clarence E, artist, h 71 Oak.
Lodge Ella A (wid Joseph H), b 263 Shelby.
Lodge Harriet N, h 433 N Penn.
Lodge James I, cashr John S Spann & Co, h 433 N Penn.
Lodge Laban L (Gray & Lodge), h 117 Woodlawn av.
Lodge Stella P, nurse City Hospital.
Loeb Louis L, ins agt, 235 Lemcke bldg, b Spencer House.
Loebenberg Abraham B, clk, h 271 E Ohio.
Loebenberg Henry, cigars, 9 S Illinois, b 271 E Ohio.
Loechle Joseph S, baker, 207 Mass av, h same.
Loehmann Charles F, painter, b 85 Weghorst.
Loeper George J, mach, b 87 Fletcher av.
Loeper Helen A, teacher Public School No 28, b 87 Fletcher av.
Loeper Jacob W, draughtsman City Civil Engineer's Office, h 87 Fletcher av.
Loeper Oliver, car builder, h 48 Nordyke av (W I).
Loeper Wm H, plumber, 327 Clifford av, h 128 N State av.
LOES JOHN, John's New Place, Pool and Sample Room, also Barber and Furnished Rooms, 102-104 S Noble, h same.
Loesche Herman, driver, h 64 Buchanan.
Loevinger Charles, driver, h 302 S Penn.
Loewer Charles, cabtmkr, h 52 Gresham.
Loftin Charles (Empey & Loftin), b 42 Ruckle.
Loftin John A, slater, h 29 Ellsworth.
Loftin Kezia (wid Almon), h 831 N Capitol av.
Loftin Mary F (wid Sample), h 73 W 9th.
Loftin Simeon, b 42 Ruckle.
Loftus James F, lab, h 29 Empire.

THE WHEN IS A WORLD BEATER.

Loftus John F, lab, b 326 W Pearl.
Loftus John J, bookbndr, b 492 S Capitol av.
Loftus Martin, lab, h 42 Haugh (H).
Loftus Martin, lab, h 326 W Pearl.
Loftus Mary (wid James), h 492 S Capitol av.
Loftus Patrick J, lab, b 492 S Capitol av.
Loftus Thomas H, painter, b 293 Virginia av.
Logan Anna E, h 325 N California.
Logan Benjamin F, mach hd, h 20 Holly av (W I).
Logan Byron C, blksmith, h 47 S Summit.
Logan Ellen (wid Thomas), b 89 Geisendorff.
Logan Ellis P, lab, h 45 Ashland (W I).
Logan Emma A, h 430 Blake.
Logan George W, lab, h 43 N McLain (W I).
Logan Henry, lab, h 612 W Michigan.
Logan Hezekiah, lab, b 430 Blake.
Logan Hugh J, bkkpr, r 228 N Illinois.
LOGAN JAMES H, Dealer in All Kinds of Staple and Fancy Groceries, and Fresh, Smoked and Salt Meats, 1149 N Illinois, h 1059 N Capitol av.
Logan John, lab, b 274 Fulton.
Logan John, lab, h 24 Grant.
Logan John A, cabtmkr, h 224½ Oliver av (W I).
Logan John B, trav agt, h 901 Broadway.
Logan John K, chief clk engr m of w P & E Ry, h 92 Spann av.
Logan John W, paperhngr, r 25½ Madison av.
Logan John S, mach hd, b 104 Agnes.
Logan Louis, hostler, r 184 Indiana av.
Logan Luke S, shoemkr, h 104 Agnes.
Logan Martin B, saloon, 199 W McCarty, h 435 S Missouri.
Logan Mary B (wid Reuben D), h 63 N East.
Logan Matthew, watchman, h 14 Oxford.
Logan Matthew J, electrician, b 14 Oxford.
Logan Michael, foreman, b 241 N West.
Logan Michael, foreman Singer Mnfg Co, h 160 S Olive.
Logan Milly L, teacher Public School No 36, b 901 Broadway.
Logan Patrick, b 24 Grant.

THE A. BURDSAL CO.
WINDOW AND PLATE
GLASS
Putty, Glazier Points, Diamonds.
Wholesale and Retail. 34 and 36 S. Meridian St.

ELECTRIC CONSTRUCTION Isolated Plants Installed. Electric Wiring and Fittings of all kinds. C. W. Meikel. Tel. 466. 96-98 E. New York St

DALTON & MERRIFIELD { LUMBER South Noble St., near E. Washington

INDIANA ELECTROTYPE CO. : BEST WORK. LOWEST PRICES.
23 WEST PEARL ST., INDIANAPOLIS, IND. JOB WORK. BOOK PLATES. BEST PATENT BASE ON THE MARKET. All Orders Promptly Filled.

KIRKHOFF BROS.,
GAS AND ELECTRIC FIXTURES
THE LARGEST LINE IN THE CITY.
102-104 SOUTH PENNSYLVANIA ST.
TELEPHONE 910.

Logan Robert, r 80 E New York.
Logan Robert H, bicycle rep, r 28 Grand Opera House blk.
Logan Robert W, blksmith, b 32 S Senate av.
Logan Samuel, butler 712 N Delaware.
Logan Scott, fireman, b 57 English av.
Logan Thomas P, mach, b 42 Grant.
Logsdon Edwin D (Middleton & Logsdon), h 132 John.
Logsdon James, lab, b 42 Smith.
Logsdon Lawrence, fruit grower, h 7 Pleasant av.
Logsdon Margaret M, artist, 363 Park av, b same.
Logsdon Martha, teacher Kindergarten No 3, h 7 Prospect.
Logsdon Wm A, carp, h w s Harris av 1 s of C C C & St L Ry (M J).
Logston Otto, lab, h 30 Bunting (H).
Logue Augustus G, stoker, b 137 Wright.
Logue George F, sawmkr, b 137 Wright.
Lohman Charles G, cigarmkr Andrew Steffen, h 397 N Brookside av.
LOHMAN CHARLES G, Druggist, 701 N Capitol av, h 702 same.
Lohman Louis F, barber, 555 E Walnut, h same.
Lohmann Henry C, mach hd, b 416 Excelsior av.
Lohning J Frank, horseshoer, r 84 E St Clair.
Lohr Anna, nurse 118 N Senate av.
Lohrman Charles G (C G Lohrman & Son), b 400 N Senate av.
Lohrman Conrad G (C G Lohrman & Son), h 400 N Senate av.
Lohrman C G & Son (Conrad G and Charles G), grocers, 400 N Senate av.
Lohrman Edward, clk, b 400 N Senate av.
Lohrman Frank, clk A Kiefer Drug Co, h 529 W Addison (N I).
Lohrman Frederick, carp, 558 W North, h same.
Lohrman Henry Q, clk, b 400 N Senate av.
Lohrman Louisa P (wid Paul), h 28 Byram pl.
Lohss Herman, dry goods, 623 S Meridian, h same.

COAL AND COKE
The W. G. Wasson Co.,
130 INDIANA AVE. TEL. 989
LIME AND LATH

Lolla Margaret (wid Monroe), h 273 Lafayette.
Lomasney Edmond H, shoemkr, b 342 S Meridian.
Lombard Albert D, b 185 Elm.
Lombard Bldg and Loan Assn, Daniel M Ransdell pres, Wm Bosson vice-pres, Hiram E Rose treas, Abe L Cook sec and mngr, 97-98 Lombard bldg.
Lombard Charles N, harnessmkr, b 185 Elm.
Lombard Charles O, driver, h 44 Dougherty.
Lombard De Otis, mach, h 185 Elm.
Lombard John A, printer, b 233 Hoyt av.
Lombard John F, cooper, h 233 Hoyt av.
LONDON GUARANTEE AND ACCIDENT CO (Limited), OF LONDON, ENGLAND, George W Pangborn Genl Agt, 704-706 Lemcke Bldg, Tel 140. (See left top lines.)
Lonergan Charles A, electrician, h 24 Columbia av.
Lonergan Michael, h 274 S Meridian.
Long, see also Lang and Lange.
Long Abraham W, lab, b 7 Astor.
Long Ada, boarding 80 S Capitol av.
LONG ALBERT E, Propr The Long Steel and Iron Roofing Co, 180-188 W 5th, Tel 1448; h 162 N Illinois.
Long Alice M (wid John H), b 116 Highland pl.
Long Allen, mach hd, h 19 Belmont av.
Long Angie K, teacher, r 205 The Shiel.
Long Anna (wid Peter), b 234 Hamilton av.
Long Arthur S, clk, b 104 Park av.
Long Benjamin F, lab, h 1661 N Capitol av.
Long Calvin, filer, h 61 E Morris.
Long Charles, lab, h 50 Church.
Long Charles H, motorman, b 792 W Washington.
Long Charles J, carp, b n w cor 22d and Central av.
Long Charles R, trav agt Murphy, Hibben & Co, h 37 Lockerbie.
Long Charles R A, clk, h 7 Henry.
Long Christian, b s s Jackson 1 w of Lincoln av (M J).
LONG DISTANCE TELEPHONE CO. See American Telephone and Telegraph Co, 14 S Meridian.
Long Druscilla F, h 69 Andrews.
Long Edgar, barber, b 250 River av (W I).
Long Edward, lab, h 26 Patterson.
Long Eli C, grainer, 177 Buchanan, h same.
Long Eli M, clk, h 70 N Liberty.
Long Enoch L, carp, h rear 353 E Market.
Long Frank M, carp, h 126 S Pine.
Long George, lab, r 233 W Washington.
Long George L, lab, b 162 Meek.
Long Granville G, shoemkr, 41 Mass av, h 78 Ft Wayne av.
Long Guy L, clk, b 104 Park av.
Long Harry, trav agt, b 134 W Ohio.
Long Harry E, clk Original Eagle, b 28 Ft Wayne av.
Long Henry, phys, 32 Mass av, h 80 W 5th.
Long Henry C, lumber, 1 Alvord, h 610 N Penn.
Long Henry G, lab, b 686 N Illinois.
Long Howard, lab, b 456 W Francis (N I).
Long James C, lab, b 1240 Bond (N I).
Long James E, fireman, b 892 W Washington.
Long James R, agt, r 194 E Washington.
Long Jennie, shorthand teacher College of Commerce, b 122 Buchanan.
Long Jeremiah J, tinner, b 250 River av (W I).

W. H. MESSENGER COMPLETE HOUSE FURNISHER
101 East Washington Street, Telephone 491

Foundry and Pattern Shop } McNamara, Koster & Co. { PHONE 1593 212-218 S. Penn. St.

Long John, baker, b 76 Kennington.
Long John, gilder, b 262 Lincoln la.
Long John, lab, b 95 Agnes.
Long John, lab, h 440 S Missouri.
Long John, patrolman, h 83 Benton.
Long John, waiter, b 201 E Washington.
Long John B, phys, 402 W New York, h same.
Long John W, h 162 Meek.
Long John W, filer, b 72 Park av.
Long Joseph, h 79 Central av.
Long Joseph J, clk, b 1240 Bond (N I).
Long Joseph T, agt Northwestern Mutual Life Ins Co, r 30 W Vermont.
Long Lutie, forewoman, b 286 N Senate av.
Long Luvicy C (wid Thomas J), b 19 Belmont av.
Long Margaret, h 138 Maple.
Long Margaret (wid James L), h 242 Indiana av.
Long Mary (wid Joseph), h n w cor 22d and Central av.
Long Mary U, dressmkr, 1661 N Capitol av, h same.
Long Merritt, driver, h 80 S Capitol av.
Long Michael Rev, h 1240 Bond (N I).
Long Minnie (wid Edwin J), b 128 Walcott.
Long Morton F, lab, b 56 S California.
Long Nannie J (wid John), h 222 N New Jersey.
Long Nicholas H, clk, h 341 E McCarty.
Long Noma O, painter, h 606 W Udell (N I).
Long Nora B, teacher Deaf and Dumb Inst.
Long Patrick, lab, h 50 S California.
Long Retta J (wid Wm), b 131½ E Washington.
Long Richard, lab, h 381 W 1st.
Long Robert D (Renihan, Long & Blackwell), h 50 Broadway.
Long Robert W, phys, 5, 156½ E Washington, h 49 Central av.
Long Samuel, engr, r 78 W South.
Long Sarah E (wid Thomas), h 456 W Francis (N I).
Long Sarah F (wid James M), h 7 Astor.
LONG STEEL AND IRON ROOFING CO THE, Albert E Long Propr, Mnfrs and Dealers in Steel and Iron Roofing, 180-188 W 5th, Tel 1448. (See adv in classified Roofers.)
Long S Lukins, driver, b rear 353 E Market.
Long Thomas J, molder, b 56 S California.
Long Thomas W, driver, h 18 Harmon.
Long Timothy, mason, h 410 S West.
Long Virenda T (wid John K), h 86 Park av.
Long Wm, car insp, b 1051 N Capitol av.
Long Wm C, city fireman, h 35 W St Joseph.
Long Wm C, painter, h 198 Elm.
Long Wm D, h 250 River av (W I).
Long Wm H, asst supt, h Central av nr Fair Grounds.
Long Wm T, livery, 227 E Wabash, h 1597 N Illinois.
Long W Ray, page Superior Court Room No 1, b 116 Highland pl.
Longanecker Ezra W, trav agt, h 536 E 7th.
Longanecker Rose D, dressmkr, 536 E 7th, h same.
Longanecker David, lab, h s s Pendleton av 2 e of Rural.
Longer Joseph, driver, h 15 Geneva.
Longerich August, plumber, b 282 E North.

Henry H. Fay,
40½ E. WASHINGTON ST.,
AGENT FOR
Insurance Co. of North America,
Pennsylvania Fire Ins. Co.

Longerich Edward, tailor, h 282 E North.
Longerich Edward jr, plumber, b 282 E North.
Longley Emily (wid John), b 293 N New Jersey.
Longshore John, trunkmkr, h 598 W Pearl.
Longshore John R, trunkmkr, h 727 S Meridian.
Longworth Andrew J, brickmkr, h 125 Division (W I).
Longworth Samuel, lab, b 125 Division (W I).
Longworth Wm M, painter, h 1259 Morris (W I).
Lonnis Frederick E, butcher, h 172 Hamilton av.
Lonsdale Helen E, stenog State Life Ins Co, b 439 College av.
Loomis Charles A, clk Indpls Foundry Co, h 52 Warman av (H).
Loomis Claudia E (wid Wm), dressmkr, h 156 S Noble.
Loomis Eleanor (wid Ruel B), b 287 S East.
Loomis Frederick M, clk Indpls Gas Co, h 409 College av.
Loomis Sallie B (wid George B), b 449 N New Jersey.
Looney Catherine (wid Michael), h 117 Huron.
Looney George L, paperhngr, h 10½ Clifford av.
Looney John F, opr Postal Tel Cable Co, b 117 Huron.
Looney Mary (wid John), b 108 Elm.
Looney Michael, plumber, b 117 Huron.
Looney Wm J, plumber, b 117 Huron.
Loos Carrie M, b 160 Newman.
Loos Philip, bkkpr Pabst Brewing Co, Indpls Branch, b 235 S Alabama.
Lop Robert, hostler, b 553 Virginia av.
Lopez Mary B (wid Solomon), b 1283 N Meridian.
Lorash Henry D, butcher, h 125 Bryan.
Lorber John, tailor, b 135 E Washington.
Lorber Regina, tailoress, b 470 N New Jersey.
Lorber Solomon, saloon, 200 Prospect, h same.
Lord Edmund, foreman, r 298 N Capitol av.

Union Casualty & Surety Co.
of St. Louis, Mo.
Employers', Public, General, Teams and Elevator Liability; also Workmen's Collective, Steam Boiler, Plate Glass and Automatic Sprinkler Insurance.
W. E. BARTON & CO., General Agents,
504 Indiana Trust Building.
LONG DISTANCE TELEPHONE 1918.

THE FRED DIETZ CO. 400 Madison Avenue. WOODEN PACKING BOXES MADE TO ORDER FACTORY AND WAREHOUSE TRUCKS. Telephone 69.

Shorthand! BUSINESS UNIVERSITY. When Bl'k. Elevator day and night. Typewriting, Penmanship, Book-keeping, Office Training free. See page 4. Est. 1850. Tel. 499. E. J. HEEB, Proprietor.

Steam Pumping Machinery { HENRY R. WORTHINGTON, 64 S. PENNSYLVANIA ST. Long Distance Telephone 284.

UNION CO-OPERATIVE LAUNDRY { (COMPOSED OF UNION LAUNDRY GIRLS.) NOS. 138, 140 AND 142 VIRGINIA AVENUE
T. E. SOMERVILLE, MANAGER—TELEPHONE 1269. INDIANAPOLIS, IND.

HORACE M. HADLEY
REAL ESTATE AND LOANS....
66 East Market Street
Telephone 1540. BASEMENT.

Loree Catherine (wid Samuel), h 276 E Merrill.
Loree Madison, trav agt Oliver Chilled Plow Wks, h 276 E Merrill.
Loree Wm C, engr m of w P C C & St L Ry Union Station, b 142 N Illinois.
Lorentz, see also Lawrence.
Lorentz Wm A (Schmeltz & Lorentz), b 568 S Meridian.
Lorenz Frederick A, letter carrier P O, h 46 Beaty.
Lorenzo Dominick, pdlr, h 21 S Liberty.
Loretz Christopher, fitter, b 146 Michigan (H).
Lorig Anna F (wid Nicholas), h 84 Downey.
Lorman George M, mach hd, b 109 N West.
Lorman Henry E, clk, b 109 N West.
Lorman Mary J (wid John F), h 109 N West.
Lorrence Flora, teacher Public School No 6, b 1203 N Meridian.
Loscent Frank, bartndr, b 336 N West.
Loscent Henry J, clk, b 336 N West.
Loscent Joseph F, fruits, 217 W Washington, b 336 N West.
Loscent Louis, driver, h 336 N West.
Losey Arthur, draughtsman, b 227 S Senate av.
Losey John, b 820 College av.
Losey Wm C, b 820 College av.
Losey Wm S, h 820 College av.
Losh Edgar, mach hd, b 40 Arbor av (W I).
Losh Frank H, mach hd, b 40 Arbor av (W I).
Losh George W, carp, h 40 Arbor av (W I).
Losh George W, harnessmkr, h 75 Hosbrook.
Losh John W, creamery, 155 W Washington, h same.
Losh Samuel, mach hd, b 40 Arbor av (W I).
Lotkey Lewis, r 260 E South.
Lots Otto B, clk, b 315 W Washington.
Lotshar Jacob R, clk When Clothing Store, h 348 N Illinois.
Lotshar Joseph H, clk The Progress Clothing Co, h 1013 N Penn.
Lott David O, condr, h 91 Quincy.
Lott Edward, motorman, h 516 Bellefontaine.
Lott James H, lawyer, b 300 N California.

Merchants' and Manufacturers Exchange
Make Collections and Commercial Reports......
J. E. TAKKEN, MANAGER,
19 Union Building, 73 West Maryland Street

Lott John T, condr, h 152 Bates.
Lott Matilda (wid John J), b 91 Quincy.
Lotz Anna M (wid George W), h 749 Chestnut.
Lotz John, harnessmkr, b 183 Johnson av.
Lotz Wm P, driver, b 183 Johnson av.
Loub Thomas, lab, h 154 Bloyd av.
Loucks Calvin R, painter, 105 English av, h same.
Loucks Charles C, printer, h 35 Andrews.
Loucks Charles E, painter, h 547 W Addison (N I).
Loucks David H, plastr, h 414 W Shoemaker (N I).
Loucks Dwight C, gasfitter, h 43 Brookside av.
Loucks Frank I, carp, h 414 W Shoemaker (N I).
Loucks Frederick, steamfitter, h 316 E Wabash.
Loucks John C, city fireman, h 44 Pleasant av.
Loucks Joseph W, carp, h 294½ Mass av.
Loucks Margaret A (wid Christopher B), b 54 Eureka av.
Loucks Oliver D, carp, h 687 Fremont (N I).
Loucks Parvin (Loucks & Jasper), b 20f Fletcher av.
Loucks Wm W, carp, b 135 Prospect.
Loucks & Jasper (Parvin Loucks, Wm C Jasper), dry goods, 333 Dillon.
Loud Martin, lab, h 161 Harmon.
Louden, see also Lowden.
Louden Andrew M, bookbndr, h 212 N West.
Louden George R, saloon, 250 S West, h 471 same.
Louden Jesse, bartndr, b 471 S West.
Louden John D, b n s Orchard av 2 e of Rural.
Louden John S, carp, h 76 Lee (W I).
Louderback Milton, tmstr, h 199½ E Washington.
Louden Martha (wid Albert), b 350 Columbia av.
Loudon George, clk N Y Store, h 1081 N Illinois.
Loughery Alvah, clk C F Meyer & Bro, b 132 N Capitol av.
Loughlin, see also Laughlin, McGlaughlin and McLaughlin.
Loughlin Hugh, lab, h 372 S Missouri.
Loughlin John M, patrolman, h 393 Indiana av.
Loughlin Michael E, insp City Civil Engineer, h 38 Center.
Loughmiller Silas D, clk Hildebrand Hardware Co, b 1514 Northwestern av (N I).
Loughrun Ulysses S, mach hd, h 158 N West.
Louis, see also Lewis.
Louis Charles W, lab, h e s Arlington av 3 n of Walnut av (I).
Louis Joseph, shoemkr, h 22 Willard.
Louis Lucy J (wid Wm S), housekpr 140 East Drive (W P).
Louis Lyman W, broker, 13 Board of Trade, h 119 E 6th.
Louis Milton O, clk Van Camp H and I Co, h 218 Fletcher av.
Louis Robert, lab, h 322 Tremont.
Louisville Henry I, photog, r 96 Eddy.

LOUISVILLE, NEW ALBANY & CHICAGO RY, George W Hayler District Pass Agt, 2 W Washington, Tel 737, Anthony J O'Reilly Commercial Agt, 1 Board of Trade Bldg, Tel 255, Local Freight Office 53 S Alabama, Tel 750.

CLEMENS VONNEGUT 184, 186 and 192 E. Washington St. | Wire Rope, Machinery, Lathes, Drills and Shapers

THE WM. H. BLOCK CO. DRY GOODS, DRAPERIES, RUGS, WINDOW SHADES.
7 AND 9 EAST WASHINGTON STREET.

Lour Andrew, brakeman, b e s Brightwood av 7 s of Willow (B).
Lourding Wm, painter, r 66½ N Penn.
Lous Nicholas, clk, r 5 Cleaveland blk.
Louthan David K, city agt, b 178 N Missouri.
Louthan May I, stenog McKee & Co, b 178 N Missouri.
Loutt Charles F, lab, h 12 N McLain (W I).
Loutt Wm H, fireman, b 12 N McLain (W I).
Love Arthur E, ins agt, b 90 Andrews.
Love Charles, waiter, r 12½ Indiana av.
Love Charles W, barber, b 48 Vincennes (W I).
Love Daniel, lab, h 260 W 6th.
Love Elijah E, condr, h 10 S Brightwood av (B).
Love Frederick K, carp, b 108½ Mass av.
Love George, tinner, h 108½ Mass av.
Love Harold, bricklyr, h 1557 Graceland av.
Love Henry, carp, h 108½ Mass av.
Love Hugh M (Brower & Love Bros), vice-pres Indpls Bleaching Co, h 184 N California.
Love James F, h 128 N Illinois.
Love John, blksmith, h s s Brookside av 3 w of Jupiter.
Love John A, transfer, b 86 Vine.
Love John F, meats, 61 E Mkt House, h 24½ Indiana av.
Love John R (Brower & Love Bros), sec and treas Indpls Bleaching Co, h 398 N Delaware.
Love Mary F (wid John), h 407 N Capitol av.
Love Morris B, lab, h 148 Geisendorff.
Love Moses, lab, b 9 Ellsworth.
Love Nelly, teacher Blind Institute.
Love Sarah A (wid Harvey N), b 148 Geisendorff.
Love Shaw C, miller, h 3 Hiawatha.
Love Thomas W, condr, h 220 Bellefontaine.
Love Wm, grocer, 150 Mass av, h 183½ same.
Love Wm J, ins agt, h 90 Andrews.
Love Wm J jr, clk, b 90 Andrews.
Love Wm S, lab, b 105 N Rural (B).
Love Wm Z, aeronaut, h 37½ Kentucky av.
Lovejoy Andrew A, baggageman, h 201 N California.
Lovejoy Artemus A, engr, b 201 N California.
Lovejoy John H, printer, h 172 Woodlawn av.
Lovejoy Sarah A, confr, 120 E Mkt House, h 201 N California.
Lovelace Andrew J, meats, 163 Hill av, h same.
Lovelace Richard L, engr, h 408 Martindale av.
Lovelace Thomas, sander, r 18 Columbia blk.
Loveless Eliza C (wid Samuel), h 150 W Michigan.
Loveless Stephen B, stenog A W Thompson, h 150 W Michigan.
Lovell Arthur E, butcher, b 1622 N Meridian.
Lovell Catherine (wid George W), b 328 E Georgia.
Lovell David A, lab, h 25 Biddle.
Lovell Elmer, lab, b 328 E Georgia.
Lovell John, lab, h 67 S Noble.
Lovell John W, h 514 W Shoemaker (N I).
Lovell Lafayette, lab, h 328 E Georgia.
Lovett Charles H, contr, 513 S New Jersey, h same.

Lovett Daniel W (F S Lovett & Co), h 861 N Penn.
Lovett F S (F S Lovett & Co), b 861 N Penn.
Lovett F S & Co (Frederick S and Daniel W Lovett), mdse brokers, 52 S Penn.
Lovett John, special agt U S Life Ins Co, h 100 Frazee (H).
Lovett Samuel J, driver, h 21 Birch av (W I).
Lovett Theresa, b 21 Birch av (W I).
Lovett Wm M, lab, h 35 Birch av (W I).
Loving George, cook, r 173 E Court.
Loving Joseph P, cook, h 33 Alvord.
Lovinger Daniel, saloon, 346 Virginia av, h same.
Lovings John M, miller, h 498 E Washington.
Low Enoch, meats, 822 W Washington, h 16 Minkner.
Low James A, grocer, 155 Ft Wayne av, h 476 Stillwell.
Low Joseph C, expressman, h 95 S West.
Low Nancy J, boarding 95 S West.
Low Thomas, barber, 137 W Washington, h 480 Newman.
Low Thomas W, watchman, h 41 Wright.
Lowden, see also Loudon.
Lowden Leonidas C, pdlr, h n s Fountain 3 w of Floral av.
Lowden Minnie W, stenog Th- -ality Building and Savings Union, r 106½ N Meridian.
Lowder Joseph, lab, b e s Commercial av 4 s of Washington av (I).
Lowder Oliver, wheelmkr, b 128 Church.
Lowder Oscar, wheelmkr, h 128 Church.
Lowder Wm, shoemkr, r 20 S Illinois.
Lowderback James, lab, h 136½ Agnes.
Lowe Benjamin, elevator opr, b 291 E Miami.
Lowe Charles G, clk N Y Store, h 104 Cornell av.
Lowe Charles J, driver, h 591 Ash.
Lowe Chastine S, coachman 28 Ft Wayne av.
Lowe Clayton F, tailor, b 272 Douglass.
Lowe Clinton V, collr County Treasurer's Office, b 272 Douglass.

GUIDO R. PRESSLER,
FRESCO PAINTER
Churches, Theaters, Public Buildings, Etc., A Specialty.
Residence, No. 325 North Liberty Street
INDIANAPOLIS, IND.

INDIANAPOLIS STEEL ROOFING AND CORRUGATING WORKS, 23 and 25 East South Street. S. D. NOEL, Proprietor.

David S. McKernan, Rooms 2-5 Thorpe Block.
REAL ESTATE AND LOANS A number of choice pieces for subdivision, or for manufacturers' sites, with good switch facilities.

DIAMOND WALL PLASTER { Telephone 1410 BUILDERS' EXCHANGE.

UNION TRANSFER AND STORAGE CO. Cor. E. Ohio St. and C., C., C. & St. L. R'y Tracks. BRICK WAREHOUSE; CLEANEST AND SAFEST STORAGE IN CITY FOR HOUSEHOLD GOODS AND MERCHANDISE.

W. McWORKMAN,

METAL CEILINGS,
ROLLING SHUTTERS,
DOORS AND PARTITIONS.

930 W. Washington St. Tel. 1118.

Lowe Dennis, lab, r 131 Douglass.
Lowe Edward, b 326 E Wabash.
Lowe Enoch A, grocer, 16 Minkner, h same.
Lowe Frederick, plastr, b 304 Blake.
Lowe George, lab, b 42 Concordia.
Lowe George P, painter, h 308 E North.
Lowe Iley C, packer, b 272 Douglass.
Lowe James C, lab, h 175 E Morris.
Lowe James D, brakeman, b 175 E Morris.
Lowe James D, lab, h 19 Minkner.
Lowe John, clk, b 334 N Illinois.
Lowe John, sergt of police, h 272 Douglass.
Lowe John, trav agt, h 93 Nebraska.
Lowe John R, draughtsman, h 1020 N Penn.
Lowe Kate, b 148 Indiana av.
Lowe Mary W (wid George), b 673 N Penn.
Lowe Nahum H, carp, 308 E North, h same.
Lowe Nahum H jr, carp, b 308 E North.
Lowe Nimrod, h 11 Minkner.
Lowe Oscar M, opr W U Tel Co, b 132 N Capitol av.
Lowe Richard H, buyer, h 276 N Alabama.
Lowe Thomas, h rear 568 W Washington.
Lowe Wm, lab, b 568 W Washington.
Lowe Wm W, h 553 N Alabama.
Lowe Woodbeck B, armature winder, h 55 Paca.
Lowel Aaron, lab, b 183 Indiana av.
Lowenthal Siegfried, clk, b 321 E Ohio.
Lowenthal Wolf, furs, 11½ W Washington, h 633 Bellefontaine.
Lowery Wm, hostler, h 266 W Court.
Lowes Albert H, foreman, h 386 N Delaware.
Lowes Clinton T, clk, b 338 N Delaware.
Lowes Helen D, teacher Public School No 5, b 338 N Delaware.
Lowes Hervey E, clk Crescent L and I Co, b 612 Central av.
Lowes James H, sec Crescent L and I Co, h 89 Park av.
Lowes James P G, clk Charles Willig, h 181 Columbia av.
Lowes Jesse E (Porter & Lowes), h e s Elm av 2 n of Washington av (I).
Lowes Louis C, b 172 E St Clair.
Lowes Martha J (wid James), b 172 E St Clair.
Lowley Ardio (wid Edwin), h 193 W South.

SEALS,
STENCILS,
STAMPS, Etc.
GEO. J. MAYER
15 S. Meridian St.
TELEPHONE 1386.

Lowman Wm H, plumber, r 12½ N Delaware.
Lowry, see also Laurie and Lawrie.
Lowry Albert, polisher, b 56 Sheffield (W I).
Lowry Albert W, dairy, w s School 1 s of Wolf pike (B), h same.
Lowry Charles A, lab, b 231 Mass av.
Lowry Charles M, salesman, h n e cor Rural and Progress av.
Lowry Charles O (Spencer & Lowry), b 124 Irwin.
Lowry Charles W, driver, r 140 E New York.
Lowry Edward H, trav agt Journal Job Printing Co, b 100 College av.
Lowry Elmer R, clk, h s w cor Laura and Washington (M J).
Lowry Eva (wid John), b 74 Lee (W I).
Lowry Ezekiel P, carp, h 867 Cornell av.
Lowry Frederick T, clk, b 100 College av.
Lowry George E, clk Indpls Gas Co, h 143 N Dorman.
Lowry George R, tel opr, b 867 Cornell av.
Lowry George W, clk, b 100 College av.
Lowry James P, trav agt Indpls Stove Co, h 124 Irwin.
Lowry James S, packer, h 304 Union.
Lowry Jennie E (wid George E), h 100 College av.
Lowry John, bartndr, b 251 E Washington.
Lowry John O, clk, b 672 College av.
Lowry Robert W, supt Journal Job Printing Co, h 228 College av.
Lowry Wm J, real est, 22 Ingalls blk, h 672 College av.
Lowry Wm W, lawyer, 57 Journal bldg, h 40 West Drive (W P).
Lowther James K, driver, h 136 Scioto.
Lowther Jay W, clk R M S, h 482 Bellefontaine.
Lowther Nimrod R (Branham & Lowther), h 333 E Miami.
Loy Amos D, carp, h 164 Hillside av.
Loy Charles V, ins agt, b 74 N Illinois.
Loy David M, tinner, 234 S Meridian, h same.
Loy Mary A (wid Amos D), h 265 River av (W I).
Loy Oscar L, lab, b 58 Ruckle.
Loy Tobias, motorman, h 58 Ruckle.
Loy Wm M C, lather, b 265 River av (W I).
Loyd, see also Lloyd.
Loyd Albert M, plastr, h 214 Elm.
Loyd Estelle, stenog Meyer & Kiser, b 388 N Alabama.
Loyd Myrtle (wid Wm), h 188 W Ohio.
Loyd Omer, letter carrier P O, h 388 N Alabama.
Loyd Richard, lab, h rear 85 River av (W I).
Lubbe Alice F (wid Edward H), h 70 Woodlawn av.
Lubbe Harry, mach, h 126 Baltimore av.
Lubbe Louisa (wid Herman H), b 727 College av.
Lubrick Harry, ironwkr, b 285 S Capitol av.
Lucas Anna E (wid Charles), b 450 N West.
Lucas Charles C, condr, h 258 Springfield.
Lucas Charles T, carp, b 293 N New Jersey.
Lucas Daniel R Rev, pastor Sixth Christian Church, h 293 N New Jersey.
Lucas Edward, cooper, b 48 Excelsior av.
LUCAS FRANCIS C, Lawyer, 86 Lombard Bldg, Tel 237; h The Milton, 30 E Pratt.
Lucas Francis M, painter, h 90 S Belmont av (W I).

A. METZGER AGENCY ESTABLISHED 1863. INSURANCE

LAMBERT GAS & GASOLINE ENGINE CO.
ANDERSON, IND. PORTABLE GASOLINE ENGINES, 2 TO 25 H. P.

Lucas George L, carp, b 46 Thomas.
Lucas Grace E, teacher, b 450 N West.
Lucas Grant, polisher, b 300 E Georgia.
Lucas Henry M, waiter, r 410 Blake.
Lucas Herbert E, clk, b 957 N Capitol av.
Lucas James, lab, b w s Burgess av 4 s of C H & D R R (I).
Lucas John, lab, h e s Rural 2 n of Belt R R (B).
Lucas Joseph W, baker, h 142 Broadway.
Lucas Mary E (wid Henry), h rear 19 Cora.
Lucas Max J, student, b 293 N New Jersey.
Lucas Omer C, chemist, b 450 N West.
Lucas Primus E, foreman, h 48 Excelsior av.
Lucas Sarah J (wid Benjamin F), b 206 Spring.
Lucas Wm, lab, h 246 S William (W I).
Luce John L, stenog, h 328 E New York.
Lucid George, caller, h 20 Roe.
Lucid John, custodian, h 358 S West.
Lucid John F, mach hd, h 280 S Senate av.
Lucid Maurice, h 363 S Missouri.
Lucid Maurice, lab, h 19 Roe.
Lucid Michael, saloon, 370 S West, h 34 Roe.
Lucid Michael A, lab, b 363 S Missouri.
Lucid Philip, butcher, h 41 Catherine.
Lucid Richard C, lab, b 363 S Missouri.
Lucke Frank L, mach, h 387 Hillside av.
Lucke John, molder, b 397 Hillside av.
Luckett Wm K, coremkr, h 136 N Pine.
Luckhardt Frederick, carp, h 149 Eureka av.
Lucky Christian F, truckman, h 25 Meek.
Ludgin Henry, lab, h 98 Kansas.
Ludington George, miller, h 13 Douglass.
Ludlow Earl T, student, b s w cor Ritter and Cherry avs (I).
Ludlow Harry A, salesman, h 253 Huron.
Ludlow John J, porter, b 97 Fayette.
Ludlow John N, fruits, E Mkt House, h 199 Pleasant.
Ludlow Julius R, trav agt George Hitz & Co, h s w cor Ritter and Cherry avs (I).
Ludlow Louis L, reporter The Indpls Sentinel, r 81 E Vermont.
Ludlow Mary J (wid Jason C), h 253 Huron.
Ludlum Edward S, baggageman, b 497 College av.
Ludlum Joseph E, solr John S Spann & Co, h 479 College av.
Ludorff Agnes (wid Louis), h 84 W North.
Ludorff Alice, photo printer, b 84 W North.
Ludorff Louis H, trav agt Francke & Schindler, b 84 W North.
Ludwig Charles G, clk, h 300 E Michigan.
Ludwig Ernest H, saloon, 77 N Alabama, h same.
Ludwig James, lab, h 948 W Vermont.
Ludwig James B, lab, h 250 Lafayette av.
Ludwig John M, r 77 N Alabama.
Ludwig Joseph, lab, h 50 Iowa.
Ludwig Joseph jr, barber, b 50 Iowa.
Ludwig Joseph G, driver, b 55 Davidson.
Ludwig Louis, milliner, 164 E Washington, h same.
Ludwig Milton S, lab, b 250 Lafayette av.
Ludwig Wm, pawnbroker, 21 N Meridian, res Evansville, Ind.
Ludwig Wm H (Lazarus & Ludwig), b 300 E Michigan.
Luebking Charles C, car insp, h 205 Coburn.
Luebking Charles H, b 619 E New York.
Luebking Charles W, b 205 Coburn.
Luebking Edward C, cutter, h 167 Spann av.
Luebking Henry C, tinner, b 205 Coburn.
Luebking Lewis C, salesman, b 167 Spann av.

Farm and City Loans
25 Years' Successful Business.
THOS. C. DAY & CO,
Rooms 325 to 330 Lemcke Building.

Luebking Wm F, carp 129 N Summit, h same.
Luedeman Bros (Herman and John F), brick mnfrs, s s Michigan av 2 e of Belt R R.
Luedeman Herman (Luedeman Bros), h s s Michigan av 2 e of Belt R R.
Luedeman John F (Luedeman Bros), h 22 Arlington.
Luedemann Diedrich H, lab, h 6 Eureka av.
Luedemann Henry H, confr, 517 Virginia av, b same.
Lueders Cornelia (Misses Lueders), h 460 N Senate av.
Lueders Eliza (Misses Lueders), h 460 N Senate av.
Lueders Louisa (Misses Lueders), h 460 N Senate av.
LUEDERS MISSES (Eliza, Louisa and Cornelia), Stamping, Embroidery Goods and Teachers of Painting, 460 N Senate av. (See adv under Stamping and Embroidery.)
Lueke Christian H, lab, h 675 S East.
Luesche Joseph, carp, h 690 Madison av.
Luessow Charles F, carp, h 10 Gresham.
Luessow Charles H, lab, h 1 Singleton.
Luessow Henry J, mach hd, b 3 Beecher.
Lueth John H, grocer, 501 S West, h same.
Lueth Wm, shoemkr, 236 S Meridian, h same.
Lueth Wm F, lab, b 501 S West.
Luft Wm, shoemkr, 504½ Bellefontaine, h same.
Luke Albert, painter, 85 Warren av (W I), h same.
Luke Jacob, molder, h rear e s English av 3 e of Belt R R.
Luke Samuel, lab, h e s English av 2 e of Belt R R.
Luke Wm R, lab, h e s English av 1 e of Belt R R.
LUKENBILL ORESTES C, Physician, 1093 E Washington, h 1003 same, Tel 1444.
Lukens Joseph O, tel opr, h 1079 W New York.

EAT
QUAKER BREAD
ASK YOUR GROCER FOR IT.
THE HITZ BAKING CO.

BICYCLES $5 DOWN. MONTHLY. Best Wheels. Best Terms. WHEELMEN'S CO. 31 W. OHIO ST. LONG DISTANCE TEL. 1855.

J. H. TECKENBROCK House, Sign and Fresco Painter, 94 EAST SOUTH STREET.

FIDELITY MUTUAL LIFE PHILADELPHIA, PA. A. H. COLLINS, Gen. Agt. Baldwin Blk. } RATES REASONABLE. SOUND BEYOND QUESTION. BUSINESS-LIKE IN PRACTICE.

Edwardsport Coal and Mining Company ROOMS 42 AND 43 WHEN BUILDING. BITUMINOUS COAL

ESTABLISHED 1876. TELEPHONE 168.
CHESTER BRADFORD,
SOLICITOR OF PATENTS,
AND COUNSEL IN PATENT CAUSES.
(See adv. page 6.)
Office:—Rooms 14 and 16 Hubbard Block, S. W. Cor. Washington and Meridian Streets, INDIANAPOLIS, INDIANA.

Lukes John F, tailor, r 27½ Monument pl.
Lukin Frederick, tmstr, h 217 Bismarck av (H).
Lull Henry, lab, h 44 Concordia.
Lumley Charles W, foreman Holliday & Wyon, h 415 S State av.
Lumley Frederick H, mach, h 22 Temple av.
Lumley Jane E (wid Wm), r 165 Prospect.
Lumley Joseph R, collarmkr, r 165 Prospect.
Lumpkin Wm E, clk, r 154 N West.
Lunan Arthur B, molder, h 200 River av (W I).
Lunau Margaret, laundress, b 288 E Morris.
Lunchford John, lab, h 363 Newman.
Lund Asher W (Danner & Lund), h 296 Prospect.
Lund Perry, patrolman, h 110 Elm.
Lundra Wm A, pdlr, h 1 Chesapeake.
Lundy Charles E, barber, 39 When bldg, h 432 S Missouri.
Lundy Grant, lab, h 129 Maxwell.
Lung Doc, laundry, 212 W Washington, h same.
Lung E, laundry, 21 Mass av, r same.
Lunkins Wm, lab, h 248 Hamilton av.
Lunsford Daniel E, lab, h 45 S Austin (B).
Lunsford Joseph McG, lab, h 264 W Court.
Lunt Joseph W (J W Lunt & Co), h 268 College av.
Lunt J W & Co (Joseph W Luht, Horace McKay), 29½ N Penn.
Lupton Charles H, bricklyr, h 249 Shelby.
Lusch Frank, porter, b 17 Meek.
Luscher Charles F, barber, 15 Hillside av, h same.
Luscher Frederick, blksmith, h 475 Lincoln av.
Luse Charles A, clk Ry Officials' and Employes' Accident Assn, h 589 Ash.
Luse Duward M, agt, h 439 N Pine.
Luse Emma R (wid Edward H), h 253½ S Capitol av.
Luse Leonard M, teacher, b 439 N Pine.
Lusk James T, inspr, h 30 McGill.
Lustig John E, saloon, 100 E South, h same.
Lustig Nicholas, bartndr, b 427 Madison av.
Luther Albert, painter, h 325 Alvord.

BUY THE BEST.
Outing BICYCLES $85
MADE BY
HAY & WILLITS MFG CO.
76 N. PENN. ST. Phone 598.

Luther Alfred J, printer, r 63 N East.
Luther Amanda (wid Albert A), h 8 Andrews.
Luther Calvin, boilermkr, h 325 Alvord.
Luther Charles A, condr, b 8 Andrews.
Luther John S, barber, h 45 Leon.
Lutkehaus Charles, brakeman, h 409 S Illinois.
Lutz Charles F, framewkr, h 532 W 22d (N I).
Lutz Christopher C, saloon, n e cor Rural and Bloyd av (B), h 26 Cushing.
Lutz Daisy, stenog, b 358 Cedar.
Lutz Eli, tmstr, h n w cor Caldwell and W North.
Lutz Frederick W, printer, h 190 E Market.
Lutz George F, clk Mutual Life Ins Co of Indiana, h 114 Woodlawn av.
Lutz George W, phys, 69½ N Illinois, b 47 N West.
Lutz Henry (Muegge & Lutz), b 349 Madison av.
Lutz Jacob, hostler, r 239 W Washington.
Lutz Jacob, painter, b 548 LaSalle.
Lutz John, lab, h 452 W 1st.
Lutz John W, bartndr, h 174 N Pine.
Lutz Joseph J, foreman, h 32 Byram pl.
Lutz Mayme, h 358 Cedar.
Lutz Michael, hostler, b 32 Byram pl.
Lutz Nicholas E, baggageman, h 482½ Stillwell.
Lutz Peter, lab, b 32 Byram pl.
Lutz Robert P, trav agt, h 91 Middle Drive (W P).
Lux George, bartndr, r 100 N Senate av.
Lux John, saloon, 219 E Washington, h same.
Lybrand Christopher C, drayman, h 917 N New Jersey.
Lybrand John W, h 177½ W Washington.
Lybrand Joseph E, buyer H P Wasson & Co, h 59 Talbott av.
Lycan Harry, student, b 166 Clinton.
Lyday Ellsworth E, lab, h s s Railroad 4 w of Central av (I).
Lyday Otis B, lab, h 135 N Liberty.
Lydy Alexander M, grocer and postmaster, 94 S Belmont av (W I), h 105 same.
Lydy George W, lab, b 105 S Belmont av (W I).
Lyke Thomas J, miller, h 940 Gent (M P).
Lyman Bement, sec and genl mngr Consumers' Gas Trust Co, h 519 N Penn.
Lyman Charles, steelblower, b 107 W South.
Lyman Joseph, fireman, r 810 Cornell av.
Lynam Elizabeth (wid Richard), boarding 5 S Station (B).
Lynam George W, driver, h 205 W Walnut.
Lynam Hattie (wid George), r 18 Fair blk.
Lynam Mary J (wid John D), b 22 Hoyt av.
Lynam Wm, lab, h 43 Beacon.
Lynch Catherine (wid Martin), h 461 S West.
Lynch Charles E, driver, b 77 Cincinnati.
Lynch Daniel C, lab, b 77 Cincinnati.
Lynch Edward M, mach, b 120 Chadwick.
Lynch Elizabeth (wid Wesley), h 470 Highland av.
Lynch Elmer E, lab, h 64 Clifford av.
Lynch Frank, lab, b 359 S Illinois.
Lynch George, grinder, h 120 Chadwick.
Lynch George, lab, h s s 7th 1 w of canal.
Lynch George B Rev, pastor Walter's A M E Zion Church, h 456 Dillon.
Lynch George W, polisher, h 34 Hillside av.
Lynch Hannah (wid Daniel), h 77 Cincinnati.
Lynch Imogene (wid James C), b 1008 N Alabama.

ROOFING MATERIAL C. ZIMMERMAN & SONS, SLATE AND GRAVEL ROOFERS, 19 SOUTH EAST STREET.

PUMPS Chain Pumps, Driven Wells and Deep Water Wells. Repairing Neatly Done. Cisterns Built. CHARLES KRAUSS', 42 S. PENN. ST. TELEPHONE 465.

Collars and Cuffs Laundered in Best of Style. Domestic or High Gloss Finish. ERTEL STEAM LAUNDRY 26 and 28 N. Senate Ave. Telephone 1089.

Lynch Jennie, mngr Woman's Exchange, r 136 N Penn.
Lynch Jeremiah, lab, h 14 McGinnis.
Lynch Jesse, watchman, r 109 N New Jersey.
Lynch John, mach, b 464 S Illinois.
Lynch John F, lab, h 379 S Missouri.
Lynch John J, fireman, b 57 Fayette.
Lynch Margaret (wid John), h 377 S Missouri.
Lynch Martin, condr, b 461 S West.
Lynch Mary, housekpr 269 S Senate av.
Lynch Mary E (wid Martin), h 464 S Illinois.
Lynch Michael, mach, b 214 Alvord.
Lynch Michael F, lab, h 469 S Capitol av.
Lynch Michael P, trav agt A Kiefer Drug Co, h 106 Highland pl.
Lynch Morris M, lab, b 77 Cincinnati.
Lynch Owen, lab, h 498 E Georgia.
Lynch Patrick, h 488 E Georgia.
Lynch Patrick H, porter, h 273 E Merrill.
Lynch Patrick J, clk, b 57 Fayette.
Lynch Robert, lab, h 270 W Maryland.
Lynch Stephen H, lab, h 576 W McLene (N I).
Lynch Thomas J, clk B J Peake, b 74 N State av.
Lynch Timothy, lab, h 269 S Senate av.
Lynch Timothy, uphlr, b 13 Lynn.
Lynch Wm A, plater, h 34 Hillside av.
Lynch Wm F, mach, h 214 Alvord.
Lynch Wm H, ins, r 183 N Capitol av.
Lynch Wm M, gasfitter, b 470 Highland av.
Lynn, see also Linn.
Lynn Adam, lab, h 164 Martindale av.
Lynn Adam A, painter, 197 W Washington, b 200 W Chesapeake.
Lynn Daniel, laundryman, h 34 Cornell av.
Lynn George A, jeweler, h 234 Martindale av.
Lynn John D, barber, h 164 Clinton.
Lynn J Raymond, clk Severin, Ostermeyer & Co, b 76 W 2d.
Lynn Lawrence E, bkkpr Anheuser-Busch Brewing Assn, b 339 Bellefontaine.
Lynn Mary E (wid Lawrence V C), h 339 Bellefontaine.
Lynn Robert, lab, h w s Earhart 2 s of Prospect.
Lynn Wesley, lab, h 53 Peru av.
Lynn Wm C, agt Nickel Plate Line, 2 Board of Trade bldg, tel 361, h 76 W 2d.
Lynn Winfield S, drug clk Browning & Son, r 1235 N Illinois.
Lynne James, flagman, h 382 E Market.
Lyon A Inloes, lumber, n e cor Home av and Alvord, h 349 College av.
Lyon John, h w s Capitol av 2 s of 30th.
Lyon John C, solr The Rough Notes Co, b 349 College av.
Lyons Almeda (wid George W), b 174 Hoyt av.
Lyons Charles W, blksmith, h 128 English av.
Lyons Cornelius G, lab, b 422 S Delaware.
Lyons Daniel, lab, h 327 S Penn.
Lyons Daniel, stoker, h 257 Union.
Lyons Daniel J, fireman, h 42 Johnson av.
Lyons Dennis, coachman 50 W 12th.
Lyons Dennis, lab, h 58 Church.
Lyons Edward T, ins agt, b 422 S Delaware.
Lyons Ella I, teacher Public School No 12, b 39 Bates.
Lyons Ellen (wid Wm H), h 39 Bates.
Lyons Grace E, stenog, b 649 College av.
Lyons James, lab, b 272 W Maryland.
Lyons James H, saloon, 1371 W Washington (M J), h same.

Richardson & McCrea, 79 East Market Street, FIRE INSURANCE, REAL ESTATE, LOANS, AND RENTAL AGENTS. Telephone 182.

Lyons John, b s s Howland 1 w of Nicholas.
Lyons John, lab, h 48 Deloss.
Lyons John, saloon, 54 S Illinois, h same.
Lyons John F, brasier, h 272 E Louisiana.
Lyons John H, lab, b 22 Seibert.
Lyons John J, lab, b 272 W Maryland.
Lyons John M, lab, h 799 E Market.
Lyons John R, lab, b 73 W 5th.
Lyons Julia A, h 73 W 5th.
Lyons Margaret (wid Armstead), h 236 Howard.
Lyons Martin, brickmolder, h 22 Seibert.
Lyons Michael W, student, b 422 S Delaware.
Lyons Patrick, lab, b 111 W South.
Lyons Patrick D, stoker, b 257 Union.
Lyons Robert H, patrolman, h 92 Fulton.
Lyons Thomas F, lab, b 62 Church.
Lyons Timothy, foreman, h 180 S Delaware.
Lyons Timothy, foreman, h 422 S Delaware.
Lyons Timothy P, stoker, b 422 S Delaware.
Lyons Wm T, boxmkr, h 250 S Linden.
Lysaght Kate (wid Terrence), h 102 Spring.
Lyster Everett, clk, b 10 Huron.
Lyster Leonard, painter, b 10 Huron.
Lytle, see also Little.
Lytle Baltzer K, bookbndr, h 6 Camp.
Lytle Edward R, collr, h 70 Laurel.
Lytle Frank T, barber, 98 W Washington, r 27 Hubbard blk.
Lytle John H, vice-pres T B Laycock Mnfg Co, h 1017 N Penn.
Lytle John Y, painter, b 1126 N Delaware.
Lytle Sallie E, r 39½ Indiana av.
Lytle Wm, lab, h 84 Fayette.
Lytle Wm, plumber, h 214 W 1st.
Lytton Jason N, carp, b 228 N Illinois.
Lyzott Albert E, painter, b s s Hoefgen la 1 w of Meridian.
Lyzott Charles W, grainer, 67 Russell av, h s s Hoefgen la 1 w of Meridian.

Mc

McAdams Alexander, lab, b 242 W Maryland.
McAdams Andrew M, painter, 8 Putnam (B), h 8 Lawn (B).
McAdams Charles W, clk, h 255 Columbia av.

SHORTHAND REPORTING...... CONVENTIONS, SPEECHES, SERMONS. COPYING ON TYPEWRITER. S. H. EAST, State Agent, THE WILLIAMS TYPEWRITER 55 Thorpe Block, 87 East Market Street.

ELLIS & HELFENBERGER Manufacturers of Iron Vases, Setees and Hitch Posts. 162-170 South Senate Ave. Tel. 958.

THE HOGAN TRANSFER AND STORAGE COMP'Y
Household Goods and Pianos Moved—Packed—Stored...... Baggage and Package Express Machinery and Safes a Specialty Cor. Washington and Illinois Sts. TELEPHONE No. 675.

Hose, Belting, Packing, Clothing, Druggists' Sundries, Bicycle Tires, Cotton Hose, Etc. New York Belting & Packing Co., L't'd.
The Central Rubber & Supply Co. 79 S. ILLINOIS ST., INDIANAPOLIS, IND. PHONES.

The Provident Life and Trust Co.
OF PHILADELPHIA.
Small Death Rate. Small Expense Rate. Safe Investments.
Insurance in force $115,000,000
D. W. EDWARDS, General Agent, 508 Indiana Trust Building.

McAdams Della (wid Henry), h 352 Union.
McAdams Harriet (wid Perry), attendant Insane Hospital.
McAdams Hugh H, painter, h 8 S Waverly (B).
McAdams James R, lab, h 74 Shade (B).
McAdams John, lab, h 15 Chadwick.
McAdams Wm A, engr, h 148 Buchanan.
McAfee Anna (wid Taylor), h rear 113 Oak.
McAfee Daniel, lab, h 231 W 3d.
McAfee Elizabeth, b 101 Hill av.
McAfee Taylor, lab, h 450 Lincoln av.
McAfee Thomas J, lab, h 199 W 2d.
McAfee Thomas J jr, lab, b 199 W 2d.
McAffee Ernest M, lab, h 16 Brett.
McAhren Mary, housekpr 39½ S Reisner (W I).
McAlexander Robert O, asst supt City Hospital, h 854 N New Jersey.
McAlister Abram, lab, r 66 N Missouri.
McAlister Albert, rubber, b 433 S West.
McAlister Daniel, lab, h 433 S West.
McAlister James, lab, h 653 W Vermont.
McAlister John A, lab, b 433 S West.
McAllester Harriet, h 127 Patterson.
McAllister, see also McCallister.
McAllister Calvin S, h 1702 Kenwood av.
McAllister Daniel J, electrician, h 130 N Summit.
McAllister James W, b 44 Eastern av.
McAllister John, contr, 442 Harrison av, h same.
McAllister John F, paperhngr, h 289½ Mass av.
McAllister Lucinda M (wid Wm), b 44 Eastern av.
McAllister Martin S, lab, h 44 Eastern av.
McAllister Minnie M, music teacher, b 1702 Kenwood av.
McAllister Owen, lab, h 272 N Senate av.
McAllister Sherman M, lab, b 35 Eastern av.
McAlpin Charles, student, b 418 N East.
McAlpin Mary E (wid John), Parkhurst Bros & Co, h 418 N East.
McAlpin Wm V, clk, b 418 N East.
McAlpine Alexander R, supt, h 223 E Walnut.
McAlpine Frank E, train disp P C C & St L Ry, h 267 E St Clair.

Julius C. Walk & Son,
Jewelers
Indianapolis.
12 EAST WASHINGTON ST.

McAlpine James H, chief train dispatcher P C C & St L Ry, h 315 Park av.
McAlyn Daniel, flagman, h 165 Bates.
McAlyn Wm E, helper, b 165 Bates.
McAnally Jesse F, bkkpr Adamant Wall Plaster Co, r 267 N New Jersey.
McAndrews Anthony, lab, h 12 Meikel.
McAndrews John B, molder, b 12 Meikel.
McAndrews Mary, grocer, 16 McCauley, b 12 Meikel.
McAREE OWEN, Grocer and Saloon, 249 English av, h same.
McArthur Anna J (wid Peter), clk Robert Keller, h 58 Johnson av.
McArthur Charles B, helper, b 58 Johnson av.
McArthur Charles S, paperruler, h 333 Blake.
McArthur George A, lab, h 162 Trowbridge (W).
McArthur James P, switchman, b 58 Johnson av.
McAtee James D, plastr, h 235 Huron.
McAuley, see also McCauley and Macauley.
McAuley Mary (wid Burrell), b 281 Chapel.
McAvoy, see also McEvoy.
McAvoy Thomas J, elocutionist, 56 Talbott blk, h 37 Fletcher av.
McBane Ellen E (wid John R), b 316 N Alabama.
McBane Jacob T, carp, h rear 356 S Delaware.
McBee Rebecca (wid Henry), h 275 W Market.
McBee Samuel, lab, h 481 W Chicago (N I).
McBeth, see MacBeth.
McBride Albert J, carp, h 56 Bates.
McBride Charles, bkkpr, b 110 Michigan (H).
McBride Charles H, b 799 Broadway.
McBride Charles M, blksmith, b 406 Virginia av.
McBride Charles S, sec and treas A Kiefer Drug Co, h 790 N Delaware.
McBride Clifford, student, b 437 N Delaware.
McBride Frank A (Syfers, McBride & Co), h 437 N Delaware.
McBride Herbert W, acct, b 799 Broadway.
McBride Ida S, sec, h 799 Broadway.
McBride James, saloon, 110 Michigan (H), h same.
McBride Jesse L, pianomkr, h 190 E Market.
McBride John, cook, b 544 S West.
McBride John, engr, b 102 N Capitol av.
McBride John, mach, b 89 N Delaware.
McBride John G, gasfitter, b 35 Ellsworth.
McBride Mary (wid Dominick), h 349 S Missouri.
McBride Otto D, lab, h 241 Newman.
McBride Robert W (McBride & Denny), h 799 Broadway.
McBride Stanley, bkkpr, b 437 N Delaware.
McBride Thomas, b 349 S Missouri.
McBride Wm, clk L S Ayres & Co, b 349 S Missouri.
McBride Wm P, clk, h 385 E Georgia.
McBRIDE & DENNY (Robert W McBride, Caleb S Denny), Lawyers, 55-58 Journal Bldg, Tel 1606.
McBroom Hugh W, patternmkr, h w s Lincoln av 3 s of Jackson (M J).
McBroom Robert M, driver, h n s Jackson 3 w of Harris av (M J).
McBroom Samuel T, lab, h s s Washington 18 w of Harris av (M J).

OTTO GAS ENGINES | BUILDERS' EXCHANGE S. W. Cor. Ohio and Penn. Telephone 535.

Becker & Son Charles Becker Jacob Becker Jr. Merchant Tailors. 21 N. Penn. St. Tel. 934

SALISBURY & STANLEY, Office, Store and Bank Fixtures a Specialty. Repairing of all kinds done on short notice. 177 Ct or Street, Indianapolis, Ind. Contractors and Builders TELEPHONE 999.

McBurney John, lab, h 293 Blake.
McCabe Cora L, dressmkr, 857 N New Jersey, b same.
McCabe David W, signwriter, h 857 N New Jersey.
McCABE DENIS REV, Pastor Holy Cross Catholic Church, h 3 Springdale Pl.
McCabe Frank, lab, b 253 Jefferson av.
McCabe George, lab, b 183 Blake.
McCabe James, Associate Justice Supreme Court of Indiana, 71 State House, res Williamsport, Ind.
McCabe John, horseshoer, b 79 E Vermont.
McCabe John, lab, b 39 N Alabama.
McCabe John, lab, b 230 W Maryland.
McCabe John P, lab, b 255½ E Washington.
McCabe John R, lab, b 183 Blake.
McCabe Matthew, confr, 15 English av, h same.
McCabe Matthew V, confr, b 15 English av.
McCabe Minnie, h 31½ Virginia av.
McCabe Thomas F, barber, 1089 E Washington, h 1151 same.
McCabe Wm G, h 183 Blake.
McCaffery Edward, horsedealer, b 34 S West.
McCaffery Hugh, butcher, b 43 S West.
McCaffery James, sawmkr, h 512 Charles.
McCaffery John, h 43 S West.
McCaffery John jr, lab, b 43 S West.
McCaffery John T, mach hd, b 16 Hadley.
McCaffery John T, sawyer, h 22 Holloway av.
McCaffery Louis, horsedealer, b 43 S West.
McCaffery James B (Lay & McCaffery), r 4, 22½ S Illinois.
McCain, see also McKain.
McCain Frederick T, student, b 162 N Illinois.
McCain James B, carp, 134 S New Jersey, b 181 same.
McCain Jesse J, clk, h 78 Laurel.
McCain John E, salesman Frank E Janes, h 1710 Kenwood av.
McCain Joseph, mess'r Indiana National Bank, b 1710 Kenwood av.
McCain Joseph C, tinner, 114 Oliver av (W I), h 112 same.
McCain Joseph H, mach, h 375 S Illinois.
McCain Mattie J, r 301 The Shiel.
McCain Warren G, mer police, h 31 Dickson.
McCain Wilfred W, printer F H Smith, b 31 Dickson.
McCain Wm F, tinner, h 210 Lexington av.
McCain Wm H, organ rep, h 410 E Walnut.
McCalip Edward L, lab, b s s Bloyd av 2 w of Shade (B).
McCalister Charles S, lab, h 399 W McLene (N I).
McCalister Mary (wid David), h 656 W Vermont.
McCallie Edward B, plumber, h 86 Keystone av.
McCallie Harlie F, fireman, b 68 Omer.
McCallie James D, custodian Union Station, h 68 Omer.
McCallie John A, carp, h 11 Omer.
McCallister, see also McAllister.
McCallister Decatur, sawmkr, h 26 Maple.
McCallister Harry E, buyer N Y Store, r 21 The Plaza.
McCallister John T, lab, h 47 W Wells (N I).
McCallister Mary (wid Wm), b 907 N New Jersey.
McCallister Wm H, lab, h 47 W Wells (N I).
McCallum, see also McCollum.

Henry H. Fay,
40½ E. WASHINGTON ST.,
FIRE INSURANCE, REAL ESTATE,
LOANS AND RENTAL AGENT.

McCallum George, molder, h 298 S Capitol av.
McCallum John, molder, h 298 S Capitol av.
McCallum Neal S Rev, h n s Downey av 1 w of University av (I).
McCalment Fletcher, clk, b 314 N West.
McCameron Charles E, driver, b 385½ E 7th.
McCameron Mary (wid John), h 385½ E 7th.
McCammack Henry T, mach hd, h 283 Christian av.
McCammel Timothy R, flagman, r 150 N Capitol av.
McCammon George W, lab, b 60 Birch av (W I).
McCammon James E, printer, h 431 N Pine.
McCammon James K, h 99 Birch av (W I).
McCammon Lewis A, trav agt The Home Stove Co, b 24 School.
McCampbell Oscar S, baggageman, h 674 S Meridian.
McCan George, porter, h 101 Howard.
McCandless George E, laundryman, h 150½ College av.
McCandless Homer, collr, b 75 E Michigan.
McCann Cortez, paperhngr, h 32 Arlington.
McCann Elwood, trav agt, h 174 E Washington.
McCann Eugene, fireman, r 32 S Gale (B).
McCann Frank J, switchman, h 412 W New York.
McCann George, lab, b rear 102 Howard.
McCann James J, barber, 1129 E Washington, h same.
McCann Josephine (wid Benjamin), b 179 W 9th.
McCann Louis H, lab, h 521 N West.
McCann Mary, b 143 E Washington.
McCann Michael, lab, h 96 Hiatt (W I).
McCann Robert A, grocer, 44 Indiana av, h 72 W New York.
McCann Samuel W, ins, h 470 N Alabama.
McCann Thomas P, lab, h 81 Meikel.
McCarter Isaac, lab, h 742 E 8th.
McCarthy Bart, sec and treas The Indpls Sentinel Co, b 79 W North.
McCarthy Charles, lab, h 511 E Georgia.
McCarthy Dennis, lab, b 511 E Georgia.

JAS. N. MAYHEW,
MANUFACTURING
OPTICIAN
LENSES AND FRAMES A SPECIALTY.
No. 13 North Meridian St., Indianapolis.

LUMBER | Sash, Door and Planing Mill Work. | Balke & Krauss Co. Cor. Market and Missouri Streets.

FRIEDGEN'S TAN SHOES are the Newest Shades Prices the Lowest. 19 North Pennsylvania St.

SAMUEL LAING General Job Work in Sheet Metal of all Kinds 72 AND 74 E. COURT STREET.

M. B. WILSON, Pres. W. F. CHURCHMAN, Cash.
THE CAPITAL NATIONAL BANK,
INDIANAPOLIS, IND.
Make collections on all points in the States of Indiana and Illinois on the most favorable rates.
Capital, - - $300,000
Surplus and Earnings, 50,000
No. 28 S. Meridian St., Cor. Pearl.

McCarthy Dora (wid Moses), h 77 E Vermont.
McCarthy Fleury, lab, h 49 Minerva.
McCarthy Frank E, finisher, b 47 Davis.
McCarthy James, condr, b 124 English av.
McCarthy Jeremiah F, saloon, 105 Harrison, h same.
McCarthy Jeremiah J, boilermkr, h 47 Davis.
McCarthy John, b 107 W South.
McCarthy John, bicycle rep, b 43 Spann av.
McCarthy John, engr, h 46 Beacon.
McCarthy John, helper, b 511 E Georgia.
McCarthy John J, engr, h 846 Cornell av.
McCarthy John T, lab, b 490 S West.
McCarthy Joseph F, finisher, b 36 Church.
McCarthy Josephine, h 490 S West.
McCarthy Louise, b 294 Broadway.
McCarthy Mary (wid Daniel), h 340 N Pine.
McCarthy Mary (wid Michael M), h 181 Woodlawn av.
McCarthy Mary (wid Wm), h 135 Davidson.
McCarthy Mary, teacher Public School No 12, b 77 Camp.
McCarthy Michael, butcher, b 230 W Maryland.
McCarthy Michael, finisher, b 490 S West.
McCarthy Patrick, h 36 Church.
McCarthy Patrick, lab, h 105 Trowbridge (W).
McCarthy Stephen, flagman, h 131 Bellefontaine.
McCarthy Thomas, clk The Bowen-Merrill Co, b 77 E Vermont.
McCarthy Thomas, engr, h 163 Spann av.
McCarthy Thomas, lab, b 63 Church.
McCarthy Thomas E, molder, b 36 Church.
McCarthy Wm C, engr, h 97 Camp.
McCarthy Wm L, insp, b 490 S West.
McCarthy Wm P, boilermkr, b 47 Davis.
McCartney Harry J, hatter, b 41 Brookside av.
McCartney Wesley L, engr, h 41 Brookside av.
McCarty Bridget, h 723 E Ohio.
McCarty Catherine (wid Dennis), h 149 Spann av.
McCarty Charles, saloon, 139 Virginia av, h 256 S Delaware.

MONEY
Loaned on Short Notice at Lowest Rates.
TUTTLE & SEGUIN,
Tel. 1168. 28 E. Market St.

McCarty Edward, lab, h 132 N Pine.
McCarty Frank, sawmkr, b California House.
McCarty Grant, lab, b 67 S Noble.
McCarty Lavina C (wid Thomas B), h 194 N Illinois.
McCarty Mary L (wid Edward), h 520 Ash.
McCarty Matthew, condr, h 129 Gresham.
McCarty Mattie E, h 140 N Alabama.
McCARTY NICHOLAS, Office 12 Hubbard Blk, Tel 1783; h 122 N Penn.
McCarty Orin B, foreman, b 229 N Penn.
McCarty Osman A, pressman, h e s Central av 3 s of Beechwood av (I).
McCarty Samuel H, janitor, h 6 St Charles.
McCarty Thomas, lab, r 300 S Capitol av.
McCarty Thomas, motorman, h 41 Vinton.
McCarty Thomas J, molder, h 13 Centennial (H).
McCarty Thomas M, engr, b 149 Spann av.
McCarty Timothy D, collr, r 172 E North.
McCarty Wm, lab, h 281 W Merrill.
McCarty Wm, lab, h 495½ S West.
McCarty Wm jr, lab, b 495½ S West.
McCarty Wm, packer, b 6 St Charles.
McCarty Wm C, engr, h 97 Camp.
McCarty Wm D, student, b 229 N Penn.
McCarty Wm H, lab, h 121 Rhode Island.
McCarver Franklin P, lab, h 146 Geisendorff.
McCary Oliver, janitor 134 N Illinois.
McCaslin George H, real est, 2½ W Washington, h 913 N New Jersey.
McCaslin Harvey W, carp, b 500 E Washington.
McCaslin Henry (McCaslin & Cavanaugh), h 342 W 1st.
McCaslin Samuel, carp, h 500 E Washington.
McCaslin & Cavanaugh (Henry McCaslin, James J Cavanaugh), grocers, 502 N West.
McCauley, see also Macauley.
McCauley Allen A, ball player, b 162 Spring.
McCauley Charles, engr, b 19 Harrison.
McCauley Christopher C, clk, b 19 Harrison.
McCauley Eugene C, ins adjuster, 11 Talbott blk, h 1207 N Penn.
McCauley Harry A, student, b 1207 N Penn.
McCauley James, lab, h 62 Grant.
McCauley Jane E (wid Christopher C), h 19 Harrison.
McCauley Mack B, lab, h 449 W Pratt.
McCauley Margaret, girls' supervisor Deaf and Dumb Inst.
McCauley Wm A, grocer, 120 Huron, h same.
McCauley Wm H, bartndr, h 162 Spring.
McCauliff Eugene H, agt Hood, Foulkrod & Co, b 30 E Pratt.
McCaw Martin J, motorman, h 404 Yandes.
McChesney Edward, baggageman, r 120 The Shiel.
McChesney George G, clk, r 298 Virginia av.
McChesney Wm G, student, b 138 N New Jersey.
McClain, see also Maclean, McCleen, McLain and McLean.
McClain Alonzo, finisher, b 13 Hester.
McClain Carl E, foreman, b 13 Hester.
McClain Charles G, brakeman, h 24 Villa av.
McClain Donald F, carp, h rear 116 N Pine.
McClain Douglas, lab, h 1 Hill.
McClain Elizabeth J, seamstress, h 78 Newman.
McClain Elmer L, lab, b 13 Hester.
McClain Frederick C, clk, b 60 S Reisner (W I).

PAPER BOXES, MANUFACTURED BY SULLIVAN & MAHAN 41 W. PEARL STREET.

DIAMOND WALL PLASTER { Telephone 1410 BUILDERS' EXCHANGE.

Fine Laundry Work our Specialty. Collars and Cuffs our Hobby. THE HOME LAUNDRY 197 S. Illinois St. Telephone 1769.

McClain Hoyt N, clk Griffiths & Potts, r 122 Irwin.
McClain Jacob, h 14 Hester.
McClain James M, fireman, h 331½ Dillon.
McClain James W jr, carp N Y Store, h 346 Columbia av.
McClain John, lab, r 172 S Missouri.
McClain Joseph T, h 447 E McCarty.
McClain Lee W, lab, r rear 478 N Penn.
McClain Levi, clk, b 170 Blake.
McClain Mary (wid George), b 266 S Penn.
McClain Richard H, janitor Public School No 20, h same.
McClain Sarah E (wid John C), h 13 Hester.
McClain Wm C, carp, 127 N Noble, h same.
McClain Wm O, carp, h 218 Spring.
McClanahan Frank, mach hd, h 239 S Olive.
McClaren, see McLaren.
McClarty Henry, lab, h 4 Howard.
McClarty Lorenzo D, lab, h 91 Darnell.
McClary Jane D, dressmkr, 264 E Miami, h same.
McClary Joseph A, broommkr, h 264 E Miami.
McClean, see also Maclean, McClain, McLain and McLeon.
McClean Archibald, lab, h 136 Elizabeth.
McCleary Alexander M, broker, 802 Majestic bldg, h 922 N Illinois.
McCleary Wm B, steelwkr, r 100 Fletcher av.
McCleaster Albert, lab, h 26 Hosbrook.
McClellan, see also McLeland.
McClellan Alonzo, phys, 104 Michigan (H), h 1070 W Vermont.
McClellan Bayard F, uphlr, h 1015 E Washington.
McClellan Frederick, rodman City Engineer, r 127 The Shiel.
McClellan George C, painter, b 1070 W Vermont.
McClellan Leonidas H, uphlr, h 334 E Miami.
McClellan Leonidas H jr, uphlr, h 112 Ramsey av.
McClellan Nancy M (wid John), b 334 E Miami.
McClellan Richard H, trav agt Fahnley & McCrea, h 130 The Shiel.
McClellan Rousseau, student, b 1070 W Vermont.
McClellan Thomas J, h s s Washington 7 e of Sherman Drive.
McClellan Wm E, packer, h 488 W 1st.
McClellan Wm R, janitor Public School No 9, h 221 Fulton.
McClellan Winona, music teacher, 334 E Miami, b same.
McClelland Charles M, carp, h 7 Frazee (H).
McClelland Edward C, mach opr The Indpls Sentinel, h 168 Johnson av.
McClelland Eliza J, laundress, h 270 Bates.
McClelland Francis M, condr, h 234 Cornell av.
McClelland Lizzie, cashr, b 241 N Pine.
McClelland Nellie, milliner, b 551 N Illinois.
McClelland Robert C, car insp, h 241 N Pine.
McClements John, lab, b 335 W Vermont.
McClimon James, carp, 235 N Pine, h same.
McClintick Wm J, yardmaster, h 74 High.
McClintock Adam R, engr, b 55 Stevens.
McClintock Denton, lab, b 191 Columbia av.
McClintock James A (Wilson & McClintock), h 561½ Virginia av.
McClintock James H, condr, h 266 Bellefontaine.
McClintock John R, plumber, h 310 Union.

FRANK NESSLER. WILL H. ROST.
FRANK NESSLER & CO.
Tailors
56 EAST MARKET ST. (Lemcke Building),
INDIANAPOLIS, IND.

McClintock Robert, lab, h 53 Greer.
McClintock Robert N, lab, h 230 Minnesota.
McClintock Thomas, clk, h 191 Columbia av.
McClintock Thomas, pdlr, b 165 S Alabama.
McClintock Thomas A, gardener, h 1776 N Illinois.
McClintock Wm, paver, h 55 Stevens.
McCloskey, see also McClusky.
McCloskey Bernard F, clk, b 194 N West.
McCloskey Bernard J, carp, b 419 E McCarty.
McCloskey James B, photog, 36½ E Washington, h same.
McCloskey James J, clk George J Marott, b 194 N West.
McCloskey John, carp, h 419 E McCarty.
McCloskey John, clk, b 519 N Senate av.
McCloskey John C, insp, h 12 Sullivan.
McCloskey John H, city dis clk P O, r 36½ E Washington.
McCloskey Maria (wid Bernard), h 194 N West.
McCloud, see also McLeod.
McCloud Alexander, painter, b 10 Huron.
McCloud David, lab, b 15 Rhode Island.
McCloud Frank, lab, b 15 Rhode Island.
McCloud Mahalah A (wid Thomas), h 207 W Vermont.
McCloud Thomas, lab, r 15 Rhode Island.
McClung Hester M, b 172 N West.
McClung Ida M, stenog, r 222½ E Washington.
McClure Alonzo, lab, h s s Orient 3 e of C C C & St L Ry (N I).
McClure Andrew J, carp, r 185 W New York.
McClure Charles S, bricklyr, h 344 Cornell av.
McClure David Z, carp, r 185 W New York.
McClure George W, carp, b 438 W Pratt.
McClure Gertrude, nurse City Hospital.
McClure Harriet, b 574 Bellefontaine.
McClure Helen N (wid John), b rear 704 N Illinois.
McClure Ira R, trav agt, h 77 Park av.
McClure Jacob H, carp, b 1655 N Senate av.
McClure John, mach, b California House.
McClure Leonidas, carp, b 438 W Pratt.

Haueisen & Hartmann
163-169 E. Washington St.
FURNITURE,
Carpets,
Household Goods,
Tin, Granite and China Wares, Oil Cloth and Shades

THE WM. H. BLOCK CO. 7 AND 9 EAST WASHINGTON STREET. DRY GOODS, MEN'S FURNISHINGS.

Fidelity and Deposit Co. of Maryland. BONDS SIGNED.—LOCAL BOARD John B. Elam, Albert Sahm, Smiley N. Chambers, John M. Spann.
GEORGE W. PANGBORN, General Agent, 704-706 Lemcke Building. Telephone 140.

Insure Your Property With FRANK K. SAWYER || 74 EAST MARKET STREET Telephone 863.

JOSEPH GARDNER,
Hot Air Furnaces
With Combination Gas Burners for Burning Gas and Other Fuel at the Same Time.
37, 39 & 41 KENTUCKY AVE. Telephone 322

McClure Lester W, mounter, h 477 S West.
McClure Phlegon T, carp, h 25 Wilcox.
McClure Rachel C (wid George H), h 438 W Pratt.
McClure Rebecca E, nurse, 195 College av, h same.
McClure Sadie, h rear 601 N Meridian.
McClure Samuel J, mer police, h 159 Alvord.
McClure Sarah (wid Samuel), b 94 Highland av.
McClure Solon, electrician, b 195 College av.
McClure Stella G, stenog Standard Oil Co, b 195 College av.
McClure Thomas, lab, h 124 N Missouri.
McClure Wm A, carp, h 48 Warren av (W I).
McClure Wm J, bricklyr, h 344 Cornell av.
McClure Wm M, porter, h 199 W 3d.
McClure Wm R, cook, h rear 704 N Illinois.
McClure Zephaniah, car rep, h 110 Columbia al.
McClurg Edward, mach, b Illinois House.
McClurg Wm, lab, h 192 W Merrill.
McCluskey, see also McCloskey.
McClusky Mary E (wid Alexander H), h 182 N State av.
McClusky Wm, motorman, b 182 N State av.
McCoin Thomas, solr, h 438 E Georgia.
McCole Henry H, tailor, h 328 W Vermont.
McColgan Wade M, driver, b 330 Douglass.
McColley Wm J, lab, b s e cor Harris av and W Washington (M J).
McCollough Frank N, barber, 10 Prospect, r 181½ S Meridian.
McColloum Joseph M, tmstr, h 37 Garden.
McCollum Andrew J, lumber, h 1472 N Illinois.
McCollum Harry W, mach hd, b 123 Hoyt av.
McCollum James F, collr C F Adams Co, h 123 Hoyt av.
McCollum John M, farmer, h 21 Pleasant.
McCollum John W, carp, h 14 Division (W I).
McCollum Joseph M, bkkpr C F Adams Co, r 308 E South.
McCollum Wm M, carp, h 149 Cottage av.
McComas George, tinner, h 169 Harmon.
McComas Milton, pdlr, b 169 Harmon.

J. S. FARRELL & CO.
Plumbing
Natural and Artificial Gas Fitting.
84 N. ILLINOIS STREET.
TELEPHONE 382.

McComb Andrew, fireman, b n w cor Michigan and State avs.
McComb David, packer, h 487 Stillwell.
McComb Edward B, feed, 59 Mass av, h 35 College av.
McComb Frank E, clk, b 35 College av.
McComb Joseph M, produce, E Mkt House, b 487 Stillwell.
McComb Minnie W, stenog Howard Kimball, b 487 Stillwell.
McComb Ozro G, trav agt, h 413 Ash.
McConaghy Joseph, clk, h 179 N Dorman.
McConaha Samuel B, lineman, b 161 Columbia av.
McConaha Wm, motorman, b 1051 N Capitol av.
McConkey Thomas C, agt, r 175 W Michigan.
McConnaughey David P, patternmkr, h 445 W Michigan.
McConnell Andrew, lab, h 147 Minerva.
McConnell Bros (Edward and Ezra), coal, 401 E Washington.
McConnell Charles A, sec Globe Machine Wks, State agt Mosler Safe Co, h 163 N Illinois.
McConnell David S, r 401 E Washington.
McConnell Edward (McConnell Bros), r 401 E Washington.
McConnell Elizabeth (wid Wm), b 459 E Georgia.
McConnell Ezra (McConnell Bros), r 401 E Washington.
McConnell Finley R, printer The Sun, h 1690 N Capitol av.
McConnell Forrest E, music teacher, 18 S Station (B), b same.
McConnell Harry, timekpr, b 335 W Vermont.
McConnell Harry J, asst cashr Kingan & Co (ltd), b 173 Bright.
McConnell Isaac W, trav agt A Kiefer Drug Co, h 18 S Station (B).
McConnell Jerome, ins agt, b 93 E Georgia.
McConnell John, carp, b 201 E Washington.
McConnell John, clk Kingan & Co (ltd), h 173 Bright.
McConnell John P, carp, 27 E Georgia, h 244 Dougherty.
McConnell John T, molder, b 197 Blake.
McConnell Kate B, stenog Van Camp H and I Co, b 78 College av.
McConnell Leander C, phys, 20 King, b same.
McConnell Lillie M, h 244 Dougherty.
McConnell Margaret (wid Stephen), b 361 S Delaware.
McConnell Mary (wid Robert F), b 1690 N Capitol av.
McConnell Mary E (wid John H), b 78 College av.
McConnell Mary E (wid John P), h 330 N New Jersey.
McConnell Sarah D (wid James), b 84 E New York.
McConnell Simpson, tmstr, b 214 Bates.
McConnell Thomas, carp, 167½ W 1st, h 509 N West.
McConney Norris J, cigars, 44 Jackson pl, h 64 W Walnut.
McConney Porter D, clk, b 64 W Walnut.
McConvay John, lab, b 240 N California.
McCool Dolphin E, canmkr, h 156 Huron.
McCool James, h 294 S Illinois.
McCool James jr, student, b 294 S Illinois.
McCool Wm, carp, h 30 Hillside av.
McCool Wm H, lab, h 8 S Linden.
McCooley Philip, lab, h 169 Bane.

IF CONTINUED to the end of its dividend period, policies of the UNITED STATES LIFE INSURANCE CO., will equal or excel any investment policy ever offered to the public. | E. B. SWIFT, Manager, 25 E. Market St.

Wm. Kotteman 89 & 91 E. Washington St. TELEPHONE 1742 Furniture

McCord Christina L (wid Benjamin R), h 33 The Windsor.
McCord Edith, student, b 175 Oliver av (W I).
McCord James F, painter, h 436 W Eugene (N I).
McCord Jeannette H, asst ticket agt I U Ry Co, b 33 The Windsor.
McCord Katherine, teacher, b 33 The Windsor.
McCord Ollie L, seamstress, h 401½ N Alabama.
McCord Sarah E (wid Samuel H), h 162 N Illinois.
McCord Thomas B, carp, h 32 Yandes.
McCord Walter W, condr, b 32 Yandes.
McCord Wm C, carp, h 1479 Northwestern av.
McCorkle Arthur I, clk, h 52½ W 7th.
McCorkle Clifford F, barber, b 207 E South.
McCorkle Henry E, boarding 306 S Meridian.
McCorkle Insco, clk, b 182 N Senate av.
McCorkle James H, clk, h 182 N Senate av.
McCorkle John P, livery, 181 Virginia av, h 207 E South.
McCorkle Marion, cigars, 97 Mass av, h 1021 N Senate av.
McCorkle Oscar J, driver, b 207 E South.
McCorkle Wm H, lab, h 34½ Malott av.
McCormack Charles W, clk, b 168 W 1st.
McCormack John L, contr, h 702 N Capitol av.
McCormack Lycurgus P, printer, h 168 W 1st.
McCormack Zuinglius K, lawyer, 72½ E Washington, h 168 W 1st.
McCormick Alvis, engr, b 122 Duncan.
McCormick Anna, teacher, b 102 S Judge Harding (W I).
McCormick Charles H, city agt Standard Oil Co, h 134 Woodlawn av.
McCormick David I, lab, h 175 Blake.
McCormick Ephraim, agt, h 260 Indiana av.
McCormick Ernest, mach, b 35 Miley av.
McCormick Frances (wid Michael), h 80 W Ohio.
McCormick Francis, carp, h 77 Oliver av (W I).
McCormick Frank E, mach, b 134 Woodlawn av.
McCormick Frank J, lab, h 344 W Maryland.
McCormick Franklin S, collr, h 114 Highland pl.
McCormick George L, mach, b 134 Woodlawn av.
McCormick Harry G, gasfitter, b 617 N West.
McCormick Harry L, agt, b 114 Highland pl.
McCORMICK HARVESTING MACHINE CO, James B Heywood Genl Agt, 67-69 S Penn, Tel 781.
McCormick Howard, artist The Indpls News, h 17 Park av.
McCormick James F, mach, h 102 S Judge Harding (W I).
McCormick Jedidiah R, carp, h 617 N West.
McCormick John, gasfitter, h 122 Duncan.
McCormick J Frank, trav agt, h 322 N Alabama.
McCormick Michael, molder, h 14 Carlos.
McCormick Newton, lab, h 35 Miley av.
McCormick Orion, lab, b 22 Merrit (H).
McCormick Otis, mach, b 122 Duncan.
McCormick Sarah E (wid Isaac N), b 17 Park av.
McCormick Stephen, lab, h 22 Merrit (H).

We Buy Municipal ~ Bonds ~
THOS. C. DAY & CO,
Rooms 325 to 330 Lemcke Bldg.

McCormick Sylva, h 68 S Summit.
McCormick Wilson J, trav agt Indpls Chair Mnfg Co, b Circle Park Hotel.
McCotter Wm, butcher, h 655 W Vermont.
McCotter Wm, lab, b 272 W Maryland.
McCoun Jack, h 104 Clifford av.
McCowan James, lab, r 279 Chapel.
McCowan Lawrence, driver, h 21 Garland (W I).
McCoy Albert, waiter The Denison.
McCoy Albert E, finisher, b e end of Vine.
McCoy Albert F, lab, h 378 Indiana av.
McCoy Bion, engr, b 142 Bates.
McCoy Callie A, housekpr, h 12 E Michigan.
McCoy Catherine, b 565 E 7th.
McCoy Celeste H (wid Wm D), h 419 N Senate av.
McCoy Charles, tmstr, b 1520 N Senate av.
McCoy Commodore P, paperhngr, b 289 Virginia av.
McCoy David, produce, 40 E Mkt House, h 336 E New York.
McCoy Elizabeth A, h 161 St Mary.
McCoy Ella B (wid Hamilton), h 275 N Delaware.
McCoy Ernest C, lab, b 29½ S Illinois.
McCoy George E E, lab, h 538 W North.
McCoy George L, lab, h 503 Sheldon.
McCoy Grant, tmstr, h n w cor Yandes and Davidge.
McCoy Harriet A, teacher Public School No 4, b 275 N Delaware.
McCoy Henry A, condr, h 224 Clifford av.
McCoy Henry B, tmstr, h 215 S Linden.
McCoy Hiram, lab, h 125 Yandes.
McCOY-HOWE CO, John B McCoy Pres, Aaron B Howe Vice-Pres, James M Mowrer Sec and Treas, Mnfg Chemists, 75, 77 and 79 W Georgia, Tel 557.
McCoy James E, musician, b 286 Virginia av.
McCoy James F, switchman, h 75 Tacoma av.
McCoy James H, lab, b 294 Douglass.
McCoy Jane (wid Wm), b 47 Camp.
McCoy Jane W (wid Samuel H), h 134 Columbia av.

EAT
QUAKER BREAD
ASK YOUR GROCER FOR IT.
THE HITZ BAKING CO.

SHOW CASES
WILLIAM WIEGEL
6 West Louisiana Street
Opp. Union Station.

CARPETS CLEANED LIKE NEW. TELEPHONE 818
CAPITAL STEAM CARPET CLEANING WORKS

BENJ. BOOTH PRACTICAL EXPERT ACCOUNTANT. Thirty years' experience. First-class credentials. Room 18, 82½ E. Washington St. Indianapolis, Ind.

The Old Reliable Sherman European Restaurant || 18 and 20 S. Meridian St. Established 1880.

ESTABLISHED 1876. TELEPHONE 168.
CHESTER BRADFORD,
SOLICITOR OF PATENTS,
AND COUNSEL IN PATENT CAUSES.
(See adv. page 6.)
Office:—Rooms 14 and 16 Hubbard Block, S.W. Cor. Washington and Meridian Streets, INDIANAPOLIS, INDIANA.

McCoy Jennie A (wid Frank T), b 248 Alvord.
McCoy John, b 112 Division (W I).
McCoy John, mach, h 301 Blake.
McCoy John B, pres McCoy-Howe Co, h 456 N New Jersey.
McCoy Manning W, carp, h e end of Vine.
McCoy Philon, lab, h 29½ S Illinois.
McCoy Robert E, hotel, 217 S Illinois.
McCoy Robert H, paperhngr, h 289 Virginia av.
McCoy Theodore, attendant Insane Hospital.
McCoy Thomas B, tmstr, h 366 Newman.
McCoy Thomas F, lab, b 125 Yandes.
McCoy Wm, lab, h 42 Concordia.
McCoy Wm, lab, h n s Fountain 4 w of Floral av.
McCoy Wm, tmstr, h 38 Maxwell.
McCoy Wm, trav agt, h 71 Central av.
McCoy Wm J, collr, b 120 W Maryland.
McCoy Wm K, car rep, h 8 Deloss.
McCracken Edward J, finisher, b 392 N West.
McCracken John C, bartndr, b 293 Bates.
McCracken Mary (wid Robert), h 210 Bright.
McCracken Ralph W, polisher, b 77 Sheffield av (H).
McCracken Robert, butcher, b 210 Bright.
McCracken Stephen G, lab, h 77 Sheffield av (H).
McCraith Augustine, sec Am Federation of Labor, r 221 E Vermont.
McCraken Wm F, trav agt, h 943 N Alabama.
McCrary John, engr, h 68 Camp.
McCrary Wade H, lab, h 25 McCauley.
McCrary Wm, coachman 978 N Penn.
McCrary Wm E, ins agt, h 83 Bright.
McCray Alonzo A, salesman Chandler & Taylor Co, h Germania av nr Michigan (H).
McCray Dicia A (wid Milton), b 147 W North.
McCray Frank, judge Marion County Criminal Court, h 722 N New Jersey.
McCray George W, contr, 81 W 11th, h same.

CORRUGATED IRON CEILINGS AND SIDING.
ALL KINDS OF REPAIRING.
O. B. ENSEY,
TELEPHONE 1562.
COR. 6TH AND ILLINOIS STREETS.

McCray John M, shoes, 256 W Washington, h 27 N West.
McCrea Addison B, clk Murphy, Hibben & Co, b 229 N Penn.
McCREA FRANK F (Richardson & McCrea), Propr Indianapolis Desk File and Paper Box Manufactory, 143½ S Meridian, h 357 Broadway, Tel 1147.
McCrea Harry C, trav agt McKee Shoe Co, b Spencer House.
McCrea James, pres Indpls Union Ry Co, res Pittsburg, Pa.
McCrea Rollin H (Fahnley & McCrea), b 357 Broadway.
McCrea Serene, h 85 N Delaware.
McCrea Wm W, salesman Fahnley & McCrea, h 1538 N Illinois.
McCready Benjamin F, gas fitter, 164 Ft Wayne av, h s e cor 24th and Central av.
McCready Charles A, clk, b s e cor 24th and Central av.
McCready Frank W, dairy, n e cor Central av and 25th, h same.
McCready James, clk Indiana National Bank, h s e cor 24th and Central av.
McCready James M, clk, h 118 Nordyke av (W I).
McCready John E, trav agt Schrader Bros, h 377 W New York.
McCready Wm T, butcher, h 492 N Senate av.
McCreary George B, mach, h 419 W 22d (N I).
McCreary John L, electrician, b 21 The Windsor.
McCreary Penrose, engr, h 846 Rembrant (M P).
McCreen Daniel J, car rep, b 80 S Brightwood (B).
McCreery Jesse, tmstr, h 127 Dearborn.
wood av (B).
McCreery Jesse, tmstr, h 127 Dearborn.
McCrisaken Daniel, lab, b 1143 E Washington.
McCrossan James A (Indpls Tool and Mnfg Co), h 273 Blake.
McCrossan Samuel, lab, h 22 Meikel.
McCullen Wm, porter Exchange Hotel (W I).
McCulley Wm W, paperhngr, h 23 N Noble.
McCulloch Guy W, lab, r 131 W 1st.
McCulloch Sarah H (wid Solomon), r 131 W 1st.
McCullough Andrew J, bookbndr, b 456 N Senate av.
McCullough Benjamin F (W J McCullough & Sons), b 53 Broadway.
McCullough Emma (wid Wm A), b 293 Kentucky av.
McCullough Franklin B, engr, h 166 W Morris.
McCullough Harry J, engr, h 476 S Missouri.
McCullough Jacob S, cashr Murphy, Hibben & Co, h 456 N Senate av.
McCullough James E (McCullough & Spaan), h 985 N Meridian.
McCullough John, buyer N Y Store, h 129 Highland av.
McCullough John G (W J McCullough & Sons), b 53 Broadway.
McCullough John S, bkkpr Indpls Coffin Co, b 456 N Senate av.
McCullough Mary (wid George), b 388 E Market.
McCullough Samuel H, engr, h 43 Henry.

TUTEWILER UNDERTAKER, No. 72 WEST MARKET STREET. TELEPHONE 216.

THE PROVIDENT LIFE AND TRUST CO. OF PHILADELPHIA. Endowment Insurance presents the double attraction of relieving manhood and middle age from anxiety and old age from want.
For particulars apply to D. W. EDWARDS, General Agent, 508 Indiana Trust Building.

McCullough Walter T, b 985 N Meridian.
McCullough Wm, mach, r 166½ W Washington.
McCullough Wm H, condr, b 1051 N Capitol av.
McCullough Wm J (W J McCullough & Sons), h 53 Broadway.
McCullough Wm J, gasfitter, h 226 W Merrill.
McCULLOUGH W J & SONS (Wm J, Benjamin F and John G), Real Estate, Rentals, Loans and Insurance, 98 E Market, Tel 1340.
McCULLOUGH & SPAAN (James E McCullough, Henry N Spaan), Lawyers, 311-317 Indiana Trust Bldg, Tel 1357.
McCullum, see McCallum.
McCune Alice (wid Thomas), b 378 W 2d.
McCune Estelle M, cashr McCune & Co, r 1131 N Meridian.
McCune George A, mach hd, h 331 Spring.
McCune Hiram B (McCune & Co), h 985 N Illinois.
McCune James F, mach hd, b 283 E Ohio.
McCune John D, motorman, h 15 Douglass.
McCune Joseph (McCune & Co), h 1131 N Meridian.
McCune Mary E (wid Thomas J), b 40 N Dorman.
McCune Mervin H, foreman, h 111 Woodlawn av.
McCUNE & CO (Hiram B McCune, Joseph T McCune), Fancy Grocers, 75 N Penn.
McCurdy, see also MacCurdy.
McCurdy Ellsworth, lab, h 74 S William (W I).
McCurdy Essie W, tmstr, h 94 Hiatt (W I).
McCurdy Francis C, packer, b 34 Hendricks.
McCurdy George W (McCurdy & Perry), h 288 N Penn.
McCurdy Halcyone, prin Kindergarten No 6, b 288 N Penn.
McCurdy Julia A, h 91 Hiatt (W I).
McCurdy Lawson A, phys, 1036 W Washington, h same.
McCurdy Olive B C, phys, 1036 W Washington, h same.
McCurdy Patrick H, condr, b 68 N Belmont av (H).
McCurdy Priscilla (wid James R), h 52 S Judge Harding (W I).
McCurdy Wm I, clk, b 288 N Penn.
McCurdy & Perry (George W McCurdy, Lorenzo N Perry), auctioneers, 139 W Washington.
McCusker Anna (wid Michael), b 997 N Capitol av.
McCuster Wm, lab, b 230 W Maryland.
McCutchan Samuel, switchman, h 299 English av.
McCutcheon George H, carp, b 82 Stevens.
McCutcheon John, plastr, b 207 W 2d.
McCutcheon John C, sec Hecla Consolidated Mining Co, h 226 N Meridian.
McCutcheon Sarah (wid Adam), h 82 Stevens.
McDade Charles, lab, h 52 Mayhew.
McDade John, coachman 816 College av.
McDade Louis B, bkkpr Fidelity B and S Union, b 537 E Ohio.
McDade Samuel, paints, 537 E Ohio, h same.
McDaniel Albert, trav agt, b 224 E Market.

THE WHEN IS A WORLD BEATER.

McDaniel Harry, finisher, b 224 E Market.
McDaniel Joseph, lab, b 11 Cleveland (H).
McDaniel Joseph E, lab, b 200 W Washington.
McDaniel Lorenzo W, h 871 N Alabama.
McDaniel McClelen, carp, h 411 Columbia av.
McDaniel Newton J, clk, h 249 Bellefontaine.
McDaniel Reason H, lab, h s e cor Ivy la and Pendleton av (B).
McDaniel Samuel W, fireman, r 105 English av.
McDaniel Wm, fireman, h 794 W Washington.
McDaniel Wm B, assembler, b 224 E Market.
McDaniels Grant, motorman, b 1063 N Capitol av.
McDermed Clarence, lab, h 100 Dougherty.
McDermed Edward, harnessmkr, h 138 S East.
McDermed Edward C, pumpmkr, b 138 S East.
McDermid Herbert M, printer, b 144 W New York.
McDermid Peter, woodwkr, h 144 W New York.
McDermott Ellen, h 253 S East.
McDermott James J, clk L E & W R R, h 591 Marlowe av.
McDermott Jeremiah D, lab, h 110 Fayette.
McDermott John P, lab, h 329 S Missouri.
McDermott Katherine (wid Michael), h 487 E Market.
McDermott Martin, clk L E & W R R, h 275 Christian av.
McDermott Robert F, insp Indpls Gas Co, h 275 Christian av.
McDermott Thomas, engr, h 487 E Market.
McDermott Thomas, lab, h 21 N California.
McDermott Wm E, clk, b 110 Fayette.
McDevitt Alonzo, trav agt, b 71 W 6th.
McDevitt Angie L (wid Levi), h 71 W 6th.
McDevitt Edward, dep clk U S Courts, h 69 W 12th.
McDevitt George, bricklyr, b 6 Henry.
McDill Bert L, clk, b 84 Vine.
McDill Mount E (wid Thomas C), h 84 Vine.

THE A. BURDSAL CO.
Manufacturers of
Paints and Colors
VARNISHES,
Brushes, Painters' and Paper Hangers' Supplies.
34 AND 36 SOUTH MERIDIAN STREET.

THEODORE F. SMITHER
COMPOSITION ROOFING MATERIALS. BEST IN THE MARKET. TELEPHONE 861. OFFICE, 151 WEST MARYLAND ST.

ELECTRICIANS | DON'T FORGET US. ALL WORK GUARANTEED. C. W. MEIKEL, Tel. 466. 96-98 E. New York St.

DALTON & MERRIFIELD { LUMBER South Noble St., near E. Washington

INDIANA ELECTROTYPE CO. :: BEST WORK. LOWEST PRICES.
23 WEST PEARL ST., INDIANAPOLIS, IND. JOB WORK. BOOK PLATES. All Orders Promptly Filled. BEST PATENT BASE ON THE MARKET.

KIRKHOFF BROS.
Steam and Hot Water Heating Apparatus,
Plumbing and Gas Fitting.
102-104 SOUTH PENNSYLVANIA ST.
TELEPHONE 910.

McDole Elizabeth A (wid Joseph), b 240 English av.
McDonal Edward, ironwkr, r 217 S Illinois.
McDonald, see also MacDonald.
McDonald Bertha (wid Wm), b 72 W 2d.
McDonald Bridget (wid James), h 572 E Michigan.
McDonald Carl A, brakeman, b 42 N State av.
McDonald Catherine (wid John F), h 147 Dougherty.
McDonald Della M, b 575 N West.
McDonald Elizabeth (wid John), b 18 Coffey (W I).
McDonald Elmer E, carp, b 136 W 1st.
McDonald Frank, polisher, b 47 Roe.
McDonald Frank L, trav agt, b 204 N Illinois.
McDonald George, blksmith, h 51 Hendricks.
McDonald George J, plastr, h 6 Wallack.
McDonald George W (McDonald & McDonald), h 377 Ash.
McDonald Henry, lab, h rear 671 N Senate av.
McDonald Holman, lab, h 129 Darnell.
McDonald Hugh, shoemkr, 32 Hill av, h 85 Yandes.
McDonald James, h 91½ Minerva.
McDonald James, h 298 S West.
McDonald James D (McDonald & McDonald), b 377 Ash.
McDonald James J, lab, b 298 S West.
McDonald James R (Ryse & McDonald), furs, 246 S Meridian, h 48 Sinker.
McDonald John, carp, h 98 Shelby.
McDonald John, fireman, h 462 Indiana av.
McDonald John, fitter, b 18 Bismarck av (H).
McDonald John C, helper, b 572 W Michigan.
McDonald John W, trav agt, h 89 Minerva.
McDonald Joseph, lab, r 200½ W Washington.
McDonald Joseph V, lab, b 884 S Meridian.
McDonald Josephine (wid Joseph E), b The Denison.
McDonald Lewis R, ins agt, b 111 E Washington.

LIME
BUILDING SUPPLIES,
Hair, Plaster, Flue Linings,
The W. G. Wasson Co.
130 INDIANA AVE. Tel. 989.

McDonald Margaret (wid Michael), b 19 N Beville av.
McDonald Martin, b 47 Roe.
McDonald Mary, h 42 S Pine.
McDonald Mary, seamstress, h 10 Warren av (W I).
McDonald Mary (wid Edward), h 15 Maple.
McDonald Mary M, stenog, b 884 S Meridian.
McDonald Milton R, transfer, 20 Roanoke, r 117 N Senate av.
McDonald Owen, lab, h 18 Bismarck av (H).
McDonald Patrick, lab, h 884 S Meridian.
McDonald Patrick A, brakeman, b 162 Harrison.
McDonald Robert, porter 124 N Alabama.
McDonald Rosa M (wid Charles), b 230 Buchanan.
McDonald Samuel J, h 586 College av.
McDonald Sherry J, propr Marion County Gazette, h 258 S New Jersey.
McDonald Solomon, janitor, h 597 N Missouri.
McDonald Thomas, engr, h 840 LaSalle (M P).
McDonald Thomas G, tmstr, h 396 N Brookside av.
McDonald Thomas W, trav agt Pearson & Wetzel, h 571 Park av.
McDonald Warren, clk, h 260 E South.
McDonald Wm, boilermkr, b 42 S Pine.
McDonald Wm, driver, b 884 S Meridian.
McDonald Wm, well driver, 275 Spring, h same.
McDonald & McDonald (George W and James D), lawyers, 96½ E Market.
McDonnell Charles, city fireman, b 281 S East.
McDonnell Edward, clk N Y Store, b 281 S East.
McDonnell Mary (wid Michael), h 281 S East.
McDonough Bridget, confr, 129 Elizabeth, h same.
McDonough Dewer B, real est, 18 Baldwin blk, h 123 E Vermont.
McDonough Frank T, trav agt, h e s Colorado 3 n of Ohio.
McDonough Owen, trav agt The Sinker-Davis Co, h 241 S Olive.
McDougal George H, boilermkr, h 108 Clifford av.
McDougal Laura H (wid James O), h 424 E Michigan.
McDougal Willard H, clk, b 452 S West.
McDougal Wm M, engr, h 11 W Sutherland (B).
McDougall Catherine, h 66 Meek.
McDougall Charles P (G P McDougall & Son), b 267 N Capitol av.
McDougall Edwin D, clk, b 43 Williams.
McDougall Eliza, b 66 Meek.
McDougall Frank W, office 62½ S Illinois, h 13 W North.
McDougall George P (G P McDougall & Son), h 267 N Capitol av.
McDougall G P & Son (George P and Charles P), furniture mnfrs, 701 S Meridian.
McDougall Louisa S (wid George), h 13 W North.
McDougall Lynn F, plumber, h 215 W 1st.
McDougall Mary, housekpr Indiana Reformatory.
McDougall Mary F (wid E Ray; S Hamilton & Co), h 43 Williams.
McDougall Richard, carp, b 120 Columbia al.
McDowell Charles B (Outland & McDowell), b 147 W North.

Parlor, Bed Room, Dining Room, Kitchen, Furniture W. H. MESSENGER, 101 E. Wash. St., Tel. 491.

ALL KINDS OF HEAVY AND LIGHT GRAY IRON CASTINGS } McNamara, Koster & Co. } Foundry and Pattern Shop
Phone 1593. 212-218 S. Penn. St.

McDowell Charles K, clk P C C & St L Ry, b 1531 N Meridian.
McDowell Cincinnatus H Rev, pastor University Place Baptist Church, pres Home Savings Assn, 629 Lemcke bldg, h 1703 N Penn.
McDowell Cull, sawyer, b 574 Ash.
McDowell Emily G, music teacher, 1531 N Meridian, b same.
McDowell Emma C (wid John A), h 450 College av.
McDowell Frederick W, student, b 450 College av.
McDowell Henry C, wall paper, 550 S Meridian, h same.
McDowell James A, lab, b 139 Downey.
McDowell Joseph G, clk, h 1531 N Meridian.
McDuffee Wm L, lab, h 510 W Udell (N I).
McDugalle Wm, driver, h 248 W Market.
McElhennen Isabella, asst librarian Indpls Public Library, b 275 Christian av.
McElrea Sarah, h 178 E North.
McElroy Carolyn M, dentist, 17 Marion blk, b 209 Broadway.
McElroy Edward, molder, b 18 Jones.
McElroy Frank, horseshoer, b 18 Jones.
McElroy Guy, miller, h 407 S Missouri.
McElroy James S, barber, h 212 E Vermont.
McElroy John, lab, h e s Earhart 1 s of Prospect.
McElroy Martha F (wid Wm), h w s Senate av 1 s of Carleton (M).
McElroy Walter, lab, b 18 Jones.
McElroy Wm H, porter, h 45 Elizabeth.
McElroy Willis, waiter, h 228 E St Clair.
McElroy Gates, h 18 Jones.
McElwain Wm P, laundry, 255 Jefferson av, h same.
McElwaine, see also McIlwain.
McElwaine Albert G, foreman, h 1738 N Capitol av.
McElwaine Calvin J, clk, b 1652 N Illinois.
McElwaine Claude M, clk The McElwaine-Richards Co, b 1652 N Illinois.
McElwaine Edward C, clk The McElwaine-Richards Co, b 1652 N Illinois.
McElwaine Ernest, printer, h 221 Hoyt av.
McElwaine Kate, h 546 N Missouri.
McElwaine Montgomery M, pres The McElwaine-Richards Co, h 1652 N Illinois.

McELWAINE-RICHARDS CO THE, Montgomery M McElwaine Pres, Melville O Haldeman Vice-Pres and Sec, George A Richards Treas, Plumbing, Steam, Gas and Water Supplies, Wrought Iron Pipe and Boiler Tubes, Natural Gas, Oil Well and Mill Supplies, 62-64 W Maryland, Tel 53.

McElwee Anna B (wid Samuel J), h 276 N Penn.
McElwee Frances M, music teacher, 276 N Penn, b same.
McElwee Ida, cashr When Clothing Store, b 35 N Pine.
McElwee John, carp, h 35 N Pine.
McElwee Thomas, foreman Nordyke & Marmon Co, h 459 E Market.
McEvoy, see also McAvoy.
McEvoy John T, condr, h 737 E Ohio.
McEvoy Mary, teacher Industrial School, h w s Central av 2 s of Grand av (I).
McEwing Wm, printer, h 166 Buchanan.
McFadden Archibald, engr, h 734 E Market.
McFadden Charles A, mach hd, b 98 Harrison.

Henry H. Fay,
40½ E. WASHINGTON ST.,
FIRE INSURANCE, REAL ESTATE,
LOANS AND RENTAL AGENT.

McFadden Edward, confr, h 419 Virginia av.
McFadden Frederick, auctioneer, b 251 S Meridian.
McFadden James, waiter, r 356 Douglass.
McFadden James S, carp, 247 Huron, h same.
McFadden John M, lab, b 98 Harrison.
McFadden John S, waiter The Denison.
McFadden Joseph M, tmstr, h 98 Harrison.
McFadden Louis, painter, b 98 Harrison.
McFadden Louisa (wid Andrew T), h 251 S Meridian.
McFadden Roscoe D, lab, b 98 Harrison.
McFadyen John, pres Indiana and Chicago Coal Co, res Latrobe, Pa.
McFall David, b 6 Wallace.
McFall Joseph, insp, r 277 S Delaware.
McFall Joseph H, mach, h 47 Russell av.
McFall Sarah M (wid James H; McFall & Wilson), h 86 N East.
McFall Wm J, bricklyr, b 309 E Ohio.
McFall & Wilson (Sarah M McFall, Mary A Wilson), boarding 86 N East.
McFarland Augustus, waiter, b 136 N Penn.
McFarland Benjamin F, salesman, h 510 E 7th.
McFarland Charlotte, h 26 E St Clair.
McFarland Edward, fireman, b 21 Walcott.
McFarland Henry C, printer, h 92 Kentucky av.
McFarland Irving, student, b 358 Home av.
McFarland John E, clk Daniel Stewart Co, b 80 W Ohio.
McFarland John F, state agt Michigan Mutual Life Ins Co, h 160 N East.
McFarland John L, sec Gibbs Cushioned Horseshoe Co, supt Railroad Transfer Co, h 94 Fletcher av.
McFarland Laura W, h 26 E St Clair.
McFarland Lavina, prin Public School No 17, b 358 Home av.
McFarland Luella A, teacher, b 134 Pleasant.
McFarland Margaret (wid Robert), h 358 Home av.
McFarland Margaret M, teacher Dist School No 2, b 134 Pleasant.

WILL GO ON YOUR BOND
American Bonding & Trust Co.
Of Baltimore, Md. Approved as sole surety by the United States Government and the different States as Sole Surety on all Forms of Bonds.
W. E. BARTON & CO., General Agents,
504 Indiana Trust Building.
LONG DISTANCE TELEPHONE 1918.

THE FRED DIETZ CO. WOODEN PACKING BOXES MADE TO ORDER FACTORY AND WAREHOUSE TRUCKS. 40 Madison Avenue. Telephone 654.

BUSINESS EDUCATION A NECESSITY. TIME SHORT. DAY AND NIGHT SCHOOL. SUCCESS CERTAIN AT THE PERMANENT, RELIABLE
Indianapolis BUSINESS UNIVERSITY

Water Works Pumping Engines { HENRY R. WORTHINGTON, 64 SOUTH PENNSYLVANIA ST. Long Distance Telephone 284.

UNION CO-OPERATIVE LAUNDRY { (COMPOSED OF UNION LAUNDRY GIRLS.) NOS. 3, 40 AND 42 VIRGINIA AVENUE. T. E. SOMERVILLE, MANAGER. TELEPHONE 8. INDIANAPOLIS, IND.

HORACE M. HADLEY
INSURANCE AND LOANS
66 E. Market Street, Basement
TELEPHONE 1540.

McFarland Mattie A, h 147 W Maryland.
McFarland Sarah A, teacher Public School No 15, b 358 Home av.
McFarland Terrence L, pdlr, r 15 Columbia blk.
McFarland Wm, h 134 Pleasant.
McFarling Julia A (wid George B), b 203 Orange.
McFarrin Mason, lab, h 161 Elizabeth.
McFeely Aaron, poultry, 599 Virginia av, h 239 Buchanan.
McFeely Frank, clk, b 239 Buchanan.
McFeely Homer, clk, b 239 Buchanan.
McFeely John, lab, b 239 Buchanan.
McFerrin Charles E, lab, b e s School 1 n of Schofield (B).
McFerrin James, lab, h e s School 1 n of Schofield (B).
McGannon Evermont J, baker, b 401 Talbott av.
McGannon John R (Buntin, Shryer & McGannon), res. Bloomfield, Ind.
McGANNON ORLANDO C, Baker and Confectioner, 401 Talbott av, h same, Tel 1619.
McGarrahan Charles A, candymkr, b 411 E Washington.
McGarrahan Thomas, confr, h rear 173 Bright.
McGarvey Charles S, plastr, 1373 W Washington (M J), h same.
McGarvey Harry J, printer, b 366 N Noble.
McGarvey Henry, carp, b 78 Cincinnati.
McGarvey Mary, b 223 Davidson.
McGarvey Wm, lab, b 84 S Wheeler (B).
McGary Andrew, baggageman, h 201 Michigan av.
McGary Mary E, grocer, 201 Michigan av, h same.
McGaughey Abbie (wid Charles A V), millinery, b 1087 N Capitol av.
McGaughey John E, dep County Clerk, h e s Commercial av 1 s of Washington av (I).
McGaughey Mary S (wid Samuel), h s s Washington av 2 w of Lake av (I).
McGaughey Moses, b e s Commercial av 1 s of Washington av (I).

COLLECTIONS
MERCHANTS' AND MANUFACTURERS' EXCHANGE
Will give you good service.
J. E. TAKKEN, Manager,
Union Building, over U. S. Pension Office.
73 West Maryland Street.

McGaughey Samuel V, student, b s s Washington av 2 w of Lake av (I).
McGauly James, plumber, 83 E Ohio, h 1107 N Senate av.
McGauly James D, clk, b 1107 N Senate av.
McGauly Rose F, bkkpr, b 1107 N Senate av.
McGaw John A, cigars, 24 N Illinois, h 166 N Senate av.
McGee, see also Magee.
McGee Addie, b 25 W New York.
McGee Anna, h 45 E North.
McGee Charles H, molder, b 1365 W Washington (M J).
McGee George, lab, b 310 E Court.
McGee George B, lab, b 7½ Concordia.
McGee George W, uphlr, h 499 Mulberry.
McGee Jasper, engr, h Shear-pike ½ mile e (B).
McGee Jennie, teacher Public School No 31, b 334 W 1st.
McGee John, clk, h 334 W 1st.
McGee John M, trav agt, h 350 N East.
McGee Kate, r 75 W Ohio.
McGee Mary A, teacher, b 334 W 1st.
McGee Mary E (wid George), h 7½ Concordia.
McGee Oliver S, plastr, h 115 Eddy.
McGee Thomas D, attendant Public Library, b 334 W 1st.
McGee Wm, live stock, b 255 N Alabama.
McGenley John J, plumber, b 107 Ash.
McGenley Patrick, lab, h 107 Ash.
McGeorge Amanda M (wid Isaac), h 130 E New York.
McGettigan Bernard M, weigher, r 466 N Meridian.
McGettigan John E, receiver The Premier Steel Wks, 16 Union bldg, r 466 N Meridian.
McGhee Enoch H, waiter, h 37 Center.
McGibeny Grace, teacher Indpls College of Music, b 546½ N Illinois.
McGibeny Hugh, teacher Indpls College of Music, h 546½ N Illinois.
McGiffin Charles S (McGiffin & Power), h 1836 N Capitol av.
McGiffin & Power (Charles S McGiffin, Peter Power), broom mnfrs, 187 W 7th.
McGILL GEORGE B, State Mngr Home Security Life Association, Rooms 334-335 Lemcke Bldg, b 169 N Illinois.
McGill Reuben, lab, h w s Earl 1 s of Belt R R.
McGill Wm, foreman, h 649 Mass av.
McGILLIARD AGENCY CO THE, Martin V McGilliard Pres, Albert W Hall Vice-Pres, J Kirk Wright Treas, Edwin Hill Sec, Insurance, 83-85 E Market, Tel 479. (See backbone and adv opp.)
McGILLIARD MARTIN V, Pres The McGilliard Agency Co and Pres Indiana Insurance Co of Indianapolis, 83-85 E Market, Tel 479; h s w cor Delaware and 7th.
McGinley Edward, lab, h 4 Chadwick.
McGinley Edward, lab, b 50 Church.
McGinley John W, janitor State House.
McGinley Patrick, lab, b 4 Chadwick.
McGinley Patrick, lab, h 50 Church.
McGinley Patrick H, lab, b 50 Church.
McGinley Timothy, lab, b 365 S Missouri.
McGinn Owen, car rep, b 17 Beacon.
McGinnis, see also Maginnis and Meginniss.

CLEMENS VONNEGUT 184, 186 and 192 E. Washington St. | BUILDERS' HARDWARE, Building Paper. Duplex Joist Hangers.

THE WM. H. BLOCK CO. DRY GOODS, DRAPERIES, RUGS, WINDOW SHADES.
7 AND 9 EAST WASHINGTON STREET.

McGinnis Annie (wid Thomas), h 517 N West.
McGinnis Charles, candymkr, b 29 Madison av.
McGinnis Charles J, bkkpr Ry Officials' and Employes' Accident Assn, h 205 Cornell av.
McGinnis Christopher N, tailor, b 517 N West.
McGinnis Clare W, clk N Y Store, b 302 Fletcher av.
McGinnis Edna P, stenog P O, b 44 Greer.
McGinnis Edward P, marker The Bates, h 279 Bright.
McGinnis Eliza (wid James), h 131 Bates.
McGinnis Fannie I (wid Wm R), h 649 Marlowe av.
McGinnis Frank, lab, b 11 Sharpe.
McGinnis Frank, lab, b 567 W North.
McGinnis Frank N, tailor, b 378 W 2d.
McGinnis Frank T, trav agt McKee Shoe Co, h 1469 N Illinois.
McGinnis George B, tailor, b 378 W 2d.
McGinnis George F, treas Union Mutual B and L Assn, h 952 N Capitol av.
McGinnis James, lab, h 11 Sharpe.
McGinnis James W, special U S Revenue agt, h 44 Greer.
McGinnis John, h 340 W Pearl.
McGinnis John A, lab, h 623 W Michigan.

McGowan Charles T, mach, b 165 S Alabama.
McGowan Ira, lab, b 425 N California.
McGowan James W, painter, h 12 Dougherty.
McGowan Lawrence, drayman Kingan & Co (ltd).
McGowan Nathan, porter, b 513 S West.
McGowan Samuel, lab, b 75 Wilson.
McGowen Charles T, car rep, h 19 W Sutherland (B).
McGrath Anna, dressmkr, b 1094 W New York.
McGrath Dennis, tmstr, h 94 Harrison.
McGrath Edward L, tailor, b 136 Fayette.

INDIANAPOLIS STEEL ROOFING

The McGilliard Agency Co.

83 and 85 East Market Street,
INDIANAPOLIS, - - - INDIANA.

FIRE, MARINE AND TORNADO INSURANCE

Represent the following reliable Companies:

Allemania Fire Insurance Co. - - - - of Pittsburg, Pa.
Citizens' Insurance Co. - - - - - of Evansville, Ind.
Central Accident Insurance Co - - - of Pittsburgh, Pa.
Firemen's Fund Insurance Co. - - - of San Francisco, Cal.
Girard Fire Insurance Co. - - - - - of Philadelphia, Pa.
Fort Wayne Insurance Co. - - - - of Fort Wayne, Ind.
Indiana Insurance Co. - - - - - of Indianapolis, Ind.
Indiana Underwriters, - - - - - of Indianapolis, Ind.
Rockford Fire Insurance Co. - - - - of Rockford, Ill.
Vernon Insurance and Trust Co. - - - of Indianapolis, Ind.
Western Underwriters, - - of Milwaukee and Freeport.

Water Works Pumping Engines { HENRY R. WORTHINGTON, 64 SOUTH PENNSYLVANIA ST. Long Distance Telephone 284.

(COMPOSED OF UNION LAUNDRY GIRLS.) NOS. 3, 40 AND 42 VIRGINIA AVENUE. TELEPHONE 8. INDIANAPOLIS, IND.

HORACE M. HADLEY
INSURANCE AND LOANS
66 E. Market Street, Basement
TELEPHONE 1540.

McFarland Mattie A, h 147 W Maryland.
McFarland Sarah A, teacher Public School No 15, b 358 Home av.
McFarland Terrence L, pdlr, r 15 Columbia blk.
McFarland Wm, h 134 Pleasant.
McFarling Julia A (wid George B), b 203 Orange.
McFarrin Mason, lab, h 161 Elizabeth.
McFeely Aaron, poultry, 599 Virginia av, h 239 Buchanan.
McFeely Frank, clk, b 239 Buchanan.
McFeely Homer, clk, b 239 Buchanan.
McFeely John, lab, b 239 Buchanan.
McFerrin Charles E, lab, b e s School 1 n

McGaughey Samuel V, student, b s s Washington av 2 w of Lake av (I).
McGauly James, plumber, 83 E Ohio, h 1107 N Senate av.
McGauly James D, clk, b 1107 N Senate av.
McGauly Rose F, bkkpr, b 1107 N Senate av.
McGaw John A, cigars, 24 N Illinois, h 166 N Senate av.
McGee, see also Magee.
McGee Addie, b 25 W New York.
McGee Anna, h 45 E North.
McGee Charles H, molder, b 1365 W Washington (M J).
McGee George, lab, b 310 E Court.
McGee George B, lab, b 7½ Concordia.
McGee George W, uphlr, h 499 Mulberry.
McGee Jasper, engr, h Shear pike ½ mile e (B).
McGee Jennie, teacher Public School No 31, b 334 W 1st.
McGee John, clk, h 334 W 1st.
McGee John M, trav agt, h 350 N East.
McGee Kate, r 75 W Ohio.
McGee Mary A, teacher, b 334 W 1st.
McGee Mary E (wid George), h 7½ Concordia.
McGee Oliver S, plastr, h 115 Eddy.
McGee Thomas D, attendant Public Library, b 334 W 1st.

THE WM. H. BLOCK CO. DRY GOODS, DRAPERIES, RUGS, WINDOW SHADES.
7 AND 9 EAST WASHINGTON STREET.

McGinnis Annie (wid Thomas), h 517 N West.
McGinnis Charles, candymkr, b 29 Madison av.
McGinnis Charles J, bkkpr Ry Officials' and Employes' Accident Assn, h 205 Cornell av.
McGinnis Christopher N, tailor, b 517 N West.
McGinnis Clare W, clk N Y Store, b 302 Fletcher av.
McGinnis Edna P, stenog P O, b 44 Greer.
McGinnis Edward P, marker The Bates, h 279 Bright.
McGinnis Eliza (wid James), h 131 Bates.
McGinnis Fannie I (wid Wm R), h 649 Marlowe av.
McGinnis Frank, lab, b 11 Sharpe.
McGinnis Frank, lab, b 567 W North.
McGinnis Frank N, tailor, b 378 W 2d.
McGinnis Frank T, trav agt McKee Shoe Co, h 1469 N Illinois.
McGinnis George B, tailor, b 378 W 2d.
McGinnis George F, treas Union Mutual B and L Assn, h 952 N Capitol av.
McGinnis James, lab, h 11 Sharpe.
McGinnis James W, special U S Revenue agt, h 44 Greer.
McGinnis John, h 340 W Pearl.
McGinnis John A, lab, h 623 W Michigan.
McGinnis John A, lab, h 623 W Vermont.
McGinnis John E, baggageman, h 209 English av.
McGinnis Margaret G (wid James S), h 462 College av.
McGinnis Matthew, lab, b 96 Bright.
McGinnis Nicholas, tailor, h 378 W 2d.
McGinnis Percy E, b 302 Fletcher av.
McGinnis Robert H, letter carrier P O, h 582 Park av.
McGinnis Thomas P, foreman Kahn Tailoring Co, h 96 Paca.
McGinnis Thomas W, tailor, b 517 N West.
McGinnis Wm, h 302 Fletcher av.
McGinty Bridget (wid Patrick), b 36 Chadwick.
McGinty Charles, barber, b 160 W McCarty.
McGinty Emma, boarding 187 S Capitol av.
McGinty Frank T, forger, b 208 Madison av.
McGinty James E, driver, h 117 Greer.
McGinty John, city fireman, h 153 W McCarty.
McGinty Kate R (wid John), h 208 Madison av.
McGinty Patrick J, carp, h 160 W McCarty.
McGinty Thomas, lab, h 187 S Capitol av.
McGinty Thomas A, barber, 397 S Capitol av, b 160 W McCarty.
McGlaughlin, see also McLaughlin.
McGlaughlin John, driver, h 24 Jones.
McGlaughlin Joseph, lab, b 268 Fletcher av.
McGlenn John, clk, b 306 Douglass.
McGlenn Michael, express, h 306 Douglass.
McGlinchey John P, fireman, r 852½ E Washington.
McGlinn Margaret (wid Patrick), h 78 W McCarty.
McGlynn John W, butcher, b 32 Church.
McGlynn Michael, lab, b 32 Church.
McGoodin Susan (wid Charles), b 502 N California.
McGovern Edward J, lab, b 87 Walcott.
McGovern Flora (wid Peter), h 75 W 13th.
McGovern Frank, horse dealer, h 179 Bright.
McGovern Frank, lab, b 890 W Washington.
McGovern John, flagman, b 217 S Illinois.
McGovern Joseph, lab, b 63 S California.
McGovern Thomas, tmstr, h 33 S California.

McGowan Charles T, mach, b 165 S Alabama.
McGowan Ira, lab, b 425 N California.
McGowan James W, painter, h 12 Dougherty.
McGowan Lawrence, drayman Kingan & Co (ltd).
McGowan Nathan, porter, b 513 S West.
McGowan Samuel, lab, b 75 Wilson.
McGowen Charles T, car rep, h 19 W Sutherland (B).
McGrath Anna, dressmkr, b 1094 W New York.
McGrath Dennis, tmstr, h 94 Harrison.
McGrath Edward L, tailor, b 136 Fayette.
McGrath Elizabeth (wid John), h 136 Fayette.
McGrath Emmett R, tailor, b 136 Fayette.
McGrath Jane (wid Dennis), h 60 Deloss.
McGrath Jennie, dressmkr, b 1094 W New York.
McGrath John, tmstr, b 60 Deloss.
McGrath John T, fireman, b 161 W South.
McGrath Mary (wid John), h 221 S West.
McGrath Mary (wid Timothy), h 82 Maple.
McGrath Michael, varnisher, h 217 Hoyt av.
McGrath Patrick, lab, b 82 Maple.
McGrath Patrick, miller, h rear 301 E Georgia.
McGrath Patrick F, plastr, b 336½ E Washington.
McGrath Philip, stoker, h 161 W South.
McGrath Robert E, tailor, b 136 Fayette.
McGrath Timothy J, molder, b 161 W South.
McGraw James, h 169 Davidson.
McGraw John, mason, h 1 Wright.
McGraw John B, plater, b 91 S Liberty.
McGraw Margaret (wid John), h 28 N California.
McGraw Terrence, tailor, h 54 Cook.
McGraw Thomas P, b 54 Cook.
McGrayel John, lab, b 483 S West.
McGreavey John L, lab, b 110 Downey.
McGreavey Owen, lab, h 110 Downey.
McGreevy John B, lab, h 299 Kentucky av.
McGregor, see also MacGregor.
McGregor Christopher, clk, h 417 N California.
McGregor James, engr, b 788 E Market.

GUIDO R. PRESSLER,
FRESCO PAINTER
Churches, Theaters, Public Buildings, Etc., A Specialty.
Residence, No. 325 North Liberty Street.
INDIANAPOLIS, IND.

INDIANAPOLIS STEEL ROOFING AND CORRUGATING WORKS, 23 and 25 East South Street. S. D. NOEL, Proprietor.

David S. McKernan, Rooms 2-5 Thorpe Block.
REAL ESTATE AND LOANS
Money to loan on real estate. Special inducements offered those having money to loan. It will pay you to investigate.

DIAMOND WALL PLASTER { Telephone 1410 BUILDERS' EXCHANGE.

UNION TRANSFER AND STORAGE CO. Cor. E. Ohio St. and C., C., C. & St. L. R'y Tracks. BEST FACILITIES FOR STORING AND TRANSFERRING MACHINERY AND MERCHANDISE.

W. McWORKMAN

FIRE SHUTTERS,
FIRE DOORS,
METAL CEILINGS.

930 W. Washington St. Tel. 1118.

McGregor John, h 325 S New Jersey.
McGregor John, Commissioner Marion County, 43 Court House, h 345 S East.
McGregor Wm, fireman, b 788 E Market.
McGregory Albert B, mnfrs' agt, 59 Commercial Club bldg, h 64 The Blacherne.
McGregory John G, clk, r 402½ S Meridian.
McGrevy James, h 254 Huron.
McGrew Effie E, b n s Bedford av near Park av.
McGrew Emma E (wid Miles J), h 98 Division (W I).
McGrew George P, engr, h 46 Randolph.
McGrew James W (J W McGrew & Co), h 36 S Judge Harding (W I).
McGrew J W & Co (James W and Olive E McGrew), feed, 857 Morris (W I).
McGrew Olive E (J W McGrew & Co), h 36 S Judge Harding (W I).
McGriff Rebecca (wid Emerson), b 231 W Vermont.
McGrigg George W, feed, 112 Hill av, h same.
McGroarty Charles J, student, b 336 S Meridian.
McGroarty Cornelius, clk Township Assessor, h 336 S Meridian.
McGroarty John, b 336 S Meridian.
McGruder, see also Magruder.
McGruder Alfred, watchman Fletcher Safe and Deposit Co, r 184½ Indiana av.
McGruder Harriet (wid Peter), h 408 Blake.
McGruder Thomas, porter, b 272 W 9th.
McGuff Edward, bkkpr, b 58 College av.
McGuff Martin, detective, h 58 College av.
McGuffey Mary B Perin, prin Knickerbacker Hall, e s Central av nr 7th.
McGuffin Charles N, switchman, h 24 Camp.
McGuffin Jennie, b 70 Oliver av (W I).
McGuffin Sarah F (wid James N), h 26 Camp.
McGuire, see also Maguire.
McGuire Anna M (wid Patrick), h w s Gale 4 n of Willow (B).
McGuire Bridget (wid John), h 119 E St Joseph.
McGuire Charles E, clk, h 264 Coburn.
McGuire Charles W, auditor, h 273 N New Jersey.

GEO. J. MAYER,
MANUFACTURER OF
SEALS
STENCILS, RUBBER STAMPS, CHECKS, BADGES, DOOR PLATES, ETC.
5 S. Meridian St., Ground Floor. TEL. 1386

McGuire Dora (wid John M), b 273 N New Jersey.
McGuire Hugh, helper, b w s Gale 2 n of Sutherland (B).
McGuire James, huckster, h 44 Clarke.
McGuire Joseph, boilermkr, b 12 N Gale (B).
McGuire Joseph A, trav agt, b Spencer House.
McGuire Martha (wid John D), b 493 S Capitol av.
McGuire Martha E (wid John M), b 273 N New Jersey.
McGuire Melissa G (wid James E), b 333 Fletcher av.
McGuire Michael P, helper, b w s Gale 2 n of Sutherland (B).
McGuire Nancy (wid Wm M), h 420 W Udell (N I).
McGuire Newton J, lawyer, 713 Lemcke bldg, h 905 Ash.
McGuire Philip H, bartndr, b 119 E St Joseph.
McGuire Samuel B, switchman, h 16 Bates al.
McGuire Thomas, blksmith, b 179 S Alabama.
McGurk Harry H, millwright, b 283 W 16th.
McGurk Joseph W, painter, h 283 W 16th.
McHaffey Israel P, lab, h 67 Foundry (B).
McHaffey James A (Turner & McHaffey), h 673 Home av.
McHaffey John S, lab, h 50 Foundry (B).
McHaffie George G, barber, h 173 Ash.
McHaffie James P, barber, 4 Woodburn av, h 197 River av (W I).
McHaffie Oscar F, janitor Public School No 10, h 173 Ash.
McHaines George, painter, b 187 S Capitol av.
McHale Harry, engr, h 95 English av.
McHale Kate, confr, 48 Church, h same.
McHale Richard M, mach, b 48 Church.
McHattie Adam, engr, h 42 Garfield pl.
McHatton Grant G, varnishmkr, h 125 Garden.
McHatton Mary J (wid Samuel S), b 125 Garden.
McHenry Harry, lab, h 243 Kentucky av.
McHenry Henry, hostler, b 64 Elm.
McHenry Marion, trav agt, b 433 N Illinois.
McHolme Robert G, clk The Wm H Block Co, h 1645 Northwestern av.
McHugh Andrew, bartndr, h 178 S Missouri.
McHugh Anthony, transfer, h 153 Dougherty.
McHugh Dennis, lab, h 33 Maple.
McHugh James, h 1101 N Meridian.
McHugh Jeremiah, lab, b 23 Abbott.
McHugh John F, pipefitter, h 3 S Beville av.
McHugh Joseph, lab, h 319 S West.
McHugh Mary E, milliner, 44 S Illinois, h 1101 N Meridian.
McHugh Michael F, molder, h 130 N Gillard av.
McHugh Thomas, saloon, 299 W Maryland, h same.
McHugh Thomas J, engr, h 159 Harrison.
McHugh Wm, lab, h 38 Grant.
McHugh Wm, lab, h 220 N Belmont av (H).
McHugh Wm F, trav agt The Indpls Millinery Co, h 213 Kentucky av.
McIlvain Wm H, drugs, 523 W Udell (N I), h 522 W Shoemaker (N I).
McIlvaine Frank, clk Van Camp H and I Co, h 14 E Michigan.
McIlwain, see also McElwaine.

A. METZGER AGENCY ESTABLISHED 1863. REAL ESTATE

LAMBERT GAS & GASOLINE ENGINE CO.
ANDERSON, IND. NATURAL GAS ENGINES.

McIlwain Kate (wid Edwin R), h 218 E Market.
McInerny Michael, gasfitter, b 359 S Illinois.
McInerny Patrick A, boarding 359 S Illinois.
McInteer Alexander, mach hd, h 319 Bates.
McIntire, see also McIntyre and MacIntire.
McIntire Benjamin, lab, r 424 Superior.
McIntire Charles, lab, h 38 State.
McIntire Charles J, lab, b 983 W Washington.
McIntire Harvey J, lab, h 100 Bloomington.
McIntire James A, painter, r 2, 143½ Virginia av.
McIntire Jesse, lab, b 38 State.
McIntire Jessie L, teacher, b 448 N New Jersey.
McIntire John C, h 1180 N Illinois.
McIntire Oliver B, real est, h 426 E 12th.
McIntire Robert W, paperhngr, h 61 Rhode Island.
McIntire Wm M, lab, b 983 W Washington.
McIntire Wm O, paperhngr, h 448 N New Jersey.
McIntosh Andrew J (A J McIntosh & Son), h 98 W Vermont.
McIntosh Arthur F, sign writer, h 298 E South.
McINTOSH A J & SON (Andrew J and Charles D), Real Estate and Loans, 66 E Market, Tel 1696.
McIntosh Charles D (A J McIntosh & Son), b 98 W Vermont.
McIntosh Eppenetus W Rev, h 298 E South.
McIntosh Frederick W, music teacher, 298 E South, h same.
McIntosh Rufus, student, b 210 N Meridian.
McIntosh Wm, millwright, h 676 S Meridian.
McIntosh Wm L, carp, h 448 W Shoemaker (N I).
McIntyre, see also McIntire and MacIntire.
McIntyre Calvin, lab, h 14 Elizabeth.
McIntyre Della (wid Lucius), h 22 Henry.
McIntyre Luella, h 344 Clinton.
McIntyre Mary E (wid Thomas), b 762 N Penn.
McKain, see also McCain.
McKAIN ARTHUR A, Pres The Indiana Mnfg Co and The American Buncher Mnfg Co, 401-405 Indiana Trust Bldg, h 928 N Alabama.
McKay, see also Mackey.
McKay Elizabeth S, housekpr 606 E Washington.
McKay Henry, barber, r 79 W Wabash.
McKAY HORACE (J W Lunt & Co), Mortgage Banker; Buys and Sells All Kinds of Municipal Bonds, 29½ N Penn, Tel 272; h 249 Broadway.
McKay John, lab, b 23 Roanoke.
McKay Martha, teacher, b 606 E Washington.
McKay Samuel, lab, h 99 N Dorman.
McKay Thomas J, lab, h 15 Clay.
McKeand John, h 226 S Noble.
McKeand Robert A, custodian Garfield Park, h same.
McKearn Anthony, condr, h 32 Warman av (H).
McKearn Thomas H, condr, h 203½ Virginia av.
McKee Arthur E, clk H T Conde Implement Co, h 188 Hoyt av.
McKee Benjamin F, lab, h 221 Cedar.
McKee Charles E, printer, h 234 E Vermont.
McKee David P, agt Economist Plow Co, r 10 Masonic Temple.

THOS. C. DAY & CO.
Financial Agents and Loans.
We have the experience, and claim to be reliable.
Rooms 325 to 330 Lemcke Bldg.

McKee Earl, printer, b 234 E Vermont.
McKee Edward L, vice-pres Indiana Natl Bank, h 765 N Penn.
McKee Isaac C, r 313 N East.
McKee James, live stock, h 425 N Penn.
McKee James A, bkkpr, h 68 W 1st.
McKee James A, ins, h 1015 N Delaware.
McKee John F (Morrow & McKee), h 20 W Walnut.
McKee Lemira E (wid Washington J), b 331 Ash.
McKee Margaret E (wid Joseph), h 23 Helen.
McKee Rachel (wid George), h 282 Christian av.
McKee Raymond E, b 180 N West.
McKee Robert S, pres McKee Shoe Co, h 616 N Meridian.
McKee Robert S (McKee & Moore), h 55 Highland pl.
McKee R Boone, with McKee Shoe Co, b 616 N Meridian.
McKEE SHOE CO, R S McKee Pres, W J McKee Sec and Treas, 102-104 S Meridian, Tel 14.
McKee Thomas J, lab, h 54 Bismarck.
McKee Thomas M (Randall & McKee), h 324½ Mass av.
McKee Wallace, porter, h 50 Bismarck.
McKee Walter A, bicycle rep, h 2 Cottage av (W I).
McKee Wm, lab, r 817 E Market.
McKee Wm, salesman M Sells & Co, b 118 W Vermont.
McKee Wm E, bkkpr Van Camp H and I Co, h 1107 N New Jersey.
McKee Wm J, sec and treas McKee Shoe Co, h 673 N Delaware.
McKee & Moore (Robert S McKee, John L Moore), ins, 54 Baldwin blk.
McKeehan Hotel, Margaret McKeehan propr, 259 Hadley av (W I).
McKeehan Margaret (wid John), propr McKeehan Hotel, 259 Hadley av (W I).
McKeever Isaac, collr, r 297 English av.
McKeever Mary (wid George), h 334 S New Jersey.

EAT
HITZ'S CRACKERS
AND CAKES.
ASK YOUR GROCER FOR THEM.

BICYCLES $5 DOWN. $1 WEEK. Best Wheels. Best Terms. WHEELMEN'S CO. 31 W. OHIO ST. LONG DISTANCE TEL. 1855.

J. H. TECKENBROCK General House Painter, 94 EAST SOUTH STREET.

FIDELITY MUTUAL LIFE—PHILADELPHIA, PA.
$75,000,000, Insurance In Force. $3,500,000, Death Losses Paid. $1,500,090, Surplus. A. H. COLLINS {General Agent, Baldwin Block.

ESTABLISHED 1876. TELEPHONE 168.
CHESTER BRADFORD,
SOLICITOR OF PATENTS,
AND COUNSEL IN PATENT CAUSES.
(See adv. page 6.)
Office:—Rooms 14 and 16 Hubbard Block, S. W. Cor. Washington and Meridian Streets, INDIANAPOLIS, INDIANA.

McKeever Mary A, prin Public School No 25, b 334 S New Jersey.
McKeever Michael, fireman, b 162 Harrison.
McKeever Thomas D, fireman, h 216 Deloss.
McKelvey Almus C, switchman, h 14 N Rural.
McKelvey Louis F, r 90 State House.
McKendry John E, h 39 Division (W I).
McKenna Edward, molder, b w s Lincoln av 1 s of Jackson (M J).
McKenna Ellen (wid James), h w s Lincoln av 1 s of Jackson (M J).
McKenna James B, insp, h w s Harris av 6 s of C C C & St L Ry (M J).
McKenna James W, molder, h 67 Traub av.
McKenna John, h 679 N Alabama.
McKenna John, lab, h 345 S Missouri.
McKenna John, huckster, b 358 S Delaware.
McKenna John S, engr, h 52 S Gale (B).
McKenna Joseph, molder, b w s Lincoln av 1 s of Jackson (M J).
McKenna Patrick, lab, h 34 S Gale (B).
McKenna Robert E, barber, 136½ W Washington, h n s Jackson 4 w of Harris av (M J).
McKenna Thomas, saloon, 1263 W Washington, b w s Lincoln av 1 s of Jackson (M J).
McKenna Thomas S, tel opr, b 34 S Gale (B).
McKenna Wm H, upfitter, b 430 E McCarty.
McKenna, George S, foreman, h 66 Kennington.
McKenzie, see also McKinsey and MacKenzie.
McKenzie Anna M, society editor The Indpls Journal, h 39 W 4th.
McKenzie Charles W, car rep, h 7 Poplar (B).
McKenzie David, h 104 W Vermont.
McKenzie Henry G, b 266 N West.
McKenzie James A, real est, h 381 College av.
McKenzie John, painter, h 76 S Wheeler (B).
McKenzie John W, clk, b 229 N West.
McKenzie Mary, mngr Woman's Dept Safety Vaults Indiana Trust Co, h 39 W 4th.

Outing BICYCLES
..MADE BY..
HAY & WILLITS MFG CO.
76 N. Pennsylvania St. Phone 598.

McKenzie Thomas, barber, r 63 N East.
McKenzie Thomas W, grocer, 502 S West, h same.
McKeon James C, fireman, b 124 English av.
McKeon John H, engr, b 124 English av.
McKeon Lawrence J, bartndr, b 240½ E Washington
McKeown Thomas, clk, b 335 W Vermont.
McKernan. see also McKiernan.
McKERNAN DAVID S, Real Estate and Loans, Rooms 2-5 Thorpe Blk, Tel 463; b Circle Park Hotel. (See right bottom lines.)
McKernan Ella (wid Louis H), b 479 N Illinois.
McKernan Francis A, b 479 N Illinois.
McKernan James, lab, h 26 Reynolds av (H).
McKernan James H, clk, h 75 W 19th.
McKernan Louisa (wid Frank S), dry goods, 869 S Meridian, h same.
McKernan Susan (wid James H), b 318 N Meridian.
McKey James, foreman, h n s Washington 5 w of Insane Hospital (M J).
McKibben Benjamin F, lab, h 42 Gatling.
McKibben Ellsworth J, tmstr, b 52 Carlos.
McKibben Wm H, driver, b 540 Charles.
McKibbons George, lab, h 405 Pleasant.
McKiernan, see also McKernan.
McKiernan Mary E (wid Warren), milliner, 12 Pembroke Arcade, h 431 N Pine.
McKiernan Warren, grocer, 397 W 2d, h same.
McKillop John P, restaurant, 313 E Washington, h same.
McKim James A, civ engr, h 1164 N Penn.
McKINLEY BROS (John G and Noah F), Funeral Directors and Embalmers, 470 Virginia av, Tel 1713.
McKinley George, blksmith, r 227 E Market.
McKinley Hugh, carriagemkr, 144 Ft Wayne av, h 306 N Pine.
McKinley John G (McKinley Bros), h 470 Virginia av.
McKinley Noah F (McKinley Bros), b 470 Virginia av.
McKinley Wesley, bicycle rep, b 306 N Pine.
McKinna James, gasfitter, b 359 S Illinois.
McKinney Addie (wid Edward), h 167 Harmon.
McKinney Alice, b 329 Virginia av.
McKinney Arthur D, adv agt, 234 Lemcke bldg, b 642 N Senate av.
McKinney Charles C, buffer, b 11 Minerva.
McKinney Clara M (wid John), h 452 N New Jersey.
McKinney Eber, lab, b 77 S Belmont av (W I).
McKinney Edward, trav agt, h 498 N Senate av.
McKinney Elizabeth (wid George), b 894 Morris (W I).
McKinney Frank, lab, h 100 Lee (W I).
McKinney Frank B, clk Lilly & Stalnaker, b 117 St Mary.
McKinney George, janitor School No 4 (W I), h 75 Shepard (W I).
McKinney George, lab, h 105 Naomi.
McKinney James, h 29 Chadwick.
McKinney John, lab, b 88 Kappus (W I).
McKinney Joseph, lab, r 202 W Maryland.
McKinney Julia A (wid John), h 117 St Mary.
McKinney Landor, gardener, h e s Belmont av 3 s of Johnson (W I).

Edwardsport Coal & Mining Co. ••••••BITUMINOUS COAL IN CAR LOADS TO DEALERS AND MANUFACTURERS. ROOMS 42 AND 43 WHEN BUILDING.

C. ZIMMERMAN & SONS | SLATE AND GRAVEL ROOFERS 19 South East Street.

DRIVEN WELLS And Second Water Wells and Pumps of all kinds at CHARLES KRAUSS', 42 S. PENN. ST., Telephone 465.

ERTEL STEAM LAUNDRY 26 and 28 N. Senate Avenue. Tel 1089 WE WILL CALL FOR AND DELIVER WORK. SATISFACTION GUARANTEED.

McKinney Lewis E, driver, h 88 Kappus (W I).
McKinney Mary (wid Thomas), h 129 Elizabeth.
McKinney Michael, lab, b 111 W South.
McKinney Morton, cook, h 22 Roanoke.
McKinney Nile, lab, b 75 Shepard (W I).
McKinney Oliver, tmstr, h 90 S William (W I).
McKinney Turner, lab, b 77 S Belmont av (W I).
McKinney Wm, carp, h 498 N Senate av.
McKinney Wm, farmer, h 77 S Belmont av (W I).
McKinney Wm, finisher, b 46 Standard av (W I).
McKinney Wm O, clk, h 57 Broadway.
McKinnick Alicia (wid Wm), b 28 Columbia al.
McKinsey, see also McKenzie.
McKinsey Anna (wid Jacob), r 23½ W Ohio.
McKinsey George W, painter, b 428 Fulton.
McKinster George, lab, h rear 180 N West.
McKinstry Albert C, polisher, h 1 Grove.
McKinstry Lafayette M, jeweler George G Dyer, b 385 W New York.
McKitrick Henry, lab, h 232 Fayette.
McKneight Andrew, clk H P Wasson & Co, r 190½ Indiana av.
McKnight Alexander A, b 451 Talbott av.
McKnight Charles H, bricklyr, h 40 N Reisner (W I).
McKown Charles B, mach, b 165 S Alabama.
McLahlan Albert G, lab, h 283 River av (W I).
McLain, see also McClain, McClean, McLean and Maclean.
McLain Charles E, lab, b 87 Birch av (W I).
McLain Charles F (James & McLain), b 537 E Ohio.
McLain Cora, nurse, r 147 N Penn.
McLain John, lab, b 187 S Capitol av.
McLain John S, clk, r 102 N Capitol av.
McLain Liberty C, M D, The H R Allen National Surgical Institute, h 710 N Alabama.
McLAIN MOSES G, Lawyer, 29-31 Thorpe Blk, Tel 1152, b The Denison.
McLaine Albert C, lab, h rear 830 S Meridian.
McLane Albert, painter, h 365 Cornell av.
McLane Elmer A, clk, b 98 Woodlawn av.
McLaran Lena A, dressmkr, 156 E St Joseph, h same.
McLaren James, supt E H Eldridge & Co, h 66 Pleasant.
McLaren John, foreman, b 66 Pleasant.
McLaren Robert, lab, b 252 Clifford av.
McLaren Wm, wireman Sanborn Electrical Co, b 230 W Ohio.
McLaughlin, see also McGlaughlin.
McLaughlin Anna K, music teacher, 99 Clifford av, b same.
McLaughlin Burke, b 280 S West.
McLaughlin Charles E, clk P C C & St L Ry, b 170 Deloss.
McLaughlin Christopher, cooper, h 164½ E Washington.
McLaughlin Edward C, uphlr, b 280 S West.
McLaughlin Ellen (wid James), b 24 Jones.
McLaughlin Elmer E, clk, b 719 N Capitol av.
McLaughlin Elmira, dressmkr, 50 Sheldon, h same.
McLaughlin Frank, mach, h 142 Nordyke av (W I).

EQUITABLE LIFE ASSURANCE SOCIETY OF THE UNITED STATES.
RICHARDSON & McCREA
Managers for Central Indiana,
79 East Market St. Telephone 182.

McLaughlin Frank, bicycle rep, 249 S Capitol av, h 122 Weghorst.
McLaughlin Frank, ins, 201 Lemcke bldg, b 154 E Ohio.
McLaughlin George D, lineman, r 45 Indiana av.
McLaughlin George H, painter, b 719 N Capitol av.
McLaughlin George W, tmstr, b 170 Deloss.
McLaughlin Greenly H Rev, h n s Michigan av 1 e of Belt R R.
McLaughlin Harry, candymkr, b 122 Weghorst.
McLaughlin Harry C, lab, b 170 Deloss.
McLaughlin Hugh, barber, r 190½ S Illinois.
McLaughlin James, lab, r 166½ W Washington.
McLaughlin John J, ironwkr, b 4 McGill.
McLaughlin John L, porter Illinois House.
McLaughlin John W, mach, b 377 S Capitol av.
McLaughlin Louis J, lab, h 119 Eddy.
McLaughlin Margaret (wid John), h 97 Fayette.
McLaughlin Margaret (wid Wm P), h 280 S West.
McLaughlin Michael, lab, h 377 S Capitol av.
McLaughlin Olin S, farmer, b n s Michigan av 1 e of Belt R R.
McLaughlin Robert C, engr, h 719 N Capitol av.
McLaughlin Samuel, produce, 177 Virginia av, b 19 Harrison av.
McLaughlin Taylor Z, lab, b 663 Madison av.
McLaughlin Thaddeus W, clk, b 99 Clifford av.
McLaughlin Thomas, h 4 McGill.
McLaughlin Thomas, bricklyr, b 252 E Washington.
McLaughlin Thomas E, mach, h 1150 E Washington.
McLaughlin Thomas F, printer Indpls Journal, b 4 McGill.
McLaughlin Thomas H, lab, h 663 Madison av.
McLaughlin Wm, foreman Indpls Gas Co, r Majestic bldg.

STENOGRAPHERS FURNISHED.
EXPERIENCED OR BEGINNERS, PERMANENT OR TEMPORARY.
S. H. EAST, State Agent,
The Williams Typewriter,
55 THORPE BLOCK, 87 EAST MARKET ST.

ELLIS & HELFENBERGER { ENTERPRISE FOUNDRY & FENCE CO. 162-170 S. Senate Ave. Tel. 958.

THE HOGAN TRANSFER AND STORAGE COMP'Y
Household Goods and Pianos Moved—Packed—Stored...... Baggage and Package Express Machinery and Safes a Specialty Cor. Washington and Illinois Sts. TELEPHONE No. 675.

Hose, Belting, Packing, Clothing, Druggists' Sundries, Bicycle Tires, Cotton Hose, Etc. New York Belting & Packing Co., L't'd.
The Central Rubber & Supply Co. PHONE 2. 79 S. ILLINOIS ST., INDIANAPOLIS, IND.

A death rate below all other American Companies, and dividends from this source correspondingly larger.
The Provident Life and Trust Company
Of Philadelphia.
D. W. EDWARDS, General Agent,
508 Indiana Trust Building.

McLaughlin Wm H, b 280 S West.
McLaughlin Wm H, foreman, h 99 Clifford av.
McLaughlin Wm S, condr, b 4 McGill.
McLean, see also Maclean, McClain, McClean and McLain.
McLean Amelia J, h 414 N Delaware.
McLean Frank W, asst supt N Y Store, h w s Talbctt av 3 s of 16th.
McLean John, carp, b 695 N Senate av.
McLean Mary A, b 597 N Illinois.
McLean Thomas, lab, b 314 E Court.
McLean Wm E, pres World B L and Inv Co, res Terre Haute, Ind.
McLeay John D, phys, 42 W Market, b 452 Tabbott av.
McLEAY J F, Druggist, 236 W Washington, Tel 526; h 452 Talbott av.
McLeay Sidney J, clk Edward C Reick, b 390 S East.
McLeay Walter, clk, b 452 Talbott av.
McLeland, see also McClellan.
McLeland George W, carp, h 276 Christian av.
McLeland Harry, collr, b 276 Christian av.
McLeland Jerome, printer, b 276 Christian av.
McLeland Oliver P, carp, 89 N Beville av, h same.
McLellen Arthur, lab, b 281 Alvord.
McLemore Robert, lab, b 173 Patterson.
McLennan James, painter, r 559 W Maryland.
McLeod, see also McCloud.
McLeod John, mach, b 14 Maria.
McLeod John, mach, h 457 W New York.
McLeod John jr, mach, b 457 W New York.
McLeran Frank W, mach, r 82½ E Washington.
McLuckie Wm, mach hd, h 291½ Kentucky av.
McMahan, see also Mahan.
McMahan David J, painter, 42 Yandes, h same.
McMahan Emma (wid John M), h 518 N New Jersey.
McMahan Franklin G, painter, b 42 Yandes.
McMahan Grant J, baggageman, b 352 Ash.
McMahan Harry, lab, b 510 S West.

Julius C. Walk & Son,
Jewelers
Indianapolis.
12 EAST WASHINGTON ST.

McMahan Samuel W, treas and mngr Western Horseman Co, phys, 26 E Ohio, h 421 N Delaware.
McMahan Thomas W, turner, h 57 Beacon.
McMahon Arthur, transfer agt Frank Bird Tranfer Co, h 102 Pleasant.
McMahon Bernard, polisher, h 9 Bell.
McMahon Frank E, pressman, b 650 N West.
McMahon John T, attendant Insane Hospital.
McMahon Mary J (wid Wm), h 622 W Francis (N I).
McMahon Matilda (wid Thomas), b 489 E Market.
McMahon Michael, lab, h 196 W Merrill.
McMahon Michael E, baggagemstr, h 650 N West.
McMahon Minnie (wid Edward), h 8½ Bellefontaine.
McMahon Nellie, housekpr 323 E North.
McMahon Patrick, bartndr, b 88 W Market.
McMahon Patrick T, lab, h 8 Chadwick.
McMahon Peter, plastr, r 227 E Market.
McMahon Wm, carp, b 323 E North.
McMain John W, cook, b 194 E Washington.
McMains Edgar M, hostler, r 170 E Court.
McManamon Andrew, mach, b 109 Church.
McManamon Bridget (wid Patrick), h 109 Church.
McManamon Catherine (wid Bryan), h 43 Elm.
McManamon Catherine (wid John), h 483 S West.
McManamon Dennis, boilermkr, h 180 Yandes.
McManamon John, coremkr, b 109 Church.
McManamon Martin, motorman, b 37 Chadwick.
McManamon Mary, forewoman Home Cracker Co, b 109 Church.
McManamon Michael, h 97 River av (W I).
McManamon Michael, boilermkr, b 141 Yandes.
McManamon Sadie F, asst bkkpr Home Cracker Co, b 109 Church.
McManaway Wm, porter, r 29 W Pearl.
McManis Clarence A, cabtmkr, h 280 Douglass.
McManis Elizabeth, printer, b 280 Douglass.
McManis Lucinda A (wid James C), b 280 Douglass.
McManis Mary E (wid Thomas B), h 45 Vine.
McMann Frances K, housekpr 75 E Michigan.
McManus Martin, whol dry goods, 48 S Capitol av, h 675 N Illinois.
McMaster John L, Judge Superior Court Room No 1, Court House, h 477 Park av.
McMaster Wm S, messenger Indiana National Bank, b 477 Park av.
McMath Benjamin, lab, h 228 W Chesapeake.
McMath Horatio G, waiter, h 275 Chapel.
McMeans Katherine, stenog Hollweg & Reese, b 539 Central av.
McMeans Robert C, clk Indiana Mutual B and L Assn, h 25 Ruckle.
McMeans Selden R, clk R M S, h 539 Central av.
McMechen Callie D, clk, b 273 N Illinois.
McMerrick Geoge, lab, b 308 W Court.
McMerrick George, lab, h 54 Smith.
McMichael Harry S, lawyer, 19 Aetna bldg, b 276 N New Jersey.
McMichael Robert W, clk, b 908 N Alabama.

OTTO GAS ENGINES | BUILDERS' EXCHANGE S. W. Cor. Ohio and Penn. Telephone 535.

Becker & Son Charles Becker Jacob Becker Jr. Merchant Tailors. 21 N. Penn. St. Tel. 934

SALISBURY & STANLEY OFFICE, STORE AND BANK FIXTURES.

McMichan Carrie L, h 72½ E Washington.
McMillan Calvin, pdlr, b 249 E Louisiana.
McMillan Elmer L, salesman, h 58 Elm.
McMillan George, pdlr, b 249 E Louisiana.
McMillan Harry, poultry, 313 W Maryland, h same.
McMillan James, lab, h 631 W Michigan.
McMillan James A, engr, r 193 W Washington.
McMillan John W, student, b w s Grand av 3 s of University av (I).
McMillan Riley S, clk, r 547 W 22d (N I).
McMillan Wm, trav agt D H Baldwin & Co, h w s Grand av 3 s of University av (I).
McMillan Wm J, nurseryman, h 58 Elm.
McMillen Charles W, brakeman, h 518 E 9th.
McMillen Hugh W, engr, r 832 Bellefontaine.
McMillen Peter, lab, h 240 W Michigan.
McMillen Peter, lab, r 679 N Senate av.
McMillen Wm, b 218 S Reisner (W I).
McMILLEN WILSON S, Genl Mngr Nichols & Shepard Co; 22 Kentucky av, Tel 985; h 173 Christian av.
McMillin Amanda A (wid James T), h 132 S Linden.
McMillin Clement T, trav agt Schnull & Co, b 132 S Linden.
McMillin Harry, clk, b 132 S Linden.
McMillin James L, barber, 665 Virginia av, b 667 same.
McMillin Martha J (wid John), b 421 N Illinois.
McMillin Mary (wid Samuel), h 74 E Vermont.
McMillin Robert S, trav agt, h w s Bellefontaine 1 n of 16th.
McMillin Samuel E, city fireman, b 132 S Linden.
McMinn Eugenia, h 173 E Washington.
McMinn George M, mach, h 172 E Pearl.
McMORROW JOHN H, Real Estate and Insurance, 2 Thorpe Blk, Tel 463; h 70 W 10th.
McMullen Charles C, driver, h 195 Fletcher av.
McMullen Claude C, clk, b 99 Lexington av.
McMullen Harry A, clk, b 3 Lexington av.
McMullen James W, carp, h w s Cornelius 1 n of Carleton (M).
McMullen John E, electrician, b 3 Lexington av.
McMullen Lydia J (wid John M), h 61 Spann av.
McMullen Sophia E, music teacher, 3 Lexington av, b same.
McMullen Samuel W, engr, h 71 N Judge Harding (W I).
McMullen Valentine S, patrolman, h 3 Lexington av.
McMullen Wm, painter, h 128 John.
McMurray, see also Murray.
McMurray Carrie B, b 325 Blake.
McMurray Columbus A, barber, r 175 W North.
McMurray James C, lab, h 751 N Senate av.
McMurray Jefferson, lab, h w s Hampton 2 s of Clifford av.
McMurray John C, lab, h 165 Elm.
McMurray Lewis H, live stock, Union Stock Yards, h 161 East Drive (W P).
McMurray Mary H (wid Robert), r 235 Mass av.
McMurray Sarah J (wid Isaac), h 162 Willow.

Henry H. Fay, 40½ E. Washington St., REAL ESTATE, AND LOAN BROKER.

McMurray Welcome B (Young & McMurray), h 14 Hall pl.
McMurry James C, h 676 College av.
McMurry James T, b 676 College av.
McMurry Joshua B, b 676 College av.
McMurtry Charles B, driver, h 5 Paca.
McNabb Frank J, lab, b n w cor Michigan and State avs.
McNabb Wm W, mach hd, b n w cor Michigan and State avs.
McNally Ann (wid Terrance), laundress, h 26 Mulberry.
McNamar America E (wid Layton S), h 423 W Francis (N I).
McNamar Cleaveland B, cabtmkr, b 423 W Francis (N I).
McNamara Frank E, printer The Indpls News, h 111 Wisconsin.
McNamara James E, collr C Maus Branch Indpls Brewing Co, h 1022 S Meridian.
McNamara John, butcher, b 49 W Raymond.
McNamara Joseph E, ship clk M O'Connor & Co, b 331 E New York.
McNAMARA, KOSTER & CO (Peter J McNamara, Louis J Koster, Richard Pierce), Foundry and Pattern Shop, 212-218 S Penn, Tel 1593. (See right top lines and p 9.)
McNamara Patrick, flagman, h 49 Raymond.
McNamara Peter J (McNamara, Koster & Co), h 395 Union.
McNAMARA WASHINGTON, Propr Co-Operative Shoe Co, 68-70 E Washington, r 81 Dearborn.
McNary Albert, lab, b 274 Blake.
McNary Angeline, h 8 Brooks.
McNaught Bessie C, dressmkr, h 4 Wendell av.
McNaught John A, engr, h 130 S State av.
McNaught Sallie A, h 221 E New York.
McNaughton Sarah J (wid Samuel W), matron City Hospital.
McNeal Charles, motorman, h 55 Hazel.
McNeal Jennie (wid Jehu), janitress, r 12, 161½ Mass av.

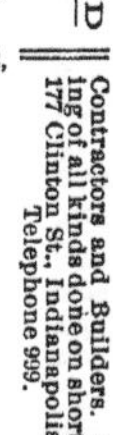

Contractors and Builders. Repairing of all kinds done on short notice. 177 Clinton St., Indianapolis, Ind. Telephone 999.

LIME, CEMENT, PLASTER FIRE BRICK AND CLAY SEWER PIPE, ETC. BALKE & KRAUSS CO., Cor. Market and Missouri Streets.

C. FRIEDGEN HAS THE FINEST STOCK OF LADIES' PARTY SLIPPERS and SHOES 19 NORTH PENNSYLVANIA ST.

SAMUEL LAING, TIN, SLATE AND STEEL ROOFING 72 AND 74 EAST COURT STREET.

M. B. Wilson, Pres. W. F. Churchman, Cash.
THE CAPITAL NATIONAL BANK,
INDIANAPOLIS, IND.
Pays Interest on Time Certificates of Deposit.
Buys and Sells Foreign Exchange at Low Rates.
Capital, - - $300,000
Surplus and Earnings, 50,000
No. 28 S. Meridian St., Cor. Pearl.

McNeal Lyman G, pressman, h 418 W 2d.
McNeal Wm H, painter, h 559½ Virginia av.
McNeely Harry A, clk, h 80 Woodlawn av.
McNeely Harry B, clk, b 18 Hall pl.
McNeely Herbert S, clk, h 1766 N Capitol av.
McNeely John B, agt I D & W Ry, h 18 Hall pl.
McNeely Wesley D, real est, h 77 S Linden.
McNees Allen H, switchman, h 52 Ash.
McNees Nettie, r 305½ E Washington.
McNeff Anna, clk, b 457 E Georgia.
McNeiliss John, lab, h 365 S Missouri.
McNeill Charles A, city agt, h 176 S Olive.
McNeley Wm M, lab, h s s Jackson 1 w of Lincoln av (M J).
McNelis Michael, trav agt, b 111 N Dorman.
McNelis Nellie A, h 111 N Dorman.
McNelis Patrick H (McNelis & Burns), propr Occidental Hotel, s e cor Illinois and Washington, h 246 N West.
McNelis & Burns (Patrick McNelis, James Burns), saloon, 19 S Illinois.
McNerney John A, lab, b 110 Hadley av (W I).
McNerney Peter J, contr, 549 Ash, h same.
McNerney Thomas, grocer, 110 Hadley av (W I), h same.
McNerney Thomas, lab, h 51 Church.
McNevin John D, boilermkr, h 263 Fletcher av.
McNevin Joseph S, boilermkr, h 66 N Belmont av (H).
McNevin Wm, printer, b 263 Fletcher av.
McNimrey Charles H, gasfitter, b 428 Indiana av.
McNimrey Frank B, hostler, r 80 W Market.
McNimrey George A, cóllr, h 428 Indiana av.
McNinnery Wm, cook, h 12 S Senate av.
McNutly Henry, carp, b 39 N Alabama.
McNulty James, insp, h 53 Bridge (W I).
McNulty Luther, b 77 Oliver av (W I).
McNulty Patrick F, lab, h 77 Oliver av (W I).
McNulty Sarah, b 26 Lynn av (W I).
McNutt Alexander, letter carrier P O, h 95 Greer.

TUTTLE & SEGUIN,
28 E. Market Street.
Fire Insurance,
Real Estate, Loan
and Rental Agents.
TELEPHONE 1168.

McNutt Alonzo D, bricklyr, h 953 S East.
McNutt Benjamin S, driver, h 41 Bismarck.
McNutt Charles, driver, b 953 S East.
McNutt George, mailing clk P O, h e s Elm av 1 n of Washington av (I).
McNutt Jennie (wid Benjamin), h 189 N East.
McNutt John, driver, b 953 S East.
McNUTT JOHN C, Librarian State Law Library, Room 64 State House, r 382 N Meridian.
McNutt Oliver P, bricklyr, h rear 296 Excelsior av.
McOuat Ellen (wid Andrew), b 206 Patterson.
McOuat Eugenia B (wid Robert L), h 162 N Meridian.
McOuat Lydia (wid David), h 70 Maxwell.
McOuat Robert L (Varney & McOuat), b 162 N Meridian.
McOuat Thomas L, city fireman, h 877 N Senate av.
McOuat Wm A, tinner, h 206 Patterson.
McPadden John (Meade & McPadden), h 319 E Washington.
McPeek Henry L, lab, h 293 E Washington.
McPeek Phineas A, lab, h 100 Sheffield av (H).
McPhail Lottie, nurse, r 149 N Penn.
McPheeters Clarke B, clk, h s e cor N Senate av and 29th.
McPheeters Thaddeus H, clk Mason's Union Life Assn, b 1101 N Senate av.
McPherson Carey C, trav agt Home Cracker Co, pres Com Trav Mutl Acc Assn, b 236 N Illinois.
McPherson George, bartndr, b 423 S Illinois.
McPherson George E, lab, h 157 Sharpe av (W).
McPherson George W, clk Wm M Clark, b 445 Martindale av.
McPherson John, lab, h 149 Harlan.
McPherson Wm, architect, b 26 Warman av (H).
McPherson Wm M, painter, 20 Sullivan, h same.
McPhetridge John M, tailor, 39 Journal bldg, h 656 College av.
McQuade Catherine, b 77 Birch av (W I).
McQuade Frank B, mach hd, b 130 Hillside av.
McQuade George n, mach hd, b 130 Hillside av.
McQuade James E, cabtmkr, b 130 Hillside av.
McQuade Patrick, mach, h 130 Hillside av.
McQuaid John F, tel opr, h 37 Ketcham (H).
McQueary James L, carp, h 44 Clark.
McQueary Sarah (wid Wilson T), h 73 W 9th.
McQueen Lewis D, barber, 76 Mass av, b Enterprise Hotel.
McQuiddy Frank T, bkkpr, h 875 N Alabama.
McQuiddy Lucy F (wid John W), b 871 N Alabama.
McQuillin Thomas, ins agt, h 71 Louise.
McQuinn Willett T, molder, h 61 Germania av (H).
McQuiston Joseph L, engr, b 9 Hoyt av.
McQuiston Wm, b 951 N Illinois.
McQuown James A, mach hd, r 7½ Shelby.
McQuown James H, harnessmkr, 11 Prospect, h same.
McRae Murdock, tailor, h 245 Kentucky av.
McReynolds John, carp, h 169 N East.
McReynolds John F, motorman, h 73 W 19th.

SULLIVAN & MAHAN Manufacturers of all kinds of PAPER BOXES 41 W. Pearl St.

DIAMOND WALL PLASTER { Telephone 1410 BUILDERS' EXCHANGE.

197 S. Illinois St. } Telephone 1769. THE HOME LAUNDRY { WORK CALLED FOR AND DELIVERED.

McRoberts John L, bartndr, h 88 N New Jersey.
McRoberts John R B, clk R M S, h 37 W Morris.
McRoberts John W, jeweler, 191 Mass av, h same.

McSHANE JOHN T, Physician, 26 E Ohio, Tel 1454; h 496 College av, Tel 652.

McShane Rose A, baker, 114 Mass av, h same.
McShanog Hugh, attendant Insane Hospital.
McShea John, helper, h 157 Columbia av.
McShea Wm F, mach, h 412 Columbia av.
McShee James P, foreman, h 619 W Eugene (N I).
McVane Jacob T, carp, h rear 356 S Delaware.
McVay Charles B, clk, h 424 Ash.
McVay Frank C, livery, h 799 N New Jersey.
McVay Horace C, clk Murphy, Hibben & Co, b 799 N New Jersey.
McVay Wm P, condr, h 169 Harrison.
McVea David, h 58 S California.
McVea Mattie, housekpr 58 S California.
McVeigh Nannie, teacher, b 132 N Capitol av.
McVeigh Sherman (Admire & McVeigh), b 132 N Capitol av.
McVey Charles P, clk B J Peake, r 780 E Market.
McVey Charles V, lab, b n s Orchard av 1 w of Rural.
McVey Charlotte, attendant Public Library, b 547 N Senate av.
McVey Elizabeth, b 225 E Ohio.
McVey Grant U, tel opr P C C & St L Ry (I), b Clifford av 7 m e of city limits.
McVey Hugh O (Rich & McVey), h 283 W Michigan.
McVey Joseph, carp, h n s Orchard av 1 w of Rural.
McVey Joseph M, h 107 Ash.
McVey Oscar L, livery, 1128 N Meridian, h 1285 same.
McVey Phoebe A (wid Frank), h 207 N Pine.
McVey Wm T, carp, h e s Good av 2 s of P C C & St L Ry (I).
McVicker Augustus, trav agt, h 228 N Capitol av.
McWater Addie, h e end of Vine.
McWhinney Louise A, h 654 N Alabama.
McWhinney Mark W P, clk, b 128 E Walnut.
McWhinney Wm L, trav agt, h 128 E Walnut.
McWhirter Felix T, real est, 70 E Market, h 720 College av.
McWhorter James W, b n s 23d 1 e of Northwestern av.
McWhorter Levi C, lab, b n s 23d 1 e of Northwestern av.
McWhorter Wm, h n s 23d 1 e of Northwestern av.
McWilliams Alonzo, lab, h 72 W Wilkins.
McWilliams Lizzie (wid Clay), h 12½ Roanoke.
McWilliams Susan I (wid George W), h 267 N New Jersey.
McWorkman Henry, b 1080 W Washington.

McWORKMAN WILLARD, Mnfr of Galvanized Iron Cornices, 930 W Washington, Tel 1118; h 1080 same. (See left top cor cards.)

FRANK NESSLER. WILL H. ROST.
FRANK NESSLER & CO.
Tailors
56 EAST MARKET ST. (Lemcke Building),
INDIANAPOLIS, IND.

M

Maag Henry, cement, h 16 Woodburn av (W I).
Maag Jacob, butcher, h 721 Chestnut.
Maahan Margaret (wid Thomas), housekpr 184 E St Clair.
Maar Henry, carp, 221 Minnesota, h same.
Maar John, sawyer, h 712 S East.
Maar Michael, carp, h 215 Minnesota.
Maas Charles, boilermkr, h 301 English av.
Maas Charles F, trav agt McKee Shoe Co, b 626 E Ohio.
Maas Charles J W, uphlr, b 169 Spann av.
Maas Frank C, clk Murphy, Hibben & Co, b 626 E Ohio.
Maas George L, lumber, h 1148 N Capitol av.
Maas Helena (wid Albert), h 301 English av.
Maas Louis, cigarmkr, h 626 E Ohio.
Maas Wm M, lab, b 251 Michigan av.
Maass George J (Jacobi & Maass), b 399 S Delaware.
Maass Henry C, grocer, 451 S Delaware, h same.
Mabb Marie, h 125 W Pearl.
Mabbitt Margaret, h rear 276 S Meridian.
Mabbitt Ores W, waiter, r 180 E Washington.
Mabe Mary (wid Willis), b 510 S Illinois.
Mabe Wm, salesman, h 510 S Illinois.
Mabee Jacob L, carp, h 279 River av (W I).
Mabrey Benjamin B, driver, h 82 Springfield.
Mabrey Charles (Mabrey & Cook), r 590 Morris (W I).
Mabrey Charles McK, barber, 180 River av (W I), b 82 Springfield.
Mabrey Henry B, bricklyr, h 24 Ethel (W I).
Mabrey & Cook (Charles Mabrey, George Cook), livery, 118 Hadley av (W I).
Mabrey Clinton, lab, b 108 N Missouri.
Macauley, see also McCauley.
Macauley Edward, brakeman, b 264 Springfield.
Macavoy Henry T, coachman 380 N Delaware.
Macbeth Dare A, trav agt, h 1202 N Illinois.
Macbeth Frank D, b 1202 N Illinois.

Haueisen & Hartmann
163-169 E. Washington St.
FURNITURE,
Carpets,
Household Goods,
Tin, Granite and China Wares, Oil Cloth and Shades

THE WM. H. BLOCK CO. 7 AND 9 EAST WASHINGTON STREET. DRY GOODS, HOUSE FURNISHINGS AND CROCKERY.

London Guarantee and Accident Co. (Ltd.) Employers', Public and Teams' Liability. Workmen's Collective Insurance and Fidelity Bonds
GEORGE W. PANGBORN, General Agent, 704-706 Lemcke Bldg. Telephone 140.

Reasonable Rates. Telephone 5. Reliable Fire Insurance. 74 E. MARKET STREET. FRANK K. SAWYER

JOSEPH GARDNER,
TIN, IRON, STEEL AND SLATE ROOFING,
GALVANIZED IRON CORNICES & SKYLIGHTS.
37, 39 & 41 KENTUCKY AVE. Telephone 322.

MacCurdy, see also McCurdy.
MacCurdy Wm C (MacCurdy & Smith), b 474 N Penn.
MacCurdy & Smith (Wm C MacCurdy, David D Smith), electric supplies, 94 N Meridian.
Macdonald, see also McDonald.
Macdonald Wm A, clk, h 87 S Linden.
MacDougall Helen, nurse, 10 Wyandot blk, r same.
Mace George W, tinner, h 134 S East.
Mace Minor, lab, b 219 N West.
Mace Wm A, trav agt, h 48 Omer.
MacFall Russell T, lawyer, 20 Fletcher's Bank bldg, r 233 E New York.
MacGregor, see also McGregor.
MacGregor Ida J (wid Joseph A), h 77 Clifford av.
Machett Charles A, trav agt Hildebrand Hardware Co, h 173 E St Joseph.
Machett Lucretia (wid Robert M), b 169 E St Joseph.
Machett Robert M, watchman, h 376 S West.
Machold Alfred G, ins agt, h 12 Sharpe.
Machold Martin, packer, h 289 E Georgia.
MacIntire, see also McIntire and McIntyre.
MacIntire Charles T, ins agt, 62 E Market, h 150 Ruckle.
MacIntyre Laselle V, opr W U Tel Co, h Malott Park, Ind.
MacIvor John C, agt, h 119 N New Jersey.
Mack, see also Meck.
Mack Amos T, trav agt Krull & Schmidt, b 77 Woodlawn av.
Mack Andrew, mach, b 109 Church.
Mack Caroline (wid Walter), h 26 Chapel.
Mack Charles W, lab, b 82 E St Clair.
Mack Dennis, lab, r 8 Warren.
Mack Dennis, lab, b 125 N West.
Mack Dominick F, boilermkr, b 143 Yandes.
Mack Edgar N, printer, b 82 E St Clair.
Mack Edward M, finisher, h 34 N California.
Mack Frederick J (F J Mack & Co), h 527 S Illinois.
Mack Frederick L, paintr, b 390 S East.

J. S. FARRELL & CO.
STEAM AND HOT WATER HEATING AND PLUMBING CONTRACTORS
84 North Illinois Street. Telephone 382.

MACK F J & CO (Frederick J Mack, Clemens Beck), House, Sign and Fresco Painters, 32 S Meridian, Tel 1726.
Mack Godfrey, painter, b 390 S East.
Mack Gustav A, fresco painter F J Mack & Co, h 97 Dunlop.
Mack James A, painter, b 10 Huron.
Mack James H, horseshoer, b 82 E St Clair.
Mack John, painter, h 82 E St Clair.
Mack John F, lab, b 104 Oliver av (W I).
Mack John F, mach hd, h 178 English av.
Mack John W, boilermkr, b 143 Yandes.
Mack Mary H (wid John), h 104 Oliver av (W I).
Mack Maurice, butcher, h 17 Chadwick.
Mack Maurice, lab, b 32 Thomas.
Mack Michael, engr, b 17 Chadwick.
Mack Rosa E (wid John), h 143 Yandes.
Mack Samuel, h 405 Highland av.
Mack Thomas P, blksmith, b 143 Yandes.
MACK WM, Carpet Cleaner and Renovator, Propr Mack's Carpet and Rug Factory, cor W 4th and canal, Tel 243; h 255 W 1st. (See adv in classified Carpet Cleaners.)
Mack Wm F, shoemkr, h 125 Church.
Mack Wm G, candymkr, b 104 Oliver av (W I).
Mackenzie, see also McKenzie.
Mackenzie Charles P, clk Kingan & Co (ltd), b 74 E Walnut.
Mackenzie David L Rev, pastor First English Evangelical Lutheran Church, h 74 E Walnut.
Mackessey Timothy, patrolman, b 195 Meek.
Mackey, see also McKay.
Mackey Albert S, carp, h 215 W Maryland.
Mackey Charles, plastr, h 88 Hadley av (W I).
Mackey George, lab, h 30 Springfield.
Mackey George, carp, h 22 Howard.
Mackey John L, carp, h 531 Jones (N I).
Mackey Lawrence E, harnessmkr, b 306 S Meridian.
Mackey Louis H, polisher, b 215 W Maryland.
Mackey Oliver H, carp, h 531 Jones (N I).
Mackey Raphael, grinder, b rear 306 E Washington.
Mackey Robert B, trucker, h 141 N Dorman.
Mackintosh, see also McIntosh.
Mackintosh Edward, lab, b 863 S Meridian.
Mackintosh George L Rev, pastor Fourth Presbyterian Church, r 909 N Delaware.
Macks Wilson M, lab, h 407 S Olive.
Maclay Elma L, teacher Knickerbacker Hall, b e s Central av nr 7th.
Maclean, see also McClain, McClean, McLain and McLean.
Maclean David A, bkkpr Parry Mnfg Co, b 132 N Capitol av.
Maclure Thomas, clk, h 32½ Miley av.
MacNab Philip, phys, 1 Ft Wayne av, h same.
MacNab Solon M, clk L E & W R R, b 1 Ft Wayne av.
Macpherson, see also McPherson.
MacPherson Alexander, painter, r Phoenix blk.
MacQuithy Harry R, photog, b 154 N New Jersey.
MacQuithy Horace P, photog, h 154 N New Jersey.
MacQuithy Lee A, foreman Parrott & Taggart Bakery, h 432 E North.

POLICIES IN UNITED STATES LIFE INSURANCE CO., offer indemnity against death, liberal cash surrender value or at option of policy-holder, fully paid-up life insurance or liberal life income. E. B. SWIFT, M'g'r, 25 E. Market St.

WM. KOTTEMAN } WILL FURNISH YOUR HOUSE COMPLETE
89 & 91 E. Washington St. Telephone 1742

SHOW CASES WILLIAM WIEGEL 6 West Louisiana Street Opp. Union Station.

MacQuithy Monroe T, student, b 154 N New Jersey.
MacQuithey Thomas S, draughtsman Dean Bros Steam Pump Works, h 189 E Ohio.
MacQuithy Victor J, painter, h 47 N East.
MacQuown Ellis, caller Union Station, h 170 E South.
MacShulse John, mer police, h 317 E North.
Macy George J, sec and treas W B Holton Mnfg Co, h 457 Bellefontaine.
Macy Harry, lab, h 33 Miley av.
Macy John S, clk, b 457 Bellefontaine.
Macy Julius L, poultry, 21 N West, h 30 Oliver av (W I).
Macy Oscar, clk, h 183 W New York.
Macy Otis, lab, b 30 Oliver av (W I).
Madaris Wm T J, tinner, 237 Mass av, h 75 Orange av.
Madden Benjamin, lab, h 117 Church.
Madden Catherine (wid Timothy), h 117 Oak.
Madden Frank, molder, h 235 E Louisiana.
Madden James, lab, h 1 Concord (H).
Madden James H, grocer, 151 Virginia av and 750 E Washington, h 150 Virginia av.
Madden John J (Thomas Madden Son & Co), h 999 N Alabama.
Madden John P, waiter, r 87 S Illinois.
Madden John W, plastr, h 64 Mayhew.
Madden Joseph J, plastr, h rear 48 Edward (W I).
Madden Joseph T, opr W U Tel Co, b 117 Oak.
Madden Mack, lab, r 171 W Wabash.
Madden Michael, clk, b 373 English av.
Madden Michael, lab, h 235 E Louisiana.
Madden Michael J, bkkpr, b 235 E Louisiana.
Madden Michael J, engr, h 184 Keystone av.
Madden Patrick J, lab, b 350 W Maryland.
Madden Robert M, foreman, h 541 W Addison (N I).
Madden Thomas (Thomas Madden, Son & Co), h 705 N Illinois.
Madden Thomas, lab, b 350 W Maryland.
Madden Thomas, Son & Co (Thomas and John J Madden, Edward J O'Reilly, Christopher A O'Connor), lounge mnfrs, English av and C C C & St L Ry.
Madden Wm J, cigarmkr, b 64 Mayhew.
Maddock Thomas E, lab, b 697 Park av.
Maddocks Charles C, lab, h 116½ Oliver av (W I).
Maddox Allen, horse dealer, h 111 N New Jersey.
Maddox Arthur C, oil dealer, 69 S Linden, h same.
Maddox Aubert W, elocutionist, b 535 Ash.
Maddox Earl O, student, b 535 Ash.
Maddox Milton F, trav agt, h 535 Ash.
Maddox Wm M, waiter, r 289½ W North.
Mader Peter, condr, h 330 Spann av.
Madex John W, barber, r 19 N Noble.
Madigan Charles A, tinner, b 39 N Alabama.
Madinger Charles (C & F Madinger), h e s Rural 5 s of Clifford av.
Madinger C & F (Charles and Frederick), dairy, e s Rural 5 s of Clifford av.
Madinger Frederick (C & F Madinger), b e s Rural 5 s of Clifford av.
Madinger Frederick, lab, b 158 Excelsior av.
Madinger Johannah M (wid John P), h 158 Excelsior av.
Madinger John G, plumber, b 153 Excelsior av.
Madinger Lena (wid Otto), h 309 E Wabash.
Madinger Wm H, lab, h 13 S Austin (B).

THOS. C. DAY & CO.
INVESTING AGENTS,
TOWN AND FARM LOANS,
Rooms 325 to 330 Lemcke Bldg.

Madinger Wm H, lab, h 140 N Rural.
Madison Almira J (wid Edwin), h 361 Spring.
Madison Bert L, h 138 Highland pl.
Madison Brewing Co, George Pfalzgraf mngr, 302 River av (W I).
Madison Caswell H, tailor, 436 Mass av, h same.
Madison Catherine (wid Anson), h 37 S McLain (W I).
Madison George A, stonecutter, h 157 Carlos.
Madison James, woodwkr, h 583 College av.
Madison James R, tel opr P C C & St L Ry, r 165 N Capitol av.
Madison Margaret M (wid Caswell), b 363 N Noble.
Madison Nelson, driver, h 188 Bird.
Madison Pulaski T, trav agt, r 119 W Maryland.
Madren Joseph P, carp, b s e cor Sheldon and 17th.
Madsen, see also Matson.
Madsen Mads P, patternmkr, h 9 Rock.
Madsen Mary M (wid Christian L F), phys, 86 N Senate av, h same.
Madsen Wm, lab, h 828 Chestnut.
Maegli Jacob, porter, r 131 W Ohio.
Maffey Frank Z, music teacher, 545 N Illinois, h same.
Magee, see also McGee.
Magee Edward, h 456 E Georgia.
Magee Edward J, driver, b 456 E Georgia.
Magee Edward R, fireman, b 33 N Beville av.
Magee James F, lab, b 456 E Georgia.
Magee John, fireman Insane Hospital.
Magee Robert W, instmtmkr, h 33 N Beville av.
Magel Anna E, grocer, 70 N Delaware, h 263 Davidson.
Magel Frank, student, h 51 Woodruff av.
Magel Henry, mngr, h 609 E Vermont.
Magel Philip, clk, h 263 Davidson.
Magennis, see also McGinnis and Megennis.
Magennis George M, brick mnfr, 310 Cypress, h same.
Magennis James, brick mnfr, e s Sherman Drive 1 n of C C C & St L Ry, h n s Prospect 1 e of Belt R R.

EAT
HITZ'S CRACKERS
AND CAKES.
ASK YOUR GROCER FOR THEM.

Capital Steam Carpet Cleaning Works
M. D. PLUNKETT Proprietor, Telephone 818

BENJ. BOOTH PRACTICAL EXPERT ACCOUNTANT. Accounts of any description investigated and audited, and statements rendered. Room 18, 82½ E. Washington St., Indianapolis, Ind.

The Best Place in the City to Get a Good Meal THE SHERMAN RESTAURANT ♦♦♦♦ 18 and 20 S. Meridian Street KERSHNER BROS., Props.

ESTABLISHED 1876. TELEPHONE 168.
CHESTER BRADFORD,
SOLICITOR OF PATENTS,
AND COUNSEL IN PATENT CAUSES.
(See adv. page 6.)
Office:—Rooms 14 and 16 Hubbard Block, S.W. Cor. Washington and Meridian Streets,
INDIANAPOLIS, INDIANA.

Magennis James E, lab, b n s Prospect 1 e of Belt R R.
Magennis Sophia, h 49 Bellefontaine.
Maggard John, lab, h 614 N West.
Maggart Joseph M, carp, h 1709 Graceland av.
Maggetts Noah, lab, h 9 Mill.
Magill Osborn L, foreman American Tribune, h 204 E McCarty.
Magill Robert J, condr, h 725 Broadway.
Magill Willis, solr, b s s Howland av 2 w of Baltimore av.
Magley Albert M, letter carrier P O, h 474 W Michigan.
Magley Lena L (wid Albert M), h 1071 N Capitol av.
Magley Lizzie (wid Jacob), h 150 Minerva.
Magner Jane H (wid Joseph T), h 529 Broadway.
Magness Alexander J, sawmkr, r 220½ S Meridian.
Magruder, see also McGruder.
Magruder Georgia L, dressmkr, 315 E Ohio, h same.
Magsam Charles M, confr, 77 Oliver av (W I), h same.
Maguire, see also McGuire.
Maguire Albert M, clk, h 574 N Penn.
MAGUIRE CHARLES, Dry Goods, 174-176 W Washington, Tel 1033; h 574 N Penn.
Maguire Charles A, contr, 42 W Market, h 73 W Vermont.
Maguire Wm G, clk, h 574 N Penn.
Mahaffey Robert G, barber, r 67 N New Jersey.
Mahalowitz Morris, confr, 416 S Meridian, h same.
Mahan, see also McMahan.
Mahan Elizabeth W (wid Archibald), h 174 Dillon.
Mahan Frank D, lab, h 123 Darnell.
Mahan Harry A, paperhngr, h rear 261 River av (W I).
MAHAN HARRY B (Sullivan & Mahan), r 370 N Meridian.
Mahan John R, engr, h 55 English av.

O. B. Ensey
SLATE, STEEL, TIN AND IRON ROOFING.
Cor. 6th and Illinois Sts. Tel. 1562

Mahan Maria (wid James), b 432 W New York.
Mahan Rosa B (wid Wm C) h 234 E Market.
Mahan Wm, farmer h s s Clifford av 1 e of Concord.
Mahaney Wm, lab, b 300 W Maryland.
Maher Edward F, opr W U Tel Co, b 468 N West.
Maher James W, turner, h 142 John.
Maher John J, opr W U Tel Co, b 468 N West.
Maher Mary E (wid John F) b 468 N West.
Maher Philip, lab b 2[illegible] W Maryland.
Maher Thomas F, [illegible]
Maher Wm A Rev, asst rector St Patrick's Church b 880 Coburn.
Maholm John S ins agt, h 23 Woodlawn av.
Malcolm Thomas A H, barber, 162 Oliver av, h 27 Garfield (W I)
Mahon John, lab, b 42 Bright.
Mahon Patrick lab h 35 Ketcham (H)
Mahone Ernest, color, b 86 E Oh[io]
Mahoney Charles engr h 114 Walcott
Mahoney Daniel bartndr, b 292 Bright.
Mahoney Daniel E, lab b 55 Ellen
Mahoney Daniel H grocer, 1069 N Capitol av, h same
Mahoney Edward J, sec Indpls Paint and Color Co h 8 Buchanan
Mahoney Ellen (wid John), h 90 Madison av.
Mahoney James D, lab, h 35 Grant
Mahoney Jeremiah shoemkr 59 Malott av, h same
Mahoney Jeremiah A, stenog L E & W R R, h 771 S Capitol av.
Mahoney John, h 10 Buchanan
Mahoney John, waiter r 90½ Mass av.
Mahoney John H, sculptor, 157 Huron, h same.
Mahoney John J, paymastr, h 573 S Capitol av.
Mahoney John T, lab b 675 S Capitol av
Mahoney Joseph J, mach hd, b 90 Madison av.
Mahoney Margaret (wid James), b 677 S S Capitol av
Mahoney Margaret A (wid James), b 31 Bradshaw.
Mahoney Martin F, patrolman, h 10 Center.
Mahoney Mary C (Union Co-Operative Laundry), b 10 Buchanan.
Mahoney Michael, produce, h 22 Buchanan
Mahoney Michael M, ins agt, h 22 Buchanan.
Mahoney Patrick, lab, b 54 S Senate av.
Mahoney Richard, uphlr, r 143 Ft Wayne av.
Mahoney Thomas, janitor, h 678 S Capitol av.
Mahoney Thomas (Mahoney & Amick), b 58 Chadwick.
Mahoney Wm, lab, h 538 S Capitol av.
Mahoney & Amick (Thomas Mahoney, Howard H Amick), saloon, 29 Virginia av.
Mahoney Lawrence S, clk, b 674 N Capitol av.
Mahorney Ann E (wid John T), h 255 W 2d.
Mahorney Gertrude A, teacher Public School No 24, b 255 W 2d.
Mahurin Guy M, student, b 401 Central av.
Mahurin Matilda L, h 303 N New Jersey.
Mahurin Melville B, trav agt, h 401 Central av.
Mahurin Melville J, trav agt, b 401 Central av.

TUTEWILER ▲ UNDERTAKER, No. 72 WEST MARKET STREET. TELEPHONE 216.

PROVIDENT LIFE AND TRUST CO. OF PHILADELPHIA. D. W. Edwards, G. A., 508 Indiana Trust Bldg. In form of policy; prompt settlement of death losses; equitable dealing with policy-holders; in strength of organization; and in everything which contributes to security and cheapness of life insurance, this company is unsurpassed.

Malbucher Joseph J, porter, h 61 Willow.
Maiden Edward F, salesman Fahnley & McCrea, b 41 N Alabama.
Maiden Ina, governess Indpls Orphan Asylum, n e cor College and Home avs.
Maiden John, h 5 English av.
Maiden Wm C, fireman, b 57 English av.
Maidens John T, condr, h 7 E Ohio.
Maids John F, lab, b w s James 1 n of Sutherland (B).
Maids John W, lab, b w s James 1 n of Sutherland (B).
Maier Charles, cornicemkr, b 218 E Market.
Maier Ernst, baker, b 15 E Washington.
Maier Joseph, cabtmkr, 58 E Washington, h same.
Maillard Albert W, grocer, 312 E 9th, h same.
Maillard Arthur, butcher, b 17 N Pine.
Maillard Marie (wid Felix), h 1 N Pine.
Main Frank M, embalmer, b 144 N Senate av.
Main Silas V, traker, b Eng av.
Main Wm, lab, b 5 W Maryland.
Maine Willis F, mngr retail dept Tuttle & Seguin, h N Illinois.
Maingault Wm E, trackman, b 111 Fletcher av.
Mains Martha M (wid John F W), h 1 E St Joseph.
Maisoll Frederick, lab, h 177 E Morris.
Maisoll Wm, dyer, 44 Virginia av, h 78 S East.
Major Anna M, mngr Enterprise Odorless Vault and Sink Cleaning Co, h 200 Elizabeth.
MAJOR JOHN L, Propr The Enterprise Odorless Vault and Sink Cleaning Co, 200 Elizabeth, h same, Tel 1075. (See adv in classified Vault Cleaners.)
Major Matilda (wid Thomas), b 26 W St Clair.
Majors Allen, cabtmkr, h 21 Indiana av.
Majors Frank, student, b 21 Indiana av.
Majors Rebecca A (wid Frank W), b 11 Hosbrook.
Makemson Wm J, lab, b 46 S Delaware.
Makepeace Alvin M, trav agt, h 95 Lexington av.
Makepeace Elizabeth, dressmkr, 95 Lexington av, h same.
Makepeace George K, carp, h 85 Sheldon.
Makepeace Horace B, Trustee Center Township, 10½ E Washington, h 48 N New Jersey.
Maker Rosalie C, dressmkr, 490 E 10th, h same.
Malcolm James F, clk, b 430 Talbott av.
Malcom Altice L, farmer, b 559 W Highland av (N I).
Malee James P, varnisher, h 120 Columbia av.
Males Calvin J, painter, h 325 N Californiа.
Males Joel F, carp, h 78 Geisendorff.
Males John T, carp, h 12 Minerva.
Maley Charles, boilermkr, h 18 Miley av.
Maley Charles F, plumber, h 28 Bridge (W I).
Maley Frank T, clk, b 251 S East.
Maley James E, h 633 N Senate av.
Maley John P, fireman, h 18 Miley av.
Maley Lawrence, car rep, h rear 609 E Washington.
Maley Michael, butcher, h 48 Bridge (W I).
Maley Patrick, flagman, h 318 W Maryland.
Maley Patrick, lab, b 633 N Senate av.

THE **WHEN** IS A WORLD BEATER.

Maley Thomas, engr, h 21 Miley av.
Malia Bridget (wid Edward), b 106 Sheffield av (H).
Malia Edward, brakeman, h 106 Sheffield av (H).
Malia Thomas, engr, h 21 Miley av.
Malick Wm F, feed, 67 N Senate av, h 8 W 8th.
Malkemus Lilian (wid Harry C), h 67 N New Jersey.
Malkus George, lab, h 113 Bismarck av (H).
Mall August W, lab, h 179 Johnson av.
Mall Charles H, lab, h 54 Chestnut.
Mall Frederick, lab, h 1 Johnson av.
Mall Wm A, lab, h 8 Columbia av.
Mallcott Alexander, packer, b 14 Church.
Mallcott Mary, bkkpr Emil Wulschner & Son, b 14 Church.
Mallery Clark E, buyer Albert Gall, h 1000 N Penn.
Mallery Newton, lab, r s w cor Allegheny and Bird.
Mallon Patrick, lab, h 119 Chadwick.
Mallory Alexander, shoemkr, r 127 Columbia al.
Mallory Charles E, supt and traffic mngr Kirgan & Co (ltd), h 151 N Illinois.
Mallory Emily (wid Henry M), b 232 Howard.
Mallory George, h rear 127 Howard.
Malloy, see also Maloy.
Malloy James, lab, b 225 Yandes.
Malloy James H, clk, r 225 Yandes.
MALLOY JAY S, Physician, 138 Mass av, Tel 738; h 273 Highland av.
Malloy John H, condr, b 117 S Illinois.
Malloy Margaret (wid Hugh), h 225 Yandes.
Malloy Matthew, rougher, h 35 E South.
Malone Abner J, mngr The Sinker-Davis Co, 112-130 S Missouri, h 124 Fletcher av.
Malone Elizabeth F, hairdresser, h 29 Wyoming.
Malone John R, barber, 58 Indiana av, h 888 N Senate av.
Malone John T, foreman, h 280 Bellefontaine.
Malone Louis, printer, b 451 W Udell (N I).
Malone Louis A, phys, 119 N New Jersey, h same.

The A. Burdsal Co. CELEBRATED **HOMESTEAD** READY MIXED PAINT. WHOLESALE AND RETAIL. 34 AND 36 SOUTH MERIDIAN STREET.

THEODORE F. SMITHER Competent and Responsible **ROOFER** Office, West Maryland St. Telephone

ELECTRIC SUPPLIES We Carry a full Stock. Prices Right. C. W. MEIKEL, Tel. 466. 96-98 E. New York St.

BENJ. BOOTH PRACTICAL EXPERT ACCOUNTANT. Accounts of any description investigated and audited, and statements rendered. Room 18, 82½ E. Washington St., Indianapolis, Ind.

The Best Place in the City to Get a Good Meal THE SHERMAN RESTAURANT 18 and 20 S. Meridian Street KERSHNER BROS., Proprs.

ESTABLISHED 1876. TELEPHONE 168.
CHESTER BRADFORD,
SOLICITOR OF PATENTS,
AND COUNSEL IN PATENT CAUSES.
(See adv. page 6.)
Office:—Rooms 14 and 16 Hubbard Block, S.W. Cor. Washington and Meridian Streets, INDIANAPOLIS, INDIANA.

Magennis James E, lab, b n s Prospect 1 e of Belt R R.
Magennis Sophia, h 49 Bellefontaine.
Maggard John, lab, h 614 N West.
Maggart Joseph M, carp, h 1769 Graceland av.
Maggetts Noah, lab, h 9 Mill.
Magill Osborn L, foreman American Tribune, h 204 E McCarty.
Magill Robert J, condr, h 725 Broadway.
Magill Willis, solr, b s s Howland av 2 w of Baltimore av.
Magley Albert M, letter carrier P O, h 474 W Michigan.
Magley Lena L (wid Albert M), h 1051 N Capitol av.
Magley Lizzie (wid Jacob), h 150 Minerva.
Magner Jane H (wid Joseph T), h 329 Broadway.
Magness Alexander J, sawmkr, r 250½ S Meridian.
Magruder, see also McGruder.
Magruder Georgia I, dressmkr, 315 E Ohio, h same.
Magsam Charles M, confr, 77 Oliver av (W I), h same.
Maguire, see also McGuire.
Maguire Albert M, clk, h 574 N Penn.
MAGUIRE CHARLES, Dry Goods, 174-176 W Washington, Tel 1633; h 574 N Penn.
Maguire Charles A, contr, 42 W Market, h 73 W Vermont.
Maguire Wm G, clk, h 574 N Penn.
Mahaffey Robert G, barber, r 67 N New Jersey.
Mahalowitz Morris, confr, 416 S Meridian, h same.
Mahan, see also McMahan.
Mahan Elizabeth W (wid Archibald), h 174 Dillon.
Mahan Frank D, lab, h 123 Darnell.
Mahan Harry A, paperhngr, h rear 261 River av (W I).
MAHAN HARRY B (Sullivan & Mahan), r 370 N Meridian.
Mahan John R, engr, h 55 English av.

O. B. Ensey
SLATE, STEEL, TIN AND IRON ROOFING.
Cor. 6th and Illinois Sts. Tel. 1562

Mahan Maria (wid James), h 432 W New York.
Mahan Rosa B (wid Wm C), h 224 E Market.
Mahan Wm, farmer, h s s Clifford av 1 e of Concord.
Mahaney Wm, lab, b 300 W Maryland.
Maher Edward F, opr W U Tel Co, b 493 N West.
Maher James W, tinner, h 163 John.
Maher John J, opr W U Tel Co, b 493 N West.
Maher Mary E (wid John F), h 493 N West.
Maher Philip, lab, b 224 W Maryland.
Maher Thomas F, mach hd, b 136 W 1st.
Maher Wm A Rev, asst rector St Patrick's Church, b 390 Coburn.
Maholm John S, ins agt, h 33 Woodlawn av.
Maholm Thomas A H, barber, 103 Oliver av, h 27 Garland (W I).
Mahon John, lab, b 82 Bright.
Mahon Patrick, lab, h 35 Ketcham (H).
Mahone Ernest, collr, b 86 E Ohio.
Mahoney Charles, engr, h 114 Walcott.
Mahoney Daniel, bartndr, b 292 Bright.
Mahoney Daniel E, lab, b 55 Ellen.
Mahoney Daniel H, grocer, 1049 N Capitol av, h same.
Mahoney Edward J, sec Indpls Paint and Color Co, h 8 Buchanan.
Mahoney Ellen (wid John), h 99 Madison av.
Mahoney James D, lab, h 35 Grant.
Mahoney Jeremiah, shoemkr, 50 Malott av, h same.
Mahoney Jeremiah A, stenog L E & W R R, h 571 S Capitol av.
Mahoney John, h 10 Buchanan.
Mahoney John, waiter, r 90½ Mass av.
Mahoney John H, sculptor, 187 Huron, h same.
Mahoney John J, paymastr, h 573 S Capitol av.
Mahoney John T, lab, b 478 S Capitol av.
Mahoney Joseph J, mach hd, b 99 Madison av.
Mahoney Margaret (wid James), b 477 S S Capitol av.
Mahoney Margaret A (wid James), b 31 Bradshaw.
Mahoney Martin F, patrolman, h 10 Center.
Mahoney Mary C (Union Co-Operative Laundry), b 10 Buchanan.
Mahoney Michael, produce, h 22 Buchanan.
Mahoney Michael M, ins agt, h 22 Buchanan.
Mahoney Patrick, lab, b 84 S Senate av.
Mahoney Richard, uphlr, r 143 Ft Wayne av.
Mahoney Thomas, janitor, h 478 S Capitol av.
Mahoney Thomas (Mahoney & Amick), h 58 Chadwick.
Mahoney Wm, lab, h 538 S Capitol av.
Mahoney & Amick (Thomas Mahoney, Howard H Amick), saloon, 29 Virginia av.
Mahoney Lawrence S, clk, b 674 N Capitol av.
Mahorney Ann E (wid John T), h 255 W 2d.
Mahorney Gertrude A, teacher Public School No 24, b 255 W 2d.
Mahurin Guy M, student, b 401 Central av.
Mahurin Matilda L, h 303 N New Jersey.
Mahurin Melville B, trav agt, h 401 Central av.
Mahurin Melville J, trav agt, b 401 Central av.

TUTEWILER UNDERTAKER, No. 72 WEST MARKET STREET. TELEPHONE 216.

PROVIDENT LIFE AND TRUST CO. OF PHILADELPHIA. D. W. Edwards, G. A., 508 Indiana Trust Bldg. In form of policy; prompt settlement of death losses; equitable dealing with policy-holders; in strength of organization; and in everything which contributes to Security and Cheapness of life insurance, this company is unsurpassed.

THEODORE F. SMITHER Competent and Responsible ROOFER Telephone 86. Off. 151 W Maryland St.

Maibucher Joseph J, porter, h 61 Willow.
Maiden Edward F, salesman Fahnley & McCrea, b 401½ N Alabama.
Maiden Ina, governess Indpls Orphan Asylum, n e cor College and Home avs.
Maiden John, h 263 English av.
Maiden Wm C, fireman, b 263 English av.
Maidens John T, condr, h 525 E Ohio.
Maids John F, lab, b w s James 6 n of Sutherland (B).
Maids John W, lab, h w s James 6 n of Sutherland (B).
Maier Charles, cornicemkr, b 218 E Market.
Maier Ernst, baker, b 135 E Washington.
Maier Joseph, cabtmkr, 338 E Washington, h same.
Maillard Albert W, grocer, 512 E 9th, h same.
Maillard Arthur, painter, b 165 N Pine.
Maillard Marie (wid Felix), h 165 N Pine.
Main Frank M, embalmer, b 144 N Senate av.
Main Silas V, brakeman, b 66 English av.
Main Wm, lab, b 326 W Maryland.
Maine Willis P, mngr real est dept Tuttle & Seguin, h 935 N Illinois.
Maingault Wm P, tankman, b 111 Fletcher av.
Mains Martha M (wid John F W), h 165 E St Joseph.
Maisoll Frederick, lab, h 177 E Morris.
Maisoll Wm, dyer, 44 Virginia av, h 258 S East.
Major Anna M, mngr Enterprise Odorless Vault and Sink Cleaning Co, h 200 Elizabeth.
MAJOR JOHN L, Propr The Enterprise Odorless Vault and Sink Cleaning Co, 200 Elizabeth, h same, Tel 1675. (See adv in classified Vault Cleaners.)
Major Matilda (wid Thomas), b 296 W St Clair.
Majors Allen, cabtmkr, h 391 Indiana av.
Majors Frank, student, b 391 Indiana av.
Majors Rebecca A (wid Frank W), b 115 Hosbrook.
Makemson Wm J, lab, b 406 S Delaware.
Makepeace Alvin M, trav agt, h 95 Lexington av.
Makepeace Elizabeth, dressmkr, 95 Lexington av, h same.
Makepeace George K, carp, h 265 Sheldon.
Makepeace Horace B, Trustee Center Township, 10½ E Washington, h 469 N New Jersey.
Maker Rosalie C, dressmkr, 490 E 10th, h same.
Malcolm James F, clk, b 430 Talbott av.
Malcom Altice L, farmer, b 559 W Highland av (N I).
Malee James P, varnisher, h 120 Columbia av.
Males Calvin J, painter, h 325 N California.
Males Joel F, carp, h 58 Geisendorff.
Males John T, carp, h 12 Minerva.
Maley Charles, boilermkr, b 18 Miley av.
Maley Charles F, plumber, h 28 Bridge (W I).
Maley Frank T, clk, b 281 S East.
Maley James E, h 633 N Senate av.
Maley John P, fireman, b 18 Miley av.
Maley Lawrence, car rep, h rear 669 E Washington.
Maley Michael, butcher, h 48 Bridge (W I).
Maley Patrick, flagman, h 318 W Maryland.
Maley Patrick, lab, b 633 N Senate av.

THE WHEN IS A WORLD BEATER.

Malěy Thomas, engr, h 21 Miley av.
Malia Bridget (wid Edward), b 106 Sheffield av (H).
Malia Edward, brakeman, h 106 Sheffield av (H).
Malia Thomas, engr, h 21 Miley av.
Malick Wm P, feed, 657 N Senate av, h 8 W 8th.
Malkemus Lilian (wid Harry C), h 67 N New Jersey.
Malkus George, lab, h 113 Bismarck av (H).
Mall August W, lab, h 179 Johnson av.
Mall Charles H, lab, h 554 Chestnut.
Mall Frederick, lab, b 179 Johnson av.
Mall Wm A, lab, h 338 Columbia av.
Mallcott Alexander, packer, b 191 Church.
Mallcott Mary, bkkpr Emil Wulschner & Son, b 191 Church.
Mallery Clark E, buyer Albert Gall, h 1000 N Penn.
Mallery Newton, lab, r s w cor Allegheny and Bird.
Mallon Patrick, lab, h 119 Chadwick.
Mallory Alexander, shoemkr, r 127 Columbia al.
Mallory Charles E, supt and traffic mngr Kingan & Co (ltd), h 951 N Illinois.
Mallory Emily (wid Henry M), b 232 Howard.
Mallory George, h rear 227 Howard.
Malloy, see also Maloy.
Malloy James, lab, b 225 Yandes.
Malloy James H, clk, r 225 Yandes.
MALLOY JAY S, Physician, 438 Mass av, Tel 738; h 273 Highland av.
Malloy John H, condr, b 117 S Illinois.
Malloy Margaret (wid Hugh), h 225 Yandes.
Malloy Matthew, rougher, h 35 E South.
Malone Abner J, mngr The Sinker-Davis Co, 112-150 S Missouri, h 124 Fletcher av.
Malone Elizabeth F, hairdresser, b 29 Wyoming.
Malone John R, barber, 58 Indiana av, h 888 N Senate av.
Malone John T, foreman, h 200 Bellefontaine.
Malone Louis, printer, b 454 W Udell (N I).
Malone Louis A, phys, 119 N New Jersey, h same.

The A. Burdsal Co. CELEBRATED HOMESTEAD READY MIXED PAINT. WHOLESALE AND RETAIL. 34 AND 36 SOUTH MERIDIAN STREET.

ELECTRIC SUPPLIES We Carry a full Stock. Prices Right. C. W. MEIKEL, Tel. 466. 96-98 E. New York St.

DALTON & MERRIFIELD { LUMBER South Noble St., near E. Washington

INDIANA ELECTROTYPE CO. : BEST WORK LOWEST PRICES.
23 WEST PEARL ST., INDIANAPOLIS, IND. JOB WORK. BOOK PLATES. BEST PATENT BASE ON THE MARKET. All Orders Promptly Filled.

KIRKHOFF BROS.,
Electrical Contractors, Wiring and Construction.
102-104 SOUTH PENNSYLVANIA ST.
TELEPHONE 910.

Malone Lucian, hostler, h 219 W Michigan.
Malone Pompey, coachman 280 Clifford av.
Malone Rollin H, waiter, r 40 N New Jersey.
Malone Rose D (wid Alva C), h 28 W Vermont.
Malone Sarah, housekpr 29 Wyoming.
Malone Sarah, dressmkr, h 29 High.
Malone Tilman H, condr, b 31 Warman av (H).
Malone Wm H, tmstr, h 146 Agnes.
Malone Wm L, clk, b 124 Fletcher av.
Maloney, see also Moloney.
Maloney James W, engr, h 480 S Capitol av.
Maloney John, attendant Insane Hospital.
Maloney John, lab, h 7 Wallace.
Maloney John, mach opr The Indpls News, h 121 Church.
Maloney Lawrence D, messenger Am Ex Co, h 52½ S Illinois.
Maloney Martin, lab, b 1000 W Washington.
Maloney Patrick, butcher, b 300 W Maryland.
Maloney Patrick, lab, b 237 W Merrill.
Maloney Patrick, lab, h 71 Spann av.
Maloney Peter, lab, h 237 W Merrill.
Maloney Robert J, h 68½ Mass av.
Maloney Robert J, supt, h 450 E Georgia.
Maloney Stephen, motorman, b 45 Vinton.
Maloney Wm, fireman, b 174 English av.
Maloney Wm, waiter, r 295 E Court.
Malott Alfred F, stenog Parry Mnfg Co, b 492 W 22d (N I).
Malott James H, real est, 94½ E Washington, h 492 W 22d (N I).
Malott Macy W, asst cashr Indiana Natl Bank, h 851 N Penn.
Malott Volney T, pres Indiana Natl Bank and John Hilt Lake Ice Co and receiver Terre Haute & Indpls R R Co, h 288 N Delaware.
Malott Wm P, h 235 N Illinois.
Maloy, see also Malloy and Meloy.
Maloy James, janitor Public School No 3, h rear 26 E Ohio.
Maloy John J, molder, h 124½ Ft Wayne av.
Maloy Kate (wid James), h 67 W McCarty.
Maloy Michael, clk, b 1 Lynn.

THE W. G. WASSON CO.,
130 Indiana Ave. Tel. 989.
STEAM
COAL
Car Lots a Specialty. Prompt Delivery.
Brazil Block, Jackson and Anthracite.

Maloy Wm A (Maloy & Egan), h 4 Lynn.
Maloy Wm J, lab, b 67 W McCarty.
Maloy & Egan (Wm A Maloy, James Egan), grocers and meats, 1 Lynn.
MALPAS CHARLES E, Druggist, 99 Indiana av, Tel 1164; h same.
Malpas Henry, sec and treas Mutl Life Ins Co of Ind, h n w cor N Meridian and 10th.
Malpas Rolla M, asst bkkpr Mutl Life Ins Co of Ind, b n w cor Meridian and 10th.
MALPAS S HERBERT, Physician, 15-16 Marion Blk, b 1052 N Alabama.
Maltby Halbert E, condr, h 6 Wendell av.
Maltby Paul B, printer, h 4 Vermont (H).
Mamlock Leon, agt, r 26 Indiana av.
Manahan John M, carp, b 36 Russell av.
Manburan Harriet N (wid Wm H), b 77 Kentucky av.
MANCHESTER JEROME J, Physician (Limited to Eye and Ear), 10 Mansur Blk, cor Washington and Alabama, h 72 Hanna.
Manee Wm W, clk James H Logan, h 1149 N Illinois.
Maness George, lab, h 816 E 9th.
Maneval Amos B, carp, h s e cor Hazel and Valley Drive.
Maney, see also Many.
Maney John, lab, b 88 Bright.
Maney John E, foreman, h 424 W Pratt.
Maney John H, clk, b 359 S Illinois.
Maney Patrick, lab, h 12 Eckert.
Mangan Mary (wid Patrick), boarding 272 W Maryland.
Mangold Frederick, saloon, 107 Prospect, h same.
Mangun George S, b 126 E Ohio.
Mangun Jennie, phys, 126 E Ohio, b same.
Manlefield Wafe, lab, h 96 Oregon.
Manien Ella A (wid John), dry goods, 444 S Meridian, h same.
Manifold George, stovefitter, b 264 S Missouri.
Manifold Mary A (wid Robert L), b 264 S Missouri.
Manifold Vinson H, mach, b 116 Cornell av.
Manion Ann, boarding 337 W Maryland.
Manion James H, clk Natl Malleable Castings Co, b 262 S Delaware.
Manion Martin, lab, h rear 63 S California.
Manion Michael, clk Daniel Stewart Co, b 108 S Illinois.
Manion Thomas F, lab, b 259 Hadley av (W I).
Manion Thomas F, molder, h 81 McGinnis.
Manion Timothy, lab, h 337 W Maryland.
MANION WM, Real Estate and Rental Agt, 262 S Delaware, h same.
Manion Wm P, tel opr, b 262 S Delaware.
Mank Mary (wid Wm), h rear 376 E Ohio.
Manke Daniel A, carp, h 29 Gresham.
Manke Reinhold, upfitter, h 447 S State av.
Mankedick Charles H F, contr, e s Auburn av 1 s of Prospect, h same.
Mankedick Wm F, tmstr, h 282 W Merrill.
Manker Allen, driver, h 21 Ashland (W I).
Manker Catherine E (wid Louis), h w s Shelby 1 s of Southern av.
Manker Frank E, phys, 85½ W Market, r same.
Manker Hutson, policeman (W I), h 23 Edward (W I).
Manker James M, lawyer, 35 Thorpe blk, r 85½ W Market.
Manker Jessie B, teacher, b w s Shelby 1 s of Southern av.

W. H. Messenger FURNITURE, CARPETS, STOVES, 101 EAST WASHINGTON ST. TEL. 491.

McNamara, Koster & Co. | Foundry and Pattern Shop, 212-218 S. PENN. ST. PHONE 1593.

Mankin Abram J, carp, h 221 N Alabama.
Mankin Elmer L, bartndr, b 450 Mass av.
Mankin Maude M, clk, b 221 N Alabama.
Manley Dennis, lab, h 76 Maple.
Manley Dennis J, sawmkr, b 76 Maple.
Manley James, lab, h 107 Meek.
Manley James E, collr Artificial Ice and Cold Storage Co, b 774 N Capitol av.
Manley Margaret (wid Percy), h 774 N Capitol av.
Manley Patrick T, engraver, b 774 N Capitol av.
Manley Thomas, boilermkr, b 76 Maple.
Manley Wm H, lab, b 206 W Walnut.
Manlove Burton E, trav agt, b 138 E Pratt.
Manlove Earl, lab, b 218 E Wabash.
Manlove Minerva J, music teacher, 318 E Pratt, h same.
Manlove Osman R, electrician, r 297 N East.
Manlove Wm E, carp, h 138 E Pratt.
Mann Alma, critic Public School No 4, b 191 Park av.
Mann Angeline L (wid Daniel), h 1113 N New Jersey.
Mann Anna L, clk Ger Am Bldg Assn, b 430 W McLene (N I).
Mann Benjamin C, waiter, b 48 Elizabeth.
Mann Calvin T, switchman, h 250 Alvord.
Mann Charles, paper dealer, 730 N Capitol av, h same.
Mann Charles O, boilermkr, b 160 Sheldon.
Mann Charles W, mach opr The Indpls News, b 1113 N New Jersey.
Mann Elmira J (wid Alfred J), h 78 Spann av.
Mann Etta J (wid Wm), h 141 W New York.
Mann George W, messenger Am Ex Co, b 75 N Pine.
Mann Harry H, painter, h 606 Cornell av.
Mann Ida A (wid Samuel), h 430 W McLene (N I).
Mann Inez E, b 486 Central av.
Mann Jacob E, bricklyr, h 609 W 22d (N I).
Mann James M, collr People's Outfitting Co, h 241 Huron.
Mann James W, saloon, 299 E Washington, h same.
Mann Jesse E, boilermkr, h 162 Sheldon.
Mann John, h 1000 W Washington.
Mann John S, lab, h 558 E 12th.
Mann John S, livery, 83 E Wabash, h same.
Mann John T, lab, h 160 Sheldon.
Mann John T, lab, b 1000 W Washington.
Mann Kate A, teacher Public School No 23, b 48 Elizabeth.
Mann Killian, jeweler, h 995 N Senate av.
Mann Knowles, bartndr, r 79 E Wabash.
Mann Martha (wid John), h 36 Huron.
Mann Martin, sec Indpls Live Stock Journal and Printing Co, r 25 Hubbard blk.
Mann Smith, clk People's Outfitting Co, h 379 N West.
Mann Theodore W, finisher, h 941 Mass av.
Mann Thomas, clk, h 609 N West.
Mann Wm, driver, h 248 S East.
Mann Wm C, mach opr The Sun, r 266 N Alabama.
Mann Willis R, h 481 W Francis (N I).
Mannalla Frank, shoemkr, 121 W Washington, h same.
Mannalla Michael A, fruits, 133 W Washington, h 118 N Capitol av.
Manners John I, phys, 380 S West, b The Bates.
Mannfeld Albert J (George Mannfeld & Sons), 336 N East.

Henry H. Fay, 40½ E. Washington St., REAL ESTATE, AND LOAN BROKER.

Mannfeld Emma L, teacher Public School No 1, b 26 Park av.
Mannfeld George (George Mannfeld & Sons), h 336 N East.
Mannfeld George N (George Mannfeld & Sons), h 7 Hall pl.
MANNFELD GEORGE & SONS (George, George N, Wm C and Albert J), Merchant Tailors, 57 N Penn.
Mannfeld Julius, tailor, h 26 Park av.
Mannfeld Wm, tailor George Mannfeld & Sons, r 15½ S Meridian.
Mannfeld Wm C (George Mannfeld & Sons), h 126 Irwin.
MANNING ALEXANDER E, Publisher and Genl Mngr Indianapolis World, 38½ S Illinois, h 528 N Meridian.
Manning Charles, mill hd, b 187 S Capitol av.
Manning Charles A, real est, 94½ E Washington, h 232 Christian av.
Manning Colonna (wid Simon), h 243 Fayette.
Manning Dennis, lab, b 207 Douglass.
Manning Frank M, clk P L Chambers, b 57 High.
Manning Frederick, r 29½ Kentucky av.
Manning Frederick, tmstr, b 330 Prospect.
Manning Harry L, painter, h n w cor Michigan and Linwood av.
Manning Hattie, teacher, b 617 W Francis (N I).
Manning James E, lab, r 80 W Market.
Manning James J, lab, b 265 W Maryland.
Manning John F, city license insp, h 128 Elizabeth.
Manning John M, tailor, h 57 High.
Manning Joseph, lab, b 165 W Maryland.
Manning Michael, clk, h 48 Hillside av.
Manning Nellie, h 234 E Washington.
Manning Peter, h 617 W Francis (N I).
Manning Robert, porter, b 243 Fayette.
Manning Stanford, porter, b 243 Fayette.
Manning Wm, tmstr, h rear 235 S Senate av.
Manning Wm E, switchman, h 172½ Virginia av.
Mannix Michael J, collr, h 141 Hoyt av.

UNION CASUALTY & SURETY CO. OF ST. LOUIS, MO.
All lines of Personal Accident and Casualty Insurance, including Employers' and General Liability.
W. E. BARTON & CO., General Agents, 504 Indiana Trust Building.
LONG DISTANCE TELEPHONE 1918.

THE FRED DIETZ CO. WOODEN PACKING BOXES MADE TO ORDER. FACTORY AND WAREHOUSE TRUCKS. 400 Madison Avenue. Telephone 654.

Indianapolis BUSINESS UNIVERSITY Leading College of Business and Shorthand. Elevator day and night. Individual instruction. Large faculty. Terms easy. Enter now. See p. 4. When Block. E. J. HEEB, President.

Water and Oil Meters { HENRY R. WORTHINGTON, 64 S. PENNSYLVANIA ST. Long Distance Telephone 284.

UNION CO-OPERATIVE LAUNDRY } NOS. 138, 40 AND 42 VIRGINIA AVENUE. (COMPOSED OF UNION LAUNDRY GIRLS.) T. E. SOMERVILLE, MANAGER — TELEPHONE 1269. INDIANAPOLIS, IND.

HORACE M. HADLEY
REAL ESTATE AND INSURANCE
66 East Market Street, Basement
TELEPHONE 1540.

Manny Marie C S, teacher Indpls College of Music, b 251 Mass av.
Manor George E, painter, h 895 S Meridian.
Mansfield Charles C, fireman, h 206 S Pine.
Mansfield Henry A (Mansfield & Allen), b 433 N Illinois.
Mansfield Lenox W, clk U S Pension Agency, b 121 E New York.
Mansfield Martin W, supt I & V Ry, Union Station, h 896 N Ilinois.
Mansfield Mary A (wid Joseph B), b 10 N Brightwood av (B).
Mansfield Michael R, condr, h 250 Bellefontaine.
Mansfield Oscar J (Keystone Co), b 194 Cornell av.
Mansfield Perry A, helper, h e s Shade 3 s of Sutherland (B).
Mansfield Robert, sec, b The Denison.
Mansfield Thomas (Mansfield & Jenkins), h 67 Stevens.
Mansfield Wm H (Keystone Co), h 194 Cornell av.
Mansfield & Allen (Henry A Mansfield, Wm C Allen), contrs, 25½ W Washington.
Mansfield & Jenkins (Thomas Mansfield, James Jenkins), horseshoers, 180 E Market.
Manshart George, carp, 198 Nebraska, h same.
Manshart George jr, carp, b 198 Nebraska.
Mansur Amelia B (wid Isaiah), h 10 E Vermont.
Mansur Charles W, b n e cor N Illinois and 24th.
Mansur Hannah A (wid Wm), h n e cor N Illinois and 24th.
Mantel Emil, saloon, 309 E Washington and 223 W Washington, h 309 E Washington.
Manther Charles A, blksmith, h 327 Alvord.
Manthey Henry, lab, h 335 Fletcher av.
Menthey Hermann F, finisher, b 152 Michigan (H).
Manuel Guy, lab, h 121 Locke.
Manufacturers' Natural Gas Co The of Indianapolis, John M Shaw pres, Hugh McK Landon sec, Frederick A W Davis treas, 75 Monument pl.

PERSONAL AND PROMPT ATTENTION GIVEN TO COLLECTIONS.
Merchants' and Manufacturers' Exchange
J. E. TAKKEN, Manager,
19 Union Building, 73 West Maryland Street.

Manville Henrietta N (wid Nicholas), h 79 Chadwick.
Manville Rufus B (Pfaff & Co), h 597 Mass av.
Manville Wm H, temperer, b 79 Chadwick.
Many, see also Maney.
Many Camille, b 11 Woodlawn av.
Many Charles J, carp, 315 Mass av, h same.
Many Charles J jr, bkkpr The Interior Hardwood Co, b 315 Mass av.
Many Clementine (wid John B), b 123 N Noble.
Many Frank C B, lab, b 117 High.
Many John B, mach, b 82 Bellefontaine.
Many John D, molder, b 188 S Senate av.
Many Julius, mach hd, h 11 Woodlawn av.
Many Lena (wid Adolph J), h 117 High.
Many Louisa (wid Charles), h 288 Fulton.
Many Robert, mach, b 315 Mass av.
Manz Michael, foreman, h 160 Willow.
Manz Michael jr, lab, b 160 Willow.
Manzer George, lab, h 754 S East.
Mauzey Edwin, driver, h 129 S Summit.
Manzey Rudolph, painter, b 160 W Maryland.
Mapes Clarence, clk R M S, h 327 S Penn.
Mapes George, lab, b 30 Thomas.
MAPES SMITH H, Physician and Druggist, 501 College av, h 514 Broadway.
Mapes Walton H, clk, b 514 Broadway.
Maple Albert, driver, h nr cor Bloyd av and Hazel.
Maple Albert M, clk, h n e cor Illinois and 1st.
Maple Alfred L (Ball & Maple), h 432 N Alabama.
Maple Andrew J, milk, h 109 Ludlow av.
Maple Archibald, tmstr, h 146 Trowbridge (W).
Maple Benjamin F, tmstr, h 125 Lincoln la.
Maple Charles W, tmstr, b 406 Bates.
Maple Edward W, lab, b 109 Ludlow av.
Maple Harry C, mach hd, h rear w s Harriet 2 n of Bloyd av (B).
Maple John, h 200 Lincoln la.
Maple John C, engr, h 129 Lincoln la.
Maple Omer S, city salesman Eli Lilly & Co, b 129 Lincoln la.
Maple Verner E, finisher, b 109 Ludlow av.
Maraman Frank, driver, h 504 N California.
Marble Edward L, condr, h 111 John.
Marble Otho D, lab, b 111 John.
Marby Louis, carp, h rear 543 E Washington.
Marcbacher Joseph, b 948 N Senate av.
MARCEAU THEODORE, Photographer, 40 N Illinois, Tel 1582; Res San Francisco, Cal.
Marchal, see also Marshall.
Marchal Rudolph, produce, E Mkt House, h 229 Ramsey av.
Marchejam George, tailor, b 237 S Delaware.
Marcy Arthur A, b 149 S East.
Marcy George L, b 149 S East.
Marcy Maud B, stenog, b 149 S East.
Marcy Theodore F, grocer, 1451 E Washington, h 149 S East.
MARCY WM T, Jeweler, 38 W Washington, h 792 N Meridian.
Marden Charles, lab, h rear 610 N West.
Mardick James W, registry clk P O Union Station, h 247 Bellefontaine.
Marer Adolph, clothing, 277 E Washington, h same.
Marer Herman, huckster, h 22 Columbia al.

CLEMENS VONNEGUT 184, 186 and 192 E. Washington St. | FOUNDRY AND MACHINISTS' SUPPLIES. "NORTON" EMERY WHEELS AND GRINDING MACHINERY.

THE WM. H. BLOCK CO. 7 AND 9 EAST WASHINGTON STREET. DRY GOODS, MILLINERY, CLOAKS AND FURS.

Marer Philip, constable, 12½ N Delaware, h 152 Davidson.
Marer Ralph L, clk Order of Chosen Friends, b 152 Davidson.
Margason Daniel H, condr, h 123 S Noble.
Margason Wm M, tmstr, h 920 Gent (M P).
Marien Peter, mason, h 21 Wyoming.
Marine Charles A, cutter, b 330 N Pine.
Marine Earl, barber, r 45 Hendricks blk.
Marine Edward O, clk, b 330 N Pine.
Marine Hester F (wid Asnah C), h 330 N Pine.
Marine Wm D, actor, b 330 N Pine.
Mariner Robert L, molder, h 5 Wacker (H).
Marion Brick Works, A W Means agt, 5 Builders' Exchange.
Marion Club, 25 E Ohio.
MARION COUNTY ASSESSOR'S OFFICE, Joseph E Boswell Assessor, 35 Court House.
MARION COUNTY AUDITOR'S OFFICE, Harry B Smith Auditor, 41 Court House, Tel 912.
MARION COUNTY CIRCUIT COURT, 45 Court House.
MARION COUNTY CLERK'S OFFICE, James W Fesler Clerk, 24-29 Court House, Tel 230.
MARION COUNTY COMMISSIONERS' OFFICE, 43 Court House, Tel 912.
Marion County Criminal Court, Court House.
Marion County Gazette, S J MacDonald propr, 22 Pembroke Arcade.
Marion County Jail, n w cor Alabama and Maryland.
Marion County Library, 55 Court House.
MARION COUNTY RECORDER'S OFFICE, Wm E Shilling Recorder, 44 Court House, Tel 912.
MARION COUNTY SHERIFF'S OFFICE, Thomas P Shufelton Sheriff, 34 Court House.
Marion County Surveyor's Office, John V Coyner Surveyor, 31 Court House.
MARION COUNTY TREASURER'S OFFICE, Wm H Schmidt Treas, 23 Court House.
Marion County Work House, s e cor 12th and Northwestern av.
Marion Gun Club, 29¼ E Market.
Marion Mnfg Co, Wm H Newby agt, threshers, 62 W Georgia.
Marion Margaret, b 1155 E Washington.
Marion Margaret (wid Joseph), b 350 Broadway.
Marion Park Hotel, Charles Behnke propr, cor Post and Vorster avs (M P).
Marion Savings Assn, 88 When bldg.
Marion Sophia (wid Oliver), b s e cor Illinois and 29th.
MARION TRUST CO THE (Capital $300,000), Frank A Maus Pres, Ferdinand Winter Vice-Pres, Henry Kothe 2d Vice-Pres and Treas, Wm T Noble Sec, s e cor Market and Monument Pl, Tel 1858. (See back cover.)
Marion Wm C jr, trav agt Indiana Bicycle Co, b The Denison.
Maris James D, carp, 1339 N Alabama, h same.
Marius Frances M, h 33 Hadley av (W I).
Mark Albert, lab, b 300 W Maryland.

PICTURES. 33 South Meridian Street. THE H. LIEBER COMPANY. ARTISTIC FRAMING. MIRRORS.

Mark Caroline (wid Nicholas), h 278 Christian av.
Mark Frank H, reporter The Indpls Journal, b 278 Christian av.
Mark Lemon B, trav agt, h 2 Ruckle.
Mark Lillie A, teacher Public School No 2, b 76 S Judge Harding (W I).
Markey James J, foreman, h 18 Ketcham.
Markey Thomas J, with Indpls Brewing Co, saloon, 255 W Washington, h 86 High.
Marking Joseph H, lab, b 312 S West.
Markle Albert, electrician, b 27 LaSalle.
Markle Frank L, engr, b 33 Eastern av.
Markle Margaret (wid Amos W), h 33 Eastern av.
Markle Thomas S, lab, b 33 Eastern av.
Markle Wallace, millwright, b 1137 Northwestern av.
Markle Wm, tinner, b 33 Eastern av.
Markley Charles F, cabtmkr, h 1702 N Capitol av.
Markley Harry, helper, h 364 N Brookside av.
Markley Harvey, lab, r 295 W 6th.
Marklin James, soldier, h 164 Brookside av.
Marklin Matthew, lab, h 313 W Pearl.
Markovich Frank, lab, h 47 Holmes av (H).
Markovits Samuel, clothing, 121 Mass av, h same.
Marks Abraham, confr, 107 E Mkt House, h 38 Maple.
Marks Benjamin H, clk, b 263 S Delaware.
Marks Benjamin S, trav agt Samuel Marks, b 289 E South.
Marks Henry, junk, 196 S Penn, h 263 S Delaware.
Marks Hiram, trav agt, h 480 W Udell (N I).
Marks Jacob, produce, E Mkt House, b 38 Maple.
Marks John, lab, b 80 S Brightwood av (B).
Marks Patrick G, helper, r 44 Poplar (B).
Marks Samuel, h 289 E South.
Marks Wm, foreman, r 44 Poplar (B).
Marks Wm J, clk Daniel Stewart Co, h 90 Stoughton av.
Markum Jacob, turner, h 121 Maple.
Markum Oscar, produce, E Mkt House, h 38 Maple.

GUIDO R. PRESSLER, FRESCO PAINTER. Churches, Theaters, Public Buildings, Etc., A Specialty. Residence, No. 325 North Liberty Street. INDIANAPOLIS, IND.

INDIANAPOLIS STEEL ROOFING AND CORRUGATING WORKS, 23 and 25 East South Street. S. D. NOEL, Proprietor.

David S. McKernan REAL ESTATE AND LOANS. Exchanging real estate a specialty. A number of choice pieces for encumbered property. Rooms 2-5 Thorpe Block.

DIAMOND WALL PLASTER { Telephone 1410 BUILDERS' EXCHANGE.

Cor. E. Ohio St. and C., C., C. & St. L. R'y Tracks. Storage of Household Goods and Pianos a Specialty. UNION TRANSFER AND STORAGE CO.

W. McWORKMAN,
Galvanized Iron Cornice Works
TIN AND SLATE ROOFING.
930 WEST WASHINGTON STREET.
TELEPHONE 1118

Marlatt Wade, plumber, b 8 Hamilton av.
Marley Charles, tinner, h 312½ W Merrill.
Marley Ellen (wid Thomas), h 127 W South.
Marley George W, huckster, h w s Linwood av 3 n of Ohio.
Marley Lena (wid Samuel T), h 105 W 6th.
Marley Michael J, tmstr, b 127 W South.
Marley Thomas E, lab, b 127 W South.
Marley Walter A, baker, 198 Columbia av, h same.
Marley Wm O, barber, h 325 W Market.
Marlin Wm S, lab, h n e cor Harrison av and Blackmore.
Marinee Jared B, carp, h 68 Columbia av.
Marlow Elliott, clk R M S, h 29 Park av.
Marlowe Albert, lab, h 153 Agnes.
Marmarowsky Albert, barber, h w s Chester av 5 n of Washington.
Marmon Daniel W, pres Indpls Light and Power Co and sec Nordyke & Marmon Co, h 518 N Delaware.
Marmon Walter C, supt, b 518 N Delaware.
Marold Wm E, tailor, h 172½ N Illinois.
Maron August, lab, h 28 Holmes av (H).
Maron Julius, lab, h 33 Warman av (H).
Marone Edith C, stenog, b 52 Greer.
Marone Elmer E, driver, h 91 Lexington av.
Marone George B, tmstr, h 52 Greer.
Marone Giuseppe, music teacher, 177 N Capitol av, h same.
Marone Joseph, tailor, b 118 N Capitol av.
Marone Mary M, housekpr 150 Bates.
Maroney Clara (wid Matthew), h 263 S West.
Maroskey Henry, porter, b 186 Blake.
Marosky Charles, carp, h 25 Tecumseh.
Marot John R, barbers' supplies, 139½ W Washington, b 222 N Delaware.
MAROTT GEORGE J, Fine Shoes, 26-28 E Washington, Tel 1487; h 241 N Alabama.
Marott George P, shoes, 16 N Penn, h 478 N Alabama.
Marott Joseph E, mngr, h 556 College av.
Marquardt Gustav H, molder, b 115 N New Jersey.

SEALS,
STENCILS,
STAMPS, Etc.
GEO. J. MAYER
15 S. Meridian St.
TELEPHONE 1386.

Marquess Gertrude T, matron Indpls Home for Friendless Women, s e cor Capitol av and 11th, h same.
Marquette Eugene O, h 859 Bellefontaine.
Marquette George, fireman, b 28 S State av.
Marquette Harry C, harnessmkr, b 47 N East.
Marquette Katharine (wid Frederick W), h 47 N East.
Marquette Louis, lab, h s e cor LaSalle and Richard (M P).
Marquette Nellie, b 44 Michigan av.
Marquis Ebenezer, paperhngr, h 363 Mass av.
Marquis Edward I, bkkpr, h 419 W Addison (N I).
Marquis Elizabeth D (wid Ebenezer), b 409 Central av.
Marquis Eugene K, asst treas Atlas Engine Wks, h 24 Ruckle.
Marquis George, express, r 566 E St Clair.
Marquis Joseph O, h 419 W Addison (N I).
Marquis Mary E (wid Charles P), h 26 Kansas.
Marquis Wm H, finisher, r 249½ W Washington.
Marquis Wm J, clk Badger Furniture Co, h 320 S Alabama.
Marr Logan G, plumber, h 111 Patterson.
Marr Thomas, cook, b 368 N New Jersey.
Marriott Clarence C, driver, b 398 Cornell av.
Marriott Elmer E, driver, b 398 Cornell av.
Marriott George A, express, h 398 Cornell av.
Marriott Walter S, clk, h 510 E 7th.
Marrow Alonzo A, pdlr, h 325 Fletcher av.
Marrow Samuel L, lawyer, 67 Ingalls blk, h 180 Pleasant.
Marrow Schuyler, mach hd, b 115 Yandes.
Marrs Eugene, hostler, r 23 Monument pl.
Marsch John A, h 11 Lynn.
Marschke August, lab, h e s McRae 1 s of Belt R R.
Marschke Carl, lab, h e s McRae 2 s of Belt R R.
Marschke Frank, lab, h e s McRae 1 n of Belt R R.
Marschke Frank, lab, h 95 New.
Marschke Frederick W, toolmkr, h 25 Gatling.
Marschke Wm J, mach, h 28 Laurel.
Marsee John L, h 203 E South.
MARSEE JOSEPH W, Dean Medical College of Indiana, Surgeon, Office Hours 3-5 P M, 106½ E New York, h 356 N New Jersey; Tel House and Office 339.
Marsee Mary D, teacher Public School No 7, b 203 E South.
Marsh Anderson R, foreman, h w s Auburn av 5 s of English av.
Marsh Anna M (wid Philo M), dressmkr, r 42½ Mass av.
Marsh Bessie, dressmkr, r 381 N Delaware.
Marsh Charles A, lab, h 122 Chadwick.
Marsh Charles H, clk Exchange Hotel (W I).
Marsh Charles H, waiter, h 119 Frazee (H).
Marsh Christopher, lab, h 290 Springfield.
Marsh Courtland, carp, h 308 N Illinois.
Marsh Daniel C, ins agt, r 11 Ryan blk.
Marsh Harmon W, chief clk I D & W Ry, b 17 S Belmont av (W I).
Marsh Henry, lab, b 290 Springfield.
Marsh Henry, shoemkr, 603 Virginia av, h 30 Lexington av.

A. METZGER AGENCY ESTABLISHED 1863. L-O-A-N-S

LAMBERT GAS & GASOLINE ENGINE CO.
ANDERSON, IND. GAS ENGINES FOR ALL PURPOSES.

Marsh Hugh L, mach opr Indpls Journal b 30 Lexington av.
Marsh Jacob M, carp, h 32 Garfield pl.
Marsh John A, lab, r 81 Muskingum al.
Marsh John J, watchman, h 64 S Judge Harding (W I).
Marsh Joseph, molder, h 371 S State av.
Marsh Mary A (wid Edward E), confr, 402 S Meridian, b 30 Lexington av.
Marsh Millard F, tmstr, h 325 Jefferson av.
Marsh Peter, lab, b 122 Chadwick.
Marsh Samuel J, printer, b 30 Lexington av.
Marsh Walter S, clk, h 1150 E Michigan.
Marsh Wm H, painter, b 30 Lexington av.
Marsh Wm M, h 279 N Meridian.
Marsh Wm S, harnessmkr, 645 S Meridian, h same.
Marshall, see also Marchal.
Marshall Albert W, treas Indpls Electrotype Foundry, h 739 N New Jersey.
Marshall Amos, housemover, 117 Yandes, h same.
Marshall Anthony (Indpls Buggy Top Co), b 707 S Meridian.
Marshall Benjamin F, lab, b 117 Yandes.
Marshall Benjamin W, tinner, b 140 N Alabama.
Marshall Catherine (wid Benjamin), h 18½ N Penn.
Marshall Catherine (wid Caspar), h 707 S Meridian.
Marshall Charles, painter, r 133 W Michigan.
Marshall Charles A, lab, b 117 Yandes.
Marshall Charles B, clk A Kiefer Drug Co, b 77 W 2d.
Marshall Charles E, tmstr, h n s Orchard av 2 e of Rural.
Marshall Charles L, mach hd, h 185 Trowbridge (W).
Marshall Charles W, undertaker, h 267 E New York.
Marshall Clarence, carver, b 421 W Eugene (N I).
Marshall David R, livery, 38 Oak, h 389 Clifford av.
Marshall Elizabeth, h 33 Willard.
Marshall Edward, lab, b rear 628 Home av.
Marshall Edward W, painter, h 173 N Pine.
Marshall Ellen (wid Edward G), b 1364 N Capitol av.
Marshall Elmer E (Cropsey & Marshall), h 125 English av.
Marshall Emma, h 41 Valley.
Marshall Firman, trav agt W J Holliday & Co, h 127 English av.
Marshall Frank E, ins agt, h 522½ E Ohio.
Marshall Frank M, carp, h 575 E 9th.
Marshall Frank N, paperhngr, h 178 E Walnut.
Marshall George, clk, h 1101 E Ohio.
Marshall George B, trav agt Tanner & Sullivan, h w s Central av 1 s of 22d.
Marshall George M, stenog Kingan & Co (ltd), h 130 Williams.
Marshall George W, coremkr, b 15 Cleveland (H).
Marshall Hannah A (wid Anson), b 127 English av.
Marshall Harry L, barber, b 522½ E Ohio.
Marshall Helen M (wid Thomas C), b 110 English av.
Marshall Henry M, foreman Pioneer Brass Works, h 448 S West.
Marshall Hiram, lab, r 1063 N Illinois.
Marshall Hiram P, insp, h 73 Woodruff av.
Marshall Ida M, nurse Asylum for Friendless Colored Children.

THOS. C. DAY & CO.
INVESTING AGENTS,
TOWN AND FARM LOANS,
Rooms 325 to 330 Lemcke Bldg.

Marshall Jacob, cabtmkr, b 128 E Merrill.
Marshall James A, painter, r 133 W Michigan.
Marshall James C, condr, h 91 Fletcher av.
Marshall James O, butler, h 219 W 2d.
Marshall Jesse G, painter, b 276 Fletcher av.
Marshall John M, lab, b 312 Indiana av.
Marshall John P, farmer, h s s Brookside av 1 e of Orchard av.
Marshall John S, horseshoer, 36 Oak, h 34 same.
Marshall John W, lab, h 1362 N Senate av.
Marshall John W, plumber, 800 N Alabama, h 1364 N Capitol av.
Marshall Joseph A (Indpls Buggy Top Co), h 381 Union.
Marshall Joseph G, mach opr The Indpls Sentinel, b 77 W 2d.
Marshall Levi, carp, h 43 Clifford av.
Marshall Louis C, trimmer, b 707 S Meridian.
Marshall Margaret (wid James H), b 218 Ramsey av.
Marshall Margaret V (wid Charles H), prin Public School No 27, h 383 Mass av.
Marshall Martha S, bkkpr Charles J Kuhn Co, b 77 W 2d.
Marshall Mary (wid Jerome B), b 220 N Capitol av.
Marshall Melville A, clk, b 35 College av.
Marshall Milam M, tmstr, h 732 Nevada.
Marshall Otis, lab, h 173 W 5th.
Marshall Robert M, h 77 W 2d.
Marshall Sarah J (wid Hiram), b w s Central av 1 s of 22d.
Marshall Sarah J (wid Walker E), h 2 Valley.
Marshall Sarah K, teacher, b w s Central av 1 s of 22d.
Marshall Sherman, coremkr, b 15 Cleveland (H).
Marshall Sidney, trav agt Atlas Engine Wks, h 681 N Capitol av.
Marshall Simon, lab, b n s 22d 2 e of Baltimore av.
Marshall Squire, lab, h 312 Indiana av.
Marshall Thomas, asst engr Deaf and Dumb Inst.
Marshall Thomas, lab, h 15 Howard.

EAT
QUAKER BREAD
ASK YOUR GROCER FOR IT.
THE HITZ BAKING CO.

BICYCLES $5 DOWN. MONTHLY. Best Wheels. Best Terms. WHEELMEN'S CO. 31 W. OHIO ST. LONG DISTANCE TEL. 1855.

J. H. TECKENBROCK | Grilles, Fretwork and Wood Carpets
94 EAST SOUTH STREET.

FIDELITY MUTUAL LIFE PHILADELPHIA, PA. A. H. COLLINS { General Agent, 52-53 Baldwin Block.

Edwardsport Coal & Mining Co. Rooms 42 and 43 When Building.

SUPERIOR BITUMINOUS COAL For Steam and Domestic . . Purposes . .

ESTABLISHED 1876. TELEPHONE 163.
CHESTER BRADFORD,
SOLICITOR OF PATENTS,
AND COUNSEL IN PATENT CAUSES.
(See adv. page 6.)
Office:—Rooms 14 and 16 Hubbard Block, S.W. Cor. Washington and Meridian Streets, INDIANAPOLIS, INDIANA.

Marshall Thomas, lab, b rear 234 W New York.
Marshall Thomas, lab, h rear 28 Sinker.
Marshall Turner T, plastr, h e s Cornelius 2 n of Carleton (M).
Marshall Violet (wid Thomas), h 284 Spring.
Marshall Wm, attendant Insane Hospital, h 522½ E Ohio.
Marshall Wm, lab, h n s 22d 2 e of Baltimore av.
Marshall Wm, lab, r 160½ W Washington.
Marshall Wm, musician, b 284 Spring.
Marshall Wm F, engr, h 130 English av.
Marshall Wm R, lab, b 312 Indiana av.
Marshall Wm T, bricklyr, h 826 S East.
Marshall Wm T, clk, b 77 W 2d.
Marshall Winfield, mach hd, b 303 Indiana av.
Marshman Minnie J (wid Thomas E), dressmkr, 318 Mass av, h same.
Marshman Wm O, mach hd, b 318 Mass av.
Marsischky Albert, lab, h 49 Ramsey av.
Marsischky Otto, lab, b s s Orchard av 1 w of Rural.
Marsischky Wm, lab, h s s Orchard av 1 w of Rural.
Marsteller Minerva B (wid Charles B), tailoress, h 31 Mulberry.
Marston Charles T, trav agt, h 222 E St Clair.
Marston Elizabeth (wid James), b 850 N Illinois.
Marston Herbert B, musician, h 186 Lexington av.
Marston Smith W, confr, 94 N Illinois, h 88 same.
Martens Herman E (Schleicher & Martens), h 533 Central av.
Martens Julius M, real est, b 148 Ruckle.
Marthens Lora V, teacher Public School No 43, b 1022 N Penn.
Martin Adslee, teacher Public School No 23, b 684 N Capitol av.
Martin Albert W, mach, b 159 Locke.
Martin Alexander, lab, h 20 Willard.
Martin Alexander E, engr, h 139 Spann av.
Martin Alford, carp, h 207 W 2d.
Martin Andrew E, supt Schools (W I), h 91 Division (W I).

HAY & WILLITS MFG CO.
76 N. PENNSYLVANIA ST.,
MAKERS
Outing BICYCLES
PHONE 598.

Martin Anna (wid Lee P), b 44 Draper.
Martin Archibald D, barber, 396 College av, h 137 Hosbrook.
Martin Arthur W, painter, b 95½ N Delaware.
Martin August F, horseshoer, r 179 W Market.
Martin Augusta H (wid Charles), b 412 Broadway.
Martin Brison, clk, h 28 Bismacrk av (H).
Martin Calvin F, clk, h 247 Hamilton av.
Martin Campbell W, trav agt, b 53 Ruckle.
Martin Charles, driver, h 134 W Maryland.
Martin Charles, tinner, h 84 Sheffield av (H).
Martin Charles A, molder, h 362 S Delaware.
Martin Charles H, switchman, h 229 S West.
Martin Charles H jr, plater, b 229 S West.
Martin Charles J, r 56 N Senate av.
Martin Charles T, tmstr, h 77 E Ray.
Martin Charles W, printer, h rear 131 Martindale av.
Martin Charles W, woodwkr, b 1 Madison av.
Martin Cicero C, phys, 151 Sanders, b same.
Martin Claude, stage hd, b 247 S Delaware.
Martin David A, actor, b 123 N Capitol av.
Martin Dora, h 112 Maple.
Martin Edgar A, actor, b 123 N Capitol av.
Martin Edna M, clk, h 362 S Delaware.
Martin Edward, butcher, b 43 S West.
Martin Edward, carp, h 16 Elliott.
Martin Edward B, carp, h 489 Broadway.
Martin Edward B Rev, State Missionary Baptist Church, h 19 Cornell av.
Martin Edward M, lab, b rear 141 St Mary.
Martin Eliza (wid Enos J), r 8 Ryan blk.
Martin Ellen N (wid Wm), h 460 Central av.
Martin Elmer, lab, h 103 Hadley.
Martin Elmer, waiter, r 18 S Senate av.
Martin Elmer E, farmer, b 83 Germania av (H).
Martin Elmer F, fireman, b 298 Fletcher av.
Martin Elwood L, engr, h 68 Tacoma av.
Martin Emil A, pres Indpls Chemical Co, h 322 College av.
Martin Ezra G, justice of peace, 154 Michigan (H), h same.
Martin Florence H (wid John C), h 53 Ruckle.
Martin Floyd W, tinner, h 159 Locke.
Martin Frances L, boarding 135 N Illinois.
Martin Frank, settlement clk Auditor of State, b 270 N Alabama.
Martin Frank E, barber, b 182 Blake.
Martin Frank H, trav agt H T Conde Implement Co, h 1136 N Penn.
Martin Frank M, candymkr, h 46 Omer.
Martin Frank S, boarding 116 Cornell av.
Martin Frank T, driver, b 256 Douglass.
Martin Frederica (wid Henry), b 25 Water.
Martin Frederick, barber, h 88 Yandes.
Martin Frederick H, brakeman, h 41 Elder av.
Martin Gary W, carp, h 1577 N Capitol av.
Martin George, brakeman, h 28 N West.
Martin George, cigarmkr, h 358 Highland av.
Martin George, cook, b 9 Ellsworth.
Martin George B, dentist, 11½ N Meridian, h 134 Tacoma av.
Martin George G, asst mngr Am Telephone and Telegraph Co, b 477 N Penn.
Martin George S, lab, b 354 Ramsey av.
Martin George W, lab, h 44 Draper.
Martin George W, teacher High School, h 260 College av.

ROOFING MATERIAL C. ZIMMERMAN & SONS, SLATE AND GRAVEL ROOFERS, 19 SOUTH EAST STREET.

DRIVEN WELLS And Second Water Wells and Pumps of all kinds at CHARLES KRAUSS', 42 S. PENN. ST., TEL. 465. REPAIRING NEATLY DONE.

Martin Gibson, lab, b 230 E Wabash.
Martin Gilbert, blksmith, e s canal nr 6th, res Ben Davis, Ind.
Mratin Grace (wid James D), h 290 Prospect.
Martin Hannah (wid Christian), b 45 Leota.
Martin Harriet (wid John H), h 83 Germania av (H).
Martin Harry, lab, h 90 Quincy.
Martin Harry D, trav agt, h 936 N Illinois.
MARTIN HARVEY B, Local Agt Glens Falls Insurance Co, 311-312 Lemcke Bldg, Tel 1740; b 1577 N Capitol av.
Martin Henry, plater, b 229 S West.
Martin Henry C, sec and treas The Rough Notes Co, h 56 The Blacherne.
Martin Henry J, driver, h 608½ Virginia av.
Martin Henry R, asst ticket agt I U Ry Co, h 25 Water.
MARTIN HERBERT R (Martin & Walker), Dentist, b 183 N Capitol av.
Martin Horace G, trav agt Hide, Leather and Belting Co, h 542 E 8th.
Martin Horace W, bkkpr, h 523 Bellefontaine.
Martin Ida M, r 400 N Illinois.
Martin James, h 29 Osgood (W I).
Martin James, lab, h 4 Brooker's al.
Martin James A, h 256 Douglass.
Martin James B, tmstr, h 22 E Ray.
Martin James H, harnessmkr, h 63½ Indiana av.
Martin James L, mach, h 313 E Georgia.
Martin Jesse H, blksmith, 123 Indiana av, h 4 Athon.
Martin John, contr, 139 N Alabama, h same.
Martin John, fireman, b 279 Christian av.
Martin John, lab, h rear 61 Maxwell.
Martin John, lab, b 67 S Noble.
Martin John, trav agt, h 394 N West.
Martin John A, engr, h 77 Fletcher av.
Martin John A, lab, h n s Sutherland 1 e of James (B).
Martin John A, motorman, h 115 Sanders.
Martin John A, phys, 58 E Ohio, h 53 Ruckle.
Martin John C, painter, h 40 N Olive.
Martin John D, clk, b 523 Bellefontaine.
Martin John E, bkkpr, h 267 E Market.
Martin John F, h w s Commercial av 4 s of Washington av (I).
Martin John G, draper, b 52 Michigan av.
Martin John H, actor, h 123 N Capitol av.
Martin John H, ironer, h 221 W. Vermont.
Martin John H, lab, h n s 8th 1 w of canal.
Martin John I, painter, h 257 Lincoln la.
Martin John M, harnessmkr, r 8 Ryan blk.
Martin John M, lab, b 77 E Ray.
Martin John S, lab, h 624 W Udell (N I).
Martin John W, lab, b 390 N California.
Martin Joseph, lab, r 167 Muskingum al.
Martin Joseph D, fireman, h 187 English av.
Martin J M, clk L E & W R R, b 155 N New Jersey.
Martin Lawrence G, uphlr, b 545 Central av.
Martin Lewis T, lab, h rear 141 St Mary.
Martin Logan, lab, h e s Earl 3 s of Belt R R.
Martin Louis E, saloon, 18 Clifford av, h 493 N East.
Martin Louis H, asst mngr The Rough Notes Co, b 56 The Blacherne.
Martin Louisa C (wid Luther R), b 10 E Michigan.
Martin Lucy A (wid Cyrus), b 231 Columbia av.
Martin Mansfield O, clk Indiana Bicycle Co, b 13 Bates.

Richardson & McCrea, REPRESENTING BEST KNOWN FIRE INSURANCE COMPANIES. Fidelity and Casualty Insurance Company of New York Represented. Telephone 182. 79 East Market St.

Martin Marion M, painter, b 220 W Merrill.
Martin Martha (wid Randolph), b 77 Lexington av.
Martin Mary, b 187 S Capitol av.
Martin Mary C, h 475 W 22d (N I).
Martin Mary E, dressmkr, 19 Cornell av, h same.
Martin Morris, engr, r 173 E Vermont.
Martin Moses M, carp, h 296 Excelsior av.
Martin Ora F, trav agt H T Conde Implement Co, h 44 Ruckle.
Martin Patrick J (Martin & Co), h 187 S Missouri.
Martin Paul F, student, b 322 College av.
Martin Preston H, grain, h 27 Vine.
Martin Rebecca A, b 271 Union.
Martin Rebecca J (wid John V), h 495 Bellefontaine.
Martin Reinhardt C L, engr, h 298 Fletcher av.
Martin Robert, bricklyr, h 293 Coburn.
Martin Robert, porter, h 185 Orange.
Martin Robert A, printer Indpls Journal, h w s Chester 3 n of Washington.
Martin Robert C, b 320 E Ohio.
Martin Robert L, painter, b 445 S Delaware.
Martin Samuel, bricklyr, h 239 Spruce.
Martin Samuel H, lineman, h 180 W Market.
Martin Samuel W, laundryman, r 522 Bellefontaine.
Martin Sidney L, driver, b 460 Central av.
Martin Stephen J, butcher, b 160 W Maryland.
Martin Thomas E, lab, b 29 Osgood (W I).
Martin Thomas F, driver, h 18 S Dorman.
Martin Thomas J, lab, b 220 W Merrill.
Martin Thomas S, grocer, 1130 E Washington, h same.
Martin Uriah, porter, r 151 Indiana av.
Martin Walter, engr, h 1193 N Capitol av.
Martin Walter G, fireman, h 222 English av.
Martin Walter M, stenog, b 447 Talbott av.
Martin Walter S, farmer, b 83 Germania av (H).
Martin Walter W, mach hd, b 256 Douglass.
Martin Wesley, lab, r 445 Blake.

The Williams Typewriter Elegant Work, Visible Writing, Easy Operation, High Speed. S. H. EAST, State Agent, 55 Thorpe Block, 87 E. Market St.

If You are not Satisfied with Your Laundry Work Give Us a Trial. . ERTEL STEAM LAUNDRY 26 and 28 N. Senate Avenue. Telephone 1089.

ELLIS & HELFENBERGER Manufacturers of IRON and WIRE FENCES 162-170 S. SENATE AVE. TEL. 958.

THE HOGAN TRANSFER AND STORAGE COMP'Y
Household Goods and Pianos Moved—Packed—Stored...... Baggage and Package Express Machinery and Safes a Specialty Cor. Washington and Illinois Sts. TELEPHONE No. 675.

Hose, Belting, Packing, Clothing, Druggists' Sundries, Bicycle Tires, Cotton Hose, Etc. New York Belting & Packing Co., L't'd.

HIGHEST SECURITY
LOWEST COST OF INSURANCE.
The Provident Life and Trust Co.
Of Philadelphia.
D. W. EDWARDS, Gen. Agent,
508 Indiana Trust Building.

Martin Wm, b 89 Indiana av.
Martin Wm, foreman, h 66 Hazel.
Martin Wm A, sawyer, h 50 Bridge (W I).
Martin Wm H, coachman, b 81 N Capitol av.
Martin Wm H, mach hd, h 197 Huron.
Martin Wm L, harnessmkr, h 247 S Delaware.
Martin Wm M, engr, h 860 Cornell av.
Martin Wm M, tailor, h 98 Ramsey av.
Martin Wm M, waiter, h 384 Clinton.
Martin Willis F, headwaiter The Grand Hotel, h 684 N Capitol av.
Martin W Vance, clk Indpls Journal, b 25 E St Joseph.
Martin & Co (Patrick J Martin, John G Ward), meats, 201 W Washington.
MARTIN & WALKER (Herbert R Martin, Wm E Walker), Dentists, 44½ N Penn.
Martindale Augusta J (wid James M), h 1107 N Delaware.
MARTINDALE CHARLES, Lawyer, 402-404 Indiana Trust Bldg, Tel 925; h 67 E 7th.
Martindale Charles C, carp, h 39 Centennial (H).
Martindale Clarence, architect, b 237 N Meridian.
Martindale Dora, dressmkr, 62 Tremont av (H), h same.
Martindale Elijah B, real est, 5 Talbott blk, h 232 N Meridian.
Martindale Elijah B jr, sec Universal Telephone Co, b 237 N Meridian.
Martindale Elzia, motorman, h 9 Quince.
Martindale George W, tel opr, h 373 Prospect.
Martindale John T, pres Universal Telephone Co, b 237 N Meridian.
Martindale Lynn B, real est, 5 Talbott blk, b 237 N Meridian.
Martindale Martha, stenog, b 62 Tremont av (H).
Martindale Robert (Robt Martindale & Co), b The Denison.

Julius C. Walk & Son,
Jewelers
Indianapolis.
12 EAST WASHINGTON ST.

MARTINDALE ROBT & CO (Robert Martindale), Real Estate, Loans and Insurance, 86 E Market, Tel 1456.
Martinek Wm, lab, b 361 W Vermont.
Martoccio Joseph M, clk Carlin & Lennox, h 187 N Liberty.
Martoccio Palma, musician, h 118 N Capitol av.
Marts Charles W, mach hd, h 21 Bridge (W I).
Marts James E, lab, h 149 Hadley av (W I).
Martyn Byron O, lab, b 40 S Belmont av (W I).
Martz Clara, h 17 Meek.
Marvel Canada H, lab, h 140 Patterson.
Marvin George E, clk C Friedgen, b 287 N Delaware.
Marvin George F, baggageman, r s w cor Illinois and Georgia.
Marvin George W, horseshoer, b 252 E Washington.
Marxer Conrad W, student, b 258 Charles.
Mascari Frank (F Mascari, Bros & Co), grocer, 41 Virginia av, h same.
Mascari F, Bros & Co (Frank, Joseph and Paul Mascari, Joseph Giuliano), commers, 47 S Delaware.
Mascari Joseph (F Mascari, Bros & Co), fruits, 23 E Mkt House, h 159 S Alabama.
Mascari Michael, clk, h 41½ Virginia av.
Mascari Paul (F Mascari, Bros & Co), fruits, E Mkt House, h 216 S East.
Mascher Freda, b 31 Palmer.
Masden Isaac J, driver, h rear 37 Center.
Mash Perry S, condr, h 15 Wendell av.
Masner George, engr, h 236 Dougherty.
Masner John, painter, h 289½ Mass av.
Masner Kruger, car insp, h 52 Bismarck av (W I).
MASON AUGUSTUS LYNCH (Mason & Latta), Pres Citizens' Street Railroad Co, h 536 N Delaware, Tel 946.
Mason Benjamin F, huckster, h 40 Excelsior av.
Mason Edward (Ropkey-Mason Engraving Co), h 726 Broadway.
Mason Edward H, porter R M S, h 401 W North.
Mason Eli, carp, h 240½ E Washington.
Mason Elizabeth D, stenog K and L of H, b 6 Hunter av (I).
Mason Elmer D, cashr Government B and L Inst, r 173 E Vermont.
Mason Frank, hackman, h 26½ N Senate av.
Mason Frederick, brakeman, r 93 N Alabama.
Mason George, hostler, r 23 Monument pl.
Mason George A, carp, h n w cor Northwestern av and Langsdale.
Mason George W, well driver, w s Northwestern av 2 n of Langsdale.
Mason Grant, well driver, 535 W Francis (N I), h same.
Mason Henry, lab, b 49 Excelsior av.
Mason Henry C, barber, 180 S Illinois, r 99½ Mass av.
Mason Hughes (Indiana Rubber Co), h 1158 N Illinois.
Mason James, barber, b 296 N California.
Mason James M, shoes, 81 Mass av, h 1158 N Illinois.
Mason John, h rear 19 Cornell av.
Mason John A, huckster, h 49 Excelsior av.
Mason John M, h 51 Ash.
Mason Kate, teacher Public School No 15, b 132 Huron.

The Central Rubber & Supply Co. PHONE 82 79 S. ILLINOIS ST., INDIANAPOLIS, IND.

OTTO GAS ENGINES | BUILDERS' EXCHANGE S. W. Cor. Ohio and Penn. Telephone 535.

Becker & Son Charles Becker Jacob Becker Jr. Merchant Tailors. 21 N. Penn. St. Tel. 934

SALISBURY & STANLEY OF BANK, STORE AND OFFICE FIXTURES, Contractors and Builders. Repairing of all kinds done on short notice. 177 C St Indianapolis, Ind. Telephone 99

Mason Martha (wid John), h 274 Fulton.
Mason Martha A (wid Ambrose D), h w s Hunter av 2 n of Washington av (I).
Mason Mary A, grocer, 289 W 6th, h same.
Mason Mary J, dressmkr, 26½ N Senate av, h same.
Mason Morton, condr, r 93 N Alabama.
Mason Moses M, polisher, r 11 S Senate av.
Mason Ralph E, foreman, b 336½ E Washington.
Mason Sophronia A, h 336½ E Washington.
Mason Thomas, supt Prudential Insurance Co of America, h 38 Lockerbie.
Mason Thomas W, driver, h 289 W 6th.
Mason Wm H, lab, h 26 Excelsior av.
Mason Wm L, huckster, h 27 Keystone av.
MASON & LATTA (Augustus Lynch Mason, Wm H Latta), Lawyers, 36-38 Journal Bldg, Tel 1767.
Masonic Advocate, Martin H Rice pub, 14 Masonic Temple.
MASONIC MUTUAL BENEFIT SOCIETY OF INDIANA, Robert S Robertson Pres, Harold C Megrew Sec and Genl Mngr, 29½ E Market, Tel 974.
Masons' Union Life Assn, Nicholas R Ruckle pres, James S Anderson sec, rooms 8 and 9 Masonic Temple.
MASSACHUSETTS BENEFIT LIFE ASSOCIATION, Daniel L Brown State Mngr, Rooms 9-10 Baldwin Blk.
Massachusetts Mutual Life Insurance Co, John F Habbe mngr, 1002 Majestic bldg.
Massay Sidney, lab, b 12 Quince.
Massey Catherine (wid George), b 76 Columbia al.
Massey Catherine R (wid Moses J), b 472 N East.
Massey Charles A, cabtmkr, h 194 Ramsey av.
Massey Everett, foreman, r 286 Mass av.
Massey Frank P, baker Parrott & Taggart, b 170 Church.
Massey James, lab, h 334 Yandes.
Massey James M, driver, r 336 N Liberty.
Massey John A, driver, b 128 Chadwick.
Massey Joseph W P, supt The Russell Lumber Co, h 501 Talbott av.
MASSEY M E, Agt The E S Dean Co, Stock Brokers, Room 51 Commercial Club Bldg, b 41 Lynn. (See adv in classified Brokers.)
Massey Roland, clk Albert Gall, b 156 N Illinois.
Massey Wm A, lab, b 194 Ramsey av.
Massillon Engine and Thresher Co The, J M Waldorf mngr, r 5 Commercial blk.
Massing Jacob P, chief of police (W I), h 62 Lynn av (W I).
Massing John, molder, h 29 Lynn av (W I).
Massing Peter, carp, h 112 Gray.
Masson Eliza T (wid James P), h 565 Ash.
Masson Jennie T, b 565 Ash.
Masson M Ross, stenog, b 565 Ash.
Masson Woodburn (Masson & Reagan), b 565 Ash.
Masson & Reagan (Woodburn Masson, Wm P Reagan), lawyers, 73 Lombard bldg.
Massonne George, foreman Michigan Lumber Co, h 286 Brookside av.
Mast George J, tinner, h 364 Fulton.
Mast Margaret (wid Samuel D), b s e cor Auburn av and Prospect.
Mast P P & Co, Fielding A Hyatt genl agt, farm implements, 100 S Capitol av.

Henry H. Fay,
40½ E. WASHINGTON ST.,
AGENT FOR
Insurance Co. of North America,
Pennsylvania Fire Ins. Co.

Masters Ezra H, photog, r Hendricks blk.
Masters George E, foreman, h 120 S Judge Harding (W I).
Masters John, lab, h 71 Lee (W I).
MASTERS JOHN L, Physician (Eye, Ear and Throat), 149 N Penn, h 724 Broadway.
Masters Minnie I, dentist, 1½ E Washington, r 271 N Alabama.
Masterson Henry, tmstr, b 398 Yandes.
Masterson Wesley C, clk Outing Bicycle Co, h 126 Woodlawn av.
Mastny Frank, watchmkr, b 34 Thomas.
Mastny Maximillian, tailor, b 34 Thomas.
Mastny Vincent, tailor, h 34 Thomas.
Matchett Eliza A (wid Richard E), h 416 Excelsior av.
Mathealy George, lab, h 124 Bryan.
Matheny Benjamin F, clk, r 101 N New Jersey.
Matheny Edna, bkkpr, b 428 W 2d.
Matheny George F, lab, b 1374 N Senate av.
Matheny John, h 141 Pleasant.
Matheny Warren, broommkr, h 428 W 2d.
Mather Alonzo J, carp, h 146 Blackford.
Mather Anna (wid John), h 344 S Olive.
Mather Daniel (Smock & Mather), h 124 E 25th.
Mather Edward G, r 82 W Washington.
Mather Wm J (Mather & Armstrong), baths, 2 Masonic Temple, h 217 N Capitol av.
Mather & Armstrong (Wm J Mather, Sig M Armstrong), barbers, 2 Masonic Temple.
Mathers Charles E, tailor, b 135 E Washington.
Mathers Henry D, plastr, b 73 Stevens.
Mathers Lewis H, mach opr Indpls Journal, h 485 Stillwell.
Mathers Mary E, music teacher, 124 E Vermont, h same.
Matheson George H, stockkpr, r 148 W Maryland.
Matheson James L, carp, h 194 Yandes.
Matheson Robert H, mach, h 125 Cornell av.
Matheson Wm A, coremkr, h 104 Martindale av.

LUMBER Sash and Doors | BALKE & KRAUSS CO., Corner Market and Missouri Sts.

Friedgen Has the BEST PATENT LEATHER SHOES AT LOWEST PRICES. 19 North Pennsylvania St.

SAMUEL LAING HOT AIR FURNACES 72 AND 74 EAST COURT STREET.

M. B. WILSON, Pres. W. F. CHURCHMAN, Cash.
The Capital National Bank,
INDIANAPOLIS, IND.
Banking business in all its branches. Bonds and Foreign Exchange bought and sold.
Interest paid on time deposits.
Checks and drafts on all Indiana and Illinois points handled at lowest rates.
No. 28 South Meridian Street, Cor. Pearl.

Mathews, see also Matthews.
Mathews Andrew J, well driver, h w s Schurman av 2 s of Wells.
Mathews Charles X, r 96 N Alabama.
Mathews Claude H, b 955 N Meridian.
Mathews Daniel, lab, h 112 Yandes.
Mathews Frank B, agt, b 123 Walcott.
Mathews Frederick, watchman, h 219 E South.
Mathews George, lab, h 58 Northwestern av.
Mathews George W, lab, h 334 Martindale av.
Mathews Harvey R, farmer, h 130 Shelby.
Mathews Henry E, notions, 13 W Washington, h 988 N Illinois.
Mathews Jacob B, molder, b 47 Haugh (H).
Mathews James C W (Mathews & Finley), h 14 Garland (W I).
Mathews John, painter, b rear 79 W North.
Mathews Joshua G, painter, b rear 149 Bellefontaine.
Mathews Marshall, waiter, h 75 Chapel.
Mathews Mary A (wid Ambrose), h 25 Woodlawn av.
Mathews May, school teacher, b 218 Cornell av.
Mathews Michael, waiter The Denison.
Mathews Sarah (wid Cyrus), h 226 N Illinois.
Mathews Silas, switchman, h 124 Chadwick.
Mathews Silas B, meats, 47 Haugh (H), h same.
Mathews Wm, lab, b 112 Yandes.
Mathews & Finley (James C W Mathews, Richard Finley), barbers, 21 S Meridian.
Mathey Alfred F, patrolman, h 90 Hosbrook.
Mathey Edward, cook, b 73 Hosbrook.
Mathey Frederick, carpet weaver, 73 Hosbrook, h same.
Mathias, see also Matthias.
Mathias Jacob, letter carrier P O, h 14 Arch.
Mathias Mary J, dressmkr, 14 Arch, h same.
Mathis James W, brazier, b 450 E Georgia.
Matillo Jerome, carp, b 115 Yandes.
Matillo John D, carp, h 583 N Rural.

Insure Against Accidents
WITH
TUTTLE & SEGUIN,
Agents for
Fidelity and Casualty Co., of New York.
$10,000 for $25. $5,000 for $12.50.
TEL. 1168. 28 E. MARKET ST.

Matillo Martin E, carp, h s s Brookside av 3 w of Waverly.
Matkin Isaac S, clk H P Wasson & Co, b 194 N West.
Matkins Noah M (Sloan & Matkins), h 1493 N Illinois.
Matley John, lab, r 170 E Court.
Matlock Charles A, janitor Industrial School, h 346 Fulton.
Matlock Charles E, mailing clk The Indpls Journal, h 24 Eastern av.
Matlock Earl O, clk Indiana National Bank, h 890 Bellefontaine.
Matlock Edith M, b 1199 Northwestern av.
Matlock Eliza (wid Wm), b 24 Eastern av.
Matlock Frank, lab, h 26 Eastern av.
Matlock Frank W, clk, b 46 Ruckle.
Matlock Fred L, clk The McGilliard Agency Co, b 46 Ruckle.
Matlock George W, broommkr, h 491 Sheldon.
Matlock James, carp, h 42 S Belmont (W I).
Matlock Louisa (wid James M), b 890 Bellefontaine.
Matlock Wm, lab, h 361 W Pearl.
Matlock Wm A, grinder, h 1199 Northwestern av.
Matracio Joseph, huckster, h 292 S Delaware.
Matson, see also Madsen.
MATSON FREDERICK E, Lawyer, 6 Fletcher's Bank Bldg, Tel 966; h 350 N New Jersey.
Matson Frederick F, clk, r 28 W New York.
Matson George I, supt Hetherington & Berner Co, h 993 N Alabama.
Matson James F, h 3 English av.
Matsumoto Ikko, jeweler, 17½ S Meridian, h 38 Highland pl.
Matt Bartholomew, h 62 Ludlow av.
Mattern August, collr Cons Coal and Lime Co, h 75 Yeiser.
Mattern Peter, h 2 Clifford av.
Mattern Wm F, painter, h n s Michigan 2 e of Sherman Drive.
Matthe Ada F, teacher Public School No 33, b 104 Brookside av.
Matthe Frederica (wid Wm), h 104 Brookside av.
Mattheus Christian, bartndr, h 349 E Morris.
Matthew Frank, horseshoer, b 92½ E South.
Matthew James, lab, h 214 S Olive.
Matthew Lee A, carp, b 214 S Olive.
Matthew Michael A, lab, b 214 S Olive.
Matthew Wilson M, agt, b 358 N Meridian.
Matthews, see also Mathews.
Matthews Albert C, clk, h 49 Hoyt av.
Matthews Albert C, ins agt, h 306 N Delaware.
Matthews Allen, mach, h 287 Shelby.
Matthews Ansel, messenger Am Ex Co, h 84 Pleasant.
Matthews Caroline, h 440 W 1st.
Matthews Charles C, brakeman, b 14 N State av.
Matthews Claude, h 273 N Illinois.
Matthews David E, condr, h 31 Temple av.
Matthews Edward P, salesman, h 512 Broadway.
Matthews Elizabeth (wid David), h 285 Kentucky av.
Matthews Elizabeth F (wid Wm B), b 179 N State av.
Matthews Ezekiel W, confr, b 559 Ash.
MATTHEWS E EDWIN, Pres Chance-Matthews Printing Co and Propr Matthews Medicine Co, h 30 Woodlawn av (formerly Elk.)

WEDDING CAKE BOXES • SULLIVAN & MAHAN 41 W. Pearl St.

DIAMOND WALL PLASTER { Telephone 1410 BUILDERS' EXCHANGE.

Best Prompt Wk. Dlvry. } THE HOME LAUNDRY 197 S. ILLINOIS ST. TEL. 1769. { Collars and Cuffs our Specialty.

Matthews E Lee, clk Bates House Pharmacy, r 28 W Vermont.
Matthews Frank, blksmith, b 92 E South.
Matthews Frank, setter, h 7 Williams.
Matthews Harvey P, fireman, b 173 S Noble.
Matthews Henry, lab, r 200½ W Washington.
Matthews Israel, lab, h 453 W Chicago (N I).
Matthews Jacob A, lab, h 287 Shelby.
Matthews Jacob F, baker, 142 E 7th, h same.
Matthews Jennie, h 22 Harrison.
Matthews John, lab, h 16 Holborn.
Matthews John C, engr, h 201 N Pine.
Matthews John E, transfer clk R M S, h 29 Ruckle.
Matthews John R, painter, 77 Torbet, h same.
Matthews John T, lab, h 148 Levison.
Matthews Joseph W, lab, h 195 W 1st.
Matthews Martha A (wid Granville M), h 225 N Liberty.
Matthews Martha J (wid Thomas J), h 122 N Liberty.
Matthews Mary (wid John R), h 22 Harrison.
Matthews Matthew, contr, 170 N New Jersey, h same.
Matthews Matthew A, condr, b 64 S State av.
Matthews Matthew D, lineman, r 174 S Capitol av.
Matthews May, h rear 431 N Pine.
MATTHEWS MEDICINE CO, E Edwin Matthews Propr, Mnfrs of Peruvian Celery, a Nerve Tonic, Peruvian Beans, a Blood Purifier, and Zura, a Female Remedy, Office 26 Woodlawn av (formerly Elk).
Matthews Miles, carp, h 78 S Reisner (W I).
Matthews Oliver W, clk, h 99 N Rural.
Matthews Samuel, lab, h 43 Elizabeth.
Matthews Sophia S (wid Horace T), h 980 N Meridian.
Matthews Thomas E, waiter, h s s Prospect 2 w of Miami.
Matthews Thomas W, saloon, 285 Kentucky av, b 31 Yeiser.
Matthews Walter J, turner, h 52 Bradshaw.
Matthew Wilbur, lab, h 102 Eureka av.
Matthews Wm (Klink & Matthews), res Bedford, Ind.
Matthews Wm, tmstr, h 102 Eureka av.
Matthews Wm H, condr, h 14 N State av.
Matthews Wm J, bricklyr, h 114 River av (W I).
Matthey Wm F, packer, h 368 W New York.
Matthias, see also Mathias.
Matthias Charles, lab, h 4 Helen (H).
Matthias Henry C, h 39 Tremont av (H).
Matthias Wm F, saloon, 123 N Belmont av (H), h 39 Tremont av (H).
Mattick Ernst F, lab, h 327 E Georgia.
Mattill Bros (Louis and John), drugs, 581 S East.
Mattill Elizabeth, h 428 S East.
Mattill John (Mattill Bros), b 428 S East.
Mattill Lavinia, b 428 S East.
Mattill Louis (Mattill Bros), h 581 S East.
Mattler Francis J, lawyer, 67 Ingalls blk, h 155 Woodlawn av.
Mattler Stephen, saloon, 298 E Washington, r same.
Mattocks Benjamin A, lab, b 523 Mulberry.
Mattocks John W, lab, b 523 Mulberry.

FRANK NESSLER. WILL H. ROST.
FRANK NESSLER & CO.

56 EAST MARKET ST. (Lemcke Building),
INDIANAPOLIS, IND.

Mattocks Wm F, shoemkr, h 523 Mulberry.
Mattox Gabriel P, bicyclemkr, h 230 N Beville av.
Mattox John W, engr, b 147 Buchanan.
Mattox Joseph M, shoemkr, h 147 Buchanan.
Matz Anthony V, bartndr, b 451 Union.
Matz John N (Matz & Matz), h 348 Blake.
Matz Joseph, mach hd, b 433 W New York.
Matz Lena, stenog, b 451 Union.
Matz Martin (Matz & Matz), h 155 Blake.
Matz Mary W (wid John), h 451 Union.
Matz Wellington, collr C F Adams & Co, b s s Johnson opp McLain (W I).
Matz & Matz (John N and Martin), saloon, 33 E Market.
Matzke Catherine G (wid Adolph), h 282 Prospect.
Matzke David F, h 207 Prospect.
Matzke Julius, meats, 72 E Mkt House, h 103 Lexington av.
Mauck Samuel M, plumber, h 62 Oak.
Maudlin Catherine (wid Joseph), h 74 Thalman av.
Mauer Christian A, driver, h 343 Bellefontaine.
Mauer Elizabeth (wid John P), h 362 Blake.
MAUER HENRY J, Grocer, 416-418 Indiana av, h same, Tel 670.
Maugenheimer Valentine, student, b 525 Talbott av.
Maul Martin, b 445 Union.
Maul Wm H, carp, 66 Middle Drive (W P), h same.
Mauler John, vinegar mnfr, h 16 Morton, h same.
Maulick Christian G, brewer, h 187 Meek.
Mauntel Christian H, teacher High School, r 26 Ft Wayne av.
Maurath Frank, bartndr, b 297 S Delaware.
Maurath Rudolph, bartndr, 297 S Delaware, b same.
Maurer Adam L, bricklyr, h 393 N New Jersey.
Maurer Charles H, driver, h n s Herbert 1 w of Gent (M P).
Maurer Edward A, mnfrs' agt, 333 Lemcke bldg, h 231 College av.

Haueisen & Hartmann
163-169 E. Washington St.
FURNITURE,
Carpets,
Household Goods,
Tin, Granite and China Wares, Oil Cloth and Shades

THE WM. H. BLOCK CO. 7 AND 9 EAST WASHINGTON STREET. DRY GOODS, HOUSE FURNISHINGS AND CROCKERY.

London Guarantee and Accident Co. (Ltd.) All forms of Liability Insurance, Workmen's Collective Insurance, Fidelity Bonds and Individual Accident Insurance.
Geo. W. Pangborn, Gen. Agent, 704-706 Lemcke Bldg. Telephone 140.

FRANK K. SAWYER, AGENT 74 East Market Street. Telephone 863.

JOSEPH GARDNER,
TIN, COPPER AND SHEET-IRON WORK AND HOT AIR FURNACES.
37, 39 & 41 KENTUCKY AVE. Telephone 322.

Maurer George F, lab, h 55 Hadley av (W I).
Maurer John, molder, h 127 Tremont av (H).
Maurer Oscar C, clk A Kiefer Drug Co, r 33 W Vermont.
Maurer Wm, bricklyr, h 101 N New Jersey.
Maurice, see also Morris.
Maurice Brother, teacher, b cor Coburn and Short.
Maurice Charles J, plumber, b 29 Fayette.
Maurice George E, clk Hollweg & Reese, b 29 Fayette.
Maurice John N, shoemkr, h 29 Fayette.
MAUS C BRANCH INDIANAPOLIS BREWING CO, Frederick C Grossart Mngr, n w cor New York and Agnes, Tel 221.
MAUS FRANK A, Pres Marion Trust Company, Crystal Ice Company and Indianapolis German Mutual Fire Insurance Company, and Vice-Pres The C Habich Company, h 28 W North, Tel 820.
Maus Magdalena (wid Casper), b 296 W New York.
Maus Mary A (wid Albert), h 434 W New York.
Maus Peter, lab, h e s Miami 2 s of Prospect.
Mauzy George, lab, b 52 S Judge Harding (W I).
Mauzy Lorenzo R, jeweler, 7 Mass av, b 143 N Alabama.
Mavity Charles K, reporter The Indpls News, b 862 N Delaware.
Mavity L Anna (wid Wm K), h 862 N Delaware.
Mavity Paul, student, b 862 N Delaware.
Mawby Jacob F, lab, b 1482 N Senate av.
Max Louis, pdlr, h 111 Eddy.
Maxey Albert, lab, h e s Sangster av 4 n of Belle.
Maxey Henry, lab, h 113 Mulberry.
Maxey James, lab, h 185 Minerva.
Maxey Leonard W, janitor K and L of H, b 74 Jones.
Maxey Lewis A, lab, h 86 Meikel.

J. S. FARRELL & CO.
STEAM AND HOT WATER HEATING FOR STORES, OFFICES, PUBLIC BUILDINGS, PRIVATE RESIDENCES, GREENHOUSES, ETC.
84 North Illinois St. Telephone 382.

Maxey Martin, lab, h 750 Brooker's al.
Maxey Rufus, lab, h 12 St Peter.
Maxey Susan (wid George), h 462 W 2d.
Maxey Timothy, policeman, b 195 Meek.
Maxfield George D, dist pass agt Wabash R R, 42 Jackson pl, h 1194 N Illinois.
Maxfield Lillian J, opr, b 1194 N Illinois.
Maxfield Rebecca D (wid George W), b 1194 N Illinois.
Maxfield Wm H, plastr, h 118 Vincennes.
Maxwell Alexina S (wid Williamson D), h 380 N Illinois.
MAXWELL ALLISON, Physician, 19 W Ohio, Tel 649; h 169 N New Jersey, Tel 290.
Maxwell Bert, b 187 N Alabama.
Maxwell Bruce W, h 1776 N Capitol av.
Maxwell Charles, lab, h 475 N Illinois.
Maxwell Charles S, clk C C C & St L Ry, b 380 N Illinois.
Maxwell Charles W, clk Ry Officials' and Employes' Accident Assn, h 36 W Michigan.
Maxwell Clifford, clk, r 36 W Michigan.
Maxwell Eli, lab, b rear 117 Birch av (W I).
Maxwell Frank A, tel opr, r 373 N Senate av.
Maxwell George W, salesman, h 1669 N Penn.
Maxwell James E, clk, r 221 N Capitol av.
Maxwell John M, h 860 N Meridian.
Maxwell Julia A (wid John C), h 277 N Capitol av.
Maxwell J Wesley Rev, pastor First M E Church (W I), h 50 William (W I).
Maxwell Maria (wid Richard H), h 28 Ft Wayne av.
Maxwell Marion, b 333 S Alabama.
MAXWELL MARVIN R, Local Freight Agt L E & W R R, h 653 N Penn, Tel 155.
Maxwell Maurice, poultry, h w s Auburn av 8 s of English av.
Maxwell Robert A, clk, b 277 N Capitol av.
Maxwell Samuel A, weigher, b 67 Ash.
Maxwell Stella, housekpr, r 205 E Market.
Maxwell Stewart W, yardmaster, h 22 W Pratt.
Maxwell Wm A, train dispatcher I D & W Ry, h 316 Bellefontaine.
Maxwell Wm E, buyer Parry Mnfg Co, b 860 N Meridian.
May Adam, h 266 Lincoln av.
May Adam J, mantel setter, b 266 Lincoln av.
May Albert D, clk, b 232 N Senate av.
May Alva C (Shellhouse & Co), h 327 Ash.
May Alvin D, collr Singer Mnfg Co, h 434 Park av.
May Amanda (wid Alvin), b 327 Ash.
May Benjamin, lab, h 5 Lafayette.
May Blanche, teacher Public School No 22, b 434 Park av.
May Charles A, agt, h 1394 Northwestern av (N I).
May Charles T, produce, E Mkt House, h s s Brookside av 2 w of Waverly av.
May Edward L, painter, 782 N Rural, h same.
May Frederick E, engr, h 37 Walcott.
May George E, lab, b 94 Mass av.
May Georgia, music teacher, 16 Blackford, h same.
May Henry, driver, h 69 N Judge Harding (W I).
May Henry H, drayman, h 290 E Merrill.
May Herman, butcher, h rear 1350 E Washington.

Prussian National Insurance Company OF STETTIN, GERMANY. ORGANIZED 1845.

United States Life Insurance Co., of New York.
E. B. SWIFT, M'g'r. 25 E. Market St.

London Guarantee and Accident Co. (Ltd.) All forms of Liability Insurance, Workmen's Collective Insurance, Fidelity Bonds and Individual Accident Insurance.
Geo. W. Pangborn, Gen. Agent, 704-706 Lemcke Bldg. Telephone 140.

FRANK K. SAWYER, AGENT 74 East Market Street. Telephone 863.
Prussian National Insurance Company OF STETTIN, GERMANY. ORGANIZED 1845.

JOSEPH GARDNER,
TIN, COPPER AND SHEET-IRON WORK AND
HOT AIR FURNACES.
37, 39 & 41 KENTUCKY AVE. Telephone 322.

Maurer George F, lab, h 55 Hadley av (W I).
Maurer John, molder, h 127 Tremont av (H).
Maurer Oscar C, clk A Kiefer Drug Co, r 33 W Vermont.
Maurer Wm, bricklyr, h 101 N New Jersey.
Maurice, see also Morris.
Maurice Brother, teacher, b cor Coburn and Short.
Maurice Charles J, plumber, b 29 Fayette.
Maurice George E, clk Hollweg & Reese, b 29 Fayette.
Maurice John N, shoemkr, h 29 Fayette.
MAUS C BRANCH INDIANAPOLIS BREWING CO, Frederick C Grossart Mngr, n w cor New York and Agnes, Tel 221.
MAUS FRANK A, Pres Marion Trust Company, Crystal Ice Company and Indianapolis German Mutual Fire Insurance Company, and Vice-Pres The C Habich Company, h 28 W North, Tel 820.
Maus Magdalena (wid Casper), b 296 W New York.
Maus Mary A (wid Albert), h 434 W New York.
Maus Peter, lab, h e s Miami 2 s of Prospec .
Mauzy George, lab, b 52 S Judge Harding (W I).
Mauzy Lorenzo R, jeweler, 7 Mass av, b 143 N Alabama.
Mavity Charles K, reporter The Indpls News, b 862 N Delaware.
Mavity L Anna (wid Wm K), h 862 N Delaware.
Mavity Paul, student, b 862 N Delaware.
Mawby Jacob F, lab, b 1482 N Senate av.
Max Louis, pdlr, h 111 Eddy.
Maxey Albert, lab, h e s Sangster av 4 n of Belle.
Maxey Henry, lab, h 113 Mulberry.
Maxey James, lab, h 185 Minerva.
Maxey Leonard W, janitor K and L of H, b 74 Jones.
Maxey Lewis A, lab, h 86 Meikel.

J. S. FARRELL & CO.
STEAM AND HOT WATER
HEATING FOR STORES, OFFICES,
PUBLIC BUILDINGS,
PRIVATE RESIDENCES,
GREENHOUSES, ETC.
84 North Illinois St. Telephone 382.

Maxey Martin, lab, h 750 Brooker's al.
Maxey Rufus, lab, h 12 St Peter.
Maxey Susan (wid George), h 462 W 2d.
Maxey Timothy, policeman, b 195 Meek.
Maxfield George D, dist pass agt Wabash R R, 42 Jackson pl, h 1194 N Illinois.
Maxfield Lillian J, opr, b 1194 N Illinois.
Maxfield Rebecca D (wid George W), b 1194 N Illinois.
Maxfield Wm H, plastr, h 118 Vincennes.
Maxwell Alexina S (wid Williamson D), h 330 N Illinois.
MAXWELL ALLISON, Physician, 19 W Ohio, Tel 649; h 169 N New Jersey, Tel 290.
Maxwell Bert, b 187 N Alabama.
Maxwell Bruce W, h 1776 N Capitol av.
Maxwell Charles, lab, h 475 N Illinois.
Maxwell Charles S, clk C C C & St L Ry, b 380 N Illinois.
Maxwell Charles W, clk Ry Officials' and Employes' Accident Assn, h 36 W Michigan.
Maxwell Clifford, clk, r 36 W Michigan.
Maxwell Eli, lab, b rear 117 Birch av (W I).
Maxwell Frank A, tel opr, r 373 N Senate av.
Maxwell George W, salesman, h 1669 N Penn.
Maxwell James E, clk, r 221 N Capitol av.
Maxwell John M, h 860 N Meridian.
Maxwell Julia A (wid John C), h 277 N Capitol av.
Maxwell J Wesley Rev, pastor First M E Church (W I), h 50 William (W I).
Maxwell Maria (wid Richard H), h 28 Ft Wayne av.
Maxwell Marion, b 333 S Alabama.
MAXWELL MARVIN R, Local Freight Agt L E & W R R, h 653 N Penn, Tel 155.
Maxwell Maurice, poultry, h w s Auburn av 8 s of English av.
Maxwell Robert A, clk, b 277 N Capitol av.
Maxwell Samuel A, weigher, b 67 Ash.
Maxwell Stella, housekpr, r 205 E Market.
Maxwell Stewart W, yardmaster, h 22 W Pratt.
Maxwell Wm A, train dispatcher I D & W Ry, h 316 Bellefontaine.
Maxwell Wm E, buyer Parry Mnfg Co, b 860 N Meridian.
May Adam, h 266 Lincoln av.
May Adam J, mantel setter, b 266 Lincoln av.
May Albert D, clk, b 232 N Senate av.
May Alva C (Shellhouse & Co), h 327 Ash.
May Alvin D, collr Singer Mnfg Co, h 434 Park av.
May Amanda (wid Alvin), b 327 Ash.
May Benjamin, lab, h 5 Lafayette.
May Blanche, teacher Public School No 22, b 434 Park av.
May Charles A, agt, h 1394 Northwestern av (N I).
May Charles T, produce, E Mkt House, h s s Brookside av 2 w of Waverly av.
May Edward L, painter, 782 N Rural, h same.
May Frederick E, engr, h 37 Walcott.
May George E, lab, b 94 Mass av.
May Georgia, music teacher, 16 Blackford, h same.
May Henry, driver, h 69 N Judge Harding (W I).
May Henry H, drayman, h 290 E Merrill.
May Herman, butcher, h rear 1350 E Washington.

United States Life Insurance Co., of New York.
E. B. SWIFT, M'g'r. 25 E. Market St.

London Guarantee and A
Geo. W. Pangborn, Gen. Agent, 704-706 Lemcke

FRANK K. SAWYER, AGENT
74 East Market Street. Telephone 8.
onal Insurance Company
GERMANY. ORGANIZED 1845.

JOSEPH GARDNER
TIN, COPPER AND SHEET
IRON WORK AND
HOT AIR FURNACES
37, 39 & 41 KENTUCKY AVE. Teleph

Maurer George F, lab, h [illegible] (W I).
Maurer John, molder, h 12 [illegible]
Maurer Oscar C, clk A Kief[illegible] 33 W Vermont.
Maurer Wm, bricklyr, h [illegible] sey.
Maurice, see also Morris
Maurice Brother, teacher [illegible] and Short.
Maurice Charles J, plumber h [illegible]
Maurice George E, clk Hollw[illegible] 29 Fayette.
Maurice John N, shoemkr, h [illegible]
MAUS C BRANCH INDIANAPOLIS BREWING CO, Frederick [illegible] Mngr, n w cor New York and [illegible] Tel 221.
MAUS FRANK A, Pres Marion [illegible] Company, Crystal Ice Company, Indianapolis German Mutual Insurance Company, and Vice-[illegible] The C Habich Company, h [illegible] North, Tel 820.
Maus Magdalena (wid Casper) [illegible] New York.
Maus Mary A (wid Albert) h [illegible] York.
Maus Peter, lab, h e s Miami [illegible] poct.
Mauzy George, lab, b 32 S Judge H[illegible] (W I).
Mauzy Lorenzo R, jeweler, 7 M[illegible] N Alabama.
Mavity Charles K, reporter Th[illegible] News, b 862 N Delaware
Mavity L Anna (wid Wm K), h 862 N [Dela]ware.
Mavity Paul, student, b 862 N Delaw[are]
Mawby Jacob F, lab, b 1452 N Senate
Max Louis, pdlr, h 111 Eddy[illegible]
Maxey Albert, [illegible] h e s [illegible] of Belle.
Maxey Henry, [illegible]
Maxey James, [illegible]
Maxey Leonar[d] [illegible] b 74 Jones.
Maxey Lewis [illegible]

TINGS
DOW SHADES

Y & CO.
S and Loans.
• • •
rience, and claim
liable.
Lemcke Bldg.

. 115 S Illinois, h 87
Public School No 7,
phy, Hibben & Co, b
cher, 201 N Liberty,
chman, h 19 S Shade
e cor Gatling and
ld Michael), h 31 Wis-
The Indpls Stove Co,
sician, h 881 Milburn
mkr, b 881 Milburn (M
n s Prospect 3 e of

clk, b 475 Broadway.
tudent, h 138 E North.
ins, h 475 Broadway.
nisher, h 416 W Udell

h 871 Milburn (M P).
d Elisha), b 264 Huron.
wid Royal H), b 37 Gar-

mach, h 462 Jackson.
grocer, 552 W Udell (N
(N I).

N, Practical and Ex-
3 N Meridian, h 38 W
right bottom cor

iter, h 227 W 2d.
ab, h 163 Martindale av.
finisher, h 622 W Francis

bkkpr, r 11½ N Meridian.
lab, h 458 Jackson.
n D, clk, h 37 Garfield pl.
b, h 46 Atlas.
mach, h 164 Jackson.

EAT
ER BREAD
GROCER FOR IT.
IITZ BAKING CO.

ET CLEANING WORKS
PHONE No. 818

WILLIAM WIEGEL
MANUFACTURER OF....
SHOW CASES
6 W. Louisiana St.
Opposite Union Station.

CHARLES MAYER & CO.

IMPORTERS AND WHOLESALE DEALERS IN

Fancy Goods, Toys, Games,

DRUGGISTS', STATIONERS' AND GROCERS' SUNDRIES.

Fancy Glass, China and Bisque Ware, Silverware, Fancy Leather and Plush Goods, Jewelry, Fans, Umbrellas, Walking Canes, Traveling Satchels, Japanese Novelties, Musical Boxes, Musical Merchandise, Fancy Hardware, Pocket and Table Cutlery, Optical Goods, Bibles, Photo., Auto. and Scrap Albums, Masks and Masquerade Trimmings.

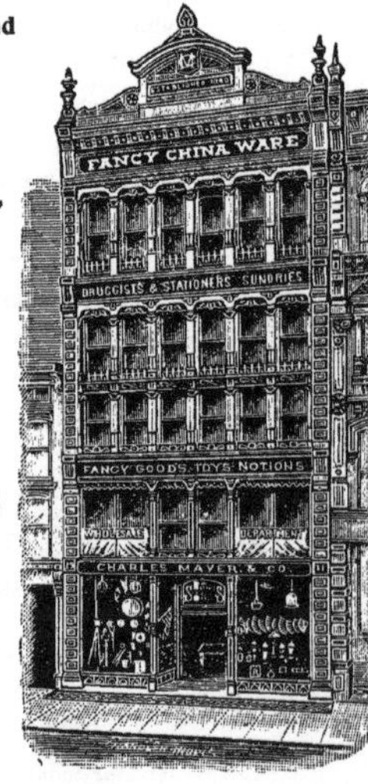

Fishing Tackle, Croquets, In and Out Door Games, Hammocks, Baseball Supplies and General Sporting Goods, Children's Carriages, Boy's Express Wagons, Doll Wagons, Velocipedes, Tricycles, Children's Chairs, Swings, Sleighs and Skates, Fireworks, Flags, Firecrackers, and FOURTH OF JULY NOVELTIES.

HOLIDAY GOODS A SPECIALTY.

Toys and Dolls an Immense Assortment,

29 and 31 W. WASHINGTON STREET,

Send for our Illustrated Catalogue of the various season goods.

Indianapolis, Ind.

WM. KOTTEMAN 89 & 91 E. Washington St. Telephone 1742 RUGS MATTINGS WINDOW SHADES

May John, engr, h 16 Singleton.
May John, lab, h 82 Muskingum al.
May John, lab, h 172 W Wabash.
May John A, lab, r 34 Howard.
May John W, lab, b 290 E Merrill.
May Joseph N, painter, r 27 W Pratt.
May Lawrence, tinner, h 204 Fletcher av.
May Louis, depot agt Adams Ex Co, h 140 Highland pl.
May Martin, reedwkr, b 249 Union.
May Melissa M, boarding 94 Mass av.
May Millard W, condr, h 32 Union.
May Pinkney J, condr, h 961 N Alabama.
May Richard C, mantel setter, b 266 Lincoln av.
May Robert H, plastr, 560 College av, h same.
May Solomon, lab, h 158 Hosbrook.
May Thomas J, lumber, h 160 S New Jersey.
May Wm W, insp, h 21 Agnes.
May Zota L, teacher, b 560 College av.
Mayberry Wm, porter, b 71 Yandes.
Mayer, see also Meier, Meyer, Mier and Myer.
Mayer Amelia dressmkr, 258 Charles, h same.
Mayer Carl F, clk Charles Mayer & Co, h 177 N Pine.
Mayer Catherine (wid Philip), h 33 Wisconsin.
Mayer Charles (Charles Mayer & Co), vice-pres A Kiefer Drug Co, h 770 N Meridian.
MAYER CHARLES & CO (Ferdinand L and Charles Mayer), Importers and Jobbers of Toys, Fancy Goods and Notions, 29-31 W Washington, Tel 84. (See adv opp.)
Mayer Cornelius, sec Insane Hospital, h 205 N Noble.
Mayer Daniel H, mach, b 19 Oriole.
Mayer David, foreman, h 82 Sullivan.
Mayer Edward C, mach, h 7 Iowa.
Mayer Elizabeth (wid Philip), b 858 S Meridian.
Mayer Esther, pawnbroker, 91 S Illinois, h 201 N Liberty.
Mayer Ferdinand L (Charles Mayer & Co), h 590 N Delaware.
Mayer Frank X, grocer, 861 S East, h same.
Mayer Frederick, clk Charles Mayer & Co, b 177 N Pine.
Mayer Frederick, trav agt, b rear 224 E Merrill.
Mayer George, mach hd, h 126 Elizabeth.
Mayer George J, mach, h 11 Barth av.
MAYER GEORGE J, Propr Capital Rubber Stamp Works, 15 S Meridian, Tel 1386; h 960 N Alabama. (See left bottom cor cards and p 5.)
Mayer George A B, teacher Public School No 1, b 205 N Noble.
Mayer Gottfried, mach hd, b 258 Charles.
Mayer Henry G, packer Pearson & Wetzel, h 114 Dunlop.
Mayer Jacob, cook, h 115 Hoyt av.
Mayer Jacob, soldier U S Arsenal.
Mayer Jacob M, trav agt, h 149 Bellefontaine.
Mayer John, cabtmkr, h 682 Chestnut.
Mayer John A, h 478 W Francis (N I).
Mayer John F, h 123 E St Joseph.
Mayer John F, salesman, h 701 S West.
Mayer John G, carp, b 19 Oriole.
Mayer Joseph, mngr, h 201 N Liberty.
Mayer Julius, trav agt, h 149 Bellefontaine.
Mayer Lee S, clk, h 1095 E Michigan.

THOS. C. DAY & CO.
Financial Agents and Loans.
We have the experience, and claim to be reliable.
Rooms 325 to 330 Lemcke Bldg.

Mayer Leopold, clothing, 115 S Illinois, h 87 N East.
Mayer Mina J, teacher Public School No 7, b 205 N Noble.
Mayer Otto C, clk Murphy, Hibben & Co, b 401 S Meridian.
Mayer Sadie, music teacher, 201 N Liberty, b same.
Mayer Samuel B, switchman, h 49 S Shade (B).
Mayer Thomas, lab, h n e cor Gatling and Sanford.
Mayer Wilhelmina (wid Michael), h 31 Wisconsin.
Mayer Xavier F, supt The Indpls Stove Co, h 327 S East.
Mayers Frank J, musician, h 881 Milburn (M P).
Mayers Wm M, cigarmkr, b 881 Milburn (M P).
Mayes Green, lab, h n s Prospect 3 e of Belt R R.
Mayfield Clifford H, clk, b 475 Broadway.
Mayfield Frank M, student, b 138 E North.
Mayfield Guilford E, ins, h 475 Broadway.
Mayhew Albert J, finisher, h 416 W Udell (N I).
Mayhew Asa, miller, h 871 Milburn (M P).
Mayhew Curney (wid Elisha), b 264 Huron.
Mayhew Fannie L (wid Royal H), b 37 Garfield pl.
Mayhew George W, mach, h 462 Jackson.
Mayhew Harry M, grocer, 552 W Udell (N I), h 578 W 22d (N I).
MAYHEW JAMES N, Practical and Expert Optician, 13 N Meridian, h 38 W St Clair. (See right bottom cor cards.)
Mayhew John, waiter, b 227 W 2d.
Mayhew John S, lab, h 163 Martindale av.
Mayhew Orlester, finisher, h 622 W Francis (N I).
Mayhew Oscar F, bkkpr, r 11½ N Meridian.
Mayhew Spencer, lab, h 458 Jackson.
Mayhew Waterman D, clk, h 37 Garfield pl.
Mayhew Wm E, lab, h 46 Atlas.
Mayhew Wm E, mach, h 164 Jackson.

EAT
QUAKER BREAD
ASK YOUR GROCER FOR IT.
THE HITZ BAKING CO.

WILLIAM WIEGEL MANUFACTURER OF.... SHOW CASES 6 W. Louisiana St. Opposite Union Station.

CARPETS AND RUGS RENOVATED.......... | CAPITAL STEAM CARPET CLEANING WORKS M. D. PLUNKETT, TELEPHONE No. 818

BENJ. BOOTH PRACTICAL EXPERT ACCOUNTANT. Complicated or disputed accounts investigated and adjusted. Room 18, 82½ E. Wash. St., Ind'p'l's, Ind.

THE SHERMAN RESTAURANT || 18 and 20 South Meridian Street KERSHNER BROS., Proprs.

ESTABLISHED 1876. TELEPHONE 168.
CHESTER BRADFORD,
SOLICITOR OF PATENTS,
AND COUNSEL IN PATENT CAUSES.
(See adv. page 6.)
Office:—Rooms 14 and 16 Hubbard Block, S.W. Cor. Washington and Meridian Streets, INDIANAPOLIS, INDIANA.

Mayhugh Isaac, engraver, b 188 Broadway.
Mayhugh Thomas G, clk Wagner Car Door Co, b 188 Broadway.
Maynard Frederick E, supt, h 27 Keith.
Maynard Jacob B, h 21 Lockerbie.
Maynard Thomas S, lab, h 75 Centennial.
Mayne Amanda M, teacher Public School No 23, r 15, 36 W Washington.
Mayne Catherine C (wid Matthew), h 92 Maple.
Mayo Abbie R (wid Edward H), h 562 N Penn.
Mayo John, waiter Hotel Oneida.
Mayo John H, porter, h 54 Davis.
MAYOR'S OFFICE, Thomas Taggart Mayor, Room 7 Basement Court House, Tel 874.
Mays Anthony, lab, h n s E Maryland 2 e of Oriental.
Mays Eva H, dresmkr, 1208 N Penn, b same.
Mays Frank, bell boy Hotel English.
Mays Isabella (wid Robert), h 186 Howard.
Mays Jennie (wid Wm D), h 213 W 2d.
Mays John, lab, b 34 Howard.
Mays Laura, h 9 Wood.
Mays Lovell, lab, r 171 E Court.
Mays Mary B (wid Elisha), h 232 N Noble.
Mays Samuel, lab, b n s E Maryland 2 e of Oriental.
Mays Susan (wid Wm), b 257 Prospect.
Mays Thomas R, lab, h 552 W Shoemaker (N I).
Mays Wm C (Bugg & Mays), b 276 E Court.
Mays Wm M, barber, b 190 N Missouri.
Maze Andrew J, lab, h 275 S Olive.
Maze George W, plater, h 195 S Olive.
Maze Harry E, polisher, h 61 Russell av.
Maze Robert L, letter carrier P O, b 173 E Market.
Maze Wm, produce, E Mkt House, h 163 Newman.
Mazelin Edward D, carp, 371 Blake, h same.
Mazo Benjamin (Lifschitz & Mazo), h 431 S Capitol av.
Mazurette Wm C, plumber, b 17 Tecumseh.
Meacham Wm, clk, h 144 Highland pl.
Mead Amelia H, stenog Gregory & Appel, r 155 N Illinois.

Metal Ceilings and all kinds of Copper, Tin and Sheet Iron work.
O. B. ENSEY,
TELEPHONE 1562.
CORNER 6TH AND ILLINOIS STS.

Mead Anna (wid John), h 18 Stevens.
Mead Anna (wid Louis), h 110 Sheffield av (H).
Mead Armstead, b 65 N Dorman.
Mead Charles, mach, r 152 W Washington.
Mead Charles H, lab, h 226 Coburn.
Mead Charles M, lab, h 94 Hillside av.
Mead Cornelius C (Mead & Adams), h 972 N Delaware.
Mead Edward B, carp, h 21 Short.
Mead Ella, laundress, h 18 Stevens.
Mead Elmer, lab, h 21 Short.
Mead James C, clk, b 94 Hillside av.
Mead Lucian D, carp, h 180 Davidson.
Mead Martha (wid Sampson), h 435 Superior.
Mead Michael, fireman, b 99 Lexington av.
Mead Oliver M P, carp, h 13 Arbor av (W I).
Mead Ormstead, h 63 N Dorman.
Mead Samuel, lab, h 295 Indiana av.
Mead Thaddeus W, agt, b 95 N Meridian.
Mead Wm A, lab, h 96 N Dorman.
Mead Wm R, lab, h 819 Mass av.
Mead Wm T, engr, h 304 E Georgia.
Mead Wm W, turner, b 94 Hillside av.
MEAD & ADAMS (Cornelius C Mead, Bert B Adams), Proprs Acme Steam Laundry, 13 N Illinois, Tel 696.
Meade Thomas F (Meade & McPadden), h 319 E Washington.
Meade & McPadden (Thomas F Meade, John McPadden), saloon, 319 E Washington.
Meadors Charles, lab, h n s Ohio 8 e of Rural.
Meadows Charles F, molder, b 239 W McCarty.
Meadows Charles S, shoes, 34 Pendleton av (B), h 50 S Stuart (B).
Meadows Frank, lab, h 23 Coburn.
Meadows Harry, molder, b 23 Coburn.
Meadows John S, city fireman, h 142 Blackford.
Meadows Wm H, carp, h 30 N West.
Meadows Zachariah, lab, h 230 W Chesapeake.
Meads Charlotta (wid Peter), h 282 Fulton.
Mealey Nellie J, h 40 The Windsor.
Means Abraham, coachman 280 N Delaware.
Means Albert F, engr, h 184 Lexington av.
Means Anderson W, agt Marion Brick Wks, h 1005 E Washington.
Means Barnett A, lab, h 37 Huron.
Means Charles H, carp, h 107 Decatur.
Means Clarence W (Means & Clarke), h 113 Brookside av.
Means Ellis D, agt, b 19 Harrison.
Means Mary J (wid Caleb), h 107 Brookside av.
Means Mary J (wid John), h 135 E North.
Means & Clarke (Clarence W Means, Charles B Clarke), lawyers, 2½ W Washington.
Meany Bridget J (wid John), h 458 E Georgia.
Meany Elizabeth, milliner, b 458 E Georgia.
Meany Josie C, milliner, 205 Virginia av, b 458 E Georgia.
Meany Mary J, b 458 E Georgia.
Meany Patrick H, lab, h 12 Eckert.
Meany Timothy F, engraver, b 458 E Georgia.
Mears Stephen, blksmith, h 345 Fletcher av.
Mears Thomas, boilermkr, b 345 Fletcher av.
Mears Wm, helper, b 345 Fletcher av.

TUTEWILER UNDERTAKER, No. 72 WEST MARKET STREET. TELEPHONE 216.

The Provident Life and Trust Co. Dividends are paid in cash and are not withheld for a long period of years, subject to forfeiture in the event of death or the termination of policy.
D. W. EDWARDS, GENERAL AGENT, 508 INDIANA TRUST BUILDING.

THEODORE F. SMITHER - GRAVEL ROOFING MATERIALS
2 and 3-Ply Ready Roofing Building Paper, etc. Best of Materials. Telephone 861. Office, 151 West Maryland St.

Measkill Leonard, baker, h 174 W 1st.
Meaux Solomon B, janitor, b 288 Bright.
Mechanics' Mutl Savings and Loan Assn No 2, George Raschig receiver, 36 Monument pl.
Mechanics' Mutl Savings and Loan Assns, Albert Rabb assignee, 61 Lombard bldg.
Meck, see also Mack.
Meck Charles W (Meck Transfer Co), h 47 Thalman av.
Meck Music Publishing Co, S Morris Meck mngr, 7 Monument pl.
Meck S Morris (Meck Transfer Co), r 252 N Senate av.
MECK TRANSFER CO (S Morris and Charles W Meck), Piano and Household Moving, Furniture Packing and Crating, 7 Monument Pl, Tel 335. (See adv in classified Transfer Companies.)
Mecum Bella F, collr M H Spades, b 140 Madison av.
Mecum Bennett, grocer, 369 S Delaware, h 140 Madison av.
Mecum John, stage hd, b 146 Madison av.
Medearis Charles W, trav agt, b 514 N New Jersey.
MEDEARIS FLETCHER C, Dealer in Watches, Diamonds and Jewelry, 11 N Penn, I O O F Building; Personal Attention to Repairing; b 514 N New Jersey.
Medearis Jefferson W, harnessmkr, 3 Cherry, h 514 N New Jersey.
Medema Peter, tmstr, h 11 Sylvan.
Medenwald Frederick M, mach, b 68 N Belmont av (H).
Medenwald Wm J, engr, h 68 N Belmont av (H).
Medert Amelia, teacher Public School No 9, b 128 N Noble.
Medert John, mngr, h s w cor Colorado and Ohio.
Medert Louis, clk R M S, h 101 N Beville av.
Medert Margaret (wid John A), h 128 N Noble.
Medias Charles, clothing, 160 Indiana av, h same.
MEDICAL COLLEGE OF INDIANA THE, Joseph W Marsee, M D, Dean, John H Oliver, M D, Treas, George J Cook, M D, Sec, n w cor Senate av and Market, Tel 443.
Medical Epitomist, Russell C Kelsey pub, 105 E Ohio.
Medical Free Press, Russell C Kelsey editor, 105 E Ohio.
Medium John, lab, b 9 Cleveland (H).
Medkirk Robert W, clk U S Pension Agency, h 218 E St Clair.
Medlam Wm O, brakeman, h 9 S Gillard av.
Medley Mayme, bkkpr, b 8 Indiana av.
Medlin George, lab, h 7 Sumner.
Medoff Frank, lab, r 32 N Senate av.
Medsker, see also Metzger and Mezger.
Medsker Irvin T, clk, b 72 Germania av (H).
Medsker John T, meats, 72 Germania av (H), h same.
Medsker Joseph, boilermkr, b 160 Sheldon.
Meehan Dennis, saloon, 168 E Washington, h 25 Dorman.
Meehan Edward H, trav agt, h 281 Spring.
Meehan Edward P, lab, h 334 E Michigan.
Meehan James, sawmkr, b 281 Spring.

THE WHEN IS A WORLD BEATER.

Meehan John F, phys, b 334 E Michigan.
Meehan Lena, stenog, b 47 Ruckle.
Meehan Michael, saloon, 159 W Washington, b 334 E Michigan.
Meek Clarence A, timekpr, b 547 Park av.
Meek David, tinner, h 335 Bicking.
Meek David M, clk, h 415 W Eugene (N I).
Meek Elmer B, caller, h 50 Warren.
Meek Florence A, music teacher, 547 Park av, b same.
Meek Florence M, stenog, b 547 Park av.
Meek Freeman A, clk, h 35 S Arsenal av.
Meek Herbert J, cabtmkr, h 19½ N Meridian.
Meek Jennie A (wid Edwin), b 297 River av (W I).
Meek John, lab, h 721 Chestnut.
Meek Lawrence S, lab, h 124 S Linden.
Meek Mary (wid Alonzo), r 28 Wyandot blk.
Meek Mary E, stenog Knight & Jillson, b 547 Park av.
Meek Nancy L (wid Jesse), b 241 N Alabama.
Meek Richard, painter, h 43 S Belmont av (W I).
Meek Robert A, clk, h 267 Fletcher av.
Meek Samuel B, lab, b 67 Nordyke av (W I).
Meeker Charles W, agt Hercules Powder Co, h 1060 E Michigan.
Meeker Curtis D, trav agt, h 65 Tacoma av.
Meeker Elizabeth J (wid Wm H), h 73 Park av.
Meeker John F, lab, h 267 Jefferson av.
Meeker Marshall, clk, h 59 E Merrill.
Meeker Wm A, cutter Kahn Tailoring Co, b 73 Park av.
Meenach Cynthia (wid Morris R), b 40 N Dorman.
Meenan Thomas, ironwkr, b 217 S Illinois.
Meenan Thomas jr, ironwkr, b 217 S Illinois.
Mees Gustav, mach hd, h 378 Coburn.
Mefford Albert B, hostler, b 725 Mass av.
Mefford Caroline C (wid Ashford L), h 298 Coburn.
Mefford Frederick R, mach hd, b 725 Mass av.
Mefford George, mach, b 93 N Gillard av.
Mefford James O, patrolman, h 169 Walcott.

The A. Burdsal Co.
Manufacturers of
STEAMBOAT COLORS
BEST HOUSE PAINTS MADE.
Wholesale and Retail.
34 AND 36 SOUTH MERIDIAN STREET.

Electric Contractors
We are prepared to do any kind of Electric Contract Work.
C. W. MEIKEL, Telephone 466.
96-98 E. New York St.

DALTON & MERRIFIELD { LUMBER South Noble St., near E. Washington

INDIANA ELECTROTYPE CO. BEST WORK. LOWEST PRICES. 23 WEST PEARL ST., INDIANAPOLIS, IND. JOB WORK. BOOK PLATES. All Orders Promptly Filled. BEST PATENT BASE ON THE MARKET.

KIRKHOFF BROS.,
Sanitary Plumbers
STEAM AND HOT WATER HEATING.
102-104 SOUTH PENNSYLVANIA ST.
TELEPHONE 910.

Mefford James W, molder, h 93 N Gillard av.
Mefford John J, engr, h 44 Ash.
Mefford Mary E (wid John J), h 725 Mass av.
Mefford Tilghman W, grocer, 200 Lexington av, h same.
Megel Balser M, clk Model Clothing Co, h 44 Eastern av.
Megel Benjamin, bartndr, b 22 Sanders.
Megel Jacob, driver, h 222 E Morris.
Megel Michael F, engr, b 22 Sanders.
Megel Regina (wid Peter), h 22 Sanders.
Meggs Thomas, lab, h 140 W 6th.
Meginniss, see also McGinnis.
Meginniss Earl C, stereotyper The Sun, b 175 Spann av.
Meginniss John W, jeweler, h 144 Hillside av.
Meginniss Nathaniel S, h 175 Spann av.
Meginniss Thomas J (Larsh & Meginniss), h 173 Newman.
Megrew Harold C, sec Masonic Mut Ben Soc, h 73 W Walnut.
Mehan Edward, mach, h 134 Newman.
Meharry Charles B, trav agt Murphy, Hibben & Co, b 600 Park av.
Meharry Frank T, trav agt The Home Stove Co, h 600 Park av.
Mehl Frederick A, millwright, h 324 W Merrill.
Mehring Luther, fertilizer mnfr, 810 S Meridian, h same.
Meid Frank, carp, h 142 S Summit.
Meier, see also Mayer, Maher, Maier, Meyer, Mier and Myer.
Meier Andrew, carp, h 219 Elizabeth.
Meier Andrew, clk, h 121 River av (W I).
Meier Anton F, carp, h 259 Shelby.
Meier Charles L, engr, h 440 E McCarty.
Meier Daniel, molder, b 219 Elizabeth.
Meier Elizabeth (wid Valentine), h 168 E Merrill.
Meier Frank, sawyer, b 168 E Merrill.
Meier Frank O, mach, h 72 Eastern av.
Meier Frederick C A, driver, h 9 Barth av.
Meier Harry C, plater, h 258½ E McCarty.
Meier Henry L, cutter, h 6 Arch.

Lime, Lath, Cement,
THE W. G. WASSON CO.
130 INDIANA AVE. TEL. 989.
Sewer Pipe, Flue Linings, Fire Brick, Fire Clay.

Meier Lewis (Lewis Meier & Co), h 3 Central av.
Meier Lewis jr, trav agt Lewis Meier & Co, b 3 Central av
MEIER LEWIS & CO (Lewis Meier, Louis F and Charles L Buschmann), Mnfrs of Pants, Overalls, Shirts and Duck Coats, 2-4 Central av and 192-200 Ft Wayne av, Tel 1213.
Meier Wm, driver, b 9 Barth av
Meier Wm, lab, b 258½ E McCarty.
Meier Wm F, lab, b 219 Elizabeth.
Meier Wm H, sec and treas The A Burdsal Co, h 121 E Michigan.
Meiere Frederick M, ins agt, h 71 Harlan.
Meighan Edward, lab, b 281 Spring.
Meigs Charles D, supt Indiana State Sunday-School Assn, h 61 Central av.
Meigs Mary L, h 409 N Penn.
Meigs Sarah T, music teacher, 409 N Penn, h same.
Meihe Charles, h 17 Birch av (W I).
Meikel, see also Michael.
Meikel Carrie, cashr, h 113 N Senate av.
MEIKEL CHARLES W, Plumber and Gas Fitter, Dealer in Gas and Electric Light Fixtures, Contractor for Electric Works, Electric Supplies and Repairs, 96-98 E New York, Tel 466; b Circle Park Hotel. (See right bottom lines.)
Meikel Edward, lab, r 253 Lincoln la.
Meikel Edward D, gasfitter, h 86 N State av.
Meikel Frederick J, floor walker, r 73 W Vermont.
Meikel George W, clk, r 73 W Vermont.
Meikle James S, lab, h 47 S West.
Meiks George H, student, r 55 Fletcher av.
Meimberg August F, supt bottling dept Indpls Brewing Co, h 261 E Morris.
Meimberg Frederick C, packer, b 157½ E Washington.
Meirim Adolph, b 174 Church.
Meisberger Joseph, lab, b 29 Lynn av (W I).
Meischke Charles, furnacewkr, h 92 Bright.
Meister Adolph G, carver, b 241 Kentucky av.
Meister Gustav, lab, h 88 Lincoln la.
Meister Oscar, pdlr, b 88 Lincoln la.
Meixner George, tinner, h e s Race 3 s of Raymond.
Meixner Max, cigarmkr, b 408 Excelsior av.
Meixner Theodore, cabtmkr, h 408 Excelsior av.
Melcher Emily (wid Henry), b 645 E Washington.
Melcher Frank T, treas Gibbs Cushioned Horseshoe Co, res Marion, Ind.
Melenz Otto, baker, b 412 S Meridian.
Melhorn Henry W, clk Am Ex Co, h 941 Ash.
Mellender Wm S, h 704 N Illinois.
Meller Ernst C, cabtmkr, b 390 S East.
Mellett Wm C, bartndr, r 259 E Vermont.
Mellinger Elizabeth A, seamstress, h 83 N Liberty.
Mellinger Theodore, painter, b cor Senate av and 27th.
Mellis John, lab, h 663 McLene (N I).
Mellon James H, clk, b 694 Madison av.
Mellon John, foreman, h 694 Madison av.
Mellon Robert, bricklyr, b 252 E Washington.
Mellon Walter, barber, 101 Patterson, b 694 Madison av.
Mellon Wm P, brakeman, h 152 Spann av.

YOUR HOMES FURNISHED BY W. H. MESSENGER 101 East Washington St. Telephone 491.

McNamara, Koster & Co. Phone 1593. ♦ 212-218 S. PENN. ST. } PATTERN MAKERS

Meloy Alfred O, molder, h 34 Bismarck av (H).
Meloy Henry C, switchman, h 28 Ashland (W I).
Melsheimer Timothy W, printer, h 29 Shriver av.
Melshimer Henry E, clk The Indpls Sentinel, r 225 N Senate av.
Melson George W, mngr California House, 184-186 S Illinois, h 189 S Illinois.
Melson Jennie, restaurant, 201 S Illinois, h 189 same.
Melton Martha E (wid Charles J), b 26 Beecher.
Melville Robert B, h 452 N West.
Melville Robert J, lab, h 245 W Maryland.
Melvin Anna, h 131 Allegheny.
Melvin John, lab, b 337 W Maryland.
Memering Casper, driver, b 247½ E Washington.
Menary Elizabeth C, nurse, 10 Wyandot blk, r same.
Mench Samuel W, agt, h 347 Columbia av.
Mendach John W, lab, h 117 Excelsior av.
Mendel Jacob, tailor, r 96 N Alabama.
Mendel Rachel (wid David), r 23½ W Washington.
MENDELL BROS (Joseph A and Wm H), Staple and Fancy Groceries, 250 W Michigan.
Mendell Charles D, painter, h 372 Cornell av.
Mendell Horatio S, fireman, b 162 Harrison.
Mendell John H, barber, 629 Madison av, h same.
Mendell Joseph A (Mendell Bros), h 250 W Michigan.
Mendell Joseph C, mach, 389 Virginia av, h same.
Mendell Nannie J, stenog Eli Lilly & Co, b 389 Virginia av.
Mendell Nettie F, bkkpr Mendell Bros, b 250 W Michigan.
Mendell Wm H (Mendell Bros), b 250 W Michigan.
Mendenhall Alice M, r 26 Cleaveland blk.
Mendenhall Alice V, sec Home Savings Assn, b 112 Park av.
Mendenhall Carl W, draughtsman S C Dark, h 1503 N Capitol av.
Mendenhall Charles W, clk, h 54 Park av.
Mendenhall Dennie J (Mendenhall, Howell & Trotter), h 425 Talbott av.
Mendenhall Elijah, phys, 184 W 3d, h same.
Mendenhall Frank F, student, h 136 Blackford.
MENDENHALL, HOWELL & TROTTER (Dennis J Mendenhall, Charles E Howell, Lemon H Trotter), Real Estate, Loans and Rentals, Room 4 Aetna Bldg, 19½ N Penn.
Mendenhall John B, agt, b 95 N Meridian.
Mendenhall John C (Hoosier Sweat Collar Co The), h 859 N Illinois.
Mendenhall Lemuel D, lab, h s w cor Grandview av and Florence (H).
Mendenhall Louis L, trav agt, r 5, 113 S Illinois.
Mendenhall Louise, h 28 W Pratt.
Mendenhall Mack, cook, r 18½ Indiana av.
Mendenhall Mary C (wid Henry W), b s e cor Walnut and Maxwell avs (I).
Mendenhall Mary R (wid Barton), b 1503 N Capitol av.
Mendenhall Melvina (wid Caleb), b 425 Talbott av.
Mendenhall Pearson, clk County Auditor, h 97 Cornell av.

Henry H. Fay, 40½ E. WASHINGTON ST., FIRE INSURANCE, REAL ESTATE, LOANS AND RENTAL AGENT.

Mendenhall Stacy E, clk Stubbins Hotel.
Mendenhall Wm C, grocer, 30 College av, h 68 Arch.
Mendenhall Wm E, druggist, b 1160 N Penn.
Menees Robert F, switchman, h 27½ N Beville av.
Menefee Austin A, molder, h 94 King av (H).
Menefee Edgar B, painter, b 170 John.
Menefee James A, painter, 170 John, h same.
Menefee James I, carp, h n w cor Tremont av and Emerich (H).
Menefee Lemuel, motorman, h 510 E 11th.
Menefee Richard L, molder, b n w cor Tremont av and Emrich (H).
Meng Elizabeth H, teacher, b 48 Jefferson av.
Meng George S, coppersmith, b 48 Jefferson av.
Meng John, florist, h 48 Jefferson av.
Menke, see Manke.
Menne John C, saloon, 406 S East, h 288 E Morris.
Mennebroeker Henry H, lab, h 798 Mass av.
Mennel John, tailor, h 24 Downey.
Menning Wm F, tailor, 121 Prospect, h 33 Harlan.
Menough Marion (wid Herman F), r 25 Ryan blk.
Mensenkamp Wm, h 62 Elm.
Menze Christian, cigarmkr, h 1700 Kenwood av.
Menze Ernst H, carp, h 239 English av.
Menzel Frederick, driver, h rear n w cor Cottage av and Wallack.
Menzel Herman, drayman, h 53 Davis.
Menzel Wm J, rec clk L E & W R R, h 19 Smithson.
Menzies James, mngr Nicoll The Tailor, h 1433 N Illinois.
Menzies Rudolph, painter, r 160 W Maryland.
Meo Antonio, fruits, 518 Virginia av and 91 E Mkt House, h 34 Valley.
Meo Rosa, h 33 Valley.
Meranda George A, condr, h 51 Temple av.

SURETY BONDS
American Bonding & Trust Co. OF BALTIMORE, MD.
Authorized to act as Sole Surety on all Bonds. Total Resources over $1,000,000.00.
W. E. BARTON & CO., General Agents, 504 Indiana Trust Building.
Long Distance Telephone 1918.

THE FRED DIETZ CO. WOODEN PACKING BOXES MADE TO ORDER FACTORY AND WAREHOUSE TRUCKS. Telephone 619 400 Madison Avenue.

Business World Supplied with Help GRADUATES ASSISTED TO POSITIONS 10,000 NOW IN GOOD SITUATIONS. TEL. 499. E. J. HEEB, PRES. Indianapolis BUSINESS UNIVERSITY

NEW YORK FILTER MFG. CO. Filters for Water-Works, Boiler Plants, Laundries, Hotels, Private Residences, Etc. | Henry R. Worthington, 64 S. Pennsylvania St. Long Distance Telephone 284.

UNION CO-OPERATIVE LAUNDRY (COMPOSED OF UNION LAUNDRY GIRLS.) NOS. 40 AND 42 VIRGINIA AVENUE. T. E. SOMERVILLE, MANAGER. TELEPHONE 19. INDIANAPOLIS, IND.

HORACE M. HADLEY
Insurance, Real Estate, Loan and Rental Agent
66 EAST MARKET STREET,
Telephone 1540. Basement.

Mercer Bros (Frank B and L Benjamin), printers, 22 Pembroke Arcade.
Mercer Clement V, contr, 46 Northwestern av, h same.
Mercer Edward R, mach hd, h 48 Arizona.
Mercer Frank B (Mercer Bros), r 285 Virginia av.
Mercer L Benjamin (Mercer Bros), r 285 Virginia av.
Mercer Mark H, engr, h 30 Traub av.
Mercer Samuel, marble setter, b 103 W South.
Mercer Wm R, contr, Hotel English, b same.
Merchant Police Headquarters, 10 Odd Fellow's blk, n e cor Washington and Penn.
MERCHANTS' DESPATCH TRANSPORTATION CO, Charles C Pierce Agt, 24 S Penn, Tel 723.
MERCHANTS' NATIONAL BANK THE, John P Frenzel Pres, Otto N Frenzel Vice-Pres and Cashier, Frederick Fahnley 2d Vice-Pres, Oscar F Frenzel Asst Cashier, s w cor Washington and Meridian, Tel 565.
MERCHANTS' AND MANUFACTURERS' EXCHANGE, Jacob E Takken Mngr, Collections and Commercial Reports, 19 Union Bldg, 63-73 W Maryland. (See left bottom cor cards.)
Meredith Albert E, sawmkr, h n w cor Broadway and 30th.
Meredith Charles, lab, b 228 W Market.
Meredith Edward H, sawmkr, h w s Broadway 2 n of 30th.
Meredith Emma S, photog, h 864 N Senate av.
Meredith Frank A, letter carrier P O, r 81½ W Market.
Meredith Franklin Rev, h 145½ Oliver av (W I).
Meredith Jane (wid Edward), h 864 N Senate av.
Meredith Joseph L, lab, h 228 W Market.
Meredith M Pearl, teacher Liberty Street Free Kindergarten, b 314 N East.

Special Detailed Reports Promptly Furnished by Us.
MERCHANTS' AND MANUFACTURERS' EXCHANGE
J. E. TAKKEN, Manager,
19 Union Building, 73 West Maryland Street.

Meredith Noah E, blksmith, 413 Chestnut, h 414 S Delaware.
Meredith Peter N, tmstr, h 529 W Washington.
Meredith Richard O, grocer, 291 W North, h 476 N West.
Meredith Samuel C, b 1033 N Capitol av.
Meredith Stephen, lab, h 43 Helen.
Meredith Wm, carp, h 22 N William (W I).
Mericle George W, engr, h 277 Fletcher av.
Mericle James E, engr, h 281 Fletcher av.
MERIDIAN LIFE AND TRUST COMPANY, James B Crawford Pres, Charles C Pierce Jr Vice-Pres and Mngr, Marcus A Jillson Treas, Andrew R Warren Sec, 432 Lemcke Bldg. (See adv opp.)
MERIDIAN STABLES, Cooper & Wood Proprs, 114-116 N Meridian, Tel 1502. (See adv in classified Livery, Boarding and Sale Stables.)
MERIDIAN STREET M E CHURCH, Rev Charles N Sims, D D, Pastor, s w cor New York and Meridian.
Meriwether John E, r 6 State House.
Merkle Charles, chemist, b 100 Pierce.
Merkle Frank, barber, b 800 S East.
Merkle George, blksmith, h 100 Pierce.
Merkle John, molder, h 792 S East.
Merkle Peter & Son, Charles G Cramer mngr, restaurant, Union Station.
Merkt August, saloon, 201 Mass av, h same.
Merkt John, bartndr, b 255 Blake.
Merkt Martin, saloon, 255 Blake, h same.
Merl Frank, clk, b 541 E Market.
Merl John R, printer, b 541 E Market.
Merl Matthias, printer, b 541 E Market.
Merl Nicholas, h 541 E Market.
Merrick John F, bartndr, b 432 National rd.
Merrick Patrick T, city foreman, b 432 National rd.
Merrick Paul, clk, h 442 E St Clair.
Merrick Richard, saloon, 432 National rd, h same.
Merrifield Charles E (Dalton & Merrifield), pres Guarantee Sav and Inv Assn, h 373 Broadway.
Merrill Carrie E, teacher Public School No 36, res Broad Ripple, Ind.
Merrill Catherine, h 227 N Capitol av.
Merrill Charles W, treas The Bowen-Merrill Co, h 581 N Illinois.
Merrill Cuyler J, painter, h 186 E St Joseph.
Merrill Edward M, lab, h 402 Jackson.
Merrill Edward S, clk, r 83 E North.
Merrill Isabella (wid Charles L), h 176 N East.
Merrill James, grinder, b 336½ E Washington.
Merrill Margaret (wid Absalom), h rear 179 N California.
Merrill Matilda F (wid Jefferson), h n s Brookside av 4 e of Orange av.
Merrill Samuel, lather, b 116 Clinton.
Merrill Wm J, clk, r 84 E North.
Merriman Edward F, r 249½ W Washington.
Merriman Horace, reedwkr, b 29 Madison av.
Merriman Rose (wid Charles F), h 11 E New York.
Merritt Frank W, cook, r 306 S Meridian.
Merritt George (George Merritt & Co), h 172 N West.

CLEMENS VONNEGUT 184, 186 and 192 E. Washington St. | CABINET HARDWARE CARVERS' TOOLS. Glues of all kinds.

The Meridian Life and Trust ....Company

ISSUES DEFINITE CONTRACTS FOR

Insurance at Natural Premium Rates and Savings and Loan Investments

Offers to borrowers all the privileges and benefits of Building Association and Life Insurance at one cost. Home Builders may thus secure their families against loss of property or savings by reason of death.

Certificates have a par value of $100 and provide for a monthly installment of fifty cents each; they are guaranteed to mature in 120 months but may be surrendered at any time with earnings up to last semi-annual dividend period.

High Grade Securities, Bonds and Mortgages
. . Bought and Sold . .

Straight Life, Accident and Accumulation Policies.

CHAS. C. PIERCE, JR., Vice-President and Manager,
FRANK D. HARGER, Secretary.

432 LEMCKE BUILDING.

THE WM. H. BLOCK CO.
DRY GOODS,
MILLINERY, CLOAKS AND FURS

HEADQUARTERS
PHOTOGRAPHIC OUTFITS
AMATEUR OR PROFESSIONAL
THE H. LIEBER COMPANY

INDIANAPOLIS STEEL ROOFING AND CORRUGATING WORKS,
23 and 25 East South Street.
S. D. NOEL, Proprietor.

DOWN.
Best Wheels.
WHEELMEN'S CO.

PRESSLER,
FRESCO PAINTER

David . McKernan
REAL ESTATE AND LOANS
THORPE BLOCK

THE WM. H. BLOCK CO. DRY GOODS, MILLINERY, CLOAKS AND FURS.
7 AND 9 EAST WASHINGTON STREET.

MERRITT GEORGE & CO (George and Worth Merritt), Woolen Mnfrs and Wool Dealers, 411 W Washington, Tel 607.
Merritt Jane, h 557 W Washington.
Merritt John, lab, b 616 Home av.
Merritt John E (Merritt & Elstun), h 485 E 9th.
Merritt Quash, lab, h e s Caroline av 1 n of Jennison.
Merritt Robert N (Robert Merritt & Co), h 450 Park av.
MERRITT ROBERT & CO (Robert N and Thomas Merritt), Genl Agts Mutual Life Insurance Co of New York, 6 Lombard Bldg, Tel 1761.
Merritt Susan, dressmkr, 118 W Vermont, h same.
Merritt Thomas (Robert Merritt & Co), res Toronto, Can.
Merritt Wm H, paperhngr, h 94 Newman.
Merritt Worth (George Merritt & Co), h 300 W New York.
Merritt & Elstun (John E Merritt, Horace H Elstun), dyers, 132 Mass av.
Merrity Richard, lab, r 24 Millard.
Merriweather Cameron, porter, b 61½ Superior.
Merriweather Wm H, lab, h 226½ Muskingum al.
Mershon Robert A, lineman, h rear 150 Madison av.
Mertz Frank W, mach hd, b 236 S West.
Mertz Frederick, cooper, b 236 S West.
Mertz Gustav, lab, b 29 Nebraska.
Mertz Hobart, h 309 English av.
Mertz Louis, polisher, b 236 S West.
Mertz Mary A, h 209 Blake.
Mertz Philip, driver, h 39 Ellsworth.
Mertz Rebecca (wid Matthias), h 236 S West.
Mertz Susan, h 15 Drake.
Merwin John, sawmkr, h 220 E Merrill.
Merwin John C, bkkpr, h 102 Johnson av.
Merz Charles, cabtmkr, h e s Zwingley 2 s of Bethel av.
Merz Charles H, shoes, 587 S Meridian, h 68 Kansas.
Merz David, meats, 401 S Meridian, h same.
MERZ FREDERICK, Insurance and Special Agt Hanover Insurance Co, 208-210 Indiana Trust Bldg, Tel 1486; h 439 S East.
Merz Frederick jr, clk George J Marott, b 439 S East.
Merz Jacob L, mngr George J Marott, h 352 Bellefontaine.
Merz John E, electrician, h 97 Oriole.
Merz John J, draper H P Wasson & Co.
Mescall Michael J, tailor, 10½ N Delaware, h 224 Randolph.
Mesker Benjamin F, agt Mass Av Depot, h 10 Woodruff av.
Mesker Edward W, agt C C C & St L Ry b 705 Chestnut.
Merz John U, draper H P Wasson & Co. h 705 Chestnut.
Merz Sophia (wid Louis), h 97 Oriole.
Mescall Catherine A, teacher, b 14 S Brightwood av (B).
Mescall James, boilermkr, b 952 W Vermont.
Mescall James J, lab, h 118 Newman.
Mescall John, lab, h 89 Newman.
Mescall John J, boilermkr, h 170 N Dorman.
Mescall Mary A (wid Joseph), h 14 S Brightwood av (B).

Mescall Mary C, teacher, b 14 S Brightwood av (B).
(B), h 14 Woodruff av.
Meskill Catherine (wid James), h 230 Fayette.
Meskill David J, uphlr, b 230 Fayette.
Meskill Elizabeth, teacher Public School No 11, b 523 N Capitol av.
Meskill James P, painter, h 178 W 2d.
Meskill James W, baker, b 230 Fayette.
Meskill Leonard, baker, h 174 W 1st.
Meskill Michael, molder, b 230 Fayette.
Meskill Patrick, painter, h 178 W 2d.
Meskill Wm D, bookbndr, h 523 N Capitol av.
Mesle Francis J, foreman Wm H Armstrong & Co, h e s Penn 1 n of Fall creek.
Mesler Charlotte, cashr Spear & Co, b 288 N Capitol av.
Mesler John, clk, h 288 N Capitol av.
Messenger Anna M, b 171 E Vermont.
MESSENGER W HORNDON, Furniture, Carpets, Stoves, Crockery, 101 E Washington and 13, 15 and 17 S Delaware, Tel 491; h 197 N Alabama. (See left bottom lines.)
Messer Frank, engr, h 29 Catherine.
Messersmith George B, lab, h 15 S Stuart (B).
Messersmith George W, caller, h 12 S Station (B).
Messersmith Robert, lab, r 244½ W Washington.
Messersmith Wm P, clk C C C & St L Ry, h 24 N Station (B).
Messham Edward P, modelmkr, h 120 Cornell av.
Messick Edward N, spl agt G W Pangborn, b 282 W New York.
Messick Jesse H, trav agt, h 249 Talbott av.
Messick John F, vice-pres Daggett & Co, h 159 East Drive (W P).
Messick John W, motorman, h 1009 N Senate av.
Messick Joseph, carp, r 148 W Maryland.
Messick Samuel W, driver, r rear 486 Central av.
Messick Thomas B, h 282 W New York.

GUIDO R. PRESSLER,
FRESCO PAINTER
Churches, Theaters, Public Buildings, Etc., A Specialty.
Residence, No. 325 North Liberty Street.
INDIANAPOLIS, IND.

INDIANAPOLIS STEEL ROOFING AND CORRUGATING WORKS, 23 and 25 East South Street. S. D. NOEL, Proprietor.

David S. McKernan REAL ESTATE AND LOANS
Houses, Lots, Farms and Western Lands for sale or trade.
ROOMS 2-5 THORPE BLOCK.

DIAMOND WALL PLASTER { Telephone 1410 BUILDERS' EXCHANGE.

Cor. E. Ohio St. and C., C., C. & St. L. R'y Tracks. ISSUE NEGOTIABLE RECEIPTS ON MERCHANDISE AND HOUSEHOLD GOODS. UNION TRANSFER AND STORAGE CO.

W. McWORKMAN,
ROOFING AND CORNICE WORKS,
930 W. Washington St. Tel. 1118.

Messick Wm T, h 447 College av.
Messing Abraham L, clk Slatts & Poe, b 285 N Delaware.
Messing Albert, lab, r 91½ E Court.
Messing Mayer Rev, rabbi Indpls Hebrew Congregation, h 285 N Delaware.
Messing Samuel, clk People's Outfitting Co, b 285 N Delaware.
Messmer Otto, brewer, b 180 E McCarty.
Messmore Jacob B, clk, r 256 N Noble.
Messner George, engr, h 236 Dougherty.
Messner Simon, b 236 Dougherty.
Metallic Manufacturing Co, Glenn G Howe pres, Wm L Higgins vice-pres, Frank Holt sec, Horace E Kinney treas, machs, 952 N New Jersey.
Metcalf Alberti C (Johnson & Metcalf), h 953 N Penn.
Metcalf Arthur B, adjuster Wyckoff, Seamans & Benedict, b 121 N Capitol av.
Metcalf Arthur B, clk, b 495 N Senate av.
Metcalf Clara G (wid Jesse), b 140 W Vermont.
Metcalf George W, carp, h 495 N Senate av.
Metcalf H Percy, piano tuner, b 448 College av.
Metcalf Kate (Ransford & Metcalf), b 1022 N Senate av.
Metcalf Mary S (wid Henry W), h 448 College av.
Metcalf Mollie (wid Charles N), r 221 N Capitol av.
Metcalf Wm H, carp, b 495 N Senate av.
Metcalfe Elenora M (wid Wm), b 517 W Highland av (N I).
Meth Charles F, solr The Snow-Church Co, r 87 N Capitol av.
Metivier Edward R, painter, b 150½ College av.
Metivier Josephine, milliner, b 150½ College av.
METROPOLITAN CYCLE CO, Samuel L Pattison Pres, John A Wilde Mngr, Bicycles, 108 Mass av. (See adv in classified Bicycle Dealers.)
METROPOLITAN LIFE INSURANCE CO OF NEW YORK, Richard D Hughes Supt, 75, 76, 77 and 80 Baldwin Blk.

GEO. J. MAYER,
MANUFACTURER OF
SEALS
STENCILS, RUBBER STAMPS, CHECKS, BADGES, DOOR PLATES, ETC.
15 S. Meridian St., Ground Floor. TEL. 1386.

Metropolitan School of Music, Franz X Arens pres, Flora M Hunter vice-pres and treas, Oliver W Pierce sec, 134 N Illinois.
Metsker Flora J (wid Henry), h 63 Peru av.
Mette Wm F, lab, b 48 S Brightwood av (B).
Mettee Hattie G, stenog H T Conde Implt Co, b 1102 N Delaware.
Metten Frank A, blksmith, h 183 N Arsenal av.
Metten Samuel A, carp, b 183 N Arsenal av.
Mettler Eugene G, supt Indpls Light and Power Co, b 299 E Merrill.
Mettler Robert H, trainer, b 299 E Merrill.
Metz Frederick H, clk, h 89 Division (W I).
Metz John, shoes, 405 Madison av, h same.
Metz Joseph, lab, r 433 W New York.
Metz Nicholas, carp, r 433 W New York.
Metzendorf Henry, gilder, h 120 Laurel.
Metzger, see also Medsker and Mezger.
METZGER ALBERT E (A Metzger Agency), Real Estate, 5 Odd Fellows' Hall, Tel 224; h 496 N Capitol av.
METZGER A AGENCY (Harry A and Albert E), Real Estate, Insurance, Loans and Steamship Agency, 5 Odd Fellows' Hall, Tel 224. (See left bottom lines.)
Metzger Benjamin, finisher, b 283 Highland av.
Metzger Bernhard, tinner, h 283 Highland av.
Metzger Carl, huckster, h 262 S Olive.
Metzger Conrad, shoes, 610 Virginia av, b 114 Buchanan.
Metzger Enoch, bricklyr, h 5 Bell.
Metzger Frank B, lumber, 36 Michigan av, h same.
Metzger George, mach, b 283 Highland av.
Metzger George D, bricklyr, b 5 Bell.
Metzger Grace, stenog U S Baking Co, b 23 Ft Wayne av.
METZGER HARRY A (A Metzger Agency), Insurance, 5 Odd Fellows' Hall, Tel 224; h 985 N Penn.
Metzger Isaac N, driver, h 812 LaSalle.
Metzger Jacob, h 301 N Capitol av.
METZGER JACOB & CO (Frederick C Wellmann), Bottlers and Dealers in Foreign and Domestic Beers, Whiskies, Wines, Porter, Mineral Waters, Champagne and Brewers of Weiss Beer; Fountains Charged; 30-32 E Maryland, Tel 407.
Metzger John, carp, h 687 Mass av.
Metzger John, lab, h 238 Lincoln la.
Metzger John, painter, r 19 S Senate av
Metzger John G, pressman, h 3 Camp.
Metzger John M, messenger Am Ex Co, h 23 Fletcher av.
Metzger Louis J, b 652 N Capitol av.
Metzger Newton, driver, h 815 LaSalle (M P).
Metzger Robert, trav agt, h 516 Dillon.
Metzger Wm F T, bricklyr, b 5 Bell.
Metzger Wilhelmina (wid Alexander), h 652 N Capitol av.
Metzler Adam E, driver, b 342 N West.
Metzler Charles E, bartndr, r 186 N Senate av.
Metzler Clarence E, lab, b 475 E St Clair.
Metzler Edward, lab, b 342 N West.
Metzler Ella, nurse, 197 N Delaware, b same.

A. METZGER AGENCY ESTABLISHED 1863. REAL ESTATE

LAMBERT GAS & GASOLINE ENGINE CO.
ANDERSON, IND. GAS AND GASOLINE ENGINES, 2 TO 50 H. P.

Metzler Jacob, grocer, 895 S Meridian, h same.
Metzler Jacob, molder, h 57 Holmes av (H).
Metzler John, h 81 N New Jersey.
Metzler John F, baker, h 285 Jefferson av.
Metzler Mary A (wid Jacob), h 342 N West.
Metzler Samuel N, phys, 7 Stewart pl, h 86 W 2d.
Metzner Emil, engraver, h 146 Central av.
Metzner Emma A, German teacher Public School No 1, b 146 Central av.
Metzner Frieda H, teacher Public School No 33, b 146 Central av.
Meunster Otto, molder, h 458 W 1st.
Meurer Albert C, capt H and L Co No 4, h 219 Virginia av.
Meuser John R, pork packer, 292 W Ray, h 385 S Meridian.
Meuser Mayme L, stenog Johnson & Metcalf, b 385 S Meridian.
Meuser Robert J, butcher, b 385 S Meridian.
Mewhinney Edward P, carver, b 126½ Newman.
Mewhinney George, cooper, h 126½ Newman.
Meyer, see also Mayer, Meier and Myer.
Meyer Adolph J (A J Meyer & Co), h 224 E Walnut.
Meyer Albert F, foreman Indpls M & C Union, h 153 Woodlawn av.
Meyer August B (A B Meyer & Co and Charles F Meyer & Bro), h 779 N Illinois.
Meyer August C, clk, h 726 S East.
MEYER A B & CO (August B and Charles F Meyer), Coal, Lime and Cement, 15-17 N Penn, Tel 516; Yards 450 N Senate av and 501 E Michigan.
Meyer A J & Co (Adolph J Meyer), real est, 33 Lombard bldg.
Meyer Bartholomew, blksmith, h 242 N Belmont av (H).
Meyer Bernhard J, cabtmkr, h 137 Church.
Meyer Bertha, b 900 Madison av.
Meyer Bros (Louis and Leo), chewing gum, 5 Pembroke Arcade.
Meyer Catherine (wid George F), h 325 N Delaware.
Meyer Charles, cabtmkr, b 137 Church.
Meyer Charles A, clk, b 656 N Alabama.
Meyer Charles A, salesman D H Baldwin & Co, b 30 W Walnut.
Meyer Charles C, carp, b 230 Davidson.
Meyer Charles F (A B Meyer & Co and Charles F Meyer & Bro), h 323 N Delaware.
Meyer Charles F, driver, b 98 Davidson.
Meyer Charles F & Bro (Charles F and August B), cigars, 15 N Penn and 30 W Washington.
Meyer Charles G, lab, h 309 English av.
Meyer Charles W, carp, 228 Elizabeth, h same.
Meyer Christian F G (C F G Meyer & Son), h 318 N Delaware.
Meyer Christian L, carp, h 98 Davidson.
Meyer Christina M (wid Frederick), h 128 Michigan av.
Meyer C F G & Son (Christian F G and Wm H), real est, 55 Baldwin blk.
Meyer Edmund L, clk, b 81 Highland av.
Meyer Edward A, clk The Gordon-Kurtz Co, h 438 S New Jersey.
Meyer Edward F, baker Parrott & Taggart, h 240 Union.
Meyer Edward H, mngr Paragon Safety Oil Co, h 163 E St Joseph.
Meyer Eleanor C (wid Charles F), h 81 Highland av.

Farm and City Loans
25 Years' Successful Business.
THOS. C. DAY & CO,
Rooms 325 to 330 Lemcke Building.

Meyer Ellen M C (wid Frederick W), h 158 Union.
Meyer Elmer U, clk, h 629 Park av.
Meyer Ernest C, barber, b 111 Greer.
Meyer Ernst R L, printer, h 154 Chestnut.
Meyer Eugene J, cook, b 547 E Vermont.
Meyer Ferdinand, barber, 834½ S Meridian, h same.
Meyer Frank, lab, b 60 Holmes (H).
Meyer Frank H, bartndr, h 479 Union.
Meyer Frank J, driver, h 146 Dougherty.
Meyer Frederick, carp, h 92 Shelby.
Meyer Frederick, finisher, h 43 Evison.
Meyer Frederick, mach hd, h 122½ N Pine.
Meyer Frederick A, saloon, 400 S Meridian, h 570 same.
Meyer Frederick C, molder, b 128 Michigan av.
Meyer Frederick G, b 192 Prospect.
Meyer Frederick H, carp, h 4 Hermann.
Meyer Frederick H, lab, b 111 Orange.
Meyer Frederick J (F J Meyer & Co), h 99 Greer.
Meyer F J & Co (Frederick J Meyer, Harry E Buddenbaum), general store, 408 S East.
Meyer George, molder, b 225 Elizabeth.
Meyer Frederick J (F J Meyer & Co), h 99 Greer.
Meyer George, sawmkr, h 108 W Ray.
Meyer George F, bkkpr A B Meyer & Co, h 656 N Alabama.
Meyer George H, bartndr, h 25 E Ray.
Meyer George J, driver, r 199 S Illinois.
Meyer George W L, h 679 S East.
Meyer Gustav, driver, h 495 S New Jersey.
Meyer Gustav J T, saloon, 74 S Delaware, h same.
Meyer Harmon, lab, b 270 E Merrill.
Meyer Harry, b 108 W Ray.
Meyer Harry, finisher, b 931 Mass av.
Meyer Henry, lab, b 480 S West.
Meyer Henry, real est, 219-220 Lemcke bldg, h 629 Park av.
Meyer Henry, saloon, 250 Highland av, h same.
Meyer Henry, tailor, h 637 Madison av.
Meyer Henry A, car rep, h 29 S Harriet (B).

EAT
HITZ'S CRACKERS
AND CAKES.
ASK YOUR GROCER FOR THEM.

BICYCLES $5 MONTHLY. Best Best Terms. WHEELMEN'S CO. 31 W. OHIO ST. LONG DISTANCE TEL. 1855.

J. H. TECKENBROCK  Painter and Decorator, 94 EAST SOUTH STREET.

FIDELITY MUTUAL LIFE—PHILADELPHIA, PA.
MATCHLESS SECURITY At LOW COST. A. H. COLLINS General Agent Baldwin Block.

Rooms 42 and 43 WHEN BUILDING.
Miners and Shippers Steam and Domestic Coal.
Edwardsport Coal & Mining Co.

ESTABLISHED 1876. TELEPHONE 168.
CHESTER BRADFORD,
SOLICITOR OF PATENTS,
AND COUNSEL IN PATENT CAUSES.
(See adv. page 6.)
Office:—Rooms 14 and 16 Hubbard Block, S. W. Cor. Washington and Meridian Streets, INDIANAPOLIS, INDIANA.

Meyer Henry B, painter, 365 Virginia av, h same.
Meyer Henry F, clk, h 664 Charles.
Meyer Henry F, clk, h 133 S Linden.
Meyer Henry F W, driver Paul H Krauss, b 158 Union.
Meyer Henry H, baker, h 227 Shelby.
Meyer Henry J, drayman, h 373 S Meridian.
Meyer Henry J, porter Murphy, Hibben & Co, h 85 Shelby.
Meyer Henry J, shoemkr, h 206 N Pine.
Meyer Herman, boilermkr, h 406 N Brookside av.
Meyer Herman H, carp, 220 N Pine, h same.
MEYER ISAAC, Mngr The Wm H Block Co, b The Denison.
Meyer Jacob M, stone cutter, h 226 Elizabeth.
Meyer John, mach hd, r 104 S Noble.
Meyer John F, watchman, h 18 Wyoming.
Meyer John H, saloon, 423 S Delaware, h 121 E McCarty.
Meyer John M, driver, h s s Lawrence 2 w of Hazel.
Meyer John P C, cigar mnfr, 86 N Illinois, h 173 W New York.
Meyer Leo (Meyer Bros), h 206 N Noble.
Meyer Louis (Meyer Bros), h 173 N East.
Meyer Louis, printer, h 154 Chestnut.
Meyer Louis C, helper, b 98 Davidson.
Meyer Louis H, turner, h 38 Elm.
Meyer Louis H C W, tailor, b 158 Union.
Meyer Louis W, mach hd, b 126 Michigan av.
Meyer Louisa (wid John F W), h 651 S Meridian.
Meyer Margaret, h rear 279 Davidson.
Meyer Margaret (wid Henry), h 931 Mass av.
Meyer Martin F, collr County Treasurer, h 805 N Alabama.
Meyer Matthew, lab, b rear 71 Maple.
Meyer Maximillian, lab, h 480 S West.
Meyer Michael, carp, h 225 Elizabeth.
Meyer Michael, mason, h 14 Mill.
Meyer Minnie (wid Wilhelm), h 245½ E Washington.

Outing BICYCLES
$85.00.
MADE AND SOLD BY
HAY & WILLITS MFG. CO.
76 N. PENNSYLVANIA ST. PHONE 598.

Meyer Otto C, baker Parrott & Taggart, h 103 Weghorst.
Meyer Peter, lab, b 863 S Meridian.
Meyer Rose (wid Matthew), h rear 71 Maple.
Meyer Solomon (Meyer & Kiser), h 152 N East.
Meyer Solomon, bkkpr, h 393 S Delaware.
Meyer Theodore, h 900 Madison av.
Meyer Theodore, cigar mnfr, 28 Minnesota, h same.
Meyer Theodore jr, salesman, h 55 Gresham.
Meyer Will H, creamery, 426 Virginia av, h same.
Meyer Wm, carp, h n s Lily 1 w of Rural.
Meyer Wm A, mach hd, b 355 S Capitol av.
Meyer Wm C, beveler, b 126 Michigan av.
Meyer Wm C, mach, h 126 Michigan av.
Meyer Wm C, porter, b 60½ S Delaware.
Meyer Wm C, watchman, h e s Sherman Drive 1 n of Washington.
Meyer Wm F, cabtmkr, 45 Mass av, r same.
Meyer Wm F C, mach hd, b 98 Davidson.
Meyer Wm H (C F G Meyer & Son), b 318 N Delaware.
Meyer Wm L, mach, b 128 Michigan av.
MEYER & KISER (Solomon Meyer, Solomon S Kiser), Real Estate and Insurance, 306 Indiana Trust Bldg.
Meyerpeter Robert H, h 140 W 11th.
Meyers, see also Miers and Myers.
Meyers Albert B, baggageman, h 31 Mulberry.
Meyers Alice (wid Frank), h 215 Bright.
Meyers Amanda (wid Frank A), h 11 Concordia.
Meyers Augustus, carp, h 22 Poplar (B).
Meyers Belle, cook City Hospital.
Meyers Bros (Flavious J and Morris H), grocers, 419 Indiana av.
Meyers Celia (wid John), h 186 W 2d.
Meyers Charles F, helper, b 11 Concordia.
Meyers Elmer I, brickmkr, b 480 W 22d (N I).
Meyers Emmett, ironwkr, r 218 E Market.
Meyers Flavious J (Meyers Bros), supt County Poor Farm, h same.
Meyers Frank, brakeman, b 92 Oliver av (W I).
Meyers Frank, brakeman, b 1100 W Washington (H).
Meyers Frederick W, mach, h 499 Martindale av.
Meyers George J, fireman, b 11 Concordia.
Meyers Henry J, lab, b 5 Grove.
Meyers Jacob C, carp, h n w cor Floral and Schurman avs (M P).
Meyers Jacob W, plumber, h 840 S Meridian.
Meyers Jennie (wid Wm), h 27½ Virginia av.
Meyers John, brickmkr, h 480 W 22d (N I).
Meyers John, waiter, r 218 E Market.
Meyers Mary (wid Herman), h 5 Grove.
Meyers Morris H (Meyers Bros), h 2 Dexter (N I).
Meyers Peter, pdlr, h 121 Rhode Island.
Meyers Wm, mach opr The Sun, b 381 Bellefontaine.
Meyers Wm H, lab, h 135 Geisendorff.
Meyrose Wm, brakeman, b 124 English av.
Mezger, see also Medsker and Metzger.
Mezger Catherine (wid David), h 610 Chestnut.
Mezger Eugene C, finisher, b 610 Chestnut.
Mezger Frank, mach, h 610 Chestnut.
Mezger Joseph W, finisher, b 366 S Alabama.
Miars George E, lab, r 167 E Vermont.

C. ZIMMERMAN & SONS SLATE AND GRAVEL ROOFERS 19 South East Street.

DRIVEN WELLS And Second Water Wells and Pumps of all kinds at CHARLES KRAUSS', 42 S. PENN. ST. TELEPHONE 465.

MICA ROOFING CO (Wm H H and Eversley Childs), P C Reilly Genl Mngr, Mnfrs and Dealers in Roofing Material and Coal Tar Products, Works s w cor Belt R R and Summit (H), Tel 1447.
Miceli Rasario, fruits, 95 E Mkt House, r 41 Virginia av.
Miceli Salvadore, fruits, 81 E Mkt House, h 56 S Alabama.
Michael Charles W, student, h 331 S Penn.
MICHAEL CLARA (wid John), Dry Goods, Notions, Staple and Fancy Groceries, 450 S Delaware, h same.
Michael David, h 927 Mass av.
Michael Josephine (wid Joseph), h 245½ E Washington.
Michael Lorie L, engr, h 83 N Gillard av.
Michael Theodore R, cabtmkr, h 119 Gillard av.
Michaelis Ernest, hatter, h 96 Maple.
Michaelis Florebert, carp, 230 E Merrill, h same.
Michaelis John, carp, h 626 N Capitol av.
Michaelis John B, b 626 N Capitol av.
Michaelis Joseph M, carp, b 281 S New Jersey.
Michaelis Morris, clk, h 10 Sharpe.
Michaelis Reuben J, b 626 N Capitol av.
Michel Arthur R, grocer, s w cor Sugar Grove and Miller avs (M P), h same.
Michel Christian, mail carrier, h s w cor Sugar Grove and Miller avs (M P).
Michel Christian C, cabtmkr, h 176 Jefferson av.
Michel John, engr, b 292 W Maryland.
Michel Theodore C, cabtmkr, b 176 Jefferson av.
Michelfelder George W, tailor, b 540 E Ohio.
Michelfelder John F, uphlr, h 48 Pleasant av.
Michelfelder John G, h 540 E Ohio.
Michelson Leopold, printer, b 93 Buchanan.
Michelson Philip F, trav agt, h 93 Buchanan.
MICHIE ALBERT, Agt Chicago Bridge and Iron Co, 6 Builders' Exchange, 35 E Ohio, Tel 970; h 636 N Alabama. (See adv in classified Contractors—Bridge.)
MICHIGAN LUMBER CO, Augustus Coburn Mngr, Lumber, Lath and Shingles, 436 E North, cor Fulton, Tel 766. (See embossed line back cover and adv opp classified Lumber Mnfrs.)
MICHIGAN MUTUAL LIFE INSURANCE CO, J F McFarland State Agt, W J Handy Cashier, 32 Journal Bldg.
Mick Edward L (W E Mick & Co), h 882 N Penn.
Mick Wm E (W E Mick & Co), h 1572 N Illinois.
MICK W E & CO (Wm E and Edward L Mick), Real Estate, Loans, Rents and Insurance, 68 E Market, Tel 601.
Mickel Edward, lab, h 151 Maple.
Mickley Henry T, mach hd, h e s Sherman Drive 4 n of Ohio.
Middaugh Isaac, lab, h 26 Standard av (W I).
Middaugh Theodore S, mach hd, b 196 N Beville av.
Middaw Arthur C, tmstr, h 246½ Bates.

RICHARDSON & McCREA,
MANAGERS FOR CENTRAL INDIANA.
EQUITABLE LIFE ASSURANCE SOCIETY
Of the United States.
79 EAST MARKET STREET,
TELEPHONE 182.

Middaw Frances (wid James W), b 214 Bates.
Middaw Wm C, switchman, h 214 Bates.
Middelton Richey S, clk Original Eagle, h 31 W St Clair.
Middelton Robert S, poultry, 188 Ft Wayne av, h 9 Ruckle.
Middlesworth, Benson, Nave & Co (Wm and Hugh Middlesworth, Adelbert S Benson, George W Nave, Abraham G Gish), live stock com, Union Stock Yards (W I).
Middlesworth Hugh (Middlesworth, Benson, Nave & Co), h 60 S Linden.
Middlesworth Wm (Middlesworth, Benson, Nave & Co), h 54 S Linden.
Middleton Albert J (Middleton & Logsdon), h 134 John.
Middleton Alfred N, h 215 Kentucky av.
Middleton Anna G (wid Calvin H), b 142 Broadway.
Middleton Catherine (wid Elijah), h w s James 7 n of Sutherland (B).
Middleton Charles, cook, h 37 Albion.
Middleton Charles N, condr, h 1156 N Capitol av.
Middleton Daniel, lab, h 8 Columbia al.
Middleton David, lab, b 564 N Senate av.
Middleton Edward W, feed stable, s s E Wabash 1 e of N Alabama, h 426 Columbia av.
Middleton Elias, hostler, r s s E Wabash 1 e of N Alabama.
Middleton George, lab, r 167 Muskingum al.
Middleton James, lab, h 76½ S West.
Middleton Joshua N, lab, h 37 Alvord.
Middleton Lucretia (wid Benjamin), h 564 N Senate av.
Middleton Wm J, opr W U Tel Co, h 441 E Ohio.
Middleton & Logsdon (Albert J Middleton, Edwin D Logsdon), broom mnfrs, rear 17 Park av.
Midland Fast Freight Line, Louis L Fellows agt, 26 S Illinois.
Miedemer Martin, lab, b 600 N Meridian.
Miegge, see Muegge.
Mieleond Irene M (wid George A), h 264 Fulton.

Typewriter-Ribbons
ALL COLORS FOR ALL MACHINES.
THE BEST AND CHEAPEST.
S. H. EAST, STATE AGENT,
The Williams Typewriter....
55 THORPE BLOCK, 87 E. MARKET ST.

ERTEL STEAM LAUNDRY
LA[illegible] AND B[illegible] IN THE STATE. PROMPT SERVICE.
26 and 28 N. Senate Ave. Tp [illegible]99.

ELLIS & HELFENBERGER Architectural Iron Work and Gray Iron Castings. 162-170 South Senate Ave. Tel. 958.

THE HOGAN TRANSFER AND STORAGE COMP'Y
Household Goods and Pianos Moved—Packed—Stored...... Baggage and Package Express Machinery and Safes a Specialty Cor. Washington and Illinois Sts. TELEPHONE No. 675.

The Central Rubber & Supply Co. ◄◆◆► Hose, Belting, Packing, Clothing, Druggists' Sundries, Bicycle Tires, Cotton Hose, Etc. New York Belting & Packing Co., L't'd. PHONE 2. 79 S. ILLINOIS ST., INDIANAPOLIS, IND.

The Provident Life and Trust Company
Of Philadelphia.
Grants Certificates of Extension to Policyholders who are temporarily unable to pay their premiums
D. W. EDWARDS, Gen. Agt., 508 Indiana Trust Bldg.

Miers, see also Mayer, Meier, Meyers and Myers.
Miers Edwin E, mach, h w s Baltimore av 2 n of 22d.
Miers James P, clk H P Wasson & Co, b 58 Barth av.
Miers Wm P, mach, h 153 Newman.
Miesel Andrew P, weaver, h 346 Blake.
Miessen Albert J, lab, b 328 E Miami.
Miessen Eliza M (wid Julius L J), h 328 E Miami.
Miessen Frederick, driver, h 290 E Louisiana.
Mifflin Jane (wid James H), h 228 N Missouri.
Miggenburg Henry B, h 48 Morton.
Mighiano Vincenzo, fruits, h 118 N Capitol av.
Mikels John R, carp, h w s Senate av 2 n of Carlton (M).
Mikesell Charles, condr, h 161½ W Washington.
Mikesell Charles M, boilermkr, r 852½ E Washington.
Mikesell Charles W, hostler, h 475 N Illinois.
Milam Charles B, engr, h 25 Minkner.
Milam George M, lab, h 65 S Reisner (W I).
Milam George O, porter, h 22 Hosbrook.
Milam James W, lab, h 577 E 8th.
Milam Susannah (wid Francis M), b 61 S Reisner (W I).
Milam Wm B, patrolman, h 23 Minkner.
Milavc John, lab, b 49 Holmes av (H).
Milberth Charles J, lab, h 209 Meek.
Milburn Christopher, lab, h 225 Huron.
Miburn Cornelius, carp, h 139 Park av.
Milburn Frank B, molder, b 546 S West.
Milburn Harry, tmstr, b 189 W Maryland.
Milburn Hugh, carp, b 139 Park av.
Milburn John L, carp, b 139 Park av.
Milburn Joseph A Rev, pastor Second Presbyterian Church, h 32 E Vermont.
Milburn Lee, carp, b 13 Park av.
Milburn Thomas W, carp, b 139 Park av.
Milburn Wm, lab, b 225 Huron.
Mildner August F, uphlr, b 492 S Missouri.
Mildner Christopher, lab, h 492 S Missouri.
Mildner George J, uphlr, b 492 S Missouri.

Julius C. Walk & Son,
Jewelers
Indianapolis.
12 EAST WASHINGTON ST.

Milender Charles E, city fireman, h 87 N Beville av.
Milender James M, painter, h 599 W Chicago (N I).
Milender Wm B, painter, h 101 S Linden.
Miles Alexander, coachman, r 334 Superior.
MILES CHARLES R, Restaurant and Furnished Rooms; Open All Night; 111 E Washington, opp Court House, h same.
Miles Clarence B, ins agt, b 432 E St Clair.
Miles Edgar, lab, h 616 Home av.
Miles Edward, janitor, r 3 Wood.
Miles Esther (wid James), h rear 169 E St Joseph.
Miles Glenn A, clk, b 7 Omer.
Miles Harry S, clk Hotel Oneida.
Miles James, lab, h 22 Sumner.
Miles James A, restaurant, h 196 N California.
Miles James H, clk The Wm H Block Co, b 49 Arbor av (W I).
Miles James W, lab, h 1205 Morris (W I).
Miles John, waiter, h 327 Tremont.
Miles John H, lab, h 41 Hendricks.
Miles Kate, h 332 Elizabeth.
Miles Marion L, lab, h 36 S Belmont (W I).
Miles N E Mrs, propr Hotel Oneida, 114-118 S Illinois.
Miles Orval E, lab, b 940 N Alabama.
Miles Richard B, clk Hotel Oneida.
Miles Richard R, clothing, 108 S Illinois, h same.
Miles Rosanna (wid John H), h 96 Nebraska.
Miles Samuel W, livery, 127 E 7th, h 940 N Alabama.
Miles Wm C, mach, b 7 Omer.
Miles Wm H, bkkpr, h 432 E St Clair.
Miles Wm J, painter, h 508 Broadway.
Miles Wm R, h 7 Omer.
Miles Wm W, cabtmkr, h 1043 N Capitol av.
Miley John S, trav agt, h 28 Tecumseh.
Miley Robert S, paperhngr, h 39 Tecumseh.
Milford James E, clk, b 347 S New Jersey.
Milford John T, millwright, 347 S New Jersey.
Milford Wm W, clk, b 347 S New Jersey.
Milharditz John, mach, r rear 31 Madison av.
Milholland, see also Mulholland.
Milholland John A, harnessmkr, h 28 W Pratt.
Milholland Wm F, sec and treas Citizens' Street Railroad Co, h 956 N Capitol av.
Milhous Charles R, engr, h 163 Prospect.
Milhous Edwin R, engr, h 62 Arch.
Milhouse Harry K, letter carrier P O, h 156 Cornell av.
Military Order Loyal Legion, Indiana Commandery, 41 When bldg.
Milks James E, mngr, h 642 E Market.
Mill Frank H, h 32 W 12th.
Millar Samuel T, supt, b 228 E North.
Millard Charles, student, b 655 N Delaware.
Millard Lydia G (wid Charles S), h 655 N Delaware.
Millard Wm, watchman, h 737 N Capitol av.
Miller, see also Moeller, Mueller and Muller.
Miller Ada E (wid Frank), b 1110 N New Jersey.
Miller Ada I (wid Richard M), h 269 N New Jersey.
Miller Adam, barber, h 227 W Vermont.
Miller Adam, cooper, b 95 S West.
Miller Adam D (A D Miller & Sons), bkkpr Globe Accident Ins Co, h 131 N Alabama.

OTTO GAS ENGINES | BUILDERS' EXCHANGE S. W. Cor. Ohio and Penn. Telephone 535.

Becker & Son Charles Becker Jacob Becker Jr. Merchant Tailors. 21 N. Penn. St. Tel. 934

SALISBURY & STANLEY • Office, Store and Bank Fixtures a Specialty. Repairing of all kinds done on short notice. 177 Clinton St. Indianapolis, Ind. • Contractors and Builders TELEPHONE 999.

Miller Adam R, agt, h 146 Elm.
Miller Agnes (wid Andrew), b 345 S East.
Miller Albert, bellman Grand Hotel.
Miller Albert, condr, b 141 Highland pl.
Miller Albert, patrolman, h 351 Mass av.
Miller Albert, shoemkr, b 41 Arizona.
Miller Albert F, uphlr, h 378 S Delaware.
Miller Albert J, drugs, 314 S Penn and 284 S West, b 280 same.
Miller Albert P (A D Miller & Sons), b 131 N Alabama.
Miller Albert R, foreman, h 111 College av.
Miller Albert S, h 26 Elm.
Miller Albert T E, lab, h 42 S Gale (B).
Miller Albert W, mach, b 241 N Liberty.
Miller Alexander, lab, h 194 W 3d.
Miller Allen, lab, h 169 Alvord.
Miller Amanda (wid Jacob), h 11 Haugh (H).
Miller Anderson, lab, r 131 Allegheny.
Miller Andrew, carp, h 948 Morris (W I).
Miller Andrew, lab, b 27 Chadwick.
Miller Andrew, lab, b 197 W Maryland.
Miller Andrew, lab, b 25 S West.
Miller Andrew H, driver, b 20 Pleasant.
Miller Andrew J, lab, h 454 W 1st.
Miller Anna, housekpr.276 N Illinois.
Miller Annie (wid Clinton), r 289½ Mass av.
Miller Annie H, dressmkr, 577 E Washington, b same.
Miller Anthony, tmstr, b 99 Lexington av.
Miller Archibald, lab, h 422 Lafayette.
Miller Archibald H, foreman Indpls Foundry Co, h 51 Nordyke av (W I).
Miller Arthur, bkkpr, b 16 Shelby.
Miller Arthur T, b 159 Buchanan.
Miller August, ironwkr, b 329 S Olive.

MILLER A D & SONS (Adam D, Claude B and Albert P), Printers and Stationers, 81 E Court, Tel 1635.

Miller Benjamin, lab, h 195 W South.
Miller Benjamin C, lawyer, r 282 N Illinois.
Miller Benjamin F, painter, b 643 S Meridian.
Miller Benjamin J, engr, h 41 Lord.
Miller Bros (Henry F and George A), carps, 179 Clinton.
Miller Bruno, lab, h 45 Parker.
Miller Caleb, foreman, b 29 School.
Miller Caroline A D (wid John D), r 7 Ryan blk.
Miller Carrie, matron Maternity Hospital, h 400 S Alabama.
Miller Cassius M, trav agt, h 556 Bellefontaine.
Miller Catherine (wid Frederick), h 41 Arizona.
Miller Catherine E (wid Sebastian S), b 26 Elm.
Miller Charles, carp, r 291 Christian.
Miller Charles, carp, b 21 Patterson.
Miller Charles, coachman 570 N Delaware.
Miller Charles, driver, h 961 S East.
Miller Charles, lab, h 6 Iowa.
Miller Charles, lab, b rear 13 McCauley.
Miller Charles, lab, r 191½ Mass av.
Miller Charles, porter, r 67 N New Jersey.
Miller Charles, porter, r 114 Roanoke.
Miller Charles, watchman, r Drover s of Indpls Abattoir.
Miller Charles A, city fireman, r 237½ Mass av.
Miller Charles A, finisher, b 95 S West.
Miller Charles A F, car rep, h 130 Temple av.
Miller Charles C, switchman, h 113 S Summit.

Henry H. Fay, 40½ E. Washington St., REAL ESTATE, AND LOAN BROKER.

Miller Charles C, vice-pres Pioneer Brass Works, b 48 Randolph.
Miller Charles E, carp, h 18 Cooper.
Miller Charles E, clk Am Ex Co, h 73 W 12th.
Miller Charles E, ins agt, h 193 College av.
Miller Charles E, trav agt, b 536 Dillon.
Miller Charles E, weighmstr, h 216 S Reisner (W I)
Miller Charles F, clk, r 192 Blackford.
Miller Charles F, clk, b 212 W New York.
Miller Charles F, mach, h 120 Lawrence.
Miller Charles F, salesman Murphy, Hibben & Co, h 681 N Illinois.
Miller Charles H, lab, h 205 Union.
Miller Charles H, molder, h 56 Cornell av.
Miller Charles J, carp, 845 E Michigan, h same.
Miller Charles L (Miller & Albrecht), h 230 Davidson.
Miller Charles P, mach hd Indpls Journal, h 3 Susquehanna.
Miller Charles S, trav agt, b 79 Astor.
Miller Charles W, lab, h 145 N Dorman.
Miller Chester C, clk, r 340½ N Delaware.
Miler Christian, tmstr, h 219 Union.
Miller Christian F, carp, 230 Davidson, h same.
Miller Christian F, tmstr, h 354 Coburn.
Miller Christian N, canmkr, b 354 Coburn.
Miller Christina (wid Anthony F), b 283 E Ohio.
Miller Claude B (A D Miller & Son), b 131 N Alabama.
Miller Claude V, packer, b 99 Quincy.
Miller Clayton J, brakeman, b 577 E Washington.
Miller Clinton, lab, h 23 Cincinnati.
Miller Charles G, foreman Natl Malleable Castings Co, b e s County rd 1 n of Michigan (H).
Miller Conrad, lab, h 77 Jones.
Miller Daniel, bricklyr, h 297½ S New Jersey.
Miller Daniel, tel opr, h 292 Christian av.
Miller Daniel A, mason, h 133½ Virginia av.
Miller Daniel Y, bartndr, h 56 Maxwell.
Miller David, hostler n w cor Washington and Gladstone av.

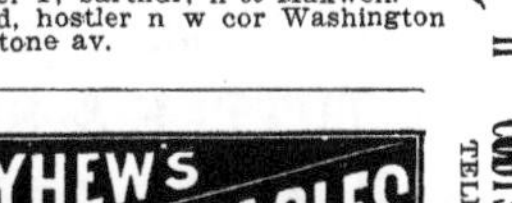

COAL AND LIME Cement, Hair, Sewer Pipe, etc. BALKE & KRAUSS CO. Cor. Missouri and Market Sts.

FRIEDGEN'S IS THE PLACE FOR THE NOBBIEST SHOES Ladies' and Gents' 19 North Pennsylvania St.

SAMUEL LAING || COPPER AND GALVANIZED IRON CORNICE MANUFACTURER
72 AND 74 E. COURT STREET. SKYLIGHTS AND VENTILATORS.

M. B. WILSON, Pres. W. F. CHURCHMAN, Cash.
THE CAPITAL NATIONAL BANK,
INDIANAPOLIS, IND.
Our Specialty is handling all Country Checks and Drafts on Indiana and neighboring States at the very lowest rates. Call and see us.
Interest Paid on Time Deposits.
28 S. MERIDIAN ST., COR. PEARL.

Miller Earl S, student, r 340½ N Delaware.
Miller Edgar L, lab, b 11 Haugh (H).
Miller Edgar S, clk R M S, b 199 Lincoln av.
Miller Edward, carp, h 394 Newman.
Miller Edward, carp, r 9 S Senate av.
Miller Edward, lab, b 241 Fayette.
Miller Edward, painter, b Ross House.
Miller Edward, porter, h 21 N Noble.
Miller Edward A R, clk P C C & St L Ry, b 283 E Ohio.
Miller Edward C, uphlr, b 602 E Vermont.
Miller Edward L, drayman, b 23 Weghorst.
Miller Edward O, clk, b 73 W 12th.
Miller Edward W, clk C H & E H Schrader, b 200 E Morris.
Miller Edward W J, bottler, b 27 Stevens.
Miller Edwin F, trav agt, r 35 W Vermont.
Miller Edwin H, clk C C C & St L Ry, h 182 Fulton.
Miller Effie, boarding 267 S Capitol av.
Miller Elijah, lab, h 1034 S Meridian.
Miller Elizabeth (wid John), r 183½ Mass av.
Miller Elizabeth (wid Wm), b 524 Jefferson av.
Miller Elizabeth A, h n w cor Wheeler and Park (B).
Miller Elizabeth E (wid Aaron), h 132 W Vermont.
Miller Elizabeth M (wid Simon R), dressmkr, 314 N East, h same.
Miller Ellen, h 18 Stevens.
Miller Elmer, baggageman, h 115 Spann av.
Miller Elmer R, trav agt, b 554 Ash.
Miller Elnathan C, painter, b 130 Windsor.
Miller Emlen F, cigars, 325 E Washington, r same.
Miller Emma (wid Frank W), r 289½ Mass av.
Miller Emma W, asst bkkpr H P Wasson & Co, b 200 E Morris.
Miller Enrique C (Baldwin, Miller & Co), h 580 N Delaware.
Miller Ephraim, carp, h 984 W New York.
Miller Ernst F, drayman, h 37 Iowa.
Miller Ernst W, carp, h 200 E Morris.
Miller Eroy, clk, h 78 S McLain (W I).
Miller Etta L, prin Public School No 28, h 919 N New Jersey.

TUTTLE & SEGUIN,
28 E. Market St. Ground Floor.
COLLECTING RENTS AND CARE OF PROPERTY A SPECIALTY.
Telephone 1168.

Miller Eugene, tester, h 191 N East.
Miller Euphemia W (wid Jacob S), h 48 N East.
Miller Everett H, carp, b e s Illinois 2 n of 30th (M).
Miller Fatima (wid Wm), b 208 Wright.
Miller Frank, boilermkr, h 1326 N New Jersey.
Miller Frank, engr, h 17 Benton.
Miller Frank, ins agt, h 84 N New Jersey.
Miller Frank, lab, h e s Temperance 1 s of English av (I).
Miller Frank, painter, h 643 S Meridian.
Miller Frank B, carp, h 162 Buchanan.
Miller Frank E, carp, h 321 Jefferson av.
Miller Frank F, coachman 622 N Alabama.
Miller Frank H T, clk, h 499½ N West.
Miller Frank J, painter, b 325 N Liberty.
Miller Frank M, barber, 903 Cornell av, b 921 same.
Miller Frank M, lab, h 89 Wright.
Miller Frank X, finisher, b 131 Fayette.
Miller Frederick, bracer, h 32 Bates al.
Miller Frederick, carp, h 567 N Senate av.
Miller Frederick, cigarmkr, r 171½ E Washington.
Miller Frederick, drayman, h 23 Weghorst.
Miller Frederick, elevator opr, r 195 N Alabama.
Miller Frederick jr, clk Francke & Schindler, h 181 Dearborn.
Miller Frederick C, lab, b 663 S Meridian.
Miller Frederick C, molder, b 23 Weghorst.
Miller Frederick D, car rep, h n w cor Sutherland and Shade (B).
Miller Frederick H, h 602 E Vermont.
Miller Frederick H, engr, h 18 Iowa.
Miller Frederick L, cabtmkr, h 286 E Wabash.
Miller Frederick M, shoemkr, h 159 Jefferson av.
Miller Frederick R, cigarmkr, b 602 E Vermont.
Miller Frederick W, carp, h 27 Stevens.
Miller Frederick W, mach, h 14 Singleton.
Miller George, engr, h 526 S Illinois.
Miller George, finisher Langsenkamp Bros' Brass Wks, h 349 Blake.
Miller George, lab, b 10 Columbia al.
Miller George, lab, r 285 S Illinois.
Miller George, painter, h 157 N State av.
MILLER GEORGE, Sample Room; Fine Wines, Whiskies and Pabst's Milwaukee Beer, 26 Columbia av, h 57 same.
Miller George, saloon, 664 S Meridian, h 845 Chestnut.
Miller George, sawmkr, b 516 S Meridian.
Miller George A (Miller Bros), b 431 E Vermont.
Miller George A, bkkpr Indpls Brewing Co, b 845 Chestnut.
Miller George A, packer, h 842 Chestnut.
Miller George B, printer, b 157 N State av.
Miller George F, clk Francke & Schindler, h 263 N Liberty.
Miller George F, dep County and City Treasurer, h n s Marlowe av bet Preston and Highland av.
Miller George H, blksmith, s w cor Cannon and Michigan av, h s s Michigan av 3 e of Auburn av.
Miller George H, bkkpr Griffith Bros, b 304 E Ohio.
Miller George H, collr, h 909 Ash.
Miller George J, foreman, h 34 Quincy.
Miller George J, helper, h 131 Fayette.
Miller George J, painter, h 731 Charles.

PAPER BOXES : SULLIVAN & MAHAN 41 W. Pearl St.

DIAMOND WALL PLASTER { Telephone 1410 BUILDERS' EXCHANGE.

If your Laundry Work is not satisfactory, try THE HOME LAUNDRY 197 S. Illinois St. Telephone 1769.

Miller George K Rev, pastor Northeast Congregational Church, h 344 Columbia av.
Miller George P, trimmer, h rear 226 E Washington.
Miller George V, salesman John M Lilly, r 340½ N Delaware.
Miller George W (G W Miller & Co), h 406 Broadway.
Miller George W, lab, b 461 S Meridian.
Miller George W, wool sorter, b 56 Maxwell.
Miller Gustin T, mach, b 149 S New Jersey.
Miller G W & Co (George W Miller, Edward Dickinson), carriagemkrs, 86 E New York.
Miller Harlan P, messenger Am Ex Co, h 551 Bellefontaine.
Miller Harry, express, h 962 N New Jersey.
Miller Harry, lab, b 659½ Virginia av.
Miller Harry C, finisher, b 948 Morris (W I).
Miller Henry E, engr, h 11 Bridge (W I).
Miller Harry P, engr, h e s LaSalle 2 n of Indiana av.
Miller Harry S, tailor, 18 S Illinois, h 474 Stillwell.
Miller Henry, cabtmkr, b 35 Howard.
Miller Henry, carpet weaver, 265 Coburn, h same.
Miller Henry, driver, h 233 Columbia av.
Miller Henry, foreman, h 523 Jefferson av.
Miller Henry, grocer, 1155 E Washington, h same.
Miller Henry, janitor, h 198 W Ray.
Miller Henry, lab, h 27 Chadwick.
Miller Henry, mach hd, r 104 S Noble.
Miller Henry, molder, h 639 W Vermont.
Miller Henry, potter, h 34 N William (W I).
Miller Henry A, drayman, h 20 William.
Miller Henry C, carp, h 110 S Summit.
Miller Henry C, lab, h 35 Howard.
Miller Henry C F, driver, b 219 Union.
Miller Henry F (Miller Bros), h 431 E Vermont.
Millert Henry J, checkman, b 227 W Vermon.
Miller Henry T, cigarmkr, h 528 S East.
Miller Henry T jr, cigarmkr, b 528 S East.
Miller Herbert C, blksmith, b 402½ S Meridian.
Miller Hiram O, candymkr, h 190 Elm.
Miller Hiram W, pres The State Bank of Indiana and Miller Steam and Gas Generator Co, h W 22d ½ mile n w of Flackville, Ind.
Miller Howard, butcher, b 29 School.
Miller Hugh T, prof Butler College, b e s Ritter av 2 s of University av (I).
Miller Hugo A, sec German International Typographical Union, h 199 Davidson.
Miller Ida L, clk Equitable Life Assurance Soc, b 473 N Delaware.
Miller Irving R, engr, h 891 N Senate av.
Miller Isaac, condr, h 187 Pleasant.
Miller Isaac F, coachman, b 567 E 8th.
Miller Jacob, h 292 Howard (W I).
Miller Jacob, carp, h 980 W New York.
Miller Jacob, carp, h 21 Patterson.
Miller Jacob, foreman John Rauch, h 288 Blake.
Miller Jacob, lab, h 110 Hosbrook.
Miller Jacob, meats, 73½ Minerva, h 675 W Vermont.
Miller Jacob jr, packer, h 643 W Vermont.
Miller Jacob, painter, h 22 N Brightwood av (B).
Miller James, carp, h rear s s Washington 4 s of Line (I).

FRANK NESSLER. WILL H. ROST.
FRANK NESSLER & CO.
Tailors
56 EAST MARKET ST. (Lemcke Building),
INDIANAPOLIS, IND.

Miller James, clk H P Wasson & Co, b 96 Walcott.
Miller James, driver, h 20 N West.
Miller James, lab, b 402 Blackford.
Miller James, lab, h 241 Fayette.
Miller James, tmstr, h 86 N New Jersey.
Miller James D, cooper, h 170 Blackford.
Miller James E, clk, b 98 Marion av (W I).
Miller James E, custodian Builders' Exchange, h 528 Bellefontaine.
Miller James H, clk, b 292 W Market.
Miller James M, carp, b 125 W Maryland.
Miller James P, bill poster, b 29 School.
Miller James P, engr, h 430 W Wells (N I).
Miller James S, carp, h rear 335 S Delaware.
Miller James U, mngr The Miller Oil Co, 23-27 McNabb, h 1145 N Penn.
Miller Jefferson P, lab, b 600 W North.
Miller John, live stock, h e s Illinois 2 n of 29th.
Miller Jemima (wid Sidney C), h 133 Wright.
Miller Jennie (wid David), h 58½ N Illinois.
Miller Jennie (wid Thomas), h 312 W Pearl.
Miller Jeremiah, lab, h 388 Clinton.
Miller Jesse, driver, b 476 W North.
Miller Jesse R, mach hd, b 99 Quincy.
Miller John, agt. r 22 W Pratt.
Miller John, carp, h 307 Shelby.
Miller John, driver, h 186 Bird.
Miller John, lab, b 115 Harrison.
Miller John, lab, h rear 669 McLene (N I).
Miller John, lab, b n e cor Michigan and Belmont av.
Miller John, lab, b 99 Minnesota.
Miller John, lab, h w s Perkins pike 2 n of Bethel av.
Miller John, lab, h 565 W Shoemaker (N I).
Miller John, lab, b 34 N William (W I).
Miller John A, buyer McKee Shoe Co, h 764 Broadway.
Miller John A, engr, b 532 E Ohio.
Miller John C, clk P C C & St L Ry, h 150 N Summit.
Miller John C, mach hd, h 9 Jefferson.
Miller John C, molder, b rear 598 N West.
Miller John D, millwright, b 500 Bellefontaine.

ACORN STOVES AND RANGES
Haueisen & Hartmann
163-169 E. Washington St.
FURNITURE,
Carpets,
Household Goods,
Tin, Granite and China Wares, Oil Cloth and Shades

THE WM. H. BLOCK CO. 7 AND 9 EAST WASHINGTON STREET. DRY GOODS, MEN'S FURNISHINGS.

The Fidelity and Deposit Co. OF MARYLAND. Bonds signed for Administrators, Assignees, Executors, Guardians, Receivers Trustees, and persons in every position of trust.
GEO. W. PANGBORN, General Agent, 704-706 Lemcke Building. Telephone 140.

INSURE YOUR PROPERTY WITH FRANK K. SAWYER

•JOSEPH GARDNER•
GALVANIZED IRON
CORNICES and SKYLIGHTS.
Metal Ceilings and Siding.
Tin, Iron, Steel and Slate Roofing.
37, 39 & 41 KENTUCKY AVE. Telephone 322.

Miller John E, carp, b 845 E Michigan.
Miller John F, r 135 W 6th.
Miller John F, carriage mnfr, 540 Dillon, h 536 same.
Miller John F, city fireman, h 167 Columbia av.
Miller John F, drayman, b 448 S Meridian.
Miller John F, inventor, h 493 W Udell (N I).
Miller John G, carp, h 149 Buchanan.
Miller John G, patternmkr, b 288 Blake.
Miller John H, h 539 Park av.
Miller John H, city fireman, h 39 E Rockwood.
Miller John H, clk, b 131 Fayette.
Miller John H, mach, h 500 Bellefontaine.
Miller John H, sawyer, h 4 Quincy.
Miller John I, lab, b 298 Blake.
Miller John J, b 184 Hill av.
Miller John J, cooper, b 170 Blackford.
Miller John J, mach, h 116 Columbia av.
Miller John J, plumber, h 192 Cherry.
Miller John M, lab, h 38 N California.
Miller John R (Indpls Drug Co), h 20 Sterling.
Miller John R, lab, b 877 Morris (W I).
Miller John R, mach hd, h 171 Highland av.
Miller John S, lab, r 141 W Washington.
Miller John S, mngr Lion Mantel and Grate House, h 485 Ash.
Miller John S, plumber, r 77½ S Illinois.
Miller John W, city fireman, h 81 W 6th.
Miller John W, condr, h 50 Omer.
Miller John W, driver, h 115 Harrison.
Miller John W, fireman, h 415 Columbia av.
Miller John W, switchman, h 23 John.
Miller John W, tel opr, b 89 Indiana av.
Miller Joseph, r 257 N Senate av.
Miller Joseph, barber, b 888 N Senate av.
Miller Joseph, brakeman, h 43 English av.
Miller Joseph, city editor German Telegraph, h 266 N East.
Miller Joseph, porter, h 86 N New Jersey.
Miller Joseph, porter, r 277 N Noble.
Miller Joseph, real est, h 1745 Graceland av.
Miller Joseph A, molder, h 160 Michigan (H).
Miller Joseph K, barber, b 192 W 3d.

J. S. FARRELL & CO.
Have Experienced Workmen and will Promptly Attend to your
PLUMBING
Repairs. 84 North Illinois Street. Telephone 382.

Miller J Clifton, cashr Kershner Bros, r 284 E Ohio.
Miller J Martin (Boyd & Miller), h 226 N Liberty.
Miller Kate (wid George), h 80 S West.
Miller Kate (wid Wm B), h 22 Cooper.
Miller Katherine (wid John), b 356 Fulton.
Miller Lafayette, janitor, h 302 Alvord.
Miller Laura M (wid Oscar F), waitress, r 94 N New Jersey.
Miller Lee B, brakeman, b 98 Marion av (W I).
Miller Lennie (Miller & Smock), b 26 Elm.
Miller Leonidas L, mason, h 85 Buchanan.
Miller LeRoy C, barber, 69 E Sutherland (B), h 3 N Station (B).
Miller Letcher, lab, h 193 W 3d.
Miller Letcher B, brakeman, b 98 Marion av (W I).
Miller Levi, blksmith, h 600 W North.
Miller Lewis G, bkkpr Henry Coburn, h 551 N Senate av.
Miller Lincoln, stairbldr, r 10½ N Delaware.
Miller Lizzie, teacher, b 500 N West.
Miller Lorin K, lab, h 221 S West.
Miller Louella, artist, h 554 Ash.
Miller Louis C, com mer, 80 S Delaware, h 159 Buchanan.
Miller Louis E F, foreman Anheuser-Busch Brewing Assn, h 605 E New York.
Miller Louis F, carp, h 46 Gatling.
Miller Louis H, finisher, h 685 Shoemaker (N I).
Miller Louis H, foreman, h 17 Harvey.
Miller Louis L, mach, h 9 Depot (B).
Miller Louis W (L W Miller & Co), b 230 Davidson.
Miller Lucien B, blksmith, h 500 N West.
Miller Luzyna (wid James), h 567 E 8th.
Miller L W & Co (Louis W Miller), bottlers, 292 E Washington.
Miller Mabel, h 168½ E Washington.
Miller Mabel B, b 176 Patterson.
Miller Mahala E (wid Minos), h 446 N East.
Miller Margaret A (wid Simon), h 402½ S Meridian.
Miller Margaret M (wid Matthew), h 149 S New Jersey.
Miller Margaret R (wid Edward T), h 577 E Washington.
Miller Martha A (wid Henry W), h 304 E Ohio.
Miller Martha J (wid George L), dressmkr, 461 S Meridian, h same.
Miller Martin, lab, b 5 Gimble.
Miller Martin L, trav agt Griffith Bros, h 123 N Liberty.
Miller Mary, h 161½ Mass av.
Miller Mary (wid Henry), h 256 N Noble.
Miller Mary (wid John), h 191 N East.
Miller Mary (wid Louis J), h 375 E Michigan.
Miller Mary E, h 111 College av.
Miller Mary M, stenog The Indiana Trust Co, b 537 Bellefontaine.
Miller Matilda M, asst bkkpr H P Wasson & Co, b 200 E Morris.
Miller Merrill, cook Kershner Bros, b 194 W 3d.
Miller Mildred, h 407 W 2d.
Miller Milton H, mer police, h 140 Davidson.
Miller Mollie, tailoress, r 13, 161½ Mass av.
Miller Murray, hostler, b s e cor Central and Washington avs (I).
Miller Nannie E (wid Newton), h 249 Fayette.
Miller Nathan G, drugs, 207 W New York, h 212 same.
Miller Nettie (wid James), h 675 Home av.

GUARANTEED INCOME POLICIES issued only by the United States Life Insurance Co.
E. B. SWIFT, Manager. 25 E. Market St.

Furniture Carpets } WM. KOTTEMAN { Stoves Ranges
89 and 91 East Washington Street. Telephone 1742.

Miller Nicholas, engr, h w s Sugar Grove av 5 s of Miller av (M P).
Miller Nicholas H, driver, h 448 N California.
Miller Noah, lab, h 1 Hendricks.
Miller Noah W, grain, h 6 Shriver av.
MILLER OIL CO THE, James U Miller Mngr, 23-27 McNabb, opp Union Station, Tel 1332. (See adv in classified Oils.)
Miller Oliver P, grocer, 1054 N Senate av, h same.
Miller Otis O, clk N Y Store, h 575 E Market.
Miller Otto, buyer N Y Store, b 999 N Capitol av.
Miller Otto, clk R M S, b 256 Prospect.
Miller Otto F, lab, b 286 E Wabash.
Miller Page, coachman 384 Park av.
Miller Paul, lab, b 1000 W Washington.
Miller Perry, baggageman, r 117 W Maryland.
Miller Peter, janitor, h 80 Adams.
Miller Peter, lab, h 77 W 1st.
Miller Peter, lab, b e s Lincoln av 4 s of C C C & St L Ry (M J).
Miller Peter C, dairy, w s Schurman av 1 n of Vorster av, h same.
MILLER PHILIP, Drugs, Medicines, Toilet Articles and Cigars, 324 Clifford av, h same, Tel 1402.
Miller Pleasant L, lab, h 501 Sheldon.
Miller Porter, lab, b 600 W North.
Miller Rachel (wid George W), b 181 Elm.
Miller Ralph, clk The Bowen-Merrill Co, b 256 Prospect.
Miller Reinhold A, musician, h 999 N Capitol av.
Miller Reinhold A jr, furnishings, 7 S Illinois, b 999 N Capitol av.
Miller Rhodes, lab, h rear 21 Cora.
Miller Richard C. trav agt, h 681 N Illinois.
Miller Robert, h 29 School.
Miller Robert, lab, b 21 Torbet.
Miller Robert F, lab, h 149 Lexington av.
Miller Rudolph, lab, b n e cor Michigan and Belmont av.
Miller Rudolph J, pdlr, h 113 S Spruce.
Miller Samantha W, journalist, h 256 Prospect.
Miller Samuel, carp, r 9 S Senate av.
Miller Samuel, driver, h 397 Blackford.
Miller Samuel, lab, h 18 Lafayette.
Miller Samuel, shoemkr, 143½ Mass av, h same.
Miller Samuel, tailor, h 154 N Liberty.
Miller Samuel, veneerer, b 29 School.
Miller Samuel F, feed, 280 W Washington, h 550 S West.
Miller Samuel H, lab, h 1032 S Meridian.
Miller Samuel H, vault cleaner, 23 S New Jersey, h 176 S Noble.
Miller Sarah, h 27 Davis.
Miller Sarah (wid Michael F), h 130 Windsor.
Miller Sarah A (wid Alfred), b 877 Morris (W I).
Miller Sarah C, dressmkr, b 461 S Meridian.
Miller Sarah E (wid Philip A), h 659½ Virginia av.
Miller Seymour, lab, h 736 N West.
Miller Simon, lab, h 685 Shoemaker (N I).
Miller Simon R, carp, h 50 Beacon.
Miller Steam and Gas Generator Co, Hiram W Miller pres, James R Henry sec and treas, 26 Kentucky av.
Miller Stephen M, baggageman, h 284 E Ohio.

We Buy Municipal
~ Bonds ~
THOS. C. DAY & CO,
Rooms 325 to 330 Lemcke Bldg.

Miller Susie, teacher Public School No 23, b 733 N West.
Miller Theodore F, lab, h 62 Roanoke.
Miller Thomas, lab, h rear 13 McCauley.
Miller Thomas, lab, b 140 W Vermont.
Miller Thomas, lab, b 34 N William (W I).
Miller Thomas, pdlr, b 18 Stevens.
Miller Thomas E, patternmkr, h 491 E 10th.
Miller Thomas F, lab, h 77 W 1st.
Miller Thomas F, molder, b 178 W South.
Miller Thomas K, carp, b 178 Brookside av.
Miller Thomas W, lab, h s s Washington 19 w of Harris av (M J).
Miller Timothy, asst clk R M S, h 256 Prospect.
Miller Valentine, sawyer, h 377 E Georgia.
Miller Valentine L, lab, b rear w s Brightwood av 2 s of Wolf pike (B).
Miller Walker, waiter, b 230 W Vermont.
Miller Walter, foreman, h 160 Wright.
Miller Warren, lab, h 162½ Indiana av.
Miller Wilkerson B, live stock, h 520 E 9th.
Miller Wm, barber, Grand Hotel, h 691 N Senate av.
Miller Wm, bartndr, b 122 Michigan (H).
Miller Wm, clk, b 265 Coburn.
Miller Wm, driver, h 37 Vinton.
Miller Wm, lab, h s w cor Calvin and Bethel av.
Miller Wm, lab, b 75 Coburn.
Miller Wm, lab, b 2 Detroit.
Miller Wm, lab, b 249 Fayette.
Miller Wm, lab, h 99 Hendricks.
Miller Wm, lab, b 602 E Vermont.
Miller Wm, mach, b 5 S Station (B).
Miller Wm, porter, h 25 Weghorst.
Miller Wm, trav agt, b 166 N Senate av.
Miller Wm A, com mer, 189 E Market, h same.
Miller Wm A, mngr, h 295 S Missouri
Miller Wm A, millwright, h 648½ College av.
Miller Wm C, clk Indpls Drug Co, r 183½ Mass av.
Miller Wm C, collr The Sun, b 221 N Capitol av
Miller Wm C, molder, h 50 S William (W I).

EAT
HITZ'S
CRACKERS
AND CAKES.
ASK YOUR GROCER FOR THEM.

WILLIAM WIEGEL { MANUFACTURER OF..... } SHOW CASES { 6 W. Louisiana St. Opposite Union Station.

TURKISH RUGS AND CARPETS RESTORED TO ORIGINAL COLORS LIKE NEW | Capital Steam Carpet Cleaning Works M. D. PLUNKETT, Telephone 818

BENJ. BOOTH PRACTICAL EXPERT ACCOUNTANT. Books Opened, Written Up, Posted and Balanced. Room 18, 82½ E. Washington St., Indianapolis, Ind.

18 and 20 S. MERIDIAN STREET || THE SHERMAN RESTAURANT || IF YOU WANT A GOOD MEAL AND HAVE IT NICELY SERVED GO TO

ESTABLISHED 1876. TELEPHONE 168.
CHESTER BRADFORD,
SOLICITOR OF PATENTS,
AND COUNSEL IN PATENT CAUSES.
(See adv. page 6.)
Office:—Rooms 14 and 16 Hubbard Block, S. W. Cor. Washington and Meridian Streets, INDIANAPOLIS, INDIANA.

Miller Wm D, painter, h 249½ E Washington.
Miller Wm E, stamp clk P O, h 1023 N Alabama.
Miller Wm F, boxmkr, b 323 S Olive.
Miller Wm F, foreman Sinker-Davis Co, b 200 E Morris.
Miller Wm F, mach, b 375 E Michigan.
Miller Wm F, shoemkr, 86 S Illinois, h 663 S Meridian.
Miller Wm G, salesman Murphy, Hibben & Co, h 530 E 8th.
Miller Wm H, carp, h 1652 Graceland av.
Miller Wm H, carp, h 106 Spring.
Miller Wm H, carp, h 135 Wright.
Miller Wm H, clk, b 845 E Michigan.
Miller Wm H, lab, h rear 381 S Olive.
Miller Wm H, mach, h w s Sugar Grove av 5 s of Miller av (W I).
Miller Wm H, mngr Klee & Coleman, h 86 Broadway.
Miller Wm H, painter, h 321 N Liberty.
Miller Wm H H (Miller & Elam), h 665 N Delaware, tel 347.
Miller Wm L, foreman, h 98 Marion av (W I).
Miller Wm L, lab, h e s Lincoln av 4 s of C C C & St L Ry (M J).
Miller Wm M, barber, b 161½ Mass av.
Miller Wm M, polisher, h 516 S Meridian.
Miller Wm M, porter, b 111 E Washington.
Miller Wm R, plastr, h 534 E Georgia.
Miller Wm S, molder, h rear 598 N West.
MILLER WM S, Saloon, 35 E Court, h same.
MILLER WM T, Genl Agt Superior Drill Co, 28 Kentucky av, h 116 Ramsey av.
Miller Willis, lab, h w s Caroline av 2 s of 17th.
Miller Willis K, student, r 340½ N Delaware.
MILLER WINFIELD, Financial Correspondent Farm Loan Department Connecticut Mutual Life Insurance Company for Ohio and Indiana, 6 Hartford Blk, 84 E Market, h 759 N Penn.

O. B. ENSEY
MANUFACTURER OF
GALVANIZED IRON CORNICE, SKYLIGHTS AND WINDOW CAPS,
TELEPHONE 1562. Cor. 6th and Illinois Sts.

Miller Wylie, roofer, h 330 Fletcher av.
Miller Zimena D, clk H P Wasson & Co, b 469 Ash.
Miller Zipporah H (wid Hugh P), b 330 Fletcher av.
Miller & Albrecht (Charles L Miller, Charles Albrecht), tinners, 208 E Washington.
MILLER & ELAM (Wm H H Miller, John B Elam), Lawyers, Rooms 2-6, 68½ E Market, Tel 241.
Miller & Smock (Lennie Miller, Della M Smock), milliners, 147 Virginia av.
Milli Frank, lab, h 32 Oriole.
Milli Louis, lab, h 17 Oriole.
Milli Reinhart, grocer, 581 Madison av, h same.
Milligan George, lab, h 8 Sheridan.
Milligan Harry J, lawyer, 68½ E Market, h 735½ N Delaware.
Milligan John, lab, h rear 267 Fayette.
Milligan Joseph, coachman, h 252 W 3d.
Milligan Lottie, r 79 Cleaveland blk.
Milligan Wm, agt, r 170 W Market.
MILLIKAN FRANK M, Special Loan Agt Northwestern Mutual Life Insurance Company of Milwaukee, Wis, 88 N Penn, Tel 1245; b The Denison.
Millikan Isaac W, contr, 17 When bldg, h 1140 N Penn.
Millikan James A, butcher, h 212 S William (W I).
Millikan John N (J N Millikan & Co), r 648 N Illinois.
Millikan J N & Co (J N and Lynn B Millikan), contrs, 17 When bldg.
Millikan Lynn B (J N Millikan & Co), h s e cor N Meridian and 9th.
Millikan Mont V, trav agt, h 554 E Ohio.
Millikan Rhoda H (wid Samuel), b 820 Park av.
Millikan Wm D, house mover, h 53 S California.
Milliken Wm L, r 60 The Blacherne.
Milliken Dennis, lab, h 247 W 5th.
Milliken Henry C, drayman Charles Mayer & Co, b 15 Mill.
Milliken John A, porter, b 247 W 5th.
Milliken Leslie, lab, b 247 W 5th.
Millikin Aaron, lab, b 3 Bryan.
Millington Thomas E, mach, b 174 John.
Millison T Rees, trav agt Clemens Vonnegut, h 455 Broadway.
Millman Anson H, dentist, 40 N Senate av, h same.
Millman Louis, bkkpr, b 349 E McCarty.
Millman Roy S, dentist, b 40 N Senate av.
Millner Wm J, r 37½ W Market.
Mills Albert H, grocer, 51 Cornell av, h same.
Mills Arthur G, engr P H Krauss, h 344 Blake.
Mills Daniel M, b 30 N William (W I).
Mills Frank R, tmstr Outing Bicycle Co, h n s Vorster av 4 e of Millburn (M P).
Mills George, huckster, b 296 Blake.
Mills George E, musician, h 186 Ash.
Mills Gertrude J, clk, b 45 S Arsenal av.
Mills Henry, driver, b 136 Martindale av.
Mills James E, engr, h 15 Athon.
Mills John, coachman, h 573 W Michigan.
Mills John D, h 384 N New Jersey.
Mills John M (The Wood Ornament Co), b 1490 N Senate av.
Mills Joseph C (Mills & Frink), h 676 McLene (N I).

TUTEWILER UNDERTAKER, NO. 72 WEST MARKET STREET. TELEPHONE 216.

PARTNERSHIP INSURANCE At low cost. By which provision is made against the pecuniary loss and embarrassment resulting from the death of a member of a firm.
Provident Life and Trust Co. of Philadelphia, D. W. EDWARDS, Gen'l Agt., 508 Indiana Trust Bldg.

THEODORE F. SMITHER, AGENT FOR WARREN'S ANCHOR BRAND —ASPHALT ROOFING— OFFICE, 151 WEST MARYLAND ST. TEL. 861.

Mills Julia A (wid Isaac), h 351 N Senate av.
Mills Lafayette, lab, h 207 W Vermont.
Mills Leander F, h 738 E 8th.
Mills Lewis, trav agt Famous Stove Co, h 30 N William (W I).
Mills Mary, cook, h 20½ N Delaware.
Mills Milton, waiter The Bates.
Mills Oscar J, mach hd, h 59 Nordyke av (W I).
Mills Pearce, brakeman, r 199 W South.
Mills Rebecca A, nurse, b 676 McLene (N I).
Mills Robert S, clk, r 282 N Illinois.
Mills Sallie A (wid Layton), h 75 S McLain (W I).
Mills Thomas P (Mills & Small), h 64 Division (W I).
Mills Wm, h 90 Patterson.
Mills Wm, meats, 128 Oliver av, h 14 Warren av (W I).
Mills Wm H, painter, h 33 Catharine.
Mills Wm R, engr, h 339 Blake.
Mills & Frink (Joseph C Mills, Edward S Frink), produce, 121 E Mkt House.
Mills & Gibb, Rolla Harris agt, dry goods, 35 W Pearl, also New York city.
MILLS & SMALL (Thomas P Mills, Samuel Small), Real Estate Brokers, Rooms 6-7, 96½ E Market, Tel 109.
Millspaugh Charles V, dairy, s s Michigan av 3 e of Belt R R, h same.
Millspaugh Edward M, tel opr, h 159 Trowbridge (W).
Millspaugh Ellsworth A, lab, h w s Auburn av 1 n of Big Four Ry.
Millspaugh George, lab, h 164 N Delaware.
Millspaugh George M, lab, h 200 N Delaware.
Millspaugh Mary A (wid David A), h 118 Trowbridge (W).
Millspaugh Wm A, foreman Natl Malleable Castings Co, b 70 Michigan (H).
Millward George, pdlr, h 201 Meek.
Milner Charles M, lab, b 169 Dougherty.
Milner Elizabeth (wid David), h 169 Dougherty.
Milner Harry W, clk, b 36 Highland pl.
Milner John W, carp, h 61 S Arsenal av.
Milner Lafayette, h 36 Highland pl.
Milner Martha M (wid Isaac L), b 24 Christian av.
Milner Wm L, contr, 1252 N Illinois, h same.
Milnor John E, clk, h 907 N Delaware.
Milnor Wm E, paperhngr, h 134 Hosbrook.
Milroy Fannie (wid Francis A), h 244½ E Washington.
Milroy Walter J, mach, b 244½ E Washington.
Milroy Wm E, mach, h 244½ E Washington.
Milstreich Emil O, lab, h 400 S Capitol av.
Milstreich Frederick, h 270 S Capitol av.
Milton Aaron, lab, b n e cor Jones and Schurman av (N I).
Milton Charles S, bricklyr, h 625 N West.
Milton Emma, b 170 Oliver av (W I).
Milton Hiram T, carp, h 48 Camp.
Milton James H, lab, h 18 Smith.
Milton Jennie (wid James H), h e s Line 5 s of Washington av (I).
Milton Wm T, tinner, h rear 48 Camp.
MILWAUKEE HARVESTER CO, S Webster Genl Agt, 6 Board of Trade Bldg.
Minardo Joseph, fruits, 19 E Mkt House, h 56 S Alabama.
Minch Amos, lab, h 28 Sheffield av.

THE WHEN IS A WORLD BEATER.

Minch Casper, carp, h 1404 Northwestern av (N I).
Minchener Katie J (wid Arthur J), boarding 46 S Capitol av.
Minchin James A, lab, h w s James 4 n of Sutherland (B).
Minderman Wm H, fireman, h rear 83 Morton.
Miner Benjamin D (Wm R Watson & Co), phys' chairs, 19 John, h 277 E Walnut.
Miner Charles H, carp, h 247 Coburn.
Miner David K, b 193 Christian av.
Miner Frederick D, abstracts, 96½ E Market, h 57 N East.
Miner Gertrude, lodging, 57 N East, h same.
Miner Herbert I, mach, h 13 Wilcox.
Miner James E, condr, h 576 N Alabama.
Miner James O, painter, b 512 Virginia av.
Miner Joshua C, lab, h 89 Holmes av (H).
Miner Loren A, clk, h 193 Christian av.
Miner Mabel, stenog, b 247 Coburn.
Miner Malinda, laundress, h 178½ Indiana av.
Miner Minnie, h 80 S Senate av.
Miner Oliver C, cigarmkr, h 24½ Indiana av.
Miner Wilford H, cigars, 150 Indiana av, b 278 Blackford.
Miner Wm C, painter, h 512 Virginia av.
MINER WM L, Rug and Mat Mnfr, 184-186 Cherry, h 81 Park av. (See adv opp classified Rugs.)
Miner Willis R, cashr County Treasurer, h 71 Broadway.
Minesinger Charles W, rec teller Merchants' National Bank, h 400 Ash.
Minesinger Mary H (wid Henry M), b 400 Ash.
Minger Albert, farmer, b n e cor Michigan and Belmont av.
Minger Elizabeth (wid John), h n e cor Michigan and Belmont av.
Minger Emil, clk, b 1386 N Senate av.
Minger Frederick, baker, h 1386 N Senate av.
Minger Frederick, dairy, s s Washington 1 e of Sherman Drive, h same.
Minger Gottfried, baker, h 1386 N Senate av.

THE A. BURDSAL CO.
WINDOW AND PLATE GLASS
Putty, Glazier Points, Diamonds.
Wholesale and Retail. 34 and 36 S. Meridian St.

ELECTRIC CONSTRUCTION Isolated Plants Installed. Electric Wiring and Fittings of all kinds. C. W. Meikel. Tel. 466. 96-98 E. New York St

DALTON & MERRIFIELD { LUMBER South Noble St., near E. Washington

INDIANA ELECTROTYPE CO. : BEST WORK LOWEST PRICES. 23 WEST PEARL ST., INDIANAPOLIS, IND. JOB WORK. BOOK PLATES. All Orders Promptly Filled. BEST PATENT BASE ON THE MARKET.

KIRKHOFF BROS.,
GAS AND ELECTRIC FIXTURES
THE LARGEST LINE IN THE CITY.
102-104 SOUTH PENNSYLVANIA ST.
TELEPHONE 910.

Minger Otto, bartndr, b 1386 N Senate av.
Minger Wm G, farmer, b n e cor Michigan and Belmont av.
Mings James M, carp, h 180 W 9th.
Minich Charles A, bkkpr, h 71 W 12th.
Minkner Catherine M (wid Wm), h n end Decatur.
Minkner Frederick H, lab, h 175 King av (H).
Minkner Minnie (wid August H W), h 15 Minkner.
Minkner Henry F, gardener, h 79 Astor.
Minkner Leo J, grocer, 51 Palmer, h same.
Minks Byron F, blksmith, b 3 Henry.
Minks Joseph M, lab, h 3 Henry.
Minks Lee W, b 3 Henry.
Minneapolis Threshing Machine Co, Justus B Parker mngr, 117 W Washington.
Minor Benjamin B, grain, 18 Board of Trade bldg, h 956 N Meridian.
Minor Charles K, lab, b 106 Prospect.
Minor Eugene V, mngr bicycle dept Lilly & Stalnaker, b 956 N Meridian.
Minor George W, lab, h 89 Martindale av.
Minor John, mer police, h 1370 N Capitol av.
Minor John W, sec and treas Sentinel Printing Co, h 111 Park av.
Minor Mary, teacher Public School No 6, b 111 Park av.
Minor Thomas J, lab, h e s Rural 5 s of Sutherland (B).
Minor Thompson J, lab, h 201 W 4th.
Minor Wm, coachman, 729 N Delaware.
MINTER ALBERT F, Manufacturer of and Dealer in Tight Barrel Staves, Circled and Square Heading, Cooperage, Etc, s end California, Tel 655; h 843 N Illinois. (See adv p 8.)
Minter Charlotte M (wid Wm H), r 265 N Capitol av.
MINTER FERDINAND, Grocer, Meat Market and Baker, s w cor Home av and Yandes, h 637 Home av.
Minter Lucy (wid Samuel), h 62 River av (W I).
Minter Mary L, grocer, 50 Yandes, h 636 Home av.

COAL AND COKE
The W. G. Wasson Co.,
130 INDIANA AVE. TEL. 989
LIME AND LATH

Minter Smith, tmstr, h 21 W 2d.
Minter Wm S, mach, b 62 River av (W I).
Minthorn Frank, clk, b 2 Cornell av.
Minthorn John J, carp, 2 Cornell av, h same.
Minton Elbert C, bridge engr C F Hunt Co, h 180 Walcott.
Minton George H, weaver, h 60 Geisendorff.
Minton Jennie, h 1 Center.
Mints Morris O, teacher, h 469 W Shoemaker (N I).
Minturn Joseph A, patent solr, 15-16 Lombard bldg, h 1140 N Illinois.
Minturn Wm M, tailor, h 508 N West.
Mirrick Paul, clk, h 442 E St Clair.
Misner Perry, lab, h 224 Madison av.
Mitchell Albert, lab, b 150 S Belmont av (W I).
Mitchell Alexander, switchman, h 124 Michigan av.
Mitchell Alexander S, teacher, b 498 N Penn.
Mitchell Alfred A, lab, h 126 Ash.
Mitchell Allen R, carp, h 76 Division (W I).
Mitchell Alonzo, lab, h 494 S West.
Mitchell Alvanus, porter, h 210 W 2d.
Mitchell Andrew, carp, h 955 N New Jersey.
Mitchell Andrew V, watchman, h 150 S Belmont (W I).
Mitchell Anna N (wid Wm), b 572 N Alabama.
Mitchell Archibald B, trav agt, h 126 E Walnut.
Mitchell Augustus C C, tubmkr, h 723 E Ohio.
Mitchell Benno V, condr, b 180 N East.
Mitchell Carlos E, turner, b 50 Standard av (W I).
Mitchell Charles, lab, h n e cor Michigan and Sharpe avs (W).
Mitchell Charles, waiter, b 229 W Washington.
Mitchell Charles B, trav agt Murphy, Hibben & Co, b Roosevelt House.
Mitchell Charles D, engr, h 4 E Sutherland (B).
Mitchell Charles H, driver, r 6, 149½ Oliver av (W I).
Mitchell Charles R, driver, h 225 Orange.
Mitchell Charles W, lab, h 161 Michigan av.
Mitchell Charles W, lab, h 34 Helen.
Mitchell Clara E (wid James L), r 279 N Capitol av.
Mitchell Colonel C, screwmkr, h 162 Fayette.
Mitchell David, cook, 26 E Michigan.
Mitchell Dora H (wid Charles R), h 179 W 2d.
Mitchell Douglass, tmstr, h 29 Roe.
Mitchell Edward C, lab, b 567 E 8th.
Mitchell Edward H, agt, b 437 E St Clair.
Mitchell Edward J, lab, b 23 Blackford.
Mitchell Elisha, lab, b Exchange Hotel (W I).
Mitchell Elwood, lab, b 1363 W Washington (M J).
Mitchell Enoch W, porter, b 126 Ash.
Mitchell Fletcher M, real est, cor W Washington and Harris av (M J), h 30 Becker (M J).
Mitchell Frank, driver, b 180 Newman.
Mitchell Frank, lab, b 433 Blake.
Mitchell Frank L, clk H P Wasson & Co, b 179 Christian av.
Mitchell Frederick, porter, r 234 S Penn.
Mitchell George, barber, 671 Madison av, r same.
Mitchell George, lab, h 24 Holborn.

W. H. MESSENGER COMPLETE HOUSE FURNISHER 101 East Washington Street, Telephone 491

Foundry and Pattern Shop } McNamara, Koster & Co. { PHONE 1593 212-218 S. Penn. St.

Mitchell George, lab, b 529 N Senate av.
Mitchell George, lab, b 20 Sheffield av (H).
Mitchell George, lineman, b 335 Jefferson av.
Mitchell George H, clk, b 437 E St Clair.
Mitchell George W, lab, h 548 Superior.
Mitchell Grant, photog, 306 River av (W I); r 301 same.
Mitchell Harrison L, picker, h 861 Rembrant.
Mitchell Harry, engr, h 98 High.
Mitchell Harry, painter, h 181 Newman.
Mitchell Harry R, sawyer, b 50 Standard av (W I).
Mitchell Henry A, lab, r 11 Ellsworth.
Mitchell Hiram, lab, b 24 Holborn.
Mitchell Horace, hostler, h 86 Torbet.
Mitchell H Lewis, clk H P Wasson & Co, b 179 Christian av.
Mitchell Isham, carp, b 21 Belmont av.
Mitchell Jacob E, carp, h 297 English av.
Mitchell James, fireman, r 117 Lexington av.
Mitchell James, fireman, b 45 Miley av.
Mitchell James, lab, h 117 Douglass.
Mitchell James, lab, h 162½ Indiana av.
Mitchell James, loans, 30 Baldwin blk, r 36½ W Washington.
Mitchell James, saloon, 258 S Missouri, h same.
Mitchell James A, lab, h 180 Newman.
Mitchell James C, finisher, h 72 Martindale av.
Mitchell James E, carp, 437 E St Clair, h same.
Mitchell James E, tmstr, b 448 Blake.
Mitchell James H, flagman, h 89 E McCarty.
Mitchell James L, lawyer, 212 Indiana Trust bldg, r 91 W Vermont.
Mitchell James M, broommkr, h 66 Yandes.
Mitchell James M, driver, h 357 English av.
Mitchell James R, lab, h 240 S Linden.
Mitchell James T, mnfrs' agt, 503 Lemcke bldg, b 400 N Illinois.
Mitchell James W, watchman, h 139 Hoyt av.
Mitchell Jesse, lab, b 105 Locke.
Mitchell John, fireman, r 117 Lexington av.
Mitchell John, lab, r 198½ W Court.
Mitchell John B, tiremkr, h 179 Harrison.
Mitchell John T M, lab, b 161 Michigan av.
Mitchell John W, broom mnfr, 240 S Linden, h 227 same.
Mitchell John W, trimmer, h 27 Shover (W I).
Mitchell Joseph A, condr, h 23 Blackford.
Mitchell Joseph R, insp, h 19 Sharpe.
Mitchell Josephine (wid Craig), h 3 Susquehanna.
Mitchell Josephine (wid Daniel), h rear 233 Fayette.
Mitchell Julius, barber, h rear 671 N Senate av.
Mitchell Julius, lab, h 31½ Columbia al.
Mitchell Kate, laundress, h 285 E Wabash.
Mitchell Laura (wid Henry), b 112 Howard.
Mitchell Levi L, watchman, h 1265 Morris (W I).
Mitchell Louis C, harnessmkr, h 12 Brett.
Mitchell Louis C, huckster, h 44 Athon.
Mitchell Luther, driver, b 190 College av.
Mitchell Lyman A, springbedmkr, b 103 Agnes.
Mitchell Margaret E, bkkpr Frank E Janes, h 23 Blackford.
Mitchell Mary (wid Jeremiah), b 529 N Senate av.
Mitchell Mary A, dressmkr, 36½ W Washington, r same.

Henry H. Fay, 40½ E. WASHINGTON ST., AGENT FOR Insurance Co. of North America, Pennsylvania Fire Ins. Co.

Mitchell Melinda, h rear 119 N Missouri.
Mitchell Nancy (wid Robert S), h 215 Orange.
Mitchell Oliver, switchman, b 180 Newman.
Mitchell Owen C, h 374 S West.
Mitchell Patrick, lab, h 379 Columbia av.
Mitchell Perry, coachman 603 N Delaware.
Mitchell Purley C, screwmkr, b 162 Fayette.
Mitchell Rebecca J (wid George G), h 400 N Illinois.
Mitchell Richard J, waiter, b 229 W Washington.
Mitchell Robert I, carp, h 173 E Walnut.
Mitchell Samuel, driver, h 198½ W Court.
Mitchell Sarah, h 29 Roe.
Mitchell Silas, lab, b 103 Geisendorff.
Mitchell Teney, lab, h 22 Sumner.
Mitchell Thomas, b 94 Columbia av.
Mitchell Thomas, hostler, h 126 N Missouri.
Mitchell Thomas J, trav agt, r 400 N Illinois.
Mitchell Thomas W, clk H P Wasson & Co, h 179 Christian av.
Mitchell Tillman M, lab, h 244 Douglass.
Mitchell Wm, coachman 734 N Meridian.
Mitchell Wm, driver, h 216 W 8th.
Mitchell Wm, foreman, h 6 Hadley av (W I).
Mitchell Wm, lab, h 7 Walker (H).
Mitchell Wm A, meats, 348 E St Clair, h 29 Clifford av.
Mitchell Wm H, lab, h 216 W 8th.
Mitchell Wm J, saloon, 154 S New Jersey, h same.
Mitchell Wm L, lab, h 50 Standard av (W I).
Mitchell Wm S, letter carrier P O, h 138 W Michigan.
Mitchell Wm S, plastr, r 141 W Washington.
Mitchell Wm T, lab, h 2 Dakota.
Mitchell Wm T, watchman, b 140 W Vermont.
Mitchell Willis D, mach hd, b 285 S Missouri.
Mitchem Valoras, cook, h 174 W 2d.
Mitrakos John G, candy, h 332 E Washington.

Union Casualty & Surety Co. of St. Louis, Mo. Employers', Public, General, Teams and Elevator Liability; also Workmen's Collective, Steam Boiler, Plate Glass and Automatic Sprinkler Insurance. W. E. BARTON & CO., General Agents, 504 Indiana Trust Building. LONG DISTANCE TELEPHONE 1918.

THE FRED DIETZ CO. WOODEN PACKING BOXES MADE TO ORDER. FACTORY AND WAREHOUSE TRUCKS. 400 Madison Avenue. Telephone 654.

Shorthand. BUSINESS UNIVERSITY. When Bl'k. Elevator day and night. Typewriting, Penmanship, Book-keeping, Office Training free. See page 4. Est. 1850. Tel. 499. E. J. HEEB, Proprietor.

HENRY R. WORTHINGTON JET and SURFACE CONDENSERS 64 S. PENN. ST. Long Distance Telephone 284.

UNION CO-OPERATIVE LAUNDRY (3D OF UNION GIRLS.) NOS. 140 AND 142 VIRGINIA AVENUE T. E. SOMERVILLE, MANAGER—TELEPHONE 129. INDIANAPOLIS, IND.

HORACE M. HADLEY
REAL ESTATE AND LOANS....
66 East Market Street
Telephone 1540. BASEMENT.

Mitschrich Herman, grocer and meats, 189 Prospect, h 100 Jefferson av.
Mitt Bartholomew, lab, h 62 Ludlow av.
Mittay Charles, lab, h 117 Lincoln la.
Mittay Edward J, lab, b 144 N Pine.
Mittay Henry A, carp, h 719 E Ohio.
Mitten Iona C, stenog Standard Oil Co, b 93 Spann av.
Mitten Louisa C (wid George A), h 93 Spann av.
Mitten Love V M (wid George D), clk, b n s Orange av 2 w of Keystone av.
Mittendorf John, ironwkr, b 285 S Capitol av.
Mittmann Frederick, grocer, 128 W Ray, h same.
Mittrach Gustav, lab, h 73 S Liberty.
Mitzenberg Mary F (wid Martin W), b 75 Norwood.
Mix Christopher, driver, h 68 Wisconsin.
Mix Frank C, mach, h 1146 E Ohio.
Mix Gustav, oils, h 68 Wisconsin.
Mix Lyman W, real est, 9 Cyclorama pl, h 63 W 12th.
Mix Oscar A, helper, b 42 Keystone av.
Mix Robert A, lab, h 42 Keystone av.
Mobley Dana L, clk, b 163 Clinton.
Mobley Grant, cooper, b 371 English av.
Mobley Harry W, cooper, h 245 W McCarty.
Mobley Hiram G, cooper, h 423 S West.
Mobley Thomas J, cooper, h 420 E Pearl.
Mock Charles, h 556 Union.
Mock George, driver, r 177 S Alabama.
Mock Henry M, plumber Knight & Jillson, h 198 Buchanan.
Mock Joseph, contr, 73 Martindale av, h same.
Mock Martin, tailor, h 127 Davidson.
Mock Thomas A, driver, h 106 Shelby.
Mock Wm H, carp, h 18 Hamilton av.
Mockford Thomas, painter, h 1593 N Illinois.
Mockford Thomas E, news agt, b 1593 N Illinois.
Mode Charles F, clk, h 232 Spring.
Mode George J W, clk, h 75 Elm.
Mode Michael, shoes, 93 E Washington, h 460 E Market.
MODEL CLOTHING CO, Saks & Co Proprs, 41-49 E Washington and 2-22 S Penn, Tel 763.

Merchants' and Manufacturers Exchange
Make Collections and Commercial Reports......
J. E. TAKKEN, MANAGER,
19 Union Building, 73 West Maryland Street

Modlein Edward, fireman, h 321 Fletcher av.
Modlin Mahlon, carp, h 105 Oliver av (W I).
Modlin Nathan L, motorman, h 1005 N Senate av.
Modlin Wm, driver, h 29 S Dorman.
Modrell Harry O, clk, r 337 N Liberty.
Moehlmann Frederick A H, checkman, h 187 Spann av.
Moehlmann Frederick H, porter, h 349 E McCarty.
Moehlmann Louis H, bkkpr Elmer E Nichols Co, b 349 E McCarty.
Moehnle Elizabeth (wid Michael), r 46 Leon.
Moehrman Rosa (wid Charles), h 13 E New York.
Moellenkamp Frederick J, b 99 Naomi.
Moellenkamp John H, lab, h 99 Naomi.
Moeller, see also Miller, Moller, Mueller and Muller.
Moeller Carl W, die cutter, h 385 Ash.
Moeller Carrie, nurse 118 N Senate av.
Moeller Christian H, carp, h n w cor Jefferson and St Peter.
Moeller Frederick A, painter, h 135 St Paul.
Moeller Henry, finisher, h 21 Holmes av (H).
Moeller Herman, driver, r 224 S Delaware.
Moeller Herman, painter, b 135 St Paul.
Moeller Mary (wid Charles), h 47 Oriental.
Moeller Wm, saloon, 175 Shelby, h same.
Moeller Wm H, lab, h 748 S East.
Moesch Elizabeth (wid Thaddeus), h e s Ethel av 1 s of 20th.
Moesch Henry W, bkkpr L W Ott Mnfg Co, h 411 S Meridian.
Moesch Julius, mach hd, b e s Ethel av 1 s of 20th.
Moeslin Joseph, cabtmkr, h 48 Wisconsin.
Moess Charles, mach, h 20 Keystone av.
Moffat Thomas (Moffat & Co), r 176½ N Alabama.
MOFFAT & CO (Thomas Moffat), Dealer in Glass, Iron, Steel and Tin Plate Mnfrs' Supplies, 402 Lemcke Bldg, Long Distance Tel 1218. (See adv p 9.)
Moffatt Ansil R, chemist, h 302 N New Jersey.
Moffett Edward D, phys, 16 W New York, h same.
Moffett Naomi C (wid Estil K), phys, 27½ Monument pl, h same.
Moffett Robert, lab, h 236 Naomi.
Moffett Winfield S (Clifford, Browder & Moffett), h 184 Broadway.
Moffitt Charles F, pres Rex Coal and Sewer Co, and sec and treas Bee Hive Paper Box Co, h 1104 N Delaware.
Moffitt Harry C, barber, h 527 W 22d (N I).
Moffitt John R, lab, h 527 W 22d (N I).
Moffitt Leroy D, carp, b 527 W 22d (N I).
Moffitt Margaret (wid John), h 108½ Mass av.
Moffitt Margaret W (wid John), b 123 Prospect.
Moffitt Wm C, lab, h 468 W McLene (N I).
Mofford Nelson, news agt, r 171 E Court.
Mogle Daniel E, grocer, 422 W 2d, h same.
Mohan James, engr, h Union Stock Yards (W I).
Mohawk Cycle Co, Horace L Hewitt sec and treas, cor Francis and Elmira (N I).
Mohler James E, lab, h 590 W Udell (N I).
Mohler John, popcorn, h 13 Arch.
Mohler John E, baker, b 194 E Washington.

CLEMENS VONNEGUT 184, 186 and 192 E. Washington St. Wire Rope, Machinery, Lathes, Drills and Shapers

THE WM. H. BLOCK CO. DRY GOODS, DRAPERIES, RUGS, WINDOW SHADES.
7 AND 9 EAST WASHINGTON STREET.

Mohler Luther, attendant Insane Hospital.
Mohler Rusha L, baker, b 13 Arch.
Mohler Samuel L, salesman, h 139 Highland pl.
Mohler Susannah (wid Henry), b 42 Eastern av.
Mohr Charles, wheelmkr, b 201 W 1st.
Mohr Emma D, German teacher Public School No 13, b 109 E St Joseph.
Mohr Henry, lithog, h 468 N West.
Mohr Jacob, pdlr, h 88 Lincoln la.
Mohr John, lab, h 201 W 1st.
Mohs Wm J A (Wm J A Mohs & Co), h 7 Shelby.
Mohs Wm J A & Co (Wm J A Mohs), dry goods and saloon, 7 Shelby.
Moir John G, student, b 166 Woodlawn av.
Moister George, millwright, h 103 Nordyke av (W I).
Moker George W, porter, h 158 Howard.
Molder Andrew, carp, h 131 Martindale av.
Molder John H, cooper, h 456 W New York.
Moldthan Albert F, clk, h 143 Meek.
Moldthan Christina (wid Christian), h 65 Buchanan.
Moling Alonzo R, lather, h 130 Yandes.
Mollenkopf George F (Rice & Mollenkopf), b w s Schurman av 1 s of Wells (N I).
Mollenkopf Louisa (wid Wm), h 114 N Dorman.
Mollenkopf Worth, lab, h 129 Windsor.
Moller, see also Miller, Moeller, Mueller and Muller.
MOLLER CARL, Wall Paper, Decorations and Window Shades, 161 E Washington, h 392 Ash.
Moller Gustav H, salesman Carl Moller, b 392 Ash.
Moller Wm G, paperhngr, h 68 Jefferson.
Molles Joseph M, lab, h e s Foundry 4 n of Willow (B).
Moloney, see also Maloney.
Moloney James H, carp, r 287 E Washington.
Moloney John, shoes, 275 S Illinois, h 643 N Senate av.
Mols Adolph, supervisor of physical culture Public Schools, h 628 Central av.
Monaghan Anthony A, sawmkr, b 68 Maple.
Monaghan Catherine (wid James), h 68 Maple.
Monaghan David J, clk, b 123 Shelby.
Monaghan John, capt Hose Co No 18, h 879 N Senate av.
Monaghan John W, sawmkr, b 68 Maple.
Monaghan Patrick H, lab, b 357 W Washington.
Monaghan Thomas F, ins agt, h 42 Barth av.
Monaghan Thomas S, trav agt, b 123 Shelby.
Monaghan Timothy, shoemkr, h 123 Shelby.
Monaghan Winnie (wid Patrick), h 317 W Washington.
Monahan Andrew, lab, b 4 Wallace.
Monahan Charles, lab, h 499 S Illinois.
Monahan Fred, lab, h 552 W Washington.
Monahan Frederick, lab, h 4 Wallace.
Monahan Hugh, driver, b 1775 Graceland av.
Monahan John, b 282 S Capitol av.
Monahan John, lab, h 166 W McCarty.
Monahan John J, lab, b 499 S Illinois.
Monahan Martin, lab, h 369 W Pearl.
Monahan Mary, housekpr 369 W Pearl.
Monahan Michael F, janitor, h 494 S Capitol av.

Monahan Rosa (wid Thomas), h 175 Duncan.
Monahan Thomas, lab, h 282 S Capitol av.
MONARCH SUPPLY CO, Grocers, 84 E Washington, Tel 1453.
Moncrief Eldo, carp, h 392 Cornell av.
Mondary Henry, lab, b 95 River av (W I).
Mondon Mary E (wid Benjamin), h 148 Eddy.
Money Charles, clk, h rear 44 Prospect.
Moneymaker Laura, b 57 Talbott av.
Monfort Alfred A, clk, h 1588 Kenwood av.
Moufort Holliday, patternmkr, b 70 Orange av.
Monfort Moses, blksmith, h 70 Orange av.
Monger Horace H, baggagemstr, h 220 Lexington av.
Monger Marshall S, condr, h 230 Hoyt av.
Monger Robert E, carp, h 89 Tremont av (H).
Monical Bedford M, molder, h 28 Warman av (H).
Monk John W, attendant Insane Hospital.
Monks John, music teacher, 369 Cornell av, h same.
Monks Leander J, associate Justice Supreme Court of Indiana, 60 State House, res Winchester, Ind.
Monks Mary J (wid John), h 630 W Francis (N I).
Monn Edwin F, feed, 207 Indiana av, h 32 Fayette.
Monn James M, clk, h 26 Fayette.
MONNINGER ALBERT D, Pharmacist, n w cor Monument Pl and Meridian, b 385 N Capitol av.
Monninger Conrad, cigars, 390 Indiana av, h 388 same.
Monninger Daniel, h 385 N Capitol av.
Monninger George, cloth coverer, h 20 Mayhew.
MONNINGER GOTTFRIED, Billiard and Sample Room, Importer of Rhine Wines, Liquors and Cigars, 101-105 N Illinois, h 377 same.
Monninger Henry, patrolman, h 391 Indiana av.

GUIDO R. PRESSLER,
FRESCO PAINTER
Churches, Theaters, Public Buildings, Etc., A Specialty.
Residence, No. 325 North Liberty Street
INDIANAPOLIS, IND.

INDIANAPOLIS STEEL ROOFING AND CORRUGATING WORKS, 23 and 25 East South Street. S. D. NOEL, Proprietor.

David S. McKernan, REAL ESTATE AND LOANS
A number of choice pieces for subdivision, or for manufacturers' sites, with good switch facilities.
Rooms 2-5 Thorpe Block.

DIAMOND WALL PLASTER { Telephone 1410 BUILDERS' EXCHANGE.

UNION TRANSFER AND STORAGE CO. Cor. E. Ohio St. and C., C., C. & St. L. R'y Tracks. BRICK WAREHOUSE; CLEANEST AND SAFEST STORAGE IN CITY FOR HOUSEHOLD GOODS AND MERCHANDISE.

W. McWORKMAN,

METAL CEILINGS,
ROLLING SHUTTERS,
DOORS AND PARTITIONS.

930 W. Washington St. Tel. 1118.

Monroe, see also Munro.
Monroe Alexander R, ins adjuster, 11 Talbott blk, h 1058 N Alabama.
Monroe Alpin F, ins agt, b 158 E 8th.
Monroe August, lab, b 11 Mill.
Monroe Calvin, lab, h 440 Martindale av.
Monroe Charles D, switchman, h 350 S West.
Monroe Clara M, stenog H T Conde Implement Co, b 88 S Linden.
Monroe Elmer E, finisher, h 131 Windsor.
Monroe George D, electrician, h 122 Newman.
Monroe Harry, student, b 304 W Market.
Monroe Henry, insp, b 95 Shelby.
Monroe John B, farmer, h 129 Yandes.
Monroe John E, cooper, h 491 W New York.
Monroe John L, stairbldr, h 44 Hill av.
Monroe John W, lab, h 304 W Market.
Monroe Lela A, stenog State B and L Assn, b 88 S Linden.
Monroe Lewis A, clk Penna Lines, r 223 E Vermont.
Monroe Louisa S, music teacher, 330 E Vermont, h same.
Monroe Margaret (wid Jesse L), h 263 Shelby.
Monroe Mary A (wid Jasper R), r 17 Ryan blk.
Monroe May, opr C U Tel Co, b 67 Minerva.
Monroe Samuel T, molder, b 263 Shelby.
Monroe Sarah T (wid John), h 67 Minerva.
Monroe Thomas F, printer, h 537 Central av.
Monroe Thomas W, sawmkr, h 152 Union.
Monroe Walter C, coremkr, b 44 Hill av.
Monroe Wm H, bricklyr, h 276 W Market.
Montague Belle (wid Edward D), b 88 S Linden.
Montague Charles, pdlr, r 77 Kentucky av.
Montague Lafayette, trav agt, h 933 N Senate av.
Montague Lester F, rep, b 933 N Senate av.
Montague Sanford, lab, h 1323 Isabelle (N I.)
Montani Anthony A (Montani Bros), b 170 N Alabama.

SEALS,
STENCILS,
STAMPS, Etc.
GEO. J. MAYER
15 S. Meridian St.
TELEPHONE 1386.

MONTANI BROS (Guy, Domenico, Anthony, Pasquale, Casper and Nicholas), Orchestra and Music Teachers, 168 N Alabama, Tel 175.
Montani Casper (Montani Bros), b 170 N Alabama.
Montani Domenico (Montani Bros), h 168 N Alabama.
Montani Ferdinand (F & I Montani), h 170 N Alabama.
Montani Ferdinand, fruits, E Mkt House, h 32 Valley av.
Montani F & I (Ferdinand and Isabella), fruits, 5 Mass av.
Montani Guy, leader Montani Bros Orchestra, h 168 N Alabama, tel 175.
Montani Isabella (F & I Montani), h 170 N Alabama.
Montani Nicholas (Montani Bros), b 170 N Alabama.
Montani Pasquale (Montani Bros); b 170 N Alabama.
Montasana Prospero, lab, b 411 E Pearl.
Montei Henry, lab, h 335 Fletcher av.
Montesano Frank, musician, h 33 Valley.
Montezuma Mill Co, Mary E Goldstine mngr, flour and feed, 100 S West.
Montgomery Amos H, molder, b 312 W Merrill.
Montgomery Anna (wid James), h 732 S Meridian.
Montgomery Arthur A, engraver, b 159 Christian av.
Montgomery Arthur M, mach opr The Indpls News, h 119 E New York.
Montgomery Catherine E (wid Henry J), h 60 Roanoke.
Montgomery Charles, farmer, h w s Northwestern av 3 n of 25th (N I).
Montgomery Charles M, carp, h 573 W Michigan.
Montgomery DeWitt C, carp, h 282 S East.
Montgomery Edward E, tmstr, h 16 Reynolds av (H).
Montgomery Ella J, teacher, b w s Northwestern av 3 n of 25th (N I).
Montgomery Elmira, teacher, b w s Northwestern av 3 n of 25th (N I).
Montgomery Francis M, mnfrs' agt, 503 Lemcke bldg, h 462 Broadway.
Montgomery Frederick, clk, r 84 S Illinois.
Montgomery George N, b w s Northwestern av 3 n of 25th (N I).
Montgomery George R, clk Holliday & Wyon, h 14 Bates.
Montgomery Harry E, lab, b 60 Roanoke.
Montgomery Isaac, driver, b 189 St Mary.
Montgomery James C, lab, b 89 Indiana av.
Montgomery Jesse, lab, b e s Bismarck 2 s of Emerich (H).
Montgomery Jordan D, lab, h 36 Howard.
Montgomery Joseph, clk, b 82 Indiana av.
Montgomery Lewis W, janitor, h 28 Journal bldg.
Montgomery Lucretia (wid Wm E), h e s Bismarck 2 s of Emrich (H).
Montgomery Marilla (wid Joseph), h 119 E New York.
Montgomery Martha (wid George B), b 426 E Georgia.
Montgomery Mary E (wid Calvin J), b 162 Bellefontaine.
Montgomery Michael, hostler 16 West Drive (W P).
Montgomery Nebraska, h 100 N Alabama.
Montgomery Oliver C, lab, b 7 W Sutherland (B).
Montgomery Oliver P, plumber, h 87 Germania av (H).

A. METZGER AGENCY ESTABLISHED 1863. INSURANCE

LAMBERT GAS & GASOLINE ENGINE CO.
ANDERSON, IND. PORTABLE GASOLINE ENGINES. 2 TO 25 H. P.

Montgomery Orville H, lab, b 7 W Sutherland (B).
Montgomery Robert E, mnfrs' agt, 736 Lemcke bldg, r 322 The Shiel.
Montgomery Robert H, clk, h 426 E Georgia.
Montgomery Russell L, lab, h 178 Agnes.
Montgomery Samuel L, b n s Northwestern av 3 n of 25th (N I).
Montgomery Seymour W, helper, h s s Bloyd av 2 w of Shade (B).
Montgomery Silas, condr, r 175 S Illinois.
Montgomery Sylvester H, tmstr, h 189 St Mary.
Montgomery Thomas J, printer, b 732 S Meridian.
Montgomery Tyra, trav agt, r 40 Kentucky av.
Montgomery Walter W, lab, h 282 Fulton.
Montgomery Wm A, gasfitter, b 426 E Georgia.
Montgomery Wm C, lab, h 476 W North.
Monticue Jesse B, mach hd, h 321 N West.
Monticue Wm B, mach, b 321 N West.
Montieth Mathias, bricklyr, h 189 Yandes.
Montoney Mathilda (wid John), b 119 Meek.
Montson Caspar, trav agt, b 411 E Pearl.

MONUMENT SAVINGS AND LOAN ASSOCIATION, Walter T Cox Pres, Wm F Churchman Treas, Henry F Stevenson Sec, 68½ E Market.

Moo Shing, laundry, 39 Virginia av.
Moody Ella, h 255½ S Delaware.
Moody Ida M, clk Joseph H Brown, b 531 E Washington.
Moody John, tmstr, b 869 S Meridian.
Moody Lorenzo D, vice-pres Indiana Sav and Inv Co, ins, 56 Coffin blk, h 127 St Mary.
Moody Mattie (wid Richard), b 175 W 6th.
Moody Robert, waiter The Bates.
Moon Albert S, student, b 688 N Illinois.
Moon Clarence C, clk, b 960 N Senate av.
Moon Clarkson H, carp, 960 N Senate av, h same.
Moon Edith, bkkpr, b 960 N Senate av.
Moon Edward T, lab, h 106 Maple.
Moon Emma J (wid George), h 622 Central av.
Moon Harry B, bricklyr, b 688 N Illinois.
Moon John M, carp, h 147 Cottage av.
Moon Lee W, asst Reporter Supreme Court, b 688 N Illinois.
Moon Melville L, car rep, h 112 Wright.
Moon Sidney R, Reporter Supreme Court, h 688 N Illinois.
Moon Sylvanus, clk Van Camp H and I Co, h 140 S Linden.
Moon Virgil O, mailing clerk P O, b 140 S Linden.
Mooney Ella, housekpr 3 Springdale pl.
Mooney Lawrence, lab, h 242 Dougherty.
Mooney Lawrence J, bkkpr D O'Brien & Co, h 40 Brookside av.
Mooney Susie (wid John), h 264 S New Jersey.
Mooney Wm A, treas Indianapolis Abattoir Co, res Columbus, Ind.
Mooney Wm J, clk A Kiefer Drug Co, h 224 Bellefontaine.
Mooney Wm P (John G Thurtle & Co), h 447 Bellefontaine.
Mooney Winifred (wid John), b 209 Douglass.
Moor Charles E, produce, 101 E Mkt House, h 138 Mass av.
Moor James F, clk, h 625 S Meridian.
Moore, see also More.

Farm and City Loans
25 Years' Successful Business.
THOS. C. DAY & CO,
Rooms 325 to 330 Lemcke Building.

Moore Aaron, lab, h 387 W New York.
Moore Addie (wid John B), h 67 Talbott av.
Moore Albert C, pdlr, h 7 Water.
Moore Albert D, cigars, 536 College av and Journal bldg, b 536 College av.
Moore Albert W, agt, h 235 W Maryland.
Moore Alfred H, asst City Engineer, h 31 N Beville av.
Moore Alice (wid John), b 368 S Delaware.
Moore Alice F (wid Alvin), h 204 Lexington av.
Moore Ambrose, h 98 Cornell av.
Moore Anderson D, molder, b 23 Bloomington.
Moore Anna, h 482 Chapel.
Moore Anna (wid Charles), b 41 Stevens.
Moore Anna M (wid Ozias), h 136 N Penn.
Moore Arminda C (wid Joseph), h 471 N New Jersey.
Moore Arthur, clk Spencer House, r 26 W New York.
Moore Arthur C, clk Moore & Co, b 920 N Illinois.
Moore Atlas, mach hd, h 25 Oriental.
Moore Belle (wid Thomas), h 173 W Vermont.
Moore Bud, lab, b 10 S Missouri.
Moore Cassius, lab, h 440 W North.
Moore Charles, hostler, b rear 855 N Illinois.
Moore Charles F, carp, h 528 W Eugene (N I).
Moore Charles G, painter, h 211½ Indiana av.
Moore Charles H (Tyndall & Moore), mngr C P Webb, h w s Euclid av 2 n of Washington.
Moore Charles J, painter, h 965 Grove av.
Moore Charles W, lab, h 314 N Missouri.
Moore Christopher C, car rep, h 53 Bloomington.
Moore Charles W, clk, b 173 W Vermont.
Moore Clemence W, clk, b 136 N Penn.
Moore Clyde T, clk Parry Mnfg Co, b 77 E McCarty.
Moore David F, barber, h 238 W Ohio.
Moore David F, carp, h 586 Morris (W I).
Moore Delta W, dairy, s w cor Sangster av and 22d, h s s 22d 1 w of Baltimore av.

EAT
QUAKER BREAD
ASK YOUR GROCER FOR IT.
THE HITZ BAKING CO.

BICYCLES $5 DOWN. $5 MONTHLY. Best Wheels. Best Terms. WHEELMEN'S CO. 31 W. OHIO ST. LONG DISTANCE TEL. 1855.

J. H. TECKENBROCK House, Sign and Fresco Painter, 94 EAST SOUTH STREET.

FIDELITY MUTUAL LIFE PHILADELPHIA, PA. A. H. COLLINS, Gen. Agt. Baldwin Blk. RATES REASONABLE. SOUND BEYOND QUESTION. BUSINESS-LIKE IN PRACTICE.

BITUMINOUS COAL ▸▸ Edwardsport Coal and Min'g Company ROOMS 42 AND 43 WHEN BUILDING.

ESTABLISHED 1876. TELEPHONE 168.
CHESTER BRADFORD,
SOLICITOR OF PATENTS,
AND COUNSEL IN PATENT CAUSES.
(See adv. page 6.)
Office:—Rooms 14 and 16 Hubbard Block, S. W. Cor. Washington and Meridian Streets, INDIANAPOLIS, INDIANA.

Moore De Witt V, draughtsman I U Ry Co, b 220 N Capitol av.
Moore Edgar L, clk, b 185 N Noble.
Moore Edward, lab, h 213 W Court.
Moore Edward, hostler, r s e cor Washington and Lake avs (I).
Moore Edward, lab, b 133 Blackford.
Moore Edward, tmstr, b 107 Locke.
Moore Edward D, chief clk Indiana Natl Bank, h 176 N East.
Moore Edward E, painter, h 43 Draper.
Moore Edward L, molder, h 26 Highland av (H).
Moore Edward V, bricklyr, h 793 E Market.
MOORE EDWIN F (W Scott Moore & Son), b 117 E Michigan.
Moore Edwin F, condr, b 20 Michigan (H).
Moore Elbert J, filer, h 204 Lexington av.
Moore Eliza J (wid Wm P), h 363 N Noble.
Moore Ella, h 56 S Noble.
Moore Ellis, lab, h rear 81 W North.
Moore Elwin O, clk, b 341 Central av.
Moore Enoch H, lumber, h 244 Michigan (H).
Moore Ernest M, collr, h e s Millburn 3 n of Humbolt (N I).
Moore Esau, lab, b 482 Chapel.
Moore Fannie S (wid Robert), b 172 Highland av.
Moore Frank, carp, b 107 Locke.
Moore Frank, lab, b 169 S Reisner (W I).
Moore Frank A, trav agt, h 34½ Hall pl.
Moore Frank B, instructor Indpls Business University, When bldg, h 226 E Ohio.
Moore Frank C, solr, h 112 S Linden.
Moore Frank D, fireman, b 71 Meek.
Moore Frank F (Terhune & Moore), h 75 Butler.
Moore Frank J, clk Indiana National Bank, h 952 N Senate av.
Moore Frederick J, steward, h 257 N Illinois.
Moore George, brakeman, b 1027 E Washington.
Moore George, car rep, h 13 N Station (B).
Moore George, motorman, h 260 Douglass.
Moore George O, clk, b 341 Central av.
Moore George O, lab, b 25 E Ray.

BUY THE BEST.
Outing BICYCLES $85
MADE BY
HAY & WILLITS MFG. CO.
76 N. PENN. ST. Phone 598.

Moore George T, bkkpr Mas Mut Ben Soc, h 19 E St Joseph.
Moore George T jr, student, b 19 E St Joseph.
Moore George T, stenog, b 290 Clifford av.
Moore George W, carp, 107 Locke, h same.
Moore George W, clk, b 498 Virginia av.
Moore George W, sexton, h 225 Muskingum al.
Moore George W, waiter, h 176 Dillon.
Moore Harriet (wid George), h 25 E Ray.
Moore Harry, lab, b 35 Malott av.
Moore Harry C, clk R M S, h w s Layman av 2 n of Washington av (I).
Moore Harry C, foreman mach shop Nordyke & Marmon Co, h 593 Bellefontaine.
Moore Harry C, trav agt John L Moore, b 372 N East.
Moore Harry F, tel opr, h 375 Prospect.
Moore Harry H, distributor, b 375 E Ohio.
Moore Harry S, student, b 145 S New Jersey.
Moore Harvey A, student, b 61 N Arsenal av.
Moore Harvey C, grocer, cor English av and Olive, h 112 S Linden.
Moore Hattie (wid Philip), h 178½ Muskingum al.
Moore Hattie A, b 304 E Market.
Moore Henry (Lanier & Moore), h 67 Howard.
Moore Henry, hostler, r 1128 N Meridian.
Moore Henry, lab, h 62 Oscar.
Moore Henry, phys, h n w cor Washington and Layman avs (I).
Moore Horace W, bkkpr Singer Mnfg Co, b 145 S New Jersey.
Moore Hugh I, tailor, b 67 S West.
Moore Ida E, dressmkr, 67 Talbott av, b same.
Moore Ivory, lab, h w s James 8 n of Sutherland (B).
Moore James, bartndr, r 148 W Maryland.
Moore James, bkkpr, b 89 Indiana av.
Moore James, lab, h 156 Michigan av.
Moore James, lab, r 427 Muskingum al.
Moore James, lab, b n w cor Reisner and Johnson (W I).
Moore James B, grocer, 2 Haugh (H), h 39 Warman av (H).
Moore James E, lab, h 56 Ludlow av.
Moore James H, bkkpr, h 611 Broadway.
Moore James H, saloon, 245 Mass av, h 431 Bellefontaine.
Moore James L, letter carrier P O, h 498 Virginia av.
Moore James L, well driver, h 143 Clarke.
Moore James M, dairy, 46 Paw Paw, h same.
Moore James T, lab, h 187½ E Washington.
Moore Jane (wid James), b 217 W Court.
Moore Jennie E (wid Frederick A), h 568 Ash.
Moore Jesse, lab, h 189 W 3d.
Moore Jesse C (Groninger & Moore), sec and treas The Universal Credit Agency, h 324 N Delaware.
Moore John, clk, b 326 S State av.
Moore John, contr, n e cor Washington and Quincy, h same.
Moore John, cook, r 12½ Roanoke.
Moore John, mngr Moore & Co, h 920 N Illinois.
Moore John A, clk P C C & St L Ry, h 29 N Rural.
Moore John B, coremkr, r 161 S William (W I).
Moore John D, switchman, h 1089 W New York.

ROOFING MATERIAL C. ZIMMERMAN & SONS, SLATE AND GRAVEL ROOFERS, 19 SOUTH EAST STREET.

PUMPS Chain Pumps, Driven Wells and Deep Water Wells. Repairing Neatly Done. Cisterns Built. CHARLES KRAUSS', 42 S. PENN. ST. TELEPHONE 465.

Coll as and Cuffs Laundered in Best of Style. Domestic or High Gloss Fi.

Moore John E, flagman, h 7 Wilcox.
Moore John F, blksmith, 114 Shelby, h 150 Cypress.
Moore John F, turner, h 27 Ashland (W I).
Moore John F L, clk, b 219 S Olive.
Moore John J, helper, b 17 Dougherty.
Moore John L (McKee & Moore), h 341 Central av.
MOORE JOHN L, Wholesale Grocer, 124-126 S Meridian, h 372 N East, Tel 402.
Moore John M, tmstr, h 397 Prospect.
Moore John N, clk, b n e cor Washington and Quincy.
Moore John O, lawyer, 92½ E Washington, h 73 Ludlow av.
Moore John W, h 35 Warman av (H).
Moore John W, carp, h 334 Yandes.
Moore John W, lab, b 510 S Illinois.
Moore John W, lab, b 284 W 6th.
Moore John W, painter, h 328 E Wabash.
Moore John W, sec and treas Indiana Tract Soc, h 175 Central av.
Moore Joseph, cooper, h 31 Sheffield (W I).
Moore Joseph, foreman, b s e cor Rural and 7th.
Moore Joseph, real est, h 536 College av.
Moore Joseph A, feed, 12 Prospect, h 1443 E Washington.
Moore Joseph M, blksmith, h 55 Johnson av.
Moore Joseph S, clk P C C & St L Ry, h 38 Walcott.
Moore Joshua M, carp, h 537 W Udell (N I).
Moore Kate, h 56 S Noble.
Moore Katharine (wid Wm), h 185 N Noble.
Moore Leonidas A, condr, h 42 Pleasant av.
Moore Louis M, city fireman, h 242 Hamilton av.
Moore Margaret, seamstress, b s e cor Olive and Orange.
Moore Margaret (wid Jacob), h 334 Yandes.
Moore Margaret (wid John J), h 138 Blackford.
Moore Mark C, boarding 129 N Illinois.
Moore Marshall, trav agt The Indpls Book and Stationery Co, h 745 N New Jersey.
Moore Martha (wid Hiram), h 35 Malott av.
Moore Martin, lab, h e s Rural 3 s of Clifford av.
Moore Mary, h 56 S Noble.
Moore Mary, teacher Public School No 10, b 471 N East.
Moore Mary A, h 493 N Meridian.
Moore Mary J (wid Cameron), h 324 N Delaware.
Moore Mary M (wid Thomas T), h 221 W Maryland
Moore Matilda A (wid John I), h 40 Warman av (H).
Moore Matthew R, supt Atlas Engine Works, h 448 Bellefontaine.
Mooore Mattie (wid John A), tailoress, h 355 S Missouri.
Moore Michael, lab, h rear 262 S Missouri.
Moore Michael H, trimmer, h 211 Davidson.
Moore Michael J, trav agt H T Conde Implement Co, h 1058 N Delaware.
Moore Michael J, trav agt The Indpls Sentinel, h e s Penn 2 s of 15th.
Moore Michael P, mach, b 17 Dougherty.
Moore Miles V, clk P L Chambers, b 170 Clinton.
Moore Myla A (wid Joseph L), h 290 Clifford av.
Moore Myrtle, b 255 W Morris.
Moore Nathan A (N A Moore & Co), h 1360 N Illinois.

Richardson & McCrea,
79 East Market Street.
FIRE INSURANCE,
REAL ESTATE, LOANS,
AND RENTAL AGENTS.
Telephone 182.

Moore Nellie C, stenog, b 129 N Illinois.
Moore Nellie M, clk W U Tel Co, b 568 Ash.
Moore Nicholas, flagman, h 17 Dougherty.
Moore Noah, porter, h 213 W Court.
MOORE N A & CO (Nathan A Moore), Grocers and Meat Market, 1-5 Indiana av, Tel 892.
Moore Olive E (wid Vivian), h w s Capitol av 5 s of 30th.
Moore Oscar, condr, h 135 N Delaware.
Moore Otis, cushionmkr, r 237 E South.
Moore Otis H, clk Joseph R Perry, b 341 Central av.
Moore Otto W, brakeman, b 54 Belmont av (H).
Moore Patrick, lab, h 50 King av (H).
Moore Patrick J, car rep, h 108 Deloss.
Moore Philip, lab, h 10 S Missouri.
Moore Ralph A, clk, b 129 N Illinois.
Moore Rebecca (wid Thomas), h 150½ College av.
Moore Remus, clk I D & W Ry, h 35 Camp.
Moore Richard, tailor, h 67 S West.
Moore Richard G, pdlr, b 211½ Indiana av.
Moore Richison, h 219 S Olive.
Moore Robert E, pres U S Saving Fund and Investment Co and treas Edwardsport Coal and Mining Co, h w s Central av 3 s of Washington av (I).
Moore Robert J, cooper, h 221 W Maryland.
Moore Robert S, h 89 S Linden.
Moore Robert W, agt James Heekin & Co, 25 W Georgia, r 259 N Illinois.
Moore Ross, student, r 106½ E New York.
Moore Sadie, h 217 W Court.
Moore Samuel, lab, h 170 Clinton.
Moore Samuel H, clk, b 363 N Noble.
Moore Samuel H, phys, 152 Virginia av, h 145 S New Jersey.
Moore Sarah (wid John), h 1401 E Washington.
Moore Sarah A, h s e cor Olive and Orange.
Moore Sarah A (wid John W), h 117 Lincoln la.
Moore Sarah E (wid John), h 255 W Morris.
Moore Shelton, lab, b 383 W New York.
Moore Sidney, lab, h 227 Muskingum al.

SHORTHAND REPORTING......
CONVENTIONS, SPEECHES, SERMONS.
COPYING ON TYPEWRITER.
S. H. EAST, State Agent,
THE WILLIAMS TYPEWRITER
55 Thorpe Block, 87 East Market Street.

ERTEL STEAM LAUNDRY 26 and 28 N. Senate Ave. Telephone 1089.

ELLIS & HELFENBERGER Manufacturers of Iron Vases, Setees and Hitch Posts. 162-170 South Senate Ave. Tel. 958

THE HOGAN TRANSFER AND STORAGE COMP'Y
Household Goods and Pianos Moved—Packed—Stored...... Baggage and Package Express Machinery and Safes a Specialty Cor. Washington and Illinois Sts. TELEPHONE No. 675.

The Central Rubber & Supply Co. PHONE 922. 79 S. ILLINOIS ST., INDIANAPOLIS, IND. ◆◆◆▶ Hose, Belting, Packing, Clothing, Druggists' Sundries, Bicycle Tires, Cotton Hose, Etc. New York Belting & Packing Co., L't'd.

The Provident Life and Trust Co.
Small Death Rate. Small Expense Rate. Safe Investments. OF PHILADELPHIA. Insurance in force $115,000,000
D. W. EDWARDS, General Agent, 508 Indiana Trust Building.

Moore Silas S, foreman Crown Hill Cemetery, h same.
Moore Simeon, waiter, h 321 W North.
Moore Sir Walter S, carp, h 394 N New Jersey.
Moore Sylvester, driver, r 88 N New Jersey.
Moore Taylor L, driver, h 553 W Washington.
Moore Terrence M, patrolman, h 324 E Miami.
Moore Thomas, h 84 S Senate av.
Moore Thomas, lab, h 776 E 10th.
Moore Thomas, phys, 22 Commercial blk, b 99 Lynn.
Moore Thomas, tailor, 7 Indiana av, b 460 E North.
Moore Thomas A, tailor, b 67 S West.
Moore Thomas C, lab, h 702 E 9th.
Moore Thomas C, mer police, h 61 N Arsenal av.
Moore Thomas C, tailor, h 460 E North.
Moore Thomas F, uphlr, h rear 43 Draper.
Moore Thomas J, boilermkr, h 522 N West.
Moore Thomas J, teacher High School, b 448 Bellefontaine.
Moore Thomas T, h 84 S Senate av.
Moore Verne, clk, b 173 W Vermont.
Moore Walter C, clk, b 383 W New York.
Moore Walter V, trav agt, h 1508 Kenwood av.
Moore Warren, tmstr, b 25 E Ray.
Moore Warren, trav agt, r 259 N Illinois.
Moore Wm, butcher, b 190 Columbia av.
Moore Wm, carp, b 79 N Alabama.
Moore Wm, hostler, b rear 855 N Illinois.
Moore Wm, packer, h 74 Madison.
Moore Wm, varnisher, b 472 S Missouri.
Moore Wm A, carp, h 402 Columbia av.
Moore Wm A, clk Badger Furniture Co, b 324 N Delaware.
Moore Wm A, painter, 127 Shepard (W I).
Moore Wm A, vice-pres H T Conde Implt Co, h 952 N Senate av.
Moore Wm C, molder, h w s Sheffield av 2 n of Clarke (H).
Moore Wm E (Moore & Dorrah), h 582 Jefferson av.
Moore Wm E, lab, b 35 Malott av.
Moore Wm F (Moore & Horan), h 176½ S Olive.

Julius C. Walk & Son, Jewelers Indianapolis. 12 EAST WASHINGTON ST.

Moore Wm J, clk, r 38½ Kentucky av.
Moore Wm J, grocer, 99 Shelby, h 91 same.
Moore Wm J, harnessmkr, b 185 N Noble.
Moore Wm O, clk Schrader Bros, h 296 E Ohio.
Moore Wm O, collr The Indiana Trust Co, h 63 Laurel.
Moore Wm P, lab, b 363 N Noble.
Moore Wm R, foreman, h 77 E McCarty.
Moore Wm R, molder, h 33 N McLain (W I).
Moore Wm R, supt Friendly Inn, h 292 W Market.
Moore Wm S, painter, h 22 S Gale (B).
Moore Wm S, student, b n e cor Washington and Quincy.
MOORE W SCOTT (W Scott Moore & Son), h 117 E Michigan.
MOORE W SCOTT & SON (W Scott and Edwin F), Architects, Rooms 12, 13 and 14 Blackford Blk, s e cor Washington and Meridian, Tel 1308. (See adv in classified Architects.)
MOORE & CO, John M Shaw Pres, Samuel Reid Vice-Pres, John Chestnutt Sec, Robert Reid Treas, John Moore Genl Business Mngr, Pork Packers, Union Stock Yards (W I), Tel 94.
MOORE & DORRAH (Wm E Moore, David S Dorrah), Contractors and Builders, 582 Jefferson av.
Moore & Horan (Wm F Moore, Michael Horan), real est, 36½ E Washington.
Moorehead George A, carp, h 25 Hoyt av.
Moorehead Jacob, porter, h 386 W 2d.
Moorehead James, tmstr, b 386 W 2d.
Moorehead John D, trav agt, h 496 W 22d (N I).
Moores Charles W (Chambers, Pickens & Moores), h 946 N Penn.
Moores Jesse R, chief insp Indpls Bureau of Inquiry and Investigation, r 387 N Senate av.
Moores Julia M (wid Charles W), h 986 N Penn.
MOORES MERRILL, Lawyer, 18½ N Penn, Tel 1157, Deputy Attorney-General State of Indiana, Room 19 State House, Tel 1300; b 986 N Penn.
Moores Ruhama (wid John A), b 387 N Senate av.
Moorhead Robert L, clk The Bowen-Merrill Co, b 928 N Meridian.
Moorhead Thomas W, whol jeweler, 146 S Meridian, h 926 N Meridian.
Moorie Mollie M, nurse City Hospital.
Moorman Allen F, waiter, b 448 E Walnut.
Moorman Calvin S, condr, h 185 Cornell av.
Moorman Charles L, trimmer, h 556 W Eugene (N I).
Moorman Elvet E, student, b s e cor Johnson and Washington avs (I).
Moorman Fannie (wid Richard), h 448 E Walnut.
Moorman Ferdinand T, elevator opr, r Lorraine bldg.
Moorman Frederick, lab, h 94 Minerva.
Moorman George, cabtmkr, b 559 W 22d (N I).
Moorman Joel H, carp, w s Central av 1 s of Beechwood av (I), h same.
Moorman John A, condr, h 146 Lynn av (W I).
Moorman John B, janitor, h Lorraine bldg.
Moorman John R, carp, h 559 W 22d (N I).

OTTO GAS ENGINES | BUILDERS' EXCHANGE S. W. Cor. Ohio and Penn. Telephone 535.

Becker & Son Charles Becker Jacob Becker Jr. Merchant Tailors. 21 N. Penn. St. Tel. 934

SALIS BRY & STANLEY. 177 Cb Set, Indianapolis, Ind. Office, Store and Bank Fixtures a Specialty. Repairing of all kinds done on short notice. Contractors and Builders TELEPHONE 999.

Moos John, bricklyr, h 103 Naomi.
Moos Philip, mason, h 72 Arizona.
Moosman Samuel, baker, 23 Palmer, h same.
Moppert Gustav A, barber, h 48 Bismarck.
Moran Daniel, lab, h 94 S Liberty.
Moran Daniel, steamfitter, h 101 Bright.
Moran Dennis, baggageman, h 630 W Vermont.
Moran Edward, lab, b 671 W Vermont.
Moran Edward A, carp, h 46 S Pine.
Moran Frank, engr, r 168½ E Washington.
Moran George E, springbedmkr, h 952 N New Jersey.
Moran Harry A, saloon, 117 S Illinois, h 1067 N Capitol av.
Moran Henry, lab, b 308 S Illinois.
Moran James J, mach, b 152 Bates.
Moran John, lab, r 200½ W Washington.
Moran John, engr, h 169 Buchanan.
Moran John, plumber, b 152 Bates.
Moran Joseph T A, clk, b 186 Davidson.
Moran Joseph W, insp, b 169 Buchanan.
Moran Katherine R, dressmkr, 186 Davidson, h same.
Moran Martin, lab, h 89 Belmont av.
Moran Martin, saloon, 50 S Illinois, h 356 same.
Moran Mary (wid Michael), b 94 S Liberty.
Moran Mary A (wid John), h 186 Davidson.
Moran Michael, b 99 Bright.
Moran Michael, lab, h 549 W Washington.
Moran Michael, saloon, 28 Michigan (H), h same.
Moran Michael C, wagonmkr, h 75 Cornell av.
Moran Patrick, foreman, h 111 W South.
Moran Patrick, lab, h 357 W Washington.
Moran Patrick F, condr, b 134 Highland pl.
Moran Patrick H, engr, h 99 Bright.
Moran Patrick J, bartndr, r 44 S West.
Moran Patrick J, tinner, h rear 472 E Washington.
Moran Patrick T, saloon, 251 W Washington, h same.
Moran Thomas, condr, b 134 Highland pl.
Moran Thomas A, meats, 6 S Station (B), h 1140 N Rural.
Moran Valentine, lab, b 314 W Maryland.
Moran Valentine, steamfitter, b 101 Bright.
Morand John E, h 396 Ash.
Moraskey Christian, foreman, h 166 Jefferson av.
Moraskey Wm, pressfeeder, b 166 Jefferson av.
Morbach Charles, dry goods, 301 S Delaware, h same.
Morbach Charles W, clk N Y Store, h 180 S Olive.
Morbach Peter, shoemkr, h 117 E Merrill.
Morck Wm O, architect, 143 Dillon, b 199 Spann av.
Mordorf Wm, lab, b 202 W Maryland.
More, see also Mohr and Moore.
More Albert E, plumber, b 516 N West.
More Philip H, piano tuner, h 516 N West.
More Sarah (wid Philip H), h 25 Ellsworth.
Moreau Jeremiah, mach, h 30 Fletcher av.
Moreland Edgar W, examiner, h 1213 N Penn.
Moreland Leland K, paperhngr, h 244 English av.
Moreland Wm L, r 264 N Capitol av.
Morey Clara, teacher Public School No 1, h 108 Frazee (H).
Morey James, harnessmkr, b 67 S Noble.
Morey Leonard, b 676 Broadway.

Henry H. Fay,
40½ E. WASHINGTON ST.,
FIRE INSURANCE, REAL ESTATE,
LOANS AND RENTAL AGENT.

Morfet Nelson, varnisher, h 614 Cornell av.
Morford Alfred C, lab, h 667½ Madison av.
Morford George U, lab, h 1365 W Washington (M J).
Morford John, gardener, h n s Washington 3 e of Line (I).
Morgan Abraham, phys, 54 Oscar, h same.
Morgan Albert, collr, h 178 Lexington av.
Morgan Anna (wid Wm), h 833 S Meridian.
Morgan Anthony, shoemkr, h 186 Elizabeth.
Morgan Augustus L, engraver, h 116 Park av.
Morgan Benjamin F Rev, pastor Oak Hill M E Church, h s w cor Miller and McLain (W I).
Morgan Benjamin J, chiropodist, 25½ W Washington, h 261 W 6th.
Morgan Benson, clk, b 143 N West.
Morgan Brazelton B, phys, b s s Washington av 2 e of Johnson av (I).
Morgan Calvin, clk, h 311 English av.
Morgan Carrie, opr C U Tel Co, b 125 Hadley av (W I).
Morgan Celina J (wid Lott E), h 598 N New Jersey.
Morgan Charles, shoemkr, 299½ W Washington, r same.
Morgan Charles C, barber, 10½ E Washington, h 182 Blake.
Morgan Charles C, lab, h 11 Bates al.
Morgan Charles Q, polisher, b 518 W Maryland.
Morgan Catherine M, waitress, h 244½ E Washington.
Morgan Daniel, lab, b 318 Fletcher av.
Morgan Dean, lab, r 229½ E Washington.
Morgan Edmund, boarding 125½ Hadley av (W I).
Morgan Edna, bkkpr, b 125½ Hadley av (W I).
Morgan Edward, clk, r 200½ W Washington.
Morgan Edward, clk, b 143 N West.
Morgan Emily (wid Wm), b 187 W 2d.
Morgan Frank, bkkpr, h 116½ N Meridian.
Morgan Frank, tailor, b Enterprise Hotel.
Morgan Frederick W, stenog Union Trust Co, res Martinsville, Ind.
Morgan George, engr, b 161 English av.

JAS. N. MAYHEW,
MANUFACTURING
OPTICIAN
LENSES AND FRAMES A SPECIALTY.
No. 13 North Meridian St., Indianapolis.

LUMBER | Sash, Door and Planing . Mill Work . | Balke & Krauss Co. Cor. Market and Missouri Streets.

FRIEDGEN'S TAN SHOES are the Newest Shades Prices the Lowest. 19 North Pennsylvania St.

SAMUEL LAING General Job Work in Sheet Metal of all Kinds 72 AND 74 E. COURT STREET.

M. B. WILSON, Pres. W. F. CHURCHMAN, Cash.
THE CAPITAL NATIONAL BANK,
INDIANAPOLIS, IND.
Make collections on all points in the States of Indiana and Illinois on the most favorable rates.
Capital, - - $300,000
Surplus and Earnings, 50,000
No. 28 S. Meridian St., Cor. Pearl.

Morgan George, feed, 70 Michigan (H), h same.
Morgan George, lab, b 272 S West.
Morgan George, lab, b rear 275 S West.
Morgan George, porter Hotel Oneida.
Morgan George H, lab, h e s Harriet 1 s of Park (B).
Morgan George W, lab, b 518 W Maryland.
Morgan Glenn, clk Natl Malleable Castings Co, b 585 Broadway.
Morgan Hannah (wid Calvin), b 249 S New Jersey.
Morgan Harry, porter, r 6 Howard.
Morgan Harry C, clk, b 116 Columbia av.
Morgan Hendricks C, bkkpr, b 116 Columbia av.
Morgan Henry, lab, h 328 Muskingum al.
Morgan Hezekiah D, mach, h 817 E Market.
Morgan Irene, dressmkr, 817 E Market, h same.
Morgan James R, h 108 Trowbridge (W).
Morgan James S, switchman, b 108 Trowbridge (W).
Morgan Jennie C (wid. James A), bkkpr, b 241 Cornell av.
Morgan Jesse, cook, r 319 E Washington.
Morgan John, finisher, b 36 Division (W I).
Morgan John, phys, 170 N Illinois, b 130 W 2d.
Morgan John F, teacher, h 1377 W Washington (M J).
Morgan John J, helper, h 326 Martindale av.
Morgan John O, engr, b 10 Hadley av (W I).
Morgan John R, filer, b n s Bethel av 3 e of Belt R R.
Morgan John S (H T Conde Implement Co), h 585 Broadway.
Morgan John W, h 427 W Highland av (N I).
Morgan Joseph N, engr, h 218 N Missouri.
Morgan Joseph R (Morgan & Morgan), b 598 N New Jersey.
Morgan Lawrence, cooper, h rear 275 S West.
Morgan Lewis, dairy e s Sherman Drive 1 s of Washington, h same.
Morgan Livingston D, tmstr, b 109 John.

MONEY
Loaned on Short Notice at Lowest Rates.
TUTTLE & SEGUIN,
Tel. 1168. 28 E. Market St.

Morgan Louis J (Morgan & Morgan), b 598 N New Jersey.
Morgan Marinda E (wid Wm J), h 66 Hadley av (W I).
Morgan Mark, shoemkr, 368 Virginia av, h same.
Morgan Martha E (wid Julius), h n s Orange av 1 e of Jefferson av.
Morgan Mary (wid George), h 51 Dougherty.
Morgan Mary G, teacher Public School No 2, b 82 N East.
Morgan Minnie C, stenog, b 178 Lexington av.
Morgan Mitchell P, lab, h 276 Alvord.
Morgan Myrta, stenog, h 419 W Addison (N I).
Morgan Nancy (wid Wm), h 278 Lafayette.
Morgan Romulus M, engr, h 10 Hadley av (W I).
Morgan Samuel, blksmith, h 29 Orange av.
Morgan Samuel D, painter, b 172 E Louisiana.
Morgan Samuel W, blksmith, h 230 Fletcher av.
Morgan Sarah (wid James), h 143 N West.
Morgan Sylvester A, sec School Board (W I), carp, 216 River av (W I), h same.
Morgan Theodore E, enlarger, h 201 S Illinois.
Morgan Thomas, baker, 349 S Delaware, h same.
Morgan Thomas, carp, h 555 W Highland av (N I).
Morgan Thomas, carp, h 106 Howard.
Morgan Thomas, cooper, b 475 Indiana av.
Morgan Walter, fireman, b 900 W Washington.
Morgan Wm, molder, b 70 Michigan (H).
Morgan Wm A, r 99 N New Jersey.
Morgan Wm A, mach, b 336 W Court.
Morgan Wm A, waiter, h 167 W Market.
Morgan Wm J, carp, h 1151 N Alabama.
Morgan Wm L, janitor, h 84 Dugdale.
Morgan Wm M, farmer, h 590 Morris (W I).
MORGAN WM V, Physician and Surgeon, 336 N Alabama, Tel 1043, h same.
MORGAN & MORGAN (Louis J and Joseph R), Lawyers, 37-38 Lombard Bldg, Tel 1584.
Morganbeck George H, mach hd, h rear 176 S New Jersey.
Morganson Daniel, brakeman, h 123 S Noble.
Moriarty Anna E, clk, b 188 Yandes.
Moriarty Bettie, h 20 Bell.
Moriarty Daniel, lab, h 20 Meikel.
Moriarty Daniel, trimmer, b 188 Yandes.
Moriarty David, tallyman, b 176 English av.
Moriarty Edward, electrician, h 134 Highland pl.
Moriarty Emma (wid Wm C), h 229 E New York.
Moriarty James, bartndr, b 374 S Delaware.
Moriarty James, lab, b 23 Bates.
Moriarty James, lab, h 42 Detroit.
Moriarty James D, saloon, 200 Virginia av, h same.
Moriarty James J, lab, b 176 English av.
Moriarty Jeremiah, lab, h 23 Bates.
Moriarty John, flagman, b 49 Williams.
Moriarty John, huckster, h 366 S Capitol av.
Moriarty John, lab, b 374 S Delaware.
Moriarty John A, stenog, b 229 E New York.
Moriarty Julia J (wid John T), h 4 Deloss.
Moriarty Maurice, lab, h 374 S Delaware.

PAPER BOXES, MANUFACTURED BY SULLIVAN & MAHAN 41 W. PEARL STREET.

DIAMOND WALL PLASTER { Telephone 1410
BUILDERS' EXCHANGE.

Fine Laundry Work our Specialty. Collars and Cuffs our Hobby. THE HOME LAUNDRY 197 S. Illinois St. Telephone 1769.

Moriarty Maurice, lab, b 18 Meikel.
Moriarty Maurice J, lab, b 176 English av.
Moriarty Michael, clk, b 188 Yandes.
Moriarty Michael, tmstr, b 252 E Washington.
Moriarty Michael J, plastr, b 4 Deloss.
Moriarty Norah (wid Patrick), h 23 Bates.
Moriarty Patrick, grocer, 227 Minnesota, h 225 same.
Moriarty Patrick F, mach hd, b 188 Yandes.
Moriarty Patrick J, helper, b 4 Deloss.
Moriarty Sylvester, cigarmkr, b 105 Minnesota.
Moriarty Thomas, lab, h 18 Meikel.
Moriarty Thomas, lab, 188 Yandes.
Moriarty Timothy J, plastr, b 4 Deloss.
Moriarty Wm, candymkr, b 511 S Illinois.
Moriarty Wm C, decorator, b 229 E New York.
Morin John L, bellboy The Bates.
Morin Margaret, forewoman Fahnley & McCrea, b 19 E Ohio.
Morise Samuel, lab, r 158 Michigan av.
Morlan Albert M, artist, 287 E Vermont, h same.
Morlan Chauncey R, b 55 Vine.
Morlan James N, h 55 Vine.
Morlan James W, driver, b 55 Vine.
Morlan Percy R, clk, b 287 E Vermont.
Morlan Ralph W, clk, b 287 E Vermont.
Morland Michael, lab, b 549 W Washington.
Morlath Edward F, plumber, b 23 Hamilton av.
Morlatt George W, lab, h 8 Hamilton av.
Morley Hannah (wid Thomas), h 226 S Missouri.
Morley John, h 55 Broadway.
Morley John M, butcher, h 19 Helen.
Morley Thomas, lab, b 226 S Missouri.
Morningstar Peter, live stock, h 527 Talbott av.
Morningstar Wm C, trav agt, b 527 Talbott av.

MORONEY DANIEL M, Druggist, 142 Michigan (Haughville), h 234 same, Tel 1788.

Moroney John R, winder, h 294 S Alabama.
Moroney Michael J, mach hd, h 78 Bicking.
Moroskey Christian, hostler, h 166 Jefferson av.
Moroskey Wm C, printer, b 166 Jefferson av.
Morre Henry C, train disp C C C & St L Ry, h 17 Rockwood.
Morrell Dora J (wid Stephen), drugs, 248 Mass av, h 237½ Mass av.
Morrell Edward C, brakeman, b 125 Prospect.
Morrell Edward N, painter, b 237½ Mass av.
Morrell Lewis H, state foreman Central Union Telephone Co, tel 43, b 383 Park av, tel 558.
Morrell Robert, lab, b rear 143 St Mary.
Morrill Joseph W, clk The Gordon-Kurtz Co, h 127 W 1st.
Morris Alfred W, brickmkr, h 64 Cleaveland blk.
Morris Allen, lab, h s s Colgrove 3 w of Mattie av.
Morris Allie M, dressmkr, 223 N Senate av, h same.
Morris Alvin M Rev, pastor Church of Christ, William street (W I), h 509 Highland av (N I).
Morris Amos I, watchman, h rear 333 S Alabama.
Morris Anna S (wid Michael), h 538 E Georgia.

FRANK NESSLER. WILL H. ROST.
FRANK NESSLER & CO.
Tailors
56 EAST MARKET ST. (Lemcke Building),
INDIANAPOLIS. IND.

Morris Anna, b 168½ E Washington.
Morris Arthur W, lawyer, h 207 E Morris.
Morris Austin J, dentist, 36½ E Washington, h 485 College av.
Morris Barbara (wid Artemus), h 207 E Morris.
Morris Catherine, h 99 Division (W I).
Morris Catherine B (wid John), h 47 Ruckle.
Morris Charles, carp, b 147 Geisendorff.
Morris Charles E, checkman L E & W R R, h 23 Ingram.
Morris Charles J, carp, b 333 Cornell av.
Morris Charles L, blksmith, h 145 Newman.
Morris Corvil A, grocer, 306 S Olive, h same.
Morris Dallas D, lab, h 608 N West.
Morris David C, trav agt, r 233 E New York.
Morris DeF Sample, mech engr, r 58 The Chalfant.
Morris Edgar A, tinner, h 26 Poplar (B).
Morris Edith (wid Asbury), h 614 Cornell av.
Morris Edith L, notions, 321 Bellefontaine, h 24 Garfield pl.
Morris Edward K (Morris Printing Co), b 917 N Delaware.
Morris Edwin E, bodymkr, h 331 S West.
Morris Edwin M, framemkr, b 207 E Morris.
Morris Elizabeth, b 65 Hadley av (W I).
Morris Elizabeth, opr C U Tel Co, b 321 N Illinois.
Morris Ellen, b 169 W 3d.
Morris Ella F (wid Luther), b 136 Columbia av.
Morris Elmer P, trav agt, h 145 Woodlawn av.
Morris Emma (wid Joseph), h 439 E Georgia.
Morris Evelyn, stenog, b 268 Central av.
Morris Frank C, printer, h 643 Park av.
Morris Franklin, engr, h 619 E 7th.
Morris George B, clk L E & W R R, b n e cor 30th and Senate av (M).
Morris George C, driver, h 333 Cornell av.
Morris George L, lab, b 42 Arch.

Haueisen & Hartmann
163-169 E. Washington St.
FURNITURE,
Carpets,
Household Goods,
Tin, Granite and China Wares, Oil Cloth and Shades

THE WM. H. BLOCK CO. DRY GOODS,
7 AND 9 EAST WASHINGTON STREET. MEN'S FURNISHINGS.

Fidelity and Deposit Co. of Maryland. BONDS SIGNED.—LOCAL BOARD John B. Elam, Albert Sahm, Smiley N. Chambers, John M. Spann.
GEORGE W. PANGBORN, General Agent, 704-706 Lemcke Building. Telephone 140.

74 EAST MARKET STREET Telephone 863.
Insure Your Property With FRANK K. SAWYER

JOSEPH GARDNER,
Hot Air Furnaces
With Combination Gas Burners for Burning Gas and Other Fuel at the Same Time.
37, 39 & 41 KENTUCKY AVE. Telephone 322

Morris Hannah J, h 24 N Noble.
Morris Harry, lab, b rear 333 S Alabama.
Morris Harry, car rep, h 72 W 19th.
Morris Harry, paperhngr, h 258 Fulton.
Morris Henry, grocer, h 375 S East.
Morris Henry, lab, b 234 Clinton.
Morris Henry, lab, b 265 Spring.
Morris Henry, trav agt, h 20 Keith.
Morris Isaac, lab, h 171 Newman.
Morris Jacob T, trimmer, h 91 Stevens.
Morris James, h 1304 N Delaware.
Morris James, bodymkr, b 217 S Illinois.
Morris James, lab, b 66 Geisendorff.
Morris James A, insp, h 134 N State av.
Morris James E, bkkpr, b 20 Keith.
Morris Jane (wid George), b 859 N Penn.
Morris James W, sec and treas Industrial Life Assn of Indpls, b 247 N Meridian.
Morris John, barber, r 35½ Kentucky av.
Morris John, bell boy The Denison.
Morris John, porter, b 412 W 2d.
Morris John F, engr, h 619 E 7th.
Morris John H, student, r 1 Ft Wayne av.
Morris John I, b 604 N New Jersey.
Morris John M, lab, h e s Lincoln av 4 n of Ida (M J).
Morris John W, filer, h 30 Ashland (W I).
Morris Joseph E, lab, h 35 N McLain (W I).
Morris Joseph H, h 3 Allfree av.
Morris Joseph H, h 22 Ft Wayne av.
Morris Joseph L, turner, h 5 Sample (W I).
Morris Julia A (wid Josiah), b 65 Agnes.
Morris Kate (wid Ernest), h 667 N Delaware.
Morris Leslie, driver, b 249 W 3d.
Morris Margaret (wid Jacob C), r 1½ Fletcher av.
Morris Martha A (wid John D), h 103 Middle Drive (W P).
Morris Martin L, surveyor C C C & St L Ry, r 173 E Vermont.
Morris Mary A (wid Harmony), b 428 Douglass.
Morris Mary A (wid Michael), h 328 Alvord.
Morris Mary C (wid Francis A), h 42 Arch.
Morris Michael, mach, b 538 E Georgia.
Morris Milton A, sec The Indpls Water Co, h 60 Central av.

J. S. FARRELL & CO.
Plumbing
Natural and Artificial Gas Fitting.
84 N. ILLINOIS STREET.
TELEPHONE 382.

Morris Minor, phys, 36 E Ohio, h 351 Broadway.
Morris Nathan (Morris, Newberger & Curtis), b 291 N Alabama.
Morris Nathaniel N, office 94 E Market, r 226 N Delaware.
MORRIS NELSON & CO, Robert H Halladay Mngr, Wholesale Meats and Provisions, 129-135 Kentucky av, Tel 954.
MORRIS, NEWBERGER & CURTIS (Nathan Morris, Louis Newberger, James B Curtis), Lawyers, 134-140 Commercial Club Bldg, Tel 87.
Morris Oliver, clk, b 746 N New Jersey.
Morris Oscar, lab, h 476 Highland av.
Morris Patrick, coachman 358 Broadway.
Morris Patrick J, lab, h 362 W Maryland.
Morris Printing Co (Wm H, Wm H jr and Edward K Morris), 467 S Illinois.
Morris Reuben, produce, 111 E Mkt House, h 13 Concordia.
Morris Samuel, pdlr, b 40 Maple.
Morris Sarah F (wid Washington), h 109 W 10th.
Morris Sheldon, clk, h 24 Garfield pl.
Morris Thomas A, lab, h 171 Newman.
Morris Thomas A, pres The Indpls Water Co, h 604 N New Jersey.
Morris Thomas O, engr m of w C C C & St L Ry, h 52 Central av.
Morris Wm, barber, 95 S West, b same.
Morris Wm B, mach, h 236 Huron.
Morris Wm C, boilermkr, h s w cor Bruce and Jackson.
Morris Wm H (Morris Printing Co), h 917 N Delaware.
Morris Wm H jr (Morris Printing Co), h 906 N Delaware.
Morris Wm H, car rep, h 72 W 19th.
Morris Wm H, molder, h 210 Coburn.
Morris Wm H, trav agt Knight & Jillson, h 11 Hall pl.
Morris Wm M, barber, b 33 Hiawatha.
Morris Wm R, lab, h 121 Division (W I).
Morris Wolfe, junk, rear 126 E Ohio, h 40 Maple.
Morrison Alexander, bkkpr Severin, Ostermeyer & Co, h 1024 N Meridian.
Morrison Anna H, artist, 27½ W Ohio, r same.
Morrison Bertha M (wid Charles E), b 193 College av.
Morrison Charles, bkkpr, h s e cor Bellefontaine and 21st.
Morrison Charles F, car bldr, h 20 S Judge Harding (W I).
Morrison Charles H, mach opr Indpls Journal, h 28 Water.
Morrison Elias, horse dealer, h 123 Maxwell.
Morrison Fannie W (wid Lewis), h 187 N Penn.
Morrison Frank, painter, r 488½ E Washington.
Morrison Frank, pres The Darmody-Morrison Co, r 318 The Shiel.
Morrison Frank A, phys, 107 N Alabama, h 324 Park av.
Morrison Frank W, finisher Emil Wulschner & Son, r 8 Eden pl.
MORRISON FRANK W, Lawyer, 7-8 When Bldg, h 466 N Penn.
MORRISON GEORGE C, Druggist, Junction Virginia av and South, h 340 E South, Tel 1150.
Morrison George R, ins agt, h 64 Oak.
Morrison Harry L, storekpr Grand Hotel.

IF CONTINUED to the end of its dividend period, policies of the UNITED STATES LIFE INSURANCE CO., will equal or excel any investment policy ever offered to the public. | E. B. SWIFT, Manager, 25 E. Market St.

Wm. Kotteman 89 & 91 E. Washington St. TELEPHONE 1742 Furniture

SHOW CASES WILLIAM WIEGEL 6 West Louisiana Street Opp. Union Station.

Morrison Henry M, ins agt, h 21 Detroit.
Morrison James, lab, r 488½ E Washington.
Morrison John, paperhngr, r 176½ E Washington.
Morrison John, sawmkr, b 15 Nordyke av (W I).
Morrison John, trav agt, b 14 Shriver av.
MORRISON JOHN B, Dentist, Iron Hall Bldg, 28 Monument Pl, h 139 Park av and Knightstown, Ind.
Morrison Lewis E, rubber goods, 4 N Meridian, h 351 N New Jersey.
Morrison Lynn A, clk The Indpls Book and Stationery Co, h 187 Broadway.
Morrison Martha (wid Samuel J), b 207 Douglass.
Morrison Martha A (wid Richard), b 221 W 2d.
Morrison Mary (wid Hugh), h 289 W Pearl.
Morrison Oliver H, lab, h 74 Bicking.
Morrison Philip, polisher, h 15 Nordyke av (W I).
Morrison Pleasant A, printer, b 90 N East.
Morrison Rolla, lab, h 316 W Morris.
Morrison Samuel A, clk S A Fletcher & Co, b n e cor Senate av and 30th (M).
Morrison Samuel D, lab, h 119 Sanders.
Morrison Samuel L, solr Robt Martindale & Co, h 1024 N Meridian.
Morrison Sheridan R, condr, h 26 Temple av.
Morrison Squire, lab, h 56 Athon.
Morrison Susan A (wid James), b 90 N East.
Morrison Walter E, barber, h 207 Douglass.
Morrison Willard R, bartndr, r 180 E Washington.
Morrison Wm, r 379 S Meridian.
Morrison Wm, b 95 N Meridian.
Morrison Wm H (W H Morrison & Co), h 199 N Penn.
Morrison Wm H, lab, h 217 Northwestern av.
Morrison W H & Co (Wm H Morrison), printers, 28 Monument pl.
Morriss James M, tinner, h 24 Detroit.
Morrissey John, lab, h 249 W South.
Morrissey John J, lab, h 146 Meek.
Morrissey John W, ironwkr, r 94 N New Jersey.
Morrissey Patrick, clk, b 249 W South.
Morrow Clifford, teacher, b rear e s Line 2 n of Washington av (I).
Morrow Elizabeth (wid John W), h 544 Superior.
Morrow Field, teacher, r 222 N Illinois.
Morrow Hamilton C, lab, h 148 Nordyke av (W I).
Morrow Janet B (wid Alfred J), h 12 Eden pl.
MORROW JOSEPH E, Physician, 203 Hadley av (W I), h same, Tel 1323.
Morrow Julius H, foreman, h 49 Barth av.
Morrow Nathaniel F, teacher Deaf and Dumb Inst, b 222 N Illinois.
Morrow Robert, b 163 Hadley av (W I).
Morrow Thomas, condr, h 179 Yandes.
Morrow Walter H, printer Wm B Burford, b rear e s Line 2 n of Washington av (I).
Morrow Walter L, agt, h rear e s Line 2 n of Washington av (I).
Morrow Wilson (Morrow & McKee), h 358 N Meridian.
MORROW & McKEE (Wilson Morrow, John F McKee), Lawyers, 38 Thorpe Blk.
Morse Aaron M, ins, h 912 N Delaware.

We Buy Municipal ~ Bonds ~
THOS. C. DAY & CO,
Rooms 325 to 330 Lemcke Bldg.

Morse Edmund L, condr, h 438 W Udell (N I).
Morse Elliott C, clk, b 519 N Alabama.
Morse Robert, cigarmkr, h 576 S West.
Morse Robert P (T J Morse & Son), h 191 N West.
Morse Thomas J (T J Morse & Son), h 193 N West.
MORSE T J & SON (Thomas J and Robert P), Genl Contractors, 2 Builders' Exchange, Tel 535.
Morse Wm, mach, h 102 Cornell av.
Morss Alethea B (wid Benjamin), b 1702 Kenwood av.
Morss Samuel E, pres The Indpls Sentinel Co, 21 N Illinois.
Mortenbeck George, mach, h rear 176 S New Jersey.
Mortensen Margaret (wid Morton P), b 444 S East.
Mortland Amelia K (wid Alexander M), h 227 N Illinois.
Mortland Anna, actress, b 227 N Illinois.
Mortland Margaret E, stenog, b 227 N Illinois.
Morton Albert, barber, r 114 Roanoke.
Morton Allie R, lab, b 50 Drake.
Morton David L, coachman, b 193 W 4th.
Morton Edward, lab, h 260 S Penn.
Morton Edwin C, baker, b 112 Brookside av.
Morton Eliza R (wid Thomas R), h 292 S East.
Morton Frank M, candymkr, h 46 Omer.
Morton George, painter, b 37 Holly av (W I).
Morton George W, carp, h 337 Alvord.
Morton James, cook, h s s Miller 1 e of Reisner (W I).
Morton James H, lab, h 70 S McLain (W I).
Morton James M Rev, pastor Antioch Baptist Church, h 193 W 4th.
Morton Jefferson, plastr, b 264 Fayette.
Morton Joseph H, clk, h 224 S William (W I).
Morton Louis, painter, h rear 299 N Pine.

EAT
QUAKER BREAD
ASK YOUR GROCER FOR IT.
THE HITZ BAKING CO.

CARPETS CLEANED LIKE NEW. TELEPHONE 818
CAPITAL STEAM CARPET CLEANING WORKS

BENJ. BOOTH PRACTICAL EXPERT ACCOUNTANT. Thirty years' experience. First-class credentials. Room 18, 82½ E. Washington St. Indianapolis, Ind.

18 and 20 S. Meridian St. Established 8.

ESTABLISHED 1876. TELEPHONE 168.
CHESTER BRADFORD,
SOLICITOR OF PATENTS,
AND COUNSEL IN PATENT CAUSES.
(See adv. page 6.)
Office:—Rooms 14 and 16 Hubbard Block, S.W. Cor. Washington and Meridian Streets, INDIANAPOLIS, INDIANA.

Morton Lucinda M (wid Oliver P), h 75 E New York.
Morton Oliver T, clk U S Circuit Court of Appeals, Chicago, b 75 E New York.
Morton Thomas, b 112 Brookside av.
Morton Thomas, mer police, h 138 Elizabeth.
Morton Wm, lab, r 374 N Missouri.
Morton Wm, painter, h n s Schofield 1 e of Foundry (B).
Morton Wm M, porter, r 56 W Washington.
Morton Wm S K, porter W H Messenger, h 331 W North.
Mosbey Henry, lab, h rear 122 N Pine.
Mosby Maria, h 339 W Market.
Mosby Wm, lab, b 285 Christian av.
Mosby Wm, lab, b 339 W Market.
Moschell Arda, teacher Public School No 41, b 209 Hadley av (W I).
Moschell Effie M, teacher Public School No 2, b 209 Hadley av (W I).
Moschell John D, millwright, h 209 Hadley av (W I).
Moschell Judson, student, b 209 Hadley av (W I).
Moser Charles A, hostler, h 36 Nebraska.
Moser George, b 187 Madison av.
Moser George jr, saloon, 187 Madison av, h same.
Moser John, well driver, b 125 E Washington.
Moser Mary (wid Hans), b 423½ Virginia av.
Moses Frank S, mach, h 490 N Alabama.
Moses Hannah E (wid Lucius W), h 87 E Michigan.
Moses Samuel, lab, h 121 Darnell.
Moses Seth F, cigarmkr, b 87 E Michigan.
Mosher Jonathan M, motorman, h 8 Allfree av.
Mosi Wm C, h 472 S Missouri.
Mosier Frank E, lab, b 234 W 23d.
Mosier Horace H, mngr loan dept Fidelity Building and Savings Union, h 37 Central av.
Mosier James W, lab, b 234 W 23d.
Moslander Norman A (W S Moslander & Son), h 866 Cornell av.

CORRUGATED IRON CEILINGS AND SIDING.
ALL KINDS OF REPAIRING.
O. B. ENSEY,
TELEPHONE 1562.
COR. 6TH AND ILLINOIS STREETS.

Moslander Wm S (W S Moslander & Son), h 864 Cornell av.
MOSLANDER W S & SON (Wm S and Norman A), Contractors and Real Estate Agts, 66½ N Penn.
Moslein Peter, mach hd, b 62 Fayette.
MOSLER SAFE CO THE, Charles A McConnell State Agt, 72-74 W Court, Tel 1811.
Mosler Samuel, baker, b 412 S Meridian.
Mosley Michael, lab, b 13 Lynn.
Mosley Robert, lab, h 12 Sheldon.
Moss Albert (Moss & Franklin), h 190 N Missouri.
Moss Charles, lab, r 374 Muskingum al.
Moss Charles A, barber, 366 E 7th, h 288 Brookside av.
Moss George, lab, b rear 29 Center.
Moss Jacob, driver Union Co-Operative Laundry, h 76 Elizabeth.
Moss James K, b 47 Paca.
Moss John, engr, h 25 Hadley.
Moss Joseph, porter, b 122 Michigan (H).
Moss Margaret F (wid John), b 409 Lexington av.
Moss Nelson M, lab, h 530 W Ontario (N I).
Moss Rollo A, barber, 241 W Washington, h 224½ same.
Moss Sophia (wid Solomon), h rear 29 Center.
Moss Wm, lab, h 47 Paca.
Moss Wm A, porter W H Messenger, h 182 Muskingum al.
Moss & Franklin (Albert R Moss, Jeremiah Franklin), barbers, 162 Indiana av.
Mossler Jesse J, clk, b 301 E New York.
Moster Mary (wid Michael), b 827 Chestnut.
Mote Percy V, brakeman, r 8 Poplar (B).
Moten Isaac, trav agt, h 224 N Belmont av (H).
Motheral George W, bridge bldr, h 58 High.
Mothershead John L, h 489 N Meridian.
Motherwell Anna, seamstress, b 46 N Senate av.
Moticka Frank, cabtmkr, h 182 Harmon.
Motley Adam, h 646 E Ohio.
Motley Armstead, lab, h 178 W 10th.
Motley Frank, lab, h 222 S William (W I).
Motley Frederick, lab, b 646 E Ohio.
Motley George, lab, h rear 195 Middle.
Motley Patience, h 318 W Court.
Mott Ceylon P, paperhngr, h 53 Temple av.
Mott Martin L, butcher, b Enterprise Hotel.
Mott Sherman, lawyer, 415 Lemcke bldg, h 88 Germania av (H).
Moulden Laura V, dressmkr, 98 Cherry, h same.
Moulden Melville B, viseman, h 98 Cherry.
Moulder Jacob, cooper, h 67 N New Jersey.
Moulin Edwin H, lab, h 109 Geisendorff.
Moulton Albert, clk, h 143 Meek.
Moulton Alfred, lab, b 51 Paca.
Moulton Andrew, clk, b 156 W Washington.
Moulton Emily C (wid Charles W), b 649 Marlowe av.
Moulton Emma, h 225 N Senate av.
Moulton Enoch, tmstr, h 11 S Gillard av.
Moulton Frank R, clk, b 327 W Michigan.
Moulton George W, carp, h 133 Windsor.
Moulton John F, car receiver, h 28 N Senate av.
Moulton Josiah F, r 152 N Senate av.
Moulton John R, tilelayr, h 73 Drake.
Moulton Lucius G, printer, h 174½ S East.
Moulton Margaret (wid James), h 51 Paca.
Moulton Milton E, painter, b 51 Paca.

The Old Pub le Sherman European Restaurant

TUTEWILER UNDERTAKER, NO. 72 WEST MARKET STREET. TELEPHONE 216.

THE PROVIDENT LIFE AND TRUST CO. OF PHILADELPHIA. Endowment Insurance presents the double attraction of relieving manhood and middle age from anxiety and old age from want.
For particulars apply to D. W. EDWARDS, General Agent, 508 Indiana Trust Building.

THEODORE F. SMITHER ROOFER
GRAVEL AND OTHER COMPOSITION
Yard, 19 W. Maryland St. Telephone 85.
Off 15 W. Maryland St.

Moulton Robert, lab, b rear 124 Broadway.
Moulton Rodman J, clk W U Tel Co, h 327 W Michigan.
Mount Algernon S, b 572 N Alabama.
Mount Charles F, trav agt, h 1165 N Penn.
Mount Charles T, carp, b 176 Douglass.

MOUNT JAMES A, Governor State of Indiana, Room 6 State House, h n w cor College av and Butler.

Mount Jesse H, clk, b 136 Prospect.
Mount Joseph M, lab, h 162 E Market.
Mount Julia A F (wid Humphrey H), h 135 Prospect.
Mount Nettie, forewoman, b 135 Prospect.
Mount Rolla, window trimmer, h 78 Bellefontaine.
Mount Thomas R, carp, h 919 Morris (W I).
Mountain Henry M, sawmkr, b 26 Carlos.
Mountain John M, policeman Union Station, h 26 Carlos.
Mountain Michael M, city fireman, h 569 S Capitol av.
Mountjoy Anthony B, lab, h e s Warren 3 s of Washington av (I).
Mountjoy Elizabeth (wid George), h 162 Martindale av.
Mountjoy Frank C, mer police, h s s Railroad 2 w of Central av (I).
Mountjoy John, h n s Rawles av 1 w of Line (I).
Mounts Charles, driver, r 116 N Meridian.
Mounts Henry M, h 450 Broadway.
Mounts Milton H, condr, h 100 English av.
Mowers George B, barber, 28 Indiana av, h 181 N California.
Mowery Harry A, clk, b 182 N Senate av.
Mowery Wm, lab, h 148 Brett.
Mowrer Amelia (wid Henry), b 260 Blake.
Mowrer George W, switchman, h 260 W Washington.
Mowrer James M, sec and treas McCoy-Howe Co, h 402 Central av.
Mowry John Q, fireman, h 84 N Gillard av.
Mowwe Anna, starcher, b 178 S Linden.
Mowwe Frank H, carp, h 177 S Linden.
Mowwe Henry C, insp, h 95 Shelby.
Mowwe Louisa (wid Henry F), h 95 Shelby.
Mowwe Margaret, starcher, h 177 S Linden.
Mowwe Otto, clk, b 95 Shelby.
Mowwe Wm F, clk N Y Store, h e s Wallack 1 n of Belt R R.
Moxey Robert, cook, r 25 S Liberty.
Moxley G Barrett, salesman A Kiefer Drug Co, b 162 N Illinois.
Moxley James T, saloon, 152 W Washington, h 184 W Ohio.
Moyer Jacob F, student, b 454 W Udell (N I).
Moylam Wm, bartndr, b 299 W Maryland.
Mozingo David C, barber, r 147 W Washington.
Mozingo John W, printer, b 2 Arch.
Mozingo Silas H, miller, h 2 Arch.
Mozka Joseph, fireman, r 252½ Mass av.
Mozo Benjamin, feed, h 431 S Capitol av.
Muchmore Charles A, printer, b 95 N Meridian.
Muchmore Isaac B, printer, b 95 N Meridian.
Mucho Christian, b 51 Woodlawn av.
Mucho Edward C, lab, h 419 Virginia av.
Mucho Frederick W, cigar mnfr, 199 E Washington, h 51 Woodlawn av.
Muecke Otto, painter, b 230 E Vermont.

MUECKE WM, House and Sign Painter, 76 Virginia av, h 230 E Vermont, Tel 1511.

Muegge Emma A (wid John D), boarding 349 Madison av.
Muegge George W, meats, 9 Prospect, h 312 Coburn.
Muegge Henry H (Muegge & Lutz), b 349 Madison av.
Muegge Herman F, lab, h 135 Lincoln la.
Muegge John D, butcher, h 138 Sheffield av (H).
Muegge & Lutz (Henry H Muegge, Henry Lutz), saloon, 349 Madison av.
Muehe Joseph, cabtmkr, b 450 S Delaware.

MUEHL SIEGMAR F, Druggist, 523 N Illinois, Tel 204; 798 N Alabama, Tel 606, and n e cor 13th and Illinois, Tel 1333; h 521 N Illinois.

Muelharsig John, mach, h rear 31 Madison av.
Mueller, see also Miller, Moeller, Moller and Muller.
Mueller Adolph, lab, h 173 Minerva.
Mueller Albert, jeweler, 48 S Illinois, h 1371 N Senate av.
Mueller Albert, lab, b 41 Arizona.
Mueller Albert C, stairbuilder, 323 Mass av, h 168 Clifford av.
Mueller Alexander F, driver, h 129 High.
Mueller Anna, dressmkr, h 49 Wallack.
Mueller Anna (wid John), h 1023 S Meridian.
Mueller Arthur, wireman Sanborn Electric Co, b 618 E Vermont.
Mueller August H, teacher, h 496 Union.
Mueller August J, patternmkr, b 93 Cornell av.
Mueller Bernhard (Mueller & Schneider), h 5 Hendricks.
Mueller Bernhard H, mach hd, h 35 Eureka av.
Mueller Carl, engraver, b 565 N West.
Mueller Carl, locksmith, h 442 S Missouri.
Mueller Carl R, butcher, h 354 Clifford av.
Mueller Catherine (wid Jacob E), h 41 Arizona.
Mueller Carrie, b 1023 S Meridian.
Mueller Charles, clk Henry J Huder, b 65 Stevens.
Mueller Charles, lab, b 323 S Olive.

THE A. BURDSAL CO.
Manufacturers of
Paints and Colors
VARNISHES,
Brushes, Painters' and Paper Hangers' Supplies.
34 AND 36 SOUTH MERIDIAN STREET.

ELECTRICIANS | DON'T FORGET US. ALL WORK GUARANTEED. C. W. MEIKEL, Tel. 466. 96-98 E. New York St.

DALTON & MERRIFIELD { LUMBER South Noble St., near E. Washington

INDIANA ELECTROTYPE CO. : BEST WORK. LOWEST PRICES.
23 WEST PEARL ST., INDIANAPOLIS, IND. JOB WORK. BOOK PLATES. BEST PATENT BASE ON THE MARKET. All Orders Promptly Filled.

KIRKHOFF BROS.
Steam and Hot Water Heating Apparatus,
Plumbing and Gas Fitting.
102-104 SOUTH PENNSYLVANIA ST.
TELEPHONE 910.

Mueller Charles, sawmkr, b 41 Arizona.
Mueller Charles A, carp, h 18 Dearborn.
Mueller Charles C, brick mnfr, w s Perkins pike 2 n of Bethel av, h n s Prospect 4 e of Belt R R.
Mueller Charles G, architect, 31 Talbott blk, b 538 E Ohio.
Mueller Charles G, coppersmith Wm Langsenkamp, h 618 E Vermont.
Mueller Charles G, drugs, 667 Virginia av, h same.
Mueller Charles H, barber, 19 Shelby, h 49 Wallack.
Mueller Charles H, stairbuilder, b 309 N Noble.
Mueller Charles H, watchmkr, 23 Virginia av, h 65 Stevens.
Mueller Charles W, finisher, b 88 Downey.
Mueller Clemens, mach, h 240 N Belmont av (H).
Mueller Conrad, genl bkkpr Merchants' Natl Bank, h 69 Lockerbie.
Mueller Conrad, mach, b 179 S Alabama.
Mueller Edward, butcher, b 1155 E Washington.
Mueller Edward H, grocer, 182 E Washington, h 305 E Market.
Mueller Emil A, bkkpr Indpls Drug Co, h 95 Walcott.
Mueller Emil R, tailor, b 1339 N Senate av.
Mueller Eugene J, teacher High School, h 23 Pleasant av.
Mueller Ferdinand A, drugs, 249 E Washington, h 233 N Liberty.
Mueller Frank C, tailor, b 485 Madison av.
Mueller Frederica G (wid John), h 53 E McCarty.
Mueller Frederick, finisher, h 82 Stevens.
Mueller Frederick, lab, b 41 Arizona.
Mueller Frederick A, stairbldr, h 561 N Senate av.
Mueller Frederick C, stairbldr, b 93 Cornell av.
Mueller Frederick G, motorman, h 279 Alvord.
Mueller George, brewer, h 64 Yeiser.
Mueller George, carp, h rear 327 E Michigan.
Mueller George, lab, r 9½ Madison av.

LIME
BUILDING SUPPLIES,
Hair, Plaster, Flue Linings,
The W. G. Wasson Co.
130 INDIANA AVE. Tel. 989.

Mueller George B, bartndr, b 6 Smithson.
Mueller George F, carp, b 262 S Illinois.
Mueller George H, clk, h 247½ N Noble.
Mueller George H, clk C C C & St L Ry, b 839 E Washington.
Mueller George H, uphlr, b 88 Downey.
Mueller George J, clk H P Wasson & Co, b 18 John.
Mueller Gustav H, rec teller Merchants' Natl Bank, b 309 N Noble.
Mueller Hannah D (wid Christian), h 88 Downey.
Mueller Harry H, saloon, 2 Ft Wayne av, h same.
Mueller Henrietta C A (wid Daniel), h 114 Yeiser.
Mueller Henry, carp, h 342 Highland av.
Mueller Henry, stairbldr, h 93 Cornell av.
Mueller Herman, boxmkr, b 41 Arizona.
Mueller's Hotel, Albert Borchardt propr, 213 S Alabama.
Mueller Ida B, music teacher, 496 Union, b same.
Mueller Jacob, cabtmkr, h 219 Columbia av.
Mueller Jacob, plumber, b 93 Cornell av.
Mueller Jacob, shoes, 565 N West, h same.
Mueller John, lab, b 342 Highland av.
Mueller John A, h 174 Bane.
Mueller John A D, stairbldr, 310 Spring, h 309 N Noble.
Mueller John F, city fireman, h 340 E Morris.
Mueller John H, clk L E & W R R, b 839 E Washington.
Mueller John H, patternmkr Atlas Engine Wks, h 148 Ruckle.
Mueller John S, packer Charles Mayer & Co, h 92 Dougherty.
Mueller Joseph, blksmith, h 129 Tremont av (H).
Mueller Joseph, lab, h 110 Hosbrook.
Mueller Joseph (wid John H), h 82 Arizona.
Mueller J Frederick, saloon, 262 S Illinois, h same.
Mueller J George (Indpls Drug Co), h 173 Central av.
Mueller Leonhard, tailor, 40 S Illinois, h 485 Madison av.
Mueller Lillie C (wid Carl B), b 69 Lockerbie.
Mueller Louis, cutter, h 105 Church.
Mueller Louis, driver, h 18 Morton.
Mueller Louis A, clk Henry J Huder, b 127 Union.
Mueller Louis N, blksmith, h 674 E St Clair.
Mueller Louisa (wid Henry), b 179 Maple.
Mueller Louisa P (wid John C H), b 309 N Noble.
Mueller Margaret (wid Charles G), h 538 E Ohio.
Mueller Margaretha (wid Peter), b 2 Ft Wayne av.
Mueller Mary (wid August), h 485 S Illinois.
Mueller Mary (wid John), h 18 John.
Mueller Mary, cook, b 37 S Delaware.
Mueller Mary A, dressmkr, b n s Prospect 4 e of Belt R R.
Mueller Mary B (wid Louis H), h 839 E Washington.
Mueller Nettie (wid Frank), h 675 Home av.
Mueller Nicholas, pump rep, h 673 S East.
Mueller Oscar, publisher, h 514 S Illinois.
Mueller Oscar G, clk Francke & Schindler, b 309 N Noble.
Mueller Otto S, tailor, b 485 Madison av.
Mueller Rudolph, chief bkkpr Indpls Brewing Co, h 343 Union.

Parlor, Bed Room, Dining Room, Kitchen, Furniture W. H. MESSENGER, 101 E. Wash. St., Tel. 491.

ALL KINDS OF HEAVY AND LIGHT GRAY IRON CASTINGS } McNamara, Koster & Co. { Foundry and Pattern Shop
Phone 1593. 212-218 S. Penn. St.

Mueller Rudolph M, teas, 61 Mass av, b 182 W Vermont.
Mueller Theodore, b 118 Dunlop.
Mueller Theodore L, mach, b e s Station 1 s of Sutherland (B).
Mueller Wilhelmina, dressmkr, b n s Prospect 4 e of Belt R R.
Mueller Wm, lab, b 366 S Alabama.
Mueller Wm, lab, h 23 Haugh (H).
Mueller Wm C, lab, h 323 S Olive.
Mueller Wm C, lineman, b 65 Stevens.
Mueller Wm H, cigarmkr, h 60 Michigan av.
Mueller Wm O, stairbldr, b 309 N Noble.
Mueller & Schneider (Bernhard Mueller, Valentine Schneider), horseshoers, 351 Madison av.
Muellerschoen Charles, propr St Charles Hotel, 27 McCrea.
Muenster Otto, molder, h 458 W 1st.
Muesel Andrew, lab, h 330 Elizabeth.
Muesing Charles, bookbndr, b 555 S Illinois.
Muesing Charles C W, tmstr, h 555 S Illinois.
Muessig Albin, molder, h 16 Haugh (H).
Muessig Charles, molder, h 26 N Judge Harding (W I).
Muggs George M, brakeman, r 62½ S Illinois.
Muhlbacher Frank X, tailor, 420 Virginia av, h same.
Muhs Frederick R, draughtsman, r 413 N Capitol av.
Muir Eugene S, brakeman, b 241 Virginia av.
Muir Henry W, trav agt The Indpls Millinery Co, h 34 N Belmont av (H).
Muir James W, trav agt The Indpls Millinery Co, h 572 N Alabama.
Muir Oran N, lawyer, 631 Lemcke bldg, b 572 N Alabama.
Muir Roland, packer, r 56 Kansas.
Muir Sidney P, salesman The Indpls Millinery Co, b 572 N Alabama.
Mulbarger Wm H, saloon, 139 River av (W I), h 97 same.
Mulcahy Michael, h 87 S Noble.
Muldoon Andrew, condr, b 113 Church.
Muldoon John, brakeman, b 113 Church.
Muldoon John, lab, r 404 S West.
Muldoon Martin, fireman, b 113 Church.
Muldoon Mary (wid Andrew), h 113 Church.
Mulhall Edward T, policeman, h 504 E Georgia.
Mulhall Judy, h 335 W Chesapeake.
Mulhall Nicholas, lab, b 335 W Chesapeake.
Mulherrin John, messenger Am Ex Co, b 268 S Penn.
Mulholland, see also Milholland.
Mulholland Alfred, brakeman, h 12 Depot (B).
Mulholland Arthur, trimmer, b 121 Minerva.
Mulholland Franklin D, clk, h 137 Geisendorff.
Mulholland Jane (wid James), b 121 Minerva.
Mull Cory, bkkpr Samuel Laing, h 332 N Senate av.
Mull David, lab, h 33 W McCarty.
Mull George F (Edenharter & Mull), r 56 The Chalfant.
Mull Jacob H, carriagemkr, h 200 N West.
Mull Leo B, clk, b 174 N Illinois.
Mull Wm A, opr W U Tel Co, h 138 E New York.
Mullally Edward, drayman, h 106 Dougherty.
Mullally Edward J, molder, b 106 Dougherty.
Mullally Harry, tel opr, b 106 Dougherty.

Henry H. Fay,
40½ E. WASHINGTON ST.,
FIRE INSURANCE, REAL ESTATE,
LOANS AND RENTAL AGENT.

Mullally John P, jeweler, 6 Monument pl, r 105 N Meridian.
Mullally Matthew A, lab, b 106 Dougherty.
Mullan Amasa J, phys, 117½ W Washington, h same.
Mullaney Patrick J, h 128 E St Joseph.
Mullen August, lab, b 60 Torbet.
Mullen Bernard, b 415 N Meridian.
MULLEN-BLACKLEDGE CO THE, Wm F Mullen Pres, Albert S Blackledge Vice-Pres and Treas, Edward M Churchman Sec, Mnfrs of Pure Food Products, Catsup, Soups, Etc, 62-66 S Alabama, Tel 1637.
Mullen Bridget (wid Malachi), h 262 S Missouri.
Mullen Burnett F, engr, h 29 McGill.
Mullen Daniel, h 427 E Vermont.
Mullen Daniel A, molder, b 82 Germania av (H).
Mullen Daniel F, clk, b 427 E Vermont.
Mullen Eugene U, painter, h 56 Kansas.
Mullen Frank, horseshoer, b 250 S Missouri.
Mullen James, bricklyr, b 187 S Capitol av.
Mullen James V, lab, b 262 S Missouri.
Mullen John, lab, b 299 W Maryland.
Mullen John, lab, b 252 S Missouri.
Mullen John, lab, h 374 S Missouri.
Mullen John, plastr, b 30 S Senate av.
Mullen John F, cashr 2d class mail P O, h 26 Dougherty.
Mullen John W, harnessmkr, b 374 S Missouri.
Mullen Joseph M, barber, b 262 S Missouri.
Mullen Katherine (wid John), h n e cor 7th and Lennox.
Mullen Leota, bkkpr, b 357 N East.
Mullen Margaret (wid John), b 269 E North.
Mullen Margaret (wid Malachi), h 252 S Missouri.
Mullen Mary (wid Michael), h 125 W South.
Mullen Michael, lab, b 40 S West.
Mullen Michael C, lab, h 269 E North.
Mullen Otis, plumber, r 69 Rockwood.
Mullen Peter, lab, h 60 Torbet.
Mullen Salathiel L, engr, h 64 Woodruff av.
Mullen Samuel S, student, b 598 N New Jersey.

WILL GO ON YOUR BOND
American Bonding & Trust Co.
Of Baltimore, Md. Approved as sole surety by the United States Government and the different States as Sole Surety on all Forms of Bonds.
W. E. BARTON & CO., General Agents,
504 Indiana Trust Building.
LONG DISTANCE TELEPHONE 1918.

THE FRED DIETZ CO.

WOODEN PACKING BOXES MADE TO ORDER
FACTORY AND WAREHOUSE TRUCKS.
400 Madison Avenue. Telephone 654.

BUSINESS EDUCATION A NECESSITY. TIME SHORT. DAY AND NIGHT SCHOOL. SUCCESS CERTAIN AT THE PERMANENT, RELIABLE
Indianapolis BUSINESS UNIVERSITY

Steam Pumping Machinery { HENRY R. WORTHINGTON, 64 S. PENNSYLVANIA ST. Long Distance Telephone 284.

UNION CO-OPERATIVE LAUNDRY (COMPOSED OF UNION LAUNDRY GIRLS.) NOS. 8, 40 AND 142 VIRGINIA AVENUE. T. E. SOMERVILLE, MANAGER — TELEPHONES — INDIANAPOLIS, IND.

HORACE M. HADLEY
INSURANCE AND LOANS
66 E. Market Street, Basement
TELEPHONE 1540.

Mullen Thomas, blksmith, b 26 Dougherty.
Mullen Thomas, condr, b 565 Ash.
Mullen Thomas, lab, b 50 S California.
Mullen Thomas, lab, b 299 W Maryland.
Mullen Thomas, mach hd, b 252 S Missouri.
Mullen Thomas O, clk Bates House Pharmacy, b 262 S Missouri.
Mullen Wm, h 455 N Senate av.
Mullen Wm, condr, r 21 S Station (B).
Mullen Wm, engr, h 407 E Washington.
Mullen Wm F, pres The Mullen-Blackledge Co, h 455 N Senate av
Mullen Wm M, clk, b 262 S Missouri.
Mullenholz Christian, mach, h 20 Wheeler.
Mullenholz Johanna (wid Peter), h 5½ Brookside av.
Mullenkamp Henry J, lab, h 99 Wyoming.
Mullens Frank, carp, r 178 S New Jersey.
Muller, see also Miller, Moeller, Moller and Mueller.
Muller Anna (wid John), h 1023 S Meridian.
Muller August, mach, h 51 Warman av (H).
Muller Bernard J, clk H P Wasson & Co, h 234 N Senate av.
Muller Bros (George and Edward), grocers, 989 S Meridian.
Muller Edward (Muller Bros), b 1023 S Meridian.
Muller George (Muller Bros), b 1023 S Meridian.
Mullerman Louise, dom 53 Woodruff av.
Mullery Martin, lab, h 47 S Gale (B).
Mullholand Edward, h 21 S Station (B).
Mullholand Emma, millinery, 65 E Sutherland (B), h 21 S Station (B).
Mullier Andrew J, engr, h 305 E McCarty.
Mullikin Wm P, carp, h 178 Brookside av.
Mullinix Ida M, b 264 E Court.
Mullinix Orris E, clk Murphy, Hibben & Co, r 63 The Windsor.
Mullins Harvey, sec and treas Acme Milling Co, h 1145 N Illinois.
Mullins James, grocer, 151 W Merrill, h same.
Mullins Wilson L, cook, h 259 Blake.
Mullis Ambrose W, b s s E Washington 1 e of Belt R R.
Mullis Charles, condr, b 1139 N Illinois.

COLLECTIONS
MERCHANTS' AND MANUFACTURERS' EXCHANGE
Will give you good service.
J. E. TAKKEN, Manager,
Union Building, over U. S. Pension Office.
73 West Maryland Street.

Mullis Joel P, lab, h rear 267 Mass av.
Mullis Rufus T (R T Mullis & Co), h 1350 N Capitol av.
MULLIS R T & CO, Dealers in Staple and Fancy Groceries, Fresh and Salt Meats, Flour, Feed, Hardware, Tin and Wooden Ware, 1348-1350 N Capitol av, cor 18th, Tel 1950.
Mulon Wm P, brakeman, h 152 Spann av.
Mulrey John J, lab, b 19 Shriver av.
Mulrey Thomas, motorman, h 19 Shriver av.
Mulrien John P, butcher, b 132 Blackford.
Mulrine James, lab, b 193 Michigan (H).
Mulrine Thomas, saloon, 165 Michigan (H), b 193 same.
Mulry James, huckster, h 173 E Louisiana.
Mulry John, horseshoer, 33 S Alabama, h 278 S Olive.
Mulry Josephine J, cashr Van Camp H and I Co, b 278 S Olive.
Mulry Laurence P, blksmith, h 42 Grant.
Mulryan John, lab, b 41 Minerva.
Mulryan John, lab, h 346 W Pearl.
Mulryan Martin, lab, h 286 W Maryland.
Mulryan Patrick, lab, b 41 Minerva.
Mulvaney James F, lab, h 266 Bates.
Mulvany Frank, foreman, h 87 Lee (W I).
Mulvey John, lab, b 252 E Washington.
Mulvihill John R, lab, b 71 Church.
Mulvihill Josephine (wid Michael P), boarding 18 Henry.
Mulvihill Michael T, lab, h 31 McGinnis.
Mulvihill Timothy, tallyman C C C & St L Ry, h 487 E Georgia.
Mumaugh Elizabeth (wid Lopez J), h 333 S Penn.
Mumford George M, lab, h 325 W 1st.
Mumford James F, clk C H & D R R, h 581 Marlowe av.
Mummenhoff Frank, pres Mummenhoff Fruit Co, h 303 Park av.
MUMMENHOFF FRUIT CO, Frank Mummenhoff Pres, 135-137 E Maryland, Tel 81.
Munce Hagerman, driver, City Hospital.
Munch Adam, waiter, r 183½ W Washington.
Munday Charles E, carp, h 54 Omer.
Munday Connor, clk Kingan & Co (ltd), b 183 Sheffield av (H).
Munday Lulu, r 131½ E Washington.
Munday Thomas J, feed, 20 Grandview av (H), h 183 Sheffield av.
Mundelle Allison B, mailing clk P O, h 248 N California.
Mundelle Robert B, asst supt mails P O, h 1119 N Penn.
Munden Jesse S, paperhngr, h 379 N West.
Munden Wm D, engr, h 227 Dillon.
Mundi Elizabeth H, stenog Indpls Brewing Co, b St Mary's Academy.
Mundy Elizabeth (wid Pleasant D), h 253 Lincoln la.
Munger Cycle Co The, Augustus Bruner pres, Anderson Bruner sec, 146 Ft Wayne av.
Mungovan Bridget (wid Michael), b 278 W New York.
Mungovan Mary J, dressmkr, 278 W New York, b same.
Municipal Engineering Co, Wm Fortune pres, 84 Commercial Club bldg.
Munier John N, fireman, h 113 Gray.
Munns George W, lab, h 990 N Senate av.
Munro, see also Monroe.
Munro David, agt, h 1283 N Meridian.

CLEMENS VONNEGUT 184, 186 and 192 E. Washington St. || BUILDERS' HARDWARE, Building Paper. Duplex Joist Hangers.

THE WM. H. BLOCK CO. DRY GOODS, DRAPERIES, RUGS, WINDOW SHADES.
7 AND 9 EAST WASHINGTON STREET.

MUNRO JAMES R, Club House and Summer Resort, 1324 Northwestern av (N I), h same.
Munro Sadie E (wid Donald R), r 36 Leon.
Munroe Jeanette M, bkkpr Peter F Bryce, b 158 E 8th.
Munsell Ezra, carriagemkr, h 6 Cornell av.
Munsell Fernando, switchman, h 69 Peru av.
Munsell Henry, b 6 Cornell av.
Munson Alvin J, lightning rods, 94 S Delaware, b 129 Park av.
Munson Charles H, b 286 N Alabama.
Munson David, h 129 Park av.
Munson David R, bkkpr, b 129 Park av.
MUNSON EDWARD A, State Agt North British and Mercantile Insurance Co of London, England, 70 E Market, Tel 1221; h 770 N New Jersey.
Munson Edward C, ins, 70 E Market, h 80 W 3d.
Munson Ezra W, carp, h w s Chester av 4 n of Washington.
Munson Grant, painter, 380 E Michigan, h same.
Munson Griffith, driver, h 365 S Capitol av.
Munson Robert, bricklyr, r 268 S Illinois.
Munson Samuel A, trav agt, b 129 Park av.
Munson Wm G, plumber, h 542 Bellefontaine.
MUNTER KEVI, Sale and Feed Stables, 45 N Alabama, Tel 583; h 234 N Delaware. (See adv in classified Sale Stables.)
Munter Saul, live stock, b 234 N Delaware.
Muntz Albert, plastr, b 82 Hosbrook.
Muntz Thomas, plastr, h 131 Elm.
Muntz Thomas F, city fireman, b 125 High.
Muntz Wm, plastr, 82 Hosbrook, h same.
Muntz Wm E, printer, b 82 Hosbrook.
Muntz Wm R, plastr, b 131 Elm.
Munzh Edward, shoemkr, 28 Sheffield av (H), h same.
Murbarger Harry E, chemist, b 423 College av.
Murbarger Samuel R, salesman, h 423 College av.
Murbarger Wm E, agt, h 423 College av.
Murdock Joseph, h 241 Davidson.
Muriel Stephen, lab, b rear 258 S Meridian.
Murman George S, attendant Insane Hospital.
Murnan Louis, lab, b 107 Sharpe av (W).
Murnan Nancy (wid George), h 107 Sharpe av (W).
Murnan Wm T, blksmith J W Buchanan, h 154 N Pine.
Murphy Albert L, paperhngr, b 67 S Shade (B).
Murphy Andrew, molder, h 178 Germania av (H).
Murphy Ann E, dressmkr, 41 Indiana av, h same.
Murphy Anna (wid Harrison), h 22 S Stuart (B).
Murphy Anna J (wid Richard), dressmkr, rear 226 E Washington, h same.
Murphy Arley R, grocer, 340 E Market, h 68 N Noble.
Murphy Augustus (R L Polk & Co), h 822 College av.
Murphy Bridget (wid Jeremiah H), h 328 S Missouri.
Murphy Bridget (wid Michael), b 76 High.
Murphy Bros (Charles E and Frederick K), dry goods, 2 N Station (B).
Murphy Frank B, student, b 240 E Ohio.

Murphy Charles E (Murphy Bros), b 22 S Stuart (B).
Murphy Charles H, mach, h 67 S Shade (B).
Murphy Charles J, mounter, h 9 Sharpe.
Murphy Charles S, clk Murphy, Hibben & Co, b 358 Central av.
Murphy Daniel, lab, h 54 Maple.
Murphy Dennis, soldier, h 116 Walcott.
Murphy Dennis A, lab, b 206 Blake.
Murphy Edward, lab, b 179 S Alabama.
Murphy Edward C, brakeman, h 139 Walcott.
Murphy Edward L (J A Murphy & Co), h 183 E Merrill.
Murphy Ellen (wid Francis), b 68 McGinnis.
Murphy Evart S, student, b 240 E Ohio.
Murphy Frank, lab, b 312 W Merrill.
Murphy Frank J, solr, b 65 Arch.
Murphy Frank M, engr, h 37 Huron.
Murphy Frank S, blksmith, h 71 N Pine.
Murphy Frank S jr, helper, b 71 N Pine.
Murphy Frederick K (Murphy Bros), b 22 S Stuart (B).
Murphy George C P, trav agt, h 194 Lexington av.
Murphy Harrison C, switchman, r 184 Bates.
Murphy Harry, bkkpr Murphy, Hibben & Co, h 28 E Michigan.
Murphy Harry, lab, b 168 Harrison.
Murphy Harry F, mach, b 41 Indiana av.
Murphy Henry, polisher, b 9 Sharpe.
Murphy Henry C, bkkpr, b 380 Talbott av.
Murphy Homer, clk, r 190½ S Illinois.
MURPHY, HIBBEN & CO (John W Murphy, Harold B Hibben, Louis Hollweg), Wholesale Dry Goods and Notions, 93-99 S Meridian, Tel 327.
Murphy James, gasfitter, h 304 W Maryland.
Murphy James, janitor, h 15, 336½ E Washington.
Murphy James A, engr, h 854 Cornell av
Murphy James D, mach, h 104 Lincoln la.
Murphy James H, motorman, b 59 Miley av.
Murphy James J, painter, b 71 N Pine.
Murphy James M, barber, h 1373 Graceland av.

GUIDO R. PRESSLER,
FRESCO PAINTER
Churches, Theaters, Public Buildings, Etc., A Specialty.
Residence, No. 325 North Liberty Street.
INDIANAPOLIS, IND.

INDIANAPOLIS STEEL ROOFING AND CORRUGATING WORKS, 23 and 25 East South Street. S. D. NOEL, Proprietor.

David S. McKernan, Rooms 2-5 Thorpe Block.
REAL ESTATE AND LOANS
Money to loan on real estate. Special inducements offered those having money to loan. It will pay you to investigate.

DIAMOND WALL PLASTER { Telephone 1410 BUILDERS' EXCHANGE.

UNION TRANSFER AND STORAGE CO. Cor. E. Ohio St. and C., C., C. & St. L. R'y Tracks. BEST FACILITIES FOR STORING AND TRANSFERRING MACHINERY AND MERCHANDISE.

W. McWORKMAN

FIRE SHUTTERS, FIRE DOORS, METAL CEILINGS.
930 W. Washington St. Tel. 1118.

Murphy James T, mach, b 164 Maple.
Murphy James W, bartndr, b 161 Bates.
Murphy James W, carp, r 249½ W Washington.
Murphy James W, painter, h 54 Lafayette av.
Murphy John, h 739 E Ohio
Murphy John, foreman, b 76 Fayette.
Murphy John, grocer, 110 John, h same.
Murphy John, lab, h 324 W 1st.
Murphy John, lab, b 30 Iowa.
Murphy John, lab, h 164 Maple.
Murphy John, lab. b 284 W Maryland.
Murphy John, lab, b 328 S Missouri.
Murphy John, lab, h 72 Morton.
Murphy John, lab, b 46 Standard av (W I).
Murphy John, lab, b 40 S West.
Murphy John B, molder, b 9 Sharpe.
Murphy John B, printer, b 72 Morton.
Murphy John E, news agt, 551 W Udell (N I), h 592 W Eugene (N I).
Murphy John F, molder, h 91 Camp.
Murphy John F, tmst, h 70 McGinnis.
Murphy John H (John H and John W Murphy), h 117 E Michigan.
Murphy John H and John W, electrical supplies, 30 E Georgia.
Murphy John J, car rep, h 35 Chadwick.
Murphy John J, clk Van Camp H and I Co, h 485 S West.
Murphy John J, engr, h 323 E Vermont.
Murphy John P, clk, h 555 S West.
Murphy John W (Murphy, Hibben & Co, John H and John W Murphy), treas C B Cones & Son Mnfg Co, h 239 N Penn.
Murphy John W, carp, h 584 S Illinois.
Murphy John W, lab, h 460 Indiana av.
Murphy John W, saloon, s s Washington 1 e of Crawfordsville rd (M J), h same.
Murphy Jonathan A (J A Murphy & Co), h 350 N Alabama.
Murphy Joseph, condr, h 45 Elder av.
Murphy Joseph, driver, h 983 W Washington.
Murphy J A & Co (Jonathan A and Edward L Murphy), com mers, 23 S Delaware.
Murphy Lafayette, lab, b 13 Warren av (W I).

GEO. J. MAYER,
MANUFACTURER OF
SEALS
STENCILS, RUBBER STAMPS, CHECKS, BADGES, DOOR PLATES, ETC.
5 S. Meridian St., Ground Floor. TEL. 1386.

Murphy Levi A, mach hd, h 600 W Eugene (N I).
Murphy Martha (wid Jesse), b 34 Clarke.
Murphy Martin, lab, b 45 Helen.
Murphy Martin F, lab, b 343 W Maryland.
Murphy Martin J (Collier & Murphy), dep City Comptroller, 1 Court House, h 94½ Ramsey av.
Murphy Mary, cook City Hospital.
Murphy Mary, stenog M O'Connor & Co, b 96 Ramsey av.
Murphy Matilda, baker, 315 Indiana av, h same.
Murphy Maurice, lab, r 27 Helen.
Murphy Merrick, engr, b 37 Huron.
Murphy Michael, lab, h 343 W Maryland.
Murphy Michael, lab, h 21 Springfield.
Murphy Michael A, lab, b 87 Maple.
Murphy Michael C, driver, b 324 W 1st.
Murphy Michael E, lab, h rear 72 Bicking.
Murphy Michael J, foreman Kingan & Co, h 81 Springfield.
Murphy Michael J, lab, h 21 Springfield.
Murphy Michael J, mounter, b 9 Sharpe.
Murphy Michael J, wheelmkr, b 164 Maple.
Murphy Nora, cook Deaf and Dumb Inst.
Murphy Oliver M, clk Indpls Gas Co, h 34 Clarke.
Murphy Patrick, lab, h 30 Iowa.
Murphy Patrick, lab, b 164 Maple.
Murphy Patrick, lab, b 17 Meikel.
Murphy Patrick, plastr, b 524 Jefferson av.
Murphy Patrick, saloon, 239 W Washington, h same.
Murphy Patrick H, brakeman, b 45 Elder av.
Murphy Patrick L, city fireman, h 253 E Washington.
Murphy Patrick M, lab, h 284 W Maryland.
Murphy Paul J, receiver, h 1023 N Penn.
Murphy Reuben W, clk Sheridan Brick Works, r 490 N Illinois.
Murphy Richard, clk, b 334 N Illinois.
Murphy Richard R, painter, r 174½ E Washington.
Murphy Rosa, cook The Denison.
Murphy Samuel, driver, h 249 W 3d.
Murphy Stephen, butcher, b 328 S Missouri.
Murphy Terrence, h 206 Blake.
Murphy Thomas, brakeman, b 14 S Brightwood av (B).
Murphy Thomas J, brakeman, r 32 S Gale (B).
Murphy Thomas J, tel opr, b 30 Iowa.
Murphy Timothy M, engr, r 153 English av.
Murphy Tobias M, ins agt, h 321 E Georgia.
Murphy Weeden B, insp, h 174 Deloss.
Murphy Wm, coachman 665 N Delaware.
Murphy Wm, gasfitter, b 237 W Maryland.
Murphy Wm, lab, b 9 Sharpe.
Murphy Wm C, foreman, b 76 Fayette.
Murphy Wm E, lab, b 52 Davis.
Murphy Wm J, h 451 Talbott av.
Murphy Wm M, painter, h 142 Fayette.
Murphy Winifred (wid James), h 9 Sharpe.
Murr Charles L, packer, b 14 Dougherty.
Murr David J, clk U S Pension Agency, h 14 Dougherty.
Murr Louis, buyer Charles Mayer & Co, h 310 N Capitol av.
Murray, see also McMurray.
Murray Abraham L, pastor Allen Chapel A M E Church, h 72 Columbia av.
Murray Allen R, foreman, b 363 W Pearl.
Murray Anna (wid Wm), h e s Gatling 3 n of Raymond.
Murray Arthur, pressfeeder, b 94 Fletcher av.
Murray Christian, cigar mnfr, 1087 E Washington, h 50 Johnson av.

A. METZGER AGENCY ESTABLISHED 1863. REAL ESTATE

LAMBERT GAS & GASOLINE ENGINE CO.
ANDERSON, IND. NATURAL GAS ENGINES.

BICYCLES $5 DOWN. $1 Best Wheels. Best Terms. WHEELMEN'S CO. 31 W. OHIO ST. LONG DISTANCE TEL. 1855.

Murray Daniel, watchman, h 654 W Francis (N I).
Murray Edwin D, trav agt, h 36 Ruckle.
Murray Elmer E, lab, h 541 Madison av.
Murray Francis, blksmith, h 69 Louise.
Murray Harvey R, paperhngr, h n w cor Baltimore av and Blackmore.
Murray James, mach, b 72 English av.
Murray James P, trav agt Fahnley & McCrea, h 495 Broadway.
Murray John, lab, r 363 W Pearl.
Murray John S, saloon, 551 Virginia av, h same.
Murray John W, barber, b 860 E Washington.
Murray Kate, typewriter, h e s Gatling 3 n of Raymond.
Murray Mary C (wid James), laundress, b 350 E Morris.
Murray Nora, h 72 English av.
Murray Oda R, tmstr, b 1006 W Washington.
Murray Oscar G, lab, b 363 W Pearl.
Murray Richard S, engr, h 260 Fletcher av.
Murray Robert C, trav agt, b 550 Chestnut.
Murray Samuel J, supt Natl Card Factory, h 60 Barth av.
Murray Samuel R, engr, h 322 E North.
Murray Thomas, lab, b 60 Torbet.
Murray Thomas, lab, h rear e s Woodside av 1 s of P C C & St L Ry (W).
Murray Thomas F, painter, h 52 Sheffield (W I).
Murray Thomas O, salesman Fahnley & McCrea, b 495 Broadway.
Murray Timothy C, trav agt McKee Shoe Co, h 567 W 22d (N I).
Murray Walter S, b 260 Fletcher av.
Murray Wm G, carp, h 363 W Pearl.
Murray Wm H, mach, h 155 Bates.
Murrell Charles H Rev, h 187 Middle Drive (W P).
Murrell Thomas J, cabtmkr, h 336½ E Washington.
Murrin Wm M, asst foreman W U Tel Co, h 64 Omer.
Murry Anna M, dresscutting school, 30 Dickson, b same.
Murry Catherine E (wid James R), h 73 Columbia av.
Murry Edward, clk W U Tel Co, b 78 Columbia av.
Murry Elizabeth, clk, b 409 Ash.
Murry Frederick, lab, b 73 Columbia av.
Murry George W, insp, h 319 Bellefontaine.
Murry James, foreman C C C & St L Ry, h w s Station 1 n of Willow (B).
Murry John D, foreman, h 75 N Beville av.
Murry John H (J H Murry & Co), h 373 Ash.
Murry J H & Co (John H Murry), lumber, 320 Lincoln av.
Murry Marie E, stenog, b 409 Ash.
Murry Mary (wid James), h 78 Columbia av.
Murry Otto M, plumber, b 30 Dickson.
Murry Theodore, tailor, b 73 Columbia av.
Murry Thomas E, tailor, b 73 Columbia av.
Murt Charles, gardener, h 52 Bluff rd.
Murt Peter, lab, h 159 W Morris.
Musard Frederick C, pipefitter, h 329 E Market.
Muse Abraham L, mach hd, h 5 Sumner.
Muse Robert H, carp, h 71 Elizabeth.
Musgrove Daniel C, brickmkr, h 170 E Morris.
Musgrove Wm H, clk, h 1339 Isabella (N I).
Mushrush John A, mach hd, h w s James 3 n of Bloyd av (B).

THOS. C. DAY & CO.
Financial Agents and Loans.
We have the experience, and claim to be reliable.
Rooms 325 to 330 Lemcke Bldg.

Musick Joseph, cigarmkr, r 175½ E Washington.
Muson Harry, lab, b 49 Excelsior av.
Muson Moses, lab, b 17 S Senate av.
Musser Albert, lab, h 83 S Liberty.
Musser Alice L (wid Wm A), h 192 Buchanan.
Musser Charles S, clk, b 192 Buchanan.
Musser Edward, bicyclemkr, b 331 E Georgia.
Musser George O, printer, h 229 E Market.
Musser Samuel, sawyer, h 102 Hill av.
Musser Thomas H, h 46 Chase (W I).
Musser Thomas O, pdlr, b 46 Chase (W I).
Musser Wm H, grinder, b 46 Chase (W I).
Mussmann Bertha, bkkpr, b 572 S Meridian.
Mussmann Diedrich, pres and treas Indpls Planing Mill Co, h 572 S Meridian.
Mussmann Frederick, mach hd, h 554 S Meridian.
Mussmann Louis, tmstr, b 554 S Meridian.
Mussmann Louis H, clk, b 490½ S Meridian.
Mussmann Louisa (wid Henry), h 490½ S Meridian.
Mussmann Wm, clk, b 554 S Meridian.
Mussmann Wm F L, clk, h 150 Church.
Muster Joseph C, boxmkr, h 124 High.
Muston Charles, sawyer, h 488 Highland av.
Mutchett Charles, clk, h 945 Bellefontaine.
Mutchett Charles L, bkkpr, h 945 Bellefontaine.
Mutchner Philip E, broker, 429 Lemcke bldg, h 377 Broadway.
Muths Andrew, lab, h 33 Bloomington.
Muths George, driver, h 40 Elizabeth.
Mutts Albert B, mach hd, h 216 E South.
Mutts Horace, clk, b 216 E South.
Mutts Sarah E (wid Jacob), h 216 E South.
Mutts Stella M, stenog, b 216 E South.
MUTUAL BENEFIT LIFE INSURANCE CO OF NEWARK, N J, Benjamin B Peck State Agt, 20-21 Fletcher's Bank Bldg, Tel 1242.
Mutual Home and Savings Assn, Wm A Rhodes sec, 72 E Market.

EAT
HITZ'S CRACKERS AND CAKES.
ASK YOUR GROCER FOR THEM.

J. H. TECKENBROCK  General House Painter, 94 EAST SOUTH STREET.

FIDELITY MUTUAL LIFE—PHILADELPHIA, PA.
$75,000,000, Insurance In Force. $3,500,000, Death Losses Paid. $1,500,090, Surplus. A. H. COLLINS {General Agent, Baldwin Block.

BITUMINOUS COAL IN CAR LOADS TO DEALERS AND MANUFACTURERS. ROOMS 42 AND 43 WHEN BUILDING. Edwardsport Coal & Mining Co.

ESTABLISHED 1876. TELEPHONE 168.
CHESTER BRADFORD,
SOLICITOR OF PATENTS,
AND COUNSEL IN PATENT CAUSES.
(See adv. page 6.)
Office:—Rooms 14 and 16 Hubbard Block, S. W. Cor. Washington and Meridian Streets, INDIANAPOLIS, INDIANA.

MUTUAL LIFE INSURANCE CO OF INDIANA, Wm R Myers Pres, Denton F Billingsley Vice-Pres, Henry Malpas Sec and Treas, John C Green Attorney, 314-322 Lemcke Bldg.
MUTUAL LIFE INSURANCE CO OF NEW YORK THE, Robert Merritt & Co Genl Agts, 6 Lombard Bldg, Tel 1761.
MUTUAL SAVINGS UNION AND LOAN ASSOCIATION THE, Martin H Rice Pres, Wm H Leedy Vice-Pres, Hiram W Miller Treas, John Schley Sec, 16 Masonic Temple.
Mutz Charles M, phys, 378 Clifford av, h same.
Muzzy Edwin B, fireman, h 24 Lynn av (W I).
Muzzy Emily E (wid Bennett), b 66 Hadley av (W I).
Muzzy Walter J, porter, h 1505 N Capitol av.
Muzzy Wm J, fireman, h 66 Hadley av (W I).
Muzzy Wm R, baggageman, b 1505 N Capitol av.
Myer, see also Mayer, Meier and Meyer.
Myer Frederick M, cook, h 143 E Merrill.
Myer John C, tel opr C C C & St L Ry, h 320 Mass av.
Myer Leopold H, towerman, b 105 N Rural (B).
Myer Wm P, h 244 S New Jersey.
Myers, see also Miers and Meyers.
Myers Albert S, lab, b 465 E Walnut.
Myers Allen, farmer, h 2000 N Meridian.
Myers Amanda, music teacher, rear 63 N East, h same.
Myers Augusta (wid Jesse), h 72 Yandes.
Myers Barbara S (wid Erastus), h 10 Warren.
Myers Benjamin F, trav agt Van Camp H and I Co, b 719 College av.
Myers Benjamin F, treas mer police, h 332 Alvord.
Myers Bernard H, blksmith, 573 W Udell (N I), h 509 W 22d (N I).
Myers Bessie, stenog, b 10 Warren.
Myers Cary A, hack driver, h 171 W Market.

Outing BICYCLES
..MADE BY..
HAY & WILLITS MFG CO.
76 N. Pennsylvania St. Phone 598.

Myers Charles A, circulator, b 525 E Washington.
Myers Charles A, clk Consumers' Gas Trust Co, h 299 W Vermont.
Myers Charles D, clk, b 561 W Francis (N I).
Myers Charles F, clk Indiana National Bank, b 2000 N Meridian.
Myers Charles H, mach, h 64 Lexington av.
Myers Charles M, engr, h 45 Bloomington.
Myers Charles R, claim agt C C C & St L Ry, b 719 College av.
Myers Christian, molder, h 271 E Market.
Myers Christina B (wid Leonard F), h 719 College av.
Myers Clarence W, mach hd, b 471 W Francis (N I).
Myers Daniel B, polisher, b 310 Virginia av.
Myers David A, lawyer, 22 Aetna bldg, h 551 Ash.
Myers David E, inventor, h 158 Madison av.
Myers Eliza (wid James C), h 500 W 22d (N I).
Myers Frank C, lab, b 332 Alvord.
Myers Frank R, clk, h 378 Martindale av
Myers George A, blksmith, r 3 Columbia blk.
Myers George E, collr, h 172 Highland av.
Myers George W, clk, b 172 Highland av.
Myers George W, lab, h 35 N McLain (W I).
Myers Harry C, engr, h 28 Elder av.
Myers Harry E, cigarmkr, b 525 E Washington.
Myers Henry, lab, r 166½ W Washington.
Myers Henry, trav agt, r 440 N Meridian.
Myers Henry C, molder, h 79 Holmes av (H).
Myers Henry D, asst mngr C F Hunt Co, h 511 W McLene (N I).
Myers Henry R, mach, h 36 Excelsior av.
Myers Herbert T, clk, b 514 N New Jersey.
Myers H Guy, draughtsman Chandler & Taylor Co, b 132 N Capitol av.
MYERS IRVIN M, Staple and Fancy Groceries, 254-256 Indiana av, h 320 N California.
Myers Jacob E, carp, h 378 Martindale av.
Myers James, solr, r 152 N Illinois.
Myers James C, collr, b 332 Alvord.
Myers James M, boarding 285 S Capitol av.
Myers James W, blksmith, h 33 N McLain (W I).
Myers Jane C (wid Amos), h 86 E Pratt.
Myers Jesse D, broker, r 3 Catterson blk.
Myers John, lab, b 77 S Liberty.
Myers John A, collr Joseph Gardner, h 27 McGill.
Myers John C (T M Hervey & Co), bkkpr McCoy-Howe Co, b 10 Warren.
Myers John E, drugs, 494 S Meridian, h same.
Myers John F, butcher, h 1118 N Delaware.
Myers John F, carp, h 594 Morris (W I).
Myers John H, tel opr, b 27 McGill.
Myers John M, turner, b 158 Madison av.
Myers John W, lab, h 465 E Walnut.
Myers Joseph A, plumber, b 171 S Olive.
Myers Joseph W, clk, h 440 S New Jersey.
Myers Lida E (wid James C), b 178 N Missouri.
Myers Louis, barber, 423½ Madison av, h 27 Dougherty.
Myers Louis E, barber, 3 Buchanan, h 6 same.
Myers Lucy C (wid Charles K), b s e cor Washington and Laura (M J).
Myers Martin, lab, h s s Washington 5 e of Line (I).

C. ZIMMERMAN & SONS | SLATE AND GRAVEL ROOFERS 19 South East Street.

DRIVEN WELLS And Second Water Wells and Pumps of all kinds at CHARLES KRAUSS', 42 S. PENN. ST., Telephone 465.

ERTEL STEAM LAUNDRY 26 and 28 N. Senate Avenue. Telephone 1089. WE WILL CALL FOR AND DELIVER YOUR WORK. SATISFACTION GUARANTEED.

Myers Mary, h 163 W Maryland.
Myers Mary A (wid Joseph), b 310 E Market.
Myers Mary E (wid James W), h 343 Blake.
Myers Mary H (wid Benjamin F), h 21 Park av.
Myers Milton S, trav agt, h 12 Eureka av.
Myers Oliver C, livery, 569 W Udell (N I), h 578 same.
Myers Oscar A, bartndr, b 438 Dillon.
Myers Peter, lab, b 67 S Noble.
Myers Philip, pdlr, h 34 McGinnis.
Myers Richard T, engr, h 12 Elder av.
Myers Robert H, carp, h 100 Cornell av.
Myers Robert H, proofreader The Indpls Sentinel, h 4 Shriver av.
Myers Samuel J, painter, h 179 Bane.
Myers Samuel O, mach hd, h 433 W McLene (N I).
Myers Samuel R, engr, h 171 S Olive.
Myers Samuel W, lab, h 158 Michigan av.
Myers Simpson P, mailing clk P O, h 27 Shriver av.
Myers Smith H, b 222 E Ohio.
Myers Theodore E, jeweler, b 514 N New Jersey.
Myers Thomas J (Sullivan & Myers), h 81 Dougherty.
Myers Wallin O, ins agt, h 181 N Alabama.
Myers Walter E, trav agt, r 218 E Market.
Myers Walter T, bricklyr, b 465 E Walnut.
Myers Wilbert T, clk Schnull & Co, h 393 S Delaware.
Myers Will I, clk, b 320 N California.
Myers Wm, h 561 W Francis (N I).
Myers Wm, blksmith, h 33 N McLain (W I).
Myers Wm, plumber, h 213 W Ohio.
Myers Wm B Rev, teacher, h rear 63 N East.
Myers Wm C (Fisher & Myers), h 228 S Noble.
Myers Wm H, carp, h 592 W Udell (N I).
Myers Wm H, insp City Engineer, b 719 College av.
Myers Wm H, meats, s w cor Sugar Grove and Miller avs, h 565 Addison (N I).
Myers Wm L, brakeman, b 38 S State av.
Myers Wm P, molder, h 35 Cleveland (H).
Myers Wm R, pres Mutual Life Ins Co of Indiana, h 992 N Meridian.
Mygrant Luella, b 45½ N Capitol av.
Myhan James H, grocer, 270 Blake, h 272 same.
Mylner Charles G, lab, h 169 Dougherty.
Mylner Elizabeth (wid David), h 169 Dougherty.
Myres Charles, lab, h 232 Ramsey av.
Myrick Orlando H, lawyer, 20½ N Delaware, b 404 S Olive.
Myrick Philip E, grain, h 237 N Senate av.
Mythen Mary A (Mythen & Garis), h 103 Dougherty.
Mythen & Garis (Mary A Mythen, Olive H Garis), milliners, 157 Virginia av.

N

Naatz Adolph E, lab, h 714 Morris (W I).
Nabauer John, porter, 49 E Washington.
Naber Benjamin E, mach, h 370 Cornell av.
Nachtrieb Margaret (wid Gottlieb), h 156 Prospect.
Nachtrieb Minnie C, h 156 Prospect.
Nacke Anthony, clk, h 270 Highland av.
Nackenhorst Frederick J, lab, h 79 Shelby.
Nackenhorst John F, trav agt Charles Mayer & Co, h 74 Barth av.
Nackenhorst Wm (Cook & Nackenhorst), b 79 Shelby.

EQUITABLE LIFE ASSURANCE SOCIETY OF THE UNITED STATES.
RICHARDSON & McCREA
Managers for Central Indiana,
79 East Market St. Telephone 182.

Naegele Frederick A, clk, b 22 Hosbrook.
Naftel Carrie P (wid Daniel), h 405 Coburn.
Nagel Albert H, foreman, h 103 Cypress.
Nagel August, r 1075 W Washington.
Nagel Wm C, engr, h 229 Olive.
NAGELEISEN BROS (Lawrence A and Wm F), Livery, Boarding and Sale Stables, 120-124 E Wabash, Tels 1108 and 831.
Nageleisen Lawrence A (Nageleisen Bros), h 277 Indiana av.
Nageleisen Wm F (Nageleisen Bros), res Piqua, O.
Naget Robert R, janitor, b 103 Cypress.
Nagle Frederick, lab, b 353 Jefferson av.
Nagle Gottfried, painter, h 561 S New Jersey.
Nagle Kate (wid Garrett), h 97 Paca.
Nagle Lawa A, dressmkr, 561 S New Jersey, h same.
Nahrup Joseph H, clk, h 293 S Alabama.
Nalis Edward J, lab, h 42 S Capitol av.
Nall James, lab, r 169 W Wabash.
Nalor James, lab, b 298 N Capitol av.
Naltner George, h 643 E Ohio.
Naltner Helene (wid Joseph), h 103 Gray.
Nankervis Charles T (J Nankervis & Son), b 13 Ludlow av.
Nankervis James (J Nankervis & Son), h 13 Ludlow av.
Nankervis J & Son (James and Charles T), bookbndrs, 18½ N Meridian.
Nankervis Susan A (wid James), h 13 Ludlow av.
Napier James, waiter, r 18½ Indiana av.
Nary Joseph, brakeman, b 23 Poplar (B).
Nash George W, phys, 402 S Illinois, h 374 same.
Nash James H, lab, h 464 W 2d.
Nash Laura B (wid Samuel), critic Kindergarten No 3, b 308 Home av.
Nash Lee T, drugs, 400 S Illinois, h 426 same.
Nash Thomas B, clk Joseph M Dwyer, r 425 Madison av.
Nash Thomas C, fireman, h 817 E Market.
Nash Wm T, genl agt N Y Life Ins Co, b 82 E Vermont.
Nassoy Frank P, baker, h 37 Carlos.

STENOGRAPHERS FURNISHED.
EXPERIENCED OR BEGINNERS, PERMANENT OR TEMPORARY.
S. H. EAST, State Agent,
The Williams Typewriter,
55 THORPE BLOCK, 87 EAST MARKET ST.

ELLIS & HELFENBERGER { ENTERPRISE FOUNDRY & FENCE CO. 162-170 S. Senate Ave. Tel. 958.

THE HOGAN TRANSFER AND STORAGE COMP'Y
Household Goods and Pianos Moved—Packed—Stored...... Baggage and Package Express Machinery and Safes a Specialty Cor. Washington and Illinois Sts. TELEPHONE No. 675.

The Central Rubber & Supply Co. Hose, Belting, Packing, Clothing, Druggists' Sundries, Bicycle Tires, Cotton Hose, Etc. New York Belting & Packing Co., L't'd. PHONE 922. 79 S. ILLINOIS ST., INDIANAPOLIS, IND.

A death rate below all other American Companies, and dividends from this source correspondingly larger.
The Provident Life and Trust Company
Of Philadelphia.
D. W. EDWARDS, General Agent,
508 Indiana Trust Building.

Natali Biaggio, pdlr, h 160 Virginia av.
Nathan Abraham, clk, b 323 N Illinois.
Nathan Fanny, dry goods, 238 W Washington, h 323 N Illinois.
Nathan Hyman B, mngr, b 323 N Illinois.
Nathan Joseph, lab, h 139 Maple.
Nathan Myer, mngr, h 323 N Illinois.
Nathan Solomon, printer, 505 N Alabama, h same.
Nathan Thomas, clk, b 323 N Illinois.
NATIONAL CASH REGISTER CO THE, Bockhoff Bros Sales Agts, Grand Hotel Blk, 65 S Illinois, Tel 418.
NATIONAL COLLECTION AGENCY, John M Eacock Pres, George J Eacock Sec, 81 Baldwin Blk.
NATIONAL ELECTRIC HEADLIGHT CO, Robert B F Peirce Pres, Edwin B Peirce Genl Mngr, Mnfrs of Locomotive Electric Headlights, 30-34 W South.
National Express Co, 5 E Washington and 145 S Meridian.
NATIONAL IDENTIFICATION CO THE, David M Geeting Pres, Albert L Willard Sec, Wm A Walker Treas, 16 Aetna Bldg, 19½ N Penn, Tel 1161.
NATIONAL MALLEABLE CASTINGS CO THE, Proprietor Indianapolis Malleable Iron Works; Resident Officers, E L Whittemore Vice-President, Charles E Brooks Assistant Treasurer, W G Griffith Sales Agent; Office and Works cor Michigan and Holmes av (Haughville), reached by Haughville cars; Long Distance Tel 51.
National Saw Guard Co, S H Collins propr, 128 Ft Wayne av.

Julius C. Walk & Son,
Jewelers
Indianapolis.
12 EAST WASHINGTON ST.

NATIONAL STARCH MANUFACTURING CO THE, Wm F Piel Sr Mngr, Starch Mnfrs, s w cor Morris and Dakota, Tel 324.
National Wall Paper Co, Samuel M Jackson agt, 136 S Illinois.
Naughton, see also Norton.
Naughton Agnes D (wid Thomas), b 36 Coburn.
Naughton Bridget (wid Patrick), h 431 Union.
Naughton Celia M, teacher Center Township District School No 7, b 385 N New Jersey.
Naughton Ella, b 431 Union.
Naughton James, fireman, h 94 Chadwick.
Naughton James, real est, b 127 W South.
Naughton James F, lab, b 10 Carlos.
Naughton Patrick, lab, h 10 Carlos.
Naughton Patrick jr, lab, b 10 Carlos.
Naughton Patrick, saloon, 351 W New York, h same.
Naughton Wm F, sawmkr, h 431 Union.
Naumann George H T, solr Consumers' Gas Trust Co, h 409 N East.
Naumann Helen F, teacher Girls' Classical School, h 407 N East.
Naumann H Th George, chemist, h 407 N East.
Nave Christian, clk, b 152 Nordyke av (W I).
Nave Frederick A, clk Ward Bros Drug Co, b 452 N New Jersey.
Nave George W (Middlesworth, Benson, Nave & Co), h 152 Nordyke av (W I).
Navin Alfred G, asst genl bkkpr Indiana Natl Bank, b 76 N Senate av.
Navin Arthur J, mngr Navin's Pharmacy No 1, 149 W Washington, b 76 N Senate av.
Navin John N, mngr Navins' Pharmacy No 2, h 316 N Illinois.
Navin Robert M, mngr Navins' Pharmacy No 3, h 124 W North.
Navins' Pharmacy No 1, Arthur J Navin mngr, 149 W Washington.
NAVINS' PHARMACY NO. 2, John N Navin Mngr, 100 E Market, cor N Delaware, Tel 383.
NAVINS' PHARMACY NO. 3, Robert M Navin Mngr, 302 N Illinois, Tel 1602.
Nay David D, clk, h 506 N Senate av.
Nay Elizabeth (wid George H J), h 139 Union.
Nay Norton D, bkkpr, b 506 N Senate av.
Naylor George B, lab, h e s Northwestern av 4 n of 24th.
Naylor Henry C, bricklyr, h 284 E Market.
Naylor James H, janitor, b 298 N Capitol av.
Naylor Lizzie N, clk, b 284 E Market.
Nead Samuel H, driver, h 90 Cherry.
Neade Michael, fireman, b 99 Lexington av.
Neal, see also O'Neal.
Neal Asbury, jeweler, 350 Blackford, h same.
Neal Bert, barber, h 144 N Illinois.
Neal Celestus, waiter, h 205 Agnes.
Neal Charles, lab, b 165 Minerva.
Neal Charles W, trimmer, b 230 W Maryland.
Neal Claret, waiter The Bates.
Neal Cyrus W, chief clk ins dept Auditor of State's Office, 39 State House, h 125 E North.
Neal Elizabeth, h 16 Willard.
Neal Harry W, tinner, h n s W Washington 2 w of Insane Hospital gate (M J).

OTTO GAS ENGINES | BUILDERS' EXCHANGE S. W. Cor. Ohio and Penn. Telephone 535.

Becker & Son Charles Becker Jacob Becker Jr. Merchant Tailors. 21 N. Penn. St. Tel. 934

SALISBURY & STANLEY

Neal James W, bus mngr Western Horseman Co, h 143 N Alabama.
Neal John, waiter, r 113 Indiana av.
Neal Louis, lab, h rear 122 W 4th.
Neal Louis, lab, r 1242 E Washington.
Neal Marcellus, prin Public School No 19, h 112 Martindale av.
Neal Nancy C, dressmkr, 71 Oak, b same.
Neal Richard W, ins agt, r 30 W Pratt.
Neal Robert W, lab, h 26 Woodside av.
Neal Russell E, trav agt, r 30 W Pratt.
Neal Sarah (wid Charles), h 71 Oak.
Neal Sarah (wid Eli), h 165 Minerva.
Neal Solon D, soldier U S Arsenal.
Neal Thomas, carp, r 306½ E Washington.
Neal Wm, waiter, b 165 Minerva.
Neal Wm M, express, h 130 Minerva.
Neal Wm S, lab, h w s Illinois 2 n of 29th.
Nealer Jacob, shoemkr, 416 Clifford av, h same.
Nealis Edward J, h 42 S Senate av.
Nealis Mary (Davis & Nealis), h 42 S Senate av.
Neall Elizabeth (wid Jonathan R), b 63 W 12th.
Neall George H, r 163 N Illinois.
Neall Samuel W, capt Chemical No 3, h 542 W Francis (N I).
NEALY H D, Draughtsman, 16 Hubbard Blk, h 159 Ramsey av, Tel 168. (See adv in classified Patent Draughtsmen.)
Near Charles H, trav agt, r 211 N Illinois.
Neate Alice (wid Robert S), b 251 S Alabama.
Neate Florence C, stenog State House Bldg Assns, b 251 S Alabama.
NEDERLAND LIFE INSURANCE CO (Limited), John T Holsinger Cashier, John A Stevenson Supt of Agts, Rooms 3, 4 and 5 Blackford Blk, s e cor Meridian and Washington.
Neeb Charles W F, mach, b 153 Johnson av.
Need John, driver, h 75 Hanway.
Need Martin, lab, h 78 Meikel.
Needham Martin, clk, r 93 N Alabama.
Needler Clara E (wid James F), h 609 Broadway.
Needler Wm H, foreman, h rear 232 S Missouri.
Needy Newton, bartndr, h 441½ Virginia av.
Neelan Patrick J, lab, h 28 Lynn.
Neeley Wesley, milkpdlr, h n w cor N Capitol av and 29th.
Neely John, butcher, h 75 Agnes.
Neely Robert J, butcher, b 75 Agnes.
Neely Thomas, saloon, 76 Kentucky av and 25 S Delaware, h 76 Kentucky av.
Neely Wm, carp, h 937 Grove av.
Neerman Alfred G, carver, b 676 E St Clair.
Neerman Christian, shoemkr, h 519 N New Jersey.
Neerman Enoch J, glass cutter, b 676 E St Clair.
Neerman Frederick W, h 70 Lockerbie.
Neerman Gustav A, assignee George V Bedell, h 676 E St Clair.
Neerman Otto S, shoes, 273 Mass av, b 676 E St Clair.
Neerman Walter S, engr, b 676 E St Clair.
Neermann Andrew C, mach hd, h 94 Hendricks.
Nees Charles F, baker, h 376 W 1st.
Nees Charles F, turner, h 683 S Meridian.
Nees Ernest, turner, h 224 Union
Nees Ernst G G jr, turner, b 224 Union.
Nees Gustavus, chairmkr, h 378 Coburn.

Henry H. Fay,
40½ E. Washington St.,
REAL ESTATE,
AND LOAN BROKER.

Neese Jesse R, tapper, b 74 Bicking.
Neesen Henry, uphlr, h 936 Madison av.
Neff Annie, h 17 Deloss.
Neff Daniel, lab, b 135 Ludlow av.
Neff David, phys, 186½ W Washington, h same.
Neff Eliza A (wid John), b 65 Quincy.
Neff Eliza C, b 201 Faytte.
Neff James R (Neff & Co), h 428 W Pratt.
Neff John W, ins agt 25½ W Washington, h 404 N West.
Neff Lee S, engr, h 106 Elm.
Neff Marion A, contr, b 253 E Washington.
Neff Richard H, insp, h 163 Michigan av.
Neff Wm, waiter, h 132 N Liberty.
Neff Wm E, dressmkr, 18½ N Meridian, b 304 Ash.
Neff Wm H, mach, h 128 Bates.
Neff Wm M, baggageman, h 65 Quincy.
Neff & Co (James R Neff), soda apparatus, 82 S Delaware.
Neffle Albert W, lab, b 279 W Merrill.
Neffle Frederick, butcher, h 279 W Merrill.
Neffle Frederick J, plumber, b 279 W Merrill.
Neffle George H, mach, h 281 S West.
Neffs Charles, lab, b 40 Parker av.
Negley Calvin, engr, h s s Pendleton av 1 e of Walker (B).
Negley Charles R, lab, b e s Brightwood av 1 n of Willow (B).
Negley David D, h 58 N Station (B).
Negley Ernest J, draughtsman, b e s Lake av 4 s of Washington av (I).
Negley George H, bicycle rep, b 58 N Station (B).
Negley Harry E, lawyer, 69 When bldg, h 39 Ingram.
Negley Homer H, tmstr, b 58 N Station (B).
Negley John, lab, b e s Brightwood av 1 n of Willow (B).
Negley Mary A (wid John), h n s Willow 2 w of Station (B).
Negley Oliver P, tel opr, r 313 E Georgia.
Negley Silas B, engr, h e s Lake av 4 s of Washington av (I).
Negley Wm H, car rep, h e s Brightwood av 1 n of Willow (B).
Neiberger Emil, driver, b 191 S Alabama.

MAYHEW
13 N. MERIDIAN STREET.

OFFICE, STORE AND BANK F[illegible]
Contractors and Builders. Repairing of all kinds done on short notice. 177 Clinton St., Indianapolis, Ind. Telephone 999.

LIME, CEMENT, PLASTER FIRE BRICK AND CLAY SEWER PIPE, ETC. BALKE & KRAUSS CO., Cor. Market and Missouri Streets.

C. FRIEDGEN HAS THE FINEST STOCK OF LADIES' PARTY SLIPPERS and SHOES 19 NORTH PENNSYLVANIA ST.

SAMUEL LAING ▸ TIN, SLATE AND STEEL ROOFING, 72 AND 74 EAST COURT STREET.

M. B. WILSON, Pres. W. F. CHURCHMAN, Cash.
THE CAPITAL NATIONAL BANK,
INDIANAPOLIS, IND.
Pays Interest on Time Certificates of Deposit.
Buys and Sells Foreign Exchange at Low Rates.
Capital, - - $300,000
Surplus and Earnings, 50,000
No. 28 S. Meridian St., Cor. Pearl.

Neiberger Flora, clk John A Craig, b 191 S Alabama.
Neiberger Lena, clk John A Craig, b 191 S Alabama.
Neiberger Valentine, lab, h 191 S Alabama.
Neidhamer, see also Niedhamer.
Neidhamer Byron B, student, b 152 Shelby.
Neidhamer John F, mach, h 152 Shelby.
Neidigh Mary C, housekpr Insane Hospital.
Neidigh Simon P, steward Insane Hospital.
Neidling, see also Niedling.
Neidling Christina (wid Louis), h 175 W 9th.
Neidling Frederick L, lab, h 175 W 9th.
Neidlinger Christian, lab, h 27 Coburn.
Neidlinger Katherine, midwife, 27 Coburn, h same.
Neidlinger Wm H (Neidlinger & Cotton), h 430 Eugene (N I).
Neidlinger & Cotton (Wm H Neidlinger, Allen W Cotton), feed, 1446 Northwestern av (N I).
Neifing Catherine (wid Nicholas), h 273 Howard.
Neiger Arthur J (Neiger & Hartwig), h 23 Davis.
Neiger Elizabeth (wid Jacob), h 291 Union.
Neiger & Hartwig (Arthur J Neiger, John H Hartwig), cistern bldrs, 175 Virginia av.
Neighbor Arthur G, b 103 Central av.
Neighbor James E, clk E C Atkins & Co, h 103 Central av.
Neighbor Robert E Rev, editor Baptist Outlook, h 103 Central av.
Neighbor Robert W, clk E C Atkins & Co, b 103 Central av.
Neighbors John H, h 235 S Senate av.
Neighbours Jane M (wid Robert), h 151 Union.
Neighbours Jeannette I, clk, b 151 Union.
Neil George, lab, b 240 N California.
Neilan Thomas H, insp, h 133 Church.
Neiligh Charles, clk H P Wasson & Co, h 189 Fletcher av.
Neill Helm, molder, h 304 Michigan (H).
Neilson John L, medical insp U S Navy, b 753 N Penn.
Neilson Andrew, tailor, 452 E North, b 99½ Mass av.
Neiman Arthur G, engraver, b 21 Arch.

TUTTLE & SEGUIN,
28 E. Market Street.
Fire Insurance,
Real Estate, Loan
and Rental Agents.
TELEPHONE 1168.

Neiman Clara J, stenog, b 318 E Market.
Neiman David M, uphlr, h 457 W Shoemaker (N I).
Neiman John S, clk, h 21 Arch.
Neiman Joseph, grocer, 301 E Washington, h same.
Neiman Thomas J, driver, h 318 E Market.
Neir, see also Nier.
Neir Louis, lab, b 213 S Alabama.
Neisler Oscar L, salesman Edward L Gross Realty Co, h 439 Talbott av.
Neiswander Harry L, lab, b 233 Alvord.
Neiswander John, switchman, h 233 Alvord.
Neiswonger Charles, agt, r 30 W Vermont.
Neiswonger Charles W, yardmaster, b 1100 W Washington.
Neitzel Albert B, finisher, b 519 E 9th.
Neitzel Charles, polisher, b 278 E Georgia.
Neitzel Charles F, finisher, b 200 S Spruce.
Neitzel John J, lab, h 519 E 8th.
Neitzel Julius, lab, h 497 E 9th.
Nelan Michael, lab, b 16 McGinnis.
Nelan Timothy F, brakeman, h 5 Depot (B).
Neligh Charles, blksmith, h w s Harris av 9 s of C C C & St L Ry (M J).
Neligh Solon H, grocer, 107 Woodburn av (W I), h 105 same.
Nell Charles R, painter, b 252 N Senate av.
Nell Edward, music teacher, 252 N Senate av, b same.
Nell Emelia (wid John B), h 252 N Senate av.
Neller George B, lab, h 128 N Dorman.
Neller Wm, lab, b 189 S Capitol av.
Neller Wm, shoemkr, h 610 N Senate av.
Nelligan Dennis, bartndr, b 263 Hadley av (W I).
Nelson Albert, mnfrs' agt, 41 Lombard bldg, b 410 N Alabama.
Nelson Albert S, finisher, b w s Ivy la 1 s of Pendleton av (B).
Nelson Amanda (wid James), b 209 Agnes.
Nelson Bird (Davidson & Nelson), h w s Ivy la 1 s of Pendleton av (B).
Nelson Charles, tailor, 803 N Illinois, h same.
Nelson Charles G, car rep, h 127 Sharpe av (W).
Nelson Charles R, supt Central Cycle Mnfg Co, h 522 Union.
Nelson Charles T, lab, r 163 W Washington.
Nelson Edmund, lab, h 372 Lafayette.
Nelson Edward F, pressman The Indpls News, h 49 Johnson av.
Nelson Elliott A, florist, cor Senate av and 27th, h same.
Nelson Elliott R, brakeman, h 1076 W Vermont.
Nelson Flora (Wm M Carothers & Co), h 1490 N Meridian.
Nelson Flora B, journalist, b 52 S State av.
Nelson Frances K (wid James W), h 81 W Walnut.
Nelson Franklin P, tel opr, h 415 Ash.
Nelson Harriet B (wid Levi), r 214 Blackford.
Nelson Henry, lab, h w s Watts 2 n of Washington.
Nelson Isaac H, lab, r 1198 Northwestern av (N I).
NELSON JAMES B, Civil Engineer, 61 Baldwin Blk, h 58 Lexington av.
Nelson James E, lab, h w s Ivy la 1 s of Pendleton av (B).
Nelson James M, trav agt, h 1490 N Meridian.
Nelson John, clk, b 196 Lincoln la.

SULLIVAN & MAHAN Manufacturers of all kinds of PAPER BOXES 41 W. Pearl St.

DIAMOND WALL PLASTER { Telephone 1410 BUILDERS' EXCHANGE.

Teleph 1769. 197 S. Illinois St. } THE HOME LAUNDRY { WORK CALLED FOR AND DELIVERED.

Nelson John, clk, h 193 Yandes.
Nelson John, condr, r 102 S Illinois.
Nelson John C, carp, h 674 W Eugene (N I).
Nelson Lewis B, clk N Y Store, h 318 Clifford av.
Nelson Martin, florist, h 352 W 22d.
Nelson Narcissa (wid Henry), b 415 Ash.
Nelson Pamelia (wid Augustus), b 170 Union.
Nelson Reuben, lab, h n s Pruitt 3 e of Fountain.
Nelson Samuel, lab, b 159 W Merrill.
Nelson Thomas, h 4 Sheridan.
Nelson Thomas H, supt Pentecost Bands, h 52 S State av.
NELSON THOMAS H, Real Estate, Rental and Loan Agt; Improved Property on Monthly Payments; as Well Own as Rent; It Costs No More; 153 W Michigan (Haughville), h 46 Bismarck av (H). (See adv in classified Real Estate.)
Nelson Thomas W, trav agt, r 28 W Vermont.
Nelson Warren, coachman 705 N Illinois.
Nelson Washington F, insp, b 200 Oliver av (W I).
Nelson Wm, clk, r 48 N West.
Nelson Wm H, baggageman, h 296 Virginia av.
Nerenberg Jacob, clothing, 272 S Illinois, h same.
Nerenberg Samuel, student, b 272 S Illinois.
Nesbitt Daniel L, tailor, 12½ Indiana av, r same.
Nesbitt Leonard, lab, h 12½ Indiana av.
Nesbitt Rachel P (wid Wm T), r 831 N Capitol av.
NESOM THOMAS (Baby Supply Mnfg Co), h 256 S East. (See adv in classified Baby Buggies and Hammocks.)
Nessen, see Nissen.
Nessler Adolph G, clk, b 102 Huron.
NESSLER FRANK (Frank Nessler & Co), h 125 Fletcher av.
NESSLER FRANK & CO (Frank Nessler, Wm H Rost), Merchant Tailors, 56 E Market. (See right top cor cards.)
Nessler George, saloon, s w cor Cruse and Michigan av, h 102 Huron.
Nessler Louis, trav agt, h 550 Eureka av.
Nessler Millie F, stenog L E & W R R, b 102 Huron.
Nestel Paul F, trav agt, h 640 N Penn.
Nester Edward, lab, h rear 31 Madison av.
Nester Henry J, packer, h 1468 N Capitol av.
Nestle George H, meats, 82 E Mkt House and 232 E Washington, b 563 E Market.
Nestle Mary M (wid John), h 563 E Market.
Netherton Charles H, weigher, h 194 S William (W I).
Nethery Joseph W, stonecutter, h 264 E 8th.
Nethery Joseph W, supt The Blacherne, h 65 same.
Neu John B, chair mnfr, 63 Arizona, h 600 S East.
Neu John E, uphlr, b 15 Dougherty.
Neu Joseph H, harnessmkr, h 489 Mulberry.
Neu Magdalena (wid Valentine), h 15 Dougherty.
Neu Mary M, dressmkr, 15 Dougherty, h same.
Neu Wm E, wheelbldr, h 15 Dougherty.

FRANK NESSLER. WILL H. ROST.
FRANK NESSLER & CO.
Tailors
56 EAST MARKET ST. (Lemcke Building),
INDIANAPOLIS, IND.

Neu Wm J, finisher, b 600 S East.
Neubacher Frank O, b 678 E Market.
Neubacher Gustav A, clk Clemens Vonnegut, b 678 E Market.
Neubacher Louis F, clk Pearson & Wetzel, b 678 E Market.
Neubacher Louis J, mach, h 678 E Market.
Neubacher Selma L, teacher Public School No 9, b 678 E Market.
Neubauer Frank, bartndr, b 507 Union.
Neubauer John, watchman, h 507 Union.
Neuberger Valentine, lab, h 191 S Alabama.
Neubling John F, helper, b 40 Highland pl.
Neubling Lewis W, mach hd, h 40 Highland pl.
Neuer John C, solr Kingan & Co (ltd), h 83 W 20th.
Neuer Wm B, cigars, 358 Mass av, h 69 W 20th.
Neuer Wm H, b 69 W 20th.
Neuert John M, blksmith, h 388 Virginia av.
Neukom Frank, h 358 W 2d.
Neukom Frank H, chairmkr, b 358 W 2d.
Neukom George C, mach, b 358 W 2d.
Neukom Wm J, bkkpr Indpls Chair Mnfg Co, b 358 W 2d.
Neumann August E, cigarmkr, b 425 S Missouri.
Neumann Caroline (wid Paul), b 30 Hendricks
Neumann Herman, lab, b 425 S Missouri.
Neumann John G (John W Neumann & Co), h Evansville, Ind.
Neumann John W (John W Neumann & Co), r 321 N New Jersey.
NEUMANN JOHN W & CO (John W and John G Neumann), Commission and Produce Merchants, 34 S Delaware, Tel 1451.
Neumann Joseph, bartndr, b 187 Madison av.
Neumann Julius R, carp, h 30 Hendricks
Neumann Minnie, stenog, b 425 S Missouri.
Neumann Rudolph, carp, b 425 S Missouri.
Neumann Rudolph F, finisher, h 21 Gresham.

Haueisen & Hartmann
163-169 E. Washington St.
FURNITURE,
Carpets,
Household Goods,
Tin, Granite and China Wares, Oil Cloth and Shades

THE WM. H. BLOCK CO. 7 AND 9 EAST WASHINGTON STREET. DRY GOODS, HOUSE FURNISHINGS AND CROCKERY.

London Guarantee and Accident Co. (Ltd.) Employers', Public and Teams' Liability, Workmen's Collective Insurance and Fidelity Bonds
GEORGE W. PANGBORN, General Agent, 704-706 Lemcke Bldg. Telephone 140.

Reliable Fire Insurance. Reasonable Rates. 74 E. MARKET STREET. Telephone 8. FRANK K. SAWYER

JOSEPH GARDNER,
TIN, IRON, STEEL AND SLATE ROOFING,
GALVANIZED IRON CORNICES & SKYLIGHTS.
37, 39 & 41 KENTUCKY AVE. Telephone 322.

Neumann Wilhelmina (wid John), h 425 S Missouri.
Neumeister Adam, shoemkr, 94 Hosbrook, h same.
Neumeister Emil A, coppersmith, b 94 Hosbrook.
Neumeister George J, tailor, b 94 Hosbrook.
Neumeister John J, clk, h 187 Elm.
Neumeyer Bernhard, b 360 N Noble.
Neumeyer Edward H, buyer Hay & Willits Mnfg Co, h 136 Broadway.
Neumeyer Julius A, clk, h 360 N Noble.
Neurenberg Richard, secondhand goods, 272 S Illinois, h same.
Neussel Charles, lab, h 59 Harrison.
Neussel Charles F W, bricklyr, b 59 Harrison.
Neussel Wm F, clk, b 204 Indiana av.
Neussinger Ludwig, lab, h 8 Hosbrook.
Nevel John, boilermkr, b 200 Bates.
Nevel Michael, cigarmkr, r 263 Fletcher av.
Nevers Joseph, mach, h 349 S Brookside av.
Nevers Wm E, mach hd, h 349 S Brookside av.
Nevill Louis, blksmith helper, h 82 W Washington.
Neville Annie (wid Judson), h 224 W Maryland.
Neville Benjamin A, molder, h 49 Haugh (H).
Neville Louis, lab, b 892 W Washington.
Nevils George, lab, b 244 W 3d.
Nevius John, condr, h 535 College av.
New Albert, clk, b 880½ N Senate av.
New Asa M, bkkpr The Home Brewg Co, h 64 N Arsenal av.
NEW ENGLAND MUTUAL LIFE INSURANCE CO OF BOSTON, Horne & Gasper Genl Agts, 400 Indiana Trust Bldg, Tel 1040.
New Frank R, real est, h 426 N Illinois.
New Harry S, vice-pres Indpls Journal Newspaper Co, h 476 N Capitol av, tel 1672.
New John C, pres Indpls Journal Newspaper Co, h 272 N Penn, tel 1558.

J. S. FARRELL & CO.
STEAM AND HOT WATER HEATING AND PLUMBING CONTRACTORS
84 North Illinois Street. Telephone 382.

New Year's Saving and Loan Assn, Berry Self pres, James H Smith sec, Franklin L Spahr treas, 36 W Washington.
New York Leather Belting Co, Henry L Whaley agt, 38 Kentucky av.
NEW YORK LIFE INSURANCE CO, Wm C Van Arsdel Mngr for Central Indiana, James A Barcus Mngr for Northern Indiana, Joseph W Harris Cashier, 200, 201 and 202 Indiana Trust Bldg, Tel 797.
NEW YORK STORE, Pettis Dry Goods Co Proprs, 25-33 E Washington, Tel 65.
Newall Alice, b 489 N Illinois.
NEWARK MACHINE CO, Granville Barnes Genl Mngr, Agricultural Implements, Room 5 Board of Trade Bldg, Tel 333.
Newball Frank, bartndr, h 507 Union.
Newbauer John H, painter, h 331 S Delaware.
Newberger Louis (Morris, Newberger & Curtis), b 428 N Capitol av.
Newberry Augustus T, agt, b 312 N California.
Newberry Laura (wid Jefferson), real est, 312 N California, h same.
Newburg Augustus H, motorman, h 563 Ash.
Newburg Charles P, mngr, h 69 Woodlawn av.
Newburg John W, trav agt, h 199 Park av.
Newby Alice L (wid John S), b 380 Park av.
Newby Alonzo B, paperhngr, b 37 Spann av.
Newby Arthur, barber, r 201 S Illinois.
Newby Arthur C, treas Indpls Chain and Stamping Co, b 968 N Capitol av.
Newby Charles R, contr, h 52 Arch.
Newby Charles T, brakeman, b 733 E Market.
Newby Elmer E, clk Schauroth & Co, r 27 Ft Wayne av.
Newby Emma, hairdresser, b 63 Howard.
Newby Emma B (wid Lawrence A), b 63 Howard.
Newby Evert, painter, b w s Union 1 s of Washington (M J).
Newby Francis A (Newby & Son), h 852 Grandview av.
Newby Guy L, brakeman, b 733 E Market.
Newby Harry B, mach, h 256 River av (W I).
Newby Jacob L, contr, 61 S Belmont (W I), h same.
Newby John, insp, h 968 N Capitol av.
Newby John, lab, h rear 392 Yandes.
Newby Joseph, lab, b 338 Martindale av.
Newby Katherine, teacher Public School No 25, b 37 Spann av.
Newby Levi E, lab, h 29 Biddle.
Newby Nathan, mach, h 730 N New Jersey.
Newby Peter, lab, h 338 Martindale av.
Newby Rachel (wid James), h 338 Martindale av.
Newby Strother E, mantel setter, h 84 N New Jersey.
Newby Thomas, r 432 W New York.
Newby Walter E (Newby & Son), real est, 57 Baldwin blk, h 852 Grandview av.
Newby Wm H, agt Marion Mnfg Co, h 21 Villa av.
Newby Wm H, loans, 224 W Washington, h 595 Ash.
Newby Wm H, watchmkr, h 37 Spann av.

POLICIES IN UNITED STATES LIFE INSURANCE CO., offer indemnity against death, liberal cash surrender value or at option of policy-holder, fully paid-up life insurance or liberal life income. E. B. SWIFT, M'g'r, 25 E. Market St.

WM. KOTTEMAN WILL FURNISH YOUR HOUSE COMPLETE
89 & 91 E. Washington St. Telephone 1742

NEWBY & SON (Francis and Walter E), Druggists, Grocers, Meat Market, Contractors and Builders, 852 Grandview av, cor 19th (old), 26th (new), Tel 1274.
Newcom Frank G, bkkpr Daniel Stewart Co, h 1289 N Meridian.
Newcomb Florence S (wid George F), asst Public Library, b 138 E St Clair.
NEWCOMB HORATIO C, Agt Travelers' Insurance Co of Hartford, Conn, 319-321 Indiana Trust Bldg, Sec The S A Haines Co, 44 N Penn, Tel 1014; h 275 N Capitol av.
Newcomb Walter C, trav agt, b 107 E St Joseph.
Newcomb Wm C, stock food mnfr. 107 E St Joseph, h same.
Newcomer Sarah E (wid Frisby S), b 22 Home av.
Newdigate Joseph, lab, h 36 Hosbrook.
Newell Abigail C (wid Henry P), h 20 E Pratt.
Newell Alice, music teacher, 489 N Illinois, h same.
Newell Arthur, cigars, 89 N Delaware, h same.
Newell Charles H, mach, h 150½ College av.
Newell Frederick, lab, b Ross House.
Newell Lyne S, r 10½ E Washington.
Newell Margaret (wid Davis), b 80 W 8th.
Newell Mary A, teacher Public School No 41, b 20 E Pratt.
Newett Frank G, harnessmkr, h 33 Sinker.
Newhall Alice R (wid George), music teacher, r 177 N Delaware.
Newhall Lucile, stenog International Typograph Union, b 30 Fletcher av.
Newhall Roberts, student, r 177 N Delaware.
Newhart Daniel, carp, h e s Shade 2 s of Sutherland (B).
Newhart Elizabeth, h 19 S Station (B).
Newhart Frederick, jeweler, 57 E Sutherland (B), b 19 S Station (B).
Newhouse Alexander, lab, h 98 S Shade (B).
Newhouse Azaraiah, marshal, h 78 S Brightwood av (B).
Newhouse Benjamin F, lab, h 423 E Pearl.
Newhouse Charles W, driver, h 337 E Wabash.
Newhouse Frederick A, grocer, 70 John, h same.
Newhouse John W, insp Indiana Bicycle Co, h 78 Meek.
Newhouse Lewis A, claywkr, h s s Bloyd av 3 w of Shade (B).
Newhouse Orpha, nurse, 785 N Illinois, r same.
Newhouse Richard, lab, b 423 E Pearl.
Newhouse Samuel E, lab, h 211½ E Washington.
Newkirk Austin T, painter, b 115 Oliver av (W I).
Newkirk Charles B, painter, b 115 Oliver av (W I).
Newkirk Frederick W, patternmkr, h 42 S Linden.
Newkirk John H, patternmkr, b 42 S Linden.
Newkirk Wm, carp, h 115 Oliver av (W I).
Newkirk Wm H, carp, b 115 Oliver av (W I).
Newland Abner L, h 18½ N Penn.
Newland Charles, lab, h 460 W Lake (N I).
Newland Edwin J, chemist, b 226 E Ohio.
Newland George, clk, b 18½ N Penn.

THOS. C. DAY & CO.
INVESTING AGENTS,
TOWN AND FARM LOANS,
Rooms 325 to 330 Lemcke Bldg.

NEWLAND HARROD C, Drugs, 90 Ft Wayne av, h same.
Newland John T, clk, b 23 E Michigan.
Newland J Guy, page Marion Circuit Court, b cor Clinton and Ohio.
Newland Lewis, photog, h 65 S Linden.
Newland Mary (wid Dallas), h 226 E Ohio.
Newland Robert A, music teacher, 23 E Michigan, h same.
Newland Robert C, teacher High School, b 557 N Senate av.
Newlin Charles E, special agt Mutual Life Ins Co, h n s Washington av 1 w of Elm av (I).
Newman Alonzo A, finisher, h 23 Frank.
Newman Charles, lab, b n e cor Brightwood av and C C C & St L Ry (B).
Newman Charles E, carp, h 33 Weghorst.
Newman Charles M, cooper, h 131 Union.
Newman Charles P, electrician, h 844 Cornell av.
Newman David, h 305 E New York.
Newman David F, collarmkr, h 327 S Missouri.
Newman David K, mach, h 207 S Linden.
Newman Frank, mach hd, h 13 Hillside av.
Newman George, lab, r 268 S Illinois.
Newman George H, carp, b 804 Cornell av.
Newman George S, contr, h 804 Cornell av.
Newman Harry L, lab, b 207 S Linden.
Newman Henry, dry goods, 372 S West, h same.
Newman Herman, shoemkr, 24 and 156 Indiana av, h Empire blk.
Newman Jacob L, supply clk L E & W R R, b 305 E New York.
Newman John B, h 408 N Delaware.
Newman John D, condr, h 124 W Ray.
Newman Lavina (wid George), h 112 Rhode Island.
Newman Louis R, h 249 N West.
Newman Mary (wid Charles), r rear 77 W North.
Newman Mary (wid John), boarding 64 S State av.
Newman Nathaniel M, lab, h e s Harriet 3 s of Park (B).
Newman Omer U, lawyer, 525 Lemcke bldg, h 370 Cedar.

EAT
HITZ'S
CRACKERS
AND CAKES.
ASK YOUR GROCER FOR THEM.

SHOW CASES | WILLIAM WIEGEL | 6 West Louisiana Street Opp. Union Station.

Capital Steam Carpet Cleaning Works
M. D. PLUNKETT Proprietor, Telephone 818

BENJ. BOOTH PRACTICAL EXPERT ACCOUNTANT. Accounts of any description investigated and audited, and statements rendered. Room 18, 82½ E. Washington St., Indianapolis, Ind.

The Best Place in the City to Get a Good Meal THE SHERMAN RESTAURANT 18 and 20 S. Meridian Street KERSHNER BROS., Proprs.

ESTABLISHED 1876. TELEPHONE 168.
CHESTER BRADFORD,
SOLICITOR OF PATENTS,
AND COUNSEL IN PATENT CAUSES.
(See adv. page 6.)
Office:—Rooms 14 and 16 Hubbard Block, S.W. Cor. Washington and Meridian Streets, INDIANAPOLIS, INDIANA.

Newman Perry, tmstr, h w s Bismarck av 1 s of Emrich (H).
Newman Peter, mach hd, h 13 Hillside av.
Newman Peter B, clk, b 327 S Missouri.
Newman Peter F W, helper, b 111 Dunlop.
Newman Peter H, hostler, h 111 Dunlop.
Newman Sarah (wid Samuel), h 58 Smith.
Newman Sarah (wid Wm T), h 148 Indiana av.
Newman Stephen B, r 1139 N Illinois.
Newman Thomas W, carp, b 806 Cornell av.
Newman Walter H, cooper, b 131 Union.
Newmier George A, carp, h 71 Fountain av.
Newnam Edward, foreman Richard H Gould, h 446 N New Jersey.
Newnam James H, trav agt Murphy, Hibben & Co, h 668 College av.
Newnam Jesse F, bricklyr, b 235 Bellefontaine.
Newnam John M, condr, h 328 Home av.
Newnam Wm F, contr, 235 Bellefontaine, h same.
Newport Clarence A, clk E C Atkins & Co, h 300 Blake.
Newport James G, painter, h 1336 N Capitol av.
Newsom Harley C, fireman, h w s Sugar Grove av 4 n of Vorster av (M P).
Newsom Isaac J, trav agt, h 1150 N Alabama.
Newsom Lysias E, tel opr C H & D R R, h 22 Newman.
Newsom Mary, h 3 Gimbel.
Newsom Sidney C, teacher Industrial School, r 282 N Penn.
Newsom Thomas C, clk, b 218 E Market.
Newsom Thomas E, mach hd, h 22 Bates.
Newton Della E (wid James I), h 251 Blake.
Newton Deloss, janitor, h 82 Kennington.
Newton Edward, lab, h 211 W Merrill.
Newton Edward, mngr Great Atlantic and Pacific Tea Co, b 204 N Illinois.
Newton Elizabeth R (wid Joseph R), b 225 W Merrill.
Newton Frances E, teacher Public School No 16, b 83 Cornell av.
Newton Gaston, lab, h cor. Clinton and Bates al.

O. B. Ensey
SLATE, STEEL, TIN AND IRON ROOFING.
Cor. 6th and Illinois Sts. Tel. 1562

Newton George R, pdlr, b 251 Blake.
Newton James A, painter, r 194 E Washington.
Newton James B, lab, h 225 W Merrill.
Newton John, tmstr, r 10 Mulberry.
Newton John, tmstr, b rear 268 S Noble.
Newton John C, millwright, h 83 Cornell av.
Newton Joseph A, engr Journal bldg, h 136 Spring.
Newton Josephine (wid Joseph T), h 441 Howard (W I).
Newton Josephine E, h 27 LaSalle.
Newton Maria S (wid Norman), h 200 N Capitol av.
Newton Mary A (wid John H), h 483 N Illinois.
Newton Mary E (wid Eugene), b 344 N Alabama.
Newton Roy, paver, b 285 S Capitol av.
Newton Thomas, bartndr, b 178 S Illinois.
Newton Van T, lab, h 25 Abbott.
Newton Willard P, filer, h 121 Kansas.
Newton Wm E, painter, r 194 E Washington.
Newton Wm K, carp, h 1 Walcott.
Newton Wm S, lab, h 297 Kentucky av.
Ney Emma B, h 833 N Capitol av.
Niblack Eliza A (wid Wm E), h 77 W North.
Nicholas Abraham R, treas American Buncher Mnfg Co, h 935 N Alabama.
Nicholas Anna, editorial writer The Indpls Journal, h 77 The Blacherne.
Nicholas Benjamin S, huckster, h 137 Ft Wayne av.
Nicholas Charles D, painter, h 184 E Morris.
Nicholas Charles E, clk, b 184 E Morris.
Nicholas Charles L, engr, h 31 Camp.
Nicholas George D, steamfitter, h 5 Camp.
Nicholas George L Rev, h 34 Lincoln la.
Nicholas Louisa (wid John D), h 665 N Penn.
Nicholas Reese K, driver, h 519 N Senate av.
Nicholas Wm, b 50 S Morris (B).
Nicholas Wm E, condr, h 644 Park av.
Nicholl Henry, cabtmkr, h 57 Downey.
Nicholl Wm, butcher, h 85 River av (W I).
Nichols Carrie R (wid Wm H), h 157 N Capitol av.
Nichols Catherine (wid Wm), b 294 E Wabash.
Nichols Charles B, printer, h 627 Marlowe av.
Nichols Charles M, broommkr, h 145 S Noble.
Nichols Charles O, clk Progress Clothing Co, b 32 S Summit.
Nichols Clarence W, clk, b 64 W 11th.
Nichols Cora E, h 99 Bates.
Nichols Edward C, janitor, h 126 Columbia al.
Nichols Edwin (A Baber & Co), h 566 N Illinois.
Nichols Ellen, mngr California House, 184 S Illinois.
Nichols Elmer E, sec and mngr Elmer E Nichols Co, h 582 Ash.
NICHOLS ELMER E CO, Mary W Malott Pres, Omer A Robertson Vice-Pres, Elmer E Nichols Sec and Mngr, Wholesale Confectioners, 74-76 S Meridian, Tel 10.
Nichols Emma J, h 222½ E Washington.
Nichols Emma R, seamstress, b 452 N New Jersey.
Nichols Francis F, transfer, h 26 Shelby.
Nichols George, lab, h 34 Lincoln la.

TUTEWILER UNDERTAKER, NO. 72 WEST MARKET STREET. TELEPHONE 216.

PROVIDENT LIFE AND TRUST CO. OF PHILADELPHIA. D. W. Edwards, G. A., 508 Indiana Trust Bldg. In form of policy; prompt settlement of death losses; equitable dealing with policy-holders; in strength of organization; and in everything which contributes to Security and Cheapness of life insurance, this company is unsurpassed.

THEODORE F. SMITHER COMPOSITION ROOFING MATERIALS. BEST IN THE MARKET. TELEPHONE 861. OFFICE, 151 WEST MARYLAND ST.

Nichols George M, clk Elmer E Nichols Co, b 34 Oliver av (W I).
Nichols James, engr, b 264 E Georgia.
Nichols James, lab, h 309 W Pearl.
Nichols James W, lab, h 477 Blake.
Nichols John, lab, b rear 13 McCauley.
Nichols John D, phys, 54 College av, b same.
Nichols John J, dentist, 37½ W Market, r same.
Nichols Josephine R (wid Edwin), h 566 N Illinois.
Nichols Leo M, clk, h 376 S Illinois.
Nichols Lewis D, bartndr, r 230 N Senate av.
Nichols Mary, r 88 N Illinois
Nichols Mary E (wid John R), h 54 College av.
Nichols Nancy (wid Addison), b 32 S Summit.
Nichols Noah S, condr, h 365 Newman.
Nichols Smith T (S T Nichols & Co), r 54 The Blacherne.
Nichols Solomon E, barber, e s Rural 2 n of Bloyd av (B), h 400 N Brookside av (B).
Nichols S T & Co (Smith T Nichols), watchmkrs' tools, 18 Hubbard blk.
Nichols Willard C, dep clk U S Courts, h 64 W 11th.
Nichols Wm, lab, b 314 W Court.
Nichols Wm H, clk, b 400 N Brookside av.
Nichols Wm H, meats, 299 Yandes, h same.
Nichols Wm W, bartndr, r 126 W New York.
Nichols Wm W, engr, h 26 S Senate av.
NICHOLS & SHEPARD CO, Wilson S McMillen Genl Mngr, Engines and Threshers, 22 Kentucky av, Tel 985.
Nicholson Adna B, painter, h 289 Springfield.
Nicholson Andrew J, carp, b 55 Ramsey av.
Nicholson Aney L (wid George F), h 74 Smith.
Nicholson Charles A, fireman, h 33 Paca.
Nicholson David, h 430 N Illinois.
Nicholson David J, car rep, h 158 Sheldon.
Nicholson Edgar J, engr, h e s Wheeler nr Morris (B).
Nicholson Elizabeth, artist, 248 Broadway, b same.
Nicholson Edward C, engr, h 50 Warren av (W I).
Nicholson Frank A, clk, b 74 Smith.
Nicholson James L, barber, h 18½ Indiana av.
Nicholson Jessie T (wid Wm T), b 449 Broadway.
Nicholson John D, trav agt, r 52½ S Illinois.
Nicholson Joseph, r 502½ E Washington.
Nicholson Lee S, registry clk P O, h 39 Williams.
Nicholson Lucy L (wid John), b 234 Prospect.
Nicholson Mary E, prin Normal Training School, b 248 Broadway.
Nicholson Meredith, editor, h 1033 N Capitol av.
Nicholson Nellie B, stenog, b 128 W Vermont.
Nicholson Percy, clk, h 114 Michigan av.
Nicholson Valentine, h 248 Broadway.
Nicholson Vernon K, painter, h 234 Prospect.
NICK THE TAILOR, (Arnold F Dold), Dyeing, Cleaning and Repairing, 78 N Illinois. (See adv opp Tailors.)

THE WHEN IS A WORLD BEATER.

NICKEL PLATE LINE, Wm C Lynn Agt, 2 Board of Trade Bldg, Tel 361.
Nickels Christian, lab, h 9 Sample (W I).
Nickens Granville, cook, h 161 Bird.
Nickerson Chester, lab, h w s Rural 2 s of 17th.
Nickerson George T, letter carrier P O, h 142 Tacoma av.
Nickerson Samuel R, lawyer, h 449½ Central av.
NICKERSON WM H, Justice of the Peace, 26 N Delaware, Tel 1640; h 588 Park av.
Nickisch Frank, lab, b 268 Yandes.
Nickum Alonzo K, boltmkr, h 176 Maple.
Nickum Charles W, baker, 75 Mass av, r same.
Nickum John R, h 26 Lockerbie.
Nickum Matilda (wid Webster A), h 52 Chadwick.
Nickum Robert D, helper, h 125 W McCarty.
Nicolai Amelia (wid Wm), h 131 Woodlawn av.
Nicolai Emmett L, paperhngr, h 190 N Dorman.
Nicolai Frank L, tel opr, b 190 N Dorman.
Nicolai Fritz A, clk, r 124 W Maryland.
Nicolai Henry, meats, 91 Mass av and 32 E Mkt House, h 89 Broadway.
Nicolai John, driver, b 190 N Dorman.
Nicolai Mary L, treas Family Dress Guide Co, h 1875 E Washington.
Nicolai Wm F, finisher, h 334 Spann av.
Nicoles Albert E, clk, b 488 Park av.
Nicoles Walter H, trav agt The Bowen-Merrill Co, h 488 Park av.
Nicoles Wm B, b 488 Park av.
Nicoli Charles A, engraver, 21 Hubbard blk, h 594 Park av.
Nicoli Lew, real est, 22 Thorpe blk, h 563 N Illinois.
Nicoll Charles B, printer, 234 Indiana av, h 629 Marlowe av.
NICOLL THE TAILOR, James Menzies Mngr, 33-35 S Illinois.

The A. Burdsal Co. CELEBRATED HOMESTEAD READY MIXED PAINT. WHOLESALE AND RETAIL. 34 AND 36 SOUTH MERIDIAN STREET.

ELECTRIC SUPPLIES We Carry a full Stock. Prices Right. C. W. MEIKEL, Tel. 466. 96-98 E. New York St.

DALTON & MERRIFIELD { LUMBER South Noble St., near E. Washington

INDIANA ELECTROTYPE CO. :: BEST WORK LOWEST PRICES.
23 WEST PEARL ST., INDIANAPOLIS, IND. JOB WORK. BOOK PLATES. All Orders Promptly Filled. BEST PATENT BASE ON THE MARKET.

KIRKHOFF BROS.,
Electrical Contractors, Wiring and Construction.
102-104 SOUTH PENNSYLVANIA ST.
TELEPHONE 910.

Nictrols Wm M, carpet layer, h 198½ N Senate av.
Niebergall George, engraver, h 229 Blackford.
Niebergall John, mach hd, h 266 N Pine.
Niece Wm, bkkpr, r 267 N New Jersey.
Nied Charles, florist, b 675 Madison av.
Niedhamer, see also Neidhamer.
Niedhamer Charles, clk, b 39 Fayette.
Niedhamer Clarence C, mach, b 39 Fayette.
Niedhamer Frederick, clk, b 39 Fayette.
Niedhamer John, mach hd, b 39 Fayette.
Niedhamer Sarah J, h 39 Fayette.
Niedlander Adne, h 170 E Merrill.
Niedlander Allen O, trav agt Griffith Bros, h 170 E Merrill.
Niedlander E Edwin, clk, b 170 E Merrill.
Niedling, see also Neidling.
Niedling Wm J, molder, h 123 Chadwick.
Niehaus Benjamin, lab, b 567 S West.
Niehaus George, lab, b 567 S West.
Niehaus George J, city fireman, h 391 S East.
Niehaus John, lab, b 567 S West.
Niehaus Joseph, lab, h 567 S West.
Niehaus Joseph R, h 76 Dunlop.
Nields Clarence W, gluer, b 181 Woodlawn av.
Nields Daniel W, chief opr Postal Tel Cable Co, h n w cor Chester av and Washington.
Nields Daniel W jr, uphlr, b n w cor Washington and Chester av.
Nielsen Carl J, lawyer, h 310 Bellefontaine.
Nielsen James, lab, h 385 W 23d.
Nielsen Peter, lab, h 176 N Belmont av (H).
Nieman Wm R, trav agt, h 672 E Market.
Nieman Wm R jr, clk H P Wasson & Co, b 672 E Market.
Niemann August, lab, h 118 Gresham.
Niemann Charles F, carp, b 322 N Pine.
Niemann Christian, plastr, h 167 E Morris.
Niemann Christian jr, foreman The Wm P Jungclaus Co, h 13 Peru av.
Niemann Christian F, carp, h 322 N Pine.
Niemann Edward C, mach, b 322 N Pine.
Niemann Elmer H, uphlr, b 322 N Pine.
Niemann Frederick C, engr, h 9 Gresham.
Niemann Frederick H, b 167 E Morris.

THE W. C. WASSON CO.,
130 Indiana Ave. Tel. 989.
STEAM
COAL
Car Lots a Specialty. Prompt Delivery.
Brazil Block, Jackson and Anthracite.

Niemann Frederick W, mach hd, h 197 Lincoln la.
Niemann Gottlieb F, clk, r 418½ Virginia av.
Niemann Harry H, mach hd, b 322 N Pine.
Niemann Henry A F, draper, b 557 S New Jersey.
Niemann Henry F, bkkpr Slatts & Poe, b 118 Gresham.
Niemann Joachim, insp, h 557 S New Jersey.
Niemann Ollie M, stenog, b 167 E Morris.
Niemann Paul, meat mkt s w cor Earhart and Prospect, h same.
Niemann Wm, carp, h 421 E Pearl.
Niemeyer Christian F, well driver, 183 Fulton, h same.
Niemeyer Frederick, driver, h 327 E Morris.
Niemeyer Frederick C, engr, h 18 Elder av.
Niemeyer Frederick W, farmer, h s s Prospect 1 w of C C C & St L Ry.
Niemeyer Henry C, molder, h s s Prospect 1 w of C C C & St L Ry.
Niemeyer Henry W, painter, h 95 W Morris.
Niemeyer Hermann, engr, h 14 Traub av.
Niemeyer Joseph, coachman Insane Hospital, h 266 E Washington.
Niemeyer Wm W, shoemkr, 539 E Washington, r 266 same.
Niemier Cornelius S, contr, 187 Lexington av, h same.
Nienaber Henry H, tailor, h 171 Pleasant.
Nienaber John H, expressman, h e s Harriet 2 s of Sutherland (B).
Nier, see also Neir.
NIER ISAAC, Wholesale Dealer in Wines, Liquors, Cigars and Tobaccos, 160 W Washington, h 405 N Alabama.
Niermann Henry F, grocer, 527 N Illinois, h 228 N Liberty.
Niermeyer Henry, shoemkr, 436 National rd, h 607 W Washington.
Nies Dora, draper, b 460 N East.
Nies Louis W, h 460 N East.
Niet Frederick, mach hd, b 75 Hanway.
Niet John tmstr, h 75 Hanway.
Nieters Anthony, clk, b Circle Park Hotel.
Niland Joseph D, lab, b 278 E Louisiana.
Niland Mary J (wid James), h 278 E Louisiana.
Niland Wm E, bricklyr, b 278 E Louisiana.
Niles Cassius M, jeweler, h 72 Tacoma av.
NILIUS CLARA, Tailoring, Cleaning, Dyeing and Repairing, 62½ S Illinois, b 510 N Senate av.
Nilius Otto (Strawmyer & Nilius), b 510 N Senate av.
Nilius Sibylla (wid Charles), h 510 N Senate av.
Nimal Wm H, restaurant, 82 E Market, h 469 same.
Nimmo Nina, bkkpr Old Wayne Mut Life Ins Co, b 154 E New York.
Nimtz Caroline (wid Charles), h 126 Wright.
Nimz Frederick M, cabtmkr, h 281 Coburn.
Nisen Lars P, packer A Kiefer Drug Co, b 426 S East.
Nissen Niels, drayman, b 37 Nebraska.
Niven Richard B, carp, h 248 Douglass.
Nix Herman, painter, b 57 Church.
Nix Robert A, supervisor German Public Schools, h 172 Clifford av.
Nixon Alexander, clk, b s e cor Waverly and Brookside avs.
Nixon Eliza J (wid Wm), h s e cor Waverly and Brookside avs.

W. H. Messenger FURNITURE, CARPETS, STOVES, 101 EAST WASHINGTON ST. TEL. 491.

McNamara, Koster & Co. | Foundry and Pattern Shop, 212-218 S. PENN. ST. . . . PHONE 1593.

Nixon Elza W, engr Robert Keller, h 76 Beaty.
Nixon Eva, h 10, 8½ Mass av.
Nixon James B, lab, h 414 E Walnut.
Nixon Lee, clk, r 15 Grand Opera House blk.
Nixon Margaret (wid John B), h 69 S Liberty
Nixon Oney, filer, b 69 S Liberty
Nixon Thomas, lab, h 108 Eddy.
Nixon Walter C, lab, h 16 S Gillard av.
Nixon Wm G, lineman, h 93 Eddy.
Noah Thomas J, news dealer, 424 Virginia av, h same.
Noble Catherine E (wid Louis F), h 423 W 2d.
Noble Charles G, mach, b 16 Traub av.
Noble Charles T, tailor, b 31 S Reisner (W I).
Noble Charles W, asst supt Prudential Life Ins Co, h 165 Clinton.
Noble Cyrus B, foreman Parrott & Taggart, h 70 Huron.
Noble Edward, stonecutter, h 17 Harrison.
Noble Frank, foreman Kingan & Co (ltd), b 300 W Maryland.
Noble Frank W, salesman, h 163 Union.
Noble George W, barber, b 17 Harrison.
Noble Harriet, teacher, r 78 The Blacherne.
Noble James R, packer, h s s Washington bet Addison and Laura (M J).
Noble Joseph E, barber, b 17 Harrison.
Noble Josephine (wid Alexander), h 297 S New Jersey.
Noble Laz (Laz Noble & Co), r 78 The Blacherne.
NOBLE LAZ & CO (Laz Noble, Columbus T Dollarhide), Booksellers and Stationers, 3 N Meridian, Tel 436.
Noble Manuel Rev, pastor M E Church, n w cor Shelby and Martin, h 3 miles s on Madison rd.
Noble Mary (wid James G), h 31 S Reisner (W I).
Noble May, music teacher, 70 Huron, b same.
Noble Nancy (wid Thomas), h 290 Springfield.
Noble Nancy M (wid James N), b 862 N Alabama.
Noble Squire, lab, h e s Race 2 s of Raymond.
Noble Thomas B (Wishard & Noble), h 955 N Capitol av, tel 257.
Noble Thomas Y, engr, h 16 Traub av.
Noble Walter T, mach, b 16 Traub av.
Noble Wm E, floorwalker, h 556 Ash.
Noble Wm T, sec Marion Trust Co, h 956 N Penn.
Noble Winston P, civil engr, h 747 N New Jersey.
NOBLESVILLE MILLING CO, S C M Horney Mngr Indianapolis Branch, Mnfrs of the Celebrated Brands Diadem and Manna Patent Flour, 132-134 Indiana av, Tel 695.
Noblets Frank, pressman, b 3 Camp.
Nock Thomas, h 37 Hosbrook.
Noe Fletcher M, pawnbroker, 64 W Market, b 530 N Illinois.
Noe Harry C, trimmer, h 435 N Pine.
Noe Harry H, mach, h 81 Buchanan.
Noe Hettie A (wid Albert M), h 530 N Illinois.
Noe James, driver, b 866 S Meridian.
Noe John B (Houton & Noe), h 178 S New Jersey.

Henry H. Fay,
40½ E. Washington St.,
REAL ESTATE,
AND LOAN BROKER.

Noe Nicholas, contr, 17 Minnesota, and livery, 864 S Meridian, b 17 Minnesota.
Noe Richard, bricklyr, b 17 Minnesota.
Noe Sa a A (wid Jephtha C), h 5½ Blackford. r h
Noe Wm M, billposter, h 167 N Pine.
Noel Belle, teacher Public School No 5, b 309 Broadway.
Noel Bros Flour Feed Co, J D Whitmore pres, S Vance B Noel sec and treas, Edmund B Noel mngr, 156 W North.
Noel Edmund B, mngr Noel Bros Flour Feed Co, h 75 E Pratt.
Noel Elizabeth B, stenog Baker & Daniels, b 235 W New York.
Noel Eugene E, music teacher, 26 Prospect, h same.
Noel James M, trav agt Standard Oil Co, h 309 Broadway.
Noel James W (Noel & Lahr), r 134 N Meridian.
Noel John M, clk, h 26 Prospect.
Noel Smallwood, b 234 W New York.
NOEL SYLVESTER D, Propr Indianapolis Steel Roofing and Corrugating Works, 23-25 E South, Tel 832; h 100 Fletcher av. (See right side lines.)
Noel S Vance B, sec Noel Bros Flour Feed Co, h 1119 N Delaware.
Noel Walter H, clk, b 26 Prospect.
NOEL & LAHR (James W Noel, Frank J Lahr), Lawyers, 411-412 Lemcke Bldg, Tel 408.
Noelke Frederick, pres Haugh-Noelke Iron Wks, h 36 Broadway.
Noelke Wm, draughtsman, b 36 Broadway.
Noell George W, driver, h 8 Coble.
Noelle Frank A, painter, h 133 N Noble.
Noelle Frank W, car rep, h 255 N Noble.
Noelle Wm F, clk, b 133 N Noble.
Noerr Frederick, mach, h 97 Sanders.
Noerr George, mach, b 97 Sanders.
Noerr Louisa (wid George), h 227 Lincoln la.
Noes, see also Nose.
Noes George, tmstr, h n s Prospect 2 e of Belt R R (N).

UNION CASUALTY & SURETY CO.
OF ST. LOUIS, MO.
All lines of Personal Accident and Casualty Insurance, including Employers' and General Liability.
W. E. BARTON & CO., General Agents,
504 Indiana Trust Building.
LONG DISTANCE TELEPHONE 1918.

THE FRED DIETZ CO. WOODEN PACKING BOXES MADE TO ORDER. FACTORY AND WAREHOUSE TRUCKS. 400 Madison Avenue. Telephone 654.

Indianapolis BUSINESS UNIVERSITY Leading College of Business and Shorthand. Elevator day and night. Individual instruction. Large faculty. Terms easy. Enter now. See p. 4. When Block. E. J. HEEB, President.

Water Works Pumping Engines { HENRY R. WORTHINGTON, 64 SOUTH PENNSYLVANIA ST. Long Distance Telephone 284.

UNION CO-OPERATIVE LAUNDRY (COMPOSED OF UNION LAUNDRY GIRLS.) NOS. 138, 140 AND 142 VIRGINIA AVENUE. TELEPHONES. INDIANAPOLIS, IND. T. E. SOMERVILLE, MANAGER

HORACE M. HADLEY
REAL ESTATE AND INSURANCE
66 East Market Street, Basement
TELEPHONE 1540.

Noffke Albert, lab, h 331 Columbia av.
Noffke Albertina (wid August), b 322 Columbia av.
Noffke August H, lab, h 328 Columbia av.
Noffke Frank F, lab, h n s Brookside av 2 e of Jupiter.
Noffke Hermann, painter. h 322 Columbia av.
Noffke Otto H, lab, h 322 Columbia av.
Noffke Wm H, painter, h 321 Columbia av.
Noeffiette Edgar, lab, 284 N Missouri.
Noffsinger Wm M, bkkpr, b 230 E North.
Noftg Charles, lab, h 40 Parker.
Noggle Henry, engr, h 11 Traub av.
Nogle Lee T, boxmkr, h 553 S Illinois.
Nohl Henry, driver, b w s Watts 1 s of Clifford av.
Nohl John, dairy, w s Watts 1 s of Clifford av, h same.
Noil Hester A (wid Andrew C), h 114 Columbia al.
Nokley Thomas, engr, b 59 E South.
Nolan Ann (wid Thomas), r 193 W Maryland.
Nolan Catherine (wid Dominick), b 27 Catharine.
Nolan Charles E, bkkpr Swift & Co, b 162 N Illinois.
Nolan Edward, driver, h 36 Drake.
Nolan Elizabeth, housekpr 308 Park av.
Nolan Johanna S (wid Timothy), h 26 Arch.
Nolan John A, butcher, b 336 W Washington.
Nolan John C, lab, b 125 W McCarty.
Nolan Josie (wid Timothy), h 26 Arch.
Nolan Margaret H (wid Michael), h 164 Deloss.
Nolan Michael, mach, h 121 Christian av.
Nolan Nicholas, lab, r 116½ W New York.
Nolan Patrick, lab, b 350 S Alabama.
Nolan Richard J, blksmith, h 125 W McCarty.
Nolan Robert M, plumber, h 355 S Missouri.
Nolan Thomas, mach, h 22 Grant.
Nolan Thomas F, lab, b 71 Peru av.
Nolan Wm, lab, h 142 Blake.
Nolan Wm H, saloon, 175 S Capitol av, h same.

PERSONAL AND PROMPT ATTENTION GIVEN TO COLLECTIONS.
Merchants' and Manufacturers' Exchange
J. E. TAKKEN, Manager,
19 Union Building, 73 West Maryland Street.

Noland Clara L (wid John W), h 685 Wells (N I).
Nole Elizabeth, h 234 W New York.
Nolen Joseph G, fruits, 213 W Washington, h 21 Blackford.
Noll Charles A, clk Gem Germent Co, b 181 St Mary.
Noll Frank J (Hanway, Bookwalter & Co), h 181 St Mary.
Noll George E, meats, 197 Virginia av, h 47 Fletcher av.
Noll Wm H, stockkpr, h 62 Maple.
Noller Gottlieb P, barber, h 230 S Missouri.
Noller Peter J, barber, h 230 S Missouri.
Nolting August C, driver, h 85 Quincy.
Nolting Frederick W, contr, 124 S State av, h same.
Nolting Gerhardt F, driver, h 55 S Summit.
NOLTING HENRY T, Sprinkling and Cement Contractor, 725 E Ohio, h same.
Nolting Henry W G, brick mnfr, e s Sherman. Drive 2 n of Washington, h 53 S Summit.
Nolting Wm F, driver, b 55 S Summit.
Nooe Charles M, press feeder, b 312 S Penn.
Nooe Charles W C, lab, b 312 S Penn.
Nooe Daniel M, press feeder, b 312 S Penn.
Nooe Lucinda (wid Daniel M), h 312 S Penn.
Noon Anthony, h 57 Maple.
Noon Dennis, motorman, h 37 Chadwick.
Noon Edward J, lab, b 183 Dougherty.
Noon James, lab, b 57 Maple.
Noon John T, lab, b 57 Maple.
Noon Mary (wid Dennis), h 424 S Missouri.
Noon Michael, bartndr, h 57 Maple.
Noon Michael, lab, b 424 S Missouri.
Noon Peter, lab, b 57 Maple.
Noon Peter H, engr, h 926 Gent (M P).
Noonan John E, lab, h 54 Oriental.
Noonan Peter E, engr, h 138 Pleasant.
NOONAN THOMAS H, Genl Mngr Central States Dispatch Fast Freight Line, Rooms 1-10 Lorraine Bldg, Tel 1396; Res Cincinnati, O.
Noone Luke F, lab, b 416 S Missouri.
Noone Michael, lab, h 416 S Missouri.
Noone Michael T, lab, b 416 S Missouri.
Noone Thomas P, lab, b 416 S Missouri.
Nooney John T, switchman, h 113 Cornell av.
Nordholt Bernhart, gardener, h e s Madison av 1 s of Palmer.
Nordman Albert, clk, b 100 Jefferson.
Nordman Frederick, bartndr, r 250 E Market.
Nordyke Addison H, pres Nordyke & Marmon Co and Commonwealth Loan and Savings Assn of Indiana, h 605 N Delaware.
Nordyke Charles E, with Nordyke & Marmon Co, h 826 Bellefontaine.
Nordyke Clayton B, clk R M S, b 235 Broadway.
Nordyke Walter A (J B Allfree Mnfg Co), h 605 N Delaware.
NORDYKE & MARMON CO, Addison H Nordyke Pres, Daniel W Marmon Sec, Amos K Hollowell Treas, Founders and Machinists, and Mnfrs of Flour Mill Machinery, Crossing I & V Ry and Morris (W I), Tel 7. **(See inside back cover.)**
Norel Frank R, chainman, h 67 John.

CLEMENS VONNEGUT 184, 186 and 192 E. Washington St. | FOUNDRY AND MACHINISTS' SUPPLIES. "NORTON" EMERY WHEELS AND GRINDING MACHINERY.

THE WM. H. BLOCK CO. DRY GOODS, MILLINERY, CLOAKS AND FURS.
7 AND 9 EAST WASHINGTON STREET.

Norisez Rosa B, dressmkr, h 84 Clifford av.
Norisez Rosalie (wid Charles), h 84 Clifford av.
Norkus Ferdinand, cabtmkr, h 61 Oriental.
Norkus Frank, carp, h 156 Keystone av.
Norman Anson, carp, b 74 Dawson.
Norman Frederick, bartndr, r 250 E Market.
Norman Isaac H, carp, 74 Dawson, h same.
Norman Jesse E, shoemkr, 10 Malott av, h 649 E 7th.
Norman Retta, h 166½ S East.
Norman Wilbur, painter, b 74 Dawson.
NORMANDIE EUROPEAN HOTEL THE, George W Koehne Propr, 101-109 S Illinois, one block north of Union Station, Tel 734.
Normann Wm, watchman, h 276 W Michigan.
Norris Alice (wid Harry), h 236 Brookside av.
Norris Arthur A, pressman, b 1323 N Delaware.
Norris Benjamin, condr, h 219 E Pleasant.
Norris Caroline, b 335 S Alabama.
Norris Ella M (wid Wm O), b 265 N Senate av.
Norris Hiram, clk U S Pension Agency, b 121 E New York.
Norris James, carp, b 194 Oliver av (W I).
Norris James C, pres The Indpls Millinery Co, h 43 Christian av.
Norris James M, lab, b 174 S William (W I).
Norris John, lab, h 125½ Susquehanna.
Norris John E, sawyer, h 150 Brookside av.
Norris John M, clk, h e s Lincoln av 6 s of C C C & St L Ry (M J).
Norris John M, shoes, 62 W Washington, h 143 N Delaware.
Norris John W, lab, b 131 Kansas.
Norris Joseph M, plastr, h 36 Sheffield (W I).
Norris Kate (wid Frank), dressmkr, 477 Blake, h same.
Norris Mary S (wid Wm E), b 1323 N Delaware.
Norris Ralph E, clk, b 484 Stillwell.
Norris Richard B, pressman, r 23 N West.
Norris Robert B, condr, h 219 Pleasant.
Norris Sarah E (wid Stephen G), b 299 Davidson.
Norris Thomas W, brakeman, h 126 Church.
Norris Willapee N, clk, h 484 Stillwell.
Norris Willard H, mach hd, h 54 Geisendorff.
Norris Wm F, painter, 170 Brookside av, h same.
Nort Frederick W, mach hd, h 55 Bridge (W I).
NORTH AMERICAN ACCIDENT ASSOCIATION, Bert L Feibleman State Agt, 35 W Market, Tel 1359.
North Ammon, lab, b 203 W 4th.
North Emily J (wid Myron), dressmkr, 761 N Senate av, h same.
North Indianapolis Cradle Works, Horace L Hewitt propr, s e cor Francis and canal (N I).
NORTH SIDE FURNITURE CO, Hayden & Spann Proprs, Upholstering and Repairing, Cash or Payments, 72 Indiana av.
NORTH SIDE LAUNDRY, Abraham & Pein Proprs, 51-53 W 7th. (See adv in classified Laundries.)

NORTH SIDE REPUBLICAN CLUB, Wesley M Gerard Pres, James Billingsley Sec, 424 College av.
Northam John M, switchman, h 1075 W Vermont.
Northcott Thomas W Rev, pastor Mapleton M E Church, h s s 30th 1 e of Illinois.
Northcott Will N, clk L E & W R R, h s s 30th 1 e of Illinois.
Northern Pacific Ry Co, John E Turner pass agt, 42 Jackson pl.
Northway Frank M, trav agt, b 638 E Vermont.
Northway George M, h 638 E Vermont.
Northway Nancy J (wid John R), b 53 Malott av.
NORTHWESTERN MILLER, Elmer E Perry Representative, 30-32 Board of Trade Bldg.
NORTHWESTERN MUTUAL LIFE INSURANCE CO OF MILWAUKEE, WIS, David F Swain Genl Agt, Frank M Millikan Special Loan Agt, 88 N Penn, Tel 1245.
Norton, see also Naughton.
Norton Charles W, clk, b 352 Ash.
Norton Frederick H, foreman, h 24 LaSalle.
Norton James R, clk The Wm H Block Co, h 557 Broadway.
Norton James W, grocer, 550 W Addison (N I), h 543 same.
Norton John H, h 352 Ash.
Norton John L, engr, h rear 20 Woodside av (W).
Norton Lester L, collr, h 191 Park av.
Norton Lucius E, bkkpr K and L of H, h 8 Hunter av (I).
NORTON PIERCE, Lawyer, 35-39 Thorpe Blk, Tel 110; h 321 Broadway.
Norton Ralph E, tel opr, b 182 Sheffield av (H).
Norton Thomas J, phys, b 151 River av (W I).
Norton Wm A, boilermkr, r 4 Walcott.
Norton Wm D, mach, b 506 W Udell (N I).

GUIDO R. PRESSLER,
FRESCO PAINTER
Churches, Theaters, Public Buildings, Etc., A Specialty.
Residence, No. 325 North Liberty Street.
INDIANAPOLIS, IND.

INDIANAPOLIS STEEL ROOFING AND CORRUGATING WORKS, 23 and 25 East South Street. S. D. NOEL, Proprietor.

David S. McKernan REAL ESTATE AND LOANS. Exchanging real estate a specialty. A number of choice pieces for encumbered property. Rooms 2-5 Thorpe Block.

DIAMOND WALL PLASTER { Telephone 1410 BUILDERS' EXCHANGE.

UNION TRANSFER AND STORAGE CO. Cor. E. Ohio St. and C., C., C. & St. L. R'y Tracks. Storage of Household Goods and Pianos a Specialty.

W. McWORKMAN,
Galvanized Iron Cornice Works
TIN AND SLATE ROOFING.
930 WEST WASHINGTON STREET.
TELEPHONE 1118.

Norvell Ulysses G, barber, h 420 W Addison (N I).
Norvell Wesley, barber, b 143 N Alabama.
Norviel Frank D, b 308 N Delaware.
Norwell Alexander C, mason, h 28 N Judge Harding (W I).
Norwood Dayton T, gas insp, h 586 N Senate av.
Norwood Elbert F, tinner, h 558 Bellefontaine.
Norwood Grace, teacher Public School No 7, b 335 N East.
Norwood Isaac N, stoker, h 310 Union.
Norwood John L, motorman, h 335 N East.
Norwood Margaret A (wid Newton N), h 590 N Senate av.
Norwood Newton S, clk, b 335 N East.
Nose, see also Noes.
Nose Rama (wid Holland), b 68 Quince.
Nose Samuel, truckman, h 68 Quince.
Notter Anthony, lab, b 8 Eckert.
Notter Frank G, lab, h 75 Kansas.
Notter Frank J, clk, b 75 Kansas.
Notter John, lab, h 23 Sharpe.
Notter Stephen, lab, h 8 Eckert.
Nottmeyer Amelia (wid Edward), b 1102 N Alabama.
Nottmeyer Christian, carp, h 293 E Ohio.
Nottmeyer Harry G, clk, b 293 E Ohio.
Nottmeyer Max, carp, b 293 E Ohio.
Nover John B, car rep, h 140 Lynn av (W I).
Nover Rose B (wid Sebastian), h 52 Broadway.
Nowland Edna G, teacher Dist School No 2, b 274 Keystone av.
Nowland Edwin R, druggist, b John H B Nowland.
Nowland John H B, h w s Waverly av 2 n of Clifford av.
Nowland Nannie G (wid Paul B L), bkkpr, b 274 Keystone av.
Nowlin Wm, driver, h 123 Clinton.
Nowling David, lab, h w s Fall Creek rd 1 n of Howland av.
Noyes Frank H, teacher Industrial School, r 401 N Penn.
Noyes Jacob, fireman, b 209 W South.
Nuckels Wm, lab, h 492½ S Meridian.

SEALS, STENCILS, STAMPS, Etc.
GEO. J. MAYER
15 S. Meridian St.
TELEPHONE 1386.

Nuebling Anna, h 257 S Delaware.
Nuebling John F, mach, b 40 Highland pl.
Nuerge Charles (Nuerge & Reinking), h 629 E Ohio.
Nuerge Wm, driver, r rear 472 E Washington.
NUERGE & REINKING (Charles Nuerge, Henry E Reinking), Carpenters and Builders; Jobbing Promptly Attended to; 629 E Ohio. (See adv in classified Carpenters.)
Nugent Andrew P, driver, h 239 S Delaware.
Nugent Catherine, b 87 S Noble.
Nugent John J, mach, h 522 W Udell (N I).
Nugent Leo, sawmkr, r 9½ Madison av.
Nugent Samuel K, molder, h 1 Frazee (H).
Nugent Wm, condr, h 24 Center.
Nugue Rosaline (wid Anton), h 606½ Virginia av.
Nuland Thomas, mach, b 133 Church.
Null Charles I, mach, h 414½ S Meridian.
Null John F, woodwkr, h 1372 Annette (N I).
Null John F jr, woodwkr, b 1372 Annette (N I).
Null Samuel L, painter, b 42 S Spruce.
Nunn Clinton, pdlr, h 100 Martindale av.
Nunn James R, lab, b 138 Elizabeth.
Nunn Robert, lab, h e s Sangster av 4 n of Belle.
Nurre Bernard T, clk H P Wasson & Co, b 115 E St Mary.
Nurre John, bkkpr, h 115 St Mary.
Nurse Augustus, lab, h 433 W Ontario (N I).
Nurse John L, lab, b 510 S Capitol av.
Nurse Thomas, lab, h 510 S Capitol av.
Nurse Thomas W, lab, h 311 S West.
Nutt Albert B, baker, b 26 E South.
Nutt Harley B M, dentist, b 413 N East.
Nutt Horace, clk Kingan & Co (ltd), b 216 S East.
Nutt James E, sub letter carrier P O, h 145 Oliver av.
Nutt James M, condr, h 103 Wright.
Nutt Sarah E (wid Jacob), h 216 E South.
Nutt Stella M, stenog Fahnley & McCrea, b 216 E South.
Nutt Wm, h 413 N East.
Nutter Green B, foreman Indpls Bicycle Co, h 34 Lexington av.
Nutter Levi, car rep, b n s Sutherland 1 w of Waverly (B).
Nutting Ada E (wid Almon F), h 112 Cornell av.
Nutting Columbia A (wid Harvey), b 335 Cornell av.
Nutz Henry, lab, b 57 Gresham.
Nutz Peter, shoemkr, 44 Michigan (H), h same.
Nutz Peter jr (Nutz & Grosskopf), h 42 Michigan (H).
NUTZ & GROSSKOPF (Peter Nutz, Adam Grosskopf), Leather and Findings, 24-26 W Maryland, Tel 1596.
Nydam Anna, teacher Public School No 20, b 453 Virginia av.
Nydegger Frederick S, turner, h 437 W Shoemaker (N I).
Nydegger Mary (wid Frederick A), b 123 Agnes.
Nye Albert E, painter, h 308 Prospect.
Nye Charles, florist, h n e cor 26th and Central av.
Nye Edward V, sawmkr, r 193½ S Illinois.
Nye Elmira, h 521 W 22d (N I).
Nye Emma (wid Benjamin F), h 181 N Noble.

A. METZGER AGENCY ESTABLISHED 1863. L-O-A-N-S

LAMBERT GAS & GASOLINE ENGINE CO.
ANDERSON, IND. GAS ENGINES FOR ALL PURPOSES.

Nye Martz W, clk, b 181 N Noble.
Nye Wm, painter, h 57½ E South.
Nye Wm J, pressman, b 717 N Senate av.
Nysewander Benjamin F, lawyer, 37½ E Washington, h 70 Middle Drive (W P).

O

Oakes Charles B, trav agt, h 1606 N Illinois.
OAKES CHARLES W, Fire Insurance, 77 E Market, Tel 1141; h w s Oriental 3 n of Michigan.
Oakes Mansur B, trav agt The Bowen-Merrill Co, b 1606 N Illinois.
Oakes Warren D, solr Charles W Oakes, h w s Oriental 3 n of Michigan.
Oakland John L, chairmkr, b 144 N Senate av.
Oakley Wm C, trav agt Francke & Schindler, b 258 N Penn.
Oaks Andrew L, hostler, b 11 Miller blk.
Oaks Bruce, hostler, h rear 317 S Alabama.
Oaks Medora C (wid Wm), h 11 Miller blk.
Oaks Oscar, hostler, b 11 Miller blk.
Oaks Wm S, driver, b 11 Miller blk.
Oaster Jesse A, clk, b 477 N Alabama.
Oates James, lab, h 5 Cleveland (H).
Oates Luke, molder, b 5 Cleveland (H).
Oates Patrick, patternmkr, b 5 Cleveland (H).
O'Banion Alexander, lab, b 273 E Court.
O'Banion Benjamin, lab, h 338 Tremont.
O'Banion George, lab, h 264 Martindale av.
O'Banion James, lab, h 273 E Court.
O'Banion Jasper W, carp, h 123 Clarke.
O'Banion Jesse F, painter, h 264 Martindale av.
O'Bannon George, roofer, h 328 W Pearl.
O'Bannon Mack, waiter, h 50 Mayhew.
O'Bannon Taylor W, bartndr, h 94 Elm.
Ober George M, phys, 92 Ash, h same.
Oberding Charles E, lab, b 30 Lynn av (W I).
Oberding Frank, finisher, b 254 Lincoln la.
Oberding George, lab, h 254 Lincoln la.
Oberding George J, finisher, b 254 Lincoln la.
Oberding Henry, molder, h 30 Lynn av (W I).
Oberding Louis P, lab, b 30 Lynn av (W I).
Obergfell Adolph I, clk, h 139 Cornell av.
Obergfell Ambrose, shoes, 559 S East, h 112 Dunlop.
Obergfell August M, cigarmkr, b 436 S Delaware.
Obergfell Emma (wid Christian), h 191 Church.
Obergfell Isadore, clk Penna Lines, h 436 S Delaware.
Obergfell John T, bartndr, h 422 Union.
Obergfell Max, driver, h 59 Downey.
Obergfell Paul, varnisher, h 126 Kennington.
Obergfell Robert, carp, h 108 Dunlop.
Oberlaender Gustav (Richard Lieber & Co), h 267 Bright.
Oberle George, lab, b 40 Tremont av (H).
Oberle Isadore, mach, h 40 Tremont av (H).
Oberlies Jacob, mach, b 78 Oriole.
Oberthur Frank, woodwkr, b 62 S Brightwood av (B).
Oberthur Peter, car rep, h 62 S Brightwood av (B).
Obleton Robert, lab, h 12 Drake
Obold Charles H, clk, b 230 S Alabama.
Obold Edward, painter, b 230 S Alabama.
Obold Frank B, storekpr Consumers' Gas Trust Co, h 230 S Alabama.

THOS. C. DAY & CO.
INVESTING AGENTS,
TOWN AND FARM LOANS,
Rooms 325 to 330 Lemcke Bldg.

Obold Howard F, turner, b 230 S Alabama.
O'Boyle Charles C, insp, h 576 N Penn.
O'Brian John, condr, h 955 N Meridian.
Obrider John, jeweler, b Enterprise Hotel.
O'Brien, see also Brian and Bryan.
O'Brien Bridget (wid John), b 464 N West.
O'Brien Catherine (wid Joseph), h 280 S Capitol av.
O'Brien Catherine (wid Michael), h 64 Maple.
O'Brien Christopher C H, h 428 W New York.
O'Brien Daniel (Daniel O'Brien & Co), h 294 Broadway.
O'Brien Daniel, bartndr, b 400 S East.
O'Brien Daniel, lab, b 280 S Capitol av.
O'Brien Daniel & Co (Daniel O'Brien), liquors, 98 S Illinois.
O'Brien Daniel W, foreman M O'Connor & Co, h 542 S Capitol av.
O'Brien David W, tel opr P C C & St L Ry, b 59 N State av.
O'Brien Dennis, b 280 S Capitol av.
O'Brien Dennis J, saloon, 102 Kentucky av, h 126 W Ray.
O'Brien Elizabeth B, bkkpr Fletcher Sanatorium, b 124 N Alabama.
O'Brien Ellen (wid Timothy), h 280 S Delaware.
O'Brien Frank, horseshoer, h 17 Russell av.
O'Brien Frank, saloon, 28 Germania av, h same.
O'BRIEN FRANK, Restaurant and Sample Room, 251-253 E Washington, Tel 836; h 27 N Senate av.
O'Brien Hannah (wid Patrick), b 280 S Capitol av.
O'Brien Henry S, reporter The Indpls News, h 16 S Judge Harding (W I).
O'Brien Honora (wid John), h 165 Harmon.
O'Brien James, bartndr, b 1020 W Washington.
O'Brien James, clk, b 240 Virginia av.
O'Brien James, molder, h 228 S Missouri.
O'Brien James A Rev, asst rector St John's Catholic Church, h 76 W Georgia
O'Brien James J, molder, b 100 N Dorman.

EAT
QUAKER BREAD
ASK YOUR GROCER FOR IT.
THE HITZ BAKING CO.

BICYCLES $5 DOWN. Best Terms. Best Wheels. WHEELMEN'S CO. 31 W. OHIO ST. LONG DISTANCE TEL. 1855.

J. H. TECKENBROCK | Grilles, Fretwork and Wood Carpets
94 EAST SOUTH STREET.

FIDELITY MUTUAL LIFE PHILADELPHIA, PA.
A. H. COLLINS { General Agent, 52-53 Baldwin Block.

SUPERIOR BITUMINOUS COAL For Steam and Domestic . . Purposes . . Edwardsport Coal & Mining Co. Rooms 42 and 43 When Building.

ESTABLISHED 1876. TELEPHONE 163.
CHESTER BRADFORD,
SOLICITOR OF PATENTS,
AND COUNSEL IN PATENT CAUSES.
(See adv. page 6.)
Office:—Rooms 14 and 16 Hubbard Block, S.W. Cor. Washington and Meridian Streets, INDIANAPOLIS, INDIANA.

O'Brien Jeremiah, furnacewkr, h 28 Wyoming.
O'Brien Jeremiah J, brakeman, b 59 N State av.
O'Brien, John, h 400 S East.
O'Brien John, h 59 N State av.
O'Brien John, clk, b 64 Maple.
O'Brien John, lab, h 176 S New Jersey.
O'Brien John, uphlr, b 280 S Delaware.
O'Brien John C, bartndr, b 196 N Senate av.
O'Brien John C, molder, h 52 Osgood (W I).
O'Brien John F, fireman, h 167 Bates.
O'Brien John F, mach hd, b 100 N Dorman.
O'Brien John H, buyer Central Cycle Mnfg Co, r 18 W New York.
O'Brien John J, city fireman, h 436 S West.
O'Brien John J, molder, b 59 S California.
O'Brien John W, bartndr, h 443 Charles.
O'Brien Joseph, woodwkr, b 280 S Capitol av.
O'Brien J Harry, clk Knight & Jillson, b 1129 N Penn.
O'Brien Louis C, oysters, 71 N Illinois, h 227 W New York.
O'Brien Margaret, dressmkr, 106 Fayette, b same.
O'Brien Margaret M, stenog, b 59 N State av.
O'Brien Margaret W (wid Philip), b 376 N Senate av.
O'Brien Mary (wid Thomas), h 65 Everett.
O'Brien Mary E, h 400 S East.
O'Brien Michael (Healy & O'Brien), h 376 N Senate av.
O'Brien Michael, carp, h 100 N Dorman.
O'Brien Michael, lab, h 233 W Merrill.
O'Brien Michael J, carver, b 181 Woodlawn av.
O'Brien Michael J, agt, h 263 S Penn.
O'Brien Michael J, janitor, h 84 Chadwick.
O'Brien Moses A, printer, b 11 Russell av.
O'Brien Patrick, lab, b 228 S West.
O'Brien Patrick, lab, b 327 Bates.
O'Brien Patrick H, lab, b 100 N Dorman.
O'Brien Patrick W, patrolman, h 117 Trowbridge (W).
O'Brien Philip (O'Brien & Lewis), h 376 N Senate av.
O'Brien Robert E, draughtsman D A Bohlen & Son, b 428 W New York.

HAY & WILLITS MFG. CO.
76 N. PENNSYLVANIA ST.,
MAKERS
Outing BICYCLES
PHONE 598.

O'Brien Sadie, h 25 N Noble.
O'Brien Thomas, engr, h 59 S California.
O'Brien Thomas, lab, h 261 Fayette.
O'Brien Thomas, lab, h 257 W McCarty.
O'Brien Thomas, lab, b 428 W New York.
O'Brien Thomas D, bartndr, b 196 N Senate av.
O'Brien Thomas F, mach, b 59 S California.
O'Brien Thomas H, bricklyr, h 94 Paca.
O'Brien Thomas M, lab, b 261 Fayette.
O'Brien Wm P, foreman, h 270 Huron.
O'Brien & Lewis (Philip O'Brien, Anderson Lewis), blksmiths, 216 W North.
Obrist Robert H, foreman, h 403 W New York.
O'Bryan Gus, Probate Commissioner, 51 Court House, h 409 Park av.
Obstfeld Henry, clothing, 229 E Washington, h same.
Obstfeld Isaac, notions, E Mkt House, h 229 E Washington.
Oburn Ellot T, foreman American Press Assn, h 239 Prospect.
O'Cain Charles, painter, h 229 W 1st.
O'Cain James, lab, b 89 McGinnis.
O'Cain Margaret (wid James), h 77 W 6th.
OCCIDENTAL HOTEL, P H McNelis Propr, s e cor Illinois and Washington, Tel 1661.
OCCIDENTAL VETERINARY REMEDY CO THE, W Riley Hart Mngr, 15-17 McNabb.
Occy Charles, fireman, b n w cor Michigan and State avs.
Ochiltree Nancy J (wid Samuel P), b 546 Jefferson av.
Ochiltree Wm D, trav agt, h 546 Jefferson av.
O'Connell, see also Connell.
O'Connell Bros (Hugh D and John M), meats, 455 E Georgia.
O'Connell Daniel, engr, h 65 N State av.
O'Connell Daniel M, printer, b 290 S Delaware.
O'Connell Hugh D (O'Connell Bros), h 451 E Georgia.
O'Connell James, h 5 Geneva.
O'Connell James, b 30 Roe.
O'Connell Johanna (wid Murty), h 290 S Delaware.
O'Connell Michael, boxmkr, r 24 N West.
O'Connell Wm K, settlement clk Auditor of State, r 116½ N Meridian.
O'Connell John M (O'Connell Bros), h 451 E Georgia.
O'Connell John M, mach, b 488 Stillwell.
O'Connell Mary (wid Daniel), h 30 Roe.
O'Connell Maurice, engr, b 30 Roe.
O'Connell Maurice J, saloon, 48 S Penn, h 67 Peru av.
O'Connell Michael, boxmkr, h 144 N Senate av, r 24 N West.
O'Connell Michael, lab, h 56 John.
O'Connell Michael J, mach, b 488 Stillwell.
O'Connell Murtagh, lab, h 488 Stillwell.
O'Connell Patrick, foreman, h 11 Peru av.
O'Connell Patrick J, tailor, r 116 N Meridian.
O'Connell Peter, lab, b 132 Blackford.
O'Connell Thomas B, bricklyr, h 27 Holmes av (H).
O'Connell Thomas M, mach, h 336 Highland av.
O'Connell Timothy C, mach, b 488 Stillwell.
O'Connor, see also Conner and Connor.
O'Connor Bernard, clk M O'Connor & Co, b 418 N Capitol av.

ROOFING MATERIAL C. ZIMMERMAN & SONS, SLATE AND GRAVEL ROOFERS, 19 SOUTH EAST STREET.

DRIVEN WELLS And Second Water Wells and Pumps of all kinds at CHARLES KRAUSS', 42 S. PENN. ST., TEL. 465. REPAIRING NEATLY DONE.

O'Connor Catherine, h 176 Huron.
O'Connor Catherine (wid Thomas), h rear 21 Buchanan.
O'Connor Charles B, salesman M O'Connor & Co, h 789 N Capitol av.
O'Connor Charles M, clk Daniel M Moroney, b 146 Michigan (H).
O'Connor Christopher A (Thomas Madden, Son & Co), h 711 N Illinois.
O'Connor Daniel, flagman, h 191 Meek.
O'Connor Daniel, lab, b rear 196 W Merrill.
O'Connor Daniel, watchman, h 1329 N Delaware.
O'Connor David, lab, b 316 Bates.
O'Connor David, lab, b 29 Grant.
O'Connor David, lab, h rear 229 S West.
O'Connor Dennis J, janitor, h 143½ Virginia av.
O'Connor Edward, tmstr, b 34 N New Jersey.
O'Connor Edward J, clk M O'Connor & Co, b 418 N Capitol av.
O'Connor Ella (wid James), b 36 Church.
O'Connor Ella F, grocer, 252 Kentucky av, h same.
O'Connor Ellen (wid Jeremiah), h 45 Minerva.
O'Connor Eugene, saloon, 300 W Maryland, h same.
O'Connor George, lab, b rear 196 W Merrill.
O'Connor George, motorman, h 47 Wright.
O'Connor Hugh D, lab, h 14½ Bates.
O'Connor James, lab, h 24 Mulberry.
O'Connor James F, foreman, h 77 King av (H).
O'Connor James F, lab, b 300 W Maryland.
O'Connor Jeremiah L, b 35 N State av.
O'Connor Jeremiah T, insp City Civil Engineer's Office, h 32 Agnes.
O'Connor John, h 29 Grant.
O'Connor John, bkkpr, h 2 College av.
O'Connor John, depot master C C C & St L Ry, h 63 Fletcher av.
O'Connor John, lab, h 288 S Delaware.
O'Connor John, lab, b 22 Everett.
O'Connor John, lab, b rear 196 W Merrill.
O'Connor John, molder, b 27 Highland av (H).
O'Connor John J, clk Parry Mnfg Co, b 35 N State av.
O'Connor John J, mach hd, b 304 S West.
O'Connor Joseph S, bkkpr M O'Connor & Co, b 418 N Capitol av.
O'Connor Martin M, checkman, h 320 Bates.
O'Connor Mary (wid Andrew), h rear 196 W Merrill.
O'Connor Mary (wid Jeremiah F), h 35 N State av.
O'Connor Mary (wid John), b 555 S West.
O'Connor Mary (wid Martin), b 257 Bates.
O'Connor Mary (wid Michael), laundress Insane Hospital, h 501 E Georgia.
O'Connor Mary (wid Michael), h 199 Bates.
O'Connor Mary (wid Michael), b 300 W Maryland.
O'Connor Mary (wid Patrick), b 798 W Washington.
O'Connor Mary (wid Thomas), h rear 380 S Delaware.
O'Connor Matthew, lab, h 395 S Capitol av.
O'Connor Maurice, h 14 Bates al.
O'Connor Maurice, clk N O'Connor & Co, b 418 N Capitol av.
O'Connor Maurice, flagman, b 260 Bates.
O'Connor Maurice P, ball player, b 260 Bates.
O'Connor Michael, h 252 Kentucky av.
O'Connor Michael, h 88 Minerva.
O'Connor Michael, b 304 S West.

Richardson & McCrea,
REPRESENTING BEST KNOWN
FIRE INSURANCE COMPANIES.
Fidelity and Casualty Insurance Company of New York Represented.
Telephone 182. 79 East Market St.

O'Connor Michael (M O'Connor & Co), h 418 N Capitol av.
O'Connor Michael, fireman, b 42 Detroit.
O'Connor Michael, flagman, h 260 Bates.
O'Connor Michael, grocer, 252 Kentucky av, h same.
O'Connor Michael, lab, b 39 N Dorman.
O'Connor Michael, lab, h 17 McGinnis.
O'Connor Michael, lab, b 103 Maple.
O'Connor Morris, lab, b 161 W McCarty.
O'CONNOR M & CO (Michael and Wm L O'Connor, James Broden), Wholesale Grocers, 47-49 S Meridian, Tel 70.
O'Connor Patrick, engr, h 36 Chadwick.
O'Connor Patrick, lab, b 126 Blackford.
O'Connor Patrick, lab, h 196 Douglass.
O'Connor Patrick, lab, b 29 Grant.
O'Connor Patrick, lab, b rear 229 S West.
O'Connor Patrick, lab, h n s Willow 3 e of Gale (B).
O'Connor Patrick, molder, b 27 Highland av (H).
O'Connor Patrick, receiving clk C C C & St L Ry, h 161 W McCarty.
O'Connor Patrick, tailor, 35½ E Washington, h 309 Indiana av.
O'Connor Patrick F, ironwkr, h 188 Blackford.
O'Connor Patrick L, shoemkr, 221 Mass av, h 300 Cornell av.
O'Connor Peter, lab, b 132 Blackford.
O'Connor Richard J, patternmkr, h 37 Agnes.
O'Connor Robert, lab, h 445 S Missouri.
O'Connor Terrence, lab, h 1311 N Delaware.
O'Connor Thomas, lab, h 495 N California.
O'Connor Thomas, lab, h 27 Highland av (H).
O'Connor Thomas, lab, b 29 Grant.
O'Connor Thomas, lab, h 165 William (W I).
O'Connor Thomas, lab, h 103 Maple.
O'Connor Thomas jr, lab, b 103 Maple.
O'Connor Thomas B, carp, h 95 Belmont av.
O'Connor Thomas F, clk C C C & St L Ry, b 1329 N Delaware.
O'Connor Thomas J, lab, b 13 Spann av.

The Williams Typewriter
Elegant Work, Visible Writing, Easy Operation, High Speed.
S. H. EAST, State Agent,
55 Thorpe Block, 87 E. Market St.

If You are not Satisfied with Your Laundry Work Give Us a Trial. ERTEL STEAM LAUNDRY 26 and 28 N. Senate Avenue. Telephone 1089.

ELLIS & HELFENBERGER Manufacturers of IRON and WIRE FENCES 162-170 S. SENATE AVE. TEL. 358.

THE HOGAN TRANSFER AND STORAGE COMP'Y
Household Goods and Pianos Moved—Packed—Stored...... Baggage and Package Express Machinery and Safes a Specialty Cor. Washington and Illinois Sts. TELEPHONE No. 675.

Hose, Belting, Packing, Clothing, Druggists' Sundries, Bicycle Tires, Cotton Hose, Etc. New York Belting & Packing Co., L't'd.
The Central Rubber & Supply Co. PHONES. 79 S. ILLINOIS ST., INDIANAPOLIS, IND.

HIGHEST SECURITY
LOWEST COST OF INSURANCE.
The Provident Life and Trust Co.
Of Philadelphia.
D. W. EDWARDS, Gen. Agent,
508 Indiana Trust Building.

O'Connor Timothy J, policeman, h 304 S West.
O'Connor Wm, clk, b 227 E South.
O'Connor Wm L (M O'Connor & Co), b 418 N Capitol av.
Octographic Review The, Rev Daniel Sommer pub, 489 W Addison (N I).
Octover Henry, pdlr, h 123 Maple.
O'Daniels Edward, steelwkr, b 46 S Capitol av.
O'Day, see also Day.
O'Day Anne (wid James), h 70 English av.
O'Day Bridget (wid Patrick), h 140 Blackford.
O'Day Edward, clk, b 140 Blackford.
O'Day George P, mach, b 1154 N Alabama.
O'Day James, bartndr, b 70 English av.
O'Day John, mach, h 1154 N Alabama.
O'Day Joseph, mach, b 1154 N Alabama.
O'Day Nellie, stenog H T Hearsey Cycle Co, b 1154 N Alabama.
O'Day Patrick, lab, b 140 Blackford.
O'Day Patrick, bricklyr, b 1012 E Washington.
O'Day Wm E, mach, b 1154 N Alabama.
Odd Fellows Mutual Aid Assn of Indiana, John F Wallick pres, David B Shideler sec Charles P Tuley treas, 2 Odd Fellows' blk.
Odd Fellows' Talisman, John Reynolds pub, 3 Odd Fellows' blk.
Oddy Thomas, bkkpr Osterman & Cooper, h 1032 W Washington.
Odee John, lab, h 507 W Maryland.
Odell Charles F, mngr Keeley Institute, 77 Commercial Club bldg, res Plainfield, Ind.
Odem Anthony, porter Occidental Hotel.
Oden Charles H, gateman, h 531 S Illinois.
Oden Harriet (wid Perry), b 430 Muskingum al.
Oden Walter S, mach, b 79 Nordyke av (W I).
Odenthal W Minor, baker, 152 E St Joseph, h same.
Oder Jared R, stonecutter, h rear 147 Bellefontaine.
Oder Ulysses G, b 524 Bellefontaine.
Oder Walter S, carp, h 58 Catharine.

Julius C. Walk & Son,
Jewelers
Indianapolis.
12 EAST WASHINGTON ST.

Odgers Wm J, lampmkr, h 439 E Georgia.
Odle David, lab, r 147 Eddy.
Odle Ernest R (Leach & Odle), h 328 Ash.
Odle Laura M (wid Adolph M), b 328 Ash.
O'Donaghue, see also Donahoe.
O'Donaghue Alexander, lab, h 55 Deloss.
O'DONAGHUE D VERY REV, Rector St Patrick's Church and Chancellor Diocese of Vincennes, h 390 Coburn.
O'Donnell, see also Donnell.
O'Donnell Albert, gear insp, b 63 E Morris.
O'Donnell Charles, foreman Kingan & Co, h 226 W South.
O'Donnell Charles, lab, b 319 S West.
O'Donnell Daniel, yardmaster, h 176 Bright.
O'Donnell Edward, wiper, b 135 Michigan av.
O'Donnell Emma (wid John), b 1148 E Ohio.
O'Donnell Harry, packer, b 135 Michigan av.
O'Donnell Hugh, lab, h 30th and L N A & C Ry.
O'Donnell James, clk, b 192 Douglass.
O'Donnell James, collr, b 587 N Capitol av.
O'Donnell James, engr, h 43 Walcott.
O'Donnell James H, lab, h 357 S West.
O'Donnell John, tmstr, h 135 Michigan av.
O'Donnell John F, insp, h 196 Blackford.
O'Donnell Joseph, mer police, h 324 Alvord.
O'Donnell Joseph F, metermkr Indpls Gas Co, h 41 Detroit.
O'Donnell Mary A (wid Wm H), h 63 E Morris.
O'Donnell M Virginia (wid James M), h 587 N Capitol av.
O'Donnell Norman, lab, b 63 E Morris.
O'Donnell Patrick, lab, b 199 W Ray.
O'Donnell Patrick D, lab, b 183 W South.
O'Donnell Patrick H, clk R M S, h 35 Minerva.
O'Donnell Patrick O, lab, h 192 Douglass.
O'Donnell Walter, clk, b 433 W New York.
O'Donnell Wm T, h 381 S Missouri.
O'Donohue Kate (wid Timothy), h 53 N Dorman.
O'Donohue Timothy, boilermkr, b 53 N Dorman.
O'Dwyer Joseph, caller, b 25 School.
Oeftering Charles, clk Power & Drake, b 112 Chadwick.
Oeftering Elizabeth M (wid George), h 112 Chadwick.
Oeftering George, butcher, h 19 Chadwick.
Oeftering Sebastian, clk, h 239 W Market.
Oehl John P, blksmith, h 245 Shelby.
Oehler Albert, painter, h 82 Russell av.
Oehler Andrew, jeweler, 20 S Delaware, h same.
Oehler Andrew jr, watchmkr, b 20 S Delaware.
Oehler Arnold, foreman, h 43 Valley.
Oehler Frederick, jeweler, b 40 N Senate av.
Oehler George H, jeweler, b 40 N Senate av.
Oehler Herman, city fireman, b 82 Russell av.
Oehler Roman, h 40 N Senate av.
Oehler Wm, watchmkr, b 20 S Delaware.
Oehri Theresa (wid Louis), h 249½ E Washington.
Oehrle Valentine, molder, r 20 S Delaware.
Oelling Rosa A (wid Wm B), b 714 Chestnut.
Oelschlager, see also Elschlager.
Oelschlager Charles A, city fireman, h s s 30th 2 e of Senate av (M).
Oelschlager Elizabeth B (wid John B), b 156 Church.

OTTO GAS ENGINES | BUILDERS' EXCHANGE S. W. Cor. Ohio and Penn. Telephone 585.

Becker & Son Charles Becker Jacob Becker Jr. Merchant Tailors, 21 N. Penn St. Tel. 934

SALISBURY & STANLEY OFF'IE, STORE AND BANK FIXTURES. Contractors and Builders. Repairing of all kinds done on short notice. 177 Clinton St, Indianapolis, Ind. Telephone 99

Oelschlager Jacob L, driver, h 756 S East.
Oestereich George J, tailor, h 62 Nebraska.
Oesterle Henry F, gardener, b 1100 S Meridian.
Oesterle John C, bottler, b 1100 S Meridian.
Oesterle Louis H, gardener, b 1100 S Meridian.
Oesterle Thomas, gardener, h 1100 S Meridian.
Oeth Cornelius E (Oeth & Kelso), r 30 Hubbard blk.
Oeth & Kelso (Cornelius E Oeth, Reuben E Kelso), watchmkrs, 30 Hubbard blk.
O'Farrell Fergus, h 77 W St Clair.
Off Albert H, draughtsman Vonnegut & Bohn, b 297 N Noble.
Off Charles C, clk Van Camp H and I Co, h 276 N Pine.
Off Christian (Christian Off & Co), h 297 N Noble.
OFF CHRISTIAN & CO (Christian and Wm F), Tinners, 230 E Washington, Tel 118.
Off Frank T, clk, b 297 N Noble.
Off Wm F (Christian Off & Co), b 297 N Noble.
Offord Frank, dressmkr, 2½ W Washington, r 26 Hubbard blk.
Offord Frederick (Offord & Willis), h 183 Mass av.
Offord & Willis (Fred Offord, Ella Willis), confrs, 183 Mass av.
Offutt Alexander, carp, r 24 Catterson blk.
Offutt Frances L, dressmkr, 219 W New York, h same.
Offutt James V, h 46 N Senate av.
Offutt John S, harnessmkr, h 219 W New York.
Offutt Sabert S (S S Offutt & Co), r 228 S Capitol av.
Offutt Sarah (wid John), h 379 Blackford.
Offutt S S & Co (Sabert S Offutt), real est, 37 Lombard bldg.
Offutt Thomas M, carp, h 274 W New York.
O'Flyng Caleb C, b 341 Broadway.
Ogan Charles, marble cutter, h 1691 Graceland av.
Ogborn Harrison, patent solr, 17 Baldwin blk, h 491 W 22d (N I).
Ogborn Wm H, lawyer, 17 Baldwin blk, h 703 Mass av.
Ogden Charles, brakeman, r 27 S Summit.
Ogden Isaac, bricklyr, r 199 S Illinois.
Ogden Joseph, ironwkr, r 118 W Maryland.
Ogden Mary R (wid Frank), b 931 N Illinois.
Ogden Walter, stamper, b 227 E South.
Ogden Wm C, lab, h 37 Gatling.
Ogle Albert A Rev, h 118 Middle Drive (W P).
Ogle Albert A jr, student, b 118 Middle Drive (W P).
Ogle Alfred L, pres Island Coal Co, h 755 N Penn.
Ogle Aurelia E (wid Francis), h 308 Blake.
Ogle Calvin R, shoemkr, h 115 Harrison.
Ogle Earl M, asst supt U S Encaustic Tile Wks, b 400 N Meridian.
Ogle Ferdinand, mach hd, h 501 W Ontario (N I).
Ogle Frederick N, mach hd, h 501 W Ontario (N I).
Ogle Jefferson D, condr, h 98 Sheffield av (H).
Ogle Oscaretta (wid James), h 6 W Chesapeake.
Ogle Robert C, bkkpr C E Coffin & Co, h 118 Middle Drive (W P).

Henry H. Fay,
40½ E. WASHINGTON ST.,
AGENT FOR
Insurance Co. of North America,
Pennsylvania Fire Ins. Co.

Ogle Robert H, pdlr, h Golden Hill.
Ogle Sanford A, carp, h 667 Mass av.
Ogle Susan (wid Wm), b 501 W Ontario (N I).
Oglesbee Rollo B, lawyer, h 11 West Drive (W P).
Oglesby Alonzo, lab, b 409 N Pine.
Oglesby Charles, lab, r 218 Indiana av.
Oglesby Daniel, lab, h 167 Bane.
Oglesby Frank T, cooper, h 409 N Pine.
Oglesby Harry, coachman 75 [illegible] Michigan.
Oglesby John H, b 871 N New Jersey.
Oglesby John H, foreman U S Encaustic Tile Wks, h 114 W New York.
Oglesby Leigh, tilesetter, b 116½ E New York.
Oglesby Susan (wid Charles), h 25 Chapel.
O'Hair Alice, prin Public School No 43, b 1156 N Alabama.
O'Hair James, h 1156 N Alabama.
O'Hair Margaret B, teacher Public School No 32, b 1156 N Alabama.
O'Hair Zella L, teacher Public School No 36, b 1156 N Alabama.
O'Hara Albert, coremkr, h 271 W Maryland.
O'Hara Alexander, coremkr, b 271 W Maryland.
O'Hara Anthony J, city fireman, b 51 McGinnis.
O'Hara Frank O, lab, h 58 Foundry (B).
O'Hara John, collr, r 72 E Vermont.
O'Hara John, stonecutter, h 76 S West.
O'Hara John W, mach hd, b 414 S Capitol av.
O'Hara Lillie F, dressmkr, 76 S West, h same.
O'Hara Martin, lab, h 314 W Maryland.
O'Hara Wm P, helper, b 58 Foundry (B).
O'Hare Frank, lab, h w s School nr Willow (B).
O'Harrow John W, clk A Kiefer Drug Co, h 46 Highland pl.
O'Haver Franklin C, die cutter, h 1364 N Illinois.
O'Haver Nathan P, tmstr, h 24 N West.
O'Haver Simon, lab, b 298 Virginia av.
O'Haver Wm, collr C F Adams & Co, h 915 W Morris (W I).

MAYHEW'S
SPECTACLES
THE BEST IN USE
SOLD ONLY AT 13 N. MERIDIAN ST.

LUMBER Sash and Doors | BALKE & KRAUSS CO., Corner Market and Missouri Sts.

Friedgen Has the BEST PATENT LEATHER SHOES AT LOWEST PRICES. 19 North Pennsylvania St.

SAMUEL LAING! HOT AIR FURNACES 72 AND 74 EAST COURT STREET.

M. B. Wilson, Pres. W. F. Churchman, Cash.

The Capital National Bank,

INDIANAPOLIS, IND.

Banking business in all its branches. Bonds and Foreign Exchange bought and sold. Interest paid on time deposits. Checks and drafts on all Indiana and Illinois points handled at lowest rates.

No. 28 South Meridian Street, Cor. Pearl.

Ohberg Richard F, tailor, h 1 Koller.
Ohlemacher Frederick J E, tailor, r 32 Stewart pl.
Ohleyer George, basket mnfr, 314 Union, h same.
Ohleyer John G, bkkpr Charles Mayer & Co, h 416 N Illinois.
Ohleyer Peter, basket mnfr, 452 S Meridian, h same.
Ohleyer Peter, clk George Wolf, h 447 S Illinois.
Ohm Louisa (wid Joseph), h 73 Pleasant.
Ohms Eliza (wid Charles), h 19 Elm.
Ohms Harry, clk, b 19 Elm.
Ohne Louisa (wid Joseph), h 73 Pleasant.
Ohr, see also Orr.
Ohr Harry M, sec and treas Adamant Wall Plaster Co, h 73 E St Joseph.
Ohr John H, ins agt, 3 Hubbard blk, h 448 N Meridian.
Ohr Martin T, vice-pres Adamant Wall Plaster Co, b 284 W Vermont.
Ohrie George, driver, h 249½ E Washington.
O'Keefe, see also Keefe.
O'Keefe Bartholomew, lab, h 47 Elm.
O'Keefe Patrick, lab, b 47 Elm.
O'Keefe Patrick, janitor, h 609 S Meridian.
O'Key Barton J, plastr, b 332 E New York.
O'Key Burton, carp, h 49 N Judge Harding (W I).
O'Key Edward, cupolatndr, h 106 Patterson.
O'Key Edward jr, baker, b 106 Patterson.
O'Key George T, porter, b 349 S New Jersey.
O'Key Henry, lab, h 47 Harris.
O'Key James D, molder, h 135 Agnes.
O'Key James M, carp, h 432 Martindale av.
O'Key John H, bricklyr, b 432 Martindale av.
O'Key Joseph B, h 609 Bellefontaine.
O'Key Joseph B, agt, h 332 E New York.
O'Key Joseph B, mach hd, h 180 Elizabeth.
O'Key Philip W, pressman, b 335 Jefferson av.
O'Key Remus B, cooper, h 18 Caldwell.
O'Key Sarah (wid Edward H), b 1541 N Meridian.

Insure Against Accidents

WITH

TUTTLE & SEGUIN,

Agents for

Fidelity and Casualty Co., of New York.

$10,000 for $25. $5,000 for $12.50.

TEL. 1168. 28 E. MARKET ST.

O'Key Wm C, saloon, 100 S East, h same.
O'Key Wm M, painter, b 432 Martindale av.
Olcott Charles A, real est, 94½ E Washington, h n s Brookside av ½ mile w of Belt R R.
Olcott Ellsworth L, clk Daniel Stewart Co, h 486 Broadway.
Old Charles W, lab, b 401 Highland av.
Old Harry V, clk Penna Lines, b 37 N Arsenal av.
Old John S, brakeman, b 30 Crawford.
OLD WAYNE MUTUAL LIFE ASSOCIATION, Lewis C Stewart Pres, Charles C Gilmore Sec, John Furnas Treas, Rooms 52-62 Commercial Club Bldg, Tel 1048.
Old Wm A, hostler, h 21 Tacoma av.
Old Wm A jr, fireman, b 21 Tacoma av.
Oldacre Mary (wid Charles), b 358 Central av.
Oldaker Benjamin J, clk, b 553 Virginia av.
Olden George, hostler, r rear 329 N West.
Olden Harry, condr, b 244 S East.
Olden Nelson, electrician, b 176 Mass av.
Oldendorf Margaret (wid Edward S), h 74 Indiana av.
Oldendorf Thoedore T, saloon, 150 N Capitol av, h same.
Oldham Harry, condr, b 103 English av.
Oldham Joseph W, clk, h 25 S Summit.
Oldham Richard W, motorman, h 408 W Shoemaker (N I).
Oldham Robert P, packer, h rear 158 Madison av.
Oldridge Charles W, engr, b 11 E Sutherland (B).
Oldridge Wm C, engr, h 11 E Sutherland (B).
Olds Charles F, trav agt, h 135 E New York.
Olds Frank S, trav agt Ry Officials' and Employes' Accident Assn, h 25 Traub av.
Olds Wesley, clk Tuttle & Seguin, b 418 Union.
Olds Wm, soap mnfr, 292 W Ray, h 418 Union.
O'Leary, see also Leary.
O'Leary Anna (wid James), h 259 S Penn.
O'Leary Anna (wid Jeremiah), boarding 268 S Penn.
O'Leary Augustine J, die sinker, h 508 S East.
O'Leary Bartholomew, lab, h 209 W McCarty.
O'Leary Bert, clk Daniel Stewart Co, h 1314 N Delaware.
O'Leary Daniel, lab, b 204 Bates.
O'Leary Edward J, boilermkr, b 65 Wyoming.
O'Leary George, gasfitter, b 359 S Illinois.
O'Leary Hanora (wid James), h 204 Bates.
O'Leary Harry J, mach, h 113 Newman.
O'Leary James, switchman, b 204 Bates.
O'Leary James E, lab, b 16 Miley av.
O'Leary Jeremiah, switchman, h e s N Dorman 1 s of Clifford av.
O'Leary John, b 16 Miley av.
O'Leary John J, lab, b 65 Wyoming.
O'Leary Margaret (wid Donald), h 106 Newman.
O'Leary Martin, grocer, 350 W Maryland, h same.
O'Leary Patrick C, grocer, 418 S West, h same.
O'Leary Timothy, foreman, h 16 Miley av.
O'Leary Wm, boilermkr, h 65 Wyoming.
O'Leary Wm F, clk, b 65 Wyoming.

WEDDING CAKE BOXES · SULLIVAN & MAHAN 41 W. Pearl St.

DIAMOND WALL PLASTER { Telephone 1410 BUILDERS' EXCHANGE.

Best Work. Prompt Delivery.

Oley Charles W, mach, b 38 Leon.
Oley Ostea, bkkpr, h 289 S Penn.
Oley Matthew, pumpmkr, h 289 S Penn.
Oley Nicholas, confr, 262 E Washington, h same.
Olges Benjamin J, lab, h s e cor Western av and Broadway av.
Oliger Elizabeth B (wid Jacob), h 200 N Pine.
Oliger Jacob C, barber, h 7 Hermann.
Olin Edwin D, baking powder, 232 S Meridian, h 399 Talbott av.
Olin Frank W, mngr The Smith Premier Typewriting Co, 76 E Market, h 360 Central av.
Olin Harry H, engr, h 235 College av.
Olin Nelson, electrician, h 235 College av.
Oliphant Charles, uphlr, h 408 W Udell (N I.)
Oliphant Nellie T (wid Millard), b 380 N Senate av.
Oliphant Wm W, uphlr, h 408 W Udell (N I).
Olive David H, clk, h 36 S Linden.
Olive Frank C, student, b 36 S Linden.
Olive John, clk, r 68 E Washington.
Olive John W, carp, 265 Huron, h same.
Olive Mary J (wid John), b 83 S Noble.
Olive Charles F, painter, h 21 Grant.
OLIVER CHILLED PLOW WORKS, Henry B Smith Mngr, Plow Mnfrs, 160 S Penn, Tel 1367.
Oliver Dandridge H, dentist, 44½ N Penn, h 272 Bellefontaine.
Oliver David, painter, h 963 S Meridian.
Oliver David J, fireman, b 963 S Meridian.
Oliver Emmett E, mach hd, b 57 Peru av.
Oliver Ernest J, mach hd, h 57 Hoyt av.
Oliver Frank M, porter, h 248 W 3d.
Oliver Fry J, lab, b s s English av 1 e of Auburn av.
Oliver George W, watchman, h 62 Tacoma av.
Oliver Hannah E (wid Abraham J), h 650 Madison av.
Oliver Harry, lab, h s e cor Rural and Sutherland (B).
Oliver James B, lab, h 187 Patterson.
Oliver John, brazier, h 42 S Liberty.
Oliver John H, phys, 14 W Ohio, h 97 E Michigan.
Oliver Mary, b 963 S Meridian.
Oliver Peter, lab, r 200½ W Washington.
Oliver Pleasant, b 190 Deloss.
Oliver Robert L, pdlr, h w s Elwood 2 s of Elizabeth.
Oliver Robert M, helper, h 146 Hillside av.
Oliver Robert T, dentist, 44½ N Penn, b 272 Bellefontaine.
Oliver Sarah S, b 622 E Washington.
Oliver Theresa J (wid Dandridge H), h 272 Bellefontaine.
Oliver Thomas I, planer, h 190 Deloss.
Oliver Wm D, lab, h 130 Newman.
Olmstead Harry W, proofreader The Indpls News, h 314 N New Jersey.
Olmstead James W, lab, b 79 W 7th.
Olmstead Minerva (wid Ulysses), b 304 S Meridian.
Olschewsky Henry C L, driver, h 2 Valley.
Olsen Carl L, patternmkr, h 46 Yeiser.
Olsen Edward, foreman Indpls Gas Co, h 50 Yeiser.
Olsen Edward jr, bricklyr, b 46 Yeiser.
Olsen Elizabeth (wid Olaf R), h 469 N Capitol av.
Olsen Emma (wid Rasmus C), h 46 Yeiser.
Olsen Ernestine M C (wid Julius), b 165 Newman.

FRANK NESSLER. WILL H. ROST.
FRANK NESSLER & CO.

Tailors
56 EAST MARKET ST. (Lemcke Building),
INDIANAPOLIS, IND.

Olsen John J, insp Indpls Gas Co, h 86 Yeiser.
Olsen John, watchman, b 88 W Ohio.
Olsen John C, fireman, b s w cor Fleet and Broadway av.
Olsen Lawrence O, mach, h 64 Wallack.
Olsen Niels P, bricklyr, h 70 Barth av.
Olsen Peter, lab, h 53 Wallack.
Olsen Peter L, tmstr, h 416 S East.
O'Mahoney John T, clk, b 176 Shelby.
O'Mahoney Patrick J, grocer, 176 Shelby, and teas, 12 E Mkt House, h 176 Shelby.
O'Malia Bridget (wid Patrick), h 46 Mayhew.
O'Malia Margaret E, clk C C C & St L Ry, b 46 Mayhew.
O'Malia Thomas P, b 46 Mayhew.
O'Malley Frank B, lab, b 34 S West.
O'Malley John O, trav agt, h 73 W 6th.
O'Malley Nona, stenog, b 207 Blake.
O'Mara Elizabeth, teacher Public School No 12, b 84 Minerva.
O'Mara James, grocer, 84 Minerva, h same.
O'Mara Jeremiah, porter, h 80 Minerva.
O'Mara Jeremiah M, patternmkr, b 247 Blake.
O'Mara John, molder, b 247 Blake.
O'Mara Joseph M, carp, b 104 Frazee (H).
O'Mara Martin, finisher, h 184 Columbia av.
O'Mara Richard, lab, h 247 Blake.
O'Meara Patrick J, cigars, s w cor Meridian and Monument pl, h 1683 N Illinois.
Onan Lizzie M, dressmkr, 362 E Market, h same.
O'Neal, see also Neal.
O'Neal Charles, engr, b 124 English av.
O'Neal Charles, trimmer, b 230 W Maryland.
O'Neal Henry A, driver, r 130 E St Clair.
O'Neal James T Rev, pastor Furnas Place M E Church, h 128 Ramsey av.
O'Neal John, lab, h 17 Ketcham (H).
O'Neal Wm F, lab, b 17 Ketcham (H).
O'Neall John H, bkkpr W E Barton & Co, h 118 E Pratt.
O'Neall Miles G (W E Barton & Co), r 504 Indiana Trust bldg.
O'Neil Charles, engr, r 53 English av.

THE HOME LAUNDRY { 197 S. ILLINOIS ST. TEL. 1769.

Haueisen & Hartmann
163-169 E. Washington St.
FURNITURE,
Carpets,
Household Goods,
Tin, Granite and China Wares, Oil Cloth and Shades

Collars and Cuffs our Specialty.

THE WM. H. BLOCK CO. 7 AND 9 EAST WASHINGTON STREET. DRY GOODS, HOUSE FURNISHINGS AND CROCKERY.

London Guarantee and Accident Co. (Ltd.) All forms of Liability Insurance, Workmen's Collective Insurance, Fidelity Bonds and Individual Accident Insurance.
Geo. W. Pangborn, Gen. Agent, 704-706 Lemcke Bldg. Telephone 140.

FRANK K. SAWYER, AGENT 74 East Market Street. Telephone 863.
Prussian National Insurance Company OF STETTIN, GERMANY. ORGANIZED 1845.

JOSEPH GARDNER,
TIN, COPPER AND SHEET-IRON WORK AND
HOT AIR FURNACES.
37, 39 & 41 KENTUCKY AVE. Telephone 322.

O'Neil Clara E, music teacher, 49 Brookside av, b same.
O'Neil Daniel H, lab, b 13 Meikel.
O'Neil James, engr, r 53 English av.
O'Neil John A, molder, h 404 S Delaware.
O'Neil Patrick, butcher, h 215 River av (W I).
O'Neil Patrick, watchman, h 164 W McCarty.
O'Neil Patrick F, butcher, b 13 Meikel.
O'Neil Wm H, h 49 Brookside av.
O'Neil Wm H, fireman, h 14 Poplar (B).
O'Neill Bridget (wid Patrick), h 186 Bates.
O'Neill Catherine, b 143 E McCarty.
O'Neill Daniel, lab, h 13 Meikel.
O'Neill Dennis, lab, h 30 Abbott.
O'Neill Esther, stamping, 8 N Penn, h 143 E McCarty.
O'Neill James, city fireman, h 168 Meek.
O'Neill John, whol flour, 428 E Ohio, h 571 N Capitol av.
O'Neill John E, foreman, h 51 Hadley av.
O'Neill John J, boilermkr, b 82 Meek.
O'Neill John J, hostler, h 22 Davis.
O'Neill John T, with Indpls Brewing Co, h 7 Traub av.
O'Neill Mary, b 143 E McCarty.
O'Neill Mary (wid Robert), h 82 Meek.
O'Neill Michael F, car insp, h 318 Bates.
O'Neill Michael F, fireman, b 168 Meek.
O'Neill Patrick E, lab, b 186 Bates.
O'Neill Robert, helper, b 82 Meek.
O'Neill Thomas, boilermkr, h 734 E 8th.
O'Neill Thomas, lab, h 164 Meek.
O'Neill Thomas F, lab, b 186 Bates.
O'Neill Timothy, watchman, h 168 Meek.
Oneita Joseph, porter, h 123 Duncan.
ONLY MANUFACTURING CO THE, Mayne C P Parker Propr. Mnfrs Fly Fishing Tackle and Artificial Bait; Fly and Trolling Worms a Specialty; 83 W Georgia.
Osterhald Herman, teacher, b 269 N California.
Oppel Richard, clk, b 322 Home av.
Oppenheim Elias, clothing, 265 E Washington, h same.

J. S. FARRELL & CO.
STEAM AND HOT WATER
HEATING FOR STORES, OFFICES,
PUBLIC BUILDINGS,
PRIVATE RESIDENCES,
GREENHOUSES, ETC.
84 North Illinois St. Telephone 382.

Oppenhemer Samuel, huckster, b 265 E Washington.
Opperman Frederick, teacher Indpls College of Music, r 13 Hutchings blk.
Oppor Frederick, lab, h e s Ivy la 4 s of Pendleton av (B).
Orbis Wm, lab, h 184 Trowbridge (W).
Orbison Charles J, lawyer, 62 Baldwin blk, b 123 Downey.
Orbison Wm H, clk, h 123 Downey.
Orcutt Asa L Rev, pastor Englewood Christian Church, h 20 Tacoma av.
Orcutt A D, ins agt, r 488½ E Washington.
Orcutt Lulu M, music teacher, 20 Tacoma av, h same.
ORDER OF CHOSEN FRIENDS, Thomas B Linn Supreme Recorder, 55, 58, 60 and 61 Commercial Club Bldg.
ORDER OF EQUITY, Wm F Lander Supreme Sec, 30 Monument Pl, Room 7, Tel 774.
Orebaugh Martin D, ins agt, h 5 Belt (W I).
O'Reilly, see also Reilly and Riley.
O'Reilly Anna I (wid Douglass), b 59 Deloss.
O'Reilly Anthony J, genl agt L N A & C Ry, 1 Board of Trade bldg, b The Denison.
O'Reilly Charles, lab, b 115 Meek.
O'Reilly Edward J (Thomas Madden, Son & Co), b 705 N Illinois.
O'Reilly Frank W, lab, h 86 Deloss.
O'Reilly Marie (wid James), b 212 S Olive.
O'Reilly Martin J, horseshoer, 301 W Washington, h 212 S Olive.
O'Reilly Michael, lab, h 350 S West.
O'Reilly Peter J, b 272 W Maryland.
O'Reilly Peter J, b 212 S Olive.
O'Reilly Wm J, lab, b 289 W Vermont.
Orf George, drugs, 578 S Capitol av, h same.
Orf Peter, bricklyr, h 578 S Capitol av.
Organizer Publishing Co, Mildred Winch mngr, 66½ N Penn.
Organizer The, Organizer Publishing Co pubs, 66½ N Penn.
ORIGINAL EAGLE CLOTHING CO, Leopold Strauss Propr, 5-7 W Washington.
O'Riley Timothy, driver, h 40 Martin.
Orlopp Bertram G (Lancaster & Orlopp), vet surg, 106 S Delaware, h 31 Greer.
Orlopp Dick A, trav agt J C Perry & Co, b 154 S Olive.
Orlopp Harry L, clk J C Perry & Co, b 154 S Olive.
Orlopp Richard A, humane insp, h 154 S Olive.
Orman Andrew, painter, h 273 E Miami.
Orman Charles, lab, b 273 E Miami.
Orman John B, lab, b 273 E Miami.
Orman Robert C, painter, h 273 E Miami.
Orme Daniel, hostler, h 246½ E Washington.
Orme Edward, attendant Insane Hospital.
Orme Francis A, driver, h 305 Fletcher av.
Orme John T, lab, h 231 Buchanan.
Ormord James W, clk, h 188 Prospect.
Ormord Joseph M, carp, h 188 Prospect.
Ormord Wesley J, clk, h 188 Prospect.
Ormsbee George W, b 165½ Michigan av.
Ormsbee Oscar L (Taylor & Ormsbee), h 165½ Michigan av.
Ormston Elmer E, lab, h 11 N Gillard av.
Orndorff Bernice F (wid David), r 14 The Shiel.
Orndorff James H, clk Consumers' Gas Trust Co, h 269 N Liberty.

United States Life Insurance Co., of New York.
E. B. SWIFT, M'g'r. 25 E. Market St.

WM. KOTTEMAN } 89 & 91 E. Washington St. Telephone 1742 { RUGS MATTINGS WINDOW SHADES

WILLIAM WIEGEL { MANUFACTURER OF . . . . } SHOW CASES { 6 W. Louisiana St. Opposite Union Station.

Orndorff Thomas, brakeman, r 137 W New York.
Orner Mary B (wid George), supt check room Union Station, b 939 Ash.
O'Rorke Robert M, foreman, r 57½ N Illinois.
O'Rorke Wm H, painter, h 537 W Washington.
Orpwood Wm H, lab, h 10 Wilcox.
Orpwood Wm H, shoemkr, h 6 Wilcox.
Orr, see also Ohr.
Orr Allan, bkkpr, h 946 N Capitol av.
Orr Belle (wid George), h 435 E St Clair.
Orr Eliza J, b 75 Clifford av.
Orr Eusebius A, condr, h 75 Clifford av.
Orr George, lab, b 300 W Maryland.
Orr Harry C, lab, h 170 E Morris.
Orr James, lab, h w s canal 1 s of 7th.
Orr Mary B (wid George W), h 435 E St Clair.
Orr Robert R, lab, b 20 Everett.
Orr Orvel, carp, h s end of Laura (M J).
Orr Wm, fireman, r 810 Cornell av.
Orr Wm B, brakeman, h 482 Stillwell.
Orsbach Louise (wid August), b Circle Park Hotel.
Ortes Peter, musician, h 206½ S Meridian.
Orth Maria S (wid Henry W), b 41 Huron.
Orthwein Christian, foreman Sander & Recker, h 38 Hendricks.
Orton Charles H, molder, h 87 Shepard (W I).
Orton Julius T Rev, pastor Olive Street Presbyterian Church, h 165 Olive.
Orton Orlando B, lawyer, h 1 Vine.
Osborn Alice C, milliner, b 84 W Vermont.
Osborn Eli A, pdlr, h 519 English av.
Osborn Elisha B, sec and treas French Chemical Wks, h 753 N New Jersey.
Osborn E F, vice-pres Indpls Union Ry Co, res Cincinnati, O.
Osborn Horace, lineman, h 111 Geisendorff.
Osborn James L, cigar mnfr, 539 W Udell (N I), h 455 W 22d (N I).
Osborn Leonard, opr C U Tel Co, b 455 W 22d (N I).
Osborn Lewis, plastr, 1143 N Alabama, h same.
Osborn Lizzie (wid George), h 41 Ellen.
Osborn Lucy E, notary public, stenog Herod & Herod, b 84 W Vermont.
Osborn Maggie (wid Wm), b 131 W McCarty.
Osborn Pauline, stenog R G Dun & Co, b 84 W Vermont.
Osborn Scott S, grocer, 302 E North, h same.
Osborn Wm, lab, b 79 Elizabeth.
Osborn Wm H, barber, h 58 Poplar (B).
Osborne Addison D, student, r 35 Grand Opera House blk.
Osborne David L, paperhngr, h 174 Eureka av.

OSBORNE D M & CO, Silas F Fleece Genl Agt, Agricultural Implements, 170 S Penn, Tel 582.

Osborne Henry C, carp, h 138 Dougherty.
Osborne Marion F, teacher Public School No 7, b 138 Dougherty.
Osburn Abraham L, broommkr, r 88 W Ohio.
Osburn Charles J, fireman, h 340 English av.
Osburn Charles N, clk, b 612 Bellefontaine.
Osburn Charles P, bkkpr, h 324 S Alabama.
Osburn Edward, cigars, s e cor 12th and Senate av, h 77 W 13th.

THOS. C. DAY & CO.
Financial Agents and Loans.
We have the experience, and claim to be reliable.
Rooms 325 to 330 Lemcke Bldg.

Osburn Edward E, bricklyr, b 612 Bellefontaine.
Osburn Frank, fireman, h 159 Fletcher av.
Osburn Sarah E (wid David M), h 612 Bellefontaine.
Osburn Wm F, fireman, h 159 Fletcher av.
Osenbach Wm, phys, 120 Michigan (H), h 101 Germania av (H).
Osgood Charles W (Osgood & Thompson), h 1549 N Meridian.
Osgood Edward C, bkkpr Kingan & Co, h 413 N Senate av.
Osgood Mason J, real est, 88 N Penn, pres Sheridan Brick Wks, h 627 N Meridian.

OSGOOD & THOMPSON (Charles W Osgood, Robert W Thompson), Lumber Dealers, 26 S Illinois, Tel 1091, and cor Vandalia and Belt R R, Tel 1416.

O'Shea, see also Shea.
O'Shea Henry B, clk, b 141 S New Jersey.
O'Shea John, engr, h 59 Deloss.
O'Shea Mary (wid Patrick), h 141 S New Jersey.
O'Shea Michael F, checkman, b 141 S New Jersey.
O'Shea Thomas, lab, b 141 S New Jersey.
Osler James G, barber, h 195 Elm.
Osmussen Osmus, lab, b w s Schurman 1 n of Vorster av (M P).
Ostendorf Henry, saloon, 81 N Illinois, h 476 Park av.
Ostendorf Henry A, h 135 W New York.
Ostendorf Louis R, mngr orchestra Empire Theater, b 135 W New York.
Ostenforth Frederick, driver, h 182 Bates.
Ostenforth Louis H, driver, b 316 N Pine.
Ostenforth Wm H, drayman, h 326 N Pine.
Osterbrink Theodore F, packer Charles Mayer & Co, h 419 S Delaware.
Osterheld Herman, teacher, b 269 N California.
Osterle Henry, bartndr, b 362 Shelby.
Osterman John (Osterman & Cooper), pres The Indpls Board of Trade, h 544 N Illinois.
Osterman & Cooper (John Osterman, Wm H Cooper), grain, 17 Board of Trade bldg.
Ostermeier Louis C, mach hd, b 5 Montana.

EAT
QUAKER BREAD
ASK YOUR GROCER FOR IT.
THE HITZ BAKING CO.

CARPETS AND RUGS RENOVATED.......... | CAPITAL STEAM CARPET CLEANING WORKS M. D. PLUNKETT, TELEPHONE No. 818

BENJ. BOOTH PRACTICAL EXPERT ACCOUNTANT. Complicated or disputed accounts investigated and adjusted. Room 18, 82½ E. Wash. St., Ind'p'l's, Ind.

18 and 20 South Meridian Street KERSHNER BROS., Proprs. THE SHERMAN RESTAURANT

ESTABLISHED 1876. TELEPHONE 168.
CHESTER BRADFORD,
SOLICITOR OF PATENTS,
AND COUNSEL IN PATENT CAUSES.
(See adv. page 6.)
Office:—Rooms 14 and 16 Hubbard Block, S.W. Cor. Washington and Meridian Streets, INDIANAPOLIS, INDIANA.

Ostermeier Mary (wid Louis), h 5 Montana.
Ostermeier Wm C, lab, b 5 Montana.
Ostermeier Carl G, clk, h 1042 E Michigan.
Ostermeyer Amelia M (wid Christian F), h 110 N Noble.
Ostermeyer Carrie, stenog Order of Chosen Friends, b 172 S Olive.
Ostermeyer Charles C, lab, h 26 Windsor.
Ostermeyer Emma (wid Charles E), h 172 S Olive.
Ostermeyer Frederick (Severin, Ostermeyer & Co), h 592 E Market.
Ostermeyer Frederick jr (Severin, Ostermeyer & Co), h 722 E Washington.
Ostermeyer Gottlieb F, lab, h 74 Kansas.
Ostermeyer Henry, lab, h 15 Woodburn av (W I).
Ostermeyer Henry, pdlr, h 79 Norwood.
Ostermeyer Henry, tmstr, h 53½ Russell av.
Ostermeyer Philippina, h 19 Meek.
Ostermeyer Wm, carp, h 260 N Noble.
Ostermeyer Wm, mach, h 19 Meek.
Ostertag Emil F, waiter, r 315 E Ohio.
Ostertag George W, candymkr, h 83 Nordyke av (W I).
Osting Louis G, lab, h 58 Jefferson.
Ostheimer Wm H, driver, h 104 Minerva.
Ostrander James, trav agt, h 246 Keystone av.
OSTROFF HENRY, Druggist, cor Central av and 9th, h 191 N New Jersey, Tel 1278.
O'Sullivan, see also Sullivan.
O'Sullivan Johanna, h 152 Meek.
O'Sullivan John F, lab, b 21 Hoyt av.
O'Sullivan Michael T, h 152 Meek.
Oswald Charles, cabtmkr, h 9 Beacon.
Oswald George A, finisher, h 18 Germania av (H).
Oswald Jacob, bartndr, h 316 W St Clair.
Oswald Katherine (wid John), h 328 Fulton.
Oswald Theodore, grocer, 376 W North, h same.
Osweiler John P, baker Parrott & Taggart, h 961 W Morris (W I).
Osweiler Joseph, b 961 Morris (W I).
Otey David, hostler, b 147 Eddy.
Otey Robert J, switchman, h 197 Hoyt av.
Otis David, lab, h 232 Belmont av (H).

Metal Ceilings and all kinds of Copper, Tin and Sheet Iron work,
O. B. ENSEY,
TELEPHONE 1562.
CORNER 6TH AND ILLINOIS STS.

O'Toole, see also Toole.
O'Toole Catherine E (wid Michael H), h 270 Douglass.
O'Toole Joseph C, marble cutter, b 270 Douglass.
O'Toole Martin, lab, h 279 W Pearl.
O'Toole Patrick, flagman, h 474 S Capitol av.
Ott Albert, flagman, b 330 E Louisiana.
Ott Albert J, clk Clemens Vonnegut, h 22 Hall pl.
Ott Bond, trav agt Pearson & Wetzel, r 356 N Meridian.
Ott Carolina, h 152 Harmon.
Ott Charles F J, uphlr N Y Store, h 155 Davidson.
Ott Charles P, cigarmkr, b 155 Davidson.
Ott Elizabeth, b 1030 N Capitol av.
Ott Ernest A, lab, h 36 Spann av.
Ott George A, lab, h 15 Greer.
Ott Henrietta, h 152 Harmon.
Ott Henry W, porter, h 286 Highland av.
Ott Jacob, sexton, h 1152 S Meridian.
Ott John, sawyer, h 43 Barth av.
Ott John, sexton, b 1152 S Meridian.
Ott John, trav agt, b 310 N Noble.
OTT L W MANUFACTURING CO, Wm F Kuhn Pres, Frank P Bailey Vice-Pres, A Kuhn Sec and Treas, Mnfrs Lounges, Rockers, Reclining Chairs and Parlor Furniture, s w cor Morris and Capitol av, Tel 636.
Ott Michael, varnisher, b 1152 S Meridian.
Ott Olive, h 376 S Alabama.
Ott Paul, lab, h 378 Jackson.
Ott Thomas B, painter, h 270 Mass av.
Otte Charles H W (Otte & Co), h 849 E Michigan.
Otte Frank H, clk The H Lieber Co, h 33 Yeiser.
Otte Harry W, clk Adams Ex Co, h 286 Highland av.
Otte Mary C, h 190 N Noble.
Otte Minnie, h 190 N Noble.
OTTE & CO (Charles H W Otte), Grocers and Meat Market, 849 E Michigan, Tel 1787.
Ottenheimer Hirsch, b 440 N New Jersey.
Otter Wm E, mach, h 17 Ketcham.
Otterbauch Louis F, engr, b 23 Russell av.
Otto Adolph, lab, h 53 Ludlow av.
Otto Albert A, h 150 Kansas.
Otto Albert C, cigarmkr, h 107 Cherry.
Otto Benjamin, sawyer, b 67 S California.
Otto Bernhart, lab, b 119 Kansas.
Otto Carl, tailor, h 428 S Missouri.
Otto Charles, bricklyr, h 52 Oriental.
Otto Edon, lab, h 22 Rural.
Otto Edward A, clk, b 107 Cherry.
Otto Eldora, h 50 Fayette.
Otto Ernst, baker, h 112 N Gillard av.
Otto E Don, tmstr, h 372 S Capitol av.
Otto Frank, cooper, h 67 S California.
Otto Frederick P, bartndr, b 16 Cherry.
OTTO GAS ENGINE WORKS THE, John Wallace, Builders' Exchange, 35 E Ohio, Tel 535. (See left bottom lines.)
Otto Henry, painter, b 18 Center.
Otto Louis E, molder, b 18 Everett.
Otto Philip, h 18 Center.
Otto Reinhold, lab, h 119 Kansas.
Otto Walter, watchman, h 8 Cleveland (H).
Otto Wm, plumber, b 52 Oriental.
Otto Wm C, mason, h 38 N Gillard av.
Otwell Harry F, driver, b 169 E Court.
Otwell Mary V (wid James), b 49 Harlan.

TUTEWILER UNDERTAKER, No. 72 WEST MARKET STREET. TELEPHONE 216.

The Provident Life and Trust Co. Dividends are paid in cash and are not withheld for a long period of years, subject to forfeiture in the event of death or the termination of policy.
D. W. EDWARDS, GENERAL AGENT, 508 INDIANA TRUST BUILDING.

THEODORE F. SMITHER ROOFER
Competent and Responsible
Telephone 861.
Office 151 West Maryland St.

Oursler Carl, student, b 910 N Alabama.
Oursler Charles W, carp, h 1251 W Washington (M J).
Oursler Lafayette, h 910 N Alabama.
Outland Alfred, barber, 6 Malott av, h 94 Yandes.
Outland Cornelius, clk, h 756 N Illinois.
Outland Edgar M, phys, 26 Mass av, h 230 E North.
Outland James E (Outland & McDowell), real est, 15½ Virginia av, h 133 College av.
Outland Virgil F, draughtsman, h 81 Bradshaw.
Outland & McDowell (James E Outland, Charles B McDowell), printers, 15½ Virginia av.
Oval Charles J (Oval & Koster), h 200 Blake.
Oval & Koster (Charles J Oval, Oscar Koster), engravers, 180 W Court.
Oval Mary A (wid Joseph), h 200 Blake.
Ovendorff Bernice (wid David), r 209 The Shiel.
Over Ewald, founder, 240 S Penn, h 411 Talbott av.
Overbay Harry C, mach, h 625 Madison av.
Overbeck Alvina (wid Wm), h 564 E 8th.
Overbeck Henry, polisher, h 95 Kansas.
Overfield Martin E, barber, 199 Hoyt av, h 189 same.
Overhiser George M, carp, h 55 S Linden.
Overhiser George M jr, clk, h 43 Villa av.
Overhiser John P, contr, 88 S Linden, h same.
Overholser Lida E, dressmkr, h 465 College av.
Overholtz James, bkkpr Wm H Armstrong & Co, h 37 W 2d.
Overman Adolphus L, salesman D H Baldwin & Co, b 249 N New Jersey.
Overman Charles M, spinner, h 108 Minerva.
Overman Elizabeth J, h 146 W New York.
Overman Elizabeth S (wid Cyrus W), h 584 Ash.
Overman Hannah C (wid Alpheus), b 415 Bellefontaine.
Overman Harry W, ins agt, 42 N Delaware, h 73 W 20th.
Overman John C, meats, 86 E Mkt House, h 193 Columbia av.
Overman John C jr, butcher, b 294 Cornell av.
Overman Joseph A, butcher, h 294 Cornell av.
Overman Mattie E, dressmkr, b e s Charles bet 31st and 32d (M).
Overman Richard B, trav agt Emil Wulschner & Son, h 100 Ruckle.
Overman Thomas P, grocer, 111 S Reisner (W I), h 50 same.
Overman Wm B (W B Overman & Co), h 356 N Meridian.

OVERMAN W B & CO (Wm B Overman), Grain Commission Brokers, 12-14 Board of Trade Bldg, Tel 533.

Overmyer Carrie E, music teacher, 62 Beaty, b same.
Overmyer Nelson F, driver, h 62 Beaty.
Overstreet George M, watchmkr, 54 Nordyke av (W I), h same.
Overstreet Louis, lab, h 20 Sumner.
Overstreet Richard B, bkkpr, r 25 W Walnut.
Overstreet Wm S, receiving teller The Capital Natl Bank, h 580 Bellefontaine.
Overton Ewing, coachman, h 40 W 1st.
Overton J Henry, tmstr, h 20 Prospect.
Overton Millard, lab, h 400 W North.

THE
WHEN
IS A WORLD BEATER.

Overton Sylvester, janitor, b 71 Hudson.
Overton Walter E, freight solr L N A & C Ry, 1 Board of Trade bldg, r 279 N Capitol av.
Overtree Augustus, driver, h 184 Douglass.
Ovold Charles H, clk, b 230 S Alabama.
Ovold Edward E, painter, b 230 S Alabama.
Ovold Frank B, mach, h 230 S Alabama.
Owen Albert P, fireman, h 732 E Washington.

OWEN BROS & CO (John and Philip Owen, John T Brush), Proprs When Clothing Store, 26-40 N Penn, Tel 482. (See right top cor cards.)

Owen Charles A, shoes, 525 W Udell (N I), h 592 W 22d (N I).
Owen Charles H, lab, b 1169 E Washington.
Owen Clarence, brakeman, h 7 Poplar (B).
Owen Edward T, sawmkr, r 159 E Washington.
Owen Emma (wid John), h 627 W Francis (N I).
Owen Frederick, porter, b 700 N Alabama.
Owen Frederick B, painter, h 3 Shriver av.
Owen Frederick C, collr, b 627 W Francis (N I).
Owen Harry, trav agt, h 225 Shelby.
Owen James, r 355 N Illinois.
Owen James, cooper, b 496 S Capitol av.
Owen James F, h 478 W Eugene (N I).
Owen John (Owen Bros & Co), res Utica, N Y.
Owen John B, drugs, 302 N Senate av, h same.
Owen Mary (wid Wm A), b 771 N Senate av.
Owen Ora T, fireman, h 79 Johnson av.
Owen Philip (Owen Bros & Co), res Utica, N Y.
Owen Walter W, canmkr, h 462 Union.
Owen Wm D, Secretary of State of Indiana, 2 State House, b The Denison.
Owen Wm E, clk, b 354 W 2d.
Owen Wm H, watchman, b 530 Jefferson av.
Owen Wm T, clk Original Eagle, r 113 S Illinois.
Owens Benjamin, lab, h rear 122 W 4th.

The A. Burdsal Co.
Manufacturers of
STEAMBOAT COLORS
BEST HOUSE PAINTS MADE.
Wholesale and Retail.
34 AND 36 SOUTH MERIDIAN STREET.

Electric Contractors
We are prepared to do any kind of Electric Contract Work.
C. W. MEIKEL. Telephone 466.
96-98 E. New York St.

DALTON & MERRIFIELD { LUMBER South Noble St., near E. Washington

INDIANA ELECTROTYPE CO. : BEST WORK. LOWEST PRICES.
23 WEST PEARL ST., INDIANAPOLIS, IND. JOB WORK. BOOK PLATES. BEST PATENT BASE ON THE MARKET.
All Orders Promptly Filled.

KIRKHOFF BROS.,
Sanitary Plumbers
STEAM AND HOT WATER HEATING.
102-104 SOUTH PENNSYLVANIA ST.
TELEPHONE 910.

Owens Benjamin, lab, h 265 N West.
Owens Charles, clk Kingan & Co (ltd), b 30 Elder av (W I).
Owens Charles, lab, b rear 258 S Meridian.
Owens Charles, lab, r 127½ Indiana av.
Owens Charles W, mach hd, h 155 Hillside av.
Owens Emma (wid John), h 159½ E Washington.
Owens Frederick, mattressmkr, h 163 Maple.
Owens Frederick jr, lab, b 163 Maple.
Owens George W, lab, h 96 S Judge Harding (W I).
Owens Ira, lab, h 354 W 2d.
Owens James, cooper, b 7 Church.
Owens James, plumber, b 388 E Market.
Owens James D, lab, b 485 Lafayette.
Owens James J, watchman, h 515 W Shoemaker (N I).
Owens John, lab, b w s Harriet 2 s of Sutherland (B).
Owens John, lab, h 507½ W Washington.
Owens John D, car rep, h w s Gale 3 n of Willow (B).
Owens John J, lab, h 515 W Shoemaker (N I).
Owens John T, mason, h 30 Elder av.
Owens Mae (wid Chasteen), h 8 Lynn.
Owens Martha (wid Timothy), b 253 S East.
Owens Mary A, boarding 225 E Market.
Owens Michael, lab, b 73 S Summit.
Owens Nicholas A, lab, h 9 Sharpe.
Owens Perry, engr, h 49 King av (H).
Owens Samuel, lab, h 553 S Meridian.
Owens Samuel, lab, h 535 Yandes.
Owens Samuel P, molder, h 535 Yandes.
Owens Sherman T, farmer, b 251 Pleasant av.
Owens Smith, shoemkr, h 283 E Wabash.
Owens Thomas, driver, h w s Elwood 3 s of Elizabeth (C P).
Owens Thomas, tmstr, b 107 W South.
Owens Thomas H, fireman, h 27 Elder av.
Owens Thomas J, lab, h 94 Columbia av.
Owens Thomas P, mach, h 383 Martindale av.
Owens Walter, porter, h 69 River ay (W I).

Lime, Lath, Cement,
THE W. G. WASSON CO.
130 INDIANA AVE. TEL. 989.
Sewer Pipe, Flue Linings, Fire Brick, Fire Clay.

Owens Wm, lab, h 625 E 7th.
Owens Wm jr, lab, b 625 E 7th.
Owens Wm H, engr, h 484 N East.
Owens Wm H, mach, h 165 Lexington av.
Owens Wm H, lab, h 79 S Reisner (W I).
Owens Wm J, barber, h 172 W New York.
Owens Wm T, h 225 E Market.
Owens Willis, lab, h 485 Lafayette.
Owings Achsha A, b 45 Bradbury.
Owings Frank E, city fireman, h 45 Bradbury.
Owings George W, h 33 Palmer.
Owings Lydia A (wid Wm), h 33 Palmer
Owings Marion W, painter, h 87 John.
Owings Mary R (wid Nathaniel J), h 640 Park av.
Owings Nathaniel, b 579 College av.
Owings Nathaniel F, insp, b 640 Park av.
Owings Sarah A (wid George W), h 53 Davidson.
Owings Wiley A, brakeman, h 120 S Summit.
Owings Wm H, lab, h 544 E Vermont.
Owsley George, lab, b 339 Douglass.
Owsley Harry, lab, b 339 Douglass.
Owsley Jane (wid David), h 339 Douglass.
Owsley Samuel, lab, b 169 W 5th.
Owsley Wm A, carp, h 57 Ramsey av.
Owsley Wm H, h 55 Ramsey av.
Oxenford John, trav agt, h 201 N Penn.

P

Paar Adolphus C F, prin German Lutheran School, h 115 N East.
Paar Edward H, student, b 115 N East.
PABST BREWING CO INDIANAPOLIS BRANCH, Wm Stumpf Mngr, 224-240 S Delaware, Tel 1291.
Pace Albert, lab, b 409 W North.
Pace George S, driver, b 653 Virginia av.
Pace Henry, lab, b n e cor English av and Sherman Drive (S)
Pace Robert L (Sanders & Pace), h n e cor English av and Sherman Drive (S).
Pace Robert C, lab, h e s Wheeler 1 s of Prospect.
Pacholke Albert, carp Insane Hospital.
Pacholke Otto, carp, h 39 S Haugh (H).
Pacific Express Co, Caleb S Phillips agt, 23 S Meridian.
Packard Ira D, pdlr, b 9 Taylor av.
Padden, see also Patten and Patton.
Padden Bridget, h 241 Bright.
Padden Edward, hostler, h 85 N New Jersey.
Padden Frank M, clk, b 241 Bright.
Padden John C, mach, b 241 Bright.
Padden Thomas, engr, b 161 English av.
Paddock Elizabeth A (wid John), h e s Downey av 1 s of University av (I).
Paddock Mary E, printer, 68 W Market, b 252 N Meridian.
Paddock Milton, printer, r 70 The Windsor.
Paddock Robert L, bkkpr, h 70 E St Clair.
Paddock Robert L jr, clk, b 70 E St Clair.
Padgett Charles, brakeman, r 36 McKim av.
Padgett James, lab, b 50 Bismarck (W I).
Padgett Wm P, mach, b e s Layman av 1 n of Washington av (I).
Padou Paul, cigar mnfr, 555 Morris (W I), h same.
Padrick Douglas, electrical engr C C C & St L Ry, h 150 Shelby.
Padrick Lewis C, carp, h 150 Shelby.
Padrick Sarah (wid Marshall), r 119 S East.
Paepke Oscar F, grocer, E Mkt House, h 166 E St Joseph.

YOUR HOMES FURNISHED BY W. H. MESSENGER 101 East Washington St. Telephone 491.

McNamara, Koster & Co. } PATTERN MAKERS
Phone 1593. ◆ 212-218 S. PENN. ST.

THE FRED DIETZ CO. WOODEN PACKING BOXES MADE TO ORDER FACTORY AND WAREHOUSE TRUCKS. 400 Madison Avenue. Telephone 654.

Paetz Alonzo W (Sligar & Paetz), h 20 The Windsor.
Paetz Benjamin S, engr Occidental Hotel.
Paetz George L (Paetz & Buennagel), h 36 Stevens.
Paetz Gustav, foreman, h 563 Madison av.
Paetz Harry C, clk, b 20 The Windsor.
Paetz Magdelena E (wid Gustav), h 131 E Merrill.
Paetz Wm, brakeman, h 435 E Georgia.
Paetz & Buennagel (George L Paetz, Jacob Buennagel), furniture mnfrs, 451 N Alabama.
Paff, see also Pfaff.
Paff Austin A, cigarmkr, b 28 N Noble.
Paff Henry B, barber, 346 E New York, b 28 N Noble.
Paff Matthew F, bricklyr, h 9 Hillside av.
Page Andrew H C, grocer, 632 N West, h 23 Brett.
Page Benjamin, lab, h 34 N Judge Harding (W I).
Page Fannie, restaurant, 187½ W 3d, h 239 same.
Page Floyd, helper, b 30 S West.
Page Frank M, carp, h 112 Ft Wayne av.
Page Frederick, lab, b 30 S West.
Page George R, shoemkr, b 121 Greer.
Page Harry, trav agt, b 318 N Meridian.
Page Isaac, lab, h 239 W 3d.
Page Jane (wid Joseph P), h 121 Greer.
Page John L, engr, h 145 S Linden.
Page John W, watchman, h 30 S West.
Page Julia L, teacher Indiana Reformatory.
PAGE LAFAYETTE F, Physician (Limited to Nose, Throat and Ear), Rooms 1-4 Marion Blk, n w cor Ohio and Meridian, h 825 N Meridian.
PAGE LIDA PURSELL, Dentist, Room 3 Commercial Blk, 53½ W Washington, h 1559 N Illinois.
Page Mattie, laundress, h rear 418 N East.
Page Robert, lab, b 239 W 3d.
Page Samuel J, fireman, b 104 Elm.
Page Thomas V (Huntington & Page), h 1699 N Illinois.
Page Wm, lab, h 10 S Judge Harding (W I).
Page Wm, lab, h 422 Muskingum al.
Page Wm H, agt, h 1559 N Illinois.
Pahud Alfred, florist, n e cor Senate av and 26th, h same.
Pain Frederick, mdse broker, 248 S Meridian, h 29 Butler.
Paine, see also Payne.
Paine Elijah D, hatter, h 580 College av.
Paine Henry W, treas Chance Matthews Printing Co, h 555 E Market.
Paine Maurice J (Paine & Co), h 226 N Delaware.
Paine Patrick, lab, b 271 W Market.
Paine Wm H, miller, h 384 W New York.
Paine & Co (Maurice J Paine), flour, 105 N Delaware.
Painter Conrad S, mach hd, h 724 S East.
Painter Frank E, clk, h 182 Fletcher av.
Painter Margaret E (wid George W), h 152 Fletcher av.
Painter Wm A, creamery, 152 Fletcher av, b same.
Painter Wm H, painter, h 493 S New Jersey.
Pake Dietrich, cigarmkr, h s e cor Mass av and Atlas.
PALACE STABLES, Frank A Beck Propr, Livery and Boarding; Fine Hacks, Coupes, Etc; 25-27 W St Clair.
Pallazzo Joseph, tailor, b 237 S Delaware.

Henry H. Fay,
40½ E. WASHINGTON ST.,
FIRE INSURANCE, REAL ESTATE,
LOANS AND RENTAL AGENT.

Pallikan Catherine (wid Wm J J), h 373 English av.
Palma Joseph, fruits, 104½ E Mkt House, h 268 S East.
Palmer, see also Parmer.
Palmer Amelia A (wid Marshall E), h 176 E St Clair.
Palmer Catherine (wid Marshall), h 70 Maxwell.
Palmer Charity, h 21 Torbet.
Palmer Charles, carp, h 204 W Walnut.
Palmer Charles L, driver, b 325½ E 7th.
Palmer Clara, music teacher, 211 Keystone av, b same.
Palmer Clarence W, lab, b e s Brookville rd 2 s of Washington.
Palmer Cora H, artist, b 401 N Penn.
Palmer Edgar H, wirewkr, h rear 604 Virginia av.
Palmer Elizabeth G (wid John J), h 401 N Penn.
Palmer Ephraim E, janitor, h 120 Osage al.
Palmer Frank, waiter, r 98 N Dorman.
Palmer Frank G, clk, b 176 E St Clair.
Palmer Frank W, foreman, h 244 Blake.
Palmer George, clk R M S, h 211 Keystone av.
Palmer Grant, h 471 W Francis (N I).
Palmer Henry A, reporter, b 441 Broadway.
Palmer James, waiter, r 113 Indiana av.
Palmer James T, painter, h 36 Russell av.
Palmer John, blksmith, h e s Brookville rd 2 s of Washington.
Palmer John E, plater, b e s Brookville rd 2 s of Washington.
Palmer John W, trav agt, h 298 Blackford.
Palmer Linnie C, bkkpr Original Eagle, b 176 E St Clair.
Palmer Louisa, h rear 80 Yandes.
Palmer Margaret, h 182 W Market.
Palmer Margaret A (wid Daniel C), h 320 E McCarty.
Palmer Marshall E, mach, b 176 E St Clair.
Palmer Mary A (wid Abraham), h 76 Chapel.
Palmer Mary B, teacher Public School No 24, b 278 Fayette.
Palmer Mary E (wid Wm), b 225 Ramsey av.

SURETY BONDS
American Bonding & Trust Co.
OF BALTIMORE, MD.
Authorized to act as Sole Surety on all Bonds.
Total Resources over $1,000,000.00.
W. E. BARTON & CO., General Agents,
504 Indiana Trust Building.
Long Distance Telephone 1918.

Business World Supplied with Help
GRADUATES ASSISTED TO POSITIONS
10,000 NOW IN GOOD SITUATIONS. TEL. 499. E. J. HEEB, PRES.
Indianapolis BUSINESS UNIVERSITY

NEW YORK FILTER MFG. CO. Filters for Water-Works, Boiler Plants, Laundries, Hotels, Private Residences, Etc. | Henry R. Worthington, 64 S. Pennsylvania St. Long Distance Telephone 284.

UNION CO-OPERATIVE LAUNDRY (COMPOSED OF UNION LAUNDRY GIRLS.) NOS. 3, 40 AND 42 VIRGINIA AVENUE. INDIANAPOLIS, IND. TELEPHONES. T. E. SOMERVILLE, MANAGER

HORACE M. HADLEY
Insurance, Real Estate, Loan and Rental Agent
66 EAST MARKET STREET,
Telephone 1540. Basement.

Palmer Miranda (wid Wm E), h 2 Wallace.
Palmer Orlando H, sec The H R Allen Nat Surg Inst, h 441 Broadway.
Palmer Oscar, lab, b 63 Superior.
Palmer Susan F (wid Osmer), b 168 Cornell av.
Palmer Thomas G, janitor, b 350 Douglass.
PALMER THOMAS W, Map Draughtsman, Room 31 Court House, h 176 E St Clair. (See adv in classified Draughtsmen.)
Palmer Walter, carp, b 553 Virginia av.
Palmer Walter, clk, b e s Brookville rd 2 s of Washington.
Palmer Wm, elev opr, h 298 Blackford.
Palmer Wm, gardener, h 128 W 5th.
Palmer Wm, lab, h 692 N Senate av.
Palmer Wm H, woodwkr, h 225 Ramsey av.
Palmer Wm T, elev opr, b 298 Blackford.
Palmes Grant, stage hd, h 14 Douglass.
Pancake Harry, waiter, r 92½ S Illinois.
Pancake Jacob F, bartndr, h 92½ S Illinois.
PANDEN BROS' ORCHESTRA (Frank, Joseph M and Louis Panden), Office 115-117 W New York. (See adv in classified Bands of Music.)
Panden Frank (Panden Bros' Orchestra), h 115 W New York.
Panden Joseph M (Panden Bros' Oschestra), h 115 W New York.
Panden Louis (Panden Bros' Orchestra), h 117 W New York.
Pangborn Eleanora (wid Henry T), h 129 Bright.
PANGBORN GEORGE W, Genl Agt London Guarantee and Accident Company and Fidelity and Deposit Company, 704-706 Lemcke Bldg, Tel 140; h 65 E 7th. (See left top lines.)
Pangborn Harry T, weaver, b 129 Bright.
Pangborn Ruany (wid Wm), b 65 E 7th.
Pangborn Wm A, condr, h 98 John.
Pangle Anna, dressmkr, 148 E St Joseph, h same.
Pangle Robert K, plumber, h 148 E St Joseph.

Special Detailed Reports Promptly Furnished by Us.
MERCHANTS' AND MANUFACTURERS' EXCHANGE
J. E. TAKKEN, Manager,
19 Union Building, 73 West Maryland Street.

Pankey Wm M, lab, h 477 W Chicago (N I).
Pankoske Frank, harness, 651 Virginia av, h 34 Bismarck.
Panse James B, patrolman, h 514 S Capitol av.
Panse Louis C, driver, h 231 Fletcher av.
PANTZER HUGO O, Surgery and Diseases of Women; Sanitarium 194 E Michigan, h same, Tel 220.
Pantzer John G, clk, h 767 S East.
Papadopulos Johannis A, confr, 105 S Illinois, r 16 Cleaveland blk.
Papas Nicholas, pdlr, b 332 E Washington.
Pape Charles W, driver, h 445 S Meridian.
Pape Frederick W, blksmith, 83 Prospect, h 66 Sanders.
Pape Wm, car insp, h 2 Weghorst.
Papenbrock Charles J, clk George J Marott, b 167 N Illinois.
Paquette Charles A, engr m of w P & E Ry, h 348 N New Jersey.
PARAGON SAFETY OIL CO, Edward H Meyer Mngr, 501 E Michigan, Tel 700.
Paramore Ada (wid John T), h 316 Highland av.
PARAMORE HEBER S, Patent Solicitor, 23 W Washington, h 623 Mass av. (See adv in Patent Solicitors.)
Paramore Hervey E (Indiana Wall Paper Co), h 625 Mass av.
Parcell, see also Purcell and Pursell.
Parcell George D, clk Pearson & Wetzel, h 184 W Vermont.
Parcels Jacob W, lab, h 121 Columbia av.
Parington John M, r 265 N Illinois.
Paris Claude, lab, h w s Chester av 1 n of Ohio.
Paris David, lab, h n s Ohio 8 e of Rural.
Paris Eugene, lab, b 13 Cooper.
Paris Harry T, lab, b 77 Chapel.
Paris Mary, nurse, h 276 N Illinois.
Paris Perry, cook, h 228 Roanoke.
Parise Leonard, pdlr, h 29 Cook.
Parisette Joseph, confr, 544 W Udell (N I), h same.
Parish, see also Parrish.
Parish James E, b 623 W Vermont.
Parish Martin, huckster, h 48 Wallack.
Parisoe Charles W, uphlr, b 433 Park av.
Park, see also Parks.
Park Billips H, carp, h 144 N Alabama.
Park Charles A, printer, h 93 Clifford av.
Park Charles E, foreman, h 94 Elm.
Park Clifford H, stenog, b 183 E Ohio.
Park Edward J, agt, b 445 E Ohio.
Park George R, saloon, 243 N Noble, b 445 E Ohio.
Park Hiram A S, phys, 445 E Ohio, h same.
Park James, h 328 Spann av.
Park James U, printer, h 130 Hoyt av.
Park Theater, 98 W Washington.
Parker Addie V, teacher, b 20 N William (W I).
Parker Albert, printer, h 74 Minerva.
Parker Albert R, trav agt, h 448 Broadway.
Parker Alfred, cooper, h 20 N William (W I).
Parker Alice A (wid Wm G), b 1776 N Capitol av.
Parker Allen C, mason, h 1203 Northwestern av.
Parker Annie (wid Walter), b 74 Hill av.
Parker Anthony, lab, h 44 Brett.
Parker Augustus G, paperhngr, h 44 Huron.
Parker Austin A, student, b 558 Park av.

CLEMENS VONNEGUT 184, 186 and 192 E. Washington St. | CABINET HARDWARE CARVERS' TOOLS. Glues of all kinds.

THE WM. H. BLOCK CO. DRY GOODS, MILLINERY, CLOAKS AND FURS. 7 AND 9 EAST WASHINGTON STREET.

INDIANAPOLIS STEEL ROOFING AND CORRUGATING WORKS, 23 and 25 East South Street. S. D. NOEL, Proprietor.

PARKER BART, Sec Board of Public Works, Room 5 Basement Court House, Tel 1789; h 30 W 12th.
Parker Charles A, clk, r 128 W Vermont.
Parker Charles A, umbrellamkr, 47 Mass av, r 80 E New York.
Parker Charles F, clk N Y Store, b 24 Gregg.
Parker Charles H, paperhngr, b 30 Vinton.
Parker Charles J W, h 452 Bellefontaine.
Parker Charles J W jr, cashr A Kiefer Drug Co, h 456 Bellefontaine.
Parker Charles R, grocer, 2 N Dorman, b 547 E Michigan.
Parker Christopher C, carp, h 475 Ash.
Parker Clarence, winder, b 396 S Alabama.
Parker Clarence E, painter, b 41 Eastern av.
Parker Claude M, salesman Murphy, Hibben & Co, b 247 N Capitol av.
Parker Clifton A (Gerhart & Co), h 578 W Addison (N I).
Parker Clinton W, clk R M S, h 1665 N Penn.
Parker David H, clk, b 24 Gregg.
Parker David L, florist, h w s Senate av 6 n of 30th (M.)
Parker David M, bicycle rep, 316 E Washington, h 68 S Noble.
Parker Dora E, grocer, 1203 Northwestern av, h same.
Parker Earl, bkkpr, r 260 E Washington.
PARKER EBEN A, Lawyer and Collector of Foreign Estates, 35½ E Washington, h 30 W 12th.
Parker Edgar, molder, b 20 N William (W I).
Parker Edward, houseman The Bates.
Parker Edward E, printer, b 24 Gregg.
Parker Edward E, student, r 124 N Meridian.
Parker Elihu M, lab, h 41 Eastern av.
Parker Elizabeth (wid Wm), h 154 Broadway.
Parker Ella O (wid Benjamin), h 45 Oak.
Parker Emma, h 336 Superior.
Parker Fannie, b 60 Talbott av.
Parker Fannie (wid Augustus), b 44 Huron.
Parker Fisher, lab, b 185 Alvord.
Parker Frank, driver, b 174 Coburn.
Parker Frank W, carp, h 738 E 7th.
Parker Frederick K, lab, b 18 Athon.
PARKER'S FURNITURE STORE, Furniture, Carpets, Stoves and House Furnishing Goods, 175, 177 and 179 W Washington, Tel 391.
Parker George, porter, r 22 W Ohio.
Parker George W, fruits, 219 W Washington, h 36 Villa av.
Parker George W, lab, h 439 Howard (W I).
Parker George W, solr N Y Life Ins Co, h 828 Bellefontaine.
Parker Harry E, blksmith, b 738 E 7th.
Parker Harvey, installment goods, 9 S Senate av, h same.
Parker Hattie, h 7 Wood.
Parker Henderson, lab, h 176 Agnes.
Parker Henrietta (wid Wilson), h 475 Ash.
Parker Henry B, clk, b 30 W 12th.
Parker Henry C, h s e cor Washington and National avs (I).
Parker Henry T, driver, b 123 W 6th.
Parker Hepsabeth (wid Wm), h 701 E Market.
Parker Isaac, driver, h 16 Mill.
Parker Isom, r 12½ Indiana av.

HEADQUARTERS PHOTOGRAPHIC OUTFITS AMATEUR OR PROFESSIONAL. THE H. LIEBER COMPANY, 33 S. MERIDIAN ST.

Parker Jacob L, mngr, h s w cor Grandview av and Merrit (H).
Parker James, blksmith, h w s Indianapolis av 2 n of Fall creek.
Parker James, brakeman, b 329 W North.
Parker James C, h 238 S Alabama.
Parker James H, lab, h rear 21 Mill.
Parker James J, lab, b 109 Locke.
Parker James R, carver, h 1376 N Capitol av.
Parker James T, lab, h 19 Bates al.
Parker John, coachman 490 N Meridian.
Parker John C, driver Charles Mayer & Co, h 122 Roanoke.
Parker John H, motorman, h 86 Germania av (H).
Parker John J, brakeman, h 396 S Alabama.
Parker John M, lab, h 205 W 2d.
Parker John T, lab, r 24 Miley av.
Parker John V, custodian Court House, h 46 Broadway.
Parker John W, clk, h 197 N West.
Parker Jonas F, h 1464 N Illinois.
Parker Joseph, lab, h 185 Alvord.
Parker Joseph, lab, b 403 W McLene (N I).
Parker Joseph R, lab, h 676½ N Senate av.
Parker Justus B, mngr Minneapolis Threshing Machine Co, h 558 Park av.
Parker Kate F (wid Robert T), stenog Hawkins & Smith, h 60 Talbott av.
Parker Lewis H, plastr, b 45 Oak.
Parker Lyman T, carp, b 7 W Chesapeake.
Parker Maria S (wid John M), h 328 Mass av.
Parker Martha (wid George W), h rear 633 N Senate av.
Parker Mary G, governess Girls' Classical School, h 345 N Penn.
Parker Mary J (wid Isaac), b 183 N Liberty.
PARKER MAYNE C P (Central Advertising Co), Propr The Only Manufacturing Co, Mnfrs Fly Fishing Tackle and Artificial Bait; Fly and Trolling Worms a Specialty; 83 W Georgia, h 505 Bellefontaine.

GUIDO R. PRESSLER, FRESCO PAINTER. Churches, Theaters, Public Buildings, Etc., A Specialty. Residence, No. 325 North Liberty Street. INDIANAPOLIS, IND.

David S. McKernan REAL ESTATE AND LOANS Houses, Lots, Farms and Western Lands for sale or trade. ROOMS 2-5 THORPE BLOCK.

DIAMOND WALL PLASTER { Telephone 1410
BUILDERS' EXCHANGE.

Cor. E. Ohio St. and C., C., C. & St. L. R'y Tracks.
ISSUE NEGOTIABLE RECEIPTS ON MERCHANDISE AND HOUSEHOLD GOODS.
UNION TRANSFER AND STORAGE CO.

W. McWORKMAN,
ROOFING AND CORNICE WORKS,
930 W. Washington St. Tel. 1118.

Parker Minnie (wid Horace), b rear 105 Locke.
Parker Moore R, huckster, h rear 294 S Missouri.
Parker Nannie (wid David H), h 24 Gregg.
Parker Oliver T, bkkpr Kothe, Wells & Bauer, b 701 E Market.
Parker Orlando M, carp, h 10 Elliott.
Parker Peter F, sawmkr, h 248 S Alabama.
Parker Quincy A, clk, r 192 W Ohio
Parker Rachel R (wid James), b 900 N New Jersey.
Parker Robert, porter The Bates
Parker Robert, carp, r 179½ Muskingum al.
Parker Samuel, tile setter, h 610 N West.
Parker Sarah (wid Joseph), b 252 W 6th.
Parker Susan, h 408 Clinton.
Paker Susan B (wid Samuel W), r 192 W Ohio.
Parker Thomas D, painter, h 43 Eastern av.
Parker Thornton, janitor, h 30 Vinton.
Parker Viola (wid LeRoy), h 395 Blackford.
Parker Wm, lab, h 178 Sheffield av (H)
Parker Wm, teacher, b 20 N William (W I).
Parker Wm A, lab, b 71 Martindale av.
Parker Wm C, condr, h 105 Andrews.
Parker Wm C, hostler, r 233 W Maryland.
Parker Wm H, lab, h e s Rural 2 n of Sutherland (B).
Parker Wm H, student, b 30 Vinton.
Parker Wm J, lab, b 322 N Tremont av (H).
Parker Wm T, trav agt, h 642 N Senate av.
Parkhill Hugh H, shirtmkr, r 95½ N Delaware.
Parkhurst Albert E, lab, h 26 Meikel.
PARKHURST BROS & CO (John W, James H and John M Parkhurst, Mary E McAlpin), Proprs of Indianapolis Bolt and Machine Works, 122-126 Kentucky av and 177-201 W Georgia, Tel 306. (See adv in classified Elevators.)
Parkhurst Daniel V, grocer, 278 Michigan (H), h same.
Parkhurst James H (Parkhurst Bros & Co), b 418 N East

GEO. J. MAYER,
MANUFACTURER OF
SEALS
STENCILS, RUBBER STAMPS, CHECKS, BADGES, DOOR PLATES, ETC.
15 S. Meridian St., Ground Floor. TEL. 1386.

Parkhurst John G, lab, h 141 Sharpe av (W).
Parkhurst John M (Parkhurst Bros & Co), h 418 N East.
Parkhurst John W (Parkhurst Bros & Co), h 107 Broadway.
Parkhurst Maggie E (wid D Alvin), confectioner, 396 Virginia av, h same
Parkhurst Wm T, lab, h 141 Sharpe av (W).
Parkin Richard, mach hd, b 1445 Northwestern av.
Parkinson Margaret (wid Wm J), b 2 Henry.
Parkison John W, mach, h 24 Maple.
Parks, see also Park.
Parks Alexander, waiter, r 156 W Washington.
Parks Anna M (wid Enoch), h 8 Howard.
Parks Jasper N, carp, h 38 Cornell av.
Parks John (Parks & Roos), h 196 N Senate av.
Parks Oscar, porter, b 8 Howard.
PARKS WM, Propr Steam Dye Works, Connected with Banner Steam Laundry, rear 322 E Washington, Tel 1121; h 136 Eddy.
Parks Wm G, lab, h 277 Bright.
Parks Wright, lab, h 228 S Linden.
Parks & Roos (John Parks, Louis A Roos), saloon, 196 N Senate av.
Parle John, soldier U S Arsenal.
Parmelee David H, clk, r 324 The Shiel.
Parmelee Edward H, clk, b 71 Highland av.
Parmelee Edward R, bkkpr Union Natl S and L Assn, h 71 Highland av.
Parmelee Harry F, contr agt Hoosac Tunnel Line, b 183 N Capitol av.
Parmelee Helen R, stenog, b 685 N Illinois.
Parmelee Mary F, dressmkr, 225 River av (W I), h same.
Parmelee Solon W, mach, h 225 River av (W I).
Parmelee Wm H, agt Hoosac Tunnel Line, 15 Union bldg, h 183 N Capitol av.
Parmer Grant, lab, h 658 N West.
Parmlee Louie (wid John R), h 685 N Illinois.
Parnell, see also Purnell.
Parnell Amanda M (wid Henry), b 30 N William (W I).
Parnell Frank, hostler, h 222 W Wabash.
Parnell Frank, lab, h 746 N West.
Parnell George, lab, h 50 Gatling.
Parnell John, lab, b 746 N West.
Parnell Jordan, coachman 878 N Delaware.
Parnell Sheridan, lab, b 746 N West.
Parnell Timothy G, lab, h 50 Gatling.
Parnham Ida E, h 525 E Washington.
Parnin Joseph E, clk U S Pension Agency, h 21 Elk.
Parr Horace E, barber, h 336 W New York.
Parr John, b 274 E Court.
Parr John C, b 213 S McLain (W I).
Parr John H, mach, b 1071 N Capitol av.
Parr Meridian N, clk, h 134 S William (W I).
Parr Sylvester, clk, b 340 Blake.
Parrington John M, printer, b 345 N Penn.
Parris Wm, lab, h e s Denny 7 n of Washington.
Parrish, see also Parish.
Parrish Amanda, h 423 E Georgia.
Parrish Clinton W, night supt P O, r 4 Hutchings blk.
Parrish Isaac, h 51 Rhode Island.
Parrish Jennie E, teacher, b 70 Arch.
Parrish Joseph R, saloon, 312 E Washington, h same.

A. METZGER AGENCY ESTABLISHED 1863. REAL ESTATE

LAMBERT GAS & GASOLINE ENGINE CO.
ANDERSON, IND. GAS AND GASOLINE ENGINES, 2 TO 50 H. P.

BICYCLES $5 DOWN. MONTHLY. Best Wheels. Best Terms. WHEELMEN'S CO. 31 W. OHIO ST. LONG DISTANCE TEL. 1855.

Parrish Lew W, letter carrier P O, b 310 E Wabash.
Parrish Nelson M, lab, h 334 W Court.
Parrish Ora J, agt, h 214 Ramsey av.
Parrott, see also Perrott.
Parrott Burton E, mngr Parrott-Taggart Bakery, 93-99 S Penn, h 682 N Alabama.
Parrott Charles W, clk, b 389 Bellefontaine.
Parrott Eugene M, cashr Parrott-Taggart Bakery, h 35 Cherry.
Parrott Harry, lab, b 77 Chapel.
Parrott Horace, h 349 N Delaware.
Parrott Mary, bkkpr Julius C Walk & Son, b 168 Blackford.
Parrott Roger, lab, b 56 McGinnis.
PARROTT-TAGGART BAKERY of The U S Baking Co, Burton E Parrott and Alexander Taggart Mngrs, 93-99 S Penn, cor Georgia, Tel 800. (See bottom edge.)
Parry, see also Peery and Perry.
Parry Charles, lab, b 187 S Capitol av.
Parry David M, pres Parry Mnfg Co, h 330 N Meridian.
Parry Edward H, mach, b 220 Fletcher av.
Parry Edward R, mngr salesman Parry Mnfg Co, h 707 N Alabama.
Parry Edward S, condr, h 398 Central av.
Parry Frederick H, butcher, h 86 S West.
PARRY MANUFACTURING CO, David M Parry Pres, St Clair C Parry Sec and Treas, Thomas H Parry Supt, Vehicle Mnfrs, 250 S Illinois, Tel 67.
Parry Permelia (wid Edward), h 21 Willard.
Parry Robert, car rep, b 1570 Kenwood av.
Parry Roger, h 1570 Kenwood av.
Parry St Clair, sec and treas Parry Mnfg Co, b 1050 N Capitol av.
Parry Thomas H, supt Parry Mnfg Co, h 1015 N Illinois.
Parry Thomas J, h 429 N Penn.
Parshall John, carp, h 405 W 2d.
Parsley Daniel, lab, h 491 W Udell (N I).
Parsley Rolla S, bartndr, b 777 N Senate av.
Parsloe Louis, carp, b 578 S West.
Parsons Clara (wid Louis), h 14 Willard.
Parsons George R, h 89 Huron.
PARSONS JOHN S, Physician, 258½ W Washington, h 524 W Maryland, Tel 1230.
Parsons John W, motorman, h 458 Central av.
Parsons Walter A, clk Original Eagle, b 120 W Maryland.
Partch Laura A, nurse City Hospital.
Partee Daniel, barber, h w s Miami 5 s of Prospect.
Partee Samuel, barber, 370 Lincoln av, h same.
Partee Wm C, constable, 88½ E Washington, h 141 Tacoma av.
Partin Joseph, lab, h 48 Haugh (H).
Partin Thomas, lab, h 52 Haugh (H).
Partlow David K (Alford & Partlow), h 81 E St Clair.
Partlow David P, lab, h 51 Foundry (B).
Partlow Ingraham F, lab, h e s Foundry 5 n of Willow (B).
Partlow James F, helper, b 44 Poplar (B).
Partlow John B, lab, h e s Brightwood av 2 n of Schofield (B).
Partlow John E, lab, b e s Brightwood av 3 n of Schofield (B).
Partlow John W, phys, 250 N Illinois, h 362 N West.

Farm and City Loans
25 Years' Successful Business.
THOS. C. DAY & CO,
Rooms 325 to 330 Lemcke Building.

Partlow Stella, cashr, r 28 W New York.
Partlow Wm H, engr, h 71 N Arsenal av.
Partlow Wm P, assembler, b 432 N East.
Partridge John S, trav agt Ward Bros Drug Co, h 522 E 9th.
Parvis George W, b 255 Bates.
Parvis Harry R, packer, h 255 Bates.
Pascall Charles, supt, h 300 Clifford av.
Pasch Albert C, lab, h 50 Arizona.
Pasch Albert G, lab, h 21 Iowa.
Pasch August W, lab, h 14 Iowa.
Pasch Charles, lab, h 74 Arizona.
Pasch Frederick A, lab, b 21 Iowa.
Pasch Herman R J, lab, h 12 Iowa.
Pasch Paul B, agt, h 23 Nebraska.
Pasch Wm H, fireman, h 114 Singleton.
Pascoe Howard, lab, b 524 E 9th.
Pasquier Charles, clk, h 402 E Michigan.
Pasquier Eugene, grocer, 143 N Delaware, h 300 Bellefontaine.
Pasquier John (Hammond & Pasquier), b 402 E Michigan.
Pasquier John B, carp, 402 E Michigan, h same.
Pasquier Julius, grocer, 148 Fletcher av, h 152 N State av.
Pass Harry, cook Sherman House.
Passehl Herman, lab, b s w cor Shade and Schofield (B).
Passehl Herman H, dairy, s w cor Shade and Schofield (B), h same.
Passmore Albert B, porter, h 414 Hanna.
Passmore Alonzo, lab, h 105 Hadley.
Passwaiter Abraham H, lab, h 368 Newman.
Passwaiter George G, carp, h 171 Columbia av.
Passwaiter John W, painter, b 171 Columbia av.
Passwater Wm E, condr, b 792 W Washington.
Patch Cynthia A (wid Horace D), b 1 Ruckle.
Patch James M, h 1 Ruckle.
Pate Benjamin, engr, h 259 E New York.
Pate John G, bricklyr, b 61 Cornell av.
Pate John H, carp, h 368 Prospect.
Pate John P, student, b 41 Madison av.
Pate Oscar E, lab, h 235 Buchanan.
Pate Theresa (wid Arbogast), b 208 W South.

EAT HITZ'S CRACKERS AND CAKES.
ASK YOUR GROCER FOR THEM.

J. H. TECKENBROCK Painter and Decorator, 94 EAST SOUTH STREET.

FIDELITY MUTUAL LIFE—PHILADELPHIA, PA.
MATCHLESS SECURITY At LOW COST. | A. H. COLLINS | General Agent Baldwin Block.

Rooms 42 and 43 WHEN BUILDING.

ESTABLISHED 1876. TELEPHONE 168.
CHESTER BRADFORD,
SOLICITOR OF PATENTS,
AND COUNSEL IN PATENT CAUSES.
(See adv. page 6.)
Office:—Rooms 14 and 16 Hubbard Block, S. W Cor. Washington and Meridian Streets, INDIANAPOLIS, INDIANA.

Patrick Bertha S. agt, b 136 Eddy.
Patten, see also Padden and Patton.
Patten Frederick U, lab, h s e cor Lafayette av and New York.
Patten Herbert A, sawmkr, b 1568 Kenwood av.
Patten James B, pres Fidelity Bldg and Savings Union, h 91 Prospect.
Patten James C, student, b 91 Prospect.
Patten Mary (wid Eugene C), b 6 Buchanan.
Patten Silas G, lab, b 67 Minerva.
Patten Sophia, b 437 N Capitol av.
Patten Wm D, mach, b 68 S Spruce.
Patten Wm T, dep treas Fidelity Bldg and Savings Union, b 91 Prospect.
Patterson, see also Pattison and Peterson.
Patterson Algernon S, real est, 12½ N Delaware, r 95½ same.
Patterson Allen A, carp, h 576 E Michigan.
Patterson Amos W, phys, 83 Mass av, h 81 Cornell av.
Patterson Andrew, clk, h 582 S State av.
Patterson Andrew J, lab, b s s English av 1 e of Auburn av.
Patterson Captain G, waiter, h 33 Ellsworth.
Patterson Carl G, student, b 1030 W Washington.
Patterson Caroline (wid Henry), h 23 Sumner.
Patterson Charles, clk, b 89 Indiana av.
Patterson Charles, lab, b 47 Warman av (H).
Patterson Charles A, carp, h 259 Fletcher av.
Patterson Charles E, bricklyr, h 50 Warman av (H).
Patterson Charles H, trainer, b 140 Mass av.
Patterson Charles T, mngr, h 519 Bellefontaine.
Patterson Clemens, dressmkr, 156 E Michigan, h same.
Patterson Cleveland H, clk, b 582 S State av.
Patterson Daniel H, fruits, E Mkt House, h 207 Davidson.
Patterson David M, trav agt Indiana Rubber Co, h 140 Mass av.

Outing BICYCLES
$85.00.
MADE AND SOLD BY
HAY & WILLITS MFG. CO.
76 N. PENNSYLVANIA ST. PHONE 598.

Patterson David W, lab, b 54 Rhode Island.
Patterson Edgar T, collr, b 1083 N Capitol av.
Patterson Edward F, lab, h 156 Madison av.
Patterson Elizabeth (wid Wm A), h 640 N Illinois.
Patterson Florence, teacher Public School No 7, b 280 E Ohio.
Patterson Frank, patternmkr, b 239 Bright.
Patterson Frank R, lab, b 742 E Ohio.
Patterson George, lab, r 123 Allegheny.
Patterson George, waiter, r 138 Elizabeth.
Patterson George C, barber, r 191½ Indiana av.
Patterson George W, watchman, h 274 Alvord.
Patterson Grace (wid John), h 362 S Illinois.
Patterson Gwyn F, clk The Capitol National Bank, b 259 Fletcher av.
Patterson Harry G, clk, b 285 N Senate av.
Patterson Harry J, finisher, h 250 W North.
Patterson Helena M, bkkpr Columbian Relief Fund Assn, b 1030 W Washington.
Patterson Henry C, cook, h 161 Agnes.
Patterson Horace, h 33 W 22d.
Patterson Hugh B, brakeman, h 65 Lexington av.
Patterson Isaac S, lab, h rear 318 E Georgia.
Patterson James, engr, b 124 English av.
Patterson James, supt Moore & Co, h 239 Bright.
Patterson James jr, molder, b 239 Bright.
Patterson James G, yardmaster, h 24 S Summit.
Patterson James R, lab, b 244½ E Washington.
Patterson Jennie H (wid R Madison), h 479 N Penn.
Patterson Jessie L, stenog S A Fletcher & Co, b 159 E Ohio.
Patterson John, engr, b 124 English av.
Patterson John, lab, h 224 Martindale av.
Patterson John L, carp, h 156 E Michigan.
Patterson John P, tinner, h 20 Birch av (W I).
Patterson John S, engr, h 66 Temple av.
Patterson John S, lab, b rear 318 E Georgia.
Patterson John W, sawyer, h 313 Spring.
Patterson Joseph, h 542 W Washington.
Patterson Joseph J, houseman 247 N Meridian.
Patterson Joseph L, supervisor Insane Hospital.
Patterson Joseph M, city fireman, b 500 E Market.
Patterson Joseph R, h 534 W Maryland.
Patterson Joseph W, molder, h 47 Warman av (H).
Patterson Josephus, lab, b 661 N Senate av.
Patterson Kate M (wid James M), b 140 Mass av.
Patterson Mary E (wid Glenn S), h 37 N Beville av.
Patterson Mary E (wid John E), h 156 Madison av.
Patterson Mary E (wid Samuel F), h 413 N Illinois.
Patterson Margaret E, janitor, h 244½ E Washington.
Patterson Moses, lab, h 40 Athon.
Patterson Oscar E, lab, b 30 Detroit.
Patterson Patsy (wid Samuel J), h n w cor North and Maxwell.
Patterson Reuben, carp, h 182 E St Clair.
Patterson Robert, h 244½ E Washington.
Patterson Robert H, bkkpr, b n w cor North and Maxwell.

Edwardsport Coal and Mining Co. Miners and Shippers Steam and Domestic Coal.

C. ZIMMERMAN & SONS | SLATE AND GRAVEL ROOFERS 19 South East Street.

DRIVEN WELLS And Second Water Wells and Pumps of all kinds at CHARLES KRAUSS', 42 S. PENN. ST. TELEPHONE 465.

Patterson Rosa (wid Isham), b 274 Alvord.
Patterson Samuel G, salesman Schnull & Co, b 413 N Illinois.
Patterson Samuel W, h 285 N Senate av.
Patterson Sarah E (wid Alonzo), h rear 23 W Ohio.
Patterson Sarah J, nurse, r 30 Wyandot blk.
Patterson Theodosia (wid John W), h 172 N New Jersey.
Patterson Thomas R, engr, b 362 S Illinois.
Patterson Vincent G, tiremkr, b 139 S East.
Patterson Walter G, livery, Union Stock Yards (W I), b 285 N Senate av.
Patterson Ward, plumber, b 66 Temple av.
Patterson Wm, h 1030 W Washington.
Patterson Wm, bricklyr, h 125 Shepard (W I).
Patterson Wm, hostler, r 233 W Maryland.
Patterson Wm, lab, r 29 Ellsworth.
Patterson Wm, lawyer, h 280 E Ohio.
Patterson Wm, saloon, 88 Malott av, h same.
Patterson Wm, sawmkr, b 362 S Illinois.
Patterson Wm A, watchman, b 500 E Market.
Patterson Wm C, clk Kingan & Co (ltd), b 280 E Ohio.
Patterson Wm G, lab, h 615 W Michigan.
Patterson Wm H, clk, r 237½ Mass av.
Patterson Wm H, coachman, b 244½ E Washington.
Patterson Wm O (Patterson & Busby), supt mails P O, h 948 N Alabama.
Patterson Wm P, clk, h 86 Vine.
Patterson & Busby (Wm O Patterson, Charles E Busby), hoop mnfrs, n w cor Biddle and Bee Line Ry.
Pattison, see also Patterson and Peterson.
Pattison Day C, student, b 512 N Illinois.
Pattison George C, student, b 512 N Illinois.
Pattison Joseph H (Phillips & Pattison), loans, 36 Monument pl, h 741 N Delaware.
Pattison Margaret L (wid Frederick R), h 167½ E Washington.
Pattison Samuel C, mach hd, h 34 Holmes av (H).
PATTISON SAMUEL L, Pres Indiana Chain Co and Pres Metropolitan Cycle Co, h 512 N Illinois, Tel 1232.
Pattison Sarah J (wid Coleman B), h 512 N Illinois.
Pattison Saressa (wid Wm E), h 149 W 8th.
Pattmann Frederick, produce, E Mkt House, h cor Raymond and Ransdell.
Patton, see also Padden and Patten.
Patton Albert, insp City Engineer, h 368 Dillon.
Patton Amanda (wid Paul), h 502½ College av.
Patton Carl, paperhngr, b 149½ Oliver av (W I).
Patton Charles D, engr, h 53 Pierce.
Patton Elmer J, tmstr, h 309 N West.
Patton George W, lab, h 211 Yandes.
Patton Harry H M, bkkpr Order of Equity, h 76 Clifford av.
Patton Henry, lab, h 695 W 22d (N I).
Patton John, lab, r 177½ W Washington.
Patton John C, printer, b 105 Fletcher av.
Patton Joseph E, car rep, h 260 English av.
Patton Lee W, lab, b 145 Columbia av.
Patton Mary J (wid Samuel M), h n s Sutherland 2 w of Shade (B).
Patton Moses, lab, b 86 S East.
Patton Robert C, carp, h 640 E 8th.
Patton Samuel G, boilermkr, h 145 Columbia av.

RICHARDSON & McCREA,
MANAGERS FOR CENTRAL INDIANA.
EQUITABLE LIFE ASSURANCE SOCIETY
Of the United States.
79 EAST MARKET STREET,
TELEPHONE 182.

Patton Thomas T A M, motorman, h 501 E 11th.
Patton Wm, polisher, h 283 W Pearl.
Patton Wm A, plastr, h 368 Dillon.
Patton Wm H, b 145 Columbia av.
Patton Wm H, lab, h 76½ Oliver av (W I).
Patton Wm H, tailor, 118½ Mass av, h 120 Christian av.
Patton Wm R, tel opr, b 105 Fletcher av.
Patzold Robert, mach, b 332 Spann av.
Paul Charles F, lab, h 1050 E Michigan.
Paul Charles M, foreman, h 1046 E Michigan.
Paul Frederick G, uphlr, b 74 Hosbrook.
Paul Joseph B, supt, h 451 N Capitol av.
Paul Leonard N, engr, r 183½ W Washington.
Paul Maria K (wid Charles H D), h 1184 N Illinois.
Paul Wilhelmina M (wid Frederick), h 74 Hosbrook.
Pauley Charles E, printer, r 314 N New Jersey.
Pauley Harry H, h 176 W Michigan.
Paulger George T, miller, h 573 W 22d (N I).
Pauli Bertha (wid Herman), h 480 S Missouri.
Pauli Henry, carp, 181 Davidson, h same.
Pauli Henry G, carp, b 181 Davidson.
Pauli Waldemar H, molder, h 136 N Gillard av.
Paulin Louis M, brakeman, b 20 Oriental.
Paulisch Rudolph W, mach, h 72 Dunlop.
Paulish Wm T, soapmkr, rear 94 English av, h same.
Paulissen George, carp, r 177 N Delaware.
Paulman, see also Pohlman.
Paulman Augustus F, sawmkr, h 164 Fletcher av.
Paulsen, see also Poulsen.
Paulsen Carl E, printer, h 55 John.
Paulsen Charles, h 555 E St Clair.
Paulsen Charles F, barber, 732 Lemcke bldg, r 138 E New York.
Paulson Erasmus, b w s Northwestern av 2 n of 25th (N I).
Paulson Frederick, trav agt, r 73 W Vermont.

Typewriter-Ribbons
ALL COLORS FOR ALL MACHINES.
THE BEST AND CHEAPEST.
S. H. EAST, STATE AGENT.
The Williams Typewriter....
55 THORPE BLOCK, 87 E. MARKET ST.

ERTEL STEAM LAUNDRY | LARGEST AND BEST IN THE STATE. PROMPT SERVICE. 26 and 28 N. Senate Ave. Telephone 19.

ELLIS & HELFENBERGER | Architectural Iron Work and Gray Iron Castings. 162-170 South Senate Ave. Tel. 958.

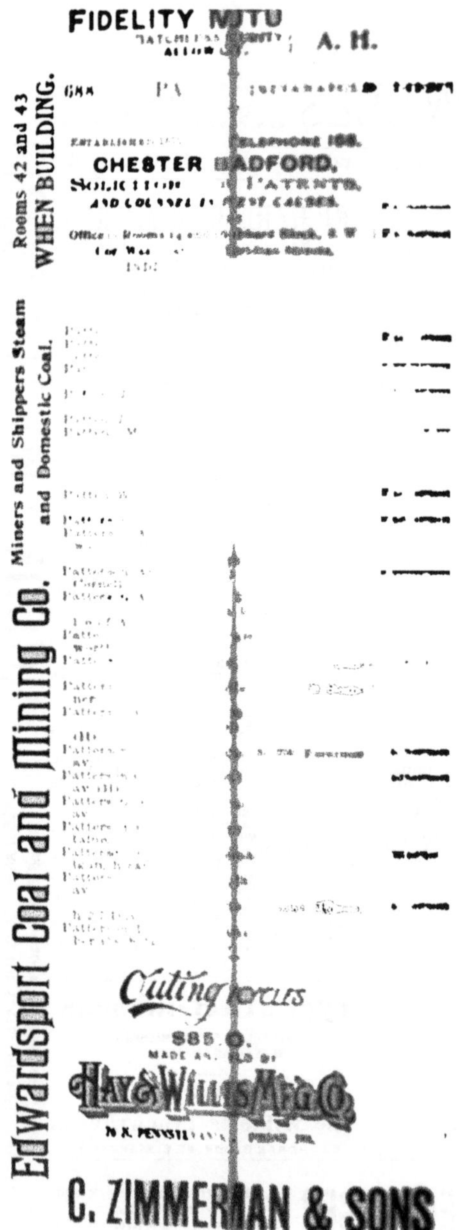
FIDELITY MUTU
A. H.
Rooms 42 and 43
WHEN BUILDING.
TELEPHONE 168.
CHESTER BADFORD,
Miners and Shippers Steam
and Domestic Coal.
Edwardsport Coal and Mining Co.
Outing
$85.0
C. ZIMMERMAN & SONS

DRIVEN WELLS And Second Water Wells and Pumps of all kinds at CHARLES KRAUSS', 42 S. PENN. ST. TELEPHONE 465.

Patterson Rosa (wid Isham), b 274 Alvord.
Patterson Samuel G, salesman Schnull & Co, b 413 N Illinois.
Patterson Samuel W, h 285 N Senate av.
Patterson Sarah E (wid Alonzo), h 23 W Ohio.
Patterson Sarah J, nurse, r 30 Wyandot blk.
Patterson Theodosia (wid John W), 172 N New Jersey.
Patterson Thomas R, engr, b 362 S Illinois.
Patterson Vincent G, tiremkr, b 139 S ...st.
Patterson Walter G, livery, Union Stock Yards (W I), b 285 N Senate av.
Patterson Ward, plumber, h 66 Temple av.
Patterson Wm, h 1030 W Washington.
Patterson Wm, bricklyr, h 125 Sheffield (W I).
Patterson Wm, hostler, r 233 W Maryland.
Patterson Wm, lab, r 29 Ellsworth.
Patterson Wm, lawyer, h 280 E Ohio.
Patterson Wm, saloon, 88 Malott av, h same.
Patterson Wm, sawmkr, b 362 S Illinois.
Patterson Wm A, watchman, b 500 E Market.
Patterson Wm C, clk Kingan & Co (ltd), b 280 E Ohio.
Patterson Wm G, lab, h 615 W Michigan.
Patterson Wm H, clk, r 237½ Mass av.
Patterson Wm H, coachman, b 24.. E Washington.
Patterson Wm O (Patterson & Busby), supt mails P O, h 948 N Alabama.
Patterson Wm P, clk, h 86 Vine.
Patterson & Busby (Wm O Patterson, Charles E Busby), hoop mnfrs, n w cor Biddle and Bee Line Ry.
Pattison, see also Patterson and Pet...
Pattison Day C, student, b 512 N Illinois.
Pattison George C, student, b 512 N Illinois.
Pattison Joseph H (Phillips & Pat...), loans, 36 Monument pl, h 741 N De...
Pattison Margaret L (wid Frederick), 167½ E Washington.
Pattison Samuel C, mach hd, ... av (H).
PATTISON SAMUEL L, Pres ... Chain Co and Pres M... Cycle Co, h 512 N Illinois.
Pattison Sarah J (wid Colem...) ... Illinois.
Pattison Saressa (wid Wm E...)
Pattmann Frederick, prod... House, h ... mond an...
Patton, see ... dden an...
Patton Al... City ... Dillon.
Patton Am... Paul) ... av.
Patton Ca... gr, ... (W I).
Patton Ch... gr, h ...
Patton El... r, h ...
Patton Ge... , h ...
Patton Ha... kpr ... h 76 Cli...
Patton He...
Patton Jo...
Patton Jo...
Patton Jo...
Patton L...
Patton M... Sutherla...
Patton Mo...
Patton R...
Patton Sa... av.

RICHARDSON & McCREA,
MANAGERS FOR CENTRAL INDIANA.
EQUITABLE LIFE ASSURANCE SOCIETY
Of the United States.
79 EAST MARKET STREET,
TELEPHONE 182.

Patton Thomas T A M, motorman, h 501 E 11th.
Patton Wm, polisher, h 283 W Pearl.
Patton Wm A, plastr, h 368 Dillon.
Patton Wm H, b 145 Columbia av.
Patton Wm H, lab, h 76½ Oliver av (W I).
Patton Wm H, tailor, 118½ Mass av, h 120 Christian av.
Patton Wm R, tel opr, b 105 Fletcher av.
Patzold Robert, mach, b 332 Spann av.
Paul Charles F, lab, h 1050 E Michigan.
Paul Charles M, foreman, h 1046 E Michigan.
Paul Frederick G, uphlr, b 74 Hosbrook.
Paul Joseph B, supt, h 451 N Capitol av.
Paul Leonard N, engr, r 183½ W Washington.
Paul Maria K (wid Charles H D), h 1184 N Illinois.
Paul Wilhelmina M (wid Frederick), h 74 Hosbrook.
Pauley Charles E, printer, r 314 N New Jer-...
... Harry H, h 176 W Michigan.
... George T, miller, h 573 W 22d (N I).
... ertha (wid Herman), h 480 S Mis-...
... enry, carp, 181 Davidson, h same.
... enry G, carp, b 181 Davidson.
... r H, molder, h 136 N Gillard ...
... brakeman, b 20 Oriental.
... W, mach, h 72 Dunlop.
... oapmkr, rear 94 English ...
... arp, r 177 N Delaware.
... Pohlman.
... F, sawmkr, h 164 ...
... oulsen.
... ter, h 55 John.
... 5 E St Clair.
... rber, 732 Lemcke bldg, ...
... w s Northwestern av ...
... av agt, r 73 W Ver-...

...-Ribbons
...LL MACHINES.
...APEST.
...ATE AGENT.
...ypewriter....
... E. MARKET ST.

ERTEL STEAM LAUNDRY
LARGEST AND BEST IN THE STATE. PROMPT ...
26 and 28 N. Senate Ave.
Telephone ...

ELLI...
Iron Work...
Castings.
...ate Ave. ...

THE HOGAN TRANSFER AND STORAGE COMP'Y
Household Goods and Pianos Moved—Packed—Stored..... Baggage and Package Express Machinery and Safes a Specialty Cor. Washington and Illinois Sts. TELEPHONE No. 675.

The Central Rubber & Supply Co. PHONE 8. 79 S. ILLINOIS ST. INDIANAPOLIS, IND. ◆◆◆◆ Hose, Belting, Packing, Clothing, Druggists' Sundries, Bicycle Tires, Cotton Hose, Etc. New York Belting & Packing Co., L't'd.

The Provident Life and Trust Company
Of Philadelphia.
Grants Certificates of Extension to Policyholders who are temporarily unable to pay their premiums
D. W. EDWARDS, Gen. Agt., 508 Indiana Trust Bldg.

Paulson Paul C, lab, h w s Northwestern av 2 n of 25th (N I).
Paulus John P, lab, b 625 N Capitol av.
Paulus Matthias, shoemkr, 137 N Noble, h same.
Paulus Peter J, clk Charles Mayer & Co, h 625 N Capitol av.
Paver Augusta W, teacher Public School No 29, b 453 Park av.
Paver John M (J M Paver & Co), h 453 Park av.
Paver John M jr, agt, b 453 Park av.
PAVER J M & CO (John M Paver), Merchandise Brokers, 82 S Penn, Tel 1755.
Paver Paul W, clk, b 453 Park av.
Pavey John W, h 77 N Beville av.
Pavey Thomas J, h 274 E St Clair.
Pawling Johnson F, ins agt, h 135 Clinton.
Paxson Augustus L, carp, 315 Mass av, h 505 Ash.
Paxton Eva F (wid Robert), dressmkr, h 148 N East.
Paxton Metteles, clk, b 148 N East.
Payne, see also Paine.
Payne Andrew F, sawyer, h 462 W Udell (N I).
Payne Anna S (wid Wm H), h 17 Short.
Payne Bettie A, h rear 140 Agnes.
Payne Charles (Craft & Payne), h 462 W Udell (N I).
Payne Clifton, coachman 795 N Penn.
Payne Daniel, lab, b 902 W Washington.
Payne Dorsey M, trav agt, h 126 Brookside av.
Payne Flora, furrier, b 53 Park av.
Payne Frank C, asst tel editor The Indpls Journal, h 1091 N Penn.
Payne Frederick L, bkkpr, b 229 N Penn.
Payne Gavin L, city editor The Indpls Journal, b 1004 N Penn.
Payne General W, lab, h 63 Howard.
Payne Henry A, mach, b 260 E Georgia.
Payne Henry K, salesman Syerup & Co, h 97 Spann av.
Payne John, lab, h 95 Sheffield av (H).
Payne John T, plumber, 63 E 14th, h 222 Howard.
Payne Joseph, clk, b 462 W Udell (N I).

Julius C. Walk & Son, Jewelers Indianapolis.
12 EAST WASHINGTON ST.

Payne Joseph F, mnfrs' agt, 44 Board of Trade bldg, h 94 Middle Drive (W P).
Payne Levona H, teacher Industrial Training School, b 240 N Alabama.
Payne Mary B (wid John G), h 1004 N Penn.
Payne Nathan, porter, h 127 Howard.
Payne Philip, mixer, h 561 E Walnut.
Payne Sarah A (wid Robert), b rear 232 N Noble.
Payne Stephen E, h 260 E Georgia.
Payne Wm, lab, h 23 S Dorman.
Payne Wm H, lawyer, 1 Talbott blk, r same.
Payne Wm V, h 63 Bismarck av (H).
Payton, see also Peyton.
Payton Andrew, lab, b 298 W St Clair.
Payton Henry, elev opr, b 39 Ellen.
Payton Noah S, lab, h 111 Shepard (W I).
Payton Wm A, lab, b 191 W 2d.
Peaberry Omer, finisher, h 264 W Michigan.
Peachee Harrison, phys, 140 S William (W I) and 42½ W Market, h 853 Bellefontaine.
Peachee Mack W, agt, h 16 Water.
Peachee Rinaldo, paperhngr, b 853 Bellefontaine.
Peacock Mary A H (wid Wm), h 314 Clifford av.
Peacock Mary H, first asst dep clk Supreme Court, b 314 Clifford av.
Peacock Samuel H, pressman The Indpls Journal, h 86 Clifford av.
Peacock Wm, lab, h E 12th 1 w of Yandes.
Peacock Wm H, mach, r 488½ E Washington.
Peacock Wm H, engr, h 314 Clifford av.
Peak Thomas, coachman 785 N Penn.
Peake, see also Peek.
Peake Alonzo W, mach, b 74 N State av.
PEAKE BENJAMIN J, Grocer, 838 E Washington, h 74 N State av.
Peake Charles E, clk, h 1448 E Washington.
Peake Freeman F, tmstr, h 136 S Olive.
Peake James R, clk, b 1448 E Washington.
Peake James T, grocer, 100 Hoyt av, meats, 97 same, h 152 N Linden.
Peake Susan J, nurse, r 133 N Penn.
Pean Robert, painter, h 1369 W Washington (M J).
Pearce, see also Peirce and Pierce.
Pearce Alphine S, clk, h 43 Ramsey av.
Pearce Arthur C, clk, b 118 Highland pl.
Pearce Charles, contr, h 374 N Illinois.
Pearce Charles W, b 374 N Illinois.
Pearce Harry W, bicycle rep, r 31 W Market.
Pearce Hiram B, clk The Pearce Pharmacy, h 140 N Senate av.
Pearce John, coachman 494 N Capitol av.
Pearce Oscar C, pressman F H Smith, h 134 Keystone av.
PEARCE PHARMACY THE, Reuben A Pearce Propr, 224 W 12th.
Pearce Reuben A, propr The Pearce Pharmacy, h 118 Highland pl.
Pearce Samuel J, printer, h 173 Dougherty.
Pearce Thornton M, clk, r 211½ E Washington.
Pearcy, see also Piercy.
Pearcy George W, lab, h 133 N Gillard av.
Pearcy Henry, hostler, h 41 Russell av.
Pearcy John K, clk, h 16 Dearborn.
Pearcy John S, driver, h 413 N Pine.
Pearcy Samuel H, h n w cor Jackson and Lincoln av (M J).
Pearl Edwin S, prin Indpls Academy for Boys, r 498 N Penn.
Pearl Wm H, teacher Indpls Academy for Boys, r 498 N Penn.

OTTO GAS ENGINES | BUILDERS' EXCHANGE S. W. Cor. Ohio and Penn. Telephone 535.

Becker & Son Charles Becker Jacob Becker Jr. Merchant Tailors. 21 N. Penn. St. Tel. 934

SALISBURY & STANLEY • Office, Store and Bar Fixtures a Specialty. Repairing of all kinds done on short notice. 177 Clinton Street, Indianapolis, Ind. • Contractors and Builders TELEPHONE 999.

Pearre Stirling E, h s s University av 3 w of Grand av (I).
Pearson, see also Pierson.
Pearson Albert W, tailor, r 55 Dearborn.
Pearson Alonzo H, packer, h 213 Douglass.
Pearson Amanda, dressmkr, 26 Traub av, h same.
Pearson Andrew, bricklyr, h 327 S New Jersey.
Pearson Charles, tmstr, h rear 111 Minerva.
Pearson Charles A, carp, b n s 17th 1 w of Capitol av.
Pearson Charles D (Pearson & Wetzell), h 400 Broadway.
Pearson Charles L, carp, 136 Harlan, h same.
Pearson Frank, b 306 E South.
Pearson George C, propr Pearson's Music House, 82-84 N Penn, h 863 N Delaware.
Pearson George W, carp, h n s 17th 1 w of Capitol av.
Pearson Harry C, clk Pearson & Wetzel, b 176 E New York.
Pearson James C, b 176 E New York.
PEARSON JOHN R, Asst to Pres Indianapolis Gas Co, h 578 N Penn.
Pearson John R, clk Pearson & Wetzel, b 176 E New York.
Pearson Julius D, drugs, 47 Virginia av, h 965 N Delaware.
Pearson Levi, lab, b 323 E Wabash.
Pearson Lewis, lab, b 325 W St Clair.
Pearson Lewis B, carp, 123 Columbia av, h same.
Pearson Margaret, laundress, h 320 E Court.
PEARSON'S MUSIC HOUSE, George C Pearson Propr, 82-84 N Penn, Tel 529.
Pearson Riley, b 1029 W Washington.
Pearson Thomas W, trav agt Tanner & Sullivan, b 176 E New York.
Pearson Wm A, foreman, h 83 Morton.
PEARSON & WETZEL (Charles D Pearson, Henry Wetzel), Wholesale China, Glass and Queensware, 119-121 S Meridian, Tel 855.
Pease Albert H, city fireman, b 20 Orange av.
Pease Catherine (wid Louis P), b 74 Park av.
Pease Charles R, timekpr, b 179 E Ohio.
Pease Harry A, trav agt, h 193 N Beville av.
Pease James L, city fireman h 75 W 6th.
Pease Theodore W (Cole & Pease), h 205 College av.
Peasley Robert B, mach, h w s Auburn av 3 s of English av (W).
Peats Charles H, lab, h 154 English av.
Peats Edward E, planer, b 154 English av.
Peats Wm E, lab, h 232 English av.
Peck Alonzo V, mach, h 440 Martindale av.
PECK BENJAMIN B, State Agt Mutual Benefit Life Insurance Co of Newark, N J, 20-21 Fletcher's Bank Bldg, Tel 1242; r 46 The Blacherne.
Peck Calvin L, plumber, 91 N Delaware, h 29 Belmont av.
Peck Charles H, buyer N Y Store, h 241 N Delaware.
Peck Charles J, cooper, h 59 Bloomington.
Peck Edward F, condr, r 124 The Shiel.
Peck Edwin C, clk, b 177 E St Clair.

Henry H. Fay, 40½ E. Washington St., REAL ESTATE, AND LOAN BROKER.

Peck Flavius J, trav agt, h 1088 N Senate av.
Peck Frank E, painter, b 37 Brookside av.
Peck Frank L, clk E C Atkins & Co, h 33 Hall pl.
Peck George I, barber, 145½ Mass av, r same.
Peck Herman L, chief clk local frt office C C C & St L Ry, b 180 E St Clair.
Peck Homer T, painter, r 235 Mass av.
Peck Irwin W, mngr Union News Co, h 659 Virginia av.
Peck Isaac N, farmer, h 37 Brookside av.
Peck Jay L, trav agt, h 953 N Alabama.
Peck Laura, millinery, 659 Virginia av, h same.
Peck Leslie E, music teacher, b 77 E Walnut.
Peck Margaret A (wid Wm), r 235 Mass av.
Peck Maria (wid Jacob), b 316 Park av.
Peck Sarah C (wid Wm J), b 82 W 2d.
Peck Thomas H S, b 177 E St Clair.
Peck Walter H, boxmkr, h 1388 Northwestern av.
Peck Walter M, polisher, h 129 Martindale av.
Peck Willard D, butter, n e cor Delaware and 10th, h 900 N New Jersey.
Peckham Alfred, mach, b 32 Drake.
Peckham Caleb H, architect, 32 Drake, h same.
Peckman Edward C, clk R M S, h 32 Division (W I).
Peckover Thomas G, polisher, h 556 W Morris.
Peddicord, see also Petticord.
Peddicord John W, picture frames, 66½ E Washington, h 1379 N Capitol av.
Peddle Charles R, b 121 E Michigan.
Peden Arthur M, yardmaster, h 770 E Market.
Peden James B, driver, h 236 Hamilton av.
Pedigo Mary E (wid Sanford) h 115 Yandes.
Pedigo Wm F, bartender, h 21 S West.
Pedlow Benjamin, mach, h 258 W 23d.
Pedlow Edward, molder, b 168 Coburn.
Pedlow Edward T, molder, h 142 Greer.
Pedlow Ella, teacher Public School No 13, b 168 Coburn.

MAYHEW'S SPECTACLES THE BEST IN USE SOLD ONLY AT 13 N. MERIDIAN ST.

COAL AND LIME Cement, Hair, Sewer Pipe, etc. BALKE & KRAUSS CO. Cor. Missouri and Market Sts.

FRIEDGEN'S IS THE PLACE FOR THE NOBBIEST SHOES Ladies' and Gents' 19 North Pennsylvania St.

SAMUEL LAING || COPPER AND GALVANIZED IRON CORNICE MANUFACTURER
72 AND 74 E. COURT STREET. SKYLIGHTS AND VENTILATORS.

M. B. WILSON, Pres. W. F. CHURCHMAN, Cash.
THE CAPITAL NATIONAL BANK,
INDIANAPOLIS, IND.
Our Specialty is handling all Country Checks and Drafts on Indiana and neighboring States at the very lowest rates. Call and see us.
Interest Paid on Time Deposits.
28 S. MERIDIAN ST., COR. PEARL.

Pedlow Harry, mach, b 168 Coburn.
Pedlow James, molder, h 173 Coburn.
Pedlow James C, blksmith, b 1061 N Senate av.
Pedlow Richard, foreman Sinker-Davis Co, h 117 Cottage av.
Pedlow Richard J, clk, b 1061 N Senate av.
Pedlow Robert J, mach, h 242 Douglass.
Pedlow Robert J, molder, h 168 Coburn.
Pee Emmet I, h 1131 N Penn.
Pee George W, trav agt, b 1131 N Penn.
Peebles James M (Peebles & Burroughs), res San Diego, Cal.
PEEBLES & BURROUGHS (James M Peebles, John A Burroughs), Physicians, Room 8, 66½ N Penn.
Peede Stella, teacher Public School No 1, b 332 E St Clair.
Peehl, see also Peele and Piel.
Peehl Louis, feed, 129 Indiana av, h 459 N Senate av.
Peek, see also Peake.
Peek Abner A, blksmith, b 19 Tremont av (H).
Peek Albert M, molder, h 13 Cleveland (H).
Peek Andrew A, b 91 Minerva.
Peek Charles E, lab, h n w cor Washington and Watts.
Peek Charles F, molder, h 148 N Belmont av (H).
Peek George W, express, h 414 S Capitol av.
Peek James, lab, b n w cor Washington and Watts.
Peek John N, attendant Insane Asylum.
Peek John W, blksmith, 116 Michigan av (H), h 19 Tremont av (H).
Peek Nathaniel T, janitor, h 145½ Oliver av (W I).
Peek Samuel M, cooper, h 66 S Belmont av (W I).
Peek Sherman W, barber, h s s 6th 1 e of Capitol av.
Peelle, see also Peehl and Picl.
Peelle John, mach, h s e cor Bailey and 29th.
Peelle Margaret F (wid Wm A), b 203 N Noble.

TUTTLE & SEGUIN,
28 E. Market St. Ground Floor.
COLLECTING RENTS AND CARE OF PROPERTY A SPECIALTY.
Telephone 1168.

Peelle Thomas, city agt, h 46 Eastern av.
Peeples James D, huckster, h 60 Gatling.
Peeples John H, fireman, h 788 E Market.
PEERLESS FOUNDRY CO (Griffith W and Wm G Williams), Founders and Machinists, 70 Meek, Tel 1598.
Peery, see also Parry and Perry.
Peery Sarah E, housekpr 163 Hoyt av.
Peery Thomas E, tmstr, h 131 N Gillard av.
Pees Charles W, barber, r 9 Grand Opera House blk.
Peffley Wm F, phys, 542 Highland av (N I), h same.
Pefley Arthur, carp, h 72 Spann av.
PeGan Arthur C, clk, b 278 E South.
PeGan Catherine (wid James), h 278 E South.
Pegg Edward, mach, r 129 Virginia av.
Pegg George A, with Diamond Wall Plaster Co, h 217 N New Jersey.
Pegg Wm J, lab, r 129 Virginia av.
Peggs Charles L, gardener, h w s Schurman 1 s of Vorster av (M P).
Peggs Frank W, mach, h 161 Yandes.
Peggs Wm L, stock examiner Bureau of Animal Industry, h 339 Jackson.
Pein George W (Abraham & Pein), h 9 Allfree.
Peine Anna C (wid John H), h 520 N Alabama.
Peine Frederick L, clk, Standard Oil Co, b 520 N Alabama.
Peine Frederick W, engr, h 177 Oliver av (W I).
Peiper Paulina (wid Louis), b 40 Wisconsin.
Peirce, see also Pearce and Pierce.
Peirce Benjamin S, driver, h 96 Keystone av.
Peirce Converse, express, h s e cor Mill and 9th.
Peirce Edwin B F, gen mngr National Electric Headlight Co, 30-34 W South, b 654 N Meridian.
Peirce George H, tel opr, b 84 W Vermont.
Peirce George L, helper, h 122 Wright.
Peirce Ira S, h 1148 E Washington.
Peirce Jasper G, pressman, h 96 Keystone av.
Peirce John H, painter, r 50 W Market.
Peirce John W, oysters, 22 S Illinois, r same.
Peirce Kathryn, dressmkr, 472 N New Jersey, h same.
Peirce Oscar C, pressman, h 134 Keystone av.
PEIRCE ROBERT B F, Receiver T St L & K C Ry, Genl Mngr I D & W Ry and Pres National Electric Headlight Co, 78 Commercial Club Bldg, Tel 1179; h 654 N Meridian, Tel 877.
Peirce Oral, pressman, b 122 Wright.
Peirce Seymour L, clk I D & W Ry, b 84 W Vermont.
Peirce Wm, r 37½ W Market.
Peirce Wm H, printer, h 85 Keystone av.
Pell Isaac, lab, b 1 Astor.
Pell John S, barber, 79 N Delaware, h 277 E Miami.
Pell Mary J (wid Isaac T), h 1 Astor.
Pellatt Joseph, evangelist, h 640 Shelby.
Pellatt Robert W, engr, h 640 Shelby.
Pellett Margaret A, draper, b 125 S Pine.
Pellett Margaret A, h 193½ E Washington.
Pellett Wm E, sub letter carrier P O, h 125 S Pine.
Pelly Wm, farmer, b e s Sherman Drive 5 n of Washington.

PAPER BOXES SULLIVAN & MAHAN 41 W. Pearl St.

DIAMOND WALL PLASTER { Telephone 1410 BUILDERS' EXCHANGE.

If your Laundry Work is not satisfactory, try THE HOME LAUNDRY 197 S. Illinois St. Telephone 1769.

Peltier Arthur L, mach, b 280 Virginia av.
Peltier Eugene T, janitor Public School No 8, h 280 Virginia av.
Pelton Chauncey W, carp, h 745 E Michigan.
Pelton Frederick, mach hd, h 164 N Pine.
Pelton Terry W, carver, h 206 Fayette.
Pemberton Robert W, carp, h 143½ Virginia av.
Pembroke Arcade, from 79 E Washington to 30 Virginia av.
PEN THE, Michael W Carr Editor and Publisher, 9-10 Cordova Bldg, 25½ W Washington.
Pence Ahija, carp, h 46 Hall pl.
Pence Caroline (wid John), h 115 Oak.
Pence George, carp, h 158 Cornell av.
Pence George, clk Cerealine Mnfg Co, b Stubbins' Hotel.
Pence George W, molder, b 47 King av (H).
Pence George W F, trav agt, h 107 Andrews.
Pence Harry O, bkkpr Daggett & Co, b 46 Hall pl.
Pence Homer R, mach, b 41 N Gillard av.
Pence Horatio S, lab, h 128 Lee (W I).
Pence John, car rep, h 41 N Gillard av.
Pence Mary A (wid Joseph), h 28 Bloomington.
Pence Nancy E (wid Joseph), h 47 King av (H).
Pence Nellie, teacher, b 47 King (H).
Pence Ray, waiter Roosevelt House.
Pence Stanley H, plumber, b 41 N Gillard av.
Pence Viola M, teacher Public School No 33, b 115 Oak.
Pence Wm H, clk M S Huey & Son, b 158 Cornell av.
Pender James H, bricklyr, b 272 W 7th.
Pendergast Albert G, bkkpr Baker & Thornton, b 53 Central av.
Pendergast Edward B, lab, h 31 Blake.
Pendergast James E, huckster, h e s Parker av 2 n of Clifford av.
Pendergast John G, h 413 N Capitol av.
Pendergast Mary B, artist, 53 Central av, b same.
Pendergast Mary J, dressmkr, 345 N Alabama, b same.
Pendergast Pamelia J (wid Enos), b 53 Central av.
Pendergast Wm, lab, h 83 John.
PENDLETON ALBERT D, Commercial Agt Vandalia Lines, 9 N Illinois, Tel 851; h 519 N Meridian.
Pendleton Hannah H, cashr New England Mut Life Ins Co, b 422 N East.
Pendleton Katherine, nurse, 197 N Delaware.
Pendleton Ralph C J, ins adjuster, h 422 N East.
Pendleton Rebecca S (wid Achilles V), h 777 N New Jersey.
Peneweit Wm H, mach, b 419 N New Jersey.
Penewit Courtland L, saloon, 49 Indiana av, h same.
Penfield Frederick F, ins agt, r 197 N Illinois.
Penhart Wm, lab, h 230 Summit (H).
Penhorwood Wm W, carp, 183 Brookside av, h same.
Penick Sidney Rev, pastor Walters Chapel, h 517 English av.
Penish Meyer, tailor, b 472 S Illinois.
Penn Gustav, florist, b 139 N Delaware.
Penn Henry, cook, h 33 Columbia al.

FRANK NESSLER. WILL H. ROST.
FRANK NESSLER & CO.
Tailors
56 EAST MARKET ST. (Lemcke Building),
INDIANAPOLIS, IND.

Penn Henry C, engr, b 30 S Gale (B).
Penn John L, lab, b 21 Belmont av.
Penn Sarah (wid John), b 21 Belmont av.
Penn Wm, lab, h 427 Clinton.
Penn Wm T, lab, h 21 Belmont av.
Pennewitt Frank, fireman, r 70 N Senate av.
Pennewitt Jesse, engr, b 287 W Michigan.
Penney Sarah N, h 220 W Merrill.
Pennicke Charles Y, painter, b 128 Huron.
Pennicke Frederick O, clk, h 113 Woodlawn av.
Pennicke John L, clk Eli Lilly & Co, h 65 Hosbrook.
Pennicke Maurice, painter, h 128 Huron.
Pennicke Maurice W, clk, b 128 Huron.
Pennicke Otto F, clk L S Ayres & Co, b 113 Woodlawn av.
Pennicke Thomas E, lab, b 128 Huron.
Pennington Ethel, stenog Providence Life and Trust Co, 508-510 Indiana Trust bldg, b 512 Bellefontaine.
Pennington Isaac, trav agt, h 512 Bellefontaine.
Pennington Joseph W, painter, 438 Talbott av, h same.
Pennington Mont R, printer, b 438 Talbott av.
Pennington Perry C, clk N Y Store, r 4 Columbia blk.
Pennington Richard T, molder, h 74 Holmes av (H).
Pennington Robert M, printer, b 438 Talbott av.
Pennington Walter, farmer, h 89 S McLain (W I).
Pennington Walter M, trav agt White Line Fast Freight, r 45 The Plaza.
Pennington Wesley J, b 1400 N Capitol av.
Pennington Wm, lab, h 18 Seibert.
Pennington Wm, lab, b 11 Willard.
Pennix Sidney lab, h 517 English av.
Pennoyer Lucretia E (wid Daniel M), b 2 Detriot.
Pennsylvania Lines, general offices n e cor Washington and Illinois, ticket offices 48 W Washington and Jackson pl.
Penny Frederick S, sawmkr, b 289 Kentucky av.

Haueisen & Hartmann
163-169 E. Washington St.
FURNITURE,
Carpets,
Household Goods,
Tin, Granite and China Wares, Oil Cloth and Shades

THE WM. H. BLOCK CO. 7 AND 9 EAST WASHINGTON STREET. DRY GOODS, MEN'S FURNISHINGS.

The Fidelity and Deposit Co. OF MARYLAND. Bonds signed for Administrators, Assignees, Executors, Guardians, Receivers Trustees, and persons in every position of trust.
GEO. W. PANGBORN, General Agent, 704-706 Lemcke Building. Telephone 140.

INSURE YOUR PROPERTY WITH FRANK K. SAWYER

•JOSEPH GARDNER•
GALVANIZED IRON
CORNICES and SKYLIGHTS.
Metal Ceilings and Siding.
Tin, Iron, Steel and Slate Roofing.
37, 39 & 41 KENTUCKY AVE. Telephone 322.

Penny Juliette (wid Isaac), b 167 Douglass.
Penrod Daniel W, poultry, E Mkt House, h 523 Martindale av.
Penrod Mary E (wid Wm R), h 168 Brookside av.
Penrod Wm H P, clk, b 168 Brookside av.
Pentecost Elmer B, h w s Commercial av 2 s of Washington av (I).
Pentecost Herald, George E Bulá mngr, Flora B Nelson editor, 52 S State av.
Pentecost Louis M, h 1401 W Rader (N I).
Pentecost Mahlon B, h 167 Cornell av.
Pentske Frederick W, mach, h 57 E Morris.
People The, James B Wilson editor and pub, 37½ Virginia av.
PEOPLE'S OUTFITTING CO, J Wineman Propr, Furniture, Carpets and House Furnishing Goods, 71-73 W Washington, Tel 1510.
Peoples Lucullus S, cook, h 24 Ellsworth.
PEORIA ATHLETIC COMPANY, F H Henning Mngr, Patee Bicycles and Athletic Goods, 58-60 N Penn, Tel 486.
Peoria & Eastern Ry, see Cleveland, Cincinnati, Chicago & St Louis Ry.
Pepper Mary A (wid George), b 1007 N Capitol av.
Pepper Wm S, miller, h 130 Carlos.
Peppler Henry, foreman, b 451 Union.
Perasuhn Henry, lab, h 70 S Belmont av (W I).
Per Due Roland C, student, h 221 Virginia av.
Pergande Charles, car rep, h 177 Pleasant.
Pergande Richard, mach, b 177 Pleasant.
Perham John W, molder, h 231 Hoyt av.
Perigo Joseph E, clk, b 201 Union.
Perigo Smith, h 5 Sylvan.
Perigo Stephen W, grocer, 201 Union, h same.
Perin James A, clk R M S, h 52½ W 7th.
Perin John F, carp, h 284 Bates.
Perine Harry D, trav agt, h 1773 N Capitol av.
Perine Horace G, clk R M S, h 38 Hall pl.
Perine Ida M, b 1996 N Meridian.

J. S. FARRELL & CO.
Have Experienced Workmen and will Promptly Attend to your
PLUMBING
Repairs. 84 North Illinois Street. Telephone 382.

Perine Mary T (wid Peter R), h 1696 N Meridian.
Perine Norman T, trav agt, h 66 Oak.
Perk Wm, dyer, b 136 Eddy.
Perkins Alice C, dressmkr, 324 Bellefontaine, h same.
Perkins Arthur D, mach opr The Indpls News, h 1250 S Meridian.
Perkins Charles H, lab, h 4 Brown.
Perkins Clarkson C (Perkins & Shockley), b 217 W Pearl.
Perkins Edgar A, proofreader The Indpls News, h 21 Gregg.
Perkins Edward L, baggageman, h 23 Hall pl.
Perkins Edward M, saw filer, h 272 Alvord.
Perkins Elizabeth (wid Charles), b 56 N State av.
Perkins Ella (wid John), h 14 Barrows.
Perkins Ells H, foreman The Indpls News, b 71 Pleasant.
Perkins Ernest E, printer, b 89 Stevens.
Perkins Frederick, lab, b s s Washington av 5 e of Line (I).
Perkins Henry L (Perkins & Shockley), h 217 W Pearl.
Perkins James W Rev, h 192 Fletcher av.
Perkins Jessie F (wid Morris), b 1677 N Penn.
Perkins John, driver, r 120 E Wabash.
Perkins John A, city fireman, h 1614 N Illinois.
Perkins John H, cigarmkr, b 473 E Georgia.
Perkins Josiah P, trav agt, b 371 N California.
Perkins Julian W, clk E C Atkins & Co, b 1558 N Meridian.
Perkins Lafayette (Hord & Perkins), h 75 E Walnut.
Perkins Lena M, r 34 Stewart pl.
Perkins Omer W, carp, h 371 N California.
Perkins Oscar G, lab, b 4 Willard.
Perkins Samuel, bartndr, b Hotel English.
Perkins Samuel E, real est, 30½ N Delaware, h 573 N Penn.
Perkins Warren J, well driver, b e s Brown 1 n of 23d.
Perkins Wm G, sawmkr, b 1558 N Meridian.
Perkins Wm H, linotype opr, h 89 Stevens.
Perkins Wm H, mason, h n w cor Ritter av and Brookville rd (I).
Perkins Wm H, motorman, h 345 Columbia av.
Perkins Wm H, sec E C Atkins & Co, h 1558 N Meridian.
Perkins Wm S, molder, h 173 W Michigan.
Perkins & Shockley (Clarkson and Henry L Perkins, Euclid Shockley), livery, 218 W Maryland.
Perkinson Edward D, boilermkr, b 243 S Senate av.
Perkinson John P, lab, b 243 S Senate av.
Perkinson Joseph H, lab, b 243 S Senate av.
Perkinson Patrick H, h 243 S Senate av.
Perlee Benjamin W, lab, b 501 S New Jersey.
Perlee Frank M, clk, h 501 S New Jersey.
Pernet Harrison W, paperhngr, b 35 Eastern av.
Perrin, see also Perin.
Perrin August, millwright, h 41 Evison.
Perrin Charles F, clk M O'Connor & Co, b 320 E Ohio.
Perrin Edwin, teas, b 661 W Eugene (N I).
Perrin George K, lawyer, 33-34 Baldwin blk, r same.
Perrin Louisa J (wid James O), h 84 Ludlow av.
Perrott, see also Parrott.

GUARANTEED INCOME POLICIES issued only by the **United States Life Insurance Co.**
E. B. SWIFT, Manager, 25 E. Market St.

Furniture Carpets } WM. KOTTEMAN { Stoves Ranges
89 and 91 East Washington Street. Telephone 1742.

Perrott Albert G, student, b 168 Blackford.
Perrott George L, bkkpr, b 168 Blackford.
Perrott Samuel V (Perrott & Gorman), h 92 Highland av.
Perrott Thomas J, pdlr, h 370 W Vermont.
Perrott Wm L, plumber, h 514 Newman.
Perrott Wm W, h 168 Blackford.
PERROTT & GORMAN (Samuel V Perrott, Patrick J Gorman), Real Estate and Loans, Room 39 Baldwin Blk.
Perry, see also Parry and Peery.
Perry Albert, lab, h 371 W North.
Perry Alfred, lab, h 60 Northwestern av.
Perry Arba T (J C Perry & Co), sec and treas Elam Mnfg Co, h 889 N Penn.
Perry Arnold D, trav pass agt C & A R R, 6 Fair blk, h 1031 N Meridian.
PERRY BROOM CO THE, James Perry Pres, Wm Perry Vice-Pres and Treas, Wm W Hammel Sec, Office 82 S Delaware, Factory e s Belt R R near Vorster av, Tel 651.
Perry Caleb, h 148 W New York.
Perry Charles, grocer, 255 S Capitol av, h same.
Perry Charles C, sec and treas Indpls Light and Power Co, h 650 N Illinois
Perry Charles E, car rep, h rear 110 English av.
Perry Charles E, driver, b 24 William.
Perry Charles W, express, h e s Arthur 1 n of Cypress.
Perry Clarence, polisher, h 329 E Georgia.
Perry Clark, mach, h 68 S Spruce.
Perry Columbus, lab, h 115 W 4th.
Perry Cora, dressmkr, 199½ Mass av, r same.
Perry Ebenezer, h rear 606 S Meridian.
Perry Edward, farmer, h s s P C C & St L Ry 2 e of Line (I).
Perry Edward, foreman, h 275 S Illinois.
Perry Edward, lab, h 67½ Russell av.
Perry Elmer E, sec and treas Indiana Millers' Mut Fire Ins Co, and Indiana agt Northwestern Miller, h 377 College av.
Perry Elzy M, tmstr, h 78 Harlan.
Perry Frances M, teacher Public School No 8, b 51 Broadway.
Perry Frank L, molder, h 147 King av (H).
Perry George H, lab, b 34 Everett.
Perry Harvey, blksmith, 329 Elizabeth, h 36 Maxwell.
Perry Henry, express, h 24 William.
Perry Homer, hostler, b rear 72 W 3d.
Perry Horace D, clk C C C & St L Ry, b 61 Elm.
Perry Isaac, engr, h 839 E Washington.
Perry Jackson, lab, b 371 W North.
Perry James, pres Perry Broom Co, h e s LaSalle 1 n of Indiana av (M P).
Perry James E, bkkpr, b e s LaSalle 1 n of Indiana av (M P).
Perry James H, b 519 N West.
Perry Jeanette (wid Matthew), b 445 S Delaware.
Perry John C (J C Perry & Co), h 667 N Delaware, tel 574.
Perry John C, bkkpr, b 125 E North.
PERRY JOSEPH R, Druggist, 200 E Washington, h 84 E Pratt.
Perry Julia A (wid Bernhard), h 34 Everett.
PERRY J C & CO (John C Perry, George C Brinkmeyer, Arba T Perry), Wholesale Grocers, 26, 28 and 30 W Georgia, Tel 406.

We Buy Municipal ~ Bonds ~
THOS. C. DAY & CO,
Rooms 325 to 330 Lemcke Bldg.

Perry Kirkman L, trav agt, h 654 N Alabama.
Perry Lorenzo N (McCurdy & Perry), b 79 W Ohio.
Perry Mary E (wid Wm L), h 124 Indiana av.
Perry Matthew, lab, h 405 Columbia av.
Perry Moses, lab, h 55 Bismarck av (W I).
PERRY ORAN, Local Freight Agt Pennsylvania Lines west of Pittsburg, Office Virginia av and Union Tracks, Tel 434; h 725 N Delaware, Tel 691.
Perry Oran, bricklyr, h 307 Yandes.
Perry Orion, driver, h 159 Elm.
Perry Samuel A, condr, h 26 N Gale (B).
Perry Sherman, flyman, b e s LaSalle 1 n of Indiana av (M P).
Perry Simon, lab, h 20 Sumner.
Perry Thomas, janitor, h 552 N Senate av.
Perry Thomas, marshal (W I), h 19 Garland (W I).
Perry Thomas H, chief engr and pur agt L E & W R R, h 51 Broadway.
Perry Wm, vice-pres and treas The Perry Broom Co, h 373 N Alabama.
Perry Wm A, b 195 W Merrill.
Perry Wm C, tmstr, h 237 Minnesota.
Perry Wm R, tmstr, h 112 N Gillard av.
Perry Willis C, barber, h 361 Douglass.
Perryman Edgar A, engr, r 113 S Illinois.
Perschbaucher Harry M, brakeman, b 131 S East.
Perschbaucher John, brakeman, b 131 S East.
Person Richard J, driver, h 40 W 1st.
Personal Property Saving and Loan Assn, J H Aufderheide pres, 4 Lombard bldg.
Personette Anne M (wid Claude C), h 5 Wilcox.
Persons Thomas, lab, b 16 Darnell.
Pertell Maurice, lab, b 224 W Maryland.
Pervear Wm H, trav agt, h 17 E North.
Peschat Frank, mach, h 84 Germania av (H).
Peterman Frank J, creamery, 445 S East, h same.
Peterman Henry (Roch & Peterman), h 479 S Missouri.

EAT HITZ'S CRACKERS AND CAKES.
ASK YOUR GROCER FOR THEM.

WILLIAM WIEGEL } MANUFACTURER OF . . . { SHOW CASES { 6 W. Louisiana St. Opposite Union Station.

TURKISH RUGS AND CARPETS RESTORED TO ORIGINAL COLORS LIKE NEW | Capital Steam Carpet Cleaning Works M. D. PLUNKETT, Telephone 818

BENJ. BOOTH PRACTICAL EXPERT ACCOUNTANT. Books Opened, Written Up, Posted and Balanced. Room 18, 82½ E. Washington St., Indianapolis, Ind.

IF YOU WANT A GOOD MEAL AND HAVE IT NICELY SERVED GO TO THE SHERMAN RESTAURANT 18 and 20 S. MERIDIAN STREET

ESTABLISHED 1876. TELEPHONE 168.
CHESTER BRADFORD,
SOLICITOR OF PATENTS,
AND COUNSEL IN PATENT CAUSES.
(See adv. page 6.)
Office:—Rooms 14 and 16 Hubbard Block, S. W. Cor. Washington and Meridian Streets, INDIANAPOLIS, INDIANA.

Peterman Otto, waiter, r 148½ W Washington.
Peterman Wm M, bartndr, r 148½ W Washington.
Peters Benjamin, steelwkr, b 232 Belmont av (H).
Peters Charles, lab, h 272 E St Clair.
Peters Clay M, trav agt, h 241 N Delaware.
Peters Eliza, h 255½ E Washington.
Peters Elizabeth (wid John), h 4 McCauley.
Peters Frederick, driver, b 148 Meek.
Peters Frederick C, mach, h 922 Gent (M P).
Peters Harry, beamer, h 6 Douglass.
Peters Henry, carp, h 37 Shelby.
Peters Henry, tel opr Postal Tel Cable Co, b 125 Blake.
Peters Ida E, teacher, b 32 W Ohio.
Peters Jennie (wid Sanford), h 26 Hosbrook.
Peters John, carp, r 26 S West.
Peters John H, lab, h 143 Harrison.
Peters John W, baker, b 76 N Alabama.
Peters Joseph, lab, h 38 Nebraska.
Peters J Christopher Rev, pastor German Evangelical Zion Church, h 32 W Ohio.
Peters Lillian M, nurse City Hospital.
Peters Louise, teacher Public School No 29, b 409 N Penn.
Peters Manson M, mach, h 809 E 9th.
Peters Mary (wid Killian), b 125 Blake.
Peters Matthias, saloon, 195 E Washington, h same.
Peters Oliver, lab, b 125 Blake.
Peters Robert, lab, h 321 Clinton.
Peters Roy, clk Emil Wulschner & Son, b 373 N Alabama.
Peters Rudolph, carver, b 450 S East.
Peters Sarah C (wid Wm), matron Deaf and Dumb Inst.
Peters Sebron C, waiter, h 356 Douglass.
Peters Sophia, h rear 333 W Morris.
Peters Stephen, stonecutter, h 15 Dawson.
Peters Wm, baker, r 77 N Alabama.
Petersdorf Gustave A, student, r 134 N Meridian.
Petersen, see also Patterson and Pattison.
Petersen Carl F, casemkr Wm Wiegel, h 28 Sanders.

O. B. ENSEY
MANUFACTURER OF
GALVANIZED IRON CORNICE, SKYLIGHTS AND WINDOW CAPS.
TELEPHONE 1562. Cor. 6th and Illinois Sts.

Petersen Henry G, clk George J Mayer, b 5 Dougherty.
Petersen Peter C, lab, h 15 Singleton.
Peterson Adrian L, polisher, b 310 Virginia av.
Peterson Andrew J, car insp, h 232 Brookside av.
Peterson Anna D (wid Charles), dressmkr, 167 N Capitol av, h same.
Peterson Arthur W, asst mngr The Indpls News, h 175 N Penn, tel 1919.
Peterson Christina (wid Hans), h 68 Yeiser.
Peterson Elizabeth (wid Nicholas), h 131 W New York.
Peterson Elmer M, electrician, h 4 Water.
Peterson Frederick, lab, h 576 W Shoemaker (N I).
Peterson George W, lab, h 1058 W Washington.
Peterson Gottfried, engr, h 122 Sheffield av (H).
Peterson Hans, tmstr, h e s Addison 2 s of Washington (M J).
Peterson James, lab, b e s Daisy 1 n of Ream.
Peterson John, polisher, b 9 Sharpe.
Peterson Lars P, lab, h 5 Dougherty.
Peterson Lycurgus L, lab, h 70 Park av.
Peterson Mary, clk, b 131 W New York.
Peterson Peter, driver, h 172 Bird.
Peterson Peter jr, foreman, b 172 Bird.
Peterson Samaria C (wid Jefferson M), h 435 N Pine.
Peterson Soren, lab, h 310 Virginia av.
Peterson Willis, engr, b 4 Water.
Petig Henry G, lab, b 85 Agnes.
Petig Johanna M (wid Charles A), h 85 Agnes.
Petit, see also Pettit.
Petit Adolph, butcher, h 278 W Market.
Pétit Alphonse L, lab, h 55 Bicking.
Petit Christopher, lab, b 292 W Maryland.
Petit George D, barber, b 41 Indiana av.
Petit Henry, barber, Central av (I), h w s Good av 3 s of Railroad (I).
Petit Joseph A, butcher, h 41 Minerva.
Petit Marshall J, driver, b 866 S Meridian.
Petit Theophile, cook, h 69 Ft Wayne av.
Petrie George H, clk, b 50 Highland pl.
Petrie James S, lab, h 407 S Olive.
Petrie John, lab, b 407 S Olive.
Petrie Robert (Pray & Petrie), h 228 Randolph.
Petrie Wm, stonecutter, h 50 Highland pl.
Petticord, see also Peddicord.
Petticord Elmer E, molder, h 349 S Alabama.
Petticord James E, lab, b 151 Church.
Petticord Nancy (wid John), h 151 Church.
Petticord Nathan S, lab, b 151 Church.
Petticrew John F, car rep, h 22 Minkner.
Pettiford Franklin, tmstr, b 602 W Michigan.
Pettiford John N, hostler, h 314 Highland av.
Pettiford Junius, lab, b 602 W Michigan.
Pettigrew Albert E, lab, h 1268 Morris (W I).
Pettigrew Charles, supt Am Steel Co, b The Bates.
Pettijohn Otto B, phys, 232 Blake, h same.
PETTIS DRY GOODS CO, A Swan Brown Pres, James A Swan Treas, George A Gay Genl Mngr, Dry Goods, Cloaks, Millinery, Notions, Carpets, Boots, Shoes, Etc, New York Store, 25-33 E Washington, Tel 65.
Pettis Frank L, clk N Y Store, h 446 Ash.

TUTEWILER UNDERTAKER, No. 72 WEST MARKET STREET. TELEPHONE 216.

PARTNERSHIP INSURANCE At low cost. By which provision is made against the pecuniary loss and embarrassment resulting from the death of a member of a firm.
Provident Life and Trust Co. of Philadelphia, D. W. EDWARDS, Gen'l Agt., 508 Indiana Trust Bldg.

THEODORE F. SMITHER - GRAVEL ROOFING M'f'r. 2 and 3-Ply Ready Roofing, Building Paper, etc. Office, 151 West Maryland St. Roof Materials.

Pettit, see also Petit.
Pettit Alonzo A, lab, h 376 E Ohio.
Pettit Cornelius B, bricylyr, h 131 Harrison.
Pettit Elijah O, condr, h 1159 N Capitol av.
Pettit Elmer, lab, b 376 E Ohio.
Pettit Hutokah, nurse 124 N Alabama.
Pettit Joseph S, agt, r 24½ Kentucky av.
Pettit Theodore W, carp, h 6 Hermann.
Pettit Wm N, bricklyr, b 131 Harrison.
Petty Calvin, lab, h 81 Bright.
Petty Clarence W, waiter, b 817 LaSalle (M P).
Petty Elmer A, porter, b 37 Beacon.
Petty Emily (wid Zachariah), h 28 Hosbrook.
Petty Frank, lineman, h 237 Spring.
Petty George, engraver, b Willow (B).
Petty George E, switchman, r 225 Michigan av.
Petty Harry E, hostler, r s w cor Allegheny and Bird.
Petty Jacob, city fireman, h 103 Martindale av
Petty James, tmstr, h 108 Ludlow av.
Petty James F, lab, b 28 Hosbrook.
Petty John W, lab, h 37 Beacon.
Petty Margaret (wid James E), h 307 Indiana av.
Petty Ransom, mach hd, h 817 LaSalle (M P).
Petty Robert I, mach hd, h n s Park 2 w of Morris (B).
Petty Wm, lab, h 354 S Meridian.
Petty Wm H, lab, b 81 Bright.
Pettycrew Wm H, embalmer Flanner & Buchanan, h 140 Fayette.
Pew, see also Pugh.
Pew Frank, tel opr, b 74 W New York.
Pew Stanley W, clk, b 113 Highland pl.
Peyton, see also Payton.
Peyton Dora M, h 197 N Illinois.
Peyton Harry, janitor, r 39 Ellen.
Pfaff, see also Paff.
Pfaff David, butcher, h 319 S Olive.
Pfaff Jacob W (Pfaff & Co), h 446 Ash.
Pfaff John A, bkkpr, b 482 Ash.
Pfaff John W, clk Assessment Bureau, b 482 Ash.
PFAFF O G, Physician and Surgeon, 134 N Penn, Tel 292; h 739 N Penn, Tel 936.
Pfaff Rosina (wid Mafious), h 173 Benton.
Pfaff Wm T, bkkpr, h 482 Ash.
Pfaff & Co (Jacob W Plaff, Wm B Huff, Rufus B Manville), wagonmkrs, 31 Cornell av.
Pfaffenberger Sarah E (wid John), h 784 N Senate av.
Pfafflin Elizabeth (wid Paul E), h 592 W Addison (N I).
Pfafflin Eugene F, clk, b 575 College av.
PFAFFLIN GROCERY CO THE, Wm Pfafflin Pres, Wm Pfafflin Jr Sec and Treas, 100 N Illinois, Tel 473.
Pfafflin Helen, agt, h 234 Spring.
Pfafflin Henry A, druggist, 402 S Delaware, b 340 N East.
Pfafflin Herman J, bkkpr D H Baldwin & Co, h 894 N Capitol av.
Pfafflin Louis, mach, h 248 N Pine.
Pfafflin Louisa J (wid Theodore A), h 182 W Vermont.
Pfafflin Otto F, clk County Recorder, h 125 Clinton.
Pfafflin Paul, janitor Indiana Trust Co, r s e cor Virginia av and Washington.
Pfafflin Theodore A, bkkpr Indpls Brewing Co, h 997 N Senate av.

THE WHEN IS A WORLD BEATER.

Pfafflin Theodore H, uphlr, h 592 W Addison (N I).
Pfafflin Wm, pres The Pfafflin Grocery Co, h 575 College av.
Pfafflin Wm jr, sec and treas The Pfafflin Grocery Co, b 575 College av.
Pfafflin Wm T, trav agt, h 234 Spring.
Pfahler Charles F, driver, h 299 Davidson.
Pfalzgraf George, mngr Madison Brewing Co, h 264 River av (W I).
Pfalzgraf Harry, bartndr, b 264 River av (W I).
Pfarer Ernst F, clk Collins T Bedford, h 10 Herman.
Pfau Charles E, trav agt James R Ross & Co, b 365 N East.
Pfau George (George Pfau & Son), h 500 N Capitol av.
Pfau George & Son (George and John G), whol liquors, 64 S Delaware.
Pfau John G (George Pfau & Son), b 500 N Capitol av.
Pfeffer Barbara (wid John), h 264 N California.
Pfeffer Charles, brakeman, h 95 Keystone av.
Pfeffer Edward C (Daily & Pfeffer), h 264 N California.
Pfeffer Leopold L (Pfeffer & Hunt), b 264 N California.
Pfeffer & Hunt (Leopold L Pfeffer, Wm H Hunt), mer brokers, 26 W Maryland.
Pfeger Frank, instrument mkr, b 81 E Vermont.
Pfeifer Bertha (wid Peter), h 177 N Pine.
Pfeifer Charles W, tel opr, h 15 Poplar (B).
Pfeifer George D, carp, h e s Lake av 7 s of Washington av (I).
Pfeifer Mary J, b 1122 N Penn.
Pfeifer Wm H, trav agt John L Moore, h 15 Halcyon blk.
Pfeiffer Edward, harnessmkr, h 109 N Dorman.
Pfeiffer Edward F, bkkpr Fairbanks, Morse & Co, r 26 The Plaza.
Pfeiffer Frederick E, bartndr, h 49 Frank.
Pfeiffer Gustave A, sec and treas Charles J Kuhn Co, h 78 Fletcher av.
Pfeiffer John F, lab, h 355 S Capitol av.

THE A. BURDSAL CO.
WINDOW AND PLATE
GLASS
Putty, Glazier Points, Diamonds.
Wholesale and Retail. 34 and 36 S. Meridian St.

ELECTRIC CONSTRUCTION Isolated Plants Installed. Electric Wiring and Fittings of all kinds. C. W. Meikel. Tel. 466. 96-98 E New York St

DALTON & MERRIFIELD { LUMBER South Noble St., near E. Washington

INDIANA ELECTROTYPE CO. BEST WORK. LOWEST PRICES. 23 WEST PEARL ST., INDIANAPOLIS, IND. JOB WORK. BOOK PLATES. BEST PATENT BASE ON THE MARKET. All Orders Promptly Filled.

KIRKHOFF BROS.,
GAS AND ELECTRIC FIXTURES
THE LARGEST LINE IN THE CITY.
102-104 SOUTH PENNSYLVANIA ST.
TELEPHONE 910.

Pfeiffer Joseph P, prin St Mary's School for Boys, h same.
Pfeiffer Michael, mach hd, h 35 Kennington.
Pfeiffer Wm G, foreman, h 18 Shriver av.
Pfeiffer Wm H H, h 235 Bright.
Pfenning Hugo W, car rep, h 9 Sharpe.
Pfieffer John, cabtmkr, h 926 Madison av.
Pfirmann Barbara (wid Conrad), h 522 S Capitol av.
Pfister Charles, cabtmkr, h 113 Excelsior av.
Pfister George C, coremkr, h 202 Oliver av (W I).
Pfisterer Frederick J, bkkpr, b 496½ N West.
Pfisterer Henry, ins agt, h 496½ N West.
PFISTERER PETER, Fire Insurance, Loans, Real Estate and Steamship Passage Agt, 103½ E Washington, h 54 Beaty.
Pfleger Elizabeth (wid Jacob), h 121 Davidson.
Pfleger Frank, mach, h 427 N Senate av.
Pfleger Frank F, lab, h 92 Keystone av.
Pfleger Henry, painter, b 121 Davidson.
Pfleger John, collr, b 27 Hermann.
Pfleger Joseph C, sewing mach, 174 E Washington, h 529 E Ohio.
Pfleger Leonard, rep, h 27 Hermann.
Pfleger Mary (wid Raymond), h 205 N State av.
Pfleging Conrad H, meats, 63 E Mkt House, h 309 Columbia av.
Pfleging Henry G A, boilermkr, b 309 Columbia av.
Pflueger George, gilder, b 236 Lincoln la.
Pflueger Joseph, carp, h 336 Lincoln la.
Pflueger Wm, lab, b 507 S West.
Pflueger Wm, horseshoer, r 169 W Market.
Pflumm John B, h 120 E Merrill.
Pflumm Oscar H, draughtsman City Civil Engineer's Office, h 227 Blackford.
Pfunder John, patternmkr, b 57 Yandes.
Phares Charles W, shoemkr, h 447 W Francis (N I).
Phares Emmett J, clk Murphy, Hibben & Co, h 30 Walcott.
Phares Eugene W, painter, h 548 LaSalle (M P).

COAL AND COKE
The W. G. Wasson Co.,
130 INDIANA AVE. TEL. 989
LIME AND LATH

Phares Martha (wid John J), h 548 LaSalle (M P).
Phebus Sarah A (wid George W), h 32½ Malott av.
Phebus Wm M, supt rest N Y Store, b 32½ Malott av.
Phelan Catherine (wid Patrick), h 369 Virginia av.
Phelan James P, b 369 Virginia av.
Phelan John, carp, h 59 Dawson.
Phelan John, switchman, h 55 Oriental.
Phelan Margaret A, bkkpr, b 61 Ft Wayne av.
Phelan Mary E, hair goods, 16½ E Washington, b 369 Virginia av.
Phelan Wm, boilermkr, h 184 Yandes.
Phelps Birdora, teacher, b 183 W New York.
Phelps Bros (Cavallie W and Samuel B), dry goods, 14 E Washington.
Phelps Cavallie W (Phelps Bros), h 225 E Walnut.
Phelps Charles W, condr, b 370 Virginia av.
Phelps Grace, clk, b 183 W New York.
Phelps Harry, cigars, 10 Monument pl, h s e cor 28th and Meridian.
Phelps John M, watchman, h 183 W New York.
Phelps Joseph A, lab, b 476 W New York.
Phelps John W, clk, b 183 W New York.
Phelps Linnie, dressmkr, 19½ N Meridian, h 183 W New York.
Phelps Mary A (wid Douglas), b 200 N Capitol av.
Phelps Milton A, lab, b 183 W New York.
Phelps Rolla M, b 7 Leota.
Phelps Samuel B (Phelps Bros), h 222 Ash.
Phelps Walter J, clk, b 183 W New York.
Phelps Walter S, mach, b 55 Bellefontaine.
Phelps Wm. H, lab, h 3 Lafayette.
Phemister Harry A, waiter, r 267 S Capitol av.
Pheneger Samuel B, lab, h w s Rural 3 n of Pope av.
PHILADELPHIA DYE HOUSE, Frank Iten Propr, 6 W Market.
Philipy Alice (wid Willard), b 284 Fletcher av.
Phillips Alexander, tmstr, h e s Manlove av 4 s of 17th.
Phillips Andrew J, carp, h 1414 Emma (N I).
Phillips Anna E (wid Wm A), h 195 N Delaware.
Phillips Arthur, coachman, r 154 Bird.
Phillips Benjamin F, lab, h 109 Orange.
Phillips Benjamin F, trav agt, h 246 Central av.
Phillips Byron J, collr, r 131 W Ohio.
Phillips Caleb S, agt United States, Pacific, B & O, and Wells Fargo & Co's Express, 23 S Meridian, h 471 N Penn.
Phillips Carrie (wid Bernhard), h 193 Virginia av.
Phillips Charles, engr, b 147 E Washington.
Phillips Charles E, condr, b 792 W Washington.
Phillips Charles O, carp, b 1414 Emma (N I).
Phillips Charles W, real est, 70 Monument pl, r 11 Halcyon blk.
Phillips Charlotte (wid Arthur), h 106 St Mary.
Phillips Cornelius B, mach hd, h 1080 W Vermont.
Phillips David M, lab, h 568 S West.
Phillips Edward, feed, 277½ Mass av, b 246 Central av.
Phillips Edward S, weigher, h 173 Blake.
Phillips Ella F (wid Charles), dressmkr, 648½ College av, h same.

W. H. MESSENGER COMPLETE HOUSE FURNISHER 101 East Washington Street, Telephone 491

Foundry and Pattern Shop } McNamara, Koster & Co. { PHONE 1593 212-218 S. Penn. St.

Phillips Elmer U, molder, h 472 W Ontario (N I).
Phillips Emanuel, lab, h 286 Spring.
Phillips Fannie E, assistant Dr G V Woolen, b 195 N Delaware.
Phillips Harry, lab, b 415 W 2d.
Phillips Harry B, canceling clk P O, b 10 Cornell av.
Phillips Harry W, cabtmkr, b 140 Lawrence.
Phillips Harry W, stenog Miller, Winter & Elam, b 76 N New Jersey.
Phillips Hattie, teacher Indiana Reformatory.
Phillips Henry, lab, h 192 N Missouri.
Phillips Henry B, carp, h 140 Lawrence.
Phillips Howard H, bkkpr, b 85 Beech.
Phillips Howard R, painter, r 161 E Ohio.
Phillips Hugh M, blksmith, h 685 E Washington.
Phillips Isaac N, lab, h 472 W Ontario (N I).
Phillips Jacob W, painter, h 828 Cornell av.
Phillips James, lab, h 103 Douglass.
Phillips James, lab, b 119 Kappus (W I).
Phillips James, lab, b n e cor 22d and Baltimore av.
Phillips James F, carp, h 44 Bellefontaine.
Phillips James F, tmstr, h 290 E Morris.
Phillips James N, tel opr, b 173 Blake.
Phillips James O, plastr, h 64 John.
Phillips Jennie, h 373 Lafayette.
Phillips Jennie A (wid Moses), h rear 73 Howard.
Phillips Jeremiah, waiter The Denison.
Phillips John, coachman 500 N Capitol av.
Phillips John, lab, b 245 W McCarty.
Phillips John, lab, h rear 18 W Michigan.
Phillips John P, ins agt, b 159½ E Washington.
Phillips John E, stage hd, b 5 Bates al.
Phillips John F, cabtmkr, h 145 Lynn av (W I).
Phillips John T, barber, r 58 N Illinois.
Phillips John W, lab, b 298 Fayette.
Phillips Joseph, bender, h 182 Harmon.
Phillips Josiah D, packer, h 582 W 22d (N I).
Phillips Leslie G, cook, r rear 18 W Michigan.
Phillips Levi A, clk, h 178 Bellefontaine.
Phillips Lois (wid Jacob), h 415 W 2d.
Phillips Mary E, laundress, b 156 S Noble.
Phillips Monroe J, examiner, r 174 E Washington.
Phillips Moses, tmstr, h s s Clifford av 2 e of Rural.
Phillips Moulton, lab, h 568 S West.
Phillips Nelson, feed, 20 S West, h 412 Addison (N I).
Phillips Nettie, nurse, b 197 N Delaware.
Phillips Ora, clk, r 119 E New York.
Phillips Philander E, contr, h 85 Beech.
Phillips Rhoda (wid Charles), h 284 Blackford.
Phillips Rufus, clk, r 2 Columbia blk.
Phillips Samuel (Phillips & Patterson), h 246 Central av.
Phillips Samuel, lab, b 225 W Vermont.
Phillips Sarah R (wid Richard), h 1080 W Vermont.
Phillips Squire C, carp, h 1066 W Vermont.
Phillips Susan J (wid Thomas), h 58 N Illinois.
Phillips Theodore, clk, h 142 Brookside av.
Phillips Thomas M, ins, h 321 Orange.
Phillips Virgil C, fireman Grand Hotel.
Phillips Warren, trav agt, h 65 E 26th.
Philips Wm, b 125½ Hadley av (W I).

Henry H. Fay,
40½ E. WASHINGTON ST.,
AGENT FOR
Insurance Co. of North America,
Pennsylvania Fire Ins. Co.

Phillips Wm, lab, b 234 Muskingum al.
Phillips Wm A, clk L S Ayres & Co, h 173 E Vermont.
Phillips Wm H, blksmith, b 58 N Illinois.
Phillips Wm H H, carp, h 10 Cornell av.
Phillips & Pattison (Samuel Phillips, Joseph H Pattison), clothing mnfrs, 198 S Penn.
Phinkston James A, lab, h 9 Center.
Phinney, see also Finney.
Phinney Claude E, mach, h 60 S Summit.
Phinney Edwin W, engr, h 66 N Arsenal av.
Phinney Francis A, mach, h 66 Gregg.
Phipps Charles, finisher, b 121 W Maryland.
Phipps Charles W, carp, h 110 Woodburn av (W I).
Phipps Edward, printer, b 110 Woodburn av (W I).
Phipps Harriet J, teacher, b 110 Woodburn av (W I).
Phipps Harry F, tel opr, r 1094 W Washington.
Phipps Kate F (wid Henry C), nurse, 150½ College av, h same.
Phipps Margaret E, dressmkr, 110 Woodburn av, h same.
Phipps Miles W, lab, b e s Daisy 1 n of Ream.
Phoenix Mutual Life Insurance Co, Edwin S Folsom gen agt, 34 Mass av.
PHYSIO-MEDICAL COLLEGE OF INDIANA, Nathan D Woodard Pres of Faculty, Collins T Bedford Sec of Faculty, n w cor North and Alabama.
Physio-Medical Journal, George Hasty editor and pub, 35 W Ohio.
Phythian Robert L, clk, h 21 Omer.
Piant George E (Guarantee Roofing Co), b Enterprise Hotel.
Piatt Richard F, trav agt J B Allfree Mnfg Co, h 702 Park av.
Picard Frank J, clk, h 132 Woodlawn av.
Picard John C, clk, b 132 Woodlawn av.
Pich Alfred M, stencil cutter, h 601 S Meridian.
Pich Frederick W, tailor, 62 Nebraska, h same.

Union Casualty & Surety Co.
of St. Louis, Mo.
Employers', Public, General, Teams and Elevator Liability; also Workmen's Collective, Steam Boiler, Plate Glass and Automatic Sprinkler Insurance.
W. E. BARTON & CO., General Agents,
504 Indiana Trust Building.
LONG DISTANCE TELEPHONE 1918.

THE FRED DIETZ CO || WOODEN PACKING BOX ES MADE TO ORDER FACTORY AND WAREHOUSE TRUCKS. 40 Madison Avenue. Telephone 65.

Shorthand! BUSINESS UNIVERSITY. When Bl'k. Elevator day and night. Typewriting, Penmanship, Book-keeping, Office Training free. See page 4. Est. 1850. Tel. 499. E. J. HEEB, Proprietor.

HENRY R. WORTHINGTON JET and SURFACE CONDENSERS 64 S. PENN. ST. Long Distance Telephone 284.

UNION CO-OPERATIVE LAUNDRY (COMPOSED OF UNION LAUNDRY GIRLS.) NOS. 138, 140 AND 142 VIRGINIA AVENUE. T. E. SOMERVILLE, MANAGER. TELEPHONE 1269. INDIANAPOLIS, IND.

HORACE M. HADLEY
REAL ESTATE AND LOANS....
66 East Market Street
Telephone 1540. BASEMENT.

Pich Martha M, teacher Public School No 28, b 62 Nebraska.
Pickard John W, photog, h 87 W 14th.
Pickard Victor, b 649½ Virginia av.
Pickart Joseph, artist, 237 N Illinois, h same.
Pickcupp James H, foreman George Merritt & Co, h 66 Camp.
Pickel Walter, lab, b 48 Northwestern av.
Picken John, sec and treas U S Encaustic Tile Wks, h 1106 N Capitol av.
Pickens Angeline (wid Edward), h 53 Johnson av.
Pickens Benjamin F, boilermkr, b 43 Tacoma av.
Pickens Rush F, b 511 N New Jersey.
Pickens Samuel O (Chambers, Pickens & Moores), h 511 N New Jersey.
Pickens Wm, lab, b 41 N Beville av.
Pickens Wm A (Pickens & Cox), h 592 Park av.
PICKENS & COX (Wm A Pickens, Linton A Cox), Lawyers, 109-111 Commercial Club Bldg, Tel 879.
Pickerill Blanche M, stenog Rehm & Van Deinse), b 474 Ash.
Pickerill Frank A, photog, h 13 N Reisner (W I).
Pickerill Wm N, lawyer, 33-36 Thorpe blk, h 474 Ash.
Pickering Elizabeth (wid Augustus), b 279 E North.
Pickett Edward H, polisher, b 49 Helen.
Pickett Elizabeth B, teacher, b 1196 N Meridian.
Pickett Isaac B, agt Brown-Manly Plow Co, h 1040 N New Jersey.
Pickett Joel W, coal, h 49 Helen.
Pickett Joseph H, tel opr, b 209 Hadley av (W I).
Pickett Michael, cooper, b 191 S Pine.
Pickett Thomas H, gasfitter, h w s Sherman Drive 2 s of Brookville rd (S).
Pickett Wilbur, clk, b 49 Helen.
Pickett Wm, lab, b 191 S Pine.
Pickle Wm P, clk, b 170 E St Joseph.
Pickrin Ferdinand, lab, h 181 W 7th.
Piehl Nicholas, lab, b 673 Union.
Piel, see also Peehl and Feelle.

Merchants' and Manufacturers Exchange
Make Collections and Commercial Reports......
J. E. TAKKEN, MANAGER,
19 Union Building, 73 West Maryland Street

Piel Anton J, lab, b 125 Williams.
Piel Charles F, supt The Natl Starch Mnfg Co and treas Indpls Mnfg Co, b 706 E Washington.
Piel Christian F, foreman, h 1038 E Michigan.
Piel Hannah L, h 125 William.
Piel Henry W, asst mngr The Natl Starch Mnfg Co, h 700 E Washington.
Piel Wm F, pres The Indiana Dry Goods Co and mngr The Natl Starch Mnfg Co, h 645 E Washington.
Piel Wm H, baker, b 125 William.
Pieper Wm, gardener, h 1195 S Meridian.
Pieper Wm F, gardener, h 756 Shelby.
Pieper Wm H C, gardener, b 756 Shelby.
Pierce, see also Pearce and Peirce.
Pierce Benjamin C (Pierce & Ingersoll), r 27½ Monument pl.
Pierce Benjamin F, shoemkr, h 404 Virginia av.
Pierce Beriah N, editor Fanciers' Gazette, h 29 Hudson.
Pierce Burt N, pres Fanciers' Gazette Co, b 29 Hudson.
Pierce Caroline E (wid John), h 21 E St Joseph.
Pierce Charles, harnessmkr, h 103 S Reisner (W I).
Pierce Charles C, agt Merchants' Despatch Transp Co, 24 S Penn, h 442 College av.
PIERCE CHARLES C JR, Vice-Pres and Genl Mngr Meridian Life and Trust Company, h 271 E St Clair.
Pierce Chesteen C, harnessmkr, b 37 S McLain (W I).
Pierce Clyde, lab, b 242 S Senate av.
Pierce Dock, lab, h 166 Minerva.
Pierce Edward, motorman, h 380 Columbia av.
PIERCE ELIZABETH V (Mrs Henry Douglas Pierce), Treas Indianapolis Propylaeum, Office and Res, 725 N Meridian.
Pierce Elmo M, mason, h 18 Garland (W I).
Pierce Frank, fireman, h 19 Decatur.
Pierce Frank M, fireman, h 50 Marion av (W I).
Pierce Frederick, stenog, b 302 N Delaware.
Pierce George, painter, h 242 S Senate av.
Pierce George W, painter, h 13 Woodlawn av.
Pierce Henry, shoemkr, h 1 Water.
PIERCE HENRY DOUGLAS (formerly Turpie & Pierce), Lawyer, United States Commissioner, Notary Public, 18½ N Meridian, Rooms 11, 12, 13 and 13½, h 725 N Meridian.
Pierce James, tmstr, h 177 N Liberty.
Pierce James E, contr agt Merchants' Despatch Transp Co, 24 S Penn, h 1027 N New Jersey.
Pierce James G, porter, b 175 S Illinois.
Pierce Jeremiah B, confr, 658 Virginia av, h same.
Pierce Jesse, electrician, r 100 N Alabama.
Pierce John W, fruits, r E Franklin blk.
Pierce Josephine, milliner, 404 Virginia av, h same.
Pierce Margaret (wid Ephraim), h rear 82 Yandes.
Pierce Martin, engr, h 49 Ash.
Pierce Mary A (wid Benjamin F), h 58 Geisendorff.
Pierce Mary E (wid Wm), h 110 Chadwick.
Pierce Minola J (wid John E), b 37 Bates.
Pierce Nathan, janitor, h 615 N Senate av.

CLEMENS VONNEGUT 184, 186 and 192 E. Washington St. | Wire Rope, Machinery, Lathes, Drills and Shapers

THE WM. H. BLOCK CO. DRY GOODS, DRAPERIES, RUGS, WINDOW SHADES.
7 AND 9 EAST WASHINGTON STREET.

Pierce Oliver W, sec Metropolitan School of Music, r 81½ W Market.
Pierce Richard (McNamara, Koster & Co), h 179 W South.
Pierce Richard, lab, h 273 Keystone av.
Pierce Ruby C, stenog Gage & Boyd, b 21 E St Joseph.
Pierce Thornton, lab, r 211½ E Washington.
Pierce Warren, lab, b 273 Keystone av.
Pierce Wesley, foreman Sentinel Printing Co, h 483 W Walnut av (N I).
Pierce Wesley, lather, h 105½ Mass av.
Pierce Wiley, lab, b 273 Keystone av.
Pierce Wm, tailor, b 615 N Senate av.
Pierce Wm C, printer, b 29 Hudson.
Pierce Wm H, molder, h 8 Thalman.
Pierce Wm H, shoemkr, b 1 Water.
Pierce & Ingersoll (Benjamin C Pierce, Albert E Ingersoll), dentists, 27½ Monument pl.
Piercy, see also Pearcy.
Piercy Frank, lab, h 221 S West.
Piercy Joseph W, exchange editor The Indpls News, h 117 E Michigan.
Piersall John H, painter, h 225 N Noble.
Pierson, see also Pearson.
Pierson Abraham M, carp, h 641 W Vermont.
Pierson Addison E, clk, b 172 N Senate av.
Pierson Albert E, city fireman, b 548 E Washington.
Pierson Albert S, clk Lilly & Stalnaker, b 978 N Penn.
Pierson Alfred, mach, h 681 W Addison (N I).
Pierson August, storekpr, h 4 Emerson pl.
Pierson Charles, lab, h 200 Agnes.
Pierson Charles A, clk L S Ayres & Co, h 534 College av.
Pierson Charles E, painter, h 18 Columbia av.
Pierson Charles H, grocer, 125 S Noble, h same.
Pierson Charles, bricklyr, b 402 Broadway.
Pierson Chiron C (J C Pierson & Son), h 22 W 14th.
Pierson David W, grocer, 304 W Maryland, h same.
Pierson Edwin H, mach, h 629 E Ohio.
Pierson Frank, bkkpr, b 79 N Olive.
Pierson Harry D, clk Robert Zener & Co, b 629 E Ohio.
Pierson Henry J, painter, h 97 Columbia av.
Pierson James, brickmkr, b 567 S Illinois.
Pierson James, carp, h 433 E Vermont.
Pierson John, broommkr, h 79 N Olive.
Pierson John C (J C Pierson & Son), h 1099 N Meridian.
Pierson John H, tmstr, h 567 S Illinois.
Pierson John W, lab, h 47 S McLain (W I).
Pierson Joseph P, lab, h 26 Brett.

PIERSON J C & SON (John C and Chiron C), Genl Contractors, 2 Builders' Exchange, Tel 535.

Pierson Levi S, h 402 Broadway.
Pierson Margaret A (wid Charles D), nurse, 39 Detroit, h same.
Pierson Martin E, h 548 E Washington.
Pierson Meade W, bkkpr Elmer E Nichols Co, h 23½ Osgood (W I).
Pierson Myrtle, stenog Central Rubber and Supply Co, b 1091 W Washington.
Pierson Olna, lab, b 567 S Illinois.
Pierson Ora C, b 402 Broadway.
Pierson Otis A, confr, b 133 Wright.
Pierson Otto C, mixer, b 304 W Maryland.
Pierson Peter, coachman 34 W 2d.

Pierson Preston, watchman, h 1091 W Washington.
Pierson Samuel D, cigars, 12 N Penn, h 181 E St Clair.
Pierson Stephen E, plastr, h 608 Miller av (M J).
Pierson Wm, collarmkr, h 179 Bradley.
Pierson Wm T, clk, r 172 N Senate av.
Pierson Wm T, student, h 252 W Michigan.
Piery Charles E, lab, r rear 110 English av.
Pietsch August, bartndr, b 201 Mass av.
Pietzuch John M, bkkpr, b 14 West Drive (W P).
Pigg Charles D, painter, h 275 Cedar.
Pigg James M, carp, h 105 English av.
Pigg Thomas, lab, h 84 Nebraska.
Pigney Jennie (wid John), b 270 N California.
Pike Daniel D, grocer, n s Washington av 1 w of Ritter av (I), h same.
Pike Elmer S, mach, h 359 Fletcher av.
Pike Frank B, lab, b 84 Maple.
Pillet Charles I, mach, b 442 Bellefontaine.
Pillet Edwin R, typewriter, h 442 Bellefontaine.
Pillet Frank H, clk Order of Chosen Friends, h 442 Bellefontaine.
Pillet Frank H jr, clk, b 442 Bellefontaine.
Pinchin Eugene A, bkkpr, r 385 N Illinois.
Pindar John H, condr, h 27 Temple av.
Pine Albert H, embalmer Charles T Whitsett, h 185½ N Senate av.
Pingpank Carl F, books, 7 S Alabama, h 74 N Liberty.
Pingpank Elise, teacher Public School No 32, b 74 N Liberty
Pink Gustav, saloon, 196 Indiana av, h same.

PINK HERMAN, Physician, Office Hours 2-4 P M and 7-8 P M, Sunday Evenings Excepted, 103 N Meridian, h same, Tel 927.

Pink Julius, clk, b 196 Indiana av.
Pink Louis, clk, r 402 S Delaware.
Pink Ricke, pres Pink Shoe Mnfg Co, h 131 N East.

GUIDO R. PRESSLER,
FRESCO PAINTER
Churches, Theaters, Public Buildings, Etc., A Specialty.
Residence, No. 325 North Liberty Street
INDIANAPOLIS, IND.

INDIANAPOLIS STEEL ROOFING AND CORRUGATING WORKS, 23 and 25 East South Street. S. D. NOEL, Proprietor.

David S. McKernan, Rooms 2-5 Thorpe Block.
REAL ESTATE AND LOANS
A number of choice pieces for subdivision, or for manufacturers' sites, with good switch facilities.

DIAMOND WALL PLASTER { Telephone 1410 BUILDERS' EXCHANGE.

UNION TRANSFER AND STORAGE CO. Cor. E. Ohio St. and C., C., C. & St. L. R'y Tracks. BRICK WAREHOUSE; CLEANEST AND SAFEST STORAGE IN CITY FOR HOUSEHOLD GOODS AND MERCHANDISE.

W. McWORKMAN,

METAL CEILINGS,
ROLLING SHUTTERS,
DOORS AND PARTITIONS.

930 W. Washington St. Tel. 1118.

Pink Shoe Mnfg Co, Ricke Pink pres, Louis Beaupre vice-pres, Simon Pink sec and treas, 25 E South.
Pink Simon, sec and treas Pink Shoe Mnfg Co, h 131 N East.
Pintzke Charles A, uphlr, b 487 S Missouri.
Pintzke Ferdinand, molder, h 23 Sinker.
Pintzke Gustav, uphlr, b 79 Kansas.
Pintzke Henry A, mach hd, h 79 Kansas.
Pintzke John G, watchman, h 487 S Missouri.
Pinyerd Uriah R, foreman J B Allfree Mnfg Co, b 137 Highland pl.
PIONEER BRASS WORKS, John H Brinkmeyer Pres, Charles C Miller Vice-Pres, Frederick A W Davis Sec, Brass Founders and Finishers, 110-116 S Penn, Tel 618.
Piper Elder W, livery, rear 642 N Illinois, h same.
Piper James C, engr Monument, h 911 Bellefontaine.
Piper Jay C, photog Marceau & Bassett, h 923 S Meridian.
Piper Margaret, h rear 108 Minerva.
Piper Wm E, agt, r 224 N Senate av.
Pipes Charles, blksmith, 517 Shelby, h e s Madeira 3 s of Prospect.
Pippert August A, lab, b 640 Chestnut.
Pippert Henry A, bartndr, b 640 Chestnut.
Pippert John, lab, h 640 Chestnut.
Pirkey Jacob H, consulting engr L E & W R R, r 185 N Delaware.
Piscator August, grinder, 86 E Georgia, r 354 S Meridian.
Piscator August jr, lab, r 354 S Meridian.
Piscator Henry, grinder, r 354 S Meridian.
Piscator Nettie, nurse, b 28 N West.
Piscator Peter, grinder, r 210½ S Meridian.
Piscator Rose, nurse 124 N Alabama.
Pitman Harry C, clk A Kiefer Drug Co, r 311 The Shiel.
Pitman Luella, stenog The Indpls Stove Co, b 691 N Capitol av.
Pitsenberger Harry M, condr, h 29 Sheffield av (H).
Pittman Frank C, carp, b 11 Cornell av.

SEALS,
STENCILS,
STAMPS, Etc.
GEO. J. MAYER
15 S. Meridian St.
TELEPHONE 1386.

Pittman Frank H (G S Pittman & Son), h 439 E Georgia.
Pittman Gideon, carp, h 66 Morton.
Pittman Greenup S (G S Pittman & Son), h 437 E Georgia.
Pittman G S & Son (Greenup S and Frank H), grocers, 439 E Georgia.
Pittman James, lab, h 89 Camp.
Pittman James, tailor, h 262 W 6th.
Pittman Wm I, engr, b 171 Woodlawn av.
Pitts Amanda E, b 3 Henry.
Pitts Dora B (wid James), b 14 Lynn.
Pitts Edgar E, waiter, b 143 E Washington.
Pitts Frank, lab, h 109 Trowbridge (W).
Pitts George W, h 695 N Senate av.
Pitts Harry, driver, r 120 E Wabash.
Pitts John H, lab, r 78 Yandes.
Pitts Minnie, h 22 Center.
Pitzer Frank A, driver, h 422 N Senate av.
Pitzer Lewis A, photog, b 263 N Senate av.
Pitzer Mary B (wid Andrew B), h 263 N Senate av.
Pitzer Watson B, clk, b 263 N Senate av.
Place Homer V, architect, h 55 William.
Place Margaret S (wid Ransom L), b 1197 N Capitol av.
Plain Ernest B, lab, h w s Line 1 s of P C C & St L Ry (I).
Plake, see also Blake.
Plake Joseph D, boilermkr, h 194 Kentucky av.
Plank August H, engr, h 515 S Meridian.
Planque Frank M, music teacher, r 291 E Ohio.
Plant Margaret (wid George T), h 282 Christian av.
Plasterer Purl C, optician, 56 N Penn, h 464 N Alabama.
Platt Edwin C, clk Indiana Car Service Assn, r 36 The Windsor.
Platt Frank W, mngr 11-13 E Washington, r 217 N Capitol av.
Platt Harry, waiter, r 42½ Kentucky av.
Platt Morris H, lather, r 138 E Pratt.
Platt Oliver S, trav agt, b 54 Arbor av (W I).
Platt Orrin W, painter, b 357 S West.
Platt Wm, mach, h 46 N Belmont av (H).
Platte Charles, attendant Insane Hospital.
Platter Amelia W, teacher High School, r 37 The Wyandot.
Platter Frank C, clk, b 162 N Noble.
Platter Herbert T, trav agt Pearson & Wetzel, h 162 N Noble.
Platterbald James, lab, b 8 W 8th.
Playfoot Albert E, blksmith, h 799 Mass av.
Plaza The, 16-24 Monument pl.
Pleckenbaum Albert, fireman, h 33 Elder av.
PLESCHNER CHARLES, Mnfr of and Dealer in Fine Harness, Saddles, Etc, 163 E Washington, h 1237 N Illinois. (See adv in classified Harness Mnfrs.)
Pleschner Maud A, bkkpr Robert Zener & Co, b 1237 N Illinois.
Pletzer Joseph, grocer, 591 Madison av, h same.
Plew Isaac C, h 887 LaSalle (M P).
Plew John L, lab, b 887 LaSalle (M P).
Plew Robert, agt, b 887 LaSalle (M P).
Plew Thomas S, lab, h 887 LaSalle (M P).
Ploch Frederick, foreman, b 293 E Ohio.
Ploeger Christian, pressman, b 318 N Noble.
Ploeger Gustav P, clk, b 476 W Francis (N I).
Ploeger John C, carp, h 318 N Noble.
Ploeger Wm J, mach, b 318 N Noble.

A. METZGER AGENCY ESTABLISHED 1863. INSURANCE

LAMBERT GAS & GASOLINE ENGINE CO.
ANDERSON, IND. PORTABLE GASOLINE ENGINES. 2 TO 25 H. P.

BICYCLES $5 DOWN. $1 Best Terms. Bet Wheels. WHEELMEN'S CO. 31 W. OHIO ST. LONG DISTANCE TEL. 1855.

Plogsterth Catherine (wid Victor), h 275 Davidson.
Plogsterth Louis W, clk, b 275 Davidson.
Plowden Martha, h 171 W 2d.
Plum Edwin A, trav agt Home Cracker Co, h 21 The Blacherne.
Plum John H, mngr Home Cracker Co, 192 S Meridian, h 998 N Alabama.
Plum John H jr, city agt Home Cracker Co, b 998 N Alabama.
Plumb Catherine (wid Joseph C), b 585 N Delaware.
Plumb Hiram H, trav agt, h 65 W Michigan.
Plummer Albert R, molder, h 123 Tremont av (H).
Plummer Benjamin F, ironwkr, h 67 Columbia av.
Plummer Charles F, painter, b 92 Greer.
Plummer Edward, condr, h 161 Columbia av.
Plummer Edwin L, draughtsman Nordyke & Marmon Co, b 96 N Alabama.
Plummer Flora B (wid Benjamin), h 56 Brookside av.
Plummer Harry, chief clk local frt office L N A & C Ry, h 171 E St Joseph.
Plummer Harry H, trav agt, b 122 Cornell av.
Plummer Hiram, real est, 93 E Market, h 122 Cornell av.
Plummer Homer L, lab, b 36 Bismarck av (H).
Plummer James W, lab, b 67 Columbia av.
Plummer James W, lab, h w s Walker 3 s of Pendleton av (B).
Plummer John T, clk, b 122 Cornell av.
Plummer Louisa (wid Gardner H), h 962 N Alabama.
Plummer Sylvester, switchman, h 52 Newman.
Plummer Wm, mach, b 32 Kansas.
Plummer Wm F, mach hd, b e s Rural 2 n of Brookside av.
Plummer Wm H, barber, h 794 W Washington.
Plummer Wm H H, finisher, h e s Rural 2 n of Brookside av.

PLUNKETT MELANCHTHON D, Propr Capital Steam Carpet Cleaning Works, s w cor 9th and Lenox (Big Four R R), h same. (See right bottom lines and adv in classified Carpet Cleaners.)

Plunkett Peter, lab, h 42 Cora.
Plymate Earl E, clk, b 796½ N Alabama.
Plymate John T, h 796½ N Alabama.
Plymouth Savings and Loan Assn, Edward Gilbert sec, 44½ N Penn.
Poe Ambrose, lab, h 60 Bismarck (W I).
Poe George M (Slatts & Poe), loans, 24 Ingalls blk, b Spencer House.
Poe Jacob F, sub letter carrier P O, h 22 Elder av.
Poe John W, h 237 Kentucky av.
Poe Louisa (wid Henry J), h rear 323 N Illinois.
Poe Susan (wid George), b 27 N Spruce.
Poe Walter, clk, h 185 River av (W I).
Poehler Anna (wid Louis C A), h 51 Gresham.
Poehler Christian, lab, h 124 Wright.
Poehler Christian F W, lab, h 780 S East.
Poehler Christian F W jr, finisher, h 54 Laurel.
Poehler Frederick W, supt The A Burdsal Co, h 31 Madison av.
Poehler Henry C F, uphlr, b 51 Gresham.

Farm and City Loans
25 Years' Successful Business.
THOS. C. DAY & CO,
Rooms 325 to 330 Lemcke Building.

Poehler Henry F, foreman C C C & St L Ry, h 64 Tacoma av.
Poehler Henry F, saloon, 297 Prospect, b 124 Wright.
Poehler Louis F, saddler, h 72 Johnson av.
Poehler Louis W, mach, b 124 Wright.
Poehler Louisa (wid Louis), b 64 Tacoma av.
Poehler Nicholas, uphlr, h 49 Gresham.
Poehler Wilhelmina (wid Wm F), h 197 Minnesota.
Poehler Wm F, lab, b 64 Tacoma av.
Poehler Wm H, clk, h 1002 W Washington.
Poenitz Robert F, lab, h 443 Harrison av.
Poer Muratt J Q, molder, h 78 N Belmont (H).
Poffinbarger Hiram, carp, 82 S Reisner (W I), h same.
Poggemeyer Frank, shoemkr, 114 N Pine, h same.
Poggemeyer John H, shoes, 492 E Washington, h same.
Pohlkotte Henry B, printer, h 139 Union.
Pohlkotte Henry C, mason, h 208 Highland av.
Pohlkotte John F, lab, b 208 Highland av.
Pohlman, see also Paulman.
Pohlman Gustave E, r 408 N New Jersey.
Pohlman John (Woodford & Pohlman), h 109 N Capitol av.
Pohlmann Julius, finisher, h 193 Lincoln la.
Poindexter Charles C, toolmkr, h 963 Cornell av.
Poindexter Robert E, mach, 25 Eddy, h 943 Ash.
Poiner Newton J, lab, h 634 W Udell (N I).
Pointer David T Rev, b 239 Shelby.
Pointer Louis, brakeman, b 29 N State av.
Pointer Mary J (wid James F), h 180 W Vermont.
Poirier Charles C, molder, h 32 Villa av.
Poirier Harry J, mach, b 32 Villa av.
Poirier John B, clk R M S, h 26 Lynn av (W I).
Poirier Wm H, city fireman, h 82 Barth av.
Poischenk Egid, lab, h s s Pansy 2 w of Floral av.
Poisel James W, lab, h 31 Everett.

EAT
QUAKER BREAD
ASK YOUR GROCER FOR IT.
THE HITZ BAKING CO.

J. H. TECKENBROCK House, Sign and Fresco Painter, 94 EAST SOUTH STREET.

FIDELITY MUTUAL LIFE PHILADELPHIA, PA. A. H. COLLINS, Gen. Agt. Baldwin Blk. RATES REASONABLE. SOUND BEYOND QUESTION. BUSINESS-LIKE IN PRACTICE.

Edwards ort Coal and Mining Company ROOMS 42 AND 43 WHEN BUILDING. BITUMINOUS COAL

ESTABLISHED 1876. TELEPHONE 168.
CHESTER BRADFORD,
SOLICITOR OF PATENTS,
AND COUNSEL IN PATENT CAUSES.
(See adv. page 6.)
Office:—Rooms 14 and 16 Hubbard Block, S. W. Cor. Washington and Meridian Streets, INDIANAPOLIS, INDIANA.

Poland Elizabeth H (wid Nicholas), h 40 N California.
Poland John, lab, b 40 N California.
Poland John, sale stable, 222 W Pearl, h rear 223 W Washington.
Poland Luther F, lab, b 95 Bradshaw.
Poland Nicholas, driver, h 64 Oliver av (W I).
Poland Wm B, asst engr m of w C C C & St L Ry, r 26 Ft Wayne av.
POLAR ICE CO, Wm P Jungclaus Pres, Lorenz Schmidt Vice-Pres, John B Ittenbach Sec, John W Schmidt Treas, Henry L Dithmer Mngr, 175-179 E Wabash, Tel 819.
Polasky Isaac, mattress mnfr, 407 S Delaware, h 289 E South.
Polcar Wm J, h 21 Meek.
Polen Albert, lab, b 37 William.
Polen Charles R, lab, h 2 Dawson.
Polen Frank, lab, b 308 E Court.
Polen John N, lab, h 37 William.
Polen Luther E, policeman Union Station, h 1107 E Ohio.
Police Station, s e cor Alabama and Pearl.
Polish Rudolph, mach, h 72 Dunlop.
Polk James T, propr Polk's Milk Depot, 325 E 7th, res Greenwood, Ind.
Polk John A, pres Indpls, Greenwood & Franklin R R, res Greenwood, Ind.
Polk John G, driver, h 28 King.
Polk Mary, b 117 Columbia al.
POLK'S MILK DEPOT, James T Polk Propr, Samuel O Dungan Mngr, 325 E 7th, Tel 1334.
Polk Paul, agt, h 118 N Meridian.
POLK R L & CO, Publishers Indianapolis City and Indiana State Directories, Rooms 23-24 Journal Bldg; Directories of all the States and Principal Cities on File for Reference. (See adv back fly leaf.)
Polk Wm E, depot agt Adams Ex Co, h 32 Sanders.
Poll Leonard, engr, b 185 W Washington.
Pollard Abraham N, tmstr, h 11 Cleveland (H).

BUY THE BEST.
Outing BICYCLES $85
MADE BY
HAY & WILLITS MFG CO.
76 N. PENN. ST. Phone 598.

Pollard Adam C, engr, h 230 S West.
Pollard Alva A, motorman, h 504 W Shoemaker (N I).
Pollard Arthur M, lab, b 504 W Shoemaker (N I).
Pollard Charles S, carp, h e s Commercial av 7 s of Washington av (I).
Pollard Daniel F, lab, h 564 W Addison (N I).
Pollard George T, painter, h n s Washington av 1 w of Ritter av (I).
Pollard Grant, lab, h 441 W Francis (N I).
Pollard Levi B, lab, h 408 S Meridian.
Pollard Marion, tmstr, h 7 Lexington av.
Pollard Sarah A (wid David), b 444 N New Jersey.
Pollard Theodore, car rep, h 128 Sheffield av (H).
Pollard Wm M, painter, h e s Commercial av 5 s of Washington av (I).
Pollester Franklin, finisher, h 60 Tremont av (H).
Pollex Ernestina (wid Henry), b 7 Iowa.
Pollitt Charles F, stenog Kingan & Co (ltd), b 512 Park av.
Pollitt Eliza (wid Francis M), h 512 Park av.
Pollock Cleveland C, lab, h 294½ Mass av.
Pollock Edward S, driver, h 215 N Senate av.
Pollock George S, trav agt, h 224 Ash.
Pollock Israel, janitor, h 129 Maple.
Pollock John G, train disp P C C & St L Ry, h 1162 N Alabama.
Pollock John L, millwright, h 57 Muskingum al.
Pollock Joseph, lab, h 23 Bates al.
Pollock Mary E, stenog, b 235 S Noble.
Pollock Ora O, cigarmkr, b 57 Muskingum al.
Pollock Stephen O, cigarmkr, h 93 Bright.
Pollock Walter J, clk, b 1162 N Alabama.
Polster Charles, saloon, 149 Indiana av, h same.
Polster Frederick, saloon, 144 Indiana av, h same.
Polster Philip, printer The Indpls Sentinel, h 266 Bright.
Pomeroy Eva (wid Samuel), h 567½ Virginia av.
Pomeroy Harry C, lab, h 567½ Virginia av.
POMEROY HENRY C, Druggist, 50 N Penn, Tel 114, h 114 St Mary.
Pomeroy James R, carp, h 969 Grove av.
Pomeroy Roy S, foreman, h 85 Woodburn av (W I).
Pomeroy Wm T, lab, b 215 Virginia av.
Pommerening August G, driver, h 449 S East.
Ponsler Charles, carp, h 90 Deloss.
Pontius Walter, driver, b 78 N Illinois.
Pool Emma (wid Willis), h 41 Guffin.
Pool Frank, lab, b 128 Columbia al.
Pool George W, hostler, b 336 Superior.
Pool James P, carp, 72 E Court, h 1423 Rader (N I).
Pool John E, lab, h 135 Howard.
Poole Adoniram J, plumber, 1553 N Illinois, h same.
Poole Bertram, packer Eli Lilly & Co, h 22 Sinker.
Poole Charles, motorman, b 1059 N Capitol av.
Poole Edward R, plumber, h 168 W Morris.
Poole Emily H, dry goods, 1553 N Illinois, h same.
Poole Frank R, h 134 E St Clair.
Poole Harriet C (wid Ambrose), b 1553 N Illinois.

ROOFING MATERIAL C. ZIMMERMAN & SONS, SLATE AND GRAVEL ROOFERS, 19 SOUTH EAST STREET.

PUMPS Chain Pumps, Driven Wells and Deep Water Wells. Repairing Neatly Done. Cisterns Built. CHARLES KRAUSS', 42 S. PENN. ST. TELEPHONE 465.

Collars and Cuffs Laundered in Best of Style. Dull or High Gloss Finish. ERTEL STEAM LAUNDRY 26 and 28 N. Senate Ave. Telephone 1089.

Poole Harry J, barber, h 132 N Alabama.
Poole John, molder, b 524 Bellefontaine.
Poole John E, h 231 Orange.
Poole Mary, dressmkr, 134 E St Clair, h same.
Poole Mary H, b 1553 N Illinois.
Poole Thomas J, porter, h 19 Wood.
Poole Wilmot S, clk, b 1553 N Illinois.
Pooley Frank R, clk, r 87 E Market.
Poor Aurelius P, h 1101 N Senate av.
Poor Emma, h n s Michigan 6 e of Sherman Drive.
Poor Henry, mach, h 139 Fayette.
Poore Charles L, clk, r 10, 16 McCrea.
Poore Marion A, mach, h 378 W 1st.
Poore Nellie M (wid Herbert M), h 28 Oxford.
Poore Patrick H, trav agt, h 861 Bellefontaine.
Poorman, see also Purman.
Poorman David S, collr Noblesville Milling Co, h 31 Fletcher av.
Pope Amos S, janitor, h 35½ Kentucky av.
Pope Christian F, dry goods, 128 Prospect, h same.
Pope Edward S, farmer, h 235 Blackford.
Pope Frederick W, blksmith, h 66 Sanders.
Pope George K, b 235 Blackford.
Pope George W, h 227 Elm.
Pope Harriet (wid John), b 149 Geisendorff.
Pope Harry J, collr The Indpls News, b 195 N West.
Pope Henry D, car insp, h 192 Prospect.
Pope Henry T, patrolman, h 195 N West.
Pope James, lab, h 436 W Chicago (N I).
Pope James P, patrolman, h 108 Elm.
Pope John, porter, b 131 Douglass.
Pope John F, driver, b 149 Geisendorff.
Pope Joseph P, cashr Hildebrand Hardware Co, h 529 Broadway.
Pope Robert A, h 75 Broadway.
Pope Sarah (wid Philip), h 218 Howard.
Pope Wm, lab, h rear s s Ohio 4 e of Watts.
Pope Wm, insp, h 2 Weghorst.
POPP GEORGE R, Teas and Fancy Groceries, 31 N Penn, Tel 119; h 178 Madison av.
Popp John, grocer, 24 English av, h same.
Popp Michael A, baker, 621 S Meridian, h same.
Poppa Eli, blksmith, h 10 Langley av.
Poppa George W, coremkr, h e s Colorado av 2 n of Ohio.
Poppe Frederick, lab, h 98 S Reisner (W I).
Poppe Wm, h 558 Virginia av.
Poppe Wm O, clk, b 558 Virginia av.
Poppenseaker August W, mach hd, h 585 W Shoemaker (N I).
Poppenseaker Gottlieb, h 682 W Fremont (N I).
Poppie Charles B, trunkmkr, b 432 N California.
Poppie Edward F, bookbndr, b 432 N California.
Poppie Mary A (wid John B), h 432 N California.
Poppie Wm G, ruler, b 432 N California.
Porr John, tailor, h 157 Davidson.
Porr Otto G, painter, b 331 W Ontario (N I).
Porr Valentine, cabtmkr, h 331 W Ontario (N I).
Porr Wm F, painter, b 331 W Ontario (N I).
Porsche Henry C, bookbndr, h 505½ S Capitol av.
Port Alexander, tailor Kahn Tailoring Co, r 53 W Merrill.
Porter Albert G, h 493 N Capitol av.
Porter Alfred, b 9 McIntyre.

Richardson & McCrea, 79 East Market Street, FIRE INSURANCE, REAL ESTATE, LOANS, AND RENTAL AGENTS. Telephone 182.

Porter Amanda (wid John), b 239 W McCarty.
Porter Anna (wid Perry G), h 1398 N Capitol av.
Porter Annie (wid Wm), b rear 176 E Washington.
Porter Arthur L (Porter & Lowes), b e s Elm av 2 n of Washington av (I).
Porter Beulah W, phys, 334 N California, h same.
Porter Beverley C, lab, h 341 W 2d.
Porter Charles A, painter, b 33 Hiawatha.
Porter Edmund D, hostler, r 80 E Court.
Porter Edward B, cashr Indiana National Bank, h 124 E Michigan.
Porter Edward D, phys, 18 When blk, h 140 E 12th.
Porter Edward N, lab, b 33 Hiawatha.
Porter Emanuel P, lab, h 21 Cora.
Porter Felix L, bkkpr Hay & Willits Mnfg Co, h 520 Broadway.
Porter Frank E, barber, 317 Virginia av, h same.
Porter George T, lawyer, 35 Ingalls blk, b 493 N Capitol av.
Porter Georgia M, music teacher, 296 N California, b same.
Porter Harry A, actor, b 658 College av.
Porter Harvey J, lab, h rear 201 W 4th.
Porter Henry C, lab, h 219 Indiana av.
Porter Isaac M, trav agt, h 1490 N Illinois.
Porter Jacob M, messenger Indiana National Bank, h 394 N California.
Porter James H, cooper, h 654 W Vermont.
Porter James H, feed, s e cor College av and 9th, h 206 Christian av.
Porter James O, tinner, r 10 N West.
Porter Jefferson D, letter carrier P O, h 334 N California.
Porter John, lab, r 290 W Market.
Porter John A, clk Township Assessor's Office, h 57 Prospect.
Porter John A, lab, h 391 S Missouri.
Porter John R, helper, h 130 S Summit.
Porter Joseph, lab, b 77 Hill av.
Porter Julia B (wid Robert), h 14 Concordia.
Porter J Austin, clk State Supt of Public Instruction, b 148 N Illinois.

SHORTHAND REPORTING...... Conventions, Speeches, Sermons. Copying on Typewriter. S. H. EAST, State Agent, THE WILLIAMS TYPEWRITER 55 Thorpe Block, 87 East Market Street.

ELLIS & HELFENBERGER Manufacturers of Iron Vases, Setees and Hitch Posts. 162-170 South Senate Ave. Tel. 958.

THE HOGAN TRANSFER AND STORAGE COMP'Y
Household Goods and Pianos Moved—Packed—Stored...... Baggage and Package Express Machinery and Safes a Specialty Cor. Washington and Illinois Sts. TELEPHONE No. 675.

Hose, Belting, Packing, Clothing, Druggists' Sundries, Bicycle Tires, Cotton Hose, Etc. New York Belting & Packing Co., L't'd.
The Central Rubber & Supply Co. 79 S. ILLINOIS ST., INDIANAPOLIS, IND. PHONE 8.

The Provident Life and Trust Co.
OF PHILADELPHIA.
Small Death Rate.
Small Expense Rate.
Safe Investments.
Insurance in force $115,000,000
D. W. EDWARDS,
General Agent, 508 Indiana Trust Building.

Porter Malcolm G, trav agt, b 191 Bellefontaine.
Porter Marjory, b 423 E Georgia.
Porter Martin, lab, h 250 W 3d.
Porter Mary E, milliner, 16½ E Washington, h 757 N Senate av.
Porter Mary J (wid Wm), h 191 Bellefontaine.
Porter Mary M, stenog, b 115 Cornell av.
Porter Nancy (wid George W), b 177 E Louisiana.
Porter Otis A, electrician Indpls Dist Tel Co, b 191 Bellefontaine.
Porter Perry G, lab, h 1363 London av.
Porter Robert P, cabtmkr, h 3 Wendell av.
Porter Roy D, lab, b 3 Wendell av.
Porter Sarah S (wid Stephen), h 115 Cornell av.
Porter Solomon S, b n w cor English av and Sherman Drive (S).
Porter Susan, b 134 N Penn.
Porter Theodore R, tailor, 16½ E Washington, h 757 N Senate av.
Porter Wm, h e s James 5 n of Sutherland (B).
Porter Wm H, printer, b 394 N California.
Porter Wm H, lab, b 485 W Ontario (N I).
Porter Wm M, painter, h 33 Hiawatha.
Porter & Lowes (Arthur L Porter, Jesse E Lowes), grocers, e s Central av 2 s of Railroad (I).
Porterfield Henry D, trav agt Ward Bros Drug Co, h 11 Vine.
Portes James, lab, r 123 Allegheny.
Portes Richard, lab, r 123 Allegheny.
Porteus Cyreinus E, mer police, h 131 Michigan av.
Portteus Theodore, trav agt, h 415 S State av.
Posey Addie (wid Herman), r 234 Clinton.
Posey Alexander R, barber, h 187 Minerva.
Posey Alexander W, trav agt, h 845 E Michigan.
Posey Charles, lab, r 16 Hiawatha.
Posey George M D, driver, b 374½ E 7th.
Posey Irene, teacher Public School No 18, h 187 Minerva.
Posey Wm G, clk, b Exchange Hotel (W I).
Posner Abraham, cigar mnfr, rear 425 Madison av, b 437 S Meridian.

Julius C. Walk & Son,
Jewelers.
Indianapolis.
12 EAST WASHINGTON ST.

Posner Fredericka (wid Morris), h 437 S Meridian.
Post Charles, lab, h rear 479 S New Jersey.
Post Charles F, clk Indiana Paper Co, b 27 E Pratt.
Post Elias E, agt, h 110 Middle Drive (W P).
Post Frank, cooper, h 45 Helen.
Post John G, cooper, h 49 Fenneman.
POST OFFICE, Albert Sahm Postmaster, s e cor Penn and Market, Tel 467.
POSTAL TELEGRAPH CABLE CO, Frank W Samuels Mngr, Office 9-11 S Meridian; Branch Offices Indiana Bicycle Co, Board of Trade, The Bates, Stock Yards, Nordyke & Marmon Co, Atlas Engine Works, Parry Mnfg Co, Indianapolis Hominy Mills, Coffin, Fletcher & Co, Fruit District, cor Delaware and Maryland, Tel 37.
Postel Charles E, painter, h 31 Evison.
Postel Edward J, lab, r 20 Roanoke.
Postel Ezra J, b 31 Evison.
Postma John, dairy, e s Perkins pike 2 n of Bethel av, h same.
Poston Claude L, bkkpr, h 24 School.
Pothast Christian, brick mnfr, n e cor Clifford and Osage avs, h same.
Pothast Henry, foreman, b n e cor Clifford and Osage avs.
Pott Charles, collr, h 127 N Arsenal av.
Pottage Benjamin C, clk, b 175 W New York.
Pottage Charles A, brazier, b 304 S Meridian.
Pottage Charles E, watchman, h 175 W New York.
Pottage Edward G, baker, b 175 W New York.
Pottage Thomas W, clk, h 304 S Meridian.
Pottenger Julia (wid Reese), b 80 S Capitol av.
Pottenger Minor J, photog, h 80 N New Jersey.
Pottenger Wm B, livery, rear 855 N Illinois, h 1007 N Illinois.
Potter Albert, clk, b 42 Arch.
Potter Albert T, buyer E C Atkins & Co, h 42 Andrews.
Potter Edward, packer, b 93 W Vermont.
Potter Frances A (wid Aaron), b 444 N East.
Potter Frank G, treas Park Theater, b 146 N Illinois.
Potter George E, h 410 Talbott av.
Potter George W, paperhngr, h 228 Northwestern av.
Potter Henry W, saloon, 103 English av, h same.
Potter Jesse W, stenog McCormick H M Co, b 39 Hudson.
Potter John A, lab, h 23 Chadwick.
Potter Joseph L (Potter & Hawekotte), h 996 N Senate av.
Potter Mary F (wid John H), h 192 W 1st.
POTTER MANUFACTURING CO THE, Potter & Hawekotte Proprs, Mnfrs of Potter Trench Machines, w s Northwestern av between W 12th and C C C & ST L Ry.
Potter Merritt A, treas E C Atkins & Co, h 444 N East.
Potter Sarah E (wid Wilson), restaurant, 265 W Washington, h 222 W Maryland.

OTTO GAS ENGINES
BUILDERS' EXCHANGE
S. W. Cor. Ohio and Penn.
Telephone 535.

Becker & Son Charles Becker Jacob Becker Jr. Merchant Tailors. 21 N. Penn. St. Tel. 934

SALISBURY & STANLEY • Office, Store and Bank Fixtures a Specialty. Repairing of all kinds done on short notice. 177 Cl Street, Indianapolis, Ind. • Contractors and Builders TELEPHONE 999.

Potter Theodore, phys, 18 E Ohio, h 518 N New Jersey.
POTTER THOMAS C, Druggist, 300 N Penn, Tel 853; h 83 E St Clair.
Potter Thomas E, hat mnfr, 26 S Capitol av, h 93 W Vermont.
Potter Thomas E jr, bkkpr, b 93 W Vermont.
Potter Wm, lab, h n s Lake 7 e of C C C & St L Ry (N I).
POTTER WM H, Photographer, 10 Claypool Blk, 9½ N Illinois, h 596 N Alabama.
Potter & Hawekotte (Joseph L Potter, Harry G Hawekotte), proprs The Potter Mnfg Co, w s Northwestern av bet W 12th and C C C & St L Ry.
Pottle Pearl D, foreman, h 119 Blake.
Pottle Samuel E, lab, b 159 Fletcher av.
Pottle Sylvester, painter, h 412 E Walnut.
Pottmann Frank, gardener, h s w cor Southern and East.
Pottmann Frederick, gardener, h s w cor Raymond and Ransdell.
Pottmann Frederick W, gardener, b s w cor Raymond and Ransdell.
Pottmann Wm, gardener, h 980 Madison av.
Potts Albert O (C and A Potts & Co), h 1219 N Penn.
Potts Alfred F (Griffiths & Potts), h 308 Home av cor Park.
Potts Amanda M (wid John W), h 27 N Gillard av.
Potts Anna E, bkkpr, b 314 W New York.
Potts Arthur M, registry clk P O Depot Branch, b 21 Ft Wayne av.
Potts Benjamin B, painter, h 385 E Ohio.
Potts Clayton, sec C and A Potts & Co, h 673 N Capitol av.
POTTS C AND A & CO, Clayton Potts Sec, Mnfrs of Clay Working Machinery, 414-428 North Branch W Washington, Tel 746.
Potts Edward F, printer, b 1766 N Capitol av.
Potts Edward G (Balfour, Potts & Doolittle), h 39 West Drive (W P).
Potts Elizabeth H (wid Oliver G), b 39 West Drive (W P).
Potts George, patternmkr, h 314 W New York.
Potts John E, trav agt, h 127 Highland av.
Potts Mary A (wid Alfred), h 199 Walcott.
Potts Mary F (wid Wm D), h s e cor Moore av and Rural.
Potts Samuel J, paperhngr, h 77 W 19th.
Potts Samuel W, molder, b 444 S East.
Potts Wm D, b 199 Walcott.
Potts Wm H, printer, h 1115 N Delaware.
Poucher Charles H C, phys, 346 E St Clair, h same.
Pouder Albert, clk, b 281 N Noble.
Pouder Ferdinand E, clk, h 281 N Noble.
Pouder Frances A E (wid Milton M), h 250 E Market.
POUDER STEWART M, Pictures, Picture Frames and Mirrors, 29 Mass av, Tel 980; h 61 Ash.
POUDER WALTER S, Bee Keepers' Supplies and Honey, 162 Mass av, Tel 468; b 121 E New York.
Poulsen, see also Paulsen.
Poulsen Lars P, tailor, 20 Kentucky av, h 415 W 22d (N I).
Poulter Henry H, meats, 307 N West, h same.

Henry H. Fay, 40½ E. WASHINGTON ST., FIRE INSURANCE, REAL ESTATE, LOANS AND RENTAL AGENT.

Poulter Henry S, clk, b 24 Brookside av.
Pounds Charles D, b 229 N Penn.
Pounds Edward, janitor, h 73 Rhode Island.
Pounds Jasper, driver, h 348 N Missouri.
Pounds John E Rev, pastor Central Christian Church, b 276 N Penn.
Pounds Mattie, b 276 N Penn.
Poundstone Alfred M, clk, h 102 Elm.
Poundstone Rosa (wid Lot), h 134 Huron.
Powderly Thomas, foreman, h 144 King av (H).
Powell Alice M (wid George), b 332 E Georgia.
Powell Alonzo (John Powell & Sons), h 1208 N Penn.
Powell America (wid James), h 224 W 7th.
Powell Amos S, painter, h 443 S East.
Powell Caroline M (wid Wm), h 225 W New York.
Powell Charles, lab, h 1038 S Meridian.
Powell Charles L, clk State B and L Assn, b 8 Warren.
Powell Charles O, bartndr, h 1329 N Capitol av.
Powell Clement H (Powell & Co), h 35 Central av.
Powell Cora (wid Jackson), h 279 Chapel.
Powell Daniel W, painter, h n w cor Sheldon and Clyde.
Powell David T, b 399 Broadway.
Powell Elihu, lab, h 287 W Merrill.
Powell Elizabeth J (wid James J), h w s Central av 1 s of Washington av (I).
Powell Enno E, clk, h 353 S State av.
Powell Frank, polisher, b 8 Warren.
Powell Frank A, ins agt, h rear 190 Bright.
Powell Frederick D, bkkpr, b 399 Broadway.
Powell George K (Powell & Harter), saloon, 132 S Illinois, h 225 W New York.
Powell George L, flagman, h 68 Yandes.
Powell George W, sec Fraternal Building-Loan Assns, h 399 Broadway.
Powell George W, wagonmkr, h 427 W Udell (N I).
Powell Green, lab, h rear 671 N Senate av.
Powell Harry, lab, b 36 Depot (B).
Powell Harry, lab, h 645 N West.
Powell James, janitor, h rear 223 Howard.

JAS. N. MAYHEW, MANUFACTURING OPTICIAN. LENSES AND FRAMES A SPECIALTY. No. 13 North Meridian St., Indianapolis.

LUMBER | Sash, Door and Planing Mill Work. | Balke & Krauss Co. Cor. Market and Missouri Streets.

FRIEDGEN'S TAN SHOES are the Newest Shades
Prices the Lowest. 19 North Pennsylvania St.

SAMUEL LAING General Job Work in Sheet Metal of all Kinds
72 AND 74 E. COURT STREET.

M. B. WILSON, Pres. W. F. CHURCHMAN, Cash.
THE CAPITAL NATIONAL BANK,
INDIANAPOLIS, IND.
Make collections on all points in the States of Indiana and Illinois on the most favorable rates.
Capital, - - $300,000
Surplus and Earnings, 50,000
No. 28 S. Meridian St., Cor. Pearl.

Powell James F, lab, h 123 Anderson.
Powell John (John Powell & Sons), res Franklin, Ind.
Powell John jr, bkkpr, b 94 S Reisner (W I).
Powell John & Sons (John, Alonzo and Ora Powell), live stock, Union Stock Yards (W I).
Powell John G, lab, b 267 S Capitol av.
Powell John M, trav agt, b 1038 S Meridian.
Powell John W, lab, b 122 Duncan.
Powell Joseph M, lab, h 428 E Georgia.
Powell Josephine, cashr, b 8 Warren.
Powell Leara E, carp, h 427 W Udell (N I).
Powell Lucinda (wid Joseph), boarding 310 E Court.
Powell Martin M, mngr Hanna Hotel.
Powell Ora (John Powell & Sons), h 158 S Judge Harding (W I).
Powell Philomene (wid Lyman B), h 8 Warren.
Powell Rebecca (wid Thomas), b 14 Woodruff av.
Powell Robert, lab, h 224 W 7th.
Powell Russell J, draughtsman, b 399 Broadway.
Powell Sarah A (wid Thomas H), h 45 Wyoming.
Powell Thomas, lab, h 238 Alvord.
Powell Thomas, mason, r 235 Mass av.
Powell Thomas G, packer, h 152 Elizabeth.
Powell Wm A, printer, h 268½ W Washington.
Powell Wm F, condr, h 504 E 11th.
POWELL & CO (Clement H Powell), Real Estate and Investments, 316-318 Indiana Trust Bldg, Tel 1240.
POWELL & HARTER (George K Powell, James B Harter), Ticket Brokers, 130 S Illinois.
Power Arthur C, carp, b 86 Huron.
Power Clarence M, gasfitter, b 1 Smithson.
Power David, barber, 233 W McCarty, h same.
Power Frank H, lab, h 521 Mulberry.
Power George J, lab, b 337 W Maryland.
Power James L, barber, b 233 W McCarty.
Power Jesse D, tmstr, b 1 Smithson.
Power Jesse T (Power & Drake), h 1036 N Alabama.

MONEY
Loaned on Short Notice at Lowest Rates.
TUTTLE & SEGUIN'
Tel. 1168. 28 E. Market St.

Power John J, lab, b 228 S West.
Power Joseph G, candymkr, b 573 S Illinois.
POWER J CLYDE, Civil Engineer; 75 Lombard Bldg, and Engineer and Supt of Public Parks, 619-625 Indiana Trust Bldg, Tel 1859; h 81 E Vermont.
Power Lucretia E (wid Jacob), h 1 Smithson.
Power Marion, carp, h 425 S Olive.
Power Marshall T, carp, h 549 S State av.
Power Michael F, clk E C Atkins & Co, h 573 S Illinois.
Power Michael L, bartndr, b 1356 N Illinois.
Power Percy O, clk, b 1036 N Alabama.
Power Peter (McGiffin & Power), b 695 N Senate av.
Power Reuben H, h 223 W 1st.
Power Robert E, carp, b 86 Huron.
Power Taylor C, clk Power & Drake, b 1036 N Alabama.
Power Wm A, bricklyr, b 86 Huron.
Power Wm G, carp, h 100 Harlan.
Power Wm J, carp, h 86 Huron.
Power Wm J, mach hd, h w s Concord 1 s of Clifford av.
POWER & DRAKE (Jesse T Power, Robert Drake), Fancy Groceries, Wines and Meat Market, 16 N Meridian, Tel 515.
Powers Benjamin, tmstr, h 4 Holborn.
Powers Bertha (wid Frank), b 122 N Senate av.
Powers Charles B, clk Taylor & Taylor, r 140 N Alabama.
Powers David J, b 103 Bismarck av (H).
Powers Delmer T, teacher, b 70 Jefferson.
Powers Ellen (wid John), h 601 S East.
Powers George, lab, h 28 Albert.
Powers Harriet A, h 565 E 7th.
Powers Isaac H, clk, h 126 Pleasant.
Powers James A, lab, b 86 Wisconsin.
Powers James A, saloon, 65 N Illinois, h 209 Fayette.
Powers James F, asst ticket agt C C C & St L Ry, 1 E Washington, h 331 E Walnut.
Powers James P, molder, b 33 Dougherty.
Powers James W, salesman Levey Bros, h 886 N Penn.
Powers John, lab, b 601 S East.
Powers John B, agt, h 70 Jefferson.
Powers John V, molder, h 33 Dougherty.
Powers Margaret (wid Patrick), b 642 E Ohio.
Powers Michael, mason, b 151 W Washington.
Powers Patrick, bricklyr, b 18 Henry.
Powers Thomas, saloon, 503 S Capitol av, h same.
Powers Thomas F saloon, 145 E Washington, h 55 N Linden.
Powers Wm J, filer, h 86 Wisconsin.
Powers Wm J, lab, b 186 W Merrill.
Poynter Louis, brakeman, b 29 N State av.
Poynter Thomas F, condr, b 261 Michigan av.
Prader Christian, carp, h 9 McGinnis.
Prahm Adolph F, foreman C C C & St L Ry, h 329 Cornell av.
Prahm Frank E, tinner, r 12 S Gale (B).
Prahm Wm F, clk, h 346 N Noble.
Prahm Wm G, tinner, b 329 Cornell av.
Praigg David T, correspondent, h 915 N Delaware.
Prall Elam G (Prall & Van Scoyoc), h 179 Columbia av.
Prall & Van Scoyoc (Elam G Prall, Charles C Van Scoyoc), dentists, 88 N Penn.

PAPER BOXES, MANUFACTURED BY SULLIVAN & MAHAN 41 W. PEARL STREET.

DIAMOND WALL PLASTER { Telephone 1410 BUILDERS' EXCHANGE.

Fine Laundry Work our Specialty. Collars and Cuffs our Hobby.

Prange Anthony, grocer, 314 Mass av, h 112 Davidson.
Prange Anthony C, b 229 N Pine.
Prange Anton H, clk, b 1087 E Michigan.
Prange Charles, grocer, 318 E Washington, h 90 Michigan av.
Prange Charles F, solr, b 193 Davidson.
Prange Edward, sec The Indiana Dry Goods Co, h 620 E Ohio.
Prange Frank H F, clk, b 112 Davidson.
Prange Frederick, h 340 E St Clair.
Prange Frederick, carp, h 289 S Illinois.
Prange Frederick, miller, 13 Davidson, h 193 same.
Prange Frederick W (Schweikle & Prange), h 23 King.
Prange George W, carp, b 289 S Illinois.
PRANGE HENRY C, Dealer in Groceries and Meats, 397-399 Bellefontaine, Tel 1653; h 54 same.
Prange Henry C (Home Lumber Co), h 315 N Pine.
Prange Henry C F, clk, h s s Sturm av 1 w of State av.
Prange John H F, clk, b 112 Davidson.
Prasse Christian (Balfour & Prasse), r 25 Shelby.
Prasse Wm H, harnessmkr, h 192 Lincoln la.
Prasuhn Herman H, carp, h 99 Hiatt (W I).
Prater Charles L, molder, b 361 Indiana av.
Prater Nicholas, driver, r 175 S Illinois.
Prater Wm H, polisher, b 361 Indiana av.
Prather Alice A, dressmkr, 108 Fayette, b same.
Prather Austin B (Prather & Co), r 27 Wyandot blk.
PRATHER BENJAMIN H (Prather & Bangs), Sec Commercial Travelers' Mutual Accident Association of Indiana, Rooms 20-21 When Bldg, h 1212 N Penn.
Prather Bertha G, h 190 N Senate av.
Prather Caroline C (wid Oscar), restaurant, 364 Mass av, h same.
Prather Enoch W, lab, b 4½ Malott av.
Prather James T, lab, b 4½ Malott av.
Prather Sarah R, teacher Public School No 29, b 199 Lincoln av.
Prather Sarah R (wid Austin B), h 199 Lincoln av.
Prather Thomas H, pdlr, h 4½ Malott av.
Prather Wesley A, mason, h 32 Tacoma av.
Prather Wm, bricklyr, h 185½ W Washington.
Prather Wm, coachman 632 N Penn.
PRATHER & BANGS (Benjamin H Prather, Wendell O Bangs), Genl Agts for Indiana of Aetna Life Insurance Company of Hartford (Accident Department), 30-31 When Bldg.
PRATHER & CO (Austin B Prather, Allen A Bowser), Real Estate and Loans, 225-226 Lemcke Bldg.
Pratt Alice R, hairdresser, h 277 Bright.
Pratt Cecelia (wid George W), b 25 S Gale (B).
Pratt Charles M, clk, h 351 S New Jersey.
Pratt Clara (wid Scott), h 351 S New Jersey.
Pratt Edmund L, engr, h 5 S Gale (B).
Pratt Frank, painter, 457 Charles, b same.
Pratt Joseph W, clk L S Ayres & Co, h 222 Fayette.

FRANK NESSLER. WILL H. ROST.
FRANK NESSLER & CO.
Tailors
56 EAST MARKET ST. (Lemcke Building),
INDIANAPOLIS. IND.

Pratt Josephine (wid George J), h 7 Beacon.
Pratt Julius F, treas Atlas Engine Wks, treas Consumers' Gas Trust Co, h 569 N Penn.
Pratt Thomas W, lab, h 277 Bright.
Pratt Wm B, h 971 N Delaware.
Pratt Wm D, propr Indiana Newspaper Union, 32 W Court, h 200 N Delaware.
Pratt Wm M, mach, b Senate Hotel.
Pray Enos E, sec Rex Coal and Sewer Co, 171 E Louisiana, h 377 Talbott av.
Pray Francis M, phys, 9 N Meridian, h 68 W Vermont.
Pray Samuel D, sec The Indpls Gas Co, h 949 N Illinois.
Pray Susannah, asst supt Indiana Reformatory.
Pray Wm (Pray & Petrie), res Knightstown, Ind.
Pray Wm H, clk Indpls Gas Co, b 129 Talbott av.
Pray & Petrie (Wm Pray, Robert Petrie), livery, 33 N Alabama.
Prayer James, porter, b 166 Osage.
Prazink Joseph, lab, b 49 Holmes av (H).
PREFERRED ACCIDENT INSURANCE CO OF NEW YORK, Evan A Bonham State Mngr, Rooms 15-16 Hartford Blk, 84 E Market.
Prehn Helmuth C, mach, h 14 S Stuart (B).
Prehn Henry, h 183 Trowbridge (W).
Prentice Emmett N, lab, b 78 Newman.
Prentice Frances (wid James), h 191 Brookside av.
Prentice Harry S, clk, b 191 Brookside av.
Prentiss James H F, bkkpr Murphy, Hibben & Co, h n e cor 32d and Charles (M).
Prentiss King, lab, b 477 W Chicago (N I).
Prentiss Rosa (wid Moses), h 48 Vincennes (W I).
Prentiss Thomas R Rev, pastor Barnes Chapel A M E Church, h 460 W Chicago (N I).
Prescott Elizabeth (wid Samuel), h 99 Shepard (W I).
Prescott Mark, lab, b 99 Shepard (W I).
Prescott Wm B, pres Internat Typograph Union, b 279 N Capitol av.

Haueisen & Hartmann
163-169 E. Washington St.
FURNITURE,
Carpets,
Household Goods,
Tin, Granite and China Wares, Oil Cloth and Shades

THE HOME LAUNDRY 197 S. Illinois St. Telephone 1769.

THE WM. H. BLOCK CO. 7 AND 9 EAST WASHINGTON STREET. DRY GOODS, MEN'S FURNISHINGS.

Fidelity and Deposit Co. of Maryland. BONDS SIGNED.—LOCAL BOARD John B. Elam, Albert Sahm, Smiley N. Chambers, John M. Spann.
GEORGE W. PANGBORN, General Agent, 704-706 Lemcke Building. Telephone 140.

74 EAST MARKET STREET Telephone 863.
Insure Your Property With FRANK K. SAWYER

JOSEPH GARDNER,
Hot Air Furnaces
With Combination Gas Burners for Burning Gas and Other Fuel at the Same Time.
37, 39 & 41 KENTUCKY AVE. Telephone 322

Presler Frank, engr, r 129 S Noble.
Presler John A, carp, r 68½ Mass av.
Pressel Charles W, mach, h 1390 Paris av.
Pressel Frederick G, clk, b 36 Bellefontaine.
Pressel George M, brickmason, h 535 W Francis (N I).
Pressel James, tmstr, h 28 Hiawatha.
Pressel Margaret (wid Thomas J), h 23 Bloomington.
PRESSEL WM H, Carpenter and Contractor, 309½ Mass av, h 36 Bellefontaine.
Presser Catherine (wid Severin), h 421 Union.
Presser Jacob I, hostler, b 421 Union.
PRESSLER GUIDO R, Fresco Painter (Exclusive), 325 N Liberty, h same. (See right bottom cor cards.)
Pressley Flats, 175 N Penn.
Pressly James A, h 49 Yandes.
Pressly John M, baker, b 485 S Meridian.
Pressly Wm F, bricklyr, b 485 S Meridian.
Pressly Wm W, contr, 485 S Meridian, h same.
Prestler George M, ins agt, h 329 E Michigan.
Preston Abraham L, phys, 73 King av (H), h same.
Preston Alfred M, propr Pythian Journal, 398 S Alabama, h same.
Preston Amanda (wid Firman), h 77 Montana.
Preston Arthur P, music teacher, 526 N Meridian, h same.
Preston Columbus P, roofer, 67 S Reisner (W I), h same.
Preston Edward W, tmstr, h 14 Hill.
Preston Elliott M, switchman, h 351 S Delaware.
Preston Emeline E (wid Moses C), b 1115 N Meridian.
Preston Francis A, car rep, h s s Pendleton av ½ mile e of (B).
Preston Frank A, teacher Industrial Training School, r 401 N Penn.
Preston Helen H (wid Wm), h 130 Cornell av.

J. S. FARRELL & CO.
Plumbing
Natural and Artificial Gas Fitting.
84 N. ILLINOIS STREET.
TELEPHONE 382.

Preston Hester (wid Wm), b 21 Detroit.
Preston John A, paperhngr, h 50 Draper.
Preston Matilda (wid Luther), b 85 N Delaware.
Preston Nell, h 215 W North.
Preston Spencer N, printer The Indpls News, h 35 Hall pl.
Preston Thomas E, sawmkr, b 351 S Delaware.
Preston Wm, saloon, 186 S Illinois, h 290 S Alabama.
Preston Wm E, lab, h 2 Wallack.
Preston Wm J, plastr, h 452 Blake.
Pretzfelder Ephraim H, clk, b 311 E New York.
Pretzfelder Isaac, clk Original Eagle, b 311 E New York.
Pretzfelder Rachel (wid Emanuel), h 311 E New York.
Preusch Anna C, stenog Indiana Bicycle Co, b 123 S Olive.
Preusch Jacob F, carp, 123 S Olive, h same.
Previett Captola (wid John H), b Illinois House.
Prewett Mack, fireman, r 27 Virginia av.
Prewett Melissa (wid Andrew J), h 147 Harlan.
Pribble John W, painter, h 566 Union.
Price Aa on S, fireman, h 405 W Addison (N I).
Price Albert, lab, h 167 Bismarck av (H).
Price Andrew J, lab, b 405 W Addison (N I).
Price Benjamin S, foreman, b 143 S East.
Price Bertha, h 175 Fulton.
Price Carl, messenger, r 289½ Mass av.
Price Charles A, driver, h 294 E Wabash.
Price Charles W, wagonmkr, h 19 Russell av.
Price Cicero W, lab, h 139 Newman.
Price Daniel M, molder, h 1069 W Michigan.
Price Edward E, bodymkr, b 392 Cornell av.
Price Edwin, coachman 845 N Illinois.
Price Elgin H, foreman, b 143 S East.
Price Elizabeth J, b 163 N Alabama.
Price Frances (wid Edward), h 98 Rhode Island.
Price Frank, waiter, h 410 W 1st.
Price Frank S, waiter, r 54 Church.
Price George W, lab, h 152 N Belmont av (H).
Price Harvey H, brickmolder, h s w cor Brookside av and Roseline.
Price Horace E, lab, h 319 Lafayette.
Price Jacob, nurse, h 143 S East.
Price Jacob W, opr W U Tel Co, b 143 S East.
Price James, lab, r 66 N Missouri.
Price James, lab, b n s Pansy 1 w of Floral av.
Price James, lab, h rear 251 W 6th.
Price John J, driver, h 189 Shelby.
PRICE JOHN J, Genl Agt Berkshire Life Insurance Co of Pittsfield, Mass, 207-208 Lemcke Bldg, h 739 N Alabama.
Price Joseph, janitor, h 203 Agnes.
Price Joseph F, lab, b 405 W Addison (N I).
Price Lehman H, trav agt, h 46 Andrews.
Price Mary (wid Pendleton P), b 519 N Alabama.
Price Mary J (wid Albert A), h rear 432 Douglass.
Price Mead N, lab, h 45 S McLain (W I).
Price Millard F, mach, h 500 Broadway.
Price Morgan A, meats, 153 E Ohio, b 155 same.
Price Nancy (wid Henry C), h 435 National rd.

IF CONTINUED to the end of its dividend period, policies of the UNITED STATES LIFE INSURANCE CO., will equal or excel any investment policy ever offered to the public. E. B. SWIFT, Manager, 25 E. Market St.

Wm. Kotteman 89 & 91 E. Washington St. TELEPHONE 1742 Furniture

SHOW CASES WILLIAM WIEGEL 6 West Louisiana Street Opp. Union Station.

Price Napoleon B, driver, h 213 E Wabash.
Price Oakley, mach, h 55 Harrison.
Price Payton, lab, b 573 E 7th.
Price Sarah M (wid Franklin), h cor E North and Bee Line Ry.
Price Sherman, watchman The Denison.
Price Stephen, boilermkr, h rear 346 Virginia av.
Price Thomas J, lab, b 405 W Addison (N I).
Price Wm, lab, r 44½ Malott av.
Price Wm, lab, h 433 National rd.
PRICE WM H, Genl Agt The Guarantors' Liability Indemnity Co of Pennsylvania, 93 Lombard Bldg, b 143 S East.
Priegnitz Anna M (wid August), h 14 Spann av.
Priegnitz Frederick N, car insp, h 119 Greer.
Priegnitz Wm, carp, h 85 Huron.
Prier, see also Pryor.
Prier George, trav agt, h 1130 N Meridian.
PRIER HENRY J, Genl Agt Aultman, Miller & Co, 75-77 W Washington, h n s E Washington 3 e of Belt R R.
Priest Charles J, condr, b 69 W 13th.
Priest John, waiter, r 283 Chapel.
Prigger Anna (wid Henry), meats, 20 E Mkt House, grocer, 336 Fulton, h same.
Prigger John H, bartndr, h 263 Spring.
Priller Hugo, carp, h 493 S Missouri.
Priller Otto G, clk, b 493 S Missouri.
Prime Mary D (wid John), h 221 W 1st.
Primer Walter, carp, b 553 Virginia av.
Primm Robert N, lab, b 516 N Senate av.
Primus David, lab, b 161 Agnes.
Primus Henry, lab, h 27 Reynolds av (H).
Primus James, driver, b 289 Indiana av.
Primus John, h 27 Reynolds av (H).
Primus John H, lab, b 27 Reynolds av (H).
Prince Boyd, soldier U S Arsenal.
Prince Edward C, fireman, b 57 Tacoma av.
Prince George W, porter, h 20 S Dorman.
Prince Harry F, clk, h 25 Bicking.
Prince Isaac, clk, b 290 Virginia av.
Prince Marion, trav agt, h 221 W 1st.
Prince Wm F, lab, h 166 Howard.
Princell George, brass molder Langsenkamp Bros' Brass Wks, h 43 Arizona.
Prindle Cynthia (wid Merwin), b 121 Pleasant.
Prindle David J, driver, h 11 Jefferson.
Prindle Romeo M, car insp, h 195 Prospect.
Pringle Charles D, lab, h 46 Kennington.
Pringle Jessie, teacher, b 377 Home av.
Pringle John L, brickmason, h 557 W Eugene (N I).
Pringle Roy K, pressman, b 557 W Eugene (N I).
Pringle Wm W, lawyer, 20½ N Delaware, h 377 Home av.
Printz Alfred W, foreman Michigan Lumber Co, h 340 N Noble.
Prinz Catherine (wid John D), h 333 N West.
Prinz Frank W, bkkpr, h 399 N West.
Prinz John G, mngr insurance dept Indiana Trust Co, h 373 N West.
Prinzel Caroline (wid Henry), h 31 Stevens.
Prinzel Henrietta (wid Henry), b 31 Stevens.
Prinzler Carl J, city salesman Clemens Vonnegut, b 173 Walcott.
Prinzler Louis, engr Deaf and Dumb Inst, h 173 Walcott.
Prinzler Louis V (Aneshaensel & Prinzler), b 173 Walcott.
Prinzler May, opr Cent U Tel Co, b 173 Walcott.

We Buy Municipal ~ Bonds ~
THOS. C. DAY & CO,
Rooms 325 to 330 Lemcke Bldg.

Prinzler Sophia (wid August), b 85 River av (W I).
Prisching Max, baker, h 379 Charles.
Pritchard Benjamin, clk, b 1071 N Capitol av.
Pritchard Edwin D, trav agt, b 853 Ash.
Pritchard Elisha, tmstr, h 533 S Capitol av.
Pritchard Evan H (Pritchard & Son), h 85 N Alabama.
Pritchard George A, student, b 1249 N Penn.
Pritchard Grace P, b 446 S Delaware.
Pritchard Henry R Rev, h 1007 N Senate av.
Pritchard James A, lawyer, 15 Baldwin blk, h 1010 N Senate av.
Pritchard John, carp, h 186 Huron.
Pritchard John E (Pritchard & Son), r 177 N Delaware.
Pritchard John E, detective, r 88 Baldwin blk.
Pritchard John M, bkkpr, b 276 N Penn.
Pritchard Mary E, h 500 E Washington.
Pritchard Medora C, dressmkr, 186 Huron, h same.
Pritchard Wm, h 166 Ash.
Pritchard Wm H, wirewkr, h 436 N East.
PRITCHARD & SON (Evan H and John E), Veterinary Surgeons), 122 E Wabash, Tel 831.
Pritchett Alice L, boarding 322 Cornell av.
Pritchett George W, saloon, 150 W Vermont, h 148½ same.
Pritchett Jeremiah N, clk, h 322 Cornell av.
Pritchett Silas C, barber, 277 E McCarty, b 265 Lafayette.
Pritchett Wm C, barber, 91 E Court, h 272 E North.
Pritsch Adolph, shoemkr, 536 S East, h same.
Pritsch Julius, shoemkr, b 536 S East.
Privitt Willis, contr and grocer, 85 Fulton, h 132 Spring.
Proal Arthur B, treas The Indpls Gas Co, res New York City.
Probert Alfred G, clk H P Wasson & Co, b 253 N Alabama.
Probert Samuel, watchman Indpls Gas Co, h 422 E New York.

EAT
QUAKER BREAD
ASK YOUR GROCER FOR IT.
THE HITZ BAKING CO.

CARPETS CLEANED LIKE NEW. TELEPHONE 818
CAPITAL STEAM CARPET CLEANING WORKS

BENJ. BOOTH PRACTICAL EXPERT ACCOUNTANT. Thirty years' experience. First-class credentials. Room 18, 82½ E. Washington St. Indianapolis, Ind.

18 and 20 S. Meridian St. Established 18

ESTABLISHED 1876. TELEPHONE 168.
CHESTER BRADFORD,
SOLICITOR OF PATENTS,
AND COUNSEL IN PATENT CAUSES.
(See adv. page 6.)
Office:—Rooms 14 and 16 Hubbard Block, S.W. Cor. Washington and Meridian Streets, INDIANAPOLIS, INDIANA.

Probert Thomas W, collr, h 381 N Delaware.
Probst Frederick, tinner, b 346 N Senate av.
Probst George J, lab, h 98 Torbet.
Probst George J jr, tinner, b 98 Torbet.
Probst Leonard M, tinner, b 98 Torbet.
Probst Wm J (Probst & Kassebaum), h 1012 N Capitol av.
PROBST & KASSEBAUM (Wm J Probst, Wm F Kassebaum), Wholesale and Retail Flour and Feed, 432 Mass av, Tel 384.
Proctor Abraham L, lab, b 22 Maple.
Proctor David, b 132 W 6th.
Proctor David W, uphlr, h 126 Weghorst.
Proctor Edmund E, engr, h 132 W 6th.
Proctor Elizabeth H (wid Wm H), h 126 Weghorst.
Proctor James (Wm Laurie & Co), h 190 College av.
Proctor Thomas (Gardner & Proctor), h 63 Ingram.
Proctor Wm, carp, h 454 S Capitol av.
Proctor Wm B, lab, b 96 Lincoln la.
Proctor Wm T, uphlr, h n w cor St Elmo and Cypress.
Proeschel George, lab, h 52 Morton.
Proeschel George, driver, b 15 Osgood (W I).
Proffit Charles W, lab, r 75 Adams.
Proffitt Jesse B, lab, h 68 Holmes av (H).
PROGRESS CLOTHING CO THE, Bliss, Swain & Co Proprs, 6-8 W Washington, Tel 1630.
PROGRESS LAUNDRY, Shaneberger & Lockwood Proprs, 322 E Washington, Tel 1121.
Promenske Theodore, molder, r 71½ N Illinois.
Prospect Savings and Loan Assn, Charles Wonnell pres, John Schley sec, Joseph W Buchanan treas, 16 Masonic Temple.
Proskopsky Charles, shoemkr, 75 W Merrill, h 432 S Capitol av.
Prosser Christian F, painter, b 35 Shelby.
Prosser Edgar M, draughtsman C C C & St L Ry, b 74 W Walnut.

CORRUGATED IRON CEILINGS AND SIDING.
ALL KINDS OF REPAIRING.
O. B. ENSEY,
TELEPHONE 1562.
COR. 6TH AND ILLINOIS STREETS.

Prosser Effie, h 331 W Washington.
Prosser Mary A (wid Joseph K), h 283 Christian av.
Prosser Ora, mach hd, b 66 Yandes.
Prosser Percy J, modeler, 470 Hanna, h 149 Madison.
Prosser Thomas E, jeweler, h 465 S West.
Prosser Wm, plastr, 150 Clifford av, h same.
Prosser Wm jr, b 150 Clifford av.
Prost John, molder, b 54 River av (W I).
Protestant Deaconess Home, 118 N Senate av.
Prothero Evan M, h 101 Bates.
Prothero Russell, mach hd, h 42 Michigan av.
Frough Almond, steam fitter, b 61 Omer.
Prough Caroline (wid Solomon), h 61 Omer.
Prough Clementia M, nurse, 197 N Delaware.
Prouse Clinton E, clk, r 16 W Michigan.
PROVIDENT LIFE AND TRUST COMPANY OF PHILADELPHIA THE, D W Edwards Genl Agt, Rooms 508-510 Indiana Trust Bldg, Tel 350. (See right top lines, left top cor cards and adv opp p 334.)
Prow Fred J (Reid & Prow), h 189 N East.
PRUDENTIAL INSURANCE COMPANY OF AMERICA, Home Office Newark, N J, Thomas Mason Supt, 33-34 Ingalls Blk.
Pruesmeier Wm, bricklyr, b 264 S Alabama.
Pruett John, express, h 47 Mayhew.
Pruett Joseph W, lab, b 165 Beacon.
Pruitt Edward E, carp, h 336½ E Washington.
Pruitt Eli J, h 562 Broadway.
Pruitt Fernandez J, b 562 Broadway.
Pruitt Hallack K, filer, h 254 Springfield.
Pruitt Harrison R, lab, h 2 Lafayette.
Pruitt Harry W, plastr, r 306 Cornell av.
Pruitt John H, plastr, h 12 Yandes.
Pruitt John M, carp, h 175 E Pearl.
Pruitt Joseph, lab, h 465½ S Meridian.
Pruitt Oran M, sec Indiana Lumber and Veneer Co, h 546 Ash.
Pruitt Wm F, clk A Selig, b 90 Columbia av.
Prunk Byron F, phys, 368 W New York, b same.
Prunk Daniel H, phys, 30 N Senate av, h 368 W New York.
Prunk Frank H (Everroad & Prunk), h 367 N California.
PRUNK HARRIET AUGUSTA MRS, Elocutionist, Principal Indiana Boston School of Elocution and Expression of Indianapolis, Professor Dramatic Art College of Music, Professor Elocution St Mary's School, h 368 W New York. (See adv p 138.)
Prunk Harry C, plumber, b 368 W New York.
Pruss Wm, student, r 228 N Capitol av.
Pryor, see also Prier.
Pryor Harry A (Larger & Pryor), h 56 N State av.
Pryor John, lab, h rear 126 W 6th.
Pryor John W, brakeman, h 38 Warren.
Pryor Martin P, feed, 98 W 7th, h 12 Hall pl.
PUBLIC LIBRARY, Eliza G Browning Librarian and Sec, s w cor Meridian and Ohio, Tel 202.
Pucciarelli Vincent, pdlr, h 17 Kentucky av.
Puckett Ellen (wid Riley), b 50 Lee (W I).

The Old Rel'ble German European Restau

TUTEWILER UNDERTAKER, No. 72 WEST MARKET STREET. TELEPHONE 216.

THE PROVIDENT LIFE AND TRUST CO. OF PHILADELPHIA. Endowment Insurance presents the double attraction of relieving manhood and middle age from anxiety and old age from want.
For particulars apply to D. W. EDWARDS, General Agent, 508 Indiana Trust Building.

THEODORE F. SMITHER, AGENT FOR WARREN'S ANCHOR BRAND —ASPHALT ROOFING— OFFICE, 151 W. MARYLAND ST. TEL. 861.

Puckett John W, lab, h 50 Lee (W I).
Pugh, see also Pew.
Pugh Albert W, h 461 S Illinois.
Pugh Charles G, clk, b 347 S State av.
Pugh Charles M, mach, h 68 Dawson.
Pugh Daniel, foreman, h 774 E Market.
Pugh Edwin B (Black & Pugh), b 1051 E Michigan.
Pugh Finley B (Bailey Mnfg Co), h 341 N Delaware.
Pugh Florence M, stenog, b 1051 E Michigan.
Pugh Frank J, driver, h 197 W Ray.
Pugh Frank W, tel opr The Sun, r 311 N Delaware.
Pugh George, attendant Insane Hospital.
Pugh George L, clk Daniel Stewart Co, h 12 Edgewood.
Pugh Isaac C, collr, h 152 Hoyt av.
Pugh James B, agt, h 1051 E Michigan.
Pugh James M, clk Wm H Armstrong & Co, h 349 N Senate av.
Pugh Jesse B (Pugh & Denney), h 177 Fletcher av.
Pugh John P, etcher, b 461 S Illinois.
Pugh John T, fireman, b 774 E Market.
Pugh Samuel W, city fireman, b 461 S Illinois.
Pugh Willard S, clk A Kiefer Drug Co, h 515 N Capitol av.
Pugh Wm E, trunkmkr, b 1051 E Michigan.
Pugh Wm R, painter, h 2 Spann av.
Pugh & Denney (Jesse B Pugh, Anna Denney), grocers, 420 Dillon.
Pugsley Cora A, b 109 Bates.
Pugsley Mary Jane (wid Richard), h 90 Bradshaw.
Puite Frank T, condr, h 4 Wendell av.
Puitt David, lab, b 229½ E Washington.
Pullen Albert J, brakeman, h s s Willow 2 e of Foundry (B).
Pullen Jane (wid Reuben), b 84 Fletcher av.
Pullen Margaret E (wid John W), b 14 Temple av.
Pullen Mary (wid Joseph), r 5½ Madison av.
Pullen Nettie, bkkpr, b 84 Fletcher av.
Pullen Wm B, meats, 117 Germania av (H), h same.
Pulley David, lab, h 9 Mill.
Pulliam Benjamin L, trav agt, h 231 Alvord.
Pulliam Elizabeth (wid George), h 503 Bellefontaine.
Pulliam George D, shoemkr, b 503 Bellefontaine.
Pulliam John F, watchman, h rear 318 E Georgia.
Pullis Eliza A (wid John), b 626 N Penn.
Pullman Palace Car Co, Timothy M Layton agt, Union Station.
Pummill Dora A, condr, h 185 E South.
Pumphrey Carl, lab, b 217 S Illinois.
Pumphrey Edward M, carp, 184 N Pine, h same.
Pumphrey George C, mach, b 184 Church.
Pumphrey Mary (wid Oliver B), h 184 Church.
Pumphrey Thomas P, clk Penna lines, h 182 Church.
Pundchu Charles G, bartndr, b 1107 E Michigan.
Pundchu Harry J, mach hd, b n w cor E Washington and Belt R R.
Pundchu Joseph, blksmith, n w cor E Washington and Belt R R, h same.
Purcell, see also Parcell and Pursell.
Purcell Charles T, lineman, b 5 Wood.
Purcell Clarence, b 252½ Mass av.
Purcell Edgar T, h 497 N Alabama.

Purcell Harry W, carp, h 123 Rhode Island.
Purcell Horace, carp, h 83 Quincy.
Purcell John H, shoemkr, 309 Mass av, h 252½ same.
Purcell Sarah J (wid Charles W), h 5 Wood.
Purcell Wm, fireman, h 26 Traub av.
Purdu James Y, lab, h 6 Hester.
Purdu John L, lab, b 6 Hester.
Purdue Alfred, lab, b 65 N East.
Purdue John B, molder, h 207 Orange.
Purdue Matthew, lab, h n s Howland av 2 e of Orchard.
Purdy Albert R, lab, b 25 Downey.
Purdy Charles W, lab, h 25 Downey.
Purdy Fred L, pres The Sun Pub Co and managing editor The Sun, h 1677 N Penn.
Purdy Jackson C, foreman, h 241 Bismarck av (H).
Purdy Lucretia (wid John C), h 6 Cleaveland blk.
Purdy Vienna, stenog Van Camp H and I Co, b 222 N Illinois.
Purdy Worthington A, carp, h 123 Trowbridge (W).
PURITAN SPRING BED CO, Frank F Rogers Pres, Melville F Shaw Sec and Treas, Mnfrs of Spring Beds, 952 N New Jersey, Tel 1883.
Purman, see also Poorman.
Purman Samuel B, asst cashr Adams Ex Co, h 132 Clifford av.
Purnell, see also Parnell.
Purnell Arthur, pressman The Indpls News, b 421 W Pratt.
Purnell George, cooper, h 336 Elizabeth.
Purnell George W, mach, b 18 Caldwell.
Purnell Martha (wid Robert K), h 90 S West.
Purnell Robert K, helper The Indpls News, b 221 W Pearl.
Pursel, see also Parcell and Purcell.
Pursel John, saloon, 810 W Washington, h same.
Pursel Joseph D, carp, h 1037 W Vermont.
Pursel Mary A (wid Daniel), h 99 Lynn.
Pursel Thomas, b 956 N Illinois.
Pursel Wm J, fireman, h w s Traub av 4 s of railroad.

THE A. BURDSAL CO.
Manufacturers of
Paints and Colors
VARNISHES,
Brushes, Painters' and Paper Hangers' Supplies.
34 AND 36 SOUTH MERIDIAN STREET.

ELECTRICIANS | DON'T FORGET US. ALL WORK GUARANTEED. C. W. MEIKEL, Tel. 466. 96-98 E. New York St.

DALTON & MERRIFIELD { LUMBER South Noble St., near E. Washington

LOWEST PRICES. BEST PATENT BASE ON THE MARKET.
INDIANA ELECTROTYPE CO. :: BEST WORK All Orders Promptly Filled.
23 WEST PEARL ST., INDIANAPOLIS, IND. JOB WORK. BOOK PLATES.

KIRKHOFF BROS.
Steam and Hot Water Heating Apparatus,
Plumbing and Gas Fitting.
102-104 SOUTH PENNSYLVANIA ST.
TELEPHONE 910.

Pursell Arthur T, electrician, 30 Mass av, b 679 College av.
Pursell Athalena A (wid Abner E), b 466 N Penn.
Pursell Elmer N, clk Van Camp H and I Co, h 463 W Walnut av (N I).
Pursell Frank S, painter, h 76 N Olive.
Pursell Harry, lab, h 129 Maxwell.
Pursell Josephine, matron Guardians' Home, s e cor Auburn av and Prospect.
PURSELL PETER M, Mantels, Grates, Furnaces, Royal Fireplace Heaters, Galvanized Iron, Tin and Slate Roofing, 30 Mass av, Tel 883; h 679 College av.
Pursell Theodore W, trav agt D P Erwin & Co, h 497 N Alabama.
Pursell Walter J, supt, h 296½ Lincoln av.
Pursley Alethea A (wid Mack), h 113 W 4th.
Pursley Benjamin, lab, b 122 Elizabeth.
Pursley Cassius, lab, b 297 River av (W I).
Purviance Harry B, clk L S Ayres & Co, b 604 E Market.
Purviance Joseph W, h 80 E St Joseph.
Purviance Richard R, clk Hildebrand Hardware Co, b 80 E St Joseph.
Purvis Alvin, engr, h 55 Catharine.
Purvis Peter W, tailor, h 289 W Michigan.
Puryear James, baker The Denison.
Puryear John A (Harris & Puryear), h 50 Camp.
Puryear Margaret J (wid Jeremiah), janitor, h n e cor Howard and 4th.
Puryear Philip M, lab, h 16 Parker.
Puryear Sidney M Rev, h 38 Lincoln la.
Pusey Robert D, clk L E & W R R, r 280 E New York.
Putnam Avery G, porter, h 177 E South.
PUTNAM COUNTY MILK CO THE, Andrew L Lockridge Propr, 12-16 N East, Long Distance Tel 1765.
Putnam James G, student, r 319 N California.
Putnam James P, supt, h 174 Coburn.
Putnam John C, agt, r 146 W New York.
Putnam Wm T, carp, h 54 Poplar (B).
Pyatt James W, grocer, 801 N Alabama, h 226 E 7th.

LIME
BUILDING SUPPLIES,
Hair, Plaster, Flue Linings,
The W. G. Wasson Co.
130 INDIANA AVE. Tel. 989.

Pyatt Wm J, engr, h 1031 W Washington.
Pyatt Wm O, baggageman, b 11 E South.
Pye Amanda H (wid John K), h 852 N New Jersey.
Pye Mary H, bkkpr The H R Allen Natl Surg Inst, b 852 N New Jersey.
Pye Wm H, trav agt Indpls Harness Co, b 252 N New Jersey.
Pyers Wm J, foreman, h 50 Fletcher av.
Pyke Benjamin F, lab, h 55 S California.
Pyle Anna C, stenog D P Erwin & Co, b 853 Ash.
Pyle Bros (Wm C and Marshall J), grocers, 294 Mass av.
Pyle Charles C, clk, b 1058 N New Jersey.
Pyle Charles R, painter, h 627 W Michigan.
Pyle Edward, molder, b 67 S Noble.
Pyle Elizabeth H, h 442 E Walnut.
Pyle Ella M, tel opr, b 1556 Graceland av.
Pyle George C, electrician, h 575 Broadway.
Pyle Marshall J (Pyle Bros), h 238 Bellefontaine.
Pyle Wm C (Pyle Bros), h 236 Cornell av.
Pyle Wm L, dairyman, h 853 Ash.
Pyle Wm N, lab, h 46 S Austin (B).
Pym Jacob F, miller, h 477 Broadway.
Pym John, lab, b 477 Broadway.
Pyne Patrick E, lab, h 498 S West.
Pynster Mary J, b 1007 N Capitol av.
Pyritz August, lab, h 122 Church.
Pythian Journal, A M Preston propr, 398 S Alabama.

Q

Quack Charles C, brick mnfr, n s Prospect 6 e of Belt R R, h same.
Quack Charles C, tinner, h 50 S Spruce.
Quack Charles W, lab, h 180 Trowbridge (W).
Quack Christian L, engr, h 25 Gresham.
Quack Christopher J, b 38 S Spruce.
Quack Wm, driver, h 38 S Spruce.
Quack Wm jr, mach hd, b 38 S Spruce.
Quack Wm C, lab, h 22 Harlan.
Quaid Anna C (wid Wm I), h 219 E North.
Quail Charlotte, dressmkr, 165 N Illinois, h same.
Quail James, lab, h rear 204 Elizabeth.
Quaintance David, medicines, 234 W Michigan, h same.
Quakenbush Benjamin, tinner, b 171 E Court.
Quakenbush Isaiah G, hostler, h 87 N New Jersey.
Qualter Michael, mach hd, b 41 Minerva.
Quandt Jacob F, plumber, h 37 S Stuart (B).
Quandt Wm H, foreman, h 40 S Gale (B).
Quarles Edward, lab, h rear 775 N Senate av.
Quarles Nathan, lab, h rear 775 N Senate av.
Quarterman John, carp, h 244½ E Washington.
Quartermaster General's Office State of Indiana, 9 State House.
Quattiocchi Salvador, pdlr, h 85 Harmon.
Quear Joseph, clk, h 558 S New Jersey.
Quear Samuel A, clk, r 247 N Capitol av.
Queisser Caroline J (wid Julius E), h 60 Highland pl.
Queisser Frank F, h 446 W Udell (N I).
Queisser Mary, h 97 N Linden.
Queisser Mary J, janitress Public School No 39, h rear 102 Pleasant av.
Queisser Oscar J, b 446 W Udell (N I).
Querry Cornelius E, cooper, h 493 W New York.

Parlor, Bed Room, Dining Room, Kitchen, Furniture W. H. MESSENGER, 101 E. Wash. St., Tel. 491.

ALL KINDS OF HEAVY AND LIGHT GRAY IRON CASTINGS } McNamara, Koster & Co. { Foundry and Pattern Shop
Phone 1593. 212-218 S. Penn. St.

Quick Austin T (E W Hoover & Co), h 820 N Alabama.
Quick Homer S, clk, h 72 W 10th.
Quick James, carp, r 169 W Market.
Quick James M, plumber, h 176 N Dorman.
Quick James M, student, r 367 N Alabama.
Quick John S, student, r 55 Fletcher av.
Quick Joseph R, tmstr, h w s Capitol av 4 s of 30th.
Quick Otho L, plumber, b 176 N Dorman.
Quick Spencer R, b 463 Park av.
Quigley Anna, milliner, 71 S Illinois, b 30 W St Clair.
Quigley Harry J, clk, b 210 Buchanan.
Quigley Homer R, clk, h 132 Cornell av.
Quigley James F, capt police, h 187 Blake.
Quigley John, h 30 W St Clair.
Quigley John A, paperhanger, h 11 Torbet.
Quigley John J, clk, h 210 Buchanan.
Quigley Wm F, buyer Van Camp H & I Co, h 404 N Illinois.
Quill John J, clk, b 360 E Morris.
Quill Leonard, clk Indpls Gas Co, h 397 Virginia av.
Quill Mary (wid John), h 332 E Louisiana.
Quill Maurice, agt, h 13 Hoyt av.
Quill Thomas, clk, b 306 E Louisiana.
Quill Thomas F (Reichwein & Quill), h 360 E Morris.
Quillin Perry, lab, r 21 Ryan blk.
Quillin Virgil N, bricklyr, h 152½ Martindale av.
Quimby John T, b 54 S Linden.
Quinlan Hannah C, h 174 W Michigan.
Quinlan John T, mach, b 244 W Washington.
Quinlan Maurice, mach hd, b 167 E South.
Quinlan Michael, flagman, h 230 Dillon.
Quinlan Michael jr, molder, b 230 Dillon.
Quinlan Patrick, h 658 W Vermont.
Quinlan Wm, lab, h 167 E South.
Quinn Alice, stenog, b 275 S Delaware.
Quinn Andrew, butler, h 180 W Michigan.
Quinn Andrew, lab, h 19 Ketcham (H).
Quinn Andrew, molder, b 67 Traub av.
Quinn Andrew J, patternmkr, b 336 W Washington.
Quinn Anthony, lab, h 228 E Merrill.
Quinn Benjamin L, painter, h 143½ Virginia av.
Quinn Bridget (wid John P), h 5 Riley blk.
Quinn Charles E, clk, b 275 S Delaware.
Quinn Edgar, plate printer Wm B Burford, b 781 N Illinois.
Quinn Edward J, lab, b 152½ W Washington.
Quinn Elizabeth (wid James), h 300 S East.
Quinn Ellen (wid Wm), b 22 S Gale (B).
Quinn Emma (wid Charles), h 21 King av (H).
Quinn Emma (wid Richard), h 781 N Illinois.
Quinn Everett, lab, h 39 W Pratt.
Quinn Harry, bricklyr, b 285 S Capitol av.
Quinn Harry, mach, b 24 N State av.
Quinn Helen M, cashr, b 336 W Washington.
Quinn Ida M, stenog, b 781 N Illinois.
Quinn James, b 427 N Capitol av.
Quinn James, lab, h 40 S West.
Quinn James M, saloon, 500 S West, h same.
Quinn James P, driver, b 83 W 20th.
Quinn John C, foreman E C Atkins & Co, h 106 N Senate av.
Quinn John F, sub letter carrier P O, h 275 S Delaware.
Quinn John P, flagman, h 275 S Delaware.
Quinn Joseph, waiter, h 15 Arch.
Quinn Lawrence, watchman, h 627 W Vermont.

Henry H. Fay,
40½ E. WASHINGTON ST.,
FIRE INSURANCE, REAL ESTATE,
LOANS AND RENTAL AGENT.

Quinn Levi, lab, h 64 Rhode Island.
Quinn Malachi F, saloon, 249 W South, h same.
Quinn Margaret (wid John), h 252½ W Washington.
Quinn Martin, butcher, h 75 Patterson.
Quinn Mary, tailoress, b 300 S East.
Quinn Mary A (wid John), r 173 Ash.
Quinn Mary E (wid Edward), h 31 W St Clair.
Quinn Matthew M, tagger Bureau of Animal Industry, h 273 W Maryland.
Quinn Michael, lab, h 336 W Washington.
Quinn Patrick, sawmkr, h 132 Blake.
Quinn Patrick J, clk, b 75 Patterson.
Quinn Patrick J, mach, b 627 W Vermont.
Quinn Patrick T, lab, h 300 S East.
Quinn Robert R, grocer, 57 Rhode Island, h same.
Quinn Roger, lab, b 300 S East.
Quinn Samuel, vice-pres and supt of agts State Life Ins Co, h 427 N Capitol av.
Quinn Thomas, umbrella rep, h 58 Cook.
Quinn Thomas F, city fireman, h 36 Mayhew.
Quinn Thomas J, foreman Kingan & Co (ltd), h 335 W Vermont.
Quinn Wm, waiter, r 75 W Ohio.
Quinn Wm D, sawmkr, b 1016 N Senate av.
Quinn Wm H, bartndr, h 268 S Delaware.
Quinn Wm J, clk, b 335 W Vermont.
Quinn Wm M, barber, 128 Indiana av, h 16 Torbet.
Quinn Winifred M, cashr, b 336 W Washington.
Quinot Wm (F G Dittman & Co), h 884 N Senate av.
Quirk Margaret (wid Patrick), b 521 S West.
Quirk Maria (wid Henry), h 234 W Wabash.
Quirk Patrick, lab, b 324 W Maryland.

R

Raab Frederick, printer, h 314 Spann av.
Raab George, waiter, h 308 S Penn.
Raab Louisa M, cook, h 308 S Penn.
Raasch Albert, mason, h 67 Spann av.

WILL GO ON YOUR BOND
American Bonding & Trust Co.
Of Baltimore, Md. Approved as sole surety by the United States Government and the different States as Sole Surety on all Forms of Bonds.
W. E. BARTON & CO., General Agents,
504 Indiana Trust Building.
LONG DISTANCE TELEPHONE 1918.

THE FRED DIETZ CO.
WOODEN PACKING BOXES MADE TO ORDER
FACTORY AND WAREHOUSE TRUCKS.
400 Madison Avenue. Telephone 695.

BUSINESS EDUCATION A NECESSITY.
TIME SHORT. DAY AND NIGHT SCHOOL.
SUCCESS CERTAIN AT THE PERMANENT, RELIABLE
Indianapolis BUSINESS UNIVERSITY

Steam Pumping Machinery { HENRY R. WORTHINGTON, 64 S. PENNSYLVANIA ST. Long Distance Telephone 284.

UNION CO-OPERATIVE LAUNDRY (OF UNION LAUNDRY GIRLS.) NOS. 38, 40 AND 42 VIRGINIA AVENUE. T. E. SOMERVILLE, MANAGER. TELEPHONE 18. INDIANAPOLIS, IND.

HORACE M. HADLEY
INSURANCE AND LOANS
66 E. Market Street, Basement
TELEPHONE 1540.

Raasch Albert jr, mason, b 67 Spann av.
Raasch Charles, lab, b 111 Spann av.
Raasch Wilhelmina (wid Frederick), h 243 English av.
Rabb Albert (Scott & Rabb), h 24 Christian av.
Rabe Herman, wood, 235 Lincoln la, h 245 same.
Rabe Paul, lab, b 245 Lincoln la.
Raber Alfred, lawyer, 312 Indiana Trust bldg, r 75 E Walnut.
Rabold Charles G, soldier U S Arsenal, h 464 Hanna.
Race Marvin E, trav agt, h 602 Bellefontaine.
Race Tunis, driver, h 310 N Pine.
Rademacher Herman J, cigarmkr, b 125 Gresham.
Rademacher John, car sealer, h 125 Gresham.
Rader Frank M, blksmith, 223 Cedar, h 216 same.
Rader George W, engr, h 119 E Merrill.
Rader Harry C, painter, b 119 E Merrill.
Rader John D, patrolman, h 386 S Olive.
Rader John J, bartndr H C Dippel, h rear 318 E Washington.
Rader Leonard E, lab, b 253 S Spruce.
Rader Phineas, agt, h 253 S Spruce.
Radowski Edward, contr, 557 Morris (W I), h same.
Radtke Carl, lab, h 18 Martha (W I).
Rafert Albert C, bkkpr Carl Moller, b 139 E Merrill.
Rafert Charles F, carp, h 134 Huron.
Rafert Charles H, carp, h e s Bradley 3 n of Ohio.
Rafert Charles W, drayman, h 99 Downey.
Rafert Christopher F, h 603 N Delaware.
Rafert Edward H, mach, h 139 E Merrill.
Rafert Emma S (Union Co-Operative Laundry), b 139 E Merrill.
Rafert Frank A, carp, h e s Bradley 2 n of Ohio.
Rafert George W, clk, b 311 S Delaware.
Rafert Henry C, carp, h 57 Omer.
Rafert Louis F, city fireman, b 530 E Georgia.
Rafert Martin E, photog, 15 Bloomington, h same.

COLLECTIONS
MERCHANTS' AND MANUFACTURERS' EXCHANGE
Will give you good service.
J. E. TAKKEN, Manager,
Union Building, over U. S. Pension Office.
73 West Maryland Street.

Rafert Otto E, clk When Clothing Store, b 311 S Delaware.
Rafert Wm H, h 311 S Delaware.
Rafert Wm H jr, clk, b 311 S Delaware.
Raffensperger Hiram C, drugs, s w cor East and South, h 280 Fletcher av.
Rafferty James E, lab, h 9 Bates al.
Rafferty Joseph, lab, b 299 W Maryland.
Rafferty Mary E (wid Timothy J), h 507½ W Washington.
Rafterty James, lab, b 297 Coburn.
Rafterty John, grocer, 187 Madison av, h same.
Raftery Michael, patrolman, h 297 Coburn.
Raftery Michael F, patternmkr, h 301 Coburn.
Raftery Michael W, blksmith, h 28 N Beville av.
Raftery Patrick, clk, b 179 W South.
Raftery Thomas, b 187 Madison av.
Raftery Thomas, lab, b 297 Coburn.
Raftery Thomas J, tmstr, h 39 Valley.
Rafton David, printer, b 169 Dougherty.
Ragan Aida, bkkpr State House Bldg Assn, b 88 Ash.
Ragan Charles A, lab, b 520 E Ohio.
Ragan John J, mach, b 520 E Ohio.
Ragan Leah M (wid Homer B), h 47 Arch.
Ragan Mary B (wid Michael), h 520 E Ohio.
Ragan Wm J, foreman, h 197 W 1st.
Ragan Zachariah, carp, h 88 Ash.
Ragland Edward M, clk, b 76 Bellefontaine.
Ragland John W, h 76 Bellefontaine.
Ragland Julia A (wid Wm L), h 420 Bellefontaine.
Raglin Louis, die cutter, b 216 Bellefontaine.
Rahe H Edward, clk, b 121 East Drive (W P).
Rahke August E (Faught & Co), saloon, cor River and Oliver avs (W I), h 196 S New Jersey.
Rahke Frances (wid George), h 5 River av (W I).
Rahm Herman, tailor, 40 Michigan (H), h same.
Rahn Leo, molder, b 23 Weghorst.
Rahn Paul, carp, h 30 Laurel.
Raible Henry A, carp, b 56 Downey.
Raible Joseph, watchman, h 655 Mass av.
Raible Margaret (wid Louis), h 56 Downey.
Rail John, engr Indpls Water Co, h 114 Church.
Railing Elmer, lab, h 51 Tacoma av.
Railroad Transfer Co, Henry G Stiles pres, Caesar A Rodney sec and treas, John L McFarland supt, cor Alabama and Virginia av.
RAILROADMEN'S BUILDING AND SAVING ASSOCIATION, David S Hill Pres, John Q Van Winkle Vice-Pres, Wm T Cannon Sec, James E Pierce Treas, Secretary's Office Union Station, Treasurer's Office 24 S Penn.
Railsback Charles, grocer, 399 N Illinois, h 846 same.
Railsback Chester A (Railsback & Son), b 187 E Ohio.
Railsback David E, bkkpr, h 474 N Senate av.
RAILSBACK EDDY A, Grocer, 404 College av, h 516 Park av, Tel 1595.
Railsback Jeremiah J, lab, h 45 McIntyre.
Railsback Lafayette D, inventor, h 115 E Ohio.
Railsback Oscar M, nurseryman, h e s Central av 2 s of 24th.

CLEMENS VONNEGUT 184, 186 and 192 E. Washington St. | BUILDERS' HARDWARE, Building Paper. Duplex Joist Hangers

THE WM. H. BLOCK CO. DRY GOODS, DRAPERIES, RUGS, WINDOW SHADES.
7 AND 9 EAST WASHINGTON STREET.

Railsback Smith H (Railsback & Son), h 187 E Ohio.
Railsback & Son (Smith H and Chester A), livery, 173 E North.
RAILWAY OFFICIALS' AND EMPLOYES' ACCIDENT ASSOCIATION, Chalmers Brown Pres, Wm K Bellis Sec and Genl Mngr, Samuel Bellis Asst Sec and Treas, 25-32 Ingalls Blk.
Rain Herman, lab, h 218 Charles.
Raine George, lab, h 21 McCauley.
Rainear Elisha H, carp, h 264 W Pearl.
Rainear Mary, r 23 Columbia blk.
Rainear Owen G, lab, b 264 W Pearl.
Rainear Robert H, sander, h 264 W Pearl.
Raines Harvey A, tel opr, h 79 S Reisner (W I).
Raines Mary J (wid George), h 219 S New Jersey.
Rainey Elizabeth, stenog Pickens & Cox, b 22 Randolph.
Rainey Harvey W, phys Insane Hospital.
Rainey Thaddeus R, clk Badger Furniture Co, h 61 Ruckle.
Rains Alvin B, mach hd, b 198 Douglass.
Rains George W, roofer, h 217½ E Washington.
Rains Hiram, sander, b 198 Douglass.
Raines Martin V, h 198 Douglass.
Raja Vincent, lab, h 73 Harmon.
Raley Henry, barber, 604 Virginia av, h 156 Hosbrook.
Rall Albert, packer, r 116½ W New York.
Ralph Richard, b w s Auburn av 6 s of English av.
Ralph Thomas S, switchman, b w s Auburn av 6 s of English av.
Ralph Wm E (Ralph & Carter), h w s Auburn av 6 s of English av.
RALPH & CARTER (Wm E Ralph, Albert B Carter), Proprs Red Clover Creamery, Butter, Lard, Dressed Poultry and Cheese, 71 N Illinois, Tel 1663.
RALSTON BOYD M, Real Estate, Rentals, Loans and Insurance, 85½ W Market, Tel 960; h 202 W 5th.
Ralston Frank J, clk Exchange Hotel (W I).
Ralston John S, broker, h 69 Christian av.
Ralston Milo M, carp, h 123 Hill av.
Ralston Walter K, mach, b 90 Bradshaw.
Ralya Wm S, sawmkr, h 613 S Meridian.
Ramazzotti Antonia (wid John), confr, 190 S Illinois, h same.
Ramazzotti Louis A, confr, 50 N Penn, b 190 S Illinois.
Rambo George H, carp, b 144 N Alabama.
Rambo Wm, agt, r 195 W South.
Rambow John G, lab, h 200 S Spruce.
Ramey Elizabeth (wid Lawrence), h 36 W St Joseph.
Ramey Elizabeth (wid Wm L), b 555 N Illinois.
Ramey Harry B, trav agt, h 403 Park av.
Ramey J Harvey, clk Indpls Fancy Grocery Co, b 36 W St Joseph.
Ramie Betsy (wid Solomon), h 169 W 3d.
Ramie Henry, lab, b 169 W 3d.
Rammler Dorothy (wid Henry J), b 42 S Linden.
Ramsay Alexander A, plumber, b 451 N West.
Ramsay Amanda H, h 122 E Ohio.
Ramsay Edward A, tel opr Union Station, h 67 W Michigan.

THE H. LIEBER COMPANY. ART EMPORIUM 33 South Meridian St. Visitors Welcome.

Ramsay Frank P, clk The Model, r 247 N Capitol av.
Ramsay John L, blksmith, h 116 Bright.
Ramsay Martin, lab, b 23 Harris.
Ramsay Walter L, plumber, 24½ N Illinois, h 451 N West.
Ramsay Wm W, plumber, b 451 N West.
Ramsey Abraham L, h 38 S State av.
Ramsey Cumings G, lab, b 13 McCauley.
Ramsey Daniel M, clk Van Camp H and I Co, h 208 River av (W I).
Ramsey David W, mach, h 578 Jefferson av.
Ramsey Edward A, ins agt, h 86 Spann av.
Ramsey Francis M, carp, h 75 Norwood.
Ramsey Harry H, mach, b 107 Walcott.
Ramsey James H, lab, b 578 Jefferson av.
Ramsey Jefferson, tmstr, r 15 Rhode Island.
Ramsey Jennie, boarding 38 S State av.
Ramsey Johanna (wid Wm), h 13 McCauley.
Ramsey John, uphlr, b 86 Spann av.
Ramsey John L, live stock, b 29 Warren av (W I).
Ramsey John W, h 260 N Illinois.
Ramsey Leah P (wid John F), h 260 N Illinois.
Ramsey Mary A (wid John H), h 107 Walcott.
Ramsey Mary E (wid Frank H), h 57½ E South.
Ramsey Matilda (wid Thomas A), h 62 Jefferson av.
Ramsey Robert H, car rep, h 407 Columbia av.
Ramsey Robert L, carp, h 45 Carlos.
Ramsey Robert R, carp, h 74 Church.
Ramsey Robert S, patternmkr, h 68 King av (H).
Ramsey Sarah, r rear 175 N Penn.
Ramsey Thomas H, clk, b 150 Jefferson av.
Ramsey Wm, bartndr, h 36 Johnson av.
Rance James, stock buyer, r 89 Indiana av.
Randall Alice, teacher Public School No 32, b 997 N Penn.
Randall Arthur J, clk, b 997 N Penn.
Randall Charles A, tubmkr, h 326 Spring.
Randall Francis M, harnessmkr, h 324 E Louisiana.

GUIDO R. PRESSLER,
FRESCO PAINTER
Churches, Theaters, Public Buildings, Etc., A Specialty.
Residence, No. 325 North Liberty Street.
INDIANAPOLIS, IND.

INDIANAPOLIS STEEL ROOFING AND CORRUGATING WORKS, 23 and 25 East South Street. S. D. NOEL, Proprietor.

David S. McKernan, Rooms 2-5 Thorpe Block. REAL ESTATE AND LOANS Money to loan on real estate. Special inducements offered those having money to loan. It will pay you to investigate.

DIAMOND WALL PLASTER { Telephone 1410 BUILDERS' EXCHANGE.

UNION TRANSFER AND STORAGE CO. Cor. E. Ohio St. and C., C., C. & St. L. R'y Tracks. BEST FACILITIES FOR STORING AND TRANSFERRING MACHINERY AND MERCHANDISE.

W. McWORKMAN

FIRE SHUTTERS,
FIRE DOORS,
METAL CEILINGS.

930 W. Washington St. Tel. 1118.

Randall Frank P, salesman W H Messenger, b 182 S New Jersey.
Randall Harry, lab, b s s Clifford av 1 w of Watts.
Randall Henry C, engr, h 210 Blake.
Randall Horace, trav agt, h 997 N Penn.
Randall James A, carp, n e cor Park av and Fleet, h same.
Randall Louis E (Randall & McKee), h 224 Ramsey av.
Randall Lucy (wid Hiram P), h 904 N Delaware.
Randall Nelson A, printer, b s s Clifford av 1 e of Watts.
Randall Otto, lab, b 165 W Merrill.
Randall Stephen M, news agt, r 67 Cleaveland blk.
Randall Theodore A (T A Randall & Co), h 642 College av.
RANDALL T A & CO (Theodore A Randall, Denton F Billingsley), Proprs The Clay Worker, 5 Monument Pl.
Randall Wm L, h 195 W Merrill.
Randall Wm T, showman, h 53½ Russell av.
Randall & McKee (Louis E Randall, Thomas M McKee), furniture, 194 Mass av.
Randerson Harriet, b 350 E New York.
Randerson Robert E, asst chief clk C C C & St L Ry, h 68 W New York.
Randolph Eliza J (wid Lot), h 50 Springfield.
Randolph Emma, h 393 Roanoke.
Randolph Harry M, condr, h 236 Blake.
Randolph Jary Rev, h w s Denny 4 n of Washington.
Randolph Laura (wid Marion DeW), restaurant, 277 Mass av, h same.
Randolph Milton S, lab, h 152 Elm.
Randolph Reuben, lab, h 531 W Maryland.
Randolph Robert, painter, h n s Michigan 4 e of Sherman Drive.
Randolph Thomas J, lab, b 50 Springfield.
Randolph Wm, lab, b 39 Ellen.
Raner Barney, wirewkr, h 217 N Senate av.
Raney Ingram B, tmstr, h 201½ English av.
Raney Mary (wid Squire A), b 70 McGinnis.
Ranger Emily A (wid John H), h 21 W 1st.

GEO. J. MAYER,
MANUFACTURER OF
SEALS
STENCILS, RUBBER STAMPS, CHECKS, BADGES, DOOR PLATES, ETC.
15 S. Meridian St., Ground Floor. TEL. 1386.

Ranje Henry, carp, b 72 Beaty.
Ranje Hugo H, painter, b 72 Beaty.
Ranje Ida M (wid Henry), h 72 Beaty.
Ranje Otto, cutter Paul H Krauss, b 72 Beaty.
Rankin Agnes R, teacher High School, b 958 N Alabama.
Rankin Barbara, h 382 W North.
Rankin Edward, brakeman, h 51 Williams.
Rankin Elisha C, clk R M S, h 958 N Alabama.
Rankin Hamilton, carp, b 219 Indiana av.
Rankin Henry, h 412 N Pine.
Rankin Louisa M, teacher, b 958 N Alabama.
Rankin Margaret M, asst matron Indiana Reformatory.
Rankin Wm F, lab, b 69 Birch av (W I).
Rankin Wm H, plastr, b 382 W North.
Rankin Wm M, engr Indpls Water Co, h 69 Birch av (W I).
Rankins George W, lab, h rear 202 Blake.
Rankins James, waiter, b 307 Fayette.
Ranlett Foster P, civil engr, r 224 N New Jersey.
Rannells Byron R, clk Indpls Gas Co, b 153 W South.
Rannells James R, shoemkr, 22 Mass av, h 153 W South.
Ranney Frank W, clk L E & W R R, h 357 College av.
Ranney Frederick W, student, b 357 College av.
Ranney Lucy M, clk, b 357 College av.
Ransdell Charles E, motorman, h 427 Ash.
Ransdell Daniel M, pres Lombard Building and Loan Assn, sec and treas American Plate Glass Co, h 672 N Alabama.
Ransdell Frank E, barber, b 201 LeGrand av.
Ransdell George B, trainer, h 187 Buchanan.
Ransdell Linney, lab, h 734 Shelby.
Ransdell Omar, clk Wm L Elder, b 201 Le Grand av.
Ransdell Peter, carp, h 201 LeGrand av.
Ransdell Wm J, clk, h 24 Hall pl.
Ransdell Wm J, clk Murphy, Hibben & Co, b 247 N Capitol av.
Ransford Nettie (Ransford & Metcalf), h 5 The Windsor.
Ransford Wm P, h 5 The Windsor.
Ransford & Metcalf (Nettie Ransford, Kate Metcalf), pubs The Eastern Star, 5 The Windsor.
Ransom Isaac N, b 481 E 9th.
Ransom John W, gasfitter, h 313 Jefferson av.
Ransom Rebecca (wid Isaac), b 11 Stoughton av.
Rapalee Charles C, painter, b 78 Bellefontaine.
Rape Charles B, barber, 14 Indiana av, r 102 N Capitol av.
Rape Sylvester P, porter, r 102 N Capitol av.
Raper Alford P, tel opr, h 1777 Graceland av.
Raper George, cigars, 19 Monument pl and The Denison, h 257 N Delaware.
Raper Jesse F, carp, r 31 Hubbard blk.
Raper Thomas, h 1768 Kenwood av.
Raphael Benjamin, clk, b 1033 N Meririan.
Raphael Goldah (wid John), b 1033 N Meridian.
Raphael Harry, milliner, 43 W Washington, h 1033 N Meridian.
Rapp Anna (wid Frederick J), h 449 N New Jersey.

A. METZGER AGENCY ESTABLISHED 1863. REAL ESTATE

LAMBERT GAS & GASOLINE ENGINE CO.
ANDERSON, IND. NATURAL GAS ENGINES.

BICYCLES $5 DOWN. $5 MONTHLY. Best Wheels. Best Terms. WHEELMEN'S CO. 31 W. OHIO ST. LONG DISTANCE TEL. 1855.

Rapp John G, collr A Kiefer Drug Co, b 449 N New Jersey.
Rappaport Fannie (wid Louis), b 60 W Merrill.
Rappaport Isaac, pdlr, h 300½ S Illinois.
Rappaport Isaac, saloon, 143 W Washington, h 56 Russell av.
Rappaport Philip, pub and editor Indiana Tribune, 18 S Alabama, h 603 N Alabama.
Rappaport Solomon S, pdlr, h 300½ S Illinois.
Rappenecker George, bartndr, r 154 W Washington.
Rapson James, carp, h 28 Depot (B).
Rarden Albert B, miller, b 134 Minerva.
Rarden James, lab, b 134 Minerva.
Rarden Joseph B, lab, b 134 Minerva.
Rarden Margaret (wid Henry), h 134 Minerva.
Rarden Margaret, cook, h 168½ E Washington.
Rardin Howard H, salesman, h 297 Cornell av.
Rardin Noble P, baker, b 297 Cornell av.
Rardon Wm, shoemkr, 135 Mass av, h 112 Singleton.
Raricks George F, car rep, b 77 Bloomington.
Raricks James J, lab, h 77 Bloomington.
Rariden Bedford W, lab, h 38 S Belmont (W I).
Rariden Emily (wid John), b 38 S Belmont (W I).
Rariden Michael, lab, h 170 S William (W I).
Rasbach Casper F W, mach, h 316 Columbia av.
Rasbach John W, plastr, b 316 Columbia av.
Raschbacher Emil L, clk Albert Gall, b 811 E Market.
Raschbacher Leonard J, shoemkr, h 811 E Market.
Raschig Daisy, stenog, b 29 Shriver av.
Raschig Edward G F, sec to supt Am Ex Co, h 72 W Michigan.
Raschig George L, sec Indpls Savings and Inv Co, real est and ins, 36 Monument pl, h 59 West Drive (W P).
Raschig Ida A (wid Reynolds), b 29 Shriver.
Raschig Jean, teacher Public School No 4, b 200 N West.
Raschig Maurice H, dentist, 8½ E Washington, h 168 N Meridian.
RASEMANN FREDERICK, Choice Liquors and Cigars, 389 N Noble, cor St Clair, h 310 N Noble.
Rasener Charles F W, mngr, h 1749 N Illinois.
Rasener Christina L (wid Wm F), h rear 331 E Ohio.
Rasener Ida C (wid Frank W), h 1150 E Michigan.
Rasener Jennie, grocer, 1749 N Illinois, h same.
Rasener Wm A, tmstr, b 125 N Summit.
Rasener Wm F, h 125 N Summit.
Rasener Wm F jr, city fireman, h 121 N Summit.
Rash Mason S, clk Model Clothing Co, h 212 Keystone av.
Rash Wm M, pdlr, r 318½ Indiana av.
Rasmussen Harry E, student, b 6 Pleasant.
Rasmussen John, tmstr, h 53 Oscar.
Rasmussen Julius, cabtmkr, h 9 Cooper.
Rasmussen Lars P, tailor, 531 W Udell (N I), h same.
Rasmussen Lillie C, milliner, b 6 Pleasant.

THOS. C. DAY & CO.
Financial Agents and Loans.
We have the experience, and claim to be reliable.
Rooms 325 to 330 Lemcke Bldg.

Rasmussen Ole, collr, h 117 Dunlop.
Rasmussen Peter, hostler, h 19 Downey.
Rasmussen Rasmus, porter, h 6 Pleasant.
Rasmussen Wm T, city agt, b 6 Pleasant.
Raspberry Wm G, lab, h 129 Patterson.
Rassfeld Dina C (wid Ferdinand), h rear 431 S Meridian.
Rassmann Charles A, clk Clemens Vonnegut, b 725 E Market.
Rassmann Dorothy (wid Charles), h 725 E Market.
Rassmann Emil C (Dyer & Rassmann), h 23 N Arsenal av.
Rassmann Otto C, bkkpr Kothe, Wells & Bauer, b 725 E Market.
Ratcliff Wm A, agt, h 96 W New York.
Ratcliffe A J, excursion agt Union Pacific System, 9 Jackson pl, r 14 E Michigan.
Ratcliffe Thomas, patternmkr, h 127 Cornell av.
Ratcliffe Thomas J, mach, h n s English av 2 w of Belt R R.
Ratcliffe Wm W, clk Adams Ex Co, h 821 N Capitol av.
Ratcliffe Xenophon, hostler 181 East Drive (W P).
Rather Isaac, lab, r 130 Allegheny.
Rathert Ethel M, b 32 W 12th.
Rathert Wm (Charles H Schwomeyer & Co), h 399 S Meridian.
Rathert Wm H, clk Sloan Drug Co, r 16 W New York.
Rathfon David M, printer, b 233 Virginia av.
Rathfon Rensen T, printer The Indpls Sentinel, b 233 Virginia av.
Rathgens John C, b 248 Yandes.
Rathsam John G, florist, 749 Broadway, h same.
Rathz Charles G, tinner, h 408½ S Meridian.
Ratliff Elizabeth (wid James), h 86 E Ohio.
Ratliff Harlan S, clk N A Moore & Co, h 444 Talbott av.
Ratliff Russell, teacher Blind Institute.
Ratti Edward G, printer, b 318 N East.
Ratti Joseph, printer, 72 S Illinois, h 318 N East.
Rau Edward D, paperhngr, h 396 N Senate av.

EAT HITZ'S CRACKERS AND CAKES.
ASK YOUR GROCER FOR THEM.

J. H. TECKENBROCK General House Painter, 94 EAST SOUTH STREET.

FIDELITY MUTUAL LIFE—PHILADELPHIA, PA.
$75,000,000, Insurance In Force. $3,500,000, Death Losses Paid. $1,500,090, Surplus. A. H. COLLINS {General Agent, Baldwin Block.

Edwardsport Coal & Mining Co. •••••• BITUMINOUS COAL IN CAR LOADS TO DEALERS AND MANUFACTURERS. ROOMS 42 AND 43 WHEN BUILDING.

ESTABLISHED 1876. TELEPHONE 168.
CHESTER BRADFORD,
SOLICITOR OF PATENTS,
AND COUNSEL IN PATENT CAUSES.
(See adv. page 6.)
Office:—Rooms 14 and 16 Hubbard Block, S. W. Cor. Washington and Meridian Streets, INDIANAPOLIS, INDIANA.

Raub Edward B (Daly & Raub), r 307 N Delaware.
Rauch Albert E, cigar mnfr, 125 Windsor, h same.
Rauch Edward J, clk John Rauch, b 327 N Capitol av.
Rauch Elizabeth (wid George), b 131 Locke.
Rauch George, b 132 Orange av.
Rauch George, cigarmkr, h 260 W Washington.
RAUCH JOHN, Mnfr and Dealer in Cigars and Tobacco, Mnfr of the Capital City Cigar, 82 W Washington, Tel 414; h 327 N Capitol av.
Rauh Charles B, furnace setter, h 318 E McCarty.
Rauh Edward J, lab, b e s Lebanon av 1 s of Brookside av.
RAUH E & SONS (Leopold, Henry and Samuel E), Hides and Fertilizer Mnfrs, Office 219 S Penn, Tel 442; Factory s e cor Gray and Belt R R.
Rauh Henry (E Rauh & Sons), treas Indpls Cabinet Works, h 224 E Ohio.
Rauh John, dairy, e s Lebanon av 1 s of Brookside av, h same.
Rauh Leopold (E Rauh & Sons), res Dayton, O.
Rauh Samuel E (E Rauh & Sons), h 675 N Capitol av.
Rausch George, lab, b 760 Madison av.
Rausch John, lab, b 905 S Meridian.
Rausch John L, cook, r 100 S Illinois.
Rausch Joseph, mach hd, h 146 Eddy.
Rausch Peter, lab, h 905 S Meridian.
Rauschen Catherine, midwife, 474 S Illinois, h same.
Rauschen Wm, lab, h 474 S Illinois.
Rauscher Anton, mach hd, h 63 Beaty.
Rauser George, driver, h 112 Harrison.
Rauser Peter E, grocer, 68 S West, h same.
Rauser Potential (wid George), b 68 S West.
Rauser Wm, barber, b 68 S West.
Rautenberg Joseph, lab, h 22 Chase (W I).
Ravencraft Francis M (C H Hart & Co), h 256½ Indiana av.
Ravenscroft Wm H, clk, h 88 Michigan av.
Rawles Abraham, carp, h 21 Walcott.

Outing BICYCLES
..MADE BY:..
HAY & WILLITS MFG CO.
76 N. Pennsylvania St. Phone 598.

Rawlings George T H, driver, b 271 N California.
Rawlings Henry O, bkkpr, h 271 N California.
Rawlings Nancy A (wid John J), b 293 N New Jersey.
Rawlinson Joseph, molder, h 85 Holmes av (H).
Rawls Edward B Rev, pastor Edwin Ray M E Church, h 88 Pleasant.
RAWLS WM S, Dentist, Room 4 Claypool Blk, 9½ N Illinois, h 242 Central av.
Ray Alfred, baggageman, h 54 Meikel.
Ray Allen, harnessmkr, h 46 Pleasant.
Ray Anderson, lab, h 88 Maple.
Ray Anna (wid John J), b 284 Highland av.
Ray Anna, teacher, b 121 East Drive (W P).
Ray Arthur M, chief clk The Bradstreet Co, b 510 Dillon.
Ray Caroline (wid Herman H), h 121 East Drive (W P).
Ray Charles, lab, r 151 W Washington.
Ray Charles W, bookbndr, b 386 Indiana av.
Ray Curtis L, carp, b 15½ S Alabama.
Ray David, wagonmkr, b 848 LaSalle (M P).
Ray Dillon B, clk, b 46 Pleasant.
Ray Edith, h 73 Kentucky av.
Ray Edmond S, mach, h 2 Shriver av.
Ray Edward H, bkkpr, b 121 East Drive (W P).
Ray Emma C (wid George), r 20 Hendricks blk.
Ray Ezra M, packer, r 185½ W Washington.
Ray Frank, lab, b 444 E 7th.
Ray Frank, lab, b 30 John.
Ray Frank, mach, b 511 W Maryland.
Ray Franklin E, phys Insane Hospital.
Ray George, carp, b 90 Sycamore.
Ray George, cook, r 12½ Indiana av.
Ray Georgiana M, music teacher, 284 Highland av, h same.
Ray Gilbert H, molder, h 644 Ontario (N I).
Ray Green, lab, h 30 John.
Ray Harry R, dyer, b 63 N Alabama.
Ray Herman H C, polisher, b 121 East Drive (W P).
Ray Hudson D, lab, h 90 Sycamore.
Ray Isaac P, carp, h 115 Christian av.
Ray James O, lab, b 473 Blake.
Ray Jennie A, bkkpr, b 26 Morton.
Ray John, lab, b s s E Washington 4 e of Belt R R.
Ray John B, carp, h 28 Dougherty.
Ray John B, lab, b 26 Morton.
Ray John F, carp, h 26 Morton.
Ray John J, painter, h 510 Dillon.
Ray John J jr, carp, h 284 Highland av.
Ray John L, shoemkr, 468 E Washington, b same.
Ray John W, office 66 E Market, h Madison rd 6 miles s of city limits.
Ray Lottie (wid James), h 252½ Mass av.
Ray Lucia H, teacher High School, b 275 N Capitol av.
Ray Mary E (wid Jacob W), h 386 Indiana av.
Ray Omer T, filer, b 195 S Pine.
Ray Oscar, lab, b s s E Washington 4 e of Belt R R.
Ray Oscar, lab, h 317 Lafayette.
Ray Oscar, lab, h rear 671 N Senate av.
Ray Otto L, brakeman, h 25 N Beville av.
Ray Rachel (wid James), h s e cor 28th and Central av.
Ray Samuel D, driver, b 252 E Georgia.
Ray Sarah J (wid George W), h 468 E Washington.

C. ZIMMERMAN & SONS | SLATE AND GRAVEL ROOFERS 19 South East Street.

DRIVEN WELLS And Second Water Wells and Pumps of all kinds at CHARLES KRAUSS', 42 S. PENN. ST., Telephone 465.

Ray Thaddeus, lab, h w s Waverly 3 n of Bloyd av (B).
Ray Thomas, lab, h 96 Torbet.
Ray Thomas B, mach, h 269½ Mass av.
Ray Timothy, flagman, h 252 E Georgia.
Ray Wm, lab, b 328 E Washington.
Ray Wm E, plastr, 54 S Austin (B), h same.
Ray Wm W, clk Indiana Paper Co, h 368 N Noble.
Rayburn Martha (wid James), h 217 E Ohio.
Rayburn May, h 230 N Senate av.
Rayburn Ross R, bricklyr, b 230 N Senate av.
Rayer R Edward, car rep, h 71 Foundry (B).
Rayle Florence D, stenog, b 429 N Senate av.
Rayls Abijah F, horse dealer, h 188 Elizabeth.
Rayls John C, coremkr, h 434 W North.
Rayls Thomas, horse dealer, b 188 Elizabeth.
Raymond Andrew, gas stationkpr, h 1207 Berlin av.
Raymond Anthony J, lab, b 228 W Georgia.
Raymond Bertha, h 222½ E Washington.
Raymond Charles, b 228 W Georgia.
Raymond Curtis B, carp, h 63 Yandes.
Raymond Edward, news agt, b 1207 Berlin av.
Raymond Harriet (wid Isaac), b 118 Ash.
Raymond Harry C, painter, h 33 S Stuart (B).
Raymond Harry W, clk, b 45 West Drive (W P).
Raymond Isaac P, cooper, h 21 Blake.
Raymond Nancy M (wid Charles S), h 228 W Georgia.
Raymond Ophir C, foreman Van Camp Packing Co, h 121 Cornell av.
Raymond Perley B, supt Adams & Williamson, h 45 West Drive (W P).
Raymond Samuel, lab, h 39 Clifford av.
Rayne Herman, molder, h 20 Oriole.
RAYNO ROLLIN PROF, Theatrical School, 130 W Ohio, h same.
Raynor Jacob R, h 123 W 4th.
Rea Albert E, painter, b 146 Clifford av.
Rea Henry S, baggageman, h 1381 N Capitol av.
Rea Samuel B, condr, h 351 Talbott av.
Rea Thomas N, baggageman, h 146 Clifford av.
Rea Wm, carp, b 126 W Vermont.
Read Annit P (wid George H), h 45½ Virginia av.
Read Charles W, painter A H Grove, h 78 Frank.
Read Daniel, lab, h 17 Howard.
Read George A, b 103 Park av.
Read Lavina H (wid Darius G), h 327½ Dillon.
Read Orville, lab, h 103 Park av.
Read Peter C, dentist, 18½ N Meridian, b 103 Park av.
Read Walter S, clk, r 76 N New Jersey.
Read Wm E, piano tuner, h 181 Lexington av.
Read Wm H, lab, b 45½ Virginia av.
Reade John H, clk Consumers' Gas Trust Co, h 35 Park av.
Reading Frank H, driver, h 310 Shelby.
Reading Isabella (wid Wm), h 310 Shelby.
Reading Wm, waiter, b 149 W South.
READING WM A, Lawyer, Rooms 3-4, 18½ N Penn, Tel 1184; h Irvington.
Ready Michael, h 76 W McCarty.

EQUITABLE LIFE ASSURANCE SOCIETY OF THE UNITED STATES.
RICHARDSON & McCREA
Managers for Central Indiana.
79 East Market St. Telephone 182.

Ready Michael J (Hayes & Ready), h 32 Central av.
Ready Patrick (Ready & Foltz), h 93 Hiatt (W I).
Ready Patrick, lab, b 9 Meikel.
Ready Patrick, lab, h 281 W Merrill.
Ready & Foltz (Patrick Ready, Alfred Foltz), painters, Car Works (W I).
Reagan Amos W, salesman M O'Connor & Co, h 445 Central av.
Reagan Charles M (Reagan & Brown), b 408 N Illinois.
Reagan Charles M, attendant Public Library, r 29 Thorpe blk.
Reagan David J, trav agt Baldwin, Miller & Co, h 573 N Senate av.
Reagan Edward, h 98 W Ohio.
Reagan Elizabeth (wid Dennis), h 27 Dickson.
Reagan John, bkkpr John L Moore, h 390 Central av.
Reagan John E, trav auditor, b 27 Dickson.
Reagan Joseph E (Baldwin, Miller & Co), h 370 College av.
Reagan Michael, tmstr, h 20 N West.
Reagan Robert R, paperhngr, h 128 W 3d.
Reagan Thomas, painter, h n w cor Euclid av and Ohio.
Reagan Wm P (Masson & Reagan), res Bridgeport, Ind.
Reagan & Brown (Charles M Reagan, Harry S Brown), lawyers, 79 Baldwin blk.
Realey Frederick, watchman, h 530 S Capitol av.
Realey George H, mach, h 500 S Capitol av.
Realey John C, lab, b 530 S Capitol av.
Ream Jacob H, lab, h e s Sherman Drive 3 n of Washington.
Ream Laura M, journalist, b 600 N Alabama.
Reardon Caroline (wid John H), r 307 N Alabama.
Reardon Charles, carp, r 16 S Senate av.
Reardon John, lab, b 179 S Alabama.
Reardon John L, lawyer, b 78 High.
Reardon Timothy O, real est, h 78 High.
Reasner, see Rasener.
Reaume Anna C (wid John A; Armstrong & Reaume), h 971 N Illinois.

STENOGRAPHERS FURNISHED.
EXPERIENCED OR BEGINNERS, PERMANENT OR TEMPORARY.
S. H. EAST, State Agent,
The Williams Typewriter,
55 THORPE BLOCK, 87 EAST MARKET ST.

ERTEL STEAM LAUNDRY 26 and 28 N. Senate Avenue. Telephone 18
WE WILL CALL FOR AND DELIVER YOUR WORK. SATISFACTION GUARANTEED.

ELLIS & HELFENBERGER { ENTERPRISE FOUNDRY & FENCE CO. 162-170 S. Senate Ave. Tel. 958.

THE HOGAN TRANSFER AND STORAGE COMP'Y
Household Goods and Pianos Moved—Packed—Stored...... Baggage and Package Express Machinery and Safes a Specialty Cor. Washington and Illinois Sts. TELEPHONE No. 675.

The Central Rubber & Supply Co. ◆◆◆ Hose, Belting, Packing, Clothing, Druggists' Sundries, Bicycle Tires, Cotton Hose, Etc. New York Belting & Packing Co., L't'd. PHONE 922. 79 S. ILLINOIS ST., INDIANAPOLIS, IND.

A death rate below all other American Companies, and dividends from this source correspondingly larger.
The Provident Life and Trust Company
Of Philadelphia.
D. W. EDWARDS, General Agent,
508 Indiana Trust Building.

Reaume Frank C, b 971 N Illinois.
Reaume George F, decorator, b 229 E New York.
Reaume Nellie (wid Joseph), r 347 N Illinois.
Rebentisch Albert J, cigar mnfr, 48 Davis, b same.
Rebentisch Henry W, cigarmkr, h 51 Johnson av.
Rebentisch Ida M (wid Charles), h 48 Davis.
Reber Charles T, printer, h 111 Bright.
Reber Christopher, brewer, h 70 Kennington.
Reber Gerhard F, jeweler, 30 Virginia av, r same.
Rebesberger Henry H, h 270 S Meridian.
Rebmann Lilly, h 168 W Chesapeake.
Rebmann Peter, lab, h 13 S Pine.
Rebmann Theodore, mach hd, b 24 Bluff rd.
Rebmann Wm H, baker, h 226 E Morris.
Recer Joseph H, patrolman, h 271 W North.
Rech Elizabeth, h 742 S Meridian.
Rech Frank G, waiter, b rear 407 S Delaware.
Rech George, ticket agt Penna Lines, h 864 E Washington.
Rech John, asst ticket agt Penna Lines, h 629 S Meridian.
Rech John E, barber, 244 E Washington, h 755 S East.
Rech Susanna (wid Nicholas), h rear 407 S Delaware.
Reckel John, driver, h 81 Palmer.
Recker Carlos, bkkpr Sander & Recker, b 238 S New Jersey.
Recker Gottfried (Sander & Recker), h 238 S New Jersey.
Recker Gustav A (Sander & Recker), h 22 W 11th.
Record Frederick R, h 51 S Reisner (W I).
Rector John A, lab, b 125 Garden.
Rector Samuel C, engr, h 291 Virginia av.
Red Clay Orchard Co, Wm A Jones pres, Wm H Cross sec, James H Smith treas, 36 W Washington.
Redd Hannah, b 18½ Indiana av.

Julius C. Walk & Son,
Jewelers
Indianapolis.
12 EAST WASHINGTON ST.

Reddehase Frederick, whol meats, 98 E Mkt House, h 64 Gatling.
Reddick Augustus H, lab, h 734 Nevada.
Reddick Charles R, trav agt, b 170 Christian.
Reddick Chauncey B, collr, b 65 Gladstone av.
Reddick Elizabeth, b 210 Newman.
Reddick Jasper N, lab, h 86 Sheldon.
Reddick Morris M, shoemkr, h 65 Gladstone av.
Reddick Richard H, lab, b 734 Nevada.
Redding Ada M, b 184 Douglass.
Redding Elizabeth (wid John), b 861 Bellefontaine.
Redding Floyd G, switchman, h 35 Tacoma av.
Redding Frank, painter, r 90 N Delaware.
Redding Harriet (wid James L), b 194 Davidson.
Redding James H, saloon, 167 Michigan (H), h same.
Redding Jeremiah, mach, 296 S Alabama, h same.
Redding Lewis, molder, b 167 Michigan (H).
Redding Wm A, lawyer, b 74 W New York.
Reddington Anna G, teacher Public School No 27, b 474 College av.
Reddington Bridget (wid Michael), h 474 College av.
Reddington John, brakeman, b 803 E Washington.
Reddington John, trimmer, b 80 Clifford av.
Reddington John H, asst sec Board of Public Works, 5 basement Court House, b 474 College av.
Reddington Michael, foreman Kingan & Co, h 206 W South.
Reder Philip, dairy, e s Waverly av 3 n of Clifford av, h same.
Redforan James, janitor, h 449 S Delaware.
Redforan John T, mach, b 419 S Delaware.
Redick Charles I, trav agt The Grocers' Mnfg Co, b 170 Christian av.
Redick De Witt A, mach, h rear 72 S Noble.
Redick Elisha T, lab, h 145 Columbia av.
Redman John, tmstr, h 96 Agnes.
Redman Oscar A, printer, b California House.
Redman Silas, clk, b 342 N Missouri.
REDMAN WM M, Special Agt Provident Life and Trust Co, 508-510 Indiana Trust Bldg, Tel 350; h w s Ritter av 7 n of Washington av (I).
Redmon James W, carp, h 11 Geneva.
Redmond Angeline, confr, E Mkt House, h 363 N New Jersey.
Redmond Ann (wid Thomas), nurse, 15 Maria, h same.
Redmond Austin H, mach hd, b 380 W 1st.
Redmond Charles, student, h 235 E Ohio.
Redmond Frank M, city fireman, r 284 Mass av.
Redmond Frank S, cigars, 24 Indiana av, h 80 W 1st.
Redmond Jeremiah, lab, h 12 Quince.
Redmond John W, tmstr, h 96 Agnes.
Redmond Margaret A (wid John F), h 88 Maxwell.
Redmond Maria (wid Paul), b s w cor Auburn av and Bethel av.
Redmond Thomas A, lab, h 34 St Peter.
Redmond Thomas F, motorman, h 754 N Illinois.
Redmond Wm E, produce, E Mkt House, h 363 N New Jersey.
Redmond Wm J, painter, b 15 Maria.
Redwine Eva (wid David), h 6 Peck.
Reece Elias, baggageman, h 339 N Noble.

OTTO GAS ENGINES | BUILDERS' EXCHANGE S. W. Cor. Ohio and Penn. Telephone 535.

Becker & Son Charly Becker Jacob Becker Jr. Merchant Tailors. 21 N. Penn. St. Tel. 934

SALISBURY & STANLEY OFFICE, STORE AND BANK FIXTURES. Contractors and Builders. Repairing of all kinds done on short notice. 177 Clinton St., Indianapolis, Ind. Telephone 999.

Reece Erven, foreman, h 153 English av.
Reece George, waiter, b 226 N Noble.
Reece John W, carp, h 13 Morgan (W I).
Reed Ada, cook, b 293 E Miami.
Reed Andrew J, engr, h 196 Cornell av.
Reed Ann (wid Jerry), b 1659 N Senate av.
Reed Anson P, h 1498 N Illinois.
Reed Benjamin, painter, r 1½ Fletcher av.
Reed Charles L, mach hd, b 520 W Addison (N I).
Reed Clara, seamstress, b 317 E Ohio.
Reed Clara O, stenog, b 38 Arbor av (W I).
Reed Clarence, ins agt, h 27 Shelby.
Reed Coley, lab, h 30 Hiawatha.
Reed Daniel A, messenger Am Ex Co, h 115 English av.
Reed Daniel W, trav agt, h 63 S Arsenal av.
Reed Edna, housekpr 80 S Reisner (W I).
Reed Edwin H, clk P C C & St L Ry, b 800 E Washington.
Reed Effie L, clk, b 180 E Morris.
Reed Eliza V (wid James P), h 317 E Ohio.
Reed Elizabeth (wid Willoughby H), b 338 N Delaware.
Reed Ellen (wid Wm), h 110 Roanoke.
Reed Frank, plastr, b e s Oakland av 1 n of Clifford av.
Reed Frank J, waiter, b rear 66 College av.
Reed George A, lab, h 29 Willard.
Reed George E, motorman, h 99 Cornell av.
Reed George T, hostler, b 306 E South.
Reed George W, lab, h 264 Fayette.
Reed George W, mantel setter, r 135 Mass av.
Reed Hal W, reporter The Indpls News, h 321 College av.
Reed Harriet M (wid David), h 96 Yandes.
Reed Harry L, gasfitter, b 317 E Ohio.
Reed Hattie E, h 226 W Pearl.
Reed Henry F, pumpmkr, h 180 E Morris.
Reed I Oscar, drugs, 501 Bellefontaine, r 583 Ash.
Reed Jacob, lab, h 210 Agnes.
Reed James, plastr, h e s Oakland av 1 n of Clifford av.
Reed James A, foreman E C Atkins & Co, h 268 Jefferson av.
Reed James E, carp, h 79 Lynn av (W I).
Reed James R, blksmith, h 10 Minkner.
Reed Jennie (wid Eleventh), h 253½ S Capitol av.
Reed John, barber, r 222 Muskingum al.
Reed John, blksmith, b 97 Division (W I).
Reed John, fireman, h rear 227 W Merrill.
Reed John, lab, b Exchange Hotel (W I).
Reed John D, clk, b 210 N Pine.
Reed John K, bricklyr, h 1308 N Delaware.
Reed John L, engr, h 43 S Gale (B).
Reed John W, painter, b 365 S East.
Reed Joseph A, blksmith, h 266 Alvord.
Reed Kate, h 75 S Senate av.
Reed Landy H, painter, h 365 S East.
Reed Lavina A (wid Reason), b 228 College av.
Reed Leon, fireman, h rear 227 W Merrill.
Reed Leon, mach hd, b 15 Nordyke av (W I).
Reed Lodie E, editor, h 112 Park av.
Reed Louis H, artist, b 299 E New York.
Reed Luke L, musician, b 317 E Ohio.
Reed Lulu, b 81 Columbia al.
Reed Martha, usher Blind Institute.
Reed Mary W (wid Enos B), h 299 E New York.
Reed Matilda (wid John), h 154 Hosbrook.
Reed Maud (wid David), h 96 Yandes.
Reed Moses A, lab, h 337 Douglass.
Reed Nancy E (wid John W), h 12 Shriver av.

Henry H. Fay, 40½ E. Washington St., REAL ESTATE, AND LOAN BROKER.

Reed Nellie V (wid Jacob F), h 196 Lincoln la.
Reed Nelson, porter, h 1 Willard.
Reed Oliver, lab, h 493 S Capitol av.
Reed Oliver, stage hd, h 230 W Market.
Reed Otto M, uphlr, b 317 E Ohio.
Reed Robert E, printer, b 23 Hosbrook.
Reed Sallie, b 116 Martindale av.
Reed Sanford, engr, h 936 Gent (M P).
Reed Sarah J (wid James A), b 248 Blake.
Reed Smith, hostler, h 574 E St Clair.
Reed Sumner W, agt, h 470 Newman.
Reed Theresa, h 61 Ellen.
Reed Thomas, lab, b 119 Ft Wayne av.
Reed Ulysses G, blksmith, h 22 Blackford.
Reed Walter C, clk J P Wimmer, b 223 E Vermont.
Reed Wm, foreman Balke & Krauss Co, h 57 Camp.
Reed Wm, proofreader Indpls Journal, h 182 Hoyt av.
Reed Wm B, lab, h 118 Lee (W I).
Reed Wm C, car rep, h 71 N Gillard av.
Reed Wm D, lab, h 196 Lincoln la.
Reed Wm H, driver, h 210 N Pine.
Reed Wm H, lab, h 182 Sheldon.
Reed Wm J, elev opr, b 61 Ellen.
Reed Wm J, porter, h 571 E 8th.
Reed Wm L, plaster, h 45 Madeira.
Reed Wm O, lab, h 349½ S Meridian.
Reed Wilson, phys, 800 E Washington, h same.
Reed Wilson H, clk, h 731 E Ohio.
Reede Frank, tmstr, b 123 Shepard (W I).
Reede John, tmstr, h 123 Shepard (W I).
Reeder Albert, lab, h n w cor Graceland av and 29th.
Reeder Arthur D, ins agt, h 356 Talbott av.
Reeder David C, lab, h 266 Martindale av.
Reeder Eliza (wid Elijah), b 180 W Ohio.
Reeder Elizabeth C (wid Charles), b 114 W Georgia.
Reeder Ephraim C, grocer, 107 Elm, h same.
Reeder Frank M, bkkpr D P Erwin & Co, h 117 Christian av.
Reeder George W, barber, b 18½ Indiana av.
Reeder Hannah A (wid Jasper), h 289 W Merrill.

13 N. MERIDIAN STREET.

LIME, CEMENT, PLASTER FIRE BRICK AND CLAY SEWER PIPE, ETC. BALKE & KRAUSS CO., Cor. Market and Missouri Streets.

C. FRIEDGEN HAS THE FINEST STOCK OF LADIES' PARTY SLIPPERS and SHOES 19 NORTH PENNSYLVANIA ST.

SAMUEL LAING ▸ TIN, SLATE AND STEEL ROOFING · 72 AND 74 EAST COURT STREET.

M. B. WILSON, Pres. W. F. CHURCHMAN, Cash.
THE CAPITAL NATIONAL BANK,
INDIANAPOLIS, IND.
Pays Interest on Time Certificates of Deposit.
Buys and Sells Foreign Exchange at Low Rates.
Capital, - - $300,000
Surplus and Earnings, 50,000
No. 28 S. Meridian St., Cor. Pearl.

Reeder Isaac F, shoes, 224 W Washington, h 450 W North.
Reeder Lucy, bkkpr, b 450 W North.
Reeder Ralph R, tinner, b 77 Columbia av.
Reel Edward, cabtmkr, r 43½ Kentucky av.
Rees Albert C, city fireman, h 167 Huron.
Rees Carl, tailor, r 185½ E Washington.
Rees George E, clk Joint Rate Assn, h 171 Michigan av.
Rees Henry, lab, b 77 Sanders.
Rees John T, h 223½ W Washington.
Rees Merritt E, insp, b 780 E Market.
Rees Robert H, com mer, 19 S Delaware, h 650 N Alabama.
Reese Annie, b 207 Alvord.
Reese Charles, painter, 175 Huron, h same.
Reese Charles W, clk Nordyke & Marmon Co, h 245 River av (W I).
Reese Clifton Y, ironwkr, h w s Caldwell 3 n of North.
Reese Edward S, bkkpr Dugdale Can Co, h 406 Central av.
Reese Ernest E, dentist, 24½ E Ohio, h 74 W Ohio.
Reese Ferdinandina (wid Charles E), h 615 N Penn.
Reese George L, porter Spencer House.
Reese George M, waiter, h 226 N Noble.
Reese Guido R, driver, h 302 Shelby.
Reese James H, lawyer, 20½ N Delaware, b 180 Eureka av.
Reese Jesse I, molder, h 16 Biddle.
Reese Joseph, painter, h 67 Huron.
Reese Joseph jr, clk, b 67 Huron.
Reese Louis C, clk Hollweg & Reese, b 615 N Penn.
Reese Mary E (wid George), h 180 Eureka av.
Reese Moses, lab, r 261½ Mass av.
Reese Murillo, music teacher, b 67 Huron.
Reese Wm, lab, h 95 Oak.
Reese Wm B, clk, r 144 N Capitol av.
Reeve Almon, wheelmkr, h 140 River av (W I).
Reeves Alvah N, clk R M S, h 339 S New Jersey.
Reeves Bertha (wid Benjamin J), r 148 W Maryland.

TUTTLE & SEGUIN,
28 E. Market Street.
Fire Insurance,
Real Estate, Loan
and Rental Agents.
TELEPHONE 1168.

Reeves Carey C, cigars, State House, h 105 Huron.
Reeves Edward, h 420 N Alabama.
Reeves Edward L, bartndr, h 281 S East.
Reeves Eli B, carp, h 1258 Morris (W I).
Reeves Elsie E, stenog Nederland Life Ins Co (ltd), b 61 Walnut.
Reeves Eugene, mach, b 285 S Capitol av.
Reeves Frank C, agt, h 1533 Kenwood av.
Reeves Frank J, bkkpr, h 297 E McCarty.
Reeves Frederick P, clk, b 646 College av.
Reeves George F, pres Indpls Electrotype Foundry, h 623 E Ohio.
Reeves George I, clk, b 863 N Illinois.
REEVES HARRY E, Brass and Wood Patternmaker, Expert in Working Models and Experimental Machinery; Will Make Any Trick or Device Wanted, 96 S Delaware, cor Georgia, Tel 121; h 276 S East. (See embossed line front cover and adv in classified Patternmakers.)
Reeves James E, nurse, 69 Mass av, h same.
Reeves Jesse W, barber, b 69 Mass av.
Reeves John S, meats, 252 Highland av, h 737 E Michigan.
Reeves Joseph R, agt, h 1585 Kenwood av.
Reeves Lewis E, paperhngr, b 1141 N Meridian.
Reeves Nettie V (wid Frank P), dressmkr, 61 Walcott, h same.
Reeves Orange D, trav agt, h 646 College av.
Reeves Richard D, b 517 N Delaware.
Reeves Richard E, clk, b 863 N Illinois.
Reeves Richard R (R R Shiel & Co), h 863 N Illinois.
Reeves Roy, cabtmkr, h 589 W Eugene (N I).
Reeves Sarah (wid Wm M), h 517 N Delaware.
Reeves Thomas P, shoemkr, 69 E 14th, h 1141 N Meridian.
Reeves Thomas P, shoemkr, 118 Michigan (H), h n w cor Grandview av and Cleveland (H).
Reeves Wm, clk, b 191 Douglass.
Reeves Wm A, lab, h 520 W Shoemaker (N I).
Reeves & Co, J George Roth mngr, threshers, 90 S Capitol av.
REGAL MANUFACTURING CO, Henry R Thomson Propr, Mnfrs of Baking Powder, Pancake Flour, Bluing and Vinegar, 269-271 E McCarty.
Regan Charles, h 22 Fletcher av.
Regan Charles jr, tallyman, b 22 Fletcher av.
Regan Elizabeth, teacher Public School No 13, b 22 Fletcher av.
Regan Ella, teacher Public School No 20, b 22 Fletcher av.
Regan Julia M (wid James), h 43 Dougherty.
Regan Wm, brakeman, h 134 S Summit.
Reger Benjamin, h 267 N Senate av.
Reger Elizabeth, teacher Public School No 3, b 267 N Senate av.
Reger Frank M, engr, h 393 N West.
Reger Henry G, cigar mnfr, 170 E Washington, h 740 E Ohio.
Reger John R, clk, b 649 E Ohio.
Reger Katharine M (wid Wm C), h 649 E Ohio.
Reger Smith F, engr, b 267 N Senate av.
Reger Wm C, foreman Indpls Cabinetmkrs' Union, b 622 E Ohio.

SULLIVAN & MAHAN Manufacturers of all kinds of PAPER BOXES 41 W. Pearl St.

DIAMOND WALL PLASTER { Telephone 1410 BUILDERS' EXCHANGE.

Regnas Arthur E, baker, b 94 W 7th.
Regula August, clk Julius A Schuller, b 163 E Morris.
Regula Julia, photog Theodore Marceau, b 46 Agnes.
Regula Sarah (wid Conrad), h 46 Agnes.
Reh Charlotte (wid Jacob), b 20 Agnes.
Rehling Anna B (wid Charles H), teacher Public School No 31, b 30 Sinker.
Rehling Charles H, foreman, h 28 S Gale (B).
Rehling Charles W, mach, b 28 S Gale (B).
Rehling Henry A, clk K and L of H, h rear 251 Virginia av.
REHLING WM C, Brick, Coal, Lime, Cement, Sewer Pipe and Flue Lining, 652 Madison av, Tel 304; h 201 E Morris.
Rehm Eugene J (Rehm & Van Deinse), h 6 Ruckle.
Rehm George H (Rehm & Van Deinse), h 388 Park av.
Rehm Jacob, cigar mkr, r 18½ S Delaware.
Rehm Ulian, framemkr, h 37 Hendricks.
REHM & VAN DEINSE (Eugene J and George H Rehm), Insurance and Real Estate, 22-23 When Bldg, Tel 733.
Rehme John E, painter, h 49 Dougherty.
Reibel Amand, harnessmkr, h 837 S Meridian.
Reibold Louis, propr The Bates, n w cor Illinois and Washington, tel 259.
Reichard Anna A (wid Benton), h 266 W Pearl.
Reichardt Charles F (Johnson & Reichardt), h 68 Park av.
Reichardt Elizabeth M (wid George J), h 136 W 1st.
Reichardt John, h 425 N East.
Reichart Philip, cabtmkr, h 75 Davidson.
Reichert Charles A, saloon, 307 Prospect, h same.
Reichert Elizabeth, housekpr, b 329 Orange.
Reichert Frederick W, baker, Parrot & Taggart, h 565 S Capitol av.
Reichert Jacob, pdlr, b 101 Maple.
Reichert Wm F, hostler, b 754 S East.
Reichman Samuel, saloon, 274 E Washington, r same.
Reichstetter Louis, mach, b 320 W 1st.
REICHWEIN'S HALL, Charles Fishinger Propr, Choice Wines, Liquors, Beer and Cigars; Garden and Club Room in Connection; 349 E Market, s w cor Noble.
Reichwein John, mason, h n w cor Concord and Pendergast (H).
Reichwein Philip (Reichwein & Quill), h 99 N Noble.
REICHWEIN & QUILL (Philip Reichwein, Thomas F Quill), Real Estate and Loans, 14 Brandon Blk, 95 E Washington.
REICK EDWARD C, Pharmacist, Deutsche Apotheke, 405 S East, Tel 1119; h 390 S East.
Reick Lena (wid Augustus), h 390 S East.
Reid Addie E (wid Erasmus), r 72 E Vermont.
Reid Arthur F, clk E B Swift, b 233½ Mass av.
Reid Austin S, carp, h 36 Leon.
REID BROS (Kenneth G and John S), Real Estate, Rentals, Loans and Insurance, 42 N Delaware, Tel 1475.

FRANK NESSLER. WILL H. ROST.
FRANK NESSLER & CO.
Tailors
56 EAST MARKET ST. (Lemcke Building),
INDIANAPOLIS, IND.

Reid Charles F, bicycles, 167 Mass av, b 507 Park av.
Reid Charlotte (wid George), dressmkr, 13 S Reisner (W I), h same.
Reid Clarence L, mach, h 253 Columbia av.
Reid Daniel G, pres Am Steel Co and treas Am Tin Plate Co, res Richmond, Ind.
Reid Edward, lab, h 206 W 1st.
Reid Frank M, salesman, b Stubbins Hotel.
Reid George W, letter carrier P O, r 72 E Vermont.
Reid Henry, lab, b 21 Torbet.
Reid Henry, porter The Denison.
Reid Jacob, hats, 7 Indiana av, r 34 S Capitol av.
Reid John, farmer, b 345 S Alabama.
Reid John, lab, h 399 S Missouri.
Reid John D (Reid & Prow), h 564 College av.
Reid John S (Reid Bros), h 70 Omer.
Reid John B, clk, b 359 S Missouri.
Reid Julia A (wid Wm I), b 434 Talbott av.
Reid Kenneth G (Reid Bros), h 63 Cherry.
Reid Lee C, agt, r 34 S Capitol av.
Reid Mae, stenog C C C & St L Ry, r 30 W Vermont.
Reid Margaret M (wid George), h 253 Columbia av.
Reid Michael, packer, h 359 S Missouri.
Reid Nancy G (wid John S), b 63 Cherry.
Reid Robert (Walkup & Reid), b 148 N Illinois.
Reid Robert, treas Moore & Co, h 675 N Alabama.
Reid Samuel, mngr Kingan & Co (ltd), h 675 N Alabama, tel 1734.
Reid Sarah B (wid John), h 117 Kappus (W I).
Reid Thomas, engr, h 55 Stevens.
Reid Wm J, buyer The Wm H Block Co, h 224 N East.
Reid Wm M, lab, b 359 S Missouri.
Reid Wm P, clk, h 76 S Judge Harding (W I).
Reid & Prow (John D Reid, Fred J Prow), dentists, 402½ College av.
Reidy Mary C (wid Maurice C), b 64 S State av.
Reidy Patrick, fireman, h 37 Tacoma av.

Haueisen & Hartmann
163-169 E. Washington St.
FURNITURE,
Carpets,
Household Goods,
Tin, Granite and China Wares, Oil Cloth and Shades

'Phone 1769. 18 Illinois St. } THE HOME LAUNDRY { WORK CALLED FOR AND DELIVERED.

THE WM. H. BLOCK CO. 7 AND 9 EAST WASHINGTON STREET. DRY GOODS, HOUSE FURNISHINGS AND CROCKERY.

London Guarantee and Accident Co. (Ltd.) Employers', Public and Teams' Liability. Workmen's Collective Insurance and Fidelity Bonds
GEORGE W. PANGBORN, General Agent, 704-706 Lemcke Bldg. Telephone 140.

Reliable Fire Insurance. Reasonable Rates. 74 E. MARKET STREET. Telephone 6.

JOSEPH GARDNER,
TIN, IRON, STEEL AND SLATE ROOFING,
GALVANIZED IRON CORNICES & SKYLIGHTS.
37, 39 & 41 KENTUCKY AVE. Telephone 322.

Reidy Timothy T, lab, h 26 Roe.
Reidy Wm, fireman, b 33 Detroit.
Reif Andrew, lab, b 138 River av (W I).
Reif Cecilia (wid Lyman), h 138 River av (W I).
Reif Frederick A, baker, h 358 E Market.
Reif George J, bkkpr, b 358 E Market.
Reifeis Charles J, brewer, h 98 Morton.
Reifeis Christian, lab, b 68 Morton.
Reifeis Christian, lab, b 559 S State av.
Reifeis Herman, lab, h 74 Morton.
Reifeis Louis C, engr, h 53 Gresham.
Reiffel Charles, meats, 213 W Washington, h 150 S Belmont av (W I).
Reiffel Charles jr, molder, b 150 S Belmont av (W I).
Reiffel Edward A, jeweler, 158 Virginia av, h same.
Reiffel George L, meats, 103 E Mkt House, h 824 Cornell av.
Reiffel Jacob, butcher, r 89½ N Delaware.
Reiffel Lillie, teacher Public School No 31, b 421 S Illinois.
Reiffel Margaret (wid Abraham), h 421 S Illinois.
Reiffel Martin, sausage mnfr, 295 W Ray, and meats, 52 E Mkt House, h 23 Russell av.
Reiffel Mary C, teacher Public School No 5, b 421 S Illinois.
Reiffel Wm E, meats, 84 E Mkt House, b 306 Douglass.
Reiley, see also O'Reilly and Riley.
Reiley Joseph L, chief clk U S Pension Agency, r 17 Commercial blk.
Reiley Thomas J, h 70 W New York.
Reilley James J, agt, h 225 Clinton.
Reilly Bernard A, brakeman, b 803 E Washington.
Reilly James, lab, h 35 S California.
Reilly James, saloon, 199 Meek, h same.
Reilly James W, clk Indpls Millinery Co, b 465 S Capitol av.
Reilly John J (Fieber & Reilly), b 465 S Capitol av.
Reilly Maurice J, clk W U Tel Co, h 465 S Capitol av.
Reilly Peter J, clk, h n e cor Beecher and Gatling.

J. S. FARRELL & CO.
STEAM AND HOT WATER HEATING AND PLUMBING CONTRACTORS
84 North Illinois Street. Telephone 382.

Reilly P C, mngr Utica Roofing Co, r 434 N Delaware.
Reilly Robert M, clk L S Ayres & Co, b 465 S Capitol av.
Reily George W, polisher, h 320 E Louisiana.
Reimann Henry F, lab, h 204 Minnesota.
Reimer Charles, drayman, b 160 Church.
Reimer Charles, porter, h 377 Union.
Reimer Charles jr, driver, b 377 Union.
Reimer Charles F, bartndr, b 323 S Olive.
Reimer Charles J, drayman, h 568 Chestnut.
Reimer Christian, porter, h 68 Arizona.
Reimer Christian, watchman, h 77 Wisconsin.
Reimer Edward, painter, b 160 Church.
Reimer Frederick C, driver, h 220 E Morris.
Reimer Frederick C, tmstr, h 88 Weghorst.
Reimer Frederick C, truckman, h 116 High.
Reimer Frederick J, lab, h 60 Kansas.
Reimer Henry, baker, b 160 Church.
Reimer Henry, sawyer, h 204 Minnesota.
Reimer Henry C, clk Francke & Schindler, b 357 Union.
Reimer Henry J, drayman, h 357 Union.
Reimer John, drayman, h 361 Union.
Reimer John, packer, h 47 Arizona.
Reimer Joseph, ironwkr, b 285 S Capitol av.
Reimer Louis, driver, h 160 Church.
Reimer Louis jr, driver, b 160 Church.
Reimer Wm, ironwkr, b 285 S Capitol av.
Reimer Wm F, porter, h 77 Wisconsin.
Rein Sigmund, draughtsman L E & W R R, r 53 Dearborn.
Reinacker Charles, molder, b 120 Kennington.
Reinacker John, clk Krag-Reynolds Co, b 120 Kennington.
Reinacker Mary (wid Jacob), h 120 Kennington.
Reinbold Jacob, lab, h 362 Highland av.
Reineberg Henry, stairbldr, h 332 S Alabama.
Reinecke Frederick, express, h 243 Union.
Reinecke Frederick jr, carp, h 57 Sinker.
Reinecke Julius F, h 56 Fletcher av.
Reiner Edward R, foreman, h 18 Union.
Reinert Adolph W, clk, b 131 W 4th.
Reinert Charles A, clk, h 95 Douglass.
Reinert Charles J, butcher, h 738 N Senate av.
Reinert Frederick G, h 131 W 4th.
Reinert Frederick G jr, clk Charles Mayer & Co, h 131 W 4th.
Reinert Gottlieb, broommkr, h 186 N Dorman.
Reinert John, foreman, h 127 W 4th.
Reinert John G (Binager & Reinert), h 69 John.
Reinert Otto, clk, b 131 W 4th.
Reinfels Charles P, cigar mnfr, 791 S East, h same.
Reinfels Henry, h 791 S East.
Reinfels Henry J jr, mach hd, h 791 S East.
REINHARD FRANCIS J, Lawyer, Rooms 5-6, 27½ S Delaware, Tel 1017; h 508 N New Jersey.
Reinhardt Andrew (Reinhardt & Brunner), h 30 Fountain.
Reinhardt Christian, lab, h 107 Trowbridge (W).
Reinhardt Edward L, printer, b 62 Maxwell.
Reinhardt Emil, locksmith, b 113 Locke.
Reinhardt John, lab, h 14 Leon.
Reinhardt John G, helper, h 178 Spann av.
Reinhardt Magdalene (wid August), b 118 Prospect.
Reinhardt Peter J, locksmith, 113 Locke, h same.

FRANK K. SAWYER

POLICIES IN UNITED STATES LIFE INSURANCE CO., offer indemnity against death, liberal cash surrender value or at option of policy-holder, fully paid-up life insurance or liberal life income. E. B. SWIFT, M'g'r, 25 E. Market St.

WM. KOTTEMAN } WILL FURNISH YOUR HOUSE COMPLETE
89 & 91 E. Washington St. Telephone 1742

SHOW CASES || WILLIAM WIEGEL || 6 West Louisiana Street Opp. Union Station.

Reinhardt Philip, lab, h 108 Patterson.
Reinhardt Robert R, paperhngr, h 62 Maxwell.
Reinhardt & Brunner (Andrew Reinhardt, Wm Brunner), saloon, Floral av 1 n of 9th.
Reinhart Catharine (wid Valentine), h 577 S Meridian.
Reinhart John, shoemkr, h s e cor Schurmann av and Fremont (N I).
Reinhart Joseph, h 34 Union.
Reinhart Leopold, mach, h 40 Dunlop.
Reinhart Louis V, mach, h 63 Downey.
Reinier Bernhard, driver, h 263½ N New Jersey.
Reinken Albert, h 9 S Gale (B).
Reinken Albert jr, tile layer, h 775 N Senate av.
Reinken Charles H, mach, h 16 S Stuart (B).
Reinken Edward, clk, b 775 N Senate av.
Reinken Henry J, saloon, 266 E Washington, h same.
Reinken Wm A, tile layer, b 775 N Senate av.
Reinkenobbe Ernest H, cigarmkr, b 1027 W Morris (W I).
Reinking Henry C, carp, b 526 E Market.
Reinking Henry E (Nuerge & Reinking), h 526 E Market.
Reinmann Reinhardt, lab, b 135 E Washington.
Reins Esther, b 165 Coburn.
Reinshagen Harry B, draughtsman Dept Public Works, r 280 E New York.
Reiring Frank E, paperhngr, b 360 E Market.
Reiring Wm J, paperhngr, b 360 E Market.
Reis George, uphlr, h 41 Grove.
Reis Henry W, bartndr, b 253 N Alabama.
Reis Katharine (wid Philip), domestic 984 N Meridian.
Reisecker Alice, teacher Public School No 4, b 204 N Illinois.
Reisert Frank, lab, h 66 Gresham.
Reising Louis, plumber, h 133 Bright.
Reising Wm T, brakeman, h 285 Fletcher av.
Reisinger Everett E, carp, h e s Baltimore av 4 n of 22d.
Reisinger James, lab, r 319 E Washington.
Reisinger Merritt H, contr, 289 E Ohio, h same.
Reisinger Nora B, clk, b 289 E Ohio.
Reisinger Otto L, clk, b 289 E Ohio.
Reisinger Samuel, blksmith, b 103 W South.
Reisinger Wesley, clk, b 145 Dougherty.
Reisner Edna M, stenog, h 241 N Capitol av.
Reisner Frederick, h 323 Union.
Reisner Frederick, car insp, h 167 Fletcher av.
Reiss Paul, blksmith, e s Illinois near 30th, h same.
Reissner Antonio, stenog German Am Bldg Assn, b 284 N West.
Reissner Frank L, clk to supt bldgs Public Schools, h 284 N West.
Reissner Herman, b 22 Shelby.
Reissner Herman jr, clk The Gordon-Kurtz Co, h 22 Shelby.
Reister Elizabeth (wid Philip), dressmkr, 467 E St Clair, h same.
Reith Joseph J, carp, h 73 Tacoma av.
Reith Wm E, painter, b 30 N West.
REITZ CHARLES & SON (Henry Reitz), Mnfrs Electrical Apparatus of Every Description and for Medical Use a Specialty, 72 Virginia av.

THOS. C. DAY & CO.
INVESTING AGENTS,
TOWN AND FARM LOANS,
Rooms 325 to 330 Lemcke Bldg.

Reitz Elizabeth (wid Charles), h 67 Woodlawn av.
Reitz Henry (Charles Reitz & Son), h 67 Woodlawn av.
Reitz Herman, electrician, b 67 Woodlawn av.
Reitz Ida, forewoman, b 67 Woodlawn av.
Reitzel Mary (wid Christian), b 419 S Illinois.
Reitzel Virle E, clk, b 40 Marion av (W I).
Reitzie John, foreman, b 325 E Ohio.
Rekmeier Charles, carp, b 65 Buchanan.
Reliance Edge Tool Co (DeHart Woodworth, George W Torrey), cor Eugene and canal (N I).
Reliford Robert, lab, h 206 W 2d.
Reller Amelia, bkkpr, b 71 W 4th.
Reller A Henry, grocer, 651 N Illinois, h 71 W 4th.
Reller Emma H, h w s Layman av 4 n of Washington av (I).
Reller Emma L (wid Wm), h w s Layman av 4 n of Washington av (I).
Remas Annie M (wid Victor R), h 270 S Noble.
Remas Isidore T, mach, h 272 S Noble.
Rembusch Nicholas, music teacher, 5 Centennial, h same.
Rembusch Peter, b 5 Centennial.
Rembusch Peter N, clk Albert Gall, h 601 Mass av.
Remetter George A, saloon, 124 N Pine, h 122 same.
Remfry James C, spec agt Mutual Life Ins Co of Newark, h 58 Cherry.
Remington Edward, pdlr, r 23 N West.
REMINGTON STANDARD TYPEWRITER, Wyckoff, Seamans & Benedict Proprs, 34 E Market, Tel 451.
Remley Amos, ironwkr, h 24 Elk.
Remley Andrew J, carp, h rear 267 Davidson.
Remley John T L, mach, h 10 S Stuart (B).
Remp George, lab, h 512 W Udell (N I).
Remsier Julia (wid Christian), b 577 S East.
Remster Charles, lawyer, 315 Indiana Trust bldg, h 13 Broadway.

EAT——
HITZ'S
CRACKERS
AND CAKES.
ASK YOUR GROCER FOR THEM.

Capital Steam Carpet Cleaning Works
M. D. PLUNKETT Proprietor, Telephone 818

BENJ. BOOTH PRACTICAL EXPERT ACCOUNTANT. Accounts of any description investigated and audited, and statements rendered. Room 18, 82½ E. Washington St., Indianapolis, Ind.

The Best Place in the City to Get a Good Meal THE SHERMAN RESTAURANT 18 and 20 S. Meridian Street KERSHNER BROS., Proprs.

ESTABLISHED 1876. TELEPHONE 168.
CHESTER BRADFORD,
SOLICITOR OF PATENTS,
AND COUNSEL IN PATENT CAUSES.
(See adv. page 6.)
Office:—Rooms 14 and 16 Hubbard Block, S.W. Cor. Washington and Meridian Streets, INDIANAPOLIS, INDIANA.

Remy Charles F, reporter Supreme Court of Indiana, room 109 State House.
Renard Emil, h 1139 W Washington (M J).
Render Sarah (wid Warren), b 442 W North.
Renforth Thomas J, miller, h 111 Minerva.
Renier Joseph H, lab, b 285 S Capitol av.
Renihan James (Renihan, Long & Blackwell and Feeney Furniture and Stove Co), h 113 N Capitol av.
Renihan James A, lab, h 31 Byram pl.
Renihan John J, blksmith, b 78 Fayette.
RENIHAN, LONG & BLACKWELL (James Renihan, Robert D Long, John J Blackwell), Undertakers, 71-73 W Market, Tel 115.
Renington Owen, lab, b 84 S Senate av.
Renker Albert, turner, b 141 Excelsior av.
Renkert Louis H, drugs, 164 W Washington, h 680 N Illinois.
Renn John H, mach, h s s Bloyd av 2 w of Shade (B).
Renn Joseph E, helper, h 32 S Morris (B).
Rennefeld Anton, uphlr, h 215½ E Washington.
Rennegarbe Frederick F, clk Christian Schrader, h 29 Bicking.
Rennegarbe Herman, driver, h 29 Villa av.
Renner Albert C, horseshoer, 24 E South, b 15 S Pine.
Renner Carl A, bartndr, h 163 E Morris.
Renner Christian, watchman, h 15 S Pine.
Renner Emma (wid Christian), h 275 Davidson.
Renner George C, packer, b 61 Downey.
Renner George W J, bkkpr, h 61 Downey.
Renner Harry C, uphlr, h 92 Lincoln la.
Renner John, lab, b 43 Ketcham (H).
Renner Litta S, masseuse, h 190 N Senate av.
Renner Regina (wid John), b 24 Haugh (H).
Renner Wm, lab, b 261 Union.
Rennett George H, mach, b e s Central av 1 s of Beechwood av (I).
Rennett Phoebe L (wid George F), h e s Central av 1 s of Beechwood av (I).
Reno Charles F, mer police, h 291 S Alabama.
Reno John, lab, h 587 W Shoemaker (N I).

O. B. Ensey
SLATE, STEEL, TIN AND IRON ROOFING.
Cor. 6th and Illinois Sts. Tel. 1562

Reno Lewis, lab, h 434 W Chicago (N I).
Reno Melissa A (wid Wm W), h 192 English av.
Reno Wm, buffer, h 89 Benton.
Rentsch Adolph, clk, h 594 N Senate av.
Rentsch Margaret (wid August F), crockery, 193 W Washington, h 295 Union.
Rentsch Edward H, h 550 E Ohio.
Rentsch Otto H, clk, b 100 Jefferson.
Rentsch Robert, grocer, 600 N Senate av, h 594 same.
Reoch David Rev, b s w cor University and Downey avs (I).
REPORTER PUBLISHING CO, Joseph T Elliott Jr Pres and Genl Mngr, Arthur F Hall Sec and Treas, Publishers The Daily Reporter, 519 Indiana Trust Bldg, Tel 54.
Reporter Supreme Court of Indiana, office 109 State House.
Republican Club House, cor River av and Morris (W I).
Republican State Central Committee, Robert E Mansfield sec, 17 Journal bldg.
Requardt Frederick W, express, h 113 Hill av.
Resch Mary A (wid Joseph), b 83 High.
Resener Anthony C, clk, h 99 N Linden.
Resener Anthony F, mason, h 120 Lexington av.
Resener Charles F W (F Dunmeyer & Co), h 321 E Vermont.
Resener Charles H, carp, h 483 Dillon.
Resener Charles H, trav agt Severin, Ostermeyer & Co, h 104 Stoughton av.
Resener Christian F, carp, 345 N Noble, h same.
Resener Christian F, shoemkr, 336 E St Clair, h same.
Resener Christian W, feed, 301 N East, h 22 Park av.
Resener Christina (wid John F), h 321 E Vermont.
Resener Clara C, tel opr, b 345 N Noble.
Resener Edward H, mach, h 626 E New York.
Resener Harry, helper, b 321 E Vermont.
Resener Henry C, clk Krag-Reynolds Co, h n s 17th 1 w of N Capitol av.
Resener Henry F, carp, h 105 Pleasant.
Resener Kate L, cashr A Metzger Agency, b 345 N Noble.
Resener Wm A, clk, h 138 Elm.
Reser Henry, lab, h 217 W Michigan.
Reser Melvin M, lab, h 496 W Ontario (N I).
Reser Wm A, clk, b 217 W Michigan.
Reserve Fund Savings and Loan Assn of Indiana, John F Wallick pres, Charles H Young sec, Winfred B Holton treas, 55-56 When bldg.
Resler Mary M (wid Frederick), h 8 Bates al.
Resler Thomas, lab, b 8 Bates al.
Resner Alva J, carp, h 133 Spann av.
Resner Edward, bricklyr, h 14 Dawson.
Resner Frederick, clk, b 99 Greer.
Resner Henry F, printer, 175 Virginia av, b 92 Dougherty.
Resner Henry J (Resner & Son), b 416 Virginia av.
Resner Henry W (Resner & Son), h 416 Virginia av.
Resner John W, plastr, b 416 Virginia av.
Resner & Son (Henry W and Henry J), shoes, 418 Virginia av.
Resnover James, lab, h 206 Dillon.
Resoner Wm L, furniture, 67 W Washington, h 115 W Vermont.

TUTEWILER UNDERTAKER, No. 72 WEST MARKET STREET. TELEPHONE 216.

PROVIDENT LIFE AND TRUST CO. OF PHILADELPHIA. D. W. Edwards, G. A., 508 Indiana Trust Bldg. In form of policy; prompt settlement of death losses; equitable dealing with policy-holders; in strength of organization; and in everything which contributes to Security and Cheapness of life insurance, this company is unsurpassed.

THEODORE F. SMITHER ROOFER
GRAVEL AND OTHER COMPOSITION
Yard, 19 W. Maryland St. Telephone 86
Office, 151 W. Maryland St.

Ressler Christian M, baggageman, h 681 Mass av.
Ressler Frederick, maltster, h 101 Eureka av.
Ressler Henry, porter, b 190 E Washington.
Ressler John A, porter, h 34 Eureka av.
Rether Ottilie, nurse 118 N Senate av.
Rethke Charles, mach, b 178 Laurel.
Rethke Wm, switchtndr, h 178 Laurel.
Rethmeier Charles, carp, b 65 Buchanan.
Rethmeier Christian W, clk, h 350 Spring.
Retterer Wm H, mach, h 898 W Washington.
Rettich Benjamin, foreman Indpls Brewing Co, b 421 S Delaware.
Reuter Ferdinand, driver, h 1127 E Washington.
Reuter Jacob, agt Jung Brewing Co, h 1017 E Washington.
Reuter Jacob, finisher, h 770 S East.
Reuter Jacob, janitor, r 32 W Ohio.
Reuter Wm G, cabtmkr, h n end Decatur.
Reutlinger Julius, clk, b 33 King.
Reutlinger Moritz, trav agt Krull & Schmidt, b 33 King.
Reuwer Henry, tailor, 63 W Market, h 165 N Noble.
Reveal Anna E (wid Thomas M), h 473 N East.
Reveal Wm O, asst postmaster, b 174 Central av.
Reveal Willis, lab, h 12 Sharpe.
Revel Wm W, engr, h 39 S Arsenal av.
REVIEW PUBLISHING CO, Publishers of National Detective and Police Review, Rooms 10-12, 96½ E Market. (See adv in classified Detective Agencies.)
REX COAL AND SEWER CO, E E Pray Sec, 171 E Louisiana, Tel 1881.
REX PORTRAIT CO, Ed H Soice Mngr, Portriats Enlarged in Crayon and Water Colors, 42 W Market.
Rexford Ann E (wid Edwin E), h 521 N New Jersey.
Rexford Edwin E, paying teller Merchants' Natl Bank, h 848 N Illinois.
Rexford Wm R, mngr Henry C Long, h 21 Butler.
Rexhouse George C, nurse, r 102 N Capitol av.
Rexroth Lona, clk, b 115 Kennington.
REXROTH LOUIS, Machinist, 125 E Pearl, h 179 E Morris.
Rexroth Mary A (wid Frederick W), h 115 Kennington.
REYER ERNEST C, Physician and Surgeon, 130 N Penn, Tel 1621; h 811 N Alabama.
Reyer Henrietta C (wid George), h 811 N Alabama.
Reyer Theodore, treas German Fire Ins Co of Indiana, h 254 N East.
Reyer Wm G, printer, h 35 Coburn.
Reynolds Belle E, bkkpr, b w s Illinois 3 n of 29th.
Reynolds Bert L, clk, b 16 Temple av.
Reynolds Byford E, brakeman, h 71 Andrews.
Reynolds Carl M, pressman The Indpls News, b 1102 N Alabama.
Reynolds Charles, weaver, b 406 Clinton.
REYNOLDS CHARLES E, Real Estate and Brokerage, 423 Ash, h same.
Reynolds Charles M, pres Krag-Reynolds Co, h 621 N Penn.

THE WHEN IS A WORLD BEATER.

Reynolds David, h 658 Broadway.
Reynolds Edna, h 255½ E Washington.
Reynolds Edward, butcher, r 218 E Market.
Reynolds Eli T, carp, h 1511 N Capitol av.
Reynolds Elizabeth, b 239 Columbia av.
Reynolds Frank, live stock agt Penna Lines, Union Stock Yards (W I), h 15 W North.
Reynolds Frank M, painter, b 268 Jefferson av.
Reynolds Frank R, clk, h 66 W 6th.
Reynolds F Foster, trav agt Odd Fellows' Talisman, b 287 N Alabama.
Reynolds George C, clk, b 24 S Station (B).
Reynolds George H, lab, h 74 Jones.
Reynolds George M, molder, h 36 Sheffield av (H).
Reynolds Hannah M (wid Wm), b 20 Grace.
Reynolds Harry F, brakeman, h 16 Temple av.
Reynolds Henry C, clk C H & D R R, h 70 Harrison.
Reynolds Hugh, h 52 Hoyt av.
Reynolds Hugh B, yardmaster P C C & St L Ry, h 78 N State av.
Reynolds Ivy L, watchmkr, b 191 N East.
Reynolds James, houseman The Denison.
Reynolds James A, waiter, b 88 W Market.
REYNOLDS JOHN, Publisher Odd Fellows' Talisman, 3 Odd Fellows' Blk, h 287 N Alabama.
Reynolds John F, clk, b 52 Hoyt av.
Reynolds John H, lab, h 110 Randolph.
Reynolds John M, h 71 Ash.
Reynolds John T, lab, h 72 Jones.
Reynolds John W, mach hd, h 51 Johnson av.
Reynolds John X, foreman Ellis & Helfenberger, h 64 Sanders.
Reynolds Josephine (wid John), h 44½ Malott av.
Reynolds Maria L (wid Joshua), toilet articles, h 244½ E Washington.
Reynolds Minnie J, h 79 W 6th.
Reynolds Nancy (wid James), h 26 Hope (B).

The A. Burdsal Co. CELEBRATED HOMESTEAD READY MIXED PAINT. WHOLESALE AND RETAIL. 34 AND 36 SOUTH MERIDIAN STREET.

ELECTRIC SUPPLIES We Carry a full Stock. Prices Right. C. W. MEIKEL, Tel. 466. 96-98 E. New York St.

DALTON & MERRIFIELD { LUMBER South Noble St., near E. Washington

INDIANA ELECTROTYPE CO. : BEST WORK LOWEST PRICES.
23 WEST PEARL ST., INDIANAPOLIS, IND. JOB WORK. BOOK PLATES. BEST PATENT BASE ON THE MARKET.
All Orders Promptly Filled.

KIRKHOFF BROS.,
Electrical Contractors, Wiring and Construction.
102-104 SOUTH PENNSYLVANIA ST.
TELEPHONE 910.

Reynolds Oscar, lab The Bates.
Reynolds Paul B, finisher, h 299½ S New Jersey.
Reynolds Roscoe M, printer, h 111 Meek.
Reynolds Samuel C, carp, h s s Walnut av 3 w of Maple av (I).
Reynolds Sarah E, h 71 Ash.
Reynolds Thompson C, carp, h 43 Temple av.
Reynolds Warren W Rev, pastor Brightwood M E Church, h 24 S Station (B).
Reynolds Washington S, lab, h 35 Omer.
Reynolds Wm, h s e cor Walnut and Maxwell avs (I).
Reynolds Wm B, grocer, 395 Blake, h 397 same.
Reynolds Wm E, wall paper, 297 Mass av, h 355 N Noble.
Reynolds Wm F, h 16 Temple av.
Reynolds Wm F, clk, h 503 N West.
Reynolds Wm L, carp, h w s Illinois 3 n of 29th.
Reynolds Wm T, painter, b 43 Temple av.
Reynolds Zachariah, shoemkr, 317 E Washington, r 315 same.
Rheinheimer Barbetta, clothing, 190 W Washington, h 230 E New York.
Rheinheimer Harriet, teacher Public School No 9, b 230 E New York.
Rheinheimer Jacob H, drayman, h 46 Elizabeth.
Rheinheimer Nathan, clk, h 230 E New York.
Rheinschild John, shoemkr, 58 Mass av, b 119 Broadway.
Rhem Catherine (wid George), h s e cor Washington av and Warren (I).
Rhem John, lab, b s e cor Washington av and Warren (I).
Rhem Lamott, lab, h 47 Wallack.
Rhinehart Joseph S, brakeman, b 100 Lynn.
Rhinehart Luella M (wid Wm E), b 88 Michigan av.
Rhinehart Nancy, h 84 W Vermont.
Rhiver George R, b 12 Oxford.
Rhiver Wm H, painter, h 12 Oxford.
Rhoades Albert, driver, b 429 N New Jersey.
Rhoades Alvah S, teacher, h e s Brightwood av 1 s of Schofield (B).

THE W. G. WASSON CO.,
130 Indiana Ave. Tel. 989.
STEAM
COAL
Car Lots a Specialty. Prompt Delivery.
Brazil Block, Jackson and Anthracite.

Rhoades Ennis, carp, h 47 Omer.
Rhoades George, watchman, r 232 Michigan (H).
Rhoades Hartley E (wid Charles), b 127 W 5th.
Rhoades John, farmer, h e s Central av 1 s of 27th.
Rhoades Otis T, tmstr, h w s Senate av 2 s of Lynn (M).
Rhoades Sarah J (wid Elisha E), h 565 Mass av.
Rhoades Thomas, farmer, h e s Central av 1 s of 27th.
Rhoades Wm H, cabtmkr, b 565 Mass av.
Rhoads Arthur, sawyer, h 100 Ash.
Rhoads Charles H, lab, b 83 Wilson.
Rhoads Charles S, supt of telegraph C C C & St L Ry, res Hartwell, O.
Rhoads Charles W, carp, h 231 W New York.
Rhoads George W, lab, h 539 W Pearl.
Rhoads Harriet N (wid Joel), b 58 Vine.
Rhoads James W, lab, b 83 Wilson.
Rhoads John P, lab, h rear 534 W Maryland.
Rhoads Taylor, pdlr, h 892 W Washington.
Rhoads Wm F, gardener, h w s Belmont av 1 s of Vandalia R R (W I).
Rhoads Wm H, tmstr, h 83 Wilson.
Rhodehamel J Wesley, bkkpr Schnull & Co, h 330 Orange.
Rhodehamel Wm G, ins agt, b 201 E Washington.
Rhodehamel Wm H, trav agt Schnull & Co, h 124 Talbott av.
Rhoden Rachel (wid Robert), h 426 Lafayette.
Rhodes Carl, coachman, h 372 N Missouri.
Rhodes Carl L, switchman, b 1100 W Washington.
Rhodes Clarence R, bkkpr S S Rhodes, b 766 N Alabama.
Rhodes Claude C, tel opr C C C & St L Ry, h 5 E Sutherland (B).
Rhodes Frank D, adv agt, h 106½ N Meridian.
Rhodes James M, b 367 N New Jersey.
Rhodes John, lab, b rear 775 N Senate av.
Rhodes John W, b 367 N New Jersey.
Rhodes John W, phys, b 642 N Capitol av.
Rhodes Kate (wid Samuel P), h 548 W Washington.
Rhodes Leslie, fireman, b 1100 W Washington.
Rhodes Mary H (wid Greenberry), h 177 Park av.
Rhodes Olive (wid John), h 101 Bloomington.
RHODES SAMUEL S, Hardware, Builders' Supplies, Etc, 178 W Washington, Tel 890; h 766 N Alabama.
Rhodes Sophia (wid John W), h 260 W 5th.
Rhodes Virginia E, b 177 Park av.
Rhodes Wm A (W A Rhodes & Co), h 444 N Meridian.
Rhodes Wm E, b 444 N Meridian.
Rhodes Wm E, carp, h 279 S Delaware.
Rhodes Wm H, engr, h 8 S Brightwood av (B).
RHODES W A & CO (Wm A Rhodes), Real Estate, Loans and Insurance, 72 E Market, Tel 765.
Rhodius George, loans, 205 Lemcke bldg, b Circle Park Hotel.
Rhodius Marie (wid George), propr Circle Park Hotel, 13 Monument pl.
Rhudy John M, lab, h 202 W 10th.

W. H. Messenger FURNITURE, CARPETS, STOVES, 101 EAST WASHINGTON ST. TEL. 491.

McNamara, Koster & Co. | Foundry and Pattern Shop, 212-218 S. PENN. ST. . . . PHONE 1593.

Rianhard Dana E, auditor Warren-Scharf Asphalt Paving Co, res New York City.
Ribble Emma A, teacher, b 101 Shelby.
Ribble Marquis de L, drugs, 101 Shelby, h same.
Ribble Walter G, repr The Hay & Willits Mnfg Co, b 229 N Penn.
Rice Adeline (wid Daniel), h 89 N Delaware.
Rice Albert G, mngr Indpls Leaf Tobacco Co, 71 E Court, h 354 N Illinois.
Rice Albert R, lab, b 332 S Missouri.
Rice Alva J, painter, b 59 Temple av.
Rice Anna A (wid Gustav), b 264 Lincoln av.
Rice Archibald, tmstr, h 144 Harlan.
Rice Benjamin, condr, b 501 E Georgia.
Rice Braid D, lab, h 300 Kentucky av.
Rice Charles W, paperhngr, h 26 W McCarty.
Rice Clarence S, mach, h 72 Sheldon.
Rice Douglas, lab, b 29 College av.
Rice Edward, painter, b 27 Prairie av.
Rice Elizabeth (wid Charles S), b 3 Bell.
Rice Ellen, b 158 N Senate av.
Rice Ernest A, driver, b 493 N New Jersey.
Rice Flora, teacher Public School No 14, b 616 E Washington.
Rice George H, collr, h 533½ Virginia av.
Rice George L H (Compton & Rice), b 172 N Delaware.
Rice Henry S, switchman, b 332 S Missouri.
Rice Herbert H, clk Nordyke & Marmon Co, b 941 N Alabama.
Rice Herman, h 616 E Washington.
Rice Hugh, waiter The Denison.
Rice Isaac, trav agt, r 311 N Delaware.
Rice James, lab, h e s Brookville rd 4 s of Washington.
Rice James W, molder, h e s Brookville rd 4 s of Washington.
Rice John, lab, h 15 Meikel.
Rice John, lab, b 332 S Missouri.
Rice John F, molder, b 10 McCauley.
Rice Lewis J, bkkpr Pioneer Brass Works, h 470 College av.
Rice Lucy (wid Wm), b 40 Summit (H).
Rice Margaret, h 127 W Maryland.
Rice Martin H, pres The Mutual Savings Union and Loan Assn, pub Masonic Advocate, 14 Masonic Temple, r 2 The Windsor.
Rice Melville L, clk, b 60 Cherry.
Rice Miller, lab, h w s Madeira 4 s of Wallace.
Rice Nancy M (wid Joel W), b 469 N Illinois.
Rice Okey J, molder, b 105 Oliver av (W I).
Rice Oliver P, pumpmkr, h 199 Woodside av (W).
Rice Patrick, lab, h 10 McCauley.
Rice Perry G (Rice & Mollenkopf), h w s Schurman av 1 s of Wells (N I).
Rice Richard A, painter, h 316 Lincoln av.
Rice Samuel J, painter, h 59 Temple av.
Rice Samuel R, lab, h 6 Andrews.
Rice Thomas J, wrapper L S Ayres & Co, b 10 McCauley.
Rice Viola S, dressmkr, 60 Cherry, h same.
Rice Wallace B, waiter, h rear 175 N Penn.
Rice Warren E, city fireman, h 469 N Illinois.
Rice Waverly F, h 60 Cherry.
Rice Welcome, condr, h 941 N Alabama.
Rice Wesley, carp, h 27 Prairie av.
Rice Wm, lab, r 82 Adams.
Rice Wm C, trav agt, h 2 The Windsor.
Rice Wm D, lab, h 332 S Missouri.

Henry H. Fay,
40½ E. Washington St.,
REAL ESTATE,
AND LOAN BROKER.

RICE WM G, Physician (Eye, Ear and Throat), Office Hours 8:30-12 M and 1:30-4 P M, 14 E Ohio, h 183 Park av.
Rice Wm H, notions, 304 Shelby, h same.
Rice Wm L, lab, b 10 McCauley.
Rice & Mollenkopf (Perry G Rice, George F Mollenkopf), dairy, w s Schurmann av 1 s of Wells (N I).
Rich James W, lab, b 33 Ellen.
Rich John W, plumber, h 793 N Capitol av.
Rich Lydia A (wid George S), h 283 W Michigan.
Rich Major, lab, h 300 Fayette.
Rich Wm S (Rich & McVey), h 3 Ruckle.
RICH & McVEY (Wm S Rich, Hugh O McVey), Pianos and Organs, Sheet Music and Musical Goods, 65 N Penn, Tel 472.
Richard Clara (wid Francis), b 399 E Georgia.
RICHARD FRANK C, Grocer, 399 E Georgia, h same.
Richard George, clk, h 468 N Senate av.
Richard Lawrence R, mach, h 59 Cornell av.
Richards Albert S, mach, b 280 Highland av.
Richards Arthur H, chief clk, h 544 Bellefontaine.
Richards Arthur H jr, bricklyr, h 500 E 11th.
Richards Augustus C, clk, r 140 W Vermont.
Richards Charles, dairy, s s Wolf pike 3 e of Baltimore av, h same.
Richards Charles H, condr, h n w cor Brookside av and Centennial.
Richards Charles H, cooper, b 17 Warren av (W I).
Richards Daniel G, cooper, h 137½ Virginia av.
Richards David S, detective, h 26 N Beville av.
Richards Edward J, clk Security Mortgage Loan Co, b 350 N Illinois.
Richards Edward R, lab, b 17 Warren av (W I).
Richards Elizabeth (wid Reuel), h 224½ W Washington.

UNIUN CASUALTY & SURETY CO.
OF ST. LOUIS, MO.
All lines of Personal Accident and Casualty Insurance, including Employers' and General Liability.
W. E. BARTON & CO., General Agents,
504 Indiana Trust Building.
LONG DISTANCE TELEPHONE 1918.

THE FRED DIETZ CO. WOODEN PACKING BOXES MADE TO ORDER. FACTORY AND WAREHOUSE TRUCKS. 40 Madison Avenue. Telephone 69.

Indianapolis BUSINESS UNIVERSITY Leading College of Business and Shorthand. Elevator day and night. Individual instruction. Large faculty. Terms easy. Enter now. See p. 4. When Block. E. J. HEEB, President.

Water and Oil Meters { HENRY R. WORTHINGTON, 64 S. PENNSYLVANIA ST. Long Distance Telephone 284.

UNION CO-OPERATIVE LAUNDRY (COMPOSED OF UNION LAUNDRY GIRLS.) NOS. 3, 40 AND 42 VIRGINIA AVENUE. T. E. SOMERVILLE, MANAGER. TELEPHONE 89. INDIANAPOLIS, IND.

HORACE M. HADLEY
REAL ESTATE AND INSURANCE
66 East Market Street, Basement
TELEPHONE 1540.

Richards Frederick, bricklyr, h s e cor Fleet and Broadway.
Richards Frederick W, proofreader The Indpls Sentinel, h 58½ W Ohio.
Richards George A, salesman, h 468 N Senate av.
Richards George A, treas The McElwaine-Richards Co, h 1020 N New Jersey.
Richards Harry, packer, b 695 N Senate av.
Richards Hugh R, b 795 N Penn.
Richards Ida B, printer, h 280 Highland av.
Richards Jefferson, lab, b w s Wallack 1 n of Pleasant run.
Richards John F, h 137 Fletcher av.
Richards John R, mach hd, h 163½ E Washington.
Richards John T, cooper, h 17 Warren av (W I).
Richards Joshua, lab, b 471 W Eugene (N I).
Richards Keziah (wid Richard), h 178 N Missouri.
Richards Louisa, teacher Indiana Reformatory, b same.
Richards Rachel (wid Abel T), b 1020 N New Jersey.
Richards Sarah (wid Jacob), h 280 Highland av.
Richards Serena H (wid Edward M), h 453 N Penn.
Richards S Roger, cashr Am Ex Co, h 892 N Capitol av.
Richards Wm A, foreman, h 471 W Eugene (N I).
Richards Wm J, mngr The Indpls News, h 795 N Penn, tel 1795.
Richards Wm L, cooper, h 44 Nordyke av (W I).
Richards Wm M, sec and treas Union Embossing Machine Co, 30-40 W South, h 417 Bellefontaine.
Richardson Ada E (wid Stoughton), h 90 Marion av (W I).
Richardson Alexander, lab, b 88 Columbia al.
Richardson Alexander C (Richardson Bros), h 157 Indiana av.
Richardson Alexander C, farmer, h 513 W Wells (N I).

PERSONAL AND PROMPT ATTENTION GIVEN TO COLLECTIONS.
Merchants' and Manufacturers' Exchange
J. E. TAKKEN, Manager,
19 Union Building, 73 West Maryland Street.

Richardson Allen L, fireman, r 4 Walcott.
Richardson Amanda (wid Ira L), h 292 E Morris.
Richardson Barzilla F, mnfrs' agt, 26 S Illinois, h 29 Laurel.
Richardson Benjamin A (Richardson & McCrea), h 30 Garfield pl.
Richardson Benjamin A jr, student, b 30 Garfield pl.
Richardson Bros (Wm W and Alexander C), saloon, 151 Indiana av.
Richardson Burt E, clk, b 253 S New Jersey.
Richardson Charles, grocer, 272 S Capitol av, h same.
Richardson Charles, lab, r 127 Columbia al.
Richardson Charles A, mach, h 92 S Wheeler (B).
Richardson Charles A, postal clk, b 268 S New Jersey.
Richardson Charles F, chaircaner, h 1 Williams.
Richardson Charles H, clk Adams Ex Co, h 1190 N Illinois.
Richardson Charles W, carp, b 57 Hoyt av.
Richardson Daisy A, lab, h 2 Margaret.
Richardson Daniel D, lab, b 7 Hoyt av.
Richardson David, lab, h 268 S New Jersey.
Richardson Edgar, clk, h 464 Ash.
Richardson Edward H, stoker, h 25 Sinker.
Richardson Edwin J, phys, h 637 Broadway.
Richardson Emma M, opr C U Tel Co, b 72 N Beville av.
Richardson Erastus, lab, b 17 N New Jersey.
Richardson Fanny L (wid Henry), b 1725 N Meridian.
Richardson Francis M, h 458½ Indiana av.
Richardson Frank, collr County Treasurer's Office, h 464 Ash.
Richardson Frank B, ironwkr, h 215 Fletcher av.
Richardson Frank J, clk H P Wasson & Co, b 272 S Capitol av.
Richardson Frank L, clk, b 57 Hoyt av.
Richardson George, lab, h n e cor Caroline av and 17th.
Richardson George A, lab, h 228 Roanoke.
Richardson Grant, mach, b 301 River av (W I).
Richardson Harry K, station agt, Indpls Gas Co, h n s Howland av 1 w of Orchard.
Richardson Harry L, shoemkr, b 165 Pleasant.
Richardson Harvey B, clk R M S, b 75 E Walnut.
Richardson Hiram F, lab, b 458½ Indiana av.
Richardson Hiram V, fruits, E Mkt House, h 156 Agnes.
Richardson Holman, horseshoer, 428 N Alabama, h 47 Villa av.
Richardson Iro W (wid Alexander), h 259 N Illinois.
Richardson James A, weigher, h 60 Marion av (W I).
Richardson James D, carp, 57 Hoyt av, h same.
Richardson James M, car rep, h 1028 Morris (W I).
Richardson James M, carp, h 42 Ash.
Richardson James M, trav agt, r 15 Ryan blk.
Richardson John H, carp, h 135 Tacoma av.
Richardson John W, lab, b 458½ Indiana av.
Richardson John W, millwright, h 154 River av (W I).
Richardson Jonathan D, b 1028 Morris (W I).

CLEMENS VONNEGUT
184, 186 and 192 E. Washington St.
FOUNDRY AND MACHINISTS' SUPPLIES. "NORTON" EMERY WHEELS AND GRINDING MACHINERY.

THE WM. H. BLOCK CO. DRY GOODS, MILLINERY, CLOAKS AND FURS.
7 AND 9 EAST WASHINGTON STREET.

Richardson Joseph, collr, h 241 E Louisiana.
Richardson Joseph, hostler, r 18 S East.
Richardson Joseph, lab, h 48 Rockwood.
Richardson Joseph R, lab, h 2 Morgan (W I).
Richardson Josephus, patrolman, h 337 Blake.
Richardson Letitia K (wid George H), h 473 W Udell (N I).
Richardson Lizzie, teacher, r 140 N Alabama.
Richardson Lorenzo D, lab, b 20 Germania av (H).
Richardson Lou C, watchman Insane Hospital.
Richardson Martha, h 253 S New Jersey.
Richardson Mary (wid Wm), h 235 W South.
Richardson Mary J, h 72 Park av.
Richardson May, restaurant, 7 The Windsor, h 8 same.
Richardson Nathan H, clk Richardson & McCrea, b 30 Garfield pl.
Richardson Otha C, painter, b 2 Margaret.
Richardson Rilla, b 8 The Windsor.
Richardson Robert B, chief clk P C C & St L Ry, h 346 Talbott av.
Richardson Robert H, grocer, 1081 E Michigan, h same.
Richardson Samuel, lab, h 679 N Senate av.
Richardson Samuel H, molder, h 48 Rockwood.
Richardson Sarah A (wid Daniel A), h 168 N Meridian.
Richardson Shelton, meats, 203 Mass av, h 16 Edward (W I).
Richardson Wilbur S, trav agt, h 1725 N Meridian.
Richardson Wm, lab, h 353 S West.
Richardson Wm H, driver, h 15 Mill.
Richardson Wm H, engr, h 108 Singleton.
Richardson Wm H, lab, b 337 Blake.
Richardson Wm I, mach hd, b 292 E Morris.
Richardson Wm L, tile setter, h 907 Cornell av.
Richardson Wm R, helper, b s s Bloyd av 2 w of Shade (B).
Richardson Wm W (Richardson Bros), h 511 W Wells (N I).
Richardson Ziba D, coremkr, b 268 S New Jersey.
RICHARDSON & McCREA (Benjamin A Richardson, Frank F McCrea), Real Estate, Loans, Rentals and Insurance, 79 E Market, Tel 182. (See right top cor cards.)
Richart Charles A, supt Builders' Exchange of Indpls, b 528 Bellefontaine.
Richart Eli J, mach hd, h 118 Clifford av.
Richart Wm T, millwright, h 46 Sterling.
Richcreek Cora I (Richcreek & Richcreek), b 156 Randolph.
Richcreek Seth M (Richcreek & Richcreek), h 156 Randolph.
RICHCREEK & RICHCREEK (Seth M and Cora I), Lawyers and Investment Brokers, 85 Baldwin Blk.
Richel Charles, restaurant, 172 E Washington, h same.
Richert Henry, baker, 348 Indiana av, h same.
Richey Charles J, blksmith, h 475 S Delaware.
Richey Edward, cook, b 9 Ellsworth.
Richey Elizabeth (wid Charles), h 231 W Chesapeake.

Richey Frank E, clk, h 305 S East.
Richey John, coachman 172 Park av.
Richey John R, clk Model Clothing Co, h 212 Ramsey av.
Richey Julius J, tinner, h 308 S East.
Richey M Alonzo, lab, b w s Morris 2 s of Division (B).
Richey Samuel H, pres Beehive Paper Box Co, h n w cor Downey av and P C C & St L Ry (I).
Richey Wm E, ins adjuster, b The Denison.
Richey Wm H, lab, b w s Morris 2 s of Division (B).
Richhart Abraham, engr, h 105 Nordyke av (W I).
Richhart Robert, mach, b 105 Nordyke av (W I).
Richie Frances A (wid Josiah A), h 75 N Pine.
RICHIE ISAAC N, Real Estate and Loans, 60 E Market, Tel 520; h 978 N Delaware.
Richmann Frank J, clk Charles W Fairbanks, h 183 St Mary.
Richmann Magdalena (wid Charles H), h 16 Fletcher av.
Richmann Wm, carp, h 212 Northwestern av.
Richmire Frederick, clk, b 399 Virginia av.
Richmire Wm, clk, b 399 Virginia av.
Richmond Alexander, lab, b 673 E 7th.
Richmond John, coachman 998 N Alabama.
Richmond John H, coachman 661 N Senate av.
Richmond Minnie (wid John), h 243 W 3d.
Richmond Monroe, lab, h 479 W Chicago (N I).
Richt Frederick C, billiard parlor, 35 E Ohio, h 469 N Senate av.
Richter Anna K, bkkpr West Side Planing Mill, b 1 Coble.
Richter Anton F, lab, b 381 Beecher.
Richter August F, painter, 14 Shelby, h same.
Richter Catherine (wid Anthony), h 381 Beecher.
Richter Charles, mach, h 178 Yandes.
Richter Charles F, clk, b 106 Greer.

GUIDO R. PRESSLER,
FRESCO PAINTER
Churches, Theaters, Public Buildings, Etc., A Specialty.
Residence, No. 325 North Liberty Street.
INDIANAPOLIS, IND.

INDIANAPOLIS STEEL ROOFING AND CORRUGATING WORKS, 23 and 25 East South Street. S. D. NOEL, Proprietor.

David S. McKernan REAL ESTATE AND LOANS. Exchanging real estate a specialty. A number of choice pieces for encumbered property. Rooms 2-5 Thorpe Block.

DIAMOND WALL PLASTER { Telephone 1410 BUILDERS' EXCHANGE.

UNION TRANSFER AND STORAGE CO. Cor. E. Ohio St. and C., C., C. & St. L. Ry Tracks. Storage of Household Goods and Pianos a Specialty.

W. McWORKMAN,
Galvanized Iron Cornice Works
TIN AND SLATE ROOFING.
930 WEST WASHINGTON STREET.
TELEPHONE 1118.

Richter Charles F, horseshoer, b 265 S Senate av.
Richter Christina (wid August), h 16 Shelby.
Richter Dora H (wid John W), h 106 Greer.
Richter Edward H, clk L E & W R R, h 86 Weghorst.
Richter Eli C, molder, b 381 Beecher.
Richter Fannie C, forewoman, b 353 N California.
Richter Frederick, h 6 Beecher.
Richter Frederick A, mason, h 64 Gresham.
Richter Frederick B, grocer, s w cor Russell av and S Illinois, h 40 Russell av.
Richter George F, h 177 Shelby.
Richter George O (Richter & Wright), h 409 W 2d.
Richter Gertrude, stenog, b 14 Shelby.
Richter Hannah, dressmkr, 417 E St Clair, h same.
Richter Harry C, bartndr, b 6 Beecher.
Richter Henry, clk, b 40 Russell av.
Richter Henry C, lab, h 265 S Senate av.
Richter Ida H, stenog, b 106 Greer.
Richter John, lab, b 121 W Garden.
Richter John A (West Side Planing Mill), h 1 Coble.
Richter John M, mach hd, b 387 Beecher.
Richter Julia L, teacher, b 379 Beecher.
Richter Katharine C (wid Anton), h 381 Beecher.
Richter Louis, foreman, h 265 Indiana av.
Richter Otto F, car insp, h 379 Beecher.
Richter Richard D, mach, b 417 E St Clair.
Richter Wm, pdlr, b 16 Shelby.
Richter Wm E, mach, b 265 S Senate av.
Richter Wm H, checkman, h 452 S East.
Richter Wm H, painter, h 156 Johnson av.
Richter Wm K, lab, h 137 Forest av.
Richter & Wright (George O Richter, John W Wright), laundry, 270 E Washington.
Richters Henry, h 353 N California.
Richwine Josephine (wid George), h 267 S Capitol av.
Richwine Wm J, motorman, h 29 Ashland (W I).
Rick Jacob, engr, h 183 Hill av.
Rickabaugh Henry M, clk, h 224 S Missouri.
Rickabaugh Peter M, carp, 50 River av (W I), h same.

SEALS, STENCILS, STAMPS, Etc. GEO. J. MAYER 15 S. Meridian St. TELEPHONE 1386.

Rickabaugh Wm M, driver, b 50 River av (W I).
Rickard Frank H, messenger, h 33 Ingraham.
Rickards Elizabeth (wid Thomas), h 314 E Market.
Rickards Wm C, patternmkr, b 314 E Market.
Ricker George, cigarmkr, h 161 E Washington.
Ricker Mary J (wid Michael), h 20 N Noble.
Ricker Wm, painter, b 10 Huron.
Rickert Benjamin, cabtmkr, b 134 Spring.
Rickert Mason, draughtsman C C C & St L Ry, b 94 N Senate av.
Rickerts Clarence J, plumber, b 56 Michigan av.
Rickerts Samuel, plastr, h 56 Michigan av.
Rickes George H, lab, h 380 Coburn.
Rickes George H jr, plumber, b 380 Coburn.
Ricketts Harry J, harnessmkr, b 237 Madison av.
Ricketts Joseph, foreman Holliday & Wyon, h 237 Madison av.
Rickman Wm M, lab, b 60 Northwestern av.
Ricks Lewis, coachman 605 E Washington.
Riddall Wm H, b s w cor Madison av and Hoefgen la.
Riddell Frank M, fencebldr, b 40 Woodlawn av.
Riddell Sarah M (wid Frank), h 40 Woodlawn av.
Riddell Wm A, confr, 269 Mass av, h same.
Riddle David A, carp, h 5 Hester.
Riddle George F, painter, b 36 St Peter.
Riddle George W, carp, h 36 St Peter.
Riddle Harry C, mach, b 5 Hester.
Ridenour Albert A, h 864 N Penn.
Ridenour Emma B, asst sec Board of School Commissioners, Library bldg, s w cor Meridian and Ohio, tel 202, h 864 N Penn.
Ridenour Martha (wid Jonathan M), h 864 N Penn.
Rider Paul, engr, r 29 S Station (B).
RIDER WM W, State Supt Central Union Telephone Co, s w cor Illinois and Ohio, Tel 43; h 352 N Meridian, Tel 1850.
Ridge Clayton H, clk, b 358 E Market.
Ridge George F, jeweler, b 68 The Windsor.
Ridge Harvey C, lab, b 43 Holly av (W I).
Ridge Jonathan J, trimmer, h 68 The Windsor.
Ridgely Henry D, supt Eli Lilly & Co, h 784 N Alabama.
Ridgeway Benjamin M, driver, h 94 Andrews.
Ridgeway Matilda M (wid Ebenezer), b 30 Fletcher av.
Ridgeway Samuel, carp, h 9 Cottage av (W I).
Ridgley Clifton D, musician, b 225 Clinton.
Ridgway Edward E, clk, r 232½ W Washington.
Ridgway Nathaniel J, tiremkr, h 179 Huron.
Ridgway Sarah B (wid John F), h 909 N Alabama.
Ridings Joseph, lab, r 13½ N Penn.
Ridle Charles, baker The Denison.
Ridlen Charles E, barber, b 104 Hoyt av.
Ridlen George F, barber, b 104 Hoyt av.
Ridlen George R, watchman, h n s Washington 1 e of Bradley.
Ridley Henry, lab, r 320 E Court.
Ridley Henry, tmstr, h 183 Meek.
Ridley Wm, lab, h 378 E Georgia.
Ridout Henry, b 353 Mass av.

A. METZGER AGENCY ESTABLISHED 1863. L-O-A-N-S

LAMBERT GAS & GASOLINE ENGINE CO.
ANDERSON, IND. GAS ENGINES FOR ALL PURPOSES.

BICYCLES $5 DOWN. MONTHLY. Best Wheels. Best Terms. WHEELMEN'S CO. 31 W. OHIO ST. LONG DISTANCE TEL. 1855.

Ridpath Albert E, lab, h 104 Ash.
Ridpath Frank A, clk, b 104 Ash.
Ridpath Frederick I, distributor, b 104 Ash.
Ridpath Henry W, phys, 370 E 7th, h 945 N New Jersey.
Riebe Christopher, pdlr, h 541 E Vermont.
Riebel David, clk F Riebel, h 27 Mayhew.
Riebel Frederick, cigars, 48 E Washington, h 425 Broadway.
Riechenmeyer Elizabeth, housekpr 115 E St Joseph.
Riechenmeyer Henry, h 115 E St Joseph.
Rieck John, lab, h 52 Iowa.
Riedel Bernhard F, filer, h 218 Deloss.
Riedel Frank, finisher, h e s Wallack 3 s of Pleasant run.
Riedel Wm, uphlr, h 50 Harlan.
Rieder George, mach, b 353 E Morris.
Rieder John, saloon, s e cor Morris and Hadley av (W I), h 353 E Morris.
Rieder John jr, cigarmkr, b 353 E Morris.
Riediker Henry, blksmith, h 179 Ramsey av.
Riedlinger Charles C, baker, 40 Gresham, h same.
Riedweg Robert, lab, h 963 S East.
Riegel Frank, sawyer, h 638 Charles.
Riegel John, b 840 Chestnut.
Riegel John jr, sawyer, h 840 Chestnut.
Rieger Leo, saloon, 577 S East, h same.
Rieger Michael, lab, h 834 Chestnut.
Rieger Oscar, pressman, b 577 S East.
Riegert John, butcher, h 24 Bluff rd.
Riegger Arnold F, sec and treas Good Mnfg Co, b 275 E New York.
Riegger Caroline (wid Edward G), h 275 E New York.
Riegger Charles H, finisher, b 213 N Dorman.
Riegger Constantine, pres Good Mnfg Co, mngr piano dept Emil Wulschner & Son, h 376 N Illinois.
Riegger Herman, cabtmkr, r 539 E Washington.
Riegger Joseph, h 213 N Dorman.
Riegger Otto, engr, h 223 N Beville av.
Riehl George, grocer, 89 Wisconsin, h same.
Riehl George R, bartndr, r 466 Chestnut.
Riehl John, cooper, h 79 Wisconsin.
Rieman Barbara J (wid Charles), florist, 1542 N Senate av, h same.
Rieman Ernst H, florist, h 225 E Morris.
Rieman Frederick A, florist, h 621 S East.
Rieman Henry W, florist, 609 S East, h same.
RIEMAN JOHN, Florist, 3 Mass av, Tel 1628; h 111 Andrews.
Rieman Otto J, florist, b 1542 N Senate av.
Riemann August, gardener, h e s Madison av 1 s of Pleasant run.
Riemenschneider Herman, r 83 N New Jersey.
Riensche Charles H, car rep, h 18 Gatling.
RIES CHRISTIAN, Sample Room, 149 Columbia av, h same, Tel 159.
Ries Conrad, grocer, 352 Dillon, h same.
RIES JOHN G, Saloon, 249 Newman, h same.
Rieser Charles J, pressman, b 606 E Vermont.
Rieser John F, lithog, b 606 E Vermont.
Rieser Philip, drayman, h 606 E Vermont.
Riesk Christian, finisher, h 186 N Belmont av (H).
Riewel John, finisher, h 176 Pleasant.
Rife Eva L (wid James M), b 84 W Vermont.
Rife Ruth, b 400 S Alabama.

THOS. C. DAY & CO.
INVESTING AGENTS,
TOWN AND FARM LOANS,
Rooms 325 to 330 Lemcke Bldg.

Riff Margaret M (wid Nicholas), h 490 N Delaware.
Riffe Nancy B, seamstress, b 19 Cornell av.
Rifner Clarence F, carp, h 1150 E Michigan.
Rifner David S, cigarmkr, b 73 N Dorman.
Rifner James M, h 70 Temple av.
Rifner Joseph C, carp, b 70 Temple av.
Rigdon Wm H, mach, r 259 N Illinois.
Rigg Herbert L, printer, h 260 Highland av.
Rigg Lydia (wid Frank), h 356 S Delaware.
Rigg Thomas H, typewriter rep, b 595 Bellefontaine.
Rigg Wm, h 595 Bellefontaine.
Riggle George W, fireman, h 14 Eldridge (N I).
Riggor Charles H, condr, h 33 Williams.
Riggs Alonzo E, lab, b 105 Hosbrook.
Riggs Charles H, printer, r 314 N New Jersey.
Riggs Charles W, lab, h 712 Morris (W I).
Riggs Frank E, trimmer, b 38 Ash.
Riggs Guy H, tailor, b 38 Ash.
Riggs James O, cupola tndr, h 186 W Merrill.
Riggs James P, ins agt, h 105 Hosbrook.
Riggs James R, engr, h 38 Ash.
Riggs Lewis A, car rep, h 142 N Gillard av.
Riggs Louisa E (wid Oscar M), h rear 224 Douglass.
Riggs Lucius H, lab, h 240 Tremont av (H).
Riggs Lucy M, dressmkr, 38 Ash, h same.
Riggs Marcellus, lab, h 871 Mass av.
Riggs Walter H, pdlr, h 2 N Sheffield (W I).
Riggs Wm G, lab, h 871 Mass av.
Rigle Andrew, engr, h 178 N Noble.
Rigler George, printer, h 245 Cornell av.
Rigler George A, tinner, b 245 Cornell av.
Rigler Wm C, tinner, h 77 Columbia av.
Rigsby Nathaniel L, h 274 Lincoln la.
Rigsby Ormal H, fireman, h 55 Bradshaw.
Rihl Charles H, bricklyr, b 127 Lincoln la.
Rihl Harry S, cooper, h 127 Lincoln la.
Rihl Martha, teacher Public School No 13, b 127 Lincoln la.
Riker Ephraim S, lab, h 93 S Liberty.
Riker Mary J, h n s Finley av 3 e of Shelby.
RIKHOFF HERMAN F, Merchant Tailor, Imported Novelties, 26 Indiana av, h 110 Andrews.

EAT
QUAKER BREAD
ASK YOUR GROCER FOR IT.
THE HITZ BAKING CO.

J. H. TECKENBROCK | Grilles, Fretwork and Wood Carpets
94 EAST SOUTH STREET.

FIDELITY MUTUAL LIFE PHILADELPHIA, PA. A. H. COLLINS { General Agent, 52-53 Baldwin Block.

Edwardsport Coal & Mining Co. Rooms 42 and 43 When Building.

SUPERIOR BITUMINOUS COAL For Steam and Domestic . . Purposes . .

ESTABLISHED 1876. TELEPHONE 163.
CHESTER BRADFORD,
SOLICITOR OF PATENTS,
AND COUNSEL IN PATENT CAUSES.
(See adv. page 6.)
Office:—Rooms 14 and 16 Hubbard Block, S.W. Cor. Washington and Meridian Streets, INDIANAPOLIS, INDIANA.

Rikhoff Herman H (J G Rikhoff & Co), h 213 N Liberty.
Rikhoff John G (J G Rikhoff & Co), res Evansville, Ind.
RIKHOFF JOHN H, Wholesale Liquors, 851 E Michigan, cor State av, Tel 1787; h 208 Randolph.
Rikhoff J G & Co (John G and Herman H Rikhoff), whol liquors, 188 S Meridian.
Rikhoff Louis A, bkkpr J G Rikhoff & Co, b 213 N Liberty.
Riley, see also O'Reilly and Reiley.
Riley Bernard, brakeman, b 803 E Washington.
Riley Callahan, watchman, b 364 W New York.
Riley Charles, lab, h 1 Douglass.
Riley Charles, lab, h 270 Hadley av (W I).
Riley Charles A Rev, h e s Commercial av 3 s of Washington av (I).
Riley Charles C, chief clk car service dept C C C & St L Ry, b 777 N New Jersey.
Riley Edgar, contr, h 479 W 22d (N I).
Riley Edward A, lab, b 52 Stevens.
Riley Edward E, bartndr, b 310 S Illinois.
Riley Elizabeth (wid Timothy), h 297 W Merrill.
Riley Ellen (wid Hugh), h 340 N Pine.
Riley Eugene, lab, b 294 Christian av.
Riley Frank H, clk, b 183 Oliver av (W I).
Riley Harry E, train despatcher Belt R R, h 47 S Reisner (W I).
Riley Harry F, filer, h 21 Maple.
Riley Hubert, b 241 S Senate av.
Riley Hugh, pressman, h 365 Spring.
Riley Isabel (wid Wm), boarding 124 English av.
Riley Jacob M, molder, b 10 Cleveland (H).
Riley James A, clk, b 3 Poplar (B).
Riley James M, miller, b 646 Herbert (M P).
Riley James Whitcomb, author and poet, h 26 Lockerbie.
Riley James W, lab, h 111 Martindale av.
Riley Jasper, lab, h 18 Blackford.
Riley Jesse R, lab, b 566 W Udell (N I).
Riley John, b 169 Maple.
Riley John, h 53½ Russell av.
Riley John, lab, b 297 W Merrill.
Riley John, lab, r 166½ W Washington.

76 N. PENNSYLVANIA ST.,
MAKERS
Outing BICYCLES
PHONE 598.

Riley John, lithog, b 340 N Pine.
Riley John, mach, h 465 Newman.
Riley John, switchman, h 38 Ashland (W I).
Riley John H, foreman E C Atkins & Co, h 310 S Illinois.
Riley John H, lab, b 465 Newman.
Riley John J, bartndr, h 55 E McCarty.
Riley John L, foreman, h 12 Cleveland (H).
Riley John T, h 55 Haugh (H).
Riley John W, h 566 W Udell (N I).
Riley John W, lab, h 183 Oliver av (W I).
Riley John W, plumber, h 268 S Alabama.
Riley John W, supt P & E Ry, n e cor Delaware and South.
Riley Joseph, driver, b 87 Meikel.
Riley Lawrence T, lawyer, 315 Indiana Trust bldg, b 1120 N Penn.
Riley Levi P, bicycle rep, 193 Mass av, h 405½ E Washington.
Riley Lewis S, lab, h 520 W Udell (N I).
Riley Alonzo, clk, h 212 E Ohio.
Riley Martha A, teacher, b 183 Oliver av (W I).
Riley Martin V, lab, h 10 Cleveland (H).
Riley Mary (wid Wm), h 241 S Senate av.
Riley Mary H, stenog, b 183 Oliver av (W I).
Riley Maurice, etcher, b 308 S Illinois.
Riley Michael, h 1120 N Penn.
Riley Michael, lab, h 350 S West.
Riley Michael E, lab, b 465 Newman.
Riley Michael F, clk, h 169 Maple.
Riley Michael F, molder, h 299 W Merrill.
Riley Michael G, lab, h 75 Church.
Riley Michael P, teacher, b 1120 N Penn.
Riley Nelson, lab, h 4 Brown av (H).
Riley Patrick J, condr, b 770 W Washington.
Riley Philip, cooper, b 209 Douglass.
Riley Robert M, molder, h 90 Maxwell.
Riley Thomas, lab, b 1 Douglass.
Riley Thomas, lab, h 42 Geisendorff.
Riley Thomas, pressman, b 340 N Pine.
Riley Thomas, stoker, h 52 Stevens.
Riley Thomas H, clk R M S, r 45 Cleaveland blk.
Riley Thomas J, wheelmkr, b 169 Maple.
Riley Thomas M, plumber, b 268 S Alabama.
Riley Wm, h 34 S Belmont (W I).
Riley Wm, lab, b 252 E Washington.
Riley Wm, lab, h 3 Poplar (B).
Riley Wm, messenger Am Ex Co, h 148 Lexington av.
Riley Wm J, clk H E Kinney, h 76 W 9th.
Riley Wm P, lab, b 224 W Maryland.
Riley Wm W, supt, r 352 N Meridian.
Rimstidt James, condr, b 69 W 13th.
Rimstidt Wm B, porter, b 437 N Pine.
Rinderknecht Charles J, mach Langsenkamp Bros' Brass Wks, h 224 Coburn.
Rinehart Martin L, clk R M S, h 8 Hall pl.
Ring Eliza (wid Armstead), b 410 E Walnut.
Ring John, lab, h 183 Dougherty.
Ring Robert B, painter, b 318 E McCarty.
Ringenberger Wm H, painter, h 502½ N West.
Ringer David F, tel opr, h 53 Poplar (B).
Ringer Henry, carp, h 47 S Gale (B).
Ringer John Q A, h 455 Park av.
Ringer Luther E, clk, b 664 E St Clair.
Ringgold Jesse H, porter, h 404 W North.
Ringland Joseph, lawyer, 65 Ingalls blk, b Enterprise Hotel.
Ringolsky Hirnon, china, 165 W Washington and junk, s e cor Maryland and Penn, h 316 S Illinois.

ROOFING MATERIAL C. ZIMMERMAN & SONS, SLATE AND GRAVEL ROOFERS, 19 SOUTH EAST STREET.

DRIVEN WELLS And Second Water Wells and Pumps of all kinds at CHARLES KRAUSS', 42 S. PENN. ST., TEL. 465. REPAIRING NEATLY DONE.

Ringolsky Jacob, clk, b 316 S Illinois.
Rink Charles B, clk Joseph A Rink, b 431 W New York.
Rink Edward A, clk Joseph A Rink, h 1017 N Senate av.
RINK JOSEPH A, Cloak and Fur Mnfr, 30-38 N Illinois, Tel 921; h 958 N Meridian; Tel 1417.
Rink Michael, clk, h 431 W New York.
Rinkel Albert J, barber, h 77 S Noble.
Rinkel Amiel G, musician, b 83 Lord.
Rinkel David J, barber, 153 E Washington, h 83 Lord.
Rinker A Dayton, patrolman, h 468 Union.
Rinker Roscoe A, frame truer, h 293 S New Jersey.
Rinne Charles H, grocer, 620 S Meridian, h 316 Union.
RINNE HERMAN E, Dealer in Fine Groceries, Teas and Coffees, 182 W Washington, Tel 1290; h 578 S Meridian.
Rinne Rudolph, trav agt Indpls Brewing Co, h 430 S New Jersey.
Rinska Charles, car insp, b 18 Gatling.
Riordan Daniel (Costello & Riordan), h 40 Concordia.
Riordan Edward, painter, b 104 Newman.
Riordan Garrett J, lab, b 40 Concordia.
Riordan John, painter, h 104 Newman.
Riordan John jr, mach, b 104 Newman.
Riordan John F, lab, b 40 Concordia.
Ripberger Charles, driver, b 828 Chestnut.
Ripberger John A, sawyer, h 409 Union.
Ripberger Joseph J, carp, h 474 Union.
Ripberger Leo A, packer, b 828 Chestnut.
Ripley Charles, mach, r 18 Hendricks blk.
Ripley Clarence, painter, h 14 Charles.
Ripley Margaret (wid Josiah), b 233 S West.
Ripley Walter W, capt Engine Co No 2, h 58 Ludlow av.
Ripley Warwick H, lawyer, 21 Thorpe blk, r 410 N Penn.
RIPLEY WM C, Clerk Board of Public Health and Charities, Room 10 Basement Court House, Tel 538; h 242 Talbott av.
Ripley Wm I, loans, 15½ Virginia av, h 242 Talbott av.
Rippetoe John A, adv solr The Indpls News, h 264 E St Clair.
Risch Frederick, carp, h 828 Chestnut.
Risch Juliana (wid Matthias), b 120 High.
Riscoll Thomas, lab, b 31 Blake.
Risdon Charles W, uphlr, h 48 N New Jersey.
Risdon Joseph A, truckman, h 55 Malott av.
Rish Benjamin F, patternmkr, h 429 Indiana av.
Rishling Benjamin F, condr, h n w cor 20th and Bellefontaine.
Risk Eugene G, brakeman, b 1316 N New Jersey.
Risk Howel, distributor, b 1316 N New Jersey.
Risk James A, collr, h 1316 N New Jersey.
Risley James M (Risley & Toon), h s w cor National av and Brookville rd (I).
Risley & Toon (James M Risley, Richard O Toon), real est, 94½ E Washington.
Risner Charles F, supt, h 183 Lambert (W I).
Rist John J, cigarmkr, r 212½ S Meridian.
Rist Sylvester S, car rep, h 48 Poplar (B).
Riston Edith (wid Archibald), h rear 422 N East.

Richardson & McCrea, REPRESENTING BEST KNOWN FIRE INSURANCE COMPANIES. Fidelity and Casualty Insurance Company of New York Represented. Telephone 182. 79 East Market St.

Riston George, lab, h s s Finley av 2 e of Shelby.
Riston Grace M, student, b 326 E 12th.
Ristow August, h 58 Hoyt av.
Ristow Frank W, lab, h 85 Spann av.
Ritchey James, artist, r 69 Mass av.
Ritchey James W, lab, h 304 W 7th.
Ritchey Preston, janitor, h 70 Cincinnati.
RITCHEY SAMUEL J, Propr Crystal Laundry, 10 Clifford av, h 779 E Washington.
Ritchie Annie L, stenog James M Winters, b 759 N Capitol av.
Ritchie Edwin G, genl agt John Hancock Mutual Life Ins Co, h 728 Broadway.
Ritchie Hannah (wid John), b 584 N Alabama.
Ritchie James A, molder, h 81 Nevada.
Ritchie John B, patternmkr, b 759 N Capitol av.
Ritchie Julia A (wid John), b 818 N Alabama.
Ritchie Mary A (wid Samuel), boarding 779 E Washington.
Ritchie Mary E, microscopist, b 759 N Capitol av.
Ritchie Robert, h 258 S Penn.
Ritchie Robert B, patternmkr, b 759 N Capitol av.
Ritchie Samuel E, mach hd, b 121 W Maryland.
Ritchie Samuel J, bkkpr, b 779 E Washington.
Ritchie Wm, foreman, h 759 N Capitol av.
Ritchlin Ernest W, h 618 W Vermont.
Riter Edward, agt, r 232½ W Washington.
Rittenhouse George L, trav agt J G Perry & Co, b 30 E Pratt.
Ritter Alvin P, trav agt, r 31½ Monument pl.
Ritter Anna C, teacher Public School No 7, b 530 S New Jersey.
Ritter Caleb L, phys, 510 Virginia av, h 146 Prospect.
Ritter Carrie L (wid Levi), h s w cor Washington and Ritter avs (I).
Ritter Charles H, uphlr, h 530 S New Jersey.

The Williams Typewriter Elegant Work, Visible Writing, Easy Operation, High Speed. S. H. EAST, State Agent, 55 Thorpe Block, 87 E. Market St.

If You are not Satisfied with Your Laundry Work Give Us a Trial . . ERTEL STEAM LAUNDRY 26 and 28 N. Senate Avenue. Telephone 19.

ELLIS & HELFENBERGER Manufacturers of IRON and WIRE FENCES 162-170 S. SENATE AVE. TEL. 958.

THE HOGAN TRANSFER AND STORAGE COMP'Y
Household Goods and Pianos. Moved—Packed—Stored...... Baggage and Package Express Machinery and Safes a Specialty Cor. Washington and Illinois Sts. TELEPHONE No. 675.

The Central Rubber & Supply Co. PHONE 922. 79 S. ILLINOIS ST., INDIANAPOLIS, IND. Hose, Belting, Packing, Clothing, Druggists' Sundries, Bicycle Tires, Cotton Hose, Etc. New York Belting & Packing Co., L't'd.

HIGHEST SECURITY
LOWEST COST OF INSURANCE.
The Provident Life and Trust Co.
Of Philadelphia.
D. W. EDWARDS, Gen. Agent,
508 Indiana Trust Building.

Ritter Christopher C, dentist, 431 Virginia av, b 70 Prospect.
Ritter Conrad J, saloon, 67 N Alabama, h 231 Davidson.
Ritter Eli F (Ritter & Baker), h 208 Central av.
Ritter Frederick, lab, h 504 Union.
Ritter Frederick O, lawyer, 408 Indiana Trust bldg, b s w cor Washington and Ritter avs (I).
Ritter Frederick W, horseshoer, h 391 Mass av.
Ritter Henry, express, h 71 Pierce.
Ritter Ida M, dressmkr, 325 E Ohio, b same.
Ritter James A, h 325 E Ohio.
Ritter Jesse B, lab, h s w cor Wolf pike and Baltimore av.
Ritter Lee R, messenger Am Ex Co, h 194 Prospect.
Ritter Levi W, collr, h 70 Prospect.
Ritter Mitchell, lab, h 323 Spring.
Ritter Paulina J, boarding 325 E Ohio.
Ritter Philip K, mach, h 649½ Virginia av.
Ritter Roscoe H, student, b 208 Central av.
Ritter Rudolph C, clk A Kiefer Drug Co, b n e cor Capitol av and 6th.
Ritter Urban, finisher, h 54 Downey.
Ritter Wm C, phys, h 36 Fletcher av.
RITTER & BAKER (Eli F Ritter, Jason E Baker), Lawyers, 45, 46 and 47 Baldwin Blk, Tel 1268.
Rittinger Elizabeth B, tailoress, b 217 E St Clair.
Ritz Andrew H, brakeman, h 38 Jefferson av.
Ritzendollar Julia A, grocer, 412 Indiana av, h same.
Ritzendollar Louis, express, h 412 Indiana av.
Ritzinger Myla F (wid John B), b 785 N Meridian.
Rivers Mary, h 14 Columbia al.
Roach David A, Sheriff Supreme and Appellate Courts, 74 State House, h 399 Ash.
Roach David M, lab, b 160 Chestnut.
Roach Edith H (wid Edmund), b 864 Bellefontaine.
Roach Frank, baggageman, h w s Chester 2 n of Washington.

Julius C. Walk & Son,
Jewelers
Indianapolis.
12 EAST WASHINGTON ST.

Roach Frank, bartndr, b 72 Church.
Roach George A, mach, h n w cor Washington and Quincy.
Roach Henry, lab, h 122 Agnes.
Roach Henry, b rear 124 Broadway.
Roach Homer J, checkman, h 20 LaSalle.
Roach John, tailor, 25 W Ohio, b 114 Meek.
Roach John C, tmstr, h 454 Martindale av.
Roach John M, hostler, b 155 Michigan (H).
Roach Jonathan J, farmer, h n w cor Washington and Quincy.
Roach Mamie F, clk Levey Bros, b 362 Coburn.
Roach Michael F, packer, h 72 Church.
Roach Michael R (Blumlein & Roach), b 101 Fayette.
Roach Patrick, lab, b 11 Douglass.
Roach Richard E, lab, h 307 W Pearl.
Roach Samuel B, b w s Chester 2 n of Washington.
Roach Sarah (wid Alva C), b 64 Prospect.
Roach Thomas, flagman, b 160 Chestnut.
Roach Thomas, molder, b 890 W Washington.
Roach Wm M, foreman, h n s Washington 2 w of Quincy.
Roache Addison L, h 593 N Penn.
Roache Addison L jr (Coe & Roache), h 77 W 3d.
Roark Albert F, motorman, b 24 Wilcox.
Roark Charles, barber, h 677 Mass av.
Roark John, painter, b 111 Malott av.
Roark Thomas P, pdlr, h 17 Osgood (W I).
Roback Amanda, dressmkr, h 734 N Senate av.
Roback Eli T, bookbndr, h 391 N Senate av.
Roback Henry H, sawyer, b 350 N Senate av.
Robards Wm T, packer, h 3 McKernan.
Robb Artemus E, condr, b 489 College av.
Robb Ernest A, motorman, b 489 College av.
Robb James W, tmstr, b 489 College av.
Robb John, tmstr, h 421 N Pine.
Robb John D, electrotype finisher, b 72 W Ohio.
Robb Nancy A, boarding 489 College av.
Robbins Alva C, tinner, h 71 Lynn av (W I).
Robbins Charles F, lawyer, 93 Lombard bldg, h 248 N Penn.
Robbins Charles M, painter, b 224 Fletcher av.
Robbins Clair E, clk P L Chambers, b 140 N East.
Robbins Corrinna E, teacher Girls' Classical School, b 466 N Penn.
Robbins Earle G, bkkpr Irvin Robbins & Co, b 12 W North.
Robbins Edward, harnessmkr, b 30 N East.
Robbins Edwin B, waiter, r 26 S West.
Robbins Elizabeth E (wid Daniel), h 30 N East.
Robbins Enos R, trav agt Daniel Stewart Co, b 581 Ash.
Robbins George E, mach, h 342 Bellefontaine.
Robbins Harry, driver, b 89 Wilson.
Robbins Hiram H, condr, h 772 W Washington.
Robbins Irvin (Irvin Robbins & Co), h 12 W North.
Robbins Irvin & Co (Irvin and Sarah A Robbins), carriage mnfrs, 32 E Georgia, tel 931.
Robbins James, lab, h 17 Minkner.
Robbins James, molder, h 120½ Oliver av (W I).
Robbins James M, trav agt, b 914 N Delaware.

OTTO GAS ENGINES | BUILDERS' EXCHANGE S. W. Cor. Ohio and Penn. Telephone 585.

Becker & Son Charles Becker Jacob Becker Jr. Merchant Tailors. 21 N. Penn. St. Tel. 934

SALISBURY & STANLEY OFFICE, STORE AND BANK FIXTURES. Contractors and Builders. Repairing of all kinds done on short notice. 177 Clinton St. Indianapolis, Ind. Tel. 999

Robbins Lydia M (wid Noah), b 37 Wilcox.
Robbins Martin (Shriner & Robbins), h 73 Wilson.
Robbins Ora J, mach, b 224 Fletcher av.
Robbins Paul G, driver, b 140 N East.
Robbins Samuel, stone contr, 848 Cornell av, h same.
Robbins Sarah A (wid Richard; Irvin Robbins & Co), h 12 W North.
Robbins Thomas H, supt, h 178 Dearborn.
Robbins Thomas M, clk I D & W Ry, b 413 N East.
Robbins Wesley, phys, 29½ W Ohio, r same.
Robbins Wm W, trav agt, h 140 N East.
Robbs Hannah F, h 194 Newman.
Roberson David J, farmer, h n w cor Tremont av and Morris (W I).
Roberson George W, gardener, h 1266 Morris (W I).
Roberson H M, lab, h 22 N Reisner (W I).
Roberson James W, tmstr, h 1270 Morris (W I).
Roberson Louis, lab, h rear 73 Howard.
Robert Frank, mach hd, h 233 W South.
Robert Jones, driver, h 18 Mill.
Roberts Alonzo, laundryman, b 1448 E Washington.
Roberts Alpheus, carp, h 11 Coble.
Roberts Ambrose B S, patternmkr, h 298 Blake.
Roberts Amos J, tmstr, h 361 W Pearl.
Roberts Andrew J, grocer, 583 W Washington, h same.
Roberts Andrew J, lab, h 596 W Maryland.
Roberts Augustus, lab, b w s Graceland av 2 s of 29th.
Roberts Belle, r 5½ Indiana av.
Roberts Benjamin, feed, s w cor Lawrence and Rural, h same.
Roberts Benjamin, tmstr, h rear 453 S Missouri.
Roberts Benjamin F, h 432 S Olive.
Roberts Bowen, lab, h 447 W 2d.
Roberts Charles, waiter, b 91 Fletcher av.
Roberts Charles R, carp, h 190 Buchanan.
Roberts Charles S, lab, h 84 Bloomington.
Roberts David, lab, h 22 Holly av (W I).
Roberts Douglas, lab, h 228 W Vermont.
Roberts Earl, lab, r 24 N West.
Roberts Edward, lab, h rear 44 Drake.
Roberts Edward, lab, b 269 N West.
Roberts Edward C, trav agt, h 94 John.
Roberts Edward L, mach, b 250 E Vermont.
Roberts Eliza (wid Wm S), h 35 Helen.
Roberts Elizabeth R (wid Wm H), dressmkr, h 157 N Alabama.
Roberts Eugene W, lab, h 202 W 6th.
Roberts Eusebius C, lab, h w s Graceland av 2 s of 29th.
Roberts Frank, confr, 266 W Washington, h same.
Roberts Frank M, bartndr, b 253 E Washington.
Roberts George, driver, h 33 Church.
Roberts George, lab, h 7 Gatling.
Roberts George A, engr, h 276 Fletcher av.
Roberts George E, harnessmkr, r 100 N Senate av.
Roberts George H, vet surg, 286 Mass av, b 20 Ruckle.
Roberts George W, polisher, b 583 W Washington.
Roberts Harry, carp, h 6 Hoyt av.
Roberts Harry W, harnessmkr, b 727 N Senate av.
Roberts Henry K, steward John Huegele, h 35 Peru av.
Roberts Hester A (wid Andrew J), h 19 Garfield pl.

Henry H. Fay,
40½ E. WASHINGTON ST.,
AGENT FOR
Insurance Co. of North America,
Pennsylvania Fire Ins. Co.

Roberts Ira W (Wagoner & Son), b 167 Hill av.
Roberts Isabel L (wid Lloyd), b 365 N East.
Roberts Ivy A, dressmkr, 298 Blake, h same.
Roberts Jackson, lab, h 72 Oscar.
Roberts James, lab, h 146 Patterson.
Roberts James, lab, h 54 Smith.
Roberts James E, h 570 N Meridian.
Roberts James W, tel opr, b 86 Harrison.
Roberts Jefferson, lab, h rear 122 Ash.
Roberts Jeremiah S, millwright, h 56 Division (W I).
Roberts Jesse H, lab, h s w cor Wolf pike and Baltimore av.
Roberts Joel J, carp, h 27 S Gale (B).
Roberts John, h 638 N Alabama.
Roberts John A Rev, h n s University av 1 e of Ritter av (I).
Roberts John A, pdlr, h 20 Ethel (W I).
Roberts John E, mach, b 195 Christian av.
Roberts John H, engr, h 188 Highland av.
Roberts John N, supt J W Lunt & Co, h 435 Central av.
ROBERTS JOHN O, Propr Plaza Apartment House, 16-24 Monument Pl, h same.
Roberts John S, clk Lyman W Louis, b 19 Garfield pl.
Roberts John S, mattressmkr, h 1031 N Penn.
Roberts John T Rev, h w s National av 1 s of P C C & St L Ry (I).
Roberts John W, harnessmkr, h 727 N Senate av.
Roberts John W, mach, h 195 Christian av.
Roberts Joseph D, trav agt, h 1679 Kenwood av.
Roberts Joseph S, trimmer, h 391 E McCarty.
Roberts Joseph T, lawyer, 51 Bloomington, h same.
Roberts Julia A (wid Wallace), h 74 Foundry (B).
Roberts Junius B, teacher High School, h 567 Park av.
Roberts J Harry, street contr, 391 E McCarty, b same.
Roberts J W, chief clk asst genl supt's office L E & W R R, h 191 N New Jersey.

MAYHEW'S SPECTACLES THE BEST IN USE SOLD ONLY AT 13 N. MERIDIAN ST.

LUMBER Sash and Doors BALKE & KRAUSS CO., Corner Market and Missouri Sts.

Friedgen Has the BEST PATENT LEATHER SHOES AT LOWEST PRICES. 19 North Pennsylvania St.

SAMUEL LAING ; HOT AIR FURNACES ..... 72 AND 74 EAST COURT STREET.

M. B. WILSON, Pres. W. F. CHURCHMAN, Cash.
The Capital National Bank,
INDIANAPOLIS, IND.
Banking business in all its branches. Bonds and Foreign Exchange bought and sold.
Interest paid on time deposits.
Checks and drafts on all Indiana and Illinois points handled at lowest rates.
No. 28 South Meridian Street, Cor. Pearl.

Roberts Lemuel (L Roberts & Son), h 252 S New Jersey.
Roberts Levi P, foreman, h 116 Trowbridge (W).
Roberts L & Son (Lemuel and Robert), stairbldrs, 177 Duncan.
Roberts Mamie G (wid Wm E), h 191 S New Jersey.
Roberts Margaret L (wid Calvin T), 18 N Reisner (W I).
Roberts Martha J (wid Nathan H), b 606 W Vermont.
Roberts Mary, h 174½ S East.
Roberts Mary (wid Thomas), h 166 Davidson.
Roberts Mary B (wid Joel), cook, r 249 S Delaware.
Roberts Mary M (wid John), h 82 W 2d.
Roberts Mayme, elocutionist, h 249 N West.
Roberts Milton G, farmer, h 250 Huron.
Roberts Montie O, carp, b 193 Fletcher av.
Roberts Myra, music teacher, 249 N West, b same.
Roberts Rachel C (wid Robert H), b 65 Arch.
Roberts Rebecca, b 426 Superior.
Roberts Richard B (Clark & Roberts), h 1031 N Penn.
Roberts Robert Rev, pastor Fletcher Place M E Church, h 308 E South.
Roberts Robert E (L Roberts & Son), b 252 S New Jersey.
Roberts Robert E, tinner, b 391 E McCarty.
Roberts Roy, mach, b 606 W Vermont.
Roberts Samuel L, trav agt, b 157 N Alabama.
Roberts Sarah (wid Jordan), h 86 Harrison.
Roberts Sarah E (wid Wm A J), b 276 W Market.
Roberts Sarah W (wid James T), h n w cor Washington and Watts.
Roberts Sheridan S, saw filer, h 11 Columbia av.
Roberts Sherman, feed, 808 W Washington, h 3 Coble.
Roberts Silas W, lab, h 9 Astor.
Roberts Thomas, polisher, h 139 Patterson.
Roberts Thomas, student, b 287 S New Jersey.

Insure Against Accidents
WITH
TUTTLE & SEGUIN,
Agents for
Fidelity and Casualty Co., of New York.
$10,000 for $25. $5,000 for $12.50.
TEL. 1168. 28 E. MARKET ST.

Roberts Thomas H, lab, h 369½ W Pearl.
Roberts Walter H, mach, h 82 Bellefontaine.
Roberts Warner D, cigarmkr, b 549 E Michigan.
Roberts Wm, brakeman, b 249 E Louisiana.
Roberts Wm, lab, b 35 Helen.
Roberts Wm, lab, b 17 Sumner.
Roberts Wm A, ins agt, h 193 Fletcher av.
Roberts Wm B, h 567 Park av.
Roberts Wm C, clk, b 157 N Alabama.
Roberts Wm E, salesman Indpls Abattoir Co, h 1332 N Delaware.
Roberts Wm H, foreman, h 26 Hoyt av.
Roberts Wm L, shoemkr, h 91 Greencastle av.
Roberts Wm P, carp, 1322 N Alabama, h same.
Roberts W Harry (W H Roberts & Co), h 30 Nordyke av (W I).
Roberts W H & Co (W Harry Roberts, George W Bone), com mer, 117 E Maryland.
Robertson Alexander M, h 480 N Meridian.
Robertson Charles E, butcher, h 116 Sheffield av (H).
Robertson Charles M, trav agt Hockett-Puntenny Piano Co, b 550 Central av.
Robertson Emma (wid Wm), h 183 Newman.
Robertson George W, mach hd, b 139 Lawrence.
Robertson Harley J, tel opr L E & W R R, b 216 Fletcher av.
Robertson Herbert B, drayman, h 97 Elm.
Robertson Jabez W, molder, h 22 King av (H).
Robertson James E, h 177 N Alabama.
Robertson James M, molder, h 39 Beason.
Robertson John, carp, h 200 W Raymond.
Robertson John A, bailiff, h 216 Fletcher av.
Robertson J Frank, phys, 1061 E Michigan, h same.
Robertson Kate, teacher, b 162 Harrison.
Robertson Lou A, lawyer, 68½ E Market, b 550 Central av.
Robertson Lucy, cook, r 219 W North.
Robertson Martha (wid Winfield), h 139 Lawrence.
Robertson May, bkkpr, b 183 Newman.
Robertson Minnie B, clk Order of Chosen Friends, b 568 N Jefferson av.
Robertson Omer A, h n s 11th 4 e of College av.
Robertson Robert S, pres Masonic Mutual Benefit Society, res Fort Wayne, Ind.
Robertson Thomas B, carp, h 138 Columbia av.
Robertson Thomas S, fireman, h 1 S Stuart (B).
Robertson Thomas W, clk, h 177 N Alabama.
Robertson Virgil F, barber, b 342 E Washington.
Robertson Webb J, city fireman, h 82 W 6th.
Robertson Wilber M, condr, h 972 N Capitol av.
ROBERTSON WILLARD, Lawyer, 625-626 Lemcke Bldg, Tel 1886; h 717 N Alabama.
Robertson Wm, mach, h 384 N West.
Robertson Wm C, agt, b 700 Chestnut.
Robertson Wm D, drayman, h 97 Elm.
Robertson Wm F, clk C C C & St L Ry, h 111 Naomi.
Robertson Wm H, condr, h 186 Buchanan.
Robertson Wm U, clk The Progress Clothing Co, h 197 N West.

WEDDING CAKE BOXES · SULLIVAN & MAHAN 41 W. Pearl St.

DIAMOND WALL PLASTER { Telephone 1410 BUILDERS' EXCHANGE.

Best Work. Prompt Delivery. } THE HOME LAUNDRY 197 S. ILLINOIS ST. TEL. 1769. } Collars and Cuffs our Specialty.

Robey Isaac, engr, h 133 Lambert (W I).
Robey John C, trav agt Parrott-Taggart Bakery, h 1095 E Ohio.
Robinette Wm W, plastr, h 276 W Court.
Robinius Edward H, collr Taylor & Taylor, b 94 English av.
Robinius Frank, janitor, h 144 Blackford.
Robinius Frank P, shoemkr, h rear 222 W Washington.
Robinius Henry H, printer, b 144 Blackford.
Robinius Michael, clk Taylor & Taylor, h 94 English av.
Robins George, lab, r 300 S Capitol av.
Robins Hamilton, confr, h 376 S Alabama.
Robins John L, bkkpr Dalton & Merrifield, b 373 Broadway.
Robinson Albert, driver, h rear 484 W North.
Robinson Albert, plumber, r 101 N New Jersey.
Robinson Albert, waiter, b 546 Superior.
Robinson Albert J, canvasser, h 1331 N Senate av.
Robinson Albert O, patrolman, h 402 N West.
Robinson Alice N (wid James W), b 46 Arch.
Robinson Alice S (wid Henry), h 14 Elliott.
Robinson Allen B (Robinson Bros), h 287 W Michigan.
Robinson Alonzo, lab, b 16 Leon.
Robinson Anna M (wid Wm J H), h 171 Woodlawn av.
Robinson Arabella (wid Wm A), h 43 Bismarck av (H).
Robinson Arie (wid Wm), b 71 Yandes.
Robinson Bancroft, cigarmkr, b 163½ E Washington.
Robinson Benjamin A, lab, h 83 Sanders.
Robinson Bros (James A and Allen B), grocers, 195 W Ohio.
Robinson Charles, lab, h 18 Church.
Robinson Charles, lab, r 29 Ellsworth.
Robinson Charles, lab, b 13 Mill.
Robinson Charles, waiter The Denison.
Robinson Charles B, filer, h 80 N Olive.
Robinson Charles D, trav agt, h 102½ Middle Drive (W P).
Robinson Charles E, adv agt, b 173 E Market.
Robinson Cyrena R, h rear e s Arlington av 2 n of Walnut av (I).
Robinson Daniel C, pres Acme Milling Co, res Boston, Mass.
Robinson David, carp, b 396 Columbia av.
Robinson Don A, broom mnfr, 163 Agnes, h same.
Robinson Edmonia (wid Berry), h 76 Chapel.
Robinson Edward, lab, r 232 W Vermont.
Robinson Edward C, janitor, h 406 W 1st.
Robinson Edward J, produce, E Mkt House, h 321 W Ontario (N I).
Robinson Elias, porter, b 291 E Miami.
Robinson Elihu, lab, h 26 W 1st.
Robinson Elizabeth, h 64 Hosbrook.
Robinson Elizabeth (wid John), h 876 N Senate av.
Robinson Elizabeth A (wid Charles D), b 102½ Middle Drive (W P).
Robinson Elizabeth Y (wid Joseph R), b 84 E Michigan.
Robinson Emma B (wid Waldo G), milliner, 233 Mass av, h same.
Robinson Emma E (wid John R), b 427 S Meridian.
Robinson Esther E (wid James B), r 9 Ryan blk.

FRANK NESSLER. WILL H. ROST.
FRANK NESSLER & CO.
Tailors
56 EAST MARKET ST. (Lemcke Building),
INDIANAPOLIS, IND.

Robinson Fanny (wid Jerome), stenog Standard Oil Co, h 66 Johnson av.
Robinson Flora, teacher Public School No 3, b 121 Elm.
Robinson Frank, teacher, r 53 Dearborn.
Robinson Frank C, bkkpr Singer Mnfg Co, h 418 Bellefontaine.
Robinson Frank F, painter, b 76 Chapel.
Robinson Frank H, pressfeeder, b 508 Charles.
Robinson Frank W, lab, h 185 Buchanan.
Robinson Frederick M, bkkpr The Gordon-Kurtz Co, res Mapleton, Ind.
Robinson Frederick S, cashr, b 970 N Delaware.
Robinson George, lab, b 34 Howard.
Robinson George W, blksmith, b 13 Fayette.
Robinson George W, mngr, h 12 The Chalfant.
Robinson George W, tmstr, h 69 Cushing.
Robinson Grant, porter, b 168 Agnes.
Robinson Guy C, trav agt, h 425 E 12th.
Robinson Harry, porter, b 116 Columbia al.
Robinson Harry, porter, b 232 W Vermont.
Robinson Harrison W, porter, b 83 Sanders.
Robinson Hayden C, clk Van Camp H and I Co, h 549 E Vermont.
Robinson Henry, carp, b 27 N Beville av.
Robinson Henry, lab, r 4 Susquehanna.
Robinson Henry, waiter, r rear 175 N Penn.
Robinson Henry F, lab, r 167 Muskingum al.
Robinson Henry F, pressman, h 508 Charles.
Robinson Isaiah, janitor, b 168 Agnes.
Robinson James, lab, h 35 Cushing.
Robinson James, lab, 624 N Penn.
Robinson James A (Robinson Bros), h 270 N California.
Robinson James B, driver, b 166 Union.
Robinson James D, porter L G Deschler, b 775 N Meridian.
Robinson James M, brakeman, h 741 E Ohio.
Robinson James M, hostler, b 63 Beaty.
Robinson James M, lab, h 303 S Penn.
Robinson James N, produce, h 121 Elm.
Robinson John, ins, h 422 Bellefontaine.
Robinson John, lab, h 385 Blackford.
Robinson John F, lab, b 36 N California.
Robinson John F, mach hd, h w s Sherman Drive 3 s of Prospect.

Haueisen & Hartmann
163-169 E. Washington St.
FURNITURE,
Carpets,
Household Goods,
Tin, Granite and China Wares, Oil Cloth and Shades

THE WM. H. BLOCK CO. 7 AND 9 EAST WASHINGTON STREET. DRY GOODS, HOUSE FURNISHINGS AND CROCKERY.

London Guarantee and Accident Co. (Ltd.) All forms of Liability Insurance, Workmen's Collective Insurance, Fidelity Bonds and Individual Accident Insurance.
Geo. W. Pangborn, Gen. Agent, 704-706 Lemcke Bldg. Telephone 140.

FRANK K. SAWYER, AGENT
74 East Market Street. Telephone 863.
Prussian National Insurance Comp'y
OF STETTIN, GERMANY. ORGANIZED 1845.

JOSEPH GARDNER,
TIN, COPPER AND SHEET-IRON WORK AND
HOT AIR FURNACES.
37, 39 & 41 KENTUCKY AVE. Telephone 322

Robinson John R, captain Chemical No 2, h 72 Elm.
Robinson John W, broker, 53½ W Washington, r 19½ N Meridian.
Robinson John W, lab, b 91 Darnell.
Robinson Joseph, cigars, 217 Indiana av, h same.
Robinson Joseph S Rev, h 37 Buchanan.
Robinson Josephine, b 84 E Michigan.
Robinson Julia, h 44 Athon.
Robinson Julius, lab, b 183 Indiana av.
Robinson Laura A, teacher Public School No 26, b 430 Ash.
Robinson Lewis, lab, r 336 Superior.
Robinson Lewis, waiter Hotel Oneida, r 189 W 9th.
Robinson Lewis P, clk Merchants' National Bank, b 970 N Delaware.
Robinson Lincoln, lab, r 34 Howard.
Robinson Louis, shoemkr, 125½ Mass av, r same.
Robinson Louis J, tel opr W U Tel Co, b 487 S Missouri.
Robinson Louisa O (wid Andrew G), h 341 Broadway.
Robinson Lucy E, teacher Deaf and Dumb Inst, b 303 N New Jersey.
Robinson McDonald, bkkpr Indiana Natl Bank, h 341 Broadway.
Robinson Malinda (wid George), h 28 Malott av.
Robinson Marcus L, engr, h 204 Spann av.
Robinson Martha E, h 75 Kentucky av.
Robinson Martin S, trav agt, h 970 N Delaware.
Robinson Mary J (wid James), h 26½ N Senate av.
Robinson Mary K (wid Rev Reuben D), h 303 N New Jersey.
Robinson Mary M (wid Jesse M), h 382 College av.
Robinson Mary Y, teacher Girls' Classical School, b 84 E Michigan.
Robinson May, h 223 Cornell av.
Robinson Milton, lab, h rear 223 Broadway.
Robinson Minnie E, stenog Indpls Chair Mnfg Co, b Frederick M Robinson.

J. S. FARRELL & CO.
STEAM AND HOT WATER
HEATING FOR STORES, OFFICES,
PUBLIC BUILDINGS,
PRIVATE RESIDENCES,
GREENHOUSES, ETC.
84 North Illinois St. Telephone 382.

Robinson Minnie M (wid Louis), h 1335 N Senate av.
Robinson Nathan, lab, h 283 S Capitol av.
Robinson Oliver, lab, b 159 W Merrill.
Robinson Otis G, clk, b 72 Elm.
Robinson Paul V, mach, b 37 Buchanan.
Robinson Rachel E, h 234 Fletcher av.
Robinson Robert, lab, r 12½ Roanoke.
Robinson Robert A, lab, b 40 N Senate av.
Robinson Robert D, phys, b Enterprise Hotel.
Robinson Royal, bkkpr, b 876 N Senate av.
Robinson Russell D, editor, b 303 N New Jersey.
Robinson Samuel, lab, b 322 Tremont.
Robinson Sarah A, h 327 W North.
Robinson Susan A (wid Anthony), b e s Auburn av 6 s of Bethel av.
Robinson Thomas, driven wells, b 502 N Senate av.
Robinson Thomas, lab, h 103 Hill av.
Robinson Thomas D, clk, b 581 Ash.
Robinson Walter L, collr, b 101 Bates.
Robinson Wesley, lab, h s s Lawrence 3 w of Hazel.
Robinson Wilbur S, phys, b 341 Broadway.
Robinson Wm, filer, h 16 Villa av.
Robinson Wm B, lab, h 176 W 1st.
Robinson Wm G, barber, 514 Virginia av, h same.
Robinson Wm H, fireman, h 200 Spann av.
Robinson Wm H, lab Insane Asylum.
Robinson Wm L, gas insp, h 478 Stillwell.
Robinson Wm O, lab, h w s Rural 7 n of 17th.
Robinson Willis B, grocer, 180 W 1st, h same.
Robinson Wilson L, lab, b 37 Buchanan.
Robinson Woodfin D, Judge Appellate Court of Indiana, 101 State House.
Robison Albert B, plumber, 202 E Ohio, r same.
Robison Charles N, bookbndr, h 215 Virginia av.
Robison Edward J, sec Fidelity Building and Savings Union, h 720 Broadway.
Robison Elvira C (wid Andrew J), h 56 Jefferson av.
Robison Harriet C (wid Philip G), h 34 Chadwick.
Robison James H, lab, h 186 Anderson.
Robison John R, tmstr, h w s Sheffield av 3 n of Clarke (H).
Robison John S, carp, h 863 Cornell av.
Robson Peter H, insp City Civil Engineer's Office, b 56 Jefferson av.
Robison Robert, carp, h 485 W Francis (N I).
Robison Samuel, lab, b n s 8th 3 w of canal.
Robison Wm, engr, h 43 N Gillard av.
Robison Wm, lab, b 125 Shepard (W I).
Robke Anthony E, eng rep, h 264 Jefferson av.
Robson Annie, laundress, h rear 236 E Wabash.
Robson Dirce, music teacher, 805 N New Jersey, b same.
Robson John K, h 71 W Walnut.
Robson Kate, prin Public School No 33, b 805 N New Jersey.
Robson Wm H, pub Indpls Trade Journal, rooms 35-36 Commercial Club bldg, tel 1284, h 805 N New Jersey.
Robuck Joseph W, caller, b 258 E Georgia.
Robuck Robert A, lab, h 258 E Georgia.
Rocap Charles E, mach, b 151 Belmont av.

United States Life Insurance Co., of New York.
E. B. SWIFT, M'g'r. 25 E. Market St.

WM. KOTTEMAN } 89 & 91 E. Washington St. Telephone 1742 { RUGS MATTINGS WINDOW SHADES

ROCH TOBIAS (Roch & Peterman), Architectural Iron and Wire Works, 125 E Pearl, between Delaware and Alabama, h 577 N West. (See adv in Architectural Iron Works.)

ROCH & PETERMAN (Tobias Roch, Henry Peterman), Mnfrs of Driven Well Points, 125 E Pearl.

Roche Charles L, lab, h s w cor Michigan and Linwood av.
Roche Elizabeth, cashr, h 415 E St Clair.
Roche Maurice, clk, b 415 E St Clair.
Roche Patrick J, dry goods, 398 Mass av, h 415 E St Clair.
Rochester Daniel, barber, r 68 N Missouri.
Rochester George, carp, b 64 Howard.
Rochester John, barber, 68 N Missouri, r same.
Rochester Mary (wid Daniel), h 22 Sheffield av (H).
Rochester Thomas, carp, h 64 Howard.
Rochford John B, lab, h 23 Abbott.

ROCHFORD JOHN J, Lawyer, 82½ E Washington, Tel 724; h 435 N East, Tel 1236.

Rochford Julia (wid James), b 266 Bates.
Rochford Michael, lab, b 326 W Vermont.
Rochford Thomas E, lab, b 266 Bates.
Rochow Carl, lab, h 10 Sycamore.
Rochow Otto C, carp, h 18 Sycamore.
Rochow Robert J, carp, 10 Sycamore, h same.
Rock Charles M, real est, h 177 E Merrill.
Rock Guy D, barber, b 257 Mass av.
Rock Hallie, clk, b 669 E Market.
Rock Ida M, music teacher, 19 N Gale (B), h same.
Rock Island Plow Co, Ira S Weisz agt, 75 W Washington.
Rock Levi M, condr, h 669 E Market.
Rock Louis M, fireman, h 19 N Gale (B).
Rockafellow Wm W, car rep, h 22 Hester.

ROCKER JOHN C, Grocer, 848 W Washington, h same.

Rocker Margaret (wid Peter), grocer, 292 W Maryland, h same.
Rocker Peter, clk, b 292 W Maryland.
Rockey Henry S, b 209 Prospect.
Rockwell George E, dist pass agt Penna Lines, h 1199 N Illinois.
Rockwood Burton L Rev, b 221 Ramsey av.

ROCKWOOD CHARLES B, Diamond Wall Plaster Co, Office 3 Builders' Exchange, Tel 1410; h 675 N Meridian.

Rockwood George O, draughtsman Rockwood Mnfg Co, b 638 N Alabama.
Rockwood Harry C, carp, b 184 E Vermont.
Rockwood Harvey A, granite, 221 Ramsey av, h same.

ROCKWOOD MANUFACTURING CO THE (American Paper Pulley Co, Wm E Rockwood), Founders and Machinists, 176-190 S Penn, Tel 944.

Rockwood Wm E (Rockwood Mnfg Co), h 638 N Alabama.
Rockwood Wm M, clk Rockwood Mnfg Co, b 638 N Alabama.
Rodabaugh Charles, baggageman, r 42 S Capitol av.
Rodecker Charlotta, tailor, b 225 E Market.
Rodefeld Frank H W, horseshoer, h 63 Omer.
Rodenbeck Christian, lab, h 242 W 23d.
Rodenbeck Henry, carp, b 48 N East.

THOS. C. DAY & CO.
Financial Agents and Loans.
We have the experience, and claim to be reliable.
Rooms 325 to 330 Lemcke Bldg.

Rodenbeck Henry, florist, h 242 W 23d.
Rodenbeck John, clk, b 242 W 23d.
Rodenberg Amelia (wid Henry), h 74 W McCarty.
Rodenberger Adolph, filer, b 539 Fremont (N I).
Rodenberger Moses, carp, h 539 Fremont (N I).
Rodenberger Samuel E, carp, h 318 E North.
Roder Ernst, clk, b 755 N West.
Roder Frederick, lab, h 112 Wisconsin.
Rodewald Henry H, bartndr, h 1 Shelby.
Rodewald John H, carp, h 48 Arbor av (W I).
Rodewald John H, clk, h 519 Virginia av.
Rodey Henry, meats, 348 E South, h same.
Rodgers Andrew J, barber, h e s Rembrant 1 s of Richard (M P).
Rodgers George W, condr, h 51 Bismarck av (H).
Rodgers Hiram D, carp, h 28 Athon.
Rodgers James H, lab, h 6½ Malott av.
Rodgers Richard B, lab, h 292 Jackson.
Rodgers Wilbur, student, b 72 W New York.
Rodgers Wm A, mach hd, h 14 Sumner.
Rodibaugh Edward S, fireman, b 640 E Ohio.
Rodibaugh Omer, b 659 N Capitol av.
Rodibaugh Phoebe (wid Adam), h 659 N Capitol av.
Rodibaugh Thomas, printer, h 733 N Capitol av.

RODNEY CAESAR A, Sec and Treas Railroad Transfer Co and Freight Agt Vandalia Line, S Capitol av and Union Ry Tracks, Tel 171; h s w cor Walnut and Arlington avs (I).

Rodocker Aaron C, clk, h 418 W Addison (N I).
Rodocker Jacob, tmstr, h e s Hillside av 5 s of 17th.
Rodtke Charles, lab, b 178 Laurel.
Rodtke Wm, lab, b 178 Laurel.
Roe John, mach, h 14 McCauley.

ROE JOHN F, Veterinary Surgeon and Dentist, 80 E Court, Tel 527; r 249½ E Washington.

Roe Maria (wid Wm), h 685 W 22d (N I).

EAT
QUAKER BREAD
ASK YOUR GROCER FOR IT.
THE HITZ BAKING CO.

WILLIAM WIEGEL { MANUFACTURER OF..... } SHOW CASES { 6 W. Louisiana St. Opposite Union Station.

CARPETS AND RUGS RENOVATED.......... | CAPITAL STEAM CARPET CLEANING WORKS M. D. PLUNKETT, TELEPHONE No. 818

BENJ. BOOTH PRACTICAL EXPERT ACCOUNTANT. Complicated or disputed accounts investigated and adjusted. Room 18, 82½ E. Wash. St., Ind'p'l's, Ind.

18 and 20 South Meridian Street || KERSHNER BROS., Proprs.

ESTABLISHED 1876. TELEPHONE 168.
CHESTER BRADFORD,
SOLICITOR OF PATENTS,
AND COUNSEL IN PATENT CAUSES.
(See adv. page 6.)
Office:—Rooms 14 and 16 Hubbard Block, S.W. Cor. Washington and Meridian Streets, INDIANAPOLIS, INDIANA.

Roe Oliver, engr, b 860 E Washington.
Roebke Henry C, drayman, h 144 Union.
Roeder Charles, drayman, h 369 Union.
Roeder Frederick, lab, b 90 N Gillard av.
Roeder Frederick W, car rep, h 90 N Gillard av.
Roeder John, saloon, 248 Davidson, h same.
Roeder John E, carp, h 107 N Noble.
Roeder John H, lab, b 369 Union.
Roeder Nicholas I, tmstr, h 100 High.
Roeder Wm H, saloon, 755 N West, h same.
Roehm Frank E, carp, b 189 S Capitol av.
Roehm George, carp, b 189 S Capitol av.
Roehm Louis, carp, b 189 S Capitol av.
Roehm Otto, carp, r 193 S Alabama.
Roembke Frederick W, car rep, h 64 Dougherty.
Roemer Elizabeth, cook, h 276 N Illinois.
Roemler Charles O, lawyer, 86 Commercial Club bldg, b 1119 N Meridian.
ROEMLER FREDERICK S, Propr The Rialto Cigar Store, 67 E Washington, Indiana Trust Bldg, b 240½ E Washington.
Roemler Otto H, cigars, 77½ N Alabama, b 240½ E Washington.
Roempke Conrad H, baker, 1558 N Illinois, h same.
Roempke Henry F, baker, 149 English av, h same.
Roempke Wm, car rep, h 26 Gatling.
Roepke, see also Ropkey.
Roepke Andrew, b 259 Prospect.
Roepke Charles F, sprinkling contr, 46 Sanders, h same.
Roepke Christian (Roepke & Weiland), h 659½ Virginia av.
Roepke Wm, lab, h 25 Shover (W I).
Roepke & Weiland (Christian Roepke, Frederick H Weiland), saloon, 661 Virginia av.
Roerer Charles, drayman, h 371 Union.
Roerer John, lab, b 371 Union.
Roerig Adam J, lab, b rear 405½ S Delaware.
Roesch Charles, lab, b 111 Spann av.
Roesch Charles, cook Circle Park Hotel.
Roesch Frank X, saloon n w cor Station and Glen Drive (B), h same.

Metal Ceilings and all kinds of Copper, Tin and Sheet Iron work.
O. B. ENSEY,
TELEPHONE 1562.
CORNER 6TH AND ILLINOIS STS.

Roesch Joseph, lab, b 37 Poplar (B).
Roesener Charles, gardener, h 944 S East.
Roesener Charles C, pressman, b 459 S Illinois.
ROESENER CHARLES F, Mngr The Home Laundry, 197 S Illinois, Tel 1769; h 94 High. (See right side lines.)
Roesener Charles H, lab, h 459 S Illinois.
Roesener Charles H, saloon, 301 Mass av, h same.
Roesener Christian H, mach, h 125 N Liberty.
Roesener Christina (wid Anthony), h 23 E McCarty.
Roesener Frederick C, clk, b 99 Greer.
Roesener Frederick W, engr, h 546 S Capitol av.
Roesener George W, pressman, b 459 S Illinois.
Roesener Harry C, mach, b 48 Yandes.
Roesener Henry A W, clk Hendricks & Cooper, b 23 E McCarty.
Roesener Henry C, driver, h 45 N Dorman.
Roesener Henry E, insp, h 48 Yandes.
Roesener Henry F, supt German General Protestant Orphans' Asylum, S State av, opp Sycamore.
Roesener Herman C, driver, b 74 W McCarty.
Roesener Lisette, matron German General Protestant Orphans' Asylum.
Roesener Sophia, seamstress, b 11 N Station (B).
Roesener Wm E, h 11 N Station (B).
Roesener Wm F, drayman, h 155 Union.
Roesener Wm F, glassbndr, b 48 Yandes.
Roesinger Wm, mach, h 370 Newman.
Roesner Wm, lab, h 11 Leota.
Roessler Caroline (wid Christian), b 34 Eureka av.
Roessler Christian, baggageman, h 681 Mass av.
Roessler John A, porter, h 34 Eureka av.
Roetter George, driver, h 318 Lincoln av.
Roetter Harry N, bicycles, 16 W Pearl, b 318 Lincoln av.
Roever Christian, puttymkr, b 268 S Penn.
Roever Hermann, harnessmkr, h 175 Union.
Rogan Dica (wid Thomas), h rear 440 Douglass.
Rogers Addison E, clk, h 72 W 6th.
Rogers Adolphus D, trav agt, h 417 Park av.
Rogers Alice (wid Isaac), h 326 W Maryland.
Rogers Allen J, engr, h 130 Chadwick.
Rogers Benjamin F (Dearinger & Rogers), h 125 N Arsenal av.
Rogers Calvin, foreman, b 1224 N Illinois.
Rogers Catherine (wid Hugh), h 340 S East.
Rogers Charles, patrolman, h 29 Brett.
Rogers Charles D, chief clk R M S, P O bldg, h 10 Ruckle.
Rogers Charles E, tel opr C C C & St L Ry, h 122 Trowbridge (W).
Rogers Clarence S, mach hd, b 321 Jefferson av.
Rogers Edwin St George (Hammond & Rogers), h 51 Madison av.
Rogers Elijah P, h 209 Broadway.
Rogers Ellen (wid Aaron), h rear e s Line 2 s of Washington av (I).
Rogers Elwood, h 298 E Market.
Rogers Emma G, music teacher, 87 Birch av (W I), b same.
Rogers Eugene, switchman, h 223 Michigan av.
Rogers Everett S, r 25 Catterson blk.

THE SHERMAN RESTAURANT

TUTEWILER UNDERTAKER, No. 72 WEST MARKET STREET. TELEPHONE 216.

The Provident Life and Trust Co. Dividends are paid in cash and are not withheld for a long period of years, subject to forfeiture in the event of death or the termination of policy.
D. W. EDWARDS, GENERAL AGENT, 508 INDIANA TRUST BUILDING.

THEODORE F. SMITHER

Rogers Frank C, finisher, h 43 Holly av (W I).
Rogers Frank C, letter carrier P O, h 52 Meikel.
Rogers Frank F, pres Puritan Spring Bed Co, h 12 West Drive (W P).
Rogers Frank W, station master Union Station, h 344 S Illinois.
Rogers Helen H, teacher Public School No 15, b 125 N Arsenal av.
Rogers Henry, mach hd, b 11 S Senate av.
Rogers Hugh, cigarmkr, b 340 S East.
Rogers Hugo, solr, b 187 Huron.
Rogers James, lab, h 143 Geisendorff.
Rogers James E, clk Kingan & Co (ltd), h 85 Geisendorff.
Rogers James G, painter, b 508 Virginia av.
Rogers James N, lumber broker, 14 Ingalls blk, h 952 N Meridian.
Rogers John, engr, h 583 Central av.
Rogers John, lab, h 37 Roe.
Rogers John A, brakeman, h 270 English av.
Rogers John J, mach hd, b 276 W Pearl.
Rogers John P, jeweler, 60 N Illinois, h same.
Rogers John W, trav agt, h 276 W Pearl.
Rogers Joseph, lab, h rear 9 Lexington av.
Rogers Joseph, lab, h 338½ S West.
Rogers Katherine P, teacher Public School No 7, b 125 N Arsenal av.
Rogers Laodicea (wid Isaac), b 404 Virginia av.
Rogers Lee, trav agt, r 82 Ft Wayne av.
Rogers Levi, engr, h 96 Randolph.
Rogers Lockey E, b 298 E Market.
Rogers Louis, boxmkr, b 326 W Maryland.
Rogers Mack C, houseman, h 68 Chapel.
Rogers Margaret, ironer, b 340 S East.
Rogers Mary J, h s s 8th 7 w of canal.
Rogers Nancy M (wid James H), h 508 Virginia av.
Rogers Olinda B, dressmkr, 87 Birch av (W I), h same.

ROGERS REBECCA W, Physician, Diseases of Women and Children, 17-20 Marion Blk, n w cor Ohio and Meridian, Tel 1763; h 209 Broadway, Tel 1631.

Rogers Roscoe C, switchman, r 32 S State av.
Rogers Samuel, lab, h 488 N Missouri.
Rogers Thomas S, cabtmkr, h 96 Duncan.
Rogers Walter, b 87 Birch av (W I).
Rogers Wm, condr, h 524 E 9th.
Rogers Wm, lab, h 74 Maxwell.
Rogers Wm, lab, b 326 W Maryland.
Rogers Wm G, h 69 Bismarck av (H).
Rogers Wm G, agt, h 22 Ingram.
Rogers Wm H, lab, b 69 Bismarck av (H).
Rogers Wm H, painter, h 1162 E Washington.
Rogge August H, carver, h 621 Mass av.
Rogge Ernst J, wagonmkr, h s s E Washington 3 e of Belt R R.
Rogge Wm F, mach, h 213 Columbia av.
Rogister George, carp, b 64 Howard.
Rogister Jane (wid George), b 64 Howard.
Rogister Thomas, carp, h 64 Howard.
Rohan Henry, lab, b 41 Hiawatha.
Rohan Honora (wid Martin), b 29 Empire.
Rohde Adolf, meats, 1094 E Washington, h same.
Rohde Wm L, baker, 125 E Mkt House, and 524 S East, h same.
Rohlmann Wm O F, cooper, h 31 Morton.
Rohman Casper, mach, r 148 W Maryland.

THE WHEN IS A WORLD BEATER.

Rohman John F, baker, h 539 Charles.
Rohr Christopher J, mach, h 18 Eckert.
Rohr Joseph C, electrician, b 293 Kentucky av.
Rohr Louisa (wid Joseph), h 293 Kentucky av.
Rohrer David, medicine mnfr, 117 Pleasant, h same.
Rohrer Susan K, b 909 N Alabama.
Rohrman John W, mach, h 159 Minnesota.
Roland Charlotte (wid Calvin J), b 9 Henry.
Roland Herman A, tinner, 284 E Merrill, h same.
Rolffs Caspar, molder, b 46 E Morris.
Rolffs Henry, lab, h 78 E Morris.
Roll Edward P (Wm H Roll's Sons), b Enterprise Hotel.
Roll Harry W (Wm H Roll's Sons), h 65 Lockerbie.
Roll Jonathan B, tmstr, h e s Line 2 s of Washington av (I).
Roll Wm H, h 475 N Penn.

ROLL'S WM H SONS (Harry W and Edward P Roll, Frank M Ruddy), Wall Papers, Fresco Painting, Fancy China, Picture Frames, Art Goods and Venetian Blinds, 103 E Washington, Tel 1377.

Roller Henry W, lab, h 222 W 22d.
Roller Jacob, mail carrier, h 249 W 22d.

ROLLER JOHN J, Choice Liquors and Cigars, also Chop House, 151 W Washington, h 235 N Liberty.

Roller Julia (wid James), h 487½ W Addison (N I).
Roller Wm, lab, r 37 Alvord.
Rollin Carroll M, clk Emil Wulschner & Son, b 139 N Penn.
Rollin Claude L, clk P & E Ry, b 275 N New Jersey.
Rollin Ella C (wid Josiah B), h 275 N New Jersey.
Rollin Eugene H, stenog P & E Ry, h 62 College av.
Rollin Sylvester A, trav agt, b 139 N Penn.
Rollings Charles F, engr Butler College, b w end Lena (I).

The A. Burdsal Co.
Manufacturers of
STEAMBOAT COLORS
BEST HOUSE PAINTS MADE.
Wholesale and Retail.
34 AND 36 SOUTH MERIDIAN STREET.

COMPOSITION ROOFING MATERIALS. BEST IN THE MARKET. TELEPHONE 861. OFFICE, 151 WEST MARYLAND ST.

Electric Contractors
We are prepared to do any kind of Electric Contract Work.
C. W. MEIKEL. Telephone 466.
96-98 E. New York St.

DALTON & MERRIFIELD { LUMBER South Noble St., near E. Washington

INDIANA ELECTROTYPE CO. BEST WORK LOWEST PRICES.
23 WEST PEARL ST., INDIANAPOLIS, IND. JOB WORK. BOOK PLATES. All Orders Promptly Filled. BEST PATENT BASE ON THE MARKET.

KIRKHOFF BROS.,
Sanitary Plumbers
STEAM AND HOT WATER HEATING.
102-104 SOUTH PENNSYLVANIA ST.
TELEPHONE 910.

Rollings Harry E, winder, b 1045 N Capitol av.
Rollings Winfield S, engr, h 1045 N Capitol av.
Rollins Ada, seamstress, h 134 N Noble.
Rollins Frank, trav agt, b 77 E Walnut.
Rollins J Frank, clk, r 24 W Walnut.
Rollins Morton, pdlr, h 1 Bryan.
Rollins Thaddeus S (Rollins & Wiltsie), h 39 Broadway.
Rollins Walter S, barber, r 128 W Vermont.
Rollins Wm K, porter, b 203 W 4th.
Rollins & Wiltsie (Thaddeus S Rollins, Charles S Wiltsie), lawyers, 71-72 Lombard bldg.
Roman Amelia (wid Matthias), h 169 Minnesota.
Roman Frank, mach hd, b 41 Minnesota.
Roman Frank G, sawyer, h 169 Minnesota.
Roman Samuel S, lab, h 188 N California.
Roman Wm M, carver, h 4 Geneva (W).
Romberg Henry F, uphlr, 45 Mass av, h 222 Coburn.
Rome Henry, waiter, r 113 Indiana av.
Romel Frederick, produce, E Mkt House, h 318 N Pine.
Romel Frederick jr, driver, b 318 N Pine.
Romer Alfred, mach, r 148 W Maryland.
Romer Benjamin F, helper, h 4 Walcott.
Romerill James H, chairmkr, b 577 E St Clair.
Rominger Henry S, pres Indpls Fancy Grocery Co, h 1232 N Penn.
Rominger Irvin T, h 374 E 15th.
Romnel Karl, carp, h n s Summit n end of Cleveland (H).
Romona Oolitic Stone Co, Hervey Bates pres, Walter Kessler vice-pres and mngr, Hervey Bates jr sec and treas, 15 Ingalls blk.
Ronan Maggie, janitress, r 106½ N Meridian.
Ronan Michael, lab, b 72 Pleasant.
Ronan Patrick, bartndr, b 146 Michigan (H).
Ronan Wm J, tel opr C H & D R R, b 109 E St Joseph.
Rondthaler Robert R, clk The A Burdsal Co, r 410 N Penn.

Lime, Lath, Cement,
THE W. G. WASSON CO.
130 INDIANA AVE. TEL. 989.
Sewer Pipe, Flue Linings, Fire Brick, Fire Clay.

Ronecker Daniel J, molder, b 168 Woodlawn av.
Ronecker Elizabeth, h 168 Woodlawn av.
Ronecker Emma, stenog, b 168 Woodlawn av.
Roney Bert, asst bkkpr L E & W R R, h 171 Prospect.
Roney Charles, clk, b 212½ S Meridian.
Roney Charles S, street contr, 302 Park av, h same.
Roney Edward, bartndr, r 52 Pendleton av (B).
Roney Henry C, street contr, 422 Park av, h same.
Roney James M, lab, h e s Carter 1 s of 30th.
Roney James M, lab, h 221 Columbia av.
Roney John, lab, b 104 Blackford.
Roney John A, painter, h 268 Fayette.
Roney John N, lab, h 271 Fayette.
Roney Joseph, lab, h 18 Mill.
Roney Oscar H, lab, h 79 Montana.
Roney Patrick, janitor, h 644 Chestnut.
Roney Patrick, lab, b 88 Bright.
Roney Wm L, train caller Union Station, h 212½ S Meridian.
Ronk Wm L, mach, h 441½ Virginia av.
Rood Henry L, trav agt Indpls Brewing Co, r 90½ Mass av.
Rooker Alfred J, painter, r 175 W Michigan.
Rooker C Della, stenog P & E Ry, b 219 Fletcher av.
Rooker Emma L (wid James I), b 731 E Ohio.
Rooker Frank, carp, h 409 Columbia av.
Rooker Frederick, painter, 424 E New York, h same.
Rooker Hugh, blksmith, h 244 N Senate av.
Rooker Rachel (wid George L D), h 127 W 22d.
Rooker Robert L, clk C C C & St L Ry, b 127 W 22d.
Rooker Samuel J, painter, h 164 Woodlawn av.
Rooker Sarah E, h 147 W North.
ROOKER WM V, Lawyer, Room 3 Brandon Blk, 95 E Washington, Tel 915; h s w cor Broadway and Bedford av.
Rooney John, lab, h 29 Blackford.
Rooney Patrick, lab, b 327 W Maryland.
Rooney Peter, mach hd, b 41 Minerva.
Rooney Wm P, condr, h 12 Lynn.
Roos Henrietta (wid John), b 299 Park av.
Roos Jacob C, meats, 616 S Meridian, h 764 same.
Roos Louis A (Parks & Roos), h 196 N Senate av.
Roos Pauline (wid Jacob), h 421½ S Delaware.
ROOSEVELT HOUSE, Milus J Bryant Propr, 80 E Ohio.
Root Charles G, genl mngr Adamant Wall Plaster Co, res Minneapolis, Minn.
Root Charles H, clk, r 44½ N Penn.
Root George R, sec and treas Standard Savings and Loan Assn, h 832 N Meridian.
Root Jay E, foreman, h 23 Shriver av.
Root Jerome B, h 511 N Illinois.
Root Joseph H, clk, h 430½ Mass av.
Root Lily M, stenog Jameson & Joss, b 512 Park av.
Root Oliver H, sec and treas Sheridan Brick Works, r 10 The Chalfant.
Root Parker H, student, b 832 N Meridian.
Root Wm R, bkkpr Standard Savings and Loan Assn, b 832 N Meridian.

YOUR HOMES FURNISHED BY W. H. MESSENGER 101 East Washington St. Telephone 491.

McNamara, Koster & Co. Phone 1593. ♦ 212-218 S. PENN. ST. PATTERN MAKERS

Roots Charles P, plumber, h 34 E Vermont.
Roper Alfred, lab, b 29 Hadley.
Roper Charles A, printer Frank H Smith, b 95½ N Delaware.
Ropkey, see also Roepke.
Ropkey Ernest C (Ropkey & Mason Engraving Co), b 188 Madison av.
Ropkey Frederick B, printer, b 188 Madison av.
Ropkey Herman F, mer police, h 188 Madison av.
Ropkey McConnell H, printer The Indpls Sentinel, b 188 Madison av.
Ropkey-Mason Engraving Co (Ernest C Repkey, Edward Mason), engravers, 24 W Maryland.
Ropp Wm E, lab, b 268 Fletcher av.
Rorax Frank, nurse, b 172 E Ohio.
Rorex George A, mach, h 61 Fayette.
Rork Thomas G, house mover, 20 Hadley, h same.
Rosa Wm H, optician Wm T Marcy, h 65 N New Jersey.
Rosasco Angelo, saloon, rear 960 N New Jersey, h same.
Rosasco John B, chainman City Civil Engineer's Office, h 86 N Dorman.
ROSBERG GUST, Merchant Tailor, 25 N Penn, h 99 N Arsenal av.
Rose Albert J, lab, h 163 Fulton.
Rose Charles, tmstr, h 349 Clifford av.
Rose Charles H, well driver, h 524 Jefferson av.
Rose Cornelia (wid August D), h 7 Riley blk.
Rose Edward H, clk Indpls Abattoir Co, h 236 S Reisner (W I).
Rose Elizabeth (wid Nathaniel), h 257 N Senate av.
Rose Emma M, h 147 Fulton.
Rose Emmet M, student, b 1149 N Meridian.
Rose Emmett L, journalist, h 57 Gatling.
Rose Everett, brakeman, h 175 Benton.
Rose Ezekiel S, b 436 Talbott av.
Rose George A, lawyer, 103½ E Washington, r same.
Rose Hattie, h 291 E Court.
Rose Herbert D, clk, b 115 High.
Rose Hiram E, sec The Government Building and Loan Institution, h 1149 N Meridian.
Rose Jennie (wid Isaac C), h 452 S Capitol av.
Rose John C, mach, b 34 S Gale (B).
Rose John G, baker, h 699 Broadway.
Rose John M, carp, b 183 Bellefontaine.
Rose John N, shoemkr, rear 1 Spann av, b 155 English av.
Rose Margaret (wid Christian B), h 299 E Court.
Rose Marie, nurse 118 N Senate av.
Rose Mary F (wid Wm), h 545 Central av.
Rose Minnie A (wid Granville O), b 339 Blake.
Rose Nathaniel A, salesman, b 860 N Meridian.
Rose Otto H, h 208 W Vermont.
Rose Phoebe J, dressmkr, 545 Central av, b same.
Rose Ralph F, trav agt, b 147 Fulton.
Rose Samuel D, lab, h 19 Centennial (H).
Rose Sarah C, b 200 Park av.
Rose Sarah J (wid Francis A), h 92 Lexington av.
Rose Thomas J, bartndr, b 541 Shelby.
Rose Wm, b 175 Benton.
Rose Wm, carp, h 615 Bellefontaine.
Rose Wm, lab, h 10 Thalman av.

Henry H. Fay, 40½ E. WASHINGTON ST., FIRE INSURANCE, REAL ESTATE, LOANS AND RENTAL AGENT.

Rose Wm A, trav agt, b 545 Central av.
Rose Zachariah T, molder, h 23 McCauley.
Roseberg Frank, carp, h 48 Villa av.
Roseberry Wm, horse trader, h 103 Sharpe av (W).
Rosebrock Charles F, carp, h 105 Sanders.
ROSEBROCK C HENRY, Abstracts of Titles, 19 Thorpe Blk, h 150 Prospect. (See back cover.)
Rosebrock Diedrich H, gardener, h 1049 S Meridian.
Rosebrock Frederick W, grocer, 666 Virginia av, h 614 same.
Rosebrock George, gardener, b 958 S East.
Rosebrock George, lab, h 197 Orange.
Rosebrock Wm, gardener, h 958 S East.
Rosebrock Wm J, clk, h 132 Orange av.
Rosebrough Florence, b 217 S Olive.
Rosebrough James A, lab, h 97 Hiatt (W I).
Rosedale Albert C, condr, h 27 Tacoma av.
Rosefield Julius, collr Elite Portrait and Frame Co, r 28½ Indiana av.
Rosemeyer Ella (wid Frederick), h e s Auburn av 2 s of Bethel av.
Rosemeyer Frederick, car insp, h 59 Jefferson.
Rosemeyer Frederick, tmstr, h 659 Fremont (N I).
Rosemeyer Henry, filer, b e s Auburn av 2 s of Bethel av.
Rosemeyer John W, driver, h 813 LaSalle (M P).
Rosemeyer Wm A, salesman Syerup & Co, h 433 E St Clair.
Rosen Henry, pdlr, b 117 Eddy.
Rosenbaum Christopher J, lab, b 35 Elm.
Rosenbaum Frank F, clk, b 35 Elm.
Rosenbaum John A, clk S A Fletcher & Co, h 170 Huron.
Rosenbaum Leopold H, insp W U Tel Co, h 481 S New Jersey.
Rosenbaum Mary (wid Christopher J), h 35 Elm.
Rosenbaum Wm F, watchman, h 27 Water.
Rosenbaum Wm F jr, clk, b 27 Water.
Rosenberg Edmund (Rosenberg & Schmidt), mngr Indpls Tent and Awning Co, h 213 Huron.

SURETY BONDS
American Bonding & Trust Co. OF BALTIMORE, MD.
Authorized to act as Sole Surety on all Bonds. Total Resources over $1,000,000.00.
W. E. BARTON & CO., General Agents, 504 INDIANA TRUST BUILDING. Long Distance Telephone 1918.

THE FRED DIETZ CO.
WBN PACKING BOXES MADE TO ORDER FACTORY AND WAREHOUSE TRUCKS. Telephone 654. 400 Madison Avenue.

Business World Supplied with Help GRADUATES ASSISTED TO POSITIONS 10,000 NOW IN GOOD SITUATIONS. TEL. 499. E. J. HEEB, PRES. Indianapolis BUSINESS UNIVERSITY

Water Works Pumping Engines { HENRY R. WORTHINGTON, 64 SOUTH PENNSYLVANIA ST. Long Distance Telephone 284.

UNION CO-OPERATIVE LAUNDRY (COMPOSED OF UNION LAUNDRY GIRLS.) NOS. 40 AND 42 VIRGINIA AVENUE. T. E. SOMERVILLE, MANAGER——TELEPHONE 1269. INDIANAPOLIS, IND.

HORACE M. HADLEY

Insurance, Real Estate, Loan and Rental Agent

66 EAST MARKET STREET,

Telephone 1540. Basement.

Rosenberg George U, tailors' trimmings, 11½ N Meridian, h 567 E Market.
Rosenberg Henry, foreman, h 54 Woodruff av.
Rosenberg John, tailor, 196 E Washington, h 320 E New York.
Rosenberg Karl, clk, b 320 E New York.
Rosenberg Samuel, lab, h rear 290 E Louisiana.
Rosenberg Samuel, sign painter, h 399½ S Capitol av.
Rosenberg & Schmidt (Edmund Rosenberg, Adam Schmidt), tents, 20 S Alabama.
Rosenberger Philip, h 583 E St Clair.
Rosendall Edward, mach hd, h 90 S Reisner (W I).
Rosenfeld Adolph, tailor, h 286½ S Illinois.
Rosenfeld Jacob, b 286½ S Illinois.
Rosengarten Charles B, h 160 Broadway.
Rosengarten Edwin H, draughtsman Thomas A Winterrowd, b 160 Broadway.
Rosengarten Harry, trav agt, b 502 S East.
Rosengarten Henry W, saloon, 333 W Morris, h same.
Rosengarten Herman, druggist, h 449 Park av.
Rosengarten Isaac, city fireman, b 502 S East.
Rosengarten Louis, h 502 S East.
Rosengarten Moses, harnessmkr, b 502 S East.
Rosengarten Nathan B, trav agt, b 502 S East.
Rosenstein John, shoemkr, 398 S Capitol av, h same.
Rosenstihl Wm R, driver, b 1140 E Washington.
Rosenthal Albert H, trav agt, b 296 E Ohio.
Rosenthal Edward D, clk, r 34 Grand Opera House blk.
Rosenthal Eugene M, clk, b 296 E Ohio.
Rosenthal Frances (wid Moses), h 296 E Ohio.
Rosenthal Joseph, clk, b 471 S East.
Rosenthal Samuel, pdlr, h s s 8th 6 w of canal.
Rosenthal Wm, trav agt, h 471 S East.
Rosenzweig Adolph, locksmith, h 66 Church.
Rosenzweig Joseph, lab, h 146 Eddy.

Special Detailed Reports Promptly Furnished by Us.

MERCHANTS' AND MANUFACTURERS' EXCHANGE

J. E. TAKKEN, Manager,

19 Union Building, 73 West Maryland Street.

Rosing Felix, carp, h 54 S Alabama.
Ross Abigail J (wid Nelson), h 138 Oliver av (W I).
Ross Ada, opr C U Tel Co, b 54 Lord.
Ross Allen, lab, b w s canal 4 s of 7th.
Ross Ambrose, carp, h 314 S Missouri.
Ross Ambrose jr, huckster, b 314 S Missouri.
Ross Andrew, lab, b 187 Bismarck av (H).
Ross Charles, news agt, r 193½ S Illinois.
Ross Charles A (The Grocers' Mnfg Co), r 241 N Delaware.
Ross Charles A, lithog, b 571 N West.
Ross Charles C, mach, h 23 King av (H).
Ross Charlotte M, b 37 Division (W I).
Ross Colonel, lab, h 19 Hill.
Ross Cyrus, lab, h s w cor Elizabeth and porter.
Ross David, phys, 136 N Penn, r same.
Ross Edward C, cutter, h 21 Concordia.
Ross Elizabeth, h 232 E Court.
Ross Elmer E, clk, b 157 Locke.
Ross Emma A (wid James), h 571 N West.
Ross Everett W, butcher, h 299 N Pine.
Ross Frank, brakeman, b 22 Detroit.
Ross Frank, gardener, h 672 W Jackson (N I).
Ross Frank, waiter, r 232½ W Washington.
Ross Fred T (Gardner Bros & Ross), b 505 Central av.
Ross Friend D, trunkmkr, h 157 Locke.
Ross George, coachman 792 N Meridian.
Ross George, lab, b 19 Hill.
Ross George J, brakeman, b 124 English av.
Ross George T, mach hd, b 175 W South.
Ross George T, porter Wm T Marcy, h 383 Lafayette.
Ross George W (G W Ross & Son), h 229 E Vermont.
Ross Guy D, paperhngr, b 62 John.
Ross G W & Son (George W and Harry C), furs, 26 E South.
Ross Hannah (wid Thomas J T), b 252 Cornell av.
Ross Harry C (G W Ross & Son), b 229 E Vermont.
Ross Harry C, steward Occidental Hotel, r 220 E Vermont.
Ross Henry, lab, h 150 Elizabeth.
Ross Henry, mach hd, h 247½ S Capitol av.
Ross House, R Wayman Ross propr, 37 McNabb.
Ross James, fireman, h 118 Blackford.
Ross James, lab, h 187 Bismarck av (H).
Ross James, hostler 750 N Meridian.
Ross James jr, barber, 124 Michigan, b 187 Bismarck av (H).
Ross James A, clk The Gordon-Kurtz Co, h 97 Greer.
Ross James B, clk, h 44 W 4th.
Ross James C, saloon, 146 Michigan (H), h same.
Ross James R (James R Ross & Co), h 505 Central av.
ROSS JAMES R & CO (James R Ross, Henry C Thomson, Henry C Knode), Wholesale Liquors, 129 S Meridian, Tel 760.
Ross James W, b 76 W 5th.
Ross Jessie, bkkpr, b 352 Union.
Ross John, plastr, h 618 W Francis (N I).
Ross John D, painter J K & H K English, h 939 Grove av.
Ross John F, gardener, h 1007 S Meridian.
Ross John F, lab, b 341 S Delaware.
Ross John T, horseshoer, b 175 W South.
Ross Johnson, painter, b 54 Lord.
Ross Joseph, driver, b 250 W Market.
Ross Joseph W, h 62 John.

CLEMENS VONNEGUT 184, 186 and 192 E. Washington St. | CABINET HARDWARE CARVERS' TOOLS. Glues of all kinds.

THE WM. H. BLOCK CO. 7 AND 9 EAST WASHINGTON STREET. DRY GOODS, MILLINERY, CLOAKS AND FURS.

Ross Lilburn, lab, b 250 W Market.
Ross Linus H, paperhngr, b 1033 W Washington.
Ross Louis A, stereotyper. The Indpls News, h 1147 N Alabama.
Ross Martha E, boarding 533 College av.
Ross Mary D, seamstress, b 1033 W Washington.
Ross Minnie, b Ross House.
Ross Merritt, engr, r 225 Michigan av.
Ross Morris M, managing editor The Indpls News, h 98 W Walnut.
Ross Oscar L, bkkpr, h 126 E 6th.
Ross Rebecca (wid Harry), b 147 Minerva.
Ross Reuben O, nurse, b 143 N Penn.
Ross Robert, carp, h 111 Newman.
Ross Robert S, molder, h 160 Trowbridge (W).
Ross Sandford H, clk, h s e cor Jones and LaSalle (N I).
Ross Sarah A (wid Jacob), b 276 Lafayette.
Ross Susan M (wid Alexander D), b 54 Lord.
Ross Thomas E, h 533 College av.
Ross Thomas J, h 175 W South.
Ross Thomas J, polisher, b 382 E Michigan.
Ross Victor G, mach, h 21 Bates al.
Ross Walter A, janitor, h 208 St Mary.
Ross Wm, lab, h 602 W Michigan.
Ross Wm, trav agt, h 27 King.
Ross Wm L, brakeman, r 184 Bates.
Ross Wm H, sawyer, h 247½ S Capitol av.
Ross Wm L, clk, r 14 Columbia blk.
Rossetter Harry F, engr, b 161 Talbott av.
Rossetter Penfield B, foreman, h 161 Talbott av.
Rossetter Thomas B, clk, h 132 Huron.
Rossetter Waldo B, salesman Charles J Kuhn Co, b 161 Talbott av.
Rossier Emil, jeweler, b 316 E North.
Rossman Paul, driver, b 293 Bates.
Rosson Amanda J, b 328 Tremont.
Rosson Frank, coachman 834 N Meridian.
Rosson James G, coachman, h 117 W 6th.
Rost Alfred J, finisher, b 21 Dougherty.
Rost August, cigarmkr, h 21 Dougherty.
Rost Conrad, lab, h n s Ohio 5 e of Rural.
Rost Daniel, grocer, 1107 E Michigan, h same.
Rost Frederick, tmstr, h n s Ohio 6 e of Rural.
Rost John, driver, h 349 Clifford av.
Rost Paul, b n s Ohio 6 e of Rural.
Rost Walter A, sawyer, b 21 Dougherty.

ROST WM H (Frank Nessler & Co), b 21 Dougherty.

Roster Ernest M, mash hd, b 81 River av (W I).
Roster James J, lab, b 81 River av (W I).
Roster John, carp, h 81 River av (W I).
Roster John E, mach hd, b 81 River av (W I).
Rosuck David, junk, 100 Eddy, h 472 S Illinois.
Roswag Benjamin, lab, b 330 E Georgia.
Roswinkel George (Wm Roswinkel & Co), h 281 N East.
Roswinkel Wm (Wm Roswinkel & Co), b 281 N East.
Roswinkel Wm & Co (Wm and George Roswinkel), shoes, 189 Mass av.
Roszell Burley G, painter, b 423 N Pine.
Roszell Charles, lab, h e s Tremont av 2 n of Grandview av (H).
Roszell Jacob E, brakeman, h 29 Detroit.
Rotach Eliene, h 1321 N Senate av.
Rotach John M, cabtmkr, b 1321 N Senate av.

Rotach Susan, milliner, b 1321 N Senate av.
Roth Adam J (Roth Bros), h 646 E Vermont.
Roth Albert, boxmkr, b 150 Carlos.
Roth Benjamin, h 177 N West.
Roth Bros (George and Adam J), grocers, 648 E Vermont.
Roth Caspar, bricklyr, h 478 Union.
Roth Charles C, trav agt Schnull & Co, h 62 Fletcher av.
Roth Charles T, mach hd, b 270 Lincoln av.
Roth Emil, lab, r w s Addison 4 s of Washington (M J).
Roth Eugene, cashr, b 200 W New York.
Roth Frederick, tinner, b 150 Carlos.
Roth George (Roth Bros), h 30 King.
Roth George, tinner, h 150 Carlos.
Roth Gilson W, engr, b 86 W 20th.
Roth Hannah (wid Abraham), b 215 W New York.
Roth Harry E, clk N Y Store, r 218 E Washington.
Roth John H, carp, h 250 S William (W I).
Roth John M, bricklyr, b 270 Lincoln av.
Roth J George, mngr Reeves & Co, h 90 S Capitol av.
Roth Leonard W, lab, h 16 Martha (W I).
Roth Martin, meats, 485 S East, h same.
Roth Martin C, meats, 428 Home av, b 485 S East.
Roth Matthew, supt The Wm P Jungclaus Co, h 270 Lincoln av.
Roth Matthew F, carver, b 270 Lincoln av.
Roth Susanna (wid John), b 646 E Vermont.
Roth Will (Roth & Young), b 787 N Alabama.

ROTH & YOUNG (Will Roth, Frank Young), Proprs The Club Stable, Livery and Hacks, 80-82 W Market, Tel 1061. (See adv in classified Liveries.)

Rothenhoefer John F, cook, h 547 E Vermont.
Rothermel Henry C, florist, h 310 Shelby.
Rothermel Silas, florist, n e cor Wheeler and Division (B), h same.
Rothert John H, grocer, 369 Virginia av, h same.

GUIDO R. PRESSLER,
FRESCO PAINTER
Churches, Theaters, Public Buildings, Etc., A Specialty.
Residence, No. 325 North Liberty Street.
INDIANAPOLIS, IND.

INDIANAPOLIS STEEL ROOFING AND CORRUGATING WORKS, 23 and 25 East South Street. S. D. NOEL, Proprietor.

David S. McKernan REAL ESTATE AND LOANS Houses, Lots, Farms and Western Lands for sale or trade. ROOMS 2-5 THORPE BLOCK.

DIAMOND WALL PLASTER { Telephone 1410 BUILDERS' EXCHANGE.

Cor. E. Ohio St. and C., C., C. & St. L. R'y Tracks. ISSUE NEGOTIABLE RECEIPTS ON MERCHANDISE AND HOUSEHOLD GOODS. UNION TRANSFER AND STORAGE CO.

W. McWORKMAN,
ROOFING AND CORNICE WORKS,
930 W. Washington St. Tel. 1118.

Rothert John H jr, clk, b 369 Virginia av.
Rothert Wm H, bottler, b 369 Virginia av.
Rothhaas James E, baggageman, h 161 Walcott.
Rothley Charles, printer, b 50 Ash.
Rothley Victor H, sec Aetna Cabinet Co, h 50 Ash.
Rothrock George W, mach hd, r 581 E St Clair.
Rothrock Louis E, plumber, b 1227 N Penn.
Rothrock Martha E, stenog, b 1227 N Penn.
Rothschild Alexander, tailor, h 247 S Pine.
Rothschild Leopold G, chief clk land dept Auditor of State, lawyer, 18½ N Penn, r 77 W Michigan.
Rottenstein Frank E, tinner, b 280 N Senate av.
ROTTLER FRANK M, The Best Selection of Harness and Turf Goods, 18 N Delaware, h 1025 N Capitol av.
Rottler John, lab, h 16 Deloss.
Roubadeaux Lavelle B, student, b 297½ Mass av.
Rough Notes, The Rough Notes Co Pubs, 79 W Market.
ROUGH NOTES CO THE, Elias C Atkins Pres, Henry C Martin Sec and Treas, Louis H Martin Asst Mngr, John C Lyon Solicitor, Insurance Publications, Mnfrs of Insurance Supplies and Office Furniture; also Publishers "Rough Notes," 79 W Market, Tel 1862.
Rouin James F, lab, h 127 W McCarty.
Round Abraham L, lab, h w s canal 3 s of 7th.
Round George, lab, b 32 Vinton.
Round Henry, cupolatndr, h 32 Vinton.
Round Wm H, lab, h 69 Sheffield av (H).
Round Wm H, lab, h 29 Thomas.
Rounder Albert O, lab, h 34 S Olive.
Rounder Alta M, lab, b 132 Hosbrook.
Rounder James A, cabtmkr, h 140 Prospect.
Rounder John N, carp, h 32 Hosbrook.
Rounder Mary C, dressmkr, 140 Prospect, h same.
Rounds Clarence E, porter, b 209 W North.

GEO. J. MAYER,
MANUFACTURER OF
SEALS
STENCILS, RUBBER STAMPS, CHECKS, BADGES, DOOR PLATES, ETC.
15 S. Meridian St., Ground Floor. TEL. 1386.

Rounds George, lab, b 350 S Alabama.
Rounds John, lab, b rear 775 N Senate av.
Rounds Joseph, lab, h 18 Cora.
Rounds Noah, lab, h rear 775 N Senate av.
Rounds Wm, lab, b rear 775 N Senate av.
Rounds Wm, lab, h 375 W North.
Roung John, lab, h 245 W Morris.
Rountree John, waiter, b 49 Torbet.
Rountree Thomas R, lab, h 85 Torbet.
Rourke Wm H, condr, h 40 Poplar (B).
Rouse Arthur E, feed, 172 Virginia av, b 129 Woodlawn av.
Rouse Bros (Thomas Rouse), whol feed, 2½ Board of Trade bldg.
Rouse Helen M (wid Randall R), b 502 N Senate av.
Rouse James H, h 1087 N Capitol av.
Rouse Mary R (wid Wyatt J), h 129 Woodlawn av.
Rouse Nancy A (wid Christopher C), h 180 Bates.
Rouse Oscar V (Wm Rouse & Son), h 257 S East.
Rouse Ralph, mach hd, b 180 Bates.
Rouse Thomas (Rouse Bros), b 43 Lord.
Rouse Walter O, clk Charles Mayer & Co, h 2 Hester.
Rouse Wm M (Wm Rouse & Son), res Acton, Ind.
Rouse Wm & Son (Oscar V and Wm M), whol feed, 72 S Delaware.
Roush Charles, dairy, e s Belmont av bet Big Four and Vandalia R R (W I), h same.
Roush Daniel, carp, h 313 Clifford av.
Roush Joel S, bartndr, b 67 Russell av.
Roush Rose E, stenog G W Pangborn, b 445 N East.
Roush Sherman R, bartndr, h 67 Russell av.
Routh Enoch B, carp, 523 College av, b same.
Routh James R, abstracts, 12½ N Delaware, h 523 College av.
Routh Milo O, tel opr, h 24 Lawn (B).
Routier Annatole B, carp, b 130 Elm.
Routier Clementine (wid Peter), h 367 Cedar.
Routier Edmond, clk, b 367 Cedar.
Routier John, mach, h 189 Elm.
Routzong Samuel, genl agt, h 88 Bellefontaine.
Rouzer Charles H, supt Columbia Club, h 724 N Illinois.
Rouzer Hal M, clk Murphy, Hibben & Co, h 335 N East.
Rover Herman E, harnessmkr, h 175 Union.
ROW GEORGE S, Physician (Limited to Eye and Ear), Office Hours 10 A M to 2 P M, 711-712 Majestic Bldg, Res Shelbyville, Ind.
Row Hines, painter, b rear 432 E St Clair.
Rowan George B, condr, b 6 Cornell av.
Rowan Margaret D, h 57½ W Maryland.
Rowand Mary J (wid Wm A), h 232 Douglass.
Rowe Alice (wid Matthew), b 65 S Summit.
Rowe Clara E (wid Louis), b 394 Cornell av.
Rowe David W, carp, h 2 Clifford av.
Rowe Davis M, boilermkr, h 176 Oliver av (W I).
Rowe Edith, b 93 N Alabama.
Rowe Edward, lab, r 148 W Maryland.
Rowe Elizabeth H (wid Wm N), h 335 Park av.
Rowe Emma J, teacher, b 335 Park av.
Rowe Francis M, blksmith, n s Michigan 3 e of Sherman Drive, h same.
Rowe George A, porter, h 734 N West.

A. METZGER AGENCY ESTABLISHED 1863. REAL ESTATE

LAMBERT GAS & GASOLINE ENGINE CO.
ANDERSON, IND. GAS AND GASOLINE ENGINES, 2 TO 50 H. P.

Rowe George W, clk, h 20 Greer.
Rowe George W, pharmacist H C Pomeroy, h 713 N Senate av.
Rowe George W, well driver, h 660 Chestnu.
Rowe Harry F, clk, h 174½ Brookside av.
Rowe Isaac N, optician, 8 N Penn, h 209 N Liberty.
Rowe John A, insp, h 210 Deloss.
Rowe John L, foreman, b 349 W Michigan.
Rowe John W, clk, b 361 Broadway.
Rowe Louis M, phys, 134 N Meridian, h same, tel 461.
Rowe Louise M, teacher, b 335 Park av.
Rowe Mary, milliner, 139 Mass av, h 209 N Liberty.
Rowe Mary E, teacher, b 335 Park av.
Rowe Matilda, b 176 Oliver av (W I).
Rowe Rebecca C (wid John R), h 131 W 2d.
Rowe Samuel P, b 27 Elder av.
Rowe Thomas P, contr, h n.w cor 23d and Central av.
Rowell Frank, clk, b 406 Virginia av.
Rowell Frederick C, r 24 Pembroke Arcade.
Rowland Bert, attendant Insane Hospital, b 417 W Eugene (N I).
Rowland Frank W, clk Murphy, Hibben & Co, b 417 W Eugene (N I).
Rowland John, grocer, 420 W North, b 338 Douglass.
Rowland Lewis, carp, h 199 Douglass.
Rowland Wm M, h 417 W Eugene (N I).
Rowland Wm R, clk W H Messenger, h 48 Pleasant.
Rowlett Edwin S, polisher, h 59 Russell av.
Rowley Benjamin, b 119 Cornell av.
Rowley Harry S, printer, b w s Garfield av 1 n of Ohio.
Rowley John, printer, h w s Garfield av 1 n of Ohio.
Rowley Nancy M (wid Samuel M), h 215 E St Clair.
Rowley Wm, phys, 119 Cornell av, h same.
Rowley Wm H, clk, h 222 E Louisiana.
Rowman Louis, lab, h 48 Gresham.
Rowney James, lab, r rear 500 E Washington.
Roy Herman J, grocer, 892 S Meridian, h same.
Roy Herman J jr, driver, b 892 S Meridian.
Royal Arcanum, Grand Council of Indiana, 43 Thorpe blk.
ROYAL SAVINGS AND LOAN ASSOCIATION, Howard Kimball Sec, 89 E Market.
Royall Octavius V, lawyer, 711-712 Lemcke bldg, r 277 Bright.
Royce George H, cashr Western Paving and Supply Co, r 6 The Chalfant.
Royle Thomas, fitter, h 54 S Stuart (B).
Roys Frank B, foreman, h 170 N Pine.
Royse Alvin O, reporter The Indpls Journal, h 132 E St Joseph.
Royse Dock, plumber, b 200 S Olive.
Royse Harry E, dep County Clerk, h 21 Dawson.
Royse James G, solr, b 200 S Olive.
Royse Walter A, asst city editor The Indpls Journal, b 200 S Olive.
Royse Wm M, trav agt, h 174 Ash.
Royse Wm T, ins agt, h 200 S Olive.
Royster Aaron R, bailiff Marion County Criminal Court, h 276 Blackford.
Royster Charles H, lab, b 1063 W Michigan.
Royster Harry, lab, r 200½ W Washington.
Royster Oliver P, farmer, h 276 Blackford.
Royster Wm L, lab, h 1063 W Michigan.
Rozeler Jacob, driver, b 464 S Capitol av.

Farm and City Loans
25 Years' Successful Business.
THOS. C. DAY & CO,
Rooms 325 to 330 Lemcke Building.

Rozier Adam E, lab, h 48 St Marie.
Rozier Edward, saloon, 101 Indiana av, h same.
Rozier George H, saloon, 50 Indiana av, h same.
Rozier John, h 1652 N Capitol av.
Rozier Percy H, cigars, 303 E Washington, r 46½ Indiana av.
Rozman Rockus, shoemkr, b 310 Indiana av.
Ruark James K, h 87 S Shade (B).
Ruark Sarah J (wid Howard J), h 29 McKim av.
Rubel Amos M, mach, h 394 Blake.
Rubel Charles, driver, h 335 W North.
Rubens George B, electrician Model Clothing Co, r 226 N Delaware.
Rubens Samuel, clothing, 60 W Washington, h 316 S Illinois.
Rubin Frederick W, engraver H C Chandler, b 61 Hoyt av.
Rubin Jacob, tel opr Fire Dept, h 61 Hoyt av.
Rubottom Florence, h 338 N Noble.
Rubottom Nerious M, engr, b 74 W New York.
Rubright Charles W, student, r 29 W Vermont.
Rubright R Dorman, clk, b 1 S Gale (B).
Rubush Benjamin C, printer, b 233 Bellefontaine.
Rubush Carter P, mason, h 329 Prospect.
Rubush Charles E, contr, 91 Woodlawn av, h same.
Rubush Elba C, clk, b 233 Bellefontaine.
Rubush Erba, mason, b 77 Woodlawn av.
Rubush George A, tmstr, h 445 Indiana av.
Rubush George E, carp, h 209 Yandes.
Rubush George W, mason, h 44 Harlan.
Rubush Harry S, finisher, b 445 Indiana av.
Rubush John T V, carp, h 862 Bellefontaine.
Rubush Joseph A, blksmith, 865 S Meridian, h 482 Union.
Rubush Preston C (Scharn & Rubush), b 233 Bellefontaine.
Rubush Thomas, brakeman, b 304 E Market.
Rubush Thomas A, tmstr, b 445 Indiana av.
Rubush Wm G, carp, h 233 Bellefontaine.
Rubush Wm M, bricklyr, b 77 Woodlawn av.

EAT
HITZ'S
CRACKERS
AND CAKES.
ASK YOUR GROCER FOR THEM.

BICYCLES $5 DOWN. MONTHLY. Best Wheels. Best Terms. WHEELMEN'S CO. 31 W. OHIO ST. LONG DISTANCE TEL. 1855.

J. H. TECKENBROCK  Painter and Decorator,
94 EAST SOUTH STREET.

FIDELITY MUTUAL LIFE—PHILADELPHIA, PA.
MATCHLESS SECURITY At LOW COST. **A. H. COLLINS** General Agent Baldwin Block.

Rooms 42 and 43 WHEN BUILDING. Edwardsport Coal and Mining Co. Miners and Shippers Steam and Domestic Coal.

ESTABLISHED 1876. TELEPHONE 168.
CHESTER BRADFORD,
SOLICITOR OF PATENTS,
AND COUNSEL IN PATENT CAUSES.
(See adv. page 6.)
Office:—Rooms 14 and 16 Hubbard Block, S. W. Cor. Washington and Meridian Streets, INDIANAPOLIS, INDIANA.

Rubush Wm R, brick contr, 77 Woodlawn av, h same.
Ruby Albert L, fireman, b 287 W Merrill.
Ruby James M, clk, h 82 Nevada.
Ruch Charles E, drugs, 150 Columbia av, h 198 Cornell av.
Ruch Henry, lab, h 369 Martindale av.
Ruckelshaus Conrad, h 202 Walcott.
Ruckelshaus Henry, grocer, 342 E St Clair, h 340 same.
Ruckelshaus John C (Fitzgerald & Ruckelshaus), b 202 Walcott.
Rucker Shiveral, painter, h 32 Davis.
Ruckersfeldt Joseph C, mach, b 33 Fletcher av.
Ruckersfeldt Mary B (wid Charles), h 33 Fletcher av.
Ruckle Nicholas R, pres Masons' Union Life Assn, h 1057 N Illinois.
Rudasel Albert B, engr, h 7 Emerson pl.
Rudasel Charles, driver, b 17 Emerson pl.
Rudasel Marilla (wid Michael), h 32 Sheffield av (H).
Rudd Gabriel N, filer, h 395 Yandes.
Rudd Henry, janitor, h 305 Alvord.
Rudd Morton E, filer, h 663 Mass av.
Rudd Ray, filer, h 68 Newman.
Ruddell Almus G, clk Ward Bros' Drug Co, b 772 N Penn.
Ruddell Mary H (wid James H), h 772 N Penn.
Ruddle Charles, fireman, b 860 E Washington.
Ruddle Daniel T, fireman, h 11 Poplar (B).
Ruddy Frank M (Wm H Roll's Sons), b 200 N Noble.
Rudisill Martin L, h 349 Park av.
Rudler Ferdinand, mach, h 50 N Brookside av.
Rudolph Henry W, mngr Interstate Art Glass Co, b 77 N Delaware.
Rudolph Charles C, trav agt, b 62 Johnson av.
Rudolph Christian, eng insp, b 107 Cornell av.
Rudolph Edward, h 62 Johnson av.
Rudolph John C, lab, h 76 Chapel.
Rudy Catherine (wid Preston), b 388 N New Jersey.

Outing BICYCLES
$85.00.
MADE AND SOLD BY
HAY & WILLITS MFG. CO.
76 N. PENNSYLVANIA ST. PHONE 598.

Rudy Richard B, salesman Emil Wulschner & Son and director When Band, h 79 Park av.
Rudy Samuel L, plumber, b 96 Prospect.
Rueb Allen F, h 11 Arch.
Ruef Elmer E, supt Bellis Cycle Co, h 524 Ash.
Ruef Wm H, mach, h 528 Ash.
Ruehl Charles, b 105 Church.
Ruehl Charles, clk, h rear 270 S Meridian.
Ruehl Edward, billiard table rep, r 43½ Kentucky av.
Ruemmele Charles F (Ruemmele & Buttler), b 850 Morris (W I).
Ruemmele Joseph, saloon, 850 Morris (W I), b same.
Ruemmele & Buttler (Charles F Ruemmele, Joseph Buttler), driven wells, 850 Morris (W I).
Ruesch Charles W, clk, h w s Station 9 n of Schofield (B).
Ruesch Ernest J, lab, b 161 Spring.
Ruesch Frederick H, watchman, h 161 Spring.
Ruff Christian, watchman, b 65 Dunlop.
Ruff Harry G, cigars, 62 Mass av, b Enterprise Hotel.
Ruff Jacob, carp, h 69 Morton.
Ruff John, driver, h 295 W Morris.
Ruff John, printer, h 112 Nebraska.
Ruff Joseph, clk Indpls Mnfrs' and Carps' Union, h 76 Morton.
Ruffin Asbury M, lab, h 429 S Illinois.
Ruffin Edward J, lawyer, b 524 N West.
Ruffin Elizabeth H (wid Charles), h 524 N West.
Ruffin Isaac W, foreman, h 431 N Senate av.
Ruffing John, clk, h 257 S Alabama.
Ruffner Mary E, seamstress, b 26 Birch av (W I).
Ruffner Strawder R, filer, h rear 126 Union.
Ruffner Wm H, clk, b 26 Birch av (W I).
Ruffner Wm M, lab, h 26 Birch av (W I).
Rufli Herman, engr, b 132 Michigan (H).
Rugan Edward, switchman, b 253 E Washington.
Rugan George, yardmaster, b 96 Chadwick.
Rugenstein Charles F, drayman, h 674 Chestnut.
Rugenstein Charles M, clk Van Camp H and I Co, h 391 Union.
Rugenstein Frederick, drayman, h 580 Chestnut.
Rugenstein Frederick H, lab, h 101 Lincoln la.
Rugenstein Frederick W, harnessmkr F L Herrington, b 105 Coburn.
Rugenstein Henry, printer, b 580 Chestnut.
Rugenstein Henry C, engr, h 59 Iowa.
Rugenstein Henry J, clk C C C & St L Ry, h 105 Coburn.
Rugenstein Henry L, driver, h 612 Chestnut.
Rugenstein Henry T, drayman, b 580 Chestnut.
Rugenstein John, h 7 Singleton.
Rugenstein Martin, engr, h 433 Union.
Rugenstein Sophia (wid Christopher), b 207 Lincoln la.
Rugenstein Sophia (wid John), h 365 Union.
Rugenstein Theodore F, checkman, h 616 Chestnut.
Rugenstein Theodore J, boilermkr, h 108 Nebraska.
Rugenstein Wm, engr, h 211 E Morris.
Rugenstein Wm, flagman, h 149 Deloss.
Rugenstein Wm C, clk, b 105 Coburn.

C. ZIMMERMAN & SONS SLATE AND GRAVEL ROOFERS **19 South East Street.**

DRIVEN WELLS And Second Water Wells and Pumps of all kinds at CHARLES KRAUSS'. 42 S. PENN. ST. TELEPHONE 465.

ERTEL STEAM LAUNDRY || LARGEST AND BEST IN THE STATE. PROMPT SERVICE. 26 and 28 N. Senate Ave. Tel 10

Rugenstein Wm H, tmstr, h 515 S Capitol av.
Rugenstein Wm M, lab, h 204 Lincoln la.
Ruggieri Michael, tailor, 237 S Delaware, h same.
Ruggles Frank, lab, b 282 W Michigan.
Ruggles Mark O, engr, h 204 W South.
Ruggles Milton C, clk, r 81 E Michigan.
Rugh Jacob I, carp, h 136 River av (W I).
Rugh Jessie E, seamstress, b 136 River av (W I).
Ruhlman Benjamin H, yard boss, b 389 E Market.
Ruhlmann George, finisher, b 18 Germania av (H).
Rule Fannie, r 244½ E Washington.
Rule Jeremiah S, carp, h n s Vorster av 2 e of Milburn (M P).
Rule John F, oiler, h 928 Gent (M P).
Rule Thomas, supt, h 515 S Illinois.
Rule Thomas J, carp, 49 Tacoma av, h same.
Rullman Edward, news agt, b 417 S Delaware.
Rullman Henry, blksmith, b 417 S Delaware.
Rumely M Co, Joseph R Shultz mngr, engines and threshers, 100 S Capitol av.
Rumford Frank L, mailing clk P O, h 62 Brookside av.
Rummel Samuel D, switchman, h 159 Spann av.
Rummseier Julia (wid Christian), b 577 S East.
Rumpf John, lab, h 245 W Morris.
Rumpler Edward C, chief clk P & E Ry, h 247 N Delaware.
Rundell Clarence C, trav agt, h 87 College av.
Runge Christian H, lab, h 60 Dunlop.
Runge J Henry, clk The Home Brewing Co, h 50 Lockerbie.
Runnels George, lab, b 85 Spring.
RUNNELS ORANGE S, Physician, 50 Monument Pl, Tel 111; Propr The Dr O S Runnels Sanatorium, 276 N Illinois, Tel 111—2 rings; h 600 N Meridian, Tel 111—3 rings. (See Sanitorium adv opp classified Physicians.)
RUNNELS SOLLIS, Physician, 38 E Ohio, Tel 1424; h 258 N Capitol av, Tel 253.
Runnels Wm, h 269½ Mass av.
Runshe Minta, stenog, b 80 Ft Wayne av.
Runyan Anthony L, condr, h 556 E 8th.
Runyan Edmond J, bkkpr Nordyke & Marmon Co, h 357 Fletcher av.
Runyan Stewart, clk, r 104 Commercial Club bldg.
Runyan Thomas, artist, 82½ N Penn, h 426 N East.
Runyan Wm A, insp City Engineer, h 54 Warren av (W I).
Runyon Archibald S, solr, h 81 Park av.
Runyon Elizabeth (wid Wm R), attendant Insane Hospital.
Runyon Frank M, mach, b 38 S State av.
Runyon George W, carp, b 23 Division (W I).
Runyon Henry S, carp, h 224 Fletcher av.
Runyon Howard A, clk Adams Ex Co, h 44 Beaty.
Runyon Sarah (wid David V), h 23 Division (W I).
Rupe James L, carp, h 503 Bellefontaine.
Rupe Hamilton N, pumps, h 787 N Delaware.

RICHARDSON & McCREA, MANAGERS FOR CENTRAL INDIANA. EQUITABLE LIFE ASSURANCE SOCIETY Of the United States. 79 EAST MARKET STREET. TELEPHONE 182.

Rupe Jesse, cook, r 92 N New Jersey.
Rupe Nancy (wid John O), b 134 Columbia av.
Rupe Veazy P, clk, h 37 Valley.
Rupe Walter F, painter, b 126 W Vermont.
Rupert Charles M, printer, 410 N Brookside av, h same.
RUPERT FRANK H, House Furnishings; Cheapest Furniture House in Town; 59 W Washington, h 435 N New Jersey.
Rupert Rudolph, h 92 Prospect.
Rupkey Henry T, driver, b 222 E Court.
Rupp John, grocer, 201 Kentucky av, h same.
Rupp Laura E, teacher German Public School No 5, b n e cor Ohio and Rural.
Rupp Theodore A, clk, b 201 Kentucky av.
Rupp Wm F, h n e cor Rural and Ohio.
Rupple John, mngr The Country Club, n w cor 30th and Michigan rd, h same.
Rusch Anna (wid Charles), h 186 E McCarty.
Rusch Bertha E, b 186 E McCarty.
Rusch Charles A, clk, b 434 N New Jersey.
Rusch Ira W, gasfitter, h 35 McGinnis.
Rusch Ira W jr, lab, b 35 McGinnis.
Ruschaupt August, filer, h 53 Bradshaw.
Ruschaupt Charles F, confr, 94 W Washington, h 19 E North.
Ruschaupt Charles F, supt, b 53 Bradshaw.
Rusche Casper, stonecutter, h 621 W Vermont.
Rusche Joseph, lab, h 109 Dunlop.
Ruschhaupt Catherine E (wid Frederick), h 640 N Penn.
Ruschke August, barber, 264 W Washington, h same.
Rush Frederick P (Frederick P Rush & Co), h 366 N Capitol av.
Rush Frederick P & Co (Frederick P Rush, George E Townley), grain, 10 Board of Trade bldg.
Rush George, condr, h 320 Fletcher av.
Rush Johannes W, butcher, h 12 S Senate av.
Rush John, h 534 S West.
Rush John, lab, h 201 Yandes.

Typewriter-Ribbons ALL COLORS FOR ALL MACHINES. THE BEST AND CHEAPEST. S. H. EAST, STATE AGENT, The Williams Typewriter.... 55 THORPE BLOCK, 87 E. MARKET ST.

ELLIS & HELFENBERGER || Architectural Iron Work and Gray Iron Castings. 162-170 South Senate Ave. Tel. 958.

THE HOGAN TRANSPER AND STORAGE COMP'Y
Household Goods and Pianos Moved—Packed—Stored...... Baggage and Package Express Machinery and Safes a Specialty Cor. Washington and Illinois Sts. TELEPHONE No. 675.

The Central Rubber & Supply Co. ♦♦♦ Hose, Belting, Packing, Clothing, Druggists' Sundries, Bicycle Tires, Cotton Hose, Etc. New York Belting & Packing Co., L't'd. PHONE 922. 79 S. ILLINOIS ST., INDIANAPOLIS, IND.

The Provident Life and Trust Company
Of Philadelphia.
Grants Certificates of Extension to Policyholders who are temporarily unable to pay their premiums
D. W. EDWARDS, Gen. Agt., 508 Indiana Trust Bldg.

Rush John F, attendant Insane Asylum.
Rusher George P, plastr, h 269 Yandes.
Rusher James W, lather, b 114 Clinton.
Rusher John T, lather, h 116 Clinton.
Rusher Wm T, lather, h 114 Clinton.
Rushton Allen C, meats, 93 E Mkt House, h 463 S Missouri.
Rushton Allen F, lab, b 2 Standard av (W I).
Rushton Caleb C, express, h 2 Yandes.
Rushton Charles B, furnace setter, b 67 S Noble.
Rushton Elizabeth J (wid Alfred), h 111 Malott av.
Rushton Gertrude (wid Douglass J), h 96 W Vermont.
Rushton Grosvenor A, lab, b 2 Yandes.
Rushton James W, mach, b 136 W 1st.
Rushton Jane (wid Allen), h 2 Standard av (W I).
Rushton John A, woodwkr, h 111 Malott av.
Rushton Otis, lab, b 2 Yandes.
Rushton Wm, mach, b 111 Malott av.
Rusie Amos W, ballplayer, b 125 Walcott.
Rusie Frederick W, condr, r 500 E Washington.
Rusie Wm A, insp City Engineer, h 125 Walcott.
Rusie Wm A jr, b 125 Walcott.
Rusk John H, wrapper L S Ayres & Co, b 117 Pleasant.
Rusk Lewis H, carp, h 153 Deloss.
Rusk Robert A, lab, r 102 S Illinois.
Rusk Tina M (wid Henry W), b 507 N Alabama.
Ruskaup Frederick, grocer, 135 N Dorman, h 129 same.
Ruskaup Henry, finisher, h 277 N Pine.
Ruskaup Wm, clk, b 129 N Dorman.
Ruske Catherine (wid Henry A), h 33 N Liberty.
Ruske Frank A, mach hd, h 597 W Udell (N I).
Ruske John F, lab, h 90 Kansas.
Russ Alonzo, waiter The Denison.
Russ Charles W, bkkpr, h 320 N Alabama.
Russ Emma M (wid George W), b 320 N Alabama.
Russ Herman, engr, r 832 Grandview av.

Julius C. Walk & Son,
Jewelers
Indianapolis.
12 EAST WASHINGTON ST.

Russ James A, b 320 N Alabama.
Russ James, barber, 127 Indiana av, b 474 W North.
Russ Jennie M, h 474 W North.
Russ Louis, waiter, b 474 W North.
Russe Christian C, car insp, h 177 Woodlawn av.
Russe Edward, driver, b 257 N California.
Russe Harry H, bkkpr, b 257 N California.
RUSSE HENRY, Wholesale and Retail Grain and Seeds, 23-25 N Capitol av, opp State House, Tel 540; h 257 N California.
Russe Wm H, clk, b 257 N California.
Russell Albert J, lab, b 50 Singleton.
Russell Allen A, stacker mnfr, 174 S Senate av, b 64 Elm.
Russell Alva, mach hd, b 215 Christian av.
Russell Benjamin, ironwkr, b 285 S Capitol av.
Russell Benjamin S, lab, b s w cor Brookside and Lebanon avs.
Russell Burrell, porter, b 276 Blake.
Russell Carrie E, h 108 Lexington av.
Russell Charles E, lab, b 34 Singleton.
Russell Charles J, filer, b 90 Columbia av.
Russell Charles W, lab, h 1352 Indianapolis av.
Russell Cyrus, lab, b 49 Rhode Island.
Russell David, molder, h 363 N Pine.
Russell Dessie, r 71½ N Illinois.
Russell Edward, lab, h 230 Roanoke.
Russell Edward F, steelwkr, h 192 W Merrill.
Russell George, lab, b 332 Indiana av.
Russell George A, lab, b 118 Rhode Island.
Russell George G, cook, r Hendricks blk.
Russell George W, carp, b 774 W Washington.
Russell George W, clk, h e s Ritter av 1 s of University av (I).
Russell George W, helper, b 363 N Pine.
Russell Hannah, cook, b 185 E Court.
Russell Harley A, mnfrs' agt, 53½ W Washington, h 64 Elm.
Russell Harry C, clk The Bowen-Merrill Co, b The Plaza.
Russell Harry C, mach, b 363 N Pine.
Russell Harvey B, mach, h w s Waverly 2 n of Bloyd av (B).
Russell Hattie, h 346 S New Jersey.
Russell Henry, packer, h 116 W Ray.
Russell Isaac, pres and treas The Russell Lumber Co, h 450 Ash.
Russell Jacob F, blksmith, h 99 Tremont av (H).
Russell James, lab, b 115 Douglass.
Russell James H, millwright, h 75 Dugdale.
Russell James W, h 34 Singleton.
Russell James W, plumber, h 90 Columbia av.
Russell Jennie M, cashr Pearson's Music House, b 346 S New Jersey.
Russell John, lab, b 115 Douglass.
Russell John C, boarding 139 N Delaware.
Russell John L, lab, h 137 Downey.
Russell John N, ins agt, 523 Lemcke bldg, r 24 W New York.
Russell John W, lab, h 163 Hadley av (W I).
Russell Logan W, farmer, h 237 Miller (W I).
Russell Lot, lab, h 276 Blake.
RUSSELL LUMBER CO THE, Isaac Russell Pres and Treas, Sidney I Russell Sec, Joseph W P Massey Supt, Lumber, Shingles and Planing Mill, Office and Yard s e cor 7th and L E & W R R, Tel 1192.

OTTO GAS ENGINES | BUILDERS' EXCHANGE S. W. Cor. Ohio and Penn. Telephone 535.

Becker & Son Charles Becker Jacob Becker Jr. Merchant Tailors. 21 N. Penn St. Tel. 934

SALISBURY & STANLEY, Office, Store and Bank Fixtures a Specialty. Repairing of all kinds done on short notice. 177 Clt or Set, Indianapolis, Ind. Contractors and Builders TELEPHONE 999.

Russell Major E, architect, b 311 S Missouri.
Russell Martin, lab, h 149 Elizabeth.
Russell Mattie A (wid Lemuel), h 139 Downey.
Russell Nicholas, cashr, b 120 S Illinois.
Russell Noah, lab, b 192 W Merrill.
Russell Otto, caller, b 37 Bloomington.
Russell Robert, lab, h 1207 Indianapolis av.
Russell Robert, lab, h 118 Rhode Island.
Russell Robert jr, porter, b 118 Rhode Island.
Russell Sadie J (wid Alva), h 282 E Court.
Russell Samuel N, paperhngr, h 183 Patterson.
Russell Sidney I, sec The Russell Lumber Co, b 450 Ash.
Russell Susan E, teacher Public School No 32, b 108 Lexington av.
Russell Thomas, finisher, b 22 Mayhew.
Russell Thomas, fireman, h 87 McGinnis.
Russell Walter, lab, h rear 180 N West.
Russell Walter, lab, b 488 W Pratt.
Russell Walter A, butcher, b 488 E Washington.
Russell Warren, mach, h rear 152 Shelby.
Russell Weldon, lab, h 210 Northwestern av.
Russell Wm, barber, b 138 Columbia.
Russell Wm, finisher, h 273 Howard.
Russell Wm, fireman, h 37 Bloomington.
Russell Wm, lab, b 278 Lafayette.
Russell Wm, motorman, h 86 Sheldon.
Russell Wm A, lab, b 34 Singleton.
Russell Wm L, motorman, h 328 Martindale av.
Russell Wm P, express, h 233 Naomi.
Russell Willis, lab, h e s Madeira 5 s of Prospect.
Russie Fred W, condr, r 500 E Washington.
Russie George (Russie & Ballard), b 44 Stevens.
Russie & Ballard (George Russie, Charles Ballard), plastrs, 44 Stevens.
Russow August C, porter, h 17 Carlos.
Rust Augustus, hostler, h s s Sutherland 3 e of Shade (B).
Rust Conrad, street sprinkling contr, 214 Cedar, h same.
Rust Conrad jr, asst bkkpr Clemens Vonnegut, h 3 Jefferson.
Rust George, motorman, h 531½ W Washington.
Rust George S, b 239 Cornell av.
Rust Herbert L, bkkpr Am Plate Glass Co, b 185 N Delaware.
Rust Zella M, sec to chief clk engr and pur dept L E & W R R, b 302 E New York.
Rustamier Francis, com mer, h 136 Nordyke av (W I).
Ruster George, engr, h 26 N Station (B).
Ruter Wm, tailor, h 79 Meikel.
Ruth Adolph, furnacewkr, b 36 Wisconsin.
Ruth Adolph A, clk, h 58 Sinker.
Ruth Charles F, bookbndr, b 58 Sinker.
Ruth Christian W Rev, h 451 Clifford av.
Ruth Henry, clk, h 307 S East.
Ruth Louis G, bkkpr Township Trustee's Office, h 472 S East.
Ruth Louis P, musician, h 83 Elizabeth.
Ruth Robert, h 36 Wisconsin.
Ruth Robert E, dry goods, 272 N Pine, h same.
Ruthart Joseph, butcher, h 161 W Morris.
Rutherford George W, produce, E Mkt House, h 244½ E Washington.
Ruthrauff Henry, lab, b 263 Shelby.
Ruthstein Selig, pdlr, b 149 Eddy.
Rutledge Carl, tel opr, b 139 Hadley av (W I).

Henry H. Fay,
40½ E. Washington St.,
REAL ESTATE,
AND LOAN BROKER.

Rutledge Elijah D (Rutledge & Spaulding), phys, 117½ W Washington, h 139 Hadley av (W I).
Rutledge Jechonias, h 154 Hoyt av.
Rutledge Thomas C, clk R M S, b 199 Lincoln av.
Rutledge Wm, lab, h 39 Elder av.
Rutledge & Spaulding (Elijah D Rutledge, John Spaulding), phys, 139 Hadley av (W I).
Rutter Harry J, lab, b 1151 E Washington.
Rutter Jennie F, phys, 1151 E Washington, h same.
Rutter Sarah (wid Benjamin F), h 543 W Addison (N I).
Rutter Wm B, mngr, h 559 W Addison (N I).
Rutz Edward J, h 63 Hadley av (W I).
Rutz Wm A, press feeder, b 63 Hadley av (W I).
Ryall Hope (wid Thomas E), h 493 W 22d (N I).
Ryall Joseph D, lab, b 493 W 22d (N I).
Ryan Abner T, brakeman, b 162 Harrison.
Ryan Annie L (wid Martin), h 331 E Louisiana.
Ryan Bridget (wid Michael), h 75 John.
Ryan Byford I, switchman, b 274 N New Jersey.
Ryan Catherine, h 43 The Windsor.
Ryan Charles J, switchman, h 14 Warren av (W I).
Ryan Clyde C, tel opr, b 274 N New Jersey.
Ryan Corrinne E, teacher Public School No 7, b 64 Beaty.
Ryan Daniel L, lab, r 163 W Washington.
Ryan Douglas E, engr, h 258½ Bates.
Ryan Edmond G, plastr, b 542 S East.
Ryan Edmund B, lab, b 113 Clinton.
Ryan Elias G, hack driver, b 95 Pleasant.
Ryan Elizabeth (wid James B), h 158 N Senate av.
Ryan E E, electrician, b 253 N Alabama.
Ryan Frank, packer, b 290 S Delaware.
Ryan Frank M, hats, 21 S Illinois, h 788 N Capitol av.
Ryan George E, h 57 Rockwood.
Ryan George W, h 99 Pleasant.
Ryan George W, sec, h 586 Broadway.
Ryan Harry B, clk, b 290 N New Jersey.

MAYHEW'S
SPECTACLES
THE BEST IN USE
SOLD ONLY AT 13 N. MERIDIAN ST.

COAL AND LIME Cement, Hair, Sewer Pipe, etc. BALKE & KRAUSS CO. Cor. Missouri and Market Sts.

FRIEDGEN'S IS THE PLACE FOR THE NOBBIEST SHOES Ladies' and Gents' 19 North Pennsylvania St.

SAMUEL LAING | COPPER AND GALVANIZED IRON CORNICE MANUFACTURER
72 AND 74 COURT STREET. SKYLIGHTS AND VENTILATORS.

M. B. WILSON, Pres. W. F. CHURCHMAN, Cash.
THE CAPITAL NATIONAL BANK,
INDIANAPOLIS, IND.
Our Specialty is handling all Country Checks and Drafts on Indiana and neighboring States at the very lowest rates. Call and see us.
Interest Paid on Time Deposits.
28 S. MERIDIAN ST., COR. PEARL.

Ryan Harry H, mach, h 111 Dougherty.
Ryan Harvey C, b 224 E Court.
Ryan Hezekiah J, grocer, 68 N Linden, h 87 Pleasant.
Ryan Horace E, clk L S Ayres & Co, h 108 Pleasant.
Ryan James, agt, h 308 E Ohio.
Ryan James, clk, b Smith's Hotel.
Ryan James, janitor, r 18 S New Jersey.
Ryan James, lab, h 13 Geneva.
Ryan James, lab, h 114 Minerva.
Ryan James F, insp Indpls Gas Co, b 231 S Senate av.
Ryan James P, brakeman, r 247½ S Capitol av.
Ryan James R (J R Ryan & Co), h 290 N New Jersey.
Ryan Jennie (wid Patrick), b 542 N Senate av.
Ryan John, h 332 Coburn.
Ryan John, h 360 S Delaware.
Ryan John, agt, b 122 N Belmont av (H).
Ryan John, boilermkr, b w s Brightwood av 4 s of Willow (B).
Ryan John, fireman, h 14 W Chesapeake.
Ryan John, lab, h 122 Douglass.
Ryan John, lab, b 272 W Maryland.
Ryan John, tmstr, h rear 79 Cornell av.
Ryan John A, driver, h 29 Hermann.
Ryan John D, clk, h 120 Cherry.
Ryan John E, lab, h 85½ N Noble.
Ryan John H, engr, h 103 N Linden.
Ryan John H, lab, b 324 W Maryland.
Ryan John J, ins agt, b 122 Belmont av (H).
Ryan John M, clk, h 342 S East.
Ryan Joseph E, carp, b 68 Ruckle.
Ryan Joseph R, sawmkr, b 122 N Belmont av (H).
Ryan Julietta E (wid Francis M), h 57 Rockwood.
Ryan J R & Co (James R Ryan), feed, 62 E Maryland.
Ryan Lawrence, lab, b 64 River av (W I).
Ryan Margaret B (wid John A), h 64 Beaty.
Ryan Mary J (wid Michael J), confr, 542 S East, h same.
Ryan Michael, engr, b n w cor Michigan and State avs.
Ryan Michael, lab, h rear 602 E St Clair.

TUTTLE & SEGUIN,
28 E. Market St. Ground Floor.
COLLECTING RENTS AND CARE OF PROPERTY A SPECIALTY.
Telephone 1168.

Ryan Michael, lab, r 189 Indiana av.
Ryan Michael, lab, h 324 W Maryland.
Ryan Michael J, tel opr P C C & St L Ry, b 73 W Georgia.
Ryan Moses J, carp, h 122 Forest av.
Ryan Nora (wid Richard), h 122 N Belmont av (H).
Ryan Patrick, lab, b 499 E Georgia.
Ryan Patrick, tmstr, h 231 S Senate av.
Ryan Patrick J (P J Ryan & Co), dep collr Internal Revenue, h 178 Park av.
Ryan Patrick J, city fireman, h 532 S Capitol av.
Ryan Patrick J, lab, b 75 John.
Ryan P J & Co (Patrick J Ryan, Edward P Fitzgerald), grocers, 650 N Capitol av.
Ryan Richard P, bartndr, b 332 Coburn.
Ryan Robert J, b 290 N New Jersey.
Ryan Robert W, carp, b 122 Forest av.
Ryan Thomas, h 341 Coburn.
Ryan Thomas, fish, 57 Russell av, h same.
Ryan Thomas F, condr, h 140 Hoyt av.
Ryan Thomas J, butcher, h 276 W McCarty.
Ryan Wm, car insp, h w s Brightwood av 4 s of Willow (B).
Ryan Wm, condr, h 226 Hamilton av.
Ryan Wm, driver, b 360 S Delaware.
Ryan Wm, molder, h 107 S Reisner (W I).
Ryan Wm B, phys, 274 N New Jersey, h same.
Ryan Wm C, lab, b 85½ N Noble.
Ryan Wm F, paperhngr, h 198 N Beville av.
Ryan Wm H, driver, h 95 Pleasant.
Ryan Wm J, usher Insane Hospital.
Ryan Wm S, lawyer, b 83 W 5th.
Rybolt Bertie W, uphlr, b 120 N Belmont av (H).
Rybolt John W, carp, h 120 N Belmont av (H).
Ryder Edward M, collr, h 435 National rd.
Ryder Joseph M, whol cigars, 145 W Washington, r 105 The Shiel.
Ryder Mary (wid Joseph), h 280¼ E Court.
Ryhn James H, musician, h 282 N Liberty.
Ryker H Custer, clk Sentinel Printing Co, b 74 Huron.
Ryker J Newton, observer U S Weather Bureau, r 250 N East.
Ryker Melvin O, bkkpr McKee Shoe Co, b 74 Huron.
Ryker Wm, porter Murphy, Hibben & Co, r 45 Clifford av.
Ryman George H, lawyer, 157½ E Washington, h same.
Rynn Margaret (wid Patrick), b 21 Fletcher av.
Ryon James S, trav agt, h 308 E Ohio.
RYSE RICHARD, Trustees' Supplies, 34 Jackson Pl, h 224 N Liberty.
Ryse Wm J (Ryse & McDonald), res Shelbyville, Ind.
Ryse & McDonald (Wm J Ryse, James R McDonald), hides, 26 E South.

S

SAAK FRANK, Florist, 124 E St Joseph. (See adv in classified Florists.)
Saalmiller John, painter, b 53 High.
Saalmiller Joseph, mach hd, b 53 High.
Sachs Edward F, driver, h 113 W 10th.
Sachs Ernst C, gasfitter, rear 302 S Illinois, h 475 Charles.
Sachs John H, cigarmnfr, 450 S Illinois, h same.
Sachs Julius C, barber, b 450 S Illinois.

PAPER BOXES SULLIVAN & MAHAN 41 W. Pearl St.

DIAMOND WALL PLASTER { Telephone 1410 BUILDERS' EXCHANGE.

If your Laundry Work is not satisfactory, try THE HOME LAUNDRY

Sachs Wm G, painter, h 105 Dunlop.
Sackett Augustin, weigher, h 351 Bellefontaine.
Sackett Cyrus O, foreman, b 169 N Noble.
Sacre Ira, lab, h 26 Merritt (H).
Sacred Heart School for Boys, cor Union and Palmer.
Sacred Heart School for Girls, cor Meridian and Palmer.
Sadlier George, horseshoer, 38 S Penn, h 1163 N Capitol av.
Saffell Albert D, clk, b 9½ Madison av.
Saffell Augustus E, mach hd, h w s Caldwell 3 s of Elizabeth.
Saffell George H, boxmkr, b 95 Yandes.
Saffell Silas B (Saffell & Sindlinger), h 95 Yandes.
Saffell Wm O (Saffell & Geider), h 9½ Madison av.
Saffell & Geider (Wm O Saffell, Charles G N Geider), grocers, 9 Madison av.
Saffell & Sindlinger (Silas B Saffell, Peter Sindlinger), box mnfrs, w end Elizabeth, office 207 W Michigan.
Sagalowsky Bros (Louis and Samuel), junk, 327 W Washington.
Sagalowsky Isaac, janitor, h 105 Eddy.
Sagalowsky Isaac, junk, 94 Eddy, h 423 S Capitol av.
Sagalowsky Jacob, pdlr, h 141 Eddy.
Sagalowsky John, pdlr, h 427 S Capitol av.
Sagalowsky Louis (Sagalowsky Bros), b 427 S Capitol av.
Sagalowsky Samuel (Sagalowsky Bros), b 427 S Capitol av.
Sagalowsky Simon, junk, 135 Eddy, h same.
Sage Addie (wid Horace), h 252½ W Washington.
Sage Buchanan, lab, h 49 Wyoming.
Sage Frederick, lab, h 361 Coburn.
Sage Henry, supt, h 24 Byram pl.
Sage Howard O, brakeman, h 71 Nordyke av (W I).
Sage James P, gasfitter, b 43 Russell av.
Sage John, molder, h 43 Russell av.
Sage John D, fireman, h 32 Depot (B).
Sage John E, lab, b 24 Byram pl.
Sage Maggie J, opr Cent U Tel Co, b 43 Russell av.
Sage Stephen G, huckster, h 110 Weghorst.
Sager Harry P, uphlr, h 135 Union.
Sahl Henry, baker, b 348 Indiana av.
Sahm Agite, carp, 105 St Mary, h same.

SAHM ALBERT, Postmaster, s e cor Penn and Market, h 407 Broadway, Tel 467.

Sahm Louis, carp, b 142 Ft Wayne av.
Sahm Ludwig, tinware, E Mkt House, h 142 Ft Wayne av.
Sailes Louis, lab, h rear 167 Johnson av.
Sains Horace, lab, h 232 Roanoke.
St Agnes Academy, 702 N Meridian.
St Anthony's School, in charge of Sisters of Providence, e s Warman av 2 s of Vermont (H).
St Charles Hotel, Charles Muellerschoen propr, 27 McCrea.
St Clair, see also Sinclair.
St Clair Charles, saloon, 79 E Wabash, h 118 W Georgia.
St Clair Colin N, mach, h 161 N State av.
St Clair Gabriel, lab, h 479 Superior.
St Clair George W, restaurant, 159 Indiana av, h 342 W North.
St Clair Henry, ball player, b 526 S West.
St Clair Wm, lab, h 526 S West.
St Clair Wm G, coremkr, b 526 S West.
St Clair Wm M, h 1391 N Senate av.

FRANK NESSLER. WILL H. ROST.
FRANK NESSLER & CO.
Tailors
56 EAST MARKET ST. (Lemcke Building),
INDIANAPOLIS, IND.

St Clair Wm N, packer, b 1391 N Senate av.
St John's Academy (under charge of the Sisters of Providence), s s Maryland bet Illinois and Capitol av.

ST JOHN'S EVANGELICAL REFORMED CHURCH, Rev Max G I Stern Pastor, s e cor Merrill and Alabama.

St John Irene, h 181 W 9th.
St John James N, grocer, 148 Mass av, h 174 Ash.
St John Leonora I (wid John), h 181 W 9th.
St John Rolla A, tankman, b 907 Cornell av.
St John's School for Boys (under charge of the Brothers of the Sacred Heart), 74 W Georgia.
St John Warren W, engr, b 12 Park av.
St Joseph's Academy, 284 N Noble.
St Joseph's Home and Industrial School, 397 S Alabama.
St Jospeh's Institute for Boys, s w cor Coburn and Short.
St Joseph's School for Boys, 321 E North.
St Mary's Academy, 73 E Maryland.
St Mary's School for Boys, rear 75 E Maryland.
St Patrick's Academy for Girls, s s Dougherty w of Short.
St Paul Quarries, Henry C Adams propr, 6 Builders' Exchange.
St Peter and St Paul School, 672 N Penn.
St Peter and St Paul School of Providence, e s Meridian 2 n of 5th.
St Vincent's Infirmary (in charge of Sisters of Charity), s e cor Delaware and South.
Sakery Wilber, tmstr, b 125 N West.
Sakewitz Karl G, cashr, b 330 N New Jersey.
Saks Andrew (Saks & Company), res New York City.
Saks Isadore (Saks & Company), res Washington, D C.

SAKS & COMPANY (Andrew and Isadore Saks), Proprs Model Clothing Co, 41-49 E Washington and 2-22 S Penn, Tel 763.

Saladin Edward, mach hd, b 37 Mayhew.

Haueisen & Hartmann
163-169 E. Washington St.
FURNITURE,
Carpets,
Household Goods,
Tin, Granite and China Wares, Oil Cloth and Shades
197 S. Telephone 1769. St.

THE WM. H. BLOCK CO. 7 AND 9 EAST WASHINGTON STREET. DRY GOODS, MEN'S FURNISHINGS.

The Fidelity and Deposit Co. OF MARYLAND. Bonds signed for Administrators, Assignees, Executors, Guardians, Receivers Trustees, and persons in every position of trust.
GEO. W. PANGBORN, General Agent, 704-706 Lemcke Building. Telephone 140.

INSURE YOUR PROPERTY WITH FRANK K. SAWYER

• JOSEPH GARDNER •
GALVANIZED IRON
CORNICES and SKYLIGHTS.
Metal Ceilings and Siding.
Tin, Iron, Steel and Slate Roofing.
37, 39 & 41 KENTUCKY AVE. Telephone 322.

Saladin Jacob, janitor, h 37 Mayhew.
Sale Willis G, turner, h 127 Brookside av.
Salemi Carl, fruits, b 157 Harmon.
Salge Henry (Salge & Kroll), h 192 Indiana av.
Salge & Kroll (Henry Salge, Wm E Kroll), bakers, 468 Indiana av.
Salinger Anton, lab, h 168 E Morris.
Salisbery Frank C, colr, r 230 N Senate av.
Salisbery James D, lab, h 19 McCauley.
Salisbery Samuel F, colr, r 144 N Capitol av.
Salisbery Wm, lab, h 131 Elizabeth.
Salisbury Percival A (Salisbury & Stanley), h 134 Bellefontaine.
SALISBURY & STANLEY (Percival A Salisbury, George W Stanley), Contractors and Builders, 177 Clinton, Tel 999. (See right side lines.)
Sallust George A, farmer, h 131 River av (W I).
Salmon Elmer, toll insp Cent U Tel Co, h 187 N Beville av.
Salmon George, lab, b 62 Geisendorff.
Salmon John, brakeman, h 51 Deloss.
Salmon John A, lab, b 23 Bismarck av (H).
Salmon Julia A (wid George), b 62 Geisendorff.
Salmon Richard S, barber, h rear 274 S Meridian.
Salmon Wm, motorman, b 1051 N Capitol av.
Salmon Wm E, lab, h 823 E 9th.
Salter Bessie I, bkkpr Model Clothing Co, b 63 W 1st.
Salter Charles W, lab, h 295 Jackson.
Salter Emma M, stenog Morris, Newberger & Curtis, b 63 W 1st.
Salter Josephine, governess Indpls Orphan Asylum.
Salter Mary L (wid Wm H), h 63 W 1st.
Salter Nora E, nurse City Hospital.
Saltmarsh Ella, attendant Public Library, b 573 Ash.
Saltmarsh Rezin F, cashr, b 573 Ash.
Saltmarsh Walter S, salesman Murphy, Hibben & Co, h 30 W Pratt.
Saltmarsh Wm L, carp, h 573 Ash.
Saltsman Robert K, lab, h 133 Tacoma av.

J. S. FARRELL & CO.
Have Experienced Workmen and will Promptly Attend to your
PLUMBING
Repairs. 84 North Illinois Street. Telephone 382.

Saltzgaber Baird, clk Union Stock Yards Co (W I).
Same Albert G, motorman, h 8 Wendell av.
Samme Wm H, plastr, h 361 Virginia av.
Sammons Eva, nurse s e cor Penn and South, h same.
Sammons Frank W, student, h s e cor Penn and South.
Sammons Mary B (wid Benjamin F), b 50 Ruckle.
Sammons Scott, fireman I D & W Ry, h 1090 W New York.
Samoniel Edward, lab, h 601 Madison av.
Sample Alexander, brakeman, h 38 Lynn.
Sample Augustus B, asst yardmaster L E & W R R, h 15 Fletcher av.
Sample Bertha A, teacher Public School No 20, b 146 Laurel.
Sample Charles P, city dis clk P O, h s s Oak av 2 e of Grand av (I).
Sample Ellen, grocer, 598 W 22d (N I), h same.
Sample Harry E, lab, h 382 N Brookside av.
Sample Ida M, dressmkr, 146 Laurel, h same.
Sample James C, carp, h 146 Laurel.
Sample Morris De F, trav agt Natl Electric Headlight Co, r 58 The Chalfant.
Sample Morton, weigher, h e s Wheeler 1 s of Sutherland (B).
Sample Riley E, switchman, b 368 N New Jersey.
Sample Robert, lab, h 176 Sheffield av (H).
Sample Robert H Rev, pastor, h w s Madeira 5 s of Prospect.
Sample Walter J, lab, h w s Dayton av 1 s of English av (I).
Sampsell Homer A, dentist, 49½ N Illinois, h 296 N Illinois.
Sampson Edward C, tel opr, h 858 Cornell av.
Sampson James, lab, h 517 W Maryland.
Sampson James J, clk, h 266 N East.
Sampson Meyer, tailor, h 145 Eddy.
Sams Allen, tmstr, h 294 Douglass.
Sams Washington M, house mover, h 216 Northwestern av.
Samson May L, stenog, b 19½ N Meridian.
Samuels Abraham L, milliner, 63 S Illinois, h 97 W Vermont.
Samuels Amelia (wid Eli), b 387 N Noble.
Samuels Bailey, milliner, b 97 W Vermont.
Samuels Charles, bellboy The Denison.
Samuels Edmond, engr, h 447 Superior.
Samuels Edward, clk, b 387 N Noble.
Samuels Frank H, stenog Kingan & Co (ltd), b 204 N Illinois.
Samuels Frank W, mngr Postal Tel Cable Co, h 1139 N Meridian.
Samuels Gertrude, bkkpr, b 387 N Noble.
Samuels Harry G, night mngr Postal Tel Cable Co, b 1139 N Meridian.
Samuels James, lab, b 430 Blake.
Samuels John, waiter, b 121 W 6th.
Samuels Louis, lab, h 85 Rhode Island.
Samuels Rosa (wid Barnett), grocer, 387 N Noble, h same.
Sanborn Abraham G, city sanitary insp, h 226 Blackford.
SANBORN ASHLEY W (Sanborn Electric Co), h 814 Ash.
SANBORN ELECTRIC CO (Gerry M and Ashley W Sanborn), Electrical Contractors, 22 E Ohio, Tel 1457. (See adv in classified Electrical Contractors and Fitters.)
Sanborn Ernest L, painter, b 226 Blackford.

GUARANTEED INCOME POLICIES issued only by the **United States Life Insurance Co.**
E. B. SWIFT, Manager. 25 E. Market St.

Furniture Carpets } WM. KOTTEMAN { Stoves Ranges
89 and 91 East Washington Street. Telephone 1742.

SANBORN GERRY M (Sanborn Electric Co), h 73 The Blacherne.
Sanborn Howard G, janitor, h 212 Bright.
Sanborn James G, miller, h 688 Chestnut.
Sanborn Thomas P, organ builder, h 255 Bellefontaine.
Sandage Wm L, toolmkr, h 156 Spann av.
Sandeborg Oscar E, condr, h 6 Wallace.
Sandefur Frederick M, wall paper, 95 Division (W I), h same.
Sandefur Oswell B, paperhngr, h 104 Woodburn av (W I).
Sander Carl G, clk, b 506 Madison av.
Sander Edgemont, clk, b 506 Madison av.
Sander Herman, blksmith, b 142 Prospect.
Sander Theodore (Sander & Recker), h 506 Madison av.
Sander Wm, helper, b 252 Union.
SANDER & RECKER (Theodore Sander, Gottfried and Gustav A Recker), Mnfrs and Dealers in Furniture, 115-119 E Washington, Mnfrs and Dealers in Office and Store Fixtures, 86-88 S Delaware, Tel 1092.
Sanders, see also Saunders.
Sanders Alexander, lab, b 325 W St Clair.
Sanders Andrew, tmstr, b 332 S State av.
Sanders Anna K (A & W Sanders), h 951 E Michigan.
Sanders A & W (Anna K and Wilhelmina L), grocers, 951 E Michigan.
Sanders Bridget (wid Wm), h 272 S West.
Sanders Caroline E, stenog Elmer E Stevenson, b 380 College av.
Sanders Ceil, waiter, h 241 W Ohio.
Sanders Charles, porter George J Marott, h 278 E Court.
Sanders Charles B, stonecutter, h 495 S West.
Sanders Charles E, mach, h 59 Hazel.
Sanders Charles G (Sanders & Spornberg), h 258 S Meridian.
Sanders Charles J, clk R M S, b 1490 N Illinois.
Sanders Daniel, coachman 1220 N Penn.
Sanders Edward D (H L Sanders & Son), b 34 Camp.
Sanders Ellis J, drayman, b 58 Greer.
Sanders Emma (wid Hugh), h rear 70 Yandes.
Sanders Frederick C, h 330 Prospect.
Sanders Frederick W, driver, b 330 Prospect.
Sanders George H, janitor, h 28 Leon.
Sanders George P, coachman, h 237 W 3d.
Sanders Harry, porter, r 241 W Ohio.
Sanders Harvey B, lab, b rear 115 Bright.
Sanders Henry C (Sanders & Pace), b 330 Prospect.
Sanders Henry L (H L Sanders & Son), gents' furngr, 18 Indiana av, h 34 Camp.
Sanders Hudson, lab, h 30 Center.
Sanders H L & Son (Henry L and Edward D), gents' furngs), 14 E Mkt House.
Sanders James, watchman, h 601 W Michigan.
Sanders James M, opr W U Tel Co, h 106 Park av.
Sanders James W, lab, b 137 Patterson.
Sanders Jane (wid John H), b 500 E 8th.
Sanders Jennie, h 325 W St Clair.
Sanders Jennie (wid Richard), b 301 N California.
Sanders Jeremiah, lab, r 23 Chapel.
Sanders Jesse A, sawmkr, h 23 Bicking.
Sanders Jesse E, painter, h 214 Madison av.
Sanders John, teacher, b 46 S Capitol av.

We Buy Municipal
~ Bonds ~
THOS. C. DAY & CO,
Rooms 325 to 330 Lemcke Bldg.

Sanders John E, bartndr, h 208 W South.
Sanders John F, bartndr, h rear 322 Prospect.
Sanders John L, trav agt, h 35 S McLain (W I).
Sanders John W, lab, h 59 Hazel.
Sanders John W, tmstr, h 215 LeGrand av.
Sanders John W, lab, h 108 River av (W I).
Sanders Joseph, shoemkr, 223 W 3d, h same.
Sanders Louis E, filer, h 70 Fulton.
Sanders Lulu (wid George), b 294 Douglass.
Sanders Margaret (wid John), grocer, 102 Columbia av, h same.
Sanders Martha (wid John), b 150 Elizabeth.
Sanders Martha J (wid Branson), h rear 115 Bright.
Sanders Mary B, music teacher, 380 College av, h same.
Sanders Mary E (wid Enoch G), h 106 Park av.
Sanders Mary E (wid Gabriel), h 21 Haugh (H).
Sanders Minnie L, dressmkr, 27 Birch av (W I), b same.
Sanders Myrtle (wid John), ironer, b 1448 E Washington.
Sanders Nancy J (wid Absalom), b 601 W Michigan.
Sanders Oliver C, clk, r 83 N Capitol av.
Sanders Oliver S, grocer, 531 W Washington, h same.
Sanders Preston, lab, b 185½ Indiana av.
Sanders Reuben H, lab, h 30 Center.
Sanders Richard J, mach, r 77½ S Illinois.
Sanders Robert W, barber, b 178½ Indiana av.
Sanders Saluda (wid Oliver S), h 27 Birch av (W I).
Sanders Samuel, lab, h 64 Thomas.
Sanders Thomas, engr, r 164 W Maryland.
Sanders Thomas A, painter, h 36 Cherry.
Sanders Thomas J, engr, h 521 W 22d (N I).
Sanders Wilhelmina L (A & W Sanders), h 951 E Michigan.
Sanders Wm, engr, r 71½ N Illinois.
Sanders Wm F, lab, h 33 Jones.
Sanders Wm F, tmstr, h 351 Charles.

EAT
HITZ'S
CRACKERS
AND CAKES.
ASK YOUR GROCER FOR THEM.

WILLIAM WIEGEL } MANUFACTURER OF.... } SHOW CASES { 6 W. Louisiana St. Opposite Union Station.

TURKISH RUGS AND CARPETS RESTORED TO ORIGINAL COLORS LIKE NEW | Capital Steam Carpet Cleaning Works M. D. PLUNKETT, Telephone 818

BENJ. BOOTH PRACTICAL EXPERT ACCOUNTANT. Books Opened, Written Up, Posted and Balanced. Room 18, 82½ E. Washington St., Indianapolis, Ind.

ESTABLISHED 1876. TELEPHONE 168.
CHESTER BRADFORD,
SOLICITOR OF PATENTS,
AND COUNSEL IN PATENT CAUSES.
(See adv. page 6.)
Office:—Rooms 14 and 16 Hubbard Block, S. W. Cor. Washington and Meridian Streets,
INDIANAPOLIS, INDIANA.

IF YOU WANT A GOOD MEAL AND HAVE IT NICELY SERVED GO TO THE SHERMAN RESTAURANT 18 and 20 S. MERIDIAN STREET

Sanders Wm L, bartndr, h 284 Martindale av.
Sanders Wm M, clk, r 181 Columbia av.
Sanders Zella (wid James R), r 31½ Virginia av.
Sanders & Pace (Henry C Sanders, Louis L Pace), creamery, 653 Virginia av.
Sanders & Spornberg (Charles G Sanders, Henry Spornberg), poultry, 303 W Washington.
Sanderson James H, saloon, 214 W 1st, h same.
Sandford James L, salesman, h 286 E St Clair.
Sandifer Fleming, lab, h 353 Lexington av.
Sandlin Charles E, waiter, b 81 W Georgia.
Sandmann Andrew J, fireman, h 414 W Wells (N I).
Sandmann Henry W, motorman, h 304 Yandes.
Sandmann Wm C, engr, h 190 Yandes.
Sands Elwood, agt, r 193 W Washington.
Sands Eva F, clk U S Pension Agency, b 325 N Illinois.
Sands Frederick, fireman, b 678 W Washington.
Sands Marshall O, fireman, h 158 Hoyt av.
Sands Newton, lab, h 103 Decatur.
Sandy James S, foreman, h 842 S Meridian.
Sandy Monticue A, jeweler, h 911 N Illinois.
Sandy Philip M, trav agt, h 227 E 8th.
Saner Jacob, bkkpr, r 145 E Merrill.
Sanford Bessie, h rear 33 Columbia al.
Sanford Frank, lab, h 541 Jones (N I).
Sanford George, lab, h 36 Hadley.
Sanford James L, trav agt Krull & Schmidt, h 286 E St Clair.
Sanford John D, engr, h 42 Beacon.
Sanford Sheridan C, trav agt, b 349 N New Jersey.
Sanford Wm H, hatter, h 539 Jones (N I).
Sanger Philip, tailor, 99 Benton, h same.
Sangernebo Alexander, molder, b 109 Brookside av.
Sangston John H, barber, w s Station 3 n of Glen Drive (B), h 36 S Station (B).
Sangston Wm J (Shaffer & Sangston), h 319 N Liberty.

O. B. ENSEY
MANUFACTURER OF
GALVANIZED IRON CORNICE, SKYLIGHTS AND WINDOW CAPS.
TELEPHONE 1562. Cor. 6th and Illinois Sts.

Sanitary Odorless Co, Lambert Krumholz propr, 36 N Delaware.
Sanks James H, driver, h 66 Oak.
Sanks Sarah R (wid George W), h 533 E Washington.
Sanks Wm W, tester, b 533 E Washington.
Sann Jacob, lab, b cor Holmes av and Michigan (H).
Sansbery Edward, lab, b 26 Chapel.
Sansbery John M, lab, h 558 W North.
Sansbury George, lab, h 100 Drake.
Santi Joseph, plumber, h 352½ Mass av.
Santa Clara Wine Co, Joseph L Schneewind sec, Myer Cohn treas, liquors, 89 N Illinois.
Santo Edward, h 214 Indiana av.
Santo Edward J, grocer, 204 Indiana av, h same.
Santo Henry, h 82 Harmon.
Santo Henry E, bottler, b 82 Harmon.
Saperstein Abraham (Saperstein Bros), b 55 Russell av.
Saperstein Bros (Jacob and Abraham), junk, 299 S Illinois.
Saperstein Iva (wid Mayer), h 131 Eddy.
Saperstein Jacob (Saperstein Bros), h 131 Eddy.
Saperstein Meyer, grocer, 55 Russell av, h same.
Sapp Anna (wid George W), h 57 Church.
Sapp George W, shoemkr, 358 Dillon, h 76 Lexington av.
Sapp Jennie E (wid Dillon), b 343 N Penn.
Sapp Thomas, foreman, h 2220 N Illinois.
Sapp Wm H, lab, b 2220 N Illinois.
Sarber Ada S (wid Wm H), h 297 E Ohio.
Sargent Albert B (M E Humphreys & Co), h 195 Walcott.
Sargent Alonzo, tmstr, h s w cor Orange and Pleasant av.
Sargent Amos M, ironwkr, b 285 S Capitol av.
Sargent Claud, ironwkr, b 285 S Capitol av.
Sargent Francis L, blksmith, h 347 W Michigan.
Sargent Harry G, b 1190 N Meridian.
Sargent Hurst H, clk Guarantee Shoe Store, b 79 W 10th.
Sargent Jacob J, packer, h 89 Shepard (W I).
Sargent James A Rev, pastor Hall Place M E Church, h 79 W 10th.
Sargent Jesse G, trav agt, b 1190 N Meridian.
Sargent Leonard S, pres Indpls Paint and Color Co, h 1123 N Meridian.
Sartor Frank, foreman, h 18 Miley av.
Sartor Scott, condr, h 91 W 14th.
Sarvis Leona (wid Alexander), b 233 W 3d.
Sassmann Wm, millwright, b 958 Sugar Grove av (M P).
Sater Emily (wid John D), h 150½ College av.
Sater George W, tmstr, h w s Madeira 6 s of Prospect.
Sater Joseph, tmstr, h w s Madeira 6 s of Prospect.
Sater Nancy, h 377 Home av.
Sattele Frank, filer, h 49 Russell av.
Sattele Frank G, lab, b 49 Russell av.
Satterfield Albert, lab, h 626 W Udell (N I).
Satterfield Enoch, lab, h e s James 2 n of Sutherland (B).
Satterlee Lewis W, painter, b 73 Lynn av (W I).
Satterthwaite Myrtellus N, engr, h 575 N Capitol av.
Sattinger Jacob (Glassman & Sattinger), h 134 Eddy.

TUTEWILER UNDERTAKER, No. 72 WEST MARKET STREET. TELEPHONE 216.

PARTNERSHIP INSURANCE At low cost. By which provision is made against the pecuniary loss and embarrassment resulting from the death of a member of a firm. Provident Life and Trust Co. of Philadelphia, D. W. EDWARDS, Gen'l Agt., 508 Indiana Trust Bldg.

THEODORE F. SMITHER Competent and Responsible ROOFER Telephone 86. Office 151 West Maryland St.

Sattler Frank, cabtmkr, b 29 Nebraska.
Sauer Anthony G, packer, h 453 Madison av.
Sauer Bernard (Sauer & Connor), h 1059 S Meridian.
Sauer Conrad, lab, h 198 Lincoln la.
Sauer Ernst, gasfitter, h 128 E 6th.
Sauer Frederick, mach, h 843 S Meridian.
Sauer George, carp, h 50 Davis.
Sauer George, dairy, w s Osage av 1 n of Clifford av, h same.
Sauer George F, mach, h 69 Downey.
Sauer John, h 27 W McCarty.
Sauer John, molder, h 109 Excelsior av.
Sauer Lena, housekpr 508 E Market.
Sauer Louis, brakeman, h 30 Jefferson av.
Sauer Margaret (wid Jacob), b w s Osage av 1 n of Clifford av.
Sauer Valentine J, shoemkr, b 198 Lincoln la.
Sauer Wm, mach, b 50 Davis.
Sauer & Connor (Bernard Sauer, Charles E Connor), proprs Central Printing Co, 83 E Court.
Sauerwein Charles A, trav agt, b 431 N Capitol av.
Sauerwein Daniel N, h 431 N Capitol av.
Sauerwein Wm E, trav agt, b 431 N Capitol av.
Saul Edgar, checkman The Denison.
Saul James T, floor walker H P Wasson & Co, b 434 S Delaware.
Saulcy Charles E, harnessmkr, h 214 N Pine.
SAULCY EUGENE, Assessor Center Township, 35 Court House, Tel 912, b 825 N Capitol av.
Saulter John T, tel opr C C C & St L Ry, r 74 W North.
Saunders, see also Sanders.
Saunders Henry R, sculptor, cor E North and Bee Line Ry, h 82 Vine.
Saunders John, carp, h 170 Bright.
Saunders John S, lab, h 30 Garland (W I).
Saunders Joseph W, lab, b 30 Garland (W I).
Saunders Miriam (wid Coleman), h 108½ Mass av.
Saunders Ruth (wid Louis), h 168 Bird.
Saunders Vauice, janitor, h 333 W North.
Sause Matthew M, driver, r 295 W 6th.
Sauter Eva (wid Frank C), b n e cor Gatling and Sanford.
Sauter Henry, saloon, 231 Shelby, h same.
Sauter Joseph, lab, h 85 Lincoln la.
Savage Albert, hostler, r 80 E Court.
Savage Edward S, mach hd, r 193 W Washington.
Savage Roderick J, fireman, h 32 S Gale (B).
Savage Wm H G, b n s Howland av 1 w of Orchard.
Saverage Edward J, painter, h 228 Columbia av.
Sawin Ira L, agt, b 325 N Illinois.
Sawyer Belle S, teacher Public School No 10, b 138 E St Clair.
Sayce George, bricklyr, b 118 W Vermont.
Sawyer Charles E, lab, r 13 Cleaveland blk.
Sawyer Charles F, mngr A W Stevens & Son, h 230 N Delaware.
Sawyer E Charles, clk Murphy, Hibben & Co, b 176 N Illinois.
SAWYER FRANK K, Agt Prussian National Insurance Co, Delaware Insurance Co, Standard Life and Accident Insurance Co, 74 E Market (ground floor), Tel 863; b 138 E St Clair. (See left side lines.)

THE WHEN IS A WORLD BEATER.

Sawyer John M (Sawyer & Jones), b 138 E St Clair.
Sawyer John S, bkkpr Frank K Sawyer, h 138 E St Clair.
Sawyer John T, clk, r 73 W Vermont.
Sawyer J Warren, real est, 215 Lemcke bldg, h 166 Bellefontaine.
Sawyer Samuel Rev, h 509 N Alabama.
Sawyer Samuel M, printer, r 190 E Market.
Sawyer Thomas, molder, h 58 Tremont av (H).
Sawyer Wm F, foreman, h 244 Douglass.
Sawyer Wm H, clk, r 73 W Vermont.
SAWYER & JONES (John M Sawyer, Louis S Jones), Brokerage and Commission, 2½ Board of Trade Bldg, Tel 658.
Saxon James F, b 9 Harvey.
Saxton Richard, lab, b 127 E Ohio.
Sayce James, lab, h 475 W Addison (N I).
Sayce Wm, bricklyr, b 475 W Addison (N I).
Sayer Philip E, lumber insp, h 237 S Olive.
Sayler Charles, lineman, b 34 S West.
Sayler Elizabeth S (wid Wm B), b 6 Fletcher av.
Sayler Wm B, printer, b 6 Fletcher av.
Sayler Ole B, mach opr The Indpls Sentinel, b 6 Fletcher av.
SAYLES CHARLES F, Insurance, Loans, Real Estate and Rental Agt, 77½ E Market, h 665 N Meridian; Tels Office 476, Res 906.
Sayles George W, tinner, h 165 Sharpe av (W).
Sayles Herman B, clk, h 27 W 4th.
Sayles Leonard, printer, h 166 Trowbridge (W).
Saylor Carrie M, teacher Public School No 35, b 427 S Meridian.
Saylor Frederick L, constable, h 25 S Gale (B).
Saylor Harvey W, lab, b 25 S Gale (B).
Saylor Jackson, h 427 S Meridian.
Saylor Louis S, city fireman, h 267 W Morris.
Saylor Samantha M (wid Henry), h 452 Mulberry.

THE A. BURDSAL CO. WINDOW AND PLATE GLASS Putty, Glazier Points, Diamonds. Wholesale and Retail. 34 and 36 S. Meridian St.

ELECTRIC CONSTRUCTION Isolated Plants Installed. Electric Wiring and Fittings of all kinds. C. W. Meikel. Tel. 466. 96-98 E New York St

DALTON & MERRIFIELD { LUMBER South Noble St., near E. Washington

INDIANA ELECTROTYPE CO. BEST WORK. LOWEST PRICES. 23 WEST PEARL ST., INDIANAPOLIS, IND. JOB WORK. BOOK PLATES. All Orders Promptly Filled. BEST PATENT BASE ON THE MARKET.

KIRKHOFF BROS.,
GAS AND ELECTRIC FIXTURES
THE LARGEST LINE IN THE CITY.
102-104 SOUTH PENNSYLVANIA ST.
TELEPHONE 910.

Saylor Theodore G, fireman, h 37 Poplar (B).
Saylor Wm J, lab, b 427 S Meridian.
Sayre Edward J, molder, h 54 King av (H).
Sayres Levi, lab, h e s Pleasant av 1 s of Belt R R.
Scahill John W, mach hd, h 41 Elizabeth.
Scales Frederick, lab, h 181 W 1st.
Scampamerto Vincenzo, fruits, 143 Mass av, h 29 Cook.
Scanlan Anthony F, collr, h 365 S West.
Scanlan Bridget (wid James), h 332 W Washington.
Scanlan Charles W, brakeman, h 170 Clifford av.
Scanlan James, driver, b 332 W Washington.
Scanlan John, condr, h 16 Elder av.
Scanlan John B, lab, h 332 W Washington.
Scanlan John P, tel opr Postal Tel Cable Co, b 31 Haugh (H).
Scanlan Michael, tinner, h 96 Bright.
Scanlan Patrick, condr, h 31 Haugh (H).
Scanlan Thomas, lab, b 332 W Washington.
Scanlon Catherine A, h 369 S Illinois.
Scanlon Frank, painter, h 324 E Miami.
Scanlon John H, mach, h 369 S Illinois.
Scanlon John T, janitor, h 76 E Walnut.
Scanlon John W, mach, h 446 Bellefontaine.
Scanlon Michael, lab, h 10 Meikel.
Scanlon Thomas, harnessmkr, b 257 Union.
Scanlon Thomas, porter The Bates.
Scanlon Thomas D, lab, b 17 Meikel.
Scanlon Wm, blksmith, b 76 E Walnut.
Scanlon Wm J, brakeman, h 313 English av.
Scantlan Frank, lab, h 324 E Miami.
Scantlin Frederica (wid John), h 79 Elizabeth.
Scantlin John R, clk, h w s Illinois 2 s of 29th.
Scarber Charles, lab, b 223 E Court.
Scarber Robert, lab, h 223 E Court.
Scarce Humphrey M, waiter, r 427 Muskingum al.
Scarlett Wm G, solr R G Dun & Co, h 335 Bellefontaine.
Scarry Mary A (wid John), h 380 N Senate av.
Scates Harry L, lab, b 134 W Ohio.
Schaad Peter, shoemkr, h 21 Weghorst.

COAL AND COKE
The W. G. Wasson Co.,
130 INDIANA AVE. TEL. 989
LIME AND LATH

Schaaf Abel, b 103 N Noble.
Schaaf Adam, tailor, h 72 Yeiser.
Schaaf Alvin W, bkkpr, b 313 E Market.
Schaaf Casper, cabtmkr, h 32 Iowa.
Schaaf Harry J, foreman Indpls Mnfrs' and Carps' Union, h 107 N Arsenal av.
Schaaf Valentine, pres and supt Indpls Mnfrs' and Carps' Union, h 313 E Market.
Schaaf Valentine, tinner, h 16 S Station (B).
Schaal John J, grinder, h 59 Greer.
Schacher Peter, tailor, h 222 Hoyt av.
Schachinger Daniel, woodwkr, h 31 Eastern av.
Schad Albert, clk N Y Store, h 16 Brookside av.
SCHAD CHARLES H, Druggist, 344 E Washington, h 542 E Ohio, Tel 528.
Schad Christian G, tailor, h 74 Cincinnati.
Schad Christian W, tmstr, h 50 Gresham.
Schad Frederick E, mach, b 50 Gresham.
Schad Frederick M (Schad & Sons), b 875 N Capitol av.
Schad George E, bookbndr Wm B Burford, b 101 Davidson.
Schad George J, finisher, h 101 Davidson.
Schad Harry E (Schad & Sons), b 875 N Capitol av.
Schad John G (Schad & Sons), h 875 N Capitol av.
Schad Louis G, carpetlyr, b 101 Davidson.
Schad Martin E, bkkpr H H Fay, b 74 Cincinnati.
Schad Matilda, b 1382 N Senate av.
Schad Rosina M (wid Gottlieb), h 101 Davidson.
Schad Theodore C, tailor, b 74 Cincinnati.
Schad & Sons (John G, Frederick M and Harry E), grocers, 700 N Capitol av.
Schadwell Maria L (wid Harrison), b 206 W 1st.
Schaefer, see also Schafer, Shafer and Shaffer.
Schaefer Andreas, cooper, h 920 Madison av.
Schaefer Augustus H, driver, b 49½ S Meridian.
Schaefer Charles, baker Parrott & Taggart, b 433 Madison av.
Schaefer Charles F, mach, b 445 W 22d (N I).
Schaefer Charles T, horseshoer, h 496½ Virginia av.
SCHAEFER C RICHARD, Physician and Surgeon, Office Hours 8-9:30 A M, 2-4 and 7-9 P M, 430 Madison av, b 329 Orange, Tel 282.
Schaefer Dora (wid Frederick W), h 10 Smith.
Schaefer Edward, polisher, b 394 S Delaware.
Schaefer Edward W, marblecutter, b 445 W 22d (N I).
Schaefer Ernest F, cabtmkr, h 126 Harlan.
Schaefer Eva, clk, h 624 N Senate av.
Schaefer Franz, collr German Telegraph, b 239 Orange.
Schaefer F Joseph, mach, h 47 Wisconsin.
Schaefer George G, clk U S Pension Agency, h 150 Lexington av.
Schaefer George J, lab, h 857 S East.
Schaefer Henry, clk W U Tel Co, b 624 N Senate av.
SCHAEFER HERMAN L, Dealer in Groceries, Meats, Fruits, Poultry, Fish, Etc, 350 W Vermont, cor Blackford, h same.
Schaefer Jacob, lab, h 5 Hendricks.

W. H. MESSENGER COMPLETE HOUSE FURNISHER 101 East Washington Street, Telephone 491

Foundry and Pattern Shop } McNamara, Koster & Co. { PHONE 1593 212-218 S. Penn. St.

Schaefer John, baker Parrott & Taggart, b 433 Madison av.
Schaefer John L, painter, h 65 Camp.
Schaefer John P, helper, b 624 N Senate av.
Schaefer Kunigunde (wid Herman E), h 580 N Senate av.
Schaefer Margaret, boarding 218 E Wabash, h same.
Schaefer Philip, carver, h 445 W 22d (N I).
Schaefer Philip, cigarmkr, h 624 N Senate av.
Schaefer Sophia (wid John), b 204 Shelby.
Schaefer Sophie (wid Charles), h 433 Madison av.

SCHAEFER WM, Mnfr of Brooms, Mops, Toy and Whisk Brooms, 218 E Wabash, h same.

Schaefer Wm, mach, b 624 N Senate av.
Schaefer Wm C, bkkpr Christian Schrader, b 10 Smith.
Schaepe Amelia (wid Carl), h 51 Tremont av (H).
Schaepe Gustave, molder, h 41 Bismarck av (H).
Schaepe John B, patternmkr, b 51 Tremont av (H).
Schaette Christian W, lab, h 625 Marlowe av.
Schaf Joseph C, pres American Brewing Co, sec and treas Crystal Ice Co and The C Habich Co, h 296 W New York.
Schafer, see also Schaefer, Shafer and Shaffer.
Schafer Agnes (wid Henry), h 197 Elizabeth.
Schafer August H, chief West Indpls Fire Dept, h 12 S Judge Harding (W I).
Schafer Charles H, bartndr, b 197 Elizabeth.
Schafer Edward T, mason, h s s Prospect 1 w of Earhart.
Schafer Ernst, saloon, n w cor English av and Pine, h same.
Schafer John, coremkr, b 920 Madison av.
Schafer John F, carp, h 30 Dougherty.
Schafer Leonhard, driver, b 197 Elizabeth.
Schafer Leopold, lab, h 4 Carlos.
Schafer Nicholas M, barber, b 30 Dickson.
Schafer Paul H, mach hd, b 580 N Senate av.
Schafer Quirin, carp, h 97 New.
Schafer Wm, grocer, 492 S Meridian, h 494 S Illinois.
Schaffenberger Wm, lab, b 304 S Meridian.
Schaffer Anna R, h 174 E Louisiana.
Schaffer Anthony F, condr, b 1071 N Capitol av.
Schaffer George A, baker, h 127 Gillard av.
Schaffer Peter, drayman, h 567 E St Clair.
Schaffer Philip, baker, r 116 Ft Wayne av.
Schaffer Wm H, janitor, h 398 W Pratt.
Schaffner, see also Shaffner.
Schaffner Carl E, polisher, b 110 Martindale av.
Schaffner Charles J, express, h 110 Martindale av.
Schaffner John, lab, h 116 Kennington.
Schaffner Louis P, yardman W G Wasson Co, h 196 W Vermont.
Schakel Andrew, finisher, b 123 S Linden.
Schakel Anton H, drayman, b 23 E McCarty.
Schakel Charles A C, car rep, h 77 Spann av.
Schakel Charles C, carp, h 262 Jefferson av.
Schakel Charles C, printer Wm B Burford, b 123 S Linden.
Schakel Charles F, lab, h 353 Jefferson av.

Henry H. Fay,
40½ E. WASHINGTON ST.,
AGENT FOR
Insurance Co. of North America,
Pennsylvania Fire Ins. Co.

Schakel Christian C, helper, b 353 Jefferson av.
Schakel Christian H, lab, h 183 N Beville av.
Schakel Frederick W, janitor Maennerchor Hall, h 181 E Washington.
Schakel Henry, lab, h 11 Atlas.
Schakel Henry C, drayman, h 34 Dawson.
Schakel Wm F, drayman, h 115 S Linden.
Schako Charles, mach, h 43 Davis.
Schako Charles, mach Outing Bicycle Co, h 60 Dougherty.
Schako Edward, mach, b 43 Davis.
Schaler George H, switchman, h 204 River av (W I).
Schaler Henry P, condr, b 69 S Noble.
Schaler Louis P, b 321 E Wabash.
Schaler Mary A (wid Henry), h 69 S Noble.
Schaler Mary L (wid Joseph A), h 583 S Illinois.
Schaler Wm H, mach, b 583 S Illinois.
Schall Vina, h 80 Cleaveland blk.
Schall Wm U, barber, h 434 Ash.
Schallenberg Frederick, chairmkr, h 604 S East.
Schaller Albert, finisher, b 26 S Stuart (B).
Schaller Charles, plastr, b s e cor Willow and Foundry (B).
Schaller Elmer, clk, b 20 Depot (B).
Schaller Lacy, plastr, b s e cor Willow and Foundry (B).
Schamsky Frank A, tailor B B Dildine, r 483 College av.
Schandle Max, bartndr, h 23 Evison.
Schandorf Herman N, engr, h 1027 W Washington.
Schandorf Martha (wid John W), h 79 W 7th.
Schane Theodore, tinner, b Marion Park Hotel (M P).
Schaner, see Shaner.
Schantz, see also Shantz.
Schantz Charles D, bartndr, h 61 E Merrill.
Scharfe Frank, ins agt, h 167 E Morris.
Scharfe Frederick, h 456 E North.
Scharff Dollie C, artist, 307 N Senate av, b same.
Scharff Nathan H, clk, b 307 N Senate av.

Union Casualty & Surety Co.
of St. Louis, Mo.
Employers', Public, General, Teams and Elevator Liability; also Workmen's Collective, Steam Boiler, Plate Glass and Automatic Sprinkler Insurance.
W. E. BARTON & CO., General Agents,
504 Indiana Trust Building.
LONG DISTANCE TELEPHONE 1918.

THE FRED DIETZ CO.
WOODEN PACKING BOXES MADE TO ORDER. FACTORY AND WAREHOUSE TRUCKS.
400 Madison Avenue. Telephone 654.

Shorthand! BUSINESS UNIVERSITY. When Bl'k. Elevator day and night. Typewriting, Penmanship, Book-keeping, Office Training free. See page 4. Est. 1850. Tel. 499. E. J. HEEB, Proprietor.

HENRY R. WORTHINGTON JET and SURFACE CONDENSERS 64 S. PENN. ST. Long Distance Telephone 284.

UNION CO-OPERATIVE LAUNDRY (COMPOSED OF UNION LAUNDRY GIRLS.) NOS. 3, 40 AND 42 VIRGINIA AVENUE T. E. SOMERVILLE, MANAGER. TELEPHONE 189. INDIANAPOLIS, IND.

HORACE M. HADLEY
REAL ESTATE AND LOANS....
66 East Market Street
Telephone 1540. BASEMENT.

Scharn John H (Scharn & Rubush), h 56 Carlos.
SCHARN & RUBUSH (John H Scharn, Preston C Rubush), Architects, 21-22 Journal Bldg. (See adv in classified Architects.)
Schatz Edward J, toolmkr, b 311 W Morris.
Schatz Henry, solr German Telegraph, b George's Hotel.
Schatz Jacob F, clk, h 311 W Morris.
Schatz Jacob F jr, clk Parry Mnfg Co, b 311 W Morris.
Schatz John H, clk, h 64 Chadwick.
Schatz Otto L, mach, h 33½ N Station (B).
Schaub Ada, h 212 E Market.
Schaub Albert, blksmith, n e cor Lafayette and Crawfordsville rds, res Emrichsville, Ind.
Schaub Andrew C, cigarmkr, h 264 Spring.
Schaub Caroline (wid Henry), h 275 Indiana av.
Schaub Charles, salesman, h 1380 N Capitol av.
Schaub Edward, musician, b 167 River av (W I).
Schaub Elizabeth (wid John), b 499 N Alabama.
Schaub Elizabeth (wid Peter), b 160 Randolph.
Schaub Frank G, mach hd, h 303 Indiana av.
Schaub Frederick E, switchman, h 1004 E Washington.
Schaub Frederick J, clk, h 217 N Noble.
Schaub Frederick L, clk, b 275 Indiana av.
Schaub George J, engr, h 351 English av.
Schaub George P, cigarmkr, h 127 Windsor.
Schaub Gustav A, clk, b 77 N Noble.
Schaub Gustav C, printer, h 105 Benton.
Schaub Henry, painter,, rear 499 N Alabama, h 65 Eastern av.
Schaub Henry J cigar mnfr, 453 E Washington, h 220 Spring.
Schaub John, saloon, 167 River av (W I), h same.
Schaub Joseph C, clk, b 167 River av (W I).
SCHAUB JOSEPH H, Sample Room, 88 E Washington, h 77 N Noble.

Merchants' and Manufacturers Exchange
Make Collections and Commercial Reports......
J. E. TAKKEN, MANAGER,
19 Union Building, 73 West Maryland Street

Schaub Leopold, brewer, h 351 E Morris.
Schaub Peter, cigarmkr, h 127 Windsor.
Schaub Robert P, ball player, b 275 Indiana av.
Schaub Wm, cigarmkr, b 264 Spring.
Schaub Wm, clk, h 499 N Alabama.
Schauer George B, mach, h s s Brookside av 2 w of Roseline.
Schaull David, tailor, r 300 S Meridian.
Schauroth & Co, Charles E Ferrell mngr, shoes, 18 E Washington.
Schebler George M, repr Emil Wulschner & Son, b 424 Union.
Schebler Joseph, watchman, h 99 Dunlop.
Scheele Frederick W, grocer, n w cor Ohio and Rural, h same.
Scheffbuch George C, flagman, h 153 Minnesota.
Scheffly Mary (wid Abraham), h 84 Ramsey av.
Scheib Andrew, lab, h 127 Downey.
Scheib John J, lab, h 23 Nebraska.
Scheib Joseph B, cooper, b 127 Downey.
Scheib Peter, saloon, 2 S Brightwood av (B), h same.
Scheich Peter, meats, 131 Davidson, h same.
Scheid Charles, cooper, h 241 Blake.
Scheid Charles, pdlr, h 95 Maxwell.
Scheid Claude, clk, b 183 E South.
Scheid John (John Scheid & Co), h 183 E South.
SCHEID JOHN & CO (John Scheid), Oysters, Fish and Game, 77 N Illinois and 67 E Market House, Tel 212.
Scheid Martin, cooper, b 241 Blake.
Scheid Wm, cooper, h 58 Minerva.
Scheideler, see also Schideler.
Scheideler Anthony Very Rev, vicar general Diocese of Vincennes and rector of St Mary's Catholic Church, h 75 E Maryland.
Scheideler Wilhelmina, housekpr 75 E Maryland.
Scheidt Edward C W, stenog Am Ex Co, b 119 Huron.
Scheidt Wm J, clk, h 119 Huron.
Scheier Frank L, poultry, E Mkt House, b 375 E New York.
Scheier John, h 375 E New York.
Scheier John C, grocer, 449 S State av, h same.
Scheier Wm C, grocer, 36 E Mkt House, b 375 E New York.
Scheigert Herman E, watchman, h 509 S Capitol av.
Scheigert Wm F, sergt of police, h 619 N Capitol av.
Schelke George, clk, r 208 N Illinois.
Schelke Wm F, bkkpr, r 208 N Illinois.
Schell Charles E, carp, h 140 Nordyke av (W I).
Schell Emma (wid Christian), h 220 Elizabeth.
Schell Henry J, carp, h 10 Poplar (B).
Schell Henry J, lithog, b 39 Elizabeth.
Schell Joseph, h 39 Elizabeth.
Schell Joseph H, lab, h 16 Hadley.
Schell Louis N, pressman, h 132 Eureka av.
Schellenberg Frederick, chairmkr, h 604 S East.
Schellenberg Rudolph, carp, h 476 N Alabama.
Scheller August, lab, h 403 W McLene (N I).
Scheller Lorenz, porter, h 278 E Michigan.
Schellert Charles R, carp, h 93 Oak.
Schellert Harry, mach, b 93 Oak.
Schellert Otto, tinner, b 93 Oak.
Schellkopf Eugene, bkkpr, b 421½ S Delaware.

CLEMENS VONNEGUT 184, 186 and 192 E. Washington St. Wire Rope, Machinery, Lathes, Drills and Shapers

THE WM. H. BLOCK CO. DRY GOODS, DRAPERIES, RUGS, WINDOW SHADES.
7 AND 9 EAST WASHINGTON STREET.

Schellschmidt Adolph, music teacher, 246 E Ohio, h same.
Schellschmidt Adolph jr, music teacher, 242 E Ohio, b 246 same.
Schellschmidt Bertha, music teacher, 246 E Ohio, b same.
Schellschmidt Conrad, musician, h 1145 N Alabama.
Schellschmidt Emma, music teacher, 246 E Ohio, b same.
Schellschmidt Pauline, music teacher, 246 E Ohio, b same.
Schelski Bruno C G, brewer, h 78 Kennington.
Schelski Erich, painter, b 89 Yandes.
Schelski George H, grocer, 268 Yandes, h same.
Schelski Theophilia (wid Gustav), h 89 Yandes.
Schenck Nancy (wid Samuel), h 15 Cleveland (H).
Schenck Samuel A, lab, h 64 Tremont av (H).
Schenck Tunis V, painter, h w s Bradley 4 n of Ohio.
Schenck Wm T, painter, h w s Bradley 4 n of Ohio.
Schendel Alfred T, bartndr, h 624 W Vermont.
Schendel Max L, bartndr, h 23 Evison.
Schendel Paul W, bartndr, b 23 Evison.
Schepper John L, car oiler, h e s Lincoln av 1 s of Ida (M J).
Schepper Mary B, cook, h 26½ N Senate av.
Scherer, see also Scherrer, Shearer and Sherer.
Scherer Charles F, molder, h 23 Downey.
Scherer Charles J, cabtmkr, h e s Rembrant av 1 n of Indiana av.
Scherer Christian L, cabtmkr, h e s Rembrant 1 n of Indiana av.
Scherer Henry M, mach, h 842 LaSalle (M P).
Scherer John, b 886 LaSalle (M P).
Scherer Margaret (wid Wm H), h 477 S New Jersey.

SCHERER SIMON P, Physician, Office Hours 9-10 A M, 2-4 and 7-8 P M, 581½ S East, h 69 High, Tels Office 1114, Res 1756.

Scherer Wm J, cabtmkr, h 24 E Morris.
Schergens August C, cabtmkr, b 115 Meek.
Schergens Henry C, jeweler, 151 E Washington, h 372 E New York.
Schering Charles F, engr, h 26 Randolph.
Schering George F, clk Theodore Stein, b 44 N Arsenal av.
Schering Matilda C, dressmkr, 44 N Arsenal av, b same.
Schering Sophia L (wid Charles H), h 44 N Arsenal av.
Scherle Wm, barber, h 186 Dearborn.
Scherrer, see also Scherer, Shearer and Sherer.

SCHERRER ADOLPH, Architect, 415-417 Indiana Trust Bldg, h 87 Union.

Scherrer Charles, chaircaner, b 91 High.
Scherrer Frank B, grocer, 53 Cushing, h same.
Scherrer Frederick W, bottler, h 694 Charles.
Scherrer George M, cigarmkr, b 91 High.
Scherrer George M, collr Francke & Schindler, b 811 Chestnut.
Scherrer John, b 91 High.
Scherrer Louis M, bottler, b 91 High.

Scherrer Michael G, janitor E Mkt House, h 811 Chestnut.
Scherrer Wilhelmina (wid John), h 91 High.
Scherzinger Helena (wid Fidel), h rear 314 Highland av.
Schetter Christopher, grocer, 300 S Penn, h 320 S Meridian.
Schetter Frederick J, lab, b 320 S Meridian.
Schetter Louis F, tel opr, h 29 Shriver av.
Scheuwecker Albert B, jeweler, 103½ E Washington, b 161 E Ohio.
Schewe August, gilder, h 603 Madison av.
Schey Charles B, harnessmkr, h 55 Iowa.
Schicketanz George J, city fireman, h 131 Prospect.
Schiel Wm, cabtmkr, h 349 Jefferson av.
Schienbein Frederick, sawmkr, h 557 E Walnut.
Schier Charles J, mason, h e s Bradley 1 n of Ohio.
Schier Conrad, cistern bldr, h 18 Yandes.
Schier John, mach, h 111½ Bismarck av (H).
Schier Otto, bricklyr, b 18 Yandes.
Schierling Charles H, bookbndr Wm B Burford, h 292 N Liberty.
Schierling Nicholas, cooper, h 292 N Liberty.
Schiesz Charles F, painter, h 22½ Wilcox.
Schiewer Charles A, cabtmkr, h 24 Quincy.
Schifferdeker Charles, saloon, 153 Davidson, h same.
Schiffling Albert, mach, 48 Virginia av, h 394 N Senate av.
Schiffling Ida H, stenog, b 394 N Senate av.
Schildmeier Benjamin, lab, b 67 N Olive.
Schildmeier Charles F W (Schildmeier & Koelling), h 312 E Market.
Schildmeier Christian L, mach, h 76 Meek.
Schildmeier Christopher C, dairy, n w cor English av and McPherson (S), h same.
Schildmeier Edward, boilermkr, h 165 Spann av.
Schildmeier Frederick, mach, b 76 Meek.
Schildmeier Johanna (wid Anthony), b 99 Fulton.
Schildmeier & Koelling (Charles F W Schildmeier, Charles C F Koelling), mer tailors, 264 E Washington.
Schildmeyer August, express, h 39 Peru av.

GUIDO R. PRESSLER,
FRESCO PAINTER
Churches, Theaters, Public Buildings, Etc., A Specialty.
Residence, No. 325 North Liberty Street
INDIANAPOLIS, IND.

INDIANAPOLIS STEEL ROOFING AND CORRUGATING WORKS, 23 and 25 East South Street. S. D. NOEL, Proprietor.

David S. McKernan, REAL ESTATE AND LOANS
A number of choice pieces for subdivision, or for manufacturers' sites, with good switch facilities.
Rooms 2-5 Thorpe Block.

DIAMOND WALL PLASTER { Telephone 1410 BUILDERS' EXCHANGE.

Cor. E. Ohio St. and C., C., C. & St. L. R'y Tracks. BRICK WAREHOUSE; CLEANEST AND SAFEST STORAGE IN CITY FOR HOUSEHOLD GOODS AND MERCHANDISE.

W. McWORKMAN,

METAL CEILINGS,
ROLLING SHUTTERS,
DOORS AND PARTITIONS.

930 W. Washington St. Tel. 1118.

Schildmeyer John, driver, b 39 Peru av.
Schill Jacob D, baker Parrott & Taggart, h 89 Coburn.
Schiller Albert, mach, h 3 N Shade (B).
Schiller Frederick W, lab, h 16 Applegate.
Schilling, see also Shilling.
Schilling Carl, lab, h 55 Hendricks.
Schilling George W, roller, h 34 McGinnis.
Schilling Herman, coachman 863 N Meridian.
Schilling Herman D, carp, b 402 S Olive.
Schilling Wm C, carp, h 402 S Olive.
Schillinger Barbara A (wid Andrew), h 115 Davidson.
Schillinger George J, clk Collins T Bedford, b 115 Davidson.
Schillinger Mary (wid George), b 329 Davidson.
Schiltges John P, dep collr Internal Revenue, h 310 E South.
Schimmel Charles, trav agt Elmer E Nichols Co, h 1265 N Meridian.
Schimmel Joseph, b 1265 N Meridian.
Schindler Caroline S (wid Robert C), h 164½ E Washington.
Schindler Oscar C, h 232 Clifford av.
Schindwolf Alois, lab, b 472 E Washington.
Schirack John A, phys, 319 N California, r same.
Schirmer Baldwin F, trav agt, h 123 Greer.
Schirmer Otto H, clk Home Stove Co, r 70 W New York.
Schisla John G, meats, 22 E Mkt House, h 616 S Meridian.
Schisla Mary (wid John), h 36 Arizona.
Schissel Christian, lab, h 374 S Capitol av.
Schissel Frederick L, lab, h 221 W Maryland.
Schissel Otto, saloon, n e cor West and Wabash, h same.
Schlaef Henry C, student, r 95 Mass av.
Schlaegel Henry E, carp, h 46 Nordyke av (W I).
Schlagle Albert B, brakeman, h 274 E Washington.
Schlake Anna (wid Wm), h 333 S New Jersey.
Schlake Wm H, bkkpr Hollweg & Reese, h 333 S New Jersey.

SEALS,
STENCILS,
STAMPS, Etc.
GEO. J. MAYER
15 S. Meridian St.
TELEPHONE 1386.

SCHLANZER BENEDICT J, Genl Contractor and Builder, Planing Mill and Wood Turning, 682 Charles, Tel 864; h 679 S Meridian. (See p 8.)
Schlanzer Benedict J jr, mach hd, b 679 S Meridian.
Schlatter Charles F, attendant Insane Asylum.
Schlechter Peter, brakeman, h 73 Leota.
Schlechty Walter A, brakeman, h 20 N Gillard av.
Schlee Charles J, engr, h 1071 W Vermont.
Schlegel Emanuel, h 140 Blake.
Schlegel Frederick, tailor, h s w cor Raymond and East.
Schlegel Frederick J, carp, b 51 Sanders.
Schlegel John, lab, h s s Ohio, 5 e of Rural.
Schlegel Katharine (wid Ferdinand), b 580 N Senate av.
Schlegel Margaret B (wid Frederick), h 51 Sanders.
Schleicher Adolf (Schleicher & Martens), h 998 N Senate av.
Schleicher Adolf jr, student, b 998 N Senate av.
Schleicher Albert F, mason, b 57 Newman.
Schleicher Charles H, printer, b 57 Newman.
Schleicher Wm, cabtmkr, h 57 Newman.
Schleicher & Martens (Adolph Schleicher, Herman E Martens), wall paper, 18 N Meridian.
Schleimer Nicholas, brewer, h 683 Union.
Schlender Herman A, clk, h 68 Christian av.
Schlenske Christian, gardener, h s e cor Southern and Madison av.
Schlenz John R, lab, h 18 Woodside av.
Schleppy John H, clk, h 31 Cherry.
Schletz Andrew H, lab, h 7 Ingram.
Schletz John A, lab, h 16 Ingram.
Schley George J, printer, h 475 Central av.
Schley Georgealice, teacher Public School No 33, b 202 Clifford av.
Schley John, sec Mutual Savings Union and Loan Assn, h 202 Clifford av.
Schlick Henry, mach, b 198 Buchanan.
Schlick Josephine (wid Henry), b 198 Buchanan.
Schliebener Herman, cabtmkr, h rear 82 S Delaware.
Schliebitz Albert, clk, b 166 E St Joseph.
Schliebitz Flora, bkkpr, b 166 E St Joseph.
Schliebitz Louisa (wid Frederick), b 166 E St Joseph.
Schloendorn Christopher C, b 681 N Alabama.
Schloss Joseph, ins agt H Seyfried, h 7 Ft Wayne av.
Schloss Mae E, stenog Spencer House, h 7 Ft Wayne av.
Schlosser John (Hart & Schlosser), res New Palestine, Ind.
Schlosser Martha (wid Robert), b 105 Minerva.
Schlotter Joseph, armature winder, h 101 Walcott.
Schlotz Charles F, lab, h 59 Haugh (H).
Schlotzhauer Adam, cabtmkr, h 109 Cherry.
Schlotzhauer Elizabeth (wid Valentine), b 634 College av.
Schlotzhauer George J, foreman, h 634 College av.
Schlotzhauer Harry A, receiving teller Indiana Natl Bank, h 313 College av.
Schludecker Fred C, lab, b 833 Chestnut.
Schludecker Leopold, tinner, b 487 S Meridian.

UNION TRANSFER AND STORAGE CO.

A. METZGER AGENCY ESTABLISHED 1863. INSURANCE

LAMBERT GAS & GASOLINE ENGINE CO.
ANDERSON, IND. PORTABLE GASOLINE ENGINES. 2 TO 25 H. P.

Schludecker Paul, carp, h 129 Kennington.
Schludecker Wm, finisher, h 833 Chestnut.
Schlueter Frederick, mach, h 183 Woodlawn av.
Schlueter Julius A, clk, h 374 W New York.
Schmakel Wm, lab, h 58 Ramsey av.
Schmalfeldt John, flagman, h 572 Chestnut.
Schmalfeldt Louis F, molder, b 572 Chestnut.
Schmalfeldt Wm H F, lab, h 10 Draper.

SCHMALHOLZ CASPAR, Wines, Liquors and Cigars, 29 S Meridian and 9 E Pearl, h 79 N East.

Schmalholz Charles O, ruler, b 556 E Market.
Schmalholz Eva (wid John), b 425 E Vermont.
Schmalholz Rudolph, harnessmkr, 278 E Washington, h 556 E Market.
Schmalholz Simon, cigarmkr, 257½ E Washington, h 425 E Vermont.
Schmalholz Wilber, clk, b 556 E Market.
Schmalz Caspar, painter, b 31 Coburn.
Schmalz George L, tailor, b 31 Coburn.
Schmalz Gideon, lab, h 10 Wisconsin.
Schmalz Robert, tailor, h 31 Coburn.
Schmalzigaug Gustav A, clk H E Frauer & Co, r 246 E Washington.
Schmedel Edward P, sawmkr, h 130 Orange av.
Schmedel Frank A, mach, b 1045 N Capitol av.
Schmedel Gustav, letter carrier P O, h 50 Woodlawn av.

SCHMEDEL HIRAM, Brush Mnfr, 420 E McCarty, h same. (See adv in classified Brush Mnfrs.)

Schmedle Samuel A, boxmkr, h 245 W South.
Schmehl Christina (wid Henry), b 19 S Dorman.
Schmeltz Jerome W (Schmeltz & Lorentz), h 568 S Meridian.
Schmeltz & Lorentz (Jerome W Schmeltz, Wm A Lorentz), jewelers, 24 S Illinois.
Schmelzer Jacob J, cabtmkr, b 143 Patterson.
Schmertz Albert C, mach hd, b 17 S Dorman.
Schmertz Edgar, cigarmkr, b 17 S Dorman.
Schmertz Minnie C, h 17 S Dorman.
Schmid, see also Schmidt, Smith and Smythe.
Schmid Amelia S, b 182 W Vermont.
Schmid B Frank, sec and treas Central Chair Co, h 900 N Capitol av.
Schmid Charles, bartndr, h 264 Fulton.
Schmid Edward C F (J C Schmid & Sons), h 1 e of 316 Bates.
Schmid Emrich, instrumentmkr, h 147 Spann av.
Schmid Frederick, sec and treas Indpls Mnfrs' and Carps' Union, h 468 N Capitol av.
Schmid Harry, lab, h 71 Smith.
Schmid John C (J C Schmid & Sons), h 244 Fletcher av.
Schmid John H (J C Schmid & Sons), h 94 Quincy.
Schmid Joseph, foreman, h 52 Prospect.
Schmid Joseph J, bkkpr J S Cruse, b 52 Prospect.
Schmid J C & Sons (John C, John H and Edward C F), stone yard, 329 Bates.
Schmid Margaret E (wid Charles H), b 244 Fletcher av.
Schmid Wm, stonecutter, h 80 Bloomington.

Farm and City Loans
25 Years' Successful Business.
THOS. C. DAY & CO,
Rooms 325 to 330 Lemcke Building.

Schmidlap Hamline (wid Lewis), b 996 N Alabama.
Schmidt, see also Schmid, Schmitt, Smith and Smythe.
Schmidt Adam (Rosenberg & Schmidt), r 173½ E Washington.
Schmidt Adolph J, plumber, h 43 S Dorman.
Schmidt Adolph R, clk, b 493 W 22d (N I).
Schmidt Albert, lab, b 370 S Illinois.
Schmidt Alonzo, clk Indpls Mnfrs' and Carps' Union, b 425 S New Jersey.
Schmidt Alvin L, phys St Vincent's Infirmary, b 162 N New Jersey.
Schmidt Anna F (wid Charles), h 432 S Meridian.
Schmidt Anthony, b 298 N West.
Schmidt Anthony, lab, h 300 W Morris.
Schmidt Anton, saloon, 362 Shelby, h same.
Schmidt Anton, saloon, 364 Virginia av, h 366 same.
Schmidt August C, tailor, 22 S Illinois, h 281 E North.
Schmidt Augustus, florist, h 1240 N Illinois.

SCHMIDT BENJAMIN F, Hardware and Groceries, 497-499 W 22d (N I), Tel 1293; h 493 same.

Schmidt Benno, cooper, h 171 Madison av.
Schmidt Bertha L, stenog, b 450 S Delaware.
Schmidt Carl, carp, h 180 Ramsey av.
Schmidt Carl, drayman, h 207 Lincoln la.
Schmidt Carl, driver, h 9 Wendell av.
Schmidt Caroline (wid Andrew), h 631 W Vermont.
Schmidt Catherine (wid Christian), h 154 Carlos.
Schmidt Cathryne, clk Nathan Kahn, b 111 Greer.
Schmidt Charles, butcher, h 273 Eureka av.
Schmidt Charles A, clk County Treasurer, h 62 W Walnut.
Schmidt Charles D, driver, h 179 Maple.
Schmidt Charles H, varnisher, b 672 Home av.
Schmidt Charles J (Krull & Schmidt), h 282 E South.
Schmidt Charles L, optician, h 1244 Bond (N I).
Schmidt Charles L, trav agt, h 531 N Alabama.

EAT
QUAKER BREAD
ASK YOUR GROCER FOR IT.
THE HITZ BAKING CO.

BICYCLES $5 DOWN. MONTHLY. Best Wheels. Best Terms. WHEELMEN'S CO. 31 W. OHIO ST. LONG DISTANCE TEL. 1855.

J. H. TECKENBROCK House, Sign and Fresco Painter, 94 EAST SOUTH STREET.

FIDELITY MUTUAL LIFE PHILADELPHIA, PA. A. H. COLLINS, Gen. Agt. Baldwin Blk. RATES REASONABLE. SOUND BEYOND QUESTION. BUSINESS-LIKE IN PRACTICE.

BITUMINOUS COAL ▸ Edwards ortp Coal and Mining Company ROOMS 42 AND 43 WHEN BUILDING.

ESTABLISHED 1876. TELEPHONE 168.
CHESTER BRADFORD,
SOLICITOR OF PATENTS,
AND COUNSEL IN PATENT CAUSES.
(See adv. page 6.)
Office:—Rooms 14 and 16 Hubbard Block, S. W. Cor. Washington and Meridian Streets, INDIANAPOLIS, INDIANA.

Schmidt Charles T, finisher, b 968 S Meridian.
Schmidt Christian H, varnisher, h 13 Carlos.
Schmidt Clarence, lab, b n s Brookville rd 2 e of Line (I).
Schmidt Conrad, yardman, b 74 Yeiser.
SCHMIDT C F BRANCH INDIANAPOLIS BREWING CO, south end Alabama, Tel 690.
Schmidt Diedrich, b 179 Maple.
Schmidt Dietrich, lab, h 44 Kennington.
Schmidt Edward, brewer, h 67 W 12th.
Schmidt Edward, painter, h 97 Nebraska.
Schmidt Edward H, florist, b 142 Hosbrook.
Schmidt Edward H (Inland Chemical Co), h 273 N Delaware.
Schmidt Edwin, painter, b 1244 Bond (N I).
Schmidt Elizabeth (wid Frederick), b 273 N Delaware.
Schmidt Elizabeth (wid Matthew), h 463 S Missouri.
Schmidt Ernst W T, driver Clemens Vonnegut, h 209 Lincoln la.
Schmidt Frank J, plumber, b 672 Home av.
Schmidt Frank X, driver, h 17 Harvey.
Schmidt Frederica (wid Adolph), h 111 Greer.
Schmidt Frederick, clk L E & W R R, b 281 E North.
Schmidt Frederick, mach, h 667 Madison av.
Schmidt Frederick H, jeweler, 32 Jackson pl, h 34 Elm.
Schmidt Frederick W, carp, h 619 E New York.
Schmidt George, clk Krull & Schmidt, h 11 Bates al.
Schmidt George, farmer, h n s Brookville rd 2 e of Line (I).
Schmidt George, meats, 666 S Meridian, h 632 S Meridian.
Schmidt George F, packer Eli Lilly & Co, b 121 Dunlop.
Schmidt George P, mach hd, b 631 W Vermont.
Schmidt Gertrude (wid Andrew), h 130 Spring.
Schmidt Gottlieb H, tailor, 640 Virginia av, h 642 same.

BUY THE BEST.
Outing BICYCLES $85
MADE BY
HAY & WILLITS MFG. CO.
76 N. PENN. ST. Phone 598.

Schmidt Gustavus W, foreman, b 136 W 1st.
Schmidt Harald, trav agt, h 425 S New Jersey.
Schmidt Helmuth, drayman, h 205 Lincoln la.
Schmidt Helmuth jr, drayman, b 205 Lincoln la.
Schmidt Henry, butcher, h 734 Shelby.
Schmidt Henry, clk, h rear 122 College av.
Schmidt Henry, clk, h e s Jones 3 s of Central av (I).
Schmidt Henry, driver, h 548 S West.
Schmidt Henry, lab, h 121 Dunlop.
Schmidt Henry, cabtmkr, b 355 S East.
Schmidt Henry, lab, b 205 Lincoln la.
Schmidt Henry, shoemkr, 366 Shelby, b 362 same.
Schmidt Henry C, butcher, h 111 Coburn.
Schmidt Henry P, carp, b 121 Dunlop.
Schmidt Herman, bartndr, b 196 Indiana av.
Schmidt Herman F, clk, h 34 Carson.
Schmidt Isaac F, clk, b 273 N Delaware.
Schmidt Jacob, h 133 Shelby.
Schmidt Jacob, h 493 S West.
Schmidt Jacob, lab, h 24 Nevada.
Schmidt Jacob, lab, b 307 Shelby.
Schmidt Jacob, lab, b 631 W Vermont.
Schmidt Jacob F, grocer, 105 Broadway, h 103 same.
Schmidt John, baker, h 62 Mayhew.
Schmidt John, driver, h 27 Yeiser.
Schmidt John A, lab, h 145 Kansas.
Schmidt John D, city agt M O'Connor & Co, b 179 Maple.
Schmidt John J, driver, h 24 Douglass.
Schmidt John J, mach hd, h 45 Barth av.
Schmidt John W, treas Polar Ice Co, h 740 N Delaware.
Schmidt Leonard H, tailor, h 60 Maple.
SCHMIDT LORENZ, Sec German Fire Insurance Co of Indiana; also Real Estate, Loan and Rental Agt, Office 27-33 S Delaware, Tel 1237; h 162 N New Jersey.
Schmidt Louis C, wheelmkr, h 685 McLene (N I).
Schmidt Louisa (wid George), b 105 Buchanan.
Schmidt Louisa H, restaurant, 24 N Delaware, h 1240 N Illinois.
Schmidt Magdalena (wid David), h 448 Indiana av.
Schmidt Maria (wid Thomas), h 322½ E Washington.
Schmidt Marie E (wid Frederick W), b 273 N Delaware.
Schmidt Mary (wid Otto), janitress, h 401 S Delaware.
Schmidt Mary A (wid Nicholas), h 327 N Pine.
Schmidt Nicholas, painter, h 455 S West.
Schmidt Oscar, clk Ger Fire Ins Co of Ind, b 162 N New Jersey.
Schmidt Oscar, clk, b n s Brookville rd 2 e of Line (I).
Schmidt Oscar W, trav agt, b 273 N Delaware.
Schmidt Otto H, mach, h 112 John.
Schmidt Paul F, barber, 69 E Washington, b 111 Greer.
Schmidt Peter, h 394 E Market.
Schmidt Peter P, plumber, b 672 Home av.
Schmidt Philip, shoemkr, 137 Ft Wayne av, h 672 Home av.
Schmidt Raphael, baker, 412 S Meridian, h same.
Schmidt Richard, b 179 Maple.
Schmidt Richard, clk, b 179 Maple.

ROOFING MATERIAL C. ZIMMERMAN & SONS, SLATE AND GRAVEL ROOFERS, 19 SOUTH EAST STREET.

PUMPS Chain Pumps, Driven Wells and Deep Water Wells. Repairing Neatly Done. Cisterns Built. CHARLES KRAUSS', 42 S. PENN. ST. TELEPHONE 465.

Collars and Cuffs Laundered in Best of Style. Domestic or High Gloss Finish

Schmidt Robert G, lab, b 414 Union.
Schmidt Rosa, h 142 Hosbrook.
Schmidt Rosina (wid John), b 137 Shelby.
Schmidt Wm, bartndr, b 968 S Meridian.
Schmidt Wm, florist, b 111 Andrews.
Schmidt Wm, huckster, r 149½ E Washington.
Schmidt Wm, surveyor, b n s Brookville rd 2 e of Line (I).
Schmidt Wm A, baker, h 470½ Virginia av.
Schmidt Wm C, bartndr, h 204 Shelby.
Schmidt Wm C, clk, b 394 E Market.
Schmidt Wm H, clk, b 399 S Delaware.

SCHMIDT WM A, Treas Marion County and City of Indianapolis, 23 Court House, h 273 N Delaware.

Schmitt Anna, b 48 Buchanan.
Schmitt Anselm, bartndr, h 89 Clifford av.
Schmitt Catherine (wid John), h 40 Arizona.
Schmitt Edward, cigarmkr, h 540 Jefferson av.
Schmitt Edward L, clk, b 434 N New Jersey.
Schmitt Edward N, painter, h 455 S West.
Schmitt Emil T, mach hd, h 94 Kansas.
Schmitt Emma, news dealer, 22 N Illinois, h 434 N New Jersey.
Schmitt Eugene A, electrician, b 105 St Mary.
Schmitt George, h 219 Spring.
Schmitt Jacob, lab, h 18 Eckert.
Schmitt John, cigar mnfr, 404 S Meridian, h same.
Schmitt Joseph, engr, h 122 Clifford av.
Schmitt Leonard, h 29 W McCarty.
Schmitt Mary, dressmkr, 404 S Meridian, h same.
Schmitt Michael J, car rep, b 89 Clifford av.
Schmitt Nicholas, lab, b 40 Arizona.
Schmitt Theobald, baker, h 404 Excelsior av.
Schmitt Wm A, mngr Emma Schmitt, h 434 N New Jersey.
Schmitt Wm H, uphlr, b 434 N New Jersey.
Schmitts Louisa, tailoress, b 504 Chestnut.
Schmitts Wm H, h 153 N Pine.
Schmitz Anna M (wid Mathias), h 679 Union.
Schmitz John, lab, b 679 Union.
Schmoe Edward H, carp, h 145 N State av.
Schmoe Louis C, carp, h 749 Nevada.
Schmoll Daniel E, cigarmkr, b 498 S Missouri.
Schmoll George Rev, h 498 S Missouri.
Schmuck, see also Smock.
Schmuck Adolph, reporter The Indpls News, h 171 N Pine.
Schmuck Emilie, teacher Public School No 14, b 171 N Pine.
Schmuck Otto L, tailor, b 171 N Pine.
Schmude Richard, finisher, b 655 Mass av.
Schmutte John F, foreman The Wm P Jungclaus Co, h 119 Kennington.
Schmutte John G, carp, b 119 Kennington.
Schnabel Christopher A, bookbndr, 46½ N Penn, h 25 Butler.
Schnabel John H, packer A Kiefer Drug Co, h 699 S Meridian.
Schnabel Oscar A, bookbndr, b 25 Butler.
Schnabel Sophia, bookbndr, b 25 Butler.
Schnable John, confr, 476 S East, h same.
Schnable Oscar, lab, b 476 S East.
Schnaible Emil M, clk, b 557 Madison av.
Schneck Luella, phys, 175 N Penn, b 124 N Alabama.
Schneeberger Frederick W, student, b 505 Madison av.
Schneewind Joseph L, sec Santa Clara Wine Co, b 410 N Delaware.

Richardson & McCrea,
79 East Market Street,
FIRE INSURANCE,
REAL ESTATE, LOANS,
AND RENTAL AGENTS.
Telephone 182.

Schneider, see also Snider and Snyder.
Schneider Albert F, tailor, b 474 S Meridian.
Schneider Amandus W, clk, b 20 Clay.
Schneider Andrew J, packer, h 20 Clay.
Schneider Anna C, b 378 Coburn.
Schneider Bertha, matron Protestant Deaconess Hospital, h 118 N Senate av.
Schneider Carolina (wid John), h 762 Charles.
Schneider Catherine (wid Michael), h 14 Clay.
Schneider Charles C, clk J S Cruse, b 285 S Olive.
Schneider Charles E, gluer, h 711 S Meridian.
Schneider Christopher J, grinder, h 147 W South.
Schneider Della, h 598½ N West.
Schneider Effie, b 134 Downey.
Schneider Eleanora, nurse 118 N Senate av.
Schneider Frank, boilermkr, h 19 Chadwick.
Schneider George, clk, h 330 S State av.
Schneider George F, mach hd, b 711 S Meridian.
Schneider George W, mach hd, h 7 Jefferson.
Schneider Harry V, helper, b 213 Coburn.
Schneider Harry W, cashr, h 20 Wyoming.
Schneider Henry L, h 302 S Penn.
Schneider Jacob, painter, h 136 Downey.
Schneider Jacob H, ins agt, h w s Newman 2 s of Stoughton av.
Schneider Jacob M, driver, h 234 E Morris.
Schneider John, sawmkr, h 38 Brett.
Schneider John B, saloon, 474 S Meridian, h same.
Schneider John C, grinder, b 134 Hosbrook.
Schneider John L, saloon, 474 S Meridian, h same.
Schneider John P, express, h 170 Prospect.
Schneider John P, mach, h 117 N Summit.
Schneider Joseph, cabtmkr, h 713 S Meridian.
Schneider Joseph, collr Indiana Reformatory, h 160 Randolph.
Schneider Joseph W, supt Indpls Brewing Co, h 179 E McCarty.
Schneider Karl, teacher Indpls College of Music, r 366 N Alabama.

SHORTHAND REPORTING......
CONVENTIONS, SPEECHES, SERMONS.
COPYING ON TYPEWRITER.
S. H. EAST, State Agent,
THE WILLIAMS TYPEWRITER
55 Thorpe Block, 87 East Market Street.

ERTEL STEAM LAUNDRY 28 and 28 N. Senate Ave. Telephone 1089.

ELLIS & HELFENBERGER Manufacturers of Iron Vases, Setees and Hitch Posts. 162-170 South Senate Ave. Tel. 958.

THE HOGAN TRANSFER AND STORAGE COMP'Y
Household Goods and Pianos Moved—Packed—Stored...... Baggage and Package Express Machinery and Safes a Specialty Cor. Washington and Illinois Sts. TELEPHONE No. 675.

The Central Rubber & Supply Co. PHONES. 79 S. ILLINOIS ST., INDIANAPOLIS, IND. Hose, Belting, Packing, Clothing, Druggists' Sundries, Bicycle Tires, Cotton Hose, Etc. New York Belting & Packing Co., L't'd.

The Provident Life and Trust Co. OF PHILADELPHIA.
Small Death Rate. Small Expense Rate. Safe Investments. Insurance in force $115,000,000
D. W. EDWARDS, General Agent, 508 Indiana Trust Building.

Schneider Louis, molder, h 173 Bane.
Schneider Louis, molder, h 378 Coburn.
Schneider Mary (wid Conrad), h 456 S East.
Schneider Mary (wid Paul), grocer, 203 Madison av, produce, 35 E Mkt House, h 203 Madison av.
Schneider Mary K (wid Conrad), h 213 Coburn.
Schneider Matilda, h 843 Chestnut.
Schneider Michael, grocer, 285 S Olive, h same.
Schneider Michael C C, mounter, h 19 Oriole.
Schneider Paul, blksmith, b 203 Madison av.
Schneider Philip H, tailor, h 1440 N Illinois.
Schneider Valentine (Mueller & Schneider), b 213 Coburn.
Schneider Valentine, tailor, h 89 Shelby.
Schneider Wm, driver, h 46 Sycamore.
Schneider Wm A, clk, h 843 Chestnut.
Schneider Wm G (Taylor & Schneider), h 52 Concordia.
Schneider Wm H F, molder, b 378 Coburn.
Schnell, see also Snell.
Schnell Elizabeth (wid Daniel), h 99 Bismarck av (H).
Schnell George D, carp, h 103 Bismarck av (H).
Schnell Henry, engr The Blacherne, h same.
Schnell Louis, waiter The Denison.
Schnell Marcus L, carp, h 91 Bismarck av (H).
Schnepf Louis, pastry cook, r 447 S Meridian.
Schnetzer Frederick, barber, h 74 W Ohio.
Schnewind Joseph L, trav agt, b 410 N Delaware.
Schnitker John H, meats, 433 E Georgia, h 431 same.
Schnull Gustav A (Schnull & Co), h 285 N Illinois, tel 814.
Schnull Henry (Schnull & Co), h 165 Central av, tel 1124.
SCHNULL & CO (Henry and Gustav A Schnull, Wm J and George G Griffin), Wholesale Grocers, 60-68 S Meridian, Tel 354.
Schober Christopher H, saloon, e s Western av 2 n of Fleet, h same.

Julius C. Walk & Son, Jewelers Indianapolis.
12 EAST WASHINGTON ST.

Schober Emil, bartndr, b e s Western av 2 n of Fleet.
Schober Wm, butcher, b 497 Madison av.
Schoch Henry, stonecutter, h 381 Fletcher av.
Schocher Wm, driver, h 54 N Belmont av (H).
Schocley James W, clk, h 140 Clarke.
Schoellkopf Eugene O, bkkpr Murphy, Hibben & Co, h 421 S Delaware.
Schoen, see also Schane.
Schoen Adam J, dyer, b n s Spann av 1 w of Auburn av.
Schoen Andrew, dyer, h n s Spann av 1 w of Auburn av.
SCHOEN BROS (Henry and John), Clothing Renovators, 29½ E Market.
Schoen Charles G, printer, h 122 Dunlop.
Schoen Edward, clk John Rauch, b 327 N Capitol av.
Schoen Henry (Schoen Bros), h s s Walnut av 2 w of Arlington av (I).
Schoen John (Schoen Bros), h 205 Hoyt av.
Schoen Joseph, agt, b 571 Virginia av.
Schoen Joseph F, cigarmkr, h 440 W Pratt.
Schoen Louis, bartndr, b 571 Virginia av.
Schoen Otto T, clk R M S, h 117 E 6th.
Schoen Sigmond, saloon, 577 Virginia av, h 571 same.
Schoenberger Edward, grocer, 676 N Senate av, b 775 same.
Schoendorf Nicholas, lab, h 532 Chestnut.
Schoeneman Emelia (wid Henry), h 448 E McCarty.
Schoeneman Engel (wid Wm), b 324 Union.
Schoeneman Frederick W, bookbndr, h 324 Union.
Schoenemann Charles H, lab, h 120 N Noble.
SCHOENEMANN JACOB H, Grocer, 185 Bismarck av (H), h same.
Schoenfeld Bernard S, clk, h 268 E St Clair.
Schoenig Joseph, lab, h 198 Meek.
Schoenkehn Andrew, polisher, h 947 Madison av.
Schoenman Isadore, ins agt, b 249 S Pine.
Schoenrogg Wm B, trav agt Syfers, McBride & Co, b 123 Coburn.
Schoenrogg Wm C, hostler, h 123 Coburn.
Schoershusen Christian H, carp, 109 Sanders, h same.
Schoessel Tillie K, dressmkr, 265 N Noble, b same.
Schoettle Christian F, clk Otto Schopp, b 485 S Illinois.
Schofield, see also Scofield.
Schofield Charles S, h 714 Broadway.
Schofield David B, farmer, h s w cor 22d and Sangster av.
Schofield Frank, livery, 180 E Wabash, h 86 S Noble.
Schofield George K, h 28½ Mass av.
Schofield George W, news agt, h e s Sangster av 2 n of Belle.
Schofield Henry, huckster, h 230 W Ohio.
Schofield Ida, teacher, r 36 Leon.
Schofield Wm, cabtmkr, b 175½ E Washington.
Schofield Wm, waiter, r 565 Broadway.
Schofield Wm A, druggist, 197 Christian av, h 630 Bellefontaine.
Scholl Charles, h 214 N Illinois.
Scholl Charles H, mach, h 159 Shelby.
Scholl Edwin R, lab, h 37 Drake.
Scholl Emilie A, notions, 117 E Mkt House, h 159 Shelby.
Scholl Jacob F, bkkpr, h 39 Agnes.
Scholl John, lab, h 18 Minkner.

OTTO GAS ENGINES | BUILDERS' EXCHANGE S. W. Cor. Ohio and Penn. Telephone 535.

Becker & Son Charles Becker Jacob Becker Jr. Merchant Tailors. 21 N. Penn St. Tel. 934

SALISBURY & STANLEY, Contractors and Builders, Office Store and Bank Fixtures & Repairing of all kinds done on short notice. 177 Clinton St. Indianapolis, Ind. TELEPHONE 99

SCHOLL LOGAN C, Propr Gem Steam Laundry, 37-39 Indiana av, b 214 N Illinois, Tel 1671.
Scholler Charles G, lab, h 171 Minnesota.
Scholler George J, barber, 511 Madison, b 171 Minnesota.
Scholler Walter T, clk, h 195 Buchanan.
Scholz Frederick J, State Treasurer, 43 State House, h 949 N Meridian.
Schomber Lewis M, fireman, h 45 Spann av.
Schomberg Edward W, finisher, h 28 Weghorst.
Schomberg Wm L, mngr Charles P Webb, h 243 N Alabama.
Schonacker Alphonzo G, city agt Sentinel Printing Co, h 165 Fayette.
Schonacker Anna D (wid Hubert), b 220 N New Jersey.
Schonacker Elizabeth, h 216 W New York.
Schonacker Hubert J, music teacher, 220 N New Jersey, h same.
Schonacker Hubert L, clk Assessment Bureau, b 165 Fayette.
Schonacker Louis, b 220 N New Jersey.
Schonacker Thomas A, plumber, b 165 Fayette.
Schonecker Andrew, dairy, s s Orchard av 1 e of Rural, h same.
Schonecker Emanuel, bartndr, r 136 Clifford av.
Schoolcraft Charles F, lab, b 9 Riley blk.
Schoolcraft Emma B (wid John F), b 1079 N Capitol av.
Schoolcraft May (wid Alexander), h rear 38 McIntyre.
Schoolcraft Nancy (wid Henry), h 9 Riley blk.
Schooler Charles, lab, b 179 Bright.
Schooler Frank P, grocer, 151 Hoyt av, h 122 same.
Schooley Benjamin F, printer, h 165 N Capitol av.
Schooley David, engr, h 37 Belmont av.
Schooley Elza, condr, b 506 Bellefontaine.
Schooley John L, lab, h 62 Ash.
Schooley Nathan R, carp, h 176 Eureka av.
Schooley Thomas, asst supt Marion County Work House.
Schoonover James S, bluing mnfr, 498 College av, h 54 Ruckle.
Schoonover Sarah (wid Stephen), b 226 N Delaware.
Schope Harry C, lab, b 41 Bismarck av (H).
Schopp Edward, brakeman, b 68 W South.
Schopp George, shoemkr, 20 S Illinois, h 68 W South.
Schopp John, lab, b 68 W South.
Schopp John, lab, r 140 Union.
SCHOPP OTTO, Druggist, 302 S Illinois, h same, Tel 1002.
Schoppe Adolph W mach hd, b 168 Dougherty.
Schoppe Edward A, mach hd, b 168 Dougherty.
Schoppe Wm A, tanner, h 168 Dougherty.
Schoppel Thomas A, cooper, r 192 S Illinois.
Schoppenhorst Amelia, dressmkr, 426 E Vermont, b same.
Schoppenhorst Frank H, bkkpr Wm Schoppenhorst, h 535 E Ohio.
Schoppenhorst Philippina (wid George H), h 426 E Vermont.
Schoppenhorst Wilhelmina C (wid Wm H), h 299 E Ohio.
SCHOPPENHORST WM, Merchant Tailor, 18 N Penn, h 317 College av.

Henry H. Fay,
40½ E. WASHINGTON ST.,
FIRE INSURANCE, REAL ESTATE,
LOANS AND RENTAL AGENT.

Schoppmann Catherine (wid Wm), b 160 Pleasant.
Schorling Albert, lab n w cor State and Willow.
Schorling Henry, collr, h 88 N New Jersey.
Schorling John, lab, b 437 N Pine.
Schorn John, driver, h 188 Indiana av.
Schorn John B, clk, h 92 Indiana av.
Schort, see also Short.
Schort Emma M, bkkpr, b 1341 N Senate av.
Schort Louisa C (wid Victor), h 1341 N Senate av.
Schort Minnie L, b 1341 N Senate av.
Schort Wm, mach hd, b 1341 N Senate av.
Schortemeier Anna, cashr, b 354 S East.
Schortemeier Elizabeth S, bkkpr, b 354 S East.
Schortemeier Henry E, grocer, 304 S East and 104 Broadway, h 354 S East.
Schory Theodore Rev, pastor St John's German Evangelical Church, h 142 Dunlop.
Schott Charles E, plumber, 58 W Maryland, b 1058 W Washington.
Schott Jacob, meats, 97 E Mkt House, h 678 Chestnut.
Schott John, lab, h 64 Chadwick.
Schott John F, clk, b 549 S West.
Schott John H, h 23 Shover (W I).
Schottle Christian, clk, b 485 S Illinois.
Schove Wm E, finisher, h 143 Ft Wayne av.
Schowe Anna (wid Frederick), h 1 Water.
Schowe Arthur, clk H Lieber Co, b 1 Water.
Schowe Catherine (wid Jacob), b 9 Gatling.
Schowe Frederick W, b 469 N Capitol av.
Schowe Frederick W, carp, h 9 Gatling.
Schowe Frederick W, trav agt Charles Mayer & Co, h 112 Middle Drive (W P).
Schowe George F, grocer, 201 Fayette, h same.
Schowe Harry, trav agt H Lieber Co, b 1 Water.
Schowe Jacob H, lab, h 9 Water.
Schowe John H, lab, b 716 Morris (W I).
Schowe Louis W, clk Albert Gall, h 69 Elm.
Schowe Margaret (wid Wm), h 530 S West.
Schowe Wm J, trav agt Charles Mayer & Co, b 13 Warren.

JAS. N. MAYHEW,
MANUFACTURING
OPTICIAN
LENSES AND FRAMES A SPECIALTY.
No. 13 North Meridian St., Indianapolis.

LUMBER | Sash, Door and Planing Mill Work. | Balke & Krauss Co. Cor. Market and Missouri Streets.

FRIEDGEN'S TAN SHOES are the Newest Shades
Prices the Lowest. 19 North Pennsylvania St.

SAMUEL LAING General Job Work in Sheet Metal of all Kinds 72 AND 74 E. COURT STREET.

M. B. WILSON, Pres. W. F. CHURCHMAN, Cash.
THE CAPITAL NATIONAL BANK,
INDIANAPOLIS, IND.
Make collections on all points in the States of Indiana and Illinois on the most favorable rates.
Capital, - - $300,000
Surplus and Earnings, 50,000
No. 28 S. Meridian St., Cor. Pearl.

Schower Wm, butcher, b 497 Madison av.
Schrader, see also Schroeder and Shrader.
Schrader Albert, car rep, h 83 Arizona.
Schrader Anthony, h 276 N Liberty.
Schrader Anthony H, clk Taylor & Taylor, h 96 Highland av.
Schrader August, lab, b 40 N Belmont av (H).
Schrader Charles H (C H & E H Schrader), r 457½ Virginia av.
Schrader Charles H, lab, h 587 W Washington.
SCHRADER CHRISTIAN, China, Glass and Queensware, 72-74 E Washington, r 107 The Shiel, Tel 1314.
SCHRADER CHRISTIAN A, Wholesale Grocer, 74-78 S Penn, Tel 1013; h 994 N Alabama, Tel 178.
SCHRADER C H & E H (Charles H and Edward H), Grocers, 154 E Washington, Tel 1641; 453-457 Virginia av, Tel 940.
Schrader Edward H (C H & E H Schrader), r 457½ Virginia av.
Schrader Fanny N (wid Henry F), h 322 N New Jersey.
Schrader Frank, lab, h 97 Bates.
Schrader Frank H, lab, b 97 Bates.
Schrader Frederick, shoes, 65 W Washington, h Brighton Beach nr Floral av.
Schrader George E, storekpr C C C & St L Ry, h 186 Deloss.
Schrader Henry, lab, h 587 W Washington.
Schrader Henry C, patrolman, h 215 Ingram.
Schrader Herman H, lab, b 40 N Belmont av (H).
Schrader Herman H, lab, b 307 N Pine.
Schrader John H, tmstr, h e s Brookville rd 4 s of Washington.
Schrader Josephine (wid Frank), housekpr 41 State.
Schrader Louisa (wid Christian H), b 171 E Merrill.
Schrader Mary M (wid Frederick), h 307 N Pine.
Schrader Rudolph S, cigarmkr, b 364 E Market.

MONEY
Loaned on Short Notice at Lowest Rates.
TUTTLE & SEGUIN,
Tel. 1168. 28 E. Market St.

Schrader Sophia (wid Charles), b 627 Marlowe av.
Schrader Sophia D (wid Charles), h 40 N Belmont av (H).
Schrader Wm, mach, b 359 S Alabama.
Schrake Henrietta, supervising prin Public School No 9, b 325 N Delaware.
Schramm Carl H, clk, b 78 E St Joseph.
Schramm John B, trav agt Pearson & Wetzel, b 78 E St Joseph.
Schramm John C A, h 78 E St Joseph.
Schramm Louis J, finisher, b 63 Peru av.
Schreck Calvin, fireman, b e s Brightwood av 7 s of Willow (B).
Schreckengost Charles W, carp, h 93 Woodruff av.
Schreckengost Elijah, carp, h 324 Cornell av.
Schreckengost Frank W, carp, h 144 Clarke.
Schreckengost Monroe, engr, b 41 Yandes.
Schreiber Alvin F, florist, h 24 N Rural.
Schreiber Barthold, baker, b 621 S Meridian.
Schreiber Frank, baker, r 450 S Delaware.
Schreiber Frederick, carp, 120 Palmer, h same.
Schreiber Theodore, collr, b 349 Orange.
Schreiner Bernhardt, molder, h 307 S Penn.
Schreiner Wm, jeweler, 427 Madison av, b 307 S Penn.
Schreyer John, salesman Frommeyer Bros, b 118 Prospect.
Schreyer John P, trav agt, h 118 Prospect.
Schroeder, see also Schrader and Shrader.
Schroeder Albert, saloon, 299 S Capitol av, h same.
Schroeder August, driver, h 87 Kansas.
Schroeder Edward, meats, 76 E Mkt House, h 23 Short.
SCHROEDER GUSTAV T, Retail Dealer in Boots and Shoes, 175 E Washington, h 1117 E Michigan.
Schroeder Max, trav agt, h 154 Bellefontaine.
Schroer Edward B, clk C C C & St L Ry, b 636 Chestnut.
Schroer Edward E, grand sec Royal Arcanum, 43 Thorpe blk, h 1639 N Illinois.
Schroer Frank H, finisher, h 43 Dunlop.
Schroer Henry H, h 591½ S Meridian.
Schroer Henry W, clk, h 219 E St Clair.
Schroer Mary J (wid Bernard), h 636 Chestnut.
Schrolucke Bertha C, stenog Indiana Bicycle Co, b 98 Yeiser.
Schrolucke John W, plater, h 98 Yeiser.
Schrolucke Wm H, grocer, 905 Madison av, h 756 S Meridian.
Schroth Henry J, baker, r 189 Elm.
Schroth Maud (wid Henry), h 42½ Malott av.
Schroth Nicholas, lab, h 87 Lord.
Schrotz Joseph, mach hd, h 245 Coburn.
Schrotz Joseph G, varnisher, b 245 Coburn.
Schrotz Leonard F, varnisher, b 245 Coburn.
Schrowe Herman, lab, h 376 S Missouri.
Schrowe Wm F, lab, h e s Wallack 2 n of Belt R R.
Schroy James A, photog, b 239 Indiana av.
Schroy Jane (wid Jeremiah), h 239 Indiana av.
Schroy Wm J, genl bkkpr Singer Mnfg Co, h 153 Cornell av.
Schrum Frank, lab, b 2 S Brightwood av (B).
Schubert Andrew, lab, b 267 S Capitol av.
Schubert Charles A, shoes, 191 Shelby, h 183 Orange.

PAPER BOXES, MANUFACTURED BY SULLIVAN & MAHAN 41 W. PEARL STREET.

DIAMOND WALL PLASTER { Telephone 1410
BUILDERS' EXCHANGE.

Schubert Frank, packer, h 15 Gresham.
Schubert Frederick, architect, h 50 Grandview av (H).
Schubert George, h 328 N West.
Schubert George A, plastr, 347 N West, h same.
Schubert Harry M, clk, b 347 N West.
Schubert John, lab, b 50 Grandview av (H).
Schubert Wm E, butcher, b 497 Madison av.
Schuch Charles H, molder, h 88 Bradshaw.
Schuch Peter A, lab, h 15 S Senate av.
Schuch Samuel, molder, h 153 King av (H).
Schuck, see also Shuck.
Schuck Anna, stenog Western Furniture Co, b 219 Coburn.
Schuck Benjamin H, fireman, h 136 Hoyt av.
Schuck Louis, brewer, h 219 Coburn.
Schuck Samuel (Schuck & Hurst), h Grandview av 2 e of city limits (H).
Schuck & Hurst (Samuel Schuck, Ernest G Hurst), real est, 144 Michigan (H).
Schuesler, see also Schussler.
Schuesler Edward, bottler, b 681 Madison av.
Schuesler Wm, saloon, 681 Madison av, h same.
Schuessler Wm F, clk The Denison, b same.
Schuh Henry, engr, h 180 Minerva.
Schuh John, h 243 E Morris.
Schuler Ambrose F, supervisor Insane Hospital.
Schuler Edward, driver, b 88 W Market.
Schuler Frank J, baker, h 186 Brookside av.
Schuler George, butcher, h 209 Dougherty.
Schuler George C, mach, h 132 Union.
Schuler Rufus, lab, h rear 289 Bright.
Schulhoff Gerhard, lab, h 378 S Illinois.
Schuller Carl H, clk L E & W R R, b 993 S Meridian.

SCHULLER JULIUS A, Importer and Dealer in Foreign and California Wines and Brandies, Wholesale and Retail, 110-112 N Meridian, h 993 N Meridian.

Schuller Theodore C, saloon, 110 N Meridian, b 993 S Meridian.
Schuller Wm J, uphlr, b 334 E Miami.
Schulmeister John F, lab, h 224 Minnesota.
Schulmeyer Bros (Wm and John), grocers, 150 St Mary.
Schulmeyer Carl W, clk S F Muehl, b 782 N Capitol av.
Schulmeyer Daniel, mason, h 50 Downey.
Schulmeyer Frederick W, h 150 St Mary.
Schulmeyer Henry, butcher, h 24 Haugh (H).
Schulmeyer Jacob, h n s Perkins pike 1 e of C C C & St L Ry.
Schulmeyer Jacob J, sawmkr, h 9 Hendricks.
Schulmeyer John, cigarmkr, b n s Perkins pike 1 e of C C C & St L Ry.
Schulmeyer John (Schulmeyer Bros), h 783 N Alabama.
Schulmeyer Louis, butcher, b 150 St Mary.
Schulmeyer Louis H, chemist, h 782 N Capitol av.
Schulmeyer Mary (wid Louis C), h 782 N Capitol av.
Schulmeyer Wm (Schulmeyer Bros), h 128 St Mary.
Schulmire Louis N, bricklyr, h 483 S East.
Schulte Alida (wid Herman), cigars, 512 S East, h same.
Schulte Angelina (wid Frank), b 299 S Alabama.

FRANK NESSLER. WILL H. ROST.
FRANK NESSLER & CO.
Tailors
56 EAST MARKET ST. (Lemcke Building),
INDIANAPOLIS, IND.

Schulte Elizabeth, folder, b 299 S Alabama.
Schulte Frederick W, lab, h 12 Singleton.
Schulte John C, trav agt, h 298 N Delaware.
Schulte Margaret (wid John), b 451 Union.
Schulte Maurice, clk Clemens Vonnegut, h 557 Morris (W I).
Schultheis Rupert, draughtsman, b 235 Cottage av.
Schultz, see also Schulz and Shultz.
Schultz Adolph, h 143 W Morris.
Schultz August, lab, h 52 Wallack.
Schultz Carl, packer, h 77 Kansas.
Schultz Carl A, lab, b 77 Kansas.
Schultz Charles, b 99 Tremont av (H).
Schultz Charles, engr, h 359 Indiana av.
Schultz Charles, music teacher, 77 E Walnut, h same.
Schultz Charles H, mach hd, h 753 S East.
Schultz Christian F, shoemkr, b 108 Weghorst.
Schultz George, lab, h 37 Maple.
Schultz George G, mach, h 640 Charles.
Schultz Herman, lab, h 16 Iowa.
Schultz Herman, lab, h 10 Wallack.
Schultz Isaac, pdlr, h 460 S Illinois.
Schultz Jacob, h 460 S Illinois.
Schultz John, h 473 W Michigan.
Schultz John H, finisher, h 804 S East.
Schultz Julius, truckman, h 109 Lincoln la.
Schultz Louis H, butcher, b 800 S East.
Schultz Louisa (wid Paul), h 888 S Meridian.
Schultz Mary, h 179 E New York.
Schultz Max M, lab, h 112 S Summit.
Schultz Paul O, lab, h 34 McRae.
Schultz Peter L, engr, h 800 S East.
Schultz Philip, b 61 Bicking.
Schultz Philip, lab, h 39 Wisconsin.
Schultz Rachel, queensware, 85 E Mkt House, h 460 S Illinois.
Schultz Tobias, tinner, h 66 Morton.
Schultz Wm, lab, b 179 E New York.
Schultz Wm, mach hd, b 16 Iowa.
Schultz Wm (Schultz & Sommer), h 106 Martindale av.
Schultz Wm A, lab, b 37 Maple.
Schultz Wm L, trav agt, h 130 Blackford.
Schultz & Sommer (Wm Schultz, Wm H Sommer), plastrs, 106 Martindale av.

ACORN STOVES AND RANGES
Haueisen & Hartmann
163-169 E. Washington St.
FURNITURE,
Carpets,
Household Goods,
Tin, Granite and China Wares, Oil Cloth and Shades

Fine Laundry Work our Specialty. Collars and Cuffs our Hobby. THE HOME LAUNDRY 197 S. Illinois St. Telephone 1769.

THE WM. H. BLOCK CO. DRY GOODS, MEN'S FURNISHINGS.
7 AND 9 EAST WASHINGTON STREET.

Fidelity and Deposit Co. of Maryland. BONDS SIGNED.—LOCAL BOARD John B. Elam, Albert Sahm, Smiley N. Chambers, John M. Spann.
GEORGE W. PANGBORN, General Agent, 704-706 Lemcke Building. Telephone 140.

74 EAST MARKET STREET Telephone 863.

JOSEPH GARDNER,
Hot Air Furnaces
With Combination Gas Burners for Burning Gas and Other Fuel at the Same Time.
37, 39 & 41 KENTUCKY AVE. Telephone 322

Schulz Albert G, mach, b 198 E Morris.
Schulz August, mach, h 198 E Morris.
Schulz Charles, clk, b 423½ Virginia av.
Schulz Frank B, lab, b 528½ S Meridian.
Schulz Henry, clk, h 282 Virginia av.
Schulz Herman H, sec and treas Balke & Krauss Co, b 272 N California.
Schulz Linda H, teacher Public School No 22, b 198 E Morris.
Schulz Louis, saloon, n s Washington 1 w of Insane Hospital (M J), h same.
Schulz Mary L (wid Albert), h 55 Davis.
Schulz Mary L, nurse, h 528½ S Meridian.
Schulz Otto, clk, b 282 Virginia av.
Schulz Otto M, printer, h rear 78 Bicking.
Schulze Walter O, lab, h 38 Water.
Schulzke Anton, lab, h 29 Applegate.
Schumacher, see also Shoemaker.
Schumacher Alexander J, clk John A Schumacher & Co, b 271 Christian av.
Schumacher Charles L, barber, b 30 Dickson.
Schumacher George, carp, h 21 Temple av.
Schumacher George jr, lab, b 21 Temple av.
Schumacher Henry, carp, b 21 Temple av.
Schumacher Henry A, foreman John A Schumacher Co, h 24 Windsor.
Schumacher John, carp, h 21 Temple av.
Schumacher John A (John A Schumacher Co), h 271 Christian av.
SCHUMACHER JOHN A CO (John A Schumacher), Contractors and Builders; also Planing Mill, 444-452 E St Clair, Tel 345.
Schumacher Max A, bkkpr John A Schumacher Co, b 271 Christian av.
Schumacher Michael (G Ittenbach & Co), h 1157 E Washington.
Schumacher Wm A, mach, b 21 Temple av.
Schumacher Wm M, mngr John A Schumacher Co, b 271 Christian av.
Schumacher Wm P, watchman, h 436 E St Clair.
Schumake Charles, lab, b 181½ S Meridian.
Schumaker Conrad H, h 71 Bismarck av (H).
Schumaker Frederick H, clk, b 71 Bismarck av (H).

J. S. FARRELL & CO.
Plumbing
Natural and Artificial Gas Fitting.
84 N. ILLINOIS STREET.
TELEPHONE 382.

Schumaker John M, driver, h 229 Fletcher av.
Schumaker Lulu, h 178 W Georgia.
Schumaker Luther M, clk H E Kinney, b 229 Fletcher av.
Schumaker Samuel E, mach, b 229 Fletcher av.
Schumaker Wm, coremkr, b 71 Bismarck av (H).
Schuman Hans, b 36 S Spruce.
Schuman Henry, clk L S Ayres & Co, h 73 Cornell av.
Schumann Henry, lab, b 47 S Spruce.
Schumann Frederick, baker, h 471 Bellefontaine.
Schumann John, lab, h 131 Cottage av.
Schumann Max, lab, h 47 S Spruce.
Schunk Henry, cooper, b 13 N California.
Schupp Henry, dairy n e cor 22d and Baltimore av, h same.
Schupp Louis, driver, b n e cor 22d and Baltimore av.
Schupp Wm, driver, b n e cor 22d and Baltimore av.
Schureman Mary W (wid Lafayette), b 295 E Ohio.
Schureman Thomas A, train dispatcher Belt R R, b 295 E Ohio.
Schurmann Bernard H, carpetlyr, h 717 S Meridian.
Schurmann Charles, sec International B and L Assn, h 78 W Michigan.
SCHURMANN EDWARD, Mngr The Androvette Glass Co, 6 Odd Fellows' Blk, Tel 1679; b The Denison.
Schurr Leonhard, jeweler, 78 Indiana av, b 76 same.
Schurr Margaret (wid Leonhard), h 76 Indiana av.
Schussler, see also Schuesler.
Schussler Abel, watchman, h 113 Spring.
Schussler Frank, meats, 28 E Mkt House, b 151 N Pine.
Schussler Stepanna, h 151 N Pine.
Schuster Joseph, tailor, h 529 E Market.
Schuster Justine, dressmkr, 131 Weghorst, h same.
Schuster Peter, fireman, h 131 Weghorst.
Schutte Charles C, pressman, r 42½ Kentucky av.
Schutte John A, woodwkr, h 108 S Noble.
Schutte Lewis H, bricklyr, h 468 Stillwell.
Schwab Charles, wagonmkr, cor 22d and Bellefontaine, b 958 Cornell av.
Schwab Charles W, bottler, h 9 Riley blk.
Schwab Frank M, sergt of police, h 413 Martindale av.
Schwab Gustav, gardener, h 1428 Schurman av (N I).
Schwab Louis, meats, 46 E Mkt House, h n s Washington 5 e of Rural.
Schwab Nicholas, produce, E Mkt House, h cor Eugene and canal (N I).
Schwabacher Joseph, agt, r 101 N New Jersey.
Schwager Charles, finisher, h 101 Agnes.
Schwager Joseph, finisher, b 101 Agnes.
Schwalb Caroline (wid Henry), h 244 N Noble.
Schwan, see Swan.
Schwanke Joseph, janitor Commercial blk, r 33 same.
Schwankhaus Benjamin G, mach, h 334 S Missouri.
Schwankhaus Frank W, mach, h 114 Douglass.
Schwankhaus Harry H, engr, h 211 Blake.
Schwankhaus Mary (wid Herman), h rear 128 Blake.

Insure Your Property With FRANK K. SAWYER

IF CONTINUED to the end of its dividend period, policies of the UNITED STATES LIFE INSURANCE CO., will equal or excel any investment policy ever offered to the public. E. B. SWIFT, Manager, 25 E. Market St.

Wm. Kotteman 89 & 91 E. Washington St. TELEPHONE 1742 Furniture

SHOW CASES WILLIAM WIEGEL 6 West Louisiana Street Opp. Union Station.

Schward Matilda (wid Leopold), confr, 356 Clifford av, h same.
Schwartz, see also Swartz.
Schwartz Augusta (wid Joseph), h 333 Alvord.
Schwartz Augustus, finisher, b 23 Maria.
Schwartz Caroline (wid Henry), h 83 Patterson.
Schwartz Charles A, tile setter, h 46 Cornell av.
Schwartz Daniel, lab, h 176 Martindale av.
Schwartz David, pdlr, h 157 Maple.
Schwartz Edward, tailor, r 174 E Washington.
Schwartz Edward H, bottler, h 23 Maria.
Schwartz Emil G, lab, h 106 Wisconsin.
Schwartz Felix, bartndr, b 606½ Virginia av.
Schwartz Harvey J, fireman, b 3 N Station (B).
Schwartz Helen (wid Peter), h 238 Spring.
Schwartz Henry, molder, h 29 Warman av (H).
Schwartz Herman C, wheelmkr, b 350 Talbott av.
Schwartz Joseph W, lab, h 146 Martindale av.
Schwartz Louis, tailor, 362 Mass av, h same.
Schwartz Martin, saloon, 589 S Meridian, h 599 same.
Schwartz Mary A (wid John), b 350 Talbott av.

SCHWARTZ MAURICE, Druggist, 350 Talbott av, cor 14th (old) or 22d (new), Tel 229; h same.

Schwartz Maurice, tinner, b 124 S Olive.
Schwartz Morris, tailor, r 120 Indiana av.
Schwartz Paul C, mach, b 135 E Washington.
Schwartz Peter H, collr Home Brewing Co, h 30 Fenneman.
Schwartz Rose, opr Cent U Tel Co, b 333 Alvord.
Schwartz Rudolph J, lab, h 41 Haugh (H).
Schwartz Samuel, clk, b 23 S West.
Schwartz Theresa H, opr Cent U Tel Co, b 333 Alvord.
Schwartz Wm A, cigarmkr, h 523 E 9th.
Schwartz Wm B, lawyer, 94½ E Washington, h 524 same.
Schwartz Wm D, house phys City Hospital, b n w cor Locke and Margaret.
Schwartz Wm K, clothing, 247 W Washington, h 23 S West.
Schwarz Elizabeth C, h 429½ S Meridian.
Schwarz John, baker, h 45 Sinker.
Schwarz John G, engr, b 40 School (B).
Schwarz Simon P Rev, asst rector Sacred Heart Church, h cor Union and Palmer.
Schwarzer Maximillian, painter, h 458 S Missouri.
Schwegel Barbara (wid Daniel), h 38 Arizona.
Schwegel Daniel, collarmkr, h 38 Arizona.
Schwegman Elizabeth, music teacher, 139 Windsor, b same.
Schwegman John C, tmstr, h 25 Harvey.
Schwegman Louis, clk, b 139 Windsor.
Schwegman Wm, grocer, s e cor Windsor and Orange av, h 139 Windsor.
Schweikle Jacob F (Schweikle & Prange), h 331 E Vermont.
Schweikle Jacob F jr, bkkpr State Bank of Indiana, b 331 E Vermont.
Schweikle & Prange (Jacob F Schweikle, Frederick W Prange), wagonmnfrs, s e cor Market and Davidson.

We Buy Municipal ~ Bonds ~
THOS. C. DAY & CO,
Rooms 325 to 330 Lemcke Bldg.

Schweinsberger Henry, packer, h 97 W Morris.
Schweitzer Charles A, barber, b 180 N Noble.
Schweitzer Frederick G Rev, pastor First Evangelical Church, h 135 N East.
Schweitzer Henry, carp, b 12 Pleasant av.
Schweitzer Jacob, carp, h 12 Pleasant av.
Schweitzer Wm, drayman, h e s Denny 5 n of Washington.
Schwenk Caroline (wid Louis), grocer, 260 Blake, h same.
Schwenk George E, clk, b 260 Blake.
Schwenzer Charles, drugs, 928 S Meridian, h same.
Schwert Charles, h 420 W 22d (N I).
Schwicho Charles S, finisher, b 1057 Madison av.
Schwicho Frederick W, butcher, h 96 Kansas.
Schwier Bros (Henry C and Charles H), grocers, 518 E Washington.
Schwier Charles H (Schwier Bros), h 516½ E Washington.
Schwier Christian F, grocer, 689 E Washington, h 693 same.
Schwier Christina S (wid Christian F), h 550 E Washington.
Schwier Frederick W, clk, h 150½ College av.
Schwier Henry, baker, h 364½ Blake.
Schwier Henry C (Schwier Bros), h 419 E Pearl.
Schwier Wm C, grocer, 1087 E Michigan, h same.
Schwing Edward, lab, h 51 Bloomington.
Schwing Henry P, car rep, h 29 Beacon.
Schwing John, butcher, b 29 Beacon.
Schwing Wm P, car rep, h 30 Everett.
Schwinge Bertram, clk, b 999 Cornell av.
Schwinge Henry, trav agt, h 999 Cornell av.
Schwockowsky Charles W, lab, h 78 Weghorst.
Schwoerer Frank C, foreman Indpls Foundry Co, h 62 W 14th.
Schwoerer John W, clk Indpls Foundry Co, b 62 W 14th.
Schwomeyer Charles, lab, b 475 Indiana av.

EAT
QUAKER BREAD
ASK YOUR GROCER FOR IT.
THE HITZ BAKING CO.

CARPETS CLEANED LIKE NEW. TELEPHONE 818
CAPITAL STEAM CARPET CLEANING WORKS

BENJ. BOOTH PRACTICAL EXPERT ACCOUNTANT. Thirty years' experience. First-class credentials. Room 18, 82½ E. Washington St. Indianapolis, Ind.

The Old Reliable Sherman European Restaurant || 18 and 20 S. Meridian St. Established 8.

ESTABLISHED 1876. TELEPHONE 168.
CHESTER BRADFORD,
SOLICITOR OF PATENTS,
AND COUNSEL IN PATENT CAUSES.
(See adv. page 6.)
Office:—Rooms 14 and 16 Hubbard Block, S.W. Cor. Washington and Meridian Streets, INDIANAPOLIS, INDIANA.

Schwomeyer Charles H (Chas H Schwomeyer & Co), h 393 S Meridian.
Schwomeyer Chas H & Co (Charles H Schwomeyer, Wm Rathert), grocers, 399 S Meridian.
Schwomeyer Christian W, packer Murphy, Hibben & Co, h 282 Coburn.
Schwomeyer Frederick, molder, h 24 Germania av (H).
Schwomeyer Gustav, lab, h rear 81 Bright.
Schwomeyer Henry, grocer and cooper, 475 Indiana av, h same.
Schwomeyer Henry jr, lab, h 26 Wilcox.
Schwomeyer Henry H, plastr, h 399½ S Capitol av.
Scofield, see also Schofield.
Scofield Joseph, b 200 Bright.
SCOFIELD, SHURMER & TEAGLE, Refiners of Superior Illuminating and Lubricating Oils, Gasoline and Naphtha, n w cor Vermont and Bee Line Ry, Tel 1062.
Scofield Silvester, h 978 N Penn.
Scott Abram L, barber, h 318 W North.
Scott Albert, clk Kingan & Co (ltd), b 158 William (W I).
Scott Albert, lab, h 51 Traub av.
Scott Albert J, mach, h 465 W 22d (N I).
Scott Albert W, messenger Am Ex Co, h 140 Mass av.
Scott Alice G (wid Adam), h 136 W Maryland.
Scott Allen, lab, b 574 E St Clair.
Scott Allen, porter, b 31 Center.
Scott Almon A, clk, h n e cor Clifford and Waverly avs.
Scott Amanda, cook, h 60 Rhode Island.
Scott Andrew, pressman The Indpls News, r 5 Astor.
Scott Anna (wid Morris), b 296 N California.
Scott Anna M, teacher, b 277 Christian av.
Scott Anna P, confr, 88 Ft Wayne av, h same.
Scott Annie (wid Owen), h 1 Wood.
Scott Arthur E, carp, r 27 Traub av.
Scott Azariah, lab, h 80 Columbia al.
Scott Belle, h 340½ E Market.

CORRUGATED IRON CEILINGS AND SIDING.
ALL KINDS OF REPAIRING.
O. B. ENSEY,
TELEPHONE 1562.
COR. 6TH AND ILLINOIS STREETS.

Scott Calvin C, motorman, h 2 Allfree av.
Scott Catharine, cook, r 205 E Market.
Scott Charles, lab, h 206 St Mary.
Scott Charles C lab, b 115 N State av.
Scott Charles E, printer, r 5 Stewart pl.
Scott Charles H, engr, h 1054 W Washington.
Scott Charles M, uphlr, b 640 E 8th.
Scott Charles P, lab, b 211 Alvord.
Scott Clarence C (Emery & Scott), r 31½ Kentucky av.
Scott Claude, clk, r 1773 N Capitol av.
Scott Clinton L, clk, b 864 N Delaware.
Scott Daniel L, mach, b 26 Newman.
Scott David, lab, h 101 Ludlow av.
Scott David C, painter, h 534 W Shoemaker (N I).
Scott David C, porter, h 203 W 2d.
Scott David I (David I Scott & Co), h 137 Bellefontaine.
SCOTT DAVID I & CO (David I Scott), Carpenters and Builders, 77½ Mass av, Tel 729.
Scott Donald G, draughtsman, h 277 Christian av.
Scott Edward, h 60 Rhode Island.
Scott Edward, waiter, r 30 Roanoke.
Scott Edward M, lab, h 55 Howard.
Scott Edward W, carp, h 478½ E Washington.
Scott Eli J Rev, h 869 Bellefontaine.
Scott Eliza (wid Crawford), h 115 N State av.
Scott Elizabeth H (wid Charles F), h 295 E Vermont.
Scott Elizabeth T (wid Robert G), h 277 Christian av.
Scott Ella, h 1556 Graceland av.
Scott Elzy L, mach hd, b 805 E Washington.
Scott Ernest F, porter, h 166 Patterson.
Scott E Harbin (W R & E H Scott), b Hotel English.
Scott Fannie (wid Isaac), h 30 Roanoke.
Scott Flora, stenog, b 30 W Walnut.
Scott Frank I, foreman Frank Bird Transfer Co, h 223 N Noble.
Scott Frank L, photog, h 15 Park av.
Scott Freeman A, brakeman, h 300 E South.
Scott George, bellboy The Denison.
Scott George, lab, b 506 S Illinois.
Scott George, waiter, b 30 Roanoke.
Scott George A (W A Scott & Sons), b 563 Broadway.
Scott George H, barber, 13 S Alabama, b 222 W Ohio.
Scott George N, etcher, b 115 N State av.
Scott George W, horse breeder, h 83 Michigan (H).
Scott Grace L, b 200 Park av.
Scott Harriet A, teacher Public School No 10, b 227 E Walnut.
Scott Harvey A, bkkpr Hogan Transfer and Parcel Delivery Co, r 123 E Ohio.
Scott Harvey B, engr, h 275 E Merrill.
Scott Hattie A (wid George H), h rear 737 N Senate av.
Scott Henry, lab, h 438 Douglass.
Scott Henry, lab, h 570 N Senate av.
Scott Herbert I, sawmkr, h 218 W St Clair.
Scott Isabella, dressmkr, 109 Agnes, h same.
Scott Jackson, well driller, h e s Baltimore av 5 s of 17th.
Scott Jacob A, sawmkr, h 115 Huron.
Scott James, porter The Denison.
Scott James, lab, h 136 N Noble.

TUTEWILER UNDERTAKER, No. 72 WEST MARKET STREET. TELEPHONE 216.

THE PROVIDENT LIFE AND TRUST CO. OF PHILADELPHIA. Endowment Insurance presents the double attraction of relieving manhood and middle age from anxiety and old age from want. For particulars apply to D. W. EDWARDS, General Agent, 508 Indiana Trust Building.

THEODORE F. SMITHER — GRAVEL ROOFING MATERIALS 2 and 3-Ply Ready Roofing, Building Paper, etc. Office, 15 West Maryland St. Tel. 861.

Scott James L, yardmaster C C C & St L Ry, h 300 E South.
Scott James R, clk m of w P C C & St L Ry, h 75 E 7th.
Scott James S, bkkpr, h 109 Broadway.
Scott James T, lab, b 115 N State av.
Scott James W, carpetlyr, h 306 E Court.
Scott Jane (wid Elijah), h 40 Howard.
Scott Jane, confr, e s Baltimore av 5 s of 17th, h same.
Scott Jennie, stenog Auditor of State, b 53 Pleasant.
Scott Jesse H, cigars, 195 Mass av, b 269 N Alabama.
Scott Joel, carp, h 52 Cornell av.
Scott John, b 227 E Walnut.
Scott John, bkkpr, h 559 N Illinois.
Scott John, engraver, h 467 Virginia av.
Scott John, jeweler, 22 Indiana av, h 385 W New York.
Scott John, lab, h 570 N Senate av.
Scott John, lab, h e s Manlove av 3 s of 17th.
Scott John D, cook, h 466 Stillwell.
Scott John E (Scott & Rabb), h 677 N Illinois.
Scott John H, canmkr, h 552 Union.
Scott John M, carp, h 27 Traub av.
Scott John P, carp, b 27 Traub av.
Scott John T, phys, 1057 E Michigan, h same.
Scott John W, h 31 Shelby.
Scott Joseph, lab, b 34 S West.
Scott Josephine K (wid James H), r 86 The Windsor.

SCOTT J M, Druggist, s e cor Illinois and 7th, h 864 N Delaware, Tel 698.

Scott Kate, b 206 Agnes.
Scott Lafayette C, tel opr I U Ry Co, b 456 N Delaware.
Scott Lewis C, patrolman, h 805 E Washington.
Scott Mabel, stenog, b 1054 W Washington.
Scott Margaret M, stenog The Indpls News, b 559 N Illinois.
Scott Marion M, saloon, 25 E Georgia, h 25 Maple.
Scott Martha (wid Wallace), h 290 Indiana av.
Scott Mary, h 52 S Summit.
Scott Mary, nurse, r 133 N Penn.
Scott Mary E (wid Henry), h 31 Center.
Scott Mary E (wid Thomas A), b 318 E Wabash.
Scott Matilda, b 206 Agnes.
Scott Morin, b 80 Columbia al.
Scott Maurice, cupolatndr, h 71 Gimbel.
Scott Nelson, train dispatcher, b 456 N Delaware.
Scott Orlando, lab, b 104 Hadley av (W I).
Scott Orrin W, blksmith, b 812 Cornell av.
Scott Oscar E, clk Hildebrand Hardware Co, b 109 Broadway.
Scott Paul R, porter, h 46 Paca.
Scott Preston, porter, b 235 W Michigan.
Scott Ray Eldon, teller Capital Natl Bank, r 376 N Illinois.
Scott Reddon, lab, h 31 Willard.
Scott Richard, barber, h 320 W Court.
Scott Robert E, dep County Clerk, b 88 Broadway.
Scott Robert F, grain, 45 Board of Trade bldg, h 944 N Senate av.
Scott Robert H, painter, 231½ E Washington, h same.
Scott Roy M, student, b 869 Bellefontaine.
Scott Samuel A, porter, b 31 Center.

THE WHEN IS A WORLD BEATER.

Scott Samuel R (W A Scott & Sons), h 576 Park av.
Scott Sarah, milliner, 16 E Washington, b 115 N State av.
Scott Sarah E (wid Marion M), h 236 S Missouri.
Scott Settie (wid George), b 51 Union.
Scott Silas J, r 232 W Georgia.
Scott Thomas B, clk Ry Officials' and Employes' Accident Assn, h 516 N New Jersey.
Scott Thomas C, grocer and meats, 376 Clifford av, h 366 same.
Scott Thomas C, janitor, h 109 Agnes.
Scott Thomas D, trav agt, r 376 N Illinois.
Scott Thomas H, lab, h 27 Cushing.
Scott Thomas J, carp, b 275 E Merrill.
Scott Walter H, barber, h 124 Allegheny.
Scott Walter P (Walter P Scott & Co), h 135 Bellefontaine.

SCOTT WALTER P & CO (Walter P Scott), Carpenters and Builders, 27 Kentucky av.

Scott Walter T, clk I D & W Ry, r 12 Fair blk.
Scott Walter W, lab, b 471 Charles.
Scott Walter W, plumber, b 559 N Illinois.
Scott Webster K, clk Indiana Bicycle Co, h 187 Orange.
Scott Wm, b 1773 N Capitol av.
Scott Wm (Daniel Stewart & Co), h 530 N Delaware.
Scott Wm, carp, 220 Mass av, h 135 Bellefontaine.
Scott Wm, painter, r 30 McGill.
Scott Wm, tmstr, b e s Baltimore av 5 s of 17th.
Scott Wm A, carp, h 399 Blake.
Scott Wm A (W A Scott & Sons), h 563 Broadway.
Scott Wm A, meats, h 53 Holly av (W I).
Scott Wm A, porter, b 254 W 6th.
Scott Wm G, clk, b 136 W Maryland.
Scott Wm H, druggist, h 366 N East.
Scott Wm M, lineman C U Tel Co, h 237 Spring.
Scott Wm P, carp, h 505 Martindale av.
Scott Wm P, lab, h 120 Roanoke.

THE A. BURDSAL CO. Manufacturers of Paints and Colors VARNISHES, Brushes, Painters' and Paper Hangers' Supplies. 34 AND 36 SOUTH MERIDIAN STREET.

ELECTRICIANS DON'T FORGET US. ALL WORK GUARANTEED. C. W. MEIKEL, Tel. 466. 96-98 E. New York St.

DALTON & MERRIFIELD { LUMBER South Noble St., near E. Washington

KIRKHOFF BROS.
Steam and Hot Water Heating Apparatus,
Plumbing and Gas Fitting.
102-104 SOUTH PENNSYLVANIA ST.
TELEPHONE 910.

Scott Wm R (W R & E H Scott), b Hotel English.
Scott Wm T, bartndr, b 60 Rhode Island.
Scott Wm W, drugs, 525 N Illinois, b 88 Broadway.
SCOTT W A & SONS (Wm A, George A and Samuel R), Proprs Indiana Screen Factory and Mnfrs Bank and Office Furniture, Store Fixtures, Counters, Shelving, Etc, 591-593 Central av, near 14th, Tel 1128. (See front cover.)
SCOTT W R & E H (Wm R and E Harbin), State Mngrs Equitable Mutual Life Association of Waterloo, Iowa, 66½ N Penn.
Scott Zaidee A, bkkpr Ward Bros Drug Co, b 81 W 2d.
SCOTT & RABB (John E Scott, Albert Rabb), Lawyers, 62-63 Lombard Bldg, Tel 237.
Scotten Alva H, h 88 Ramsey av.
Scotten David, h 88 Ramsey av.
Scotten Washington T, carp, h 23 Arbor av (W I).
SCOTTISH RITE A AND A, Joseph W Smith Sec, 29-37 S Penn.
Scotton Albert B, trav agt, h 45 Huron.
Scotton Herod L, stairbldr, h 18 N William (W I).
Scotton Wm E, grocer, 413 W Addison (N I), h same.
Screes Albert E, butcher, b 163 Hill av.
Screes Walter T, grocer, n e cor Willow and Hope (B), h 44 School (B).
Scribben James, lab, b 350 S Alabama.
Scribner Albert G, huckster, h 462 W McLene (N I).
Scrimsher Carl F, supt H P Wasson & Co, h 269 E St Clair.
Scrimsher Iva M, teacher Public School No 33, b 629 Bellefontaine.
Scrimsher Jasper W, carp, h 629 Bellefontaine.
Scriven Mary V (wid Gardner R), b 112 Hoyt av.
Scriven Michael, lab, h 35 Valley.

LIME
BUILDING SUPPLIES,
Hair, Plaster, Flue Linings,
The W. G. Wasson Co.
130 INDIANA AVE. Tel. 989.

Scroggins Daisy O, opr C U Tel Co, b 240 Virginia av.
Scroggins Dalton, clk, b 240 Virginia av.
Scroggins Jennie (wid George), h 184 Bright.
Scruggs Dora B, grocer, h 577 Bellefontaine.
Scrugham George W, painter, h 252½ Mass av.
Scudder Edward D, engr, h 585 W Washington.
Scudder Henry, pdlr, b 709 Mass av.
Scudder James R, engr, h 23 Birch av (W I).
Scudder Jane (wid Wm), b 36 W Ohio.
Scudder John, livery, 36 W Ohio, h same.
Scudder Mary E (wid Edward D), h 152 College av.
Scudder Matte E, sec Hoosier Packing Co, b 152 College av.
Scudder Oliver E, filer, h 73 N Judge Harding (W I).
Scudder Sophronia C, h 77 Lee (W I).
Scudder Wm L, polisher, h 62 Sheffield (W I).
Scudder Willis L, stereotyper The Indpls Journal, b 152 College av.
Scull Wm O, paperhngr, h 443 Ash.
Sculley Catherine, dressmkr, b 128 E Merrill.
Sculley Edward P, driver, b 128 E Merrill.
Sculley Johanna (wid Michael), h 128 E Merrill.
Scullin Thomas F (Scullin & Myers), r 327 Lemcke bldg.
SCULLIN & MYERS (Thomas F Scullin, Thomas J Myers), Proprs Indianapolis Pattern Works, 101 S Penn.
Scully John P, lab, b 23 Patterson.
Scully Matthew J, clk Consumers' Gas Trust Co, h 748½ E Washington.
Scully Michael, lab, h 23 Patterson.
Seales Edward P, driver, b 83 W 20th.
Sealiff Thomas, r 472½ E Washington.
Seaman Elizabeth (wid Charles T), h 434 W Shoemaker (N I).
Seaman Myron D, clk The Wm H Block Co, h 511 E 7th.
Seamans Joseph R, patrolman, h 434 W Shoemaker (N I).
Seaner Frank, gasfitter, b 332 E Miami.
Seaner George, mason, h 332 E Miami.
Seaner George H, cigarmkr, h 128 Spring.
Seaner John E, elevator opr, b 332 E Miami.
Seaner Wm, baker, b 332 E Miami.
Search Charles H, brakeman, b 594 Morris (W I).
Search Thomas, carp, h 67 Vine.
Searcy Lester, packer, b 106 River av (W I).
Searcy Wm, bellboy The Bates.
Searle Scott H, druggist, h 71 Gregg.
Searles Jasper, foreman, h 185 Fayette.
Searls Henry M, gasfitter, r 174½ W Washington.
Searls Wm, h 193½ S Illinois.
Searls Wm H, barber, h 193½ S Illinois.
Sears Andrew L, bricklyr, h 71 Quince.
Sears Bridget (wid Thomas), h 61 Fletcher av.
Sears Burrell R, lab, h e s Sheldon 1 n of Clyde.
Sears Claude M, bkkpr Indiana Paper Co, b 38 W St Joseph.
Sears George T, clk, b 61 Fletcher av.
Sears George W, clk, b 28 Lawn (B).
Sears Henry E, driver, h 1 Guffin.
Sears Jacob, lab, b 575 Highland av (N I).
SEARS JOHN W, Justice of the Peace, 91½ E Court, h 28 Lawn (B).

INDIANA ELECTROTYPE CO. :: BEST WORK. LOWEST PRICES.
23 WEST PEARL ST., INDIANAPOLIS, IND. JOB WORK. BOOK PLATES. BEST PATENT BASE ON THE MARKET.
All Orders Promptly Filled.

Parlor, Bed Room, Dining Room, Kitchen, Furniture W. H. MESSENGER, 101 E. Wash. St., Tel. 491.

ALL KINDS OF HEAVY AND LIGHT GRAY IRON CASTINGS } McNamara, Koster & Co. Phone 1593. 212-218 S. Penn. St. } Foundry and Pattern Shop

Sears Martin F, bartndr, b 118 Meek.
Sears Mary (wid Thomas), h 118 Meek.
Sears Oscar W, chemist A Kiefer Drug Co, r 440 N Meridian.
Sears Robert B, trav agt Wm B Burford, b 38 W St Joseph.
Sears Ross G, presser, b 28 Lawn (B).
Sears Walter C, repairer Outing Bicycle Co, b 28 Lawn (B).
Sears Wm A, clk, h 61 Fletcher av.
Seasongood, Stix, Krouse & Co, Jonas F Johnson agt, clothing, 146 S Meridian.
Seaton Henry D, porter, h 450 Blake.
Seaton Lawson (Vanderwood & Seaton), h 174½ Indiana av.

SEATON WM D, Hatter, Agt for Dunlap Hats, 27 N Penn, h 235 Park av.

Seaton Wm H, phys, 44 E Ohio, h 235 Park av.
Seay Isaac S, turner, h 67 Maxwell.
Sebastian Delmar H, clk Model Clothing Co, h 31 N Spruce.
Sebastian Irvin H, h 1055 W Michigan.
Sebastian Tabitha A (wid John C), h 34 S Arsenal av.
Sebastian Wm, carp, r 175 W Ohio.
Sebato John, cabtmkr, b 506 W Udell (N I).
Sebel Adolph, shoes, 253 W Washington, h same.
Sebern Elizabeth H (wid James W), h 619 N Meridian.
Sebern Horace E, contr, b 619 N Meridian.
Sebern John S, cigars, 93 S Illinois, b 455 N Meridian.
Sebern Julia (wid Samuel), b 455 N Meridian.
Sebern Mary J (wid Harrison A), b 359 Jefferson av.
Sebern Wm S, clk, b 619 N Meridian.
Sebold John, sawmkr, b rear 405½ S Delaware.
Sebree John E, molder, h 79 Marion av (W I).
Seburn Harvey T, foreman, h 39 E McCarty.
Seburn Wm, supt, h 865 N Alabama.
Sechrist John, lab, h 79 Springfield.
Sechrist John G, coremkr, b 79 Springfield.
Seckelson Emelia (wid Jacob M), h 120 Elm.
Secor Sidney B, foreman Carlon & Hollenbeck, h 137 St Mary.
Secord Norval A, salesman Pearson's Music House, h 518 Talbott av.
Secrest Bates H, stenog Hide, Leather and Belting Co, b 25 Shelby.
Secrest Carrie F, music teacher, 25 Shelby, h same.
Secrest Charles R (Bowen & Secrest), r 17 Fair blk.
Secrest Nathan A, horse trader, h 25 Shelby.
Secretary of State's Office, Wm D Owen Secretary of State, 2 State House.
Secrist George H, saloon, 190 Dillon, b 188 same.
Secrist Henry A, confr, r 5 Miller blk.
Secrist John, bartndr, b 188 Dillon.
Secrist Perry, architect, b 134 Spring.
Secttor Lester, saloon, 131 E Washington, h 257 N Liberty.

SECURITY MORTGAGE LOAN CO, 207-209 Indiana Trust Bldg.

Security Savings and Loan Association, Kenneth G Reid sec, 42 N Delaware.
Sedam Alexander H, trav agt, h 404 Cornell av.

Henry H. Fay,
40½ E. WASHINGTON ST.,
FIRE INSURANCE, REAL ESTATE,
LOANS AND RENTAL AGENT.

Sedam James E, bricklyr, h 882 Milburn (M P).
Sedam John E, dairy, e s Cornelius 1 n of 30th (M), h same.
Sedam Philip, farmer, h e s N Senate av 1 n of 29th.
Sedan Anna (wid Charles), h 139 Eddy.
Sedan Frank, lab, b 139 Eddy.
Sedan Thomas, lab, b 139 Eddy.
Sedenburg Albert, plumber, b 255½ E Washington.
Sedenburg Wm, lab, b 277 E Washington.
Sedwick Benjamin F, clk, b 933 N Illinois.
Sedwick Charles W, clk, h 993 N Penn.
Sedwick James B (A Baber & Co), h 933 N Illinois.
Sedwick James B jr, bkkpr, h 822 Ash.
See Harry P, finisher, b 67 S Reisner (W I).
See John W, blksmith, h 223 S McLain (W I).
Seebah Peter, clk, h 105 Tremont av (H).
Seeds Cordelia A (wid George W), b 57 Lexington av.
Seeds Russel M, chief clk Secretary of State, h 181 East Drive (W P).
Seegmiller Frederick, h 874 N Delaware.
Seegmiller Wilhelmina, supervisor of drawing Public Schools, b 874 N Delaware.
Seehofer Frank, cabtmkr, h rear 251 Virginia av.
Seehofer Joseph, clk, b rear 251 Virginia av.
Seek Herman, porter Murphy, Hibben & Co, h rear 281 S New Jersey.
Seel George J, finisher, h 668 S East.
Seele Christian J (Franke & Seele), h 199 Prospect.
Seeley Edward N, plumber H A Goth, h 71 Cincinnati.
Seeley George C, fixturehngr, b 308 N Liberty.
Seeley Henry C, h 308 N Liberty.
Seeley Henry C jr, tinner, b 308 N Liberty.
Seeley Wm F, carp, b 308 N Liberty.
Seely Jane W, h 195 College av.
Seely Martin W, lab, r 410 E Walnut.
Seely Susan (wid Martin), h 27 Alvord.
Seely Theophilus A, h 44 Hosbrook.
Seeman Anna, nurse, 294½ Mass av, h same.

WILL GO ON YOUR BOND
American Bonding & Trust Co.
Of Baltimore, Md. Approved as sole surety by the United States Government and the different States as Sole Surety on all Forms of Bonds.
W. E. BARTON & CO., General Agents,
504 Indiana Trust Building.
LONG DISTANCE TELEPHONE 1918.

THE FRED DIETZ CO. WOODEN PACKING BOXES MADE TO ORDER. FACTORY AND WARE HOUSE TRUCKS. 40 Madison Avenue. Telephone 654.

BUSINESS EDUCATION A NECESSITY. TIME SHORT. DAY AND NIGHT SCHOOL. SUCCESS CERTAIN AT THE PERMANENT, RELIABLE Indianapolis BUSINESS UNIVERSITY

NEW YORK FILTER MFG. CO. Filters for Water-Works, Boiler Plants, Laundries, Hotels, Private Residences, Etc. | Henry R. Worthington, 64 S. Pennsylvania St. Long Distance Telephone 284.

UNION CO-OPERATIVE LAUNDRY (COMPOSED OF UNION LAUNDRY GIRLS.) NOS. 8, 40 AND 42 VIRGINIA AVENUE. T. E. SOMERVILLE, MANAGER. TELEPHONE 1269. INDIANAPOLIS, IND.

HORACE M. HADLEY
INSURANCE AND LOANS
66 E. Market Street, Basement
TELEPHONE 1540.

Seeman Carrie, nurse, 294½ Mass av, h same.
Seeman Josephine, nurse, 294½ Mass av, h same.
Seery Thomas F, mach, h 61 Lexington av.
Seesenguth Charles G, cabtmkr, h s w cor Orange av and Windsor.
Sefton George, condr, r 22 N Brightwood av (B).
Segal Jacob, tailor, 274 S Illinois, h same.
Segar Elias L, sec Brown Straw Binder Co, h 303 E New York.
Segar Elizabeth (wid Lewis), h 247 N Liberty.
Segar Henry D, trav agt, b 440 N New Jersey.
Segar Rachel, asst prin Public School No 9, b 247 N Liberty.
Segar Simon, clk, b 247 N Liberty.
Segar Solomon L, collr, b 247 N Liberty.
Seger Jonathan M, h 239 N Illinois.
Seguin Edward S R (uttle & Seguin), h 26 E Michigan.
Sehrt Frederick, clk, b 30 S Senate av.
Seiberling J F & Co, Hugh E Larrimer agt, farm impts, 38 Kentucky av.
Seibert, see also Siebert.
Seibert Charles W, painter, b 638 W 22d (N I).
Seibert Cicero, city fireman, b 751 N Capitol av.
Seibert Edward J W, mach hd, b 66 Morton.
Seibert Ferdinand C, painter, 209 N Pine, h same.
Seibert George W, loans, h 1479 N Illinois.
Seibert George W jr, sec and treas Fulmer-Seibert Co, h 185 S New Jersey.
Seibert Henry, painter, 71 Peru av, h same.
Seibert Henry G, clk Am Ex Co, b 528 S East.
Seibert Henry J, h 78 Arizona.
Seibert Ida M, dressmkr, 36½ W Washington, h same.
Seibert Jacob T, lab, h n s Vorster av 1 e of Milburn (M P).
Seibert Mary E (wid Hiram), h 143 Pleasant.
Seibert Royal S, city fireman, h 107 Newman.

COLLECTIONS
MERCHANTS' AND MANUFACTURERS' EXCHANGE
Will give you good service.
J. E. TAKKEN, Manager,
Union Building, over U. S. Pension Office.
73 West Maryland Street.

Seibert Samuel M, h 638 W 22d (N I).
Seibert Thomas B, woodwkr, h 655 W 22d (N I).
Seibert Walter W, clk, h 1473 N Illinois.
Seibold John, cabtmkr, h 735 S Meridian.
Seid Charles C, mach hd, h 165 Blake.
Seidelman Henry C, mach, b 391 Bellefontaine.
Seidensticker Adolph (Florea & Seidensticker), b 377 N East.
Seidensticker Charles A, clk, b 224 S East.
Seidensticker George (Florea & Seidensticker), h 193 N Noble.
Seidensticker Louis H, tailor, 70 S Austin (B), h same.
Seidensticker Margaret (wid Frederick), h 224 S East.
Seidensticker Minna (wid Adolph), h 377 N East.
Seidensticker Oswald, clk Ger Fire Ins Co of Ind, h 459 Bellefontaine.
Seidensticker Wm C, saloon, 233 S East, b 224 same.
Seiders Charles W, attendant Insane Hospital.
Seiders Wm H, h 410 Broadway.
Seifer Joseph A, toolmkr, h 67 S Noble.
Seifer Louis, lab, h 220 Columbia av.
Seifert, see also Seyfort.
Seifert Eugene J, lab, h 180 Columbia av.
Seifert George, driver, h 148 Laurel.
Seifert John, lab, h 793 Mass av.
Seifert Joseph, lab, h 36 Chadwick.
Seifert Joseph, lab, h 11 Gresham.
Seifert Odelia (wid John), b 180 Columbia av.
Seifert Philip, lab, b 493 S West.
Seifert Wm L, bkkpr The Denison, b same.
Seigle, see also Siegel.
Seigle Edward H, tmstr, h 24 Dearborn.
Seigle Wm H, candymkr, b 24 Dearborn.
Seilaff, see Sielaff.
Seiler Gertrude (wid Saffel), b 64 Shelby.
Seiler Joseph F, butcher, b 64 Shelby.
Seinbrueggs Frank, blksmith, h 136 Lee (W I).
Seiner Charles F (Cooney, Seiner & Co), tinware, 87 E Mkt House, h 269 E New York.
Seiter Christopher, saloon, 476 E Washington, h same.
Seiter Kasimir, cooper, h 100 Union.
Seitz Charles, lab, h 259 Reisner.
Seitz Charles, saloon, 1100 E Washington, h same.
Seitz Frederick, baker, r 524 S East.
Seitz Jacob, baker Blind Inst, h 227 Coburn.
Seitz Jacob, butcher Insane Hospital.
Seitz Laura, teacher Public School No 39, b 227 Coburn.
Seitz Mary, stenog Emil Wulschner & Son, h 227 Coburn.
Seitz Wm R, bartndr, b 1100 E Washington.
Selb Matthias, saloon, 577 S Capitol av, h same.
Selby Edward, condr, h 148 Randolph.
Selby Francis M, fruits, 151 Hoyt av, h same.
Selby Mabelle, stenog, b 151 Hoyt av.
Selby Mary F (wid Joshua D), h 112 Blackford.
Selch Cornelius A, fireman, h 29 Hoyt av.
Selden Mary E (wid Frank), b 41 Fayette.
Self Albert L, clk Kahn Tailoring Co, b 225 E North.
Self Berry, clk Kahn Tailoring Co, h 225 E North.

CLEMENS VONNEGUT 184, 186 and 192 E. Washington St. | BUILDERS' HARDWARE, Building Paper. Duplex Joist Hangers

THE WM. H. BLOCK CO. 7 AND 9 EAST WASHINGTON STREET. **DRY GOODS,** DRAPERIES, RUGS, WINDOW SHADES.

Self David A, pressman, h 264 Fletcher av.
Self Herbert A, clk Kahn Tailoring Co, b 225 E North.
Self James D, clk, b 47 Woodruff pl.
Selig Abram (mngr), shoes, 20 N Penn, h 224 N Alabama.
Selig Augusta, dry goods, 170 W Washington, h 18 E Pratt.
Selig Herbert, clk Abram Selig, b 224 N Alabama.
Selig Jacob L, clk Abram Selig, b 224 N Alabama.
Selig Leopold, mngr, h 18 E Pratt.
Selig Moses, dry goods, 109 S Illinois, h 461 N Capitol av.
Selig Solomon K, trav agt, h 303 E Market.
Seligson Bernard, furrier, r 11½ W Washington.
Selking Charles H, wheelmkr, h 169 S Reisner (W I).
Selking Elizabeth (wid Wm), h 22 N Noble.
Selking Lovina (wid Wm), b 39 S McLain (W I).
Selking Wm L, finisher, h 39 S McLain (W I).

SELLARS ALBERT H, City Pass and Ticket Agt L E & W R R, 26 S Illinois, h 194 Broadway, Tel 1091.

Sellars Amanda B, teacher, r 171 N Capitol av.
Sellars Charles A (American Toilet Supply Co), sec National Harness Mnfg Co, r 28½ Mass av.
Selleck Roda E, teacher High School, r 30 W Vermont.
Seller Thomas P, phys, s e cor Ruth and Washington (M J), h same.
Sellers Blaine H, dentist, 29½ S Illinois, h 1696 N Illinois.
Sellers Charles A, clk Daniel Stewart Co, h 47 Andrews.
Sellers Daniel, stoves, 247 Indiana av, h 27 S Pine.
Sellers George, clk, h 134 Ruckle.
Sellers Jackson, lab, h rear 737 N Senate av.
Sellers John, collr, h 219 Douglass.
Sellers John, engr, b n s 8th 2 w of canal.
Sellers Marshall A, lab, h 48 Holloway av.
Sellers Richard, gasfitter, 129 Mass av, h same.
Sellers Samuel N, dentist, r 29½ S Illinois.
Sellers Sarah J, clothing, 129 Mass av, h same.
Sellers Wm T, books, 21 Virginia av, h 33 Ashland (W I).
Sellers Wm W, h 113 N Illinois.
Sellinghausen Louis F, motorman, h 27 Nebraska.
Sellmeyer Henry C, grocer, 350 E New York, h same.
Sells Abram, lab, h rear 24 Mulberry.
Sells Corwin P, bkkpr, b 982 N Meridian.
Sells Harry G, salesman M Sells & Co, h 207 College av.
Sells Michael (M Sells & Co), pres Indpls Packing and Rendering Co, h 982 N Meridian.

SELLS M & CO (Michael Sells, T Smith Graves), Live Stock Commission, Union Stock Yards (W I), Tel 21.

Selman Andrew G, phys, 680 E Washington, h same.

Selvage Charles B, packer, h 663 W Eugene (N I).
Selvage Edward L, bkkpr Atlas Engine Wks, b 706 Ash.
Selvage Jane E (wid John F), h 706 Ash.
Selvage Joseph W, bkkpr, h 605 Broadway.
Selvage Sarah E (wid Luther P), b 178 Virginia av.
Selvage Wm J, clk, h 593 W Eugene (N I).
Selwin John, h 86 S Shade (B).
Selzer Charles, blksmith, b 146 Lexington av.
Selzer Jacob, watchman, h 106 Michigan (H).
Selzer John, mach, h 48 Nebraska.
Selzer John, finisher, h 622 S East.
Selzer Maria (wid Carl), b 559 S State av.
Selzer Nicholas, barber, 247 E Morris, h 294 same.
Selzer Stephen, mach hd, b 622 S East.
Seman Joseph W, lab, h 89 Germania av (H).
Semans Thomas J, 28½ E Market, h 292 Clifford av.
Semmler Henry, tailor, 216 S Olive, h same.
Semon Herbert A, clk, b 464 N East.
Semones Wm, lab, h 402½ College av.
Senate Hotel, Emma H Karstetter propr, 50½ N Senate av.
Senefeld John P, clk Van Camp H and I Co, h 355 Fletcher av.
Seneff Jacob A, lab, h 54 Sheffield (W I).
Senff Arthur C, harnessmkr, h 269 N Noble.
Senges Philip H, lithog Wm B Burford, h 228 E McCarty.
Sengstock Charles A, foreman, h 292 W Morris.
Sengstock Dorothea, grocer, 292 W Morris, h same.
Sengstock Henry A, clk, b 292 W Morris.
Senior Charles D, switchman, h 145 Spann av.
Senior Ellen T (wid Zachariah), h 110 Hadley av (W I).
Senn Jacob, lab, b 152 Michigan (H).
Sennett Earle J M, clk, b 852 Bellefontaine.
Sennett John W, miller, h 1276 Northwestern av (N I).

GUIDO R. PRESSLER,
FRESCO PAINTER
Churches, Theaters, Public Buildings, Etc., A Specialty.
Residence, No. 325 North Liberty Street.

INDIANAPOLIS STEEL ROOFING AND CORRUGATING WORKS, 23 and 25 East South Street. S. D. NOEL, Proprietor.

DIAMOND WALL PLASTER { Telephone 1410 BUILDERS' EXCHANGE.

UNION TRANSFER AND STORAGE CO. Cor. E. Ohio St. and C., C., C. & St. L. R'y Tracks. BEST FACILITIES FOR STORING AND TRANSFERRING MACHINERY AND MERCHANDISE.

W. McWORKMAN

FIRE SHUTTERS,
FIRE DOORS,
METAL CEILINGS.

930 W. Washington St. Tel. 1118.

Senour Alfred W, baking powder, 92 E South, b n e cor Alabama and South.
Senour George R, foreman F R Jennings, r 156 Chestnut.
Senour Jackson, lab, h 184 Dougherty.
Senour Marion, lab, h 628 N West.
Senour Robert, h 36 Sheldon.
Senour Wm, clk, b 200 W New York.
Sensitive Governor Co, John R Allen pres, Oliver M Allen sec, bicycles, 100 S Capitol av.
Senti George R, ins agt, r 126 E 14th.
SENTINEL PRINTING CO, Wm S Fish Pres, Charles E Haugh Vice-Pres, John W Minor Sec and Treas, Book and Job Printers, 75, 77 and 79 W Market, Tel 503.
Sento, see Santo.
Sephus Minerva J (wid Joseph), b w s Caroline av 1 n of Hillside av.
Serff John H, ins adjuster, h 280 College av.
Sering Emmett G, lab, h n s 22d 1 w of Baltimore av.
Sering McKendra, mach, h 141 Shelby.
Sering Mathew T, mach hd, b 141 Shelby.
Sering Samuel, clk, b 108 Bright.
Seringer Ura (wid George), r 42 S Capitol av.
Serinski Moses, pdlr, h 129 Eddy.
Serles Berton D, clk, r 265 N Illinois.
Serrin James S, phys, 381 N New Jersey, h same.
Serriu Wm Y, trav agt, b 381 N New Jersey.
Server Augustus, lab, b 123 Hosbrook.
Servers Wm O, carp, h 34 Standard av (W I).
Service Sarah (wid Henry), h 114 Prospect.
Servoss George L, phys, 44 E Ohio, h 648½ College av.
Seth Joshua M, coachman, h 53 High.
Settegast Dora R (wid Wm J), b 1152 N Penn.
Settle Fielding T, boilermkr, h 30 Temple av.
Settle Jaco A, vulcanizer, b 283 E Georgia.
Settle Jesse E, clk, b w end University av (I).

GEO. J. MAYER,
MANUFACTURER OF
SEALS
STENCILS, RUBBER STAMPS, CHECKS, BADGES, DOOR PLATES, ETC.
5 S. Meridian St., Ground Floor. TEL. 1386.

Settle Jesse J, painter, h 136 Shelby.
Settle Mary A, supt ladies' hall Butler College, h same.
Settle Myron C, student, b w end University av (I).
Settles C Carr, bartndr, r 255 N West.
Settles John L, lab, b s w cor Railroad and Good av (I).
Settles John S, h s w cor Railroad and Good av (I).
Settles Louis, lab, h w s Madeira 4 s of Prospect.
Setzen Wm, shoemkr, 321 E Washington, h same.
Seuel Emanuel D, clk Merchants' Natl Bank, b 262 E Ohio.
Seuel Peter Rev, pastor German Evangelical Lutheran Trinity Church, h 262 E Ohio.
Seuel Theodore H, clk Severin, Ostermeyer & Co, h 180 Highland av.
Seuffert Henry J, mach, b 11 Jefferson av.
Seuffert Margaret (wid John G), h 11 Jefferson av.
Severence Charles V, carp, h Raymond and J M & I R R.
Severence Frederick C, painter, h 195½ E Washington.
Severin Henry (Severin, Ostermeyer & Co), h 573 N Meridian.
Severin Henry jr (Severin, Ostermeyer & Co), b 573 N Meridian.
SEVERIN, OSTERMEYER & CO (Henry Severin, Frederick Ostermeyer, Julius Wocher, Frederick Ostermeyer Jr, Henry Severin Jr), Wholesale Grocers, 51-53 S Meridian, Tel 15.
Severn Joseph, lab, b 25 S West.
Severns Edmond P, grocer, 148 Bloyd av, h 464 Bellefontaine.
Severson John P, messenger Am Ex Co, r 220½ S Meridian.
Sevier Milton, barber, h 120 Elizabeth.
Sewall Elmer C, buyer McKee Shoe Co, h 373 Park av.
Sewall May Wright (wid Theodore L), prin Girls' Classical School, h 343 N Penn.
Seward Arthur R, visitor Township Trustee's Office, h 276 S Delaware.
Seward Catherine (wid Elias H), h 128 Fletcher av.
Seward George B, tmstr, h 469 Ash.
Seward Martha (wid Samuel), b 44 Beaty.
Sewell Edward, switchman, h 6 Detroit.
Sewell John, baker, b 103 English av.
Sexton Johanna (wid John), h 213 Deloss.
Sexton John, proofreader, r 52½ S Illinois.
Sexton Mary M, stenog Brown-Ketcham Iron Works, b 213 Deloss.
Sexton Peter, lab, h 193 Hoyt av.
Sexton Thomas, mach, b 213 Deloss.
Sexton Timothy, clk C C C & St L Ry, b 193 Hoyt av.
Sextroh Henry W, bartndr, h 75 Union.
Seybold James H, marble cutter August Diener, h 9 Sylvan.
Seyffert Herman C, carp, h 137 S Olive.
Seyfort, see also Seifert.
Seyfort Louis, painter, h 47 Bates.
SEYFRIED HENRY, Insurance, 29 N Penn, h 71 Sanders.
Seyfried Jacob, clk, b 130 W Ray.
Seyfried John W, lab, b 346 Blake.
Seyfried Joseph C, molder, h 580 S Illinois.
Seyfried Mary, stenog H Seyfried, b 130 W Ray.
Seyfried Michael, mngr Indpls Storage and Transfer Co, b 130 W Ray.

A. METZGER AGENCY ESTABLISHED 1863. REAL ESTATE

LAMBERT GAS & GASOLINE ENGINE CO.
ANDERSON, IND. NATURAL GAS ENGINES.

Seyfried Rosalia (wid Henry), h 130 W Ray.
Seyler Frederick L, clk H Lieber Co, b 335 S New Jersey.
Seyler Nicholas, cigarmkr, h 335 S New Jersey.
Seymour Alonzo, janitor, b 312 E Court.
Seymour Anna (wid Wm G), h 449 W Michigan.
Seymour John W, switchman, h 67 Lynn av (W I).
Seymour Margaret, h 25 Ellsworth.
Seymour Nathaniel A Rev, pastor New Bethel Baptist Church, h rear 601 N Meridian.
Seytter Paul, collr, h 621 Marlowe av.
Shackleton Joseph P, patternmkr, h 64 Prospect.
Shackleton Wm H, supt Consumers' Gas Trust Co, treas Am Medical College, h 223 College av.
Shadbourne Maria (wid Madison), h rear 971 N Delaware.
Shade Fannie G (wid Reuben), h 166 W Georgia.
Shafer, see also Schaefer and Schafer.
Shafer Ada H, stenog Allison Coupon Co, b 319 S Alabama.
Shafer Alice, b 76 Beaty.
Shafer Harvey G, millwright, h 42 S State av.
Shafer Jacob, cooper, b 125 N West.
Shafer Martin J, mach, h 33 Evison.
Shaff, see also Schaaf.
Shaff Benjamin F, clk, h 146 W Vermont.
Shaffer Adolphus C, patrolman, h 280 Blake.
Shaffer Amasa, b 162 Walcott.
Shaffer Benjamin F, plumber, b 172 Pleasant.
Shaffer Carl E, electrician, b 430 Ash.
Shaffer Charles A, clk L S Ayres & Co, h 1184 N Illinois.
Shaffer Charles C, mach, h 92 Tremont av (H).
Shaffer Charles J, clk When Clothing Store, h 135 Hoyt av.
Shaffer Edward L, clk, h 59 Elm.
Shaffer Frank, plumber, b 172 Pleasant.
Shaffer Frank I, mach, h 1024 N Senate av.
Shaffer George W (Shaffer & Sangston), h 256 N East.
Shaffer George W, clk, h 1024 N Senate av.
Shaffer Harry, mach, h 875 Cornell av.
Shaffer Hayes R, electrician, b 280 Blake.
Shaffer Jacob, b 17 Holly av (W I).
Shaffer Jacob R, bartndr, h 165 Clinton.
Shaffer John D, helper, h 690 W Shoemaker (N I).
Shaffer John W, blksmith, h 80 Germania av (H).
Shaffer Maude, b 222½ E Washington.
Shaffer Nancy A (wid Jacob), h 79 N Liberty.
Shaffer Nellie B, music teacher, b 430 Ash.
Shaffer Newton, patrolman, h 141 Greer.
Shaffer Oscar C, carver, b s s Washington av 1 e of Downey av (I).
Shaffer Sarah L, h 175 W Michigan.
Shaffer Wallace F, clk, h 27 Park av.
Shaffer Walter M, contr, 172 Pleasant, h same.
Shaffer Wm, armature winder, b 280 Blake.
Shaffer Wm C, horseshoer, b 560 Ash.
Shaffer Wm H, horseshoer, 138 E 7th, h 560 Ash.
Shaffer & Sangston (George W Shaffer, Wm J Sangston), barbers, 205 Mass av.
Shaffner, see also Schaffner.
Shaffner Asa, cabtmkr, h 215½ E Washington.

THOS. C. DAY & CO.
Financial Agents and Loans.
We have the experience, and claim to be reliable.
Rooms 325 to 330 Lemcke Bldg.

Shaffner Lydia (wid Jacob), b 403 Pleasant.
Shake Charles C, fireman, b 112 N Dorman.
Shake Homer C, clk, h 125½ Oliver av (W I).
Shake Ira H, drugs, 125 Oliver av (W I), h 129 same.
Shake John P, lab, h 158 Madison av.
Shake Robert, lab, r 83 Cleaveland blk.
Shake Wm A, b 88 S Judge Harding (W I).
Shalamsky David, clk, b 233 E Washington.
Shallcross John, hostler, r 267 W Pearl.
Shallcross Thomas T, blksmith, h 496 Bellefontaine.
Shallcross Wm E, helper, h 496 Bellefontaine.
Shallenberger Alexander, contr, h 468 N Delaware.
Shallenberger Jacob M, janitor, b 32 Byram pl.
Shalls Earl, molder, b 169 Lexington av.
Shanahan Bartholomew, sawmkr, h 87 Maple.
Shanahan John J, condr, h 90 Spann av.
Shane, see also Schoen.
Shane Albert, lab, b 948 W Vermont.
Shane Alexander, supervisor of bridges and bldgs C C C & St L Ry, h 85 College av.
Shane Jerome R, express, h 103 S William (W I).
Shane Vida I (wid James E), clk C C C & St L Ry, h 7 Leota.
Shaneberger Albert H, trav agt W J Holliday & Co, b 81 W 2d.
Shaneberger Edgar L, civil engr, b 81 W 2d.
Shaneberger Edgar T, clk, b 326 N Senate av.
Shaneberger Ezra, clk, h 326 N Senate av.
Shaneberger Georgia M (wid Wm A), h 46 Bellefontaine.
Shaneberger Harry W, clk C C C & St L Ry, b 46 Bellefontaine.
Shaneberger Harvey F, foreman, h 214 W New York.
Shaneberger Lydia A, h 81 W 2d.
Shaneberger Roy C (Shaneberger & Lockwood), b 326 N Senate av.
Shaneberger & Lockwood (Roy C Shaneberger, Charles S Lockwood), proprs Progress Laundry, 322 E Washington.

EAT HITZ'S CRACKERS AND CAKES.
ASK YOUR GROCER FOR THEM.

BICYCLES $5 ... Best Wheels. WHEELMEN'S CO. 31 W. OHIO ST. LONG DISTANCE TEL. 1855.

J. H. TECKENBROCK General House Painter, 94 EAST SOUTH STREET.

FIDELITY MUTUAL LIFE—PHILADELPHIA, PA.
$75,000,000, Insurance In Force. $3,500,000, Death Losses Paid. $1,500,090, Surplus. A. H. COLLINS {General Agent, Baldwin Block.

BITUMINOUS COAL IN CAR LOADS TO DEALERS AND MANUFACTURERS. ROOMS 42 AND 43 WHEN BUILDING. Edwardsport Coal & Mining Co.

ESTABLISHED 1876. TELEPHONE 168.
CHESTER BRADFORD,
SOLICITOR OF PATENTS,
AND COUNSEL IN PATENT CAUSES.
(See adv, page 6.)
Office:—Rooms 14 and 16 Hubbard Block, S.W. Cor. Washington and Meridian Streets, INDIANAPOLIS, INDIANA.

Shaner Elmer, molder, b 157 Sheldon.
Shaner George A, paperhngr, h 73 Montana.
Shaner James W, paperhngr, h 175 Hill av.
Shaner Mary (wid Andrew C), h 157 Sheldon.
Shaner Warren A, paperhngr, b 157 Sheldon.
Shank Carlin H, clk C H & E H Schrader, b 519 Ash.
Shank Clara L, teacher Public School No 15, b n e cor Washington av and Line (I).
Shank Flora E, state sec Young Women's Christian Assn, 139 N Meridian, b n e cor Washington av and Line (I).
Shank Harry R, plumber, b 168 Mass av.
Shank, Joseph F, painter, h 587 S East.
Shank Samuel, h 519 Ash.
Shank Samuel H, student, b n e cor Washington av and Line (I).
Shank Samuel L, clk, b 519 Ash.
Shank Sarah F (wid John M), h 168 Mass av.
Shank Theophilus M, agt, h 76 Torbet.
Shank Wm H H, meats, s e cor Central av and Railroad (I), and 7 E Mkt House, h n e cor Washington av and Line (I).
Shanks James, lab, b 183 W South.
Shannon Bartholomew, mach, h 87 Maple.
Shannon Charles E, basketmkr, b 171 Davidson.
Shannon James E Rev, pastor First United Brethren Church, h 244 Keystone av.
Shannon Martin E, saloon, 1204 E Washington, h same.
Shannon Mattie, wrapper, b 338 N Noble.
Shannon Myra, bkkpr Western Horseman Co, b 260 Brookside av.
Shannon Samuel S, collr, h 149 N Penn.
Shannon Smith D, b 450 E Georgia.
Shannon Thomas E, barber, h 450 E Georgia.
Shannon Timothy, watchman, h 232 Prospect.
Shannon Wm, helper, h 182 Muskingum al.
Shannon Wm C, fireman, h 291 Fletcher av.
Shannon Wm F, produce, 7 E Mkt House, h 260 Brookside av.
Shannon Wm T, teacher Blind Institute.

Outing BICYCLES
..MADE BY..
HAY & WILLITS MFG CO.
76 N. Pennsylvania St. Phone 598.

Shantz, see also Schantz.
Shantz Harry D, clk U S Ex Co, h 115 Greer.
Shapero Benjamin, shoemkr, 327 E Washington, r same.
Shapland Harry, dyer, 131 N Meridian, h same.
Share Charles K, ins agt, h 27 Butler.
Share George K, h 27 Butler.
Share Louis A, novelties, cor Hanway and J M & I R R, b 27 Butler.
Sharits Frank G, clk, b 111 E Washington.
Sharkey John, engr, b 57 W Raymond.
Sharkey John H, clk C C C & St L Ry, b 289 English av.
Sharkey John J, special police Indiana Trust Co, h 57 Fayette.
Sharkey Martin J, foreman, h 218 W Georgia.
Sharkey Michael, boilermkr, h 289 English av.
Sharkey Michael, condr, r 259 Michigan av.
Sharkey Wm H, fireman, r 86 S State av.
Sharp Benjamin F, lab, h 139 Ft Wayne av.
Sharp Charles M, caller, h 47 English av.
Sharp, Clara F, boarding 325 S Meridian.
Sharp Daniel H, broommkr, h 381 W 2d.
Sharp Eva E, trimmer, b 168 E North.
Sharp Emmett S, cigarmkr, h 472 W Ontario (N I).
Sharp George, cigarmkr, h e s Range 1 s of Washington.
Sharp George, lab, h 288 Douglass.
Sharp Harry C, paperhngr, h 83 Paca.
Sharp Harry L, clk George J Marott, h 357 S Alabama.
Sharp Irwin, lab Blind Inst.
Sharp John C, contr, 85 Paca, h same.
Sharp Joseph, lab, b n s Howland av 2 e of Orchard.
Sharp Mary J, h 288 Fulton.
Sharp Mary J (wid Wm), h 167 W Market.
Sharp Stephen, engr, h 257 S Alabama.
Sharp Stephen O, tabletmkr, h 123 Nordyke av (W I).
Sharp Walter M, broommkr, b 381 W 2d.
Sharp Wm F, lab, h 528 W North.
Sharp Wm O, lumber, h 325 S Meridian.
Sharpe Andrew W, cigarmnfr, 353 S East, h same.
Sharpe Elizabeth C (wid Thomas H), h 850 N Penn.
Sharpe Harriet E (wid Calvin L), teacher Public School No 29, h 513 Broadway.
Sharpe James N, janitor, h 9 Center.
Sharpe Joseph K, real est, h 770 N Penn.
Sharpe Joseph K jr, sec and treas Am Buncher Mnfg Co and Indiana Mnfg Co, 401-405 Indiana Trust bldg, h 680 N Delaware.
Sharpe Randolph G, chief clk Central Union Tel Co, h 823 N Capitol av, tels, office 43, res 1702.
Sharpe Wm E, trav agt Atlas Engine Wks, b 850 N Penn.
Sharper Alfred W, bkkpr Mut Life Ins Co of Indiana, h 61 Prospect.
Sharpless Charles W, grocer, 550 Ash, h same.
Sharrard Newton I, clk, h 96 Chadwick.
Shartel Benjamin F, cigarmkr, h w s Range 1 s of Washington.
Shartle Ellis Y (R S Foster & Co), h 333 N New Jersey.
Sharts Sarah E (wid Wm), h 562 Park av.
Sharts Walter D, painter, h 432 E Vermont.
Shattuck Charles M, trav agt Holliday & Wyon, h 469 Bellefontaine.

C. ZIMMERMAN & SONS | SLATE AND GRAVEL ROOFERS 19 South East Street.

DRIVEN WELLS And Second Water Wells and Pumps of all kinds at CHARLES KRAUSS', 42 S. PENN. ST., Telephone 465.

ERTEL STEAM LAUNDRY 26 and 28 N. Senate Avenue. Tel. 18 ►► WE WILL CALL FOR AND DELIVER YOUR WORK. SATISFACTION GUARANTEED.

Shattuck Flora, stenog H P Wasson & Co, b 453 Ash.
Shauck Wm L, millwright, h 48 S William (W I).
Shaughnessy James T, lab, b 234 S West.
Shaughnessy John, clk, b 8 Huron.
Shaughnessy Joseph, boilermkr, h 42 Bicking.
Shaughnessy Michael, trucker, h 48 Concordia.
Shaughnessy Rose (wid John), h 46 Bicking.
Shaughnessy Thomas J, lab, h 72 Bicking.
Shaughnessy Wm, boilermkr, b 46 Bicking.
Shaw Albert, lab, b 172 S Missouri.
Shaw Alice (wid Martin), h 3 N Haugh (H).
Shaw Alphonso (Hawkins & Shaw), h Sherman House.
Shaw Augustus D, yardmaster, h 67 Ash.
Shaw Benjamin C, supt registry div P O, h 15 Dearborn.
Shaw Benjamin F, driver, h 202 Spann av.
Shaw Charles, lab, h 35 Cincinnati.
Shaw Charles G, clk County Recorder, b 67 Ash.
Shaw Christina (wid Robert), h w s Walker 1 s of Pendleton pike (B).
Shaw Corey H, driver Union Co-Operative Laundry, b 125 W Pratt.
SHAW DECORATING CO (Edward H Shaw), Wall Paper, 106-108 N Meridian. (See adv in classified Wall Paper.)
SHAW EDWARD H (Shaw Decorating Co), h 21 Morrison.
Shaw Eliza L (wid Daniel J), h 449 Talbott av.
Shaw Elizabeth, housekpr, b 25 Miley av.
Shaw Elmer, lab, b 111 E Washington.
Shaw Emerson, tmstr, h 1358 Indianapolis av.
Shaw Emsley H, dry goods, 466 Virginia av, h s e cor Dillon and Pleasant.
Shaw Frank M, trav agt, h 193 E South.
Shaw Frank S, veneerer, b 220 N East.
Shaw Hamilton, cook, r 12 Roanoke.
Shaw Harvey, lab, r 2 Susquehanna.
Shaw Harvey, cook, b rear 73 Howard.
Shaw James, clk, r 133½ E Washington.
Shaw James, coremkr, b 3 N Haugh (H).
Shaw James H, clk, b 277 N Delaware.
Shaw James M, agt, r 23 Indiana av.
Shaw Jeannette P, teacher High School, b 21 Morrison.
Shaw John, gardener, h rear e s Rural 1 n of Michigan.
Shaw John, dep marshal, h 18 King av (H).
Shaw John F, clk, r 10 Masonic Temple.
Shaw John G, clk Sherman House.
Shaw John J, painter, h 6 S Brightwood av (B).
Shaw John M, bkkpr The Shaw Decorating Co, b 21 Morrison.
Shaw John M, pres Moore & Co and mngr Kingan & Co (ltd), h 268 Park av.
Shaw John N, clk, b s e cor Dillon and Pleasant.
Shaw John W, lab, h 48 S Austin (B).
Shaw John W, tel opr, h 1076 W New York.
Shaw Kossuth N (Shaw & Vinson), b 98 Highland av.
Shaw Margaret A (wid Jeremiah), b 106 Minerva.
Shaw Martin, coremkr, b 3 N Haugh (H).
Shaw Melville F, sec and treas Puritan Spring Bed Co, h 180 East Drive (W P).
Shaw Nicias E, foreman, h 151 Belmont av.
Shaw Oran W, molder, b 390 W North.

EQUITABLE LIFE ASSURANCE SOCIETY OF THE UNITED STATES.
RICHARDSON & McCREA
Managers for Central Indiana,
79 East Market St. Telephone 182.

Shaw Pertle, lab, h 210 Newman.
Shaw Philip J, buyer N Y Store, b 495 Talbott av.
Shaw Rebecca A (wid John), h 143 Sharpe av (W).
Shaw Richard, lab, r 234 W Wabash.
Shaw Richard J, yardmaster, h 102 Stoughton av.
Shaw Robert, lab, b 337 W Maryland.
Shaw Robert D, fireman, b w s Walker 1 s of Pendleton av (B).
Shaw Rockford, clk L E & W R R, b Sherman House.
Shaw Samuel, dyer, h 472 W New York.
Shaw Thomas, molder, b 3 N Haugh (H).
Shaw Wm L, opr W U Tel Co, b 132 N Capitol av.
Shaw & Vinson (Kossuth N Shaw, Frank J Vinson), gents' furngs, 55 N Penn.
Shawber John, restaurant, 73 N Alabama, r same.
Shawhan Clare E, clk Home Savings Assn, r 24 W Walnut.
Shawhan Lorenzo R, mail clk L E & W R R, r 24 W Walnut.
Shawver Aruas P, agt, h 48 Prospect.
Shawver Emma (wid Christopher J), b 922 Ash.
Shayne Daniel, salesman J L Kavanagh, b The Bates.
Shea, see also O'Shea.
Shea Anna, b 108 Chadwick.
Shea Bartholomew, lab, b 301 Bates.
Shea Catherine, b 92 Phipps.
Shea Catherine N, h 19 W Pratt.
Shea Christina (wid Michael), b 933 N Meridian.
Shea Cornelius, packer, b 18 Henry.
Shea Cornelius, lab, h 314 S West.
Shea Cornelius jr, lab, b 314 S West.
Shea Daniel, boilermkr, h 20 Henry.
Shea Dennis, boilermkr, b 84 Chadwick.
Shea Dennis, brakeman, b 30 McKim av.
Shea Dennis, lab, b 301 Bates.
Shea Dennis B, weigher, b 275 English av.
Shea Ella M, dressmkr, b 30 McKim av.
Shea Ellen (wid Daniel), h 196 Bates.
Shea Ellen (wid Michael), h 30 McKim av.
Shea Emma, b 186 W South.

STENOGRAPHERS FURNISHED.
EXPERIENCED OR BEGINNERS, PERMANENT OR TEMPORARY.
S. H. EAST, State Agent,
The Williams Typewriter,
55 THORPE BLOCK, 87 EAST MARKET ST.

ELLIS & HELFENBERGER { ENTERPRISE FOUNDRY & FENCE CO. 162-170 S. Senate Ave. Tel. 958.

THE HOGAN TRANSFER AND STORAGE COMP'Y
Household Goods and Pianos Moved—Packed—Stored...... Baggage and Package Express Machinery and Safes a Specialty Cor. Washington and Illinois Sts. TELEPHONE No. 675.

The Central Rubber & Supply Co. ◆◆◆ Hose, Belting, Packing, Clothing, Druggists' Sundries, Bicycle Tires, Cotton Hose, Etc. New York Belting & Packing Co., L't'd. PHONE 2. 79 S. ILLINOIS ST., INDIANAPOLIS, IND.

A death rate below all other American Companies, and dividends from this source correspondingly larger.
The Provident Life and Trust Company
Of Philadelphia.
D. W. EDWARDS, General Agent,
508 Indiana Trust Building.

Shea Emma, h 17 Wood.
Shea Florance, lab, h 13 Lynn.
Shea Frank, gilder, h 33 Willow.
Shea Frank P, mach, b 196 Bates.
Shea George A, mach, h 797 E Market.
Shea Henry W, fruits, 276 W Washington, h 270 W Court.
Shea James, blksmith, h 407 Highland.
Shea James, carp, h 486 S Capitol av.
Shea James, lab, b 314 S West.
Shea James A, grinder, h 156 S Noble.
Shea James L, clk, h 415 E Georgia.
Shea James L, tallyman C C C & St L Ry, h 113 S Illinois.
Shea Jeremiah, city fireman, h 476 S Capitol av.
Shea Jeremiah, lab, h 126 Blackford.
Shea Jeremiah, lab, b 87 Leota.
Shea Johanna (wid Thomas R), h 26 Arch.
Shea John, foreman, h 275 English av.
Shea John, grocer, 200 W South, h 277 S Missouri.
Shea John, lab, h 511 S Capitol av.
Shea John, lab, h 17 Grant.
Shea John, lab, b 87 Leota.
Shea John, lab, b rear 24 Woodside av (W).
Shea John, shoemkr, 210 S Capitol av, h same.
Shea John D, lab, b 247 S Missouri.
Shea John E, helper, b 275 English av.
Shea John F, mach, b 126 Blackford.
Shea John J, clk, b 407 Highland av.
Shea Joseph E, switchman, h 33 Detroit.
Shea Julia (wid Dennis), h 247 S Missouri.
Shea Kate (wid Andrew), matron Union Station, h 2 Henry.
Shea Michael, b 407 Highland av.
Shea Michael, clk, b 277 S Missouri.
Shea Michael, lab, b 30 McKim av.
Shea Michael, lab, b 34 S West.
Shea Michael J, boilermkr, b rear 24 Woodside av (W).
Shea Michael J, fireman, b 258 Bates.
Shea Michael J, fireman, b 773 E Market.
Shea Nancy M, h 19 W Pratt.
Shea Nellie T, laundress, b 312 Coburn.
Shea Patrick, butcher, b 247 S Missouri.
Shea Patrick, lab, h 198 English av.
Shea Patrick, lab, h 74 Morton.

Julius C. Walk & Son,
Jewelers
Indianapolis.
12 EAST WASHINGTON ST.

Shea Patrick, switchman, h 84 S Noble.
Shea Roger, butcher, b 314 S West.
Shea Thomas, blksmith, h 773 E Market.
Shea Thomas, lab, h 322 Bates.
Shea Thomas, lab, h 355 Virginia av.
Shea Thomas, lab, b 314 S West.
Shea Thomas, lab, h rear 24 Woodside av (W).
Shea Timothy, lab, h 501 E Georgia.
Shea Timothy J, twistmkr, b 773 E Market.
Shea Timothy T, barber, b 360 E Washington.
Shea Wm, helper, h 342 N Pine.
Sheaf Edward, trav agt, r 45 Indiana av.
Sheahan Mary, h 84 Lexington av.
Shear Charles, bicycle rep, b 26 S Senate av.
Shear Clara, nurse, r 147 N Penn.
Shear Frank Z, clk Cerealine Mnfg Co, b 224 Douglass.
Shear Wm J, molder, b 267 S Capitol av.
Shearer, see also Scherer, Scherrer and Sherer.
Shearer Daniel, carp, h 577 E St Clair.
Shearer Henry, molder, h 34 Centennial (H).
Shearer Lottie B, b 65 Columbia av.
Shearer Mary C, teacher Public School No 6, b 908 N Delaware.
Shearer Minnie (wid James A), h 18½ N Penn.
Shearer Samuel H, supt and engr Western Paving and Supply Co, h 1002 N Alabama.
Shearer Thomas H, express, h 38 S Stuart (B).
Shearer Thomas J, carp, 363 N Pine, h same.
Shearer Wm D, lather, h 95 Malott av.
Shearer Wm L, switchman, b 363 N Pine.
Sheares Harriet E (wid Claiborne), r rear 175 N Penn.
Shearman John D, clk Van Camp Packing Co, h 1033 N New Jersey.
Shearman John R, clk The S A Haines Co, b 1033 N New Jersey.
Shears Mack, porter, b 324 Tremont.
Shedd Edwin H, clk L E & W R R, r 49 The Chalfant.
Shedd Mary M, music teacher, 74 When bldg, r 217 E Ohio.
Shedd Susan H (wid Edwin R), b 903 Broadway.
Sheehan Albert C, lather, b 366 E Market.
Sheehan Catherine (wid Timothy T), h w s Hanna 1 n of Campbell.
Sheehan Daniel W, engr, h 159 Meek.
Sheehan Dowdell, brakeman, b 1 Madison av.
Sheehan Ernest W, lab, b 366 E Market.
Sheehan Eugene, contr, b w s Hanna 1 n of Campbell.
Sheehan James, engr, h 36 Foundry (B).
Sheehan James, lab, h 15 Birch av (W I).
Sheehan Jeremiah, insp City Engineer, b 46 Russell av.
Sheehan John, contr, b w s Hanna 1 n of Campbell.
Sheehan John, lab, b 486 E Georgia.
Sheehan John, switchman, h 48 N Station (B).
Sheehan Mary (wid Daniel), h 237 S West.
Sheehan Mary (wid Dennis), h 486 E Georgia.
Sheehan Mary (wid Timothy), h 257 Bates.
Sheehan Naomi E (wid Nathan), h 366 E Market.
Sheehan Thomas, city agt Mut Sav Union and Loan Assn, h 322 W New York.
Sheehan Timothy, lab, h 91 Spann av.
Sheehan Timothy B, stoker, b 416 S Delaware.

OTTO GAS ENGINES | BUILDERS' EXCHANGE S. W. Cor. Ohio and Penn. Telephone 535.

Becker & Son Charles Becker Jacob Becker Jr. Merchant Tailors. 21 N. Penn. St. Tel. 934

SALISBURY & STANLEY OFFICE, STORE, AND BANK FIXTURES. Contractors and Builders. Repairing of all kinds done on short notice. 177 Clinton St., Indianapolis, Ind. Telephone 999.

Sheehan Timothy C, lab, h 14 S Austin (B).
Sheehan Timothy D, lab, h 153 Bates.
Sheehan Timothy, mach, b 126 N Dorman.
Sheehan Timothy M, lab, b 257 Bates.
Sheehan Walter A, lab, b 366 E Market.
Sheehan Wm J, fireman, b 14 S Austin (B).
Sheehy Andrew, uphlr, b 195 W McCarty.
Sheehy Daniel, engr, b 124 English av.
Sheehy Edward P, molder, h 168 King av (H).
Sheehy James, lab, b 195 W McCarty.
Sheehy John, butcher, b 195 W McCarty.
Sheehy John J, engr, h 58 English av.
Sheehy Robert, brick mason, h 195 W McCarty.
Sheehy Wm E, foreman, h 163 E Ohio.
Sheeley David G, fireman, h 40 Lord.
Sheeley Michael, b 177 N West.
Sheely Calvin U, porter, h 52 Tacoma av.
Sheely Oliver P, carp, h w s Rambrant 2 n of Indiana av.
Sheets Charles E, carp, h 378 Union.
Sheets Charles W, buyer N Y Store, h 478 N Penn.
SHEETS CHARLES W, Livery and Boarding Stable, in rear of 475 N Illinois, h 475 same, Tel 1543.
Sheets Christie L, h 478 N Penn.
Sheets Edward D, engr, h 192 N State av.
Sheets George, lab, h 457 Charles.
SHEETS HARRY, Genl Agt Gaar, Scott & Co, 414 N West, h same, Tel 1750.
Sheets Harry, mach, b 192 N State av.
Sheets Harry N, clk, r 313 N East.
Sheets Harvey, mach, b 414 N West.
Sheets Peter, driver, h 471 E Georgia.
Sheets Samuel, lab, h 59 Bismarck av (W I).
Sheets Wm C, drugs, 840 W Washington, h same.
Sheets Wm O, clk, h 187 Yandes.
Sheetz Fred H, foreman Knight & Jillson, r 96 W New York.
Sheffield John, lather, b s w cor Lexington av and Frank.
SHEFFIELD SAW WORKS, E C Atkins & Co Proprs, 202-206 S Illinois, Tel 55.
Sheffield Wm H, car rep, h 58 Beacon.
Sheible Daniel R, clk, r 36 Grand Opera House blk.
Shekell Edward R, stenog L E & W R R, h 94 Hanna.
Shelby Benjamin F, attendant Insane Hospital.
Shelby Calvin F, lather, h 240 Yandes.
Shelby Clarence L, lather, b 240 Yandes.
Shelby Edgar, lab, b 382 Indiana av.
Shelby George W, dairy, s s W 20th 2 e of Northwestern av, h same.
Shelby Millard, motorman, b 240 Yandes.
Shelby Walter V, dairy, w s Brightwood av 2 s of Wolf pike (B), h same.
Shelby Wm, plastr, h 54 Catherine.
Shelby Wm P, condr, h 376 E 10th.
Sheldon Edward A, vice-pres Indpls Engine Co, res Oswego, N Y.
Shelkey, see Schelke.
Shellady Samuel E, millwright, h 46 Pleasant av.
Shellburn Jacob F, packer, h 972 Sugar Grove av (M P).
Shelley Earl, insp, b 382 N Meridian.
Shelley Isaac, h 382 N Meridian.
Shelley Isaac O, lab, h 9 Morgan (W I).
Shelley John D, salesman Krag-Reynolds Co, h 499 Bellefontaine.

Henry H. Fay, 40½ E. Washington St., REAL ESTATE, AND LOAN BROKER.

Shelley Linden G, printer, h 1199 N Capitol av.
Shelley Samuel S, h 101 Fayette.
Shelley Wm O, clk Progress Clothing Co, b 326 N Senate av.
Shellhouse Conrad H (Shellhouse & Co), h 153 E Ohio.
Shellhouse Frank M, b 153 E Ohio.
Shellhouse Wm S (W S Shellhouse & Co), b 153 E Ohio.
Shellhouse W S & Co (Wm S Shellhouse, Ida B Alyea), grocers, 99 N Alabama.
SHELLHOUSE & CO (Conrad H Shellhouse, Alva C May, Anthony F Kleinschmidt), Builders' Supplies, Hardware, Paints, Oils, Glass, Lime, Cement, Etc, 271-275 E Washington, Tel 514.
Shelton Charles S, huckster, b 563 E Market.
Shelton David F, brakeman, h 253 English av.
Shelton Edward N, lab, b 323 W North.
Shelton Edwin E, real est, b 524 W McLene (N I).
Shelton Ernest L, lab, h 539 S Capitol av.
Shelton Frank B, farmer, h 93 Hadley av (W I).
Shelton George H, mach hd, b 98 Division (W I).
Shelton Henry H, engr, h 323 W North.
Shelton James, porter, r rear 175 N Penn.
Shelton James N, clk Township Assessor's Office, h 291 Douglass.
Shelton John, porter, r 406 Blackford.
Shelton John F, lab, h 436 W Wells (N I).
Shelton John P, tmstr, h 104 Locke.
Shelton Joseph R, h 62 Hoyt av.
Shelton Leighton L, trav agt, h 524 W McLene (N I).
Shelton Reuben, lab, h 274 Lafayette.
Shelton Reuben B, musician, b 323 W North.
Shepard Adam, tinner, r 491 W Addison (N I).
Shepard Boynton, lab, r 336 Superior.
Shepard Carlos F, bkkpr, h 720 E Ohio.
Shepard Christopher, paperhngr, r 491 W Addison (N I).

MAYHEW 13 N. MERIDIAN STREET.

LIME, CEMENT, PLASTER FIRE BRICK AND CLAY SEWER PIPE, ETC. BALKE & KRAUSS CO., Cor. Market and Missouri Streets.

C. FRIEDGEN HAS THE FINEST STOCK OF LADIES' PARTY SLIPPERS and SHOES 19 NORTH PENNSYLVANIA ST.

SAMUEL LAING, TIN, SLATE AND STEEL ROOFING, 72 AND 74 EAST COURT STREET.

M. B. WILSON, Pres. W. F. CHURCHMAN, Cash.

THE CAPITAL NATIONAL BANK,

INDIANAPOLIS, IND.

Pays Interest on Time Certificates of Deposit.
Buys and Sells Foreign Exchange at Low Rates.

Capital, - - $300,000
Surplus and Earnings, 50,000

No. 28 S. Meridian St., Cor. Pearl.

Shepard Frank R, real est, 79 E Market, b 772 N Alabama.
Shepard Frederick K, dep Auditor of Marion County, 41 Court House, h 13 West Drive (W P).
Shepard Henry, lab, h 428 Clinton.
Shepard James H, lab, h rear 337 E Wabash.
Shepard Jonathan T, millwright, h 215 Huron.
Shepard Kate (wid Abner H), dressmkr, 92 Lexington av, h same.
SHEPARD SILAS M, Lawyer, 50-51 Baldwin Blk, Tel 1012; h 772 N Alabama.
Shepard Silas M jr, lumber, 51 Baldwin blk, b 772 N Alabama.
Shephard Alice M, cook, b 982 N Meridian.
Shepherd Albert S, lab, h 28 Everett.
Shepherd Boyden H, lab, b 277 Chapel.
Shepherd Charles F, switchman, b 503 N Alabama.
Shepherd Christie, engr, b Hotel English.
Shepherd Claudia, music teacher, b 60 Birch av (W I).
Shepherd Clyde F, driver, h 4 Cottage av (W I).
Shepherd David M, policeman, h 740 Chestnut.
Shepherd Edward J, finisher, h 44 Harrison.
Shepherd Edward W, helper, b 68 Camp.
Shepherd Emma B, school teacher, h 336 Yandes.
Shepherd Frank H, foreman Beveridge Paper Co, h 274 W New York.
Shepherd Frank, lab, h e s Baltimore av 3 s of 17th.
Shepherd Harry, polisher, b 306 S Meridian.
Shepherd Henry E, barber, 121 Oliver av (W I), h 119 same.
Shepherd Henry L, tailor, h 84 Fulton.
Shepherd Henry V, saloon, 840 E Washington, h 549 E Market.
Shepherd James, lab, r 135 Allegheny.
Shepherd James H, h 25 Short.
Shepherd James McB, h 121 N Senate av.
Shepherd John H, driver, h 60 Birch av (W I).
Shepherd John P, porter, h 336 Yandes.

TUTTLE & SEGUIN,

28 E. Market Street.

Fire Insurance,
Real Estate, Loan
and Rental Agents.

TELEPHONE 1168.

Shepherd John R, jeweler, 431 S Meridian, h same.
Shepherd Mary (wid John), b e s Range 1 s of Washington.
Shepherd Mary F (wid John S), b 72 Temple av.
Shepherd Orpha J, cook, b 21 Chapel.
Shepherd Oscar H, yardmaster, h 72 Temple av.
Shepherd Wm D, lawyer, b 99 Highland pl.
Shepp Benjamin F, h 1139 Northwestern av.
Shepp Jacob F, h 41 Omer.
Shepp Loren, lab, h 1282 Northwestern av (N I).
Sheppard Adam, cooper, b 272 W Maryland.
Sheppard Albert, cook, h 85 Eddy.
Sheppard Anna (wid Jacob T), b 270 Spring.
Sheppard Byron, tmstr, h 32 Bicking.
Sheppard Callie (wid George W), medicines, 50½ S Illinois, h same.
Sheppard Charles, mach, h 123 English av.
Sheppard George W, foreman, r 106½ N Meridian.
Sheppard Henry H, clk Murphy, Hibben & Co, h e s N Senate av 4 n of 27th.
Sheppard Joseph A, constable, 26 N Delaware, b 140 Madison av.
Sheppard Thomas C, h 197 Walcott.
Sheppard Wm C, tinner, 541 W Udell, h 487½ W Addison (N I).
Sheppard Wm W, harnessmkr, 444 E Washington, h 64 Johnson av.
Sheppard Wm W jr, painter, b 64 Johnson av.
Shepper John, car insp, h e s Lincoln av 10 s of C C C & St L Ry (M J).
Shepperd Cora B, officer Indiana Reformatory, b same.
Shepperd John, carp, h 363 Bellefontaine.
Shepperd Joseph F, clk N Y Store, b 363 Bellefontaine.
Sherbert Wm, lab, h 533 Jones (N I).
Sherer, see also Scherer, Scherrer and Shearer.
Sherer Adam G, shoemkr, h 192 Kentucky av.
Sherer Adam W, com mer, 122 E Maryland, h 1014 E Washington.
Sherer Edward (Laakmann & Sherer), h 362 W 1st.
Sherer Francis J, pdlr, h 186 W Vermont.
Sherer Frank, stenog, b 224 Douglass.
Sherer Frank P, fruits, E Mkt House, h 226 Oliver av (W I).
Sherer John L, tinner, h 196 Kentucky av.
Sherer Joseph M, grocer, 231 W Ohio, b 192 Kentucky av.
Sherer Julia A (wid Joseph), h 224 Douglass.
Sherer Mamie, grocer, 191 W South, h 196 Kentucky av.
Sheresefsky Hyman, clk, b 65 W McCarty.
Sheresefsky Mary (wid Louis), grocer, 400 S Capitol av, h 65 W McCarty.
Sherfey Frank R, clk Knight & Jillson, b 267 N Alabama.
Sherfey Mary A (wid Wm H), h 267 N Alabama.
Sherfey Thomas R (Sherfey & Holler), h 68 Ruckle.
Sherfey & Holler (Thomas R Sherfey, Philip W Holler), horseshoers, 83 S Penn.
Sherfy Benjamin B, farmer, h s s Lena 4 w of Parker (I).
Sherfy Charles P, clk The Indpls Book and Stationery Co, b s s Lena 4 w of Parker (I).

SULLIVAN & MAHAN Manufacturers of all kinds of PAPER BOXES 41 W. Pearl St.

DIAMOND WALL PLASTER { Telephone 1410 BUILDERS' EXCHANGE.

Telephone 1769. 197 S. Illinois St. } THE HOME LAUNDRY { WORK CALLED FOR AND DELIVERED.

Sheridan Bernard, clk R M S, h 8 Camp.
SHERIDAN BRICK WORKS, Mason J Osgood Pres, Oliver H Root Sec and Treas, 88 N Penn, Tel 1896.
Sheridan Cornelius, clk, h s s Washington nr Belmont av.
Sheridan John, chief dining dept Insane Hospital, h 88 Sheffield av (H).
Sheridan John H, molder, h 487 N California.
Sheridan Joseph, b 146 Belmont av (H).
Sheridan Louis, h 178 W 7th.
Sheridan Mary (wid John), h 300 W St Clair.
Sheridan Michael, ins agt, b 65 Church.
Sheridan Patrick, lab, b 124 Agnes.
Sheridan Rachel C, teacher Public School No 22, h 223 Park av.
Sheridan Wm, grocer, 399 N West, h same.
Sherkins Gustav, cabtmkr, b 115 Meek.
Sherlock Daniel H, lab, h 302 Michigan (H).
Sherlock Henry W, lab, h 36 Grove.
Sherlock John W, mach, h 16 Wilcox.
Sherman, see also Schurmann.
Sherman Alice V, teacher Public School No 15, b 442 Broadway.
Sherman Ann D, h 237 Columbia av.
Sherman Charles, lab, b 896 W Washington.
Sherman Charles J, trav agt, h 124 E St Joseph.
Sherman Edward H, clk, h 23 W McCarty.
Sherman Emily J (wid Willis G), h 939 N Penn.
Sherman Herman E, b 459 S Meridian.
Sherman House, Hawkins & Shaw proprs, n e cor Louisiana and McCrea, tel 1900.
Sherman Jacob, condr, h 896 W Washington.
Sherman John S, clk U S Pension Agency, h 442 Broadway.
Sherman Matilda (wid LeRoy), b 239 W McCarty.
Sherman Miller, baggageman, h 153 Cottage av.
Sherman Nathaniel S asst mngr Union News Co, b 459 S Meridian.
Sherman Nellie, h 100 S Senate av.
Sherman Oscar E, mngr Union News Co, 193 S Illinois, h 459 S Meridian.
Sherman Paul, harnessmkr F L Herrington, r 29 Hutchings blk.
SHERMAN'S RESTAURANT, Kershner Bros Proprs, 18-20 S Meridian, Tel 197. (See left side lines and opp classified Restaurants.)
Sherman Rosella M, h 452 Mulberry.
Sherman Sylvester A, mach hd, h 34 Larch.
Sherman Wm, lab, h 27 Church.
Sherman Wm B, clk, b 39 Newman.
Sherrard Richard F, attendant Insane Asylum.
Sherrick David E, trav agt, b 138 E Pratt.
Sherrill Leonard M, cooper, h 453 W New York.
Sherry Cora, h 305½ E Washington.
Sherwood Anson W, agt, r 351 N Senate av.
Sherwood Francis M, restaurant, 90 S Illinois, h 24 Dearborn.
Sherwood George E, furnace setter, h 68 Hill av.
Sherwood Henry A, tailor, b 24 Dearborn.
Sherwood Isaac R, pres Western Horseman Co, res Canton, O.
SHERWOOD JOHN B, Lawyer, 84-85 Lombard Bldg, Tel 1698; b 147 N New Jersey.
Sherwood Sarah (wid Anson), b 206 Yandes.

FRANK NESSLER. WILL H. ROST.
FRANK NESSLER & CO.
Tailors
56 EAST MARKET ST. (Lemcke Building),
INDIANAPOLIS, IND.

SHERWOOD WALLACE, Commercial Printer, 29 S Delaware, h 224 Huron.
Sherwood Wm O, carp, h 222 N Illinois.
Sherwood Wm P, mach, h 206 Yandes.
Shetzley Julius C, lab, h 388 Highland av.
Shewman Jacob S, mason, h w s Maple av 2 n of Washington av (I).
Shewman John, lab, h w s Central av 1 s of C H & D R R (I).
Shewmon John A, lab, h 10 Sumner.
Shewmon Wm A, motorman, h 479 E 9th.
Shey Charles, harnessmkr, h 55 Iowa.
Shey Francis M, trav agt, h 9 Paca.
Shick Frederick, lab, b 94 Bright.
Shideler, see also Scheideler.
Shideler Charlotte M (wid Isaac M), h 186 E St Joseph.
Shideler David B, mngr Equitable Life Assurance Society for Southwestern Indiana, 600-603 Indiana Trust bldg, h 1012 N Penn.
Shideler David L, clk, h 187 Ash.
Shideler Edwin F, com mer, h e s Sutherland av 2 n of 20th.
Shideler Fannie B (wid John W), music teacher, b n s Eastern av 1 e of Grand av (I).
Shideler John E (Tutewiler & Shideler), h 949 N Alabama.
Shiel Frederick, carp, h 349 Jefferson av.
Shiel Michael E, sec, h 82 Hoyt av.
Shiel Roger R (R R Shiel & Co), h 551 N Meridian.
Shiel R R & Co (Roger R Shiel, Richard R Reeves), live stock, Union Stock Yards (W I).
Shiel The, 120-122 N Illinois and 25 Indiana av.
Shield Wm, lab, h 136 Geisendorff.
Shields Aaron, lab, h n s 8th 2 w of canal.
Shields Cain M, h 102 Greer.
Shields Carrie B, bkkpr, b 149 Hoyt av.
Shields Columbus, driver, h 14 Hiawatha.
Shields Daniel T, attorney Fahnley & McCrea, h 209 College av.
Shields Edward, mach, b 334 S Alabama.
Shields Edward, lab, b 14 Hiawatha.
Shields Elmer E, artist, 62½ E Washington, h 149 Hoyt av.

ACORN STOVES AND RANGES
Haueisen & Hartmann
163-169 E. Washington St.
FURNITURE,
Carpets,
Household Goods,
Tin, Granite and China Wares, Oil Cloth and Shades

THE WM. H. BLOCK CO. 7 AND 9 EAST WASHINGTON STREET. DRY GOODS, HOUSE FURNISHINGS AND CROCKERY.

London Guarantee and Accident Co. (Ltd.) Employers', Public and Teams' Liability. Workmen's Collective Insurance and Fidelity Bonds
GEORGE W. PANGBORN, General Agent, 704-706 Lemcke Bldg. Telephone 140.

FRANK K. SAWYER || Reliable Fire Insurance. Reasonable Rates. 74 E. MARKET STREET. Telephone 8.

JOSEPH GARDNER,
TIN, IRON, STEEL AND SLATE ROOFING,
GALVANIZED IRON CORNICES & SKYLIGHTS.
37, 39 & 41 KENTUCKY AVE. Telephone 322.

Shields Felix G, foreman, h 676 Vorster av (M P).
Shields Frederick B, barber, 254 Highland av, h same.
Shields George W, tmstr, h 109 Hosbrook.
Shields Hugh, h 806 Cornell av.
Shields James C, helper, h 16 Ketcham.
Shields John, molder, b 102 Greer.
Shields John A, painter, b 30½ N Reisner (W I).
Shields John W, b 311 N Delaware.
Shields Joseph M, painter, 30½ N Reisner (W I), h same.
Shields Lester C, clk, b 1150 E Washington.
Shields Louis D, stenog, h 83 N New Jersey.
Shields Manford A, condr, b 806 Cornell av.
Shields Mary, h 311 N Delaware.
Shields Robert, blksmith, b 500 Columbia av.
Shields Robert, mach, b 334 S Alabama.
Shields Samuel, lab, h 136 Newman.
Shields Sarah A, h 31 E St Joseph.
Shields Thomas C, asst yardmaster P C C & St L Ry, h 1150 E Washington.
Shields Walter, lab, h 334 S Alabama.
Shields Walter, lab, h 224 Naomi.
Shields Walter R, butcher, r 58½ W Ohio.
Shields Wm, fireman, r 872 Cornell av.
Shifley Wm, lab, r 66 N Missouri.
Shigley Frederick W, creamery, 38 Hill av, h n s 17th 1 e of Hillside av.
Shill Wm F, agt, b 223 W Maryland.
Shillabeer Ernst, sec junior dept Y M C A, h 188 Eureka av.
Shilling, see also Schilling.
Shilling Clara (wid Robert), h 496 N West.
Shilling Edward E, clk County Recorder, h 319 N West.
Shilling Elmer S, clk County Recorder, h 21 Camp.
Shilling Richard L, trunks, 55 W Washington, r 45½ N Capitol av.
Shilling Stephen A, foreman, h 532 Bellefontaine.
Shilling Thomas S, clk County Recorder, h 197 Fayette.
Shilling Wesley H, trav agt Ward Bros Drug Co, b 496 N West.

J. S. FARRELL & CO.
STEAM AND HOT WATER HEATING AND PLUMBING CONTRACTORS
84 North Illinois Street. Telephone 382.

SHILLING WM E, Recorder of Marion County, 44 Court House, Tel 914; h 237 N West.
Shimer Charles B (Shimer & Allen), r 451 N New Jersey.
Shimer Charles O, farmer, h w s National av 1 s of Brookville rd (I).
Shimer Corydon R, farmer, h s s Brookville rd 1 w of Line (I).
Shimer Elias N, car rep, h 40 N Station (B).
Shimer Harry W, clk, b 174 S Olive.
Shimer James T, bkkpr Bowen-Merrill Co, b s s Brookville rd 1 w of Line (I).
Shimer Nelson R, h w s Auvergne av 1 s of Fletcher av (I).
Shimer Richard O, letter carrier P O, h 233 Michigan av.
Shimer Richard T, clk R M S, h 174 S Olive.
Shimer Thomas N, lab Insane Asylum.
Shimer Wm R, farmer, h s s Brookville rd 1 w of National av (I).
Shimer & Allen (Charles B Shimer, Linton R Allen), lawyers, 636 Lemcke bldg.
Shimp Emma C (wid Wm R), h 598 E St Clair.
Shimp Joseph T, clk, b 598 E St Clair.
Shimp Wm T, carp, h s s Schofield 2 w of Shade (B).
Shinault Daniel, lab, h 429 Clinton.
Shindle Rebecca V (wid Sample F), h 914 N Delaware.
Shindler, see Schindler.
Shindoff John, engr, r 5 McCormick.
Shine Bros (Wm jr and John), saloon, 112 W Ray.
Shine Cornelius, lab, h 23 Meikel.
Shine Eugene, lab, b 71 Church.
Shine John (Shine Bros), h 65 Church.
Shine John, lab, b 31 McGinnis.
Shine Michael, lab, b 71 Church.
Shine Patrick, lab, b 31 McGinnis.
Shine Thomas, lab, b 71 Church.
Shine Wm, h 71 Church.
Shine Wm jr (Shine Bros), b 71 Church.
Shingler Edward, contr, 900 Ash, h same.
SHINGLER, HANN & CO (Robert Shingler, Otis C Hann), Genl Insurance Agts and Real Estate, 92-93 Baldwin Blk, Tel 1922.
Shingler John O, clk E C Atkins & Co, h 530 Jefferson av.
Shingler Robert (Shingler, Hann & Co), h 901 Ash.
Shingler Wm, lab, h 698 Park av.
Shingler Wm H, engr, h 21 Russell av.
Shingleton, see also Singleton.
Shingleton Charles, brakeman, b 88 Spann av.
Shingleton Elizabeth M (wid DeWitt C), b 290 Bates.
Shingleton Henry W lab, h 88 Spann av.
Shingleton Mary A (wid Clarence D), grocer, 290 Bates, h same.
Shingleton Roland T, lab, h 72 Laurel.
Shingleton Wm M, condr, b 88 Spann av.
Shinkle Charles, engr, b 150 Madison.
Shinkle Henry C, lab, h 150 Madison.
Shinkle John, lab, b 150 Madison.
Shinn Alva C, lather, b 366 E Market.
Shinn Alva O, city fireman (W I), b 904 Morris (W I).
Shinn Ernest, hostler, b 366 E Market.
Shinn John H, lab, h n w cor Hanna and E Michigan.
Shinn Lora, teacher School No 4 (W I), b 904 Morris (W I).
Shinn Naomi E (wid Nathan), h 366 E Market.

POLICIES IN UNITED STATES LIFE INSURANCE CO., offer indemnity against death, liberal cash surrender value or at option of policy-holder, fully paid-up life insurance or liberal life income. E. B. SWIFT, M'g'r, 25 E. Market St.

WM. KOTTEMAN } WILL FURNISH YOUR HOUSE COMPLETE
89 & 91 E. Washington St. Telephone 1742

SHOW CASES | WILLIAM WIEGEL | 6 West Louisiana Street Opp. Union Station.

Shinn Roscoe E, lab, h 94 S Reisner (W I).
Shinn Wm J, clk, h 904 Morris (W I).
Shipley Harry C, molder, h 138 S East.
Shipley John L, lab, h 328 W Court.
Shipley Talbott B, mason, h 26 Paca.
Shipley Thomas, mason, b 26 Paca.
Shipley Wm H, mason, b 26 Paca.
Shipman Charles, brakeman, h 36 Oriental.
Shipman Clara (wid Samuel), b 129 Michigan av.
Shipman Everett N, salesman, b 339 Alvord.
Shipman George W, agt, h w s Talbott 1 s of 22d.
Shipman George W, brakeman, h 58 Temple av.
Shipman George W, cooper, h 217 Douglass.
Shipman John, lab, b 373 E Georgia.
Shipman John L, lab, h 339 Alvord.
Shipman Levin T, lab, h 373 E Georgia.
Shipman Uriah H, cooper, b 217 Douglass.
Shipman Wheeler M, cooper, b 217 Douglass.
Shipman Wm, driver, h n s Prospect 2 e of Belt R R.
Shipman Wm K, engr, h 129 Michigan av.
Shipp George, lab, b 45 Ellen.
Shipp Joseph P, h 540 N Delaware.
Shipp Joseph V, clk, h w s Lake av 2 s of Washington av (I).
Shipp Mary C (wid Sandford C), b 699 N Senate av.
Shipp Richard, engr, h 306 Prospect.
Shipp Samuel M, trav agt Hendrickson, Lefler & Co, r 29 Wyandot blk.
Shipp Thomas R, student, b w s Lake av 2 s of Washington av (I).
Shipp Wm D, porter, b 306 Prospect.
Shireman Wm A, trav agt Schnull & Co, h 991 N Penn.
Shires George S, trav agt, b 36 Ruckle.
Shirk Clara L, stenog, b 111 N New Jersey.
Shirk Georgia A (wid John M), h 111 N New Jersey.
Shirk Rose (wid Milton), h 167 W 1st.
Shirk Samuel S, driver, h 61 Barth av.
Shirley Abraham S, bkkpr, h 503 Talbott av.
Shirley Bertram L, trav agt, b 855 Bellefontaine.
Shirley Daniel, b 28 Becker (M J).
Shirley Frederick T, insp, h 25 Garfield pl.
Shirley Foster, clk J A Shirley, b 855 Bellefontaine.
Shirley Harlan T, lab, h 29 McCormick.
Shirley John R, janitor, h 39 Church.
Shirley Joseph A, real est, 701 Lemcke bldg, h 855 Bellefontaine.
Shirley Russell V, waiter, r 88½ N Illinois.
Shirlocke Charles, attendant Insane Hospital.
Shirrell Leonard M, cooper, h 453 W New York.
Shissler Joseph, carp, h 557 Bellefontaine.
Shive Henry, bridgebldr, r 127 W Maryland.
Shiveley Daniel, cook, r 12½ Indiana av.
Shiveley Joseph, porter Occidental Hotel.
Shiveley Stella, cook, r 155 N Illinois.
Shiverick Charles H, clk, b 433 N Illinois.
Shobe Anna (wid Hugh), b 9 Lafayette.
Shobe Clement D, lab, b 438 E 7th.
Shobe Edward, clk U S Arsenal.
Shobe George, lab, b 438 E 7th.
Shobe Hugh F, lab, b 438 E 7th.
Shobe Lucy (wid Luther) h 438 E 7th.
Shobe Price, lab, h 95 Nebraska.
Shockency Stephen, molder, h 199 Sheffield (H).
Shockley Celestia A (wid James M), h 477 W Udell (N I).

THOS. C. DAY & CO.
INVESTING AGENTS,
TOWN AND FARM LOANS,
Rooms 325 to 330 Lemcke Bldg.

Shockley Charles N, pres Aetna Cabinet Co, h 192 Oliver av (W I).
Shockley Euclid (Perkins & Shockley), b 217 W Pearl.
Shockley Grace, cashr Schauroth & Co, b 447 W Udell (N I).
Shockley Nancy (wid John), b 89 Germania av (H).
Shoecraft Frances C, teacher Girls' Classical School, b 768 N Penn.
Shoemaker, see also Schumacher.
Shoemaker August, mach, b s s Pansy 4 w of Floral av.
Shoemaker Boston, carp, h 182 Newman.
Shoemaker Charles J, h 165 Walcott.
Shoemaker Frederick W, coremkr, b 14 Dearborn.
Shoemaker George F, driver, h 163 Lexington av.
Shoemaker Henry F, teacher Indpls College of Music, h 420½ Mass av.
Shoemaker James W, plastr, h 88 N New Jersey.
Shoemaker John C, pres Union Mutual B and L Assn, h 923 N Illinois.
Shoemaker John F, cabtmkr, h 14 Dearborn.
Shoemaker Karl L, driver, h 41 S Austin (B).
Shoemaker Samuel A, phys, r 133 W Michigan.
Shoemaker Thomas B, tinner, h 162 Spann av.
Shoemaker Walter D, clk, b 15 Dearborn.
Shoemaker Wm, lab, r 264 Bates.
Shoemaker Wm H, fireman, r 92 Lexington av.
Shoemaker Wm J, mach, h 27 St Peter.
Shoemaker Wm R, carp, rear 313 E Georgia, h 36 Bates al.
Shoff Wm R, engr, h 593 W Shoemaker (N I).
Shoffner Jennie, nurse, b 197 N Delaware.
Shommer Henry, bartndr, b 288 E Morris.
Shoobridge Alfred J, driver, h 242 E St Clair.
Shoobridge Charles, grocer, 30 Pendleton av (B), h same.

EAT——
HITZ'S
CRACKERS
AND CAKES.
ASK YOUR GROCER FOR THEM.

Capital Steam Carpet Cleaning Works
M. D. PLUNKETT Proprietor, Telephone 818

BENJ. BOOTH PRACTICAL EXPERT ACCOUNTANT. Accounts of any description investigated and audited, and statements rendered. Room 18, 82½ E. Washington St., Indianapolis, Ind.

The Best Place in the City to Get a Good Meal THE SHERMAN RESTAURANT ♦♦♦♦ 18 and 20 S. Meridian Street KERSHNER BROS., Proprs.

ESTABLISHED 1876. TELEPHONE 168.
CHESTER BRADFORD,
SOLICITOR OF PATENTS,
AND COUNSEL IN PATENT CAUSES.
(See adv. page 6.)
Office:—Rooms 14 and 16 Hubbard Block, S.W. Cor. Washington and Meridian Streets,
INDIANAPOLIS, INDIANA.

Shook Andrew, driver, b 326 E Wabash.
Shook Claude, clk, b 450 W 22d (N I).
Shook Edgar, lab, b 1059 W Vermont.
Shook Elias, grocer, 153 N Capitol av, h 450 W 22d (N I).
Shook George, lab, h 133 Lambert (W I).
Shook George, mach, b 325 E Ohio.
Shook John, lab, h 422 Newman.
Shook John H, plumber, b 9 Warren.
Shook John N, lab, h 111 Columbia av.
Shook Jonathan, papermkr, h 1059 W Vermont.
Shook Wm, h 133 Lambert (W I).
Shoptaugh Jacob A, confr, 154 Virginia av, h 54 Oak.
Shorb Hattie M, cashr W H Ballard, b 301 E Ohio.
Shorb Jeannette C (wid Henry C), h 301 E Ohio.
Shorb Wm C, ice creammkr, b 301 E Ohio.
Shore John A, lab, h 17 Sharpe.
Shores Joseph B, lab, h 424½ W North.
Shores Zachariah, janitor, b 203 W 2d.
Short, see also Schort.
Short Albert N, music teacher, 226 Yandes, h same.
Short Cora L (wid John C), grocer, 420 W Michigan, h same.
Short Etta (wid Charles), h 215 W South.
Short Frank M, clk, b 22 Keith.
Short Jennie (wid Robert), h 97 Douglass.
Short Jesse E, ins agt, h 22 Keith.
Short Louisa C (wid Victor), b 1341 N Senate av.
Short Major, shoemkr, 6 S Missouri, h 292 Huron.
Short Mamie, b 138 S William (W I).
Short Walter, painter, h 432 E Vermont.
Short Willard N, drugs, 49 S Illinois, r same.
Short Wm G, clk L E & W R R, b 165 N Alabama.
SHORTHAND TRAINING SCHOOL, S H East Principal and Mngr, 49-55 Thorpe Blk.
Shorton Richard, shoemkr, b 100 S Reisner (W I).
Shortridge Charles, bartndr, b 430 Virginia av.

O. B. Ensey
SLATE, STEEL, TIN AND IRON ROOFING.
Cor. 6th and Illinois Sts. Tel. 1562

Shortridge Charles H, boxmkr, b 58 Barth av.
Shortridge Ella W, cashr Sloan Drug Co, b 387 Bellefontaine.
Shortridge Frank A, mach, h 537 Bellefontaine.
Shortridge Mary E (wid Wm), h 259 E Vermont.
Shortridge Willard, dentist, 60 Baldwin blk, r 7 Vinton blk.
Shortridge Wm C, b 111 E Washington.
Shortt James A, draughtsman, r 378 N Meridian.
Shott Artie M (wid Simon M), boarding 131 S East.
Shotts, see also Schott.
Shotts Henry, lab, b 101 Maple.
Shotwell Charles A, grain, 18 Board of Trade bldg, h s w cor Cherry and Lawn avs (I).
Shotwell John, carp, h 851½ S Meridian.
Shotwell Oliver, lab, b 851½ S Meridian.
Shoup Emil, agt, b 32 S Senate av.
Shouse David C, lab, h 154 Lee (W I).
Shover Amos F (Browder & Shover), h 768 N New Jersey.
Shover Barton R, electrician, b 591 Broadway.
SHOVER CHARLES E, Storage and Heavy Transfer, 180-188 E Wabash, h 179 E Ohio, Tel 657.
Shover Clara A, bkkpr, b 26 The Blacherne.
SHOVER GARRETT H, Carriage and Wagon Mnfr, 172 E Market, Tel 806; h 591 Broadway.
Shover James E, contr, 125 N Alabama, h 26 The Blacherne.
Shover Oran D, livery, 282 E Washington, h 117 N East.
Shovey Augustus, lab, h 24 S Rural.
Showalter Francis L, carp, h e s New Jersey 1 n of 21st.
Showalter Samuel, h 258 Indiana av.
Showecker Job, cooper, h 48 Sheffield av (W I).
Showers David L, blksmith, h 440 S Delaware.
Showers Maud E (wid Charles H), b 27 E Pratt.
Shrader, see also Schrader and Schroeder.
Shrader Arnold E, b 45 W 2d.
Shrader Daniel, messenger Am Ex Co, h 477 E 9th.
Shrader Oscar E, grain, h 45 W 2d.
Shreve David R, feather renovator, s s Sturm av 1 e of Arsenal av, h same.
Shreve Enzor C, brakeman, h 230 English av.
Shreve Jessie (wid John W), b 299 Spann av.
Shreve Margaret L (wid Joseph H), h 189 Johnson av.
Shreve Roland R, lab, h s s Sturm av 1 e of N Arsenal av.
Shreve Wm D, bkkpr Van Camp H and I Co, h 189 Johnson av.
Shrewsbury Charles W, contr, 87 Hoyt av, h same.
Shrewsbury Worthus, plastr, b 87 Hoyt av.
Shriner, see also Schreiner.
Shriner Charles T (Shriner & Robbins), h 483 S Missouri.
Shriner Ida, h 27½ Virginia av.
Shriner & Robbins (Charles T Shriner, Martin Robbins), horseshoers, 428 Charles.
Shriver Robert, pres J B Allfree Mnfg Co, res Cumberland, Md.

TUTEWILER UNDERTAKER, No. 72 WEST MARKET STREET. TELEPHONE 216.

PROVIDENT LIFE AND TRUST CO. OF PHILADELPHIA. D. W. Edwards, G. A., 508 Indiana Trust Bldg. In form of policy; prompt settlement of death losses; equitable dealing with policy-holders; in strength of organization; and in everything which contributes to Security and Cheapness of life insurance, this company is unsurpassed.

THEODORE F. SMITHER, AGENT FOR WARREN'S ANCHOR BRAND ASPHALT ROOFING. OFFICE, 151 WEST MARYLAND ST. TEL. 861.

Shroebel Frances, h e s Arlington av 1 n of Washington av (I).
Shroyer Harry, student, r 282 N Senate av.
Shrub Ella L (wid Calvin A), b 651½ N Senate av.
Shryer Mark H (Buntin, Shryer & McGannon), h 412 Talbott av.
Shuck, see also Schuck.
Shuck Andrew, driver, b 66 N Noble.
Shuck Jesse, lab, r 227 Hadley av (W I).
Shue Joseph T, lab, b 610½ Virginia av.
Shue Stewart F, cabtmkr, h 610½ Virginia av.
Shue Wm S, bartndr, h 55 Willow.
Shuey Frank, electrician, h 407 E Washington.
Shufelton Harry W, mach, b 149 Park av.
Shufelton Margaret A (wid Henry C), h 149 Park av.
SHUFELTON THOMAS P, Sheriff Marion County, 34 Court House, h County Jail.
Shufflebarger Wm, lab, b 304 S Meridian.
Shufflebarger Wm H, shoemkr, h 56 Deloss.
Shugert Edgar K, bkkpr, b 228 Ramsey av.
Shugert Frank W, mach, b 228 Ramsey av.
Shugert Worley C, yardmaster, h 228 Ramsey av.
Shugrue, see also Sughrue.
Shugrue Daniel, lab, h 324 Bates.
Shugrue Daniel C, lab, b 283 Bates.
Shugrue Margaret, b 73 S Summit.
Shugrue Patrick, lab, b 890 W Washington.
Shugrue Thomas, lab, h 73 S Summit.
Shuler Lawrence S, h 983 N Illinois.
Shull David, tailor, b 300 S Meridian.
Shulse John M, mer police, h 317 E North.
Shultie Benjamin, engraver, b 235 Cottage av.
Shultz, see also Schultz and Schulz.
Shultz Jay O, printer, b 590 College av.
Shultz Homer, brakeman, h 281 N Noble.
Shultz Joseph R, mngr M Rumely Co, 100 S Capitol av, h 1016 N Penn.
Shultz Melissa (wid Joseph), b 861 N Delaware.
Shumar John C, driver, r 28 Hutchings blk.
Shumate Clara, r 24 Columbia blk.
Shumate Elmer F, coremkr, b 44 Warman av (H).
Shumate Myrtle P, bkkpr Home Cracker Co, b 453 N Penn.
Shumm Lillian G (wid Wm H), h 158 Spann av.
Shunterman Minnie W, stenog, b 345 N Alabama.
Shuppert Frank, lab, b 188 Meek.
Shuppert Michael, lab, h 423 N Pine.
Shute Alfred S, carp, h 138 Winchester.
Shute Hamlin L, builders' material, 35 Talbott blk, b 174 N Illinois.
Shutt Jacob F, h 41 Omer.
Shutt Mary A (wid Harry), h 50 Hosbrook.
Shutt Samuel C, engr Court House, b 107 Cornell av.
Shutte Charles, lab, r 86 N Senate av.
Shutters Harrison, wheelmkr, b 297 River av (W I).
Sibley Anderson, tmstr, h 390 Alvord.
Sichelstiel Aloysius J, tinner, h 560 Union.
Sickel John E, cabtmkr, h 59 College av.
Sickels Frederick S, clk W U Tel Co, h 272 E Walnut.
Sickels Henry C, chief clk W U Tel Co, h 1083 N Illinois.
Sickels Wm H Rev, h 351 N East.
Sickford George A, novelty mnfr, 62 W Ohio, h 419 N East.

THE WHEN IS A WORLD BEATER.

Sickle Edward, cook The Denison.
Sickler Edward E, h 28 Morrison.
Sickler Isaac H, h 506 N Meridian.
Sickles Catherine A, teacher, b 351 N East.
Sickles Clara, bookbndr Wm B Burford, r 103 The Shiel.
Sicko David, h 329 Tremont.
Sicks Thomas S, plumber, h 192 Cherry.
Siddall Frances M, stenog, b 784 N Penn.
Siddall Melinda A (wid James P), h 227 E Louisiana.
Siddall Wm H, asst foreman Indpls Journal, h 93 Lexington av.
Siddle Henry, lab 330 N Meridian.
Sidener James B, trav agt Hide, Leather and Belting Co, h 439 Broadway.
Sidener Merle, reporter The Sun, h 107 Irwin.
Sides Edwin, mattressmkr, b 115 Chadwick.
Sides Wm A, carp, h 431 E St Clair.
Sidow Albert F, trav agt, h 280 N Noble.
Siebe Wm F, molder, h 256 Alvord.
Siebert, see also Seibert.
Siebert Henry J, painter, h 80 S Dorman.
Siebert Wm G, fireman, h 146 Randolph.
Sieboldt Anna (wid Herman), h 166 N Noble.
Sieboldt John A, sawmkr, h 407 S Delaware.
Sied Charles E, lab, h 155 Blake.
Sied Hattie, dressmkr, 1003 N Senate av, b same.
Sied Wm, h 1003 N Senate av.
Siegel Harris, shoemkr, 311 E Washington, h same.
Siegel Louis, pdlr, h 185 N Pine.
Siegfried Julia, phys, 65 W Ohio, r same.
Siegle Elizabeth, dressmkr, b 244 N Noble.
Siegle Ralph, clk, b 244 N Noble.
Siegle Sarah, dressmkr, b 244 N Noble.
Siegler Esther (wid Lebewald), b 53 Union.
Siegman Henry, mach, h 131½ Newman.
Siegmound James, lab, h n w cor James and Bloyd av (B).
Siegmund Charles, carp, h 125 Downey.
Siegmund Henry D, plastr, h 388 Columbia av.
Siegmundt Harry A, clk, r 224½ Kentucky av.
Sielaff August, h rear 472 E Washington.

The A. Burdsal Co. CELEBRATED HOMESTEAD READY MIXED PAINT. WHOLESALE AND RETAIL. 34 AND 36 SOUTH MERIDIAN STREET.

ELECTRIC SUPPLIES We Carry a full Stock. Prices Right. C. W. MEIKEL, Tel. 466. 96-98 E. New York St.

DALTON & MERRIFIELD { LUMBER South Noble St., near E. Washington

INDIANA ELECTROTYPE CO. ••• BEST WORK LOWEST PRICES.
23 WEST PEARL ST., INDIANAPOLIS, IND. JOB WORK. BOOK PLATES. BEST PATENT BASE ON THE MARKET. All Orders Promptly Filled.

KIRKHOFF BROS.,
Electrical Contractors, Wiring and Construction.
102-104 SOUTH PENNSYLVANIA ST.
TELEPHONE 910.

Sielaff Charles O, lab, h 1 Eureka av.
Sielaff Herman J, motorman, h 417 Harrison av.
Sielken Herman H, clk Charles Mayer & Co, r 860 N New Jersey.
Sielken H Louis, mngr H Lieber Co, h 858 N New Jersey.
Sielken Marianne, teacher German Public School No 10, b 858 N New Jersey.
Siem Henry, meats, 633 Madison, h same.
Siemon Charles W, sawyer, b 312 S Penn.
Siener Jacob, bkkpr Indpls Brewing Co, r 145 E Maryland.
Siersdorfer Albert, clk Louis Siersdorfer, b 293 E South.
Siersdorfer Edward A, clk Louis Siersdorfer, h 137 Spann av.
Siersdorfer Frank, clk Louis Siersdorfer, b 263 N Senate av.
Siersdorfer Joseph G, clk Louis Siersdorfer, h 92 English av.
SIERSDORFER LOUIS, Boots and Shoes, 27 W Washington, h 293 E South.
Siersdorfer Louis, trav agt, h 480 N Senate av.
Siessl, see also Sissle.
Siessl John B, saloon, 135 E Washington, h same.
Siesz Joseph, lab, h 251 W Morris.
Sigelen Christian A, mnfrs' agt, h 133 Hoyt av.
Sigler Frank M, h 204 College av.
SIGLER GEORGE A, Physician, cor Central av and 9th, h 404 Central av.
Sigmond Jacob, molder, b e s Brown av 2 n of Michigan (H).
Sikes Joseph, lab, h rear w s canal 1 n of 6th.
Silbernagel John, wagonmkr, h 43 Wisconsin.
Silcox Schuyler C, driver, h 155 Minnesota.
Siler Daniel W, lab, h 508 W McLene (N I).
Siler Frank A, lab, b 561 W Francis (N I).
Siler John W, mach, h 672 W Eugene (N I).
Siler Josephine, seamstress, b 525 E 8th.
Siler Lewis H, porter, r 29 S Illinois.

THE W. C. WASSON CO.,
130 Indiana Ave. Tel. 989.
STEAM

Car Lots a Specialty. Prompt Delivery.
Brazil Block, Jackson and Anthracite.

Siler Martha A (wid Enos C), h 525 E 8th.
Siler Sophia (wid Daniel), b 672 W Eugene (N I).
Siles Louis A, lab, h 167 Johnson av.
Sills George W, mach hd, h 209 S Linden.
Silsby Charles A, miller, h 42 Belmont av (H).
Silva Una F (wid Edward), b 72½ Indiana av.
Silver Leroy J, sub letter carrier P O.
Silver Robert, trav agt, h 521 Park av.
Silver Wm F, carp, 29 Tacoma av, h same.
Silverman Eli, pdlr, h 106 Eddy.
Silvers Austin H (Silvers Bros), h 181 Alvord.
Silvers Bros (Walter B and Austin H), wagonmkrs, 454 Mass av.
Silvers Elmer E, printer, r 137 Virginia av.
Silvers Walter B (Silvers Bros), h 502 Park av.
Silvers Wm C, b 181 Alvord.
Silverstein Abraham, tailor, 317 E Washington, h same.
Silvester, see also Sylvester.
Silvester Wm B, b 579 N Penn.
Silvester Wm R N, h 597 N Penn.
Silvey Hilary L, lab, h 142 Clarke.
Silvey John H, lab, h s e cor Willow and Foundry (B).
Silvey Presley, lab, h 9 Lawn (B).
Silvey Presley A, lab, h s e cor Willow and Foundry (B).
Silvey Travis A, lab, h 22 Ludlow av.
Silvey Wm H, b s e cor Willow and Foundry (B).
Silvius Ellis T (Thurman & Silvius), h 589 Broadway.
Silvius James M, cooper, b 547 E Michigan.
Silz John P, lab, b 201 Orange.
Silz Wm F, b 113 S Spruce.
Simco Louisa, b 147 Minerva.
Simco Philip, hostler, r 23 Monument pl.
Simco Wm, lab, h 480 Chapel.
Simco Wm, porter, h 47 Agnes.
Simkins Frank O, broommkr, h 262 Spring.
Simmelink Harry B, trav frt agt P & E Ry, r 232 The Shiel.
Simmendinger John P, clk, b 290 W Washington.
Simmes Charles E, carp, b 26 Grace.
Simmes Edward C, carp, 26 Grace, h same.
Simmonds Fernandez M (Leonard & Simmonds), h 287 N Penn.
Simmons Albert N, bricklyr, b 230 Buchanan.
Simmons Alonzo J, clk Consumers' Gas Trust Co, h 23 Camp.
Simmons Anderson Rev, pastor First Baptist Church (N I), h 65 Cornell av.
Simmons Artemus G (O D Hardy & Co), h 240½ E Washington.
Simmons Benjamin F, h 19 School.
Simmons Calvin, engr, b 194 Kentucky av.
Simmons Charles T, clk, h 9 Hall pl.
Simmons Charles W, lab, h w s Samoa 1 s of Mass av.
Simmons Daniel, trav agt, b 109 Broadway.
Simmons Edward, porter, h 539 E 7th.
Simmons Emily (wid Wm Price), h 179 Tremont av (H).
Simmons George G, printer, b 13 Cooper.
Simmons Harry, clk, h 261 Virginia av.
Simmons John, waiter The Bates.
Simmons John A, agt West Shore Fast Freight Line, 1 E Washington, b 19 School.
Simmons John G, grocer, 150 English av, h 137 same.

W. H. Messenger FURNITURE, CARPETS, STOVES, 101 EAST WASHINGTON ST. TEL. 491.

McNamara, Koster & Co. | Foundry and Pattern Shop, 212-218 S. PENN. ST. . . . PHONE 1593.

Simmons Joseph L, lab, h 63 Ludlow av.
Simmons Julius G, lab, b 179 Tremont av (H).
Simmons Moses, lab, h 82 Columbia al.
Simmons Nellie P, stenog D H Baldwin & Co, b 1009 N Penn.
Simmons Oliver M, com agt, 19½ N Meridian, b 392 W Pratt.
Simmons Paul B, bicycle rep, 818 N Illinois, b 9 Hall pl.
Simmons Sarah E (wid Albert A), b 230 Buchanan.
Simmons Shade, lab, h 98 Rhode Island.
Simmons Silas E, mach, b 289 Virginia av.
Simmons Thomas, janitor, b 8 Miller blk.
Simmons Thomas J Rev, b 434 Central av.
Simmons Wm A, bricklyr, h 230 Buchanan.
Simms, see also Sims.
Simms Allen C, clk County Treasurer, h 209 Agnes.
Simms Caroline (wid Jeffrey), laundress, h 573 Mass av.
Simms Edmund K, plastr, h 227 E Market.
Simms Frank M, engr, h 765 E Washington.
Simms James N, medicine mnfr, 127½ Indiana av, r same.
Simms Joseph M, carp, h 69 Villa av.
Simms Lewis, driver, b 399 N Illinois.
Simms Lucy (wid James), h 6 Lafayette.
Simms Susan, b 138 Martindale av.
Simms Thomas J, lab, b 136 N Dorman.
Simms Wm H, barber, 768½ S East, h 1 Gimbel.
Simon Abraham, plumber, b 399 S Illinois.
Simon Adolph H, driver, h 12 Wisconsin.
Simon Charles, driver, b 266 E Wabash.
Simon Charles C, carp, h 72 N Gillard av.
Simon Christopher G, blksmith, b 215 W South.
Simon Emil F, finisher, b 22 Sheldon.
Simon Frederick A, clk Hollweg & Reese, h 241 Madison av.
Simon Frederick W, grocer, 188 N Noble, h same.
Simon George, lab, b 266 E Wabash.
Simon Goodman, grocer, 399 S Illinois, h same.
Simon Gustav J, candymkr, b 503 S New Jersey.
Simon Henry, mach, h 143 E Merrill.
Simon Henry A, gasfitter, h 270 S Alabama.
Simon Henry L, finisher, h 148 Dougherty.
Simon Henry O, shoemkr, b 1038 E Michigan.
Simon Henry W, mach, b 369 N Noble.
Simon Herman A, candymkr, b 503 S New Jersey.
Simon Jacob, lab, b 234 W New York.
Simon Louis, bartndr, b 270 S Illinois.
Simon Louis P, mach, 199 S Meridian, h 132 N Noble.
Simon Magnus, h 503 S New Jersey.
Simon Martin, lab, r 104 S Noble.
Simon Mary (wid Charles), h 266 E Wabash.
Simon Robert J, plumber H A Goth, b 317 W Morris.
Simon Wm, waiter, b 683 N Senate av.
Simon Wm A, meats, 2 E Mkt House, h 84 Weghorst.
Simonds John, blksmith, r 41 Indiana av.
Simons Charles H, mngr Swift & Co, b 159 Christian av.
Simons Emma, dressmkr, 427 Talbott av, h same.
Simons Harvey L, painter, h 6 Madison.
Simons Orin L, painter, h rear 328 Alvord.
Simons Rachel (wid Wm), h 173 Harmon.

Henry H. Fay, 40½ E. Washington St., REAL ESTATE, AND LOAN BROKER.

Simons Susan S (wid Martin), h 27 Alvord.
Simons Thomas L, lab, b 427 Talbott av.
Simons Victor A, switchman, b 27 Alvord.
Simons Wm, waiter Grand Hotel.
Simonsen Albert, carp, h 68 Buchanan.
Simonsen Gustav, clk Progress Clothing Co, h 1125 N Penn.
Simonson Newton A, engr, h w s National av 1 s of C H & D R R (I).
Simpson Arthur J, bkkpr, b 917 N New Jersey.
Simpson Charles, lab, b 25 Patterson.
Simpson Charles, mach hd, b 280 Archer.
Simpson Charles A, tailor, h 380 Union.
Simpson Charles F, woodwkr Indpls Pattern Wks, b 380 Union.
Simpson Edgar M, clk N Y Store, b 511 Broadway.
Simpson Edward C, lawyer, h 1144 N Delaware.
Simpson Elizabeth (wid John), h 1050 W Washington.
Simpson Elizabeth D, housekpr 368 W New York.
Simpson Elliott, lab, h 427 Lafayette.
Simpson Frank E, mach hd, b 319 N Noble.
Simpson George P, bookbndr, b 674 N Capitol av.
Simpson George W, lab, r 83 N Capitol av.
Simpson George W, musician, h 405 W 2d.
Simpson Harry, plumber, b 398 Martindale av.
Simpson Henry, lab, b 189 W 9th.
Simpson James M, musician, r 40 S Capitol av.
Simpson John, mason, h w s Hanna 2 n of E Michigan.
Simpson John R, grocer, 179 N East, h 177 same.
Simpson Lucetta (wid James L), dressmkr, 96 S East, h same.
Simpson Margaret (wid Richard), h 82 W North.
Simpson Margaret M (wid John), b 674 N Capitol av.
Simpson Maria (wid James P), b 209 Hoyt av.
Simpson Mary (wid James L), b 167 W Washington.

UNIUN CASUALTY & SURETY CO. OF ST. LOUIS, MO. All lines of Personal Accident and Casualty Insurance, including Employers' and General Liability. W. E. BARTON & CO., General Agents, 504 Indiana Trust Building. LONG DISTANCE TELEPHONE 1918.

THE FRED DIETZ CO. WOODEN PACKING BOXES MADE TO ORDER. FACTORY AND WAREHOUSE TRUCKS. 400 Madison Avenue. Telephone 654.

Indianapolis BUSINESS UNIVERSITY Leading College of Business and Shorthand. Elevator day and night. Individual instruction. Large faculty. Terms easy. Enter now. See p. 4. When Block. E. J. HEEB, President.

Water and Oil Meters { HENRY R. WORTHINGTON, 64 S. PENNSYLVANIA ST. Long Distance Telephone 284.

UNION CO-OPERATIVE LAUNDRY } (COMPOSED OF UNION MEMBERS.) NOS. 138, 140 AND 142 ... AVENUE. T. E. SOMERVILLE, MANAGER. TELEPHONE 1269. INDIANAPOLIS, IND.

HORACE M. HADLEY
REAL ESTATE AND INSURANCE
66 East Market Street, Basement
TELEPHONE 1540.

Simpson Nettie, teacher Public School No 13, b 209 Hoyt av.
Simpson Oliver, lab, h 280 Highland av.
Simpson Robert L, lab, h 75 Meikel.
Simpson Samuel S, clk R M S, h 479 N Meridian.
Simpson Sarah, smstrs, b 29 Shover (W I).
Simpson Sarah (wid John), b 627 E Vermont.
Simpson Thomas J, spl police, h 62 Beacon.
Simpson Wm, clk, b 347 W Washington.
Simpson Wm, engr, r 154 N New Jersey.
Simpson Wm, photog, 94½ E Washington, h 579 Marlowe av.
Simpson Wm B, tinner, h 209 Hoyt av.
Simpson Wm M, ins agt, h 511 Broadway.
Simpson Wm O, engr, r 126 E New York.
Sims, see also Simms.
Sims Augustus A, condr, h 286 Virginia av.
Sims Austin, lab, b 2 Holborn.
Sims Bessie, h 11 Mill.
Sims, Charles, lab, b n s 8th 3 w of canal.
Sims Charles B, plumber Holmes & Co, h 630 Virginia av.
Sims Charles E, trav agt, h 747½ N New Jersey.
SIMS CHARLES N REV, Pastor Meridian Street Methodist Church, h 25 W New York.
Sims Charles W, lab, h 33 Reynolds av (H).
Sims Dudley, carp, h n s 8th 3 w of canal.
Sims Frank, lab, b 1169 E Washington.
Sims Frank B, carp, b 102 Frazee (H).
Sims George, lab, b 33 Reynolds av (H).
Sims George W, lab, r 291 Christian av.
Sims Henry W, paperhngr, b 179 Hill av.
Sims Israel, lab, h 179 Hill av.
Sims James A, roofer, h s w cor 26th and Central av.
Sims Jefferson F, janitor, r 36 Bird.
Sims Jefferson T, cooper, b 66 Warren av (W I).
Sims John, lab, h 32 Parker.
Sims John, lab, h w s James 3 s of Sutherland (B).
Sims John D, lab, h 483 Martindale av.
Sims John M (Heaton, Sims & Co), res Knightstown, Ind.

PERSONAL AND PROMPT ATTENTION GIVEN TO COLLECTIONS.
Merchants' and Manufacturers' Exchange
J. E. TAKKEN, Manager,
19 Union Building, 73 West Maryland Street.

Sims John M, carp, h 102 Frazee (H).
Sims John S, coachman, h 4 Peck.
Sims John W, driver, h 131 N Pine.
Sims Martin, lab, h 89 Newman.
Sims Martin V, cooper, b 102 Frazee (H).
Sims Oscar W, lab, b 179 Hill av.
Sims Robert, carp, h 489 Martindale av.
Sims Robert H, lab, h 23 Roanoke.
Sims Thomas, coachman 174 Central av.
Sims Thomas, lab 264 N Capitol av.
Sims Thomas, lab, h 5 Peck.
Sims Wm E, waiter, h 465 Union.
Sims Wm H, barber, h 27 Columbia al.
Sinclair, see also St Clair.
Sinclair Alexander, foreman Kingan & Co (ltd), b 335 W Vermont.
SINCLAIR ROBERT S, Mngr Kingan & Co, h 122 W Michigan, Tel 597.
Sinden Amanda (wid Jesse), h 75 River av (W I).
SINDLINGER BROS (Peter and Charles), Meat Market, 100 N Illinois, Tel 473.
Sindlinger Charles (Sindlinger Bros), h 132 W North.
Sindlinger Eva (wid Gottlieb), h 309 Fletcher av.
Sindlinger George, meats, 204 Prospect, h 379 S State av.
SINDLINGER PETER (Sindlinger Bros; Saffel & Sindlinger), Wholesale and Retail Meats, 207 W Michigan, and Stalls 25-26 E Market House, b 213 W Michigan, Tel 860.
Sine Charles B, carp, h 231 College av.
Sine Frank E, condr, h 574 Park av.
Sinex Charles B, floor mngr N Y Store, b 138 E St Joseph.
Sing Hop, laundry, 75 N Illinois.
Sing Lee, laundry, 295 Mass av.
Sing Pang, laundry, 125 Mass av.
Sing Wah, laundry, 143 E Washington.
Singer Anna D, clk W E Stevenson & Co, b 168 St Mary.
Singer George P, hostler, h 168 St Mary.
Singer Isaac, pdlr, h 256 S Meridian.
Singer Jacob, gents' furngs, 224 E Washington, h same.
SINGER MANUFACTURING CO THE, Jacob Fox Mngr, Sewing Mechines, 72-74 W Washington, Tel 1418.
Singer Meta (wid George), h 399 S East.
Singer Wm F, steelwkr, b 46 S Capitol av.
Singleton, see also Shingleton.
Singleton Arthur F, bkkpr, h 275 E Walnut.
Singleton Charles, brakeman, b 157 Lexington av.
Singleton Edward E, dry goods, 149 Shelby, h same.
Singleton Elizabeth K (wid Alonzo H), b 651 S Meridian.
Singleton Harvey, lab, r 36 Roanoke.
Singleton Henry, lab, h 157 Lexington av.
Singleton Jane (wid Price), h 1764 N Illinois.
Singleton Lovell, lab, h 1764 N Illinois.
Singleton Martha (wid John W), r 27½ Monument pl.
Singleton Richard (Cooper & Singleton), billiards, 117 Ft Wayne av, b 221 W Michigan.
Singleton Theodore W, foreman, h 298 E St Clair.
Singleton Wm, lab, h 291 Bright.
Sinick John W, switchtndr, h 27 S Station (B).
Sink Francis C, tmstr, h 150 River av (W I).

CLEMENS VONNEGUT
184, 186 and 192 E. Washington St.
FOUNDRY AND MACHINISTS' SUPPLIES. "NORTON" EMERY WHEELS AND GRINDING MACHINERY.

THE WM. H. BLOCK CO. DRY GOODS, MILLINERY, CLOAKS AND FURS. 7 AND 9 EAST WASHINGTON STREET.

Sink Hiram T, carp, 553 E Michigan, h same.
Sink Wm H, electrician, b 150 River av (W I).
SINKER-DAVIS CO THE, James H Hooker Pres, Henry R Bliss Sec and Treas, Abner J Malone Supt, Founders and Machinists, 112-150 S Missouri, Tel 415.
Sinker Henry B, driver, h 716 Chestnut.
Sinker John, gardener, h 942 Madison av.
Sinker John, lab, h 693 Chestnut.
Sinker John, lab, h 908 Madison av.
Sinks Emory, driver, h w s Harris av 3 s of W Washington (M J).
Sinks E Barton, stenog J H Dilks, b Sherman House.
Sinks James M, h 208 Bright.
Sinks Laura (wid George), b 1018 N Penn.
Sinnott Michael J, lab, h 27 Hendricks.
Sinnott Nicholas M, trav agt Murphy, Hibben & Co, h 245 Central av.
SIPE JACOB C, Wholesale Mnfg and Retail Jeweler, 4 Waverly Bldg, 18½ N Meridian, b The Bates.
Sipf Carrie (wid Wm E), b 108 Keystone av.
Sipf Christian E, harnessmkr, b 201 Douglass.
Sipf Frederick, harnessmkr, 268 W Washington, h 201 Douglass.
Sipf Walter, baker, h 201 Douglass.
Sirp Frederick, carp, h 89 Hoyt av.
Sirp Frederick H, mach hd, b 89 Hoyt av.
Sirp George, painter, h 139 St Paul.
Sirp George H, sawyer, h 33 N Spruce.
Sirp Richard, lab, h 226 Shelby.
Sirp Sarah, dressmkr, 520 Shelby, h same.
Sirp Wm, meats, 81 E Mkt House, h 142 Buchanan.
Sisk Alpheus E, b w s Sugar Grove av 3 s of Miller av (M P).
Sisk George W, mngr, h 288 N New Jersey.
Sisk Wm B, millwright, h w s Sugar Grove av 3 s of Miller av (M P).
Sisloff Clara I, stenog, b 383 Bellefontaine.
Sisloff Gamaliel S, molder, h 383 Bellefontaine.
Sisloff Jesse S, bookbndr Wm B Burford, b 383 Bellefontaine.
Sissenguth Dietrich C, tel opr, b 181 E Washington.
Sissenguth Wm C, mach, b 23 Larch.
Sissle, see also Siessl.
Sissle George A Rev, h 210 Columbia av.
Sissle Martha A, teacher Public School No 18, h 210 Columbia av.
Sisson Ernest R, student, r 227 N Liberty.
Sisson Wm, lab, h 1622 N Meridian.
Sisson Wm J, trav agt D P Erwin & Co, h 17 Butler.
Sisters of the Good Shepherd, Sister Mary or St Ursula Schaw superioress, 57 W Raymond.
Sisters of Providence, St John's Academy, s s Maryland bet Illinois and Capitol av.
Sisters of St Francis, 73 E Maryland.
Sites George A, yard foreman C C C & St L Ry, h 13 S Station (B).
Sites Jacob P, h rear 137 E Pratt.
Sites Orrin M, clk, b rear 137 E Pratt.
Sitzmann John, cabtmkr, b 71 Park av.
Skaggs Alfred T, lab, b 593 W Maryland.
Skaggs Jefferson, lab, h 541 W Pearl.
Skaggs Jefferson jr, lab, b 541 W Pearl.
Skaggs Robert H, lab, h 1 Minerva.
Skaggs Robert H, mach hd, h 593 W Maryland.

PICTURES · MIRRORS. THE H. LIEBER COMPANY. 33 South Meridian Street. Artistic Framing.

Skeen Fanny, attendant Insane Hospital.
Skelly Robert H, lab, h 14 Water.
Skelton Elizabeth E, h 344½ E St Clair.
Sketten George W, porter, r 548 Superior.
Skibbe August, carp, h 52 Cook.
Skidmore Jennie, h 256½ W Washington.
Skidmore John A, pressman The Indpls News, h 87 Highland pl.
Skidmore Joseph R, brakeman, b 256½ W Washington.
Skiles Henry, clk, b 245 W 5th.
Skiles Mary A (wid Thomas H), b 98 Middle Drive (W P).
Skillen Eleanor S, prin Public School No 34, b 526 N Capitol av.
Skillen James, h 526 N Capitol av.
Skillen Jennie C, teacher Public School No 17, b 526 N Capitol av.
Skillen Samuel W, baggageman, h 113 Coburn.
Skillman James C, baggageman, h 43 Fletcher av.
Skillman P Victor, modelmkr, h 330 N New Jersey.
Skillman Wm T, lab, b 43 Fletcher av.
Skillmon David J, janitor, h 240 Huron.
Skinner Allison, driver, h 10 Harrison.
Skinner Bessie F (wid Oscar T), h 170 Cornell av.
Skinner Charles H, fireman, h 3 Depot (B).
Skinner Ebenezer T, tmstr, h 1167 E Ohio.
Skinner Edward, lab, h 63 Eastern av.
Skinner Eli, lab, h rear 472 E Washington.
Skinner Flora A (wid Gilbert A), h 27 W 22d.
Skinner Henderson, lab, h 7 Ellsworth.
Skinner Henderson jr, porter, b 7 Ellsworth.
Skinner James A, lab, h 63 Eastern av.
Skinner Joseph, cook Deaf and Dumb Inst.
Skinner Lewis B (Smith & Skinner), h 17 Tecumseh av.
Skinner Nancy (wid Dennis), h 120 Columbia al.
Skinner Nathaniel M, h 87 Tremont av (H).
Skinner Oliver D, painter, h 69 Columbia av.
Skinner Thomas J, paperhngr, b 5, 602½ E Washington.

GUIDO R. PRESSLER
FRESCO PAINTER
Churches, Theaters, Public Buildings, Etc., A Specialty.
Residence, No. 325 North Liberty Street.
INDIANAPOLIS, IND.

INDIANAPOLIS STEEL ROOFING AND CORRUGATING WORKS, 23 and 25 East South Street. S. D. NOEL, Proprietor.

David S. McKernan REAL ESTATE AND LOANS. Exchanging real estate a specialty. A number of choice pieces for encumbered property. Rooms 2-5 Thorpe Block.

DIAMOND WALL PLASTER { Telephone 1410 BUILDERS' EXCHANGE.

UNION TRANSFER AND STORAGE CO. Cor. E. Ohio St. and C., C., C. & St. L. R'y Tracks. Storage of Household Goods and Pianos a Specialty.

W. McWORKMAN,
Galvanized Iron Cornice Works
TIN AND SLATE ROOFING.
930 WEST WASHINGTON STREET.
TELEPHONE 1118.

Skinner Thomas M, hostler, r 180 E Wabash.
Slack Albert, barber, n s Michigan 5 e of Sharpe av (W), b 141 Sharpe av (W).
Slack Harry S, clk C C C & St L Ry, h 16 Union.
Slack Louis B, bicycle rep, h 279 W Michigan.
Slack Louis E, student, b 135 W Michigan.
Slack Oliver P, filer, h 178 E Vermont.
Slackman Hodges, lab, b 391 W 2d.
Slager Willis E, contr, h 35 Clarke.
Slagle George, plastr, b 609 W Pearl.
Slagle Scott, lab, r 38 Oak.
Slaick Albert L, carp, h 140 E New York.
Slannery Sallie, b 127 Palmer.
Slate Henry T, policeman, h 59 Bradshaw.
Slate Pamelia A (wid Benjamin F), h 54 Bradshaw.
Slate Henry, patrolman, h 59 Bradshaw.
Slate Wm F, mach, b 59 Bradshaw.
Slater Cicero C, lab, h 97 Bates.
Slater Jacob H, pres State Capitol Inv Assn, h 375 Central av.
Slater Lucius N, tmstr, h 176 W 7th.
Slatery Edwin S, coremkr, b 118 Tremont av (H).
Slatery George P, coremkr, b 118 Tremont av (H).
Slatery James C, mach, h 118 Tremont av (H).
Slaton Lucinda J (wid Samuel), h 274 Blake.
Slatter George W, lather, h 47 Peru av.
Slattery Johanna W (wid Wm), h 505 E Georgia.
Slattery John, engr, b 505 E Georgia.
Slatts Wm C (Slatts & Poe), loans, 24 Ingalls blk, h 78 N New Jersey.
SLATTS & POE (Wm C Slatts, George M Poe), Ticket Brokers, 122 S Illinois, Tel 362.
Slaughter Alonzo T, lather, b 146 River av (W I).
Slaughter Benjamin V, switchman, h 105 Brookside av.
Slaughter George B, switchman, h 1091 W New York.
Slaughter Henry, carp, h w s Central av 2 s of Beechwood av (I).

SEALS,
STENCILS,
STAMPS, Etc.
GEO. J. MAYER
15 S. Meridian St.
TELEPHONE 1386.

Slaughter James C, plastr, h 146 River av (W I).
Slaughter John, lab, r 186 N California.
Slaughter Joseph, electrician, h 101 Walcott.
Slaughter Mary E (wid Milton A), b 105 Brookside av.
Slaughter Milton A, boilermkr, h 5½ Brookside av.
Slaughter Wm, lab, h n s Sutherland 2 e of James (B).
Slauter Henry K, mngr H T Hearsey Cycle Co, h 128 Brookside av.
Slauter Mary M (wid John W), b 124 Brookside av.
Slaven Edward, driver, b 235 W Market.
Slavin Michael, medicines, 62½ S Illinois, h 51 Drake.
Slavin Minelma L, bkkpr, b 51 Drake.
Slayback Lawrence O, clk Polar Ice Co, r 93 N Alabama.
Slayman George, lab, h 319 W Maryland.
Sleabener Herman, janitor, h rear 76 S Delaware.
Slean Peter, bricklyr, b 135 N Illinois.
Slee George F, trav agt, h 880 Bellefontaine.
Sleepir George, hostler, r 189 E Wabash.
Sleet Ida (wid Henry), h 367 S East.
Sleet James C, lab, h 120 Darnell.
Sleet John, lab, h rear 165 Minerva.
Sleet John H, clk Chandler & Taylor Co, b 367 S East.
Sleeth Amanda (wid George M), h 108 Ramsey av.
Sleeth Coke, lab, b 108 Ramsey av.
Sleeth James J, lab, b 108 Ramsey av.
Sleeth John, lab, h 159 Woodside av (W).
Sleeth John W, lab, h 143 Sharpe av (W).
Sleeth Wm, printer, b 108 Ramsey av.
Sleight Edward, watchman, h 43 Rockwood.
Sleight Elizabeth (wid John), h 295 S East.
Sleight John W, printer, 25 W Georgia, b 43 Rockwood.
Sleight Richard N, checkman Penna lines, h 538 S Meridian.
Sleight Wm, lab, h 408 Coburn.
Sleight Wm T, driver, b 408 Coburn.
Slemmer Charles H, mngr W U Tel Co, Union Stock Yards (W I), b 652 College av.
Slemmer Edward B, brakeman, b 652 College av.
Slemmer Mary L (wid Thomas B), h 652 College av.
Slemmons Lena (wid Wm), b 482 Superior.
Slevin Edward, checkman, b 317 S Delaware.
Slevin Frank, restaurant, 38 Jackson pl, b 317 S Delaware.
Slevin Marie (wid James), h 317 S Delaware.
Slick Charles, driver, b 15 Osgood (W I).
Slick Minnie (wid Joseph), b 198 Buchanan.
Slider Charles C, carp, h 20 Lawn (B).
Slider Charles E, presser, b 10 Lawn (B).
Slider Daniel D, mach hd, h 10 Lawn (B).
Slider Thomas, lab, h 190 Shelby.
Slider Wm T, mach, h 655 N Capitol av.
Slifer Harry O, barber, 54 Clifford av, h 483½ Stillwell.
Sligar Jesse W (Sligar & Paetz), b 118 E Pratt.
Sligar & Paetz (Jesse W Sligar, Alonzo W Paetz), laundry, 141 N Delaware.
Slinger Alardus C, clk Frederick M Herron, r 214 S Olive.
Slinger Julia (wid John I), h 122 Laurel.
Slinkard Stephen W, live stock, h 973 N Delaware.

A. METZGER AGENCY L-O-A-N-S ESTABLISHED 1863.

LAMBERT GAS & GASOLINE ENGINE CO.
ANDERSON, IND. GAS ENGINES FOR ALL PURPOSES.

Slinker Joseph, waiter, h 75 Hudson.
Sliter Henry L, cutter, h 1744 N Capitol av.
Slivey Wm, watchman, h 149 Clarke.
Sloan Alfred F, produce, b 751 Shelby.
Sloan Andrew J, tmstr, b 123 Huron.
Sloan Charles E, bkkpr The Indiana Mnfg Co, h 1349 N Illinois.

SLOAN DRUG CO, George W Sloan Pres, C B Sloan Vice-Pres, George B Sloan Sec and Treas, 22 W Washington, Tel 187.

Sloan Emory T, carp, h 41 S Linden.
Sloan Frank J, sawyer, h 119 Yandes.
Sloan Frank M, city fireman, b 536 N Senate av.
Sloan George B, sec and treas Sloan Drug Co, r 326 N Meridian.
Sloan George G, trav agt Schrader Bros, r 326 N Illinois.
Sloan George W, pres Sloan Drug Co, h 304 N Meridian.
Sloan Harry M, foreman, h 213 Fletcher av.
Sloan Hattie E, bkkpr Parry Mnfg Co, b 77 Huron.
Sloan James A, lab, b 536 N Senate av.
Sloan James D, painter, h 77 Huron.
Sloan James J, mach, h 339 Bates.
Sloan James K (Sloan & Matkins), h 536 N Senate av.
Sloan John, plumber, b 536 N Senate av.
Sloan John, tmstr, h 123 Huron.
Sloan John J, broommkr, h 53 Camp.
Sloan Mary F (wid Wm), h e s Commercial av 4 s of Washington av (I).
Sloan Mary L, clk, b 41 S Linden.
Sloan Oliver B, poultry, 31 E Mkt House, h 170 Spann av.
Sloan Robert R (Leonard & Sloan), h Michigan av 6 miles e of city.
Sloan Robinson, plumber, b 536 N Senate av.
Sloan Thomas J, grocer, 150 Walcott, h 148 same.

SLOAN & MATKINS (James K Sloan, Noah M Matkins), Stair Builders and Mnfrs of Grilles, Fret Work, Etc; Special Attention Given to Orders; Estimates Furnished; s e cor 7th and L E & W R R, Tel 1192. (See adv in classified Stair Builders.)

Sloan Warren R, city fireman, h 185 Hoyt av.
Sloan Wm G, produce, h s e cor Shelby and Bradbury.
Sloan Wm M, broommkr, h 427 W 22d (N I).
Sloan Wm W, plumber, b 136 N Senate av.
Slocomb Hannah A (wid Charles P), h 67 Middle Drive (W P).
Slocum Carmelia M (wid Eli), b 263 Keystone av.
Slocum Clarence W, agt Mass Mutual Life Ins Co, h 1227 N Meridian.
Slocum Edward W, bartndr, r 116½ N Meridian.
Slocum Ella, dressmkr, 4 Sheldon, h same.
Slocum Philip J, teacher, h 248 Keystone av.
Slocum Sarah C, dressmkr, 257 Lincoln la, h same.
Slocum Stewart H, student, h 248 Keystone av.
Sloski Abraham, lab, b 129 Eddy.
Sloss Van Buren, lab, h 69 Ludlow av.
Slough Carrie M, teacher, b e s Clyde av 1 n of English av (I).
Slough George W, farmer, h e s Clyde av 1 n of English av (I).

THOS. C. DAY & CO.
INVESTING AGENTS,
TOWN AND FARM LOANS,
Rooms 325 to 330 Lemcke Bldg.

Slough Harry H, printer Wm B Burford, h e s Linwood av 1 n of Ohio.
Sluder Isaac, lab, h 1327 Isabella (N I).
Sluder Joseph, gasfitter, h 187 W New York.
Slupesky Frank, pdlr, h 415 Union.
Slusher James N, cooper, h 78 S West.
Slusher Thomas E, grocer, 106 S William (W I), h same.
Sluss John W phys, 346 E St Clair, h 59 Ruckle.
Slusser Warren J, confr, 79 Mass av, h same.
Slutsky Henry S, jeweler, 22 Indiana av, h 286½ S Illinois.
Small, see also Smoll.
Small Charles A, sawmkr, h w s Rural 1 n of S Brookside av.
Small Clarence E, carp, h 3 Hester.
Small Daniel J, bkkpr, b 41 College av.
Small David, slater, h 79 N Dorman.
Small Dennis, barber, b 4 Walcott.
Small Edward, motorman, h 112 Blackford.
Small Eli B, h 348 Cornell av.
Small Ella M, bkkpr Wm H Robson, b 113 Meek.
Small Hattie E (wid Jerome N), h 113 Meek.
Small Hattie R, bkkpr, b 113 Meek.
Small Henry A, clk, b 41 College av.
Small Herbert, storekpr, h 120 Wright.
Small Isabella (wid Henry), h 41 College av.
Small James S, salesman Edward L Gross Realty Co, r 156 W Washington.
Small Millicent J, teacher, b 90 Division (W I).
Small Patrick, b 4 Walcott.
Small Samuel (Mills & Small), h 90 Division (W I).
Small Theodore C, cook, b 217 Orange.
Small Wm H, carp, h 217 Orange.
Smalley Edward, driver, h 274 W 7th.
Smalley James L, trav agt, h 473 Highland av.
Smallwood Charles C, boxmkr, h 75 Coburn.
Smallwood Charles E, lab, h 61 John.
Smallwood Edgar N, barber, 904 W Washington, b 898 same.
Smallwood Frank M, clk R M S, h 465 Park av.

EAT
QUAKER BREAD
ASK YOUR GROCER FOR IT.
THE HITZ BAKING CO.

BICYCLES $5 DOWN. $1 Best Wheels. Best Tr. WHEELMEN'S CO. 31 W. OHIO ST. LONG DISTANCE TEL. 1855.

J. H. TECKENBROCK | Grilles, Fretwork and Wood Carpets
94 EAST SOUTH STREET.

FIDELITY MUTUAl

SUPERIOR BITUMINOUS COAL For Steam and Domestic . . Purposes . . Edwardsport Coal & Mining Co. Rooms 42 and 43 When Building.

ESTABLISHED 1876. TELEPHONE
CHESTER BRADFORD
SOLICITOR OF PATEN
AND COUNSEL IN PATENT CAUSE
(See adv. page 6.)
Office:—Rooms 14 and 16 Hubbard Block,
Cor. Washington and Meridian Streets.
INDIANAPOLIS, INDIANA.

Smallwood Frank S, draughtsman, Yeiser.
Smallwood Joseph, molder, b 218 E Mor
Smart James D, painter, h 200 W 5th.
Smart Mary J (wid Charles), b 115 Co av.
Smart Nancy M (wid Joseph T), h 50½ ford av.
Smart Wm C, switchman, h 115 Cornell
Smead, see also Snead.
Smead Benjamin F, brakeman, h 877 M (W I).
Smead Leona E, bkkpr, b 34 Detroit.
Smead Wm H, yardmaster Belt R R, Nordyke av (W I).
Smear Wm, cabtmkr, h 67 Langley av.
Smelser George M, clk, b 200 N Capito
Smelser John A, oils, h 391 Bellefontai
Smelser Josephine, boarding 391 Belle taine.
Smelser May, stenog Wyckoff, Seamai Benedict, b 21 Park av.
Smelser Timothy C, pipefitter, h 39 Gil av.
Smeltzer Albert S, lab, h 470 W Mcl (N I).
Smiley Beriah J, horse dealer, h 60 N den.
Smiley Casius C, clk Geo W Stout, b 2 Illinois.
Smiley Edward A, lab, b 79 Norwood.
Smiley Hannah J (wid Frank M), Greer.
Smiley John, saloon, 151 W McCarty, Norwood.
Smiley Michael, mer police, h 79 Norw
Smiley Michael F, lab, b 79 Norwood.
Smiley Robert H, trav agt, r 28 Ft W av.
Smiley Thomas E, collr The Indpls tinel, h 330 E St Clair.
Smiley Thomas G, chief clk P & E R 275 N Delaware.
Smiley Wilber C, harnessmkr, b 284 S I
Smith, see also Schmid, Schmidt, Sch and Smythe.
Smith Abraham H, engr, h 247 N East.
Smith Abram, pdlr, h 33 Maxwell.
Smith Abram, janitor City Hospital.

ROOFING

Smith Bridget J (wid Peter J), h 58 N Brightwood av (B).
Smith Bonaparte, fireman, b 564 W Washington.
Smith Burton, lab, b 22 Center.
Smith Burton M, trav agt, b 231 N New Jersey.
SMITH CAREY L, Lawyer, 419-420 Lemcke Bldg, b 1400 N Capitol av.
Smith Carlisle M, timekpr P O, b 163 Talbott av.
Smith Caroline (wid Alonso), boarding 235 E Court.
Smith Caroline R, teacher Deaf and Dumb Inst, b 725 E Washington.
Smith Carter, elev opr, b 259 Blake.
Smith Carter, lab, b 33 Athon.
Smith Catherine (wid John), h 76 Fayette.
Smith Cecil J, trav agt, h 895 N Delaware.
Smith Celia (wid John), h 18 Maple.
Smith Charles, lab, b 306 Blackford.
Smith Charles, lab, h 234 Howard.
Smith Charles, lab, b 15 Rhode Island.
Smith Charles, cook, h 286 Lafayette.
Smith Charles, lab, b 34 Sheffield av (H).
Smith Charles, lab, b 30 Sheffield av (H).
Smith Charles, mach hd, h 486 English av.
Smith Charles, shoemkr, r 75 W Merrill.
Smith Charles, lab, h rear s s Washington 2 e of Line (I).
Smith Charles A, boilermkr, b 96 N Dorman.
Smith Charles A, clk The A Burdsal Co, b 1101 N Alabama.
Smith Charles A, lab, h w s Auburn av 4 s of English av.
Smith Charles B, condr, h 535 Bellefontaine.
Smith Charles C, lab, b 25 Beacon.
Smith Charles C, lab, h 265 N Noble.
Smith Charles D, waiter, h 293 N Delaware.
Smith Charles E, h 116 Ft Wayne av.
Smith Charles F, pres Indiana Bicycle Co, h 678 N Delaware.
Smith Charles F, student, r 84 E North.
Smith Charles H, carp, b 417 E Washington.
Smith Charles H, credit man Murphy, Hibben & Co, h 40 Huron.
Smith Charles L, barber, 33 W Market, r same.
Smith Charles L, clk, b 135 W Michigan.
Smith Charles L, horse dealer, b 7 Paca.
Smith Charles L L, mach, h 32 S State av.
Smith Charles M, carp, h 73 Gregg.
Smith Charles O, butcher, h 17 Centennial (H).
Smith Charles P, artist, b 276 N Penn.
Smith Charles R, coremkr, b 9 Cleveland (H).
Smith Charles S, h 352 Talbott av.
Smith Charles T, lab, h 294 Douglass.
Smith Charles T, mach hd, h 629 N West.
Smith Charles W (Duncan, Smith & Hornbrook), h 79 E Pratt.
Smith Charles W, farmer, h n end Belmont av (H).
Smith Charles W, lab, b 62 Bates.
Smith Charles W, lab, b 126 Williams.
Smith Charles W, porter, h 112 Columbia al.
Smith Christina C (wid Frederick), b 46 Water.

Te.

Smith
Smith
lum.
Smith C
Smith C
Smith C
SMITH C
Deer S
same. C
and Wi
Smith Colu
Smith Cora
SMITH, CH
David CH
Real Estat.
monds and
als. 10 Fair
Smith Cyrus A
Smith Cyrus M,
pl, h n s U
av (I).
Smith Daniel
31 Highland
Smith David
N Illinois.
Smith David
Smith David
Smith Davi
Smith Davi
Smith, Day
Lorey D.
chair mnfr
Smith Denn
Smith Dillar
of Auburn
Smith Dora A
Smith Dudley
av (H).
Smith Dwight
Smith Earl C
Johnson av.
Smith Earl C
same.
Smith Edmund
land, h 1 Cana
Smith Edward
Smith Edward
Smith Edward,

The Williams Ty

Elegant Work, ble
Easy Operation, gh S

S. H. EAST, Sta
55 Thorpe Block, E.

ELLIS & HELFENBERGER { Manufactu IRON and WIR 162-170 S. SENATE

FIDELITY MUTUAL LIFE PHILADELPHIA, PA. A. H. COLLINS { General Agent, 52-53 Baldwin Block.

Edwardsport Coal & Mining Co. Rooms 42 and 43 When Building.

ESTABLISHED 1876. TELEPHONE 163.
CHESTER BRADFORD,
SOLICITOR OF PATENTS,
AND COUNSEL IN PATENT CAUSES.
(See adv. page 6.)
Office:—Rooms 14 and 16 Hubbard Block, S.W. Cor. Washington and Meridian Streets, INDIANAPOLIS, INDIANA.

Smallwood Frank S, draughtsman, h 70 Yeiser.
Smallwood Joseph, molder, b 218 E Morris.
Smart James D, painter, h 200 W 5th.
Smart Mary J (wid Charles), b 115 Cornell av.
Smart Nancy M (wid Joseph T), h 50½ Clifford av.
Smart Wm C, switchman, h 115 Cornell av.
Smead, see also Snead.
Smead Benjamin F, brakeman, h 877 Morris (W I).
Smead Leona E, bkkpr, b 34 Detroit.
Smead Wm H, yardmaster Belt R R, h 147 Nordyke av (W I).
Smear Wm, cabtmkr, h 67 Langley av.
Smelser George M, clk, b 200 N Capitol av.
Smelser John A, oils, h 391 Bellefontaine.
Smelser Josephine, boarding 391 Bellefontaine.
Smelser May, stenog Wyckoff, Seamans & Benedict, b 21 Park av.
Smelser Timothy C, pipefitter, h 39 Gillard av.
Smeltzer Albert S, lab, h 470 W McLene (N I).
Smiley Beriah J, horse dealer, h 60 N Linden.
Smiley Casius C, clk Geo W Stout, b 204 N Illinois.
Smiley Edward A, lab, b 79 Norwood.
Smiley Hannah J (wid Frank M), h 53 Greer.
Smiley John, saloon, 151 W McCarty, b 79 Norwood.
Smiley Michael, mer police, h 79 Norwood.
Smiley Michael F, lab, b 79 Norwood.
Smiley Robert H, trav agt, r 28 Ft Wayne av.
Smiley Thomas E, collr The Indpls Sentinel, h 330 E St Clair.
Smiley Thomas G, chief clk P & E Ry, b 275 N Delaware.
Smiley Wilber C, harnessmkr, b 284 S East.
Smith, see also Schmid, Schmidt, Schmitt and Smythe.
Smith Abraham H, engr, h 247 N East.
Smith Abram, pdlr, h 33 Maxwell.
Smith Abram, janitor City Hospital.

76 N. PENNSYLVANIA ST., MAKERS Outing BICYCLES PHONE 598.

Smith Adda M (wid Pawhattan D), boarding 860 E Washington.
Smith Adolphus H, lab, h 28 Cleveland (H).
Smith Albert (Circle Transfer Co), h 36 Torbet.
Smith Albert, asst supt Parry Mnfg Co, h 265 S Illinois.
Smith Albert, bkkpr Internat Typograph Union, b 889 N Senate av.
Smith Albert, coachman 270 N Illinois.
Smith Albert, lab, b 17 Margaret.
Smith Albert, lab, h 192 Spann av.
Smith Albert C, barber, b 248 S East.
Smith Albert E, letter carrier P O, h 7 Schriver av.
Smith Albert P, b 79 E Pratt.
Smith Albert R, caller, h 321 Bates.
Smith Albert R, driver, h 571 S West.
Smith Albion, trav agt, h 672 E Washington.
Smith Alexander, lab, h 121 W 4th.
Smith Alfred, carp, h 180 Lexington av.
Smith Allen F, patrolman, h 67 W 11th.
Smith Alma E, stenog, b 202 Randolph.
Smith Almer D, lab, b 323 W Michigan.
Smith Alonzo, waiter, h 223 Howard.
Smith Alonzo Greene (Smith & Korbly), h 800 N Penn.
Smith Alva A, lab, h e s Austin 2 s of Sutherland (B).
Smith Alvie O, feed, 151 Columbia av, b 302 same.
Smith Anderson, lab, b 285 Christian av.
Smith Andrew, clk S A Fletcher & Co, h 82 N Noble.
Smith Andrew J, lab, h 119 Cottage av.
Smith Anna, h 20½ N Delaware.
Smith Anna, h 49 Hiatt (W I).
Smith Anna E (wid Hamilton), h 16 Windsor.
Smith Anna M, h 354 Fulton.
Smith Anna T (wid Wm C), h 438 N Meridian.
Smith Arley, electrician, b 180 E Washington.
Smith Arthur, attendant Insane Asylum.
Smith Arthur, tinner, 18 N Senate av, h 280 same.
Smith Arthur B, lab, h 19 Russell av.
Smith Arthur D, student, r 179 E New York.
Smith Arthur T, clk Taylor & Smith, b 352 Broadway.
Smith August C, cutter Louis Adam, h 15 Tacoma av.
Smith Aurelius, trav agt F H Smith, b 431 W 22d (N I).
Smith A Judson, bkkpr Indpls Ice Co, h 139 W Michigan.
Smith Barbara (wid Charles), h 79 Drake.
Smith Bartley, phys, 137 S William (W I), h same.
Smith Bedford F, engr, h 111 Fletcher av.
Smith Belle N (wid Eli), b 599 Ash.
Smith Benjamin, huckster, h 563 S Illinois.
Smith Benjamin, lab, b 234 W New York.
Smith Benjamin, mason, r 73 Maxwell.
Smith Benjamin F, piano tuner, 257 Highland av, h same.
SMITH BENJAMIN R, Livery and Boarding Stable; also Wholesale and Retail Flour and Feed, 4-8 Prospect, h 129 S Olive, Tel 219.
Smith Benjamin T, jeweler, b 820 N Illinois.
Smith Benjamin W, engr, h 571 E 9th.
Smith Bertha, teacher Industrial School, b 21 Ketcham.

SUPERIOR BITUMINOUS COAL For Steam and Domestic . . Purposes . .

ROOFING MATERIAL C. ZIMMERMAN & SONS SLATE AND GRAVEL ROOFERS, 19 SOUTH EAST STREET.

DRIVEN WELLS And Second Water Wells and Pumps of all kinds at CHARLES KRAUSS', 42 S. PENN. ST., TEL. 465. REPAIRING NEATLY DONE.

Smith Bertha, stenog Wm L Taylor, b 72 Tacoma av.
Smith Bertha V, bkkpr, b 771 N Senate av.
Smith Bertrand L, mailing clk P O, h 66½ N Delaware.
Smith Beryman, flagman, h 216 Yandes.
Smith Bridget J (wid Peter J), h 58 N Brightwood av (B).
Smith Bonaparte, fireman, b 564 W Washington.
Smith Burton, lab, b 22 Center.
Smith Burton M, trav agt, b 381 N New Jersey.
SMITH CAREY L, Lawyer, 419-420 Lemcke Bldg, b 1400 N Capitol av.
Smith Carlisle M, timekpr P O, b 163 Talbott av.
Smith Caroline (wid Alonzo), boarding 295 E Court.
Smith Caroline R, teacher Deaf and Dumb Inst, b 725 E Washington.
Smith Carter, elev opr, b 359 Blake.
Smith Carter, lab, b 33 Athon.
Smith Catherine (wid John), h 76 Fayette.
Smith Cecil J, trav agt, h 895 N Delaware.
Smith Celia (wid John), h 18 Maple.
Smith Charles, lab, b 308 Blackford.
Smith Charles, lab, h 234 Howard.
Smith Charles, lab, b 15 Rhode Island.
Smith Charles, cook, h 395 Lafayette.
Smith Charles, lab, b 24 Sheffield av (H).
Smith Charles, lab, b 20 Sheffield av (H).
Smith Charles, mach hd, h 485 English av.
Smith Charles, shoemkr, r 75 W Merrill.
Smith Charles, lab, h rear s s Washington 2 e of Line (I).
Smith Charles A, boilermkr, b 90 N Dorman.
Smith Charles A, clk The A Burdsal Co, b 1101 N Alabama.
Smith Charles A, lab, h w s Auburn av 4 s of English av.
Smith Charles B, condr, h 535 Bellefontaine.
Smith Charles C, lab, b 25 Beacon.
Smith Charles C, lab, h 265 N Noble.
Smith Charles D, waiter, h 293 N Delaware.
Smith Charles E, h 116 Ft Wayne av.
Smith Charles F, pres Indiana Bicycle Co, h 678 N Delaware.
Smith Charles F, student, r 84 E North.
Smith Charles H, carp, b 417 E Washington.
Smith Charles H, credit man Murphy, Hibben & Co, h 40 Huron.
Smith Charles L, barber, 33 W Market, r same.
Smith Charles L, clk, b 135 W Michigan.
Smith Charles L, horse dealer, b 7 Paca.
Smith Charles L L, mach, h 32 S State av.
Smith Charles M, carp, h 73 Gregg.
Smith Charles O, butcher, h 17 Centennial (H).
Smith Charles P, artist, b 276 N Penn.
Smith Charles R, coremkr, b 9 Cleveland (H).
Smith Charles S, h 352 Talbott av.
Smith Charles T, lab, b 294 Douglass.
Smith Charles T, mach hd, h 629 N West.
Smith Charles W (Duncan, Smith & Hornbrook), h 79 E Pratt.
Smith Charles W, farmer, h n end Belmont av (H).
Smith Charles W, lab, b 62 Bates.
Smith Charles W, lab, b 126 Williams.
Smith Charles W, porter, h 112 Columbia al.
Smith Christina C (wid Frederick), b 46 Water.

Richardson & McCrea, REPRESENTING BEST KNOWN FIRE INSURANCE COMPANIES. Fidelity and Casualty Insurance Company of New York Represented. Telephone 182. 79 East Market St.

Smith Cicero S, painter, b 75 Hill av.
Smith Clarence C, attendant Insane Asylum.
Smith Clarence W, lab, r 477 W Lake (N I).
Smith Clement T, lab, b 119 Cottage av.
Smith Clinton R, carp, h 14 Osgood (W I).
SMITH COLLINS H, Mnfr Window and Door Screens, 70 Columbia av, h same. (See adv in classified Door and Window Screens.)
Smith Columbus, lab, h 119 W 6th.
Smith Cora (wid Wm), b 193 Hillside av.
SMITH, CURTIS & CO (Earl C Smith, David Cline, Hamilton C Curtis), Real Estate; Loans on Realty, Diamonds and all Chattels; also Rentals, 10 Fair Blk.
Smith Cyrus A, trav agt, h 228 Clifford av.
Smith Cyrus M, mnfrs' agt, 28 Monument pl, h n s University av 1 w of Central av (I).
Smith Daniel G, solr N Y Life Ins Co, h 31 Highland pl.
Smith David D (MacCurdy & Smith), r 169 N Illinois.
Smith David H, foreman, h 320 E Ohio.
Smith David K, lab, h 23 E 26th.
Smith David W, bartndr, h 133 E New York.
Smith David W, lab, h 501 N California.
Smith, Day & Co, ltd, (Charles A Smith, Lorey D, Charles and Walter L Day), chair mnfrs, 76 Shelby.
Smith Dennis, coachman 751 N Penn.
Smith Dillard, lab, b s s English av 1 e of Auburn av.
Smith Dora, h 142 Indiana av.
Smith Dudley J, driver, h 174 N Belmont av (H).
Smith Dwight G, clk, b 293 N Delaware.
Smith Earl C (Smith, Curtis & Co), h 34 Johnson av.
Smith Earl C, phys, 44 Clifford av, b 94 same.
Smith Edmund T, com mer, 127 E Maryland, h 1 Camp.
Smith Edward, b 286 E Vermont.
Smith Edward, barber, 310 Blake, h same.
Smith Edward, cook, h 444 S Illinois.

The Williams Typewriter Elegant Work, Visible Writing, Easy Operation, High Speed. S. H. EAST, State Agent, 55 Thorpe Block, 87 E. Market St.

If You are not Satisfied with Your Laundry Work Give Us a Trial. . ERTEL STEAM LAUNDRY 26 and 28 N. Senate Avenue. Telephone 1089.

ELLIS & HELFENBERGER Manufacturers of IRON and WIRE FENCES 162-170 S. SENATE AVE. TEL. 358.

THE HOGAN TRANSPER AND STORAGE COMP'Y
Household Goods and Pianos Moved—Packed—Stored...... Baggage and Package Express Machinery and Safes a Specialty Cor. Washington and Illinois Sts. TELEPHONE No. 675.

Hose, Belting, Packing, Clothing, Druggists' Sundries, Bicycle Tires, Cotton Hose, Etc. New York Belting & Packing Co., L't'd.
The Central Rubber & Supply Co. PHONES 79 S. ILLINOIS ST., INDIANAPOLIS, IND.

HIGHEST SECURITY
LOWEST COST OF INSURANCE.
The Provident Life and Trust Co.
Of Philadelphia.
D. W. EDWARDS, Gen. Agent,
508 Indiana Trust Building.

Smith Edward, lab, r 84 Maple.
Smith Edward, lab, r 166 W Washington.
Smith Edward, waiter, r 18½ Indiana av.
Smith Edward A, bkkpr, b 247 N East.
Smith Edward A, mach hd, h 400½ S Meridian.
Smith Edward A, music teacher, 149 Hosbrook, h same.
Smith Edward B, dyer, 24 Monument pl, h 664 Bellefontaine.
Smith Edward F, buyer Shellhouse & Co, h 121 E Michigan.
Smith Edward H, carp, h 183 Jefferson av.
Smith Edward H, clk, h 233 W Washington.
Smith Edward J, blksmith, h 90 N Dorman.
Smith Edward J, engr, h 182 Woodlawn av.
Smith Edward J, mach, b 89 Indiana av.
Smith Edward W, salesman Crescent Oil Co, r 31½ Indiana av.
Smith Edwin E, clk, h 72 Wright.
Smith Elisha C, baggageman, b Ross House.
Smith Eliza (wid George), h 112 Rhode Island.
Smith Elizabeth (wid James), h 514 N West.
Smith Elizabeth A (wid Josiah), h 280 Indiana av.
Smith Elizabeth E, stenog, b 155 N Illinois.
Smith Elizabeth G (wid Ebenezer), h 213 E Ohio.
Smith Elizabeth M (wid Richard W), nurse City Hospital.
Smith Elizabeth S (wid Wm T), h e s Sherman Drive 1 n of Washington.
Smith Ella, h 111 Buchanan.
Smith Ella (wid Jesse), h 147 Eddy.
Smith Ella (wid Wm), b 25 Roanoke.
Smith Ella M, music teacher, 594 E St Clair, h same.
Smith Ella M, bkkpr Monarch Supply Co, b 72 Ft Wayne av.
Smith Ellen (wid George W), b 7 Paca.
Smith Ellen (wid Washington), b 352 Virginia av.
Smith Elmer, mach, h 296 Columbia av.
Smith Elmer E, baggageman, h 187 S Alabama.
Smith Elmer O, clk R M S, h 1110 N Delaware.

Julius C. Walk & Son,
Jewelers
Indianapolis.
12 EAST WASHINGTON ST.

Smith Elmer S, motorman, b 149 King av (H).
Smith Elmore, lab, b 215 W 3d.
Smith Elwood, car rep, b 8 N Brightwood av (B).
Smith Emil, umbrella rep, h 246 Madison av.
Smith Emma, h 12 Maria.
Smith Emma (wid Augustus), h 202 Randolph.
Smith Emma (wid Simon), housekpr e s Oakland av 1 n of Clifford av.
Smith Emma C, h 91 N Delaware.
Smith Emma L (wid Wm T), h 287 E Market.
Smith Emma R (wid Charles M), h 359 Blake.
Smith Ernest A, clk, b n s University av 1 w of Central av (I).
Smith Ernest A, lab, h 42 Brett.
Smith Ernest W, b 186 Minerva.
Smith Ervin, lab, h 90 Yandes.
Smith Estelle E, bkkpr Jersey Bulletin, b 323 W Michigan.
Smith Etta, h 264 E Georgia.
Smith Eugene A (Harold V Smith & Co), h 106 St Mary.

SMITH'S EUROPEAN HOTEL, O H Smith Propr, 190-198 E Washington, Tel 983.

Smith Evangeline M, record clk Insane Hospital.
Smith Eveline (wid Isaac E), h 41 Depot (B).
Smith Everett L, weigher, h 192 Lexington av.
Smith Fernando C, foreman, h 595 S State av.
Smith Finley, condr, r 20 N West.
Smith Fitzhugh W, b rear 122 College av.
Smith Florence, h 44 Harris.
Smith Florian O (Wm Q Smith & Co), b 730 N New Jersey.
Smith Florine Rev, b 90 Yandes.
Smith Fountain P (F P Smith & Co), h 270 N West.
Smith Frances, h 170 Muskingum al.
Smith Frances (wid Jacob), nurse, 23 Dawson, b same.
Smith Francis, loans, h n w cor 3d and Capitol av.
Smith Francis E, ins agt, h 68 Downey.
Smith Frank, barber, h 17 Springfield.
Smith Frank, bartndr, r 71½ N Illinois.
Smith Frank, bartndr, h 212 E Market.
Smith Frank, carp, b 190 Fayette.
Smith Frank, carp, b 166 Minerva.
Smith Frank, clk The Wm H Block Co, b 321 N Illinois.
Smith Frank, driver, b 62 Bates.
Smith Frank, helper, b s w cor Rader and Francis (N I).
Smith Frank, lab, h 227 N California.
Smith Frank, lab, b 342 N Missouri.
Smith Frank, lab, b 230 W 2d.
Smith Frank C, foreman, h 138 W Michigan.
Smith Frank D, fireman, h 54 Gresham.
Smith Frank E, clk, b 121 E Michigan.
Smith Frank E, cooper, h 105 Weghorst.
Smith Frank E, grocer, 825 N Illinois, h 781 N New Jersey.
Smith Frank E A, clk, b 339 N Penn.
Smith Frank F, attendant Insane Hospital.
Smith Frank G, flagman, b 139 E Morris.
Smith Frank H, clk Cerealine Mnfg Co, h 259 Talbott av.
Smith Frank H, huckster, h 400 W Pratt.

OTTO GAS ENGINES | BUILDERS' EXCHANGE S. W. Cor. Ohio and Penn. Telephone 535.

THE HOGAN TRANSFER AND STORAGE COMP'Y
Household Goods and Pianos Moved—Packed—Stored...... Baggage and Package Express Machinery and Safes a Specialty Cor. Washington and Illinois Sts. TELEPHONE No. 675.

Hose, Belting, Packing, Clothing, Druggists' Sundries, Bicycle Tires, Cotton Hose, Etc. New York Belting & Packing Co., L't'd.
The Central Rubber & Supply Co. PHONE 922. 79 S. ILLINOIS ST., INDIANAPOLIS, IND.

HIGHEST SECURITY
LOWEST COST OF INSURANCE.
The Provident Life and Trust Co.
Of Philadelphia.
D. W. EDWARDS, Gen. Agent,
508 Indiana Trust Building.

Smith Edward, lab, r 84 Maple.
Smith Edward, lab, r 166 W Washington.
Smith Edward, waiter, r 18½ Indiana av.
Smith Edward A, bkkpr, b 247 N East.
Smith Edward A, mach hd, h 400½ S Meridian.
Smith Edward A, music teacher, 149 Hosbrook, h same.
Smith Edward B, dyer, 24 Monument pl, h 664 Bellefontaine.
Smith Edward F, buyer Shellhouse & Co, h 121 E Michigan.
Smith Edward H, carp, h 183 Jefferson av.
Smith Edward H, clk, h 233 W Washington.
Smith Edward J, blksmith, h 90 N Dorman.
Smith Edward J, engr, h 182 Woodlawn av.
Smith Edward J, mach, b 89 Indiana av.
Smith Edward W, salesman Crescent Oil Co, r 31½ Indiana av.
Smith Edwin E, clk, h 72 Wright.
Smith Elisha C, baggageman, b Ross House.
Smith Eliza (wid George), h 112 Rhode Island.
Smith Elizabeth (wid James), h 514 N West.
Smith Elizabeth A (wid Josiah), h 280 Indiana av.
Smith Elizabeth E, stenog, b 155 N Illinois.
Smith Elizabeth G (wid Ebenezer), h 213 E Ohio.
Smith Elizabeth M (wid Richard W), nurse City Hospital.
Smith Elizabeth S (wid Wm T), h e s Sherman Drive 1 n of Washington.
Smith Ella, h 111 Buchanan.
Smith Ella (wid Jesse), h 147 Eddy.
Smith Ella (wid Wm), b 25 Roanoke.
Smith Ella M, music teacher, 594 E St Clair, h same.
Smith Ella M, bkkpr Monarch Supply Co, b 72 Ft Wayne av.
Smith Ellen (wid George W), b 7 Paca.
Smith Ellen (wid Washington), b 352 Virginia av.
Smith Elmer, mach, h 296 Columbia av.
Smith Elmer E, baggageman, h 187 S Alabama.
Smith Elmer O, clk R M S, h 1110 N Delaware.

Julius C. Walk & Son,
Jewelers
Indianapolis.
12 EAST WASHINGTON ST.

Smith Elmer S, motorman, b 149 King av (H).
Smith Elmore, lab, b 215 W 3d.
Smith Elwood, car rep, b 8 N Brightwood av (B).
Smith Emil, umbrella rep, h 246 Madison av.
Smith Emma, h 12 Maria.
Smith Emma (wid Augustus), h 202 Randolph.
Smith Emma (wid Simon), housekpr e s Oakland av 1 n of Clifford av.
Smith Emma C, h 91 N Delaware.
Smith Emma L (wid Wm T), h 287 E Market.
Smith Emma R (wid Charles M), h 358 Blake.
Smith Ernest A, clk, b n s University av 1 w of Central av (I).
Smith Ernest A, lab, h 42 Brett.
Smith Ernest W, b 186 Minerva.
Smith Ervin, lab, h 90 Yandes.
Smith Estelle E, bkkpr Jersey Bulletin, b 323 W Michigan.
Smith Etta, h 264 E Georgia.
Smith Eugene A (Harold V Smith & Co), h 106 St Mary.
SMITH'S EUROPEAN HOTEL, O H Smith Propr, 190-198 E Washington, Tel 983.
Smith Evangeline M, record clk Insane Hospital.
Smith Eveline (wid Isaac E), h 41 Depot (B).
Smith Everett L, weigher, h 192 Lexington av.
Smith Fernando C, foreman, h 595 S State av.
Smith Finley, condr, r 20 N West.
Smith Fitzhugh W, b rear 122 College av.
Smith Florence, h 44 Harris.
Smith Florian O (Wm Q Smith & Co), b 730 N New Jersey.
Smith Florine Rev, b 90 Yandes.
Smith Fountain P (F P Smith & Co), h 270 N West.
Smith Frances, h 170 Muskingum al.
Smith Frances (wid Jacob), nurse, 23 Dawson, b same.
Smith Francis, loans, h n w cor 3d and Capitol av.
Smith Francis E, ins agt, h 68 Downey.
Smith Frank, barber, h 17 Springfield.
Smith Frank, bartndr, r 71½ N Illinois.
Smith Frank, bartndr, h 212 E Market.
Smith Frank, carp, b 190 Fayette.
Smith Frank, carp, b 166 Minerva.
Smith Frank, clk The Wm H Block Co, b 321 N Illinois.
Smith Frank, driver, b 62 Bates.
Smith Frank, helper, b s w cor Rader and Francis (N I).
Smith Frank, lab, h 227 N California.
Smith Frank, lab, b 342 N Missouri.
Smith Frank, lab, b 230 W 2d.
Smith Frank C, foreman, h 138 W Michigan.
Smith Frank D, fireman, h 54 Gresham.
Smith Frank E, clk, b 121 E Michigan.
Smith Frank E, cooper, h 105 Weghorst.
Smith Frank E, grocer, 825 N Illinois, h 781 N New Jersey.
Smith Frank E A, clk, b 339 N Penn.
Smith Frank F, attendant Insane Hospital.
Smith Frank G, flagman, b 139 E Morris.
Smith Frank H, clk Cerealine Mnfg Co, h 259 Talbott av.
Smith Frank H, huckster, h 400 W Pratt.

OTTO GAS ENGINES | BUILDERS' EXCHANGE S. W. Cor. Ohio and Penn. Telephone 535.

WE HAVE THE BEST : : | STEEL AND COPPER PLATE
WE DO THE BEST : : : : : | ENGRAVING and
WE MAKE THE BEST : : | EMBOSSING.

LETTER HEADS, ENVELOPES, CARDS AND SOCIETY PAPER ALL DONE IN FIRST-CLASS STYLE.

PRICES IN KEEPING.

FRANK H. SMITH

Twenty-two North Pennsylvania St.

LEADER IN

. . Commercial Printing . .

OF ALL KINDS.

Fine Stationery and Office Supplies.

BLANK BOOKS.

Becker & Son Charles Becker Jacob Becker Jr. Merchant Tailors. 21 N. Penn. St. Tel. 934

SMITH FRANK H, Mnfg Stationer, Copper Plate Engraver, and Book and Job Printer, 22 N Penn, b The Denison. (See adv opp.)
Smith Frank J, cook, h 12 Hadley.
Smith Frank J, engr, h 28 Standard av.
Smith Frank L, brakeman, h 85 N Alabama.
Smith Frank M, carp, h w s Allfree av 2 s of Marlette Drive.
Smith Frank M, trav agt, b 430 College av.
Smith Frank P, foreman, h 655 N Capitol av.
Smith Frank S, condr, h 168 Lexington av.
Smith Frank X, lab, b 571 S West.
Smith Frederick, clk, b 90 Andrews.
Smith Frederick, lab, r 102 N Capitol av.
Smith Frederick, lab, h 414½ S Capitol av.
Smith Frederick, lab, b 506 E Georgia.
Smith Frederick C, bkkpr, b 138 W Michigan.
Smith Frederick W, driver Charles J Kuhn Co, b 516 Park av.
Smith Frederick W, lineman, h 33 Meek.
Smith F P & Co (Fountain P and Z Jane Smith), china, 45 N Illinois.
Smith George, lab, h 174 Agnes.
Smith George, lab, h 178 N Belmont av (H).
Smith George, lab, h 2 Edward (W I).
Smith George, lab, h 125 Maxwell.
Smith George, lab, b rear 234 W New York.
Smith George, lab, b 95 S West.
Smith George, mach hd, b 1675 Graceland av.
Smith George, stairbldr, h 240 Ash.
Smith George C, h 287 Huron.
Smith George C, foreman, h 565 W Highland av (N I).
Smith George D, polisher, h 139 Locke.
Smith George E, clk, b 228 Christian av.
Smith George E, painter, b 68 Harrison.
Smith George F, barber, 268 E Washington, h same.
Smith George F, carp, 89 Spann av, h same.
Smith George F, clk, r 115 N New Jersey.
Smith George G, trav agt A Kiefer Drug Co, h 519 Broadway.
Smith George H, condr, h 95 Decatur.
Smith George H, lab, h e s St Paul 1 s of Stanton av.
Smith George J, lab, h 9 Cleveland (H).
Smith George L, trav agt, h 517 Broadway.
Smith George M, polisher, h 85 Dugdale.
Smith George O, contr, 27 Villa av, h same.
Smith George R, mach, b 58 N Brightwood av (B).
Smith George R, painter, b 254 W Pearl.
Smith George R, trav agt, b 121 E Michigan.
Smith George T, finisher, h 544 S West.
Smith George W, b 126 E Vermont.
Smith George W, condr, b 306 Fletcher av.
Smith George W, lab, b 272 W Court.
Smith George W, lab, h 365 W Ontario (N I).
Smith George W, meats, 3 E Mkt House, h 177 E Market.
Smith George W, news agt, h 63 Cincinnati.
Smith George W, tmstr, h 30 Hadley.
Smith George W B, bkkpr, h 15 E Ohio.
Smith Giles L, bkkpr, h 265 N California.
Smith Glenn, electrician, b 135 W Michigan.
Smith Goldwin J, bkkpr E A Strong, h 88 E Pratt.
Smith Green A, gasfitter, h 77 Cornell av.
Smith Hardes A, attendant Insane Hospital.
Smith Harley B, contr, h 99 Hendricks.
Smith Harold O, treas Indpls Rubber Co, h s s Washington av 1 e of Central av (I).

Henry H. Fay,
40½ E. WASHINGTON ST.,
AGENT FOR
Insurance Co. of North America,
Pennsylvania Fire Ins. Co.

Smith Harold V (Harold V Smith & Co), b 577 N Capitol av.
SMITH HAROLD V & CO (Harold V and Eugene A Smith), Electrical Engineers and Contractors, 90 E Market, Tel 1913. (See adv in classified Electrical Contractors.)
Smith Harriet (wid Christian M), b 34 Bellefontaine.
Smith Harry, coachman 294 N Meridian.
Smith Harry, cook, r 257 N Senate av.
Smith Harry, driver, b 91 N Delaware.
Smith Harry, finisher, h 378 S East.
Smith Harry, framemkr, b 1675 Graceland av.
SMITH HARRY B, Auditor of Marion County, 41 Court House, h 696 N Alabama, Tels Office 912, Res 92.
Smith Harry C, bkkpr Island Coal Co, h 1023 N Meridian.
Smith Harry E, carp, h n s Pruitt 2 e of Fountain.
Smith Harry E, condr, h 443 N New Jersey.
Smith Harry P, condr, h 25 Williams.
Smith Harry W, mach, b 454 E Georgia.
Smith Harvey B, lab, h 317 Columbia av.
Smith Harvey S, opr W U Tel Co, h 178 N Capitol av.
Smith Hattie N, b 21 Ketcham.
Smith Hattie V, r 77 Kentucky av.
Smith Henry, lab, h rear 671 N Senate av.
SMITH HENRY, Saloon and Restaurant, 39-41 N Illinois, h 416 N Illinois, Tel 1078.
Smith Henry, watchman, h 506 E Georgia.
Smith Henry B, mngr Oliver Chilled Plow Wks and South Bend Iron Wks, 160 S Penn, h 309 N Delaware, tel 1367.
Smith Henry C, marble cutter, h 135 W Michigan.
Smith Henry F, engr, h 51 Hoyt av.
Smith Henry G, condr, h 95 Decatur.
Smith Henry J, waiter, r 287 N California.
Smith Henry L, genl mngr Indpls Greenwood & Franklin R R, h 165 Park av.
Smith Henry L, farmer, h s s English av 1 e of Auburn av.

MAYHEW'S SPECTACLES
THE BEST IN USE
SOLD ONLY AT 13 N. MERIDIAN ST.

SALISBURY & STANLEY OFFICE, STORE AND BANK FIXTURES.

LUMBER Sash and Doors BALKE & KRAUSS CO., Corner Market and Missouri Sts.

Friedgen Has the BEST PATENT LEATHER SHOES AT LOWEST PRICES. 19 North Pennsylvania St.

SAMUEL LAING : HOT AIR FURNACES 72 AND 74 EAST COURT STREET.

M. B. WILSON, Pres. W. F. CHURCHMAN, Cash.
The Capital National Bank,
INDIANAPOLIS, IND.
Banking business in all its branches. Bonds and Foreign Exchange bought and sold.
Interest paid on time deposits.
Checks and drafts on all Indiana and Illinois points handled at lowest rates.
No. 28 South Meridian Street, Cor. Pearl.

Smith Henry M (Smith & Skinner), h 91 Woodruff av.
Smith Henry M, mach, h 25 Beacon.
Smith Henry N, grocer, 302 Columbia av, h same.
Smith Henry W, clk C C C & St L Ry, b 188 Huron.
Smith Herman, clk A Burdsal Co, b 193 E Morris.
Smith Herman, clk Daniel Stewart Co, h e s Bluff rd 2 s of Belt R R.
Smith Herman F, clk, h 46 Water.
Smith Hiram B, lab, b 431 W 22d (N I).
Smith Homer B, presser, b 68 Harrison.
Smith Horace E (Hawkins & Smith), h 578 N Penn, tel 1303.
Smith Hurtly H, bkkpr, b 1070 N Capitol av.
Smith Ida, forewoman, r 213 S Pine.
Smith Ida (wid John J), h 293 W Michigan.
Smith Ida P, janitor Liberty Street Free Kindergarten, h 81 S Liberty.
Smith Irvin, electrician, b 135 W Michigan.
Smith Irvin C, lab, b 302 Columbia av.
Smith Irving J, reporter, b 678 N Delaware.
Smith Isaac, lab, h 2 Anderson.
Smith Isaac, lab, r 37½ Kentucky av.
Smith Isaac B, baggageman, h rear 61 Johnson av.
Smith Isaac E, porter, r 66 N Missouri.
Smith Isaac N, b w s Waverly av 1 n of Pope av.
Smith Isaac N, huckster, h 458 W Shoemaker (N I).
Smith Israel J, dairyman, h e s Lincoln av 11 s of C C C & St L Ry (M J).
Smith Jacob, driver, h 220 W 8th.
Smith Jacob, lab, h 31 California.
Smith Jacob, porter, h 125 Osage al.
Smith Jacob F, lab, h 716 W Morris (W I).
Smith Jacob K, h 122 Lambert (W I).
Smith Jacob K, huckster, h w s Caldwell 2 s of Elizabeth.
Smith Jacob L, porter, h 23 Dawson.
Smith Jacob W, sec The Indpls Board of Trade, 38 Board of Trade bldg, h 942 N Alabama.
Smith James, brakeman, b 36 S Gale (B).
Smith James, chemist, b 130 Minerva.

Insure Against Accidents
WITH
TUTTLE & SEGUIN,
Agents for
Fidelity and Casualty Co., of New York.
$10,000 for $25. $5,000 for $12.50.
TEL. 1168. 28 E. MARKET ST.

Smith James, lab, b 390 N California.
Smith James, lab, h rear w s Ivy la 4 s of Pendleton av.
Smith James A, carp, h 45 Tacoma av.
Smith James A, mach, h 12 Elliott.
Smith James B, plumber, b 428 E North.
Smith James E, tmstr, h 291 Sheffield av (H).
Smith James F, sawyer, h 514 Addison (N I).
Smith James F, watchman, h 68 Harrison.
Smith James H (J H Smith & Co), asst sec New Year S and L Assn, h 379 Park av.
Smith James H, cooper, h 454 E Georgia.
Smith James J, lab, h 66 Chadwick.
Smith James J, lineman, b 8 McCauley.
Smith James L, clk A Kiefer Drug Co, h 1070 N Capitol av.
Smith James L, printer, h 7 Hoyt av.
Smith James L, woodwkr, h 393½ Indiana av.
Smith James M, coremkr, b 216 Yandes.
Smith James P, condr, h 1028 N New Jersey.
Smith James P, painter, b 58 N Brightwood av (B).
Smith James R, brakeman, h 473 S Delaware.
Smith James R, brakeman, h 25 Temple av.
Smith James T, h 303 Prospect.
Smith James T, lab, b 347 S East.
Smith James W, clk, b 39 Greer.
Smith James W, lab, h 183 Keystone av.
Smith James W, lab, h 554 W Washington.
Smith James W, tmstr, h 1474 Schurmann av (N I).
Smith Jane (wid Henry H), h 80 W 8th.
Smith Jarrett, waiter, h 105 Rhode Island.
Smith Jay D, uphlr, h 69 Kansas.
Smith Jean, painter, r 155½ Indiana av.
Smith Jean N, lab, r 234 E Wabash.
Smith Jeanette D (wid Amos G), b 242 Central av.
Smith Jennie (wid Edwin), h 1449 N Illinois.
Smith Jeremiah, tmstr, b 430 E McCarty.
Smith Jeremiah, waiter The Bates.
Smith Jesse, cooper, b 277 Mass av.
Smith Jesse, mach, h 270 S Meridian.
Smith Jesse J, asst prin Public School No 11, b 1101 N Alabama.
Smith John, b 188 Huron.
Smith John, r 115 N Illinois.
Smith John, b 243 Newman.
Smith John, r 20 N West.
Smith John, bricklyr, b 272 W Maryland.
Smith John, butcher, b 828 E Washington.
Smith John, cooper, b 272 W Court.
Smith John, lab, b 303 Deloss.
Smith John, lab, b 320 W 1st.
Smith John, lab, b w s Illinois 1 s of 35th (M).
Smith John, lab, r 449 W 2d.
Smith John, molder, b 8 McCauley.
Smith John, motorman, b 115 Highland pl.
Smith John, patternmkr, b 656 W Vermont.
Smith John, waiter, r 232 W North.
Smith John A, b 172 Coburn.
Smith John A, b 932 Gent (M P).
Smith John A, lab, h 175 W 5th.
Smith John A, mach hd, b 216 Yandes.
Smith John B, lab, h rear 143 S New Jersey.
Smith John C, clk, b 501 W Francis (N I).
Smith John C, treas Indpls Fancy Grocery Co, h 745 College av.
Smith John C, woodwkr, h 355 S Meridian.
Smith John E, h 103 N Capitol av.
Smith John E, h s s Railroad 1 e of Central av (I).

WEDDING CAKE BOXES · SULLIVAN & MAHAN 41 W. Pearl St.

Smith John E, janitor, h 204 Agnes.
Smith John Ed, pres Indpls Rubber Co, h s s Washington av 1 e of Central av (I).
Smith John F, car rep, h 41 S Gale (B).
Smith John F, carp, h 94 Division (W I).
Smith John F, driver, b 76 Fayette.
Smith John F, engr, b 55 Division (W I).
Smith John F, lab, h 732 S East.
Smith John H, carp, h 1200 Rural.
Smith John H, condr, b 340½ E Market.
Smith John H, lab, h 584 W Francis (N I).
Smith John H, watchman, h 193 E Morris.
Smith John H S, bkkpr, b 430 College av.
Smith John L, lab, h 63 Lexington av.
Smith John N, clk, h 574 Broadway.
Smith John O, polisher, b 420 S West.
Smith John P, salesman Murphy, Hibben & Co, h 167 Hoyt av.
Smith John R, boilermkr, h 90 N Dorman.
Smith John R, lab, h 477 W Lake (N I).
Smith John S, h 408 W 2d.
Smith John S, express, h 163 Talbott av.
Smith John S, ice creammkr, h 134 Cornell av.
Smith John T, lab, h 647 Mass av.
Smith John T, prin Public School No 24, h 90 Martindale av.
Smith John W (J W Smith & Son), h 366 N Alabama.
Smith John W, bkkpr H P Wasson & Co, h 163 N Alabama.
Smith John W, engr, b 93 Spann av.
Smith John W, lab, h 13 Cooper.
Smith John W, lab, h 666 W Eugene (N I).
Smith John W, mach hd, h 34 Tacoma av.
Smith John W, porter, h 62 Bates.
Smith John W, tmstr, h 726 Shelby.
Smith John W, trav agt Wm B Burford, r 84 E North.
Smith Jordan, lab, h 5 Gimbel.
Smith Jordan A, lab, r 220 W Wabash.
Smith Joseph, car insp, h 303 Deloss.
Smith Joseph, clk N A Moore & Co, h 116½ Fayette.
Smith Joseph, clk, r 130 W Vermont.
Smith Joseph, newsdealer, 56 N Illinois, h same.
Smith Joseph, polisher, h 420 S West.
Smith Joseph A, tmstr, h 1 Gardners la.
Smith Joseph G, lab, h s e cor Harriet and Sutherland (B).

SMITH JOSEPH W, Agt Erie Despatch, 46 W Washington, b 1070 N Capitol av, Tel 517.

Smith Joseph W, lab, h 31 Warman av (H).
Smith Julia (wid Thomas), b 308 Blackford.
Smith Julia A (wid Thomas), b 298 N Capitol av.
Smith Julius J, tinner, b 101 N Alabama.
Smith J Cumming Rev, pastor Tabernacle Presbyterian Church, n e cor Meridian and 2d.
Smith J Hamilton, printer, h 16 Windsor.

SMITH J H & CO (James H Smith), Real Estate, Rental and Insurance, 36 W Washington.

Smith J W & Son (John W and Lou W), bakers, 121 Ft Wayne av.
Smith Koran, lab, h 256 S Meridian.
Smith Lambertine H, real est, b 170 Martindale av.
Smith Lansing F (Tichenor & Smith), b The Plaza.
Smith Laura A, exchange editor The Indpls Sentinel, b 1101 N Alabama.
Smith Laura M (wid Wm), h 10 Elizabeth.
Smith Leah (wid Elisha C), b 75 Gimbel.

FRANK NESSLER. WILL H. ROST.
FRANK NESSLER & CO.
Tailors
56 EAST MARKET ST. (Lemcke Building),
INDIANAPOLIS, IND.

Smith Leah (wid Joseph), b 296 Blake.
Smith Leander H, lab, h 32 Samoa.
Smith Lee, h rear 169 W 5th.
Smith Lee, houseman The Bates.
Smith Lee, lab, h 122 Elizabeth.
Smith Lee O, music teacher, b 221 N Capitol av.
Smith Lemuel W, molder, b 170 Martindale av.
Smith Leon R, solr, b 290 N Pine.
Smith Leroy B, molder, h 158 Columbia av.
Smith Lewis A, lab, h 1 Margaret.
Smith Lilian G, teacher Public School No 11, b 276 N Penn.
Smith Lon, welldriver, b 277 Mass av.
Smith Lorenzo, lab, h 356 Martindale av.
Smith Lot, lab, b 631 W Michigan.
Smith Lou W (J W Smith & Son), h 434 N East.
Smith Louis F, clk Badger Furniture Co, h 35 Ingraham.
Smith Louis J, blksmith, h 58 N Brightwood av (B).
Smith Louis S, pres The Home Benefit Assn, h 1062 W Vermont.
Smith Louisa (wid Benjamin K), h 193 Hillside av.
Smith Lucinda (wid Stephen), b 258 W 5th.
Smith Lucius J, case hardener, r 90 N Senate av.
Smith Luella (wid Jesse), h 147 Eddy.
Smith Margaret (wid Fred), b 33 Meek.
Smith Margaret (wid John B), h 281 Christian av.
Smith Maria, h 443 Blake.
Smith Marion C, condr, h 77 Hoyt av.
Smith Marion F, cooper, h 429 McLene (N I).
Smith Mark A, mer police, h 330 Yandes.
Smith Mark C, h 889 N Senate av.
Smith Marmaduke D, elev opr, b 269 E Market.
Smith Martha E, clk C C C & St L Ry, b 383 Mass av.
Smith Martha J, phys, 208 N Alabama, h same.
Smith Martin, lab, b rear 82 Yandes.
Smith Martin M, motorman, h 118 Columbia av.

ACORN STOVES AND RANGES
Haueisen & Hartmann
163-169 E. Washington St.
FURNITURE,
Carpets, Household Goods,
Tin, Granite and China Wares, Oil Cloth and Shades

THE HOME LAUNDRY 197 S. ILLINOIS ST. TEL. 1769. ...st Work. ...ompt Delivery. Collars and C... our Specialty.

THE WM. H. BLOCK CO. 7 AND 9 EAST WASHINGTON STREET. DRY GOODS, HOUSE FURNISHINGS AND CROCKERY.

London Guarantee and Accident Co. (Ltd.) All forms of Liability Insurance, Workmen's Collective Insurance, Fidelity Bonds and Individual Accident Insurance.
Geo. W. Pangborn, Gen. Agent, 704-706 Lemcke Bldg. Telephone 140.

FRANK K. SAWYER, AGENT 74 East Market Street. Telephone 863.
Prussian National Insurance Company OF STETTIN, GERMANY. ORGANIZED 1845.

JOSEPH GARDNER,
TIN, COPPER AND SHEET-IRON WORK AND
HOT AIR FURNACES.
37, 39 & 41 KENTUCKY AVE. Telephone 322.

Smith Mary (wid Almarion), h s s Lena 2 w of Parker (I).
Smith Mary (wid Frank), h 94 Bright.
Smith Mary (wid Jackson), b 878 N Delaware.
Smith Mary (wid Lawrence), h 72 Davidson.
Smith Mary (wid Patrick), h 222 W 22d.
Smith Mary (wid Wm), b 38 S State av.
Smith Mary, asst phys Insane Hospital.
Smith Mary, clk, b 111 Buchanan.
Smith Mary E, h 643 S Meridian.
Smith Mary E (wid Gilbert B), h 771 N Senate av.
Smith Mary F (wid Frank M), b 440 Blake.
Smith Mary J, h rear 121 Agnes.
Smith Matilda (wid John), h rear 130 Newman.
Smith Michael F, ins agt, h 423 W Pratt.
Smith Michael S, lab, b 8 McCauley.
Smith Milon F, filer, h 35 Ingram.
Smith Minnie, h 230 W Ohio.
Smith Miriam, b 95 Malott av.
Smith Mitchell, coachman, h e s Muskingum al 4 n of 1st.
Smith Mosby, lab, h 59 Oriental.
SMITH M M, Druggist, 44-46 Clifford av, Tel 1778, h 94 same.
Smith Nancy (wid George), h 112 Rhode Island.
Smith Nancy (wid Julius J), h 1101 N Alabama.
Smith Nancy E (wid James R), h 8 Minerva.
Smith Nathan W, engr, h 10 Springfield.
Smith Nelson G, phys, 44 Clifford av, h 94 same.
Smith Nelson K, lab, h 431 W 22d (N I).
Smith Noah D, lab, h 107 Maple.
Smith Omer T, painter, h 26 Larch.
Smith Orin S, hostler, r 83 E Wabash.
Smith Orvel H, propr Smith's European Hotel and bakery, 190-198 E Washington.
Smith Oscar, clk Lilly & Stalnaker, h s s Bloyd av 1 w of Fountain.
Smith Oscar R, h 228 Christian av.
Smith Otis D, uphlr, b 119 Cottage av.
Smith Patrick, lab, h 333 W Maryland.
Smith Patrick C, h 138 E St Joseph.
Smith Pearl, h 210 W Ohio.

J. S. FARRELL & CO.
STEAM AND HOT WATER HEATING FOR STORES, OFFICES, PUBLIC BUILDINGS, PRIVATE RESIDENCES, GREENHOUSES, ETC.
84 North Illinois St. Telephone 382.

Smith Perry C, trav agt, b 1400 N Capitol av.
Smith Peter, h w s Meridian 1 s of 38th (M).
Smith Peter F, lab, b 17 Keystone av.
Smith Philip J Rev, h 485 Ontario (N I).
Smith Philip T, porter P & E Ry, r 232 W North.
SMITH PREMIER TYPEWRITER CO THE, Frank W Olin Mngr, 76 E Market, Tel 1211.
Smith Ralph, bookbndr, b s w cor Rader and Francis (N I).
Smith Ralph K, teller S A Fletcher & Co, h 1045 N Alabama.
Smith Raphael, lab, h 180 Tremont av (H).
Smith Richard, postmaster North Indpls, h 501 W Francis (N I).
Smith Richard R, lab, h 106 Yandes.
Smith Richard S, lab, h 342 Martindale av.
Smith Riley E, cashr Ind Bicycle Co, h 39 Newman.
Smith Robert, printer, b 214 Fulton.
Smith Robert A, prin Public School No 41, h 178 Clifford av.
Smith Robert C, student, b 942 N Alabama.
SMITH ROBERT E, Lawyer, 13 Baldwin Blk, h 189 N Noble.
Smith Robert L, r 85½ W Market.
SMITH ROBERT L, Toy and Regalia Trunk Mnfr, 244 Indiana av, b 280 same.
Smith Robert M, bkkpr Bowen-Merrill Co, r 65 State House.
Smith Robert M, motorman, h 437 W New York.
Smith Rosalind (wid James H), b 195 College av.
Smith Roscoe, lab, h 137 Lincoln la.
Smith Rose, h 170 W New York.
Smith Rose (wid James), b 36 S Gale (B).
Smith Royal B M, lab, h 150½ Columbia av.
Smith Ruple D, asst State Law Library, r 66 State House.
Smith Ruth A (wid Samuel W), b 447 Central av.
Smith Samuel (The Webb-Jameson Co), h 167 John.
Smith Samuel, lab, h 277 Chapel.
Smith Samuel D, dentist, 240 E Ohio, h asme.
Smith Samuel H, marshal, h w s Line 2 s of P C C & St L Ry (I).
Smith Samuel J, bricklyr, b 183 Yandes.
Smith Samuel M, fireman, h 18 S Gillard av.
Smith Samuel O, lab, h e s Sherman Drive 1 n of Washington.
Smith Samuel S, h 170 Martindale av.
Smith Samuel S, trav agt, h 565 S State av.
Smith Samuel W, agt Deere, Mansur & Co, h 447 Central av.
Smith Sarah (wid Aaron C), h 28 Cincinnati.
Smith Sarah (wid John), h 363 Mass av.
Smith Sarah (wid John), b 7 Ruckle.
Smith Sarah (wid Shelton W), b 573 W Michigan.
Smith Sarah A, seamstress, h 169 E Court.
Smith Sarah C, b s e cor Auburn av and Prospect.
Smith Sarah E (wid John), b 6 Dawson.
Smith Sarah F, h 121 E Michigan.
Smith Sarah J (wid Charles W), h 352 W 2d.
SMITH SARAH M (wid Moses), Groceries, 1281 Annette, h 450 W Wells (N I).

United States Life Insurance Co., of New York.
E. B. SWIFT, M'g'r. 25 E. Market St.

Smith Scott, lab, h 23 Reynolds av (H).
Smith Scott W, pdlr, h 43 Drake.
Smith Septimus H, publr The Woodworker, s e cor Monument pl and Meridian, h 38 Fletcher av.
Smith Sidney T, painter, h 426 S Olive.
Smith Silas, lab, h 18 Reynolds av (H).
Smith, Solomon S, harnessmkr, r 229 E South.
Smith Stephen, lab, h 446 E Walnut.
Smith Stephen N, driver, h 20 S Linden.
Smith Sue J, dry goods, 304 Mass av, h 228 Christian av.
Smith Susan (wid John), b 200 Clifford av.
Smith Sylvester E, lab, b 71 Elizabeth.

SMITH THEODORE W, Analytical Chemist, 23 W Ohio, h 416 E McCarty. (See adv in classified Chemists—Analytical.)

Smith Theresa H (wid Weller B), h 577 N Capitol av.
Smith Thomas, lab, r 35½ Kentucky av.
Smith Thomas, porter, b 10½ E Washington.
Smith Thomas E, clk, r 224 E New York.
Smith Thomas F, mach hd, b 243 Newman.
Smith Thomas F, lab, b 14 Carlos.
Smith Thomas F jr, lab, b 8 McCauley.
Smith Thomas F, saloon, Sherman House, h 117 W Maryland.
Smith Thomas J, brakeman, r 233 Cedar.
Smith Thomas S, city fireman, h 162 Yandes.
Smith Virgil A, painter, h 1250 S Meridian.
Smith Wallace R, floor mngr N Y Store, h 44 S State av.
Smith Walter, phys, 63 Oliver av (W I), h same.
Smith Walter, mach, b 285 S Capitol av.
Smith Walter F, clk Enterprise Hotel.
Smith Walter S, mason, h 147 Hillside av.
Smith Walter S, paperhngr, h 111 Lambert (W I).
Smith Washington C, carp, b 125 E Washington.
Smith Willard A, pressman F H Smith, b 431 W 22d (N I).
Smith Willard P, insp City Engineer, r 5½ Indiana av.
Smith Wm, h s s Washington av 1 e of Maple av (I).
Smith Wm, clk, b 1101 N Alabama.
Smith Wm, clk, b 56 N Illinois.
Smith Wm, clk, h 13 Torbet.
Smith Wm, clk, r 262½ E Washington.
Smith Wm, clk, b 514 N West.
Smith Wm, condr, b 304 E Market.
Smith Wm, driver, b 20 Mill.
Smith Wm, driver, h 197 Minnesota.
Smith Wm, lab, b n s Brookville rd 4 s of Washington.
Smith Wm, lab, h s s Finley av 1 e of Shelby.
Smith Wm, lab, r 201 S Illinois.
Smith Wm, lab, b 31 Jones.
Smith Wm, lab, b e s Rural 6 s of Sutherland (B).
Smith Wm, lineman, r 228 N Capitol av.
Smith Wm, mer police, h 121 Agnes.
Smith Wm, tmstr, b w s Harris av 2 s of W Washington (M J).
Smith Wm, tmstr, h 65 Agnes.
Smith Wm, trav agt Standard Oil Co, h 131 E St Joseph.
Smith Wm A, h 243 Newman.
Smith Wm A, bricklyr, b 307 E Court.
Smith Wm A, grocer, 2 Camp, h same.
Smith Wm A, uphlr, h 100 Clifford av.
Smith Wm C, mach hd, h 55 Division (W I).

THOS. C. DAY & CO.
Financial Agents and Loans.
We have the experience, and claim to be reliable.
Rooms 325 to 330 Lemcke Bldg.

Smith Wm C, solr, h 97 Malott av.
Smith Wm D, butcher, h 330 W 1st.
Smith Wm D, flagman, h 221 Alvord.
Smith Wm D, saloon, 79 N Illinois, h 272 E Miami.
Smith Wm E, student, b 41 Madison av.
Smith Wm F, blksmith, h 294½ Mass av.
Smith Wm H (Taylor & Smith), h 352 Broadway.
Smith Wm H, engr, h 23 Douglass.
Smith Wm H, grocer, 320 S West, h same.
Smith Wm H, janitor Public School No 5, h 24 N California.
Smith Wm H, journalist, h 406 Talbott av.
Smith Wm H, lab, h 421 Muskingum al.
Smith Wm H, plastr, 276 Brookside av, h same.
Smith Wm H, tailor, 24 S Illinois, r 347 N Illinois.
Smith Wm J (Brown & Smith), h 78 Arbor av (W I).
Smith Wm J, lab, h 52 Beacon.
Smith Wm J, painter, h 7 W Sutherland (B).
Smith Wm J, wheelmkr, h 70 Miller (W I).
Smith Wm L, buyer N Y Store, h 465 Ash.
Smith Wm L, cook, h 78 Columbia al.
Smith Wm M, lab, h rear s s English av 3 e of Belt R R.
Smith Wm P, clk, b 334 N Illinois.
Smith Wm P, clk Penna Lines, b 162 N Senate av.
Smith Wm P, civil engr, 594 E St Clair, h same.
Smith Wm P, driver, r 326 E South.
Smith Wm Q (Wm Q Smith & Co), h 1400 N Capitol av.
Smith Wm Q & Co (Wm Q and Florian O Smith), roofers, 140 E 7th.
Smith Wm T, engr, h 290 N Pine.
Smith Wm T, motorman, h 27 Cornell av.
Smith Willis S, carp, h 59 Holloway av.
Smith Wirt C, lawyer, 42 Baldwin blk, h 136 Walcott.
Smith Zemro A, associate editor The Indpls Journal, h 131 Home av.
Smith Z Jane (F P Smith & Co), h 270 N West.

EAT
QUAKER BREAD
ASK YOUR GROCER FOR IT.
THE HITZ BAKING CO.

WILLIAM WIEGEL } MANUFACTURER OF..... } SHOW CASES } 6 W. Louisiana St. Opposite Union Station.

CARPETS AND RUGS RENOVATED.......... | CAPITAL STEAM CARPET CLEANING WORKS M. D. PLUNKETT, TELEPHONE No. 818

BENJ. BOOTH PRACTICAL EXPERT ACCOUNTANT. Complicated or disputed accounts investigated and adjusted. Room 18, 82½ E. Wash. St., Ind'p'l's, Ind.

18 and 20 South Meridian Street KERSHNER BROS., Proprs. THE SHERMAN RESTAURANT

ESTABLISHED 1876. TELEPHONE 168.
CHESTER BRADFORD,
SOLICITOR OF PATENTS,
AND COUNSEL IN PATENT CAUSES.
(See adv. page 6.)
Office:—Rooms 14 and 16 Hubbard Block, S.W. Cor. Washington and Meridian Streets,
INDIANAPOLIS, INDIANA.

SMITH & KORBLY (Alonzo Greene Smith, Charles A Korbly), Lawyers, 602-606 Indiana Trust Bldg, Tel 95.
Smith & Skinner (Henry M Smith, Louis B Skinner), plumbers, 106 Mass av.
Smitha Cassius, coachman, h 172 W 1st.
Smitha Elmer A, lawyer, 71 Lombard bldg, b 1101 N New Jersey.
Smitha Homer G, tel opr, b 1101 N New Jersey.
Smitha Rebecca, h 529½ N Illinois.
Smitha Wm B, trav agt, h 1101 N New Jersey.
SMITHER HENRY C, Agt Trinidad Asphalt Composition; Gravel Roofer, Dealer in Roofing Material and Contractor for Asphalt Mastic Paving, 169 W Maryland, h 422 N New Jersey. (See adv opp classified Roofing Material.)
Smither Mary H (wid Willis), b 190 Spann av.
Smither Otho W, fireman, b 564 W Washington.
SMITHER THEODORE F, Treas Builders' Exchange of Indianapolis, Gravel and Composition Roofer, Dealer in Building Paper and Roofing Materials; also Agt for Warren's Amber Brand Asphalt Roofing, 151 W Maryland, h 532 Park av, Tel 861. (See right side lines.)
Smitherman George, tmstr, h 242 S Linden.
Smitherman Wm, huckster, b 275 S Olive.
Smithey Ellen (wid John), carpet weaver, s s Railroad 3 w of Central av (I), h same.
Smithey John F, grocer, 100 Columbia av, h same.
Smithey Leonard W, h 153 Martindale av.
Smithey Samuel C, lab, b s s Railroad 3 w of Central av (I).
Smithey Wm, butcher, b 215 W South.
Smithson Grant, letter carrier P O, h 39½ S Reisner.
Smithurst John W, janitor, h 4 Cleveland blk.

Metal Ceilings and all kinds of Copper, Tin and Sheet Iron work.
O. B. ENSEY,
TELEPHONE 1562.
CORNER 6TH AND ILLINOIS STS.

Smithurst Wm J, janitor, h 209 Virginia av.
Smock, see also Schmuck.
Smock Abraham, lab, h 83 Lee (W I).
Smock Abraham E, horseshoer, b 1 Smithson.
Smock Abram, lab, h 314 Jefferson av.
Smock Austin F, painter, b 202 Coburn.
Smock Celia, supt Door of Hope Rescue Home, h 84 N Alabama.
Smock Charles E, bkkpr Parrott-Taggart Bakery, h 269 S New Jersey.
Smock Charles P, shoemkr, 20 Prospect, h same.
Smock Cornelius B, carp, h 90 Keystone av.
Smock David J, constable, h 55 Spann av.
Smock Della M (Miller & Smock), h 147 Virginia av.
Smock Eliza H, boarding 229 N Penn.
Smock Ernest, painter, b 55 Spann av.
Smock Ernest E, paperhngr, h 202 Coburn.
SMOCK FERDINAND C, Genl Contractor, Office Builders' Exchange, s w cor Penn and Ohio, h 503 Park av.
Smock Frank, brakeman, h 26 Elder av.
Smock Gabriel A, lab, b 314 Jefferson av.
Smock George A, lab, h 283 E Court.
Smock George C, constable, h 130 Elm.
Smock George W, drayman, h 145 Cottage av.
Smock Hanford E, clk, b 549 Central av.
Smock Homer, agt, r 12½ N Delaware.
Smock Homer M (Batty & Co), b 1241 N Illinois.
Smock Howard, salesman, h 915 N New Jersey.
Smock Howard A (Fetters & Smock), h 12 Brookside av.
Smock Ira C, carp, b 29 Clifford av.
Smock Isaac N, letter carrier P O, h 229 N Penn.
Smock James W, bkkpr Goverment B and L Inst, h 1241 N Illinois.
Smock Jesse R, tinner, h 42 McIntyre.
Smock John, lab, h 391 S Missouri.
Smock John S, cooper, h 55 S California.
Smock Lewis G, express, b 121 Frazee (H).
Smock Lovia P (wid Wm A), b 782 N New Jersey.
Smock Marcellus L, messngr Am Ex Co, h 100 Ramsey av.
Smock Marcellus L jr, musician, b 172 Ramsey av.
Smock Omer G, carp, b 202 Coburn.
Smock Orleana (wid Peter D), b 17 Woodlawn av.
Smock Richard M, asst adjutant and asst quartermstr genl Dept of Indiana G A R, 25 State House, h 549 Central av.
Smock Thaddeus S, lab, h 569 Shelby.
Smock Thomas, lab, h 106 Blackford.
Smock Thomas B (Smock & Berringer), b 258 Hendricks blk.
Smock Walter R, driver, h 110 Keystone av.
Smock Wm, lab, b 314 Jefferson av.
Smock Wm A, h 51 Beacon.
Smock Wm C (Smock & Mather), h e s Delaware 1 n of 10th.
Smock Wm M, collr, h 427 Talbott av.
Smock & Berringer (Thomas B Smock, Wm H Berringer), printers, 15 S Alabama.
SMOCK & MATHER (Wm C Smock, Daniel Mather), Real Estate, Loans and Insurance, 32 N Delaware.
Smoll Louis, saloon, s e cor Hazel and Lawrence, h same.

TUTEWILER UNDERTAKER, No. 72 WEST MARKET STREET. TELEPHONE 216.

Smoll Oscar E D, mach hd, b 88 Michigan av.
Smoot Edward J, h 381 N California.
Smoot Jesse, engr, h 109 Sheffield av (H).
Smoot John H, cook, r 165 Indiana av.
Smoot Joshua, molder, b 78 Sheffield av (H).
Smoot Lucy A (wid Adam N), h 296 N California.
Smoot Martha A (wid Winfield), h 128 W 4th.
Smoot Murat, lab, b 78 Sheffield av (H).
Smoot Richard M, farmer, h 78 Sheffield av (H).
Smorzka Joseph, city fireman, r 284 Mass av.
Smothers Nancy A (wid Samuel G), restaurant, 165 Indiana av, h same.
Smullen Avery, lab, b 155 Harrison.
Smullen Lafayette, lab, h 155 Harrison.
Smyser Myrtle L, teacher Public School No 33, b 129 E Pratt.
Smyth, see also Schmid, Schmidt and Smith.
Smyth Catherine K (wid Andrew), h 96 Bates.
Smyth Noah B, brakeman, h 28 Poplar (B).
Smyth Wm H, engr, b 96 Bates.
SMYTHE ELMER A, Dentist, 9-10 Talbott Blk, b 1039 N Capitol av.
Smythe Hugh, foreman, b 450 Mass av.
Smythe Lizzie, dressmkr, 294 N Penn, h same.
Smythe Oscar, lab, h 74 Springfield.
Smythe Victor, polisher, b 294 N Penn.
SMYTHE WM H, Grand Sec Grand Lodge F and A Masons and Grand Commandery K T, Masonic Temple, s e cor Washington and Capitol av, h 1039 N Capitol av, Tel 1056.
Snapp Anna, b 258½ E McCarty.
Snapp Robert, tmstr, h s w cor Indianapolis av and 16th.
Snapp Sarah J, clk Kingan & Co (ltd), h 258 E McCarty.
Snapp Thomas J, engr, h 194 N Dorman.
Snapp Wm H, driver, h 254 E McCarty.
Snavely Charles, jeweler, 183 W Washington, h same.
Snavely Martin, grocer, 209 W Washington, h 113 N West.
Snead, see also Smead.
Snead Henry, lab, h 135 Howard.
Snead Lizzie, h rear 132 W 1st.
Snedeker John, cheesemkr, b 19 S Senate av.
Snedeker Wm, poultry, b 30 S Senate av.
Sneed George, lab, h 132 Columbia al.
Sneedman Louis, huckster, b 134 Maple.
Snell, see also Schnell.
Snell Eliza R, h rear 80 Spann av.
Snell Ellen (wid Lafayette), h 232 W Vermont.
Snell Isaac T, lab, b 229 W 3d.
Snell Joseph T, blksmith, r 313 N East.
Snell Lafayette W, waiter, h 17 Mill.
Snell Oliver M, molder, h 262 English av.
Snell Royal P, blksmith, h 126 Lawrence.
Snelling Robert, lab, h e s Ivy la 3 s of Pendleton av (B).
Snideman Adam H, mach, h 21 Clifford av.
Snider, see also Schneider and Snyder.
Snider Albert, saloon and restaurant, 63 N Alabama, h same.
Snider Albert H, state agt Columbus Buggy Co, 12-14 Monument pl, h 1204 N Illinois.
Snider Benjamin F, cooper, r 146 Blackford.
Snider Bertha M, teacher, b 616 Virginia av.

THE
WHEN
IS A WORLD BEATER.

Snider Charles M, cooper, h 2 Minerva.
Snider Frances (wid James), b 510 E Georgia.
Snider George, engr, h 127 N Liberty.
Snider George W, propr Hide, Leather and Belting Co, h 575 N Penn.
Snider Harry K, trav agt, h 145 S Olive.
Snider John, lab, b 60 Holmes av (H).
Snider John L, baker, b 173 E Market.
Snider John M, helper, b 510 E Georgia.
Snider Lizzie, b cor Russell av and S Illinois.
Snider Luceta, dressmkr, 85 Davidson, h same.
Snider Mary E (wid Charles D), h 616 Virginia av.
Snider Oliver N, grocer, 52 Langley av, h 50 same.
Snider Thomas M, butter, r 182 E Washington.
Snider Wm W, trav agt, h 251 Virginia av.
Snitgen Amelia, b 508 E Georgia.
Snitgen Rosina K (wid J Wm), b 508 E Georgia.
Snitman Louis, produce, E Mkt House, h 134 Maple.
Snoddy Carrie, teacher, b 174 S William (W I).
Snoddy Elizabeth H (wid John M), h 174 S William (W I).
Snoddy John D, mach, b 174 S William (W I).
Snodgrass James, clk P C C & St L Ry, h 70 N State av.
Snook Walter C, carp, h 125 Columbia av.
Snow Alpheus H, lawyer, h 166 N Meridian.
SNOW-CHURCH CO THE, E R Vazeille Mngr, Law and Collections, 112 Commercial Club Bldg, Tel 879. (See adv in classified Collection Agts.)
Snow Ebenezer, lab, h 274 S Capitol av.
Snow Jacob H (J H Snow & Co), b The Bates.
SNOW J H & CO (Jacob H Snow), Consulting Mechanical Engineers and Manufacturing for Inventors, Rooms 33-35 Cordova Bldg, 25 W Washington, and 187-195 S Meridian.

The A. Burdsal Co.
Manufacturers of
STEAMBOAT COLORS
BEST HOUSE PAINTS MADE.
Wholesale and Retail.
34 AND 36 SOUTH MERIDIAN STREET.

THEODORE F. SMITHER ROOFER
GRAVEL AND OTHER COMPOSITION
Yard, 19 W. Maryland St. Telephone 861.
Office, 15 W. Maryland St.

Electric Contractors
We are prepared to do any kind of Electric Contract Work.
C. W. MEIKEL. Telephone 466.
96-98 E. New York St.

DALTON & MERRIFIELD { LUMBER South Noble St., near E. Washington

INDIANA ELECTROTYPE CO. : BEST WORK LOWEST PRICES.
23 WEST PEARL ST., INDIANAPOLIS, IND. JOB WORK. BOOK PLATES. BEST PATENT BASE ON THE MARKET.
All Orders Promptly Filled.

KIRKHOFF BROS.,
Sanitary Plumbers
STEAM AND HOT WATER HEATING.
102-104 SOUTH PENNSYLVANIA ST.
TELEPHONE 910.

Snow Wm, bricklyr, b 182 N Belmont av (H).
Snowden Dora, lab, h 40 Brett.
Snowden Frank, lab, h 267 Yandes.
Snowden James P, tmstr, h e s Bismarck av 5 n of Morris (W I).
Snowden Jesse, phys, 422 W Addison (N I), h same.
Snowden John W, contr, 130 Lynn av (W I), h same.
Snowden Joseph M, livery, 272 W Washington, h 230½ same.
Snowden Thomas, clk, b 224 E St Clair.
Snowden Walter, carp, h 49 Bismarck (W I).
Snowden Wm R, lab, h 422 W Addison (N I).
Snyder, see also Schneider and Snider.
Snyder Carrie, r 85 N Delaware.
Snyder Charles A, painter, 425 E St Clair, h same.
Snyder Charles W, bkkpr M S Huey & Son, h 468 Bellefontaine.
Snyder Clara E (wid James A W), b 1443 E Washington.
Snyder Daniel W, woodwkr, b 490 Stillwell.
Snyder Dennis F, foreman, h 119 S Noble.
Snyder Edward, canmkr, b 437 S Illinois.
Snyder Edward J, clk Clemens Vonnegut, h 28 S Arsenal av.
Snyder Ella H, stenog Military Order Loyal Legion, b 468 Bellefontaine.
Snyder Emily M (wid David E), b 27 Home av.
Snyder Ernest, hostler, h 29 Bynum pl.
Snyder Frederick M (F M Snyder & Co), b 41 Yandes.
Snyder F M & Co (Frederick M Snyder, Pearl A Havelick), contrs, 68½ E Market.
Snyder George, foreman Indpls Brewing Co, h 350 S New Jersey.
Snyder George E, stenog Am Ex Co, b 29 W Vermont.
Snyder George R, molder, b 760 S East.
Snyder Harry, hostler, b 350 S New Jersey.
Snyder Harry, lab, b 22 Springfield.
Snyder Harry B, clk County Treasurer, h 77 Middle Drive (W P).

Lime, Lath, Cement,
THE W. G. WASSON CO.
130 INDIANA AVE. TEL. 989.
Sewer Pipe, Flue Linings, Fire Brick, Fire Clay.

Snyder Harry T, coachman 605 N Delaware.
Snyder Henrietta (wid Stephen), h 437 S Illinois.
Snyder Henry, lab, b 307 Columbia av.
Snyder Henry, wagonmkr, h 490 Stillwell.
Snyder Henry M, engr, h 226 Fletcher av.
Snyder Irvin P, miller, h 21 Singleton.
Snyder James W, b e s Lincoln av 9 s of C C C & St L Ry (M J).
Snyder Jessie, h 209 W Market.
Snyder John D, printer, b 437 S Illinois.
Snyder John S, polisher, h 356½ Clifford av.
Snyder Lee, mach hd, h 568 Union.
Snyder Leroy E, blksmith, h s s Jackson 2 w of Lincoln av (M J).
Snyder Lev Tull, car rep, h 436 E Vermont.
Snyder Lucas, lab, h 307 Columbia av.
Snyder Margaret (wid Jackson), h 100 Rhode Island.
Snyder Margaret (wid John), dressmkr, 54 Chadwick, h same.
Snyder Mary, h 295 E Georgia.
Snyder Michael H, genl mngr Advance Thresher Co, 3 Masonic Temple, tel 1615, h 390 Bellefontaine.
Snyder Oliver H, mach, h 621 E Vermont.
Snyder Robert, lab, b 100 Rhode Island.
Snyder Robert B, cabtmkr, h w s Ethel av 2 s of 17th.
Snyder Thomas L, b 306 W Maryland.
Snyder Wm, tmstr, h 78 N New Jersey.
Snyder Wm H, bkkpr D W Williamson & Co, b 621 E Vermont.
Snyder Wm H, finisher, b 437 S Illinois.
Snyder Wm J, grocer, 200 Hoyt av, h same.
Snyder Wm K, cooper, h 306 W Maryland.
Snyder Wm T, carp, h 35 Johnson av.
Sobhe, see also Zobbe.
Sobhe Charles, carp, h 247 N Pine.
Sobbe Henry, driver, b 519 Virginia av.
Socialer Turnverein, n e cor Michigan and New Jersey.
Socks Daniel, painter, b 67 S Noble.
Socwell Bros (Wm P and M Spencer), grocers, 240 E Washington.
Socwell Henry M, h 294 E Market.
Socwell M Spencer (Socwell Bros), h 57 Davidson.
Socwell Samuel H, grocer, 99 Mass av, h 228 N Alabama.
Socwell Wm P (Socwell Bros), b 294 E Market.
Soehner Charles J, salesman Fahnley & McCrea, h 91 W Vermont.
Sogemeier August, meats, 21 E Mkt House, h 667 S Meridian.
Sogemeier Wm, poultry, 665 S Meridian and 165 W Pearl, and produce, 5 E Mkt House, h 667 S Meridian.
Sogemeier Wm jr, clk, b 667 S Meridian.
Sohl Levi, h 358 Central av.
Sohn George, finisher, h 423 Union.
Sohn John, blksmith, h 74 Yeiser.
Sohn John M, clk, h 430 W North.
Soice Edward H, mngr Rex Portrait Co, 42 W Market, h same.
Soice Walter M, bkkpr, b 42 W Market.
Sokol Sarah (wid Samuel), grocer, 283 S Capitol av, h same.
Soland John B, mach, b 40 Thomas.
Soland Victor, carp, h 40 Thomas.
Solberg Sarah J (wid Charles), b 435 N New Jersey.
Solenberg Robert J, lab, h 258 Highland av.
Sollers Mary B, nurse, b 141 E Pratt.
Solliday John, lab, b 86 S Noble.
Solomon Abraham, clk, b 229 E Ohio.

YOUR HOMES FURNISHED BY W. H. MESSENGER 101 East Washington St. Telephone 491.

McNamara, Koster & Co. Phone 1593. ◆ 212-218 S. PENN. ST. } PATTERN MAKERS

THE FRED DIETZ CO. WOODEN PACKING BOXES MADE TO ORDER. FACTORY AND WAREHOUSE TRUCKS. 40 Madison Avenue. Telephone 654.

Solomon David, second hand goods, 141½ Mass av, h same.
Solomon Esther M, stenog Mutual Life Ins Co of Ind, b 339 E Market.
Solomon George A (Dreyfoos & Co), h 222 E Walnut.
Solomon Henry, ticket broker, 25 S Illinois, b 229 E Ohio.
Solomon Hyman, pdlr, h 89 W Morris.
Solomon Jacob C, mngr Americus Club, b 339 E Market.
Solomon Jesse F, trav agt, b 339 E Market.
Solomon Joseph, pawnbroker, 25 S Illinois, h 229 E Ohio.
Solomon Morris, auctioneer, 78 E Washington, h 339 E Market.
Solomon Sarah (wid Henry), b 339 E Market.
Solomon Sarah (wid Isaac), b 201 N Liberty.
Solon Michael, lab, h 42 S Capitol av.
Solon Michael J, lab, r 590 Morris (W I).
Solsbury La Rude, foreman, h 112 Division (W I).
Solsbury Naomi A, grocer, n e cor Woodburn av and Division, h 112 Division (W I).
Soltau John A, grocer, 104 Davidson, h same.
Soltau Peter W, trav agt, h 597 Marlowe av.
Soltau Wm A, clk, b 104 Davidson.
Somers Anna J, stenog Atlas Engine Wks, b 125 Cornell av.
Somers Ralph K, trav agt, b 30 E Pratt.
Somerville Arthur E, mach, b 449 E Washington.
Somerville Elmore W, clk R M S, h 284 Fletcher av.
Somerville Henry, lab, h 12 Wilcox.
Somerville James, supt and engr Indpls Gas Co, h 378 N Meridian.
Somerville James L, bkkpr Hendricks & Cooper, b 378 N Meridian.
Somerville John M, clk S A Fletcher & Co, h 70 The Blacherne.
Somerville Melville I, fireman, b 284 Fletcher av.
Somerville Theodore E, mngr Union Co-Operative Laundry, h 302 E South.
Somerville Tilford D, saloon, 449 E Washington, h same.
Somerville Walter S, clk, b 378 N Meridian.
Sommer, see also Summer.
Sommer August K, drayman, h 33 E McCarty.
Sommer Charles W, grocer, 139 W 3d, h same.
Sommer Chester W, student, b 454 W Udell (N I).
Sommer Daniel Rev, pub The Octographic Review, h 454 W Udell (N I).
Sommer Edward W, clk Paul H Krauss, b 33 E McCarty.
Sommer Edwin, clk, b 302 Prospect.
Sommer Franklin E, student, b 454 W Udell (N I).
Sommer Frederick, editor The Octographic Review, h 501 W Highland av (N I).
Sommer Herman, baker James P Bruce, h 32 S Dorman.
Sommer Louis, saloon, 302 Prospect, h same.
Sommer Wm E, bkkpr M O'Connor & Co, h 33 E McCarty.
Sommer Wm H (Schultz & Sommer), h 55 Yandes.
Sommerfield Wm, h 64 S Noble.
Sommerlad Christian, trav agt, r 285 S Illinois.

Henry H. Fay, 40½ E. WASHINGTON ST., FIRE INSURANCE, REAL ESTATE, LOANS AND RENTAL AGENT.

Sommerlad Christopher, dairy, 1057 Madison av, h same.
Sommerlad Otto L, driver, b 1057 Madison av.
Sommers August, molder, h 239 Huron.
Sommers Frank E, mach, h 39 Everett.
Sommers Harry B, clk, b 501 S West.
Sommers John H, engr, h 25 Miley av.
Sonderegger Frank J, b 49 N Brightwood av (B).
Sondermann, see also Sundermann.
Sondermann Frederick, carp, h 178 Prospect.
Sondermann Ottilie, teacher, b 178 Prospect.
Sonnefield Henry W, paperhngr, r 26½ N Senate av.
Sonnefield Wm, engr, h 50 Jefferson av.
Sonnenberger Jacob J, janitor, h 233 E Market.
Sonnenberger Samuel, clk, b 233 E Market.
Sonnenschmidt Carl (Junge & Sonnenschmidt), b s s Brookville rd 1 w of P C C & St L Ry (S).
Sonntag John, finisher, h 17 Dunlop.
Sonntag John H jr, dep Treasurer of State, h 30 E Pratt.
Soper Oscar A, sub letter carrier P O, h 40 Birch av (W I).
Soper Wm C, h 100 Vincennes (W I).
Sorden Albert W, trav agt, b 82 Ft Wayne av.
Sorey Alvin K, hostler, b 74 N Illinois.
Sorgenfrei Otto, butcher, r 135 E Washington.
Sorhage Carl H, cigarmkr, b 461 S Meridian.
Sorhage Henry C, cigar mnfr, 161 Virginia av, h 43 Fletcher av.
Sorrell Alexander, lab, h 143 Sharpe av (W).
Sorrells George, painter, r 143½ N Delaware.
Sorters Charles G, constable, b 48 N California.
Sortwell George W, mach, h 153 Locke.
Souder Ellen R, h 340 N Meridian.
Souder Louis B, presser, b 130 W Pratt.
Souder Luther B, clk, b 130 W Pratt.
Souder Solomon, lab, b 84 S Wheeler (B).
Souders O Otis, mngr Bates House Pharmacy, b 312 College av.
Souers, see also Sauer.

SURETY BONDS——— American Bonding & Trust Co. OF BALTIMORE, MD. Authorized to act as Sole Surety on all Bonds. Total Resources over $1,000,000.00. W. E. BARTON & CO., General Agents, 504 INDIANA TRUST BUILDING. Long Distance Telephone 1918.

Business World Supplied with Help GRADUATES ASSISTED TO POSITIONS 10,000 NOW IN GOOD SITUATIONS. TEL. 499. E. J. HEEB, PRES. Indianapolis BUSINESS UNIVERSITY

Water Works Pumping Engines { HENRY R. WORTHINGTON, 64 SOUTH PENNSYLVANIA ST. Long Distance Telephone 284.

UNION CO-OPERATIVE LAUNDRY (COMPOSED OF UNION LAUNDRY GIRLS.) NOS. 38, 40 AND 42 VIRGINIA AVENUE. TELEPHONE 8. INDIANAPOLIS, IND. T. E. SOMERVILLE, MANAGER

HORACE M. HADLEY

Insurance, Real Estate, Loan and Rental Agent

66 EAST MARKET STREET,

Telephone 1540. Basement.

Souers Andrew, h 241 E Louisiana.
Souers Joseph, blksmith, h 241 E Louisiana.
Souers Joseph, tobacconist Indpls Tobacco Wks, b 241 E Louisiana.
Soughley Michael, lab, b n w cor Michigan and State avs.
Soule Charles E, printer, h 8 Cleaveland blk.
Soult Albert E, florist, b 30 Beecher.
Soult Frank L, florist, b 65 Wallack.
Sourbeer Edward G, clk, b s e cor McLene and Rader (N I).
Sourbeer John R, grocer, s e cor McLene and Rader (N I), h same.
Sourbeer Walter S, engr, h 173 Church.
Sourwine Edgar A, condr, h 232 Yandes.
Sourwine Elizabeth (wid Samuel), h 46 N Station (B).
Sourwine George, janitor, h 487 Union.
Sourwine Jacob, horseshoer, 1217 Morris (W I), h 18 Sheffield (W I).
South Albert, mach, b 73 Gimbel.
South Allison G, printer, h 20 Hall pl.
South Bend Chilled Plow Co, D T Bennett agt, 5 Board of Trade bldg.
SOUTH BEND IRON WORKS, Henry B Smith Mngr, Plow Mnfrs, 160 S Penn, Tel 1367.
South Benjamin F, carp, h 22 Henry.
South Charles C, driver, b 414 W 2d.
South Ellen (wid Daniel), h 414 W 2d.
South Erastus O, harness, 188 Indiana av, h 22 Fayette.
South Harry, mach hd, h 382 W 2d.
South Henry, lab, h w s Lee 1 n of Johnson (W I).
South John, mach, h 123 Buchanan.
South Lawrence H, furnace setter, b 126 E Ohio.
South Lizzie A (wid James M), boarding 126 E Ohio.
South Oliver E, harnessmkr, h 22 Fayette.
South Otto E, clk, b 414 W 2d.
South Walter W, miller, h 19 Henry.
Southall John E, cook, h 56 Fayette.
Southard Alpheus L, butcher, h 512 W Maryland.
Southard Charles T, trav agt, h 552 Ash.

Special Detailed Reports Promptly Furnished by Us.

MERCHANTS' AND MANUFACTURERS' EXCHANGE

J. E. TAKKEN, Manager,

19 Union Building, 73 West Maryland Street.

Southard George, h 99 Ruckle.
Southard John A, painter, h 118½ Mass av.
Southard Lena, teacher Public School No 41, b 99 Ruckle.
Southard Lot, printer, b 129 N Alabama.
Southerd Lydia F (wid James), h 156 Prospect.
Southern Express Co, John J Henderson agt, 25 S Meridian.
Southern Jacob T, mngr, h 525 N Capitol av.
Southern James E, cutter, h 45½ Brookside av.
Southern John S, janitor, r rear 100 E Michigan.
Southern Thomas J, agt, h 525 N Capitol av.
Southern Wm J, lab, r 286 Mass av.
Southman Laura (wid Luther), h 537 Fremont (N I).
Southside Dispensary, George A Broady supt, 588 Virginia av.
Southwick Byron T, agt, h 67 N New Jersey.
Southworth Martin O, electrician, h 61 The Blacherne.
Sowders David (Sowders & Edwards), b 80 S West.
Sowders Edward, fish, h 126 Spring.
Sowders James M, fish, 237 W Washington, h 66 Woodlawn av.
Sowders John, ball player, h 2 N Dorman.
Sowders Rinaldo, fish, 64 E Mkt House, b 80 S West.
Sowders Wm M (Egan & Sowders, fish, 36 E Mkt House, h 70 N Liberty.
Sowders & Edwards (David Sowders, Jet D Edwards), fish, 596 Virginia av.
Sowle Charles, brakeman, b 274 S Penn.
Spaan, see also Spahn and Spann.
Spaan Henry N (McCullough & Spaan), h 858 N Meridian.
Spacke Frederick W, foreman Sinker-Davis Co, b 110 Dunlop.
Spacke George H, mach, b 110 Dunlop.
Spacke Henry, brewer, h 532 E Georgia.
Spacke Mary (wid Frederick), h 110 Dunlop.
Spacke Mary (wid Philip), h 500 S East.
Spacy Alvin E, cook, h 295 E New York.
Spade Joseph J, bartndr, b 17 Harrison.
Spades John, uphlr, b 204 E Morris.
Spades Josephine H (wid Jacob C), h 307½ N West.
Spades Michael H, office 55 W Market, h 300 N Meridian.
Spaerle August, lab, b 506 E Washington.
Spaethe Benjamin E, jeweler, rear 550 W Udell (N I), r same.
Spafford Lynn H, asst bkkpr Daniel Stewart Co, b 77 E Walnut.
Spafford Thomas E, gas insp, 155 Michigan (H), h 118 King av (H).
Spahn, see also Spaan and Spann.
Spahn Charles, helper, h n s Lily 4 e of Rural.
Spahn John, lab, h e s Hazel 2 s of Lawrence.
Spahr Charles E, salesman Fahnley & McCrea, h 159 Cornell av.
Spahr Franklin L, bkkpr and cashr Fahnley & McCrea, h 30 Broadway.
Spahr George L, clk, h 115 Bright.
Spahr George W, lawyer, 95 E Washington, h 470 Ash.
Spahr John, lab, b Marion Park Hotel (M P).
SPAHR JOHN H (Agt), Propr Grand Opera House Livery Stables, 75 E Wabash, Tel 102; h 1337 N Illinois. (See adv in classified Livery.)

CLEMENS VONNEGUT 184, 186 and 192 E. Washington St. || CABINET HARDWARE CARVERS' TOOLS. Glues of all kinds.

Spahr John M, clk, h 95 Bright.
Spahr John O (Spahr & Kingsbury), h 1343 N Illinois.
Spahr Louis F, foreman, h 1355 N Senate av.
Spahr Mary K, stenog, b 1337 N Illinois.
Spahr Wm H, real est, r 69 Mass av.
Spahr & Kingsbury (John O Spahr, John H Kingsbury), lawyers, 215 Indiana Trust bldg.
Spain Herman T, trav agt D H Baldwin & Co, h 404 Talbott av.
Spain Rebecca (wid Pleasant), b 427 Talbott av.
Spalding, see also Spaulding.
Spalding Mary (wid Peter), h 218 Howard.
Spalding Samuel, lab, b rear 474 N California.
Spalding Wm H, wagonmkr, h 625 E Ohio.
Spangenberger Anna, b 270 S Capitol av.
Spangenberger Charles L, cigarmkr, b 81 W McCarty.
Spangenberger Louis C, cigar mnfr, 560 S Illinois, h same.
Spangenberger Peter, bartndr, h 357 Spring.
Spangenberger Philip, tmstr, h 81 W McCarty.
Spangenberger Philip A, cigarmkr, b 81 W McCarty.
Spangler Charles, molder, b 46 Russell av.
Spangler Charles L, toolmkr, h 130 W Michigan.
Spangler Eugene P, bkkpr, b 17 Halcyon blk.
Spangler Franklin J, salesman Nelson Morris & Co, h 24 Roanoke.
Spangler John T, mach hd, h 48 Hadley av (W I).
Spann, see also Spaan and Spahn.
Spann Charles B (Hayden & Spann), b 182 S New Jersey.
Spann Edward, tmstr, h 54 Langley av.
Spann Henry J (John S Spann & Co), b 163 N Penn.
Spann John M (John S Spann & Co), h 25 West Drive (W P).
Spann John S (John S Spann & Co), h 163 N Penn.
SPANN JOHN S & CO (John S, Thomas H, John M and Henry J Spann), Real Estate, Insurance, Loans and Rental Agts, 84-86 E Market, Tel 133.
Spann Thomas H (John S Spann & Co), h 502 N Delaware.
Spannoeth Christian F, lab, h 43 Iowa.
Spannuth Ernst, lab, h 307 English av.
Spargur Eliza (wid Reuben W), b 61 Walcott.
Spargur Morgan A, lab, h 113 Naomi.
Sparks Andrew S, driver, h 669 Wells (N I).
Sparks Charles H, r 25 Hutchings blk.
Sparks David W, grocer, 385 W North, h same.
Sparks Emma, h 114 Darnell.
Sparks Everett L, plastr, h 472 Sheldon.
Sparks Francis M, plastr, h 136 Cornell av.
Sparks George I, plumber, b 110 S Summit.
Sparks Guy L, clk Eli Lilly & Co, h 87 Sanders.
Sparks Harry D, barber, r 22 Hutchings blk.
Sparks James B, cook, h 65 The Windsor.
Sparks John W, lab, h 65 Maxwell.
Sparks Judith (wid Jesse), b 224 N Senate av.
Sparks Marion T, clk, b n e cor Grandview and Belmont avs (H).
Sparks Martha A, prin Center Twp Dist School No 7, b 375 Home av.

HEADQUARTERS
PHOTOGRAPHIC OUTFITS
AMATEUR OR PROFESSIONAL
THE H. LIEBER COMPANY
33 S. MERIDIAN ST.

Sparks Mary E, teacher, h 375 Home av.
Sparks Ora, brakeman, h 128 S State av.
Sparks Stella, h 69½ Indiana av.
Sparks Wiley A, mach, h 84 Kappus (W I).
Sparks Wm J, blksmith, h 373 S Capitol av.
Sparrow Benjamin F, miller, h 181 Maple.
Spatts Stoughton F, clk, h 87 Broadway.
Spaugh Mae A, dressmkr, 273 E North, b same.
Spaugh Ralph H, student, b 164 E New York.
Spaugh Solomon W, carp, h 273 E North.
Spaulding, see also Spalding.
Spaulding Charles, lab, b 101 N Senate av.
Spaulding David, produce, b 79 N Alabama.
Spaulding Edward, lab, b 120 Yandes.
Spaulding Emma M, h 217 E Wabash.
Spaulding James H, cook, h 49 Torbet.
Spaulding John (Rutledge & Spaulding), h 233 Hadley av (W I).
Spaulding John L, b 28 Ft Wayne av.
Spaulding Lucinda (wid Thomas), h 130 Anderson.
Spaulding Ralph, restaurant, 22 Prospect, h same.
Spaulding Ralph, lab, h 41 Hiawatha.
Spaulding Richard, engr Hartford blk, h same.
Spaulding Thomas, lab, b 119 Ft Wayne av.
Spaulding Wm, b 233 Hadley av (W I).
Spaulding Wm, lab, b 167 S Alabama.
Spaulding Wm, lab, b 528 W North.
Spaulding Wm E, painter, h 141 Ludlow av.
Speake Gardner W, painter, h 1740 Kenwood av.
Speake Joseph M, painter, h e s Capitol av 2 s of 30th.
Speake Joseph M jr, clk, b 1740 Kenwood av.
Speake Louis E, clk, h 276 E St Clair.
Speake Thomas, b 276 E St Clair.
Speany Willis W, watchman, h 445 E McCarty.
Spear Edwin H (Spear & Co), h 29 E Pratt.
SPEAR & CO (Edwin H Spear), Genl Agts Computing Scale Co of Dayton, Ohio, and Indiana Graphophone Co, 50, 51 and 52 When Bldg. (See adv in Talking Machines.)

GUIDO R. PRESSLER,
FRESCO PAINTER
Churches, Theaters, Public Buildings, Etc., A Specialty.
Residence, No. 325 North Liberty Street.
INDIANAPOLIS, IND.

INDIANAPOLIS STEEL ROOFING AND CORRUGATING WORKS, 23 and 25 East South Street. S. D. NOEL, Proprietor.

David S. McKernan | REAL ESTATE AND LOANS
Houses, Lots, Farms and Western Lands for sale or trade.
ROOMS 2-5 THORPE BLOCK.

DIAMOND WALL PLASTER { Telephone 1410 BUILDERS' EXCHANGE.

UNION TRANSFER AND STORAGE CO. Cor. E. Ohio St. and C., C., C. & St. L. R'y Tracks. ISSUE NEGOTIABLE RECEIPTS ON MERCHANDISE AND H USEH LD GOODS.

W. McWORKMAN,
ROOFING AND CORNICE WORKS,
930 W. Washington St. Tel. 1118.

Spearing Albert H, mach, b 325 E Walnut.
Spearing Frederick, patrolman, h 325 E Walnut.
Spearing Wm H, uphlr, b 325 E Walnut.
Spearman David K, tmstr, h 24 Barth av.
Spears, see also Speer and Spier.
Spears Henry A, h 665 N Penn.
Spears James, watchman, b 507 S West.
Spears James C, lab, b 507 S West.
Spears John M, mer police, h 1943 N Senate av.
Spears Joshua, janitor, h 8 Center.
Spears Mary, b 665 N Penn.
Spears Solomon, lab, r 331 W North.
Spears Wm I, trav agt, h 76 Cornell av.
Specht Adolph, condr, b 770 W Washington.
Specht Emma, b 23 Yandes.
Specht Ferdinand O, barber, h 23 Yandes.
SPECIALTY MANUFACTURING CO, Thomas Bemis Pres, J B Dill Sec and Treas, Pattern and Model Makers, 193 S Meridian, Tel 843. (See adv opp classified Photographers.)
Speck Victor E, cook, b 107 S Illinois.
Speckin Charles, mach, h 306 Yandes.
Speckmann Ferdinanda (wid Henry), b 1402 N Illinois.
Speckmann George, cigarmkr, b 1351 E Washington.
Speckmann Henry, grocer, 128 E Mkt House, h 76 W 19th.
Speckmann Wm H, cigarmkr, h 1351 E Washington.
Speddy Robert G, filer, h 531 S New Jersey.
Speece Lizzie (wid Thomas), h 67 Ingraham.
Speece Wm, well driver, b 54 Langley av.
Speer, see also Spears and Spier.
Speer James W, carp, h 148 King av (H).
Speer Wilkinson B, trav agt, h 42 Hall pl.
Speers Harry A O, buyer Kingan & Co (ltd), b 228 E North.
Speiser Adam, carp, h 171 W Morris.
Spellman Adolph R, tailor Kahn Tailoring Co, h 354 S Illinois.
Spellman George M, lumber insp, h 25 W 22d.
Spellman Mary (wid Thomas), h 49 Oak.

GEO. J. MAYER,
MANUFACTURER OF
SEALS
STENCILS, RUBBER STAMPS, CHECKS, BADGES, DOOR PLATES, ETC.
15 S. Meridian St., Ground Floor. TEL. 1386.

Spellman Riley, clk, r 171 W Market.
Spellman Samuel D, h 975 N Penn.
Spellmire Joseph H, bkkpr J L Farrell & Co, h 207 The Shiel.
Speltz Peter D, carp, h 221 Elizabeth.
Spelz Joseph S, lab, h 134 N Noble.
Spence Alexander, lab, h 61 Temple av.
Spence Jacob, engr, h 332 S New Jersey.
Spence Joseph B, watchman, h 78 High.
Spence Wm J, condr, h 474 Highland av.
Spence Wm O, uphlr, b 332 S New Jersey.
Spencer Alexander T, condr, h 131 W 1st.
Spencer Benjamin D, lab, b 116 Ramsey av.
Spencer Cecil S, trav agt, r 440 N Meridian.
Spencer Charles H, sec to mayor, 7 basement Court House, r 76 W Walnut.
Spencer Charles N, trav agt, h 57 Talbott av.
Spencer Commodore, lab, b 519 W McLene (N I).
Spencer David E, supt Udell Woodenware Wks, h 1502 Northwestern av (N I).
Spencer Ellen J, clk U S Pension Agency, b 974 N Delaware.
Spencer Eunice (wid Nathan), b 27 N West.
Spencer George, mach, b 439 E Georgia.
Spencer Harry M, driver, b 179 Douglass.
Spencer Henry G, bkkpr Kingan & Co (ltd), h n e cor 17th and N Senate av.
Spencer Herbert J, baker, h 166 Ash.
SPENCER HOUSE, Henry W Lawrence Propr, n w cor Illinois and Louisiana, Tel 546.
Spencer Jacob, lab, b 331 Hillside av.
Spencer Jacob J, lab, h w s Ivy la 1 s of Pendleton av (B).
Spencer James K, carp, h 331 Hillside av.
Spencer Jennie (wid Frank), h 17 Beacon.
Spencer Jerome, cabtmkr, h 614 W Eugene (N I).
Spencer John M (Spencer & Lowry), h 1241 E Washington.
Spencer Joseph B, fireman, h 36 Warren.
Spencer Kate H, dressmkr, 218 Indiana av, h same.
Spencer Leander, b 439 E Georgia.
Spencer Lou (wid Charles), h 215 N Senate av.
Spencer Louisa C (wid Charles), b 149 Hoyt av.
Spencer Marie M (wid Charles), dressmkr, 39 W Washington, h 76 W Walnut.
Spencer Martin V B, agent U S Pension Agency, 67 W Maryland, h 974 N Delaware.
Spencer Rae, stenog, b 420 N Illinois.
Spencer Robert H, driver, h 179 Douglass.
Spencer Robert H, lab, b 71 Harlan.
Spencer Samuel J, lab, h 218 Indiana av.
Spencer Wm, baker, h 166 Ash.
Spencer Wm H, checkman, h 343 E McCarty.
Spencer Wm H, pipefitter, h 447 W Michigan.
Spencer Wm W (Van Vorhis & Spencer), h 174 E Walnut.
Spencer & Lowry (John M Spencer, Charles O Lowry), phys, 1241 E Washington.
Spengel Philip H, butcher, h 427 S West.
Spenny Charles, engr, h 120 N Dorman.
Spering Christina (wid John), h 98 Yeiser.
Sperling Abraham, foreman, h 39 Peru av.
Spering Edward B, lab, b 98 Yeiser.
Sperr George J, meats, 387 Fulton, h 427 E St Clair.

A. METZGER AGENCY ESTABLISHED 1863. REAL ESTATE

LAMBERT GAS & GASOLINE ENGINE CO.
ANDERSON, IND. GAS AND GASOLINE ENGINES, 2 TO 50 H. P.

BICYCLES $5 DOWN. MONTHLY. Best Wheels. Best Tr. WHEELMEN'S CO. 31 W. OHIO ST. LONG DISTANCE TEL. 1855.

Sperr Jacob, lab, b 213 S Alabama.
Sperr Michael, b n s Lily 4 e of Rural.
Sperr Michael G, butcher, h 135 Geisendorff.
Sperry Lovina H (wid Ira A), b 291 Park av.
Spesshardt Samuel C, clk George J Marott, h 385 S East.
Speth John, uphlr, b rear 204 E Morris.
Speth Joseph, mach hd, h 913 S Meridian.
Speth Magdalena (wid Peter), h rear 204 E Morris.
Spicer Alta M, nurse, r 245 N Delaware.
Spicer Emma E (wid James A), h 576 W Francis (N I).
Spicer Ernest W, bkkpr Natl Malleable Castings Co, h 84 W 9th.
Spicer Eva L, stenog, b 197 N Delaware.
Spicer James B, bkkpr, b 576 W Francis (N I).
Spicer James T, tmstr, h 244½ E Washington.
Spiece Elmer, brakeman, b e s Brightwood av 7 s of Willow (B).
Spiegel Augustus F, h 219 N Liberty.
Spiegel George M, trav agt, h 1138 N Alabama.
Spiegel Henry L, fretwork, 316 E Vermont, h 220 same.
Spiegel Mary A, teacher Public School No 1, b 219 N Liberty
Spiegel Wm C (Indpls Pulley Mnfg Co), h 171 N Noble.
Spielberger Jacob, grocer, 260 Howard (W I), h same.
Spielhoff Henry (H Spielhoff & Son), h 191 Coburn.
Spielhoff H & Son (Henry and Wm F), carps, 189 Coburn.
Spielhoff Laura, stenog, b 190 Coburn.
Spielhoff Wm F (H Spielhoff & Son), h 256 Coburn.
Spielman Don J, painter, b 103 W South.
Spielman George, bartndr, r 69 S Liberty.
Spier, see also Spear and Speer.
Spier Elizabeth (wid Frederick), h 494 E Washington.
Spier Ella (Spier Sisters), b 494 E Washington.
Spier John F, grocer, 494 E Washington, h 539 E Market.
Spier Sisters (Ella and Sophia), dressmkrs, 494 E Washington.
Spier Sophia (Spier Sisters), b 494 E Washington.
Spilker John F, lab, h 12 Thalman av.
Spillman Clarence, sawmkr, b 55 Palmer.
Spillman Mary (wid Thomas), h 49 Oak.
Spillman Thornton P, lab, h 202 W 5th.
Spillman Wm G, harness, 365 S Delaware, h 365½ same.
Spillman Wm O, carriagemkr, h 26 Bicking.
Spilman Oliver P, clk Indpls Union Ry Co, h 4 The Windsor.
SPINK MARY A, Physician, 124 N Alabama, h same, Tel 381.
Spinner Edmund H, foreman Pabst Brewing Co, Indpls Branch, h 240 S Delaware.
Spinner Mary (wid Matthias), h 240 S Delaware.
Spires Adolphus, lab, h 286 Douglass.
Spires Catherine, h rear 9 Elizabeth.
Spitler David A, agt, h 387 Indiana av.
Spitz Richard, brakeman, b 107 Walcott.
Spitz Victor J, brakeman, b 107 Walcott.
Spitzfaden Charles A, bartndr, h 124 Hosbrook.
Spitzfaden Peter, saloon, 201 Virginia av, h 294 E South.

Farm and City Loans
25 Years' Successful Business.
THOS. C. DAY & CO,
Rooms 325 to 330 Lemcke Building.

Spitzfaden Wm P, saloon, s w cor Madeira and Prospect, h w s Earhart 1 s of Prospect.
Spitznagel Joseph L, barber, 454 S Meridian, h same.
Spitznagel Leopold, saloon, 920 S Meridian, h same.
Siptznagel Wm L, cabtmkr, h 918 S Meridian.
Splann James, tmstr, h 91 S West.
Splann Joseph F, engraver, b 91 S West.
Splann Thomas, condr, h 277 S Noble.
Splann Timothy, chief detective, h 58 S West.
Splann Timothy, lab, h 367 E Market.
Splann Timothy, lab, b 43 S West.
Splann Wm F, trimmer, b 91 S West.
Spoerle August, lab, b 506 E Washington.
Spohr J George, shoes, 37 N Illinois, h 74 E Pratt.
Sponager John, trav agt, h 615 E Vermont.
Sponenberger Peter, condr, r 249½ E Washington.
Spong Thomas E, transfer clk R M S, h 274 Highland av.
Sponnet Gustav, lab, b 43 Iowa.
Sponsel Charles, sawyer, b 42 Davis.
Sponsel Henry, saloon, 345 Madison av, h same.
Sponsel Henry G, clk Robert Keller, h 108 Yeiser.
Sponsel Wm G, butcher, h 404 Madison av.
Spoon Frank P, mach hd, h 810 E 9th.
Spoon Harry O, mach, h 6 S Waverly (B).
Spoon Orval H, lab, b 159 Newman.
Spoon Wm A, lab, h 159 Newman.
Spoon Wm T, lab, b 159 Newman.
Spooner Frank W, opr W U Tel Co, b 1093 E Ohio.
Spooner Jesse, porter, b 111 E Washington.
Spooner John C, real est, 10½ N Delaware, h 1093 E Ohio.
Spooner Samuel H, lawyer, 6 Fletchers' Bank bldg, h 31 E St Joseph.
Spornberg Henry (Sanders & Spornberg), r 17 Columbia blk.
Spotts Charles C, mach, h 165 Jefferson av.
Spotts Stanton H, clk, h 847 N Penn.
Spotts Stoughton F, clk, h 87 Broadway.

EAT
HITZ'S
CRACKERS
AND CAKES.
ASK YOUR GROCER FOR THEM.

J. H. TECKENBROCK Painter and Decorator, 94 EAST SOUTH STREET.

FIDELITY MUTUAL LIFE—PHILADELPHIA, PA.
MATCHLESS SECURITY At LOW COST. | A. H. COLLINS | General Agent Baldwin Block.

Rooms 42 and 43 WHEN BUILDING.

ESTABLISHED 1876. TELEPHONE 168.
CHESTER BRADFORD,
SOLICITOR OF PATENTS,
AND COUNSEL IN PATENT CAUSES.
(See adv. page 6.)
Office:—Rooms 14 and 16 Hubbard Block, S. W. Cor. Washington and Meridian Streets,
INDIANAPOLIS, INDIANA.

Spotts Wm, grain dealer, b 87 Broadway.
SPOTTVOGEL THE (German, Sunday), Gutenberg Co, Publishers, 27 S Delaware, Tel 269.
Sprague Charles, finisher, h 232 Shelby.
Sprague Edgar B, bailiff Superior Court Room No 2 Court House, h 519 N Francis (N I).
Sprague Henry H, pres H H Sprague Co, h 27 Lockerbie.
Sprague H H Co, Henry H Sprague pres, Frank J Le Moyne sec and treas, gas meter mnfrs, 30 W South.
Sprague Julia E (wid Frank), b 232 Shelby.
Sprague Roger A, lawyer, 138 Woodlawn av, h same.
Sprague Sigel F, carp, b 690 N Illinois.
Sprandel George, chairmkr, h 550 N Senate av.
Sprandel Herman F, bkkpr Indpls Mnfrs' and Carps' Union, b 276 N Senate av.
Sprankel George, blksmith, h 213 Hamilton av.
Sprankel Margaret (wid Christopher), h 213 Hamilton av.
Sprankel Matilda E, dressmkr, 213 Hamilton av, b same.
Sprankle Alfred H, agt, r 77½ S Illinois.
Sprankle Walter S, piano teacher, h 220 E St Clair.
Sprankle Webster, fireman, h 118 River av (W I).
Spratt Elzie, lab, b 227 Howard.
Spratt Emma, h 3 Margaret.
Spratt George, driver, b 59 Lincoln la.
Spratt John H, money delivery clk U S Ex Co, h s e cor Valley Drive and Ludlow av.
Spratt Nellie (wid John), h 227 Howard.
Spratt Walter S, foreman, h 163 Woodlawn av.
Spray Wm P, mach, h 17 N William (W I).
Sprecher Peter, driver, h 344 Indiana av.
Spreen Wm C, cabtmkr, h 181 Yandes.
Spreng Albert F, grocer, 75 E Mkt House, h 723 Mass av.
Spreng Caroline F (wid Adam), h 292 E Miami.

Spreng Edward, clk, b 292 E Miami.
Spreng Wm F, clk, b 292 E Miami.
Sprenger Anthony F, clk Robert Keller, r 5 Shelby.
Sprengpfeil Henry, saloon, 190 Kentucky av, h 170 S Missouri.
Sprey John, varnisher, h 52 Martindale av.
Sprey John J, mach, h 44 Holloway av.
Spring Max, bookbndr, b Circle Park Hotel.
Springer Albert J, dairy, n w cor Brookside and Lebanon avs, h same.
Springer Amos H, stairbldr, w s Hubbard 1 s of Clifford av, h same.
Springer Carroll D, city agt John Rauch, h 797 N New Jersey.
Springer Edgar, stenog, b 28 Broadway.
SPRINGER FRANCIS M, Attorney at Law, Room 12, Ingalls Blk, h 236 Union.
Springer George, carp, b 860 E Washington.
Springer George W, molder, h 452 S Delaware.
Springer George W, motorman, h 8 Wallace.
Springer Harry M, baker, b 165 Michigan av.
Springer Henry, molder, h 97 Bismarck.
Springer Isaac, pres Indpls Basket Co, h 195 N Alabama.
Springer Jacob M, b 1490 N Meridian.
Springer Jacob M, carp, h 324 E Wabash.
Springer James E, trav agt Thomas C Day & Co, h 544 Central av.
Springer Jesse, driver, r 5-7, 149½ Oliver av (W I).
Springer John E, mach, b 196 Fayette.
Springer John M, patternmkr, h 566 Shelby.
Springer Joseph, patternmkr, b 366 N East.
Springer Judah, h 10 Brookside av.
Springer Levi, carp, b 894 W Washington.
Springer Lulu M, bkkpr, b 28 Broadway.
Springer Martin B, molder, h w s Brightwood av 2 n of Schofield (B).
Springer Martha J, dressmkr, 324 E Wabash, h same.
Springer Morris, h 894 W Washington.
Springer Nathan A, turner, h 162 Nordyke av (W I).
Springer Nathan U, carp, h 196 Fayette.
Springer Otto C, lab, h 8 Everett.
Springer Ruth M (wid Isaac), h 28 Broadway.
Springer Wm E, clk Parry Mnfg Co, b 28 Broadway.
Springer Wm E, lab, h rear 352 Mass av.
Springer Wm G, carp, h 165 Michigan av.
Springer Wm H, molder, h 97 Bismarck av (H).
Springer Wm, watchmkr Julius C Walk & Son, r 233 N Delaware.
Springsteen Abraham H, clk When Clothing Store, b 433 N Illinois.
Springsteen Harry A, plumber, b 79 E Vermont.
Springsteen Harry R (Springsteen & James), h 34 Cherry.
Springsteen Jefferson, painter, b 105 N Linden.
Springsteen John W, trav agt, b 126 E Ohio.
Springsteen Mary A (wid Abram), b 34 Cherry.
Springsteen Robert E, with Model Clothing Co, h 73 W 3d.
Springsteen & James (Harry R Springsteen, Wm E James), laundry, 504 Bellefontaine.
Sprinkle David, meats, w s Harris av 1 s of W Washington (M J), h s w cor Harris av and Jackson (M J).

Edwardsport Coal and Mining Co. Miners and Shippers Steam and Domestic Coal.

C. ZIMMERMAN & SONS | SLATE AND GRAVEL ROOFERS 19 South East Street.

DRIVEN WELLS And Second Water Wells and Pumps of all kinds at CHARLES KRAUSS', 42 S. PENN. ST. TELEPHONE 465.

Sproesser Frederick, mach hd, h 303 Bright.
Sprole Margaret M (wid Wm T), b 914 Broadway.
Sproston Margaret M (wid Richard), h 340½ E Market.
Sproston Richard W, timekpr, h 85 Meikel.
Sproul Wm P, lab, h 496 S Illinois.
Sproule James E, storekpr Insane Hospital; h 502 N Illinois.
Sproule James E jr, salesman A Kiefer Drug Co, b 502 N Illinois.
Sproule Mary F (wid Robert S), h 27 E Pratt.
Sproule Wm K, insp of customs, h 502 N Illinois.
Sproule Wm K jr, collr The State Bank of Indiana, b 502 N Illinois.
Sproule Wm S, h 27 E Pratt.
Sprow George W, lab, h 508 W Maryland.
Sprow John, lab, b 508 W Maryland.
Spruance Alexander P, mngr glue works Kingan & Co (ltd), h 954 N Penn.
Spry John F, lab, h 16 Hill.
Spurgeon Milton, roll man, b Marion Park Hotel (M P).
Spurgeon Thomas R, tel opr C C C & St L Ry, r 325 S Alabama.
Spurgin Tilghman, lab, h 281 River av (W I).
Spurlin Reese, waiter, r 229 W Washington.
Spurlock Robert R, real est, b 478 N Brookside av.
Spurrier Charles C, lab, h 66 Torbet.
Spurrier Charles W, plastr, b 343 Mass av.
Spurrier Claude C, bkkpr Major Taylor, b 461 S Meridian.
Spurrier Dennis, cooper, b 461 S Meridian.
Spurrier Edith, stenog Globe Accident Ins Co, b 379 N Alabama.
Spurrier Francis H, trav agt, h 1135 N Delaware.
Spurrier James L, clk, b 119 W 1st.
Spurrier Vennis, cooper, b 461 S Meridian.
Squibb Robert, carp, h 10 Lafayette.
Squires Frank M, engr, h 326 Spring.
Squires George, motorman, b 5 Wallace.
Squires George W, trav agt, h 309 E Ohio.
Squires Rebecca, b 53 Bloomington.
Staab Andreas, butcher, h 57 Bridge (W I).
Staab Andreas jr, butcher, h 77 S Reisner (W I).
Staab Frank X, engr, h 1004 W Washington.
Staab Nicholas, lab, b 57 Bridge (W I).
Staats Alpheus S, attendant Insane Hospital, h 67 Tremont av (H).
Staats Andrew F, h 61 Spann av.
Staats George B, chief clk I & V Ry, h 599 Ash.
Staats Henry, cook, r 77½ S Illinois.
Staats Julius, lab, b 61 Spann av.
Staats Louisa S (wid Abram), h 424 N Meridian.
Staats Margaret C (wid George D), b 10 E Michigan.
Staats Wm N, mach hd, h 186 Prospect.
Stacey George C, salesman Peoria Athletic Co, h 336 Clifford av.
Stacey Henry, h 629 N Capitol av.
Stacey Herbert H, b 629 N Capitol av.
Stacey Ottie (wid John), b 396 S West.
Stacey Ottilie, b 5 W Chesapeake.
Stack Michael K (Bannon & Co), r 130 N Senate av.
Stackhouse Carrie A, bkkpr The Home Stove Co, b 754 Broadway.
Stackhouse Clandine A, h Ritter av (I).
Stackhouse Henry M, sec Comstock & Coonse Co, b 754 Broadway.

RICHARDSON & McCREA,
MANAGERS FOR CENTRAL INDIANA.
EQUITABLE LIFE ASSURANCE SOCIETY
Of the United States.
79 EAST MARKET STREET,
TELEPHONE 182.

Stackhouse Hugh Rev, pastor Methodist Protestant Church, h 377 Dillon.
Stackhouse Isaac N, h 754 Broadway.
Stacy Eugene E, state sec Y M C A, h 1162 N Penn.
Stacy Milton H, finisher, h 1213 N Capitol av.
Stader Elizabeth (wid Peter), b 135 Hosbrook.
Stader Robert E, lab, b 135 Hosbrook.
Stadtlander Frank A, condr, h 159 Hoyt av.
Stadtlander Frederick C, switchman, h 212 Lexington av.
Staehle Louisa (wid Wm), b 260 S Alabama.
Staehle Wilhelmina, grocer, 260 S Alabama, h same.
Staercker Philip, shoemkr, h 276½ Coburn.
Staff Peter, engr, h 27 S Shade (B).
Stafford Albert, butcher, h 163 Ft Wayne av.
Stafford Archibald, painter, b 163 Ft Wayne av.
Stafford Archibald S, painter, r 359 N Senate av.
Stafford Charles A, phys, 24 E Ohio, h 491 N Senate av.
Stafford Dora M (wid Jonathan W), b 179 E New York.
STAFFORD EARL E, Propr Indiana Illustrating Co and Publisher The Indiana Woman, 49½ N Illinois, Tel 1077; b 491 N Senate av. (See adv in classified Engravers.)
Stafford Hattie, h 118 Ash.
Stafford James, lab, b 27 Columbia al.
Stafford James, porter, h 433 Blake.
Stafford Lydia (wid Columbus), b 400 W Udell (N I).
Stafford Mary E (wid Selman), h 500 N Senate av.
Stafford Otta L, h 359 N Senate av.
Stafford Shelby, mach, h 132 W Vermont.
Stafford Wm H, blksmith, h 173 N State av.
Stafford Wm T, lab, h 381 N Senate av.
Stage Caroline (wid Wm B), h 643 E 7th.
Stagg Daniel E, music teacher, 64 W 6th, h same.

Typewriter-Ribbons
ALL COLORS FOR ALL MACHINES.
THE BEST AND CHEAPEST.
S. H. EAST, STATE AGENT,
The Williams Typewriter....
55 THORPE BLOCK, 87 E. MARKET ST.

ERTEL STEAM LAUNDRY
LA[illegible] AND B[illegible] IN THE STATE. PROMPT SERVICE.
26 and 28 N. Senate Ave. Telephone 1089.

ELLIS & HELFENBERGER Architectural Iron Work and Gray Iron Castings. 162-170 South Senate Ave. Tel. 958.

THE HOGAN TRANSFER AND STORAGE COMP'Y
Household Goods and Pianos Moved—Packed—Stored...... Baggage and Package Express Machinery and Safes a Specialty Cor. Washington and Illinois Sts. TELEPHONE No. 675.

The Central Rubber & Supply Co. ◆◆◆ Hose, Belting, Packing, Clothing, Druggists' Sundries, Bicycle Tires, Cotton Hose, Etc. New York Belting & Packing Co., L't'd. PHONE 922. 79 S. ILLINOIS ST., INDIANAPOLIS, IND.

The Provident Life and Trust Company
Of Philadelphia.
Grants Certificates of Extension to Policyholders who are temporarily unable to pay their premiums
D. W. EDWARDS, Gen. Agt., 508 Indiana Trust Bldg.

Stagg Wm F, trav agt, b 64 W 6th.
Staggs Charles J, dentist, n s Sutherland 1 w of Station (B), b 170 Christian av.
Staggs Sarah E (wid John), h 170 Christian av.
Stahl Benjamin E, lab, b 174 Columbia av.
Stahl Charles C, lab, h 174 Columbia av.
Stahl Edward, lab, b 1027 E Washington.
Stahl Frederick, grocer, 330 N Noble, h same.
Stahl Frederick M, lab, b 174 Columbia av.
Stahl Harry, b 200 Bright.
Stahl Louis J, painter, r 172 W Washington.
Stahl Louise (wid George), h 683 Mass av.
Stahl Margaret (wid Frank), h 57 Harlan.
Stahl Nicholas G, barber, 193 Virginia av, h 57 Harlan.
Stahlberger Frederick, lab, h 25 S Dorman.
Stahle John, carp, b 135 E Washington.
Stahlhut Charles, varnisher, b 770 S East.
Stahlhut Charles A, clk, h 37 Temple av.
Stahlhut Charles F, carp, h 35 Temple av.
Stahlhut Elizabeth (wid Julius), h 43 Spann av.
Stahlhut Emma, dressmkr, 228 Fulton, b same.
Stahlhut Frederick, lab, h e s Webb 1 n of Raymond.
Stahlhut Frederick C, grocer, 199 Mass av, h 295 N East.
Stahlhut Frederick J, painter, h 1359 N Capitol av.
Stahlhut Frederick W, carp, h 229 N Pine.
Stahlhut John, mach, b 43 Spann av.
Stahlhut Julius, coppersmith, b 43 Spann av.
Stahlhut Wm C, mach, b 43 Spann av.
Stahr Hans F, clk, b 444 S East.
Stahr Joseph, r 170 E Vermont.
Staib Mary, nurse, r 102 N Capitol av.
Stake Charles, engr, h 41 S Arsenal av.
Stake Charles T, beamer, b 99 Blake.
Stake John W, city fireman, b 99 Blake.
Stake Joseph, finisher, h 489 Ash.
Stalcup Charles G, clk Oliver P Miller, h 176 W 9th.
Stalcup Henry R, lab, h 282 W Market.
Stalcup John B, trav agt, h 320 E St Clair.

Julius C. Walk & Son,
Jewelers
Indianapolis.
12 EAST WASHINGTON ST.

Staley Belle (wid Wm), r 304 N Senate av.
Staley Bernard A, framemkr, h 123 Spring.
Staley Charles P, restaurant, 86 W Washington, h 635 Broadway.
Staley Erhardt, h 602 Bellefontaine.
Staley Frank M, mngr retail dept Indiana Bicycle Co, h 472 Bellefontaine.
Staley Franklin E, carp, h w s Station 5 n of Schofield (B).
Staley Hiram, lab, b rear 175 S East.
Staley John S, well driver, 268 W Merrill, h same.
Staley John W, cooper, b 280 E Louisiana.
Staley Michael C, drugs, 441 Virginia av, h 448 E McCarty.
Staley Thomas, motorman, h 26 Arbor av (W I).
Staley Wm R, clk, r 69½ W Market.
Stalhut Frederick W, carp, h 638 N Capitol av.
Stallard Albert, express, h 138 W 9th.
Stallard Isaac, lab, h n s Orchard 1 e of Rural.
Stallard James M, tuner D H Baldwin & Co, h 471 E 9th.
Stallard Joseph, tmstr h s w cor Caroline av and 17th.
Stallard Thomas, tmstr, b n s Orchard 1 e of Rural.
Stallo Joseph, tailor, b 165 N Noble.
Stalnaker Frank D (Lilly & Stalnaker), treas Guardian S and L Assn, h 1055 N Illinois.
Stalnaker Gabriel W, grocer, 207 W Washington, h 215 W Pearl.
Stalnaker Olive L, cashr Lilly & Stalnaker, b 1055 N Illinois.
Stalnaker Orion F, trav agt Hendrickson, Lefler & Co, h 378 Ash.
Stambaugh Henry J, helper, h 11 Brown (W).
Stamm David H, contr, 57 Haugh (H), h same.
Stamm Henry, carp, h 77 Bismarck av (H).
Stamm Jacob, carp, h 81 Bismarck av (H).
Stamm James, bricklyr, h 27 State.
Stamm James, carp, h 61 Bloomington.
Stamm John B, carp, h 90 Eureka av.
Stamm John R, bricklyr, h n e cor Holmes and Grandview avs (H).
Stamm John W, lab, b 57 Haugh (H).
Stammel Edward W, clk, h 210 Huron.
Stammer Charles, baker, h 39 Yeiser.
Stamp Thomas, engr, b 430 E McCarty.
Stamper Mabel C, stenog Dickson & Beaning, b 85 College av.
Stanbery Charles E, motorman, h 576 W Washington.
Stanbery James V, agt Trader's Despatch, h 109 Talbott av.
Stanbrough Otis G, lab, h 1671 N Senate av.
Stanbury Francis T, carp, h 31 Orange av.
STANDARD DRY KILN CO THE, Albert T Bemis Pres, Wm P Hussey Vice-Pres, Robert Elliott Sec and Treas, Mnfrs Brick and Lumber Driers, 184 S Meridian, Tel 571.
STANDARD LIFE AND ACCIDENT INSURANCE CO OF DETROIT, C A Timewell Mngr, 62 E Market (Lemcke Bldg.)
STANDARD OIL CO, Joseph W Fromeyer Mngr, n w cor Pine and Lord, Tel 79.
Standard Rope and Twine Co, Alexander L Sykes agt, 9 Board of Trade.
Standard Saving and Loan Assn of Indianapolis, C Henry Rosebrock sec, 88½ E Washington.

OTTO GAS ENGINES | BUILDERS' EXCHANGE S. W. Cor. Ohio and Penn. Telephone 535.

Becker & Son Charles Becker Jacob Becker Jr. Merchant Tailors. 21 N. Penn. St. Tel. 934

SALISBURY & STANLEY. Office, Store and Repairing of all kinds done on short notice. Bank a Specialty. 177 Clinton Street, Indianapolis, Ind. Contractors and Builders TELEPHONE 999.

Standard Savings and Loan Assn of Indiana, Braxton Baker pres, George R Root sec and treas, 27 Thorpe blk.
Standard Wheel Co, cor Morris and Belt R R (W I).
Standfield Frank, motorman, h 73 W 13th.
Stanfield Zeph, barber, b 73 W 13th.
Standifer Joshua C, carp, 700 Park av, h same.
Staneart Ansel C, painter, h 226 Hoyt av.
Staneart George O, painter, b 226 Hoyt av.
Stanford David, lab, h 374 Muskingum al.
Stanford Frederick O, clk, r 10½ N Delaware.
Stanford Perkins W, ins agt, b 396 Broadway.
Stanford Philip A, driver, h 97 Ramsey av.
Stanford Sylvester, mach hd, h 6 Mansur blk.
Stange Emil R, foreman foundry Nordyke & Marmon Co, h 1097 N Capitol av.
Stanger Peter, watchmkr George G Dyer, h 292 E South.
Stangler Henry, pressman, b 333 E Georgia.
Stanislaus Brother, teacher, b cor Coburn and Short.
Stanley Albert, florst, b 328 W 23d.
Stanley Arthur E, lineman, h 108 Blackford.
Stanley Charles A, clk, h 53 Barth av.
Stanley Charles E, finisher, h 123 Lexington av.
Stanley Charles H, mach hd, h 25 Osgood (W I).
Stanley Clarence B, clk The A Burdsal Co, b 967 N Delaware.
Stanley Clinton, driver, r 27 Grand Opera House blk.
Stanley Crutchfield F, lab, b 191 N East.
Stanley Edward, clk, b cor Noble and Huron.
Stanley Edward, waiter, b 467 E St Clair.
Stanley Edward I, lab, b 721 N Illinois.
Stanley Eleanor (wid Reuben), b 83 N Rural.
Stanley Elias L, barber, r rear 139 St Mary.
Stanley Frank, carp, h 90 S Shade (B).
Stanley Frank P, carp, 44 S Morris (B), h same.
Stanley George W (Salisbury & Stanley), pres Builders' Exchange, h 967 N Delaware.
Stanley Henry H, engr, b 467 E St Clair.
Stanley James, bartndr, h 147 Columbia av.
Stanley John, lab, h 30 S Morris (B).
Stanley John J, asst supt Prudential Ins Co, h 96 Clifford av.
Stanley John J, clk R M S, h 33 Ruckle.
Stanley John M, phys, r 224 The Shiel.
Stanley Josephine, dressmkr, 68½ N Delaware, h same.
Stanley Levi D, Associated Press, The Indpls Journal, r 224 The Shiel.
Stanley Lewis F, car rep, h w s Shade 6 s of Pendleton av (B).
Stanley Peter, musician, r rear 331 E Michigan.
Stanley Sylvester M, cabtmkr, h e s Lincoln av 5 s of C C C & St L Ry (M J).
Stanley Wm W, carp, 289 Excelsior av, h same.
Stanridge George, pdlr, h 52½ Marion av (W I).
Stansberry Catherine B, stenog, b 444 N New Jersey.
Stansbury James, lab, h rear 671 N Senate av.
Stansbury Wm, mach hd, h 306 Howard (W I).

Henry H. Fay, 40½ E. Washington St., REAL ESTATE, AND LOAN BROKER.

Stansifer John F, opr W U Tel Co, h 443 N Meridian.
Stanton Ambrose P (Stanton & Denny), h 523 N Delaware.
Stanton Chalkley A, clk Ward Bros Drug Co, b 461 N Alabama.
Stanton Elwood, fruits, 98 E Mkt House, h 461 N Alabama.
Stanton Howard M (Stanton & Denny), b 523 N Delaware.
Stanton John, lab, b 150 W 8th.
Stanton John W, painter, h 355 Virginia av.
Stanton Louisa, music teacher, 217 E Ohio, r same.
Stanton Louise, teacher Public School No 41, b 588 N Alabama.
Stanton Mary A (wid Wm B), h 375 S Capitol av.
Stanton Patrick, lab, b 150 W 8th.
Stanton Robert, pdlr, r 26 S West.
Stanton Robert G, clk Universal Credit Agency, b 145 Cottage av.
Stanton Sarah, stenog, b 375 S Capitol av.
Stanton Sarah G (wid John B), h 66 Birch av (W I).
Stanton Thomas, lab, h 150 W 8th.
Stanton Thomas jr, foreman, b 150 W 8th.
Stanton Wm, clk, h 126 Lee (W I).
Stanton Wm W, bottler, b 375 S Capitol av.
Stanton Willis, lab, h 308 E Court.
STANTON & DENNY (Ambrose P Stanton, Austin Flint Denny, Howard M Stanton), Lawyers, Rooms 8, 9 and 10 Aetna Bldg, 19½ N Penn, Long Distance Tel 1911.
Stanwood Sophia (wid Frederick), h 44 S William (W I).
Stapelkemper John H, carver, h 1378 N Capitol av.
Stapelkemper Wm, clk, b 1378 N Capitol av.
Staples John M, molder, r 209 W Ohio.
Staples John R, carp, h 442 W Wells (N I).
STAPLES WM A, Architect, 55 Baldwin Blk, h 442 W Wells (N I).
Staples Zachary T, optician James N Mayhew, h 60 Greer.

MAYHEW'S SPECTACLES THE BEST IN USE SOLD ONLY AT 13 N. MERIDIAN ST.

COAL AND LIME Cement, Hair, Sewer Pipe, etc. BALKE & KRAUSS CO. Cor. Missouri and Market Sts.

FRIEDGEN'S IS THE PLACE FOR THE NOBBIEST SHOES Ladies' and Gents' 19 North Pennsylvania St.

SAMUEL LAING || COPPER AND GALVANIZED IRON CORNICE MANUFACTURER
72 AND 74 E. COURT STREET. SKYLIGHTS AND VENTILATORS.

M. B. WILSON, Pres. W. F. CHURCHMAN, Cash.
THE CAPITAL NATIONAL BANK,
INDIANAPOLIS, IND.
Our Specialty is handling all Country Checks and Drafts on Indiana and neighboring States at the very lowest rates. Call and see us.
Interest Paid on Time Deposits.
28 S. MERIDIAN ST., COR. PEARL.

Stapleton Thomas F, clk, h 409 W New York.
Stapleton Thomas J, clk, h 219 S Missouri.
Stapp Abraham H, gardener, h n s Ohio av 3 w of Elm av (I).
Stapp Charles C, barber, r 175 W North.
Stapp Emma R (wid Thomas B), b 739 N Capitol av.
Stapp George R, condr, h 739 N Capitol av.
Stapp Mary J (wid James H), h 64 Belmont av (H).
STAR SAVINGS AND LOAN ASSOCIATION, Horace M Hadley Pres, Henry H Fay Sec, 40½ E Washington.
STAR STORE, Efroymson & Wolf Proprs, Dealers in Dry Goods, Boots, Shoes, Cloaks, Millinery, Etc, 194-198 W Washington, Tel 1744.
Starbrock Edward J, pressman, b 488 S East.
Starbrock Frederick, wheelmkr, h 488 S East.
Starbuck Abbott G, h 217 English av.
Starbuck Leroy B, h 16 Quince.
Stark Alexander, lab, h 275 Bright.
Stark Christian, wagonmkr, h 412 College av.
Stark Edward J, student, b 111 N New Jersey.
Stark Edward L, photog, h 144 St Mary.
Stark Edward T, lab, b 48 Haugh (H).
Stark Frank, lab, b 119 King.
Stark George F, cabtmkr, h 22 S William (W I).
Stark Gustav A, carver, b 534 E Ohio.
Stark Gustav G, sec Indpls Cabtmkrs' Union, h 534 E Ohio.
Stark Henry, clk, b 169 Bright.
Stark Ira G, trav agt McCormick H M Co, h 539 Ash.
Stark Ira L, lab, b 48 Haugh (H).
Stark James O, huckster, h 76 McGinnis.
Stark John C (Stark & Hill), h 412 College av.
Stark John C jr, bkkpr, b 412 College av.
Stark John H, canmkr, h 552 Union.
Stark Joseph G, bkkpr, h 864 Broadway.
Stark Louisa (wid Herman), h 169 Bright.

TUTTLE & SEGUIN,
28 E. Market St. Ground Floor.
COLLECTING RENTS AND CARE OF PROPERTY A SPECIALTY.
Telephone 1168.

Stark Miletus, photog, h 144 St Mary.
Stark Otto, artist, 17 Hartford blk, b 534 E Ohio.
Stark Reinhold, painter, 122 S Pine, h same.
Stark Robert, marble cutter, b 534 E Ohio.
Stark Sarah, teacher Blind Inst.
Stark Simpson, lab, h 40 Guffin.
Stark Thomas C, photog, h 143½ N Delaware.
Stark & Hill (John C Stark, Conrad Hill), horseshoers, 3 John.
Starke Emma, nurse City Hospital.
Starkey Alva O, lab, b 31 N McLain (W I).
Starkey Harry, artist, h 44 Osgood (W I).
Starkey John H, lab, b 31 N McLain (W I).
Starkey Wm E, gardener, h 200 S Belmont av (W I).
Starkey Wm H, condr, b 145 Bellefontaine.
Starks Alexander W, lab, h 275 Bright.
Starks John, lab, h s w cor Auburn and Bethel avs.
Starling Clinton E, condr, h 59 Miley av.
Starling John W, barber, r 175 W North.
Starr Charles A, carp, h rear 242 S Senate av.
Starr Charles C, insp, b 430 E McCarty.
Starr Charles M, bkkpr C C C & St L Ry, h 787 N Capitol av.
Starr Christopher, lab, h 32 Water.
Starr John C, boilermkr, h 13 Minkner.
Starr Moses L, b 787 N Capitol av.
Starr Susan (wid Philemon J), h 430 E McCarty.
Starry Ida, b 272 N Meridian.
Startsman Wm H, clk, h 183 N Liberty.
Startz Andrew J, foreman, h 41 Standard av (W I).
STATE BANK OF INDIANA THE, Hiram W Miller Pres, David A Coulter Vice-Pres, James R Henry Cashier, Bates House corner, Tel 1203.
STATE BUILDING AND LOAN ASSOCIATION OF INDIANA THE, Henry T Conde Pres, Nicholas R Ruckle Vice-Pres, Frank H Hovey Sec and Treas, 31 S Penn, Tel 154.
STATE CAPITOL INVESTMENT ASSOCIATION, Jacob H Slater Pres, John Furnas Sec, J Wesley Smith Treas, O H Hovey Supt of Agts, 26-27 When Bldg.
State Fair Grounds, n s 30th e of L N A & C Ry.
State Geological Museum, r 126 State House.
State Geologist's Office, Willis S Blatchley geologist, 89 State House.
State House, n s Washington bet Capitol and Senate avs.
STATE HOUSE BUILDING ASSOCIATIONS OF INDIANA, John S Lazarus Pres, Hillis F Hackedorn Sec, 211-213 Indiana Trust Bldg, Tel 1807.
STATE HOUSE DIME ASSOCIATION OF INDIANA, John S Lazarus Pres, Hillis F Hackedorn Sec, 211-213 Indiana Trust Bldg, Tel 1807.
STATE LAW LIBRARY, John C McNutt Librarian, Rooms 64-65 State House.
STATE LIBRARY, Emma L Davidson Librarian, Room 47 State House.
STATE LIFE INSURANCE CO THE, Andrew M Sweeney Pres, Samuel Quinn Vice-Pres and Supt of Agts, Wilbur S Wynn Sec, 515-520 Lemcke Bldg, Tel 1873.

PAPER BOXES SULLIVAN & MAHAN 41 W. Pearl St.

DIAMOND WALL PLASTER { Telephone 1410 BUILDERS' EXCHANGE.

If your Laundry Work is to suit

State Superintendent of Public Instruction, David M Geeting supt, 27 State House.
State Supreme and Appellate Courts, State House.
STATE SUPREME AND APPELLATE COURTS CLERK'S OFFICE, Alexander Hess Clerk, Room 17 State House.
Staten Elizabeth (wid Smith), h 374½ E 7th.
Staten Louisa H (wid Joseph), h 208 Middle.
Staton Isham, carp, h 173 W 6th.
Staton James A, packer, b 173 W 6th.
Staton John W, weigher, h 204 Oliver av (W I).
Staton Joseph T, waiter, h 173 W 6th.
Staton Nancy A (wid George W), h 280 Indiana av.
Statt John R, lab, b 48 Osgood (W I).
Staub Charles P, milling, h 871 Bellefontaine.
STAUB JOHN W, Merchant Tailor, 63 N Penn, Tel 1294; b 200 N Noble.
Staub Joseph, insp, b 59 Johnson av.
Staub Magdalene (wid Joseph), h 200 N Noble.
Staub Nicholas F, carp, h 131 E Merrill.
Staub Oliver B, fireman, h 59 Johnson av.
Staub Sebastian, tmstr, h 156 Davidson.
Stauball Eliza (wid David), b s w cor Auburn and Bethel avs.
Stauball Wm, lab, b s w cor Auburn and Bethel avs.
Staubbs James E, cook The Bates.
Stauch George E, miller, h 108 N Dorman.
Stauch John, lab, h 281 N Pine.
Stauffer Ella, clk, b 113 N West.
Staus Gustavus, mach, h 110 Willow (B).
Staver Jacob, huckster, h 164 S Olive.
Staver John E, clk Syerup & Co, h 164 S Olive.
Staver Thomas M, uphlr, b 164 S Olive.
Stayton Thomas N, agt, r 193 W Washington.
Steading John H, switchman, b 714 E Washington.
Steadman Annie, h 247½ E Washington.
Steadman Francis M, waiter, r 192 W Merrill.
Stearn Jacob F, carp, h 373 W Vermont.
Stearne Wm H, custodian State Fair Grounds, h same.
Stearns Carl A, b 20 Garfield pl.
Stearns Eliza R, h 455 Central av.
Stearns Frank J, bartndr B B Jearl, h 455 Central av.
Stearns Lizzie J, critic Public School No 29, b 20 Garfield pl.
Stebbins Sarah A (wid John), b 247 S Delaware.
Steblein Aloysius, lab, b 128 Blake.
Stechhan Frank W, h 321 College av.
Stechhan Henrietta (wid Louis), b 321 College av.
Stechhan Otto, pres Ger Am Bldg Assn and sec and treas Indpls Drop Forging Co, h 25 Christian av.
Steck Andrew, lab, h 94 Torbet.
Steck Henry C, meats, 116 Patterson, h same.
Stecken Wm, lab, b 291 W Morris.
Steckt Frederick, lab, b 244 Fayette.
Steckt Henry, lab, h 244 Fayette.
Stedtfeld Harry F, bkkpr Merchants' Natl Bank, b 290 E South.
Stedtfeld Henry, baker, h 290 E South.
Stedtfeld Louis, lab, h 15 Iowa.
Stedtfeld Walter C G, clk, b 290 E South.

FRANK NESSLER. WILL H. ROST.
FRANK NESSLER & CO.
Tailors
56 EAST MARKET ST. (Lemcke Building),
INDIANAPOLIS, IND.

Steeb Charles, stone cutter, h 107 River av (W I).
Steeb Charles C, mach, b 107 River av (W I).
Steeb Elizabeth (wid Moritz), h w s S Meridian 2 s of Belt R R.
Steeb John, tinner, 813 S East, h same.
Steed Mary E (wid Milton), h 212 Alvord.
Steeg Charles S, brakeman, h 63 Walcott.
Steeg John L F, supt money order div P O, h 207 Dougherty.
Steeg Martha, stenog M S Huey & Son, b 63 Walcott.
Steeg Wm L, agt, b 207 Dougherty.
Steele Allen, lab, b 40 Clay.
Steele Charles, b 31 Cherry.
Steele Cromwell A, foreman David I Scott & Co, h 33 Leon.
Steele Edward A, mach hd, h 84 Oliver av (W I).
Steele Frank, mill hd, b 187 S Capitol av.
Steele Homer O, supreme deputy Natl Frat Union, h 32 Coffey (W I).
Steele James N, sol agt Empire Fast Freight Line, h 60 Ruckle.
Steele James W, attendant Insane Asylum.
Steele Jasper, lab, b 26 Meikel.
Steele Lucy (wid Marshall), h 170 Minerva.
Steele Marion, h 921 N Delaware.
Steele Nancy (wid Moses), b 341 W Market.
Steele Preston, driver, h rear 359 Blake.
Steele Rembrandt, student, b n e cor Penn and 7th.
Steele Robert, lab, b 133 Fulton.
Steele Samuel J, brakeman, h 46 S Gale (B).
Steele Shirley, student, b n e cor Penn and 7th.
Steele Theodore C, artist, n e cor Penn and 7th, h same.
Steele Thomas J, managing editor The Indpls Journal, h 347 N East.
Steele Ulysses G, clk, h 347 N Illinois.
Steele Wm F, driver, h 40 Clay.
Steele Wm T, h 727 N Delaware.
Steelsmith John A, trav agt, h 170 Sheffield av (H).
Steely Harry R, clk, b 180 E Vermont.
Steely John N, clk The Sinker-Davis Co, h 180 E Vermont.

Haueisen & Hartmann
163-169 E. Washington St.
FURNITURE,
Carpets,
Household Goods,
Tin, Granite and China Wares. Oil Cloth and Shades

THE HOME LAUNDRY
197 S. Illinois St. Telephone 15

The Fidelity and Deposit Co. OF MARYLAND. Bonds signed for Administrators, Assignees, Executors, Guardians, Receivers, Trustees, and persons in every position of trust. GEO. W. PANGBORN, General Agent, 704-706 Lemcke Building. Telephone 140.

INSURE YOUR PROPERTY WITH FRANK K. SAWYER

•JOSEPH GARDNER•
GALVANIZED IRON
CORNICES and SKYLIGHTS.
Metal Ceilings and Siding.
Tin, Iron, Steel and Slate Roofing.
37, 39 & 41 KENTUCKY AVE. Telephone 322.

Steely Thomas, clk The Sinker-Davis Co, b 180 E Vermont.
Steen Anders, lab, h 164 Trowbridge (W).
Steep Elizabeth (wid Peter), h 968 S Meridian.
Steeple John H, driver, h 546 Superior.
Steffe Marie, German teacher Public School No 25, b 302 N Capitol av.
Steffen Albert, insp, h 289 Highland av.
Steffen Albert jr, sawyer, b 289 Highland av.
STEFFEN ANDREW, Cigar Mnfr, 220 E Washington, Tel 1600; h same.
Steffen Anton, baker, 102 Prospect, h same.
Steffen Charles L, clk A Kiefer Drug Co, b 218 E Washington.
Steffen Elizabeth (wid Charles), h 52 Sullivan.
Steffen John C, printer, h 351 N Noble.
Steffen Joseph, engr, h 506 S Capitol av.
Steffen Nicholas, shoemkr, b 185 Elm.
Steffen Peter J, engr, h 506 S Capitol av.
Steffen Wm A, cigarmkr, h 656 Chestnut.
Steffens Elizabeth F (wid Ernest F), b 191 Blake.
Steffey Gideon W, trav agt Indpls Chair Mnfg Co, h 126 N Summit.
Steffey Gladys M, stenog Ind Children's Home Soc, b 126 N Summit.
STEGEMEIER HENRY, Restaurant, 19 N Illinois, h 248 N West.
Stegemeier Richard, cashr Henry Stegemeier, b 248 N West.
Stegner Louis M, carp, 565 W Eugene (N I).
Stego Herman, driver, b 79 Spruce.
Stehlin August H, mach hd, h 1 Elizabeth.
Stehlin Caroline (wid Martin), h 498 N West.
Stehlin George, saloon, 300 N West, h same.
Stehlin John H, saloon, 462 N West, h same.
Stehlin Oscar H, city fireman, b 498 N West.
Stehlin Wm F, lab, b 498 N West.
Stehr August, lab, b 84 Downey.
Steibing Theodore F, lab, h 31 Riley blk.
Steidel Frank, gluer, h 402 Brookside av.
Steidle George, mach, h 155 Minerva.

J. S. FARRELL & CO.
Have Experienced Workmen and will Promptly Attend to your
PLUMBING
Repairs. 84 North Illinois Street. Telephone 382.

Steidle John B, bookbndr, b 341 N Liberty.
Steidle Joseph H, gasfitter, b 341 N Liberty.
Steidle Paulina M (wid John B), h 341 N Liberty.
Steidle Peter P, tailor, b 341 N Liberty.
Steierberg Charles W, h 57 Dunlop.
Steierberg Charles W jr, carp, b 57 Dunlop.
Steiert Edith A, bkkpr People's Outfitting Co, b 410 Ash.
Steiert John B, mach, h 410 Ash.
Steiert John H, mach, b 410 Ash.
Steiert Wm, mach, h 70 N East.
Stein, see also Stine.
Stein Albert, contracting agt Blue Line, h 492 College av.
Stein Andrew, lab, b 164 Trowbridge (W).
Stein Andrew J, watchman, h 46 Edward (W I).
Stein Edward, fireman, r 209 W South.
Stein Edward V, chairmkr, b 644 N Senate av.
Stein Emma, bkkpr, r 123 E Ohio.
Stein Ferdinand, barber, 123 W South, h same.
Stein John C, painter, b 123 W South.
Stein Joseph, shoemkr, b 82 Russell av.
Stein Louis, lab, b 312 W Morris.
Stein Mary E, dressmkr, 123 W South, h same.
Stein Minnie (wid Wm), h 644 N Senate av.
STEIN THEODORE, Pres German Fire Insurance Co, Abstracter of Titles, also Loans, 229-230 Lemcke Bldg, Tel 1760; h 230 Central av.
Stein Willard H, lumber, b 46 Edward (W I).
Stein Wm, clk, b 392 Broadway.
Stein Wm T, clk, r 402 College av.
Steinbauer Elizabeth (wid Leonard), b 25 Davis.
Steinbauer John, lab, h 947 S East.
Steinbauer Simon C, mach hd, h 2 Gatling.
Steinberg Myer, pdlr, h 146 Eddy.
Steinberger George W, ironwkr, h 505 S Illinois.
Steinberger Gustav, brakeman, r 57½ W Maryland.
Steiner Albert, blksmith, h 65 River av (W I).
Steiner Charles C, bartndr, h 568 Morris (W I).
Steiner John, b 86 Wisconsin.
Steiner Kate E (wid Wm E), h 109 N New Jersey.
Steiner Louis, lab, b 312 W Morris.
Steinert John G Rev, pastor First German Reformed Church, h 341 E Ohio.
Steinhagen Christopher L, harnessmkr, h 272 S Olive.
Steinhagen Wm, teacher Industrial School, b 272 S Olive.
Steinhauer Edward, clk, b 381 S Meridian.
Steinhauer Frederick, transfer clk R M S, h 174 E South.
Steinhauer Frederick jr, printer, h 302 E McCarty.
Steinhauer Michael C, coal, 201 Bates, h 1000 N Capitol av.
Steinhauser Eliza (wid Bruno A), h 84 Michigan av.
Steinhilber Anna J (wid Martin), h 316 Fulton.
Steinhilber Emil, clk Paul H Krauss, h 239 E Walnut.
Steining Frank A, blksmith, h 94 Duncan.
Steinkrueger Christina (wid August), h 569 E Washington.

GUARANTEED INCOME POLICIES issued only by the **United States Life Insurance Co.** E. B. SWIFT, Manager. 25 E. Market St.

Furniture Carpets } WM. KOTTEMAN { Stoves Ranges
89 and 91 East Washington Street. Telephone 174.

Steinkuehler Casper H, watchman, h 85 Johnson av.
Steinkuehler Frederick J, mach, b 85 Johnson av.
Steinkuehler Henry R, mach hd, h 365 N Pine.
Steinle Charles R, packer, h 133 E McCarty.
Steinmann Carl, saloon, 346 E Washington, h 18 N Noble
Steinmann John, tailor, 15 Buchanan, h same.
Steinmann John G, mach, h 3 Buchanan.
Steinmark Joseph R, boilermkr, h rear 43 Hadley av (W I).
Steinmark Mary (wid Louis N), b 110 Ludlow la.
Steinmetz Charles, molder, b 54 Hosbrook.
Steinmetz Frederick, engr, h 677 Union.
Steinmetz Henry S, blksmith, h 196 Shelby.
Steinmetz Jacob J, meats, 71 E Mkt House, h 364 Jackson.
Steinmetz Jacob J jr, meats, 70 E Mkt House, b 364 Jackson.
Steinmetz John, h 54 Hosbrook.
Steinmetz John, condr, b 792 W Washington.
Steinmetz John A, engr, h 921 S Meridian.
Steinmtez John F, ammoniamkr, h 143 S Olive.
Steinmetz Nicholas, helper, h 681 Union.
Steinmetz Rudolph, coachman, r 326 Clifford av.
Steinmeyer Bertha, dressmkr, b n s Brookville rd 1 e of Line (I).
Steinmeyer Frederick, drayman, h 849 Chestnut.
Steinmeyer Helen (wid Christian), h n s Brookville rd 1 e of Line (I).
Steinmeyer John T, toolmkr, b 369 Union.
Steinruck Edward, bottler, b 220 Deloss.
Steinruck John F, driver, h 220 Deloss.
Steinruck Joseph, patrolman, h 287 E Miami.
Steinwenter Charles E, clk Elliott & Butler, h 468 N West.
Stelhorn Charles G, lab, b 222 N New Jersey.
Stelhorn Charles O, painter, b 668 E St Clair.
Stelhorn Christian F, b 306 N Noble.
Stelhorn Edward C, pipefitter, h 35 Draper.
Stelhorn Frederick W, carp, h 668 E St Clair.
Stelhorn George C, bkkpr Bertermann Bros, h 306 N Noble.
Stelhorn Harry, lab, b 668 E St Clair.
Stelhorn Harry C, driver, b 668 E St Clair.
Stelhorn Louis W, carp, h 423 Highland av.
Steller James H, janitor, r 39 Talbott blk.
Steller Rebecca (wid Frederick), h 5½ Brookside av.
Steller Wm G M, lab, b 5½ Brookside av.
Stellwagen John, saloon, 488 S Illinois, h same.
Stellwagen John jr, bartndr, b 488 S Illinois.
Stelting Alfred D, mach, h 243 Bright.
Stelting Augustus, h 109 Douglass.
Stelting Cora (wid Wm), b 334 Douglass.
Stelting Elizabeth (wid Lawrence), h 334 Douglass.
Stelting John W, pipefitter, b 109 Douglass.
Stelzel Arthur L, baker, h 280 Coburn.
Stelzel John, barber, 374 E Ohio, h 386 same.
Stelzel Walter T, sewer W H Messenger, b 386 E Ohio.
Stein John H, architect, 51 Ingalls blk, h 258 N Penn.
Stemen Clara, dressmkr, 127 W 7th, h same.
Stemen Joseph G, guard Marion County Work House, h 127 W 7th.

We Buy Municipal ~ Bonds ~
THOS. C. DAY & CO,
Rooms 325 to 330 Lemcke Bldg.

Stemen Walter S, paperhngr, r 30 Commercial blk.
Stempfel Theodore C, bkkpr The Indiana Trust Co, h 118 St Mary.
Stenecker Henry, driver, h 689 Chestnut.
Stengel George, butcher, h 52 Wallack.
Stengel John B, lab, h 14 Applegate.
Stenger Leopold, lab, h 234 Dougherty.
Stenger Peter, h 234 Dougherty.
Stenzel Charles E, clk, b 211 N Noble.
Stenzel Frank C, barber, h 211 N Noble.
Stenzel Theodore E, clk A B Ault & Co, b 211 N Noble.
Stephan Charles, engr, b 760 S East.
Stephan John G, agt, h 76 Dougherty.
Stephen Joseph Z, mnfrs' agt, 92 S Illinois, h 727 N New Jersey.
Stephen Ray J, clk The Gordon-Kurtz Co, b 727 N New Jersey.
Stephens Andrew J, policeman, h 151 Fayette.
Stephens Asbury M, fireman, h 173 W Michigan.
Stephens Charles W, frt receiver Penna Lines, h 118 Wright.
Stephens Eli, mach, r 179 Dearborn.
Stephens Henry W, engr, h 80 S Missouri.
Stephens Jasper J, saloon, 32 S Brightwood av (B), h 8 S Gale.
Stephens John F, boilermkr, n w cor Georgia and Missouri, h 110 Prospect.
Stephens John M, hostler, h 335 N West.
Stephens Joseph D, pressman, h 451 S State av.
Stephens Lewis, attendant Insane Asylum.
Stephens Lewis, mach, r 179 Dearborn.
Stephens Mary (wid Frederick), h 33½ W South.
Stephens Maud, bkkpr, b 110 Prospect.
Stephens Peter J, plumber, h 272 S West.
STEPHENS PHOTO SUPPLY CO, Rufus E Stephens Mngr, Dealers in Photographic Goods of all Kinds, 19 Mass av.
Stephens Robert B, boilermkr, b 110 Prospect.
Stephens Roscoe, brakeman, r 12 Warren.
Stephens Rufus E, sewing machines, 19 Mass av, h 669 N Alabama.

EAT HITZ'S CRACKERS AND CAKES.
ASK YOUR GROCER FOR THEM.

WILLIAM WIEGEL } MANUFACTURER OF .... SHOW CASES { 6 W. Louisiana St. Opposite Union Station.

TURKISH RUGS AND CARPETS RESTORED TO ORIGINAL COLORS LIKE NEW | Capital Steam Carpet Cleaning Works M. D. PLUNKETT, Telephone 818

BENJ. BOOTH PRACTICAL EXPERT ACCOUNTANT. Books Opened, Written Up, Posted and Balanced. Room 18, 82½ E. Washington St., Indianapolis, Ind.

ESTABLISHED 1876. TELEPHONE 168.
CHESTER BRADFORD,
SOLICITOR OF PATENTS,
AND COUNSEL IN PATENT CAUSES.
(See adv. page 6.)
Office:—Rooms 14 and 16 Hubbard Block, S. W. Cor. Washington and Meridian Streets, INDIANAPOLIS, INDIANA.

Stephens Samuel, h 319 S Alabama.
Stephens Samuel D, restaurant, 38 W 13th, h same.
Stephenson, see also Stevenson.
Stephenson Amos W, carp, h 74 Temple av.
Stephenson Barbara E (wid James A), h 113 Dunlop.
Stephenson Benjamin M, car rep, h 191 Fletcher av.
Stephenson Charles, engr, b 892 W Washington.
Stephenson Charles O, collr, b 26 Ruckle.
Stephenson Deane C, clk Kingan & Co (ltd), h 494 S New Jersey.
Stephenson Dolie (wid George T), h 422 Superior.
Stephenson Frank M, h 13 The Windsor.
Stephenson Frederick W, paperhngr, h 35 Spann av.
Stephenson George E, mach opr Indpls Journal, h 57 Barth av.
Stephenson George J, trav agt, h 391 S Delaware.
Stephenson George W, lab, h 277 Springfield.
Stephenson Jeremiah, lab, b 263½ N New Jersey.
STEPHENSON JOHN C, Physician, 324 Clifford av, h 193 Ramsey av, Tel 1402.
Stephenson John E, trav agt, h 998 N Penn.
Stephenson John W, plastr, b 54 S Austin (B).
Stephenson Joseph, mach, r 191 W Market.
Stephenson Lena, dressmkr, 277 Springfield, h same.
Stephenson Libbie J (wid James S), b 494 S New Jersey.
Stephenson Louisa (wid Malchus), r 9 Cleaveland blk.
Stephenson Malinda J (wid John W), h 277 Springfield.
Stephenson Martha J (wid Reuben), h 541 W Shoemaker (N I).
Stephenson Perry, clk Illinois House, r 190½ S Illinois.
Stephenson Robert, lab, b 187 S Capitol av.
Stephenson Robert, lab, h 291½ Kentucky av.

O. B. ENSEY
MANUFACTURER OF
GALVANIZED IRON CORNICE, SKYLIGHTS AND WINDOW CAPS.
TELEPHONE 1562. Cor. 6th and Illinois Sts.

Stephenson Robert E, mach, b 277 Springfield.
Stephenson Samuel, lab, r 16 W North.
Stephenson Samuel L, saddler, h 185 Pleasant.
Stephenson Wm E, lab, h 113 Dunlop.
Stephenson Wm B, carp, b 74 Temple av.
Stepney Laura (wid James M), b 334 W North.
Stepp Isaac, lab, h 191 Alvord.
Stepp Nelson, lab, h 120 Bryan.
Sterk Charles, teacher, b 95 N Meridian.
Stern Aaron, letter carrier P O, b 125 Davidson.
Stern Aaron R, bookbndr, b 287 N Noble.
Stern Abraham, agt, h 125 Davidson.
Stern Edward, tailor, b 742 E Washington.
Stern Jesse, tmstr, h n s 30th 3 e of Illinois (M).
Stern John, r 149½ E Washington.
Stern Leon, clk Penna lines, b 125 Davidson.
STERN MAX G I REV, Pastor St John's Evangelical Reformed Church, h 159 E Merrill.
Stern Robert, clk, h 287 N Noble.
Sternberger Frank, tmstr, h 50 Singleton.
Sterne Albert E, phys, 75 E Michigan, h same.
Sterns Henry, agt, h 898 N New Jersey.
Sterrett Maria (wid Frank), h 235 W 3d.
Sterrett Samuel, lab, h 112 Columbia av.
Sterzik Edwin A, designer, h 512 W Eugene (N I).
Steth Joseph A, lab, h 138 S New Jersey.
Stettler Frederick, baker, b 346 S East.
Stettler Gottfried G, baker, 346 S East, h same.
Stetzel Charles H, filer, h 98 Paca.
Stetzel Frances (wid Joseph I), h 143 Bates.
Stetzel Frank I, finisher, b 143 Bates.
Stetzel Joseph I, fireman, b 143 Bates.
Steuber Henry C, painter, h 5 Hamilton av.
Stevens Anna, dressmkr, 50½ S Illinois, h same.
Stevens Augusta, nurse City Hospital.
STEVENS A W & SON, Charles F Sawyer Mngr, Farm Implements, 8 Board of Trade Bldg, Tel 1892.
Stevens Benjamin F, tinner, h 29 Helen.
Stevens Bion R, police, h 160 Hillside av.
Stevens Charles A Rev, A B, instructor Butler College, b n s University av 2 w of Downey av (I).
Stevens Charles H, saloon, 408 Blake, h 229 Elizabeth.
Stevens Charles W, motorman, h 206 S Olive.
Stevens Edward, lab, h 18 Bates.
Stevens Edward M, bricklyr, r 18 Arch.
Stevens Eliza A (wid Henry), h 51 S Austin (B).
Stevens Eliza A (wid Wm M), h 29 Prospect.
Stevens Ella N (wid Thaddeus M), h 253 S New Jersey.
Stevens Frank, trav agt, r 158 N New Jersey.
Stevens Frank H, clk, b 40 Marion av (W I).
Stevens George E, brakeman, b 274 S Penn.
Stevens George W, molder, h 13 Haugh (H).
Stevens Grace (wid George), h 166½ S East.
Stevens Harry C, bartndr, r 192 Blackford.
Stevens Henry, lab, b 51 S Austin (B).
Stevens Henry C, wall paper, 496 N Senate av, h same.
Stevens Hulda B (wid Henry K), h 274 S Penn.
Stevens Jacob S, condr, b 274 S Penn.

18 and 20 S. MERIDIAN STREET || THE SHERMAN RESTAURANT || IF YOU WANT A GOOD MEAL AND HAVE IT NICELY SERVED GO TO

TUTEWILER UNDERTAKER, NO. 72 WEST MARKET STREET. TELEPHONE 216.

PARTNERSHIP INSURANCE At low cost. By which provision is made against the pecuniary loss and embarrassment resulting from the death of a member of a firm.
Provident Life and Trust Co. of Philadelphia, D. W. EDWARDS, Gen'l Agt., 508 Indiana Trust Bldg.

THEODORE F. SMITHER

Stevens James, bellboy The Bates.
Stevens James A, lab, b rear 327 S Alabama.
Stevens James H Rev, b e s Lake av 4 s of Washington av (I).
Stevens James N, policeman, h 50½ S Illinois.
Stevens James V, ironwkr, b 88 W Ohio.
Stevens James V, lab, b 72 Hazel.
Stevens John, barber, 171 Elizabeth, h same.
Stevens John, grocer, 1 Buchanan, h same.
Stevens John E, helper, h 1 Geneva (W).
Stevens John, lab, b 275 W Market.
Stevens John H, lab, b rear 327 S Alabama.
Stevens John Q, gasfitter, 29 Prospect, h same.
Stevens Joseph P, lab, h 175 Meek.
Stevens Lizzie, h 350 N Missouri.
Stevens Mary (wid John), h 37½ W Market.
Stevens Mary E, nurse, 252½ Mass av, h same.
Stevens Orie L, student, b 253 S New Jersey.
Stevens Richard S, hostler, h 97 Geisendorff.
Stevens Robert, lab, h 34 Chadwick.
Stevens Robert C, draughtsman Atlas Engine Works, r 16 W New York.
Stevens Thomas, cooper, b 125 N West.
Stevens Thomas, lab, b 29 Helen.
Stevens Thomas A, lab, h rear 327 S Alabama.
Stevens Walter G, paperhngr, b 496 N Senate av.
Stevens Wm, dairy, 103 Naomi, h same.
Stevens Wm, tilemkr, h s w cor Burton av and McLene (N I).
Stevens Wm H, shoemkr, h 288 N Senate av.
Stevens Wm S, plastr, h 1396 N Capitol av.
Stevens Wm W, b 186 W Vermont.
Stevenson, see also Stephenson.
Stevenson Albert A, clk, b 569 Central av.
Stevenson Alonzo J, watchman, h 159 Yandes.
Stevenson Arnold L, porter, b 106 Locke.
Stevenson Augusta L, teacher Public School No 14, b s s Washington av 2 e of Central av (I).
Stevenson Benjamin C, real est, 86 Lombard bldg, b 704 N Penn.
Stevenson Charles, motorman, b 150 Cornell av.
Stevenson Charles F, bkkpr, h 5½ Indiana av.
Stevenson Charles F, engr, b 95 Blake.
Stevenson Charles N, trav agt, h 569 Central av.
Stevenson David W, clk Hildebrand Hardware Co, h 62 Ruckle.
Stevenson David W, cooper, h 8 Minerva.
STEVENSON ELMER E, Lawyer, 703, 707 and 708 Lemcke Bldg, Tel 296; b 374 Park av.
Stevenson Emma F, h 106 Locke.
Stevenson Everett W, lab, b 191 Spann av.
Stevenson Frank, condr, r 269 E Washington.
Stevenson Frank J, b s s Washington av 2 e of Central av (I).
Stevenson Franklin F, carp, b 1028 S Meridian.
Stevenson Henry, porter, h 174½ Indiana av.
STEVENSON HENRY F, Lawyer and Sec Lawyers' Loan and Trust Co, 68½ E Market, h 995 N Alabama.

THE WHEN IS A WORLD BEATER.

Stevenson Howard, lab, h 10 Chadwick.
Stevenson James, h s s Washington av 2 e of Central av (I).
Stevenson James, lawyer, 86 Lombard bldg, h 950 N Illinois.
Stevenson James D, b 708 N Alabama.
Stevenson John, lab, r 275 W Market.
Stevenson John, trav agt, h 940 N Meridian.
Stevenson John A, supt agts Nederland Life Insurance Co (ltd), b Hotel English.
Stevenson John L, carp, h s w cor Lexington av and Frank.
Stevenson John W, lab, h 402 Bates.
Stevenson Lee H, insp, h 447 Charles.
Stevenson Margaret (wid Worth), h 93 N Alabama.
Stevenson Rebecca J (wid Alexander C), h 704 N Penn.
Stevenson Robert, lab, b 187 S Capitol av.
Stevenson Robert C, mech engr, r 16 W New York.
Stevenson Robley D, humorist The Indpls Journal, h 84½ N Illinois.
Stevenson Russell A clk, b 735 N Illinois.
Stevenson Samuel, porter, h rear 18 W North.
Stevenson Waverly S, broommkr, b 191 S Linden.
Stevenson Wm, carp, h 191 S Linden.
Stevenson Wm, lab, h 449 Howard (W I).
Stevenson Wm C, driver, b 1028 S Meridian.
Stevenson Wm E, tmstr, b 191 S Linden.
STEVENSON WM E (W E Stevenson & Co), Treas Lawyers' Loan and Trust Co, h 708 N Alabama.
Stevenson Wm M, bkkpr Indpls Gas Co, h 729 College av.
Stevenson Wilms, lab, h 344 Yandes.
STEVENSON W E & CO (Wm E Stevenson), Real Estate and Loan Brokers, 74 E Market, Tel 1288.
Stevers Charles, roll man, b 646 Herbert (M P).
Steward Charles W, blksmith, b 177 Mass av.
Steward E Eugene, drugs, 1052 N Senate av, h same.

THE A. BURDSAL CO.
WINDOW AND PLATE
GLASS
Putty, Glazier Points, Diamonds.
Wholesale and Retail. 34 and 36 S. Meridian St.

COMPOSITION ROOFING MATERIALS. BEST IN THE MARKET. TELEPHONE 861. OFFICE, 15 WEST MARYLAND ST.

ELECTRIC CONSTRUCTION Isolated Plants Installed. Electric Wiring and Fittings of all kinds. C. W. Meikel. Tel. 466. 96-98 E New York St

DALTON & MERRIFIELD { LUMBER South Noble St., near E. Washington

INDIANA ELECTROTYPE CO. BEST WORK LOWEST PRICES. 23 WEST PEARL ST., INDIANAPOLIS, IND. JOB WORK. BOOK PLATES. All Orders Promptly Filled. BEST PATENT BASE ON THE MARKET.

KIRKHOFF BROS.,
GAS AND ELECTRIC FIXTURES
THE LARGEST LINE IN THE CITY.
102-104 SOUTH PENNSYLVANIA ST.
TELEPHONE 910.

Steward Henrietta (wid Jackson), h 338 W North.
Steward Ida, h 115 Geisendorff.
Steward John H, waiter The Bates.
Steward John W, lab, h 29 Ellen.
Steward Leotis, lab, b 61½ Superior.
Steward Thomas M, barber, 410 Indiana av, r 504 N California.
Steward Wm, lab, b 338 W North.
Stewart Abner C, lab, b w s Illinois 3 n of 28th.
Stewart Albert, lab, h 124 Yandes.
Stewart Albert, molder, b 245 W South.
Stewart Alexander F, live stock, h n w cor Bruce and Yandes.
Stewart Alexander M (Emil Wulschner & Son), h 22 W St Clair.
Stewart Alfred, lab, b 400 W North.
Stewart Allen, janitor, h 143 S Linden.
Stewart Ananias, lab, h 562 W Addison (N I).
Stewart Anderson, lab, b 207 W Vermont.
Stewart Angeline J (wid James), h 268 Fulton.
Stewart Annetta, h 30 W Walnut.
Stewart Archibald D, chainmkr, h n w cor Bruce and Yandes.
Stewart Arthur L, teacher, b 445 N California.
Stewart Augustus, elev opr, b 25 Howard.
Stewart Calder C, barber, h 522 Jefferson av.
Stewart Catherine (wid Charles E), b 379 E Georgia.
Stewart Catherine (wid Madison), h 478 Lincoln av.
Stewart Charles A, clk C C C & St L Ry, h 521 N Senate av.
Stewart Charles E, buyer N Y Store, h 232 College av.
Stewart Charles G, managing editor The Indianapolis Sentinel, h 357 N Illinois.
Stewart Charles H, printer, h 26 W 1st.
Stewart Clarence, elev opr, b 26 W 1st.
STEWART DANIEL CO (John N and M S Carey, Wm and M S Scott), Wholesale Druggists, 42-50 S Meridian, Tel 66.
Stewart David, coachman 330 Broadway.

COAL AND COKE
The W. G. Wasson Co.,
130 INDIANA AVE. TEL. 989
LIME AND LATH

Stewart David, lab, h 124 Yandes.
Stewart Edgar, clk, b 954 N Meridian.
Stewart Edward, lab, h 66 N Senate av.
Stewart Edward, porter, b 311 Indiana av.
Stewart Edward C, brakeman, h 46 N Belmont av (H).
Stewart Edwin, lab, b 402 W McLene (N I).
Stewart Elise M, asst matron Indpls Orphan Asylum, n e cor College and Home avs.
Stewart Eliza (wid Alfred), h 400 W North.
Stewart Elizabeth, h rear 228 S Missouri.
Stewart Elizabeth (wid Judson A), h 41 Sinker.
Stewart Elliott S, carp, h 663 W 22d (N I).
Stewart Elmer E (Johnson & Stewart), b 409 W 22d (N I).
Stewart Ernest A, carp, h 466 Highland av.
Stewart Frank, barber, 67 E 14th, b 1322 N Alabama.
Stewart Frank, lab, h 403 W Addison (N I).
Stewart Frank, plumber, b 112 Buchanan.
Stewart Frank C (Stewart, Stewart & Stewart), h 32 Hall pl.
Stewart Frank C, yard clk C C C & St L Ry, b 348 S Alabama.
Stewart Garland R, clk, h 849 N Illinois.
Stewart George, driver, b 311 Indiana av.
Stewart George P, waiter, r 321 W North.
Stewart George W, agt, r 101 Bates.
Stewart George W, lab, h 25 Howard.
Stewart Hamilton, lab, h 445 W Francis (N I).
Stewart Harry J, tinner, b 41 Sinker.
Stewart Helen T, h 99 N New Jersey.
Stewart Henrietta, h rear 77 W North.
Stewart Henry, switchman, b 112 Buchanan.
Stewart Horace G, mach hd, b 246 N Tremont av (H).
Stewart Hugh P, real est, h 344 W 2d.
Stewart Jacob M, painter, h 622 E 10th.
Stewart James, bkkpr, b 533 N Alabama.
Stewart James, clk, h 953½ Wilcox.
Stewart James, lab, h rear 234 W New York.
Stewart James A, janitor, h 139 Hosbrook.
Stewart James A, lab, h 8 Hadley.
Stewart James D, lab, h s s Winchester 3 w of Mattie av.
Stewart James H, barber, 327 W Washington, r same.
Stewart James M, car rep, h 14 Depot (B).
Stewart James T, bkkpr, r 35 W Vermont.
Stewart James W, coachman 358 Park av.
Stewart James Y, b 59 Pleasant.
Stewart Jane (wid John), b n w cor Yandes and Bruce.
Stewart John, carp, 75 Susquehanna, h 211 Cornell av.
Stewart John, lab, h 276 E Washington.
Stewart John, lab, h 275 Yandes.
Stewart John, mach, h n w cor Bruce and Yandes.
Stewart John, plumber, 32 Monument pl, h 203 Coburn.
Stewart John B, carp, 267 N Noble, h same.
Stewart John D, carp, h n e cor Bethel av and Perkins pike.
Stewart John F, mach, h n w cor Bruce and Yandes.
Stewart John W, saloon, 126 E Wabash, h same.
Stewart Jonathan carp, h 349 N East.
Stewart Joseph C (Electrical Construction Co), h 188 Walcott.
Stewart Joseph H, electrician Insane Hospital, h s s Jackson 5 w of Lincoln av (M J).
Stewart Julia A (wid Wm), b 223 Clinton.

W. H. MESSENGER COMPLETE HOUSE FURNISHER 101 East Washington Street, Telephone 491

Foundry and Pattern Shop } McNamara, Koster & Co. { PHONE 1593 212-218 S. Penn. St.

Stewart June, b 42½ Malott av.
Stewart Kate (wid Robert), h 130 N Pine.
Stewart Lewis, bellboy, b 25 Howard.
Stewart Lewis C, pres Old Wayne Mutual Life Assn, phys, 522 Jefferson av, b same.
Stewart Lola M (wid George), h 65 Cincinnati.
Stewart Louis, brakeman, h 98 Fulton.
Stewart Louisa (wid Wm), h 311 Indiana av.
Stewart Margaret (wid Joseph W C), boarding 308 S Illinois.
Stewart Martha A (wid Daniel), h 530 N Delaware.
Stewart Martha C, h 226 N Meridian.
Stewart Martin, lab, b 165 S Alabama.
Stewart Mary A (wid John H), sec U S Lounge Mnfg Co, h 735 N Meridian.
Stewart Mary R, solr The McGilliard Agency Co, b 30 W Walnut.
Stewart Melton, carp, h 17 McCauley.
Stewart Moses, bellboy, h 25 Howard.
Stewart Nannie, dressmkr, 267 N Noble, h same.
Stewart Newell H, trav agt Indpls Drug Co, b 401 N Delaware.
Stewart Obadiah, lab, b 478 Lincoln av.
Stewart Patrick, painter, h n s 7th 2 w of canal.
Stewart Peter, meats, 668 Virginia av, b same.
Stewart Phila L, h 321 W North.
Stewart Place, s e cor Illinois and Ohio.
Stewart Robert F, carp, h 402 W McLene (N I).
Stewart Samuel D, collarmkr, b 64 Yandes.
Stewart Sarah E (wid Horace R), h 246 Tremont av (H).
Stewart, Stewart & Stewart (Frank C, Willis B and Wm R), phys, 85 E Ohio.
Stewart Theresa (wid John), h 112 Buchanan.
Stewart Thomas, mach, b 488 N West.
Stewart Wm, hostler 126 E Michigan.
Stewart Wm, lab, b rear 77 W North.
Stewart Wm, waiter, r 3 Wood.
Stewart Wm D, plastr, h 348 S Alabama.
Stewart Wm F, clk, h 825½ N Illinois.
Stewart Wm G, sawyer, h 193½ E South.
Stewart Wm L, mach hd, h 64 Yandes.
Stewart Wm R (Stewart, Stewart & Stewart), h 443 Central av.
Stewart Wm T, coachman 649 N Penn.
Stewart Wm W, lab, h 168 Howard.
Stewart Willis B (Stewart, Stewart & Stewart), h 415 College av.
Stiarwalt Van Buren B, real est, 51 Baldwin blk, h 69 Vine.
Stibing Henry P, fireman, b 36 Agnes.
Stibing Wm T, engr, h 36 Agnes.
Stich Anthony H, driver Clemens Vonnegut, h 11 Stevens pl.
Stich Florebert, h 281 S New Jersey.
Stich Joseph A, clk Clemens Vonnegut, b 281 S New Jersey.
Stickan Herman, lab, b 196 Orange.
Stickel John F, baggageman, h 177 Hoyt av.
Sticken Wm, lab, b 291 W Morris.
Stickley John, brakeman, h 1072 W Vermont.
Stickney Ida M (Clesson R), critic Public School No 1, h 20 Garfield pl.
Stieff Wm F, reporter German Telegraph, h 33 Stevens.
Stiegelmeyer Edward F, cabtmkr, h 79 N Pine.
Stiegelmeyer George, clk, h 394 S Delaware.
Stiegelmeyer George H, cabtmkr, h 119 Fulton.

Henry H. Fay,
40½ E. WASHINGTON ST.,
AGENT FOR
Insurance Co. of North America,
Pennsylvania Fire Ins. Co.

Stiegelmeyer John E, fireman, b 142 Prospect.
Stiegelmeyer John R, mach, b 142 Prospect.
Stiegelmeyer Wm G turner, h 142 Prospect.
Stiegemeier Henry R, clk, b 125 Greer.
Stiegemeier Rudolph, watchman, h 125 Greer.
Stiegliz Anton, coachman 630 E Washington.
Stiegmann George C F, clk, b 122 Spring.
Stienecker Alvin, gardener, b n e cor Ransdell and Southern av.
Stienecker Anna (wid Ernst), h 222 Union.
Stienecker Edward, gardener, b n e cor Ransdell and Southern av.
Stienecker Frank, carp, b n e cor Ransdell and Southern av.
Stienecker Frank E H, molder, b 222 Union.
Stienecker George, lab, b n e cor Ransdell and Southern av.
Stienecker George, porter, h 557 Madison av.
Stienecker Henry F, driver, b 222 Union.
Stienecker Henry W, carp, b n s Ohio 1 e of Belt R R.
Stienecker Herman H, gardener, h n e cor Ransdell and Southern av.
Stienecker John H, lab, b 222 Union.
Stienecker Wm, drayman, b 222 Union.
Stienecker Wm G, lab, b n s Ohio 1 e of Belt R R.
Stienning Frank A (Co-operative Carriage and Wagon Co), h 94 Duncan.
Stienstra Klass, lab, h 237 S Linden.
Stierle Gallus, grocer, 49 Draper, h 18 Arthur.
Stierle Gustav, butcher, b 540 Virginia av.
Stiers Wm, driver, b 350 N Senate av.
Stiers Wm, lab, b 105 Decatur.
Stierwalt Daniel C, lab, b 72 S McLain (W I).
Stierwalt Frank, clk L S Ayres & Co, b 68 S Judge Harding (W I).
Stierwalt James L, lab, h 72 S McLain (W I).
Stierwalt John M, chairmkr, h 68 S Judge Harding (W I).

Union Casualty & Surety Co.
of St. Louis, Mo.
Employers', Public, General, Teams and Elevator Liability; also Workmen's Collective, Steam Boiler, Plate Glass and Automatic Sprinkler Insurance.
W. E. BARTON & CO., General Agents,
504 Indiana Trust Building.
LONG DISTANCE TELEPHONE 1918.

THE FRED DIETZ CO. WOODEN PACKING BOXES MADE TO ORDER FACTORY AND WAREHOUSE TRUCKS. 400 Madison Avenue. Telephone 654.

Shorthand! BUSINESS UNIVERSITY. When Bl'k. Elevator day and night. Typewriting, Penmanship, Book-keeping, Office Training free. See page 4. Est. 1850. Tel. 499. E. J. HEEB, Proprietor.

Steam Pumping Machinery { HENRY R. WORTHINGTON, 64 S. PENNSYLVANIA ST. Long Distance Telephone 284.

UNION CO-OPERATIVE LAUNDRY { NOS. 138, 140 AND 42 VIRGINIA AVENUE. (COMPOSED OF UNION LAUNDRY GIRLS.) T. E. SOMERVILLE, MANAGER. TELEPHONE 1269. INDIANAPOLIS, IND.

HORACE M. HADLEY
REAL ESTATE AND LOANS....
66 East Market Street
Telephone 1540. BASEMENT.

Stierwalt Orion F, clk, b 68 S Judge Harding (W I).
Stigerman Alfred lab, r 69 Mass av.
Stigernoven Carl, painter, b 430 National rd.
Stigger Ella M, h 334 W North.
Stiles Elizabeth (wid George W), b 22 Osgood (W I).
Stiles Frederick H, clk, b 238 Virginia av.
STILES HENRY G, Pres Railroad Transfer Co and Genl Agt Freight Dept C H & D R R, 2 W Washington, Tel 737; h 238 Virginia av.
Stiles Irwin A, phys, 16 E Ohio, r same.
Stiles James, shoemkr, h 154 Madison av.
Stiles Louisa A (wid Otis B), b 911 N Capitol av.
Stiles Margaret, b 379 S Missouri.
Stiles Taylor, carp, b 391 W 2d.
Stille Henry E, gents' furngs, 30 Hill av, h 59 Columbia av.
Stillinger John W, dairy, 7 Downey av (H), h same.
Stills Granville, plastr, h n w cor Nicholas and English av.
STILLSON JOSEPH O, Physician (Limited to Eye and Ear), 245 N Penn, Tel 713; h same.
Stillwell Mary D, prin Public School No 36, b s w cor 17th and Broadway.
STILTZ JAMES P, Grocer, 800 N Senate av, h same.
Stiltz Rolla P, clk, h 788 N Senate av.
Stilwell Ann (wid George W), b Hanna Hotel.
Stilwell Frank L, letter carrier P O, h 123 Highland pl.
Stilwell Harry H, bartndr, b 127 E Ohio.
Stilwell Henry S, painter, h 72 Omer.
Stilwell Matthew B, grocer, 263 W Washington, h same.
Stilwell Samuel T, porter, h 353 E St Clair.
Stilwell Thomas J, wireman, b 235 W Vermont.
Stilz Anna C (wid Frederick), h 35 Pleasant.

Merchants' and Manufacturers Exchange
Make Collections and Commercial Reports......
J. E. TAKKEN, MANAGER,
19 Union Building, 73 West Maryland Street

Stilz Anna M (wid George J), h 2 Edgewood.
Stilz Charles B, chief clk I U Ry Co, h 208 Wright.
Stilz Frederick D (Webber & Co), b 59 Vine.
Stilz George A, asst ticket agt I U Ry Co, h 2 Edgewood.
Stilz George H, bkkpr Albert Gall, b 59 Vine.
Stilz John E, bkkpr A Kiefer Drug Co, b 59 Vine.
Stilz John G, drugs, 191 E Washington, h 59 Vine.
Stilz Wm F, clk Hitz Baking Co, b 35 Pleasant.
Stilz Wm F, vice-pres Indpls Terra Cotta Co, res Philadelphia, Pa.
Stimmel Marcus, h 951 N Capitol av.
Stimpson Elizabeth J (wid Henry A), h 70 W Vermont.
Stimson Joseph B, car insp, r 47 English av.
Stine, see also Stein.
Stine Charles P, finisher, h 32 Sinker.
Stine David L, dentist, 27 Talbott blk, r same.
Stinger Harry W, clk, b 18 Osgood (W I).
Stinnett Elijah W, h 113 S Belmont av (W I).
Stinson Alexander M, polisher Emil Wulschner & Son, h 52 Dougherty.
Stinson Frederick C, agt, b 456 S Alabama.
Stinson James J, bricklyr, h 6 Henry.
Stinson John, lab, h s s Brookville rd 2 w of Ritter av (I).
Stinson Lula, b 79 W Morris.
Stinson Paris B, clk, h 456 S Alabama.
Stipp Isaac B, motorman, h 100 Lynn.
Stire Francis H, salesman Emil Wulschner & Son, h 146 Ruckle.
Stires Harriet, b 122 College av.
Stirk David P, limbmkr, h 118 N East.
Stirks Matilda, seamstress, r 69 N East.
Stith Robert H, waiter, h 131 Ft Wayne av.
Stitt Emma P (wid Tilgman G), h 579 E 7th.
Stitz Frederick, cigar mnfr, 18 McKim av, h same.
Stitzel John, driver, r 41 S Delaware.
Stivers Wm D, plastr, h 320 W 1st.
Stiving Philip H, hostler, b 36 Agnes.
Stiving Wm T, engr, h 36 Agnes.
Stizelberger Henry, moldmkr, b 1 S Gale (B).
Stizelberger Jacob, modelmkr, b 1 S Gale (B).
Stobaugh Wilson S, blksmith, h 10 S Waverly (B).
Stock Henry J, h 19 Coburn.
Stock James, baker, h 45 Yeiser.
Stock John, live stock, r 77 N New Jersey.
STOCK YARDS PRINTING CO. See Indianapolis Live Stock Journal and Printing Co.
Stockdale Benjamin, finisher, b 201 E Washington.
Stockdeal Joseph, tmstr, h 567½ Virginia av.
Stockdell John M, car rep, h 287 Springfield.
Stockdell Thomas J, cooper, h 487 Highland av.
Stocker Charles, cook, h 422 E Pearl.
Stocker George, cook, h 422 E Pearl.
Stocker Isaac, tmstr, h 241 S Reisner (W I).
Stocker Wm H, drugs, 500 E Washington, h same.
Stockhamp Frederick W, lab, h 7 Birch av (W I).
Stocking Roswell W, mach, r 19 N Arsenal av.

CLEMENS VONNEGUT 184, 186 and 192 E. Washington St. | Wire Rope, Machinery, Lathes, Drills and Shapers

THE WM. H. BLOCK CO. DRY GOODS, DRAPERIES, RUGS, WINDOW SHADES.
7 AND 9 EAST WASHINGTON STREET.

Stocking Thomas M, bookbndr, h cor 47th and Light av.
Stockman George W, weighmaster, h 363 E McCarty.
STOCKMAN LOUIS S, Druggist, 251-253 N Illinois, Tel 1025; r 250 same.
Stockton Cread, janitor, r 125 Hillside av.
Stockton George P, clk, r 275 W Market.
Stockton, Gillespie & Co (Washington W Stockton, Bryant W Gillespie, Chauncey H Clark, Joseph F Clay), live stock com, Union Stock Yards (W I).
Stockton Hattie, h 16 Columbia al.
STOCKTON SARAH, Physician, 227 N Delaware, h same, Tel 1498.
Stockton Washington W (Stockton, Gillespie & Co), h 76 S McLain (W I).
Stockton Wm W, clk I D & W Ry, h 1079 W Vermont.
Stockwell Arthur O, paperhngr, b 247 Bates.
Stockwell John H, mnfrs' agt, 92 S Illinois, h 3 Broadway.
Stockwell Othello O, paperhngr, b 247 Bates.
Stockwell Palmer R, clk Indpls Light and Power Co, h 26 Newman.
Stockwell Tillman W, tmstr, h 247 Bates.
Stoddard Charles E, lab, h 37 Division (W I).
Stoddard Dwight L, carp, h 210 W Raymond.
Stoddard Elmer, h 8 S Judge Harding (W I).
Stoddard Eva H, teacher Public School No 8, b 354 Talbott av.
Stoddard Percy F, h 120 Fletcher av.
Stoddard Samuel P, cigars, 51 W Washington, h 1688 N Capitol av.
Stoddard Susan J, b 354 Talbott av.
Stoddard Wm R, millwright, h 215 Ramsey av.
Stodghill Harry J, lab, b 92 Spring.
Stodghill Sarah E, dressmkr, 92 Spring, h same.
Stodler Henry, student, r 77½ S Illinois.
Stoeffler August, mach hd, h 381 W 23d.
Stoeffler Henry C, clk, b 381 W 23d.
Stoeffler Wm, gardener, h 381 W 23d.
Stoeffler Wm jr, bartndr, h 117 Davidson.
Stoehr George F, presser, h n w cor Gale and Schofield (B).
Stoelting Charles, lab, b 377 E Michigan.
Stoelting Charles A, lab, h 86 Fulton.
Stoelting Frank G, chairmkr, h 67 Quincy.
Stoelting Lena (wid Christian G), h 377 E Michigan.
Stoelting Louis C, clk The Gordon-Kurtz Co, b 667 E Washington.
Stofer Frank W, lab, b 1040 W Washington.
Stofer George, engr, r 34 S State av.
Stofer Ulysses S G, switchman, h 476 S West.
Stoffregen Elizabeth, teacher German Public School No 4, b 252 N California.
Stogsdill John H, towerman, h 38 Poplar (B).
Stogsdill Mandivill E, motorman, h 44 Marion av (W I).
Stogsdill Marion, mach, b 3 Allfree.
Stogsdill Sarah (wid Jacob M), h 20 N Spruce.
Stokely Sarah A (wid Benjamin), h 164 N Pine.
Stokes Charlotte A (wid Howard A), h 713 E Market.
Stokes Edwin F, teacher Public School No 40, b 300 E North.

THE H. LIEBER COMPANY. IMPORTERS. ARTISTS' MATERIALS. Fine Brushes, Canvas, Colors, STUDIES. 33 S. MERIDIAN ST.

Stokes Frederick A, student, b 300 E North.
Stokes Jacob C, painter, h 80 Willow.
Stokes James, watchman, h e s Shade 3 n of Sutherland (B).
Stokes James B, b 276 W McCarty.
Stokes John, polisher, b 171 S Reisner (W I).
Stokes John W, clk A Kiefer Drug Co, h 140 E North.
Stokes Joseph T, prescription clk The J N Hurty Pharmacy Co, r 84 E New York.
Stokes Lemuel, h 300 E North.
Stokes Lottie, h 242 Indiana av.
Stokes Mary (wid Thomas), b 37 Vinton.
Stokes Thomas B, trav auditor, h 1148 N Delaware.
Stokes Thomas D, tel opr, h 245½ E Washington.
Stokes Thomas D, florist, b 357 Coburn.
Stokes Wm A, lab, b 171 S Reisner (W I).
Stoliker Ambrose F, lab, h 561 W Addison (N I).
Stoll, see also Stahl.
Stoll George C, journalist, b 135 N Illinois.
Stoll George W, mach, b 29 Larch.
Stoll Henry C, uphlr, b 74 S Spruce.
Stoll Herman, carp, b 123 S Spruce.
Stoll Jacob, cabtmkr, h 19 Windsor.
Stoll John, lab, b 407 Newman.
Stoll John, mach hd, h 389 Martindale av.
Stoll John J, bartndr, b 389 Martindale av.
Stoll Joseph, r 126 E Ohio.
Stoll Michael, carp, h 123 S Spruce.
Stoll Michael jr, cigar mnfr, 428 Virginia av, b 123 S Spruce.
Stolp Charles L, lab, h 10 Singleton.
Stolp Ernest, produce, E Mkt House, b 10 Singleton.
Stolte Albert, painter, h 962 S Meridian.
Stolte George E, engr, h 10 Water.
Stolte Henry, saloon, 249 W Maryland, h 64 Stevens.
Stolte Wm F, h 35 Shelby.
Stolz Charles H, packer, b 457 Madison av.
Stolz Frank, clk, h 595 Marlowe av.
Stolz George J, pressman, b 457 Madison av.
Stolz John A, driver, h 457 Madison av.
Stone Annison, lab, h 185 W 9th.
Stone Arthur M, trimmer, b 869 N New Jersey.

GUIDO R. PRESSLER,
FRESCO PAINTER
Churches, Theaters, Public Buildings, Etc., A Specialty.
Residence, No. 325 North Liberty Street
INDIANAPOLIS, IND.

INDIANAPOLIS STEEL ROOFING AND CORRUGATING WORKS, 23 and 25 East South Street. S. D. NOEL, Proprietor.

David S. McKernan, Rooms 2-5 Thorpe Block.
REAL ESTATE AND LOANS
A number of choice pieces for subdivision, or for manufacturers' sites, with good switch facilities.

DIAMOND WALL PLASTER { Telephone 1410 BUILDERS' EXCHANGE.

UNION TRANSFER AND STORAGE CO. & E. Ga 10 St. and C., C., C. & St. L. R'y Tracks. BRICK WAREHOUSE; CLEANEST AND SAFEST STORAGE IN CITY FOR HOUSEHOLD GOODS AND MERCHANDISE.

W. McWORKMAN,

METAL CEILINGS, ROLLING SHUTTERS, DOORS AND PARTITIONS.
930 W. Washington St. Tel. 1118.

Stone Caroline E (wid Earl S), h 74 W New York.
Stone Charles H, tmstr, h 8 Highwater.
Stone Charles S, agt Robert Zener & Co, b 627 N Illinois.
Stone Charles T, mnfrs' agt, h 869 N New Jersey.
Stone Daniel E, trav agt, h 134 Cornell av.
Stone Daniel O, boarding 578 W Udell (N I).
Stone Edith, h 94 S East.
Stone Emmsuiredell, waiter, r 154 Bird.
Stone George T, mason, b 176 E New Jersey.
Stone George W, b 24 Miley av.
Stone Guy A, clk, h 174 E St Joseph.
Stone Henrietta A (wid Oliver P), b 316 Broadway.
Stone Henry, lab, h 8 Hiawatha.
Stone James, lab, b 229 W Washington.
Stone James I, furniture, 69 W Washington, h 213 W 10th.
Stone Jefferson D, barber, 145 Mass av, h 372½ Muskingum al.
Stone John, saloon, 115 Ft Wayne, h same.
Stone John, special agt, h 359 College av.
Stone John E, trav agt, b 174 E St Joseph.
Stone John H, lab, h 24 N Judge Harding (W I).
Stone John S, foreman, h 134 Cornell av.
Stone John W, engr, r 19 N Arsenal av.
Stone John W, phys, 1549 N Capitol av, h same.
Stone J Blake, bkkpr Indiana National Bank, b 627 N Illinois.
Stone Leonard, switchman, h 382 Columbia av.
Stone Lillian, stenog American Plate Glass Co, b 72 E Vermont.
Stone Louis H, porter George W Stout, h 819 LaSalle (M P).
Stone Lucy J (wid George P), h 72 E Vermont.
STONE LYNN E, Agt Central States Dispatch Fast Freight Line, Room 1 Lorraine Bldg, Tel 1396; h 320 N Illinois.
Stone Mary C, phys, 1549 N Capitol av, h same.
Stone Richard, painter, b California House.

SEALS, STENCILS, STAMPS, Etc. GEO. J. MAYER 15 S. Meridian St. TELEPHONE 1386.

Stone Ruby, bkkpr, b 143 N West.
Stone R French, phys, 250 N Illinois, h 294 N Capitol av.
Stone Thomas J, lab, h 5 Oriole.
Stone Wm B, dentist, b 72 E Vermont.
Stone Wm C, painter, h 235 Madison av.
Stone Wm H, ironwkr, b 181 S New Jersey.
Stonebarger Clara B, clk Supt Public Schools, b 619 N Illinois.
Stonebarger Emily, h 619 N Illinois.
Stonecifer Herbert L, student, b 236 E Vermont.
Stoneman Charles G, watchman, h 256 Howard (W I).
Stoneman Walter E, condr, h 91 Oliver av (W I).
Stoner Albert D, clk L E & W R R, h 172 Brookside av.
Stoner Charles C, clk, h 198½ N Senate av.
Stoner Harry, clk, h 171 Mass av.
Stoner Henry, lab, b 58 S Gale (B).
Stoner Peter J, lab, b 162 Michigan (H).
Stoney Ira L, painter, b 278 English av.
Stoney Wm W, car rep, h 278 English av.
Stookey Oliver, lab, h 30 Thomas.
Stoops James P, janitor Public School No 32, h 58 W 12th.
Stoops Kate E, h 122 N Liberty.
Stoops Mary E, dressmkr, 122 N Liberty, b same.
Stoops Rufus P, mach, b 54 N Belmont av (H).
Storch Adam E, blksmith, h 44 N Belmont av (H).
Storch Louis A E, phys, 680 S Meridian, h 8 Carlos.
Storer Emil, bkkpr C Friedgen, b 287 N Delaware.
Storm Elizabeth (wid John), h 1000 S Meridian.
Storm Herman, lab, b 359 S Illinois.
Storm Richard, lab, b 1000 S Meridian.
Stormer Edward J, draughtsman Vonnegut & Bohn, b 222 N Illinois.
Storms Earl W, blksmith, b w s Poplar 1 n of Putnam (B).
Storms Ezra R, baggageman, h 453 E McCarty.
Storms Guy T, brakeman, h 28 Poplar (B).
Storms Harry E, b 487 E Market.
Storms Margaret, h 487 E Market.
Storms Thomas W, brakeman, h 332 Fletcher av.
Storts John W, mach, b s w cor Union and Jackson (M J).
Storts Joseph L, lab, b s w cor Union and Jackson (M J).
Storts Nancy J (wid Joseph B), h s w cor Union and Jackson (M J).
Storts Perry M, lab, b s w cor Union and Jackson (M J).
Stortz John A, butcher, r 323 W Washington.
Story Abraham L, agt, h 21 Fletcher av.
Story Sarah E (wid Wm), b 188 Fayette.
Stossmeister Wm, trav agt, h 54 W Shoemaker (N I).
Stott Andrew J, student, b 169 N Illinois.
Stott Anna M, r 37 The Windsor.
Stott Edward G, salesman Fahnley & McCrea, h 311 Union.
Stott John H, toolmkr, h 548 Broadway.
Stott Margaret (wid Isaiah), h 321 Union.
Stott Thomas, mason, h 53 English av.
Stott Wm T, pres Indpls Baptist Pub Co, res Franklin, Ind.
Stouch Harry, broker, 21 W Maryland, r 257 N Delaware.
Stoud Elmer, bkkpr, h 208 Dougherty.

A. METZGER AGENCY ESTABLISHED 1863. INSURANCE

LAMBERT GAS & GASOLINE ENGINE CO.
ANDERSON, IND. PORTABLE GASOLINE ENGINES. 2 TO 25 H. P

Stough Wm L, printer, r 45 Indiana av.
Stout Alexander A, lab, b 425 N California.
Stout Alice, fruits, 110 E Mkt House, b 425 N California.
Stout Allen, lab, r 156 W Washington.
Stout Amanda, produce, E Mkt House, b 425 N California.
Stout Benjamin, lab, h 425 N California.
Stout Benjamin F, with G W Stout, b 777 N Meridian.
Stout Charles E, clk, h 109 Bright.
Stout Edward E (H Stout & Co), h 126 W North.
Stout Edward T, motorman, b 109 Hosbrook.
Stout Edwin J, mach, h 20 Minkner.
Stout Elizabeth M (wid Benjamin G), b 751 N Capitol av.
Stout Ella M, smstrs, b 409 Ash.
Stout Frank, clk, b 244 Douglass.
Stout Furman, h 209 N Penn.
Stout George, miller, h 108 N Dorman.
Stout George R, produce, 174 E Wabash, b 105 N Alabama.
Stout George W, h e s Capitol av 1 n of 29th.
Stout George W, vault cleaner, 107 Hosbrook, h same.
STOUT GEORGE W, Wholesale Grocer, 107-109 S Meridian, Tel 20; h 777 N Meridian.
Stout Harry (H Stout & Co), b 751 N Capitol av.
Stout Harry W, janitor, b 218 E Wabash.
Stout Harvey B, real est, 31 W Market, h 108 Highland pl.
Stout Henry, b 209 N Penn.
Stout Hiram W, engr, h 86 N Senate av.
Stout Horace A, bkkpr, b 382 S Illinois.
Stout Horace A, switchman, h 1643 N Illinois.
Stout Howard F V, attendant Insane Hospital.
Stout Huldah A (wid Oliver B), wall paper, 62 N Illinois, h 236 E Market.
Stout H & Co (Harry and Edward E Stout), shoes, 184 W Washington, 242 E Washington, 68 Mass av and 98 Indiana av.
Stout Ira H, h 109 Hosbrook.
Stout Ira W, bartndr, b 109 Hosbrook.
Stout John B, h 211 W New York.
Stout John H Rev, h 19 Russell av.
Stout John W, h 536 E 8th.
Stout Madison, clk Ry Officials' and Employes' Accident Assn, h 211 W New York.
Stout Mary C (wid John R), b 327 N Illinois.
Stout Monroe, lab, b 165 Indiana av.
Stout Remsen, engr, h 382 S Illinois.
Stout Reuben A, carp, h 182 N Belmont av (H).
Stout Richard K, garbage, b 109 Hosbrook.
Stout Ross H, lab, b 425 N California.
Stout Thomas L, detective, h 17 Minerva.
Stout Thomas O, h 272 E South.
Stout Wesley A, saloon, 178 S Illinois, h same.
Stout Wm, lab, b 109 Hosbrook.
Stout Wm F, plastr, h 381 S Meridian.
Stoutenbery Elizabeth, phys, 345 N Senate av, r same.
Stovell Robert, lab, b 98 Division (W I).
Stover Alonzo W, draughtsman, b 346 Chestnut.
Stover Daniel Rev, h 195 Miller (W I).
Stover Harold B, tel opr, b 132 N Capitol av.
Stowe Wm B, fireman, h 105 Fletcher av.

Farm and City Loans
25 Years' Successful Business.
THOS. C. DAY & CO,
Rooms 325 to 330 Lemcke Building.

STOWERS EARNEST C, Druggist, 546 W Udell (N I), b 471 W Francis (N I).
Stowers Jesse L (Stowers & Jones), h 22 Stewart pl.
Stowers & Jones (Jesse L Stowers, Lewis L Jones), tailors, 95 S Illinois.
Stoy Cyrus S, clk U S Pension Agency, b Hotel English.
Strack Anton, mach hd, h 88 High.
Strack Charles, saloon, 427 Madison av, h same.
Strack Frank, h 176 Virginia av.
Strack Ignatz, cigar mnfr, 379 S Delaware, h same.
Strack Joseph, lab, b 379 S Delaware.
Strack Philip, real est, 155 Columbia av, h s s Brookside av 2 w of Jupiter.
Strack Wm, carpets, 176 Virginia av, h same.
Strack Wm L, lab, b 88 High.
Strader Henry, b 9½ Sharpe.
Stradford Frank, coachman 521 N Meridian.
Stradford John B, barber, 506 N West, h 219 same.
Stradling David W, b 454 Central av.
Stradling George W, contr carp, 454 Central av, h same.
Straffa John J, fruits, 69 E Mkt House, r 227 E Washington.
Strahl Louisa, b 61 E South.
Strahl Nathaniel E, lab, b 31 Jefferson av.
Strahl Oliver M, polisher, h 114 Deloss.
Strain Hazel, b 768 Charles.
Strain Joseph F, lab, h 77 Cushing.
Strain Louis M, barber, 395 S Delaware, h same.
Strain Wm E, barber, 131 Hadley av (W I), h 22 Nordyke av (W I).
Strain Wm F, engr, h 24 Ashland (W I).
Straka Emanuel J, tailor, b Circle Park Hotel.
Straley Ingo, dressmkr, 99 Malott av, h same.
Straley Simon, mach hd, h 99 Malott av.
Strall Mary (wid James), h 349½ N California.
Strange Fannie (wid James), h 24 Chapel.
Strange James, lab, b 332 Indiana av.

EAT
QUAKER BREAD
ASK YOUR GROCER FOR IT.
THE HITZ BAKING CO.

BICYCLES $5 DOWN. Best Wheels. Best Terms. WHEELMEN'S CO. 31 W. OHIO ST. LONG DISTANCE TEL. 1855.

J. H. TECKENBROCK House, Sign and Fresco Painter, 94 EAST SOUTH STREET.

FIDELITY MUTUAL LIFE, PHILADELPHIA, PA. A. H. COLLINS, Gen. Agt. Baldwin Blk. RATES REASONABLE. SOUND BEYOND QUESTION. BUSINESS-LIKE IN PRACTICE.

Edwardsport Coal and Mining Company ROOMS 42 AND 43 WHEN BUILDING. BITUMINOUS COAL

ESTABLISHED 1876. TELEPHONE 168.

CHESTER BRADFORD,
SOLICITOR OF PATENTS,
AND COUNSEL IN PATENT CAUSES.
(See adv. page 6)
Office:—Rooms 14 and 16 Hubbard Block, S W Cor. Washington and Meridian Streets, INDIANAPOLIS, INDIANA

Strange Lydia (wid A[illegible]) h [illegible]
Strange Wm, lab, h [illegible] H [illegible] Nicholas.
Strangmeier, Frederick G, [illegible] 177 Shelby, h same.
Strangmeier Louisa (wid Fr[illegible]) [illegible] Shelby.
Strangmeier Wm, car rep, h [illegible]
Strassner Frederick L, engr [illegible]
Strassner George J, driver [illegible]
Strate Charles F, blksmith [illegible] M Lain (W I).
Stratford Alfred, phys, [illegible] 227 E Louisiana.
Stratford Anna B, [illegible] prin [illegible] No 2, b 606 E Washington.
Stratford Caroline A (wid [illegible]) [illegible] Dickson.
Stratford Elizabeth L, [illegible] No 1, b 606 E Washington.
Stratman Emmett C, mach, [illegible] son av.
Stratman Frank H, bartndr [illegible] Randolph.
Stratman Henry, lab, h [illegible]
Stratman Henry W, driver [illegible]
Strattan Edward D, mach, [illegible]
Stratton Alice (wid Lemon M[illegible])
Stratton James, mason, h 12 M[illegible]
Stratton Joseph W, lab, h [illegible] N [illegible] av (N I).
Stratton Kate, laundress Deaf [illegible] Inst.
Stratton Rufus M, salesman F[illegible] & M Crea, h 280 N Penn.
Straub Frank, foreman Natl Star [illegible] Co, h 655 S Meridian.
Straub Frank jr, engr, h [illegible] W[illegible]
Straub John, clk, h [illegible] S M[illegible]
Straub Vincent, shoemkr, [illegible] S [illegible] same.
Straughan Harry, tuner, h [illegible] W[illegible] av (W I).
Straughan Martha L (wid H[illegible]) Woodburn av (W I).
Straughan Wilbur, carp, h [illegible] (W I).
Strausburg Albert P, molder [illegible] N[illegible]
Strauss Joseph S, clk, h [illegible] N M[illegible]

BUY THE BEST.
Outing BICYCLES $85
MADE BY
HAY & WILLITS MFG. CO.
76 N. PENN. ST. Phone 598.

[illegible] proper Original Eagle [illegible] W Washington, h [illegible] N [illegible]
[illegible] h 609 S East.
[illegible] mach, h 122 E Georgia.
[illegible] h 316 Ash.
[illegible] (wid Wm) [illegible]
[illegible]
[illegible] A [illegible] 71 S Me[illegible]
[illegible]
[illegible] (Wm F Strawmyer, [illegible] 17 M[illegible] ment pl
[illegible] h Lilly & S[illegible]
[illegible] J clk Lilly & S[illegible]
[illegible] Court
[illegible] 121½ Ft Wayne av
[illegible] porter [illegible] W [illegible]
[illegible] Shelby [illegible]
[illegible] and Sprinkling Office, [illegible]
[illegible] (wid James A), [illegible] N Dela[illegible]
[illegible]
[illegible] Margaret (wid Ja[illegible]) h [illegible]
[illegible] Garfield av [illegible]
[illegible] (wid A[illegible]) h 1027 E [illegible]
[illegible] (wid Wm), h 641 S Mer[illegible]
[illegible] M patrolman, h [illegible] Bradshaw
[illegible] h 655 S [illegible]
[illegible] h 655 S East
[illegible] watchmkr, [illegible] S Illin[illegible]
[illegible] h [illegible] Locke
[illegible] packer, h [illegible] W Wash[illegible]
[illegible] h 23 Lents
[illegible] M barber [illegible] E 7th, h 3[illegible]
[illegible] h 321 Mass av
[illegible] W porter, h 329 Spring
[illegible] h 354 W Market.
[illegible] Joseph W, bookbndr, h 32[illegible] Belle[illegible]
[illegible] lab, h 128 Sharpe av
[illegible] clk, h 32[illegible] E [illegible]
[illegible] h 120 Christian av
[illegible] cashr Kingan & [illegible]
[illegible] blk.
[illegible] h 325 E Washing[illegible]
[illegible] W, h 100 E North
[illegible] baker, 320 N Senate av.
[illegible] F, printer, h 320 N Senate
[illegible] Frederick J sec Gutenberg Co
[illegible]
[illegible] plastr, h 322 N Pine.
[illegible] Herman F feed, s e cor Walnut
[illegible] & St L Ry, h 320 N Senate av
[illegible] John F baker, h 320 N Senate
[illegible] M plastr, h 335 Highland av.
[illegible] Xavier, carp, h 21 Hendricks.
[illegible] Elizabeth, h 12[illegible] Excelsior av.
[illegible] Carl, lab, h 41 Draper

ROOFING MATERIAL C. ZIMMERMAN & SONS, SLATE AND GRAVEL ROOFERS, 19 SOUTH EAST STREET.

Chain Pumps, Driven Wells and Deep Water Wells. Repairing Neatly Done. Cisterns Built.
CHARLES KRAUSS',
42 S. PENN. ST. TELEPHONE 466.

Collars and Cuffs Laundered in Best of Style.
Domestic or High Gloss Finish.

Richardson & McCrea,
79 East Market Street.
FIRE INSURANCE,
REAL ESTATE, LOANS,
AND RENTAL AGENTS.
Telephone 182.

STUBBEL BROS (George J and Wm R), Wholesale Dealers in Poultry, Butter and Eggs, 112-114 W Washington. Tel (Bell) 1812. Warerooms 407 Washington av

k W, porter, h 173
Wm C, tmstr, 29½ N Penn, h
Holmes av (H).
Holmes av (H).
Gent (M P).
h 942 Gent (M P).
mkr, h 122 E Ohio.
Wm, h 72½ S Illinois.
h 227 E South.
mkr The Sinker-Davis
teacher 41½ N Ala-
Lawn (B).
Lawn (B).
h 74 W Wilkins.
N Senate av.
dressmkr,
N Alabama,
lawyer, 172 Huron, h
Watson),
STUBBINS EUROPEAN HOTEL THE, Stubbins & Watson Props, n e cor Illinois and Georgia. Tel 1371.
A Stubbins,
Stubbins
Illinois and
Yandes.
Hill av.
Thorpe blk,
Bellefontaine.
h 474 Park av.
Raymond 1 e of
h 189 W Mary-
Shelby.
h 771 Shelby.

STUBBS & PULLEN (Robert H Stubbs, Shelby B Pullen), Real Estate, Room 3, 25½ E Market. Tel

ERTEL STEAM LAUNDRY
26 and 28 N. Senate Ave.
Telephone 1089.

SHORTHAND REPORTING......
S. H. EAST, State Agent,
THE WILLIAMS TYPEWRITER
Thorpe Block, 87 East Market Street.

ELLIS & HELFENBERGER
Manufacturers of Iron Vases, Setees and Hitch Posts.
162-170 South Senate Ave. Tel. 958.

FIDELITY MUTUAL LIFE PHILADELPHIA, PA. A. H. COLLINS, Gen. Agt. Baldwin Blk. RATES REASONABLE. SOUND BEYOND QUESTION. BUSINESS-LIKE IN PRACTICE.

BITUMINOUS COAL ▸▸ Edwards ort Coal and Mining Company ROOMS 42 AND 43 WHEN BUILDING.

ESTABLISHED 1876. TELEPHONE 168.
CHESTER BRADFORD,
SOLICITOR OF PATENTS,
AND COUNSEL IN PATENT CAUSES.
(See adv. page 6.)
Office:—Rooms 14 and 16 Hubbard Block, S. W. Cor. Washington and Meridian Streets, INDIANAPOLIS, INDIANA.

Strange Lydia (wid Alonzo), b 221 Elm.
Strange Wm, lab, b s s Howland 1 w of Nicholas.
Strangmeier, Frederick G, music teacher, 177 Shelby, h same.
Strangmeier Louisa (wid Frederick), h 177 Shelby.
Strangmeier Wm, car rep, b 25 Villa av.
Strassner Frederick L, engr, b 55 Kansas.
Strassner George J, driver, h 22 Rock.
Strate Charles F, blksmith, h 93 S McLain (W I).
Stratford Alfred, phys, 166 Virginia av, h 227 E Louisiana.
Stratford Anna B, asst prin Public School No 2, b 606 E Washington.
Stratford Caroline A (wid Isaac W), b 25 Dickson.
Stratford Elizabeth I, teacher Public School No 1, b 606 E Washington.
Stratman Emmett C, mach hd, h 25 Johnson av.
Stratman Frank H, bartndr, b 148 Randolph.
Stratman Henry, lab, h 148 Randolph.
Stratman Henry W, driver, h 309 S East.
Strattan Edward D, mach hd, h 473 Blake.
Stratton Alice (wid Lemon M), h 426 E 15th.
Stratton James, mason, h 12 McGinnis.
Stratton Joseph W, lab, h 1220 Northwestern av (N I).
Stratton Kate, laundress Deaf and Dumb Inst.
Stratton Rufus M, salesman Fahnley & McCrea, h 280 N Penn.
Straub Frank, foreman Natl Starch Mnfg Co, h 655 S Meridian.
Straub Frank jr, engr, h 116 Wisconsin.
Straub John, clk, b 655 S Meridian.
Straub Vincent, shoemkr, 443 S Illinois, h same.
Straughan Harry, tinner, b 95 Woodburn av (W I).
Straughan Martha L (wid Henry), b 95 Woodburn av (W I).
Straughan Wilbur, carp, h 73 Lynn av (W I).
Strausburg Albert R, molder, h W 22d (N I).
Strauss Joseph S, clk, b 382 N Meridian.

BUY THE BEST.
Outing BICYCLES $85
MADE BY
HAY & WILLITS MFG. CO.
76 N. PENN. ST. Phone 598.

Strauss Leopold, propr Original Eagle Clothing Co, 5-7 W Washington, h 1022 N Meridian.
Strauss Lippman, b 469 S East.
Strauss Eugene L, mach, h 332 E Georgia.
Strawbridge George, insp, b 216 Ash.
Strawders Julia (wid Wm), h n s 8th 1 w of canal.
Strawders Morris, lab, b n s 8th 1 w of canal.
Strawmyer John A, harnessmkr, 471 S Meridian, h same.
Strawmyer Wm P (Strawmyer & Nilius), b 510 N Senate av.
Strawmyer & Nilius (Wm P Strawmyer, Otto Nilius), harness, 17 Monument pl.
Strayer Andrew E, engr, h 13 S Gale (B).
Strebel George, clk Lilly & Stalnaker, h 124 Laurel.
Strebel George J, clk Lilly & Stalnaker, h 124 Laurel.
Street Commissioner s Office, 14 Court House.
Street John, lab, r 121½ Ft Wayne av.
Street Peter W, porter, h 444 E Walnut.
Street Richard N, watchman, h 156 Sheffield av (H).
Street Sweeping and Sprinkling Office, 12 Court House.
Street Mary J (wid James A), h 175 N Delaware.
Streggow, see Strigro.
Streicher Margaret (wid Jacob), h 16 Cherry.
Streight John, h w s Garfield av 1 n of Washington.
Streight Lavina (wid Abel D), h 1867 E Washington.
Streight May G (wid Wm), b 661 S Meridian.
Streit Jesse M, patrolman, h 57 Bradshaw.
Streit Otto P, tinner, b 625 S East.
Streit Peter, foreman, h 625 S East.
Streng Andrew J, watchmkr, 24½ S Illinois, h 608½ Virginia av.
Strens Ferdinand, carbldr, h 76 Lockerbie.
Stribling John C, packer, h 186½ W Washington.
Stricker Anna C, b 73 Leota.
Stricker Frank M, barber, 154 E 7th, h 34 Byram pl.
Stricker Henry O, lab, h 581 Mass av.
Strickland Allen W, porter, h 269 Spring.
Strickland Harry C, b 254 W Market.
Strickland Joseph W, bookbndr, h 252 Bellefontaine.
Strickland Lyman, lab, h 125 Sharpe av (W).
Strickland Orion D, clk, b 252 Bellefontaine.
Strickland Smith H, clk, h 119 Christian av.
Strickland Thomas, cashr Kingan & Co (ltd), r 31 Hutchings blk.
Strickler Eli, bricklyr, h 755 E Washington.
Strickler John W, b 140 E North.
Striebeck Charles, baker, 350 N Senate av, h same.
Striebeck Conrad F, printer, b 350 N Senate av.
Striebeck Frederick J, sec Gutenberg Co, h 55 S Dorman.
Striebeck Harry, plastr, b 282 N Pine.
Striebeck Herman F, feed, s e cor Walnut and C C C & St L Ry, b 350 N Senate av.
Striebeck John F, baker, b 350 N Senate av.
Striebeck Paul M, plastr, h 255 Highland av.
Striblein Xavier, carp, h 21 Hendricks.
Strieby Elizabeth, h 127 Excelsior av.
Striggo Carl, lab, h 41 Draper.

ROOFING MATERIAL C. ZIMMERMAN & SONS, SLATE AND GRAVEL ROOFERS, 19 SOUTH EAST STREET.

PUMPS Chain Pumps, Driven Wells and Deep Water Wells. Repairing Neatly Done. Cisterns Built. CHARLES KRAUSS', 42 S. PENN. ST. TELEPHONE 465.

Collars and Cuffs Laundered in Best of Style. Domestic or High Gloss Finish. ERTEL STEAM LAUNDRY 26 and 28 N. State Ave. Telephone 1089.

Striggo Christina (wid John), b 42 Smithson.
Striggo Christopher F, lab, h 79 S Spruce.
Striggo Herman F, hackman, b 79 S Spruce.
Striggo John A, lab, h 226 Minnesota.
Strigler Jacob J, mach, h 353 Fletcher av.
Stringer George C, carp, h 145 Oliver av (W I).
Stringer Lydia (wid Eli), b 145 Oliver av (W I).
Stringer Thomas D, city fireman, h 435 W New York.
Stringer Wm H, h 428 N Senate av.
Stripp Frank J, condr, h 329 E Market.
Strissinger Jacob, lab, h s s Sturm av 1 e of Arsenal av.
STROBEL BROS (George J and Wm R), Wholesale Dealers in Poultry, Butter and Eggs, 412-414 W Washington, Tell (Bell) 1612; Warerooms 405-407 Washington av.
Strobel George J (Strobel Bros), h 50 Oliver av (W I).
Strobel John G, bartndr, b 11 Shelby.
Strobel Wm R (Strobel Bros), b 50 Oliver av (W I).
Stroble John, restaurant, 87 S Illinois, h 51 Union.
Stroble John W, cashr, b 51 Union.
Strode Roger A, h 75 Norwood.
Stroele Frederick, cabtmkr, h 515 E Georgia.
Strohmeyer Dietrich F, baker, 222 W Washington, h same.
Strome Marion H, barber, 470 E Washington, h same.
Strong Clarence W, bkkpr, b 223 W New York.
Strong Edward A, plumber, 92 E Market, h 71 Dougherty.
Strong Elisha L, supt Rockwood Mnfg Co, h n w cor LaSalle and Indiana av (M P).
Strong George W, salesman Wm B Burford, h 41 Hudson.
Strong John, sawyer, h 12 Lord.
Strong Minnie V (wid Thomas T), h 72 W 4th.
Strong Nora (wid Henry), h 648 E Ohio.
Strong Thomas D, foreman, h 74 Hoyt av.
Stropes James R, brakeman, b 320 E St Clair.
Stropes James T, condr, h 625 E New York.
Stropes Sarah E (wid Wm P), b 823 E Market.
Strother Albert E, lab, h 14 Woodburn av (W I).
Strother Wm, tmstr, h 14 Martha (W I).
Strothers Albert, bellboy, b 27 Center.
Strothers George W, porter, b 27 Center.
Strothers Joseph, lab, b 27 Center.
Stroud Silas R, mach hd, h 1314 Rader (N I).
Stroud Wm, engr, b n w cor Michigan and State avs.
Strough Joseph H, lab, h 16 S Waverly (B).
Strouse Robert H (Strouse & Fullen), h 108½ Mass av.
STROUSE & FULLEN (Robert H Strouse, Shelby D Fullen), Real Estate, Room 3, 25½ E Market, Tel 1797.
Struble Clarence E, clk, b s s Howland av 2 w of Baltimore av.
Struby Laura (wid Henry), h 301 N Capitol av.
Struckman Henry, mach, h 107 Germania av (H).

Richardson & McCrea, 79 East Market Street, FIRE INSURANCE, REAL ESTATE, LOANS, AND RENTAL AGENTS. Telephone 182.

Struckmann Frederick W, porter, h 173 Union.
Struckmann Wm C, tmstr, 29½ N Penn, h 106 Randolph.
Struna Anton, lab, b 49 Holmes av (H).
Struna Frank, lab, b 49 Holmes av (H).
Strupe Thomas J, lab, h 930 Gent (M P).
Strupe Thomas S, lab, h 942 Gent (M P).
Stuard Frank, umbrella mkr, b 122 E Ohio.
Stuard Nellie (wid Wm), h 52½ S Illinois.
Stuart Angus C E, teacher, h 227 E South.
Stuart Ellis V, time kpr The Sinker-Davis Co, b 172 Huron.
Stuart Emma L, music teacher, 401½ N Alabama, b same.
Stuart Frederick C, lab, b 18 Lawn (B).
Stuart George, mach hd, h 18 Lawn (B).
Stuart James W, barber, h 74 W Wilkins.
Stuart Katherine A, b 178 N Senate av.
Stuart Martha A (wid John C F), dressmkr, 401½ N Alabama, b same.
Stuart Orion D, actor, b 401½ N Alabama.
Stuart Romus F, lawyer, 172 Huron, h same.
Stuart Wm, h 170 S Olive.
Stubbins Archibald A (Stubbins & Watson), h Stubbins European Hotel.
STUBBINS EUROPEAN HOTEL THE, Stubbins & Watson Proprs, n e cor Illinois and Georgia, Tel 1371.
Stubbins & Watson (Archibald A Stubbins, Samuel N Watson), proprs Stubbins European Hotel, n e cor Illinois and Georgia, tel 1371.
Stubbs Allen S, mach, h 35 Yandes.
Stubbs Charles, lab, h 70 Oscar.
Stubbs Edgar A, cutter, b 79 Hill av.
Stubbs George W, lawyer, 33-36 Thorpe blk, h 82 Randolph.
Stubbs Harvey, ins agt, h 524 Bellefontaine.
Stubbs India, teacher, b 35 Yandes.
Stubbs Joseph H, trav agt, h 474 Park av.
Stuck Christian, lab, h n s Raymond 1 e of Madison av.
Stuck David B, bartndr, h 189 W Maryland.
Stuck Edward, lab, h 551 Shelby.
Stuck George, lab, h 551 Shelby.

SHORTHAND REPORTING...... CONVENTIONS, SPEECHES, SERMONS. COPYING ON TYPEWRITER. S. H. EAST, State Agent, THE WILLIAMS TYPEWRITER 55 Thorpe Block, 87 East Market Street.

ELLIS & HELFENBERGER Manufacturers of Iron Vases, Setees and Hitch Posts. 162-170 South Senate Ave. Tel. 958.

THE HOGAN TRANSFER AND STORAGE COMP'Y
Household Goods and Pianos Moved—Packed—Stored...... Baggage and Package Express Machinery and Safes a Specialty Cor. Washington and Illinois Sts. TELEPHONE No. 675.

Hose, Belting, Packing, Clothing, Druggists' Sundries, Bicycle Tires, Cotton Hose, Etc. New York Belting & Packing Co., L't'd.
The Central Rubber & Supply Co. 79 S. ILLINOIS ST., INDIANAPOLIS, IND. PHONE 922.

The Provident Life and Trust Co.
OF PHILADELPHIA.
Small Death Rate. Small Expense Rate. Safe Investments.
Insurance in force $115,000,000
D. W. EDWARDS,
General Agent, 508 Indiana Trust Building.

Stuck Henry W, driver, b 40 N East.
Stuck James M, baker, h 45 Yeiser.
Stuck James W, lab, h 406 W Wilkins.
Stuck James W jr, filer, b 406 W Wilkins.
Stuck Jane E (wid Peter), b rear 313 S Olive.
Stuck Matthias A, boilermkr, h 40 N East.
Stuck Peter F, driver, h rear 313 S Olive.
Stuck Robert, baker, b 199 E Morris.
Stuck Robert G, brickmkr, h 199 E Morris.
Stuck Wm H, shoemkr, 122 S Olive, h same.
Stucker Jacob H, dairy, n e cor 25th and Central av, h same.
Stuckey Charles F, bartndr, h 36 Quincy.
Stuckey Christina (wid Charles H), h 114 Fulton.
Stuckey Frank, lab Insane Asylum.
Stuckey Oliver, lab, b 30 Thomas.
Stuckmeyer August, meats, 24 E Mkt House, h 400 Virginia av.
Stuckmeyer Caroline (wid John H), b 557 Madison av.
STUCKMEYER CHARLES H, City Clerk, Room 6 Basement Court House, Tel 542; Meat Market, 29 English av, h 67 English av.
Stuckmeyer Edward A (J H and E A Stuckmeyer), h 115 Prospect.
Stuckmeyer John H (J H and E A Stuckmeyer), h 557 Madison av.
STUCKMEYER J H & E A (John H and Edward A), Druggist and Pharmacists, Deutsche Apotheke, cor Madison av and Dunlop, Tel 1162, and cor Prospect and Laurel, Tel 1137.
Stuckmeyer Wm H, carp, h 162 S Linden.
Stuckwisch Frederick W, patternmkr, b 49 Arbor av (W I).
Stuckwisch Henry R, mach, b 49 Arbor av (W I).
Stuckwisch Rudolph M, carp, h 49 Arbor av (W I).
Stuckwisch Oliver H, mach hd, b 49 Arbor av (W I).
Stucky Edward W, druggist, 11 N Illinois, h 243 Central av.

Julius C. Walk & Son,
Jewelers
Indianapolis.
12 EAST WASHINGTON ST.

STUCKY THOMAS E, Physician, Office Hours 9-10 A M, 12-2 and 7-8 P M, 580 N Alabama, Tel 1721; h same.
Studer Victor, painter, 235 S Linden, h same.
Studt John H, carp, h n w cor Brookland and Progress avs.
Study Horace G, lawyer, b 1005 N Illinois.
Stueber Henry C, painter, h 5 Hamilton av.
Stuecker Frederick R, painter, 399 S East, h same.
Stufflebene John W, lab, h 101 Lawrence.
Stuffiebiem Eugene, painter, h 50 Hazel.
Stuhlfaut John H, switchman, h 129 N Liberty.
Stukey Rufus J, pres Ind H and Sav Assn, h 439 Park av.
Stull John E, fireman, b 124 English av.
Stultz Albert E, lab, h 76½ Oliver av (W I).
Stultz Hurkie A, cabtmkr, b 84 Columbia av.
Stultz John W, mach hd, h 84 Columbia av.
Stultz Sarah (wid John J), b 84 Columbia av.
Stultz Wiley, lab, b 46 Standard av (W I).
Stultz Wm F, carp, h 601 W Francis (N I).
Stumon James M, musician, h 297 Sheffield av (H).
Stumpf Grace, bkkpr Stumpf & Thiele, h s s Lena 3 w of Parker (I).
Stumpf Henry, engr, b 136 W 1st.
Stumpf Henry A (Stumpf & Thiele), h s s Lena 3 w of Parker (I).
Stumpf John W, tinner, b 213 S Alabama.
Stumpf John J, mason, h 21 John.
Stumpf Martin, butcher, h 55 Sanders.
Stumpf Wm, mngr Pabst Brewing Co, Indianapolis Branch 224-240 S Delaware, h 288 Fletcher av.
STUMPF & THIELE (Henry A Stumpf, Louis C Thiele), Furnace Mnfrs, 19-21 N Capitol av, Tel 1495.
Stumph Albert H, clk, b 54 Bradshaw.
Stumph Caroline (wid John B), h 6 Ruckle.
Stumph Christina C (wid John R), h 54 Bradshaw.
Stumph Conrad, cigarmkr, h 256 Highland av.
Stumph George, lab, h 10 Edgewood.
Stumph George W, cigarmkr, h 43 Peru av.
Stumph Henry, mason, h 576 E St Clair.
Stumph Henry B, lab, h 103 N Dorman.
Stumph Henry B, mach, h 915 S Meridian.
Stumph Henry C, cutter, b 10 Edgewood.
Stumph Herman W, clk, b 256 Highland av.
Stumph James H, bookbndr, h 29 Larch.
STUMPH JOHN B, h 35 N Pine.
Stumph John E, mach hd, b 256 Highland av.
Stumph John H, lab, h 46 S Reisner (W I).
Stumph John J, carp, h 99 Buchanan.
Stumph Valentine A, collr, h 54 Bradshaw.
Stumph Wm H, bookbndr, b 576 E St Clair.
Stumph Wm L, draughtsman, b 6 Ruckle.
Stunden Katherine A, teacher Public School No 12, b 367 N West.
Stunden Patrick, express, h 367 N West.
Stuppy Adam, molder, h 98 Tremont av (H).
Stuppy Michael, molder, h 109 Tremont av (H).
Sturgeon Ambrose, lab, b 1 Rathbone.
Sturgeon Charles M, mach hd, h 289½ Mass av.
Sturgeon David, lab, h 168 Clinton.

OTTO GAS ENGINES | BUILDERS' EXCHANGE S. W. Cor. Ohio and Penn. Telephone 535.

Sturgeon Elizabeth (wid Hume), h 1 Rathbone.
Sturgeon Elmer R, painter, h 812 E 9th.
Sturgeon Maggie, opr C U Tel Co, b 42 Athon.
Sturgeon Wm B, lab, b 1 Rathbone.
Sturgeon Wm I, lab, b 42 Athon.
Sturges Eugene M, agt, h rear 87 Cornell av.
Sturges Wm, painter, h 700 E 9th.
Sturgis James W, trav agt, h 247 N Delaware.
Sturm August, huckster, h 110 Nebraska.
Sturm Frederick C, agt, h 268 Excelsior av.
Sturm Helene G, teacher Industrial Training School, b 87 Fletcher av.
Sturm John, driver, h 761 Madison av.
Sturm Richard, finisher, b 1000 S Meridian.
Sturm Roy C, paperhngr, h 154 Excelsior av.
Sturtevant Arthur H, h 247 N Meridian.
Sturzenegger John, h cor School and Wolf pike (B).
Sturzenegger John, packer N Y Store, b 11 Minkner.
Stute Mary A (wid John B), h 359 E Market.
Stuter Halcy, brakeman, h 371 E Georgia.
Stutphin Isaac V, pres Beveridge Paper Co, res Cincinnati, O.
Stutsman Elmer E, agt, b 72 W Ohio.
Stutsman David T, blksmith, h 124 Newman.
Stutsman Frank W, mngr, r 194 E Washington.
Stutsman Harry, b 124 Newman.
Stutsman Jacob H, grocer, 449 Central av, h same.
Stutsman James M, letter carrier P O, h 17 Cooper.
Stutsman Joseph A, agt, h 1698 N Illinois.
Stutsman Lewis W, clk, b 449 Central av.
Stutzel Minnie, h 317½ E Washington.
Stutzenberger John W, trav agt, h 1114 N Delaware.
Stuvel Benjamin, lab, h 47 Evison.
Stwain Wm, janitor, b 140 N Gillard av.
Styer Charles, h 365 Park av.
Styer David H, clk, b 4 S Waverly (B).
Styer Martin R, collr, b 315 E Merrill.
Styer Samuel (Styer & Leatherman), h n s Wolf pike 1 w of School (B).
Styer & Leatherman (Samuel Styer, Aaron Leatherman), dairy, n s Wolf pike 1 w of School (B).
Styers Charles F, ironwkr, h 40 Bellefontaine.
Styers George, condr, b 44 Poplar (B).
Suart John B, grocer, 509 E 7th, h same.
Suart Wm S, clk, b 509 E 7th.
Sublette James M, supt, h 107 Blake.
Suby John, student, b 43 Beaty.
Suckfiel Emma (wid Ferdinand), h 555 W Washington.
Sudbrock Anna (wid Henry), h 314 N Noble.
Sudbrock Arthur F, clk, b 314 N Noble.
Sudbrock Frank H, treas The Indiana Dry Goods Co, b 645 E Washington.
Sudbrock Herman, lab, b 277 Keystone av.
Sudbrock Walter, clk, b 314 N Noble.
Sudbury Alonzo, tel opr, b 188 Pleasant.
Suding Benjamin, huckster, h 1030 Madison av.
Sudkamp Henry, gardener, h 1051 Madison av.
Sudler James B, finisher, h 236 W Michigan.
Sudler Nancy B (wid Wallace L), b 236 W Michigan.
Sudmann Henry L, express, h 54 Yeiser.

Henry H. Fay,
40½ E. WASHINGTON ST.,
FIRE INSURANCE, REAL ESTATE,
LOANS AND RENTAL AGENT.

Sudmeyer Charles H, wagonmkr, 862 S Meridian, h S Meridian 1½ miles s of Belt R R.
Sudmeyer Wm F, driver, h 3 Geneva.
Sudres John F, porter, b 385 N Capitol av.
Suess Charles A, tailor, h 189 E Washington.
Suess Edward M, mach, b 350 N Noble.
Suess Frederick, mach, b 22 Stevens.
Suess Gustav C J, barber, b 312 N Noble.
Suess Joseph, confr, 606 Virginia av, h same.
Suess Joseph, lab, h 251 W Morris.
Suess Joseph, condr, h 312 N Noble.
Suess Louis C, printer, b 32 Lynn av (W I).
Suess Martin, patternmkr, h 350 N Noble.
Suess Max B, tailor, 189½ E Washington, h 22 Stevens.
Suesz Charles M, clk, h 331 N East.
Suesz Frederick W, cigarmkr, h 95 Oriole.
Suesz Mary (wid Gottfried), h s e cor Rural and Lily.
Suesz Otto J T, uphlr, b s e cor Rural and Lily.
Suesz Wm G, butcher, b s e cor Rural and Lily.
Suffrins Charles A, printer, 42 W Market, h 36 Greer.
Suffrins Nancy M (wid David), h 1 Dougherty.
Sugden John S, cabtmkr, h 356½ Clifford av.
Suggs Wm, lab, h 36 Lincoln la.
Sughrow Michael, lab, h 130 Meek.
Sughrue, see also Shugrue.
Sughrue Lawrence, lab, h 29 Holly av (W I).
Suher Herman W, bricklyr, h 276 Highland av.
Suhr August C, lab, b 42 Maple.
Suhr Charles A, grinder, h 42 Maple.
Suhr Charles G, blksmith, b 118 Church.
Suhr Franklin P, sawyer, b 352 S Meridian.
Suhr Frederick, contr, 536 S Illinois, h same.
Suhr Frederick, drayman, h 118 Church.
Suhr Frederick jr, painter, b 118 Church.
Suhr Frederick W, car rep, h 444 S Missouri.
Suhr Henry W, driver, b 214 Minnesota.

JAS. N. MAYHEW,
MANUFACTURING
OPTICIAN
LENSES AND FRAMES A SPECIALTY.
No. 13 North Meridian St., Indianapolis.

SBURY & STANLEY • 177 Ca Set, Indianapolis, Ind. • Contractors and Builders
Office, Store and Bank Fixtures a Specialty. Repairing of all kinds done on short notice.
TELEPHONE 999.

LUMBER | Sash, Door and Planing . Mill Work . | Balke & Krauss Co. Cor. Market and Missouri Streets.

FRIEDGEN'S TAN SHOES are the Newest Shades
Prices the Lowest. 19 North Pennsylvania St.

SAMUEL LAING General Job Work in Sheet Metal of all Kinds
72 AND 74 E. COURT STREET.

M. B. WILSON, Pres. W. F. CHURCHMAN, Cash.
THE CAPITAL NATIONAL BANK,
INDIANAPOLIS, IND.
Make collections on all points in the States of Indiana and Illinois on the most favorable rates.
Capital, - - $300,000
Surplus and Earnings, 50,000
No. 28 S. Meridian St., Cor. Pearl.

Suhr John, baker Parrott & Taggart, b 103 English av.
Suhr Harry M (wid Henry), h 23 Gresham.
Suhr Wm, car insp, h 214 Minnesota.
Suhre Albert J, carp, b 46 Standard av (W I).
Suhre Edward F, student, b 46 Yandes.
Suhre Elizabeth M (wid August E), h 8 Detroit.
Suhre Frank F, carp, b 46 Yandes.
Suhre Henry C, contr, 46 Yandes, h same.
Suhre Henry W, driver, h 125 Kansas.
Suhre Lizzie M, b 143 Hadley av (W I).
Suits Bert C, gearmkr, b 219 S Capitol av.
Suits Henry M, woodwkr, h 219 S Capitol av.
Suitt James B, b s e cor Central and Washington avs (I).
Sulgrove Adah, teacher Public School No 28, b 457½ Virginia av.
Sulgrove Edwin R, etcher The Indpls News, h 48 Beaty.
Sulgrove Eli L, harnessmkr, h 41 Birch av (W I).
Sulgrove Frank, uphlr, b 41 Birch av (W I).
Sulgrove George W, letter carrier P O, h 176 Blackford.
Sulgrove Henry J, harnessmkr, h 457½ Virginia av.
Sulgrove James W, clk The Gordon-Kurtz Co, h 180 E St Clair.
Sulgrove Joseph B, mach opr, b 71 E St Clair.
Sulgrove Leslie M, lab, b 136 Church.
Sulgrove Martha J (wid Jerome), b 396 W Pratt.
Sulgrove Milton M, harnessmkr, h 60½ S Illinois.
Sulgrove Norman R, clk H L Schaefer, b 176 Blackford.
Sullivan, see also O'Sullivan.
Sullivan Achilles V, lab, h 39 Sheffield (W I).
Sullivan Addison L, cabtmkr, h 153 Shelby.
Sullivan Ann (wid Timothy), h 84 Russell av.
Sullivan Bertha M, dressmkr, h 98 W 1st.
Sullivan Beverly W, dentist, 190 Cherry, h same.

MONEY
Loaned on Short Notice at Lowest Rates.
TUTTLE & SEGUIN,
Tel. 1168. 28 E. Market St.

Sullivan Bridget (wid James), h 47 Roe.
Sullivan Bridget (wid John), h 7 Bates.
Sullivan Bridget (wid Timothy), h 335 N Pine.
Sullivan Bridget, saloon, 301 Bates, h same.
Sullivan Bryan, lab, b 271 W Merrill.
Sullivan Budd, boilermkr, b 112 Meek.
Sullivan Catherine, h 142 Meek.
Sullivan Catherine R, stenog Indpls Brewing Co, b 581 Shelby.
Sullivan Charity (wid John B), b 86 Highland pl.
Sullivan Charles, mason, b California House.
Sullivan Charles A, clk, h 37 Temple av.
Sullivan Charles E, clk H P Wasson & Co, b 178 Huron.

SULLIVAN CHARLES H (Sullivan & Mahan), h 220 Keystone av.

Sullivan Charles S, tel opr, b 31 Williams.
Sullivan Clarence G, clk, h 335 S Alabama.
Sullivan Cornelius, lab, b 180 N Dorman.
Sullivan Cornelius W, plastr, b 84 Russell av.
Sullivan Daniel, b 124 Meek.
Sullivan Daniel, h 55 S Pine.
Sullivan Daniel, engr, h 166 Walcott.
Sullivan Daniel, lab, b 153 Bates.
Sullivan Daniel, lab, b 584 E St Clair.
Sullivan Daniel, lab, h 112 Meek.
Sullivan Daniel, lab, h 100 Warren av (W I).
Sullivan Daniel jr, brakeman, b 100 Warren av (W I).
Sullivan Daniel B (Kenney & Sullivan), h 241 W Maryland.
Sullivan Daniel H, trav agt, h 227 Christian av.
Sullivan Daniel J, condr, h 12 Peck.
Sullivan Daniel J, lab, b 441 S West.
Sullivan David J, lab, b 231 W Merrill.
Sullivan Deborah, h 175 N Capitol av.
Sullivan Dennis, lab, h 271 W Merrill.
Sullivan Dennis, saloon, 114 Agnes, h same.
Sullivan Dennis J, clk, r 219 N Capitol av.
Sullivan Dennis M, h 217 Hoyt av.
Sullivan Edward J, lab, b 335 N Pine.
Sullivan Ella A, clk, b 84 Russell av.
Sullivan Ellen (wid Daniel), h 99 Madison av.
Sullivan Eugene, lab, h 83 Meikel.
Sullivan Eugene, lab, h 70 S West.
Sullivan Francis J H, stenog Natl Malleable Castings Co, h 104 N Belmont av (H).
Sullivan Frank, plastr, b 118 W Vermont.
Sullivan Frank H, bartndr, b 251 W Morris.
Sullivan Frank L, mngr traffic dept Indpls Brewing Co, b 18 Fletcher av.
Sullivan Frank W, trav agt, b 821 College av.
Sullivan Frederick R, contr agt West Shore Fast Freight Line, h 68 W 1st.
Sullivan George L, ins agt, h 413 Excelsior av.
Sullivan George R (Tanner & Sullivan), h 418 N Meridian.
Sullivan George T, r 24 School.
Sullivan George W, lab, h 14 Mill.
Sullivan Harry E, mach, b 190 Cherry.
Sullivan Henry H, coachman, h 158 Spring.
Sullivan Henry M, lab, h 72 Sheffield av (H).
Sullivan Isaac R, mach, h 284 Sheffield av (H).
Sullivan James, bartndr, b 114 Agnes.
Sullivan James, ironwkr, r 164 W Maryland.
Sullivan James, lab, b 162 English av.
Sullivan James, lab, b rear 162 Meek.

PAPER BOXES, MANUFACTURED BY SULLIVAN & MAHAN 41 W. PEARL STREET.

DIAMOND WALL PLASTER { Telephone 1410 BUILDERS' EXCHANGE.

Fine Laundry Work our Specialty. Collars and Cuffs our Hobby. THE HOME LAUNDRY 19 S. Ill St. Telephone 1769.

Sullivan James, lab, h 368 S Capitol av.
Sullivan James, lab, b 90 Spann av.
Sullivan James, tmstr, h 227 Hamilton av.
Sullivan James jr, lab, b 441 S West.
Sullivan James F, fireman, b 29 Davis.
Sullivan James L, lab, h 441 S West.
Sullivan James S, janitor, h 177 Muskingum al.
Sullivan Jeremiah, gasfitter, b 359 S Illinois.
Sullivan Jeremiah, lab, h 162 English av.
Sullivan Jesse, h 33 Iowa.
Sullivan Johanna (wid Daniel), h 81 Quincy
Sullivan John, janitor, b 348 S West.
Sullivan John, lab, b 138 Columbia al.
Sullivan John, lab, h 3 Douglass.
Sullivan John, lab, b 162 English av.
Sullivan John, lab, h 285 S West.
Sullivan John, lab, b 441 S West.
Sullivan John, lab, b 52 Tremont av (H).
Sullivan John, mail clk, b 190½ S Illinois.
Sullivan John, steamfitter, r 80 N New Jersey.
Sullivan John jr, lab, b 285 S West.
Sullivan John C, lab, b w s Lincoln av 1 s of Jackson (M J).
Sullivan John D, lab, h 301 Bates.
Sullivan John D, lab, h 442 S West.
Sullivan John E, cashr, r 194½ E Washington.
Sullivan John H, lab, b 339 S Alabama.
Sullivan John J, car rep, h 40 Pierce.
Sullivan John J, condr, h 179 Lexington av.
Sullivan John J, lab, b 289 Bates.
Sullivan John J, molder, b 84 Russell av.
Sullivan John L, city fireman, b 7 Bates.
Sullivan John L, lab, h 67 Church.
Sullivan John L, lab, b 315 S Missouri.
Sullivan John M, clk, b 77 River av (W I).
Sullivan John M, trav agt, h 459 S Delaware.
Sullivan John O, lab, h 315 S Missouri.
Sullivan John R, switchman, h 1084 W New York.
Sullivan Jordan, lab, h 667½ Madison av.
Sullivan Joseph P, attendant Insane Hospital.
Sullivan Julia (wid Michael), b 43 Benton.
Sullivan Kate, laundress Deaf and Dumb Inst.
Sullivan Lemuel M, feed, 261 W Washington, h 636 Broadway.
Sullivan Leslie T, cutter, h 34 Stevens.
Sullivan Louisa L, dressmkr, h 98 W 1st.
Sullivan Luther, lab, b 31 Williams.
Sullivan Margaret, r 124 E Ohio.
Sullivan Martin, helper, b 81 Quincy.
Sullivan Mary (wid Eugene), b 258 Bates.
Sullivan Mary (wid James), h 108½ Mass av.
Sullivan Mary (wid John), h 52 Tremont av (H).
Sullivan Mary (wid Martin), h 509 E Georgia.
Sullivan Mary (wid Patrick), b 18 Meikel.
Sullivan Mary, laundress, b 290 S Delaware.
Sullivan Mary E (wid Daniel), b 81 Quincy.
Sullivan Mary J, cook N Y Store, b 177 Muskingum al.
Sullivan Maurice, boilermkr, b 112 Meek.
Sullivan Maurice, mach, h 77 River av (W I).
Sullivan May, stenog Pierce Norton, b 229 E Ohio.
Sullivan Michael, lab, h 89 Deloss.
Sullivan Michael, lab, b 162 English av.
Sullivan Michael, lab, b 485 S West.
Sullivan Michael, lab, b 52 Tremont av (H).
Sullivan Michael, lab, r 175 W Ohio.
Sullivan Michael, tmstr, b 59 N Dorman.

FRANK NESSLER. WILL H. ROST.
FRANK NESSLER & CO.
Tailors
56 EAST MARKET ST. (Lemcke Building),
INDIANAPOLIS, IND.

Sullivan Michael B, mach, b 203 Meek.
Sullivan Michael F, lab, b 285 S West.
Sullivan Michael R, lab, b 118 Deloss.
Sullivan Michael T, lab, b 22 Concordia.
Sullivan Nora M, clk, b 176 Harrison.
Sullivan Patrick, bartndr, b 450 Mass av.
Sullivan Patrick, clk, b 285 S West.
Sullivan Patrick, lab, h 73 Dougherty.
Sullivan Patrick, lab, b 34 Oriental.
Sullivan Patrick, lab, b 188 W Merrill.
Sullivan Patrick, stoker, h 35 Catharine.
Sullivan Patrick J, clk, b 552 S West.
Sullivan Patrick J, clk, h 283 W Merrill.
Sullivan Patrick W, lab, h 348 S West.
Sullivan Peter, h 326 N California.
Sullivan Peter, boilermkr, h 48 Miley av.
Sullivan Peter, paperhngr, h 378½ W New York.
Sullivan Reazin L, ins agt, r 8½ Bellefontaine.
Sullivan Rebecca (wid Matthew), b 417 S Missouri.
Sullivan Reginald H, student, b 253 N Capitol av.
Sullivan Richard A, observer U S Weather Bureau, b 76 E New York.
Sullivan Richard H, blksmith, s e cor Glen Drive and Shade (B), h 17 S Stuart (B).
Sullivan Stella, stenog, b 636 Broadway.
Sullivan Stephen J, lab, b 301 Bates.
Sullivan Thomas, lab, b 58 Church.
Sullivan Thomas, lab, h 22 Concordia.
Sullivan Thomas H, cashr, b 77 River av (W I).
Sullivan Thomas L, lawyer, 77-78 Lombard bldg, h 253 N Capitol av.
Sullivan Timothy, hostler, h 203 Meek.
Sullivan Timothy, lab, b 298 S Capitol av.
Sullivan Timothy, lab, b 52 Tremont av (H).
Sullivan Timothy F, tel opr, b 112 Meek.
Sullivan Timothy J, policeman Insane Hospital.
Sullivan Wm, coachman, h 223 W 6th.
Sullivan Wm, lab, b 417 S Missouri.
SULLIVAN WM A, Commercial Agt C C C & St L Ry, 1 E Washington, h 18 Fletcher av.
Sullivan Wm B, barber, h 94 N East.

Haueisen & Hartmann
163-169 E. Washington St.
FURNITURE,
Carpets,
Household Goods,
Tin, Granite and China Wares, Oil Cloth and Shades

THE WM. H. BLOCK CO. 7 AND 9 EAST WASHINGTON STREET. DRY GOODS, MEN'S FURNISHINGS.

Fidelity and Deposit Co. of Maryland. BONDS SIGNED.—LOCAL BOARD John B. Elam, Albert Sahm, Smiley N. Chambers, John M. Spann.
GEORGE W. PANGBORN, General Agent, 704-706 Lemcke Building. Telephone 140.

74 EAST MARKET STREET Telephone 8.
Insure Your Property With FRANK K. SAWYER

JOSEPH GARDNER,
Hot Air Furnaces
With Combination Gas Burners for Burning Gas and Other Fuel at the Same Time
37, 39 & 41 KENTUCKY AVE. Telephone 322

Sullivan Wm B, engr, h 127 Columbia av.
Sullivan Wm J, brakeman, h 31 Williams.
Sullivan Wm L, paperhngr, h 378½ W New York.
Sullivan Wm O, lab, h 214 N Senate av.
Sullivan Wm R, cabtmkr, h 241 Hamilton av.
SULLIVAN & MAHAN (Charles H Sullivan, Harry B Mahan), Mnfrs of all Kinds of Paper Boxes, 41 W Pearl, Tel 719. (See left bottom lines.)
Suman Charles W, trav agt Schnull & Co, r 320 N Illinois.
Sumey Edward, porter, h 280 Spring.
Sümler Wm, produce, E Mkt House, h 455 W Pratt.
Summers, see also Sommer.
Summers Gilbert G, foreman, h 387 N California.
Summers Harry E, plumber, b 387 N California.
Summers Jesse, sec Am Building and Loan Assn, h n s Oak av 3 e of Central av (I).
Summers Maria M (wid Daniel R), b 315 Ash.
Summers Mary J (wid Nathan), h s e cor Zwingley and Bethel av.
Summers Wm E, clk, h 670 E Market.
Summit John M, clk, h 227 N West.
Summitt Sarah A (wid John), h 146 S Judge Harding (W I).
Summons Harrison, lab, h 12 Parker.
Sumner Dempsey, lab, h 338 Hillside av.
Sumner Osbert R, bkkpr Schnull & Co, b 948 N Penn.
Sumner Wm F, lab, h 329 Hillside av.
Sumner Wm J, salesman Schnull & Co, h 157 Cornell av.
Sumpter Charles, lab, h 329 Sharpe av (W).
Sun Building, Loan and Investment Co, Charles F Coffin pres and treas, John Green sec, 12½ N Delaware.
SUN PUBLISHING CO THE, Fred L Purdy Pres, Andrew C Keifer Vice-Pres and Treas, Oel L Thayer Sec, Publishers The Sun, 79 E Ohio, Tel 880.

J. S. FARRELL & CO.
Plumbing
Natural and Artificial Gas Fitting.
84 N. ILLINOIS STREET.
TELEPHONE 382.

SUN THE, Sun Publishing Co Proprs, 79 E Ohio, Tels Office 880, Editorial Rooms 620.
SUNDAY JOURNAL THE, The Indianapolis Journal Newspaper Co Publishers, n e cor Monument Pl and Market, Tel 238; Editorial Rooms 86.
Sunderland Bert F, baker Parrott & Taggart, b 22 S Dorman.
Sunderland Charles E, carp, h 22 S Dorman.
Sunderland Elizabeth C, h 506½ E Washington.
Sunderland George E, helper, h 34 Morris (B).
Sunderland Peter J, carp, 274 Spring, h same.
Sundermann Gottlieb H, lab, h 791 Mass av.
Superintendent of Public Instruction, 27 State House.
Superior Court Room 1, Court House.
Superior Court Room 2, Court House.
Superior Court Room 3, Court House.
SUPERIOR DRILL CO THE, Wm T Miller Genl Agt, 28 Kentucky av.
Supper Charles F, painter, h 57 Downey.
Supper Christian A, lab, h 28 Hendricks.
Supreme Court of Indiana, 67 State House.
Surber Charles, clk, r 100 N Senate av.
Surber Claud C, printer, b 119 N Illinois.
Surber David J, tmstr, h 24 Reynolds av (H).
Surber Ernest, lab, b 24 Reynolds av (H).
Surber George C, clk, b 27 Prospect.
Surber Henry A, adv agt, 40½ S Illinois, r 100 W Ohio.
Surber James M, lab, h 27 Prospect.
Surber Mary E (wid Clay), h 119 N Illinois.
Surber Thomas, lab, h 104 W Vermont.
Surbey Edith D, teacher Public School No 28, b 335 E South.
Surbey Jacob S (Surbey & Amt), h 335 E South.
Surbey & Amt (Jacob S Surbey, George Amt), grocers, 199 Virginia av.
Surdam Oliver, well driver, b 122 Blackford.
Surdam Orlando, lab, b 25 Maria.
Surface Charles F, adv agt, 401 Indiana Trust bldg, h 749 N New Jersey.
Surface Gilbert G, carp, b 157 Elm.
Surface Mattie, waiter, r 106½ N Meridian.
Surface Melville R, clk, h 157 Elm.
SURGICAL INSTITUTE WILSON, Charles A Wilson, M D (Faculty Prize, Medical College of Ohio, 1879), Propr, 81 W Ohio.
Surveyor of Customs' Office, George R Tanner, surveyor, 3d floor P O bldg.
Sury Frank, lab, h 255½ E Washington.
Sury Lavina (wid Harvey), b 135 S Summit.
Sussman Isaac, bartndr, b 51 Russell av.
Sussman Louis, saloon, 205 W Ohio, h same.
Sussman Max, clk, b 251 N Liberty.
Sussman Wolf, saloon, 304 S Ilinois, h same.
Sutcliffe John A, phys, 6 Baldwin blk, r 297 N Delaware.
Suter Henry, carp, b Germania House.
Suter James A, clk H P Wasson & Co, h 1192 N Meridian.
Suter Norris C, b 1192 N Meridian.
Suter Wm, filer, h 1256 Morris (W I).
Sutfin Wm, miller, b 175½ E Washington.
Sutherland Edward, b 59 E McCarty.
Sutherland Emma D (wid Wm H), h 271 Bright.

IF CONTINUED to the end of its dividend period, policies of the UNITED STATES LIFE INSURANCE CO., will equal or excel any investment policy ever offered to the public. E. B. SWIFT, Manager, 25 E. Market St.

Wm. Kotteman 89 & 91 E. Washington St. TELEPHONE 1742 Furniture

Sutherland George B, tmstr, h 27 Barth av.
Sutherland James H, medicine mnfr, b 820 College av.
Sutherland James W, tailor, b 850 N New Jersey.
Sutherland Levi (The Burns Chemical Co), h 59 E McCarty.
Sutherland Lillington D, driver, h 240 Bright.
Sutherland Matilda (wid James W), b 240 Bright.
Sutherland Perry, carp, h 225 Sheldon.
Sutherland Ray L, trav agt, b 462 W New York.
Sutherland Sylvanus, driver, b 59 E McCarty.
Suthers Thomas, driver, b 175 W Ohio.
Sutphen George, painter, h 87 John.
Sutphen James, painter, h 326 Mass av.
Sutphen Thomas, boilermkr, h 85 Spring.
Sutphen Thomas J, lab, b 33 Dougherty.
Sutter Emma (wid Frederick), h 178 S Senate av.
Sutter George W, ice, h 286 W 6th.
Sutter Jacob C, lab, h 164 S Linden.
Sutterfield John T, grinder, h 83 Woodburn av (W I).
Sutton Charles A, carp, h 424 E St Clair.
Sutton Charles W, sec Arthur Jordan Co, h 76 E Vermont.
Sutton George E, cook, b 69 N Alabama.
Sutton Herbert L, bkkpr, b 82 E Vermont.
Sutton John A, clk, b 44 Hall pl.
Sutton Joseph M, h 82 E Vermont.
Sutton Morton, presser, h 416 W Francis (N I).
Sutton Ross P, butcher, h 16 Columbia blk.
Sutton Wm D, foreman, h 533 W Eugene (N I).
Svendsen Christina (wid Rasmus), h 998 S Meridian.
Svendsen Hans, sawmkr, b 998 S Meridian.
Svendsen Wm C, mach, h 1 s of Belt e s of Bluff rd.
Swafford Abraham L, blksmith, h 52 Torbet.
Swails Charles A, brakeman, h 189 Spann av.
Swails Francis M W, painter, b 171 Spann av.
Swails James W (Francis & Swails), h e s Sheffield 1 n of Morris (W I).
Swaim Claude M, painter, b 201 E Washington.
Swaim Frank A, trav agt, h 753 Broadway.
Swaim Harry O, clk Indpls Fire Inspection Bureau, b 11 English av.
Swaim James B, fireman, b 11 English av.
Swaim John S, brakeman, b 11 English av.
Swaim Philadelphia (wid Traugott), h 11 English av.
Swain Albertus, furniture, b 869 N Penn.
Swain Carl B, trav agt, b 449 College av.
Swain Carrol E, bkkpr Chandler & Taylor Co, h 41 Fletcher av.

SWAIN DAVID F, Genl Agt Northwestern Mutual Life Insurance Co of Milwaukee, Wis, Frank M Millikan Special Loan Agt, 88 N Penn, Tel 1245; h 73 E Michigan.

Swain Fremont, phys, 334 N New Jersey, b same.
Swain George B (Central Advertising Co), b Sherman House.
Swain George G, bkkpr W H Messenger, h 1129 N Meridian.

We Buy Municipal ~ Bonds ~
THOS. C. DAY & CO,
Rooms 325 to 330 Lemcke Bldg.

Swain George H, stereotyper The Indpls News, h 286 N Alabama.
Swain Joseph H, plumber, b 224 W New York.
Swain Mary J (wid James P), h 312 W Merrill.
Swain Rachel, phys, 334 N New Jersey, h same.
Swain Rufus, clk Chandler & Taylor Co, h 334 S State av.
Swain Thomas A (Bliss, Swain & Co), h 992 N Penn.
Swain Thomas P, trav agt Hendrickson, Lefler & Co, h 447 College av.
Swain Victor A, b 224 W New York.
Swain Wm M, solr, h 45 Andrews.
Swain Zell C, student, b 28½ Indiana av.
Swan Anna H, h 15 Bismarck av (H).
Swan Benjamin C, grocer, 551 W 22d (N I), h same.
Swan Cassius, r 226 N Illinois.
Swan Edward, molder, b 349 S Alabama.
Swan Edwin J, electrician, h 510 Ash.
Swan Frank, lab, r 84 S Illinois.
Swan Frederick A, bkkpr, b 510 Ash.
Swan George B, clk, b 551 W 22d (N I).
Swan George H, carp, h 22 N Judge Harding (W I).
Swan James A, treas Pettis Dry Goods Co, res New York city.
Swan James M, bkkpr Sentinel Printing Co, h 552 W Eugene (N I).
Swan John H, trav agt, h 997 N Capitol av.
Swan John R, salesman Carlin & Lennox, r 78 W Maryland.

SWAN JOSEPH C, Druggist, 547 W 22d (N I), h same, Tel 1946.

Swan Orin H, clk, b 551 W 22d (N I).
Swan Wm, lab, r 137½ Virginia av.
Swan Wm A, foreman, b 31½ Virginia av.
Swan Wm E, brakeman, b 90 Belmont av (H).
Swanburg Lynn, lab, h 671 Shelby.
Swanigan Sampson, lab, h 116 Ash.
Swank Alvin G, printer, b 1079 N Capitol av.
Swann Ann E (wid Morris), b 73 W 20th.
Swann Wm F, engr, h 142 Davidson.

EAT
QUAKER BREAD
ASK YOUR GROCER FOR IT.
THE HITZ BAKING CO.

SHOW CASES || WILLIAM WIEGEL || 6 West Louisiana Street Opp. Union Station.

CARPETS CLEANED LIKE NEW. TELEPHONE 818
CAPITAL STEAM CARPET CLEANING WORKS

BENJ. BOOTH PRACTICAL EXPERT ACCOUNTANT. Thirty years' experience. First-class credentials. Room 18, 82½ E. Washington St. Indianapolis, Ind.

The Old Reliable Sherman European Restaurant || 18 and 20 S. Meridian St. Established 1880.

ESTABLISHED 1876. TELEPHONE 168.
CHESTER BRADFORD,
SOLICITOR OF PATENTS,
AND COUNSEL IN PATENT CAUSES.
(See adv. page 6.)
Office:—Rooms 14 and 16 Hubbard Block, S.W. Cor. Washington and Meridian Streets, INDIANAPOLIS, INDIANA.

Swanson Alfred, car rep, b 92 S Shade (B).
Swanson Gustav, car rep, h 92 S Shade (B).
Swanson John, bricklyr, b 272 W Maryland.
Swanson Otto, coachman 548 N Meridian.
Swanston Wm, master mechanic P C C & St L Ry, h 69 Middle Drive (W P).
Swartling Lorenz, janitor Public School No 31, h 95 Lincoln la.
Swarts Amelia, b 129 S Olive.
Swartz, see also Schwartz.
Swartz Frank, driver, h 794 N Illinois.
Swartz Myer, dressmkr, h 546 N Illinois.
Swauger Frank P, plastr, b 808 E Washington.
Swauger Henry T, switchman, h 808 E Washington.
Swauger James L, polisher, b 808 E Washington.
Swauger John E, polisher, h 808 E Washington.
Sweed John A, watchman, b 72 Fulton.
Sweeney Alonzo B, baker, h 214 N Senate av.
Sweeney Ambrose, b 268 S Meridian.
Sweeney Andrew A, sawmkr, b 426 S Capitol av.
Sweeney Andrew M, pres The State Life Ins Co, h 854 N Illinois.
Sweeney Anna M, usher Insane Hospital.
Sweeney Benjamin W, lab, h 249 E Louisiana.
Sweney Charles H, mailing clk The Indpls Journal, b 80 Elizabeth.
Sweeney Daniel A, clk, h 390 S Capitol av.
Sweeney Daniel E, lab, h 93 Quincy.
Sweeney Daniel J, lab, h 443 S West.
Sweeney Dennis, janitor, h 158 Huron.
Sweeney Dennis, lab, b 9 Concordia.
Sweeney Eliza M (wid John W), h 156 Yandes.
Sweeney Ellen (wid Frank), h 302 Coburn.
Sweeney Hugh, h 268 S Meridian.
Sweeney James G, janitor, h 283 Chapel.
Sweeney Jeremiah, h 217 S West.
Sweeney John, lab, h 9 Concordia.
Sweeney John, molder, b 31 Maple.
Sweeney John, mounter, b 217 S West.
Sweeney John H, engr The Indpls Journal, h 80 Elizabeth.

CORRUGATED IRON CEILINGS AND SIDING.
ALL KINDS OF REPAIRING.
O. B. ENSEY,
TELEPHONE 1562.
COR. 6TH AND ILLINOIS STREETS.

Sweeney Katharine, attendant Insane Hospital.
Sweeney Martha A (wid Ashley), h 207 W Ohio.
Sweeney Mary, housekpr 240 N Capitol av.
Sweeney Michael, b 854 N Illinois.
Sweeney Michael, trimmer, b 230 W Maryland.
Sweeney Peter, lab, b 107 W South.
Sweeney Robert L, fireman, r 172 N East.
Sweeney Samuel, barber, h 249 E Louisiana.
Sweeney Sarah, h 281 Indiana av.
Sweeney Sarah (wid Patrick), b 60½ S Illinois.
Sweeney Sarah, boarding 249 E Louisiana.
Sweeney Thomas, barber, h 249 E Louisiana.
Sweeney Thomas, lab, b 217 S West.
Sweeney Thomas H, molder, h 102 Harrison.
Sweeney Thomas P, watchman, h 92 Minerva.
Sweeney Wiley R, lab, h 672 Wells (N I).
Sweeney Wm, agt, h 54 McGinnis.
Sweeney Wm, lab, b 217 S West.
Sweeney Wm G, lab, r 164 W Maryland.
Sweeney W Allison, editor The World, h 778 S East.
Sweenie Arthur W, trav agt, b 62 W 12th.
Sweenie George H, clk, b 62 W 12th.
Sweenie Hattie, dressmkr, 232-233 Lemcke bldg, h 62 W 12th.
Sweenie Ida B, music teacher, b 62 W 12th.
Sweenie James, yardmaster, h 157 Spann av.
Sweenie John, bkkpr, h 62 W 12th.
Sweesy John, r 199 S Illinois.
Sweet Cuba H, bkkpr, b 477 N New Jersey.
Sweet Edward W, produce, h w s Gladstone av 1 n of Washington.
Sweet Elizabeth, stenog, b 477 N New Jersey.
Sweet Frances D, teacher Public School No 26, b 863 Bellefontaine.
Sweet Frank E, clk, b 416 N Penn.
Sweet George, mach, h 3 Omer.
Sweet George H, condr, h rear 277 Blake.
Sweet Lucy E, b 863 Bellefontaine.
Sweet Marcy E (wid David G), h 863 Bellefontaine.
Sweet Mary F (wid George W), dressmkr, 40 N East, b same.
Sweet Matilda (wid John), h 477 N New Jersey.
Sweet Oliver B, clk, h 876 Bellefontaine.
Sweet Samuel B, genl freight agt L E & W R R, h 416 N Penn.
Sweet Wm O, plastr, r 8 Columbia blk.
Sweetland Henry, transfer, 34 S Penn, h 234 W 5th.
Sweetman Wm A, tuner D H Baldwin & Co, h e s Elm av 3 n of Washington av (I).
Sweets Elizabeth A, clk U S Pension Agency, b 155 N Illinois.
Sweetser George M, collr, h 862 N Alabama.
Sweigert John W, marble cutter, h e s Western av 2 n of 22d.
Sweir Wm, cabtmkr, h 13 Langley av.
Swenson Kahrn (wid Peter), b 300 Cornell av.
Swhear Herman W, lab, h 276 Highland av.
Swick Adaline, h 81 E Michigan.
Swick Clyde, clk, b 81 E Michigan.
Swick Harry, driver, b 81 E Michigan.
Swift Adam, lab, r 191 W Market.
Swift Charles H, lab, b 439 E Georgia.
Swift Edwin S, opr W U Tel Co, h 886 Bellefontaine.

TUTEWILER UNDERTAKER, No. 72 WEST MARKET STREET. TELEPHONE 216.

THE PROVIDENT LIFE AND TRUST CO. OF PHILADELPHIA. **Endowment Insurance** presents the double attraction of relieving manhood and middle age from anxiety and old age from want.
For particulars apply to D. W. EDWARDS, General Agent, 508 Indiana Trust Building.

THEODORE F. SMITHER Competent and Responsible ROOFER Telephone 861. 95 W. St.

SWIFT ELIAS B, Mngr United States Life Insurance Co, 25 E Market, Tel 1797; h 1551 Northwestern av. (See left bottom lines.)
Swift Fremont E, electrician, h 356 S Delaware.
Swift Harry E, varnisher, h 72 S Pine.
Swift Henry, lab, h 322 S East.
Swift Hugh R, lab, h 138 Patterson.
Swift Huldah (wid Robert), h 439 E Georgia.
Swift Joseph W, lab, h 472 W Francis (N I).
Swift Lucius B, lawyer, 2 Hubbard blk, h 26 Irwin.
Swift Newton E, teacher Indpls College of Music, r 40 W St Joseph.
SWIFT & CO, Charles H Simons Mngr, Wholesale Meats and Provisions, 123-127 Kentucky av, Tel 29.
Swigert Earl, page Public Library, b 561 N Illinois.
Swigert Edith E, notary public, 18 Union bldg, b 561 N Illinois.
Swigert Elizabeth, dressmkr, 160 S New Jersey, b same.
Swigert Ernest, clk, b 561 N Illinois.
Swigert Harry, b 561 N Illinois.
Swigert Joseph O, pension agt, 18 Union bldg, h 561 N Illinois.
Swigert Sarah (wid Michael), r 160 S New Jersey.
Swiggett Bert, enameler, b 236 Douglass.
Swiggett Carlton E, tailor, h 1538 N Penn.
Swiggett Charles H, trav agt, h 930 N Meridian.
Swiggett Charles P, carp, h 50 Elizabeth.
Swiggett Frederick S, printer The Indpls News, b 236 Douglass.
Swiggett Orville K, printer, b 54 Columbia av.
Swiggett Rose, waitress City Hospital.
Swiggett Samuel A, cutter, r 311 The Shiel.
Swiggett Thomas P, carp, h 236 Douglass.
Swiggett Walter F, tailor, h 279 N Meridian.
Swihart James T, bricklyr, h 301 W Pearl.
Swihart Wm H, lab, h rear 428 S East.
Swim Ida, b 965 N Delaware.
Swindelle J Lindsey, stenog F P Rush & Co, b 670 E Market.
Swindler George W, insp, h 82 Warren av (W I).
Swine Breeders' Journal, The Morris Printing Co pubs, 467 S Illinois.
Swineford Harry, paperhngr, b 271 N Noble.
Swineford Robert, riveter, b 82 E St Clair.
Swing Anna N, b 50 W 12th.
Swing George W, bookbndr, b 50 W 12th.
Swing Wm W jr, trav agt, b 50 W 12th.
Swink James M, pressman, h 5 Sumner.
Swisher Alzina, boarding house 46 Russell av.
Swisher Anthony, lab, h 10 Edward (W I).
Swisher Arthur, engr, h 4 S Gale (B).
Swisher Harriet, h 46 Russell av.
Swisher James C, lineman, h 244 S Missouri.
Swisher Otto A, electrician, h 84 Division (W I).
Swisher Philip, lab, b 136 Scioto.
Swisher Richard, b 48 Russell av.
Swisher Wm F, h 1584 Kenwood av.
Swoboda Charles N, lab, b 20 Arthur.
Swoboda John, cabtmkr, b 527 W Francis (N I).
Swoboda Joseph, cabtmkr, h 132 Yandes.
Swoboda Joseph A, cabtmkr, h 20 Arthur.
Swoboda Martin J, lab, b 132 Yandes.
Swope Albert, lab, b 97 Oliver av (W I).

THE WHEN IS A WORLD BEATER.

Swope Jesse K, harnessmkr, b 284 S East.
Swope Joseph, h 284 S East.
Swope Mary E (wid Addison), grocer, 249 River av (W I), h same.
Swope Wm A, livestock, h 97 Oliver av (W I).
Swope Wm J, lab, h 101 Bloomington.
Syders Dallas C, clk, b 80 W 12th.
Syders Philip B, trav agt, h 80 W 12th.
Syers David, brakeman, b 111 Yandes.
Syerup Charles (Syerup & Co), h 255 N East.
Syerup Henry C, clk Syerup & Co, h 229 N Beville av.
Syerup Herman, driver, h 23 Sylvan.
Syerup Lisette (wid Henry), h 257 N East.
SYERUP & CO (Charles Syerup, George Vondersaar), Commission Merchants, 22-24 S Delaware, Tel 279.
Syfers James A, trav agt, r 31½ Indiana av.
Syfers, McBride & Co (Rufus K Syfers, Frank A McBride), whol grocers, 78 S Meridian.
Syfers Rufus K (Syfers, McBride & Co), h 348 N Capitol av.
Sykes Alexander L, agt Standard Rope and Twine Co, b 400 N Illinois.
Sykes Martha L (wid Elias), b 115 W 6th.
Sykes Wm, lab Roosevelt House.
Sylvester, see also Silvester.
Sylvester Aaron, foreman Putnam County Milk Co, h 80 N Beville av.
Sylvester James A, carp, h 79 S McLain (W I).
Sylvester Marion A, carp, h 4 S Belmont (W I).
Sylvester Wm H, driver, h 56 Greer.
Sym Jane (wid James), h 346 S New Jersey.
Sym Margaret, h 346 S New Jersey.
Symmes Henry H, pres H H Symmes & Co, b 657 College av.
SYMMES H H CO, Henry H Symmes Pres, Bert E Symmes Treas, Carl Koechlin Sec, Asphalt and Pitch Roofing, and Asphalt and Cement Paving, 39 S Alabama, Tel 1563.
Symmonds Edward, car rep, b 1060 W Vermont.

THE A. BURDSAL CO.
Manufacturers of
Paints and Colors
VARNISHES,
Brushes, Painters' and Paper Hangers' Supplies.
34 AND 36 SOUTH MERIDIAN STREET.

ELECTRICIANS DON'T FORGET US. ALL WORK GUARANTEED. C. W. MEIKEL, Tel. 466. 96-98 E. New York St.

DALTON & MERRIFIELD { LUMBER South Noble St., near E. Washington

INDIANA ELECTROTYPE CO. ⁝ BEST WORK. LOWEST PRICES.
23 WEST PEARL ST., INDIANAPOLIS, IND. JOB WORK. BOOK PLATES. All Orders Promptly Filled. BEST PATENT BASE ON THE MARKET.

KIRKHOFF BROS.
Steam and Hot Water Heating Apparatus,
Plumbing and Gas Fitting.
102-104 SOUTH PENNSYLVANIA ST.
TELEPHONE 910.

Symons Samantha, dressmkr, 166 N Alabama, h same.
Syphers Willis, lab, h 616 S West.

T

Tabbe Wilhelmina (wid Charles), h 543 E Washington.
Tabert Albert, lab, h 329 English av.
Tacke Christian F W, lab, h 923 Madison av.
Tacoma Laundry, 141 N Delaware.
Tacoma Reno, uphlr, h 8 Dawson.
Taffe Catherine N, teacher, b 296 Clifford av.
Taffe George A, doorman police station, h 30 N New Jersey.
Taflinger Thomas J, condr, h 11 Wendell av.
Taft O H & F E, Willis E Hutchason mngr, dentists, 25½ W Washington.
Taggart Alexander, mngr Parrott-Taggart Bakery, 93-99 S Penn, h 384 Park av.
Taggart George, lab, h 308 Coburn.
Taggart Hannibal, driver, h rear 436 W North.
Taggart Joseph, baker, 51 E Mkt House, h 1100 N Meridian.
TAGGART THOMAS, Pres The Grand Hotel Co, Mayor City of Indianapolis, Room 7 Basement Court House, Tel 874; h 410 N Capitol av, Tel 666.
Tague, see also Teague.
Tague Archibald, lab, b 330 E Georgia.
Tague Frank, condr, r 201 S Illinois.
Tague George C, slater, h 257 W Ray.
Tague James McG, pressfeeder, b 232 Madison av.
Tague Jonathan, lab, b 257 W Ray.
Tague Thomas M, packer, h 232 Madison av.
TAISEY FRED R, Dept Agt Lamson Consolidated Store Service Co, 31½ Virginia av, h 179 Brookside av. (See adv under classified Cash Carriers.)

LIME
BUILDING SUPPLIES,
Hair, Plaster, Flue Linings,
The W. G. Wasson Co.
130 INDIANA AVE. Tel. 989.

TAKKEN JACOB E, Mngr The Merchants' and Manufacturers' Exchange, Collections and Commercial Reports, 19 Union Building, over U S Pension Office, 63-73 W Maryland. (See left bottom cor cards.)
Talbert, see also Tolbert.
Talbert Edgar C, clk Indiana Car Service Assn, b 187 St Mary.
Talbert Edward, restaurant, 166 Indiana av, h 121 W 6th.
Talbert Jesse, clk Frank E Walcott, b 179 Blackford.
Talbert Leander A, lab, h n w cor 4th and Lafayette.
Talbert Lindley A, painter, h 187 St Mary.
Talbert Samuel A, contr, 179 Blackford, h same.
Talbert Wm, lab, h 202 Oregon.
Talbert Ella (wid Everett), h 30 E Pratt.
Talbot Elsie D, seamstress, b 568 Ash.
Talbot Howard M, clk Indiana Natl Bank, h 178 Christian av.
Talbot Joseph C, bkkpr, h 178 Christian av.
Talbot Richard L, real est, 44 Thorpe blk, h 178 Christian av.
Talbot Richard L jr, cashr State B and L Assn, h 74 Christian av.
Talbott Anna (wid George), b 20 S Dorman.
Talbott Burt B, condr, h 93 N State av.
Talbott Charles W, paperhngr, b 409 W New York.
Talbott Chase C, bartndr, h 73 S West.
Talbott Frank M, real est, 61½ N Penn, h 884 same.
Talbott Frank M, vice-pres Indpls Basket Co, h 625 N Illinois.
Talbott George, foreman, b 625 N Illinois.
Talbott George H, broker, h 870 N Penn.
Talbott Henry, tmstr, h 10 McIntyre.
Talbott Henry J Rev, presiding elder West Indpls District M E Church, h 197 College av.
Talbott Henry M (Dickson & Talbott), h 884 N Penn.
Talbott Henry N, lab, b 226 Michigan (H).
Talbott Herschel B, clk R M S, r 23 Ft Wayne av.
Talbott John, lab, h 594 E 10th.
Talbott John A, lab, b 503 E 11th.
Talbott John H, medical examiner Penna Lines, Union Station, h 675 N Illinois.
Talbott John W, lab, h 226 Michigan (H).
Talbott Julia (wid Henry), h 120 Elizabeth.
Talbott Lutitia, b 441 E Ohio.
Talbott Margaret (wid Worthington), h 409 W New York.
Talbott Nathan H, lab, b 226 Michigan (H).
Talbott Richard, lab, h 411 Muskingum al.
Talbott Sarah A, dressmkr, 25 Birch av (W I), h same.
Talkenberg Bernard, turner, b 188 Shelby.
Talkington Albert, fireman, b 860 E Washington.
Tall Houston H, florist, b 1531 N Illinois.
Tall Persifor F, cementwkr, b 1531 N Illinois.
Tall Wm R, cement contr, h 1531 N Illinois.
Tallant Alexander Q, agt, h 85 Middle Drive (W P).
Tallentire James M, mach, b 199 Fletcher av.
Tallentire Lewis E, clk, b 199 Fletcher av.
Tallentire Thomas, foreman, h 199 Fletcher av.
Tallentire Thomas jr, insp, h 223 Fletcher av.
Tallentire Wm G, chief tel opr Fire Dept, h 165 S East.

Parlor, Bed Room, Dining Room, Kitchen, Furniture W. H. MESSENGER, 101 E. Wash. St., Tel. 491.

ALL KINDS OF HEAVY AND LIGHT GRAY IRON CASTINGS } McNamara, Koster & Co. { Foundry and Pattern Shop
Phone 1593. 212-218 S. Penn. St.

Talley Robert, mach hd, h 176 Muskingum al.
Talliaferro Wm, brakeman, h 15 Belmont av.
Tally Richard, bartndr, r 218 E Market.
Talmadge Wm J, clk Am Ex Co, h 62 The Blacherne.
Talmage Frank J, condr, h 21 Keith.
Tamblyn Henry W, mach, h 41 S Summit.
Tamblyn John F, mach, h 424 E Vermont.
Tamm August, dairy, 336 Hillside av, h same.
Tamm August jr, dep City Clerk, room 2 basement Court House, h 6 Water.
Tamm August C, collr Clemens Vonnegut, b 6 Water.
Tamm Peter, lab, b 600 S West.
Tandy Samuel, bellboy The Bates.
Taney Charles A, clk, b 209 Indiana av.
Taney Michael, carp, h 209 Indiana av.
Tangney Mary (wid Dennis), h 175 Bane.
Tangney Robert P, r 71½ N Illinois.
Tangston Nathan, lab, h 5 Susquehanna.
Tankston Carrie E, h 352 W North.
Tanner Abraham, lab, h 575 E 8th.
Tanner Albert, actor, b 269 Fayette.
Tanner Charles, lab, h 35 Stevens.
Tanner Frank, lab, r 60 S Delaware.
Tanner Frank, lab, h 39 Thalman av.
Tanner George G (Tanner & Sullivan), Surveyor of Customs, P O bldg, h 250 N Capitol av.
Tanner Isaac W, lab, h 13 Margaret.
Tanner Jackson, lab, r rear 70 Yandes.
Tanner Jacob L, lab, h 39 Clifford av.
Tanner James W, hostler, h 117 Clinton.
Tanner Maria L (wid Gordon), r 250 N Capitol av.
Tanner Minnie D, dressmkr, 39 Clifford av, h same.
Tanner Thomas H (Circle Transfer Co), b 13 Margaret.
TANNER & SULLIVAN (George G Tanner, George R Sullivan), Wholesale Tinners' Supplies, 116-118 S Meridian, Tel 429.
Tanquary James R, clk R M S, h 1288 N New Jersey.
Tansel Benjamin, tmstr, b 52 S Judge Harding (W I).
Tansel Minos, livery, 202 W Washington, h 11 Emerson pl.
Tansel Patie, lab, r 186 N California.
Tansey Charles A, lab, h 22 Thomas.
Tansy Hamet H, private U S Army, b 25½ N Illinois.
Taphorn John H, mach hd, h 255 Shelby.
Tapking Henry H, supt Indpls Cabinetmakers' Union, b 123 N New Jersey.
Tapking John F, mach hd, h 123 N New Jersey.
Tapking Wilhelmina (wid Frederick H), h 432 N Delaware.
Tapp Wm P, b 210 Douglass.
Tappert Gustav, butcher, h 44 S Austin (B).
Tarkington Booth N, b 598 N Penn.
Tarkington Jesse C, agt, h 26 E St Clair.
Tarkington John S, mngr Fletcher's Safe Deposit Co, h 598 N Penn, tel 969.
Tarkington Joseph E, city dis clk P O, b 286 E Vermont.
Tarkington Ransom A, lab, b 53 Athon.
Tarkington Wm S R, supt Daniel Stewart Co, h 477 N Capitol av.
Tarlton Charles S, sec, b 631 College av.
Tarlton James A, salesman George W Stout, h 631 College av.
Tarlton James A jr, clk L S Ayres & Co, h 427 E 7th.

Henry H. Fay,
40½ E. WASHINGTON ST.,
FIRE INSURANCE, REAL ESTATE,
LOANS AND RENTAL AGENT.

Tarlton Roberta, clk, b 534 Broadway.
Tarlton Will M, butcher, h 429 E 12th.
Tarpenning Charles T, tinner, h 312 Shelby.
Tarpey Bridget (wid Malachi), h 31 S West.
Tarpey Ellen (wid John), h 146 Belmont av (H).
Tarpey Patrick J, lab, b 31 S West.
Tarpey Thomas, bartndr, b 249 W South.
Tarpey Wm W, lab, b 146 Belmont av (H).
Tarrants Joseph, lab, h 296 Blake.
Tasch Philip, shoemkr, h 282 Spring.
Tasker Amanda, laundress, h 424 Superior.
Taskey Otto, bricklyr, h 465½ S Meridian.
Tastum Jacob, tilemkr, b 1139 N Illinois.
Tate James L, mach, r 59 Columbia av.
Tate John W, carp, b 160 Cornell av.
Tate Warren T, h 144 N East.
Tatman Edward, driver, b 36 Sheldon.
Tatman Francis M, cooper, h 467 W New York.
Tattersall Alice C, teacher Public School No 34, b 459 N West.
Tattersall Anna B, teacher Public School No 16, b 459 N West.
Tattersall Joseph, h 459 N West.
Tauer Paul, mach, h 145 Patterson.
Taux Carl, painter, h 5½ Brookside av.
Tavenor Edward F, lab, h 118 Chadwick.
Taylor Addie (wid George J), h 144 E McCarty.
Taylor Albert, bkkpr, h 1132 N Delaware.
Taylor Albert, lab, h 508 Superior.
Taylor Albert, tmstr, h 90 Maple.
Taylor Alexander, barber, h 122 Allegheny.
Taylor Alexander, lab, h rear 775 N Senate av.
Taylor Alfred A, letter carrier P O, h 1135 N Alabama.
Taylor Alfred R, cashr Taylor & Taylor, b 287 Park av.
Taylor Alice R (wid David M), r 31 E St Joseph.
Taylor Allen T, lab 323 Lafayette.
Taylor Alonzo W (Taylor & Taylor), h 1229 N Penn.
Taylor Alphonso J, student, h 20 Cornell av.
Taylor Amos, lab, b 323 W Market.
Taylor Andrew, clk, b 131 W Ohio.

WILL GO ON YOUR BOND
American Bonding & Trust Co.
Of Baltimore, Md. Approved as sole surety by the United States Government and the different States as Sole Surety on all Forms of Bonds.
W. E. BARTON & CO., General Agents,
504 Indiana Trust Building.
LONG DISTANCE TELEPHONE 1918.

THE FRED DIETZ CO.
WOODEN PACKING BOXES MADE TO ORDER
FACTORY AND WAREHOUSE TRUCKS.
400 Madison Avenue. Telephone 654.

BUSINESS EDUCATION A NECESSITY.
TIME SHORT. DAY AND NIGHT SCHOOL.
SUCCESS CERTAIN AT THE PERMANENT, RELIABLE
Indianapolis BUSINESS UNIVERSITY

HENRY R. WORTHINGTON JET and SURFACE CONDENSERS 64 S. PENN. ST. Long Distance Telephone 284.

UNION CO-OPERATIVE LAUNDRY (COMPOSED OF 80 N LAUNDRY GIRLS.) NOS. 38, 40 AND 42 VIRGINIA AVENUE. T. E. SOMERVILLE, MANAGER TELEPHONE 18. INDIANAPOLIS, IND.

HORACE M. HADLEY
INSURANCE AND LOANS
66 E. Market Street, Basement
TELEPHONE 1540.

Taylor Anna (wid Wm), h 256½ E McCarty.
Taylor Anna, stenog, h w s Central av 2 s of Grand av (I).
Taylor Annie, h 32 Bird.
Taylor Annie, agt, r 28½ Indiana av.
Taylor Armstead, carp, h 222 W 4th.
Taylor Arthur, mach Indpls Pattern Wks, b 544 E Washington.
Taylor Arthur H, bkkpr S A Fletcher & Co, h 129 East Drive (W P).
Taylor Arthur H, collr, h 100 Walcott.
Taylor Arthur J, teacher High School, h 1443 N Illinois.
Taylor Arthur L, mach, b 544 E Washington.
Taylor Augustus L, lab, b 100 Concord (H).
Taylor Belle (wid George M), nurse, 266 N East, h same.
Taylor Benjamin, h 566 N Senate av.
Taylor Bert, hostler, b 32 Bird.
Taylor Bessie G, teacher Public School No 28, b 203 Huron.
Taylor Braxton, lab, h 308 W Court.
Taylor Bruce R, clk U S Atty, r 28½ Indiana av.
Taylor B Alexander, barber, h 122 Allegheny.
Taylor Carl A, clk, h 1222 N Penn.
Taylor Catherine (wid Marshall W), b 257 W 6th.
Taylor Catherine A (wid James T), h 176 Martindale av.
Taylor Cecelia C (wid Wm H), b 70 Temple av.
Taylor Charles, lab, h 227 Howard.
Taylor Charles A, gasfitter, h 56 Excelsior av.
Taylor Charles A, lab, b 106 Yandes.
Taylor Charles B Rev, h 63 Beaty.
Taylor Chalres E, lab, h 466 N West.
Taylor Charles E, student, r 367 N Alabama.
Taylor Charles F, lab, b 219 E Wabash.
Taylor Charles H (Taylor & Ormsbee), h 165½ Michigan av.
Taylor Charles H, lab, b 239 W 3d.
Taylor Charles H, mach hd, b 55 Palmer.
Taylor Charles P, deputy U S Marshal, b 280 E St Clair.

COLLECTIONS
MERCHANTS' AND MANUFACTURERS' EXCHANGE
Will give you good service.
J. E. TAKKEN, Manager,
Union Building, over U. S. Pension Office.
73 West Maryland Street.

Taylor Charles W, coachman, r 49 Tecumseh.
Taylor Charles W, plastr, h 239 Sheldon.
Taylor Clara A (wid Wm O), h 434 N Delaware.
Taylor Clarence, lab, b 75 Shepard (W I).
Taylor Corwin M, tinner, h 164 Elizabeth.
Taylor Daniel, lab, h rear 17 Center.
Taylor David, lab, b 207 W 6th.
Taylor David J, h 247 Bright.
Taylor Earl B, ins agt, h 432 S Illinois.
Taylor Edgar S, bkkpr, b 9 Cherry.
Taylor Edith G, stenog, b 881 N Senate av.
Taylor Edward A, mach, b 71 Peru av.
Taylor Edward A, trav agt Taylor & Smith, b 336 Central av.
Taylor Edward C, checkman, h 124 Hoyt av.
Taylor Edward R, lab, h 409 Newman.
Taylor Elizabeth A (wid Israel), h 280 E Market.
Taylor Elizabeth R (wid Alfred A), h 287 Park av.
Taylor Fillmore E, boilermkr, h 320 Coburn.
Taylor Flora (wid James W), b 125 E Washington.
Taylor Frank, lab, b 125½ Hadley av (W I).
Taylor Frank H, storekpr The Bates.
Taylor George, driver, h 9 Ingram.
Taylor George, driver, h rear 122 N Pine.
Taylor George, lab, h 575 Mass av.
Taylor George, lab, b 115 Meek.
Taylor George, lab, b rear 33 Woodlawn av.
Taylor George, insp, h 39 Nebraska.
Taylor George, porter, b 389 Blackford.
Taylor George, tmstr, b 204 Elm.
Taylor George, trav agt, r 5½ Indiana av.
Taylor George R, trav agt, h 525 Broadway.
Taylor George W, brakeman, h 422 S State av.
Taylor George W, brakeman, h 43 Williams.
Taylor George W, carp, h 203 Huron.
Taylor Gilbert, lab, h 1156 Northwestern av (N I).

TAYLOR HAROLD, Lawyer, 302-304 Indiana Trust Bldg, Tel 265; h 749 N Penn.

Taylor Harrison, driver, h s w cor 13th and Big Four Ry.
Taylor Harry, lab, b 209 W North.
Taylor Harry, lab, b 323 W Market.
Taylor Harry N, printer, h 498 N West.
Taylor Harriet B, h 336½ E Washington.
Taylor Henry, hostler 540 Virginia av.
Taylor Henry, janitor, r 28 Catterson blk.
Taylor Henry, lab, r 286 Douglass.
Taylor Henry, lab, h 263 Lafayette.
Taylor Henry, lab, b 82 Martindale av.
Taylor Henry M, plastr, h 483 W Ontario (N I).
Taylor Hugh L Mc, special examiner U S Pension Bureau, r 197 N Alabama.
Taylor Irenius C, stairbldr, h 544 E Washington.
Taylor Irving, porter, r 82 Ft Wayne av.
Taylor Isaac, architect, h 83 E Michigan.
Taylor Jacob, lab, h 487 S Capitol av.
Taylor James, tmstr, h 17 Mulberry.
Taylor James, janitor, b 107 Muskingum al.
Taylor James, supt Rockwood Mnfg Co, h n s E Washington 2 e of Belt R R.
Taylor James A, student, h 28 Cornell av.
Taylor James E, optician N Y Store, r 279 N Capitol av.
Taylor James H, phys, 2 The Chalfant, h 632 N Penn.

CLEMENS VONNEGUT 184, 186 and 192 E. Washington St. | BUILDERS' HARDWARE, Building Paper. Duplex Joist Hangers

THE WM. H. BLOCK CO. DRY GOODS, DRAPERIES, RUGS, WINDOW SHADES.
7 AND 9 EAST WASHINGTON STREET.

Taylor James L, h 387 N Senate av.
Taylor James M (Taylor & Lane), h n e cor Bismarck and Grandview avs (H).
Taylor James R, brakeman, r 15 Russell av.
Taylor James W, city fireman, h 14 Meikel.
Taylor Jane B (wid John F), h n s Walnut 1 w of Maple av (I).
Taylor Jason C, watchmkr, h 1437 N Illinois.
Taylor Jennie R, artist, 435 Park av, h same.
Taylor Jenny, h 169 W McCarty.
Taylor Jeremiah, bartndr, h 255 N West.
Taylor John, tmstr, h 24 Wisconsin.
Taylor John D, lab, b 855 S East.
Taylor John F, clk, r 32 Hutchings blk.
Taylor John G, stair-bldr, b 46 Bellefontaine.
Taylor John, b rear 33 Woodlawn av.
Taylor John, lab, h 281 Chapel.
Taylor John, lab, h 230 W 5th.
Taylor John, lab, h 480 W North.
Taylor John, lab, b 48 Pendleton av (B).
Taylor John, insp Kingan & Co (ltd), h 91 Bright.
Taylor John H, lab, h rear 127 E St Joseph.
Taylor John T, driver, b 480 W North.
Taylor John W, clk, h 73 Indiana av.
Taylor Joseph, lab, h 211 W Ohio.
Taylor Joseph, lab, h rear 86 S Noble.
Taylor Joseph, lab, h 38 Thomas.
Taylor Joseph B, contr, h 881 N Senate av.
Taylor Joseph L, printer, h 88 Broadway.
Taylor Joseph M, letter carrier P O, h 435 Park av.
Taylor Joseph M, opr W U Tel Co, h 409 Central av.
Taylor Julia (wid Thomas), h 195 Middle.
Taylor Julia A (wid Richard), h 228 W 7th.
Taylor Laura, b 102 N Missouri.
Taylor Laura N (wid David), b rear 177 Park av.
Taylor Laura (wid John), h 6 Lafayette.
Taylor Lillie (wid Wm), b 119 W 4th.
Taylor Lloyd, finisher, b 147 Dougherty.
Taylor Louis H, carp, b 76 N Gillard av.
Taylor Louisa M (wid Wm G), h 147 Dougherty.
Taylor Lulu M, stenog C C C & St L Ry, b 50 Lexington av.

TAYLOR MAJOR, Propr Excelsior Steam Laundry, 2-6 Masonic Temple, S Capitol av, Tel 249; h 683 N Alabama.

Taylor Margaret (wid Rev Frank), h 22½ Hall pl.
Taylor Margaret C (wid John W), h 701 N Alabama.
Taylor Mary (wid Wm), h 269 Fayette.
Taylor Mary E, h rear 355 Blake.
Taylor Mary E, h w s Central av 2 s of Grandview av (I).
Taylor Mary E (wid Wiley F), h 323 W Market.
Taylor Mary J (wid Thomas), h 207 W 6th.
Taylor Mary W (wid Wm), b 208 Middle.
Taylor Nellie F, stenog C C C & St L Ry, b 203 Huron.
Taylor Nettie, r 106½ N Meridian.
Taylor Newton M, lawyer, 444 Lorraine bldg, h 9 Cherry.
Taylor Oliver I, clk, b 176 Martindale av.
Taylor Ora C, mach, b 124 Hoyt av.
Taylor Oscar C, b 50 Lexington av.
Taylor Oscar S, phys, 22 W Ohio, b 1134 N Alabama.
Taylor Philip, lab, b 16 Columbia al.

Taylor Phoebe (wid George), h 100 Rhode Island.
Taylor Retta (wid Frank), b 124 Blackford.
Taylor Richard C, butler 622 N Meridian.
Taylor Robert, lab, b 391 Blackford.
Taylor Robert, waiter, h rear 17 Center.
Taylor Robert A, h 1134 N Alabama.
Taylor Robert A, lab, b 144 E McCarty.
Taylor Robert G, printer, h 100 Broadway.
Taylor Robert L, clk Boyd, Besten & Langen Co, b 525 Broadway.
Taylor Robert L, lab, b w s Hillside av 1 s of 17th.
Taylor Sadie (wid Albert), h 106 Prospect.
Taylor Samuel (Taylor & Co), b 455 N Meridian.
Taylor Samuel, lab, h rear 169 E St Joseph.
Taylor Samuel, lab, r rear 162 E North.
Taylor Samuel, packer, h 369 W New York.
Taylor Samuel jr, lab, b 369 W New York.
Taylor Samuel L (Taylor & Schneider), h 424 S State av.
Taylor Sandy F, chief clk C C C & St L Ry, h 11 Stoughton av.
Taylor Seth, trav agt, b 262 W Michigan.
Taylor Smith, painter, h 29 Atlas.
Taylor Sophia (wid Charles), h rear 106 Prospect.
Taylor Stephen, driver, h 310 W Pratt.
Taylor Stephen R, express, h 206 Northwestern av.
Taylor Thomas, lab, b 397 Blackford.
Taylor Thomas, patternmkr, b 188 S Senate av.
Taylor Thomas J, b 42 Chase (W I).
Taylor Thomas J, carriagemkr, h 273 N Noble.
Taylor Thomas P, huckster, b 209 Minnesota.
Taylor Van, mach hd, h 534 W Francis (N I).
Taylor Walter, lab, b 38 Thomas.
Taylor Wichard, lab, r 11 Ellsworth.
Taylor Wm, lab, b rear 18 Bismarck.
Taylor Wm, lab, h rear 15 Cornell av.
Taylor Wm, lab, r 74 Mayhew.
Taylor Wm, lab, b 23 N New Jersey.
Taylor Wm, lab, h rear 518 Virginia av.
Taylor Wm, h 76 N Gillard av.

GUIDO R. PRESSLER,
FRESCO PAINTER
Churches, Theaters, Public Buildings, Etc., A Specialty.
Residence, No. 325 North Liberty Street.
INDIANAPOLIS, IND.

INDIANAPOLIS STEEL ROOFING AND CORRUGATING WORKS, 23 and 25 East South Street. S. D. NOEL, Proprietor.

David S. McKernan, Rooms 2-5 Thorpe Block.
REAL ESTATE AND LOANS
Money to loan on real estate. Special inducements offered those having money to loan. It will pay you to investigate.

DIAMOND WALL PLASTER { Telephone 1410 BUILDERS' EXCHANGE.

UNION TRANSFER AND STORAGE CO. E. Ohio St. and C., C., C. & St. L. R'y Tracks. BEST FACILITIES FOR STORING AND TRANSFERRING MACHINERY AND MERCHANDISE.

W. McWORKMAN

FIRE SHUTTERS,
FIRE DOORS,
METAL CEILINGS.

930 W. Washington St. Tel. 1118.

Taylor Wm, janitor, h 269 Fayette.
Taylor Wm, lab, b 761 Brooker's al.
Taylor Wm A (Taylor & Smith), h 336 Central av.
Taylor Wm A, cook, h 254 W 6th.
Taylor Wm A, printer The Indpls News, h 170 Elm.
Taylor Wm A, switchman, h 346 S Alabama.
Taylor Wm C, carp, h 42 Chase (W I).
Taylor Wm D, lab, h 30 Willard.
Taylor Wm F, painter, h 50 Lexington av.
Taylor Wm F, printer Indpls Journal, h 263 Huron.
Taylor Wm G, lab, b 216 Yandes.
Taylor Wm G, sec Mechanics' Mut S and L Assn, chief clk and supt motive power C C C & St L Ry, h 53 Woodruff av.
Taylor Wm H, h 10 Detroit.
Taylor Wm H, barber, r 39 Hosbrook.
Taylor Wm H, lab, h 209 W North.
Taylor Wm H, switchman, h 60 S State av.
Taylor Wm H, tinner, h 176 Elm.
Taylor Wm J, waiter, r 180 Muskingum al.
TAYLOR WM L, Lawyer, 18½ N Penn, Tel 317; h 125 E New York.
Taylor Wm M, clk, b 91 Bright.
Taylor Wm M, mach, h 1140 E Washington.
Taylor Wm M, vice-pres and treas Chandler & Taylor Co, b 679 N Delaware.
Taylor Wm W, ins agt, b 220 N Capitol av.
Taylor Witcher, barber, r 35½ Kentucky av.
Taylor Zachariah, carp, h 855 S East.
Taylor Zachariah, chiropodist, 17 McCauley, h same.
TAYLOR & CO (Samuel Taylor), Real Estate, Loans, Stocks, Bonds and Insurance, 5 Talbott Blk.
TAYLOR & LANE (James M Taylor, Harry J Lane), Druggists, n e cor Bismarck and Grandview avs (H).
Taylor & Ormsbee (Charles H Taylor, Oscar L Ormsbee), grocers, 167 Michigan av.
TAYLOR & SCHNEIDER (Samuel L Taylor, Wm G Schneider), Merchant Tailors, 22 Monument Pl.

GEO. J. MAYER,
MANUFACTURER OF
SEALS
STENCILS, RUBBER STAMPS, CHECKS, BADGES, DOOR PLATES, ETC.
5 S. Meridian St., Ground Floor. TEL. 1386.

TAYLOR & SMITH (Wm A Taylor, Wm H Smith), Leather, Findings, Belting, Hose and Mill Supplies, 137-139 S Meridian, Tel 412.
TAYLOR & TAYLOR (Alonzo W Taylor), Carpets, Draperies and Shades, 30-36 S Illinois, Tel 871.
Teachnor Abraham, lab, h 38 Wallace.
Teaford Lillian I, boarding e s Brightwood av 7 s of Willow (B).
Teague, see also Tague.
Teague Albert, student, b 259 Virginia av.
Teague Albert E, phys, 86 N Senate av, h same.
Teague Andrew F, clk R M S, h 184 Woodlawn av.
Teague Charles U, uphlr, b 145 Hadley av (W I).
Teague Franklin, lab, h 145 Hadley av (W I).
Teague Lewis, lab, h 35 Drake.
Teague Mabel, grand mistress of records and correspondence Rathbone Sisters, h 86 N Senate av.
Teague Nellie, b 170 Nordyke av (W I).
Teal Benjamin F, bartndr, r s w cor East and Market.
Teal Mary L (wid Alfred), b 284 Martindale av.
Teal Walter V, clk, h 135 E North.
Teale John E, printer, b 40½ S Illinois.
Tean John, carp, b 27 Empire.
Teaney Catherine, boarding 944 Gent (M P).
Teaney Charles L, lab, b 944 Gent (M P).
Teaney George, lab, b 944 Gent (M P).
Teas Edward Y, florist, w s Elm av 1 n of Washington av (I), h same.
Teas Frederick E, clk, b w s Elm av 1 n of Washington av (I).
Teas Mary M, music teacher, w s Elm av 1 n of Washington av (I), b same.
Teaster Charles H (F P Teaster & Son), b 407 Newman.
Teaster Finley P (F P Teaster & Son), h 407 Newman.
Teaster F P & Son (Finley P and Charles H), produce, 176 E Wabash.
Teats Herman, agt, h 24 W New York.
Techentin Frederick, clk, b 964 N Capitol av.
Techentin Henry (Techentin & Freiberg), h 964 N Capitol av.
TECHENTIN & FREIBERG (Henry Techentin, John Freiberg), Harness and Saddle Makers, 14 N Delaware.
Teckenbrock Christopher H, blksmith, h 32 Henry.
Teckenbrock Edward, painter, b 74 W McCarty.
Teckenbrock Henry W, car insp, h 74 W McCarty.
TECKENBROCK JOHN H, Genl Painter and Decorator, Paperhanger and Dealer in Grille and Fret Work, Wood Carpets, Etc, 94 E South, h 43 Standard av (W I). (See right bottom lines and adv in classified Painters.)
Teckenbrock Wm E, clk, h 239 S Alabama.
Tedeman Frederick, truckman, h 169 Pleasant.
Tedrow Catherine (wid David F), h 286 Christian av.
Tedrow Eunice, b 1007 N Capitol av.
Tedrowe Charles W, clk McCormick H M Co, h 286 E Morris.

A. METZGER AGENCY ESTABLISHED 1863. REAL ESTATE

LAMBERT GAS & GASOLINE ENGINE CO.
ANDERSON, IND. NATURAL GAS ENGINES.

Tedrowe Isaac P, h 59 Barth av.
Tedrowe Joseph T, h 1160 N Meridian.
Teeguarden Daniel, carp, h 16 Sharpe.
Teeguarden Wm R, mach, h 141 Hosbrook.
Teel Adna A, trav agt The Sinker-Davis Co, b Spencer House.
Teeny Fannie (wid Wesley), b 41 Elm.
Teepe August H, lab, h 53 Hosbrook.
Teepe Dinah (wid Herman), b 360 Virginia av.
Teepe George H, molder, h 360 Virginia av.
Teeple Ames, condr, r 353½ E Market.
Teeple John, engr Insane Hospital.
Teeters Amanda, h 291 E Miami.
Teeters Charles, lab, h 218 Howard.
Teeters Edward W, weaver, b 291 E Miami.
Teeters George W, grocer, 480 W Chicago (N I), h 478 same.
Teeters Irene (wid Jerry), h 471 Charles.
Teeters Richard, lab, h 159½ Agnes.
Teetor Abraham L, patent solr, h 1062 N Senate av.
Tefft Hannah E (wid Albert), h 169 Columbia av.
Tefft Wm A, carp, b 169 Columbia av.
Tegtmeier Gerhard L, b 188 Highland av.
Tehan Catherine (wid Wm), h rear 162 Meek.
Tehan Dennis F, painter, h 395 S Capitol av.
Teichert Paul E, musician, h 250 W Market.
Teine Christian, grocer, 217 W 8th, h same.
Teine Christian jr, pdlr, h 219 W 8th.
Teiney Christian, shoemkr, h 84 N Brookside av.
Teipen Anton, filler, h 561 S West.
Teipen Bernard A H, lab, h 38 Carlos.
Teipen Henry J, lab, h 38 Fenneman.
Teitelbaum Julius, tailor, r 269½ E Washington.
Telford Henry B, agt, h 277 Prospect.
Telgener Henry A, trav agt, h 299 S East.
Teljohann Henry, h 22 Vinton.
Tellas Jeremiah, tmstr, h s w cor Jackson and Addison (M J).
Tellas John T, fireman, h 211 Kentucky av.
Tellefson Andrew, salesman Henry R Worthington, b 297 E Market.
Teller John E, driver, b 111 E Washington.
Teller Mary (wid John), h 447 N California.
Tellkamp Anna, grocer, 36 Ramsey av, b same.
Tellkamp Catherine M (wid John H), h 36 Ramsey av.
Tellkamp Henry J, clk Daniel Stewart Co, h 1104 E Michigan.
Temman Charles F, painter, b 140 Newman.
Temman Wm, painter, h 140 Newman.
Temperley Clara B, boarding 283 E Georgia.
Temperley Dorcas (wid John R), b 214 Keystone av.
Temperley George R, h 44 Highland pl.
Temperley Harry H, whol meats, Indpls Abattoir, h 167 Church.
Temperley John R, carp, h 283 E Georgia.
Temperley Ralph, butcher, b 125½ Hadley av (W I).
Temple Henry, lab, b 50 Concordia.
Temple Alonzo F, lab, h 129 W New York.
Temple Carter, patrolman, h 186 Minerva.
Temple Edward J, lab, r 148 W Maryland.
Temple George W, lab, b 184 Minerva.
Temple John L, lab, b 49 Rhode Island.
Temple John P, h 227 N California.
Temple Samuel L, carp, b 160 W Maryland.
Temple Sidney, engr, h 384 E Michigan.
Temple Walter J, engr, h 389 W Vermont.
Temple Wm W, switchman, h 20 Iowa.

THOS. C. DAY & CO.
Financial Agents and Loans.
We have the experience, and claim to be reliable.
Rooms 325 to 330 Lemcke Bldg.

Templeton Aaron D, h 72 Harrison.
Templeton Boyd W, bkkpr Samuel P Hamilton, b 455 Ash.
Templeton Leroy, farmer, h 272 N California.
Templeton Maurice J, clk, h 225 Fletcher av.
Templeton Wm E, grand jury bailiff Sheriff's Office, h 455 Ash.
Teney Frank, lab, h 189 Indiana av.
Teney Stephen W, blksmith, 12 Michigan (H), h 22 Wilcox.
Ten Eyck Charles G, enameler, b 279 Douglass.
Ten Eyck Frank, cutter, b 279 Douglass.
Teneyck John, h 120 Indiana av.
Ten Eyck John, engr, h 279 Douglass.
Ten Eyck Richard F, shoemkr, 338 W Washington, h 369 W Vermont.
Teneyck Samuel H, salesman Gem Garment Co, h n w cor 30th and Meridian (M).
Ten Eyck Sarah A (wid Nelson), h e s Colorado av 1 n of Washington.
Ten Eyck Walter F, tailor, b 369 W Vermont.
Tennant Alexander F, clk, h 18 Lexington av.
Tenner Andreas, saloon, 499 S West, h same.
Tenner Frederick W, driver, h 519 S New Jersey.
Tenner John, clk, b 499 S West.
Tenney George S, fireman, h 69 Leota
Tenney Wm W, bkkpr Lilly Varnish Co, b 380 N Illinois.
TENNIS ALVA R, Chief Clerk Genl Agt's Office Erie Railroad Co, 46 W Washington, h 373 N Penn.
Tennis Wm H, gen agt Erie Railroad Co, 46 W Washington, h 373 N Penn.
Terhune Avery C, printer, b 124 E Washington.
Terhune Charles O, printer, h 61 N New Jersey.
Terhune Garrett, lab, h 122 S Summit.
Terhune George B, printer, r 220 N Capitol av.

EAT
HITZ'S CRACKERS
AND CAKES.
ASK YOUR GROCER FOR THEM.

BICYCLES $5 DOWN. MONTHLY. Best Wheels. Best Terms. WHEELMEN'S CO. 31 W. OHIO ST. LONG DISTANCE TEL. 1856.

J. H. TECKENBROCK General House Painter, 94 EAST SOUTH STREET.

FIDELITY MUTUAL LIFE—PHILADELPHIA, PA.
$75,000,000, Insurance In Force. $8,500,000, Death Losses Paid. $1,500,090, Surplus. A. H. COLLINS {General Agent, Baldwin Block.

BITUMINOUS COAL IN CAR LOADS TO DEALERS AND MANUFACTURERS. ROOMS 42 AND 43 WHEN BUILDING. Edwardsport Coal & Mining Co.

ESTABLISHED 1876. TELEPHONE 168.
CHESTER BRADFORD,
SOLICITOR OF PATENTS,
AND COUNSEL IN PATENT CAUSES.
(See adv. page 6.)
Office:—Rooms 14 and 16 Hubbard Block, S.W. Cor. Washington and Meridian Streets, INDIANAPOLIS, INDIANA.

Terhune Harry V, cashr, h 300 E New York.
Terhune Pearl, clk, b 122 S Summit.
Terhune Sarah (wid John), h 300 E New York.
Terhune Thomas J (Terhune & Moore), h 670 N Penn.
TERHUNE & MOORE (Thomas J Terhune, Frank F Moore), Lawyers, 404-406 Lemcke Bldg.
TERRE HAUTE BREWING CO, Maurice Donnelly Mngr, 148 S West, Tel 1664.
Terre Haute & Indianapolis R R Co, Volney T Malott receiver, 1006 Majestic bldg.
Terrell, see also Tyrrell.
Terrell Albert, lab, b 110 Ludlow av.
Terrell Beecher J (Thompson & Terrell), h w s Central av 2 s of Washington av (I).
Terrell Charles, lab, h 14 Ellen.
Terrell John J, blksmith, h 10 Lord.
Terrell Maverick, student, b 263 N Senate av.
Terrell Millie J, teacher Liberty Street Free Kindergarten, r 28 E New York.
Terrell Samuel N, lab, b 10 Lord.
Terrell Sarah E (wid Wm H H), h 486 Highland av (N I).
Terry Albert, foreman E C Atkins & Co, h 13 Columbia av.
Terry Charles J, foreman, h 69 S McLain (W I).
Terry Charles T, engr, b 28 S State av.
Terry George B, carp, r 579 Morris (W I).
Terry Henry M, bricklyr, b rear 362 Douglass.
Terry Horace D, clk, b 61 Elm.
Terry Isham, porter, b 28 Ellsworth.
Terry Lena (wid Frederick), b 187 S Illinois.
Terry Lincoln A, bkkpr, h 249 W New York.
Terry Lizzie J (wid John D), b 567 E Market.
Terry Mary A, h 61 Elm.
Terry Mary A (wid Wm R), b 28 Yandes.
Terry Oliver W, fireman, h 218 Randolph.
Terry Robert S, lab, h 166 Olive.

..MADE BY..
HAY & WILLIS MFG CO.
76 N. Pennsylvania St. Phone 598.

Terry Segious (wid Wm H), h 117 Columbia al.
Terry Thomas B, condr, h 186 N California.
Terwilliger Anson M, mach hd, h 519 W Eugene (N I).
Tesson Charles A, carver, h 36 Yandes.
Test Bertha (wid Charles), h 81 W Vermont.
Test Charles E, pres Inpls Chain and Stamping Co, h 98 Middle Drive (W P).
Test John C (W M Bird jr & Co), b 81 W Vermont.
Tetaz Henry L, huckster, h 352 Bellefontaine.
Tetaz Margaret, h e s Lake av 3 s of Washington av (I).
TETER HIRAM, Pres Union Insurance Co, Lawyer, 309-310 Lemcke Bldg, h 567 Broadway.
Teufel Flora (wid Gottfried), h 212 Madison av.
Teufel John, uphlr, b 212 Madison av.
Teuteberg Andrew H, grocer, 1249 E Washington, h same.
Tevebaugh Edward H, lab, h 197 Bates.
Tevebaugh Harry W, clk Penna lines, h 67 Hosbrook.
Tevebaugh Wm F, carp, h 3 Leota.
Tevis Charles S, clk Daniel Stewart Co, h w s Layman av 3 n of Washington av (I).
Tevis John S Rev, h 70 W 9th.
Tevis Milton J, mach hd, h 524 W Wells (N I).
Tevis Tillie (wid Joseph), h 10 Columbia al.
Texas Express Co, John J Henderson agt, 25 S Meridian.
Texton David R, foreman, r s s Railroad 1 e of Central av (I).
Thacker James L, carp, h 158 S William (W I).
Thaeter John A, gasfitter, h 1725 Graceland av.
Thaldorf George, lab, h 54 Cleaveland blk.
Thale Bernard M, lithog, h 222 Blackford.
Thale Bernardina (wid Bernard), b 944 N Delaware.
Thale Henry A, farmer, b 871 N Penn.
Thale Henry H, lithog, h 871 N Penn.
Thale John H, lithog, h 458 E Michigan.
Thale John W, bkkpr, b 871 N Penn.
Thale Joseph B, lithog, h 944 N Delaware.
Thalhamer Henry J, clk George J Mayer, b 327 S East.
Thalman Charles E, clk, b 29 Clifford av.
Thalman Harry, clk, b 29 Clifford av.
Thalman Isaac, b 553 E Washington.
Thamlan John, grocer, 29 Clifford av, h same.
Thalman John I, grocer, 661 W Eugene (N I), h same.
Tharp, see also Thorp.
Tharp Abraham B, clk, h w s Layman av 1 n of Washington av (I).
Tharp Charles W, b 292 E Morris.
Tharp Everett, carp, h 953 Wilcox.
Tharp George H, carp, h 242 Lafayette av.
Tharp James P, village marshal (H), h 18 Warman av (H).
Tharp Leonard, lab, b 18 Warman av (H).
Thatch Wm, waiter, r 3 Wood.
Thatcher Alva O, clk P C C & St L Ry, b 61 Tacoma av.
Thatcher Elwood, waiter, r 151 W Washington.
Thatcher Frank S, printer, b 151 High.
Thatcher Gertrude, teacher Public School No 25, b 151 High.
Thatcher Holman C, printer, b 151 High.
Thatcher James C, agt, h 26½ N Senate av.

C. ZIMMERMAN & SONS | SLATE AND GRAVEL ROOFERS 19 South East Street.

DRIVEN WELLS And Second Water Wells and Pumps of all kinds at CHARLES KRAUSS', 42 S. PENN. ST., Telephone 465.

ERTEL STEAM LAUNDRY 26 and 28 N. Senate Avenue. Telephone 1089. WE WILL CALL FOR AND DELIVER YOUR WORK. SATISFACTION GUARANTEED.

Thatcher James H, well driver, 151 High, h same.
Thatcher Jasper W, janitor Public School No 13, h 222 Buchanan.
Thatcher John C, molder, b 151 High.
Thatcher Sherman, bartndr, h 92 N New Jersey.
Thatcher Thomas T, carp, h e s Illinois 1 s of 30th.
Thau August B, baker, r 524 S East.
Thau Bernhardt, baker, 81 Hosbrook and 123 E Mkt House, h 81 Hosbrook.
Thau Gustav, baker, h 76 Hosbrook.
Thau John, b 81 Hosbrook.
Thayer Albert, coal, 2 John, h 379 Mass av.
Thayer Daniel W, trav agt, h 311 E Market.
Thayer Edward H (Thayer & Vannatta), h 190 E Morris.
Thayer Frank, clk, b 311 E Market.
Thayer Frank C, solr, h 211 E Ohio.
Thayer George W B, lab, h w s School 1 n of Wolf pike (B).
Thayer Ira K, student Holtzman & Leathers, b 375 Mass av.
Thayer Mary A (wid Daniel), h 311 E Market.
Thayer May S (wid Lee C), stenog F B Davenport, b 82 Randolph.
Thayer Nancy R (wid Daniel V), b 916 N New Jersey.
Thayer Oel L, sec Sun Publishing Co, h 159 Johnson av.
Thayer & Vannatta (Edward H Thayer, Daniel D Vannatta), furniture, 133 E Washington.
Theamann Herman H, veneer cutter, h 323 E Walnut.
Theil Albert, lab, h 155 Church.
Theil Paul, clk, b 155 Church.
Theis Charles A, trav agt The Home Stove Co, h 318 N Alabama.
Theis Henry C, molder, h 106 Torbet.
Theis Joseph E, mach, h 88 John.
Theis Mary, dressmkr, 88 John, h same.
Theising Frank, painter, b n s E Washington 5 e of Belt R R.
Theising Gustave M, carp, h 541 Jefferson av.
Theising Henry A, shoemkr, 150 Agnes, h same.
Theising Thomas A, lab, b 150 Agnes.
Thelen Charles, uphlr, h 132 N Dorman.
Theurer Frank, lab, b 317 W Morris.
Theurer J George, lab, h 317 W Morris.
Thicksten Emerson C, clk, b 142 Hoyt av.
Thicksten Nathan E, clk, b 142 Hoyt av.
Thicksten Thomas E, cutter, b 142 Hoyt av.
Thicksten Wm W, gateman Union Station, h 142 Hoyt av.
Thiecke Ella, dressmkr, 112 Spann av, h same.
Thiecke Ella M, teacher Public School No 15, b 320 E McCarty.
Thiecke Mary A (wid John A), b 320 E McCarty.
Thiecke Rudolph P, harnessmkr, h 483 S New Jersey.
Thiecke Wm D, lab, h 212 S Linden.
Thiel Henry L, turner, h 121 Palmer.
Thiel John H, finisher, b 121 Palmer.
Thiele Albert R, gasfitter, b 473 N Illinois.
Thiele Arthur E, lab, b 17 Grant.
Thiele Emil, butcher, h 159 Fayette.
Thiele Herman, cabtmkr, b 159 Fayette.
Thiele Herman E, clk, b 473 N Illinois.
Thiele Louis C (Stumpf & Thiele), b 473 N Illinois.
Thiele Mary (wid Herman), h 473 N Illinois.

EQUITABLE LIFE ASSURANCE SOCIETY OF THE UNITED STATES. RICHARDSON & McCREA Managers for Central Indiana, 79 East Market St. Telephone 182.

Thiele Oliver W, furnace setter, b 473 N Illinois.
Thielmann Charles, hardware, 144 College av, h 55 Omer.
Thiemann Frederick H, mach, h 23 Larch.
Thieme Louis, carp, 490 E Washington, h 115 Meek.
Thienes Henry, cigarmkr, h 204 Clifford av.
Thienes Peter, printer, h 479 N Alabama.
Thiesing Charles J, lab, h 48 Langley av.
Thiesing Henry H, mach hd, b 28 Hillside av.
Thiesing Louis A, lab, h 28 Hillside av.
Thiesing Wm F, foreman, h 129 N Gillard av.
Thisselle Wm J, teacher Industrial School, h 191 Blake.
Thistlethwaite Clemens, clk Sloan Drug Co, r 400 N Illinois.
Thistlethwaite Margaret A (wid Wm), h 204 W New York.
Thixton Thomas E, cutter, b 142 Hoyt av.
Thoeny John J, cashr Clemens Vonnegut, b e s Bluff rd 1 s of Pleasant run.
Thoman Anthony, tiremkr, h 78 Benton.
Thoman Clemens H, clk, b 567 S East.
Thoman Peter, clk, b 567 S East.
Thomas Ada C (wid James G), h 524 N Capitol av.
Thomas Aimee A, bkkpr, b 106 College av.
Thomas Albert, bricklyr, h 70 Hill av.
Thomas Albert D, asst treas L E & W R R, h 19 West Drive (W P).
Thomas Albert M, lab, b 133 W Michigan.
Thomas Andrew, lab, h 1474 N Senate av.
Thomas Anna M (wid Elias B), h 212 Hoyt av.
Thomas Archibald C, salesman J C Perry & Co, b 115 N Noble.
Thomas Arthur C, paymaster L E & W R R, h 157 East Drive (W P).
Thomas Arthur S, tel opr, b 82 Hosbrook.
Thomas Benjamin E, creamery, 256 Blake, h 262 same.
Thomas Benjamin F, watchman, h 68 Minerva.
Thomas Busch R, barber, h 115 W 6th.
Thomas Catherine (wid Robert), b 170 Cornell av.

STENOGRAPHERS FURNISHED. EXPERIENCED OR BEGINNERS, PERMANENT OR TEMPORARY. S. H. EAST, State Agent, The Williams Typewriter, 55 THORPE BLOCK. 87 EAST MARKET ST.

ELLIS & HELFENBERGER { ENTERPRISE FOUNDRY & FENCE CO. 162-170 S. Senate Ave. Tel. 958.

THE HOGAN TRANSFER AND STORAGE COMP'Y
Household Goods and Pianos Moved—Packed—Stored...... Baggage and Package Express Machinery and Safes a Specialty Cor. Washington and Illinois Sts. TELEPHONE No. 675.

Hose, Belting, Packing, Clothing, Druggists' Sundries, Bicycle Tires, Cotton Hose, Etc. New York Belting & Packing Co., L't'd.
The Central Rubber & Supply Co. PHONES 79 S. ILLINOIS ST.: INDIANAPOLIS, IND.

A death rate below all other American Companies, and dividends from this source correspondingly larger.
The Provident Life and Trust Company
Of Philadelphia.
D. W. EDWARDS, General Agent,
508 Indiana Trust Building.

Thomas Charles, cook, h 182 W 2d.
Thomas Charles, tinner, 476 W Michigan, h 141 Minerva.
Thomas Charles E, lab, n 54 S Belmont av (W I).
Thomas Charles E, patternmkr, b 68 Minerva.
Thomas Charles H, real est, 10½ N Delaware, h 321 S Olive.
Thomas Charles S, porter, b 445 W 1st.
Thomas Clarence C, decorator, h 217 Virginia av.
Thomas Crawford, carp, 1324 N Alabama, h same.
Thomas Cyrus H, stairbldr, h 37 Ingraham.
Thomas Daniel A, lab, b 217 W Court.
Thomas David F, lab, h 568 W Michigan.
Thomas Edward, lab, b 359 S Illinois.
Thomas Edward, lab, b 272 W Maryland.
Thomas Edward, lab, b 198 Middle.
Thomas Edward A, lab, b 568 W Michigan.
Thomas Edwin C, phys, 235 Blake, h same.
Thomas Eli W, dairy, e s Dayton av 1 s of English av (I), h same.
Thomas Elisha, b 411 W North.
Thomas Eliza E (wid John), h 219 N Alabama.
Thomas Ervin D, tmstr, b 156 Johnson (W I).
Thomas Evan C, bkkpr, b 38 West Drive (W P).
Thomas Ezra E, lineman, b 95 N Meridian.
Thomas Fannie (wid Oliver E), h 69 N Liberty.
Thomas Francis M, lab, h 433 Mulberry.
Thomas Frank, engr, h s s Vorster av 1 w of Milburn (M P).
Thomas Frederick D, porter, b 169 W 5th.
Thomas Frederick L, bkkpr Van Camp Packing Co, h 241 Central av.
Thomas George, carp, r 205½ W Ohio.
Thomas George, lab, b 156 Johnson (W I).
Thomas George, lab, b 172 E Louisiana.
Thomas George, porter, b 114 Agnes.
Thomas George A, tinner, h n w cor Sheffield and Grandview av (H).
Thomas George B, lab, h 72 Hazel.
Thomas George H, b 144 Blackford.
Thomas George W, agt, h 268 E Pearl.

Julius C. Walk & Son,
Jewelers
Indianapolis.
12 EAST WASHINGTON ST.

Thomas George W, blksmith, h 103 W South.
Thomas Harry C, pressman, b 219 W St Clair.
Thomas Harry E, yardmaster, h 340 Fletcher av.
Thomas Harry H, mach, h 293 Cornell av.
Thomas Harry S, b 276 N Capitol av.
Thomas Harry S, miller, h 162 Blake.
Thomas Henry, lab, h 172 Agnes.
Thomas Henry, lab, b 28 Standard av (W I).
Thomas Henry, lab, h 244 W 3d.
Thomas Henry, molder, r 193 W Washington.
Thomas Henry, porter, b 82 Talbott.
Thomas Henry A, lab, b 57 Smith.
Thomas Henry E, bkkpr Indiana School Book Co, b 276 N Capitol av.
Thomas Henry P, mer police, h 106 College av.
Thomas Herman B, trav agt, h 1318 N Capitol av.
Thomas Horace J, clk, h 70 Hoyt av.
Thomas Howard, barber, b 103 W South.
Thomas Jacob H, lab, h 28 N Judge Harding (W I).
Thomas James, lab, h 173 Alvord.
Thomas James, lab, b 34 St Paul.
Thomas James, lab, h 436 Blake.
Thomas James, lab, h 165 W 2d.
Thomas James, lab, b 225 W Vermont.
Thomas James, porter, b 178 S Illinois.
Thomas James A (Leonard & Thomas), b 181 S Illinois.
Thomas James A, bricklyr, h 166 Fayette.
Thomas James E, lab, b 173 Alvord.
Thomas James E, clk W U Tel Co, h 38 East Drive (W P).
Thomas James H, janitor, h 18 Brett.
Thomas James H, carp, r 44½ N Penn.
Thomas James W, lab, h 176 S Missouri.
Thomas Jeremiah, driver, h 82 Martindale av.
Thomas Jesse A, asst Henry W Tutewiler, r 42 Hubbard blk.
Thomas Jesse C, lab, h 876 S Meridian.
Thomas John, foreman Hogan Transfer and Storage Co, h 206½ S Meridian.
Thomas John, lab, r 173 E Court.
Thomas John, lab, h s s 8th 3 w of canal.
Thomas John, lab, b 1 Guffin.
Thomas John, lab, b 219 N West.
Thomas John, pres Hecla Consolidated Mining Co, b 750 N Meridian.
Thomas John, express, h 257 Prospect.
Thomas John, weighmaster, b 55 S McLain (W I).
Thomas John A, molder, b Illinois House.
Thomas John C, grocer, 247 N Noble, h 115 same.
Thomas John H, bartndr, b Senate Hotel.
Thomas John H, lab, b 450 Lincoln av.
Thomas John M, tmstr, h 156 Johnson (W I).
Thomas John R, painter, h 32 Hiawatha.
Thomas John S, timekpr Atlas Engine Works, h 331 Yandes.
Thomas John W, lab, b 173 Alvord.
Thomas John W, uphlr, b 876 S Meridian.
Thomas Joseph, lab, h 400 Yandes.
Thomas Joseph P E, salesman Murphy, Hibben & Co, h 450 Central av.
Thomas Joseph T, dyer, 57 Indiana av, h 219 W St Clair.
Thomas Julius, lab 608 Central av.
Thomas Lelia M, stenog The McGilliard Agency Co, b 219 N Alabama.
Thomas Lewis A, engr, h 231 Virginia av.

OTTO GAS ENGINES | BUILDERS' EXCHANGE S. W. Cor. Ohio and Penn. Telephone 535.

Becker & Son Charles Becker Jacob Becker Jr. Merchant Tailors. 21 N. Penn. St. Tel. 934

Thomas Linnie, h rear 273 S West.
Thomas Lizzie (wid Zachariah T), grocer, 55 S McLain (W I), h same.
Thomas Louis D, clk, h 235 E Ohio.
Thomas Louis P, carp, h 39 Blake.
Thomas Luke C, lab, b 207 W 4th.
Thomas Marcus H, student, b 212 Hoyt av.
Thomas Marion C, driver, b 176 S Missouri.
Thomas Marshal, lab, h 324 W Court.
Thomas Martha A (wid James C), h 256½ Indiana av.
Thomas Martha E (wid James W), h 350 N West.
Thomas Martin, lab, b 244 W 3d.
Thomas Mary (wid Henry), b 749 N Senate av.
Thomas Mary A (wid Wm T), h 193 College av.
Thomas Mary J, milliner L S Ayres & Co, b 486 College av.
Thomas Mason, carp, h 185½ Indiana av.
Thomas Minnie M, h 91 Highland pl.
Thomas Minnehaha, teacher, b e s Dayton av 1 s of English av (I).
Thomas Nelson, lab, h 254 S William (W I).
Thomas Olive P (wid James), b 679 College av.
Thomas Oliver H, dentist, h 67 Hudson.
Thomas Oscar G, printer, h 34 N Beville av.
Thomas Oscar H, mach, b 106 College av.
Thomas Richard, sec and treas Cerealine Mnfg Co, b The Denison.
Thomas Robert, h 265 Howard.
Thomas Robert P, painter, h 45 Drake.
Thomas Samuel, bellman, b 26 Roanoke.
Thomas Samuel, lab, h 331 Yandes.
Thomas Samuel S, baggageman, h 69 N State av.
Thomas Sanford E, ins agt, h e s Colorado av 2 n of Washington.
Thomas Stephen H, lab, h 92 Newman.
Thomas Traugott, cabtmkr, h 611 Mass av.
Thomas Viretta E (wid Charlton), nurse 100 Stoughton av, b same.
Thomas Walter K K, bkkpr, b 115 N Noble.
Thomas Walter S, clk, b 229 Virginia av.
Thomas Wm, agt, h 902 W Washington.
Thomas Wm, cabtmkr, b 611 Mass av.
Thomas Wm, lab, b 27 Hosbrook.
Thomas Wm, lab, b 218 E Wabash.
Thomas Wm A, trav agt, h 175 W Michigan.
Thomas Wm C, lab, b 265 Howard.
Thomas Wm C, tmstr, b 156 Johnson (W I).
Thomas Wm E, barber, 141 Cornell av, h same.
Thomas Wm F, bartndr, h 264 E Wabash.
Thomas Wm H, carp, h 77 S West.
Thomas Wm H, clk Hecla Consolidated Mining Co, h 420 College av.
Thomas Wm H, phys, 285 Virginia av, h same.
Thomas Wm I, foreman, b 95 N Meridian.
Thomas Wm J, lab, b e s Dayton av 1 s of English av (I).
Thomas Wm J, tmstr, h 176 S Missouri.
Thomas Wm S, clk Indiana Natl Bank, h 1324 N Alabama.
Thomas Winfield S, engr, h 27 Greer.
Thomas W Marshall, sec and genl mngr The Indiana Retail Merchants' Assn, h 96 Ramsey av.
Thomes Elmer, lab, r 222 W 8th.
Thompson, see also Thomson.
Thompson Abijah P, pdlr, h 120 Duncan.
Thompson Abraham, driver, h 295 Shelby.

Henry H. Fay,
40½ E. Washington St.,
REAL ESTATE,
AND LOAN BROKER.

Thompson Alexander, lab, b 237 W Maryland.
Thompson Alexander E, carp, h 251 S Capitol av.
Thompson Alfred, mach hd, h 664 E St Clair.
Thompson Alice, h 117 Roanoke.
Thompson Andrew, barber, r 111 Indiana av.
Thompson Andrew, lab, h 189 W 3d.
Thompson Anna (wid Charles A), tailoress, b 170 Union.
Thompson Anna, author, b 36 Leon.
Thompson Anson H, agt, h 1518 Kenwood av.
Thompson Arthur R, lab, b 483 Virginia av.
Thompson Atlas, b 208 River av (W I).
Thompson Atlas M, painter, h 19 Woodburn av (W I).
Thompson Augustin S, grocer, 221½ W Washington, h 230½ same.
Thompson Augustus W, carp, h 171½ E Washington.
Thompson Beauford, lab, h 395 Roanoke.
Thompson Catherine, h 16 Sullivan.
Thompson Catherine (wid Eli), h 9 Hester.
Thompson Catherine (wid Peleg), h 287 Indiana av.
Thompson Charles C, engr, h 174 Laurel.
Thompson Charles G, lab, h 74½ Mayhew.
Thompson Charles G, saloon, 1400 Northwestern av (N I), h same.
Thompson Charles L, trav agt, h 48 Cherry.
Thompson Charles N (Carson & Thompson), h 874 N Penn.
Thompson Charles N, switchman, h 166 Hoyt av.
Thompson Clarence, lab, b 75 Rhode Island.
Thompson Clarence W, driver, h 76 Hill av.
Thompson Claude C, clk, b 53 Dearborn.
Thompson Claude W, retoucher, h 8½ N Penn.
Thompson Clifford A, condr, b 105 Patterson.
Thompson Crayton W, carp, h 176 N Missouri.
Thompson C Frank, lab, b 271 S Delaware.
THOMPSON DANIEL A, Physician (Eye and Ear), 22 W Ohio, h 1114 N Penn.

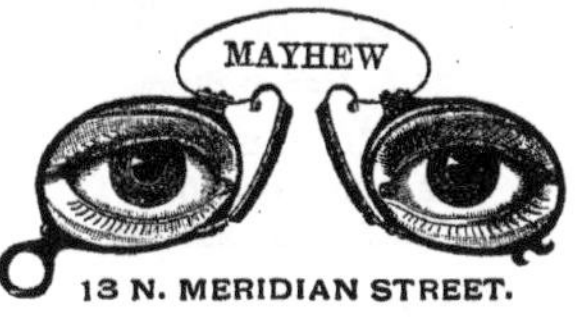

SALISBURY & STANLEY
Office, Store and Bank Fixtures.
Contractors and Builders. Repairing of all kinds done on short notice. 177 Clinton St., Indianapolis, Ind. Telephone 909.

LIME, CEMENT, PLASTER FIRE BRICK AND CLAY SEWER PIPE, ETC. BALKE & KRAUSS CO., Cor. Market and Missouri Streets.

C. FRIEDGEN HAS THE FINEST STOCK OF LADIES' PARTY SLIPPERS and SHOES 19 NORTH PENNSYLVANIA ST.

SAMUEL LAING ▸ TIN, SLATE AND STEEL ROOFING 72 AND 74 EAST COURT STREET.

M. B. WILSON, Pres. W. F. CHURCHMAN, Cash.

THE CAPITAL NATIONAL BANK,

INDIANAPOLIS, IND.

Pays Interest on Time Certificates of Deposit.
Buys and Sells Foreign Exchange at Low Rates.

Capital, - - $300,000
Surplus and Earnings, 50,000

No. 28 S. Meridian St., Cor. Pearl.

Thompson Daniel E, handlemkr, r 5½ Shelby.
Thompson Daniel I, b 36 Hendricks.
Thompson David, tmstr, b 1366 N Senate av.
Thompson David, tmstr, h 21 Woodburn av (W I).
Thompson Edgar L, clk, b 280 Bright.
Thompson Edmond, mach hd, b 124 Weghorst.
Thompson Edward, clk H P Wasson & Co, h 560 E Market.
Thompson Edward, trav agt, b 203 N West.
Thompson Edward C, banker, h s e cor Downey and University avs (I).
Thompson Edward J, h 167 E Vermont.
Thompson Edward M, fireman, h 263 English av.
Thompson Edward P, sec Board of Regents, State Soldiers' and Sailors' Monument, 93 State House, h 278 Central av.
Thompson Edwin S, carp, h rear 312 S Missouri.
Thompson Elizabeth (wid Henry), h 1366 N Senate av.
Thompson Ella, h 12 McCauley.
Thompson Ella E, teacher Public School No 27, b 666 E St Clair.
Thompson Ellen F (wid John A), h 164 Johnson av.
Thompson Elwood C, condr, h 29 W McCarty.
Thompson Ernest R, lab, b 21 Alvord.
Thompson Eugene, waiter The Bates.
Thompson Eugene C, feed, 317 Mass av, h 239 Ramsey av.
Thompson Everett J, lab, h 113 Harrison.
Thompson Evert M, pres and treas Handle-Hoop Tub Co, h 629 N Illinois.
Thompson Flora L (wid Joseph E), h rear 16 Sullivan.
Thompson Frances, teacher Deaf and Dumb Inst, b 273 N Illinois.
Thompson Frank, brakeman, b 57 English av.
Thompson Frank E, insp, h 140 Walcott.
Thompson Frank M, motorman, b 370 Cornell av.
Thompson Frank V, brakeman, b 57 English av.

TUTTLE & SEGUIN,

28 E. Market Street.

Fire Insurance,
Real Estate, Loan
and Rental Agents.

TELEPHONE 1168.

Thompson Frederick, clk, b 203 N West.
Thompson George, gardener, h 946 S East.
Thompson George, lab, h 117 N Missouri.
Thompson George, tmstr, b 1366 N Senate av.
Thompson George B, steward Spencer House.
Thompson George C W, h 8½ N Penn.
Thompson George E, plastr, b 1148 E Ohio.
Thompson George H, mach hd, h 24 Edward (W I).
Thompson George R, lab, h 294 S Missouri.
Thompson George W, carp, h w s Central av 1 s of Grand av (I).
Thompson George W, carp, h 9 Hester.
Thompson George W, janitor, r 5 E Washington.
Thompson Gideon B, state editor The Indpls News, h 460 College av.
Thompson Harry G, weighmaster, b 280 Bright.
Thompson Harvey, tmstr, b w s Baltimore av 2 n of 22d.
Thompson Harvey M, clk, h cor 6th and West.
Thompson Henry, lab, h 192 N Missouri.
Thompson Henry, lab, r 244 W 3d.
Thompson Henry B, lab, h 94 N Dorman.
Thompson Henry F, real est, r 9 Wyandot blk.
Thompson Henry H Rev, h 61 Harlan.
Thompson Henry H, collr, h 45 Indiana av.
Thompson Henry H, lab, h 394 Yandes.
Thompson Henry J, barber, r 111 Indiana av.
Thompson Hibben H, fireman, h 164 Johnson av.
Thompson Howard T, clk R M S, h 125 Irwin.
Thompson Hugh C, engr, h 181 S William (W I).
Thompson Ida, laundress, h 160 Bird.
Thompson James B, brass founder, h 33 Holmes av (H).
Thompson James C, clk, b 53 Dearborn.
Thompson James D, driver, h 276 River av (W I).
Thompson James E, clk, h 231 Hadley av (W I).
Thompson James H, lab, h 46 King av (H).
THOMPSON JAMES L, Physician (Eye and Ear), 22 W Ohio, h 97 E Michigan.
Thompson James M, lab, b 251 W Morris.
Thompson James N, blksmith, h 112 Singleton.
Thompson James R, mach hd, b 124 Weghorst.
Thompson James S (Lawrence & Thompson), h 927 N Alabama.
Thompson James W, brakeman, h 35 McKim av.
Thompson James W, lab, b 121 S Spruce.
Thompson Jane (wid Portan), h 162 Howard.
Thompson Jefferson, lab, h 220 Yandes.
Thompson Jesse L, press feeder, b 29 W McCarty.
Thompson John, driver, h 21 Alvord.
Thompson John, lab, h 199 S Belmont av (W I).
Thompson John, lab, b 205 Douglass.
Thompson John, lab, b 181 S William (W I).
Thompson John, presser, b 18 Bates.
Thompson John A, h 38 Drake.
Thompson John F, carp, h 55 Langley av.
Thompson John H, lab, h 149½ King av (H).

SULLIVAN & MAHAN Manufacturers of all kinds of PAPER BOXES 41 W. Pearl St.

DIAMOND WALL PLASTER { Telephone 1410 BUILDERS' EXCHANGE.

Telephone 1769. 197 S. Illinois St. } THE HOME LAUNDRY { WORK CALLED FOR AND DELIVERED.

Thompson John H, patternmkr, h e s Lincoln av 5 s of Jackson (M J).
Thompson John M Rev, h 569 S State av.
Thompson John W, brakeman, h 35 McKim av.
Thompson John W, lab, b 21 Alvord.
Thompson Joseph, grocer, 227 W Michigan, b 229 same.
Thompson Joseph, huckster, h 271 S Delaware.
Thompson Julia, b 1000 N Meridian.
Thompson Kate A, teacher Industrial School, r 86 Fletcher av.
Thompson Laura, h 29 W McCarty.
Thompson Lawrence, lab, h 21 Columbia al.
Thompson Lawrence M, carp, h 53 Division (W I).
Thompson Lee F, polisher, h 24 Abbott.
Thompson Lewis, coachman 935 N Meridian.
Thompson Lewis C, furniture, 293 Christian av, h 53 Bellefontaine.
Thompson Lollie (wid Daniel), b 39 Malott av.
Thompson Lovina M, nurse, h 92 Cornell av.
Thompson Lucinda (wid Wm J), h 417 Coburn.
Thompson Lydia A (wid Uriah), h 44 Bradshaw.
Thompson Maro R, clk, h 1560 N Capitol av.
Thompson Marshall O, lab, b 203 N West.
Thompson Martin, cooper, h 581 W 22d (N I).
Thompson Mary, h 23 Rhode Island.
Thompson Mary (wid Frank), h 152 Maple.
Thompson Mary (wid John), h 33 Johnson av.
Thompson Mary A (wid Lewis O), b 194 N Illinois.
Thompson Mary F (wid Wm H) h 280 Bright.
Thompson Matthew, lab, h 320 Blake.
Thompson Millard, hostler, r 267 W Pearl.
Thompson Milton F, clk State Statistician, b 122 E Pratt.
Thompson Moses bicycle rep, n w cor Michigan and Bismarck av (H), h same.
Thompson Myrtle M, stenog Henry R Worthngton, h Broad Ripple, Ind.
Thompson Oliver N, carp, h 38 Miley av.
Thompson Omer J, clk, h 44 Bradshaw.
Thompson Perry, waiter, h 220 Indiana av.
Thompson Ralph R, clk, b rear 18 Sullivan.
Thompson Raymond C, clk, b 460 College av.
Thompson Rebecca C (wid George W), h 53 Dearborn.
Thompson Richard N, porter h 312 W Pratt.
Thompson Robert, student, r 82 E Michigan.
Thompson Robert A, h 203 N West.
Thompson Robert G, lab, b 294 S Missouri.
Thompson Robert W (Osgood & Thompson), h 53 Bellefontaine.
Thompson Rollie, tmstr, h 381 Martindale av.
Thompson Samuel, lab, h 9 Rose.
Thompson Samuel H, tinner, h 530 S East.
Thompson Sarah (wid James), b 122 W Maryland.
Thompson Sarah A (wid Staples B), b 560 E Market.
Thompson Sarah E (wid Wm), b cor 6th and West.
Thompson Sarah H (wid Edwin J) b 36 S Judge Harding (W I).

FRANK NESSLER. WILL H. ROST.
FRANK NESSLER & CO.
Tailors
56 EAST MARKET ST. (Lemcke Building),
INDIANAPOLIS, IND.

Thompson Sarah H, dressmkr, 423 Muskingum al, h same.
Thompson Savannah P, butcher, h w s Caroline av 1 n of Hillside av.
THOMPSON SIMEON J, Chief Indiana Bureau of Statistics, Room 33 State House, h 122 E Pratt.
Thompson Squire, stockbuyer, h 463 W Addison (N I).
Thompson Stiles E, aeronaut, b 36 Osgood (W I).
Thompson Thomas, driver, h s s Wilcox 3 w of river.
Thompson Thomas, lab, b 1366 N Senate av.
Thompson Thomas J, clk L E & W R R, h 143 N Alabama.
Thompson Thomas L (Thompson & Terrell), h s e cor Washington and Johnson avs (I).
Thompson Thomas L, pres Central Chair Co, h 940 N Capitol av.
Thompson Walter C, paperhngr, 359 Coburn, h same.
Thompson Walter H, checkman, h 67 Orange.
Thompson Walter J, lab, h 191 W 3d.
Thompson Wm, bellman Grand Hotel.
Thompson Wm, carp, h 132 Hosbrook.
Thompson Wm, cooper, h 855 Rembrant.
Thompson Wm, feed, 100 Ft Wayne av, h 890 N Senate av.
Thompson Wm, fireman, b 20 Orange av.
Thompson Wm A, lab, h 106 Singleton.
Thompson Wm B, city fireman, b 370 Cornell av.
Thompson Wm B, clk H P Wasson & Co, b 560 E Market.
Thompson Wm C, lawyer, 35 Baldwin blk, h e s Illinois 2 n of 29th.
Thompson Wm C, phys, h 73 W Ohio.
Thompson Wm E, huckster, h 577 E 7th.
Thompson Wm H, blksmith, h 294 E Merrill.
Thompson Wm H, janitor, h 356 W 2d.
Thompson Wm H, lineman, h 688 E Market.
Thompson Wm H, student, b 236 E Vermont.

Haueisen & Hartmann
163-169 E. Washington St.
FURNITURE,
Carpets,
Household Goods,
Tin, Granite and China Wares, Oil Cloth and Shades

THE WM. H. BLOCK CO. 7 AND 9 EAST WASHINGTON STREET. DRY GOODS, HOUSE FURNISHINGS AND CROCKERY.

London Guarantee and Accident Co. (Ltd.) Employers', Public and Teams' Liability. Workmen's Collective Insurance and Fidelity Bonds
GEORGE W. PANGBORN, General Agent, 704-706 Lemcke Bldg. Telephone 140.

Reasonable Rates. Reliable Fire Insurance. 74 E. MARKET STREET. Telephone 8. FRANK K. SAWYER

JOSEPH GARDNER,
TIN, IRON, STEEL AND SLATE ROOFING,
GALVANIZED IRON CORNICES & SKYLIGHTS.
37, 39 & 41 KENTUCKY AVE. Telephone 322.

Thompson Wm J, janitor, h 959 N New Jersey.
Thompson Wm L, lab, r 318 W North.
Thompson Wm O, lab, b w s Caroline av 1 n of Hillside av.
Thompson Wm R, h 96 W New York.
Thompson Wm S, lumber insp, h 666 E St Clair.
Thompson Wm S, molder, h 277 River av (W I).
Thompson Willis, janitor, h 331 Alvord.
Thompson Willis H, clk, b 203 N West.
THOMPSON & TERRELL (Thomas L Thompson, Beecher J Terrell), Physicians, n w cor Central av and P C C & St L Ry (I).
Thoms Albert H, sec The Fred Dietz Co, h 752 N New Jersey.
Thoms Ella, milliner, h 48 N East.
Thoms Frederick W, packer, h 19 S Dorman.
Thoms George R, mach, h 644 E Ohio.
Thoms Henry E, clk Indpls Mnfg Co, h 178 Union.
Thoms Herman E (H E Frauer & Co), h 624 E Ohio.
Thoms Mathilda (wid Frederick W), h 76 N East.
Thomsen Thomas C, carp, h 10 Spann av.
Thomson, see also Thompson.
Thomson Albert F, mach, b 213 Blake.
Thomson Alexander, engr, h 1065 W Washington.
Thomson Alexander W, grain, 34 Board of Trade, h 590 College av.
Thomson Amanda, h 194 Cherry.
Thomson Bessie A, solr, b 194 Cherry.
Thomson Charles M, city agt Home Cracker Co, b 447 N New Jersey.
Thomson Claude L, mach, b 194 Cherry.
THOMSON COMPRESSED YEAST CO, Henry R Thomson Propr, 269-271 E McCarty.
Thomson Elizabeth (wid James), h 590 College av.
Thomson Ella M, bkkpr Regal Mnfg Co, b 515½ S New Jersey.

J. S. FARRELL & CO.
STEAM AND HOT WATER
HEATING AND PLUMBING
CONTRACTORS
84 North Illinois Street. Telephone 382.

Thomson Guy R, boilermkr, b 194 Cherry.
Thomson Henry, b 515½ S New Jersey.
Thomson Henry C (James R Ross & Co), h 944 N Alabama.
Thomson Henry R, propr Regal Mnfg Co and Thomson Compressed Yeast Co, r 558 S New Jersey.
Thomson James E, bleacher, h 213 Blake.
Thomson Jennie C, music teacher, b 194 Cherry.
Thomson John A, lab, h 119 Bright.
Thomson John W, condr, h 478 Highland av.
Thomson Richard M, grocer, 315 W Washington, h same.
Thomson Margaret J (wid Hugh), h 515½ S New Jersey.
Thomson Maud M, solr, b 194 Cherry.
Thoren Charles H, mach, h 234 Shelby.
Thormyer George, h e s Lake av 5 s of Washington av (I).
Thorn Charles P, baggageman, r 117 S Illinois.
Thorn Ellen E (wid Wm), b 94 Broadway.
Thorn Jennie (wid Charles), h 154 Madison av.
Thorn Wm, chief clk comm agt Vandalia Lines, b 94 Broadway.
Thornberg Jesse S, painter, h 288 Highland av.
Thornberry Adeline, stenog, b 191 S East.
Thornberry Charles, tmstr, b 182 S William (W I).
Thornberry George L, carp, b 406 Virginia av.
Thornberry John, hostler, r 23 Monument pl.
Thornberry John R, cigarmkr, b 176 E South.
Thornberry Sarah E (wid Thomas B), h 182 S William (W I).
Thornberry Susan (wid George), h 176 E South.
Thornberry Wm M, finisher, h 682 E St Clair.
Thornbrough Henry, carp, h 37 Decatur.
Thornburg Alva A, polisher, b 164 Coburn.
Thornburg George D, clk, b 90 Fulton.
Thornburg James F, bkkpr, h 278 E St Clair.
Thornburg Joseph A, carp, 313 Mass av, h same.
Thornburg Oliver M, brakeman, h 311 S Penn.
Thornburg Samuel, carp, b 313 Mass av.
Thornburg Sarah (wid Jonathan), h 164 Coburn.
Thornburg Wm W, produce, E Mkt House, h n end Maxwell av (I).
Thornburgh John W, car rep, h 114 Wright.
THORNBURGH THOMAS R, Druggist, 190 Ft Wayne av, h 731 N New Jersey, Tel 195.
Thornburrow Wm D, trav agt, r 203 N Illinois.
Thorne Charles, restaurant, 60 W Market, h 33 Stewart pl.
Thorne John C, butcher, h 596 N West.
Thorne John R, carp, h 1136 N New Jersey.
Thorne Joseph, butcher, b 596 N West.
Thorne Marcus O, painter, 217 Buchanan, h same.
Thorne Samuel A, driver, h 32 Rhode Island.
Thorne Vinton S, porter, r 10 Athon.
Thorne Wm, clk, h 740 S East.
Thornell Harriet M (wid Nathaniel), h 30 N Beville av.

POLICIES IN UNITED STATES LIFE INSURANCE CO., offer indemnity against death, liberal cash surrender value or at option of policy-holder, fully paid-up life insurance or liberal life income. E. B. SWIFT, M'g'r, 25 E. Market St.

WM. KOTTEMAN 89 & 91 E. Washington St. Telephone 1742 WILL FURNISH YOUR HOUSE COMPLETE

SHOW CASES WILLIAM WIEGEL 6 West Louisiana Street Opp. Union Station.

Thornsbrough Luella (wid John F), h 88 Holmes av (H).
Thornton Albert B, barber, r 15 Russell av.
Thornton Benjamin T, detective, h 295 Bright.
Thornton Charles, lab, r 237 E South.
Thornton Charles E, pres Indiana Society for Savings, h 236 Broadway.
Thornton Delia, h 168½ E Washington.
Thornton Edith S, waiter, r 230½ E Washington.
Thornton Elizabeth (wid Edward), h w s canal 4 s of 7th.
Thornton Essie M, h 295 Bright.
Thornton Frank, lab, h w s Northwestern av 4 s of 30th (N I).
Thornton Henry C (Baker & Thornton), h 811 N Delaware.
Thornton James S, molder, h 184 Tremont av (H).
Thornton John, lab, b n s 8th 2 w of canal.
Thornton Joseph, b 159 W McCarty.
Thornton Leonard, cook, b 369 Lafayette.
Thornton Margaret (wid John), h 108 N Missouri.
Thornton Melinda I (wid Daniel T), h 274 College av.
Thornton Sarah (wid John), b 42 College av.
Thornton Thomas F, molder, h 10 Wilcox.
Thornton Wm, patternmkr, b 46 S Capitol av.
Thornton Wm W (Blackledge & Thornton), h 1011 N Delaware.
Thorp, see also Tharp.
Thorp Frank, lab, b e s James 6 n of Sutherland (B).
Thorp Henry, lab, h 108 Shepard (W I).
Thorp Jesse, janitor, b 113 Kappus (W I).
Thorp John, plumber, h 386 W North.
Thorp John H, presser, h 88 W Ohio.
Thorp Robert, lab, h e s James 6 n of Sutherland (B).
Thorp Smith, lab, h 139 Davidson.
Thorpe Alfred, barber, r 25 S West.
Thorpe Block Savings and Loan Assn, J Kirk Wright sec, 83 E Market.
Thorpe Sandford, dynamo tndr, h rear 211 Kentucky av.
Thrasher Samuel L, motorman, h 120 Cleveland (H).
Thrasher Wm M, prof Butler College, h s s Washington av 2 e of Cherry av (I).
Thrift Delilah (wid Jesse), b 31 Center.
Thrift Edward J, waiter, h 108½ Mass av.
Throckmorton Ora E, student, h 125 Elm.
Throm Alois, cook, b 60 S Delaware.
Throm Frank, varnisher, h 410 Harrison av.
Throm Herman, framer, b rear 10 Gatling.
Throm John, butcher, r 310 E Market.
Throm Joseph, butcher, h 327 Columbia av.
Throm Katherine (wid Louis), h 23 Gresham.
Throne David, clk, r 8 Catterson blk.
Thrun Wilhelmina (wid Wm), h e s Wallack 1 s of Pleasant run.
Thrush George A, carp, h 636 Home av.
Thrush Harry J, mer police, h 120 Greer.
Thrush Ora T, lineman, b 319 S Meridain.
Thudium Harry O, pres The Gutenberg Co, h 416 N New Jersey.
Thuemmler Harriet M (wid Edward), h 91 Highland pl.
Thuerer George, lab, b 317 W Morris.
Thumann August, carp, h 165 N Noble.
Thumma Silas W, carp, h 618 W Eugene (N I).
Thurman Albert, waiter, h rear 177 N West.
Thurman Charles W, lab, b 17 Sumner.

THOS. C. DAY & CO.
INVESTING AGENTS,
TOWN AND FARM LOANS,
Rooms 325 to 330 Lemcke Bldg.

Thurman Fuel Burner Co, John S Thurman pres, Ellis T Silvius sec, 44 When bldg.
Thurman James, waiter, r 322 N Liberty.
Thurman James R, coachman 710 N Meridian.
Thurman John S (Thurman & Silvius), b 939 N Penn.
Thurman Wm, lab, b 564 N Senate av.
Thurman & Silvius (John S Thurman, Ellis T Silvius), patent attorneys, 44 When bldg.
Thurston Charles, lab, b 156 N West.
Thurston George W, carp, h 456 E Washington.
Thurston John W, harnessmkr, h 672 S Meridian.
Thurston Vallorous, mach hd, h 67 Camp.
Thurtle John G (John G Thurtle & Co), sec Ingalls Land Co, h 225 N New Jersey.
THURTLE JOHN G & CO (John G Thurtle and Wm P Mooney), Architects, 57 Ingalls Blk. (See adv in classified Architects.)
Thuston Henry, lab, b 121 Darnell.
Thuston Howard, lab, h 121 Darnell.
Thuston Jeffery, lab, h 434 W 2d.
Thuston Thomas, lab, b 121 Darnell.
Tibbets Charles, carp, b s e cor Sheldon and 17th.
Tibbets Samuel, carp, h s e cor Sheldon and 17th.
Tibbetts Augustus, fruit grower, h n s Haughey av opp Cornelius (M).
Tibbetts Walter L, ins agt, r 208 N Illinois.
Tibbott Anna, teacher Public School No 6, h w s Ritter av 8 n of Washington (I).
Tibbott David, h w s Ritter av 8 n of Washington av (I).
Tibbott Everard F, stenog, h w s Grand av 5 s of University av (I).
Tibbott John L, clk I & L M Brown, b w s Ritter av 8 n of Washington av (I).
Tibbott Vida C, teacher, b w s Ritter av 8 n of Washington av (I).
Tibbs Daniel W (Tolin, Totten, Tibbs & Co), h 349 Michigan (H).
Tibbs John, driver, b 294 Douglass.
Tibbs Thomas, clk, h 162 S Judge Harding (W I).

EAT HITZ'S CRACKERS AND CAKES.
ASK YOUR GROCER FOR THEM.

Capital Steam Carpet Cleaning Works
M. D. PLUNKETT Proprietor, Telephone 818

BENJ. BOOTH PRACTICAL EXPERT ACCOUNTANT. Accounts of any description investigated and audited, and statements rendered. Room 18, 82½ E. Washington St., Indianapolis, Ind.

The Best Place in the City to Get a Good Meal THE SHERMAN RESTAURANT ♦♦♦♦ 18 and 20 S. Meridian Street KERSHNER BROS., Proprs.

ESTABLISHED 1876. TELEPHONE 168.
CHESTER BRADFORD,
SOLICITOR OF PATENTS,
AND COUNSEL IN PATENT CAUSES.
(See adv. page 6.)
Office:—Rooms 14 and 16 Hubbard Block, S.W. Cor. Washington and Meridian Streets, INDIANAPOLIS, INDIANA.

Tice Beatrice E, teacher Public School No 28, b 14 Warren.
Tice Harry L, carp, b 394 Bellefontaine.
Tice Lewis, carp, h 394 Bellefontaine.
Tice Wm H, mach E C Atkins & Co, h 14 Warren.
Tichenor Edward A, h 63 Drake.
Tichenor John C (Tichenor & Smith), h 110 Cherry.
Tichenor & Smith (John C Tichenor, Lansing F Smith), pubs, 23½ W Ohio.
Tiehen Garrett H, special police Indiana Natl Bank, h 49 Barth av.
Tiedeman John H, lab, h 511 N West.
Tielking Henry W, contr, 343 S State av, h same.
Tiemann Mary, seamstress, h 540 S New Jersey.
Tierney Elizabeth, h 385 S Illinois.
Tierney Martin E, h 385 S Illinois.
Tierney Michael, trimmer, b 120 Columbia av.
Tierney Michael J, patternmkr, h 385 S Illinois.
Tieste Eliza M (wid August), b 85 Clifford av.
Tietz Wm, agt, h 576 Morris (W I).
Tiffany Claude J, stenog, b 130 W 2d.
Tihm Christopher, pensioner, h 83 Davidson.
Tilbury Matthew, lab, b 121 Maxwell.
Tilden Charles, tel insp, b 168 N Meridian.
Tilden John W, mngr, h 63 Buchanan.
Tilford Emily (wid Milton C), b 317 N New Jersey.
Tilford John C, foreman I U Ry Co, h 582 Morris (W I).
Tilford John O, coachman 982 N Meridian.
Tilford Joseph M, b w s Ritter av 4 n of Washington av (I).
Tilford Maxwell J, pressman, b 474 N Alabama.
Tilford Samuel E, bailiff Superior Court No 3, h 474 N Alabama.
Tilford Wm, lab, h 442 W Chicago (N I).
Tilford Wm, lab, h 8 Peck.
Tilford Wm, coachman, h rear 130 N Penn.
Tilghman Charles A, confr, 21 Prospect, h same.
Tilghman Frank E, engr, b 104 Ash.

O. B. Ensey
SLATE, STEEL, TIN AND IRON ROOFING.
Cor. 6th and Illinois Sts. Tel. 1562

Tilghman Isabella E, confr, 531 E Washington, h same.
Tilley Charles H, h rear 251 Michigan (H).
Tilley Kathryn C, stenog, b 497 N East.
Tilley Rebecca C (wid James), h 497 N East.
Tilley Tunis T, grocer, 130 E Mkt House, h 160 Brookside av.
Tillins Philip, lab, h 779 E Market.
Tillman Agnes (wid Samuel), h 36 Cornell av.
Tillman Daniel, lab, b 159 W Merrill.
Tillman Emanuel, lab, h 16½ McIntyre.
Tillman Frank, lab, h 64 Dawson.
Tillman Frank, lab, r 28 Roanoke.
Tillman Henry, porter, r rear 81 W North.
Tillotson Charles, driver, r 242 Indiana av.
Tillotson Charles E, creamery, 370 Virginia av, h same.
Tillson Wm L, bkkpr, h 181 E South.
Tilly Edward E, clk, h 460 W New York.
Tilly Fanny (wid Herman), b 401 Madison av.
Tilly Herman F, porter, h 523 Madison av.
Tilly Joseph G, mngr Herancourt Brewing Co, h 209 N Noble.
Tilney Aley D, teacher Kindergarten No 7, b 23 E St Joseph.
Tilson Anna M (wid Michael), b 281 Huron.
Tilson Frank M, trimmer, b 36 S Capitol av.
Tilson Harvey, yardman, h 273 E Washington.
Tilson Kate E, teacher, b 325 S Meridian.
Tilton Charles S, insp C U Tel Co, b 168 N Meridian.
TIMBERLAKE ARTHUR, Druggist, 400 College av, Tel 263; h 423 E 7th.
Timberlake Charles, electrician, b 423 E 7th.
Timberlake Jackson, lab, r 182 W Market.
Timberlake Joseph B, barber, r 39 Ellen.
Timblin Elvi L, lab, h 44 Thalman av.
Timblin Lee E, woodwkr, h 32 Centennial.
Timewell Catherine (wid James), b 73 Highland pl.
Timewell Charles A, mngr Standard Life and Accident Ins Co of Detroit, 62 E Market, h 73 Highland pl.
Timman Wm H, painter, b 273 E Court.
Timmerman August, carp, h 40 Chadwick.
Timmerman Herman H, lab, h 81 Nordyke av (W I).
Timmerman Louisa, b 194 Minnesota.
Timmon, see Temman.
Timmonds Ann C (wid Charles W), h 270½ W Washington.
Timmons Bert, clk, h 433 W 22d (N I).
Timmons Charles W, clk, b 44½ S Illinois.
Timmons Emma (wid Richard), b 30 Grant.
Timmons George, lab, b 34½ Malott av.
Timmons George A, lab, h 8½ Malott av.
Timmons Melissa (wid Thomas F), h 514 W Shoemaker (N I).
Timmons Monroe W, painter, h 34½ Malott av.
Timms Harvey N, h 1249 N Penn.
Timons Charles, lab, h 46 Rockwood.
Timons Martha J (wid George), h 46 Rockwood.
Tincher Alfred B, bkkpr, b 204 N Illinois.
Tincher Earl L, lab, b 445 W Udell (N I).
Tincher James R, brakeman, h e s Brightwood av 2 s of Schofield (B).
Tincher Wm E, carp, h 445 W Udell (N I).
Tindall Walter B, condr, h 28 Gregg.
Tindel George M, horseshoer, h 32 Reynolds av (H).
Tindel Korah, barber, r 458 W New York.
Tinder Hattie, h 133 W Michigan.
Tinder John, lab, h 420½ W Michigan.

TUTEWILER UNDERTAKER, No. 72 WEST MARKET STREET. TELEPHONE 216.

OF PHILADELPHIA.
D. W. Edwards, G. A., 508 Indiana Trust Bldg.
in everything which contributes to Security and Cheapness of life insurance, this company is unsurpassed.

THEODORE F. SMITHER

Tinder Wm, lab, h 1251 Schurman av (N I).
Tindolph Frank D, clk, b Stubbins Hotel.
Tindolph Sarah M (wid Allen), b Stubbins Hotel.
Tingle George W, mach, b 108 Yandes.
Tingle John E, clk R M S, h 628 Park av.
Tingle Joseph T, lab, h 108 Yandes.
Tingle Newton, lab, b e s Ivy la 3 s of Pendleton av (B).
Tingle Wm S, lab, b 120 Yandes.
Tingley Frank B, lab, h 398 S Alabama.
Tinker Polly S (wid James), h 239 Columbia av.
Tinkey Calvin, lab, h 80 Sheffield av (H).
Tinkey Ira, lab, b 80 Sheffield av (H).
Tinney Thomas H, printer, h 373 N Senate av.
Tinsley Frank C, phys, 402 Mass av, h 118 Brookside av.
Tinsley Isaac, lab, h 463 Mulberry.
Tinsley Wm W, lab, b 206 S William (W I).
Tipps James, lab, h 83 Holmes av (H).
Tipton Charles A, saloon, 60 Mass av, r same.
Tipton James L, letter carrier P O, h 26 Osgood (W I).
Tipton John H, clk R M S, h 403 Broadway.
Tires Wm, tiremkr, b rear 306 E Louisiana.
Tisch Louis J, printer, h 559 Union.
Tisch Stanislaus T, tailor, 834 S Meridian, h same.
Tischmacher Rem, brakeman, b 51 N State av.
Titus Earl M, barber, b 285 Chapel.
Titus Egbert, barber, r 285 Chapel.
Titus Eliza (wid Richard), b 112 Martindale av.
Titus John, lab, b 274 W New York.
Titus John C, trav agt, h 865 N Delaware.
Tivenan Michael P, saloon, 402 S Capitol av, r same.
Tobert Herman, b 107 Trowbridge (W).
Tobias Wm S, mach, h 406 Newman.
Tobin Albert L, news agt, r 193½ S Illinois.
Tobin Cynthia (wid George), b 609 W Pearl.
Tobin Dennis, trav agt D O'Brien & Co, b 477 N Illinois.
Tobin Frank E, boilermkr, b 154 W McCarty.

TOBIN JAMES, Genl Contractor and Builder, cor Kentucky av and Merrill, h 462 S West.

Tobin John W, grocer, 400 S West, h same.
Tobin Joseph (Tobin & Harrison), h 650 N Senate av.
Tobin Mary (wid John), grocer, 335 S Delaware, h same.
Tobin Mary (wid Wm D), h 384 Coburn.
Tobin Thomas, h 154 W McCarty.
Tobin Wm, capt Headquarters Fire Dept, h 173 W Morris.
Tobin & Harrison (Joseph Tobin, Charles A Harrison), saloon, 650 N Senate av.
Todd Annie, h 334 W Washington.
Todd Charles W, mach, h 175 E South.
Todd Douglas P, molder, h 437 E Francis (N I).
Todd Elizabeth (wid Perry), b 31 Tremont av (H).
Todd James W, lab, h 95 Meikel.
Todd John M (John M Todd & Co), h 179 Bellefontaine.

TODD JOHN M & CO (John M Todd), Real Estate, Mortgage Loans and Insurance, 7 Ingalls Blk, s w cor Penn and Washington, Tel 1022.

Todd Joseph, barber, h 406 Bright.
Todd Joseph, engr, h 104½ Indiana av.

THE
WHEN
IS A WORLD BEATER.

Todd Joseph, porter, h 406 Blackford.
Todd Julia A (wid Henry), b 317 W North.

TODD L L, Physician, 19 W Ohio, Tel 649; h 294 N Alabama, Tel 566.

Todd Margaret M (wid Charles N), h 597 N Illinois.
Todd Marie C, teacher Public School No 10, b 179 Bellefontaine.

TODD NEWTON, Insurance, Loans, Rentals, Stocks and Bonds, 7 Ingalls Blk, s w cor Penn and Washington, Tel 1022; h 778 N Penn.

Todd Samuel B, attendant Insane Hospital.
Todd Stephen, r 94 N Senate av.
Todd Susan, teacher Public School No 2, b 294 N Alabama.
Todd Wm E, bkkpr, h 82 Temple av.
Todhunter Thomas S, paperhngr, h 13 Hall pl.
Toeppe Wilhelmina (wid Charles), h rear 539 E Washington.
Toien Charles, diecutter, h 764 Charles.
Tola Henry, clk, b 72 Downey.
Tola Wm F, stonemason, h 72 Downey.
Tolbert, see also Talbert.
Tolbert Harry, lab, h w s Auburn av 1 s of Prospect.
Tolds Orlando, lab, h 319 Hillside av.

TOLEDO BRIDGE CO THE, Daniel Lesley Agt, Room 42 When Blk, Tel 1916. (See adv in classified Bridge Contractors.)

Toler John T, driver, h 950 W Vermont.
Tolin Alfred H, sub letter carrier P O, h 97 N Rural (B).
Tolin Alexander B (Tolin, Totten, Tibbs & Co), mayor of West Indpls, h 120 Nordyke av (W I).
Tolin Benton T, clk, h 301 Prospect.
Tolin Jacob W, barber, b 56 Martindale av.
Tolin Sanford S, letter carrier P O, h 236 E Merrill.
Tolin, Totten, Tibbs & Co (Alexander B Tolin, John J Totten, Daniel W Tibbs, John B Harrell), live stock com, Union Stock Yards (W I).

The A. Burdsal Co.
CELEBRATED
HOMESTEAD
READY MIXED PAINT.
WHOLESALE AND RETAIL.
34 AND 36 SOUTH MERIDIAN STREET.

ROOFING MATERIALS
2 and 3-Ply Roofing, Building Paper, etc. Roof Materials.
Telephone 88. Office, 14 West Maryland St.

ELECTRIC SUPPLIES We Carry a full Stock. Prices Right.
C. W. MEIKEL,
Tel. 466. 96-98 E. New York St.

DALTON & MERRIFIELD { LUMBER South Noble St., near E. Washington

INDIANA ELECTROTYPE CO. : BEST WORK LOWEST PRICES. 23 WEST PEARL ST., INDIANAPOLIS, IND. JOB WORK. BOOK PLATES. All Orders Promptly Filled. BEST PATENT BASE ON THE MARKET.

KIRKHOFF BROS.,
Electrical Contractors, Wiring and Construction.
102-104 SOUTH PENNSYLVANIA ST.
TELEPHONE 910.

Tolin Wm, dep constable Carl Habich, h 1112 N Rural.
Toliver Spencer, laundryman, h 236 W Wabash.
Toll Curt, supervisor of physical culture Public Schools, b 623 S Meridian.
Tolle Henry C, motorman, h 180 W 7th.
Toller Joseph, lab, b 407 Olive.
Tolles Catherine O (wid George), b 62 Poplar (B).
Tolley Wm V, phys, 745 N Senate av, h same.
Tolliver Annie, h 309 N California.
Tolliver Charles, janitor, r 182 E Washington.
Tolliver Edward, bellboy Hotel English.
Tolliver John, porter, b 146 Michigan (H).
Tolliver John B, lab, h 403 W North.
Tolliver Lawrence, lab, 333 N Capitol av.
Tolliver Lewis, express, h 85 Camp.
Tolliver Monroe B, lab, b 173 Alvord.
Tolly James A, salesman Stockton, Gillespie & Co, b 251 Howard (W I).
Tomamichel Joseph J, molder, h 567 Shelby.
Tomasko Johanna (wid Wenzel), b 261 Yandes.
Tomasko Joseph, mach, h 261 Yandes.
Tomlin James H, pres Equitable State B and L Assn, res Shelbyville, Ind.
Tomlin John A, lab, h 495 W Francis (N I).
TOMLIN WM S, Physician, n e cor Illinois and North, h same, Tel 1602.
Tomlinson Agnes, b 169 S William (W I).
Tomlinson Benjamin F, yardmaster, h 169 S William (W I).
Tomlinson Charles C, pension agt, h 32 Miley av.
Tomlinson Charles W, barber, h 436 E St Clair.
Tomlinson Edwin J, billposter, b 169 S William (W I).
Tomlinson Eston F, carp, h 436 E St Clair.
Tomlinson Florin E, paperhngr, h 1728 Graceland av.
Tomlinson George, meats, 102 Shepard (W I), h 104 same.
Tomlinson George H, patrolman, h 62 Smith.

THE W. C. WASSON CO.,
130 Indiana Ave. Tel. 989.
STEAM
COAL
Car Lots a Specialty. Prompt Delivery.
Brazil Block, Jackson and Anthracite.

Tomlinson George I, h 21 N Spruce.
Tomlinson George W, farmer, h n w cor Tremont and Grandview avs (H).
Tomlinson Hall, n e cor Market and Delaware.
Tomlinson Henry A, condr, b 92 Agnes.
Tomlinson Henry C, carp, h 22 Bismarck av (H).
Tomlinson James M, phys, 28½ E Ohio, b 410 N Meridian.
Tomlinson John W (Benjamin C Wright & Co), h Madison av 2 miles s of city limits.
Tomlinson John W, trimmer, b 21 N Spruce.
Tomlinson Jonathan, lab, r 190 E Market.
Tomlinson Listus S, boilermkr, h 17 N Gale (B).
Tomlinson Matthew, paperhngr, h 47 Helen.
Tomlinson Milton, lab, b Perry C Tomlinson.
Tomlinson Perry C, tmstr, h s w cor Ruth and Jackson (M J).
Tomlinson Samuel J Rev, h s e cor Houston and Cherry avs (I).
Tomlinson Samuel M, lab, h 52 Kappus (W I).
Tomlinson Thomas C, millwright, h 1815 N Senate av.
Tomlinson Virginia R, phys, 169 S William (W I), b same.
Tomlinson Wm J, paperhngr, h 47 Helen.
Tompkins Alexander K, plumber, h 537 W Addison (N I).
Tompkins Andrew T, foreman bindery Carlon & Hollenbeck, h 420 N Illinois.
Tompkins Charles C, clk, h 145 S Noble.
Tompkins Charles W, porter, b 157 Minerva.
Tompkins Clarissa (wid Ezra), h 532 W Addison (N I).
Tompkins Edmund W, drugs, 165 Mass av, r 161½ same.
Tompkins Edward G, lab, b 157 Minerva.
Tompkins Edward O, trav agt, h 382 Union.
Tompkins Frank P, clk, h n s Washington 2 e of Colorado av.
Tompkins James H F, drugs, n w cor Central av and P C C & St L Ry, (I), h n e cor Grand and Oak avs (I).
Tompkins Jennie M, dry goods, 539 W Addison (N I), h 537 same.
Tompkins John R, clk, b n e cor Grand and Oak avs (I).
Tompkins Washington, lab, h 157 Minerva.
Tompkins Wm F, car rep, b 157 Minerva.
Tompkins Wm H, lab, h 216 Huron.
Tone Alfred J, h 23 S Liberty.
Toner Frank P, clk Kingan & Co (ltd), b 59 Chadwick.
Toner George C, carp, h 52 Arbor av (W I).
Toner James, printer, b 240 N California.
Toner Samuel J, bkkpr, b 59 Chadwick.
Toney Edward, motorman, h 475 W Francis (W I).
Tongat Andrew M, hostler, b 5 Williams.
Tongat Maigie M, h 5 Williams.
Tony Wm, lab, h 220 E Wabash.
Toohey Michael, carp, h 268 S Capitol av.
Toohill Patrick, flagman, h 474 S Capitol av.
Toohill Richard, watchman Insane Hospital.
Toohill Thomas P, opr W U Tel Co, b 474 S Capitol av.
Toohill Wm, clk, h 474 S Capitol av.
Toole, see also O'Toole.
Toole Edward, motorman, b 792 W Washington.
Toole Isabell (wid Samuel), h 67 Malott av.
Toole Joseph, boilermkr, b 69 Birch av (W I).

W. H. Messenger FURNITURE, CARPETS, STOVES, 101 EAST WASHINGTON ST. TEL. 491.

McNamara, Koster & Co. | Foundry and Pattern Shop, 212-218 S. PENN. ST. . . . PHONE 1593.

Toole Mary (wid Joseph), h 3 Beacon.
Toole May, h 232 W Market.
Toole Peter M, mach, h 4 Lord.
Tooley Harry C, patternmkr, b 111 Highland pl.
Tooley Ida M, stenog, b 111 Highland pl.
Tooley James M, painter, h 131 Nordyke av (W I).
Tooley John E, cornicemkr, b 36 S Capitol av.
Tooley Mary J (wid Wm H), h 111 Highland pl.
Toombs Wm, lab, h 245 W McCarty.
Toombs Wm F, lab, h 68 Chadwick.
Toomey, see also Tumey.
Toomey Anna M, clk, b 259 Coburn.
Toomey Margaret (wid Jeremiah), h 259 Coburn.
Toomey Margaret, housekpr 173 N Capitol av.
Toomey Michael W (Toomey & Dwyer), b 259 Coburn.
Toomey & Dwyer (Michael W Toomey, Joseph J Dwyer), saloon, 17 Monument pl.
Toon Charles, plumber, 1541 Kenwood av, h 1540 N Illinois.
Toon Curtis, clk, b 167 Woodlawn av.
Toon Eliza J (wid Martin S), h 561 E Washington.
Toon George G, city fireman, b 561 E Washington.
Toon Lewis C, lab, b 561 E Washington.
Toon Richard O (Risley & Toon), b 561 E Washington.
Toon Wm G, driver, h 167 Woodlawn av.
TOOPS EMORY D, Mnfr Safety Gates for Elevators, 1201 N Penn, h same.
Topey Wm, plumber, b 165 S Alabama.
Topf Augusta (wid Albert), h rear 407 S Delaware.
Toph Harry, clk The Wm H Block Co, b 31 Frank.
Toph Joseph H, painter, h 31 Frank.
Topham Frederick P, polisher, b 131 Locke.
Topmiller Frank H, music teacher, 66 English av, b same.
Topp Alexander O, gardener, b 1640 N Illinois.
Topp Charles, dairy, s s Shearer pike 1 w of Belt R R (B), h 450 Clifford av.
Topp Charles C, driver, b Charles Topp.
Topp Frank, b Charles Topp.
Topp Frederick, gardener, h 1640 N Illinois.
Topp Frederick W, gardener, b 1640 N Illinois.
Torbet Wirt H, condr, b 465 Bellefontaine.
Torrence Anna R, teacher Public School No 24, b 1203 N Meridian.
Torrence Flora E, teacher Public School No 6, b 1203 N Meridian.
Torrence John, h 1744 Kenwood av.
Torrence Lydia J (wid John), h 1203 N Meridian.
Torrence Miriam J (wid Wm P), h 263 Shelby.
Torrey George W (Reliance Edge Tool Co), h 368 N Senate av.
Totman Samuel T, policeman Insane Hospital.
Totten John, lab, b 306 Lambert (W I).
Totten John J (Tolin, Totten, Tibbs & Co), h 114 Nordyke av (W I).
Totten Thomas B, carp, h 306 Lambert (W I).
Totten Wm, lab, b 306 Lambert (W I).
Totten Wm A, live stock, h 170 Broadway.
Touber Sanders, lab, r rear 311 E North.
Toup Robert S, trimmer, r 155 E Ohio.

Henry H. Fay, 40½ E. Washington St., REAL ESTATE, AND LOAN BROKER.

Toup Wm K, foreman Parry Mnfg Co, r 155 E Ohio.
Tousey Edward A, trav agt, h 83 W 5th.
Tousey Eudora (wid Wood G), h 359 N Illinois.
Tousey Louise A (wid George), h 737 N Meridian.
Tousey Omer, trav agt, h 440 N Meridian.
Tousey Wm E, h 999 N Senate av.
Tousley Penelope M, b 222 N Illinois.
Tousley Wm G, engr, h 216 W McCarty.
Tout Asa, brickmason, h 219 Fayette.
Tout George W, lab, b 25 Helen.
Tout Robert D, trav agt, b 45 Warren.
Tout Wilkinson M, h 928 N Delaware.
Tower Mary, supervisoress Insane Hospital.
Tower Paul, mach, h 145 Patterson.
Towles Alfred N, phys, s s Railroad 1 e of Central av (I), h n s University av 1 w of Downey av (I).
Towles Frederick M, clk, b Alfred N Towles.
Towne Frank F, printer, h 80 Walcott.
Townley George E (Frederick P Rush & Co), h 358 Broadway.
Townley Morris, student, b 358 Broadway.
Townsend Addison M, riding bailiff Sheriff's Office, h 844 S Meridian.
Townsend Allen E, clk, b 564 Ash.
Townsend Asenath C (wid Jesse N), b 364 College av.
TOWNSEND BROS (Thomas E and Robert D), Lime, Cement and Builders' Materials, 41 S Alabama, Tel 452.
Townsend Charles, engr, h 956 N Senate av.
Townsend Caesar C Rev, presiding elder A M E Church, h e s Baltimore av 1 n of Hillside av.
Townsend Charles S, trav agt, h e s Addison 4 s of Washington (M J).
Townsend Edna S, b 461 N Alabama.
Townsend Elmer E, engr, h 52 Belmont av (H).
Townsend Franklin, lineman, h 648 W Washington.
Townsend James, mach, b 229 W Washington.

UNION CASUALTY & SURETY CO. OF ST. LOUIS, MO. All lines of Personal Accident and Casualty Insurance, including Employers' and General Liability. W. E. BARTON & CO., General Agents, 504 Indiana Trust Building. LONG DISTANCE TELEPHONE 1918.

THE FRED DIETZ CO. WOODEN PACKING BOXES MADE TO ORDER. FACTORY AND WAREHOUSE TRUCKS. 400 Madison Avenue. Telephone 654.

Indianapolis BUSINESS UNIVERSITY Leading College of Business and Shorthand. Elevator day and night. Individual instruction. Large faculty. Terms easy. Enter now. See p. 4. When Block. E. J. HEEB, President.

NEW YORK FILTER MFG. CO. Filters for Water-Works, Boiler Plants, Laundries, Hotels, Private Residences, Etc. | Henry R. Worthington, 64 S. Pennsylvania St. Long Distance Telephone 284.

UNION CO-OPERATIVE LAUNDRY (COMPOSED OF UNION LAUNDRY GIRLS.) NOS. 138, 140 AND 142 VIRGINIA AVENUE. T. E. SOMERVILLE, MANAGER—TELEPHONE 1269. INDIANAPOLIS, IND.

HORACE M. HADLEY
REAL ESTATE AND INSURANCE
66 East Market Street, Basement
TELEPHONE 1540.

Townsend James A, tailor, h 431 College av.
Townsend James J, trav agt, h 379 W 2d.
Townsend Julia A (wid James), b 219 W Merrill.
Townsend Marion, carp, b 956 N Senate av.
Townsend Mary E (wid Wm), h 302 E South.
Townsend Robert D (Townsend Bros), h 564 Ash.
Townsend Samuel A, clk P & E Ry, h 224 E 7th.
Townsend Thomas E (Townsend Bros), h 287 Hillside av.
TOWNSHIP ASSESSOR'S OFFICE, Eugene Sauley Assessor Center Township, 35 Court House, Tel 912.
TOWNSHIP TRUSTEE'S OFFICE, Horace B Makepeace Trustee, 10½ E Washington, Tel 782.
Townsley Oliver H, clk R M S, h 143 Davidson.
Trabue Curran, molder, h rear e s Sherman Drive 2 s of Washington.
Trabue Jackson A, engr, h e s Judge Harding 1 s of Washington (W I).
Trabue Margaret (wid Curran), h w s Perkins pike 4 n of Bethel av.
Trabue Peter, lab, h e s Wheeler 2 s of Prospect.
Tracey Louis, tinner, r 193 W Washington.
Tracey Thomas W, lab, h 637 N West.
Tracey Ulysses G, barber, 493½ W 22d (N I), h 420 W Addison (N I).
Tracy Alonzo, waiter, r 275 W Market.
Tracy Frank W, undertaker Collier & Murphy, b 541 S West.
Tracy James J, lab h 22 Roe.
Tracy James O, trav agt, r 247 N Capitol av.
Tracy John, lab, b 27 Helen.
Tracy John A, cook, r 275 W Market.
Tracy John M, lab, b 541 S West.
Tracy Thomas, lab, h 541 S West.
Tracy Thomas jr, lab, b 541 S West.
Trader Harry H, agt, h 56 S William (W I).

PERSONAL AND PROMPT ATTENTION GIVEN TO COLLECTIONS.
Merchants' and Manufacturers' Exchange
J. E. TAKKEN, Manager,
19 Union Building, 73 West Maryland Street.

Traders' Despatch, James V Stanbery agt, 23 Board of Trade bldg.
Trager John J, fireman, h 172 Lexington av.
Trager Louis lab, b 189 S Capitol av.
Trager Louisa (wid John), h 172 Lexington av.
Trager Wm W, fireman h 27 Oriental.
Trailor Jeremiah, lab, h 19 Cora.
Train Alice (wid George), r 144 W New York.
Tramer Elias, clk Clemens Vonnegut, h 19 Morrison.
Trankner Richard, porter, r 198 W Washington.
Transou Sarah (wid Calvin A), b 66 Huron.
Traphagen Frank E, clk, b 150 N Illinois.
Trapp Charles A, lab, h 327 E Georgia.
Traquair George E, paperhngr, h 49 Empire.
Trask George K, railroad editor The Indpls Journal, h 815 N Meridian.
Trask Walter C, checkman, h 297 N East.
Trattner Moses, bartndr, h 243 W Maryland.
Trattner Samuel, clk, b 243 W Maryland.
Traub Alfred H, b 1094 W Washington.
Traub Benjamin, clk Emil Wulschner & Son, b 23 S Station (B).
Traub Catherine F (wid Jacob) h 1094 W Washington.
Traub Charles, lab h 327 E Georgia.
Traub Charles G, trav agt, h 190 Bright.
Traub George C, bkkpr, b 208 Douglass.
TRAUB GEORGE F, Druggist, 252 W Washington, Tel 961; h same.
Traub Jacob J, clk R M S, h 23 S Station (B).
Traub John, mason, b 723 N Senate av.
Traub Sarah E, h 252 W Washington.
Traub Wm H, real est, 1085 W Vermont, h same.
Trauber Sanders, lab, b 38 Oak.
Traugott Joachim, saloon, 174 River av (W I), h same.
Traugott Louis, saloon, 1206 Morris (W I), h same.
Traugott Michael, bartndr, b cor Meridian and Merrill.
Traut, see also Trout.
Traut Charles A barber, 561 S East, h 43 Russell av.
Traut John, h 354 S Meridian.
Trautwein, see also Troutwine.
Trautwein John C, baggageman, h e s N Senate av 2 s of 29th.
Trautwine Hannah D (wid John H), h 281 Bright.
Trautwine Wm S, motorman, h 127 Blake.
TRAVELERS' INSURANCE CO OF HARTFORD, CONN, Horatio C Newcomb City Agt, 319-321 Indiana Trust Bldg.
Travers Patrick, driver, b 61 Beaty.
Travers Peter T, gas insp, h 204 Coburn.
Travis Abraham, lab, h 21 Sumner.
Travis Albert, watchman, h 78 Yandes.
Travis Charles E, solr, r 154 Broadway.
Travis Charles F, condr, b 78 Yandes.
Travis Eli E, chief route agt Am Ex Co, b 204 N Illinois.
Travis Harry E, carp, h 272 Brookside av.
Travis Lewis M, bottler, b 78 Yandes.
Trayford George, plastr, 452 Clifford av, h same.
Traylor Boman H, student, b 39 E McCarty.
TRAYLOR MARION H, Architect, 57 Baldwin Blk, s w cor Market and Delaware, Tel 1274; h 524 Park av. (See adv in classified Architects.)

CLEMENS VONNEGUT 184, 186 and 192 E. Washington St. | FOUNDRY AND MACHINISTS' SUPPLIES. "NORTON" EMERY WHEELS AND GRINDING MACHINERY.

Traylor Rose, bkkpr, b 432 N East.
Traylor Sarah J (wid Jessamine G W), h 432 N East.
Traylor Wm H, carp, h 47 Cornell av.
Treadway Charles T, molder, h 23 Sheffield av (H).
Treat Atwater J (A J Treat & Son), h 297 N Meridian.
TREAT A J & SON (Atwater J and Edward L), Merchant Tailors, 24 N Penn, Tel 180.
Treat Charles S, condr, h 478 W Shoemaker (N I).
Treat Edward L (A J Treat & Son), b 297 N Meridian.
Treat Hiram B, clk, h 25 N Reisner (W I).
Treat Louis F, attendant Insane Hospital.
Treat Wm B F Rev, b 81 Pleasant.
Trees Alonzo S, carp, h 40 Pleasant av.
Trees Irvin W, phys, 124 Prospect, h 122 same.
Trees Roland A, teacher Industrial Training School, h 78 W 10th.
Treeter Bros (Peter H and Henry M), driven wells, rear 9 Lexington av.
Treeter George, mason, h 32 N Olive.
Treeter Henry M (Treeter Bros), b 79 S Liberty.
Treeter John C, mason, h 36 S Spruce.
Treeter Louisa (wid John), h 79 S Liberty.
Treeter Peter H (Treeter Bros), r rear 9 Lexington av.
Trefry Edward, bricklyr, h 766 Charles.
Trefz George E, carp, b 1329 E Washington.
Trefz Jacob F, dairy, 1329 E Washington, h same.
Trefz Wm J, carp, h 215 Orange.
Trego Frederick, lab, b 548 W Washington.
Treher Mallie M, bkkpr, b 214 W New York.
Treitschke Wm M, salesman, h 370 N West.
Thembley Martha (wid George D), h 1071 N Capitol av.
Tremor Francis F, finisher, h 101 Woodburn av (W I).
Tremp Alexander E, foreman, h 128 Blackford.
Trenary David F, student, b 124 N Capitol av.
Trenary Ethel, opr C U Tel Co, b 124 N Capitol av.
Trenary John W, engr, h 9 Crawford.
Trenary Julia M (wid James V R), h 124 N Capitol av.
Trenary Walter O, clk P C C & St L Ry, h 44 Yandes.
Trenck Frederick C, genl agt Ellis & Helfenberger, h 47 Laurel.
Trenck Frederick C, lab, h 170 W Morris.
Trendelman Christian F, lab, h 30 Lynn.
Trendelman Frederick, flagman, h 33 N Dorman.
Trendelman Frederick, lab, h 9 Orchard av.
Trendelman Harry, instmkr, b 33 N Dorman.
Trendelman John H, lab, b 30 Lynn.
Trent Archibald, janitor, h 71 Hudson.
Trent James A, lab, b 11 Iowa.
Trent John, b 88 Maple.
Trent John C, teacher High School, h 1130 N Delaware.
Trent Mary E (wid Alexander), h 11 Iowa.
Trentman Edward, engr The Denison.
Treon Martin L, lab, h 316 S Missouri.
Tresemer August F, mach, h 162 Woodlawn av.
Treser Charles H, butcher, b n w cor Carleton and Senate av (M).
Treser Wm L, butcher, h n w cor Carleton and Senate av (M).

33 SOUTH MERIDIAN STREET. PICTURES. THE H. LIEBER COMPANY. ARTISTIC FRAMING. MIRRORS.

Tresice Alfaretta, b 264 S New Jersey.
Tresler David L, carp, h 827 E 9th.
Tresslar Emery A, produce, 62 E Mkt House, h 318 Fletcher av.
Tretton James, stonemason, h 12 McGinnis.
Treuhann Frank, cigar mnfr, 762 S Meridian, h same.
Treuhann Frank J, mach hd, b 762 S Meridian.
Trevan Henry, lab, b rear 24 W North.
Trevan John, lab, h rear 24 W North.
Trevan Lewis, janitor, b rear 24 W North.
Trevan Mary (wid Henry), b 323 Clinton.
Tribble Abraham, porter, h 354 Douglass.
Tribble Louis, lab, r 66 N Missouri.
Triber Wm, saloon, 149 Dunlop, h same.
Trickett Alice C, tailor, b 332 E St Clair.
Trickett Louise K (wid Thomas S), h 332 E St Clair.
Trieb Andrew, polisher, h 501 S Meridian.
Trieb Henry, paperhngr, h 31 Lynn av (W I).
Trieb Louis, lab, b Exchange Hotel (W I).
Trieb Wm, lab, b 466 Union.
Trieselman Christian, clk, h 156 W McCarty.
Trieselmann Henry F, carp, h 53 Sanders.
Trietsch George, real est, h 428 N East.
Trigg Samuel, lab, b 234 Clinton.
Triggs James M (Combs & Triggs), h 493 Madison av.
Trimble Adam, blksmith, b 15 S Station (B).
Trimble Adelbert, helper, b 15 S Station (B).
Trimble Armour, lab, b 121 W Maryland.
Trimble Elizabeth J (wid Joseph), h 15 N Station (B).
Trimble Elmer E, car rep, h 15 N Station (B).
Trimble Mary I, dressmkr N Y Store, r 29 The Shiel.
Trimble Minnie, h 219 E Georgia.
Trimble Wm H, painter, h e s Brightwood av 8 s of Willow (B).
Trimmer Barbara A (wid Wm), b 12 Wilcox.
Trimmer Clara M, r 90½ Mass av.
Trimpe Bernard A (J H Trimpe & Son), h 116 Minerva.

GUIDO R. PRESSLER
FRESCO PAINTER
Churches, Theaters, Public Buildings, Etc., A Specialty.
Residence, No. 325 North Liberty Street.
INDIANAPOLIS, IND.

INDIANAPOLIS STEEL ROOFING AND CORRUGATING WORKS, 23 and 25 East South Street. S. D. NOEL, Proprietor.

David S. McKernan REAL ESTATE AND LOANS. Exchanging real estate a specialty. A number of choice pieces for encumbered property. Rooms 2-5 Thorpe Block.

DIAMOND WALL PLASTER { Telephone 1410 BUILDERS' EXCHANGE.

UNION TRANSFER AND STORAGE CO. Cor. E. Ohio St. and C., C., C. & St. L. R'y Tracks. Storage of Household Goods and Pianos a Specialty.

W. McWORKMAN,
Galvanized Iron Cornice Works
TIN AND SLATE ROOFING.
930 WEST WASHINGTON STREET.
TELEPHONE 1118.

Trimpe Diana (wid Benjamin), h 446 N West.
Trimpe Henry M, letter carrier P O, h 14 Holloway av.
Trimpe John A, carver, b 238 Blackford.
Trimpe John B, foreman, b 446 N West.
Trimpe John H (J H Trimpe & Son), h 238 Blackford.
Trimpe John H, cigarmkr, b 446 N West.
Trimpe J H & Son (John H and Bernard A), shoes, 162 Indiana av.
Trindle James S, clk, h 1137 N Penn.
Trindle John M, condr, h 288 Union.
Tripp Albert A, pres Union Transfer and Storage Co, res North Vernon, Ind.
Tripp Albert E (Austin & Tripp), res Allisonville, Ind.
Tripp Edward W, engr, h 77 Spann av.
Tripp Ernest H, sec and treas Union Transfer and Storage Co, h 87 Middle Drive (W P).
Triquimia Medical Co, George J Langsdale mngr, 129 E Pratt.
Trissel David O, carp, h 767 E Washington.
Trissel Frank R, repairer, b 767 E Washington.
Trobaugh Charles, lab, h 70 Tacoma av.
TRON WM, Propr The Kingston Saloon, 17 N Illinois, Tel 706; h 1329 N Capitol av, Tel 1266.
Trone Peter B, trav agt, b 716 Broadway.
Trosky Charles L, mach, b 573 E 9th.
Trosky Frank H, plumber, b 573 E 9th.
Trosky Frederick W, shoemkr, 156 E 7th, h 573 E 9th.
Trosky Louise, cashr Equitable Savings and Loan Assn, b 573 E 9th.
Trost Frank, gardener, h w s N Illinois 3 n of 28th.
Trost John, molder, h 54 River av (W I).
Trotcky Solomon, dry goods, 219 Howard (W I), h same.
Troth John W, clk, h 20 Osgood (W I).
Trott Barbara (wid John), r 236 N Illinois.
Trotter Charles H, clk Ewart Mnfg Co, h 274 Michigan (H).
Trotter Edgar H, bkkpr, h 567 Central av.
Trotter James F, lab, h 164 W Michigan.

SEALS,
STENCILS,
STAMPS, Etc.
GEO. J. MAYER
15 S. Meridian St.
TELEPHONE 1386.

Trotter Lemon H (Mendenhall, Howell & Trotter), r 28 Ft Wayne av.
Trotter Levi M, lab, h 179 N Dorman.
Trotter Oscar (Helt & Trotter), h 151 River av (W I).
Trotter Wm O, stock dealer, h n e cor Concord and Michigan (H).
Troughton Thomas J, molder, b 108 S Judge Harding (W I).
Troup John B, carp, h 12 Downing av (H).
Trout, see also Traut.
Trout Elizabeth (wid Oscar), h 124 Lexington av.
Trout Eleanora (wid Joshua), h 218 S New Jersey.
Trout Frank, collr, h 21 Bismarck av (H).
Trout Henry H, pdlr, h 9 Minerva.
Trout Leroy, engr, h 105 N Noble.
Trout Samuel W, salesman Krag-Reynolds Co, h 100 Highland pl.
Trout Wm H, h 389 S State av.
Trout Wm S, trav agt, h 16 W Michigan.
Troutman Abner, lab, h 115 N Missouri.
Troutman Agnes (wid Benjamin), h 92 Yandes.
Troutman Beecher, mngr Hay & Willits Mnfg Co, b 117 E 6th.
Troutwine, see also Trautwein.
Troutwine Martha A (wid Andrew), h 320 N Alabama.
Trowbridge Charles Reeve, state editor The Indpls Sentinel, r 320 The Shiel.
Trowbridge Eva W (wid Roger R), r 320 The Shiel.
Trowbridge Frank E, r 320 The Shiel.
Troxel Henry J, lab, h 40 Maxwell.
Troxell Eliza V (wid Joseph R), h 275 N East.
Troy Frank E, condr, h 464 W Shoemaker (N I).
Troy John, lab, b Germania House.
Troy John F, furnacewkr, b 41 Davis.
Troy J Wm, insp Indiana Car and Foundry Co, h 75 Nordyke av (W I).
Troy Russell B, clk, h 14 Allfree.
Troyer Stephen W, pastor Lincoln Av M E Church, h 477 Lincoln av.
Trucks Theodore, blksmith, r 1 Riley blk.
Trucksess Emma E, h 203 W South.
Trucksess Frederick, watchman, h 263 W Morris.
Trucksess John J, meats, E Mkt House, h 365 W New York.
Trucksess Lilly M, h 203 W South.
Trucksess Talbot B, hostler, h rear 353 W Morris.
Trucksess Theodore, horseshoer, 151 W Maryland, r 1 Riley blk.
Trueasch George A, lab, h 164 Dougherty.
Trueblood Georgie, stenog, b 907 N New Jersey.
Trueblood Hezekiah L, painter, h 907 N New Jersey.
Trueblood Sylvester C, bkkpr J D Adams & Co, h 506 Central av.
Truehart Elijah, barber, 69 N Alabama, r same.
Truelove Wm, lab, b 86 S East.
Trueman Susan, stenog The Bowen-Merrill Co, b 429 N New Jersey.
Truemper Charles J, tents, 330 S East and saloon e s Northwestern av nr canal, h e s Northwestern av 1 n of 30th.
Truesdale Fannie (wid Edward), h 197 W 3d.
Truex Grant I, lab, h 101 Sheffield av (H).
Truex Isaac C, lab, b 101 Sheffield av (H).
Truitt Edgar F, bricklyr, h 183 Yandes.
Truitt Loren E, lab, b 619 Virginia av.

A. METZGER AGENCY ESTABLISHED 1863. L-O-A-N-S

LAMBERT GAS & GASOLINE ENGINE CO.
ANDERSON, IND. GAS ENGINES FOR ALL PURPOSES.

Truitt Peter, confr, 619 Virginia av, h same.
Trulock George W, switchman, h 30 Chase (W I).
Trulock John F, clk, b 91 Bright.
Trulock John W, switchman, h 51 N Judge Harding (W I).
Trulock Martha, h 28 Warren av (W I).
Trulock Mary, b 301 S West.
Trulock Wm J, condr, h 46 Coffey (W I).
Truman Sarah G (wid Stephen G), h 82 Chestnut.
Trusler Albert C, real est, b 106 Middle Drive (W P).
Trusler Charles L, supt McCoy-Howe Co, b 280 N Penn.
Trusler Ira T, student, h 314 Bellefontaine.
Trusler Otway, insp, b 314 Fletcher av.
Trusler Preston C, sec and treas Indiana Construction Co, h 314 Fletcher av.
Trusler Robert N, trav agt, b 706 N Illinois.
Trusler Sarah E (wid Gilbert), h 706 N Illinois.
Trusler Thomas J, lawyer, 10½ N Delaware, h 106 Middle Drive (W P).
Trusty Thomas, lab, h 61 W Morris.
Tschaegle Alexander, cabtmkr, h 62 S Spruce.
Tschaegle Louis, cigarmkr, b 62 S Spruce.
Tschaegle Theophil, mach, b 62 S Spruce.
Tschentscher Adelheid (wid Rudolph C), h 175 E Market.
Tschentscher Gertrude C, clk The H Lieber Co, b 175 E Market.
Tschirschnitz Charles, cook, b e s Northwestern av nr canal.
Tubbs James, b 23 Athon.
Tucker Alice G, clk C C C & St L Ry, b 325 S Alabama.
Tucker Arkansas (wid Andrew J), h 112 W Vermont.
Tucker Caroline, seamstress, b 112 W Vermont.
Tucker Charles, h 569 E 8th.
Tucker Charles, coachman 891 N Penn.
Tucker Charles, lab, r 218 E Market.
Tucker Charles S, adv solr The Indpls Journal, b 121 E North.
Tucker Charles W, barber, 824 N Illinois, h 117 W 5th.
Tucker Clarence, actor, b 112 W Vermont.
Tucker David, porter, h 292 Yandes.
Tucker Dorcas, dressmkr, 101 N Senate av, h same.
Tucker Elizabeth (wid Wm H), matron Pentecost Bands, 52 S State av.
Tucker Ella C, bkkpr, b 113 Greer.
Tucker Ella L, teacher Public School No 31, b 365 Talbott av.
Tucker Ernest, r 98 W Ohio.
Tucker Florence (wid Wm), b 198 Newman.
Tucker Florence A, stenog Western Horseman Co, b 446 S Delaware.
Tucker George E S, carp, h 313 Cedar.
Tucker George O, real est, r 72 E Vermont.
Tucker George W, janitor, h 577 Mass av.
Tucker George W, phys, 158 Michigan (H), h same.
Tucker George W, trav agt, h 446 S Delaware.
Tucker Hannibal S, gloves, 10 E Washington, h 121 E North.
Tucker Jesse H, sawyer, h 113 Greer.
Tucker John I, lab, h 179 Meek.
Tucker Joseph, lab, h rear 381 S Olive.
Tucker Josephine E, dressmkr, 113 Greer, h same.
Tucker Lou (wid Joseph), h 40 Scioto.
Tucker Mary (wid George C), h 96 S East.

THOS. C. DAY & CO.
INVESTING AGENTS,
TOWN AND FARM LOANS,
Rooms 325 to 330 Lemcke Bldg.

Tucker Mary S (wid Erwin W), b 365 Talbott av.
Tucker Milo A, sawmkr, h 95 Woodburn av (W I).
Tucker Minetta, bkkpr Albert E Buchanan, b 36 W Michigan.
Tucker Sarah H (wid Richard S), h 64 English av.
Tucker Sarah J, h 285 Christian av.
Tucker Sarah S (wid John), b 631 Park av.
Tucker Wm, lab, r 338 Superior.
Tucker Wm, packer, b 80 S Capitol av.
Tucker Wm, patternmkr, h 266 Blackford.
Tucker Wm, waiter The Bates.
Tucker Wm H, pres Tucker & Dorsey Mnfg Co, h 122 Fletcher av.
Tucker Wm M, storekpr, h 327 S Alabama.
Tucker Wm M, waiter, r 577 Mass av.
Tucker & Dorsey Mnfg Co, Wm H Tucker pres, Robert L Dorsey sec and treas, hardware specialties, s w cor State av and Bates.
Tuckson Wm, porter, r 22 S Delaware.
Tudor Henry T, b 197 N West.
Tudor John W, cabtmkr, h 115 Clarke.
Tudor Wm H, boilermkr, h 380 W North.
Tuemme Paul, clk, b 196½ Ft Wayne av.
Tuft Anna (wid Wm), h 436 Superior.
Tuley Charles P, trav agt, h w s Ritter av 5 n of Washington av (I).
Tull Alton W, plumber, b 141 Fayette.
Tull John H, painter, h 141 Fayette.
Tull Wm, engr, b 22 S State av.
Tull Wm G, dentist, r 28½ Mass av.
Tull Wm H, b 518 Broadway.
Tulley Louis W, grocer, 720 S East, h 718 same.
Tullis Alexander J, cigarmkr, h 264 E Ohio.
Tullis Elmer R, metal polisher, h cor Russell av and S Illinois.
Tullis James H, insp, h 190 Oliver av (W I).
Tullis Wm K, clk, h 76 Bradshaw.
Tully Edward, lab, b 230 W Maryland.
Tully Edward M, trav agt Van Camp H and I Co, h 345 Talbott av.
Tumey, see also Toomey.
Tumey Andrew T, watchman, h 452 Chestnut.
Tunelius J Charles, bkkpr, b 174 N Illinois.

EAT
QUAKER BREAD
ASK YOUR GROCER FOR IT.
THE HITZ BAKING CO.

BICYCLES $5 { DOWN. MONTHLY. } Best Wheels. Best Terms. { WHEELMEN'S CO. 31 W. OHIO ST. LONG DISTANCE TEL. 1855.

J. H. TECKENBROCK | Grilles, Fretwork and Wood Carpets
94 EAST SOUTH STREET.

FIDELITY MUTUAL LIFE PHILADELPHIA, PA. A. H. COLLINS General Agent, 52-53 Baldwin Block.

Edwardsport Coal & Mining 6. Rooms 42 and 43 When Building.
SUPERIOR BITUMINOUS COAL For Steam and Domestic . . Purposes . .

ESTABLISHED 1876. TELEPHONE 168.
CHESTER BRADFORD,
SOLICITOR OF PATENTS,
AND COUNSEL IN PATENT CAUSES.
(See adv. page 6.)
Office:—Rooms 14 and 16 Hubbard Block, S.W. Cor. Washington and Meridian Streets, INDIANAPOLIS, INDIANA.

Turacki John, shoemkr. b 141½ Mass av.
Turk Charles L, fireman, b 37 Newman.
Turk Frank J, lawyer, b 37 Newman.
Turk Joseph P, mach opr, b 348 E Morris.
Turk John, lab, h 348 E Morris.
Turk Peter, lab, h 23 S Liberty.
Turk Stephen, lab, h e s Perkins pike 1 s of Prospect.
Turk Wm C, bricklyr, h 37 Newman.
Turk Wm D, pressman, b 348 E Morris.
Turley Henry, clk, b 878 Bellefontaine.
Turley Milton, carp, h 1074 W Vermont.
Turley Noble, student, b 46 S Capitol av.
Turner Adolph, carver, h 131 Blake.
Turner Albert M, barber, b 185 W 5th.
Turner Allen L, tinner, b 21 Bright.
Turner Alvin H, supt Turner Zephyr Furnace Co, b 58½ W Ohio.
Turner Annais, h 268 Mass av.
Turner Benjamin E, clk, b 75 Highland pl.
Turner Caroline (wid Joseph), h 261 Lafayette.
Turner Charles, lab, b 196 Huron.
Turner Charles B, h 211 N Illinois.
Turner Charles E, porter, b 185 W 5th.
Turner Chauncey L, h 827 N Meridian.
Turner Darius, tmstr, b 120 Elizabeth.
Turner David, lab, h 334 Superior.
Turner David J, drayman, b 331 Clinton.
Turner Edward, lab, b 131 Howard.
Turner Edward, molder, b 310 N Pine.
Turner Eliza (wid John), b 153 Agnes.
Turner Elizabeth, dressmkr, b 615 N Senate av.
Turner Emma (wid Burton), b 124 Columbia al.
Turner Evelyn L W C (wid Joseph M), h 9 Wood.
Turner Frances (wid Nathan), b 257 W 5th.
Turner Frank D, fireman, h 279 S Senate av.
Turner Frederick, lab, b 185 W 5th.
Turner George, waiter, r rear 359 Blake.
Turner George L, cabtmkr, h 9 Peru av.
Turner George L, trav agt, r 77½ E Market.
Turner Gilbert, lab, h 84 W 8th.
Turner Grace (wid Ephraim), h 20 Seibert.
Turner Grant, lab, b s s Finley av 3 e of Shelby.

HAY & WILLITS MFG CO.
76 N. PENNSYLVANIA ST.,
MAKERS
Outing BICYCLES
PHONE 598.

Turner Henry C, clk Consumers' Gas Trust Co, h 580 Park av.
Turner Henry C, contr, 298 Fayette, h same.
Turner Henry C, waiter, r 267 S Capitol av.
Turner Isom, lab, h 13 Alvord.
Turner Jacob, lab, b 115 Meek.
Turner James, h n s University av 2 w of Central av (I).
Turner James, coachman 750 N Meridian.
Turner James, hostler, h 337 W North.
Turner James, lab, b 4 Holborn.
Turner James E, lab, h 400½ S Capitol av.
Turner James L, nurse, h 185 W 5th.
Turner James M (Turner & McHaffey), h 20 Yandes.
Turner John, lab, b 62 Bismarck (W I).
Turner John, lab, h rear 16 Center.
Turner John, lab, r 66 N Missouri.
Turner John, lab, r 430 Superior.
Turner John D, clk Penna Lines, h 392 N Alabama.
Turner John E, pass agt Northern Pacific Ry, 42 Jackson pl.
Turner John H, cigarmkr, h 77 N Pine.
Turner John J, letter carrier P O, h 279 N Liberty.
Turner John L, lab, h 239 S Capitol av.
Turner Joseph, lab, h 97 Darnell.
Turner Josephine (wid John), baker, 427 E Vermont, h same.
Turner Major W, roofer, h 33 S Dorman.
Turner Martin, lab, h 221 E Wabash.
Turner Mary (wid Nathan), h 228½ N Missouri.
Turner Pleasant, lab, h 132 Downey.
Turner Robert, lab, h 185 W 2d.
Turner Robert L, tinner, 25 Kentucky av, h 43 N Rural.
Turner Robert O, foreman, h 256 W Michigan.
Turner Samuel G, lab, h rear 279 S Senate av.
Turner Sarah (wid George), h 12½ Roanoke.
Turner Sarah E (wid Marcus I), h 190 Hoyt av.
Turner Sarah L (wid George A), boarding 70½ N Delaware.
Turner Sophia, cook, h 267 Spring.
Turner Stanton H, tel opr Fire Dept, h 222 Muskingum al.
Turner Thaddeus, lab, b 4 Brown.
Turner Thomas, lab, r 94 Bright.
Turner Thomas J, cook, h 839 S Meridian.
Turner Thomas J, driver, r rear 422 N East.
Turner Ulsey, lab, b 24 Sheffield av (H).
Turner Wm, lab, b 23 Athon.
Turner Wm, lab, h s s Finley av 3 e of Shelby.
Turner Wm, lab, r 15 Rhode Island.
Turner Wm A, mach hd, h 199 W Ray.
Turner Wm H, driver, b 228 N Delaware.
Turner Wm H, pres Turner Zephyr Furnace and Stove Co, h 58½ W Ohio.
Turner Wm Hyde, sec Turner Zephyr Furnace and Stove Co, h 76 W 4th.
Turner Wm J, lab, h 131 Howard.
Turner Wm J, janitor, b 615 N Senate av.
Turner Wm S, designer U S Encaustic Tile Wks, b 827 N Meridian.
Turner Wm W, clk, b 309 N Pine.
TURNER ZEPHYR FURNACE AND STOVE CO, Wm H Turner Pres, Wm Hyde Turner Sec, Newton M Taylor Treas, Alvin H Turner Supt, 94-100 Kentucky av and 81 S Senate av.
Turner & McHaffey (James M Turner, James A McHaffey), grocers, 49 Yandes.

ROOFING MATERIAL C. ZIMMERMAN & SONS SLATE AND GRAVEL ROOFERS, 19 SOUTH EAST STREET.

DRIVEN WELLS And Second Water Wells and Pumps of all kinds at CHARLES KRAUSS', 42 S. PENN. ST., TEL. 465. REPAIRING NEATLY DONE.

Turney Amos, lab, r 175 E Market.
Turney Loama E, student, r 367 N Alabama.
Turney Thomas, driver, b rear 422 N East.
Turnham John G, driver, h 175 St Marie.
Turpie David, United States Senator, h 173 N Capitol av.
Turpin Alfred P, motorman, h 24 Cleveland (H).
Turpin Arthur J, mach, h 42 Clarke.
Turpin George W, miller, r 101 Bates.
Turpin Harrison G, b 35 Wilcox.
Turpin John F, gasfitter, h 52 Nordyke av (W I).
Turpin Mahala A (wid Asa), b 147 Union.
Turpin Mary E (wid James), h 42 Clarke.
Turpin W Wallace, cloth coverer, b 20 N William (W I).
Turrell Anna E, stenog Stanton & Denny, b 330 College av.
Turrell Evalynne (wid Richard S), h 636 Park av.
Turrell Wm S, clk, h 330 College av.
Turrell Willard S, lab, b 330 College av.
Tush Wm H, farmer, h 643 College av.
Tussey Delia V, dressmkr, 126 E New York, r same.
Tutewiler Charles W (Tutewiler & Shideler), h 411 Park av.
TUTEWILER HARRY D, Undertaker, 72 W Market, Tel 216; h 1105 N Delaware.
TUTEWILER HENRY W, Undertaker, 72 W Market, Tel 216; h 401 N Senate av, Tel 441. (See left bottom lines.)
Tutewiler James, farmer, h n s Brookville rd 1 e of P C C & St L Ry (S).
Tutewiler Mary J (wid Henry), h 85 Mass av.
TUTEWILER & SHIDELER (Charles W Tutewiler, John E Shideler), Mngrs Equitable Life Assurance Society of the United States for Western Indiana, 601-603 Indiana Trust Bldg, Tel 1143.
Tuthill Benjamin, clk C C C & St L Ry, h 195 Davidson.
Tutt John C, proofreader The Indpls Sentinel, b 21 Lockerbie.
Tutt Reuben, lab, h 222 W 8th.
Tuttle Alvin E, floorlyr, b n s Orange av 2 e of Jefferson av.
Tuttle Annie, laundress, h rear 236 E Wabash.
Tuttle Armenia B (wid Reuben B), h 945 N Illinois.
Tuttle Calvin, driver, b n s Orange av 2 e of Jefferson av.
Tuttle Charles A, lab, h 154 Lee (W I).
Tuttle Clark C, mngr retail dept The Hay & Willits Mnfg Co, h 222 Davidson.
Tuttle Edward C, painter, h 646 N Senate av
Tuttle Edward J, foreman, h 1699 Graceland av.
Tuttle Elmer W, printer, h 411 W Michigan
Tuttle Herman C (Tuttle & Seguin), h 1660 N Illinois.
Tuttle John E, packer, r 269 N Alabama.
Tuttle Julia A (wid Perry E), b 222 Davidson.
Tuttle Marvin H, foreman H C Bauer Engraving Co, r 81 W North.
Tuttle Mary A (wid Benjamin F), h 326 N Meridian.
Tuttle Milton B, clk The Grand Hotel.

Richardson & McCrea, REPRESENTING BEST KNOWN FIRE INSURANCE COMPANIES. Fidelity and Casualty Insurance Company of New York Represented. Telephone 182. 79 East Market St.

Tuttle Orrin, city fireman, h 645 N Senate av.
Tuttle Richard B, clk, b 945 N Illinois.
Tuttle Riley J, lab h 825 E 9th.
Tuttle Sarah J (wid Gaylord P) b 801 N New Jersey.
Tuttle Thomas F, spec agt Orient Ins Co, h 267 N East.
Tuttle Walter C, music teacher, 136 W Vermont, b 645 N Senate av.
Tuttle Wm, mach hd, h n s Orange av 2 e of Jefferson av.
TUTTLE & SEGUIN (Herman C Tuttle, Edward S R Seguin), Real Estate, Insurance, Loans and Rentals, 28 E Market, Tel 1168. (See left bottom cor cards.)
Tweed Charles E, tel opr W U Tel Co, h 1027 Morris (W I).
Twente John H, soldier, h 14 Hamilton av.
Twente Louis G, furniture, 122 Ft Wayne av, h 122½ same.
Twente Mollie, h 137 Shepard (W I).
Twente Wm F, furniture, 219 Mass av, h same.
TWENTIETH CENTURY RUG CO THE, Wm L Miner Propr, 184-186 Cherry. (See adv opp classified Rugs.)
Twichell Alice E, phys, 268 Brookside av, b same.
TWINAME JAMES E, Bailiff Marion Circuit Court, 45 Court House, h n w cor Barth av and Roll.
Twiname John J, contr, h 850 Park av.
Twine Lee, cook, r 170 Bird.
Twine Millie (wid Richard), h 196 Newman.
Twine Warren S, lab, b 196 Newman.
Twines David, driver, h 30 W 1st.
Twines Harvey, lab, h 484 Superior.
Twines Joseph, lab, h 125 Ft Wayne av.
Twyman Edwin B, printer F H Smith, h 233 E Ohio.
Twyman Henry D, whitewasher, h 8 Cornell av.
Twyman James E, chief mailing clk The Indpls Journal, h 112 College av.

The Williams Typewriter Elegant Work, Visible Writing, Easy Operation, High Speed. S. H. EAST, State Agent, 55 Thorpe Block, 87 E. Market St.

If You are not Satisfied with Your Laundry Work Give Us a Trial. ERTEL STEAM LAUNDRY 26 and 28 N. Se Avenue. Telephone 18.

ELLIS & HELFENBERGER { Manufacturers of IRON and WIRE FENCES 162-170 S. SENATE AVE. TEL. 358.

THE HOGAN TRANSPER AND STORAGE COMP'Y
Household Goods and Pianos Moved—Packed—Stored..... Baggage and Package Express Machinery and Safes a Specialty Cor. Washington and Illinois Sts. TELEPHONE No. 675.

The Central Rubber & Supply Co. PHONE 2. 79 S. ILLINOIS ST., INDIANAPOLIS, IND. Hose, Belting, Packing, Clothing, Druggists' Sundries, Bicycle Tires, Cotton Hose, Etc. New York Belting & Packing Co., L't'd.

HIGHEST SECURITY
LOWEST COST OF INSURANCE.
The Provident Life and Trust Co.
Of Philadelphia.
D. W. EDWARDS, Gen. Agent,
508 Indiana Trust Building.

Twyman Marcellus M, packer, h 21 Cornell av.
Twyman Margaret, h 233 E Ohio.
Twyman Thomas lab, h 154 Belmont av (H).
Tyer Charles W, engr, h 156 N Pine.
Tyer Wm mach, h 137 N Gillard av.
Tyers George H, cooper, h 287½ E Washington.
Tyler Cynthia A (wid John), b 532 Chestnut.
Tyler Albert W, painter, h 92 S West.
Tyler Charles B, confr, b 91 Harmon.
Tyler Charles M, clk Kingan & Co (ltd), h 468 W 22d (N I).
Tyler Charles W, clk, b 468 W 22d (N I).
Tyler Clifford H, collr Central Union Telephone Co, b 162 N Illinois.
Tyler Ferdinand W, printer Indpls Journal, r 10 The Windsor.
Tyler Frank S, hardware, 186 Virginia av, h 193 Buchanan.
Tyler Joseph, lab, b 156 Michigan av.
Tyler Joseph E, clk, b 420 Udell (N I).
Tyler Joseph M, carp, h 28 S Judge Harding (W I).
Tyler Judson, mach, b 122 E Ohio.
Tyler Lambert D (Griggs & Tyler), h 21 Cherry.
Tyler Lucy A (wid George), b 108 Maple.
Tyler Mary C (wid Oliver), h 468 W 22d (N I).
Tyler Matilda, b 232 W Vermont.
Tyler Robert E, clk N Y Store, b 527 Broadway.
Tyler Spofford E, b 412 N East.
Tyler Theodore M, foreman, h 63 Hoyt av.
Tyler Walter, waiter, r 104 W South.
Tyler Wm, tmstr, h 108 Maple.
Tyler Wm H, clk Model Clothing Co h 67 Martindale av.
Tynan John A, mach, h 256 S Meridian.
Tynan Mary A, dressmkr, 256 S Meridian, h same.
Tyndall Robert H (Tyndall & Moore) b w s Euclid av 2 n of Washington.
Tyndall & Moore (Robert H Tyndall, Charles H Moore), grocers, e s Garfield av 2 n of Washington.
Tyner Charles C, plumber, h e s Tremont av 4 s of Clark (H).

Julius C. Walk & Son,
Jewelers
Indianapolis.
12 EAST WASHINGTON ST.

Tyner Charles G, express, h 478 Bellefontaine.
Tyner Charles L, barber, 39 E Market, h 107 Fayette.
Tyner Charles W clk, b 478 Bellefontaine.
Tyner Christian G, clk N Y Store, b 478 Bellefontaine.
Tyner Edward E, packer, h 45½ Virginia av.
Tyner Elbert T, bartndr, r 168½ E Washington.
Tyner Elijah H, mach, h 32 Crawford.
Tyner Frank (Boicourt, Tyner & Co), b 182 E North.
Tyner Frank, watchman, b 26½ N Senate av.
Tyner Franklin P, bartndr, r 168½ E Washington.
Tyner James, tmstr, h 484 N California.
Tyner Lemuel F, brakeman, r 19 N Arsenal av.
Tyner Thomas E, condr, h 103 Geisendorff.
Tyner Wm, clk, b 264 W Michigan.
Tyner Wm jr, mach, b 71 English av.
Tyner Wm B, condr, h 71 English av.
Tyre Griffin, well driver, b 190 N East.
Tyre Lizzie, h 65 W Georgia.
Tyree Charles W, lab, h 27 Hiawatha.
Tyree Charles jr, lab, b 27 Hiawatha.
Tyree Charles, lab, b 172 N New Jersey.
Tyree Jasper, driver, b 27 Hiawatha.
Tyrrell, see also Terrell.
Tyrrell Alexander, flagman, b 133 Lynn av (W I).
Tyrrell Frank, clk, b 22 Garland (W I).
Tyrrell Harry M, lab, b 22 Garland (W I).
Tyrrell Nancy J (wid Alexander), h 22 Garland (W I).
Tysinger George W, meats, 71 Cherry, h 102 Broadway.

U

Udell Calvin G jr, asst sec Y M C A, h 544 W Francis (N I).
UDELL EUGENE, Agt Indianapolis Gas Co, 544 W Addison (N I), Tel 1736; h 542 same.
Udell Wm C, mach, h 550 W Addison (N I).
Udell Woodenware Works, Albert A Barnes propr, n w cor Addison and Emma (N I).
Uden Thomas, lab, h rear 363 S Olive.
Uebelacker Frank, saloon, 1205 S Meridian, h same.
Uebele Carl, packer Charles Mayer & Co, h 72 Cincinnati.
Uebele Fritz, baker, b 72 Cincinnati.
Uhl Calvin M, motorman, h 32 S Senate av.
Uhl Charles H, pres Indpls Live Stock Journal and Ptg Co, res Evansville, Ind.
Uhl Edward H, agt, b 755 N Capitol av.
Uhl Frank A, meats, 53 E Mkt House, h 31 Kansas.
Uhl John, meats, 351 Dillon, h 365 same.
Uhl John C, clk, b 365 Dillon.
Uhl Louis, meats, 534 S Meridian, h same.
Uhl Peter, cigarmkr, h 755 N Capitol av.
Uhl Regina (wid John), h 31 Kansas.
Ulery Charles H, tmstr, h 35 Harris av (M J).
Ulery Edward, blksmith, h 501½ W Washington.
Ulery John, baggageman, h 235 W Market.
Ullery Martha (wid Allen), h 21 Meikel.
Ullery Wm G, fireman, h 50 Temple av.
Ulmer George W, lab, b rear e s Woodside av 1 s of P C C & St L Ry (W).
Ulmer Henry C, mach, h rear e s Woodside av 1 s of P C C & St L Ry (W).

OTTO GAS ENGINES | BUILDERS' EXCHANGE S. W. Cor. Ohio and Penn. Telephone 535.

JOHN H. HOLLIDAY, President. ADDISON C. HARRIS, Vice-Pres.
HENRY EITEL, 2d Vice-Pres. and Treas. H. C. G. BALS, Secretary.

* DIRECTORS *

Charles H. Brownell, Peru.	Sterling R. Holt.
S. A. Culbertson, New Albany.	George Kothe.
Thos. C. Day.	Henry C. Long.
I. C. Elston, Crawfordsville.	Volney T. Malott.
Addison C. Harris.	Edward L. McKee.
John H. Holliday.	Sam. E. Rauh.

. . The . .
Union Trust Company

68 E. MARKET STREET, INDIANAPOLIS.

Capital, $600,000.00
Surplus, $60,000.00

Stockholders' Additional Liability, $600,000.00.

The Union Trust Company is organized under a special law which requires a guarantee of ample financial responsibility, and establishes a state supervision. It must be examined twice a year by the Auditor of State, and may be examined any time he pleases. The safeguards of law thus thrown about it assure correct management. It is authorized to act as executor and guardian, administrator, assignee, receiver or trustee under wills or by appointment of court, and can do business, as a rule, more efficiently and economically than an individual. Its stockholders are liable for twice the amount of their stock.

It acts as agent and trustee in any matter of business, and as financial depository for Building Associations and other corporations.

It buys and sells securities, deals in county and municipal bonds, loans money on mortgage and collateral security.

It furnishes bonds for executors, administrators and guardians in any county in the State. It is a legal depository for court and trust funds.

Interest allowed on deposits of money, which may be made at any time and withdrawn after notice or at a fixed date, and will be entitled to interest for the whole time they remain with the Company.

Executors, Administrators or Trustees of Estates will find this Company a convenient depository for money. It does not receive deposits payable on demand, nor does it do a banking business. Lends money on Farms.

Charges Moderate.

Becker & Son Charles Becker Jacob Becker Jr. Merchant Tailors. 21 N. Penn. St. Tel. 934

Ulmer James W, lab, b rear e s Woodside av 1 s of P C C & St L Ry (W).
Ulmer Oscar, b 152 Michigan (H).
Ulrey David J, engr, h 261 W Pearl.
Ulrich Frank, driver, r rear 472 E Washington.
Ulrich Frederick P, bartndr, h cor Capitol av and Garden.
Ulrich George, fireman, h 1040 W Washington.
Ulrich Harry, clk L S Ayres & Co, b 167 Fayette.
Ulrich John, litho-engraver Wm B Burford, h 237 Blackford.
Ulrich John G, clk L S Ayres & Co, h 167 Fayette.
Ulrich Margaret F, b 250 S Capitol av.
Ulrich Otto, lab, h 141 Sheffield av (H).
Ulrich Thomas D, trav agt, h 152 Bellefontaine.
Ulrich Wm, lab, h 379 Fletcher av.
Ulsas Leonard, lab, h 58 Arizona.
Umberger Henry, mach hd, b 165 S Alabama.
Umbright Arsinoe, boarding 22 S State av.
Umbright Ernest J, baker, h 22 S State av.
Umphrey Clarinda (wid Absalom), b 18 Arbor av (W I).
Umphrey Louis, foreman Natl Starch Mnfg Co, h 118 Wisconsin.
Umsteadter David M, clk, h 164 Lexington av.
Unavy Frank T, tailor, b 31 Madison av.
Underhill Abraham V, clk Murphy, Hibben & Co, h 21 Elm.
Underhill Sarah W, h 455 N Capitol av.
Underwood Addison, canmkr, b 564 Union.
Underwood Andrew, lineman, h 75 Stevens.
Underwood Edson S, painter, h 95½ N Delaware.
Underwood Elizabeth (wid James M), h 564 Union.
Underwood George, condr, h 36 Dearborn.
Underwood George R, molder, h 386 Columbia av.
Underwood Henry, lab, h 165 S William (W I).
Underwood James A, lab, h 102 Hadley av (W I).
Underwood James W, clk, b 894 S Meridian.
Underwood Joseph H, waiter, h 302½ N Senate av.
Underwood Madison, canmkr, b 564 Union.
Underwood Samuel, lab, h s s Pansy 1 w of Floral av.
Underwood Wm, student, r 19 Russell av.
Underwood Wm H, lab, h 165 S William (W I).
Ungar Philip, saloon, 98 Russell av, h same.
Unger Charles W, driver, h 123 St Mary.
Unger Christian, brewer, h 58 Dunlop.
Unger Jeremiah, carp, 119 Hoyt av, h same.
Unger Joseph, lab, h 316 Excelsior av.
Unger Mary, h 138 Kennington.
Ungerer Bernard, shooting gallery, 129 W Washington, r same.
Ungericht Herman, baker, b 277 S Alabama.
Ungericht John, barber, h 470 N West.
Ungericht Wm F, agt, h 650½ N West.
UNION CASUALTY AND SURETY CO OF ST LOUIS, MO, W E Barton & Co Genl Agts, 504 Indiana Trust Bldg, Long Distance Tel 1918. (See right bottom cor cards.)
Union Construction Co, David C Bryan pres and mngr, 236 Lemcke bldg.

Henry H. Fay,
40½ E. WASHINGTON ST.,
AGENT FOR
Insurance Co. of North America,
Pennsylvania Fire Ins. Co.

UNION CO-OPERATIVE LAUNDRY, Theodore E Somerville Mngr, 138-144 Virginia av, Tel 1269. (See left side lines.)
UNION EMBOSSING MACHINE CO, Edward S De Tamble Pres, Wm M Richards Sec and Treas, Mnfrs of Drop Carving Machines and Dies, 30-40 W South, Tel 1513.
Union Insurance Co The, Hiram Teter pres, Fred W Alexander sec, 423 Lemcke bldg.
UNION LINE, John C Wood Agt, 28-29 Commercial Club Bldg, Tel 277.
UNION MUTUAL BUILDING AND LOAN ASSOCIATION, John C Shoemaker Pres, Albert Gall Vice-Pres, James E Franklin Sec, George F McGinnis Treas, 87 W Market.
UNION NATIONAL SAVINGS AND LOAN ASSOCIATION OF INDIANAPOLIS, Charles F Griffin Pres, A B Gates 1st Vice-Pres, Adolph Schleicher 2d Vice-Pres, Nicholas Ensley Sec, Capital National Bank Treas, 65 E Ohio, Tel 1369.
Union News Co, Oscar E Sherman mngr, 193 S Illinois.
UNION PUBLISHING CO, Elbert T Howe Mngr, Subscription Books, 29 Baldwin Blk.
UNION TRANSFER AND STORAGE CO, Albert A Tripp Pres, James A Green Vice-Pres, Ernest H Tripp Sec and Treas, n e cor E Ohio and C C C & St L Ry, Tel 725. (See left side lines.)
UNION TRUST CO THE, John H Holliday Pres, Henry C G Bals Sec, Henry Eitel 2d Vice-Pres and Treas, 68 E Market, Tel 1576. (See front cover.)
United States Army Recruiting Service, Capt Ralph W Hoyt recruiting officer, 25½ N Illinois.
United States Arsenal, Major A L Varney commandant, n end Arsenal av.

MAYHEW'S SPECTACLES THE BEST IN USE SOLD ONLY AT 13 N. MERIDIAN ST.

SALISBURY & STANLEY OFFICE, STORE AND BANK FIXTURES. Contractors and Builders. Repairing of all kinds done on short notice. 177 Clinton St., Indianapolis, Ind. Telephone 999.

LUMBER Sash and Doors BALKE & KRAUSS CO., Corner Market and Missouri Sts.

Friedgen Has the BEST PATENT LEATHER SHOES AT LOWEST PRICES. 19 North Pennsylvania St.

SAMUEL LAING : HOT AIR FURNACES 72 AND 74 EAST COURT STREET.

M. B. WILSON, Pres. W. F. CHURCHMAN, Cash.
The Capital National Bank,
INDIANAPOLIS, IND.
Banking business in all its branches. Bonds and Foreign Exchange bought and sold.
Interest paid on time deposits.
Checks and drafts on all Indiana and Illinois points handled at lowest rates.
No. 28 South Meridian Street, Cor. Pearl.

UNITED STATES ARTISTIC CO (Herbert M and Winthrop R Adkinson), Embossed Wood Mnfrs, 166 S New Jersey.

UNITED STATES BAKING CO, Parrott-Taggart Bakery, 93-99 S Penn, Tel 800. (See bottom edge.)

UNITED STATES BUILDING AND LOAN INSTITUTION (Capital $2,000,000), Caleb N Lodge Sec, 721-722 Lemcke Bldg.

United States Bureau of Animal Industry, Joseph C Roberts insp in charge Kingan & Co.

UNITED STATES CASUALTY CO OF NEW YORK, Daniel F Fleener Genl Agt, 427-428 Lemcke Bldg.

United States Circuit Court, Wm A Woods Judge, P O bldg.

United States Commissioner's Office, 29½ N Penn.

United States Courts Clerk's Office, Noble C Butler Clerk, P O bldg.

United States Custom House, George G Tanner Surveyor, P O bldg.

United States Deputy Internal Revenue Collector's Office, 2d floor P O bldg.

United States District Attorney's Office, Frank B Burke Attorney, P O bldg.

United States District Court, John H Baker Judge, P O bldg.

UNITED STATES ENCAUSTIC TILE WORKS, John J Cooper Pres, Jackson Landers Vice-Pres, John Picken Sec and Treas, cor 7th and Big Four Ry, Tel 950.

UNITED STATES EXPRESS CO, Caleb S Phillips Agt, 23 S Meridian, Tel 378; Union Depot, Tel 370.

UNITED STATES INTERNAL REVENUE OFFICE, Wm H Bracken Collr, P O Bldg, Tel 505.

UNITED STATES LIFE INSURANCE CO OF NEW YORK, Elias B Swift Mngr, 25 E Market, Tel 1797. (See left bottom lines.)

Insure Against Accidents
WITH
TUTTLE & SEGUIN,
Agents for
Fidelity and Casualty Co., of New York.
$10,000 for $25. $5,000 for $12.50.
TEL. 1168. 28 E. MARKET ST.

United States Lounge Mnfg Co, Samuel H Collins pres, K G Stewart vice-pres, M A Stewart sec, 128 Ft Wayne av and 25 N Illinois.

United States Marshal's Office, Wm H Hawkins marshal, 29½ N Penn.

UNITED STATES PENSION AGENCY, Martin V B Spencer Agt, 67 W Maryland, Tel 1309.

United States Playing Card Co, Samuel J Murray supt, cor Gatling and Belt R R.

United States Railway Mail Service, Charles D Rogers chief clk, P O bldg.

United States Saving Fund and Investment Co, Robert E Moore pres, Elisha H Hall sec, 42 Lorraine bldg.

United States Secret Service, Thomas B Carter agt, 29½ N Penn.

UNITED STATES SPECIAL EXAMINERS PENSION BUREAU, P O Bldg, Tel 1309.

United States Weather Bureau, Charles F R Wappenhans local forecast official, 905-907 Majestic bldg.

UNITED STATES WRINGER CO, Isaac H Hendershot Mngr, Installment Goods, 19 Indiana av.

UNIVERSAL CREDIT AGENCY THE OF INDIANAPOLIS, Harry S Holton Pres, James E Neighbor Vice-Pres, Jesse C Moore Sec and Mngr, Mercantile Reports, 90-91 Baldwin Blk, Tel 740.

Universal Telephone Co, John T Martindale pres, Elijah B Martindale jr sec, 86 E Market.

University of Indianapolis, Allen M Fletcher pres, George E Hunter sec, Herman Lieber treas, assembly rooms Commercial Club.

Unser Charles, lab, b 152 Michigan (H).

Unsworth Edwin, agt, h 33 Lynn av (W I).

Unversaw Albert H, carp, h e s McRae 2 n of Belt R R.

Unversaw Andrew J, butcher, h 934 Madison av.

Unversaw Andrew J. cooper, h 306 W Market.

Unversaw Charles G, clk R M S, h 80 Pleasant.

Unversaw Edward, huckster, r 224 Bright.

Unversaw Elizabeth (wid Andrew), h 347 S Alabama.

Unversaw Ernst M, butcher, b 13 Dougherty.

Unversaw Frank A, carp, h 190 Minnesota.

Unversaw George, lab, b 650 Madison av.

Unversaw John J, lab, h 7 Peck.

Unversaw John N, meats, 83 E Mkt House, h 13 Dougherty.

Unversaw John W, carp, h 58 Buchanan.

Unversaw Leonard, butcher, b 1112 N Senate av.

Unversaw Louis F, porter, h 422 W Shoemaker (N I).

Unverzagt Herman H, gardener, h 1382 Schurman av (N I).

Unverzagt John H, gardener, h 1382 Schurman av (N I).

Updegraff Edward T, tmstr, h 120 Douglass.

Updegraff George W, shoemkr, 191 Virginia av, h same.

Updegraff Jacob, pdlr, h 142 Lynn av (W I).

Updegraff John W, porter, 171 W Washington.

Updegraff Julius, shoemkr, 908 W Washington, h same.

WEDDING CAKE BOXES · SULLIVAN & MAHAN 41 W. Pearl St.

Updike Caleb G, lab, h 177 Minnesota.
Updike Samuel B, lab, b 403 Coburn.
Updike Samuel H, plastr, h 403 Coburn.
Updyke John, h 16 Dawson.
Updyke Susan M, b 16 Dawson.
Upfold Emily L, b 546 N Meridian.
Upham Albert S, clk C C C & St L Ry, h 18 Arch.
Uphaus Herman, cigarmkr, b 8 Wisconsin.
Uphaus Mary A (wid Henry), midwife, 8 Wisconsin, h same.
Uphaus Victor, varnisher, b 8 Wisconsin.
Upton Bluford H, lab, h 103 S New Jersey.
Upton Harley S, clk Browning & Son, h 50 The Chalfant.
Upton Willard, lab, b 103 S New Jersey.
Uratanar John, lab, b 60 Holmes av (H).
Urey Wm B, carp, h 47 Russell av.
Urhland Olga, nurse 118 N Senate av.
Urlevicz Joseph, lab, h 555 Union.
Urlevicz Joseph jr, canmkr, b 555 Union.
Urmston Guy, stenog, b 657 College av.
Urmston Sarah (wid Stephen E), h 657 College av.
Urschel Lewis P, mngr, b 165 N Alabama.
Uter Edward C, clk Van Camp H and I Co, b 242 Blackford.
Uter Robert L, butcher, h 242 Blackford.
Utley Harvey, lab, b 201 E Washington.
Utt John R, lab, h 149 S Spruce.
Utter James G, printer, r 191 Fletcher av.
Utterback Anna K (wid Wm A), b 777 N New Jersey.
Utterbach Hezekiah, lab, h 860 Milburn (M P).
Utz John, lab, h 731 Charles.

V

Vacker Anton J, lab, h 571 Charles.
Vacker John, blksmith, h 33 Clay.
Vacker John, molder, b 571 Charles.
Vacker Louisa (wid Frederick), h w s Station 6 n of Schofield (B).
Vahey James, boys' supervisor Deaf and Dumb Inst.
Vahle Edward H, mach, h 176 Highland av.
Vahle Harry, bill clk Tanner & Sullivan, b 313 N Noble.
Vahle Henry, lab, h 313 N Noble.
Vahle Henry H, carp, 44 Walcott, h same.
Vahle Herman H, carp, h 180 Fulton.
Vahle Herman H, carp, h 48 Sterling.
Vahle Herman H jr, carp, h 25 Windsor.
Vahle Wm A, mach, b 180 Fulton.
Vail Flora E, music teacher 1208 N Penn, b same.
Vail Homer J, trav agt, r 272 N Senate av.
Vail John D, clk, h 19 S West.
Vail John H, bkkpr, h 79 W 5th.
Vail John W, trav agt Parrott-Taggart Bakery, b 790 N Illinois.
Vail Mary B, teacher Industrial Training School, b 448 College av.
Vail Robert A (Vail Seed Co), b 731 E Washington.
VAIL SEED CO (Robert A Vail, Wm H Kelly, Wm A Eshbach), Wholesale and Retail Seeds and Bulbs, 96 N Delaware, Tel 145.
Vail Sidney J, teacher Deaf and Dumb Inst, h 731 E Washington.
Vail Wm B, printer, b 225 E Market.
VAJEN-BADER CO THE, Willis C Vajen Pres and Mngr, Fire Equipment Mnfrs, Room 15, 88 N Penn.
Vajen Charles T, real est, 20 Thorpe blk, b 128 N Meridian.

FRANK NESSLER. WILL H. ROST.
FRANK NESSLER & CO.
Tailors
56 EAST MARKET ST. (Lemcke Building),
INDIANAPOLIS. IND.

Vajen Frank, clk, b 128 N Meridian.
Vajen John H, h 128 N Meridian.
VAJEN'S REAL ESTATE EXCHANGE, Willis C Vajen, 88 N Penn.
Vajen Willis C (Vajen's Real Estate Exchange), pres and mngr The Vajen-Bader Co, 88 N Penn, h 22 E Vermont.
VALDENAIRE JOHN J, Lumber, Sash, Doors and Blinds, Pumps and Hardware, s s Glen Drive 2 w of Gale (B), h s s Glen Drive 2 e of Shade (B).
Valdes Elizabeth (wid Raymond), h 77 Cincinnati.
Valentine Andrew J, lab, b 562 W North.
Valentine Charles, painter, b 643 S Meridian.
Valentine Charles, tmstr, h 197 Middle.
Valentine Hugh H, plastr, r 81 Muskingum al.
Valentine Isom, tmstr, h e s James 4 n of Sutherland (B).
Valentine James W, tmstr, h 60 Ludlow av.
Valentine Jennie, h 28 N West.
Valentine Jeremiah, lab, h 562 W North.
Valentine Lafayette, lab, h 82 Meikel.
Valentine Michael, spinner, b 28 N West.
Valentine Samuel, lab, h 102 Torbet.
Valentine Thomas J, spinner, b 28 N West.
Valinetz Louis, optician, h 447 S Capitol av.
Valley Wm, bricklyr, h 47 Holly av (W I).
Vallowe Wm H, clk A E Dochez, b 179 Dearborn.
Valodin Charles M (Dye, Valodin & Co), h 490 W Highland av (N I).
Valodin John F, clk, b 490 W Highland av (N I).
Valodin Wm A, bkkpr, h 26 S Reisner (W I).
Van Anda Henry C, teller The Indiana Trust Co, b 48 W North.
Van Arsdale Bros (Miles S and Leslie C), druggists, 1059 E Michigan.
Van Arsdale Diana (wid Abraham B), h 36 Sullivan.
Van Arsdale Edgar, lab, b 36 Sullivan.
Van Arsdale Leslie C (Van Arsdale Bros), res Plainfield, Ind.

ACORN STOVES AND RANGES
Haueisen & Hartmann
163-169 E. Washington St.
FURNITURE,
Carpets,
Household Goods,
Tin, Granite and China Wares, Oil Cloth and Shades

st Work. ompt Delivery. } THE HOME LAUNDRY 197 S. ILLINOIS ST. TEL. 1769. { Collars and Cuffs our Specialty.

THE WM. H. BLOCK CO. 7 AND 9 EAST WASHINGTON STREET. DRY GOODS, HOUSE FURNISHINGS AND CROCKERY.

London Guarantee and Accident Co. (Ltd.) All forms of Liability Insurance, Workmen's Collective Insurance, Fidelity Bonds and Individual Accident Insurance.
Geo. W. Pangborn, Gen. Agent, 704-706 Lemcke Bldg. Telephone 140.

FRANK K. SAWYER, AGENT 74 East Market Street. Telephone 863.
Prussian National Insurance Company OF STETTIN, GERMANY. ORGANIZED 1845.

JOSEPH GARDNER,
TIN, COPPER AND SHEET-IRON WORK AND
HOT AIR FURNACES.
37, 39 & 41 KENTUCKY AVE. Telephone 322.

Van Arsdale Miles S (Van Arsdale Bros), r 1059 E Michigan.
Van Arsdale Wade H, agt, b 36 Sullivan.
Van Arsdall Marion, fence mnfr, 222 Ramsey av, h same.
Vanarsdall Wm C, plastr, 554 S Illinois, h same.
Van Arsdel Gilbert A, mach hd, b 566 W Udell (N I).
Van Arsdel Melvina (wid Abram B), h 466 W Shoemaker (N I).
Van Arsdel Wm C, mngr Central Ind N Y Life Ins Co, h 702 College av.
Van Arsdell Joseph B, miller, h 208 Huron.
Vanatta Joel D, barber, 366 Mass av, h 14 Stoughton av.
Van Benthusen Aaron, b 858 E Washington.
Van Benthusen Edward, lab, b 73 Malott av.
Van Benthusen Harry B, clk, b 73 Malott av.
Van Benthusen Henry J, pdlr, h 73 Malott av.
Van Benthusen John J, carp, h 184 Eureka av.
Van Bergen Wm H, carp, h 68 W 6th.
Van Blarcom Newton P, meats, 51 Mass av, h 262 N Alabama.
Van Blaricum George F, lab, b 269 Kentucky av.
Van Blaricum George M, blksmith, h 233 Blake.
Van Blaricum Jacob S, lab, h 217 S Reisner (W I).
Van Blaricum James, student, b 55 N State av.
Van Blaricum Sanford, clk, b 385 W New York.
Van Buren Albert A (D H Baldwin & Co), res Louisville, Ky.
Van Buren Harriet S (wid James), b 746 N Alabama.
Van Buren Martin L, hostler, h 180 Howard.
VAN BUREN WM A, Lawyer, 18½ N Penn, Tel 1137; h 746 N Alabama.
Van Buskirk Grace, teacher Public School No 29, b 375 Home av.

J. S. FARRELL & CO.
STEAM AND HOT WATER
HEATING FOR STORES, OFFICES,
PUBLIC BUILDINGS,
PRIVATE RESIDENCES,
GREENHOUSES, ETC.
84 North Illinois St. Telephone 382.

Van Buskirk Harry W, collr, r 342 N Illinois.
Van Buskirk John, trav agt, r 31 The Wyandot.
Van Buskirk Joseph L, condr, h 249 Blake.
Van Camp Albert A, clk Van Camp H and I Co, h 100 Bright.
Van Camp Cortland, pres Van Camp H and I Co, h 714 N Delaware.
Van Camp Elmer S, clk, b 1018 N Penn.
Van Camp Frank, condr, b 1100 Washington (H).
Van Camp Frank, sec and treas Van Camp Packing Co, h 940 N Penn.
Van Camp George, supt Van Camp Packing Co, h 1018 N Penn.
Van Camp Gilbert C, pres Van Camp Packing Co, h 926 N Meridian.
VAN CAMP HARDWARE AND IRON CO, Cortland Van Camp Pres, David C Bergundthal Sec and Treas, Wholesale Hardware, 78-82 S Illinois, Tel 425.
Van Camp Hester J (wid Gilbert), b 926 N Meridian.
Van Camp John, carp, 164½ E Washington, h same.
VAN CAMP JOSEPH A, Agt The Geiser Mnfg Co, 73 W Maryland, h 131 W St Clair.
VAN CAMP PACKING CO, Gilbert C Van Camp Pres, Frank Van Camp Sec and Treas, Fruit Packers, 300-400 Kentucky av, Tel 816.
Van Camp Raymond P, bkkpr Van Camp H and I Co, b 714 N Delaware.
Van Camp Samuel, cigars, 428 Virginia av, h 383 Coburn.
Van Camp Wm, lab, b 421 National rd.
Vance Arthur E, carp, h 467 W Shoemaker (N).
Vance Charles M, lab, h 595 W Shoemaker (N I).
Vance Charles W, lab, b 174 Sheldon.
Vance Edward A, carp, h 322 S New Jersey.
Vance Edward P, clk, b 322 S New Jersey.
Vance Ella F (wid David F), b 162 N Illinois.
Vance Herman E, clk Hendricks & Cooper, h 26 W 11th.
Vance Howard E, mach, b 322 S New Jersey.
Vance Lewis T, foreman Indpls Rubber Co, h 171 Park av.
Vance Louis P, hostler, h 25½ Mass av.
Vance Orin J, molder, h 132 Lynn av (W I).
Vance Susanna B (wid Thomas), h 327 E Vermont.
Vance Thomas Rev, h s s Burgess av 2 s of C H & D Ry (I).
Vance Wm, lab, b 174 Sheldon.
Van Cleave Alva E, stenog, b 529 E Washington.
Vancleave Bazil, tmstr, h 127 Hillside av.
Van Cleave Charles, driver, b 211 W Market.
Van Cleave Edgar S, woodwkr, b 36 Osgood (W I).
Van Cleave George E, poultry, E Mkt House, h 207 Bismarck av (H).
Van Cleave Jacob, lab, b s w cor Samoa and Mass av.
Van Cleave James W, engr, h 36 Osgood (W I).
Vancleave Jasper R, ins agt, h 90 Shelby.
Vancleave Thomas I, butcher, h 375 N Senate av.

United States Life Insurance Co., of New York.
E. B. SWIFT, M'g'r. 25 E. Market St.

WM. KOTTEMAN } 89 & 91 E. Washington St. Telephone 1742 { RUGS MATTINGS WINDOW SHADES

WILLIAM WIEGEL } MANUFACTURER OF.... } SHOW CASES } 6 W. Louisiana St. Opposite Union Station.

Van Dake Helen M (wid H St John), h 170 E North.
Vandalia Line, see Pennsylvania Lines.
Vandawalker Daniel M, pub, 13 Marion blk, h 183 Ash.
Vandegrift Martha E (wid Harry), h 1022 N Penn.
Van Deinse Anton J, pres A J Van Deinse & Co, h 50 Ft Wayne av.
Van Deinse A J & Co, Anton J Van Deinse pres, ins, 219 Lemcke bldg.
Van Deinse Marie, teacher Public School No 27, b 77 E St Joseph.
Van Deinse Peter, clk Rehm & Van Deinse, b 50 Ft Wayne av.
Van Deman Joshua H, farmer, h 157 Pleasant.
Vandeman Joshua L, lab, h 99 Douglass.
Van Deman Nathaniel A, trav agt, h 27 Laurel.
Van Deman Ordo L, farmer, b 157 Pleasant.
Van Deman Roy L, student, b 157 Pleasant.
Van Denbrook Levi, lab, r 164 W Maryland.
Vanderpool Dominick, h 31 LeGrand av.
Vanderpool Dominick jr, student, b 31 LeGrand av.
Vanderpool Wm, harness, 226 E Washington, b 31 LeGrand av.
Vanderwood Wm (Vanderwood & Seaton), h 174 Indiana av.
Vanderwood & Seaton (Wm Vanderwood, Lawson Seaton), restaurant, 174 Indiana av.
Van Deusen Kate (wid Chauncey), h 326 E South.
Vandeventer Edward, carp, b 51 Hosbrook.
Vandeventer Margaret M (wid Wm), h 51 Hosbrook.
Vandiver Benjamin F, shoemkr, 197½ River av (W I), h 105 Birch av (W I).
Vandiver Bros (Wm N and Clarence E), feed, 488 Virginia av.
Vandiver Clarence E (Vandiver Bros), b 169 Huron.
Vandiver Wm N (Vandiver Bros), h 169 Huron.
Vandivier James S, carp, h 69 Lynn av (W I).
Vandivier John C, plastr, h 106 River av (W I).
Vandivier John W Rev, pastor Church of Christ, h 583 W 22d (N I).
Vandivier Mary, b 135 Hadley av (W I).
Vandivier Peter, h 10 Arizona.
Van Doren Wm A, musician, b 68 W New York.
Van Dorin Harvey L, b 120 Mass av.
Van Dorn Margaret (wid Wm C), h 98 N Dorman.
Van Dorn Wm C, driver, b 168 E North.
Van Dyke David Rev, evangelist, h 1514 Northwestern av (N I).
Van Dyke John, coachman 1015 N Penn.
Van Dyke Wm W, real est, 227 Lemcke bldg, b 11 Ketcham.
Van Dyne Eugene, clk, b 271 Bright.
Van Eaton Charles L, engr, h 157 Hoyt av.
Van Every David C, b 188 Ramsey av.
Van Every Michael T, clk, h 125 John.
Vanfleet Hartford, carp, b 341 E South.
Van Gorder Harry, supervisor C C C & St L Ry, h 204 Hoyt av.
Vanguard Cycle Co, John A Kurtz pres, Wm T Barnes sec and treas, 106 N Penn.
Van Harlingen John R, train disp P C C & St L Ry, h 60 W Walnut.
Van Hoff Henry L (Fraser Bros & Van Hoff), h 625 N Penn.

THOS. C. DAY & CO.
Financial Agents and Loans.
We have the experience, and claim to be reliable.
Rooms 325 to 330 Lemcke Bldg.

Van Horn Abel F, lab, h e s Brown 1 n of 23d.
Van Horn Albert H, painter, h 190 River av (W I).
Van Horn Arthur R, lab, h 34 Wisconsin.
Van Horn Charles F, painter, h 11 Ellsworth.
Van Horn Edward E, painter, h 28 Marion av (W I).
Van Horn Francis M, painter, h 28 Marion av (W I).
Van Horn Henry, fireman, h 8 Traub av.
Van Horn Ida M (wid John C), h 276 N New Jersey.
Van Horn Joseph A, plumber, b e s Brown 1 n of 23d.
Van Horn Marion, lab, b 173 Harmon.
Van Horn May, h 209 W Court.
Van Horn Otto C, bkkpr, b 56 Johnson av.
Van Horn Reuben J, mach, h 22 S State av.
Van Horn Stephen D, lab, h 614 Miller av (M P).
Van Horn Thomas M, mnfrs' agt, 49 Board of Trade bldg, h 105 Highland pl.
Van Hummell Henry, phys, 60 Monument pl, b 262 N Meridian.
VAN HUMMELL QUINCY, M D, Medical Director Indianapolis Infirmary, 60 Monument Pl, h 262 N Meridian.
Vanier Anna M (wid Bazil H), h 348 Union.
Vankirk Wm F, brakeman, b 99 Lexington av.
Vanlandingham Charles E, mach hd, h 11 Arbor av (W I).
Van Landingham Jennie (wid Albert H), h 256 N Senate av.
Van Laningham Bashaba (wid Milton), b 1145 Northwestern av.
Van Laningham Livingston D, lab, b 17 S Waverly (B).
Van Laningham Mary P, stenog Howard Cale, b 286 Keystone av.
Van Laningham Pearl T, engr, h 520 Ash.
Van Laningham Minerva, h 286 Keystone av.
Vanlund John A, electrotyper, b 379 S Meridian.
Van Meter Frank M, pressman, h 16 Henry.

EAT
QUAKER BREAD
ASK YOUR GROCER FOR IT.
THE HITZ BAKING CO.

CARPETS AND RUGS RENOVATED.......... | CAPITAL STEAM CARPET CLEANING WORKS M. D. PLUNKETT, TELEPHONE No. 818

BENJ. BOOTH PRACTICAL EXPERT ACCOUNTANT. Complicated or disputed accounts investigated and adjusted. Room 18, 82½ E. Wash. St., Ind'p'l's, Ind.

18 and 20 South Meridian Street KERSHNER BROS., Proprs. THE SHERMAN RESTAURANT

ESTABLISHED 1876. TELEPHONE 168.
CHESTER BRADFORD,
SOLICITOR OF PATENTS,
AND COUNSEL IN PATENT CAUSES.
(See adv. page 6.)
Office:—Rooms 14 and 16 Hubbard Block, S. W. Cor. Washington and Meridian Streets, INDIANAPOLIS, INDIANA.

Vannatta Daniel D (Thayer & Vannatta), b 188 Walcott.
Van Natta Harry B, phys City Dispensary, 32 E Ohio.
Van Natta James, livery, 175 E Michigan, h 108½ Mass av.
Van Natta James S, h 203 N Illinois.
Van Ness Stephen A, clk C C C & St L Ry, h 31 The Windsor.
Van Ness Wesley S, trimmer, h 13 Hosbrook.
Van Nostran Wm H, engr, h 123 Lynn av (W I).
Vannostrand Sidney J, tmstr, h 110 Singleton.
Vannote Charles A, roofer, b 163 W South.
Vannote Hannah (wid Alfred), h 163 W South.
Vannote John S, carp, h 10 Sharpe.
Vannoy John, bartndr, b 600 W 22d (N I).
Van Noy Samuel O, engr, h 72 Sugar Grove av (M P).
Vannoy Wm, lab, h 600 W 22d.
Van Nuys Adalaska, trav agt, h 69 W 7th.
Vanosdol Nathan A, condr, h 165 Yandes.
Van Pelt Edward M, plumber, h rear 28 Prospect.
Van Pelt Frank D, trav agt, h 620 E Washington.
Van Pelt George A, h 186 E Michigan.
Van Pelt Ira S, fruits, E Mkt House, h 70 S Pine.
Van Pelt Sutton B, feed, 41 N Alabama, h 547 Central av.
Van Plake Alexander, woodturner, h rear 71 River av (W I).
Van Scholck Sarah (wid Wm), h 228 N Illinois.
Van Scoyoc Charles C (Prall & Van Scoyoc), r 53 Dearborn.
Van Scoyoc Frank, brakeman, h 78 S Dorman.
Van Scoyoc John, trimmer, b 78 S Dorman.
Van Scoyoc Jonathan M, painter, b 78 S Dorman.
Van Scyoc Charles, clk N A Moore & Co, b 132 N Capitol av.
Vanscyoc Jacob, lab, h 7 Lawn (B).
Van Sickle Aaron, carp, h 1111 N Delaware.

Metal Ceilings and all kinds of Copper, Tin and Sheet Iron work,
O. B. ENSEY,
TELEPHONE 1562.
CORNER 6TH AND ILLINOIS STS.

Van Sickle Andrew, mach, b 224 Union.
Van Sickle Belinda (wid Daniel A), b 439 Park av.
Van Sickle Earl R, clk, b 1129 N Penn.
Van Sickle Elizabeth teacher, h 15 Omer.
Van Sickle Frank M, printer, b 15 Omer.
Van Sickle George W, grocer, 30 Clifford av, h 399 Talbott av.
Van Sickle James W, clk, b 4 Brookside av.
Van Sickle John A, huckster, b w s Bradley 4 n of Ohio.
Vansickle Mamie, h 525 Roanoke.
Van Sickle Mary A (wid Joseph) h 551 S Illinois.
Van Sickle Myrtle, stenog, b 274 N Alabama.
Van Sickle Orange W, mach, h 32 Clark.
Van Sickle Sarah J (wid Lewis A), h 15 Omer.
Van Siclen Phoebe (wid Ferdinand), b 356 Bellefontaine.
Van Skiver Charles C, filer, h 255 Deloss.
Van Slack Alvin H, lab, b Ellen Van Slack.
Van Slack Ellen (wid Nathan), h e s Woodside av 1 s of P C C & St L Ry (W).
Van Slack Nathan F, lab, b Ellen Van Slack.
Van Slyke Clara B, h 182 E Washington.
Van Slyke Mary J, milliner, 414 S Meridian, h 95 Bookside av
Van Slyke Sarah J (wid Peter C), h 95 Brookside av.
Van Slyke Stephen, patternmkr, r 45½ Virginia av.
Van Stan John, shoemkr, 66 W 7th, h 47 Yeiser.
Van Stan John W, polisher, b 47 Yeiser.
Van Stan Thomas, bricklyr, h 17 Gresham.
VANSYCKLE ADVERTISING CO THE, G W Vansyckle Pres and Mngr, Distributing, Card and Sign Tacking, Country Advertising and Sign Painting, Rooms 9-10 McDougall Bldg, opp Grand Hotel. (See adv in classified Advertising Agents.)
Vansyckle George W, pres and mngr The Vansyckle Advertising Co, 9-10 McDougall bldg, h 358 S East.
Van Sycle Frank, lab, b 304 S Meridian.
Van Tassell Elizabeth (wid Parker A), h 353½ E Market.
Van Tilburgh Charles R, bkkpr, b 180 W Ohio.
Van Tilburgh John B, h 180 W Ohio.
Van Trees Joseph W, photog, 41 Palmer, h same.
Van Treese Alonzo, painter, h 431 W Udell (N I).
Van Treese Joseph H, painter, h 1655 N Senate av.
Van Tress Benjamin F, trav agt, h 885 N Senate av.
Van Tress Minnie, b 18 Orange av.
Van Tuyl Amelia (wid Abram), h 429 E St Clair.
Van Tuyl George, clk C C C & St L Ry, h 70 N Senate av.
Van Tuyl Harry, fireman, b 70 N Senate av.
Van Voorhees George R, clk, h 1008 N Alabama.
Van Vorhis Flavius J (Van Vorhis & Speucer) h 276 N Senate av.
Van Vorhis Sara C (wid Isaac M), b 276 N Senate av.
VAN VORHIS & SPENCER (Flavius J Van Vorhis, Wm W Spencer), Lawyers, Rooms 20-24 Baldwin Blk, Tel 489.

TUTEWILER UNDERTAKER, NO. 72 WEST MARKET STREET. TELEPHONE 216.

The Provident Life and Trust Co. Dividends are paid in cash and are not withheld for a long period of years, subject to forfeiture in the event of death or the termination of policy.
D. W. EDWARDS, GENERAL AGENT, 508 INDIANA TRUST BUILDING.

THEODORE F. SMITHER, AGENT FOR WARREN'S ANCHOR BRAND—ASPHALT ROOFING—OFFICE, 151 WEST MARYLAND ST. TEL. 861.

Van Wie Avery, city salesman Cerealine Mnfg Co, h 44 Andrews.
Van Wie Daniel D, trav agt, h 216 E Market.
Van Wie Frank L, clk, b 216 E Market.
Van Wie Homer H, bkkpr, h 227 N West.
Van Wie Jesse S, clk Clemens Vonnegut, h 60 W 14th.
Van Wie Raphael, city dis clk P O, h 50 Andrews.
Van Winkle Henry C, mngr The George Co, b 350 N Alabama.
Van Winkle John Q, genl supt C C C & St L Ry, n e cor Delaware and South, h 232 Central av.
Van Wye Frank, carp, h 673 Mass av.
Van Wylich Wm, printer, r 555 E Market.
Van Zandt Henry L, lab, b 845 S East.
Van Zandt John H, clk Hendrickson, Lefler & Co, b 45 Spann av.
Van Zandt Martha A (wid Samuel A), h 845 S East.
Van Zandt Wilbur, packer, b 845 S East.
Van Zandt Wood, mach, b n e cor Michigan and Sherman Drive.
Vanzant Frank, lab, h 399 Yandes.
Vanzant Isaac N, helper, h 885 Mass av.
Van Zant James G, clk, h 398 Columbia av.
Van Zant John W, carrier, b 885 Mass av.
Van Zant Wm M, bartndr, r 77 N Alabama.
Van Zant Worthington, grocer, 249 Davidson, h 279 same.
Varin George, toilet articles, 37½ W Washington, h 158 Johnson av.
Varley Anderson E, porter R M S, h 35 Henry.
Varner Frank M, clk, b 45 Laurel.
Varner John F, h 45 Laurel.
Varner Joseph B, mach, h 35 Cleaveland blk.
VARNEY A L MAJOR, Commandant U S Arsenal, n end Arsenal av, h same, Tel 633.
Varney Gordon E (Varney & McOuat), b U S Arsenal.
Varney Theodore, draughtsman, b U S Arsenal.
VARNEY & McOUAT (Gordon E Varney, Robert L McOuat), Electrical Engineers and Mnfrs' Agts, 75 E Market, Tel 849. (See adv in classified Electrical Engineers.)
Varon Annie L (wid Joseph), b 726 N Capitol av.
Varon Joseph, engr, h 20½ Henry.
Vasbinder John A, lineman, h 138 Hosbrook.
Vater Thomas J, contr, 299 Bellefontaine, h same.
Vaughan Almon T, condr, h 1025 N Senate av.
Vaughan Dennis, carp, 206 E Washington, h same.
Vaughan Edith (wid Thomas N), h 595 Mass av.
Vaughan Edward, tmstr, h 211½ E Washington.
Vaughan Ethel (wid James), h 307 E Court.
Vaughan Frank, lab, h e s Wheeler 3 s of Prospect.
Vaughan George A, brakeman, h 259 Michigan av.
Vaughan George W, clk W H Messenger, h 281 N Noble.
Vaughan John, lab, r 86 Columbia al.
Vaughan Martin, lab, b e s Wheeler 3 s of Prospect.

THE WHEN IS A WORLD BEATER.

Vaughn Calvin C, electrician, h 366 S Illinois.
Vaughn Frances (wid George), h 227 Howard.
Vaughn Frank A, yard clk C C C & St L Ry, h 333 S Meridian.
Vaughn George, porter, h 168 Muskingum al.
Vaughn Halet L, clk U S Ex Co, b 243 E South.
Vaughn James W, optician, h 40 Ash.
Vaughn James W, saloon, 167 Indiana av, h 518 N West.
Vaughn Lewis, janitor, h 558 Muskingum al.
Vaughn Lucy, b rear 135 E Pratt.
Vaught George W, express, h 313 Alvord.
Vaught James B, filer, b 115 W South.
Vaught Rufus, h 115 W South.
Vaught Wm T, filer, b 115 W South.
Vaus Rose (wid Oliver), h 1137 Northwestern av.
Vewter James M, mach, r 149½ Oliver av (W I).
Vawter James M, lab, h 15 N California.
VAZEILLE ETIENNE R, Lawyer, Mngr The Snow-Church Co, 112 Commercial Club Bldg, r 28 Ft Wayne av.
Veach Albert F, tmstr, b 3 Madeira.
Veach Benjamin, lab, b 1440 Rader (N I).
Veach Deering S, painter, b 289 Virginia av.
Veach Eliza (wid James), h 1440 Rader (N I).
Veach Harry L, painter, h 163 John.
Veach Horace G (Veach & Didion), h 151 Meek.
Veach John, lab, b 1440 Rader (N I).
Veach Joshua, barber, h 399 W Udell (N I).
Veach Wm W, plumber, b e s Bond 1 n of Chicago (N I).
Veach & Didion (Horace G Veach, Alpha Didion), plumbers, 93 Mass av.
Veale Ellis W, electric belts, h 31 Standard av (W I), h same.
Veaman Emma, r 106½ N Meridian.
Veatch Benjamin F, car rep, h 460 E Washington.
Veatch Charles W, painter, b 167 N Noble.
Veatch Edgar, lab, b 126 Newman.
Veatch Travis S, lab, h 126 Newman.

The A. Burdsal Co.
Manufacturers of
STEAMBOAT COLORS
BEST HOUSE PAINTS MADE.
Wholesale and Retail.
34 AND 36 SOUTH MERIDIAN STREET.

Electric Contractors | We are prepared to do any kind of Electric Contract Work. C. W. MEIKEL, Telephone 466. 96-98 E. New York St.

DALTON & MERRIFIELD { LUMBER South Noble St., near E. Washington

INDIANA ELECTROTYPE CO. : BEST WORK. LOWEST PRICES.
23 WEST PEARL ST., INDIANAPOLIS, IND. JOB WORK. BOOK PLATES. BEST PATENT BASE ON THE MARKET. All Orders Promptly Filled.

KIRKHOFF BROS.,
Sanitary Plumbers
STEAM AND HOT WATER HEATING.
102-104 SOUTH PENNSYLVANIA ST.
TELEPHONE 910.

Veeder Harry, mach, h 332 Martindale av.
Vegara Leonardo, music teacher, 221 N Capitol av, r same.
Vehling Carrie, clk, b 53 Harrison.
Vehling Charles A, joiner, h 46 Preston.
Vehling Christopher H G, mach, h 241 S Alabama.
Vehling C F Wm, asst ticket agt I U Ry Co, h 547 E Ohio.
Vehling Ernst, mach, h 38 Iowa.
Vehling Frederick, car insp, h 186 Trowbridge (W).
Vehling Frederick, shoes, 331 Dillon, h 53 Harrison.
Vehling Frederick W, h 191 E South.
Vehling Henry C, undertaker, 390 Virginia av, h same.
Vehling Henry J, mach, b 536 E Ohio.
Vehling Henry W C, mach hd, h 536 E Ohio.
Vehling John F, plater, b 536 E Ohio.
Vehling Louis C, driver, b 191 E South.
Vehling Wm C, driver, b 536 E Ohio.
Vehling Wm H, plastr, e s Waverly av 2 n of Clifford av, h same.
Veit Vitus, lab, h n s Pansy 2 w of Floral av.
Veitch Rolland T, real est, 711-712 Lemcke bldg, b 5 Pressley Flats.
Venable Albert, tmstr, h s w cor Manlove av and 17th.
Venable America (wid Thomas), b 202 Yandes.
Venable Charles C, condr, b 501½ Bellefontaine.
Venable David E, carp, h 462 W Shoemaker (N I).
Venable David L, lab, h 64 Chapel.
Venable Ellen (wid Thomas), b 751 N Senate av.
Venable Eugenia S, cook, h 30 Beecher.
Venable George, tmstr, h e s Western av 5 n of 22d.
Venable George W, lab, h 204 Yandes.
Venable Henry C, lab, h 187 Alvord.
Venable Isom, tmstr, h 77 Hill av.
Venable James, waiter, h 409 Muskingum al.
Venable James M, tmstr, b e s Western av 5 n of 22d.

Lime, Lath, Cement,
THE W. G. WASSON CO.
130 INDIANA AVE. TEL. 989.
Sewer Pipe, Flue Linings, Fire Brick, Fire Clay.

Venable John, tmstr, b 17 Willard.
Venable Judge T, cook, r 294 Bright.
Venable Noble, driver, h 30 Bird.
Venable Phoebe (wid Henry), h 294 Bright.
Venable Thomas, lab, h rear 36 Central av.
Venall John, hatter, r 55 Dearborn.
Veney James C, lab, h 223 Clinton.
Venis Frank A, lab, h 257 Columbia av.
Venn Alexander J, clk L S Ayres & Co, h 898 N Capitol av.
Venn George S, bkkpr Dean Bros' Steam Pump Works, b 372 N Meridian.
Verbarg Charles W, porter, h 236 Huron.
Verbarg George W, motorman, h 1091 N Senate av.
Verdon Charles A, tailor, h 13 Woodlawn av.
Veregge Albert J, tinner, h 223 Alvord.
Veregge Clarence, clk, h 278 E Miami.
Veregge Walter H, carp, h 81 N Dorman.
Veregge Wm, carp, b 278 E Miami.
Verity Stephen T, musical insts, 62 Virginia av, h 60 Woodlawn av.
VERNON INSURANCE AND TRUST CO, The McGilliard Agency Co Genl Agts, 83-85 E Market, Tel 479. (See backbone and opp p 588.)
Vernon Marion R, condr, h 574 W 22d (N I).
Vernon Samuel, porter Sherman House.
Verry George W, tinner, h 530 W Shoemaker (N I).
Vert Elizabeth A (wid Daniel), h 169 W Market.
Vert Milton R, horseshoer, h 79 Division (W I).
Vertrees John, lab, h 177 Valley Drive.
Vesper John L, tailor, r 54 Hubbard blk.
Vesper Joseph, lab, b 161 Gresham.
Vess Mary M, h 77 W Ohio.
Vest Benjamin F, carp, b 86 Newman.
Vest John W, condr, h 469 N Meridian.
Vestal Ada (wid Virgil A), h 1387 London av.
Vestal Allan P, dep County Clerk, b 138 Madison av.
Vestal Charles E, trav agt A Kiefer Drug Co, h 244 Davidson.
Vestal Everett J, clk, h 56 Lord.
Vestal Foster M, shoes, Central av (I), h 32 S Reisner (W I).
Vestal Harry L, cashr Kershner Bros, r 27 Ft Wayne av.
Vestal Henry L, carp, h 27 Ft Wayne av.
Vestal John, clk, h 138 Mass av.
Vestal John N, printer, h 195 Sheffield av (H).
Vestal Sidney, paperhngr, h 65 King av (H).
Vestal Wm H, brakeman, b 475 E Market.
Vestbinder Bert, printer F H Smith, b 328 Shelby.
Vester John L, tailor, r 54 Hubbard blk.
Vester Philip, miller, b 235 S Alabama.
Veth Charles O, ironwkr, h 5 Emerson pl.
Vetor Anna G (wid John), h 332 Martindale av.
Vetter John C, h 8 Hadley av (W I).
Vetter John J (Carter & Vetter), r 124 W Maryland.
Vetter Oscar O, varnisher, b 95 Geisendorff.
Vetter Reinhold E, lab, b 279 S West.
Vetter Rudolph G, harnessmkr, h 882 S East.
Vial Elizabeth P (wid James M), h 2 Pleasant.
Vial James M (Caird, Vial & Co), b 2 Pleasant.
Vial John B, clk, h 445 S Olive.
VIAVI CO THE, Dr Eva A Cropper Mngr, Suite 9, 68½ E Market.

YOUR HOMES FURNISHED BY W. H. MESSENGER 101 East Washington St. Telephone 491.

Vice David J, polisher, h 98 Russell av.
Vice Nellie (wid Andrew J), r 254½ W Washington.
Vickers Mansfield, lab, h 62 Church.
Vickers Percy B, trav agt, h 1782 N Illinois.
Vickers Randolph, pressfeeder, b 69 W 20th.
Vickery Catharine (wid Absalom), h 99 Quincy.
Victor Elijah, carp, h 183 Bellefontaine.
Victor Frederick C (F C Victor & Co), b 250 Howard.
Victor F C & Co (Frederick C Victor), printers, 26 N Delaware.
VICTOR HENRY, Propr Mozart Hall Saloon and Restaurant, 37-39 S Delaware, h same.
Victor Henry R, clk, b 250 Howard.
Victor John A, grocer, 598 N West, b 250 Howard.
Victor Julius A, grocer, 275 Howard, h 250 same.
Viehmann Mary (wid Morton), b 86 McGinnis.
Vielhaber Amelia, dressmkr, 386 S East, b same.
Vielhaber Daniel, shoes, 212 E Washington, h 386 S East.
Vielhaber Frederick D, clk, b 386 S East.
Vielhaber Otto H, butcher, b 386 S East.
Vieira Alice S (wid Emanuel J), b 99 Bates.
Vieweg August V, h 201 Blake.
Viewegh Ernest, mach, h 70 Morton.
Vigus Wm J Rev, dist supt American Bible Society, h 1143 N Meridian.
Viles Shepard, hostler, b rear 233 S West.
Villa Joseph, lab, h 306½ E Washington.
Villiers Walter H, real est, 108 Oliver av (W I), h 106 same.
Vincent Albert S, clk, h 44 Hall pl.
Vincent Ann B (wid Henry B), h 272 E Market.
Vincent Anna Laura, notary public, stenog Kern & Bailey, h 44 Hall pl.
Vincent Antionnette (wid Thomas E), h 94 Kappus (W I).
Vincent Archibald S, mach hd, b 507½ W Washington.
Vincent Charles F, clk, h 31 Ludlow av.
Vincent Cuthbert, pub American Nonconformist, also Farm Record, 70 E Ohio, h same.
Vincent Edgar R, trav agt, h 596 Central av.
Vincent Elizabeth C, printer, b 163 Sharpe av (W).
Vincent Isaac A, b 596 Central av.
Vincent John, hostler, h 66 N Noble.
Vincent John H, driver, h 27 S Linden.
Vincent John M, oil, 358 Jefferson av, h same.
Vincent John R, carp, 22 S New Jersey, h 163 Sharpe av (W).
Vincent Mary L (wid Henry C), h 53 Pleasant.
Vincent Susan C, b 272 E Market.
Vincent Theodore A, cook, h 372 N Senate av.
Vincent Wm H, carp, 163 Sharpe av (W), h same.
Vincent Wm H jr, carp, 22 S New Jersey, h 267 E Market.
Vinch Michael, bkkpr, h 160 Virginia av.
Vinch Nunzio, grocer, 160 Virginia av, h same.
Vinch Vincent, pdlr, h 160 Virginia av.
Vinnedge Albert J, clk, b 890 N Alabama.
Vinnedge Charles A, auditor Indpls Union Ry Co, Union Station, h 68 Beaty.

Henry H. Fay,
40½ E. WASHINGTON ST.,
FIRE INSURANCE, REAL ESTATE,
LOANS AND RENTAL AGENT.

Vinnedge George E, clk, b 890 N Alabama.
Vinnedge Harry D, clk, b 890 N Alabama.
Vinnedge John A, insp Indpls Gas Co, h 890 N Alabama.
Vinnedge Kate Y (wid Joseph D), b 206 N Delaware.
Vinnedge Lawrence A, h 595 Broadway.
Vinson Charles W, painter, h 285 Keystone av.
Vinson Ebenezer D, painter, h 550 Jefferson av.
Vinson Erastus, carp, h 98 Highland av.
Vinson Frank J (Shaw & Vinson), h 1218 N Penn.
Vinson James, driver, b 609 N Senate av.
Vinson John Rev, pastor Church of God, h 4 Leonard.
Vinson John L, clk N Y Store, h 53½ Temple av.
Vinson Lula, teacher Public School No 14, b 98 Highland av.
Vinson Mark M, lab, b 550 Jefferson av.
Vinson Mary J (wid Wm), h 5 Leonard.
Vinson Monroe M, carp, h 125 Frazee (H).
Vinson Victor V, mach, h 402 W Pratt.
Vinzant Joseph F, condr, h 180 N Illinois.
Violet Eli, lab, b 26 Sheffield av (H).
Violet George C, lab, h 343 Jefferson av.
Violet Stephen, h 26 Sheffield av (H).
Violet Wm, lab, b 343 Jefferson av.
Virt Cornelius, b 81 Johnson av.
Virt Edward E, fireman, h 81 Johnson av.
Virt John W, brakeman, h 785 E Market.
Virt Josephine E (wid John), b 402 Clifford av.
Vito Vincent, fruits, 106 S Illinois, b 33 Valley.
Vittemore John V, trav agt, b 598 N Illinois.
Vittemore Mary E, h 598 N Illinois.
Vliet Argle R, barber, b 168 E St Joseph.
Vliet John E, trav agt, h 165 Ft Wayne av.
Vliet Wm C, barber, 158 Ft Wayne av, h 168 E St Joseph.
Voegeli Gerfas, carp, h 751 S East.
Voegtle Oscar S, collr Jacob Metzger & Co, h 80 Palmer.
Voelker Charles W, janitor, h 269 Highland av.

SURETY BONDS
American Bonding & Trust Co.
OF BALTIMORE, MD.
Authorized to act as Sole Surety on all Bonds.
Total Resources over $1,000,000.00.
W. E. BARTON & CO., General Agents,
504 INDIANA TRUST BUILDING.
Long Distance Telephone 1918.

THE FRED DIETZ CO.
WOODEN PACKING BOXES MADE TO ORDER.
FACTORY AND WAREHOUSE TRUCKS.
40 Madison Avenue. Telephone 654.

Business World Supplied with Help
GRADUATES ASSISTED TO POSITIONS
10,000 NOW IN GOOD SITUATIONS. TEL. 499. E. J. HEEB, PRES.
Indianapolis BUSINESS UNIVERSITY

Water and Oil Meters { HENRY R. WORTHINGTON, 64 S. PENNSYLVANIA ST. Long Distance Telephone 284.

UNION CO-OPERATIVE LAUNDRY } (COMPOSED OF UNION LAUNDRY GIRLS.) NOS. 8, 40 AND 42 VIRGINIA AVENUE. T. E. SOMERVILLE, MANAGER —— TELEPHONE 1269. INDIANAPOLIS, IND.

HORACE M. HADLEY
Insurance, Real Estate, Loan and Rental Agent
66 EAST MARKET STREET,
Telephone 1540. Basement.

Voelker George J, driver, h 160 Buchanan.
Voelker Henry J W, lab, b 269 Highland av.
Vogel Andrew, lab, b 11 Dawson.
Vogel Bertha, teacher German Public School No 15, b 30 West Drive (W P).
Vogel Carl F, lab, h 519 S West.
Vogel Conrad E, clk, b 451 S Delaware.
Vogel Frederica (wid George), produce, E Mkt House, h 439 S Delaware.
Vogel Frederick, mach, h 68 Bicking.
Vogel Henry, h 535 E Market.
Vogel Henry C, uphlr, h 51 Arbor av (W I).
Vogel Wm C, driver, h 102 Gray.
Vogler Samuel E, electrician, b 32 N Liberty.
Vogler Wm, lab, b 713 S East.
Vogler Wm H Rev, pastor College av Moravian Church, h 901 Broadway.
Voglesong Frederick, lab, h 19 Gresham.
Voglesong George E, shoes, 299 Mass av, h 70 College av.
Vogt Carl B, musician, b 222 E Ohio.
Vogt Frederick C, messr P O, h 111 N Noble.
Vogt Frederick J, h 12 Hollis.
Vogt Frederick W, clk, h 12 Hollis.
Vogt George R, clk, b 222 E Ohio.
Vogt Harry F, musician, b 222 E Ohio.
Vogt Henry G, pressfeeder, b 432 S State av.
Vogt Marie (wid Bernhard J), h 222 E Ohio.
Vogt Michael, mason, b s s Walnut 3 w of Belt R R.
Voight George H, foreman Home Brewing Co, h 466 Union.
Voigt Christiana (wid Louis), b 900 Madison av.
Voigt Henry F, bartndr, b 620 N Illinois.
Voigt Henry W, h 620 N Illinois.
Voigt Richard M, attendant Insane Hospital.
Volderauer Charles, lab, h 378½ W New York.
Volderauer John, tmstr, h 1163 Northwestern av.
Volderauer Richard, h 1155 Northwestern av.
Volkening Charles, lab, b 196 Lincoln la.
Volkening Christian F (C F Volkening & Co), h 665 N Capitol av.

Special Detailed Reports Promptly Furnished by Us.
MERCHANTS' AND MANUFACTURERS' EXCHANGE
J. E. TAKKEN, Manager,
19 Union Building, 73 West Maryland Street.

Volkening C F & Co (Christian F Volkening), com mers, 43 S Delaware.
Volkening Louisa (wid Charles), h 196 Lincoln la.
Volkert Henry J, stenog, b 476 S New Jersey.
Volkert John, baker, b 45 Wyoming.
Volkert Julius, lab, h 125 Gray.
Volkert Melchior A, clk, h 476 S New Jersey.
Volkert Theodore H, bkkpr, b 476 S New Jersey.
VOLKSBLATT THE (German, Weekly), Gutenberg Co Publishers, 27 S Delaware, Tel 269.
Vollmer Annie M, cashr H F Haynes, r 123 E Ohio.
Vollmer Barthold, janitor, b n w cor Palmer and Union.
Vollmer Daniel G, bartndr, h 251 Fayette.
Vollmer Frank X, jeweler, 855 S Meridian, h n w cor Palmer and Union.
Vollmer John, produce, E Mkt House, h 292 N Pine.
Vollmer Samuel M, lab, h 37 Johnson av.
Vollrath Adolph, butcher, b rear 633 Madison av.
Vollrath Charles A, grocer, 575 Madison av, h same.
Vollrath Emil C, clk, b 575 Madison av.
Vollrath Herman G, meats, 101 E Mkt House, h 130 Kennington.
Volmar George J, painter, h 68 W McCarty.
Volmar John B, painter, 68 W McCarty, h same.
Volpp Charles F, mason, h 65 Gresham.
Volpp Christian F, mason, h 10 Morton.
Volpp Wm, mason, h 588 Chestnut.
Volrath John C, mach, b 742 S East.
Volrath Louis, carp, 742 S East, h same.
Voltz Clara (wid Anthony), h 431 S State av.
Voltz John, porter Circle Park Hotel.
Volunteers The, 35 S Illinois.
Volz Anthony H, hostler, h 23 Agnes.
Volz Charles, lab, h 175 Minnesota.
Volz Charles A, mngr The Guarantee Shoe Store, b 886 N Capitol av.
Volz Frank, painter, h 593 Mass av.
Volz Frank G, clk, h 886 N Capitol av.
Volz Henry A, saddler, h 34 Agnes.
Volz Jacob, lab, b 334 Douglass.
Volz Nicholas B, mach hd, h 632 W Eugene (N I).
Volz Quirin, harness, 169 W Washington, h 603 N Meridian.
Von Burg Albert, printer, h 64 S Arsenal av.
Vonburg Bernard, patternmkr, h 65 Tremont av (H).
Vonburg Clement, foreman, h 83 Sheffield av (H).
Von Burg Edward C, tailor, h 1200 Madison av.
Von Burg Frank T H, lab, b 420 E Vermont.
Von Burg George L, glasswkr, b 420 E Vermont.
Von Burg James F, tailor, b 83 Sheffield av (H).
Von Burg John S, molder, h 420 E Vermont.
Von Burg Joseph J, tailor, 261 Mass av, b 420 E Vermont.
Von Burg Martha J, music teacher, 83 Sheffield av (H), b same.
Von Burg Wm C, patternmkr, h 284 Brookside av.
Von Cannon Wm A, trav agt, b 223½ E North.

CLEMENS VONNEGUT
184, 186 and 192 E. Washington St.
CABINET HARDWARE
CARVERS' TOOLS. Glues of all kinds.

THE WM. H. BLOCK CO. 7 AND 9 EAST WASHINGTON STREET. MILLINERY, CLOAKS AND FURS.

Vondersaar Anna M (wid John), h 774 Charles.
Vondersaar Edwin L, uphlr, b 904 N New Jersey.
Vondersaar Frank H, mach hd, h 19 Buchanan.
Vondersaar George (Syerup & Co), h 384 N Alabama.
Vondersaar John J, florist, 675 Madison av, h same.
Vondersaar Wendel, blksmith, 904 N New Jersey, h same.
Vondersaar Wm, sawyer, h 103 Dunlop.
Von Hake Carl, pres Indpls Coffin Co, h 358 Park av.
Von Jelgerhois Bernard, produce, E Mkt House, h cor Prospect and Auburn av.
Vonnegut Bernard (Vonnegut & Bohn and Clemens Vonnegut), h 342 Home av.

VONNEGUT CLEMENS (Clemens, Clemens Jr, Bernard, Franklin and George Vonnegut), Hardware, 184, 186 and 192 E Washington, Tel 589. (See left bottom lines.)

Vonnegut Clemens (Clemens Vonnegut), h 504 E Market.
Vonnegut Clemens jr (Clemens Vonnegut), sec and treas Indpls Coffin Co, h 224 Broadway.
Vonnegut Franklin (Clemens Vonnegut), vice-pres Indpls Coffin Co, h 508 E Market.
Vonnegut George (Clemens Vonnegut), h 182 N East.

VONNEGUT & BOHN (Bernard Vonnegut, Arthur Bohn), Architects, 608-610 Indiana Trust Bldg, Tel 875.

Von Spreckelson Albert H, carp, h 737 E Michigan.
Von Spreckelson Edward O, carp, b 749 E Michigan.
Von Spreckelson John A, foreman, h 378 Highland av.
Von Spreckelson Rebecca (wid John), h 749 E Michigan.
Von Tesmar Otto, janitor Medical College of Indiana, r n w cor Senate av and Market.
Von Willer Wm, lab, b Wm E Von Willer.
Von Willer Wm E, lab, h s s Bloyd av 2 w of Shade (B).
Voorhees Jacob, plastr, h 58 Arch.
Voorhees Mary J (wid Abram L), h 407 N Capitol av.
Voorhees Richard, produce, 90 E Mkt House, and grocer, 350 Yandes, h same.
Vordermark Frederick, carp, h w s Bradley 1 n of Ohio.
Vordermark George, mach hd, b w s Bradley 1 n of Ohio.
Vordermark John P, bartndr, h 999 S Meridian.
Vordermark Wm, chairmkr, b 16 Warren av (W I).
Vore Delbert F, condr, h 1077 W Vermont.
Vore Jennie, dressmkr, 1077 W Vermont, h same.
Vores Peter W, lab, h 170 Yandes.
Vorget Magdalena, h 22 Dougherty.
Vorhees Belle, h 298 W St Clair.
Vories Hervey D, sec and treas Equitable State B and L Assn, h 179 N Penn.
Voris Wm C (Clark, Wysong & Voris), h 471 College av.
Voris Wm D, carp, h 425 E 7th.
[illegible] lab, h 195 Middle.

HEADQUARTERS PHOTOGRAPHIC OUTFITS AMATEUR OR PROFESSIONAL THE H. LIEBER COMPANY, 33 S. MERIDIAN ST.

Vornehm Benjamin, lab, h n s McCormick 1 e of Miley av.
Vornehm Henry, lab, b 38 Everett.
Vornehm Joseph F, mason, h 90 Bloomington.
Vornehm Mary (wid Andrew), h 38 Everett.
Vornheder Frederick J, plumber, h 317 English av.
Vornheder Margaret E (wid Henry), h 315 English av.
Vornholt Henry J, grocer, 108 Weghorst, h same.
Voss Jay G, real est, 35 W Market, b 225 N Penn.
Voss Dennis, lab, h 160 Harmon.
Voss Emil, die sinker, b 623 S Meridian.
Voss John, condr, b 90 Belmont av (H).
Voss Tarquinia L, h 251 Broadway.
Votaw Artemisia (wid Henry), h 354 Indiana av.
Votaw Clarence E, clk R M S, h 378 N Alabama.
Votaw Herman O (Laport & Votaw), b 354 Indiana av.
Votz Minnie, h 63 W Georgia.
Vought John E, proofreader The Indpls Journal, b 914 N Delaware.
Vowles Robert, coachman 152 N Meridian.

W

Wabash Railroad, George D Maxfield pass agt, 42 Jackson pl.
Wabnetz Louis, meats, 99 E Mkt House, h n s Ohio 2 e of Rural.

WACHS WM, Wood Turner, rear 252 S New Jersey, Tel 668; h 172 Blake. (See adv in classified Wood Turners.)

Wachsmann Charles H, carver, h 112 Patterson.
Wachsmann Julius, musical insts, 70 Virginia av, h 338 S Alabama.
Wachsmann Paul, music teacher, 70 Virginia av, b 338 S Alabama.
Wachstetter Albert J, b 947 S East.
Wachstetter Alfred J, mach, b 72 N Senate av.

GUIDO R. PRESSLER, FRESCO PAINTER Churches, Theaters, Public Buildings, Etc., A Specialty. Residence, No. 325 North Liberty Street.

INDIANAPOLIS STEEL ROOFING AND CORRUGATING WORKS, 23 and 25 East South Street. S. D. NOEL, Proprietor.

DIAMOND WALL PLASTER { Telephone 1410 BUILDERS' EXCHANGE.

UNION TRANSFER AND STORAGE CO. Cor. E. Ohio St. and C., C., C. & St. L. R'y Tracks. ISSUE NEGOTIABLE RECEIPTS ON MERCHANDISE AND HOUSEHOLD GOODS.

W. McWORKMAN,
ROOFING AND CORNICE WORKS,
930 W. Washington St. Tel. 1118.

Wachstetter Anna (wid Gottlieb), h 502 Park av.
Wachstetter Bros (Robert C and Wm S), saloon, 56 Indiana av.
Wachstetter Charles, cigars, Board of Trade bldg, h 179 W Market.
Wachstetter Charles H, bkkpr Kahn Tailoring Co, b 147 N West.
Wachstetter Edward J, barber, 41 McCrea, h 111 Chadwick.
Wachstetter Flora, stenog Thomas C Day & Co, b 72 N Senate av.
Wachstetter Frederick, bartndr, b 40 Fayette.
Wachstetter George W, blksmith, h 133 Columbia av.
Wachstetter Henry, city fireman, b 223 Douglass.
Wachstetter Jacob, tmstr, h 270 Bright.
Wachstetter Jacob J, h 72 N Senate av.
Wachstetter Robert C (Wachstetter Bros), r Iron blk.
Wachstetter Sarah A (wid John), h 40 Fayette.
Wachstetter Stella, printer, b 165 N Capitol av.
Wachstetter Wm S (Wachstetter Bros), h 310 N California.
Wachtel John, lab, h 49 Hendricks.
Wachter Anna M (wid Louis), h 438 Mulberry.
Wachter Charles, cabtmkr, h 32 Guffin.
Wack Charles, mach, h 222 W Washington.
Wacker August W, butcher, h 606 Chestnut.
Wacker Edward C, clk, b 140 Michigan (H).
Wacker John, meats, 140 Michigan (H), h same.
Wacker Karl, butcher, 21 Tremont av (H), h same.
Wacuvik Joseph, filer, h 52 Morton.
Waddell Edward R, barber, h 154 S New Jersey.
Waddell Elijah J, collr, h 203 Ash.
Waddell Minor T, clk, b 203 Ash.
Waddle Baxter M, lab, h 67 Harrison.
Waddle Charles, printer, r 161½ Mass av.
Waddle Curtice H, clk, b 5 Ruckle.
Waddle Edward S, assembler, b 33 Davis.
Waddle Howell (Waddle & Dugdale), h 5 Ruckle.

GEO. J. MAYER,
MANUFACTURER OF
SEALS
STENCILS, RUBBER STAMPS, CHECKS, BADGES, DOOR PLATES, ETC.
15 S. Meridian St., Ground Floor. TEL. 1386.

Waddle & Dugdale (Howell Waddle, Benjamin H Dugdale), real est, 433 Lemcke bldg.
Waddles Charles, waiter, r 1½ Wood.
Waddy Henry A, clk, b 131 Madison.
Waddy Herbert O, grocer, 50 Clifford av, h 25 Newman.
Waddy John B, clk, h 131 Madison.
Waddy Percy A, clk, h 54 Brookside av.
Wade Anna P (wid Patrick J), b 560 E 8th.
Wade Benjamin F, contr, h 79 Howard.
Wade Carney, student, b 116 Martindale av.
Wade Enos T, cigars, 25½ Virginia av, h 274 W New York.
Wade Francis H, poultry, E Mkt House, h 71 Eastern av.
Wade George H, b 678 W Washington.
Wade George W, driver, h 79 Howard.
Wade Henry C, trav agt, b 130 Broadway.
Wade James, lab, b 567 Bellefontaine.
Wade James E, bookbndr, h 146 Bellefontaine.
Wade Jethro, baker, r 20 S Delaware.
Wade Landy V, lab, b 29 College av.
Wade Lee, lab, b 228 W Chesapeake.
Wade Mary A (wid David), h 130 Broadway.
Wade Ohio L, lumber, h 371 College av.
Wade Olive J, bkkpr, b 320 E Ohio.
Wade Patrick S, messenger Am Ex Co, h 567 Bellefontaine.
Wade Walker, cook, h 22 Sumner.
Wade Wm H, clk, b 174 W New York.
Wade Wm T, h e s Station 2 n of Schofield (B).
Wadkins Hayden, lab, h rear 604 N West.
Wadkins Wm, barber, r 165 Indiana av.
Wadlington James H, barber, r 18½ Indiana av.
Wadsworth Ariel, lab, h 70 S Noble.
Wadsworth John, driver, b 70 S Noble.
Wadsworth Robert D, letter carrier P O, h 54 Arch.
Waechter Ferdinand, lab, b 31 Poplar.
Wagar Harry A, foreman Dalton & Merrifield, h 9 N Gillard av.
Wagenfeld Henry, watchman, h 35 Iowa.
Wager Zella, stenog, b 9 N Gillard av.
Waggener Albert H, trav pass agt C & N W Ry, 7 Jackson pl.
Waggener Hannibal, grocer, 191 W 3d, h same.
Waggoner Benjamin E, baker, 266 Mass av, h 23 Park av.
Waggoner Benjamin E jr, b 23 Park av.
Waggoner Caroline, grocer, 21 Tremont av (H), h 39 Helen.
Waggoner David, lab, h 127 Sheffield av (H).
Waggoner James F, baggageman, h 34 Dearborn.
Waggoner Jane A (wid John L), h 59 King.
Waggoner Lewis H, clk, b 23 Park av.
Waggoner Sheldon, clk, h 39 Helen (H).
Waggoner Thomas, lab, h 478 W Lake (N I).
Waggoner Washington, lab, h 83 Torbet.
Waggoner Wm R, carp, h 431 W Francis (N I).
Waggy Edward, engr, h 567 W Udell (N I).
Wagner Abram, bkkpr E C Atkins & Co, h 238 Central av.
Wagner Anna (wid Henry G), h 91 Kansas.
Wagner Bernard, carp, h 50 Iowa.
Wagner Calvin D, barber, b 111 Trowbridge (W).
Wagner Car Door Co, H Rieman Duval pres, Charles S Lewis sec and treas, 3 Ingalls blk.
Wagner Caroline M (wid Frederick C), h 120 N Pine.

A. METZGER AGENCY ESTABLISHED 1863. REAL ESTATE

LAMBERT GAS & GASOLINE ENGINE CO.
ANDERSON, IND. GAS AND GASOLINE ENGINES, 2 TO 50 H. P.

Wagner Charles H, lab, h 257 Coburn.
Wagner Charles J, h 730 E 8th.
Wagner Conrad, carp, b 8 Singleton.
Wagner Daniel A, brakeman, h 111 Trowbridge (W).
Wagner Elizabeth (wid Charles), shoes, 855 S Meridian, h 859 same.
Wagner Eva (wid John), h 859 S Meridian.
Wagner Everett, sec World B, L and I Co, h 14 West Drive (W P).
Wagner Frederick, driver, b 222 Union.
Wagner Frederick C, lab, h 204 Union.
Wagner George, b 23 Hendricks.
Wagner George, tmstr, h 900 Shelby.
Wagner Henry, h 268 River av (W I).
Wagner Henry H, driver, b 204 Union.
Wagner Jacob, h 438 S East.
Wagner John, farmer, h rear s e cor Line and P C C & St L Ry (I).
Wagner John jr, lab, b rear s e cor Line and P C C & St L Ry (I).
Wagner John, grocer, h 851 S Meridian, h 870 same.
Wagner John, lab, h 26 St Marie av.
Wagner John W, lab, b 268 River av (W I).
Wagner Joseph, b 618 W Vermont.
Wagner Joseph, asst mkt master E Mkt House, h 512 Dillon.
Wagner Joseph C, mach, b 44 Poplar (B).

WAGNER JOSEPH H, Groceries, Meats, Hardware and Queensware, s e cor William and Howard (W I), h 461 Union.

Wagner Martin, lab, h rear 568 W Washington.
Wagner Otto, clk Clemens Vonnegut, h 364 Home av.
Wagner Otto F, varnisher, b 204 Union.
Wagner Otto R, toolmkr, h 8 Singleton.
Wagner Palace Car Co, Frank W Hadlock agt, Union Station.
Wagner Peter, saloon, 858 S Meridian, h same.
Wagner Theodore A, phys, 94 N Delaware, h 349 Broadway.
Wagner Wm, car insp, h 147 Harmon.
Wagner Wm C, lab, h 527 W Udell (N I).
Wagner Wm F, lab, b 204 Union.
Wagner Wm H, printer, 46½ N Penn, b 91 Kansas.
Wagoner David L, waiter, r 331 Superior.
Wagoner John V, bkkpr Williams & Flickinger, b 35 W Vermont.
Wagoner Marcellus L (Wagoner & Son), h 167 Hill av.
Wagoner Samuel R, lab, h 73 Yandes.
Wagoner Sarah E (wid Wm R), b 10 Pleasant av.
Wagoner Wm H, agt, h 19 Beacon.
Wagoner & Son (Marcellus L Wagoner, Ira W Roberts), meats, 167 Hill av.
Wagschal Louis, foreman, h 341 S Delaware.
Wahl Andrew, clk Albert Gall, h 113 S Noble.
Wahl Andrew H, clk, h 118 Bright.
Wahl Frederick, cabtmkr, h 260 Coburn.
Wahl Frederick W, tel opr, b 260 Coburn.
Wahl John N, lab, b 113 S Noble.
Wahlerman Wm, lab, h 1 Sample (W I).
Waidlick Ernest H, clk, h 264 S Capitol av.
Wainscott Cameron, plumber, r 249½ W Washington.
Wainscott Frank M, carp, h 249½ W Washington.
Wainscott Lavina (wid Amos), h 213 S McLain (W I).

Farm and City Loans
25 Years' Successful Business.
THOS. C. DAY & CO,
Rooms 325 to 330 Lemcke Building.

Wainwright John F, bkkpr Richardson & McCrea, b 46 Bellefontaine.
Wainwright Lucius M, pres Central Cycle Mnfg Co, r 81½ W Market.
Waite, see also Wayt.
Waite Albert, painter, b 202 W Maryland.
Waite Calista A (wid Benjamin T), b 114 St Mary.
Waite George R, lab, b 546 S West.
Waite Gordon, filer, h 546 S West.
Waite Jefferson, baker, r 20 S Delaware.
Waite Oliver S, molder, b 546 S West.
Waite Volney B, carp, h 419 N California.
Waits Abraham, lab, h 41 Harlan.
Waitzmann Otto, supt foreign dept Kingan & Co (ltd), b 408 N Illinois.
Wakefield Adam Rev, pastor African M E Zion Church, h 356 Blackford.
Wakefield Benjamin, lab, h 27 Hosbrook.
Wakefield David, r 23 N West.
Wakefield Henry, lab, b 1 Darwin.
Wakefield John F, lab, b 86 Sheldon.
Wakefield Lulu, h 506 S Illinois.
Wakefield Mary B (wid Henry), h 229 Elizabeth.
Wakeland Ida M, b 127 W Maryland.
Walch, see also Walsh, Welch and Welsh.
Walch Caroline (wid Bonifacious), dyer, 17 Meek, h same.
Walcott, see also Wolcott.
Walcott Benjamin D, pres and treas Indpls Terra Cotta Co, h 777 N Penn.
Walcott Charles H, loans, 66 E Market, h 512 N Meridian.
Wald Adolph, cigarmkr, 237 N Liberty, b same.
Wald Edward J, helper, b 680 E St Clair.
Wald John H, condr, h 680 E St Clair.
Wald Louisa, b 487 Madison av.
Wald Oliver R, hardware, 591 S Meridian, h 298 Union.
Walden Elias, farmer, h n w cor 21st and New Jersey.
Walden Elizabeth (wid Wm), h 124 Columbia al.
Walden George, lab, h rear e s English av 2 e of Belt R R.
Walden Henry, lab, b 462 W Chicago (N I).

EAT
HITZ'S CRACKERS
AND CAKES.
ASK YOUR GROCER FOR THEM.

BICYCLES $5 DOWN. Best Wheels. Best Terms. WHEELMEN'S CO. 31 W. OHIO ST. LONG DISTANCE TEL. 1855.

J. H. TECKENBROCK Painter and Decorator, 94 EAST SOUTH STREET.

FIDELITY MUTUAL LIFE—PHILADELPHIA, PA.
MATCHLESS SECURITY At LOW COST. A. H. COLLINS General Agent Baldwin Block.

Edwardsport Coal and Mining Co. Miners and Shippers Steam and Domestic Coal. Rooms 42 and 43 WHEN BUILDING.

ESTABLISHED 1876. TELEPHONE 168.
CHESTER BRADFORD,
SOLICITOR OF PATENTS,
AND COUNSEL IN PATENT CAUSES.
(See adv. page 6.)
Office:—Rooms 14 and 16 Hubbard Block, S. W. Cor. Washington and Meridian Streets, INDIANAPOLIS, INDIANA.

Walden James H, barber, b 525 N Senate av.
Walden Lewis S, solr N Y Life Ins Co, h e s Ritter av 1 n of University av (I).
Walden Robert R (Robert R Walden & Son), h 186 S Olive.
Walden Robert R & Son (Robert R and Robert W), hardware, 818 E Washington.
Walden Robert W (Robert R Walden & Son), b 186 S Olive.
Walden Sylvester G, engr, h 266 Howard (W I).
Walden Grant, paperhngr, b 124 Columbia al.
Walden Wayne, plastr, h w s Senate av 1 s of Lynn (M).
Walden Wm, carp, r 305½ E Washington.
Walden Wm A, lab, h 260 W Washington.
Walden Wm O, packer, h 260 W Washington.
Walden Wm O, lab, b 105 Naomi.
Walden Wm W, summons clk Sheriff's office, h 122 Columbia al.
Waldenmeier Bertha, midwife, 33 Barth av, h same.
Waldenmeier John H, lab, h 33 Barth av.
Walder Sophia (wid Jacob), r 52 Michigan av.
Walding Richard, hostler, r Union Stock Yards (W I).
Waldkoetter John F, cabtmkr, h 13 Pleasant av.
Waldman Louis, agt, h 505 S Capitol av.
Waldo Andrew M, tel opr L N A & C Ry, h 233 Hoyt av.
Waldo John P, chief train disp C C C & St L Ry, h 120 Highland pl.
Waldon James B, carp, h 628 Ontario (N I).
Waldorf John M, mngr Massillon Engine and Trestle Co, res South Bend, Ind.
Waldorff Nancy (wid John M), h 172 S Missouri.
Waldron George M, condr, h 104 Lexington av.
Waldron Thomas, brickmason, b 1 Carlos.
Waldruck Wm, tmstr, h 270 Union.
Wales Edward A, bkkpr, h 1367 N Illinois.
Wales George R, bkkpr, b 250 College av.

Outing BICYCLES
$85.00.
MADE AND SOLD BY
HAY & WILLITS MFG CO.
76 N. PENNSYLVANIA ST. PHONE 598.

Wales Louis H, trav agt, h 50 The Blacherne.
Wales Ruama W, teacher Public School No 14, b 250 College av.
Wales Samuel W, lime, 387 Mass av, h 250 College av.
Walk Carl F (Julus C Walk & Son), b 175 N West.
Walk Charles J, butcher, h 177 Church.
Walk Julius C (Julius C Walk & Son), h 175 N West.
WALK JULIUS C & SON (Julius C and Carl F), Jewelers and Silversmiths, 12 E Washington, Tel 127. (See left bottom cor cards.)
Walk Louis, lab b 177 Church.
Walker Aaron Rev, h 1350 Annette (N I).
Walker Abraham, lab, h 196 Huron.
Walker Albert, lab, r 142 S East.
Walker Alva J, h 40 S Liberty.
Walker Arthur L, drugs, 201 S Pine, h 207 same.
Walker Barclay, music teacher, Brenneke bldg, h 1632 N Meridian.
Walker Beulah B (wid Bertram), trimmer, b 593 Bellefontaine.
Walker Charles G, clk, h 167 Pleasant.
Walker Charles M, associate editor The Indpls Journal, h 76 W 3d.
Walker Claire A, h 76 W 3d.
Walker Cora B, music teacher, 169 Prospect, h same.
Walker Curtis L, trav agt, r 203 N Illinois.
Walker Daniel, lab, b 30 Torbet.
Walker David, lab, h s s 7th 1 w of canal.
Walker Edward A, h 810 N Delaware.
Walker Edward B, lab, h 135 Patterson.
Walker Edward B, waiter, h 341 Olive.
Walker Edward M, trav agt, h 420 S Delaware.
Walker Edward P, candymkr, h 108 Cornell av.
WALKER EDWIN T, Druggist, 1164 E Washington, h same.
Walker Ellen E, milliner, r 5 Halcyon blk.
Walker Elmer, lab, h 171 Harmon.
Walker Elmer, lab, h rear 310 E Washington.
Walker Emily (wid John), h 189 Bell.
Walker Emily L (wid John), r 480 W Francis (N I).
Walker Evelena R, evangelist, h 341 Olive.
Walker Francis M, lab, h 1131 E Michigan.
Walker Frank B, b 130 N Penn.
Walker Frank E, clk Indpls B and S Co, b 42 Arch.
Walker Frank S, mngr Union Transfer and Storage Co, h 173 E Vermont.
Walker George, lab, b 117 Indiana av.
Walker George A, clk, b 95 Brookside av.
Walker George W, collr Indpls Plumbing Co, b 120 Spring.
Walker George W, transfer, 34 Monument pl, h 522 N California.
Walker Gratten, lab, h 31 Jones.
Walker Greenberry, tmstr, h w s Caroline av 2 n of 17th.
Walker Hannah (wid John T), h 292 Fletcher av.
Walker Harry, mach, r 204 W South.
WALKER HARRY A, Saloon, 75 E Court, h 80 W Vermont.
Walker Harvey B, tel opr Postal Tel Cable Co, h 22 Oxford.
Walker Helen, stenog Russel M Seeds, b 407 N Illinois
Walker Henderson, lab, h rear 251 W 6th.

C. ZIMMERMAN & SONS | SLATE AND GRAVEL ROOFERS 19 South East Street.

DRIVEN WELLS And Second Water Wells and Pumps of all kinds at CHARLES KRAUSS'. 42 S. PENN. ST. TELEPHONE 465.

Walker Henry, lab, h 246 English av.
Walker Harry M, r 143½ Virginia av.
Walker Isaac N, phys, 130 N Penn, h same.
Walker Ivan N, h 557 N Capitol av.
Walker Jacob, barber, 251 W 6th, h 213 same.
Walker James W, lab, h 142 Hill av.
Walker Jesse L, mach hd, h 90½ S Capitol av.
Walker John, waiter, r rear 273 S Illinois.
Walker John A, engr, h 188 Brookside av.
Walker John C phys, b 130 N Penn.
Walker John G, plastr, r 88 W Ohio.
Walker John T, carp, 167 Pleasant, h same.
Walker Joseph B, ins agt, r 32 The Plaza.
Walker Judge, lab, h 381 Blackford.
Walker Julia, h 350 W North.
Walker Julietta (wid Wm G), r 281 Christian av.
Walker Kate (wid Wm), h 117 Indiana av.
Walker Layton C, supt loans State B and L Assn, b 557 N Capitol av.
WALKER LOUIS C, Attorney at Law, 55-56 Lombard Bldg, 24½ E Washington, Tel 643; h 785 N Delaware.
Walker Martha J (wid Green S), h 745 Brooker's al.
Walker Mary (wid Scott), h 115 Torbet.
Walker Merle N A, asst State Prosecuting Attorney, lawyer, 31 Lombard bldg, h 37 W Vermont.
Walker Mollie A, stenog Union Embossing Machine Co, b 249 Blake.
Walker Myra J (wid Wm F), h 377 S State av.
Walker Napoleon, lab, h 15 Rhode Island.
Walker Nellie, stenog, r 155 N Illinois.
Walker Robert D, cook, r 27 Fayette.
Walker Robert E, clk, h 62 W 13th.
Walker Rollin F, h 169 Prospect.
Walker Rufus J, bicycle rep, r 88 Mass av.
Walker Solomon, h rear 163 St Mary.
Walker Spencer, lab, b 189 Bell.
Walker Susan (wid Alexander), b 736 N West.
Walker Thomas, lab, h n w cor Tremont av and Emrich (H).
Walker Thomas, waiter, r 284 Blackford.
Walker Thomas R, clk McKee Shoe Co, h 340 N Capitol av.
Walker Walter F, grocer, 550 Bellefontaine, h 548 same.
Walker Walter H, tel opr, b 35 S Arsenal av.
Walker Walter L, piano tuner, h s e cor 7th and Illinois.
Walker Werden, cook The Bates.
Walker Wm, lab, h n w cor Tremont av and Emrich (H).
Walker Wm, waiter, b 33 Ellsworth.
Walker Wm A, sec Globe Accident Ins Co, h 540 Central av.
Walker Wm A, trav agt McCoy-Howe Co, b 402 Central av.
Walker Wm D, trav agt, h 406 Bellefontaine.
WALKER WM E (Martin & Walker), Dentist, b 183 N Capitol av.
Walker Wm J, motorman, h 142 Hill av.
Walker Wm P, painter, h 101 Sharpe av (W).
Walkup Francis H (Walkup & Reid), b 148 N Illinois.
Walkup & Reid (Francis H Walkup, Robert Reid), mnfrs' agts, 14 Hartford blk.
Wall Albert, bkkpr, r 34 S Capitol av.
Wall Arthur H, painter, h 54 Osgood (W I).

RICHARDSON & McCREA, MANAGERS FOR CENTRAL INDIANA. EQUITABLE LIFE ASSURANCE SOCIETY Of the United States. 79 EAST MARKET STREET, TELEPHONE 182.

Wall David, brakeman, b e s Brightwood av 7 s of Willow (B).
Wall David, phys, 59 Indiana av, h 339 W Vermont.
Wall Edward, engr, h 60 Stevens.
Wall Edward G, die sinker, b 256 W 23d.
Wall Elizabeth S (wid Joseph), b 72 W New York.
Wall Frances E, teacher Public School No 1 (H), b 111 Bismarck av (H).
Wall Frank B, mach, b 54 Osgood (W I).
Wall Frederick W, mngr dressmkg dept H P Wasson & Co, h 232 N Alabama.
Wall George, engr, h 256 W 23d.
Wall George A, printer, b 54 Osgood (W I).
Wall Harry A, lab, b 256 W 23d.
Wall Henry A, dentist, r 74 W New York.
Wall James W, tmstr, h 103 Sheffield av (H).
Wall John, phys, b 232 N Alabama.
Wall John F, paperhngr, r 271 Mass av.
Wall John M, lawyer, 51 Lombard bldg, b 339 W Vermont.
Wall John P, brakeman, h 93 Belmont av.
Wall Mary (wid Thomas), b 60 Stevens.
Wall Mary C, laundress, h 277 Spring.
Wall Michael, engr, h 157 Bates.
Wall Richard F, engr, h 111 Bates.
Wall Sarah J (wid Rev James S), h 111 Bismarck av (H).
Wall Thomas, lab, h 60 Stevens.
Wall Wm O, sawmkr, h 218 E Morris.
Wall Wm W, lab, h 218 E Morris.
Wallace Addie M, stenog, b 78 W 1st.
Wallace Albert, lab, b 594 E 10th.
Wallace Albert H, mach Sanborn Electric Co, b 551 Broadway.
Wallace Alexander, polisher, h 583 S East.
Wallace Andrew, b 25 Yeiser.
Wallace Bertha, h 321 E Wabash.
Wallace Catherine S, notions, 328 Mass av, h same.
Wallace Charles C, engr, r 234 Fletcher av.
Wallace David, chief dep Treas of Marion County and City of Indpls, 23 Court House, r 71 The Blacherne.
Wallace Elizabeth, h 12 Bates al.
Wallace Emma (wid Wm H), h 68 Holloway av.

Typewriter-Ribbons ALL COLORS FOR ALL MACHINES. THE BEST AND CHEAPEST. S. H. EAST, STATE AGENT, The Williams Typewriter.... 55 THORPE BLOCK, 87 E. MARKET ST.

ERTEL STEAM LAUNDRY LARGEST AND BEST IN THE STATE. PROMPT SERVICE. 26 and 28 N. Senate Ave. Telephone 18.

ELLIS & HELFENBERGER Architectural Iron Work and Gray Iron Castings. 162-170 South Senate Ave. Tel. 958.

THE HOGAN TRANSPER AND STORAGE COMP'Y
Household Goods and Pianos Moved—Packed—Stored..... Baggage and Package Express Machinery and Safes a Specialty. Cor. Washington and Illinois Sts. TELEPHONE No. 675.

Hose, Belting, Packing, Clothing, Druggists' Sundries, Bicycle Tires, Cotton Hose, Etc. New York Belting & Packing Co., L't'd.
The Central Rubber & Supply Co. PHONE 922. 79 S. ILLINOIS ST., INDIANAPOLIS, IND.

The Provident Life and Trust Company
Of Philadelphia.
Grants Certificates of Extension to Policyholders who are temporarily unable to pay their premiums
D. W. EDWARDS, Gen. Agt., 508 Indiana Trust Bldg.

Wallace Frank H, etcher, b 68 Cypress.
Wallace Frank S, bookbndr, h 51 Omer.
Wallace George, engr, h 659½ Virginia av.
WALLACE GEORGE E, Real Estate, 77½ E Market, h 77 Johnson av.
Wallace George W, watchman, r 52½ Indiana av.
Wallace Georgie E (wid Benjamin), h 318 E Court.
Wallace Gilbert L, carp, h 436 W 2d.
Wallace Harriet E, asst prin Public School No 4, b 250 College av.
Wallace Harry R, patrolman, b 192 Hoyt av.
WALLACE HENRY L, Agt The Blacherne, n w cor Meridian and Vermont, Tel 1183; h 737 N Penn.
Wallace Howard, lab, b 152 Maple.
Wallace Jacob J, engr, b 97 S Noble.
Wallace James H, janitor Public School No 7, h 53 Concordia.
Wallace James M, mach, h 379 Fletcher av.
WALLACE JOHN, The Otto Gas Engine Works, Builders' Exchange, 35 E Ohio, Tel 535; h 551 Broadway. (See left bottom lines.)
Wallace John B, finisher, b 159 N Pine.
Wallace John B, saloon, n w cor Holmes av and Frazee (H), h same.
Wallace John H, lab, h 4 Hiawatha.
Wallace John K P, salesman, h 53 Greer.
Wallace John L, foreman Indpls Foundry Co, b 137 Prospect.
Wallace Johnston, saloon, 64 Malott av, h same.
Wallace Lew jr, lawyer, 139 Commercial Club bldg, h 124 W 2d.
Wallace Lucinda (wid Peter), nurse, 881 Mass av, b same.
Wallace Maggie (wid Samuel), b 36 W Michigan.
Wallace Mary A (wid James), b 914 N Senate av.
Wallace Matilda (wid Thomas), b 63 Maxwell.
Wallace Nellie, h 27 Erie.
Wallace Perry, clk The McElwaine-Richards Co, h 379 College av.

Julius C. Walk & Son, Jewelers Indianapolis.
12 EAST WASHINGTON ST.

Wallace Robert, lab, b 363 E McCarty.
Wallace Ross H, collr clk Indiana Natl Bank, b 525 N Alabama.
Wallace Samuel, bricklyr, h 63 Vine.
Wallace Samuel L, acct, h 525 N Alabama.
Wallace Samuel M, letter carrier P O, b 192 Hoyt av.
Wallace Sarah E, teacher Public School No 29, b 63 Vine.
Wallace Sarah J (wid Wm J), h 192 Hoyt av.
Wallace Thomas, lab, h 6 Brown av (H).
Wallace Thomas, lab, h rear 44 Yandes.
Wallace Thomas L, millwright, h 525 Highland av (N I).
Wallace Wm B, mach, h 159 N Pine.
Wallace Wm C, mach, h 387 Fletcher av.
Wallace Wm P, clk R M S, h 379 College av.
Walle Albert M, packer, b 120 Davidson.
Walle John A, lab, h 14 Clay.
Walle Joseph A, mach hd, b 120 Davidson.
Walle Joseph W, mach, b 214 E Morris.
Walle Matthew, blksmith, h 337 S Meridian.
Walle Matthew, horseshoer, h 120 Davidson.
Walle Wm, lab, h 13 N California.
Wallen Carl, condr, b 75 W 13th.
Wallen Green B, condr, h 642 N Capitol av.
Wallener Louis, optician, h 447 S Capitol av.
Waller Bernhard, shoemkr, 153 Indiana av, h 293 N California.
Waller Bernhard jr, shoemkr, 40 W 13th, h 1147½ N Illinois.
Waller Charles, uphlr, b 293 N California.
Waller George, cabtmkr, h 664 McLene (N I).
Waller Wm, shoemkr, b 293 N California.
Wallers Alfred, mach, h 71 Johnson av.
Wallet Lulie J, printer The Ensign, b 143 Greer.
Wallet John A, bartndr, h 281 Huron.
Wallick Earl V, driver, h 320 Fulton.
WALLICK JOHN F, Supt Western Union Telegraph Co, 19 S Meridian, Tel 236; h 496 N Meridian, Tel 184.
Wallick John G, clk W U Tel Co, b 496 N Meridian.
Wallick Martin H, asst bkkpr The McGilliard Agency Co, b 496 N Meridian.
Wallick Samuel G, tel opr W U Tel Co, b 476 N Illinois.
Walling Charles, uphlr, h 726 N Senate av.
Walling Harry, cigarmkr, b 34 N New Jersey.
Wallingford Charles A, architect, 44 Coffin blk, b 247 N Meridian.
Wallington James, barber, r 18½ Indiana av.
Wallis Ernest, salesman Emil Wulschner & Son, h 327 E McCarty.
Wallis Theodore, teacher, h 389 S New Jersey.
Wallmann Anna (wid Henry), h e s Randell 1 s of Pleasant run.
Wallmann Frederick, tailor, h s s Downey 2 w of Wright.
Wallmann Wm, tailor, h s s Downey 2 w of Wright.
Walls Albert B, carp, h 294½ Mass av.
Walls Charles H, showman, h 520 W Wells (N I).
Walls Henry, restaurant, 44 W Washington, r 85½ W Market.
Walls John F, paperhngr, b 269 Mass av.
Walls John W, molder, h 49 Bismarck (H).
Walls Louis, music teacher, rear 66 E Michigan, b same.
Walls Van S, lab, h 103 Sheffield av (H).
Wallsmith Marcellus J E, lab, h w s Austin 5 s of Sutherland (B).

OTTO GAS ENGINES | BUILDERS' EXCHANGE S. W. Cor. Ohio and Penn. Telephone 535.

Becker & Son Charles Becker Jacob Becker Jr. Merchant Tailors. 21 N. Penn. St. Tel. 934

Walmsley Charles S, mach, h 433 Martindale av.
Walmsley David C, draughtsman, h 433 Martindale av.
Walpole Luke, justice of peace, 12½ N Delaware, h 410 N Illinois.
Walpole Martin, cooper, h 113 Patterson.
Walrad Lucilla E, h 1092 E Washington.
Walrath Albert E, brakeman, h 172 Prospect.
Walsh, see also Welch and Welsh.
Walsh Agnes M, teacher Public School No 2 (H), b 175 Sheffield av (H).
Walsh Alice S, stenog H D Pierce and notary public, 12, 18½ N Meridian, b 175 Sheffield av (H).
Walsh Arthur J, porter, r 159 E Ohio
Walsh Clara E (wid John), cigars, 16 S Illinois, h 62½ same.
Walsh Daniel, lab, b 84 S Senate av.
Walsh Eliza (wid Thomas), h 175 Sheffield av (H).
Walsh Frank J, clk, b 74 Stevens.
Walsh Hamilton J, brakeman, h 25 Walcott.
Walsh Harry J, salesman, b 127 W 2d.
Walsh James, clk, r 130 N Senate av.
Walsh James, clk Hollweg & Reese, b 74 Stevens.
WALSH JAMES A, Stenographer and Notary Public, 14-16 Hubbard Blk, b 265 N Senate av.
Walsh James C, grocer, 621 Virginia av, h same.
Walsh John, clk, b 97 Hosbrook.
Walsh John, tailor, h 127 W 2d.
Walsh John C, h 97 Hosbrook.
Walsh John J, buyer N Y Store, r 130 N Senate av.
Walsh John R, tailor, b 346 S Missouri.
Walsh Joseph, shoemkr, b 193 W Washington.
Walsh Julia (wid Patrick), h 346 S Missouri.
Walsh Margaret (wid Thomas), b 220 Douglass.
Walsh Matthew P, painter, 386 Fulton, h same.
Walsh Maurice, janitor Public School No 26, h 132 Martindale av.
Walsh Michael, lab, b 450 Mass av.
Walsh Michael J, brakeman, b 25 Walcott.
Walsh Patrick, h 674 N Capitol av.
Walsh Patrick, lab, h rear 186 W Merrill.
Walsh Patrick W, engr, h 413 W Howard (W I).
Walsh Peter, lab, h 25 Sharpe.
Walsh Richard, foreman, h 124 Agnes.
Walsh Thomas W, engr, h 364 W New York.
Walsh Wm J, tailor, h 524 S Illinois.
Walsman Delores, b 305 S Delaware.
Walsman Edward F, clk N Y Store, b 123 Davidson.
Walsman Edward H, uphlr, b 163 Fletcher av.
Walsman Frederick, lab, h 89 N Delaware.
Walsman Frederick C, cook, b 123 Davidson.
Walsman Frederick E, mattressmkr, b 288 N Liberty.
Walsman James H, cook, b 73 N Alabama.
Walsman John P, marker, b 52 Tacoma av.
Walsman Wm, cabtmkr, h 163 Fletcher av.
Walson Benjamin, lab 250 N Meridian.
Walter Catherine, laundress, h rear 407 S Delaware.
Walter Charles G, riding bailiff Sheriff's Office, h e s Hillside av 4 s of 17th.
Walter David, barber, b 156 Minerva.

Henry H. Fay,
40½ E. Washington St.,
REAL ESTATE,
AND LOAN BROKER.

Walter Esther (wid Edward), h 65 High.
Walter Emma, stenog American Tin Plate Co, b 65 High.
Walter Frederick, clk, h 578 S Illinois.
Walter Frederick P, decorator, h 319 Prospect.
Walter George, h 815 S East.
Walter George, caller Fahnley & McCrea, b 578 S Illinois.
Walter George H, bartndr, h 452 Charles.
Walter Henry, lab, b 233 W 3d.
Walter Herman J, saloon, 100 S Noble, h same.
Walter Horace, barber, b 59 S Illinois.
Walter Jacob, finisher, b 578 S Illinois.
Walter James, molder, h 581 S Illinois.
Walter James P (Blair, Baker & Walter), h Crawfordsville, Ind.
Walter John, shoemkr, h 578 S Illinois.
Walter John A, feed, 252 Mass av, r same.
Walter John E, lab, h e s Hillside av 6 s of 17th.
Walter John W, mach, h 99 Ramsey av.
Walter Lewis C, propr Indiana Wire Wks, h 71 W 7th.
Walter Philip, h rear 407 S Delaware.
Walter Sophie (wid Jacob), h 52 Michigan av.
Walter Wm H, trav agt, h 6 Fletcher av.
Walterhouse Gillam N, clk, b 141 E Pratt.
Walterhouse Louisa B, nurse, b 141 E Pratt.
Walterhouse Sarah M (wid Thomas S), h 141 E Pratt.
Walterman Charles F, stonecutter, h 959 N Senate av.
Walters America E, h 630 Virginia av.
Walters Benjamin, cook, b e s Central av nr 7th.
Walters Christian F, carp, h 735 E Michigan.
Walters Curry, lab, b rear 362 Douglass.
Walters David E, brakeman, h 20 S Pine.
Walters DeWitt C, driver, h 65½ Beaty.
Walters Edward, painter, r 19 S West.
Walters Eva, teacher Industrial Training School, b 21 Church.
Walters Frank C, carp, h 735 E Michigan.
Walters Frederick W, wagonmkr, h 607 Madison av.

SALISBURY & STANLEY • Office, Store and Bank Fixtures a Specialty. Repairing of all kinds done on short notice. 177 Clinton Street, Indianapolis, Ind. • Contractors and Builders TELEPHONE 999.

FRIEDGEN'S IS THE PLACE FOR THE NOBBIEST SHOES Ladies' and Gents' 19 North Pennsylvania St.

SAMUEL LAING || COPPER AND GALVANIZED IRON CORNICE MANUFACTURER
72 AND 74 E. COURT STREET. SKYLIGHTS AND VENTILATORS.

M. B. WILSON, Pres. W. F. CHURCHMAN, Cash.
THE CAPITAL NATIONAL BANK,
INDIANAPOLIS, IND.
Our Specialty is handling all Country Checks and Drafts on Indiana and neighboring States at the very lowest rates. Call and see us.
Interest Paid on Time Deposits.
28 S. MERIDIAN ST., COR. PEARL.

Walters George, coachman 729 N Meridian.
Walters George, coal, 218 W Pearl, h same.
Walters George C, toolmkr, h 578 Ash.
Walters George W, ins agt, b 630 Virginia av.
Walters Gustav C, carp, b 735 E Michigan.
Walters Harriet (wid DeWitt C), h 281 Jefferson av.
Walters Harry, lab, h 507 E 11th.
Walters Harry A, mach hd, b 578 Ash.
Walters Harry C, mach, b 607 Madison av.
Walters Harry S, grocer, 53 Maxwell, h same.
Walters Henry, cabtmkr, h 735 E Michigan.
Walters Henry, tmstr, r 183½ W Washington.
Walters Herman J, lab, h 229 E South.
Walters Jacob H, foreman, h 234 English av.
Walters James, roller, b 277 S Penn.
Walters Jennie A, h 336½ E Washington.
Walters John, plastr, h rear 362 Douglass.
Walters John, h 1025 W Washington.
Walters John P, lab, h s w cor Auburn and English av.
Walters Julia A (wid Frank), h 40 Sullivan.
Walters Mary G (wid John E), h 219 Fletcher av.
Walters Mason, trimmer, b 1092 N Senate av.
Walters Nellie, h 46 Cleaveland blk.
Walters Otto R, baker Parrott & Taggart, b 735 E Michigan.
Walters Richard J, clk Indpls Chair Mnfg Co, r 168 W Michigan.
Walters Thomas, driver, b 21 Church.
Walters Thomas C, bricklyr, b rear 362 Douglass.
Walters Wm A, clk, h 205 S Pine.
Walters Wm H, b 234 English av.
Walters Wm H, driver, r 57½ E South.
Walters Wm Z, driver, h 281 Jefferson av.
Walthall Frank, lab, h e s Miami 6 s of Prospect.
Walthall Hannah (wid Charles), b 241 Orange.
Walthall Maria (wid John), b Frank Walthall.
Walther Franklin, janitor, h 115 Fayette.

TUTTLE & SEGUIN,
28 E. Market St. Ground Floor.
COLLECTING RENTS AND CARE OF PROPERTY A SPECIALTY.
Telephone 1168.

Waltke Frederick W, mngr When bldg, 34 When bldg, r same.
Waltman Henry A, mach, h 392 Columbia av.
Walton Alba, boilermkr, b 46 Russell av.
Walton Charles, candymkr, h 457 Mulberry.
Walton Estella R, b 571 E 9th.
Walton George B, com mer, 48 S Delaware, h 461 College av.
Walton James P, h 244½ E Washington.
Walton James S, trav agt Standard Oil Co, h 35 Dearborn
Walton King, lab, h 26 Seibert.
Walton Thomas C, poultry, b 15 Shriver av.
Walton Wm H, carp, h 60 Hoyt av.
Waltz Andrew, lab, h 125 S East.
Waltz Andrew E, drayman, b 125 S East.
Waltz Daniel, carp, h 88 Sheldon.
Waltz Frederick L, foreman E C Atkins & Co, h 88 Church.
Waltz George, butcher, r 232 E Washington.
Waltz Harry, sawmkr, b 24 Harmon.
Waltz Mary (wid Frank), h 24 Harmon.
Waltz Sarah A, dressmkr, 88 Sheldon, h same.
Waltz Solomon F, millwright, h 128 High.
Wambach Joseph, h 221 Fletcher av.
Wambach Wm, h 221 Fletcher av.
Wambaugh Clara L, h e s Muskingum al 2 n of 1st.
Wambaw Anna, r 116½ W New York.
Wambsgauss Frederick Rev, pastor St Paul's German Evangelical Lutheran Church, h 391 S New Jersey.
Wammick Wm, porter, h 529 N Senate av.
Wampler Augustus W, waiter, b 107 S Illinois.
Wampler James W, stock examiner Bureau of Animal Industry, b s s Moore av 1 e of Dearborn.
Wampler John, clk, h s s Moore av 1 e of Dearborn.
Wampler Wm B, carp, r 291 E New York.
Wampner Andrew, insp, h 44 Williams.
Wampner George A, contr, 26 Dawson, h same.
Wampner John H, drayman, h 139 Lexington av.
Wamsley Charles O, molder, h 342 Douglass.
Wamsley Frank, plastr, b 407½ Indiana av.
Wamsley Mary A (wid Harvey), h 244½ Indiana av.
Wamsley Oscar A, lab, h 215 Douglass.
Wamsley Rebecca A (wid Wm), h 407½ Indiana av.
Wamsley Samuel L (Wamsley & Holmes), h 294 N California.
Wamsley Willard L, city fireman, h 232 S Alabama.
Wamsley & Holmes (Samuel L Wamsley, David J Holmes), horseshoers, 116 W Maryland.
Wanamaker Car Scale Co The, Harry E Drew pres, John W Chipman sec, Albert G Cox treas, 46 Thorpe blk.
Wanamaker Charles B, supt Globe Machine Wks, h 187 Pleasant.
Wands Eliza S, stenog J S Cruse, b 57 Greer.
Wands James W, mngr J S Cruse, h 133 Pleasant.
Wands John, shoemkr, 237 E Washington, h same.
Wands Robert H, shoemkr, b 237 E Washington.
Wands Wm (Indiana Electrotype Foundry), phys, 6 Baldwin blk, h 330 E Vermont.

PAPER BOXES SULLIVAN & MAHAN 41 W. Pearl St.

DIAMOND WALL PLASTER { Telephone 1410
BUILDERS' EXCHANGE.

If your Laundry Work is not satisfactory, try THE HOME LAUNDRY 197 S. Illinois St. Telephone 178

Wands Wm R, mngr Hoosier Mnfg Co, 192 S Illinois, h 181 Lexington av.
Wanee Charles H, clk, b 71 Oak.
Wangbigler George, glass beveler, h 50 Sanders.
Wangelin Ida, stenog Ger Fire Ins Co of Ind, b 39 Highland pl.
Wanger Solomon, shoemkr, 84 Indiana av, h same.
Wankel Conrad, boilermkr, b 333 S Penn.
Wankel George, tankman, h 145 Harrison.
Wann James H, blksmith, h 24 N Judge Harding (W I).
Wanner Andrew J, lab, b 268 Fletcher av.
Wanner Peter F, clk R M S, r 11 The Plaza.
Wantland Wm F, molder, h 55 Sheffield (W I).
Wappenhans Charles F R, local forecast official U S Weather Bureau, r 63 Ingalls blk.
WARBURTON CHARLES S, Supt Loans Massachusetts Mutual Life Insurance Co, 1002 Majestic Bldg, Tel 839; h 168 E St Clair, Tel 1153.
Warchold Frank, lab, b 87 Nebraska.
Ward Adelaide J, seamstress, h 251 Bellefontaine.
Ward Albert E, mach, h e s Sherman Drive 2 n of Ohio.
Ward Albert L Rev, h e s Good av 4 s of Railroad (I).
WARD ALBERT O, Physician, 189 Virginia av, h 102 Woodlawn av.
Ward Alva C, bkkpr N Y Store, b e s Sherman Drive 1 n of Michigan.
Ward Anthony, saloon, 11 Russell av, h same.
Ward Anthony jr, bartndr, b 11 Russell av.
Ward Boswell, pres Ward Bros Drug Co, h 387 N New Jersey.
WARD BROS' DRUG CO, Boswell Ward Pres, Claire S Dearborn Sec, Marion Ward Treas, Wholesale Druggists, 72 S Meridian, Tel 215.
Ward Burt C, clk, b 1016 N Penn.
Ward Carey J, carp, e s Sherman Drive 1 n of Michigan, h same.
Ward Catherine (wid Wm), b 13 Hoyt av.
Ward Charles, barber, r 161 Indiana av.
Ward Charles, trainer Hay & Willitts Mnfg Co, b 229 N Penn.
Ward Charles W, bricklyr, b 127 Meek.
Ward Charles W, clk, r 30 Hendricks blk.
Ward Clarence V, student, b 102 Woodlawn av.
Ward Clinton C, lab, h 286 N Missouri.
Ward Daniel, helper, b 91 John.
Ward Daniel, lab, b 88 Meikel.
Ward Daniel, motorman, b 75 W 13th.
Ward Delancy L, ex mess, h 155 N Capitol av.
Ward Edward, hostler, b cor McLain and Howard (W I).
Ward Edward, porter, b 671 N Senate av.
Ward Emma, h 220 E Court.
Ward Francis A, asst custodian State House, h 87 S West.
Ward Frank, bartndr, b 1349 N Capitol av.
Ward Frank E, clk, b 452 Central av.
Ward Frank M, novelty mnfr, 178 E Louisiana, h 388 Broadway.
Ward Frank M, fireman, h 177 English av.
Ward Frederick, letter carrier P O, h 100 Yeiser.
Ward George, clk U S Pension Agency, b 1653 Kenwood av.

FRANK NESSLER. WILL H. ROST.
FRANK NESSLER & CO.
Tailors
56 EAST MARKET ST. (Lemcke Building),
INDIANAPOLIS, IND.

Ward George L, papermkr, h 44 Haugh (H).
Ward George W, mach, b 177 Mas sav.
Ward George W jr, mach, b 177 Mass av.
Ward Harvey L, trav agt, h 423 N Capitol av.
Ward Hattie E, b 325 N Illinois.
Ward Henry, lab, h 454½ S Capitol av.
Ward Henry, lab, h 30 Holborn.
Ward Henry C, brakeman, h 44 Michigan av.
Ward Henry R, janitor, h 31 Tremont av (H).
Ward Hugh, h 329 N New Jersey.
Ward James, lab, b 159 W McCarty.
Ward James E, expressman, h 493 N New Jersey.
Ward James L, painter, h 118 Cook.
Ward Jesse, lab Exchange Hotel (W I).
Ward John, carp, h rear 25 Nordyke av (W I).
Ward John, lab, h n w cor Reisner and Johnson (W I).
Ward John, millwright, h 15 Nordyke av (W I).
Ward John, supt, h 1186 N Illinois.
Ward John F, clk C C C & St L Ry, n e cor South and Delaware, res Perry twp.
Ward John F, clk, b 322 S New Jersey.
Ward John G (Martin & Co), h 554 Virginia av.
Ward John N, carp, h 8 Oxford.
Ward John P, grocer, 23 Astor, h same.
Ward John S, tailor, b 12 Elizabeth.
Ward Joseph H, student, b 291 W Michigan.
Ward Leah H (wid Wm), b 136 Cornell av.
Ward Luke, lab, b 57 S California.
Ward Kate, bkkpr Union Co-Operative Laundry, b 130 N Senate av.
Ward Kate, laundress, h 17 N New Jersey.
Ward Marion, treas Ward Bros' Drug Co, h 274 N Alabama.
Ward Mary (wid Patrick A), h 130 N Senate av.
Ward Mary D, seamstress, h 251 Bellefontaine.
Ward Mary E (wid Henry B), h 227 Hadley av (W I).
Ward Mary J (wid Samuel P), b 38 Warren av (W I).

Haueisen & Hartmann
163-169 E. Washington St.
FURNITURE,
Carpets,
Household Goods,
Tin, Granite and China Wares, Oil Cloth and Shades

The Fidelity and Deposit Co. OF MARYLAND. Bonds signed for Administrators, Assignees, Executors, Guardians, Receivers, Trustees, and persons in every position of trust. GEO. W. PANGBORN, General Agent, 704-706 Lemcke Building. Telephone 140.

INSURE YOUR PROPERTY WITH FRANK K. SAWYER

•JOSEPH GARDNER•
GALVANIZED IRON
CORNICES and SKYLIGHTS.
Metal Ceilings and Siding.
Tin, Iron, Steel and Slate Roofing.
37, 39 & 41 KENTUCKY AVE. Telephone 322.

Ward Michael, lab, h 114 Hadley av (W I).
Ward Michael, lab, h 78 Willow.
Ward Nancy (wid Daniel), h 91 John.
Ward Nathan, lab, r 29 Hiawatha.
Ward Nathan T, patrolman, h 10 Hiawatha.
Ward Nathan W, lab, b 10 Hiawatha.
Ward Nora A, stenog Internat Typograph Union, b 554 Virginia av.
Ward Otis J, clk, h 502 N Senate av.
Ward Patrick, saloon, 832 W Washington, h same.
Ward Patrick W, saloon, 669 N Senate av, h 1103 N Delaware.
Ward Pompey, lab, h 556 N Senate av.
Ward Richard B, real est, h 1203 Northwestern av.
Ward Sarah, h 84 S East.
Ward Sarah (wid John), b 402 Bates.
Ward Stephen J (Ward & Co), b 130 N Senate av.
Ward Theresa I, teacher, b 130 N Senate av.
Ward Thomas (Ward & Co), h 338 Douglass.
Ward Thomas, brick insp, h 12 Elizabeth.
Ward Thomas W, bartndr, b 671 N Senate av.
Ward Timothy F, tel opr, h 123 Fayette.
Ward Walter D, barber, 193 Shelby, h 156 Minerva.
Ward Wm, cabtmkr, h 659 W Eugene (N I).
Ward Wm, pictures, 42 N Penn, h 237 N Delaware.
Ward Wm H, books, 89 S Illinois, r Stubbins Hotel.
Ward Zachary T, plastr, h s s Walnut av 1 w of Maple av (I).
Ward & Co (Stephen J and Thomas Ward), pawnbrokers, 11 N Meridian.
Wardell Edward, barber, r 144 N Capitol av.
Warden Frederick, lab, b 619 W Pearl.
Warden Samuel, well driver, b 61 E South.
Warder, Bushnell & Glessner Co, Oliver P Bair mngr, farm impits, 96 S Capitol av.
Wardrip Ida, h 191½ E Washington.
Wardrop Christy, h 167 W Washington.
Wardwell Harry E, mach, b 63 Nordyke av (W I).
Wardwell Ralph, lab, h 63 Nordyke av (W I).
Ware Charles A, patrolman, h 23 Elk.

J. S. FARRELL & CO.
Have Experienced Workmen and will Promptly Attend to your
PLUMBING
Repairs. 84 North Illinois Street. Telephone 382.

Ware David, b 23 Elk.
Ware David, brickmkr, h 76 Willow.
Ware David jr, mach, b 76 Willow.
Ware George A, barber, 98 Prospect, r 108 same.
Ware James R, lab, h 328 English av.
Ware Jasper, lab, b 314 E Court.
Ware John, lab, h 261 S Senate av.
Ware John jr, uphlr, b 261 S Senate av.
Ware Joseph E, insp, h 41 S West.
Ware Thomas A, lab, h 328 English av.
Ware Thomas F, barber, b 328 English av.
Ware Wm, lab, h 358 Douglass.
Warfel Frank E, carp, b 86 E Ohio.
Warfield Charles, brickmason, b rear 633 N Senate av.
Warfield Edward, bricklyr, b rear 633 N Senate av.
Warfield Harry, coachman 410 N Capitol av.
Warfield Nellie (wid Charles), h 302½ N Senate av.
Warfield Parker, lab, h 226 Martindale av.
Warfield Wm, lab, b 429 Clinton.
Warfield Wm, lab, h 116 Darnell.
Warfield Wm, lab, h 560 Jefferson av.
Warfield Wm, lab, h w s Northwestern av 3 s of 30th (N I).
Warford Walter S, foreman The Sun, h 423 E 12th.
Waring John H, barber, 515 E 8th, h 72 Yandes.
Waring Semira H (wid Wm P), h 127 St Mary.
Warmack Charles W, lab, h 15 Center.
Warmack John, lab, h 564 W North.
Warmack Peter, lab, h 620 Home av.
Warmack Queen, h 19 Columbia.
Warmack Wm H, porter R M S, h 529 N Senate av.
Warman, Black, Chamberlain & Co (Enoch Warman, George W Black, Jenner H Chamberlain, James C Davis), sale stable, Union Stock Yards.
Warman Enoch (Warman, Black, Chamberlain & Co), h 588 N Alabama.
Warman Franklin E, b 588 N Alabama.
Warman Phoebe J, b 1140 W Washington (H).
Warmburg James, lab, h 50 Colgrove av.
Warmeling Charles T, baker, 175 Madison av, h same.
Warmeling Ernest, driver, b 175 Madison av.
Warmeling Henry, mach, h 175 Madison av.
Warmeling Rudolph F, mattress mnfr, 177 Madison, h 239 same.
Warmouth George W, lawyer, 14 Fletcher's Bank bldg, b 1304 N Delaware.
Warnburg Charles T, brickmkr, h w s Sylvan 1 s of Sycamore.
Warne Charles F, r 165 W Pearl.
Warne Joseph B (E P Fulmer & Co), h 16 W Michigan.
Warne Joseph B, clk McKee Shoe Co, h 66 W 11th.
Warneke Henry, shoemkr, rear 202 Hoyt av, b 271 Prospect.
Warner, see also Werner.
Warner Abel L, stairbldr, h 67 Sheffield av (W I).
Warner Catharine A (wid Thomas D), b 86 Clifford av.
Warner Charles, clk R M S, b 325 N Illinois.
Warner Charles T, mach Indpls Journal, b 86 Clifford av.
Warner Cortice M (C M Warner & Co), b 572 N Penn.

GUARANTEED INCOME POLICIES issued only by the United States Life Insurance Co. E. B. SWIFT, Manager. 25 E. Market St.

Furniture Carpets } WM. KOTTEMAN { Stoves Ranges
89 and 91 East Washington Street. Telephone 1742.

WARNER C M & CO (Cortice M and Otis H Warner), Wholesale and Retail Cigars, Tobacco, Etc, n e cor Washington and Meridian.
Warner David, candymkr, b 92 W Ohio.
Warner David, lab, h 293 E Washington.
Warner Edward P, lab, r 5½ Madison av.
Warner Elward W, trav agt, h 412 N Delaware.
Warner Florence (wid Charles G), h 517 W Shoemaker (N I).
Warner Frank, brakeman, h 30 Eastern av.
Warner Frank J, h rear 408 Union.
Warner Frank J, mach, h 421 Charles.
Warner Henry H, lab, b 416 Union.
Warner Herman E, printer, h 517 W Shoemaker (N I).
Warner John, b 224 E St Clair.
Warner John, engr, h 51 S Gale (B).
Warner John, lab, b w s Earhart 8 s of Prospect.
Warner John A, collr, h 435 Ash.
Warner John A, pressman The Indpls Journal, b 908 N Senate av.
Warner John T, mach, h 416 Union.
Warner Joseph C, electrician, h e s Ritter av 1 n of University av (I).
Warner Margaret E, r 193 W Washington.
Warner Mitchel L, butcher, h 14 Sharpe.
Warner Otis H (C M Warner & Co), h 136 W 1st.
Warner Peter, clk R M S, r 21 The Plaza.
Warner Roscoe C, agt, h 173 E South.
Warner Silas, lab, h w s Earhart 8 s of Prospect.
Warner Willard H, canmkr, b 108 Hosbrook.
Warner Wm F, mach, h 188 Minnesota.
Warner Wm S, letter carrier P O, h 634 E Vermont.
Warning Benjamin, mach, r 19 N Arsenal av.
Warnke John H, cigarmkr, b 196 Oliver av (W I).
Warnke Sophia (wid Henry), h 196 Oliver av (W I).
Warnock John J, mach, h 60 Poplar (B).
Warren Alonzo, engr, h 462 E North.
Warren Andrew R, trav agt, h 34 E Pratt.
Warren Calvin M, policeman, h 720 Ash.
Warren Cathedine, teacher, b 420 Union.
Warren Charles E (Justice & Warren), h 136 Brookside av.
Warren Daniel, gasfitter, b 39 N Alabama.
Warren Daniel, sawmkr, b 94 S Liberty.
Warren Daniel F, opr W U Tel Co, b 611 S Meridian.
Warren George S, sec Indpls Elevator Co, h 369 N Capitol av.
Warren Henry, lab, h 98 Hiatt (W I).
Warren Hugh, driver, b 226 Oliver av (W I).
Warren James A, driver, h 714 S Meridian.
Warren John, lab, h 318 E Court.
Warren John R, carp, h 29 Windsor.
Warren Kate, teacher Public School No 22, b 420 Union.
Warren Mary (wid Michael), b 94 S Liberty.
Warren Matilda (wid Isaiah), b 70 Oliver av (W I).
Warren Michael, lab, b 420 Union.
Warren Miles, janitor Park Theater, r same.
Warren Minnie F, clk When Clothing Store, h 143 N Alabama.

We Buy Municipal ~ Bonds ~
THOS. C. DAY & CO,
Rooms 325 to 330 Lemcke Bldg.

WARREN-SCHARF ASPHALT PAVING CO, Wm R Warren Pres, Frederick W White Treas, Dana E Riankard Auditor, S Whinery Vice-Pres, Henry R Bradbury Sec, Henry C Adams Agt, 6 Thorpe Blk, Tel 1541.
Warren Timothy, lab, h 611 S Meridian.
Warren Wm R, pres Warren-Scharf Asphalt Paving Co, res New York City.
Warren Wm T, car rep, h 50 S Morris (B).
Warren Wm W, bricklyr, h 28 N Noble.
Warrenburg Charles T, lab, h 1 Sylvan.
Warrenburg Edward L, painter, b 515 English av.
Warrenburg Gilbert, mach hd, b 297 River av (W I).
Warrenburg James, fireman, h s s Colgrove av 1 e of Shelby.
Warrenburg John, finisher, b 51 Sheffield (W I).
Warrenburg John, tmstr, h 515 English av.
Warrenburg Viola, boarding 297 River av (W I).
Warrenburg Thomas A, clk, h n s Michigan av 3 e of Sharpe av (W).
Warrenburg Walter F, lab, b 30 Hillside av.
Warrenburg Wm, tmstr, h 7 Sylvan.
Warrenburg Wm M, wheelmkr, h 297 River av (W I).
Warrick Edward H, grocer, 252 Highland av, b 737 E Michigan.
Warrington Charles H, printer, h 49 Bradshaw.
Warrington Jesse, draughtsman Nordyke & Marmon Co, h 159 Union.
Warrum Henry, lawyer, 312 Indiana Trust bldg, h 522 College av.
Warstat John, lab, r 4 Erie.
Warth Alice, teacher Public School No 20, b 204 N Illinois.
Warth Nathaniel G, asst state supt Central Union Telephone Co, tel 43, h 204 N Illinois, tel 136.
Warweg August H, gardener, h 936 S East.
Warweg Christian, gardener, h w s Watts 2 s of Clifford av.
Warweg Dorothy (wid Christian), h 936 S East.

EAT
HITZ'S CRACKERS
AND CAKES.
ASK YOUR GROCER FOR THEM.

WILLIAM WIEGEL } MANUFACTURER OF.... } SHOW CASES } 6 W. Louisiana St. Opposite Union Station.

BENJ. BOOTH PRACTICAL EXPERT ACCOUNTANT. Books Opened, Written Up, Posted and Balanced. Room 18, 82½ E. Washington St., Indianapolis, Ind.

THE SHERMAN RESTAURANT || S. MERIDIAN STREET 18 and 20
IF YOU WANT A GOOD MEAL AND HAVE IT NICELY SERVED GO TO

ESTABLISHED 1876. TELEPHONE 168.
CHESTER BRADFORD,
SOLICITOR OF PATENTS,
AND COUNSEL IN PATENT CAUSES.
(See adv. page 6.)
Office:—Rooms 14 and 16 Hubbard Block, S.W. Cor. Washington and Meridian Streets, INDIANAPOLIS, INDIANA.

Warweg Henry, lab, b w s Watts 2 s of Clifford av.
Warweg Wilhelmina (wid Henry), h w s Watts 3 s of Clifford av.
Washburn Anson, student, b 809 N Meridian.
Washburn Benjamin F, lab, h e s Gladstone av 1 n of Washington.
Washburn Clara E, prin Public School No 11, b 809 N Meridian.
Washburn Hamer T, supt Billiard Rooms Grand Hotel, b same.
Washburn Horace A, engr, h 27 Spann av.
Washburn James L, trav agt, h 134 East Drive (W P).
Washburn Landy, h 39 N McLain (W I).
Washburn Mary J, h 7 W Chesapeake.
Washburn Samuel A, engr, h 27 Spann av.
Washington Anderson, lab, b 10 Elizabeth.
Washington Charles, porter, r 70 W Maryland.
Washington Club, 715 E Washington.
Washington Edward, lab, r 70 W Maryland.
Washington Edward, lab, b 164 Osage.
Washington Edward, waiter, r 18½ Indiana av.
Washington George, lab, r 225 W Ohio.
Washington George, lab, h 512 S West.
Washington George S, lab, h 140 W 9th.
Washington James G, gardener, h n s 23d 1 w of N Senate av.
Washington John M, tailor, 66½ N Penn, h s s Prospect 2 e of Belt R R.
Washington Joseph, waiter The Bates.
Washington Katherine E, instructor The Singer Mnfg Co, b s s Prospect 2 e of Belt R R.
Washington Larkin, brickmkr, h 14 Smithson av.
WASHINGTON LIFE INSURANCE CO OF NEW YORK, Clifford Arrick State Agt, 68 E Market, Tel 1576.
Washington Loyd, lab, h 164 Osage.
Washington Samuel, lab, h 378 Lafayette.
Washington Sarah, h 2 Holborn.
Washington Sarah, h 218 N West.

O. B. ENSEY
MANUFACTURER OF
GALVANIZED IRON CORNICE, SKYLIGHTS AND WINDOW CAPS,
TELEPHONE 1562. Cor. 6th and Illinois Sts.

WASHINGTON SAVINGS AND LOAN ASSOCIATION, Jesse J M La Follette Pres, Charles F Coffin Vice-Pres, John W Hall Sec, George Benedict Treas, 18, 19 and 20 Aetna Bldg.
Washington Susan (wid George), h rear 775 N Senate av.
Washington Wm H, porter, h s s Prospect, 2 e of Belt R R.
Wasman George, lab, h 490½ E Washington.
Wassert Gottlieb, lab, h 128 Excelsior av.
WASSON CHARLES K, Real Estate and Loans; also Notary Public, 24 S Penn, Tel 723; h 798 N New Jersey.
Wasson Charles P, b 115 Hosbrook.
Wasson Ethelbert E, opr W U Tel Co, r 115 Huron.
Wasson George E, mach, b 73 Hudson.
Wasson Harry, lab, b 334 Spann av.
Wasson Harry D, lab, b 174 W 7th.
Wasson Hiram P (H P Wasson & Co), h 606 N Delaware.
WASSON H P & CO (Hiram P Wasson), Dry Goods, Notions, Carpets, Millinery and Dressmaking, 12-18 W Washington, Tel 1830.
Wasson James A, painter, h rear 14 Mulberry.
Wasson John F, tmstr, h 174 W 7th.
Wasson Mary E (wid John H), dressmkr, h 375 E Ohio.
Wasson Wm G, pres and treas The W G Wasson Co, h 81 Middle Drive (W P).
WASSON W G CO, Wm G Wasson Pres and Treas, Joseph F Jacquemin Sec, Dealer in Builders' Supplies, Coal, Coke and Lime, 130 Indiana av, Tel 989. (See left bottom cor cards and adv in classified Cement and Lime.)
Waterbury Charles M, h 491 Broadway.
Waterman Christian F H, sec and treas Haugh-Noelke Iron Works, h 280 E Market.
Waterman Frederick W, car rep, h 303 English av.
Waterman Herman H, blksmith, 1199 Michigan av, h n s Michigan av 1 e of Woodside av.
Waterman Lewis R, trav agt, h 22 The Chalfant.
Waterman Luther D, phys, b The Denison.
Waters, see also Watters.
Waters Charlotte L, janitress, r 9 Columbia blk.
Waters Daniel, lab, b 56 Tremont av (H).
Waters Emanuel M, lab, h 111 Kappus (W I).
Waters Frank, lab, h 119 Bryan.
Waters Frank R, clk Leyendecker & Waters, b 824 Ash.
Waters George, lab, b 301 Indiana av.
Waters Harry E, h s e cor 28th and Meridian.
Waters George B, coachman 729 N Meridian.
Waters John J, lab, b 511 S West.
Waters Leah H (wid Wm), h 506 W Udell (N I).
Waters Marion F, painter, h 271 S Illinois.
Waters Maurice, clk, h 511 S West.
WATERS ROBERT, Real Estate and Rental Agt, 10 Monument Pl, Tel 1055; h 101 Andrews.
Waters Samuel D, steamfitter, r 265½ W Washington.

TUTEWILER UNDERTAKER, NO. 72 WEST MARKET STREET. TELEPHONE 216.

PARTNERSHIP INSURANCE At low cost. By which provision is made against the pecuniary loss and embarrassment resulting from the death of a member of a firm.
Provident Life and Trust Co. of Philadelphia, D. W. EDWARDS, Gen'l Agt., 508 Indiana Trust Bldg.

THEODORE F. SMITHER GRAVEL AND OTHER COMPOSITION ROOFER Yard, 180 W. Maryland St. Telephone 861. Office, 151 W. Maryland St.

Waters Samuel R (Leyendecker & Waters), h 824 Ash.
Waterson, see also Watterson.
Waterson Fianna (wid John), h 105 Locke.
Waterson Lucian, bartndr, h 97 W 7th.
Waterson Marshall F, bartndr, b 780 N Senate av.
Watkins Arthur W, lab, b 1358 N Senate av.
Watkins Benjamin, lab, b 225 Columbia av.
Watkins Burleigh B, ins agt, h 29 Centennial.
Watkins Caroline (wid Abraham), b 277 Chapel.
Watkins Charles W, clk, h 1147½ N Illinois.
Watkins Clara D, teacher Public School No 18, b 185 Columbia av.
Watkins Eugene, waiter, r 79 W Wabash.
Watkins Eustace H, stripper, b 1 Susquehanna.
Watkins George T, printer, h 486½ Stillwell.
Watkins George W, janitor Public School No 24, h n e cor North and Agnes.
Watkins Harry, cook, b 190 W 4th.
Watkins Houston E, twistmkr, r 1 Susquehanna.
Watkins James H, harnessmkr, b 29 Madison av.
Watkins James H, mach hd, h 583 Mass av.
Watkins John P, asst mngr Mass Ben Life Assn, 9 Baldwin blk, h 323 College av.
Watkins Lewis, lab, h 225 Columbia av.
Watkins Manson, lab, h 185 Columbia av.
Watkins Mary L (wid Wm T), dressmkr, 172 Ramsey av, h same.
Watkins Mattie, boarding 142 N Illinois.
Watkins Oscar L, trav agt, h 45 The Blacherne.
Watkins Queen Ann (wid Joseph), h 201 Belmont av (H).
Watkins Raymond L, clk John T Dye, b 258 N Penn.
Watkins Wm C, fireman, h 47 Temple av.
Watkins Wm H, mngr Indpls Base Ball Club, b Grand Hotel.
Watkins Wm H B, barber, b 163 Indiana av.
Watson Benjamin, coachman 250 N Meridian.
Watson Benjamin F, musician, b 132 W 6th.
Watson Benjamin F (Ewbank & Watson), h 26 Stoughton av.
Watson Blanche E, music teacher, 26 Stoughton av, h same.
Watson Charles C, drugs, 511 Virginia av, h same.
Watson Charles M, mach, h 120½ Woodlawn av.
Watson Charles T, painter, 309 N Pine, h same.
WATSON CHAUNCEY R, Agt Blue Line, 1 Board of Trade Bldg, h 1200 N Meridian.
Watson Cora M, b 73 W Vermont.
Watson Delbert O, lab, b e s Brightwood av 2 n of Schofield (B).
Watson Edward, lab, h s w cor School and Spencer (B).
Watson Edward S, trav agt, h 104 Walcott.
Watson Edwin A, cashr Putnam County Milk Co, b 32 Oriental.
Watson Elbridge C, grocer, 100 Keystone av, h same.
Watson Elizabeth (wid George), h e s Illinois 1 n of 35th.
Watson Elmer W, painter, h 310 Excelsior av.
Watson Estes D, switchman, h 218 E South.
Watson George, foreman Consumers' Gas Trust Co, r 157 E Ohio.

THE WHEN IS A WORLD BEATER.

Watson George C, motorman, h 17 Cornell av.
Watson George W, bricklyr h 135 N Alabama.
Watson George W, engr, b 220 N Missouri.
Watson Harry F, clk, r 466 N Alabama.
Watson Hayden P, h 220 N Capitol av.
Watson Henrietta, h 35 Willard.
Watson Henry, lab, h 390 N Brookside av.
Watson Ivin F, clk, h 135 Keystone av.
Watson James, engr, h 159 Bates.
Watson James, mach, b 5 Concordia.
Watson James E, engr, h 231 Elm.
Watson James T C, clk R M S, h 1108 N Delaware.
Watson Jasper, driver, h 77 N Liberty.
Watson Jehu M, grocer, 91 Columbia al, h same.
Watson John, bricklyr, b 135 N Alabama.
Watson John, carp, h 629 N West.
Watson Joseph S, h 226 E Ohio.
Watson Julia K, teacher Public School No 10, b 77 E St Joseph.
Watson Martha J (wid James M), h 511 Virginia av.
Watson Mary (wid Thomas), h 48 N West.
Watson Mary J (wid James F), h 32 Oriental.
Watson Mary J (wid Thomas N) h 112 Ash.
Watson Matilda C (wid Willis), h n w cor Ritter and University avs (I).
Watson Newton H, motorman, h 265 E North.
Watson Nona, retoucher, b 220 N Capitol av.
Watson Oliver P, welldriver, r 271 Mass av.
Watson Oliver W, lab, b 32 Oriental.
Watson Philemon M, b 754 N Delaware.
Watson Rchard, lab, h e s Illinois 1 n of 35th.
Watson Robert, lab, b 23 Roanoke.
Watson Rosa A (wid John C), h 388 E Market.
Watson Samuel E, tmstr, h 287 Keystone av.
Watson Samuel N (Stubbins & Watson), b Stubbins European Hotel.
Watson Sarah D (wid Amos), b 603 N West.
Watson Sarah F, h 220 N Missouri.

THE A. BURDSAL CO.
WINDOW AND PLATE
GLASS
Putty, Glazier Points, Diamonds.
Wholesale and Retail. 34 and 36 S. Meridian St.

ELECTRIC CONSTRUCTION Isolated Plants Installed. Electric Wiring and Fittings of all kinds. C. W. Meikel. Tel. 466. 96-98 E. New York St

DALTON & MERRIFIELD { LUMBER South Noble St., near E. Washington

INDIANA ELECTROTYPE CO. : BEST WORK LOWEST PRICES.
23 WEST PEARL ST., INDIANAPOLIS, IND. JOB WORK. BOOK PLATES. All Orders Promptly Filled. BEST PATENT BASE ON THE MARKET.

KIRKHOFF BROS.,
GAS AND ELECTRIC FIXTURES
THE LARGEST LINE IN THE CITY.
102-104 SOUTH PENNSYLVANIA ST.
TELEPHONE 910.

Watson Sarah M (wid Thomas N), h 293 E Miami.
Watson Thomas lab, b 122 Ash.
Watson Wm, lab, b 332 W Washington.
Watson Wm E, policeman Insane Hospital.
Watson Wm O, farmer, b 51 S Austin (B).
Watson Wm R (Wm R Watson & Co), b 324 N Noble.
Watson Wm R & Co (Wm R Watson, Benjamin D Miner), bicycles, 48 N Delaware.
Watt John W Elder, pres Indiana Tract Society, h 175 Central av.
Watt Wm H, phys, 100 Mass av, h 163 Clinton.
Watters, see also Waters.
Watters Albert L, mngr Bellis Cycle Co, r 272 N Meridian.
Watters Bert, lab, b 99 Maxwell.
Watters Harry, lab, h 507 E 11th.
Watters James, molder, h 99 Maxwell.
Watters Laura B W, supervisoress Insane Hospital.
Watters Patrick J, asst phys Insane Hospital.
Watters Robert, lab, h 99 Maxwell.
Watters Wm S, foreman, h 175 E Louisiana.
Watters Wm W, h 78 S Belmont (W I).
Watterson, see also Waterson.
Watterson Mary (wid James), r 47 Elm.
Watterson Minnie F, bkkpr Indpls Light and Power Co, b 277 N Capitol av.
Watts Aaron H, mach hd, h 609 W Francis (N I).
Watts Albert, lab, h 350 Douglass.
Watts Burton F, lawyer, 92½ E Washington, h 235 E Vermont.
Watts Clarence V, clk W E Mick & Co, b 286 E St Clair.
Watts David R, collr W H Ballard, b 180 E Washington.
Watts Edwin C, draughtsman L E & W R R, r 76 N East.
Watts Ephraim A, lab, b 141 W Washington.
Watts George W, b 180 E Washington.
Watts George W jr, restaurant, 180 E Washington, h same.
Watts Harrison, lab, h 54 S Belmont (W I).

COAL AND COKE
The W. G. Wasson Co.,
130 INDIANA AVE. TEL. 989
LIME AND LATH

Watts Haden M, grocer, 548 W Udell (N I), h 546½ same.
Watts Henry W, lab, h 289 E Miami.
Watts Hillary G, pressman, h 68 Ash.
Watts Howard, condr, h 20 Blackford.
Watts Ira E, printer, b 284 E Michigan.
Watts Jacob W (The Wood Ornament Co), h 458 W Udell (N I).
Watts James, trav agt, b 127 Dearborn.
Watts James B, clk H T Conde Implement Co, h 63 Ellen.
Watts James H, stairbldr, h 284 E Michigan.
Watts John, porter, h 422 Blake.
Watts John E, carp, h 137 Yandes.
Watts Joseph A, painter, b 33 Catherine.
Watts Louis N, trav agt, b 580 College av.
Watts Nina, nurse 124 N Alabama.
Watts Samuel, lab, h rear 268 S Noble.
Watts Thomas L, lab, b 145 Columbia av.
Watts Ulysses S, printer, b 379 S Merdian.
Watts Wm D, agt, b 252 E Washington.
Watts Wm F, lab, h 573 E 7th.
Watts Wm H, collr, b 158 N West.
Watz Helena, clk, b 869 S Meridian.
Watz Louis, blksmith, 965 S Meridian, h 938 Madison av.
Waugh Daniel A, mach, h 401 Highland av.
Waugh George E, printer The Indpls News, b 150 N Illinois.
Waughtel Bertha, b 227 W Merrill.
Wauglin Otto J, trav agt, h 39 Highland pl.
Way James K P, lab, h 147 Lambert (W I).
Wayland Charles W, sawyer, h 358 Coburn.
Wayman Bertie M, h rear 176 E Washington.
Wayman Laura B (wid Joseph M), r 224 E Ohio.
Waymire Milton E, carp, h 21 N Dorman.
Wayne Charles L (Charles L Wayne & Co), h 23 The Blacherne.
WAYNE CHARLES L & CO (Charles L Wayne, John H Dilks), Hardware, Wood Mantels and Grates, 61-63 W Washington, Tel 173.
Wayne John, cook, h 362 W Vermont.
Wayt, see also Waite.
Wayt Charles W, fireman, h 105 Decatur.
Wayt Jacob, motorman, r 230½ W Washington.
Wayt James B, millwright, h 23 Beacon.
Waywood Anthony, turner, h 110 Kennington.
Waywood Frank, turner, h 112 Kennington.
Weadon Bruce C, contracting agt Erie Despatch, 46 W Washington, h 501 N Senate av.
Weadon Frank M, chief clk engr maintenance of way C C C & St L Ry, h Churchman's pike.
Weadon Frank P, theatrical mngr, h 153 Park av.
Weadon George A, trav agt Fahnley & McCrea, h 355 E 8th.
Weakley Jeremiah A, tinner, 317 W Washington, h 179 W New York.
Weakley Robert P, tinner, h e s Becker 2 s of Washington (M J).
Weakley Walter P, coachman 273 N Illinois.
Weakley Wm H, collr, h 207 Virginia av.
Weakly George W, opr W U Tel Co, h 343 E South.
Wear Wm, doortndr, b 358 Douglass.
Wease Mary, dressmkr, 137 Martindale av, b same.
Wease Wm H, lab, h 137 Martindale av.
Wease Wm H, tmstr, h 281 Yandes.
Weatherinton Allen W, porter, b 408 N New Jersey.

W. H. MESSENGER COMPLETE HOUSE FURNISHER 101 East Washington Street, Telephone 491

Foundry and Pattern Shop } McNamara, Koster & Co. { PHONE 1593 212-218 S. Penn. St.

Weatherly Albert, lab, h 135 Columbia av.
Weatherly Charles G, blksmith, b 98 Kappus (W I).
Weathers Anna (wid Lewis), h 231 Columbia av.
Weathers Enoch, b 328 Ash.
Weathers George A, lab, h 326 Superior.
Weathers George W, lab, b 335 E Miami.
Weathers Jackson, cook, b 285 Christian av.
Weathers James, patents, 340 E Washington, h 125 Michigan av.
Weathers John, lab, b 55 Wallack.
Weathers John, switchman, r 249½ W Washington.
Weathers Lafayette D, clk Spencer House, h w s Harris av 7 s of C C C & St L Ry (M J).
Weathers Louis, lab, h 446 W North.
Weathers Perry, bricklyr, h w s Cushing 2 s of 17th.
Weathers Richard, lab, h 126 Bryan.
Weathers Wm J, tmstr, h 335 E Miami.
Weaver Alonzo G, fireman, h 25 Bloomington.
Weaver Amos C, h 435 Talbott av.
Weaver Annie E (wid Wm), h 12 Garland (W I).
Weaver Arthur, carp, b 887 Milburn (M P).
Weaver Benjamin C, carp, b 315 Virginia av.
Weaver Charles F, city agt Nelson Morris & Co, h 48 Henry.
Weaver Charles H, agt, h 60 Ingram.
Weaver Henry L, trav agt, h 1692 Graceland av.
Weaver Charles M, cabtmkr, h 528 W Addison (N I).
Weaver Charles M, carp, h 315 Virginia av.
Weaver Charles W, baker, 164 W 12th, h same.
Weaver Cleon L, condr, b 792 W Washington.
Weaver Elizabeth (wid John W), h 196 W Ohio.
Weaver Frank, bricklyr, h 563 E 7th.
Weaver Frank, coachman 484 N Penn.
Weaver George, contr, 559 E 7th, h same.
Weaver George A, bricklyr, h 388 Bellefontaine.
Weaver George R, train disp Belt R R, h 1667 N Capitol av.
Weaver George W, lab, h 69½ W Market.
Weaver Harry, janitor Public School No 27, h 468 Park av.
Weaver Harry E, bricklyr, h 558 Bellefontaine.
Weaver Harry T, mach, h 46 N Rural.
Weaver Hart B, bkkpr, h 122 N Senate av.
Weaver Henry A, fireman, b 860 E Washington.
Weaver Howard, stenog, b 406 N Alabama.
Weaver Jackson, lab, b 214 N Illinois.
Weaver James, lab, h rear 228 E Merrill.
Weaver James, shoemkr, 118 Mass av, b 119 Cornell av.
Weaver James M, cabtmkr, h 599 W Udell (N I).
Weaver James M, lab, h 3 Kaufman pl.
Weaver Johanna (wid George), b 539 W Udell (N I).
Weaver John, driver, h 319 E Louisiana.
Weaver John, molder, b 12 Garland (W I).
Weaver John B, carp, h 439 W Addison (N I).
Weaver John D, insp, h 30 N Gillard av.
Weaver John F, driver, b 170 E South.
Weaver Lawrence J, painter, b 45 Barth av.
Weaver Letta, bkkpr C Henry Rosebrock, b 150 Prospect.

Henry H. Fay,
40½ E. WASHINGTON ST.,
AGENT FOR
Insurance Co. of North America,
Pennsylvania Fire Ins. Co.

Weaver Lizzie, h 195 W Vermont.
Weaver Louisa E, confr, 822 N Illinois, h 56½ W 7th.
Weaver Lydia, b 1449 N Illinois.
Weaver Nancy A (wid Orange R), h 74 Pleasant.
Weaver Ozro D (O D Weaver & Co), h 857 N Illinois.
Weaver O D & Co (Ozro D Weaver, Charles E Bannwarth), grain, 21 Board of Trade bldg.
Weaver Richard, farmer, h Sellar's farm (W I).
Weaver Robert, boilermkr, b 12 Garland (W I).
Weaver Robert L, brazier, h w s LaSalle 2 n of Vorster av (M P).
Weaver Rufus, lab, h 298 Indiana av.
Weaver Susan (wid George F), b 1100 N Meridian.
Weaver Thomas W, car rep, h 7 N Station (B).
Weaver Urban R (Wood-Weaver Printing Co), h 431 Talbott av.
Weaver Walter W, carp, b 528 W Addison (N I).
Weaver Wm, fireman, b 860 E Washington.
Weaver Wm E, carp, h 439 W Addison (N I).
Weaver Wm R, lab, b 359 S Illinois.
Weaver Wilson H, ornamenter, h 798 S East.
Webb Alice (wid Peter), h 44½ Malott av.
Webb Amanda (wid Sewell R), h 46 Thomas.
Webb Anna, asst bkkpr McCoy-Howe Co, b s s Washington 12 w of Harris av (M J).
Webb Anna F (wid Thomas), h 85 Union.
Webb Arthur H, clk S A Fletcher & Co, h 436 Park av.
Webb Benjamin L, treas Bellis Cycle Co, h 822 N Meridian.
Webb Charles A, pres The Webb-Jameson Co, coal, 222 S Meridian, h 22 Bismarck av.
WEBB CHARLES P, Ticket Broker, 5 and 128 S Illinois, Tel 300; h 954 N Meridian.
Webb Clayton A, tmstr, h 89 Wilson.
Webb Courtland D, trav agt Daniel Stewart Co, h 8 The Chalfant.

Union Casualty & Surety Co.
of St. Louis, Mo.
Employers', Public, General, Teams and Elevator Liability; also Workmen's Collective, Steam Boiler, Plate Glass and Automatic Sprinkler Insurance.
W. E. BARTON & CO., General Agents,
504 Indiana Trust Building.
LONG DISTANCE TELEPHONE 1918.

THE FRED DIETZ CO. OF
WOODEN PACKING BOXES MADE TO FACTORY AND WAREHOUSE TRUCKS.
400 Madison Avenue. Telephone 654.

Shorthand! BUSINESS UNIVERSITY. When Bl'k. Elevator day and night. Typewriting, Penmanship, Book-keeping, Office Training free. See page 4. Est. 1850. Tel. 499. E. J. HEEB, Proprietor.

Water Works Pumping Engines { HENRY R. WORTHINGTON, 64 SOUTH PENNSYLVANIA ST. Long Distance Telephone 284.

UNION CO-OPERATIVE LAUNDRY { (COMPOSED OF UNION LAUNDRY GIRLS.) NOS. 38, 40 AND 42 VIRGINIA AVENUE. T. E. SOMERVILLE, MANAGER—TELEPHONE 1269. INDIANAPOLIS, IND.

HORACE M. HADLEY
REAL ESTATE AND LOANS....
66 East Market Street
Telephone 1540. BASEMENT.

Webb David, lab, h 235 Orange.
Webb David B, condr, h 18 Arbor av (W I).
Webb Dorothea, opr C U Tel Co, h 1365 W Washington.
Webb Edward S, trav agt, h 26 Warman av (H).
Webb Elizabeth A (wid John D), h 181 E Merrill.
Webb Ella A, milliner, 66 N Illinois, h 418 N California.
Webb Ellen C (wid Richard), b 39 E McCarty.
Webb Elwood P, lab, b 843 S East.
Webb Frank B, engr, h 843 S East.
Webb Harry, lab, h 408 W Addison (N I).
Webb Henry, blksmith, b s s Washington 5 w of Harris av (M J).
Webb Henry E, lab, h 121 S Spruce.
Webb Henry W, painter, h 179 S William (W I).
Webb Henry W, watchman, h 446 Indiana av.
Webb Homer C (Faulkner & Webb), b 85 Union.
Webb Ira C, painter, h 418 N California.
Webb Isaiah, collr John S Spann & Co, h 244 Central av.
Webb James A, lab, h 222 Oliver av (W I).
Webb James C, drugs, cor W Washington and Harris av (M J), h same.
Webb James H, lab, h 65 Oliver av (W I).
WEBB-JAMESON CO THE (Charles A Webb, Walter Jameson, Samuel Smith), Building and Safe Movers, 222 S Meridian, Tel 356. (See adv in classified House Movers.)
Webb John P, clk H P Wasson & Co, h 81 W 3d.
Webb John R, lab, b 222 Oliver av (W I).
Webb John W, molder, h 79 Nevada.
Webb Leonidas E, blksmith, n s Washington 1 w of Crawfordsville rd (M J), h 1365 W Washington.
Webb Liberty (wid John D), h 181 E Merrill.
Webb Mary (wid Henry), h 23 Alvord.
Webb Mary A, h 26 Chadwick.
Webb Mary E (wid Thomas F), b 193 N Beville av.

Merchants' and Manufacturers
Make Exchange
Collections and
Commercial Reports......
J. E. TAKKEN, MANAGER,
19 Union Building, 73 West Maryland Street

Webb Mary E (wid Thomas S), b 11 Woodruff av.
Webb Matilda, b 320 E Court.
Webb Melinda C (wid Joshua), b 452 Chestnut.
Webb Nellie W, teacher Public School No 17, b 85 Union.
Webb Obadiah, lab, h 22 Riley blk.
Webb Olive V (wid James C), dressmkr, 70½ N Delaware, h same.
Webb Orville L (Webb & Co), h 193 N Beville av.
Webb Ova, lab, r 300 W Washington.
Webb Peter, mach, b 108 Shepard (W I).
Webb Richard, lab, b 128 Columbia al.
Webb Robert, lab, h 51 Weghorst.
Webb Sarah E (wid John W), b 15 Division (W I).
Webb Valorous D, tel opr, r 17 S Station (B).
Webb Wm, engr, h 140 Oliver av (W I).
Webb Wm W, b 1373 W Washington (M J).
Webb Wm W (Webb & Co), h 11 Woodruff av.
Webb & Co (Orville L and Wm W Webb, John C Fullenwider), real est, 9-10 When bldg.
Webber Benjamin F, barber, h 215 Alvord.
Webber Charles, b 192 W Ohio.
Webber Charles R, blksmith, h 471 Lincoln av.
Webber Charles R, hat mnfr, 202 S Meridian, r 16 The Plaza.
Webber Elizabeth (wid Frederick), h n s Grandview av 2 w of Tremont av (H).
Webber Frank H, hostler, h 102 Meek.
Webber George H, blksmith, h 144 S East.
Webber Gustave, painter, h 9 Lynn.
Webber Henry, lab, b n e cor Michigan and Belmont av.
Webber James H (Webber & Co), h 721 Broadway.
Webber John F, clk, h 8 Leon.
Webber John S, tmstr, h 1332 N Senate av.
Webber Levator A, hatter, r 75½ Mass av.
Webber Levi, cook, h 125 N Noble.
Webber Thomas A, barber, h 60 Howard.
Webber Wm, fireman, b 860 E Washington.
WEBBER & CO (James H Webber, Frederick D Stilz), Real Estate, Loans, Insurance and Rentals, 91 E Market, Tel 716.
Weber Adam C, watchman, h 490 S Missouri.
Weber Albert, clk, h 151 John.
Weber Albert, lab, b 1717 N Senate av.
Weber Albert C, clk, b 546 Bellefontaine.
Weber Albert T, printer, b 178 Mass av.
Weber Amelia (wid Adam), h 297 S Alabama.
Weber Amelia (wid Theodore F), h 89 Benton.
Weber August W, molder, h w s Sherman Drive 1 s of Brookville rd (S).
Weber Charles, mach, h 31 Holmes av (H).
Weber Charles A, carp, 33 William, h same.
Weber Charles E, clk U S Pension Agency, h 70 Beaty.
Weber Christina (wid Wm), b 150 Church.
Weber Clara O (wid Albert), b 396 S Alabama.
Weber Edward J, trav agt M O'Connor & Co, b 45 N William (W I).
Weber Elizabeth, clk, b 297½ Virginia av.
Weber Ferdinand F, carver, b 42 Thomas.
Weber Frank, b 45 N William (W I).
Weber Frank C, clk Schrader Bros, b 17 Alvord.

CLEMENS VONNEGUT
184, 186 and 192 E. Washington St.
Wire Rope, Machinery, Lathes, Drills and Shapers

THE WM. H. BLOCK CO. DRY GOODS, DRAPERIES, RUGS, WINDOW SHADES.
7 AND 9 EAST WASHINGTON STREET.

Weber Frank G, condr, h 221 N Capitol av.
Weber Frank L, saloon, 186 Blake, h same.
Weber Frederick, lab, h 31 Barth av.
Weber Frederick, saloon, 115 Agnes, h same.
Weber Frederick J, jeweler, 426 Mass av, h 546 Bellefontaine.
Weber Frederick J, motorman, h 326 Lincoln av.
Weber Frederick W, mach, h 122 Tremont av (H).
WEBER GEORGE M, Druggist, 99 N Illinois, Tel 1099; h 101 The Shiel.
Weber Harry A (Zimmer & Co), h 297 S Alabama.
Weber Helen V, teacher, b 221 N Capitol av.
Weber Henry, filer, h 511 S Illinois.
Weber Henry jr, filer, b 511 S Illinois.
Weber Henry, piano finisher D H Baldwin & Co, h 70 Sheldon.
Weber Jacob B, trav agt M O'Connor & Co, b 575 College av.
Weber Jacob F, clk, h 222 N Noble.
Weber John, dairy, s s Finley av 2 e of Shelby, h same.
Weber John, saloon, 50 N Noble, h same.
Weber John A, clk, h 17 Alvord.
Weber John H, drayman, h 460 Mulberry.
Weber John T, lab, b 37 Ashland (W I).
Weber John V, mach hd, h 36 Lynn.
Weber John W, clk The Bowen-Merrill Co, h 174 N Illinois.
Weber John W, porter, h 313 Indiana av.
Weber Joseph, lab, h 29 Yeiser.
Weber Joseph F Rev, rector Church of the Assumption, h 45 N William (W I).
Weber Leo, engr, h s e cor LaSalle and Richard (M P).
Weber Leonard, lab, b s s Finley av 2 e of Shelby.
Weber Louis, baker, h 209 Meek.
Weber Louis, barber, h 127 Weghorst.
WEBER LOUIS, Saloon, 570 W Addison (N I), h 568 same.
Weber Louis H, foreman Home Cracker Co, h 421 Madison av.
Weber Magdalena (wid Frederick), h 366 N Noble.
Weber Oswald T, stove mounter, h 330 E Louisiana.
Weber Paul, molder, h 33 Cleveland (H).
Weber Peter, lab, h 319 S Missouri.
Weber Peter, molder, h 32 Oliver av (W I).
Weber P Otho, clk U S Pension Agency, r 221 N Capitol av.
Weber Rinehart (T J Hamilton & Co), h 106 W Ray.
Weber Susan (wid David H), h 717 N Senate av.
Weber Wilbur, cigarmkr, b 106 W Ray.
Weber Wm, carp, r 330 E Louisiana.
Weber Wm, florist, h 44 N Rural.
Weber Wm, lab, b 256 W 7th.
Weber Wm C, letter carrier P O, h 257 Shelby.
Weber Wm G, finisher, h 574 S Illinois.
Weber & Zimmer (Harry A Weber, Louis A Zimmer), dry goods, 198 Virginia av.
Webster Ada F, h 36 S New Jersey.
Webster Anna (wid Abner), b 706 N Illinois.
Webster Anna (wid Roll), b 28 Oregon.
Webster Charles, lab, r 130 Allegheny.
Webster Charles E, grocer, 40 Pleasant, h same.
Webster Charles H, clk R M S, h 106 Keystone av.
Webster Charles T, printer, h 451 N California.

Webster Frances M (wid James), h 45 Arch.
Webster George C, pres Chester Oil Co, h 574 College av.
Webster George E, b 21 Bates al.
Webster George W, mach hd, h 59 E Morris.
WEBSTER HARRY C, Genl Mngr American Detective Agency, Rooms 12-15, 96½ E Market, h 80 Sullivan. (See adv in classified Detective Agencies.)
Webster Hayden P, ruler, b 451 N California.
Webster Helen (wid George C), b 987 N Penn.
Webster Joseph H, h 125 E St Clair.
Webster Justus D, grinder, h 81 Wisconsin.
WEBSTER SIMEON, Genl Agt Milwaukee Harvester Co, 6 Board of Trade Bldg, Tel 1902; h 957 N Capitol av.
Webster Simon, lab, b 154 Hosbrook.
Webster Wm H (Webster & White), h 124 S East.
WEBSTER & WHITE (Wm H Webster, Edward F White), Attorneys at Law, 37½ E Washington.
Wechsler Charles, meats, 752 N Capitol av, h same.
Wechsler David, butcher, h 424 S Illinois.
Wechsler Emil, meats, 59 E Mkt House, b 424 S Illinois.
Wechsler Henry, meats, 25 W McCarty, h same.
Wechsler Louis, butcher, h 22 Minnesota.
Wechsler Wm W, clk H P Wasson & Co, h 429 Union.
Wecker Abraham, tailor, h 742 E Washington.
Weckerly Dora E (wid Conrad), h 72 Minerva.
Weckerly Wm R, tinner, h 70 Minerva.
Weddell James M, engr, h 35 N Arsenal av.
Weddington Mary S (wid Nathan), b 265 S East.
Weddle Andrew D, contr carp, 191 Oliver av (W I), h same.
Weddle Chapman, carp, b 104 Frazee (H).
Weddle Darius, carp, b 104 Frazee (H).

GUIDO R. PRESSLER,
FRESCO PAINTER
Churches, Theaters, Public Buildings, Etc., A Specialty.
Residence, No. 325 North Liberty Street
INDIANAPOLIS, IND.

INDIANAPOLIS STEEL ROOFING AND CORRUGATING WORKS, 23 and 25 East South Street. S. D. NOEL, Proprietor.

David S. McKernan, Rooms 2-5 Thorpe Block.
REAL ESTATE AND LOANS
A number of choice pieces for subdivision, or for manufacturers' sites, with good switch facilities.

DIAMOND WALL PLASTER { Telephone 1410 BUILDERS' EXCHANGE.

UNION TRANSFER AND STORAGE CO., 6 E. Ohio St. and C., C., C. & St. L. R'y Tracks. BRICK WAREHOUSE; CLEANEST AND SAFEST STORAGE IN CITY FOR HOUSEHOLD OR MERCHANDISE.

W. McWORKMAN,

METAL CEILINGS,
ROLLING SHUTTERS,
DOORS AND PARTITIONS.
930 W. Washington St. Tel. 1118.

Weddle David W, mach hd, b 681 Madison av.
Weddle Jennie M (wid Oscar M), h 119 N Gillard av.
Weddle Joseph A, carp, h 1091 W Michigan.
Weddle Milton G, carp, h 104 Frazee (H).
Weddle Oscar M, mach hd, b 119 Gillard av.
Wedel Frederick A, fireman, h 115 S Summit.
Wedewen Edward, lab, h 203 Minnesota.
Wedewen Emil, lab, h 89 Minnesota.
Wedge Isaac, lab, h 25 S McLain (W I).
WEEBER CHARLES F, Propr Germania House, 200 S Meridian.
Weeber Christopher, blksmith, 6 Jefferson av, h 151 same.
Weed Henry J, b 480 N Meridian.
Weedfall John A, cabtmkr, b 471 W Francis (N I).
Weedmer David, temperer, h 146 S William (W I).
Weegmann Carl H, music teacher, 1 Halcyon blk, r same.
Weekley Clarence, painter, b California House.
Weekley Walter, driver, b 276 Chapel.
Weeks, see also Wickes.
Weeks Edith E, clk, b 83 W Walnut.
Weeks Frank W, chief clk Penna Lines, h 227 E Walnut.
Weeks Harry C, carp, h 122 Maple.
Weeks Henry, lab, b 636 Home av.
Weeks John, harnessmkr, h 45 Madison av.
Weeks Joseph, bartndr, h 25 Stewart pl.
Weeks Sebern W, harness cutter, h 45 Madison av.
Weeks Thomas E, switchman, h 57 Miley av.
Weelburg George F (Coburn & Weelburg), h 322 Prospect.
Weelburg Margaret (wid Henry), h 54 Buchanan.
Weer Harlan A, carp, h 16 N Rural.
Weesner Benajah, carp, h 1683 N Senate av.
Weesner Elwood P, gardener, h w end of Church (I).
Weesner Josephine, dressmkr, 156½ E Washington, b Elwood P Weesner.

SEALS,
STENCILS,
STAMPS, Etc.
GEO. J. MAYER
15 S. Meridian St.
TELEPHONE 1386.

Weesner Leander W, carp, h 229 N New Jersey.
Weesner Micajah, b 1683 N Senate av.
Weesner Theodore M, clk, b w end Church (I).
Wefler Jacob E, mach, h 8 Sheldon.
Wegenfeld Henry, watchman, h 35 Iowa.
Wegenhardt George, horseshoer, b Germania House.
Wegener Frederick C E, timekpr, b 222 Union.
Weghorn Annie M (wid George), h 78 Belmont av (H).
Weghorn John P, fireman, b 78 Belmont av (H).
Weghorst Albert C, nailer, b 211 Lincoln la.
Weghorst Charles H, gardener, h s s Downey 1 w of Wright.
Weghorst Elizabeth, h 194 N Noble.
Weghorst Frederick W, broker, 52 Virginia av, h 64 Buchanan.
Weghorst Geroge W, uphlr, h 11 Iowa.
Weghorst Henry, gardener, h 713 S East.
Weghorst Henry jr, gardener, b 713 S East.
Weghorst Henry H, gardener, h 1768 N Illinois.
Weghorst Herman, lab, h 211 Lincoln la.
Weghorst Herman H, mach, h 57 Gresham.
Weghorst Wm, gardener, h 776 Madison av.
Weghorst Wm H, clk, h 130 Harlan.
Wegman Adolph, b 85 N Delaware.
Wegner Henry C, mach hd, h 60 Saunders.
Wehinger Martin, shoemkr, 438 S Delaware, h same.
WEHKING CHARLES F, Brick Contractor, 427 S New Jersey, h same, Tel 1861.
Wehle Lucas, shoemkr, 274 W 1st, h same.
Wehle Minnie M (wid Theodore C), h 255 N Alabama.
Wehlerman Frederick W, foreman Parrott & Taggart, h 90 Fletcher av.
Wehlerman Herman, engr, h 325 W Market.
Wehling Charles, driver, h 117 Kennington.
Wehling Christine K, bkkpr, b 127 W St Clair.
Wehling Henry C, uphlr, b 160 Prospect.
Wehling Pauline C (wid Charles H), h 127 W St Clair.
Wehrel Frank J, clk, b 238 Yandes.
Wehrer Elizabeth (wid John), h 4 Erie.
Wehrle Maurice, attendant Insane Hospital.
Wehrley Charles W, foreman, h 50 King av (H).
WEHRMAN ERNEST A, Physician, Rooms 7-8 Marion Blk, h 1004 N Alabama.
Wehrman Julius O, student, b 1004 N Alabama.
Weibel Adolph E, foreman Parrott-Taggart Bakery, h 635 Marlowe av.
Weibel Charles, lab, b rear 333 W Morris.
Weibel Rudolph A, baker, b 635 Marlowe av.
Weibke, see Wiebke.
Weible John, patrolman, r 4 24½ Kentucky av.
Weickman Wm, jeweler, h 170 Chestnut.
Weidemann John A, lab, h 192 Coburn.
Weidgenant Wm J, clk, b 175 E New York.
Weidig Helen C, dressmkr, 426 E St Clair, b same.
Weidig Wilhemina, h 426 E St Clair.
Weidler Jesse B, clk Indpls Stove Co, h 251 Shelby.
Weidman Louis, saloon, 136 Clifford av, h 135 Excelsior av.

A. METZGER AGENCY ESTABLISHED 1863. INSURANCE

LAMBERT GAS & GASOLINE ENGINE CO.
ANDERSON, IND. PORTABLE GASOLINE ENGINES, 2 TO 25 H. P.

Weidner David, temperer, h 146 S William (W I).
Weiffenbach Frederick, bkkpr, h 79 Oriole.
Weiffenbach Gustave, clk Hide, Leather and Belting Co, b 79 Oriole.
Weighing and Inspection Bureau, John B Eckman, supt, 42 Board of Trade bldg.
Weiglein Frederick H, harnessmkr, h 454 S West.
Weihl Sydney J, trimmer, b 106 Spann av.
Weiker Henry, driver, h 384 E Market.
Weikert Edgar E, R R adv agt, 6 Fair blk, h 549 Broadway.
Weikert Harriet R (wid Joseph), b 549 Broadway.
Weikert Harry E, mach, h 381 N Illinois.
Weil Adam, boilermkr, h 13 Belmont av.
Weil Frederick, bartndr, h 83 Englsh av.
Weil Isadore, agt, r 175 Elm.
Weil Joseph, h 206 Douglass.
Weil Louis, saloon, 12 Shelby, h 36 Water.
Weilacher Andrew, porter, b n w cor English av and Pine.
Weilacher Frank, bartndr, h 154 Agnes.

WEILACHER JOHN, Saloon, 92 E Washington, h 389 N West.

Weilacher John G J, clk Indpls Brewing Co, b 380 Indiana av.
Weiland Anton F C, painter, h 183 Lexington av.
Weiland Charles C, lab, b 56 N Arsenal av.
Weiland Charles C W, finisher, b 134 Union.
Weiland Christian F, b 134 Union.
Weiland Emma E, stenog, b 495 S Meridian.
Weiland Frederick H (Roepke & Weiland), h 45 Lexington av.
Weiland Henry C, clk, h 233 Fulton.
Weiland Henry H, car rep, h 108 English av.
Weiland John W, b 45 Lexington av.
Weiland Wm C, grocer, 495 S Meridian, h same.
Weiland Wm H, painter, h 167 Lexington av
Weiler Abraham, h 283 E Market.
Weiler John, waiter, r 34 Gresham.
Weilhammer Michael, tinner, h 311 Orange.
Weill Harry, bkkpr E Rauh & Sons, b 327 E Market.
Weill Max, trav agt E Rauh & Sons, h 327 E Market.
Weimar John G, chief engr Kingan & Co, h 86 Camp.
Weimer George, timekpr The Bates.
Weimer Nicholas, lab, b s s Finley av 2 e of Shelby.
Weimer Peter, baker, b 179 S Alabama.
Weinberg Benjamin F, engr, h 473 Ash.
Weinberger Albert J, clk Herman J Weinberger, b 88 Union.
Weinberger Edwin, mngr Weinberger's European Hotel, 10-14 W Louisiana.

WEINBERGER'S EUROPEAN HOTEL, Herman Weinberger Propr, 10-14 W Louisiana.

WEINBERGER HERMAN, Propr Weinberger's European Hotel, 10-14 W Louisiana, h 88 Union.

Weinberger Louis, tailor, 19 Kentucky av, h same.
Weinbrecht Daniel M, coremkr, h 22 Germania av (H).
Weinbrecht Jacob, lab, h 81 Germania av (H).

Farm and City Loans
25 Years' Successful Business.
THOS. C. DAY & CO,
Rooms 325 to 330 Lemcke Building.

Weinbrecht John G, saloon, 134 Michigan (H), h same.
Weinbrenner Albert, driver, b n w cor 22d and Baltimore av.
Weindel John B, tailor, h 393 E Michigan.
Weinert Wm C, tinner, b 132 N Capitol av.
Weinfeld Joseph, clk, b 98 Eddy.
Weingart Wm, meats, 258 S Delaware, h same.
Weinke, see also Wienke.
Weinke August, lab, h 776 S East.
Weinke Herman N, mach hd, b 776 S East.
Weinke Julius, lab, h 776 S East.
Weinland Edwin D, tinner, h e s Western av 1 n of 22d.
Weinland James G, tinner, h 76 Harrison.
Weinland Rufus C, clk R P Daggett & Co, b n e cor 22d and College av.
Weinland R Earl, mach, b 76 Harrison.
Weinman, see also Wineman.
Weinman Herman, bartndr, h 360 E Market.
Weinman Joseph E, clk, b 66 Cornell av.
Weinmann John, clk L S Ayres & Co, h 591 College av.
Weinmann John C, clk L S Ayres & Co, b 591 College av.
Weir Alonzo, lab, h 239 W Maryland.
Weir Anna, teacher Public School No 12, b 1115 N New Jersey.
Weir Clarence E, lawyer, 137 Commercial Club bldg, h 157 Johnson av.
Weir David H, foreman, b 1115 N New Jersey.
Weir Edwin C, asst supt city delivery P O, b 1115 N New Jersey.
Weir Elizabeth E (wid Walter), h 1115 N New Jersey.
Weir Elmer E, clk Parry Mnfg Co, b 1115 N New Jersey.
Weir Everett L, bkkpr, b 22 Hoyt av.
Weir George W, sec Blue Flame Oil Burner Co, h 22 Hoyt av.
Weir John, brakeman, b 1027 E Washington.
Weir John F, condr, h 558 Broadway.
Weir Samuel, detective, h 39 Oliver av (W I).
Weir Wm, marble wks, rear 105 E Washington, r 115 E Washington.

EAT
QUAKER BREAD
ASK YOUR GROCER FOR IT.
THE HITZ BAKING CO.

BICYCLES $5 DOWN. $1 Best Wheels. Best Terms. WHEELMEN'S CO. 31 W. OHIO ST. LONG DISTANCE TEL. 1855.

J. H. TECKENBROCK House, Sign and Fresco Painter, 94 EAST SOUTH STREET.

FIDELITY MUTUAL LIFE PHILADELPHIA, PA. A. H. COLLINS, Gen. Agt. Baldwin Blk. } RATES REASONABLE. SOUND BEYOND QUESTION. BUSINESS-LIKE IN PRACTICE.

BITUMINOUS COAL ▸▸ Edwardsport Coal and Mining Company ROOMS 42 AND 43 WHEN BUILDING.

ESTABLISHED 1876. TELEPHONE 168.
CHESTER BRADFORD,
SOLICITOR OF PATENTS,
AND COUNSEL IN PATENT CAUSES.
(See adv. page 6.)
Office:—Rooms 14 and 16 Hubbard Block, S. W. Cor. Washington and Meridian Streets, INDIANAPOLIS, INDIANA.

Weirick Drue (wid Wm), h 71 Park av.
Weirick Henry L, fireman, h 26 Johnson av.
Weirick Lewis, h 5½ Brookside av.
Weis, see also Weiss, Weise and Wise.
Weis Andrew J, bkkpr, b 735 S East.
Weis Anna M (wid John), h 343 N Delaware.
Weis Charles E, jeweler, 258 W Washington, h 343 N Delaware.
Weis Charles F, h 1008 N Capitol av.
Weis Charles F, clk, h 25 Dickson.
Weis Felix, furnaces, 269 English av, h same.
Weis Jacob P, engr, h 617 S Meridian.
Weis Margaret (wid Peter), h 735 S East.
Weis Michael, helper, b Peter Weis.
Weis Peter, lab, h e s Miama 5 s of Prospect.
Weis Richard, uphlr, b Peter Weis.
Weis Wm, baggageman, r 225 Michigan av.
Weisbrod George, uphlr, b 681 S Meridian.
Weise Lucy (wid Andrew), h n e cor Sangster av and Belle.
Weisenberg Wilbur, carp, h 167 Benton.
Weisenberger Frank (Barnett & Weisenberger), h s s Ohio 3 e of Rural.
Weisenborn Frank A, butcher, h 54 Maxwell.
Weisenburger Louis, mngr Murphy, Hibben & Co, h 731 N Delaware.
Weisenheimer Frederick L, cabtmkr, h 496 W New York.
Weiser Curtis A, mach, h 108 Fayette.
Weiser Emmett E, driver, h 170 N Pine.
Weismantel Frank, baker, b 222 W Washington.
Weismueller Annie (wid Jacob), b 18 McKim av.
Weiss, see also Weis, Weise and Wise.
Weiss Anna (wid John L), h 223 E Morris.
Weiss Christian, driver, r 416 W Washington.
Weiss Christian G, genl agt Ger Am Bldg Assn, h 18 E Michigan.
Weiss John G, brewer, h 190 Orange.
Weiss Karl C, student, b 18 E Michigan.
Weiss Paul T H, bartndr, h 455 Mulberry.
Weiss Theodore M, drugs, 198 Mass av, b 18 E Michigan.

BUY THE BEST.
Outing BICYCLES $85
MADE BY
HAY & WILLITS MFG. CO.
76 N. PENN. ST. Phone 598.

WEISS WM G, Dealer in Choice Wines, Liquors and Cigars, 13 S Meridian, h 221 E Morris.

Weisshaar Francis X, brazier, b 184 Dillon.
Weisshaar Jacob, lab, h 105 Lincoln la.
Weisshaar John, shoemkr, 184 Dillon, h same.
Weisshaar Joseph F, stonecutter, h 184 Dillon.
Weissmueller Frank, lab, b 267 S Capitol av.
Weist Carl G, mach, h 25 Prairie av.
Weist John F, lab, h 117 Lawrence.
Weist Wm H, tmstr, h 10 Cooper.
Weisz Ira S, agt Rock Island Plow Co, h 232 N Illinois.
Weitzel Louis P, baker, 269 W Washington, h same.
Weizeman, see also Wiseman.
Weizeman Alfred D, horseshoer, h 162 N Pine.
Weizeman Eliza J (wid John M), b 162 N Pine.
Welch, see also Walsh and Welsh.
Welch Bartholomew, lab, h rear 188 W Merrill.
Welch David, chiropodist, r 6 Miller blk.
Welch David, mach, b 16 McCauley.
Welch Frank E, clk, h 203 Northwestern av.
Welch George, fireman, b 1 S Gale (B).
Welch Harry, foreman, b 16 McCauley.
Welch Isaac N, chiropodist, 6 Miller blk, r same.
Welch Jackson W, fireman, b s e cor Gale and Sutherland (B).
Welch James, lab, r 200½ W Washington.
Welch James L, agt, h 171 Davidson.
Welch Johanna (wid James), h 207 Meek.
Welch John, chiropodist, r 6 Miller blk.
Welch John, vault cleaner, 5 Arthur, h same.
Welch John A, tel opr I D & W Ry, h 97 S Reisner (W I).
Welch John R (Welch & Carlon), h 778 N Illinois.
Welch Lawrence, engr, b 73 W Georgia.
Welch Mary (wid David), h 16 McCauley.
Welch Mary E (wid Samuel), b 203 Northwestern av.
Welch Newell D, foreman, h 138 Huron.
Welch Patrick, lab, b 16 McCauley.
Welch Robert, motorman, b 98 Sheffield av (H).
Welch Samuel, tmstr, h 17 Willard.
Welch Sherman, lab, h 54 Church.
Welch Thomas, fireman, h 183 Douglass.
Welch Thomas E, lab, b 441 S West.
Welch Wm, lab, b 183 Douglass.
Welch Wm H, trav agt, h 249 Central av.
Welch Wm P, brakeman, r 233 Cedar.
Welch Wm S, clk Stubbins Hotel, h 54 Church.

WELCH & CARLON (John R Welch, John Carlon), Real Estate and Insurance Agts, 34 Monument Pl, Tel 1531.

Weldon John M, lab, h 28 Ketcham (H).
Weldon Thomas, painter, 119 Fulton, h same.
Welk Albert G, brakeman, h 140 S Summit.
Wellbaum Alonzo E, condr, b 10 Sumner.
Weller Byron, lab, b 38 Nordyke av (W I).
Weller Clemen V, molder, b 38 Nordyke av (W I).
Weller Frederick, pdlr, r 23 N West.
Weller Gilbert J, molder, h 147 Hadley av (W I).

ROOFING MATERIAL C. ZIMMERMAN & SONS, SLATE AND GRAVEL ROOFERS, 19 SOUTH EAST STREET.

WELLER HARRY D, Dentist, 11-12 Marion Blk, n w cor Meridian and Ohio, r 359 N Illinois.
Weller James A, molder, h 72 Smith.
Weller John B, painter, b 79 N Liberty.
Weller Joseph C, molder, b 147 Hadley av (W I).
Weller Margaret, h 185½ E Washington.
Weller Wm, h 38 Nordyke av (W I).
Weller Wm W, mach, b 38 Nordyke av (W I).
Welling Emma E (wid John S), h 34 N New Jersey.
Welling Frankie L, mngr, b 70 W New York.
Welling Harry O, cigarmkr, b 34 N New Jersey.
Welling Henry C, carp, 127 Spring, h same.
Welling Wm W, collr, h 802 N New Jersey.
Wellman Frederick, hostler, h 473 S New Jersey.
Wellman Frederick G, bartndr, b 360 W Vermont.
Wellman Howard G, hostler, h 360 W Vermont.
Wellman Jeremiah L, carp, h w s National av 3 s of Washington av (I).
Wellman Richard G, clk, h 360 W Vermont.
Wellmann Frederick C (Jacob Metzger & Co), h 222 Madison av.
Wellmann Wm, sec The H Lieber Co, b 623 S Meridian.
Wells Ada B, h 349 W Michigan.
Wells Alexander E, mngr Famous Stove Co, h 1107 N Penn.
Wells Amanda (wid Lee), h 65 Rhode Island.
Wells Amanda E (wid Albert S), h 155 E Ohio.
Wells Amelia H (wid Graham A), h 181 N New Jersey.
Wells Andrew J, letter carrier P O, h 31½ Monument pl.
Wells Anna, dressmkr, r 418 Union.
Wells Annie, restaurant, 16 Indiana av, h 22½ same.
Wells Benjamin, lab, h w s Earl 1 s of Belt R R.
Wells Bessie, physical director Young Women's Christian Assn, b 114 Broadway.
Wells Charles, lab, b 191 W 4th.
Wells Charles, lab, b 252 W 22d.
Wells Charles A, ins agt, h 78 N Olive.
Wells Charles W (Kothe, Wells & Bauer), h 931 N Illinois.
Wells Charles W, woodwkr, h 1387 N Capitol av.
Wells Christian D (C Wells & Bro), h 130 W New York.
Wells Claude E, elev opr, b 750 N Illinois.
Wells C & Bro (Christian D and Wm H), lumber, 113 S Illinois.
Wells David N, lab, b 1155 Michigan av.
Wells Don D, clk, h 158 Agnes.
Wells Dudley, polisher, b 108 Cherry.
Wells Edmond, shoemkr, r 411 E Washington.
Wells Edward D, porter, h 279 Fayette.
Wells Edward H, cigars, 43 N Illinois, h 26 W New York
Wells Eleanor, teacher Public School No 10, b 1107 N Penn.
Wells Eli, bricklyr, b 50½ Clifford av.
Wells Elizabeth (wid Wm), b 76 Bates.
Wells Elza, lab, h rear 671 N Senate av.
Wells Emma S, b 540 Central av.
Wells, Fargo & Co's Express, Caleb S Phillips agt, 23 S Meridian.
Wells Frank, lab, h 479 W Ontario (N I).

Richardson & McCrea,
79 East Market Street,
FIRE INSURANCE,
REAL ESTATE, LOANS,
AND RENTAL AGENTS.
Telephone 182.

Wells Frank, trav agt E C Atkins & Co, h 623 Park av.
Wells Frank W, b 107 Dunlop.
Wells George, coppersmith Wm Langsenkamp, r 96 E Georgia.
Wells George, grocer, 247 S Capitol av, h 379 S Meridian.
Wells George, lab, h 456 W McLene (N I).
Wells George W, lab, h 195 W 3d.
Wells Hannah (wid Wm), b 87 Woodlawn av.
Wells Harry C, carp, h 87 Woodlawn av.
Wells Henry J, lab, h rear 217 S New Jersey.
Wells Henry T, lab, b 130 Anderson.
Wells Imogene B, stenog Chandler & Taylor Co, b 282 N Alabama.
Wells Isaac H, ins agt, h 696 Addison (N I).
Wells James H, barber Union Station, h 73 Howard.
Wells James H, lab, h rear 217 S New Jersey.
Wells James J, contr, h 750 N Illinois.
Wells James R, condr, b rear 72 W McCarty.
Wells James S, lab, h 107 Dunlop.
Wells John, boilermkr, h 132 Forest av.
Wells John B, millwright, h 5 Cooper.
Wells John T, real est, h 469 Virginia av.
Wells Joseph B, mnfrs' agt, h 23 Keith.
Wells Lewis, lab, h 22 Traub av.
Wells Livingston D, trav agt, b 931 N Illinois.
Wells Lucy (wid Peter), h 40 Locke.
Wells Mack, driver, r 278 Chapel.
Wells Mahlon, carp, h 98 Concord (H).
Wells Margaret (wid James), h rear 72 W McCarty.
Wells Marguerite I, nurse, 10 Wyandot blk, r same.
Wells Mark T, asst cashr Equitable Life Assurance Society, r 28 The Marquette.
Wells Martin L Rev, h 36 Dickson.
Wells Merit, dentist, 18 W Ohio, h 114 Broadway.
Wells Michael, coachman 400 N Meridian.
Wells Milton D, clk, h 93 Dougherty.
Wells Nancy C (wid Wm A), h 4 N Dorman.

SHORTHAND REPORTING......
CONVENTIONS, SPEECHES, SERMONS.
COPYING ON TYPEWRITER.
S. H. EAST, State Agent,
THE WILLIAMS TYPEWRITER
55 Thorpe Block, 87 East Market Street.

...llars and Cuffs Laundered in Best of Style. Dull or High Gloss Finish.

ERTEL STEAM LAUNDRY
26 and 28 N. Senate Ave. Telephone 1089.

Manufacturers of Iron Vases,

THE HOGAN TRANSFER AND STORAGE COMP'Y
Household Goods and Pianos Moved—Packed—Stored...... Baggage and Package Express Machinery and Safes a Specialty Cor. Washington and Illinois Sts. TELEPHONE No. 675.

Hose, Belting, Packing, Clothing, Druggists' Sundries, Bicycle Tires, Cotton Hose, Etc. New York Belting & Packing Co., L't'd. The Central Rubber & Supply Co. 79 S. ILLINOIS ST., INDIANAPOLIS, IND. PHONE 8.

The Provident Life and Trust Co.
OF PHILADELPHIA.
Small Death Rate. Small Expense Rate. Safe Investments.
Insurance in force $115,000,000
D. W. EDWARDS,
General Agent, 508 Indiana Trust Building.

Wells Nathan, coachman, h 748 Brooker's al.
Wells Nellie, teacher Public School No 17, b 85 Union.
Wells Nellie G, teacher Public School No 16, h 114 Broadway.
Wells Oliver C M, soldier U S Arsenal.
Wells Oscar L, helper, h 427 Highland av.
Wells Richard A, motorman, h 14 Allfree av.
Wells Richard W, lab, h 40 Locke.
Wells Robert, clk, b 469 Virginia av.
Wells Robert S, clk, r 82 N Illinois.
Wells Robert W, driver, b 1520 N Senate av.
Wells Sarah A (wid Henry M L), b 26 W New York.
Wells Sarah E, teacher, b 1107 N Penn.
Wells Sera D, nurse, 36 Dickson, b same.
Wells Stella, music teacher, 36 Dickson, b same.
Wells Talitha (wid Abram), b 231 Columbia av.
Wells Thomas, lab, b rear 77 W North.
Wells Thomas J, lab, b 1155 Michigan av.
Wells Thomas W, carp, 1518 N Senate av, h 1520 same.
Wells Wade H, lab, h 151 Woodside av (W).
Wells Wesley, lab, h 63 Superior.
Wells Wm B, clk, h 282 N Alabama.
Wells Wm C, lab, b 85 Spring.
Wells Wm F, h 931 N Illinois.
Wells Wm H (C Wells & Bro), b 130 W New York.
Wells Wilson, tmstr, h 1520 N Senate av.
Wells Worthy, tmstr, b 176 Patterson.
WELMAN SALEM P, Attorney at Law, 425-426 Lemcke Bldg, Tel 1847; h 297 N Alabama.
Welsh, see also Walsh and Welch.
Welsh Amanda C (wid George), h 1105 N Meridian.
Welsh Bridget (wid Michael), h 58 McGinnis.
Welsh Charles S, trav agt, b Stubbins Hotel.
Welsh Daniel J, fireman, b 110 Davidson.
Welsh Daniel M, uphlr, b 58 McGinnis.
Welsh David, lab, h 421½ National rd.

Julius C. Walk & Son,
Jewelers
Indianapolis.
12 EAST WASHINGTON ST.

Welsh Ella (Union Co-operative Laundry), h 58 McGinnis.
Welsh Emma (wid Michael), h 195 Columbia av.
Welsh James, engr, h 223 English av.
Welsh James, janitor St John's Academy, b same.
Welsh James E, foreman, h 231 W Merrill.
Welsh James M, engr, h 253 Bates.
Welsh John, driver, r rear 27 Camp.
Welsh John, lab, b 605 W Vermont.
Welsh John, motorman, b 281 W Pearl.
Welsh John, switchman, b 424 S Delaware.
Welsh John J, h 110 Davidson.
Welsh Katie E (Union Co-operative Laundry), h 58 McGinnis.
Welsh Martin, lab, r 142 S East.
Welsh Mary (wid Patrick), h e s Perkins pike 1 s of C C C & St L Ry.
Welsh Mary D (wid Michael), boarding 99 Lexington av.
Welsh Mary (wid John), h 424 S Delaware.
Welsh Maurice, boilermkr, b 424 S Delaware.
Welsh Maurice B, molder, h 110 Davidson.
Welsh Michael, bartndr, b 396 S Illinois.
Welsh Michael, boilermkr, b 505 E Georgia.
Welsh Michael, lab, r 58 W Merrill.
Welsh Michael, varnisher, b 650 E 8th.
Welsh Patrick, lab, h 25 Patterson.
Welsh Patrick, lab, b 281 W Pearl.
Welsh Richard P, foreman, h 426 Union.
Welsh Thomas, b 181 E Merrill.
Welsh Thomas, trav agt, r 24 S Penn.
Welsh Thomas E, clk, h 1441 N Illinois.
Welsh Thomas M, lab, b 343 W Maryland.
Welsh Timothy, lab, h 32 Bismarck av (H).
Welsh Wm, lab, b 424 S Delaware.
Welsh Wm J, boilermkr, b 110 Davidson.
Welshans Bertrand, boilermkr, b 226 English av.
Welshans Wm H, switchman, h 226 English av.
Welty Charles M, barber, r 148 W Maryland.
Wemmer, see also Wimmer.
Wemmer George, blksmith, h 41 Iowa.
Wempe Frank, trav agt, h 23 Gatling.
Wempner Christian F, carp, h 32 Spann av.
Wempner George, bricklyr, h 28 Dawson.
Wempner Henry, b 309 S East.
Wempner Henry C F, barber, r 193½ E Washington.
Wempner Wm C, driver, h 153 Prospect.
Wencke Michael, mach hd, 82 Ludlow av.
Wencke Wm F, lab, h 82 Ludlow av.
Wendel Alexander, carp, h 167 Laurel.
Wendhausen Frederick W, tailor, h 79 Downey.
Wendler Clemens A, dairy, e s Sherman Drive 1 s of Prospect, h same.
Wendling Albert, gilder, h 62 Downey.
Wendling Theobold jr, clk, h 10 Dawson.
WENELL JOHN A, Practical Hatter, 73 S Illinois, h 55 Dearborn. (See adv in classified Hatters.)
Wenning Bernhart, lab, h 1040 Madison av.
Wenner Christine, teacher Public School No 25, b 47 Pleasant av.
Wenner Dora, teacher Public School No 20, b 47 Pleasant av.
Wenner John J, h 47 Pleasant av.
Wenner Otis, clk, b 136 W 1st.
Wenner Wm, finisher, h 951 E Michigan.
Wenning Dick, gardener, h 980 Madison av.
Wenning Frederick B, finisher, b 700 Chestnut.
Wenning Herman, lab, h 700 Chestnut.

OTTO GAS ENGINES
BUILDERS' EXCHANGE S. W. Cor. Ohio and Penn. Telephone 535.

Becker & Son Charles Becker Jacob Becker Jr. Merchant Tailors. 21 N. Penn. St. Tel. 934

SALISBURY & STANLEY. Office, Store and Bank Fixtures a Specialty. Repairing of all kinds done on short n. 177 Clint or Street, Indianapolis, Ind. Contractors and Builders TELEPHONE 999.

Wenning John F, framemkr, b 980 Madison av.
Wenning Wm J, painter, b 700 Chestnut.
Wensley James L, meats, 42 E Mkt House, h 96 Keystone av.
Wenslow Edward, painter, b 128 Chadwick.
Wentling Levi L, weighmaster, r 11 Catterson blk.
Wentworth Ella E (wid George), b 181 E St Clair.
Wentz Kate, teacher Industrial Training School, b 569 Central av.
Wenz Elizabeth A (wid Wm), h 218 Dougherty.
Wenz George W, carp The Indpls News, h 220 Dougherty.
Wenz George W jr, mach, b 220 Dougherty.
Wenz Louis P, patternmkr, b 220 Dougherty.
Wenzel Frederick P F, clk Consumers' Gas Trust Co, h 468 S East.
Wenzel Juhus L, janitor, h 202 W Walnut.
Wenzler Andrew S, lab, b 148 Hosbrook.
Wenzler Charles M, pressman, b 1069 W New York.
Wenzler Constantine, foreman, h 1069 W New York.
Wenzler Simon, carp, h 148 Hosbrook.
Werbe Charles B, carp, h 614 S Meridian.
Werbe Edwin F G, driver, h 184 E Court.
Werbe Fredericka (wid Ferdinand), b 175 N West.

WERBE GEORGE A, Cigars, Tobacco and Smokers' Supplies, 98 N Penn, h 74 W 4th.

Werbe Henry, tinner, b 75 Dearborn.
Werbe Henry G, salesman Julius C Walk & Son, h 807 N Delaware.
Werbe Wm F, grinder J P Wimmer, h 28 Harrison.
Werchold Johanna, h 53 Hendricks.
Werheiser Morris C, sawmkr, h 107 Douglass.
Werk Albert, draughtsman, b 190 N West.
Werking Charles E, lab, h 199 N West.
Werking James B, lab, b 39 Drake.
Werking Jonathan, cooper, h 137 Bright.
Werking Phoebe R (wid Isaac A), h 39 Drake.
Wernbeck Wilhelmina M (wid George M), b 9 Atlas.
Werner, see also Warner and Woerner.
Werner Albert, mach hd, b 46 Smithson.
Werner August W, clk, h 720 S East.
Werner Charles P, mach opr Indpls Journal, h 108½ Mass av.
Werner Christian, truckman, h 27 Weghorst.
Werner Emil, uphlr, b 46 Smithson.
Werner Ernest F, draughtsman Vonnegut & Bohn, h 540 S New Jersey.
Werner John, cabtmkr, h 358 Spring.
Werner John, dairy, e s Lebanon av 3 n of Clifford av, h same.
Werner Vincent, carp, h 46 Smithson.
Werner Wm F, drug clk Sloan Drug Co, r 330 E Louisiana.
Wernert Charles I, porter R M S, h 325 N Illinois.
Werning Benjamin C, lab, h 19 N Arsenal av.
Werning Joseph, driver, h 82 Elizabeth.
Wernsang Joseph, mach, h 657 Mass av.
Wernsing Joseph G, lab, h 82 Elizabeth.
Wernsing Andrew, lab, b 865 Madison av.
Wernsing Augustus J, horseshoer, b 209 N Pine.

Henry H. Fay,
40½ E. WASHINGTON ST.,
FIRE INSURANCE, REAL ESTATE,
LOANS AND RENTAL AGENT.

Wernsing George W (Wernsing & Haenggi), h 628 E New York.
Wernsing Herman F, mach hd, b 121 Kennington.
Wernsing John W, city fireman, h 836 S Meridian.
Wernsing & Haenggi (George W Wernsing, Theophilus Haenggi), stair builders, 628 E New York.
Wert, see also Wirt.
Wert Edwin A, vice-pres The Gordon-Kurtz Co, h 181 Christian av.
Werther Maria (wid Wm), h 358 E New York.
Wertman Frank, dairy, e s Rural 3 n of Brookside av, h same.
Werts Noah S, farmer, h n e cor Clifford and Lebanon avs.
Wertz, see also Wirtz and Wurtz.
Wertz Charles G, sawmkr, h 39 N State av.
Wertz Edward, student, b 41 Madison av.
Wertz Hannah (wid Benton), h 266 W Pearl.
Wesbey Charles E, capt Hose Co No 14, h n w cor Capitol av and 22d.
Wesbey Dora, b 83 N Capitol av.
Wesbey Elizabeth (wid Ephraim), b n w cor Capitol av and 22d.
Wescott, see also Westcott.
Wescott Martha (wid Bergen B), h 224 N Senate av.
Weser Edith E, music teacher, 641 E Vermont, b same.
Weser Philip (Weser & Collins), h 633 E Vermont.
Weser & Collins (Philip Weser, John W Collins), saloon, 812 E Washington.
Wesling Christian F, carp, h 93 Greencastle av.
Wesling Edward C F, carp, h 303 N Pine.
Wesp Henry H, agt, h 14 Hermann.
Wesp John L, grocer, 467 N California, h same.
Wessel Henry, carp, h 36 S Stuart (B).
Wessel Henry, roller, b 187 S Capitol av.
Wessel Louis J, clk, b 195 E South.
Wessel Theodore H, tinner, b 36 N Stuart (B).
Wessel Wm, mach hd, b 203 Minnesota.
Wessler John, plastr, b 559 S State av.

JAS. N. MAYHEW,
MANUFACTURING
OPTICIAN
LENSES AND FRAMES A SPECIALTY.
No. 13 North Meridian St., Indianapolis.

LUMBER | Sash, Door and Planing . Mill Work . | Balke & Krauss Co. Cor. Market and Missouri Streets.

FRIEDGEN'S TAN SHOES are the Newest Shades Prices the Lowest. 19 North Pennsylvania St.

SAMUEL LAING General Job Work in Sheet Metal of all Kinds 72 AND 74 E. COURT STREET.

M. B. WILSON, Pres. W. F. CHURCHMAN, Cash.
THE CAPITAL NATIONAL BANK,
INDIANAPOLIS, IND.
Make collections on all points in the States of Indiana and Illinois on the most favorable rates.
Capital, - - $300,000
Surplus and Earnings, 50,000
No. 28 S. Meridian St., Cor. Pearl.

Wessling Henry, saloon, 199 Hoyt av, h same.
Wessling Louis, trav agt, b 1725 N Meridian.
Wessling Louis A, b 70 N East.
Wesson Moore M, car rep, h e s Concord 1 n of Michigan (H).
West Alexander, painter, h 958 Grove av.
West Alfred, lab, b 103 Blake.
West Andrew J, lab, h 11 Valley Drive.
West Caswell, lab, h 464½ W 2d.
West Charles, turner, h 956 Grove av.
West Charles W, lab, b e s Concord 3 s of Michigan (H).
West Crampton, lab, b 295 W Merrill.
West David, painter, b 956 Grove av.
West David W, engr C H & D R R, h 28 Woodlawn av.
WEST DISINFECTING CO, Mnfr Chloro-Napholeum and Carbolized Powders, 7 Monument Pl. (See adv in classified Disinfectants.)
West Edward C, brakeman, r 852½ E Washington.
West Edward E, bkkpr Marion Trust Co, h 956 N Delaware.
West Elmer E, driver, b 322 Cornell av.
West Enos D, brakeman, h 222 Lexington av.
West Evelyn, teacher Public School No 41, b 546 Highland av (N I).
West Frank, clk, b 174 N Illinois.
West Frank, lab, b 322 Cornell av.
West Frank, lab, b 195 W Merrill.
West Frank, plumber, h 163 W Vermont.
West Frederick, lab, h rear 11 Bates.
West Frederick B, student, r 217 E Ohio.
West George W, lab, h 147 Madison.
West Harry K, brakeman, h 57 Leota.
West James, carp, b 86 N East.
West James, lab, h 295 W Merrill.
West James, tmstr, h 84 Sheldon.
West John, h 546 Highland av (N I).
West John, engr, h 17 Spann av.
West John, packer, h 198 Newman.
West John R, engr, h 52 Yandes.
West Louisa, stenog Parry Mnfg Co, b 302 N Delaware.
West Luther H, lab, h 294 W St Clair.

MONEY
Loaned on Short Notice at Lowest Rates.
TUTTLE & SEGUIN,
Tel. 1168. 28 E. Market St.

West Mabel, teacher Public School No 36, b 546 Highland av (N I).
West Millie (wid Saul), h 229 W 3d.
West Peter, lab, h 334 Hillside av.
West Robert A, painter, b 1308 N Delaware.
West Shore Fast Freight Line, John A Simmons agt, 1 E Washington.
WEST SIDE PLANING MILL CO (Conrad Draut, John A Richter, Milledge A Baker), 1000 W New York, Tel 1668.
West Silas F, fireman, h 184 Huron.
West Solomon, lab, h 479 Lafayette.
West Stephen E, fireman, h 33 Decatur.
West Tennessee Spoke and Lumber Co, David E Allen pres, 658 N Alabama.
West Thomas, polisher, h 301½ E Washington.
West Thomas J, h 327½ E Washington.
West Walter W, condr, h 131 Elm.
West Wm, carp, h 281 Alvord.
West Wm, lab, b 105 Locke.
West Wm, lab, b 394 W North.
West Wm B (Zeisler & West), h 51 Warren av (W I).
West Wm D, lab, b 128 W 4th.
West Wm T, h 65 Ingraham.
West Wm W, tmstr, h 228 W 1st.
Westcott, see also Wescott.
Westcott Edgar R, printer Indpls News, h 12 Roanoke.
Westenberg John M, carp, h 155 John.
Westerbeck John, lab, h rear 244 Michigan (H).
Westerfield Ellen (wid Charles), h e s Rural 4 n of Sutherland (B).
Westerfield Herman, car rep, h 190 Fulton.
Westerhausen August E, mach, h 10 Henry.
WESTERN CREOSOTING CO, P C Reilly Mngr, cor Merritt and Belt R R n of Michigan.
WESTERN FURNITURE CO, Wm L Hagedorn Pres, Charles Fearnaught Sec and Treas, Madison av opp S Delaware, Tel 438.
Western Horseman Co, I R Sherwood pres, A E Harlan sec, S W McMahan treas and genl mngr, pubs The Western Horseman, 49 Monument pl.
Western Horseman The, Western Horseman Co, pubs, 49 Monument pl.
WESTERN PAVING AND SUPPLY CO THE, Volney W Foster Pres, Amos H Perkins Mngr, Samuel H Shearer Supt and Engineer, 39 Ingalls Blk, Tel 57; Yards and Works cor Indiana av and Michigan, Tel 380.
WESTERN UNION TELEGRAPH CO, John F Wallick Supt, Tel 236; Mahlon D Butler Mngr; General Office 19 S Meridian, Tels 24 and 25; Branches: Board of Trade Bldg, Union Station, Union Stock Yards, Kingan & Co, The Denison, Grand Hotel, Mass av Station, 27 S Delaware, Lemcke Bldg and 370 W Washington.
Westfall Ida B, teacher, b 95 Oliver av (W I).
Westfall Wm H, mngr Henry Smith, r 18 The Shiel.
Westfield August W, painter, h 1349 N Senate av.
Westfield Mary, baker, 138 E Mkt House, h 1349 N Senate av.

PAPER BOXES, MANUFACTURED BY SULLIVAN & MAHAN 41 W. PEARL STREET.

DIAMOND WALL PLASTER { Telephone 1410 BUILDERS' EXCHANGE.

Fine Laundry Work our Specialty. Gll as and Cuffs our Hobby. THE HOME LAUNDRY 197 S. Illinois St. Telephone 1769.

Westing Frederick H, clk, b 616 E Washington.
Westing Gustav H, trav agt, h 616 E Washington.
Weston James F, sawmkr, h s e cor Illinois and 29th.
Weston Wm W, contr, b Illinois House.
Westover Charles W, foreman, h 66 Marion av (W I).
Westover Jonathan M, b 355 S Meridian.
Westover Leland R, janitor, r 67 W Maryland.
Westover Wm H, band sawyer, h 1236 Madison av.
Westpfahl Catherine (wid Frederick), b 154 Carlos.
Westpfahl Sophia (wid Theodore), h 530 S West.
Westphal Henry, h 141 Wisconsin.
Westphal Louis, huckster, h 530 S Illinois.
Westphal Martin, lab, h s s Ohio 2 e of Rural.
Wetcel Frederica (wid Wm), h 146 Davidson.
Wetcske Adolph, bricklyr, h 32 Chadwick.
Wetherill Matilda J (wid Henry), r 69 Mass av.
Wetherwault Alexander, mach, b 6 Cornell av.
Wetsell Harry P, clk Kingan & Co (ltd), b 899 N Delaware.
Wetsell Mary S (wid Harry P), h 899 N Delaware.
Wetter Albert J, lab, h 85 Wisconsin.
Wetter Charles, baker, b 85 Wisconsin.
Wetter Wm C, sawfiler, h 85 Wisconsin.
Wettrick Edward G, tmstr, h 12 Hartford.
Wetzel Anna (wid Peter), h rear 333 W Morris.
Wetzel Christian A, mach, h 103 Meek.
Wetzel Christian G, driver, h 477 S East.
Wetzel Harrison, condr, b 150 Cornell av.
Wetzel Henry (Pearson & Wetzel), h 200 N Meridian.
Wetzel Henry, mason, h 40 Wallack.
Wetzel Henry A, bartndr, h rear 333 W Morris.
Wetzel Herman, bkkpr Pearson & Wetzel, b 285 N Illinois.
Wetzel Orren L, h 133 E North.
Wewer Bernard Rev, asst rector Sacred Heart Church, h n w cor Union and Palmer.
Weybright David W, carp, h 968 W New York.
Weyenberg Peter C, contr, 12 Hamilton av, h same.
Weymouth Sallie M (wid Amos H), h 9 Rhode Island.
Weyreter Ernest, horseshoer, h 39 Davis.
Whalen, see also Whelan.
Whalen Dennis, flagman, h 269 S Capitol av.
Whalen Dennis J, clk, b 80 Minerva.
Whalen James, lab, b California House.
Whalen John, cooper, h 9 Elwood.
Whalen John, lab, h Burgess av (I).
Whalen Joseph, waiter Hotel Oneida.
Whaley Charles O, clk, b 327 S Olive.
Whaley Harry L, agt Chicago Belting Co, h 585 Marlowe av.
Whaley James H, painter, h 32 Bradshaw.
Whaley John W, wheelbldr, h 57 Barth av.
Whaley Nancy (wid James H), h 327 S Olive.
Whaley Robert E, ins agt, h 134 Shelby.
Whaley Wm J, wheelmkr, b 327 S Olive.
Whallon James I, clk L E & W R R, h 42 Highland pl.

FRANK NESSLER. WILL H. ROST.
FRANK NESSLER & CO.
Tailors
56 EAST MARKET ST. (Lemcke Building),
INDIANAPOLIS, IND.

Wharton Charles L, mach hd, h 476 N Senate av.
Wharton Frank B, lab, b 258 E Georgia.
Wharton George A, tmstr, h n s Michigan av 2 e of Woodside av (W).
Wharton Jeremiah, lab, h 338 Tremont.
Wharton John E, attendant Insane Asylum.
Wharton John M, clk, h 1153 E Washington.
Wharton Joseph W, real est, 96½ E Market, r 94 N Illinois.
Wharton Oscar, hostler, b 338 Tremont.
Wharton Wm T, b 32 S State av.
Whearley Clifford E, bookbndr, b 27½ Monument pl.
Whearley Jacob, baker, h 27½ Monument pl.
Wheat Benjamin C, cashr Indiana Soc for Savings, h 320 E Miami.
Wheat Charles W, engr, h 320 E Miami.
Wheat James, painter, r 197½ E Washington.
Wheat John, lab, b 162 Elizabeth.
Wheatcraft Charles O, florist, 1541 N Capitol av, h same.
Wheatley Franklin, baggageman, h 40 Cleveland (H).
Wheatley George, motorman, b 1028 W Washington.
Wheatley Harry, lab, b 216 Alvord.
Wheatley Harry A, brakeman, b 40 Cleveland (H).
Wheatley Harry H, supt Marion County Work House.
Wheatley John M, b 960 N Alabama.
Wheatley John N, miller, h 72 Cypress.
Wheatley Joseph W, condr, h 216 Alvord.
Wheatley Thomas, b 40 Cleveland (H).
Wheatley Wm J, watchman, h 332 Yandes.
Wheatley Wm T, driver, h 512 S Illinois.
Wheaton Perry, lab, h 456 Mulberry.
Wheaton Samuel, lab, h rear 233 S West.
Wheeler Addison A, clk, r 200½ W Washington.
Wheeler Albert J, trav agt, h 963 N Senate av.
Wheeler Amanda J (wid Sewell W), h 94 N New Jersey.

ACORN STOVES AND RANGES
Haueisen & Hartmann
163-169 E. Washington St.
FURNITURE,
Carpets,
Household Goods,
Tin, Granite and China Wares, Oil Cloth and Shades

THE WM. H. BLOCK CO. 7 AND 9 EAST WASHINGTON STREET. DRY GOODS, MEN'S FURNISHINGS.

Fidelity and Deposit Co. of Maryland. BONDS SIGNED.—LOCAL BOARD John B. Elam, Albert Sahm, Smiley N. Chambers, John M. Spann.
GEORGE W. PANGBORN, General Agent, 704-706 Lemcke Building. Telephone 140.

74 EAST MARKET STREET Telephone 5. Insure Your Property With FRANK K. SAWYER

JOSEPH GARDNER,
Hot Air Furnaces
With Combination Gas Burners for Burning Gas and Other Fuel at the Same Time.
37, 39 & 41 KENTUCKY AVE. Telephone 322

Wheeler Arden E, mach, b 959 S East.
Wheeler Charles H, porter, h 27 Hadley.
Wheeler Charles S, pressman, b 55 Laurel.
Wheeler Charles W, butcher, h 6 S Judge Harding (W I).
Wheeler Dressed Beef Co (Wm H and Hillis A Wheeler, Joseph F Feelemyer), Indpls Abattoir (W I).
Wheeler Edgar, lab, b 344 Clinton.
Wheeler Edward, packer, r 200½ W Washington.
Wheeler Edward, patrolman, h 152 Clifford av.
Wheeler Elizabeth (wid John H), h 319 Virginia av.
Wheeler Elizabeth (wid Wm), b 236 S Missouri.
Wheeler Emma A (wid Henry), h 14 Hadley av (W I).
Wheeler Ephraim B, h 55 Laurel.
Wheeler Harry W, clk, b 892 Morris (W I).
Wheeler Hillis A (Wheeler Dressed Beef Co), h 892 Morris (W I).
Wheeler Ira D, tiremkr, b 346 Bates.
Wheeler Jennie (wid David H), h 344 Clinton.
Wheeler John L, lab, h 11 Sumner.
Wheeler Julius L, lab, b 80 Oliver av (W I).
Wheeler Kate L, stenog John M Bailey, b 55 Laurel.
Wheeler Lawrence T, ins agt, h 252 Cornell av.
Wheeler Leonard, b 28 Reynolds av (H).
Wheeler Samuel W, lab, h 28 Reynolds av (H).
Wheeler Walter H, student, b 179 Broadway.
Wheeler Walter R, engr, h 106 John.
Wheeler Walter S, clk, r 28 N Senate av.
Wheeler Wm A, bicycle mnfr, 94 Ft Wayne av, h 299 Broadway.
Wheeler Wm B, engr, h 55 Oak.
Wheeler Wm H (Wheeler Dressed Beef Co), h 890 Morris (W I).
Wheeler Wm H, lab, h 364 W North.
Wheeler Wm N, attendant Insane Asylum.
Wheeler Wm V, supt, h 179 Broadway.
Wheeler Wilson D, driver, h 19 N William (W I).

J. S. FARRELL & CO.
Plumbing
Natural and Artificial Gas Fitting.
84 N. ILLINOIS STREET.
TELEPHONE 382.

WHEELMEN'S CO, Ben L Darrow Propr, Wholesale and Retail Dealers in Bicycles and Bicycle Sundries, 31 W Ohio, Tel 1855. (See right side lines.)
WHEELMEN'S GAZETTE, Ben L Darrow Editor and Publisher, 31 W Ohio, Tel 1855. (See right side lines.)
Wheelock Lyman T, clk h 139 S William (W I).
Wheelock Wm B, vice-pres L S Ayres & Co, h 656 N Delaware.
Wheet Charles, lab, h 463 Mulberry.
Whelan, see also Whalen.
Whelan John E, mach, h 486 Highland av.
Whelan Rose (wid Thomas S), h 486 Highland av.
Whelan Wm E, engr, h 348 E St Clair.
Whelden Joseph E, gents' furngs, 85 N Penn, h 1019 same
When Band, George E Mills leader, 70½ E Court.
WHEN CLOTHING STORE, Owen Bros & Co Proprs, 26-40 N Penn, Tel 482. (See right top cor cards.)
Wherritt Wm F, bkkpr, h 33 W Vermont.
Wherry Scott J, mach, h 9 N Gale (B).
Whetstine Edward, toolmkr, b 263 Bates.
Whetstine Jacob A, fireman, b 263 Bates.
Whetstine John, mach, h 375 Fletcher av.
Whetstine John W, mach, b 263 Bates.
Whetstine Martha H (wid Perry C), h 263 Bates.
Whetstine Michael, lab, h 224 Hoyt av.
Whetstine Oscar, lab, b 224 Hoyt av.
Whetstone Gideon W, plastr, h 84 Camp.
Whiffing Ada, h 167 N Illinois.
Whiffing Robert A, lab, h 56 Tremont av (H).
Whinery Samuel, vice-pres Warren-Scharf Asphalt Paving Co, res Cincinnati, O.
Whipple Joseph M, mach, h rear 281 River av (W I).
Whisennand Catherine J (wid James), h 347 S East.
Whisler Grover, brakeman, r e s Brightwood av 9 s of Willow (B).
Whisner James H, clk, b 210 English av.
Whisner Joseph H, carp, h 210 English av.
Whistleman Bernhard, lab, b 128 Blake.
Whistler Augustus H, paymaster Atlas Engine Wks, r 551 Ash.
Whistler Richard R, finisher, b 533 S Capitol av.
Whitacre Wm, baker, b Illinois House.
Whitaker Anna (wid John B), h 221 Fletcher av.
Whitaker Charles F, jeweler, 32 N Delaware, h 426 E 15th.
Whitaker Francis J, carp, h 120 Raymond.
Whitaker George B, feed, 645 Virginia av, h 35 Woodlawn av.
Whitaker Hendricks V, driver, b 224½ W Washington.
Whitaker Horatio S, cooper, b 224½ W Washington.
Whitaker Ida M, confr, 406 College av, h same.
Whitaker James H, h 192 Woodlawn av.
Whitaker John, driver, h rear 54 Davis.
Whitaker Lawrence, carp, h 630 E St Clair.
Whitaker Sarah A (wid Joshua), b 141 Sharpe av (W).
Whitaker Susan A (wid Smith B), h 224½ W Washington.
Whitaker Wm H, driver, r 649 Virginia av.
Whitaker Wm H, tmstr, h 69 S Arsenal av.

IF CONTINUED to the end of its dividend period, policies of the UNITED STATES LIFE INSURANCE CO., will equal or excel any investment policy ever offered to the public. | E. B. SWIFT, Manager, 25 E. Market St.

Wm.Kotteman 89 & 91 E. Washington St. TELEPHONE 1742 Furniture

SHOW CASES WILLIAM WIEGEL 6 West Louisiana Street Opp. Union Station.

Whitcomb Charles E, painter, b 268 W 5th.
Whitcomb George E, trav agt, b 566 N Penn.
Whitcomb Harry A, paperhngr, h 542 N Senate av.
Whitcomb Jerome G, h 566 N Penn.
WHITCOMB LARZ A, Lawyer, 725-726 Lemcke Bldg, h 56 The Chalfant.
Whitcomb Lewis E, painter, h 689 W Shoemaker (N I).
Whitcomb Mary, dressmkr, 145 Fayette, h same.
Whitcomb Mary M (wid Edward A), h 268 W 5th.
Whitcomb Theodore C, ins, 60 E Market, h n e cor Michigan and Bright.
White, see also Whyte.
White Adelaide (wid Wm H), h 64 Oak.
WHITE AHIRA R, M D, Pres White Chemical Co and Mnfr Proprietary Medicines, 190 S Meridian, h 450 N East.
White Albert, waiter, b 182 Muskingum al.
White Albert A, lab, b 51 Hope (B).
White Albert O, buttermkr, h 22 Gregg.
White Alfred, lab, h 118 Martindale av.
White Alice, h 45 Maple.
White Alice, dressmkr, h 108½ Mass av.
White Alma C, music teacher, 395 Bellefontaine, h same.
White Amory G, lab, h 32 Gresham.
White Arthur C, city editor The Indpls Sentinel, h 22 The Blacherne.
White Belle, b 526 S East.
White Benedict, trav agt B L Blair & Co, b 379 N Penn.
White Benjamin, cook, h 165 W Chesapeake.
White Benjamin F, eng insp, h School (B).
White Birney K, restaurant, 271 Mass av, h same.
White Catherine, h 34 Warman av (H).
White Catherine (wid John), b 774 E Washington.
White Charles A, meats, rear 152 Lexington av, h 112 same.
White Charles A, soldier U S Arsenal.
White Charles B, agt, h 257 N East.
White Charles F, carp, h 22 Warman av (H).
White Charles G, grocer, E Mkt House, h 230 Bright.
White Charles I (White & Co), b 705 E Market.
White Charles L, trav agt, b 257 N East.
White Chemical Co, Ahira R White pres, mnfrs Tamazula chewing gum, 190 S Meridian.
White Clara, h 26 Chapel.
White Conyers A, oils, 69 S Linden, h same.
White Daniel, coachman 284 N Meridian.
White Daniel, lab, b 28 Roanoke.
White Dora, h 236 E Wabash.
White Edmund, janitor, r 56 Thorpe blk.
White Edmund J, watchman, h 108 Roanoke.
White Edward, brakeman, r 4 S Station (B).
White Edward F (Webster & White), b 705 E Market.
White Edwin F, clk The Indpls News, h 290 E St Clair.
White Edwin J, lab, b 25 N Beville av.
White Edwin M, musician Empire Theater, b 135 E New York.
White Elbert A, helper, h School (B).
White Eliza A wid Robert W), dry goods, 512 W Addison (N I), h same.

We Buy Municipal ~ Bonds ~

THOS. C. DAY & CO,
Rooms 325 to 330 Lemcke Bldg.

White Ernest F, clk, b 630 E Washington.
White Francis M, butcher, h 21 McGinnis.
White Frank, lab, h 180 Sheffield av (H).
White Frank, mach, r 294½ Mass av.
White Frank C, chief dep clk Indiana Supreme Court, h 579 Park av.
White Frank L, plumber, h 432 W McLene (N I).
White Frank M, grocer, E Mkt House, b 287 Douglass.
White Frederick, lab, b 153 Agnes.
White Frederick W, condr, h 61 W 14th.
White Frederick W, treas Warren-Scharf Asphalt Paving Co, res New York city.
White Gardner T, mngr S H Knox & Co, h 242 N Alabama.
White George, h rear 169 Lexington av.
White George, lab, b 126 Ash.
White George, lab, h 45 Lee (W I).
White George C, clk, b 658 College av.
White George E, lineman, b 64 Oak.
White George W, trav agt, h 658 College av.
White Guy E, mach hd, b 79 Hill av.
White Harry O, bkkpr Wm B Burford, h 273 N New Jersey.
White Harry L, clk, r 84 E New York.
White Harry W, clk, b 224 Bright.
White Herman B, salesman E C Atkins & Co, b 45 Arch.
White Hiram C, shoemkr, h 38 Rhode Island.
Wh te Horace B, brakeman, b 705 E Market.
White Hughes W, tailor, 56½ N Illinois, h 224 Bright.
White Ida L, grocer, 198-200 N Senate av, h 390 N West.
White Isaac G, b 39 W Pratt.
White James, h 217 S East.
White James, porter Hanna Hotel.
White James D, cigars, 43 Mass av, h same.
White James E, butcher, h 23 N Reisner (W I).
White James E, ins agt, h 1538 N Capitol av.
White James F, mngr, h 130 N Senate av.
White James L, condr, h 42 N State av.
White James W (White & Harrison), b 109 John.

EAT
QUAKER BREAD
ASK YOUR GROCER FOR IT.
THE HITZ BAKING CO.

CARPETS CLEANED LIKE NEW. TELEPHONE 818
CAPITAL STEAM CARPET CLEANING WORKS

BENJ. BOOTH PRACTICAL EXPERT ACCOUNTANT. Thirty years' experience. First-class credentials. Room 18, 82½ E. Washington St. Indianapolis, Ind.

The Old Red Mle Sherman European Restaurant || 18 and 20 S. Meridian St. Established 8.

ESTABLISHED 1876. TELEPHONE 168.
CHESTER BRADFORD,
SOLICITOR OF PATENTS,
AND COUNSEL IN PATENT CAUSES.
(See adv. page 6.)
Office:—Rooms 14 and 16 Hubbard Block, S.W. Cor. Washington and Meridian Streets, INDIANAPOLIS, INDIANA.

White James W, lab, h 43 Depot (B).
White Jane (wid Henry), h 182 Muskingum al.
White Jeremiah, lab, h s s 8th 2 w of canal.
White Joel B, farmer, h 705 E Market.
White John, clk, b 86 E Ohio.
White John, electrician, h 162 E Morris.
White John, lab, h 25 Everett.
White John, lab, h 621 N Senate av.
White John, waiter, r 27 Fayette.
White John D, painter, r 22 Ryan blk.
White John F, ballplayer, b 79 John.
White John F, mngr Indiana Labor Leader, 25 S Delaware, h 162 Hoyt av.
White John F, printer, h 169 Lexington av.
White John H Right Rev, Bishop of the Diocese of Indiana, h 242 N Penn.
White John J, boilermkr, b 507 E Georgia.
White John L, car rep, h 51 Hope (B).
White John Q, paperhngr, h 150 Bellefontaine.
White John W, carp, 163 Davidson, h same.
White John W, clk, r 233 W Maryland.
White John W, weigher, h 68 Bates.
White Joseph M, brakeman, h 109 Bates.
White Joseph P, plumber, b 253½ S Delaware.
White Julia, h 25 Columbia al.
White Lee A, porter, b 409 N Pine.
White Lena, h 166 W Chesapeake.
White Levi W, meats, 543 W Udell (N I), h 406 W Shoemaker (N I).
White Line Fast Freight, Louis J Blaker agt, 1 E Washington.
White Lois A, sec Christian Woman's Board of Missions, b 172 N New Jersey.
White Marcellus, watchman, h 6 Lawn (B).
White Marshall, confr, b 96 Lexington av.
White Mary, r 115 N Illinois.
White Mary (wid Joseph), h 395 Bellefontaine.
White Mary (wid Nicholas), h 98 Dunlop.
White Mary A, h 181 Meek.
White Mary A (wid Nathaniel G), h 155 Spann av.
White Mary E (wid Marshall), b 181 College av.
White Michael, lab, b 94 Deloss.

CORRUGATED IRON CEILINGS AND SIDING.
ALL KINDS OF REPAIRING.
O. B. ENSEY,
TELEPHONE 1562.
COR. 6TH AND ILLINOIS STREETS.

White Michael C, lab, h 262½ E Georgia.
White Michael R, car rep, h 79 John.
White Milton, lab, b e s Hubbard 3 s of Clifford av.
White Minnie, stenog Edenharter & Mull, b 195 N East.
White Nicholas, engr, b 98 Dunlop.
White Oakley M, clk Murphy, Hibben & Co, b 430 E McCarty.
White Oliver, lab, b 41 Ellen.
White Oliver G, car rep, h 47 S Austin (B).
White Omer, lather, h 661 W 22d (N I).
White Paul H, draughtsman Indiana Bicycle Co, h 18 The Chalfant.
White Patrick, tmstr, r 2 McGill.
White Patrick A, chief clk Spencer House.
White Pompey, lab, b 308 E Court.
White Remmy, bellboy The Bates.
White Ribbon House, Frances G Clark propr, 95 N Meridian.
White Richard, lab, b 273 Lafayette.
White Richard, lab, h 910 Madison av.
White Riley, condr, h 17 Beech.
White Riley F, clk N Y Store, h 1049 E Michigan.
White Rosini, pdlr, b 155 Harmon.
White Rush, mngr, h 390 N West.
White Samuel, h 8 Haugh (H).
White Samuel, lab, h 407 W North.
White Samuel, lab 122 N Penn.
White Samuel A, contr, 79 Hill av, h same.
White Sarah E (wid Martin), h 250½ S Meridian.
White Susan M, genl sec Young Women's Christian Assn, b 801 N New Jersey.
White Thomas, fireman, b 860 E Washington.
White Thomas G, carriages, 30 S Penn, r 113 N Illinois.
White Thomas H, billiards, 16 Prospect, h 75 Fayette.
White Thomas J, express, h 104 Chadwick.
White Walter S, lab, h 39 Poplar (B).
White Wayman T, janitor, h 56 Thorpe blk.
White Wm, bricklyr, h 56 Eureka av.
White Wm, condr, b 115 Highland pl.
White Wm, engr, b 116 Spann av.
White Wm lab, b 14 Reynolds av (H).
White Wm, plastr, h 65 S East.
White Wm A, electrotyper, h 127 Agnes.
White Wm A, polisher, h 119 Locke.
White Wm A, lab, h 93 Woodburn av (W I).
White Wm E, dentist, 228 W Michigan, b 192 W 1st.
White Wm E, painter, r 250½ S Meridian.
White Wm F, lab, h 64 Holmes av (H).
White Wm H, carp, h 192 Bellefontaine.
White Wm H, confr, 213 Howard (W I), h same.
White Wm H, cook, h 730 N West.
White Wm R, agt, h 39 Jones.
White Wm R, condr, h 177 Columbia av.
White Wm S driver, b 294 Douglass.
White Wm S, plastr, h 175 Elizabeth.
White Wm T, h 384 N Senate av.
White Wm T, lab, h 26 Roanoke.
White Wm T, lab, r 72 W Ohio.
White & Co (Charles I White), printers, 37½ Virginia av.
WHITE & HARRISON (James W White, James Harrison), Contractors, 109 John.
Whitebread Catherine (wid Peter), h 681 S Meridian.
Whitebread George, uphlr, b 661 S Meridian.
Whitecotton Benton H, bricklyr, h 589 Mass av.

TUTEWILER UNDERTAKER, No. 72 WEST MARKET STREET. TELEPHONE 216.

OF PHILADELPHIA. from anxiety and old age from want.
For particulars apply to D. W. EDWARDS, General Agent, 508 Indiana Trust Building.

THEODORE F. SMITHER

Whitecotton Charles W, condr, h 961 N Alabama.
Whitecotton John, policeman, h 330 N California.
Whiteford James, lab, h 18 N Haugh (H).
Whitehall Alexander L, h 1047 E Michigan.
Whitehead Anna J (wid Moses S), h 612 N Illinois.
Whitehead Bertha M, stenog, b 523 Central av.
Whitehead Dallas, lab, h 27 McCauley.
Whitehead Edward B, engr, h 76 John.
Whitehead Felix G, carp, r 180 W Vermont.
Whitehead Francis M, carp, h n s Herbert 2 w of Gent (M P).
Whitehead Harry L, b 523 Central av.
Whitehead Herbert L, b 612 N Illinois.
Whitehead John B, bkkpr American Press Assn, h 86 Hoyt av.
Whitehead John K, blksmith, h 592 Morris (W I).
Whitehead John R, grocer, 36 Crawford, h same.
Whitehead Louis, lab, h 49 Prospect.
Whitehead Louise I, teacher Public School No 8, b 86 Hoyt av.
Whitehead Nancy J (wid Murphy), h 44 Cleaveland blk.
Whitehead Thomas J, carp Insane Asylum.
Whitehead Wm, car rep, h Sutherland (B).
Whitehead Wm, lab, h Addison (M J).
Whitehead Wm C, h 523 Central av.
Whiteley Clay, h 933 N Meridian.
Whiteley George, h 24 W 11th.
Whiteley John, paperhngr, h 60 Church.
Whiteman John H, policeman, h 161 Cornell av.
Whiteman John W, h 108 King av (H).
Whiteman Omer S, student, b 197 N Illinois.
Whitenack David S, h 227 E 7th.
Whitenack Frederick D, lab, b 275 E Ohio.
Whitenack Ida M, stenog The McGilliard Agency Co, b 227 E 7th.
Whitenack Nannie E, cashr P B Ault & Co, b 227 E 7th.
Whitesell Arthur, clk, h 142 Blackford.
Whitesell Arthur A, constable, 26 N Delaware, h 314 Yandes.
Whitesell Charles J, lab, b 190 N East.
Whitesell Charles L, carp, h 12 Cornell av.
Whitesell Samuel M, lab, b 407 Newman.
Whiteside Dora E, b 434 E St Clair.
Whiteside Fielding A, lab, b 144 Madison av.
Whiteside George, tmstr, b 370 Union.
Whiteside James, carp, r 212 E Market.
Whiteside Omer T, lab, b 138 N Pine.
Whiteside Wm H, trav agt, b 18 Arch.
Whiteside Wm J, mdse broker, 27½ S Delaware, h 434 E St Clair.
Whiteside Wm T, lab, h 138 N Pine.
Whitfield Allen, lab, b rear 309 E Washington.
Whitfield Amanda, h e s Hubbard 3 s of Clifford av.
Whitfield Bright, lab, h 807 Mass av.
Whitfield Carey, lab, h 623 E 7th.
Whitfield Eliza, h rear 309 E Washington.
Whitfield Henry, lab, h w s Indianapolis av 2 s of 16th.
Whitfield Nellie (wid Bristowe), h s w cor Indianapolis av and 16th.
Whitford Harry G, clk, b 1 Hanway.
Whitford Henry T, lab, h 1 Hanway.
Whiting Francis E, plumber, h 395 N California.
Whiting James G, actor, b 225 English av.
Whiting Thomas B, trav agt The A Burdsal Co, b 174 N Illinois.

THE WHEN IS A WORLD BEATER.

Whiting Timothy M, h 1750 N Meridian.
Whitinger Jacob, car rep, h 8 N Brightwood av (B).
Whitley Albert, lab, h 288 Alvord.
Whitlock Charles, lab, h 598 E 10th.
Whitlock Claude, opr W U Tel Co, r 222 N Capitol av.
Whitlock Daisy, h 53½ Russell av.
Whitlock Frank M Rev, pastor Fellowship Congregational Church, h 599 Central av.
Whitlock Frederick B, salesman Natl Malleable Castings Co, b 294 N Meridian.
Whitlock George E, lab, h 116 Rhode Island.
Whitlock George N, foreman, h 482 Highland.
Whitlock Harry E, clk, b 421 E Georgia.
Whitlock James H, painter, h 29 Crawford.
Whitlock James H, painter, h 421 E Georgia.
Whitlock John, lab, h 744 N West.
Whitlock John H, clk Great Atlantic and Pacific Tea Co, h 64 Bates.
Whitlock Margaret (wid Michael), h 11 Guffin.
Whitlock Michael, lab, b 598 E 10th.
Whitlock Pearl, cutter, b 29 Crawford.
Whitlock Pinkie, b 63 Brookside av.
Whitlock Wilbert, insp, h 103 Woodburn av (W I).
Whitlock Wm T, foreman, b 421 E Georgia.
Whitlock Wm W, mach, h 63 Brookside av.
Whitman Barbara (wid John), b 129 Locke.
Whitman George, patternmkr, b 129 Locke.
Whitman John H, mer police, h 161 Cornell av.
Whitman Sarah J (wid Daniel), b 164 Brookside av.
Whitmore J D, pres Noel Bros Flour Feed Co, res Dayton, O.
Whitmore Samuel A, contr, h 97 Andrews.
Whitney Asbury, lab, h 257 Prospect.
Whitney Elizabeth (wid Theophilus D), h 28 Center.
Whitney George W, clk H P Wasson & Co, h 383½ Indiana av.
Whitney Harry, lab, h 28 Center.
Whitney James, hostler n s Washington 1 e of Sherman Drive.
Whitney John A, lab, b 28 Center.
Whitney John E, lab, b 106 Minerva.

THE A. BURDSAL CO.
Manufacturers of
Paints and Colors
VARNISHES,
Brushes, Painters' and Paper Hangers' Supplies.
34 AND 36 SOUTH MERIDIAN STREET.

COMPOSITION ROOFING MATERIALS. BEST IN THE MARKET. TELEPHONE 861. OFFICE, 151 WEST MARYLAND ST.

ELECTRICIANS | DON'T FORGET US. ALL WORK GUARANTEED. C. W. MEIKEL, Tel. 466. 96-98 E. New York St.

DALTON & MERRIFIELD { LUMBER South Noble St., near E. Washington

INDIANA ELECTROTYPE CO. :: BEST WORK. LOWEST PRICES.
23 WEST PEARL ST., INDIANAPOLIS, IND. JOB WORK. BOOK PLATES. BEST PATENT BASE ON THE MARKET. All Orders Promptly Filled.

KIRKHOFF BROS.
Steam and Hot Water Heating Apparatus,
Plumbing and Gas Fitting.
102-104 SOUTH PENNSYLVANIA ST.
TELEPHONE 910.

Whitney John M, foreman, h 106 Minerva.
Whitney Nelson, lab, b 13 Ellsworth.
Whitney Oscar M, trav agt, r 297 N East.
Whitney Richard B, h 221 E North.
WHITNEY WILLISTON H, State Agt White and Middleton Gas and Gasoline Engines, and Dealer in Gas Regulators, 74 Virginia av, h 116 Belmont av (H).
Whitridge Frederick, broommkr, b 180 W 7th.
Whitridge Harry R, clk, b 282 Douglass.
Whitridge Ola D, h 282 Douglass.
Whitridge Samuel, painter, h 180 W 7th.
Whitridge Samuel jr, painter, b 180 W 7th.
Whitridge Wm, painter, b 180 W 7th.
Whitsett A Noble, bkkpr Charles T Whitsett, b 1094 N Meridian.
WHITSETT CHARLES T (Successor to C E Kregelo & Whitsett), Funeral Director, 123-125 N Delaware, Office Tel 564; h 1094 N Meridian, Tel 570.
Whitsett John W, b 1094 N Meridian.
Whitsit Benjamin C, bricklyr, h 1323 N Delaware.
Whitsit Caroline M (wid John A), h 809 N Meridian.
Whitsit George L, bricklyr, h 80 Laurel.
Whitsit Gertrude B, teacher, b 1323 N Delaware.
Whitsit Jennie S (wid Jesse S), h 22 Pleasant.
Whitsit John, cabtmkr, b 160 Prospect.
Whitsit Martha L (wid Courtland E), h 160 Prospect.
Whitsitt Edward K, engr, h 374 Cedar.
Whitson Courtney B, b 82 E North.
Whitson Tobias, yardmaster, h 112 Bates.
Whitson Wm, h 1745 N Meridian.
Whitson Wm H, blksmith, h 574 Jefferson av.
Whittaker, see also Whitaker.
Whittaker George, lab, r rear 33 S Alabama.
Whittaker Ida (wid Allen N), h 178 S New Jersey.
Whittaker Joshua E, ins agt, h 118 S Summit.

LIME
BUILDING SUPPLIES,
Hair, Plaster, Flue Linings,
The W. G. Wasson Co.
130 INDIANA AVE. Tel. 989.

Whittaker Wm E, baker, b Illinois House.
Whitted Annie (wid John V), confr, 391 W New York, h same.
Whitted Mary C (wid John), grocer, 146 Elizabeth, h same.
Whittemore Edward L, vice-pres Natl Malleable Castings Co, res Toledo, O.
Whitten Massie (wid Doc), h 1224 Northwestern av (N I).
Whittenburg Elbert E, mach, h 192 Columbia av.
Whittenburg Smith R, ironwkr, b 82 Michigan av.
Whittier David L, h 624 N Penn.
Whittinghill John C, mer police, h 36 Yandes.
Whittinghill Wm L, lawyer, 19 Baldwin blk, h 49 Malott av.
Whittlesey Elizabeth K (wid Stephen L), r 5½ Shelby.
Whittlesey Vernon K, plumber, r 5½ Shelby.
Whitty John M, laundry, 60 W Maryland, h same.
Whitworth Sampson, lab, h 187 W 3d.
Whorton, see Wharton.
Whyte, see also White.
Whyte Johanna, stenog Ry Officials' and Employes' Accident Assn, b 637 E Ohio.
Whyte John M, janitor, h 637 E Ohio.
Wich Barbara (wid Andrew), b 121 Blake.
Wich Henry, baker, 121 Blake, h same.
Wichman Charles C L, h 52 Dougherty.
Wichmann Anton, lab, h 28 Iowa.
Wick Albert, lab, h 149 Kansas.
Wick Alice B, reference asst Public Library, b 178 Christian av.
Wickard Franklin E, meats, 49 E Mkt House, h 323 Yandes.
Wickard John B, h 552 Broadway.
Wickard Joseph, h 547 Park av.
Wickard Willard S, mngr J H Murry & Co, b 373 Ash.
Wickenhoefer Ernest E, tailor, h 325 Coburn.
Wickens Jerusha, stenog, b 22 Vinton.
Wicker Lindsey, lab, b 252 W 22d.
Wicker Mary A, student, b 46 Cushing.
Wickers Henry E, lab, h 48 Keystone av.
Wickers Wm H, lab, h 279 English av.
Wickersham Wm A, engr, h 46 Warren av (W I).
Wickes, see also Weeks.
Wickes George F, painter, h 50 Lafayette av.
Wickes Wm E, driver, h 774 W Washington.
Wickham George E, carp, h 27 Empire.
Wickliff Mary E (wid Tolly), h 341 Tremont.
Wickliff Peter, porter, h 96 Howard.
Wicks Charles H, clk, r 9 S Senate av.
Wicks Maud A, supt training department City Hospital.
Wicks George W, mach hd, b 105 N Rural (B).
Widgeon Wm E, foreman, b Sherman House.
Widner Samuel, h 96 Yeiser.
Widner Samuel, lab, r rear 176 E Washington.
Widolff Charles B, lab, h 105 Blake.
Wiebke Charles H, car rep, h 19 Tecumseh.
Wiebke Charles H jr, trav agt Severin, Ostermeyer & Co, h 848 LaSalle (M P).
Wiebke Edward A C, plumber, b 19 Tecumseh.
Wiebke Frederick, carp, h 145 John.
Wiebke Frederick, lab, b 439 E Ohio.

Parlor, Bed Room, Dining Room, Kitchen. Furniture W. H. MESSENGER, 101 E. Wash. St., Tel. 491.

ALL KINDS OF HEAVY AND LIGHT GRAY IRON CASTINGS } McNamara, Koster & Co. } Foundry and Pattern Shop
Phone 1593. 212-218 S. Penn. St.

Wiebke Frederick jr, clk Charles Mayer & Co, b 145 John.
Wiebke Henry F, car rep, b 19 Tecumseh.
Wiedenhaupt Albert, sawyer, h 151 Deloss.
Wiedenhaupt August G, lab, h 93 Kansas.
Wiedenhaupt Charles, lab, b 93 Kansas.
Wiedenhaupt Elmer, lab, h 151 Deloss.
Wiedenhaupt Herman, mach, h 677 S East.
Wiedenhaupt Herman, mach hd, h 458 E North.
Wiedenhorn Wm R, baker Parrott & Taggart, h 78 Dunlop.
Wiedmann Frank, mach, h 261 Yandes.
Wiegand Anthony (Wiegand & Son), h 844 N Illinois.
Wiegand Catherine M (wid John G), h 447 S Meridian.
Wiegand Conrad, lab, b 241 Lincoln la.
Wiegand Frank, barber, b 241 Lincoln la.
Wiegand George B (Wiegand & Son), b 844 N Illinois.
Wiegand John W, patternmkr, h 189 Bright.
Wiegand Lula M, bkkpr, b 447 S Meridian.
Wiegand Michael, lab, h 241 Lincoln la.
Wiegand Wm, filer, h 114 Minerva.
Wiegand Wm W, clk, b 67 English av.
WIEGAND & SON (Anthony and George B), Florists, 838 N Illinois, Tel 183.
WIEGEL WM, Mnfr of Show Cases, 6 W Louisiana, h 108 Greer. (See right side lines and adv in Classified Show Case Mnfrs.)
Wiegman Frank H, mach hd, b 209 Fletcher av.
Wiegman Oscar C, opr W U Tel Co, b 209 Fletcher av.
Wiegman Sophia M (wid Christian), h 209 Fletcher av.
Wiehenstroth Margaret (wid Christopher), h 591 Madison av.
Wiellmann Jacob, h w s Rural 2 n of S Brookside av.
Wieman Thomas, lab, h 61 Jones.
Wiemann Henry F, bkkpr Slatts & Poe, b 118 Gresham.
Wiemann John, clk, h 594 College av.
Wienke, see also Weinke.
Wienke Otto E, finisher, h 179 Pleasant.
Wienke Wm, farmer, h n s 30th 2 e of Northwestern av (M).
Wienke Wm, shoemkr, 179 Pleasant, b same.
Wienke Wm F, plumber, b 277 N Pine.
Wierhake Louisa (wid Wm), h rear 428 S East.
Wiese, see also Weis, Weiss and Wise.
Wiese Andrew H, car insp, h 1248 E Michigan.
Wiese Anton (H C Wiese & Co), res Cumberland, Ind.
Wiese Charles C H, clk, b 35 N East.
Wiese Charles F W, clk P C C & St L Ry, b 1248 E Michigan.
Wiese Charles H, h 283 E Ohio.
Wiese Christian, undertaker, 39 N East, h 35 same.
Wiese Frederick C F, driver, h 122 Fulton.
Wiese Frederick P, tel opr C C C & St L Ry, h 52 Depot (B).
Wiese George D, canmkr, h 104 Dunlop.
Wiese Henry, carp, h 62 N Arsenal av.
Wiese Henry, carp, h 30 Lincoln la.
Wiese Henry C (H C Wiese & Co), h w s Lake av 3 s of Washington av (I).
Wiese H C & Co (Henry C and Anton Wiese), lumber, 1208 E Washington.

Henry H. Fay,
40½ E. WASHINGTON ST.,
FIRE INSURANCE, REAL ESTATE,
LOANS AND RENTAL AGENT.

Wiese John, boilermkr, h 72 Holloway av.
Wiese Julia (Wiese & Fuehring), b 62 N Arsenal av.
Wiese Theodore C, mach, b 62 N Arsenal av.
Wiese Wm F, lab, h rear 23 Palmer.
Wiese Wm W, clk C C C & St L Ry, b 62 N Arsenal av.
Wiese & Fuehring (Julia Wiese, Emma Fuehring), milliners, 405 E Washington.
Wiethe Henry J, collr J S Cruse, b 66 Fletcher av.
Wiggam Carlton, city agt, h 196 Lexington av.
Wiggam Martha J (wid Hiram), r 177 Shelby.
Wiggam Travanion, city agt, h 145 Minerva.
Wiggins Bessie B, grocer, 480 W Michigan, h 116 Minerva.
Wiggins Charles, lab, h 109 Decatur.
Wiggins Charles F, coremkr, h 8 Minkner.
Wiggins Clinton, carp, r 225 N Senate av.
Wiggins Coleman H, tmstr, h w s Rembrant 3 n of Indiana av (M P).
Wiggins Dudley H, clk The Indpls Stove Co, b 75 E St Joseph.
Wiggins Dulania S, student, r 106½ E New York.
Wiggins Henry D, mach, h 272 W New York.
Wiggins Howard, clk, r 35 The Chalfant.
Wiggins Irvin M, condr, h 185 Fletcher av.
Wiggins Mount V, buyer The Bowen-Merrill Co, h 276 Bellefontaine.
Wiggins Norman A, clk, h 324 E North.
Wiggins Sarah H (wid Joseph), society editor The Indpls Sentinel, h 75 E St Joseph.
Wigginton David T, carp, 22 Elk, h same.
Wiggs Russell C, clk N Y Life Ins Co, b 81 Fletcher av.
Wiggs Wheeler, h 81 Fletcher av.
Wigley Henry A, carp, h 42 N California.
Wigson Wm G, soldier U S Arsenal.
Wikel Henry A, lab, h 1060 W Vermont.
Wikel Henry H, physical director Y M C A, r 270 N Delaware.
Wiker Charles E, trimmer, h 383 S Illinois.
Wiker Daniel L, carp, h 54 Kansas.

WILL GO ON YOUR BOND
American Bonding & Trust Co.
Of Baltimore, Md. Approved as sole surety by the United States Government and the different States as Sole Surety on all Forms of Bonds.
W. E. BARTON & CO., General Agents,
504 Indiana Trust Building.
LONG DISTANCE TELEPHONE 1918.

THE FRED DIETZ CO. WOODEN PACKING BOXES MADE TO ORDER. FACTORY AND WAREHOUSE TRUCKS. 400 Madison Avenue. Telephone 654.

BUSINESS EDUCATION A NECESSITY. TIME SHORT. DAY AND NIGHT SCHOOL. SUCCESS CERTAIN AT THE PERMANENT, RELIABLE
Indianapolis BUSINESS UNIVERSITY

HENRY R. WORTHINGTON JET and SURFACE CONDENSERS 64 S. PENN. ST. Long Distance Telephone 284.

UNION CO-OPERATIVE LAUNDRY (COMPOSED OF LAUNDRY GIRLS.) NOS. 38, 40 AND 42 VIRGINIA AVENUE
T. E. SOMERVILLE, MANAGER—TELEPHONE 1269. INDIANAPOLIS, IND.

HORACE M. HADLEY
INSURANCE AND LOANS
66 E. Market Street, Basement
TELEPHONE 1540.

Wilberger Jane E (wid Gilbert), h 123 W 6th.
Wilberger Louisa, h 278 Fayette.
Wilberger Thompson, lab, h 506 N California.
Wilch Catharine (wid Christian), b 337 Central av.
Wilcox Andrew J, circulator The Sun, h 77 W 7th.
Wilcox Esther A, violin teacher, b 77 W 7th.
Wilcox George H, b 22 Ruckle.
Wilcox Henry P, painter, h 42 English av.
Wilcox Louis F, agt, h 437 E Washington.
Wilcox Nancy E (wid David H), h w s Mill 1 n of 10th.
Wilcox Olin C, trav agt, h 569 N Senate av.
Wilcox Thomas F, mach, h 56 Cushing.
Wilcox Wm W (Wilcox & Judd), h 22 Ruckle.
Wilcox & Judd (Wm W Wilcox, Wm F Judd), plumbers, 146 Mass av.
Wilcoxon Levi, salesman John L Moore, h 96 Andrews.
Wild David, clothing, 215 E Washington, h same.
Wild George, lab, b 266 S West.
Wild John, mach hd, h 266 S West.
Wild John F (Campbell, Wild & Co), res Anderson, Ind.
Wild Louis, clothing, 211 E Washington, h same.
Wild Morris, clk, b 533 Ash.
Wilde Edwin, sawmkr, b 575 S Illinois.
WILDE JOHN A, Bicycles, Mngr Metropolitan Cycle Co and Agt Remington Wheels, 108 Mass av, Tel 979; h 57 Oriental.
Wilde John A, sawmkr, b 575 S Illinois.
Wilde John H, foreman E C Atkins & Co, h 575 S Illinois.
Wilde Urban K, clk, b 575 S Illinois.
Wilder Eloise (wid Charles), b 1089 N Illinois.
Wildhack Wm A, auditor L E & W R R, h 201 Broadway.
Wilding Edgar E W, clk L E & W R R, b 123 N East.

COLLECTIONS
MERCHANTS' AND MANUFACTURERS' EXCHANGE
Will give you good service.
J. E. TAKKEN, Manager,
Union Building, over U. S. Pension Office.
73 West Maryland Street.

Wilding George, clk R R Bennett, b 123 N East.
Wilding Harry, printer, b 627 E Vermont.
Wilding Herbert, bkkpr, b 627 E Vermont.
Wilding John, printer, h 545 E Vermont.
Wilding Josephine (wid Charles), h 123 N East.
Wilding Robert, mach, h 627 E Vermont.
Wildman James A (Wildman & Glover), h 415 N Penn.
Wildman & Glover (James A Wildman, John B Glover), real est, 19 Talbott blk.
Wildner Charles, lab, b e s Senate av 2 s of 26th.
Wildofsky Albert, pdlr, b 95 Eddy.
Wildofsky Samuel, janitor, h 95 Eddy.
Wildrick Wm D, lab, h 370 Union.
Wildridge George G, dyer, b 1531 N Capitol av.
Wildridge Wm, dyer, h 1531 N Capitol av.
Wilertt George, brakeman, b 29 N State av.
Wiles Addie M, teacher Public School No 9, b 199 Broadway.
Wiles Adolph, driven wells, 1242 E Washington, res Greenfield, Ind.
WILES DANIEL H, Money and Loan Broker, Stocks, Bonds and Mortgage Loans, 46½ N Penn, h 199 Broadway.
Wiles Ernest M, buyer Murphy, Hibben & Co, h 737 N Delaware.
Wiles Frank M, asst phys Insane Hospital.
Wiles Frederick, bartndr, r 83 English av.
Wiles Frederick B, clk, b 199 Broadway.
Wiles Nellie F, h 424 N Delaware.
Wiles Sarah A (wid Christian H), h 46 King av (H).
Wiles Theodore, painter, h 23 Vine.
Wiles Thomas H, clk Natl Malleable Castings Co, b 46 King (H).
Wiles Walter W, clk Kingan & Co (ltd), h 97 Woodburn av (W I).
Wiles Wm, driver, r rear 27 Camp.
Wiles Winifred H, h 424 N Delaware.
Wiley, see also Willey and Wylie.
Wiley Alfred, r 5½ Indiana av.
Wiley Alonzo, printer, b 10 Hall pl.
Wiley Charles H, mach, b 12 Temple av.
Wiley Cordelia (wid Frank A), h 199 W South.
Wiley David, boilermkr, b 228 S West.
Wiley David G, sec Indpls Electrotype Foundry, 17-25 W Georgia, h 221 N East.
Wiley Edward A, watchmkr, h 307 E St Clair.
Wiley Edward E, mngr C F Adams Co, b 10 Hall pl.
Wiley Eleanor J (wid Lewis C), h 10 Hall pl.
Wiley Eliza G (wid Wm Y), b 240 N Penn.
Wiley Emmett H, trav agt Tanner & Sullivan, h 489 W Francis (N I).
Wiley Fay, h 118 W Georgia.
Wiley Francis M, trav agt, h 291 N Liberty.
Wiley Frederick H, office, room 1, 68½ E Market, b 240 N Penn.
Wiley Frederick W, tailor, r 55 Dearborn.
Wiley Harry, helper, b 532 E 8th.
Wiley Inez E (wid George), dressmkr, 27 Grove, h same.
Wiley James M, painter, b 532 E 8th.
Wiley Jesse, b 248 Yandes.
Wiley John A, blksmith, b 532 E 8th.
Wiley Joseph, lab, b e s Northwestern av 1 n of 30th.
Wiley Lucinda T (wid George M), h 464 W Madison (N I).
Wiley Mary E (wid Harrison), h 12 Temple av.

CLEMENS VONNEGUT 184, 186 and 192 E. Washington St. BUILDERS' HARDWARE, Building Paper. Duplex Joist Hangers

Wiley Ulric Z, Judge Appellate Court of Indiana, 114 State House.
Wiley Wm A, bkkpr McKee Shoe Co, h 25 Pleasant.
WILEY WM T, Expert Linotype Operator on Book Work, 75 W Market, h 12 Stoughton.
Wilgus Wm, grocer, 928 S Meridian, h same.
Wilharm Charles, car insp, h 150 S Spruce.
Wilharm Christian H, mach, b 150 S Spruce.
Wilharm Christian W, buyer, b 265 S Alabama.
Wilharm Henry W, clk, b 516½ E Washington.
Wilharm Sophia (wid Christian), h 265 S Alabama.
Wilhelm Albert L, car rep, h 26 S Austin (B).
Wilhelm Charles E, lab, h 35 Samoa.
Wilhelm Frederick, clk, h 54 S Arsenal av.
Wilhelm George, finisher, b 625 Madison av.
Wilhelm Louisa A (wid George K), b 108 Cornell av.
Wilhelm Sophia (wid Carl), b 538 S New Jersey.
Wilhelm Theresa (wid Casper), h 625 Madison av.
Wilhelm Wm H, bkkpr Insane Hospital.
Wilhite Hattie E, clk U S Pension Agency, h 126 W Vermont.
Wilhite James, barber, 112 Howard, h same.
Wilhite John R, clk, h 88 S Judge Hardinf (W I).
Wilhite Mary A (wid Herbert), h 286 W 6th.
Wilhite Mary J (wid John W), h 108 S Judge Harding (W I).
Wilhite Noah H, jeweler, 131 William (W I), h 10 Martha (W I).
Wilhite Wm, coachman 927 N Alabama.
Wilhite Wm A, motorman, h 33 Warren av (W I).
Wilkening Frederick A, asst bkkpr Tanner & Sullivan, b 283 Davidson.
Wilkening Henry, jeweler Julius C Walk & Son, h 41 McKim av.
Wilkens, see also Wilkins.
Wilkens Albert H, clk, b 109 Ruckle.
Wilkens Harley J, clk Parry Mnfg Co, b 109 Ruckle.
Wilkens Henry C, mach, b 109 Sanders.
Wilkens John A, ins agt, h 109 Ruckle.
Wilkerson Albert, constable, h 65 S Shade (B).
Wilkerson Thomas C, cashr Levey Bros, b 886 N Penn.
Wilkes Earl D, clk L E & W R R, r 155 N New Jersey.
Wilkes Wm M, clk, h 636 Marlowe av.
Wilkey John W, driver, h 532 W Washington.
Wilking Charles J, boxmkr, h 119 Blake.
Wilking Charles T, foreman, h 117 Blake.
Wilking Frederick C, bartndr, b 16 Greer.
Wilking Henry, uphlr, b 16 Greer.
Wilking Henry P M, uphlr, h 55 Dearborn.
Wilking Louisa (wid Henry), h 16 Deloss.
Wilking Mary (wid Henry), h 16 Greer.
Wilking Otto A, uphlr, b 16 Greer.
Wilkins, see also Wilkens.
Wilkins Charles F, fireman, h 92 Oliver av (W I).

Wilkins Charles H, carp, h 1398 N Senate av.
Wilkins Clarence E, fireman, h 1 S Beville av.
Wilkins Clarence H, painter, h 859 Cornell av.
Wilkins Cooper W, clk, b 174 N Illinois.
Wilkins Eva (wid Thomas W), b 474 Highland av.
Wilkins Frank, city fireman, h 22 W 22d.
Wilkins Frank, mach, b 350 Columbia av.
Wilkins Frank S, butcher, h 10 E Michigan.
Wilkins Harry, hostler, h rear 21 Park av.
Wilkins John, lab, b 746 N Senate av.
Wilkins John, lab, b 420 W 22d (N I).
Wilkins John D, lab, h 3 Concord (H).
Wilkins John H, oiler, b w s Sugar Grove av 4 n of Vorster av (M P).
Wilkins John R, farmer, h 853 Milburn (M P).
Wilkins Joseph B, insp, h 1083 N Capitol av.
Wilkins Mary F (wid James E), h 409 W Addison (N I).
Wilkins Moses, mach, h 205 Blake.
Wilkins Noble O, mach, h 379 W 2d.
Wilkins Paul, clk, b 561 N Alabama.
Wilkins Wm A, reporter, h 561 N Alabama.
Wilkins Wm C, clk Penna Lines, h 143 W Michigan.
Wilkins Wm C, engr, b 151 Harrison.
Wilkins Wm F, bartndr, h 134 N Dorman.
Wilkins Wm H, driver, h 111 W 10th.
Wilkins Wm S, clk, b 561 N Alabama.
Wilkins Wm S, lab, h 111 W 10th.
Wilkinson Allen A (Greer-Wilkinson Co), h 852 N Penn.
Wilkinson Charles, baker, b 142 E 7th.
Wilkinson Charles L, clk, b 17 Pleasant.
Wilkinson Edgar B, phys, 201 Majestic bldg, b 524 N Senate av.
Wilkinson Edmond, lab, b 550 N Missouri.
Wilkinson Fidela M (wid Daniel), h 1100 N Senate av.
Wilkinson George, lab, b 159 W Merrill.
Wilkinson Herbert, porter, r 34 Bird.
Wilkinson John, tailor, 18½ N Meridian, h 1210 N Illinois.

GUIDO R. PRESSLER,
FRESCO PAINTER
Churches, Theaters, Public Buildings, Etc., A Specialty.
Residence, No. 325 North Liberty Street.
INDIANAPOLIS, IND.

DIANAPOLIS STEEL ROOFING AND CORRUGATING WORKS, 23 and 25 East South Street. S. D. NOEL, Proprietor.

David S. McKernan,
Rooms 2-5 Thorpe Block.
REAL ESTATE AND LOANS
Money to loan on real estate. Special inducements offered those having money to loan. It will pay you to investigate.

DIAMOND WALL PLASTER : Telephone 1410 BUILDERS' EXCHANGE.

UNION TRANSFER AND STORAGE CO. Cor. E. Ohio St. and C., C., C. & St. L. R'y Tracks

W. McWORKMAN

FIRE SHUTTERS
FIRE DOORS
METAL CEILINGS

[illegible] E. Washington St. Tel. [illegible]

[illegible]

GEO. J. MAYER
[illegible]
SEALS
[illegible]
[illegible] Meridian St. Ground Floor. Tel. [illegible]

A. METZGER AGENCY REAL ESTATE ESTABLISHED 1863.

LAMBERT GAS & GASOLINE ENGINE CO.
ANDERSON, IND. NATURAL GAS ENGINES

THOS. G. DAY & CO.

BICYCLES $85

EAT HITZ'S CRACKERS AND CAKES
ASK YOUR GROCER FOR THEM.

J. H. TECKENBROCK

DIAMOND WALL PLASTER { Telephone 1410 BUILDERS' EXCHANGE.

Cor. E. Ohio St. and C., C., C. & St. L. R'y Tracks. BEST FACILITIES FOR STORING AND TRANSFERRING MACHINERY AND MERCHANDISE.
UNION TRANSFER AND STORAGE CO.

W. McWORKMAN

FIRE SHUTTERS,
FIRE DOORS,
METAL CEILINGS.
930 W. Washington St. Tel. 1118.

Wilkinson Mary (wid Emanuel), b 545 Bellefontaine.
Wilkinson Pearl, coachman 673 N Delaware.
Wilkinson Perle (wid Arthur), supervisor of music, Public Schools, h 27 Morrison.
Wilkinson Philip, lawyer, 68 Lombard bldg, b 1100 N Senate av.
Wilkinson Samuel W, clk, b 527 Broadway.
Wilkinson Wm A, clk L E & W R R, h 527 Broadway.
Wilkison Junius, chairmkr, b 456 Mulberry.
Wilkison Rebecca (wid Wm), h 286 N New Jersey.
Wilkison Wm H, musician, b 286 N New Jersey
Wilks Oscar, blksmith, r 247½ E Washington.
Will Elizabeth (wid Frederick), h 172 Meek.
Will John J, cigarmkr, h 28 Larch.
Will Louis G, h 89 Stevens.
Willard Albert B, bkkpr, h 20 W 12th.
WILLARD ALBERT L, Sec National Identification Co, 19½ N Penn, h 1720 N Illinois.
Willard Charles, hostler, r 2 N Brightwood av (B).
Willard Deaf Mute Club, 41 Board of Trade bldg.
Willard Edward, pdlr, h 405 Indiana av.
Willard Eugene A, attendant Insane Asylum.
Willard Frances S, bkkpr George Merritt & Co, r 440 N Meridian.
Willard Harry S, clk, h 457 W Highland av (N I).
Willard Winifred H, bkkpr, b 20 W 12th.
Willbrandt Emil, h 581 N Capitol av.
Willbrandt Otto, clk, b 581 N Capitol av.
Willcox Anna, h 208 W St Clair.
Willcox Louis M, clk, b 208 W St Clair.
Willcox Wm H, bkkpr, b 208 W St Clair.
WILLCOX & GIBBS, Automatic Sewing Machine, 108 N Penn.
Willcuts Ann (wid John), h 417 E Washington.
Willem Jacob, bartndr, b n e cor West and Wabash.

GEO. J. MAYER,
MANUFACTURER OF
SEALS
STENCILS, RUBBER STAMPS, CHECKS, BADGES, DOOR PLATES, ETC.
5 S. Meridian St., Ground Floor. TEL. 1386

Willett Amanda E (wid Edward W), h 322 E Market.
Willett Clara (wid Wm), h 67 Dougherty.
Willett Edwin C, waiter, r 175 W Michigan.
Willett Elmer F, carp, b 86 Hosbrook.
Willett Frank M, cabtmkr, b 67 Dougherty.
Willett Henry G, lab, h 447 W Chicago (N I).
Willett Jesse E, tmstr, h 473 Highland av.
Willett Joseph, brakeman, b 23 Detroit.
Willett Lyman F, carp, b 113 Naomi.
Willett Mary A (wid Henry C), h 86 Hosbrook.
Willett Wm A, lab, b 174 Trowbridge (W).
Willett Wm J, clk, h 28 Clay.
Willey, see also Wiley and Wylie.
Willey Charles L, foreman, Outing Bicycle Co, b 453 W New York.
Willey George, attendant Insane Hospital.
Willey Mary J (wid John R), h 401 Blackford.
Willey Samuel, lab, h 3 Wilcox.
Willey Sylvester, h 704 Chestnut.
Willey Walter L, student, b 121 E New York.
Willhoff George J, car rep, h 83 English av.
Willhoff Lawrence J, foreman, b 83 English av.
Williams Abraham, lab, h 3 Carter.
Williams Ada M (wid Pollard), b 177 W 2d.
Williams Adney, gardener Insane Hospital.
Williams Albert, engr, h 445 Charles.
Williams Albert, lab, h 570 W McLene (N I).
Williams Albert E, clk Penna Lines, b 162 N Illinois.
Williams Albert O, lab, b 236 Brookside av.
Williams Albert R, lab, b 889 Morris (W I).
Williams Albertus, bkkpr Moffat & Co, r 178 N Alabama.
Williams Alcade, tel opr, h 207 Cornell av.
Williams Alexander, lab, b 38 Locke.
Williams Allan H, molder, h 4 Cleveland (H).
William Allen, lab, h e s Bismarck av 3 n of Emrich (H).
Williams Allen, lab, h 418 Superior.
Williams Alpha M, clk, h 47 Clifford av.
Williams Alphonso, clk, b 374 W Vermont.
Williams Alvarado L, bartndr, h 37 Peru av.
Williams Amanda (wid Wm), h 391 W 2d.
Williams Amelia (wid James H), dressmkr, h n s Brookside av 2 w of Atlas.
Williams Anderson, cook, h 299 Bright.
Williams Andrew J, boilermkr, h 9 Poplar (B).
Williams Angeline (wid Thomas H), b 143 Huron.
Williams Anna, laundress, b 435 Superior.
Williams Anna (wid Isaac), h 32 Detroit.
Williams Annie M, h 616 W Michigan.
Williams Archibald C, ins agt, b 106 Bates.
Williams Archibald L, driver, h w s Ritter av 3 n of Washington av (I).
Williams Ariadne F (wid John C), h 7 Elizabeth.
Williams Augustus A, tailor, h 170 Union.
WILLIAMS AUGUSTUS W, Rug, Silk Curtain and Carpet Mnfr, 169 Mass av, Tel 1074; h 142 Greer.
Williams Au Vern V, clk, h 53 Park av.
Williams Benjamin, lab, h 67 N Dorman.
Williams Benjamin A S, clk, b 42 The Windsor.
Williams Benjamin F, trav agt, h 1002 N Penn.

A. METZGER AGENCY ESTABLISHED 1863. REAL ESTATE

Williams Bertrand T, clk The Indpls News, b 833 N Meridian.
Williams Broady, lab, h w s James 3 n of Sutherland (B).
Williams Bros (Wilford M, James L and Lemuel G), washing tea, 214 S Meridian.
Williams Bruce, porter, b 198 W 2d.
Williams Carmi P (Williams & Flickinger), h 1116 N Penn.
Williams Catharine G, bkkpr, b 927 N Meridian.
Williams Catherine J (wid Charles A), h 617 Madison av.
Williams Charles, car insp, h 150 S Spruce.
Williams Charles C, glass, 149 S Meridian, b The Bates.
Williams Charles E, bricklyr, h 324 N Noble.
Williams Charles E, lab, h 61 Lynn av (W I).
Williams Charles F Rev, pastor South Calvary Baptist Church, h 55 Maple.
Williams Charles F, tel opr, h 923 Shelby.
Williams Charles G, coachman s e cor Meridian and 8th.
Williams Charles J, painter, b 139 N Delaware.
Williams Charles L, lab, h 488 Newman.
Williams Charles O, h 79 Birch av (W I).
Williams Charles R, editor The Indpls News, h 833 N Meridian.
Williams Charles R, insp, h 913 Morris (W I).
Williams Charles T, clk, b 1365 N Capitol av.
Williams Chester P, b 250 Talbott av.
Williams Christopher, mach, b 150 Spruce.
Williams Clara J, teacher Public School No 9, b 654 Park av.
Williams Clare I, tel opr C C C & St L Ry, b 239 S Alabama.
Williams Clarence, lab, h rear 10 Lafayette.
Williams Clement, lab, b 204 Elm.
Williams Clementine (wid John), h 119 Roanoke.
Williams Coleman, driver, h 416 Superior.
Williams Cora, nurse, b 39 W St Joseph.
Williams Cora (wid Edgar), h 200 Jefferson av.
Williams Crawford H, jeweler, 145 W Washington, h 38 N Reisner (W I).
Williams Cynthia A (wid James W), h 374 W Vermont.
Williams Daniel, lab, h 310 W Court.
Williams Daniel G, trav agt, h 1044 N Capitol av.
Williams David A (D A Williams & Co), h 816 College av.
Williams David E, condr, h 162 Huron.
Williams DeWitt, lab, b 180 Agnes.
Williams Dudley W, butcher, b 190 E Market.
Williams D A & Co (David A Williams, James H Billingsley), com mers, 131 E Maryland.
Williams Edgar, barber, r 294½ Mass av.
Williams Edgar H, mngr, h s s Washington 5 e of Sherman Drive.
Williams Edith M, teacher Public School No 36, b 1002 N Penn.
Williams Edward, tmstr, r 156 W Washington.
Williams Edward, waiter, r 163 Bird.
Williams Edward, painter, b 147 Locke.
Williams Edward A, driver, b 41 Valley.
Williams Edward L, coremkr, h 103 Belmont av.
Williams Edward W, trimmer, b 139 N Delaware.

THOS. C. DAY & CO.
Financial Agents and Loans.
We have the experience, and claim to be reliable.
Rooms 325 to 330 Lemcke Bldg.

Williams Edwin, mach, b 1365 N Capitol av.
Williams Edwin L, h 12 Pleasant.
Williams Eleanor F, teacher Public School No 8, b 1002 N Penn.
Williams Elijah E, condr, h 80 Columbia av.
Williams Eliza (wid Joseph), b w s Rural 1 n of Clifford av.
Williams Elizabeth, artist, h 178 N Alabama.
Williams Ella, h 188 W Court.
Williams Ella P (wid Jesse S), h 331 Bates.
Williams Ellsworth, driver, h 21½ Chapel.
Williams Elmer C, waiter, r 177½ W Washington.
Williams Elmer R, restaurant, 315 E Washington, h same.
Williams Elvira M (wid August), h 142 Greer.
Williams Elza, driver, h 372 N Missouri.
Williams Emanuel, driver, r 36 Roanoke.
Williams Emma A, h 173 W Michigan.
Williams Emma D (wid Philip), h 421 N Illinois.
Williams Emory H, lab, b 450 S West.
Williams Esther H (wid Albert), h 143 St Mary.
Williams Ethel, h rear 222½ E Washington.
Williams Eugene (Williams & Greene), r rear 685 N Delaware.
Williams Fannie, h 140 Maple.
Williams Fannie M (wid James F), h 537 Virginia av.
Williams Fernandez C, paperhngr, h 234 W Michigan.
Williams Frank, b n w cor Gale and Willow (B).
Williams Frank, lab, b 344 Columbia av.
Williams Frank, lab, b 310 W Court.
Williams Frank B, painter, b 25 N Station (B).
Williams Frank G, lab, h 443 W Francis (N I).
Williams Frank W, city dist clk P O, b 250 Talbott av.
Williams Frank W, patternmkr, b 34 Brett.
Williams Frederick, lab, b 119 Ft Wayne av.
Williams Frederick R, carp, h 36 Birch av (W I).

EAT
HITZ'S
CRACKERS
AND CAKES.
ASK YOUR GROCER FOR THEM.

BICYCLES $5 DOWN. MONTHLY. Best Wheels. Best Terms. WHEELMEN'S CO. 31 W. OHIO ST. LONG DISTANCE TEL. 1855.

J. H. TECKENBROCK General House Painter, 94 EAST SOUTH STREET.

FIDELITY MUTUAL LIFE—PHILADELPHIA, PA.
$75,000,000, Insurance In Force. $3,500,000, Death Losses Paid. $1,500,090, Surplus. A. H. COLLINS {General Agent, Baldwin Block.

BITUMINOUS COAL IN CAR LOADS TO DEALERS AND MANUFACTURERS. ROOMS 42 AND 43 WHEN BUILDING. Edwardsport Coal & Mining Co.

ESTABLISHED 1876. TELEPHONE 168.
CHESTER BRADFORD,
SOLICITOR OF PATENTS,
AND COUNSEL IN PATENT CAUSES.
(See adv. page 6.)
Office:—Rooms 14 and 16 Hubbard Block, S.W. Cor. Washington and Meridian Streets, INDIANAPOLIS, INDIANA.

Williams George, r 143½ N Delaware.
Williams George, clk, b 1388 Paris av.
Williams George, lab, r 122 Agnes.
Williams George, lab, h 180 Agnes.
Williams George lab, b 67 N Dorman.
Williams George, lab, h 177 W 2d.
Williams George E, lab, h 573 E 8th.
Williams George L, motorman, h 217 S New Jersey.
Williams George S, b 1388 Paris av.
Williams George W, lab, b 281 N Pine.
Williams Gottlieb, carp, h 175 S Reisner (W I).
Williams Grace P, teacher, b 421 N Illinois.
Williams Griffith W (Peerless Foundry Co), b 147 Bates.
Williams Hannah (wid John), b 79 Birch av (W I).
Williams Hanover W, junk, 448 Blake, h same.
Williams Harrison H, h 616 W Michigan.
Williams Harrison, lab, b 229½ E Washington.
Williams Harry, janitor, b 671 N Senate av.
Williams Harry, lab, h 605 Madison av.
Williams Harry, switchman, h 810 Cornell av.
Williams Harry D, fireman, h Stuart (B).
Williams Harry N, foreman Indiana Bicycle Co, h 66 Dawson.
Williams Harry R, bkkpr J B Allfree Mnfg Co, h 48 Andrews.
Williams Harry T, lab, h 262 Martindale av.
Williams Hattie, r 84 Cleaveland blk.
Williams Helena C, teacher Public School No 10, b 654 Park av.
Williams Henry, lab, h 177½ Muskingum al.
Williams Henry, lab, h rear 66 College av.
Williams Henry jr, waiter, b rear 66 College av.
Williams Henry B, lab, b 32 N McLain (W I).
Williams Henry C, carp, h 223 Hoyt av.
Williams Henry J, lab, h w s Rural 1 n of Clifford av.
Williams Herman H, brakeman, h 21 Jefferson av.
Williams Homer D, supt American Steel Co, b 272 N Meridian.

76 N. Pennsylvania St. Phone 598.

Williams Hubbard W, painter, h 84 Wallack.
Williams H Jerome, mngr Church Press Assn, 734 Lemcke bldg, h 18 Park av.
Williams Irving, r 194 N Illinois.
Williams Isaac, lab, b 65 Cornell av.
Williams Isaac, lab, h n w cor Park and Morris (B).
Williams Isaac N, mer police, b 42 Davis.
Williams Isabel, h rear 23 Athon.
Williams Jackson tinner, r 23 N West.
Williams Jacob R, saloon, 102 Howard, h same.
Williams James, driver, h 82 Fayette.
Williams James, express, b 557 W Washington.
Williams James, lab, h 399 Blackford.
Williams James A, carp, h 250 Talbott av.
Williams James A, tmstr, h 943 S East.
Williams James D, lab, h 137 Elizabeth.
Williams James E, motorman, h 1145 Northwestern av.
Williams James E, paperhngr, h 1388 Paris av.
Williams James F, lab, b 63 Rhode Island.
Williams James H, lab, h 30 Hiatt (W I).
WILLIAMS JAMES L (Williams Bros), Physician, Eye, Ear and Throat a Specialty, 36 E Ohio, h 798 N Capitol av.
Williams Jane, h 481 W Ontario (N I).
Williams Jennie, h 116 Columbia al.
Williams Jennie J, clk U S Pension Agency, b 421 N Illinois.
Williams Jeremiah, lab, h 15 Sumner.
Williams Jeremiah, lab, h rear 19 Center.
Williams Jesse, lab, b n w cor Park and Morris (B).
Williams Jesse E, brakeman, b 30 Crawford.
Williams Jesse M, photog, 88 Paca, h same.
Williams John, clk, h 107 Benton.
Williams John, driver, h 15 Center.
Williams John, foreman John H Spahr, r 75 E Wabash.
Williams John, lab, h 1 Center.
Williams John, lab, h 170 E Court.
Williams John, lab 677 N Illinois.
Williams John, lab, h 43 Maple.
Williams John, lab, b rear 61 Maxwell.
Williams John, lab, h rear 484 W North.
Williams John, lab, h 6 Sheridan.
Williams John A, driver, h 465 Mulberry.
Williams John C, mach, h 76 Bloomington.
Williams John E, clk, b 397 Blake.
WILLIAMS JOHN G, Attorney, 407-413 Indiana Trust Bldg, Tel 1936; h 287 Park av.
Williams John H, agt, h 147 Union.
Williams John H, carp, h 77 Minerva.
Williams John H, coachman 303 Park av.
Williams John H, painter, h 282 E Miami.
Williams John H N, molder, b 100 Bismarck av (H).
Williams John I, brakeman, b 38 S State av.
Williams John J, bricklyr, b 252 E Washington.
Williams John J, ins, h 1375 N Capitol av.
Williams John L, porter, h 116 Martindale av.
Williams John M, h 233 N Pine.
Williams John M, engr, b 729 E Market.
Williams John N, lab, h 150 Trowbridge (W).
Williams John O, mach, h 1130½ E Washington.
Williams John R, lab, h 3 Center.

C. ZIMMERMAN & SONS | SLATE AND GRAVEL ROOFERS 19 South East Street.

DRIVEN WELLS And Second Water Wells and Pumps of all kinds at CHARLES KRAUSS', 42 S. PENN. ST., Telephone 465.

Williams John T, barber, 504 College av, h 217 Cornell av.
Williams John T, brakeman, h 24 Temple av.
Williams John T, engr, h 302 Cornell av.
Williams John T, janitor, h 23 Omer.
Williams John W, carp, h 174 W Morris.
Williams John W, spec agt The McGilliard Agency Co, h 1026 N Penn.
Williams Joseph, carp, h 433 Home av.
Williams Joseph A, filer, h 67 N Olive.
Williams Joseph J, clk, h 28 Maple.
Williams Joseph M, boilermkr, h 25 N Station (B).
Williams Joseph N, lab, h 150 Trowbridge (W).
Williams Joseph W, tmstr, h 123 Weghorst.
Williams Kate, teacher Public School No 14, b s s Washington 5 e of Sherman Drive.
Williams Keziah A (wid Caleb S), b 36 King av (H).
Williams Lafayette, engr, h 1034 W Washington.
Williams Landonia B (wid John), teacher Public School No 19, h 518 N West.
Williams Lee H, salesman The McElwaine-Richards Co, h 25 Henry.
Williams Lemuel G (Williams Bros), h 22 Byram pl.
Williams Lewis, lab, h 507 Mulberry.
Williams Lillie, h 23½ Harris.
Williams Lloyd, mach, h 263 Alvord.
Williams Louis, restaurant, 195 S Illinois, h 401 Columbia av.
Williams Louis E, paperhngr, b s e cor Washington and Addison (M J).
Williams Lucinda (wid Charles S), b 25 N Station (B).
Williams Lucy (wid Alexander), h 38 Locke.
Williams Luther, tel opr I U Ry Co, h 48 Lexington av.
Williams Mack, driver, b 166 W 2d.
Williams Margaret (wid John), h 232 W Market.
Williams Margaret (wid Robert), h 57 Fayette.
Williams Margaret A (wid Edward P), h 743 E Michigan.
Williams Maria L (wid David N), h 308 N Pine.
Williams Marshall, coachman 674 N Delaware.
Williams Martha, restaurant, 64 Indiana av, h same.
Williams Martha G (wid David B), h 53 Prospect.
Williams Mary, laundress, h 27 Fayette.
Williams Mary E (wid Benjamin A), millinery, 356 Mass av, h same.
Williams Mary J (wid Ransom T), h 218 Bright.
Williams Mary L (wid Myron B), b 110 Talbott av.
Williams Mary L, music teacher, 200 N Capitol av, b same.
Williams Matthew, ironwkr, b 285 S Capitol av.
Williams Millicent (wid Edmond), h 91 Newman.
Williams Minerva, b 37 English av.
Williams Moses, lab, h 863 Mass av.
Williams Moses A, lab, h 420 Hanna.
Williams M Ray, agt Northwestern Mutual Life Ins Co, h e s Grand av 2 s of University av (I).
Williams Nancy A (wid Daniel W), h 503 N Alabama.

EQUITABLE LIFE ASSURANCE SOCIETY OF THE UNITED STATES.
RICHARDSON & McCREA
Managers for Central Indiana,
79 East Market St. Telephone 182.

Williams Nettie (wid Clarence E), h 121 W Vermont.
Williams Nicholas McC, clk, h 551 N Illinois.
Williams Noel W, lawyer, 103½ E Washington, r same.
Williams Oliver, brakeman, b 151 Virginia av.
Williams Oliver H P, b 70 Mayhew.
Williams Onis, lab, b 7 Elizabeth.
Williams Orland, painter, h 508 N West.
Williams Oscar, driver, b 61 Maxwell.
Williams Pearl, h 22 Tuxedo.
Williams Peter A, h s s Railroad 1 e of Central av (I).
Williams Philip, brakeman, b 54 N Belmont av (H).
Williams Phygellus, tmstr, h e s Rural 3 n of Sutherland (B).
Williams Plymouth, tmstr, b 7 Elizabeth.
Williams Porter F, lab, h 415 Howard (W I).
Williams Randolph, h s e cor Washington and Addison (M J).
Williams Randolph, lab, r 323 Clinton.
Williams Rees R, engr, b 439 S Illinois.
Williams Reuben, huckster, h 143 Huron.
Williams Reuben, lab, h s s 9th 2 e of Mill.
Williams Richard, boilermkr, h 79 Lockerbie.
Williams Richard, lab, b 312 W Court.
Williams Robert E, grocer, 501 E 7th, h 537 same.
Williams Robert T, janitor, h 122 N Meridian.
Williams Rosa (wid McClary), dressmkr, 246 N Illinois, h same.
Williams Roxie, condr, h 80 Columbia av.
Williams Rufus, lab, b 321 Blake.
Williams Rufus H, molder, h 100 Bismarck av (H).
Williams Samuel P, lab, h e s Rural 1 n of Sutherland (B).
Williams Samuel W, lab, b 245 W 5th.
Williams Sarah (wid Charles C), r 139 N Meridian.
Williams Schuyler C, b 1002 N Penn.
Williams Schuyler S, clk, h 37 Catharine.
Williams Seneca, lab, h 54½ Mayhew.
Williams Stephen, lab, h 116 Martindale av.

STENOGRAPHERS FURNISHED.
EXPERIENCED OR BEGINNERS, PERMANENT OR TEMPORARY.
S. H. EAST, State Agent,
The Williams Typewriter,
55 THORPE BLOCK, 87 EAST MARKET ST.

ERTEL STEAM LAUNDRY 26 and 28 N. Senate Avenue. Tel. 1348. WE WILL CALL FOR AND DELIVER YOUR WORK. SATISFACTION GUARANTEED.

ELLIS & HELFENBERGER { ENTERPRISE FOUNDRY & FENCE CO. 162-170 S. Senate Ave. Tel. 958.

THE HOGAN TRANSPER AND STORAGE COMP'Y
Household Goods and Pianos Moved—Packed—Stored...... Baggage and Package Express Machinery and Safes a Specialty Cor. Washington and Illinois Sts. TELEPHONE No. 675.

The Central Rubber & Supply Co. PHONE 922. 79 S. ILLINOIS ST., INDIANAPOLIS, IND. Hose, Belting, Packing, Clothing, Druggists' Sundries, Bicycle Tires, Cotton Hose, Etc. New York Belting & Packing Co., L't'd.

A death rate below all other American Companies, and dividends from this source correspondingly larger.
The Provident Life and Trust Company Of Philadelphia.
D. W. EDWARDS, General Agent,
508 Indiana Trust Building.

Williams Susan, h 285 W North.
Williams Taylor, hostler J H Spahr, r 75 E Wabash.
Williams Thaddeus K, trav agt, h 340½ E Market.
Williams Thomas, lab, h rear 17 Cornell av.
Williams Thomas, lab, h 312 W Court.
Williams Thomas A, lab, b 194 W Ray.
Williams Thomas J, carp, h 450 S West.
Williams Thomas M, brakeman, b 1127 E Washington.
Williams Thomas T, brakeman, h 617 Madison av.
Williams Thomas T, bricklyr, h 364 S Olive.
Williams Thomas W, waiter, r 323 W North.
WILLIAMS TYPEWRITER, S H East State Agt, 55 Thorpe Blk. (See right bottom cor cards.)
Williams Vastine W, foreman, h 109 Sharpe av (W).
Williams Wallace, lab, h rear 29 W Michigan.
Williams Wallace, lab, h e s Race 5 s of Raymond.
Williams Walter, waiter, h 200 W 1st.
Williams Walter B, cook 373 Ash.
Williams Walter D, solr Kingan & Co, h 307 N Pine.
Williams Walter O, asst supt E C Atkins & Co, b 110 Talbott av.
Williams Watkin H, mach, h 1365 N Capitol av.
Williams Wilford M (Williams Bros and Williams & Hunt), h 702 N Illinois.
Williams Wm, condr, h 60 W 13th.
Williams Wm, lab, b 32 Detroit.
Williams Wm, lab, h 201 Northwestern av.
Williams Wm, lab, h 765 E 10th.
Williams Wm, soap mnfr, 273 W McCarty, h 474 S Illinois.
Williams Wm C, clk U S Pension Agency, h 127 S Olive.
Williams Wm E, b 127 S Olive.
Williams Wm E, lab, h s s 9th 1 w of canal.
Williams Wm F (Hoosier Sweat Collar Co), h 927 N Meridian.
Williams Wm G (Peerless Foundry Co), b 147 Bates.

Julius C. Walk & Son, Jewelers Indianapolis.
12 EAST WASHINGTON ST.

Williams Wm H, hack driver 83 E Wabash, b 173 W Ohio.
Williams Wm H, lab, h 21 Gatling.
Williams Wm H, student, h 571 W Highland av (N I).
Williams Wm H, trav agt, h 64 N Gale (B).
Williams Wm L, collr N Y Store, h 262 Huron.
Williams Wm L, lab, h 85 Trowbridge (W).
Williams Wm M, butcher, h 407 E 17th.
Williams Wm M, clk, h 407 Harrison av.
Williams Wm M, cook, h rear 82 Yandes.
Williams Wm O, phys, 36 King av (H), h same.
Williams Wm P, lab, h 9 Poplar (B).
Williams Wm R, letter carrier P O, h 654 Park av.
Williams Wm R, reporter, b 249 Bellefontaine.
Williams Wm T, lab, b 310 W Court.
Williams Wm W, mach, b 374 W Vermont.
Williams Winston F, wheelmkr, h 27 Buchanan.
Williams Wright, driver, r 199 S Illinois.
Williams Zachariah, express, h 92 Torbet.
Williams Zwinglius R, lab, h 127 Darnell.
WILLIAMS & FLICKINGER (Carmi P Williams, Elmer E Flickinger), State Agts John Hancock Mutual Life Insurance Co, 95-96 Lombard Bldg, Tel 1588.
Williams & Greene (Eugene Williams, Lewis W Greene), barbers, 48 Malott av.
Williams & Hunt (Wilford M Williams, Mary C Hunt), soap mnfrs, 701 S West.
Williamson Alfred M, clk, b 92 Andrews.
Williamson Bessie M, stenog Lewis C Walker, b 424 Virginia av.
Williamson Charles, foreman, h w s La Salle 2 n of Brett (M P).
Williamson Charles D, lab, h 433 Virginia av.
Williamson Clinton, clk, h 1090 W Vermont.
Williamson David A, bkkpr, h 15 N Reisner (W I).
Williamson Dwight W (D W Williamson & Co), h 224 Park av.
Williamson D W & Co (Dwight W and Otis E Williamson), veneer mnfrs, 52 John.
Williamson Edmund, engr, h 65 N Judge Harding (W I).
Williamson Edward C, painter, h 150 N Belmont av (H).
Williamson Edward R, tel insp, b 41 Barth av.
Williamson Elizabeth (wid Wm), h 78 Dugdale.
Williamson Emma, h 121 E Ohio.
Williamson Felix, janitor, h 62 Howard.
Williamson Frances M (wid Marshall D), b 224 Park av.
Williamson George W, painter, b 41 Barth av.
Williamson George W, plastr, h n e cor Parker and Clifford avs.
Williamson Henry E, agt, h 37 Jefferson av.
Williamson Iza, officer Indiana Reformatory.
Williamson James A, engr, b 1035 W Washington.
Williamson James O, printer Indpls Journal, h 297 E McCarty.
Williamson John, mach, r 211 N Illinois.
Williamson John H, lab, b 165 Coburn.
Williamson John M, livery, 78 N Alabama, butter, 88 E Mkt House, h 92 Andrews.
Williamson John W, carp, b 630 E St Clair.
Williamson John W, phys, 15 Commercial blk, r same.

OTTO GAS ENGINES | BUILDERS' EXCHANGE S. W. Cor. Ohio and Penn. Telephone 535.

Becker & Son Charles Becker Jacob Becker Jr. Merchant Tailors. 21 N. Penn. St. Tel. 934

Williamson Joseph H, carp, h 41 Barth av.
Williamson Louis, lab, h 528 W North.
Williamson Mary, dressmkr, 165 Coburn, b same.
Williamson Minerva S (wid Levi B), b 79 Lexington av.
Williamson Oliver E, City Clerk (W I), h 92 Kappus (W I).
Williamson Orpheus C, switchman, h 118 Windsor.
Williamson Otis E (D W Williamson & Co), h 477 Ash.
Williamson Robert C, watchman, h 89 Columbia av.
Williamson Samuel H, boarding 1100 W Washington (H).
Williamson Samuel M, lab, b 89 Columbia av.
Williamson Samuel T, mach, h 79 Lexington av.
Williamson Sarah, h 421½ National rd.
Williamson Sheridan, plastr, 108 Clifford av, b same.
Williamson Sophronia (wid James), h 165 Coburn.
Williamson Wallace C, driver, h 213½ Mass av.
Williamson Warren, patternmkr, h 531 W Highland av (N I).
Williamson Wm, lab, r 276 Fayette.
Williamson Wm L, switchman, h 145 Sheffield av (H).
WILLIG CHARLES, Furniture, Carpets and House Furnishing Goods, 79 W Washington, Tel 1808; h 237 E South.
Willig Henrietta (wid Daniel), h 163 St Mary.
Willing Hermon S, printer, b 52 S State av.
Willis Albert C, cooper, h 6 Minerva.
Willis Albert H, bricklyr, h 602 E St Clair.
Willis Amanda (wid Jackson), h 10 Roanoke.
Willis Andrew J, h rear 50 Coffey (W I).
Willis Anthony, driver, h 43 Hosbrook.
WILLIS CASSIUS M C, Undertaker, 184 Indiana av, Tel 1173; h 283 N California.
WILLIS CHARLES W, Bicycle Instructor Bellis Bicycle Co, 27 Ingalls Blk, r 19 E North.
Willis Edward, lab, h 119 Kappus (W I).
Willis Ella (Offord & Willis), h 1116 N Penn.
Willis Frank, hostler, h 77 Chapel.
Willis Frederick B, tinner, b 448 Indiana av.
Willis Frederick I, supt H T Hearsey Cycle Co, h 939 N Alabama.
Willis George, messenger U S Ex Co, r 250 E Market.
Willis George, waiter, h 195 W 3d.
Willis George W, lab, b 189 Patterson.
Willis Gilbert, lab, h 442 E 7th.
Willis Harry, driver, h 151 Spann av.
Willis Jasper, driver, r 152 W Washington.
Willis Jonathan, tinner, 448 Indiana av, h same.
Willis Lee, lab, b 120 Patterson.
Willis May, teacher, b 448 Indiana av.
Willis Peyton, lab, h 186 Agnes.
Willis Richard, lab, b 40 Locke.
Willis Wm, cooper, h 120 Patterson.
Willits, see also Willett.
Willits Charles B (M A Willits & Co), h 452 Blake.
Willits Clinton, cooper, b 89 Patterson.
Willits Ellis J, storekpr, h 69 W 19th.
Willits Jehu L, carp, b 69 W 19th.
Willits Josiah C, carp, h 89 Patterson.

Henry H. Fay,
40½ E. Washington St.,
REAL ESTATE,
AND LOAN BROKER.

Willits Mary A (M A Willits & Co), h 452 Blake.
Willits M A & Co (Mary A and Charles B Willits), wall paper, 236 W Washington.
Willits V Burton, mngr The Hay & Willits Mnfg Co, h 129 Talbott av.
Willits Walter R, hostler, h 36 N New Jersey.
Willkosky Frank, pdlr, h 132 Maple.
Willmann Charles, lab, h 88 Agnes.
Willmann Wm, coachman 1179 N Illinois.
Willms Wm, tailor, h 29 Shelby.
Willoeby Maria T (wid George), h 1027 N Senate av.
Willoughby Charles A, agt, r 10½ N Delaware.
Willoughby Clara, bkkpr, b 182 Lexington av.
Willoughby Sherman S, carp, h e s Lake av 9 s of Washington av (I).
Willoughby Willis S, engr, h 39 Gatling.
Wills Arthur G L, foreman, h 250 E McCarty.
Wills Bernard, engr, h 475 E Vermont.
Wills Charles A, salesman Fahnley & McCrea, h 218 Ramsey av.
Wills Edgar W, bkkpr, h 50 Randolph.
Wills George, lab, b 74 Sheffield (H).
Wills James A, blksmith, h 72 Sheffield (W I).
Wills John F, cutter, h 119 Patterson.
Wills John W, ins, r 130 W Vermont.
Wills Nora (wid Otto), h 72 Cleaveland blk.
Wills Wm, pedal bldr, b 56 Laurel.
Wills Willis W, carp, h 56 Laurel.
Willsey Eugene, baggageman, h 234 Prospect.
Willsey Henry J, policeman, h 164 Prospect.
Willsey Lewis B, driver, h 4 Hester.
Willsey Wm F, carp, h 62 William.
Willson, see also Wilson.
Willson Elizabeth E (wid Joseph), h 449 College av.
Willson Mary E, prin Public School No 23, b 449 College av.
Willson Victoria A, prin Public School No 18, b 449 College av.
Willy Mary J (wid John R), h 401 Blackford.

SALISBURY & STANLEY
OF ICE, SAFE AND BANK FIXTURES.
Contractors and Builders. Repairing of all kinds done on short notice. 177 Clinton St., Indianapolis, Ind. Telephone 999.

LIME, CEMENT, PLASTER FIRE BRICK AND CLAY SEWER PIPE, ETC. BALKE & KRAUSS CO., Cor. Market and Missouri Streets.

C. FRIEDGEN HAS THE FINEST STOCK OF LADIES' PARTY SLIPPERS and SHOES 19 NORTH PENNSYLVANIA ST.

SAMUEL LAING ▸ TIN, SLATE AND STEEL ROOFING 72 AND 74 EAST COURT STREET.

M. B. WILSON, Pres. W. F. CHURCHMAN, Cash.
THE CAPITAL NATIONAL BANK,
INDIANAPOLIS, IND.
Pays Interest on Time Certificates of Deposit.
Buys and Sells Foreign Exchange at Low Rates.
Capital, - - $300,000
Surplus and Earnings, 50,000
No. 28 S. Meridian St., Cor. Pearl.

Wilmans Francis A, phys, 60 Monument pl, r same.
Wilmington Anna E, music teacher, 184 Brookside av, b same.
Wilmington Arthur W, chief clk L E & W R R, b 124 E St Mary.
Wilmington Edward N, salesman Fahnley & McCrea, b 184 Brookside av.
Wilmington Eliza A (wid Edward M), h 124 St Mary.
Wilmington George A, printer, h 35 N Spruce.
Wilmington James N, finisher, b 124 St Mary.
Wilmington Oscar N, carp, h 184 Brookside av.
Wilmington Roseline M (wid Levi F), h 111 Brookside av.
Wilmot Alferetta C, teacher Public School No 31, b 373 Coburn.
Wilmot Frank L, confr, 78 N Illinois, r same.
Wilner George, florist, b e s Capitol av 2 s of 30th.
Wilson, see also Willson.
Wilson Albert, bodymkr, b 206 Lexington av.
Wilson Albert, tmstr, h e s Arlington av 4 n of Walnut av (I).
Wilson Albert C, lab, h s s Walnut 2 w of Sherman Drive.
Wilson Albert H, carp, h 1091 E Ohio.
Wilson Alexander, lab, b 167 Bismarck av (H).
Wilson Alexander C, huckster, h 544 E New York.
Wilson Alice (wid Harry H), b 232 Douglass.
Wilson Allen, lab, b 206 W 1st.
Wilson Alma W, artist, 1303 N Delaware, h same.
Wilson Almon E, engr, h 22 Brett.
Wilson Alonzo W, sawmkr, h 34 Brett.
Wilson Amelia (wid James D), grocer, 33 N East, b same.
Wilson Amos L, phys, 823 N Illinois, h 27 W 11th.
Wilson Andrew B, trav agt A W Stevens & Son, h 454 N California.

TUTTLE & SEGUIN,
28 E. Market Street.
Fire Insurance,
Real Estate, Loan
and Rental Agents.
TELEPHONE 1168.

Wilson Andrew J, farmer, h w s Good av 2 s of Railroad (T).
Wilson Andrew T, finisher, h 82 Oliver av (W I).
Wilson Andrew W, h 512 N New Jersey.
Wilson Ann G (wid Charles G), b 266 S Senate av.
Wilson Anna (wid John), h 72 Maple.
Wilson Anna A (wid James), b 127 E St Joseph.
Wilson Anna V (wid Junius), dressmkr, 98 Fulton, h same.
Wilson Arthur, clk, b 567 E Market.
WILSON ARTHUR N, Loans, 9, 156½ E Washington, b 76 N Arsenal av.
Wilson Asa B, lab, h 206 Lexington av.
Wilson Augustus, barber, h 232 E Pearl.
Wilson A E, trav agt, r 316 N Meridian.
Wilson Benjamin, express, h 307 Alvord.
Wilson Benjamin, porter The Denison.
Wilson Benjamin F, engr, h 313 Fletcher av.
Wilson Benjamin F, mer police, h 81 Maple.
Wilson Benjamin F, saloon, 116 S Reisner (W I), h same.
Wilson Benjamin I, lab, b 50 Locke.
Wilson Bert, lab, h 1091 E Ohio.
Wilson Calvin N, engr, h 134 Spann av.
Wilson Charles, clk George R Popp, h 51 Spann av.
Wilson Charles, painter, r 141 N Alabama.
Wilson Charles A, engr, h 100 Hiatt av (W I).
WILSON CHARLES A, M D (Faculty Prize Medical College of Ohio, 1879), Orthopedic Surgeon Wilson Surgical Institute, 81 W Ohio, h same.
Wilson Charles E, finisher, h 16 Shriver av.
Wilson Charles E, Governor's private sec, 6 State House, res Lebanon, Ind.
Wilson Charles E, painter, h 143½ Virginia.
Wilson Charles E, trav agt, h 129 E Walnut.
Wilson Charles F, lab, r 173 W Michigan.
Wilson Charles F, painter, h 756 N Illinois.
Wilson Charles H, hostler, r 30 S Penn.
Wilson Charles H, paperhngr, h 108½ Mass av.
Wilson Charles L, phys, 81 W Ohio, res Lawrence, Ind.
Wilson Charles T, clk, b 33 N East.
Wilson Charles W, tmstr, h 178 S Lee (W I.)
Wilson Charles W, grocer, 13 E Mkt House, h 35th and Central av.
Wilson Christopher C Rev, pastor Tabernacle Baptist Church, h 89 Rhode Island.
Wilson Clarence N, lab, h 118 Clinton.
Wilson Claude A, painter, h 20 Elder av.
Wilson Cora, stenog, b 444 Central av.
Wilson Daniel, lab, h 474 E 9th.
Wilson Daniel P, b 1326 N New Jersey.
Wilson Daniel W, lab, b 341 W Maryland.
Wilson David, carp, b 11 E South.
Wilson Delia (wid Thomas), h 65 Martindale av.
Wilson De Motte, teacher, h w s Brook 1 s of Church (I).
Wilson Donaldson A, fireman, b 103 Prospect.
Wilson Dudley K, creamery, 1 Fletcher av, b 109 S Noble.
WILSON EDGAR H, Druggist, 1 Bates, Tel 1071; h 342 E South.
Wilson Edmond G, clk, h 734 Ash.

SULLIVAN & MAHAN Manufacturers of all kinds of PAPER BOXES 41 W. Pearl St.

DIAMOND WALL PLASTER { Telephone 1410 BUILDERS' EXCHANGE.

Telephone 1798. 19 S. Ill St. } THE HOME LAUNDRY { WORK CALLED FOR AND DELIVERED.

Wilson Edward L, h 14 Reynolds av (H).
Wilson Edwin, lab, b 37 Drake.
Wilson Edwin C, shoecutter, b 512 N New Jersey.
Wilson Elizabeth (wid Caswell), b 137 Fletcher av.
Wilson Elizabeth, janitress, h 252½ Mass av.
Wilson Elmer L, grocer, 60 Jefferson av, h 40 same.
Wilson Emma J (wid John), janitress Halcyon blk.
Wilson Emma L (wid Walter B), h 268 N Alabama.
Wilson Emmett W, finisher, b 16 Shriver av.
Wilson Ernest, lab, h 10½ Clifford av.
Wilson Ernest, lab, b 53 Peru av.
Wilson Eugene M, mailing clk P O, b 333 N Illinois.
Wilson Eulah G, stenog, b 165 Ft Wayne av.
Wilson Everett F, lab, b s end Temperance (I).
Wilson Everett R, clk, r 173 E South.
Wilson Fannie M, boarding 162 Harrison.
Wilson Francenia A (wid Wm W), h s s Railroad 2 e of Central av (I).
Wilson Frank, baker The Bates.
Wilson Frank, cabtmkr, h 71 Villa av.
Wilson Frank, detective, h 491 E Market.
Wilson Frank, painter, h 756 N Illinois.
Wilson Frank E, clk R M S, r 27 Ft Wayne av.
Wilson Frank H, sec to genl supt C C C & St L Ry, n e cor Delaware and South, b 491 E Market.
Wilson Frank I, trav agt, b 134 W Ohio.
Wilson Frank M, lab, b 162 Harrison.
Wilson Frankie B (wid James A), h 100 N Senate av.
Wilson Franklin T, cooper, h 40 Everett.
Wilson George, lab, r 17 W Pearl.
Wilson George, tmstr, h e s James 1 n of Bloyd av (B).
Wilson George C, mach, h 129 Buchanan.
Wilson George T, lab, b 65 Martindale av.
Wilson George W, carp, r 149 S New Jersey.
Wilson George W, fireman, h 213 S Pine.
Wilson Georgetta (wid Joseph C), b 99 N State av.
Wilson Hannah (wid Elam), h 27 Jefferson av.
Wilson Harley A, engr, h 8 Brown av (H).
Wilson Harriet, nurse, 27 Warren av (W I), h same.
Wilson Harry, lab, b 268 Lafayette.
Wilson Harry B, clk L E & W R R, b 176 N East.
Wilson Harry H, clk L S Ayres & Co, b 734 Ash.
Wilson Harry W, mach, h 5½ Brookside av.
Wilson Harvey, lab, r 16 Center.
Wilson Harvey, molder, h 5 Frazee (H).
Wilson Hayes, lab, b 65 Martindale av.
Wilson Henrietta (wid Frank), h 165 Ft Wayne av.
Wilson Henry, r 75 W Ohio.
Wilson Henry, lab, b 326 Tremont.
Wilson Henry, lab, h e s Concord 3 s of Michigan (H).
Wilson Henry H, janitor, b 23 Omer.
Wilson Herbert C, stonecutter, b 268 W Vermont.
Wilson Hinson, driver, h 109 S Noble.
Wilson Homer H, clk Hildebrand Hardware Co, b 164 Fayette.

FRANK NESSLER. WILL H. ROST.
FRANK NESSLER & CO.
Tailors
56 EAST MARKET ST. (Lemcke Building),
INDIANAPOLIS, IND.

Wilson Horace D, carp, b 28 Byram pl.
Wilson Howard, carp, h 217 W 8th.
Wilson Ira, b rear 23 Center.
Wilson Isaac, carp, b e s Waverly 1 s of Sutherland (B).
Wilson Isaac B, lab, b s end Temperance (I).
Wilson Jacob M, hostler, h 3 Gardner's la.
Wilson James, r 102 S Illinois.
Wilson James, carp, h 228 N Senate av.
Wilson James, clk, b 190 N Missouri.
Wilson James, produce, b 46 S Capitol av.
Wilson James A, molder, h 215 Hoyt av.
Wilson James B, barber, b 11 E South.
WILSON JAMES B, Editor and Publisher The People, 37½ Virginia av, h same.
Wilson James B, lab, h 238 W Market.
Wilson James B, trav agt Murphy, Hibben & Co, b 269 E St Clair.
Wilson James C, ins agt, b 1525 N Meridian.
Wilson James E, filer, h 438 Mass av.
Wilson James F (Coughlin & Wilson), b 494 N Penn.
Wilson James F, patrolman, h 394 S East.
Wilson James F, pressman, b 166 E Michigan.
Wilson James G, carp, h 36 Brett.
Wilson James H, sec The Indpls Book and Stationery Co, h 818 N Alabama.
Wilson James H, sec and treas Daggett & Co, h 466 N Meridian.
Wilson James N, h 252½ Mass av.
Wilson James W, actor, h 163½ E Washington.
Wilson James W, lab, h 104 John.
Wilson Jamison H, trav agt, r 144 E New York.
Wilson Jefferson M, grocer, 31 Traub av, h 2 same.
Wilson Jeremiah S, porter, b 793 N Senate av.
Wilson Jesse E, clk, b 105 Greer.
Wilson Johanna (wid Highland), h 345 N Alabama.
Wilson John, h 28 Roanoke.
Wilson John, clk, r 269 E St Clair.
Wilson John, dairy, s s Brookville rd 2 w of P C C & St L Ry (S), h same.

Haueisen & Hartmann
163-169 E. Washington St.
FURNITURE,
Carpets,
Household Goods,
Tin, Granite and China Wares, Oil Cloth and Shades

THE WM. H. BLOCK CO. 7 AND 9 EAST WASHINGTON STREET. DRY GOODS, HOUSE FURNISHINGS AND CROCKERY.

London Guarantee and Accident Co. (Ltd.) Employers', Public and Teams' Liability. Workmen's Collective Insurance and Fidelity Bonds
GEORGE W. PANGBORN, General Agent, 704-706 Lemcke Bldg. Telephone 140.

FRANK K. SAWYER || Reliable Fire Insurance. Reasonable Rates.
74 E. MARKET STREET. Telephone 8.

JOSEPH GARDNER,
TIN, IRON, STEEL AND SLATE ROOFING,
GALVANIZED IRON CORNICES & SKYLIGHTS.
37, 39 & 41 KENTUCKY AVE. Telephone 322.

Wilson John, foreman Kingan & Co, r 175 W New York.
Wilson John, lab, b 230 Roanoke.
Wilson John, lab, b 144 N Senate av.
Wilson John, lab, h 616 N West.
Wilson John, painter, h 133 Elizabeth.
Wilson John A, b 26 Brett.
Wilson John A, blksmith, h 73 Villa av.
Wilson John C, lab, h 28 N Belmont av (H).
Wilson John C, lab, h 80 Meikel.
Wilson John E, tel opr, b 116 Cornell av.
Wilson John F, painter, h 646 E 8th.
Wilson John G, lab, r 76 N New Jersey.
Wilson John G, stock breeder, 131 N Meridian, res Lawrence, Ind.
Wilson John H, h 268 W Vermont.
Wilson John H, lawyer, 38½ E Washington, r 174 E Ohio.
Wilson John H, saloon, 396 S Illinois, h same.
Wilson John J, lab, b 265 W Washington.
Wilson John L, clk R M S, h 446 E McCarty.
Wilson John McC, baker Parrott & Taggart, h 270 S Senate av.
WILSON JOHN R, Lawyer, Rooms 11-12 Aetna Bldg, 19½ N Penn, Tel 588; h 174 Central av.
Wilson John S, carp, 599 Park av, h same.
Wilson John S, brakeman, b 2 Traub av.
Wilson John T, clk R M S, r 40 Lorraine bldg.
Wilson John T, plastr, h 697 Park av.
Wilson John W, boarding 333 N Illinois and 173 E Market.
Wilson John W Rev, pastor Mayflower Congregational Church, h 914 N New Jersey.
Wilson John W, plastr, h 113 Sharpe av (W).
Wilson Joseph, bracemkr, h 366 N West.
Wilson Joseph R (Wilson & Son), h 15 S Senate av.
Wilson Josephine (wid Lorenzo D), h 68½ Mass av.
Wilson J Russell, cashr Peoria Rubber and Mnfg Co, b 27 The Windsor.
Wilson Kate C, teacher Public School No 26, h 18 Cornell av.

J. S. FARRELL & CO.
STEAM AND HOT WATER HEATING AND PLUMBING CONTRACTORS
84 North Illinois Street. Telephone 382.

Wilson Laura (wid Alfred), h rear 1379 N Senate av.
Wilson Leon, mach hd, b 40 Everett.
Wilson Levi, plastr, h 88 Willow.
Wilson Lew E, carp, h 27 Jefferson av.
Wilson Lewis, lab, h 189 Alvord.
Wilson Lewis, mach hd, h 38 McIntyre.
Wilson Lyda, h 288 Indiana av.
Wilson Mack S, hostler, b 295 E Court.
Wilson Margaret A, h 134 W Ohio.
Wilson Margaret E (wid James), h 179 W Vermont.
Wilson Margaret E, boarding 11 E South.
Wilson Martin E, collr, h 546½ E Ohio.
Wilson Mary (wid Jordan), h 442 Superior.
Wilson Mary (wid Wm), h 246 English av.
Wilson Mary, seamstress Insane Asylum.
Wilson Mary A (McFall & Wilson), h 86 N East.
Wilson Mary A (wid Thomas), h 233 Clinton.
Wilson Mary B, housekpr 81 Nordyke av (W I).
Wilson Mary C (wid Thomas), b 1506 Northwestern av (N I).
Wilson Mary E, b 224½ W Washington.
Wilson Mary E (wid Fleming L), h w s Hillside av 1 s of 17th.
Wilson Mary F (wid Wm), h 418 Blake.
Wilson Mary L, bkkpr Capital Life Ins Co of Ind, b 23 Ft Wayne av.
Wilson Maze L, bill clk Fahnley & McCrea, b 105 Greer.
WILSON MEDFORD B, Pres The Capital National Bank, h 684 N Delaware, Tel 1799.
Wilson Melvin L, grocer, 1091 E Michigan, h same.
Wilson Minerva J, h rear 23 Center.
Wilson Morton I, bartndr, h 30th and L N A & C Ry.
Wilson M Belle, stenog Van Camp H and I Co, b 268 N Alabama.
Wilson Nan M (wid Emory), h 164 Fayette.
Wilson Nancy (wid James B), h 33 Bismarck av (H).
Wilson Nathaniel J (Wilson & Son), h 13 S Senate av.
Wilson Nellie M, stenog, b 164 Fayette.
Wilson Newton Rev, h w s National av 4 s of Washington av (I).
Wilson Nicholas A, driver, h 28 Dawson.
Wilson Olive, usher Deaf and Dumb Inst.
Wilson Oliver E, furniture, h 51 Mayhew.
Wilson Oliver T, trav agt Judson & Hanna, h 400 W Udell (N I).
Wilson Omar, A B, prin preparatory school Butler College, h w s Ritter av 4 n of Washington av (I).
Wilson Orin E, attendant Insane Asylum.
Wilson Oscar, bellboy The Bates.
Wilson Oscar H, cooper, h 3 Geneva.
Wilson Oscar H, plumber, b 266 S Senate av.
Wilson Otto H, tmstr, h e s Concord 3 s of Michigan (H).
Wilson Oto J, clk C C C & St L Ry, h 179 W Vermont.
Wilson Rachel A (wid Richard), h 359 Cornell av.
Wilson Ralph E, barber, b 646 E 8th.
Wilson Ralph W E, phys City Dispensary, 32 E Ohio, b 76 N Arsenal av.
Wilson Randolph, carp, h 281 S Missouri.
Wilson Ray S, clk I D & W Ry, b 144 E New York.
Wilson Richard, coachman 1490 N Illinois.
Wilson Richard, lab, h 268 Lafayette.

POLICIES IN UNITED STATES LIFE INSURANCE CO., offer indemnity against death, liberal cash surrender value or at option of policy-holder, fully paid-up life insurance or liberal life income. **E. B. SWIFT, M'g'r, 25 E. Market St.**

SHOW CASES

Wilson Richard M, clk Model Clothing Co, h 304 Ash.
Wilson Rilla E, teacher, b 17 N William (W I).
Wilson Robert, lab, b n s 8th 3 w of canal.
Wilson Robert H, clk, h 431 Clifford av.
Wilson Robert W, lab, b 68 Fountain.
Wilson Sabina E, h 116 Walcott.
Wilson Sallie H (wid Isaac H), h 374 Park av.
Wilson Samuel, porter N Y Store, h 300 Alvord.
Wilson Samuel, lab, h 166 W McCarty.
Wilson Samuel H, lab, h 245 W Addison (N I).
Wilson Samuel H, painter, h 8 Geneva.
Wilson Samuel J, rental mngr C E Coffin & Co, h 134 Broadway.
Wilson Samuel W, blksmith, h 31 Clay.
Wilson Sedonia W (wid Frank S), h 166 E Michigan.
Wilson Sidney G, ship clk John L Moore, h 307 Fletcher av.
Wilson Spencer W, lab, b 646 E 8th.

WILSON SURGICAL INSTITUTE, Charles A Wilson, M D (Faculty Prize Medical College of Ohio, 1879), Propr, 81 W Ohio.

Wilson Susan J, tailor, 571 E Washington, h same.
Wilson Sylvester, lab, b e s Illinois 1 n of 35th.
Wilson Sylvester, plumber, h 368 E Morris.
Wilson Theodore E, lab, h e s Harriet 3 s of Park (B).
Wilson Thomas, glassblower, h 128 John.
Wilson Thomas C, hostler, r Union Stock Yards (W I).
Wilson Thomas K, lab, h 544 E New York.
Wilson Thomas W, painter, b 8 Geneva.
Wilson Walker, lab, h 281 Indiana av.
Wilson Walter B, molder, h 590 W North.
Wilson Walter W, letter carrier P O, b 333 N Illinois.
Wilson Wealtha A, teacher Public School No 29, b 599 Park av.
Wilson Weldon, porter, r 1004 N New Jersey.
Wilson Wesley (Wilson & McClintock), h 368 E Morris.

WILSON WILBORN, Attorney at Law, Room 1, 12½ N Delaware, h 36 N Reisner (W I).

Wilson Wm, lab, h 35 Ellen.
Wilson Wm, lab, h 122 Osage al.
Wilson Wm, lab, h 594 E 10th.
Wilson Wm, molder, h 30 Bismarck av (H).
Wilson Wm, motorman, h 967 Grove av.
Wilson Wm A, car rep, b 8 N Brightwood av (B).
Wilson Wm D (James A Johnson & Co), agt Lackawanna Fast Freight Line, h 83 Fletcher av.
Wilson Wm D, horseshoer, 58 W Merrill, h 410 S Delaware.
Wilson Wm E, bkkpr, b 166 E Michigan.
Wilson Wm F, farmer, h s end Temperance (I).
Wilson Wm F, lab, h 12 Sylvan.

WILSON WM F, Staple Groceries and Meats, 380-382 E 9th, h 518 Broadway.

Wilson Wm G, mngr The Grand Hotel, h 1506 Northwestern av (N I).
Wilson Wm H, clk Kahn Tailoring Co, b 129 E Walnut.

THOS. C. DAY & CO.
INVESTING AGENTS,
TOWN AND FARM LOANS,
Rooms 325 to 330 Lemcke Bldg.

Wilson Wm H, painter, h 456 S Capitol av.
Wilson Wm H, policeman, h 95½ N Delaware.
Wilson Wm H, supt glue wks Kingan & Co, h 47 Brett.
Wilson Wm H, trav agt, b 129 E Walnut.
Wilson Wm J, bartndr, h 1 Wilson.
Wilson Wm M, h 103 Ft Wayne av.
Wilson Wm M, trav agt Schauroth & Co, h 441 College av.
Wilson Wm N, clk, h 98½ Russell av.
Wilson Wm P, lab, b 23 Sinker.
Wilson Wm Pitt, office 8 Baldwin blk, h 496 Bellefontaine.
Wilson Wm R, lab, b 226 W 2d.
Wilson Wm R, turner, b e s Concord 3 s of Michigan (H).
Wilson Wm T, mach, b 454 N California.
Wilson Wm W, clk R M S, b 734 Ash.
Wilson Wilmer, student, b w s National av 4 s of Washington av (I).
Wilson Winchester T, h 198 River av (W I).
Wilson Wood L, copy editor The Indpls News, h 1525 N Meridian.
Wilson Zerilda, h 76 N Arsenal av.
Wilson Zilpa A (wid Orin G), h 27 Jefferson av.
Wilson & McClintock (Wesley Wilson, James A McClintock), plumbers, 561 Virginia av.
Wilson & Son (Nathaniel J and Joseph R), blksmiths, 190 W Pearl.
Wilstack Joseph H, plumber, b 140 N Alabama.
Wilt Daniel, lab, h rear 47 Omer.
Wilt Daniel F, lab, b rear 47 Omer.
Wilt Jacob C, carp, b 25 Prairie av.
Wilt John, lab, h 266 S West.
Wilt Ward L, clk, h 60 Temple av.
Wilts George, lab, h rear 33 Columbia al.
Wiltse Anson B, mngr Central Loan Co, 7-8 Talbott blk, h 527 E Washington.
Wiltshire Andrew P, h 953 Cornell av.
Wiltshire David A, bicyclemkr, b 61 N Linden.
Wiltshire Meyers W, lab, h 301½ E Washington.
Wiltshire Scott G, cooper, h 61 N Linden.

EAT——
HITZ'S
CRACKERS
AND CAKES.
ASK YOUR GROCER FOR THEM.

WILLIAM WIEGEL
6 West Louisiana Street
Opp. Union Station.

Capital Steam Carpet Cleaning Works
M. D. PLUNKETT Proprietor, Telephone 818

BENJ. BOOTH PRACTICAL EXPERT ACCOUNTANT. Accounts of any description investigated and audited, and statements rendered. Room 18, 82½ E. Washington St., Indianapolis, Ind.

The Best Place in the City to Get a Good Meal ♦♦♦♦ THE SHERMAN RESTAURANT ♦♦♦♦ 18 and 20 S. Meridian Street KERSHNER BROS., Proprs.

ESTABLISHED 1876. TELEPHONE 168.
CHESTER BRADFORD,
SOLICITOR OF PATENTS,
AND COUNSEL IN PATENT CAUSES.
(See adv. page 6.)
Office:—Rooms 14 and 16 Hubbard Block, S. W.
Cor. Washington and Meridian Streets,
INDIANAPOLIS, INDIANA.

WILTSIE CHARLES S, Prosecuting Attorney Marion County, 73 Court House; Private Office 71-72 Lombard Bldg, Tel 1589; h 614 E Washington.
Wiltsie Lydia (wid George), b 614 E Washington.
Wimberley James M, engr, h 211½ E Washington.
Wimmer, see also Wemmer.
Wimmer Charles, lab, h 150 Sheffield av (H).
Wimmer David, flagman, b 906 Morris (W I).
Wimmer Elbert L Rev, pastor East Park M E Church, h 104 N Beville av.
Wimmer Eli M, marble cutter, b 324 W Vermont.
Wimmer George, engr, h 220 Newman.
Wimmer George W, lab, b 150 Sheffield av (H).
Wimmer Gilbert B, clk Kingan & Co (ltd), h 324 W Vermont.
Wimmer Helena M (wid Jacob), h 41 Iowa.
Wimmer John, engr, h 329 Yandes.
WIMMER JOHN P, Optician, 14 N Penn, h 1287 N Meridian.
Wimmer Malinda J (wid Wm), h 532 E Ohio.
Winans Louis C, clk, r 26 Ryan blk.
Winans Lucinda T (wid Wm M), h 275 Highland av.
Winch Mildred, mngr Organizer Pub Co, b 112 Park av.
Winchell Austin, clk, h 928 Morris (W I).
Winchester Francis O, confr, 476 S Meridian, h same.
Winchester John S, clk, b 476 S Meridian.
Winchester Wilbur F, trav agt Hendricks & Cooper, h 1089 N Illinois.
Windhorst Anna M (Armbruster & Windhorst), h 219 N Pine.
Windhorst August C, wagonmkr, h 899 Madison av.
Windhorst Wm, lab, h 59 William.
Windsor Mary, b 24 Columbia al.
Windsor Joseph, r 23 N West.
Windsor The, s w cor Illinois and Market.

O. B. Ensey
SLATE, STEEL, TIN AND IRON ROOFING.
Cor. 6th and Illinois Sts. Tel. 1562

Winebrener Alfred A, tmstr, b 22d and Baltimore av.
Wineman, see also Weinman.
Wineman Joseph, propr People's Outfitting Co, h 1098 N Illinois.
Wineman Minerva J (wid John), h 472 S West.
Wineman Thomas J, watchman, h 61 Jones.
Winenow John H, carp, h 26 Depot (B).
Wines Abner G, h 126 E North.
Wines Charles, painter, h 464 W Francis (N I).
Wines Thomas, lab, b 187 S Capitol av.
Wing Fannie F, h 178 E Washington.
Wing Henry M, creamery, 276 Dillon, h same.
Wingate Edwin H, carp, h 446 College av.
Wingate Ferdinand H, trav agt Central Rubber and Supply Co, h 998 N Meridian.
Wingate Frederick W, clk, r 226 N Delaware.
Wingate Wm L, bkkpr, h 579 College av.
Wingenroth Carl, mach, h 272 Yandes.
Winger Jacob, cigarmkr, r 60 S Delaware.
Wingerter Edward W, cigars, 66 S Illinois, b 57 Church.
Wingfield John B, clk, h 541 Bellefontaine.
Wingfield Thomas, fireman, b 341 W Market.
Winings Daniel P, salesman Krag-Reynolds Co, h 820 N Penn.
Winings Jesse R, lab, h 11 Wilcox.
Winkel Frank W, mach, h 123 John.
Winkel Peter, mach opr The Indpls Sentinel, h 645 Marlowe av.
Winkelhaus Andrew, painter, b 406 Virginia av.
Winkelhaus Charles L, paperhngr, b 406 Virginia av.
Winkelhaus George O, cigarmkr, b 179 S Alabama.
Winkelhaus John, clk Charles Willig, b 406 Virginia av.
Winkelhaus Philip G, painter, h 78 Dougherty.
Winkelman Herman, cabtmkr, b 53 N Judge Harding (W I).
Winkelman Paul, mattressmkr, b 53 N Judge Harding (W I).
Winkelman Simon, tailor, b 115 Mass av.
Winkelman Wm E, lab, h 182 S Reisner (W I).
Winkelman Wm E, mattressmkr, b 53 N Judge Harding (W I).
Winkenhofer Leon, clk Fraternal B and L Assn, b 419 Ash.
Winkenhofer Otto, bkkpr Fraternal B and L Assn and notary public, 51 Journal bldg, h 419 Ash.
Winkle Charles W, lab, h 217 Mass av.
Winkle George W, lab, b 415 N East.
Winkle Henry, lab, h 415 N East.
Winkle Jesse J, carp, h 275 W Washington.
Winkle Mary E (wid Samuel), h 444 W Eugene (N I).
Winkler David G, saloon, 201 Ft Wayne av, h 16 Cherry.
Winkler Dicy A (wid Richard), b 740 E Washington.
Winkler Erbie, painter, h 293 E Washington.
Winkler George M, mach, h 278 Highland av.
Winkler Joseph, clothing, 306 E Washington, h same.
Winkler Mary A (wid Michael), b 278 Highland av.
Winkler Wallace W, fireman, h 740 E Washington.

TUTEWILER ▲ UNDERTAKER, No. 72 WEST MARKET STREET. TELEPHONE 216.

Winkles Charles W, foreman, h 130 S East.
Winlock Charles, lab, b 69 Quince.
Winlock Henry, lab, h 54 Arthur.
Winn, see also Wynn.
Winn Charles, paperhngr, h 632 Home av.
Winn David, lab, h 111 Indiana av.
Winn James W, patrolman, h 203 W 3d.
Winn Lucius C, trav agt, h 134 N Penn.
Winn Lucius G, bicycle locks, 26 Ingalls blk, b 134 N Penn.
Winn Mary (wid James), h 285 S Missouri.
Winn Thomas F, asst supt Prud Ins Co, b 164 N Illinois.
Winn Willis, lab, b 174 S Missouri.
Winneg Frederick, sawyer, h 66 Arizona.
Winnia Edward H, collr, b 226 N Liberty.
Winningham Jesse W, trav agt, r 335 N Liberty.
WINONA ASSEMBLY AND SUMMER SCHOOL, Rev Solomon C Dickey, D D, Sec and Genl Mngr, 36 When Bldg.
WINONA PUBLISHING CO, Henry S Dickey Mngr, Publishers The Inter-Synod, 36 When Bldg.
Winpenny Christian (wid Wm), h 429 Ash.
Winpenny Ellen E, artist, b 429 Ash.
Winpenny George W, lawyer, 19 Baldwin blk, b 429 Ash.
Winrow Samuel, lab, r 111 Indiana av.
Winscom Wm W, clk, b 162 N Illinois.
Winscott Frank H, clk, b 170 Christian av.
Winship Benjamin F, clk, h 523 Broadway.
Winship Wilbur H, clk, b 523 Broadway.
Winslow Edward, painter, b 117 N Missouri.
Winslow Ezra E, waiter, b 223 W Vermont.
Winslow Frank, ironwkr, r 94 N New Jersey.
Winslow Henry O, clk George J Marott, h 355 E Market.
Winslow Hezekiah K, engr, h 19 Spann av.
Winslow Seth B, engr, b 57 English av.
WINSLOW WM W, Pres Capitol Paving and Construction Co and Genl Agt Wrought Iron Bridge Co, 1 Hubbard Blk, s w cor Washington and Meridian, Tel 1190; h 950 N Meridian. (See adv p 10.)
Winstead John, lather, h 25½ S Alabama.
Winston Joseph H, b 229 W Washington.
Winston Martin A, blksmith, b 138 Mass av.
Winston Wm, molder, h 82 Germania av (H).
Winte Henry D, adv clk The Indpls Sentinel, r 270 N Delaware.
Winter Carl G, phys, 40 E Ohio, h 489 Madison av.
WINTER CHARLES R, Sanitary Plumber and Gas Fitter, 162 Ft Wayne av, h w s Central av 2 n of 23d. (See adv in classified Plumbers.)
Winter Clarence, student, b 699 N Meridian.
Winter David W, molder, h s w cor Fernway and Paw Paw.
WINTER FERDINAND, Lawyer, 802-804 Majestic Bldg, Tel 1935; h 699 N Meridian, Tel 1187.
Winter George W, mach hd, h 85 Wilson.
Winter Gottfried, carp, h 436 Charles.
Winter Henry, grocer, 51 Yandes, h same.
Winter Henry F, watchman, h 97 Nordyke av (W I).

THE
WHEN
IS A WORLD BEATER.

Winter Hiram O, mngr, h 83 Highland pl.
Winter Jacob H, local cashr Adams Ex Co, h 9 Pleasant.
Winter James C, mach, h 198 Fayette.
Winter James M, b 198 Fayette.
Winter John, pressman Wm B Burford, h 68 N Beville av.
Winter John A, painter, h 209 Prospect.
Winter John H, turner, h 350½ W Vermont.
Winter Lars, lab, h 135 Downey.
Winter Mary, teacher Public School No 28, h 20 Dawson.
Winter Mary (wid David W), h 96 Lawrence.
Winter Thomas, student, b 699 N Meridian.
Winter Wm A, carver, h 382 N Senate av.
Winter Wm E, carp, h 30 Depot (B).
Winter Winfield S, molder, b 96 Lawrence.
Wintergerst Adam, lab, h 114 Blackford.
Wintergerst John A, packer, h 43 Hendricks.
Wintermute Alger B, agt, b 760 N Illinois.
Winterroth Edward O A, clk W J Holliday & Co, h 117 Yeiser.
Winterrowd James, clk, h 88 Woodlawn av.
WINTERROWD THOMAS A, Architect, 75-76 Lombard Bldg, 24½ E Washington, Tel 1730; h 480 Central av. (See adv in classified Architects.)
Winterrowd Wm P, salesman Daggett & Co, h 141 Woodlawn av.
WINTERS ARCHIAS E, Printer and Editor The Ensign and The Zig-Zag Cycler, 33 Talbott Blk, r 29 same. (See adv opp classified Newspapers.)
Winters Charles, agt, r 180 Christian av.
Winters Edward L, bricklyr, b 769 Chestnut.
Winters Frank, lab, b 48 N West.
Winters George, h 466 N Meridian.
Winters George C, plater, b 122 Blackford.
Winters Henry, turner, h 350½ W Vermont.
WINTERS JAMES M, Lawyer, 4-5 Fletcher's Bank Bldg, Tel 496; h 270 N Illinois.

The A. Burdsal Co.
CELEBRATED
HOMESTEAD
READY MIXED PAINT.
WHOLESALE AND RETAIL.
34 AND 36 SOUTH MERIDIAN STREET.

THEODORE F. SMITHER Competent and Responsible ROOFER
Office, 151 West Maryland St. Telephone 86

ELECTRIC SUPPLIES We Carry a full Stock. Prices Right. C. W. MEIKEL, Tel. 466. 96-98 E. New York St.

DALTON & MERRIFIELD { LUMBER South Noble St., near E. Washington

INDIANA ELECTROTYPE CO. :: BEST WORK. LOWEST PRICES.
23 WEST PEARL ST., INDIANAPOLIS, IND. JOB WORK. BOOK PLATES. All Orders Promptly Filled. BEST PATENT BASE ON THE MARKET.

KIRKHOFF BROS.,
Electrical Contractors, Wiring and Construction.
102-104 SOUTH PENNSYLVANIA ST.
TELEPHONE 910.

Winters John N, city fireman, h 301 Fletcher av.
Winters Philip C, bricklyr, h 769 Chestnut.
Winters Stephen S, car rep, h 4 E Willow (B).
Winters Wm H, molder, h 122 Blackford.
Wintersmith Gabriel, lab, h 10 Holborn.
Winton Sarah E (wid George), h 426 Superior.
Wire Fence Supply Co The, John B Cleaveland mngr, 329 Mass av.
Wireman Fannie S, clk The Wm H Block Co, b 282 Douglass.
Wirick Michael, foreman, h 213 W McCarty.
Wirker Reinhold, lab, h n e cor Berlin av and 20th.
Wirt, see also Wert.
Wirt John B, baker, 8 Indiana av, h same.
Wirthlin Alice E, clk Carlin & Lennox, b 31 W Vermont.
Wirtz Frederick, polisher, b 286 E Louisiana.
Wirtz George, lab, h 104 Douglass.
Wirtz Harry A, mach, b 343 Fletcher av.
Wirtz Henry J, blksmith, h 343 Fletcher av.
Wirtz Jacob F, blksmith, 225 W Pearl, h 507 W Washington.
Wirtz John W, uphlr, h 29 S Station (B).
Wisby Alonzo L, condr, h 402 Yandes.
Wischmeier Charles H, yard clk, h 70 Hanna.
Wischmeier Henry C W, plumber, b 70 Hanna.
Wischmeyer Henry G W, blksmith, h 30 Sanders.
Wischmeyer Martin, clk, b 765 S East.
Wischmeyer Wm, gardener, h e s Randell 3 s of Pleasant run.
Wisdom Edward, tmstr, b 129 Howard.
Wisdom Elizabeth (wid Joseph A), h 129 Howard.
Wise, see also Weis, Weiss and Wiese.
Wise Albert A, supt, h 160 E St Joseph.
Wise August, lab, h 356 Fulton.
Wise Axel A, foreman, h 492 W Udell (N I).
Wise Charles A, bricklyr, h 562 W 22d (N I).
Wise Charles L, bricklyr, h 492 W Udell (N I).

THE W. G. WASSON CO.,
130 Indiana Ave. Tel. 989.
STEAM
COAL
Car Lots a Specialty. Prompt Delivery.
Brazil Block, Jackson and Anthracite.

Wise Daniel H, carp, h 174 Hoyt av.
Wise Della, tel opr, b 132 W New York.
Wise Edward A, mach hd, b 332 Elizabeth.
Wise Harry A, restaurant, 143 E Washington, h same.
Wise Harry H, finisher, h 608 W Udell (N I).
Wise Herbert, fireman, b 28 S State av.
Wise Jennie, h 163 N Capitol av.
Wise John, lab, r 152 W Washington.
Wise John, waiter, b 313 E Miami.
Wise John A, lab, b 332 Elizabeth.
Wise John R, condr, r 175 S Illinois.
Wise Laura B, b 313 E Miami.
Wise Louis B, clk, r 50 Monument pl.
Wise Mary (wid John), b 599 W Pearl.
Wise Oscar O, lab, h 492 W Udell (N I).
Wise Robert J, tel opr, b 48 Warren.
Wise Thomas, h 48 Warren.
Wise Thomas H, driver, b 48 Warren.
Wise Wm H, baggageman, h 21 S Dorman.
Wisehart Wm H, student, h 280 E Merrill.
Wiselogel Frederick G, mech engr, h 10 Union.
Wiselogel Robert F, mech engr, b 10 Union.
Wiseman, see also Weizemann.
Wiseman George, lab, h 15 Springfield.
Wiseman Isaac L, lawyer, 12½ N Delaware, h 182 Prospect.
Wiseman Margaret, h 249½ W Washington.
Wiseman Robert A, engr, h 116 Meek.
Wiseman Simon R, driver, b 166 Beacon.
Wiseman Walter F, driver, h 166 Beacon.
Wiseman Wellington M, motorman, h 242 Yandes.
WISHARD ALBERT W, Lawyer and 2d Res Vice-Pres American Surety Co of New York, Rooms 106-108 Commercial Club Bldg, Tel 1539; h 264 N Capitol av.
Wishard George W (Thos C Day & Co), h 1042 N Illinois.
Wishard Ralph W, billposter, h 6 Emerson pl.
Wishard Susan L (wid James H), b 955 N Capitol av.
Wishard Wm H (Wishard & Noble), h 264 N Capitol av, tel 1574.
WISHARD WM N, Physician, Office Hours 9 A M to 12:30 P M, Sundays 2-3 P M, 18 E Ohio, h 311 N Capitol av; Tel Office 1231; Res 1574.
WISHARD & NOBLE (Wm H Wishard, Thomas B Noble), Physicians, Rooms 5-7, 37½ W Market.
Wishmeier Charles H, trimmer, b 300 N Pine.
Wishmeier Christian F, car insp, b 300 N Pine.
Wishmeier Christina M (wid Charles F), h 300 N Pine.
Wishmeier Wm F, car rep, h 610 E Vermont.
Wishmeyer Christian, lab, h 57 King.
Wishmeyer Frederick, cooper, h 326 W Maryland.
Wishmier Andrew J, foreman, h s s Jackson 3 w of Lincoln av (M J).
Wishmier Harry T, clk H P Wasson & Co, b s w cor State and Everett.
Wishmier Henry G W, hostler, h s w cor State and Everett.
Wismiller Anna (wid Jacob), b 18 McKim av.
Wisser Frederick, cigarmkr, 172 S Linden, b same.
Wisser John, h 172 S Linden.
Wissman George F (J H Wissman & Son), b 147 Deloss.

W. H. Messenger FURNITURE, CARPETS, STOVES, 101 EAST WASHINGTON ST. TEL. 491.

McNamara, Koster & Co. | Foundry and Pattern Shop, 212-218 S. PENN. ST. . . . PHONE 1593.

Wissman John H (J H Wissman & Son), h 147 Deloss.
Wissman J H & Son (John H and George F), planing mill, n w cor Hall and Moore av.
Witham Samuel L, phys, 33½ S Station (B), r same.
Withem Edmund J, blksmith, h 195 Yandes.
Witherby Wesley W, finisher, h 551 S New Jersey.
Withers Amanda (wid Thomas), b 236 W 3d.
Withmar Wm, trav agt, b 350 N Illinois.
Withrow Real M, tilemkr, h 607 W Francis (N I).
Withrow Thomas F, lab, b 596 Morris (W I).
Withrow Wm, mach hd, h 170 Nordyke av (W I).
Withrow Wm H H, h 596 Morris (W I).
Witkowski Herman, lab, h 32 N Judge Harding (W I).
Witman Clinton, carp, b 101 Bradshaw.
Witman Harry H, driver, b 101 Bradshaw.
Witman James E, lineman Postal Tel Co, r 11 S Meridian.
Witman Mary M (wid Henry N), h 101 Bradshaw.
Witt Albert W, lab, h 16 Keystone av.
Witt Anna (wid Gottlieb), b 447 S State av.
Witt Benjamin, lab, h 124 Eureka av.
Witt Charles, lab, b 179 Johnson av.

WITT GUSTAV C, Saloon and Mnfr of Fine Cigars (Blue Label Goods), 251 Michigan av, h same.

Witt James A, lab, h 590 W Addison (N I).
Witt Lazarus, phys, 449 S Capitol av, h same.
Witte, see also Witty.
Witte Frederick, driver, h 504 Union.
Witte Henry, carp, h 22 Yandes.
Witte Marie (wid Edward G), h 31 E McCarty.
Wittenburg Albert, meats, 30 E Mkt House, h 131 S Linden.
Wittenberg Charles, trav agt, h 460 N Delaware.
Wittenburg ...ian, nurse 124 N Alabama.
Wittenring Henry, cigar mnfr, 196 Orange, h same.
Wittendorfer Frank A, clk, b 117 Spring.
Wittendorfer Frederick W, meats, 75 E Mkt House, b 117 Spring.
Wittendorfer Leonard, butcher, h 117 Spring.
Wittenmeier George, saloon, 881 Morris (W I), h same.
Wittenmeier John, painter, 829 Chestnut, h same.
Witter Emma A (wid Hiram F), r 305 N Senate av.
Witthoft August, turner, h 79 Rockwood.
Witthoft Charles, foreman, b 165 S East.
Witthoft Frederick, h 325 Indiana av.
Witthoft Frederick jr, saloon, 329 Indiana av, b 325 same.
Witthoft George H, driver, h 3 Paca.
Witthoft Louisa (wid Henry), h 165 S East.
Wittlin Albert, tailor George Mannfeld & Sons, h 217 Coburn.
Wittlin Otto, driver, b 217 Coburn.
Wittlinger George L, asst ticket agt I U Ry Co, h 439 E Georgia.
Wittmer Eliza (wid David), b 857 N New Jersey.
Wittmer George F, pres G F Wittmer Lumber Co, h n s E Washington 1 e of Belt R R.

Henry H. Fay, 40½ E. Washington St., REAL ESTATE, AND LOAN BROKER.

WITTMER G F LUMBER CO, George F Wittmer Pres, John A Dugan Treas, and Frank H Ewers Sec, n e cor E Washington and Belt R R, Tel 1758.

Witty James H, wire works, 47 S Illinois, h 334 Clifford av.
Witty John B (Coons & Witty), h 248 Talbott av.
Wocher Adolph G, clk S A Fletcher & Co, b 179 St Mary.
Wocher Charles A, teller S A Fletcher & Co, b 179 St Mary.
Wocher Frank F, teller S A Fletcher & Co, h 373 E 19th.

WOCHER JOHN, Insurance, Real Estate, Loans and Rentals, Aetna Bldg, 19½ N Penn, Tel 295; h 505 N Delaware, Tel 889.

Wocher Julius (Severin, Ostermeyer & Co), h 681 N Alabama.
Wocher Regina (wid John), h 179 St Mary.
Wocher Wm F, mngr John Wocher, h 179 St Mary.
Wodtke Henry, harnessmkr, h 235 W McCarty.
Wodtke Herman H, blksmith, h 228 W McCarty.
Woechter Ferdinand, lab, b 31 Poplar.
Woehrmeier George, waiter, r 29½ S Illinois.
Woelfle Charles E, carp, b 269 W Market.
Woelfle Wm, millwright, h 269 W Market.
Woelz Edward A, collr The Indpls News, b 128 Highland pl.
Woelz Henry L, mngr Acme Cloak and Suit Co, 6 Indiana av, h 477 E Vermont.
Woelz Louisa (wid Charles A), h 128 Highland pl.
Woempner Henry, h 309 S East.
Woerlen Albert, asst florist Insane Hospital.
Woerner, see also Warner and Werner.
Woerner Anton, bartndr, h 8 W Morris.
Woerner Augustus L, collr, h 205 N West.
Woerner Charles, chemist, b 156 W Pratt.
Woerner Charles A, clock rep Julius C Walk & Son, h 922 Ash.

UNION CASUALTY & SURETY CO. OF ST. LOUIS, MO.
All lines of Personal Accident and Casualty Insurance, including Employers' and General Liability.
W. E. BARTON & CO., General Agents, 504 Indiana Trust Building.
LONG DISTANCE TELEPHONE 1918.

THE FRED DIETZ CO. WOODEN PACKING BOXES MADE TO ORDER. FACTORY AND WAREHOUSE TRUCKS. 400 Madison Avenue. Telephone 654.

Indianapolis BUSINESS UNIVERSITY Leading College of Business and Shorthand. Elevator day and night. Individual instruction. Large faculty. Terms easy. Enter now. See p. 4. When Block. E. J. HEEB, President.

Steam Pumping Machinery { HENRY R. WORTHINGTON, 64 S. PENNSYLVANIA ST. Long Distance Telephone 284.

UNION CO-OPERATIVE LAUNDRY { NOS. 138, 140 AND 142 VIRGINIA AVENUE. (COMPOSED OF UNION LAUNDRY GIRLS.) T. E. SOMERVILLE, MANAGER — TELEPHONE 1269. INDIANAPOLIS, IND.

HORACE M. HADLEY
REAL ESTATE AND INSURANCE
66 East Market Street, Basement
TELEPHONE 1540.

Woerner Charles F, vice-pres Central Chair Co, h 934 N Illinois.
Woerner Frank, brewer, h 36 Sanders.
Woerner Frank W, patent draughtsman, 415-418 Lemcke bldg, res Kokomo, Ind.
Woerner John W, meats, 1424 Northwestern av (N I), h same.
Woerner Joseph A, saloon, 499 N Senate av, h same.
Woerner Louis, dairy, 693 Jones (N I), h same.
Woerner Lulu R, h 219 Dillon.
Woerner Mary (wid Alois), h 156 W Pratt.
Woerner Oscar F, clk, h 454 Indiana av.
Woerner Theodore, grocer, 494 N Senate av, h same.
Woerner Wilhelmina (wid Ludwig), h 231 W Michigan.
Woerner Wm C, clk, b 1424 Northwestern av (N I).
Woersdorfer August, tailor, h 452 S Missouri.
Woessner George C, city sanitary insp, h 3 Cress.
Woessner Henry F (Jacob Woessner & Sons), h 275 Huron.
Woessner Jacob (Jacob Woessner & Sons), h 540 Virginia av.
Woessner Jacob & Sons (Jacob, Wm L and Henry F), grocers, 540 Virginia av.
Woessner John C, butcher, b 151 N Pine.
Woessner Rosinda (wid John), b 540 Virginia av.
Woessner Wm, butcher, h 174 E Morris.
Woessner Wm L (Jacob Woessner & Sons), b 540 Virginia av.
Wohlecke Andrew, mach, h 685 Mass av.
Wohlfeld Benjamin, furrier, b 633 Bellefontaine.
Wohlfeld Julius, furrier, 11½ W Washington, h 633 Bellefontaine.
Woirhaye James R, blksmith, h 133 N Summit.
Wolcott, see also Walcott.
Wolcott Elizabeth (wid James H), b 109 Geisendorff.
WOLCOTT FRANK E, Druggist, 378 W New York, Tel 536; and 849 La Salle, Tel 536—3 rings; h 372 W New York.

PERSONAL AND PROMPT ATTENTION GIVEN TO COLLECTIONS.
Merchants' and Manufacturers' Exchange
J. E. TAKKEN, Manager,
19 Union Building, 73 West Maryland Street.

Woldt Anna, dressmkr, b 79 Fletcher av.
Woldt Charles, stock dealer, b 79 Fletcher av.
Woldt Wm, carp, h 79 Fletcher av.
Wolf, see also Woolf and Wulf.
Wolf August, pdlr, h 563 S Capitol av.
Wolf Bernard, painter, b 449 Charles.
Wolf Caroline (wid Joseph), h 219 Buchanan.
Wolf Charles, lab, b 14 Dougherty.
Wolf Charles, lab, h 141 Harmon.
Wolf Charles W, lab, b 131 Spann av.
Wolf Daniel, saloon, 152 Michigan (H), h same.
Wolf Edward, carp, h e s Lake av 8 s of Washington av (I).
Wolf Edward B, mach, h 185 Madison av.
Wolf Edwin A, painter, 2 Kentucky av, h 449 Charles.
Wolf Elias, driver, h 274 S Noble.
Wolf Elihu, ins agt, h 577 Shelby.
Wolf Elizabeth (wid Philip H), h 171 E Merrill.
Wolf Francis M, bartndr, r 298 N Capitol av.
Wolf Frank R, clk, b 325 S Penn.
Wolf Frederick, butcher, b 122 Bright.
Wolf Frederick H, foreman, h 93 Sanders.
Wolf George, b 577 Shelby.
Wolf George, carp, h 489 S New Jersey.
WOLF GEORGE, Real Estate, Loans and Insurance, 221-222 Lemcke Bldg, Tel 1926; h 923 N Delaware. (See adv in classified Real Estate.)
Wolf Harry S (H S Wolf & Co), h 530 Dillon.
Wolf Harvey S, well driver, b 14 Dougherty.
Wolf Henry, lab, r 11 Shelby.
Wolf Henry, mach, h w s Rural 1 s of Orchard av.
Wolf Herman, uphlr, r 193 W Washington.
WOLF H S & Co (Harry S Wolf), Carriage Painting of all Kinds, Hacks a Specialty, 477-479 S Delaware. (See adv in classified Carriage and Wagon Makers.)
Wolf Jacob C, motorman, b 81 E McCarty.
Wolf James, lab, b 568 W Michigan.
Wolf John, cigar mnfr, 28 N Delaware, h 325 S Penn.
Wolf John, lab, h n e cor Hope and Willow (B).
Wolf John, molder, h 38 N Haugh (H).
Wolf John D, lab, h rear 472 E Washington.
Wolf John H, trav agt, h 533 E 7th.
Wolf Joseph, fireman, h 82 S William (W I).
Wolf Joseph, grocer, cor LaSalle and Humboldt av, h same.
Wolf Lee, cigar mnfr, 30 Larch, h same.
Wolf Louis (Efroymson & Wolf), h 330 S Meridian.
Wolf Louis, lab, h 131 Spann av.
Wolf Louisa M (wid Jacob), confr, 81 E McCarty, h same.
Wolf Maria M (wid Christian F), h 344 N Noble.
Wolf Mason O, b 27 Columbia av.
Wolf Matilda (wid Otto), b 30 Larch.
Wolf Michael, clk, b 325 S Penn.
Wolf Minnie, h 108½ Mass av.
Wolf Moses, cigarmkr, b 325 S Penn.
Wolf Valentine C, saloon, 330 Clifford av, h same.
Wolf Walter W, condr, h 27 Columbia av.
Wolf Wm O, lab, b 44 Kennington.

CLEMENS VONNEGUT || FOUNDRY AND MACHINISTS' SUPPLIES. "NORTON" EMERY WHEELS AND GRINDING MACHINERY.
184, 186 and 192 E. Washington St.

Wolfanger John, barher, 611 Virginia av, h same.
Wolfard Ellen (wid Daniel), b 166 Walcott.
Wolfard George W, mach, h 883 Mass av.
Wolfe Andrew J, painter, h 506½ E Washington.
Wolfe Anna E (wid Wm G), music teacher, 187 Columbia av, b same.
Wolfe Benjamin, coremkr, b 29 King av (H).
Wolfe Charles D, harnessmkr, h 286 Bates.
Wolfe George H, pressman Indpls News, b 282 E Merrill.
Wolfe Harry P, lab, h 49 Pierce.
Wolfe Jerusha (wid Isaac), b 41 Indiana av.
Wolfe John M, painter, h 126 Elm.
Wolfe Keziah, r 225 Shelby.
Wolfe Lemond G F, clk, r 430 Broadway.
Wolfe Mary J (wid Jacob M), h 508 Bellefontaine.
Wolfe Odie I, coremkr, b 29 King av (H).
Wolfe Penelope L (wid George), teacher, r 430 Broadway.
Wolfe Sarah E (wid Samuel), h 29 King av (H).
Wolfert Peter, lab, h 48 W Raymond.
Wolff Albert C, mach, h 181 Jefferson av.
Wolff Charles, mach, h 398 Jackson.
Wolff Francis X, grocer, n e cor Garfield av and Washington, h same.
Wolfgang Lewis, carp, h e s Rural 2 n of Progress av.
Wolfinger Charles, engr, b 99 Lexington av.
Wolfkiel Perry, engr, r 17 S Senate av.
Wolfla Charles D, painter, h w s Bradley 2 n of Washington.
Wolfla Frank, lab, b 609 W Washington.
Wolfla Henry D, weighmaster, h 183 Minerva.
Wolfley George, lab, r 38 Springfield.
Wolfolk Frederick D, porter, b 304 Alvord.
Wolfolk Taylor, lab, h 304 Alvord.
Wolford John, b 45 Paca.
Wolfram Albert T, clk, h 201 N New Jersey.
Wolfram Charles A, stoves, 197 E Washington, b 201 N New Jersey.
Wolfram Clara D (wid Christian A), h 176 E Michigan.
Wolfred Charles, mach, h 304 N Brookside av.
Wolfred Charles T, mach, b 304 N Brookside av.
Wolfred George R, polisher, b 304 N Brookside av.
Wolfred Wm G, mach, b 304 N Brookside av.
Wollenweber Charles L, carp, 119 Maxwell, h 115 same.
Wolley Ira J, motorman, h 29 N State av.
Wolridge Clara (wid John), h 23 N New Jersey.
Wolsifter Christina (wid John), h 959 S Meridian.
Wolsiffer Frank J, janitor Public School No 33, h 125 Stoughton av.
Wolsiffer John, saloon, 827 S Meridian, h same.
Wolsiffer Joseph, lab, h 648 S Illinois.
Wolsiffer Mary (wid Joseph), h 121 Kennington.
Womack Albert A, h 470 Park av.
Womack John, lab, h 564 W North.
Womack Robert H, lab, h 70 Mayhew.
Woman's Christian Temperance Union of Indiana, Lena M Beck pres, Mary E Balch sec, Luella F McWhirter treas, 66½ N Penn.

WOMAN'S DEPT SAFETY VAULTS, Indiana Trust Bldg, s e cor Virginia av and Washington, Tel 36. (See front cover, adv opp and opp classified Insurance Agts.)
Woman's Exchange, Laura F Hodges pres, notions, 125 N Penn.
Woman's Relief Corps National Headquarters, Agnes Hitt pres, Ida S McBride sec, 41 When bldg.
WOMEN'S INDUSTRIAL ASSOCIATION FOR PRACTICAL PROGRESS, Louise L Lawrence Pres, Elsie Collins Sec, 6, 156½ E Washington.
Wonder Elizabeth (wid Howshield), h 66 Hosbrook.
Wonder Henry, lab, h 52 Sinker.
Wonder John P, b 66 Hosbrook.
Wonderly Mary (wid Henry), h 146 Davidson.
Wonders George, carp, h 119 Hosbrook.
Wonnell Charles, blksmith, 248 S Delaware, h 160 Laurel.
Wonnell Harry W, blksmith, h 95 Malott av.
Wonnell Louisa (wid John A), b 124 W 5th.
Wonnell Mary E, housekpr 20 N State av.
Wood, see also Woods.
Wood Albert, carp, h 367½ W Pearl.
Wood Albert, lab, h 46 Cushing.
Wood Alexander, h 550 Broadway.
Wood Alford, engr, b 245 E Market.
Wood Alonzo E, lab, b 131 Kansas.
Wood Amelia S (wid George M), h 131 Kansas.
Wood Andrew B, h 91 Marion av (W I).
Wood Benjamin F, mach hd, h 76 Frank.
Wood Charles, blksmith, b 149½ Oliver av (W I).
Wood Charles A, engr, h 112 Randolph.
Wood Charles H (Cooper & Wood), h 224 N Meridian.
Wood Daniel, gluer, b 67 Oliver av (W I).
Wood Daniel, lab, b 177 River av (W I).
Wood Daniel L, h 417 N Penn.
Wood Daniel M, dentist, 223 Indiana Trust bldg, h 72 Highland pl.

GUIDO R. PRESSLER,
FRESCO PAINTER
Churches, Theaters, Public Buildings, Etc., A Specialty.
Residence, No. 325 North Liberty Street.
INDIANAPOLIS, IND.

INDIANAPOLIS STEEL ROOFING AND CORRUGATING WORKS, 23 and 25 East South Street. S. D. NOEL, Proprietor.

David S. McKernan REAL ESTATE AND LOANS. Exchanging real estate a specialty. A number of choice pieces for encumbered property. Rooms 2-5 Thorpe Block.

DIAMOND WALL PLASTER { Telephone 1410 BUILDERS' EXCHANGE.

Cor. E. Ohio St. and C., C., C. & St. L. R'y Tracks. Storage of Household Goods and Pianos a Specialty. UNION TRANSFER AND STORAGE CO.

W. McWORKMAN,
Galvanized Iron Cornice Works
TIN AND SLATE ROOFING.
930 WEST WASHINGTON STREET.
TELEPHONE 1118.

Wood David B, real est, h 552 Bellefontaine.
Wood Dicy A (wid Jacob P), h 336½ E Washington.
Wood Edmonson R, carp, h 555 Bellefontaine.
Wood Edson T, bkkpr Singer Mnfg Co, h 53 The Blacherne.
Wood Edward M (Blume & Co), h 1137 N Meridian.
Wood Emsley H, real est, h 665 Park av.
Wood Francis G, carp, h 556 Muskingum al.
Wood Frank, lab, h 214 W 8th.
Wood Frank, waiter, r 55 Hendricks blk.
Wood Frank G, chief clk The Singer Mnfg Co, h 62 Talbott av.
Wood Frank W, mngr Indiana Chain Co, h 1027 N Alabama.
Wood George W (Hendricks & Wood), h 120 Clifford av.
Wood Georgianna, h 30 Torbet.
Wood Harry N, h 187 N Penn.
Wood Harry R, carp, h 90 N New Jersey.
Wood Hazard, coachman 850 N Meridian.
Wood Heman, r 183 N Capitol av.
Wood Henry F, molder, h 264 S Missouri.
Wood Herbert S, teller Indiana Natl Bank, h 417 N Penn.
WOOD HORACE F, Livery, 23 Monument Pl, Tel 1097; h 848 N Penn.
Wood Jacob S, h 385 N Illinois.
Wood James A, lab, b 131 Kansas.
Wood James C, trav agt, h 383 N Senate av.
Wood James H, brakeman, h 9 Minkner.
Wood James W, watchman, h 124 Bates.
Wood John, b 592 Morris (W I).
Wood John, driver, b 185 W New York.
Wood John, lab, h 621 W 22d (N I).
Wood John B, bkkpr Singer Mnfg Co, h 79 W 3d.
Wood John B, supt George Merritt & Co, h 946 N Alabama.
Wood John C, agt Union Line, 28 Commercial Club bldg, h 85 Middle Drive (W P).
Wood John F, h 555 College av.
Wood John F (Wood-Weaver Printing Co), h 419 Talbott av.
Wood John M, fireman, h 17 Crawford.

SEALS, STENCILS, STAMPS, Etc.
GEO. J. MAYER
15 S. Meridian St.
TELEPHONE 1386.

Wood John M, grocer, s e cor Concord and Michigan (H), h same.
Wood John M, grocer, 168 Hillside av, h same.
Wood Joseph G, lab, h 570 W Washington.
Wood Levi, phys, 282 Lincoln av, h same.
Wood Lydia (wid Thomas), h 379 Fletcher av.
Wood Martin L, messenger Am Ex Co, r 88½ S Illinois.
Wood Mary (wid Richard), h 322 Mass av.
Wood Morton E, chainman, b 555 Bellefontaine.
Wood Morton H, produce, b 385 N Illinois.
Wood Newton, clk, b 168 Hillside av.
Wood Nicholas P, b 407 W 2d.
Wood Norris P, mach, b 391 Bellefontaine.
WOOD ORNAMENT CO THE (Casper Kleifgen, John M Mills, Jacob W Watts), Mnfrs of Artistic Furniture, Show Cases, Etc, rear 544 W Addison (N I), Tel 1736. (See adv in classified Furniture Mnfrs.)
Wood Pleasant, lab, b 288 Douglass.
Wood Richard G, clk David S McKernan, h 322 Mass av.
Wood Sarah (wid James D), h 689 Shelby.
Wood Sarah R, b 124 Bates.
Wood Walter A Harvester Co, John B Kennedy mngr, 68 S Capitol av.
WOOD-WEAVER PRINTING CO (John F Wood, Urban R Weaver), Book and Job Printers, 116 N Delaware, Tel 1437. (See adv in classified Printers.)
Wood Wm, lab, r 422 Muskingum al.
Wood Wm A, driver, h 934 Gent (M P).
Wood Wm D, harnessmkr, b 550 Broadway.
Wood Wm E, b 79 W 3d.
Wood Wm H, lab, h 177 River av (W I).
Wood Wm H, real est, 10½ N Delaware, h 94 Oliver av (W I).
Wood Winfield S, real est, h 322 Mass av.
Wood-Worker The, Septimus H Smith pub, s e cor Monument pl and Meridian.
Woodall Allen E, b 243 N Alabama.
Woodall Emma E (wid Aquilla), b 243 N Alabama.
Woodall Jennie N, h 178 E Washington.
Woodard, see also Woodward.
Woodard Charles M, cutter, h 403 College av.
Woodard Harnie E, optician, 16 E Washington, h 269 Keystone av.
Woodard Hiliary, mach hd, h 26 Thomas.
Woodard Johnson, coachman 994 N Meridian.
Woodard Nathan D, phys, 24 Mass av, h 960 N Penn.
Woodard Sanders, coachman 843 N Illinois.
Woodard Warren, b 70 S Spruce.
Woodbeck Frank, lab, b 792 W Washington.
Woodbeck Theodore, boarding 792 W Washington.
Woodbridge Frank (H G Caldwell & Co), r 188 N Capitol av.
Woodbridge Wm W, trav agt Fahnley & McCrea, h 1126 N Meridian.
Woodburn James H, phys, 372 N Capitol av, h same.
Woodbury Granville, messenger, h 151 Cornell av.
Woodbury Preston N, ins, h 1157 N Meridian.
Woodcock Wm, painter, h 33 Sullivan.

A. METZGER AGENCY ESTABLISHED 1863. L-O-A-N-S

LAMBERT GAS & GASOLINE ENGINE CO.
ANDERSON, IND. GAS ENGINES FOR ALL PURPOSES.

BICYCLES $5 DOWN. MONTHLY. Best Wheels. Best Terms. WHEELMEN'S CO. 31 W. OHIO ST. LONG DISTANCE TEL. 1855

Woodcock Wm W, lab, h 180 Blackford.
Wooden Cicero, waiter, r 123 W Vermont.
Wooden James, lab, h 299 Shelby.
Wooden John A, porter, h 411 W North.
Wooden Thomas, lab, h 297 Shelby.
Wooden Wm, lab, b 411 W North.
Wooden Wright, lab, b 299 Shelby.
Woodfall Jordan, lab, h 186 Howard.
Woodfill Robert L, oils, h 385 Bellefontaine.
Woodfolk Cornelius, lab, h 269 Lafayette.
Woodfolk Taylor, lab, h 156 Michigan av.
Woodford Charles, express, h 239 Blake.
Woodford George A (Woodford & Pohlman), h 861 N Illinois.
WOODFORD & POHLMAN (George A Woodford, John Pohlman), Wholesale Wines and Liquors, 143 S Meridian, Tel 1020.
Woodfork Burrell, driver, h rear 143 St Mary.
Woodfork George, lab, h 186 Howard.
Woodfork Hattie, b 184 Minerva.
Woodgate Frederick, soldier, h 684 E St Clair.
Woodman Alfred E, mngr Rug Dept H P Wasson & Co, h 31 The Blacherne.
Woodring Allen, lab, h 116 Elizabeth.
Woodring Claude, huckster, b 116 Elizabeth.
Woodruff Albert H, driver, r 6, 502½ E Washington.
Woodruff Ezra B, helper, h 54 Ingraham.
Woodruff Joab H, supervisor of penmanship Public Schools, h 596 Broadway.
Woodruff John F, draughtsman P C C & St L Ry, h 131 East Drive (W P).
Woodruff John H, trimmer, b 1092 N Senate av.
Woodruff John Q, city fireman, h 467 Stillwell.
Woodruff Nancy E, asst matron Rescue Mission Home, h 49 E South.
Woodruff Nettie (wid Wm C), h 33 W St Clair.
Woodruff Vance, barber, 67 S Illinois, r s e cor Park and Cherry.
Woodruff Wm, clk Charles Mayer & Co, b 1092 N Senate av.
Woods, see also Wood.
Woods Albert O, lab, b 135 Forest av.
Woods Alice (wid George), h 340 Martindale av.
Woods Belle I, h 76 N New Jersey.
Woods Catherine (wid Thomas), b 50 Chadwick.
Woods Charles, lab, h 648 N West.
Woods Charles, steelwkr, b 95 S West.
Woods Charles E, meats, 488 E Washington, h same.
Woods Charles W, lab, h 249½ W Maryland.
Woods Clarence, waiter, r 255 N West.
Woods Edward, lab, b e s Earl 2 s of Belt R R.
Woods Edward, lab, h 47 Hosbrook.
Woods Eliza A, h 158 Fayette.
Woods Elmer E, clk Bates House Pharmacy, b 123 N Capitol av.
Woods Floyd A, lawyer, 18½ N Penn, r 28 The Chalfant.
Woods Ford, genl frt agt P & E Ry, n e cor Delaware and South, b 372 N Capitol av.
Woods Frank, motorman, b 24 Brookside av.
Woods Franklin B, lab, r 488½ E Washington.
Woods George, driver, b 6 Gimbel.
Woods George A, head waiter Kershner Bros, h 418 S State av.
Woods George S, molder, h 95 River av (W I).
WOODS GEORGE W, Lawyer, 6 Aetna Bldg, 19½ N Penn, h 74 College av.
Woods Harry M, collr, h 225 W 1st.
Woods Henry, lab, h 149 Elizabeth.
Woods Homer A, stenog, b 158 Fayette.
Woods James B, cabtmkr, b 128 Bates.
Woods James M, trav agt, b 1135 N Meridian.
Woods John, lab 376 N Capitol av.
Woods John, porter The Bates.
Woods John W, carp, 135 Forest av, h same.
Woods John W, lab, b rear 54 Davis.
Woods Kate S (wid Marshall C), h 910 N Delaware.
Woods Lee, trav agt, r 28½ Indiana av.
Woods Louis, lab, r 15 Rhode Island.
Woods Luke, lab, h 311 Yandes.
Woods Martha J (wid Philip M), h 57 Warren av (W I).
Woods Martin, lab, h 125 Hillside av.
Woods Mary (wid Anthony), h 206 Elm.
Woods Nannie, b 75 N Pine.
Woods Patrick H, opr Postal Tel Cable Co, h 31 Carlos.
Woods Robert, lab, h 22 Sumner.
Woods Robert E, ins agt, h 155 Woodside av (W).
Woods Robert S, carp, h 6 Gimbel.
Woods Thomas, elev opr The Denison.
Woods Thomas, lab, b 200 Agnes.
Woods Thomas, lab, h e s Earl 2 s of Belt R R.
Woods Thomas L, molder, h 158 Nordyke av (W I).
Woods Wm, molder, b 63 Bismarck av (H).
Woods Wm A, Judge U S Circuit Court, P O bldg, b The Denison.
Woods Wm C, polisher, h 444 W Francis (N I).
Woods Wm T, tmstr, h 14 Coffey (W I).
Woodson Silas W, molder, h 18 Everett.
Woodward, see also Woodard.
Woodward Charles A, trav agt, h 602 Central av.

THOS. C. DAY & CO.
INVESTING AGENTS,
TOWN AND FARM LOANS,
Rooms 325 to 330 Lemcke Bldg.

EAT
QUAKER BREAD
ASK YOUR GROCER FOR IT.
THE HITZ BAKING CO.

J. H. TECKENBROCK | Grilles, Fretwork and Wood Carpets
94 EAST SOUTH STREET.

FIDELITY MUTUAL LIFE PHILADELPHIA, PA. A. H. COLLINS { General Agent, 52-53 Baldwin Block.

Edwardsport Coal & Mining Co. Rooms 42 and 43 When Building.
SUPERIOR BITUMINOUS COAL For Steam and Domestic . . Purposes . .

ESTABLISHED 1876. TELEPHONE 168.
CHESTER BRADFORD,
SOLICITOR OF PATENTS,
AND COUNSEL IN PATENT CAUSES.
(See adv. page 6.)
Office:—Rooms 14 and 16 Hubbard Block, S.W. Cor. Washington and Meridian Streets,
INDIANAPOLIS, INDIANA.

Woodward Hubbard, engr, h 435 E Washington.
Woodward James, lab, b 36 Sheffield av (H).
Woodward James B, lab, h 36 Sheffield av (H).
Woodward Relly M, phys, b 602 Central av.
Woodward Robert A, coremkr, b 36 Sheffield av (H).
Woodward Sheldon G, trav agt, h 7 Ruckle.
Woodward Vestal W, buyer D P Erwin & Co, h 370 College av.
Woodward Wm, patrolman, h 551 Jefferson av.
Woodward Willis J, saloon, 18 S Delaware, h 680 W Washington.
Woodworth De Hart (Reliance Edge Tool Co), h 1105 N Penn.
Woodworth Hannah (wid Henry J), b 20 Broadway.
Woodworth Nellie, photog, b 20 Broadway.
Woodworth Orson H, lawyer, h 20 Broadway.
Woodworth Robert B, civil engr, r 308 N Illinois.
Woodworth Walter J, photog, b 20 Broadway.
Woody Angeline S, teacher Public School No 29, b 495 Ash.
Woody Ellen M (wid Samuel N), h 495 Ash.
Woody John, motorman, h 145½ Oliver av (W I).
Woody John A, foreman, h 34 Sinker.
Woody Mahlon P, mach hd, h 485 W 22d (N I).
Woody Orla A, clk R M S, b 495 Ash.
Woody Wm T, mach, b 495 Ash.
Woodyard Albert J, helper, h 12 Cooper.
Woodyard Charles H, harnessmkr, r 15 E New York.
Woodyard Edward, h 105 N Rural (B).
Woodyard John, h e s Arlington av 2 n of Walnut av (I).
Woof Charles, b 345 N Alabama.
WOOLEN GREEN V, Physician, 20 W Ohio, Tel 1493; h 50 W 12th.
Woolen Keziah, h 121 N Capitol av.
Woolery Freeman R, mach, h 296 Union.

76 N. PENNSYLVANIA ST.,
MAKERS
Outing BICYCLES
PHONE 598.

Wooley Josephine, vestmkr, h 106½ N Meridian.
Woolf, see also Wolf and Wulf.
Woolf Charles, lab, b 345 N Alabama.
Woolf Marcus, saloon, 139 E Washington, h 284 E New York.
Woolfolk Clarine, b 44 W North.
Woolfolk Elizabeth, h 159 Elizabeth.
Woollen Anna S (wid Wm I), b 922 N Senate av.
Woollen Evans (Woollen & Woollen), sec Commercial Club, h 772 N Penn.
Woollen Evermont M M A, lab, h 109 Germania av (H).
Woollen Harry, sec and treas The Herdrich-Woollen Machine Co, b 828 N Penn.
Woollen Herbert M, b 721 N Illinois.
Woollen Milton A, vice-pres Arthur Jordan Co, h 721 N Illinois.
Woollen Wm W (Woollen & Woollen), h 828 N Penn.
Woollen Wm Wesley, h 172 E Ohio.
Woollen & Woollen (Wm W and Evans), lawyers, 130 Commercial Club bldg.
Woolley Charles F, condr, h 161 Bates.
Woolley Oliver W, painter, h 90 E McCarty.
Woolling Joseph H, mngr, h 384 N New Jersey.
Woolls Albert E, carp, h s e cor Bruce and Jackson.
Woolridge Charles, lab, b 20 Church.
Woolridge Perry, coachman 530 N Delaware.
Woolsey Clarence J, ins agt, h 18 Allfree av.
Woolwine Blueford, tmstr, b 22 Ingram.
Woolwine Howard, tmstr, h 19 Ingram.
Wooten Allen, bellboy The Bates.
Wooten Ferney, lab, h e s Lancaster av 3 n of Clifford av.
Wooten George R, brakeman, h 35 Jefferson av.
Wooten John L, lab, h 84 N Olive.
Wooton Office Desk Co The, John T Dickson pres, Lewis V Horton sec, cor Malott and Columbia avs.
Wootton Howard W, clk, b 319 Virginia av.
Worcester Charles J, engr, h 247 S Senate av.
Worden Hector, trav agt, h 61 Clifford av.
Worden Samuel, b 61 E South.
Workman Anna L, bkkpr Am B and L Assn, b 174 Elm.
Workman Charles A, molder, h 63 King av (H).
Workman Edward S, molder, b 19 Warman av (H).
Workman George H, driver, h 567 Mass av.
Workman George W, watchman, b 567 Mass av.
Workman Harden T, lab, h 169 Sheffield av (H).
Workman Pascal N, engr, h 174 Elm.
Workman Robert M, mach hd, b 917 S Meridian.
Workman Rosina S (wid Wm G), b 22 King.
Workman Samuel M, assembler, b 917 S Meridian.
Workman Silas A, canmkr, h 917 S Meridian.
Workman Thomas J, plastr, h 11 Grove.
Workman Wm A (Wright & Workman), b 22 King.
Workman Wm L, driver, h 20 Gregg.
Worland Albert J, harnessmkr, h 155 Shelby.
Worland Clara E, printer, h 124 Huron.

ROOFING MATERIAL C. ZIMMERMAN & SONS SLATE AND GRAVEL ROOFERS, 19 SOUTH EAST STREET.

DRIVEN WELLS And Second Water Wells and Pumps of all kinds at CHARLES KRAUSS', 42 S. PENN. ST., TEL. 465. REPAIRING NEATLY DONE.

If You are not Satisfied with Your Laundry Work Give Us a Trial. ERTEL STEAM LAUNDRY 26 and 28 N. Senate Avenue. Telephone 1089.

Worland John T, hostler, b 123 E McCarty.
World Building, Loan and Investment Co, Wm E McLean pres, Everett Wagner sec, Wm H Armstrong treas, 36½ W Washington.
Worley Frank C, yardmaster, h 826 Cornell av.
Worley Henry A, blksmith, h 136 Forest av.
Worley John A, fireman, h 87 Benton.
Worley John B, clk, b 630 S Meridian.
Worley Wm, lab, h 438 Martindale av.
Worley Wm H, switchman, h 808 Cornell av.
Worm Albert R, meats, 113 Oliver av (W I), h same.
Wormser Jacob, grocer, 143 Maple, h same.
Wormser Jessie L, stenog, b 395 E McCarty.
Wormser Nathan, barber, 117 S Illinois, h 395 E McCarty.
Wormwood Joseph I, molder, h 50 N California.
Worrell Charles E, bkkpr, b 125 Prospect.
Worrell Edward, brakeman, h 128 N Missouri.
Worrell Elizabeth (wid Wm), b 93 Fletcher av.
Worrell Elizabeth (wid Wm), h 476 N Illinois.
Worrell Frank L, tel opr, b 125 Prospect.
Worrell Jasper S, lab, h 247 Michigan (H).
Worrell John, dep chief Indiana Bureau of Statistics, res Clayton, Ind.
Worrell Preston L, carp, h 125 Prospect.
Worth Alfred, musician, b 86 E Ohio.
Worth Charles F, special agt Singer Mnfg Co, h 1671 Kenwood av.
Worth Eugene, dentist, b 1671 Kenwood av.
Worth George, carp, h 108 Eddy.
Worth John H, barber, h 256 W Pearl.
Worth Nathan, b 204 N Illinois.
Worth Virginia B, b 488 Park av.
Worthington Allen W, tel opr, b 408 N New Jersey.
Worthington Charles E, lab, b e s Miami 3 s of Prospect.
Worthington Ernest B, clk, h 487 Dillon.
Worthington George, letter carrier P O, b 127 Darnell.
Worthington Guy O, b 408 N New Jersey.
WORTHINGTON HENRY R, D H Chester Mngr, Mnfr of Steam Pumps, Water and Oil Meters, Condensers and Water Filters, 64 S Penn, Tel 284. (See left top lines.)
Worthington Howard G, driver, h 74 Hill av.
WORTHINGTON ROBERT, Contractor and Builder; Stores and Offices Remodeled, 45 Mass av, h 850 Cornell av.
Worthington Sarah A, dressmkr, 74 Hill av, h same.
Worthington Wm H, clk, h 291 E Ohio.
Worthy Albert, lab, b 390 N California.
Wortman Charles, brick contr, 33 Villa av, h same.
Worttmann Henry, express, h 207 English av.
Woywod Anthony, carver, b 110 Kennington.
Woywod Emma (wid Jerome), b 126 Kennington.
Woywod Ferdinand, driver, b 110 Kennington.
Woywod Frank, h 110 Kennington.
Woywod Frank jr, mach hd, h 112 Kennington.

Richardson & McCrea, REPRESENTING BEST KNOWN FIRE INSURANCE COMPANIES. Fidelity and Casualty Insurance Company of New York Represented. Telephone 182. 79 East Market St.

Wrade Charles C, truckman, h 67 Barth av.
Wrade Christian, lab, h 406 S Olive.
Wrade Henry, mounter, b 67 Barth av.
Wrangham John B, cashr Euitable Life Assurance Society, h 473 N Delaware.
Wrassman George, lab, h 488½ E Washington.
Wrassman John F, car rep, h 91 N Beville av.
Wratenal Johan, lab, h Sheffield (H).
Wray Charles, painter, h 19 Elm.
Wray Harvey, lab, b 19 Elm.
Wray Henry, watchman, h 80 Bates.
Wray Wm W, trav agt Pearson & Wetzel, b 354 Talbott av.
Wrege Arthur J, stenog, b 199 Cornell av.
Wren Anna, dressmkr, 167 W 1st, b same.
Wren Dennis J, insp City Civil Engineer's Office, h 68 Gregg.
Wren Edward, blksmith, b 494 Chestnut.
Wren Ellen (wid Edward), b 494 Chestnut.
Wren Frank E, collarmkr, b 66 N Noble.
Wren George B, helper, h 23 Foundry (B).
Wren James J, baggageman, b 22 Elm.
Wren John J, letter carrier P O, h 183 Church.
Wren John T, gasfitter, b 355 S Capitol av.
Wren Mary (wid John), h 22 Elm.
Wren Michael, plumber, b 355 S Capitol av.
Wren Michael E, engr, b 22 Elm.
Wren Nora (wid Thomas), h 355 S Capitol av.
Wren Thomas, lab, h 1 Henry.
Wren Thomas A, engr, h 65 S Summit.
Wren Thomas J, helper, b 193 W South.
Wren Wm A, horseshoer, 496 Virginia av, h same.
Wrenick James, clk, b 187 Columbia av.
Wright Adelia R (wid Thomas), h rear 175 St Mary.
Wright Addie, teacher Public School No 4, b 80 W St Clair.
Wright Albert, lab, b rear 175 St Mary.
Wright Albert J, tmstr, h 244 S Capitol av.
Wright Alice (wid Daniel), h 16 Hiawatha.
Wright Alonzo, mach hd, h 408 N Brookside av.
Wright Amanda O, dressmkr, 97 Cherry, h same.

The Williams Typewriter Elegant Work, Visible Writing, Easy Operation, High Speed. S. H. EAST, State Agent, 55 Thorpe Block, 87 E. Market St.

ELLIS & HELFENBERGER { Manufacturers of IRON and WIRE FENCES 162-170 S. SENATE AVE. TEL. 358.

THE HOGAN TRANSFER AND STORAGE COMPANY

The Central Rubber & Supply Co.

OTTO GAS ENGINES

THE HOGAN TRANSFER AND STORAGE COMP'Y
Household Goods and Pianos Moved—Packed—Stored...... Baggage and Package Express Machinery and Safes a Specialty Cor. Washington and Illinois Sts. TELEPHONE No. 675.

Hose, Belting, Packing, Clothing, Druggists' Sundries, Bicycle Tires, Cotton Hose, Etc. New York Belting & Packing Co., L't'd.

HIGHEST SECURITY
LOWEST COST OF INSURANCE.
The Provident Life and Trust Co.
Of Philadelphia.
D. W. EDWARDS, Gen. Agent,
508 Indiana Trust Building.

Wright Andrew, lab, b 15 Stevens.
Wright Anna (wid Charles E), b The Denison.
Wright Anna M (wid Quincy A), h 119 Meek.
Wright Anna P, stenog E C Atkins & Co, b 299 Broadway.
Wright Arthur L (Wright & Workman), h 109 N Arsenal av.
Wright Asbury P, carp, h s w cor Lena and Parker (I).
Wright Augustus G, roadmaster, h 309 Ash.
Wright Barton M, trav agt, r 152 N Senate av.
Wright Benjamin C (Benjamin C Wright & Co), h w s Central av 1 n of 30th.
Wright Benjamin C, mach, b 746 N New Jersey.
WRIGHT BENJAMIN C & CO (Benjamin C Wright, John W Tomlinson), U S Claim Attorneys, 29½ N Penn.
Wright Benjamin F, clk Masonic Mutual Benefit Society, h 305 E Ohio.
Wright Cager M, pumpmkr, 63 Shelby, h same.
Wright Cassius E, lab, b s w cor Brookside and Lebanon avs.
Wright Charles, r 45 Indiana av.
Wright Charles, lab, h 97 Cherry.
Wright Charles, lab, h n s Ohio 8 e of Rural.
Wright Charles, lab, b 254 W 5th.
Wright Charles, porter, b 324 Tremont.
Wright Charles, waiter The Denison.
Wright Charles A, baggageman, b 309 Ash.
Wright Charles C, engraver, h 50 Eastern av.
Wright Charles E, phys, b The Denison.
Wright Charles J, undertaker, b 139 N Delaware.
Wright Charles S, bkkpr Indpls Gas Co, h 590 Broadway.
Wright Charles W, h 184 E St Clair.
Wright Charles W, collr Charles T Whitsett, r 123 N Delaware.
Wright Charles W, roofer, b 135 E Washington.
Wright Daniel D, lab, h 33 Hendricks.

Julius C. Walk & Son,
Jewelers
Indianapolis.
12 EAST WASHINGTON ST.

Wright David L, custodian Monument, r 44 State House.
Wright Douglas, engr, h 258½ Bates.
Wright Earl M, trav agt, b 71 Madison av.
Wright Edna S, bkkpr Boyd, Besten & Langen Co, b 60 W 5th.
Wright Edward, tmstr, b 831 E Market.
Wright Elden L, lab, h 359 S Delaware.
Wright Eliza A (wid Charles W), h 204 Elm.
Wright Elizabeth (wid Hayden S), b 512 S Meridian.
Wright Elmer, driver, h e s Sherman Drive 3 s of Washington.
Wright Elmer D, student, h 367 N Alabama.
Wright Emma L, h 20 Oxford.
Wright Ernest, pumpmkr, h 63 Shelby.
Wright Fay, clk G W Stout, h 34 Birch av (W I).
Wright Francis M (wid John M), h 317 E St Clair.
Wright Francis S (wid Willis W), h 382 Clifford av.
Wright Frank, framemkr, b 87 Birch av (W I).
Wright Frank, lawyer, b Senate Hotel.
Wright Frank A, paperhngr, h 494 N Missouri.
Wright Frank C, express, h 15 Leota.
Wright Frank M, planing mill, n w cor Ohio and Belt R R, h n s E Ohio 7 e of Rural.
Wright Frank M, ruler, h 297 W Vermont.
Wright Franklin Y, motorman, h 40 Harlan.
Wright George, collr, b 334 N Illinois.
Wright George, phys, 37½ W Market, h 49 Cottage av (W I).
Wright George, tiremkr, b 235 S Noble.
Wright George C, supt, b 346 N Pine.
Wright George E, carp, h e s Madeira 4 s of Prospect.
Wright George L, mason, b 539 Highland av (N I).
Wright George P, clk R M S, h 214 Walcott.
Wright George W, h 831 E Market.
Wright Granville S, lawyer, supreme treas Order of Equity, 29½ N Penn, h cor Central av and 35th.
Wright Hamilton S, mach hd, h 95½ N Delaware.
Wright Harry, motorman, r 71 W 13th.
Wright Harry C, mach, h 83 Springfield.
Wright Harry M, foreman, h 200 Woodlawn av.
Wright Harry P, mach, b 571 N Penn.
Wright Harry W, trav agt, b 59 Pleasant.
Wright Harvey A, mince meat mnfr, 69 Indiana av, h 69 W New York.
Wright Harvey W, clk Lilly & Stalnaker, b 382 Clifford av.
Wright Henry, lab, h 730 S East.
Wright Henry B, cook, h 135 Virginia av.
Wright Herman A, carp, b 524 Chestnut.
Wright Howard, carp, b e s Northwestern av nr canal.
Wright Isaac H, lab, h rear 91 Cornell av.
Wright Ivy E, clk, b 20 Oxford.
Wright Jacob, carp, b 61 E South.
Wright Jacob M, lab, h 566 W McLene (N I).
Wright James F, trav agt, h 77 N Olive.
Wright James M, lab, h 76 Dugdale.
Wright James M, lab, h 758 Madison av.
Wright James S, condr, b 489 College av.
Wright James T, h 29 E St Joseph.
Wright James W, cooper, h 249 S Senate av.

The Central Rubber & Supply Co. PHONE 922. 79 S. ILLINOIS ST., INDIANAPOLIS, IND.

OTTO GAS ENGINES | BUILDERS' EXCHANGE S. W. Cor. Ohio and Penn. Telephone 535.

Becker & Son Charles Becker Jacob Becker Jr. Merchant Tailors, 21 N. Penn. St. Tel. 934

SALISBURY & STANLEY OFFICE, STORE AND BANK FIXTURES. Contractors and Builders. Repairing of all kinds done on short notice. 177 Clinton St., Indianapolis, Ind. Telephone 999.

Wright James W, lab, b 524 Chestnut.
Wright Jesse, farmer, h 690 N Illinois.
Wright Jessie S (wid Frank), nurse, 189 Johnson av, b same.
Wright Joel L (J L Wright & Co), b 567 College av.
Wright John A, city agt D P Erwin & Co, h 59 Pleasant.
Wright John B, carp, h 61 E South.
WRIGHT JOHN C, Office Room 1 Wright's Market Street Blk, 68½ E Market, Tel 1497; h 30 E Vermont.
Wright John H, creamery, 669 E Washington, h same.
Wright John H, mngr The Diamond Steam Laundry and Toilet Supply Co, h 83 W 10th.
Wright John L, lab, b 512 S Meridian.
Wright John S, bkkpr Henry C Adams, b 382 Clifford av.
Wright John S, botanist, r 225 N Capitol av.
Wright John W (Richter & Wright), h 241 Douglass.
Wright John W, contr, 172 Laurel, h same.
Wright John W, lab, b 106 Lincoln la.
Wright John W, motorman, h 719 Mass av.
Wright Joseph, molder, h 949 Morris (W I).
Wright Joseph H, porter, b 49 Cottage av (W I).
WRIGHT J KIRK, Treas The McGilliard Agency Co, Sec Indiana Insurance Co of Indianapolis, and Thorpe Block Savings and Loan Association, 83-85 E Market, Tel 479; h 397 N Alabama.
WRIGHT J L & CO (Joel L, Worth and Wilbur T Wright), Real Estate Agts, 48 When Blk.
Wright Laura A (wid Thomas W), h 567 College av.
Wright Leve G, lab, h 106 Lincoln la.
Wright Lewis G, plumber, b 539 E Ohio.
Wright Lewis J, woodwkr, h 51 Wyoming.
Wright Louis J, lab, h 512 S Meridian.
Wright Louisa A (wid George W), furn rooms 190½ S Illinois.
Wright Lovina M (wid Walter W), h 539 Highland av (N I).
Wright Magnetic Medicine Co, Willis H Wright pres, Charles R Miles vice-pres, Nannie B Miles sec and treas, 111½ E Washington.
Wright Martha (wid Henry B), b 569 Union.
Wright Mary D (wid John), b 41 Indiana av.
Wright Mary E (wid Joseph), h 260 S Missouri.
Wright Matthew D, lab, h 578 W McLene (N I).
Wright Morris P, b 270 Central av.
Wright Newton B, trav agt, h 538 Bellefontaine.
Wright Owen S, clk Natl Malleable Castings Co, h 51 King av (H).
Wright Parvin, h 270 Central av.
Wright Parvin F, mach, b 166 E Michigan.
Wright Peter M, cigars, Court House, h 539 E Ohio.
Wright Richard, bookbndr, r 22 Hubbard blk.
Wright Robert, coachman 599 N Penn.
Wright Roy, horseshoer, b 79 E Vermont.
Wright Sallie A (wid Benjamin H), h 746 N New Jersey.
Wright Sarah J (wid George), h e s Linwood av 1 n of Washington.
Wright Sheffield H, h 75 18th.

Henry H. Fay, 40½ E. WASHINGTON ST., AGENT FOR Insurance Co. of North America, Pennsylvania Fire Ins. Co.

Wright Silas D, shoemkr, h 26 Singleton.
Wright Stephen I, molder, h 78 Marion av (W I).
Wright Susanna (wid Wm), h 209 N Liberty.
Wright Thomas A, clk R M S, h 175 Oliver av (W I).
Wright Thomas B, printer, h 22 Harmon.
Wright Thomas G, foreman, h 64 S Summit.
Wright Thomas G, grocer, 9 E Mkt House, h 122 N Summit.
Wright Thomas H, carp, h 524 Chestnut.
Wright Thomas W, grocer, 284 W Washington, h same.
Wright Thornton, lab, b 16 Hiawatha.
Wright Virgil M, trav agt, h 112 Keystone av.
Wright Walter B, b 270 Central av.
Wright Walter C, b 49 Cottage av (W I).
Wright Wilbur T (J L Wright & Co), b 567 College av.
Wright Wm, mach, h 80 S Shade (B).
Wright Wm A, porter N Y Store, h 217 Alvord.
Wright Wm C, molder, h e s Lincoln av 9 s of C C C & St L Ry (M J).
Wright Wm H, clk, h 205 Sheldon.
Wright Wm H, lab, b 259 Hadley av (W I).
Wright Wm H, trav agt Severin, Ostermeyer & Co, r 1235 N Illinois.
Wright Wm L, lumber, rear 310 E Washington, h 495 Dillon.
Wright Wm M, phys, 134 N Penn, r same.
Wright Wm S, electrotyper, b 169 W Market.
Wright Wm S, lab, h 15 Carlos.
Wright Willis H, pres Wright Magnetic Medical Co, h 430 W Shoemaker (N I).
Wright Willis N, condr, h 30 Crawford.
Wright Worth (J L Wright & Co), b 177 Park av.
Wright Zerelda (wid Wm G), h 47 Draper.
Wright Zilpha A (wid Alfred), h 204 Elm.
WRIGHT & WORKMAN (Arthur L Wright, Wm A Workman), Wood Workers, 440 E Ohio.
Wrinck John W, h 215 Christian av.

MAYHEW'S SPECTACLES THE BEST IN USE SOLD ONLY AT 13 N. MERIDIAN ST.

LUMBER Sash and Doors BALKE & KRAUSS CO., Corner Market and Missouri Sts.

Friedgen Has the BEST PATENT LEATHER SHOES AT LOWEST PRICES. 19 North Pennsylvania St.

SAMUEL LAING! HOT AIR FURNACES 72 AND 74 EAST COURT STREET.

M. B. WILSON, Pres. W. F. CHURCHMAN, Cash.
The Capital National Bank,
INDIANAPOLIS, IND.
Banking business in all its branches. Bonds and Foreign Exchange bought and sold.
Interest paid on time deposits.
Checks and drafts on all Indiana and Illinois points handled at lowest rates.
No. 28 South Meridian Street, Cor. Pearl.

Wrinkle David M, trav agt, b 361 Ramsey av.
Wrinkle Elisha, h 361 Ramsey av.
Wrinkle James S, trav agt, b 361 Ramsey av.
Writesman John, lab, b 71 Oak.
Writesman Wm H, mach hd, h 585 Mass av.
Wroblinsky Thomas, lab, h 95 Woodruff av.
WROUGHT IRON BRIDGE CO, Builders of Iron, Wood, Combination Railroad, Highway and City Bridges, Wm W Winslow Genl Agt, 1 Hubbard Blk, s w cor Meridian and Washington, Tel 1190. (See adv p 10.)
Wuelfing Eugene, asst bkkpr The H Lieber Co, h 423 Highland av.
Wuelfing Hugo, bkkpr Francke & Schindler, h 86 Stoughton av.
Wuensch Frank J, barber, b 33 Water.
Wuensch George, carver, h 619 S Meridian.
Wuensch Mary (wid Frederick), h 33 Water.
Wuensch Oscar, mach, h 84 Wisconsin.
Wuerffel Frederick, h 325 Bates.
Wuerffel Johanna, h 325 Bates.
Wulf, see also Wolf.
Wulf Frederick (Wulf & Bishoff), res Cumberland, Ind.
Wulf Gottlieb W, wagonmkr, r 185 Prospect.
Wulf & Bishoff (Frederick Wulf, Jacob Bishoff), whol meats, 8 E Mkt House.
Wulff Johanna (wid Conrad C), saloon, s w cor Morris and Nordyke av (W I), h same.
Wulfson Isidor, second hand goods, 296 E Washington, h same.
Wulle George H, lab, b 58 School (B).
Wulle John G, carp, h 58 School (B).
Wulschner Emil (Emil Wulschner & Son), h 410 N Meridian.
WULSCHNER EMIL & SON (Emil Wulschner, Alexander M Stewart), Pianos, Organs, Musical Merchandise, Sheet Music and Books, 78-80 N Penn, Tel 885.

Insure Against Accidents
WITH
TUTTLE & SEGUIN,
Agents for
Fidelity and Casualty Co., of New York.
$10,000 for $25. $5,000 for $12.50.
TEL. 1168. 28 E. MARKET ST.

Wulsin Clarence (D H Baldwin & Co), h 712 N Meridian.
Wulsin Lucius (D H Baldwin & Co), res Cincinnati, O.
Wulzen Charles F, butcher, h 2 Gardner's la.
Wulzen Charles W, well sinker, 58 Mayhew, b same.
Wulzen Dora, housekpr 535 E Market.
Wulzen Kate, dressmkr, h 3, 502½ E Washington.
Wundram Anna, h 662 S Meridian.
Wundram Anna (wid Wm), h 40 Wisconsin.
Wundram Emil, clk, h 664 S Meridian.
Wundram Louis, shoemkr, 554 S Meridian, h 43 Kansas.
Wundram Louis jr, chairmkr, h 370 Coburn.
Wundram Wm, grocer, 662 S Meridian, h 31 Wisconsin.
Wundram Wm W, lab, b 43 Kansas.
Wunschel Frederick C, clk, r Hendricks blk.
Wunschel Louis, brewer, h 476 E Washington.
Wurfel George, blksmith, h 20 N Rural.
Wurgler Anna C, bkkpr G Adolph Wurgler, b 343 Coburn.
Wurgler George J, mach, h 275 Fletcher av.
WURGLER G ADOLPH, Real Estate, Rentals and Loans; also Notary Public, Rooms 2-3, 88½ E Washington, h 343 Coburn.
Wurgler G Adolph jr, plumber, 88½ E Washington, h 81 Lexington av.
Wurster Ernst, meats, 579 Madison av, h same.
Wurth Catherine (wid David), h 902 S Meridian.
Wurth Frederick, lab, b 902 S Meridian.
Wurth Louis T, lab, h 51 Agnes.
Wurtz, see also Wertz and Wirtz.
Wurtz Catherine E (wid Michael M), laundress, h 247 Madison av.
Wurtz Charles E, engraver Indiana Illustrating Co, b 104 Wisconsin.
Wurtz Flora, b 104 Wisconsin.
Wurtz Joseph W, saloon, 125 W Washington, r 219 E Washington.
Wurtz Michael, blksmith, h 104 Wisconsin.
Wurtz Peter W, bartndr, r 1014 S Meridian.
Wurz John W, baker, b 56 Morton.
Wyant Mott, bricklyr, b 477 Stillwell.
Wyatt Charles, mach hd, b 256 S Capitol av.
Wyatt Charles W, lab, b 29 S Summit.
Wyatt Frank J, condr, h 47 Brookside av.
Wyatt George, lab, b 89 S Liberty.
Wyatt George W, bartndr, h 29 S Summit.
Wyatt Harrison N, lawyer, 113½ E Washington, h 127 E Washington.
Wyatt Jacob, car rep, h 226½ W Washington.
Wyatt Joseph F, motorman, h 71 W 13th.
Wyatt Louisa, h 89 S Liberty.
Wyatt Luther N, foreman, h 116 S Olive.
Wyatt Perry S, lab, h 85 S Liberty.
Wyatt Robert C, lab, b 45 Birch av (W I).
Wyckoff Albert C, watchman, h w s Rural 2 n of Lily.
Wyckoff John C, carp, h 99 Fountain av.
Wyckoff Rolla, lab, h s e cor Tremont and Schurmann av (W I).
Wyckoff Samuel B, watchman, h w s Rural 1 n of Lily.
WYCKOFF, SEAMANS & BENEDICT (Incorporated), Proprs Remington Typewriter, George E Field Mngr, 34 E Market, Tel 451.

WEDDING CAKE BOXES · SULLIVAN & MAHAN 41 W. Pearl St.

DIAMOND WALL PLASTER (BUILDERS' EXCHANGE.

Best Work. Prompt Delivery. } THE HOME LAUNDRY 197 S. ILLINOIS ST. TEL. 1769. { Collars and Cuffs our Specialty.

Wyckoff Stanley, creamery, 177 Virginia av, h 1007 N Illinois.
Wylie, see also Wiley and Willey.
WYLIE ANDREW, Dealer in Books and Stationery, 13 N Penn, h 37 Benton.
WYLIE BRUCE M, Physician, 503 S Meridian, h same, Tel 1297.
Wylie Ellen J (wid Charles), h 444 Cornell av.
Wylie John, lab, b 217 S Illinois.
Wyllie Robert C, salesman, h 22 Tuxedo.
Wyman Edward, clk, h 112 N Noble.
Wyman Kate M (wid Charles W), h 193 Cornell av.
Wyman Margaret A (wid Henry K), news dealer, 406 Virginia av, h same.
Wyman Wm C, fireman, b 193 Cornell av.
Wymond Charles F, b 284 N Capitol av.
Wymond Harry A, broker, 227 Lemcke bldg, h 405 N Illinois.
Wynn Frank B, phys, 18 E Ohio, h 39 Christian av.
Wynn John G, electrician, b 27 LaSalle (M P).
Wynn Malachi, lab, b 246 W Washington.
Wynn Peter F, janitor State House.
WYNN WILBUR S, Sec The State Life Insurance Co, 515-520 Lemcke Bldg, h 735 N Delaware.
Wynn Wm D, stoker, h 120 S New Jersey.
Wynne Oliver A, clk, h 224 Clinton.
Wynne Thomas A, supt Indpls Light and Power Co, b 385 N New Jersey.
Wyon Albert F (Holliday & Wyon), h 728 N New Jersey.
Wyon John F, trav agt Holliday & Wyon, h 1392 N Capitol av.
Wyper Alexander, lab, b 614 W Vermont.
Wyper James, watchman, h 614 W Vermont.
Wyrich Jacob G, coachman, h 64 Roanoke.
Wysong Alva P, clk, b 631 Park av.
Wysong Annie, h 631 Park av.
Wysong Bedford C, clk, b 557 Bellefontaine.
Wysong Benjamin F (Clark, Wysong & Voris), h 80 S Reisner (W I).
Wysong Charles, bricklyr, h 296 Coburn.
Wysong David M, engr, h 31 N State av.
Wysong Edna D, stenog, b 557 Bellefontaine.
Wysong George, bricklyr, h 285 Broadway.
Wysong Marcus D, clk, b 557 Bellefontaine.
Wysong Oliver, bricklyr, b 39 N Alabama.
Wysong Reese, clk, b 631 Park av.
Wysong Thomas, mason, h 166 Woodlawn av.
Wysong Wm J, mason, b 166 Woodlawn av.

Y

Yagen Matthew, carp, h 50 Hosbrook.
Yager Charles, carp, b 1329 E Washington.
Yager Marion, fireman, h 86 Bates.
Yager Peter, lab, h 72 Torbet.
Yagerlenner Charles C, clk P C C & St L Ry, h 25½ N Gillard av.
Yagerlenner George F, helper, h 180 Pleasant.
Yagerlenner Samuel A, insp, b 25½ Gillard av.
Yakey Charles, basketmkr, b 86 N East.
Yakey Wm, trav agt John L Moore, b St Charles Hotel.
Yancey Alexander C, mach hd, b 1363 Emma (N I).
Yancey Bragg, lab, h 212 W 10th.
Yancey John, lab, h n e cor Northwestern av and 9th.

FRANK NESSLER. WILL H. ROST.
FRANK NESSLER & CO.
Tailors
56 EAST MARKET ST. (Lemcke Building),
INDIANAPOLIS, IND.

Yancey Orville J, dairy, w s Brightwood av 1 s of Wolf pike (B), h same.
Yancey Otto E, basketmkr, b 1169 E Washington.
Yancey Thomas L, mach hd, h 1363 Emma (N I).
Yancey Wirt L, mach hd, h 1363 Emma (N I).
Yandes George B, vice-pres Indiana Natl Bank, office, 12 Hubbard blk, h 84 E Michigan.
Yandes Simon, office, 5 Ingalls blk, b Grand Hotel.
Yanker Frank B, clk, b 172 Indiana av.
Yankuner Abraham, clk Kahn Tailoring Co, b 172 Indiana av.
Yankuner Frank B, clk, b 172 Indiana av.
Yankuner Harry, clk, b 172 Indiana av.
Yankuner Louis M, clk, b 172 Indiana av.
Yankuner Nathan, clothing, 172 Indiana av, h same.
Yanthis George W, tmstr, h 37 Hiawatha.
Yanzer Sarah J (wid Jacob), h 423 Chestnut.
Yarber Franklin, lab, h 410 N Brookside av.
Yard Sallie (wid Stephen), r 9½ Madison av.
Yaryan Harry R, clk Penna Lines, b 162 S Illinois.
Yaryan Jerome J, foreman, h 50 Athon.
Yaryen John J, carp, h e s Northwestern av 1 n of 24th.
Yaryen Sylvester A, lab, h 53 N Brightwood av (B).
Yates Emmett, condr, r 888 W Washington.
Yates Francis M, lab, h 7 Cottage av (W I).
Yates James L, foreman, h 168 Laurel.
Yates John C, carp, h 436 Chestnut.
Yates John R, b Hanna Hotel.
Yates Rina M (wid Arnold E), h 168 E North.
Yeager Calvin W, mach, b 28 School.
Yeager Caroline (wid Casper), h 138 N Dorman.
Yeager Elias, shoemkr, 224 S Linden, h same.
Yeager Frank R, lab, b 138 N Dorman.
Yeager Frederick W, lab, h 40 School (B).
Yeager George F, drugs, 297 Virginia av, h same.

ACORN STOVES AND RANGES
Haueisen & Hartmann
163-169 E. Washington St.
FURNITURE,
Carpets,
Household Goods,
Tin, Granite and China Wares, Oil Cloth and Shades

THE WM. H. BLOCK CO. 7 AND 9 EAST WASHINGTON STREET. DRY GOODS, HOUSE FURNISHINGS AND CROCKERY.

London Guarantee and Accident Co. (Ltd.) All forms of Liability Insurance, Workmen's Collective Insurance, Fidelity Bonds and Individual Accident Insurance.
Geo. W. Pangborn, Gen. Agent, 704-706 Lemcke Bldg. Telephone 140.

FRANK K. SAWYER, AGENT 74 East Market Street. Telephone 863.
Prussian National Insurance Company OF STETTIN, GERMANY. ORGANIZED 1845.

JOSEPH GARDNER,
TIN, COPPER AND SHEET-IRON WORK AND
HOT AIR FURNACES.
37, 39 & 41 KENTUCKY AVE. Telephone 322.

Yeager Minnie A, h 156 Chestnut.
Yeager Nathaniel E, waiter, h 33 E South.
Yeager Obanyan, lab, h 6 Lafayette.
Yeager Peter J, gasmkr, h 72 Torbet.
Yeager Zachariah, lab, h 86 Bates.
Yealey Henry, packer, b 55 Columbia av.
Yeamans Otto, sawmkr, b 319 S Meridian.
Yearns John B, saloon, 129 S Noble, h same.
Yeaton Frederick A, foreman W U Tel Co, h n w cor 16th and Ash.
Yeaton Susan D (wid Lendell B), teacher Public School No 29, b 589 Broadway.
Yeaw Marshall S, barber, 33 W 1st, r 483 N Illinois.
Yeazell Otway R, carp, h 1074 W New York.
Yeazell Sherman B, lab, b 426 Cornell av.
Yeazell Wm A, insp, h Harris av (M J).
Yercer M W, phys, r 81 W Michigan.
Yerkes Florence, nurse City Hospital.
Yetter Christian G, cabtmkr, h 22 Weghorst.
Yetter Frederick C, uphlr, h 97 Kansas.
Yetter Magdalena (wid Gottfried), h 618 S East.
Yewell Elizabeth (wid Solomon), b 571 E 9th.
Yike Joseph, lab, h 261 River av (W I).
Yingling Wm H, trav agt W J Holliday & Co, r 84½ N Illinois.
Yockey John F, carp, h 82 Park av.
Yocum Charles, painter, b 323 N Liberty.
Yocum Charles A, shoemkr, 372 E 7th, h 559 Broadway.
Yocum Ellen (wid Daniel J), b 21 Sharpe.
Yocum George W, locksmith, 262 Mass av, b 36 Ash.
Yocum Samuel H, h 36 Ash.
Yocum Thomas, painter, h 323 N Liberty.
Yoder Henry D, sec and treas Blanton Milling Co, r 68 W Vermont.
Yoerg Catherine (wid Peter), h 31 Deloss.
Yoerg Henry, finisher, h 31 Deloss.
Yoh Ludoskia (wid Frank R), h 630 N Senate av.
Yohn Eliza S (wid James C), h 206 N Delaware.
Yoke Charles R, student, b 131 Fletcher av.

J. S. FARRELL & CO.
STEAM AND HOT WATER HEATING FOR STORES, OFFICES, PUBLIC BUILDINGS, PRIVATE RESIDENCES, GREENHOUSES, ETC.
84 North Illinois St. Telephone 382.

Yoke George J, farmer, h w s Shelby 1 s of Southern av.
Yoke Nelson, supervising prin Public School No 7, h 131 Fletcher av.
Yoke Richason A, farmer, h w s Shelby 2 s of Southern av.
Yontz Eugene, lab Deaf and Dumb Inst.
Yontz Manford D, trav agt Wm B Burford, h 81 W 10th.
Yooter Willis, lab, h 24 Columbia al.
Yorfer Louis, pdlr, h 565 S Capitol av.
Yorger Charles, meats, 582 Virginia av, h same.
Yorger Clemens C, lab, h 126 Williams.
Yorger Harry C, mach, h 226 Dillon.
Yorger Louis, city agt, h 43 Vinton.
Yorger Thomas L, butcher, h 13 Woodlawn av.
York Albert S, fireman, h 242 English av.
York Andrew J, lab, h 87 Woodburn av (W I).
York Asbury, cashr U S Ex Co, h 667 Park av.
York Charles, fireman, b 124 Lexington av.
York Charles C, confr, b 431 E McCarty.
York Edward O, confr, h 4 Holmes.
York Edwin D, mess Am Ex Co, h 394 Union.
York Ella, cook, h 143½ Virginia av.
York Florence S, stenog, b 431 E McCarty.
York Harry B, clk, h 482 W Shoemaker (N I).
York Harry F, mach hd, h 265 S East.
York Harry W, mess Am Ex Co, b 394 Union.
York John E, oil, h w s Ritter av 1 n of Washington av (I).
York John M, engr, h 327 Fletcher av.
York Joseph A, lab, b 190 N East.
York Joseph W, lab, h 629 W Eugene (N I).
York Mahala, r 17 Wyandot blk.
York Margaret J, h 27½ W Ohio.
York Nathaniel W, contr, b 431 E McCarty.
York Thaddeus E, tel opr, b 394 Union.
York Thomas L, hostler, r 30 S Penn.
York Wm, fireman, r 872 Cornell av.
York Wm G, h 431 E McCarty.
Yorn John A, h 429 N New Jersey.
Yorn Louis H, lab, h 556 S Illinois.
Yost Elizabeth, h 04 W Georgia.
Yost George W R, clk W U Tel Co, h 354 Cedar.
Yosten Herman, coachman 401 Madison av.
Yott Frank H, mach, h 177 Blake.
Youart Margaret R (wid John M), h 23 E 26th.
Youel Ernest H, mngr Globe Advertising Co and sec Indiana Collection Bureau, b 278 N East.
Youel Louisa M (wid Robert D), h 278 N East.
Younce Harvey J, lab, h n e cor Willow and Gale (B).
Younce John F, flue welder, h 59 N Gale (B).
Younce Mary J (wid Philip), b n e cor Willow and Gale (B).
Young, see also Yung.
Young Adolph, mach hd, h 714 S East.
Young Albert, lab, b 75 Rhode Island.
Young Albert, mach, b 945 S East.
Young Albert C, lab, b 28 Seibert.
Young Alfred T, foreman, h 26 Bismarck.
Young Alice C, cashr, b 179 Huron.
Young America E (wid Wm H), h 319 N Noble.
Young Andrew G, asst gent frt agt L E & W R R, h 107 Ruckle.
Young Archibald A (Young & McMurray), h 948 N Capitol av.

United States Life Insurance Co., of New York.
E. B. SWIFT, M'g'r. 25 E. Market St.

WM. KOTTEMAN } 89 & 91 E. Washington St. Telephone 1742 { RUGS MATTINGS WINDOW SHADES

WILLIAM WIEGEL { MANUFACTURER OF.... } SHOW CASES { 6 W. Louisiana St. Opposite Union Station.

Young Austin L, student, b s e cor Keystone and Brookside avs.
Young Barbara, h rear 236 E Wabash.
Young Benjamin, cushionmkr, b 27 Ingram.
Young Benjamin, tmstr, h 28 Seibert.
Young Benjamin L, switchtndr, h 180 E South.
Young Beverly, mach hd, h 191 Bell.
Young Bloomer T, b 642 N Capitol av.
Young Calvin J, draughtsman, h 186 N New Jersey.
Young Charles, barber, r 21 Fayette.
Young Charles, cabtmkr, h 619 Mass av.
Young Charles H, sec Reserve Fund S and L Assn, h 71 Highland pl.
Young Christian C, lab, b 50 Preston.
Young Christopher, lab, h 134 Yandes.
Young Daniel W, lab, b 121½ Newman.
Young Daniel W, student, h 166 Clinton.
Young Du Bois, mach hd, h 485 E 9th.
Young Edgar E, mach hd, h 214 Buchanan.
Young Edward, coachman 49 Central av.
Young Edward K, brakeman, h 1094 W New York.
Young Edwin E, clk, h 374 W Vermont.
Young Emma J (wid Merritt T), h 642 N Capitol av.
Young Frank (Roth & Young), h 787 N Alabama.
Young Frank, student, b 28 Seibert.
Young Frank H, mnfr's agt, 3 Board of Trade bldg, h 212 Ash.
Young Frederick G, bkkpr, r 121 E New York.
Young Frederick P, glass beveler, b 619 Mass av.
Young George, coachman 856 N Meridian.
Young George B, trav agt, h s e cor Keystone and S Brookside avs.
Young George F, tailor, 34 Indiana av, h 1064 N Senate av.
Young George J, billiards, 78 N Delaware, h 219 Ramsey av.
Young George W, car rep, h 144 N Gillard av.
Young George W, dairyman, 8 Highland pl, h same.
Young Horace G, hides, 2 St Peter, h same.
Young Howard L, lab, h 15 Henry.
Young Ira W, lab, h 25 N Beville av.
Young Isaac, b 268 Fulton.
Young Jacob, lab, h 50 Preston.
Young Jacob C, draughtsman, h 186 N New Jersey.
Young James, blksmith, h 26 Riley blk.
Young James, lab, h 475 Charles.
Young James H, prin Public School No 37, h 226 N Noble.
Young James R, bkkpr, h 570 Jefferson av.
Young James S, coachman 739 N Penn.
Young Jefferson W, lab, b 121½ Newman.
Young Jeanette (wid Christian), h 945 S East.
Young John, bartndr, h 308 N Senate av.
Young John, coachman 810 N Meridian.
Young John A, mach, h 55 Nordyke av (W I).
Young John A, stone dresser, h 15 Bridge (W I).
Young John D, bricklyr, h 618 E New York.
Young John F, driver, h 120 S State av.
Young John F, hostler, h 256 Fayette.
Young John F, mngr, h 787 N Alabama.
Young John G, bricklyr, h 447 W Pratt.
Young John H, trav agt, b 980 N Illinois.
Young John O, saloon, 252 S Capitol av, h 119 Trowbridge (W).
Young John W, lab, h 75 Drake.
Young John W, lab, r 228 N Noble.

THOS. C. DAY & CO.
Financial Agents and Loans.
We have the experience, and claim to be reliable.
Rooms 325 to 330 Lemcke Bldg.

Young Johnson E, carp, b 642 N Capitol av.
Young Joseph, baker, h rear 176 E Washington.
Young Joseph H, mach, h 262 E Georgia.
Young Leonard L, mach hd, b 24 Ingram.
Young Leslie C, attendant Insane Hospital.
Young Lewis, lab, h w s Burgess av 2 s of C H & D Ry (I).
Young Margaret (wid Alexander), h 121½ Newman.
Young Martha J (wid Henry), h 119 Trowbridge (W).
Young Mary (wid Jacob), h 75 Rhode Island.
Young Mary (wid John), h 17 Sumner.
YOUNG MEN'S CHRISTIAN ASSOCIATION, Wm T Brown Pres, O H Palmer Sec, Theodore A Hildreth Genl Sec, 29-37 N Illinois, Tel 1414.
Young Men's Savings and Loan Assn, J A Kebler pres, H A Weber sec, H J Budenz treas, 2 Thorpe blk.
Young Michael A, phys, 244½ E Washington, h 451 E Market.
Young Nancy (wid Richard), h 21 Mill.
Young Nettie (wid Christian), h 945 S East.
Young Nora B, teacher, b 155 N Illinois.
Young Orange, porter, h 208 Northwestern av.
Young Owen, coachman 1134 N Meridian.
Young People's Journal, George F Bass editor, 105 Commercial Club bldg.
Young Plummer P, grocer, 506 E 9th, h 482 same.
Young Richard B, lab, h 408 W North.
Young Richard M, lab, h 24 Ingram.
Young Richard N, contr, 96 Oliver av (W I), h same.
Young Robert M, motorman, b 150 Cornell av.
Young Robert R, student, b 186 N New Jersey.
Young Samuel, condr, h 433 Ash.
Young Samuel B, finisher, h n e cor Hazel and Lawrence.
Young Schuyler C, clk Van Camp H and I Co, b 179 Huron.

EAT
QUAKER BREAD
ASK YOUR GROCER FOR IT.
THE HITZ BAKING CO.

CARPETS AND RUGS RENOVATED.......... | CAPITAL STEAM CARPET CLEANING WORKS M. D. PLUNKETT, TELEPHONE No. 818

BENJ. BOOTH PRACTICAL EXPERT ACCOUNTANT. Complicated or disputed accounts investigated and adjusted. Room 18, 82½ E. Wash. St., Ind'p'l's, Ind.

18 and 20 South Meridian Street KERSHNER BROS., Proprs. THE SHERMAN RESTAURANT

ESTABLISHED 1876. TELEPHONE 168.
CHESTER BRADFORD,
SOLICITOR OF PATENTS,
AND COUNSEL IN PATENT CAUSES.
(See adv. page 6.)
Office:—Rooms 14 and 16 Hubbard Block, S.W. Cor. Washington and Meridian Streets, INDIANAPOLIS, INDIANA.

Young Shad R, jeweler, h 186 N New Jersey.
Young Squire, lab, h 266 Fayette.
Young Thomas, cook, h 187 W 3d.
Young Thomas J, phys, 18½ N Meridian, r same.
Young Vincent J, student, b 326 N Illinois.
Young Walter K, clk L E & W R R, b 107 Ruckle.
Young Wesley A, lab, b 525 N Senate av.
Young Wm, driver, r 247 Fayette.
Young Wm, fireman, b 269 Springfield.
Young Wm A, carp, h s e cor 26th and Central av.
Young Wm A, pastor Seventh Day Adventist Church, h 98 Cherry.
Young Wm D, lab, h 575 N West.
Young Wm F, porter, h 169 W 6th.
Young Wm G, collection clk The Capital Natl Bank, h 767 N Alabama.
Young Wm H, bartndr, r 137½ Virginia av.
Young Wm H, carp, b 1349 N Capitol av.
Young Wm H, trimmer, h 339 S Delaware.
Young Wm J, molder, h 75 Drake.
Young Wm L, phys, 121 S Noble, h same.
Young Winthrop, h 179 Huron.
Young Women's Christian Association, 139 N Meridian.
Young Zacharia, lab, b 221 W 3d.
YOUNG & McMURRAY (Archibald A Young, Welcome B McMurray), Merchant Tailors, 12-14 N Meridian, Tel 1648.
Youngerman Albert A, etcher, h 74 Cypress.
Youngerman August, mach hd, h 734 Shelby.
Youngerman Conrad W, tool mnfr, 176 Dearborn, h 220 S Reisner (W I).
Youngerman Henry, mach hd, h 560 Shelby.
Youngerman Wm A, patternmkr, h Harris av (M J).
Youngman Charles, meats, 705 E Washington, h same.
Youngman Daniel, bartndr, b 762 E Washington.
Youngman George S, lab, h 144 Blackford.
Youngman Wm S, saloon, 762 E Washington, h same.

Metal Ceilings and all kinds of Copper, Tin and Sheet Iron work.
O. B. ENSEY,
TELEPHONE 1562.
CORNER 6TH AND ILLINOIS STS.

Younk Jackson, blksmith, h n s Willow 4 w of Brightwood av (B).
Younk John, lab, h w s School 2 n of Spencer (B).
Younk Wm E, lab, b w s School 2 n of Spencer (B).
Yount Benjamin F, lab, h 31 Palmer.
Yount Daniel, grocer, 200 S Pine, h 93 English av.
Yount Edward J, mach, h 341 Yandes.
Yount Enoch T, motorman, h 438 Cornell av.
Yount Frank H, clk, h 602 College av.
Yount Frederick G, civil engr, b 316 Ash.
Yount Horace J, mach, h 333 Yandes.
Yount Jesse M, electrician, b 316 Ash.
Yount Mary A (wid John M), h 316 Ash.
Yount Oscar G, clk Order of Chosen Friends, b 450 Bellefontaine.
Yount Thomas J, chief clk Order of Chosen Friends, h 450 Bellefontaine.
Yount Webb D, foreman, h 35 Cornell av.
Yount Wm C, motorman, b 1007 N Illinois.
Yount Wm H, motorman, h 481 E 9th.
Yount Wm T, brakeman, b 213 W Maryland.
Youree Bailey, lab, b 254 W 5th.
Youree John, lab, h 254 W 5th.
Youree Wm, lab, h 252 W 5th.
Youse Frank L, trav agt D H Baldwin & Co, h 368 Talbott av.
Youse John F, tinner, h 1152 N Alabama.
Youse Lucy, teacher Public School No 9, b 1152 N Alabama.
Youtsey Laura E, teacher, b 207 Huron.
Youtsey Mary J (wid Thomas), h 207 Huron.
Youtsey Sarah C, teacher Public School No 20, b 207 Huron.
Youtsey Wm M, bartndr, r 71 W Michigan.
Yowell George C, trav agt Francke & Schindler, r 215 N Illinois.
Yule Edward, driver, b 100 W 1st.
Yule James, teacher Industrial Training School, h 21 Leota.
Yule Margaret A (wid Samuel T), h 100 W 1st.
Yule Wm (Yule & Hartman), h 200 Highland av.
Yule & Hartman (Wm Yule, Frederick W Hartman), horseshoers, 25 N Liberty.
Yuncker Charles J, trav agt, b 213 N Liberty.
Yuncker Jacob C, real est, r 134 N Meridian.
Yuncker Leo E, bkkpr, r 69½ W Market.
Yung, see also Young.
Yung Gustav A, cabtmkr, h 619 Mass av.
Yung Henry, shoemkr, 160 Ft Wayne av, b 134 Yandes.
Yunker John, engr, b 22 S State av.
Yux Anton, uphlr, h 174 N Missouri.
Yux Apollonia (wid Joseph), b 174 N Missouri.

Z

Zabel Charles G, cabtmkr, h 521 E Ohio.
Zabel Emil, clk A Metzger Agency, b 521 E Ohio.
Zabelle Leo, finisher, h 530 W Eugene (N I).
Zaenglein John C, sawmkr, h 23 Hill.
Zahl Charles, blksmith, 259 Shelby, h 8 Beecher.
Zaiser Edward, stencilcutter, b 183 E Morris.
Zaiser Lenoir O, stampmkr, b 183 E Morris.
Zaiser Lenoir T F, stencilcutter, 21½ W Washington, h 183 E Morris.
Zaiser Wm H, stampmkr, b 183 E Morris.
Zanker John, lab, h 18 Hartford.

TUTEWILER UNDERTAKER, NO. 72 WEST MARKET STREET. TELEPHONE 216.

The Provident Life and Trust Co. Dividends are paid in cash and are not withheld for a long period of years, subject to forfeiture in the event of death or the termination of policy.
D. W. EDWARDS, GENERAL AGENT, 508 INDIANA TRUST BUILDING.

THEODORE F. SMITHER - GRAVEL ROOFING MATERIALS
2 and 3-Ply Ready Roofing, Building Pap er etc. Roof Materials. Telephone 861. 169 West Maryland St.

Zapf Frederick, saloon, 80 W Washington, h same.
Zapf Philip, saloon, 42 Virginia av, h same.
Zaring Amzi C, driver, h 99 Camp.
Zaring Claudius R, plastr, 121 Williams, h same.
Zaring Leander B, plastr, h 100 Camp.
Zaring Louie M, grocer, 100 Camp, h same.
Zaring Robb E Rev, pastor Hyde Park M E Church, h 1771 N Illinois.
Zarwell August F Rev, pastor Second German M E Church, h 329 N Spruce.
Zarzi Peter, lab, h rear 31 Madison av.
Zastezemski Samuel, lab, h 321 W Maryland.
Zawatzky Anthony, glazier, h 32 Leon.
Zearing Albert F, bkkpr, b 631 Mass av.
Zearing Frances C (wid Henry H), h 631 Mass av.
Zebell Leving T, finisher, h 479 W Highland av (N I).
Zebink Joseph, lab, h 49 Holmes av (H).
Zeeck Adam P, lab, h 38 S Gale (B).
Zehr Andrew, h 425 Union.
Zehringer Hannah (wid Frank), h 59 S Dorman.
Zehringer Josephine, h 165 Fulton.
Zehrung Isaac S, lab, h 50 Bismarck (W I).
Zeien Anna M (wid Joseph), h 813 Chestnut.
Zeien Joseph, blksmith, h 696 Chestnut.
Zeien Joseph, saloon, 859 S East, h same.
Zeien Matthew, lab, b 79 Downey.
Zeien Peter, lab, h 157 Minnesota.
Zeiher Frank G, uphlr, b 594 E St Clair.
Zeisler Wm (Zeisler & West), b 52 Warren av (W I).
Zeisler & West (Wm Zeisler, Wm B West), plumbers, rear 51 Warren av (W I).
Zell Theodore W, bkkpr, h S Meridian beyond limits.
Zell Walter, clk, h 64 William.
Zeller Felix, coachman, h 130 E St Joseph.
Zeller Mary, h 256 E Georgia.
Zener Clarence M (Robert Zener & Co), b 316 College av.
Zener Robert (Robert Zener & Co), h 316 College av.

ZENER ROBERT & CO (Robert and Clarence M Zener), Insurance Agts, 10-15 Talbott Blk, n w cor Penn and Market, Tel 522.

Zenor John, painter, b 467 S Missouri.
Zepf Barbara (wid Matthias), h 357 E McCarty.
Zeph David, cigarmkr, h 770 Chestnut.
Zepp Charles N, engr, h 44 Arch.
Zeppruitt Joseph, lab, b n w cor Station and Glen Drive (B).
Zerbe Clinton D, printer, h 101 N New Jersey.
Zernicke Carl, shoemkr, rear 764 S East, h 243 Lincoln la.
Zernicke Theresa (wid Carl); b 243 Lincoln la.
Zessin August, lab, h 276 Martindale av.

ZEUMER JENNIE M, State Cashier Fidelity Mutual Life Insurance Co, 52-53 Baldwin Blk, b 42 Woodlawn av.

Ziegel Edward F, coll teller Merchants' Natl Bank, h 1131 N Delaware.
Ziegel Margaret M (wid Louis), h 63 W 14th.
Ziegler Adolph G, b 129 Kansas.
Ziegler August F, cabtmkr, h 129 Kansas.
Ziegler Carl, cabtmkr, h 419 S Illinois.
Ziegler Catherine (wid Rudolph), h 127 Kansas.
Ziegler Charles, h 97 S Noble.

THE WHEN IS A WORLD BEATER.

Ziegler Ernest L, clk C F Meyer & Bro, b 129 Kansas.
Ziegler Frank J, carp, h 33 W Morris.
Ziegler Frederick W, cabtmkr, b 129 Kansas.
Ziegler Henry, locksmith, 221 Mass av, h same.
Ziegler Henry T, carp, h 430 Chestnut.
Ziegler John T, painter, b 36 S Capitol av.
Ziegler Louis C, fruits, 182 S Illinois, h same.
Ziegler Louisa (wid August), b 250 S Capitol av.
Ziegler Margaret, b Circle Park Hotel.
Ziegler Max H, clk, b 97 S Noble.
Ziegler Rebecca A, boarding 430 Chestnut.
Ziegler Sarah A, notions, 150 E 7th, h 97 S Noble.
Ziegler Wm H, lab, b 134 Douglass.
Ziegner Charles, finisher, b 101 Agnes.
Ziegner Oscar G (Ziegner & Ensley), h 30 Cornell av.
Ziegner Roscoe C, lab, b 30 Cornell av.
Ziegner & Ensley (Oscar G Ziegner, Wm A Ensley), feed, 460 Virginia av.
Zier Abraham, produce, E Mkt House, h 85 W Morris.
Zietlow Wilhelmina (wid Frederick), b 24 Quincy.
Zigrosser Hugo A (D A Bohlen & Son), r 409 N Alabama.

ZIG-ZAG CYCLER THE, Cycler Printing Co Publishers, 33 Talbott Blk. (See adv opp classified Newspapers).

Zimmer Cecilia (wid Ferdinand), h 123 E Merrill.
Zimmer Edward C, clk, b 123 E Merrill.
Zimmer Ferdinand H, clk H P Wasson & Co, b 123 E Merrill.
Zimmer George D, clk, h 391 N Senate av.
Zimmer George F (Zimmer & Co), b 123 E Merrill.
Zimmer Harry E, drugs, 82 E Washington, h 19 E St Joseph.
Zimmer Henry, lab, h 12 Morton.
Zimmer Henry W, clk, b 295 S Delaware.
Zimmer Henry W, paperhngr, 16 Clay, h same.
Zimmer Joseph F, clk, b 295 S Delaware.

The A. Burdsal Co.
Manufacturers of
STEAMBOAT COLORS
BEST HOUSE PAINTS MADE.
Wholesale and Retail.
34 AND 36 SOUTH MERIDIAN STREET.

Electric Contractors
We are prepared to do any kind of Electric Contract Work.
C. W. MEIKEL. Telephone 466.
96-98 E. New York St.

DALTON & MERRIFIELD { LUMBER South Noble St., near E. Washington

INDIANA ELECTROTYPE CO. ::: BEST WORK. LOWEST PRICES. 23 WEST PEARL ST., INDIANAPOLIS, IND. JOB WORK. BOOK PLATES. All Orders Promptly Filled. BEST PATENT BASE ON THE MARKET.

KIRKHOFF BROS.,
Sanitary Plumbers
STEAM AND HOT WATER HEATING.
102-104 SOUTH PENNSYLVANIA ST.
TELEPHONE 910.

Zimmer Louis A (Zimmer & Co and Weber & Zimmer), b 123 E Merrill.
Zimmer Mary E (wid Peter), grocer, 293 S Delaware, h 295 same.
Zimmer & Co (George F and Louis A Zimmer, Harry A Weber), dry goods, 1 Shelby.
Zimmerla Arthur J, mach, b 103 Ft Wayne av.
Zimmerla Jennie A (wid Daniel), h 103 Ft Wayne av.
Zimmerman Albert, lab, h 143 Fulton.
Zimmerman Andrew, mach hd, b 101 Church.
Zimmerman Anna (wid Christian E), h 291 S East.
Zimmerman Charles (C Zimmerman & Sons), b 566 E Washington.
Zimmerman Charles, butcher, b 207 W Michigan.
Zimmerman Charles, mngr Empire Theater, n w cor Delaware and Wabash, r same.
Zimmerman Charles L, clk Henry J Huder, h 34 S Arsenal av.
Zimmerman Christopher (C Zimmerman & Sons), h 566 E Washington.
Zimmerman Conrad, mach hd, b 101 Church.
ZIMMERMAN C & SONS (Christopher, Charles and Walter), Slate and Genl Roofers and Roofing Materials, 19-21 S East, Tel 1753. (See left bottom lines.)
Zimmerman Dean, clk The Bowen-Merrill Co, b 124 E Ohio.
Zimmerman Elizabeth (wid John), h 101 Church.
Zimmerman Frederick, lab, h n w cor Vorster and Sugar Grove avs (M P).
Zimmerman Frederick D, clk, h 57 Greer.
Zimmerman George, h 25 Dickson.
Zimmerman Grant, paperhngr, h 17 Woodlawn av.
Zimmerman Jacob, lab, h 102 Downey.
Zimmerman Jacob N, books, 305 Virginia av, h 327 W Ontario (N I).
Zimmerman John, driver, h rear 727 S Meridian.
Zimmerman John F, saloon, 131 W Washington, h 93 Dunlop.

Lime, Lath, Cement,
THE W. G. WASSON CO.
130 INDIANA AVE. TEL. 989.
Sewer Pipe, Flue Linings, Fire Brick, Fire Clay.

Zimmerman John W, h 318 Union.
Zimmerman Josephine E (wid Henry C), h 105 Davidson.
Zimmerman Josh, propr Globe Excelsior Wks, 19 S East, h 560 E Washington.
Zimmerman Matthias, driver, h 79 Patterson.
Zimmerman Matthias S, harnessmkr, b 57 Greer.
Zimmerman Perry, trav agt, r 121 E Michigan.
Zimmerman Richard N, lab 526 N Meridian.
Zimmerman Walter (C Zimmerman & Sons), b 566 E Washington.
Zims Elizabeth (wid Joseph), cook, 567 N Illinois.
Zingler Frank L, baker, h 80 Erie.
Zink George, lab, h 24 Weghorst.
Zink Henry, lab, b 267 S Capitol av.
Zink James L, physical director Butler College, h e s National av 2 s of Washington av (I).
Zink John G, fireman, b 208 Fayette.
Zink Joseph, cabtmkr, h 46 Davis.
Zink Leopold, butcher, b 475 Indiana av.
Zinkand Adam, coremkr, h 5 N Haugh (H).
Zinkand Wm, attendant Insane Hospital, h 5 N Haugh (H).
Zinn Peter, trav agt, h 74 College av.
Zinn Robert E, bkkpr, b 74 College av.
Zinsmeister Michael, condr, h 36 Tecumseh.
Zintel Michael, contr, 23 Tompkins, h same.
Zion Alonzo A, supt Indpls Union Ry Co, b Grand Hotel.
Zion Amelia J, stenog, b 155 N Illinois.
Zion George A, lab, h 653 Wells (N I).
Zion George H, coachman, h 324 Tremont.
Zion Harry F, engr, h 165 Nordyke av (W I).
Zion Homer C, brakeman, h 20 N Reisner (W I).
Zion John L S, lab, b 745 Brooker's al.
Zion Matthew O, bartndr, b 519 E Ohio.
Zion Thomas J, trav agt, h 519 E Ohio.
Zion Wm, gateman, b 519 E Ohio.
Zisener Paul M, clk N Y Store, h 523 E Ohio.

ZITZLAFF CHARLES J, Physician, Office Hours 8:30-10 A M, 2-4 P M and 7-8 P M, 273 E McCarty, Tel 1119; h 387 S New Jersey.

Zobbe Bros (Charles F and Christian), grocers, 192 W Washington.
Zobbe Charles F (Zobbe Bros), h 35 Prospect.
Zobbe Christian (Zobbe Bros), h 330 S Alabama.
Zobbe Wm F, clk Schrader Bros, h 330 S Alabama.
Zoffmann Rudolph, mach, h 821 S East.
Zolezzi Anthony F, baggageman, h 125 E New York.
Zolezzi Carrie G, nurse, 125 E New York, b same.
Zoller Albert, clk Charles Mayer & Co, b 316 N Meridian.
Zoller Edmund, lawyer, h 299 W 7th.
Zoller Frederick W, painter, h 269 W Merrill.
Zoller John A, car insp, h 984 S Meridian.
Zollinger Julius, grocer, 100 N State av, h same.
Zollinger Magdalena M (wid Henry), b 114 S State av.
Zollman John, uphlr, h 74 Frank.
Zollner Charles H, meats, 290 W Washington, h same.
Zook Charles A, lab, h 162 Johnson (W I).

YOUR HOMES FURNISHED BY W. H. MESSENGER 101 East Washington St. Telephone 491.

McNamara, Koster & Co. Phone 1593. ◆ 212-218 S. PENN. ST. } PATTERN MAKERS

Zook Grant, tilemkr, h. 6 Martha (W I).
Zook John C, carp, h w s Kenwood av 1 s of 30th.
Zook Jonas L, lab, b 77 S Belmont av (W I).
Zook Moses B, carp, r 205 E Market.
Zook Wm L, agt, h 145 Miller (W I).
Zorn George H, grocer, 200 Wright, b same.
Zorn Julius, lab, h 200 Wright.
Zorniger George, mach hd, h 587 W Ontario (N I).
Zorniger John, cigars, e s Lulu 3 n of Udell (N I), r same.
Zoschke Charles, baker, b 14 Keystone av.
Zoschke Herman, butcher, b 540 E Washington.
Zoschke Julius J, lab, h 14 Keystone av.
Zschech Anna B (wid Gustavus), b 999 N Capitol av.
Zschech Elizabeth (wid Frederick M), h 90 Union.
Zschech Henry E, lab, b 90 Union.
Zschech John C, saloon, 401 S Delaware, b 90 Union.
Zschech Otto H, helper, b 90 Union.
Zuber Minda (wid John), h 439 Union.
Zulick Wm R, trav agt, r 28 W Vermont.
Zumpfe Edgar O, bkkpr, b 401 Park av.
Zumpfe Emil, music teacher, 401 Park av, h same.

ZUMPFE'S ORCHESTRA, Wm A Zumpfe Leader, Office 4 Lombard Bldg.

Zumpfe Wm A (Aufderheide & Zumpfe), leader Zumpfe's Orchestra, h 605 N Alabama.
Zwick Albert F, bkkpr Charles Krauss, b 222 N East.
Zwick Charles F, mach, h 40 Tacoma av.
Zwick Edward K, finisher, b 222 N East.
Zwick Frederick C, clk, h 30 N Gillard av.
Zwick Henry, carp, h 42 Tacoma av.

Henry H. Fay,
40½ E. WASHINGTON ST.,
FIRE INSURANCE, REAL ESTATE,
LOANS AND RENTAL AGENT.

Zwick Henry F, clk, b 40 Tacoma av.
Zwick Wm F, tailor, h 222 N East.
Zwicker Frederick, maltster, h 331 Orange.
Zwicker Frederick jr, trav agt, b 331 Orange.
Zwicker Matilde, teacher Public School No 3, b 331 Orange.
Zwissler Adam, uphlr, b 33 Oriental.
Zwissler Mary J, dressmkr, 33 Oriental, h same.

SURETY BONDS
American Bonding & Trust Co.
OF BALTIMORE, MD.
Authorized to act as Sole Surety on all Bonds.
Total Resources over $1,000,000.00.
W. E. BARTON & CO., General Agents,
504 INDIANA TRUST BUILDING.
Long Distance Telephone 1918.

THE FRED DIETZ CO. WOODEN PACKING BOXES MADE TO ORDER. FACTORY AND WAREHOUSE TRUCKS. 400 Madison Avenue. Telephone 654.

DIRECTORY BORROWERS

WE RECEIVE many complaints from our patrons to the effect that they are bothered so much by **BORROWERS.** These parties are not the private citizen nor the stranger in the city, who steps in, looks at the Directory and goes out, but merchants, business and professional men, who need a Directory every day of the year, yet who are too close-fisted to buy one.

These same individuals are the ones that borrow your Directory "just for a minute," which, in the majority of cases, means a day or perhaps a week, unless you remember that they have it and send for it.

These same borrowers will tell the Directory canvasser that he has "no use for a Directory," that he "knows everybody," and, vice versa, "everybody knows him."

Business World Supplied with Help
GRADUATES ASSISTED TO POSITIONS
10,000 NOW IN GOOD SITUATIONS. TEL. 499. E. J. HEEB, PRES.
Indianapolis BUSINESS UNIVERSITY

INCORPORATED 1885.

ESTABLISHED 1870.

R. L. POLK & CO.

GAZETTEER and DIRECTORY

PUBLISHERS.

PUBLISHERS OF GAZETTEERS AND BUSINESS DIRECTORIES

FOR THE STATES OF

ILLINOIS, WEST VIRGINIA, CALIFORNIA,
MICHIGAN, KENTUCKY, WASHINGTON,
PENNSYLVANIA, INDIANA, COLORADO,
NEW JERSEY, IOWA, WYOMING,
MINNESOTA,, WISCONSIN, NEW MEXICO,
MONTANA TEXAS, UTAH,
DAKOTA, MARYLAND, NEVADA,
KANSAS, OREGON, ARIZONA,
MISSOURI, TENNESSEE, ARKANSAS
ALABAMA, PROVINCE OF ONTARIO, IDAHO,
MEDICAL AND SURGICAL REGISTER OF THE UNITED STATES,
DENTAL REGISTER OF THE UNITED STATES.
ARCHITECTS' AND BUILDERS' DIRECTORY OF THE UNITED STATES.

AND CITY DIRECTORIES

—FOR—

Baltimore, Md.; Detroit, Grand Rapids, Saginaw, Bay City, Jackson, Lansing, Muskegon, Port Huron, Sault Ste. Marie, Ann Arbor, Ypsilanti, Kalamazoo, Flint, Alpena, Cheboygan and Big Rapids, Mich.; Toledo, Columbus, Zanesville, Findlay, Newark and Lima, Ohio; Atlanta Columbus and Augusta, Ga.; Birmingham and Montgomery, Ala.; Memphis and Knoxville, Tenn.; Indianapolis and Fort Wayne, Ind.; St. Paul, Minneapolis and Duluth, Minn.; Ashland, Oshkosh and Eau Claire, Wis.; Des Moines, Sioux City and Dubuque, Iowa; Portland, Ore.; Stockton, Cal.; Bismarck, Mandan and Sioux Falls, Dak.; Butte, Mont.; Seattle, Tacoma, Spokane Falls and Walla Walla, W.; Salt Lake City, Utah; London, Hamilton and Toronto, Ont.; Puget Sound; and Marine Directory of the Great Lakes.

Head Office, 40 to 44 Larned St. West, Detroit, Mich.

OFFICES:

St. Louis, Mo., 904 Olive Street.
Chicago, Ill., 122 La Salle Street.
Philadelphia, Pa., Ledger Building, corner Chestnut and Sixth Streets.
Toledo, Ohio, 306 Madison Street.
Columbus, Ohio, 49 North High Street.
Baltimore, Md., 112 North Charles Street.
St. Paul, Minn., National German American Bank Building.
Minneapolis, Minn., 257 First Avenue South.
Des Moines, Iowa, 410 Iowa Loan and Trust Building.
Toronto, Ont., 18 Wellington, E.
Portland, Ore., First National Bank Building.
Atlanta, Ga., Chamber of Commerce.
San Francisco, Cal., 606 Montgomery Street.
Memphis, Tenn., 341 Second Street.
Salt Lake City, Utah.

Indianapolis Office, Rooms 23 and 24 Journal Building.

DIAMOND

WALL PLASTER

◆◆◆◆◆◆

A PURE SELENITIC CEMENT MORTAR FOR PLASTERING PURPOSES, EMPLOYING WHITE LEAD AND OIL AS RETARDERS. IT IS IN EVERY WAY SUPERIOR TO BEST LIME MORTAR AS REGARDS.

TENSILE STRENGTH,
TOUGHNESS, HARDNESS,
DURABILITY AND FIRE AND
WATER-PROOFING QUALITIES,

BESIDES BEING LESS IN FIRST COST THAN OLD STYLE LIME MORTAR PREPARED BY OLD STYLE METHODS.

IN ONE HOUR AFTER USING IT MAY SAFELY BE

PAINTED, TINTED OR PAPERED

Thus saving the weeks of time required by lime mortar to harden.

DIAMOND PLASTER is a complete cement, requiring the addition of water only to prepare it for immediate use, and since 1890, when it was first introduced in Indianapolis, it has been furnished to over 6,000 dwellings, store-rooms, etc. For further information, apply to

DIAMOND WALL PLASTER COMPANY,

C. B. ROCKWOOD, Manager.

OFFICE, BUILDERS' EXCHANGE. **TELEPHONE 1410.**

R. L. POLK & CO.'S

Indianapolis City Directory.

1897.

CLASSIFIED BUSINESS DIRECTORY.

Headings marked thus (*) are special, and are only inserted when specially contracted for.

ABATTOIRS.

Indianapolis Abattoir Co, cor Morris and White river (W I).

*ABSTRACT EXAMINERS.

Rosebrock C Henry, 19 Thorpe Blk. (See back cover.)

ABSTRACTS OF TITLES.

Brown I & L M, 66 E Market.
Coval & Lemon, 96½ E Market.
Elliott & Butler, 84 E Market.
Knapp Wm W, 8 Baldwin blk.
Miner Frederick D, 96½ E Market.
Rosebrock C Henry, 19 Thorpe Blk. (See back cover.)
Routh James R, 12½ N Delaware.
Stein Theodore, 229-230 Lemcke Bldg.

ACADEMIES.

See Colleges, Schools, Etc.

*ACCOUNTANTS.

Booth Benjamin, Room 18, 82½ E Washington. (See left top lines.)
Indianapolis Business University, When Bldg, N Penn, opp Post Office, E J Heeb Propr. (See front cover, right bottom lines and p 4.)

*ADAMANT PLASTER.

Adamant Wall Plaster Co of Indiana, Office and Factory cor Phipps and J M & I R R.

ADVERTISING AGENTS.

Cassell & Karnatz, 52½ S Illinois.
Central Advertising Co, 83 W Georgia.
Globe Advertising Co, 303 Indiana Trust Bldg.
Hodges Edward R, 29½ W Ohio.
Humphreys George H, 31 Lombard bldg.
McKinney Arthur D, 234 Lemcke bldg.
Surber Henry A, 40½ S Illinois.
Surface Charles F, 401 Indiana Trust bldg.
Vansyckle Advertising Co The, 9-10 McDougall Bldg. (See adv.)

Vansyckle Advertising Co.
Established 1889.
DISTRIBUTING, SAMPLING, SIGN TACKING, ETC.
62½ S. Illinois St., Suite 9-10 (Opp. Grand Hotel), INDIANAPOLIS, IND.
Local Members International Ass'n of Distributers.
G. W. VANSYCKLE, Manager.

AGRICULTURAL IMPLEMENTS.

Advance Thresher Co, 3 Masonic Temple.
American Buncher Mnfg Co, 212 S Penn.
Aultman Co The, 3 Board of Trade bldg.
Aultman, Miller & Co, 75 W Washington.
Avery Planter Co, 45 Kentucky av.
Brown-Manly Plow Co, 170 S Penn.
Brown Straw Binder Co, 39 E South.
Case J I Threshing Machine Co, 42 Kentucky av.
Conde H T Implement Co, 27-33 N Capitol av.
Deere, Mansur & Co, 75 W Washington.
Deere & Co, 75 W Washington.
Deering Harvester Co, 192 W Market.
Economist Plow Co, 10 Masonic Temple.
Frick Company The, 28 Kentucky av.
Gaar, Scott & Co, Harry Sheets Genl Agt, 414 N West.
Gale Mnfg Co, 117 W Washington.
Geiser Mnfg Co The, 73 W Maryland.
Gordon & Harmon, 75 W Washington.
Holton W B Mnfg Co, 177 E Washington.
Huber Mnfg Co The, 40 Kentucky av.
Huntington & Page, 78 E Market. (See adv p 5.)
Indiana Mnfg Co The, 401-405 Indiana Trust bldg.
Janesville Machine Co, 75 W Washington.
Kenney & Sullivan, 3 Board of Trade bldg.
McCormick Harvesting Machine Co, 67-69 S Penn.

David S. McKernan | REAL ESTATE AND LOANS
Houses, Lots, Farms and Western Lands for sale or trade.
ROOMS 2-5 THORPE BLOCK.

DIAMOND WALL PLASTER { Telephone 1410 BUILDERS' EXCHANGE.

UNION TRANSFER AND STORAGE CO. Cor. E. Ohio St. and C., C., C. & St. L. R'y Tracks. ISSUE NEGOTIABLE RECEIPTS ON MERCHANDISE AND HOUSEHOLD GOODS.

Agricultural Implements—Con.
Marion Mnfg Co, 62 W Georgia.
Massillon Engine and Thresher Co, 5 Commercial blk.
Mast P P & Co, 100 S Capitol av.
Milwaukee Harvester Co, 6 Board of Trade bldg.
Minneapolis Threshing Machine Co, 117 W Washington.
Newark Machine Co The, 5 Board of Trade bldg.
Nichols & Shepard Co, 22 Kentucky av.
North Indpls Cradle Wks, s e cor Francis and canal (N I).
Oliver Chilled Plow Wks, 160 S Penn.
Osborne D M & Co, 170 S Penn.
Plano Mnfg Co, 1 Cleaveland blk.
Potter Mnfg Co The, w s Northwestern av bet W 12th and Big Four Ry.
Reeves & Co, 90 S Capitol av.
Rock Island Plow Co, 75 W Washington.
Rumely M Co, 100 S Capitol av.
Russell Allen A, 174 S Senate av.
Seiberling J F & Co, 38 Kentucky av.
South Bend Chilled Plow Co, 5 Board of Trade bldg.
South Bend Iron Wks, 160 S Penn.
Stevens A W & Son, 8 Board of Trade bldg.
Superior Drill Co The, 28 Kentucky av.
Warder, Bushnell & Glessner Co, 96 S Capitol av.
Wood Walter A Harvester Co, 68 S Capitol av.

*AIR PUMPS.

Worthington Henry R, 64 S Penn. (See left top lines.)

ALE AND BEER BOTTLERS.

See Bottlers.

APARTMENT HOUSES.

Blacherne The, n w cor Meridian and Vermont.
Chalfant The, n w cor Penn and Michigan.
Plaza The, 16-24 Monument pl.
Pressley Flats, 175 N Penn.
Shiel The, 122 N Illinois and 27 Indiana av.

ARCHITECTS.

Bartel Samuel G, 88 Germania av (H).
Bates Charles Edgar, 323-324 Lemcke Bldg. (See adv.)

CHARLES EDGAR BATES,
ARCHITECT,
323-324 LEMCKE BUILDING,
INDIANAPOLIS.

Bohlen D A & Son, 95 E Washington.
Bowman Wm N, 13-14 Ingalls blk.
Brubaker Samuel H, 37½ E Washington. (See adv.)

SAMUEL H. BRUBAKER,
ARCHITECT
Fire-Proof and Slow Burning Construction a Specialty.
Rooms 11 and 12, 37½ East Washington Street,
INDIANAPOLIS, IND.

Carter Fletcher, 427 Lemcke bldg.
Christian Theodore R, 364 Ramsey av.
Church Andrew S, 352 Ramsey av.
Daggett R P & Co, 28-32 Marion Blk. (See adv.)

R. P. DAGGETT. JAMES B. LIZIUS.
ESTABLISHED 1868.
R. P. DAGGETT & CO.,
Architects.
Offices, Nos. 28 to 32, Fifth Floor, Marion Block, N. W. Cor. Meridian and Ohio Streets.
TELEPHONE 619.
Cost of buildings erected after our plans during the last twenty-eight years OVER SEVEN MILLION DOLLARS.
Send for List of References.

Dark Stephen C, 31-32 Cordova Bldg. (See adv.)

S. C. DARK,
PRACTICAL ARCHITECT AND SUPERINTENDENT.
Plans and Specifications Furnished on Short Notice.
Cordova Building. 25 West Washington St.

Foltz Herbert W, 49-50 Ingalls Blk. (See adv.)

HERBERT W. FOLTZ
ARCHITECT
Rooms 49-50 Ingalls Block
S. W. Cor. Washington and Pennsylvania Sts.

Fryberger John, 68 Temple av.
Gibson Louis H, 84 E Market.

A. METZGER AGENCY ESTABLISHED 1863. REAL ESTATE

LAMBERT GAS & GASOLINE ENGINE CO.
ANDERSON, IND. GAS AND GASOLINE ENGINES, 2 TO 50 H. P.

Hastings Samuel A, 33 W Market. (See adv.)

S. A. HASTINGS,
Architect and Superintendent
Plans Executed and Estimates Furnished.
Reasonable Prices for All Work.
33 West Market Street. INDIANAPOLIS.

Hendrickson Henry C, 68½ E Market.
Krutsch & Laycock, 25½ W Washington.
McPherson Wm R, 26 Warman av (H).

Moore W Scott & Son, Rooms 12, 13 and 14 Blackford Blk, s e cor Washington and Meridian. (See adv.)

TELEPHONE NO. 1308.
W. SCOTT MOORE & SON,
Architects.
Rooms 12, 13, 14 Blackford Block,
S. E. Cor. Washington and Meridian Streets.

Morck Wm O, 143 Dillon.
Mueller Charles G, 31 Talbott blk.
Peckham Caleb H, 32 Drake.

Scharn & Rubush, 21 Journal Bldg. (See adv.)

J. H. SCHARN. P. C. RUBUSH.
SCHARN & RUBUSH,
ARCHITECTS AND SUPERINTENDENTS
21 AND 22 JOURNAL BUILDING,
INDIANAPOLIS, IND.

Scherrer Adolph, 415-417 Indiana Trust bldg.

Staples Wm A, 55 Baldwin Blk. (See adv.)

W. A. STAPLES,
PRACTICAL
Architect and Superintendent,
REASONABLE PRICES FOR ALL WORK.
Rooms 55 and 55½ Baldwin Blk., Indianapolis.

Stem John H, 51 Ingalls blk.

Thurtle John G & Co, 57 Ingalls Blk. (See adv.)

JOHN G. THURTLE,
Architect and Superintendent
57 AND 68 INGALLS BLOCK,
INDIANAPOLIS, IND.

Traylor Marion H, 57 Baldwin Blk, s w cor Market and Delaware. (See adv.)

MARION H. TRAYLOR,
ARCHITECT
57 BALDWIN BLOCK
INDIANAPOLIS, INDIANA.

Vonnegut & Bohn, 608 Indiana Trust bldg.
Wallingford Charles A, 44 Coffin blk.

Winterrowd Thomas A, 75-76 Lombard Bldg. (See adv.)

THOS. A. WINTERROWD,
ARCHITECT,
Rooms 75-76 Lombard Building,
Telephone 1730. INDIANAPOLIS, IND.

*ARCHITECTS' SUPPLIES.

Lieber H Co The, 33 S Meridian. (See right top cor cards.)

*ARCHITECTURAL IRON WORKS.

Ellis & Helfenberger, 162-168 S Senate av. (See right bottom lines.)
Hetherington & Berner Co, 19-27 W South.
Roch Tobias, 125 E Pearl. (See adv.)

T. ROCH
ARCHITECTURAL IRON AND WIRE WORKS
125 East Pearl Street, Indianapolis, Ind.
Bet. Delaware and Alabama Sts.
Mnfrs. of all Kind of Fences. Repairs promptly attended to and Satisfaction Guaranteed.

Wrought Iron Bridge Co, Wm W Winslow Genl Agt, 1 Hubbard Blk. (See adv p 10.)

BICYCLES $5 DOWN. MONTHLY. Best Wheels. Best Terms. WHEELMEN'S CO. 31 W. OHIO ST. LONG DISTANCE TEL. 1855.

J. H. TECKENBROCK  Painter and Decorator,
94 EAST SOUTH STREET.

FIDELITY MUTUAL LIFE—PHILADELPHIA, PA.
MATCHLESS SECURITY At LOW COST. A. H. COLLINS General Agent Baldwin Block.

Edwardsport Coal and Mining Co. Miners and Shippers Steam and Domestic Coal. Rooms 42 and 43 WHEN BUILDING.

*ARSENIC.

Moffat & Co, 402 Lemcke Bldg. (See adv p 9.)

*ART EMPORIUMS.

Lieber H Co The, 33 S Meridian. (See right top cor cards.)

*ART ENGRAVERS.

Indiana Illustrating Co, s e cor Market and Illinois. (See adv opp Engravers.)

*ART GLASS.

Interstate Art Glass Co, Henry W Rudolf Genl Mngr, 77-81 N Delaware.

*ART STAINED GLASS.

Black John, Office 159 Mass av, Factory 222 E Michigan.

ARTIFICIAL LIMB MANUFACTURERS.

Haywood Alfred, 61 S Illinois.

ARTISTS.

Baker Manville W, 265 N New Jersey.
Brazington Wm C, 63 Ingalls blk.
Cahill Thomas B, 619 Virginia av.
Cary Kittie I, 151 N Illinois.
Colman Samuel A, 302½ N Senate av.
Crossman Elizabeth A, 1285 N Meridian.
Day Laura H, 176 N California.
Dennis James W, 25 Marion blk.
Doty Clara, 19 Greer.
Elbreg Mary E, 48 Ash.
Fertig Charles D, 326 Mass av.
Fetsch Carl P, 3 Williams.
Forsyth Wm, 132 Fletcher av.
Geiger Melchior, 91 Hoyt av.
Gross Phoebe M, 149 Hosbrook.
Gruelle Richard B, 35 Coffin blk.
Hahn Josephine B, 409 S Delaware.
Hahn Queena J, w s Denny 1 n of Ohio.
Hammer Frank E, 77½ S Illinois.
Hann Sarah A, 178 N Alabama.
Hatton Thomas F, 19 Greer.
Howard Kate, 116½ N Meridian.
Hoyt Addie, 178 Huron.
Ingraham Ellen M, 265 N Capitol av.
Jackson James H, 382 College av.
Jameson Elizabeth M, 413 Ash.
King Emma B, 188 N Illinois.
Knodle Frederick S, 395 Central av.
Kohn Joseph, 44½ N Penn.
Lewis Harry S E, 18½ N Meridian.
Lodge Charles E, 71 Oak.
Logsdon Margaret, 363 Park av.
Lueders Misses, 460 N Senate av. (See adv in Stamping and Embroidery.)
Morlan Albert M, 287 E Vermont.
Morrison Anna H, 27½ W Ohio.
Nicholson Elizabeth, 248 Broadway.
Palmer Cora H, 401 N Penn.
Pendergast Mary B, 53 Central av.
Pickart Joseph, 237 N Illinois.
Reed Louis H, 299 E New York.
Runyan Thomas, 82½ N Penn.
Scharff Dollie C, 307 N Senate av.
Shields Elmer E, 62½ E Washington.
Stark Otto, 17 Hartford blk.
Steele Theodore C, n e cor Penn and 7th.
Taylor Jennie R, 435 Park av.
Tooley James M, 131 Nordyke av (W I).
Williams Elizabeth, 178 N Alabama.
Wilson Alma A, 1303 N Delaware.
Winpenny Ellen E, 429 Ash.

*ARTISTS' MATERIALS.

Lieber H Co The, 33 S Meridian. (See right top cor cards.)

Mayer Charles & Co, 29-31 W Washington. (See adv opp p 615.)

*ASPHALT PAVING.

Symmes H H Co, 39 S Alabama.

*ASPHALT ROOFING.

Smither Henry C, 169 W Maryland. (See adv opp Roofing Material.)

Smither Theodore F, 151 W Maryland. (See right side lines.)

Symmes H H Co, 39 S Alabama.

Zimmerman C & Sons, 19-21 S East. (See left bottom lines.)

*ATHLETIC GOODS.

Peoria Athletic Co, 58-60 N Penn.

AUCTION AND COMMISSION.

Beebe & Brown, 132 Commercial Club bldg.
Carter & Vetter, 252 E Washington.
McCurdy & Perry, 139 W Washington.
Solomon Morris, 78 E Washington.

AWNING AND TENT MNFRS.

Eberhardt & Co, 80 S Capitol av.
Griffin Jeremiah A, 175 Clinton.
Indianapolis Tent and Awning Co, 20 S Alabama.
Jenner Leopold A, 89 N Delaware.
Rosenberg & Schmidt, 20 S Alabama.
Truemper Charles J, 330 S East.

*AXLE GREASE.

Miller Oil Co The, 23-27 McNabb. (See adv in Oils.)

BABY BUGGY MANUFACTURERS.

Baby Supply Mnfg Co, 256 S East. (See adv in Hammocks.)

Baby Supply Mnfg. Co.,
Manufacturers of
Safety Hammocks,
Folding Baby Cabs,
Etc.
THOMAS NESOM, Mngr., No. 256 South East Street.

Indianapolis Mnfg Co, s w cor Madison av and Ray.

*BABY CARRIAGES—RETAIL.

Haueisen & Hartmann, 163-169 E Washington. (See right bottom cor cards.)

*BADGES.

Kinklin Richard, 240-242 E Washington. (See adv in Costumers.)

Mayer Charles & Co, 29-31 W Washington. (See adv opp p 615.)

Mayer George J, 15 S Meridian. (See left bottom cor cards and p 5.)

C. ZIMMERMAN & SONS | SLATE AND GRAVEL ROOFERS 19 South East Street.

DRIVEN WELLS And Second Water Wells and Pumps of all kinds at CHARLES KRAUSS', 42 S. PENN. ST. TELEPHONE 465.

ERTEL STEAM LAUNDRY LARGEST AND BEST IN THE STATE. PROMPT SERVICE. 26 and 28 N. Senate Ave. Telephone 1089.

BAKERS—WHOLESALE.

Bryce Peter F, 14-16 E South.
Hitz Baking Co The, 68-70 S Delaware. (See right bottom cor cards.)
Home Cracker Co, 192-194 S Meridian.
Parrott-Taggart Bakery of the U S Baking Co, 93-99 S Penn, cor Georgia. (See bottom edge.)

BAKERS AND CONFECTIONERS.

Aebker Christopher H, 149 Prospect.
Bane Jane, 614½ S East.
Baumann David, 365 Indiana av.
Baumann Frederick, 336 Indiana av.
Baumann Peter F, rear 336 Indiana av.
Beaty John R, 207 Virginia av.
Beck Conrad, 671 E Washington.
Beck Frederick D, 34 E Mkt House and 311 Mass av.
Brackmeier George O, 180 Virginia av.
Bromm Christian, 17 Shelby.
Bruce James P, 598-600 Virginia av. (See adv.)

JAMES P. BRUCE,
Baker, Confectioner
—AND—
....FANCY GROCER....
598-600 VIRGINIA AVENUE.

Bruner Henry E, 94 W 7th.
Buck Sylvester T, 437 Madison av.
Covert Wm T, 105 Agnes.
Crow Rebecca, E Mkt House.
Culmann John, 614 N Senate av.
Dame Eliza, 374 E 7th.
Dauch David J, 187 Elizabeth.
Dietz August, 44 Pendleton av (B).
Doty Taylor E, 267 Mass av.
Eckert Jacob, 614 S East.
Feucht Paul, 28 King av (H).
Flickinger Frederick W, 32 Singleton.
Gerold Ignatz, 29 Meek.
Giezendanner Wm, n e cor Schurmann and Vorster avs (M P).
Giezendanner Wm jr, 104 Yandes.
Gilpin Joseph P, 385 Clifford av.
Gleason Major K, 947 Ash.
Griffith Robert W, 86 E Georgia.
Guy James C, 269 Mass av.
Hahn Jacob, 409 S Delaware
Haug August, 421 S Meridian.
Haunss Frederick, 363 Shelby.
Herrmann George H, 285 E Washington.
Hespelt Charles D, 372 Virginia av.
Hetz Frederick, 68 N Penn.
Hill Holman T, w s Watts 1 n of Michigan.
Hilpert Rudolph W, 473 S Meridian.
Hinshaw & Baker, 142 Broadway.
Hunter May F, 293 Mass av.
Irving Joseph L, 503 College av.
Jaehnke Edward, 642 S Meridian.
Jones Ralph H, e s Capitol av 3 s of 30th.
Kane Henry, 63 E Mkt House.
Kiesel John, 507 N West.
King August, 135 E Mkt House.
Knight Mary, 140 E Mkt House.
Kopp Ernestine, 351 E Market.
Lauler Joseph, 230 W McCarty.
Loechle Joseph, 207 Mass av.
Luedemann Henry H, 517 Virginia av.
McGannon Orlando C, 401 Talbott av.
McShane Rose A, 114 Mass av.
Marley Walter A, 198 Columbia av.
Matthews Jacob F, 142 E 7th.
Minter Ferdinand, s w cor Home av and Yandes.
Moosman Samuel, 23 Palmer.
Morgan Thomas, 349 S Delaware.
Murphy Matilda, 315 Indiana av.
Nickum Charles W, 75 Mass av.
Odenthal Minor, 152 E St Joseph.
Oley Nicholas, 262 E Washington.
Popp Michael A, 621 S Meridian.
Richert Henry, 348 Indiana av.
Riedlinger Charles C, 40 Gresham.
Roempke Conrad H, 1558 N Illinois.
Roempke Henry F, 149 English av.
Rohde Wm L, 125 E Mkt House and 524 S East.
Salge & Kroll, 468 Indiana av.
Schmidt Raphael, 412 S Meridian.
Scott Anna P, 88 Ft Wayne av.
Smith Orvel H, 194 E Washington.
Smith J W & Son, 121 Ft Wayne av.
Steffen Anton, 102 Prospect.
Stettler Gottfried G, 346 S East.
Striebeck Charles, 350 N Senate av.
Strohmeyer Dietrich F, 222 W Washington.
Taggart Joseph, 51 E Mkt House.
Thau Bernhardt, 123 E Mkt House and 81 Hosbrook.
Truitt Peter, 619 Virginia av.
Turner Josephine L, 427 E Vermont.
Waggoner Benjamin E jr, 266 Mass av.
Warmeling Charles T, 175 Madison av.
Weaver Charles W, 164 W 12th.
Weitzel Louis P, 269 W Washington.
Westfield Mary, 138 E Mkt House.
Wich Henry, 121 Blake.
Wirt John B, 8 Indiana av.

BAKING POWDER MANUFACTURERS.

Climax Baking Powder Co, 124 E Maryland.
Grocers' Mnfg Co The, 80 S Penn.
Holland & Donahue, 135 Church.
Linegar Thomas F, 31 W South.
Olin Edwin D, 232 S Meridian.
Regal Mnfg Co, 269-271 E McCarty.
Senour Alfred W, 92 E South.

*BANDS OF MUSIC.

Panden Bros' Orchestra, 115-117 W New York. (See adv.)

PANDEN BROS'
ORCHESTRA
Office and Residence,
115 to 117 West New York Street.
Music Furnished for all Occasions.

ELLIS & HELFENBERGER Architectural Iron Work and Gray Iron Castings. 162-170 South Senate Ave. Tel. 958.

THE HOGAN TRANSFER AND STORAGE COMP'Y
Household Goods and Pianos Moved—Packed—Stored...... Baggage and Package Express Machinery and Safes a Specialty Cor. Washington and Illinois Sts. TELEPHONE No. 675.

Hose, Belting, Packing, Clothing, Druggists' Sundries, Bicycle Tires, Cotton Hose, Etc. New York Belting & Packing Co., L't'd.

Bands of Music—Continued.
Second Regiment Infantry, Indiana Legion, Band and Orchestra, Alfred Houghton Band Master, 383 E New York. (See adv.)

Music furnished for Concerts, Balls, Parties, Picnics, Parades, Funerals, Etc., on short notice.
HOUGHTON'S
Military Band and Orchestra,
Prof. A. Houghton, Band Master,
383 East New York St., INDIANAPOLIS, IND.

When Band, 70½ E Court.

*BANK AND OFFICE FIXTURES.
Scott W A & Sons, 591-593 Central av. (See adv front cover.)

BANKS AND BANKERS.
Capital National Bank The, Commercial Club Bldg. (See backbone and left top cor cards.)
Fletcher S A & Co, 30-34 E Washington.
Indiana National Bank, s e cor Virginia av and Penn.
Indianapolis National Bank, Edward Hawkins Receiver, 607-609 Indiana Trust Bldg.
Marion Trust Co The, s e cor Market and Monument Pl. (See back cover.)
Merchants' National Bank The, s w cor Washington and Meridian.
State Bank of Indiana The, Bates House corner.
Union Trust Co The, 68 E Market. (See front cover opp Insurance and opp p 867.)

*BANNERS.
Kinklin Richard, 240½ E Washington. (See adv in Costumers.)

*BAR FIXTURES.
Killinger George W, s w cor Market and Missouri. (See adv in Saloons.)
Laing Samuel, 72-74 E Court. (See left side lines.)

BARBERS.
Adair Horace, 216 W Washington.
Albertsmeyer Herman C, 153 Prospect.
Alcazar, 30 W Washington.
Alderson James W, 338 S West.
Allen John D, 322 Clifford av.
Anderson John F, 108 Ft Wayne av.
Andress Lan S, s e cor 9th and Yandes.
Artis Eli, 145 W Merrill.
Bader Elizabeth, 320 E Washington.
Baker Albert J, 508 E Washington.
Baker David M, Hotel English.
Balch Percy, 287 Mass av.
Ballard James W, 108 Michigan (H).
Bany Bros, 97 E South.
Bany Edmund, 105 Harrison.
Becker Charles T, 548 S East.
Becker Edward J, 760 S East.
Beltz F P & Son, 29 S Illinois.
Bentley George P, 104 Mass av.
Bernloehr George, 1 English av.
Berry Bros, 205 Indiana av.
Black Charles S, 206 S Meridian.
Blakemore Harvey, 169 Virginia av.
Blume Guy E, 64 Michigan (H).
Blumlein & Roach, s e cor Washington and Illinois.
Bolander Alma E, 628 E 9th.
Bond Thomas J, 1560 N Illinois.
Bonesteel Wm C, 606 S Meridian.
Boss Adolph, 356 Dillon.
Bowers Henry, 205 E Washington.
Boyd Robert E, 814 E Washington.
Brady Thomas J, 304 Blake.
Bramkamp Wm H, 146 Fletcher av.
Breeding James A, 64 N Illinois.
Brewer Albert H, 75 N Alabama.
Brown Charles, 342 E Washington.
Brown Christopher C, 441 W Michigan.
Brown James A, 174 Virginia av.
Brummell Robert D, Union Stock Yards (W I).
Buchanan Wm T, 1 Michigan (H).
Buckner Alexander, 206 W Washington.
Bundy Charles E, 197 W Washington.
Campbell Len, 115½ Mass av.
Carpenter Perry, 299 W Washington.
Cass Ray D, 29 N Illinois.
Castor Hiram C, 288 Mass av.
Cave Omer, 123 Ft Wayne av.
Chapman Harry, 325 E Washington.
Christian Joseph C, 78 E Ohio.
Circle Park Barber Shop, 15 Monument Pl.
Clark Horace A, 357 Virginia av.
Cohen Joseph, 306 S Illinois.
Coleman Naldo R, 96 Russell av.
Corbin Wm H, 142 S Illinois.
Cottom George M, 168 E Washington.
Crabb Keller E, 64 Virginia av.
Craven Charles G, 103 Indiana av.
Cress Henry, 247 Mass av.
Crutcher Henry, 186 W 7th.
Curtis Harry E, 290 Mass av.
Dale Salathiel B, 554 W Udell (N I) and 216 E Washington.
Darling Charles, 13 Mass av.
Dehoney James R, 596 N West.
Dingman Frederick D, 452 W New York.
Dodson Elmer E, 103 S Noble.
Dugan Bernard W, rear 370 S West.
Dungey James R, 37½ Virginia av.
Duzan Samuel, 94 S Belmont av (W I).
Edmondson Milton J, 116 Agnes.
Elsasser Rudolph, 125 Belmont av.
Evans Wm G, 160 W 12th.
Farner Abraham, 247 W South.
Farrell Daniel E, 80 W South.
Fernkas John, 195 Howard (W I).
Field Sanford E, 307 Mass av.
Fields John F, 1555 N Illinois.
Fisher John, 412 Virginia av.
Floyd Wm T, 20 Indiana av.
Funke Anthony, 586 S Meridian.
Gardner Napoleon P, 1 S Meridian.
Givens Samuel G, 46 Virginia av.
Givens Wm E, 517 Virginia av.
Gordon Albert E, 179 S Illinois.
Grafford Leonard, 35 Kentucky av.
Grandjean Frank, 439 Virginia av.
Green John S, 81 E Wabash.
Griffin Henry N, h 78 S Judge Harding (W I).
Grist Jeremiah A, 13 S Illinois.
Gross Andrew L, 289 W Maryland.

The Central Rubber & Supply Co. PHONE 922. 79 S. ILLINOIS ST., INDIANAPOLIS, IND.

OTTO GAS ENGINES | BUILDERS' EXCHANGE S. W. Cor. Ohio and Penn. Telephone 535.

lward, rear 586 Morris (W I).
'aesar, rear 249 English av.
enry, 347 E Market.
H, 340 W Washington.
Bros, 29 Monument pl.
Oliver M, 858 Morris (W I).
ichard, 270 W Washington.
everley, 261½ Mass av.
ham H, 14 Michigan (H).
John W, 806 W Washington.
enry, 100 E Market.
Harry J, rear 501 College av.
larence A, 105 Harrison.
arl A, 347 Madison av.
harles W, 541 Shelby.
'm A, 161 W Washington.
an F, 323 Clifford av.
'm L, 151½ Michigan (H).
George W, 52 E Washington.
an James H, 490 S Illinois.
Elijah T, 50 S West.
Andrew, 17 Pembroke Arcade.
y & Jelf, 9 Indiana av.
gar A, 147 W Washington.
Frank P, 175 Virginia av.
John W, 161 Indiana av.
Wm H, 196 Prospect.
Charles, 188 Madison av.
m Henry, 853 S Meridian.
George D, 42 W 13th.
James O, 1111 E Michigan.
Reddin, 497½ S West.
Tarlton L, 181 S Meridian.
dward S, s s Washington 20 w of av (M J).
ichard, 694 N Capitol av.
eter A, 347 Madison av.
m, 618 N Senate av.
Martin L, 504 N West.
Willis A, 814 N Illinois.
lward S, 446 Mass av.
vell, 548 W Addison (N I).
ohn G, 55 Mass av.
eorge L, 18 N Illinois.
Nicholas L, rear 501 College av.
ar Gustave A, 403 S Meridian.
orge P, 447 E Washington.
& Moore, 91 N Penn.
& Votaw, 354 Indiana av.
Hezekiah K, 42 Indiana av.
Wm G, 545 W Udell (N I).
Charles B, 166½ W Washington.
& Kerr, 46 N Delaware.
an, 104 S Noble.
Louis F, 555 E Walnut.
omas, 137 W Washington.
Charles E, 39 When bldg.
Charles F, 15 Hillside av.
rank T, 98 W Washington.
Thomas F, 1089 E Washington.
James J, 1129 E Washington.
ugh Frank, 10 Prospect.
Thomas A, 397 S Capitol av.
James P, 4 Woodburn av (W I).
a Robert E, 1361½ W Washington

James L, 665 Virginia av.
Lewis D, 76 Mass av.
Charles McK, 180 River av (W I).
Thomas A H, 103 Oliver av (W I).
John R, 58 Indiana av.
Archibald, 396 College av.
Henry C, 180 S Illinois.
& Armstrong, 2 Masonic Temple.
& Finley, 21 S Meridian.
Rudolph, 297 S Delaware.
Walter, 101 Patterson.
John H, 629 Madison av.
erdinand, 834½ S Meridian.

Miller Frank M, 903 Cornell av.
Miller LeRoy C, 69 E Sutherland (B).
Miller Wm, Grand Hotel.
Mitchell George, 671 Madison av.
Morgan Charles C, 10½ N Delaware.
Morris Wm M, 95 S West.
Moss Charles A, 366 E 7th.
Moss Rollie A, 241 W Washington.
Moss & Franklin, 162 Indiana av.
Mowers George B, 28 Indiana av.
Mueller Charles H, 19 Shelby.
Myers Louis, 423½ Madison av.
Myers Louis E, 3 Buchanan.
Nichols Solomon E, e s Rural 2 n of Bloyd av (B).
O'Meara Patrick J, s w cor Meridian and Monument pl.
Outland Alfred, 6 Malott av.
Overfield Martin E, 199 Hoyt av.
Paff Henry B, 346 E New York.
Partee Samuel, 370 Lincoln av.
Paulsen Charles F, 732 Lemcke bldg.
Peck George I, 145½ Mass av.
Pell John S, 79 N Delaware.
Peters Mathias, 193 E Washington.
Petit Henry, n w cor Central av and P C C & St L Ry (I).
Porter Frank E, 317 Virginia av.
Power David, 233 W McCarty.
Pritchett Silas C, 277 E McCarty.
Pritchett Wm H, 91 E Court.
Quinn Wm M, 128 Indiana av.
Raley Henry, 604 Virginia av.
Rape Charles, 14 Indiana av.
Rech John E, 244 E Washington.
Rinkel David, 153 E Washington.
Robinson Wm G, 514 Virginia av.
Rochester John, 68 N Missouri.
Ross James, 124 Michigan (H).
Ruschke August, 264 W Washington.
Russ James W, 127 Indiana av.
Sangston John H, w s Station 3 n of Glen Drive (B).
Schmidt Paul F, 69 E Washington.
Scholler George J, 511 Madison av.
Scott George H, 13 S Alabama.
Selzer Nicholas, 247 E Morris.
Shaffer & Sangston, 205 Mass av.
Shepherd Henry E, 121 Oliver av (W I).
Shields Frederick B, 254 Highland av.
Simms Wm H, 768½ S East.
Slack Albert, n s Michigan av 5 e of Sharp av (W).
Slifer Harry O, 54 Clifford av.
Smallwood Edgar N, 904 W Washington.
Smith Charles L, 33 W Market.
Smith Edward, 310 Blake.
Smith George F, 268 E Washington.
Spitznagel Joseph L, 454 S Meridian.
Stahl Nicholas G, 193 Virginia av.
Stein Ferdinand, 123 W South.
Stelzel John, 374 E Ohio.
Stevens John, 171 Elizabeth.
Steward Thomas M, 410 Indiana av.
Stewart Frank, 67 E 14th.
Stewart James H, 327 W Washington.
Stille Henry E, 30 Hill av.
Stone Jefferson D, 145 Mass av.
Stradford John B, 506 N West.
Strain Louis M, 395 S Delaware.
Strain Wm E, 131 Hadley av (W I).
Strome Marion H, 470 E Washington.
Thomas Wm E, 141 Cornell av.
Tracey Ulysses G, 493½ W 22d (N I).
Traut Charles, 561 S East.
Truehart Elijah, 69 N Alabama.
Tucker Charles W, 824 N Illinois.
Tyner Charles L, 39 E Market.
Vanatta Joel D, 366 Mass av.

FRIEDGEN'S IS THE PLACE FOR THE NOBBIEST SHOES Ladies' and Gents' 19 North Pennsylvania St.

COPPER AND GALVANIZED IRON CORNICE MANUFACTURER

SKYLIGHTS AND VENTILATORS.

Barbers—Continued.
Vliet Wm C, 158 Ft Wayne av.
Wachstetter Edward J, 41 McCrea.
Walker Jacob, 251 W 6th.
Ward Walter D, 193 Shelby.
Ware George A, 98 Prospect.
Waring John H, 515 E 8th.
Wells James H, Union Station.
Willhite James, 112 Howard.
Williams John T, 504 College av.
Williams & Green, 48 Malott av.
Wolfanger John, 611 Virginia av.
Woodruff Vance, 67 S Illinois.
Wormser Nathan, 117 S Illinois.
Yeaw Marshall S, 33 W 1st.

BARBERS' SUPPLIES.

Grab Charles G, 64 S Illinois.
Marot John R, 139½ W Washington.
Mayer Charles & Co, 29-31 W Washington. (See adv opp p 615.)

***BASE BALL SUPPLIES.**

Mayer Charles & Co, 29-31 W Washington. (See adv opp p 615.)

BASKET MANUFACTURERS.

Indianapolis Basket Co, 482 E New York.
Ohleyer George, 314 Union.
Ohleyer Peter, 452 S Meridian.

***BATH TUBS.**

Hussey & Baker, 116 N Delaware. (See adv in Plumbers.)

***BATHS.**

Harmon Matthew H, w s Holmes av 1 s of Michigan (H). (See adv.)
Haughville Mineral Well and Bath House, w s Holmes av 1 s of Michigan (H). (See adv.)

M. H. HARMON, Proprietor.
HAUGHVILLE MINERAL WELL AND SANITARIUM,
Haughville—Indianapolis, Ind.
Sanitarium and Park is on Haughville Electric Car Line, one-half square south from corner Michigan St. and Holmes Ave. Cars run every ten minutes.

Mather Wm J, 2 Masonic Temple.

***BEDDING MANUFACTURERS.**

Hirschman Jacob C (estate of), 69-71 N New Jersey.

***BEE KEEPERS' SUPPLIES.**

Pouder Walter S, 162 Mass av.

BEEF PACKERS.

See Packers—Pork and Beef.

BELL MANUFACTURERS.

Hoffman Irenius M, w s Watts 2 n of Michigan.

***BELTING CLOTHS.**

Nordyke & Marmon Co, crossing I & V Ry and Morris (W I). (See inside back cover.)

BELTING MANUFACTURERS AND DEALERS.

Central Rubber and Supply Co The, 79 S Illinois. (See left side lines.)
Chicago Belting Co, 38 Kentucky av.
Miller Oil Co The, 23-27 McNabb. (See adv in Oils.)
New York Leather Belting Co, 38 Kentucky av.
Nordyke & Marmon Co, crossing I & V Ry and Morris (W I). (See inside back cover.)

BENT WOOD WORKS.

Gillette Oscar S, s w cor Bloyd av and Morris (B).

BICYCLE CHAIN MNFRS.

Indiana Chain Co, cor 15th and Belt R R.
Metallic Mnfg Co, 950-960 N New Jersey.

BICYCLE DEALERS.

Bird W M Jr & Co, Rambler Bicycles, 29 E Market.
Clemens W Frank, 36 Mass av.
Conde H T Implement Co, 27-33 N Capitol av.
Darrow Ben L, 31 W Ohio. (See right side lines.)
Fisher C G & Co, 64 N Penn.
Forslund Peter A, 417 Virginia av.
Haines S A Co The, 44 N Penn.
Hay & Willits Mnfg Co The, 76 N Penn. (See left bottom cor cards.)
Hearsey H T Cycle Co, 116-118 N Penn.
Indiana Bicycle Co (retail dept), 100 N Penn.

DIRECTORIES OF ALL THE STATES AND PRINCIPAL CITIES ON FILE FOR REFERENCE AT OUR OFFICE.

R. L. POLK & CO.
23-24 JOURNAL BLDG.

SAMUEL LAING 72 AND 74 E. COURT STREET.

PAPER BOXES SULLIVAN & MAHAN 41 W. Pearl St.

DIAMOND WALL PLASTER { Telephone 1410 BUILDERS' EXCHANGE.

WATCH
THE TRINITY
BUILT BY FOWLER.
WRITE FOR CATALOGUE.
METROPOLITAN CYCLE CO.
STATE AGENTS.
108 MASSACHUSETTS AVE.

Metropolitan Cycle Co, 108 Mass av. (See adv.)
Peoria Athletic Company, 58-60 N Penn.
Pfleger Joseph C, 174 E Washington.
Reid Charles F, 167 Mass av.
Watson Wm R & Co, 48 N Delaware.
Wheelmen's Co, Ben L Darrow Propr, 31 W Ohio. (See right side lines.)
Wilde John A, 108 Mass av.

*BICYCLE INSTRUCTORS.

Willis Charles W, 27 Ingalls blk.

BICYCLE MANUFACTURERS.

Bellis Cycle Co, office 27 Ingalls blk, factory 124 S Penn.
Central Cycle Mnfg Co, 238-240 S Meridian.
Hay & Willits Mnfg Co The, 76 N Penn. (See left bottom cor cards.)
Indiana Bicycle Co, 67-99 S East.
Mohawk Cycle Co, cor Francis and Elmira (N I).
Munger Cycle Co The, 146 Ft Wayne av.
Sensitive Governor Co, 100 S Capitol av.
Vanguard Cycle Co, 106 N Penn.
Wheeler Wm A, 94 Ft Wayne av.
Wheelmen's Co, Ben L Darrow Propr, 31 W Ohio. (See right side lines.)

BICYCLE REPAIRERS.

Ahlders Bernard E, 539 S Meridian.
Benton Justin H, 86 E Georgia.
Boeckling Arthur A, 65 W 7th.
Caird, Vial & Co, 16 Monument pl.
Clingler Albert G, 63 Indiana av.
Davis Louis J, 18 N West.
Dynes & Greig, 96 N Delaware.
Hay & Willits Mnfg Co The, 76 N Penn. (See left bottom cor cards.)
Lawson Joseph F, 255 W Washington.
McLaughlin Frank, 249 S Capitol av.
Parker David M, 316 E Washington.
Pfleger Joseph C, 174 E Washington.
Resner Henry F, 175 Virginia av.
Riley Levi P, 193 Mass av.
Roetter Harry N, 16 W Pearl.
Simmons Paul B, 818 N Illinois.
Thompson Moses, n w cor Michigan and Bismarck av (H).
Wheelmen's Co, Ben L Darrow Propr, 31 W Ohio. (See right side lines.)

*BICYCLE SUNDRIES.

Central Rubber and Supply Co The, 79 S Illinois. (See left side lines.)
Davis Mnfg Co, 68½ E Market.
Haines S A Co The, 44 N Penn.
Hay & Willits Mnfg Co The, 76 N Penn. (See left bottom cor cards.)
Peoria Athletic Company, 58-60 N Penn.
Wheelmen's Co, Ben L Darrow Propr, 31 W Ohio. (See right side lines.)
Winn Lucius G, 26 Ingalls blk.

BILL POSTERS.

Indianapolis Bill Posting Co, 61½ N Penn.
Vansyckle Advertising Co The, 9-10 McDougall Bldg. (See adv in Advertising Agts.)

If your Laundry Work is not satisfactory, try THE HOME LAUNDRY 197 S. Telephone 15 St 16.

THE WM. H. BLOCK CO. 7 AND 9 EAST WASHINGTON STREET. DRY GOODS, MEN'S FURNISHINGS.

The Fidelity and Deposit Co. OF MARYLAND. Bonds signed for Administrators, Assignees, Executors, Guardians, Receivers Trustees, and persons in every position of trust.
GEO. W. PANGBORN, General Agent, 704-706 Lemcke Building. Telephone 140.

INSURE YOUR PROPERTY WITH FRANK K. SAWYER

BILLIARD ROOMS.

Bates The, n w cor Illinois and Washington.
Chambers Perlee L, 59 N Penn.
Cooper & Singleton, 499 W Shoemaker (N I).
Emminger Joseph, 11 Monument pl.
Grand Hotel The, s e cor Illinois and Maryland.
Huff Andrew L, 40 Pendleton av.
Lang Samuel, 140 S Illinois.
Richt Frederick C, 35 E Ohio.
Singleton Richard, 117 Ft Wayne av.
White Thomas H, 16 Prospect.
Young George J, 78 N Delaware.

BILLIARD TABLE MANUFACTURERS.

Brunswick-Balke-Collender Co The, 138-140 S Illinois.

*BIRD CAGES.

Mayer Charles & Co, 29-31 W Washington. (See adv opp p 615.)

BIRD DEALERS.

Klepper Charles F, 133 Mass av.

*BITUMINOUS COAL.

Edwardsport Coal and Mining Co, 42-43 When Bldg. (See left side lines and adv in Coal Miners.)

BLACKSMITHS.

Ambuhl J F, 125 W 18th.
Arbuckle James F, s e cor Pendleton av and Rural.
Atkinson Newman, 5 Hillside av.
Barger G T, 1352 N Senate av.
Bernd Bros, 69-71 W Morris.
Boyd John M, 3 N Judge Harding (W I).
Buergelin Willis E, 1364 Northwestern av (N I).
Dilges Jacob, n e cor Rural and Clifford av.
Foreman Milton, 345 Indiana av.
Forshee George W, 222 Mass av.
Francis & Swails, s w cor Indiana av and Locke.
Gates Cecil H, w s Maple av 1 n of Washington av (I).
Gilbert Charles R, e s Lancaster av 2 n of Clifford av.
Gilbert Martin, cor 6th and Northwestern av.
Greenwell Charles H, s e cor College av and 9th.
Harrison John G, 236 E Michigan.
Hawkins Samuel, 185 Prospect.
Hellmann Peter L, 576 W Michigan.
Hessong J Wm, s e cor Meridian and 30th.
Johnson & Stewart, 1438 Northwestern av (N I).
Karrer George W, 120 Hill av.
Karrer Wm E, 368 Lincoln av.
Kealing James A, 1440 E Washington.
Keppler James, s e cor Washington and National avs (I).
Kieser Frank A, 643 Shelby.
Kurts & Kenton, 442 Douglass.
Martin Gilbert, e s canal opp 6th.
Martin Jesse H, 123 Indiana av.
Meredith N E, 413 Chestnut.
Miller George H, s w cor Cannon and Michigan av.
Moore John F, 114 Shelby.
Myers Bernard H, 573 W Udell (N I).
Neuert John M, 378 Virginia av.
O'Brien & Lewis, 216 W North.
Pape Frederick W, 83 Prospect.
Peek John W, 116 Michigan (H).
Perry Harvey, 329 Elizabeth.
Pipes Charles, 517 Shelby.
Pundchu Joseph, n w cor E Washington and Belt R R.
Rader Frank M, 223 Cedar.
Reiss Paul, e s Illinois near 30th.
Rowe Francis M, n s Michigan 3 e of Sherman Drive.
Rubush Joseph A, 865 S Meridian.
Schaub Albert, n e cor Lafayette and Crawfordsville rds.
Sullivan Richard H, s e cor Glen Drive and Shade (B).
Teney Stephen W, 12 Michigan (H).
Vondersaar Wendel, 904 N New Jersey.
Waterman Herman H, 1199 Michigan av.
Watz Louis, 965 S Meridian.
Webb Leonidas E, n s Washington 1 w of Crawfordsville rd (M J).
Weeber Christopher, 6 Jefferson av.
Wilson & Son, 190 W Pearl.
Wirtz Jacob F, 225 W Pearl.
Wonnell Charles, 248 S Delaware.
Zahl Charles, 359 Shelby.

BLANK BOOK MANUFACTURERS.

(See also Book Binders.)

Baker & Thornton, 38 S Meridian.
Burford Wm B, 21 W Washington. (See adv opp p 230.)
Carlon & Hollenbeck, s e cor Monument Pl and Meridian. (See adv opp p 244.)
Indianapolis Printing Co, 37-39 Virginia av.
Levey Bros & Co, 19 W Maryland. (See adv opp p 561.)
Smith Frank H, 22 N Penn. (See adv opp p 803.)

BLEACHERS.

Indianapolis Bleaching Co, e bank of White river n of National rd.

*BLUE PRINTS.

Nealy H D, 16 Hubbard Blk. (See adv in Patent Draughtsmen.)

BLUING MANUFACTURERS.

Labadie Louis P, 1 Cress.
Regal Mnfg Co, 269-271 E McCarty.
Schoonover James S, 500 College av.

BOARDING HOUSES.

Alkire Christina, 75 E Walnut.
Ayers Lucetta, 86 E Ohio.
Bailey John E, n w cor Michigan and State avs.
Baldwin Ebenezer, 1 S Gale (B).
Ball Jessie M, 68 S State av.
Ballinger Linnie A, 205 E Market.
Ballow Elizabeth, 232 S Capitol av.
Bannan Richard, 171 E Court.
Berry George W, 176 S New Jersey.
Brecount Eveline, 23 Poplar (B).
Brown George W, 76 E New York.
Brown Thomas B, 127 E Ohio.
Burbank Lizzie L, 148 N Illinois.
Burges Mary A, 169 N Noble.
Burgett Enoch D, 36 S Capitol av.
Campbell Mary A, 29 Madison av.
Cartwright Frederick, 132 W Ohio.

GUARANTEED INCOME POLICIES issued only by the United States Life Insurance Co.
E. B. SWIFT, Manager. 25 E. Market St.

Furniture Carpets } WM. KOTTEMAN { Stoves Ranges
89 and 91 East Washington Street. Telephone 1742.

WILLIAM WIEGEL } MANUFACTURER OF.... } SHOW CASES { 6 W. Louisiana St. Opposite Union Station.

Chenoweth Jennie, 181 N Delaware.
Clark Sarah A, 184 E Vermont.
Cross Rachel, 889 Morris (W I).
Coble Mary A, 189 S Capitol av.
Cochran Effie N, 1139 N Illinois.
Collinge Robert, 88 W Ohio.
Collins Anna M, 28 S State av.
Compton Samuel M, 172 N Delaware.
Copeland Martha F, 125 W Maryland.
Cox Martha G, 275 E Ohio.
Cronkhite Apollos B, 272 N Meridian.
Crooker C Edward, 287 S Penn.
Cullen Mary, 107 W South.
DeHaven Hattie L, 319 S Meridian.
Demaree Alice J, 98 N Alabama.
Donavon Grace A, 41 Madison av.
Duncan Carrie, 118 S Judge Harding (W I).
Engesser John, 128 Blake.
Faulkner Alice M, 342 S Meridian.
Fennell Retta, 181 S New Jersey.
Findlay George, 165 S Alabama.
Fling Mary, 34 S West.
Fodrea Emeline, 121 E New York.
Ford Wm A, 224 W New York.
Fraley Mollie E, 227 S Senate av.
Frauer May E, 24 Brookside av.
Fuller Edward P, State Fair Grounds.
Graham Nancy, 159 W Merrill.
Halffin Elizabeth A, 310 E Wabash.
Harris George W, 66 N Missouri.
Hayden Emma L, 182 S New Jersey.
Heart Sarah, 42 N New Jersey.
Hedges Sarah A, 83 N Capitol av.
Hennessy Elizabeth, 171 S New Jersey.
Henry Caroline, 252 E Washington.
Hernly Amos B, 166 N Delaware.
Hickman Mary, 230 S Penn.
Higgins Margaret, 646 Herbert.
Hiteshue Fannie A, 183 E Ohio.
Hittle Lulu G, 132 E Walnut.
Hollingsworth Lucinda, 144 N Senate av.
Horton Minnie, 193 S Alabama.
Hunter Bessie, 132 N Capitol av.
Ittenbach Mary A, 235 S Alabama.
James Annie, 39 N Alabama.
Jennings John Q A, 301 River av (W I).
Jennings Thomas J, 46 Standard av (W I).
Johnson Frank H, 156 N Illinois.
Johnson Hattie E, 184 N Capitol av.
Kegley Emma B, 862 Cornell av.
Kinney Margaret, 79 E Vermont.
Kretsch Anna M, 179 S Alabama.
Kydna Rose, 138 Mass av.
Landry Sylvester, 285 S Illinois.
Layden Ollie J, 263 S Penn.
Leonard Minnie, 6 Cornell av.
Long Ada, 80 S Capitol av.
Low Nancy J, 95 S West.
Lynam Elizabeth, 5 S Station (B).
McCorkle Henry E, 306 S Meridian.
McFall & Wilson, 86 N East.
McGinty Emma, 187 S Capitol av.
McInerny Patrick A, 359 S Illinois.
Mangan Mary, 272 W Maryland.
Manion Ann, 337 W Maryland.
Martin Frances L, 135 N Illinois.
Martin Frank S, 116 Cornell av.
May Melissa M, 94 Mass av.
Miller Effie, 267 S Capitol av.
Minchener Katie J, 46 S Capitol av.
Moore Mark C, 139 N Illinois.
Morgan Edmund, 125½ Hadley av (W I).
Muegge Emma A, 349 Madison av.
Mulvihill Josie, 18 Henry.
Myers James M, 285 S Capitol av.
Newman Mary, 64 S State av.
O'Leary Anna, 268 S Penn.
Owens Mary A, 225 E Market.
Pottage Thomas W, 304 S Meridian.
Powell Lucinda, 310 E Court.
Pritchett Alice L, 322 Cornell av.
Ramsey Jennie, 38 S State av.
Reichardt Elizabeth, 136 W 1st.
Riley Isabel, 124 English av.
Ritchie Mary A, 779 E Washington.
Ritter Paulina, 325 E Ohio.
Robb Nancy A, 489 College av.
Ross Martha E, 533 College av.
Russell John, 139 N Delaware.
Schaefer Margaret, 218 E Wabash.
Schmedle Sarah, 245 W South.
Sharp Clara F, 325 S Meridian.
Shott Artie M, 131 S East.
Smelser Josephine, 391 Bellefontaine.
Smith Adda M, 860 E Washington.
Smith Caroline, 295 E Court.
Smock Eliza H, 229 N Penn.
South Lizzie A, 126 E Ohio.
Stafford Ota L, 736 N Capitol av.
Stewart Margaret, 308 S Illinois.
Stone Daniel O, 578 W Udell (N I).
Sweeney Sarah, 249 E Louisiana.
Swisher Alzina, 46 Russell av.
Teaford Lillian I, e s Brightwood av 7 s of Willow (B).
Teaney Catherine, 944 Gent (M P).
Temperley Clara B, 283 E Georgia.
Thomas Martha A, 103 W South.
Umbright Arsinoe, 22 S State av.
Vaughn Frank A, 41 Madison av.
Warrenburg Viola, 297 River av (W I).
Watkins Mattie, 142 N Illinois.
Welsh Mary D, 99 Lexington av.
Williamson Samuel H, 1100 W Washington (H).
Wilson Fannie M, 162 Harrison.
Wilson John W, 333 N Illinois and 173 E Market.
Wilson Maggie E, 11 E South.
Woodbeck Theodore, 792 W Washington.
Woodward Willis J, 678 W Washington.
Ziegler Rebecca A, 430 Chestnut.

BOARDING STABLES.

See Livery and Sale Stables.

*BOATS.

Mayer Charles & Co, 29-31 W Washington. (See adv opp p 615.)

BOILER COMPOUND MNFRS.

Griggs Joseph E, 22 Ingalls blk.
Jennings Milton, 177 S Illinois.

*BOILER FEED PUMPS.

Worthington Henry R, 64 S Penn. (See left top lines.)

*BOILER FILTERS.

Worthington Henry R, 64 S Penn. (See left top lines.)

TURKISH RUGS AND CARPETS RESTORED TO ORIGINAL COLORS LIKE NEW | Capital Steam Carpet Cleaning Works M. D. PLUNKETT, Telephone 818

BENJ. BOOTH PRACTICAL EXPERT ACCOUNTANT. Books Opened, Written Up, Posted and Balanced. Room 18, 82½ E. Washington St., Indianapolis, Ind.

IF YOU WANT A GOOD MEAL AND HAVE IT NICELY SERVED GO TO THE SHERMAN RESTAURANT 18 and 20 S. MERIDIAN STREET

P. W. KENNEDY. J. P. CONNAUGHTON.

Capital City Steam Boiler and Sheet Iron Works.

Telephone 1748.

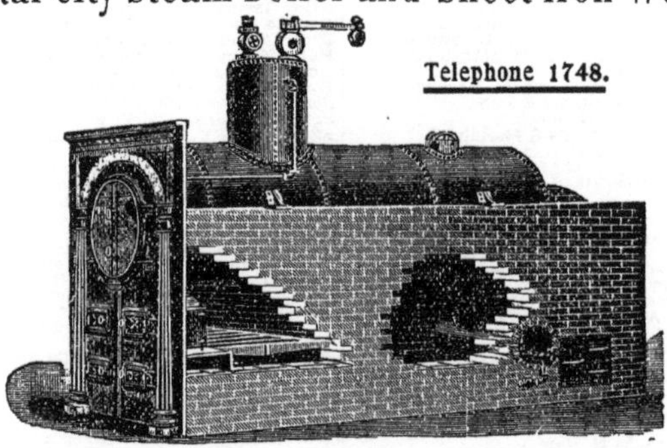

Kennedy & Connaughton

MANUFACTURERS OF

BOILERS AND TANKS

Boilers Built to Order, Water Tanks, Smoke Stacks, Breechings, Fire Fronts, Grate Bars, Etc. REPAIRING A SPECIALTY.

207 and 209 S. Illinois St., Indianapolis, Ind.

BOILERMAKERS.

Capital City Steam Boiler and Sheet Iron Works, 207-209 S Illinois. (See adv.)

Cruse Bros, 284 S Capitol av.

Kennedy & Connaughton, 207-209 S Illinois. (See adv.)

Stephens John F, n w cor Georgia and Missouri.

BOLT AND NUT MNFRS.

Indianapolis Bolt and Machine Works, 122-126 Kentucky av. (See adv in Elevator Mnfrs.)

*BOLTING CLOTHS.

Nordyke & Marmon Co, crossing I & V Ry and Morris (W I). (See inside back cover.)

*BONDS—SURETY.

American Bonding and Trust Co of Baltimore City, W E Barton & Co Genl Agts, 504 Indiana Trust Bldg. (See right bottom cor cards.)

Fidelity and Deposit Co of Maryland, George W Pangborn Genl Agt, 704-706 Lemcke Bldg. (See left top lines.)

London Guarantee and Accident Co (Limited) of London, England, George W Pangborn Genl Agt, 704-706 Lemcke Bldg. (See left top lines.)

*BONDS—SURETY FOR ADMINISTRATORS, GUARDIANS AND EXECUTORS.

Indiana Trust Co The, Indiana Trust Bldg, s e cor Washington and Virginia av. (See front cover, opp p 487 and opp Insurance Agts.)

Marion Trust Co, s e cor Market and Monument Pl. (See back cover.)

Union Trust Co, 68 E Market. (See front cover and opp p 867.)

BOOK BINDERS AND BLANK BOOK MANUFACTURERS.

Baker & Thornton, 38 S Meridian.

Brandt A G & Co, 64 S Penn.

TUTEWILER UNDERTAKER, No. 72 WEST MARKET STREET. TELEPHONE 216.

PARTNERSHIP INSURANCE At low cost. By which provision is made against the pecuniary loss and embarrassment resulting from the death of a member of a firm.
Provident Life and Trust Co. of Philadelphia, D. W. EDWARDS, Gen'l Agt., 508 Indiana Trust Bldg.

THEODORE F. SMITHER, AGENT FOR WARREN'S ANCHOR BRAND —ASPHALT ROOFING— OFFICE, 151 WEST MARYLAND ST. TEL. 861.

Burford Wm B, 21 W Washington. (See adv opp p 230.)
Carlon & Hollenbeck, s e cor Monument Pl and Meridian. (See adv opp p 244.)
Gierke Wm F A, 408½ S East.
Levey Bros & Co, 19 W Maryland. (See adv opp p 561.)
Nankervis J & Son, 18½ N Meridian.
Schnabel Christopher A, 46½ N Penn.
Smith Frank H, 22 N Penn. (See adv opp p 803.)

*BOOK ILLUSTRATING.

Indiana Illustrating Co, s e cor Market and Illinois. (See adv opp Engravers.)

BOOKS AND STATIONERY—WHOLESALE.

Indianapolis Book and Stationery Co The, 75 S Meridian.

BOOKS AND STATIONERY—RETAIL.

Allison Enos Co The, 92 N Meridian.
Baker & Thornton, 38 S Meridian.
Blair B L & Co, 23 W Maryland.
Bowen-Merrill Co The, 9-11 W Washington.
Burford Wm B, 21 W Washington. (See adv opp p 230.)
Cathcart, Cleland & Co, 6 E Washington.
Crouse Francis M, 38 N Delaware.
Crowell Melvin E, 24 E Market.
Epworth League Headquarters, 19 Pembroke Arcade.
George Co The, 11 Mass av.
Iske Frederick C, 329 S New Jersey.
Krieg Bros, 62 S Illinois.
Levey Bros & Co, 19 W Maryland. (See adv opp p 561.)
Noble Laz & Co, 3 N Meridian.
Pingpank Carl F, 7 S Alabama.
Sellers Wm T, 21 Virginia av.
Ward Wm H, 89 S Illinois.
Wylie Andrew, 13 N Penn.
Zimmerman Jacob N, 305 Virginia av.

BOOTS AND SHOES—WHOLESALE AND MANUFACTURERS.

Hendricks & Cooper, 85-87 S Meridian.
McKee Shoe Co, 102-104 S Meridian.
Pink Shoe Mnfg Co, 25 E South.

BOOTS AND SHOES—RETAIL.

Aldag Louis, 679 E Washington.
Barnard Frederick, 3 S Illinois.
Barr Wm H, 228 E Washington.
Bolin Sidney J, 509½ S West.
Brill Albert, 314 E Washington.
Brown Frank E, 156 E Washington.
Burk John E, 102 S Reisner (W I).
Camplin Richard S, 71 E Washington.
Cox Francis M, 310 Indiana av.
Crane Stephen D (agt), 162 Virginia av.
Dammeyer Bros, 247 E Washington.
Davies Jacob, 119 Mass av.
Ehrensperger J A & Co, 188 W Washington.
Fleischmann John L, 151 Prospect.
Florsheim Milton S, 50 E Washington.
Fox Oliver A, 68 E Washington.
Friedgen Cornelius, 19 N Penn. (See left top lines.)
Gelman Adolph H, 126 Indiana av.
Gift Benjamin F, 442 Mass av.
Gisler George, 650 Virginia av.
Glickert John, 306 S West.
Green James B, 178 Virginia av.
Green John B, 680 N Senate av.
Grover R B & Co, 40 E Washington.
Guarantee Shoe Store The, 50 N Illinois.
Gumbinsky Jacob, 153 W Washington.
Haag Anthony A, 186 Indiana av.
Habermann Gustav A, 1095 E Washington.
Harris Wm B, 51 W Washington.
Hart John C, 10 N Penn.
Hart Wm, 460 S Meridian.
Hart & Schlosser, 39 W Washington.
Heine Christian H, 479 Virginia av.
Henschen Adam H, 526 S Meridian.
Hill Paul C, 204 W Washington.
Horuff & Sons, 188-190 Virginia av.
Ioor Charles J, 162 W Washington.
Karle Joseph C, 73 E Washington.
Karst E Frank, 360 Mass av.
Keller Robert, 570-578 S East.
Kistner Charles C, 83 S Illinois.
Koeckert Max P, 345 S Delaware.
McCray John M, 256 W Washington.
Marott George J, 26-28 E Washington.
Marott George P, 16 N Penn.
Mason James M, 81 Mass av.
Meadows Charles S, 34 Pendleton av (B).
Merz Charles H, 587 S Meridian.
Metz John, 405 Madison av.
Metzger Conrad, 610 Virginia av.
Mode Michael, 93 E Washington.
Moloney John, 275 S Illinois.
Mueller Jacob, 565 N West.
Neerman Otto S, 273 Mass av.
Norris John M, 62 W Washington.
Nutz Peter, 44 Michigan (H).
Obergfell Ambrose, 559 S East.
O'Connor Patrick L, 221 Mass av.
Owen Charles A, 525 W Udell (N I).
Pettis Dry Goods Co, 25-33 E Washington.
Poggemeyer John H, 492 E Washington.
Reeder Isaac F, 224 W Washington.
Resner & Son, 418 Virginia av.
Roswinkel Wm & Co, 139 Mass av.
Schauroth & Co, 18 E Washington.
Schrader Frederick, 65 W Washington.
Schroeder Gustav T, 175 E Washington.
Schubert Charles A, 191 Shelby.
Sebel Adolph, 253 W Washington.
Selig Abram (mngr), 20 N Penn.
Siersdorfer Louis, 27 W Washington.
Spohr J George, 37 N Illinois.
Stout H & Co, 98 Indiana av, 64 Mass av, 184 W Washington and 242 E Washington.
Trimpe J H & Son, 162 Indiana av.
Updegraff Julius, 908 W Washington.
Vehling Frederick, 331 Dillon.
Vestal Foster M, w s Central av 5 s of Railroad (I).
Vielhaber Daniel, 212 E Washington.
Voglesong George E, 299 Mass av.
Wagner Elizabeth, 855 S Meridian.

BOOT AND SHOEMAKERS.

Alloways & Co, 28 Mass av.
Arndt August F, 217 E Morris.
Arschafsky Harris, 283 E Washington.
Bany Simon, 832 E Market.
Beaupre James, 291 Prospect.
Berdel John, 269 W McCarty.
Berg Michael, 370½ S West.

ELECTRIC CONSTRUCTION Isolated Plants Installed. Electric Wiring and Fittings of all kinds. C. W. Meikel. Tel. 466. 96-98 E New York St

DALTON & MERRIFIELD { LUMBER South Noble St., near E. Washington

INDIANA ELECTROTYPE CO.; BEST WORK. LOWEST PRICES. All Orders Promptly Filled. 23 WEST PEARL ST., INDIANAPOLIS, IND. JOB WORK. BOOK PLATES. BEST PATENT BASE ON THE MARKET.

Boot and Shoemakers—Continued.

Bertel John, 269 W McCarty.
Borgerding Frank H, 356 S New Jersey.
Boyd Addison E, 144 Howard (W I).
Brisky Moses L, 29 W Ohio.
Brossel Hubert, 78 N Illinois.
Burcham Joseph E, 163 Virginia av.
Burkhardt John J, 104 N Noble.
Burnett John A, rear 71 Minerva.
Busch Charles A, 495 College av.
Busch Christian, s s Washington 17 w of Harris av (M J).
Carey Wm, 52 W Georgia.
Chives Enos B, 19 Clifford av.
Chives James A, 247 Indiana av.
Co-Operative Shoe Co, 68-70 E Washington.
Crawley Hiram C, 183 S Meridian.
Crolf Abraham, 45 Mass av.
Davis Samuel, 275 E Washington.
Dieter Ernest, 57 College av.
Dorsey Ezra, 86 Lincoln la.
Eblein John, 143 S New Jersey.
Eckert Wm, 119 Mass av.
Estabrook Wm W, 509 E 7th.
Eymann John H, 33 Monument pl.
Fields James M, rear 50 S West.
Fischer George, 100 Hill av.
Fitzpatrick Hugh L, 411 Indiana av.
Ford Michael, 71 Camp.
Friedgen Cornelius, 19 N Penn. (See left top lines.)
Gakstatter Philip, 74 W 1st.
Galbraith Richard, 734 E 7th.
Gehrke Christian F, 151 Mass av.
Geiger Gottlieb, 253 Highland av.
Gisler George H, 650 Virginia av.
Graderlein Ernest, 315 Shelby.
Greiner John, 226 Prospect.
Griffin Wm H, 152 W North.
Grimes Aaron R, 27¼ Monument pl.
Guenther Casimir, 696 N Capitol av.
Hague Joseph F, 184 Blake.
Hanvey Alexander, 12 Ft Wayne av.
Harding John L, 139 Oliver av (W I).
Harper Frank C, 53 N Illinois.
Harris Jacob, 283 E Washington.
Harris Lee, 193 Mass av.
Hartley Thomas S, 107 Harrison.
Hartmann Oswald, 250 Davidson.
Harves Bros, 235 W Washington.
Hasenstab Alois, 33 Kennington.
Haskerl Charles H, 181 Madison av.
Haug Charles G, 102 Ft Wayne av.
Hedges Wm H, 48 S Illinois.
Heidenreich Edward, 583 Morris (W I).
Heilman Frederick, 94 Russell av.
Helwig Jacob, 847 E Michigan.
Herntschier Anton, 3 Cherry.
Hill Henry, 34 Monument pl.
Hofer Edward G, 155 Virginia av.
Hoffmann Henry, 231½ S Delaware.
Horuff & Sons, 188-190 Virginia av.
Howard James P, 207 S Noble.
Hutchins George A, 10½ Prospect.
Jenkins David A, 521 E 9th.
Jenson Jacob, 951 S Meridian.
Johannes John, 27 Minnesota.
Jolly John, 287 Howard (W I).
Jones Ellis, 103 Oliver av (W I).
Jones John B, 176 Indiana av.
Joyce Thomas, 171 Virginia av.
Judkins Wm, rear 251 English av.
Kaler Jacob E, 743 N Capitol av.
Kappeler Anthony E, 103 Ash.
Kaser Edward H, 310 E Washington.
Kathmann Bernard, 5 Indiana av.
Kettler Henry W, 317 Clifford av.
Kingsley James, 63 E Sutherland (B).
Kistner Henry, 460 S Delaware.
Klein John, 275 E Georgia.
Koch George, 329 S East.
Koenig Charles, 476 S East.
Kremer John, rear 501 College av.
Kronovsek Kancian, 355 S Capitol av.
Krug Frederick B, rear 115 Agnes.
Krug Karl, 48 Virginia av.
Kurtz John G, 47 Kentucky av.
Langer Charles, 268 Bates.
Lee Andrew, 33 Camp.
Levi Harris, 191 S Illinois.
Locke Wm T, 1547 N Illinois.
Long Granville G, 41 Mass av.
Lueth Wm, 236 S Meridian.
Luft Wm, 504½ Bellefontaine.
McDonald Hugh, 32 Hill av.
Mahoney Jeremiah, 50 Malott av.
Mannalla Frank, 121 W Washington.
Marsh Henry, 603 Virginia av.
Miller Samuel, 143½ Mass av.
Miller Wm F, 86 S Illinois.
Morgan Charles, 299½ W Washington.
Morgan Mark, 368 Virginia av.
Munzh Edward, 28 Sheffield av (H).
Nealer Jacob, 416 Clifford av.
Neumeister Adam, 94 Hosbrook.
Newman Herman, 24 and 156 Indiana av.
Niemeyer Wm W, 539 E Washington.
Niermeyer Henry, 436 National rd.
Norman Jesse E, 10 Malott av.
Paulus Matthias, 137 N Noble.
Poggemeyer Frank, 114 N Pine.
Pritsch Adolph, 536 S East.
Proskopsky Charles, 75 W Merrill.
Purcell John H, 309 Mass av.
Rannells James R, 22 Mass av.
Rardon Wm, 135 Mass av.
Ray John L, 468 E Washington.
Reeves Thomas P, 69 E 14th.
Reeves Thomas P, 118 Michigan (H).
Reinhart John, s e cor Schurmann av and Fremont (N I).
Resener Christian F, 336 E St Clair.
Reynolds Zachariah, 317 E Washington.
Rheinschild John, 58 Mass av.
Robinson Louis, 125½ Mass av.
Rose John N, rear 1 Spann av.
Rosenstein John, 398 S Capitol av.
Sanders Joseph, 223 W 3d.
Sapp George W, 358 Dillon.
Schives Enos B, 19 Clifford av.
Schmidt Henry, 366 Shelby.
Schmidt Philip, 137 Ft Wayne av.
Schopp George, 20 S Illinois.
Setzen Wm, 321 E Washington.
Shapero Benjamin, 327 E Washington.
Shea John, 210 S Capitol av.
Short Major, 6 S Missouri.
Siegel Harris, 311 E Washington.
Smock Charles P, 20 Prospect.
Staercker Philip, 276½ Coburn.
Straub Vincent, 443 S Illinois.
Stuck Wm H, 122 S Olive.
Ten Eyck Richard F, 338 W Washington.
Theising Henry A, 150 Agnes.
Trosky Frederick W, 156 E 7th.
Updegraff George W, 191 Virginia av.
Vandiver Benjamin F, 197½ River av (W I).
Van Stan John, 66 W 7th.
Waller Bernhard, 153 Indiana av.
Waller Bernhard jr, 40 W 13th.
Wands John, 237 E Washington.
Wanger Solomon, 84 Indiana av.
Warneke Henry, rear 202 Hoyt av.
Weaver James, 118 Mass av.
Wehinger Martin, 438 S Delaware.
Wehle Lucas, 274 W 1st.

W. H. MESSENGER COMPLETE HOUSE FURNISHER 101 East Washington Street, Telephone 491

THE FRED DIETZ CO.

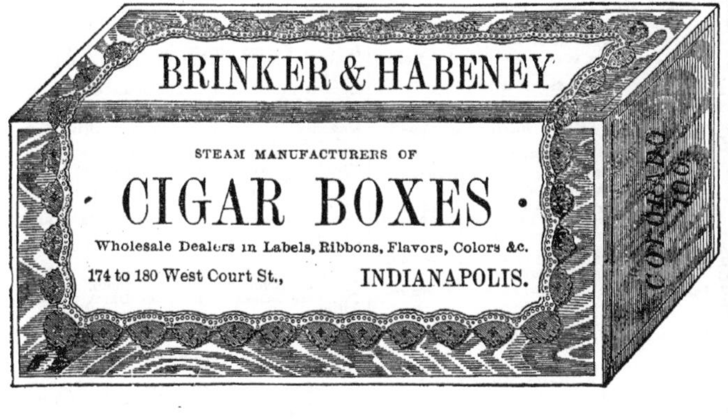

BRINKER & HABENEY
STEAM MANUFACTURERS OF
CIGAR BOXES
Wholesale Dealers in Labels, Ribbons, Flavors, Colors &c.
174 to 180 West Court St., INDIANAPOLIS.
COLORADO
100

Weisshaar John, 184 Dillon.
Wienke Wm, 179 Pleasant.
Wundram Louis, 554 S Meridian.
Yeager Elias, 224 S Linden.
Yocum Charles A, 372 E 7th.
Yung Henry, 160 Ft Wayne av.
Zornige Charles, rear 764 S East.

*BOTTLERS.

Lieber, Rich & Co (All Kinds of Carbonated Beverages and Distilled Waters), cor New York and Agnes.
Klee & Coleman (All Kinds of Carbonated Beverages), 227-229 S Delaware.

BOTTLERS—ALE AND BEER.

American Brewing Co, 175-197 W Ohio.
Anheuser-Busch Brewing Association, Jacob L Bieler Mngr Indianapolis Branch, 454-458 E Ohio.
Habich C Co The, 187 W Ohio.
Home Brewing Co of Indianapolis, cor Cruse and Wilson.
Indianapolis Brewing Co, 25 High.
Lieber P Branch Indpls Brewing Co, 514 Madison av.
Metzger Jacob & Co, 30-32 E Maryland.
Miller L W & Co, 292 E Washington.
Pabst Brewing Co Indianapolis Branch, 224-240 S Delaware.
Schmidt C F Branch Indpls Brewing Co, s end Alabama.
Terre Haute Brewing Co, Maurice Donnelly Mngr, 148 S West.

BOX MANUFACTURERS—CIGAR.

Brinker & Habeney, 174-180 W Court. (See adv.)

BOX MANUFACTURERS—PACKING.

Ballweg & Co, cor Wilkins and Pogue's run.
Brandt Frederick W, 85 S California.
Brunson H C & Co, s e cor St Clair and canal.
Dietz Fred Co The, 370-406 Madison av. (See right side lines and p 10.)
Saffell & Sindlinger, w end Elizabeth.

BOX MANUFACTURERS—PAPER.

Bee Hive Paper Box Co, 78½ W Washington.
Sullivan & Mahan, 41 W Pearl. (See left bottom lines.)

*BOYS' WAGONS.

Mayer Charles & Co, 29-31 W Washington. (See adv opp p 615.)

BRASS FOUNDERS.

Dean Bros' Steam Pump Works, 1st near cor Senate av. (See adv p 3.)
Howe Louis C, s e cor Michigan and Warman av (H).

WOODEN PACKING BOXES MADE TO ORDER
FACTORY AND WAREHOUSE TRUCKS.
400 Madison Avenue. Telephone 654.

Shorthand! BUSINESS UNIVERSITY. When Bl'k. Elevator day and night. Typewriting, Penmanship, Book-keeping, Office Training free. See page 4. Est. 1850. Tel. 499. E. J. HEEB, Proprietor.

NEW YORK FILTER MFG. CO.
Filters for Water-Works, Boiler Plants, Laundries, Hotels, Private Residences, Etc.

Henry R. Worthington,
64 S. Pennsylvania St.
Long Distance Telephone 284.

UNION CO-OPERATIVE LAUNDRY (COMPOSED OF UNION LAUNDRY GIRLS.) NOS. 3, 40 AND 142 VIRGINIA AVENUE.
T. E. SOMERVILLE, MANAGER— TELEPHONE 1269. INDIANAPOLIS, IND.

Brass Founders—Continued.

Langsenkamp Bros' Brass Works, 90-92 E Georgia. (See adv p 7.)

Pioneer Brass Works, 110-116 S Penn.

***BRASS GOODS.**

Reeves Harry E, 96 S Delaware, cor Georgia. (See embossed line front cover and adv in Patternmakers.)

***BREAD—WHOLESALE.**

Hitz Baking Co The, 68-70 S Delaware. (See right bottom cor cards.)

Parrott-Taggart Bakery of the U S Baking Co, 93-99 S Penn, cor Georgia. (See adv bottom edge.)

***BREAKFAST CEREALS—WHOLESALE AND RETAIL.**

Janes Frank E, 107-113 N Delaware.

BREWERS.

American Brewing Co, 175-197 W Ohio.

Anheuser-Busch Brewing Association, Jacob L Bieler Mngr Indianapolis Branch, 454-458 E Ohio.

Herancourt Brewing Co, 61 S Liberty.

Home Brewing Co of Indianapolis The, cor Cruse and Wilson.

Indianapolis Brewing Co, 25 High.

Jung Brewing Co The, cor Dillon and C C C & St L Ry.

Lieber P Branch Indpls Brewing Co, 514 Madison av.

Madison Brewing Co, 302 River av (W I).

Maus C Branch Indpls Brewing co, n w cor New York and Agnes.

Metzger Jacob & Co (Berliner Weiss Beer), 30-32 E Maryland.

Pabst Brewing Co Indianapolis Branch, 224-240 S Delaware.

Schmidt C F Branch Indpls Brewing Co, s end Alabama.

Terre Haute Brewing Co, Maurice Donnelly Mngr, 148 S West.

***BREWERY PUMPS.**

Worthington Henry R, 64 S Penn. (See left top lines.)

***BRICK DEALERS.**

Balke & Krauss Co, cor Missouri and Market. (See right bottom lines.)

Wasson W G Co The, 130 Indiana av. (See left bottom cor cards and adv in Cement and Lime.)

***BRICK—FIRE.**

Moffat & Co, 402 Lemcke Bldg. (See adv p 9.)

BRICK MACHINERY.

Fletcher Stephen K, 45 Ingalls blk.

BRICK MANUFACTURERS.

Adams Brick Co The, 2 Builders' Exchange.

Bremer Frederick, e s Sherman Drive 2 s of Prospect.

Brooks Noah, w s Sherman Drive 1 s of Clifford av.

Eilering Richard, s s Bethel av 2 e of Zwingley.

Flack Joseph F, 52 Mass av.

Indiana Paving Brick Co, 46½ N Penn.

Johnson John J, s e cor Mass and Peru avs.

Luedeman Bros, s s Michigan av 2 e of Belt R R.

Magennis George M, 310 Cypress.

Magennis James, e s Sherman Drive 1 n of Big 4 Ry.

Marion Brick Works, 5 Builders' Exchange.

Mueller Charles C, w s Perkins pike 2 n of Bethel av.

Nolting Henry W G, e s Sherman Drive 2 n of Washington.

Pothast Christian, n e cor Clifford and Osage avs.

Quack Charles C, n s Prospect 6 e of Belt R R.

Rehling Wm C, 652 Madison av.

Sheridan Brick Works, 88 N Penn.

Twiname James E, n w cor Barth av and Roll.

***BRIDGE BUILDERS—IRON.**

Adams J D & Co, 30 Jackson Pl, opp north entrance to Union Station.

Wrought Iron Bridge Co, Wm W Winslow Genl Agt, 1 Hubbard Blk. (See adv p 10.)

Indianapolis Bolt and Machine Works, 122-126 Kentucky av. (See adv in Elevator Mnfrs.)

***BRIDGE CONTRACTORS.**

(See also Contractors—Bridge.)

Chicago Bridge and Iron Co, 6 Builders' Exchange, 35 E Ohio. (See adv in Contractors—Bridge.)

Toledo Bridge Co The, Daniel Lesley Agt, 42 When Bldg. (See adv.)

THE
Toledo Bridge Company
ESTABLISHED 1867.
Steel and Iron Highway and Railway
BRIDGES
Steel Roof Trusses and Buildings.
DANIEL LESLEY, AGENT,
Room 42 When Bldg. Telephone 1916.

Wrought Iron Bridge Co, Wm W Winslow Genl Agt, 1 Hubbard Blk. (See adv p 10.)

BROKERS—BOND.

Campbell, Wild & Co, 205 Indiana Trust bldg.

Day Thos C & Co, 325-330 Lemcke Bldg. (See right top cor cards.)

CLEMENS VONNEGUT
184, 186 and 192 E. Washington St.

Wire Rope, Machinery, Lathes, Drills and Shapers

THE E. S. DEAN COMPANY
Room 51 Commercial Club Building.
STOCKS AND GRAIN
ORIGINATORS OF DEAN'S SAFE SYSTEM OF SPECULATION.
M. E. MASSEY, Representative.

Hawkins George M, 303-308 Lemcke bldg.
Indiana Trust Co The, Indiana Trust Bldg, s e cor Washington and Virginia av. (See front cover, opp p 487 and opp Insurance Agts.)

BROKERS—CIGAR.

Elam Edwin M, 89 S Meridian.
Phelps Harry E, 10 Monument pl.
Stouch Harry, 21 W Maryland.

BROKERS—GENERAL.

Haskell Joseph E, 19½ N Meridian.
Mutchner Philip E, 429 Lemcke bldg.
Wymond Harry A, 227-228 Lemcke bldg.

*BROKERS—GRAIN.

(See also Grain Dealers.)

Dean E S Co The, 51 Commercial Club Bldg. (See adv.)

*BROKERS—INSURANCE.

Metzger A Agency, 5 Odd Fellows' Hall. (See left bottom lines.)

BROKERS—INVESTMENT.

Bryan David C, 236 Lemcke Bldg.
Day Thos C & Co, 325-330 Lemcke Bldg., (See right top cor cards.)
Dean E S Co The, 51 Commercial Club Bldg. (See adv.)
Frenzel Bros, s w cor Washington and Meridian.
Indiana Trust Co The, Indiana Trust Bldg, s e cor Washington and Virginia av. (See front cover, opp p 487 and opp Insurance Agts.)

BROKERS—MERCHANDISE.

Applegate W A & Co, 32 S Meridian.
Conner Wm R, 25 W Georgia.
Dietz Charles L, 52 Virginia av.
Garrard T J & Son, 21 W Maryland.
Heath Corydon A, 37 E Maryland.
Holland Theodore F, 74 S Meridian.
Howland H H & Co, 36 Commercial Club bldg.
Jennings Francis R, 66½ W Maryland.
Jones John W & Co, 200 S Capitol av.
Kahn David & Co, 131 Commercial Club bldg.
Leib Edward H, 76 S Meridian.
Lovett F S & Co, 52 S Penn.
McCleary Alexander M, 802 Majestic bldg.
Pain Frederick, 248 S Meridian.
Paver J M & Co, 82 S Penn.
Pfeffer & Hunt, 26 W Maryland.
Robinson John W, 53½ W Washington.
Sawyers & Jones, 2½ Board of Trade bldg.
Shearman J D, Room 13, 17½ S Meridian.
Weghorst Frederick W, 52 Virginia av.
Whiteside Wm J, 27½ S Delaware.

BROKERS—MONEY.

Wiles Daniel H, 46½ N Penn.

BROKERS—PAPER AND TWINE.

Hubbard Wm H, 3 Hubbard blk.

BROKERS—STOCK.

Greene James & Co, 227-228 Lemcke Bldg.
Lawyers' Loan and Trust Co, 68½ E Market. (See adv top edge and opp p 555.)

*BROKERS—STOCK AND GRAIN.

Dean E S Co The, 51 Commercial Club Bldg. (See adv.)
Kinsey L A Co The, Commercial Club bldg.

*BROKERS—STOCKS, BONDS, GRAIN AND PROVISIONS.

Forest W E "Fluctuation System," 77½ E Market. (See adv p 9.)

BROKERS—TICKET.

See Ticket Brokers.

BROOM MANUFACTURERS.

Bass Charles O, 516 Ash.
Binager & Reinert, n e cor St Clair and Bee Line Ry.

INDIANAPOLIS STEEL ROOFING AND CORRUGATING WORKS, 23 and 25 East South Street. S. D. NOEL, Proprietor.

David S. McKernan, REAL ESTATE AND LOANS
A number of choice pieces for subdivision, or for manufacturers' sites, with good switch facilities.
Rooms 2-5 Thorpe Block.

DIAMOND WALL PLASTER { Telephone 1410 BUILDERS' EXCHANGE.

UNION TRANSFER AND STORAGE CO. Cor. E. Ohio St. and C., C., C. & St. L. R'y Tracks. BRICK WAREHOUSE; CLEANEST AND SAFEST STORAGE IN CITY FOR HOUSEHOLD GOODS AND MERCHANDISE.

Broom Manufacturers—Continued.
McGiffin & Power, 187 W 7th.
Middleton & Logsdon, rear 17 Park av.
Mitchell John W, 240 S Linden.
Perry Broom Co The, 82 S Delaware.
Robinson Don A, 163 Agnes.
Schaefer Wm, 218 E Wabash.

BRUSH MANUFACTURERS.

Aldag Paint and Varnish Co The, 222 E Washington. (See adv in Paints.)
Burdsal A Co The, 34-36 S Meridian. (See right bottom cor cards.)
Indianapolis Brush Mnfg Co, rear 736 W Washington.
Laitner Louis, 27 Cleveland (H).
Schmedel Hiram, 420 E McCarty. (See adv.)

HIRAM SCHMEDEL, MANUFACTURER OF BRUSHES No. 420 East McCarty St., INDIANAPOLIS All Kinds of Machinery Brushes Made to Order.

*BUGGY TOP MANUFACTURERS.

Indianapolis Buggy Top Co, 119 N Alabama.

BUILDERS.

See Carpenters, Contractors and Builders.

*BUILDERS' HARDWARE.

Vonnegut Clemens, 184-192 E Washington. (See left bottom lines.)

*BUILDERS' MATERIAL.

Balke & Krauss Co, cor Missouri and Market. (See right bottom lines.)
Dalton & Merrifield, 30-50 S Noble, near E Washington. (See left top lines.)
Diamond Wall Plaster Co, Office 3 Builders' Exchange, Factory E North and Bee Line Ry. (See top lines and opp p 941.)
Indianapolis Manufacturers' and Carpenters' Union, 38-42 S New Jersey. (See adv p 2.)
Indianapolis Steel Roofing and Corrugating Works, 23-25 E South. (See right side lines.)
Michigan Lumber Co, 436 E North, cor Fulton. (See embossed line back cover and adv opp Lumber.)
Rhodes Samuel S, 178 W Washington.
Shute Hamlin L, 35 Talbott blk.
Smither Henry C, 169 W Maryland. (See adv opp Roofing Material.)
Smither T F, 151 W Maryland. (See right side lines.)
Townsend Bros, 41 S Alabama.
Wasson W G Co The, 130 Indiana av. (See left cor cards and adv in Cement and Lime.)

The W. G. Wasson Co.
LIME, LATH, SEWER PIPE,
Flue Linings, Fire Brick, Coal and Coke.
Telephone 989. 130 Indiana Ave.

*BUILDING PAPER.

Smither Henry C, 169 W Maryland. (See adv opp Roofing Material.)
Smither T F, 151 W Maryland. (See right side lines.)
Vonnegut Clemens, 184-186 E Washington. (See left bottom lines.)

*BUILDING, SAVING AND LOAN ASSOCIATIONS.

(See also Miscellaneous Directory.)

Aetna Savings and Loan Association, 89 E Market.
American Building and Loan Association of Indiana, 42-43 Lombard Bldg.
Commonwealth Loan and Savings Association of Indiana, 18½ N Meridian.
Crescent Loan and Investment Co, 63-64 When Bldg.
Fidelity Building and Savings Union, 81-83 W Market.
Fraternal Building-Loan Associations, 51-52 Journal Bldg.
German-American Building Association of Indiana, 100 N Delaware.
Government Building and Loan Institution The, 31 Journal Bldg.
Guardian Savings and Loan Association, 70 E Market.
Indiana Mutual Building and Loan Association, 32 E Market.
Indiana Savings and Investment Co of Indianapolis, 90 E Market.
Indiana Society for Savings, 214-218 Lemcke Bldg.
Indianapolis Savings and Investment Co, 36 Monument Pl.
International Building and Loan Association, 83 E Market.

A. METZGER AGENCY ESTABLISHED 1863. INSURANCE

LAMBERT GAS & GASOLINE ENGINE CO.
ANDERSON, IND. PORTABLE GASOLINE ENGINES. 2 TO 25 H. P.

Meridian Life and Trust Company, 432 Lemcke Bldg. (See adv opp p 620.)
Monument Savings and Loan Association, 68½ E Market.
Mutual Savings Union and Loan Association The, 16 Masonic Temple.
New Year Saving and Loan Association, 36 W Washington.
Reserve Fund Savings and Loan Association of Indiana, 55-56 When Bldg.
State Building and Loan Association, 31 S Penn.
State Capitol Investment Association, 26-27 When Bldg.
State House Building Associations of Indiana, 211-213 Indiana Trust Bldg.
State House Dime Association of Indiana, 211-213 Indiana Trust Bldg.
Union Mutual Building and Loan Association, 87 W Market.
United States Building and Loan Institution, 721-722 Lemcke Bldg.
Washington Savings and Loan Association, 18, 19 and 20 Aetna Bldg, 19½ N Penn.

*BULBS.

Huntington & Page, 78 E Market. (See adv p 5.)

*BURLAPS.

Vonnegut Clemens, 184-186 E Washington. (See left bottom lines.)

*BUSINESS COLLEGES.

(See also Colleges and Schools.)

Indianapolis Business University, When Bldg, N Penn (Bryant & Stratton and Indianapolis Business Colleges Consolidated), E J Heeb Propr. (See front cover, right bottom lines and p 4.)

BUTCHERS.

See Meat Markets.

BUTTER, EGGS AND CHEESE.

Balfour, Potts & Doolittle, 28 S Delaware.
Cross Frank P, 105 E Mkt House.
Groff Henry F, 142 E Mkt House.
Groff N B & Son, 97 N Delaware and 43 E Mkt House.
Hart C H & Co, 44 E Mkt House.
Haworth Albert C, 38 E Mkt House.
Heath Wm A, 29 S Delaware.
Kerr John M L, 17 E Mkt House.
Kohnle George F, 61 Indiana av.
Lewellen Wm H, 24½ E Mkt House.
Peck Willard D, n e cor Delaware and 10th.
Williamson John M, 88 E Mkt House.

*CABINET HARDWARE.

Vonnegut Clemens, 184-186 E Wash-

Wiegel Wm, 6 W Louisiana. (See right side lines and adv in Show Case Mnfrs.)

*CALCIUM LIGHT SUPPLIES—OXYGEN AND HYDROGEN GAS.

Indianapolis Calcium Light Co, rear 126 W Maryland and 127 W Pearl.

CANDY MANUFACTURERS.

See Confectioners.

*CANNED GOODS.

Shearman J D, Room 13, 17½ S Meridian.

CANNING FACTORIES.

Henry T L & Co, n w cor St Clair and C C C & St L Ry.
Van Camp Packing Co, 300-400 Kentucky av.

CAR MANUFACTURERS.

Indiana Car and Foundry Co, Hadley av s of Belt R R (W I).

CAR DOOR MANUFACTURERS.

Wagner Car Door Co, 3 Ingalls blk.

*CARBONATED BEVERAGES.

Klee & Coleman, 227-229 S Delaware.
Lieber Rich & Co (also Distilled Water), cor New York and Agnes.

*CARPENTERS—GENERAL.

Salisbury & Stanley, 177 Clinton. (See right side lines.)

CARPENTERS, CONTRACTORS AND BUILDERS.

(See also Contractors.)

Agee Wm A, n w cor Bismarck and Miller (W I).
Alisch John A, 136 Spann av.
Anderson Charles, 28 N New Jersey.
Anderson George, 180 E Court.
Aufderheide Henry, 234 N Pine.
Bagley Wm R, 180 E Court.
Baker Joseph T, 30 Tacoma av.
Baptist John H, 61 Yandes.
Barnhill Jacob W, 200 W Pearl.
Barrett Jesse S, 379 Ash.
Beard Alvin G, 950 Ash.
Beerman August, 102 Dunlop.
Beermann Louis, 38 Davis.
Bender Conrad, 180 W 5th.
Berry James A, 1 Hester.
Bertels George, 107 Lexington av.
Bowlen Leonidas, n s Ohio 9 e of Rural.
Bowling John H, 176 Spann av.
Bowman Wm H, 132 Christian av.

BICYCLES $5 DOWN. MONTHLY. Best Wheels. Best Terms. WHEE 31 W LONG D

FIDELITY MUTUAL LIFE PHILADELPHIA, PA. A. H. COLLINS, Gen. Agt. Baldwin Blk. RATES REASONABLE. SOUND BEYOND QUESTION. BUSINESS-LIKE IN PRACTICE.

BITUMINOUS COAL ▸▸ Edwardsport Coal and Mining Company ROOMS 42 AND 43 WHEN BUILDING.

Carpenters, Etc.—Continued.
Cauldwell E H & Co, 147 Ash. (See adv.)

E. H. CAULDWELL & CO.
Contractors and Builders
All orders for Counters, Shelving, Screens and Job Work promptly attended to. Estimates Furnished.
147 ASH STREET.

Chapman Thomas S, 38 Camp.
Clements George, 494 Madison av.
Clements Peter, 679 Madison av.
Cline Benjamin F, 573 Broadway.
Cloud Jonathan, 40 Standard av (W I).
Cloud & Co, 246 Virginia av.
Cochran Wm A, 322 Union.
Cochrane Samuel W, 424 N Senate av.
Cole James A, 148 Harlan.
Cook Nicholas J, 34½ S Penn.
Cox George H, 155 English av.
Craig Herman T, 452 E Market.
Curtis Charles W, 191 N New Jersey.
Davis Harvey L, 73 W 19th.
Despo Alfred O, 200 Fletcher av.
Dollman Henry L, 66 E Market and 25 William.
Duchemin Elias P, 325 S Meridian.
Dunn George E, 128 King av (H).
Earp Henry, 214 Fletcher av.
Edwards Richard, 15 S Alabama.
Eickman Henry C, 40 N Gillard av.
Elder Joseph I, 110 S Judge Harding (W I).
Elliott Joel T, 89 Oliver av (W I).
Evans Jesse A, 194 Oliver av (W I).
Evans Marion, 1079 Morris (W I).
Everett Andrew J, 38 Eastern av.
Fatout Warren, 28 Mass av.
Faught Abram E, 26 Ruckle.
Fesler Wm B, 290 Union.
Field Omri T, 120 Ramsey av.
Fife Wm, 461 N East.
Fish Louis C, n s Orange av 1 e of Ramsey av.
Fisher & Myers, 71 W Michigan.
Fitchie Michael G, 868 N Senate av.
Flowers Thomas J, 333 Bates.
Fontaine Willard M, 60 Walcott.
Francis David T, 437 E Vermont.
Freeland James A, 96 Lee (W I).
Freund Matthew W, 508 N West.
Fryberger Charles W, 70 Temple av.
Gant Jesse, 547 E Michigan.
Gay Henry E, 248 Indiana av.
George Benjamin F, 297 E Market.
Gilkey Oliver B, 248 Virginia av.
Gisler John U, 114 Greer.
Grant Benjamin F, 50 Arbor av (W I).
Gray Robert, 78 E St Clair.
Green Isaac, 60 N New Jersey.
Groves David F, 131 Madison av.
Grube John H, 296 S Illinois.
Ham Joseph M, 446 S Olive.
Hamilton Charles L, 119 Spann av.
Hardacre John, 9 Cornell av.
Harrell Adolph, 105 Patterson.
Harris Charles E, 122 Wright.
Harris George W, 70 Pleasant.
Harris Jesse, 240 Oliver av (W I).
Hawkey Stanton W, 1181 N Illinois.
Hedlund John W, rear 21 Kentucky av.
Helm Adam, 283 E North.
Helms Henry, 364 N Pine.
Henschen Wm H, 259 S East.
Hereth Peter P, 501 Broadway.
Hertz Martin, 213 Hoyt av.
Hicks Wm W, 221 Buchanan.
Hoereth John G, 263 N East.
Hoffert Daniel S, 394 Highland av.
Hogue Henry H, w s Rural 2 n of Orchard av.
Hopkins Charles H, 210 Fletcher av.
Hubbard Wm F, e s Illinois 1 n of 30th.
Hughes Joseph A, 45 S Wheeler (B).
Hurd James E, 577 W Addison (N I).
Hurley Wm H, 579 E St Clair.
Indianapolis Manufacturers' and Carpenters' Union, 38-42 S New Jersey. (See adv p 2.)
Jameson Thomas H, Builders' Exchange.
Jeffries James S, 293 Davidson.
Johnson James A, 170 Woodlawn av.
Jones Jewett W, 12 Arbor av (W I).
Jordan Henry H, 26 Ludlow av.
Joslin Sylvanus, 210 Highland av.
Kattau Wm H, 151 Harrison.
Kiel Edward F, 361 N Noble.
Kiel Henry C, 168 Prospect.
Kirch Jacob, 26 Sanders.
Kiser Wm A, 29 William (W I).
Kottlowski Charles T, 220 S Noble.
Kraas Wm, 209 E Morris.
Lakin Edward J, 75 Lily.
Lather John, w s Northwestern av 1 s of 30th.
Laycock Charles F, 401 E McCarty.
Lehr Philip, 367 N Noble.
Lohrman Frederick, 558 W North.
Lemaire Antoinette, 305 Bright.
Lovett Charles H, 513 S New Jersey.
Lowe Nahum H, 308 E North.
Luebking Wm F, 129 N Summit.
McCain James B, 134 S New Jersey.
McClain Wm C, 127 N Noble.
McClimon James, 235 N Pine.
McConnell John P, 27 E Georgia.
McConnell Thomas, 167½ W 1st.
McCormack John L, 702 N Capitol av.
McFadden James S, 247 Huron.
McLain Wm O, 218 Spring.
McLeland George W, 276 Christian av.
McLeland Oliver P, 89 N Beville av.
Maar Henry, 221 Minnesota.
Maguire Charles A, 42 W Market.
Manshart George, 198 Nebraska.
Many Charles J, 315 Mass av.
Maris James D, 1339 N Alabama.
Maul Wm H, 66 Middle Drive (W P).
Mazelin Edward D, 371 Blake.
Meyer Charles W, 228 Elizabeth.
Meyer Herman H, 220 N Pine.
Michaelis Florebert, 230 E Merrill.
Miller Bros, 179 Clinton.
Miller Charles J, 845 E Michigan.
Miller Christian F, 230 Davidson.
Milner Wm L, 1252 N Illinois.
Minthorn John J, 2 Cornell av.
Mitchell James E, 437 E St Clair.
Mock Joseph, 73 Martindale av.
Moon Clarkson H, 960 N Senate av.
Moore George W, 107 Locke.
Moore & Dorrah, 582 Jefferson av.
Moorman Joel H, w s Central av 1 s of Beechwood av (I).
Morgan Sylvester, 216 River av (W I).
Moslander W S & Son, 66½ N Penn.
Neumann Julius R, 30 Hendricks.
Newby Jacob L, 61 S Belmont av (W I).
Newby & Son, 852 Grandview av.
Newman George S, 806 Cornell av.

ROOFING MATERIAL C. ZIMMERMAN & SONS, SLATE AND GRAVEL ROOFERS, 19 SOUTH EAST STREET.

NUERGE & REINKING,

CARPENTERS AND BUILDERS

JOBBING PROMPTLY ATTENDED TO.

Shop, 629 East Ohio St., Indianapolis, Ind.

Norman Isaac H, 74 Dawson.
Nuerge & Reinking, 629 E Ohio. (See adv.)
Olive John W, 265 Huron.
Overhiser John P, 88 S Linden.
Pasquier John B, 402 E Michigan.
Pauli Henry, 181 Davidson.
Paxson Augustus L, 315 Mass av.
Pearson Charles L, 136 Harlan.
Pearson Lewis B, 123 Columbia av.
Penhorwood Wm W, 183 Brookside av.
Poffinbarger Hiram, 82 S Reisner (W I).
Pool James P, 72 E Court.
Pressel Wm H, 309½ Mass av.
Pressly Wm W, 485 S Meridian.
Preusch Jacob F, 123 Olive.
Privett Willis, 85 Fulton.
Pumphrey Edward M, 184 N Pine.
Radowski Edward, 557 Morris (W I).
Randall James A, n e cor Park av and Fleet.
Reisinger Merritt H, 289 E Ohio.
Resener Christian F, 345 N Noble.
Richardson James D, 57 Hoyt av.
Rickabaugh Peter M, 50 River av (W I).
Robins Irvin & Co, 32 E Georgia.
Roberts Wm P, 1322 N Alabama.
Rochow Robert J, 10 Scyamore.
Routh Enoch B, 523 College av.
Rubush Wm G, 233 Bellefontaine.
Rule Thomas J, 49 Tacoma av.
Sahm Agit, 105 St Mary.
Salisbury & Stanley, 177 Clinton. (See right side lines.)
Schlanzer Benedict J, 682 Charles. (See adv p 8.)
Shoershusen Christian H, 109 Sanders.
Schreiber Frederick, 120 Palmer.
Schrimsher Jasper W, 629 Bellefontaine.
Schumacher John A & Co, 444-452 E St Clair.
Scott David I & Co, 77½ Mass av.
Scott Walter P & Co, 27 Kentucky av.
Scott Wm, 220 Mass av.
Scott W A & Sons, 591-593 Central av. (See front cover.)
Sharp John C, 85 Paca.
Shearer Thomas J, 363 N Pine.
Shoemaker Boston, 182 Newman.
Shoemaker Wm R, rear 313 E Georgia.
Silver Wm F, 29 Tacoma av.
Simmes Edward C, 26 Grace.
Sink Hiram T, 553 E Michigan.
Smith George F, 89 Spann av.
Snowden John W, 130 Lynn av (W I).
Spielhoff H & Son, 189 Coburn.
Standifer Joshua C, 700 Park av.
Stanley Frank P, 44 S Morris (B).
Stanley Wm W, 289 Excelsior av.
Stewart John B, 267 N Noble.
Stradling George W, 454 Central av.
Suhr Frederick, 536 S Illinois.
Suhre Henry C, 46 Yandes.
Sunderland Peter J, 274 Spring.
Talbert Samuel A, 179 Blackford.
Thieme Louis, 490 E Washington.
Thomas Crawford, 1324 N Alabama.
Thornburg Joseph A, 313 Mass av.
Thumann August, 361 E New York.
Tice Henry L, 394 Bellefontaine.
Tobin James, cor Kentucky av and Merrill.
Unger Jeremiah, 119 Hoyt av.
Vahle Henry H, 44 Walcott.
Van Camp John, 164½ E Washington.
Vaughan Dennis, 206 E Washington.
Vincent John R, 22 S New Jersey.
Vincent Wm H, 163 Sharpe av (W).
Vincent Wm H jr, 22 S New Jersey.
Volrath Louis, 742 S East.
Walker John T, 167 Pleasant.
Ward Carey J, e s Sherman Drive 1 n of Michigan.
Weber Charles A, 33 William.
Weddle Andrew D, 191 Oliver av (W I).
Welling C Henry, 127 Spring.
Wells Thomas W, 1518 N Senate av.
White John W, 163 Davidson.
Wigginton David T, 22 Elk.
Wilson John S, 599 Park av.
Wollenweber Charles L, 119 Maxwell.
Woods John W, 135 Forest av.
Worthington Robert, 45 Mass av.

ERTEL STEAM LAUNDRY
26 and 28 N. Senate Ave. Telephone 1089.
fs Laundered in Best of Style.
c or High Gloss Finish.

ELLIS & HELFENBERGER
Manufacturers of Iron Vases, Setees and Hitch Posts.
162-170 South Senate Ave. Tel. 958

THE HOGAN TRANSFER AND STORAGE COMP'Y
Household Goods and Pianos Moved—Packed—Stored...... Baggage and Package Express Machinery and Safes a Specialty Cor. Washington and Illinois Sts. TELEPHONE No. 675.

MACK'S
Carpet and Rug Factory
CARPETS CLEANED TO LOOK LIKE NEW, 3c. PER YARD.
We Have the Reputation of Doing the Best Work in the City.
Beautiful Rugs made of old Carpets, per yd....75c.
Rug Carpets woven, per yd.......... .... 10c.
FACTORY: FOURTH AND CANAL. Telephone 243.

The Capital Steam Carpet Cleaning Works,
M. D. PLUNKETT, Proprietor.
Cor. Ninth and Lennox Sts.,
(Big Four R. R.)
Phone 818.
EXCLUSIVELY Carpet Cleaning Works.
8,000 Feet Floor Space.
Capacity 3,000 Yards Daily.
NO BEATING—NO TEARING.

The Central Rubber & Supply Co. ◄◆◆► Hose, Belting, Packing, Clothing, Druggists' Sundries, Bicycle Tires, Cotton Hose, Etc. New York Belting & Packing Co., L't'd.
PHONE 922. 79 S. ILLINOIS ST., INDIANAPOLIS, IND.

CARPET CLEANERS.

Capital Steam Carpet Cleaning Works The, M D Plunkett Propr, cor 9th and Lenox (Big Four Ry). (See right bottom lines and adv.)
Howard Liberty, n w cor St Clair and canal.
Mack Wm, cor W 4th and canal. (See adv.)
Plunkett Melanchthon D, Propr Capital Steam Carpet Cleaning Works, cor 9th and Lenox (Big Four Ry). (See right bottom lines and adv.)

CARPET WEAVERS.

Braendlein Henry J, 376 Coburn.
Cooper John O, 223 Mass av.
Haggard Esther I, 79 Shepard (W I).
Mathey Frederick, 73 Hosbrook.
Miller Henry, 265 Coburn.
Smithey Ellen, s s Railroad 3 w of Central av (I).
Williams Augustus W, 169 Mass av.

CARPETS, OIL CLOTHS, ETC.

Gall Albert, 17-19 W Washington.
Gallahue Philip M (whol), 40 W Market.
Haueisen & Hartmann, 163-169 E Washington. (See right bottom cor cards.)
Kotteman Wm, 89-91 E Washington. (See right top lines.)
Messenger W Horndon, 101 E Washington and 13, 15 and 17 S Delaware. (See left bottom lines.)
Pettis Dry Goods Co, 25-33 E Washington.
Strack Wm, 176 Virginia av.
Taylor & Taylor, 30-36 S Illinois.
Wasson H P & Co, 12-18 W Washington.
Willig Charles, 79 W Washington.

*CARPET AND RUG MNFRS.

Mack Wm, cor W 4th and canal. (See adv.)
Miner Wm L, 184-186 Cherry. (See adv opp Rugs.)

*CARRIAGE BODY MANUFACTURERS.

Hampton Jehiel B, 112 S East.

CARRIAGE PAINTERS.

Wolf H S & Co, 477-479 S Delaware. (See adv.)

OTTO GAS ENGINES | BUILDERS' EXCHANGE S. W. Cor. Ohio and Penn. Telephone 535.

Becker & Son Charles Becker Jacob Becker Jr. Merchant Tailors. 21 N. Penn. St. Tel. 934

HENRY GLATTFELDER,
H. S. WOLF & CO.,
WM. H. BARNHART,

CARRIAGE AND WAGON MAKERS,

Repairs of all Kinds. Painting a Specialty.

477 and 479 SOUTH DELAWARE STREET.

Lamson Consol'd Store Service Co.

MANUFACTURES ABOVE TWENTY DIFFERENT STYLES OF

PARCEL, CASH, BALL, ELECTRIC, CABLE, DOUBLE WIRE, SPRING, GRAVITY AND PNEUMATIC

CASH AND PARCEL CARRYING DEVICES

We Shall be Pleased to Quote SALE AND LEASE PRICES.

F. R. TAISEY, Department Agent. Office, 31½ Virginia Ave., Indianapolis.

*CARRIAGE PAINTS.

Burdsal A Co The, 34-36 S Meridian. (See right bottom cor cards.)

*CARRIAGE PLATES.

Mayer George J, 15 S Meridian. (See left bottom cor cards and p 5.)

*CARRIAGE REPOSITORIES.

Comstock & Coonse Co, 193-199 S Meridian.
Conde H T Implement Co, 27-33 N Capitol av.
Fisk H C & Son, 12-14 Monument pl.
Johr Augustus J, 154 E Ohio.
White Thomas G, 30 S Penn.

CARRIAGE AND WAGON MNFRS.

(See also Blacksmiths.)

Abright Charles F, 211 W Vermont.
Barnhart Wm H, 479 S Delaware.
Beltz Frank P, 100 W Market.
Bernd Bros, 69 W Morris.
Black Charles H, 44 E Maryland.
Bohmie John M, 180 E Pearl.
Buchanan Joseph W, 302 E Washington.
Burgan J C & Co, 114 E Ohio.
Co-Operative Carriage and Wagon Co, 115 N Alabama.
Guedelhoefer John, 102 Kentucky av.
Hartman & Bulmahn, 220 E South.
Helfer Edward T, 37-41 N Capitol av.
Helfrich Adam H, 380 W Washington.
Kramer Jacob J, 213-215 E Market.
McKinley Hugh, 144 Ft Wayne av.
Miller George W & Co, 86 E New York.
Miller John F, 540 Dillon.
Parry Manufacturing Co, 250 S Illinois.
Pfaff & Co, 31 Cornell av.
Robbins Irvin & Co, 32 E Georgia.
Schwab Charles, cor 22d and Bellefontaine.
Schweikle & Prange, s e cor Market and Davidson.
Shover Garrett H, 172 E Market.
Silvers Bros, 454 Mass av.
Sudmeyer Charles H, 862 S Meridian.

*CARVERS' TOOLS.

Vonnegut Clemens, 184-186 E Washington. (See left bottom lines.)

*CASH CARRIERS.

Lamson Consolidated Store Service Co. 31½ Virginia av. (See adv.)

CASH REGISTERS.

National Cash Register Co The, Grand Hotel Blk, 65 S Illinois.

CATSUP AND SOUP MANUFACTURERS.

Mullen-Blackledge Co The, 62-66 S Alabama.

*CEDAR SHINGLES.

Byrd Joseph W, 323 Lemcke Bldg. (See adv opp Lumber Mnfrs and Dealers.)

LUMBER | Sash, Door and Planing Mill Work. | Balke & Krauss Co. Cor. Market and Missouri Streets.

SALISBURY & STANLEY • Office Store and Bar Fixtures a Specialty. Repairing of all kinds done on short notice. 177 Clinton Street, Indianapolis, Ind. • Contractors and Builders TELEPHONE 999.

FRIEDGEN'S TAN SHOES are the Newest Shades
Prices the Lowest. 19 North Pennsylvania St.

SAMUEL LAING General Job Work in Sheet Metal of all Kinds
72 AND 74 E. COURT STREET.

*CEILING AND SHEET METAL WORK.

Ensey O B, cor 6th and Illinois. (See left bottom cor cards.)
McWorkman Willard, 930 W Washington. (See left top cor cards.)

*CEMENT AND LIME.

(See also Lime, Cement and Plaster).
Balke & Krauss Co, cor Market and Missouri. (See right bottom lines.)
Moffat & Co, 402 Lemcke Bldg. (See adv p 9.)
Wasson W G Co The, 130 Indiana av. (See left cor cards and adv.)

THE W. G. WASSON CO.
American and Imported
Portland Cements, Louisville Cement,
TELEPHONE 989.
Office and Yards, 130 Indiana Ave.

*CEMETERY FENCING.

Ellis & Helfenberger, 162-168 S Senate av. (See right bottom lines.)

CEREALINE MANUFACTURERS.

Cerealine Mnfg Co, 950 Gent (M P).

CHAIN MANUFACTURERS.

Ewart Mnfg Co, cor Michigan and Holmes av (H).
Indpls Chain and Stamping Co, cor Senate av and Georgia.

CHAIR MANUFACTURERS.

Central Chair Co, s w cor Georgia and Missouri.
Frye Henry, 1 Fayette.
Indianapolis Chair Mnfg Co, n w cor New York and Ellsworth.
Neu John B, 63 Arizona.
Smith, Day & Co, 76 Shelby.

*CHECKS.

Mayer George J, 15 S Meridian. (See left bottom cor cards and p 5.)

CHEMISTS—ANALYTICAL.

Hurty John N, 8 Hutchings blk.
Smith Theodore W, 23 W Ohio. (See adv.)

T. W. SMITH, Chemist,
Analytical
Laboratory.

EXPERT
ANALYSIS
MADE OF
WATER, MILK, FOOD STUFF, BEVERAGES, Etc.
23 West Ohio Street, Indianapolis, Ind.

CHEMISTS—MANUFACTURING.

Duden August & Co, 51 Huron.
Indianapolis Chemical Co, 543 Madison av.
Inland Chemical Co, 126-130 W Maryland.
Jackson B F & Co, rear 71 Ash.
Lilly Eli & Co, 132-140 E McCarty.
McCoy-Howe Co, 75-79 W Georgia.

CHEWING GUM MANUFACTURERS.

Fitch A M & Co, 79 Ft Wayne av.
Meyer Bros, 27 S Meridian.
White Chemical Co, 190 S Meridian.

*CHILDREN'S CARRIAGES.

Mayer Charles & Co, 29-31 W Washington. (See adv opp p 615.)

*CHIMNEY PIPE.

Balke-Krauss Co, cor Missouri and Market. (See right bottom lines.)
Wasson W G Co The, 130 Indiana av. (See left bottom cor cards and adv in Cement and Lime.)

CHINA, GLASS AND QUEENSWARE—WHOLESALE.

Frommeyer Bros, 24 S Meridian.
Hollweg & Reese, 82-98 S Meridian.
Pearson & Wetzel, 119-121 S Meridian.

CHINA, GLASS AND QUEENSWARE—RETAIL.

Cusack John T, 103 S Illinois.
Davis Clara, 136 Minerva.
Frommeyer Bros, 24 S Meridian.
Kaufman Morris D, 173 W Washington.
Mayer Charles & Co, 29-31 W Washington. (See adv opp p 615.)
Messenger W Horndon, 101 E Washington and 13, 15 and 17 S Delaware. (See left bottom lines.)
Rentsch Margaret, 193 W Washington.
Ringolsky Himon, 165 W Washington.
Schrader Christian, 71-74 E Washington.
Schultz Rachel, 85 E Mkt House.
Smith F P & Co, 45 N Illinois.

CHIROPODISTS AND MANICURES.

Braley Charles H, 77 W Ohio.
Buzan Mollie A, 25½ W Washington.
Eliker Mary E, 4 Mass av.
Evans Ada P Mme, over 2½ W Washington. (See adv in Hair Goods.)
Lewis Solomon H, 235 Mass av.
Morgan Benjamin J, 25½ W Washington.
Taylor Zachariah, 17 McCauley.
Welch Isaac N, 6 Miller blk.

*CHLORO-NAPTHOLEUM.

West Disinfecting Co, 7 Monument Pl. (See adv in Disinfectants.)

*CIGAR BOX MANUFACTURERS.

Brinker & Habeney, 174-180 W Court. (See adv in Box Mnfrs—Cigar.)

CIGAR MANUFACTURERS.

Anschuetz Edward, 548 Virginia av.
Auerbach Mark, 78 N Illinois.
Aufderheide Gottfried, 52 Hillside av.
Babcock Adrian, 105½ Mass av.

PAPER BOXES, MANUFACTURED BY SULLIVAN & MAHAN 41 W. PEARL STREET.

DIAMOND WALL PLASTER { Telephone ... BUILDERS' EXCHANGE

Baggerly Charles W, 78 W Maryland.
Baker Jacob, 195 Virginia av.
Barasch Leon, 233 E Washington.
Becker Jacob, 47 Iowa.
Benzing Charles W, 666½ S Meridian.
Bertelsman Charles, 264 Mass av.
Bleistein Adam, 128 N Noble.
Bourgonne Stephen B, 140 Union.
Burns Gerrone W, 252 Blake.
Burns Wm F, 8 Indiana av.
Buser John P, 142 River av (W I).
Christoph Wm F, 85 Kansas.
Coffin Wm J, 72 Frank.
Colter George R, 139 Virginia av.
Coxe John, 262 W Washington.
Dalton Thomas J, 659 N Senate av.
Earles Silas J, 46 Kappus (W I).
Echols Wm A, 289 Mass av.
Engilman Isaac M, 34 Hubbard blk.
Feld Oscar P, n e cor Michigan and canal.
Flora John, 35 Tecumseh.
Foerster Adolph E, 759 S East.
Frank Abraham H, 340 W Washington.
Franz George L, 395 N Brookside av.
Franz Wm, 27 Yandes.
Gartlein John F, 123 Windsor.
Gebhardt Henry, 353 E McCarty.
Gessert Frank W, 429 S State av.
Gest George I & Sons, 328 Hillside av.
Grenwald Sam, rear 333 Jefferson av.
Grund George W, 636 Virginia av.
Haehl Cornelius, 128 Orange av.
Hamilton T J & Co, 43 Kentucky av and 177-179 W Maryland.
Harms Arthur E, 507 Broadway.
Harms August C, 534 Broadway.
Harms Herman P, 292 E Washington.
Harms Martha, 77 W Walnut.
Heede Henry, 254 Bates.
Heeg Charlotte, 208 E Morris.
Jeffery Julian F, 122 Ft Wayne av.
Jennings Theodore H, rear 56 Newman.
Jonas Wm F, 549 S West.
Keller Anton, 86 Stevens.
Kiefer Rudolph C, 102 Michigan (H).
Kistner Henry jr, 71 Yeiser.
Kluge Gustav, 425 S Delaware.
Koehler John F, 214 Hamilton av.
Koeniger George J, 124 Kennington.
Kornfeld Henry and Lena, 208 N Pine.
Kretsch Charles P, 221 S Alabama.
Kretsch Peter, 9 Gresham.
Larsh & Meginniss, 353 E St Clair.
Meyer Gustav J T, 74 S Delaware.
Meyer John P C, 86 N Illinois.
Meyer Theodore, 28 Minnesota.
Mucho Frederick W, 199 E Washington.
Murray Christian, 1087 E Washington.
Osborn James L, 539 W Udell (N I).
Padou Paul, 555 Morris (W I).
Posner Abraham, rear 425 Madison av.
Rauch Albert E, 125 Windsor.
Rauch John, 82 W Washington.
Rebentisch Albert J, 48 Davis.
Reger Henry G, 170 E Washington.
Reinfels Charles P, 791 S East.
Sachs John A, 450 S Illinois.
Schaub Henry J, 453 E Washington.
Schmalholz Simon, 257½ E Washington.
Schmitt John, 404 S Meridian.
Sharpe Andrew W, 353 S East.
Sorhage Henry C, 161 Virginia av
Spangenberger Louis, 560 S Illinois.
Steffen Andrew, 220 E Washington.
Stitz Frederick, 18 McKim av.
Stoll Michael, 428 Virginia av.
Strack Ignatz, 379 S Delaware.
Treuhann Frank, 762 S Meridian.
Wald Adolph, 237 N Liberty.
Wells Edward H, 43 N Illinois.
Wisser Frederick, 172 S Linden.
Witt Gustav C, 251 Michigan av.
Wittenbring Henry, 196 Orange.
Wolf John, 28 N Delaware.
Wolf Lee, 30 Larch.

CIGARS AND TOBACCO—WHOLESALE.

Berkowitz Armin, 484 E Washington.
Craig Henry J, 15 Indiana av.
Hitt D C & J B, 32 S Meridian.
Judson & Hanna, 21 W Maryland.
Kaufman B & Son, 168 W Washington.
Metzger Jacob & Co, 30-32 E Maryland.
Meyer Charles F & Bro, 15 N Penn.
Ryder Joseph M, 145 W Washington.
Warner C M & Co, n e cor Washington and Meridian.

CIGARS AND TOBACCO—RETAIL.

Adam Herman F, 15 N Illinois.
Alcazar, 30 W Washington.
Alford Ambrose A, 21 S Meridian.
Axtell Samuel P, 144 S Meridian.
Balk Lizzie E Mrs, 80 E Market.
Barckdall Daniel, 666 W Washington.
Barrett Solomon, 90 E South.
Beltz F P & Son, 29 S Illinois.
Bradford James M, Commercial Club bldg.
Brown Robert P, 137 River av (W I).
Campbell Arthur B, 2 Malott av.
Chambers Perlee L, 56 W Washington and 59 N Penn.
Clark Edward A, 150 Mass av.
Collins Emanuel, 179 Indiana av.
Coombs Wm H, 15 Virginia av.
Costigan Frank, Occidental Hotel.
Crabb Keller E, 64 Virginia av.
Dearth John P, 303 Virginia av.
Denson Charles W, 149½ Mass av.
Deschler Louis G, 51 N Penn and The Bates.
DeVoss Samuel H, 308 Virginia av.
Doherty James, 60 S Illinois.
Feetman Solomon, 586 W Washington.
Frazee Stephen J, 67 S Illinois.
George Henry S, 33 McCrea.
Giblin Elizabeth J, 200 W Chesapeake.
Grau Julius jr, 366 Blake.
Hollenbeck Frank B, Stubbins Hotel.
Joss George N, 82 Indiana av.
Kiemeyer Wm, 76 E Washington.
King John, 215½ W Washington.
Kriel Wm C, 898 N Illinois.
Lewis George S, 102 Mass av.
Loebenberg Henry, 9 S Illinois.
McConney Norris J, 44 Jackson pl.
McCorkle Marion, 97 Mass av.
McGaw John A, 24 N Illinois.
Meyer Charles F & Bro, 15 N Penn and 30 W Washington.
Miller Emlen F, 325 E Washington.
Miner Wilford H, 150 Indiana av.
Monninger Conrad, 390 Indiana av.
Moore Albert D, Journal bldg and 536 College av.
Neuer Wm B, 358 Mass av.
Newell Arthur, 89 N Delaware.
O'Meara Patrick J, s w cor Meridian and Monument pl.
Osburn Edward, n e cor 12th and Senate av.
Pierson Samuel D, 12 N Penn.
Raper George, The Denison and 19 Monument pl.
Redmond Frank S, 24 Indiana av.
Reeves Carey, State House.
Riebel Frederick, 48 E Washington.

Fine Laundry Work our Specialty. Collars and Cuffs our Hobby. THE HOME LAUNDRY 197 S. Illinois St. Telephone 1769.

THE WM. H. BLOCK CO. 7 AND 9 EAST WASHINGTON STREET. DRY GOODS, MEN'S FURNISHINGS.

FRIEDGEN'S TAN SHOES are the Newest Shades
Prices the Lowest. 19 North Pennsylvania St.

SAMUEL LAING General Job Work in Sheet Metal of all Kinds
72 AND 74 E. COURT STREET.

*CEILING AND SHEET METAL WORK.

Ensey O B, cor 6th and Illinois. (See left bottom cor cards.)
McWorkman Willard, 930 W Washington. (See left top cor cards.)

*CEMENT AND LIME.

(See also Lime, Cement and Plaster).
Balke & Krauss Co, cor Market and Missouri. (See right bottom lines.)
Moffat & Co, 402 Lemcke Bldg. (See adv p 9.)
Wasson W G Co The, 130 Indiana av. (See left cor cards and adv.)

THE W. G. WASSON CO.
American and Imported
Portland Cements, Louisville Cement,
TELEPHONE 989.
Office and Yards, 130 Indiana Ave.

*CEMETERY FENCING.

Ellis & Helfenberger, 162-168 S Senate av. (See right bottom lines.)

CEREALINE MANUFACTURERS.

Cerealine Mnfg Co, 950 Gent (M P).

CHAIN MANUFACTURERS.

Ewart Mnfg Co, cor Michigan and Holmes av (H).
Indpls Chain and Stamping Co, cor Senate av and Georgia.

CHAIR MANUFACTURERS.

Central Chair Co, s w cor Georgia and Missouri.
Frye Henry, 1 Fayette.
Indianapolis Chair Mnfg Co, n w cor New York and Ellsworth.
Neu John B, 63 Arizona.
Smith, Day & Co, 76 Shelby.

*CHECKS.

Mayer George J, 15 S Meridian. (See left bottom cor cards and p 5.)

CHEMISTS—ANALYTICAL.

Hurty John N, 8 Hutchings blk.
Smith Theodore W, 23 W Ohio. (See adv.)

T. W. SMITH, Chemist,
Analytical Laboratory.

EXPERT ANALYSIS MADE OF
WATER, MILK, FOOD STUFF, BEVERAGES, Etc.
23 West Ohio Street, Indianapolis, Ind.

CHEMISTS—MANUFACTURING.

Duden August & Co, 51 Huron.
Indianapolis Chemical Co, 543 Madison av.
Inland Chemical Co, 126-130 W Maryland.
Jackson B F & Co, rear 71 Ash.
Lilly Eli & Co, 132-140 E McCarty.
McCoy-Howe Co, 75-79 W Georgia.

CHEWING GUM MANUFACTURERS.

Fitch A M & Co, 79 Ft Wayne av.
Meyer Bros, 27 S Meridian.
White Chemical Co, 190 S Meridian.

*CHILDREN'S CARRIAGES.

Mayer Charles & Co, 29-31 W Washington. (See adv opp p 615.)

*CHIMNEY PIPE.

Balke-Krauss Co, cor Missouri and Market. (See right bottom lines.)
Wasson W G Co The, 130 Indiana av. (See left bottom cor cards and adv in Cement and Lime.)

CHINA, GLASS AND QUEENSWARE—WHOLESALE.

Frommeyer Bros, 24 S Meridian.
Hollweg & Reese, 82-98 S Meridian.
Pearson & Wetzel, 119-121 S Meridian.

CHINA, GLASS AND QUEENSWARE—RETAIL.

Cusack John T, 103 S Illinois.
Davis Clara, 136 Minerva.
Frommeyer Bros, 24 S Meridian.
Kaufman Morris D, 173 W Washington.
Mayer Charles & Co, 29-31 W Washington. (See adv opp p 615.)
Messenger W Horndon, 101 E Washington and 13, 15 and 17 S Delaware. (See left bottom lines.)
Rentsch Margaret, 193 W Washington.
Ringolsky Himon, 165 W Washington.
Schrader Christian, 71-74 E Washington.
Schultz Rachel, 85 E Mkt House.
Smith F P & Co, 45 N Illinois.

CHIROPODISTS AND MANICURES.

Braley Charles H, 77 W Ohio.
Buzan Mollie A, 25½ W Washington.
Eliker Mary E, 4 Mass av.
Evans Ada P Mme, over 2½ W Washington. (See adv in Hair Goods.)
Lewis Solomon H, 235 Mass av.
Morgan Benjamin J, 25½ W Washington.
Taylor Zachariah, 17 McCauley.
Welch Isaac N, 6 Miller blk.

*CHLORO-NAPTHOLEUM.

West Disinfecting Co, 7 Monument Pl. (See adv in Disinfectants.)

*CIGAR BOX MANUFACTURERS.

Brinker & Habeney, 174-180 W Court. (See adv in Box Mnfrs—Cigar.)

CIGAR MANUFACTURERS.

Anschuetz Edward, 548 Virginia av.
Auerbach Mark, 78 N Illinois.
Aufderheide Gottfried, 52 Hillside av.
Babcock Adrian, 105½ Mass av.

PAPER BOXES, MANUFACTURED BY SULLIVAN & MAHAN 41 W. PEARL STREET.

DIAMOND WALL PLASTER { Telephone 1410 BUILDERS' EXCHANGE.

Fine Laundry Work our Specialty. Coll as and Cfs our Hobby.

Baggerly Charles W, 78 W Maryland.
Baker Jacob, 195 Virginia av.
Barasch Leon, 233 E Washington.
Becker Jacob, 47 Iowa.
Benzing Charles W, 666½ S Meridian.
Bertelsman Charles, 264 Mass av.
Bleistein Adam, 128 N Noble.
Bourgonne Stephen B, 140 Union.
Burns Gerrone W, 252 Blake.
Burns Wm F, 8 Indiana av.
Buser John P, 142 River av (W I).
Christoph Wm F, 85 Kansas.
Coffin Wm J, 72 Frank.
Colter George R, 139 Virginia av.
Coxe John, 262 W Washington.
Dalton Thomas J, 659 N Senate av.
Earles Silas J, 46 Kappus (W I).
Echols Wm A, 289 Mass av.
Engilman Isaac M, 34 Hubbard blk.
Feld Oscar P, n e cor Michigan and canal.
Flora John, 35 Tecumseh.
Foerster Adolph E, 759 S East.
Frank Abraham H, 340 W Washington.
Franz George L, 395 N Brookside av.
Franz Wm, 27 Yandes.
Gartlein John F, 123 Windsor.
Gebhardt Henry, 353 E McCarty.
Gessert Frank W, 429 S State av.
Gest George I & Sons, 328 Hillside av.
Grenwald Sam, rear 333 Jefferson av.
Grund George W, 636 Virginia av.
Haehl Cornelius, 128 Orange av.
Hamilton T J & Co, 43 Kentucky av and 177-179 W Maryland.
Harms Arthur E, 507 Broadway.
Harms August C, 534 Broadway.
Harms Herman P, 292 E Washington.
Harms Martha, 77 W Walnut.
Heede Henry, 254 Bates.
Heeg Charlotte, 208 E Morris.
Jeffery Julian F, 122 Ft Wayne av.
Jennings Theodore H, rear 56 Newman.
Jonas Wm F, 549 S West.
Keller Anton, 86 Stevens.
Kiefer Rudolph C, 102 Michigan (H).
Kistner Henry jr, 71 Yeiser.
Kluge Gustav, 425 S Delaware.
Koehler John F, 214 Hamilton av.
Koeniger George J, 124 Kennington.
Kornfeld Henry and Lena, 208 N Pine.
Kretsch Charles P, 221 S Alabama.
Kretsch Peter, 9 Gresham.
Larsh & Meginniss, 353 E St Clair.
Meyer Gustav J T, 74 S Delaware.
Meyer John P C, 86 N Illinois.
Meyer Theodore, 28 Minnesota.
Mucho Frederick W, 199 E Washington.
Murray Christian, 1087 E Washington.
Osborn James L, 539 W Udell (N I).
Padou Paul, 555 Morris (W I).
Posner Abraham, rear 425 Madison av.
Rauch Albert E, 125 Windsor.
Rauch John, 82 W Washington.
Rebentisch Albert J, 48 Davis.
Reger Henry G, 170 E Washington.
Reinfels Charles P, 791 S East.
Sachs John A, 450 S Illinois.
Schaub Henry J, 453 E Washington.
Schmalholz Simon, 257½ E Washington.
Schmitt John, 404 S Meridian.
Sharpe Andrew W, 353 S East.
Sorhage Henry C, 161 Virginia av
Spangenberger Louis, 560 S Illinois.
Steffen Andrew, 220 E Washington.
Stitz Frederick, 18 McKim av.
Stoll Michael, 428 Virginia av.
Strack Ignatz, 379 S Delaware.
Treuhann Frank, 762 S Meridian.
Wald Adolph, 237 N Liberty.
Wells Edward H, 43 N Illinois.
Wisser Frederick, 172 S Linden.
Witt Gustav C, 251 Michigan av.
Wittenbring Henry, 196 Orange.
Wolf John, 28 N Delaware.
Wolf Lee, 30 Larch.

CIGARS AND TOBACCO—WHOLESALE.

Berkowitz Armin, 484 E Washington.
Craig Henry J, 15 Indiana av.
Hitt D C & J B, 32 S Meridian.
Judson & Hanna, 21 W Maryland.
Kaufman B & Son, 168 W Washington.
Metzger Jacob & Co, 30-32 E Maryland.
Meyer Charles F & Bro, 15 N Penn.
Ryder Joseph M, 145 W Washington.
Warner C M & Co, n e cor Washington and Meridian.

CIGARS AND TOBACCO—RETAIL.

Adam Herman F, 15 N Illinois.
Alcazar, 30 W Washington.
Alford Ambrose A, 21 S Meridian.
Axtell Samuel P, 144 S Meridian.
Balk Lizzie E Mrs, 80 E Market.
Barckdall Daniel, 666 W Washington.
Barrett Solomon, 90 E South.
Beltz F P & Son, 29 S Illinois.
Bradford James M, Commercial Club bldg.
Brown Robert P, 137 River av (W I).
Campbell Arthur B, 2 Malott av.
Chambers Perlee L, 56 W Washington and 59 N Penn.
Clark Edward A, 150 Mass av.
Collins Emanuel, 179 Indiana av.
Coombs Wm H, 15 Virginia av.
Costigan Frank, Occidental Hotel.
Crabb Keller E, 64 Virginia av.
Dearth John P, 303 Virginia av.
Denson Charles W, 149½ Mass av.
Deschler Louis G, 51 N Penn and The Bates.
DeVoss Samuel H, 308 Virginia av.
Doherty James, 60 S Illinois.
Feetman Solomon, 586 W Washington.
Frazee Stephen J, 67 S Illinois.
George Henry S, 33 McCrea.
Giblin Elizabeth J, 200 W Chesapeake.
Grau Julius jr, 366 Blake.
Hollenbeck Frank B, Stubbins Hotel.
Joss George N, 82 Indiana av.
Kiemeyer Wm, 76 E Washington.
King John, 215½ W Washington.
Kriel Wm C, 898 N Illinois.
Lewis George S, 102 Mass av.
Loebenberg Henry, 9 S Illinois.
McConney Norris J, 44 Jackson pl.
McCorkle Marion, 97 Mass av.
McGaw John A, 24 N Illinois.
Meyer Charles F & Bro, 15 N Penn and 30 W Washington.
Miller Emlen F, 325 E Washington.
Miner Wilford H, 150 Indiana av.
Monninger Conrad, 390 Indiana av.
Moore Albert D, Journal bldg and 536 College av.
Neuer Wm B, 358 Mass av.
Newell Arthur, 89 N Delaware.
O'Meara Patrick J, s w cor Meridian and Monument pl.
Osburn Edward, n e cor 12th and Senate av.
Pierson Samuel D, 12 N Penn.
Raper George, The Denison and 19 Monument pl.
Redmond Frank S, 24 Indiana av.
Reeves Carey, State House.
Riebel Frederick, 48 E Washington.

THE HOME LAUNDRY 19 S. Ill St Telephone 1769.

THE WM. H. BLOCK CO. 7 AND 9 EAST WASHINGTON STREET. DRY GOODS, MEN'S FURNISHINGS.

Fidelity and Deposit Co. of Maryland. BONDS SIGNED.—LOCAL BOARD John B. Elam, Albert Sahm, Smiley N. Chambers, John M. Spann.
GEORGE W. PANGBORN, General Agent, 704-706 Lemcke Building. Telephone 140.

74 EAST MARKET STREET Telephone 863.
Insure Your Property With FRANK K. SAWYER

Cigars, Etc.—Retail—Continued.
Robinson Joseph, 217 Indiana av.
Roemler Frederick S, 67 E Washington.
Roemler Otto H, 77½ N Alabama.
Rozier Percy H, 303 E Washington.
Ruff Harry G, 62 Mass av.
Schulte Alida, 512 S East.
Scott Jesse H, 195 Mass av.
Sebern John S, 93 S Illinois.
Stoddard Samuel P, 51 W Washington.
Van Camp Samuel, 428 Virginia av.
Wachstetter Charles, Board of Trade bldg.
Wade Enos T, 25½ Virginia av.
Walsh Clara E, 16 S Illinois.
Warner C M & Co, 2 E Washington.
Werbe George A, 98 N Penn.
White James D, 43 Mass av.
Wingerter Edward W, 66 S Illinois.
Wright Peter M, Court House.
Zorniger John, e s Lulu 3 n of Udell (N I).

CISTERN BUILDERS.

See Well and Cistern Builders.

CIVIL ENGINEERS AND SURVEYORS.

Baker E Brown, 225 Lemcke bldg.
Brown Charles C, 225 Lemcke bldg.
Central Engineering Co, 225 Lemcke bldg.
Christian Frederick E, 364 Ramsey av.
Defrees Morris M, 62 Ingalls blk.
Fatout Hervey B, Room 1, 30½ N Delaware. (See adv.)

HERVEY B. FATOUT
SURVEYOR AND
CIVIL ENGINEER
ROOM 1, SECOND FLOOR VON HAKE BLOCK,
30½ N. DELAWARE ST.

Hadley Artemus N, 23 Talbott blk.
Nelson James B, 61 Baldwin Blk.
Power J Clyde, 75 Lombard bldg.
Smith Wm P, 594 E St Clair.

***CLAY WORKING MACHINERY.**

Potts C and A & Co, 414 North branch W Washington.

***CLOAKS.**

Acme Cloak and Suit Co, 6 Indiana av.
Ayres L S & Co, 33-37 W Washington.
Block Wm H Co The, 7-9 E Washington. (See right top and bottom lines.)
Boyd, Besten & Langen Co, 39 E Washington.
Brosnan James Y, 52 N Illinois.
Pettis Dry Goods Co, 25-33 E Washington.
Rink Joseph A, 30-38 N Illinois.

***CLOTHES CLEANERS.**

(See also Dyers and Scourers.)
Nick The Tailor, 78 N Illinois. (See adv opp Tailors.)

CLOTHING—WHOLESALE AND MANUFACTURING.

Bailey Mnfg Co, 196 S Meridian.
Cones C B & Son Mnfg Co, 12 N Senate av.
Excelsior Shirt Mnfg Co, 27 W Pearl.
Meier Lewis & Co, 2-4 Central av.
Phillips & Patterson, 198 S Penn.

CLOTHING—RETAIL.

Abstine Israel, 239 E Washington.
Baumann Sarah, 166½ W Washington.
Borinstein Abraham, 233 E Washington.
Brunswick & Kahn, 3 E Washington.
Budweitsky Joseph, 293 E Washington.
Cohen Simon, 592 Virginia av.
Conrad Owen J, 70-72 Mass av.
Davis David, 231 E Washington.
Dudley G J & Co, 669 Virginia av.
Finkelstein Louis, 422 S Meridian.
Frankfort Henry, 107 Mass av.
Gelman Samuel, 178 Indiana av.
Globe Clothing Co The, 97-99 E Washington.
Goldberger Joseph, 117 Mass av.
Goldstein Joseph, 115 Mass av.
Gramling & Son, 35 E Washington.
Greenbaum Abraham, 182 Indiana av.
Gundelfinger Benjamin, 72 W Washington.
Josefsberg Abraham, 54 Indiana av.
Kahn Nathan, 580-582 S East.
Kantrowitz Bros, 10 W Washington.
Kauffman Louis H, 185 E Washington.
Kauffman Max, 158 Indiana av.
Keller Robert, 570-578 S East.
Klein Henry, 189 E Washington.
Levey Anna R, 279 E Washington.
Libowitz Abraham, 207 E Washington.
Marer Adolph, 277 E Washington.
Markovits Sam, 121 Mass av.
Mayer Leopold, 115 S Illinois.
Medias Charles, 160 Indiana av.
Miles Richard R, 108-110 S Illinois.
Model Clothing Co, 41-49 E Washington.
Nerenberg Jacob, 272 S Illinois.
Obstfeld Henry, 229 E Washington.
Oppenheim Elias, 265 E Washington.
Original Eagle Clothing Co, 5-7 W Washington.
Progress Clothing Co The, 6-8 W Washington.
Rheinheimer Barbetta, 190 W Washington.
Rubens Samuel, 60 W Washington.
Schwartz Wm K, 247 W Washington.
Seasongood, Stix, Krouse & Co, 146 S Meridian.
Sellers Sarah J, 129 Mass av.
When Clothing Store, 26-40 N Penn. (See right top cor cards.)
Wild David, 215 E Washington.
Wild Louis, 211 E Washington.
Winkler Joseph, 306 E Washington.
Yankuner Nathan, 172 Indiana av.

***CLOTHING—RUBBER—WHOLESALE AND RETAIL.**

Central Rubber and Supply Co The, 79 S Illinois. (See left side lines.)

***COAL—BITUMINOUS.**

Edwardsport Coal and Mining Co, 42-43 When Bldg. (See left side lines and adv in Coal Miners.)

***COAL GAS.**

Otto Gas Engine Works The, Builders' Exchange, 35 E Ohio. (See left bottom lines.)

IF CONTINUED to the end of its dividend period, policies of the UNITED STATES LIFE INSURANCE CO., will equal or excel any investment policy ever offered to the public. | E. B. SWIFT, Manager, 25 E. Market St.

Wm. Kotteman 89 & 91 E. Washington St. TELEPHONE 1742 Furniture

SHOW CASES || WILLIAM WIEGEL || 6 West Louisiana Street Opp. Union Station.

*COAL MINERS.

Edwardsport Coal and Mining Co, 42-43 When Bldg. (See left side lines and adv.)

Edwardsport Coal and Mining Co.
Miners of Steam and Domestic Coal in Car Load Lots.
Telephone 1916. Office, Rooms 42-43 When Blk.

*COAL TAR PRODUCTS.

Mica Roofing Co, s w cor Belt R R and Summit.
Smither Henry C, 169 W Maryland. (See adv opp Roofing Material.)
Smither Theodore F, 151 W Maryland. (See right side lines.)

*COAL—WHOLESALE.

Edwardsport Coal and Mining Co, 42-43 When Bldg. (See left side lines and adv in Coal Miners.)

COAL, WOOD AND COKE.

Anderson Mads P, 381-385 Cedar.
Baille Hamilton, rear 148 S West.
Balke & Krauss Co, cor Market and Missouri. (See right bottom lines.)
Batty & Co, 301 Indiana Trust bldg.
Benner Wm J, 185 W 7th.
Bugg & Mays, 294 E Washington.
Cloud Henry F, 587 W McLene (N I).
Consolidated Coal and Lime Co, 13 Virginia av.
Dell Frank M, 378 E Washington.
Dobson James, 265 Michigan av.
Eaglesfield Wm Co, s w cor Alvord and 9th.
Edward Charles, 50 Sheffield (W I).
Edwardsport Coal and Mining Co, 42-43 When Bldg. (See left side lines and adv in Coal Miners.)
Friendly Inn, 290 W Market.
Gansberg Bros, 368 Shelby.
Goepper Frederick, n s Jackson 1 w of Harris av (M J).
Greenen Joseph W, 70 S State av.
Greenen J W & Son, 825 E Washington.
Gresh Wm H & Co, s e cor Peru and Mass avs.
Indianapolis Coal and Feed Co, cor Kentucky av and Merrill.
Indiana & Chicago Coal Co, 8 Fair blk.
Island Coal Co, 5 Hartford blk.
Jefferson James, 259 E Washington.
McConnell Bros, 401 E Washington.
Meyer A B & Co, 15-17 N Penn, 450 N Senate av and 501 E Michigan.
Quinn Robert R, 57 Rhode Island.
Rabe Herman, 235 Lincoln la.
Rehling Wm C, 652 Madison av.
Rex Coal and Sewer Co. 171 E Louisiana.
Steinhauer Michael C, 201 Bates.
Thayer Albert, 2 John.
Thompson Wm, 100 Ft Wayne av.
Walters George, 218 W Pearl.
Wasson W G Co The, 130 Indiana av. (See left bottom cor cards and adv in Cement and Lime.)
Webb Charles A, 222 S Meridian.

COFFEE AND SPICE MILLS.

Champion Coffee and Spice Mills, 31-33 E Maryland.
Grocers Mnfg Co The, 80 S Penn.

COFFEES AND TEAS.

See Teas and Coffees.

COFFIN MANUFACTURERS.

Indianapolis Coffin Co The, 188 E Washington.

COLLAR MANUFACTURERS.

See Horse Collar Manufacturers.

*COLLECTION AGENTS.

American Collecting and Reporting Assn, 41-42 Baldwin blk.
Bradstreet Co The, n w cor Meridian and Washington.

DIRECTORIES OF ALL THE STATES AND PRINCIPAL CITIES ON FILE FOR REFERENCE AT OUR OFFICE.

R. L. POLK & CO.

23-24 JOURNAL BLDG.

CARPETS CLEANED LIKE NEW. TELEPHONE 818
CAPITAL STEAM CARPET CLEANING WORKS

BENJ. BOOTH PRACTICAL EXPERT ACCOUNTANT. Thirty years' experience. First-class credentials. Room 18, 82½ E. Washington St. Indianapolis, Ind.

The Old Reliable Sherman European Restaurant || 18 and 20 S. Meridian St. Established 1880.

BRONTE M. AIKINS. SALEM P. WELMAN. GEO. H. BRACKNEY.

THE CENTRAL LAW UNION

LAW AND COLLECTIONS

COLLECTIONS FROM RETAIL HOUSES NOT SOLICITED.

425 and 426 Lemcke Building, Indianapolis, Ind.

TELEPHONE 1847.

REFERENCES:

Reid, Murdock & Co., Chicago, Ill.
Rouse, Hazard & Co., Peoria, Ill.
Murphy, Hibben & Co., Indianapolis, Ind.
E. C. Atkins & Co., Indianapolis, Ind.
J. C. Perry & Co., Indianapolis, Ind.
Van Camp Hardware and Iron Co., Indianapolis, Ind.
Indianapolis Stove Co., Indianapolis, Ind.
Udell Works, Indianapolis, Ind.
Innis, Pearce & Co., Rushville, Ind.
Hulman & Co., Terre Haute, Ind.
Studebaker Bros.' Mfg. Co., South Bend, Ind.
Coquillard Wagon Works, South Bend, Ind.
Wayne Knitting Mills, Ft. Wayne, Ind.
Hartman Manufacturing Co., Vincennes, Ind.
Rogers Shoe Co., Toledo, O.
Geo. F. Dana & Co., Cincinnati, O.
Morris Woodhull, Dayton, O.
Davis Sewing Machine Co., Dayton, O.
F. & L. Kahn & Bros., Hamilton, O.
Stratton & Terstegge, Louisville, Ky.
McSherry Manufacturing Co., Middletown, O.

Depository, State Bank of Indiana.

THE SNOW CHURCH CO.

LAW AND COLLECTIONS

Telephone 879. 112 Commercial Club Bldg.

COMMERCIAL LAW. Attachments; replevins; supplementary proceedings; chattel mortgages; mechanics' liens; proof of claims, and filing them with receivers and assignees; questions arising on negotiable paper; assigned claims; transfers in fraud of creditors; and the application of the best legal remedies to effect collection of claims from dishonest debtors, all over the United States.

Collection Agents—Continued.

Central Law Union The, 425-426 Lemcke Bldg. (See adv.)

Dun R G & Co, 18½ N Meridian.

Indiana Collection Bureau, 303 Indiana Trust Bldg.

Indianapolis Collecting and Reporting Agency, 39-40 Journal Bldg. (See adv opp p 488.)

Merchants' and Manufacturers' Exchange, Jacob E Takken Mngr, 19 Union Bldg, 63-73 W Maryland. (See left bottom cor cards.)

National Collection Agency, 81 Baldwin Blk.

Simmons Oliver M, 19½ N Meridian.

Snow-Church Co The, 112 Commercial Club Bldg. (See adv.)

***COLLEGES, SCHOOLS, ETC.**

(See also Miscellaneous Directory.)

Butler College, Irvington. (See adv opp p 235.)

Indiana Boston School of Elocution and Expression of Indianapolis, Mrs Harriet A Prunk Principal, 368 W New York. (See adv in Miscellaneous Directory.)

Indianapolis Business University, When Bldg, N Penn (Bryant & Stratton and Indianapolis Business Colleges Consolidated), E J Heeb Propr. (See front cover, right bottom lines and p 4.)

TUTEWILER UNDERTAKER, No. 72 WEST MARKET STREET. TELEPHONE 216.

THE PROVIDENT LIFE AND TRUST CO. OF PHILADELPHIA. Endowment Insurance presents the double attraction of relieving manhood and middle age from anxiety and old age from want.
For particulars apply to D. W. EDWARDS, General Agent, 508 Indiana Trust Building.

THEODORE F. SMITHER ROOFER
GRAVEL AND OTHER COMPOSITION
Yard, 19 W. Maryland St. Telephone 861.
Off, 15 W. Maryland St.

COMMERCIAL AGENCIES.

See Mercantile Agencies.

COMMISSION MERCHANTS.

Adams L F & Co, 36 S Delaware.
Applegate Lauren F, 90 S Delaware.
Blumberg John, 133 E Maryland.
Blume & Co, 52 Virginia av.
Gold S N & Co, 49 S Delaware.
Grim M W & Sons, 17 S Alabama.
Hitz George & Co, 30-32 and 68-70 S Delaware.
Jose Victor R, 41 S Delaware.
Larossa Frank, 116 E Maryland.
Mascari F Bros & Co, 47 S Delaware.
Miller Louis C, 80 S Delaware.
Miller Wm A, 189 E Market.
Mummenhoff Fruit Co, 135-137 E Maryland.
Murphy J A & Co, 23 S Delaware.
Neumann John W & Co, 34 S Delaware.
Rees Robert H, 19 S Delaware.
Roberts W H & Co, 117 E Maryland.
Sherer Adam W, 122 E Maryland.
Smith Edmund T, 127 E Maryland.
Syerup & Co, 22-24 S Delaware.
Volkening C F & Co, 43-45 S Delaware.
Walton George B, 48 S Delaware.

CONFECTIONERS—WHOLESALE AND MANUFACTURING.

Aughinbaugh Wm M, 1149 N Alabama.
Daggett & Co, 18-20 W Georgia.
Darmody-Morrison Co The, 84 S Penn.
Downey Charles E, 255 E Washington.
Jenkins & Co, 84 E Georgia.
Krull & Schmidt, 52 S Penn.
Nichols Elmer E Co, 74-76 S Meridian.
Robertson & Nichols, 62 S Penn.

CONFECTIONERS—RETAIL.

Anterelli Louis, 308 E Washington.
Apple Anna L, 750 N Senate av.
Aughinbaugh Charles P, 8 Malott av.
Barckdall Daniel, 666 W Washington.
Batley Celia D, e s Lulu 4 n of Udell (N I).
Birchman Wm, 36 Hill av.
Brom Christian, 20 E Mkt House.
Bruce James P, 598-600 Virginia av. (See adv in Bakers.)
Buck Sylvester T, 60 Indiana av.
Carter Charles E, 59 N Illinois.
Coltrain Jarrett N, 15 Madison av.
Coval Nathaniel, 810 E Washington.
Cox Isaac S, 88 Mass av.
Craig John A, 20 E Washington.
De Trani Francesco, 227 E Washington.
Doolittle Joseph P, E Mkt House.
Dukes Mary A, 410 N West.
Juliano Antonio, 287 E Washington.
Dushman Minnie, 298 S Illinois.
Evison Harry, 70 Indiana av.
Faulkner Rhoda, 144 Elizabeth.
Filardo Gabriel, 368 Mass av.
Floros Peter, 45 W Washington.
Geiger Leonard F, 348 Virginia av.
Gandolfo Nicolo, 214 E Washington.
Giuliano Antonio, 287 E Washington.
Grund Wm, 427 N Illinois.
Hanrahan Nellie, 59 E South.
Hill Henrietta, 221 W Ohio.
Hoeltke Anna S C, 328 Mass av.
Howe Wm M, 147 E 7th.
Ihndris Neatha, 156 Martindale av.
Iversen Christian, 309 N West.
Jenkins & Co, 96 Mass av.
Keith Mary, 150 S William (W I).
Kellenberger Peter B, 33 Mass av.
Kelley Ileane, e s Capitol av 3 s of Ray.
King John, 215½ W Washington.
Kroll Amelia E, 468 Indiana av.
Kruger Mathilde, 99 Madison av.
Laughner Wm J, 72 N Illinois.
Leeds George, 27 E Mkt House.
Lemontree Frank, 424 S Meridian.
Lewis Casper, 126 Oliver av (W I).
Lobraico Joseph, 90 N Illinois.
Lovejoy Sarah A, 120 E Mkt House.
McCabe Matthew, 15 English av.
McDonough Bridget, 129 Elizabeth.
McHale Kate, 48 Church.
Magsam Charles M, 77 Oliver av (W I).
Mahalowitz Morris, 416 S Meridian.
Marks Abraham, 107 E Mkt House.
Marsh Mary A, 402 S Meridian.
Marston Smith W, 94 N Illinois.
Minter Ferdinand, s w cor Home av and Yandes.
Offord & Willis, 183 Mass av.
Parisette Joseph, 544 W Udell (N I).
Parkhurst Maggie E, 396 Virginia av.
Pierce Jeremiah B, 658 Virginia av.
Popadopulos Johannis A, 105 S Illinois.
Ramazzotti Antonia, 190 S Illinois.
Ramazzotti Louis, 50 N Penn.
Redmond Angeline, E Mkt House.
Riddell Wm A, 269 Mass av.
Roberts Frank, 266 W Washington.
Ruschaupt Charles F, 94 W Washington.
Ryan Mary J, 542 S East.
Schnable John, 476 S East.
Schward Matilda, 356 Clifford av.
Scott Jane, e s Baltimore av 5 s of 17th.
Shoptaugh Jacob A, 154 Virginia av.
Slusser Warren J, 79 Mass av.
Suess Joseph, 606 Virginia av.
Tilghman Charles A, 21 Prospect.
Tilghman Isabella E, 531 E Washington.
Weaver Louisa E, 822 N Illinois.
Whitaker Ida M, 406 College av.
White Wm H, 213 Howard (W I).
Whitted Annie, 391 W New York.
Winchester Francis O, 476 S Meridian.
Wilmot Frank L, 78 N Illinois.
Wolf Louisa M, 81 E McCarty.

CONTRACTORS—BRICK.

Dennis Peter, 36 Buchanan.
Dreier Ernest, 112 English av.
Ellis Hiram R, 16 Hamilton av.
Fearey John, 477 N East.
Fiscus Andrew J, 254 Alvord.
Hanway Samuel, e s Senate av 1 s of 28th.
Heintz Valentine, 1 Hermann.
Larison John H, 222 Prospect.
Martin John, 139 N Alabama.
Newman Wm F, 235 Bellefontaine.
Noe Nicholas, 17 Minnesota.
Rowe Thomas P, n w cor 23d and Central av.
Rubush Charles E, 91 Woodlawn av.
Rubush Wm R, 77 Woodlawn av.
Smith George O, 27 Villa av.
Stamen David H, 57 Haugh (H).
Twiname John J, 850 Park av.
Vater Thomas J, 299 Bellefontaine.
Wampner George H, 26 Dawson.
Weaver George, 559 E 7th.
Wehking Charles F, 427 S New Jersey.
Weyenberg Peter C, 12 Hamilton av.
Wortman Charles M, 33 Villa av.
Zintel Michael, 23 Tompkins.

ELECTRICIANS DON'T FORGET US. ALL WORK GUARANTEED.
C. W. MEIKEL,
Tel. 466. 96-98 E. New York St.

DALTON & MERRIFIELD { LUMBER South Noble St., near E. Washington

INDIANA ELECTROTYPE CO. BEST WORK LOWEST PRICES.
All Orders Promptly Filled.
23 WEST PEARL ST., INDIANAPOLIS, IND. JOB WORK. BOOK PLATES. BEST PATENT BASE ON THE MARKET.

CONTRACTORS—BRIDGE.

Chicago Bridge and Iron Co, 6 Builders' Exchange. (See adv.)

CHICAGO
BRIDGE AND IRON CO.
Engineers and Contractors
MANUFACTURERS OF
METAL FOR STRUCTURES.
HORACE E. HORTON, PRES.
ALBERT MICHIE, Agent,
Builders' Exchange. INDIANAPOLIS.

Fife Wm, 461 N East.
Hunt C F Co, 92 S Illinois.
Jackson James H, 84 E North.
Toledo Bridge Co The, Daniel Lesley Agt, Room 42 When Bldg. (See adv in Bridge Contractors.)
Wrought Iron Bridge Co, Wm W Winslow Genl Agt, 1 Hubbard Blk. (See adv p 10.)

*CONTRACTORS—CEMENT.

Coldwell H G & Co, 74 E Market.
Davidson Wm J, 186 Dougherty.
Dearinger & Rogers, rear 313 E Georgia.
Dunn Francis M, 563 Park av.
Keller Julius, 7 Pembroke Arcade.
Lingenfelter Frank C, 12 Pleasant.
McAllister John, 442 Harrison av.
Niemier Cornelius S, 187 Lexington av.
Nolting Frederick W, 124 S State av.
Nolting Henry T, 725 E Ohio.
Shingler Edward, 900 Ash.
Snyder F M & Co, 68½ E Market.

CONTRACTORS—GENERAL.

Browder & Shover, 54 Ingalls blk.
Cauldwell E H & Co, 147 Ash. (See adv in Carpenters.)
Davis Felix, 154 Bird.
Dunn James O, 91 Germania av (H).
Fletcher Horace H, 7 Lorraine bldg.
Hoosier Construction Co, 301 Indiana Trust bldg.
Hoss Jacob D A, 92 Baldwin blk.
Indiana Construction Co, 103½ E Washington.
Kattau Wm, 151 Harrison.
Lewis Edward, 306 E South.
McNerney Peter J, 549 Ash.
Mansfield & Allen, 25½ W Washington.
Millikan Isaac W, 17 When bldg.
Millikan J N & Co, 17 When bldg.
Morse T J & Son, 2 Builders' Exchange.
Nuerge & Reinking, 629 E Ohio. (See adv in Carpenters.)
Pearce Charles, 374 N Illinois.
Pierson J C & Son, 2 Builders' Exchange.
Salisbury & Stanley, 177 Clinton. (See right side lines.)
Schlanzer Benedict J, 682 Charles. (See adv p 8.)
Scott W A & Sons, 591-593 Central av. (See front cover.)
Shover James E, 125 N Alabama.
Smock Ferdinand C, 503 Park av.
Tobin James, cor Kentucky av and Merrill.
Union Construction Co, 236 Lemcke bldg.
White & Harrison, 109 John.
Young Richard N (gas mains), 96 Oliver av (W I).

*CONTRACTORS—IRON.

Chicago Bridge and Iron Co, 6 Builders' Exchange, 35 E Ohio. (See adv in Contractors—Bridge.)

CONTRACTORS—MILL.

Nordyke & Marmon Co, crossing I & V Ry and Morris (W I). (See inside back cover.)

CONTRACTORS—PAVING.

Buntin, Shryer & McGannon, 421 Lemcke bldg.
Capitol Paving and Construction Co, 1 Hubbard Blk, s w cor Washington and Meridian.
Indiana Bermudez Asphalt Co, 25-26 Baldwin blk.
Smither Henry C (Asphalt Mastic for Floors), 169 W Maryland. (See adv opp Roofing Material.)
Warren-Scharf Asphalt Paving Co, 6 Thorpe blk.
Western Paving and Supply Co The, 39 Ingalls blk.

CONTRACTORS—PLASTERING.

Abernathy Justus, 29 Palmer.
Allison Joseph E, 148 Woodlawn av.
Amick Charles P, 1202 Morris (W I).
Anderson Martin C, 41 Hoyt av.
Beltz Jacob, 85 Stevens.
Boring Edward E, 400 W 1st.
Boring Ephraim, 345 N West.
Brown J Wyley, 192 Hillside av.
Burch John A, 200 St Marie.
Burnett George C, 266 S Penn.
Burnett Seth, 105 N Gillard av.
Burton Joseph E, 612 W Eugene (N I).
Cramer Winfield S, 206 Fletcher av.
Crouch George W, 113 Woodlawn av.
Dunlap Joseph A, 200 Elm.
Enright Joseph J, e s Lebanon av 2 s of Pope av.
Ernst Joseph, 1 Builders' Exchange.
Fortney Charles P, 275 Alvord.
Gilleland Charles H, 235 Columbia av.
Grove Wm R, 947 Morris (W I).
Hamilton James W, 218 E South.
Harris Thomas W, 1148 E Ohio.
Humphrey Charles B, 82 Paca.
Hutson Albert W, 151 Clarke.
Junghans Gustav C, 241 Eureka av.
Kingham John A, 22 Sheldon.
Laporte Wm S, 33 Johnson av.
McAtee James D, 235 Huron.
McGarvey Charles S, 1373 W Washington (M J).
Mackey Charles, 88 Hadley av (W I).

Parlor, Bed Room, Dining Room, Kitchen, Furniture W. H. MESSENGER, 101 E. Wash. St., Tel. 491.

ALL KINDS OF HEAVY AND LIGHT GRAY IRON CASTINGS } McNamara, Koster & Co. { Foundry and Pattern Shop
Phone 1593. 212-218 S. Penn. St.

May Robert H, 560 College av.
Muntz Wm, 82 Hosbrook.
Nieman Christian, 167 E Morris.
Osborn Lewis, 1143 N Alabama.
Prosser Wm, 150 Clifford av.
Pruitt John H, 12 Yandes.
Ray Wm E, 54 S Austin (B).
Russie & Ballard, 44 Stevens.
Schubert George A, 347 N West.
Shultz & Sommer, 106 Martindale av.
Shaffer Walter M, 172 Pleasant.
Shrewsbury Charles W, 87 Hoyt av.
Slaughter James C, 146 River av (W I).
Smith Wm H, 276 Brookside av.
Sparks Francis M, 136 Cornell av.
Sullivan Cornelius W, 84 Russell av.
Trayford George, 452 Clifford av.
Vanarsdall Wm C, 554 S Illinois.
Vehling Wm H, e s Waverly av 2 n of Clifford av.
Wells James J, 750 N Illinois.
Williamson George W, n e cor Parker and Clifford avs.
Williamson Sheridan, 108 Clifford av.
Wilson John T, 697 Park av.
Zaring Claudius R, 121 Williams.

*CONTRACTORS—ROOFING.

Gardner Joseph, 37-41 Kentucky av. (See left top cor cards.)
Indianapolis Steel Roofing and Corrugating Works, 23-25 E South. (See right side lines.)
Laing Samuel, 72-74 E Court. (See left side lines.)
Long Steel and Iron Roofing Co The, 180-186 W 5th. (See adv in Roofers.)
McWorkman Willard, 930 W Washington. (See left top cor cards.)
Smither Henry C, 169 W Maryland. (See adv opp Roofing Material.)
Zimmerman C & Sons, 19-21 S East. (See left bottom lines.)

CONTRACTORS—SEWER.

Bossert Wm, 7 Pembroke Arcade.
Brillhart Claud I, 130 Michigan av.
Fulmer-Seibert Co, 27-28 Baldwin blk.
Gansberg Wm F, 35 S Linden.
Hanahan Edward P, 43 Elm.
Indiana Construction Co, 103½ E Washington.
Herron Samuel F, 265 W 6th.
Hussey & Baker, 116 N Delaware. (See adv in Plumbers.)
Matthews Matthew, 170 N New Jersey.
Mercer Clement V, 46 Northwestern av.
Mercer Wm R, Hotel English.
Rex Coal and Sewer Co, 171 E Louisiana.
Turner Henry C, 298 Fayette.

CONTRACTORS—STONE.

Dammel Michael W, 75 Downey.
Fritz Peter, 70 Stevens.
Hanway Thomas, e s Senate av 1 s of 28th.
Holle Herman C, 343 E Market.
Ittenbach G & Co, 150 Harrison.
Koss & Fritz, 1 Builders' Exchange.
Moos Philip, 72 Arizona.
Petrie Wm, 50 Highland pl.
Robbins Samuel, 848 Cornell av.
Tielking Henry W, 343 S State av.

CONTRACTORS—STREET.

Abbett Wm H, 896 S Meridian.
Bennett George W, 509 Talbott av.
Cooper Joseph K, 341 Talbott av.
Drake Robert B, 526 N Brookside av.
Dunning Robert P, 426 N California.
Flaherty Michael, 120 W Ray.
Foley Daniel, 52 English av.
Haywood David A, 302 Park av.
Hendricks Wm H, 254 Mass av.
Hudson James W, 319 Union.
Kennington Bros, 455 S Delaware.
Indiana Construction Co, 103½ E Washington.
Lackey Frank E, 15 Elliott.
McCray George W, 81 W 11th.
Mankedick Charles H F, e s Auburn av 1 s of Prospect.
Moore John, n e cor Washington and Quincy.
Roberts J Harry, 391 E McCarty.
Roney Charles S, 302 Park av.
Roney Henry C, 422 Park av.
Smith Harley B, 59 Hendricks.

CONTRACTORS—STREET CLEANING.

Fuehring Bros, 545 E Ohio.
Indianapolis Street Cleaning Co, 112 N Penn.

CONTRACTORS—STREET SPRINKLING.

Fuehring Bros, 545 E Ohio.
Nolting Frederick W, 124 S State av.
Nolting Henry T, 725 E Ohio.
Roepke Charles F, 46 Sanders.
Rust Conrad, 214 Cedar.

COOPERS.

Blair Failey, 2 Ingalls blk.
Brandt Frederick W, 85 S California.
Burton Wm H, 487 W New York.
Hill G W & Son, 110 S East.
Indiana Cooperage Co, 315 Bates.
Koehring Bernhard, 38 Cincinnati.
Minter Albert F, south end California. (See adv p 8.)
Schwomeyer Henry, 475 Indiana av.

*COOPERS' TOOLS.

Vonnegut Clemens, 184-186 E Washington. (See left bottom lines.)

*COPPER CORNICES.

Laing Samuel, 72-74 E Court. (See left side lines.)

COPPERSMITHS.

Laugsenkamp Wm, n w cor Delaware and Georgia. (See adv p 7.)

CORDAGE AND TWINES.

Standard Rope and Twine Co, 9 Board of Trade.

*CORNICE MANUFACTURERS.

Ensey O B, cor 6th and Illinois. (See left bottom cor cards.)
Gardner Joseph, 37-41 Kentucky av. (See left top cor cards.)
Laing Samuel, 72-74 E Court. (See left side lines.)
McWorkman Willard, 930 W Washington. (See left top cor cards.)

THE FRED DIETZ CO. || WOODEN PACKING BOXES MADE TO ORDER FACTORY AND WAREHOUSE TRUCKS. 400 Madison Avenue. Telephone 69.

BUSINESS EDUCATION A NECESSITY. TIME SHORT. DAY AND NIGHT SCHOOL. SUCCESS CERTAIN AT THE PERMANENT, RELIABLE Indianapolis BUSINESS UNIVERSITY

Water Works Pumping Engines { HENRY R. WORTHINGTON, 64 SOUTH PENNSYLVANIA ST. Long Distance Telephone 284.

UNION CO-OPERATIVE LAUNDRY (COMPOSED OF LAUNDRY GIRLS) NOS. 138, 140 VIRGINIA AVENUE. T. E. SOMERVILLE, MANAGER. TELEPHONE 1269. INDIANAPOLIS, IND.

*CORNSHELLER MANUFACTURERS.

Nordyke & Marmon Co, crossing I & V Ry and Morris (W I). (See inside back cover.)

*CORRUGATED IRON.

Ensey O B, cor 6th and Illinois. (See left bottom cor cards.)
Gardner Joseph, 37-41 Kentucky av. (See left top cor cards.)
Indianapolis Steel Roofing and Corrugating Works, 23-25 E South. (See right side lines.)
Laing Samuel, 72-74 E Court. (See left side lines.)
McWorkman Willard, 930 W Washington. (See left top cor cards.)

COSTUMERS.

Barnett Julia, 288 N Liberty.
Kinklin Richard, 240-242 E Washington. (See adv.)

Masquerade Suits and Wigs To Rent —AT— R. Kinklin's, 240-242 East Washington St.

COUPON MANUFACTURERS.

Allison Coupon Co, 69 W Georgia.

*CRACKER MANUFACTURERS.

Hitz Baking Co The, 68-70 S Delaware. (See right bottom cor cards.)
Parrottt-Taggart Bakery of the U S Baking Co, 93-99 S Penn, cor Georgia. (See bottom edge.)

CREAMERIES.

Deputy Bros, 231 Mass av.
Fox Caroline, 424 W North.
Frazee Joseph, rear 152 Lexington av.
Furnas Robert W, 112-114 N Penn.
Guyer Wm & Sons, 1096 E Washington.
Hill Benjamin F, 291 Mass av.
Hinshaw & Baker, 142 Broadway.
Indianapolis Creamery, 52 Mass av.
Kealing Samuel, 533 N Illinois.
Kingsley Royal R, 267 W Washington.
Losh John W, 155 W Washington.
Meyer Will H, 426 Virginia av.
Painter Wm A, 152 Fletcher av.
Peterman Frank J, 445 S East.
Putnam County Milk Co The, 12-16 N East.
Sanders & Pace, 653 Virginia av.
Shigley Frederick W, 38 Hill av.
Thomas Benjamin E, 256 Blake.
Tillotson Charles E, 370 Virginia av.
Wilson Dudley K, 1 Fletcher av.
Wing Henry M, 276 Dillon.
Wright John H, 669 E Washington.
Wyckoff Stanley, 177 Virginia av.

CREOSOTE MANUFACTURERS.

Western Creosoting Co, Creosoters of all Kinds of Timber, cor Merrit and Belt R R, n of Michigan.

*CROCKERY.

(See also China, Glass and Queensware.)

Block Wm H Co The, 7-9 E Washington. (See right top and bottom lines.)

*CROQUET SETS.

Mayer Charles & Co, 29-31 W Washington. (See adv opp p 615.)

*CUPOLA BLOCKS.

Wasson W G Co The, 130 Indiana av. (see left cor cards and adv in Cement and Lime.)

*CUTLERY.

Linke Hermann, 197 S Meridian.
Mayer Charles & Co, 29-31 W Washington. (See adv opp p 615.)
Piscator August, 86 E Georgia.

CUTLERY—POCKET AND TABLE.

Vonnegut Clemens, 184-186 E Washington. (See left bottom lines.)

DAIRIES.

Alexander Robert, n s Wolf pike 1 e of School (B).
Bernhardt George, 60 W Raymond.
Billingsley Judson J W, w s Orchard 1 n of Howland av.
Bisig & Lange, e s Sherman Drive 1 s of Brookville rd (S).
Bradford Algernon, 72 Michigan (H).
Brown Ernest M, n w cor 22d and Baltimore av.
Brown George T, n s Bethel av 1 e of Auburn av.
Bunnell Julius C, s e cor Wolf pike and Baltimore av.
Casady Robert, n w cor Clifford and Waverly avs.
Caylor Edward A, s w cor Brookside and Waverly avs.
Clements John B, 20 W 20th.
Conroy John, n w cor Brookside and Waverly avs.
Coonse Harvey W, n s Washington 2 s of Quincy.
Craig James R, 309 S Brookside av.
Darrah Samuel F, w s Colorado av 3 n of Ohio.
Darrah Thomas, w s Garfield av 2 n of Ohio.
Dawson Thomas B, e s Hubbard 1 s of Clifford av.
Evans Cheek P, n e cor Ritter av and Brookville rd (I).
Finley Frank, e s Belmont 2 s of Johnson (W I).
Frazee Alva E, 178 Sheffield av (H).
Green Isaac A, 747 N Capitol av.
Green Wm, 30th and L N A & C Ry.
Harmening Wm H, w s Auburn av 2 s of Belt R R.
Hartman Henry C, w s LaSalle 1 s of P C C & St L Ry.
Heckmann Louis, 149 Wisconsin.
Hinesley Charles E, w s N Illinois 1 n of 29th.

CLEMENS VONNEGUT 184, 186 and 192 E. Washington St. | BUILDERS' HARDWARE, Building Paper. Duplex Joist Hangers

THE WM. H. BLOCK CO. DRY GOODS, DRAPERIES, RUGS, WINDOW SHADES.
7 AND 9 EAST WASHINGTON STREET.

Hoover Forest G, n e cor Broadway and 22d.
Huggler John W, n w cor Watts and Clifford av.
Kirsch Magdalen M, 31 New.
Lancaster Charles D, s s E Washington 4 e of Belt R R.
Lehr John E, s s Clifford av 1 e of Watts.
Lowry Albert W, w s School 1 s of Wolf pike (B).
McCready Frank W, n e cor Central av and 25th.
Madinger C & F, e s Rural 5 s of Clifford av.
Miller Peter C, w s Schurmann av 1 n of Vorster av.
Millspaugh Charles V, s s Michigan av 3 e of Belt R R.
Minger Frederick, s s Washington 1 e of Sherman Drive.
Moore Delta W, s w cor Sangster av and 22d.
Moore James M, 46 Paw Paw.
Morgan Lewis, e s Sherman Drive 1 s of Washington.
Nohl John, w s Watts 1 s of Clifford av.
Passehl Herman H, s w cor Shade and Schofield (B).
Postma John, e s Perkins pike 2 n of Bethel av.
Rauh John, e s Lebanon av 1 s of Brookside av.
Reder Philip, e s Waverly av 3 n of Clifford av.
Rice & Mollenkopf, w s Schurmann av 1 s of Wells (N I).
Richards Charles, s s Wolf pike 3 e of Baltimore av.
Sauer George, w s Osage av 1 n of Clifford av.
Schildmeier Christopher C, n w cor English av and McPherson (S).
Schonecker Andrew, s s Orchard av 1 e of Rural.
Schupp Henry, n e cor 22d and Baltimore av.
Sedam John C, e s Cornelius 1 n of 30th.
Shelby George W, s s 20th 2 e of Northwestern av.
Shelby Walter V, w s Brightwood av 2 s of Wolf pike (B).
Smith Israel J, e s Lincoln av 11 s of C C C & St L Ry (M'J).
Sommerlad Christopher, 1057 Madison av.
Springer Albert J, n w cor Brookside and Waverly avs.
Stevens Wm, 103 Naomi.
Stillinger John W, 7 Downing av (H).
Stucker Jacob H, n e cor 25th and Central av.
Styer & Leatherman, n s Wolf pike 1 w of School (B).
Tamm August, 336 Hillside av.
Thomas Eli W, e s Dayton av 1 s of English av (I).
Topp Charles, s s Shearer pike 1 w of Belt R R (B).
Trefz Jacob F, 1329 E Washington.
Weber John, s s Finley av 2 e of Shelby.
Wendler Clemens A, e s Sherman Drive 1 s of Prospect.
Werner John, e s Lebanon av 3 n of Clifford av.
Wertman Frank, e s Rural 3 n of Brookside av.
Wilson John, s s Brookville rd 2 w of P C C & St L Ry (S).
Woerner Louis, 693 Jones (N I).
Yancey Orville J, w s Brightwood av 1 s of Wolf pike (B).
Young George W, 8 Highland av (H).

DANCING ACADEMIES.

Aldrich Mary C, The Propylaeum.
Brenneke David B, n w cor Illinois and North.
Gresh Benneville F, 181 E Washington.
Rayno Rollin, 130 W Ohio.

*DECORATORS.

Teckenbrock John H, 94 E South. (See right bottom lines and adv in Painters.)

DENTAL DEPOTS.

Bodine J E & Co, 27 Monument pl.
Fox & Garhart Specialty Co, 88 N Penn.
Herriott Juliet I, 110 N Penn.

DENTISTS.

Addison Stanley L, 302½ N Senate av.
Albrecht Maurice, 61 Ingalls blk.
Anderson Eli W, 37½ E Washington.
Baily Jesse S, 18 E Ohio.
Blakeman Robert I, 6 Marion blk.
Bonniwell Wm A, 66½ N Penn.
Britton Oscar F, 28½ E Ohio.
Buchanan Albert E, 33 When bldg.
Byram John Q, n w cor Central av and P C C & St L Ry (I).
Conover George R, 852½ E Washington.
Couchman James B, 3 Grand Opera House blk.
Coughlin & Wilson, 44½ N Penn.
Cravens Junius E, 24 Marion blk.
Culver Raymond E, 262 E South.
Davidson Thomas H, 10 Marion blk.
Deputy Addison C, 91 Lombard bldg.
Earhart Perry W, 16½ E Washington.
Earhart Sylvester F, 16½ E Washington.
Everts Charles C, 8½ N Penn.
Faries Timothy C, 108 Hoyt av.
Farnsworth Theodore W, 11 Stewart pl.
Fox Arthur, 45 Holly av (W I).
Gant Wm A, 40½ E Washington.
Gates Willard W, 1 Odd Fellows' blk.
George Joseph H, 414 Lemcke bldg.
Gilman Frank L, 653½ N Senate av.
Green Dental Rooms, 8 Stewart pl, s e cor Illinois and Ohio.
Hacker Thomas S, 28½ E Ohio.
Hamilton Frank A, 24 Marion blk.
Heckard Wm A, 14 W Ohio.
Heiskell Wm L, 76½ E Market.
Helms Louis A, 37½ W Washington.
Herron Alexander P, 95 N Delaware.
Hohl Charles F, 12 Park av.
House David A, 28½ E Ohio.
Hovey Alvin J, 509-510 Lemcke bldg.
Jameson Alexander, 20 W Ohio.
Kahlo Harry C, 60 Journal bldg.
Kimberlin Thomas A, 136 N Penn.
Kunkel Wm M, 52 Clifford av.
Lange Frank A, 155 Mass av.
Lloyd Mary C, 19 Fletcher's Bank bldg.
McElroy Carolyn M, 20 Marion blk.
Martin George B, 11½ N Meridian.
Martin & Walker, 44½ N Penn.
Master Minnie I, 1½ E Washington.
Milman Anson H, 40 N Senate av.
Morris Austin J, 36½ E Washington.
Morrison John B, 28 Monument pl.
Nichols John J, 37½ W Market.
Oliver Dandridge H, 44½ N Penn.
Oliver Robert T, 44½ N Penn.

INDIANAPOLIS STEEL ROOFING AND CORRUGATING WORKS, 23 and 25 East South Street. S. D. NOEL, Proprietor.

David S. McKernan, Rooms 2-5 Thorpe Block.
REAL ESTATE AND LOANS
Money to loan on real estate. Special inducements offered those having money to loan. It will pay you to investigate.

DIAMOND WALL PLASTER { Telephone 1410
BUILDERS' EXCHANGE.

Cor. E. Ohio St. and C., C., C. & St. L. R'y Tracks.
BEST FACILITIES FOR STORING AND TRANSFERRING MACHINERY AND MERCHANDISE.
UNION TRANSFER AND STORAGE CO.

T. E. HALLS, Gen. Manager. J. R. MOORES, Chief Inspector. W. O. MYERS, Supt. Inquiry Div.

THE

Indianapolis Bureau of Inquiry and Investigation

None But Experienced Operatives Employed.

All Communications Strictly Confidential. Faithful Service. Reliable Reports.

This Bureau makes a specialty of all classes of investigations, such as Looking up Evidence, Examining Testimony, Tracing Missing Witnesses, Searching for Lost Heirs, Investigating Frauds, Working up Criminal Cases, Mysterious Disappearances, Forgeries or Robberies on Banks or Mercantile Houses, Railways, Corporations or Private Parties; Returns Fugitives from Justice, Locates Thefts and Shortages, Inspects Dishonest Employes; Furnishes Operatives to Detect Pilfering from Stores or Business Houses, Watchmen for Buildings or other purposes.

All cases given close and careful attention.

No Divorce Cases Taken, or Anything that will Interfere with the Marital Relations.

Correspondents in all parts of the United States and Canada.

General Offices, Rooms 68 and 69 Ingalls Block.

Dentists—Continued.

Page Lida Pursell, 3 Commercial blk.
Pierce & Ingersoll, 27½ Monument pl.
Prall & Van Scoyoc, 88 N Penn.
Raschig Maurice H, 8½ E Washington.
Rawls Wm S, 9½ N Illinois.
Read Peter C, 18½ N Meridian.
Reese Ernest E, 24½ E Ohio.
Reid & Prow, 402½ College av.
Ritter Christopher C, 431 Virginia av.
Sampsell Homer A, 49½ N Illinois.
Sellers Blaine H, 29½ S Illinois.
Shortridge Willard P, 60 Baldwin blk.
Smith Samuel D, 240 E Ohio.
Smythe Elmer A, 9-10 Talbott blk.
Staggs Charles J, n s Sutherland 1 w of Station (B).
Stine David L, 27 Talbott blk.
Sullivan Beverly W, 190 Cherry.
Taft O H & F E, 25½ W Washington.
Weller Harry D, 12 Marion blk.
Wells Merit, 18 W Ohio.
White Wm E, 228 W Michigan.
Wood Daniel M, 223 Indiana Trust bldg.

***DESIGNERS.**

Bauer H C Engraving Co The, 23 W Washington. (See adv opp Engravers.)
Bowley George J, 14 Yohn Blk, n e cor Meridian and Washington. (See adv in Wood Engravers.)
Indiana Illustrating Co, s e cor Market and Illinois. (See adv opp Engravers.)
Nealy H D, 16 Hubbard Blk. (See adv in Patent Draughtsmen.)

***DESIGNERS—MACHINERY.**

Jacob & Co, s w cor Georgia and Penn. (See adv in Pattern and Model Makers.)
Specialty Manufacturing Co, 193 S Meridian. (See adv opp Photographers.)

DESK MANUFACTURERS.

Indianapolis Cabinet Works, cor Malott and Columbia avs.
Lane Wm B, 167 Bane.
Lunt J W & Co, 29½ N Penn.
Wooton Office Desk Co The, cor Malott and Columbia avs.

DETECTIVE AGENCIES.

American Detective Agency, Rooms 10-13, 96 E Market. (See adv.)
Hopson Isaac P, 88 Baldwin blk.
Indianapolis Bureau of Inquiry and Investigation, Rooms 68-69 Ingalls Blk. (See adv.)

***DIAMOND WALL PLASTER.**

Diamond Wall Plaster Co, Office 3 Builders' Exchange, Factory cor E North and Bee Line Ry. (See top lines and opp p 941.)

A. METZGER AGENCY ESTABLISHED 1863. REAL ESTATE

American Detective Agency,

CAPT. H. C. WEBSTER, Gen. Mgr.

Rooms 11-15, 96½ East Market Street, Indianapolis, Ind.

(PHOENIX BLOCK.)

Fidelity.

Secrecy.

Accuracy.

Fidelity.

Secrecy.

Accuracy.

This agency makes no **EXPERIMENTS** at the expense of its patrons, as it engages only experienced operatives.

Every kind of detective service promptly rendered.

Reports giving the truth, and nothing but the truth.

All cases receive **CAPT. WEBSTER'S** personal attention.

Facilities for the achievements of good results will not suffer by comparison with those of any other agency.

Civil, criminal, mercantile, railway, express, municipal, insurance, patent, mechanical and individual cases undertaken, and secrecy, fidelity and accuracy guaranteed.

ESTABLISHED 1889.

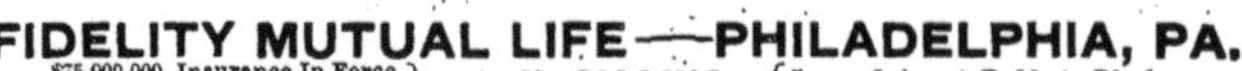
FIDELITY MUTUAL LIFE—PHILADELPHIA, PA.
$75,000,000, Insurance In Force. $3,500,000, Death Losses Paid. $1,500,090, Surplus. } A. H. COLLINS {General Agent, Baldwin Block.

Surveys Made
THOS. W. PALMER.
Maps & Plats of every Description neatly & accurately executed.
TOPOGRAPHICAL DRAUGHTSMAN
BLUE PRINTS AND TRACINGS A SPECIALTY.
REFERENCES: INDIANAPOLIS GAS CO. INDIANAPOLIS WATER CO. R. F. CATTERSON & SON. AUDITOR MARION COUNTY.
ROOM 31 COURT HOUSE.
INDIANAPOLIS.

BITUMINOUS COAL IN CAR LOADS TO DEALERS AND MANUFACTURERS. ROOMS 42 AND 43 WHEN BUILDING.
Edwardsport Coal & Mining Co.

*DIAMONDS.

Walk Julius C & Son, 12 E Washington. (See left bottom cor cards.)

*DIE SINKERS.

Mayer George J, 15 S Meridian. (See left bottom cor cards and p 5.)

Specialty Manufacturing Co, 193 S Meridian. (See adv opp Photographers.)

*DIES.

Mayer George J, 15 S Meridian. (See left bottom cor cards and p 5.)

*DIRECTORY PUBLISHERS.

Polk R L & Co, 23-24 Journal Bldg. (See back fly leaf.)

*DISINFECTANTS—CARBOLATED LIME.

West Disinfecting Co, 7 Monument Pl. (See adv.)

Chloro-Naptholeum
WORLD RENOWNED
ANTISEPTIC, DISINFECTANT, VERMICIDE,
Used for 50 Years. Invaluable about the Household.
West Disinfecting Co., 7 Monument Place.

*DOLLS AND DOLL OUTFITS.

Mayer Charles & Co, 29-31 W Washington. (See adv opp p 615.)

*DOOR MAT MANUFACTURERS.

Miner Wm L, 184-186 Cherry. (See adv adv opp Rug Mnfrs.)

*DOOR AND WINDOW SCREEN MNFRS.

C. H. SMITH
Swings and Fly Screens
MADE TO ORDER,
70 Columbia Avenue.

*DRAPERIES.

Badger Furniture Co, 75-77 E Washington and 20-24 Virginia av.

Block Wm H Co The, 7-9 E Washington. (See right top and bottom lines.)

Duvall Charles E, 44 N Illinois.

DRAUGHTSMEN.

Allen Bros, 61 Baldwin blk.

Bell Thompson R, 64 Ingalls Blk. (See adv in Patent Attorneys.)

Indiana Illustrating Co, s e cor Market and Illinois. (See adv opp Engravers.)

Jacob & Co, s w cor Georgia and Penn. (See adv in Pattern and Model Makers.)

Jones Horace B, 415-418 Lemcke Bldg. (See adv in Mechanical Engineers.)

Nealy H D, 16 Hubbard Blk. (See adv in Patent Draughtsmen.)

Palmer Thomas W, Room 31 Court House. (See adv.)

Reeves Harry E, 96 S Delaware, cor Georgia. (See embossed line front cover and adv in Pattern Makers.)

Specialty Manufacturing Co, 193 S Meridian. (See adv opp Photographers.)

*DRESS CUTTING SCHOOLS.

Murry Anna M, 30 Dickson.

C. ZIMMERMAN & SONS | SLATE AND GRAVEL ROOFERS 19 South East Street.

DRIVEN WELLS And Second Water Wells and Pumps of all kinds at CHARLES KRAUSS', 42 S. PENN. ST., Telephone 465.

ERTEL STEAM LAUNDRY 26 and 28 N. Senate Avenue. Telephone 1089. WE WILL CALL FOR AND DELIVER YOUR WORK. SATISFACTION GUARANTEED.

DRESS AND CLOAK MAKERS.

Achenbach Sadie C, 66 W New York.
Adams Jane, 267 N Noble.
Adams Maggie E, 16 Haugh (H).
Adel Mildred C, 559 Highland av (N I).
Albin Emma, 380 S East.
Alexander Carrie, 25½ W Washington.
Allen Ella, 832 E 9th.
Allgire Augusta W M, 205 E Ohio.
Andrews Stella M, 45 Russell av.
Armbruster & Windhorst, 25½ W Washington.
Aspinwall Annie, 28½ Indiana av.
Austin Elizabeth A, 128 Nordyke av (W I).
Ayres L S & Co, 33-37 W Washington.
Bakemeier Emma, 475 Virginia av.
Baker Georgia, 37½ W Washington.
Banke Elizabeth, 218 Olive.
Banta Louisa J, 43 Bates.
Barrett Sarah E, 34 Elder av.
Bartliner Josephine, 55 Vine.
Bauer Rosa, 22 Kansas.
Baumhoefer Matilda, 796½ N Alabama.
Beard Urbana C, 123 N Illinois.
Becker Barbara, 305 S Penn.
Beerbower Mary E, 11 Broadway.
Behrendt Anna L, 59 High.
Bidwell Elizabeth, 24 Pleasant av.
Biebinger Mary A, 94 N East.
Bishop Sarah, 373 W Vermont.
Blair Flora A, 197 N Illinois.
Blalock-Jones Matilda A, 217½ Mass av.
Bloomer Mary E, 296 Blackford.
Blount May L, 11 S Senate av.
Bonham Nettie M, 236½ S Meridian.
Boone Mollie A, 210 Madison av.
Booth Minnie, 122 Indiana av.
Brewer Marie S, 364 N California.
Brimm Sallie H, 170 Madison av.
Brink Lina, 504 S East.
Brower Ellen M, 443 E Ohio.
Brown Margaret E, 263½ N New Jersey.
Brown Nancy A, 484 W North.
Bruce Ida B, 173 Hadley av (W I).
Brumfield Martha, 266 Indiana av.
Brummell Anna L, 53 Fayette.
Burke Corinne, 61 Cornell av.
Burke Mary, 5½ Blackford.
Burks Cora, n w cor Michigan and Bismarck av (H).
Burnett Dora M, 266 S Penn.
Burns Christine, 577 W Michigan.
Burns Elizabeth, 187 Hoyt av.
Cahill Mary, 414 S Meridian.
Cahill Mary A, 217 W Michigan.
Calvert Mary E, 195 Bellefontaine.
Cameron Sarah E, 200 E St Joseph.
Carter Hattie, 25 Elm.
Carter Mattie, 306½ E Washington.
Carvin Hannah E, 473 Stillwell.
Case Alice T, 32 S Spruce.
Catt Sarah, 466 S Illinois.
Chapel Anna, 158 N Senate av.
Clark Alice J, 244½ E Washington.
Clark Alice M, 47 Peru av.
Clark Hattie, 252 E Washington.
Clark Nannie A, 306 N Delaware.
Colclazier Mary, 134 N Liberty.
Cole Isabel, 507 E Market.
Colson Elnora, 548 Chestnut.
Comer Mary E, 224 Ramsey av.
Condrey Rose, 428 Douglass.
Cottingham Cynthia A, 96 W 1st.
Cotton Jennie, 331 E South.
Coultis America, 50 Ruckle.
Curtis Nellie, 36 Fayette.
Cushing Isabelle, 85 Hoyt av.
Daniels Phoebe J, 152 E 7th.
Dantzer Mary P, 270 Douglass.
Davis Margaret A, 463 S Meridian.
Davis Martha E, 420 E Pearl.
Davis Mary H, 26 Wilcox.
Davis Virginia E, s s Oak av 1 e of Central av (I).
Delaney Frances B, 388 S Capitol av.
Denton Mary R, 145½ W Washington.
Dickerson Belle K, 1129 N Delaware.
Dickert Jane E, 271 Union.
Dill Emily, 239 Shelby.
Dillenbeck Carrie M, 217 Dougherty.
Dillman Ella J, 28 Evison.
Disher Mary C, 731 N Illinois.
Doran Josephine, 18½ N Meridian.
Dowling Mary A, 311 N California.
Downs Ida, 148 W Maryland.
Dunbar Nancy, 25½ W Washington.
Duncan Minnie O, 444 Indiana av.
Durfeld Angelica A, 308 Blake.
Early Jennie E, 414 Clifford av.
Earsom Alice E, 156 E St Joseph.
Edwards Emma, 163 S East
Ellis Annie, 319 S Meridian.
Ely Lillie, 173 Mass av.
Ennis Lotta, 7, 113 S Illinois.
Ennis Tillie A, 6½ E Washington.
Erzinger Mary A, 344 N Pine.
Estabrook Jane C, 433 Ash.
Evans Fannie L, 446 N East.
Evans Meda, 410 N Penn.
Farnham Jerusha, 75 W 5th.
Fate Laura B, 21 S Alabama.
Favors Josephine, 188 Meek.
Ferguson Jennie M, 330 E Louisiana.
Ferguson Matilda, 131 Indiana av.
Ferguson M J & A A, 103 N Beville av.
Ferringer Carrie R, 401 Blake.
Fetrow Nellie A, 234 E Louisiana.
Fitch Mary J, 19½ N Meridian.
Flannery Mary E, 104½ Broadway.
Fleck Rosa A, 24 King.
Fletcher Anna E, 46 Hill av.
Flynn Annie, 338 N Noble.
Folckemmer Lucy, 60 Brookside av.
Folger Jessie E, 99 Ash.
Ford Susan L, 357 Blake.
Frazier Martha, 281 N East.
Frobeinus Kunigunda, 345 W Michigan.
Gadd Annie E, 454 S Delaware.
Gardner Mary J, 273 E Court.
Gibson Lucinda, 105 Minerva.
Gilbert Esther M, rear 161 E St Mary.
Gimbel Katherine, 20 Morton.
Girick Isaac, 53 Russell av.
Givan Mary E, 124 Columbia av.
Gobin Mary F, 430 Broadway.
Godley Mary T, 395 Ash.
Goetz Anna T, 350 Indiana av.
Goodin Maud, 108½ Mass av.
Gordon Mary, 4 Hadley.
Goul Sadie J, 68 Huron.
Graham Mary B, 25½ W Washington.
Graham Sarah E, 246 S East.
Green Mattie, 35 Alvord.
Green Minnie, 18 Commercial blk.
Griffin Mary, 49½ N Illinois.
Grubbs Deborah A, 1 Jefferson.
Grummann Mary, 237 S Noble.
Guedel Kate, 176 E Morris.
Guinea Sadie A, 440 Blake.
Haas Mary, 223 S Capitol av.
Haggard Laura B, 361 E Market.
Hamill Kate E, 403 S Olive.
Hamilton Mary E, 161 E Ohio.
Hamilton Susan A, 564 W Shoemaker (N I).
Hannah Laura, 23 W St Clair.

ELLIS & HELFENBERGER { ENTERPRISE FOUNDRY & FENCE CO. 162-170 S. Senate Ave. Tel. 958.

THE HOGAN TRANSFER AND STORAGE COMP'Y
Household Goods and Pianos Moved—Packed—Stored...... Baggage and Package Express Machinery and Safes a Specialty Cor. Washington and Illinois Sts. TELEPHONE No. 675.

Hose, Belting, Packing, Clothing, Druggists' Sundries, Bicycle Tires, Cotton Hose, Etc. New York Belting & Packing Co., L't'd.

Dress and Cloak Makers—Con.
Hanrahan K & E, 19 Commercial blk.
Harris Eliza, 191½ Indiana av.
Harrod Joel E, 9 Pembroke Arcade.
Hart Sarah E, 682 E Market.
Hawkins Elvina, 390 E Market.
Hawkins Jennie E, 199 N East.
Hays Louella, 16 Stevens pl.
Heidenreich Rena, 69 N East.
Heller Marie M, 105 N Meridian.
Helm Iva A, 133½ Martindale av.
Hendricks Josephine C, 362 Talbott av.
Henry Mary E, 602½ N West.
Hensley Vina, 247 N West.
Hereth Gertrude E, 160 Davidson.
Herr Ida B, 113 E St Joseph.
Hill Ida M, 453 Ash.
Hill Olive M, 123 Cornell av.
Hill Sarah L, 529 E Washington.
Hobbs Sarah E, 165 Hoyt av.
Holcomb Sarah, 239 Blackford.
Holmes Mary A, 223 W Maryland.
Howden Alice J, 373 E Ohio.
Hoy Zella A, 122 Mass av.
Huder Louisa, 529 Ash.
Hurt Essie F, 362 Douglass.
Hunt Mary J, 499 N West.
Ingalls Frances, 519 N Alabama.
Jacks Rose, 11 Paca.
Jackson Martha, 34 N East.
Jackson Mary O, 395 S Capitol av.
Jenkins Dora A, 490 E 10th.
Jessup Lydia A, 50 Division (W I).
Johnson Julia E, 317 N Alabama.
Johnson Martha J, 139 St Mary.
Johnston Walter C, 18½ N Meridian.
Jones Ella, 87 Coburn.
Katzenbach Rebecca B, 58 Ingalls blk.
Keene Annabelle, 383 Fletcher av.
Kelly Emma R, 25 S Summit.
Kelly Kate, 11, 113 S Illinois.
Kemnitz Henrietta, 46 Michigan av.
Keogh Anna, 291 S East.
Kerins Anna C, 137 Harrison.
Kersey Emma, 1261 W Washington (M J).
Kersey Priscilla, 182 Fulton.
Kiel Ida, 168 Prospect.
Kinder Adeline, 180 Mass av.
King Mary C, 463 E Walnut.
Kittley Ottilie H, 289 W Michigan.
Kleinsmith Clara, 294 E Ohio.
Klink Elizabeth, 233 E Morris.
Kraft Babette, 196 Elizabeth.
Kuerst Alvina, 51 Beaty.
Lacy Lou J, 195 W Vermont.
Lanahan Mary, 15 Benton.
Langbein Mary, 511 College av.
Lawyer Amy D, 400½ N Senate av.
Lee Mary E, 151 Walcott.
Lehr Maria, 442 S Delaware.
Lemmen Emily, 22 Fletcher's Bank bldg.
Light Elizabeth L, 5½ Indiana av.
Lipps Anna M, 496½ S Meridian.
Loch Sisters, 356 E Market.
Long Mary U, 1661 N Capitol av.
Longanecker Rosie D, 536 E 7th.
McCabe Cora L, 857 N New Jersey.
McClary Jane D, 264 E Miami.
McLaran Lena A, 158 E St Joseph.
McLaughlin Elmira, 50 Sheldon.
Magruder Georgia J, 315 E Ohio.
Makepeace Elizabeth, 95 Lexington av.
Maker Rosalie C, 490 E 10th.
Marshman Minnie J, 318 Mass av.
Martin Mary E, 19 Cornell av.
Martindale Dora, 62 Tremont av (H).
Mason Mary J, 26½ N Senate av.
Mathias Mary J, 14 Arch.
Mayer Amelia, 258 Charles.
Mays Eva H, 1208 N Penn.
Merritt Susan, 118 W Vermont.
Miller Annie H, 577 E Washington.
Miller Elizabeth M, 314 N East.
Miller Martha J, 461 S Meridian.
Mitchell Mary A, 36½ W Washington.
Moore Ida E, 67 Talbott av.
Moran Katherine R, 186 Davidson.
Morgan Irene, 817 E Market.
Morris Allie M, 225 N Senate av.
Moulden Laura V, 98 Cherry.
Mungoran Mary J, 278 W New York.
Murphy Ann, 41 Indiana av.
Murphy Anna J, rear 226 E Washington.
Nagle Lawa A, 561 S New Jersey.
Neal Nancy C, 71 Oak.
Neff Wm E, 18½ N Meridian.
Neu Mary M, 15 Dougherty.
Norris Kate, 477 Blake.
North Emily J, 761 N Senate av.
O'Brien Margaret, 106 Fayette.
Offord Frank, 2½ W Washington.
Offutt Frances L, 219 W New York.
O'Hara Lillie F, 76 S West.
Onan Lizzie M, 362 E Market.
Pangle Anna, 148 E St Joseph.
Parmelee Mary F, 225 River av (W I).
Patterson Clements, 156 E Michigan.
Paxton Eva F, 148 N East.
Pearson Amanda, 26 Traub av.
Peirce Kathryn, 472 N New Jersey.
Pendergast Mary J, 345 N Alabama.
Perkins Alice C, 324 Bellefontaine.
Perry Cora, 199½ Mass av.
Peterson Anna D, 167 N Capitol av.
Phelps Linnie, 19½ N Meridian.
Phillips Ella F, 648½ College av.
Phipps Margaret E, 110 Woodburn av (W I).
Poole Mary, 134 E St Clair.
Prather Alice A, 108 Fayette.
Pritchard Medora C, 186 Huron.
Quail Charlotte, 165 N Illinois.
Reeves Nettie V, 61 Walcott.
Reid Charlotte, 13 S Reisner (W I).
Reister Elizabeth, 467 E St Clair.
Rice Viola S, 60 Cherry.
Richter Hannah, 417 E St Clair.
Riggs Lucy M, 38 Ash.
Ritter Ida M, 325 E Ohio.
Roberts Elizabeth R, 157 N Alabama.
Roberts Ivy, 298 Blake.
Rogers Olinda B, 87 Birch av (W I).
Rose Phoebe J, 545 Central av.
Rounder Mary C, 140 Prospect.
Sample Ida M, 146 Laurel.
Sanders Minnie L, 27 Birch av (W I).
Schering Matilda C, 44 N Arsenal av.
Schmitt Mary, 404 S Meridian.
Schoessel Tillie K, 265 N Noble.
Schoppenhorst Amelia, 426 E Vermont.
Schuster Justine, 131 Weghorst.
Scott Isabella, 109 Agnes.
Seibert Ida M, 36½ W Washington.
Shepard Kate, 92 Lexington av.
Sied Hattie, 1003 N Senate av.
Siegle Elizabeth, 244 N Noble.
Simons Emma, 427 Talbott av.
Simpson Lucetta, 96 S East.
Sirp Sarah, 520 Shelby.
Slocum Ella, 4 Sheldon.
Slocum Sarah C, 257 Lincoln la.
Smythe Lizzie, 294 N Penn.
Snider Lucetta, 85 Davidson.
Spaugh Mae A, 273 E North.
Spencer Kate H, 218 Indiana av.
Spencer Marie M, 39 W Washington.
Spier Sisters, 494 E Washington.
Sprankel Matilda E, 213 Hamilton av.

The Central Rubber & Supply Co. PHONE 922. 79 S. ILLINOIS ST., INDIANAPOLIS, IND.

OTTO GAS ENGINES | BUILDERS' EXCHANGE S. W. Cor. Ohio and Penn. Telephone 535.

Becker & Son Charles Becker Jacob Becker Jr. Merchant Tailors. 21 N. Penn St. Tel. 934

SALISBURY & STANLEY OFFICE, STORE AND BANK FIXTURES.

Springer Martha J, 324 E Wabash.
Stahlhut Emma, 228 Fulton.
Stanley Josephine, 68½ N Delaware.
Stein Mary C, 123 W South.
Stemen Clara, 127 W 7th.
Stephenson Lena, 277 Springfield.
Stevens Anna, 50½ S Illinois.
Stewart Nannie, 267 N Noble.
Stodghill Sarah E, 92 Spring.
Stoops Mary E, 122 N Liberty.
Straley Ingo, 99 Malott av.
Stuart Martha A, 401½ N Alabama.
Sweenie Hattie, 232-233 Lemcke bldg.
Sweet Mary F, 40 N East.
Swigert Lizzie, 160 S New Jersey.
Symons Samantha, 166 N Alabama.
Talbott Sarah A, 25 Birch av (W I).
Tanner Minnie D, 39 Clifford av.
Thiecke Ella, 112 Spann av.
Theis Mary, 88 John.
Thompson Sarah H, 423 Muskingum al.
Tucker Dorcas, 101 N Senate av.
Tucker Josie E, 113 Greer.
Tussey Delia V, 126 E New York.
Tynan Mary A, 256 S Meridian.
Vielhaber Amelia, 386 S East.
Vore Jennie, 1077 W Vermont.
Waltz Sarah A, 88 Sheldon.
Wasson H P & Co, 12-18 W Washington.
Watkins Mary L, 172 Ramsey av.
Wease Mary, 137 Martindale av.
Webb Olive V, 70½ N Delaware.
Weesner Josephine, 11, 156½ E Washington.
Weidig Helen C, 426 E St Clair.
Whitcomb Mary, 145 Fayette.
Wiley Inez E, 27 Grove.
Williams Rosa, 246 N Illinois.
Williamson Mary, 165 Coburn.
Wilson Anna V, 98 Fulton.
Woldt Anna, 79 Fletcher av.
Worthington Sarah A, 74 Hill av.
Wren Anna, 167 W 1st.
Wright Amanda O, 97 Cherry.
Zwissler Mary J, 33 Oriental.

*DRIER MANUFACTURERS—BRICK AND LUMBER.

Standard Dry Kiln Co, 184 S Meridian.

*DRIVEN WELL POINT MNFRS.

Roch & Peterman, 125 E Pearl.

*DRIVEN WELLS.

(See also Well and Cistern Builders.)
Krauss Charles, 42 S Penn. (See right top lines.)

*DROP CARVING MACHINE MNFRS.

Union Embossing Machine Co, 30-40 W South.

*DROP FORGINGS.

Indianapolis Drop Forging Co, s w cor Hanway and J M & I R R.

DRUGGISTS—WHOLESALE.

Bedford Collins T, 2 Indiana av.
Indianapolis Drug Co, 21-25 E Maryland.
Kiefer A Drug Co, 101-105 S Meridian.
McManus Martin, 48 S Capitol av.
Stewart Daniel Co, 42-50 S Meridian.
Ward Bros Drug Co, 72 S Meridian.

DRUGGISTS—RETAIL.

Baird Wm H, s e cor Michigan and Highland av.
Barmm Charles E, 452 Mass av.
Baron Bros, 703 E Washington.
Bates House Pharmacy (Open all Night), 54 W Washington; Branch 767 S East.
Baughman Carrie P, 500 N Alabama.
Baughman John & Co, 248 Mass av.
Becker Wm L, cor Hadley av and York (W I).
Bedford Collins T, 2 Indiana av.
Blodau Robert P, 102 Indiana av.
Bolin Roger M, 552 S West.
Borst George F, cor Meridian and Russell av.
Bourgonne Otto S, 399 S Capitol av.
Bowens Adrian, 316 S West.
Brehm Bernhard, 400 Mass av.
Broich Charles H, 588 S Meridian.
Brown Helena C, 1310 N Capitol av.
Browning & Son, 15 W Washington.
Bryan James W, n e cor Illinois and Jackson pl.
Bullington Frank L, n s Washington 1 e of Sherman Drive.
Burrage Charles R, 131 Mass av.
Carson John H, n e cor 30th and Illinois.
Carter Frank H, 298 Mass av.
Caskey J B & Son, 1 N Station (B).
Caulkins Aloc M, 109 E Washington.
Chambers Bros, 199 Howard (W I).
Clary Alonzo E, 102 Hoyt av.
Coffman Jacob, 540 S East.
Collins Thomas E, 52 Indiana av.
Cook Charles A, 361 Shelby.
Coons Wm I, w s Central av 1 s of Railroad (I).
Darrah Walter H, 1099 E Washington.
Deitch Othello L, 158 River av (W I).
Deitch Otto A, 880 W Washington.
Dechez A E & Co, 82 Mass av.
Dorey Edward R, 144 College av.
Driggs Nathaniel S, 850 E Washington.
Dudley F & Co, 600 Central av.
Dwyer Joseph M, 425 Madison av.
Eads Robert I, 100 E New York.
Eichrodt Charles W, s e cor West and 1st.
Elliott Joel T, 1201 Northwestern av.
Enners Edward H, 150 N Noble.
Erdelmeyer Frank, 489 N New Jersey.
Evans Mary C, 1299 N Meridian.
Eyster A M, 602 N Senate av.
Field Claude, 400 Bellefontaine.
Firquin Wm, 50 N Senate av.
Fisher George C, 402 College av.
Frauer H E & Co, 246 E Washington.
Frey F Joseph, 752 E Washington.
Fritz John P, 355 Virginia av.
Gable Lewis A, 828 N Illinois.
GAULD A B & BRO, 499 W Addison (N I).
Gauld John D, 201 Indiana av.
Givens Charles W, 27 Clifford av.
Grahn Edward G, 143 Cornell av.
Graves Gilbert H, 630 N West.
Grover Drug Co, 199 S Illinois.
Haag Julius A, 87 N Penn.
Haag Louis E, 302 Mass av, cor College av.
Hadley Bros, 317 Indiana av.
Hahn Charles C, n e cor Hadley av and Morris (W I).
Hall Frank A, 901 Morris (W I).

...ing of ...Co and Builders. Repairing of all kinds done on short notice. 177 ... St, Indianapolis, Ind. Telephone 99.

LIME, CEMENT, PLASTER FIRE BRICK AND CLAY SEWER PIPE, ETC. BALKE & KRAUSS CO., Cor. Market and Missouri Streets.

C. FRIEDGEN HAS THE FINEST STOCK OF LADIES' PARTY SLIPPERS and SHOES 19 NORTH PENNSYLVANIA ST.

SAMUEL LAING ▸ TIN, SLATE AND STEEL ROOFING, 72 AND 74 EAST COURT STREET.

Druggists—Retail—Continued.
Hampton Rufus C, 2 Hill av.
Hayes Lewis C, 152 Indiana av.
Heims Isaac N, 51 N Illinois.
Hobart Wm, 327 Dillon.
Holmes L W & Co, 352 Clifford av.
Hoshour Ed S, 650 College av.
Hoss Jacob V, n e cor Glen Drive and Gale (B).
Huder Henry J, 52-54 E Washington.
Hurty J N Pharmacy Co The, 102-104 N Penn.
Izor Bros, 259 W Washington.
Jobes George O, 417 Indiana av.
Johnson Wm H, 30 S Station (B).
Johnston John F, 401 N Illinois.
Jones C & Son, 101 N Delaware.
Keegan Frank, 1552 N Illinois.
Keenan James H, 151 Michigan (H).
Keller Conrad, 680 S Meridian.
Kern Walter H, 452 E Michigan.
Klepper Wm H, 100 Mass av.
Klingensmith Isaiah L, 502 College av.
Kloth Rudolph D, 100 Prospect.
Kluge Herman W, 202 Hoyt av.
Kolling Charles F, 205 Prospect.
Lamberson & Hackleman, Forest av and 20th (old).
Lambert Charles W, 448-450 W Michigan.
Lambert Minerva, 1132 E Washington.
Lay & McCaffrey, 186 W Washington.
Lehrritter Hugo H, 149 Fletcher av cor Grove.
Lender Gustav, 254 N Noble.
Lichty Mary, 398 Talbott av.
Lohman Charles G, 701 N Senate av.
Lohss Herman, 623 S Meridian.
McIlvain Wm H, 523 W Udell (N I).
McLeay J F, 236 W Washington.
Malpas Charles E, 99 Indiana av.
Mapes Smith H, 501 College av.
Mattill Bros, 581 S East.
Miller Albert J, 314 S Penn and 248 S West.
Miller Nathan G, 207 W New York.
Miller Philip, 324 Clifford av.
Monninger Albert D, n s Monument pl and N Meridian.
Morell Dora J, 248 Mass av.
Moroney Daniel M, 142 Michigan (H).
Morrison George C, junction Virginia av and South.
Muehl Siegmar F, 523 N Illinois, 798 N Alabama and 1147 N Illinois.
Mueller Charles G, 667 Virginia av.
Mueller Ferd A, 249 E Washington.
Myers John E, 494 S Meridian.
Nash Lee T, 400 S Illinois.
Navin's Pharmacy No 1, 149 W Washington.
Navin's Pharmacy No 2, 100 E Market.
Navin's Pharmacy No 3, 302 N Illinois.
Newby & Son, rear 852 Grandview av.
Newland Harrod C, 90 Ft Wayne av.
Orf George, 578 S Capitol av.
Ostroff Henry, cor Central av and 9th.
Owen John B, 302 N Senate av.
Pearce Pharmacy The, 224 W 12th.
Pearson Julius D, 47 Virginia av.
Perry Joseph R, 200 E Washington.
Pfafflin Henry A, 402 S Delaware.
Pomeroy Henry C, 50 N Penn.
Potter Thomas C, 300 N Penn.
Raffensperger Hiram C, s w cor East and South.
Reed I Oscar, 501 Bellefontaine.
Reick Edward C, 405 S East.
Renkert Louis H, 164 W Washington.
Ribble Marquis de L, 101 Shelby.
Ruch Charles E, 150 Columbia av.
Schad Charles H, 344 E Washington.
Schofield Wm A, 197 Christian av.
Schopp Otto, 302 S Illinois.
Schwartz Maurice, 350 Talbott av.
Schwenger Charles, 928 S Meridian.
Scott J M, s e cor Illinois and 7th.
Scott Wm W, 525 N Illinois.
Shake Ira H, 125 Oliver av (W I).
Sheets Wm C, 840 W Washington.
Short Willard N, 49 S Illinois.
Sloan Drug Co, 22 W Washington.
Smith M M, 46 Clifford av.
Staley Michael C, 441 Virginia av.
Steward E Eugene, 1052 N Senate av.
Stilz John G, 191 E Washington.
Stocker Wm H Dr, 500 E Washington.
Stockman Louis S, 251-253 N Illinois.
Stowers Earnest C, 546 W Udell (N I).
Stuckmeyer J H & E A, 557 Madison av and 115 Prospect.
Stucky Edward W, 11 N Illinois.
Swan Joseph C, 547 W 22d (N I).
Taylor & Lane, n e cor Bismarck and Grandview avs (H).
Thornburgh Thomas R, 190 Ft Wayne av.
Timberlake Arthur, 400 College av.
Tompkins Edmund W, 165 Mass av.
Tompkins James H F, n w cor Central av and P C C & St L Ry (I).
Traub George F, 252 W Washington.
Van Arsdale Bros, 1059 E Michigan.
Walker Arthur L, 201 S Pine.
Walker Edwin T, 1164 E Washington.
Watson Charles C, 511 Virginia av.
Webb James C, cor W Washington and Harris av (M J).
Weber George M, 99 N Illinois.
Weiss Theodore M, 198 Mass av.
Wilson Edgar H, 1 Bates.
Wolcott Frank E, 378 W New York and 849 LaSalle.
Yeager George F, 297 Virginia av.
Zimmer Harry E, 82 E Washington.

*DRUGGISTS' SUNDRIES.

Central Rubber and Supply Co The, 79 S Illinois. (See left side lines.)
Mayer Charles & Co, 29-31 W Washington. (See adv opp p 615.)

DRY GOODS—WHOLESALE.

Erwin D P & Co, 106-114 S Meridian and 5-13 McCrea.
Hood, Foulkrod & Co, 17½ McCrea.
McManus Martin, 48 S Capitol av.
Mills & Gibbs, 35 W Pearl.
Murphy, Hibben & Co, 93-99 S Meridian.

DRY GOODS—RETAIL.

Armitstead Mary E, 36 Malott av.
Ayres L S & Co, 33-37 W Washington.
Berry James E, 201 Hoyt av.
Binzer Solomon, 286 S Illinois.
Block Wm H Co The, 7-9 E Washington. (See right top and bottom lines.)
Brady James J, 911 S Meridian.
Breadheft Henry D, 319 Clifford av.
Brosnan Bros, 39 S Illinois.
Cathro Elizabeth, 579 N West.
Chitwood Maria J, 241 English av.
Cohen Bros, 230 W Washington.
Cotter Elizabeth, 130 N Belmont av (H).
Craig James, 190 Indiana av.
Deer John W, 131 William (W I).

SULLIVAN & MAHAN Manufacturers of all kinds of PAPER BOXES 41 W. Pearl St.

DIAMOND WALL PLASTER { Telephone 1410 BUILDERS' EXCHANGE.

Telephone 1769. 197 S. Illinois St. } THE HOME LAUNDRY { WORK CALLED FOR AND DELIVERED

Ebner Adolph, 136 Michigan (H).
Efroymson Jacob, 462 S Meridian.
Efroymson & Wolf, 194-198 W Washington.
Fox Caroline, 424 W North.
Glick August, 211 W Washington.
Glick Henry, 254 W Washington.
Green Agnes H, 692 N Senate av.
Groves Helen J M, 378 E 9th.
Hahn Orville L, 31 S Station (B).
Handlon Catherine, 376 Blake.
Helpman May E, 211 Prospect.
Hempleman Laura B, 563 S Meridian.
Heyer Oscar, 698 Home av.
Hoenig Margaretha, 458 S Meridian.
Hohlt Frederick W, 133 Hadley av (W I).
Indiana Dry Goods Co The, 158-160 E Washington.
Kahn Nathan, 580-582 S East.
Kean Thomas P, 816 E Washington.
Keller Robert, 570-578 S East.
Keller & Gamerdinger, 248-250 E Washington.
Kingston Samuel, 192 Virginia av.
Kingston Samuel H, 786 S East.
Knight Jasper N, s w cor Illinois and 30th.
Koss Charles W, 403 S Delaware.
Laurie Wm & Co, 15-19 N Meridian.
Lizius Augusta, 1156 E Washington.
Lohss Herman, 623 S Meridian.
Loucks & Jasper, 333 Dillon.
McKernan Louisa, 869 S Meridian.
Maguire Charles, 174-176 W Washington.
Manien Ella A, 444 S Meridian.
Mauer Henry J, 518 Indiana av.
Meyer F J & Co, 408 S East.
Michael Clara, 450 S Delaware.
Mohs Wm J A & Co, 11 Shelby.
Morbach Charles, 301 S Delaware.
Murphy Bros, 2 N Station (B).
Nathan Fanny, 238 W Washington.
Newman Henry, 372 S West.
Pettis Dry Goods Co, 25-33 E Washington.
Phelps Bros, 14 E Washington.
Poole Emily H, 1553 N Illinois.
Pope Christian F, 128 Prospect.
Roche Patrick J, 398 Mass av.
Ruth Robert E, 272 N Pine.
Selig Augusta, 170 W Washington.
Selig Moses, 109-111 S Illinois.
Shaw Emsley H, 466 Virginia av.
Singleton Edward E, 149 Shelby.
Smith Sue J, 304 Mass av.
Star Store, 194-198 W Washington.
Thomas John C, 249 N Noble.
Tompkins Jennie M, 539 W Addison (N I).
Trotcky Solomon, 219 Howard (W I).
Traugott Joachim, 174 River av (W I).
Wasson H P & Co, 12-18 W Washington.
Weber & Zimmer, 198 Virginia av.
White Eliza A, 512 W Addison (N I).
Ziegler Sarah A, 152 E 7th.
Zimmer & Co, 1 Shelby.

*DUMB WAITERS.

Hoffman C D & Co, 29 Kentucky av. (See adv in Elevators.)

DYERS AND SCOURERS.

Brill John C, 95 N Illinois and 38 Mass av.
Conover Wm F, 336 E Market.
Emmare & Gayler, 8½ E Washington.
Foulks Anna, 299 Virginia av.
Iten Frank, 21 Monument pl.
Kendall John A, 43 Mass av.
Kendall Mary, 25 Mass av.
Keystone Co, 17 Mass av.
Lewis Abram T, 127 Indiana av.
Maisoll Wm, 44 Virginia av.
Merritt & Elstun, 132 Mass av.
Nick The Tailor, 78 N Illinois. (See adv opp Tailors.)
Nilius Clara, 62½ S Illinois.
Parks Wm, rear 322 E Washington.
Philadelphia Dye House, 6 W Market.
Schoen Bros, 29½ E Market.
Shapland Henry, 131 N Meridian.
Smith Edward B, 24 Monument pl.
Thomas Joseph T, 57 Indiana av.
Walch Caroline, 17 Meek.

*DYNAMOS, AND MOTOR MNFRS.

Commercial Electric Co, cor Merrill and Willard.
Jenney Electric Motor Co, Belt R R and Panhandle crossing.
Varney & McOuat, 75 E Market. (See adv opp Electrical Engineers.)

*EASTER NOVELTIES.

Mayer Charles & Co, 29-31 W Washington. (See adv opp p 615.)

*ELECTRIC APPARATUS.

Indianapolis District Telegraph Co The, 15 S Meridian. (See adv in Electric Supplies.)
Sanborn Electric Co, 22 E Ohio. (See adv in Electrical Contractors.)
Varney & McOuat, 75 E Market. (See adv.)

*ELECTRIC BELT MANUFACTURERS.

Veale Ellis W, 31 Standard av (W I).

*ELECTRIC CONSTRUCTION.

Kirkhoff Bros, 102-104 S Penn. (See left top cor cards.)
Meikel Charles W, 96-98 E New York. (See right bottom lines.)
Sanborn Electric Co, 22 E Ohio. (See adv in Electrical Contractors.)

*ELECTRIC CONTRACTORS.

Indianapolis District Telegraph Co The, 15 S Meridian. (See adv in Electric Supplies.)
Kirkhoff Bros, 102-104 S Penn. (See left top cor cards.)
Meikel Charles W, 96-98 E New York. (See right bottom lines.)
Sanborn Electric Co, 22 E Ohio. (See adv in Electrical Contractors.)

THE WM. H. BLOCK CO. 7 AND 9 EAST WASHINGTON STREET. DRY GOODS, HOUSE FURNISHINGS AND CROCKERY.

London Guarantee and Accident Co. (Ltd.) Employers', Public and Teams' Liability, Workmen's Collective Insurance and Fidelity Bonds
GEORGE W. PANGBORN, General Agent, 704-706 Lemcke Bldg. Telephone 140.

FRANK K. SAWYER || Reliable Fire Insurance. Reasonable Rates. 74 E. MARKET STREET. Telephone 863.

Electric Contractors—Continued.
Smith Harold V & Co, 90 E Market. (See adv.)

HAROLD V. SMITH & CO.
Electrical Engineers and Contractors
Wiring and General Construction. Estimates Furnished.
Telephone 1913.
90 EAST MARKET STREET.

***ELECTRIC FANS.**
Sanborn Electric Co, 22 E Ohio. (See adv in Electrical Contractors.)
Varney & McOuat, 75 E Market. (See adv.)

***ELECTRIC HEAT REGULATORS.**
Kirkhoff Bros, 102-104 S Penn. (See left top cor cards.)

ELECTRIC LIGHT COMPANIES.
Indianapolis Light and Power Co, 24 Monument pl.

***ELECTRIC REPAIRS.**
Indianapolis District Telegraph Co The, 15 S Meridian. (See adv.)
Meikel Charles W, 96-98 E New York. (See right bottom lines.)
Sanborn Electric Co, 22 E Ohio. (See adv.)
Varney & McOuat, 75 E Market. (See adv.)

ELECTRIC SUPPLIES.
Faradizer Co The, 513 Majestic bldg.
Fryer & Fleming, 27 Monument pl.
MacCurdy & Smith, 94 N Meridian.
Meikel Charles W, 96-98 E New York. (See right bottom lines.)
Murphy John H & John W, 30 E Georgia.
Sanborn Electric Co, 22 E Ohio. (See adv.)
Varney & McOuat, 75 E Market. (See adv.)

***ELECTRIC WIRING.**
Kirkhoff Bros, 102-104 S Penn. (See left top cor cards.)
Meikel Charles W, 96-98 E New York. (See right bottom lines.)
Sanborn Electric Co, 22 E Ohio. (See adv.)
Smith Harold V & Co, 90 E Market. (See adv.)

***ELECTRICAL CONTRACTORS AND FITTERS.**
Kirkhoff Bros, 102-104 S Penn. (See left top cor cards.)
Sanborn Electric Co, 22 E Ohio. (See adv.)

SANBORN ELECTRIC CO.
ELECTRICAL CONTRACTORS AND FITTERS
Special Agents

WIRES.
WE USE NOTHING BUT FIRST-CLASS MATERIAL and GUARANTEE ALL WORK.
22 E. Ohio St.
Telephone 1457

Varney & McOuat, 75 E Market. (See adv.)

***ELECTRICAL ENGINEERS.**
Varney & McOuat, 75 E Market. (See adv opp.)

ELECTRICAL EQUIPMENTS.
Varney & McOuat, 75 E Market. (See adv.)

DIRECTORIES OF ALL THE STATES AND PRINCIPAL CITIES ON FILE FOR REFERENCE AT OUR OFFICE.

R. L. POLK & CO.
23-24 JOURNAL BLDG.

POLICIES IN UNITED STATES LIFE INSURANCE CO., offer indemnity against death, liberal cash surrender value or at option of policy-holder, fully paid-up life insurance or liberal life income.
E. B. SWIFT, M'g'r, 25 E. Market St.

G. E. VARNEY. R. L. McOUAT.

Varney & McOuat

ELECTRICAL ENGINEERS

No. 75 East Market Street

Electrical Supplies,
Wiring and General
Construction,
Electric Light,
Power and
Mining Plants.

WE ARE AGENTS FOR

"Buckeye" Incandescent Lamps

TELEPHONE 849.

BENJ. BOOTH PRACTICAL EXPERT ACCOUNTANT. Accounts of any description investigated and audited, and statements rendered. Room 18, 82½ E. Washington St., Indianapolis, Ind.

The Best Place in the City to Get a Good Meal ✦✦ THE SHERMAN RESTAURANT ✦✦ 18 and 20 S. Meridian Street KERSHNER BROS., Proprs.

MESSENGER BOYS.
ERRANDS.
DISTRIBUTION.

RELIABLE

ELECTRIC BELLS,
BURGLAR ALARMS,
ELECTRIC GAS LIGHTING,

Electric Motors, Dynamos,

Electric Light Supplies,
Reliable Incandescent Construction.

Private Telephones and Telephone Exchanges Installed Complete.

THE

Indianapolis District Telegraph COMPANY,

C. C. Hatfield, Pres't. INCORPORATED 1885. John T. Brush, Sec'y.

15 S. Meridian St. Telephone 123.

*ELECTRICAL SUPPLIES.

Indianapolis District Telegraph Co The, 15 S Meridian. (See adv.)
Sanborn Electric Co, 22 E Ohio. (See adv.)

ELECTRICIANS.

Electrical Construction Co, 116 N Delaware.
Hartung Edward C, 5 Cyclorama pl.
Indianapolis District Telegraph Co The, 15 S Meridian. (See adv.)
Meikel Charles W, 96-98 E New York. (See right bottom lines.)
Reitz Charles & Son, 72 Virginia av.
Sanborn Electric Co, 22 E Ohio. (See adv.)
Smith Harold V & Co, 90 E Market. (See adv.)
Varney & McOuat, 75 E Market. (See adv.)

ELECTROTYPE FOUNDRIES.

Benedict Geo H & Co, 175 S Clark St, Chicago, Ill. (See adv opp Engravers.)
Indiana Electrotype Co, 23 W Pearl. (See left side lines.)
Indianapolis Electrotype Foundry, 17-25 W Georgia.

*ELEVATOR EXPERTS.

Cryan John, 96 S Delaware. (See adv.)

ELEVATOR GATE MANUFACTURERS.

Elder James M, 1205 N Illinois.

*ELEVATOR GATES—AUTOMATIC.

Indiana Elevator Gate Co, 1205 N Illinois.

ELEVATOR MANUFACTURERS.

Cryan John, 96 S Delaware. (See adv.)
Hoffman C D & Co, 29 Kentucky av. (See adv.)
Indianapolis Bolt and Machine Works, 122-126 Kentucky av and 177-201 W Georgia. (See adv.)
Nordyke & Marmon Co, crossing I & V Ry and Morris (W I). (See inside back cover.)
Varney & McOuat, 75 E Market. (See adv in Electrical Engineers.)

*ELEVATOR REPAIRERS.

Cryan John, 96 S Delaware. (See adv.)

ELOCUTIONISTS.

Cogswell Anna P, 283 Douglass.
Hamilton Mary W, 142 N Illinois.
McAvoy Thomas J, 56 Talbott blk.
Prunk Harriet Augusta Mrs, 368 W New York. (See adv p 138.)

*EMBALMERS.

Tutewiler Henry W, 72 W Market. (See left bottom lines.)

TUTEWILER UNDERTAKER, No. 72 WEST MARKET STREET. TELEPHONE 216.

JOHN CRYAN

Elevator Erecting and Repairing

A SPECIALTY.

Thoroughly Familiar with the Construction of "THE CRANE," "THE HALE," "THE STANDARD," "THE REEDY" and all other makes of Passenger and Freight Elevators.

ALL REPAIRS DONE PROMPTLY AND PROPERLY AT ANY TIME MOST CONVENIENT TO PROPRIETOR

Elevator Supplies of all Kinds in Stock

REFERENCES: LEADING BUSINESS MEN OF INDIANAPOLIS.

96 South Delaware Street, Corner Georgia Street

TELEPHONE 121. **INDIANAPOLIS, IND.**

Indianapolis Elevator and Millwright Shop

C. D. HOFFMAN & CO.

PASSENGER AND FREIGHT HIGH GRADE ELECTRIC ELEVATORS.

ALL KINDS MACHINERY ERECTING. SHAFTING HANGERS AND PULLEYS. REPAIRING ALL KINDS OF ELEVATORS.

OFFICE AND SHOP, 29 KENTUCKY AVENUE, INDIANAPOLIS, IND.

INDIANAPOLIS

Bolt and Machine Works,

MANUFACTURERS OF

Improved Freight Elevators

Electric, Steam or Hand Power.

Machinery and Castings made to order. Pulleys, Shafting, Hangers and all kinds of Bolts, Rods, Etc.

Parkhurst Bros. & Co., Proprs.

TELEPHONE 306. **122 to 126 Kentucky Ave.**

DALTON & MERRIFIELD { LUMBER South Noble St., near E. Washington

INDIANA ELECTROTYPE CO. : BEST WORK LOWEST PRICES. All Orders Promptly Filled.
23 WEST PEARL ST., INDIANAPOLIS, IND. JOB WORK. BOOK PLATES. BEST PATENT BASE ON THE MARKET.

***EMBOSSED WOOD MANUFACTURERS.**

United States Artistic Co, 166 S New Jersey.

EMBOSSING MACHINE MNFRS.

Union Embossing Machine Co, 30-40 W South.

***EMERY WHEELS AND GRINDING MACHINERY.**

Vonnegut Clemens, 184-186 E Washington. (See left bottom lines.)

EMPLOYMENT OFFICES.

Bartholomew Deborah S, 30½ N Delaware.
Hough Ora B, 95½ N Delaware.
Hugle L E, 23 W Ohio.

ENCAUSTIC TILE.

United States Encaustic Tile Works, cor 7th and C C C & St L Ry.

***ENGINEERS—MECHANICAL.**

Jones Horace B, 415-418 Lemcke Bldg. (See adv in Mechanical Engineers.)

***ENGINES AND BOILERS.**

Atlas Engine Works, n e cor 9th and Martindale av.
Chandler & Taylor Co, 370 W Washington.
Indianapolis Engine Co, n e cor Bloyd and Hillside avs.
Lambert Gas and Gasoline Engine Co, Anderson, Ind. (See right top lines.)
Otto Gas Engine Works The, 3 Builders' Exchange. (See left bottom lines.)

ENGRAVERS.

(See also Wood Engravers.)

Bauer H C Engraving Co The, 23 W Washington. (See adv opp.)
Benedict Geo H & Co, 175-177 S Clark St, Chicago, Ill. (See adv.)
Bowley George J, Room 14 Yohn Blk, n e cor Meridian and Washington. (See adv in Wood Engravers.)
Burford Wm B, 21 W Washington. (See adv opp p 230.)
Indiana Illustrating Co, s e cor Market and Illinois. (See adv opp.)
Kamber Amadee, 11½ N Meridian.
Levey Bros & Co, 19 W Maryland. (See adv opp p 561.)
Mayer George J, 15 S Meridian. (See left bottom cor cards and adv p 5.)
Nicoli Charles A, 21 Hubbard blk.
Oval & Koster, 180 W Court.
Ropkey-Mason Engraving Co, 24 W Maryland.
Smith Frank H, 22 N Penn. (See adv opp p 803.)

***ENGRAVERS—ALL METHODS.**

Benedict Geo H & Co, 175-177 S Clark St, Chicago, Ill. (See adv.)

***ENGRAVERS—COPPER PLATE AND STEEL.**

Burford Wm B, 21 W Washington. (See adv opp p 230.)
Levey Bros & Co, 19 W Maryland. (See adv opp p 561.)
Smith Frank H, 22 N Penn. (See adv opp p 803.)

***ENGRAVERS—HALF TONE.**

Bauer H C Engraving Co The, 23 W Washington. (See adv opp.)
Indiana Illustrating Co, s e cor Market and Illinois. (See adv opp.)

***ENGRAVERS—LITHO.**

Burford Wm B, 21 W Washington. (See adv opp p 230.)
Indianapolis Lithographic Co, F A Heuss Propr, 95 E South.
Levey Bros & Co, 19 W Maryland. (See adv opp p 561.)

***ENGRAVERS—METAL.**

Mayer George J, 15 S Meridian. (See left bottom cor cards and p 5.)

***ENGRAVERS—PHOTO.**

Bauer H C Engraving Co The, 23 W Washington. (See adv opp.)
Indiana Illustrating Co, s e cor Market and Illinois. (See adv opp.)

***ENGRAVERS—PROCESS.**

Indiana Illustrating Co, s e cor Market and Illinois. (See adv opp.)

***ENGRAVERS—WOOD.**

Bauer H C Engraving Co The, 23 W Washington. (See adv opp.)
Bowley George J, Room 14, Yohn Blk, n e cor Meridian and Washington. (See adv in Wood Engravers.)
Burford Wm B, 21 W Washington. (See adv opp p 230.)
Chandler Henry C, 47½ N Illinois, s e cor Market. (See adv.)

H.C.CHANDLER
WOOD AND PROCESS
ENGRAVER
ENGRAVINGS FOR ALL ILLUSTRATIVE PURPOSES
S.E.Cor.Illinois & Market Streets.
INDIANAPOLIS,IND.

Levey Bros & Co, 19 W Maryland. (See adv opp p 561.)

***ENGRAVERS—ZINC.**

Bauer H C Engraving Co The, 23 W Washington. (See adv opp.)

***ENGRAVINGS AND ETCHINGS.**

Lieber H Co The, 33 S Meridian. (See right top cor cards.)

EXCELSIOR MANUFACTURERS.

Globe Excelsior Wks, 19 S East.
Johnson Jesse B, 366 W Market.

W. H. Messenger FURNITURE, CARPETS, STOVES, 101 EAST WASHINGTON ST. TEL. 491.

INDIANAPOL S, I

DALTON & MERRIFIELD | LUMBER South Noble St., near E. Washington

INDIANA ELECTROTYPE CO. BEST WORK LOWEST PRICES. 23 WEST PEARL ST., INDIANAPOLIS, IND. JOB WORK. BOOK PLATES. All Orders Promptly Filled. BEST PATENT BASE ON THE MARKET.

*EMBOSSED WOOD MANUFACTURERS.

United States Art ... New Jersey

EMBOSSING MACHINE WORKS.

Union Embossing M ... South

*EMERY WHEELS AND GRINDING MACHINERY.

Vonnegut Clemens, 184 ... Washington. (See left bottom lines.)

EMPLOYMENT OFFICES.

Bartholomew Deborah ...
Hough Ora H ...
Hugle L L, 23 W ...

ENCAUSTIC TILE.

United States E... Wks, cor 7th and C C C & St L ...

*ENGINEERS—MECHANICAL.

Jones Horace B, 418-419 Lemcke Bldg. (See adv in Mechanical Engineers.)

*ENGINES AND BOILERS.

Atlas Engine Works ... Martindale av
Chandler & Taylor ... Washington
Indianapolis Engine ... and Hillside av
Lambert Gas and Gasoline Engine Co, Anderson, Ind. (See right ... lines.)
Otto Gas Engine Works The, Builders' Exchange. (See left bottom lines.)

ENGRAVERS.

(See also W...)

Bauer H C Engraving Co The, 23 W Washington. (See adv opp.)
Benedict Geo H & Co, 175-177 ... St, Chicago, Ill. (See adv ...)
Bowley George J, Room 14 ... Bldg, n e cor Meridian and Washington. (See adv in Wood Engravers.)
Burford Wm B, 21 W Washington. (See adv opp p 230.)
Indiana Illustrating Co, ... Market and Illinois. (See adv opp.)
Kamber Amadee ... N M...
Levey Bros & Co, 19 W Maryland. (See adv opp p 561.)
Mayer George J, 15 S Meridian. (See left bottom cor cards and p ...)
Nicoll Charles A, 21 Hall ...
Oval & Koster 160 W ...
Ropkey-Mason Engraving ... W Maryland.
Smith Frank H, 22 N Penn. (See adv opp p 563.)

*ENGRAVERS—ALL METHODS.

Benedict Geo H & Co, 175-177 Clark St, Chicago, Ill. (See adv ...)

*ENGRAVERS—COPPER PLATE AND STEEL.

Burford Wm B, 21 W Washington. (See adv opp p 230.)

Levey Bros & Co, 19 W Maryland. (See adv opp p 561.)
Smith Frank H, 22 N Penn. (See adv opp p 563.)

*ENGRAVERS—HALF TONE.

Bauer H C Engraving Co The, 23 W Washington. (See adv opp.)
Indiana Illustrating Co, s e cor Market and Illinois. (See adv opp.)

*ENGRAVERS—LITHO.

Burford Wm B, 21 W Washington. (See adv opp p 230.)
Indianapolis Lithographic Co, F A Heuss Propr, 95 E South.
Levey Bros & Co, 19 W Maryland. (See adv opp p 561.)

*ENGRAVERS—METAL.

Mayer George J, 15 S Meridian. (See left bottom cor cards and p 5.)

*ENGRAVERS—PHOTO.

Bauer H C Engraving Co The, 23 W Washington. (See adv opp.)
Indiana Illustrating Co, s e cor Market and Illinois. (See adv opp.)

*ENGRAVERS—PROCESS.

Indiana Illustrating Co, s e cor Market and Illinois. (See adv opp.)

*ENGRAVERS—WOOD.

Bauer H C Engraving Co The, 23 W Washington. (See adv opp.)
Bowley George J, Room 14, n e cor Meridian and Washington. (See adv in Wood Engravers.)
Burford Wm B, 21 W Washington. (See adv opp p 230.)
Chandler Henry C, 67½ ... cor Market. (See adv.)

H. C. CHANDLER Wood and Photo ENGRAVER

Levey Bros & Co, 19 ... (See adv opp p 561.)

*ENGRAV...

Bauer H C Engrav... Washington. ...

*ENGRAVIN...

Lieber H Co The ... right top cor ...

EXCELSIOR ...

Globe Excelsior ... Jones ...

W. H. Messenger FURNITURE ... 101 EAST ...

HALF-TONE FROM PHOTOGRAPH

MADONNA

H. C. BAUER ENG. CO.
23 WEST WASHINGTON STREET
INDIANAPOLIS

The Indiana Illustrating Company

Telephone 1077

47 AND 49 NORTH ILLINOIS STREET, CORNER MARKET,
INDIANAPOLIS, INDIANA.

Half-Tones, Zinc-Etching and Designing

CUTS BY ALL METHODS. UP-TO-DATE IDEAS

The oldest process engraving house in Indiana. We make engravings by all methods. Work of the highest order and turned out quickly. Parties wishing bids on catalogue work should write us. We compete with New York and Chicago houses on quality and quickness of production, but our prices are lower.

Advertise in

The Indiana Woman

The largest and handsomest illustrated weekly in the world for the money. Two dollars per year.

Circulation, over 4,000 in Indianapolis alone and growing.

Rates very reasonable. Address

The Indiana Woman,

49 North Illinois Street, Indianapolis, Ind.

E. E. STAFFORD, PUBLISHER.

REASONABLE RELIABLE AND PROMPT.
Geo. H. Benedict & Co.
Designers
Engravers
BY ALL METHODS AND
Electrotypers
175
177-
CLARK
STREET
CHICAGO
ILL. U.S.A.
FACILITIES·CAPACITY AND QUALITY·UNEXCELLED.
B

Steam Pumping Machinery { HENRY R. WORTHINGTON, 64 S. PENNSYLVANIA ST. Long Distance Telephone 284.

UNION CO-OPERATIVE LAUNDRY { NOS. 138, 40 AND 42 VIRGINIA AVENUE. (COMPOSED OF UNION LAUNDRY GIRLS.) —T. E. SOMERVILLE, MANAGER— TELEPHONE 1269. INDIANAPOLIS, IND.

*EXPERIMENTAL MACHINERY.

Indianapolis Pattern Works, Scullin & Myers Proprs, 101 S Penn.

Jacob & Co, s w cor Georgia and Penn. (See adv in Pattern and Model Makers.)

Reeves Harry E, 96 S Delaware, cor Georgia. (See embossed line front cover and adv in Pattern Makers.)

Specialty Manufacturing Co, 193 S Meridian. (See adv opp Photographers.)

*EXPERT ACCOUNTANTS.

Booth Benjamin, Room 18, 82½ E Washington. (See left top lines.)

Indianapolis Business University, When Bldg, N Penn (Bryant & Stratton and Indianapolis Business Colleges Consolidated), E J Heeb Propr. (See front cover, right bottom lines and p 4.)

EXPRESS COMPANIES.

Adams Express Co, 25 and 147 S Meridian.
American Express Co, 5 E Washington and 145 S Meridian.
Baltimore & Ohio Express Co, 23 S Meridian.
Great Northern Express Co, 5 E Washington and 145 S Meridian.
National Express Co, 5 E Washington and 145 S Meridian.
Pacific Express Co, 23 S Meridian.
Southern Express Co, 25 S Meridian.
Texas Express Co, 25 S Meridian.
United States Express Co, 23 S Meridian.
Wells, Fargo & Co, 23 S Meridian.

*EYE GLASSES.

Mayhew James N, 13 N Meridian. (See right bottom cor cards.)

*FANCY CHINA AND GLASSWARE.

Mayer Charles & Co, 29-31 W Washington. (See adv opp p 615.)

*FANCY GOODS.

Kipp Bros Co, 37-39 S Meridian.

Mayer Charles & Co, 29-31 W Washington. (See adv opp p 615.)

*FANCY HARDWARE.

Mayer Charles & Co, 29-31 W Washington. (See adv opp p 615.)

*FANS—MANUFACTURERS.

Specialty Manufacturing Co, 193 S Meridian. (See adv opp Photographers.)

*FEATHER DUSTERS.

Mayer Charles & Co, 29-31 W Washington. (See adv opp p 615.)

*FEATHER DYERS—OSTRICH.

Columbian Feather Cleaning and Dyeing Establishment, 147 Mass av. (See adv p 8.)

FEATHER RENOVATORS.

DuBois Benjamin F, 116 Mass av.
Shreve David R, s s Sturm av 1 e of Arsenal av.

*FEATHERS.

Hirschman Jacob C (Estate of), 69-71 N New Jersey.

*FELT ROOFING.

Zimmerman C & Sons, 19-21 S East. (See left bottom lines.)

FENCE MANUFACTURERS.

(See also Iron and Wire Fences.)

American Truss Fence Co, 11-13 W Pearl.

Cleaveland Fence Co, Office 21 Biddle, Factory 18-22 same.

Ellis & Helfenberger, 162-168 S Senate av. (See right bottom lines.)

Indianapolis Fence Co, Office 15 Thorpe Blk.

Van Arsdall Marion, 222 Ramsey av.

FERTILIZER MANUFACTURERS.

Dockweiler & Kingsbury, 67 S Meridian.

Huntington & Page, 78 E Market. (See adv p 5.)

Indianapolis Desiccating Co, s e cor Madison av and Lincoln la.
Kalter Albert E, 418 W Washington.
Kaufman S & Sons, 1½ E Washington.
Mehring Luther, 810 S Meridian.
Rauh E & Sons, 219 S Penn.

*FINANCIAL AGENTS.

Day Thos C & Co, 325-330 Lemcke Bldg. (See right top cor cards.)

Indiana Trust Co The, Indiana Trust Bldg, s e cor Washington and Virginia av. (See front cover, adv opp p 487 and opp Insurance Agts.)

Lawyers' Loan and Trust Co, 68½ E Market. (See top edge and adv opp p 555.)

Marion Trust Co, s e cor Market and Monument Pl. (See back cover.)

Union Trust Co The, 68 E Market. (See front cover, adv opp Insurance and opp p 867.)

*FIRE BRICK AND FIRE CLAY.

Balke & Krauss Co, cor Missouri and Market. (See right bottom lines.)

Moffat & Co, 402 Lemcke Bldg. (See adv p 9.)

Wasson W G Co The, 130 Indiana av. (See left bottom cor cards and adv in Cement and Lime.)

*FIRE ENGINES.

Indianapolis Engine Co, n e cor Bloyd and Hillside avs.

FIRE EQUIPMENT MNFRS.

Vajen-Bader Co The, 88 N Penn.

*FIRE HOSE.

Central Rubber and Supply Co The, 79 S Illinois. (See left side lines.)

CLEMENS VONNEGUT 184, 186 and 192 E. Washington St. | FOUNDRY AND MACHINISTS' SUPPLIES. "NORTON" EMERY WHEELS AND GRINDING MACHINERY.

THE WM. H. BLOCK CO. DRY GOODS, MILLINERY, CLOAKS AND FURS.
7 AND 9 EAST WASHINGTON STREET.

ESTABLISHED 1869.

FRANK SAAK,

FLORIST No. 124 EAST ST. JOSEPH ST.,
Between Alabama and Delaware.
Cut Flowers, Decorations, Fancy Designs. Funerals and Parties Supplied on Short Notice.

INDIANAPOLIS STEEL ROOFING AND CORRUGATING WORKS, 23 and 25 East South Street. S. D. NOEL, Proprietor.

*FIRE INSPECTION BUREAUS.

Indianapolis Fire Inspection Bureau, 18-20 Journal bldg.

*FIRE PROOF SHUTTERS AND DOORS.

McWorkman Willard, 930 W Washington. (See left top cor cards.)

*FIRE PUMPS.

Worthington Henry R, 64 S Penn. (See left top lines.)

*FIRE WORKS AND FLAGS.

Mayer Charles & Co, 29-31 W Washington. (See adv opp p 615.)

*FISHING TACKLE.

Mayer Charles & Co, 29-31 W Washington. (See adv opp p 615.)

*FISHING TACKLE MNFRS.

Only Mnfg Co The, 83 W Georgia.

FLORISTS AND NURSERYMEN.

Alcazar, 30 W Washington.
Aughinbaugh Edward L, 1572 N Meridian.
Bertermann Bros, 85 E Washington (30 Pembroke Arcade), and 1370 E Washington.
Braendlein Martin, e s Senate av 2 s of 26th.
Butcher Ellen, 84 E Mkt House and n end Maxwell av (I).
Craft Charles O, 1541 N Capitol av.
Fohl Bernie A, n w cor Senate av and 30th (M).
Fohl John R, 1149 N New Jersey.
Glaubke Wm A, w s Carter 1 s of 30th.
Grande John, 322 Shelby.
Harritt Rolla F, E Mkt House.
Hartje John, 1633 N Illinois.
Heidenreich John J, s w cor Applegate and Morton.
Hukriede & Son, 495 S State av and 528 Virginia av.
Junge & Sonnenschmidt, s s Brookville rd 1 w of P C C & St L Ry (S).
Lange & Son, 1044 S Meridian.
Larsen Mary J, 328 W 23d.
Lilly Bros, 682 N Senate av.
Nelson Elliott A, cor Senate av and 27th.
Pahud Alfred, n e cor Senate av and 26th.
Rathsam John G, 749 Broadway.
Rieman Barbara J, 1542 N Senate av.
Rieman Henry W, 609 S East.
Rieman John, 3 Mass av.
Rothermel Silas, n e cor Wheeler and Division (B).
Saak Frank, 124 E St Joseph. (See adv.)
Teas Edward Y, w s Elm av 1 n of Washington av (I).
Vondersaar John J, 675 Madison av.
Wheatcraft Charles O, 1541 N Capitol av.
Wiegand & Son, 838 N Illinois.

*FLOUR MILL MACHINERY.

Nordyke & Marmon Co, crossing I & V Ry and Morris (W I). (See adv inside back cover.)

David S. McKernan REAL ESTATE AND LOANS. Exchanging real estate a specialty. A number of choice pieces for encumbered property. Rooms 2-5 Thorpe Block.

DIAMOND WALL PLASTER { Telephone 1410 BUILDERS' EXCHANGE.

Cor. E. Ohio St. and C., C., C. & St. L. R'y Tracks.
Storage of Household Goods and Pianos a Specialty.
UNION TRANSFER AND STORAGE CO.

FLOUR MILLS.

Acme Milling Co, 352 W Washington.
Bachman Valentine, n w cor Madison av and Ray.
Blanchard Ida M, e s Highland av 1 s of Clifford av.
Blanton Milling Co, 200 W Maryland.
Evans George T, 452 W Washington.
Prange Frederick, 13 Davidson.

FLOUR AND FEED—WHOLESALE.

Ferger Charles, 45 Virginia av.
Hockensmith Harry E, 478 E Washington.
Janes Frank E, 107-113 N Delaware.
McComb Edward B, 57 Mass av.
Montezuma Mill Co, 100 S West.
Noblesville Milling Co, 132 Indiana av.
O'Neill John, 428 E Ohio.
Paine & Co, 105 N Delaware.
Probst & Kassebaum, 432 Mass av.
Rouse Bros, 2½ Board of Trade bldg.
Rouse Wm & Son, 72 S Delaware.
Ryan J R & Co, 62 E Maryland.
Smith Benjamin R, 4-8 Prospect.

FLOUR AND FEED—RETAIL.

Amos Henry J, 21 Oriental.
Bischoff & Fisse, s e cor Rural and Belt R R (B).
Brownell Charles C, 148 Blake.
Bursott John W, 263 Indiana av.
Campbell Wm B, 2 Malott av.
Catt L A & Co, 192-194 W Maryland.
Cloud Henry F, 587 W McLene (N I).
Cummings Matthew M, 62 N Delaware.
Dehne Charles & Bro, 26 N Liberty.
Dittman F G & Co, 746 N Senate av.
Elder Leonard M, 368 E 7th.
Fahrion J George, 373 S Delaware.
Fisher Charles, 306 Virginia av.
Francis Thomas E, 237 Blake.
Furgason Francis M, 636 N West.
Gentry Jeremiah, 25 Marion av (W I).
George Charles A, 1114 E Washington.
Geyer Samuel, 177 Indiana av.
Ging Benjamin F, e s National av 5 s of Washington av (I).
Haney Scott, n w cor Court and Missouri.
Hitz Jesse E, 78 S Delaware.
Hockensmith Harry E, 478 E Washington.
Houton & Noe, n w cor Pine and Noble.
Howard & Davidson, 502 E Washington.
Huntington & Page, 78 E Market. (See adv p 5.)
Indianapolis Coal and Feed Co, cor Kentucky av and Merrill.
Janes Frank E, 107-113 N Delaware.
Justice & Warren, 1547-1549 N Illinois.
Keller Robert, 570-578 S East.
Kenipe James M, 90 E South.
Laughlin Dennis, 318 Indiana av.
Lipschitz & Mazo, 92 Russell av.
McGrew J W & Co, 857 Morris (W I).
McGrigg George W, 112 Hill av.
Malick Wm P, 657 N Senate av.
Miller Samuel F, 280 W Washington.
Monn Edwin F, 207 Indiana av.
Moore Joseph A, 12 Prospect.
Morgan George, 70 Michigan (H).
Mullis R T, 1350 N Capitol av.
Munday Thomas J, 20 Grandview av (H).
Neidlinger & Cotton, 1446 Northwestern av (N I).
Noel Bros' Flour Feed Co, 156 W North.
Peehl Louis, 129 Indiana av.
Phillips Edward, 277½ Mass av.
Phillips Nelson, 20 S West.
Porter James H, s e cor College av and 9th.
Probst & Kassebaum, 432 Mass av.
Pryor Martin P, 98 W 7th.
Resener Christian W, 301 N East.
Roberts Benjamin, s w cor Lawrence and Rural.
Roberts Sherman, 808 W Washington.
Rouse Arthur E, 172 Virginia av.
Smith Alvie O, 151 Columbia av.
Smith Benjamin R, 4-8 Prospect.
Streibeck Herman F, s e cor Walnut and Big Four tracks.
Sullivan Lemuel M, 261 W Washington.
Thompson Eugene C, 317 Mass av.
Thompson Wm, 100 Ft Wayne av.
Vandiver Bros, 488 Virginia av.
Van Pelt Sutton B, 41 N Alabama.
Walter John A, 252 Mass av.
Whitaker George B, 645 Virginia av.
Ziegner & Ensley, 460 Virginia av.

*FLUE LINING.

Balke & Krauss Co, cor Market and Missouri. (See right bottom lines.)
Wasson W G Co The, 130 Indiana av. (See left cor cards and adv in Cement and Lime.)

*FLUE PIPES.

Balke & Krauss Co, cor Market and Missouri. (See right bottom lines.)
Wasson W G Co The, 130 Indiana av. (See left cor cards and adv in Cement and Lime.)

*FLY SCREENS.

Indiana Screen Factory, 591-593 Central av, near 14th. (See front cover.)

*FOREIGN COLLECTIONS.

Metzger A Agency, 5 Odd Fellows' Hall. (See left bottom lines.)

*FOREIGN EXCHANGE.

Metzger A Agency, 5 Odd Fellows' Hall. (See left bottom lines.)

*FORGES.

Vonnegut Clemens, 184-186 E Washington. (See left bottom lines.)

*FOUNDERS—BRASS.

Dean Bros' Steam Pump Works, 1st near cor Senate av. (See adv p 3.)

*FOUNDERS—IRON.

Dean Bros' Steam Pump Works, 1st near cor Senate av. (See adv p 3.)
Ellis & Helfenberger, 162-168 S Senate av. (See right bottom lines.)
McNamara, Koster & Co, 212-218 S Penn. (See right top lines and p 9.)
Over Ewald, 240-246 S Penn.

FOUNDERS AND MACHINISTS.

Capital City Steam Boiler and Sheet Iron Works, 207-209 S Illinois. (See adv in Boilermakers.)
Dean Bros' Steam Pump Works, 1st near cor Senate av. (See adv p 3.)

A. METZGER AGENCY ESTABLISHED 1863. L-O-A-N-S

LAMBERT GAS & GASOLINE ENGINE CO.
ANDERSON, IND. GAS ENGINES FOR ALL PURPOSES.

Ellis & Helfenberger, 162-168 S Senate av. (See right bottom lines.)
Haugh-Noelke Iron Wks, cor Palmer and J M & I R R.
Hetherington & Berner Co, 19-27 W South.
Indianapolis Bolt and Machine Works, 122-126 Kentucky av. (See adv in Elevator Mnfrs.)
Indianapolis Foundry Co, Judge Harding s of Washington.
Kennedy & Connaughton, 207-209 S Illinois. (See adv in Boilermakers.)
Leonard & Thomas, 171 River av (W I).
Langsenkamp Bros' Brass Works, 90-92 E Georgia. (See adv p 7.)
McNamara, Koster & Co, 212-218 S Penn. (See right top lines and p 9.)
Nordyke & Marmon Co, crossing I & V Ry and Morris (W I). (See inside back cover.)
Peerless Foundry Co, 70 Meek.
Pioneer Brass Works, 110-116 S Penn.
Rockwood Mnfg Co, 176-190 S Penn.
Sinker-Davis Co The, 112-150 S Missouri.
Specialty Manufacturing Co, 193 S Meridian. (See adv opp Photographers.)

***FOUNTAIN PEN MANUFACTURERS.**

Allison James A, 5 Stewart Pl.

***FRAMES AND MOULDINGS.**

Lieber H Co The, 33 S Meridian. (See right top cor cards.)

FREIGHT LINES.

See Transportation Lines.

***FRESCO PAINTERS.**

Pressler Guido R, 325 N Liberty. (See right bottom cor cards.)
Shaw Decorating Co, 106-108 N Meridian. (See adv in Wall Paper.)

FRUITS.

Allison Wm J, 266½ W Washington.
Amick George L, 143 E Mkt House.
Asmus Louis, 2 Louisiana.
Beard Alfred E, E Mkt House.
Blue Bros, cor Illinois and 38th.
Catalani Frank, n e cor Washington and Illinois.
Clark Luther, 73 E Mkt House.
Corci Peter, 49 S Illinois.
Delorenzo Dominick, 90 E Mkt House.
DeMartine Antonio A, 124 S Illinois.
Dottolo Frederick, 41 E Mkt House.
Duncan Robert, 119 E Mkt House.
Dunlea Arthur, E Mkt House.
Eaton Obadiah, 96 E Mkt House.
Fieder Samuel, E Mkt House.
Foppiana John, 11 S Illinois.
Fosatti John, 85 S Illinois.
Gemmer Wm, E Mkt House.
Glick Henry, 47 E Mkt House and 292 Virginia av.
Goodwin Harry E, 214 Blackford.
Gregori Mansuel, 76 S Illinois.
Hallett Andrew J, 55 E Mkt House.
Hart Charles H, 49 E Mkt House.
Herman Samuel, 215 W Washington.
Hess Charles W, E Mkt House.
Hoosier Packing Co, 183 W Pearl.
Indiana Fruit Co, 66 E Market.
Jardini Paul, 38 E Mkt House.
Juliano Antonio, 287 E Washington.
Keehn Hiram W, 99 E Mkt House.
Larossa Frank, 67 E Mkt House.
Loscent Joseph F, 217 W Washington.
Ludlow John N, E Mkt House.
Mannalla Michael A, 133 W Washington.
Mascari Joseph, 23 E Mkt House.
Mascari Paul, E Mkt House.
Meo Antonio, 91 E Mkt House and 518 Virginia av.
Miceli Rosario, 95 E Mkt House.
Miceli Salvadore, 81 E Mkt House.
Minardo Joseph, 19 E Mkt House.
Montani F & I, 5 Mass av.
Morris Wolf, E Mkt House.
Nolen Joseph G, 213 W Washington.
Palma Joseph, 104½ E Mkt House.
Parker George W, 219 W Washington.
Patterson David H, E Mkt House.
Richardson Hiram V, E Mkt House.
Scampamerto Vincenzo, 143 Mass av.
Selby Francis M, 151 Hoyt av.
Shea Henry W, 276 W Washington.
Sherer Frank P, E Mkt House.
Stanton Elwood, 97 E Mkt House.
Stout Alice, 110 E Mkt House.
Straffa John J, 69 E Mkt House.
Van Pelt Ira S, E Mkt House.
Vito Vincent, 106 S Illinois.
Ziegler Louis C, 182 S Illinois.

***FUEL.**

Edwardsport Coal and Mining Co, 42-43 When Bldg. (See left side lines and adv in Coal Miners.)

***FUEL GAS.**

Otto Gas Engine Works The, Builders' Exchange, 35 E Ohio. (See left bottom lines.)

FUNERAL DIRECTORS.

Bennett Warren G, 20 Michigan (H).
Blanchard Frank A, 99 N Delaware.
Britton Charles O, 51 Indiana av, Ryan blk.
Collier & Murphy, 59 W Maryland.
Donovan Benjamin C, 40 Division (W I).
Flanner & Buchanan, 172 N Illinois.
Grinsteiner Bros, 276 E Market.
Herrmann George, 26 S Delaware.
Irvin & Adams, 97 N Illinois and 37 W Ohio.
Kregelo D & Son, 69 N Illinois.
McKinley Bros, 470 Virginia av.
Renihan, Long & Blackwell, 71-73 W Market.
Tutewiler Henry W, 72 W Market. (See left bottom lines.)
Vehling Henry C, 390 Virginia av.
Whitsett Charles T, 123-125 N Delaware.
Wiese Christian, 39 N East.
Willis Cassius M C, 184 Indiana av.

***FUR GOODS.**

Ayres L S & Co, 33-37 W Washington.

BICYCLES $5 DOWN. $5 MONTHLY. Best Terms. WHEELMEN'S CO 31 W. OHIO ST. LONG DIS 1855.

J. H. TECKENBROCK | Grilles, Fretwork and Wood Carpets
94 EAST SOUTH STREET.

FIDELITY MUTUAL LIFE PHILADELPHIA, PA. A. H. COLLINS { General Agent, 52-53 Baldwin Block.

Edwardsport Coal & Mining Co. Rooms 42 and 43 When Building.

FURNACE MANUFACTURERS.

Bailey L Foster, mngr, 33 W Market.
Gardner Joseph, 37-41 Kentucky av. (See left top cor cards.)
Kruse & Dewenter, 223-225 E Washington.
Pursell Peter M, 30 Mass av.
Stumpf & Thiele, 19-21 N Capitol av.
Turner Zephyr Furnace and Stove Co, 94-100 Kentucky av and 81 S Senate av.
Weis Felix, 269 English av.

***FURNACES—HOT AIR.**

Abel & Doyle, 31 Indiana av. (See adv p 5.)
Laing Samuel, 72-74 E Court. (See left side lines.)

***FURNITURE CRATERS AND PACKERS.**

Anderson Mads P, 381-385 Cedar.
Meck Transfer Co, 7 Monument Pl. (See adv in Transfer Companies.)

FURNITURE MANUFACTURERS AND DEALERS.

(See also Cabinet Makers.)

Advance Mnfg Co, n e cor Sheldon and Pike.
Aetna Cabinet Co, 168 W Georgia.
Anderson Mads P, 381-385 Cedar.
Badger Furniture Co, 75-77 E Washington and 20-24 Virginia av.
Baker Bros, 141 Mass av.
Bernstein Joseph, 187 W Washington.
Boone Frank M, 141 E Washington.
Born Valentine, 62 E Washington.
Brade Otto, 486 Virginia av.
Clune Michael, 700 S Meridian.
Cummings Richard, 25 Madison av.
Davis Lambert D, 300 W Washington.
Davis Lewis B, 405 Virginia av.
Elder Wm L, 43-45 S Meridian.
Emrich Furniture Co The, 190 W Morris.
Feeney Furniture and Stove Co, 76-78 W Washington.
Geyer & Haehl, 682 Charles.
Griffin Isom, 180 Indiana av.
Haueisen & Hartmann, 163-169 E Washington. (See right bottom cor cards.)
Hutchinson Albert, 178 E Washington.
Indianapolis Cabinetmakers' Union, n w cor Market and Pine.
Indianapolis Church Furniture Co, s e cor Shelby and Martin.
Indianapolis Lounge Co, cor Hanway and J M & I R R.
Iske Bros, 105 E Washington.
Jensen Andrew, 567 Virginia av.
Killinger George W, s w cor Market and Missouri. (See adv in Saloons.)
Koch Christian, 198 E Washington.
Koch John, 464 Virginia av.
Koesters Charles G, 456 S Meridian.
Kotteman Wm, 89-91 E Washington. (See adv right top lines.)
Kramer Mnfg Co, s e cor Merrill and New Jersey.
Lauter Herman, Washington and N Judge Harding (W I).
Laycock T B Mnfg Co, n w cor 1st and canal.
Lunt J W & Co, 29½ N Penn.
McDougall G P & Son, 701-705 S Meridian.
Madden Thomas, Son & Co, English av and Big Four Ry.
Messenger W Horndon, 101 E Washington and 13, 15 and 17 S Delaware. (See left bottom lines.)
North Side Furniture Co, 72 Indiana av.
Ott L W Mnfg Co, s w cor Morris and Capitol av.
Paetz & Buennagel, 451 N Alabama.
Parker's Furniture Store, 175-179 W Washington.
People's Outfitting Co, 71-73 W Washington.
Pettis Dry Goods Co, 25-33 E Washington.
Randall & McKee, 224 Ramsey av.
Resoner Wm L, 67 W Washington.
Rupert Frank H, 59 W Washington.
Sander & Recker, 115-119 E Washington.
Stone James I, 69 E Washington.
Thompson Lewis C, 293 Christian av.
Twente Wm F, 219 Mass av.
United States Lounge Mnfg Co, 128-134 Ft Wayne av and 25-27 N Illinois.
Western Furniture Co, Madison av opp S Delaware.
Willig Charles, 79 W Washington.
Wood Ornament Co The, rear 544 W Addison (N I). (See adv.)

The Wood Ornament Co.,
MANUFACTURERS OF
ARTISTIC FURNITURE,
Drug Fixtures and Show Cases.
Telephone 1736. North Indianapolis, Ind.

World's Fair, 101-113 W Washington.

***FURNITURE MOVERS.**

Hogan Transfer and Storage Co The, s w cor Washington and Illinois and cor Delaware and Georgia. (See left top lines and adv in Transfer Companies.)
Meck Transfer Co, 7 Monument Pl. (See adv in Transfer Companies.)
Indianapolis Storage and Transfer Co, 370-372 S Delaware. (See back cover.)

***FURNITURE REPAIRERS.**

Crosby Michael, 351-353 S Meridian.
Fetters & Smock, 124 Mass av.

FURS.

Block Wm H Co The, 7-9 E Washington. (See right top and bottom lines.)
Kaufman Solomon, 21½ W Washington.
McDonald James R, 246 S Meridian.
Ross G W & Son, 26 E South.
Wohlfeld Julius, 11½ W Washington.

GALVANIZED IRON CORNICE MNFRS.

Ensey O B, cor 6th and Illinois. (See left bottom cor cards.)

SUPERIOR BITUMINOUS COAL For Steam and Domestic . . Purposes . .

ROOFING MATERIAL C. ZIMMERMAN & SONS SLATE AND GRAVEL ROOFERS, 19 SOUTH EAST STREET.

DRIVEN WELLS And Second Water Wells and Pumps of all kinds at CHARLES KRAUSS', 42 S. PENN. ST., TEL. 465. REPAIRING NEATLY DONE.

If You are not Satisfied with Your Laundry Work Give Us a Trial. ERTEL STEAM LAUNDRY 26 and 28 N. Senate Avenue. Telephone 1089.

Humphreys M E & Co, rear 119 S East.
Laing Samuel, 72-74 E Court. (See left side lines.)
McWorkman Willard, 930 W Washington. (See left top cor cards.)
Purcell Peter M, 30 Mass av.

***GARDENERS' SUPPLIES.**

Huntington & Page, 78 E Market. (See adv p 5.)

GARMENT MNFRS—LADIES' AND CHILDREN'S.

Gem Garment Co, 17-23 W Pearl.

GAS COMPANIES.

Consumers' Gas Trust Co, 43-49 N Capitol av.
Indianapolis Gas Co The, n e cor Penn and Maryland.
Indiana Natural and Illuminating Gas Co, 49 S Penn.
Manufacturers' Natural Gas Co, 75 Monument pl.

***GAS ENGINEERS.**

Lambert Gas and Gasoline Engine Co, Anderson, Ind. (See right top lines.)
Otto Gas Engine Works The, Builders' Exchange, 35 E Ohio. (See left bottom lines.)

***GAS ENGINES.**

Lambert Gas and Gasoline Engine Co, Anderson, Ind. (See right top lines.)
Otto Gas Engine Works The, Builders' Exchange, 35 E Ohio. (See left bottom lines.)
White & Middleton, W H Whitney State Agt, 74 Virginia av.

***GAS FITTERS.**

(See also Plumbers, Steam and Gas Fitters.)
Boyd Alonzo, 816 N Illinois. (See adv in Plumbers.)
Farrell J S & Co, 84 N Illinois. (See left bottom cor cards.)
Kirkhoff Bros, 102-104 S Penn. (See left top cor cards.)
Meikel Charles W, 96-98 E New York. (See right bottom lines.)

GAS GENERATORS.

Miller Steam and Gas Generator Co, 26 Kentucky av.

***GAS GRATES.**

Lilly Jno M, 78-80 Mass av. (See adv p 8.)

GAS METER MANUFACTURERS.

Sprague H H Co, 30-40 W South.

***GAS REGULATORS.**

Whitney Williston H, 74 Virginia av.

***GAS AND ELECTRIC LIGHT FIXTURES.**

Farrell J S & Co, 84 N Illinois. (See left bottom cor cards.)
Meikel Charles W, 96-98 E New York. (See right bottom lines.)

***GAS AND GASOLINE ELECTRIC LIGHTING PLANTS.**

Lambert Gas and Gasoline Engine Co, Anderson, Ind. (See right top lines.)

***GAS AND GASOLINE ENGINES.**

Lambert Gas and Gasoline Engine Co, Anderson, Ind. (See right top lines.)
Otto Gas Engine Works The, Builders' Exchange, 35 E Ohio. (See left bottom lines.)

***GASOLINE.**

Lambert Gas and Gasoline Engine Co, Anderson, Ind. (See right top lines.)
Otto Gas Engine Works The, Builders' Exchange, 35 E Ohio. (See left bottom lines.)

***GASOLINE ENGINES.**

Lambert Gas and Gasoline Engine Co, Anderson, Ind. (See right top lines.)
Otto Gas Engine Works The, Builders' Exchange, 35 E Ohio. (See left bottom lines.)

***GATE MANUFACTURERS.**

Toops Emory D, 1201 N Penn.

GENTS' FURNISHING GOODS.

(See also Clothing.)
Adams Bert B, 13 N Illinois.
Ault P B & Co, 38 E Washington.
Barkalow Albert V, 20 Pembroke Arcade.
Block Wm H Co The, 7-9 E Washington. (See right top and bottom lines.)
Brill Albert, 314 E Washington.
Gelman Eli, 227 W Washington.
Iglick Rose, 298 S West.
Krause Harry W, 285 Mass av.
Krause Reinhold, 127 E Washington.
Krauss Moses, 604 N Senate av.
Krauss Paul H, 44-46 E Washington.
Lefkowitz Jacob, 166 E Washington.
Leonard E L & Co, 69 S Illinois.
Miller Reinhold A jr, 7 S Illinois.
Sanders Henry L, 18 Indiana av.
Sanders H L & Son, 14 E Mkt House.
Shaw & Vinson, 55 N Penn.
Singer Jacob, 224 E Washington.
Stille Henry E, 30 Hill av.
Whelden Joseph E 85 N Penn.
When Clothing Store, 26-40 N Penn. (See right top cor cards.)

***GLASS.**

(See also Paints, Oils and Glass.)
Aldag Paint and Varnish Co The, 222 E Washington. (See adv in Paints and Oils.)
American Plate Glass Co, 65-68 When bldg.
Androvette Glass Co The, 6 Odd Fellows' blk.
Black John, 159 Mass av.
Burdsal A Co The, 34-36 S Meridian. (See right bottom cor cards.)
Hamilton Harry E, 18 Pembroke Arcade.
Williams Charles C, 149 S Meridian.

ELLIS & HELFENBERGER Manufacturers of IRON and WIRE FENCES 162-170 S. SENATE AVE. TEL. 958.

THE HOGAN TRANSFER AND STORAGE COMP'Y
Household Goods and Pianos Moved—Packed—Stored...... Baggage and Package Express Machinery and Safes a Specialty Cor. Washington and Illinois Sts. TELEPHONE No. 675.

The Central Rubber & Supply Co. Hose, Belting, Packing, Clothing, Druggists' Sundries, Bicycle Tires, Cotton Hose, Etc. New York Belting & Packing Co., L't'd. 79 S. ILLINOIS ST., INDIANAPOLIS, IND. PHONE 92

***GLASS—ART, STAINED AND ORNAMENTAL.**

Burdsal A Co The, 34-36 S Meridian. (See right bottom cor cards.)
Interstate Art Glass Co, Henry W Rudolf Genl Mngr, 77-81 N Delaware.

***GLASS—CATHEDRAL.**

Burdsal A Co The, 34-36 S Meridian. (See right bottom cor cards.)

***GLASS MANUFACTURERS' SUPPLIES.**

Moffat & Co, 402 Lemcke Bldg. (See adv p 9.)

***GLASS—PLATE.**

Burdsal A Co The, 34-36 S Meridian. (See right bottom cor cards.)

***GLASS—WINDOW.**

Burdsal A Co The, 34-36 S Meridian. (See right bottom cor cards.)

***GLASSWARE—BOHEMIAN.**

Mayer Charles & Co, 29-31 W Washington. (See adv opp p 615.)

***GLAZIERS' SUPPLIES.**

Burdsal A Co The, 34-36 S Meridian. (See right bottom cor cards.)

***GLOVES.**

Block Wm H Co The, 7-9 E Washington. (See right top and bottom lines.)
Tucker Hannibal S, 10 E Washington.

***GLUE—ALL KINDS.**

Burdsal A Co The, 34-36 S Meridian. (See right bottom cor cards.)
Vonnegut Clemens, 184-186 E Washington. (See left bottom lines.)

GLUE MANUFACTURERS.

Kingan & Co, McIntyre and West.

GRAIN DEALERS.

Bales Solomon D, Union Stock Yards (W I).
Bassett & Co, 33 Board of Trade bldg.
Brown Eli P & Co, 25 Board of Trade bldg.
Faught & Co, 18½ N Meridian.
Foster R S & Co, 47 Board of Trade bldg.
Hammer Charles L, 68 E Wabash.
Hixson Walter B, 49 Board of Trade bldg.
Johnson C H & Co, 16 Board of Trade bldg.
Kinney Horace E, 20-22 Board of Trade bldg.
Louis Lyman W, 13 Board of Trade bldg.
Minor Benjamin B, 18 Board of Trade bldg.
Osterman & Cooper, 17 Board of Trade bldg.
Overman W B & Co, 12-14 Board of Trade bldg.
Rush Frederick P & Co, 10 Board of Trade bldg.
Scott Robert F, 45 Board of Trade bldg.
Shotwell Charles A, 18 Board of Trade bldg.
Thomson Alexander W, 34 Board of Trade bldg.
Weaver O D & Co, 21 Board of Trade bldg.

GRAIN ELEVATORS.

Indianapolis Elevator Co, 11 Board of Trade bldg.

***GRANITE.**

Diener August, 243 E Washington; Branch Works opp east entrance Crown Hill Cemetery. (See adv front edge and opp Monuments.)

***GRAPHOPHONES.**

Indiana Graphophone Co, 49-52 When Bldg. (See adv in Talking Machines.)

***GRAVEL ROOFERS.**

Smither Henry C, 169 W Maryland. (See adv opp Roofing Material.)
Smither T F, 151 W Maryland. (See right side lines.)
Zimmerman C & Sons, 19-21 S East. (See left bottom lines.)

GRILLE AND FRET WORKS.

Baumhofer Bros, 163 Lambert (W I).
Spiegel Henry L, 316 E Vermont.
Teckenbrock John H, 94 E South. (See right bottom lines and adv in Painters.)

GROCERS—WHOLESALE.

Indianapolis Fancy Grocery Co, 60 S Penn.
Kothe, Wells & Bauer, 128-130 S Meridian.
Krag-Reynolds Co, 31-33 E Maryland.
Moore John L, 124-126 S Meridian.
O'Connor M & Co, 47-49 S Meridian.
Perry J C & Co, 26-30 W Georgia.
Schnull & Co, 60-68 S Meridian.
Schrader Christian A, 74-78 S Penn.
Severin, Ostermeyer & Co, 51-53 S Meridian.
Stout George W, 107-109 S Meridian.
Syfers, McBride & Co, 78-80 S Meridian.

GROCERS—RETAIL.

Alexander Wm H, 451 W 1st.
Algeo Samuel, 49 Clifford av.
Allen Lucy, 300 River av (W I).
Allison John C, 1411 Annette (N I).
Amick Louisa J, 1202 Morris (W I).
Anderson Addison L, 113 Ft Wayne av.
Anderson Samuel, 97 Maple.
Ankenbrock C Wm, 326 Clifford av.
Armitstead James C, 36 Malott av.
Arnholter Henry jr, 564 Virginia av.
Arnold Wm A E, 534 Park av.
Artist Everett D, n s Sutherland 1 e of Rural (B).
Austin & Son, 852 E Washington.
Avery Guy C, 13 E Mkt House.
Ayers James C, n e cor Washington and Denny.
Backemier Charles H, 429 W Pratt.
Baggott Thomas, 479 W Michigan.
Bailey James L, 326 S Olive.
Bailie Samuel F, 32 Agnes.
Baker Doras J, n w cor Washington and Crawfordsville rd (M J).
Baker Elmer A, 303 Shelby.
Baker Robert A, 71 Pendleton av (B).
Baldus Caroline, 42 Pendleton av.
Balz Frederick, 400 N West.
Barnum Wm W, 200 E Market.
Barthel Bros, 540 E Washington.
Bauer Conrad, 148 N Capitol av.

OTTO GAS ENGINES | BUILDERS' EXCHANGE S. W. Cor. Ohio and Penn. Telephone 535.

Becker & Son Charles Becker Jacob Becker Jr. Merchant Tailors. 21 N. Penn St. Tel. 934

Baumann Laura, 449 Columbia av.
Bechert Ferdinand W, 296 S West.
Beck Henry, 280 S Olive.
Beck Otto C, 94 Indiana av.
Becker Julius D, 679 S East.
Beckerich Bros, 648 College av.
Behr Lena, 139 Cornell av.
Behymer Frank, 302 Yandes.
Bell Miletus F, 349 Yandes.
Bernhart John L, 38 Dunlop.
Beskin Henry, 118 Indiana av.
Biebinger Jacob, n s 30th 2 e of Illinois (M).
Bistline Henry E, 187 S Illinois.
Blackwell & Gates, n e cor N Delaware and 10th.
Bloemker Ernst W, 602 E New York.
Bloom Samuel, 28 S Station (B).
Bloomer Lewis H, 68 N Delaware.
Bogert Charles C, 26 Minerva.
Bolander Samuel P, 398 College av.
Bolin George, 101 Shepard (W I).
Bolin Margaret E, 1173 E Washington.
Bolin Roger M, 552 S West.
Bolser John W, 113 River av (W I).
Bonke Robert R, 152 Church.
Boring Jennie, 400 W 1st.
Born Frederick, 3 Shelby.
Bornemeier Herman, 157 High.
Boyce John E, 265 Lincoln la.
Boylan Thomas, 53 Church.
Bradshaw Wm A, 2 N Brightwood av (B).
Brandes Herman F, s e cor Madeira and Prospect.
Brandt Christian F W, 543 E Washington.
Brattain John W, 414 W New York.
Brennan Patrick, 326 S State av.
Bretz Adam, 106 S Illinois.
Brinkman Anton C, 765 S East.
Brown Helena C, 1310 N Capitol av.
Brown Henry L, 356 Indiana av.
Brown Wm L, 125 Lynn av (W I).
Buddenbaum Bros, 2 Fletcher av.
Buddenbaum & Heller, 327 Prospect.
Burgess Alvin B, 252 N Noble.
Burgess Benjamin F, 143 Newman.
Burnett Bros, 138 Michigan (H).
Burnett Levi M, 71 Minerva.
Burns Kate, 184 Fayette.
Buschmann August, 148-150 College av.
Buschmann Wm & Co, 192-200 Ft Wayne av.
Buser Charles O, 250 Yandes.
Bushong Deniza, 225 W Walnut.
Caldwell Benjamin F, 188 W 7th.
Caldwell James, 65 E 14th.
Callahan John, 152 Johnson (W I).
Callahan John P, 109 Lexington av.
Callahan John R, 101 S Reisner (W I).
Callis Joseph, 183 Elizabeth.
Calvin Otha F, 203 W Washington.
Campbell Chester E, 59 Howard.
Camphausen Louisa, 53 River av (W I).
Carr Hannah, 296 S Missouri.
Chamberlin Hannah J, 242 Oliver av (W I).
Cheely & Son, s e cor Washington and Addison (M J).
Christensen Hans, 80 Tremont av (H).
Clark Charles L, 4 N Station (B).
Clay Andrew J, 549 Shelby.
Clem Aaron, 86 Christian av.
Clifton Benjamin, 355 Indiana av.
Clifton C W & Co, 80 Ft Wayne av.
Coen John J, 50 S Capitol av.
Cohen Marcus, 127 Eddy.
Compton & Rice, 49 Mass av.
Condron Michael, 124 N Belmont av (H).
Connor John, 362 S West.
Cook Frederick W jr, 593 Madison av.
Cook John, 899 Morris (W I).
Cook & Nackenhorst, 622 Virginia av.
Cornet Bros, 500 College av.
Costello Jeremiah, 401 S Capitol av.
Cotton Isaac M, 1158 E Washington.
Coval Bros, 61 S West.
Crabill Bros, 400 Talbott av.
Crabtree Lovell B, 352 Mass av.
Craft & Payne, 426 W Udell (N I).
Craig & Co, 75 Oliver av (W I).
Cramer Wm E, 59 E Mkt House.
Cranor Andrew J, n s Vorster av 1 w of Belt R R (M P).
Cron Adam, 449 Newman.
Cross Amelia M, 140 Spring.
Crouch Addison M, 31 Clifford av.
Cullen Joseph A, 120 Oliver av (W I).
Cummings Matthew M, 62 N Delaware.
Dailey Harry C, 56 Kentucky av.
Dammeyer Bros, 247 E Washington.
Dannie Catherine A, 207 Davidson.
Darter James K P, n w cor Illinois and 30th (M).
Davis Benjamin N, 526 N Senate av.
Day Walter S, 158 W Washington.
Delaney Hannah M, 301 S West.
Derry Edward H, 1381 W Washington (M J).
DeVersey Elizabeth, 697 S Meridian.
DeWitt Wm L, 877 Cornell av.
Dickert Norbert A, 271 Union.
Diefenbach Jacob, 210 W 1st.
Dillinger John, 31 Cooper.
Diettman F G & Co, 750 N Capitol av.
Dodd James A, 184 Hill av.
Doenges Casper, 436 S Meridian.
Donahue Jeremiah, 249 W McCarty.
Donlon Ellen, 901 N Senate av.
Dougherty Albert U, 28 Meikel.
Downie Samuel C, 289 Prospect.
Doyle E X & Co, 401 Mass av.
Dugan Martin M, 571 W Michigan.
Dunmeyer F & Co, 15 E Mkt House.
Dunn Clement T, 148 Brookside av.
Dunn Joseph, 297 S Illinois.
Eagle John H, 340 N Delaware.
Earhart George W, 188 S William (W I).
Earhart Wm I, 412 W North.
Eck Teterick, 62 Michigan (H).
Edwards Jerome B, 444 Mass av.
Egan & Son, 53 Holmes av (H).
Egelhoff Margaret, s s Prospect 3 e of Madeira.
Egelus Frederick W, 49 N Brightwood av (B).
Elliott Bros, 255 Keystone av.
Elstun Emma, 1027 E Washington.
Elwarner Wm, 503 E 7th.
Emden Sophia, 250 E Ohio.
Emrich Jacob A, n e cor Lafayette and Crawfordsville rds.
Erath Frank X, 398 Bellefontaine.
Erber Frances, 81 Louise.
Erbrich August, 147 Fletcher av.
Erhart Barbara, 681 Madison av.
Essig Thomas, 7 Roseline.
Essigke Wm F, 129 Hadley av (W I).
Evans Isabell E, n e cor Grandview and Belmont avs (H).
Feller John, 33 Harris av (M J).
Felton Sylvander, 179 W 12th.
Fenneman Edward W, 299 N Senate av.
Finn Daniel W, 501 S Capitol av.
Fisher George P, 453 Central av.
Fisher James W, 59 Beacon.
Fitzgerald Anna, 182 Meek.
Flaherty Michael O, 349 Fletcher av.
Flaskamp Fred, 126 Hillside av, cor 8th.
Flickinger Wendel, cor Sugar Grove and Miller avs (M P).

SALISBURY & STANLEY OFFICE, STORE AND BANK FIXTURES.
and Builders. Repairing of all kinds done on short notice. 177 Clinton St., Indianapolis, Ind. Tel 99

LUMBER Sash and Doors | BALKE & KRAUSS CO., Corner Market and Missouri Sts.

Friedgen Has the BEST PATENT LEATHER SHOES AT LOWEST PRICES. 19 North Pennsylvania St.

SAMUEL LAING : HOT AIR FURNACES 72 AND 74 EAST COURT STREET.

Grocers—Retail—Continued.
Foltz Anthony, 38 S Reisner (W I).
Forrest & Coolman, 353 W New York.
Foss Bros, Wells opp C C C & St L Depot (N I).
Fowler Anna J, 226 Howard.
Fox Lawrence P, 2 Carlos.
Franklin Moses, 301 Fayette.
French Eugene R, n s Michigan av 4 e of Sharpe av (W).
Frick Charles, 752 N Senate av.
Friedrichs Louis, 75 W McCarty.
Fritsch Joseph, 438 Clifford av.
Fuerst Charles J, 479 S New Jersey.
Fuerst Joseph F, 573 S Meridian.
Fulton Wm B, s w cor Cornell av and 22d.
Furgason John A, 306 N Illinois.
Galloway George E, 290 E Washington.
Gaston Edward, 49-53 Kentucky av.
Geisel Jennie, s e cor Clifford av and Rural.
Geltmeier Henry, 200 Orange.
Gemmer Wesley, 37 E Mkt House.
George Isaac L, 826 N Illinois.
Gibbons Charles W, 499 W McLene (N I).
Gibbons James, 241 W McCarty.
Giberson Lewis W, 951 W Michigan.
Gibson James W, 656 N West.
Gillum Granville N, w s Denny 1 n of Washington.
Gilman Benjamin, 276 S Illinois.
Given John A, 30 Indiana av.
Goe Margaretta C, n w cor Central av and P C C & St L Ry (I).
Goldman David, 282 S Illinois and 350 S Meridian.
Gordon Edward R, 852 LaSalle.
Gottwalles Joseph M, 122 Patterson.
Graf Gottfried, 228 E Morris.
Graham Wm R, 106 S Linden.
Graves Thomas, 524 S Brookside av.
Gray Cyrus E, 201 English av.
Griffin May M, 211 W McCarty.
Gross & Co, 243 Mass av.
Grubb Norval D, 118 Oliver av (W I).
Gunter Wm M, s w cor Washington and Lake avs (I).
Haeberle Wm A, n w cor Brookside av and Jupiter.
Hagedorn Henry, 564 Morris (W I).
Hagelskamp George, 50 Prospect.
Hahn Adam, 113 S William (W I).
Halstead James H, 133 Martindale av.
Hamill Patrick, 404 W Washington.
Hamilton John M, 60 Fountain.
Hamilton S & Co, 9 Lynn.
Hammel George J, 110-112 Mass av, 215-217 N Alabama.
Hammer Christian, 251 Yandes.
Hammond & Pasquier, 316 Virginia av.
Haneman John F, 186 Hillside av.
Hansen Jacob, 150 Spann av.
Hansen Peter, 258 E McCarty.
Hansen Soren, 768 S East.
Hardey & Gausepohl, 150 Madison av.
Hardy Niles, 296 Howard (W I).
Hardy Samuel E, 891 Mass av.
Harrah Thomas C, 98 Kappus (W I).
Harrigan Cornelius A, 457 E Georgia.
Hartmann August, 412 N West.
Harwood James W, 2 Howard.
Hatton George W, 179 Elm.
Hauck Edward L, 441 N Illinois.
Hawes Charles L, 115 Birch av (W I).
Hawkins Jesse F, 50 S Belmont (W I).
Hedges Wm H, 1061 W Washington.
Hedrick George W, 199 Shelby.
Heidt George, 442 Indiana av.
Heller Wm J, 149 Oliver av (W I).
Helt & Trotter, 151 River av (W I).
Henderson Mary D, 143 E 7th.
Hergt Frederick W, 119 Prospect.
Herman Henry S, 59 W Morris.
Hermanny Andrew, 150 Blake.
Hervey Gilford P, 533 W Addison (N I).
Hess Casper, 507 Madison av.
Hilgemeier Christian H, 360 Shelby.
Hinners Christian T, 301 N Pine.
Hinshaw Catharine F, 510 S West.
Hirth Bridget, 1020 W Washington.
Hirwatz Charles, 432 S Capitol av.
Hoban Hopkins E, 384 Dillon.
Hodson Joseph, 452 Newman.
Hofacker Gottlob, 73 N Liberty.
Hoffman Alva R, 211 Christian av.
Hoffman Wm H, 1650 N Capitol av.
Hoffmark Simeon, 473 E St Clair.
Hofherr Frederick C, 505 Madison av.
Hofmann Philip H, n w cor Lawrence and Rural.
Hofmeister Henry, 75 Hill av.
Holland Edward, 428 S West.
Hollowell Calvin L, 603 E Washington.
Holt Hiram S, 430 National rd.
Holtzman Henry A, 186 Shelby.
Homuth Edward, 564 E St Clair.
Hoover Perry, 235 Cornell av.
Hoover Wm W, 408 Indiana av.
Hosbrook Frank, cor Prospect and S State av.
Houppert Frank, 101 Meek.
House Ernest L, 201 Columbia av.
Hoy Joseph, 368 Blake.
Hubert George C, 152 Martindale av.
Huffman Charles W, 1-3 Hillside av.
Hughes John A, 939 Mass av.
Humphrey John W, 314 Indiana av.
Jackson Maud, 231 S Delaware.
Jacobi & Maass, 397-399 S Delaware.
Jacobs Piety, 76 Oliver av (W I).
James & McLain, 537 E Ohio.
Janes Frank E, 107-113 N Delaware.
Jeffers Charles F, 2 S Belmont (W I).
Jelf Isaac L, 151 Martindale av.
John Paul R, 547 S West.
Johnson Elhanon, 502 W Addison (N I).
Johnson Virgil H, 109 E Mkt House.
Johnson W Frank, 145 Buchanan.
Johnson & Reichardt, 421 N East.
Jones Dennis G, 1200 Northwestern av (N I).
Jones Elijah, 21 Sheffield av (H).
Jones George D & Co, 43 E North.
Jones Hester C, 812 W Washington.
Jones Thomas E, 43 Torbet.
Jones Wm E & Co 52 Marion av (W I).
Justice & Warren, 1547 N Illinois.
Kaesberg Mathias, 70 High.
Kahan Morris, 231 W Washington.
Kahl Charles, 373 W Michigan.
Kahle Frederick C, 607 W Michigan.
Kaiser August, 459 Sheldon.
Karibo Frederick, 63 N Brightwood av (B).
Kaser David G, 494 W North.
Kashner Alonzo R, 578 E 7th.
Keers George W, 532 W North.
Kehlbeck Herman F, 195 E South.
Keller Robert, 570-578 S East.
Kelly James M, 201 Bellefontaine.
Kerr John F, 98 Woodlawn av.
Kerz Nickolaus, 591 W Michigan.
Kidd John D, 3 Holmes av (H).
Kiefer Valentine, 191 Indiana av.
Kimmel Albert A, 307 E 8th.
King Bernard, 168 Elizabeth.
King Warren, 495 W Addison (N I).
Kinister Wm H, 100 Paca.

WEDDING CAKE BOXES · SULLIVAN & MAHAN 41 W. Pearl St.

DIAMOND WALL PLASTER { Telephone 1410 BUILDERS' EXCHANGE.

Best Work. Prompt Delivery. } THE HOME LAUNDRY 197 S. ILLINOIS ST. TEL. 1769. { Collars and Cuffs our Specialty.

Kinney Otto, 287 Coburn.
Kirk Joseph H, 448 W North.
Kiser Harter, 152 N East.
Klein Jacob, 130 Davidson.
Klingensmith Reuben, 182 Sheffield av (H).
Koehler Louis C, 138 Buchanan.
Koehler Wm F, 346 Clifford av.
Kolb Wm F, 151 Davidson.
Koplan Solomon, 143 Eddy.
Kreitlein George F, mngr, 250 W Washington.
Krome August, n e cor Market and Delaware.
Kuhlman Charles A, 72 Newman.
Kuhn Charles J Co, 49 N Illinois.
Laatz Henry, 94 Dougherty.
Lahman August, 505 N West.
Lange & Son, 104 Bismarck av (H).
Langsdale Rebecca A, 295 E Georgia.
Lawrence Arthur V, 175 Howard.
Leck & Co, 54 W 7th.
Lee Henry H, 34 W Washington, 250 Virginia av, 7-9 N Penn and 1 Madison av.
Lehr Louis, 475 S Illinois.
Lensmann Henry J, 562 Shelby.
Leser John jr, 331 W Morris.
Lewis A & Co, 401 N Alabama.
Lewis Wm H, 203 Bellefontaine.
Lichtenauer Fred, 609 W Washington.
Lichtenberg John, 552 S Capitol av.
Lichtenberg Wm E, 300 E Ohio.
Liening Anton, 160 Keystone av.
Lindemann Frank, 210 E Washington.
Linton & Co, 1551 N Illinois.
Lippert Margaret, 301 S East.
Little Bros, 1202 E Washington.
Logan James H, 1149 N Illinois.
Lohrman C G & Son, 400 N Senate av.
Love Wm, 150 Mass av.
Low James A, 155 Ft Wayne av.
Lowe Enoch, 16 Minkner.
Lueth John H, 501 S West.
Lydy Alexander M, 94 S Belmont av (W I).
McAndrews Mary, 16 McCauley.
McAree Owen, 249 English av.
McCann Robert A, 44 Indiana av.
McCaslin & Cavanaugh, 502 N West.
McCauley Wm A, 120 Huron.
McCune & Co, 75 N Penn.
McGary Mary E, 201 Michigan av.
McKenzie Thomas W, 502 S West.
McKiernan Warren, 397 W 2d.
McNerney Thomas, 110 Hadley av (W I).
Maass Henry C, 451 S Delaware.
Madden James H, 151 Virginia av and 750 E Washington.
Magel Anna E, 70 N Delaware.
Mahoney Daniel H, 1049 N Capitol av.
Maillard Albert W, 512 E 9th.
Maloy & Egan, 1 Lynn.
Marcy Theodore F, 1451 E Washington.
Martin Thomas S, 1130 E Washington.
Mascari Frank, 41 Virginia av.
Mason Mary A, 289 W 6th.
Mauer Henry J, 416 Indiana av.
Mayer Frank X, 861 S East.
Mayhew Harry M, 552 W Udell (N I).
Mecum Bennett, 369 S Delaware.
Mefford Tilghman W, 200 Lexington av.
Mendell Bros, 250 W Michigan.
Mendenhall Wm C, 30 College av.
Meredith Richard O, 291 W North.
Metzler Jacob, 895 S Meridian.
Meyer F J & Co, 408 S East.
Meyers Bros, 419 Indiana av.
Michael Arthur R, s w cor Sugar Grove and Miller avs (M P).
Michael Clara, 450 S Delaware.
Miller Henry, 1155 E Washington.
Miller Oliver P, 1054 N Senate av.
Milli Reinhart, 581 Madison av.
Mills Albert H, 51 Cornell av.
Minkner Leo J, 51 Palmer.
Minter Ferdinand, s w cor Home av and Yandes.
Mitschrich Herman, 189 Prospect.
Mittmann Frederick, 128 W Ray.
Mogle Daniel E, 422 W 2d.
Monarch Supply Co, 84 E Washington.
Moore James B, 2 Haugh (H).
Moore N A & Co, 1-5 Indiana av.
Moore Wm J, 99 Shelby.
Moriarty Patrick, 227 Minnesota.
Morris Corvil A, 366 S Olive.
Mueller Edward H, 182 E Washington.
Muller Bros, 989 S Meridian.
Mullins James, 151 W Merrill.
Mullis R T & Co, 1350 N Capitol av.
Murphy Arley R, 340 E Market.
Murphy John, 110 John.
Myers Bros, 419 Indiana av.
Myers Irvin M, 256 Indiana av.
Myhan James H, 270 Blake.
Neiman Joseph, 301 E Washington.
Neligh Solon H, 107 Woodburn av (W I).
Newby & Son, rear 852 Grandview av.
Newhouse Fred A, 70 John.
Niermann Henry F, 527 N Illinois.
Norton James W, 550 W Addison (N I).
O'Connor Ella F, 252 Kentucky av.
O'Leary Martin, 350 W Maryland.
O'Leary Patrick C, 418 S West.
O'Mahoney Patrick J, 176 Shelby.
O'Mara James, 84 Minerva.
Osborn Scott S, 302 E North.
Oswald Theodore, 376 W North.
Otte & Co, 849 E Michigan.
Overman Thomas P, 111 S Reisner (W I).
Page Andrew H C, 632 N West.
Parker Charles R, 2 N Dorman.
Parker Dora E, 1203 Northwestern av.
Parkhurst Daniel V, 278 Michigan (H).
Pasquier Eugene, 143 N Delaware.
Pasquier Julius, 148 Fletcher av.
Peake Benjamin J, 838 E Washington.
Peake James T, 100 Hoyt av.
Perigo Stephen W, 201 Union.
Perry Charles, 255 S Capitol av.
Pfaffiin Grocery Co The, 100 N Illinois.
Pierson Charles H, 125 S Noble.
Pierson David W, 304 W Maryland.
Pike Daniel D, n s Washington av 1 w of Ritter av (I).
Pittman G S & Son, 439 E Georgia.
Pletzer Joseph, 591 Madison av.
Popp George R, 31 N Penn.
Popp John, 24 English av.
Porter & Lowes, e s Central av 2 s of Railroad (I).
Power & Drake, 16 N Meridiau.
Prange Anthony, 314 Mass av.
Prange Charles, 318 E Washington.
Prange Henry C, 399 Bellefontaine.
Prigger Anna, 336 Fulton.
Privitt Willis, 85 Fulton.
Pugh & Denney, 420 Dillon.
Pyatt James W, 801 N Alabama.
Pyle Bros, 294 Mass av.
Quinn Robert R, 57 Rhode Island.
Raftery John, 187 Madison av.
Railsback Charles, 399 N Illinois.
Railsback Eddy A, 404 College av.
Rasener Jennie, 1149 N Illinois.
Rauser Peter E, 68 S West.
Reeder Ephraim C, 107 Elm.
Reller A Henry, 651 N Illinois.
Rentsch Robert, 600 N Senate av.
Reynolds Wm B, 395 Blake.
Richard Frank C, 399 E Georgia.

THE WM. H. BLOCK CO. 7 AND 9 EAST WASHINGTON STREET. DRY GOODS, HOUSE FURNISHINGS AND CROCKERY.

London Guarantee and Accident Co. (Ltd.) All forms of Liability Insurance, Workmen's Collective Insurance, Fidelity Bonds and Individual Accident Insurance.
Geo. W. Pangborn, Gen. Agent, 704-706 Lemcke Bldg. Telephone 140.

FRANK K. SAWYER, AGENT 74 East Market Street. Telephone 863.

Grocers—Retail—Continued.

Richardson Charles, 272 S Capitol av.
Richardson Robert H, 1081 E Michigan.
Richter Frederick B, cor Russell av and Illinois.
Riehl George, 89 Wisconsin.
Ries Conrad, 352 Dillon.
Rinne Charles H, 620 S Meridian.
Rinne Herman E, 182 W Washington.
Ritzendollor Julia, 412 Indiana av.
Roberts Andrew J, 583 W Washington.
Robinson Bros, 197 W Ohio.
Robinson Willis B, 180 W 1st.
Rocker John C, 848 W Washington.
Rocker Margaret, 292 W Maryland.
Rosebrock Frederick W, 666 Virginia av.
Rost Daniel, 1107 E Michigan.
Roth Bros, 648 E Vermont.
Rothert John H, 369 Virginia av.
Rowland John, 420 W North.
Roy Herman J, 892 S Meridian.
Ruckelshaus Henry, 342 E St Clair.
Rupp John, 201-203 Kentucky av.
Ruskaup Frederick, 135 N Dorman.
Ryan Hezekiah J, 68 N Linden.
Ryan P J & Co, 650 N Capitol av.
Saffell & Geider, 7-9 Madison av.
St John James N, 148 Mass av.
Sample Ellen, 598 W 22d (N I).
Samuels Rosa, 387 N Noble.
Sanders A & W, 951 E Michigan.
Sanders Margaret, 102 Columbia av.
Sanders Oliver S, 531 W Washington.
Santo Edward J, 201 Indiana av.
Saperstein Meyer, 55 Russell av.
Schad & Sons, 700 N Capitol av.
Schaefer Herman L, 350 W Vermont.
Schafer Wm, 492 S Meridian.
Scheele Frederick W, n w cor Ohio and Rural.
Scheier John C, 449 S State av.
Scheier Wm C, 36 E Mkt House.
Schelski George H, 268 Yandes.
Scherrer Frank B, 53 Cushing.
Schetter Christopher, 300 S Penn.
Schmidt Benjamin F, 497 W 22d (N I).
Schmidt Jacob F, 103 Broadway.
Schneider Mary, 203 Madison av.
Schneider Michael, 285 S Olive.
Schoenberger Edward, 676 N Senate av.
Schoenemann Jacob H, 185 Bismarck av (H).
Schooler Frank P, 151 Hoyt av.
Schortemeier Henry E, 104 Broadway and 304 S East.
Schowe George F, 201 Fayette.
Schrader C H & E H, 154 E Washington and 453-457 Virginia av.
Schrolucke Wm, 905 Madison av.
Schulmeyer Bros, 150 St Mary.
Schwegman Wm, s e cor Windsor and Orange av.
Schwenk Caroline, 260 Blake.
Schwier Bros, 518 E Washington.
Schwier Christian F, 689 E Washington.
Schwier Wm C, 1087 E Michigan.
Schwomeyer Charles H & Co, 399 S Meridian.
Schwomeyer Henry, 475 Indiana av.
Scott Thomas C, 376 Clifford av.
Scotton Wm E, 413 W Addison (N I).
Screes Walter T, n e cor Willow and Hope (B).
Sellmeyer Henry C, 350 E New York.
Sengstock Dorothea, 292 W Morris.
Severns Edmond P, 148 Bloyd av.
Sharpless Charles W, 550 Ash.
Shea John, 200 W South.
Shellhouse W S & Co, 99 N Alabama.
Sherer Joseph M, 231 W Ohio.
Sherer Mamie, 191 W South.
Sheresefsky Mary, 400 S Capitol av.
Sheridan Wm, 399 N West.
Shingleton Mary A, 290 Bates.
Shoobridge Charles, 30 Pendleton av (B).
Shook Elias, 153 N Capitol av.
Short Cora C, 420 W Michigan.
Simmons John G, 150 English av.
Simon Frederick W, 188 N Noble.
Simon Goodman, 399 S Illinois.
Simpson John R, 179 N East.
Sloan Thomas J, 150 Walcott.
Slusher Thomas E, 106 S William (W I).
Smith Frank E, 825 N Illinois.
Smith Henry N, 302 Columbia av.
Smith Sarah M, 1281 Annette (N I).
Smith Wm A, 2 Camp.
Smith Wm H, 320 S West.
Smithey John F, 100 Columbia av.
Snavely Martin, 209 W Washington.
Snider Oliver N, 52 Langley av.
Snyder Wm J, 200 Hoyt av.
Socwell Bros, 240 E Washington.
Socwell Samuel H, 99 Mass av.
Sokol Sarah, 283 S Capitol av.
Solsbury Naomi, n e cor Woodburn av and Division (W I).
Soltau John A, 104 Davidson.
Sommer Charles W, 139 W 3d.
Sourbeer John R, s e cor McLene and Rader (N I).
Sparks David W, 385 W North.
Speckmann Henry, 128 E Mkt House.
Spielberger Jacob, 260 Howard (W I).
Spier John F, 494 E Washington.
Spreng Albert F, 75 E Mkt House.
Staehle Wilhelmina, 260 S Alabama.
Stahl Frederick, 330 N Noble.
Stahlhut Frederick C, 199 Mass av.
Stalnaker Gabriel W, 207 W Washington.
Stevens John, 1 Buchanan.
Stierle Gallus, 49 Draper.
Stiltz James P, 800 N Senate av.
Stilwell Matthew B, 263 W Washington.
Stutsman Jacob H, 449 Central av.
Suart John B, 509 E 7th.
Surbey & Amt, 199 Virginia av.
Swan Benjamin C, 551 W 22d (N I).
Swope Mary E, 249 River av (W I).
Taylor & Ormsbee, 167 Michigan av.
Teeters George W, 480 W Chicago (N I).
Teine Christian, 217 W 8th.
Tellkamp Anna, 36 Ramsey av.
Teuteberg Andrew H, 1249 E Washington.
Thalman John, 29 Clifford av.
Thalman John I, 661 W Eugene (N I).
Thomas John C, 249 N Noble.
Thomas Lizzie, 55 S McLain (W I).
Thompson Augustin S, 221½ W Washington.
Thompson Joseph, 227 W Michigan.
Thomson Richard M, 315 W Washington.
Tilley Tunis T, 130 E Mkt House.
Tobin John W, 400 S West.
Tobin Mary, 335 S Delaware.
Tulley Louis W, 720 S East.
Turner & McHaffey, 49 Yandes.
Tyndall & Moore, e s Garfield av 2 n of Washington.
Van Pelt Sutton B, 41 N Alabama.
Van Sickle George W, 30 Clifford av.
Van Zant Worthington, 249 Davidson.
Victor John A, 598 N West.
Victor Julius A, 275 Howard.
Vinch Nunzio, 160 Virginia av.
Vollrath Charles A, 575 Madison av.
Voorhees Richard, 350 Yandes.

Prussian National Insurance Comp'y OF STETTIN, GERMANY. ORGANIZED 1845.

United States Life Insurance Co., of New York.
E. B. SWIFT, M'g'r. 25 E. Market St.

WM. KOTTEMAN } 89 & 91 E. Washington St. Telephone 1742 { RUGS MATTINGS WINDOW SHADES

WILLIAM WIEGEL { MANUFACTURER OF.... } SHOW CASES { 6 W. Louisiana St. Opposite Union Station.

Vornholt Henry J, 108 Weghorst.
Waddy Herbert O, 50 Clifford av.
Waggener Hannibal, 191 W 3d.
Waggoner Caroline, 21 Tremont av (H).
Wagner John, 851 S Meridian.
Wagner Joseph H, s e cor William and Howard (W I).
Walker Walter F, 550 Bellefontaine.
Walsh James C, 621 Virginia av.
Walters Harry S, 53 Maxwell.
Ward John P, 23 Astor.
Warrick Edward H, 252 Highland av.
Watson Elbridge C, 100 Keystone av.
Watson Jehu M, 91 Columbia al.
Watts Haden M, 548 W Udell (N I).
Webster Charles E, 40 Pleasant.
Weiland Wm C, 495 S Meridian.
Wells George, 247 S Capitol av.
Wesp John L, 467 N California.
White Charles G, C E Mkt House.
White Frank M, 1 E Mkt House.
White Ida L, 198 N Senate av.
Whitehead John R, 36 Crawford.
Whitted Mary C, 146 Elizabeth.
Wiggins Bessie B, 480 W Michigan.
Wilgus Wm, 928 S Meridian.
Williams Robert E, 501 E 7th.
Wilson Amelia, 33 N East.
Wilson Charles W, B E Mkt House.
Wilson Elmer L, 60 Jefferson av.
Wilson Jefferson M, 31 Traub av.
Wilson Melvin L, 1091 E Michigan.
Wilson Wm F, 380 E 9th.
Winter Henry, 51 Yandes.
Woerner Theodore, 494 N Senate av.
Woessner Jacob & Sons, 540 Virginia av.
Wolf Joseph, cor LaSalle and Humbolt av.
Wolff Francis X, n e cor Garfield av and Washington.
Wood John M, s e cor Concord and Michigan (H).
Wood John M, 168 Hillside av.
Woods Charles E, 488 E Washington.
Wormser Jacob, 143 Maple.
Wright Thomas G, 9 E Mkt House.
Wright Thomas W, 284 W Washington.
Wundram Wm, 662 S Meridian.
Young Plummer P, 506 E 9th.
Yount Daniel, 200 S Pine.
Zaring Louie M, 100 Camp.
Zimmer Mary E, 293 S Delaware.
Zobbe Bros, 192 W Washington.
Zollinger Julius, 100 N State av.
Zorn George H, 200 Wright.

*GROCERS' SPECIALTIES.

French Chemical Works, 22 S Alabama.
Grocers' Mnfg Co The, 80 S Penn.

*GROCERS' SUNDRIES.

Mayer Charles & Co, 29-31 W Washington. (See adv opp p 615.)

*GUNS AND AMMUNITION.

Habich Gustave, 62 W Market.
Leauty August, 81 W Washington.

*GYMNASIUM GOODS.

Mayer Charles & Co, 29-31 W Washington. (See adv opp p 615.)

*HACK LINES.

Bird Frank Transfer Co, General Office 24 Pembroke Arcade; Branches 115 N Delaware, Bates House and Union Station. (See adv in Omnibus Lines; also in Transfer Companies and p 192.)

HAIR GOODS.

Donnell Dollie, 19½ N Meridian.
Elbertson Marie A, 11 Madison av.
Evans Ada P, over 2½ W Washington. (See adv.)

HAIR PARLORS.

All the new novelties received regularly at Mme. Evans', successor to Mrs. A. S. Fowler. Special attention is paid to dressing hair for parties and entertainments. Orders by mail promptly attended to. Hair dressers sent out of the city by engagement. Ladies, when in the city, please call and investigate.
Madam Evans is a graduate in Chiropodist Work. Instant and painless relief from corns, bunions and ingrowing nails.

MADAM EVANS,
Successor to Mrs. A. S. Fowler,
2½ WEST WASHINGTON STREET,
INDIANAPOLIS, IND.

Hastings Clara W, 37½ W Washington.
Jackson E B & D W, 2½ W Washington.
Kinzly Herman H, 46 N Illinois.
Knox George L, 20 N Illinois.
Phelan Mary E, 16½ E Washington.
Varin George, 37½ W Washington.

*HAIR—PLASTERERS'.

Wasson W G Co The, 130 Indiana av. (See left bottom cor cards and adv in Builders' Material; also in Cement and Lime.)

*HAMMOCKS AND OUTING TENT MANUFACTURERS.

Baby Supply Manufacturing Co, 256 S East. (See adv p 7 and in Baby Buggy Mnfrs.)

BABY SUPPLY MNFG. COMPANY
Manufacturers of
SAFETY HAMMOCKS,
FOLDING BABY CABS, Etc.
Thos. Nesom, Mgr.
No. 256 South East St.

*HAMMOCKS.

Mayer Charles & Co, 29-31 W Washington. (See adv opp p 615.)

*HARDWARE—BUILDERS'.

Vonnegut Clemens, 184-186 E Washington. (See left bottom lines.)

HARDWARE—WHOLESALE.

Francke & Schindler, 35 S Meridian.
Hildebrand Hardware Co, 52 S Meridian.
Holliday W J & Co, 59-61 S Meridian.
Layman & Carey Co, 63 S Meridian.
Van Camp Hardware and Iron Co, 78-82 S Illinois.
Vonnegut Clemens, 184-186 E Washington. (See left bottom lines.)

CARPETS AND RUGS RENOVATED.......... | CAPITAL STEAM CARPET CLEANING WORKS M. D. PLUNKETT, TELEPHONE No. 818

BENJ. BOOTH PRACTICAL EXPERT ACCOUNTANT. Complicated or disputed accounts investigated and adjusted. Room 18, 82½ E. Wash. St., Ind'p'l's, Ind.

THE SHERMAN RESTAURANT || 18 and 20 South Meridian Street KERSHNER BROS., Proprs.

Charles Pleschner

Dealer in and Manufacturer of

FINE HARNESS AND SADDLERY

TURF AND HORSE FURNISHING GOODS, WHIPS, BLANKETS, TRUNKS AND TELESCOPES.

163 East Washington Street.

HARDWARE-RETAIL.

Carter John W, 296 Mass av.
Combs & Triggs, 496 Madison av.
Everroad & Prunk, 170 Indiana av.
Francke & Schindler, 35 S Meridian.
Franke & Seele, 199 Prospect.
Gardner & Proctor, 13 Shelby.
Herdman Carrie M, 418 W Michigan.
Hildebrand Hardware Co, 52 S Meridian.
Hoss Walter S, 860 Morris (W I).
Johnson Wm C, 249 W Washington.
Koehring B & Son, 530-532 Virginia av.
Lauck John, 496 S Meridian.
Lilly & Stalnaker, 64 E Washington.
Rhodes Samuel S, 178 W Washington.
Schmidt Benjamin F, 499 W 22d (N I).
Shellhouse & Co, 271-275 E Washington.
Thielmann Charles, 144 College av.
Tyler Frank S, 186 Virginia av.
Valdenaire John J, s s Glen Drive 2 w of Gale (B).
Vonnegut Clemens, 184-186 E Washington. (See left bottom lines.)
Waggoner Caroline, 21 Tremont av (H).
Wagner Joseph H, s e cor William and Howard (W I).
Wald Oliver R, 591 S Meridian.
Walden Robert R & Son, 818 E Washington.
Wayne Charles L & Co, 61 W Washington.

***HARDWOOD CARPETS.**

Interior Hardwood Co The, Mnfrs, 317 Mass av.

***HARDWOOD LUMBER.**

Byrd Joseph W, 323 Lemcke Bldg. (See adv opp Lumber Mnfrs and Dealers.)
Huey M S & Son, 551 Mass av. (See adv p 5.)

HARNESS AND SADDLE MANUFACTURERS AND DEALERS.

Arnholter Henry, 572 Virginia av.
Coxley Joseph, 585 Morris (W I).
Craven Riley, 64 W 7th.
Hagedon Charles, 53 Mass av.
Herrington Frank L, 81 E Market. (See adv opp p 450.)
Holliday & Wyon, 96-100 S Penn.
Indianapolis Harness Co, 10-16 McCrea and 38 E South.
King James, 256 Mass av.
Kutsch John A, 263 Mass av.
McDonald Hugh, 32 Hill av.
McQuown James H, 11 Prospect.
Marsh Wm S, 645 S Meridian.
Medaris Jefferson W, 3 Cherry.
Pankoske Frank, 651 Virginia av.
Pleschner Charles, 163 E Washington. (See adv.)
Rottler Frank M, 18 N Delaware.
Schmalholz Rudolph, 278 E Washington.
Sheppard Wm W, 440 E Washington.
Sipf Frederick, 268 W Washington.
South Erastus O, 188 Indiana av.
Spillman Wm G, 365-367 S Delaware.
Strawmyer John A, 471 S Meridian.
Strawmyer & Nilius, 17 Monument pl.
Techentin & Freiberg, 14 N Delawer.
Vanderpool Wm, 226 E Washington.
Volz Quirin, 169 W Washington.

***HATTERS.**

Wenell John A, 73 S Illinois. (See adv.)

JOHN A. WENELL,
Practical Hatter
73 South Illinois St., Indianapolis.
Silk and stiff hats made to order. Old hats made new in the latest styles, and all kinds of repairs on gentlemen's hats. Trimmings to match any color. ☞Silk hats blocked or ironed while you wait.

HATS—MANUFACTURERS AND PRESSERS.

De Puy Wm, 47 Mass av.
Potter Thomas E, 26 S Capitol av.
Webber Charles R, 202 S Meridian.

HATS, CAPS AND FURS—WHOLESALE.

Hendrickson, Lefler & Co, 89 S Meridian.
Henley, Eaton & Co, 58 S Meridian.

HATS, CAPS AND FURS—RETAIL.

Dalton Hat Co, 64 W Washington.
Danbury Hat Co, 8 E Washington.

TUTEWILER UNDERTAKER, No. 72 WEST MARKET STREET. TELEPHONE 216.

The Provident Life and Trust Co. Dividends are paid in cash and are not withheld for a long period of years, subject to forfeiture in the event of death or the termination of policy.
D. W. EDWARDS, GENERAL AGENT, 508 INDIANA TRUST BUILDING.

THEODORE F. SMITHER Competent and Responsible ROOFER
Office, 151 W Maryland St. Telephone 86

Globe Clothing Co The, 97-99 E Washington.
Helstein Simon F, 25 W Washington.
Kleinsmith Wm E, 23 W Washington.
Lowenthal Wolf, 11½ W Washington.
Original Eagle Clothing Co, 5-7 W Washington.
Progress Clothing Co The, 6-8 W Washington.
Reid Jacob, 7 Indiana av.
Ryan Frank M, 21 S Illinois.
Seaton Wm D, 27 N Penn.
When Clothing Store, 26-40 N Penn. (See right top cor cards.)

*HAY CARRIERS.

Vonnegut Clemens, 184-186 E Washington. (See left bottom lines.)

*HAY—WHOLESALE AND RETAIL.

Janes Frank E, 107-113 N Delaware.

HEADLIGHT MANUFACTURERS.

National Electric Headlight Co, 30-34 W South.

*HERBALISTS.

Bumgardner John, 108 E Mkt House.

HIDES AND PELTS.

Allerdice Joseph & Co, 128 Kentucky av.
Rauh E & Sons, 219 S Penn.
Ryse & McDonald, 26 E South.
Young Horace G, 2 St Peter.

*HITCHING POSTS.

Ellis & Helfenberger, 162-170 S Senate av. (See right bottom lines.)

*HOISTING MACHINERY.

Vonnegut Clemens, 184-186 E Washington. (See left bottom lines.)

*HOLIDAY GOODS.

Mayer Charles & Co, 29-31 W Washington. (See adv opp p 615.)

*HOMEOPATHIC PHARMACIES.

Frietzsche John U, 62 E Ohio.

HOMINY MANUFACTURERS.

Indianapolis Hominy Mills, cor Madison av and Palmer.

*HONEY AND BEESWAX.

Hardwick George W, E E Mkt House.

HOOP MANUFACTURERS.

Patterson & Busby, n w cor Biddle and Bee Line Ry.

HORSE COLLAR MANUFACTURERS.

Hoosier Sweat Collar Co The, s w cor Alvord and 8th.
Indianapolis Harness Co, 10-16 McCrea and 38 E South.

*HORSE GOODS.

Herrington Frank L, 81 E Market. (See adv opp p 450.)

HORSESHOERS.

(See also Blacksmiths.)

Beatty Albert J, 675 N Senate av.
Brown Robert A, 29 Bird.
Bucker Henry, 18 Cherry.
Carfield John R, 210 S Meridian.
Clark John T, 98 Kentucky av.
Colwell Faires, 424 Mass av.
Connor John, Union Stock Yards (W I).
Connor Michael O, 56 W Wabash.
Costello & Riordan, 108 E Wabash.
Cox George M, 108 Belmont av (W I).
Crowe Wm M, 87 Hadley av (W I).
Danner Charles F, 860 S Meridian.
Danner & Lund, 68 W 7th.
Dell Wm A, 595 Morris (W I).
Disher Thomas G, 378 E 7th.
Drum Charles, 25 S William (W I).
Egan Dennis, 112 N Delaware.
Egelhoff Henry, 901 Madison av.
Emrich Clarence, 25 N New Jersey.
Fells Harry J, 446 E Washington.
Foreman J M & Co, 285 W Washington.
Garr Thomas W, 463 Central av.
Gibbs Cushioned Horseshoe Co, 67 N Capitol av.
Glattfelder Henry, 477 S Delaware.
Hill Henry C, 297 W Washington.
Holmes & Carey, 82 W Wabash.
Izor Frank S, 1 Susquehanna.

MAYHEW'S SPECTACLES
THE BEST IN USE
SOLD ONLY AT 13 N. MERIDIAN ST.

Electric Contractors
We are prepared to do any kind of Electric Contract Work.
C. W. MEIKEL. Telephone 466.
96-98 E. New York St.

DALTON & MERRIFIELD { LUMBER South Noble St., near E. Washington

INDIANA ELECTROTYPE CO. : BEST WORK. LOWEST PRICES.
23 WEST PEARL ST., INDIANAPOLIS, IND. JOB WORK. All Orders Promptly Filled.
BOOK PLATES. BEST PATENT BASE ON THE MARKET.

Jockey Club Shoeing Shop
Horses Called For and Delivered.
86 EAST ST. CLAIR ST.
TELEPHONE 1216.

Positively no heavy draught horses wanted. We shoe light roadsters, private coach horses, livery, delivery, saddle, trotters and pacers. Every description of hand-made shoes done in the best manner and at short notice. Free consultation and examination. *FRANK F. JACOBS.*

Horseshoers—Continued.

Jacobs Frank F, 86 E St Clair. (See adv.)
King & Knight, 60 Virginia av.
Lancaster & Orlopp, 106 S Delaware.
Mansfield & Jenkins, 180 E Market.
Marshall John S, 36 Oak.
Mueller & Schneider, 351 Madison av.
Mulry John, 33 S Alabama.
O'Reilly Martin J, 301 W Washington.
Renner Albert C, 24 E South.
Richardson Holman, 428 N Alabama.
Sadlier George, 38 S Penn.
Schwartz Wm K, 243 W Washington.
Shaffer Wm H, 138 E 7th.
Sherfey & Holler, 83 S Penn.
Shriner & Robbins, 428 Charles.
Sourwine Jacob, 1217 Morris (W I).
Stark & Hill, 3 John.
Trucksess Theodore, 151 W Maryland.
Wamsley & Holmes, 116 W Maryland.
Wilson Wm D, 58 W Merrill.
Wren Wm A, 496 Virginia av.
Yule & Hartman, 25 N Liberty.

***HOSE.**

Central Rubber and Supply Co The, 79 S Illinois. (See left side lines.)

HOSPITALS.

See Miscellaneous Directory.

***HOT AIR FURNACES.**

Laing Samuel, 72-74 E Court. (See left side lines.)

***HOT WATER HEATING AND VENTILATING.**

Kirkhoff Bros, 102-104 S Penn. (See left top cor cards.)

***HOT WATER AND STEAM HEATING.**

Farrell J S & Co, 84 N Illinois. (See left bottom cor cards.)

HOTELS.

American Hotel, 84 S Illinois.
Bates The, n w cor Illinois and Washington.
California House, 184-186 S Illinois.
Capital House, 193 W Washington.
Circle Park Hotel, 13 Monument pl.
Denison The, s e cor Penn and Ohio.
Enterprise Hotel, 82½ Mass av.
Erven Isaac G, 78-80 W Maryland.
Exchange Hotel, Union Stock Yards (W I).
Field Richard A, 35 W Georgia.
George's Hotel, 201 E Washington.
Germania House, 200 S Meridian.
Grand Hotel The, s e cor Illinois and Maryland.
Hanna' Hotel, 63 N Alabama.
Hotel English, w s Monument pl, bet Market and Meridian.
Hotel Oneida, 108-116 S Illinois.
Illinois House, 181-185 S Illinois.
James House, 39 N Alabama.
Jefferson House, 59-63 E South.
McCoy Robert E, 217 S Illinois.
McKeehan Hotel, 259 Hadley av (W I).

YOUR HOMES FURNISHED BY W. H. MESSENGER 101 East Washington St. Telephone 491.

McNamara, Koster & Co. Phone 1593. 212-218 S. PENN. ST. PATTERN MAKERS

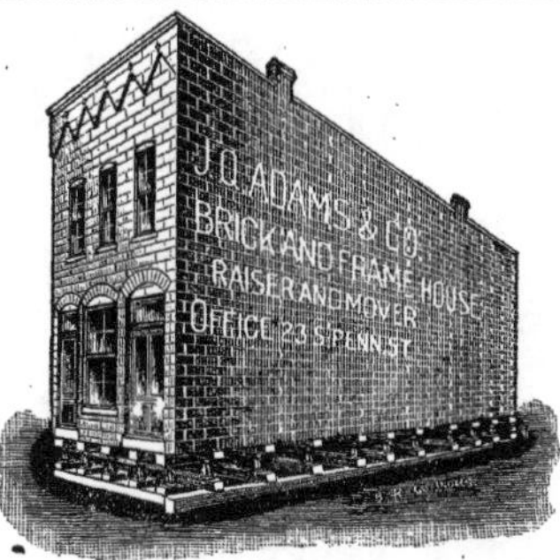

J. Q. Adams & Co.
House Raisers and Movers
Also Contractors for Moving Safes and Heavy Machinery.
Office, 26 Virginia Avenue
Yards, 211 E. Market St.
TELEPHONE 1217.

Marion Park Hotel, cor Post and Vorster av (M P).
Mueller's Hotel, 213 S Alabama.
Normandie European Hotel The, 101-109 S Illinois.
Occidental Hotel, s e cor Illinois and Washington.
Roosevelt House, 80 E Ohio.
Ross House, 37 McNabb.
St Charles Hotel, 27 McCrea.
Senate Hotel, 50½ N Senate av.
Sherman House, n e cor Louisiana and McCrea.
Smith's European Hotel, 190-200 E Washington.
Spencer House, n w cor Illinois and Louisiana.
Stubbins European Hotel, n e cor Illinois and Georgia.
Weinberger's European Hotel, 10-14 W Louisiana.
White Ribbon House, s e cor Meridian and Ohio.

*HOUSE FURNISHING GOODS.

Block Wm H Co The, 7-9 E Washington. (See right top and bottom lines.)
Griggs & Tyler, 118 N Meridian.
Haueisen & Hartmann, 163-169 E Washington. (See right bottom cor cards.)
Kotteman Wm, 89-91 E Washington. (See right top lines.)
Messenger W Horndon, 101 E Washington and 13, 15 and 17 S Delaware. (See left bottom lines.)
Parker's Furniture Store, 175-179 W Washington.
People's Outfitting Co, 71-73 W Washington.
Rupert Frank H, 59 W Washington.
Willig Charles, 79 W Washington.

HOUSE MOVERS.

Adams J Q & Co, 26 Virginia av. (See adv.)
Conover Wm, 297 W Washington.
Marshall Amos, 117 Yandes.
Roark Thomas G, 20 Hadley.

. FOR .
Lists of Names
ANY
Trade
Business
Profession or
Pursuit
ADDRESS
R. L. Polk & Co.
23-24 JOURNAL BLDG.

THE FRED DIETZ CO. WOODEN PACKING BOXES MADE TO ORDER. FACTORY AND WAREHOUSE TRUCKS. 400 Madison Avenue. Telephone 654.

Business World Supplied with Help
GRADUATES ASSISTED TO POSITIONS
10,000 NOW IN GOOD SITUATIONS. TEL. 499. E. J. HEEB, PRES.
Indianapolis BUSINESS UNIVERSITY

HENRY R. WORTHINGTON JET and SURFACE CONDENSERS
64 S. PENN. ST.
Long Distance Telephone 284.

UNION CO-OPERATIVE LAUNDRY (COMPOSED OF UNION LAUNDRY GIRLS.) NOS. 138, 140 AND 142 VIRGINIA AVENUE. TELEPHONE 1269. INDIANAPOLIS, IND. T. E. SOMERVILLE, MANAGER

THE WEBB-JAMESON CO.

Building Movers

SAFES, BOILERS AND SMOKE STACKS MOVED AND RAISED.

BRICK HOUSES A SPECIALTY.

TELEPHONE 356. 222 S. MERIDIAN ST., INDIANAPOLIS.

House Movers—Continued.
Webb-Jameson Co The, 222 S Meridian. (See adv.)

ICE CREAM.

Ballard Wm H, 102 N Delaware.
Furnas Robert W, 112-114 N Penn.
Grave Dora, 572 Shelby.
Kealing Samuel, 531-533 N Illinois.
Putnam County Milk Co The, 12-16 N East.

ICE MANUFACTURERS AND DEALERS.

Armstrong E J & J W, 223 W Walnut.
Artificial Ice and Cold Storage Co, 197 W New York.
Benner Wm J, 185 W 7th.
Budd Wm S, n w cor 6th and canal.
Crystal Ice Co, 181 W Ohio.
Hall John S, 70 Elizabeth.
Hilt John Lake Ice Co, 82½ E Washington.
Holt Ice and Cold Storage Co The, n e cor North and canal.
Polar Ice Co, 175-179 E Wabash.

*ILLUSTRATING COMPANIES.

Indiana Illustrating Co, s e cor Market and Illinois. (See adv opp Engravers.)

*INK DIES.

Mayer George J, 15 S Meridian. (See left bottom cor cards and p 5.)

*INK PADS.

Mayer George J, 15 S Meridian. (See left bottom cor cards and p 5.)

*INK—STENCILS.

Mayer George J, 15 S Meridian. (See left bottom cor cards and p 5.)

*INSTALLMENT GOODS.

Adams C F Co, 93 N Illinois.
American Wringer Co, 27 Indiana av.
Beard W R & Co, 20 S Alabama.
Conroy A J & Co, 23 Indiana av.
Parker Harvey, 9 S Senate av.
United States Wringer Co, 19 Indiana av.

INSURANCE ADJUSTERS.

Scott David I, 77½ Mass av.

INSURANCE AGENTS.

Adams Joseph, 40½ Kentucky av.
Ainsworth Frank B, 35 Talbott blk.
Alexander & Co, 423-424 Lemcke bldg.
Armstrong James M, 48 Journal bldg.
Barnitt James L, 31 Lombard bldg.
Barton W E & Co, 504 Indiana Trust Bldg. (See right bottom cor cards.)
Bates Charles A, 19 Monument pl.
Batt Horace M, 31½ Virginia av.
Benton Walter P, 7 Ingalls blk.
Bland Wm I, 42 W Market.
Bond Pleasant, 412 Indiana Trust bldg.
Bonham Evan A, 15-16 Hartford Blk.
Brown Daniel L, 9 and 10 Baldwin blk.
Buchanan James A, 214 Lemcke bldg.
Canfield Woods P, 155 Michigan (H).
Clark Robert L, 20½ N Delaware.
Coe & Roache, 300 Indiana Trust Bldg.
Coffin C E & Co, 90 E Market.

CLEMENS VONNEGUT
184, 186 and 192 E. Washington St.
CABINET HARDWARE
CARVERS' TOOLS. Glues of all kinds.

INDIANA TRUST COMPANY

CAPITAL, $1,000,000.00.

INDIANAPOLIS.

OFFICES: INDIANA TRUST BUILDING.

WRITES FIRE INSURANCE

ATTENDS TO EVERYTHING IN CONNECTION WITH REAL ESTATE.

COLLECTS RENTS. PAYS TAXES.

MAKES REPAIRS.

Safety Deposit Vaults.

J. P. FRENZEL, President.
FREDERICK FAHNLEY, First Vice-President.
E. G. CORNELIUS, Second Vice-President.
JOHN A. BUTLER, Secretary.
JOHN G. PRINZ, Manager Insurance Department.

DIRECTORS.

FREDERICK FAHNLEY.
ALBERT LIEBER.
JAMES F. FAILEY.
O. N. FRENZEL.
F. G. DARLINGTON.
J. P. FRENZEL.
EDWARD HAWKINS.
E. G. CORNELIUS.
H. W. LAWRENCE.
WM. F. PIEL.
CHARLES B. STUART.

HENRY R. WORTHINGTON JET and SURFACE CONDENSERS 64 S. PENN. ST.

THE WEBB-JAMESON CO.

Building Movers

SAFES, BOILERS AND SMOKE STACKS MOVED AND RAISED.

BRICK HOUSES A SPECIALTY.

TELEPHONE 356. 2 S. MERIDIAN ST., INDIANAPOLIS.

House Movers

Webb-Jameson Co

ridian. (See adv.)

ICE CREAM

Ballard Wm H

Furnas Robert W

Grave Dora

Kealing Samuel

Putnam County Milk

ICE MANUFACTURERS AND DEALERS

Armstrong E J & J W

Artificial Ice and

New York

Benner Wm J

Budd Wm S

Crystal Ice Co

Hall John S.

Hilt John Lake

Holt Ice and

cor North

Polar Ice Co.

*ILLUSTRATING COMPANIES.

Indiana Illustrating Co.

ket and Illinois. (See adv

gravers.)

*INK DIPS

Mayer George J. 13 S Meri

left bottom cor cards and

*INK PADS.

Mayer George J. 13 S Meri

left bottom cor cards and

CLEMENS VONNEGUT

ATTEN
IN C
R

COLLECTS

FIRE INSURANCE

ONLY THE BEST COMPANIES REPRESENTED BY

INDIANA TRUST COMPANY

Patrons of this Company can place with it their property with the feeling that it will be

PROPERLY INSURED

With the same scrupulous care and complete financial responsibility which is offered with every undertaking of the Company.

REAL ESTATE.

This Company acts as general or special agent in taking care of real estate. It attends to

MAKING REPAIRS,
COLLECTING RENTS,
PAYING TAXES,
DRAWING LEASES,
WRITING INSURANCE.

Interest allowed on deposits, which may be made at any time, and withdrawn upon notice or at a fixed date.

Financial depository for Building Associations and other corporations.

Acts as surety on bonds of administrators, executors and guardians in any county in the State.

Legal depository for court and trust funds.

INDIANA TRUST COMPANY,

Offices in Company's Building, Cor. Washington Street and Virginia Avenue,

LONG DISTANCE TELEPHONE No. 36.

THE WM. H. BLOCK CO. DRY GOODS, MILLINERY, CLOAKS AND FURS.
7 AND 9 EAST WASHINGTON STREET.

Collins A H, 52-53 Baldwin Blk. (See left top lines.)
Coons & Witty, 15 When bldg.
Craft W H & Co, 47½ N Illinois.
Davenport Frank B, 727-728 Lemcke bldg.
De Witt Carroll L, 311 Lemcke bldg.
Edwards D W, 508-510 Indiana Trust Bldg. (See right top lines, left top cor cards and opp p 334.)
Faber Samuel E, 7 Ingalls blk.
Fay Henry H, 40½ E Washington. (See right top cor cards.)
Feibleman Bert L, 35 W Market.
Fleener Daniel F, 427-428 Lemcke bldg.
Folsom Edwin S, 34 Mass av.
Foster Edgar J, 25 E Market.
Frankel Jacob, 90 Lombard bldg.
Gilbert Edward, 44½ N Penn.
Gilpatrick George H, 54 When bldg.
Gregory & Appel, 96 E Market.
Habbe John F, 1002 Majestic bldg.
Hadley Horace M, 66 E Market. (See left top cor cards.)
Hanes George T, 45-46 Lorraine bldg.
Harden Tyre N, 125 E Walnut.
Harlan Isaac N, 36 N Delaware.
Hoover E W & Co, 718 Lemcke bldg.
Horne & Gasper, 400 Indiana Trust bldg.
Hughes Richard D, 75-80 Baldwin blk.
Indiana Association of Underwriters, 4 Hartford blk.
Indiana Trust Co The, Indiana Trust Bldg, s e cor Washington and Virginia av. (See front cover, opp p 487 and opp Insurance Agts.)
Ingram John C, 345 Park av.
Jones A Cary, 234 Lemcke bldg.
Keen W Witcher, 319 Indiana Trust bldg.
Klum Robert L, 19½ N Penn.
Kohne Benjamin F, 118 N Illinois.
Lambert John S, 11 When bldg.
Landis Hiram F, 135 Virginia av.
Lawrence & Thompson, 62 E Market.
Leigh Wm F, 60 Baldwin blk.
Loeb Louis L, 235 Lemcke bldg.
McCullough W J & Sons, 98 E Market.
McDowell Cincinnatus H, 629-630 Lemcke bldg.
McGill George B, 334 Lemcke bldg.
McGilliard Agency The, 83-85 E Market. (See backbone and opp p 588.)
McKee & Moore, 54 Baldwin blk.
McLaughlin Frank, 201 Lemcke bldg.
MacIntire Charles T, 62 E Market.
Marion Trust Co The, s e cor Market and Monument Pl. (See back cover.)
Martindale Robt & Co, 86 E Market.
Merritt Robert & Co, 6 Lombard bldg.
Merz Frederick, 208-210 Indiana Trust bldg.
Metzger A Agency, 5 Odd Fellows' Hall. (See left bottom lines.)
Meyer & Kiser, 306 Indiana Trust bldg.
Moody Lorenzo D, 56 Coffin blk.
Munson Edward A, 70 E Market.
Munson Edward C, 70 E Market.
Neff John W, 25½ W Washington.
Newcomb Horatio C, 319-321 Indiana Trust bldg.
Oakes Charles W, 77 E Market.
Ohr John H, 3 Hubbard blk.
Overman Harry W, 42 N Delaware.
Pangborn George W, 704-706 Lemcke Bldg. (See left top lines.)
Peck Benjamin B, 20-21 Fletcher's Bank bldg.
Pfisterer Peter, 103½ E Washington.
Prather & Bangs, 30-31 When bldg.
Price John J, 207-208 Lemcke bldg.
Price Wm H, 93 Lombard bldg.
Rehm & Van Deinse, 22-23 When Bldg.
Reynolds C E & Co, 10 Monument pl.
Richardson & McCrea, 79 E Market. (See right top cor cards.)
Russell John N, 523 Lemcke bldg.
Sawyer Frank K, 74 E Market. (See left side lines.)
Sayles Charles F, 77½ E Market.
Scott W R & E H, 66½ N Penn.
Seyfried Henry, 29 N Penn.
Shideler David B, 603 Indiana Trust bldg.
Shingler, Hann & Co, 92-93 Baldwin Blk.
Smith J H & Co, 36 W Washington.
Smock & Mather, 32 N Delaware.
Spann John S & Co, 84-86 E Market.
Swain David F, 88 N Penn.
Swift Elias B, 25 E Market. (See left bottom lines.)
Timewell Charles A, 62 E Market.
Todd Newton, 7 Ingalls blk.
Tutewiler & Shideler, 601 Indiana Trust bldg.
Tuttle & Seguin, 28 E Market. (See left bottom cor cards.)
Union Trust Co The, 68 E Market. (See front cover and opp p 867.)
Van Deinse A J & Co, 219-220 Lemcke bldg.
Welch & Carlon, 34 Monument pl.
Whitcomb Theodore C, 60 E Market.
Williams & Flickinger, 95-96 Lombard bldg.
Wocher John, 19½ N Penn.
Wolf George, 221-222 Lemcke Bldg. (See adv in Real Estate.)
Zener Robert & Co, 10-15 Talbott blk.

INSURANCE ASSOCIATIONS.

Indianapolis Fire Inspection Bureau, 18-20 Journal bldg.

INSURANCE COMPANIES—ACCIDENT—HOME.

Capitol Life Insurance Co of Indiana, 29 N Penn. (See adv opp p 243.)
Columbian Relief Fund Assn, 409-410 Lemcke bldg.
Commercial Travelers' Mutual Accident Association of Indiana; Preferred Accident Insurance at Cost; Membership Fee $3.00; 20-21 When Bldg.
Globe Accident Insurance Co, 15-19 Aetna Bldg, 19½ N Penn. (See adv back cover.)
Railway Officials' and Employes' Accident Association, 25-32 Ingalls Blk.

INDIANAPOLIS STEEL ROOFING AND CORRUGATING WORKS, 23 and 25 East South Street. S. D. NOEL, Proprietor.

David S. McKernan REAL ESTATE AND LOANS
Houses, Lots, Farms and Western Lands for sale or trade.
ROOMS 2-5 THORPE BLOCK.

DIAMOND WALL PLASTER { Telephone 1410 BUILDERS' EXCHANGE.

UNION TRANSFER AND STORAGE CO. Cor. E. Ohio St. and C., C., C. & St. L. R'y Tracks. ISSUE NEGOTIABLE RECEIPTS ON MERCHANDISE AND H USDH LD GOODS.

*INSURANCE COMPANIES—ACCIDENT—FOREIGN.

Aetna Life Insurance Co of Hartford, Conn (Accident Dept), Prather & Bangs Genl Agts for Indiana, 30-31 When Bldg.

Fidelity and Casualty of New York, Indiana Trust Co Agts, s e cor Washington and Virginia av. (See front cover and opp p 487 and opp.)

Fidelity and Casualty Co of New York, Richardson & McCrea Agts, 79 E Market. (See right top cor cards.)

Fidelity and Casualty Co of New York, Tuttle & Seguin Agts, 28 E Market. (See left bottom cor cards.)

London Guarantee and Accident Co (Limited) of London, England, George W Pangborn Genl Agt, 704-706 Lemcke Bldg. (See left top lines.)

North American Accident Association, Bert L Feibleman State Agt, 35 W Market.

Preferred Accident Insurance Co of New York, E A Bonham State Mngr, 15-16 Hartford Blk.

Richardson & McCrea, 79 E Market. (See right top cor cards.)

Standard Life and Accident Insurance Co of Detroit, Frank K Sawyer Agt, 74 E Market. (See left side lines.)

Travelers' Insurance Co of Hartford, Conn, H C Newcomb City Agt, 319-321 Indiana Trust Bldg.

Union Casualty and Surety Co of St Louis, Mo, W E Barton & Co Genl Agts, 504 Indiana Trust Bldg. (See right bottom cor cards.)

United States Casualty Co of New York, Daniel F Fleener Genl Agt, 427-428 Lemcke Bldg.

INSURANCE COMPANIES—AUTOMATIC SPRINKLER.

Union Casualty and Surety Co of St Louis, Mo, W E Barton & Co Genl Agts, 504 Indiana Trust Bldg. (See right bottom cor cards.)

*INSURANCE COMPANIES—ELEVATOR—FOREIGN.

Fidelity and Casualty Co of New York, A Metzger Agency Agts, 5 Odd Fellows' Hall. (See left bottom lines.)

Fidelity and Casualty Co of New York, Richardson & McCrea Agts, 79 E Market. (See right top cor cards.)

Fidelity and Casualty of New York, Tuttle & Seguin Agts, 28 E Market. (See left bottom cor cards.)

London Guarantee and Accident Co (Limited) of London, England, George W Pangborn Genl Agt, 704-706 Lemcke Bldg. (See left top lines.)

Union Casualty and Surety Co of St Louis, Mo, W E Barton & Co Genl Agts, 504 Indiana Trust Bldg. (See right bottom cor cards.)

*INSURANCE COMPANIES—EMPLOYERS' LIABILITY—FOREIGN.

Fidelity and Casualty of New York, Indiana Trust Co Agts, s e cor Washington and Virginia av. (See front cover and opp p 487.)

Fidelity and Casualty of New York, A Metzger Agency Agts, 5 Odd Fellows' Hall. (See left bottom lines.)

Fidelity and Casualty Co of New York, Richardson & McCrea Agts, 79 E Market. (See right top cor cards.)

Fidelity and Casualty of, New York, Tuttle & Seguin Agts, 28 E Market. (See left bottom cor cards.)

Guarantors' Liability Indemnity Co of Pennsylvania, Wm H Price Genl Agt, 93 Lombard Bldg.

London Guarantee and Accident Co (Limited) of London, England, George W Pangborn Genl Agt, 704-706 Lemcke Bldg. (See left top lines.)

Travelers' Insurance Co of Hartford, Conn, H C Newcomb City Agt, 319-321 Indiana Trust Bldg.

Union Casualty and Surety Co of St Louis, Mo, W E Barton & Co Genl Agts, 504 Indiana Trust Bldg. (See right bottom cor cards.)

INSURANCE COMPANIES—FIDELITY BONDS.

American Bonding and Trust Co of Baltimore City, W E Barton & Co Genl Agts, 504 Indiana Trust Bldg. (See right bottom cor cards.)

INSURANCE COMPANIES—FIRE AND MARINE—HOME.

Associated Underwriters, Indiana Trust Co, s e cor Washington and Virginia av. (See front cover, opp p 487 and opp Insurance Agts.)

Citizens' Insurance Co of Ft Wayne, Ind, The McGilliard Agency Co Genl Agts, 83-85 E Market. (See backbone and opp p 588.)

Ft Wayne Insurance Co of Ft Wayne, Ind, The McGilliard Agency Co Genl Agts, 83-85 E Market. (See backbone and opp p 588.)

German Fire Insurance Co of Indiana, 27-33 S Delaware.

German Fire Insurance Co of Indiana, Indiana Trust Co Agts, s e cor Washington and Virginia av. (See front cover, opp p 487 and opp Insurance Agts.)

Indiana Insurance Co of Indianapolis, The McGilliard Agency Co Genl Agts, 83-85 E Market. (See backbone and opp p 588.)

Indiana Millers' Mutual Fire Ins Co, 32 Board of Trade bldg.

Indiana Underwriters' Insurance Co, The McGilliard Agency Co Genl Agts, 83-85 E Market. (See backbone and opp p 588.)

A. METZGER AGENCY REAL ESTATE ESTABLISHED 1863.

THE UNION TRUST COMPANY

In its Insurance Department

Is prepared to write policies upon all classes of property. It also insures plate glass and against losses by burglary, including personal injuries inflicted by burglars.

COMPANIES REPRESENTED

	ASSETS
North British and Mercantile, of England,	$3,833,132
Palatine, of England, - - -	2,836,236
Norwich Union, of England, - -	2,170,234
Caledonian, of Scotland, - - -	2,015,904
Traders, of Chicago, - - - -	1,747,792
Hamburg-Bremen, of Germany, -	1,422,723
AND	
Thuringia, of Germany, - - -	10,000,000

CLIFFORD ARRICK, MANAGER

Office, 68 East Market Street

TELEPHONE 1576

LAMBERT GAS & GASOLINE ENGINE CO.
ANDERSON, IND. GAS AND GASOLINE ENGINES, 2 TO 50 H. P.

Indianapolis German Mutual Fire Insurance Co, 7, 156½ E Washington.

Union Insurance Co The, 423-424 Lemcke bldg.

Vernon Insurance and Trust Co of Indianapolis, Ind, The McGilliard Agency Co Genl Agts, 83-85 E Market. (See backbone and opp p 588.)

***INSURANCE COMPANIES—FIRE AND MARINE—FOREIGN.**

Allemania Insurance Co of Pittsburg, Pa, The McGilliard Agency Co Genl Agts, 83-85 E Market. (See backbone and opp p 588.)

American Central Insurance Co of St Louis, Mo, Tuttle & Seguin Agts, 28 E Market. (See left bottom cor cards.)

Boston Marine Insurance Co of Boston, Robt Martindale & Co Agts, 86 E Market.

British America Assurance Co of Toronto, Canada, Richardson & McCrea Agts, 79 E Market. (See right top cor cards.)

Buffalo Commercial of Buffalo, N Y, A Metzger Agency Agts, 5 Odd Fellows' Hall. (See left bottom lines.)

Buffalo German of Buffalo, N Y, A Metzger Agency Agts, 5 Odd Fellows' Hall. (See left bottom lines.)

Caledonian of Scotland, Union Trust Co Agts, 68 E Market. (See front cover and opp p 867.)

Delaware Insurance Co of Philadelphia, Frank K Sawyer Agt, 74 E Market. (See left side lines.)

Detroit Fire and Marine Insurance Co of Detroit, Mich, Richardson & McCrea Agts, 79 E Market. (See right top cor cards.)

Fireman's Fund Insurance Co of San Francisco, The McGilliard Agency Co Genl Agts, 83-85 E Market. (See backbone and opp p 588.)

Franklin Fire Insurance Co of Philadelphia, Horace M Hadley Agt, 66 E Market. (See left top cor cards.)

Franklin Fire Insurance Co of Philadelphia, George Wolf Agt, 221-222 Lemcke Bldg. (See adv in Real Estate.)

Germania of New York, A Metzger Agency Agts, 5 Odd Fellows' Hall. (See left bottom lines.)

Girard Fire Insurance Co of Philadelphia, Pa, The McGilliard Agency Co Genl Agts, 83-85 E Market. (See backbone and opp p 588.)

Glens Falls Insurance Co, Carroll L De Witt Special Agt, Harvey B Martin Local Agt, 311-312 Lemcke Bldg.

Grand Rapids Insurance Co of Michigan, Tuttle & Seguin Agts, 28 E Market. (See left bottom cor cards.)

Greenwich Insurance Co of New York, Robt Martindale & Co Agts, 86 E Market.

Hamburg-Bremen Fire Insurance Co of Germany, Richardson & McCrea Agts, 79 E Market. (See right top cor cards.)

Hamburg-Bremen Fire Insurance Co of Germany, Union Trust Co Agts, 68 E Market. (See front cover and opp p 867.)

Insurance Co of North America, Philadelphia, Pa, Henry H Fay Agt, 40½ E Washington. (See right top cor cards.)

Insurance Co of North America, Richardson & McCrea Agts, 79 E Market. (See right top cor cards.)

Manchester of Manchester, England, A Metzger Agency Agts, 5 Odd Fellows' Hall. (See left bottom lines.)

Merchants' Insurance Co of Newark, N J, Richardson & McCrea Agts, 79 E Market. (See right top cor cards.)

North British and Mercantile, Union Trust Co Agts, 68 E Market. (See front cover and opp p 867.)

Northern Assurance Co of London, Indiana Trust Co Agts, s e cor Washington and Virginia av. (See adv front cover, opp p 487 and opp Insurance Agts.)

Norwich Union of England, Horace M Hadley Agt, 66 E Market. (See left top cor cards.)

Norwich Union of London, England, Union Trust Co Agts, 68 E Market. (See front cover and opp p 867.)

Palatine Insurance Co of Manchester, England, Indiana Trust Co Agts, s e cor Washington and Virginia av. (See front cover and opp p 487.)

Palatine Insurance Co of Manchester, England, Union Trust Co Agts, 68 E Market. (See front cover and opp p 867.)

Pennsylvania Fire Insurance Co of Philadelphia, Pa, Henry H Fay Agt, 40½ E Washington. (See right top cor cards.)

Phenix Insurance Co of Brooklyn, N Y, Richardson & McCrea Agts, 79 E Market. (See right top cor cards.)

Philadelphia Underwriters of Philadelphia, Pa, Indiana Trust Co Agts, s e cor Washington and Virginia av. (See front cover, opp p 487 and opp Insurance Agts.)

Philadelphia Underwriters of Philadelphia, Pa, Richardson & McCrea Agts, 79 E Market. (See right top cor cards.)

Phoenix Insurance Co of Hartford, Tuttle & Seguin Agts, 28 E Market. (See left bottom cor cards.)

Prussian National of Stettin, Germany, Frank K Sawyer Agt, 74 E Market. (See left side lines.)

Queen Insurance Co of America, Robt Martindale & Co Agts, 86 E Market.

Rockford Fire Insurance Co of Rockford, Ill, The McGilliard Agency Co Genl Agts, 83-85 E Market. (See backbone and opp p 588.)

BICYCLES $5 DOWN. Best Terms. WHEELMEN'S CO 31 W. OHIO ST. LONG DISTANCE TEL. 1855.

J. H. TECKENBROCK Painter and Decorator, 94 EAST SOUTH STREET.

FIDELITY MUTUAL LIFE—PHILADELPHIA, PA.
MATCHLESS SECURITY At LOW COST. } A. H. COLLINS { General Agent Baldwin Block.

Rooms 42 and 43 WHEN BUILDING.
Miners and Shippers Steam and Domestic Coal.
Edwardsport Coal and Mining Co.

Insurance Companies—Fire and Marine—Foreign—Continued.

Rockford Fire Insurance Co of Rockford, Ill, Tuttle & Seguin Agts, 28 E Market. (See left bottom cor cards.)

Svea Assurance Co of Gothenburg, Sweden, Tuttle & Seguin Agts, 28 E Market. (See left bottom cor cards.)

Thuringia of Germany, Union Trust Co Agts, 68 E Market. (See front cover and opp p 867.)

Traders' of Chicago, Union Trust Co Agts, 68 E Market. (See front cover and opp p 867.)

Union Marine of Liverpool, England, Richardson & McCrea Agts, 79 E Market. (See right top cor cards.)

Western Assurance Co of Toronto, Canada, Richardson & McCrea Agts, 79 E Market. (See right top cor cards.)

Western Underwriters' Association of Chicago, Tuttle & Seguin Agts, 28 E Market. (See left bottom cor cards.)

Western Underwriters' Association, Composed of Milwaukee Mechanics' Insurance Co of Milwaukee, Wis, and German Insurance Co of Freeport, Ill, The McGilliard Agency Co Genl Agts, 83-85 E Market. (See backbone and opp p 588.)

Williamsburgh City of Brooklyn, N Y, A Metzger Agency Agts, 5 Odd Fellows' Hall. (See left bottom lines.)

INSURANCE COMPANIES—GENERAL LIABILITY.

Union Casualty and Surety Co of St Louis, Mo, W E Barton & Co Genl Agts, 504 Indiana Trust Bldg. (See right bottom cor cards.)

INSURANCE COMPANIES—GUARANTEE—FOREIGN.

American Bonding and Trust Co of Baltimore City, W E Barton & Co Genl Agts, 504 Indiana Trust Bldg. (See right bottom cor cards.)

Fidelity and Deposit Co of Maryland, George W Pangborn Genl Agt, 704-706 Lemcke Bldg. (See left top lines.)

London Guarantee and Accident Co (Limited) of London, England, George W Pangborn Genl Agt, 704-706 Lemcke Bldg. (See left top lines.)

INSURANCE COMPANIES—IDENTIFICATION.

National Identification Co, 16 Aetna Bldg.

INSURANCE COMPANIES—INDEMNITY BOND.

American Bonding and Trust Co of Baltimore City, W E Barton & Co Genl Agts, 504 Indiana Trust Bldg. (See right bottom cor cards.)

INSURANCE COMPANIES—LIABILITY OF TEAMS.

Union Casualty and Surety Co of St Louis, Mo, W E Barton & Co Genl Agts, 504 Indiana Trust Bldg. (See right bottom cor cards.)

INSURANCE COMPANIES—LIFE—HOME.

Capitol Life Insurance Co of Indiana, 29 N Penn. (See adv opp p 243.)

Columbian Relief Fund Assn, 409-410 Lemcke bldg.

German American Savings Life Assn, 718 Lemcke bldg.

Home Benefit Assn of Indianapolis, Ind, 67 Ingalls blk.

Indiana Indemnity Co, 147 Mass av.

Industrial Life Association of Indianapolis, Ind, Rooms 1, 2 and 3 Hartford Blk.

Masonic Mutual Benefit Society, 29½ E Market.

Masons' Union Life Assn, 8-9 Masonic Temple.

Meridian Life and Trust Company, 432 Lemcke Bldg. (See adv opp p 620.)

Mutual Life Insurance Co of Indiana, 314-322 Lemcke Bldg.

Odd Fellows' Mutual Aid Assn of Indiana, 2 Odd Fellows' blk.

Old Wayne Mutual Life Association, 52-62 Commercial Club Bldg.

State Life Insurance Co, 515-520 Lemcke Bldg.

*INSURANCE COMPANIES—LIFE—FOREIGN.

Aetna Life Insurance Co of Hartford, Conn, R W Kempshall & Co Mngrs, James A Buchanan Special Agt, 214 Lemcke Bldg.

Berkshire Life Insurance Co of Pittsfield, Mass, John J Price Genl Agt, 207-208 Lemcke Bldg.

Connecticut Mutual Life Insurance Co, Charles P Greene Genl Agt, 76 Commercial Club Bldg.

Covenant Mutual Life Association of Galesburg, Ill, J M Armstrong State Mngr, 48 Journal Bldg.

Equitable Life Assurance Society of the United States, 601-603 Indiana Trust Bldg.

Equitable Life Assurance Society of New York, Richardson & McCrea Agts, 79 E Market. (See right top cor cards.)

Equitable Life Assurance Society of the United States, Tutewiler & Shideler Mngrs for Western Indiana, 601 Indiana Trust Bldg.

Equitable Life Insurance Co of Iowa, C H McDowell Genl Agt, 629-630 Lemcke Bldg.

Equitable Mutual Life Association of Waterloo, Iowa, W R and E H Scott State Mngrs, 66½ N Penn.

Fidelity Mutual Life Insurance Co of Philadelphia, A H Collins State Mngr, 52-53 Baldwin Blk. (See left top lines.)

C. ZIMMERMAN & SONS | SLATE AND GRAVEL ROOFERS 19 South East Street.

DRIVEN WELLS And Second Water Wells and Pumps of all kinds at CHARLES KRAUSS', 42 S. PENN. ST. TELEPHONE 465.

Germania Life Insurance Co of New York, W H Coburn State Mngr, Room 4 Odd Fellows' Blk.

Germania of New York, A Metzger Agency Agts, 5 Odd Fellows' Hall. (See left bottom lines.)

Hancock John Mutual Life Insurance Co of Boston, Williams & Flickinger State Agts, 95-96 Lombard Bldg.

Home Security Life Association of Saginaw, Mich, George B McGill State Mngr, Rooms 334-335 Lemcke Bldg.

Massachusetts Benefit Life Association, Daniel L Brown State Agt, Rooms 9-10 Baldwin Blk.

Metropolitan Life Insurance Co of New York, Richard D Hughes Supt, 75-80 Baldwin Blk.

Michigan Mutual Life Insurance Co, J F McFarland State Agt, W J Handy Cashier, 32 Journal Bldg.

Mutual Benefit Life Insurance Co of Newark, N J, Benjamin B Peck State Agt, 20-21 Fletcher's Bank Bldg.

Mutual Life Insurance Co of Kentucky, Louisville, Ky, Jacob Frankel State Agt, 90 Lombard Bldg.

Mutual Life Insurance Co The of New York, Robert Merritt & Co Genl Agts, 6 Lombard Bldg.

Nederland Life Insurance Co (Ltd), John T Holsinger Cashier, Rooms 3, 4 and 5 Blackford Blk, s e cor Meridian and Washington.

New England Mutual Life Insurance Co of Boston, Mass, Horne & Gasper Genl Agts, 400 Indiana Trust Bldg.

Northwestern Mutual Life Insurance Co of Milwaukee, Wis, D F Swain Genl Agt Life Dept, Frank M Millikan Special Loan Agt, 88 N Penn.

Phoenix Mutual Life Insurance Co, Edwin S Folsom Genl Agt, 34 Mass av.

Provident Life and Trust Co of Philadelphia The, D W Edwards Genl Agt, 508-510 Indiana Trust Bldg. (See right top lines and left top cor cards and opp p 334.)

Prudential Insurance Co of America, Home Office Newark, N J, Thomas Mason Supt, 33-34 Ingalls Blk.

Travelers' Insurance Co of Hartford, Conn, H C Newcomb City Agt, 319-321 Indiana Trust Bldg.

United States Life Insurance Co of New York, Elias B Swift Mngr, 25 E Market. (See left bottom lines.)

Washington Life Insurance Co of New York, Clifford Arrick State Agt, 68 E Market.

*INSURANCE COMPANIES—PLATE GLASS—FOREIGN.

Fidelity and Casualty Co of New York, Indiana Trust Co Agts, s e cor Washington and Virginia av. (See front cover, opp p 487 and opp Insurance Agts.)

Fidelity and Casualty Co of New York, Richardson & McCrea Agts, 79 E Market. (See right top cor cards.)

Fidelity and Casualty Co of New York, Tuttle & Seguin Agts, 28 E Market. (See left bottom cor cards.)

Metropolitan of New York, A Metzger Agency Agts, 5 Odd Fellows' Hall. (See left bottom lines.)

Union Casualty and Surety Co of St Louis, Mo, W E Barton & Co Genl Agts, 504 Indiana Trust Bldg. (See right bottom cor cards.)

INSURANCE COMPANIES—PUBLIC LIABILITY.

Union Casualty and Surety Co of St Louis, Mo, W E Barton & Co Genl Agts, 504 Indiana Trust Bldg. (See right bottom cor cards.)

INSURANCE COMPANIES—STEAM BOILER.

Fidelity and Casualty Co of New York, Richardson & McCrea Agts, 79 E Market. (See right top cor cards.)

Union Casualty and Surety Co of St Louis, Mo, W E Barton & Co Genl Agts, 504 Indiana Trust Bldg. (See right bottom cor cards.)

INSURANCE COMPANIES—STEAM BOILER INSPECTION.

Hartford Steam Boiler Inspection and Insurance Co, Indiana Trust Co Agts, s e cor Washington and Virginia av. (See front cover, opp p 487 and opp Insurance Agts.)

*INSURANCE COMPANIES—SURETY BONDS—FOREIGN.

American Bonding and Trust Co of Baltimore City, W E Barton & Co Genl Agts, 504 Indiana Trust Bldg. (See right bottom cor cards.)

American Surety Co of New York, Albert W Wishard 2d Res Vice-Pres, Rooms 106-108 Commercial Club Bldg.

Fidelity and Casualty Co of New York, A Metzger Agency Agts, 5 Odd Fellows' Hall. (See left bottom lines.)

Fidelity and Casualty Co of New York, Richardson & McCrea Agts, 79 E Market. (See right top cor cards.)

Fidelity and Deposit Co of Maryland, George W Pangborn Genl Agt, 704-706 Lemcke Bldg. (See left top lines.)

London Guarantee and Accident Co (Limited) of London, England, George W Pangborn Genl Agt, 704-706 Lemcke Bldg. (See left top lines.)

INSURANCE COMPANIES—WORKINGMEN'S COLLECTIVE LIABILITY.

Union Casualty and Surety Co of St Louis, Mo, W E Barton & Co Genl Agts, 504 Indiana Trust Bldg. (See right bottom cor cards.)

ERTEL STEAM LAUNDRY || LARGEST AND BEST IN THE STATE. PROMPT SERVICE. 26 and 28 N. Senate Ave. Telephone 18

ELLIS & HELFENBERGER || Architectural Iron Work and Gray Iron Castings. 162-170 South Senate Ave. Tel. 958.

THE HOGAN TRANSFER AND STORAGE COMP'Y
Household Goods and Pianos Moved—Packed—Stored..... Baggage and Package Express Machinery and Safes a Specialty Cor. Washington and Illinois Sts. TELEPHONE No. 675.

Hose, Belting, Packing, Clothing, Druggists' Sundries, Bicycle Tires, Cotton Hose, Etc. New York Belting & Packing Co., L't'd.
The Central Rubber & Supply Co. 79 S. ILLINOIS ST., INDIANAPOLIS, IND. PHONE 2.

*INSURANCE SUPPLIES.

Rough Notes Co The, 79 W Market.

*INVESTMENT BANKERS AND BROKERS.

Coffin C E & Co, 90 E Market.
Day Thos C & Co, 325-330 Lemcke Bldg. (See right top cor cards.)
Indiana Trust Co The, Indiana Trust Bldg, s e cor Washington and Virginia av. (See front cover, opp p 487 and opp Insurance Agts.)
Lawyers' Loan and Trust Co, 68½ E Market. (See top edge and opp p 555.)
Marion Trust Co The, s e cor Market and Monument Pl. (See back cover.)
Metzger A Agency, 5 Odd Fellows' Hall. (See left bottom lines.)
Union Trust Co The, 68 E Market. (See front cover and opp p 867.)

*IRON CASTINGS.

Indianapolis Foundry Co, Judge Harding s of Washington.

*IRON—CORRUGATED.

Indianapolis Steel Roofing and Corrugating Works, 23-25 E South. (See right side lines.)
Laing Samuel, 72-74 E Court. (See left side lines.)

*IRON GRATING AND CRESTING.

Ellis & Helfenberger, 162-168 S Senate av. (See right bottom lines.)

*IRON ROOFING.

Indianapolis Steel Roofing and Corrugating Works, 23-25 E South. (See right side lines.)
Long Steel and Iron Roofing Co The, 180-186 W 5th. (See adv in Roofers.)
Moffat & Co, 402 Lemcke Bldg. (See adv p 9.)

*IRON VASES.

Ellis & Helfenberger, 162-168 S Senate av. (See right bottom lines.)

*IRON WORKS.

Brown-Ketcham Iron Works, Michigan (H).

IRON AND STEEL—WHOLESALE.

Hazen Co The, 807 Majestic bldg.

*IRON AND STEEL MNFRS' SUPPLIES.

Moffat & Co, 402 Lemcke Bldg. (See adv p 9.)

*IRON AND WIRE FENCES.

Cleaveland Fence Co, Factory 18-22 Biddle, Office 21 Biddle.
Ellis & Helfenberger, 162-168 S Senate av. (See right bottom lines.)
Indianapolis Fence Co, Office 15

*JAPANESE NOVELTIES.

Mayer Charles & Co, 29-31 W Washington. (See adv opp p 615.)

*JEWELERS.

(See also Watches, Clocks and Jewelry.)
Walk Julius C & Son, 12 E Washington. (See left bottom cor cards.)

JEWELERS—MANUFACTURING.

Craft & Koehler, 27½ S Meridian.
Dyer George G, 18½ N Meridian.
Matsumoto Ikko, 2, 17½ S Meridian.
Sipe Jacob C, 18½ N Meridian.

JUNK DEALERS.

Bernstein Joseph, 189 Indiana av.
Borinstein A, 109-115 S East.
Buechert Frederick, 212 W McCarty.
Cohen Alexander, 359 W Washington.
Cohen Harris, 291 W Washington.
Edwards Wm H, 81 Norwood.
Falender S & Co, 92 Eddy.
Finkelstein Solomon, 167 Madison av.
Griffey Wm, 18 Wright.
Hughes Thomas, rear 131 E Washington.
Hyman Louis, 428 W Washington.
Marks Henry, 196 S Penn.
Morris Wolfe, rear 126 E Ohio.
Ringolsky Himon, s e cor Maryland and Penn.
Rosuck David, 100 Eddy.
Sagalowsky Bros, 427 W Washington.
Sagalowsky Isaac, 94 Eddy.
Sagalowsky Simon, 135 Eddy.
Saperstein Bros, 299 S Illinois.
Williams Hanover W, 448 Blake.

JUSTICES OF THE PEACE.

Clark Charles A, 88½ E Washington.
Habich Carl, 96 E Court.
Hay Frank M, 80½ E Market.
Lockman Wm S, 34 N Delaware.
Martin Ezra G, 154 Michigan (H).
Nickerson Wm H, 26 N Delaware.
Pentecost Elmer B, w s Commercial av 2 s of Washington (I).
Sears John W, 91½ E Court.
Walpole Luke, 12½ N Delaware.

*LADIES' FURNISHING GOODS.

Clune John, 13 E Washington.
Haerle Wm, 4 W Washington.

*LAGOS PALM OIL.

Moffat & Co, 402 Lemcke Bldg. (See adv p 9.)

*LATH.

Balke & Krauss Co, cor Market and Missouri. (See right bottom lines.)
Dalton & Merrifield, 30-50 S Noble. (See left top lines.)
Wasson W G Co The, 130 Indiana av. (See left cor cards and adv in Cement and Lime.)

LAUNDRIES.

Abraham & Pein, 51-53 W 7th. (See adv.)
Acme Steam Laundry, 13 N Illinois.

OTTO GAS ENGINES | BUILDERS' EXCHANGE S. W. Cor. Ohio and Penn. Telephone 535.

Becker & Son Charles Becker Jacob Becker Jr. Merchant Tailors. 21 N. Penn. St. Tel. 934

SALISBURY & STANLEY • Office, Store and Bank Repairing of all kinds done on short notice. 177 Clinton Street, Indianapolis, Ind. • Contractors and Builders TELEPHONE 999.

J. B. ABRAHAM. GEO. W. PEIN.

North Side Laundry

51-53 WEST SEVENTH ST.

OUR SPECIALTIES:
GOOD WORK.
PROMPT DELIVERY.

INDIANAPOLIS.

American Toilet Supply Co, 26 S Illinois. (See adv in Toilet Supply Companies.)
Armstrong Laundry, 70 S Illinois and 126-130 W Maryland.
Christy Wm W, 367 Blake.
Crystal Laundry, 10 Clifford av.
Diamond Steam Laundry and Toilet Supply Co, 146 Ft Wayne av.
Domestic Laundry, 73 N Illinois.
Ertel Steam Laundry, 26-28 N Senate av. (See right side lines.)
Excelsior Steam Laundry, 2-6 Masonic Temple.
Gem Steam Laundry, 37-39 Indiana av.
Gun Charles, 565 Virginia av.
Heath Samuel, 147 Mass av.
Home Laundry The, 197 S Illinois. (See right side lines.)
Krauss Paul H, 44-46 E Washington.
Lee Hop, 12 and 189 Indiana av.
Lee Jim, 241 W Washington.
Lee Quong, 118 N Delaware.
Lee Quong Sing, 66 Indiana av.
Lee Sing, 226 E Washington.
Lung Doc, 212 W Washington.
Lung E, 21 Mass av.
McElwain Wm P, 255 Jefferson av.
Moo Shing, 39 Virginia av.
North Side Laundry, 51-53 W 7th. (See adv.)
Progress Laundry, 322 E Washington.
Ritchey Samuel J, 10 Clifford av.
Richter & Wright, 270 E Washington.
Sing Hop, 75 N Illinois.
Sing Lee, 295 Mass av.
Sing Pang, 125 Mass av.
Sing Wah, 143 E Washington.
Sligar & Paetz, 141 N Delaware.
Springsteen & James, 504 Bellefontaine.
Union Co-Operative Laundry, 138-144 Virginia av. (See left side lines.)
Whitty John M, 60 W Maryland.

*LAUNDRY FILTERS.

Worthington Henry R, 64 S Penn. (See left top lines.)

*LAW BOOK PUBLISHERS.

Bowen-Merrill Co The, 9-11 W Washington.

*LAWN GUARDS.

Ellis & Helfenberger, 162-168 S Senate av. (See right bottom lines.)

*LAWN MOWERS.

Vonnegut Clemens, 184-186 E Washington. (See left bottom lines.)

*LAWN SWINGS.

Mayer Charles & Co, 29-31 W Washington. (See adv opp p 615.)

*LAWN TENNIS.

Mayer Charles & Co, 29-31 W Washington. (See adv opp p 615.)

LAWYERS.

Adkinson Wm P, 113½ E Washington.
Aikins Bronte M, 425-426 Lemcke Bldg.
Alford & Partlow, 37 Baldwin blk.
Allison Charles H, 214-218 Lemcke bldg.
Arbaugh Archibald M, 50 S Meridian.
Ashby Samuel, 68½ E Market.
Atkinson & Knipp, 521-523 Lemcke bldg.
Averill Charles E, 33-36 Thorpe blk.
Aydelotte Wm M, 504 Lemcke bldg.
Ayres & Jones, 500-502 Indiana Trust Bldg.
Bailey John M, 37½ E Washington.
Bailey Wm E, 20½ N Delaware.
Baird John W, 19½ N Meridian.
Baker James P, 29 Thorpe blk.
Baker & Daniels, 9, 10 and 11 Ingalls blk.
Bamberger Edwin L, 37 Journal bldg.
Bamberger Ralph, 11 Aetna bldg.
Bartholomew Pliny W, 11-12 College av.
Bastian Willits A, 57 Journal bldg.
Batchelor George E, 5 Hubbard blk.
Beck Henry A, 419-420 Lemcke bldg.
Beckett Wymond J, 68½ E Market.
Bell Joseph E, 77-78 Lombard bldg.
Benedict & Benedict, 33-34 Lombard bldg.
Beveridge Albert J, 18½ N Penn.
Bickel Harrison C, 82½ E Washington.
Black & Pugh, 57-58 Lombard bldg.
Blackledge & Thornton, 634-635 Lemcke bldg.
Blair & Vazeille, 112 Commercial Club Bldg.
Bloomer Isaac L, 33-34 Baldwin blk.

COAL AND LIME Cement, Hair, Sewer Pipe, etc. BALKE & KRAUSS CO. Cor. Missouri and Market Sts.

FRIEDGEN'S IS THE PLACE FOR THE NOBBIEST SHOES Ladies' and Gents' 19 North Pennsylvania St.

SAMUEL LAING || COPPER AND GALVANIZED IRON CORNICE MANUFACTURER
72 AND 74 E. COURT STREET. SKYLIGHTS AND VENTILATORS

Lawyers—Continued.
Boice Augustin, 18½ N Meridian.
Booth John S, 77½ E Market.
Bosson Wm, 81-83 Lombard bldg.
Bowles Duane H, 625-626 Lemcke bldg.
Bowlus John W, 26 N Delaware.
Bowser Harry, 46 Lombard bldg.
Bradbury Daniel M, 403 Lemcke bldg.
Bradford Chester, 14-16 Hubbard Blk. (See left top cor cards, p 6 and opp Patent Solicitors.)
Bradwell Isaac N, 32 Thorpe blk.
Bragg Thomas F, 10½ N Delaware.
Branthoover Frank M, 87 Baldwin blk.
Brown Arthur V, 12-13 Fletcher's Bank bldg.
Brown Edgar A, 88-90 Lombard bldg.
Brown Herbert P, 719-720 Lemcke bldg.
Brown Wm T, 216-218 Indiana Trust bldg.
Buenting Lueppo D, 27½ S Delaware.
Bullock Henry W, 95 E Washington.
Bynum Wm D, 534-535 Lemcke bldg.
Cady Frederick W, 8½ N Penn.
Cale Howard, 68½ E Market.
Calvert George C, 18½ N Penn.
Canine Fred L, 11-12 Baldwin blk.
Carnahan James R, 54 Journal bldg.
Carroll Charles P, 12 Fletcher's Bank bldg.
Carson Oliver H, 88 Lombard bldg.
Carson & Thompson, 525-528 Lemcke Bldg.
Carter George, 94½ E Washington.
Central Law Union The, 425-426 Lemcke Bldg. (See adv in Collection Agts.)
Chambers Ferdinand, 18½ N Penn.
Chambers, Pickens & Moores, 602-610 Lemcke bldg.
Claypool Jefferson H, 14 Talbott blk.
Claypool & Claypool, 1-2 Blackford blk.
Clifford, Browder & Moffett, 72½ E Washington.
Coburn John, 531 Lemcke bldg.
Coffin Charles F, 15-19 Aetna bldg.
Cole Albert B, 17 Thorpe blk.
Coleman Lewis Austin, 81 Baldwin blk.
Collier Joseph, 215 Indiana Trust bldg.
Compton Charles E, 111 Commercial Club bldg.
Cooper Charles M, 51 Lombard bldg.
Cotter James A C, 74 S Meridian.
Cox Henry C, 47 Thorpe blk.
Cox Millard F, 7-8 When bldg.
Cravens Thomas S, 18½ N Penn.
Cropsey & Marshall, 529-530 Lemcke bldg.
Cutter Frank C, 1 Fletcher's Bank bldg.
Dailey Hezekiah, 95 E Washington.
Daly & Raub, 11-13 Aetna bldg.
Daniels Milton H, 110 English av.
Davidson Robert F, 609 Lemcke bldg.
Davis Arthur G, 38 Thorpe blk.
De Haas Charles L, 729-731 Lemcke bldg.
Deitch Guilford A, 26 Thorpe blk.
Dickey Alfred E, 9 Ingalls blk.
Dickey Almon H, 91½ E Court.
Dickey Edward T, 4 Lombard bldg.
Dixon Sterling P, 30½ N Delaware.
Dowling Henry M, 506 Indiana Trust bldg.
Dryer Charles A, 408 Indiana Trust bldg.
Duncan, Smith & Hornbrook, 76½ E Washington.
Durham & Erganbright, 629-630 Lemcke bldg.
Dye John T, 101-102 Commercial Club Bldg.
Dye Wm H, 507 Indiana Trust Bldg.
Edenharter & Mull, 204-206 Indiana Trust bldg.
Elliott & Elliott, 9-10 Fletcher's Bank bldg.
Estabrook Gay R, 95 E Washington.
Everett Harmon J, 92½ E Washington.
Ewbank & Watson, 12 Brandon Blk, 95 E Washington.
Fairbanks Charles W, 37 Ingalls blk.
Feibleman Charles B, 90 E Court.
Feibleman Isidore, 139 Commercial Club bldg.
Finch & Finch (The Law of Insurance a Specialty), 26, 28 and 30 Thorpe Blk.
Fishback & Kappes, 631-633 Lemcke bldg.
Fitzgerald & Ruckelshaus, 37-40 Journal bldg.
Florea & Seidensticker, 27½ S Delaware.
Forkner Samuel, 19 Baldwin blk.
Foster Frank S, 536 Lemcke bldg.
Galvin George W, 18½ N Penn.
Gates & Hume, 801 Majestic bldg.
Gavin & Davis, 903-904 Majestic bldg.
Gooding David S, 47 Thorpe blk.
Grant Amandus N, 419-420 Lemcke bldg.
Gray Pierre, 39 Thorpe blk.
Green John C, 314 Lemcke bldg.
Griffiths & Potts, 713-719 Lemcke bldg.
Groninger & Moore, 323-325 Indiana Trust bldg.
Grubbs Daniel W, 9 Cyclorama pl.
Haas Schuyler A, 531-533 Lemcke bldg.
Hadley Alonzo M, 62½ E Washington.
Hadley Cash C, 711-712 Lemcke bldg.
Hadley Hugh H, 44 Lorraine bldg.
Hammond & Rogers, 17-18 Fletcher's Bank bldg.
Hamrick Jesse D, 35½ E Washington.
Hanna Thomas, 5-6, 18½ N Penn.
Harding & Hovey, 51-54 Lombard bldg.
Harlan Levi P, 62½ E Washington.
Harper James W, 212 Indiana Trust bldg.
Harrington & Carlon, 515-517 Indiana Trust bldg.
Harris Addison C, 1-3 Fletcher's Bank bldg.
Harrison Benjamin, 68½ E Market.
Hasely Charles R, 15½ Virginia av.
Hatch Aretas W, 14 Talbott blk.
Haughey & Coleman, 48 Thorpe blk.
Hawkins & Smith, 303-308 Lemcke bldg.
Hay Linn D, 307-309 Indiana Trust bldg.
Heinrichs Wm F, 15 Ingalls blk.
Hendricks Caroline P, 501 Indiana Trust bldg.
Herod & Herod, 14-17 Fletcher's Bank Bldg.
Hill James T V, 10½ N Delaware.
Hines Fletcher S, 4 Franklin Insurance bldg, 25 E Market.
Hobbs Robert D, 58-59 Baldwin blk.
Hollett John E, 502 Indiana Trust bldg.
Holstein, Barrett & Hubbard, 84 E Market.
Holtzman & Leathers, 34-35 Journal bldg.
Hood Arthur M (H P Hood & Son), 68½ E Market. (See adv in Patent Attorneys.)
Hopkins Murat W, 20-21 Fletcher's Bank bldg.
Hord Horace B, 431 Lemcke bldg.
Hord & Perkins, 504, 505 and 506 Lemcke bldg.
Howe Daniel Wait, 5-9 Hubbard blk.
Hynes Amos P, 5 Brandon blk.
Iles Orlando B, 35 Lombard bldg.
Irvin Wm, 69 When bldg.
Jacoby Elias, 37 Ingalls blk.

PAPER BOXES : SULLIVAN & MAHAN 41 W. Pearl St.

DIAMOND WALL PLASTER { Telephone 1410 BUILDERS' EXCHANGE.

Jameson & Joss, 5-7 Brandon blk.
Jenkins John C, 18½ N Penn.
Johnson Marquis L, 10½ N Delaware.
Johnson Thomas E, 35½ E Washington.
Jones J Lyman, 701 Lemcke bldg.
Jordan Henry C, 713 Lemcke bldg.
Jordan Wm H, 211 Lemcke bldg.
Julian & Julian, 12½ N Delaware.
Kahn Sylvan W, 90-92 Baldwin blk.
Kealing John W, 46 Lombard bldg.
Kealing & Hugg, 95 E Washington.
Keith Ernest R, Rooms 1-3, 38½ E Washington.
Keith Robert B, 68½ E Market.
Kern & Bailey, 1, 2, 3, 4 and 7. 8½ N Penn.
Ketcham Wm A, 6 Fletcher's Bank bldg and 19-21 State House.
Kinney Collie E, 55 N Illinois.
Knefler & Berryhill, 82½ E Washington.
LaFuze Samuel D, 68 Lombard bldg.
Lamb & Hill, 507-513 Indiana Trust bldg.
Lazarus & Ludwig, 303 Indiana Trust bldg.
Leach & Odle, 13-14 Lombard bldg.
Lecklider John T, 11½ N Meridian.
Leyendecker & Waters, 308 Indiana Trust bldg.
Littleton Frank L, 9 Fletcher's Bank bldg.
Lockwood Virgil H, 415-418 Lemcke Bldg. (See adv in Patent Attorneys.)
Lodge Caleb N, 719-720 Lemcke bldg.
Lowry Wm W, 57 Journal bldg.
Lucas Francis C, 86 Lombard bldg.
McBride & Denny, 55-58 Journal bldg.
McCormack Zuinglius K, 72½ E Washington.
McCullough & Spaan, 311-317 Indiana Trust bldg.
McDonald & McDonald, 96½ E Market.
McGuire Newton J, 713 Lemcke bldg.
McKay Horace, 29½ N Penn.
McLain Moses G, 29-31 Thorpe blk.
McMichael Harry S, 19 Aetna bldg.
MacFall Russell T, 20 Fletcher's Bank bldg.
Manker James M, 35-39 Thorpe blk.
Marrow Samuel L, 67 Ingalls blk.
Martindale Charles, 402-404 Indiana Trust bldg.
Mason & Latta, 36-38 Journal Bldg.
Masson & Reagan, 73 Lombard bldg.
Matson Frederick E, 6 Fletcher's Bank bldg.
Mattler Francis J, 67 Ingalls blk.
Means & Clarke, 2½ W Washington.
Miller & Elam, 68½ E Market.
Milligan Harry J, 68½ E Market.
Mitchell James L, 212 Indiana Trust bldg.
Moore Frank F, 611 Lemcke bldg.
Moore John O, 92½ E Washington.
Moores Merrill, 18½ N Penn.
Morgan & Morgan, 37-38 Lombard Bldg, 24½ E Washington.
Morris, Newberger & Curtis, 134-140 Commercial Club bldg.
Morrison Frank W, 7-8 When bldg.
Morrow & McKee, 38 Thorpe blk.
Mott Sherman, 415 Lemcke bldg.
Muir Oran N, 631 Lemcke bldg.
Myers David A, 22 Aetna bldg.
Myrick Orlando H, 20½ N Delaware.
Negley Harry E, 69 When bldg.
Newman Omer U, 525 Lemcke bldg.
Noel & Lahr, 411-412 Lemcke bldg.
Norton Pierce, 35-39 Thorpe blk.
Nysewander Benjamin F, 37½ E Washington.
Ogborn Wm H, 17 Baldwin blk.
Orbison Charles J, 62 Baldwin blk.
Parker Eben A, 35½ E Washington.
Payne Wm H, 1 Talbott blk.
Perrin George K, 33-34 Baldwin blk.
Pickens & Cox, 109-111 Commercial Club bldg.
Pickerill Wm N, 33-36 Thorpe blk.
Pierce Henry Douglas, 11, 12, 13 and 13½, 18½ N Meridian.
Porter George T, 35 Ingalls blk.
Pringle Wm W, 20½ N Delaware.
Pritchard James A, 15 Baldwin blk.
Raber Alfred, 312 Indiana Trust bldg.
Reading Wm A, 18½ N Penn.
Reagan & Brown, 79 Baldwin blk.
Reese James H, 20½ N Delaware.
Reinhard Francis J, 27½ S Delaware.
Remster Charles, 215 Indiana Trust bldg.
Richcreek & Richcreek, 85 Baldwin blk.
Riley Lawrence T, 315 Indiana Trust bldg.
Ringland Joseph, 65 Ingalls blk.
Ripley Warwick H, 21 Thorpe blk.
Ritter Frederick O, 408 Indiana Trust bldg.
Ritter & Baker, 45-47 Baldwin blk.
Robbins Charles F, 93 Lombard bldg.
Roberts Joseph T, 51 Bloomington.
Robertson Lou A, 68½ E Market.
Robertson Willard, 625-626 Lemcke bldg.
Rochford John J, 82½ E Washington.
Roemler Charles O, 86 Commercial Club bldg.
Rollins & Wiltsie, 71-72 Lombard bldg.
Rooker Wm V, 95 E Washington.
Rose George A, 103½ E Washington.
Rothschild Leopold G, 18½ N Penn.
Royall Octavius V, 711-712 Lemcke bldg.
Ruffin J Edward, 112 Commercial Club bldg.
Ryman George H, 157½ E Washington.
Schwartz Wm B, 94½ E Washington.
Scott & Rabb, 62-63 Lombard bldg.
Seyfried Henry, 29 N Penn.
Shepard Silas M, 50-51 Baldwin blk.
Shepherd Wm D, 99 Highland pl.
Sherwood John B, 84 Lombard bldg.
Shimer & Allen, 636 Lemcke bldg.
Smith Carey L, 419-420 Lemcke bldg.
Smith Robert E, 13 Baldwin blk.
Smith Wirt C, 41 Baldwin blk.
Smith & Korbly, 602-606 Indiana Trust bldg.
Smitha Elmer A, 71 Lombard bldg.
Snow-Church Co The, 112 Commercial Club Bldg. (See adv in Collection Agts.)
Spahr George W, 95 E Washington.
Spahr & Kingsbury, 215 Indiana Trust bldg.
Spooner Samuel H, 6 Fletcher's Bank bldg.
Sprague Roger A, 138 Woodlawn av.
Springer Francis M, 12 Ingalls blk.
Stanton & Denny, 8, 9 and 10 Aetna bldg.
Stevenson Elmer E, 703-708 Lemcke bldg.
Stevenson Henry F, 68½ E Market.
Stevenson James, 86 Lombard bldg.
Stuart Romus F, 172 Huron.
Stubbs George W, 33-36 Thorpe blk.
Sullivan Thomas L, 77-78 Lombard bldg.
Swift Lucius B, 2 Hubbard blk.
Taylor Harold, 302-304 Indiana Trust Bldg.
Taylor Newton M, 44 Lorraine bldg.
Taylor Wm L, 18½ N Penn.
Terhune & Moore, 404-406 Lemcke Bldg.
Teter Hiram, 309-310 Lemcke bldg.
Thompson Wm C, 35 Baldwin blk.
Trusler Thomas J, 10½ N Delaware.

If your Laundry Work is not satisfactory, try THE HOME LAUNDRY 19 S. Illinois St. Telephone 16.

THE WM. H. BLOCK CO. 7 AND 9 EAST WASHINGTON STREET. DRY GOODS, MEN'S FURNISHINGS.

The Fidelity and Deposit Co. OF MARYLAND. Bonds signed for Administrators, Assignees, Executors, Guardians, Receivers, Trustees, and persons in every position of trust.
GEO. W. PANGBORN, General Agent, 704-706 Lemcke Building. Telephone 140.

INSURE YOUR PROPERTY WITH FRANK K. SAWYER

Lawyers—Continued.
Van Buren Wm A, 18½ N Penn.
Van Vorhis & Spencer, 20-24 Baldwin blk.
Walker Lewis C, 55-56 Lombard bldg.
Walker Merle N A, 31 Lombard bldg.
Wall John M, 51 Lombard bldg.
Wallace Lew jr, 139 Commercial Club bldg.
Warmouth George W, 14 Fletcher's Bank bldg.
Warrum Henry, 312 Indiana Trust bldg.
Watts Burton F, 92½ E Washington.
Webster & White, 37½ E Washington.
Weir Clarence E, 137 Commercial Club bldg.
Welman Salem P, 425-426 Lemcke Bldg.
Whitcomb Larz A, 725-726 Lemcke bldg.
Whittinghill Wm L, 19 Baldwin blk.
Wilkinson Philip, 68 Lombard bldg.
Williams John G, 407-413 Indiana Trust bldg.
Williams Noel W, 103½ E Washington.
Wilson John H, 38½ E Washington.
Wilson John R, 11-12 Aetna bldg.
Wilson Wilborn, 12½ N Delaware.
Wiltsie Charles S, 71-72 Lombard bldg.
Winpenny George W, 19 Baldwin blk.
Winter Ferdinand, 802-804 Majestic bldg.
Winters James M, 4-5 Fletcher's Bank bldg.
Wiseman Isaac L, 12½ N Delaware.
Wishard Albert W, 264 N Capitol av.
Woods Floyd A, 18¼ N Penn.
Woods George W, 19¼ N Penn.
Woollen & Woollen, 130 Commercial Club bldg.
Wright Granville S, 29½ N Penn.
Wyatt Harrison N, 113½ E Washington.

LEAF TOBACCO.
See Tobacco—Leaf.

LEATHER AND FINDINGS.
Hide, Leather and Belting Co, 125 S Meridian.
Holliday & Wyon, 96 S Penn.
Nutz & Grosskopf, 24-26 W Maryland.
Taylor & Smith, 137-139 S Meridian.

***LETTER FILE MANUFACTURERS.**
Lane Wm B, 160 Bane.

***LIGHTNING ROD MANUFACTURERS.**
Munson Alvin J, 94 S Delaware.

LIME, CEMENT AND PLASTER.
Balke & Krauss Co, cor Market and Missouri. (See right bottom lines.)
Consolidated Coal and Lime Co, 13 Virginia av.
Ingalls Lime Co, 436 Lemcke bldg.
Meyer A B & Co, 15-17 N Penn.
Rex Coal and Sewer Co, 171 E Louisiana.
Wales Samuel W, 387 Mass av.
Wasson W G & Co, 130 Indiana av. (See left bottom cor cards and adv in Cement and Lime.)

***LINE ENGRAVING.**
Indiana Illustrating Co, s e cor Market and Illinois. (See adv opp Engravers.)

***LINOTYPE OPERATORS.**
Wiley Wm T, 75 W Market.

***LINSEED OIL MANUFACTURERS.**
Evans Linseed Oil Works, 4 Ingalls blk.

LITHOGRAPHERS.
Burford Wm B, 21 W Washington. (See adv opp p 230.)
Indianapolis Lithographing Co, F A Heuss Propr, 95 E South.

LIVE STOCK COMMISSION.
Allen Stephen T, Union Stock Yards (W I).
Baber A & Co, Union Stock Yards (W I).
Beck George C, Union Stock Yards (W I).
Blair, Baker & Walter, Union Stock Yards (W I).
Brunson George R, Union Stock Yards (W I).
Capital Live Stock Commission Co, Union Stock Yards (W I).
Clark, Wysong & Voris, Union Stock Yards (W I).
Coburn & Weelburg, Union Stock Yards (W I).
Cook Robert B, Union Stock Yards (W I).
Dye, Valodin & Co, Union Stock Yards (W I).
Jeffery, Fuller & Co, Union Stock Yards (W I).
Kahn A & Son, Union Stock Yards (W I).
McMurray Lewis H, Union Stock Yards (W I).
Middlesworth, Benson, Nave & Co, Union Stock Yards (W I).
Powell John & Sons, Union Stock Yards (W I).
Sells M & Co, Union Stock Yards (W I).
Shiel R R & Co, Union Stock Yards (W I).
Stockton, Gillespie & Co, Union Stock Yards (W I).
Tolin, Totten, Tibbs & Co, Union Stock Yards (W I).

LIVERY, BOARDING AND SALE STABLES.
Adams & Son, 239 W Pearl.
Aldrich Frank, 277 W Washington.
Armstrong & Carmony, 80 E Court.
Barnett & Weisenberger, rear 478 N Penn.
Beck Frank A, 27 W St Clair.
Bird Frank Transfer Co, 24 Pembroke Arcade, 115 N Delaware, The Bates and Union Station. (See adv p 192; also in Omnibus Lines; also in Transfer Companies.)
Bohannon Ambrose G, 855 E Michigan.
Brock Thomas, 407 Virginia av.
Brown Theodore E, 163 W Washington.
Brown & Jones, 276-278 E Washington.
Carter Wm E, 233 W Maryland.
Catt L A & Co, 192-194 W Maryland.
Clancy Charles L, rear 224 N Meridian.
Coble George jr, 48 Pendleton av (B).
Cook George, 30 S Penn.
Cooper & Wood, 114-116 N Meridian. (See adv.)
Dearth Wm L, rear 162 E North.
Earhart David, 671 Madison av.
Eaton Marion, 25 W 7th.
Foudray Edgar E, 19 Bismarck av (H).
Fournace John B, 70 Kentucky av.
Gardner Anson J, 408 College av.
Gilbreath John S, 130 Christian av.
Girton Charles, 187 Indiana av.
Goodin & Davenport, 137 Hudson.
Gould Richard H, 132 E St Clair.

GUARANTEED INCOME POLICIES issued only by the United States Life Insurance Co.
E. B. SWIFT, Manager. 25 E. Market St.

Furniture Carpets } WM. KOTTEMAN { Stoves Ranges
89 and 91 East Washington Street. Telephone 1742.

WILLIAM WIEGEL } MANUFACTURER OF ...... } SHOW CASES { 6 W. Louisiana St. Opposite Union Station.

E. A. COOPER.
C. H. WOOD.
Telephone 1502.
THE MERIDIAN LIVERY AND BOARDING STABLE
LAUDAUS, BROUGHAMS, COACHES, CABRIOLETS, Traps and Fine Light Livery.
114, 116, 118 North Meridian St., INDIANAPOLIS.
PARTICULAR ATTENTION PAID TO BOARDING HORSES.

Grand Opera House Livery Stables, 75 E Wabash. (See adv.)
Green & Co, 69 W Market.
Grothe & Son, 40 E Maryland.
Haensel E Robert, 189 E Wabash.
Hannemann Albert, rear 137 E Pratt.
Haney Scott, n w cor Missouri and Court.
Henry & Son, 240 W Pearl.
Herrmann George, 26 S Delaware.
Hollingsworth Zeph, 267 W Pearl.
Holloway Cornelius B, 22 Cherry.
Hommown John, 30 Roanoke.
Hyatt Charles F, 26 W Merrill.
Jacobs Parmenas C, s e cor Washington and Lake avs (I).
Jennings Francis R, 70 W Maryland.
Johnson Caleb R, rear 1 Fayette.
Kessler George, 200 W Pearl.
Kinney Ray L, 440 E Washington.
Lang Herman, 170 E Court.
Leonard & Sloan, 541 Virginia av.
Long Wm T, 227 E Wabash.
McCorkle John P, 181 Virginia av.
McVey Oscar L, 1128 N Meridian.
Mabrey & Cook, 118 Hadley av (W I).
Mann John S, 83 E Wabash.
Marshall David R, 38 Oak.

Meridian Stables, 114-116 N Meridian. (See adv.)

Middleton Edward W, s s Wabash 1 e of Alabama.
Miles Samuel W, 127 E 7th.

Munter Kevi, 45 N Alabama. (See adv in Sale Stables.)

Murphy Patrick, 239 W Washington.
Myers Oliver C, 569 W Udell (N I).
Nageleisen Bros, 120-124 E Wabash.
Noe Richard, 864 S Meridian.
Patterson Walter G, Union Stock Yards (W I).
Perkins & Shockley, 218 W Maryland.
Piper Elder W, rear 642 N Illinois.
Poland John, 222 W Pearl.
Pottenger Wm B, rear 855 N Illinois.
Pray & Petrie, 33 N Alabama.
Railsback & Son, 173 E North.
Roberts George H, 286 Mass av.

DIRECTORIES OF ALL THE STATES AND PRINCIPAL CITIES ON FILE FOR REFERENCE AT OUR OFFICE.

R. L. POLK & CO.
23-24 JOURNAL BLDG.

TURKISH RUGS AND CARPETS RESTORED TO ORIGINAL COLORS LIKE NEW | Capital Steam Carpet Cleaning Works M. D. PLUNKETT, Telephone 818

BENJ. BOOTH PRACTICAL EXPERT ACCOUNTANT. Books Opened, Written Up, Posted and Balanced. Room 18, 82½ E. Washington St., Indianapolis, Ind.

THE SHERMAN RESTAURANT 18 and 20 S. MERIDIAN STREET

Livery, Etc., Stables—Continued.
Roth & Young, 80 W Market. (See adv.)
Schofield Frank, 180 E Wabash.
Scudder John, 36 W Ohio.
Sheets Charles W, rear 475 N Illinois.
Shover Oran D, 282 E Washington.
Smith Benjamin R, 4-8 Prospect.
Snowden Joseph M, 272 W Washington.
Spahr John H (Agt), 75 E Wabash. (See adv.)
Tansel Minos, 202 W Washington.
Van Natta James, 175 E Michigan.
Warman, Black, Chamberlain & Co, Union Stock Yards (W I).
Williamson John M, 78 N Alabama.
Wood Horace F, 23 Monument pl.

***LOANS—PERSONAL PROPERTY.**

Central Loan Co, 7-8 Talbott Blk.
Gausepohl Edward J, Room 4, 2½ W Washington.
Household Loan Association, 44 Lombard Bldg.
Indiana Mortgage Loan Co, 4 Lombard Bldg.
Security Mortgage Loan Co, 207-209 Indiana Trust Bldg.

***LOANS.**

(See also Real Estate.)

Aldrich Joshua H, 25 Thorpe blk.
Archer Frank P, 10 Thorpe blk.
Aufderheide Wm, 37½ E Washington.
Barnitt James L, 31 Lombard bldg.
Bennett Robert R, 44 Lombard bldg.
Boice & Dark, 18½ N Meridian.
Boyd Wm H, 63 Baldwin blk.
Boyd & Miller, 63 Baldwin blk.
Britton Charles O, 12 Fletcher's Bank bldg.
Byram, Cornelius & Co, 15 Thorpe blk.
Catterson R F & Son, 24 Kentucky av.
Central Loan Co, 11½ N Meridian.
Coe & Roache, 300 Indiana Trust Bldg.
Coffin C E & Co, 90 E Market.
Cranor John H, 723 Lemcke bldg.
Day Thos C & Co, 325-330 Lemcke Bldg. (See right top cor cards.)
Eckman Russell, 40 Board of Trade bldg.
Fay Henry H, 40½ E Washington. (See right top cor cards.)
Gausepohl Edward J, 2½ W Washington.
Gorsuch Charles W, 305 Indiana Trust bldg.
Greene James & Co, 227-228 Lemcke bldg.
Gregory & Appel, 96 E Market.
Hadley Horace M, 66 E Market. (See left top cor cards.)
Hann John B, 323 Lemcke bldg.
Hubbard Walter J, 211-212 Lemcke bldg.
Indiana Trust Co The, Indiana Trust Bldg, s e cor Washington and Virginia av. (See front cover, opp p 487 and opp Insurance Agts.)
Kramer Charles T, 723 Lemcke bldg.
Lawyers' Loan and Trust Co, 68½ E Market. (See top edge and opp p 555.)
McCullough W J & Sons, 98 E Market.
McIntosh A J & Son, 66 E Market.
McKay Horace, 29½ N Penn.
McKernan David S, 2-5 Thorpe Blk. (See right bottom lines.)
Marion Trust Co The, s e cor Market and Monument Pl. (See back cover.)
Martindale Robt & Co, 86 E Market.
Metzger A Agency, 5 Odd Fellows' Hall. (See left bottom lines.)
Miller Winfield, 6 Hartford Blk, 84 E Market.
Mitchell James, 30 Baldwin blk.
Nelson Thomas H, 153 Michigan (H). (See adv in Real Estate.)
Newby Wm H, 224 W Washington.
Pattison Joseph H, 36 Monument pl.
Poe George M, 24 Ingalls blk.
Reynolds C E & Co, 10 Monument pl.
Rhodius George, 215 Lemcke bldg.
Richardson & McCrea, 79 E Market. (See right top cor cards.)
Ripley Wm I, 15½ Virginia av.
Schmidt Lorenz, 33 S Delaware.
Security Mortgage Loan Co, 209 Indiana Trust bldg.
Slatts Wm C, 24 Ingalls blk.
Smith, Curtis & Co, 10 Fair blk.
Smock & Mather, 32 N Delaware.
Spann John S & Co, 84-86 E Market.
Stein Theodore, 229-230 Lemcke Bldg.
Tuttle & Seguin, 28 E Market. (See left bottom cor cards.)
Union Trust Co, 68 E Market. (See front cover, opp p 867 and opp Insurance Agts.)
Walcott Charles H, 66 E Market.
Wilson Arthur N, 9, 156½ E Washington.
Wolf George, 221-222 Lemcke Bldg. (See adv in Real Estate.)

LOCK MANUFACTURERS.

Keyless Lock Co, 81 Newman.

LOCKSMITHS AND BELL HANGERS.

Budd Frank, 321 Clifford av.
Fitch Wm H, 35 Indiana av.
Isensee Albert T, 31 Monument Pl. (See adv.)

A. ISENSEE, Jr.,
Locksmith and Bellhanger
KEYS OF ALL KINDS.
Locks Picked, Repaired and Altered
31 MONUMENT PLACE.

Reinhardt Peter J, 113 Locke.
Yocum George W, 262 Mass av.
Ziegler Henry, 221 Mass av.

***LOOKING GLASSES.**

Lieber H Co The, 33 S Meridian. (See right top cor cards.)

LOUNGE MANUFACTURERS.

See Furniture Manufacturers.

IF YOU WANT A GOOD MEAL AND HAVE IT NICELY SERVED GO TO

TUTEWILER UNDERTAKER, NO. 72 WEST MARKET STREET. TELEPHONE 216.

WILL ROTH. J. FRANK YOUNG.

THE CLUB STABLES

FINE

LIVERIES AND CARRIAGES

RUBBER TIRE BROUGHAMS
AND LIGHT RIGS.

Special Attention to Boarders.
Horses Kept on Ground Floor.

TEL. 1061

80 AND 82 W. MARKET ST.

Hacks can be called by Indianapolis District Telegraph Co's Boxes.

ROTH & YOUNG, Proprietors.

JOHN H. SPAHR, Agt.,

Grand Opera House

and Empire

Livery, Sale AND Boarding Stables

TELEPHONE 102.

Horses Bought and Sold. 75 E. Wabash St., Indianapolis.

DALTON & MERRIFIELD { LUMBER South Noble St., near E. Washington

INDIANA ELECTROTYPE CO. BEST WORK. LOWEST PRICES. 23 WEST PEARL ST., INDIANAPOLIS, IND. JOB WORK. BOOK PLATES. All Orders Promptly Filled. BEST PATENT BASE ON THE MARKET.

LUMBER—HARDWOOD.

Balke & Krauss Co, cor Missouri and Market. (See right bottom lines.)
Byrd Joseph W, 323 Lemcke Bldg. (See adv opp Lumber Mnfrs and Dealers.)
Dalton & Merrifield, 30-50 S Noble, near E Washington. (See left top lines.)
Indianapolis Manufacturers' and Carpenters' Union, 38-42 S New Jersey. (See adv p 2.)
Interior Hardwood Co The, Manufacturers, 317 Mass av.
Michigan Lumber Co, 436 E North, cor Fulton. (See embossed line back cover and adv opp.)

LUMBER MANUFACTURERS AND DEALERS.

(See also Planing Mills.)

Bachman Frederick M, s e cor Madison av and Lincoln la.
Balke & Krauss Co, cor Market and Missouri. (See right bottom lines.)
Brooks Bartholomew D, Morris and Belt R R (W I).
Buddenbaum Lumber Co, s e cor New York and Pine.
Bugbee Ira B, s e cor Lincoln av and L E & W R R.
Burnet & Lewis, 553 Dillon.
Byrd Joseph W, 323 Lemcke Bldg. (See adv opp.)
Capitol Lumber Co, 331-335 Mass av.
Carter, Lee & Co, 995 W Washington.
Christian J E & Co, 475 E Michigan.
Christian Thomas J, 71 Alvord.
Clark John W, 79 Alvord.
Coburn Henry, cor Kentucky av and Georgia.
Dalton & Merrifield, 30-50 S Noble, near E Washington. (See left top lines.)
Dickson James C (agt), 480 E Michigan.
Eichholtz George W, 95 E Market.
Fatout M K & Son, 463 E St Clair.
Foster Lumber Co, n w cor St Clair and N Senate av. (See adv in Planing Mills.)
Fraser Bros & Van Hoff, 41 Michigan av.
Gage & Boyd, 336 Lemcke bldg.
Gladden Lumber Co, 133 Commercial Club bldg.
Green-Wilkinson Co, 477 E Michigan.
Griffin Ransom, 21 W Maryland.
Hale James, 136 S Illinois.
Hamilton Wm A, 143 Dillon.
Herrmann Henry, 213 S Penn.
Home Lumber Co, 460-474 E Michigan.
Indianapolis Manufacturers' and Carpenters' Union, 38-42 S New Jersey. (See adv p 2.)
Isgrigg James A, n w cor Senate av and 5th.
Jackson Andrew M, 47½ N Illinois.
Jungclaus Wm P Co The, 317 Mass av.
Knight W W & Co, 84 E Market.
Landers & Donnelly, 148 S West.
Long Henry C, 1 Alvord.
Lyon A Inloes, n e cor Home av and Alvord.
Metzger Frank B, 36 Michigan av.
Michigan Lumber Co, 436 E North, cor Fulton. (See embossed line back cover and adv.)
Murry J H & Co, 320 Lincoln av.
Osgood & Thompson, 26 S Illinois and cor Vandalia and Belt R R (W I).
Rogers James N, 14 Ingalls blk.
Russell Lumber Co The, s e cor 7th and L E & W R R.
Shepard Silas M jr, 51 Baldwin blk.
Valdenaire John J, s s Glen Drive 2 w of Gale (B).
Wells C & Bro, 113 S Illinois.
Wiese H C & Co, 1208 E Washington.
Wittmer G F Lumber Co, n e cor Washington and Belt R R.
Wright Wm L, rear 310 E Washington.

*MACHINE SHOPS.

McNamara, Koster & Co, 212-218 S Penn. (See right top lines and p 9.)

*MACHINERY DEALERS.

Vonnegut Clemens, 184-186 E Washington. (See left bottom lines.)

*MACHINERY—EXPERIMENTAL.

Jacob & Co, s w cor Georgia and Penn. (See adv in Pattern and Model Makers.)

*MACHINERY MOVERS.

Hogan Transfer and Storage Co The, s w cor Washington and Illinois. (See left top lines and adv in Transfer Companies.)

*MACHINISTS' LATHES.

Vonnegut Clemens, 184-186 E Washington. (See left bottom lines.)

*MACHINISTS' TOOLS.

Vonnegut Clemens, 184-186 E Washington. (See left bottom lines.)

MACHINISTS AND MACHINERY.

(See also Founders and Machinists.)

Castle O H, 19 W South.
Chandler & Taylor Co, 360 W Washington.
Globe Machine Works, 72-74 W Court.
Green Thomas L, 331 Mass av.
Hall Albert B, 126 W Maryland.
Herdrich-Woollen Machine Co The, 329 Mass av.
Hoffman C D & Co, 29 Kentucky av.
Hoosier Canning Machinery Co, s w cor Louisiana and McGill.
Howard Michael E, 174 S Senate av.
Indianapolis Bolt and Machine Works, 122-126 Kentucky av. (See adv in Elevator Mnfrs.)
Indianapolis Tool and Mnfg Co, 15-17 McNabb.
Jacob & Co, s w cor Georgia and Penn. (See adv in Pattern and Model Makers.)
Keys John T, 110 W Maryland.
Koss Louis, 254-256 S Penn.
Larger & Pryor, 79 S Senate av.
Leonard & Dyer, 18½ N Meridian.
Mendell Joseph C, 389 Virginia av.

W. H. MESSENGER COMPLETE HOUSE FURNISHER 101 East Washington Street, Telephone 491

A SPECIALTY

436 East North St., Cor. Fulton St.

Telephone 766.

Cella & Geis, 23 W Ohio. | LePage John P 1552 Northwestern av (N

J. W. BYRD

Wholesale Lumber

(CAR LOAD LOTS TO THE TRADE ONLY.)

WHITE AND YELLOW PINE SHINGLES,
SASH, DOORS AND BLINDS.

SPECIALTIES:

Capitol Lumber Co, 331-335 Mass av.
Carter, Lee & Co, 995 W Washington

(See left top lines and adv in Transfer Companies)

Foundry and Pattern Shop } McNamara, Koster & Co. { PHONE 1593 212-218 S. Penn. St.

Nordyke & Marmon Co, crossing I & V Ry and Morris (W I). (See inside back cover.)
Pioneer Brass Works, 110-116 S Penn.
Poindexter Robert E, 25 Eddy.
Potter Mnfg Co, 440-444 E Ohio.
Potts C and A & Co, 414-428 north branch W Washington.
Redding Jeremiah, 296 S Alabama.
Reeves Harry E, 96 S Delaware, cor Georgia. (See embossed line front cover and adv in Patternmakers.)
Rexroth Louis, 125 E Pearl.
Schiffling Albert, 48 Virginia av.
Simon Louis P, 199 S Meridian.
Specialty Manufacturing Co, 193 S Meridian. (See adv opp Photographers.)

*MALLEABLE IRON FOUNDERS.

National Malleable Castings Co The, cor Michigan and Holmes av (H).

*MANICURES.

(See also Chiropodists and Manicures.)
Evans Ada P, over 2½ W Washington. (See adv in Hair Goods.)

*MANTEL MANUFACTURERS.

Huey M S & Son, 551 Mass av. (See p 5.)

MANTELS AND GRATES.

Balke & Krauss Co, cor Missouri and Market. (See right bottom lines.)
Cella & Geis, 23 W Ohio.
Hopkins Linn B, 145 N Delaware.
Huey M S & Son, 551 Mass av. (See p 5.)
Lilly Jno M, 78-80 Mass av. (See adv p 8.)
Lion Mantel and Grate House, 114 N Delaware.

MANUFACTURERS' AGENTS.

Baldwin Frank M, 83 Baldwin blk.
Bassett Walter B, 18½ N Meridian.
Benton Howard H, 86 Lombard bldg.
Brodbeck H C & Co, 146 S Meridian.
Brown Marcus L, 6 Builders' Exchange.
Burton James M, 1½ E Washington.
Coleman Herbert B, 503 Lemcke bldg.
Condit & Arnold, 35 W Pearl.
Cooper Charles, 66½ N Penn.
Curtis Caswell B, 114 Commercial Club bldg.
Edgerton Dixon, 77 E Market.
Ellis James, 6 Indiana av.
Fishback Frank S, 32 S Meridian.
Foreman George, 34 W Maryland.
Gallahue Phoenix M, 40 W Market.
Gallahue Warren C, 40 W Market.
Gillett Welby H, 333 Lemcke bldg.
Gookin George F, 59 Commercial Club bldg.
Helvie Charles E, 92 S Illinois.
Holland & Essex, 198 S Meridian.
Hunt Edward A, 503 Lemcke bldg.
Keltenbrun James J, 333 Lemcke bldg.
Kurtz John A, 143½ S Meridian.
Liebert Charles G S, 143½ S Meridian.
McGregory Albert B, 59 Commercial Club bldg.
Maurer Edward A, 333 Lemcke bldg.
Meyer Bros, 5 Pembroke Arcade.
Mitchell James T, 503 Lemcke bldg.
Montgomery Frank M, 503 Lemcke bldg.
Montgomery Robert E, 736 Lemcke bldg.
Nelson Albert, 41 Lombard bldg.
Payne Joseph F, 44 Board of Trade bldg.
Richardson Barzilla F, 26 S Illinois.
Russell Harley A, 53½ W Washington.
Shearman J D, 13, 17½ S Meridian.
Siegelen Christian A, 133 Hoyt av.
Smith Cyrus M, 28 Monument pl.
Stephen Joseph Z, 92 S Illinois.
Stockwell John H, 92 S Illinois.
Taisey Frederick R, 31½ Virginia av.
Van Horn Thomas M, 49 Board of Trade bldg.
Varney & McOuat (Electrical), 75 E Market. (See adv opp Electrical Engineers.)
Walkup & Reid, 14 Hartford blk.
Young Frank H, 3 Board of Trade bldg.

*MAP DRAUGHTSMEN.

Palmer Thomas W, Room 31 Court House. (See adv in Draughtsmen.)

MARBLE AND GRANITE DEALERS AND WORKS.

Boicourt, Tyner & Co, 121 N Delaware.
Diener August, 243 E Washington; Branch Works opp east entrance Crown Hill Cemetery. (See front edge and adv opp Monuments.)
Farrell Michael H, 208 W Washington.
Goth & Co, 157 Mass av.
Heinsdale's N C Sons' Granite Co The, 709-710 Lemcke bldg.
Krumshield Louis P, 112 E Ohio.
LePage John P, 1552 Northwestern av (N I).
Rockwood Harvey A, 221 Ramsey av.
Weir Wm, rear 105 E Washington.

*MASKS AND MASQUERADE TRIMMINGS.

Mayer Charles & Co, 29-31 W Washington. (See adv opp p 615.)

*MAT MANUFACTURERS.

Miner Wm L, 184-186 Cherry. (See adv opp Rugs.)

*MATTRESS MANUFACTURERS.

Hirschman Jacob C (estate of), 69-71 N New Jersey.
Warmeling Rudolph, 177 Madison av.
Palasky Isaac, 407 S Delaware.

*MEAT MARKET SUPPLIES.

Vonnegut Clemens, 184-186 E Washington. (See left bottom lines.)

MEATS—WHOLESALE.

Beck Wm, 187 E Washington and 79-80 E Mkt House.
Bryan D & Sons, Indpls Abattoir (W I).
Crawford Stephen M, Indpls Abattoir (W I).
Gardner Charles J, Vandalia R R and river.
Indianapolis Abattoir Co, Morris and White river (W I).
Morris Nelson & Co, 129-135 Kentucky av.
Reddehase Frederick, 98 E Mkt House.
Sindlinger Peter, 207 W Michigan.

THE FRED DIETZ CO.
WOODEN PACKING BOXES MADE TO ORDER
FAN AND WAREHOUSE TRUCKS.
40 Madison Avenue. Telephone 69

Shorthand! BUSINESS UNIVERSITY. When Bl'k. Elevator day and night. Typewriting, Penmanship, Book-keeping, Office Training free. See page 4. Est. 1850. Tel. 499. E. J. HEEB, Proprietor.

Water and Oil Meters { HENRY R. WORTHINGTON, 64 S. PENNSYLVANIA ST. Long Distance Telephone 284.

UNION CO-OPERATIVE LAUNDRY { OF UNION LAUNDRY GIRLS.) AND 142 VIRGINIA AVENUE. T. E. SOMERVILLE, MANAGER — TELEPHONE 1269. INDIANAPOLIS, IND.

Meats—Wholesale—Continued.
Swift & Co, 123-127 Kentucky av.
Temperley Harry H, Indpls Abattoir (W I).
Wheeler Dressed Beef Co, Indpls Abattoir (W I).
Wulf & Bishoff, 8 E Mkt House.

MEAT MARKETS.
(See also Grocers.)

Aisenbrey Charles W, 25 Virginia av.
Ankenbrock C Wm, 328 Clifford av.
Arnold Herman G, 502 S Capitol av.
Arnold Wm A E, 534 Park av.
Balz John M, 60 W 7th.
Barnum Wm W, 196 E Market.
Barthel Albert, 754 E Washington.
Barthel Bros, 540 E Washington.
Bauchle Charles F, 429 Madison av.
Beck Otto C, 94 Indiana av.
Beck Wm, 187 E Washington and 79-80 E Market House.
Beckerich Bros, 648 College av.
Beyer John, 414 W North.
Birk Martin J, 298 N West.
Bittrich Wm S, 56 E Mkt House.
Blackman Joseph B, 19 E Mkt House.
Blackman Lloyd J, 95 E Mkt House.
Bloemker Ernst W, 602 E New York.
Blythe Harry F, 58 E Mkt House.
Boecher Henry, 549 N West.
Boettcher Frederick, 77 E Mkt House.
Brady Charles H, 104 E Mkt House.
Braendlein Paul, 91 E Mkt House and 38 Gresham.
Brown Wm L, 125 Lynn av (W I).
Buddenbaum & Heller, 327 Prospect.
Burgess Alvin B, 252 N Noble.
Burton Wm I, 158 E 7th.
Buschmann August, 148 College av.
Buschmann Wm & Co, 192-200 Ft Wayne av.
Buser Charles O, 250 Yandes.
Buser Daniel T, 392 College av.
Bussey & Dietz, 903 N Senate av.
Carney Bros, 773 N Illinois.
Carr Hannah, 296 S Missouri.
Caton Edward G, 102 E Mkt House.
Chaplin Edward, 78 E Mkt House.
Coleman Henry, 402 S West.
Condron Michael, 124 N Belmont av (H).
Cook Joseph, 55 E Mkt. House.
Cooke James, 47 E Mkt House.
Coombs Curtis C, 440 Mass av.
Cornet Bros, 498-500 College av.
Crabb John S, 493 W Addison (N I).
Craig & Co, 75 Oliver av (W I).
Crather Thomas H, 11 E Mkt House.
Crook John W, 578 E St Clair.
Davis Samuel, 43 E Mkt House.
DeHart Pauline, 401 W Udell (N I).
Delaney Hannah M, 303 S West.
Derleth George, 234 W McCarty.
Derleth Wm, 50 E Mkt House and 189 W Washington.
Deshler John jr, 31 E Mkt House.
Dicks Harry E, 32 Indiana av.
Dicks Ilva A, 197 Mass av and 27 E Mkt House.
Dietz Theodore, 453½ Central av.
Dittman F G & Co, 748 N Capitol av.
Dobrowitz Henry, 51 Russell av.
Doughty Ernest M, 304 N Illinois.
Douglass Robert, 193 Howard (W I).
Eacret John D, 24 Michigan (H).
Edwards Jerome B, 444 Mass av.
Ehmann Gustav, 28½ King av (H).
Eicher John N, 34 E Mkt House.
Evans Isabell E, n e cor Grandview and Belmont avs (H).
Fauple Henry, 151 N Noble.
Fenneman Edward W, 299 N Senate av.
Feuchter Christian, 51 E Mkt House.
Fielder Edward G, 48 E Mkt House.
Filz Frank, 23 E Mkt House.
Fischer August, 293 Coburn.
Fischer Joseph, 74 E Mkt House.
Flaskamp Fred, 126 Hillside av cor 8th.
Fleckhammer Charles W, 33 E Mkt House.
Flick Jacob, 846 W Washington.
Fowler George, 226 Howard.
Fox Henry S, 495 W 22d (N I).
Fox Lawrence P, 2 Carlos.
Funk Edgar A, 85 E Mkt House.
Galloway George E, 290 E Washington.
Gardner Charles J, 47 N Illinois.
Gaston Edward, 49-53 Kentucky av.
Geis Jacob, 292 E Georgia.
Geldermann Henry G, 62 E Mkt House.
Gemmer Gideon, 461 Virginia av.
Gill Richard, 202 W South.
Gisler Conrad, 812 S East.
Glassman & Sattinger, 37 Russell av.
Goll Christian, 377 Blake.
Graf Gottfried, 228 E Morris.
Graham Wm R, 106 S Linden.
Grund Wm, 18 E Mkt House.
Gutfleisch George, 1 Paca.
Hagedorn Henry, 564 Morris (W I).
Hahn Adam, 113 S William (W I).
Hahn Jacob, 909 Morris (W I).
Hamilton James R, 1 E Mkt House.
Hamilton S & Co, 9 Lynn.
Hammel George J, 110-112 Mass av and 215-217 N Alabama.
Hammond & Pasquier, 316 Virginia av.
Hardey & Gausepohl, 150 Madison av.
Hastings Robert, 45 E Mkt House.
Hebble Frank W, 252 Indiana av.
Heckman D P & Sons, 549 W 22d (N I) and 4 E Mkt House.
Heid John F, 1017 S Meridian and 6 E Mkt House.
Heidt George, 442 Indiana av.
Heimbach John, 1348 N Capitol av.
Heinrich Christian F, 576 N Senate av.
Heitkam Henry J, 350 Virginia av.
Heller Wm J, 149 Oliver av (W I).
Hergt Charles A, 834 E Washington.
Hergt Frederick W, 117 Prospect.
Hilgemeier Bros, 60 E Mkt House and n e cor Raymond and Applegate.
Hotz John, 796 N Senate av.
Hotz Wm F, 502 Bellefontaine.
Howell Thomas F, 152 English av.
Howes Charles A, 154 Blake.
Hubert Michael, 527 S Capitol av.
Isenflamm Edward, 258 S Alabama.
Isherwood Mahlon W, 54 Marion av (W I).
Jaffe Isaac, 221½ W Washingtoon.
James & McLain, 537 E Ohio.
Jaus Wm, 902 S Meridian.
Johnson Frank M, 57 E Mkt House.
Jones Clinton, 96 E Mkt House.
Jones George D & Co, 41 E North.
Jones & Son, 106 Prospect.
Jung Louis, 340 Mass av.
Justice & Warren, 1547 N Illinois.
Kahan Morris, 231 W Washington.
Kashner Alonzo R, 578 E 8th.
Keller Robert, 570-578 S East.
Kiser Gottlieb, 150 N East.
Kneer Charles J, rear 150 Spann av.
Koehler Wm F, 346 Clifford av.
Kramer & Hurrle, 287 S Delaware.
Kuhn Calvin L, 100 E Mkt House.
Kuntz Martin C, 610 N Senate av.

CLEMENS VONNEGUT 184, 186 and 192 E. Washington St. | Wire Rope, Machinery, Lathes, Drills and Shapers

THE WM. H. BLOCK CO. DRY GOODS, DRAPERIES, RUGS, WINDOW SHADES.
7 AND 9 EAST WASHINGTON STREET.

La Rue Gordon A, 550 Bellefontaine.
Lichtenberg Christian F, 201 Shelby.
Lichtenberg Wm, 300 E Ohio.
Liehr Peter, 247 Davidson.
Linnaman John, n s Bloyd av 2 w of Harriet (B).
Linton & Co, 1551 N Illinois.
Logan James H, 1149 N Illinois.
Love John F, 61 E Mkt House.
Lovelace Andrew J, 163 Hill av.
Low Enoch, 822 W Washington.
Lueth John H, 501 S West.
McDougall & Hamilton, 9 Lynn.
McGary Mary E, 201 Michigan av.
Maass Henry C, 451 S Delaware.
Mahoney Daniel H, 1049 N Capitol av.
Maloy & Egan, 1 Lynn.
Martin & Co, 201 W Washington.
Mathews Silas B, 47 Haugh (H).
Matzke Julius, 72 E Mkt House.
Mecum Bennett F, 152 Madison av.
Medsker John T, 72 Germania av (H).
Merz David, 401 S Meridian.
Meyer F J & Co, 408 S East.
Miller Jacob, 73½ Minerva.
Miller Oliver P, 154 W 12th.
Mills Wm, 128 Oliver av (W I).
Minter Ferdinand, s w cor Home av and Yandes.
Mitchell Wm A, 348 E St Clair.
Mitschrich Herman, 100 Jefferson.
Montani Ferdinand, E Mkt House.
Moore N A & Co, 1-5 Indiana av.
Moran Thomas A, 6 S Station (B).
Muegge George W, 9 Prospect.
Mullis R T & Co, 1348-1350 N Capitol av.
Murphy Arley R, 342 E Market.
Myers Wm H, s w cor Sugar Grove and Miller avs (N I).
Neligh Solon H, 107 Woodburn av (W I).
Nestle George H, 82 E Mkt House and 232 E Washington.
Newby & Son, rear 852 Grandview av.
Nichols Wm H, 297 Yandes.
Nicolai Henry, 32 E Mkt House and 91 Mass av.
Niemann Paul, s w cor Earhart and Prospect.
Noll George E, 197 Virginia av.
O'Connell Bros, 455 E Georgia.
Otte & Co, 849 E Michigan.
Overman John C, 86 E Mkt House.
Peake James T, 97 Hoyt av.
Perigo Stephen W, 201 Union.
Pfleging Conrad A, 63 E Mkt House.
Poulter Henry H, 307 N West.
Power & Drake, 16 N Meridian.
Prange Frederick, 348 E St Clair.
Prange Henry C, 397-399 Bellefontaine.
Price Morgan A, 153 E Ohio.
Prigger Anna, 20 E Mkt House.
Pullen Wm B, 117 Germania av (H).
Railsback Edward A, 404 College av.
Reeves John S, 252 Highland av.
Reiffel Charles, 213 W Washington.
Reiffel George L, 103 E Mkt House.
Reiffel Martin, 52 E Mkt House.
Reiffel Wm E, 84 E Mkt House.
Richardson Charles, 272 S Capitol av.
Richardson Shelton, 203 Mass av.
Robinson Bros, 195-197 W Ohio.
Rodey Henry, 348 E South.
Rohde Adolph, 1094 E Washington.
Roos Jacob C, 616 S Meridian.
Roth Martin, 485 S East.
Roth Martin C, 428 Home av.
Rupp John, 203 Kentucky av.
Rushton Allen C, 93 E Mkt House.
Ruskaup Frederick, 135 N Dorman.
Schad & Sons, 698 N Capitol av.
Schaefer Herman L, 350 W Vermont.
Schafer Wm, 492 S Meridian.
Scheich Peter, 131 Davidson.
Schmidt George, 666 S Meridian.
Schmitker John H, 433 E Georgia.
Schott John, 97 E Mkt House.
Schroeder Edward, 76 E Mkt House.
Schulmeyer Bros, 150 St Mary.
Schussler Frank, 28 E Mkt House.
Schwab Louis, 46 E Mkt House.
Schwier Bros, 516 E Washington.
Scott Thomas C, 376 Clifford av.
Shank Wm H H, s e cor Central av and Railroad (I) and 7 E Mkt House.
Shea John, 200 W South.
Sheresefsky Mary, 398 S Illinois.
Shisla John G, 22 E Mkt House.
Siem Henry, 633 Madison av.
Simon Wm A, 2 E Mkt House.
Simpson John R, 179 N East.
Sindlinger Bros, 100 N Illinois.
Sindlinger George, 204 Prospect.
Sindlinger Peter, 207 W Michigan.
Sirp Wm, 81 E Mkt House.
Smith George W, 3 E Mkt House.
Smithey John F, 100 Columbia av.
Sogemeier August, 21 E Mkt House.
Sperr George J, 387 Fulton.
Sprinkle David, w s Harris av 1 s of W Washington (M J).
Steck Henry C, 116 Patterson.
Steinmetz Jacob J, 71 E Mkt House.
Steinmetz Jacob J jr, 70 E Mkt House.
Stewart Peter, 668 Virginia av.
Stuckmeyer August, 24 E Mkt House.
Stuckmeyer Charles H, 29 English av.
Swope Mary E, 249 River av (W I).
Thomas John C, 363 E Michigan.
Tobin John W, 400 S West.
Tomlinson George, 102 Shepard (W I).
Trucksess John J, E Mkt House.
Turner & McHaffey, 49 Yandes.
Tysinger George W, 71 Cherry.
Uhl Frank A, 53 E Mkt House.
Uhl John, 351 Dillon.
Uhl Louis, 534 S Meridian.
Unversaw John N, 83 E Mkt House.
Van Blarcom Newton P, 51 Mass av.
Van Sickle George W, 30-32 Clifford av.
Vollrath Herman G, 101 E Mkt House.
Wabnetz Louis, 99 E Mkt House.
Wacker John, 140 Michigan (H).
Wacker Karl, 21 Tremont av (H).
Wagner John, 851 S Meridian.
Wagner Joseph H, s e cor William and Howard (W I).
Wagoner & Son, 167 Hill av.
Wechsler Charles, 752 N Capitol av.
Wechsler Emil, 59 E Mkt House.
Wechsler Henry, 25 W McCarty.
Weingart Wm, 258 S Delaware.
Wensley James L, 42 E Mkt House.
White Charles A, rear 152 Lexington av.
White Ida L, 198 N Senate av.
White Levi W, 543 W Udell (N I).
Whitehead John R, 36 Crawford.
Wickard Franklin E, 49 E Mkt House.
Wilson Jefferson M, 31 Traub av.
Wilson Wm F, 382 E 9th.
Winter Henry, 51 Yandes.
Wittenburg Albert, 30 E Mkt House.
Wittendorfer Frederick W, 75 E Mkt House.
Woerner John W, 1424 Northwestern av (N I).
Wood Charles E, 488 E Washington.
Wood John M, 168 Hillside av.
Worm Albert R, 113 Oliver av (W I).
Wurster Ernst, 579 Madison av.
Yorger Charles, 582 Virginia av.
Youngman Charles, 705 E Washington.
Zollner Charles H, 290 W Washington.

INDIANAPOLIS STEEL ROOFING AND CORRUGATING WORKS, 23 and 25 East South Street. S. D. NOEL, Proprietor.

David S. McKernan, REAL ESTATE AND LOANS
Rooms 2-5 Thorpe Block. A number of choice pieces for subdivision, or for manufacturers' sites, with good switch facilities.

DIAMOND WALL PLASTER { Telephone 1410 BUILDERS' EXCHANGE.

UNION TRANSFER AND STORAGE CO. Cor. E. Ohio St. and C., C., C. & St. L. R'y Tracks. BRICK WAREHOUSE; CLEANEST AND SAFEST STORAGE IN CITY FOR HOUSEHOLD GOODS AND MERCHANDISE.

*MECHANICAL DRAUGHTSMEN.

Bell Thompson R, 64 Ingalls Blk. (See adv in Patent Attorneys.)
Jacob & Co, s w cor Georgia and Penn. (See adv opp Pattern and Model Makers.)
Nealy H D, 16 Hubbard Blk. (See adv in Patent Draughtsmen.)

*MECHANICAL ENGINEERS.

Bell Thompson R, 64 Ingalls Blk. (See adv in Patent Attorneys.)
Jones Horace B, 415-418 Lemcke Bldg. (See adv.)

HORACE B. JONES, B. S.,
MECHANICAL ENGINEER AND DRAUGHTSMAN,
415-418 LEMCKE BUILDING.
LONG DISTANCE TELEPHONE 1103.

Snow J H & Co, 25 W Washington and 187-195 S Meridian.

MECHANICAL EXPERTS.

Hood H P & Son, 68½ E Market. (See adv in Patent Attorneys.)

MEDICAL COLLEGES.

See Miscellaneous Directory.

*MEDICINAL WATER MNFRS.

Lieber Rich & Co (Carlsbad, Ems, Vichey, Lithia, Etc; also Distilled Water), cor New York and Agnes.

MEDICINE MANUFACTURERS.

Cash L E & H M, 853 E Michigan.
Cole James H, 71 Indiana av.
Gustin Esom B, 182 Huron.
Haas Joseph, 56 S Penn.
Harlan Hiempsal L, Liver, Kidney and Rheumatic Cure, 477 N Meridian.
Hull A J Medical Co, 451 Virginia av.
Matthews Medicine Co, 26 Woodlawn av (formerly Elk.)
Occidental Veterinary Remedy Co, 15-17 McNabb.
Rohrer David, 117 Pleasant.
Simms James N, 127½ Indiana av.
Sheppard Callie, 50½ S Illinois.
Slavin Michael, 62½ S Illinois.
Triquima Medical Co, 129 E Pratt.
Viavi Co The, 68½ E Market.
White Ahira R, 190 S Meridian.
Wright Magnetic Medicine Co, 111½ E Washington.

*MEN'S FURNISHINGS.

When Clothing Store, 26-40 N Penn. (See right top cor cards.)

MERCANTILE AGENCIES.

Bradstreet Co The, n w cor Meridian and Washington.
Dun R G & Co, 18½ N Meridian.
Indianapolis Collecting and Reporting Agency, 39-40 Journal Bldg. (See adv opp p 488.)
Merchants' and Manufacturers' Exchange, Jacob E Takken Mngr, 19 Union Bldg, 63-73 W Maryland. (See left bottom cor cards.)
Universal Credit Agency The of Indianapolis, 90-92 Baldwin blk.

*MERCANTILE ENGRAVING.

Indiana Illustrating Co, s e cor Market and Illinois. (See adv opp Engravers.)

MERCHANDISE BROKERS.

See Brokers—Merchandise.

*MERCHANT TAILORS.

(See also Tailors.)

Adam Louis, 17 Virginia av.
Becker & Son, 21 N Penn. (See right top lines.)
Dildine Bert B, 64 E Market.
Egan & Co, 22 Pembroke Arcade.
Fleming Thomas W, 68 Indiana av.
Frenk & Birk, 70 N Penn.
Gramling P & Son, 35 E Washington.
Hotz George, 124 S Illinois.
Hurrle Ignatz, 4 Pembroke Arcade.
Kahn Tailoring Co, 22 E Washington.
Lalley Bros, 5 N Meridian.
Lalley John, 437 Virginia av.
Landgraf Norbert, 83 N Penn.
Mannfeld George & Sons, 57 N Penn.
Nessler Frank & Co, 56 E Market. (See right top cor cards.)
Nicoll The Tailor, 33-35 S Illinois.
Rikhoff Herman F, 26 Indiana av.
Rosberg Gust, 25 N Penn.
Rosenberg John, 196 E Washington.
Schildmeier & Koelling, 264 E Washington.
Schoppenhorst Wm, 18 N Penn.
Staub John W, 63 N Penn.
Taylor & Schneider, 22 Monument pl.
Treat A J & Son, 24 N Penn.
When Clothing Store, 26-40 N Penn. (See right top cor cards.)
Young & McMurray, 12-14 N Meridian.

*MESSENGER SERVICE.

Indianapolis District Telegraph Co The, 15 S Meridian. (See adv in Electrical Supplies.)

*METAL CEILINGS.

Ensey O B, cor 6th and Illinois. (See left bottom cor cards.)
Gardner Joseph, 37-41 Kentucky av. (See left top cor cards.)
McWorkman Willard, 930 W Washington. (See left top cor cards.)

A. METZGER AGENCY ESTABLISHED 1863. INSURANCE

LAMBERT GAS & GASOLINE ENGINE CO.
ANDERSON, IND. PORTABLE GASOLINE ENGINES. 2 TO 25 H. P.

BICYCLES $5 DOWN. MONTHLY. Best Wheels. Best Terms. WHEELMEN'S CO 31 W. OHIO ST. LONG DISTANCE TEL. 1855.

MIDWIVES.

Bernloehr Margaret, 153 Meek.
Clarke Jennie E, 462 S Illinois.
Frantzreb Theresa, 11 Smithson.
Gardner Anna M, 194 E Morris.
Neidlinger Katherine, 27 Coburn.
Rauschen Catherine, 474 S Illinois.
Uphaus Mary A, 8 Wisconsin.
Waldenmeier Bertha, 33 Barth av.

*MILL FURNISHINGS.

Nordyke & Marmon Co, crossing I & V Ry and Morris (W I). (See inside back cover.)

*MILL MACHINERY AND GEARING.

Indianapolis Pulley Mnfg Co, 372-374 E Michigan. (See adv in Pulley Mnfrs.)

Nordyke & Marmon Co, crossing I & V Ry and Morris (W I). (See inside back cover.)

*MILL SUPPLIES.

Atkins E C & Co, 202-216 S Illinois.

Central Rubber and Supply Co The, 79 S Illinois. (See left side lines.)

Nordyke & Marmon Co, crossing I & V Ry and Morris (W I). (See inside back cover.)

*MILL WORK.

Indianapolis Manufacturers' and Carpenters' Union, 38-42 S New Jersey. (See adv p 2.)

*MILLINERS' TRIMMINGS.

Aneshaensel Walter, 143½ S Meridian.

MILLINERY—WHOLESALE.

Fahnley & McCrea, 140-142 S Meridian, 39-41 McCrea and 8 W Louisiana.
Griffith Bros, 132 S Meridian.
Indianapolis Millinery Co, 15-19 McCrea.

MILLINERY—RETAIL.

Ayres L S & Co, 33-37 W Washington.

Baker Bertha, 214 E Washington.
Baker & Hartbeck, 378 S East.
Bell Alma C, 172 Columbia av.
Black Hannah M, 23½ W Washington.

Block Wm H Co The, 7-9 E Washington. (See right top and bottom lines.)

Bollinger Mamie J, 89 Mass av.
Bowman Ella, 28 S Illinois.
Brace Minta, 39 W Washington.
Brian Eveline, 58 N Illinois.
Brininstool Carrie, 1556 N Illinois.
Buttz Pearl D, 54 Mass av.
Catellier Leda, 1 Putnam (B).
Clune John, 11-13 E Washington.
Cody Minnie B, 46 N Illinois.
Crawley Lillie M, 428 S Meridian.
Croft Fannie M, 83 Mass av.
Daglish & Brownlee, 240 Indiana av.
Dietrichs M & Co, 10 E Washington.
Drake Emma G, 472 Virginia av.
Drudy Winifred V, 173 E Washington and 131 N Noble.
Falk Nannie P, 47 S Illinois.
Figg Mamie T, 42 N Illinois.
Finley Sarah J, 622 N Senate av.
Frankmoelle Gertrude, 39 E Washington.
Gaupen Louisa, 617 Virginia av.
Greer Anna, 42 S Illinois.
Grothaus Caroline R, 229 E Morris.
Groves Virginia, 378 E 9th.
Hempleman Laura B, 563 S Meridian.
Hutchason Ella, 10 W Market.
Johnston Elizabeth, 484 Virginia av.
Jones Emma L, 1071 E Michigan.
Joss Mary E, 80 Indiana av.
Lange Theresa, 187 Mass av.
Ludwig Louis, 164 E Washington.
McHugh Mary E, 44 S Illinois.
McKernan Mary E, 12 Pembroke Arcade.
Meany Josie C, 205 Virginia av.
Miller & Smock, 147 Virginia av.
Mullholland Emma, 65 E Sutherland (B).
Mythen & Garis, 157 Virginia av.
Peck Laura, 659 Virginia av.

Pettis Dry Goods Co, 25-33 E Washington.

Pierce Josephine, 404 Virginia av.
Porter Mary E, 16½ E Washington.
Quigley Anna, 71 S Illinois.
Raphael Harry, 43 W Washington.
Robinson Emma B, 233 Mass av.
Rowe Mary, 139 Mass av.
Samuels Abraham L, 63 S Illinois.
Scott Sarah, 16 E Washington.
Van Slyke Mary J, 414 S Meridian.

Wasson H P & Co, 12-18 W Washington.

Webb Ella A, 66 N Illinois.
Wiese & Fuehring, 405 E Washington.
Williams Mary E, 356 Mass av.

*MILLSTONE MANUFACTURERS.

Nordyke & Marmon Co, crossing I & V Ry and Morris (W I). (See inside back cover.)

*MILLWRIGHTS.

Hoffman C D & Co, 29 Kentucky av. (See adv in Elevators.)

Jacob & Co, s w cor Georgia and Penn. (See adv opp Pattern and Model Makers.)

Nordyke & Marmon Co, crossing I & V Ry and Morris (W I). (See inside back cover.)

MINCEMEAT MANUFACTURERS.

Herman Henry L, 80 E Maryland.
Wright Harvey A, 69 Indiana av.

*MINE PUMPS.

Worthington Henry R, 64 S Penn. (See left top lines.)

*MINERAL SPRINGS.

Harmon Matthew H, w s Holmes av 1 s of Michigan (H). (See adv in Baths.)

MINERAL WATER MANUFACTURERS.

(See also Bottlers.)

Klee & Coleman, 227-229 S Delaware.

Lieber Rich & Co (also Distilled Waters), cor New York and Agnes.

J. H. TECKENBROCK House, Sign and Fresco Painter, 94 EAST SOUTH STREET.

FIDELITY MUTUAL LIFE PHILADELPHIA, PA. A. H. COLLINS, Gen. Agt. Baldwin Blk. RATES REASONABLE. SOUND BEYOND QUESTION. BUSINESS-LIKE IN PRACTICE.

BITUMINOUS COAL ▸▸ Edwardsport Coal and Mining Company ROOMS 42 AND 43 WHEN BUILDING.

MINING COMPANIES.

Edwardsport Coal and Mining Co, 42-43 When Bldg. (See left side lines and adv in Coal Miners.)
Hecla Consolidated Mining Co, 63½ E Market.

*MIRRORS.

Interstate Art Glass Co, Henry W Rudolf Genl Mngr, 77-81 N Delaware.
Killinger George W, s w cor Market and Missouri. (See adv in Saloons.)

*MODEL MAKERS.

Jacob & Co, s w cor Georgia and Penn. (See adv opp Pattern and Model Makers.)

JACOB & CO.
MAKERS OF PATTERNS
Models and Experimental Work.
102 S. Pennsylvania St., Cor. Georgia

McNamara, Koster & Co, 212-218 S Penn. (See right top lines and p 9.)
Reeves Harry E, 96 S Delaware, cor Georgia. (See embossed line front cover and adv in Patternmakers.)
Specialty Manufacturing Co, 193 S Meridian. (See adv opp Photographers.)

SPECIALTY MFG. CO.
Pattern and Modelmakers
MACHINISTS AND GENERAL MANUFACTURERS.
187 to 195 South Meridian Street.
(See Adv. Opposite Photographers.)

*MOLDINGS AND FRAMES.

Kautsky Wenzel, 125 E Morris.
Lieber H Co The, 33 S Meridian. (See right top cor cards.)

*MONUMENTS.

Diener August, 243 E Washington; Branch Works opp east entrance Crown Hill Cemetery. (See adv front edge and adv opp.)

*MORTAR COLORS.

Wasson W G Co The, 130 Indiana av. (See left bottom cor cards and adv in Cement and Lime.)

*MORTGAGE LOANS.

Coffin C E & Co, 90 E Market.
Day Thos C & Co, 325-330 Lemcke Bldg. (See right top cor cards.)
Fay Henry H, 40½ E Washington. (See right top cor cards.)
Gregory & Appel, 96 E Market.
Indiana Trust Co The, Indiana Trust Bldg, s e cor Washington and Virginia av. (See front cover, adv opp p 487 and opp Insurance Agts.)
Lawyers' Loan and Trust Co, 68½ E Market. (See adv top edge and opp p 555.)
McKernan David S, 2-5 Thorpe Blk. (See right bottom lines.)
Metzger A Agency, 5 Odd Fellows' Hall. (See left bottom lines.)
Miller Winfield, 6 Hartford Blk.
Richardson & McCrea, 79 E Market. (See right top cor cards.)
Security Mortgage Loan Co, 207-209 Indiana Trust Bldg.
Spann John S & Co, 86 E Market.
Tuttle & Seguin, 28 E Market. (See left bottom cor cards.)

*MOTORS—MANUFACTURERS.

Specialty Manufacturing Co, 193 S Meridian. (See adv opp Photographers.)

*MUSIC BOXES.

Mayer Charles & Co, 29-31 W Washington. (See adv opp p 615.)

MUSIC TEACHERS.

Archbold Charles E, 25 N Spruce.
Bahr Paul, 572 E Washington.
Barmeier Henrietta, 867 N New Jersey.
Barnhart Emma, 220 E Louisiana.
Barus Carl, 243 N East.
Bates Eliza E, 182 Brookside av.
Beard Arthur, 72 E Vermont.
Beissenherz Henry D, 529 N Alabama.
Belcher Thomas W S, 147 N Penn.
Berns Augustus F, 304 N New Jersey.
Biddle Stephen I, 519 N Alabama.
Black James S, 10 E 7th.
Bockstahler Alma R, 410 S Illinois.
Boyd Mary L, 238 N West.
Brock Elizabeth S, 23 Hosbrook.
Brown Tunstall Q, 169 W 5th.
Church Luretta M, 137 N Arsenal av.
Clemmer Eugenie P, 130 N Illinois.
Coulter Bertha A, 189 Fayette.
Creasy Maud, 292 E South.
Cress Wm H, s e cor Brookside av and Atlas.
Dame Daisy, 374 E 7th.
Dehne Robert A W, 435 E McCarty.
De LaTour Marie, 191 N New Jersey.
Donley Wm H, 42 W Market.
Dunnington Adeline J, 92 Eureka av.
Dwyer Mary E, 36 Coburn.
Eckert George R, 87 N State av.
Ehricke Charles, 298 Lincoln av.
Elbreg Beatrice V, 48 Ash.
Ernestinoff Alexander, 1119 N Meridian.
Estabrook Wm C, 447 Talbott av.
Evans Thomas W L, 90 Hoyt av.
Ferguson W Sinks, 143 Dougherty.
Ferrall Josephine, 241 Indiana av.
Gard Samuretta V, 121 E Ohio.
Golden Margaret J, rear 448 S East.
Gough Elizabeth I, 72 E Maryland.
Guntermann Joseph, 34 School.
Hamilton Mary F, 1261 E Washington.

ROOFING MATERIAL C. ZIMMERMAN & SONS, SLATE AND GRAVEL ROOFERS, 19 SOUTH EAST STREET.

The above cut represents my Branch Works at the

EAST ENTRANCE CROWN HILL CEMETERY.

Main Works and Office,

243 EAST WASHINGTON ST.,

Where a full line of

GRANITE AND MARBLE MONUMENTS

Is constantly on view.

AUGUST DIENER.

FIDELITY MUTUAL LIFE
PHILADELPHIA, PA.
A. H. COLLINS, Gen. Agt. [illegible]

RATES REASONABLE.
SOUND BEYOND QUESTION.
BUSINESS-LIKE IN PRACTICE.

Edwardsport Coal and Mining Company
ROOMS 42 AND 43 WHEN BUILDING.

BITUMINOUS COAL

*MINING COMPANIES.

Edwardsport Coal and Mining Co, 42-43 When Bldg. (See [illegible] side lines and adv in Coal Miners.)

[illegible] Consolidated Mining Co, [illegible] E Market.

*MIRRORS.

Interstate Art Glass Co, [illegible] Rudolf Genl Mngr, [illegible]

Killinger George W, [illegible] Market and Missouri. (See adv in Saloons.)

*MODEL MAKERS.

Jacob A Co, [illegible] and Penn. (See adv opp Pattern and Model Makers.)

JACOB & CO.
MAKERS OF PATTERNS
Models and Experimental Work.
102 S. Pennsylvania St., cor. Georgia

McNamara, Koster & Co, 212-218 S Penn. (See right top [illegible] p [illegible])

Reeves Harry F, [illegible] Georgia. (See [illegible] front cover and adv in Patternmakers.)

Specialty Manufacturing Co, 193 S Meridian. (See adv opp Photographers.)

SPECIALTY MFG. CO.
Pattern and Modelmakers
Machinists an[illegible]
187 to 195 South Meridian Street.
(See Adv. Oppos[illegible])

*MOLDINGS AND FRAMES.

Kautsky Wenzel [illegible]

Lieber H Co The, 33 S Meridian. (See right top cor cards.)

*MONUMENTS.

Diener August, 243 E Washington; Branch Works opp [illegible] entrance Crown Hill Cemetery. (See adv front edge and adv opp.)

*MORTAR COLORS.

Wasson W G Co The, [illegible] Indiana av. (See left bottom cor [illegible] and adv in Cement and Lime.)

*MORTGAGE LOANS.

Coffin C E & Co, 90 E Market.

Day Thos C & Co, 325-330 Lemcke Bldg. (See right top cor cards.)

Fay Henry H, 40½ E Washington. (See right top cor cards.)

Gregory & Appel, 96 E Market.

Indiana Trust Co The, Indiana Trust Bldg, s e cor Washington and Virginia av. (See front cover, adv opp p 507 and opp Insurance Agts.)

Lawyers' Loan and Trust Co, 68½ E Market. (See adv top edge and opp p 555.)

McKernan David S, 2-5 Thorpe Blk. (See right bottom lines.)

Metzger A, Agency, 5 Odd Fellows' Hall. (See left bottom lines.)

Miller Winfield, 6 Hartford Blk.

Richardson & McCrea, 79 E Market. (See right top cor cards.)

Security Mortgage Loan Co, 207-209 Indiana Trust Bldg.

Spann John S & Co, 86 E Market.

Tuttle & Seguin, 28 E Market. (See left bottom cor cards.)

*MOTORS—MANUFACTURERS.

Specialty Manufacturing Co, 193 S Meridian. (See adv opp Photographers.)

*MUSIC BOXES.

Mayer Charles & Co, 29-31 W Washington. (See adv opp p 611.)

MUSIC TEACHERS.

[illegible]

[illegible]TERIAL C. Z[illegible]

EAST ENTRANCE C OWN HILL CEMETERY

243 EAST WASHINGTON

a full line of

GRANITE AND

PUMPS Chain Pumps, Driven Wells and Deep Water Wells. Repairing Neatly Done. Cisterns Built. CHARLES KRAUSS', 42 S. PENN. ST. • TELEPHONE 465.

Collars and Cuffs Laundered in Best of Style. Domestic or High Gloss Finish.

Hebble George M, 398 N California.
Hess Anna, 173 E South.
Hill Clara L, 5 Ruckle.
Hoar John H, 121 Chadwick.
Houghton Alfred, 383 E New York. (See adv in Bands of Music.)
Houppert Anna, 103 Meek.
Hume Charles W, 136 E St Joseph.
Hume Clay A B, 136 E St Joseph.
Hyatt Carrie A, 6 Lincoln av.
Isensee Clara A, 37 W St Joseph.
Isensee Thirza O, 228 N California.
Jaeger Minnie I, 20 King.
Jaillet Adelaide C, 222 Keystone av.
Jeffries Evelyn, s s University av 3 w of Downey av (I).
Joiner Martha E, 414 Talbott av.
Jones Laura B, 430 N Senate av.
King Mollie, 251 N Liberty.
Koepper Lucy A, 25 Leota.
Koerner Anna, 30 Hall pl.
Krugmann Ida, 200 N West.
Kunz Helena, 339 E McCarty.
Leckner Max, 359 N Penn.
McAllister Minnie M, 1702 Kenwood av.
McClellan Winona, 334 E Miami.
McConnell Forest E, 18 S Station (B).
McDowell Emily G, 1531 N Meridian.
McElwee Frances M, 276 N Penn.
McIntosh Frederick W, 298 E South.
McLaughlin Anna K, 99 Clifford av.
McMullen Sophia E, 3 Lexington av.
Maffey Frank Z, 545 N Illinois.
Manlove Minerva J, 138 E Pratt.
Marone Giuseppe, 177 N Capitol av.
Mathers Mary E, 124 E Vermont.
May Georgia, 16 Blackford.
Mayer Sadie, 201 N Liberty.
Meek Florence A, 547 Park av.
Meigs Sarah T, 409 N Penn.
Metropolitan School of Music, 134 N Illinois.
Monks John, 369 Cornell av.
Monroe Louisa S, 330 E Vermont.
Montani Anthony, 168 N Alabama.
Montani Domenico, 168 N Alabama.
Montani Guy, 168 N Alabama.
Mueller Ida B, 496 Union.
Myers Amanda, rear 63 N East.
Nell Edward, 252 N Senate av.
Newell Alice, 489 N Illinois.
Newhall Alice R, 177 N Delaware.
Newland Robert A, 23 E Michigan.
Noble May, 70 Huron.
Noel Eugene E, 26 Prospect.
O'Neil Clara E, 49 Brookside av.
Orcutt Lulu M, 20 Tacoma av.
Overmyer Carrie E, 62 Beaty.
Palmer Clara, 211 Keystone av.
Porter Georgia M, 296 N California.
Preston Arthur P, 526 N Meridian.
Prunk Harriet Augusta Mrs, 368 W New York. (See adv p 138.)
Ray Georgiana M, 284 Highland av.
Rembusch Nicholas, 5 Centennial.
Roberts Myra, 249 N West.
Robson Dirce, 805 N New Jersey.
Rock Ida M, 19 N Gale (B).
Rogers Emma G, 87 Birch av (W I).
Sanders Mary B, 380 College av.
Schellschmidt Adolph, 246 E Ohio.
Schellschmidt Adolph jr, 242 E Ohio.
Schellschmidt Bertha, 246 E Ohio.
Schellschmidt Conrad, 1145 N Alabama.
Schellschmidt Emma, 246 E Ohio.
Schellschmidt Pauline, 246 E Ohio.
Schneider Karl, 366 N Alabama.
Schonacker Hubert J, 220 N New Jersey.
Schultz Charles, 77 E Walnut.
Schwegman Elizabeth, 139 Windsor.
Secrest Carrie F, 25 Shelby.
Shedd Mary M, 74 When bldg.
Shideler Fannie B, n s Eastern av 1 e of Grand av (I).
Short Albert N, 226 Yandes.
Smith Edward A, 149 Hosbrook.
Smith Ella M, 594 E St Clair.
Stagg Daniel E, 64 W 6th.
Stanton Louisa, 217 E Ohio.
Strangmeier Frederick G, 177 Shelby.
Stuart Emma L, 401½ N Alabama.
Teas Mary M, w s Elm av 1 n of Washington av (I).
Thomson Jennie C, 194 Cherry.
Topmiller Frank H, 66 English av.
Tuttle Walter C, 136 W Vermont.
Vail Flora E, 1208 N Penn.
Vegara Leonardo, 221 N Capitol av.
Von Burg Martha J, 83 Sheffield av (H).
Wachsmann Paul, 338 S Alabama.
Walker Barclay, Brenneke bldg.
Walker Cora B, 169 Prospect.
Walls Louis, rear 66 E Michigan.
Watson Blanche E, 26 Stoughton av.
Weegmann Carl H, 1 Halcyon blk.
Wells Maud L, 282 N Alabama.
Wells Stella, 36 Dickson.
Weser Edith E, 641 E Vermont.
White Alma C, 395 Bellefontaine.
Williams Mary L, 200 N Capitol av.
Wilmington Anna E, 184 Brookside av.
Wolfe Anna E, 187 Columbia av.
Zumpfe Emil, 401 Park av.

MUSIC AND MUSICAL MERCHANDISE.

(See also Pianos and Organs.)
Conrad Owen J, 72 Mass av.
Conrath Joseph, 195 Virginia av.
Estey-Camp Music House, 254 Mass av. (See adv in Pianos and Organs.)
Henninger G & E, 35 Virginia av.
Mayer Charles & Co, 29-31 W Washington. (See adv opp p 615.)
Meck Music Publishing Co, 7 Monument pl.
Verity Stephen T, 62 Virginia av.
Wachsmann Julius, 70 Virginia av.

*NATURAL GAS FITTERS.

Boyd Alonzo, 816 N Illinois. (See adv in Plumbers.)
Farrell J S & Co, 84 N Illinois. (See left bottom cor cards.)
Meikel Charles W, 96-98 E New York. (See right bottom lines.)

*NETTING.

Vonnegut Clemens, 184-186 E Washington. (See left bottom lines.)

NEWS DEALERS.

(See also Books and Stationery.)
Bertelsman Wm, 264 Mass av.
Christy Samuel A, 259 Mass av.
Day Harry A, 100 Meek.
Deschler Louis G, The Bates.
Hicks Richard L, 127 W Washington.
Housel Thomas, 71 Mass av.
Lawrence Cyrus W, Hotel English.
Murphy John E, 551 W Udell (N I).
Noah Thomas J, 424 Virginia av.
Schmitt Emma, 22 N Illinois.
Smith Joseph, 56 N Illinois.
Union News Co, 193 S Illinois.
Winchester Francis O, 476 S Meridian.
Wyman Margaret A, 406 Virginia av.

ERTEL STEAM LAUNDRY 26 and 28 N. Sa Ave. Telephone 1089.

ELLIS & HELFENBERGER Manufacturers of Iron Vases, Setees and Hitch Posts. 162-170 South Senate Ave. Tel. 958.

THE HOGAN TRANSFER AND STORAGE COMP'Y
Household Goods and Pianos Moved—Packed—Stored...... Baggage and Package Express Machinery and Safes a Specialty Cor. Washington and Illinois Sts. TELEPHONE No. 675.

Hose, Belting, Packing, Clothing, Druggists' Sundries, Bicycle Tires, Cotton Hose, Etc. New York Belting & Packing Co., L't'd.

*NEWSPAPER ILLUSTRATING.

Indiana Illustrating Co, s e cor Market and Illinois. (See adv opp Engravers.)

*NEWSPAPERS.

(See also Miscellaneous Directory.)

Agricultural Epitomist, 21½ W Washington.
American Tribune, 46-47 Journal Bldg.
Daily Reporter The, 519 Indiana Trust Bldg.
Ensign The, A E Winters Editor, 33 Talbott Blk. (See adv opp.)
German Telegraph (Daily except Sunday), 27 S Delaware.
Indiana Woman The, 49½ N Illinois.
Indianapolis Journal The (Daily, Sunday and Weekly), n e cor Monument Pl and Market.
Indianapolis Live Stock Journal, Union Stock Yards (W I).
Indianapolis News The (Daily except Sunday), 32 W Washington.
Indianapolis Sentinel The (Daily, Sunday and Weekly), 21-23 N Illinois.
Indianapolis Trade Journal, 35-36 Commercial Club Bldg.
Little Folks (Monthly), Little Folks Publishing Co Publishers, 5, 42 W Market.
Mutual Investor The (Monthly), Investor Printing and Publishing Co Publishers, 537 Lemcke Bldg.
National Detective and Police Review, Rooms 10-12, 96½ E Market. (See adv in classified Detective Agencies.)
Spottvogel The (German, Sunday), 27 S Delaware.
Sun The (Daily), 79 E Ohio.
Volksblatt (German, Weekly), 27 S Delaware.
Wheelmen's Gazette, Ben L Darrow Publisher, 31 W Ohio. (See right side lines.)
Zig-Zag Cycler (Weekly), Cycler Printing Co Publishers, 33 Talbott Blk. (See adv opp.)

*NICKEL PLATERS.

Vonnegut Clemens, 184-186 E Washington. (See left bottom lines.)

*NITRATE OF SODA.

Moffat & Co, 402 Lemcke Bldg. (See adv p 9.)

*NOTARIES PUBLIC.

Batchelor George H, 5 Hubbard blk.
Curtis James B, 139 Commercial Club bldg.
Drapier Wm H Jr, 29½ E Market.
Feibleman Isidore, 139 Commercial Club bldg.
Frey Adolph, 196 Elizabeth.
Gauld Adam A, 550 W Udell (North Indianapolis.)
Hadley Horace M, 66 E Market. (See left top cor cards.)
Hanna Gertrude, 18½ N Penn.
Hervey Bessie, 18½ N Penn.
Howe Daniel Wait, 5-9 Hubbard blk.
Korbly Charles A jr, 604 Indiana Trust bldg.
McKernan David S, 2-5 Thorpe Blk. (See right bottom lines.)
Metzger Albert E, 5 Odd Fellows' Hall. (See left bottom lines.)
Metzger Harry A, 5 Odd Fellows' Hall. (See left bottom lines.)
Morris Nathan, 139 Commercial Club bldg.
Newberger Louis, 140 Commercial Club bldg.
Osburn Lucy E, 14 Fletcher's Bank bldg.
Pierce Henry Douglas, 11, 12, 13 and 13½, 18½ N Meridian.
Pierce James E, 24 S Penn.
Pugh Edwin B, 57-58 Lombard bldg.
Rosebrock C Henry, 19 Thorpe Blk. (See back cover.)
Swigert Edith E, 18 Union bldg.
Tuttle Herman C, 28 E Market. (See left bottom cor cards.)
Vincent Anna Laura, 8½ N Penn.
Wallace Lew jr, 139 Commercial Club bldg.
Walsh Alice S, 18½ N Meridian.
Walsh James A, 14-16 Hubbard blk.
Wasson Charles K, 24 S Penn.
Winkenhofer Otto, 51 Journal bldg.
Wolf George, 221-222 Lemcke bldg.
Wurgler G Adolph, 88½ E Washington.

*NOTARY PUBLIC SEALS.

Mayer George J, 15 S Meridian. (See left bottom cor cards and p 5.)

NOTIONS—WHOLESALE.

Kipp Bros Co, 37-39 S Meridian.
Mayer Charles & Co, 29-31 W Washington. (See adv opp p 615.)
Murphy, Hibben & Co, 93-99 S Meridian.

NOTIONS—RETAIL.

Abright Catherine, 139 E Mkt House.
Ahlders Ahlrich, 539 S Meridian.
Anderson Leman C, 177 W 12th.
Ayres L S & Co, 33-37 W Washington.
Bannon & Co, 26 N Illinois.
Block Wm H Co The, 7-9 E Washington. (See right top and bottom lines.)
Burgoyne Frank, 5 Madison av.
Chambers James, 159 E Washington.
Clark Emma, 17 Hillside av.
Craig Eva, 136 Minerva.
Crombatch Marcus, 13 E Mkt House.
Davenport Anna, 184 Virginia av.
Elbreg George W, 26 English av.
Eminger Ira D, 652 Virginia av.
Farber Annie, 115 E Mkt House.
Gibs Max, E Mkt House.
Goldman David, 97 E Mkt House.
Haerle Wm, 4 W Washington.
Halbing Anna, 290 W Morris.
Hamilton Thomas D, E Mkt House.
Hanna Anna R, 452 S Meridian.
Harrison Catherine, 144 Blake.
Hawes Charles L, 115 Birch av (W I).
Hereth George L, 508 N West.
Hertz Magdaline, 15 E Mkt House.

The Central Rubber & Supply Co. ◆◆◆ PHONE 922. 79 S. ILLINOIS ST., INDIANAPOLIS, IND.

OTTO GAS ENGINES | BUILDERS' EXCHANGE S. W. Cor. Ohio and Penn. Telephone 535.

ADVERTISING. PRINTING.

"THE ENSIGN"

Is a weekly paper published at 33 Talbott Block.
The Ensign has advertising space for sale.
The Ensign is Four years old.
The Ensign is prepared to do Job Printing.
The Ensign Respectfully solicits a call from you when you want

ADVERTISING OR **JOB PINTING.**

THE ENSIGN

33 Talbott Block,
N. W. corner Pennsylvania and Market Streets.
(OPPOSITE POST OFFICE)
Indianapolis - - - - - Ind.

THE ZIG ZAG CYCLER,

A BICYCLE MAGAZINE.

When an advertiser wishes to place his goods before the younger class of wheelmen he will find a most excellent medium in

THE ZIG ZAG CYCLER

Founded 1890. Send us your address. Samples Free.
ARCHIAS E. WINTERS EDITOR AND MANAGER.

THE ZIG ZAG CYCLER,

33 Talbott Block,
[OPPOSITE POST OFFICE] N. W. corner Pennsylvania and Market Sts.
Indianapolis, - - - Ind.

Advertising. Printing.

Becker & Son Merchant Tailors

SALISBURY & STANLEY

[illegible] Augusta, [illegible] E Mkt House
[illegible] Bros, [illegible] N
[illegible] S H & Co, 24 W Wash [illegible]
[illegible] Louis C, [illegible] W [illegible]
[illegible] Mary E, [illegible] N West
[illegible] Misses, [illegible] N Senate av. (See adv in Stamping.)
[illegible] Henry E, 12 W Wash [illegible]
[illegible] Charles A Co, 29-31 W Washington. (See adv opp p 615.)
[illegible] Clara [illegible] S [illegible]
[illegible] Edith [illegible]
[illegible] Isaac [illegible] E Mkt House
[illegible] Dry Goods Co, 25-33 E Washington.
[illegible] Wm H, 304 Shelby
[illegible] Emilie A [illegible] E Mkt H[illegible]
[illegible] Catherine S [illegible] Mass av
[illegible] Exchange 125 N Penn
[illegible] Sarah A, [illegible] S [illegible]

NOVELTY MANUFACTURERS.

[illegible] Novelty Manufacturing [illegible] Chestnut.
[illegible] Harris & Co [illegible] Baldwin blk
[illegible] & Nelson, [illegible] av [illegible] Belt R R (B)
[illegible] George A, [illegible] W Ohio
[illegible] Frank M (mechan[illegible]) [illegible] E [illegible]

NURSERYMEN.

(See also Florists and Nurserymen [illegible])

Burkhart Harvey A & Sons, [illegible] N Meridian. (See adv opp p 232.)

NURSES.

[illegible] Sarah, 351 Mass av
[illegible] Mary P, [illegible] Spring
[illegible] Sarah E, [illegible] Fulton
[illegible] Ada, [illegible] E St Clair
[illegible] Margaret L, [illegible] Cornell av
[illegible] Elizabeth, [illegible] S Delaware
[illegible] May D, [illegible] Virginia av
[illegible] Wm, [illegible] Enterprise Hotel
[illegible] Veronica, [illegible] S Meridian
[illegible] Lucy, [illegible] Miller blk
[illegible] Theresa M, [illegible] S Meridian
[illegible] Frederica, 191 Coburn
[illegible] Sarah, 256 Virginia av
[illegible] Agnes J, [illegible] Walcott
[illegible] Ray A, 242 E Vermont
[illegible] Stella S, 242 E Vermont
[illegible] Elizabeth P, [illegible]
[illegible] Fanny E, [illegible] Cornell av
[illegible] Charlotte E, [illegible] College av
[illegible] Anna, [illegible] E Morris
[illegible] Ella T, [illegible] N Penn
[illegible] Kate, [illegible] N Illinois
[illegible] Minnie W, [illegible] E North
[illegible] Mary L, 10 Wyandot blk
[illegible] Blanche, [illegible] S Alabama
[illegible] Mary E, 66 Hill av
[illegible] Anna, [illegible] Mass av
[illegible] Ella H, 10 Wyandot blk
[illegible] Mary F, [illegible] The Shiel
[illegible] Joseph, [illegible] Mass av
[illegible] John G, [illegible] Oak
[illegible] Susan E, 18 Wyandot blk
[illegible] Mary A, [illegible] S Meridian
[illegible] Nora, 444 N New Jersey
[illegible] Rebecca E, [illegible] College
[illegible] Helen, 10 Wyandot
[illegible] Elizabeth, 10 Wyandot blk
[illegible] Ella, [illegible] N Delaware

[illegible] N Illinois
[illegible] College av
[illegible] N Detroit
[illegible] Mass av
[illegible] Penn and South
[illegible] Mass av
[illegible] Mass av
[illegible] Mass av
[illegible] Dawson
[illegible] Mass av
[illegible] N East
[illegible] Brighton av
[illegible] Mass av
[illegible] Pratt
[illegible] 10 Wyandot blk
[illegible]
[illegible] Warren av (W I)
[illegible] St Joseph av
[illegible] New York

OCULISTS AND AURISTS.

(See also Physicians.)

Adams H Alden, 21 W Ohio.
Heath Frederick C, 19 W Ohio.
Manchester Jerome J, 10 Mansur Blk, cor Washington and Alabama.
[illegible] Wm G, [illegible] Ohio
Stillson Joseph O, 245 N Penn.
[illegible] W Ohio
[illegible] W Ohio
[illegible] E Ohio

OFFICE DESKS.

Katteman Wm, 89-91 E Washington. (See right top lines.)

OFFICE FURNITURE AND FIXTURES.

Hough Notre Co The, 70 W Market.

OFFICE AND BAR FURNITURE AND FIXTURES.

Killinger George W, s w cor Market and Missouri. (See adv in Saloons.)
Salisbury & Stanley, 177 Clinton. (See right side lines.)

OFFICIAL REPORTERS.

[illegible] P O bldg
[illegible] & C[illegible], [illegible] Court House
[illegible] & Metcalf, [illegible] Court House

OIL BURNER MANUFACTURERS.

[illegible] Oil Burner Co, [illegible] N Delaware

OIL CLOTHS.

Block Wm H Co The, 7-9 E Washington. (See right top and bottom lines.)

OILS—ILLUMINATING AND LUBRICATING.

A[illegible] Oil Co, 41 Lemcke bldg
Brooks Oil Co, 188 E Michigan.
Burdsal A Co The, 34-36 S Meridian. (See right bottom cor cards.)
[illegible] Co, [illegible] Lombard bldg
[illegible] Christopher H, [illegible] W Chesapeake
[illegible] E South
[illegible] Mfg Co, [illegible] S Illinois
[illegible] Oil Tank Line, cor Oliver av and [illegible] (W I)

Office, Store and Bank Fixtures of all Kinds Specialty [illegible] Street, Indianapolis [illegible]

Contractors and Builders TELEPHONE 9[illegible]

LUMBER | Sash, Door and Planing Mill Work. Balke & Krauss Co. Cor. Market and Missouri Streets.

Becker & Son Charles Becker Jacob Becker Jr. Merchant Tailors. 21 N. Penn St. Tel. 934

SALISBURY & STANLEY · Office, Store and Bank Fixtures a Specialty. Repairing of all kinds done on short notice. 177 Clinton St. Indianapolis, Ind. · Contractors and Builders TELEPHONE 99.

Jackman Augusta, 131 E Mkt House.
Jereissati Bros, 48 N Illinois.
Knox S H & Co, 24 W Washington.
Larsen Louis C, 556 W Udell (N I).
Lockstand Mary E, 750 N West.
Lueders Misses, 460 N Senate av. (See adv in Stamping.)
Mathews Henry E, 13 W Washington.
Mayer Charles & Co, 29-31 W Washington. (See adv opp p 615.)
Michael Clara, 450 S Delaware.
Morris Edith L, 321 Bellefontaine.
Obstfeld Isaac, E Mkt House.
Pettis Dry Goods Co, 25-33 E Washington.
Rice Wm H, 304 Shelby.
Scholl Emilie A, 117 E Mkt House.
Wallace Catherine S, 328 Mass av.
Woman's Exchange, 125 N Penn.
Ziegler Sarah A, 97 S Noble.

NOVELTY MANUFACTURERS.

Cresshull Novelty Manufacturing Co, 596 Chestnut.
Cripe, Harris & Co, 82 Baldwin blk.
Davidson & Nelson, s s Bloyd av 1 e of Belt R R (B).
Sickford George A, 62 W Ohio.
Ward Frank M (mechanical), 178 E Louisiana.

*NURSERYMEN.

(See also Florists and Nurserymen.)

Burkhart Harvey A & Sons, 492 S Meridian. (See adv opp p 232.)

NURSES.

Armstrong Sarah, 261 Mass av.
Austin Mary P, 215 Spring.
Cain Sarah E, 28 Evison.
Carr Ada, 583 E St Clair.
Cloud Margaret L, 18 Cornell av.
Cronnon Elizabeth, 275 S Delaware.
Currie May D, 285 Virginia av.
Daggy Wm, b Enterprise Hotel.
Dasohler Veronica, 851½ S Meridian.
Deischer Lucy, 7 Miller blk.
Delaney Theresa M, 465½ S Meridian.
Dippel Frederica, 191 Coburn.
Earnest Sarah, 285 Virginia av.
Espy Agneese J, 25 Walcott.
Eberingham Ray A, 242 E Vermont.
Eberingham Stella S, 242 E Vermont.
Gerard Elizabeth P, 108 Cornell av.
Gerard Fanny E, 108 Cornell av.
Glasscock Charlotte E, 29 College av.
Gorius Anna, 185 E Morris.
Gregoire Ella T, 1025 N Penn.
Harmuth Kate, 529½ N Illinois.
Hays Minnie W, 223½ E North.
Henchman Mary L, 10 Wyandot blk.
Hover Blanche, 357 S Alabama.
Hunter Mary E, 66 Hill av.
Johns Anna, 294½ Mass av.
Keene Ella H, 10 Wyandot blk.
Kelley Mary F, 303 The Shiel.
Kingham Joseph, 253 Mass av.
Koerner John G, 59 Oak.
Lanham Susan E, 18 Wyandot blk.
Lawrence Mary A, 465½ S Meridian.
Lee Nora, 444 N New Jersey.
McClure Rebecca E, 195 College av.
MacDougall Helen, 10 Wyandot blk.
Minary Elizabeth, 10 Wyandot blk.
Meztler Ella, 197 N Delaware.
Newhouse Orpha, 685 N Illinois.
Phipps Kate F, 150½ College av.
Pierson Margaret A, 39 Detroit.
Redmond Ann, 15 Maria.
Reeves James E, 69 Mass av.
Sammons Eva, s e cor Penn and South.
Seeman Anna, 294½ Mass av.
Seeman Carrie, 294½ Mass av.
Seeman Josephine, 294½ Mass av.
Smith Frances, 23 Dawson.
Stevens Mary E, 252½ Mass av.
Taylor Belle, 266 N East.
Thomas Viretta, 100 Stoughton av.
Wallace Lucinda, 881 Mass av.
Walterhouse Louisa B, 141 E Pratt.
Wells Marguerite I, 10 Wyandot blk.
Wells Sera D, 36 Dickson.
Wilson Harriet, 27 Warren av (W I).
Wright Jessie S, 189 Johnson av.
Zolezzi Carrie G, 125 E New York.

*OCULISTS AND AURISTS.

(See also Physicians.)

Adams H Alden, 21 W Ohio.
Heath Frederick C, 19 W Ohio.
Manchester Jerome J, 10 Mansur Blk, cor Washington and Alabama.
Rice Wm G, 14 E Ohio.
Stillson Joseph O, 245 N Penn.
Thompson Daniel A, 22 W Ohio.
Thompson James L, 22 W Ohio.
Williams James L, 36 E Ohio.

*OFFICE DESKS.

Kotteman Wm, 89-91 E Washington. (See right top lines.)

*OFFICE FURNITURE AND FIXTURES.

Rough Notes Co The, 79 W Market.

*OFFICE AND BAR FURNITURE AND FIXTURES.

Killinger George W, s w cor Market and Missouri. (See adv in Saloons.)
Salisbury & Stanley, 177 Clinton. (See right side lines.)

OFFICIAL REPORTERS.

Evans Rowland, P O bldg.
Garber & Carpenter, 51 Court House.
Johnson & Metcalf, 81 Court House.

*OIL BURNER MANUFACTURERS.

Blue Flame Oil Burner Co, 87 N Delaware.

*OIL CLOTHS.

Block Wm H Co The, 7-9 E Washington. (See right top and bottom lines.)

OILS—ILLUMINATING AND LUBRICATING.

Acme Oil Co, 401 Lemcke bldg.
Brooks Oil Co, 488 E Michigan.
Burdsal A Co The, 34-36 S Meridian. (See right bottom cor cards.)
Chester Oil Co, 51 Lombard bldg.
Corcoran Christopher H, 192 W Chesapeake.
Crescent Oil Co, 34 E South.
Hoosier Mnfg Co, 192 S Illinois.
Indiana Oil Tank Line, cor Oliver av and Judge Harding (W I).

LUMBER | Sash, Door and Planing . Mill Work . | Balke & Krauss Co. Cor. Market and Missouri Streets.

FRIEDGEN'S TAN SHOES are the Newest Shades
Prices the Lowest. 19 North Pennsylvania St.

SAMUEL LAING General Job Work in Sheet Metal of all Kinds
72 AND 74 E. COURT STREET.

Oils—Illuminating and Lubricating—Continued.

Maddox Arthur C, 69 S Linden.
Miller Oil Co The, 23-27 McNabb. (See adv.)

THE MILLER OIL CO.,
Dealers in Mill Supplies, Oils, Lubricating Greases, Felt Roofing and Scale Solvent.
Circular Saws, Rubber and Leather Belting, Emery Wheels, Files, Wood and Iron Pulleys, Oil Cups.
23, 25 AND 27 McNABB ST.,
Tel. 1332. Opp. Union Station,
INDIANAPOLIS, IND.

Paragon Safety Oil Co, 501 E Michigan.
Scofield, Shurmer & Teagle, n w cor Vermont and Bee Line Ry.
Standard Oil Co, n w cor Lord and Pine.
Vincent John H, 358 Jefferson av.
White Conyers A, 69 S Linden.

***OMNIBUS LINES.**

Bird Frank Transfer Co, General Office 24 Pembroke Arcade; Branches 115 N Delaware, Bate House and Union Station. (See adv in Transfer Companies, p 192 and below.)

FRANK BIRD TRANSFER CO.
General Office, 24 Pembroke Arcade.
Offices { Union Station. 115 North Delaware and Bates House.
Stable, 115 North Delaware.
Order by Telephone Day or Night. | Baggage Checked at Residence | Carriages for Parties, Weddings, Depot, etc.
Telephone 534.

***OPTICAL GOODS.**

Mayer Charles & Co, 29-31 W Washington. (See adv opp p 615.)
Mayhew James N, 13 N Meridian. (See right bottom cor cards.)

OPTICIANS.

Gold & Adler, 61 S Illinois.
Lando Leo, 93 N Penn.
Mayhew James N, 13 N Meridian. (See right bottom cor cards.)
Plasterer Purl C, 56 N Penn.
Rowe Isaac N, 8 N Penn.
Wimmer John P, 14 N Penn.
Woodward Harnie E, 16 E Washington.

***ORCHESTRAS.**

Montani Bros, 168 N Alabama.
Panden Bros, 115-117 W New York.
Zumpfe's Orchestra, 4 Lombard bldg.

***ORGAN MOTORS.**

Tuerk Hydraulic Power Co, 39 Dearborn St, Chicago, Ill.

***ORTHOPEDISTS.**

Garr Benjamin T, 463 Central av.

***OSTRICH FEATHER DYERS.**

Failles Charles, 28 S Illinois.

***OUTDOOR GAMES.**

Mayer Charles & Co, 29-31 W Washington. (See adv opp p 615.)

OVERALL MANUFACTURERS.

Brown Louis, 82 N Liberty.
De Bush John W, 292 Mass av.
Harseim Robert G, 202 S Meridian.
Meier Lewis & Co, 2-4 Central av.

OYSTERS, FISH AND GAME.

Clark Wm M, 178 E Wabash.
Egan & Sowders, 286 E Washington.
Fulton Fish Market, 61 N Illinois.
Haag Bros, 168 Indiana av.
Heinlein John jr, 193 Indiana av.
Kamps Frank G, 40 Virginia av.
Kernel Frank J, 410 S Meridian.
Linus Daniel A, 63 Mass av and 92 E Mkt House.
O'Brien Louis C, 71 N Illinois.
Peirce John W, 22 S Illinois.
Ryan Thomas, 57 Russell av.
Scheid John & Co, 77 N Illinois and 67 E Mkt House.
Sowders James M, 237 W Washington.
Sowders Rinaldo, 64 E Mkt House.
Sowders Wm, 36 E Mkt House.
Sowders & Edwards, 596 Virginia av.

***PACKAGE DELIVERY.**

Indianapolis Storage and Transfer Company, 370-372 S Delaware. (See back cover.)

PACKERS—BEEF AND PORK.

Coffin, Fletcher & Co, n s Ray w of West.
Kingan & Co (ltd), w end Maryland.
Meuser John R, 292 W Ray.
Moore & Co, Union Stock Yards (W I).
Reiffel Martin, 295 W Ray.

PACKING BOX MANUFACTURERS.

Dietz Fred Co The, 370-406 Madison av. (See right side lines and p 10.)

***PACKING—STEAM.**

Central Rubber and Supply Co The, 79 S Illinois. (See left side lines.)

***PAINT MANUFACTURERS.**

Burdsal A Co The, 34-36 S Meridian. (See right bottom cor cards.)
Indianapolis Paint and Color Co, 40, 42, 44, 46 and 48 Mass av. (See adv in Paints and Oils.)

***PAINTERS—CARRIAGE.**

Brooks Jesse, 325 N Noble.
La Rue Clarence L, 302 Excelsior av.
Wolf H S & Co, 479 S Delaware.

***PAINTERS—FRESCO.**

Fertig & Kevers, 8 W Market. (See adv.)
Mack F J & Co, 32 S Meridian.
Pressler Guido R, 325 N Liberty. (See right bottom cor cards.)

PAPER BOXES, MANUFACTURED BY SULLIVAN & MAHAN 41 W. PEARL STREET.

DIAMOND WALL PLASTER { Telephone 1410 BUILDERS' EXCHANGE.

JOS. R. ADAMS,
177 CLINTON STREET,
PAINTER
SPECIAL ATTENTION GIVEN TO
GRAINING, CALCIMINING, TINTING AND GLAZING.
Telephone 999. INDIANAPOLIS.
Residence, 891 North Pennsylvania Street.

Teckenbrock John H, 94 E South. (See right bottom lines and adv.)

PAINTERS—HOUSE AND SIGN.

Adams Joseph R, 177 Clinton. (See adv.)

Andrews Earnest L, 70½ E Court.
Ante Louis, cor Meridian and Russell av.
Avery Edwin L, 167½ W 1st.

Ballmann J Henry, 60 E Ohio.

Boller Peter, 282 N Pine.
Bowe James C, 32 S Meridian.
Brommer Frederick, rear 524 E Washington.
Brown George W, 29 Keith.
Burges Edward, 325 Davidson.
Burrows Wm H, 176½ N Missouri.
Capen Philip M B, 110 Ludlow av.
Cleaveland Calvin C, 15 S Meridian.
Clements Harry B, 194 Davidson.
Cook Thomas V, 36 Monument pl.
Daily & Pfeffer, 66 W Market.
Denny Owen L, e s Nicholas 1 s of Howland.
Derleth Michael, 31 Downey.
Ellig Bernard E, 204 E Morris.

English J K & H K, 143½ N Delaware.

Fatout J Noble, 4 Cyclorama Pl.

Fertig & Kevers, 8 W Market. (See adv.)

Established 1850.
FERTIG & KEVERS
(Successors to Frank Fertig.)
PAINTERS,
8 W. Market St. 'Phone 120.

Fowler George I, 904 N Delaware.
Gill James D, 174 Lexington av.
Gioscio John, 170 N Alabama.
Grove Albert H, 94 E Market.
Grover Wm, 50 Dawson.
Guinan Matthew, 477 S Capitol av.
Gustin Wm J, 26 Water.
Hallock Samuel D, 71½ Lockerbie.
Hamilton J W, 34½ S Penn.
Hilsabeck Judson A, 231 Yandes.
Hilsabeck Wm A, 52 S Belmont (W I).
Hofmann Charles, 419 Madison av.
Holmes Leslie S, 382 E Michigan.
Horn Charles W, 65 Mass av.
Huxley Joseph, 17½ Virginia av.
Israel James N, 20 Douglass.
Jaqueth Burnham G, 185 W New York.
Johnson Harry, 175¼ S East.
Johnson Wm A, 545 Ash.
Kaiser August, 459 Sheldon.
Kaley Henry L, 58 Brookside av.
King Eli, 259 Keystone av.
Klanke August, 275 Coburn.
Lange Louis L, 472 Union.
LaRue Willis E, 70½ E Court.
Lewis Charles W, 216 W North.
Long Eli C, 177 Buchanan.
Loucks Calvin R, 105 English av.
Luke Albert, 85 Warren av (W I).
Lynn Adam A, 197 W Washington.
Lyzott Charles W, 67 Russell av.
McAdams Andrew M, 8 Putnam (B).
McMahan David J, 42 Yandes.
McPherson Wm M, 20 Sullivan.

Mack F J & Co, 32 S Meridian.

Macpherson Alexander, 94 E Market.
Matthews John R, 77 Torbet.
May Edward S, 782 N Rural.
Menefee James A, 170 John.
Meyer Henry B, 365 Virginia av.
Muecke Wm, 76 Virginia av.
Munson Grant, 380 E Michigan.
Norris Wm F, 170 Brookside av.
Pennington Joseph W, 438 Talbott av.
Pratt Frank, 457 Charles.
Ready & Foltz, Car Works (W I).
Reese Charles, 175 Huron.
Richter August F, 14 Shelby.
Rooker Frederick, 424 E New York.
Rupert Charles M, 410 N Brookside av.
Schaub Henry, rear 499 N Alabama.
Scott Robert H, 231½ E Washington.
Seibert Ferdinand C, 209 N Pine.
Seibert Henry, 71 Peru av.
Shields Joseph M, 30½ N Reisner (W I).
Snyder Charles A, 425 E St Clair.
Stark Reinhold, 122 S Pine.
Studer Victor, 235 S Linden.
Stuecker Frederick R, 399 S East.
Swain George B, 21 S Meridian.

Fine Laundry Work our Specialty. Collars and Cuffs our Hobby. || THE HOME LAUNDRY || 197 S. Illinois St. Telephone 1769.

THE WM. H. BLOCK CO. 7 AND 9 EAST WASHINGTON STREET. DRY GOODS, MEN'S FURNISHINGS.

Fidelity and Deposit Co. of Maryland. BONDS SIGNED.—LOCAL BOARD John B. Elam, Albert Sahm, Smiley N. Chambers, John M. Spann.
GEORGE W. PANGBORN, General Agent, 704-706 Lemcke Building. Telephone 140.

74 EAST MARKET STREET Telephone 863.

J. H. TECKENBROCK
94 EAST SOUTH STREET
PAINTER AND DECORATOR
Graining, Glazing, Varnishing, Calcimining, Tinting and Paper Hanging,
INDIANAPOLIS, IND.

Insure Your Property With FRANK K. SAWYER

Painters—House and Sign—Con.

Teckenbrock John H, 94 E South. (See right bottom lines and adv.)
Thorne Marcus O, 217 Buchanan.
Volmar John B, 68 W McCarty.
Walsh Matthew P, 386 Fulton.
Watson Charles T, 309 N Pine.
Weldon Thomas, 119 Fulton.
White Samuel A, 79 Hill av.
Wittenmeier John, 829 Chestnut.
Wolf Edwin A, 2 Kentucky av.

*PAINTERS—SIGN.

Adams Joseph R, 177 Clinton. (See adv.)

*PAINTERS' SUPPLIES.

Aldag Paint and Varnish Co The, 222 E Washington. (See adv in Paints and Oils.)
Burdsal A Co The, 34-36 S Meridian. (See right bottom cor cards.)
Indianapolis Paint and Color Co, 40, 42, 44, 46 and 48 Mass av. (See adv in Paints and Oils.)

*PAINTS—ROOFING.

Smither Henry C, 169 W Maryland. (See adv opp Roofing Material.)
Smither Theodore F, 151 W Maryland. (See right side lines.)

PAINTS AND OILS.

Aldag Paint and Varnish Co The, 222 E Washington. (See adv.)

The Aldag Paint and Varnish Co.
DEALERS IN
PAINTERS' SUPPLIES
OILS, VARNISHES, BRUSHES AND GLASS.
222 E. Washington St. Telephone 334

Burdsal A Co The, 34-36 S Meridian. (See right bottom cor cards.)
Indianapolis Paint and Color Co, 40, 42, 44, 46 and 48 Mass av. (See adv.)

Indianapolis Paint and Color Co.
Manufacturers and Grinders of
STRICTLY PURE PAINTS AND COLORS
40 to 48 Massachusetts Ave. Phone 1770.

Indianapolis Steel Roofing and Corrugating Works, 23-25 E South. (See right side lines.)
Lake Charles N, 208 S Meridian.
McDade Samuel, 537 E Ohio.
Shellhouse & Co, 271-275 E Washington.
Smither Henry C, 169 W Maryland. (See adv opp Roofing Material.)
Smither Theodore F, 161 W Maryland. (See right side lines.)

*PANELED STEEL CEILING AND SHEET METAL WORK.

McWorkman Willard, 930 W Washington. (See left top cor cards.)

*PAPER.

Bowen-Merrill Co The, 9-11 W Washington and 10-12 W Pearl.

PAPER MANUFACTURERS.

Beveridge Paper Co, cor Maryland and Geisendorff.
Indiana Paper Co, 27 E Maryland.

PAPER—WHOLESALE.

Fisher Moses P, 131 S Meridian.
Lesh C P Paper Co, 85 W Market.

*PAPER BOX MANUFACTURERS.

Indianapolis Desk File and Paper Box Manufactory, 143½-145 S Meridian.
Sullivan & Mahan, 41 W Pearl. (See left bottom lines.)

IF CONTINUED to the end of its dividend period, policies of the UNITED STATES LIFE INSURANCE CO., will equal or excel any investment policy ever offered to the public. E. B. SWIFT, Manager, 25 E. Market St.

Wm. Kotteman 89 & 91 E. Washington St. TELEPHONE 1742 Furniture

SHOW CASES ‖ WILLIAM WIEGEL ‖ 6 West Louisiana Street Opp. Union Station.

E. A. DEARINGER,

Paper Hanger and Decorator

PRICES REASONABLE. WORK GUARANTEED.

Orders Solicited. 118 Ft. Wayne Avenue, Indianapolis.

U. S. and Foreign

PATENTS

Procured for Inventors by **T. R. BELL,** Mechanical Engineer and Patent Solicitor. New and special machinery designed and inventions perfected. Working drawings at lowest rates consistent with careful work. **BLUE PRINTING** at very reduced rates. **All classes of light or heavy machinery carefully constructed at lowest contract prices.** Call on

T. R. BELL, 64 Ingalls Block.

PAPERHANGERS.

Ammeroth August, 412 Union.
Avels Henry, 359 S Alabama.
Berdel Carl, 45 Beaty.

Dearinger Edward A, 118 Ft Wayne av. (See adv.)

Jachmann Wm F, 413 E Washington.

Shaw Decorating Co, 106-108 N Meridian. (See adv in Wall Paper.)

Teckenbrock John H, 94 E South. (See right bottom lines and adv in Painters.)

Thompson Walter C, 359 Coburn.
Zimmer Henry W, 16 Clay.

*PAPERHANGERS' SUPPLIES.

Burdsal A Co The, 34-36 S Meridian. (See right bottom cor cards.)

*PARQUETRY FLOORS.

Interior Hardwood Co The, Manufacturers, 317 Mass av.

PASTE MANUFACTURERS.

Altenberger Frederick W, 137 W Maryland.

*PATENT ATTORNEYS.

Bell Thompson R, 64 Ingalls Blk. (See adv.)

Bradford Chester, 14-16 Hubbard Blk. (See left top cor cards, p 6 and opp Patent Solicitors.)

Herod Wm P, 14-17 Fletcher's Bank Bldg.

CARPETS CLEANED LIKE NEW. TELEPHONE 818
CAPITAL STEAM CARPET CLEANING WORKS

BENJ. BOOTH PRACTICAL EXPERT ACCOUNTANT. Thirty years' experience. First-class credentials. Room 18, 82½ E. Washington St. Indianapolis, Ind.

The Old Reliable Sherman European Restaurant || 18 and 20 S. Meridian St. Established 1880.

H. P. HOOD. *30 YEARS' EXPERIENCE.* A. M. HOOD, Late Examiner U. S. Pat. Office.

H. P. HOOD & SON,

Patents and Patent Law,

Attorneys and Consulting Experts in Infringement Suits.

EXPERT WITNESSES IN PATENT LITIGATION.

We give special attention to the preparation and presentation of applications for patents in this and all foreign countries.

Both members of the firm have a practical mechanical training and a wide experience in patent matters.

29-30 Wright's Block, 68½ East Market St.

V. H. LOCKWOOD,

PATENT AND TRADE MARK LAWYER.

Have Practiced in the United States and State Courts and the Patent Office for the Past Eleven Years.

U. S. AND FOREIGN PATENTS procured promptly and with broad and legal claims. Expert draughtsmen in the office. Terms very reasonable. References in any locality furnished on application.

OPINIONS AS TO the **VALIDITY OF PATENTS** and **INFRINGEMENTS** prepared. **CONTRACTS** relating to patents prepared or construed. Full set of Patent Office Reports and a complete patent law library in the office.

PATENT LITIGATION a specialty.

Long Distance Telephone 1103. Rooms 415-418 Lemcke Bldg., opp. Post-Office.

SOME REFERENCES.

Adams & Williamson, Indianapolis.
Commercial Electric Co., Indianapolis.
Crowell Apparatus Co., Indianapolis.
Good Mfg. Co., Indianapolis.
Hay & Willits, Indianapolis.
Indianapolis Drug Co., Indianapolis.
Indianapolis Electric Co., Indianapolis.
Indianapolis Excelsior Mfg. Co., Indianapolis.
Indianapolis Harness Co., Indianapolis.
Indianapolis Street Cleaning Co., Indianapolis.
Thos. Madden, Son & Co., Indianapolis.
McElwaine-Richards Co., Indianapolis.
Maus & Bretney Co., Indianapolis.
Mendenhall & Williams, Indianapolis.
Munger Bicycle Mfg. Co., Indianapolis.
Murphy, Hibben & Co., Indianapolis.
Pioneer Brass Co., Indianapolis.
Puritan Spring Bed Co., Indianapolis.
Pyle Electric Headlight Co., Indianapolis.
Rockwood Mfg. Co., Indianapolis.
U. S. Camera Co., Indianapolis.
Van Camp Packing Co., Indianapolis.
The Hudnut Co., Terre Haute, Ind.
Geo. Memmer & Co., Terre Haute, Ind.
LaFayette Bridge Co., LaFayette, Ind.
Champion Mfg. Co., Richmond, Ind.
The F. & N. Mfg. Co., Richmond, Ind.
Marion Flint Glass Co., Marion, Ind.
Marion Stove Co., Marion, Ind.
American Shaft Holder Co., Wabash, Ind.
Rex Mfg. Co., North Manchester, Ind.
Turner Mfg. Co., Lagrange, Ind.
Greenfield Iron and Nail Works, Greenfield, Ind.
Scott Automatic Boiler Feeder Co., Louisville, Ky.

Patent Attorneys—Continued.

Hood H P & Son, 29-30 Wright Blk. (See adv.)

Jacob & Co, s w cor Georgia and Penn. (See adv in Pattern and Model Makers.)

Lockwood Virgil H, 415-418 Lemcke Bldg. (See adv.)

PATENT SOLICITORS.

Bell Thompson R, 64 Ingalls Blk. (See adv.)

Bradford Chester, 14-16 Hubbard Blk. (See left top cor cards, P 6 and opp.)

Hood H P & Son, 29-30 Wright Blk. (See adv.)

TUTEWILER UNDERTAKER, No. 72 WEST MARKET STREET. TELEPHONE 216.

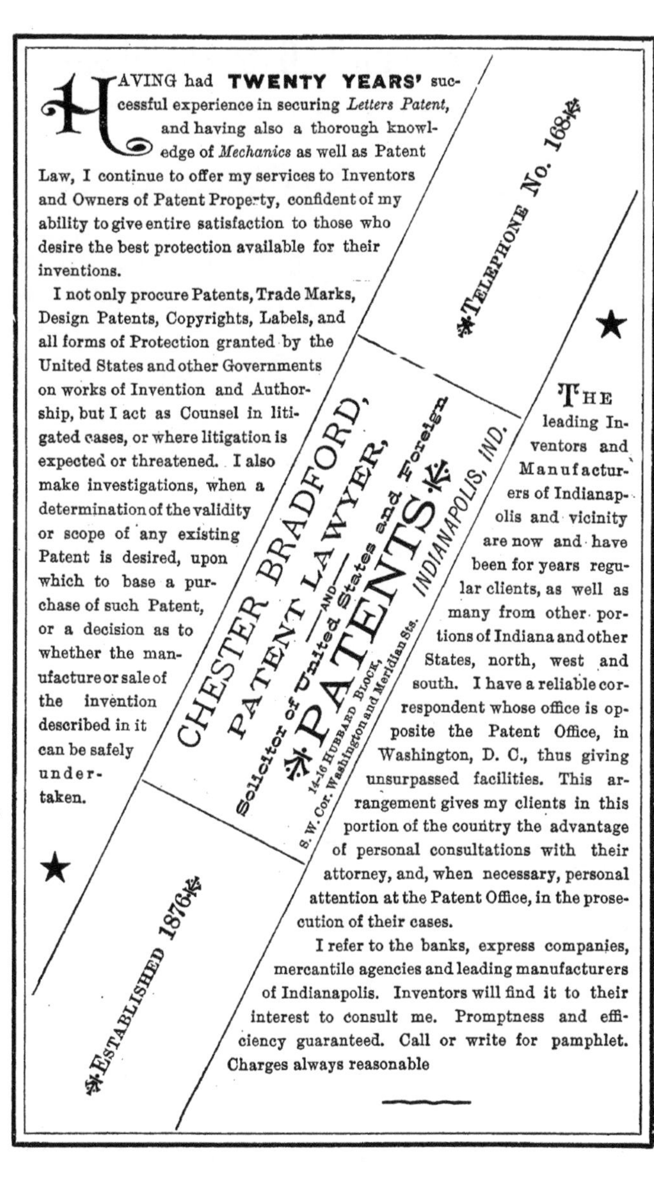
HAVING had TWENTY YEARS' successful experience in securing *Letters Patent*, and having also a thorough knowledge of *Mechanics* as well as Patent Law, I continue to offer my services to Inventors and Owners of Patent Property, confident of my ability to give entire satisfaction to those who desire the best protection available for their inventions.
I not only procure Patents, Trade Marks, Design Patents, Copyrights, Labels, and all forms of Protection granted by the United States and other Governments on works of Invention and Authorship, but I act as Counsel in litigated cases, or where litigation is expected or threatened. I also make investigations, when a determination of the validity or scope of any existing Patent is desired, upon which to base a purchase of such Patent, or a decision as to whether the manufacture or sale of the invention described in it can be safely undertaken.
Telephone No. 168
CHESTER BRADFORD,
PATENT LAWYER,
—AND—
Solicitor of United States and Foreign
PATENTS
14-16 HUBBARD BLOCK,
S. W. Cor. Washington and Meridian Sts.
INDIANAPOLIS, IND.
Established 1876
THE leading Inventors and Manufacturers of Indianapolis and vicinity are now and have been for years regular clients, as well as many from other portions of Indiana and other States, north, west and south. I have a reliable correspondent whose office is opposite the Patent Office, in Washington, D. C., thus giving unsurpassed facilities. This arrangement gives my clients in this portion of the country the advantage of personal consultations with their attorney, and, when necessary, personal attention at the Patent Office, in the prosecution of their cases.
I refer to the banks, express companies, mercantile agencies and leading manufacturers of Indianapolis. Inventors will find it to their interest to consult me. Promptness and efficiency guaranteed. Call or write for pamphlet. Charges always reasonable

DALTON & MERRIFIELD { LUMBER South Noble St., near E. Washington

H. D. NEALY, DRAUGHTSMAN,
DRAWINGS OF EVERY DESCRIPTION. ENGRAVINGS BY ALL METHODS. PATENT & MECHANICAL WORK A SPECIALTY.
HUBBARD BLOCK, COR. MERIDIAN & WASHINGTON STREETS
LONG DISTANCE TELEPHONE 168. P. O. BOX 10.
Indianapolis, Ind.

HEBER S. PARAMORE
SOLICITOR OF UNITED STATES AND FOREIGN
PATENTS
TRADE-MARKS, DESIGN PATENTS, COPYRIGHTS and LABELS
Prompt and Careful Personal Attention to all Business. Skilled Associate in Washington. Reasonable Terms. Best References.
23 West Washington Street, Indianapolis.

Patent Solicitors—Continued.

Jacob & Co, s w cor Georgia and Penn. (See adv opp Pattern and Model Makers.)

Lockwood Virgil H, 415-418 Lemcke Bldg. (See adv in Patent Attorneys.)

Minturn Joseph A, 15-16 Lombard bldg.

Ogborn Harrison, 17 Baldwin blk.

Paramore Heber S, 23 W Washington. (See adv.)

Snow J H & Co, 25½ W Washington.

Specialty Manufacturing Co, 193 S Meridian. (See adv opp Photographers.)

Thurman & Silvius, 44-46 When bldg.

*PATENT DRAUGHTSMEN.

Nealy H D, 16 Hubbard Blk. (See adv.)

Woerner Frank W, 415-418 Lemcke Bldg.

*PATENTS.

Bell Thompson R, 64 Ingalls Blk. (See adv.)

Bradford Chester, 14-16 Hubbard Blk. (See left top cor cards, p 6 and opp Patent Solicitors.)

Hood H P & Son, 29-30 Wright Blk. (See adv.)

Jacob & Co, s w cor Georgia and Penn. (See adv in Pattern and Model Makers.)

Lockwood Virgil H, 415-418 Lemcke Bldg. (See adv in Patent Attorneys.)

Specialty Manufacturing Co, 193 S Meridian. (See adv opp Photographers.)

Weathers James, 340 E Washington.

PATTERN AND MODEL MAKERS.

JACOB & CO.
MAKERS OF PATTERNS
Models and Experimental Work.
102 S. Pennsylvania St., Cor. Georgia

Duncan J R & Co, 168 W Georgia.

Indianapolis Pattern Works, Scullin & Myers Proprs, 101 S Penn.

Jacob & Co, s w cor Georgia and Penn. (See adv.)

McNamara, Koster & Co, 212-218 S Penn. (See right top lines and p 9.)

Parlor, Bed Room, Dining Room, Kitchen, Furniture W. H. MESSENGER, 101 E. Wash. St., Tel. 491.

INDIANA ELECTROTYPE CO. ●●● BEST WORK. LOWEST PRICES.
All Orders Promptly Filled.
23 WEST PEARL ST., INDIANAPOLIS, IND. JOB WORK. BOOK PLATES. BEST PATENT BASE ON THE MARKET.

JACOB & CO.

102 South Pennsylvania Street,
Corner Georgia.

PATTERN AND MODEL MAKERS

Patterns in Wood or Metal.

OLDEST
AND MOST
RELIABLE
NONE BUT THE BEST
MECHANICS
EMPLOYED.

JACOB & CO.,

102 S. Pennsylvania St., Cor. Georgia, INDIANAPOLIS, IND.

SEE OTHER SIDE.

JACOB & CO.

Pattern and Model Makers.

READ CAREFULLY.

To Factories, Foundries, Etc.

You are using machinery that can be improved.

You desire working drawings, blue prints, plans, specifications, etc.

We can design and build you special machinery, make your drawings, blue prints, etc.

You are caused frequently to witness certain parts of your machinery broken, and must have broken parts replaced at once.

You use heavy machinery, pulleys, gears, etc. If they break, ship them to us and we will make pattern and casting, finish casting and send same to you at earliest possible moment.

If you have large gears, etc., that are liable to break, send us word and we will come and make drawings, then furnish pattern, casting, etc., as desired.

We make patterns of every description, in either wood or metal, for cast iron, malleable iron, brass, steel, etc.

We have one of the largest pattern and model shops in the West.

We make a specialty of large bevel and spur gears up to fourteen feet in diameter.

We have special room prepared for experimental work, and all improvements made by us while working on such work become the property of the inventor employer.

An inventor should take out a caveat on his invention, and then have the invention made practical, and apply for letters patent in its complete working order, thus saving much expense and giving a more valuable invention. All this we can do, having many years' experience in this line.

Write us for full information.

See other side of this sheet.

JACOB & CO.,
102 South Pennsylvania St., Corner Georgia,
INDIANAPOLIS, IND.

SEE OTHER SIDE.

ALL KINDS OF HEAVY AND LIGHT GRAY IRON CASTINGS } McNamara, Koster & Co. { Foundry and Pattern Shop
Phone 1593. 212-218 S. Penn. St.

Reeves Harry E, 96 S Delaware, cor Georgia. (See embossed line front cover and adv.)

H. E. REEVES
Wood and Metal Pattern
AND MODEL MAKER.
Inventors Assisted. Fine Machinery and Apparatus Made and Repaired. Aluminum Work a Specialty,
96 South Delaware Street
Tel. 121. Indianapolis, Ind.
(See Embossed Line, Front Cover.)

Specialty Manufacturing Co, 193 S Meridian. (See adv opp Photographers.)

SPECIALTY MFG. CO.
Pattern and Model Makers
MACHINISTS AND GENERAL MANUFACTURERS.
187 to 195 South Meridian Street.
(See Adv. Opposite Photographers.)

PAVING—ASPHALT.

Symmes H H Co, 39 S Alabama.

*PAVING COMPANIES.

Capitol Paving and Construction Co, 1 Hubbard Blk, s w cor Washington and Meridian.

PAVING CONTRACTORS.

See Contractors—Paving.

PAWNBROKERS.

Cohen Hyman, 31 S Illinois.
Conlen John A, 57 W Washington.
Conlen Patrick, 14 Pembroke Arcade.
Drozdowitz Michael, 149 E Washington.
Ludwig Wm, 21 N Meridian.
Mayer Esther, 91 S Illinois.
Noe Fletcher M, 64 W Market.
Solomon Joseph, 25 S Illinois.
Ward & Co, 11 N Meridian.

PEN MANUFACTURERS.

Allison James A, 5 Stewart Pl.

*PENMANSHIP.

Indianapolis Business University, When Bldg, N Penn, E J Heeb Propr. (See front cover, right bottom lines and p 4.)

PENSION AGENTS AND ATTORNEYS.

Fitzgerald & Delp, 47 Journal Bldg. (See adv.)

F. N. FITZGERALD. OTTO DELP.
WE ARE RELIABLE
FITZGERALD & DELP
SUCCESSORS TO
P. H. Fitzgerald Claim Agency
Pensions under the Old or New law. No Pension—no Pay. Place your claim with us, as our system is the best. Rm. 47 Journal Bldg., Indianapolis.

Holt Henry, 77½ E Market.
Swigert Joseph O, 8 Union bldg.
Wright Benjamin C & Co, 29½ N Penn.

*PHONOGRAPHS.

Brown Wm G, 26 Pembroke Arcade.
Indiana Graphophone Co, 49-52 When Bldg. (See adv in Talking Machines.)

*PHOTO—LITHOGRAPHERS.

Burford Wm B, 21 W Washington. (See adv opp p 230.)

. FOR .
Lists of Names
ANY
Trade
Business
Profession or
Pursuit
ADDRESS
R. L. Polk & Co.
23-24 JOURNAL BLDG.

THE FRED DIETZ CO. WOODEN PACKING BOXES MADE TO ORDER FACTORY AND WAREHOUSE TRUCKS. 400 Madison Avenue. Telephone 654.

BUSINESS EDUCATION A NECESSITY. TIME SHORT. DAY AND NIGHT SCHOOL. SUCCESS CERTAIN AT THE PERMANENT, RELIABLE Indianapolis BUSINESS UNIVERSITY

Water Works Pumping Engines { HENRY R. WORTHINGTON, 64 SOUTH PENNSYLVANIA ST. Long Distance Telephone 284.

UNION CO-OPERATIVE LAUNDRY (COMPOSED OF UNION LAUNDRY GIRLS.) NOS. 138, 40 AND 42 VIRGINIA AVENUE TELEPHONE 89 INDIANAPOLIS, IND. T. E. SOMERVILLE, MANAGER

PHOTOGRAPHERS.

Allison James B, 113 Mass av.
Bennett J Wesley, 38½ E Washington.
Biddle Frederick S, 16½ E Washington.
Bosard Edgar M, 164 Virginia av.
Brandenburger Bros, 65 S Linden.
Brown Albert, 72½ E Washington.
Brown Charles, 121 W Washington.
Bryant Kate, 88 S Illinois.
Clark James H, 66 E Washington.
Crippen Ira L, 278 English av.
Dryer George W, 96½ S Illinois.
Faradizer Co The, 511-512 Lemcke bldg.
Hardy O D & Co, 240½ E Washington.
Harrod Joel E, 62½ Virginia av.
Keeter Joseph P, 214 W Washington.
Keeter Rufus G, 6½ E Washington.
Koehler & Bishop, 62½ E Washington.
Lacey Frank M, 126 Mass av.
McCloskey James B, 36½ E Washington.
Marceau Theodore, 40 N Illinois.
Mitchell Grant, 306 River av (W I).
Potter Wm H, 10 Claypool Blk, 9½ N Illinois.
Rafert Martin E, 19 Bloomington.
Simpson Wm, 94½ E Washington.
Van Trees Joseph W, 41 Palmer.
Williams Jesse M, 88 Paca.

*PHOTOGRAPHERS' SUPPLIES.

Lieber H Co The, 33 S Meridian. (See right top cor cards.)
Stephens Photo Supply Co, 19 Mass av.

*PHOTOGRAVURES.

Burford Wm B, 21 W Washington. (See adv opp p 230.)

PHYSICIANS.

Abbett Charles H, 31½ Virginia av.
Abbett Francis M, 15½ Virginia av.
Abbott Albert L, 252 Bright.
Adams H Alden (Eye, Ear and Nose), 21 W Ohio.
Alexander James T, 175½ Shelby.
Alexander Joseph C, 123 S Noble.
Allen Horace R jr, n w cor Ohio and Capitol av.
Allen Wm P, 297½ Mass av.
Anderson Don A, 402 Virginia av.
Anderson James E, 3 Grand Opera House blk.
Anthony Emanuel, 90 Mass av.
Anthony E Grove, 92 Mass av.
Anthony James A, 405 College av.
Bacon Hattie C, 9½ Fletcher av.
Baker Frank W, 31 W Market.
Baker John J, 37½ W Market.
Ball Addison W, 132 Columbia av.
Ball Cutler T, 29½ W Ohio.
Ballard Joseph H, 108 Hill av.
Barnes Dawson E, 3 West Drive (W P).
Barnes Henry F, 1215 N Penn.
Barnhill John F (Limited to Nose, Throat and Ear), 516-518 Indiana Trust Bldg.
Beamouth Fanando A, 123 W Vermont.
Beard Elisha, 31½ Virginia av.
Beck Wm S, 42 W Market.
Becker Frank C, 592 Morris (W I).
Bedford Collins T, 185 Mass av.
Bell Guido, s w cor N East and E Ohio.
Bell Leonard, s w cor N East and E Ohio.
Benepe John L, 209-210 Lemcke Bldg.
Benham John F, 914 Morris (W I).
Berauer Joseph M, 557½ Madison av.
Bigger Richard F, 102 N Alabama.
Bigger Robert H, 102 N Alabama.
Bigger R H & R F, 429 Virginia av.
Biggins James M, 117½ W Washington.
Billman Gustus S, 643 Virginia av.
Birket Charles T, 187 Columbia av.
Bistline Arvilla M, 394 N New Jersey.
Blu Uriah L, 65 Indiana av.
Bonham Alfred N, 201 The Majestic.
Booz J Jordan, 128 W New York.
Boswell James F, e s Sutherland av 1 n of 20th.
Bowers Isaac H, 803 E Washington.
Boyd James T, 76 E Ohio.
Boynton Charles S, 164 E New York.
Brayton Alembert W, 26½ E Ohio.
Brennan Edward J, 240 N Capitol av.
Brennan Vincent G, 240 N Capitol av.
Brigham Edwin B, 153 Columbia av.
Brill James H, 310 N New Jersey.
Brown Benjamin A, 59 E Sutherland (B).
Brown Eli F, 296 E Michigan.
Brown John R, 8 Sterling.
Browning Wm J, 19 W Ohio.
Brubaker & Ayres, 1-5 Fair blk.
Brunning Charles E, 101 Coburn.
Bryan Thomas N, 346 E South.
Bryson Rachel A, 434 Mass av.
Buehler Jacob, 120 E McCarty.
Bula Rolla W, 33 W Ohio.
Burckhardt Louis, 18 E Ohio.
Butler Wm H, 599 N Senate av.
Bye Benjamin F, 170 N Illinois.
Bye Charles E, 170 N Illinois.
Bye David M, 170 N Illinois.
Bye Wm O, 170 N Illinois.
Cain John C, 57 King av (H).
Caldwell W Hampton, 143 N Penn.
Campbell Levi S, 65 Indiana av.
Canfield Benton V, 325 Virginia av.
Carey George A E, 413 College av.
Carroll Robert J, 276 S Meridian.
Carson John H, cor Illinois and 30th.
Carson & Geddes, 22 S Reisner (W I).
Carter Charles A, 122 W Maryland.
Carter James, 210 Prospect.
Carvin James M, 113 S Illinois.
Cary Elmer E, 151 N Illinois.
Casebeer Jacob B, 173 Bellefontaine.
Castor Hiram C, 288 Mass av.
Charlton Fred R, 16 E Ohio.
Chavis Wm M, 187½ Mass av.
Chitwood George R, 31 N East.
Clark Andrew J, 338 N New Jersey.
Clark Edmund D, 14 W Ohio.
Clark Wm H, 27½ Monument pl.
Clarke Henry P, 2 Mansur blk.
Clarke Wm B, 645 N Senate av.
Cleaveland Charles F, 425 N Capitol av.
Clemmer Ferd O, 130 N Illinois.
Clevenger Wm F, 19 E Ohio.
Cline Lewis C (Limited to Throat, Nose and Ear), 42 E Ohio.
Cole Albert M, 173 N Penn.
Cole James J, 507 E Market.
Coleman James M, 187 Shelby.
Combs George W, 30 E Ohio.
Comingor John A, 34 When bldg.
Compton Joshua A (Homeopathic), 75 E Ohio.
Cook George J, 18 W Ohio.
Cook Matthew D, 20 Thalman av.
Cooke Benjamin J, 228 W Michigan.
Courtney Thomas E, 501 Virginia av.

CLEMENS VONNEGUT 184, 186 and 192 E. Washington St. | BUILDERS' HARDWARE, Building Paper. Duplex Joist Hangers

THOS. BEMIS, President. SEE BOTH SIDES OF THIS SHEET. J. B. DILL, Sec'y and Treas.

SPECIALTY MFG. CO.

187-189-191-193-195 South Meridian St., INDIANAPOLIS, IND.

TELEPHONE 843.

We manufacture Machinery and Specialties of all kinds, make Patterns in Wood or Metal, Models and Working Drawings. We assist Inventors in completing their inventions; our ideas and views are given free on application. We do our work by contract or by the hour, to suit our customers.

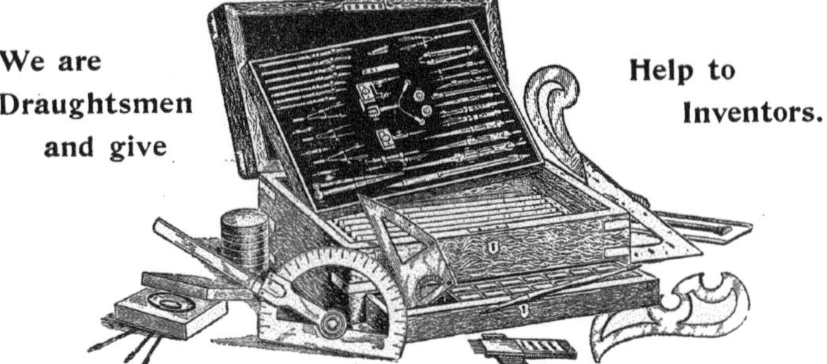

We are
Draughtsmen
and give
Help to
Inventors.

The very first thing you should do after inventing anything is to have a working drawing made of it, and find out what it can be made for. If you find it is a success, take out a patent on it, and if it is a failure you do not want a patent.

We solicit patents and successfully prosecute applications that have been rejected in the hands of attorneys or others not familiar with the patent practice.

We Manufacture and Sell Patents of all kinds
on Royalty or Commission.
We Make all kinds of Models.
We Furnish Light Gearing and Chains.
SPECIALTY MFG. CO. - INDIANAPOLIS, IND.

We furnish castings of Steel, Malleable Iron, Cast Iron, Brass; Belts Metal, Bike Metal, Mahaffie Steel, etc. Send for prices and information. Close prices on all work and promptness guaranteed.

SEE BOTH SIDES OF THIS SHEET.

Triumph Exhaust Fan.

Triumph Water Blow Fan.

FANS

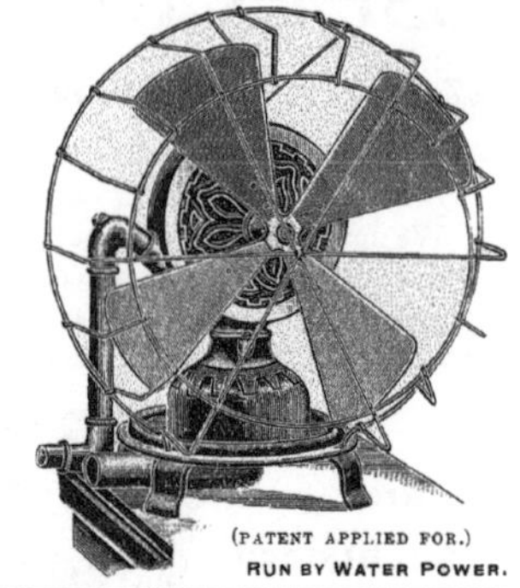

(PATENT APPLIED FOR.)
RUN BY WATER POWER.

VENTILATING FANS OF EVERY DESCRIPTION.

We are the only Fan Manufacturers in Indiana. Send for Catalogue.

Specialty Mfg. Co.

THOS. BEMIS, President.
J. B. DILL, Sec'y and Treas.
TELEPHONE 843.

187-189-191-193-195 South Meridian St., INDIANAPOLIS, IND.

We manufacture Electric Ceiling Fans, Triumph Water Counter Column Fans, Ceiling Fans for belt power, Triumph Water Floor Column Fans, Triumph Exhaust Fans, Triumph Water Blow Fans, and all kinds of Motors for running machinery.

Specialty Water Motor.

For running Fans and Light Machinery.

Specialty Ceiling Fan.

The only Fan made of Malleable Iron. Handsomely finished in Maroon Enamel.

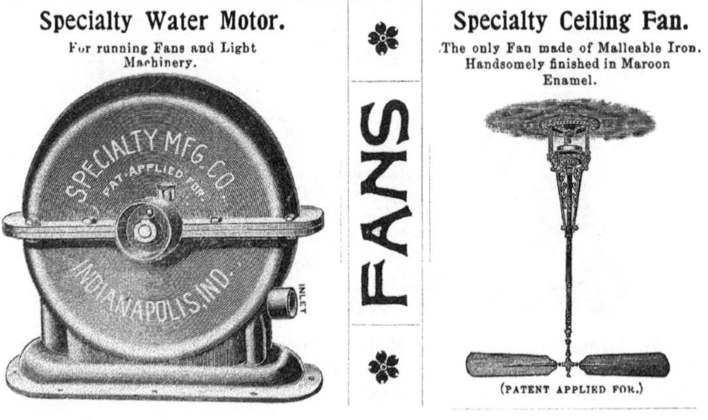

(PATENT APPLIED FOR.)

THE WM. H. BLOCK CO. DRY GOODS, DRAPERIES, RUGS, WINDOW SHADES.
7 AND 9 EAST WASHINGTON STREET.

Cox Ira E, 469 W Addison (N I).
Crans James T, 243 Jefferson av.
Crist Daniel O, 22 W Ohio.
Crose Samuel E, 117½ W Washington.
Crow Charles R, 32 Monument pl.
Culver Dudley M, 410 Virginia av.
Culver Thomas M, 379 S Meridian.
Cunningham Henry S, 85½ W Market.
Curryer Wm F, 40 E Ohio.
Curtis John E, 1056 W Washington.
Daniels Annie E, 55 N State av.
Daugherty John H, w s Central av 3 s of Railroad (I).
Davis Emily, 125 Lambert (W I).
Davis Eugene J, 399 College av.
Davis Joel R, 125 Lambert (W I).
Dedmon James E, 327-329 The Shiel.
DeHaas Thomas W, 36 W 13th.
Deitch Oscar S, 2 Bloomington.
Deitch Othello L, 158 River av (W I).
Dellett Jacob, 77½ S Delaware.
Denson Henry A, 16 E Ohio.
Dickerson George L, 80 Dawson.
Dowell George W, 618 W 22d (N I).
Dunlap John M, 19 W Ohio.
Dunlavy Ira E, 493 College av.
Dunning Lehman H, 249 N Alabama.
Durham Charles O, 302 S Illinois.
Earp Samuel E, 24½ Kentucky av.
Eastman Joseph, 197 N Delaware.
Eastman Joseph R, 197 N Delaware.
Eastman Thomas B, 197 N Delaware.
Edenharter George F, Central Indiana Hospital for Insane.
Edwards Samuel G, 501 N West.
Eisenbeiss Erastus M, 254½ W Washington.
Elbert Samuel A, 104 Indiana av.
Eskew Howell T, 33 W Ohio.
Ewing Calvin K, 24 E Ohio.
Falk Frederick, 47½ S Illinois.
Farnsworth Theodore W, 11 Stewart pl.
Ferguson Charles E, City Hospital.
Ferguson Frank C, 208 N Alabama.
Ferree Shadrach L, 725 E Washington.
Field Martin H, 1 Broadway.
Fisher Amos W, 35 W Ohio.
Fisk J Guard, cor 19th and Bellefontaine.
Fletcher Calvin I, 369 S Meridian.
Fletcher Wm B, 124 N Alabama.
French Benjamin F, 884 N Capitol av.
French Martha J, 113 Highland pl.
Funk James B, 436 Talbott av.
Furniss Henry W, 92 W New York.
Furniss Sumner A, 92 W New York.
Gabe Harry E, 539 Virginia av.
Galloway Clinton E, 444 Central av.
Gardner Jesse S, 25 N Illinois.
Garshwiler Wm P, 4 Hill av.
Garstang Reginald W, 142 Mass av.
Garver John J, 126 N Meridian.
Garver Wm R, 426 Talbott av.
Gaseway Thomas O, 369 Newman.
Gaston John M, 147 N New Jersey.
Gaylord Harry G, 19 Prospect.
Geddes Thomas, 24 S Reisner (W I).
Geis John F, 105 N New Jersey.
Gentle Luke M, 19 W Ohio.
George & George, 1-4 Baldwin blk.
Graham Alois B, 107 N Alabama.
Gray Wm, 50½ S Illinois.
Haag Emil A, 138 Park av.
Hadley Evan, 136 N Penn.
Haggard Ernest M, 95 Mass av.
Hagood Louis M, 135 W 6th.
Hammer Nathan L, 277 Douglass.
Hanable Charles A, 624 Central av.
Harold Cyrus N, 451 College av.
Hart Millard M, 1550 N Illinois.
Harvey Jesse B, 152 W 12th.
Haslep Marie, 16 The Windsor.
Hasty George, 35 W Ohio.
Haynes John R, 264 N Illinois.
Haynes Wm H, n w cor 7th and Illinois.
Hays Franklin W, 19 E Ohio.
Hazleton Elizabeth E, 4 Ash.
Hazelton Frederick Q, 4 Ash.
Heath Frederick C (Eye and Ear), 19 W Ohio.
Helming Herman F, 606 S East.
Helming Theodore W, 606 S East.
Hervey Edwin V, 744 Shelby.
Hervey James W, 744 Shelby.
Hibbs James I, 46 Hoyt av.
Hicks Joseph M, 171 E Washington.
Hinshaw Thomas M, 142 Broadway.
Hobbs Alice L, 199 N Illinois.
Hodges Edward F, 2 W New York.
Hodgin Edward E, rear 901 Cornell av.
Hollingsworth John S, 92 Oliver av (W I).
Holman Charles C, 124 Oliver av (W I).
Hoover John E, 541 E Washington.
Hoskins Walter D, 186½ Ft Wayne av.
House George H F, 1563 N Illinois.
Houser J A & S K, 21½ W Maryland.
Howard Edward, 223 N Illinois.
Howard Lewis N, 62½ S Illinois.
Howe Wm F, 168 Bellefontaine.
Hutchins Frank F, 409 N Alabama.
Irick George W, 40½ Kentucky av.
Jameson Henry, 28 E Ohio.
Jameson Patrick H, 28 E Ohio.
Jeffries Wm E, 456 Virginia av.
Jenkins John G, n w cor Ohio and Capitol av.
Jeter Frank, 52 Michigan (H).
Johnson Wm H, 30 S Station (B).
Johnston Charles E, 95 Mass av.
Jones Homer I, 58 E Ohio.
Jordan John S, 36 W Washington.
Jordan Thomas, 99 Bates.
Kahler Charles E, 720 E Ohio.
Kahlo George D, 60 Journal bldg.
Kahn David L, 867 N Meridian.
Karstetter Wm B, 471 W 22d (N I).
Kayne Jennie A, e s Waverly 1 s of Sutherland (B).
Keller Amelia R, 352 S Meridian.
Kelsey Russell C, 105 E Ohio.
Kendrick Wm H, 73 N East.
Kennedy John Y, 194 N East.
Kennedy Samuel A, 133 Fayette.
Kimberlin Albert C, 136 N Penn.
Kindleberger Wm H, 18 W Ohio.
Kitchen John M, 44½ N Penn.
Kluge Herman W, 202 Hoyt av.
Knerr Charles B, 858 E Washington.
Knox Edwin S, 323 S State av.
Koch Alice H, 758 N Senate av.
Kolmer John, 203 N Illinois.
Krug H Stewart, n w cor Ohio and Capitol av.
Lake M Elizabeth, 276 N Alabama.
Lambert John A, 146 E 7th.
Lash Hugh M, 18 E Ohio.
Laycock Reuben T, 107 Bates.
Leatherman A Lincoln, 132 N Alabama.
Leathers Douglas A, 125 College av.
Leeth M Cortez, 53½ W Washington.
Lewis Edwin R, 131 N Meridian.
Lewis James C, 215 Cornell av.
Lockridge John E, 37½ W Washington.

INDIANAPOLIS STEEL ROOFING AND CORRUGATING WORKS, 23 and 25 East South Street. S. D. NOEL, Proprietor.

David S. McKernan, Rooms 2-5 Thorpe Block.
REAL ESTATE AND LOANS
Money to loan on real estate. Special inducements offered those having money to loan. It will pay you to investigate.

. . . THE . . .

Dr. O. S. Runnels Sanatorium

276 NORTH ILLINOIS STREET

Indianapolis, Ind.

Established in 1890

The building is commodious, easily accessible and conforms in all its appointments to the demands of a home set apart for the restoration of the broken in health.

CONSERVATIVE WORK A SPECIALTY

Homœopathic Medication, Massage, Electricity, the Rest Cure, and every known means of recuperation employed to their fullest extent. Resort to surgical operations only after failure of all other available methods. Good cooking and a liberal table for convalescents. Graduate nurses only. Visiting physicians always welcome. Correspondence solicited.

The Runnels Private Hospital

Was established in 1890 by O. S. Runnels, A. M., M. D., 276 North Illinois Street, to meet the requirements of the best services attainable in surgical and gynecological practice. After an extensive surgical experience of twenty years under the most favorable conditions possible in the various public hospitals, hotels and homes, Dr. Runnels recognized the need of better service than could be thus commanded. Finding it impossible to secure the best results in the unfavorable environment of the old order, the service was transferred to the private hospital where everything has been specialized to the highest degree.

NATURAL APTITUDE AND LONG EXPERIENCE HAS PLACED DR. RUNNELS IN THE FRONT RANK OF THE BEST SURGEONS.

FIDELITY MUTUAL LIFE—PHILADELPHIA, PA.
$75,000,000, Insurance In Force. $3,500,000, Death Losses Paid. $1,500,090, Surplus. A. H. COLLINS {General Agent, Baldwin Block.

BITUMINOUS COAL IN CAR LOADS TO DEALERS AND MANUFACTURERS. ROOMS 42 AND 43 WHEN BUILDING. Edwardsport Coal & Mining Co.

Physicians—Continued.
Long Henry, 32 Mass av.
Long John B, 402 W New York.
Long Robert W, 5, 156½ E Washington.
Lukenbill Orestes C, 1093 E Washington.
Lutz George W, 69½ N Illinois.
McClellan Alonzo, 104 Michigan (H).
McConnell Leander C, 20 King.
McCurdy Lawson A, 1036 W Washington.
McCurdy Olive B C, 1036 W Washington.
McLain Liberty C, n w cor Ohio and Capitol av.
McLeay John D, 42 W Market.
McMahan Samuel W, 26 E Ohio.
McShane John T, 26 E Ohio.
Mac Nab Philip, 1 Ft Wayne av.
Madsen Mary M, 86 N Senate av.
Malloy Jay S, 438 Mass av.
Malone Louis A, 119 N New Jersey.
Malpas S Herbert, 15-16 Marion Blk.
Manchester Jerome J, 10 Mansur blk.
Mangun Jennie, 126 E Ohio.
Manker Frank E, 85½ W Market.
Manners John I, 380 S West.
Mapes Smith H, 501 College av.
Maple Alfred L, 29½ W Ohio.
Marsee Joseph W, 106½ E New York.
Martin Cicero C, 151 Sanders.
Martin John A, 58 E Ohio.
Masters John L, 149 N Penn.
Maxwell Allison, 19 W Ohio.
Mendenhall Elijah, 184 W 3d.
Metzler S N, 7 Stewart pl.
Moffett Edward D, 16 W New York.
Moffett Naomi C, 27½ Monument pl.
Moore Samuel H, 152 Virginia av.
Moore Thomas, 22 Commercial blk.
Morgan Abraham, 54 Oscar.
Morgan John, 170 N Illinois.
Morgan Wm V, 336 N Alabama.
Morris Minor, 36 E Ohio.
Morrison Frank A, 107 N Alabama.
Morrow Joseph E, 203 Hadley av (W I).
Mullan Amasa J, 117½ W Washington.
Mutz Charles M, 378 Clifford av.
Nash George W, 402 S Illinois.
Neff David, 186½ W Washington.
Nichols John D, 54 College av.
Ober George M, 92 Ash.
Oliver John H, 124 N Meridian.
Osenbach Wm, 120 Michigan (H).
Ostroff Henry, cor Central av and 9th.
Outland Edgar M, 26 Mass av.
Page Lafayette F, 1-4 Marion blk.
Pantzer Hugo O (Surgery and Diseases of Women), 194 E Michigan.
Park Hiram A S 445 E Ohio.
Parsons John S, 258½ W Washington.
Partlow J Wesley, 250 N Illinois.
Patterson Amos W, 83 Mass av.
Peachee Harrison, 42½ W Market.
Peebles & Burroughs, 66⅛ N Penn.
Peffley Wm F, 542 W Highland av (N I).
Pettijohn Otto B, 232 Blake.
Pfaff O G, 134 N Penn.
Pink Herman, 103 N Meridian.
Porter Beulah W, 334 N California.
Porter Edward D, 18 When blk.
Potter Theodore, 18 E Ohio.
Poucher Charles H C, 346 E St Clair.
Preston Abraham L, 73 King av (H).
Prunk Byron F, 368 W New York.
Prunk Daniel H, 30 N Senate av.
Rainey Harvey W, Insane Asylum.
Ray Franklin E, Insane Asylum.
Reed Wilson, 800 E Washington.
Reyer Ernest C, 130 N Penn.
Ridpath Henry W, 370 E 7th.
Rice Wm G (Eye, Ear and Throat), 14 E Ohio.
Ritter Caleb L, 510 Virginia av.
Robbins Wesley, 29½ W Ohio.
Robertson J Frank, 1061 E Michigan.
Rogers Rebecca W, 17-20 Marion blk.
Ross David, 136 N Penn.
Row George S (Limited to Eye and Ear), 711-712 Majestic Bldg.
Rowe Louis M, 134 N Meridian.
Rowley Wm, 119 Cornell av.
Runnels Orange S, 50 Monument Pl. (See Sanatorium adv opp.)
Runnels Sollis, 38 E Ohio.
Rutledge & Spaulding, 139 Hadley av (W I).
Rutter Jennie F, 1151 E Washington.
Ryan Wm B, 274 N New Jersey.
Schaefer C Richard, 430 Madison av.
Scherer Simon P, 581½ S East.
Schirack John A, 319 N California.
Schmidt Alvin L, St Vincent's Infirmary.
Schneck Luella, 175 N Penn.
Seaton Wm H, 44 E Ohio.
Seller Thomas P, s e cor Ruth and W Washington (M J).
Selman Andrew G, 680 E Washington.
Selman Andrew J, 680 E Washington.
Servoss George L, 44 E Ohio.
Siegfried Julia, 65 W Ohio.
Sigler George A, cor Central av and 9th.
Sluss John W, 346 E St Clair.
Smith Bartley, 137 S William (W I).
Smith Earl C, 44 Clifford av.
Smith Martha J, 208 N Alabama.
Smith Mary, Insane Asylum.
Smith Nelson G, 44 Clifford av.
Smith Walter, 63 Oliver av (W I).
Snowden Jesse, 422 W Addison (N I).
Spencer & Lowry, 1241 E Washington.
Spink Mary A, 124 N Alabama.
Stafford Charles A, 24 E Ohio.
Stephenson John C, 324 Clifford av.
Sterne Albert E, 75 E Michigan.
Stewart Lewis C, 522 Jefferson av.
Stewart, Stewart & Stewart, 85 E Ohio.
Stiles Irwin A, 16 E Ohio.
Stillson Joseph O (Eye and Ear), 245 N Penn.
Stockton Sarah, 227 N Delaware.
Stone John W, 1549 N Capitol av.
Stone Mary C, 1549 N Capitol av.
Stone R French, 250 N Illinois.
Stoutenbery Elizabeth, 345 N Senate av.
Storch Louis A E, 680 S Meridian.
Stratford Alfred, 166 Virginia av.
Stucky Thomas E, 580 N Alabama.
Sutcliffe John A, 6 Baldwin blk.
Swain Fremont, 334 N New Jersey.
Swain Rachel, 334 N New Jersey.
Talbott John H, Union Station.
Taylor James H, 2 The Chalfant.
Taylor Oscar S, 22 E Ohio.
Teague Albert E, 86 N Senate av.
Thomas Edwin C, 235 Blake.
Thomas Wm H, 285 Virginia av.
Thompson Daniel A, 22 W Ohio.
Thompson James L, 22 W Ohio.
Thompson & Terrell, n w cor Central av and P C C & St L Ry (I).
Tinsley Frank C, 402 Mass av.
Todd L L, 19 W Ohio.
Tolley Wm V, 745 N Senate av.
Tomlin Wm S, n e cor Illinois and North.

C. ZIMMERMAN & SONS | SLATE AND GRAVEL ROOFERS 19 South East Street.

DRIVEN WELLS And Second Water Wells and Pumps of all kinds at CHARLES KRAUSS', 42 S. PENN. ST., Telephone 465.

ERTEL STEAM LAUNDRY 26 and 28 N. Senate Avenue. Telephone 19
WE WILL CALL FOR AND DEIVER YOUR WORK. SATISFACTION GUARANTEED.

W. H. HENDRICKS. GEO. W. WOOD.

ESTEY-CAMP MUSIC HOUSE

HIGH GRADE

PIANOS AND ORGANS.

PIANOS.

DECKER BRO'S, ESTEY, CAMP, ARION.

ORGANS.

ESTEY, CAMP, AND OTHERS.

MUSICAL MERCHANDISE.

TUNING AND REPAIRING A SPECIALTY.

144 MASSACHUSETTS AVENUE.

Tomlinson James M, 28½ E Ohio.
Tomlinson Virginia R, 169 S William (W I).
Towles Alfred N, s s Railroad 1 e of Central av (I).
Trees Irvin W, 122 Prospect.
Tucker George W, 158 Michigan (H).
Twichell Alice E, 268 Brookside av.
Van Hummell Henry, 60 Monument pl.
Van Hummell Quincy, 60 Monument Pl.
Wagner Theodore A, 94 N Delaware.
Walker Isaac N, 130 N Penn.
Wall David, 59 Indiana av.
Wands Wm, 6 Baldwin blk.
Ward Albert O, 189 Virginia av.
Watt Wm H, 100 Mass av.
Watters Patrick J, Insane Asylum.
Wehrman Ernest A, 7-8 Marion blk.
White Ahira R, 190 S Meridian.
Wiles Frank M, Insane Asylum.
Wilkinson Edward B, 201-202 The Majestic.
Williams James L, 36 E Ohio.
Williams Wm O, 36 King av (H).
Williamson John W, 15 Commercial blk.
Wilmans Francis A, 60 Monument pl.
Wilson Amos L, 823 N Illinois.
Wilson Charles A, M D, Orthopedic Surgeon, Wilson Surgical Institute, 81 W Ohio.
Wilson Charles L, 81 W Ohio.
Winter Carl G, 40 E Ohio.
Wishard Wm N, 18 E Ohio.
Wishard & Noble, 5-7, 37½ W Market.
Witham Samuel L, 33½ S Station (B).
Witt Lazarus, 449 S Capitol av.
Wood Levi, 282 Lincoln av.
Woodard Nathan D, 24 Mass av.
Woodburn James H, 372 N Capitol av.
Woolen George V, 20 W Ohio.
Wright George, 37½ W Market.
Wright Wm M, 134 N Penn.
Wylie Bruce M, 503 S Meridian.
Wynn Frank B, 18 E Ohio.
Young Michael A, 244½ E Washington.
Young Thomas J, 18⅛ N Meridian.
Young Wm L, 121 S Noble.
Zitzlaff Charles J, 273 E McCarty.

PHYSICIANS' CHAIRS.

Allison Wm D Co, 85 E South.
Clark & Roberts, 114 N Delaware.
Miner Benjamin D, 19 John.

*PIANO MOVERS.

Indianapolis Storage and Transfer Co, 370-372 S Delaware. (See back cover.)
Meck Transfer Co, 7 Monument Pl. (See adv in Transfer Companies.)

*PIANO TUNERS.

Heim John R, 559 E St Clair.
Humann John H, w s Commercial av 3 s of Washinton av (I).
Smith Benjamin F, 257 Highland av.

*PIANOS AND ORGANS.

Baldwin D H & Co, 95-99 N Penn.
Carlin & Lennox, 31 E Market.
Estey-Camp Music House, 144 Mass av. (See adv.)
Pearson's Music House, 82-84 N Penn.
Rich & McVey, 65 N Penn.
Wulschner Emil & Son, 78-80 N Penn.

ELLIS & HELFENBERGER { ENTERPRISE FOUNDRY & FENCE CO. 162-170 S. Senate Ave. Tel. 958.

THE HOGAN TRANSFER AND STORAGE COMP'Y
Household Goods and Pianos Moved—Packed—Stored...... Baggage and Package Express Machinery and Safes a Specialty Cor. Washington and Illinois Sts. TELEPHONE No. 675.

The Central Rubber & Supply Co. ◆◆◆ Hose, Belting, Packing, Clothing, Druggists' Sundries, Bicycle Tires, Cotton Hose, Etc. New York Belting & Packing Co., L't'd. PHONE 922. 79 S. ILLINOIS ST.: INDIANAPOLIS, IND.

C. C. FOSTER, Pres. *A. P. HENDRICKSON, Vice-Pres.* *O. P. ENSLEY, Sec-Treas.*

Foster Lumber Company,

PLANING MILL.

The largest and best equipped Planing Mill in the State. Make a specialty of hardwood interior finish, veneered doors, grilles, mantels, stairways and hardwood floors.

Estimates furnished upon application for delivery at any part of State. Large stock of dry lumber always on hand.

Long Distance Telephone 254. Lumber Yard and Planing Mill, 402 to 420 N. Senate Ave.

PICKLE AND SAUCE MNFRS.

Archdeacon Wm, 248 S Meridian.
Baum Pickle Co, 201 Lemcke Bldg.
Campbell George D Co The, 593 to 599 E Washington.
Faulkner & Webb, 18 E Mkt House.
Frauer Anna, 93 E Mkt House.
Heinz H J Co, 33 S Delaware.
Indianapolis Pickling and Preserving Co, 200 S Penn.

*PICNIC AND EXCURSION WAGONS.

Hogan Transfer and Storage Co The, s w cor Washington and Illinois. (See left top lines and adv in Transfer Companies.)

PICTURE FRAME AND MOLDING MANUFACTURERS.

Ballweg Charles F, 109½ E Washington.
Lieber H Co The, 33 S Meridian. (See right top cor cards.)
Pouder Stewart M, 29 Mass av.

PICTURES AND FRAMES.

Elite Portrait and Frame Co, 68½ E Market.
Garman & Kane, 17 Stewart pl.
Graeter Louis V, 13 Madison av.
Herman B H & Co, 66 N Penn.
Kautsky Wenzel, 125 E Morris.
Lieber H Co The, 33 S Meridian. (See right top cor cards.)
Messenger W Horndon, 101 E Washington and 13, 15 and 17 S Delaware. (See left bottom lines.)
Peddicord John W, 66½ E Washington.
Rex Portrait Co, 42 W Market.
Ward Wm, 42 N Penn.

*PIPE AND TUBING.

Chester Pipe and Tube Co The, 203 Majestic bldg.

*PIPES—BRIAR AND MEERSCHAUM.

Mayer Charles & Co, 29-31 W Washington. (See adv opp p 615.)

PLANING MILLS.

(See also Lumber Manufacturers and Dealers.)
Balke & Krauss Co, cor Market and Missouri. (See right bottom lines.)
Bedell George V, 399 E Market.
Brooks Bartholomew D, Morris and Belt R R (W I).
Coburn Henry, cor Kentucky av and Georgia.
Eaglesfield Wm C, s w cor Alvord and 9th.
Eldridge E H & Co, 174 S New Jersey.
Fatout M K & Son, 443-463 E St Clair.
Foster Lumber Co, n w cor St Clair and N Senate av. (See adv.)
Huey M S & Son, 551 Mass av. (See adv p 5.)
Indianapolis Manufacturers' and Carpenters' Union, 38-42 S New Jersey. (See adv p 2.)
Indianapolis Planing Mill Co, s w cor Meridian and Wilkins.
Kattau Wm H, 151 Harrison.
Russell Lumber Co The, s e cor 7th and L E & W R R.
Schlanzer Benedict J, 682 Charles. (See adv p 8.)
Scott Wm A & Sons, 591-593 Central av. (See front cover.)
West Side Planing Mill Co, 1000 W New York.
Wissman J H & Son, n w cor Hall and Moore av.
Wright Frank M, n w cor Ohio and Belt R R.

*PLASTER.

Balke & Krauss Co, cor Market and Missouri. (See right bottom lines.)
Diamond Wall Plaster Co, Office 3 Builders' Exchange, Factory cor E North and Bee Line Ry. (See top lines and adv opp p 941.)

*PLASTER MANUFACTURERS.

Adamant Wall Plaster Co of Indiana, cor Phipps and J M & I R R.

OTTO GAS ENGINES | BUILDERS' EXCHANGE S. W. Cor. Ohio and Penn. Telephone 535.

Becker & Son Charles Becker Jacob Becker Jr. Merchant Tailors. 21 N. Penn. St. Tel. 934

Diamond Wall Plaster Co, Office 3 Builders' Exchange, Factory cor E North and Bee Line Ry. (See top lines and adv opp p 941.)

PLASTERERS.

See Contractors—Plastering.

PLASTERERS' HAIR.

Balke & Krauss Co, cor Market and Missouri. (See right bottom lines.)
Independent Hair Co The, 219 S Penn.
Wasson W G Co The, 130 Indiana av. (See left bottom cor cards and adv in Cement and Lime.)

*PLASTERERS' SUPPLIES.

Wasson W G Co The, 130 Indiana av. (See left bottom cor cards and adv in Cement and Lime.)

*PLATE GLASS.

Burdsal A Co The, 34-36 S Meridian. (See right bottom cor cards.)
Indianapolis Paint and Color Co, 40, 42, 44, 46 and 48 Mass av. (See adv in Paints and Oils.)

*PLATERS—GENERAL.

Conley Bros, 17 W Pearl.
Davis & Nealis, 92 S Delaware.
Dick George W, 33 Virginia av.

*PLAYING CARDS.

Mayer Charles & Co, 29-31 W Washington. (See adv opp p 615.)
United States Playing Card Co, s w cor Gatling and Belt R R.

PLOW MANUFACTURERS.

(See also Agricultural Implements.)

Oliver Chilled Plow Works, 160 S Penn.

PLUMBERS, STEAM AND GAS FITTERS.

Adolph Jacob S, 175 College av.
Albright Frank A, 60 S Judge Harding (W I).
Aneshaensel C & Co, 102 N Meridian.
Aneshaensel & Prinzler, 145 Virginia av.
Arthur John, 238 Indiana av.
Barton Frank, 15 Edward (W I).
Boyd Alonzo, 816 N Illinois. (See adv.)
Buchner Augustus J, 62 Virginia av.

A. BOYD,
Plumbing

Natural and Artificial
GAS FITTING
AND DEALER IN
GAS FIXTURES.
All Kinds of Pump Work Attended To.
ALL ORDERS WILL RECEIVE PROMPT ATTENTION.
816 NORTH ILLINOIS STREET.
Telephone 1618.
INDIANAPOLIS, IND.

SALISBURY & STANLEY
OFFICE, STORE AND BANK FIXTURES.
Contractors and Builders. Repairing of all kinds done on short notice. 177 Clinton St., Indianapolis, Ind. Telephone 999.

LIME, CEMENT, PLASTER FIRE BRICK AND CLAY SEWER PIPE, ETC. BALKE & KRAUSS CO., Cor. Market and Missouri Streets.

C. FRIEDGEN HAS THE FINEST STOCK OF LADIES' PARTY SLIPPERS and SHOES 19 NORTH PENNSYLVANIA ST.

SAMUEL LAING, TIN, SLATE AND STEEL ROOFING 72 AND 74 EAST COURT STREET.

T. L. CARLETON,
SANITARY PLUMBING.
TELEPHONE 261. GAS AND STEAM FITTING, SEWER WORK.
6 Central Avenue, Indianapolis.

HUSSEY & BAKER,
FINE PLUMBING.
SEWER CONTRACTORS.
TEL. 1437. 116 N. DELAWARE ST.

Plumbers, Etc.—Continued.
Carleton Thomas L, 6 Central av. (See adv.)
Carothers Wm M & Co, 62 W 7th.
Caswell Wm H, 305 E Washington.
Clarke & Sons, 98 N Delaware.
Clifford & Arnold, 67 Indiana av.
Craig Andrew J, 197 W Maryland.
Curry Solomon L, 173 N Pine.
Dahz George F W, 17 Edward (W I).
Dunn John C, 63 N Illinois.
Enders & Kopp, 506 E Washington.
Exler Wm H, 22 Michigan (H).
Farrell J S & Co, 84 N Illinois. (See left bottom cor cards.)
Foley Bros & Co, 84 Mass av.
Franklin Philip, 468 Muskingum al.
Feaney Bros, 26 Virginia av.
Gehle Frederick, 472 E Washington.
Goth Herman A, 487 N New Jersey.
Gundelfinger Benno, 461 Central av.
Gunn Wm, 23 S Alabama.
Haslinger Joseph F, 73 Mass av.
Harris Walter B, 1547 N Illinois.
Healy & O'Brien, 57 W Maryland.
Hermann Oscar, 376 E 7th.
Holmes & Co, 92 E Market.
Holtmann Charles, 348 E New York.
Hudson Henry T, 435 Madison av.
Hussey & Baker, 116 N Delaware. (See adv.)
Indianapolis Plumbing Co, 9 Mass av.
Jacob Milton C, 118 N East.
Johnson Charles A, 35 W Market.
Keyser George W, 91 N Illinois.
Kirkhoff Bros, 102-104 S Penn. (See left top cor cards and adv.)
Knight & Jillson, 75-77 S Penn.
Krauss Charles, 42 S Penn. (See right top lines.)
Loeper Wm H, 327 Clifford av.
McCready Benjamin F, 164 Ft Wayne av.
McGauly James, 83 E Ohio.
Marshall John W, 800 N Alabama.
Meikel Charles W, 96-98 E New York. (See right bottom lines.)
Payne John T, 63 E 14th.
Peck Calvin L, 91 N Delaware.
Poole Adoniram J, 1553 N Illinois.
Ramsay Walter L, 24½ N Illinois.
Robinson Albert, 202 E Ohio.
Ruemmele & Buttler, 850 Morris (W I).
Sachs Ernest C, rear 302 S Illinois.
Schott Charles E, 58 W Maryland.
Sellers Richard, 129 Mass av.
Stevens John Q, 29 Prospect.
Stewart John, 32 Monument pl.
Strong Edward A, 92 E Market.
Toon Charles, 1541 Kenwood av.
Veach & Didion, 93 Mass av.
Wilcox & Judd, 146 Mass av.
Wilson & McClintock, 561 Virginia av.
Winter Charles R, 162 Ft Wayne av. (See adv.)

CHAS. R. WINTER,
Sanitary Plumber and Gas Fitter
Natural Gas Fitting a Specialty.
Job Work Promptly Attended To.
No. 162 Fort Wayne Ave., Indianapolis.

SULLIVAN & MAHAN Manufacturers of all kinds of PAPER BOXES 41 W. Pearl St.

DIAMOND WALL PLASTER { Telephone 1410 BUILDERS' EXCHANGE.

24 Years' Practical Experience. J. H. KIRKHOFF, Gas and Fuel Oil Engr.. GEO. F. KIRKHOFF, Plumber. CHAS. F. KIRKHOFF, Steam and Hot Water Fitter.

KIRKHOFF BROS.

STEAM AND HOT WATER HEATING.

SANITARY PLUMBERS AND GAS FITTERS

ELECTRICAL CONSTRUCTION, FIXTURES, ETC.

PHONE 910. 102 and 104 South Pennsylvania St.

Telephone 1769. 197 S. Illinois St. } THE HOME LAUNDRY { WORK CALLED FOR AND DELIVERED.

Wurgler G Adolph jr, 83½ E Washington.
Zeisler & West, rear 51 Warren av (W I).

*PLUMBERS' SUPPLIES.

Berry Bros, 374 Shelby.
Good Mnfg Co, 28 Monument pl.
McElwaine-Richards Co The, 62-64 W Maryland.

*POCKET AND TABLE CUTLERY.

Mayer Charles & Co, 29-31 W Washington. (See adv opp p 615.)

POLISH MANUFACTURERS.

Burns Chemical Co The, 24 S New Jersey.
Hoffman George W, 295 E Washington.

*POLISHING AND BUFFING WHEELS.

Vonnegut Clemens, 184-186 E Washington. (See left bottom lines.)

PORK PACKERS.

See Packers—Pork and Beef.

*PORTABLE GASOLINE ENGINES.

Lambert Gas and Gasoline Engine Co, Anderson, Ind. (See right top lines.)

*PORTABLE MILLS.

Nordyke & Marmon Co, crossing I & V Ry and Morris (W I). (See inside back cover.)

*PORTLAND CEMENT.

Moffat & Co, 402 Lemcke Bldg. (See adv p 9.)

POTTERIES.

Cochran Robert, 566 W Washington.

*POULTRY—WHOLESALE.

Strobel Bros, 412-414 W Washington.

POULTRY DEALERS.

Arnold Thomas, E Mkt House.
Budd J R & Co, 283 W Washington.
Chastain John A T, E Mkt House.
Clare Wm, E Mkt House.
Cottrell Thomas, 355 W Washington.
Day Worthington W, E Mkt House.
Dixon Albert, 172 W Maryland.
Ellerman Samuel E, 205 Ft Wayne av.
Freiberg Henry, 127 E Mkt House.
Fry James R, 319 Virginia av.
Hamm Robert L, 440 Mass av.
Howard Frank O, 196 W Maryland.
Hulse Wm C, E Mkt House.
Janes Albert, 1½ E Mkt House.
Kemper Marion B, 65 E Mkt House.
Kiel Henry H, 638 Virginia av.
Klingstein Otto, 53½ Prospect.
McFeely Aaron, 599 Virginia av.
McMillan Harry, 313 W Maryland.
Macy Julius, 21 N West.
Middleton Robert S, 188 Ft Wayne av.
Penrod Daniel W, E Mkt House.
Ralph & Carter, 71 N Illinois.
Sanders & Spornberg, 303 W Washington.
Scheler Frank L, E Mkt House.
Sloan Oliver B, E Mkt House.
Sogemeier Wm, 665 S Meridian and 165 W Pearl.
Stout George R, 174 E Wabash.
Strobel Bros, 412-414 W Washington.
Teaster F P & Son, 176 E Wabash.
Van Cleave George E, E Mkt House.
Wade Francis H, E Mkt House.

*POULTRY NETTING.

Vonnegut Clemens, 184-186 E Washington. (See left bottom lines.)

POWDER.

Hercules Powder Co, 21½ W Maryland.

PRINTERS—BOOK AND JOB.

Baker & Thornton, 38 S Meridian.
Blandford Bertha, 40½ S Illinois.
Bradford Hunter, 92 E Court.
Braun Julius, 149 Virginia av.
Buennagel George J, 95½ E South.
Burford Wm B, 21 W Washington. (See adv opp p 230.)
Canfield Wm S, 31 Virginia av.
Carlon & Hollenbeck, s e cor Monument Pl and Meridian. (See adv opp p 244.)
Castor Bros, 77 Mass av.
Central Printing Co, 83 E Court.
Chance-Matthews Printing Co, 32½ W Washington.
Cole Wm H, 80½ E Market.
Cycler Printing Co, 33 Talbott Blk. (See adv opp Newspapers.)
Drapier Wm D, 78½ S Delaware.
Engle F E & Son, 16 N Delaware.
Fulmer E P & Co, 75 E Market.

THE WM. H. BLOCK CO. 7 AND 9 EAST WASHINGTON STREET. DRY GOODS, HOUSE FURNISHINGS AND CROCKERY.

London Guarantee and Accident Co. (Ltd.) Employers', Public and Teams' Liability. Workmen's Collective Insurance and Fidelity Bonds
GEORGE W. PANGBORN, General Agent, 704-706 Lemcke Bldg. Telephone 140.

Reliable Fire Insurance. Reasonable Rates. FRANK K. SAWYER 74 E. MARKET STREET. Telephone 8.

Printers—Book and Job—Con.

Gutenberg Co The (German and English), 27 S Delaware.
Hale Frank R, 32½ Clifford av.
Hammer Emmett J, 124 E New York.
Hampton John E & Wm W, 67 W Georgia.
Harrison Thomas G, 84 E Court.
Hasselman Printing Co, 126-130 W Maryland.
Hendricks Wm G, 37 W Market.
Indianapolis Live Stock Journal and Printing Co, Union Stock Yords (W I).
Indianapolis Printing Co, 37-39 Virginia av.
Journal Job Printing Co, 126-130 W Maryland.
Kelley Patrick J, 37 Virginia av.
King John B, 286 Jefferson av.
Kiser Charles L, 280 River av (W I).
Leech Herbert E, 95½ E South.
Levey Bros & Co, 19 W Maryland. (See adv opp p 561.)
Mercer Bros, 22 Pembroke Arcade.
Miller A D & Sons, 81 E Court.
Morris Printing Co, 467 S Illinois.
Morrison W H & Co, 28 Monument pl.
Nathan Solomon, 505 N Alabama.
Nicoll Charles B, 234 Indiana av.
Outland & McDowell, 15½ Virginia av.
Rappaport Philip, 18 S Alabama.
Ratti Joseph, 72 S Illinois.
Resner Henry F, 175 Virginia av.
Sentinel Printing Co, 75-79 W Market.
Sherwood Wallace, 29 S Delaware.
Sleight John W, 25 W Georgia.
Smith Frank H, 22 N Penn. (See adv opp p 803.)
Smock & Berringer, 15 S Alabama.
Suffrins C A, 42 W Market.
Victor F C & Co, 26 N Delaware.
Wagner Wm H, 46½ N Penn.
White & Co, 37½ Virginia av.
Winters Archias E, 33 Talbott Blk. (See adv opp Newspapers.)
Wood-Weaver Printing Co, 116 N Delaware. (See adv.)

Wood-Weaver Printing Co.,
116 North Delaware St.
Telephone 1437.
All kinds of Printing done in first-class style, on short notice and at reasonable prices.
Your patronage asked.

***PRINTERS' PRESS WORK.**

Fulmer E P & Co, 94 E Court.
Indianapolis Printing Co, 37-39 Virginia av.

PRODUCE.

Adams Oscar O, E Mkt House.
Alexander Wm, E Mkt House.
Arnold Martitia C, 39 E Mkt House.
Austin Mary, 132 E Mkt House.
Austin Mary P, 132 E Mkt House.
Backmeyer Henry, E Mkt House.
Baskin Harry, E Mkt House.
Bauer Charles, 130 High.
Bayer Harry, E Mkt House.
Becker Charles, E Mkt House.
Bevis Andrew J, E Mkt House.
Beyer Meyer, E Mkt House.
Bott Edward D, 35 E Mkt House.
Bumb Charles H, E Mkt House.
Butcher George L, E Mkt House.
Carlisle Mary J, 103 E Mkt House.
Clifton John G & Son, 94 E Mkt House.
Craven John, 33 E Mkt House.
Cress John V, E Mkt House.
Davis James C, E Mkt House.
Eliker Wm H, 39 E Mkt House.
Ellwanger Daniel F, E Mkt House.
Fry Ephraim, E Mkt House.
Gerhart & Co, 3 E Mkt House.
Gieseking Gottlieb, 11 E Mkt House.
Gieseking Katherine, 11 E Mkt House.
Haberer Matthias, E Mkt House.
Hines Andrew, 122 E Mkt House.
Hines Andrew jr, E Mkt House.
Hitz George & Co, 30-32 and 68-70 S Delaware.
Hole Albert T, E Mkt House.
Jauldiner Vincent, E Mkt House.
Jones Charles W, 61 E Mkt House.
Kahle Frederick, E Mkt House.
Keach James L, 62 S Delaware.
Kimberlin Jacob R, 82 E Mkt House.
King Samuel, 79 E Mkt House.
Kohnle George F, 61 Indiana av.
Kruse Christian, 86 E Mkt House.
Kuhns Benjamin F, 78 E Mkt House.
Lovell John W, E Mkt House.
McComb Joseph M, E Mkt House.
McCoy David, 40 E Mkt House.
McLaughlin Samuel, 177 Virginia av.
Marchal Rudolph, E Mkt House.
Marks Abraham, E Mkt House.
Marks Jacob, E Mkt House.
Markum Oscar, E Mkt House.
May Charles T, E Mkt House.
Maze Wm, E Mkt House.
Mehollowitz Morris, E Mkt House.
Mills & Frink, 121 E Mkt House.
Moor Charles, 101 E Mkt House.
Morris Reuben, 111 E Mkt House.
Morris Wolf, E Mkt House.
Pattmann Frederick, E Mkt House.
Redmond Wm E, E Mkt House.
Robinson Edward, E Mkt House.
Romel Frederick, E Mkt House.
Rutherford George W, E Mkt House.
Schneider Mary, 35 E Mkt House.
Schwab Nicholas, E Mkt House.
Shannon Wm F, 7 E Mkt House.
Snitman Louis, E Mkt House.
Sogemeier Wm, 5 E Mkt House.
Stolp Ernest, E Mkt House.
Stout Amanda, E Mkt House.
Stout George R, 174 E Wabash.
Sumler Wm, E Mkt House.
Teaster F P & Son, 176 E Wabash.
Thornburg Wm W, E Mkt House.
Tresslar Emery A, 62 E Mkt House.
Vogel Fredericka, E Mkt House.
Vollmer John, E Mkt House.
Von Jelgerhois Bernard, E Mkt House.
Voorhees Richard, 90 E Mkt House.
Zier Abraham, E Mkt House.

PROVISION BROKERS.

See Brokers—Provision.

***PUBLIC ACCOUNTANTS.**

Booth Benjamin, Room 18, 82½ E Washington. (See left top lines.)

POLICIES IN UNITED STATES LIFE INSURANCE CO., offer indemnity against death, liberal cash surrender value or at option of policy-holder, fully paid-up life insurance or liberal life income. E. B. SWIFT, M'g'r, 25 E. Market St.

WM. KOTTEMAN } WILL FURNISH YOUR HOUSE COMPLETE
89 & 91 E. Washington St. Telephone 1742

SHOW CASES | WILLIAM WIEGEL | 6 West Louisiana Street Opp. Un. Sta.

W. C. SPIEGEL. F. HOFFMAN.

INDIANAPOLIS PULLEY MFG. CO.,

(*Successors to The Suter-Linder Pulley Mfg. Co.*)

MANUFACTURERS OF

Patent Wood Split Pulleys.

Telephone 1626. 372 and 374 East Michigan St.

PUBLISHERS.

(See also Subscription Book.)

American Tribune Co, 46-47 Journal bldg.
Baker Charles, 39 Virginia av.
Bell Wm A, 66½ N Penn.
Billingsley John J W, 19 Talbott blk.
Bowen-Merrill Co The, 9-11 W Washington and 10-12 W Pearl.
Bramwood John W, 29½ E Market.
Brown & Smith, 291 River av (W I).
Callen Frank J, 83 E Court.
Carlon & Hollenbeck, s e cor Monument Pl and Meridian. (See adv opp p 244.)
Carr Michael W, 25½ W Washington.
Clark Wm F & Wm F jr, 25 Cyclorama pl.
Collier Peter F, 93 N Delaware.
Cycler Printing Co, 33 Talbott Blk. (See adv opp Newspapers.)
Darrow Ben L, 31 W Ohio. (See right side lines.)
Douglass Wm W, 11½ N Meridian.
Drapier Wm H, 78½ S Delaware.
Epitomist Publishing Co, 21½ W Washington.
Family Dress Guide Co, 6, 156½ E Washington.
Fanciers' Gazette Co, 49 Virginia av.
Gutenberg Co, 27 S Delaware.
Hasty George, 35 W Ohio.
Heeb Publishing Co, 81 When Bldg.
Indiana Baptist Publishing Co, 68 Baldwin blk.
Indiana Farmer Co, 30½ N Delaware.
Indiana Medical Journal Publishing Co, 18 W Ohio.
Indiana Newspaper Union, 32 W Court.
Indiana Pharmacist Publishing Co, 107 E Ohio.
Indiana School Book Co, Publishers and Contractors of Indiana State Series School Text Books, 605 Indiana Trust Bldg.
Indianapolis Journal Newspaper Co, n e cor Monument Pl and Market.
Indianapolis Live Stock Journal and Printing Co, Union Stock Yards (W I).
Indianapolis News Co The, 32 W Washington.
Indianapolis Sentinel Co The, 21-23 N Illinois.
Investor Printing and Publishing Co, 537 Lemcke bldg.
Jenkins Dennis H, 76 S Illinois.
Journal Job Printing Co, 126-130 W Maryland.
Kelsey Russell C, 105 E Ohio.
Little Folks Publishing Co, 5, 42 W Market.
Magill Osborne L, 10½ N Delaware.
Manning Alexander E, 40½ S Illinois.
Morris Printing Co, 467 S Illinois.
Municipal Engineering Co, 84 Commercial Club bldg.
Organizer Publishing Co, 66½ N Penn.
Polk R L & Co (Directory), 23-24 Journal Bldg. (See back fly leaf.)
Preston Alfred M, 398 S Alabama.
Pritchard John E, 87 Baldwin blk.
Randall T A & Co, 5 Monument pl.
Ransford & Metcalf, 5 The Windsor.
Reporter Publishing Co, 519 Indiana Trust bldg.
Review Publishing Co, 96½ E Market.
Reynolds John, 3 Odd Fellows' blk.
Rice Martin H, 14 Masonic Temple.
Robson Wm H, 35-36 Commercial Club Bldg.
Rough Notes Co The, 79 W Market.
Smith Frank H, 22 N Penn. (See opp p 803.)
Smith Septimus H, s e cor Monument pl and Meridian.
Sommer Daniel Rev, 489 W Addison (N I).
Stafford Earl E, 49½ N Illinois.
Sun Publishing Co, 79 E Ohio.
Vandawalker Daniel M, 13 Marion blk.
Wilson James B, 37½ Virginia av.
Winona Publishing Co, 36 When bldg.

*PULLEY MANUFACTURERS.

American Paper Pulley Co (Rockwood Mnfg Co), 176-190 S Penn.
Indianapolis Pulley Mnfg Co, 372-374 E Michigan. (See adv.)
Rockwood Mnfg Co (American Paper Pulley Co), 176-190 S Penn.

PUMP MANUFACTURERS AND DEALERS.

Boyd Martindale, 45 Mass av.
Comstock & Coonse Co, 193-199 S Meridian.
Dean Bros' Steam Pump Works, 1st near cor Senate av. (See adv p 3.)
Hasket Elijah, rear 80 S Delaware.

Capital Steam Carpet Cleaning Works
M. D. PLUNKETT Proprietor, Telephone 818

BENJ. BOOTH PRACTICAL EXPERT ACCOUNTANT. Accounts of any description investigated and audited, and statements rendered. Room 18, 82½ E. Washington St., Indianapolis, Ind.

The Best Place in the City to Get a Good Meal THE SHERMAN RESTAURANT ♦♦♦♦ 18 and 20 S. Meridian Street KERSHNER BROS., Proprs.

Pump Manufacturers and Dealers—Continued.
Hughes Nelson R, 27 N Capitol av.
Krauss Charles, 42 S Penn. (See right top lines.)
Worthington Henry R, 64 S Penn. (See left top lines.)
Wright Cager M, 63 Shelby.

***PUMPING MACHINERY.**

Worthington Henry R, 64 S Penn. (See left top lines.)

***PUMPING MACHINERY—GAS AND GASOLINE.**

Lambert Gas and Gasoline Engine Co, Anderson, Ind. (See right top lines.)

***PUNCHES AND DIES.**

Specialty Manufacturing Co, 193 S Meridian. (See adv opp Photographers.)

RAG CARPET MANUFACTURERS.

Miner Wm L, 184-186 Cherry. (See adv opp Rugs.)

RAILROAD SUPPLIES.

Central Rubber and Supply Co The, 79 S Illinois. (See left side lines.)
Indianapolis Switch and Frog Co, 37 Ingalls blk.

RAILROADS.

See Miscellaneous Directory.

***RAZOR MANUFACTURERS.**

Linke Hermann, 197 S Meridian.

REAL ESTATE.

Andrew John B, 236 E Morris.
Arbuckle M & Son, 62 E Market.
Aufderheide & Zumpfe, 4 Lombard bldg.
Bailey Andrew J, 94½ E Washington.
Ballard Granville M, 19 Talbott blk.
Barnitt James L, 31 Lombard bldg.
Beville Henry H, 2½ W Washington.
Boeckling A R & Co, 59-60 When bldg.
Boeckling George A, 59 When bldg.
Boice & Dark, 18½ N Meridian.
Bolen Daniel W, 38 When bldg.
Bolton Frank T, 36 N Delaware.
Booth & Johnson, 77½ E Market.
Bowen & Secrest, 17 Fair blk.
Boyles Michael W, 98 E Market.
Braden Robert B, 77 E Market.
Brouse Charles W & Co, 66½ E Market.
Caldwell & Deacon, 52 Journal bldg.
Campbell Henry C, 435 Lemcke bldg.
Carroll & Copeley, 299 S Missouri.
Carter & Boatright, 13 Baldwin blk.
Catterson R F & Son, 24 Kentucky av.
Cline Wm, 12½ N Delaware.
Coffin C E & Co, 90 E Market.
Cole & Pease, 18 Baldwin blk.
Coulter David A, 94 E Market.
Craft W H & Co, 47½ N Illinois.
Craig John F, 104 Michigan (H).
Crawford Wm T, 72½ E Washington.
Cregg John C, 94½ E Washington.
Crews John W, n w cor Walnut and Northwestern av (N I).
Cross Charles M & Co, 19½ N Meridian.
Cruse James S, 92 E Market.
Dale Charles A, 18½ N Penn.
Davidson Dorman N, 15 Baldwin blk.
Davis Marks C, 47½ N Illinois.
Day Thos C & Co, 325-330 Lemcke Bldg. (See right top cor cards.)
Denny Albert W, 30 N Delaware.
De Souchet Augustus M, 231 Lemcke bldg.
Dunkle Alfred W, 22 Thorpe blk.
Dyer & Rassmann, 31 Monument pl.
Empey & Loftin, 37½ W Washington.
Fay Henry H, 40½ E Washington. (See right top cor cards.)
Fieber & Reilly, 84 E Market.
Gearhard Charles P, 66½ N Penn.
Gordon Wm, 219-220 Lemcke bldg.
Gorsuch Charles W, 305 Indiana Trust bldg.
Greene James & Co, 227-228 Lemcke Bldg.
Gregory & Appel, 96 E Market.
Grover Arthur B, 436 Lemcke bldg.
Hadley Horace M, 66 E Market. (See left top cor cards.)
Hamilton Francis W, 31 Lombard bldg.
Hammons Wm H, 24 Thorpe blk.
Harris Emma P, 82 Baldwin blk.
Heard John, 924 Morris (W I).
Hilgenberg Christian A, 27 W Ohio.
Hobbs Wm H, 70 E Market.
Holman Daniel B, 550 Chestnut.
Hoover Wm H, 146 Pleasant.
Hutchinson Charles L, 178 E Washington.
Indiana Land Co, 236 Lemcke bldg.
Indiana Trust Co The, Indiana Trust Bldg, s e cor Washington and Virginia av. (See front cover, opp p 487 and opp Insurance Agts.)
Ingalls Land Co, 436 Lemcke bldg.
Kellogg Henry C, 67 S Penn.
Kreber Joseph J, 434 Lemcke bldg.
Kropp Jacob, 12½ N Delaware.
Lail George H, 38 When bldg.
Lemcke Julius A, 231 Lemcke bldg.
Lemon Daniel A, 55 N Illinois.
Lowry Wm J, 22 Ingalls blk.
McCaslin George H, 2½ W Washington.
McCullough W J & Sons, 98 E Market.
McDonough Dewar B, 18 Baldwin blk.
McIntosh A J & Son, 66 E Market.
McKernan David S, Rooms 2-5, Thorpe Blk. (See right bottom lines.)
McMorrow John H, 2 Thorpe blk.
McWhirter Felix T, 70 E Market.
Malott James H, 94½ E Washington.
Manion Wm, 262 S Delaware.
Manning Charles A, 94½ E Washington.
Marion Trust Co The, s e cor Market and Monument Pl. (See back cover.)
Martindale Elijah B, 5 Talbott blk.
Martindale Lynn B, 5 Talbott blk.
Martindale Robt & Co, 86 E Market.
Mendenhall, Howell & Trotter, 4 Aetna bldg.
Metzger A Agency, 5 Odd Fellows' Hall. (See left bottom lines.)
Meyer A J & Co, 33 Lombard bldg.
Meyer C F G & Son, 55 Baldwin blk.
Meyer Henry, 219-220 Lemcke bldg.
Meyer & Kiser, 306 Indiana Trust bldg.
Mick W E & Co, 68 E Market.

TUTEWILER UNDERTAKER, NO. 72 WEST MARKET STREET. TELEPHONE 216.

PROVIDENT LIFE AND TRUST CO. OF PHILADELPHIA. D. W. Edwards, G. A., 508 Indiana Trust Bldg. In form of policy; prompt settlement of death losses; equitable dealing with policy-holders; in strength of organization; and in everything which contributes to Security and Cheapness of life insurance, this company is unsurpassed.

THEODORE F. SMITHER
COMPOSITION ROOFING MATERIALS. BEST IN THE MARKET. TELEPHONE 861. OFFICE, 151 WEST MARYLAND ST.

GEORGE WOLF,
Real Estate, Loans and Insurance,
Agent FRANKLIN FIRE INSURANCE CO. of Philadelphia.
NOTARY PUBLIC. TELEPHONE 1926.
Rooms 221-222 Lemcke Building.

Mills & Small, 96½ E Market.
Mitchell Fletcher M, cor W Washington and Harris av (M J).
Mix Lyman W, 9 Cyclorama pl.
Moore & Horan, 36½ E Washington.
Moslander W S & Son, 66½ N Penn.
Nelson Thomas H, 153 Michigan (H). (See adv.)

THOMAS H. NELSON,
Real Estate, Rental and Loan Agent,
153 West Michigan St., Haughville, Ind.
A man's home is his castle. As well own as rent; it costs no more.
Best Additions. Improved and unimproved property in all parts of town to suit all people and purses.

Newberry Laura, 312 N California.
Newby Walter E, 57 Baldwin blk.
Nicoli Lew, 22 Thorpe blk.
Offutt S S & Co, 37 Lombard bldg.
Olcott Charles A, 94½ E Washington.
Osgood Mason J, 88 N Penn.
Outland James E, 15½ Virginia av.
Patterson Algernon S, 12½ N Delaware.
Perkins Samuel E, 30½ N Delaware.
Perrott & Gorman, 39 Baldwin blk.
Pfisterer Peter, 103½ E Washington.
Phillips Charles W, 70 Monument pl.
Plummer Hiram, 93 E Market.
Powell & Co, 316-318 Indiana Trust bldg.
Prather & Co, 225-226 Lemcke bldg.
Ralston Boyd M, 85½ W Market.
Raschig George L, 36 Monument pl.
Red Clay Orchard Co, 36 W Washington.
Rehm & Van Deinse, 22-23 When bldg.
Reichwein & Quill, 95 E Washington.
Reid Bros, 42 N Delaware.
Reynolds Charles E, 423 Ash.
Rhodes W A & Co, 72 E Market.
Richardson & McCrea, 79 E Market. (See right top cor cards.)
Richie Isaac N, 60 E Market.
Risley & Toon, 94½ E Washington.
Sawyer J Warren, 214 Lemcke bldg.
Sayles Charles F, 77½ E Market.
Schmidt Lorenz, 27-33 S Delaware.
Schuck & Hurst, 144 Michigan (H).
Shepard Frank R, 79 E Market.
Shingler, Hann & Co, 92-93 Baldwin blk.
Shirley Joseph A, 701 Lemcke bldg.
Smith, Curtis & Co, 10 Fair blk.
Smith J H & Co, 36 W Washington.
Smock & Mather, 32 N Delaware.
Spann John S & Co, 84-86 E Market.
Spooner John C, 10½ N Delaware.
Stevenson Benjamin C, 86 Lombard bldg.
Stevenson W E & Co, 74 E Market.
Stiarwalt Van Buren B, 51 Baldwin blk.
Stout Harvey B, 31 W Market.
Strack Philip, 155 Columbia av.
Strouse & Fullen, 25½ E Market.
Talbott Frank M, 61½ N Penn.
Talbott Richard L, 44 Thorpe blk.
Taylor & Co, 5 Talbott blk.
Thomas Charles H, 10½ N Delaware.
Todd John M & Co, 7 Ingalls blk.
Traub Wm H, 1085 W Vermont.
Tuttle & Seguin, 28 E Market. (See left bottom cor cards.)
Vajen Charles T, 20 Thorpe blk.
Vajen's Real Estate Exchange, 88 N Penn.
Van Dyke Wm W, 227-228 Lemcke bldg.
Veitch Rolland T, 711-712 Lemcke bldg.
Villiers Walter H, 108 Oliver av (W I).
Voss Jay G, 35 W Market.
Waddle & Dugdale, 433 Lemcke bldg.
Wallace George E, 77½ E Market.
Wasson Charles K, 24 S Penn.
Waters Robert, 10 Monument Pl.
Webb & Co, 9-10 When bldg.
Webber & Co, 91 E Market.
Welch & Carlon, 34 Monument pl.
Wharton Joseph W, 96½ E Market.
Wildman & Glover, 19 Talbott blk.
Wocher John, 19½ N Penn.
Wolf George, 221-222 Lemcke Bldg. (See adv.)
Wood Wm H, 40 N Delaware.
Wright J L & Co, 48 When bldg.
Wurgler G Adolph, 88½ E Washington.

*RED MORTAR.

Balke & Krauss Co, cor Market and Missouri. (See right bottom lines.)
Wasson W G Co The, 130 Indiana av. (See left bottom cor cards and adv in Cement and Lime.)

*REFRIGERATORS.

Messenger W Horndon, 101 E Washington and 13, 15 and 17 S Delaware. (See left bottom lines.)

*REGALIA AND BADGES.

Mayer George J, 15 S Meridian. (See left bottom cor cards and p 5.)

ELECTRIC SUPPLIES We Carry a full Stock. Prices Right. C. W. MEIKEL, Tel. 466. 96-98 E. New York St.

DALTON & MERRIFIELD { LUMBER South Noble St., near E. Washington

INDIANA ELECTROTYPE CO. : BEST WORK LOWEST PRICES. 23 WEST PEARL ST., INDIANAPOLIS, IND. JOB WORK. BOOK PLATES. All Orders Promptly Filled. BEST PATENT BASE ON THE MARKET.

***REGISTERS AND VENTILATORS.**

Vonnegut Clemens, 184-186 E Washington. (See left bottom lines.)

RENDERING WORKS.

Indianapolis Packing Works and Rendering Co, Union Stock Yards (W I).

***RENTAL AGENTS.**

Coffin C E & Co, 90 E Market.
Fay Henry H, 40½ E Washington. (See right top cor cards.)
Greene James & Co, 227-228 Lemcke Bldg.
Gregory & Appel, 96 E Market.
Hadley Horace M, 66 E Market. (See left top cor cards.)
Indiana Trust Co The, Indiana Trust Bldg, s e cor Washington and Virginia av. (See front cover, opp p 487 and opp Insurance Agts.)
Lawyers' Loan and Trust Co, 68½ E Market. (See adv top stencil and opp p 555.)
McCullough W J & Sons, 98 E Market.
Marion Trust Co The, s e cor Market and Monument Pl. (See back cover.)
Metzger A Agency, 5 Odd Fellows' Hall. (See left bottom lines.)
Nelson Thomas H, 153 Michigan (H). (See adv in Real Estate.)
Richardson & McCrea, 79 E Market. (See right top cor cards.)
Spann John S & Co, 84-86 E Market.
Tuttle & Seguin, 28 E Market. (See left bottom cor cards.)
Waters Robert, 10 Monument Pl.

RESTAURANTS.

Banks Wesley S, 31 Kentucky av.
Beasley Henry, 155 Indiana av.
Beaupre Mary A, 141 W Washington.
Bechtel Jacob, 328 E Washington.
Bowen Wm E, 1085 E Washington.
Bradshaw John W, 56 S Illinois.
Burnett Lee, 100 W Washington.
Burris Thomas & Son, 125 E Washington.
Carpenter Clark, 88 W Market.
Clarke Good H, 98 N Illinois.
Coble George jr, 50 Pendleton av (B).
Coley Wm E, 191 W Washington.
Commercial Club Restaurant, Commercial Club Bldg.
Corya Louis W, 135 Hadley av (W I).
Crutcher Henry, 182 W 7th.
Cubel Mary, 315 E Washington.
Curry George W, 234 Indiana av.
Cutts John H, 1412 Lulu (N I).
Deady Margaret, 66 N Delaware.
Dimock Daniel J, 25 S Penn and 74 N Illinois.
Duchene Charles, 411 E Washington.
Dwinnell & Jontz, 75 N Delaware.
Elite Cafe, 120-122 N Illinois.
Fehlinger John, 147 E Washington.
Foster Robert M, 94-96 E Washington.
Gable Clyde C, 110 E Wabash.
George Richard J, 120 S Illinois.
Gessler Jacob, 128 E Wabash.
Gilchrist Minerva M, 14 S Station (B).
Graham Wm E, 185 W Washington.
Hamilton Julia, 186 W 3d.
Harris Lou, 183 Indiana av.
Haynes Horace F, 62 N Penn and 72 N Delaware.
Hays Charles S, 178 S Illinois.
Helm Wm H, 257 Mass av.
Hilliker Alpha W, 46 N Penn.
Huegele John, 60 E Washington.
Hunter James T, 229 W Washington.
Hunter Lucy, 119 Ft Wayne av.
Hunter Silas W, 104 S Illinois.
Hyde Nelson J, 59 S Illinois.
Jackson Charles W, 336 Indiana av.
Johnson Alice, 223 W Ohio.
Johnson Frank O, 16-18 Monument pl.
Kemp Phoenicia J, 69 N Alabama.
Kershner Bros, 18-20 S Meridion. (See left side lines.)
Koehler Albert, 128 E Wabash.
Lang Herman, 240 W Washington.
Lee Harry, 210 W Washington.
McKillop John P, 313 E Washington.
Melson Jennie, 201 S Illinois.
Merkle Peter & Son, Union Station.
Miles Charles R, 111 E Washington.
Millner James W, 35 E Market.
Moran Harry A, 117 S Illinois.
Nimal Wm H, 82 E Market.
O'Brien Frank, 253 E Washington.
Page Fannie, 187½ W 3d.
Potter Sarah E, 265 W Washington.
Prather Caroline C, 360 Mass av.
Randolph Laura, 277 Mass av.
Richardson May, 7 The Windsor.
Richel Charles, 172 E Washington.
Roller John J, 151 W Washington.
St Clair George W, 159 Indiana av.
Schmidt Louisa H, 24 N Delaware.
Shawber John, 73 N Alabama.
Sherman's Restaurant, 18-20 S Meridian. (See left side lines.)
Sherwood Francis M, 90 S Illinois.
Slevin Frank, 38 Jackson pl.
Smith Henry, 39 N Illinois.
Smith Orvel H, 194 E Washington.
Smothers Nancy A, 165 Indiana av.
Snider Albert, 65 N Alabama.
Spaulding Ralph, 22 Prospect.
Staley Charles P, 86 W Washington.
Stegemeier Henry, 19 N Illinois.
Stephens Samuel D, 38 W 13th.
Stroble John, 87 S Illinois.
Thorne Charles, 60 W Market.
Tolbert Edward, 166 Indiana av.
Vanderwood & Seaton, 174 Indiana av.
Walls Henry, 44 W Washington.
Watts George W jr, 180 E Washington.
Wells Annie, 16 Indiana av.
White Birney K, 271 Mass av.
Williams Elmer, 315 E Washington.
Williams Louis, 195 S Illinois.
Williams Martha, 64 Indiana av.
Wise Harry A, 143 E Washington.

***ROAD MACHINERY.**

Adams J D & Co, 30 Jackson Pl, opp north entrance to Union Depot.

***ROOFERS—ASPHALT.**

Smither Henry C, 169 W Maryland (See adv opp Roofing Material.)
Symmes H H Co, 39 S Alabama.
Zimmerman C & Sons, 19-21 S East (See left bottom lines.)

ROOFERS—ASPHALT MASTIC.

Smither Henry C, 169 W Maryland (See adv opp Roofing Material.)

W. H. Messenger FURNITURE, CARPETS, STOVES, 101 EAST WASHINGTON ST. TEL. 491

McNamara, Koster & Co. | Foundry and Pattern Shop, 212-218 S. PENN. ST. . . . PHONE 1593.

CONTRACTORS FOR "AAT" ROOFING, GRAVEL ROOFING, AND CEMENT WALKS, Old Roofs Examined and Estimates Given Free of Charge.

GEO. E. PIANT. A. E. DOCHEZ.
THE GUARANTEE ROOFING COMPANY,

THE FI

DEALERS IN

THE OLD RELIABLE

Sherman Restaurant

18 and 20 South Meridian Street

(Established 1880.)

THE BEST PLACE IN THE CITY
TO GET A GOOD MEAL AT A REASONABLE PRICE.
ALL KINDS OF GAME IN SEASON.

KERSHNER BROS., Proprietors.

ROOFERS—COPPER.

Laing Samuel, 72-74 E Court. (See left side lines.)

*ROOFERS—FELT.

Zimmerman C & Sons, 19-21 S East. (See left bottom lines.)

Indiana Paint and Roofing Co, 27-29 Muskingum.

Indianapolis Steel Roofing and Corrugating Works, 23-25 E South. (See right side lines.)

Laing Samuel, 72-74 E Court. (See left side lines.)

Long Steel and Iron Roofing Co The, 180-186 W 5th. (See adv.)

ES MADE TO OR TRUCKS. Telephone 654.

Indianapolis BUSINESS UNIVERSITY Leading College of Business and Shorthand. Elevator day and night. Individual instruction. Large faculty. Terms easy. Enter now. See p. 4. When Block. E. J. HEEB, President.

DIANA
EST PEARL ST.

Dwinnell & Jontz, 75 N Delaware.
Elite Cafe, 120-122 N Illinois.
Fehlinger John, 147 E Washington.
Foster Robert M, 94-96 E Washington.
Gable Clyde C, 110 E Wabash.
George Richard J, 120 S Illinois.
Gessler Jacob, 128 E Wabash.
Gilchrist Minerva M, 14 S Station (B).
Graham Wm E, 185 W Washington.
Hamilton Julia, 186 W 3d.

Smither Henry C, 169 W Maryland.
(See adv opp Roofing Material.)
Symmes H H Co, 39 S Alabama.
Zimmerman C & Sons, 19-21 S East.
(See left bottom lines.)

ROOFERS—ASPHALT MASTIC.

Smither Henry C, 169 W Maryland.
(See adv opp Roofing Material.)

McNamara, Koster & Co. | Foundry and Pattern Shop, 212-218 S. PENN. ST. . . . . PHONE 1593.

CONTRACTORS FOR
"AAT" ROOFING,
GRAVEL ROOFING,
AND
CEMENT WALKS,
Old Roofs Examined and Estimates Given Free of Charge.
DEALERS IN
ALL KINDS OF ROOFING MATERIAL.

GEO. E. PIANT. A. E. DOCHEZ.
THE GUARANTEE ROOFING COMPANY,
OFFICE:
Telephone 1345. 82 MASSACHUSETTS AVE.

THE LONG
Steel and Iron Roofing Co.
MANUFACTURERS AND DEALERS IN
STEEL, IRON ROOFING, SIDING AND CEILING.
ALSO, SLATE AND TIN ROOFING AND GALVANIZED IRON WORK.
REPAIR AND JOB WORK PROMPTLY ATTENDED TO.
TELEPHONE 1448. 180 to 186 West Fifth St.
A. E. LONG, PROPRIETOR.

*ROOFERS—COMPOSITION.

Smither Henry C, 169 W Maryland. (See adv opp Roofing Material.)
Smither Theodore F, 151 W Maryland. (See right side lines.)
Zimmerman C & Sons, 19-21 S East. (See left bottom lines.)

ROOFERS—COPPER.

Laing Samuel, 72-74 E Court. (See left side lines.)

*ROOFERS—FELT.

Zimmerman C & Sons, 19-21 S East. (See left bottom lines.)

ROOFERS—GENERAL.

Ensey O B, cor 6th and Illinois. (See left bottom cor cards.)
Gardner Joseph, 37-41 Kentucky av. (See left top cor cards.)
Guarantee Roofing Co The, 82 Mass av. (See adv.)
Indiana Paint and Roofing Co, 27-29 Muskingum.
Indianapolis Steel Roofing and Corrugating Works, 23-25 E South. (See right side lines.)
Laing Samuel, 72-74 E Court. (See left side lines.)
Long Steel and Iron Roofing Co The, 180-186 W 5th. (See adv.)

Indianapolis BUSINESS UNIVERSITY Leading College of Business and Shorthand. Elevator day and night. Individual instruction. Large faculty. Terms easy. Enter now. See p. 4. When Block. E. J. HEEB, President.

THE FRED DIETZ CO. || WOODEN PACKING BOXES MADE TO ORDER. FACTORY AND WAREHOUSE 40 Madison Avenue. Telephone 654.

Steam Pumping Machinery { HENRY R. WORTHINGTON, 64 S. PENNSYLVANIA ST. Long Distance Telephone 284.

UNION CO-OPERATIVE LAUNDRY (COMPOSED OF UNION LAUNDRY GIRLS.) NOS. 3, 40 AND 42 VIRGINIA AVENUE. T. E. SOMERVILLE, MANAGER. TELEPHONE 18. INDIANAPOLIS, IND.

Roofers—General—Continued.
McWorkman Willard, 930 W Washington. (See left top cor cards.)
Preston Columbus P, 67 S Reisner (W I).
Sims James A, s w cor 26th and Central av.
Smither Henry C, 169 W Maryland. (See adv opp Roofing Material.)
Smither Theodore F, 151 W Maryland. (See right side lines.)
Zimmerman C & Sons, 19-21 S East. (See left bottom lines.)

***ROOFERS—GRAVEL.**

Guarantee Roofing Co The, 82 Mass av. (See adv.)
Smither Henry C, 169 W Maryland. (See adv opp Roofing Material.)
Smither Theodore F, 151 W Maryland. (See right side lines.)
Zimmerman C & Sons, 19 S East. (See left bottom lines.)

***ROOFERS—IRON.**

Ensey O B, cor 6th and Illinois. (See left bottom cor cards.)
Gardner Joseph, 37-41 Kentucky av. (See left top cor cards.)
Indianapolis Steel Roofing and Corrugating Works, 23-25 E South. (See right side lines.)
Long Steel and Iron Roofing Co The, 180-186 W 5th. (See adv.)
McWorkman Willard, 930 W Washington. (See left top cor cards.)

***ROOFERS' MATERIAL.**

Smither Henry C, 169 W Maryland. (See adv opp Roofing Material.)
Smither Theodore F, 151 W Maryland. (See right side lines.)
Zimmerman C & Sons, 19-21 S East. (See left bottom lines.)

***ROOFERS—PITCH.**

Smither Henry C, 169 W Maryland. (See adv opp Roofing Material.)
Smither Theodore F, 151 W Maryland. (See right side lines.)
Symmes H H Co, 39 S Alabama.
Zimmerman C & Sons, 19 S East. (See left bottom lines.)

***ROOFERS—SLATE.**

Ensey O B, cor 6th and Illinois. (See left bottom cor cards.)
Gardner Joseph, 37-41 Kentucky av. (See left top cor cards.)
Laing Samuel, 72-74 E Court. (See left side lines.)
Long Steel and Iron Roofing Co The, 180-186 W 5th. (See adv.)
McWorkman Willard, 930 W Washington. (See left top cor cards.)
Zimmerman C & Sons, 19-21 S East. (See left bottom lines.)

***ROOFERS—SLATE AND TIN.**

Smith W Q & Co, 140 E 7th.
Zimmerman C & Sons, 19-21 S East. (See left bottom lines.)

***ROOFERS—STEEL.**

Gardner Joseph, 37-41 Kentucky av. (See left top cor cards.)
Indianapolis Steel Roofing and Corrugating Works, 23-25 E South. (See right side lines.)
Laing Samuel, 72-74 E Court. (See left side lines.)
Long Steel and Iron Roofing Co The, 180-186 W 5th. (See adv.)
McWorkman Willard, 930 W Washington. (See left top cor cards.)

***ROOFERS—TIN.**

Abel & Doyle, 31 Indiana av. (See adv p 5.)
Ensey O B, cor 6th and Illinois. (See left bottom cor cards.)
Gardner Joseph, 37-41 Kentucky av. (See left top cor cards.)
Laing Samuel, 72-74 E Court. (See left side lines.)
Long Steel and Iron Roofing Co The, 180-186 W 5th. (See adv.)
McWorkman Willard, 930 W Washington. (See left top cor cards.)

***ROOFERS—TRINIDAD ASPHALT.**

Smither Henry C, 169 W Maryland. (See adv opp Roofing Material.)

***ROOFING CONTRACTORS.**

(See also Contractors—Roofing.)
Zimmerman C & Sons, 19-21 S East. (See left bottom lines.)

***ROOFING MATERIAL.**

Smither Henry C, 169 W Maryland. (See adv opp.)
Smither Theodore F, 151 W Maryland. (See right side lines.)
Zimmerman C & Sons, 19-21 S East. (See left bottom lines.)

***ROOFING MATERIAL MNFRS.**

Mica Roofing Co, s w cor Belt R R and Summit (H).

ROPE AND TWINE MANUFACTURERS.

Standard Rope and Twine Co, 38 Kentucky av.

***RUBBER CLOTHING—WHOLESALE AND RETAIL.**

Central Rubber and Supply Co The, 79 S Illinois. (See left side lines.)

RUBBER GOODS.

Central Rubber and Supply Co The, 79 S Illinois. (See left side lines.)
Indiana Rubber Co, 127 S Meridian.
Indianapolis Rubber Co, 301-309 E Georgia.
Mayer Charles & Co, 29-31 W Washington. (See adv opp p 615.)
Morrison Lewis E, 4 N Meridian.

CLEMENS VONNEGUT 184, 186 and 192 E. Washington St. | FOUNDRY AND MACHINISTS' SUPPLIES. "NORTON" EMERY WHEELS AND GRINDING MACHINERY.

ROOFING....

MANUFACTURER AND DEALER IN

COMPOSITION ROOFING MATERIALS
BUILDING AND SHEATHING FELT
ASBESTOS FIRE PROOF FELT

Asphalt

COAL TAR, PITCH, ROOFING FELT

MOTH PROOF FELT.

2 AND 3 PLY ASPHALT }
2 AND 3 PLY COAL TAR } READY ROOFING.

ALSO PUT ON

Coal Tar Pitch and Felt }
Asphalt and Crescent Brand Felt } GRAVEL ROOFING.

ASPHALT MASTICE FOR ROOFING.

ASPHALT MASTICE FOR FLOORS AND WALKS, ETC.

H. C. SMITHER, Agent

169 West Maryland Street

TELEPHONE 937. **——Indianapolis.**

DIAMOND WALL PLASTER { Telephone 1410 BUILDERS' EXCHANGE.

UNION TRANSFER AND STORAGE CO. Cor. E. Ohio St. and C., C., C. & St. L. R'y Tracks. Storage of Household Goods and Pianos a Specialty.

RUBBER STAMPS.

Capital Rubber Stamp Works, 15 S Meridian. (See left bottom cor cards and opp p 5.)
Feintuch Wm, 134 Eddy.

*RUBBER TYPE.

Mayer George J, 15 S Meridian. (See left bottom cor cards and p 5.)

*RUG MANUFACTURERS.

Cooper J O & Co, 223 Mass av.
Lemaire Antoinette, 305 Bright.
Miner Wm L, 184-186 Cherry. (See adv opp.)
Twentieth Century Rug Co The, 184-186 Cherry. (See adv opp.)
Williams Augustus W, 169 Mass av.

SADDLE AND HARNESS MNFRS.

(See also Harness and Saddle Mnfrs.)
Herrington Frank L, 81 E Market. (See adv opp p 450.)

SADDLERY HARDWARE—WHOLESALE.

Gordon-Kurtz Co The, 143 S Meridian.

*SAFE DEPOSIT COMPANIES.

(See also Banks and Bankers.)
Fletcher's Safe Deposit Co, 30-34 E Washington.
Indiana Trust Co The, Indiana Trust Bldg, s e cor Washington and Virginia av. (See front cover, adv opp p 487 and opp Insurance Agts.)

*SAFE EXPERTS.

Isensee Albert T, 31 Monument Pl. (See adv below and in Locksmiths.)

A. ISENSEE, Jr.
LOCK AND SAFE EXPERT
Office and Bank Safes Opened and Repaired. Combination Changed.
31 MONUMENT PLACE.

*SAFE MOVERS.

Adams J Q & Co, 26 Virginia av. (See adv in House Movers.)
Hogan Transfer and Storage Co The, s w cor Washington and Illinois and cor Delaware and Georgia. (See left top lines and adv in Transfer Companies.)
Webb-Jameson Co The, 222 S Meridian. (See adv in House Movers.)

SAFES.

Mosler Safe Co, Charles A McConnell State agt, 72-74 W Court.

*SAFETY VAULTS.

Indiana Trust Co The, Indiana Trust Bldg, s e cor Washington and Virginia av. (See front cover, opp p 487 and opp Insurance Agts.)

*SALE STABLES.

(See also Livery Stables.)
Munter Kevi, 45 N Alabama. (See adv.)

K. MUNTER,
Feed, Sale and Exchange Stable
45 NORTH ALABAMA STREET,
(Opposite East Side of Court House.)
Draft, Carriage and Driving Horses Constantly on hand, also, a good supply of Mules.
Team Horses and Mules Hired by the Day.
TELEPHONE 583.

SALOONS.

Ackelow Herman, 269 Hadley av (W I).
Adams Clay F, 187 W 3d.
Agnew John T, 52 S Illinois.
Albertsmeyer Charles H, 155 Prospect.
Aldred Frederick H, 38 W Market.
Allman Haman B, 67 Russell av.
Altmann Herman, 586 Morris (W I).
Arens Frank J, 249 E Morris.
Arnouil Louis, 253 S West.
Austin James J, 199 W Merrill.
Baaske Charles T, 20 N Delaware.
Bacher Herman, 26 S Missouri.
Baily Samuel, 164 Indiana av.
Bain John R, 101 S Noble.
Baist John R, 2 Warman av (H).
Baldus Joseph, 250 N Noble.
Balfour & Prasse, 559 Virginia av.
Bany Peter, 257 E washington.
Barnes Wm J, 353 W Washington.
Bauer Theodore, 298 W Washington.
Beattey Wm, 541 Shelby.
Berkowitz Armin, 484 E Washington.
Berkowitz Ignatz, 1102 E Washington.
Bernauer Edward E, 430 Virginia av.
Bernhart Frederick, 76 S Delaware.
Bernhart John, 423 S Meridian.
Bleckwell Frederick, 528 E 9th.
Bohn Joseph, n s Grandview av nr Germania av (H).
Bolser Gilbert, 251 Columbia av.
Bonner Paul, 201 W South.
Borchert August, 425 S Delaware.
Borgmann Wm, 359 Virginia av.
Bottler Julius, 233 S Delaware.
Boylan Michael T, 300 S Capitol av.
Brandt Fred, 44 W Washington.
Brinkman Joseph H, 195 Shelby.
Britton Charles O, 234 E Washington.
Brochhausen Swebert J, 2 Buchanan.
Brown G Charles, 66 Shelby.
Buechsenmann Martin, 288 W 6th.
Burkhart Louis, 1 Madison av.
Burns Gerrone W, 24 N Delaware.
Burns James, 263 Hadley av (W I).
Bush John, 172 W Washington.
Buthe Augustus L, 171 W Washington.
Caldwell Benjamin F, 186 W 7th.
Campbell Daniel, 471 E St Clair.
Carpenter Clark, 86 W Market.
Carson Calvin, 176 Elizabeth.
Cavett Henry, Union Stock Yards (W I).
Chamberlin James E, 1321 Northwestern av.
Clark Elliott D, 274 W Washington.
Click John, 349 English av.

A. METZGER AGENCY ESTABLISHED 1863. L-O-A-N-S

"The Progressive, Up-to-Date and Un-X-Ld Weavers"

INDIANAPOLIS, 1897.

In soliciting a bid for your patronage, we beg to say that we are determined to adhere to the "high standard" of excellence in manufacture which has made the reputation of

"The 20th Century Rugs."

We weave them! There is no doubt about it. "There are none better," and but few as good. We've always made the best, and are going right ahead doing so. We are proud of **"The 20th Century Rugs,"** so you can be. We've said we have the right weaves, and we are sure we've the RIGHT STYLES. Styles count as well as weaves.

WE'VE BOTH.

"The 20th Century Rugs" are in vogue and have a reputation for originality, stability and absolute worth—honest worth. "Merit tells." Why, of course, there are others, but none to compare in style and quality with **"The 20th Century Rugs,"** unequaled for

ARTISTIC EFFECT AND MODERATE IN COST.

They are made from your old carpets (any and all kinds), which are thoroughly cleansed and deodorized.

REMEMBER!

"BRAN-NOO" Rugs, Mats, Druggets, Runners (Hall Rugs), Stair Strips, are strictly hand-made—insures for them a lasting durability.

THINK!

"MAK-NU" Rugs from your old carpets. Made in all sizes with an extra heavy pile.

NO GOOD RUG SO LOW PRICED.
NO LOW PRICED RUG SO GOOD.

The 20th Century Rug Co.

WM. L. MINER, Proprietor.

FACTORY, 184 AND 186 CHERRY STREET,
One Block West of Massachusetts Avenue Depot (New East Tenth St.)

DIAMONI

RUBI
Capital Rubbe
Meridian. (Se
and opp p 5.)
Feintuch Wm, 1

*RU
Mayer George
left bottom

*RUG M
Cooper J O & C
Lemadro Antoin
Miner Wm
adv opp.)
Twentieth Ce
186 Cherry.
Williams Augu

SADDLE A
(See also H
Herrington
(See adv op

SADDLERY

Gordon-Kurtz

*SAFE I
(See als
Fletcher's S
Washingto
Indiana Tr
Bldg, s e
ginia av.
p 487 and

Isensee A
(See adv I

A.

LC

NSFER AND STORAGE CO.
Cor. E. Ohio St. and C., C., C. & St. L. R'y Tracks.
Storage of Household Goods and Pianos a Specialty.

VELLS And Second Water Wells and Pumps of all kinds at CHARLES KRAUSS', 42 S. PENN. ST., TEL. 465. REPAIRING NEATLY DONE.

St Clair Charles, 79 E Wabash.
S[illegible]lerson James H, 214 W 1st.
Santo Edward J, 204 Indiana av.
S[illegible]ter Henry, 231 Shelby.
Schaefer Ernst, n w cor English av and Pine.
Schaub John, 167 River av (W I).
Schaub Joseph H, 88 E Washington.
S[illegible]h Peter, 2 S Brightwood av (B).
S[illegible]terdeker Charles, 153 Davidson.
S[illegible]ssel Otto, cor West and Wabash.
S[illegible]malholz Casper, 29 S Meridian and 9 E Pearl.
Schmidt Anton, 362 Shelby.
Schmidt Anton, 364 Virginia av.
S[illegible]der John B, 474 S Meridian.
S[illegible]n Sigmond, 577 Virginia av.
Schroeder Albert, 299 S Capitol av.
S[illegible]ster Wm, 681 Madison av.
Schuller Theodore C, 110 N Meridian.
Schulz Louis, n s Washington 1 w of Insane Hospital (M J).
Schwartz Martin, 580 S Meridian.
Scott Marion M, 25 E Georgia.
S[illegible]rist George H, 190 Dillon.
S[illegible]tor Lester, 131 E Washington.
S[illegible]nsticker Wm C, 233 S East.
S[illegible]er Christopher, 476 E Washington.
S[illegible]z Charles, 1100 E Washington.
S[illegible] Matthias, 577 S Capitol av.
S[illegible]on Martin E, 1204 E Washington.
Shepherd Henry V, 840 E Washington.
S[illegible]e Bros, 112 W Ray.
S[illegible] John B, 135 E Washington.
S[illegible]ey John, 151 W McCarty.
S[illegible] Henry, 41 N Illinois.
S[illegible]h Thomas F, Sherman House.
S[illegible] Wm D, 79 N Illinois.
S[illegible] Wm H, 322 S West.
S[illegible] Louis, s e cor Hazel and Lawrence.
S[illegible]r Albert, 63 N Alabama.
Somerville Tilford D, 449 E Washington.
S[illegible]r Louis, 322 Prospect.
S[illegible]tzfaden Peter, 201 Virginia av.
S[illegible]tzfaden Wm P, s w cor Madeira and Prospect.
S[illegible]agel Leopold, 920 S Meridian.
S[illegible]sel Henry, 345 Madison av.
S[illegible]gpfeil Henry, 190 Kentucky av.
S[illegible]lin George, 590 N West.
S[illegible]lin John H, 462 N West.
S[illegible]mann Carl, 316 E Washington:
S[illegible]wagen John, 488 S Illinois.
S[illegible]ns Jasper J, 32 S Brightwood av (B).
Stevers Charles H, 408 Blake.
Stewart John W, 126 E Wabash.
S[illegible] Henry, 249 W Maryland.
S[illegible] John, 115 Ft Wayne av.
S[illegible] Wesley A, 178 S Illinois.
S[illegible]k Charles, 427 Madison av.
Sullivan Bridget, 201 Bates.
Sullivan Dennis, 114 Agnes.
Sussman Louis, 205 W Ohio.
Sussman Wolf, 304 S Illinois.
[illegible]ner Andreas, 499 S West.
Thompson Charles G, 1400 Northwestern av (N I).
Tipton Charles A, 60 Mass av.
Tiveman Michael P, 402 S Capitol av.
Tobin & Harrison, 650 N Senate av.
Toomey & Dwyer, 17 Monument pl.
Traugott Joachim, 174 River av (W I).
Traugott Louis, 1206 Morris (W I).
Triber Wm, 149 Dunlop.
Tron Wm, 17 N Illinois.
Truemper Charles J, e s Northwestern av nr canal.
[illegible]belacker Frank, 1205 S Meridian.

If You are not Satisfied with Your Laundry Work Give Us a Trial . . || ERTEL STEAM LAUNDRY || 26 and 28 N. Senate Avenue. Telephone 1089.

[illegible]BERGER { Manufacturers of IRON and WIRE FENCES 162-170 S. SENATE AVE. TEL. [illegible]98.

LAMBERT GAS & GASOLINE ENGINE CO.
ANDERSON, IND. GAS ENGINES FOR ALL PURPOSES.

BICYCLES $5 DOWN. MONTHLY. Best Wheels. Best Terms. WHEELMEN'S CO. 31 W. OHIO ST. LONG DISTANCE TEL. 1855.

G. W. KILLINGER,

Cold Storage Architect and Refrigerator Builder.
MANUFACTURER OF
STORE, OFFICE AND BAR FIXTURES.
IMPORTER OF
French and Belgian Mirrors,
Plain and Beveled.
Office and Factory,
Corner Market and Missouri Streets,
Warerooms,
141 Virginia Avenue,
INDIANAPOLIS, INDIANA.

Coble George jr, 52 Pendleton av (B).
Coleman Henry, 723 N Senate av.
Coleman Patrick A, 59 Beacon.
Conner John F, 286 S West.
Costello Michael, 490 S Meridian.
Coyle Bernard, 849 S Meridian.
Coyle Derby, 240 W Maryland.
Crone Jacob, 74 N Delaware.
Cronin James A, 73 W McCarty.
Danke Albert, 250 S Meridian.
Davis Patrick, 101 Patterson.
Davy John, 169 Michigan (H).
Deluse George, 20 Kentucky av.
Deluse John P, 99 E South.
Denison Casino Co The, 81 N Penn.
Denning Charles B, 1008 E Washington.
Dietz Theodore A, 299 S Delaware.
Dinnin Samuel E, 100 E Washington.
Dippel Henry C, 60 N Delaware.
Di Trani Nicoli, 125 E Maryland.
Duffey James, 157 W McCarty.
Dugan Daniel, 200 W Washington.
Dugan John, 38 Michigan (H).
Duncan Robert, 340 Blake.
Dwyer James J, 820 W Washington.
Ebner John, 154 W Washington.
Egerton Charles, 280 S Illinois.
Ellerkamp Christian, 183 Prospect.
Emery & Scott, 33 Kentucky av.
Emhardt John, 781 S East.
Emminger Joseph, 11 Monument pl.
Emrich John C, s e cor Lafayette and Crawfordsville rd.
Ems Frederick W, 293 Bates.
Engle Daniel W, 101 S Illinois.
Essmann Louis N, 29 W Pearl.
Essman Wm L, 185 S Illinois.
Fair David, 793 N Senate av and n w cor 30th and L N A & C Ry.
Falender Julius, 300 S Illinois.
Farrington Wyatt L, 275 W Washington.
Federspill Michael, 27 S Illinois.
Feeny Timothy, 252 W New York.
Ferris John E, 90 W Washington.
Fessler David, 180 E McCarty.
Finitzer John, 184 W 1st.
Finn Michael, 252 S West.
Fishinger Charles, 349 E Market.
Flynn Wm, 114 W Ray.
Ford Michael, 113 Agnes.
Fournace John B, 129 W Maryland.
Friedrich Max, 764 S East.
Fritsch Martin, 428 Clifford av.
Funck Frank, 71 Wyoming.
Gallagher Patrick B, 195 W Washington.
Galm Michael, 628 Virginia av.
Gally Julius M, 149 Ft Wayne av.
Gardner John G, 189 S Reisner (W I).
Gasper John B, 53 N Penn.
Gasper Joseph, 68 Virginia av.
Gassert Gottlieb, 464 S Delaware.
Gaston Edward, 49-53 Kentucky av.
Gates Joseph W, 687 E Washington.
Gaul Frederick W, 404 S West.
Gavin Timothy, 336 S West.
Germania House, 200 S Meridian.
Gillispie John, 291 W Maryland.
Gisler Frank, 185 E Washington.
Glitzenstein Charles, 286 W Washington.
Gorman Frank, 175 S Illinois.
Graebner John, 307 Shelby.
Graham John, 151 Elizabeth.
Grand Hotel, s e cor Illinois and Maryland.
Grau Bros, 364 Blake.
Greathouse Archibald, 10 Indiana av.
Green Herbert W, 67 N Penn.
Greenman Jacob, 109 Mass av.
Gruenert J Henry, 59-63 E South.

J. H. TECKENBROCK | Grilles, Fretwork and Wood Carpets
94 EAST SOUTH STREET.

FIDELITY MUTUAL LIFE PHILADELPHIA, PA. A. H. COLLINS { General Agent, 52-53 Baldwin Block.

Edwardsport Coal & Mining Co. Rooms 42 and 43 When Building.
SUPERIOR BITUMINOUS COAL For Steam and Domestic . . Purposes . .

Saloons—Continued.
Grunwald Joseph, 428 Mass av.
Haberern Michael, 504 N West.
Hafner August H, 323 W Washington.
Hafner John V, 1246 E Washington.
Hagerty Frank H, 250 Columbia av.
Hamill Patrick, 404 W Washington.
Hamlin James D, 312 Blake.
Harmening Christian H, 12 N Delaware.
Harrington Wm J, 199 S Capitol av.
Haubrich Adam, 64 N Delaware.
Heess Conrad, 330 Mass av.
Hefferman Thomas J, 84 W Market.
Hegarty James H, 438 National rd.
Heid Jacob, 403 Clifford av.
Heier Fred F, 18-20 S New Jersey.
Heinlein John, 199 Indiana av.
Heitkam John W, 184 W 7th.
Helms August jr, 2 Lexington av.
Henn Alois, 627 Madison av.
Henry George A, 296 E Georgia.
Henry Jacob B, 176 E Washington.
Hertz Frank M, 251 English av.
Hess Casper, 507 Madison av.
Hett John M, 342 National rd.
Hignight James R, 598 Virginia av.
Hild Wm, n w cor Blake and New York.
Hill Wade, 233 W Ohio.
Hinnenkamp Frederick, 149 N Noble.
Hirth Bridget, 1020 W Washington.
Hitzelberger Albert, W McLene and canal (N I).
Hoereth Conrad, 600 S West.
Hoffbauer Joseph G, 1 Orange av.
Hoffbauer Philip J, 107 Hill av.
Hofherr Frederick C, 505 Madison av.
Hofmann Otto, 470 S Meridian.
Holmes Thomas J, 75 S West.
Hotel Oneida, 114-118 S Illinois.
Huegele John, 60 E Washington.
Hughes John, 122 Michigan (H).
Hurley Charles H, 33 Kentucky av.
Hurley Timothy, 102 S Illinois.
Hurt James F, 185 Tremont av (H).
Ilg Frederick, 23 Virginia av.
Illinois House, 181-185 S Illinois.
Jackson Charles W, 338 Indiana av.
Jacobs Abraham, 270 S Illinois.
Jay James E, 45 W Pearl.
Jearl Benjamin B, 58 N Delaware.
Jones Edward L, 105 Mass av.
Kampman Henry W, 124 E Wabash.
Kaufman B & Son, 168 W Washington.
Keating Joseph F, 132 Michigan (H).
Keller George J, 243 Hadley av (W I).
Keller Julius, 38 Virginia av.
Keller Ottmar, 113 E Washington.
Kelly John J, 151 English av.
Kelly Malachi L, 246 W Washington.
Kennedy Michael R, 49 S West.
Kerr Gilford T, 81 S Illinois.
Kerr & Irie, 82 N Delaware and 88 W Washington.
Kersting Benjamin, 288 W Washington.
Kiley Philip, 450 Mass av.
Kinander Charles, 510 E 9th.
King John W, 37 N Alabama.
Kissel C Fred, s e cor Capitol av and 18th and 30th and main entrance State fair grounds.
Kistner John, 198 W Washington.
Kleine Henry, 265 Mass av.
Knarzer George, 60 S Delaware.
Koerner Valentine, 1050 S Meridian.
Kolb Frederick W, 21 Kentucky av.
Kolcheck George, 813 N Capitol av.
Kolker Henry A, 451 E Washington.
Kremp Frederick, 49 N Alabama.
Kroeckel Frederick, 590 S Meridian.
Krupp John, 341 S Penn.
Kuechler John, 514 E Washington.
Lanahan Daniel J, 44 S West.
Lange Leonard, rear 104 Bismarck av (H).
Langenberg Henry W, 22 N Delaware.
Lawrence Henry W, n w cor Illinois and Louisiana.
Lehrritter Conrad, 349 Indiana av.
Leible Herman, 270 Howard (W I).
Lenaghan John N, 453 S West.
Lenaghan Neal E, 100 S Illinois.
Lentz Herman, 390 W North.
Lenzen Wm S, 120 E Maryland.
Leukhardt Gottlieb, 102 N Noble.
Levy Myer, 220 W Washington.
Lichtenauer Frederick, 611 W Washington.
Loes John, 102 S Noble.
Logan Martin B, 199 W McCarty.
Lorber Solomon, 200 Prospect.
Louden George R, 250 S West.
Lovinger Daniel, 346 Virginia av.
Lucid Michael, 370 S West.
Ludwig Ernest H, 77 N Alabama.
Lustig John E, 100 E South.
Lutz Christopher C, n e cor Rural and Bloyd av (B).
Lux John, 219 E Washington.
Lyons James H, 1371 W Washington (M J).
Lyons John, 54 S Illinois.
McAree Owen, 249 English av.
McBride James, 110 Michigan (H).
McCarthy Jeremiah F, 105 Harrison.
McCarty Charles, 256 S Delaware.
McHugh Thomas, 299 W Maryland.
McKenna Thomas, 1263 W Washington (M J).
McNelis & Burns, 19 S Illinois.
Madden James H, 748 E Washington.
Mahoney & Amick, 29 Virginia av.
Mangold Frederick, 107 Prospect.
Mann James W, 299 E Washington.
Mantel Emil, 309 E Washington and 223 W Washington.
Markey Thomas J, 255 W Washington.
Martin Louis E, 18 Clifford av.
Matthews Thomas W, 285 Kentucky av.
Matthias Wm F, 123 N Belmont av (H).
Mattler Stephen, 298 E Washington.
Matz & Matz, 33 E Market.
Mauer Henry J, 316 Indiana av.
Meade & McPadden, 319 E Washington.
Meehan Dennis, 16? E Washington.
Meehan Michael, 159 W Washington.
Menne John C, 406 S East.
Merkt August, 201 Mass av.
Merkt Martin, 255 Blake.
Merrick Richard, 432 National rd.
Meyer Frederick A, 400 S Meridian.
Meyer Gustave J T, 74 S Delaware.
Meyer Henry, 250 Highland av.
Meyer John H, 423 S Delaware.
Miller George, 26 Columbia av.
Miller George, 664 S Meridian.
Miller Wm S, 36 E Court.
Mitchell James, 258 S Missouri.
Mitchell Wm J, 154 S New Jersey.
Moeller Wm, 175 Shelby.
Mohs Wm J A & Co, 7 Shelby.
Monninger Gottfried, 101-105 N Illinois.
Moore James H, 245 Mass av.
Moran Harry A, 119 S Illinois.
Moran Martin, 50 S Illinois.
Moran Michael, 28 Michigan (H).
Moran Patrick T, 251 W Washington.
Moriarty James D, 200 Virginia av.
Moser George jr, 187 Madison av.
Moxley James T, 152 W Washington.
Muegge & Lutz, 349 Madison av.

ROOFING MATERIAL C. ZIMMERMAN & SONS SLATE AND GRAVEL ROOFERS, 19 SOUTH EAST STREET.

DRIVEN WELLS And Second Water Wells and Pumps of all kinds at CHARLES KRAUSS', 42 S. PENN. ST., TEL. 465. REPAIRING NEATLY DONE.

Mueller Harry H, 2 Ft Wayne av.
Mueller J Frederick, 262 S Illinois.
Muellerschoen Charles, 27 McCrea.
Mulbarger Wm H, 139 River av (W I).
Mulrine Thomas, 165 Michigan (H).
Munro James R, 1324 Northwestern av (N I).
Murphy John W, s s Washington 1 e of Crawfordsville rd (M J).
Murphy Patrick, 239 W Washington.
Murray John S, 531 Virginia av.
Naughton Patrick, 351 W New York.
Neely Thomas, 76 Kentucky av and 25 S Delaware.
Nessler George, s w cor Cruse and Michigan av.
Nolan Wm H, 175 S Capitol av.
O'Brien Dennis J, 102 Kentucky av.
O'Brien Frank, 28 Germania av (H).
O'Brien Frank, 251 E Washington.
O'Connell Maurice J, 48 S Penn.
O'Connor Eugene, 300 W Maryland.
Okey Wm C, 100 S East.
Oldendorf Theodore T, 150 N Capitol av.
Ostendorf Henry, 81 N Illinois.
Park George R, 243 N Noble.
Parks & Roos, 196 N Senate av.
Parrish Joseph R, 312 E Washington.
Patterson Wm, 88 Malott av.
Peneweit Courtland L, 49 Indiana av.
Peters Mathias, 195 E Washington.
Pink Gustav, 196 Indiana av.
Poehler Henry F, 297 Prospect.
Polster Charles, 149 Indiana av.
Polster Frederick, 144 Indiana av.
Potter Henry W, 103 English av.
Powell George K, 132 S Illinois.
Powers James A, 65 N Illinois.
Powers Thomas, 503 S Capitol av.
Powers Thomas F, 145 E Washington.
Preston Wm, 186 S Illinois.
Pritchett George W, 150 W Vermont.
Pursel John, 810 W Washington.
Quinn James M, 500 S West.
Quinn Malachi F, 249 W South.
Rahke August E, cor River and Oliver avs (W I).
Rappaport Isaac, 143 W Washington.
Rasemann Frederick, 389 N Noble.
Redding James H, 167 Michigan (H).
Reichert Charles A, 307 Prospect.
Reichman Samuel, 274 E Washington.
Reichwein's Hall, 349 E Market.
Reilly James, 199 Meek.
Reinhardt & Brunner, Floral av 1 n of 9th.
Reinken Henry J, 266 E Washington.
Remetter George A, 124 N Pine.
Richardson Bros, 151 Indiana av.
Rieder John, s e cor Morris and Hadley av (W I).
Rieger Leo, 577 S East.
Ries Christian, 149 Columbia av.
Ries John G, 249 Newman.
Ritter Conrad J, 67 N Alabama.
Roeder John, 248 Davidson.
Roeder Wm H, 755 N West.
Roepke & Weiland, 661 Virginia av.
Roesch Frank X, n w cor Station and Glen Drive (B).
Roesener Charles H, 301 Mass av.
Roller John J, 151 W Washington.
Rosasco Angelo, rear 960 N New Jersey.
Rosengarten Henry W, 333 W Morris.
Ross James C, 146 Michigan (H).
Rost Daniel, 1107 E Michigan.
Rozier Edward, 101 Indiana av.
Rozier George H, 50 Indiana av.
Ruemmele Joseph, 850 Morris (W I).
Ruskaup Frederick, 135 N Dorman.
St Clair Charles, 79 E Wabash.
Sanderson James H, 214 W 1st.
Santo Edward J, 204 Indiana av.
Sauter Henry, 231 Shelby.
Schafer Ernst, n w cor English av and Pine.
Schaub John, 167 River av (W I).
Schaub Joseph H, 88 E Washington.
Schieb Peter, 2 S Brightwood av (B).
Schifferdeker Charles, 153 Davidson.
Schissel Otto, cor West and Wabash.
Schmalholz Casper, 29 S Meridian and 9 E Pearl.
Schmidt Anton, 362 Shelby.
Schmidt Anton, 364 Virginia av.
Schneider John B, 474 S Meridian.
Schoen Sigmond, 577 Virginia av.
Schroeder Albert, 299 S Capitol av.
Schuesler Wm, 681 Madison av.
Schuller Theodore C, 110 N Meridian.
Schulz Louis, n s Washington 1 w of Insane Hospital (M J).
Schwartz Martin, 589 S Meridian.
Scott Marion M, 25 E Georgia.
Secrist George H, 190 Dillon.
Secttor Lester, 131 E Washington.
Seidensticker Wm C, 233 S East.
Seiter Christopher, 476 E Washington.
Seitz Charles, 1100 E Washington.
Selb Matthias, 577 S Capitol av.
Shannon Martin E, 1204 E Washington.
Shepherd Henry V, 840 E Washington.
Shine Bros, 112 W Ray.
Siessl John B, 135 E Washington.
Smiley John, 151 W McCarty.
Smith Henry, 41 N Illinois.
Smith Thomas F, Sherman House.
Smith Wm D, 79 N Illinois.
Smith Wm H, 322 S West.
Smoll Louis, s e cor Hazel and Lawrence.
Snider Albert, 63 N Alabama.
Somerville Tilford D, 449 E Washington.
Sommer Louis, 302 Prospect.
Spitzfaden Peter, 201 Virginia av.
Spitzfaden Wm P, s w cor Madeira and Prospect.
Spitznagel Leopold, 920 S Meridian.
Sponsel Henry, 345 Madison av.
Sprengpfeil Henry, 190 Kentucky av.
Stehlin George, 300 N West.
Stehlin John H, 462 N West.
Steinmann Carl, 346 E Washington.
Stellwagen John, 488 S Illinois.
Stephens Jasper J, 32 S Brightwood av (B).
Stevens Charles H, 408 Blake.
Stewart John W, 126 E Wabash.
Stolte Henry, 249 W Maryland.
Stone John, 115 Ft Wayne av.
Stout Wesley A, 178 S Illinois.
Strack Charles, 427 Madison av.
Sullivan Bridget, 301 Bates.
Sullivan Dennis, 114 Agnes.
Sussman Louis, 205 W Ohio.
Sussman Wolf, 304 S Illinois.
Tenner Andreas, 499 S West.
Thompson Charles G, 1400 Northwestern av (N I).
Tipton Charles A, 60 Mass av.
Tivenan Michael P, 402 S Capitol av.
Tobin & Harrison, 650 N Senate av.
Toomey & Dwyer, 17 Monument pl.
Traugott Joachim, 174 River av (W I).
Traugott Louis, 1206 Morris (W I).
Triber Wm, 149 Dunlop.
Tron Wm, 17 N Illinois.
Truemper Charles J, e s Northwestern av nr canal.
Uebelacker Frank, 1205 S Meridian.

If You are not Satisfied with Your Laundry Work Give Us a Trial. ERTEL STEAM LAUNDRY 26 and 28 Indiana Avenue. Telephone 19.

ELLIS & HELFENBERGER { Manufacturers of IRON and WIRE FENCES 162-170 S. SENATE AVE. TEL. 958.

THE HOGAN TRANSFER AND STORAGE COMP'Y
Household Goods and Pianos Moved—Packed—Stored...... Baggage and Package Express Machinery and Safes a Specialty Cor. Washington and Illinois Sts. TELEPHONE No. 675.

Hose, Belting, Packing, Clothing, Druggists' Sundries, Bicycle Tires, Cotton Hose, Etc. New York Belting & Packing Co., L't'd.
The Central Rubber & Supply Co. PHONE 82 79 S. ILLINOIS ST., INDIANAPOLIS, IND.

Saloons—Continued.
Ungar Philip, 98 Russell av.
Vaughn James W, 167 Indiana av.
Victor Henry, 37-39 S Delaware.
Vollrath Charles A, 577 Madison av.
Wachstetter Bros, 56 Indiana av.
Wagner Peter, 858 S Meridian.
Walker Harry A, 75 E Court.
Wallace John B, n w cor Holmes av and Frazee (H).
Wallace Johnston, 64 Malott av.
Walter Herman J, 100 S Noble.
Ward Anthony, 11 Russell av.
Ward Patrick, 832 W Washington.
Ward Patrick W, 671 N Senate av.
Weber Frank L, 186 Blake.
Weber Frederick, 115 Agnes.
Weber John, 50 N Noble.
Weber Louis, 570 W Addison (N I).
Weidman Louis, 136 Clifford av.
Weil Louis, 12 Shelby.
Weilacher John, 92 E Washington.
Weinberger Herman, 14 W Louisiana.
Weinbrecht John G, 134 Michigan (H).
Weiss Wm G, 13 S Meridian.
Weser & Collins, 812 E Washington.
Wessling Henry, 199 Hoyt av.
Williams Jacob R, 102 Howard.
Wilson Benjamin F, 116 S Reisner (W I).
Wilson John H, 396 S Illinois.
Winkler David G, 201 Ft Wayne av.
Witt Gustav C, 251 Michigan av.
Wittenmeier George, 881 Morris (W I).
Witthoft Frederick jr, 329 Indiana av.
Woerner Joseph A, 499 N Senate av.
Wolf Daniel, 152 Michigan (H).
Wolf Valentine, 330 Clifford av.
Wolsiffer John, 827 S Meridian.
Woodward Willis J, 18 S Delaware.
Woolf Marcus, 139 E Washington.
Wulff Johanna, s w cor Morris and Nordyke av (W I).
Wurtz Joseph W, 125 W Washington.
Yearns John B, 129 S Noble.
Young John O, 252 S Capitol av.
Youngman Wm S, 762 E Washington.
Zapf Frederick, 80 W Washington.
Zapf Philip, 42 Virginia av.
Zeien Joseph, 859 S East.
Zimmerman John F, 131 W Washington.
Zschech John C, 401 S Delaware.

***SANATORIUMS.**

Dunning Lehman H (Diseases of Women and Abdominal Surgery), 249 N Alabama.
Eastman Joseph, 197 N Delaware.
Fletcher Wm B, 124 N Alabama.
Keeley Institute, Plainfield, Ind.
Pantzer Hugo O (Surgery and Diseases of Women), 194 E Michigan.
The Dr O S Runnels Sanatorium, 276 N Illinois, Tel 422. (See adv opp Physicians.)

***SAND.**

Balke & Krauss Co, cor Missouri and Market. (See right bottom lines.)
Wasson W G Co The, 130 Indiana av. (See left bottom cor cards and adv in Cement and Lime.)

***SANITARY PLUMBERS.**

Kirkhoff Bros, 102-104 S Penn. (See left top cor cards.)

***SASH, DOORS AND BLINDS.**

(See also Lumber; also Planing Mills.)
Balke & Krauss Co, cor Market and Missouri. (See right bottom lines.)
Byrd Joseph W, 323 Lemcke Bldg. (See adv opp Lumber Mnfrs and Dealers.)
Dalton & Merrifield, 30-50 S Noble. (See left top lines.)
Foster Lumber Co, n w cor St Clair and N Senate av. (See adv in Planing Mills.)
Indianapolis Manufacturers' and Carpenters' Union, 38-42 S New Jersey. (See adv p 2.)
Michigan Lumber Co, 436 E North, cor Fulton. (See embossed line back cover and adv opp Lumber Mnfrs.)
Valdenaire John J, s s Glen Drive 2 w of Gale (B).

***SAVINGS BANKS.**

Indiana Trust Co, Indiana Trust Bldg, s e cor Washington and Virginia av. (See front cover, adv opp p 487 and opp Insurance Agts.)
Lawyers' Loan and Trust Co, 68½ E Market. (See top edge and adv opp p 555.)

SAW MANUFACTURERS.

Atkins E C & Co, 202-216 S Illinois.
Barry W B Saw and Supply Co, 132-134 S Penn.
Farley Thomas, 19 McNabb.
National Saw Guard Co, 128-134 Ft Wayne av.

SAW MILLS.

See Lumber Manufacturers.

SCALE MANUFACTURERS.

Fairbanks, Morse & Co, 100 S Meridian.
Wanamaker Car Scale Co, 46 Thorpe blk.

***SCALE MNFRS—COMPUTING.**

Computing Scale Co of Dayton, O, Spear & Co Genl Agts, 50, 51 and 52 When Bldg.

SCHOOLS.

See Colleges, Schools, Etc.

***SCHOOL SUPPLIES.**

Baker & Thornton, 38 S Meridian.
Mayer Charles & Co, 29-31 W Washington. (See adv opp p 615.)

***SCREEN DOORS AND WINDOWS.**

Indiana Screen Factory, 591-593 Central av near 14th. (See front cover.)
Smith Collins H, 70 Columbia av. (See adv in Door and Window Screens.)

***SCREENS.**

Vonnegut Clemens, 184-186 E Washington. (See left bottom lines.)

OTTO GAS ENGINES | BUILDERS' EXCHANGE S. W. Cor. Ohio and Penn. Telephone 535.

Becker & Son Charles Becker Jacob Becker Jr. Merchant Tailors. 21 N. Penn. St. Tel. 934

SALISBURY & STANLEY OFFICE, STORE AND BANK FIXTURES.

SCULPTORS.

Dunkinson John D, 17 Bell.
Lindenberg Herman A, 49 S Shade (B).
Mahoney John H, 187 Huron.
Saunders Henry R, cor E North and Bee Line Ry.

*SEALS.

Mayer George J, 15 S Meridian. (See left bottom cor cards and p 5.)

SECOND HAND BOOKS.

See Books and Stationery.

SECOND HAND GOODS.

Barrett Haiman, 272 and 281 E Washington.
Bartholomew Silas T, 277 E Washington.
Bernstein Joseph, 235 E Washington.
Boone Frank M, 141 E Washington.
Clune James M, 209 E Washington.
Crosby Michael, 467 S Meridian.
Eldridge Job, 275 Mass av.
Goldberg Bennett, 217 E Washington.
Klein Henry, 189 E Washington.
Lawson Scott, 289 Christian av.
Solomon David, 141½ Mass av.
Thayer & Vannatta, 133 E Washington.
Twente Louis G, 122 Ft Wayne av.
Winkler Joseph, 141 Mass av.
Wulfson Isidor, 296 E Washington.

*SEEDS.

Conde H T Implement Co, 27-33 N Capitol av.
Everitt J A Seedsman, 50 N Delaware and 121-123 W Washington.
Huntington & Page, 78 E Market. (See adv p 5.)
Lee Charles E, 145 E Mkt House.
Russe Henry, 23-25 N Capitol av.
Vail Seed Co, 96 N Delaware.

*SEWER PIPE.

Adams J D & Co, 30 Jackson Pl, opp north entrance to Union Station.
Balke & Krauss Co, cor Market and Missouri. (See right bottom lines.)
Duncan Samuel E, 157 Mass av.
Wasson W G Co The, 130 Indiana av. (See left bottom cor cards and adv in Cement and Lime.)

SEWING MACHINES.

Brown Elmer E, 194 Virginia av.
Carey Benjamin F, 211 W Washington.
Kaiser Wm, 654 Virginia av.
Pfleger Joseph C, 174 E Washington.
Singer Mnfg Co The, 72-74 W Washington.
Stephens Rufus E, 19 Mass av.
Willcox & Gibbs, 108 N Penn.

*SHEET IRON WORKS.

Abel & Doyle, 31 Indiana av. (See adv p 5.)
Capital City Steam Boiler and Sheet Iron Works, 207-209 S Illinois. (See adv in Boilermakers.)
Ensey O B, cor 6th and Illinois. (See left bottom cor cards.)
Kennedy & Connaughton, 207-209 S Illinois. (See adv in Boilermakers.)

*SHEET METAL ROOFERS.

Laing Samuel, 72-74 E Court. (See left side lines.)

*SHEET METAL WORKS.

Ensey O B, cor 6th and Illinois. (See left bottom cor cards.)
Gardner Joseph, 37-41 Kentucky av. (See left top cor cards.)
Laing Samuel, 72-74 E Court. (See left side lines.)
McWorkman Willard, 930 W Washington. (See left top cor cards.)

SHINGLE MANUFACTURERS.

Clay Shingle Co, 1 Ingalls blk.

*SHIRT MANUFACTURERS.

Grafftey, Ault & Co, 38 E Washington.
Harding Altus M, 18½ N Meridian.
Harris Henry W, 277 N East.

SHOEMAKERS.

See Boot and Shoe Makers.

SHOOTING GALLERIES.

Ungerer Bernard, 129 W Washington.

*SHORTHAND SCHOOLS.

Indiana Shorthand College, Consolidated Indianapolis Business University, When Bldg, E J Heeb Propr. (See front cover, right bottom lines and p 4.)
Indianapolis Business University, When Bldg, N Penn (Bryant & Stratton and Indianapolis Business Colleges Consolidated), E J Heeb Propr. (See front cover, right bottom lines and p 4.)
Shorthand Training School, 49-55 Thorpe Blk.

*SHOW CASE MANUFACTURERS.

Wiegel Wm, 6 W Louisiana. (See right side lines and adv.)

WILLIAM WIEGEL,
Manufacturer of Fine
Show Cases and Glass Counters
No. 6 West Louisiana Street,
Opposite East End Union Railroad Station.

*SILVERSMITHS.

Walk Julius C & Son, 12 E Washington. (See left bottom cor cards.)

SINGLETREE MANUFACTURERS.

Hall George B, cor Judge Harding and Vandalia R R (W I).

*SKATES AND SLEIGHS.

Mayer Charles & Co, 29-31 W Washington. (See adv opp p 615.)

...ors and Builders. Repairing of all kinds done on short notice. 177 Clinton St, Indianapolis, Ind. Telephone 999

LUMBER Sash and Doors BALKE & KRAUSS CO., Corner Market and Missouri Sts.

Friedgen Has the BEST PATENT LEATHER SHOES AT LOWEST PRICES. 19 North Pennsylvania St.

SAMUEL LAING! HOT AIR FURNACES 72 AND 74 EAST COURT STREET.

*SKYLIGHTS.

Ensey O B, cor 6th and Illinois. (See left bottom cor cards.)

Gardner Joseph, 37-41 Kentucky av. (See left top cor cards.)

Laing Samuel, 72-74 E Court. (See left side lines.)

McWorkman Willard, 930 W Washington. (See left top cor cards.)

*SLATE ROOFERS.

(See also Roofers.)

McWorkman Willard, 930 W Washington. (See left top cor cards.)

Zimmerman C & Sons, 19-21 S East. (See left bottom lines.)

*SMOKERS' ARTICLES.

Mayer Charles & Co, 29-31 W Washington. (See adv opp p 615.)

SOAP MANUFACTURERS.

Andrews Edgar C, Drover s of Morris st bridge (W I).
Bergmann Francis J, 251 W Morris.
Hinkle Leonard, 174 W Market.
Hoosier Mnfg Co, 192 S Illinois.
Olds Wm, 292 W Ray.
Paulish Wm T, 94 English av.
Williams Wm, 273 W McCarty.
Williams & Hunt, 701 S West.

*SOAP POWDER MANUFACTURERS.

Elam Mnfg Co, 26-30 W Georgia.

*SODA ASH.

Moffat & Co, 402 Lemcke Bldg. (See adv p 9.)

SODA APPARATUS MNFRS.

Neff & Co, 82 S Delaware.

*SODA WATER MANUFACTURERS.

(See also Mineral Water Mnfrs.)

Metzger Jacob & Co, 30-32 E Maryland.

*SPECTACLES AND EYEGLASSES.

Mayhew James N, 13 N Meridian. (See right bottom cor cards.)

SPOKE MANUFACTURERS.

Indiana Spoke Co, 658 N Alabama.
West Tennessee Spoke and Lumber Co, 658 N Alabama.

*SPORTING GOODS.

Hay & Willits Mnfg Co The, 76 N Penn. (See left bottom cor cards.)

Mayer Charles & Co, 29-31 W Washington. (See adv opp p 615.)

SPRING BED MNFRS.

Laycock T B Mnfg Co, n w cor 1st and canal.
Puritan Spring Bed Co The, 952 N New Jersey.

*SPRING AND SUMMER TOYS.

Mayer Charles & Co, 29-31 W Washington. (See adv opp p 615.)

*STAIR BUILDERS.

(See also Carpenters and Contractors.)

Indianapolis Manufacturers' and Carpenters' Union, 38-42 S New Jersey. (See adv p 2.)

Mueller Albert C, 323 Mass av.
Mueller John A D, 310 N Noble.
Roberts L & Son, 177 Duncan.

Salisbury & Stanley, 177 Clinton. (See right side lines.)

Sloan & Matkins, s e cor 7th and L E & W R R. (See adv.)

Sloan & Matkins,
STAIR BUILDERS.
Manufacturers of Grilles, Fretwork, Etc.
Special attention to orders, and Estimates Furnished.
443-463 E. St. Clair St. Telephone 677

Springer Amos M, w s Hubbard 1 s of Clifford av.
Watts James H, rear 321 E Michigan.
Wernsing & Haenggi, 628 E New York.

STAMPING AND EMBROIDERY.

Lueders Misses, 460 N Senate av. (See adv.)

MISSES LUEDERS
DEALERS IN
Materials for Embroidering, Lace, Braids, Etc.
STAMPING
A SPECIALTY.
Lessons Given in Needle Work and Painting.
460 North Senate Avenue.

O'Neill Esther, 8 N Penn.

STARCH MANUFACTURERS.

National Starch Mnfg Co The, s w cor Morris and Dakota.

*STATIONERS—WHOLESALE.

Baker & Thornton, 38 S Meridian.

Bowen-Merrill Co The, 9-11 W Washington.

Burford Wm B, 21 W Washington. (See adv opp p 230.)

Indianapolis Printing Co, 37-39 Virginia av.

WEDDING CAKE BOXES · SULLIVAN & MAHAN 41 W. Pearl St.

DIAMOND WALL PLASTER { Telephone 1410 BUILDERS' EXCHANGE.

Levey Bros & Co, 19 W Maryland. (See adv opp p 567.)

Smith Frank H, 22 N Penn. (See adv opp p 803.)

*STATIONERS—MANUFACTURING.

Smith Frank H, 22 N Penn. (See opp p 803.)

*STATIONERS' SUNDRIES.

Mayer Charles & Co, 29-31 W Washington. (See adv opp p 615.)

*STATUARY—MARBLE.

Diener August, 243 E Washington; Branch Works opp east entrance Crown Hill Cemetery. (See front edge and adv opp Monuments.)

STAVE AND HEADING MNFRS.

Balke & Krauss Co, cor Missouri and Market. (See right bottom lines.)

Blair & Failey, 2 Ingalls blk.

Minter Albert F, s end California. (See adv p 9.)

*STEAM PUMPS.

Dean Bros' Steam Pump Works, 1st near cor Senate av. (See adv p 3.)

Worthington Henry R, 64 S Penn. (See left top lines.)

*STEAM, WATER AND GAS SUPPLIES.

Knight & Jillson, 75 S Penn.

*STEAM AND GAS FITTERS.

(See also Plumbers, Steam and Gas Fitters.)

Farrell J S & Co, 84 N Illinois. (See left bottom cor cards.)

Hussey & Baker, 116 N Delaware. (See adv in Plumbers.)

Kirkhoff Bros, 102-104 S Penn. (See left top cor cards.)

*STEAM AND HOT WATER HEATING.

Farrell J S & Co, 84 N Illinois. (See left bottom cor cards.)

Kirkhoff Bros, 102-104 S Penn. (See left top cor cards.)

*STEAMSHIP LINES.

CUNARD, WHITE STAR, AMERICAN, NORTH GERMAN LLOYD, HAMBURG, ANTWERP, FRENCH LINE, ANCHOR, RED STAR OF ANTWERP AND ALLAN LINE, A Metzger Agency Agts, 5 Odd Fellows' Hall. (See left bottom lines.)

*STEAMSHIP PASSAGE.

Frenzel Bros, s w cor Washington and Meridian.

Metzger A Agency, 5 Odd Fellows' Hall. (See left bottom lines.)

STEEL MANUFACTURERS.

American Steel Co, cor Senate av and W Merrill.

Gould Steel Co, 143½ S Meridian.

*STEEL ROOFING.

Indianapolis Steel Roofing and Corrugating Works, 23-25 E South. (See right side lines.)

Long Steel and Iron Roofing Co The, 180-186 W 5th. (See adv in Roofers.)

McWorkman Willard, 930 W Washington. (See left top cor cards.)

*STEEL STAMPS.

Mayer George J, 15 S Meridian. (See left bottom cor cards and p 5.)

*STENCIL CUTTERS.

Mayer George J, 15 S Meridian. (See left bottom cor cards and p 5.)

Zaiser Lenoir T F, 21½ W Washington.

STENOGRAPHERS.

Baker Mamie C, 601 Indiana Trust bldg.
Bowser Allen A, 225 Lemcke bldg.
Bryan Alma L Mrs, 135 E Pratt.
Evans Rowland, P O bldg.
Garber & Carpenter, 51 Court House.
Hardy & Hansen, 501 Lemcke bldg.

Indianapolis Business University, When Bldg, N Penn (Bryant & Stratton and Indianapolis Business Colleges Consolidated), E J Heeb Propr. (See front cover, right bottom lines and p 4.)

Johnson & Metcalf, 81 Court House.
Jones Adelaide E, 702 Lemcke bldg.

Shorthand Training School, 49-55 Thorpe Blk.

Van Laningham Mary P, 24, 68½ E Market.

*STENOGRAPHIC INSTITUTES.

Indianapolis Business University, When Bldg, N Penn (Bryant & Stratton and Indianapolis Business Colleges Consolidated), E J Heeb Propr. (See front cover, right bottom lines and p 4.)

STOCK YARDS.

Union Stock Yards, crossing I & V and Belt R R (W I).

*STONE CRUSHERS.

Adams J D & Co, 30 Jackson Pl, opp north entrance to Union Depot.

STONE QUARRIES.

Bedford Indiana Stone Co, 25-26 Baldwin blk.
Romona Oolitic Stone Co, 15 Ingalls blk.
St Paul Quarries, 6 Builders' Exchange.

STONE YARDS.

Goddard Samuel, Kentucky av and White River.
Ittenbach G & Co, 150 Harrison.
Klinck & Matthews, Kentucky av and White river.
Schmid J C & Sons, 329 Bates.

Best Work. Prompt Delivery. { THE HOME LAUNDRY 197 S. ILLINOIS ST. TEL. 1769. { Collars and Cuffs our Specialty.

THE WM. H. BLOCK CO. 7 AND 9 EAST WASHINGTON STREET. DRY GOODS, HOUSE FURNISHINGS AND CROCKERY.

London Guarantee and Accident Co. (Ltd.) All forms of Liability Insurance, Workmen's Collective Insurance, Fidelity Bonds and Individual Accident Insurance.
Geo. W. Pangborn, Gen. Agent, 704-706 Lemcke Bldg. Telephone 140.

Prussian National Insurance Company OF STETTIN, GERMANY. ORGANIZED 1845. FRANK K. SAWYER, AGENT 74 East Market Street. Telephone 863.

STORAGE.

Anderson Mads P, 381-385 Cedar.
Hamilton Sanford P, 11 S Alabama.
Harris & Puryear, 76-78 W New York.
Hogan Transfer and Storage Co The, s w cor Washington and Illinois. (See left top lines and adv in Transfer Companies.)
Indianapolis Storage and Transfer Co, 370-372 S Delaware. (See back cover.)
Indianapolis Warehouse Co, 265 S Penn.
Shover Charles E, 180-188 E Wabash.
Union Transfer and Storage Co, n e cor E Ohio and C C C & St L Ry. (See left side lines.)

*STORE FIXTURES.

Salisbury & Stanley, 177 Clinton. (See right side lines.)
Scott W A & Sons, 591-593 Central av. (See front cover.)

*STORE SERVICE.

Lamson Consolidated Store Service Co, 31½ Virginia av. (See adv in Cash Carriers.)

*STORE AND OFFICE FIXTURES.

Killinger George W, s w cor Market and Missouri. (See adv in Saloons.)
Salisbury & Stanley, 177 Clinton. (See right side lines.)

STOVE MANUFACTURERS.

Famous Stove Co, 135 S Meridian.
Home Stove Co The, 79 S Meridian.
Indianapolis Stove Co The, 71-73 S Meridian.
Turner Zephyr Furnace and Stove Co, 94-100 Kentucky av and 81 S Senate av.

STOVE REPAIRERS.

Hellstern August A, 289 E Washington.

*STOVES AND RANGES.

Kotteman Wm, 89-91 E Washington. (See right top lines.)
Messenger W Horndon, 101 E Washington and 13, 15 and 17 S Delaware. (See left bottom lines.)

STOVES AND TINWARE.

(See also Hardware.)

Efroymson Harry, 157 E Washington.
Haueisen & Hartmann, 163-169 E Washington. (See right bottom cor cards.)
Sahrn Ludwig, E Mkt House.
Seiner Charles F, 87 E Mkt House.
Sellers Daniel, 247 Indiana av.
Wolfram Charles A, 197 E Washington.

*STRAW STACKER MNFRS.

Indiana Manufacturing Co, Office 401-405 Indiana Trust Bldg, Factory cor I & St L R R and Missouri.

SUBSCRIPTION BOOK PUBLISHERS.

Bowen-Merrill Co The, 9-11 W Washington.
Collier Peter F, 93 N Delaware.
Cox Eugene T, 17 Talbott blk.
Douglass Robert, 11½ N Meridian.
Union Publishing Co, 29 Baldwin blk.

*SURETY COMPANIES.

Fidelity and Deposit Co of Maryland, George W Pangborn Genl Agt, 704-706 Lemcke Bldg. (See left top lines.)
London Guarantee and Accident Co (Limited) of London, England, George W Pangborn Genl Agt, 704-706 Lemcke Bldg. (See left top lines.)
Marion Trust Co The, s e cor Market and Monument Pl. (See back cover.)

*SURGEONS.

Castor Hiram C, 288 Mass av.
Eisenbeiss Erastus M, 254½ W Washington.
Falk Frederick, 47½ S Illinois.
Jameson Henry, 28 E Ohio.
Jameson Patrick H, 28 E Ohio.
Marsee Joseph W, 106½ E New York.
Pantzer Hugo O (Surgery and Diseases of Women), 194 E Michigan.
Schaefer C Richard, 430 Madison av.

SURGICAL INSTITUTES.

Allen H R National Surgical Institute The, n w cor Ohio and Capitol av, opp State House.
Electro Cure Institute, 29½ W Ohio.
Indianapolis Infirmary, 60 Monument Pl. (See adv.)
Indianapolis Medical and Surgical Institute, 60 Monument Pl. (See adv.)
Wilson Surgical Institute, Charles A Wilson, M D (Faculty Prize Medical College of Ohio, 1879), Propr, 81 W Ohio.

SURGICAL INSTRUMENT MNFRS.

Armstrong Wm H & Co, 77 S Illinois.

SUSPENDER MANUFACTURERS.

Indianapolis Suspender Co, 144-150 S Meridian.

SYRUP REFINERS.

Barton Wm H, 501 W Washington.

*TACKLE BLOCKS.

Vonnegut Clemens, 184-186 E Washington. (See left bottom lines.)

TAILORS.

(See also Clothing and Merchant Tailors.)

Anderberg Martin, 29½ N Penn.
Anderberg Nils, 43 Hubbard blk.
Andrews the Tailor, s e cor Illinois and Washington.
Barry John, 29 Indiana av.
Becker & Son, 21 N Penn. (See right top lines.)
Brautigam John M, 149 Mass av.
Butterworth Charles W L, 18½ N Penn.
Caldwell Oscar, 50½ S Illinois.

United States Life Insurance Co., of New York.
E. B. SWIFT. M'g'r. 25 E. Market St.

WM. KOTTEMAN } 89 & 91 E. Washington St. Telephone 1742 { RUGS MATTINGS WINDOW SHADES

WILLIAM WIEGEL { MANUFACTURER OF..... } SHOW CASES { 6 W. Louisiana St. Opposite Union Station.

Diseases Treated and Cured by the Indianapolis Infirmary.

Class One—Chronic Diseases of the Nose, Throat and Lungs. Catarrh treated by our new method. Thousands cured.

Class Two—Chronic Diseases of the Eye and Ear.

Class Three—Chronic Diseases of the Heart, Stomach, Liver and Kidneys.

Class Four—Chronic Diseases of the Rectum and Bladder. Piles and Rupture cured without the knife.

Class Five—Chronic Diseases of Men and Women.

Class Six—Chronic Diseases of the Nervous System.

Class Seven—Deformities of the Human Body. We manufacture all kinds of apparatus and appliances in our own shops at Infirmary.

20th Century Discovery

X-RAY AND OZONE INHALATION

Combined destroy Tubercle Baccilli and Cure Consumption, discovered by the Scientists of this Infirmary. Examinations with

The Largest X-Ray Apparatus in the World.

The Largest Fluoroscope ever made.

No more groping in the dark.

No more experimental cutting.

We invite the medical profession to bring their obscure medical and surgical cases for examination, and know positively what is wrong before treatment is commenced.

Women's Dep't in charge of Lady Specialist.

STAFF OF EXPERT SPECIALISTS.

Thirty beds for patients. Established 1869.

Hours, 8 to 8. **Telephone 1434.**

Indianapolis Infirmary, 60 Monument Place, Indianapolis, Ind.

Q. VAN HUMMELL, M. D., Medical Director.

Carlson Gustav, 27 Commercial blk.
Christensen Christian, 99½ Mass av.
Cotter James, 8½ E Washington.
Demaree Claude R, 12 Commercial blk.
Demaree & Fisse, 41 Virginia av.
Denker Charles, 594 Virginia av.
Dippel Charles L, 420 S Meridian.
Erdman David, 97 N Meridian.
Fette Conrad F, 205 S Noble.
Foster Edward, 8 Monument pl.
Gerstner Anthony J, 171 E Washington.
Glaescher Frederick, 159 Virginia av.
Gramling Wm C, 96 N Illinois.
Hahn Margaret, 264 S Illinois.
Heidenreich John J, 20 Commercial blk.
Henninger Frederick W, 336 E Market.
Kelly Patrick J, 1098 E Washington.
Keystone Co, 17 Mass av.
Klass John, 746 Chestnut.
Kleinschmidt Frederick, 442 E Georgia.
Kline Leo, 59 Ingalls blk.
Koenig Maurice, 81 N Delaware.
Kribs Edward J, 177 S Illinois.
Kribs Jacob, 181½ S Meridian.
Kunz Joseph F, 459 S Meridian.
Leppert Leopold, 79 E Washington.
McPhetridge John M, 39 Journal bldg.
Madison Caswell H, 436 Mass av.
Menning Wm F, 121 Prospect.
Mescall Michael J, 10½ N Delaware.
Miller Harry S, 18 S Illinois.
Moore Thomas, 7 Indiana av.
Mueller Leonhard, 40 S Illinois.
Muhlbacher Frank, 420 Virginia av.
Nelson Andrew, 452 E North.
Nelson Charles, 803 N Illinois.
Nesbitt Daniel L, 12½ Indiana av.

DIRECTORIES OF ALL THE STATES AND PRINCIPAL CITIES ON FILE FOR REFERENCE AT OUR OFFICE.

R. L. POLK & CO.

23-24 JOURNAL BLDG.

CARPETS AND RUGS RENOVATED.......... | CAPITAL STEAM CARPET CLEANING WORKS M. D. PLUNKETT, TELEPHONE No. 818

BENJ. BOOTH PRACTICAL EXPERT ACCOUNTANT. Complicated or disputed accounts investigated and adjusted. Room 18, 82½ E. Wash. St., Ind'p'l's, Ind.

18 and 20 South Meridian Street KERSHNER BROS., Proprs. THE SHERMAN RESTAURANT

INDIANA GRAPHOPHONE CO.

SPEAR & CO., General Agents,

49, 50, 51, 52 WHEN BUILDING.

Talking Machines,

Records, Supplies, Etc.

Slot Machines sold on Monthly Payments. Send for full descriptive catalogue. ☞ Agents wanted.

Tailors—Continued.

Nessler Frank & Co, 56 E Market. (See right top cor cards.)
Nick The Tailor, 78 N Illinois. (See adv opp.)
O'Connor Patrick, 35½ E Washington.
Patton Wm H, 118½ Mass av.
Pich Frederick W, 62 Nebraska.
Porter Theodore R, 16½ E Washington.
Poulsen Lars P, 20 Kentucky av.
Rahm Herman, 40 Michigan (H).
Rasmussen Lars P, 531 W Udell (N I).
Reuwer Henry, 63 W Market.
Roach John, 25 W Ohio.
Ruggieri Michael, 237 S Delaware.
Sanger Philip, 99 Benton.
Schmidt August C, 22 S Illinois.
Schmidt Gottlieb H, 640 Virginia av.
Schwartz Louis, 362 Mass av.
Segal Jacob, 274 S Illinois.
Seidensticker Louis H, 70 S Austin (B).
Semmler Henry, 216 S Olive.
Silverstein Abraham, 317 E Washington.
Smith Wm H, 24 S Illinois.
Steinmann John, 15 Buchanan.
Stowers & Jones, 95 S Illinois.
Suess Max B, 189½ E Washington.
Fisch Stanislaus T, 834 S Meridian.
Von Burg Joseph J, 261 Mass av.
Washington John M, 66¼ N Penn.
Weinberger Louis, 19 Kentucky av.
White Hughes W, 56½ N Illinois.
Wilkinson John, 18½ N Meridian.
Wilson Susan J, 571 E Washington.
Young George F, 34 Indiana av.

TAILORS' TRIMMINGS.

Rosenberg George U, 11½ N Meridian.

*TALKING MACHINES.

Indiana Graphophone Co, 50, 51 and 52 When Bldg. (See adv.)

TANNERS.

Gray Frank, S Belmont av s of Johnson (W I).

TAXIDERMISTS.

Noe Fletcher M, 64 W Market.

TEAS AND COFFEES.

(See also Grocers.)

Coffy Adelbert B, 130 Mass av.
Courtney Zachary T, 122 Mass av.
Ganote Edwin M, 100 Mass av.
Great Atlantic and Pacific Tea Co The, 20 W Washington and 152 E Washington.
Heekin James & Co, 25 W Georgia.
Lee Henry H, 34 W Washington, 250 Virginia av, 7-9 N Penn and 1 Madison av.
Mueller Rudolph M, 61 Mass av.
O'Mahoney Patrick J, 12 E Mkt House.

TELEGRAPH COMPANIES.

Postal Telegraph Cable Co, 9-11 S Meridian.
Western Union Telegraph Co, 19 S Meridian.

*TELEGRAPH INSTITUTES.

Indianapolis Business University, When Bldg, N Penn (Bryant & Stratton and Indianapolis Business Colleges Consolidated), E J Heeb Propr. (See front cover, right bottom lines and p 4.)

TELEPHONE COMPANIES.

American Telephone and Telegraph Co, 14 S Meridian and 131 W 22d.
Central Union Telephone Co, s w cor Illinois and Ohio.
Universal Telephone Co, 86 E Market.

*TELEPHONE MANUFACTURERS.

Elliott Larkin V, 690 N Capitol av.

*TENTS—WHOLESALE.

Mayer Charles & Co, 29-31 W Washington. (See adv opp p 615.)

TENTS

See Awnings and Tents.

TERRA COTTA MANUFACTURERS.

Indianapolis Terra Cotta Co, s w cor Bloyd av and Morris (B).

THEATERS.

Empire Theater, n w cor Delaware and Wabash.
English's Opera House, n s Monument pl bet Market and Meridian.
Grand Opera House, 73 N Penn.
Park Theater, 98 W Washington.

TUTEWILER UNDERTAKER, No. 72 WEST MARKET STREET. TELEPHONE 216.

"NICK The Tailor"

THE OLD CLOTHES RENOVATOR

If you try him you will find his WORK FIRST-CLASS AND PRICES REASONABLE.

Fine Repairing a Specialty.

Overcoats Shortened to Latest Style.

SUITS MADE TO ORDER FROM $12.00 Up

Suits Cleaned and Pressed, - - 50 Cents
Pants Pressed with Crease, - - 15 Cents

AT

78 NORTH ILLINOIS ST.

DALTON & MERRIFIELD { LUMBER South Noble St., near E. Washington

INDIANA ELECTROTYPE CO. ••• BEST WORK. LOWEST PRICES. 23 WEST PEARL ST., INDIANAPOLIS, IND. JOB WORK. BOOK PLATES. BEST PATENT BASE ON THE MARKET. All Orders Promptly Filled.

TICKET BROKERS.

Gerard "The Ticket Man," s w cor Washington and Illinois.
Goldberg Abe H, 112 S Illinois.
Hervey T M & Co, 15 S Illinois.
Powell & Harter, 130 S Illinois.
Slatts & Poe, 122 S Illinois.
Solomon Henry, 25 S Illinois.
Webb Charles P, 5 and 128 S Illinois.

*TILE—FLOOR AND HEARTH.

Diener August, 243 E Washington; Branch Works opp east entrance Crown Hill Cemetery. (See front edge and adv opp Monuments.)
Huey M S & Son, 551 Mass av. (See adv p 5.)
Lilly Jno M, 78-80 Mass av. (See adv p 8.)
United States Encaustic Tile Works, cor 7th and Big Four Ry.

TIN CAN MANUFACTURERS.

Dugdale Can Co, S Meridian and Belt R R.

TIN PLATE MANUFACTURERS.

American Tin Plate Co The, 805, 806 and 807 Majestic bldg.

*TIN PLATE MNFRS' SUPPLIES.

Moffat & Co, 402 Lemcke Bldg. (See adv p 9.)

TINNERS.

(See also Stoves and Tinware.)

Abel & Doyle, 31 Indiana av. (See adv p 5.)
Bakemeyer Andrew H, 359 Indiana av.
Baker & Fleehart, 141 Ash.
Betts Howell T, rear 457 W Eugene (N I).
Bouvy Julius H, 533 Virginia av.
Branham & Lowther, 294 E Washington.
Braughton McCullough C, 250 Mass av.
Brown Joseph H, 18 Prospect.
Cooney Seiner & Co, 17 E South.
Cox Richard, 516 E 7th.
Crompton Ebenezer R, 86 Mass av.
Donnan Wallace, 74 Mass av.
Ehrich Wm G, 63 W Washington.
Enders C F August, 506 E Washington.
Ensey O B, cor 6th and Illinois. (See left bottom cor cards.)
Eschenbach Moritz, 605 Madison av.
Francis James B, 392 E Michigan.
Gardner Joseph, 37-41 Kentucky av. (See left top cor cards.)
Gauss Charles A, 67 Russell av.
Gerkin John, 1547 N Illinois.
Gurley Schuyler C, 67½ W Georgia.
Hersh Jacob, 278 W Washington.
Hoover J J & Son, 485 S Delaware.
Kalb John, 751 N Illinois.
Laing Samuel, 72-74 E Court. (See left side lines.)
Laut H W & Co, 350 E South.
Loy David M, 234 S Meridian.
McCain Joseph C, 114 Oliver av (W I).
McWorkman Willard, 930 W Washington. (See left top cor cards.)
Madaris Wm T J, 237 Mass av.
Miller & Albrecht, 208 E Washington.
Off Christian & Co, 230 E Washington.
Roland Herman A, 284 E Merrill.
Sheppard Wm C, 541 W Udell (N I).
Smith Arthur, 18 N Senate av.
Steeb John, 813 S East.
Thomas Charles, 471 W Michigan.
Turner Robert L, 43 N Rural.
Weakley Jeremiah A, 317 W Washington.
Willis Jonathan, 448 Indiana av.

*TINNERS' SUPPLIES.

Tanner & Sullivan, 116-118 S Meridian.

*TITLE EXAMINERS.

Rosebrock C Henry, 19 Thorpe Blk. (See back cover.)

*TOBACCO—LEAF.

Gray & Lodge, 25-27 W Pearl.
Indianapolis Leaf Tobacco Co, 71 E Court.
Kavanagh James L, 54 S Penn.
Levy Percival, 81 E Court.

TOBACCO MANUFACTURERS.

Cheely George W, 41 Belmont av.
Hardy Charles T, 480 E Washington.
Indianapolis Tobacco Works, 35-37 S Alabama.

*TOILET ARTICLES.

Mayer Charles & Co, 29-31 W Washington. (See adv opp p 615.)

*TOILET SUPPLY COMPANIES.

American Toilet Supply Co, 26 S Illinois. (See adv.)

American
TOILET SUPPLY
Company

Towels and Toilet Supplies for Offices, Stores, Hotels, Saloons, Restaurants and Barber Shops.

Office, 26 South Illinois Street.

'PHONE 1091.

*TOMBSTONES.

Diener August, 243 E Washington; Branch Works opp east entrance Crown Hill Cemetery. (See front edge and adv opp Monuments.)

TOOL MANUFACTURERS.

Chapin Edward J, 500 W Washington.
Dearinger Frank B, rear 313 E Georgia.
Reliance Edge Tool Co, cor Eugene and canal (N I).
Youngerman Conrad W, 176 Dearborn.

YOUR HOMES FURNISHED BY W. H. MESSENGER 101 East Washington St. Telephone 491.

McNamara, Koster & Co. Phone 1593. 212-218 S. PENN. ST. PATTERN MAKERS

*TOOLS.

Vonnegut Clemens, 184-186 E Washington. (See left bottom lines.)

TOYS—WHOLESALE.

Mayer Charles & Co, 29-31 E Washington. (See adv opp p 615.)

*TOYS—RETAIL.

Haueisen & Hartmann, 163-169 E Washington. (See right bottom cor cards.)

TRANSFER COMPANIES.

Anderson Mads P, 381-385 Cedar.
Behrent Charles F, 199 Harrison.
Bird Frank Transfer Co, General Office 24 Pembroke Arcade; Branches 115 N Delaware, Bates House and Union Station. (See adv.)

FRANK BIRD TRANSFER CO.
General Office, 24 Pembroke Arcade.
Offices { Union Station. 115 North Delaware and Bates House.
Stable, 115 North Delaware.
Order by Telephone Day or Night. | Baggage Checked at Residence | Carriages for Parties, Weddings, Depot, etc.
Telephone 534.

Circle Transfer Co, 90 W Market.
Dumas James T, 27 Bicking.
Green & Co, 63-69 W Market.
Hamilton Sanford P, 11 S Alabama.
Harris & Puryear, 76-78 W New York.

Hogan Transfer and Storage Co The, s w cor Washington and Illinois. (See left top lines and adv.)

HOGAN
TRANSFER AND STORAGE CO.
Household Goods and Pianos Moved, Packed and Stored. | Baggage and Package Express. Machinery and Safes a Specialty.
OFFICES { Delaware & Georgia Sts. Washington & Illinois Sts. Phone 675

Indianapolis Storage and Transfer Co, 370-372 S Delaware. (See back cover.)

Jenkins John, 11 N Alabama.
Koepke Frederick, 504 Chestnut.
Lehman's Transfer Office, 19 Monument pl.
McDonald Milton R, 20 Roanoke.

Meck Transfer Co, 7 Monument Pl. (See adv.)

Meck's Transfer Co.
PIANO AND
HOUSEHOLD MOVING.
Furniture Crating and Packing a Specialty.
Baggage and General Transfer.
Draying of all kinds.
Special attention given to the Freight Depots.
Phone 335. Office, 7 Circle.

Railroad Transfer Co, cor Alabama and Virginia av.
Reinecke Frederick, 243 Union.
Shover Charles E, 180-188 E Wabash.
Sweetland Henry, 42 E Maryland.
Union Transfer and Storage Co, n e cor E Ohio and C C C & St L Ry. (See left side lines.)
Walker George W, 34 Manument pl.

TRANSPORTATION LINES.

Blue Line, 1 Board of Trade bldg.
Central States Dispatch Fast Freight Line, 1 Lorraine bldg.
Commerce Despatch Line, 1011-1012 Majestic bldg.
Empire Fast Freight Line, 67 W Maryland.
Erie Despatch, 46 W Washington.
Hoosac Tunnel Line, 15 Union bldg.
Kanawha Despatch, n e cor Delaware and South.
Lackawanna Fast Freight Line, 71 W Maryland.
Lake Erie & Western R R, Local Freight Office 53 S Alabama. (See opp inside back cover.)
Lake Shore-Lehigh Valley Route, n e cor Delaware and South.
Merchants' Despatch Transportation Co, 24 S Penn.
Midland Fast Freight Line, 26 S Illinois.
Nickel Plate Line, 2 Board of Trade bldg.
Traders' Despatch, 23 Board of Trade bldg.
Union Line, 28-29 Commercial Club bldg.
West Shore Fast Freight Line, 1 E Washington.
White Line Fast Freight, 1 E Washington.

*TRAVELING SATCHELS.

Mayer Charles & Co, 29-31 W Washington. (See adv opp p 615.)

*TREES AND PLANTS.

Burkhart Harvey A & Sons, 492 S Meridian. (See adv opp p 232.)

*TRUCKS (FOR FACTORIES AND WAREHOUSES.)

Dietz Fred Co The, 370-406 Madison av. (See right side lines and adv p 10.)

THE FRED DIETZ CO. WOODEN PACKING BOXES MADE TO ORDER FACTORY AND WAREHOUSE TRUCKS. 40 Madison Avenue. Telephone 654.

Business World Supplied with Help
GRADUATES ASSISTED TO POSITIONS
10,000 NOW IN GOOD SITUATIONS. TEL. 499. E. J. HEEB, PRES.
Indianapolis BUSINESS UNIVERSITY

NEW YORK FILTER MFG. CO. Filters for Water-Works, Boiler Plants, Laundries, Hotels, Private Residences, Etc.
Henry R. Worthington, 64 S. Pennsylvania St. Long Distance Telephone 284.

UNION CO-OPERATIVE LAUNDRY (OF UNION LAUNDRY GIRLS.) NOS. 38, 40 AND 42 VIRGINIA AVENUE. TELEPHONES 1269. INDIANAPOLIS, IND. T. E. SOMERVILLE, MANAGER

TRUNK MNFRS AND DEALERS.

Bogert James & Sons, 40 W Washington.
Morrison Lewis E, 2 N Meridian.
Shilling Richard L, 55 W Washington.
Smith Robert L, 244 Indiana av.

*TRUNK MOVERS.

Hogan Transfer and Storage Co The, s w cor Washington and Illinois and cor Delaware and Georgia. (See left top lines and adv in Transfer Companies.)

TRUST COMPANIES.

Fidelity and Deposit Co of Maryland, George W Pangborn Genl Agt, 704-706 Lemcke Bldg. (See left top lines.)
Indiana Trust Co The, Indiana Trust Bldg, s e cor Washington and Virginia av. (See front cover, opp p 487 and opp Insurance Agts.)
Lawyers' Loan and Trust Co, 68½ E Market. (See adv top edge and opp p 555.)
Marion Trust Co The, s e cor Market and Monument Pl. (See back cover.)
Union Trust Co The, 68 E Market. (See front cover and opp p 867.)

*TRUSTEES' SUPPLIES.

Ryse R, 34 Jackson pl.

TUB MANUFACTURERS.

Handle-Hoop Tub Co, s w cor St Clair and C C C & St L Ry.

*TURF GOODS.

Herrington Frank L, 81 E Market. (See adv opp p 450.)

*TURNERS—METAL.

Reeves Harry E, 96 S Delaware, cor Georgia. (See embossed line front cover and adv in Patternmakers.)

*TURNERS—WOOD.

Huey M S & Son, 551 Mass av. (See adv p 5.)
Indianapolis Manufacturers' and Carpenters' Union, 38-42 S New Jersey. (See adv p 2.)
Reeves Harry E, 96 S Delaware, cor Georgia. (See embossed line front cover and adv in Patternmakers.)

*TYPEWRITER SUPPLIES.

Bird W M jr & Co, 29 E Market.
Remington Standard Typewriter, Wyckoff, Seamans & Benedict, 34 E Market.
Williams Typewriter, S H East State Agt, 55 Thorpe Blk. (See right bottom cor cards.)

*TYPEWRITING.

Indianapolis Business University, When Bldg, N Penn, E J Heeb Propr. (See front cover, right bottom lines and p 4.)

*TYPEWRITING MACHINES.

Bird W M Jr & Co (Densmore Typewriters), 29 E Market.
Remington Standard Typewriter, Wyckoff, Seamans & Benedict, 34 E Market.
Smith Premier Typewriter Co The, 76 E Market.
Williams Typewriter, S H East State Agt, 55 Thorpe Blk. (See right bottom cor cards.)

TYPEWRITING MACHINES FOR RENT.

Remington Standard Typewriters, Wyckoff, Seamans & Benedict, 34 E Market.

UMBRELLA DEALERS AND REPAIRERS.

Block Wm H Co The, 7-9 E Washington. (See right top and bottom lines.)
Clark James H, 11 Indiana av.
Gunther Charles W, 21 Pembroke Arcade and 56 Mass av.
Harity Patrick, 43 Virginia av.
Parker Charles A, 47 Mass av.

*UNDERTAKERS.

(See also Funeral Directors.)
Tutewiler Henry W, 72 W Market. (See left bottom lines.)

*UNDERWRITERS' FIRE PUMPS.

Worthington Henry R, 64 S Penn. (See left top lines.)

UNITED STATES COMMISSIONERS.

Ayres Alexander C, 500-502 Indiana Trust bldg.
Moores Charles W, 602-610 Lemcke bldg.
Morris Nathan, 134-140 Commercial Club bldg.
Pierce Henry Douglas, 11-13, 18½ N Meridian.
Taylor Harold, 302-304 Indiana Trust bldg.
Van Buren Wm A, 18½ N Penn.

UPHOLSTERERS.

Block Wm H Co The, 7-9 E Washington. (See right top and bottom lines.)
Fetters & Smock, 124 Mass av.
Gray Mary, 149 N Delaware.
Hudson Simeon T, 135 Mass av.
Iske Bros, 105 E Washington.
Jones Cassius M C, 287 Christian av.
Romberg Henry F, 45 Mass av.

*VALENTINES.

Mayer Charles & Co, 29-31 W Washington. (See adv opp p 615.)

VARNISH MANUFACTURERS.

Indianapolis Varnish Co, s e cor Ohio and Pine.
Lilly Varnish Co, 10 Rose.

*VARNISHES.

Aldag Paint and Varnish Co The, 222 E Washington. (See adv in Paints and Oils.)

CLEMENS VONNEGUT 184, 186 and 192 E. Washington St.
CABINET HARDWARE CARVERS' TOOLS. Glues of all kinds.

THE WM. H. BLOCK CO. DRY GOODS, MILLINERY, CLOAKS AND FURS.
7 AND 9 EAST WASHINGTON STREET.

INDIANAPOLIS VETERINARY INFIRMARY
18-24 South East Street, Corner Pearl.
Equipped with all MODERN IMPROVEMENTS, such as Elevators, Soaking and Bathing Stalls, Operating Tables, Slings, Etc., that modern skill and science can produce. Capacity for 25 head of horses. Calls made to all parts of the city, day or night.
DISEASES OF DOGS A SPECIALTY.
OFFICE TELEPHONE 905.
RESIDENCE TELEPHONE 1798.
L. A. GREINER, V. S., Proprietor.

INDIANAPOLIS STEEL ROOFING AND CORRUGATING WORKS, 23 and 25 East South Street. S. D. NOEL, Proprietor.

Indianapolis Paint and Color Co, 40, 42, 44, 46 and 48 Mass av. (See adv in Paints and Oils.)

VAULT CLEANERS.

Abbott George, 171 S Alabama.
Buhneing Ernest, 32 N Delaware.
Enterprise Odorless Vault and Sink Cleaning Co, 200 Elizabeth. (See adv.)

THE ENTERPRISE
ODORLESS
Vault and Sink Cleaning Co.
200 ELIZABETH STREET,
TEL. 1675. INDIANAPOLIS, IND.
John L. Major, Proprietor. Anna M. Major, Mgr.

Krumholz Lambert, 36 N Delaware. (See adv.)

L. KRUMHOLZ, Proprietor.
The SANITARY ODORLESS CO.
PRIVIES, VAULTS AND SINKS.
Office, 36 North Delaware St., Baldwin Block.
Residence, 177 Union Street.
DISINFECTANTS FREE OF CHARGE.

Lanktree James W, 18 Baldwin blk.
Miller Samuel H, 23 S New Jersey.
Stout George W, 107 Hosbrook.
Welch John, 5 Arthur.

VENEER MANUFACTURERS.

Adams & Williamson, s e cor Clifford av and Bee Line Ry.
Indiana Lumber and Veneer Co, cor L E & W R R and 15th.
Williamson D W & Co, 52 John.

*VENTILATING ENGINEERS.

Kirkhoff Bros, 102-104 S Penn. (See left top cor cards.)

*VENTILATORS.

Gardner Joseph, 37-41 Kentucky av. (See left top cor cards.)
Laing Samuel, 72-74 E Court. (See left side lines.)
McWorkman Willard, 930 W Washington. (See left top cor cards.)

*VETERINARY DENTISTS.

Roe John F, 80 E Court.

VETERINARY SURGEONS.

Anderson David E, 266 E Washington.
Craig Wm B, 23 Monument pl.
Creeden Joseph A, 550 Virginia av.
Edwards Wm, 134 W Pearl.
Elliott & Erganbright, 83 E Wabash.
Greiner Louis A, 18-24 S East. (See adv.)
Indianapolis Veterinary Infirmary, 18-24 S East. (See adv.)
Orlopp Bertram G, 106 S Delaware.
Pritchard & Son, 122 E Wabash.
Roberts George H, 286 Mass av.
Roe John F, 80 E Court.

VINEGAR MANUFACTURERS.

Campbell George D Co The, 593-599 E Washington.
Grocers' Mnfg Co The, 80 S Penn.
Huffman Wm D, 24 Dunlop.
Mauler John, 16 Morton.
Regal Mnfg Co, 269-271 E McCarty.

*WALKING CANES.

Mayer Charles & Co, 29-31 W Washington. (See adv opp p 615.)

WALL PAPER AND WINDOW SHADES.

Amthor Wm L, 454 Virginia av.
Coppock Bros, 187 Virginia av and 15 Pembroke Arcade.
Gall Albert, 17-19 W Washington.
Indiana Wall Paper Co, 82-84 Virginia av.
Jacoby Edward T, 27 Mass av.
Knickerbocker James B, 40½ Kentucky av.
McDowell Henry C, 550 S Meridian.
Moller Carl, 161 E Washington.
National Wall Paper Co, 136 S Illinois.
Reynolds Wm E, 297 Mass av.
Rolls Wm H Sons, 103 E Washington.
Sandefur Frederick M, 95 Division (W I).

David S. McKernan | REAL ESTATE AND LOANS
Houses, Lots, Farms and Western Lands for sale or trade.
ROOMS 2-5 THORPE BLOCK.

DIAMOND WALL PLASTER { Telephone 1410
BUILDERS' EXCHANGE.

UNION TRANSFER AND STORAGE CO. Cor. E. Ohio St. and C., C., C. & St. L. R'y Tracks.
ISSUE NEGOTIABLE RECEIPTS ON MERCHANDISE AND HOUSEHOLD GOODS.

Shaw Decorating Co.,

WALL PAPERS

PAPER HANGINGS, Fabric Effect.

TAPESTRIES, High Class Results.

FRESCOING, RELIEF WORK, In all Materials.

106 and 108 North Meridian Street.

Wall Paper, Etc.—Continued.

Schleicher & Martens, 18 N Meridian.
Shaw Decorating Co, 106-108 N Meridian. (See adv.)
Stevens Henry C, 496 N Senate av.
Stout Huldah A, 62 N Illinois.
Taylor & Taylor, 30-36 S Illinois.
Willits M A & Co, 236 W Washington.

*WALL PLASTER MANUFACTURERS.

Adamant Wall Plaster Co of Indiana, cor Phipps and J M & I R R.
Diamond Wall Plaster Co, Office 3 Builders' Exchange, Factory cor E North and Bee Line Ry. (See top lines and opp p 941.)

*WAREHOUSES.

Indianapolis Storage and Transfer Co, 370-372 S Delaware. (See back cover.)
Union Transfer and Storage Co, n e cor E Ohio and C C C & St L Ry. (See left side lines.)

*WAREHOUSE TRUCKS.

Dietz Fred Co The, 370-406 Madison av. (See right side lines and adv p 10.)

WARP MILLS.

Brower & Love Bros, e bank of White river n of National rd.

*WASHING COMPOUND.

Williams Bros, 214 S Meridian.

WATCHES, CLOCKS AND JEWELRY—WHOLESALE.

Baldwin, Miller & Co, 31-34 Commercial Club bldg.
Haase Mamie, 17½ S Meridian.
Heaton, Sims & Co, 17 W Maryland.
Moorhead Thomas W, 146 S Meridian.

WATCHES, CLOCKS AND JEWELRY—RETAIL.

Alverson Harlan, 547 W 22d.
Bernloehr Christopher, 324 S Meridian.
Bishop Henry H, 580 Virginia av.
Bryant Frank L, 89 Mass av.
Burgheim Henry D, 41 W Washington.
Burns Wm F, 8 Indiana av.
Campbell Milton T, 134 Mass av.
Comstock Horace A, 16 E Washington.
Conrad Owen J, 70-72 Mass av.
Crane Isaiah C, 135 Virginia av.
Dittrich Edward A, 182 Virginia av.
Ducas Fannie, 115 W Washington.
Dyer George G, 18½ N Meridian.
Eisele Emma, 81 E Washington.
Feller Louis, 218 E Washington.
Gardner Bros & Ross, 56 N Penn.
Ginn John T, 260 W Washington.
Gray & Gribben, 92 N Illinois.
Hempleman Isaac L, 563 S Meridian.
Herron Frederick M, 4 E Washington.
Jerusalem Robert B, 236 W Washington.
Johnson Horace, 21 Mass av.
Kelso Reuben E, 820 N Illinois.
Kiefer L F & Son, 86 N Penn.

A. METZGER AGENCY ESTABLISHED 1863. REAL ESTATE

LAMBERT GAS & GASOLINE ENGINE CO.
ANDERSON, IND. GAS AND GASOLINE ENGINES, 2 TO 50 H. P.

McRoberts John W, 191 Mass av.
Marcy Wm T, 38 W Washington.
Matsumoto Ikko, 17½ S Meridian.
Mauzy Lon R, 7 Mass av.
Mayhew James N, 13 N Meridian. (See right bottom cor cards.)
Medearis Fletcher C, 11 N Penn.
Mueller Albert, 48 S Illinois.
Mueller Charles H, 23 Virginia av.
Mullally John P, 6 Monument pl.
Neal Asbury, 350 Blackford.
Newhart Frederick, 57 E Sutherland (B).
Oehler Andrew, 20 S Delaware.
Oeth & Kelso, 30 Hubbard blk.
Overstreet George M, 54 Nordyke av (W I).
Reber Gerhard F, 30 Virginia av.
Reiffel Edward A, 158 Virginia av.
Rogers John P, 60 N Illinois.
Schergens Henry C, 151 E Washington.
Scheuroecker Albert B, 103½ E Washington.
Schmeltz & Lorentz, 24 S Illinois.
Schmidt Frederick H, 32 Jackson pl.
Schreiner Wm, 427 Madison av.
Schurr Leonhard, 78 Indiana av.
Scott John, 22 Indiana av.
Shepherd John R, 431 S Meridian.
Sipe Jacob C, 18½ N Meridian.
Slutsky Henry S, 22 Indiana av.
Snavely Charles, 183 W Washington.
Spaethe Benjamin E, rear 550 W Udell (N I).
Streng Andrew J, 24½ S Illinois.
Vollmer Frank X, 855 S Meridian.
Walk Julius C & Son, 12 E Washington. (See left bottom cor cards.)
Weber Frederick J, 426 Mass av.
Weis Charles E, 258 W Washington.
Whitaker Charles F, 32 N Delaware.
Wilhite Noah H, 131 William (W I).
Williams Crawford H, 145 W Washington.
Wimmer John P, 14 N Penn.

WATCHMAKERS' TOOLS AND SUPPLIES.

Nichols S T & Co, 18 Hubbard blk.

WATER FILTERS—PRESSURE AND GRAVITY.

Worthington Henry R, 64 S Penn. (See left top lines.)

***WATER GAS.**

Lambert Gas and Gasoline Engine Co, Anderson, Ind. (See right top lines.)
Otto Gas Engine Works The, 3 Builders' Exchange, 35 E Ohio. (See left bottom lines.)

***WATER METERS.**

Tuerk Hydraulic Power Co, 39 Dearborn St, Chicago, Ill.
Worthington Henry R, 64 S Penn. (See left top lines.)

***WATER WORKS MACHINERY.**

Dean Bros' Steam Pump Works, 1st near cor Senate av. (See adv p 3.)
Worthington Henry R, 64 S Penn. (See left top lines.)

***WEAVERS.**

Miner Wm L, 184-186 Cherry. (See adv opp Rugs.)

***WEISS BEER BREWERS.**

Metzger Jacob & Co (Berliner Weiss Beer), 30-32 E Maryland.

***WELL BUILDERS.**

Krauss Charles, 42 S Penn. (See right top lines.)

WELL AND CISTERN BUILDERS.

Austin & Tripp, 31 W Maryland.
Bishop Lewis P, 391 N New Jersey.
Brady George W, 473 Lincoln av.
Butler Job, 171 S Reisner (W I).
Butts Frank C, 133 Indiana av.
Clark Henry H, 136 Martindale av.
Davis Joseph T & Co, 289 W Vermont.
Dolby James H, 81 W 7th.
Durbon Charles R, 103 Yeiser.
Gardner Samuel M, 72 E Court.
Gordon Charles F, 205 E Washington.
Gray John E, 57 Maxwell.
Kiker John C, 32 N Delaware.
Krauss Charles, 42 S Penn. (See right top lines.)
Lewis Preston J, 237 W 7th.
McDonald Wm, 275 Spring.
Mason George W, Northwestern av 2 n of Langsdale.
Mason Grant, 535 Francis (N I).
Neiger & Hartwig, 175 Virginia av.
Niemeyer Christian F, 183 Fulton.
Ruemmele & Buttler, 850 Morris (W I).
Staley John S, 268 W Merrill.
Thatcher James H, 151 High.
Treeter Bros, rear 9 Lexington av.
Wiles Adolph, 1242 E Washington.
Wright John W, 172 Laurel.
Wulzen Charles W, 58 Mayhew.

WHEEL MANUFACTURERS.

Anderegg Christian, cor Osgood and Vandalia R R (W I).
Cushion Car Wheel Co The, 143½ S Meridian.
Standard Wheel Co, cor Morris and Belt R R (W I).

***WHEELS.**

Vonnegut Clemens, 184-186 E Washington. (See left bottom lines.)

***WHITE LEAD.**

Burdsal A Co The, 34-36 S Meridian. (See right bottom cor cards.)

***WHITE SAND.**

Wasson W G Co The, 130 Indiana av. (See left bottom cor cards and adv in Cement and Lime.)

WILLOW WARE.

Compton, Ault & Co, 82 S Penn.

***WINDOW GLASS.**

Indianapolis Paint and Color Co, 40, 42, 44, 46 and 48 Mass av. (See adv in Paints and Oils.)

***WINDOW GUARDS.**

Ellis and Helfenberger, 162-168 S Senate av. (See right bottom lines.)

BICYCLES $5 DOWN. Best Wheels. WHEELMEN'S CO. 31 W. OHIO ST. LONG DISTANCE TEL. 1855.

J. H. TECKENBROCK  Painter and Decorator, 94 EAST SOUTH STREET.

FIDELITY MUTUAL LIFE—PHILADELPHIA, PA.
MATCHLESS SECURITY At LOW COST. } A. H. COLLINS { General Agent Baldwin Block.

Rooms 42 and 43 WHEN BUILDING. Miners and Shippers Steam and Domestic Coal. Edwardsport Coal and Mining Co.

*WINDOW SCREENS.

Indiana Screen Factory, 591-593 Central av near 14th. (See front cover.)

*WINDOW SHADES.

Block Wm H Co The, 7-9 E Washington. (See right top and bottom lines.)

WINES AND LIQUORS—WHOLESALE.

Bos Jacob (estate of), 35-37 S Delaware.
Ciener Isaac, 167 W Washington.
Cohn Myer, 33 W Ohio.
Duncan Robert, 340 Blake.
Eckhouse Bros, 56 S Meridian.
Feldkamp Reinhard W, 267 E Washington.
Groenwoldt & Behringer, 84 S Delaware.
Hancock Charles E, 82 Monument pl.
Hayes & Ready, 123 S Meridian.
Hitzelberger Albert, W McLene and canal (N I).
Kaufman B & Son, 168 W Washington.
Koepper Christian, 35 E Maryland.
Metzger Jacob & Co, 30-32 E Maryland.
Nier Isaac, 160 W Washington.
O'Brien Daniel & Co, 98 S Illinois.
Pfau George & Son, 64 S Delaware.
Rikhoff John H, 851 E Michigan.
Rikhoff J G & Co, 188 S Meridian.
Ross James R & Co, 129 S Meridian.
Santa Clara Wine Co, 89 N Illinois.
Schmalholz Casper, 29 S Meridian.
Schuller Julius A, 110-112 N Meridian.
Woodford & Pohlman, 143 S Meridian.

*WIRE CLOTH.

Vonnegut Clemens, 184-186 E Washington. (See left bottom lines.)

*WIRE FENCE MANUFACTURERS.

Cleaveland Fence Co, Factory 18-22 Biddle, Office 21 Biddle.
Ellis & Helfenberger, 162-168 S Senate av. (See right bottom lines.)
Indianapolis Fence Co, Office 15 Thorpe Blk.

*WIRE ROPES.

Vonnegut Clemens, 184-186 E Washington. (See left bottom lines.)

WIRE WORKS.

Fachmann Herman W, 77 N Delaware.
Hollenbeck T P & Son, 32 S Meridian.
Indiana Wire Works, 70½ W Court.
Witty James H, 47 S Illinois.

*WOOD ALCOHOL.

Moffat & Co, 402 Lemcke Bldg. (See adv p 9.)

*WOOD CARPETS.

Interior Hardwood Co The, Manufacturers, 317 Mass av.
Teckenbrock John H, 94 E South. (See right bottom lines and adv in Painters.)

*WOOD DEALERS.

Anderson Mads P, 381-385 Cedar.
Balke & Krauss Co, cor Missouri and Market. (See right bottom lines.)

*WOOD ENGRAVERS.

(See also Engravers.)

Bauer H C Engraving Co The, 23 W Washington. (See adv opp Engravers.)
Bowley George J, Room 14 Yohn Blk, n e cor Meridian and Washington. (See adv.)

GEORGE J. BOWLEY,
Designer and Wood Engraver
First-class Work at Reasonable Prices.
All Work Done When Promised.
Room 14 Yohn Bldg., Northeast Cor. Washington and Meridian Sts.

Chandler Henry C, 47½ N Illinois, s e cor Market. (See adv in Engravers—Wood.)

*WOOD MOULDINGS.

United States Artistic Co, 166 S New Jersey.

WOOD ORNAMENT MANUFACTURERS.

Wood Ornament Co, 452 W Addison (N I). (See adv in Furniture Mnfrs.)
(See adv in Furniture Mnfrs.)

*WOOD SPLIT PULLEYS.

Indianapolis Pulley Mnfg Co, 372-374 E Michigan. (See adv in Pulley Mnfrs.)

WOOD TURNERS.

Cummings Marshall F, 87 E South.
Schlanzer Benedict J, 682 Charles. (See adv p 8.)
Share Louis A, Hanway and J M & I R R.
Wachs Wm, rear 252 S New Jersey. (See adv.)

WM. WACHS,
WOOD TURNER
Newels, Balusters, Columns, Etc., Etc.
Telephone 668. Rear 252 S. New Jersey.

Wright & Workman, 440 E Ohio.

C. ZIMMERMAN & SONS | SLATE AND GRAVEL ROOFERS
19 South East Street.

DRIVEN WELLS And Second Water Wells and Pumps of all kinds at CHARLES KRAUSS'. 42 S. PENN. ST. TELEPHONE 465.

WOODEN AND WILLOW WARE.

Tucker & Dorsey Mnfg Co, s w cor State av and Bates.
Udell Woodenware Works, n w cor Addison and Emma (N I).

WOODEN AND WILLOW WARE—FANCY.

Mayer Charles & Co, 29-31 W Washington. (See adv opp p 615.)

WOOLEN MILLS.

Geisendorff C E & Co, 402 National rd.
Merritt George & Co, 411 W Washington.

WRENCH MANUFACTURERS.

Indianapolis Wrench and Stamping Co, 96 S Delaware.

***WROUGHT IRON PICKET FENCING.**

Ellis & Helfenberger, 162-168 S Senate av. (See right bottom lines.)

YEAST MANUFACTURERS.

Fleischmann & Co, 213 S Illinois.
Hawes Judson S, 11 N Alabama.
Thomson Compressed Yeast Co, 269 and 271 E McCarty.

***ZINC ETCHING.**

Bauer H C Engraving Co The, 23 W Washington. (See adv opp Engravers.)

Indiana Illustrating Co, s e cor Market and Illinois. (See adv opp Engravers.)

WE RECEIVE many complaints from our patrons to the effect that they are bothered so much by **BORROWERS.** These parties are not the private citizen nor the stranger in the city, who steps in,

ERTEL STEAM LAUNDRY || LARGEST AN
26 and

FIDELITY MUTUAL LIFE—PHILADELPHIA, PA.
MATCHLESS SECURITY AT LOW COST. A. H. COLLINS General Agent Baldwin Block.

Rooms 42 and 43 WHEN BUILDING.
Edwardsport Coal and Mining Co. Miners and Shippers Steam and Domestic Coal.

*WINDOW SCREENS.

Indiana Screen Factory, 801-03 Central av near 11th. (See front cover.)

*WINDOW SHADES.

Block Wm H Co The, 7-9 E Washington. (See right top and bottom lines.)

WINES AND LIQUORS—WHOLESALE.

Bos Jacob (estate of) ... S Meridian.
Clener Isaac, 167 W Wash...
Cohn Myer, 23 W Ohio
Duncan Robert, 340 Lake
Eckhouse Bros 54 S Mer
Feldkamp Reinhard W, 26 ... ington
Groenwoldt & Behringer ...
Hancock Charles F 52 M...
Hayes & Ready, 121 S M...
Hitzelberger Albert W M... canal (N I)
Kaufman H & Son 106 W W...
Koepper Christian ... E M...
Metzger Jacob & Co, 30-32 Maryland.
Nier Isaac, 1... W Wa...
O'Brien Daniel & Co ... S I...
Pfau George & Son ... S D...
Rikhoff John H, 54 E M...
Rikhoff J G & Co 1... S M...
Ross James R & Co 1... S M...
Santa Clara Wine Co ... N I...
Schmalholz Casper ... S M...
Schuller Julius A, 1... N M...
Woodford & Pohlman, 1... S ...

*WIRE CLOTH.

Vonnegut Clemens, 184-186 E Washington. (See left bottom lines.)

*WIRE FENCE MANUFACTURERS.

Cleveland Fence Co, Factory 18-22 Biddle, Office 21 Biddle.
Ellis & Helfenberger, 162-168 Senate av. (See right bottom lines.)
Indianapolis Fence Co, (See 15 Thorpe Blk.

*WIRE ROPES.

Vonnegut Clemens, 184-186 E Washington. (See left bottom lines.)

WIRE WORKS.

Fachmann Herman W, 7... N ...
Hollenbeck T P & Son 32 S M...
Indiana Wire Works, 5... W ...
Witty James H, 67 S Illinois

*WOOD ALCOHOL.

Moffat & Co, 102 Lemcke Bldg (See adv p 9.)

*WOOD CARPETS.

Interior Hardwood Co The, Manufacturers, 317 Mass av.
Teckenbrock John H, 94 E South. (See right bottom lines and adv Painters.)

*WOOD DEALERS.

Anderson Wade P, 201-205 Cedar.
Balke & Krauss Co, cor Missouri and Market. (See right bottom lines.)

*WOOD ENGRAVERS.

(See also Engravers.)

Bauer H C Engraving Co The, 23 W Washington. (See adv opp Engravers.)
Bowley George J, Room 14 Yohn Blk, n e cor Meridian and Washington. (See adv.)

GEORGE J. BOWLEY,
Designer and Wood Engraver
First-class Work at Reasonable Prices.
All Work Done When Promised.
Room 14 Yohn Bldg., Northeast Cor. Washington and Meridian Sts.

Chandler Henry C, 47½ N Illinois, s e cor Market. (See adv in Engravers—Wood.)

*WOOD MOULDINGS.

United States Artistic Co, 166-8 N... Jersey.

WOOD ORNAMENT MANUFACT...

Wood Ornament Co, 432 W... (N I). (See adv in Furnitu... (See adv in Furniture...

*WOOD SPLIT ...

Indianapolis Pulley ... E Michigan. (See ... Mnfrs.)

WOO...

Cummings Mar...
Schlanzer Ben... (See adv p ...
... A...
Wachs Wm... (See adv.)

W...
WO...
Tel...
W...
N& S...

DRIVEN W

DIR

REASONABLE
RELIABLE AND
PROMPT
Geo. H.
Benedict
& Co.
Designers
Engravers
BY ALL METHODS AND
Electrotypers
175
177-
CLARK
STREET
CHICAGO
ILL. U.S.A.
FACILITIES·CAPACITY AND
QUALITY·UNEXCELLED.
B

INCORPORATED 1885.

ESTABLISHED 1870.

R. L. POLK & CO.

GAZETTEER and DIRECTORY

PUBLISHERS.

PUBLISHERS OF GAZETTEERS AND BUSINESS DIRECTORIES

FOR THE STATES OF

ILLINOIS, MICHIGAN, PENNSYLVANIA, NEW JERSEY, MINNESOTA, MONTANA, DAKOTA, KANSAS, MISSOURI, ALABAMA, WEST VIRGINIA, KENTUCKY, INDIANA, IOWA, WISCONSIN, TEXAS, MARYLAND, OREGON, TENNESSEE, PROVINCE OF ONTARIO, CALIFORNIA, WASHINGTON, COLORADO, WYOMING, NEW MEXICO, UTAH, NEVADA, ARIZONA, ARKANSAS, IDAHO,

MEDICAL AND SURGICAL REGISTER OF THE UNITED STATES,
DENTAL REGISTER OF THE UNITED STATES.
ARCHITECTS' AND BUILDERS' DIRECTORY OF THE UNITED STATES.

AND CITY DIRECTORIES

—FOR—

Baltimore, Md.; Detroit, Grand Rapids, Saginaw, Bay City, Jackson, Lansing, Muskegon, Port Huron, Sault Ste. Marie, Ann Arbor, Ypsilanti, Kalamazoo, Flint, Alpena, Cheboygan and Big Rapids, Mich.; Toledo, Columbus, Zanesville, Findlay, Newark and Lima, Ohio; Atlanta Columbus and Augusta, Ga.; Birmingham and Montgomery, Ala.; Memphis and Knoxville, Tenn.; Indianapolis and Fort Wayne, Ind.; St. Paul, Minneapolis and Duluth, Minn.; Ashland, Oshkosh and Eau Claire, Wis.; Des Moines, Sioux City and Dubuque, Iowa; Portland, Ore.; Stockton, Cal.; Bismarck, Mandan and Sioux Falls, Dak.; Butte, Mont.; Seattle, Tacoma, Spokane Falls and Walla Walla, W.; Salt Lake City, Utah; London, Hamilton and Toronto, Ont.; Puget Sound; and Marine Directory of the Great Lakes.

Head Office, 40 to 44 Larned St. West, Detroit, Mich.

OFFICES:

St. Louis, Mo., 904 Olive Street.
Chicago, Ill., 122 La Salle Street.
Philadelphia, Pa., Ledger Building, corner Chestnut and Sixth Streets.
Toledo, Ohio, 306 Madison Street.
Columbus, Ohio, 49 North High Street.
Baltimore, Md., 112 North Charles Street.
St. Paul, Minn., National German American Bank Building.
Minneapolis, Minn., 257 First Avenue South.
Des Moines, Iowa, 410 Iowa Loan and Trust Building.
Toronto, Ont., 18 Wellington, E.
Portland, Ore., First National Bank Building.
Atlanta, Ga., Chamber of Commerce.
San Francisco, Cal., 606 Montgomery Street.
Memphis, Tenn., 341 Second Street.
Salt Lake City, Utah.

Indianapolis Office, Rooms 23 and 24 Journal Building.

Lake Erie & Western R. R. Co.

Ft. Wayne, Cincinnati & Louisville R. R.
Northern Ohio Railway Co.

NATURAL GAS ROUTE

THE POPULAR SHORT LINE

..........BETWEEN..........

Peoria, Bloomington, Chicago, St. Louis, Springfield, Lafayette, Frankfort, Muncie, Portland, Lima, Findlay, Fostoria, Fremont, Sandusky, Akron, Indianapolis, Kokomo, Peru, Rochester, Plymouth, LaPorte, Michigan City, Ft. Wayne, Hartford, Bluffton, Connersville and Cincinnati, making direct connections for all points

EAST, WEST, NORTH & SOUTH.

THE ONLY LINE TRAVERSING THE

GREAT NATURAL GAS and OIL FIELDS

Of Ohio and Indiana, giving the patrons of this Popular Route an opportunity to witness the grand sight from the train as they pass through. Great fields covered with tanks, in which are stored millions of gallons of Oil, Natural Gas wells shooting their flames high in the air, and the most beautiful cities, fairly alive with Glass and all kinds of factories.

We furnish our patrons with Elegant Reclining Chair Cars Free on day trains, and L. E. & W. Palace Sleeping and Parlor Cars on night trains, at very reasonable rates.

Direct connections to and from Cleveland, Buffalo, New York, Boston, Philadelphia, Baltimore, Pittsburg, Washington, Kansas City, Denver, Omaha, Portland and San Francisco, and all points in the United States and Canada.

This is the popular route with the ladies on account of its courteous and accommodating train officials, and with the commercial traveler and general public for its comforts, quick time and sure connections. For any further particulars call on or address any ticket agent.

GEO. L. BRADBURY, Vice-President and General Manager.
CHAS. F. DALY, General Passenger and Ticket Agent.
INDIANAPOLIS, INDIANA.

8226

ESTABLISHED 1851.

NORDYKE & MARMON MILL WORKS

[Take any Street Car from Hotels or Union Depot to Stock Yards.]

FOUNDERS AND MACHINISTS

And Manufacturers from the Raw Material of Flouring Mill Machinery.

ROLLER MILLS,
PORTABLE MILLS,
PURIFIERS,
GRAIN MACHINERY,
ELEVATOR WORK,
BRAN DUSTERS,
CENTRIFUGAL BOLTS,
MILLSTONES,
PULLEYS,
GEARING AND SHAFTING.

WE KEEP IN STOCK

Bolting Cloth

AND ALL GRADES OF
WOVEN WIRE, LEATHER
AND GUM BELTING.

Take Stock-Yard Street Cars

Marion Trust Co.

CAPITAL, $300,000.

ACTS AS EXECUTOR, ADMINISTRATOR, GUARDIAN, TRUSTEE OR ASSIGNEE.

PAYS INTEREST ON TIME DEPOSITS.

OFFICES, S. E. COR. MONUMENT PLACE AND MARKET ST.

C. HENRY ROSEBROCK,

ABSTRACTS OF TITLES

To Real Estate in [illegible] ...vancer.

OFFICE, ROOM 19 [illegible] ...ARKET ST.

NOTARY PUBLIC ALWAYS IN OFFICE. [illegible] ...POLIS IND.

Indianapolis St[illegible] Com[illegible]pany

370 AND 3[illegible] SOUT[illegible] STREET.

Moving an[illegible] Storage

HOUSEHO[illegible] GOODS, PIAN[illegible]S, MERCHANDISE AND [illegible]

Telephone 1049.

[illegible] have [illegible] ONLY VANS in the City. Warehouses New and Modern.

GLOBE ACCIDENT INSURANCE COMPANY

Of Indianapolis, Ind.

WRITES ALL CLASSIFICATIONS

The Company has paid over $50,000 in claims in the past four years. For all information address the Secretary,

TELEPHONE 1161. W. A. WALKER, 15 and 19 Ætna Building.

Lightning Source UK Ltd.
Milton Keynes UK
UKHW031341031218
333390UK00012B/676/P